D0067996

BLOOMSBURY
CROSSWORD
SOLVER'S
DICTIONARY

Consultant Editor
Anne Stibbs

Editor
Stephen Curtis

BLOOMSBURY

A BLOOMSBURY REFERENCE BOOK

Consultant Editor
Anne Stibbs

Editor
Stephen Curtis

Market House Books
John Daintith

Text Processing
Katy McAdam
Edmund Wright

Editorial Team
Sandra Anderson
Lesley Brown
Ann-Marie Imbornoni
Charlotte Regan
Ian M. Spackman

First edition published in Great Britain 2003
This edition published in the United States of America 2004

Bloomsbury Publishing Plc, 38 Soho Square, London W1D 3HB

Bloomsbury Reference titles are distributed
in the United States of America by
Independent Publishers Group, 814 N. Franklin St., Chicago, IL 60610
1-800-888-4741
www.ipgbook.com

Copyright © Bloomsbury Publishing Plc 2003, 2004

Publisher's note
This dictionary includes material based on text in the
Bloomsbury Thesaurus (© Bloomsbury Publishing Plc 1993, 1997) and
Bloomsbury Crossword Companion (© Bloomsbury Publishing Plc 1996).

All rights reserved. No part of this publication may be reproduced in any form
or by any means without the prior written permission of the publishers.

ISBN 1 904970 02 8

All papers used by Bloomsbury Publishing are natural, recyclable products
made from wood grown in well-managed forests. The manufacturing processes
conform to the environmental regulations of the country of origin.

Text computer typeset by Bloomsbury
Printed in the United States of America by Quebecor World Fairfield

Introduction

The solver of crossword puzzles needs access to a whole range of information in order to crack clues, and there is a respectable tradition of using reference books to help find solutions. Most crossword enthusiasts keep a general English dictionary to hand and often a thesaurus and encyclopedia as well. The compilers of this crossword dictionary have used these and other resources to put together a particularly useful book in which all these kinds of information are combined in a single place. The solutions it includes can be used to solve all types of crossword clue: a brief summary of these follows.

Although word games and puzzles are as old as language itself, the crossword puzzle is a relatively new invention. The first recognizable modern crossword—using numbered clues and a grid for the answers—was published in 1913 in the *New York World* newspaper. Puzzles of this type became extremely popular in the United States in the 1920s and eventually spread to Britain and most other countries. The London *Times* published its first puzzle in 1930. For many years the *New York Times* refused to publish crosswords (as well as comic strips) but eventually capitulated, first publishing a Sunday puzzle in 1942 and a daily puzzle in 1950. Today, almost all newspapers and many other periodicals contain a crossword of some sort.

Despite the many different formats taken by crosswords over the past 90 years, there are only two basic types: noncryptic puzzles and cryptic puzzles. In noncryptic puzzles the clue is straightforward. Often, the answer is simply a synonym of the clue, i.e., a word or phrase having the same (or similar) meaning. Crosswords of this type also often require encyclopedic knowledge: "capital of Belgium"; "Roman god of war"; "breed of rabbit"; etc. In such "quick crosswords," as they are often called, an element of ambiguity is often introduced by the very brevity of the clues; the clue *base* (7), for example, could have as its solution "bedrock," "support," or "ignoble." However, there is usually only one set of answers that fits the grid in the completed puzzle.

In cryptic crosswords, which are less common than noncryptic crosswords in the United States, the approach is less straightforward. The clues are, in a sense, riddles that have to be solved to get the answer, and certain conventions have evolved for writing cryptic clues. Most cryptic clues have three distinct parts:

a)   a *definition*—a word or phrase that gives the meaning of the answer (in noncryptic puzzles this is usually the whole of the clue).

b)   one or more *indicators*—key words or phrases that provide instructions to the reader. For example, "formerly" may indicate that the answer (or part of the answer) takes the form of an archaic word.

c)   the *working material* of the clue—the word or words to which the indicators apply.

Often, however, the boundaries between these parts are by no means distinct—sometimes, for example, the entire clue provides the definition, within which are embedded indicators and working material. The solution to a cryptic clue can be an anagram, a hidden word embedded in the clue, a reversed or split word from the clue, a palindrome (a word that reads the same backward and forward), a shortening of a word in the clue, or a homophone (a word that sounds the same as a word in the clue).

In this dictionary solutions to clues are presented in an easily accessible way. The crossword solver simply has to look up a keyword from the clue in the dictionary (which is arranged alphabetically). Here, each headword is followed by a list of words that may provide an important step towards a solution. These are not restricted to simple synonyms but contain obscure and old-fashioned words, associated words, literary and historical allusions, and names of people and places. For ease of reference, these words are arranged first according to length (with a maximum of 15 letters), and then alphabetically. The number of letters in the words are given in bold, so the user knows exactly where to start looking in the entry.

A special feature of this dictionary is the inclusion of several thousand phrases consisting of two or more words. These are listed at the end of entries after all one-word solutions, and are introduced by the heading PHRASES.

> **Arkansas 2** AR; **4** pine (tree); **11** mockingbird (bird); PHRASES: **3, 6, 4** The people rule (motto); **5, 7** apple blossom (flower); **6, 4** Little Rock (capital); **7, 5** Natural State (nickname).

This clear layout and combination of headwords and phrases should provide all crossword enthusiasts with the tools they need to tackle even the toughest clue.

Anne Stibbs

A

A 3 ace, age, key, one, per, top; **4** acre, alto, ante; **5** adult, upper; **6** annual; **7** America, article; **8** advanced; **9** anonymous.

aardvark 3, 4 ant bear.

Aaron's beard 4, 2, 6 rose of Sharon.

AB 7 Alberta.

abaca 6, 4 Manila hemp.

abalone 5 ormer *UK*; PHRASES: **3, 5** ear shell.

abandon 3 end; **4** deny, dump, halt, stop; **5** abort, ditch, leave, scorn, spurn, waive; **6** cancel, desert, refuse, reject; **7** discard, forsake, license, neglect; **8** wildness; **11** unrestraint; **12** intemperance, recklessness; **15** uninhibitedness; PHRASES: **4, 2** give up; **4, 3** call off; **4, 3, 2** walk out on; **5, 3** throw out; **5, 4** throw away; **5, 6** leave behind; **7, 2** dispose of.

abandonment 7 leaving; **9** desertion. *See also* **abandon**

abase 5 abash, crush, lower; **6** debase, demean, reduce; **7** degrade; **8** belittle, diminish; **9** denigrate, humiliate, subjugate; PHRASES: **3, 4** put down; **4, 2** dump on, trip up; **4, 4** take down; **5, 3** bring low.

abasement 7 putdown; **10** abnegation; **11** degradation, denigration, deprecation, humiliation, subjugation; **12** belittlement. *See also* **abase**

abash 5 shame; **7** mortify; **14** discountenance.

abate *See* **decrease**

abattoir *See* **slaughterhouse**

abbreviate 3 cut; **6** reduce; **7** abridge, curtail, shorten; **8** condense, truncate; PHRASES: **3, 5** cut short.

abbreviation 7 acronym; **9** reduction; **10** abridgment, truncation; **11** contraction, curtailment; PHRASES: **5, 4** short form.

Abdias 7 Obadiah.

abdicate 7 abandon; **8** renounce; PHRASES: **4, 2** give up; **4, 4** hand over, step down.

abduct 5 seize; **6** kidnap; **7** capture; PHRASES: **5, 3** carry off.

abduction 6 kidnap; **7** capture, seizure, slavery; **10** kidnapping; PHRASES: **8, 3** carrying off.

Abe 7, 7 Abraham Lincoln.

Aberdeen 5 Angus; **7** terrier; PHRASES: **7, 4** Granite City.

aberrant 3 odd; **7** deviant, unusual; **8** abnormal, atypical, peculiar; **9** anomalous, eccentric, irregular.

aberration 7 anomaly; **9** deviation; **11** abnormality, peculiarity; **12** irregularity.

abet 3 aid; **4** back, help, urge; **6** assist, incite; **7** connive, support; **9** encourage.

abhorrent *See* **hateful**

abide 4 bear, live, stay; **5** dwell, lodge, stand; **7** stomach; **8** tolerate.

ability 4 bent, gift; **5** flair, grasp, knack, range, reach, savvy, skill; **6** genius, talent; **7** compass, fitness, mastery; **8** aptitude, capacity, efficacy, facility; **9** attribute, endowment, potential, resources; **10** capability, competence, efficiency; **11** proficiency; **12** effectuality, potentiality; **13** effectiveness, qualification; PHRASES: **3, 4, 5** the real thing; **3, 5, 5** the right stuff; **4, 2, 5** what it takes; **4-3** know-how; **5, 7** green fingers; **6, 3** native wit; **6, 6** street smarts.

abject 4 meek; **6** humble; **7** extreme; **8** hopeless; **9** miserable; **11** deferential.

abjure 4 deny; **7** abstain; **8** forswear, renounce; PHRASES: **4, 2** give up.

ablaze 5 afire; **6** alight; **7** burning; PHRAS-

ES: 2, 4 on fire; **2, 6** in flames.

able 5 adept; **6** bright, clever, gifted, rating, seaman; **7** capable, skilled; **8** talented; **9** competent; **10** proficient; **11** intelligent.

ablutions 4 lick, wash; **6** lavage, plunge, toilet; **7** bathing, cleanup, dipping, hygiene, rinsing *UK*, shampoo, soaking, soaping, washing; **8** bathroom, lavation, toilette; **PHRASES: 4, 3, 5, 2** wash and brush up *UK*.

abnegation 6 denial; **9** disavowal, rejection; **11** repudiation; **12** renunciation; **14** relinquishment; **PHRASES: 4-6** self-denial; **4-9** self-restraint, self-sacrifice.

abnormal 3 odd; **5** queer; **6** mutant; **7** deviant, strange, unsound, unusual; **8** aberrant, atypical, peculiar; **9** anomalous, irregular, malformed, perverted, unnatural.

abnormality 5 fault; **6** defect, oddity; **7** anomaly, oddness; **9** aberrance, deformity, deviation; **10** aberration, perversion; **11** malfunction; **12** irregularity, malformation.

abode 4 home; **8** domicile, dwelling; **9** residence.

abolish 3 end; **4** stop; **9** eliminate, eradicate; **PHRASES: 2, 4, 4** do away with.

abolition 6 ending; **11** elimination, eradication; **12** obliteration.

abolitionist 4 Howe (Julia Ward), Howe (Samuel Gridley), Mott (Lucretia), Rose (Ernestine), Weld (Theodore Dwight); **5** Brown (John), Soule (Silas), Stowe (Harriet Beecher), Truth (Sojourner); **6** Grimke (Angelina Emily), Lowell (James Russell), Lowell (Maria White), Tappan (Arthur), Tubman (Harriet); **7** Clemens (Samuel), Emerson (Ralph Waldo), Garrett (Thomas John), Lovejoy (Elijah), Stanton (Elizabeth Cady), Thoreau (Henry David); **8** Douglass (Frederick), Franklin (Benjamin), Garrison (William Lloyd), Phillips (Wendell); **PHRASES: 5, 4, 5** Uncle Tom's Cabin; **11, 4** Huckleberry Finn; **11, 8** Underground Railroad.

abominable 4 vile; **5** awful; **7** hateful; **8** dreadful; **10** horrendous.

Abominable Snowman 4 yeti; **7** Bigfoot; **9** Sasquatch.

abominate *See* **hate**

abomination 6 hatred; **7** dislike, eyesore, outrage, scandal; **8** atrocity, disgrace, loathing; **9** revulsion; **10** repugnance.

aboriginal, aborigine 5 local, Maori; **6** native; **10** indigenous; **13** autochthonous.

abort 3 end; **4** halt, quit, stop; **5** crash, erase; **6** cancel, delete, logoff, logout; **7** abandon; **9** bootstrap, terminate; **PHRASES: 4, 1, 4** call a halt; **4, 3** call off; **4, 9** stop midstream; **5, 3** break off.

abortive *See* **futile**

abound 4 teem; **5** swarm; **6** throng; **11** proliferate.

about 1 c; **2** ca, on, re; **5** astir, circa, close; **6** almost, around, nearby, nearly; **7** apropos, roughly; **9** regarding; **10** concerning; **11** approaching; **13** approximately; **PHRASES: 2, 3, 5, 2** of the order of; **2, 3, 6, 2** in the region of; **2, 3, 7, 2** on the subject of; **2, 3, 8** in the vicinity; **2, 7** as regards; **2, 8, 2** in relation to; **3-1-3** vis-à-vis; **3, 3, 3** not far off; **4, 2** nigh on *UK*; **4, 2, 4** more or less; **4, 9, 2** with reference to; **5, 2, 3** going on for *UK*; **7, 8** roughly speaking; **9, 4** something like.

about-face 5 shift; **9** backtrack, turnabout; **10** revolution, turnaround *UK*; **14** transformation; **PHRASES: 1-4** U-turn; **3, 6** sea change; **4, 5** back trail; **5-4** about-turn *UK*, volte-face; **5-5-4** right-about-face; **6, 2, 4** change of tack; **6, 2, 5** change of heart.

about-turn *See* **about-face**

above 4 atop, over; **6** beyond; **9** exceeding.

above (get above oneself) 7 presume; **PHRASES: 4, 2** lord it; **6, 4, 5** forget one's place; **8, 3, 4** overstep the mark.

ABR 8 abridged.

abrade 3 rub; **4** bark, gnaw, rasp; **5** chafe, graze, grind, scuff; **6** scrape, strike; **7** roughen, scratch; **PHRASES: 4, 4** gnaw away.

abrasive 4 file, rude; **5** gruff, harsh, rough, sharp; **6** coarse, grainy; **7** brusque, rasping; **8** scratchy; **9** sandpaper; **10** aggressive, glasspaper, unfriendly; **11** insensitive; **13** argumentative; **PHRASES: 4, 4** nail file; **5, 5** emery board, emery paper.

abreast 5 level; **6** beside; **PHRASES: 2, 4** up with; **4, 2, 4** side by side.

abridge *See* **shorten**

abridgement 6 digest, reduce; **7** cutdown; **9** reduction; **12** condensation.

abroad 7 foreign; **8** overseas; **9** elsewhere.

abrogate 5 annul; **6** recant, repeal, revoke; **7** abolish, disavow, nullify, rescind, retract; **9** repudiate.

abrogation 6 denial; **8** apostasy, negation; **9** abolition, annulment, disavowal; **10** abnegation, retraction, revocation; **11** recantation, repudiation, rescindment; **12** cancellation; **13** nullification.

abrupt 4 curt, rude; **5** brief, brisk, gruff, hasty, quick, rapid, sharp, short, terse; **6** rushed, snappy, sudden; **7** brusque, offhand; **8** snappish; **9** irascible; **10** unexpected, unforeseen; PHRASES: **5-8** shorttempered.

abscess 4 boil, sore; **7** pustule; **8** eruption; **9** carbuncle.

abscond 3 cut, fly; **4** flee, skip; **5** elope; **6** decamp, defect, desert, escape, vanish; **7** vamoose; **9** disappear; **13** dematerialize; PHRASES: **2, 1, 4** do a bunk *UK*; **2, 4** go AWOL; **2, 7** go missing *UK*; **3, 3** run off; **3, 3, 4** fly the nest; **3, 4** run away; **4, 3** bunk off *UK*, make off; **4, 4** jump ship; **4, 5** play hooky; **4, 6** play truant; **5, 3** break out, skive off.

absence 4 lack, none, want; **6** dearth, nobody; **7** nullity, unbeing; **8** nihility, nonbeing; **9** emptiness, nonentity, privation, unreality; **10** deficiency; **11** absenteeism, nonpresence; **12** nonexistence; **13** nonappearance, nonoccurrence; PHRASES: **2-3** no-one; **3, 1, 3** not a one; **3, 1, 7, 3** not a blessed one; **4, 1, 3** nary a one, ne'er a one; **4, 3** time off; **5, 1, 3** never a one.

absent 3 out; **4** away, gone, null, void; **5** vague; **6** unreal, vacant; **7** lacking, missing, vacuous; **9** deficient; **11** inattentive, nonexistent, preoccupied, unavailable; **12** nonattendant, nonoccurrent; PHRASES: **2, 5, 6** in short supply; **3, 4** far away; **3, 7** not present; **6-6** absent-minded.

absentee 6 skiver *UK*, truant; **7** runaway; **8** defector, deserter; **9** absconder, defaulter, nonperson; PHRASES: **2-4** no-show; **7, 6** missing person.

absently 7 blankly, emptily; **8** dreamily, hollowly; **12** abstractedly, distractedly; PHRASES: **2, 5** by proxy; **2, 8** in absentia. *See also* **absent**

absent-minded 10 stargazing; **11** daydreaming; **13** woolgathering; PHRASES: **2, 1, 5, 5** in a brown study; **3, 2, 5** out to lunch; **3, 4, 2** not with it; **4, 2, 7** lost in thought.

absent oneself 4 exit; **5** leave; **6** depart, retire, vacate; **7** retreat; **8** withdraw; PHRASES: **3, 3** bow out; **4, 3** slip out; **4, 4** slip away;

4, 5 take leave; **5, 3** sneak out; **5, 3, 5** leave the scene.

absolute 4 firm, pure, rule, unit, zero; **5** final, fixed, given, music, pitch, total, utter, value; **6** decree, entire; **7** alcohol, certain, perfect, supreme; **8** ablative, complete, definite, humidity, judgment, majority, monarchy, outright, resolved; **9** magnitude, principle, threshold, unbounded, unlimited, unmovable; **10** conclusive, unmodified; **11** fundamental, temperature, unequivocal, unqualified; **12** unchangeable; **13** unadulterated, unconditional; **14** unquestionable; PHRASES: **3-3-3** out-and-out.

absolute ruler *See* **ruler**

absolution 6 pardon; **9** acquittal, atonement, discharge; **10** redemption; **11** condonation, deliverance, exculpation, exoneration, forgiveness, vindication; **14** reconciliation, rehabilitation.

absolve 4 free; **5** clear, remit; **6** acquit, assoil, cancel, excuse, pardon; **7** deliver, dismiss, forgive, release; **8** liberate; **9** discharge, exculpate, exonerate, vindicate; PHRASES: **3, 3** let off; **3, 3, 3, 4** let off the hook; **3, 4** set free; **5, 4, 4** clear one's name; **5, 5** sweep clean; **5, 6** start afresh.

absorb 3 mop, rub; **4** blot, grip, rapt, soak, swab, wipe; **5** admit, amuse, brush, grasp, learn; **6** adsorb, digest, engage, getter, osmose, sponge; **7** attract, engross, immerse, realize, riveted, sputter; **8** enthrall, interest, permeate; **9** captivate, fascinate, recognize, spellbind; **10** assimilate, infiltrate, understand; **11** incorporate, internalize; PHRASES: **3, 2** mop up, sop up; **4, 2** blot up, seep in, soak in, soak up, suck up, take in, take up, wipe up; **5, 2** drink up.

absorbed 7, 2 wrapped up. *See also* **absorb**

absorbent 6 porous, spongy; **7** osmotic, soaking; **8** bibulous, blotting, pervious; **9** adsorbent, digestive, ingestive, permeable, spongeous; **10** absorptive, penetrable; **12** assimilative.

absorption 7 osmosis, seeping; **8** blotting, interest, raptness, sorption, sponging; **9** digestion, immersion, inclusion; **10** absorbency, adsorption, engagement; **11** captivation, combination, fascination; **12** amalgamation, assimilation, enthrallment; **13** concentration, incorporation, preoccupation.

abstain 5 hedge, spare; **6** desist, temper; **7** forbear, refrain; **8** forswear, moderate, withdraw, withhold; PHRASES: **2, 7** do without, go without; **3, 2, 3, 5** sit on the fence; **3, 4, 5** not take sides; **3, 5** not touch; **3, 7** not indulge; **4, 2** give up, pass up; **4, 3, 5** kick the habit; **4, 4** hold back; **4, 4, 7** pull one's punches; **4, 7** deny oneself, stay neutral.

abstemious 7 Spartan; **9** abstinent; **10** forbearing; PHRASES: **2, 5, 3, 5** on bread and water; **4-7** self-denying; **7, 4** without food.

abstinence 10 abstention, asceticism, moderation, refraining, temperance; **11** forbearance, forswearing; PHRASES: **4-6** self-denial; **4-9** self-restraint; **4-10** self-discipline.

abstinent 3 dry; **5** sober; **7** ascetic; **8** teetotal; **9** temperate; **10** abstemious.

abstract 4 noun; **6** mental, précis, remove, select; **7** abridge, extract, isolate, shorten, summary; **8** academic, condense, separate, synopsis, theorize; **9** summarize; **10** abridgment, conceptual, immaterial, intangible; **11** conjectural, hypothesize, nonconcrete, speculative, theoretical; **12** hypothetical, intellectual; **13** conceptualize, expressionism, nonfigurative; PHRASES: **4, 3** take out; **5, 7** short version.

abstraction 4 idea; **6** notion; **7** concept, removal, thought; **9** construct, deduction, vagueness; **10** dreaminess, extraction, withdrawal; **11** daydreaming, pensiveness; **13** preoccupation.

abstruse See **obscure**

absurd 5 empty, silly; **6** futile, hollow; **7** bizarre, strange; **8** farcical; **9** illogical, ludicrous, pointless; **10** irrational, ridiculous; **11** incongruous, meaningless, nonsensical, purposeless; **12** preposterous.

abundance 6 plenty, wealth; **9** profusion. See also **abundant**

abundant 4 rich; **5** ample; **6** lavish; **7** copious, profuse; **9** plentiful; **11** overflowing; **13** superabundant; PHRASES: **4, 4, 6** more than enough.

abuse 5 swear; **6** insult, misuse, molest; **7** cruelty, exploit, insults; **8** maltreat, mistreat, swearing, violence; **10** manipulate; **11** mishandling; **12** exploitation, maltreatment, manipulation, mistreatment; PHRASES: **3-5** ill-treat; **3-9** ill-treatment.

abuser 4 thug; **8** polluter; **9** loudmouth; **10** desecrator; PHRASES: **4-6** wife-beater.

Abu Simbel 8 Ipsambul.

abusive 3 bad; **4** evil, foul, rude; **5** cruel, rough; **7** harmful, impious, profane, vicious, violent; **8** damaging, forceful, sadistic, wasteful; **9** barbarous, injurious, insulting, obnoxious, offensive, perverted; **10** fraudulent, oppressive, outrageous; **11** extravagant; **12** exploitative.

abut 4 bump, join, meet; **5** bound, clash, crash, reach, touch; **6** adjoin, attach, border, couple; **7** conjoin, connect, contact, impinge, overlap; **8** converge, neighbor; **9** interface, intersect; **10** amalgamate; PHRASES: **2, 4, 2** be next to; **2, 8, 2** be adjacent to; **3, 4** run into; **3, 9** lie alongside; **4, 2** link up; **5, 2** verge on.

abyss See **gulf**

abyssal 8 plutonic.

Abyssinia 8 Ethiopia.

AC 7 account; **8** actinium; **11** aircraftman UK; PHRASES: **3, 4** new line (Italian: a capo).

acacia 6 locust; PHRASES: **3, 6** gum arabic.

academia 7 academe; **8** literati; **10** illuminati, university; **14** intelligentsia; PHRASES: **6, 2, 7** groves of academe; **8, 5** academic world; **8, 7** academic circles.

academic 3 don UK; **4** moot; **5** tutor; **6** school; **7** bookish, college, learned, preachy, scholar, teacher; **8** abstract, lecturer, literary, studious; **9** professor, scholarly; **10** researcher, scholastic, university; **11** educational, pedagogical, theoretical; **12** hypothetical, intellectual; PHRASES: **9, 9** assistant professor, associate professor.

academy 5 Royal; **6** French, school; **7** college; **8** military; **12** conservatory; **13** conservatoire; PHRASES: **4, 6** arts school; **7, 6** private school.

Academy Award 4 Song; **5** Actor, Oscar, Sound; **6** Makeup; **7** Actress; **9** Directing; **14** Cinematography; PHRASES: **3, 9** Art Direction; **4, 6, 5, 4** Live Action Short Film; **4, 7** Best Picture, Film Editing; **5, 7, 7** Sound Effects Editing; **5, 9** Dance Direction; **6, 7** Visual Effects; **7, 6** Costume Design; **7, 7, 10** Writing Adapted Screenplay; **7, 8, 4** Foreign Language Film; **7, 8, 10** Writing Original Screenplay; **8, 5, 4** Animated Short Film; **8, 5, 5** Original Music Score; **8, 7** Animated Feature; **10, 5** Supporting Actor; **10, 7** Supporting Actress; **11, 7** Documentary Feature.

acajou 6 cashew.

acanthous 7 spinous.

accelerate 3 lap, run; **4** bolt, dash, pass, rush; **5** hurry, spurt; **6** hasten, outrun, spring, sprint; **7** outpace, quicken, scamper; PHRASES: **2, 6** go faster; **3, 1, 4, 2** get a move on; **3, 2, 3** let it rip; **3, 4, 4, 4** put one's foot down; **4, 2** open up, step up; **4, 2, 2** step on it; **4, 2, 3, 3** step on the gas; **4, 2, 3, 4** pick up the pace, step up the pace; **4, 2, 5** pick up speed; **4, 3** dart off, dash off, tear off; **4, 3, 8** open the throttle; **4, 5** jump ahead; **4-5** fasttrack; **5, 2** speed up; **5, 3** shake off; **5, 6** leave behind; **5, 8** leave standing; **6, 5** gather speed, thrust ahead; **6, 7** spring forward; **6, 8** gather momentum, impart momentum; **8, 5** increase speed.

acceleration 3 zap, zip; **4** dive, jump, leap, rush, whiz, zing, zoom; **5** bound, burst, drive, swoop, vroom; **6** canter, gallop, pounce, spring, sprint, swoosh, thrust; **7** getaway, impetus, impulse, rushing, scamper, tantivy; **8** changeup, hurrying; **9** hastening; **10** quickening; PHRASES: **5, 2** speed up; **5, 2, 5** burst of speed; **5, 2, 6** burst of energy; **5, 4** power dive; **6, 5** flying start; **8, 2** speeding up, stepping up; **8, 4** headlong rush.

accent 4 alif, ayin, beat, burr; **5** acute, breve, caron, drawl, grave, hacek, tilde, trill, twang; **6** ablaut, brogue, hamzah, macron, ogonek, stress, umlaut; **7** cedilla, lisping, stridor; **8** dieresis, emphasis, heighten, nasality; **9** diacritic, diaeresis *UK*, emphasize, highlight; **10** accentuate, apostrophe, circumflex, inflection, intonation, prominence; **11** enunciation; **12** accentuation; **13** pronunciation; PHRASES: **3, 6, 2** put stress on; **4, 2, 5** tone of voice; **4, 6, 2** give weight to; **4, 9, 2** draw attention to; **11, 4** diacritical mark.

accentuate *See* **emphasize**

accept 2 OK; **4** bear, pass, take; **5** admit, adopt, agree, allow; **6** accede, assent, assume, endure, ratify; **7** believe, condone, consent, endorse, license, receive; **8** sanction, shoulder, tolerate; **9** acquiesce, authorize, recognize, undertake; **10** understand; **11** acknowledge, countenance; PHRASES: **3, 2, 4** put up with; **3, 3** say yes; **4, 2** take on; **4, 3, 2-5** give the go-ahead; **4, 4, 7** give one's consent; **5, 2, 4** agree to take; **5, 10** grant permission; **6-5** rubber-stamp; **6, 8** resign yourself.

acceptance 6 assent, belief; **7** receipt; **8** approval, credence, currency; **9** accession, agreement, reception, rejection, tolerance; **10** toleration; **11** concurrence, recognition; **12** acquiescence; **14** acknowledgment.

accepted 6 normal; **8** expected, received; **9** customary; **11** established, traditional; **12** conventional; PHRASES: **4-7** time-honored.

access 4 door, gate, open, pass, path, read, road; **5** entry, trail; **6** direct, entrée, random; **7** channel, contact, pathway; **8** approach, entrance, footpath, retrieve; **9** admission; **10** admittance, passageway, sequential; PHRASES: **3, 2** log on, way in; **3, 4** get into; **4, 2** call up; **4, 6, 2** gain ~ to; **5, 2, 3** right of way; **5, 2, 5** right of entry; **6, 4** bridle path; **8, 6** stepping stones.

accessible 4 main, open; **5** clear, handy; **6** genial, nearby, simple, smooth; **7** affable, bridged, through, trodden; **8** arterial, friendly; **9** available, reachable, welcoming; **10** connecting, manageable; **12** approachable; **13** communicating; **14** comprehensible, understandable; **15** straightforward; PHRASES: **2, 4** at hand, to hand; **4, 2, 3** easy to use; **4-8** user-friendly; **6, 5** within reach; **6, 7** easily reached.

accession 6 accord, assent; **7** consent; **8** takeover, transfer; **9** agreement, elevation, promotion; **10** assumption, attainment, changeover, compliance, succession; **11** appointment, concurrence, inheritance; **12** inauguration; PHRASES: **5, 4** entry upon; **6, 4** taking over; **6, 6** taking office.

accessories 3 bib, obi; **4** belt, mask, muff, sash, wrap; **5** aegis, apron, cabas, dhoti, ephod, pinny *UK*, purse, scarf, shawl; **6** braces *UK*, cestus, peplum, shades, tippet; **7** armband, baldric, balteus, dopatta, handbag, parasol, scogger, sporran; **8** cincture, codpiece; **9** bandoleer, surcingle, wristband; **10** cummerbund, sunglasses; **11** spatterdash *UK*; **12** handkerchief; **13** accouterments, paraphernalia; PHRASES: **3, 4** tie tack; **3, 6, 4** sam browne belt; **4, 3** bolo tie, head bag; **4-5** chin-cloth; **5, 4** cinch belt; **6, 4, 5** camel's hair shawl; **6, 5** clutch purse, rubber apron, sewing apron; **7, 8** ostrich feathers; **8, 3** shoulder pad; **8, 5** bungalow apron. *See also* **clothes, jewelery**

accessory 7 abettor, fixture, partner; **8** addition; **10** accomplice, decoration. *See also* **accessories**

accidental 6 chance; 7 unlucky; 9 unplanned; 10 calamitous, disastrous, fortuitous, unintended; 11 inadvertent, involuntary, unfortunate; 12 infelicitous, manslaughter; 13 unintentional.

acclaim 4 clap, hail, hand, roar; 5 bravo, cheer, honor, paean, stamp, whoop; 6 cheers, encore, huzzah, praise; 7 applaud, commend, hosanna, ovation, plaudit, whistle; 8 applause, approval, cheering, clapping, handclap, stamping; 9 whistling; 10 hallelujah; 11 acclamation, approbation, compliments; 12 commendation, handclapping; PHRASES: 3-3, 6 hip-hip hurrah; 3, 4 big hand; 4, 3 root for; 5, 2, 8 round of applause; 5, 3, 4 raise the roof, shout for more; 5, 5 shout bravo; 5, 6 three cheers; 5, 7 throw flowers; 7, 4 curtain call; 8, 7 standing ovation.

accolade *See* tribute

accommodate 4 help, hold, seat; 5 adapt, house, lodge; 6 adjust, assist, billet, oblige; 7 contain, quarter; 11 acclimatize, familiarize; PHRASES: 2, 2, 7 be of service; 2, 3, 6, 3 be big enough for; 3, 2 put up; 3, 4, 2 get used to; 4, 4, 2, 4 find ways to help; 4, 4, 3 have room for; 4, 8, 3 have capacity for.

accompaniment 7 adjunct, garnish; 8 addition, coagency, trimming; 9 accessory, auxiliary, chaperone, symbiosis; 10 supplement; 11 association, coexistence, combination, conjunction; 12 cohabitation, concomitance.

accompany 4 lead; 5 guide; 6 attend, concur, convoy, escort; 7 garnish; 8 coincide; 9 chaperone, symbiosis; 10 complement, supplement; PHRASES: 2, 4 go with; 2, 4, 2, 4 be tied in with; 2, 5, 4 go along with; 2, 6, 4 be linked with; 2, 8, 4 go together with; 4, 4 come with, side dish; 4, 4, 4 keep time with; 6, 4 belong with.

accompanying 9 accessory, attendant, attending, belonging; 10 additional, associated, background, collateral, contextual, incidental; 11 concomitant, corequisite; 12 cocurricular; 13 complementary, supplementary; PHRASES: 3-2 add-on.

accomplish 2 do; 3 win; 6 attain, finish; 7 achieve, realize, succeed; 8 complete; PHRASES: 3, 4 get done; 4, 3 pull off; 5, 3 carry out; 5, 5 bring about.

accomplished 4 able; 5 adept; 6 expert, gifted; 7 capable, skilled; 8 skillful, talented; 10 consummate, proficient.

accord 3 fit; 4 deal, give, pact; 5 allow, match, peace, unity; 6 afford, bestow, comply, confer, permit, render, treaty; 7 concede, concert, concord, empathy, harmony, rapport; 8 affinity, identity, sympathy; 9 accedence, agreement, closeness, communion, concourse, consensus, empathize, mutuality, unanimity; 10 acceptance, accordance, compliance, compromise, concession, confluence, correspond, settlement, similarity, solidarity; 11 concordance, concurrence; 12 acquiescence, capitulation; 13 accommodation, compatibility; 14 reconciliation; PHRASES: 3, 4 one mind; 3, 5 one voice; 3, 6 vox populi; 4, 6 team spirit; 4-10 like-mindedness; 5, 4 agree with; 5, 6 happy family; 6, 2, 5 esprit de corps; 7, 2, 5 meeting of minds; 8, 4 identify with.

accord (in accord) 6 agreed, united; 8 agreeing, amicable, together, unitedly; 9 accepting, accordant, compliant, complying, conceding, concerted, confluent, congenial, unanimous; 10 communally, compatible, concessive, concordant, concurrent, consenting, harmonious; 11 acquiescent, consentient, empathizing, reconciling, sympathetic; 12 compromising, conciliatory, frictionless, reconcilable; 13 accommodating; PHRASES: 2, 3 at one; 2, 3, 4 of one mind; 2, 4 en bloc; 2, 5 en masse; 2, 7 en rapport, in concert; 2, 9 by consensus; 3, 3 nem. con.; 3, 8 all together; 4, 3, 5 with one voice; 4, 5 like sheep; 4-6 like-minded; 11, 4 identifying with.

accordingly 2 so; 4 ergo, thus; 5 hence; 6 whence; 8 suitably; 9 fittingly, therefore, wherefore, wherefrom; 12 consequently; 13 appropriately; 15 correspondingly; PHRASES: 2, 1, 6 as a result; 2, 4, 3 in that way; 2, 4, 4 at that rate, in that case; 2, 4, 6 on that ground; 2, 7, 4 it follows that; 2, 11 in consequence; 3, 4, 6 for that reason; 4, 4 like that; 4, 5, 2 that being so.

according to rule 13 traditionally; 14 conventionally; PHRASES: 2, 3, 4 by the book.

accordion 7-3 squeeze-box.

accost 4 stop; 5 hound; 6 detain; 8 approach, confront.

account 3 NOW, tab; 4 bank, bill, book, cash, cost, post; 5 check, debit, enter, entry, joint, short, slate, story, tally, trust, value; 6

budget, charge, credit, excuse, fiddle, garble, reason, record, report; **7** balance, capital, control, current, deposit, drawing, expense, savings, version; **8** checking, estimate, register, relation, suspense; **9** narrative; **10** journalize; **11** arrangement, description, explanation; **13** justification; **14** interpretation; PHRASES: **4, 3, 5** keep the books; **4, 8** keep accounts; **5, 2** write up; **5, 4** carry over, write down; **5, 7** carry forward.

account (on account) 2, 3, 3 on the tab; **2, 3, 4** on the bill; **2, 3, 5** on the slate; **2, 6** on credit.

accountant 2 c.a.; **3** CPA; **4** turf; **6** bursar, purser; **7** actuary, auditor, cashier; **9** chartered, paymaster, treasurer; **10** bookkeeper; **11** storekeeper; **12** statistician; PHRASES: **4, 7** bean counter.

account book 5 books; **6** ledger; **7** daybook, journal, records; **8** bankbook, cashbook, passbook, register; **9** checkbook; PHRASES: **5-4, 4** petty-cash book.

accounted 5 saved, spent; **6** billed, costed; **7** audited, debited, settled, tallied; **8** balanced, credited, invoiced, received, recorded; **9** deposited; **10** registered; PHRASES: **7, 7** carried forward.

accounting 5 audit, score, tally; **6** fiscal; **8** creative, economic, itemized; **9** actuarial, budgetary, bursarial, computing, financial, reckoning; **10** commercial; **11** accountable, bookkeeping, calculating, calculation, computation, enumeration, inventorial, statistical; **12** arithmetical, mathematical.

accumulation 5 hoard, stock, store; **6** growth; **7** accrual, buildup, deposit; **9** accretion, gathering; **10** collection.

accuracy 5 rigor, truth; **6** acuity, detail, nicety; **8** delicacy, fidelity, pedantry, pinpoint, rigidity, squaring, subtlety, trimming; **9** precision; **10** definition, exactitude, micrometry, perfection, refinement; **12** accurateness; **13** documentation; PHRASES: **2-2** hi-fi; **4, 8** high fidelity; **4-9** hair-splitting; **4, 10** fine adjustment; **7, 5** perfect pitch.

accurate 2 OK; **3** apt, set; **4** dead, even, fine, just, nice, true; **5** exact, plumb, right; **6** square, strict; **7** correct, defined, perfect, precise, refined, squared, trimmed; **8** absolute, delicate, detailed, faithful, flawless, pedantic, pinpoint, rigorous, straight, truthful, verbatim; **9** faultless; **10** definitive, fastidious, meticulous, scientific, scrupulous; **11** documentary, microscopic, punctilious;

PHRASES: **3-7** nit-picking.

accurately 2, 1, 1 to a T; **2, 1, 4** to a hair; **2, 1, 6** to a nicety; **2, 2, 5** to be exact; **2, 3, 3, 6** to the nth degree; **2, 3, 4** by the book, on the mark, on the nose; **2, 3, 6** on the button, to the letter; **2, 3, 8** in all respects; **2, 5, 6** in every detail; **4, 1, 4** tout à fait *UK*; **4, 2** just so; **4-2** bang-on, dead-on, spot-on *UK*; **4, 3, 4** word for word; **4, 5** dead right; **4-5** well-aimed; **4-7** word-perfect; **4-9** hair-splitting; **5, 2** plumb on; **5-5** point-blank; **6, 2, 6** letter by letter; **8, 2** straight up. *See also* **accurate**

accurate person 6 pedant; **8** quibbler; PHRASES: **3-6** nit-picker; **4-8** hair-splitter.

accurate thing 7 quibble; **9** metronome; **10** micrometer; PHRASES: **3, 5** mot juste; **4, 2, 3** hole in one; **4, 4** fine line; **4, 6** dead center, fine detail; **4, 11** nice distinction; **5-3** bull's-eye; **5, 6** finer points; **5, 7** legal quibble; **6, 4** proven fact; **6, 5** atomic clock; **10, 4** documented fact.

accursed 5 awful, fated; **6** damned, doomed; **7** hateful; **8** horrible, terrible; **9** appalling; PHRASES: **3-5** ill-fated; **3-7** ill-starred.

accusation 4 case, suit; **5** blame, claim, count; **6** action, arrest, charge, plaint; **7** booking, lawsuit, summons; **8** accusing, citation, evidence, gravamen, reproach; **9** complaint; **10** allegation, imputation, indictment, litigation; **11** impeachment, implication, insinuation, prosecution; **12** denunciation; **13** countercharge, incrimination, recrimination; PHRASES: **4, 4** true bill; **5, 4** court case.

accuse 3 sue, try; **4** book, cite, narc, sing; **5** blame, fault; **6** allege, arrest, charge, impute, indict, snitch, squeal, summon; **7** arraign, censure, impeach, witness; **8** complain, denounce, litigate, reproach; **9** implicate, inculpate, insinuate, prosecute; **10** denunciate; **11** incriminate, recriminate, stoolpigeon; **13** countercharge; PHRASES: **3, 2, 5** put on trial; **3, 3, 5, 2** lay the blame on; **3, 3, 6, 2** put the finger on; **3, 5, 2** lay blame on; **4, 2** haul up; **4, 3, 4** blow the gaff; **4, 3, 7** blow the whistle; **4, 7** bear witness, file charges; **5, 1, 7** bring a lawsuit, serve a summons; **5, 1, 8** serve a citation; **5, 1, 9** lodge a complaint; **5, 3, 4, 2** throw the book at; **5, 3, 6** point the finger; **5, 4, 1, 4** serve with a writ; **5, 6** bring action; **5, 7** bring charges; **5, 10** bring litigation; **6, 7** inform against.

accused (be accused) 5, 2, 3, 4 stand

in the dock; **5, 5** await trial; **5, 7** stand accused; **6, 7** defend oneself; **7, 1, 7** receive a summons.

accused person 7 culprit, suspect; **8** prisoner; **9** defendant; **10** respondent; **13** correspondent; PHRASES: **6, 3** marked man; **6, 5** guilty party.

accuse falsely 5 frame, libel; **6** defame; **7** slander; **10** calumniate; **12** misrepresent; PHRASES: **4, 2, 1, 6** cook up a charge; **4, 3, 8** fake the evidence; **5, 2, 1, 6** trump up a charge; **5, 8** plant evidence; **6, 7** commit perjury; **7, 7** perjure oneself.

accuser 2 DA; **4** fink, narc; **5** grass *UK*, sneak *UK*; **6** canary, snitch; **7** charger, libeler, stoolie; **8** claimant, indicter, informer, libelant, litigant, opponent, perjurer, snitcher, squealer, telltale; **9** appellant, denouncer, impeacher, plaintiff; **10** challenger, confronter, criticizer, petitioner, prosecutor, supergrass *UK*, talebearer, tattletale; **11** complainant, faultfinder; **12** incriminator; PHRASES: **5, 2, 1, 4** party to a suit; **5, 6** stool pigeon; **5, 7** false witness; **7-6** whistle-blower; **7, 7** hostile witness.

accustomed 4 used; **10** acquainted, habituated.

ace 1 I; **3** one, top; **4** card, star; **5** pilot, super; **6** expert, victor, winner; **7** leading; **8** champion, topnotch; **9** brilliant, excellent, wonderful; PHRASES: **3, 6** top player; **5-4** first-rate; **5-5** world-class.

acetum 7 vinegar.

ache 4 hurt, long, pain, want, wish; **5** smart, sting, throb, yearn; **6** desire, twinge.

achieve 2 do; **4** gain; **5** reach; **6** attain; **7** fulfill, prosper, realize, succeed; **8** complete; **10** accomplish; PHRASES: **2, 10** be successful; **3, 2, 3, 3** get to the top; **3, 5** get ahead, get there; **4, 2** make it; **4, 3** pull off; **4, 3, 5** make the grade; **4, 4** make good; **5, 3** carry out; **5, 3, 3** reach the top.

achievement 4 feat; **6** making; **7** success, triumph; **9** accession; **10** completion; **11** realization; **14** accomplishment; PHRASES: **3-6** ten-strike.

Achilles 4 heel; **6** tendon.

aching 4 ache, achy, itch, pain, sore; **5** throb; **6** desire, pining, tender; **7** longing, painful; **8** yearning.

acid 3 LSD; **4** drop, hard, rain, rock, soil, sour, tart, test, weak; **5** acrid, basic, green, harsh, Lewis, sharp, tangy; **6** acidic,

barbed, biting, bitter, lemony, saline, strong, unripe; **7** acerbic, caustic, cutting, dibasic, mineral, mordant, neutral, organic, pungent; **8** alkaline, critical, hydrated, protonic, tribasic, vinegary; **9** acidulous, anhydrous, monobasic; **10** acidulated, amphoteric, carboxylic; **11** unsweetened.

acknowledge 3 nod; **4** hail, wave; **5** admit, allow, grant, greet, react, reply; **6** accept, answer, credit, rejoin, retort, return, salute; **7** concede, confess, confirm, respond; **9** attribute, recognize; **10** appreciate; PHRASES: **3, 2** own up.

acknowledgement 3 nod; **4** hail, RSVP, wave; **5** reply; **6** answer, retort, return, salute; **7** receipt, tribute; **9** rejoinder; **10** salutation; **12** appreciation.

acme *See* **peak**

acolyte 4 aide; **6** helper; **7** devotee; **8** adherent, disciple, follower; **9** assistant, attendant, supporter.

acquiescence 6 assent; **7** consent, pliancy; **8** docility; **9** agreement, obedience; **10** acceptance, compliance, pliability, submission, submissive; **11** amenability; **12** tractability; **14** persuadability.

acquiescent 6 docile; **7** pliable; **8** amenable, obedient, yielding; **9** accepting, agreeable, assenting, compliant, tractable; **10** consenting, submissive; **11** persuadable.

acquire 3 buy, get; **4** gain, heap, pile, pool, save; **5** amass, bunch, catch, glean, hoard, learn, stack; **6** attain, obtain, secure; **7** accrete, collect, develop, harvest, procure; **8** assemble, cumulate, purchase; **9** stockpile; **10** accumulate, assimilate; PHRASES: **3, 2** dig up; **3, 4, 5, 2** get your hands on; **3, 5, 2** get ahold of; **3, 8** get together; **4, 2** come by, pick up, pile up, save up, take up; **5, 2** round up, scare up, stock up; **5, 4** store away; **6, 2** gather in; **6, 8** gather together, scrape together.

acquit 4 free; **5** clear, quash, spare; **6** excuse, exempt, pardon; **7** absolve, dismiss, forgive, justify, release, respite; **8** abrogate, liberate, reprieve; **9** discharge, exculpate, exonerate, vindicate; PHRASES: **3, 2** let go; **3, 3** get off, let off; **3, 3, 3** let off the hook; **4** set free; **3, 5, 7** not press charges; **4, 3** find for; **4, 3, 6** find not guilty; **5, 10** grant absolution; **7, 7** dismiss charges.

acrid 5 harsh, sharp; **6** bitter; **7** caustic, choking, cutting, pungent; **9** vitriolic; **10**

unpleasant.

acrimony 5 spite; 6 grudge, malice, rancor; 8 aversion, soreness, sourness; 9 animosity, hostility; 10 bitterness, resentment; 11 peevishness; 14 unfriendliness, vindictiveness; PHRASES: 3, 4 ill will; 3, 5 bad blood; 3, 7 bad feeling, ill feeling.

acrobat 7 gymnast, tumbler; 11 entertainer, funambulist; 13 contortionist; PHRASES: 6, 9 circus performer; 7, 6 trapeze artist UK.

across 7 athwart; 9 crossways, crosswise; 10 diagonally; 12 transversely; PHRASES: 4, 4, 2, 4 from side to side.

act 4 bill, deed, exit, feat, mime, play, ploy, riot, wage, work; 5 doing, enact, feign, feint, labor, mimic, stamp, stunt; 6 action, appear, behave, commit, costar, decree, direct, happen, manage; 7 attempt, execute, exploit, fulfill, imitate, operate, perform, portray, pretend, proceed, replace, statute; 8 function, maneuver, practice, pretense, transact; 9 dissemble, dramatize, enactment, implement, improvise, influence, interfere, intervene, legislate, officiate, personify, prosecute, represent, undertake; 10 accomplish, administer, commission, manipulate, masquerade, perpetrate, understudy; 11 achievement, impersonate, participate, performance, undertaking; 12 administrate; 13 entertainment; PHRASES: 2, 2 be in, go as; 2, 2, 6 be in charge; 2, 6 be active; 2, 8 do business; 3, 2 get on; 3-2 put-on; 3, 2, 2 ham it up, put it on; 3, 4, 5 ply one's trade; 3, 4, 8 put into practice; 3, 5 get going; 3, 8 get cracking; 4, 1, 4, 2 have a hand in, play a part in; 4, 2 deal in, pose as, take on; 4, 2, 2, 4 have to do with; 4, 2, 6 make an effort; 4, 3 show off, take off, work for; 4-3 play-act; 4, 3, 4 play the lead; 4, 3, 4, 2 play the part of; 4, 4 deal with; 4-4 role-play; 4, 4, 2 take care of, take part in; 4, 5 play about UK, take steps; 4, 6 fool around, lark around, take action, take effect; 4-6 play-acting; 4, 9, 2 take advantage of; 5, 2 carry on; 5, 3 carry out, speak for; 5, 3, 6 tread the boards; 5, 7 carry through; 6, 7 acquit oneself; 7, 1, 6 produce a result; 7, 2 indulge in; 7, 2, 6 produce an effect; 7, 7 comport oneself, conduct oneself; 8, 7 militate against.

act (not act) 3 die; 4 idle, loaf, quit, rest, rust, stop, wait; 5 avoid, cease, coast, defer, delay, drift, glide, pause, relax, slide, watch; 6 desist, ignore, repose, unwind; 7 abstain, despair, neglect, refrain; 8 stagnate, tolerate, vegetate; 9 disregard, freewheel; 13 procrastinate; PHRASES: 2, 7 do nothing; 2, 8 be inactive; 3, 2, 3, 5 sit on the fence; 3, 2, 4, 5 sit on one's hands; 3, 3 put off; 3, 3, 2, 3 not bat an eye; 3, 4 let pass, lie dead, lie idle, sit back; 3, 4, 5 let well alone; 3, 5 let alone, not budge, sit tight; 3, 6 lie fallow; 4, 1, 5, 3 turn a blind eye; 4, 2 give up, look on, pass up; 4, 3 keep mum; 4, 3, 2 keep out of; 4, 3, 3 wait and see; 4, 3, 4 live and let live; 4, 3, 4 pass the buck; 4, 4 hang fire, kill time; 4, 4, 4 bide one's time; 4, 4, 5 kick one's heels; 4, 5 keep quiet, stay still; 4, 7 stay neutral; 5, 2 stand by; 5, 3, 4 watch and wait; 5, 5 leave alone, tread water; 6, 4 gather dust.

acting 3 cue; 4 busy, exit, mime; 5 aside, drama; 6 active, byplay, heroic, hoking, Method; 7 charade, interim, mimesis, mimicry, mummery; 8 artistic, business, creative, dramatic, dumbshow, militant; 9 enactment, operative, portrayal, temporary; 10 masquerade, substitute; 11 histrionics, industrious, interactive, performance, personation, showmanship; 13 impersonation, improvisation; 14 interpretation, representation; PHRASES: 2, 3, 5 up and doing; 2, 4 at work; 2, 6 in action; 2, 7 in harness; 2, 9 in operation; 3, 5 the stage; 3, 7 the theater; 4, 7 star quality; 5-2 stand-in; 5, 5 stage fever; 5, 6 stage fright; 5, 7 stage whisper; 5, 8 stage business, stage presence; 10, 4 performing arts.

actinomycosis 5, 3 lumpy jaw.

action 4 case, deed, feat, move, play, raid, suit, work; 5 drama, force, group, labor, power, steps, swing; 6 agency, battle, combat, motion, policy, praxis, replay, stroke; 7 attempt, lawsuit, process, program, routine, warfare; 8 behavior, campaign, conflict, dogfight, endeavor, fighting, measures, movement, painting, skirmish, stations; 9 committee, direction, enactment, encounter, influence, militancy, operation, potential, procedure; 10 commission, engagement; 11 achievement, performance, proceedings, transaction; 14 accomplishment, administration, implementation; PHRASES: 5, 10 legal proceeding.

action (take action) 3 man, use; 4 crew, move; 5 cause, drive, power, treat, wield; 6 employ, handle, manage; 7 execute, process, procure, service, support, sustain; **8** maintain, maneuver; **9** implement; **10** manipulate; PHRASES: **3, 2** get to; **3, 4** act upon, get done; **4, 4** bear upon, deal with, make with, play upon, work upon UK.

activate 4 boot; **5** cause, start; **6** launch, prompt; **7** actuate, provoke, trigger; **8** generate, initiate, motivate; **9** galvanize, influence, stimulate; PHRASES: **3, 2** rev up; **3, 2, 6** set in motion; **3, 3** set off; **4, 2** plug in, turn on, wind up; **4, 4** make work; **4-5** kick-start; **4, 6** make active, make happen; **5, 2** start up; **5, 3** spark off; **5, 3, 4** light the fuse; **5, 3, 5** apply the match; **5, 3, 6** press the button; **5, 4, 4** bring into play; **5, 4, 5** bring into force; **5, 4, 6** bring into action, bring into effect; **5, 5** start going; **6, 2** switch on; **7, 3** trigger off.

active 4 able, fast, gleg, keen, list, live, spry; **5** agile, alert, alive, awake, brisk, eager, fussy, going, nippy, quick, ready, smart; **6** ardent, engagé, fierce, frisky, lively, moving, nimble, prompt, speedy, strong; **7** coltish, dynamic, engagée UK, fervent, nervous, running, service, volcano, wakeful, warlike, willing, working, zealous; **8** agitated, animated, forceful, frenetic, frenzied, involved, militant, resolute, restless, vigilant, vigorous, watchful; **9** activated, committed, effective, energetic, excitable, incessant, operative, sprightly, strenuous, unceasing; **10** functional, practicing, vocabulary; **11** expeditious, functioning, hyperactive, interactive, operational, overwrought; PHRASES: **2, 3, 2** on the go; **2, 3, 5** on the alert; **2-3-6** up-and-coming; **2, 4, 4** on one's toes; **2, 5** in force; **2, 6** in action; **2-7** go-getting; **4-6** able-bodied.

active (be active) 2 do; **3** act, fly, run; **4** blow, dash, flow, fume, fuss, move, race, rage, rise, roar, rush, stir; **5** burst, hurry, spurt, surge; **6** bother, bustle, hasten, hustle, scurry; **7** agitate, bluster, explode, rampage; **8** scramble, squabble; PHRASES: **2, 2, 3, 5** be up and doing; **3, 2** get up; **3, 4** run riot; **4, 2** wake up; **4, 3, 2** come and go; **4, 3, 5** rise and shine; **4, 4** move fast.

activism 8 sedition, uprising; **9** crusading, militancy; **10** engagement; **11** involvement, politicking; PHRASES: **2-7** do-gooding; **4, 8** mass movement; **6, 6** direct action, social action; **7, 8** popular movement; **9, 6** political action.

activist 5 agent; **7** realist; **8** achiever, advocate, lobbyist, militant, objector; **9** formalist, motivator, protester; **10** campaigner, naturalist; **13** expressionist; **14** constructivist.

activity 4 stir, work; **5** hobby, whirl; **6** action, bustle, career, flurry, tumult, vortex; **7** pastime, pursuit, turmoil; **8** business, endeavor, interest, movement; **9** agitation, commotion, maelstrom; **10** excitation, occupation, recreation; **11** disturbance, stimulation; PHRASES: **2-2** to-do; **4, 3** much ado; **5, 6** great doings; **6-2** goings-on; **7, 7** leisure pursuit; **7, 8** leisure interest.

actor 3 ham; **4** diva, icon, idol, lead, star; **5** extra, lovie; **6** artist, luvvie UK, mummer, player; **7** actress, artiste, darling, farceur, Roscius, speaker, standby, starlet, support, trouper; **8** comedian, narrator, prologue, thespian; **9** performer, presenter UK, superstar, tragedian; **10** comedienne, improviser, understudy; **11** barnstormer, pantomimist, tragedienne; **13** supernumerary; PHRASES: **4, 4** film star UK; **4-5** look-alike; **4, 6** body double; **5-2** stand-in; **5, 4** movie star; **5, 5** prima donna; **5, 7** jeune premier; **5-7** actor-manager, spear-carrier; **5, 9** stage performer; **7, 3** leading man; **7, 4** leading lady, matinée idol; **9, 5** character ~; **10, 5** supporting ~.

actress *See* **actor**

actual *See* **real**

actuality 4 fact; **5** truth; **7** reality; **9** certainty, existence; **10** factuality; **11** historicity; **12** authenticity, practicality; PHRASES: **3, 4, 5** the real thing, the real world; **4, 3, 3** here and now; **4, 4** real fact, real life; **6, 4** actual fact.

acumen 6 wisdom; **7** insight; **8** judgment; **10** shrewdness; **11** penetration.

acupressure 7 shiatsu.

acupuncture 11 stylostixis.

acute 4 deep, keen; **5** eager, sharp; **7** extreme, fervent, intense; **8** distinct; **10** compelling, compulsive.

AD 13 advertisement; PHRASES: **4, 2, 3, 4** year of our Lord (Latin: anno Domini).

adamant 8 obdurate; **9** obstinate, unbending; **10** inflexible, unyielding.

adapt 3 fit; **4** bend, vary; **5** alter, amend, score; **6** adjust, change, modify, revise, rework; **7** arrange, compose, fashion, qualify; **8** moderate; **9** acclimate; **11** acclimatize, choreograph, familiarize, orchestrate;

PHRASES: 3, 1, 4, 3 get a feel for; **3, 4, 2** get used to; **4, 4, 4** find your feet; **6, 2** settle in.

adaptable **6** pliant; **7** passive, willing; **8** flexible, obedient, yielding; **9** compliant, malleable, resilient; **10** responsive, submissive; **11** complaisant; **13** accommodating.

add **3** sum, tot; **5** affix, annex, carry, count, raise, swell, tally, times, total, unite; **6** accrue, adjoin, append, attach, borrow, burden, expand, extend, flavor, impose, insert, prefix, season, suffix; **7** accrete, augment, combine, compute, conjoin, engraft, enhance, enlarge, garnish, improve, include, overlay, plaster, preface, subjoin; **8** decorate, increase, multiply, ornament, totalize; **9** aggregate, calculate, embellish, factorize, integrate, intensify, interject, interpose, introduce; **10** complement, supplement; **11** agglutinate, interpolate, superimpose; **PHRASES: 3, 2** lay on, let in, mix in, pin to, put in, sum up, tag on, tot up; **3, 4** mix with; **4, 2** heap on, pile on *UK*, tack on, take in, tote up; **4, 3, 8** one's two penn'orth.

addendum *See* **addition**

adder's-tongue **8, 6** dogtooth violet.

addicted **6** hooked; **9** obsessive; **PHRASES: 4-9** drug-dependent.

addictive **8** clinging, haunting, narcotic; **9** besetting; **11** psychedelic; **14** hallucinogenic; **PHRASES: 4-7** mind-blowing; **5-7** habit-forming.

addition **2** PS *UK*; **3** sum; **4** coda, load, toll; **5** count, extra, tally, total; **6** addend, augend, burden, insert; **7** accrual, adjunct, codicil; **8** addendum, additive, appanage, appendix, increase, postlude, tallying, totaling; **9** accession, accessory, accretion, admixture, affixture, afterword, aggregate, appendage, extension, inclusion, increment, insertion, prefixion, subscript, suffixion, summation, surcharge; **10** annexation, attachment, complement, imposition, postscript, supplement; **11** calculation, computation, enlargement, subjunction, suffixation; **12** accumulation, augmentation, continuation, interjection, postposition, prolongation, supervention; **13** agglutination, interposition, reinforcement, superaddition, superposition; **15** superimposition, supplementation; **PHRASES: 3-2** add-on; **5, 4** extra load; **6, 2** adding up; **6, 8** adding together; **7, 2** totting up *UK*.

additional **4** more; **5** added, bonus, extra, other; **6** annexd; **7** adjunct, another, further,

surplus; **8** additive, adjoined, attached, included, inserted, prefixed; **9** accretive, auxiliary, subjoined; **10** adjunctive, collateral, subsidiary; **11** conjunctive, superfluous; **12** accretionary, adscititious, adventitious, interpolated, supplemental; **13** agglutinative, complementary, supplementary; **PHRASES: 3, 7** yet another.

additional item **2** PS *UK*; **3** ell, PPS, tab, tag; **4** coda, flap, tail, wing; **5** affix, annex, envoy, frill, infix, lapel, patch, rider, sauce; **6** adverb, border, edging, ending, finish, fringe, lappet, lining, prefix, suffix, ticket; **7** adjunct, codicil, garnish, padding; **8** addendum, addition, additive, appendix, dressing, epilogue, footnote, leftover, outhouse, stuffing; **9** adjective, component, corollary, flavoring, interlude, seasoning, tailpiece, trappings, trimmings; **10** additament, annotation, attachment, conclusion, decoration, garnishing, inflection, ingredient, intermezzo, marginalia, postscript; **11** aftereffect, furnishings; **12** contribution; **13** accouterments, interpolation, ornamentation, reinforcement; **14** interlineation; **PHRASES: 3-2** add-on; **3, 3, 9** all the trimmings; **3, 5** the works; **3, 7** the fixings; **4, 5** side issue; **4, 6** side effect; **5, 2, 3, 4** icing on the cake; **5-4** carry-over; **8, 4** marginal note; **9, 5** finishing touch; **10, 4** additional part.

additionally **3** and, too; **4** also, else, more, plus; **5** extra; **6** beside; **7** besides, despite, further, jointly; **8** moreover; **9** including; **11** furthermore; **12** cumulatively; **PHRASES: 2, 1, 3** as a tip; **2, 1, 9** as a lagniappe; **2, 3** on top; **2, 3, 4** on the side; **2, 3, 4, 4** at the same time; **2, 4** as well, to boot; **2, 6** et cetera; **2, 8** in addition; **3, 2, 2** and so on; **3, 2, 5** and so forth; **3, 2, 7** not to mention; **3, 3, 4** for all that; **3, 5** let alone; **3, 10** not forgetting; **4, 3, 5** over and above; **4, 3, 7** into the bargain; **4, 4** even with; **4, 5, 2** with knobs on; **4, 8** with interest; **9, 2** inclusive of. *See also* **additional**

address **4** home, talk; **6** direct, earful, homily, report, screed, sermon, speech, tackle, tirade; **7** declaim, deliver, forward, lecture, oration, reading, recital; **8** diatribe, dispatch, domicile, harangue, jeremiad, location, mouthful, perorate; **9** discourse, invective, philippic, residence, sermonize, speechify, statement; **10** allocution, apostrophe, recitation; **11** declamation, pontificate, rodomontade; **12** apostrophize, disquisition, presentation; **PHRASES: 3-5** tubthump; **4, 1, 4** give a talk; **4, 1, 6** make a speech; **4, 1, 7** give a lecture; **4, 2** talk to; **4, 2, 4** take in hand; **4, 3, 5** take the floor; **4, 4** deal with; **4, 5** hold forth; **5, 2** speak to; **6, 2** preach at; **6, 6** formal speech, public speech; **8, 6** prepared speech.

address oneself to 9 undertake; PHRASES: **2, 2, 3** go in for; **4, 2** take up; **5, 7, 2** apply oneself to; **6, 2** engage in; **6, 7, 2** devote oneself to.

adept *See* **skillful**

adequate 3 apt, fit; **4** able; **5** ample; **6** enough, plenty; **7** capable; **8** passable, suitable; **9** competent, tolerable; **10** acceptable, sufficient; **11** appropriate; **12** satisfactory; PHRASES: **2, 2, 3, 4** up to the mark.

adhere 3 fit, hug; **4** grip, hold, obey, stay; **5** clasp, cling, grasp, stick; **6** clinch, cohere, follow, freeze, remain; **7** embrace, observe, squeeze; **8** condense, solidify; **9** coagulate; PHRASES: **4, 2** hold on, keep to; **4, 4** hold fast; **4, 4, 2** take hold of; **4, 8** hang together, hold together; **5, 2** abide by, stand by; **5, 4** stick onto; **5, 4, 4** stick like glue; **5, 5** close ranks, stick close; **5, 6** twine around; **6, 2** cleave to; **6, 4** freeze onto.

adherent 4 buff; **6** member, shadow, zealot; **7** devotee, fanatic, servant; **8** believer, follower, parasite, retainer; **9** appendage, dependent, satellite, supporter; **10** aficionada, aficionado, enthusiast; PHRASES: **6-2** hanger-on; **6, 5** sticky label; **7, 3** chewing gum.

adhesion 4 grip, hold; **5** union, unity; **7** bonding, linkage, welding; **8** cohesion, sticking; **9** coherence, soldering; **10** attachment, connection, continuity, stickiness; **11** cementation, congealment; **12** adhesiveness, cohesiveness; **13** agglomeration, agglutination, concentration, connectedness, consolidation; **14** conglomeration, indivisibility, inseparability; PHRASES: **7, 8** holding together; **8, 5** sticking power.

adhesive 3 gum, tar, wax; **4** clay, glue, lime, lute, size; **5** close, dense, gluey, gummy, paste, putty, resin, solid, tacky; **6** bonded, cement, chicle, gluten, mastic, mortar, solder, sticky, viscid; **7** sessile, viscous; **8** birdlime, clinging, coherent, cohesive, concrete, fixative, flypaper; **9** colloidal, Sellotape™, skintight, superglue; PHRASES: **4-2-4** side-by-side; **4, 3** guar gum; **4-3** Band-Aid; **4, 4** fish glue; **5, 5** epoxy resin; **5-6** close-packed; **5-7** close-fitting; **6, 4** Scotch tape, sticky tape; **6-7** figure-hugging *UK*; **7, 3** sealing wax; **7, 4** masking tape; **8, 4** ~ tape; **8, 7** sticking plaster *UK*.

adipocere 5-3 grave-wax.

adjacent 4 near, next; **5** close; **6** joined, nearby; **7** liminal, meeting; **8** abutting, flanking, touching; **9** adjoining, bordering; **10** connecting, contiguous, continuous, juxtaposed, tangential; **11** coterminous, interactive, interfacial, neighboring; **12** conterminous; PHRASES: **3-2-3** end-to-end; **4-2-4** face-to-face, nose-to-nose, nose-to-tail, side-by-side; **4, 4** next door; **5-2-4** cheek-by-jowl; **5-2-5** elbow-to-elbow; **6-2-6** bumper-to-bumper.

adjoining *See* **adjacent**

adjourn 3 end; **4** stop; **5** defer, delay; **6** finish; **7** suspend; **8** postpone; PHRASES: **5, 3** break off.

adjudicator *See* **judge**

adjunct 4 aide; **8** addition; **9** assistant, secretary; **10** attachment; PHRASES: **3-2** add-on; **4-2-4** aide-de-camp. *See also* **part of speech**

adjust 4 bend, vary; **5** adapt, alter, amend, tweak; **6** attune, change, modify; **7** correct; **8** regulate; PHRASES: **4-4** fine-tune; **6, 4** fiddle with.

adjutant *See* **assistant**

administer 4 rule; **5** apply; **6** anoint, govern, infuse, ingest, inhale, inject, insert; **7** implant, instill, perfuse, swallow; **8** organize; **9** inoculate; PHRASES: **4, 2** take in.

administration 5 admin, board, staff; **6** bosses, quango *UK*; **7** cabinet, council; **9** committee, employers, executive, paperwork; **10** government, management, presidency; **11** directorate, supervision; **12** dispensation, organization; PHRASES: **6, 3** doling out, giving out, meting out; **7, 3** dealing out, handing out.

administrator 7 manager, officer; **8** director, governor, overseer; **10** bureaucrat, proprietor, supervisor; **12** commissioner.

admirable 4 good; **6** worthy; **8** laudable, splendid; **9** deserving, estimable, excellent, marvelous, venerable; **10** creditable, worthwhile; **11** commendable, meritorious; **12** praiseworthy.

admiral 3 red; **4** rear, vice; **5** fleet, white.

admiration 3 awe; **4** love; **5** favor, honor; **6** credit, esteem, fealty, homage, liking, regard, wonder; **7** respect, worship; **8** approval, prestige; **9** adoration, adulation, affection, gratitude, obeisance, reverence; **10** popularity, veneration; **11** approbation, idolization, recognition; **12** appreciation; **14** acknowledgment; PHRASES: **4, 6** high regard; **4, 7** good opinion, hero worship.

admired 6 prized; **7** popular, revered; **8** esteemed; **9** respected, venerated; **11** appreciated; PHRASES: **2, 4, 4** in good odor; **2, 4, 6** in high esteem; **2, 6** in demand; **4-5** well-liked; **4, 7, 2** well thought of; **4-8** well-regarded.

admirer 3 fan; **5** lover; **6** rooter; **7** devotee, fanatic, groupie; **8** follower; **9** supporter; **10** aficionada, aficionado, enthusiast; PHRASES: **3, 4** fan club; **4-9** hero-worshiper; **10, 4** supporters' club.

admiringly 7 eagerly, readily; **8** lovingly; **9** favorably, longingly, willingly; **10** desirously, yearningly; **11** approvingly; **12** passionately; **14** empathetically; **15** sympathetically; PHRASES: **4, 4** with love.

admission 3 fee; **4** pass, visa; **5** entry, price; **6** access, avowal, charge, permit, ticket; **8** entrance, passport; **9** statement; **10** admittance, confession, deposition, disclosure, permission, profession; **11** declaration, immigration, importation; **14** acknowledgment; PHRASES: **4-4, 6** open-door policy; **5, 2, 5** right of entry; **5, 3** entry fee; **6, 5** ticket price; **8, 3** entrance fee.

admit 3 own; **4** avow; **5** allow, grant, state; **6** affirm, assent, avouch, depose, import, insert, permit; **7** concede, confess, declare, include, receive, welcome; **11** acknowledge; PHRASES: **3, 2** let in, own up; **3, 4** let pass; **4, 2** take in; **4, 3, 4, 2** open the door to; **4, 3, 7** open the hatches; **4, 4, 5, 2** open one's heart to; **4, 5** come clean; **4, 6** give access; **5, 2** allow in, bring in; **5, 6** allow access, plead guilty.

admittance 5 entry; **6** access, import; **8** entrance; **9** admission; **11** importation; PHRASES: **5, 2, 5** right of entry; **6, 2** taking in.

admixture 3 dye, hue; **4** blot, dash; **5** color, pinch, smack, stain, tinge, touch; **6** flavor, strain, streak; **7** element, modicum, smidgen, soupçon; **8** infusion, tincture; **10** ingredient, sprinkling.

admonition 6 rebuke; **7** caution, warning; **8** reproach; **9** reprimand.

adolescent *See* **juvenile**

adopt 5 agree; **6** accept, assume; **7** approve, embrace, espouse; **9** implement; **11** appropriate; PHRASES: **3, 2, 4, 3** use as one's own; **4, 2** take on, take up; **5, 7, 2** avail oneself of.

adoptive 4 step; **5** legal; **7** adopted; **8** adopting; **9** adoptable; **12** appropriable, appropriated; **13** appropriating.

adoration 6 esteem; **7** respect, worship; **9** adulation, reverence; **10** admiration; **11** idolization; **13** glorification; PHRASES: **4, 6** high regard.

adore 4 love; **5** enjoy; **6** admire, esteem, revere; **7** adulate, glorify, idolize, respect, worship.

adorn 4 gild; **7** enhance, garnish; **8** beautify, decorate, ornament, prettify, titivate; **9** embellish.

adornment 8 ornament, richness, trimming; **10** decoration, enrichment, ornateness, titivation; **11** enhancement; **13** embellishment, ornamentation; **14** beautification, prettification.

adrenaline 11 epinephrine.

Adrianople 6 Edirne.

adrift 4 free, lost; **5** loose; **7** aimless; **8** drifting, floating; **9** wandering; **11** purposeless; **13** directionless; PHRASES: **2, 5** in limbo; **2, 5, 4** at loose ends.

adroit *See* **skillful**

adult 4 ripe; **5** elder; **6** mature, senior; **9** developed; **11** experienced; PHRASES: **2, 4, 5** in full bloom, in one's prime; **4-5** full-grown; **5-2** grown-up.

adultery 5 amour; **6** affair; **7** liaison; **8** cheating, intrigue; **10** cuckolding, infidelity; **11** concubinage; **14** unfaithfulness; PHRASES: **3-6** two-timing.

adulthood 7 manhood, oldness; **8** majority, maturity, ripeness; **9** seniority, womanhood; **10** maturation; PHRASES: **3, 3** old age; **5, 2, 4** prime of life; **5, 4** later life; **6, 3** middle age.

advance 3 fee; **4** copy, gain, lift, loan, poll, rise; **5** ahead, guard, sally; **6** ascent, expand, notice, spread; **7** booking, enhance, further, improve, proceed, success; **8** increase, progress; **9** elevation, expansion, promotion; **10** enterprise, furthering, innovation, preferment, prosperity; **11** achievement, advancement, development, enhancement, furtherance, improvement;

12 encroachment; PHRASES: **2, 5** go ahead; **2, 7** go forward *UK*; **3-2** leg-up; **4, 2** move on; **4, 5** move ahead; **4, 7** down payment, move forward, take forward; **5, 2** build up, press on; **5, 2, 5** money up front; **5, 7** early payment, press forward; **6, 6** ground gained.

advantage 3 pro; **4** boon, edge, gain, help, lead, odds, plus; **5** favor, start; **6** points; **7** benefit, vantage; **8** handicap; **11** improvement; PHRASES: **3, 2, 3, 4** ace in the hole; **3-9** one-upmanship; **4, 4** whip hand; **4, 5** head start; **4, 8** pole position; **5, 2, 7** coign of vantage; **5, 4** trump hand, upper hand; **6, 5** flying start, inside track; **6, 8** seeded position; **7, 5** vantage point; **7, 6** vantage ground *UK*.

advantage (have an advantage) 6 outwit; **8** outshine, outstrip, outthink; **11** outmaneuver.

advent 4 dawn; **5** start; **7** arrival; **9** beginning; PHRASES: **6, 2** coming on.

adventurer 7 pioneer, voyager; **8** explorer, investor, traveler; **9** buccaneer, innovator; **10** speculator; **11** opportunist, trailblazer; **12** entrepreneur, swashbuckler; PHRASES: **7, 6** fortune hunter.

adventurous 4 bold, game, rash; **5** brave; **6** daring; **8** carefree, gambling; **9** audacious, foolhardy; **10** courageous; **11** venturesome; **13** adventuresome; PHRASES: **4-6** risk-taking; **6-6** danger-loving; **6-7** thrill-seeking.

adversary *See* **opponent**

adverse 3 bad, ill; **4** cold, dire, hard, poor; **5** bleak; **6** doomed, gloomy, tragic, unwell; **7** harmful, hostile, ominous, opposed, ruinous; **8** contrary, dreadful, opposing, sinister; **9** declining, difficult, miserable, unhelpful; **10** disastrous, unpleasant; **11** conflicting, destructive, detrimental, troublesome, undesirable, unfavorable; **12** antagonistic, inauspicious, oppositional, unpropitious, unsuccessful; **13** unsympathetic; **15** disadvantageous; PHRASES: **2, 1, 3, 3** in a bad way; **2, 4, 4, 4** on one's last legs; **2, 4, 5** in poor shape; **2, 4, 6** in poor health; **2, 7** in trouble; **2, 7, 2** up against it; **2, 10** in opposition; **2, 12** in difficulties; **3, 5, 4** not doing well.

adversity 4 bane, evil, pain, ruin; **5** cares, curse, death, worry; **6** blight, burden, cancer, danger, defeat, downer, injury, misery, mishap, plague, plight, rebuff, sorrow, threat, trials; **7** decline, illness, retreat, sadness, scourge, setback, travail, worries; **8** accident, calamity, casualty, comedown, disaster, distress, downfall, hardship, pressure, struggle, troubles; **9** bleakness, dejection, emergency, suffering; **10** affliction, desolation, difficulty, misfortune, opposition, visitation; **11** catastrophe, despondency, destitution, humiliation, predicament; **12** homelessness, misadventure, wretchedness; **13** deterioration; PHRASES: **3, 2, 7** cup of sorrows; **3, 4** bad news, ill wind, raw deal, the pits; **3, 5** the worst; **4, 3** lost war; **4, 4** cold wind; **4, 6** dark clouds, lost battle, poor health; **5, 2, 4** cross to bear; **5, 3, 4** gloom and doom; **5, 6** storm clouds; **5, 10** harsh conditions; **6, 3** bitter cup; **6, 4** bitter pill, living hell; **7, 5** trouble ahead; **7, 8** natural disaster; **8, 7** terminal illness; **10, 4** unrequited love.

adversity (cause adversity) 3 hex; **4** jinx, sink; **6** burden, defeat, injure, voodoo; **7** oppress, trouble; **8** overload; **9** humiliate; **10** overburden; PHRASES: **4, 3** make ill; **5, 2, 8** cause an accident; **5, 4** weigh down; **5, 7** cause trouble; **6, 8** create problems.

adversity (in adversity) 5 sadly; **6** poorly; **7** bleakly; **9** adversely, harmfully, miserably, unhappily, unluckily; **10** contrarily, dreadfully, grievously, tragically; **11** unfavorably; **12** accidentally, disastrously; **13** detrimentally, unfortunately; **14** inauspiciously, unpropitiously, unsuccessfully; PHRASES: **2, 8** by accident; **2, 12** by misadventure; **4, 3, 2, 5** from bad to worse.

adversity (person in adversity) 4 dupe, prey; **5** loser, tramp; **6** martyr, victim; **8** bankrupt, sufferer, underdog, weakling; **9** destitute, scapegoat; **11** unfortunate; PHRASES: **2-5** no-hoper; **3, 4** bag lady, sad sack; **4-3-3** down-and-out; **4, 4** lame duck, poor risk; **4, 5** born loser; **4, 6** poor person, poor wretch; **6, 2, 4** victim of fate; **8, 6** homeless person.

adversity (time of adversity) 6 winter; PHRASES: **3, 5** bad patch, bad spell, bad times; **4, 5** hard times; **4, 6** lean period; **5, 3** rainy day; **5, 5** rough patch.

advertisement 2 ad; **4** bill, blad, plug; **5** blurb, flier, flyer; **6** advert *UK*, banner, insert, notice, poster, teaser; **7** affiche, leaflet, placard, preview, trailer; **8** brochure, circular, handbill, hoarding *UK*, pamphlet, personal; **9** billboard, insertion; **10**

commercial; **11** advertorial; **12** announcement; PHRASES: **4, 2** want ad; **4, 3** puff job; **4-3** hand-out; **4, 5** puff piece; **5, 2** small ad; **6, 5** notice board *UK*, Yellow Pages *UK*; **7, 5** display board; **8, 5** sandwich board; **10, 2** classified ad.

advertising 2 PR *UK*; **4** hype; **6** mailer; **7** billing; **8** ballyhoo, flackery; **9** marketing, promotion, publicity; **11** publicizing; **13** advertisement; PHRASES: **4, 4** hard sell, soft sell; **5, 9** sales promotion; **6, 4** direct mail; **6, 9** public relations; **7, 6** Madison Avenue.

advice 3 aid, nod, tip; **4** hint, rede; **5** aside; **6** wisdom; **7** caution, counsel, opinion, pointer, precept, therapy, warning; **8** advising, briefing, guidance; **9** direction; **10** admonition, assistance, guidelines, indication, intimation, moralizing, submission, suggestion; **12** intelligence, notification, prescription; **13** communication, encouragement; **14** recommendation; PHRASES: **3-3** tip-off; **4, 2, 3, 3** word in the ear; **4, 2, 3, 4** word to the wise; **4, 2, 5** word of mouth; **5, 2, 6** words of wisdom; **5, 10** moral injunction; **6, 2, 6** pearls of wisdom; **7, 4** passing word.

advisable 4 wise; **7** logical, politic, prudent; **8** sensible, suitable; **9** desirable, expedient, judicious, practical, sagacious; **10** worthwhile; **11** recommended; **13** recommendable.

advise 4 help, tell, urge, warn; **5** brief, guide, opine, press, teach; **6** charge, direct, enjoin, exhort, inform, notify, prompt; **7** apprise, caution, command, commend, counsel, propose, suggest, support; **8** advocate, champion, propound; **9** encourage, patronize, prescribe, recommend; **11** countenance; PHRASES: **3, 2** put to; **3, 4** let know; **4, 2, 4** take in hand; **4, 5** make aware; **5, 3** argue for, plump for; **5, 4** think best; **5, 6** offer advice; **5, 7** offer counsel.

adviser 4 aide, guru, sage; **5** guide, judge, tutor; **6** critic, Egeria, expert, friend, helper, lawyer, mentor, Nestor, oracle, pastor, priest; **7** analyst, arbiter, padrino, referee, teacher; **8** advocate, attorney, busybody, cicerone, minister, prompter, reminder; **9** barrister *UK Can*, cornerman, counselor, estimator, motivator, ombudsman, solicitor; **10** arbitrator, confidante, consultant, prescriber; **11** recommender; **14** troubleshooter; **15** psychotherapist; PHRASES: **4, 3** wise man; **4-4, 6** back-seat driver; **4, 6** best

friend; **5, 5** Dutch uncle; **5, 7** legal counsel; **6-5** advice-giver; **6, 6** social worker; **6, 7** public inquiry; **6, 9** select committee; **7, 7** student council; **9, 6** intrusive person.

advising 7 warning; **8** advisory, didactic, monitory; **9** hortative, hortatory; **10** admonitory, cautionary, counseling, dissuasive, moralizing, persuasive; **11** encouraging, informative, instructive; **12** consultative, deliberative, prescriptive; **14** recommendatory.

advocate 4 back, lord, urge; **5** judge; **6** backer, devil's, lawyer, patron, preach; **7** promote, sponsor, support; **8** activist, attorney, believer, champion, exponent, promoter; **9** encourage, proponent, recommend, supporter; **10** campaigner; **11** recommender; PHRASES: **2, 2, 5, 2** be in favor of; **9, 6** favorable critic.

aeolian 4 harp, mode; **8** deposits.

Aeolian Islands 6, 7 Lipari Islands.

aerate 4 beat, whip; **5** spray, whisk; **6** aerify, expose; **7** atomize, freshen, perfume; **8** etherize, fluidize, fumigate; **9** carbonate, deodorize, oxygenate, ventilate; **11** hydrogenate; PHRASES: **3-4** air-cool; **3, 7** let breathe; **3-9** air-condition.

aeration 5 yeast; **6** airing, leaven; **7** ferment; **9** leavening; **10** freshening; **11** ventilation; **12** fermentation; PHRASES: **7, 5** raising agent.

aerial 6 midair; **7** antenna, buoyant; **8** airborne, floating, inflated; **9** flatulent, pneumatic; PHRASES: **2-6** in-flight; **5-2** blown-up; **5, 6** above ground.

aerogastria 3, 8 gas gangrene.

aeronautical 7 avionic; **9** aerobatic; **11** aerodynamic.

aeronautics 8 avionics; **10** aerobatics; **14** aeroballistics, bioaeronautics; PHRASES: **4-6** aero-optics; **8, 6** aircraft design.

aesthetic 6 visual; **8** artistic; **9** appealing, beautiful.

AF 3, 5 air force.

affable *See* **genial**

affair 5 issue; **6** matter; **7** concern; **8** business; **9** situation.

affect 3 act; **4** fake; **5** adopt, alter, shape, touch, upset; **6** assume, change, grieve, impact, modify, soften; **7** concern, disturb, imitate, involve, pretend; **8** distress; **9** influence; PHRASES: **3, 2** end in, put on; **6, 2**

result in.

affectation 4 airs; 5 habit, quirk, trait; 7 bombast, fustian; 8 artifice, boasting; 9 eloquence, hyperbole, loftiness, mannerism, pomposity, showiness, turgidity; 10 flatulence, Johnsonese, orotundity, pretension; 11 convolution, diffuseness, ostentation, rodomontade; 12 affectedness, exaggeration, extravagance; 13 artificiality, overstatement; 14 characteristic, circumlocution; 15 pretentiousness; PHRASES: 4, 4 high tone; 5, 4 empty talk, false show; 5, 5 false front; 7, 2, 4 putting on airs; 7, 3 showing off.

affected 4 posh *UK*; 5 moved, puffy, showy; 6 chichi, ironic, mouthy, stagey, swanky; 7 changed, stilted, touched; 8 boastful, ironical, mannered, precious, specious; 9 conceited, unnatural; 10 artificial, histrionic, theatrical; 11 euphemistic, exaggerated, pretentious; 12 meretricious; 13 sanctimonious; PHRASES: 2-2-2 la-di-da; 3, 4, 3, 4 all piss and wind; 3, 4, 3, 5 all wind and water; 4-5 high-flown; 4-9 self-conscious; 6, 2 puffed up; 6-2-5 tongue-in-cheek.

affection 3 PDA; 4 love; 6 liking, regard; 8 fondness; 10 attachment, friendship, tenderness; 11 amorousness.

affectionate 4 fond, kind, warm; 6 caring, loving, wooing; 7 amorous; 8 courting, familiar, fondling, friendly, spooning; 9 caressing; 10 coquettish; 11 flirtatious, sentimental; 13 demonstrative; PHRASES: 5-5 lovey-dovey.

affiliate 4 join, link; 6 member; 7 connect, partner; 9 associate, colleague.

affiliation *See* **association**

affinity 7 empathy, kinship; 8 likeness, sympathy; 10 attraction, similarity; 11 resemblance; 14 correspondence; PHRASES: 6, 7 fellow feeling *UK*.

affirm 3 say; 4 aver, avow; 5 speak, state, swear, utter, vouch; 6 assert, attest, submit, uphold; 7 confirm, declare, profess; 8 announce, proclaim; 9 enunciate, establish, pronounce; 10 asseverate; PHRASES: 3, 4 set down; 3, 7 put forward; 4, 1, 9 make a statement; 4, 2, 1, 5 live by a creed; 4, 3, 4 give the word; 4, 4, 3 have one's say; 4, 5, 2 give voice to; 5, 1, 9 issue a manifesto; 7, 1, 5 release a paper.

affirmation 6 avowal; 8 averment; 9 assertion, statement; 11 attestation, declaration; 12 asseveration.

affirmative 8 agreeing, positive; 9 affirming, assenting, assertive, favorable; 10 conclusive, supportive, validatory; 11 affirmatory, declarative, declaratory, enunciatory, predicative; 12 annunciatory, confirmatory, proclamatory.

affirmatively 10 absolutely, definitely; 11 undoubtedly; 12 emphatically, indisputably; 13 categorically, unequivocally; 14 unquestionably; PHRASES: 4, 8 with emphasis. *See also* **affirmative**

affirmer 4 ally; 5 vower; 7 assurer, pledger, sponsor, swearer, witness; 8 advocate, asserter, champion, declarer, endorser, promoter, ratifier, seconder, verifier; 9 announcer, attestant, certifier, discloser, guarantor, professor, supporter, testifier; 10 eyewitness, proclaimer; 12 corroborator; 13 authenticator; PHRASES: 4-5 oath-taker; 5, 2, 8 tower of strength.

afflict 3 mar, vex; 4 harm; 5 blast, decay, upset, worry; 6 affect, blight, bother, burden, infest, plague, wither; 7 shrivel, torment, trouble; 8 distress; PHRASES: 6, 4 strike down.

afflicted 3 ill, sad; 4 hurt, sick, sore; 6 struck; 7 injured, plagued, wounded, wracked; 8 affected, stricken, troubled; 9 aggrieved, depressed, disturbed, miserable, sorrowful, suffering, tormented; 10 distressed; 11 traumatized; PHRASES: 4, 3 laid low; 5-8 grief-stricken.

affliction 3 woe; 4 harm, hurt, loss, pain, pest, ruin, sore; 5 abuse, angst, death, grief, trial, wound; 6 blight, burden, damage, injury, malady, misery, plague, sorrow; 7 disease, illness, malaise, problem, scourge, tragedy, trouble; 8 accident, calamity, casualty, disaster, distress, fatality, hardship, sickness, weakness; 9 adversity, annoyance, complaint, infirmity, malignity, suffering; 10 depression, difficulty, discomfort, imposition, malignancy, misfortune, pestilence, visitation; 11 catastrophe, destruction, harmfulness, hurtfulness, infestation, painfulness; PHRASES: 4, 3 hard row; 6, 4 bitter pill, mortal blow; 6, 7 mental illness; 7, 4 running sore.

affluence *See* **prosperity**

afford 4 give; 5 allow, offer; 7 present, provide; PHRASES: 3, 3 pay for.

affront 4 slur; 5 upset; 6 injury, insult, offend, slight; **7** outrage.

afraid (be afraid) *See* **dread**

African 4 lily; **6** violet; **8** mahogany.

African lily 10 agapanthus.

African violet 11 saintpaulia.

Afrikaans 4, 5 Cape Dutch.

after 4 like; **5** later; **6** behind; **9** afterward, following, hereafter, regarding; **10** henceforth, subsequent; **11** hereinafter; **12** henceforward, subsequently; PHRASES: **1, 2** à la; **2, 3, 4, 2** to the rear of; **2, 3, 4, 3, 2** in the same way as; **2, 3, 5, 2** in the style of, on the heels of, on the trail of; **2, 3, 6, 2** in the manner of; **2, 4, 2** as soon as; **2, 5, 2** in quest of; **2, 6, 2** in search of; **2, 7, 2** in pursuit of; **2, 9, 2** in imitation of; **4, 2** next to; **4, 3, 2** from now on; **5, 4** later than; **7, 2, 4** bearing in mind.

afterlife 3 Dis; **4** hell, Styx; **5** Hades, Sheol; **6** heaven; **8** paradise; **9** hereafter; **10** afterworld, underworld; PHRASES: **4, 5** next world; **4, 5, 5** life after death; **6, 5** spirit world; **7, 4** eternal life; **7, 5** Stygian shore; **7, 6** Elysian fields; **8, 5** Abraham's bosom.

aftermath 6 legacy, result, upshot; **7** fallout, outcome, spinoff; **8** hangover; **9** byproduct *UK*; **10** aftershock, aftertaste; **11** aftereffect; **12** consequences *UK*, repercussion.

afternoon 2 PM, p.m.; **3** tea; **6** siesta; **7** matinée; **12** postmeridian; PHRASES: **3-4** pipemma *UK*; **5, 7** early evening.

afterthought 2 PS *UK*; **5** extra; **8** addendum, addition, epilogue; **10** postscript; **15** reconsideration; PHRASES: **6, 7** second thought.

AG 6 silver.

again 3 bis; **4** anew; **5** ditto; **6** afresh, encore; PHRASES: **2, 4** da capo; **3, 1, 6, 4** for a second time; **3, 4, 5** all over ~; **4, 3, 3** from the top; **4, 3, 5** from the start; **4, 4** once more; **4, 5** once ~, over ~; **4, 7** from scratch; **5, 4** twice over; **7, 4** another time.

against 1 V; **4** anti; **6** beside, versus; **7** hostile, opposed; **8** critical, touching; **9** alongside; PHRASES: **2, 8, 2** in contrast to; **2, 10, 2** in opposition to; **3, 2, 5** not in favor; **4, 2** next to; **7, 2** counter to; **8, 2** adjacent to, compared to, contrary to.

agapanthus 7, 4 African lily.

age 3 eon, era; **4** fade, gray, rust, time; **5** decay, epoch, phase, ripen, stage, times, wizen, years; **6** mature, mellow, molder,

period, weaken, wither; **7** crumble, decline, shrivel, wrinkle; **8** lifespan, lifetime, timespan; **9** decompose; **11** deteriorate; PHRASES: **2, 2, 3** go to pot; **2, 2, 4** go to seed; **3, 2** get on; **4, 2** grow up; **4, 2, 4** time of life; **4, 3** burn out, grow old; **4, 4, 5** pass one's prime; **4, 5** grow older, turn white; **7, 2, 5** advance in years.

aged 3 old; **5** anile, hoary, lined; **6** senile; **7** ancient, antique, elderly, matured, ripened, wizened; **8** decrepit, moribund, wrinkled; **9** doddering, geriatric, shriveled, venerable; PHRASES: **3, 2, 3, 5** old as the hills; **3, 2, 10** old as Methuselah; **4, 2** past it; **4, 4, 5** past one's prime; **4-6** gray-haired; **4-9** well-preserved; **5, 3** grown old; **5-6** white-haired; **8, 2, 5** advanced in years.

ageless 8 dateless, immortal; **9** deathless.

agency 4 news; **5** press; **6** bureau, outfit, travel; **7** charity, society, support; **8** activity; **10** assistance, employment; **11** advertising; **12** organization.

agent 3 law, rep; **4** doer, free, land, tool; **5** brief, cause, crown, envoy, means, press, proxy; **6** broker, consul, dealer, deputy, double, driver, estate, legate, pander, secret; **7** agentry, attaché, contact, manager, officer, trustee, wetting; **8** delegate, diplomat, emissary, employer, executor, mediator, merchant, minister, operator, producer, reducing, shipping, stimulus; **9** barrister *UK Can*, executive, executrix, influence, middleman, operative, oxidizing; **10** ambassador, arbitrator, disclosing, forwarding, instrument, matchmaker, negotiator, substitute, wholesaler; **11** functionary, perpetrator; **12** commissioner, intermediary, practitioner; **13** administrator; **14** representative; PHRASES: **2-7** go-between; **4, 6** vice consul; **6-7** consul-general; **7, 5** driving force.

age-related 6 ageist; **12** gerontologic.

aggravate 3 vex; **5** annoy; **6** deepen, madden, pester, worsen; **7** augment, enhance, inflame, magnify, provoke; **8** heighten, increase, irritate; **9** frustrate, infuriate, intensify; **10** exacerbate, exaggerate, exasperate; PHRASES: **3, 2, 2** rub it in; **3, 3, 6, 2** fan the flames of; **3, 4, 4, 2, 2** rub one's nose in it; **4, 5** make angry, make worse; **5, 2, 1, 4** bring to a head.

aggravating 7 grating; **9** vexatious. *See also* **aggravate**

aggravation 5 aggro *UK*; **6** bother, hassle; **7** trouble; **9** deepening, worsening; **10** difficulty, irritation; **11** enhancement; **12** augmentation, exacerbation; **15** intensification.

aggregate 3 sum; **4** mass; **5** amass, total, whole; **6** gather; **7** amassed, collect, combine; **8** combined; **10** accumulate, collection, collective, cumulative.

aggression 5 anger; **6** attack; **7** assault; **8** invasion, violence; **9** hostility, offensive, onslaught; **10** antagonism; **12** belligerence.

aggressive 5 pushy, rowdy; **7** hawkish, hostile, violent; **8** clashing, forceful, hardline, inimical, militant, opposing; **9** assertive, bellicose, insistent, litigious, truculent; **10** determined, jingoistic, pugnacious, unfriendly; **11** belligerent, destructive, provocative, quarrelsome, threatening; **12** antagonistic, disputatious; **13** argumentative; **14** uncompromising; **15** confrontational; PHRASES: **4-7** hard-hitting; **5-7** blood-thirsty.

aggressor *See* **attacker**

agile 5 alert, lithe; **6** bright, nimble, supple; **9** sprightly; PHRASES: **5-6** clear-headed; **5-8** quick-thinking.

aging 6 waning; **7** graying, sinking; **8** moribund; **9** declining, senescent, weakening; PHRASES: **2, 3, 4** on the wane; **5, 4** going gray; **7, 2** getting on; **7, 2, 4** running to seed; **7, 3** growing old.

agitate 3 mix, wag; **4** beat, rile, stir, toss, wave, whip; **5** churn, rouse, shake, swirl, upset, whisk, worry; **6** excite, paddle, ruffle, rumple; **7** disturb, fluster, flutter, perturb, protest, trouble; **8** advocate, brandish, campaign, disquiet, flourish; **10** discompose, disconcert, perturbate; **11** demonstrate; PHRASES: **3, 2** hop up; **4, 2** work up; **4, 2, 7** stir up opinion; **4, 5** move about; **4, 6** move around; **5, 2** churn up, shake up; **5, 3, 6** muddy the waters.

agitated 4 edgy; **5** nervy *UK*, tense, upset; **6** shaken, uneasy; **7** anxious, excited, frantic, hopping, jittery, leaping, nervous, ruffled, shocked, twitchy, unquiet; **8** confused, flurried, restless, stressed, troubled, unsteady; **9** disturbed, flustered, perturbed, unsettled; **10** distressed; **11** discomposed, embarrassed; **12** disconcerted; PHRASES: **2, 1, 6** in a lather; **6, 2** shaken up, worked up; **7, 2** stirred up.

agitation 4 flap, stir; **5** panic, upset, worry; **6** dither, unease; **7** anxiety, jitters, protest, tension; **8** activism, disquiet, distress, edginess; **9** jerkiness, jumpiness, nerviness, worriment; **10** excitement; **11** butterflies, disquietude, disturbance, nervousness; **12** collywobbles, discomposure, perturbation, unsteadiness; **13** confrontation, demonstration, embarrassment; PHRASES: **5-2** shakeup; **6-7** heebie-jeebies.

agitator 5 churn, whisk; **6** beater, paddle; **8** activist, vibrator; **9** demagogue, dissenter, eggbeater, firebrand, protester; **10** campaigner; PHRASES: **6-6** rabble-rouser; **7, 6** soapbox orator.

aglow *See* **glowing**

agnomen 8 nickname.

agnostic 6 unsure; **7** doubter, skeptic; **8** doubting; **9** skeptical, uncertain; **10** questioner; **11** nonbeliever, unconvinced; PHRASES: **8, 6** doubting Thomas.

ago 4 back, past; **5** since; **6** before; **10** previously.

agony 3 woe; **4** aunt, pain; **6** column; **7** anguish, torment, torture; **8** distress; **10** heartbreak.

agree 3 fix; **4** echo; **5** allow, ditto, grant, match, unite; **6** accede, accept, affirm, assent, comply, concur, decide, permit, ratify, settle; **7** approve, concede, confirm, consent, support, welcome; **8** coincide, complete, contract; **9** acquiesce, harmonize, subscribe; **10** correspond; PHRASES: **2, 2, 6** be in accord; **2, 3, 4** be the same; **2, 5, 4** go along with; **3, 2** tie in; **3, 3** say yes; **3, 3, 2** see eye to eye; **5, 9** reach agreement.

agreeable 4 good; **7** affable, amiable, willing; **8** amenable, friendly, pleasant, pleasing, suitable; **9** compliant, congenial, enjoyable; **10** acceptable, concordant, delightful, harmonious, satisfying; **11** comfortable, pleasurable; **15** unobjectionable; PHRASES: **2, 4, 6** to your liking; **2, 6** in accord.

agreement 4 bond, deal, pact; **5** peace, terms, truce, union, unity; **6** accord, assent, pledge, treaty, unison; **7** bargain, compact, concord, consent, harmony, promise; **8** approval, blessing, contract, covenant; **9** consensus, unanimity; **10** acceptance, accordance, collective, compliance, compromise, conformity, consonance, gentlemen's, permission, settlement; **11** arrangement, concurrence, cooperation, willingness; **12** acquiescence; **13** understanding; PHRASES: **6, 2** thumbs up.

agricultural 5 rural; **6** farmed, rustic; **7** bucolic, georgic, peasant; **8** agrarian, agrestic *UK*, geoponic, pastoral, praedial; **9** agronomic; **10** cultivated; **11** agrological, undeveloped.

agriculture 4 mano; **5** ejido, milpa; **6** lister, remuda, stover; **7** farming, feedbag; **8** agrology, agronomy, estancia, fencerow, rareripe, rototill; **9** cowperson, equalizer, farmwoman, geoponics, husbandry, newground, rancheria; **10** agronomics, cornhusker, ecofarming, rototiller; **11** agrarianism, agrobiology, agroecology, agrogeology, agroscience, cornhusking, cultivation, sheepherder, whiffletree; **12** agribusiness, agroforestry; **13** agroecosystem, sharecropping; PHRASES: **4, 5** back forty; **4, 7** crop growing; **4, 10** food production; **5, 4** truck farm; **5, 7** mixed farming; **5, 9** rural economics; **6, 5** cattle guard; **6, 7** arable farming; **7, 7** factory farming, organic farming.

agriculturist 6 farmer, grower, raiser, tiller, yeoman; **7** breeder, crofter, granger, grazier *UK*, planter, rancher; **8** ranchero, ranchman; **9** cattleman; **10** agrologist, agronomist, cultivator, husbandman, kibbutznik; **11** smallholder, stockkeeper; **12** sharecropper, stockbreeder; **13** agrobiologist, agroecologist, agrogeologist; **15** agriculturalist; PHRASES: **3, 7** tea planter; **4, 6** beef farmer, dirt farmer, hill farmer; **5, 6** dairy farmer, fruit farmer, sheep farmer, stock farmer, truck farmer; **6, 5** barley baron; **6, 6** arable farmer, tenant farmer; **6, 7** coffee planter; **7, 6** peasant farmer.

ahead 5 early; **6** before, onward; **7** forward; **10** beforehand; **11** prematurely; PHRASES: **2, 3, 4** in the lead, to the fore; **2, 3, 5** to the front; **2, 3, 6** in the future; **2, 3, 9** at the forefront; **2, 4** to come; **2, 5** in front, up front; **2, 7** in advance; **3, 2, 2** yet to be; **4, 3, 6** into the future; **5, 2** ~ of; **6, 3, 4** across the line; **7, 2** further on.

Al 6 tiptop; PHRASES: **5, 5** first class.

aid 4 abet, back, help; **5** first, legal; **6** assist, relief, rescue, succor; **7** foreign, hearing, promote, relieve, salvage, service, support, sustain; **8** teaching; **9** encourage; **10** assistance, facilitate; **12** emancipation; **13** encouragement; PHRASES: **4, 7, 2** give support to; **7, 4** helping hand. *See also* **abet**

aid (in aid of) 2, 3, 7, 2 in the service of; **2, 6, 2** on behalf of; **3, 3, 4, 2** for the sake of.

aid climbing 7 pegging; PHRASES: **3, 8** peg climbing.

aide 6 helper; **7** adviser; **9** assistant, supporter.

aikido 3 kyu, uke, ura; **4** tori; **5** grade, ikkyo, omote, throw; **6** bokken, nikkyo, sankyo, yonkyo; PHRASES: **2, 4** jo kata; **2, 6** jo suburi; **3, 2, 5** ken no kamae; **3, 6** ken suburi; **4, 2** kumi jo; **4, 5** kumi tachi; **4, 6** kote gaeshi; **5, 4** irimi nage, shiho nage, tachi dori; **6, 4** kaiten nage, tenchi nage.

ail 4 pain; **6** affect, suffer; **7** trouble; **8** distress; PHRASES: **2, 3** be ill; **2, 4** be sick.

ailanthus 4-2-6 tree-of-heaven.

aim 3 try; **4** goal, mark, mean, plan, plot, seek, want, wish; **5** drift, level, point, train; **6** aspire, design, direct, intend, intent, object, reason, scheme, target, toward; **7** propose, purpose; **8** ambition, endeavor; **9** intention, objective, overreach; **10** aspiration; PHRASES: **2, 3** go for; **3, 3** bid for, try for; **3, 4, 6, 2** set one's sights on; **3, 5** get ideas; **4, 2** zero in; **4, 3** head for, work for; **5, 2** dream of, focus on, point at, point to; **5, 7** point towards *UK*; **6, 2** aspire to; **6, 3** strive for; **6, 5** strive after; **8, 7** overstep oneself.

aim at 3 woo; **5** court; PHRASES: **2, 5** be after; **5, 3** steer for; **5, 4** swarm over; **5, 7, 2** throw oneself at; **6, 3** strive for; **6, 4, 4** pursue one's ends; **6, 4, 5** pursue one's goals.

aimless 6 futile, random; **7** useless; **9** arbitrary, desultory, haphazard, pointless, worthless; **11** purposeless; **13** directionless, indeterminate; **15** inconsequential.

air 3 bag, bed, gun, sky; **4** aura, hole, lift, look, mail, mass, mile, pump, raid, shot, sock, song, tell, tone, tune, vent; **5** brake, ether, force, ozone, rifle, scout, shaft, space, spray, valve; **6** aerate, bridge, expose, heaven, jacket, letter, manner, melody, oxygen, pocket, reveal, welkin; **7** bladder, cushion, declare, express, feeling, hostess, marshal, officer, quality, traffic, turbine; **8** announce, corridor, proclaim, terminal; **9** broadcast, circulate, commodore, publicize, ventilate; **10** appearance, atmosphere, impression; **12** conditioning; PHRASES: **4, 6** make public; **4-7** vice-marshal; **6, 4** vacuum tube.

air attack 6 strafe; **7** bombing; PHRASES: **3-3** ack-ack; **3, 4** air raid; **3-5, 7** low-level bombing; **3, 6** air strike; **4, 3** bomb run; **4-7** dive-bombing; **4-8** bomb-dropping; **5, 9** laser targeting; **6, 5** tracer flare; **6, 7** carpet bombing; **7, 6** missile strike; **7, 7** suicide bombing; **8, 7** kamikaze bombing, tactical bombing.

air bladder 5 float; PHRASES: **4, 7** swim bladder.

aircraft 3 fin, jet; **4** kite, STOL, tail, VTOL, wing; **5** blimp, cabin, plane, rotor; **6** bomber, copter, glider, rudder; **7** aileron, airfoil, airship, balloon, biplane, chopper, cockpit, shuttle; **8** aerostat, airliner, airplane, autogiro, concorde, fuselage, joystick, rotodyne, seaplane, skiplane, triplane, turbofan, turbojet, zeppelin; **9** aeroplane *UK*, autopilot, dirigible, monoplane, propeller, sailplane, tailplane, taxiplane, turboprop; **10** helicopter, hovercraft, hydroplane, microlight *UK*, paraglider; **13** convertiplane, stratocruiser, undercarriage; PHRASES: **3-3, 7** hot-air balloon; **3, 5** air brake; **3, 6** jet engine; **4-3** jump-jet; **4, 4** nose cone; **4, 5** nose wheel, tail rotor; **4, 6** hang glider; **4-6** wide-bodied; **5-3** jumbo-jet; **5, 5** light plane; **5, 8** light ~ *UK Can*; **6, 4** flight deck; **6-4** flying-boat; **6, 6** puddle jumper; **6, 7** flying machine, helium balloon; **6, 8** flight recorder; **7, 4** landing gear; **7-4-3** heavier-than-air, lighter-than-air; **7-5** freight-plane; **8, 4** ejection seat; **9, 3** executive jet; **9, 5** passenger plane. *See also* **military aircraft**

aircraft personnel 4 crew; **5** flyer, pilot; **6** purser; **7** aircrew, aviator, captain, steward; **8** observer; **9** navigator; **10** groundcrew, pathfinder, stewardess; **12** aircraftsman; PHRASES: **2-5** co-pilot; **3, 7** air hostess *UK*; **4, 5** test pilot; **5, 7** first officer; **6, 8** flight engineer, ground engineer.

air force 3 RAF *UK*; **4** USAF, WRAF *UK*; PHRASES: **3, 3** air arm; **3, 5** air corps; **5, 3, 3** Fleet Air Arm *UK*; **5, 3, 5** Royal Air Force *UK*; **6, 5** flying corps.

airman 4 para; **6** gunner, Wingco; **7** aircrew; **8** observer; **9** airperson, navigator; **10** bombardier, dropmaster; **11** paratrooper; PHRASES: **2-5** co-pilot; **3, 4-7** air vice-marshal *UK*; **3, 5, 7** air chief marshal *UK*, air force officer; **3, 7** air marshal; **3, 9** air commodore *UK*; **4, 5** crew chief; **4, 9** wing commander; **5, 7** group captain, pilot officer *UK*; **5, 10** chief technician *UK*; **6, 5** bomber pilot, ground staff *UK*; **6, 7** flying officer *UK*, master aircrew; **6, 8** flight sergeant *UK*;

7, 5 fighter pilot; **8, 6** squadron leader *UK*; **8, 7** sergeant aircrew; **9, 6** parachute troops.

airport 5 apron; **6** hangar, ramper, runway; **7** airbase, airpark, airside, taxiway; **8** airdrome, airfield, airstrip, clearway *UK*, landside, terminal; PHRASES: **3, 7** air station; **4, 2** sock in; **4, 8** hard standing; **6, 4** flight line; **7, 5** baggage claim, control tower, landing field, landing strip.

airship 5 blimp; **7** balloon; **8** zeppelin; **9** dirigible.

airway 7 airline; PHRASES: **3, 4** air lane; **3, 5** air route; **3, 7** air network; **3, 8** air corridor; **6, 4** flight lane.

airy 3 gay; **4** aery, open; **5** fresh, light, roomy; **6** aerial, blithe, casual, flimsy; **7** airlike, buoyant, exposed; **8** aeriform, carefree, ethereal, rarefied, spacious; **10** aeriferous, nonchalant; **11** atmospheric, unconcerned; **12** lighthearted; PHRASES: **13** insubstantial.

aisle *See* **passageway**

Aix-la-Chapelle 6 Aachen.

AKA 4, 5, 2 also known as.

akin *See* **similar**

Alabama 2 AL; **8** camellia (flower); **10** Montgomery (capital); **12** yellowhammer (bird); PHRASES: **2, 4, 6, 3, 6** We dare defend our rights (motto); **5, 2, 5** Heart of Dixie (nickname); **8, 4** southern pine (tree); **12, 5** Yellowhammer State (nickname).

alarm 3 SOS; **4** bell, call, fear, fire, horn, ring; **5** alert, blast, dread, false, flare, light, panic, scare, shock, shout, siren, upset, worry; **6** alarum, beacon, fright, Klaxon, mayday, signal, terror, tocsin; **7** anxiety, terrify, unnerve, warning; **8** distress, frighten; **9** agitation; PHRASES: **4, 4** code blue; **5, 5** smoke detector; **6, 6** danger signal; **7-4** trumpet-call; **8, 6** distress signal.

alarm (raise the alarm) 5 alert, knell, scare; **6** arouse, scream; **7** startle; **8** frighten; PHRASES: **3, 4** cry wolf; **3, 4, 6** cry blue murder; **4, 2, 9** call an ambulance; **4, 3, 3, 5** turn out the guard; **4, 3, 4** ring the bell; **4, 3, 6** call the police; **4, 3, 7** blow the whistle.

Alaska 2 AK; **6** Juneau (capital); PHRASES: **4, 6-2-3** wild forget-me-not (flower); **4, 8, 5** Last Frontier State (nickname); **5, 2, 3, 6** North to the future (motto); **5, 6** sitka spruce (tree); **6, 9** willow ptarmigan (bird).

albatross 6 burden; **9** hindrance, millstone; **10** impediment; **11** encumbrance; **PHRASES: 6, 4** gooney bird.

album 2 CD, LP; **4** book, tape; **6** folder, record; **8** cassette; **PHRASES: 5, 5** photo ~; **9, 5** autograph ~.

Alcides 8 Hercules.

alcohol 4 amyl, wood; **5** allyl, butyl, ethyl, grain; **6** lauryl, methyl; **7** ethanol, rubbing; **8** absolute; **PHRASES: 7, 2, 4** spirits of wine.

alcoholic drink 3 ale, cup, rum, rye; **4** beer, grog, hops, mild, ouzo, raki, vino, wine; **5** booze, drink, hooch, juice, negus, plonk, punch, stout, toddy, vodka; **6** arrack, bitter, cassis, caudle, eggnog, frappé, liquor, poison, porter, posset *UK*, poteen, redeye, rotgut, Scotch; **7** alcohol, alcopop, aquavit, Bacardi™, bourbon, cordial, liqueur, spirits, whiskey; **8** absinthe, advocaat, apéritif, cocktail, Drambuie™; **9** Cointreau™, grenadine, hippocras, moonshine; **10** shandygaff, usquebaugh; **11** boilermaker; **PHRASES: 3, 3, 5** Tom and Jerry; **3, 4** jug wine, keg beer *UK*, May wine, pop wine; **3, 5** hot toddy, rum punch, Tia Maria™; **3, 7** rye whiskey; **4, 3** dark rum *UK*, pale ale, real ale *UK*; **4, 4** bock beer, home brew, near beer; **4, 5** hard cider; **4, 6** malt liquor; **4, 10** John Barleycorn; **5, 2, 4** water of life; **5, 2, 6** crème de menthe; **5, 3** light rum, white rum; **5, 4** craft beer; **5, 5** mixed drink; **5, 7** Dutch courage, Irish whiskey; **6, 3** claret cup, strong ale; **6, 4** mulled wine; **6, 7** bonded whiskey, Scotch whiskey; **7, 3** bathtub gin, Jamaica rum; **7, 4** mother's ruin; **7, 7** bourbon whiskey; **8, 3** demerara rum, mountain dew.

alcoholism 3 DT's; **7** jimjams, tremors; **10** dipsomania; **PHRASES: 3, 7** the horrors; **4, 9** pink elephants; **5, 7** drink problem *UK*; **6-7** heebie-jeebies; **7, 5** alcohol abuse; **8, 7** delirium tremens.

alcove *See* **recess**

ale 4 real; **6** ginger.

alert 4 tell, warn; **5** alarm, aware, siren; **6** notify, signal; **7** warning; **8** forewarn, prepared, vigilant, watchful; **9** attentive; **PHRASES: 3, 5** red ~.

alfalfa 7 lucerne; **PHRASES: 6, 5** purple medic.

alfilaria 6 clover.

alfresco *See* **outdoor**

alga 3 mat, red; **4** kelp; **5** brown, fucus,

green, wrack; **6** lichen, tangle; **7** seaweed; **8** gulfweed, rockweed; **9** stonewort, symbiotic; **10** phycobiont; **11** thallophyte; **12** bladderwrack; **13** phytoplankton; **14** eutrophication; **PHRASES: 3, 4** red tide; **3, 7** sea lettuce; **4, 4** frog spit, pond scum; **5, 4** Irish moss; **5, 5** algal bloom.

algae 3 red; **5** brown, green; **7** isokont; **8** algology; **9** phycology; **10** algologist, Cyanophyta, Phaeophyta, phaeophyte, Rhodophyta, rhodophyte; **11** Chlorophyta, chlorophyte, Chrysophyta, chrysophyte, phycologist, Xanthophyta, xanthophyte; **13** cyanobacteria; **PHRASES: 4-5** blue-green; **6-5** golden-brown, yellow-green.

algal product 4 agar, miru; **5** algin, kombu; **8** alginate; **12** stromatolite; **PHRASES: 5, 5** laver bread *UK*.

algebra 3 set; **4** ring; **5** field, group; **6** linear; **7** Boolean; **8** abstract; **12** propositions.

algebraic expression 4 term; **6** braces *UK*; **7** unknown; **8** binomial, brackets, constant, variable, vinculum; **9** invariant, parameter; **10** expression, polynomial; **11** coefficient, parentheses; **PHRASES: 4, 4** root sign; **5, 8** angle brackets; **6, 8** square brackets; **7, 8** unknown quantity.

algorithm 7 fractal; **9** iteration, recursion; **PHRASES: 3, 2, 5** set of rules; **4-2-4** step-by-step.

alias 3 a.k.a.; **9** pseudonym; **PHRASES: 3, 2, 5** nom de plume; **3, 4** pen name; **4, 5, 2** also known as; **4, 6** also called; **5, 4** stage name; **7, 4** assumed name.

alibi 6 excuse, reason; **7** account, defense; **11** explanation.

alien 7 Martian, strange, unknown, unusual; **8** stranger; **9** foreigner, immigrant; **10** outlandish, unfamiliar; **PHRASES: 5, 7** space invader; **8, 5** resident ~.

alight 4 land, rest, stop; **5** perch; **6** ablaze, settle; **7** blazing, burning, descend; **8** dismount; **PHRASES: 2, 4** on fire; **2, 6** in flames; **3, 3** get off, get out.

align 4 ally; **5** curve, slope; **7** subtend, support; **8** converge, inscribe; **9** affiliate, associate, intersect; **PHRASES: 4, 2** line up; **4, 2, 4** line up with; **4, 4** make even, side with; **4, 8** make parallel, make straight; **5, 4, 4** bring into line.

alive 4 full, live; **5** alert, aware, awash, perky, quick, vital; **6** active, extant, living, packed, reborn; **7** animate, buzzing, hopping, jumping, kicking, teeming, vibrant; **8** animated, blooming, bustling, existent, swarming, thriving, vivified; **9** breathing, conscious, energetic, enlivened, incarnate, sensitive, surviving, vivacious; **10** interested; **11** flourishing; PHRASES: **2, 3, 5** in the flesh; **2, 4** in life; **3, 4** not dead; **4, 2** with us; **4, 2, 4** full of life; **5, 6** above ground; **5, 9** still breathing; **9, 2, 4** tenacious of life.

alkaloid 7 aconite, cocaine, coniine, quinine; **8** atropine, caffeine, morphine; **10** colchicine, papaverine, strychnine.

alkane 8 kerosene, paraffin.

alkene 7 olefine.

all 4 each, very; **5** total, whole; **6** entire, wholly; **7** totally; **8** entirely, everyone; **9** everybody; **10** altogether, completely, everything; PHRASES: **2, 4, 8** le tout ensemble; **3, 3** the lot; **3, 3, 3** one and ~; **3, 3, 5** ~ the world; **3, 5** the total, the whole, the world; **3, 5, 3** the whole lot; **3, 5, 5** the whole world; **3, 6** the entire; **3, 8** the complete; **3, 9** the aggregate; **4, 3, 5, 3** each and every one; **5, 3** every bit, every one; **5, 3, 5** Alpha and Omega; **5, 6, 3** every single one.

all-around 5 grand; **8** sweeping; **9** inclusive, versatile; **10** everywhere; **11** exceptional; **12** multifaceted; PHRASES: **2, 3, 5** on all sides; **3-9** all-inclusive; **5-5** large-scale.

allegation *See* **claim**

allege *See* **claim**

allegiance 4 duty; **6** comity, fealty, homage; **7** loyalty, respect; **8** devotion, fidelity; **9** adherence; **10** commitment, dedication, submission; **12** faithfulness.

allergy 4 hate; **7** dislike; **8** aversion, distaste, reaction; **9** antipathy; **11** sensitivity.

alleviate *See* **ease**

alley 5 blind; PHRASES: **7** bowling.

alley-oop! 4, 3 lift off!; **4-5** upsy-daisy!.

alliance 3 mob; **4** axis, band, bloc, bond, crew, gang, holy, link, pact, team; **5** bunch, combo, group, guild, posse, trust, union; **6** cartel, league, merger, treaty, triple; **7** synergy; **8** grouping; **9** agreement, coalition, collusion, community, concordat; **10** connection, consortium, conspiracy, convention, federation, fellowship; **11** affiliation, association, cooperation, partnership; **12** amalgamation, relationship; **13** collaboration, consolidation; PHRASES: **3-2** tie-up; **4-2** hook-up; **9, 2** trade agreement; **6, 4** Warsaw

Pact; **6, 7** Triple Entente *UK*; **7, 7** entente society; **7, 8** entente cordiale.

alliance (form an alliance) 4 ally; **5** coact, unite; **6** cowork; **7** collude, conjoin, partner; **8** conspire; **9** affiliate, synergize; **10** fraternize; **11** collaborate; PHRASES: **2, 2, 7** be in cahoots; **4, 2** gang up, team up; **4, 4** join with, side with; **4, 8** pull together; **7, 4** combine with; **9, 4** associate with.

alliance (in alliance) 9 federally; **11** corporately; PHRASES: **2, 6** in league; **2, 7** in cahoots; **2, 11** in partnership; **4, 2, 4** hand in hand; **5, 2, 4** cheek by jowl.

allied 4 akin; **5** joint; **6** bonded, joined, linked, merged, united; **7** aligned, related, similar; **8** coactive, combined, conjoint, synergic; **9** colluding, combining, connected, corporate, fraternal, partnered; **10** affiliated, associated; **11** amalgamated; **12** contributing; **13** collaborative; PHRASES: **2, 9** in communion.

alligator pear 7 avocado.

allocated 5 dealt; **7** divided; **8** allotted, assigned; **9** earmarked; **11** apportioned, distributed; PHRASES: **6, 3** shared out.

allocation 5 share; **7** portion, sharing; **8** division; **9** allotment, allotting, allowance, partition, provision; **10** assignment, dispensing, earmarking; **11** appointment, demarcation, subdivision; **12** apportioning, delimitation, distribution; **13** apportionment; PHRASES: **6, 3** doling out; **7, 3** dealing out, sharing out; **8, 2** divvying up; **10, 3** parcelling out.

allot 3 cut; **4** deal, give; **5** allow, limit, share, split; **6** assign, divide, ration; **7** delimit, earmark, prorate; **8** allocate, dispense; **9** apportion, demarcate, designate, subdivide; **10** distribute; PHRASES: **3, 5** set aside; **4, 3** deal out, dish out, dole out, mete out; **5, 2** carve up, divvy up; **5, 3** share out *UK*; **6, 3** parcel out; **6, 6** spread around; **7, 3** portion out.

allow 3 let; **5** admit, agree, allot, grant; **6** accept, permit; **7** concede, consent; **8** tolerate; **9** apportion; **11** acknowledge.

allowed 8 accepted, approved, forgiven, indulged, pardoned; **9** permitted; **10** authorized, legitimate, recognized, sanctioned.

alloys 5 brass, steel; **6** babbit, bronze, pewter, solder; **7** amalgam; **8** gunmetal; **10** superalloy; **11** cupronickel, electrotype; PHRASES: **4, 4** cast iron; **4, 5** type metal; **5, 5**

misch metal, muntz metal, rose's metal, wood's metal; **6, 6** German silver, silver solder; **8, 6** phosphor bronze; **9, 5** admiralty metal, britannia metal, stainless steel.

all right **2** OK; **3** fit, yes; **4** fair, fine, good, okay, safe, sure, well; **6** agreed; **7** healthy; **8** balanced, passable, passably, pleasing, suitable, unharmed; **9** certainly, obviously, uninjured; **10** acceptable, acceptably, positively, reasonable, reasonably; **12** satisfactory; **14** satisfactorily; PHRASES: **2-2** so-so; **2, 2, 3** up to par; **2, 3, 4** in the pink; **2, 3, 5** by all means; **2, 4, 6** in good health; **2, 6** of course; **2, 7** no problem; **3, 5** all there; **4, 2, 8** fair to middling; **4, 3, 5** safe and sound; **4, 6** fair enough, good enough; **5, 3, 4** alive and well; **7, 1, 5** without a doubt.

allspice **7** pimento; PHRASES: **7, 6** Jamaica pepper.

all the time **4** ever; **5** while; **6** always, during, whilst *UK*; **7** forever; **9** endlessly, meanwhile; **10** constantly, repeatedly; **11** continually, incessantly, permanently; PHRASES: **2, 3, 7** in the interim; **2, 3, 8** in the meantime; **3, 1, 4** for a time; **3, 1, 6** for a season; **3, 2, 3** day by day; **3, 2, 3, 3** day in day out; **3, 3** for now; **3, 3, 4, 5** for the time being; **3, 3, 8** for the duration; **3, 5** all along; **3, 5, 4** the whole time; **3, 7** all through; **4, 2, 4, 3** week in week out; **4, 3, 2, 3** from day to day; **4, 3, 4, 2** from the word go; **4, 3, 5** from the start; **4, 3, 6** from the outset; **7, 6** between whiles.

allure **4** draw, pull; **5** charm; **6** appeal; **7** glamour; **8** charisma; **9** seduction; **10** attraction, enticement, temptation; **11** fascination; **13** seductiveness; PHRASES: **3, 6** sex appeal; **4-2** come-on; **6, 9** animal magnetism.

alluring *See* **appealing**

ally **4** join; **5** align; **6** friend, helper; **7** connect, partner; **9** affiliate, assistant, associate, supporter.

almanac **6** manual; **8** calendar, handbook, yearbook; **9** directory; **12** encyclopedia; PHRASES: **9, 4** reference book.

almighty **7** immense, massive, supreme; **8** enormous, gigantic; **10** invincible, omnipotent; **11** omnipresent; PHRASES: **3-8** all-powerful.

alms *See* **charity**

aloe **7, 5** century plant.

aloes **9** eaglewood.

alone **4** lone, solo; **5** aloof, apart; **6** lonely; **7** forlorn, insular, unaided; **8** deserted, detached, forsaken, isolated, lonesome, separate, solitary, uniquely; **9** abandoned, reclusive, separated, withdrawn; **10** friendless; **13** companionless, independently, unaccompanied; PHRASES: **2, 3, 3** on its own; **2, 4, 3** on one's own, on one's tod; **2, 4, 4** on one's Jack; **2, 4, 8** on one's lonesome; **2, 6** by itself; **3, 2** per se; **3, 2, 7** all by oneself; **6-8** single-handedly; **7, 4** without help.

aloneness **7** privacy; **8** solitude; **9** isolation, seclusion; **10** detachment, insularity.

along **6** beside; **9** alongside; PHRASES: **2, 3, 4, 2** by the side of; **4, 2** next to; **8, 2** adjacent to.

alongside (be alongside) **4** edge, face; **5** flank, skirt; PHRASES: **2, 4, 2** be next to; **4, 2, 2** side up to; **5, 4, 2, 4** stand side by side.

aloof **4** cold; **5** proud; **6** remote, snooty; **7** distant; **8** detached, isolated, reserved, separate, solitary; **10** antisocial, unfriendly, unsociable; **11** independent, indifferent, standoffish; **14** unapproachable; PHRASES: **3, 5** set apart.

aloud **6** loudly; **7** audibly, clearly, noisily; **8** verbally; **10** distinctly, noticeably; PHRASES: **3, 4** out loud.

alpha **3** ray; **5** chief, first, helix; **6** rhythm; **7** leading, primary; **8** centauri, dominant, particle; **9** important.

alphabet **3** ABC *UK*, IPA; **4** ABCs; **5** Greek, kanji, Roman, runic; **6** Arabic, Hebrew, script; **7** Braille, futhark, letters, symbols; **8** Cyrillic, hiragana, ideogram, katakana, phonetic; **9** cuneiform, pictogram, syllabary; **13** hieroglyphics; PHRASES: **7, 6** writing system; **7, 8** initial teaching; **8, 6** phonetic symbol; **9, 3** character set.

Alsatian **6, 8** German shepherd.

also **3** and, too; **8** likewise, moreover; **9** similarly; **11** furthermore; **15** correspondingly; PHRASES: **2, 4** as well; **2, 8** in addition.

altar **3** boy; **4** dais, slab; **5** bench, cloth, table.

alter **4** turn, vary; **5** adapt, amend, cause, emend, renew, shift; **6** adjust, affect, change, detour, divert, modify, reform, remold, revise, rework; **7** commute, convert, correct, deviate, remodel, reorder, reshape, rewrite; **8** innovate, modulate, relocate; **9** diversify, fluctuate, influence, modernize, rearrange; **10** redecorate, reorganize; **11** restructure.

altercation *See* **argument**

alternate 4 vary; **5** other, proxy, swing; **6** backup, double, rotate; **7** another, reserve; **8** exchange; **9** different, fluctuate, oscillate, surrogate, vacillate; **10** substitute; **11** alternating, alternative, interchange, intersperse; **13** complementary; PHRASES: **5-2** stand-in; **5, 5** every other; **5, 6** every second.

alternation 6 change; **8** rotation; **10** repetition; **11** fluctuation, interchange.

alternation of generations 11 metagenesis; **13** heterogenesis.

alternative 3 sub; **5** locum, scrub; **6** change, choice, option; **7** reserve, unusual; **8** redshirt; **9** alternate, different, surrogate; **10** discretion, substitute, understudy, unorthodox; **11** nonstandard, replacement; **12** substitution; **14** unconventional; **16** counterhegemonic; PHRASES: **5, 6** locum tenens, pinch hitter; **7, 2, 6** freedom of choice; **8, 3** whipping boy.

alternatively 2 or; **6** either; **7** instead; **9** otherwise; PHRASES: **2, 3, 5, 4** on the other hand; **2, 10** as substitute; **3, 3** per pro; **4, 5** then again. *See also* **alternative**

althaea 4, 2, 6 rose of Sharon.

altimeter 7 compass, sextant; **8** calipers, gyrostat; **9** gyroscope; **10** micrometer, theodolite; **11** gyrocompass; PHRASES: **7, 5** vernier scale.

altitude *See* **height**

altruistic *See* **unselfish**

always 2 ay; **3** e'er; **4** ever; **7** forever; **9** eternally; **10** constantly; PHRASES: **3, 3, 4** all the time.

AM 7 morning; PHRASES: **6, 5** Albert Medal.

amalgamate *See* **merge**

amaryllis 10, 4 belladonna lily.

amateur 6 shoddy, unpaid; **7** dabbler, leisure; **8** slapdash; **9** layperson; **10** dilettante; **11** substandard; **12** recreational; **14** unprofessional; **15** nonprofessional; PHRASES: **4-4** part-time.

amaze 3 awe; **4** stun; **5** floor, shock; **6** boggle; **7** astound, impress, stagger, startle, stupefy; **8** astonish, gobsmack, surprise; **9** dumbfound; **11** flabbergast; PHRASES: **2, 1, 8** be a surprise; **4, 4** bowl over; **4, 5** take aback; **5, 3, 1, 4** knock for a loop; **5, 3, 3**

knock for six *UK*; **5, 10** leave speechless; **6, 4** strike dumb.

amazed 4 agog, awed; **9** awestruck; **10** speechless; **13** thunderstruck. *See also* **amaze**

amazement 5 shock; **6** wonder; **8** surprise; **10** admiration; **11** incredulity; **12** astonishment, bewilderment, stupefaction.

ambiance 4 feel, mood; **7** setting; **10** atmosphere; **11** environment.

ambiguity 5 doubt; **7** opacity; **8** haziness; **9** obscurity, vagueness; **11** uncertainty; **12** abstruseness.

ambiguous 4 hazy; **5** vague, wooly; **6** woolly; **7** complex, unclear; **8** abstruse, involved; **9** confusing, equivocal, uncertain; **10** indefinite; **11** complicated.

ambition 3 aim; **4** goal; **5** dream, drive; **6** desire; **9** objective; **10** aspiration, motivation; **13** determination.

ambitious 5 pushy; **8** ruthless; **9** energetic; **10** determined; **11** adventurous, impractical, speculative, unrealistic; **13** overconfident; PHRASES: **2, 3, 4** on the make; **3, 3** out for; **6-6** single-minded.

ambrosia 8 beebread.

ambush 4 trap; **6** waylay; **9** ambuscade, bushwhack; PHRASES: **3, 2, 4** lie in wait; **4, 2, 8** take by surprise; **5, 2, 2** creep up on; **6, 2** pounce on; **6, 4** spring upon; **8, 6** surprise attack.

ameliorate 5 amend; **6** better, enrich; **7** perfect, upgrade.

amenable 4 open; **6** pliant; **7** pliable, willing; **8** biddable; **9** agreeable, compliant, tractable; **10** responsive; **11** cooperative, persuadable.

American 1 A; **2** GI, US; **4** aloe, plan, Yank; **5** cloth, eagle, Samoa; **6** cheese, Indian, Yankee; **8** football; **10** Revolution; **11** Americanist; PHRASES: **5, 3** Uncle Sam.

American Indian *See* **Native American**

American Revolution 3 DAR (Daughters of the American Revolution), Lee (Richard Henry); **5** Adams (John), Adams (Samuel), Boone (Daniel), Henry (Patrick), Paine (Thomas), Stark (John); **6** Arnold (Benedict), Camden (Battle of), Monroe (James), Quebec (Battle of), Revere (Paul); **7** Concord, Cowpens (Battle of), Danbury, Hancock (John), Trenton

(Battle of); **8** Burgoyne (John), Franklin (Benjamin), Hamilton (Alexander), Loyalist, Monmouth (Battle of), Saratoga (Battle of), Savannah (Siege of), Yorktown, Yorktown (Battle of); **9** Lexington, minuteman, Princeton (Battle of), Vincennes (Battle of); **10** Bennington (Battle of), Brandywine (Battle of), Charleston (Siege of), Germantown, Germantown (Battle of), Kosciuszko (Thaddeus), Washington (George); **11** Continental, Ticonderoga, Ticonderoga (Battle of); **12** Hillsborough; PHRASES: **2, 7** La Fayette (Marquis de); **4, 5** Blue Licks (Battle of); **4, 6** Long Island (Battle of); **4, 10** Fort Washington (Battle of); **5, 3** Louis XVI; **5, 5** Stony Point (Battle of); **5, 6, 8** Olive Branch Petition; **5, 7** Eutaw Springs (Battle of); **5, 8** King's Mountain (Battle of); **6, 3** George III; **6, 3, 5** Boston Tea Party; **6, 4** Bunker Hill, Bunker Hill (Battle of); **6, 6** Yankee Doodle; **7, 3** Valcour Bay (Battle of); **8, 4** Freeman's Farm (Battle of); **8, 7** Saratoga Springs; **9, 3, 7** Lexington and Concord (Battle of); **11, 4** Continental Army; **11, 8** Continental Congress.

amiability **8** civility, courtesy; **9** geniality; **10** affability, cordiality, kindliness, politeness; **11** amicability, sociability; **12** congeniality, friendliness; **13** agreeableness; PHRASES: **4, 5** good humor; **4, 6** good nature.

amiable *See* **amicable**

amicable **4** kind; **6** polite; **7** cordial, likable; **8** friendly, sociable; **9** agreeable, compliant, congenial; **10** harmonious; **11** acquiescent; **12** conciliatory; **13** accommodating; PHRASES: **4-7** good-humored, good-natured.

amid **2** in; **6** amidst, during, within; PHRASES: **2, 3, 4, 4, 2** at the same time as; **2, 3, 6, 2** in the course of; **5, 4** along with.

amidst **4** amid; **5** among; PHRASES: **2, 3, 5, 2** in the midst of; **2, 3, 6, 2** in the middle of; **2, 6** at random; **3, 2, 5** out of order; **5, 4** among many, inter alia; **5, 5** inter alios; **5, 6** among others; **7, 5** between races.

amino acid **5** kinin; **7** cystine, kalidin, peptide; **9** dipeptide, essential; **10** bradykinin, tripeptide; **11** polypeptide; **12** nonessential, oligopeptide; PHRASES: **5, 4** imino acid; **7, 4** peptide bond; **9, 4** disulfide bond.

amiss **5** wrong; **7** wrongly; **8** mistaken; **9** erroneous, incorrect; **10** mistakenly; **11** erroneously, incorrectly; **13** inappropriate; **15** inappropriately.

ammeter **9** voltmeter, wattmeter; **11** stroboscope; **12** electrometer, galvanometer, magnetometer, oscilloscope; **13** potentiometer.

ammunition **3** dud, wad; **4** ammo, ball, bomb, flak, live, shot, slug; **5** blank, round, shell; **6** bullet, dumdum, pellet, powder; **7** grenade, missile; **8** buckshot, canister, shrapnel; **9** cartouche, cartridge, grapeshot, mitraille; **10** cannonball, projectile; PHRASES: **3-3** ack-ack; **4, 4** case shot; **4-5, 6** softnosed bullet; **5, 4** chain shot, round shot, small shot; **5, 5** baton round *UK*; **5, 9** blank cartridge, spent cartridge; **6, 6** rubber bullet; **7, 6** plastic bullet; **9, 4** cartridge belt, cartridge case, cartridge clip; **9, 6** expanding bullet.

amnesty **6** pardon; **8** reprieve; **9** remission; **11** forgiveness.

amorous **3** coy; **4** sexy; **5** horny, randy; **6** ardent, erotic, flirty, loving, moping, sexual, tender; **7** amatory, excited, longing, lustful, melting, mooning; **8** desirous, enamored, romantic, yearning; **9** emotional, erogenous, seductive; **10** infatuated, lascivious, passionate; **11** flirtatious, sentimental; **12** affectionate.

amount **3** few, lot, sum; **4** dose, heap, hunk, lake, less, load, mass, mess, more, most, pack, part, some; **5** batch, bunch, chunk, floor, least, limit, piece, quota, share, stint, total, whack; **6** dosage, extent, packet, parcel, quorum, ration, volume; **7** dribble, expanse, fewness, portion, quantum; **8** addition, decrease, fraction, increase, majority, minority, pittance, quantity, somewhat; **9** aggregate, extension; **11** subtraction.

amount owing **4** bill; **5** score, tally; **7** account, arrears, deficit; **9** overdraft; **10** defaulting; **11** foreclosure, receivables; PHRASES: **4, 3** back pay; **4, 4** back rent; **5-3** write-off; **6, 6** frozen assets; **6, 7** frozen balance; **7, 2, 3** balance to pay; **7, 7** overdue payment.

amphetamine **5** speed, whizz.

amphibian **3** eft, olm; **4** frog, newt, toad; **5** siren; **6** anuran, apodan, froggy; **7** axolotl, caudate, paddock, toadish, urodele, xenopus; **8** bullfrog, froglike, limbless, mudpuppy, newtlike, tailless, toadlike; **9** caecilian, neotenous; **10** batrachian, hellbender, natterjack *UK*, salamander, salientian; **12** salamandrian; PHRASES: **3, 5** mud puppy; **4, 4** cane toad, tree frog, wood frog; **4, 10** fire salamander; **5, 3** congo eel; **5, 4** hairy frog; **5, 10** tiger salamander; **6, 4** clawed frog, horned toad; **6, 6** spring peeper; **7, 4** goliath frog, midwife toad *UK*; **7, 10** spotted salamander; **9, 4** spadefoot toad; **10, 4** natterjack toad.

amphitheater 4 bowl, dome, ring; **5** arena; **7** stadium; **10** auditorium. *See also* **building**

ample 4 rife; **6** enough, galore, plenty; **7** copious, liberal, profuse; **8** abundant, adequate; **9** plenteous, plentiful; **10** sufficient; **13** superabundant; PHRASES: **2, 9** in abundance, in profusion.

amplified 8 expanded, extended.

amplifier 2 PA; **8** bullhorn; **9** megaphone; **11** loudspeaker.

amplify 4 flow, gush; **5** swell; **6** detail, dilate, expand, extend, repeat, waffle; **7** augment, clarify, develop, enlarge, magnify; **8** increase, lengthen, protract; **9** elaborate, expatiate, intensify, reiterate; **10** strengthen; **13** particularize; PHRASES: **2, 4, 6** go into detail; **3, 2** add to; **3, 3** pad out; **3, 8** wax eloquent; **6, 2** ramble on; **7, 2** enlarge on; **7, 4** enlarge upon.

amuse 5 charm; **6** absorb, divert; **7** engross; **8** distract, interest; **9** entertain.

amusement 3 fun; **4** glee; **5** hobby, mirth; **7** pastime, pursuit; **8** hilarity, pleasure; **9** diversion, enjoyment, merriment; **10** recreation; **13** entertainment.

amusing 4 zany; **5** comic, droll, funny, wacky, witty; **7** comical; **8** humorous; **9** diverting, hilarious; **12** entertaining.

amylum 6 starch.

anachronism 5 relic; **8** archaism, dinosaur, holdover, leftover, survival, survivor; **9** misdating, mistiming.

anachronistic 5 dated, passé; **7** archaic; **8** misdated, obsolete, outdated, outmoded; **10** antiquated; **11** obsolescent; PHRASES: **3-2-4** out-of-date; **3-9** old-fashioned.

analgesia 5 salve; **6** arnica; **7** anodyne, aspirin, codeine, morphia; **8** dullness, hypnosis, laudanum, morphine, nepenthe, Novocain™, numbness; **9** ibuprofen, lidocaine, paralysis, pethidine; **10** anesthesia, meperidine, painkiller; **11** acupuncture, paracetamol, unawareness; **12** painlessness; **13** insensibility, insensitivity; PHRASES: **4, 6** pain relief; **4, 8** pain reliever; **4-9** pain-relieving; **4, 10** pain management; **7, 5** nitrous oxide; **8, 3** laughing gas.

analgesic 7 dulling, numbing; **9** analgesia, deadening, demulcent, ibuprofen, paralysis, pethidine; **10** anesthetic, palliative; **11** painkilling. *See also* **analgesia**

analogous 4 akin, like; **7** related, similar; **8** parallel; **10** comparable, equivalent, metaphoric.

analogy 6 simile; **8** allegory, analogue, likeness, metaphor, parallel; **10** comparison, similarity; **11** correlation, equivalence, resemblance; **14** correspondence.

analyse *See* **examine**

analysis 7 inquiry, testing; **8** scrutiny; **9** breakdown; **10** assessment, evaluation; **11** examination, exploration, qualitative; **12** quantitative; **13** consideration, investigation, psychotherapy; **14** psychoanalysis.

analyst 6 expert; **9** predictor; **10** forecaster; **12** psychiatrist; **13** psychoanalyst; **15** psychotherapist; PHRASES: **4, 7** city ~ *UK*; **6, 7** market ~.

analytic 7 logical; **8** critical, rational, reasoned; **10** analytical *UK*, diagnostic, equivalent, methodical, stationary, systematic; **11** neutralized, questioning; **12** quantitative, standardized; **13** investigative.

anarchic 4 wild; **5** heady; **6** unruly; **7** chaotic, lawless, radical, rampant, riotous, willful; **8** confused; **9** unbridled; **10** anarchical, disordered, disorderly, headstrong, rebellious, ungoverned; **11** anarchistic, disobedient; **12** disorganized, uncontrolled, unrestrained; **13** insubordinate, irresponsible, revolutionary, unaccountable, undisciplined; PHRASES: **3, 2, 7** out of control; **3-3-3** dog-eat-dog.

anarchism 8 nihilism; **11** syndicalism.

anarchist 5 rebel; **6** anarch; **7** radical; **8** assassin, mutineer, nihilist; **9** guerrilla, ochlocrat, terrorist; **10** antinomian, subversive; **11** seditionary, syndicalist; **13** revolutionary.

anarchistic 8 anarchic; **10** nihilistic; **13** revolutionary, syndicalistic; **14** antigovernment.

anarchy 4 coup; **5** chaos; **6** mutiny; **7** misrule, turmoil; **8** disorder, sedition; **9** anarchism, overthrow, rebellion; **10** revolution, subversion, unruliness; **11** interregnum, lawlessness, unrestraint; **12** dethronement, disobedience, indiscipline; **15** disorganization, insubordination; PHRASES: **2, 9** no authority; **3, 2, 3, 6** law of the jungle; **3, 3** mob law; **3-3-3** dog-eat-dog; **3, 4** mob rule; **4, 5** coup d'état; **5, 2, 6** reign of terror; **5, 3** lynch law; **5, 6** power vacuum.

anatomy 4 form; **6** makeup; **8** analysis; **9** framework, histology, structure; **10** dissection, morphology; **11** comparative, composition, examination; **13** investigation; PHRASES: **5, 9** gross structure; **6, 9** tissue structure.

ancestor 4 Adam, sire; **8** forebear; **9** precursor, primitive, prototype; **10** antecedent, forefather, forerunner, progenitor; **11** predecessor.

ancestry 6 origin; **7** descent, lineage; **8** heritage; **10** extraction.

anchor 3 fix; **4** moor, ring; **5** affix; **6** attach, fasten, secure; **9** anchorman, announcer, presenter *UK*; **10** newscaster, newsreader *UK*; **11** anchorwoman, broadcaster, commentator; **12** anchorperson.

ancient 2 Ur; **3** old; **5** Greek, hoary, olden; **6** lights, primal; **7** antique, archaic, history; **8** monument, obsolete, outdated, primeval; **10** antiquated, primordial; **11** prehistoric; **12** antediluvian; PHRASES: **3-3** age-old; **3-9** old-fashioned.

anciently 2, 4 of yore; **2, 5, 4** in olden days.

and 4 also, next, then, with; **8** moreover; **9** afterward; **11** furthermore; PHRASES: **2, 4, 2** as well as; **2, 8** in addition; **2, 8, 2** in addition to; **4, 2, 4** what is more; **5, 4** along with; **7, 4** coupled with.

android 5 robot; **6** bionic, cyborg; **7** machine; **8** humanoid; **9** automaton.

anecdote 4 tale; **5** story; **6** sketch; **9** narration, narrative.

anesthetic 4 drug; **5** ether, local, opium; **6** downer; **7** cocaine, general, numbing; **8** hypnosis, hypnotic, laudanum, narcotic, nepenthe, sedating, sedative; **9** analgesic, deadening, halothane, novocaine *UK*, pethidine, soporific; **10** lignocaine, painkiller; **11** acupuncture, barbiturate, painkilling, somniferous; **12** tranquilizer; PHRASES: **8, 5** knockout drops.

anesthetize 4 numb, stun; **5** blunt; **6** benumb, deaden, freeze, sedate; **7** concuss, stupefy; **8** etherize; **11** desensitize; PHRASES: **3, 2, 5** put to sleep; **3, 3** put out; **3, 5** put under; **5, 3** knock out.

angel 4 cake, dust, food; **5** falls, hell's, putto, shark, Uriel; **6** backer, cherub, fallen, patron, powers, seraph, spirit; **7** Gabriel, Lucifer, Michael, Raphael, sponsor, thrones, virtues; **9** archangel, celestial, financier, guarantor, messenger; **10** benefactor, destroying; **11** dominations; **14** principalities; PHRASES: **5, 2, 4** ~ of love; **5, 2, 5** ~ of death, ~ of light; **5, 9** choir invisible, fairy godmother; **7, 4** angelic host; **8, 4** heavenly host; **8, 5** guardian ~, heavenly being; **9, 2, 3** messenger of God.

angelfish 7 scalare.

angelic 4 good, kind, pure; **6** caring, divine; **7** saintly; **8** adorable, beatific, cherubic, innocent, seraphic, virtuous.

angel shark 8 monkfish.

anger 3 fit, ire, irk; **4** fury, heat, huff, rage, rile; **5** annoy, paddy, scene, storm, swear, tizzy, wrath; **6** choler, dander, enrage, madden, raging, temper; **7** ferment, incense, outrage, passion, provoke, tantrum; **8** irritate, outburst, paroxysm, shouting, violence; **9** aggravate, annoyance, crossness, explosion, infuriate, vehemence; **10** convulsion, exasperate, irritation, resentment, sullenness; **11** bellicosity, indignation; **12** belligerence, snappishness, wrathfulness; PHRASES: **3-3** cat-fit; **4-2** blow-up; **4-3** duck-fit; **4, 5** spit tacks; **5-2** flare-up; **5, 4** blind fury, blind rage; **6, 4** raging fury; **6, 7** temper tantrum.

angle 3 net; **4** apex, bank, bend, bias, cant, cast, fish, hook, hour, lean, spin, tilt, turn, warp; **5** acute, bevel, miter, plane, plate, point, right, seine, slant, slope, trawl, troll, twist; **6** camber, corner, dogleg, obtuse, reflex, vertex, zigzag; **7** bracket, incline, oblique, outlook, salient; **8** approach, critical, dihedral, exterior, interior, junction, latitude; **9** elevation, intersect, longitude, reentrant, subtended, viewpoint; **10** circumflex, depression; **11** perspective; **12** intersection; **13** complementary, perpendicular; PHRASES: **3, 1, 3** tie a fly; **3-4** fly-fish; **4, 2** reel in; **4, 3, 4** bait the hook; **4-4** spin-cast; **4-5** knee-joint; **5, 1, 3** dress a fly; **5, 2, 4** point of view; **5, 6** sharp corner; **7, 4** hairpin bend *UK*; **8, 6** opposite angles; **9, 6** alternate angles.

angled 6 square; **7** cuneate, diamond, faceted, scalene; **9** cuneiform, decagonal, hexagonal, octagonal, polygonal, prismatic, pyramidal; **10** decahedral, heptagonal, pentagonal, polyhedral, rhomboidal, triangular, trilateral; **11** rectangular; **12** quadrangular; **13** perpendicular, quadrilateral.

angler 6 fisher; **8** Compleat; **9** fisherman; **10** trawlerman; PHRASES: **3-6** fly-fisher.

angling 4 bait, bite, cast, chum, worm; **5** bread, catch, skish; **6** baited, bottom, coarse, fished, ground, insect, maggot, mayfly, minnow, strike; **7** baiting, casting, dapping, dressed, fishing, harness, jointed, natural, sinking, trolled; **8** mooching, spinning, trolling, trotting; **9** ledgering; **10** artificial; PHRASES: **3-3, 7** dry-fly fishing, wet-fly fishing; **3-4, 7** big-game fishing; **3, 7** ice fishing; **3-7** fly-fishing; **4-3, 7** deep-sea fishing; **4-3, 8** deep-sea trolling; **4, 7** bait casting, bait fishing, game fishing, surf fishing; **4-7** spin-casting; **5-5** fixed-spool, rubby-dubby; **5, 6** chair socket; **5, 7** float fishing, match fishing, still fishing; **5-7** beach-casting, strip-casting; **6, 4** ground bait; **6, 7** coarse fishing *UK*; **7, 3** natural fly; **8, 5** accuracy event, distance event, throwout level; **9, 5** turntable chair.

angling terms 3 dun, fly, net, rod, tag, tip; **4** barb, cast, gaff, hemp, hook, lead, line, lure, plug, pole, reel, shot, tail, worm; **5** creel, float, floss, joker, leger, quill, spoon, whisk; **6** caster, hackle, maggot, marker, palmer, pinkie, priest, slider, spigot, squatt, strike, zoomer; **7** antenna, bristle, dapping, dubbing, plummet, spinner, waggler; **8** freeline, legering, swingtip; **9** bloodworm, disgorger, quivertip; **11** paternoster; PHRASES: **3, 3** dry fly, wet fly; **3, 4** rod rest, rod ring; **4, 3** bale arm, keep net; **4-3-3** hair-and-fur; **4, 4** back shot, dead bait, line bite, stop knot; **4, 6** snap tackle, swim feeder; **4-6** foul-hooked, whip-finish, wing-cutter; **4, 7** bait dropper; **5, 4** blued hook, cloud bait, gorge bait, micro shot, midge hook, roach pole, tying silk; **5, 5** stick float; **5, 6** devon minnow; **5-6** dough-bobbin; **6, 4** caddis hook, coffin lead, double hook, ground bait; **6, 5** bubble float, loaded float; **7, 3** fly-body fur, landing net; **7, 4** arlesey bomb, gallows tool, sparkle body; **7, 5** sliding float; **8, 4** barbless hook; **8, 6** blockend feeder; **9, 3** parachute fly; **10, 4** multiplier reel.

angry 3 mad, PO'd; **5** cross, irate, livid, rabid, ratty; **6** fierce, fuming, heated, huffed, ireful, raging, savage; **7** angered, annoyed, berserk, boiling, burning, cursing, enraged, foaming, furious, hopping,

roaring, violent; **8** choleric, frenzied, gnashing, growling, incensed, outraged, sizzling, snapping, swearing, wrathful; **9** bellicose, indignant, irritated, rampaging, sulfurous; **10** aggravated, aggressive, apoplectic, implacable, infuriated, smoldering, stuttering; **11** belligerent, exasperated; PHRASES: **2, 1, 4** in a huff, in a stew; **2, 1, 5** in a strop *UK*; **2, 4, 7** in high dudgeon; **3, 2** het up *UK*; **3, 4, 4** red with rage; **3, 4, 5** red with anger; **3-8** bad-tempered; **6, 3** seeing red; **6, 7** beside oneself; **7, 3** browned off *UK*, hopping mad.

angry (be angry) 4 boil, burn, fret, fume, lour, rage, rant, rave, stew; **5** broil, chafe, glare, growl, lower, scowl, snarl, storm; **6** glower, seethe, simmer, sizzle; **7** bluster, quarrel, rampage, smolder; **9** fulminate; PHRASES: **2, 7** go berserk; **3, 2, 5** cut up rough; **4, 1, 5** make a scene; **4, 2** take on; **4, 2, 1, 3** kick up a row; **4, 2, 3, 5** foam at the mouth; **4, 2, 4** kick up dirt; **4, 3, 4** rant and rave; **4, 5** look black; **4, 7** look daggers; **5, 1, 3** throw a fit; **5, 1, 3-3** throw a cat-fit; **5, 1, 6** throw a wobbly; **5, 2** carry on; **5, 3, 4** raise the roof; **5, 4** raise Cain, raise hell; **5, 4, 4** stamp one's foot; **6, 1, 5** create a scene; **7, 4** breathe fire.

angry (become angry) 6 bridle, ignite; **7** bristle, explode; PHRASES: **2, 3, 3, 4, 3** go off the deep end; **2, 5** go spare; **2, 6** go postal; **2, 9** go ballistic; **3, 3** bug out, let fly, see red, wig out; **3, 3, 3, 6** fly off the handle; **3, 3, 4** hit the roof; **3, 4, 1, 4** fly into a rage; **3, 4, 6, 2** get one's dander up, get one's monkey up; **4, 1, 4** blow a fuse; **4, 1, 6** blow a gasket; **4, 1, 10** have a hemorrhage; **4, 4** boil over; **4, 4, 3** blow one's lid; **4, 7** lose control; **4, 8** lose patience; **5, 1, 7** throw a tantrum; **5, 2** flare up; **5, 3** freak out; **5, 4, 5** flush with anger.

angry (make angry) 4 huff; **6** enrage, madden; **7** envenom; **8** ulcerate; **9** aggravate, infuriate; PHRASES: **3, 3** put out; **4, 3, 3** push too far; **5, 2, 3, 4** drive up the wall; **5, 3** brown off.

anguish *See* **suffering**

angular 4 bent, bony, thin; **5** gaunt, gawky, lanky, rangy; **6** forked, hooked; **7** jointed, mitered; **8** cornered; **9** bifurcate, doglegged; PHRASES: **5-8** sharp-cornered.

angular measurement 5 trine; **6** square; **7** sextant, sextile, sundial; **8** geometry, quadrant, quincunx, quintile; **10** biquintile, goniometer, goniometry, opposition, protractor, theodolite; **12** trigonometry; PHRASES: **1-6** T-square; **3, 6** set square; **4-7** semi-sextile; **5, 6** bevel square.

angwantibo 5 potto.

animal 4 bird, dumb, fish, host, prey, worm; **5** beast, being, biped, brute, swine, zooid; **6** grazer, insect, mammal, rights, rodent, vector; **7** browser, critter, kingdom, mollusk, monster, protist, reptile, spirits, varmint; **8** chordate, creature, omnivore, organism, parasite, predator, symbiont; **9** amphibian, arthropod, carnivore, commensal, gastropod, herbivore, husbandry, intuitive, magnetism, marsupial, protozoan, quadruped, scavenger; **10** animalcule, vertebrate; **11** bloodsucker, insectivore, instinctive, instinctual; **12** ectoparasite, endoparasite, invertebrate; PHRASES: **4-5** meat-eater; **4, 6** dumb friend; **5-5** flesh-eater; **5, 6** furry friend; **6, 6** filter feeder; **8, 5** creeping thing.

animal (adjectives describing animals) 4 wild; **5** feral, tamed; **6** marine, social; **7** aquatic, benthic, bipedal, diurnal, pelagic, zooidal; **8** arboreal, chordate, colonial, littoral, solitary; **9** commensal, nocturnal, parasitic, symbiotic; **10** omnivorous, planktonic, predacious, vertebrate; **11** animalcular, carnivorous, herbivorous, quadrupedal, terrestrial; **12** bloodsucking, domesticated, invertebrate; **13** ectoparasitic, endoparasitic, insectivorous.

animal covering 3 fur, kid; **4** calf, fell, hair, hide, mink, pelt, skin; **5** conch, sable, scale, scalp, scute, shell, suede; **6** cocoon, cortex, ermine, eschar, eyelid, fleece, lorica; **7** chamois, cuticle, doeskin, leather, morocco, pigskin, plumage, rawhide, scallop; **8** buckskin, carapace, feathers; **9** chrysalis, clamshell, epidermis, horsehide, operculum; **10** chinchilla; **11** saddlecloth; PHRASES: **5, 4** outer skin; **5, 5** snail shell; **5, 7** horse blanket; **6, 4** beaver pelt; **6, 5** oyster shell, turtle shell.

animal cry 3 baa, bay, mew, moo, yap; **4** bark, bell, hiss, howl, meow UK, purr, roar, snap, wail, woof, yawl, yawp, yelp, yowl; **5** bleat, growl, neigh, snarl; **6** bellow, whinny; PHRASES: **3-3** hee-haw; **6, 4** mating call; **7, 3** warning cry.

animal-fearing 9 zoophobic.

animal food and feeding 3 hay; **4** bale, bran, corn, nuts, oats; **5** grain, grass, straw; **6** acorns, barley, clover, fodder, forage, silage; **7** alfalfa, haylage, lucerne, pasture; **8** birdseed, fishmeal, molasses, pigswill UK, saltlick; **9** feedstuff, pasturage, provender; **11** chickenfeed; PHRASES: **3, 4** dry feed; **4, 5** malt culms; **5, 4** beech mast; **5-4, 4** sugar-beet pulp; **5, 5** dried grass; **6, 4** cattle cake UK, rabbit food; **6, 5** flaked maize; **7, 5** brewers' yeast; **10, 4** cottonseed cake.

animal home 3 den, pen, run, sty; **4** cage, drey, form, lair, sett; **5** couch, earth, hutch, lodge, pound, stall; **6** burrow, corral, covert, stable.

animalian 4 dumb, zoic; **6** animal, brutal; **7** beastly, bestial, brutish; **8** animalic, subhuman; **9** beastlike; **10** zoomorphic; **11** animalistic; **13** theriomorphic; **14** therianthropic; PHRASES: **6-4** animal-like.

animal killer 6 poison; **7** knacker, matador, picador; **8** ratsbane, toreador; **9** germicide, pesticide, vermicide; **11** bullfighter, insecticide, rodenticide; **12** slaughterman UK; **14** vivisectionist. *See also* **hunter**

animal killing 4 cull; **7** lemming; **8** knackery; **11** vivisection; **12** slaughtering; **13** extermination; PHRASES: **5, 6** blood sports; **5, 8** whale beaching; **8, 5** Gadarene swine; **9, 4** selective cull. *See also* **hunting**

animal-loving 9 zoophilic.

animals 2 ai; **3** ape, ass, bat, cat, dog, elk, fox, gnu, hog, kob UK, pig, rat, yak; **4** anoa, bear, cavy, deer, game, gaur, goat, hare, ibex, kudu, lion, lynx, mink, mole, mule, oryx, paca, pika, puma, saki, seal, sika UK, tahr, titi, urus, vole, wolf, zebu; **5** addax, beast, bison, bongo, camel, chiru, civet, coati, coney, coypu, dhole, dingo, drill, eland, fauna, fossa, gayal, genet, goral, hinny, horse, hutia, hyena, hyrax, indri, kiang, koala, lemur, liger, llama, loris, moose, mouse, nyala, okapi, oribi, otter, ounce, panda, potto, ratel, sable, saiga, serow, sheep, shrew, skunk, sloth, stoat, tapir, tiger, tigon, whale, zebra; **6** agouti, alpaca, aoudad, argali, auroch, baboon, badger, beaver, bobcat, cattle, chital UK, colugo, cougar, coyote, cuscus, desman, donkey, dugong, duiker, ermine, fennec, ferret, fisher, galago, gelada, gerbil, gibbon, gopher, grison, guenon, hyaena, impala, jackal, jaguar, jerboa, langur, margay, marmot, marten, monkey, nilgai, numbat UK, nutria, ocelot, olingo, onager, possum, rabbit, rodent, serval, sifaka, tenrec, tiglon, vervet, vicuna, walrus, wapiti, weasel, wisent, wombat; **7** acouchi, banteng, bighorn, blesbok, buffalo, caracal, caribou, chamois, cheetah, colobus, dasyure, dolphin, echidna, felidae, gazelle, gemsbok, gerenuk, giraffe, glutton, gorilla, grampus, guanaco, gymnure, hamster, lemming, leopard, linsang, macaque, mammoth, manatee, markhor, meerkat, mouflon, muskrat, narwhal, noctule, opossum, panther, peccary, polecat, primate, raccoon, rorqual, sealion, siamang, souslik, tamarin, tamarou, tarsier, wallaby, warthog, wildcat, zorilla; **8** aardvark, aardwolf, Animalia, anteater, antelope, babirusa, bontebok *UK*, bushbaby, bushbuck, cachalot, capybara, chipmunk, dormouse, elephant, entellus, hedgehog, kangaroo, kinkajou, mandrill, mangabey, marmoset, mongoose, muskrats, musquash, pangolin, platypus, porpoise, reedbuck, reindeer, ruminant, squirrel, steinbok, talapoin, tamandua, viscacha, wallaroo, wildlife; **9** armadillo, bandicoot, binturong, blackbuck, chickaree, dromedary, groundhog, hamadryas, monotreme, pachyderm, phalanger, porcupine, pronghorn, prosimian, sitatunga, solenodon, springbok, thylacine, waterbuck, wolverine, woodchuck; **10** angwantibo, bottlenose, cacomistle, chevrotain, chimpanzee, chinchilla, chiroptera, cottontail, hartebeest, jackrabbit, jaguarundi, rhinoceros, springhaas *UK*, wildebeest; **11** barbastelle *UK*, douroucouli, pipistrelle, spermophile; **12** hippopotamus, klipspringer; PHRASES: **3, 3** red fox, sea cow; **3-3** aye-aye, dik-dik; **3, 4** big game, red deer, roe deer; **3, 5** sea otter, sei whale; **3, 8** rat kangaroo *UK*, red squirrel; **4, 2** musk ox; **4, 2, 3** fish of the sea, fowl of the air; **4, 3** blue fox, cane rat, mole rat, moon rat, pack rat; **4, 4** axis deer, gray wolf, mule deer, musk deer, wild boar; **4, 5** blue whale, deer mouse, palm civet, tree shrew; **4-5, 4** star-nosed mole; **4, 6** pine marten *UK*; **4, 6, 4** Père david's deer; **4, 7** snow leopard; **4, 8** gray squirrel, roan antelope, tree kangaroo *UK*; **5, 3** fruit bat, Irish elk, water rat; **5, 4** black bear, brown bear, mouse deer, small game, water vole *UK*; **5-4** orang-utan *UK*; **5, 5** black widow, field mouse, honey mouse *UK*, otter shrew, pilot whale, right whale, sperm whale, water shrew *UK*, white whale; **5, 6** honey badger; **5-6, 4** black-tailed deer, white-tailed deer; **5, 7** water buffalo; **5, 8** royal antelope, sable

antelope; **5, 10** white rhinoceros; **6, 3** arctic fox, desert rat, flying fox, guinea pig, pampas cat, silver fox; **6, 4** arctic hare, banana slug, fallow deer, harbor seal, hooded seal, Indian pony, timber wolf; **6, 5** flying lemur, killer whale; **6, 6** pocket gopher; **6, 7** dorcas gazelle; **6, 8** flying squirrel, ground squirrel; **6, 9** flying phalanger; **7, 3** barbary ape, Pallas's cat *UK*, pouched rat, prairie dog, raccoon dog, vampire bat; **7, 4** barking deer *UK*, grizzly bear, leopard seal, prairie wolf; **7, 5** harvest mouse *UK*, jumping mouse; **7, 7** clouded leopard; **8, 3** kangaroo rat, serotine bat; **8, 4** elephant seal, mountain goat, mountain lion; **8, 5** humpback whale, snowshoe hares; **8, 6** mountain beaver; **9, 3** horseshoe bat *UK*; **9, 4** marsupial mole, Tasmanian wolf; **9, 5** Tasmanian devil; **10, 3** anthropoid ape.

animal science 7 zoology, zoonomy, zootomy; **8** ethology, zoometry; **9** mammology, zoography; **10** embryology, entomology, malacology; **11** herpetology, ichthyology, ornithology; **12** paleontology, paleozoology, parasitology, protozoology, sociobiology, zoochemistry, zoogeography, zoopathology; **13** helminthology; PHRASES: **6, 7** marine biology.

animal welfare 3 zoo; **5** RSPCA *UK*; **11** reservation, zootechnics; **12** dolphinarium; **13** thremmatology; PHRASES: **4, 7** game reserve *UK*; **6, 4** safari park; **8, 4** wildlife park.

animal welfarist 3 vet; **8** zoophile; **12** veterinarian; **15** conservationist, thremmatologist; PHRASES: **3, 5** cat lover, dog lover, pet owner; **3-6** zoo-keeper; **4, 3** hunt sab; **4, 6** game warden *UK*; **4, 8** hunt saboteur *UK*; **6, 5** animal lover.

animate 4 live, stir; **5** alive, rouse; **6** living; **7** enliven; **9** breathing; PHRASES: **5, 2** liven up *UK*; **5, 2, 4** bring to life; **5-3-5** flesh-and-blood.

animation 4 life; **5** vigor; **6** energy; **7** cartoon; **8** vibrancy; **10** liveliness, simulation; **12** animatronics. *See also* **drawing**

animosity 6 enmity, hatred, rancor; **7** dislike; **8** acrimony, loathing; **9** hostility; **10** antagonism, bitterness, resentment; PHRASES: **2, 4, 4** no love lost; **3, 4** ill will; **3, 5** bad blood; **3, 7** bad feeling, ill feeling.

ankh 4, 6 crux ansata.

anklebone 5 talus.

annihilate 4 beat, kill, nuke, rout, veto; **5**

abort, annul, crush; **6** defeat, murder, negate, thrash; **7** conquer, destroy, nullify; **8** vaporize; **9** eradicate, overpower, overwhelm; **10** extinguish, invalidate, obliterate; **11** exterminate; PHRASES: **3, 2, 3, 2** put an end to; **4, 3** wipe out.

annihilation 3 end; **4** rout, veto; **6** defeat, murder; **10** extinction; **11** destruction, dissolution, elimination, eradication, liquidation; **12** invalidation, obliteration; **13** extermination.

anniversary 6 annual, Easter, yearly; **7** jubilee, Metonic, secular; **8** birthday; **9** Christmas, Hallowe'en; **10** centennial, millennial, millennium; **11** celebration; **12** bicentennial, Thanksgiving, tricentenary; **13** commemoration, commemorative; **15** sesquicentenary; PHRASES: **2, 10, 3** St Valentine's Day; **3, 2, 8** day to remember; **3, 3** May Day; **3, 5, 3** New Year's Day; **3, 6, 5** Guy Fawkes Night; **4, 3** flag day, gala day, high day *UK*, holy day, name day; **4, 7** ruby wedding *UK*; **5, 3** feast day, field day, great day, Labor Day *UK*, poppy day; **5, 5, 3** April Fools' Day; **6, 2, 4** Fourth of July; **6, 3** Boxing Day, Canada Day, saint's day; **6, 7** golden jubilee *UK*, golden wedding *UK*, silver jubilee, silver wedding; **7, 3** Father's Day, Mother's Day, special day; **7, 7** diamond jubilee, diamond wedding; **8, 3** Bastille Day, Memorial Day; **9, 3** Armistice Day, Australia Day *UK*; **12, 3** Independence Day.

annotate 4 mark, note; **5** gloss; **7** explain; **8** inscribe; PHRASES: **4, 2** mark up; **4, 5, 2** make notes on; **7, 2** comment on.

annotation 4 mark, note; **5** gloss; **6** legend; **8** appendix, exegesis, footnote, variorum; **10** commentary, marginalia; **11** explanation; PHRASES: **7, 4** textual note; **8, 4** marginal note.

annotative 8 critical; **9** editorial; **10** glossarial; **11** explanatory.

announcement 6 notice; **7** message; **9** statement; **11** declaration; **12** proclamation.

announcer 4 host; **6** anchor; **8** coanchor; **10** newsreader *UK*; **11** broadcaster.

annoy 3 bug, irk, vex; **4** goad, nark, rile; **5** anger, peeve, tease; **6** bother, enrage, hassle, madden; **7** provoke; **8** irritate; **9** aggravate, displease, frustrate, infuriate; **10** antagonize, exasperate; PHRASES: **3, 2, 4, 6** get on one's nerves; **3, 3** put out; **4, 3** hack off *UK*; **5, 3** drive mad *UK*; **6, 3** cheese off

UK; **6-3-4** nickel-and-dime.

annoyance 4 pest; **5** anger; **6** bother, hassle; **8** vexation; **10** irritation; **11** aggravation, displeasure, frustration, indignation, provocation; **12** exasperation.

annoyed *See* **angry**

annual ring 4, 4 tree ring; **6, 4** growth ring.

annul 3 end; **6** cancel; **7** nullify, rescind; **8** dissolve; **9** terminate; **10** invalidate; PHRASES: **3, 2, 3, 2** put an end to; **4, 3** call off; **4, 4, 3, 4** make null and void.

annulment 8 negation; **11** dissolution, elimination, termination; **12** cancellation, invalidation; **13** nullification.

anodyne 4 tame; **5** bland; **7** calming, insipid, neutral; **8** relaxing, settling, soothing; **9** analgesic, deadening; **10** comforting, palliative; **11** inoffensive, painkilling; PHRASES: **4-9** pain-relieving.

anoint 3 oil, rub; **5** baste, cream, salve, slick, smear; **6** smooth, spread; **7** massage, unguent; **9** embrocate; PHRASES: **4, 3, 4** pour oil upon.

anointing of the sick 7, 7 extreme unction.

anointment 7 unction; **9** inunction *UK*; **11** chrismation.

anon *See* **soon**

anonymity 1 X; **4** Anon.; **5** alias; **7** privacy, secrecy; **8** dullness; **9** blandness, obscurity, pseudonym; **11** concealment; **12** facelessness, namelessness, ordinariness; **14** indistinctness, insignificance; PHRASES: **2, 4** no name; **3, 2, 5** nom de plume; **3, 4** pen name; **4, 4** code name; **5, 4** stage name; **7, 4** assumed name; **7, 7** unknown country, Unknown Warrior; **7, 8** unknown quantity.

anonymous 6 secret; **7** unknown; **8** everyday, nameless, unsigned; **10** mysterious; **11** unspecified; **12** unidentified; **13** indistinctive, unexceptional; **15** undistinguished; PHRASES: **3, 2, 3, 4** run of the mill.

another time 4 soon, then; **5** later; **6** mañana; **7** earlier, someday; **8** sometime, tomorrow; **9** yesterday; PHRASES: **2, 3, 4** in the past; **2, 3, 6** in the future; **3, 2, 3, 6** not at the moment; **3, 2, 5, 4** one of these days; **3, 3** not now; **3, 4** any time; **3, 5** not today; **4, 4, 1, 4** once upon a time; **4, 5, 4** some other time; **6, 2, 5** sooner or later.

answer 3 key; **5** react, reply, solve; **6** rejoin, remedy, retort, return; **7** confirm, counter, fulfill, resolve, respond, riposte, satisfy; **8** backtalk, comeback, reaction, repartee, response, solution; **9** rejoinder; **10** responsion; **11** acknowledge; PHRASES: **3, 3** way out; **4, 4** back talk, come back; **5, 8** witty repartee.

answer (in answer) 9 echoingly; **10** reactively; **11** defensively, reflexively; **12** reciprocally, responsively; **13** dialectically, interactively, retroactively, reverberantly; **14** antithetically; **15** argumentatively, interchangeably; PHRASES: **2, 5** in reply; **2, 7** in defense; **2, 8** in response; **2, 12** in conversation.

answerability 4 duty; **9** liability; **10** obligation; **14** accountability, responsibility.

answerable 6 liable; **7** dutiful, obliged; **8** beholden, blamable; **10** chargeable, obligatory, punishable; **11** accountable, responsible; PHRASES: **4-5** duty-bound; **5, 10** under obligation.

answerably 7 instead; PHRASES: **2, 4** in lieu; **2, 5** in place. *See also* **answerable**

answer back 4 sass; **5** argue, cheek, react, rebut; **6** object, refute, retort; **7** confute, counter, respond, riposte; **8** backtalk; **9** interject, vindicate; **10** contradict; **12** counterblast; **13** countercharge; PHRASES: **2, 4** be rude; **3, 3** lip off; **4, 2** butt in; **4, 4** come back, talk back; **5, 3** mouth off; **5, 4** shout down.

answerer 6 solver, talker; **7** decoder, replier; **8** objector; **9** addressee, defendant; **10** respondent; **11** interviewee; **12** interlocutor; **13** correspondent.

answer for 5 atone; **7** endorse, replace; **8** deputize; **9** represent; PHRASES: **2, 6, 3** be liable for; **2, 8, 3** be punished for; **3, 2, 6, 2** act on behalf of; **3, 3** pay for; **4, 2** back up; **4, 3, 3** take the rap; **4, 6, 3** make amends for; **5, 2, 3** stand in for, stand up for; **5, 3** speak for, vouch for *UK*; **6, 3** appear for.

answering 8 insolent, replying, returned; **10** respondent, responding, responsive; **12** backtalkting.

answer to 4 twin; **5** agree, match, tally; **7** conform, require; **8** parallel; **9** correlate; **10** correspond; **11** reciprocate.

ant 3 red; **4** army, bear, bird, fire, heap, hill, wood; **5** eater, emmet, slave, white; **6** amazon, flying, formic, velvet, worker; **7** bulldog, pharaoh, pismire, soldier, termite; **9** carpenter, legionary; **10** leafcutter; PHRAS-ES: **5-6** slave-making.

antagonist *See* **rival**

antagonize 4 rile; **5** annoy, grate, upset; **6** enrage, madden, poison; **7** incense, provoke; **8** alienate, disunite, embitter, estrange, irritate, nauseate; **9** aggravate, infuriate; PHRASES: **3, 4, 4, 2** get your back up; **3, 7** set against; **5, 7** cause offense.

ant bear 8 aardvark.

anteater 6 numbat *UK*; **7** echidna; **8** pangolin.

antenna 4 beam, dish, horn, loop, whip, Yagi; **5** probe; **6** aerial, dipole, feeler; **7** whisker; **8** director, radiator, tentacle; **9** receiving, reflector; **10** projection; **11** directional; **12** protuberance, transmitting; **15** omnidirectional; PHRASES: **4-4** long-wire; **6, 6** folded dipole.

anterior 4 fore; **5** front; **6** before, sooner; **7** earlier, leading; **8** foremost.

ant hill 9 formicary.

anthology *See* **collection**

anthracite 4, 4 hard coal.

anthropological 10 anatomical, ecological, ethnogenic; **11** demographic; **12** craniometric, ethnographic, ethnological, sociological; **13** anthropogenic, craniological, functionalist, structuralist; **14** anthropometric, anthroposcopic, craniometrical; **15** ethnoscientific.

anthropological concept 5 taboo; **7** descent, kinship; **10** matriarchy, patriarchy; **11** matrilineal, patrilineal; **12** diffusionism; **13** consanguinity, functionalism, structuralism; PHRASES: **3, 3** age set.

anthropologist 11 craniologer, demographer, ethnogenist, ethnologist; **12** ethnographer; **13** craniometrist; **15** anthropometrist.

anthropology 6 social; **8** cultural, economic, folklore, humanism, physical, symbolic; **9** ethnogeny, ethnology, mythology, sociology; **10** biological, craniology, demography, somatology; **11** craniometry, ethnography; **12** anthropogeny; **13** anthropometry, anthroposophy *UK*; **14** anthropography; **15** anthropogenesis, ethnomusicology, humanitarianism; PHRAS-ES: **5, 7** human ecology, human studies; **5, 9** human geography; **7, 2, 3** science of man.

anthropophagite 8 cannibal.

anticipate 5 await; **6** expect; **7** foresee,

predict, preempt, preface; **8** forecast; **9** forestall; PHRASES: **2, 2, 7** do in advance; **4, 3** hope for, long for, wait for; **4, 3, 3** jump the gun; **4, 7, 2** look forward to; **5, 5** think ahead; **5, 6** think likely.

anticipation (in anticipation) 2, 1, 7 as a prelude; **2, 1, 11** as a preliminary; **2, 11** in preparation.

anticyclone 4 high.

antidote 4 cure; **6** answer, remedy; **7** antigen; **8** antibody, medicine, sedative, solution; **9** antiserum, antitoxin, febrifuge, vermifuge; **10** antibiotic, corrective; **11** antipyretic; **13** anticoagulant, antihistamine, antispasmodic, counterpoison; **14** anticonvulsant, countermeasure; **15** counterirritant.

antifreeze 6 deicer; PHRASES: **8, 6** ethylene glycol.

antimony 7 stibium.

antipathy See **opposition**

antipope 4 John; **5** Donus, Felix, Linus; **6** Philip, Victor; **7** Amadeus, Gregory, Guibert, Hadrian, Michael, Paschal; **8** Adalbert, Benedict, Boniface, Eulalius, Honorius, Nicholas, Novatian, Theodore; **9** Anacletus, Callixtus, Celestine, Dioscorus, Sylvester, Theodoric, Ursicinus, Valeriano; **10** Anastasius, Hippolytus, Laurentius, Theofylact; **11** Christopher, Constantine.

antiquarian 8 archaist; **9** antiquary; **10** antecedent, classicist; **11** medievalist; **12** paleographer; **13** archaeologist; PHRASES: **7, 6** antique dealer.

antiquarianism 8 archaism; **11** archaeology, medievalism, paleography.

antiquarianize 6 exhume; **8** archaize, excavate; PHRASES: **3, 2, 3, 4** dig up the past; **4, 4** look back; **5, 4** trace back.

antiquated 5 dated, passé, stale; **7** outworn; **8** obsolete, outdated, outmoded; **10** fossilized; PHRASES: **3, 2, 4** out of date; **3, 3** old hat; **3-9** old-fashioned; **4, 4** long past; **4-5** moth-eaten; **6, 3, 5** behind the times.

antique See **old**

antiquity 5 decay, relic; **7** antique, cobwebs, remains; **8** artifact; **11** ancientness; **13** primitiveness; PHRASES: **3, 7, 4** the distant past; **4, 3, 2, 4** time out of mind; **4, 10** time immemorial; **5, 4** olden days; **5, 5** olden times; **6, 4** bygone days; **7, 4** distant past; **7, 5** ancient times.

antiseptic 4 pure, tame; **5** bland, clean; **7** insipid, sterile; **9** colorless; **13** antibacterial, uninteresting; **14** uncontaminated.

antisocial 3 shy; **7** harmful; **8** reserved; **10** disruptive, rebellious, unfriendly, unsociable; **11** belligerent; **12** disagreeable; **13** inconsiderate.

antithesis See **opposite**

anvil 5 incus.

any 3 one; **4** each, some; **5** every; **6** anyone; **7** anybody, several; **8** anything, slightly *UK*, somewhat, whatever; **9** whichever; PHRASES: **2, 3** at all; **2, 3, 5** in the least.

any (not any) See **nothing**

anyhow 4 well; **6** anyway; **7** besides; **11** nonetheless; **12** nevertheless; PHRASES: **2, 3, 4** at any rate, in any case; **2, 5** at least; **3, 4** all over; **3, 4, 3, 4** all over the shop *UK*; **3, 4, 3, 5** all over the place; **4-4** pell-mell; **4-5** arsy-versy *UK*; **5-5** topsy-turvy; **5, 5, 3** every which way; **5-6** harum-scarum; **6-4** upside-down; **6-7** helter-skelter.

anyway 4 well; **6** anyhow; **7** besides; **10** regardless; **11** nonetheless; **12** nevertheless; PHRASES: **2, 3, 4** at any rate, in any case; **2, 6, 4** no matter what.

AP 6, 1, 4 before a meal (Latin: *ante prandium*).

apart 4 rent; **5** cleft, riven, split; **6** broken, cloven; **7** asunder, distant; **8** brokenly, separate, sundered; **9** dispersed, divergent, radiating, scattered, shattered *UK*; **10** separately; **11** divergently; **14** interstitially; **15** discontinuously; PHRASES: **2, 1, 8** at a distance; **2, 3, 4** to one side; **2, 4** in bits, to bits; **2, 6** in pieces, to shreds; **2, 7** to tatters; **2, 9** at intervals; **2, 11** to smithereens; **3, 2** cut up; **3, 3, 2** off and on; **3, 3, 4** now and then; **3, 3, 5** now and again; **3, 8** not together; **4, 4, 4** limb from limb; **5, 2, 5** every so often.

apartment 5 suite; **6** studio; **9** penthouse; PHRASES: **9, 7** ~ complex.

apathetic 4 lazy; **5** aloof, bored; **8** listless, lukewarm, resigned; **9** impassive, lethargic; **10** dispirited; **11** indifferent, unconcerned; **12** noncommittal, uninterested; PHRASES: **2, 4, 2, 4, 3** no will of one's own; **4-5** easy-going.

apathy 5 ennui; **7** boredom; **8** lethargy; **9** inertness, passivity, unconcern; **12** indifference; **14** dispiritedness; PHRASES: **4-11** half-heartedness.

ape 4 copy; 5 mimic; 6 mirror, monkey, parrot; 7 imitate; 11 impersonate.

aperture *See* opening

apex *See* top

aphorize 6 remark; 7 observe, proverb; 8 moralize, theorize; 13 epigrammatize; PHRASES: 4, 1, 6 coin a phrase.

Aphrodite 6 Urania.

aplomb *See* assurance

apocalyptic 7 ruinous; 11 cataclysmic; 12 catastrophic; PHRASES: 4-5 doom-laden *UK.*

apologetic 5 sorry; 6 rueful; 8 contrite, pleading; 9 defensive, justified, regretful, repentant; 10 remorseful, vindicated; 11 justifiable; PHRASES: 2, 7 in defense.

apologize 4 fast, pray; 5 atone, offer; 6 defend, pacify, repent; 7 appease, confess, explain; 10 conciliate, propitiate; PHRASES: 2, 7 do penance; 3, 3, 2, 5 say one is sorry; 3, 5 say sorry; 3, 6 beg pardon; 3, 8 act contrite; 3, 11 beg forgiveness; 4, 2, 7 make an apology; 4, 3, 2, 4 come cap in hand; 4, 6 make amends; 5, 2, 8 offer an oblation; 7, 6 express regret.

apology 6 excuse; 7 defense, fasting, penance, regrets, remorse, stopgap; 8 pretense; 9 cleansing, imitation, penitence; 10 confession, contrition, repentance; 11 austerities, explanation; 12 purification; 13 justification; 14 acknowledgment; PHRASES: 3, 2, 5 bed of nails; 3, 2, 10 act of contrition; 3, 5 mea culpa; 4, 5 hair shirt; 4, 7 poor example; 4, 10 poor substitute; 5, 8 burnt offering, peace offering; 6-7 breast-beating; 6, 8 votive offering; 8, 6 pathetic excuse; 11, 3 penitential act.

apostasy 7 perfidy; 8 betrayal; 9 defection, desertion, recreancy, treachery; 10 conversion; PHRASES: 5, 4 going over; 7, 7 turning traitor; 7, 8 turning renegade.

apostatize 6 betray, defect, desert, switch; 8 blackleg; 11 collaborate; PHRASES: 2, 4 go over; 3, 3, 4, 4 let the side down; 4, 4, 4 turn one's coat; 4, 7 turn traitor; 4, 8 turn renegade; 5, 3, 5 cross the floor; 5, 4 cross over; 6, 4 switch over; 6, 5 change sides.

apostle 7 devotee; 8 advocate, champion, disciple, follower, promoter; 9 messenger, proponent, supporter; 10 missionary.

apparatus 3 kit; 4 gear; 6 device, gadget, method, system, tackle; 9 mechanism, operation; 11 arrangement.

apparent 5 clear, plain; 7 evident, obvious, outward, present, seeming, visible; 8 external, specious; 9 deceptive, imaginary; 10 noticeable, ostensible; 11 perceptible, superficial.

apparently 8 avowedly; 9 allegedly; 10 manifestly; 11 purportedly; PHRASES: 2, 3, 4, 2, 2 on the face of it; 2, 3, 7 on the surface; 2, 4 in fact; 2, 5 at sight, on sight; 2, 5, 4 it seems that; 2, 5, 5 at first blush, at first sight; 2, 6, 2, 2 it sounds as if; 2, 7, 4 it appears that; 4, 5 into sight; 5, 3, 2, 4 rumor has it that. *See also* apparent

apparition *See* ghost

appeal 3 ask; 4 call, plea, urge; 5 charm, plead, tempt; 6 allure; 7 attract, request; 8 interest, petition; 9 fascinate, influence; 10 attraction; 11 application; 14 attractiveness.

appealing 7 likable; 8 alluring, charming, engaging, hypnotic, magnetic, mesmeric, pleasing, tempting; 9 affecting, emotional, inspiring, seductive; 10 attractive, compelling, motivating, suggestive; 11 charismatic, encouraging, fascinating, interesting; 12 irresistible.

appeal to 6 invoke; 7 entreat; 8 petition; PHRASES: 4, 2 pray to; 5, 2 apply to.

appear 2 be; 3 act; 4 grow, look, loom, open, play, seem, show; 5 begin, exist, occur; 6 arrive, attend, emerge, happen, mirror; 7 imitate, perform, reflect; 8 manifest, resemble; 11 materialize; PHRASES: 2, 4 be seen; 2, 5 be found, be there; 2, 7 be present; 3, 2 pop up; 3, 3 pop out; 4, 1, 4 play a part; 4, 2 crop up, roll up, show up, turn up; 4, 2, 2 look as if, seem to be; 4, 2, 5 come to light; 4, 2, 8 make an entrance; 4, 3 come out, leak out; 4, 3, 3 meet the eye; 4, 3, 4 give the idea; 4, 4 look like, seem like; 4, 4, 2 take part in; 4, 4, 4 come into view; 4, 4, 5 come into focus, come into sight; 4, 5 come forth; 5, 2, 5 heave in sight; 5, 5 break forth; 5, 7 shine through.

appear (something that appears) 4 pose; 5 ghost, guise, image, sight; 6 mirage, vision; 7 chimera, phantom, seeming, specter; 8 disguise, epiphany, hologram, illusion, pretense; 9 ectoplasm, emanation, semblance, spectacle; 10 apparition, revelation; 13 hallucination; PHRASES: 5-5 afterimage.

appearance 4 face, form, look, mien; 5

birth, debut, front, guise, image, issue, onset, shape; **6** advent, aspect, coming, façade, format, growth, launch, manner, veneer; **7** arising, arrival, bearing, contour, dawning, opening, outline, outside, persona, profile, release, surface; **8** entrance, exterior, features, premiere, presence; **9** beginning, emergence, formation, semblance, unfolding; **10** attendance, dimensions, embodiment, expresion, impression, revelation, silhouette; **11** incarnation, physiognomy, publication, superficies; **12** introduction, presentation; **13** manifestation; **14** superficiality; **15** characteristics, materialization; PHRASES: **5, 5** outer shell; **5, 9** first screening; **6, 7** public persona; **7, 2** opening up; **7, 4** outward show; **7, 5** issuing forth.

appear guilty 5 blush; **7** stammer; PHRASES: **4, 8** look sheepish.

appease 4 calm; **6** pacify, settle, soothe; **7** assuage, mollify, placate; **10** conciliate.

appeaser 3 wet; **4** wimp; **5** gofer, grunt, mouse, slave, toady; **6** coward, menial; **7** doormat, quitter, servant; **8** groveler, pacifier, pushover; **9** defeatist, sycophant; **11** conciliator; PHRASES: **5-4** brown-nose; **5-5** brown-noser.

appendage 4 limb; **6** feeler, member; **7** adjunct; **8** addition; **9** accessory, extremity; **10** attachment, projection; PHRASES: **3-2** add-on.

appetite 4 wish; **5** binge, greed, taste; **6** desire, famine, hunger, thirst; **7** bolting, craving, gorging, passion; **8** bingeing, feasting, gluttony, gobbling, guzzling, keenness, voracity; **9** devouring, eagerness; **10** enthusiasm, hungriness, overeating, starvation; **11** gourmandism, inclination, thirstiness, wolfishness; **12** gormandizing; **13** voraciousness; **14** overindulgence; PHRASES: **3, 3** pig out; **4, 2, 3** need to eat; **5, 7** empty stomach; **6, 3, 4** desire for food; **8, 7** stuffing oneself.

appetizer 6 dainty, morsel, nibble, sample, taster, tidbit; **7** sampler, soupçon, starter, tasting; **8** apéritif, delicacy, sampling; **9** foretaste; **12** introduction; PHRASES: **4, 7** hors d'oeuvre; **5, 6** bonne bouche *UK*; **5, 7** sneak preview.

applaud 4 clap, yell; **5** cheer, shout; **6** admire, praise; **7** approve, support; **12** congratulate.

applauder 7 cheerer, clapper; **8** claqueur; **11** cheerleader.

applause 4 hand; **6** praise; **7** ovation, support; **8** approval, clapping; **11** approbation; **12** appreciation.

apple 3 big, may, oak; **4** crab, isle, jack, love, rose; **5** adam's, sauce, thorn; **6** balsam, bitter, brandy, butter; PHRASES: **5, 5** candy ~.

application 3 bid, DTP, TEX, use; **4** MIDI, wimp; **5** claim, usage; **6** editor, effort, tender, window; **7** purpose, request; **8** database, devotion, function; **9** appliance, attention, diligence, relevance; **10** submission; **11** spreadsheet; **12** presentation, solicitation; **13** concentration; PHRASES: **4, 4** hard work; **4, 6** text editor; **4, 10** word processing; **6, 7** window manager; **7, 8** network database; **8, 7** spelling checker.

apply 3 ask, use; **5** smear; **6** affect, employ, relate; **7** concern, operate, pertain, request, utilize; PHRASES: **2, 8** be relevant; **3, 2** put on, rub on; **6, 2** spread on.

appoint 4 hire, pick; **5** agree; **6** assign, choose, employ, select; PHRASES: **4, 2** sign up, take on.

appointment 3 job; **4** date, post; **6** choice, office; **7** meeting, opening; **8** position; **9** selection; **10** engagement, nomination, rendezvous.

appreciate 4 rise, soar; **5** grasp, value; **7** realize; **8** escalate; **10** understand; PHRASES: **2, 8, 3** be grateful for, be thankful for.

appreciation 4 rise; **5** grasp, sense; **6** growth, thanks; **8** approval, increase, pleasure; **9** enjoyment, gratitude, inflation; **10** admiration, escalation, obligation, perception; **13** comprehension, understanding.

apprehend *See* **catch**

apprehension 5 worry; **6** arrest; **7** anxiety, capture, seizure; **9** detention; **11** trepidation. *See also* **apprehensive**

apprehensive 6 uneasy; **7** anxious, nervous; **10** suspicious.

approach 3 way; **4** hail, line, loom, near; **5** greet, slant, style; **6** accost, attack, handle, manage, method, salute, tackle, tactic, toward, waylay; **7** advance, attempt, contact; **8** attitude, consider, driveway; **10** buttonhole; **11** approximate, methodology; **13** confrontation; PHRASES: **2, 7, 2** be similar to; **3-2** run-up; **3, 2, 5, 4** get in touch with; **3, 5** set about; **4, 2** call to, draw up, talk to; **4, 2, 2** come up to; **4, 2, 6** line of attack; **4, 4** come near, deal with, draw near; **4, 5** come close;

4, 6, 5 come within reach; **4, 7** move towards *UK*; **4, 7, 4** make contact with; **5, 2** speak to, verge on; **5, 3** sound out; **6, 4** parley with; **8, 4** converse with; **9, 3** narrowing gap; **9, 6** collision course.

approaching 6 coming, future; **7** inbound, nearing, pending; **8** imminent, incoming, oncoming; **9** advancing, impending, potential; **11** forthcoming, inwardbound.

appropriate 3 apt; **4** take; **5** right, seize; **6** assume; **7** fitting; **8** apposite, suitable; **14** misappropriate; PHRASES: **4, 4** take over.

approvable 8 passable; **10** acceptable; **11** permissible; **12** satisfactory.

approval 2 OK; **3** nod; **4** seal, vote, wink; **6** assent, esteem, liking, praise; **7** backing, consent, license, mandate, support; **8** advocacy, blessing, sanction; **9** agreement; **10** acceptance, admiration, imprimatur, permission; **11** approbation, benediction, endorsement; **12** acquiescence, appreciation, championship, satisfaction; **13** authorization; **14** recommendation; PHRASES: **2-5** go-ahead; **3-2** say-so; **5, 5** green light; **6, 2** thumbs up; **6, 5** rubber stamp; **6, 9** formal agreement.

approval (meet with approval) 4 pass; **7** satisfy; PHRASES: **3, 6** win praise; **4, 2, 2, 7** come up to scratch; **4, 3, 4** pass the test; **4, 5** find favor; **4, 6** gain credit, pass muster.

approve 2 OK; **4** like, okay, pass; **5** agree, allow, favor, grant, prize, value; **6** accept, admire, esteem, permit, ratify; **7** certify, commend, consent, endorse, respect, support; **8** sanction; **9** authorize; **10** greenlight; PHRASES: **4, 2, 5** find no fault; **4, 4** hold with; **5, 3, 4, 2** think the best of; **5, 4, 2** think well of; **5, 6, 2** think highly of; **6, 6** regard highly.

approving 7 content, fulsome; **8** admiring, positive; **9** adulatory, favorable, laudatory, lionizing, panegyric, satisfied; **10** eulogistic, flattering, respectful, uncritical; **11** acclamatory, approbatory, encomiastic, sympathetic; **12** appreciative, appreciatory, commendatory; **13** complimentary.

approximation *See* **estimate**

apt 4 able; **5** prone, quick; **6** likely; **7** capable, fitting, skilled, tending; **8** apposite, inclined, suitable; **9** competent, pertinent; **11** appropriate.

aptitude 4 bent, gift, turn; **5** flair, knack, skill; **6** genius, talent; **7** ability, faculty; **8** ca-

pacity, instinct, tendency; **9** endowment; **10** propensity; **11** inclination; **13** qualification; PHRASES: **3, 3** ear for, eye for; **4-3** knowhow; **5, 7** green fingers; **6, 7** innate ability; **7, 3** feeling for.

AQ 5 water (Latin: aqua).

aquatic animal 4 fish, seal; **5** coral, krill, larva, whale; **6** nekton, sponge; **7** bivalve, dolphin, octopus; **8** cetacean, plankton, starfish; **9** jellyfish, shellfish; **10** cephalopod, cuttlefish, echinoderm; **11** zooplankton; **12** coelenterate; PHRASES: **6, 6** marine animal, marine mammal.

aquilegia 9 columbine.

AR 5 queen (Latin: Anna Regina).

Arabian camel 9 dromedary.

arable farming 11 monoculture; **12** monocropping; PHRASES: **3, 7** dry farming; **4, 7** tank farming, tree farming; **4, 8** crop rotation; **4, 9** crop husbandry; **5-3-4** slash-and-burn; **5, 7** fruit farming; **5, 8** plant breeding; **5, 10** Green Revolution; **6, 9** market gardening.

arachnid 4 mite, tick; **6** acarid, spider; **7** redback; **8** scorpion; **9** tarantula; **10** harvestman; PHRASES: **4, 4** soft tick; **4, 6** bird spider, wolf spider; **5, 5** black widow; **5, 6** money spider *UK*, water spider *UK*; **5, 7, 6** brown recluse spider; **5, 8** false scorpion; **6-3, 6** funnel-web spider; **6-8** pseudo-scorpion; **7, 6** jumping spider; **8, 6** trapdoor spider.

arachnological 12 acarological.

arachnologist 11 acarologist.

arbiter 6 leader; **7** example; **8** mediator; **9** authority, influence; **10** arbitrator, negotiator; **12** intermediary; PHRASES: **2-7** go-between; **4, 5** role model.

arbitrary 6 chance, random; **9** illogical; **10** subjective, uninformed.

arbitrator *See* **judge** *See* **mediator**

arboretum 6 pinery; **7** orchard, pinetum; PHRASES: **4, 7** tree nursery.

arboricultural 12 dendrologous; **13** dendrological, silvicultural.

arc *See* **curve**

arcade 4 mall, nave; **5** aisle, penny, prado, video; **6** loggia, parade *UK*; **7** gallery, pergola, portico, walkway; **8** cloister, seafront, shopping; **9** amusement, colonnade, esplanade, promenade, triforium; **10** ambulatory, passageway; PHRASES: **7, 3** covered way.

arcane 4 deep; 6 hidden, secret; 8 esoteric; 10 mysterious.

arch 3 arc, bow; 4 bend, keel, ogee, skew; 5 acute, curve, false, roman, sweep, Tudor; 6 basket, corbel, fallen, gothic, lancet, Norman, raking; 7 archway, cunning, doorway, knowing, playful, pointed, portico, rampant, roguish, rounded; 8 catenary, strainer; 9 arcuation, curvature, depressed, horseshoe, parabolic, segmental, triumphal, zygomatic; 10 elliptical, semicircle, shouldered; 11 mischievous; 12 semicircular; PHRASES: 3, 8 two centered; 4, 2, 6 anse de panier; 4-8 four-centered.

archaeological 12 epigraphical, paleological; 13 Egyptological, Sumerological; 14 Assyriological, paleobotanical, paleographical.

archaeologist 10 epigrapher; 11 paleologist; 12 Egyptologist, paleographer, Sumerologist; 13 Assyriologist, paleobotanist; 14 paleobiologist, paleoecologist, paleontologist, paleozoologist.

archaeology 6 marine; 9 epigraphy, paleology; 10 Egyptology, industrial, Sumerology; 11 Assyriology, fossilology, paleobotany, paleography, prehistoric; 12 paleobiology, paleoecology, paleozoology; 14 paleogeography.

archaic 5 early; 7 disused, primary; 8 original, primeval; 9 ancestral, classical; 10 historical, immemorial; PHRASES: 3-2-4 out-of-date; 3-7 old-worldly; 3-9 old-fashioned.

arched 4 bent; 5 bowed, domed, round; 6 curved; 7 arcuate, rounded, vaulted; 8 arcuated.

archer 5 Cupid, Diana, Orion; 6 bowman, hunter, Nimrod; 7 Artemis; 8 marksman; 11 Sagittarius; PHRASES: 5, 4 Robin Hood UK; 7, 4 William Tell.

archetype See **model**

architect 3 Pei (I. M.); 4 Adam (Robert), Hunt (Richard Morris), Kahn (Louis I.), Wren (Sir Christopher); 5 Aalto (Alvar), civil, Gaudí (Antoni), Hoban (James), Jones (Inigo), mason, McKim (Charles Follen), naval, Soane (Sir John), Stone (Edward Durell), White (Stanford); 6 Breuer (Marcel), Foster (Norman), Fuller (R. Buckminster), Upjohn (Richard), Vasari (Giorgio), Wright (Frank Lloyd); 7 Bernini (Gianlorenzo), builder, creator, founder, Gilbert (Cass), Gropius (Walter), Johnson (Philip), Latrobe (Benjamin Henry), Lutyens (Sir Edwin), planner, Renwick (James), Venturi (Robert); 8 Bramante (Donato), Bulfinch (Charles), Bunshaft (Gordon), designer, domestic, engineer, inventor, military, Niemeyer (Oscar), Palladio (Andrea), Saarinen (Eero), Saarinen (Eliel), Sullivan (Louis); 9 draftsman, Hawksmoor (Nicholas), landscape, Vitruvius; 10 industrial, Mackintosh (Charles Rennie), originator, Richardson (H. H.); 11 Churriguera (José Benito), draftswoman; 12 Brunelleschi (Filippo), draftsperson, Michelangelo; PHRASES: 2, 9 Le Corbusier; 4, 3, 3, 4 Mies van der Rohe (Ludwig); 5, 5 prime mover, stone mason, Tange Kenzo; 6, 7 master builder; 8, 2, 5 Leonardo da Vinci.

architectural features and terms 3 bow, hip, rib; 4 anta, base, beak, beam, case, coin, cope, dado, naos, neck, pier, roof, wall; 5 ancon, attic, cella, floor, gable, groin, quoin, story, truss; 6 arcade, ashlar, concha, coping, corbel, cordon, cupola, fascia, filler, finial, frieze, haunch, impost, invert, lintel, loggia, louver, louvre, module, podium, squint, string, taenia, window; 7 astylar, balcony, bolster, capital, ceiling, cornice, fantail, frustum, landing, lantern, lunette, necking, portico, rooftop, rotunda, tambour; 8 capstone, casement, chapiter, cymatium, epistyle, extrados, fenestra, gorgerin, housetop, intrados, keystone, pediment, prostyle, shafting, spandrel, springer, stringer, tympanum, voussoir; 9 copestone, dripstone, fastigium, headstone, penthouse, ridgepole, stairhead, vestibule; 10 ambulatory, architrave, cantilever, fenestella, propylaeum; 11 entablature, rustication; 12 frontispiece; PHRASES: 4-7, 4 load-bearing wall; 5, 3 gable end; 5, 4 cheek wall; 5, 6 oriel window; 6, 5 coping stone; 6, 6 lancet window; 7, 4 curtain wall, picture rail UK Can; 7, 6 lantern cupola; 7, 7 picture molding; 10, 4 nonbearing wall.

architecture 4 cusp, herm; 5 Doric, Ionic, order, Tudor; 6 Empire, Gothic, Norman, rococo, taenia, Tuscan; 7 annulet, Baroque, Bauhaus, crocket, entasis, federal, Grecian, meander, moderne, Moorish, Mudéjar; 8 colonial, dogtooth, Georgian, graphics, Jacobean, lanceted, pediment, triglyph; 9 brutalism, brutalist, Byzantine, classical, Composite, Decorated, Gothicism, guilloche, mannerism, modernism, modernist, multifoil, Palladian, Victorian; **10** architrave, classicism, Corinthian, Federation *UK*; flamboyant, Florentine, minimalist, postmodern, Romanesque, skiagraphy, transition, vernacular; **11** cinquecento, Elizabethan, entablature, Normanesque, perspective, Renaissance; **12** construction, ecclesiology, neoclassical; **13** perpendicular; **14** architectonics; **17** intercolumniation; PHRASES: **3, 4** art deco; **3-6** neo-Gothic; **3, 7** art nouveau, bed molding; **4, 4** high tech; **4, 6** rose window; **5, 4** onion dome, strap work; **5, 5** Doric order, Ionic order; **5, 7** Early English; **6, 4** lancet arch; **6, 7** Gothic revival, Gothic Revival; **6, 10** French provincial; **7-4** wedding-cake; **9, 4** horseshoe arch; **9, 12** Decorated ~; **10, 5** Corinthian order.

architrave 8 epistyle.

archive 4 file; **6** record; **7** library; **8** document; **13** documentation.

arctic 3 fox; **4** char, hare, tern; **6** circle, frigid, frozen, willow; **7** glacial, subzero; **8** freezing.

Arctic 5 igloo, Ocean; **6** Circle, Eskimo; **7** iceberg, Siberia; **8** snowline; **9** Antarctic; **10** permafrost; PHRASES: **4, 5** snow house; **5, 4** North Pole, South Pole; **6, 4** frigid zone.

ardent *See* **passionate**

ardour *See* **passion**

arduous 9 laborious, punishing, strenuous.

area 4 acre, belt, goal, gray, zone; **5** field, range, theme, topic; **6** corner, county, domain, extent, locale, parish, region, sphere; **7** borough, enclave, expanse, hectare, penalty, service, subject; **8** district, division, province, township, vicinity; **9** catchment, community, specialty; **10** speciality *UK*; **12** municipality, neighborhood; PHRASES: **2-2** no-go.

arena 5 field, pitch *UK*; **6** ground; **7** funplex, stadium; **10** showground *UK*; PHRASES: **6, 6** sports ground *UK*.

argent 6 silver.

argentum 6 silver.

argot 5 idiom, slang; **6** jargon, speech; **7** dialect.

arguable 4 moot; **7** dubious; **8** doubtful; **9** debatable, uncertain, undecided, unsettled; **10** disputable; **11** contentious, problematic; **12** questionable; **13** controversial; PHRASES: **3, 4, 7** far from certain; **4, 2, 8** open to question.

arguably 5 maybe; **7** perhaps; **8** possibly; **9** plausibly; **10** contrarily; **14** hypothetically; PHRASES: **2, 3, 5, 4** on the other hand; **2, 3, 8** on the contrary.

argue 3 row; **4** feud, spar, spat, tiff; **5** brawl, claim, clash, fight, scrap; **6** argufy, bicker, debate, hassle, object, reason, tussle; **7** contend, contest, dispute, dissent, gainsay, protest, quarrel, quibble, rupture, wrangle; **8** conflict, disagree, maintain, squabble, struggle; **9** altercate; **10** contradict, polemicize; **11** remonstrate; PHRASES: **2, 2, 3** go to war; **2, 2, 5** go to court; **4, 1, 4** make a case; **4, 2, 1, 3** kick up a row; **4, 2, 1, 6** kick up a shindy; **4, 2, 5-3** kick up bobsydie *NZ*; **4, 3** fall out; **4, 5** have words, lock horns.

arguer 6 jurist, lawyer; **7** casuist, debater, pleader, sophist; **8** advocate, disputer, litigant, polemist, reasoner, wrangler; **9** barrister *UK Can*, disputant, firebrand, litigator, plaintiff, proponent, quarreler; **10** polemicist.

argument 3 row, war; **4** feud, fray, rift, spat, tiff; **5** brawl, claim, clash, fight, scrap, split; **6** barney *UK*, debate, dustup, fracas, hassle, ruckus, rumpus, schism, shindy, strife, tussle; **7** discord, dispute, polemic, quarrel, ruction, scuffle, wrangle; **8** conflict, exchange, squabble, struggle; **9** bickering; **10** contention, difference, donnybrook, fisticuffs; **11** altercation, controversy; **12** disagreement; PHRASES: **2-2** todo; **2-6** go-around; **3-2** run-in, set-to; **4, 2, 9** line of reasoning; **4-5** argy-bargy *UK*; **4, 8** open conflict; **5, 2, 1, 6** storm in a teacup; **5-3** bobsy-die; **5, 4** blood feud; **7-3** falling-out; **8, 5** slanging match *UK*.

argumentative 5 testy; **7** awkward, grouchy, polemic, stroppy *UK*; **8** choleric, contrary, factious; **9** disputing, fractious, litigious, querulous; **10** dissenting; **11** belligerent, dialectical, dissentious, quarrelsome; **12** cantankerous, disputatious; **13** controversial; **15** confrontational; PHRASES: **6-7** rabble-rousing.

arise 5 begin, occur, start; **6** appear, ascend, evolve, happen, uprear; **7** surface; **8** commence; PHRASES: **2, 3, 6, 2** be the result of; **2, 6, 2** be caused by; **2, 10** be upstanding; **3, 2** get up; **3, 2, 4, 4** get to your feet; **3, 3, 2, 3** get out of bed; **4, 2** come up, crop up, jump up, leap up, rise up; **4**, **2**, **4** come to pass; **4**, **2**, **4**, **4** jump to one's feet, leap to one's feet; **4**, **4** come from, stem from; **4**, **5** take place; **4**, **7** lift oneself; **4**, **7**, **2** pull oneself up; **5**, **2** stand up; **6**, **4** result from.

aristocracy **4** nobs; **5** elite, toffs; **6** gentry; **7** dukedom, earldom, peerage; **8** lordship, nobility; **9** baronetcy, viscounty; **10** gentlefolk, viscountcy; PHRASES: **4**, **5** beau monde; **4**, **7** high society; **5**, **2**, **3**, **5** peers of the realm *UK*; **5**, **3**, **6** lords and ladies *UK*; **5**, **5** upper class, upper crust; **6**, **5** ruling class; **6**, **6** ancien régime, landed gentry.

aristocrat(ic) *See* **noble**

Arizona **2** AZ; **7** Phoenix (capital); PHRASES: **3**, **8** God enriches (motto); **4**, **5** palo verde (tree); **5**, **6**, **5** Grand Canyon State (nickname); **6**, **4** cactus wren (bird); **7**, **6**, **7** saguero cactus blossom (flower).

Arkansas **2** AR; **4** pine (tree); **11** mockingbird (bird); PHRASES: **3**, **6**, **4** The people rule (motto); **5**, **7** apple blossom (flower); **6**, **4** Little Rock (capital); **7**, **5** Natural State (nickname).

armadillo **10** pichiciego.

armed force **4** file, rank, wing; **5** corps, fleet, squad, troop; **6** column, detail, flight, outfit; **7** battery, brigade, company, phalanx, platoon, section; **8** division, flotilla, regiment, squadron; **9** battalion; **10** detachment; PHRASES: **4**, **5** task force; **9**, **5** auxiliary fleet.

armed forces **3** men, SAS (Special Air Service); **4** army, base, levy, line, navy, rear, wing; **5** draft, staff; **6** armada, detail, forces, Guards, patrol, picket, sentry, troops; **7** marines, militia, vedette; **8** armament, garrison, military, recruits, reserves, sentinel, services, vanguard; **9** frontline, personnel, rearguard, spearhead; **10** commandoes, detachment, effectives, paratroops; **11** auxiliaries, contingents, mercenaries; **12** replacements; **13** servicemember; **14** reinforcements; PHRASES: **3**, **5** air force; **4**, **3**, **4** thin red line; **4**, **5** task force; **4**, **6** base troops; **5**, **4** field army; **5**, **5** coast guard, night watch; **5**, **6** corps d'élite, night patrol, shock troops, storm troops; **5**, **7** first echelon; **6-5** combat-ready; **7-3** arrière-ban; **7**, **4** general levy; **7**, **5** advance party, defense force; **7**, **6** assault troops, Special Forces; **9**, **5** guerrilla force; **9**, **6** household troops *UK*, parachute troops.

armor **4** coif, helm, jack, mail; **5** armet, busby, crest, culet, shako, shell, skull, visor; **6** beaver, bracer, bridle, byrnie, camail, casque, cassis, celate, cheeks, crenel, crinet, cuisse, gorget, greave, gusset, hagbut *UK*, helmet, lorica, scutum, shield, tabard, target, umbril; **7** baldric, buckler, corslet, crupper, cuirass, cuisses, defense, epaulet, frontal, hackbut, harness, hauberk, panache, panoply, placard, poitral, surcoat, testudo; **8** armature, arquebus, baldrick, bardings, bascinet, bearskin, brassard, burgonet, chausses, corselet, covering, gauntlet, jambeaux, pectoral, plastron; **9** backplate, habergeon; **10** brigandine, lambrequin, protection; **11** breastplate, breaststrap; **13** reinforcement; PHRASES: **3**, **3** tin hat; **3**, **5** cod piece; **4**, **2**, **4** coat of mail; **4**, **2**, **5** suit of ~; **4**, **4** buff coat; **4**, **5** jack boots; **4**, **6** flak jacket; **5**, **3** siege cap; **5-3** elbow-cop; **5**, **4** chain mail, lance rest *UK*; **5-5** steelplate; **5**, **6** steel helmet; **6**, **4** banded mail, barrel helm; **6**, **7** arming doublet; **11**, **4** bulletproof vest.

armored cavalry **4** tank; **6** Panzer; **7** Leopard; **10** Challenger; PHRASES: **4**, **11** tank transporter; **7**, **3** armored car; **7**, **8** armored division.

armpit **6** axilla.

arms **4** guns, side; **5** order, small; **7** archery, canting *UK*, gunnery, missile, weapons; **8** armament, heraldic, musketry, rocketry, weaponry; **9** armaments, artillery, missilery, munitions; **10** bowmanship, escutcheon.

arms race **13** proliferation; PHRASES: **3-7** gun-running; **4**, **5** arms trade; **4**, **7** arms traffic.

army **2** TA (Territorial Army); **3** mob; **4** band, host, mass; **5** crowd, field, horde, sally; **6** church, legion, throng, troops; **7** militia, regular; **8** military, soldiers, standing; **9** conscript, mercenary, multitude, salvation, volunteer; **11** territorial; **12** professional; PHRASES: **4**, **5** Home Guard *UK*; **5**, **6** armed forces; **7**, **5** defense force.

army ranks **4** foot, peon; **5** cadet, major; **6** gunner, sapper, Zouave; **7** captain, colonel, general, officer, pioneer, private; **8** chasseur, corporal, sergeant; **9** brigadier *UK*; **10** bombardier, lieutenant; **11** footslogger, infantryman; PHRASES: **3-2-4** man-at-arms; **3**, **5** the ranks; **4**, **3**, **4** rank and file; **4**, **7** foot soldier; **5**, **3** merry men; **5**, **7** major general; **5-7** field-marshal; **5-8** lance-corporal; **6, 6** cannon fodder; **6, 7** common soldier; **7-6** machine-gunner; **7, 7** gallant company, warrant officer; **8, 6** enlisted person; **9, 3** artillery man.

army unit 4 band, file, line, rank, unit; **5** array, corps, group, party, squad, troop; **6** cohort, column, decury, detail, legion, square; **7** battery, brigade, century, company, maniple, phalanx, platoon, section; **8** division, infantry, regiment, squadron; **9** battalion; **10** detachment; PHRASES: **4, 5** army corps; **4, 8** foot regiment, line infantry; **5, 7** heavy brigade, light brigade, rifle brigade; **5, 8** light infantry; **6, 8** panzer division; **7, 5** medical corps; **7, 8** armored division, cavalry regiment.

aroma *See* **smell**

aromatic 5 musky; **7** piquant, pungent, scented; **8** fragrant, redolent.

around 1 c; **2** ca; **4** here, near, over; **5** about; **6** across, almost, nearby, nearly; **7** present, roughly; **8** covering; **9** available; **10** everywhere, throughout; **11** surrounding; **13** approximately; PHRASES: **2, 3, 4** in the area; **2, 3, 5, 2** in the order of *UK*; **2, 3, 6, 2** in the region of; **2, 3, 8** in the environs, in the vicinity; **3, 4** all over; **3, 4, 3, 5** all over the place; **3, 5** all round *UK*; **4, 2, 4** give or take, more or less; **4, 3, 5** here and there; **4, 4** near here; **4, 5** just about; **5, 2** close to; **5, 2, 3** going on for *UK*; **5, 4** round here *UK*; **7, 8** roughly speaking.

arousal 6 thrill, urging; **10** excitement; **11** provocation, stimulation.

arouse 4 stir, wake, whet; **6** awaken, excite, thrill; **7** agitate, animate, enliven, impress, inflame, produce, provoke, quicken; **8** activate; **9** galvanize, stimulate, titillate; **10** invigorate; PHRASES: **4, 2** wake up; **5, 1, 3, 5** touch a raw nerve; **5, 1, 9** cause a sensation.

arquebus 6 hagbut *UK*; **7** hackbut.

arrange 3 fix, set; **4** plan, pose; **5** align, array, group, order, place, range, space; **6** locate, settle; **7** compose, display, dispose, marshal; **8** allocate, assemble, organize, schedule, transact; **9** negotiate, structure; **10** coordinate; **11** orchestrate; PHRASES: **3, 2** fix up, set up; **3, 2, 5** put in order; **3, 3** lay out, set out; **3, 4, 5** put into shape; **3, 8** put together; **4, 2** line up; **4, 5** make terms; **4, 5, 3** make plans for; **5, 3** space out; **5, 5, 2** shake hands on; **6, 2, 5** reduce to order.

arrangement 4 bond, deal, pact, plan, pose; **5** array, group; **6** layout, pledge, treaty; **7** compact, display, placing; **8** arraying, assembly, contract, covenant, disposal, grouping, ordering, position; **9** agreement, alignment, arranging, placement, procedure, provision, structure; **10** collection, convention, groundwork, marshaling, settlement; **11** composition, disposition, preparation, structuring, transaction; **13** understanding; **14** prearrangement; PHRASES: **7, 2, 5** putting in order.

arrangement (make arrangements) 4 plan; **6** devise, manage; **7** prepare; **8** contrive, organize, schedule; **10** prearrange.

array 4 garb, line, rank; **5** align, drape, dress, group, order, range, style; **6** attire, bedeck, clothe; **7** apparel, arrange, display, dispose, exhibit, pattern, regalia; **8** clothing, grouping, organize; PHRASES: **3, 2, 5** put in order; **3, 3** lay out, set out; **4, 2** line up; **4, 3** deck out; **6, 3** string out.

arrival 5 debut, entry, guest, onset; **6** advent, caller, coming, influx; **7** advance, incomer *UK*, visitor; **8** approach, entrance, newcomer; **9** beginning, emergence; **10** appearance, occurrence.

arrive 3 hit; **4** come, land; **5** enter, reach; **6** appear, attain, emerge; **7** succeed; **9** disembark; PHRASES: **2, 10** be successful; **3, 2** bob up, pop up; **3, 4** hit town; **3, 5** get there; **4, 2** blow in, come to, drop in, make it, pull in, roll up, show up, turn up; **4, 3** work out; **4, 4** make your mark; **4, 11** gain recognition; **6, 2** decide on.

arriving 8 incoming. *See also* **arrive**

arrogance 5 pride; **7** conceit, egotism; **13** condescension; **14** overconfidence; PHRASES: **4-10** self-importance. *See also* **arrogant**

arrogant 4 bold, smug; **5** proud; **6** brazen, chesty, uppish, uppity; **7** egotism, haughty; **8** superior; **9** bigheaded, bodacious, conceited, egotistic; **11** overweening; **12** presumptuous, supercilious; **13** condescending, overconfident; PHRASES: **4-9** self-important, self-satisfied.

arrogate 5 claim; **6** assume; **11** appropriate; **14** misappropriate; PHRASES: **3, 5, 2** lay claim to.

arrow 4 barb, bolt, dart, sign; **5** shaft; **6** cursor, symbol; **7** missile, pointer; **8** signpost; **9** indicator; **10** projectile; PHRASES: **4, 4**

road sign.

arsenal 5 cache, stash, store; 6 armory; 7 battery, caisson, gunroom; 8 magazine, resource; 10 collection; PHRASES: 3, 4 gun rack; 4, 4 ammo dump; 4, 5 arms depot; 6, 3 powder keg; 6, 4 powder horn; 6, 5 powder flask, weapon store; 6-5 bullet-pouch; 6, 6 powder barrel; 6, 8 powder magazine; 9, 4 cartridge belt; 9, 5 munitions store; 10, 3 ammunition box; 10, 4 ammunition dump, ammunition room, ammunition ship; 10, 5 ammunition chest.

arsenopyrite 9 mispickel.

art 2 op; 3 pop; 4 Dada, deco, fine, form; 5 batik, black, craft, knack, noble, paper, skill; 6 cubism, design, talent; 7 ability, Baroque, drawing, etching, Fauvism, graphic, kinetic, mosaics, nouveau, plastic, realism; 8 ceramics, futurism, painting, tapestry; 9 enameling, engraving, Mannerism, modernism, sculpture, symbolism, vorticism; 10 classicism, commercial, conceptual, decoration, decorative, embroidery, industrial, minimalism, surrealism, virtuosity; 11 calligraphy, lithography, performance, photography, pointillism, Renaissance, Romanticism, woodcarving; 13 expressionism, impressionism, postmodernism; 14 constructivism; PHRASES: 3, 6, 4 the visual arts; 3-12 Pre-Raphaelitism; 4, 3, 6 arts and crafts; 5, 4 beaux arts; 7, 5 stained glass.

arteries 5 aorta, iliac, renal, ulnar; 6 radial, tibial; 7 carotid, femoral, hepatic; 8 brachial, thoracic; 9 pulmonary; 10 innominate, mesenteric, subclavian.

artery 4 line, road; 5 route; 7 channel, pathway.

artful 3 sly; 6 dodger; 7 devious; 8 craftful; 9 ingenious.

art gallery 4 MoMA (New York); 6 Louvre (Paris), SFMOMA (San Francisco), Uffizi (Florence); 9 Hermitage (St. Petersburg); 10 Guggenheim (New York); 12 Metropolitan (New York); PHRASES: 3, 9, 2, 7 Art Institute of Chicago; 4, 6 Tate Modern (London); 4, 6, 2, 3 High Museum of Art (Atlanta); 4, 7 Tate Britain (London); 5, 3, 5 Museo del Prado (Madrid); 5, 6 Musée d'Orsay (Paris); 5, 10, 10 Peggy Guggenheim Collection (Venice); 6, 2, 6, 3 Museum of Modern Art (New York); 8, 7 National Gallery (London); 10, 6 Guggenheim Museum (Bilbao).

arthropod 4 crab; 5 prawn; 6 insect, isopod, shrimp, slater; 7 copepod, cyclops, daphnia, gribble, limulus, lobster, seafood; 8 amphipod, arachnid, barnacle, chilopod, crawfish, crayfish, diplopod, myriapod; 9 cirripede, shellfish, trilobite; 10 crustacean, eurypterid, tardigrade; 11 branchiopod, branchiuran; 12 onychophoran; PHRASES: 3, 3 sow bug; 3, 4 pea crab; 4, 3 pill bug; 4, 4 land crab, sand flea; 4, 5 fish louse, wood louse; 4, 6 sand hopper, seed shrimp; 5, 4 water bear, water flea; 5, 5 water louse *UK*, whale louse; 5, 6 brine shrimp, fairy shrimp; 5, 7 spiny lobster; 5, 8 acorn barnacle, goose barnacle; 6, 4 hermit crab, robber crab, spider crab; 6, 6 mantis shrimp, mussel shrimp; 7, 4 fiddler crab; 7, 6 opossum shrimp, tadpole shrimp; 7, 8 stalked barnacle; 8, 6 skeleton shrimp; 9, 4 horseshoe crab.

arthropodous 7 jointed; 8 crablike; 9 arachnoid, insectile; 10 arachnidan, crustacean, shrimplike; 11 chelicerate; 13 entomological; 14 arachnological; PHRASES: 6-4 insect-like, spider-like.

Arthurian legend 3 Kay; 4 Bors; 5 Ector, Grail; 6 Arthur, Avalon, Gawain, Merlin; 7 Camelot, Galahad, Igraine, Mordred, Viviane; 8 Agravain, Lancelot, Morgause, Percival; 9 Excalibur, Guinevere; PHRASES: 5, 9 Uther Pendragon; 6, 2, 3 Morgan le fay.

article 1 a; 2 an; 3 the; 4 item, puff, term; piece, thing; 6 clause, column, exposé, leader *UK*, notice, object, review; 7 leading, section; 8 artifact, critique, definite; 9 editorial, paragraph; 10 commentary, indefinite; 11 stipulation; PHRASES: 5-2 write-up; 5, 2, 7 piece of writing.

articulate 3 say; 5 clear, lucid, speak, state, utter, voice; 6 convey, fluent; 7 express, jointed; 8 coherent, eloquent; 9 enunciate, formulate, pronounce, verbalize; 11 communicate; 13 communicative; PHRASES: 3, 4, 5 put into words; 4-6 well-spoken.

articulation 6 speech; 7 diction, gesture, voicing; 8 delivery; 9 elocution, phonation, utterance; 10 expression; 11 enunciation, formulation; 12 vocalization; 13 communication, pronunciation, verbalization.

artifice 3 lie; 4 ploy; 5 trick; 6 deceit; 7 cunning; 8 pretense, trickery; 9 deception; 10 artfulness; PHRASES: 7, 2, 4 sleight of hand.

artificial 4 fake, mock, sham; 5 bogus, dummy, false, phony *UK*, quasi; 6 phoney, pseudo; **7** feigned, pretend, virtual; **8** specious, spurious; **9** contrived, imitation, insincere, pretended, simulated, synthetic, unnatural; **11** counterfeit, respiration; **12** insemination, intelligence; PHRASES: **2-6** so-called; **3-2** put-on; **3-4** man-made.

artificial intelligence 8 robotics; **11** cybernetics; **13** neurocomputer; PHRASES: **4, 6** game theory; **4-7** game-playing; **5, 5** fuzzy logic; **6, 3** neural net; **6, 6** expert system.

artificiality 9 imitation, phoniness; **10** pretension, simulation; **11** affectation, insincerity; **12** affectedness; **14** inauthenticity; **15** pretentiousness; PHRASES: **4-6** playacting; **7, 7** virtual reality.

artillery 4 arms, guns; **6** firing; **7** cannons, gunnery, weapons; **8** missiles, musketry, weaponry; **9** armaments, howitzers; **10** ballistics.

artisan 5 mason, smith, tiler; **6** artist, carver, cooper, cutter, fitter, forger, gasman, joiner, master, potter, sawyer, tailor, tinker, turner, weaver, welder, wright; **7** builder, jeweler, painter, plumber, spinner; **8** clothier, gunsmith, mechanic, thatcher, tinsmith; **9** architect, artificer, carpenter, craftsman, decorator, goldsmith, locksmith, machinist, plasterer, repairman, tradesman; **10** apprentice, blacksmith, bricklayer, clockmaker, journeyman, shipwright, technician, wainwright, watchmaker, woodworker; **11** craftswoman, craftworker, electrician, metalworker, needlewoman, shipbuilder, silversmith, wheelwright; **12** craftsperson, housebuilder; **14** handicraftsman; PHRASES: **4-7** boatbuilder; **5-6** glass-blower; **5-7** coach-builder; **7-5** cabinet-maker; **7, 6** skilled worker.

artist 2 RA *UK*; **6** cubist, drawer, limner, master; **7** artisan, artiste, copyist, dadaist, doodler, graphic; **8** animator, designer, enameler, pavement, sculptor, sidewalk, sketcher; **9** craftsman, draftsman, performer; **10** cartoonist, commercial, delineator, pastellist; **11** academician, entertainer, illuminator, illustrator, miniaturist, portraitist; **12** caricaturist; PHRASES: **6, 6** modern master. *See also* **painter**

artistic 5 artsy; **6** scenic; **8** creative, esthetic, stylized; **9** inventive, painterly; **10** decorative, statuesque; **11** atmospheric, imaginative, picturesque; **12** illustrative; PHRASES: **5-6** artsy-fartsy; **5-7** artsy-craftsy.

artistic structure 5 theme, unity; **6** design, rhythm; **7** balance, subject; **11** composition; **12** choreography; **13** structuralism.

artistry 3 art; **5** flair, skill, taste, virtu; **6** genius, talent; **7** ability, mastery; **8** artiness; **9** brushwork, invention, technique; **10** creativity; **11** composition, imagination, originality, perspective; **12** skillfulness; **13** craftsmanship, draftsmanship, inventiveness, painterliness; **14** foreshortening; PHRASES: **5-10** artsy-craftiness, artsy-fartsiness.

artist's materials 3 ink, pen; **4** oils, size; **5** chalk, easel, gesso, model, paper, salon; **6** crayon, ground, medium, paints, pastel, pencil, sitter, studio; **7** atelier, gouache, palette, solvent, spatula, subject, tempera, thinner, varnish; **8** airbrush, charcoal, fixative, paintbox, pigments, spraygun; **9** distemper, mahlstick, maulstick, siccative, sketchpad, stretcher; **10** paintbrush, scratchpad, sketchbook, turpentine; **11** watercolors; PHRASES: **3, 5** art paper *UK*, oil paint; **5, 4** paint tube; **5, 6** white spirit *UK*; **6, 5** Claude glass; **6, 6** camera lucida; **6, 7** camera obscura; **7, 5** drawing frame, drawing paper, palette knife, picture frame.

artless 6 simple; **7** natural; **9** guileless, ingenuous, unworldly.

art of war 4 plan; **5** march; **7** gunnery, tactics; **8** campaign, maneuver, planning, strategy, warcraft; **9** Annapolis, logistics, Sandhurst *UK*; **10** airmanship, ballistics, seamanship, siegecraft; **11** generalship, soldiership; **13** fortification; PHRASES: **3, 3** Sun Tzu; **3, 4** war game; **4, 2, 6** plan of battle; **5, 8** grand strategy, rifle practice; **8, 5** training drill.

arts 6 visual; **7** graphic, liberal; **10** performing.

arum 5 calla.

as 4 when; **5** since, while; **6** during, whilst *UK*; **7** because; PHRASES: **2, 3, 6, 2** at the moment of; **4, 4** just when; **6, 4** seeing that; **11, 4** considering that.

as a rule 6 mainly, mostly; **7** chiefly, usually; **8** commonly, normally *UK*; **9** generally; **10** habitually, ordinarily; **11** customarily; PHRASES: **2, 2, 4, 4** as is one's wont; **2, 3, 4** in the main; **2, 3, 5** on the whole; **2, 5, 2, 3** as often as not; **2, 7** in general; **3, 3, 4, 4** for the most part; **4, 2, 3, 4** most of the time.

ascend 4 lift, rise, soar; **5** arise, climb,

mount, scale, spire; **6** aspire, spiral; **8** levitate, upstream; **9** culminate; PHRASES: **2, 2** go up; **3, 2** get up; **4, 2** come up, grow up, rise up; **4, 6** move upward; **4, 7** curl upwards; **5, 2** swarm up, sweep up; **5, 3, 3** reach the top; **5, 3, 6** reach the zenith.

ascender 4 lark; **5** eagle; **6** rocket, soarer; **7** climber, skylark; **8** alpinist, cragsman *UK*, laverock *UK*; **9** skyrocket; **10** foretopman; **11** mountaineer, steeplejack; PHRASES: **4, 7** rock climber.

ascending 5 steep; **6** ascent, rising, uphill, upward; **7** soaring; **8** climbing, mounting, uplifted, upturned; **9** retroussé, uparching; PHRASES: **2, 3, 9** in the ascendant; **6-2** turned-up; **6, 6** upward motion.

ascent 4 rake, rise; **5** angle, climb, grade, slope; **6** rising, uphill, uprise; **7** incline, scaling, upslope *UK*; **8** gradient, mounting, upcoming; **9** ascension, elevation; **10** assumption, levitation; PHRASES: **6, 6** upward motion.

ascent (means of ascent) 5 steps; **6** perron, stairs; **7** landing; **8** escalier, stairway; **9** companion, staircase; **10** backstairs; **12** companionway; PHRASES: **4, 6** fire escape; **6, 2, 6** flight of stairs; **6, 3, 6** treads and risers.

ascertain 5 learn; **8** discover; **9** determine; PHRASES: **4, 3** find out; **4, 7** make certain.

ascetic 6 frugal; **7** austere, puritan, spartan; **8** celibate, penitent; **9** abstainer, abstinent; **10** abstemious.

ascribe 6 assign, credit; **9** attribute; PHRASES: **3, 4, 2** put down to.

as follows 4 last; **6** lastly; **8** secondly; PHRASES: **2, 4, 3** in this way; **2, 6, 5** in second place.

ash 3 can; **4** bone, dust, slag, soda; **5** blond; **6** embers; **7** cinders, residue; **8** mountain; **9** Wednesday.

ashamed 7 abashed, humbled; **8** hesitant; **9** mortified, reluctant, unwilling; **10** humiliated; **11** embarrassed.

Asian pear 5 nashi *UK*.

aside 4 away; **5** apart; **6** remark; **7** tangent, whisper; **8** excluded, excursus, sideways, sidewise; **9** departure, excursion, soliloquy, undertone; **10** digression, separately; **11** disregarded, parenthesis; **13** interposition; **15** notwithstanding; PHRASES: **2, 3, 4** on the side, to one side, to the side; **2-4** by-play; **2,**

7 in reserve; **3, 2, 3, 3** out of the way; **7, 7** mumbled comment.

askew 4 awry; **6** aslant; **8** cockeyed; **9** crookedly, obliquely, skewwhiff *UK*; **10** diagonally; PHRASES: **2, 1, 7** on a tangent; **2, 2, 5** at an angle; **2, 3, 4** on the bias; **3, 2, 4** out of line; **3, 2, 6** out of kilter; **3, 6** off center.

ask for forgiveness 9 apologize; PHRASES: **3, 6** beg pardon; **5, 9** offer apologies.

asleep 4 dead, numb; **7** napping; **8** benumbed, sleeping; **10** slumbering; PHRASES: **5, 6** sound ~.

asp 5 aspen; PHRASES: **6, 5** horned viper.

asparagus 12 sparrowgrass.

aspect 3 air; **4** item, look, mien, part, side, view; **5** datum, facet, phase, point, trait; **6** detail, factor; **7** bearing, element, feature, outlook; **8** demeanor, position, property; **9** attribute, viewpoint; **10** appearance, expression, standpoint; **11** countenance; **14** characteristic; PHRASES: **4, 4** dark side; **5, 4** cruel side, funny side.

aspect (description of) 4 ugly; **5** plain; **6** homely; **9** beautiful, decorated, unsightly; **10** attractive, decorative; **11** fashionable; **12** unattractive; **13** unfashionable; PHRASES: **3-7** ill-dressed *UK*; **4, 2, 3, 3** easy on the eye; **4-7** well-dressed.

aspen 3 asp; PHRASES: **9, 6** trembling poplar.

aspersion 4 slur; **5** smear; **6** slight; **7** calumny, slander; **8** innuendo; **9** criticism; **10** accusation, defamation; **13** disparagement; PHRASES: **9, 6** slighting remark.

asphalt *See* **tar**

aspirant 6 seeker; **7** hopeful, longing, wannabe; **8** desirous, yearning; **9** ambitious, applicant, candidate, contender; PHRASES: **2-7** go-getting; **5-2** would-be.

aspirate 5 sound, voice; **6** remove; **7** extract; **9** enunciate, pronounce; **10** articulate; PHRASES: **4, 3** draw out, suck out.

aspiration 3 aim, end; **4** goal, want, wish; **5** dream; **6** desire, target, Utopia, vision; **7** fantasy; **8** ambition; **9** intention, objective; PHRASES: **4, 5** high hopes; **5-6-4** cloud-cuckoo-land; **5, 8** fool's paradise; **7, 2, 3, 3** castles in the air; **7, 2, 5** castles in Spain; **8, 4** promised land.

aspire 3 aim; **4** seek, want, wish; **5** await, dream; **6** desire, expect; **10** anticipate;

PHRASES: **4, 7, 2** look forward to.

ass 3 Ned; **4** fool, Jack, mule; **5** burro, hinny, idiot, Jenny, Neddy; **6** donkey.

assail 5 beset; **6** attack, berate, revile; **7** assault; **9** criticize; PHRASES: **3, 4** lay into; **3, 5** set about.

assassin *See* **killer**

assault 3 hit, mug; **4** raid; **5** blitz; **6** assail, attack, batter, onrush, sortie, strike; **7** beating, mugging; **8** stabbing, storming; **9** incursion, offensive, onslaught; PHRASES: **3, 4** lay into; **3, 5** set about; **4, 2** beat up.

assay 3 try; **4** test; **6** assess; **7** analyze, attempt, examine; **8** endeavor, evaluate; **9** undertake.

assemblage 3 set; **5** batch, crowd, group, hoard; **6** throng; **8** assembly, grouping; **9** congeries, gathering, stockpile; **10** collection; **11** aggregation; **12** accumulation, congregation; **13** agglomeration; **14** conglomeration.

assemble 4 heap, herd, make, mass, meet, pile; **5** amass, build, group, hoard, mound, stack, store; **6** gather, muster; **7** collect, compile, connect, convene, marshal; **8** shepherd; **9** aggregate, construct, stockpile; **10** accumulate, congregate; **11** agglomerate, manufacture; PHRASES: **3, 2** set up; **3, 8** fit together, put together; **4, 8** come together, draw together, pull together; **5, 2** build up, round up; **5, 8** bring together, group together.

assembler 8 convener *UK*, herdsman, shepherd; PHRASES: **7-2** whipper-in.

assembly 3 set; **4** army, band, bloc, body, club, gang, team, trio, wing; **5** bunch, choir, corps, crowd, fleet, force, group, nonet, octet, party, rally; **6** chorus, muster, septet, sextet; **7** brigade, collage, company, council, general, meeting, montage, quartet, quintet, society; **8** audience, conclave, congress, erection, flotilla, grouping, national, regiment, squadron, symphony, unlawful; **9** aggregate, anthology, community, gathering, orchestra, syndicate; **10** assemblage, collecting, collection, compendium, confluence, consortium, government; **11** aggregation, association, combination, compilation, corporation, fabrication, legislative, legislature, manufacture; **12** conglomerate, congregation, mobilization; **13** agglomeration; **14** conglomeration; **15** representatives; PHRASES:

3, 8 air squadron; **3-8** get-together; **6, 8** coming together; **7, 8** fitting together, joining together, putting together; **11, 4** legislative body.

assent 3 nod; **5** agree, allow, grant; **6** accede, comply, concur, permit; **7** approve, concede, consent; **8** approval, sanction; **9** acquiesce, agreement; **10** acceptance; **11** affirmation, concurrence; **12** acquiescence, confirmation; PHRASES: **2, 5, 4** go along with; **3, 3** say yes.

assert 5 state; **6** defend, uphold; **7** declare, profess; **8** maintain, proclaim; **9** emphasize; PHRASES: **6, 2** insist on.

assertive 4 bold, firm; **5** blunt, plain, pushy; **6** driven; **7** assured, decided, forward, pointed; **8** decisive, dogmatic, emphatic, explicit, forceful, incisive, positive, vehement, vigorous; **9** confident, insistent, outspoken; **10** aggressive, peremptory, pontifical; PHRASES: **2, 8** ex cathedra; **3, 8** not negative; **4-7** self-assured; **4-9** self-assertive, self-confident.

assertive (be assertive) 4 push; **6** insist; PHRASES: **3, 2** say so; **3, 4, 3, 3** lay down the law; **3, 6, 5** use strong words; **5, 2, 6** brook no denial; **5, 3** speak out.

assertiveness 5 drive, oomph, vigor; **8** chutzpah; **9** assurance, vehemence; **10** confidence, insistence; PHRASES: **3-2-3-2** get-up-and-go; **4-9** self-assertion; **6, 5** strong words. *See also* **assertive**

assess 5 judge, value; **6** review; **8** appraise, consider, estimate, evaluate; **9** calculate.

asset 7 benefit, holding; **8** property, resource, strength; **9** advantage; **10** possession; PHRASES: **4, 5** plus point *UK*.

assiduity 4 care; **5** labor; **7** stamina; **8** industry; **9** attention, diligence; **10** intentness, resolution; **11** application, devotedness, painstaking; **12** perseverance, stickability, tirelessness; **13** assiduousness, concentration, determination, laboriousness, perfectionism; **15** industriousness; PHRASES: **4, 4** hard work.

assiduous 7 careful; **8** diligent, sedulous, thorough; **10** meticulous; **11** industrious, painstaking; **13** conscientious.

assign 4 give, send; **5** allot; **6** deploy, detail; **7** appoint, ascribe, consign; **8** allocate, delegate, dispense, disperse, motivate, transfer; **9** apportion, designate; **11** requisition; PHRASES: **4, 3** dole out; **4, 4** hand over; **5, 1, 6** allot a billet.

assignment 3 job; **4** duty, role, task; **7** project; **8** position, transfer; **10** allocation, delegation, obligation; **11** appointment, consignment.

assimilate 5 adapt, coach, drill, imbue, learn, teach, train; **6** absorb, adjust, digest, school; **7** conform, embrace, espouse, implant, instill; **8** instruct; **9** integrate; **10** naturalize, understand; **11** acclimatize, incorporate; **12** indoctrinate, rehabilitate; PHRASES: **2-7** re-educate *UK*; **3, 2** fit in; **4, 2** take in; **5, 2** blend in.

assist 3 aid; **4** abet, back, ease, help; **7** replace, succeed, support; **9** reinforce; PHRASES: **4, 1, 4** give a hand, lend a hand; **4, 3** help out; **5, 2, 3** stand in for; **8, 3** deputize for; **10, 3** understudy for.

assistant 2 PA *UK*; **3** sub; **4** aide, hand, help, pawn, pimp, vice; **5** agent, slave; **6** deputy, helper, intern, junior, lackey, pander, puppet; **7** midwife, servant, trainee; **8** adjutant, handmaid, mediator, procurer; **9** associate, secondary, secretary; **10** amanuensis; **11** subordinate; **12** intermediary; PHRASES: **2-7** go-between; **3, 6** man Friday; **4-2-4** aide-de-camp; **4-3** cat's-paw.

associate 3 kin; **4** ally, clan, join, kith, link, meet, yoke; **5** crony, tribe, unite; **6** adhere, couple, escort, fellow, friend, hobnob, junior, liaise, minion, relate; **7** cohabit, combine, comrade, conjoin, connect, consort, kinsman, network, partner; **8** confrère, coworker, relation, relative; **9** assistant, colleague, companion, correlate, interface, socialize, underling; **10** accomplice; **11** confederate, subordinate; **12** acquaintance; **13** coconspirator; PHRASES: **2, 6, 4** go around with; **2, 8, 4** be involved with; **4, 2** gang up, pair up, team up; **4-2-5** hand-in-glove; **4, 8** join together; **5, 4, 4** spend time with; **5, 8** group together; **6, 4** assort with; **6, 6** family member, fellow worker; **8, 7** business partner.

associated 7 related; **9** attendant; **11** concomitant, inseparable; **12** accompanying; **13** supplementary; PHRASES: **5, 2, 7** thick as thieves.

association 4 club, link; **5** group, guild, nexus, union; **6** cartel, fusion, memory, merger; **7** company, liaison, merging, network, society; **8** alliance, overtone, relation, sorority; **9** alignment, coalition, syndicate; **10** attachment, connection, consortium, federation, fellowship, fraternity, friendship, sisterhood; **11** affiliation, brotherhood, combination, connotation, corporation, integration, intercourse, involvement, partnership, unification; **12** amalgamation, conglomerate, organization, relationship; **13** communication, confederation, confraternity, consolidation, incorporation; PHRASES: **3-2** tie-in, tie-up; **4-2** hook-up; **5, 5** labor union, trade union.

association of ideas 4 free; **5** clang; **11** synesthesia; **12** transference; **13** reinforcement.

assorted 5 mixed; **6** divers, motley, sundry, varied; **7** diverse, various; **9** checkered, multiform; **10** allotropic; **11** diversiform; **12** multicolored, multifaceted, multifarious, multipurpose, polymorphous; **13** kaleidoscopic, miscellaneous; **14** heteromorphous; PHRASES: **2, 3, 5** of all sorts; **2, 4, 5** of many kinds; **3, 3, 6** all and sundry.

assortment 5 group, range; **6** medley, motley; **7** mixture, variety; **9** allotropy; **10** collection, hodgepodge, hotchpotch *UK*, miscellany; **11** variegation; **12** multiformity, multiplicity; **14** heteromorphism; PHRASES: **4, 3, 4** odds and ends; **5, 3** mixed bag.

assuage 4 ease; **6** lessen, soften; **7** appease; **8** moderate.

assume 4 fake; **5** feign; **6** affect, deduce; **7** presume, suppose; **8** simulate; **10** presuppose; PHRASES: **3, 2** put on; **4, 2** take on, take up.

assumption *See* **supposition**

assurance 4 oath, word; **5** poise; **6** aplomb, pledge; **7** promise, warrant; **9** composure, guarantee; **10** confidence, equanimity; **11** affirmation, reassurance; PHRASES: **4-8** self-reliance; **4-10** self-confidence, self-possession.

assure *See* **guarantee**

assured 4 cool, sure; **6** poised; **7** certain; **8** composed; **9** confident; **10** guaranteed; **13** authoritative; PHRASES: **4-9** self-confident, self-possessed; **6, 8** beyond question.

assuredly 6 indeed, really, surely; **9** certainly; **12** indisputably; PHRASES: **2, 2, 4** to be sure; **2, 5** in truth; **3, 4** for sure; **3, 7** for certain; **4, 6** sure enough; **4, 9** most certainly. *See also* **assured**

astern 3 aft; **5** abaft; **6** behind; **8** backward; PHRASES: **2, 3, 4** at the back, at the rear, to the rear; **2, 7** in reverse.

asteroid **9** planetoid; PHRASES: **5, 6** minor planet.

asteroids **4** Amor, Aten, Eros, Hebe, Iris, Juno; **5** Ceres, Vesta; **6** Adonis, Apollo, Chiron, Hermes, Hygiea, Icarus, Pallas; **7** Astraea, Eunomia, Hidalgo; **8** Achilles; **10** Euphrosyne.

astir **2** up; **5** alive, awake; **6** active, moving; **7** aroused; **8** stirring; PHRASES: **2, 3, 5** up and about.

astonish *See* **surprise**

astonishment *See* **surprise**

astray **4** awry, lost; **6** adrift; PHRASES: **3, 3, 4** off the mark; **3, 4** off beam; **3, 5** off track; **3, 6** off course, off target; **4, 2, 3, 4** wide of the mark.

astronaut **8** spaceman; **9** cosmonaut, rocketeer; **10** spacewoman; PHRASES: **5, 8** space traveler.

astronautics **12** cosmonautics; **15** bioastronautics; PHRASES: **5, 7** space science; **5, 8** space medicine, space research; **5, 10** space technology.

astronomer **8** observer; **9** stargazer; **11** cosmogonist, cosmologist; **14** astrophysicist; PHRASES: **5, 9** space scientist; **5, 10** radio ~; **10, 5** ~ royal.

astronomical **4** huge, vast; **5** lunar, solar; **6** astral, cosmic, starry; **7** immense, stellar; **8** cometary, enormous, galactic, heavenly, infinite, meteoric, sidereal, telluric; **9** boundless, celestial, excessive, extremely, planetary, tellurian; **10** asteroidal, exorbitant, meteoritic, telescopic; **11** astronautic, terrestrial; **12** cosmological, extramundane, heliocentric, interstellar; **13** astronautical, astrophysical, extragalactic, intergalactic, spectrometric; **14** interplanetary; PHRASES: **3-4** sky-high; **4-7** star-studded.

astronomically **9** extremely; **11** exceedingly; **12** inordinately, meteorically, prodigiously; **13** exceptionally; PHRASES: **7, 3, 4** through the roof. *See also* **astronomical**

astronomical unit **6** parsec; PHRASES: **5, 4** solar mass; **5-4** light-year.

astronomy **5** radar, radio; **7** optical; **8** infrared; **9** cosmogony, cosmology; **10** astrometry, exobiology, stargazing; **11** astrobotany; **12** astrobiology, astrogeology, astrophysics; **13** astrodynamics; **14** astrochemistry; PHRASES: **1-3** X-ray; **4, 8** star watching; **5-3** gamma-ray; **5, 7** space science.

asylum **5** haven; **6** refuge; **7** shelter; **8** security; **9** sanctuary; **10** protection; PHRASES: **4, 5** safe haven.

asymmetric **6** uneven; **7** crooked; **8** lopsided; **9** contorted, different, imperfect, irregular, misshapen; **13** unsymmetrical.

at a price **2, 3, 4, 2** to the tune of; **2, 3, 6, 2** to the amount of.

athlete **5** boxer, champ, coach, hiker, judge, miler, racer; **6** fencer, jumper, kegler, player, runner, soccer, walker; **7** acrobat, amateur, gymnast, harrier, hurdler, ironman, judoist, leaguer, Olympic, puncher, starter, thrower, tumbler, vaulter; **8** champion, foilsman, grappler, medalist, pugilist, sprinter, wrestler; **9** contender, cricketer, gladiator, ironwoman, letterman, sportsman, strongman; **10** challenger, competitor, contestant, decathlete, footballer, ironperson, jujitsuist, marathoner, racewalker, timekeeper; **11** funambulist, heptathlete, participant, pentathlete, sportswoman; **12** letterwinner, professional, sportsperson, weightlifter; **13** steeplechaser; PHRASES: **3-6, 6** all-around player; **3-7** all-rounder *UK*; **3-8** all-American; **4, 6** high jumper, long jumper, team member; **4-6** shot-putter; **4-7** blue-chipper, pole-vaulter; **4, 8** gold medalist, sumo wrestler; **5, 6** broad jumper; **6-2** runner-up; **6, 6** triple jumper; **6, 7** discus thrower; **6-7** hammer-thrower; **7, 7** javelin thrower; **8, 6** baseball player, football player, marathon runner.

athletic **3** fit; **6** sporty; **7** healthy; **8** physical; PHRASES: **2, 4, 5** in good shape.

at home **4** easy, sure; **5** comfy; **7** capable, relaxed, skilled; **8** familiar; **9** competent, confident; **10** accustomed, proficient; **11** comfortable, experienced; **13** knowledgeable; PHRASES: **2, 4** at ease; **2, 7** in control; **4, 2** used to.

atmosphere **3** air, CFC, sky; **4** aura, feel, mood, tone; **5** ether, upper, vibes; **6** milieu; **7** feeling, heavens; **8** ambiance, overtone; **9** character, pollutant, pollution, undertone; **11** environment; **12** surroundings; PHRASES: **11, 4** atmospheric dust.

atmosphere (atmospheric layers) **7** stratum; **9** exosphere; **10** ionosphere, mesosphere, tropopause; **11** chemosphere, ozonosphere, photosphere, stratopause, troposphere; **12** stratosphere, thermosphere; **15** substratosphere; PHRASES: **1, 6** D region, E region, F region; **3, 5, 4** Van Allen belt; **5, 5** ozone layer; **5, 10** lower atmosphere, outer atmosphere, upper atmosphere; **8, 5** Appleton layer; **9, 5** Heaviside layer.

atmospheric 5 moody; **7** ambient; **9** adiabatic, advective, radiative; **10** convective, isothermal; **11** distinctive, geostrophic, ionospheric, situational, supercooled; **12** tropospheric; **13** stratospheric; PHRASES: **2, 3, 3** in the air; **4, 2, 9** full of character.

atmospheric process 9 advection, radiation; **10** absorption, convection, reflection, saturation, scattering; **11** evaporation, sublimation; **12** condensation, supercooling; PHRASES: **4, 8** heat transfer; **4, 9** heat transport; **5, 7** water balance; **6, 7** energy balance.

atom 3 bit, jot; **4** iota; **5** grain; **6** proton; **7** glimmer, neutron, nucleon, nucleus; **8** electron, molecule, particle, subshell; PHRASES: **1-8** d-electron, f-electron, p-electron, s-electron; **4, 4** tiny part; **6, 9** atomic structure; **8, 5** electron shell.

atomic 3 age; **4** heat, mass, pile; **5** clock, power; **6** energy, number, theory, volume, weight; **7** nuclear; **8** cocktail; **9** structure; **11** fissionable; **13** thermonuclear.

atonality 6 series; **9** cacophony, serialism; **10** dissonance; **11** discordance, dodecaphony; PHRASES: **4, 2, 7** lack of harmony; **4, 3** note row; **6-4, 5** twelve-note scale, twelve-tone scale.

atone 5 repay; **6** answer, redeem, repair, suffer; **7** appease, expiate, rectify, redress, requite, satisfy; **9** apologize, indemnify, reconcile; **10** compensate, conciliate, propitiate, recompense; PHRASES: **2, 7** do penance; **3, 3, 7** pay the forfeit, pay the penalty; **3, 4** pay back; **3, 4, 4** pay one's dues; **3, 5** say sorry *UK*; **4, 2** make up; **4, 4** make good; **4, 5** make right; **4, 6** make amends; **6, 2** square it; **6, 6** square things.

atonement 5 quits; **6** amends; **7** apology, payment, penance, redress, wergild; **8** requital, squaring; **9** expiation, indemnity, penitence, quittance, repayment; **10** punishment, recompense, redemption, reparation; **11** restitution; **12** compensation, conciliation, propitiation, satisfaction; **13** rectification; **15** indemnification; PHRASES: **3, 3, 2, 3** eye for an eye; **5, 5** blood money.

atoner 8 expiator, penitent, repenter; **9** scapegoat; **10** flagellant; PHRASES: **8, 3** whipping boy.

atoning 5 sorry; **7** lustral; **8** contrite, oblatory, penitent, piacular; **9** expiatory, purgative, repentant; **10** apologetic, lustrative, reparatory; **11** penitential, purgatorial, restitutive, restitutory, sacrificial; **12** compensatory, lustrational, penitentiary, propitiatory; **14** reconciliatory; PHRASES: **6, 6** making amends.

atrocity *See* **violence, violence (instance of violence)**

attach 3 fix; **4** join; **5** award; **6** accord, assign, fasten; **7** ascribe, connect; **9** attribute.

attachment 4 bond; **5** extra; **6** regard; **8** addition; **9** accessory, affection; **10** connection, friendship, supplement; PHRASES: **3-2** add-on.

attack 3 hit, mug, ram; **4** bout, dose, hunt, hurt, push, raid, rape, rush, slur; **5** abuse, argue, begin, blitz, drive, foray, force, harry, libel, occur, onset, pound, smear, spasm, spell; **6** affect, ambush, assail, bother, charge, damage, engage, harass, infect, mangle, molest, pincer, ravish, savage, strike, tackle, thrust, verbal; **7** advance, assault, barrage, bombard, calumny, censure, decrial, mugging, slander, torture, violate; **8** argument, boarding, confront, disagree, enfilade, incident, outbreak, surprise, violence; **9** aspersion, cannonade, criticism, criticize, hostility, incursion, injustice, offensive, onslaught, pugnacity; **10** aggression, blitzkrieg, defamation, harassment, revilement; **11** bellicosity, bombardment, denigration; **12** belligerence, condemnation, denunciation, intimidation, vilification; **13** confrontation, disparagement; PHRASES: **2, 3** go for; **2, 4, 3** go over the top; **3, 2** set to; **3, 2, 8** act of violence; **3, 4** lay into; **3-5** ill-treat; **3, 7** fly against; **4, 2** beat up, pile in, take on, turn to; **4, 4** foul play; **5, 2** start on; **5, 3, 6** sound the charge; **5, 7** armed robbery; **6, 4** strike down; **8, 7** indecent assault.

attack (successfully) 4 beat, burn, kill; **5** board, carry, storm; **6** breach, corner, invade, ravage, scorch; **7** capture, grapple, overrun, torture, trample; **8** escalade, overcome; **9** offensive, overpower, overwhelm, slaughter, terrorize; **10** overmaster; PHRASES: **2, 2, 3, 7** go on the rampage; **3, 4** run down; **3, 5** lay waste; **4, 2, 5** take by storm;

4, 4 ride down, take over; **5, 2** burst in; **5, 2, 3** bring to bay; **5, 5** wreak havoc; **5, 7** break through.

attacker 3 foe; **4** hawk; **5** enemy; **6** bomber, killer, mugger, raider, rapist, sniper; **7** invader, stormer *UK*, warrior; **8** assassin, besieger, crusader, murderer; **9** aggressor, assailant, blockader, escalader, guerrilla, spearhead, terrorist; **10** antagonist, bombardier; **12** sharpshooter; PHRASES: **3, 3** air ace, top gun; **4, 6** dive bomber; **5, 7** storm trooper; **6, 5** strike force; **7, 5** fighter pilot; **9, 5** attacking force.

attacking 5 cruel; **6** bloody, brutal, raging, savage; **7** berserk, brutish, violent; **8** frenzied; **9** barbarous; **11** destructive; **12** bloodthirsty.

attain 5 reach; **6** manage; **7** achieve, realize; **10** accomplish; PHRASES: **6, 2** arrive at.

attainable 8 possible; **9** realistic; **10** accessible, achievable; **12** approachable; PHRASES: **3-2-4** get-at-able; **6, 5** within reach.

attempt 2 go; **3** aim, bid, try; **4** bash *UK*, leap, move, seek, shot, stab, step; **5** crack, debut, essay, offer, whack, whirl; **6** effort, gambit, strain, tackle; **8** endeavor, struggle; PHRASES: **3, 2** aim to; **4, 1, 2** have a go; **4, 3** dead set, good try, last bid, last try; **4, 4** best shot, last shot, swan song; **4, 6** best effort; **5-2-5-3** catch-as-catch-can; **7, 6** valiant effort.

attempter 5 trier; **6** bidder; **7** essayer, fighter, quester, striver; **8** activist, inquirer, lobbyist; **9** contender, struggler, volunteer; **10** adventurer, challenger, contestant, contractor; **12** entrepreneur, experimenter.

attempting 4 game; **9** ambitious; **11** venturesome; **12** enterprising; PHRASES: **7, 7** nothing daunted.

attempt the impossible 3, 3, 1, 7 try for a miracle; **3, 3, 3, 4** cry for the moon; **4, 2, 5** walk on water; **4, 4, 3, 4** turn back the tide; **4, 4, 4** turn back time; **5, 3, 4** catch the wind; **5, 4** waste time.

attend 4 view; **5** focus, watch; **6** follow, listen, shadow; **7** observe, witness; **8** spectate; **11** concentrate, participate; PHRASES: **2, 7** be present; **3, 2, 2** sit in on; **3, 5** tag along; **3, 9** pay attention; **4, 2** join in, look on, show up, turn up, wait on; **4, 2, 2** look in on; **4, 3** hang out; **4, 4** take part; **4, 4, 4, 2** keep your mind on; **4, 6** hang around; **5, 2** stand by; **5, 4, 4** apply your mind; **5, 5** think about; **5, 10**

dance attendance; **6, 3, 4** report for duty; **7, 7** present oneself.

attendance 5 court, crowd, dance, suite; **7** cortege, retinue, turnout; **8** audience, presence; **9** entourage; **10** appearance; PHRASES: **5, 7** being present; **6, 7** number present.

attendant 4 aide, maid, page; **5** guard, guide, usher, valet; **6** barman *UK*, batman, busboy, butler, caddie, carhop, duenna, escort, flight, linked, minder *UK*, porter, potboy, redcap, server, skycap, squire, waiter; **7** barkeep, barmaid *UK*, bellboy, bellhop, hostess, janitor, pageboy, related, steward, swamper; **8** cavalier, chaperon, outrider, waitress, watching; **9** assistant, barkeeper, barperson, bartender, bodyguard, bootblack, caretaker, concierge, connected, groomsman, protector, resultant, sommelier, waitstaff; **10** associated, bridesmaid, consequent, headwaiter, salesclerk, stewardess, waitperson; **11** concomitant; **12** accompanying; PHRASES: **2, 4** on hand; **2, 10** in attendance; **3, 3** bus boy; **4, 2, 5** maid of honor; **4, 3** best man; **4, 5** coat check; **4, 6** ring bearer; **4, 7** wine steward; **4, 9** shop assistant *UK*; **5, 4** cabin crew, truck stop; **5, 6** staff member; **6, 1** maître d'; **6, 2, 5** matron of honor; **6, 6** maitre d'hotel.

attention 4 care; **6** notice, regard; **7** concern, thought; **8** courtesy, devotion, interest, kindness; **9** awareness; **11** finickiness, helpfulness, mindfulness; **12** watchfulness; **13** attentiveness, concentration, consideration; **14** responsiveness, thoughtfulness.

attentive 4 wary; **5** alert; **7** careful, mindful; **8** diligent, sedulous, studious, vigilant, watchful; **9** assiduous, observant; **10** meticulous; **11** circumspect.

attentive (be attentive) 4 note; **6** notice, regard; **8** consider; PHRASES: **3, 9** pay attention; **4, 3** care for; **5, 4** hover over; **5, 10** dance attendance.

attentive person 5 lover; **6** suitor; **7** scholar; **8** chaperon, examiner.

attenuate 6 dilute, lessen, reduce; **8** decrease, diminish.

attest 5 prove; **6** verify; **7** confirm; **11** corroborate; **12** substantiate; PHRASES: **4, 3** bear out.

attestant 4 ally; **6** backer; **7** assurer, sponsor, witness; **8** advocate, affirmer, asserter, promoter, seconder; **9** affirmant, announcer, confessor, guarantor, supporter, testifier; **12** corroborator; PHRASES: **4-5** oath-taker.

attire *See* **clothes, dress**

attitude 4 bent, bias, mind, mood, pose, tone, vein, view; **5** humor; **6** genius, stance; **7** bearing, leaning, opinion, posture, thought; **8** boldness, carriage, defiance, penchant; **9** arrogance, brashness, character, insolence, prejudice, proneness, readiness, viewpoint; **10** partiality, proclivity, propensity; **11** disposition, inclination; **12** idiosyncrasy, predilection, preparedness; **13** assertiveness; **14** predisposition, susceptibility; PHRASES: **4, 2, 4** cast of mind, turn of mind; **4, 3** mind set; **5, 2, 4** point of view.

attorney 5 crown; **8** district; **11** prosecuting.

attract 3 tug; **4** drag, draw, move, pull; **5** charm; **6** adduct, appeal, entice, induce, invite; **7** enchant; **8** interest, persuade; **9** fascinate, influence, magnetize, spellbind; PHRASES: **5, 8** bring together.

attract attention 4, 9 draw attention; **5, 3, 3, 2** catch the eye of.

attraction 3 tug; **4** itch, lure, pull; **5** charm; **6** allure, desire; **8** affinity, sympathy; **9** magnetism; **10** temptation; **11** fascination; **12** desirability; **14** attractiveness.

attractive 4 cute, sexy; **5** dishy, hunky; **6** comely, lovely, pretty; **7** winning; **8** alluring, charming, enticing, fetching, handsome, inviting, magnetic, pleasing, stunning, tempting; **9** appealing, beautiful, seductive; **11** captivating, charismatic, fascinating; **12** irresistible; PHRASES: **3-8** eye-catching; **4-7** good-looking, nice-looking.

attractive man 4 beau, dish, hunk; **5** pinup; **6** Adonis, looker; **7** charmer; **9** dreamboat; **10** studmuffin; PHRASES: **5, 3** cover boy, dream man.

attractive woman 4 lulu; **5** belle, dream, jewel, pearl; **6** beauty, looker, vision; **7** dazzler, smasher *UK*; PHRASES: **3, 3** boy toy; **5, 2, 3, 4** belle of the ball; **5, 4** pinup girl; **5, 6** femme fatale; **5, 7** bobby dazzler; **6, 5** beauty queen.

attune 5 adapt; **6** adjust; **8** accustom; **11** accommodate.

atypical *See* **different**

AU 4 gold.

aubergine 8 eggplant.

auction *See* **sale**

audacious 4 bold; **5** brave, risky; **6** cheeky, daring; **7** assured, blatant; **8** fearless, flagrant, impudent; **9** foolhardy, unabashed; **10** courageous; **11** brazenfaced; **13** overconfident.

audacity 4 guts *UK*; **5** cheek, nerve, pluck; **6** bottle *UK*, daring, hubris, mettle; **7** bravery, courage; **8** blatancy; **9** assurance, impudence; **13** audaciousness. *See also* **audacious**

audibility 5 noise, sound; **7** clarity; **8** loudness; **9** acoustics; **12** distinctness; **14** discernibility, perceptibility; PHRASES: **7, 5** decibel level.

audience 7 hearing, meeting, viewers; **9** interview, listeners, onlookers; **10** addressees, spectators; **11** appointment; **12** consultation.

audio device 2 CB (Citizens' Band radio), CD, PA (public-address system); **3** amp, bug; **4** call, disc, disk *UK*, mike, tape; **5** asdic *UK*, audio, pager, phone, radar, radio, sonar; **6** mobile, pickup, record; **7** bleeper *UK*, handset, headset, speaker, wiretap; **8** bullhorn, cassette, cellular, earpiece, intercom, receiver, wireless; **9** amplifier, earphones, megaphone, telephone; **10** connection, headphones, microphone, radiopager, radiophone; **11** answerphone, loudspeaker, stethoscope, transceiver; **12** echolocation; **13** amplification; **14** radiotelephone; **3, 7** ear trumpet; **4, 3** boom box, deaf aid *UK*; **4, 5** cell phone, talk radio; **4-6** loud-hailer; **4, 8** tape recorder; **5, 4** vinyl disc; **6, 5** mobile phone; **6-6** walkie-talkie; **6, 7** ghetto blaster, volume control; **7, 3** hearing aid; **7, 4** compact disc; **8, 6** personal stereo; **10, 5** transistor radio.

audit 4 list; **5** check; **6** assess, review; **7** catalog *UK*, examine, inspect; **8** accounts, appraise; **9** appraisal, catalogue *UK*, inventory; **10** inspection; **11** stocktaking; PHRASES: **4, 5** take stock.

auditorium 3 box, pit; **4** hall, loge; **5** foyer; **6** circle, heaven, stalls; **7** balcony, gallery, parquet, seating, theater; **8** fauteuil, paradise, parterre; **9** mezzanine; **10** proscenium; **12** amphitheater; PHRASES: **3, 4** box seat, the gods; **3, 6** box office; **4, 6** back stalls; **5, 2, 5** front of house *UK*; **5, 3** royal box, stage box; **5, 5** opera house; **5, 6** dress circle, front stalls, upper circle; **6, 7** peanut gallery; **7, 4** concert hall, lecture hall; **9, 6** orchestra stalls *UK*.

auditory *See* **aural**

augment 3 add; 4 grow; 5 boost, widen; 6 dilate, expand, extend, spread; 7 advance, amplify, broaden, develop, enlarge, improve, inflate; 8 escalate, increase, mushroom, snowball; 9 intensify; 10 appreciate, strengthen; 11 proliferate; PHRASES: 3, 2, 6 put on weight; 4, 2, 5 rise in price; 4, 6 gain height, gain weight; 5, 1, 9 reach a crescendo.

augmentation 4 rise; 5 raise; 6 growth, spread; 7 advance; 8 dilation, increase, widening; 9 crescendo, expansion, increment, inflation, spreading; 10 betterment, broadening, escalation; 11 development, enlargement, improvement; 12 appreciation; 13 amplification; 15 intensification; PHRASES: 3, 8 pay increase; 4, 2, 5 gain in value; 5, 8 price increase.

Auld Reekie 9 Edinburgh.

aura 3 air; 5 force; 7 quality; 10 appearance, atmosphere.

aural 5 audio, radio; 7 audient, hearing, musical; 8 acoustic, auditory, wireless; 9 attentive, auricular, broadcast, listening; 10 telephonic; 11 audiovisual, radiophonic; PHRASES: 3, 4 all ears.

aurally 5 aloud; 7 audibly; 8 hearably; 14 telephonically; PHRASES: 2, 3 by ear; 2, 3, 5 on the radio; 3, 4 out loud; 6, 5 within range; 6, 7 within earshot, within hearing.

aureole 4 halo; 6 corona.

auricula 5-3 bear's-ear.

aurora 8 borealis; 9 australis; PHRASES: 5, 6 polar lights; 7, 7 auroral display; 8, 6 northern lights, southern lights.

aurora borealis 8, 6 northern lights.

auspice *See* **omen**

auspicious 4 fair, rosy; 5 clear, lucky; 6 bright, likely; 7 hopeful; 9 cloudless, favorable, fortunate, opportune, potential, promising; 10 optimistic, propitious; 11 encouraging; 12 providential; PHRASES: 4, 2, 7 full of promise; 4, 2, 9 full of potential.

auspicious (be auspicious) 5 bless, favor; PHRASES: 3, 4 bid fair; 4, 4 bode well; 5, 2 shine on, smile on; 5, 4 augur well.

austere *See* **severe**

austerity 7 economy, gravity; 8 scarcity, severity, shortage; 10 simplicity; PHRASES: 4-6 self-denial.

authentic 4 echt, pure, real, true; 5 pukka, solid, sound, valid; 6 dinkum *Aus and NZ*; 7 genuine, natural, sincere; 8 accurate, faithful, official, original, patented, reliable, rightful, sterling, truthful, uncopied, verified; 9 undoubted; 10 dependable, hallmarked, inimitable, legitimate; 11 copyrighted, trademarked, trustworthy; 13 authenticated, unadulterated; 14 unquestionable; PHRASES: 4, 4 bona fide; 4, 6 sure enough; 6-2-3 honest-to-God; 6-4, 5 twenty-four karat.

authenticate 4 mark, seal; 5 check, prove, stamp; 6 attest, clinch, ratify, second, uphold, verify; 7 certify, confirm, endorse, sustain; 8 validate; 9 ascertain, establish, indenture, reinforce; 11 corroborate, demonstrate; 12 substantiate; PHRASES: 4, 2 back up; 4, 3 bear out; 6, 3, 6 settle the matter.

authenticity 2 it; 5 truth; 6 purity; 7 reality; 8 solidity, validity; 10 legitimacy; 13 inimitability; PHRASES: 2, 8 no illusion; 2, 9 no imitation; 3, 1, 4 not a fake; 3, 4, 5 the real McCoy, the real thing, the very thing; 8, 6 sterling silver. *See also* **authentic**

author 4 bard, poet, scop; 5 skald; 6 fabler, penman, rhymer, scribe, source, writer; 7 creator, diarist, elegist, poetess; 8 annalist, essayist, fabulist, inventor, jongleur, lyricist, novelist, satirist, trouvère; 9 balladeer, dramatist, historian, poetaster, rhymester, sonneteer, versifier, wordsmith; 10 allegorist, biographer, chronicler, dramaturge, journalist, librettist, originator, playwright, rhapsodist, troubadour; 11 mythologist, novelettist, storyteller; 12 dithyrambist, screenwriter; 14 autobiographer; 15 historiographer; PHRASES: 4, 4 epic poet, lake poet; 4, 8 poet laureate; 4, 10 Lost Generation; 5, 6 crime writer; 7, 6 fiction writer; 8, 4 dramatic poet, pastoral poet, romantic poet.

authoritarian (be authoritarian) 4 boss; 5 drill; 7 oppress; 8 dominate, domineer; 9 subjugate, tyrannize; 10 discipline; PHRASES: 3, 4, 3 lay down the law; 4, 2, 3, 4 lead by the nose; 4, 2, 4 lord it over; 4, 3 play god; 4, 3, 3, 4 hold all the aces; 4, 3 call the tune; 4, 3, 5 rule the roost, wear the pants; 4, 3, 8 wear the trousers *UK*; 5, 3, 4 crack the whip; 7, 2 dictate to.

authoritative 4 firm; 5 bossy, legal; 6 lawful, lordly, mighty, potent, ruling, senior, strong; **7** leading, learned, supreme; **8** absolute, coercive, dominant, imposing, official, powerful, puissant, reliable, rightful, superior; **9** confident, empowered, governing, imperious, masterful, respected; **10** commanding, definitive, dependable, imperative, legitimate, overruling, peremptory, preeminent; **11** controlling, domineering, influential, predominant, trustworthy; **13** authoritarian, knowledgeable; PHRASES: **2**, **3**, **4** at the helm; **2**, **3**, **5** at the reins, at the wheel; **2**, **3**, **6** in the saddle; **2**, **5** in power; **2**, **6** in charge; **2**, **7** ex officio, in command, in control; **2**, **9** in authority; **4-6** high-handed; **4-9** self-assertive.

authoritativeness 5 clout; **6** weight; **7** command, majesty; **8** position, solidity, standing, validity; **9** authority, greatness, influence, knowledge; **10** confidence; **11** credibility, reliability; **13** dependability; PHRASES: **4-9** self-assertion. *See also* **authoritative**

authority 3 law; **4** buff, rule, sway, writ; **5** board, clout, might, power, reign, right, trust; **6** agency, charge, expert, permit, source, weight; **7** ability, charter, command, control, license, mandate, mastery, potency, royalty, warrant; **8** citation, dominion, evidence, hegemony, legality, strength, warranty; **9** direction, dominance, influence, knowledge, patronage, puissance *UK*, seniority, supremacy; **10** absolutism, ascendancy, confidence, consultant, conviction, domination, experience, governance, government, leadership, legitimacy, management, permission, specialist, suzerainty; **11** constituted, corporation, prerogative, sovereignty, superiority; **13** authorization; **14** administration; PHRASES: **3-2** say-so; **3**, **4**, **4** the whip hand; **3**, **5**, **4** the upper hand; **5**, **5** legal power; **5**, **7** purse strings; **6**, **5** divine right, hidden power; **6**, **7** expert witness; **7**, **6** eminent domain; **8**, **5** absolute power.

authority (be an authority on) 4 know; PHRASES: **4**, **3**, **5** know all about, know the ropes; **4**, **4**, **2**, **5** know back to front *UK*; **4**, **4**, **5** know one's stuff; **4**, **6**, **3** know inside out; **10**, **2** specialize in.

authority (grant authority) *See* **authorize**

authority (have authority) 4 lead, rule, sway; **5** judge, power, reign; **6** compel, direct, govern, impose, manage, police; **7** command, control; **8** dominate; **9** influence, legislate; **10** administer, manipulate; **11** predominate; PHRASES: **3**, **2**, **3**, **6** sit on the throne; **4**, **3**, **5** call the shots, rule the roost; **4**, **3**, **7** call the signals; **4**, **4** hold sway; **4**, **5** have power, keep order, pull wires; **4**, **7** pull strings; **4**, **8** pass judgment; **4**, **10** rule absolutely; **5**, **7** reign supreme; **5**, **9** wield authority; **7**, **4** preside over; **8**, **5** exercise power.

authority (person of authority) 2 MP (Member of Parliament); **3** cop, MEP (Member of the European Parliament); **4** beak, boss, dean, exec, guru, head, jefe, king, pope, sage, whip; **5** bobby, chief, judge, mayor, queen, rabbi, ruler, swami; **6** bigwig, bishop, consul, copper, despot, leader, mentor, Senate, tyrant; **7** emperor, empress, manager, marshal, monarch, premier, primate, provost, sheriff, teacher; **8** autocrat, cardinal, dictator, director, educator, governor, mayoress *UK*, official, superior; **9** authority, commander, constable, executive, patrician, policeman, president, principal, proconsul, seneschal, sovereign; **10** archbishop, archdeacon, chancellor, headmaster, magistrate; **11** Congressman, policewoman; **12** commissioner, headmistress; **13** Congresswoman; **14** representative; PHRASES: **3**, **3** top dog; **3**, **4** big shot; **3**, **5** big wheel; **3**, **6** big cheese; **4**, **3** wise man; **4**, **6** head honcho; **4**, **10** vice chancellor; **5**, **6** heavy hitter; **5**, **8** prime minister; **6**, **7** consul general; **7**, **6** cabinet member; **8**, **2**, **5** minister of state; **8**, **7** military officer.

authority (place of authority) 6 palace, prison; **7** capital; **8** Congress; **9** classroom, courtroom, Whitehall; **10** Parliament, Washington; **11** Westminster; PHRASES: **3**, **4** the Hill; **3**, **5**, **5** the White House; **3**, **7** the Capitol; **6**, **3** Number Ten *UK*; **6**, **7** police station; **7**, **4** Capitol Hill; **7**, **6** Downing Street; **8**, **4** military base, military unit.

authority (take authority) 5 usurp; **6** accede; **7** succeed; **9** overthrow; PHRASES: **4**, **1**, **4**, **5** lead a coup d'état; **4**, **3**, **4** take the helm; **4**, **4** take over; **4**, **5** gain power; **4**, **7** take control; **5**, **1**, **4**, **5** stage a coup d'état; **5**, **3**, **6** mount the throne, usurp the throne; **5**, **5** seize power, usurp power; **6**, **3**, **6** ascend the throne; **6**, **7** assume command.

authorization 5 leave; **6** charge, permit; **7** consent, mandate; **8** approval, sanction; **9** agreement, patronage; **10** commission, permission; **11** appointment, endorsement; **PHRASES: 3, 2-5** the go-ahead; **7, 6** letters patent.

authorize 2 OK; **4** okay; **5** allow, elect; **6** anoint, charge, depute, enable, permit, ratify, select; **7** appoint, approve, charter, empower, entitle, license, mandate, warrant; **8** accredit, delegate, legalize, sanction; **10** commission, consecrate, legitimate; **PHRASES: 4, 5** make legal; **4, 10** give permission; **5, 9** grant authority.

authorized 5 legal; **6** lawful; **8** official; **9** certified, chartered.

auto 3 car; **6** driver; **7** driving.

autocrat 6 despot, tyrant; **8** dictator; **13** authoritarian.

autocratic 5 bossy; **8** despotic; **9** arbitrary, imperious; **10** tyrannical; **11** dictatorial, domineering, overbearing; **13** authoritarian.

Autocue 12 Teleprompter; **PHRASES: 5, 5** idiot board.

autodidactic 10 perceptive; **PHRASES: 4-6** self-taught; **4-8** self-schooled.

automatic 5 pilot; **6** preset, reflex, repeat; **7** robotic, routine; **8** habitual, mindless; **9** automated, impulsive; **10** inevitable, mechanical, mechanized, programmed, unthinking; **11** instinctive, involuntary, unconscious; **12** transmission.

autonomy 10 discretion; **11** sovereignty; **12** independence; **PHRASES: 4, 4** free will; **4-4** self-rule; **4-10** self-government.

autopsy 8 analysis, necropsy; **10** debriefing, dissection, postmortem; **11** examination.

autumn 4 fall; **5** close; **6** golden, season; **7** decline, equinox, harvest; **8** autumnal; **10** Michaelmas; **11** culmination; **PHRASES: 4, 2, 3, 4** fall of the leaf; **4, 3** back end; **5, 2, 5** point of Libra; **6, 6** Indian summer; **7, 4** harvest moon, harvest time *UK*, hunter's moon.

autumn crocus 7 saffron; **PHRASES: 5, 6** naked ladies *UK*; **6, 7** meadow saffron.

auxiliary 7 support; **9** assisting, secondary; **10** supporting; **13** supplementary.

AV 3, 5 the Bible (Authorised Version).

avail *See* **benefit**

availability 6 plenty; **8** disposal, nearness, vicinity; **9** handiness, immediacy, proximity, readiness; **11** convenience, propinquity, sufficiency; **12** neighborhood; **13** accessibility, obtainability; **PHRASES: 9, 6** immediate circle.

available 2 on; **4** here, near; **5** close, handy, ready, there; **6** nearby, plenty, vacant; **7** offered; **9** immediate; **10** accessible, convenient, obtainable, sufficient; **PHRASES: 2, 2, 3** to be had; **2, 3** on tap; **2, 4** at hand, on hand, to hand; **2, 10** in attendance; **5, 2** close by; **5, 2, 4** ready to hand; **5, 4, 4** under one's nose; **6, 5** within reach; **8, 2** standing by.

avalanche 4 fall, mass; **5** flood, slide; **8** increase, quantity; **PHRASES: 4, 4** snow slip.

avant-garde 3 van; **6** modish, trendy; **8** advanced, vanguard; **11** fashionable; **12** trendsetting; **PHRASES: 1, 2, 4** à la mode; **2-3** in-set; **2-5** in-crowd, in-group; **3, 3, 4** all the rage; **3, 10** new generation; **4, 2** with it; **4, 10** next generation; **5, 10** young generation; **7, 5** advance guard.

avarice 5 greed; **7** avidity; **8** cupidity; **11** materialism; **12** covetousness; **15** acquisitiveness.

avaricious 6 greedy; **8** grasping; **9** deceptive, predatory, rapacious; **10** possessive; **11** acquisitive; **12** extortionate, manipulative; **PHRASES: 4, 1, 8** like a predator; **4, 7** with avarice.

AVE 6 avenue.

Ave Maria 4, 4 Hail Mary.

avenge 6 punish; **7** redress, requite, revenge; **9** retaliate; **PHRASES: 3, 4** hit back; **3, 4, 2** get back at; **4, 3, 5** even the score; **4, 9** take vengeance.

avenger 7 nemesis; **8** punisher; **10** retaliator, vindicator.

aventurine 8 sunstone; **9** goldstone.

avenue 3 way; **4** road; **6** chance, street; **7** opening; **9** boulevard; **11** opportunity, possibility.

average 3 par; **4** fair, mean, mode, norm, rule, type; **5** class, halve, model, stock, usual; **6** common, median, normal, wonted; **7** classic, current, general, generic, measure, popular, regular, routine, typical; **8** accepted, everyday, familiar, habitual, mediocre, middling, normalcy, ordinary, orthodox, standard; **9** customary, normality, normative, prevalent, universal, yardstick; **10** accustomed, commonness, conformity, generality, middlebrow, prevailing, prevalence, regularity, regulation; **11** familiarity, indifferent, predominant, traditional; **12** conventional, ordinariness, predominance, universality, unremarkable; **14** representative; **15** conventionality; PHRASES: **2-2** so-so; **2, 2, 3, 6, 2** be in the region of; **2, 4, 2, 4** be more or less; **2, 5, 2** be close to; **2, 6** be around; **3-2-3-4** run-of-the-mill; **3, 3, 6, 3** the way things are; **3, 5** the usual; **3, 6, 3** the common lot; **3, 8** the ordinary; **5-5** fifty-fifty; **5, 5, 7** grade point ~; **6-3-5** across-the-board; **6, 7** garden variety; **7, 3** general run; **10, 4** arithmetic mean.

average (be average) **7** conform, prevail; **11** predominate; PHRASES: **3, 2** get by; **3, 5, 1, 4** not cause a stir; **4, 2** make do.

average (make average) **5** halve, level; **6** bisect, divide, equate; **7** balance; **8** allocate, equalize; **9** normalize; **10** distribute, generalize, regularize; **11** standardize; PHRASES: **2, 5** go Dutch; **2, 6** go halves; **4, 3** even out; **5, 2** level up; **5, 3** share out; **6, 1, 7** strike a balance; **6, 3** smooth out.

average (on average) **5** about; **6** mainly, mostly; **7** broadly, chiefly, overall, roughly, usually; **8** commonly, normally UK; **9** generally, routinely, typically; **10** altogether, habitually, ordinarily; **13** predominantly; PHRASES: **2, 1, 4** as a rule; **2, 1, 5** as a whole, at a guess; **2, 1, 7, 4** as a general rule; **2, 3, 4, 3** in the long run; **2, 3, 5** as per usual, by and large, on the whole; **2, 7** in general, on balance; **3, 2, 3** all in all; **3, 3, 4, 4** for the most part; **4, 2, 4** more or less; **4, 5** just about; **5, 5** round about; **7, 8** broadly speaking, roughly speaking.

average person **6** common, masses, people; **8** everyman; **10** everywoman; **11** proletariat; PHRASES: **2, 3** GI Joe; **2, 7** Mr Average; **3, 2, 3, 6** man in the street; **3, 4** Joe Blow, Joe Soap UK; **3, 4, 3, 5** Tom Dick and Harry; **3, 4, 4** boy next door; **3, 6** hoi polloi, Joe Public UK; **4, 1, 6** John Q. Public; **4, 3, 4** rank and file; **5, 4** plain Jane; **6, 4** common folk; **6-5** second-rater; **7, 7** working classes; **8, 3** ordinary Joe.

aversion See **dislike**

avert **4** foil, stop; **5** avoid, deter; **6** hinder; **7** deflect, obviate, prevent; **8** obstruct; **9** forestall; PHRASES: **4, 3** ward off; **4, 4** turn away; **4, 5** turn aside.

avian **5** birdy, goosy; **6** oscine, owlish, ratite; **7** corvine, hawkish, singing, turdine; **8** anserine, aquiline, birdlike, crowlike, dovelike, perching, rasorial; **9** columbine, galliform, hirundine, passerine, predatory, raptorial, vulturine; **10** anseriform, cuculiform, flightless, psittacine, strigiform, struthious; **11** columbiform, fringilline, passeriform; **12** gallinaceous, psittaciform; **14** struthioniform.

aviation **6** flight, flying, glider, sortie; **7** airdrop, airlift, airmail, gliding, payload, skyjack; **8** paradrop, pilotage, piloting; **10** aerobatics, skywriting; **11** aeronautics; **12** aerodynamics; PHRASES: **3, 3** jet lag; **3, 6** air travel; **3, 8** air corridor; **4, 7** crop dusting; **5, 6** mercy flight UK; **6, 6** flying circus, flying doctor UK; **9, 6** scheduled flight.

aviation terms **3** dip; **4** drag, rake, STOL, VTOL; **7** flyover, flypast, gremlin, loading; **8** downwash, driftage, flameout, wingspan; **9** footprint, sweepback; **10** aerotowing, feathering, slipstream, turbulence; **11** airsickness; PHRASES: **3, 4** air flow, air miss; **3, 6** air pocket; **4-2** hook-up; **4, 5** wind shear; **4, 6** bird strike, load factor, wind tunnel; **4, 7** wing loading; **8, 4** boarding card UK, parasite drag.

aviator **5** flier, flyer, pilot; **7** copilot, steward; **8** aeronaut, observer; **9** navigator; **10** groundcrew, pathfinder, stewardess; **12** aircraftsman; PHRASES: **3, 7** air hostess UK; **6, 8** ground engineer; **6, 9** flight attendant.

avid See **keen**

avocado **9, 4** alligator pear.

avoid **3** cut; **4** duck, shun, snub; **5** avert, dodge, elude, evade, leave, skirt; **6** bypass, escape, eschew, ignore; **7** prevent; **8** hesitate, preclude, sidestep; **9** forestall; **10** circumvent; PHRASES: **3, 3, 2** get out of; **3, 5** get round UK, let alone; **4, 1, 5, 3** turn a blind eye; **4, 2** pass up; **4, 3** hold off; **4, 3, 2** keep out of; **4, 3, 5, 3** look the other way; **4, 4** keep away, keep from, stay away, turn away; **4, 5** keep clear, turn aside; **4-8** cold-shoulder; **5, 4** stand back; **5, 5** stand aloof, stand apart, stand clear, steer clear.

avoidable **8** needless; **9** stoppable; **11** unnecessary.

avoidance **4** snub; **7** dodging, evasion; **8** averting, escaping, eschewal, shunning, stopping; **9** bypassing, hindrance; **10** abstention, prevention, refraining; **11** obstruction; **12** anticipation, forestalling; **13** circumvention; PHRASES: **4, 5** wide berth; **4, 8** cold shoulder, safe distance; **7, 3** holding off.

avoider 5 idler; 6 coward, dodger, evader, possum, skiver, truant; 7 dreamer, escapee, escaper, ostrich, quitter, refugee, runaway, shirker, skulker, slacker; 8 absentee, deserter, escapist, fugitive, renegade, shrinker; 9 abstainer; 10 nondrinker, nonrealist, teetotaler; 11 sidestepper; 12 scrimshanker; PHRASES: 3, 6 tax evader; 4, 5 gold brick; 4, 7 gold bricker; 5, 6 draft dodger; 9, 6 displaced person.

avoiding 3 shy; 6 hidden, hiding, hunted, latent; 7 elusive, escaped, evasive, neutral, passive, runaway; 8 blinking *UK*, cowering, fugitive, inactive, skulking, slippery, taciturn; 9 apathetic, blenching, equivocal, flinching, reluctant, shrinking, unwilling; 10 preventive; 11 uncommitted; 12 noncommittal; 13 unforthcoming; PHRASES: 2, 3, 3 on the lam; 2, 3, 9 on the defensive; 3-2-5 fly-by-night; 3, 8 not involved; 4, 2, 5 hard to catch.

avoirdupois weight 3 ton; 4 dram, gram, kilo; 5 carat, ounce, pound, stone; 6 drachm; 7 scruple; 11 pennyweight; 13 hundredweight; PHRASES: 4, 6 troy weight; 6, 6 atomic weight; 9, 6 molecular weight.

await 4 loom, near; 6 expect; PHRASES: 2, 2, 5 be in store; 3, 2, 4 lie in wait; 3, 5 lie ahead; 4, 2 wait on.

awake 2 up; 4 wide; 5 alert, aware; 6 roused; 7 aroused, wakeful; 8 stirring; 9 conscious; PHRASES: 2, 3, 4 on the ball; 2, 3, 6 up and around; 4, 2 wake up.

awake (not awake) 4 dozy; 5 dopey; 6 asleep, dozing, drowsy, sleepy, torpid; 7 dormant, resting, sedated, yawning; 8 comatose, dreaming, sleeping; 9 somnolent, soporific; 10 hypnotized, insensible, slumberous; 11 aestivating, hibernating, unconscious; 13 anaesthetized; PHRASES: 3, 4 out cold; 4, 2, 3, 5 dead to the world; 4, 6 fast asleep; 4-6 half-asleep; 5-4 heavy-eyed; 5, 6 sound asleep; 6, 3 flaked out; 7, 3 nodding off.

awaken 4 stir, wake; 5 evoke, force, impel, rouse, tempt; 6 arouse, compel, elicit, excite, foment, hasten, incite, induce, kindle, manage; 7 inspire, promote, provoke; 8 initiate, motivate; 9 encourage, influence, stimulate; 11 precipitate; PHRASES: 3, 2 get up; 5, 2 bring on; 5, 3 bring out, spark off, touch off; 7, 3 trigger off.

award 4 gift, give; 5 endow, grant, honor, prize; 6 bestow, reward; 7 present, verdict;

8 decision, judgment; 10 settlement.

aware 5 alert; 7 mindful; 8 informed; 9 attentive, concerned, conscious; 10 interested, responsive; 11 experienced; 13 knowledgeable.

away 3 off, out; 4 fled, gone, left, lost; 5 aloof, apart, flown, right, while; 6 absent; 7 asunder, distant, missing, nowhere; 8 departed, vamoosed, vanished; 9 absconded, distantly, elsewhere; 11 disappeared; 14 dematerialized; PHRASES: 2, 4 on tour; 2, 5 on leave; 2, 8 on furlough, on vacation; 2, 10 on sabbatical; 3, 2, 4 out of town; 3, 2, 5 out of sight; 3, 3, 8 off the premises; 3, 4 not here; 3, 5 not there.

awe 4 fear; 5 dread; 6 fright, terror, wonder; 7 respect; 8 surprise; 9 amazement; 10 admiration; PHRASES: 11 trepidation.

awe-inspiring 6 august; 8 imposing; 9 important; 10 impressive; 13 authoritative.

awkwardly 7 gawkily, ineptly; 8 clumsily, gauchely, uneasily; 10 annoyingly; 11 gracelessly, inelegantly, ponderously; 12 cumbersomely; 13 uncomfortably; 14 inconveniently; PHRASES: 4-11 self-consciously.

awkwardness 6 unease; 9 gawkiness, ineptness; 10 clumsiness, difficulty, discomfort, gaucheness, inelegance, uneasiness; 12 discomfiture, stubbornness, ungainliness, unwieldiness; 13 embarrassment, gracelessness; PHRASES: 4, 2, 4 lack of ease; 4, 2, 5 lack of grace, lack of skill.

awkward situation 6 bother, shtook; 7 dispute; 12 disagreement; PHRASES: 3, 5 bad patch; 4, 2, 6 spot of bother; 4, 2, 7 spot of trouble; 4, 5 hard times; 6, 6 sticky wicket.

AWOL 4 gone; 6 absent, truant, wanted *UK*; 7 missing; 9 deserting; 10 absconding.

awry 5 amiss, askew, wrong; 6 aslant, astray, skewed; 7 crooked, muddled, twisted; 8 cockeyed; 9 skewwhiff *UK*; PHRASES: 3, 2, 2, 6, 2 not as it should be; 3, 2, 4 out of true; 3, 2, 6 out of kilter; 3, 4 off beam; 3-6 off-center.

ax 3 cut; 4 fire; 7 dismiss; 8 downsize; PHRASES: 3, 2 let go; 3, 3 lay off; 3, 4 cut back; 4, 4 slim down; 4, 9 make redundant *UK*; 5, 4 scale down. *See also* **tool, weapons**

axilla 6 armpit.

axiom *See* **maxim**

axis 4 bloc; 6 league; 8 alliance; 10 federation; 11 partnership.

axle 3 hub, pin, rod; 4 axis, nave, pole; 5 hinge, pivot, shaft; 6 gimbal, hotbox, pintle, swivel; 7 bearing, bushing, distaff, fulcrum, gudgeon, journal, mandrel, radiant, spindle; 8 trunnion; 9 headstock; PHRASES: 4, 7 ball bearing; 5, 7 bevel bearing; 6, 7 needle bearing, roller bearing, thrust bearing; 7, 3 journal box.

aye *See* yes

Ayers Rock 5 Uluru.

Azania 5, 6 South Africa.

azote 8 nitrogen.

azoth 7 mercury.

B

B **3** key; **4** bass, bill, note; **5** black; **6** bishop; **8** Bachelor; PHRASES: **9, 4** secondary road.

BA **6** barium, degree; PHRASES: **7, 7** British Airways; **8, 2, 4** Bachelor of Arts.

babble **3** hum; **4** buzz; **5** drone; **6** gabble, hubbub, murmur, mutter; **7** blather, chatter, prattle.

baby **3** kid, tot, war; **4** babe, blue, boom, love, talk; **5** buggy, child, lover, spoil, sprog *UK*, sugar, tooth; **6** coddle, cosset, infant, pamper, rhesus, rugrat; **7** newborn; **8** carriage, snatcher; **11** cradleboard, mollycoddle, overprotect; PHRASES: **4, 2, 4** babe in arms; **4, 4** fuss over; **4-4** test-tube; **5-5** anklebiter *UK*; **9, 7** receiving blanket.

baby carriage **4** pram *UK*; **6** walker; **8** stroller; **9** Portacrib, pushchair *UK*; **12** perambulator *UK*; PHRASES: **4, 5** baby buggy; **4, 6** baby walker *UK*.

back **3** ebb; **4** door, down, help, hind, rear, rest, room, seat, wane, yard; **5** light, spine; **6** assist, behind, boiler, burner, ladder, marker, matter, recede; **7** country, finance, passage, regress, reverse, subside, support; **8** backbone, backward, hindmost, rearmost, rearward, straight; **9** encourage, vertebrae; **10** retrogress; PHRASES: **2, 2, 3, 3** go to bat for; **2, 3, 4** to the rear; **2, 8** go backward; **3, 6** get behind; **4, 4** ally with, side with; **4, 8** move backward; **5, 2** stand by, stick by; **5, 2, 3** stick up for; **5, 4** align with; **5, 6** stand behind *UK*; **6, 6** spinal column; **7, 3** provide for; **9, 6** vertebral column.

backbone **4** prop; **5** spine; **6** pillar; **7** courage, stamina, support; **8** mainstay; **9** fortitude, vertebrae; PHRASES: **5, 5** moral fiber; **6, 6** spinal column.

backer *See* **supporter**

background **6** family, milieu; **7** setting; **8** backdrop; **10** experience, upbringing; **11** environment; **12** surroundings; **13** circumstances.

backhander *See* **bribe**

backslide **5** lapse; **6** revert; **7** regress, relapse; PHRASES: **2, 4, 3, 5** go down the tubes; **4, 4** slip back.

backslider **7** failure; **8** apostate, deserter; **9** defaulter; **10** recidivist; **12** transgressor; PHRASES: **2-5** no-hoper.

backsliding **10** recidivism.

backtalk **8** rudeness; **9** impudence; **10** cheekiness, disrespect; **12** impertinence.

backward **3** shy; **5** timid; **6** astern, toward; **7** bashful; **8** hesitant, rearward, retiring; **9** diffident, hindwards, reluctant; **10** regressive, retrograde; **13** retrogressive; PHRASES: **2, 3, 4** to the rear; **2, 7** in reverse; **3, 5, 3** the wrong way; **3, 5, 3, 5** the wrong way round; **4, 2, 5** back to front *UK*; **4, 2, 5, 3, 7** back to where one started; **7, 3, 4** towards the back *UK*, towards the back *UK*, towards the rear *UK*; **9, 11** rearwards reflexively.

backward and forward **2, 3, 3** to and fro; **2, 3, 4** up and down; **4, 3, 5** back and forth; **4, 4, 2, 4** from side to side.

backwards **6** toward.

backwoods *See* **wilderness**

bacon **3** ham; **4** back, side; **5** green; **6** Danish, flitch, gammon, rasher, smoked; **7** streaky; **8** Canadian, sowbelly, unsmoked; PHRASES: **4, 4** salt pork; **5, 4** belly pork *UK*; **6, 3** boiled ham, middle cut.

bad **3** off; **4** base, evil, grim, news, poor, sour; **5** acute, awful, black, blood, cruel, faith, grave, gross, harsh, inept, lands, nasty, stale, worse, worst, wrong; **6** clumsy, faulty, flawed, guilty, horrid, putrid, rancid, rotten, severe, sinful, uneasy, unjust, unruly, wicked; **7** abysmal, adverse, ashamed, beastly, corrupt, crooked, decayed, ghastly, harmful, heinous, illegal, immoral, naughty, noisome, noxious, ruinous, serious, tedious, testing, unhappy, vicious, wayward, willful; **8** accursed, annoying, contrite, criminal, damaging, decaying, depraved, dreadful, gruesome, hopeless, horrible, horrific, inferior, pathetic, penitent, ruthless, shocking, terrible; **9** appalling, dangerous, debauched, defective, deficient, dishonest, execrable, imperfect, merciless, obnoxious, regretful, repentant, shameless, unhealthy, unlikable; **10** abominable, apologetic, burdensome, delinquent, horrendous, lamentable, remorseful, unpleasant, villainous; **11** decomposing, disobedient, incompetent, intolerable, mischievous, prejudicial, substandard, troublesome, unendurable, unspeakable; **12** disagreeable, irredeemable, unmanageable, unscrupulous; **13** objectionable; PHRASES: **2, 4** no good; **3, 4** not nice; **3-6** ham-fisted; **4-6** cack-handed *UK*; **4-11** life-threatening.

bad conduct 4 vice; **7** badness; **8** mischief, rudeness, vileness; **10** misconduct, wickedness; **11** boorishness, discourtesy, misbehavior, naughtiness, selfishness; **12** monkeyshines; **14** ungraciousness.

bad feeling 4 envy, fury, rage; **5** spite; **6** grudge, hatred, rancor; **7** dislike; **8** acrimony, jealousy; **9** animosity; **10** antagonism, bitterness, resentment; **11** intolerance; **12** spitefulness; PHRASES: **3, 4** ill will; **3, 5** bad blood, bad vibes; **4, 8** hard feelings.

badge 3 pin; **5** clasp; **6** brooch, emblem, symbol; **8** insignia.

badger 5 harry, press, ratel; **6** harass, hassle, pester, plague; PHRASES: **2, 2, 2** go on at *UK*.

bad luck *See* **luck**

badly behaved 3 cad, git; **4** boor, lout, rude; **6** unruly, wicked; **7** asshole *UK*, boorish, bounder, naughty, selfish, wayward; **8** criminal, impolite; **9** obnoxious; **10** immoralist, ungracious; **11** disobedient, mischievous; **12** discourteous, unmanageable; **13** inconsiderate; PHRASES: **3-4** ill-bred; **3-8** ill-mannered; **7, 2** playing up; **7, 5** naughty child.

bad-mannered 4 rude; **5** crude, lippy, saucy; **6** cheeky, coarse, savage, vulgar; **7** abusive, boorish, caddish, cursing, loutish,

uncouth; **8** churlish, impudent, insolent, swearing; **9** barbarian, irascible, offensive, truculent, unrefined; **10** uncultured, unmannerly; **11** impertinent; **12** obstreperous, unchivalrous; PHRASES: **3-4** ill-bred; **3-8** ill-mannered; **4-7** foul-mouthed.

bad manners 3 lip; **5** cheek, sauce; **8** rudeness; **9** crudeness, grossness, impudence, insolence, vulgarity; **10** coarseness, impatience, incivility, misconduct, truculence; **11** boorishness, caddishness, discourtesy, loutishness; **12** churlishness, impertinence, impoliteness; **13** offensiveness; **14** unmannerliness; PHRASES: **3-8** illbreeding; **4, 2, 8** want of chivalry; **5, 8** gross behavior, scant courtesy.

badminton 3 IBF (International B~ Federation), net; **4** bird, shot; **5** court, drive, fault, smash; **6** racket, server; **7** shuttle; **8** feathers, receiver; **9** tramlines; **10** battledore; **11** shuttlecock; PHRASES: **2, 4** in side; **3, 4** out side; **3, 5** net posts; **4-4** drop-shot; **6, 4** center line; **7, 7** plastic shuttle.

badness 3 sin; **4** evil, vice; **5** crime, wrong; **6** horror; **7** cruelty; **8** distress, villainy; **9** annoyance, depravity, injustice; **10** dishonesty, illegality, immorality; **11** abomination; **15** irredeemability.

bad person 3 rat; **4** bane, hood, ogre, pimp, rake, thug; **5** brute, bully, cheat, crook, felon, fiend, ghoul, hussy, Judas, knave, louse, rogue, scamp, skunk, snake, swine, thief; **6** baddie, Hitler, killer, lecher, outlaw, rapist, rascal, robber, rotter, sadist, savage, sinner, Stalin, tyrant; **7** bounder, culprit, hoodlum, lowlife, monster, outcast, pervert, stinker, traitor, villain, wastrel, wrong'un *UK*; **8** assassin, betrayer, criminal, evildoer, gangster, hooligan, murderer, offender, poisoner, profaner, quisling, recreant, renegade, Satanist, swindler; **9** cutthroat, desperado, kidnapper, miscreant, pedophile, racketeer, reprobate, scoundrel, terrorist, wrongdoer; **10** blackguard, blasphemer, degenerate, lawbreaker, malefactor, profligate; **11** rapscallion, undesirable; **12** pornographer, streetwalker, transgressor, troublemaker; PHRASES: **3, 3** bad egg, bad lot *UK*, hit man; **3, 4** bad news; **3, 5** bad fairy; **3, 9** bad influence; **4, 2, 3, 5** scum of the earth; **4-2-4** ne'er-do-well; **4-3-7** good-for-nothing; **4, 4** call girl, lost soul; **4, 5** lost sheep; **4, 6** evil genius, gang member, holy terror *UK*; **4, 7** drug peddler; **4, 8** mass murderer, ugly customer; **5, 2, 3, 5** snake in the grass; **5, 2, 7** dregs of society; **5-3** gross-out; **5, 5** black sheep; **5, 6** hired killer; **5, 9** devil incarnate; **5, 10** devil worshipper; **6, 5** fallen angel, fallen woman, rotten apple; **6, 6** serial killer; **7, 7** mafioso mobster; **8, 3** prodigal son; **8-5** mischief-maker; **9, 6** homicidal maniac.

bad taste *See* **vulgarity**

bad-tempered *See* **irritable**

baffle *See* **confuse**

bag 3 air, bum *UK*, ice, sac, sag, tea; **4** blue, body, case, golf, grab, grip, grow, keep, poke, sack, take, tote; **5** catch, claim, doggy, jiffy, mixed, money, paper, pouch, purse, seize, shoot, snare; **6** bundle, clutch, coffee, duffel, kitbag *UK*, occupy, school, sponge, sports, string, tucker *UK*; **7** capture, carrier *UK*, evening, feedbag, freezer, handbag, holdall *UK*, mailbag, nosebag, plastic, postbag *UK*, reserve, satchel, shopper *UK*, sporran, weekend; **8** backpack, carryall, knapsack, lavender, reticule, rucksack, shopping, shoulder, sleeping; **9** carpetbag, container, gladstone, haversack, overnight, saddlebag; **10** diplomatic, pocketbook, receptacle; **PHRASES: 8, 4** shopping cart; **10, 5** diplomatic pouch.

bagatelle *See* **trifle**

baggage 4 bags, case, gear, pack; **5** cases, trunk; **6** kitbag *UK*, valise; **7** daysack, holdall *UK*, luggage; **8** backpack, carryall, knapsack, rucksack, suitcase; **9** briefcase, carrycase, haversack, portfolio; **10** belongings; **11** portmanteau; **PHRASES: 5, 4** money belt; **6, 4** travel case, vanity case; **7, 4** attaché case.

bail 4 bond; **6** surety; **7** payment; **8** security.

bailiff 5 agent; **6** factor; **7** evictor, steward; **8** overseer; **12** dispossessor; **PHRASES: 3, 7** law officer; **5, 7** legal officer; **6, 7** estate manager.

bait 4 draw, lure; **5** taunt, tease, tempt; **6** entice, harass; **7** attract, torment; **10** attraction, enticement, inducement, temptation.

bake 3 sun; **4** boil, burn, cook, fire, heat, kiln; **5** roast, toast; **6** bleach, harden, scorch; **7** swelter; **8** overheat; **PHRASES: 3, 3** dry out; **3-3** sun-dry.

balance 4 rest; **5** argue, poise, weigh; **6** assess, debate, offset, settle, square, steady; **7** compare, discuss, residue, surplus; **8** consider, equalize, evaluate; **9** calculate, re-mainder, stability, stabilize; **10** steadiness; **11** equilibrium; **PHRASES: 3, 2, 6** set of scales; **4, 2** even up; **4, 2, 5** keep in place; **4, 3** even out; **4, 6** hold steady, keep steady, stay poised; **4, 7** keep upright; **5, 2** weigh up *UK*; **5, 4** what's left; **8, 6** weighing scales *UK*; **8, 7** weighing machine.

balcony 5 lanai; **6** circle, loggia; **7** gallery, terrace, veranda; **PHRASES: 3, 4** the gods *UK*; **5, 4** upper tier *UK*; **5, 6** upper circle.

bald 4 bare, thin, worn; **5** blunt, frank, plain; **6** direct, simple, smooth; **8** hairless, receding; **9** unadorned; **10** baldheaded *UK*, threadbare; **15** straightforward; **PHRASES: 4, 2, 3** thin on top.

balderdash *See* **nonsense**

baldness 5 baldy; **8** alopecia, skinhead; **9** calvities, premature; **PHRASES: 4, 2, 4** lack of hair; **4, 4** hair loss. *See also* **bald**

bale *See* **bundle**

balk 6 recoil; **8** hesitate; **PHRASES: 4, 4** draw back, pull back; **4, 5** stop short.

ball 3 boy, orb; **4** bead, blob, bowl, cock, dart, game, golf, puck, shot, wood *UK*; **5** globe, rugby, valve; **6** bobble *UK*, marble, pellet, soccer, sphere, tennis; **7** bearing, cricket, droplet, floater, globule; **8** football, snowball, spheroid; **PHRASES: 5, 6** field hockey; **7, 5** curling stone.

ballad 4 poem, song; **9** narrative; **PHRASES: 4, 4** folk song.

ballast 4 bulk; **6** weight; **7** balance; **10** makeweight, stabilizer.

ballet 4 bras, demi, jeté, plié, posé, saut, solo, tutu, volé; **5** arqué, barre, battu, beats, brisé, collé, coupé *UK*, dance, décor, élève, fondu, ligne, passé, piqué, pivot, porté, rosin, sauté, serré, tendu, tombé; **6** aplomb, attack, baissé, ballon, cambré, chainé, changé, chassé, croisé, dégagé, détiré, devant, écarté, éffacé, élancé, entrée, épaulé, étendu, étoile, failli, jarret, modern, monter, penché, pointe, relevé, retiré, voyagé; **7** allongé, arrondi, attaque, balancé, ballong, bourrée, dancing, danseur, déboité, deboulé, échappé, emboité, étendre, fouetté, glissée, jarreté, leotard, maillot, marquer, poisson, ramassé, retombé, Russian, sissone, soutenu, taqueté; **8** assemblé, attitude, ballonné, ballotté, batterie, cabriole, cagneaux, coryphée, danseuse, déboulés, derrière, détourné, glissade, pistolet, renversé, romantic, serpette, spotting, stulchik, tonnelet; **9** arabesque, ballabile, classical, développé, élévation, entrechat, enveloppé, équilibre, hortensia, juponnage, limbering, marcheuse, pirouette, raccourci, révérence, revoltade; **10** battements, changement, enlèvement, épaulement, soubresaut, taqueterie; **11** contretemps, soubresauté; **12** choreography, enchaînement, gargouillade; **13** choreographer; **14** divertissement; PHRASES: **1, 5** à terre; **3, 2, 4** pas de chat, pas de deux; **3, 2, 6** pas de basque; **3, 5** toe dance; **4, 2, 4** coup de pied; **4, 4** back bend; **5, 2, 4** tours en l'air; **5, 2, 6** corps de ~; **6, 5** modern dance; **6, 8** closed position.

ballet companies 5, 6 Royal Ballet; **6, 7** Ballet Rambert.

ballets 7 Giselle; **8** Coppelia; PHRASES: **3, 9** Les Sylphides; **3, 10** The Nutcracker; **4, 4** Swan Lake.

balloon 5 bloat, pilot, swell, trial; **6** expand, helium; **7** barrage, distend, inflate; **9** dirigible; **10** inflatable; PHRASES: **3-3** hot-air; **4, 2** blow up; **4, 3** puff out.

ballot 4 poll, vote; **6** survey; **7** canvass, consult; **8** election; PHRASES: **6, 6** secret ~.

balm 3 oil; **4** wash; **5** cream, salve; **6** balsam, cerate, lotion, relief, solace; **7** comfort, eyewash, lanolin, unguent; **8** cosmetic, liniment, ointment, Vaseline™; **9** emollient; **10** palliative, petrolatum; **11** consolation, embrocation, moisturizer; PHRASES: **4, 5** face cream.

bamboozle 3 con; **5** cheat, trick; **6** bemuse, puzzle; **7** confuse, deceive, perplex; **8** bewilder, hoodwink.

ban 2 no; **3** bar; **4** curb, veto; **5** brake, debar, order, taboo; **6** forbid, outlaw; **7** abolish, embargo, exclude; **8** disallow, prohibit, sanction; **9** interdict, proscribe; **10** disqualify, injunction; **11** prohibition, restriction.

banal *See* **commonplace**

banana(s) 3 oil; **4** skin; **5** split; **8** republic.

band 3 big, duo, mob; **4** belt, crew, gang, jazz, pipe, sash, trio; **5** brass, choir, combo, crowd, dance, group, octet, posse, range, steel, strap, strip; **6** collar, energy, fillet, girdle, ribbon, rubber, septet, sextet, string, stripe; **7** bandage, elastic, quartet, quintet, stretch; **8** citizens', ensemble, headband, mariachi, neckband; **9** bandoleer, bellyband, frequency, orchestra, waistband; **10** cummerbund, tourniquet; **11** sinfonietta; PHRASES: **3, 5** pop group *UK*.

bandage 3 Ace; **4** bind; **5** cover, dress; **7** binding; **8** compress, dressing; **9** strapping.

bandit *See* **robber**

bandore 7 pandora, pandore.

band together 5 unite; **7** combine; **9** associate; **10** amalgamate; PHRASES: **3, 8** get together; **4, 2** fall in, gang up, join up, link up, team up; **4, 6** join forces; **4, 8** club together.

bane 5 curse; **6** blight, bother; **8** nuisance; **10** irritation.

baneberry 4, 11 herb Christopher *UK*.

bang 3 hit, zap; **4** bash, blow, boom, bump, peal, shot, slam, thud, wham; **5** blast, burst, crack, crash, knock, pound, round, salvo, smash, thump, whack; **6** batter, hammer, report, rumble, volley; **7** blowout, collide, explode, resound, thunder; **8** backfire, detonate; **9** discharge, explosion; **10** detonation; **11** thunderclap; PHRASES: **4, 2** blow up; **4, 2, 7** clap of thunder; **5, 4** sonic boom; **6-4** pistol-shot.

banging 9 deafening, explosive; **10** thunderous; PHRASES: **3-9** ear-splitting.

banish *See* **eject**

bank 3 fog, pay, rim, row; **4** bill, card, cash, data, draw, edge, heap, lean, mass, pile, pool, rate, save, side, soil, tilt, veer; **5** array, blood, cache, clerk, group, hoard, mound, piggy, pitch, shore, slope, sperm, stack, stock, store; **6** border, encash *UK*, invest, memory; **7** account, central, deposit, incline, manager, reserve, savings; **8** clearing, discount, exchange, merchant, national, pawnshop, withdraw; **9** annuities, liquidate, reservoir, statement, stockpile; **10** commercial, depository, embankment, extinguish; **11** cooperative, pawnbroker's; **12** accumulation; PHRASES: **3, 2** pay in, put in; **4, 1, 5** cash a check; **4, 2** cash in; **4, 2, 2** have an account; **5, 1, 5** write a check; **6, 5** credit union; **6, 6** credit bureau; **7, 5** finance house; **7, 7** finance company; **7, 7, 5** Federal Reserve Board; **8, 7** friendly society *UK*.

bankrupt 4 bust, poor; **5** broke; **6** ruined; **9** insolvent, liquidate, overdrawn, penniless; **10** impoverish; PHRASES: **2, 3, 3** in the red; **5, 3** bleed dry, clean out, clear out *UK*.

banner *See* **sign**

banquet *See* **feast**

banter 3 wit; **4** joke, mock; **5** tease; **6** joking; **7** mockery, teasing; **8** repartee; PHRAS-ES: **4, 3, 2** make fun of, poke fun at.

baobab 6, 5 monkey bread.

bar 3 ban, but, inn, pub *UK*; **4** bolt, code, lock, milk, pole, rail, sand, wine; **5** block *UK*, chart, color, court, debar, graph, ingot, inner, local *UK*, outer, shaft, staff; **6** bodega, casino, coffee, except, fasten, forbid, hinder, impede, public, saloon, secure, stripe, tavern; **7** barrier, barroom, exclude, mitzvah, prevent, shebeen, singles; **8** hostelry, obstruct, prohibit, restrain, restrict, sinister; **9** barricade, billiards, excluding, hindrance, nightclub, roadhouse, speakeasy; **10** horizontal, impediment; **11** obstruction, restriction; PHRASES: **1-4** B-girl; **3, 2, 3, 3** get in the way; **4, 3** keep out; **4, 5** juke joint; **5, 3** close off; **5, 4** apart from; **5, 5** blind tiger; **7, 4** country club; **8, 4** watering hole; **8, 5** drinking place.

barb 3 dig, tip; **4** gibe, hook, spur; **5** spike, sting, taunt, thorn; **6** insult; **7** prickle.

barbaric 5 cruel; **6** brutal, fierce; **7** vicious; **9** ferocious.

Barbary ape 5 magot.

barbed 4 acid; **5** cruel, snide, spiky, spiny; **6** hispid, hooked, thorny, unkind; **7** acerbic, bearded, bristly, cutting, hirsute, hurtful, pointed, prickly, stubbly, unkempt, unshorn; **8** bristled, scratchy, taunting, unshaven; **9** bristling, mustached, sarcastic; **10** barbellate; **11** bewhiskered.

bard 4 poet; **8** composer, songster; **9** versifier, wordsmith.

bare 4 mere, nude, show; **5** basic, blank, clear, empty, naked, plain, scant, stark; **6** barren, expose, meager, measly, reveal, severe, simple; **7** austere, display, uncover; **9** unadorned, unclothed, uncovered, undressed.

bargain 3 bid, low; **4** APEX (Advance Purchase Excursion), deal, pact, sale, snip *UK*; **5** cheap, offer, steal, trade; **6** accord, barter, broker, charge, dicker, haggle, higgle, outbid, tender; **7** dumping *UK*, overbid, preempt, reduced, rejects, seconds, wrangle; **8** contract, covenant, giveaway, huckster, railcard *UK*, stickler, underbid; **9** agreement, incentive, negotiate; **10** travelcard; **11** arrangement, inexpensive; PHRASES: **3, 4** bus pass *UK*, cut rate; **3-4, 4** car-boot sale, off-peak fare; **3, 5** cut price; **3, 6** bon marché; **4, 2** push up; **4, 3** good buy; **4, 4** beat

down, fire sale, good deal, half fare; **4, 5** sale goods; **4, 6** loss leader; **4-6** rock-bottom; **5, 2** agree to, shake on; **5-3-3, 4** bring-and-buy sale *UK*; **5, 3, 4** wheel and deal; **5, 6** cheap ticket; **6, 3** settle for; **6, 4** garage sale, jumble sale; **6-5, 4** second-class fare; **6, 6** season ticket; **7, 4** economy fare, rummage sale, standby fare; **7, 5** special offer, special price; **7-8** bargain-basement; **8, 5** basement price; **9, 4** clearance sale.

bargain hunter 5 miser; **7** Scrooge, sponger; **9** skinflint; **10** freeloader; PHRASES: **4-7** gate-crasher; **5-4** cheap-jack; **5-7** penny-pincher.

bargaining 3 WTO (World Trade Organization); **4** GATT (General Agreement on Tariffs and Trade); **6** buyout, merger, tender; **8** contract, haggling, higgling, takeover; **9** agreement, greenmail; **11** negotiation; PHRASES: **5-7** horse-trading; **5, 9** trade agreement.

barge 4 push, rush; **5** burst, elbow, surge.

barking deer 7 muntjac.

barley 4 wine; **5** sugar, water.

barn 3 owl; **4** byre *UK*, door, shed; **5** dance, store; **6** stable; **7** cowshed; **8** outhouse.

barometer 5 gauge; **7** aneroid, mercury; **9** barograph, flowmeter, indicator; **10** hydrometer, hygrometer, statoscope; **12** weatherglass; PHRASES: **8, 5** pressure gauge.

barometric 8 isobaric; **9** udometric; **10** isothermal; **11** anemometric, atmospheric, barographic, hygrometric; **12** anemographic, hygrographic, pluviometric, thermometric; **13** psychrometric, thermographic; **14** meteorological.

baroque 6 ornate; **8** overdone; **9** elaborate; **10** decorative, flamboyant, ornamental; **11** exaggerated; PHRASES: **4-3-3** over-the-top.

barrage 3 dam; **4** bank, dike, hail; **5** flood, salvo, storm; **6** volley; **9** fusillade, onslaught; **10** embankment, outpouring; **11** bombardment.

barred 5 lined; **6** banded, banned, fenced, meshed, secure; **7** grilled, striped; **8** debarred, excluded, streaked; **12** disqualified.

barrel 3 keg, tub, vat; **4** butt, cask.

barrel organ 4, 5 hand organ; **6, 5** street piano.

barrel vault 5, 5 wagon vault; **6, 5** tunnel

vault.

barren 5 bleak, harsh, stark; 7 sterile; 8 desolate; 9 infertile; 10 unfruitful; 12 inhospitable, unproductive.

barricade 3 bar; 5 block; 6 cordon, secure; 7 barrier, fortify; 8 blockade, obstruct; 11 obstruction; 13 fortification.

barrier 3 dam; 4 boom, dike, moat, mole, wall, weir; 5 block, ditch, fence, jetty, levee, sonic, sound, spike; 6 abatis, buffer, bunker, condom, laager, paling, zareba; 7 bulwark, caltrop, parapet, rampart; 8 blockade, obstacle, palisade, stockade; 9 barricade, diaphragm, earthwork, hindrance, roadblock; 10 breakwater, breastwork, difficulty, embankment, impediment, portcullis; 11 obstruction, prophylaxis; PHRASES: 3, 4 sea wall; 4, 7 Iron Curtain; 5, 4 brick wall, razor wire, stone wall; 5, 5 crash crush; 6, 4 barbed wire, Berlin Wall; 7-2-5 chevaux-de-frise; 7, 4 Maginot Line; 8, 4 Hadrian's Wall; 8, 5 electric fence, sticking point; 9, 4 Siegfried Line; 9, 5 stumbling block.

barrister 6 lawyer; 8 advocate, attorney, defender; 9 counselor.

barrow 4 cart, hill, long, tomb; 5 mound; 7 trailer, trolley *UK Can*, tumulus; 8 handcart, pushcart; 11 wheelbarrow; PHRASES: 6, 5 burial mound.

barter *See* **exchange**

barytes 5, 4 heavy spar.

base 3 air, fix; 4 data, deck, pier, root; 5 basal, basic, basis, first, floor, found, Lewis, metal, nadir, stand; 6 alkali, anchor, bottom, center, create, ground, lowest, origin, plinth, sordid, source; 7 basilar, bedrock, ignoble, immoral, organic, radical, squalid, station, support; 8 diacidic, flooring, inherent, pavement, pedestal, platform, underlie, underpin; 9 construct, essential, establish, fundament, inorganic, prisoner's, triacidic, undermost, underside, vestigial; 10 bottommost, foundation, monoacidic, nethermost, pyrimidine, quaternary, substratum, supporting, underlayer, underlying; 11 fundamental, rudimentary; 12 dishonorable, disreputable, headquarters; PHRASES: 3, 3 sea bed; 3, 5 sea floor, sea level; 4, 6 main office, weak alkali; 4-6 rock-bottom; 5, 3 river bed; 5, 5 ocean floor; 5, 8 floor covering; 6, 5 lowest point; 6-5 ground-level; 6, 6 strong alkali; 8, 5 starting point.

baseball 3 bat, cap, MLB (Major League Baseball), MVP, out; 4 balk *UK*, base, bunt, foul, save, walk; 5 coach, field, pitch, plate, score, swing; 6 aboard, batter, dugout, hitter, inning, runner, slider, stands, strike; 7 battery, bullpen, catcher, college, diamond, fielder, infield, manager, pitcher, sidearm, starter; 8 ballpark, fadeaway, outfield, slugfest; 9 bleachers, infielder, stickball; 10 outfielder, substitute; PHRASES: 2, 5, 9 St. Louis Cardinals; 3, 1, 3 hit a fly; 3, 2 pop up; 3, 3 fly out; 3-3 fly-out, put-out, tag-out; 3-4 All-Star; 3, 4, 4 New York Mets; 3, 4, 7 New York Yankees; 3, 5 box score, run bases; 3-5 off-speed; 3, 5, 6 San Diego Padres; 3, 6 big league; 3-6 one-bagger; 3, 7, 7 Los Angeles Dodgers; 3-8 All-American; 3, 9, 6 San Francisco Giants; 4, 2, 4 Hall of Fame; 4, 3 foul off, home run; 4-3 dust-off; 4, 3, 5 load the bases; 4, 4 fast ball, home base; 4, 5 chin music, hard pitch, home stand, left field, soft pitch, wild pitch; 4, 6 base runner, bush league; 4, 7 left fielder; 4, 9 fair territory, foul territory; 5, 1, 3 catch a fly, score a run; 5, 3 force out, throw out; 5-3 forceout, throw-out; 5, 3, 5, 4 Tampa Bay Devil Rays; 5, 4 force play, slide home; 5, 5 right field; 5, 6 Annie Oakley, major league, minor league, World Series; 5, 7 right fielder, Texas Rangers; 5, 9 world champions; 6-1, 6 Triple-A league; 6-3 strike-out; 6, 3, 3 Boston Red Sox; 6, 4 double play, gopher ball, pepper game, stolen base, strike zone, triple play; 6, 4, 6 Kansas City Royals; 6, 5 center field, circus catch; 6, 6 Little League; 6-6 double-header; 6, 7 center fielder; 6, 8 middle position; 7, 3 infield fly; 7, 4 Chicago Cubs, knuckle ball; 7, 4, 4 Toronto Blue Jays; 7, 5, 3 Chicago White Sox; 7, 6 Altanta Braves, Anaheim Angels, Detroit Tigers, Houston Astros; 7, 7 Florida Marlins; 7, 8 Seattle Mariners; 7, 9 Oakland Athletics; 7, 12 Arizona Diamondbacks; 8, 5 Montreal Expos; 8, 6 American League, National League; 8, 7 Colorado Rockies, slugging average; 9, 5 Minnesota Twins; 9, 6 Baltimore Oriole; 9, 7 Cleveland Indians, Milwaukee Brewers; 10, 4 Cincinatti Reds; 10, 7 Pittsburgh Pirates; 12, 8 Philadelphia Phillies.

baseball player 4 Bell (James "Cool Papa"), Cobb (Ty), Mack (Connie), Mays (Willie), Rose (Pete), Ruth (Babe), Ryan (Nolan), Sosa (Sammy); 5 Aaron (Hank), Bench (Johnny Lee), Berra (Yogi), Grove

(Lefty), Maris (Roger), Paige (Leroy Robert "Satchel"), Young (Cy); **6** Gehrig (Lou), Gibson (Josh), Koufax (Sandy), Mantle (Mickey), Palmer (Jim), Ripken (Cal Jr.); **7** Clemens (Roger), Hornsby (Rogers), Jackson (Joseph Jefferson "Shoeless Joe"), Johnson (Walter), Johnson (William "Judy"), McGwire (Mark David), Stengel (Casey); **8** Clemente (Roberto), DiMaggio (Joe), Durocher (Leo), Robinson (Brooks), Robinson (Jackie), Williams (Ted); **9** Mathewson (Christy); **10** Charleston (Oscar).

baseboard 8 mopboard; **9** washboard.

basely 6 humbly; **10** unworthily; **13** subordinately, subserviently.

bash 3 hit; **4** ball, blow, bump, dent, gala; **5** clout, dance, knock, party, prang *UK*, punch, smash, thump, whack; **7** condemn; **9** criticize; **11** celebration.

bashful 3 coy, shy; **5** timid; **6** chaste, demure, modest; **8** blushing, confused, reserved, reticent, retiring, timorous; **9** diffident, withdrawn; PHRASES: **4-9** self-conscious.

bashfulness 6 virtue; **7** modesty, reserve; **8** chastity, timidity; **9** reticence; **10** diffidence; **13** shamefastness; **14** shamefacedness. *See also* **bashful**

basic 3 key; **7** central; **9** essential, principal; **10** elementary; **11** rudimentary, undeveloped; **15** straightforward.

basically 11 essentially; **13** fundamentally.

basilisk 10 cockatrice.

basin 4 sink; **8** washbowl; **9** washbasin; PHRASES: **4, 5** hand ~.

bask 5 enjoy, savor; **6** lounge, relish; **7** recline; **9** luxuriate.

basket 3 bag, log; **4** case, chip, hilt, reed, rush, skep *UK*, trug *UK*, wire; **5** chair, creel, fruit, linen, maker, Moses, weave; **6** flower, hamper, picnic, pollen, punnet *UK*, wicker; **7** carrier *UK*, clothes, laundry, pannier; **8** bassinet, shopping; **10** wastepaper; **11** breadbasket, wastebasket; PHRASES: **6, 6** market ~, picnic hamper; **8, 4** shopping cart.

basketball 3 cut, NBA (National B~ Association), net, rim, sub; **4** dunk, FIBA (Fédération Internationale de Basketball), foul, goal, hack, pass, shot, trip, walk, WNBA (Women's National B~ Association); **5** biddy, block, court, draft, drive, guard, pivot, press, shoot, timer, whish; **6** basket, center, hanger, jersey, passer, pickup, rookie, scorer, screen, travel, umpire; **7** blocker, college, dribble, forward, quarter, rebound, referee, shooter; **8** hoopster, swingman; **9** backboard, rebounder; **10** substitute; PHRASES: **3, 2** tip in; **3-2** tip-in; **3-3** All-Pro; **3, 4** air ball, low post; **3, 4, 6** New York Knicks; **3, 6, 4** New Jersey Nets; **3, 7, 5** San Antonio Spurs; **3, 7, 7** New Orleans Hornets; **3, 7, 8** Los Angeles Clippers; **3-8** All-American; **4, 2, 4** Hall of Fame; **4, 3** foul out; **4, 4** bank shot, dead ball, dunk shot, free shot, held ball, high post, hook pass, hook shot, jump ball, jump shot, live ball, slam dunk, Utah Jazz; **4-4** goal-tend; **4, 5** back court, free throw; **4-5** shot-clock; **4, 7** zone defense; **4, 7, 6** Losa Angeles Lakers; **5, 3** pivot man; **5, 4** alley ball, draft pick, Dream Team, field goal, loose ball, Miami Heat; **5, 5** front court; **5-5** biddy-biddy *UK*; **6, 4** bounce pass, center line; **6, 5** center court, sudden death; **6, 5, 8** Golden State Warriors; **6, 7** Boston Celtics, Denver Nuggets; **6, 9** Dallas Mavericks; **7, 4** Phoenix Suns, scoring desk; **7, 5** Altanta Hawks, Chicago Bulls, Orlando Magic; **7, 6** Indiana Pacers; **7, 7** Detroit Pistons, Houston Rockets, running offense, Toronto Raptors; **7, 9** Memphis Grizzlies; **7, 11** Seattle SuperSonics; **8, 4** baseball pass; **8, 5, 7** Portland Trail Blazers; **9, 5** Milwaukee Bucks; **9, 7** Charlotte Bobcats; **9, 9** Cleveland Cavaliers; **9, 12** Minnesota Timberwolves; **10, 4** possession ball; **10, 5** Sacramento Kings; **10, 7** Washington Wizards; **12, 5** Philadelphia 76ers.

basketball player 4 Bird (Larry); **5** Cousy (Bob), Lemon (Meadowlark), O'Neal (Shaquille); **6** Bryant (Kobe), Cowens (Dave), Erving (Julius), Jordan (Michael), McHale (Kevin), Parish (Robert), Thomas (Isiah); **7** Bradley (Bill), Johnson (Magic), Russell (Bill); **8** Havlicek (John), Naismith (James); **11** Chamberlain (Wilt); PHRASES: **5-6** Abdul-Jabbar (Kareem).

basking shark 8 sailfish.

bass 3 sea; **4** deep, rock; **5** black, stone; **6** double, ground, string; **7** figured, walking; **8** thorough; **10** largemouth, smallmouth; PHRASES: **3-7** low-pitched; **4-5** deep-toned; **4-6** deep-voiced.

bass viol 5, 2, 5 viola da gamba; **6, 4** double bass.

bastard measles 7 rubella.

baste 3 hem, sew; 4 bash, seam, tack; 5 cover, thump; 6 grease, stitch, thrash; 7 clobber, drizzle, moisten; 8 saturate.

bastion 7 bulwark, defense, rampart, support; 8 defender, mainstay; 10 stronghold; 13 fortification.

Basuto 5 Sotho.

Basutoland 7 Lesotho.

bat 3 cut, hit, pad; 4 ball, club, edge, flap, hook, lift, loft, play, pull, seam, slam, slog, wink; 5 blink, block, drive, force, fruit, glide, guide, score, shank, shine, slice, smash, snick, sweep; 6 batter, glance, paddle, player, racket, spline, strike, volley, willow; 7 batsman, flicker, flutter, receive, vampire; 8 straight; 9 batswoman *UK*, cricketer *UK*, horseshoe; 11 pipistrelle; 13 insectivorous; PHRASES: 3, 2, 2 pad up to; 3, 4 new ball, old ball; 6, 3 flying fox, square cut; 6, 4 raised seam; 6, 8 flying squirrel.

batata 5, 6 sweet potato.

Batavia 7 Holland, Jakarta.

batch 3 lot, set; 5 bunch, group; 11 consignment.

bath 3 bed, hip, hot, mud, sun, tin, tub, vat; 4 bowl, chap *UK*, cold, cube, salt, sink, soak, tank, wash; 5 basin, baths, bidet, blood, chair, salts, sauna, steam, stone, vapor; 6 bubble, douche, plunge, shower, sponge; 7 bathtub, blanket, eyebath, hipbath, Jacuzzi™, thermae, Turkish, washtub; 8 bathroom, footbath, sitzbath, swimming, washbowl, washroom; 9 immersion, washbasin, washstand; 10 natatorium, sudatorium; PHRASES: 3, 3 hot tub; 5, 3, 4 basin and ewer; 5, 3, 7 basin and pitcher; 6, 5 public baths; 7, 4 kitchen sink; 7, 5 Turkish baths; 7, 8 immerse yourself; 8, 4 swimming pool; 8, 5 swimming baths *UK*.

bathe 3 dip; 4 dunk, lave *UK*, soak, soap, swim, wash; 5 rinse, steep; 6 douche, drench, lather, paddle, shower; 7 immerse, shampoo; 8 inundate, submerge; PHRASES: 2, 3, 1, 3 go for a dip; 4, 1, 4 have a bath, take a bath.

bathroom 3 Men; 5 gents *UK*, Women; 6 ladies, Ladies; 8 washroom; 9 amenities, cloakroom *UK*, garderobe, Gentlemen; PHRASES: 4, 4 Men's Room; 6, 4 powder room, Women's Room; 6, 4, 4 little boys' room; 6, 5, 4 little girls' room; 6, 11 public convenience *UK*; 7, 7 comfort station; 8, 4

smallest room.

bathymetric 5 sonar; 7 probing; 11 bathometric; 13 oceanographic.

bathymetry 10 bathometry; 12 displacement, echolocating, echolocation, oceanography; PHRASES: 4, 8 echo sounding; 5, 8 depth sounding.

baton *See* **rod**

battalion 4 mass; 5 crowd, horde; 6 throng; 9 multitude.

batter 3 bat, hit; 4 maim; 5 pound, thump; 6 attack, player, thrash; 7 assault, batsman; 9 batswoman *UK*, brutalize, cricketer *UK*.

battery 3 run, set; 6 series; 8 sequence; 10 succession; PHRASES: 7-3, 7 lithium-ion ~.

battle 2 do; 3 cry, try, war; 4 fire, fray, give, join, line; 5 blitz, brush, clash, drive, fight, mêlée *UK*, order, rally, royal, scrap, shoot, stand; 6 action, attack, charge, combat, engage, fracas, resist, strive, tussle; 7 contend, contest, cruiser, crusade, defense, dispute, fatigue, pitched, scuffle, wrangle, wrestle; 8 campaign, conflict, confront, dogfight, shootout, skirmish, struggle; 9 collision, defensive, encounter, offensive; 10 engagement; 13 confrontation; PHRASES: 2, 2, 3 go to war; 2, 4, 3, 3 go over the top; 3, 2 dig in; 3, 5 air fight; 4, 1, 5 make a stand; 4, 2, 5 come to blows; 4, 3, 4 beat the drum; 4, 4 open fire; 5, 1, 8 stage a shootout; 5, 2, 3 fight it out; 5, 3, 6 sound the charge; 5, 8 armed conflict.

battleground 5 bulge, front; 6 pocket, sector; 7 salient; 9 beachhead, frontline; 10 bridgehead; 11 battlefield; PHRASES: 3, 4 war zone; 5, 2, 6 field of battle; 5, 2, 8 field of conflict; 6, 4 combat zone, firing line; 7, 2, 3 theater of war; 7, 5 killing field.

batty *See* **eccentric**

bauble 3 toy; 5 charm, trash; 6 doodad, gewgaw, rattle, tinsel, trifle; 7 bibelot, novelty, trinket; 8 frippery, gimcrack, ornament, trumpery; 9 bagatelle, plaything; 10 decoration, knickknack; PHRASES: 4-1-4 bric-a-brac; 5, 3 small toy.

Bavaria 6 Bayern.

bawdy *See* **ribald**

bawl 3 cry, sob; 4 howl, roar, wail, weep, yell; 5 shout; 6 shriek; 7 screech.

bay 3 cry, rum, yap; 4 bark, cove, howl, leaf, lynx, tree, wail, woof, yelp; 5 haven, inlet; 6 alcove, harbor, recess, street, window; **7** cubicle, loading; **9** anchorage; **11** compartment; PHRASES: **7, 6** natural harbor.

bay lynx 6 bobcat.

bayonet 4 stab; **5** knife; **6** impale. *See also* **weapons**

bazaar 4 souk; **6** market; **11** marketplace; PHRASES: **3-4, 4** car-boot sale; **4, 2, 4** sale of work *UK*; **4, 6** flea market; **5-3-3, 4** bring-and-buy sale *UK*; **6, 4** jumble sale; **7, 4** rummage sale.

BC 3, 5 old times; **6, 6** before Christ.

be 4 live, stay; **5** ensue, exist, occur, stand; **6** befall, happen, remain; **7** coexist, located, present, subsist; **8** situated; **9** transpire; PHRASES: **4, 2, 4** come to pass; **4, 5** come about, have being, take place.

BE 9 beryllium.

beach 4 ball, boys, sand; **5** buggy, coast, shore; **6** strand; **7** seaside; **8** seashore; **9** coastline, shoreline.

beachwear 5 thong; **7** maillot; **8** flippers, sundress; **10** sunglasses; **11** leisurewear; PHRASES: **3, 4** wet suit; **5, 4** beach robe; **6, 4** diving mask; **6, 7** summer clothes. *See also* **clothes, swimwear**

beacon 4 fire, sign; **5** alarm, flare, radio; **6** signal; **7** belisha, bonfire, example, guiding *UK*, warning; **11** inspiration; **13** encouragement; PHRASES: **6, 2, 4** symbol of hope; **7, 7** shining example.

bead 4 blob, drip, drop; **7** droplet, globule.

beak 5 judge.

beaker 3 cup, mug; **5** glass; **7** tankard, tumbler.

beam 3 ray, RSJ *UK*; **4** emit, glow, grin; **5** joist, shine, smile; **6** girder, lumber, rafter, timber; **7** radiate, sunbeam.

bean 3 wax; **5** cocoa, shell, tonka; **6** coffee; **7** jumping. *See also* **pulse**

bean curd 4 tofu.

bear 3 ant, hug, sun; **5** abide, allow, black, bring, brook, brown, carry, great, honey, koala, polar, sloth, stand, stick, teddy, water, white, wooly, yield; **6** accept, assume, convey, create, endure, evince, garden, kodiak, little, native, suffer, woolly; **7** develop, display, exhibit, grizzly, produce, stomach, support, sustain, undergo; **8** cinnamon, shoulder, tolerate; **9** transport, withstand; **11** countenance; PHRASES: **2, 7** go through; **3, 2, 4** put up with; **4, 5, 2** give birth

to; **5, 4, 5** bring into being; **5, 5** bring forth; **6, 2** submit to; **10, 4** spectacled ~.

beard 4 bush; **6** accost, goatee; **7** stubble; **8** confront, whiskers; **9** challenge; PHRASES: **6, 4** facial hair.

bear down on 5 press; **6** accost, charge, squash, thrust; **7** depress, detrude; **8** approach, suppress; PHRASES: **4, 2** lean on; **4, 4** draw near, hold down, keep down, push down; **5, 2** march on, press on, weigh on; **5, 2, 2** close in on; **5, 4** press down; **7, 2** advance on; **8, 2** converge on.

bearing 2 NE, NW, SE, SW; **3** ENE, ESE, NNE, SSW, WNW, WSW; **4** line, mien, path, tack, true; **5** drift, route, tenor, track, trend; **6** course, effect, impact, manner, stance, thrust, vector; **7** beeline, compass, heading, posture; **8** attitude, behavior, carriage, demeanor, tendency; **9** direction, influence, relevance; **10** connection, deportment; **11** comportment, inclination, orientation; PHRASES: **7, 7** compass reading; **8, 6** relative course.

beast *See* **animal**

beast of burden 2 ox; **3** ass; **4** mule, sled; **5** burro, camel, husky, llama; **6** donkey; **7** sumpter; **8** elephant; **9** dromedary, packhorse; **12** draughthorse; PHRASES: **4, 6** pack animal; **6, 3** sledge dog.

beat 3 hit, mix, tap; **4** bang, blow, cane, dead, drum, flog, lash, lick, rout, whip, whup, wing; **5** baste, blend, break, crush, flail, knead, knock, outdo, pound, pulse, punch, smash, spank, tempo, throb, thump, tired, weary, whisk; **6** batter, bruise, crunch, defeat, hammer, Mersey, outrun, pummel, rhythm, strike, stroke, thrash, wallop; **7** circuit, flutter, pitapat, pulsate, scrunch, surpass, trounce, vibrate; **8** drumming, lambaste, outclass, outshine, outstrip, overcome; **9** exhausted, overwhelm, palpitate, pulsation, pulverize, throbbing; **10** outperform; **11** outdistance, palpitation; PHRASES: **2, 3, 6, 4** go one better than; **2, 6, 4** do better than; **3, 2** had it; **3, 2, 4** fit to drop *UK*; **3, 3, 6, 2** get the better of; **3-5** dog-tired; **4, 3** worn out; **4, 4** mash thud; **5, 3** tired out.

beaten 7 crushed, trodden; **8** defeated; **9** conquered, flattened; **10** compressed, vanquished.

beau 3 fop; **5** dandy, swell; **6** poseur, squire, steady, suitor; **7** admirer *UK*, peacock; **9** boyfriend.

beautician 6 barber; 7 crimper; 8 coiffeur; 9 coiffeuse; 10 manicurist, pedicurist; 11 cosmetician, hairdresser; 12 trichologist; PHRASES: 4-2, 6 make-up artist; 4-7 hair-stylist; 7, 7 plastic surgeon.

beautiful 4 fair, fine, lush; 5 bonny; 6 bright, comely, lovely, pretty, scenic, superb; 8 charming, esthetic, gorgeous, handsome, pleasing, striking, stunning, tasteful; 9 beauteous, exquisite, glamorous, Junoesque, wonderful; 10 attractive, delightful; 11 picturesque; 15 pulchritudinous; PHRASES: 4-4 well-made; 4-7 good-looking.

beautify 5 adorn, primp, prink; 6 revamp; 7 bejewel, enhance; 8 decorate, prettify, titivate; 9 embellish, glamorize, transform; 10 redecorate; 11 transfigure; PHRASES: 4, 1, 8 give a facelift *UK*; 4, 2 doll up, tart up *UK*; 7, 2 smarten up.

beauty 4 spot; 5 peach, pearl, queen, salon, sleep; 6 looker, upside; 7 bathing, benefit, cracker *UK*, smasher *UK*; 8 knockout, splendor; 9 advantage, humdinger; 10 camberwell, loveliness, prettiness; 12 magnificence; 14 attractiveness; PHRASES: 4, 5 good looks.

beaver 4 toil, work; 5 labor; 6 castor; 9 persevere; PHRASES: 4, 2 keep at; 4, 4 plug away.

because 2 as; 3 for; 5 since.

Bechuanaland 8 Botswana.

beckon 4 sign; 6 signal, summon; 7 gesture; 8 indicate.

become 4 suit; 5 befit; 7 convert, develop, enhance, flatter; PHRASES: 4, 4 turn into.

becoming 3 apt; 6 pretty; 7 fitting; 8 charming, fetching, suitable; 9 befitting; 10 attractive, flattering; 11 appropriate.

bed 3 air, cot, day, kip, pay, pit, zee; 4 band, base, bunk, camp, crib, form, plot, rest, sack, seam, sofa, twin; 5 berth, cover, divan, duvet, floor, futon, layer, linen, patch, plant, quilt, sheet, strip, water; 6 border, bottom, canopy, cradle, double, Empire, flower, ground, jacket, litter, oyster, seabed, single, spread; 7 bedding, blanket, feather, hammock, paneled, stratum, truckle, trundle, valance; 8 bassinet, bedsheet, bedstead, canopied, Colonial, coverlet, foldaway, riverbed; 9 bedspread, comforter, couchette, davenport, eiderdown, footboard, headboard, Portacrib; 10 bedclothes, pillowcase; 11 counterpane; PHRASES: 4, 3

bunk ~, sofa ~; 4-4 king-size; 4, 6 dust ruffle; 4-6 four-poster; 5-3 apple-pie; 5-4 queen-size; 5, 6 Moses basket *UK*; 6, 4 pillow sham; 6, 5 fitted sheet; 6, 6 chaise longue; 8, 5 mattress cover; 9, 5 patchwork quilt.

bedeck *See* **decorate**

Bedloe's Island 7, 6 Liberty Island.

bedspread 5 cover, quilt, throw; 8 coverlet; 9 eiderdown; 11 counterpane.

bedstead 3 bed; 4 base; 5 frame.

bee 4 hive; 5 drone, honey, mason, queen; 6 bumble, mining, worker; 8 spelling; 9 carpenter; 10 leafcutter.

beebread 8 ambrosia.

beef 3 leg, rib; 4 carp, moan, neck, rump, shin; 5 blade, brawn, chuck, flank, gripe, round, sinew, whine; 6 grouse, muscle, whinge *UK*; 7 brisket, chunter *UK*, grumble, sirloin, topside *UK*; 8 complain, topround; 9 bellyache, complaint, entrecôte; 10 silverside *UK*, tenderloin; 11 Porterhouse; PHRASES: 1-4 T-bone; 4, 3 back rib, best end *UK*; 5, 5 short plate; 5, 6 filet mignon; 6, 5 fillet steak.

Beelzebub 4, 2, 3, 5 Lord of the Flies.

beer 3 ale; 4 bock, root; 5 small, stout; 6 ginger, kaffir, porter, spruce.

beetle 3 bug; 4 dart, scud; 5 hurry, roach; 6 chafer, scurry, weevil; 7 scuttle; 9 cockroach, whirligig; 10 cockchafer; PHRASES: 3, 6 dor ~, oil ~; 4, 6 bark ~, boll weevil, corn chafer, dung ~, june ~, leaf ~, rove ~, stag ~; 5, 6 click ~, grain weevil, tiger ~, water ~; 6, 6 carpet ~, diving ~, ground ~, scarab ~, sexton ~; 7, 6 blister ~, burying ~, goliath ~, soldier ~; 8, 6 ambrosia ~, colorado ~, darkling ~, hercules ~, tortoise ~. *See also* **insects**

befall *See* **happen**

before 2 by; 3 ere, pre; 4 ante, fore; 5 afore; 6 facing; 7 earlier; 8 formerly; 10 beforehand, previously; PHRASES: 2, 3, 4 in the past; 2, 5, 2 in front of; 2, 7 in advance; 5, 2 ahead of, prior to; 6, 4 sooner than; 8, 2 previous to.

before now 3 yet; 7 already; 8 hitherto; 10 heretofore, previously; PHRASES: 2, 2, 3 up to now; 2, 2, 4, 4 up to this time; 2, 2, 4, 6 up to this moment; 2, 3 as yet, by now; 2, 4, 5 ex post facto; 3, 7 not anymore; 4, 3 till now; 5, 3 until now.

befriend 4 help; 6 assist; 7 support; PHRASES: 2, 6, 4 go around with; 2, 8, 4 be friendly with; 3, 2, 3, 4 hit it off with; 3, 2, 4 get to know; 3, 7 win friends; 3, 10 get acquainted; 4, 2 warm to; 4, 2, 4 take up with; 4, 4, 2 take care of; 4, 5 look after; 4, 7 make friends; 4, 7, 4 keep company with; 4, 9 make overtures; 5, 3, 3 break the ice; 6, 4 hobnob with; 10, 4 fraternize with.

befuddle *See* **confuse**

beg 5 plead, whine; 6 favors; 7 beseech, entreat, implore, request, solicit, wheedle; 10 supplicate; PHRASES: 3, 3 ask for.

beget *See* **cause**

beggar 3 bum; 4 defy, hobo; 5 tramp; 6 busker *UK*, cadger, defeat, exceed; 7 moocher, sponger, surpass, vagrant; 8 confound, vagabond; 9 mendicant, scrounger; 10 freeloader, panhandler; PHRASES: 2, 6 be beyond; 5, 7 rough sleeper; 6-2 hanger-on; 8, 6 homeless person; 9, 5 mendicant friar.

beggarly 4 mean; 5 cheap, dirty, seedy; 6 hungry, ragged, shabby, slummy; 7 patched, raggedy, scruffy, squalid; 8 barefoot, homeless, starving, tattered, underfed; 9 mendicant; 10 threadbare; 11 dilapidated, shelterless; PHRASES: 2, 3, 6 on the street; 2, 4 in rags; 3, 2, 6 out at elbows; 4, 2, 4 gone to ruin; 4-2-4 down-at-heel; 4-3-3 down-and-out.

beggary 4 rags, slum; 6 famine, hunger; 7 squalor, tatters; 8 meanness; 9 poorhouse, seediness, workhouse; 10 mendicancy, raggedness, shabbiness; 12 beggarliness, dilapidation, homelessness.

begin 4 dawn, open; 5 arise, debut, start; 6 create, launch, unveil; 8 activate, commence, initiate, premiere; 9 establish, instigate, originate; 10 inaugurate; PHRASES: 3, 2 set up; 3, 2, 5 set in train *UK*; 3, 2, 6 set in motion; 3, 3 set off; 3, 4, 2 get down to; 3, 5, 3 get under way; 4, 3 kick off; 4, 4, 5 come into being; 4, 5, 2 give birth to; 5, 2 start on; 5, 4, 5 bring into being; 6, 2 embark on.

beginner 1 L; 3 deb; 4 tyro; 5 pupil; 6 novice, rookie; 7 fresher *UK*, learner, recruit, student, trainee; 8 freshman, initiate, neophyte; 9 debutante, greenhorn; 10 apprentice, tenderfoot; 11 probationer; PHRASES: 3, 3 new boy; 3, 4 new girl.

beginning 4 dawn; 5 birth, debut, early, first, onset, start; 6 launch, outset; 7 dawning, initial, newborn, opening, primary; 8 creation, outbreak, premiere; 9 formative, inaugural; 10 initiation, initiative, initiatory; 11 instigation; 12 commencement, inauguration, introduction; PHRASES: 3-2 get-go; 3, 3 day one; 5, 5 first night; 5, 7 grand opening; 5-7 house-warming; 6, 3 square one; 6, 6 maiden voyage.

beginning (from the beginning) 2, 3 ab ovo; 2, 6 ab initio; 2, 7 ab origine; 4, 3, 4, 2 from the word go; 4, 3, 5 from the first; 4, 7 from scratch.

beginning (in the beginning) 9 initially; 10 originally; PHRASES: 2, 3, 4, 5 at the very start.

begrudge *See* **resent**

behave 3 act; 4 work; 7 perform; PHRASES: 3, 3, 4 toe the line; 4, 3, 5 obey the rules.

behavior 5 deeds; 7 actions, manners; 10 activities; 11 performance.

behead *See* **decapitate**

behind 5 after, later.

being (bring into being) 4 form, make; 5 cause, reify; 6 create, devise, invent; 7 compose, realize; 9 actualize.

Belau 5, 7 Palau Islands.

belch 3 gas; 4 burp, wind; 5 eruct; 6 flatus, hiccup; 9 windiness; 10 eructation, flatulence; PHRASES: 3, 3 let rip; 4, 3 blow off, drop one; 5, 4 break wind.

belief 4 idea, view; 5 angle, creed, faith, trust, truth; 6 notion, stance, theory; 7 opinion, premise, surmise, thought; 8 attitude, credence, judgment; 9 certainty, intuition, viewpoint; 10 acceptance, confidence, conviction, hypothesis, impression, persuasion, standpoint; 11 proposition, supposition; PHRASES: 5, 2, 4 point of view.

believable 5 sound; 6 likely; 7 sincere, tenable; 8 credible, possible, probable, reliable; 9 authentic, plausible, realistic; 10 acceptable, convincing, dependable, persuasive, reasonable; 11 trustworthy; PHRASES: 4, 2, 4 true to life.

believe 3 buy; 4 deem, hold, know; 5 judge, opine, think, trust; 6 accept, affirm, credit; 7 confess, declare, imagine, profess, suppose, swallow; 8 consider, maintain; PHRASES: 2, 7, 2 be certain of; 4, 3 fall for; 4, 3, 7 take for granted; 4, 5, 2 have faith in; 4, 7 rest assured; 5, 2 count on, swear by; 6, 2 depend on; 6, 2, 4 accept as true.

believe (be believed) 4, 8 find credence; **4, 10** gain acceptance.

believe (make someone believe) **4** dupe; **7** convert, deceive; **8** convince, persuade; **9** brainwash; **10** evangelize; **11** proselytize; **12** indoctrinate; PHRASES: **3, 4** win over; **4, 2** take in; **6, 3, 4** spread the word.

believer **3** fan, nun; **4** monk; **5** deist, hajji; **6** mystic, theist; **7** convert, devotee, pilgrim; **8** advocate, disciple, follower, sanyasin; **9** supporter; **10** churchgoer, conformist, worshipper *UK*; **11** communicant; **13** contemplative.

believer (in a nonmaterial world) **6** medium; **7** animist, Kantian, psychic; **8** Hegelian, idealist; **9** occultist, Platonist, solipsist; **12** spiritualist *UK*; PHRASES: **3-9** Neo-Platonist; **4, 6** mind reader; **7, 5** crystal gazer; **7, 6** fortune teller.

belittle *See* **disparage**

Belize **7, 8** British Honduras.

bell **3** jar; **4** buoy, hand, ring, tent; **5** alarm, chime, metal, sheep; **6** bronze, buzzer, church, diving, lutine, school, silver, sleigh, tinkle *UK*; **7** heather, passing, sanctus; **8** doorbell; **10** canterbury *UK*.

belladonna lily **9** amaryllis.

bellflower **9** campanula.

bellicose **7** warlike; **9** combative; **10** aggressive, pugnacious; **11** belligerent, quarrelsome; **13** argumentative; **15** confrontational.

bellicosity **8** jingoism, Ramboism; **9** militancy, pugnacity; **10** aggression, chauvinism, militarism, patriotism; **12** expansionism; PHRASES: **3, 5** war fever; **5, 2, 5** might is right; **5, 5, 5** might makes right; **5-8** saber-rattling; **8, 6** fighting spirit. *See also* **bellicose**

belligerency **7** wartime; **9** militancy; **11** hostilities; PHRASES: **4, 2, 3** time of war; **5, 2, 3** state of war; **5, 2, 5** state of siege; **6, 2, 4** resort to arms; **8, 2, 3** outbreak of war.

belligerent *See* **aggressive**

bellow *See* **shout**

bellwort **9** campanula.

belly **3** gut; **4** flop; **5** dance, laugh, tummy; **6** middle; **7** abdomen, stomach.

belonging **8** inherent, integral; **9** essential, intrinsic; **11** appurtenant, fundamental; PHRASES: **4, 2** part of.

beloved **3** pet; **4** dear; **5** liked, loved; **6** adored, prized; **7** admired, darling, revered; **8** esteemed, favorite, regarded; **9** cherished, preferred, treasured; **10** sweetheart; PHRASES: **4, 2, 4, 5** dear to one's heart; **4-5** much-loved, well-liked; **5, 4, 5** after one's heart.

below **5** lower, under; **7** beneath; **10** underneath; PHRASES: **4, 4** less than.

belt **3** fan, hit, tie; **4** band, beat, line, race, ring, rush, sash, seat; **5** bible, black, green, hurry, punch, strap, sword, thump; **6** attach, buckle, copper, cotton, fasten, garter, girdle, ribbon, safety, secure, strike, stripe, thrash; **8** chastity, conveyor, Lonsdale; **9** cartridge, restraint, suspender; **10** cummerbund; **11** stockbroker.

beluga **5, 5** white whale.

bemuse **4** daze, drug; **5** addle, blunt, stump; **6** baffle, fuddle, muddle, puzzle; **7** confuse, flummox, mystify, obscure, perplex; **8** bewilder, confound; **12** anaesthetize.

bench **3** pew; **4** form, seat; **5** front, king's, stall; **7** counter, worktop; **8** treasury; **9** workbench.

benchmark **5** level; **6** target; **8** standard; **9** yardstick.

bend **3** arc, bow; **4** arch, coil, curl, fold, loop, oval, turn, wave; **5** crook, curve, stoop, twist; **6** camber, circle, corner, crease, detour, spiral; **8** crescent, meniscus, parabola; **9** curvature, hyperbola, roundness; **10** undulation; PHRASES: **1-4** U-turn; **1-5** S-curve; **4, 4** lean over; **6, 9** change direction.

beneath *See* **below**

benediction *See* **approval**

benefactor **5** angel, genie; **6** backer, patron; **7** sponsor; **8** tutelary; **12** benefactress; **14** philanthropist; PHRASES: **4-6** well-wisher; **5, 9** fairy godmother; **6, 5** patron saint; **8, 5** guardian angel.

beneficial **6** useful; **7** gainful, helpful; **8** beatific, edifying, positive, remedial, salutary, valuable; **9** expedient, favorable, improving; **10** beneficent, profitable, propitious, worthwhile; **11** therapeutic; **12** advantageous, constructive; PHRASES: **2, 3** of use.

beneficiary **4** heir; **5** owner, payee; **6** coheir; **7** devisee, heiress, heritor, legatee; **8** assignee, receiver; **9** inheritor, recipient; **11** inheritress; PHRASES: **4-2-3** heir-at-law; **4, 2, 4** next in line; **4, 8** heir apparent; **4, 11** heir presumptive.

benefit 3 aid, pay, use; 4 boon, gain, gift, help; 5 avail, child, grant, serve; 6 behalf, family, fringe, injury, profit, return, reward; 7 advance, bestead, further, housing, payment, promote, subsidy, welfare; 8 interest, sickness; 9 advantage, allowance, maternity; 10 betterment, fundraiser, invalidity, prosperity, usefulness; 11 disablement, edification, improvement; 12 unemployment; 13 profitability, supplementary; 14 worthwhileness; PHRASES: 2, 4, 2 do good to; 3, 3 pay off; 4, 5 bear fruit; 4-5 well-being; 5, 3, 4 serve one well; 5, 7 bring results; 6, 4 common good, public good, public weal; 7, 5 charity event.

benevolence 4 love, pity; 5 grace, mercy; 6 toward; 8 altruism, bonhomie, goodness, goodwill, humanity, kindness; 9 benignity, geniality, tolerance; 10 affability, amiability, compassion, cordiality, generosity, humaneness, kindliness; 11 forgiveness, helpfulness, magnanimity, mindfulness, munificence; 13 brotherliness, consideration, courteousness; 14 benevolentness, thoughtfulness; 15 humanitarianism; PHRASES: 4-11 good-naturedness, kind-heartedness UK; 5, 2, 3 grace of God; 5, 2, 4 heart of gold; 6, 7 fellow feeling UK; 6, 8 loving kindness; 9, 4 brotherly love.

benevolent 4 good, kind; 6 benign, caring, decent, genial, giving, humane, kindly, loving; 7 affable, amiable, cordial, helpful, lenient; 8 fatherly, friendly, generous, maternal, motherly, obliging, paternal, sisterly, sociable, tolerant; 9 brotherly, courteous, forgiving, fraternal, indulgent; 10 altruistic, beneficent, charitable, empathetic, munificent, neighborly, solicitous, thoughtful; 11 considerate, sympathetic; 12 affectionate; 13 compassionate, philanthropic; PHRASES: 4-5 well-meant; 4-7 good-humored, good-natured, kind-hearted UK, well-meaning; 4-8 well-disposed; 4-11 well-intentioned.

benevolent (be benevolent) 4 love; 5 nurse; 6 oblige; 7 comfort, forgive, indulge, relieve, support; 8 tolerate; 9 empathize, encourage; 10 sympathize, understand; 11 accommodate; PHRASES: 4, 4 mean well, wish well; 4, 7 show concern; 5, 4 treat well.

benighted 4 evil, grim; 5 blind, murky, shady; 6 arcane, dismal, gloomy, hidden, mystic, occult, secret, somber, wicked; 7 cryptic, obscure, ominous, shadowy; 8 esoteric, ignorant, menacing, sinister; 9 oblivious; 10 forbidding, mysterious; 13 disadvantaged, unenlightened.

benign 4 kind; 6 caring, gentle, kindly; 10 benevolent.

Benin 7 Dahomey.

benjamin 9 spicebush.

bent 3 set; 5 bowed, flair; 6 curved, talent; 7 corrupt, crooked, decided, twisted; 8 criminal, resolved; 9 dishonest; 10 determined; 11 inclination.

bequeath 4 give, will; 5 grant, leave; 6 bestow, confer, donate; 8 transfer; PHRASES: 4, 2 pass on; 4, 4 hand down.

berate 4 lash, rail; 5 abuse, scold; 6 assail, attack, rebuke; 8 harangue, lambaste; 9 criticize, reprimand; PHRASES: 3, 4 lay into; 4, 3 bawl out, tell off; 4, 3, 4, 3 read the riot act; 4, 5 skin alive; 5, 2 shout at; 5, 3, 4, 2 throw the book at; 5, 4 pitch into; 6-4 tongue-lash.

bereavement 4 loss; 5 grief; 6 sorrow; 8 mourning.

berg 8 mountain.

Bermuda 3 rig; 5 grass; 6 shorts; 8 triangle.

berserk 3 mad; 4 wild; 5 crazy; 7 bananas, bonkers; 10 irrational; PHRASES: 3, 2, 5 out to lunch; 3, 2, 7 out of control; 3, 3, 4, 3 off the deep end; 6, 3, 4 around the bend.

berth 4 dock, land, moor; 5 wharf; 7 mooring; PHRASES: 4, 2 come in; 7, 5 landing place.

beseech See **beg**

beset 5 annoy; 6 assail, attack, hamper, harass; 7 plagued, trouble; 8 harassed UK, overcome, surround; 9 overwhelm, tormented; 11 overwhelmed.

beside 2 by; 4 near; 5 close; 8 adjacent; 9 adjoining, alongside; 10 contiguous; 12 contiguously, continuously, tangentially; PHRASES: 2, 3, 4, 2 at the side of; 2, 7 in contact; 2, 13 in juxtaposition; 3, 2, 3 end to end; 4, 2 next to; 4, 2, 4 face to face, nose to tail, side by side; 5, 2, 4 cheek by jowl.

besiege 5 beset; 6 invest; 7 enclose; 8 blockade, encircle, surround; 9 beleaguer, overwhelm; PHRASES: 3, 2 hem in; 3, 5, 2 lay siege to; 6, 3 starve out.

bespeak *See* **signify**

bespectacled 10 farsighted; 11 near-sighted; PHRASES: 4-4 four-eyed; 4-7 near-sighted; 5-7 short-sighted.

best 3 ace, boy, end, man, max, top; 4 girl, main, most, peak, pick, plum, tops; 5 chief, crack, cream, elite, first, outdo, prime; 6 choice, defeat, finest, flower, record, seller, tiptop, unique, utmost; 7 capital, highest, maximum, optimum, paragon, perfect, primary, supreme, surpass, topmost, winning; 8 cardinal, champion, crowning, dominant, flawless, foremost, greatest, overcome, peerless, platinum, topnotch, ultimate, unbeaten; 9 essential, matchless, nonpareil, paramount, principal, supremacy, unequaled, unmatched, unrivaled; 10 inimitable, invincible, perfection, preeminent, prevailing, triumphant, unbeatable, victorious; 11 predominant, superlative, supernormal, unmatchable, unsurpassed; 12 incomparable, preponderant, quintessence, transcendent, unparalleled; 13 unsurpassable; 14 quintessential, transcendental, unapproachable; PHRASES: 1, 3, 5 a cut above; 3, 2, 4, 5 out of this world; 3-4 all-time; 3, 4, 4, 2 the last word in; 3, 5 top marks; 3-6 top-ranked; 3-7 top-ranking; 4-5 gold-medal; 4, 6 sans pareil; 4-6 blue-ribbon; 4-7 best-selling; 5, 1 Grade A; 5, 2, 3, 4 cream of the crop; 5, 2, 3, 5 jewel in the crown; 5-4 first-rate; 5-5 first-class; 5-7 chart-busting, chart-topping, world-beating; 5, 8 nulli secundus; 5-8 grand-champion; 6, 2, 4 second to none; 6-3 number-one; 6, 7 beyond compare; 6, 8 record breaking; 7, 4, 2 nothing like it; 7, 5 without equal.

bestow *See* **bequeath**

bet 4 ante, plan; 5 stake, think, wager; 6 choice, expect, gamble, option; 7 believe; 8 consider; 9 candidate; 10 anticipate; 11 alternative; PHRASES: 3, 5, 2 put money on.

betray 3 con, rat; 4 blab, dupe, hoax, leak, sham, sing; 5 cheat, cozen, fraud, peach, split, sting, trick; 6 delude, reveal, squeal; 7 deceive, forsake, mislead, swindle; 8 disclose, flimflam, misguide; 11 stoolpigeon; 12 tergiversate; PHRASES: 2, 8 be disloyal; 3, 4 let down, let slip; 4, 2 tell on; 4, 3, 4, 4 give the game away; 4, 4 give away, hand over; 4, 5 name names, play false; 5, 3 blurt out; 5, 3, 5 spill the beans; 6, 2 inform on; 6-5 double-cross; 11, 2 stoolpigeon up.

betrothal 4 pact; 5 troth; 7 compact, promise; 10 engagement.

better 4 well; 5 outdo; 6 appeal, exceed; 7 enhance, surpass; 8 improved, outshine, outstrip, superior; 9 captivate, healthier, radically; 10 ameliorate, improvably, recovering, remedially; 13 progressively, restoratively; PHRASES: 2, 3, 4 on the mend; 2, 4, 6 in good health; 7, 2 improve on.

better (get better) 4 mend, rise; 5 rally, ripen, study; 6 ascend, evolve, mature, mellow, reform, revive; 7 advance, develop, improve, prosper, recover, succeed; 8 fructify, increase, progress; 10 convalesce, recuperate; PHRASES: 2, 4 do well; 2, 8 go straight; 4, 1, 8 make a comeback; 4, 2 make it, pick up; 4, 2, 3 make it big; 4, 2, 3, 5 rise in the world; 4, 3, 5 make the grade; 4, 3, 6 turn the corner; 4, 4 make good; 4, 4, 1, 3, 3 feel like a new man; 4, 4, 4 mend one's ways; 4, 5 bear fruit; 4, 7 make headway; 4, 8 make progress; 4, 9, 2 take advantage of; 6, 2 profit by; 7, 7 improve oneself.

between 4 amid; 5 among; 7 flanked, joining, linking; 10 concerning, connecting.

between (between times 7 interim; 8 interwar; 10 interlunar; 11 intercalary; 12 interglacial, intermediate.

bevel 4 cant.

beverage *See* **drink**

bewilder *See* **confuse**

bewitch 3 hex; 4 jinx; 5 charm, curse; 6 incant; 7 bedevil, enchant, possess; 8 demonize, entrance; 9 fascinate, hypnotize, mesmerize, spellbind; PHRASES: 3, 5, 5 say magic words; 4, 1, 4 wave a wand; 4, 1, 10 ride a broomstick; 4, 6 cast spells.

bewitched 5 hexed; 6 cursed, jinxed; 7 charmed, haunted, spooked; 9 bedeviled, enchanted, entranced, possessed; 10 fascinated, hypnotized, mesmerized, spellbound; PHRASES: 3-6 hag-ridden.

Bharat 5 India.

bhindi 5, 6 lady's finger.

bias 4 bent; 5 angle, slant, twist; 8 jaundice; 9 prejudice; 10 favoritism, partiality, preference, subjective; 13 preconception; 14 predisposition.

biased 4 bent; 6 unfair; 7 partial; 10 predispose, subjective. *See also* **bias**

Bible 4 Holy; PHRASES: 4, 4 Good Book; 4, 5 King James; 7, 8, 7 Revised Standard Version; **8, 8, 7** American Standard Version.

Bible (books) 3 Job; 4 Acts, Amos, Ezra, Joel, John, Jude, Luke, Mark, Ruth; 5 Hosea, James, Jonah, Kings, Micah, Nahum, Peter, Titus, Tobit; 6 Baruch, Daniel, Esdras, Esther, Exodus, Haggai, Isaiah, Joshua, Judges, Judith, Psalms, Romans, Samuel, Wisdom; 7 Ezekiel, Genesis, Hebrews, Malachi, Matthew, Numbers, Obadiah, Susanna, Timothy; 8 Habakkuk, Jeremiah, Nehemiah, Philemon, Proverbs; 9 Ephesians, Galatians, Leviticus, Maccabees, Zechariah, Zephaniah; 10 Chronicles, Colossians, Revelation; 11 Corinthians, Deuteronomy, Philippians; 12 Ecclesiastes, Lamentations; 13 Thessalonians; 14 Ecclesiasticus; PHRASES: 3, 3, 3, 6 Bel and the dragon; 3, 4, 2, 6 The rest of Esther; 4, 2, 7 Song of Solomon.

biblical characters 3 Eve, Job, Lot; 4 Abel, Adam, Baal, Cain, Esau, John, Luke, Mark, Mary, Noah, Paul, Ruth, Saul; 5 Aaron, David, Enoch, Herod, Isaac, Jacob, James, Jesus, Jonah, Judah, Moses, Peter, Sarah, Simon, Titus; 6 Andrew, Daniel, Elijah, Elisha, Esther, Gideon, Isaiah, Israel, Joseph, Joshua, Martha, Miriam, Nathan, Philip, Pilate, Salome, Samson, Samuel, Thomas; 7 Abraham, Absalom, Barabas, Delilah, Ephraim, Ezekiel, Gabriel, Goliath, Ishmael, Jezebel, Lazarus, Matthew, Michael, Rebekah, Solomon, Stephen, Timothy; 8 Barabbas, Benjamin, Caiaphas, Hezekiah, Jeremiah, Jonathan, Matthias; 9 Bathsheba, Nathaniel, Nicodemus; 10 Belshazzar, Methuselah; 11 Bartholomew; 14 Nebuchadnezzar; PHRASES: 4, 3, 7 John the Baptist; 5, 8 Judas Iscariot.

bicker *See* **argue**

bicycle 3 ATB, BMX; 4 bike, clip, fork, gear, pump; 5 brake, chain, crank, cycle, frame, pedal, spoke, trike, wheel; 6 fender, racing *UK*, saddle, safety, tandem; 7 chopper, clanger, pannier, toeclip, trishaw; 8 crossbar, minibike, mudguard *UK*, rickshaw, roadster, tricycle, unicycle; 9 kickstand, monocycle, saddlebag, trailbike; 10 boneshaker *UK*, chainguard, derailleur, handlebars, velocipede, wheelwoman; 11 quadricycle, wheelperson; PHRASES: 3-2-3-3 sit-up-and-beg; 3-7 two-wheeler; 4-4 pushbike *UK*; 4, 5 iron horse; 4, 10 drop handlebars; 5-8 penny-farthing *UK*; 6, 7 tandem ~; 7, 5 folding cycle; 8, 4 mountain bike; 8, 6 training wheels.

bid 3 try; 4 seek, tell; 5 offer, order; 6 direct, effort, submit, tender; 7 attempt, command, proffer, propose; 8 endeavor, proposal; 9 undertake; 10 submission; 11 proposition, undertaking.

bier *See* **stand**

big 3 Ben, end, top; 4 band, bang, deal, deep, high, huge, mega, shot, tall, time, vast, wide; 5 adult, Apple, baggy, beefy, broad, bulky, elder, giant, grand, great, heavy, jumbo, large, lofty, massy, older, roomy, stick, wheel; 6 Bertha, bumper, cheese, dipper, mighty, screen; 7 brother, hulking, immense, mammoth, massive, monster, outsize, soaring, spanker, titanic, whopper; 8 almighty, behemoth, business, colossal, elephant, enormous, generous, gigantic, imposing, infinite, mastodon, spacious, towering, whopping; 9 capacious, Cyclopean, extensive, ginormous, humongous, important, leviathan, limitless, monstrous, overgrown, overlarge, oversized; 10 commodious, cumbersome, Gargantuan, megalithic, monumental, prodigious, stupendous, thundering *UK*, tremendous, voluminous; 11 gigantesque, macroscopic, mountainous, significant, substantial; 12 astronomical; 13 comprehensive; 14 Brobdingnagian; PHRASES: 2, 3 of age; 3-5 man-sized; 4, 4 King Kong; 4-4 full-size, king-size, life-size; 4-5 fair-sized, full-blown, full-grown, full-scale; 5-2 grown-up; 5, 2, 4 large as life; 5-4 queen-size; 5, 5 extra large; 5-5 large-scale; 6-4 family-size; 6, 4, 4 larger than life; 7-4 economy-size.

big (be big) 4 bulk, loom, soar; 5 tower; PHRASES: 4, 5 loom large.

big (become bigger) 3 bud, fan, fat, wax; 4 grow, rise; 5 belly, bloat, bloom, breed, build, bulge, flare, plump, shoot, splay, swell, widen; 6 branch, dilate, expand, extend, fatten, flower, ramify, sprawl, spread, sprout, thrive, unfold; 7 amplify, augment, balloon, blossom, broaden, burgeon, develop, distend, enlarge, greaten, inflate, magnify, outgrow, stretch; 8 flourish, increase, lengthen, multiply, mushroom, overgrow, snowball; 9 crescendo, germinate, procreate, pullulate, reproduce; 11 hypertrophy, overdevelop; PHRASES: 3, 2, 6 put on weight; 3, 3 fan out; 4, 2 grow up; 4, 3 draw out, fill out; 5, 2 shoot up; 5, 3 plump out; 6, 2 spring up; 6, 3 branch out, spread out; 8, 2, 4 increase in size.

bigger 5 grown, puffy, tumid; 6 fatted, fatter, flared, larger, mature, padded, raised, spread, turgid; 7 bloated, dilated, splayed, stuffed, swelled, swollen, widened; 8 elevated, enlarged, expanded, extended, fattened, inflated, unfolded; 9 amplified, augmented, broadened, developed, dispersed, distended, dropsical, edematous, increased, magnified, outspread, stretched; 10 heightened, incrassate, lengthened, overweight, widespread; 12 outstretched; 13 hypertrophied, overdeveloped; PHRASES: 4-4 wide-open; 4-5 fullblown, full-grown; 5-2 blown-up, built-up; 5-3 drawn-out; 5, 5 fully grown; 5, 7 fully fledged; 5, 9 fully developed; 6, 2 puffed up; 6-2 pumped-up; 6-3 spread-out; 9, 3 stretched out.

bigger (make bigger) 4 cube, fuel, grow, hike, open, pump, rear; 5 bloat, boost, breed, build, erect, exalt, flare, plump, raise, splay, stoke, stuff, swell, widen; 6 climax, deepen, dilate, double, enlist, enrich, expand, extend, fatten, ramify, sprawl, spread, square, triple; 7 amplify, augment, broaden, develop, distend, elevate, enhance, enlarge, glorify, inflate, magnify, prolong, stretch, thicken; 8 condense, disperse, energize, escalate, heighten, increase, lengthen, maximize, multiply, redouble; 9 aggravate, culminate, duplicate, intensify, propagate, quadruple, reproduce, stimulate; 10 accelerate, aggrandize, exacerbate, exaggerate, invigorate, supplement; PHRASES: 3, 2 hot up *UK*; 3, 3 fan out, pad out; 3, 4, 2 add fuel to; 4, 2 beef up, blow up, bump up, fill up, heat up, jack up, jazz up, puff up, step up; 5, 2, 1, 4 bring to a head; 5, 2, 3, 4 bring to the boil; 5, 4, 6 raise one's sights; 8, 2, 4 increase in size.

bighorn 8, 5 mountain sheep.

bigness 8 enormity, grandeur; PHRASES: 4, 4 full size, life size; 4, 6 full growth.

bigot 3 pig; 4 Nazi; 5 jingo; 6 ageist, racist, sexist; 7 diehard, elitist, fanatic, fascist; 8 jingoist, partisan; 9 dogmatist, extremist, homophobe, racialist, xenophobe; 10 chauvinist, misandrist, misogynist; 12 superpatriot; 14 fundamentalist; PHRASES: 4-6 anti-Semite; 4, 10 male chauvinist; 5-6 witchhunter.

big person 4 hulk, ogre; 5 Atlas, giant,

Titan; 6 Amazon, ogress, Typhon; 7 Cyclops, Goliath; 8 colossus, giantess, Hercules; 9 Gargantua; 10 Pantagruel, Polyphemus; 14 Brobdingnagian; PHRASES: 3, 8 man mountain.

big wheel 6, 5 Ferris wheel.

bigwig 2 MD *UK*; 3 BTO, VIP; 4 head, lion, sage, star; 5 catch, chief, mogul, noble; 6 biggie, expert, leader, tycoon; 7 grandee, kingpin, magnate, notable; 8 favorite, mandarin, somebody, superior, superman; 9 godfather, personage; 10 aristocrat, notability; 11 heavyweight, personality; PHRASES: 2, 3 Mr Big, Mr. Big; 3, 3 big gun; 3, 4 big fish, big name, big shot; 3, 5 big Chief, big Daddy, big noise, big timer, big wheel, top brass; 3, 6 big cheese; 3, 9 big enchilada; 4, 2, 3, 5 lord of the manor, salt of the earth; 4, 4-1-4 high muck-a-muck; 5, 3 brass hat; 5, 5 prima donna; 5, 6 first fiddle; 5, 10 grand panjandrum; 6, 2, 7 pillar of society; 7, 5 leading light; 7-6 wheeler-dealer; 9, 4 uncrowned king.

bijou *See* compact

bile 6 spleen; 7 vitriol; 8 sourness; 10 bitterness; 12 irritability.

bilge 3 mud; 4 base, hold, hull, keel, silt, tank; 5 trash; 6 bottom, bowels, drivel, sludge; 7 garbage, rubbish; 8 effluent, interior, nonsense; PHRASES: 5, 5 ~ water.

bilingual 6 diglot, fluent; 8 polyglot; 12 multilingual.

bill 3 fee, old, sum; 4 beak, debt, menu; 5 books, carte *UK*, debit, mouth, price, score, tally, total; 6 amount, charge, damage, demand, docket, double, ledger, reform, tariff; 7 account, Buffalo, invoice, measure, receipt; 8 document, mandible, manifest, petition, proposal, treasury; 9 overdraft, reckoning, statement; 11 proposition, receivables; 13 accommodation; PHRASES: 4, 2, 4 ~ of fare; 4, 2, 6 ~ of lading; 4, 4 wine list; 5, 4 price list; 7, 5 account books; 8, 4 shopping list.

billet 6 shelter, station; 8 lodgings, quarters; 11 accommodate; 14 accommodations; PHRASES: 5, 5 guest house; 8, 5 boarding house.

billiards 3 cue; 4 club, coup, miss, pool, rest, spot; 5 baize, break, chalk, plain, screw; 6 cannon, French, hazard, marker, miscue, pocket, safety, string, stroke; 7 cushion, English, referee, striker, stroked; 8

centered, crotched, numbered, pocketed, triangle; **9** nominated, snookered; PHRASES: **2-3** in-off *UK*; **2, 4** in balk; **3, 1** the D; **3, 1, 4** pot a ball; **3, 4** cue ball; **3, 6** top pocket; **4, 4** balk line, bank shot, dead ball, kiss shot; **4-4** full-ball, half-ball; **4, 5** long loser; **4, 6** push stroke, spot stroke; **4, 7** balk cushion; **5, 4** eight ball, massé shot, white ball; **5, 9** carom ~; **6, 3, 4** pocket the ball; **6, 4** center line, center spot, object ball; **6, 6** bottom pocket, center pocket, direct cannon; **7, 4** pyramid spot; **8, 4** billiard spot, numbered ball; **8-4** straight-rail.

billow 3 ebb; **4** comb, curl, dash, flow, foam, peak, puff, rise, roll, rush, toss, waft, wave; **5** break, bulge, cloud, crash, froth, heave, surge, swell, swirl; **6** riffle, ripple; **7** balloon, inflate; **8** mushroom, undulate; PHRASES: **3, 3, 4** ebb and flow; **4, 2** flow in; **4, 3, 4** rise and fall; **5, 3, 4** catch the wind; **5, 4** surge back.

bin 4 silo; **6** basket; **7** dustbin *UK*; **9** container; PHRASES: **5, 3** waste ~ *UK*; **6, 3** litter ~ *UK*; **7, 3** garbage can, rubbish ~ *UK*, storage ~.

binary 4 code, dual, form, star, twin; **5** digit; **6** double, number; **7** twofold; **8** notation; **9** dualistic; PHRASES: **3-4** two-part.

bind 3 jam, tie; **4** bolt, grip, join, lock, moor, rope, yoke; **5** chain, clamp, lasso, latch, leash, truss, unite; **6** attach, batten, coerce, compel, fasten, fetter, oblige, secure, tether; **7** combine, connect, dilemma, impasse, manacle, padlock, require, shackle; **8** handcuff, quandary; **9** constrain; **11** predicament; PHRASES: **5, 9** tight situation.

binding 3 tie; **4** band, trim; **5** cover, strip, truss; **6** edging; **8** required; **9** fastening, mandatory, necessary, stitching; **10** attachment, compulsory, obligatory.

binge 4 orgy; **5** gorge, spree; **6** bender, overdo; **7** indulge, rampage, splurge; **9** brannigan; **11** overindulge; PHRASES: **3, 3** pig out.

bingo 6-6 housey-housey *UK*.

biochemical 6 living; **7** enzymic, natural, organic; **8** anabolic, chemical, hormonal; **9** catabolic, metabolic; **10** biological; **12** bioenergetic, biomolecular, biosynthetic; **14** photosynthetic.

biochemistry 10 enzymology; **11** biomolecule; **12** biosynthesis; **13** bioenergetics, biotechnology, endocrinology.

biographer 6 author, writer; **8** profiler; **9** historian; **10** researcher; **14** autobiographer.

biography 2 CV *UK*; **4** life, past; **5** story; **6** memoir, résumé; **7** account, memoirs, profile; **11** experiences; **13** autobiography; PHRASES: **4, 5** life story.

Bioko 8, 2 Fernando Po.

biological 4 life; **5** birth; **6** bionic, biotic, living; **7** generic, genetic, natural, organic; **8** adoptive, bionomic, specific; **9** biometric, botanical, endocrine, taxonomic; **10** anatomical, ecological, systematic, zoological; **11** biochemical, biophysical, cytological, virological; **12** evolutionary, histological; **13** embryological, immunological, morphological, physiological; **15** bacteriological.

biological function 3 sex; **5** birth, sight, smell, taste, touch; **7** coition, hearing; **8** delivery; **9** breathing, fertility, pregnancy, viability; **10** conception, copulation, fatherhood, motherhood, parenthood; **11** confinement, procreation, propagation, respiration; **12** reproduction; PHRASES: **10, 5** biological clock.

biotic 9 symbiotic; **10** biogenetic, biological, bioplastic; **12** biogenetical, protoplasmic, protoplastic.

birch 3 rod; **4** cane, flog, lash, whip; **5** stick; **6** strike, switch, thrash.

birds 3 hen, jay, moa, pie, web; **4** cock, coot, dodo, dove, fowl, game, gull, hawk, kite, rook, sora, wren; **5** brant, buteo, capon, eagle, early, flier, hobby, junco, macaw, mynah, ouzel, quail, robin, scaup, swift, table; **6** birdie, chough, condor, cuckoo, dipper, dunlin, falcon, hoopoe, kakapo, martin, merlin, oriole, osprey, parrot, parson, peewit, pepper, phoebe, pigeon, raptor, roller, scoter, strike, toucan, towhee, trogon, turaco, turkey, willet; **7** anhinga, antbird, bustard, buzzard, catbird, cowbird, creeper, dunnock *UK*, fantail, flicker, gadwall, gallows, goshawk, grackle, harrier, hoatzin, jacamar, kestrel, kinglet, limpkin, manakin, migrant, oilbird, peacock, peafowl, quetzal, redhead, redpoll, redwing, rooster, tanager, touraco, vulture, warbler, waxbill, waxwing, widgeon, wryneck; **8** avifauna, bateleur, birdlife, bluebird, bobolink, bobwhite, caracara, cardinal, cockatoo, curassow, elephant, gamebird, grosbeak, hornbill, killdeer, lovebird, lyrebird, megapode, nightjar, nuthatch, ovenbird, oxpecker, parakeet, pheasant, redstart, rifleman, surfbird, thrasher, titmouse, wheatear, whipbird, wildfowl, woodcock; **9** blackbird, blackpoll, bowerbird, brambling, broadbill, chickadee, cockatiel, crossbill, fieldfare, friarbird, frogmouth, goldfinch, goosander, gyrfalcon, migratory, mousebird *UK*, nighthawk, partridge, ptarmigan, riflebird, sapsucker, secretary, solitaire, trumpeter; **10** budgerigar, bufflehead, canvasback, chiffchaff, honeyeater, kookaburra, meadowlark, nutcracker, saddleback, sandgrouse, tailorbird, turtledove, woodpecker; **11** gnatcatcher, hummingbird, lammergeier, mockingbird, treecreeper, waterthrush, woodcreeper; **12** capercaillie, honeycreeper, whippoorwill, yellowthroat; PHRASES: **3-4, 3** saw-whet owl; **3-5** bee-eater; **3-6, 9** red-winged blackbird; **3-10, 4** red-shouldered hawk; **4, 2, 3, 3** fowl of the air; **4, 2, 7** bird of passage; **4, 2, 8** bird of paradise; **4, 3** blue jay, hawk owl; **4, 4** fish crow, fish hawk, rock dove, rock wren, wood duck; **4, 5** bald eagle, snow goose; **4, 6** blue grouse, pine siskin, sage grouse, surf scoter, wood pigeon, wood thrush; **4-6, 4** ring-billed gull, ring-necked duck; **4, 7** Rock Cornish, song sparrow, tree sparrow, wood warbler; **4, 8** sage thrasher; **4-8, 8** rose-breasted grosbeak; **4-8, 11** ruby-throated hummingbird; **5, 4** ruddy duck, sedge wren; **5-4, 10** three-toed woodpecker; **5, 5** harpy eagle, honey guide, snowy egret; **5-5** brain-fever; **5, 6** black grouse, house martin; **5-6, 6** white-winged scoter; **5-6, 7** rough-winged swallow, sharp-tailed sparrow; **5, 7** black vulture, marsh harrier; **5-7, 4** sharp-shinned hawk; **5-7, 7** white-crowned sparrow; **5-8, 7** white-throated sparrow; **5, 10** hairy woodpecker; **6, 4** common loon, guinea fowl, jungle fowl, mallee fowl *UK*; **6, 5** Canada goose, golden eagle, purple finch; **6, 6** hermit thrush, homing pigeon, purple martin, spruce grouse, varied thrush; **6, 7** purple grackle, vesper sparrow, yellow warbler; **6-7, 7** yellow-shafted flicker; **6-7, 9** yellow-bellied sapsucker; **6, 8** tufted titmouse; **6-8, 4** yellow-breasted chat; **6, 9** purple gallinule, upland sandpiper; **7, 3** screech owl; **7, 4** sparrow hawk; **7, 5** chimney swift; **7, 7** bearded vulture, griffon vulture, painted bunting, prairie chicken, seaside sparrow; **7, 9** roseate spoonbill, spotted sandpiper; Wilson's phalarope; **8, 3** Steller's jay; **8, 4** laughing gull, mourning dove, umbrella bird, Virginia rail; **8, 5** American eagle, sandhill crane, warbling vireo, whooping crane; **8, 6** northern oriole; **8, 7** chipping sparrow, laughing jackass, northern harrier; **8, 8** mountain bluebird; **9, 4** harlequin duck; **9, 6** Baltimore oriole, feathered friend, passenger pigeon, peregrine falcon; **10, 6** loggerhead shrike; **12, 7** prothonotary warbler. *See also* **flightless bird, owl, songbird, water bird**

bird song 3 caw, coo; **4** hiss, hoot, note, peep; **5** cheep, chirp, cluck, croak, quack, trill, tweet, whoop; **6** gobble, squawk, squeak, warble; **7** chatter, chirrup, screech, twitter; **8** chirping, woodnote; PHRASES: **2-4, 2-4** tu-whit tu-whoo *UK*; **4-1-6-3** cock-a-doodle-doo; **4, 6** dawn chorus; **5-5** tweet-tweet.

Birmingham 9 Brummagem *UK*.

birth 4 dawn, rate; **5** labor, natal, start; **6** origin, outset; **7** control, genetic; **8** delivery, founding, nativity; **9** beginning, formation, naissance; **11** certificate, confinement, parturition; **12** commencement.

birth control 3 IUD; **4** coil, IUCD *UK*, loop, pill; **6** condom, johnny, rubber, sheath; **7** femidom; **8** minipill; **9** diaphragm; **10** spermicide; **11** precautions; **12** prophylactic; **13** contraception, contraceptive; PHRASES: **5, 3** Dutch cap; **6, 6** French letter *UK*, rhythm method; **6, 8** family planning.

birthday 4 suit; **9** honors; **9** birthdate; **11** anniversary; PHRASES: **4, 2, 5** date of birth.

biscuit 3 dog, tea; **4** soda; **5** water; **6** cookie; **7** bourbon; **8** captain's.

bisexual 2-3 bi-guy.

bistort 9 snakeroot.

bit 3 tad; **4** drop, jiff, part, spot; **5** crumb, jiffy, piece, scrap, skosh, slice, speck, trace, while; **6** minute, moment, morsel, second; **7** smidgen; **8** fragment.

BIT 6, 5 binary digit.

bite 3 nip; **4** chew, gnaw, hurt, maul, tang; **5** piece, prick, sting, taste, wound; **6** attack, nibble; **8** mouthful, piquancy, puncture, tartness; **9** spiciness.

biting 4 cold; **7** acerbic, cutting, mordant; **8** freezing, piercing, scathing, stinging; **9** sarcastic, satirical.

bits and pieces 4 rags; **6** debris, rubble, scraps, things; **7** clobber *UK*, filings, moraine, parings, tatters; **8** detritus, leavings, oddments, peelings, shavings; **9** clippings, leftovers; **10** belongings; **11** knickknacks, miscellanea; PHRASES: **4-1-4** bric-a-brac; **4, 3, 4** bits and bobs *UK*, odds and ends; **8, 6** disjecta membra.

bitter 3 end, icy, raw; **4** acid, cold, sour; **5** acrid, angry, apple, harsh, polar, sharp; **6** acidic, arctic, biting, orange; **7** cutting, glacial, hostile, pungent, vicious; **8** freezing, piercing, stinging, vehement, virulent; **9** indignant, principle, rancorous, resentful; **10** astringent, embittered; **11** acrimonious; PHRASES: **4, 4, 2** hard done by *UK*.

bitterness 4 bile, gall; **5** anger, spite, venom; **6** grudge, rancor, spleen; **7** acidity, vitriol; **8** acerbity, acrimony, asperity, cynicism, mordancy; **9** animosity, hostility, mordacity, virulence; **10** causticity, resentment; **11** astringency, indignation; PHRASES: **3, 7** ill feeling; **4, 5** sour taste; **5, 6** sharp tongue; **6, 5** bitter taste; **6, 7** biting comment; **7, 5** caustic reply.

bittersweet 8 poignant, touching; **9** nostalgic; **11** sentimental; PHRASES: **5, 10** woody nightshade.

bitumen *See* **tar**

bivalve 9 pelecypod; **13** lamellibranch.

bivouac 4 tent; **6** encamp; **7** shelter.

bizarre *See* **strange**

black 3 All, art, box, eye, fly, ice, ink, jet, Rod, sad, Sea, tie; **4** bean, bear, belt, bile, bird, body, book, coal, dark, ebon, head, hell, hole, inky, jack, mark, mass, monk, soot, spot, swan; **5** angry, berry, board, death, dusky, ebony, friar, frost, hills, ivory, japan, jetty, large, magic, Maria, murky, night, penny, pitch, raven, sable, sheep, sooty, Watch, widow; **6** beetle, bottom, carbon, coffee, forest, gloomy, grouse, market, niello, pepper, pitchy, Prince, somber, spruce, velvet; **7** country, currant, diamond, economy, melanin, obscure, panther, shadowy, swarthy, thunder, treacle; **8** blacking, blackish, hopeless, menacing, midnight, molasses, mournful, platinum; **9** lampblack, Mountains, nigrosine; **10** fuliginous, nightshade, nigrescent, silhouette; **11** threatening; PHRASES: **3, 2, 6** ace of spades; **8, 7** mourning clothes.

blackball *See* **exclude**

blackbird 5 merle, ouzel.

black box 6, 8 flight recorder.

black diamond 4 coal; **9** carbonado.

black earth 9 chernozem.

blacken 3 ink, tan; **4** blot, burn, char, slur; **5** dirty, japan, libel, singe, sully; **6** darken, deepen, defame, malign, niello, smirch, smudge, suntan, vilify; **7** asperse, begrime, slander; **8** besmirch; **9** blackball, blacklist, denigrate; PHRASES: **5, 3, 2** speak ill of.

black-eyed pea 6 cowpea.

blackfish 5, 5 pilot whale.

blackguard *See* **scoundrel**

black-haired 8 brunette; PHRASES: **4-6** dark-haired, dark-headed; **5-4** black-eyed; **5-6** black-locked, raven-haired.

blackhead 3 zit; **4** spot; **6** comedo, pimple; PHRASES: **7, 4** blocked pore.

black-hearted 4 evil; **6** wicked; **7** heinous; **9** nefarious; **10** villainous; **12** blackguardly.

blackjack 5-2-2 vingt-et-un.

black lead 8 graphite.

black letter 6 Gothic.

blackmail 5 bribe, exact; **6** extort; **7** bribery, extract; **9** extortion; **10** corruption, extraction; **12** intimidation; PHRASES: **4, 2, 6** hold to ransom.

blackness 4 dark, dusk, fury; **5** anger, color, depth, gloom, night; **6** checkr, menace, shadow, temper; **7** pigment; **8** melanism, Negroism; **9** darkening, hostility, melanosis, nigritude, pessimism; **10** aggression, depression, melancholy, resentment; **11** chiaroscuro, despondency, nigrescence, obscuration; **12** belligerence, pigmentation; PHRASES: **4, 4** deep tone; **4, 5** dark color; **5-3-5** black-and-white.

blackout 4 veto; **7** embargo, seizure; **8** collapse, shutdown; **10** censorship; **11** suppression; PHRASES: **5, 3** power cut; **5, 7** power failure; **8, 3** fainting fit *UK*.

Black Sea 6, 3 Euxine Sea; **6, 7** Pontus Euxinus.

bladder campion 7 cowbell.

blade 3 fin; **4** edge, sail, vane; **9** propeller; PHRASES: **5-4** knife-edge; **5, 5** razor ~.

blaeberry 12 whortleberry.

blame 5 fault, guilt; **6** accuse, charge, earful, impugn, impute, rebuke, rocket, sermon; **7** censure, chiding, condemn, lecture, reproof, upbraid, wigging *UK*; **8** denounce, reproach, scolding; **9** carpeting, complaint, criticize, liability, reprehend, reprimand, stricture; **10** accusation, admonition; **11** castigation, culpability, incriminate, recriminate; **12** admonishment, chastisement, condemnation, denunciation, reprehension; **13** recrimination; **14** responsibility; **15** blameworthiness; PHRASES: **4, 2, 4** take to task; **4, 2, 4, 3** flea in one's ear; **4, 5, 4** find fault with; **4, 6** home truths; **4, 11** hold accountable, hold responsible; **5, 2, 4, 4** piece of one's mind; **5, 4** black mark; **5, 5, 2** think badly of; **7-2** talking-to; **7-3** telling-off *UK*, ticking-off *UK*; **8-4** dressing-down.

blameless *See* **innocent**

blameworthy *See* **guilty**

bland *See* **insipid**

blank **4** bare, void; **5** check, clean, clear, empty, plain, total, utter, verse, white; **6** barren, vacant; **7** amnesic, Lethean, vacuous; **8** absolute, complete, outright; **9** cartridge, downright, forgetful, impassive, perplexed; **11** unmitigated, unqualified; **15** uncomprehending; PHRASES: **5-6** empty-headed; **6-6** absent-minded.

blanket **4** bath; **5** cover, drape, total; **6** afghan, carpet, encase, finish, stitch, swathe; **7** obscure, overlay; **8** absolute, complete, covering, coverlet, electric; **9** bedspread, extensive, unlimited, wholesale; **10** overspread; **13** comprehensive; PHRASES: **6-3-5** across-the-board; **8, 7** Mackinaw ~.

blankness **3** gap; **6** vacuum; **7** amnesia, vacancy, vacuity; **8** blackout; **9** confusion; **10** forgetting; **11** nothingness; **12** bewilderment, indifference; **15** incomprehension; PHRASES: **4, 2, 6** loss of memory; **5, 5** empty space, total blank; **6, 5** mental block. *See also* **blank**

blarney **3** oil; **4** bunk; **5** charm, salve, smarm; **6** bunkum, drivel; **7** flannel *UK*; **8** flattery, nonsense; PHRASES: **4, 4** soft soap; **5-4** sweet-talk; **6, 2** butter up, soften up; **6, 4** smooth talk; **7, 5** honeyed words; **7, 7** honeyed phrases.

blaspheme *See* **curse**

blast **4** boom, burn, gust; **5** blare, flare, flash; **6** attack, blight, damage, vilify; **7** blister, censure, explode, resound; **8** demolish, detonate, lambaste; **9** criticize, disfigure, explosion; **10** detonation; PHRASES: **4, 2** blow up.

blatant **5** crude, lurid; **6** brazen, patent, vulgar; **7** obvious, flagrant, manifest; **9** barefaced, obtrusive, shameless; **10** deliberate; **11** extravagant, transparent, unconcealed.

blather **6** babble, drivel, jabber; **7** blabber, chatter, prattle.

blaze **4** burn, fire, glow, rage; **5** flash, glare; **7** inferno; **9** intensity; **10** combustion; **13** conflagration.

bleach **3** dye; **4** fade, pale, tint; **5** color; **6** blanch, blench, whiten; **7** lighten; **8** peroxide; **10** decolorize; PHRASES: **4, 5** lose color.

bleak **4** bare, cold, drab; **5** harsh; **6** futile, gloomy, wintry; **7** austere, forlorn; **8** dejected, doubtful, hopeless; **9** cheerless, miserable; **11** downhearted, unwelcoming; **12** disheartened.

bleed **4** milk; **5** drain, wring; **6** bloody, extort, fleece; **7** deplete, exploit, squeeze; **9** nosebleed; **10** hemorrhage; PHRASES: **4, 5** lose blood, shed blood; **5, 4** blood loss; **5, 5** spill blood.

bleeding **4** flow; **6** bloody, bruise; **8** bruising, petechia; **9** hematuria, hemorrhea, nosebleed; **10** ecchymosis, hemophilia, hemoptysis, hemorrhage; **11** hematemesis; PHRASES: **5, 4** blood loss.

bleep **4** beep, call, page, tone; **5** alert, noise, sound; **6** signal; **7** contact.

blemish **3** mar; **4** flaw, mark, ruin, scar, soil, spot, wart; **5** crack, fault, fleck, smear, spoil, stain, taint; **6** blotch, damage, deface, defect, deform, impair, injure, pimple, smudge; **7** distort, tarnish, vitiate; **8** discolor, misshape, mutilate; **9** disfigure; **12** imperfection; **13** discoloration, disfigurement.

blemished **8** discolor, shopworn; **9** defective, imperfect; **10** shopsoiled. *See also* **blemish**

blench **6** blanch, falter, flinch, recoil; **7** lighten; **8** hesitate; PHRASES: **2, 4** go pale.

blend **3** mix; **4** meld; **5** merge, stain, unify; **6** fusion, merger, mingle; **7** amalgam, combine, mixture, pervade; **8** emulsify; **9** composite, integrate, penetrate; **10** amalgamate, assortment; **11** combination, intermingle; PHRASES: **5, 8** bring together.

blende **10** sphalerite.

bless **4** back, laud; **5** extol; **6** hallow; **7** approve, endorse, support; **8** sanctify, sanction; **10** consecrate.

blessing **7** consent, miracle; **8** approval, sanction; **10** dedication, permission; **11** approbation, benediction; **12** consecration; **14** sanctification; PHRASES: **6, 2, 4** stroke of luck.

blight 4 blot, ruin, scar; **5** stain; **6** impair; **9** disfigure; **10** affliction; **13** disfigurement.

blind 3 bat, gut; **4** blur, date, mask, mole, spot; **5** alley, snake, stone, visor; **6** awning, canopy, darken, dazzle, roller, screen, strike; **7** blinker, deceive, eclipse, eyeless, Freddie, obscure; **8** bedazzle, hoodwink, staggers, stamping, unseeing, venetian; **9** amaurotic, blindfold, sightless, unsighted; **10** camouflage, registered, visionless; **12** glaucomatous; PHRASES: **4-5** snow-blind; **6, 5** window shade; **6-8** vision-impaired; **7, 5** lacking sight.

blind (be blind) 5 blink, grope; **6** squint; PHRASES: **3, 3** not see; **3, 5** see badly; **3, 6** see double; **4, 4, 3** feel one's way; **4, 4, 5** lose one's sight; **5, 3** black out.

blind (be blind to) 6 ignore; **8** overlook; **9** disregard; PHRASES: **4, 1, 5, 3** turn a blind eye; **4, 2** wink at; **4, 2, 6, 2** take no notice of; **4, 3, 5, 3** look the other way; **4, 4** look away; **4, 4, 4** drop one's eyes; **4, 4, 4, 2** shut one's eyes to; **5, 2** blink at; **5, 4, 4** avert one's gaze.

blind (blind to) 7 unaware; **8** ignorant; **9** benighted, blinkered, oblivious, unmindful; **11** thoughtless, unconcerned, unconscious, unobservant; **12** imperceptive, undiscerning; **13** inconsiderate, unenlightened; PHRASES: **2, 3, 4** in the dark.

blinded 7 dazzled; **9** blindfold, blinkered; **11** blindfolded; PHRASES: **4-5** snow-blind.

blinding 6 bright, strong, superb; **7** amazing, glaring; **8** dazzling, striking, stunning; **9** darkening, deceptive, obscuring; **10** bedazzling, misleading; **11** outstanding; **13** extraordinary.

blindly 9 blindfold; PHRASES: **2, 3** by ear; **2, 4** by feel; **2, 5** by touch; **7, 7** without looking.

blindness 4 snow; **5** river, stone; **8** ablepsia, blackout, cataract, darkness, glaucoma, rashness, trachoma; **9** amaurosis; **12** carelessness, heedlessness, recklessness; **13** impetuousness; PHRASES: **4, 2, 5** lack of sight; **4, 2, 6** loss of vision; **5-3** white-out; **8, 6** impaired vision; **9, 2, 3** inability to see. *See also* **blind**

blindness (figurative) 9 disregard, ignorance, prejudice, unconcern; **11** unawareness; **13** benightedness, obliviousness; **15** thoughtlessness, unconsciousness; PHRASES: **3-2-4** fly-by-wire; **5, 3** blind eye; **5, 4** blind side, blind spot; **5, 6** blind flying.

blindworm 8 slowworm.

blink 4 wink; **5** flash; **6** signal; **7** flicker, twinkle; PHRASES: **3, 2, 6** bat an eyelid.

blinker 5 cover, patch, smoke; **6** façade, screen; **7** curtain, eclipse; **8** blinders, covering, eyepatch; **9** blindfold; **10** camouflage.

blinkered 5 blind; **6** narrow; **7** insular, limited, unaware; **8** ignorant; **9** benighted, oblivious, unmindful; **11** thoughtless, unconscious, unobservant; **12** imperceptive, undiscerning; **13** unenlightened; PHRASES: **6-6** narrow-minded; **6-7** inward-looking.

blister 4 burn, pack, rust, sore; **5** blood, bulge, erupt; **6** beetle, bubble; **8** eruption, swelling; **9** suppurate; PHRASES: **5, 2** swell up; **5, 3** break out.

blitz 3 hit; **4** bomb, tidy; **5** blast, clean; **6** attack; **7** barrage, bombard; **9** offensive, onslaught; **10** blitzkrieg; **11** bombardment; PHRASES: **5, 2** focus on; **5-3** clear-out *UK*.

bloater 8 buckling *UK*.

blob 3 dot; **4** dash, daub, spot; **6** pimple, smudge, splash; **7** globule, splotch.

bloc *See* **alliance**

block 3 bar, dam, ice, jam, sun, tin; **4** band, cake, clog, hunk, lump, mass, part, slab, snag, stop, trip, unit, vote, wall, wing, wood, zone; **5** brick, choke, chunk, delay, deter, fence, flats *UK*, heart, ingot, piece, stall, tower, wedge; **6** breeze, cavity, hamper, hinder, impede, letter, mental, module, office, oppose, picket, region, saddle, sector, shower, strike, tablet, thwart, toilet; **7** diagram, embargo, expanse, prevent, release, section, stretch; **8** blockade, building, cylinder, deadlock, obstruct, printing, protract, sabotage, sampling, starting *UK*; **9** apartment, cellblock, extension, frustrate, intervene, stumbling; **10** bottleneck, filibuster; **11** malfunction; **13** inconvenience, psychological; PHRASES: **3, 2** gum up; **3, 2, 3** get in the way; **3, 2, 3, 5** gum up the works; **4, 2** trip up, wall up; **4, 3** lock out; **4, 3, 4** play for time; **4, 4** hold back; **5, 1, 9** reach a stalemate; **5, 2, 7** reach an impasse; **5, 4, 5** cramp one's style; **5, 7** cause trouble; **6, 5** cinder ~.

blockage 3 jam; **5** snarl; **6** logjam; **7** impasse; **10** bottleneck; **11** obstruction; PHRASES: **5-2** snarl-up *UK Can*.

blocked 6 barred, choked, closed,

curbed, jammed; **7** clogged; **8** burdened, indebted; **9** congested, deterrent, hazardous; **10** accidental, deadlocked, gridlocked, impassable, obstructed, overloaded, regulatory, restrained; **11** restraining, unnavigable; **12** backbreaking, bureaucratic, impenetrable, inconvenient, overburdened; **14** malfunctioning; PHRASES: **2, 1, 3** in a fix; **2, 1, 6** in a corner, in a pickle; **2, 1, 10** at a standstill; **2, 2, 7** at an impasse; **2, 3, 3** in the way; **2, 4** in debt; **3, 4** not easy; **5-5** heavy-laden; **6, 2** bunged up *UK*, choked up; **6-2** fenced-in, walled-in; **7, 2** plugged up, stopped up; **7, 4** saddled with.

blood **3** bad, kin, red; **4** bank, bath, blue, cell, clan, clot, feud, gore, heat, race, test, type; **5** bull's, count, donor, fluke, group, ichor, money, serum, sport, stock, whole, young; **6** claret, family, orange, origin, plasma, venous, vessel; **7** antigen, brother, descent, dextran, dragon's, kinfolk, kinship, lineage, opsonin, pudding; **8** ancestry, antibody, arterial, globulin, heritage, pedigree, platelet, pressure, relation, relative; **9** genealogy, household, leucocyte, leukocyte, lifeblood, phagocyte, poisoning; **10** extraction, hemoglobin, lymphocyte, thrombosis; **11** bloodmobile, bloodstream, circulation, erythrocyte, isoantibody, transfusion; PHRASES: **1, 5, 6** O ~ groups; **2, 6** Rh factor; **2-8** Rh-negative, Rh-positive; **3, 5, 4** red ~ cell; **4, 5** body fluid; **5, 5, 4** white ~ cell; **6, 6** Rhesus factor; **8, 7** clinical dextran; **9, 6** synthetic plasma.

blood disease **6** anemia; **8** leukemia, lymphoma; **10** hemophilia, hemorrhage; **11** thalassemia; PHRASES: **8, 6** aplastic anemia.

bloodless **3** wan; **4** pale; **5** white; **6** anemic, pallid; **8** peaceful; **10** nonviolent; **13** nonaggressive.

blood poisoning **10** septicemia.

bloodstone **10** heliotrope.

bloody **4** gory; **5** hemal, hemic; **7** injured, wounded; **8** bleeding; **9** bloodshot, hemogenic; **10** hemophilic, sanguinary; **11** ensanguined, incarnadine, sanguineous; **12** bloodstained; PHRASES: **5-9** blood-spattered.

bloom **3** bud; **4** glow, tint; **5** tinge; **6** flower, thrive; **7** blossom, prosper; **8** flourish; **10** coloration.

bloomer **7** blossom.

bloomers **7** panties; **9** underwear.

blooming **2-3-6** up-and-coming; **2, 5** in

bloom; **2, 6** in flower. *See also* **bloom**

blooper **4** slip; **5** error, gaffe; **6** howler; **7** blunder, mistake; PHRASES: **4, 3** faux pas; **8, 4** Freudian slip.

blossom *See* **bloom**

blot **4** mark, ruin, spot; **5** spoil, stain; **6** pimple; **7** blemish, tarnish; **9** disfigure.

blotchy **6** marked, pimply; **7** dappled, freckly, mottled, spotted; **9** blemished; **10** pockmarked.

blot on the landscape *See* **eyesore**

blouse *See* **shirt**

blow **3** box, cut, dab, dig, fan, hit, jab, pat, rap, tap; **4** bang, bash, belt, biff, body, bonk, boot, butt, clop, cuff, dash, dent, dint, drub, gust, howl, jolt, kick, lash, poke, prod, puff, punt, push, rage, roar, sigh, slam, slap, slog, slug, stir, swat, veer, waft, wail, whip; **5** blast, brunt, brush, chuck, clout, crack, drive, flick, heave, knock, nudge, plunk, pound, press, punch, shock, shove, smack, sough, spank, spend, stamp, stomp, swing, swipe, thump, upset, waste; **6** buffet, exhale, fillip, hustle, joggle, jostle, murmur, stress, strike, stripe, stroke, thrust, thwack, wallop; **7** bluster, cocaine, freshen, setback, whisper, whistle; **8** cannabis, squander; **9** sideswipe; **10** misfortune; **14** disappointment; PHRASES: **4, 2, 3** kick in the teeth; **4, 4** drop kick; **5, 4** throw away; **5-4** knock-back *UK*; **6, 5** sucker punch; **7, 4** fritter away.

blower **5** whale.

blowfish **6** puffer.

blowfly **10** bluebottle.

blown up **5** hyped; **6** bombed; **7** bloated, swelled, swollen, wrecked; **8** enlarged, inflated, overdone; **9** distended; **10** demolished; **11** exaggerated; PHRASES: **3-6** air-filled; **6-2** puffed-up, pumped-up; **6-3** burned-out *UK*.

blow up **4** fill; **5** blast, storm, swell, wreck; **6** expand; **7** amplify, balloon, destroy, distend, enlarge, explode, flatten, inflate, magnify; **8** demolish, detonate, dynamite, increase; **9** dramatize, embellish, embroider, fulminate, overstate; **10** exaggerate; PHRASES: **2, 3** go mad *UK*; **2, 7** be furious; **2, 9** go ballistic; **3, 3, 3, 6** fly off the handle; **3, 3, 4** hit the roof; **3, 4, 1, 4** fly into a rage; **4, 1, 4** blow a fuse; **4, 1, 6** blow a gasket; **4, 2** lose it, puff up, pump up; **4, 3** fill out; **4, 4, 3** blow your top, flip your lid, lose your rag *UK*; **4, 4, 4** lose your cool; **4, 4, 6** lose your temper; **4, 6** make larger; **5, 2** flare up.

bludgeon 3 hit; **4** bash, beat, club, cosh *UK*, mace; **5** bully, staff; **6** batter, coerce, compel, cudgel, hammer, strike; **7** sandbag; **8** bulldoze; **9** truncheon; **10** intimidate; **11** steamroller; PHRASES: **5, 6** blunt weapon; **7-6** knuckle-duster; **8, 3** baseball bat; **9, 3** battering ram.

blue 3 bag, fox, gum, jay, low, sad, sky, tit; **4** baby, bell, bice, bird, bleu, chip, ciel, crab, cyan, dark, deep, down, funk, iris, mold, moon, navy, Nile, pale, saxe, vein, woad; **5** azure, berry, beryl, blood, grass, green, jeans, light, perse, peter, print, royal, Saxon, slate, smalt, smoke, steel, stone, whale; **6** bright, cheese, cobalt, cyanic, devils, ensign, French, indigo, murder, Oxford, pencil, powder, riband, ribbon, velvet; **7** Antwerp, gentian, obscene, peacock, Stilton, unhappy; **8** cerulean, dejected, downcast, eggshell, electric, hyacinth, midnight, Prussian, sapphire, Wedgwood; **9** Cambridge, depressed, Mountains, turquoise; **10** aquamarine, cornflower, kingfisher, melancholy; **11** hyacinthine, ultramarine; PHRASES: **3, 2** fed up; **3, 4** sea ~; **3-5** air-force; **4, 2, 3, 5** down in the dumps; **4-3** duck-egg; **4, 4, 4** ball park ~; **5, 4** alice ~, cadet ~, delph ~, dutch ~, wally ~; **5, 6** lapis lazuli; **6-2-3** forget-me-not; **6-3** robin's-egg; **6, 4** French navy, marine ~, petrol ~ *UK*, zenith ~; **7, 4** gobelin ~, horizon ~; **8, 4** overseas ~; **10, 4** periwinkle ~.

bluebell 8 harebell; PHRASES: **4, 8** wild hyacinth, wood hyacinth.

blueberry 11 huckleberry.

bluebill 5 scaup.

bluebottle 7 blowfly; **9** policeman.

blue cod 8 patutuki; **10** pakirikiri; PHRASES: **4, 3** rock cod *UK*.

blue ground 10 kimberlite.

blue-pencil 4 edit.

blueprint 4 plan; **5** draft; **6** design, scheme; **7** drawing, outline, program; **8** proposal; **9** cyanotype.

blueweed 6, 7 viper's bugloss.

bluff 3 con, lie; **4** fake, hill, loud, sham; **5** cliff, mound, trick; **6** cheery, hearty; **7** pretend; **8** headland, hillside, pretense; **10** forthright; PHRASES: **5-6** plain-spoken.

bluish 5 livid; **7** bruised; **8** caesious, cyanosed, cyanotic, freezing; PHRASES: **4, 2, 3, 4** blue in the face; **4, 4, 4** blue with cold; **5-3-4** black-and-blue.

blunder 3 err; **4** boob *UK*, goof, muff, slip, trip; **5** boner, error, fluff, gaffe; **6** bobble, bungle, career, howler; **7** bloomer *UK*, blooper, clanger *UK*, misstep, mistake, stagger, stumble; **8** flounder; **9** gaucherie; PHRASES: **3-2** mix-up; **3, 2, 5** get it wrong; **3-3** boo-boo; **4, 1, 7** make a mistake; **4, 2** cock up, foul up, mess up, slip up; **4, 3** faux pas, pig's ear; **5-2** balls-up *UK*, botch-up *UK*, louse-up, screw-up; **6, 4** banana skin *UK*; **7, 5** glaring error.

blundering *See* **clumsy**

blunt 4 bate, curt, dull, flat, snub, stub, turn, worn; **5** bated, bluff, frank, plain, round; **6** abrupt, candid, dampen, direct, dulled, lessen, obtund, smooth, soothe, square, stubby; **7** blunted, curving, flatten, rounded, unedged; **8** diminish, edgeless, moderate, smoothed; **9** flattened, outspoken, pointless, unpointed; **10** forthright; **11** unsharpened; **14** uncompromising; **15** straightforward; PHRASES: **2, 3, 5** to the point; **2-8** no-nonsense; **4, 3, 4, 3** take the edge off; **4-5** dull-edged; **8-7** straight-talking.

blunt instrument 3 ram; **4** club, cosh *UK*, foil, mace; **5** lathi, staff, stave, stick; **6** cudgel, hammer; **7** sandbag, spatula; **8** bludgeon; **9** blackjack, knobstick, truncheon, warhammer; **10** knobkerrie, shillelagh; **12** quarterstaff; PHRASES: **4, 9** life preserver; **5, 8** brass knuckles; **7-6** knuckle-duster; **8, 3** baseball bat; **9, 3** battering ram.

bluntness 6 candor; **7** honesty.

blur 4 blob, blot, haze; **5** cloud, smear; **6** blotch, smudge; **7** confuse, distort, obscure; **9** fuzziness; **10** distortion.

blurb *See* **description**

blush 5 color, flush; **6** redden; **7** crimson; PHRASES: **2, 3** go red.

blushing 3 coy, red, shy; **5** ruddy, timid; **6** modest; **7** awkward, flushed, nervous; **8** sheepish; **10** shamefaced; **11** embarrassed; PHRASES: **3-5** red-faced *UK*; **4-9** self-conscious. *See also* **blush**

bluster 4 blow, gust, puff, rage, rant, waft; **5** bully; **7** protest; **8** harangue, threaten.

blustery *See* **windy**

board 4 beam, food, full, half, live, meal, room, slat, stay; 5 above, draft, emery, idiot, lodge, panel, patch, plank, sheet; 6 diving, embark, lumber, notice, school, timber, wobble; 7 circuit, drawing, ironing, running; 8 bulletin, cribbage, draining, managers, sandwich, skirting, sounding; 9 admiralty, catchment, chipboard, committee, hardboard, millboard; 10 commission, fiberboard, floorboard, linerboard, strawboard, sustenance; 11 beaverboard, nourishment, refreshment; 12 plasterboard; 13 particleboard; 14 containerboard; PHRASES: 8, 5 advisory group; 10, 4 management team.

boarding 5 house; 6 school.

boardsailing 11 windsurfing.

boast 4 brag, crow, hype, rant, rave; 5 claim, enjoy, swank, vaunt; 7 bombast, display, flatter, inflate, possess; 8 huckster, overrate, oversell; 9 assertion; 10 overpraise, pretension; PHRASES: 3, 2, 2 lay it on; 3, 2, 2, 5 lay it on thick; 3, 4, 3, 4 fly your own kite UK; 3, 5, 2 lay claim to; 3-5, 5 out-Herod Herod; 4, 2, 2 pile it on; 4, 3 show off; 4, 4, 2 make much of; 4-7 self-glorify; 5, 8, 2 pride yourself on.

boastful 4 vain; 5 cocky, proud; 6 elated, swanky; 7 blatant, pompous, swelled; 8 affected, arrogant, bragging, immodest, inflated, prideful; 9 bigheaded, bombastic, bumptious, conceited, strutting; 10 complacent, swaggering, ungracious; 11 opinionated, overweening, pretentious; 12 ostentatious; 15 exhibitionistic; PHRASES: 4-2-3 know-it-all; 4, 2, 7 full of oneself; 4-9 self-conceited, self-important, self-satisfied; 4-10 self-glorifying; 4-11 self-opinionated; 5-2 stuck-up; 5-4 smart-assd; 5-5 smart-aleck; 6, 2 puffed up; 7, 2, 4 putting on airs; 7-6 swollen-headed.

boastfulness 4 side; 5 pride, swank; 7 bravado, conceit, heroics; 8 bragging, machismo; 9 arrogance, dramatics, immodesty, showiness; 11 histrionics, ostentation; 13 exhibitionism, theatricality; 14 sensationalism; PHRASES: 4-7 self-conceit, self-display; 4-10 self-importance; 6-3, 5 puffed-out chest; 7, 3 showing off. *See also* **boastful**

boat 3 HMS UK, USS; 4 deck, race, ship; 5 canal, craft, drill, gravy, sauce, train; 6 bateau, dinghy, flying, narrow, people, rowing, vessel; 7 joeboat, sailing, sharpie, torpedo, wanigan; 8 fireboat, johnboat, mackinaw, mosquito, sneakbox; 9 rumrunner.

boatman 5 rower; 6 bargee, Charon, punter UK; 7 oarsman, paddler, sculler; 8 bargeman, canoeist, ferryman, waterman; 9 gondolier, wherryman, yachtsman; PHRASES: 6, 5 galley slave.

bob 3 bow, dip, jog, nod; 4 duck; 6 bobble, curtsy; 9 genuflect.

bobbin *See* **reel**

bobble 3 bob, dip, jog, nod.

bobby 3 pin; 4 calf; 5 socks.

bobcat 4 lynx; 7 wildcat.

bobsled 3 bob, run; 4 axle, drag, hood, lift, loop, luge; 5 brake, cable, steer, sweep; 6 bobrun, runner; 7 cowling, lifting, lugeing; 8 dragging, skeleton, steering, toboggan; 9 bobsledge, bobsleigh UK; PHRASES: 3-4 out-wick; 4, 4 luge race; 6, 3 Cresta Run; 8, 5 toboggan chute.

bodily *See* **physical**

body 4 area, blow, bulk, dead, form, hull, mass, shop; 5 build, frame, group, image, party, stiff; 6 amount, cavity, corpse, corpus, figure, supply, warmer; 7 cadaver, carcass, essence, popping, remains, society; 8 building, deceased, language, majority, physique, quantity, snatcher, stocking; 9 corporate, reservoir; 10 federation; 11 association; 12 organization; PHRASES: 4, 4 main part; 5, 5 lion's share; 6, 4 better part.

body fluid 3 pee, pus, wee; 4 milk, tear; 5 blood, chyle, edema, humor, ichor, lymph, mucor, mucus, rheum, semen, serum, sweat, tears, urine; 6 dropsy, matter, phlegm, plasma, saliva; 7 spittle, synovia; 8 teardrop; 9 colostrum, discharge, excrement, hydrocele, lactation; 10 leukorrhea; 11 suppuration; 12 perspiration; PHRASES: 6, 5 serous fluid; 7, 4 mother's milk; 7, 5 gastric juice; 9, 4 menstrual flow.

bodyguard 5 guard; 6 escort; 8 guardian; 9 attendant.

BOF 9, 2, 4 beginning of file.

bog 3 fen, oak; 4 mire, moss, rush; 5 marsh, swamp; 6 cotton, myrtle, orchid; 7 fenland UK; 8 asphodel, quagmire, standard; 9 marshland.

boggle *See* **confuse**

bogus 4 sham; 5 phony UK; 6 phoney; 8 spurious; 11 counterfeit.

bohemian 6 hippie; 7 offbeat; 8 carefree; 11 alternative, freethinker; 13 nonconformist; 14 unconventional; PHRASES: 4, 6 free spirit.

boil 3 fry; 4 bake, burn, cook, cyst, fume, heat, rage, sore, spot, stew; 5 broil, grill, poach, roast, ulcer; 6 bubble, pimple, seethe, simmer; 7 abscess, swelter; 8 furuncle, overheat, swelling; PHRASES: 2, 5 be angry, be irate.

bold 4 font, loud; 5 brash, brave, heavy, vivid; 6 brassy, brazen, bright, cheeky, daring; 7 forward, valiant; 8 boldface, intrepid, typeface; 9 audacious, confident; 10 courageous; 11 conspicuous, unflinching; PHRASES: 4-5 bold-faced; 4-7 self-assured.

boldness 4 sass; 5 cheek, front UK, nerve, sauce, valor; 6 bottle UK, daring; 7 bravado, bravery, courage; 8 audacity, chutzpah; 9 arrogance, impudence; 10 confidence, effrontery; PHRASES: 4-9 self-assurance; 5, 4 brass neck UK. See also **bold**

bole 4 stem; 5 stalk, trunk.

bolide 8 fireball.

bollard See **post**

bolt 3 bar, pin, rod, run; 4 down, gulp, lock, wolf; 6 devour, fasten, gobble, secure; PHRASES: 4, 2 lock up.

bomb 3 car; 4 atom, buzz, fail, fire, flop, mail, mine, nail, nuke, pile, time; 5 blast, blitz, prang UK, shell, smoke, stink; 6 atomic, attack, bundle, carpet, cobalt, flying, fusion, letter, napalm, petrol, rocket; 7 assault, barrage, bombard, cluster, explode, fallout, fission, grenade, neutron, nuclear, plaster, torpedo; 8 flounder, hydrogen, landmine; 9 bombshell, doodlebug, pineapple, radiation; 10 disappoint, incendiary; 11 blockbuster; 13 fragmentation, radioactivity; PHRASES: 1-4 A-bomb, H-bomb; 3, 3, 6 hit the target; 3, 4 lay eggs, tin fish; 4, 3, 7 drop the payload; 4, 4 fall flat; 4, 7 hand grenade; 5, 4 booby trap, Greek fire; 5, 6 depth charge; 6, 4 limpet mine; 7, 8 Molotov cocktail; 8, 4 acoustic mine, magnetic mine; 8, 5 mushroom cloud; 9, 6 explosive device.

bombard 4 bomb; 5 blast, flood, shell; 6 assail, shower; 7 barrage, overrun; 8 inundate; PHRASES: 4, 4, 2 open fire on.

bombast 4 hype; 7 bluster, fustian; 8 bragging, flattery; 9 pomposity; 10 chauvinism; 11 affectation, huckstering, verboseness; 13 magniloquence; 14

grandiloquence; PHRASES: 3, 3 hot air; 6, 5 purple prose.

bombastic 6 raving; 7 pompous, ranting, verbose; 8 affected, boastful, boasting, bragging; 10 overrating; 11 pretentious; 12 magniloquent; 13 grandiloquent; PHRASES: 4-6 long-winded; 4-10 self-glorifying.

Bombay 6 Mumbai.

bon 3 mot UK, ton; 6 vivant, voyage.

bonanza 5 bonus; 7 jackpot; PHRASES: 3, 2, 4 pot of gold UK; 4, 4 gold mine; 6, 2, 4 stroke of luck.

bond 3 fix, tie; 4 bail, bind, glue, join, link, oath, pair, word; 5 affix, stick, union, unite; 6 adhere, attach, cement, double, granny, income, patent, pledge, relate, single, triple; 7 charter, connect, English, Flemish, peptide, promise; 8 chemical, contract, covalent, covenant, hydrogen, metallic, security, treasury, warranty; 9 guarantee; 10 attachment, connection, friendship; 11 herringbone; 12 relationship; 13 electrovalent, qualification; PHRASES: 3, 2 get on; 3, 2, 3 hit it off; 5, 4 title deed.

bone 3 ash, hip, jaw, rib; 4 back, heel, idle, long, meal, shin, ulna; 5 ankle, anvil, cheek, china, costa, crazy, femur, funny, hyoid, ilium, incus, nasal, pubis, skull, spine, talus, thigh, tibia, vomer, wrist; 6 breast, cannon, carpal, carpus, coccyx, coffin, collar, cuboid, fetter, fibula, hallux, hammer, pelvis, rachis, radius, sacrum, splint, stapes, tarsal, tarsus; 7 cranium, ethmoid, frontal, humerus, ischium, kneecap, kneepan, malleus, mastoid, maxilla, patella, phalanx, scapula, sternum, stirrup; 8 clavicle, mandible, parietal, scaphoid, sesamoid, sphenoid, temporal, tympanic, vertebra; 9 calcancus, cartilage, maxillary, occipital, phalanges, zygomatic; 10 astragalus, innominate, metacarpal, metacarpus, metatarsal, metatarsus; PHRASES: 6, 6 spinal column; 8, 3 floating rib; 8, 5 shoulder blade; 9, 6 vertebral column.

bonfire See **fire**

bonny 6 lovely, pretty; 8 handsome; 10 attractive; PHRASES: 4-7 good-looking.

bonus 5 extra; 6 reward; 7 benefit, handout; 8 addition, gratuity, windfall; 9 advantage; PHRASES: 7, 5 signing ~.

boob 3 mug UK; 4 dupe, fool; 6 sucker; PHRASES: 4, 3 fall guy. See also **chest**

booby 4 trap; 5 hatch, prize.

book 3 end; 4 club, hymn, open, tome; 5 black, novel, order, token; 6 closed, engage, ledger, phrase, prayer, record, volume; 7 reserve, statute, talking; 8 cookbook, domesday, doomsday, hardback, register, softback; 9 hardcover, paperback, reference, softcover; 10 manuscript; 11 commonplace; PHRASES: 4, 2, 3 sign up for; 7, 4 chapter ~.

bookmark 4 flag.

Book of Changes 1, 5 I Ching.

boom 3 arm; 4 bang, beam, grow, pole, rise, roar, soar; 6 bellow, growth, report, rocket, rumble; 7 bracket, resound, thunder, upsurge; 8 affluent, increase, thriving; 9 expansion; 10 prosperous, successful.

boon 4 help; 5 bonus; 7 benefit, godsend; 9 advantage.

boor *See* **lout**

boost 4 lift; 6 uplift; 7 enhance, improve, support; 8 increase; 9 encourage; 11 enhancement, improvement; PHRASES: 7, 4 helping hand.

bootless *See* **useless**

borax 6 tincal.

border 3 bed, hem, rim; 4 abut, bind, edge; 5 frame, limit, skirt, touch, verge; 6 adjoin, fringe, margin; 7 confine, conjoin; 8 boundary, frontier; 9 flowerbed, perimeter, periphery; 10 borderline, herbaceous; 13 circumference; PHRASES: 2, 4, 2 be next to; 2, 7, 2 be bounded by; 2, 8, 2 be adjacent to; 3, 9 run alongside; 5, 2 verge on.

borderline 6 border; 7 unclear; 8 boundary, disputed, doubtful, frontier, marginal; 9 uncertain.

bore 4 glut; 5 drill, gouge, rigid, stiff; 6 pierce, tunnel; 8 nuisance; 9 penetrate, perforate; PHRASES: 2, 5 to death, to tears; 4, 1, 4, 2 make a hole in. *See also* **boring (be boring)**

borecole 4 kale.

bored 5 jaded, rigid, sated, stiff, tired, weary; 6 dreary, sullen; 7 wearied; 8 fatigued, satiated; 12 dissatisfied, uninterested; 13 disinterested; PHRASES: 2, 5 to death, to tears; 3, 2 fed up; 4, 2 sick of; 4, 3, 5, 2 sick and tired of; 5, 2, 6 tired of living; 5-5 world-weary; 7, 3 cheesed off *UK*.

boredom 5 ennui; 6 tedium; 7 aridity, fatigue, humdrum, languor, satiety; 8 banality, longueur, monotony, sameness; 9 prolixity, weariness; 10 boringness, inactivity, insipidity, uniformity; 11 Weltschmerz; 12 indifference; PHRASES: 4, 2, 8 lack of interest; 4, 2, 9 lack of enjoyment, lack of variation; 5-9 thumb-twiddling; 6, 6 devil's tattoo; 7, 5 taedium vitae *UK*. *See also* **bored, boring**

boring 3 dry; 4 arid, blah, drab, dull, flat, slow; 5 banal, plain, prosy, stale, trite; 6 deadly, draggy, dreary, prolix, stodgy, stuffy; 7 cloying, humdrum, insipid, irksome, prosaic, tedious, uniform; 8 boresome, disliked, dragging, drilling, overlong, suburban, tiresome, wearying; 9 soporific, unvarying, wearisome; 10 invariable, lackluster, languorous, monotonous, pedestrian, repetitive, unexciting, unreadable; 11 commonplace, repetitious, unenjoyable, uninspiring; 13 uninteresting; PHRASES: 2, 7 ad nauseam; 3, 2, 4 dry as dust; 4-6 long-winded; 4-7 mind-numbing; 5, 3 drawn out; 5-5 world-weary; 5, 5, 5 yadda yadda yadda; 5-8 sleep-inducing.

boring (be boring) 3 irk; 4 cloy, drag, dull, jade, pall, sate, tire; 5 weary; 6 repeat; 7 fatigue, satiate; PHRASES: 2, 2, 3, 2 go on and on; 4, 2 harp on; 4, 2, 5 bore to death, bore to tears; 4, 5 bore stiff; 4, 7 lack variety; 5, 2 drone on; 5, 3 never end.

boring person 4 bore, drag, drip, nerd, pain, pest; 5 dweeb, moper; 6 anorak, bummer, egoist, misery, wanker *UK*; 7 bromide, egotist, killjoy; 11 buttonholer; 12 trainspotter; PHRASES: 3, 6 Mrs Grundy; 3, 7 wet blanket; 4, 2, 3, 3 pain in the ass; 4, 2, 3, 4 pain in the neck; 5-2-3-3 stick-in-the-mud.

boring thing 3 rut; 4 bind, drag; 5 chore, snore; 6 bummer, downer; 7 bromide; 8 monotony; 9 treadmill; 10 grindstone, yawnsville; PHRASES: 3, 8 old chestnut; 4, 2, 4 time to kill; 4, 2, 4, 5 time on one's hands; 4, 3, 5 same old story; 4, 6 dull speech; 5-4, 4 twice-told tale; 6, 6 broken record; 8, 4 assembly line, conveyor belt.

born 2 by; 3 née; 5 sired; 6 dammed, foaled, innate, native; 7 dropped, hatched, natural, newborn, spawned; 8 begotten, fathered, mothered, produced, untaught; 9 intuitive; 10 congenital; 11 instinctive; PHRASES: 3, 2 out of.

born (be born) 5 begin; PHRASES: 4, 5, 6 draw first breath; 4, 6 draw breath; 5, 6 fetch breath.

borough 4 area; 8 district, division; 12

municipality.

borrow 3 beg, bum, use; 4 copy, hock, pawn; 5 cadge, mooch, steal; 6 derive, pirate, sponge; 8 scrounge; 10 plagiarize; 11 appropriate; PHRASES: 4, 3, 2 make use of; 5, 1, 4 float a loan; 5, 7 touch someone; 6, 1, 4 secure a loan; 7, 5 request money; 7, 6 request credit; 9, 1, 4 negotiate a loan.

borrower 4 ower; 6 cadger, debtor, pirate; 7 pledger, sponger; 8 imitator; 9 mortgagor; 10 plagiarist; PHRASES: 6, 4 credit user.

borrowing 7 advance; 8 drawdown; PHRASES: 4, 9 loan agreement; 4, 11 loan application, loan transaction; 5-7 money-raising; 6, 2, 6 buying on credit; 7, 2 hitting up; 9, 4 repayment plan.

boschvark 7 bushpig.

bosom 4 best, firm; 5 close, heart, midst; 6 center; 7 dearest, embrace, special. *See also* chest

boss 4 head; 5 chief; 7 manager; 10 supervisor; PHRASES: 4, 6 give orders.

Boston ivy 8, 7 Virginia creeper.

botanical 5 bushy, hardy, mossy, plant, woody; 6 annual, fruity, grassy; 7 botanic, scrubby, shrubby, vegetal, verdant, wilting; 8 biennial, blighted; 9 perennial, succulent, verdurous; 10 ecological; 11 algological; 12 phytological; 13 dendrological, horticultural, phytochemical; PHRASES: 4, 2, 4 gone to seed; 4-5 half-hardy.

botch 4 flop, ruin; 5 spoil; 6 cockup *UK*, damage, fiasco; 7 failure; 8 disaster; PHRASES: 2, 5 do badly; 4, 1, 4, 2 make a mess of.

botched 4 poor; 6 failed, ruined; 7 bungled, spoiled; 8 inferior, slipshod; 11 substandard; PHRASES: 6, 2 messed up.

bother 3 ado, nag; 6 badger, harass, nettle, pester, plague; 7 disturb, perturb, trouble; 9 importune; 13 inconvenience.

bo tree 6 peepul.

Botswana 12 Bechuanaland.

bottle 3 jug; 4 beer, milk, tree, vial, wine; 5 flask, gourd, klein, party, phial; 6 brandy, carafe, carboy, flagon, magnum, Nansen, spirit; 7 canteen, feeding, thermos; 8 calabash, decanter, demijohn, jeroboam, rehoboam, wineskin; 9 balthazar; 10 methuselah; PHRASES: 3, 5 hip flask; 3-5 hotwater.

bottlebrush 11 callistemon.

bottle gourd 8 calabash.

bottom 3 bed, end; 4 base, foot, line; 5 floor, house, limit; 6 drawer, lowest; 9 extremity, lowermost, underside; 10 bottommost, foundation, nethermost, underbelly, underneath; 12 substructure.

bough *See* branch

bought 6 bribed; 7 charged; 8 bribable, ransomed, redeemed; 9 emptional, purchased; 11 purchasable; PHRASES: 4, 3 paid for; 5, 6 worth buying.

boulder *See* rock

bounce 3 bob; 4 jump; 5 bound, eject, evict, expel; 6 bobble, recoil, spring; 7 rebound; PHRASES: 5, 3 throw out; 6, 2 spring up; 6, 4 spring back.

bouncing Betty 8 soapwort.

bouncy 6 lively; 7 elastic, playful, pliable, springy; 9 energetic; 12 effervescent.

bound 3 hop; 4 abut, jump, leap, sure, tied; 5 skirt, touch, vault, yoked; 6 adjoin, border, bounce, forced, spring; 7 assured, certain, chained, clamped, lassoed, obliged, secured; 8 battened, destined, fettered, required, shackled, tethered; 9 compelled, harnessed, obligated; 10 guaranteed, handcuffed, inevitable; 11 constrained, unavoidable; PHRASES: 2, 4, 2 be next to; 2, 8, 2 be adjacent to; 2, 10, 2 be contiguous to.

boundary 3 rim; 4 edge, wall; 5 fence, hedge, limit; 6 border, margin, screen; 7 barrier; 8 frontier; 9 barricade, outskirts, perimeter, periphery; 10 borderline; PHRASES: 2-2 ha-ha; 4, 7 Iron Curtain; 5-5, 4 Mason-Dixon Line; 6, 4 Berlin Wall; 8, 4 dividing line.

boundary marker 4 line; 5 fence, hedge, river; 8 latitude; 9 longitude; 10 checkpoint; PHRASES: 4, 2, 3, 4 line in the sand; 4, 4 time zone; 9, 4 partition wall.

bountiful 6 giving; 7 copious, liberal, profuse; 8 abundant, generous; 9 plentiful; 10 munificent, openhanded.

bounty 3 tip; 4 gift; 5 price, prize; 6 plenty, reward; 7 douceur, payment, premium; 8 gratuity; 9 abundance, baksheesh, pourboire, trinkgeld; 10 generosity.

bouquet 4 posy; 5 aroma, bunch, scent, smell, spray; 7 nosegay, perfume; 9 fragrance.

bourgeois 5 staid; 10 conformist; 11 reactionary; **12** conservative, conventional; **13** unadventurous; **14** traditionalist; PHRAS-ES: **6-5** middle-class.

bout 3 fit; **5** fight, match, round, spasm, spell, stint; **7** contest, seizure, session; **8** paroxysm; PHRASES: **5, 6** short period.

boutonniere 5 spray; **6** flower; **7** corsage.

bow 3 arc, bob, nod, sag, tie; **4** arch, bend, duck, kink, knot, lean, legs, long, prow; **5** cross, curve, droop, kneel, lower, stern, stoop, sweep, yield; **6** accept, cringe, Cupid's, curtsy, deform, grovel, kowtow, revere, salaam, window; **9** genuflect, obeisance; PHRASES: **3, 8** pay respects; **4, 4** bend over; **4, 5** kiss hands; **7, 4, 4** incline one's head.

bowfin 7 dogfish.

bowl 3 cut, lob; **4** ball, cast, dish, dust, hurl, rice, roll, seam, sink, spin, toss, turn, wood *UK*; **5** basin *UK*, boule, chuck, fling, pitch; **6** bounce, careen, career, crater, crease, finger, hollow, krater, mixing, valley, vessel, yorker *UK*; **7** begging, overarm; **8** boundary, goldfish, overhand, underarm; **9** container, underhand, washbasin; **10** depression; PHRASES: **3, 1, 5** lay a block; **3, 2** run in; **3-5** leg-break *UK*, off-break; **4, 1, 4** fire a shot; **4, 1, 5** play a frame; **4, 3** take out; **4, 3, 4** pick the seam, roll the jack, tilt the ~; **4, 5** roll along; **5, 1, 5** score a spare; **5, 1, 6** score a strike; **7, 3, 4** release the ball; **7, 5** pudding basin *UK*.

bowler 5 derby; **6** tenpin.

bowling 3 end, mat, pin, pit; **4** ball, bank, bias, bowl, foul, head, hook, lane, rink, wood; **5** alley, curve, ditch, frame, kitty, spare, split, swing; **6** backup, curved, gutter, hooked, strike, tenpin, triple, turkey; **7** duckpin; **8** duckpins, ninepins, skittles *UK*; **9** backboard; **10** candlepins; **11** rangefinder; PHRASES: **3, 4** pin spot; **3-6** pin-setter; **4, 3** head pin; **4, 4** foul line; **4-4** four-step; **4, 6** ball return; **4, 7** rear cushion; **6, 4** gutter ball, gutter shot; **6-7** follow-through; **9, 5** converted split.

box 2 TV; **3** can, hit, tin; **4** case, coin, cool, deed, Esky *UK*, fuse, jury, pack, safe, seat, shoe, spar, tick; **5** black, booth, caddy, check, chest, crate, elder, fight, frame, glove, pleat, punch, snuff, telly *UK*, thump, voice; **6** ballot, camera, carton, casket, coffer, coffin, girder, goggle, letter, locker, number, office, pillar, punnet *UK*, sentry,

signal, spring, strong, tinder, window, wrench; **7** confine, cubicle, jewelry, package, penalty, spanner *UK*, witness; **8** canister, dispatch, junction, matchbox, moneybox; **9** cardboard, Christmas, container, enclosure, rectangle, telephone; **10** ammunition, eucalyptus, prizefight, television; **11** compartment, sarcophagus; PHRASES: **3, 3** tin can; **3, 5** tea chest *UK*; **4, 1, 5** land a punch; **5, 6** small screen; **9, 4** cigarette case.

boxer 3 pug; **5** champ; **6** hooker, jabber, second; **7** amateur, fighter, manager, Olympic, puncher, referee, slugger, trainer; **8** champion, pugilist, southpaw; **10** challenger; **11** titleholder; **12** prizefighter, professional; PHRASES: **5, 8** world champion; **8, 7** sparring partner.

boxing 2 KO; **3** bob, jab, TKO, WBA (World B~ Association); **4** bell, butt, hook, left, ring, slug, spar; **5** block, count, cross, dance, feint, fight, glove, match, parry, punch, purse, right, ropes, round, rules, swing; **6** corner, shadow, shorts, stance; **8** decision, footwork, knockout, pugilism, straight, uppercut; **9** knockdown, scorecard, technique; **10** fisticuffs, prizefight; **13** prizefighting; PHRASES: **3-3, 5** one-two punch; **3, 5, 3, 4** hit below the belt; **4, 5** bolo punch; **5, 1, 5** throw a fight; **5, 5** fixed fight; **5, 6** point system; **6, 5** rabbit punch, Sunday punch; **8, 3** punching bag; **8, 6** sparring helmet.

boxing weight divisions 9 flyweight; **11** heavyweight, lightweight; **12** bantamweight, middleweight, welterweight; **13** cruiserweight, featherweight; PHRASES: **5-9** light-flyweight.

boy 3 lad, old, son, tar; **4** ball, best, rent; **5** altar, Bevin, bucko, cabin, child, teddy, youth; **6** barrow, errand, office; **8** teenager, whipping; **9** principal, schoolboy, youngster; PHRASES: **4-4** blue-eyed; **4-6, 3** fairhaired ~; **5, 3** young man *UK*.

boycott *See* **embargo**

boyfriend 3 boy; **4** beau, date, dish, hunk, mate; **5** groom, lover; **6** Adonis, escort, fiancé, steady, suitor, toyboy; **7** partner; **8** beefcake; **10** bridegroom, sweetheart; PHRASES: **4, 6** male friend; **4, 7** main squeeze; **5, 3** lover boy; **5, 5** sugar daddy.

Boz 7 Dickens.

BR 6 trains; PHRASES: **7, 4** British Rail.

bra *See* **underwear**

brace 4 pair, prop; 5 batch, brood, strut; 6 litter; 7 bracket, support; 13 reinforcement.

bracing 4 cold; 5 brisk; 7 healthy; 11 stimulating; 12 invigorating.

bracken 5 brake.

bracket 3 set; 4 band, join, link, prop, stay; 5 brace, group, range, strut; 6 cohort, relate; 7 connect, support; 9 associate.

brag 4 crow; 5 boast, swank; 7 swagger; PHRASES: 4, 3 show off, talk big.

bragging 5 cocky; 8 arrogant, boastful, boasting; 9 arrogance, conceited; PHRASES: 3, 3 hot air; 4-9 self-important.

braid 3 net, web; 4 bind, lace, mesh, trim; 5 plait, skein, twist, weave; 6 fringe, thread; 7 crochet, entwine, fishnet, lattice, macramé, network, pigtail, tatting, tracery, trellis, webbing; 8 espalier, filigree, fretwork; 9 arabesque, interlace; 10 intertwine, interweave, wickerwork; PHRASES: 4, 6 cat's cradle; 7, 3 spider's web.

brain 2 IQ; 4 head, loaf, mind, nous, stem, wave, wits; 5 death, drain, fever; 6 genius, noddle; 7 egghead, prodigy; 8 brainbox *UK*, cerebrum; 9 intellect; 10 mastermind; 12 intellectual; 13 understanding; PHRASES: 4, 2, 7 seat of thought; 4, 6 gray matter; 5, 5 upper story; 6, 5 common sense.

brainless *See* **foolish**

brain-teaser 4 code, maze; 5 rebus; 6 cipher, riddle, teaser; 7 anagram, charade, decoder, tangram; 8 acrostic; 9 conundrum, crossword, labyrinth; 10 cryptogram; 12 cryptography; 13 hieroglyphics; PHRASES: 4-6 word-puzzle; 7, 6 Chinese puzzle.

brake 3 air; 4 curb, disc, disk *UK*, drum, shoe, slow; 5 fluid, light; 6 damper, lining; 7 bracken, control; 8 shooting; 9 deterrent, hydraulic, parachute, restraint; 10 constraint, decelerate, horsepower, limitation; 11 centrifugal; 14 discouragement; PHRASES: 3, 2 let up; 6, 5 reduce speed; 7, 5 coaster ~.

branch 3 arm; 4 area, bole, fork, leaf, limb, side, slip, spur, stem, turn, twig, wing; 5 bough, calyx, field, petal, scion, sepal, shoot, split, spray, sprig, stalk, stump, topic, torso, trunk; 6 anther, aspect, divide, domain, office, outlet, ramify, sphere, stamen, sucker, switch; 7 diverge, foliage, leaflet, tendril, turnoff; 8 division, offshoot,

separate; 9 bifurcate, tributary; 10 department, trifurcate; 11 subdivision; 12 ramification; PHRASES: 4, 4 side road; 4, 6 area office; 6, 4 flower head; 6-5 spread-eagle.

branching 7 forking; 8 crossing; 10 crossroads; 11 bifurcation; 12 arborescence, arborization, intersection, ramification, trifurcation.

brand 4 call, kind, make, mark, name, sort, type; 5 class, image, label, stamp, style; 6 leader, marque; 7 imprint, product, variety; 8 classify, describe; 9 trademark; 10 categorize; 14 identification; PHRASES: 5, 4 trade name; 11, 4 identifying mark.

brandish *See* **wield**

brandy 4 snap; 6 bottle, butter.

brash 4 loud; 6 brazen, garish; 8 arrogant; 10 aggressive; 12 presumptuous; PHRASES: 4-9 self-confident.

Brasov 6 Stalin; 9 Kronstadt.

brass 3 hat; 4 band, gall, neck; 5 cheek, nerve, tacks; 7 rubbing; 8 boldness, chutzpah, farthing; 9 arrogance, brashness, impudence; 13 assertiveness; PHRASES: 4-9 self-assurance.

Bratislava 7 Pozsony; 9 Pressburg.

bravado 4 show; 6 daring; 7 bluster, heroics, swagger; 8 audacity, boldness, bonhomie, defiance, machismo; 11 braggadocio, presumption.

brave 4 bear, bold, defy, face; 5 macho; 6 daring, endure, heroic, plucky; 7 doughty, gallant, valiant; 8 confront, fearless, intrepid; 9 audacious; 10 courageous; PHRASES: 4, 2 take on; 5, 2, 2 stand up to.

bravo! 3 bis; 4 more; 6 encore, hurrah; PHRASES: 4, 4 hear hear, well done.

brawl 5 clash, fight; 6 affray, tussle; 7 scuffle, wrestle; PHRASES: 5-2 punch-up *UK Can.*

brawn *See* **strength**

bray 3 cry; 4 bark, call, rasp; 5 grate, neigh, snort, sound; 6 bellow, whinny.

breach 4 hole, rift; 5 break, crack, flout; 7 fissure, opening, rupture, violate; 8 betrayal, defiance, division, infringe; 9 penetrate, violation; 10 contravene, separation; 12 estrangement, infringement; 13 contravention; PHRASES: 3, 7 get through; 5, 7 break through.

bread 3 nan, nut, rye; 4 beer, cash, corn,

dosh *UK*, flat, food, malt, naan, pita, puri, roti, rusk *UK*, soda; **5** bialy, black, brown, crumb, crust, daily, dough, fried, funds, lolly *UK*, matzo, money, moola, toast, wheat, white; **6** awendo, potato, raisin, sippet, sliced; **7** awendaw, challah, chapati, crouton, finance, granary, hoecake, rations, toastie *UK*; **8** ciabatta, cornpone, focaccia, poppadom, tortilla; **9** schnecken, sourdough; **10** johnnycake, sustenance, wholewheat; **11** nourishment; **12** pumpernickel; **PHRASES: 3, 5** pan dulce; **4, 4** corn pone; **4, 5** corn ~, hush puppy, milk toast; **4, 7** hush puppies; **5, 2, 8** means of survival; **5, 5** brown ~, Melba toast, spoon ~; **6-3** banananut; **6, 4** kaiser roll; **6, 5** batter ~, Boston brown, French toast; **7, 5** anadama ~; **8, 5** cinnamon toast. *See also* **loaf**

breadbasket 7 stomach.

breadth 4 beam, size, span; **5** gauge, girth, range, scale, scope, space, splay, width; **6** extent, leeway, radius; **7** caliber, expanse; **8** coverage, diameter, dilation, fullness, latitude, wideness, wingspan; **9** ampleness, amplitude, broadness, thickness, tolerance; **11** catholicity, handbreadth; **12** spaciousness; **13** expansiveness, extensiveness; **PHRASES: 5-10** broad-mindedness.

breadthwise 6 across; **7** athwart; **8** sideways; **9** broadside, broadways, crossways, crosswise, widthways; **11** breadthways; **12** transversely; **PHRASES: 3, 3, 3, 6** all the way across.

break 3 end, tea, top; **4** beat, even, fail, halt, rest, rout, stop, trip; **5** crack, crash, crush, dance, lunch, pause, relax, sever, smash, solve, space, split, start; **6** breach, chance, coffee, decode, defeat, exceed, hiatus; **7** destroy, disobey, disturb, getaway, holiday *UK*, opening, respite, rupture, shatter, surpass, unravel, violate, weekend; **8** breather, collapse, decipher, disclose, fracture, infringe, vacation; **9** breakdown, cessation, disregard, interrupt, overwhelm; **10** contravene, disruption, unscramble; **11** opportunity; **12** intermission, interruption; **13** discontinuity; **PHRASES: 2, 2, 6, 2** be in breach of; **2, 8** be revealed; **3, 2** leg up, way in; **3, 3** get out; **3, 4** cut into; **3-4** sit-down; **3, 4, 4, 2** put your feet up; **4, 1, 8** take a breather; **4, 2, 4** take it easy; **4, 3** leak out, time off; **4, 4** take five; **4, 4, 3** have time out; **4, 6** make public; **4, 7** stop working; **6, 5** become known; **6, 6** become public.

breakable *See* **brittle**

breakdown 4 halt; **7** failure, rundown, summary; **8** analysis, collapse; **9** cessation; **10** dissection; **12** interruption; **14** classification.

breaker *See* **wave**

breakfast cereal 4 bran; **5** brose *UK*, grits, gruel; **6** brewis, muesli; **7** granola, oatmeal; **8** porridge *UK*; **10** cornflakes; **PHRASES: 4, 6** bran flakes; **5, 4** wheat germ. *See also* **cereal**

breakneck *See* **quick**

break up 5 smash; **7** adjourn, atomize, crumble; **8** disperse; **12** disintegrate.

breakwater 4 mole, pier; **5** groin; **8** causeway; **PHRASES: 3, 4** sea wall; **6, 4** harbor wall.

breastbone 7 sternum.

breastplate 8 plastron.

breath 4 gasp, gush, pant, puff, sigh, waft; **5** draft; **7** current; **10** exhalation, inhalation.

breathe *See* **respire**

breathlessness *See* **panting**

bred 5 grown; **PHRASES: 8-2** fattened-up.

breed 4 farm, kind, rear, type; **5** cause, class, raise; **6** create, strain; **7** produce, variety; **8** generate, multiply; **9** procreate, propagate, reproduce; **PHRASES: 4, 6** have babies; **5, 2** bring up; **5, 5** bring about.

breeding 3 dam; **4** sire, stud; **7** manners; **8** pedigree, purebred, studbook; **9** bloodline, education; **10** background, refinement, upbringing; **12** conformation, thoroughbred; **PHRASES: 4, 7** good manners; **6, 8** social standing; **7, 5** blooded horse.

breeze 4 gust, waft, wind; **5** cinch; **6** doddle *UK*; **8** walkaway, walkover; **PHRASES: 5, 2, 4** piece of cake; **5, 4** light wind; **6, 4** child's play, gentle wind.

breezy 5 blowy, brisk, fresh, gusty, windy; **6** cheery; **8** blustery, cheerful, flippant; **9** windswept; **12** lighthearted.

brethren 4 open; **5** elder; **8** Plymouth; **9** exclusive.

brew 3 mix; **4** grow, home, loom, make; **5** blend, drink, steep; **6** infuse, potion; **7** concoct, develop, distill, ferment, mixture, prepare; **8** beverage, cocktail, infusion, threaten; **10** concoction; **11** combination; **PHRASES: 4, 2** blow up; **6, 5** gather force.

bribe 3 oil, tip; **4** bung *UK*; **6** carrot, entice, grease, induce, payoff, reward, square, suborn; **7** corrupt, payment; **8** kickback, persuade; **9** baksheesh, incentive, sweetener; **10** backhander *UK*, enticement, inducement; PHRASES: **3, 3** buy off, pay off; **3, 3, 4** oil the hand; **4, 6** pork barrel; **5, 4** slush fund; **6, 3, 4** grease the palm.

bribery 10 corruption, enticement, inducement, subornment; **11** subornation.

brick *See* **block**

brickbat 6 insult; **7** comment; **9** criticism; **10** suggestion; **11** insinuation.

brickwork *See* **fabric**

bridal party 4 page; **5** bride, groom, usher; **7** pageboy; **9** attendant; **10** bridegroom, bridesmaid; PHRASES: **4, 2, 5** maid of honor; **4, 3** best man; **5-6** train-bearer; **6, 4** flower girl.

bride *See* **wife**

bridge 3 air, tie; **4** arch, beam, bond, deck, ford, join, land, lift, link, pier, road, rope, snow, span, toll, turn; **5** board, canal, cards, ferry, fixed, pivot, swing, truss; **6** arched, Bailey, flying, girder, rubber, skewed, square; **7** auction, balance, bascule, catwalk, channel, clapper, conduit, connect, flyover *UK*, gangway, movable, passage, pontoon, railway *UK Can*, rainbow, through, trestle, viaduct, walkway; **8** abutment, aqueduct, causeway, concrete, contract, floating, flooring, humpback, overpass, railroad; **9** associate, duckboard, duplicate, gangplank; **10** cantilever, connection, drawbridge, footbridge, pedestrian, suspension, Wheatstone; **11** association, transporter; **12** counterpoise, overcrossing; PHRASES: **3, 4** way over; **3-6** box-girder; **3, 8** tie together; **4-4** four-deal; **5-6** cable-stayed, plate-girder; **6, 4** single span; **8, 4** multiple span; **8-4** vertical-lift; **8, 6** stepping stones.

bridgeboard 3, 6 cut string.

bridle 4 curb; **7** bristle, control, prickle; **8** restrain; PHRASES: **3, 5** get angry; **4, 2** rein in; **4, 2, 5** keep in check; **6, 7** become annoyed.

brief 4 task, tell; **5** coach, drill, groom, pithy, remit *UK*, short, teach, train; **6** digest, direct, duties, inform, orders, update; **7** concise, educate, mandate, mission, outline, passing, prepare, summary; **8** abstract, briefing, fleeting, instruct, succinct; **9** ephemeral, momentary; **10** assignment, guidelines, transitory; **11** instruction, prep-

aration; **12** epigrammatic; PHRASES: **2, 3, 5** to the point; **4, 2** fill in; **5, 2, 2, 4** bring up to date; **5-4** short-term; **5-5** short-lived; **6, 5** ground rules.

brief (be brief) 4, 2, 3, 5 come to the point.

brief (in brief) 2, 1, 3, 5 in a few words; **2, 1, 4** in a word; **2, 1, 8** in a nutshell; **2, 5** in short.

briefing 5 drill; **6** update; **7** meeting, seminar; **8** exercise, training; **9** education, novitiate; **10** conference; **11** instruction; **12** consultation; **14** apprenticeship; PHRASES: **5, 10** press conference; **8, 7** updating session.

brigade 4 boys', crew, fire, gang, team, unit; **5** group; **10** contingent; **13** International.

bright 5 clear, fiery, happy, light, lurid, perky, quick, smart, sunny, vivid; **6** ablaze, aflame, alight, brainy, clever, flashy, garish, lively, upbeat; **7** blazing, flaming, glaring, intense, shining, spangly; **8** blinding, cheerful, dazzling, diamanté, flashing, glinting, glittery, positive, sequined, sparking, splendid, tinselly; **9** brilliant, effulgent, sparkling, twinkling; **10** flamboyant, glittering, optimistic; **11** coruscating, fluorescent, intelligent, resplendent; **13** kaleidoscopic, scintillating; PHRASES: **3-7** Day-Glo™; **5-6** sharp-witted.

brighten 6 uplift, vivify; **7** animate, enhance, enliven, gladden, hearten, improve, lighten; **8** revivify; **10** exhilarate, illuminate, revitalize; PHRASES: **3, 2** add to; **4, 3** jazz up, look up, perk up; **4, 3, 2, 2** snap out of it; **4, 6** feel better, make better; **4, 7** make lighter; **4, 8** make brighter; **5, 2** cheer up, liven up *UK*.

brightness 5 glare; **6** luster; **8** optimism; **9** happiness, intensity, sunniness; **10** brilliance, cheeriness; **12** illumination. *See also* **bright**

brilliance 6 genius, talent, wisdom; **9** intensity; **10** luminosity. *See also* **brilliant**

brilliant 5 clear, smart, vivid; **6** bright, clever, gifted, superb; **7** intense, radiant; **8** dazzling, gleaming, inspired, luminous, skillful, talented, virtuoso; **9** excellent, marvelous, sparkling, wonderful; **11** magnificent.

brimstone 6 sulfur; **7** sulphur *UK*.

bring 3 get; **4** earn, give, make, pass, take; **5** beget, carry, cause, fetch; **6** convey, create, effect; **7** command, produce; **8** generate; **9** transport; PHRASES: **2, 3, 5, 2** be the cause of; **3, 2** end in; **4, 2** lead to; **4, 3** sell for; **4, 5** take along; **4, 6** make happen; **6, 2** result in.

bring (be brought) 4, 2, 4 come to hand.

bring back 3 get; **4** send; **5** chase, evoke, fetch, renew; **6** assign, commit, deport, obtain, recall, retain, return, revive, secure; **7** entrust, procure, replace, restore; **8** reawaken, rekindle, retrieve; **9** extradite, recapture, reinstate; PHRASES: **2, 3** go for; **2, 5** go after; **3, 5** run after; **4, 2** hand on, pass on, pick up; **4, 3** call for; **5, 2, 4** bring to mind; **5, 3, 5** fetch and carry; **5, 5** chase after; **6, 2** summon up.

bring down 3 dip; **4** deck, duck, fell, sink; **5** couch, douse, drown, floor, souse, upset; **6** defeat, depose, humble, plunge, topple; **7** depress, overset, scuttle, subvert, torpedo; **8** demolish, dethrone, overturn, submerge; **9** overthrow; **11** spreadeagle; PHRASES: **3, 3** lay out; **4, 2, 3, 6** send to the bottom; **4, 4** bowl over; **4, 8** send headlong; **5, 4** knock down, knock over, shoot down; **5, 5** seize power.

brink 3 lip, rim; **4** brim, edge; **5** point, verge; **6** border; **9** precipice, threshold.

briny 4 salt; **5** drink, salty; **6** saline, salted; **8** brackish.

brisk 4 cold, cool, curt, fast; **5** quick, rapid; **6** abrupt; **7** brusque, hurried; **9** energetic, impatient; **10** refreshing; **11** stimulating; **12** invigorating.

brisling 5 sprat.

bristle 4 brim, hair, rise, teem; **5** spike, spine; **6** bridle, hackle, object; **7** prickle, stiffen, stubble; **8** overflow; PHRASES: **2, 4** be full; **2, 5, 4** be thick with; **2, 9** be resentful; **3, 5** get angry; **5, 2** stand up; **6, 5** become erect.

Bristol 7 Channel, fashion.

British dish 6 haggis, mutton; **7** kippers; **8** porridge; PHRASES: **3, 3, 3, 4** eel pie and mash; **4-1-6** cock-a-leekie; **4-2-3-4** toad-in-the-hole; **4, 3, 5** fish and chips; **5, 4** Dover sole, Irish stew, roast beef; **5, 5** mixed grill; **5, 7** Welsh rarebit; **6, 3, 6** bubble and squeak; **6, 5** Scotch broth; **6, 6** smoked salmon; **7, 3** cottage pie; **7, 3, 4** bangers and mash; **7, 4** jellied eels; **8, 7** devilled kidneys; **9, 3** shepherd's pie; **9, 4** Aylesbury duck.

British Honduras 6 Belize.

British money 4 note, pony, quid; **5** fiver, oncer, penny, piece, pound; **6** archer, monkey, nicker, tenner; **7** smacker; **8** twopence; PHRASES: **3, 5** new penny; **5, 4** pound coin; **5, 5** fifty pence; **6, 5** twenty pence; **7, 7** decimal coinage.

brittle 4 hard, torn, weak; **5** crazy, crisp, flaky, frail, rigid, short, split, stiff; **6** broken, crispy, dainty, flimsy, papery; **7** chipped, cracked, crumbly, crushed, fissile, flaking, fragile, friable, powdery; **8** breaking, bursting, chipping, cracking UK, crackled, crumbled, delicate, gimcrack, scissile, tearable, unsteady; **9** breakable, crackable, crumbling, crushable, explosive, frangible, inelastic, shattered UK, splintery, splitting; **10** shattering, tumbledown, vulnerable; **11** dilapidated, shatterable, splintering; **13** insubstantial; PHRASES: **4, 9** like parchment; **5, 2, 5** ready to break; **5-4** wafer-thin; **5-5** jerry-built.

brittle (be brittle) 4 chip, snap; **5** break, burst, crack, crash, craze, crush, flake, split; **6** shiver; **7** crumble, explode, shatter; **8** fracture, fragment, splinter; **12** disintegrate; PHRASES: **4, 2, 6** fall to pieces; **4, 3** chip off, give way, snap off; **4, 4** wear thin; **5, 3** break off.

brittleness 5 split; **7** breakup, frailty; **8** breaking, cracking, delicacy, scission; **9** crumbling, fissility, fragility, splitting; **10** friability; **11** splintering; **12** breakability, crushability, frangibility, inelasticity; **13** deterioration, vulnerability; PHRASES: **8, 5** delicate state.

brittle thing 5 balsa, glass, slate; **6** bubble, icicle, lamina, pastry; **7** crystal, pottery, snowman; **8** eggshell, piecrust; **9** matchwood, parchment, porcelain; **10** glasshouse UK, greenhouse, windowpane; PHRASES: **3, 4** old bone; **3, 5** old paper; **4, 3** thin ice; **4, 4** dead leaf; **4, 5** rice paper; **4, 6** sand castle; **5, 2, 5** house of cards.

broad 3 big; **4** bean, deep, full, jump, lake, mere, open, seal, wide; **5** ample, arrow, baggy, clear, gauge, heavy, large, plain, roomy, splay, thick, woman; **6** church, flared; **7** general, inexact, sketchy, splayed, visible; **8** distinct, spacious, unsubtle; **9** broadcast, expansive, extensive, imprecise; **10** pronounced, transverse, widespread; **11** approximate, distinctive, transparent; **13** comprehensive; PHRASES: **2, 4, 2, 1, 5** as wide as a truck; **3-8** far-reaching; **3-12** all-encompassing; **4-3** wide-set; **4-4** wide-open; **4-5** wide-angle; **4-6** wide-screen, wide-spaced; **4-7** wide-ranging; **4-8** bell-bottomed; **6-3** spread-out.

broad (be broad) 5 flare, splay; **6** extend.

broad bean 5, 4 horse bean.

broadbill 9 swordfish.

broadcast 3 air, sow; **4** news, play, show, soap; **5** drama, relay, rerun, shout, strew; **6** airing, screen, sitcom, sports, spread; **7** concert, diffuse, program, scatter; **8** announce, disperse, newscast, newsreel, telethon, televize, transmit; **9** advertise, docudrama, publicize, recording; **10** commercial, distribute, miniseries, sportscast, travelogue; **11** disseminate, documentary, infomercial; **12** infotainment, transmission; PHRASES: **3, 3** put out; **4-2** call-in; **4, 4** game show, quiz show, talk show; **4, 5** make known, news flash, soap opera; **5-2** phone-in *UK Can*; **7, 4** reality show; **7, 6** current events; **8, 7** makeover program.

broadcaster 2 DJ, MC (master of ceremonies); **4** disk *UK*, host; **5** emcee; **6** anchor, deejay; **7** compere; **8** reporter; **9** anchorman, announcer, informant, newswoman, presenter *UK*; **10** journalist, newscaster, newsreader *UK*; **11** anchorwoman, commentator, telegrapher; **12** anchorperson; **13** televangelist; PHRASES: **4, 6** disc jockey; **5, 8** radio operator; **7, 4** talking head; **8, 6** question master *UK*.

broaden 4 open; **5** widen; **6** dilate, expand, extend, spread; **7** diverge, enlarge, thicken; **8** increase; PHRASES: **4, 5** make wider.

broadly 6 mostly; **7** roughly; **9** obscenely; PHRASES: **2, 3, 5** by and large, on the whole. *See also* **broad**

broad-minded 4 open; **6** candid, direct; **7** liberal; **8** explicit, unbiased; **9** impartial, unbigoted; **12** unprejudiced; **13** disinterested; PHRASES: **4-6** open-minded; **4-8** free-thinking.

broad-mindedness 7 freedom; **10** liberality; PHRASES: **12** impartiality. *See also* **broad-minded**

brogue *See* **accent**

broil 4 cook; **5** brown; **7** griddle; **10** rotisserie.

broke *See* **bankrupt**

broken 6 beaten, faulty, licked; **7** crushed, wrecked; **8** defeated, dejected; **9** defective, faltering, fractured, imperfect; **10** fragmented; **11** inoperative; **14** malfunctioning; PHRASES: **3, 2, 5** out of order.

broker *See* **trader**

bronze *See* **sculpture**

brooch *See* **pin**

brood 4 fret, kids, mope; **5** issue, worry, young; **6** clutch, family, litter; **7** progeny; **8** children, ruminate; **9** offspring; PHRASES: **5, 2** dwell on.

brook 4 beck *UK*, burn *UK*; **5** allow, river; **6** accept, stream, suffer; **7** rivulet; **8** tolerate; PHRASES: **3, 2, 4** put up with.

brothel 5 house; **6** bagnio; **8** bordello, cathouse; **9** honkytonk; **10** bawdyhouse; PHRASES: **3, 5** red light; **4, 5** juke house; **7, 6** massage parlor; **8, 4** knocking shop *UK*; **10, 5** disorderly house *UK*.

brother 3 big, lay; **4** br'er; **5** blood; **6** member; **7** comrade; **9** associate, colleague.

brow *See* **summit**

brown 3 bay, dun, fry, nut, owl, tan; **4** buff, burn, char, dark, ecru, fawn, foxy, peat, roan, sear; **5** beige, broil, camel, cocoa, grill, hazel, henna, honey, khaki, light, liver, mocha, mousy, ocher *UK*, ochre *UK*, rusty, sepia, shirt, singe, snake, study, tawny, toast, umber; **6** auburn, bistre, bomber, bronze, coffee, copper, maroon, russet, sorrel, suntan, tanned *UK*, walnut; **7** biscuit, bronzed, caramel, coppery, embrown, fulvous, fuscous, oatmeal, Vandyke; **8** Bismarck, brunette, chestnut, cinnamon, cupreous, mahogany, mushroom; **9** champagne, chocolate, suntanned; **10** rubiginous; **11** ferruginous; **12** butterscotch; PHRASES: **3, 5** raw umber; **3, 6** raw sienna; **4, 2, 4** café au lait; **4-7** rust-colored; **5, 5** burnt umber, congo ~, flesh color; **5, 6** burnt almond, burnt sienna; **5-7** snuff-colored; **7, 5** logwood ~; **10, 5** caledonian ~.

brown thing 3 fat, rot; **4** bear, belt, coal, rice; **5** algae, betty, bread, paper, sugar, trout; **6** coffee, toffee; **7** brownie, caramel, freckle, lignite; **8** cinnamon, demerara *UK*; **9** chocolate, muscovado; **10** brownstone; **12** butterscotch; PHRASES: **4-5** seal-point (Siamese cat); **4, 6** fall colors; **5, 6** burnt almond; **6, 6** autumn colors; **7, 3** Burmese cat; **7, 4** tobacco leaf; **9-5** chocolate-point (Siamese cat); **10, 5** wholewheat bread.

browse 4 look, surf; 6 cruise, glance, peruse.

brucellosis 5, 5 Malta fever; 8, 5 undulant fever.

bruise 4 bump, hurt, mark, welt; 6 damage, injure; 8 discolor; 13 discoloration; PHRASES: 5, 3 black eye.

brunette 4 dark; 5 brown, raven.

brush 4 coat; 5 besom, broom, clear, graze, groom, scrub, sweep, touch; 6 scrape, stroke; 7 contact, meeting, sweeper; 8 skirmish; 9 encounter; 10 whiskbroom; 12 disagreement; 13 confrontation; PHRASES: 4, 5 corn broom, yard broom; 5, 5 stick broom.

brusque 4 curt; 5 brisk, rough; 6 abrupt; 7 offhand.

Brussels 4 lace; 6 carpet, sprout.

brutal 5 cruel, harsh, rough; 6 fierce, severe; 7 callous, vicious; 8 pitiless, ruthless; 11 insensitive.

brute 4 thug; 5 beast, bully, swine; 6 animal; 7 monster; 8 creature.

bryozoan 8 polyzoan; 9 ectoproct; PHRASES: 3, 3 sea mat.

BSE 3, 3, 7 mad cow disease.

bubble 3 car, gum; 4 bath, boil, fizz, foam, pack, suds; 5 float, froth, spray, spume; 6 gurgle, lather, memory, mousse, simmer, sponge; 7 balloon, chamber, ferment, soufflé, sparkle; 8 meringue; 9 spindrift; 10 effervesce; PHRASES: 3, 6 air pocket; 3, 7 air bladder.

bubbly 5 fizzy, foamy; 6 bouncy, frothy, lively, yeasty; 7 aerated, fizzing; 8 animated, cheerful; 9 sparkling, vivacious; 10 carbonated; 12 effervescent; PHRASES: 4, 2, 4 full of life.

buccaneer See **pirate**

Buchmanism 5, 10 Moral Rearmament.

buck 4 jump, kick, rear; 5 blame, bound, fault, fever, guilt; 6 oppose, rabbit, resist, spring; 8 sawhorse; 9 liability; 11 culpability; 14 responsibility; PHRASES: 2, 7 go against; 3, 2, 3, 4, 2 fly in the face of; 4, 3 kick out; 5, 7 stand against.

buckle 4 clip, fold; 5 bulge, catch, clasp, close; 6 fasten, secure; 7 crumple; 8 collapse, fastener; 9 fastening; PHRASES: 4, 2 cave in.

bucolic See **rural**

bud 4 grow; 5 bloom, gemma, shoot; 6 apical, flower, sprout, winter; 7 blossom, burgeon, gemmule, lateral; 8 axillary, dormancy, flourish, terminal; 9 gemmation, outgrowth; 11 gemmulation; 12 adventitious; PHRASES: 4, 3 open out.

bud (in the bud) 2, 3, 7 in its infancy; 2, 6 in embryo.

buddleia 9, 4 butterfly bush.

budge See **move**

budgerigar 8 lovebird.

budget 4 cost, plan; 5 cheap, funds; 7 account; 8 accounts, finances; 10 economical, reasonable; 11 inexpensive; PHRASES: 3-6 low-priced; 4, 10 make provisions; 9, 4 financial plan.

buff 3 fan, rub; 5 shine; 6 expert, polish; 7 burnish; 10 enthusiast; 11 connoisseur; PHRASES: 3, 2 rub up UK.

buffer 3 pad; 5 cloak, cover; 6 bumper, defend, screen, shield; 7 barrier, bulwark, curtain, cushion, defense, protect; 9 safeguard; 10 camouflage; PHRASES: 5, 8 shock absorber.

buffet 4 bang, rock; 5 knock, pound; 6 batter.

buffoon 3 wag, wit; 4 fool; 5 clown, japer, joker, tease; 6 jester, teaser; 7 farceur; 8 comedian, humorist; 9 prankster; 11 wisecracker; PHRASES: 9, 5 practical joker.

bug 3 fly, irk, sow; 4 germ, June, lace, pest, pill; 5 annoy, error, fault, mealy, virus; 6 bother, chinch, croton, madden, shield, squash; 7 cabbage, gremlin, kissing, microbe, mistake, problem, wiretap; 8 assassin, creature, irritate; 9 bacterium, infection, infuriate, lightning; 13 microorganism; PHRASES: 3, 2 spy on; 6, 2, 2 listen in on; 6-6 creepy-crawly; 9, 6 listening device.

buggy 4 baby, cart, pram UK; 5 beach, swamp; 7 vehicle; 8 stroller; 9 pushchair UK; 12 perambulator UK; PHRASES: 4, 8 baby carriage.

bugleweed 9 horehound.

build 4 body, join, make, size; 5 erect, shape; 6 create, figure; 8 assemble, physique; 9 construct; PHRASES: 3, 2 put up; 3, 8 put together.

building 4 line, pile, roof, shop, wall, wing; 5 block, frame, gable, hotel, house, porch, store, tower; 6 castle, church, façade, garage, listed, office, prison, school, soffit, window; 7 balcony, carbarn, chimney, cottage, doorway, edifice, eyesore, factory, feedlot, society, stadium, theater, veranda; **8** buttress, corncrib, elevator, erection, exterior, frontage, hospital, ratables, spouting, teardown; **9** apartment, bunkhouse, carbuncle, colonnade, elevation, escalator, guttering *UK*, stairwell, structure, townhouse, vestibule, warehouse; **10** auditorium, multistory, quadraplex, quadriplex, quadruplex, skyscraper, smokestack; **12** construction, semidetached; PHRASES: **3-4** low-rise, mid-rise; **3, 5** box stall, fun house, row house; **4-2** walkup; **4-4** high-rise; **4, 6** fire escape, rain gutter; **4-8** half-timbered; **5, 4** strip mall; **5, 5** field house, ranch house, tower block *UK*; **6-5** single-story; **6, 8** office ~; **6, 9** garden apartment; **7, 4** parking ramp; **7, 5** chapter house, polling place; **7, 7** country cottage, housing project; **7, 11** housing development; **8, 5** detached house, medicine lodge, terraced house *UK*; **8, 7** thatched cottage; **10, 5** department store.

bulge **3** arc, bud; **4** boil, boss, bubo, bump, bust, corn, cyst, hump, knob, knot, lens, lump, nose, tits, wart; **5** balls, boobs, bosom, edema, pecks, rocks, swell, tumor; **6** biceps, breast, bubble, bunion, button, expand, muscle, nipple; **7** beergut, blister, papilla; **8** erection, knockers, mammilla, pectoral, protrude, swelling; **9** carbuncle, pregnancy, testicles; **10** projection, prominence; **12** protuberance; PHRASES: **2, 7** be swollen; **4, 2** puff up; **4, 3** puff out; **5, 3** stick out.

bulging **4** full; **7** bloated, stuffed, swelled, swollen; **8** overfull, swelling; **9** distended; **10** protruding; **11** overstuffed, protuberant.

bulk **4** body, form, hulk, mass, size; **6** volume, weight; **8** majority, vastness *UK*; **9** immensity, substance; PHRASES: **4, 4** main part; **7, 4** greater part, largest part.

bull **2** ox; **3** run; **4** nose; **5** edict, snake, steer; **6** decree; **7** bullock, mastiff, session, terrier; **10** encyclical; **11** instruction; **12** proclamation; PHRASES: **5, 6** papal decree.

bullbat **9** nighthawk.

bulldoze **4** raze; **5** bully, clear, level; **6** coerce; **7** flatten; **8** bludgeon, browbeat, demolish.

bulletin **6** update; **7** journal; **9** newspaper, statement; **10** communiqué, newsletter, periodical; **11** publication; **12** announcement; PHRASES: **4, 4** news item; **4, 6** news report; **4,**

7 news summary; **5, 7** press release.

bullfight **7** corrida, matador, picador; **8** toreador.

bullion **3** bar; **4** gold; **5** ingot; **6** billon, nugget, silver; **8** electrum, platinum; PHRASES: **5, 4** false gold, fool's gold, solid gold, white gold; **5, 6** solid silver; **6, 5** yellow metal; **8, 5** precious metal.

bull snake **6** gopher.

bully **4** beef, thug; **6** badger, harass, hassle, hector, tyrant; **7** torment; **8** browbeat, frighten; **9** aggressor, persecute, terrorize, tormentor; **10** intimidate, persecutor; **11** intimidator.

bulwark **6** buffer; **7** defense, rampart; **8** buttress; **9** barricade, earthwork, safeguard; **10** embankment, protection; **13** fortification.

bumble **6** lumber, mumble, murmur, mutter; **7** blunder, stagger, stumble, stutter; **8** hesitate.

bumblebee **9** humblebee.

bump **3** hit, jar; **4** bang, jerk, jolt, lump, thud; **5** bulge, crash, knock, smash, thump; **6** bounce, bruise, jounce, strike, wallop; **7** collide; **8** accident, swelling; **9** collision, contusion; PHRASES: **4, 4** slam into; **5, 4** crash into, smash into.

bumpy **5** jerky, lumpy, rough; **6** bouncy, choppy, rutted, uneven; **7** jarring, jolting; **8** potholed; **9** turbulent; **13** uncomfortable.

bun **6** cookie.

bunch **3** lot, set; **4** crew, gang, posy, team; **5** clump, crowd, group, spray; **6** gather, huddle; **7** bouquet, cluster, corsage, nosegay; **8** assembly; **10** collection; PHRASES: **5, 8** crowd together.

bundle **3** wad; **4** bale, bolt, crop, hank, pack, push, roll, rush; **5** batch, bunch, hurry, sheaf, shove, skein, truss; **6** hustle, packet *UK*, quiver; **7** fortune, hassock, hayrick *UK*, package, tussock; **8** haystack; PHRASES: **3, 5** big money.

bung **4** cork, plug; **7** stopper.

bungle **4** ruin; **5** bodge *UK*, botch, spoil; **9** mismanage; PHRASES: **2, 5** do badly; **4, 1, 4, 2** make a hash of; **4, 2** mess up.

bungling **4** flop, flub, mess, miss, muff; **5** botch, error, fluff, gaffe, inept; **6** clumsy, cockup *UK*, foozle, fumble, gauche, mishit, misuse; **7** failure, misfire, mistake, useless; **8** bumbling, misthrow, shambles, travesty;

9 maladroit, overthrow; **10** amateurish, blundering, infelicity, unskillful; **11** inattention, incompetent, mishandling, misjudgment; **12** indiscretion, tactlessness; **13** butterfingers, noncompletion; **14** misapplication; **15** thoughtlessness; PHRASES: **3, 3** bad job, off day; **3, 4** own goal *UK*; **3, 4, 5** too many cooks; **3-6** ham-fisted; **4-2** foul-up; **4, 3** faux pas, pig's ear; **4, 4** poor show; **4, 5** lost labor; **4-5, 5** wild-goose chase; **4, 6** dog's dinner; **4, 8** half measures; **4, 9** pale imitation; **5-2** balls-up *UK*; **6, 6** missed chance, wasted effort; **7, 5** dropped catch.

bunk 3 bed; **5** berth; **6** drivel, humbug; **7** garbage, rubbish; **8** nonsense; **9** couchette, gibberish; PHRASES: **6, 3** single bed.

bunkum *See* **nonsense**

buoy 3 can; **4** bell, life, spar; **5** float; **6** marker; **7** sustain; **8** breeches, maintain; PHRASES: **4, 2** hold up, prop up; **4, 6** keep afloat; **12, 3** navigational aid.

buoyant 5 happy, light, tough; **6** afloat, jaunty; **8** carefree, cheerful, flexible, floating; **9** resilient, resistant; **10** optimistic.

burble 4 gush; **6** babble, bubble, murmur, ramble, ripple, splash; **7** blather; PHRASES: **2, 2, 5** go on about.

burbot 7 eelpout.

burden 3 tax; **4** duty, load, onus, yoke; **5** cargo, debts, drain, theme, topic, worry; **6** charge, lumber *UK*, saddle, weight; **7** problem, subject, trouble; **8** encumber, handicap, mortgage; **9** albatross, liability, millstone; **10** affliction, dependants, dependents, imposition, obligation; **11** encumbrance; **14** responsibility; PHRASES: **4, 5** last straw; **4, 6** dead weight; **5, 2, 4** cross to bear; **5, 4** weigh down; **5, 8** white elephant; **6, 4** saddle with; **7, 6** subject matter.

bureau 4 desk, unit; **6** agency, office; **10** department, escritoire; PHRASES: **7, 4** writing desk; **7, 5** writing table.

bureaucrat *See* **official**

burgeon 3 bud; **5** bloom; **6** flower; **7** blossom, prosper; **8** flourish, multiply, mushroom; **11** proliferate.

burglar *See* **thief**

burgle *See* **rob**

burial 3 urn; **4** pyre, tomb; **5** grave, myrrh, vault; **6** casket, coffin, morgue, natron; **7** funeral; **8** catacomb, mortuary; **9** committal, cremation, crematory, embalming, inter-ment; **10** entombment, inhumation; **11** crematorium, sarcophagus; **12** incineration; **13** mummification; PHRASES: **2, 3** at sea; **4-5** dead-house; **5-4** mummy-case; **7, 4** funeral pile; **7, 5** charnel house.

buried 6 hidden; **7** covered, dormant, inhumed; **8** coffined, cremated, embalmed, entombed, interred, secreted; **9** concealed, forgotten, mummified, repressed *UK*, submerged; **10** suppressed; **11** underground; PHRASES: **2, 3, 5** in the grave; **3, 4, 5** six feet under; **4, 2, 4** laid to rest; **5, 6** below ground.

Burkina-Faso 5, 5 Upper Volta.

burlesque 4 mock, skit; **5** spoof; **6** parody; **7** lampoon; **8** travesty; **10** caricature; PHRASES: **4, 3, 2** make fun of.

burn 3 gut, use; **4** fire, fume, glow, hurt, sear; **5** blaze, blush, brand, color, flame, flare, scald, shine, singe, smoke, sting, torch; **6** expend, ignite, injury, kindle, redden, scorch, tingle; **7** blacken, blister, calcine, consume, crackle, cremate, smolder, twinkle; **8** overcook, vaporize; **9** carbonize, cauterize; **10** incinerate; PHRASES: **2, 1, 5** to a crisp; **2, 1, 6** to a cinder; **2, 2, 2, 6** go up in flames; **2, 2, 4** be on fire; **2, 3** go red; **2, 3, 5** at the stake; **2, 3, 6** to the ground; **2, 6** be ablaze; **3, 1, 5, 2** put a match to; **3, 2, 4** set on fire; **3, 4, 2** set fire to; **3, 6** set alight; **5, 4** catch fire; **5, 4, 6** burst into flames; **6, 2, 5** reduce to ashes.

burned 5 shale, umber; **6** almond, cooked, sienna; **8** offering. *See also* **burn**

burner 3 jet; **4** back, heat, lime, spit; **5** broil, flame, grill, stove; **6** bunsen; **7** griddle, toaster; **8** barbecue.

burning 3 hot, red; **5** vital; **6** ablaze, ardent, strong, tingly, urgent; **7** blazing, crucial, febrile, fervent, flaming, flushed, painful, prickly; **8** feverish, smarting, stinging; **9** important; **10** passionate, smoldering, sweltering; **11** significant; PHRASES: **2, 4** on fire; **3-3** red-hot; **3-9** all-consuming; **5, 3** fiery hot; **6, 3** piping hot; **7, 3** boiling hot.

burrow 3 den, dig; **4** hole, lair; **5** delve; **6** cuddle, nestle, nuzzle, search, tunnel, warren; **7** channel, snuggle; **8** excavate, hideaway, scrabble; **11** investigate; PHRASES: **3, 3** dig out; **4, 2** cozy up.

burst 4 gush, gust, rush; **5** erupt, spout, spurt; **7** rupture, torrent; **8** eruption, fracture; **12** disintegrate; PHRASES: **5, 3** break out; **5, 4** break open, split open.

bury 4 hide, keen; **5** cover, inter, mourn, plant; **6** bemoan, embalm, entomb, grieve, inhume, lament; **7** conceal, cremate, mummify, secrete; **8** eulogize, submerge; **10** incinerate; PHRASES: **3, 2, 3, 5** lay in the grave; **3, 2, 3, 6** put in the ground; **3, 2, 4** lay to rest; **3, 3** lay out; **3, 3, 2, 5** put out of sight; **3, 3, 4, 5** put six feet under; **4, 1, 7** sing a requiem; **4, 3** deep six; **4, 3, 5** toll the knell; **5, 3, 4** lower the body; **7, 2, 5** consign to earth.

bus 3 boy; **4** lane, stop; **5** carry, coach; **6** convey, travel; **7** journey, omnibus, shelter; **9** charabanc *UK*, transport; **10** trolleybus; **14** transportation; PHRASES: **6, 6** double decker, single decker.

bush 5 plant, scrub, shrub, wilds; **6** calico, cotton, native, needle; **7** burning, orchard, outback; **8** creosote, savannah; **9** bouvardia, butterfly, cranberry, scrubland; **10** gooseberry, strawberry; PHRASES: **9, 5** flowering shrub.

bush baby 6 galago.

bushpig 9 boschvark.

business 3 bid, big, hum, job; **4** firm, post, sale, show, task, work; **5** event, issue, sales, trade, wages; **6** affair, matter, merger, métier, office, sphere; **7** beehive, calling, company, concern, damages, dealing, postage, problem, salvage, selling, venture; **8** busyness, commerce, dealings, industry, interest, overhead, position, vocation, wharfage, workshop; **9** corporate, patronage, situation, ultimatum, utilities; **10** commercial, enterprise, freightage, lighterage, occupation, production, profession; **11** corporation, marketplace, partnership, transaction, undertaking; **12** conglomerate, occupational, organization, professional; **13** establishment, multinational, transnational; **14** responsibility; PHRASES: **2-2** to-do; **2, 8** no sinecure; **3-3** buy-out; **4, 2, 8** hive of activity, hive of industry; **4, 5** fair offer, firm price; **4, 6** high street; **5-2, 5** start-up costs; **5, 5** final offer, legal costs; **5, 7** heavy traffic; **6, 5** asking price; **6, 8** office supplies; **7, 5** madding crowd, running costs, special offer; **7, 7** freight charges; **8, 3** takeover bid.

buss 4 kiss.

bust 4 raid; **5** break, burst, model, smash, torso; **6** arrest, broken, figure, ruined, search, statue; **7** capture, seizure, shatter; **8** fracture; **9** apprehend, sculpture; PHRASES: **3, 2** had it; **3, 2, 5** out of order; **3, 7** not working; **4, 8** take prisoner; **6, 4** police raid.

bustle 4 stir; **5** hurry; **8** activity, movement; **9** commotion; PHRASES: **2, 2, 3, 2** be on the go; **2, 4** be busy; **4, 6** rush around; **4, 8** busy yourself.

busy 3 bee; **4** full, hard; **5** afoot, astir; **6** active, beaver, hectic, lively, tiring; **7** engaged, harried, humming; **8** bustling, diligent, employed, eventful, hustling, occupied, slogging; **9** demanding, pottering, puttering; **10** overworked; **11** industrious, unavailable; **12** overemployed; PHRASES: **2, 3, 2** on the go; **2, 3, 4** on the make, on the move, on the trot; **2, 3, 5** up and doing; **2, 4** at work; **2, 4, 5** in full swing; **2, 6** in demand; **2, 7** in harness; **4, 2, 2** hard at it; **4, 2, 4** hard at work; **4, 2, 8** full of activity; **4-7** hardworking; **5, 7** fully engaged; **5, 8** fully occupied; **6, 3, 5** coming and going.

busy (be busy) 3 hum; **6** thrive; **7** prosper; **8** progress; PHRASES: **3, 4, 4** not have time; **4, 2, 1, 5** live in a whirl; **4, 3, 3, 4** join the rat race; **4, 5** rise early; **4, 6** keep moving; **4, 8** make progress.

but 3 bar; **5** rider; **6** except; **7** however, proviso; **8** although; **9** condition, excluding, objection, provision; **12** nevertheless; PHRASES: **2, 3, 8** on the contrary; **4, 3** save for; **5, 4** other than.

butcher 4 kill, ruin; **5** botch, spoil; **6** killer, murder, slayer; **8** murderer; **9** slaughter; **11** exterminate, slaughterer; **12** exterminator; PHRASES: **4, 1, 4, 2** make a hash of, make a mess of.

butchery 7 carnage, killing; **9** bloodshed, slaughter; **14** slaughterhouse.

butt 3 end, hit, keg, ram, tub, vat; **4** base, bump, cask, drum, dupe, fool, jest, joke, stub; **5** stock, stump; **6** barrel, object, stooge, strike, target, victim; **9** cigarette, container, scapegoat; PHRASES: **4, 3** fall guy; **4, 4** easy mark, fair game; **4, 5** Aunt Sally *UK*; **5, 7** knock against; **6, 2, 3** figure of fun *UK*; **8, 3** straight man; **8, 5** laughing stock *UK*.

butter 4 bean; **6** muslin.

butterfish 6 marari; **9** greenbone.

butterfly bush 8 buddleia.

butterfly weed 8 milkweed; PHRASES: **8, 4** pleurisy root.

butternut 5, 6 white walnut.

buttocks 4 tail; **5** booty, nates; **11** callipygous.

button 3 key; 4 knob; 5 close; 6 fasten, switch; PHRASES: 2, 2 do up; 4, 6 push ~.

buttonhole 4 grab; 6 accost, corner, waylay; 8 confront.

buttress 4 prop; 7 support; 9 reinforce, structure; 10 strengthen; 13 reinforcement; PHRASES: 4, 2 prop up; 6, 8 flying ~.

buy 4 deal; 6 obtain; 7 acquire, bargain, procure; 8 purchase; 11 acquisition; PHRASES: 3, 3 pay for.

buy back 6 ransom, redeem; 10 repurchase.

buyer beware 6, 6 caveat emptor.

buying 3 COD; 7 bidding, bullish; 8 haggling, shopping; 9 investing, marketing; 10 bargaining, preemptive, purchasing, redemptive; 11 acquisitive, speculative; 12 teleshopping; PHRASES: 3, 1, 4 for a song; 3-5 cut-price UK; 4, 2, 8 cash on delivery.

buy off 5 bribe; 6 induce, square, suborn; 7 corrupt; PHRASES: 3, 3 pay off; 3, 4, 5, 2 pay hush money to.

buzz 3 hum, saw; 4 bell UK, bomb, call, high, hiss, kick, lift, news, rasp, ring UK, talk, whir, word; 5 drone, grate, noise, rumor, whine; 6 gossip, hubbub, murmur, thrill, tinkle UK; 7 whisper; 9 bombinate UK; 10 stridulate; 11 information; PHRASES: 4, 2, 5 word of mouth; 5, 4 phone call; 9, 4 telephone call.

BW 5, 3, 5 black and white.

by 3 via; 4 gone, near, past; 6 before, beside; 7 through; PHRASES: 2, 1, 6, 2 as a result of; 2, 5, 2 ~ means of; 3, 5, 4 not later than; 4, 2 next to; 6, 4 sooner than.

bye See goodbye

bygone See former

bypass 5 avoid; 8 sidestep; PHRASES: 2, 6 go around; 3, 5 get round UK.

byword 5 axiom; 6 saying, slogan; 7 epitome, proverb; 10 embodiment; PHRASES: 5, 6 catch phrase; 7, 7 perfect example, shining example.

byzantine 7 complex, devious; 8 scheming, tortuous; 9 deceitful, intricate, secretive, underhand; 10 convoluted; 11 complicated.

C

C 4 note; 5 about, circa, clubs; 6 carbon; 7 Celsius, century; 10 centigrade; PHRASES: 3, 7 one hundred.

cab 4 hack, taxi; 5 cabin; 7 cockpit, hackney, minicab *UK*, taxicab; 11 compartment; PHRASES: 4, 3 hire car; 7, 8 hackney carriage *UK*.

cabal 4 plot, unit; 5 group; 6 scheme; 7 faction, section; 9 collusion; 10 connivance, conspiracy.

cabaret 3 bar; 4 club, show; 9 burlesque, nightclub, nightspot; PHRASES: 5, 4 floor show.

cabbage 4 cole, kale.

cabin 3 hut; 4 room; 5 berth, lodge; 6 chalet; 7 cottage, cubicle; 8 bungalow; 9 stateroom; 11 compartment.

cabinet 4 case, desk, unit; 5 chest, hutch, shelf; 6 bureau, closet, drawer, fridge, lowboy; 7 armoire, cassone, commode, council, dresser, freezer, highboy, shelves, tallboy *UK*, whatnot; 8 bookcase, credenza, cupboard, wardrobe; 9 bookshelf, davenport, secretary, sideboard; 10 breakfront, canterbury *UK*, dishwasher, escritoire, secretaire; 12 refrigerator; PHRASES: 4, 4 wall unit; 4, 5 hope chest; 5, 2, 7 chest of drawers; 6, 4 fitted unit; 6, 7 double dresser, filing ~; 6, 8 corner cupboard; 7, 4 display case, kitchen unit, writing desk.

cable 2 TV; 4 cord, lead, rope, wire; 10 television; PHRASES: 2-2 co-ax.

cableway 7 gondola, telpher, wireway; 8 monorail; 9 funicular; PHRASES: 3, 3 ski tow; 3, 4 ski lift; 4, 7 wire ropeway; 5, 4 chair lift.

cache 4 hide; 5 hoard, store; 7 reserve, secrete; 10 collection; 12 accumulation.

cackle *See* **laugh**

cacophony 3 din, row; 5 Babel, noise; 6 bedlam, clamor, hubbub, racket, tumult, uproar; 7 discord, turmoil, yowling; 9 harshness, stridency; 10 disharmony, dissonance, hullabaloo; 11 discordance, pandemonium; 12 caterwauling, katzenjammer, unmusicality; PHRASES: 4, 6 cat's chorus; 4, 7 cat's concert.

cad *See* **rogue**

CAD 8 drafting, graphics.

cadaver *See* **corpse**

caddy *See* **container**

cadence 4 lilt, pace; 5 pulse, tempo; 6 accent, rhythm, stroke; 10 inflection, intonation, modulation.

cage 3 pen; 4 coop; 5 crate; 7 confine, enclose, impound; 8 birdcage; 9 enclosure; PHRASES: 4, 2 coop up.

cagebird 6 budgie, canary, parrot; 8 cockatoo, parakeet, songster; 10 budgerigar; PHRASES: 5, 4 mynah bird.

cajole 4 coax; 5 court, toady; 6 entice; 7 flatter, wheedle; 8 blandish, inveigle, persuade; PHRASES: 3, 5 get round *UK*; 4, 2, 2 make up to, suck up to *UK*; 5-4 sweet-talk; 5, 5 curry favor.

Cajun 4 okra; 5 gumbo; 6 boudin, Creole, French, zydeco; 7 Acadian, cuisine, etoufée, trinity; 8 Acadiana, chaurice, crawfish; 9 andouille, jambalaya, sassafras.

cake 3 bar, bun, mud, oil, wad; 4 barm, cube, fish, flan, loaf, lump, puff, rock, roll, salt, slab, tart; 5 angel, block, cover, donut, fancy, genoa, jelly, lardy, layer, pound, tipsy, torte; 6 cotton, Danish, dundee, eccles, éclair, gateau, johnny, marble, muffin, parkin *UK*, pastry, simnel, sinker, sponge, tablet; 7 ashcake, banbury, beignet, brownie, congeal, cruller, cupcake, encrust, fritter, madeira, pancake, strudel, wedding; 8

brownies, doughnut, flapjack, macaroon, sandwich, seedcake, turnover; **9** coagulate, fruitcake, madeleine; **10** Battenburg, cheesecake, coffeecake, ladyfinger, pontefract; **11** gingerbread; PHRASES: **3, 4** jam tart; **3, 4, 3** key lime pie; **3, 5** egg bread; **3, 8** jam doughnut; **4, 2, 8** pain au chocolat; **4, 3** Bath bun *UK*, yule log; **4, 5** barm brack *UK*; **4-6** self-rising; **5, 2, 5** maids of honor; **5, 3** apple pie, chess pie, mince pie, pecan pie; **5, 4** angel ~, fudge ~, jelly roll, lardy ~ *UK*, petit four, pound ~, spice ~, sweet roll, Swiss roll *UK*; **5, 4, 4** angel food ~, angel food ~ *UK*; **5, 6** black bottom; **5, 6, 3** sweet potato pie; **5, 6, 4** Black Forest ~; **5, 7** apple fritter, peach cobbler; **6, 4** carrot ~, coffee ~ *UK*, Dundee ~ *UK*, Eccles ~ *UK*, sponge ~; **6, 4, 4** devil's food ~; **6-4, 4** upside-down ~; **6, 5, 3** Boston cream pie; **6, 6** Danish pastry; **7, 3** Chelsea bun *UK*, coconut pie, pumpkin pie, whoopie pie; **7, 4** Madeira ~ *UK*, wedding ~; **7, 6** English muffin; **8, 4** Bakewell tart *UK*, birthday ~, cinnamon roll, doughnut hole; **9, 4** chocolate ~, Christmas ~ *UK*; **9, 6** chocolate gateau.

calcium hydroxide **6, 4** slaked lime.

calcium oxide **9** quicklime.

calculate **4** tell; **5** count, gauge, score, solve, tally; **6** assess, cipher, figure, reckon; **7** compute, foresee, measure, predict; **8** estimate, evaluate, numerate, quantify; **9** determine; **10** anticipate; **11** guesstimate; PHRASES: **4, 1, 5** keep a count; **4, 3** dope out, work out; **5, 2** notch up, weigh up *UK*; **6, 3** figure out.

calculation **3** sum; **4** sums *UK*; **6** answer, design, result; **7** algebra, control, cunning; **8** addition, analysis, calculus, division, equation, estimate, figuring, geometry, scheming, totaling; **9** algorithm, intention, inversion, logarithm, reckoning, reduction; **10** assessment, estimation, numeration, shrewdness; **11** computation, determining, deviousness, enumeration, integration, permutation, subtraction; **12** trigonometry; **13** approximation, extrapolation, interpolation; **14** multiplication, transformation; **15** differentiation.

calculative **9** actuarial, computing, numerical; **10** estimative, numerative; **11** calculating, computative, enumerative, quantifying, statistical; **13** computational, psephological.

calculator **6** abacus, teller; **7** abacist,

counter; **8** computer, pollster, reckoner; **9** estimator; **10** enumerator; PHRASES: **4, 8** cash register; **5, 4** score card; **5, 5** tally stick; **6-5** census-taker; **6, 7** adding machine; **7, 5** Napier's bones.

calculus **5** stone; **8** analysis; **10** concretion; **11** integration; **15** differentiation.

calendar **3** log, PDA; **4** Ides; **5** diary *UK*, Nones; **6** agenda; **7** Calends, program; **8** schedule; **9** Gregorian, programme *UK*, timetable *UK*; PHRASES: **3, 4** New Year; **4, 5** time table; **4, 7** year planner; **8, 7, 9** personal digital assistant; **11, 4** appointment book.

caliber **4** bore, size; **5** gauge; **6** talent; **7** ability, measure, quality; **8** capacity, diameter; **10** competence.

California **2** CA; **5** poppy (flower); **6** Eureka (I have found it) (motto); **10** Sacramento (capital); PHRASES: **6, 5** Golden State (nickname); **10, 4** C~ wren (bird); **10, 7** C~ redwood (tree).

call **3** ask, bid, cry, dub, say; **4** buzz, dial, hail, name, page, plea, ring *UK*, song, term, yell; **5** label, phone, photo, shout, sound, visit; **6** appeal, beckon, demand, gather, invite, scream, summon; **7** arrange, baptize, convene, entitle, exclaim, request, verdict; **8** assemble, birdsong, christen, decision, describe, identify, judgment, nickname, organize; **9** telephone; **10** assessment, invitation; PHRASES: **2, 2, 3** go to see; **3, 1, 5** pay a visit; **3, 2** pop in, set up; **3, 3** cry out; **4, 1, 4** give a bell *UK*, give a buzz *UK*; **4, 2** drop in, hail as, look in, look up, stop by; **4, 3** stop off; **4, 6** come around; **5, 2** phone up *UK*.

calla **4** arum.

caller **5** guest; **6** friend; **7** visitor.

callous **4** cold, dour, grim, hard; **5** cruel, gruff, harsh, rough, stern, stony, tough; **6** flinty, rugged, severe, steely; **7** austere; **8** gloating, hardened, obdurate, pitiless, ruthless, uncaring, ungentle; **9** calloused, heartless, merciless, unfeeling, unnatural; **11** hardhearted, insensitive; **13** unsympathetic; PHRASES: **4, 2, 5** hard of heart; **4-4** cold-eyed; **4-7** cold-blooded, cold-hearted; **5-7** flinthearted, stony-hearted, thick-skinned; **6-4** steely-eyed; **6-7** marble-hearted.

call together **5** rally; **6** gather, muster, summon; **7** collect, convene, convoke, marshal; **8** assemble, mobilize; PHRASES: **5, 2** round up.

calm **4** cool, ease, even, lull, mild; **5** abate,

peace, quell, quiet, still, stoic; **6** pacify, placid, serene, soothe; **7** appease, quieten *UK*, relaxed, subside, unmoved; **8** calmness, composed, coolness, detached, peaceful, serenity, stoicism, tranquil; **9** collected, composure, quietness, stillness, unruffled, unworried; **10** untroubled; **11** tranquility, unemotional, unflappable, unflustered, unperturbed; **13** dispassionate, imperturbable; PHRASES: **2, 4** at ease; **4, 4** ~ down; **4-5** sang-froid; **5, 5, 3** stiff upper lip; **6, 4** settle down; **7, 4** quieten down *UK*; **7, 7** lacking emotion.

caltrop 4, 7 star thistle; **5, 8** water chestnut.

calumet 5, 4 peace pipe.

Calvary 8 Golgotha.

camaraderie *See* **friendship**

Cambria 5 Wales.

camelopard 7 giraffe.

camera 3 box; **4** cine; **5** flash, gamma, Kodak™, movie; **7** obscura, pinhole; **8** Polaroid™; **9** camcorder; **10** Instamatic™; **11** videocamera; PHRASES: **3, 7** box Brownie; **5, 5** photo booth.

camouflage 4 hide, mask; **6** façade; **7** conceal, mimicry, obscure; **8** disguise; **11** concealment; PHRASES: **4-2** make-up; **5-2** cover-up; **5, 6** smoke screen.

camp 4 base, site, tent; **5** David, group, gulag, oflag; **6** clique, stalag; **7** cohorts, faction, meeting; **8** vacation; **9** followers; **10** encampment, supporters; PHRASES: **5, 3** sleep out.

campaign 4 push, work; **5** drive, fight; **7** canvass, crusade; **8** movement; **9** operation; **11** electioneer.

campanology 4 peal; **6** change; **8** carillon, handbell; **9** grandsire; PHRASES: **4, 7** bell ringing; **6, 7** change ringing.

campanula 8 bellwort; **10** bellflower.

camphire 5 henna.

can 3 bog, loo *UK*, may, pot, tin *UK*; **4** able, gaol, jail, john, stir; **5** billy *UK*; **6** prison, toilet, vessel; **8** bathroom; **9** destroyer; PHRASES: **2, 4** is able.

canal 3 cut; **4** duct, Erie, root, Suez, tube; **5** Grand; **6** Panama, seaway; **7** channel, passage, Welland; **8** waterway; **9** Haversian; **10** alimentary, Caledonian, Mittelland; **12** semicircular.

canary 4 bird, seed; **6** singer, yellow; **11** stoolpigeon.

cancel 3 cut; **4** kill, stop, void; **5** annul, erase, quash; **6** abjure, censor, deface, delete, efface, negate, recall, recant, reject, remove, renege, repeal, revoke, waiver; **7** abandon, abolish, destroy, expunge, nullify, rescind, retract, reverse, scratch, suspend; **8** abrogate, disallow, overrule, renounce, reprieve, withdraw; **9** eliminate, repudiate, terminate; **10** annihilate, invalidate, obliterate; **11** countermand; PHRASES: **2, 4, 4** do away with; **3, 5** set aside; **4, 3** blot out, call off, wipe out; **4, 4, 3, 4** make null and void; **5, 3** black out, cross out, scrub out, write off; **6, 3** strike out; **8, 3** scribble out.

cancel out 4 undo; **6** cancel, efface, negate, offset, refute; **7** balance, nullify; **8** equalize; **10** contradict, counteract, neutralize; **11** countermand, countervail; **12** counterorder, counterpoise, counterweigh; **14** counterbalance; PHRASES: **3, 4, 4** cut both ways; **4, 3, 6, 2** turn the tables on; **4, 4, 4** work both ways; **4, 7** work against; **5, 2, 7** weigh up against; **5, 7** weigh equally.

cancer 4 bane, crab, evil, pest; **5** tumor; **6** blight, canker, growth, menace, plague; **7** disease, sarcoma, scourge; **8** leukemia, melanoma, neoplasm; **9** carcinoma; **10** corruption, malignancy; **11** epithelioma; PHRASES: **3, 3, 1** the big C; **6, 5** benign tumor; **9, 5** cancerous tumor, malignant tumor; **9, 6** cancerous growth.

candid 4 open; **5** blunt, frank; **6** chatty, honest; **7** sincere, upfront; **8** straight, truthful; **9** outspoken, revealing; **10** forthright, indiscreet, unreserved; **11** forthcoming, informative; **13** communicative; **15** straightforward.

candidate (be a candidate) 3 run; **5** stand; PHRASES: **3, 3, 5** bid for votes; **5, 3, 4** enter the race; **5, 7** offer oneself; **7, 2, 6** contest an office; **7, 5** solicit votes.

candle-tree 3, 6 wax myrtle.

candy 4 chew, mint; **5** fudge, taffy; **6** bonbon, comfit, jujube, piñata, toffee; **7** caramel, confect, gumdrop, jimmies, praline; **8** licorice; **9** chocolate; **10** gobstopper *UK Can*, jawbreaker, peppermint; **11** marshmallow; **12** butterscotch; **13** confectionery; PHRASES: **4, 5** hard ~, rock ~; **5, 4** jelly bean; **5, 5** penny ~; **6, 5** cotton ~; **8, 7** licorice allsort; **9, 3** chocolate bar.

candy store 5, 4 sweet shop.

cane 3 hit; **4** beat; **5** staff, stick; **6** bamboo, punish, rattan, strike, thrash, wicker; PHRAS-ES: **5, 4** sword ~; **7, 5** walking stick.

cane sugar 7 sucrose.

Canicula 6 Sirius.

canine 3 cur, dog; **5** doggy, hound, pooch; **7** doggish, doglike, mongrel.

canker *See* **evil**

cannabis 3 pot; **4** blow, hash, hemp; **5** ganja.

canned 5 drunk, taped; **6** tinned *UK*; **8** recorded; **9** conserved, preserved, synthetic; **10** artificial, reproduced; **11** prerecorded.

canoe 4 waka; **5** kayak; **6** dugout, paddle.

canoeing 3 bow; **4** deck, gate, keel, seat, well; **5** kayak, stern, sweep; **6** decked, paddle, stroke, thwart; **7** cockpit, gunwale, jamming, paddled; **8** faltboat, foldboat, pushover, stopping; **9** catamaran, outrigger; **11** centerboard, watercourse; PHRASES: **1, 6** J stroke; **1-6** V-bottom; **3, 6** bow stroke; **4, 4** keel lock; **4, 6** draw stroke; **5, 6** sweep stroke; **6, 4** Eskimo roll; **6-5** double-ended; **6, 6** slalom racing; **6-6** double-bladed, single-bladed; **7, 3** shaking out; **7, 3, 5** locking the blade; **7, 6** jamming stroke; **8, 4** cruising hook; **8, 6** cruising stroke, pushover stroke, stopping stroke.

canon 4 code; **7** charter; **8** rulebook; **12** bibliography, constitution; **13** jurisprudence; PHRASES: **7, 4** statute book.

canopy 3 top; **4** roof; **5** blind, cover, crown; **6** awning; **7** shelter; **8** covering.

cant 3 tip; **4** heel; **5** bevel, lingo, slang; **6** humbug, jargon, patois; **7** blather, clichés; **8** tokenism; **9** corniness, hypocrisy, triteness; **10** banalities, platitudes, vernacular; **11** insincerity; **12** commonplaces; PHRASES: **3, 7** lip service; **4, 5** list argot.

cantaloupe 4, 5 rock melon *UK*.

canter 3 jog, run; **4** trot; **6** gallop, sprint.

canton *See* **region**

canvass 4 poll, test; **5** stump; **6** survey; **8** campaign, research; **11** electioneer, investigate; PHRASES: **4, 2, 7** drum up support; **7, 5** solicit votes.

cap 3 lid, top, wax; **4** plug, stop; **5** check, cover, crown, dutch *UK*, excel, limit, outdo, watch; **6** better, juliet, shaggy; **7** capital, ceiling, control, improve, stopper, surpass;

8 outshine, regulate, restrain, restrict; **9** restraint, threshold; **11** restriction.

capability *See* **ability**

capable 3 apt; **4** able, deft; **5** abled, ready; **6** proper, worthy; **8** skillful; **9** competent, efficient, masterful; **10** acceptable, proficient; **11** appropriate.

capacity 4 role, room, size; **5** skill, space; **6** office, talent, volume; **7** ability; **8** aptitude, function, position; **10** capability, dimensions; **14** responsibility.

cape 3 Cod; **4** Horn, ness; **5** point, Verde, Wrath; **8** headland; **9** peninsula; **10** promontory. *See also* **cloak**

caper 4 jump, lark, leap; **5** dance, jaunt; **6** antics, cavort, frolic; **8** escapade; **9** adventure.

capital 2 A1; **3** hub; **4** good, head, Lima, Riga, Rome; **5** block, funds, goods, great, money, Paris, stock, super; **6** center, wealth; **9** principal, resources; **12** headquarters.

capitalist 8 consumer, investor; **9** financier; **10** commercial, industrial; **11** consumerist; **12** entrepreneur; **13** industrialist; **14** businessperson; **15** entrepreneurial.

capital punishment 6 noyade; **7** burning, drawing, gassing, hanging, purging, stoning; **8** drowning, genocide, lynching, massacre, shooting; **9** beheading, execution, garroting, injection, martyrdom, poisoning, slaughter; **10** garrotting, impalement, lapidation; **11** crucifixion, decollation; **12** decapitation, guillotining; **13** electrocution, martyrization, strangulation; PHRASES: **3, 9** the Holocaust; **4-2-2** auto-dafé; **4, 9** mass execution; **5, 3** lynch law; **5, 7** death penalty; **5, 8** death sentence, Final Solution; **7, 5** flaying alive; **8, 5** traitor's death; **8, 6** judicial murder.

caprice 3 fad; **4** whim; **5** fancy, quirk; **6** levity, notion, whimsy; **7** faddism *UK*, impulse; **8** mischief; **9** frivolity, giddiness; **10** fickleness, fitfulness, quirkiness; **11** faddishness, flightiness, fretfulness, inconstancy, instability, pettishness, playfulness, uncertainty, variability, waywardness; **12** eccentricity, fecklessness, freakishness, irascibility, whimsicality; **13** arbitrariness, changeability, frivolousness, inconsistency, unreliability; **14** capriciousness, changeableness, coquettishness; **15** flirtatiousness; PHRASES: **4, 2, 1, 3** drop of a hat;

5-10 light-mindedness; **6, 2, 5** flight of fancy.

capricious 3 mad; **5** crazy, faddy *UK*, fluid, giddy, moody, weird; **6** chancy, fickle, fitful, mobile, quirky, random, wanton; **7** erratic, faddish, flighty, fretful, mutable, offbeat, playful, wayward, willful; **8** captious, contrary, fanciful, feckless, flexible, freakish, perverse, prankish, quixotic, skittish, unstable, variable, volatile, wavering; **9** aleatoric, arbitrary, crotchety, eccentric, fantastic, frivolous, haphazard, humorsome, impulsive, irascible, mercurial, uncertain, whimsical; **10** changeable, coquettish, hysterical, inconstant, motiveless, particular, refractory, unexpected, unreliable; **11** flirtatious, fluctuating, mischievous, purposeless; **12** inconsistent, unreasonable; **13** idiosyncratic, irresponsible, temperamental, undisciplined, unpredictable; **14** featherbrained; PHRASES: **3, 4, 3, 4** now that now this; **5-6** light-minded.

capricious (be capricious) 4 vary; **5** flirt, tease; **6** change, coquet; **9** fluctuate, vacillate; PHRASES: **4, 3, 3, 4** blow hot and cold; **4, 3, 6** chop and change, pick and choose; **4-4** flip-flop; **6, 2, 1, 4** submit to a whim; **6, 4** trifle with.

capsize 3 tip; **4** heel, list; **6** careen; **8** overturn; PHRASES: **4, 4** keel over, roll over, turn over; **4, 6** turn turtle.

capsule 3 pod; **4** case, pill, seed; **5** shell; **6** casing, tablet; **7** lozenge; **9** container.

captain 4 boss, head, lead; **5** chief; **6** leader, manage; **7** skipper; PHRASES: **4, 6** take charge.

caption 5 title; **6** footer, header, legend, slogan; **7** cutline, heading, outline, summary; **8** subtitle; **10** indication; **11** description.

captious 5 petty; **7** devious, trivial; **8** critical, pedantic; **9** confusing; **10** misleading, nitpicking; **11** bewildering; **12** disingenuous.

captivate 5 charm; **7** attract, enchant; **8** entrance; **9** fascinate.

captive 4 rapt; **6** intent; **7** hostage; **8** confined, detainee, enslaved, internee, prisoner; **9** attentive; **10** fascinated, imprisoned, spellbound; PHRASES: **2, 6** in prison; **6, 2** locked up; **8, 2, 3** prisoner of war.

captivity *See* **imprisonment**

capture 4 gain, take, trap; **5** catch, seize; **6** arrest, attain, detain, obtain, secure; **7** acquire, confine, ensnare, portray, seizure; **8** describe, imprison; **9** apprehend, detention, summarize; **11** encapsulate; **12** apprehension, imprisonment; PHRASES: **3, 2** sum up; **4, 2** pick up; **4, 4, 2** grab hold of.

car 2 GT; **3** bus, Jag; **4** auto, bomb, Fiat, Ford, heap, limo, Mini, Seat; **5** buggy, cabin, coach, coupe, coupé *UK*, crate, motor *UK*, Rolls, sedan, wagon; **6** banger *UK*, estate, jalopy, ragtop, saloon *UK*, tourer, wheels *UK*; **7** compact, flatcar, gondola, minivan, Pullman, racecar, railcar, sleeper, vehicle; **8** carborne, carriage, dragster, motorcar, roadster, runabout; **9** couchette, hatchback, hoppercar, limousine, mailcoach; **10** automobile, pimpmobile, rattletrap; **11** convertible; PHRASES: **3, 3** hot rod; **3, 5** low rider; **3, 6** tin lizzie; **3-6** low-loader *UK*, off-roader; **4-2-4** four-by-four; **4, 5** tank wagon; **5, 3** stock ~; **5-4, 5** fixed-head coupé; **5, 5** stick shift; **5-7** three-wheeler; **6, 3** guard's van *UK*, muscle ~; **6, 7** people carrier *UK*; **7, 4** stretch limo; **7, 5** station wagon; **7, 8** railway carriage *UK*.

caracal 4 lynx; PHRASES: **6, 4** desert lynx.

caravan 5 group; **6** column, convoy, parade; **9** cavalcade, motorcade; **10** procession; PHRASES: **4, 5** line fleet.

carbohydrate 5 sugar; **6** aldose, hexose, ketose, octose, starch, triose; **7** heptose, pentose, tetrose; **8** furanose, glycerin, glycerol, inositol, mannitol, pyranose, sorbitol; **9** cellulose, digitalin, glucoside, glycoside, hemiketal; **10** saccharide; **12** disaccharide; **14** monosaccharide.

carbuncle *See* **spot**

carcass *See* **corpse**

card 1 A, J, K, Q; **2** ID; **3** ace, wag; **4** club, cove, jack, king, pass, show, vote; **5** deuce, heart, joker, queen, spade, tarot, trump; **6** ticket; **7** diamond; **8** postcard.

card games 3 bid, cut, fit, loo, pan, pot, rum, run; **4** acol, ante, brag, call, cull, deal, deck, fold, game, hand, hold, jass, klob, lead, pack, pair, pass, ruff, shoe, slam, snap, spit, trey, vint, void; **5** alert, bingo, boure, cards, cinch, comet, darda, dummy, entry, flush, guard, honor, limit, omber, ombre, pedro, pitch, poker, poque, prial, raise, rebid, rummy, samba, stack, table, whist, yukon; **6** banker, boston, bridge, casino, chemmy, double, écarté, eights, euchre, gaigel, gerber, julepe, kicker, length, misfit, piquet, pochen, pokino, quinze, revoke, rubber, sevens *UK*, smudge, system, tenace, timing, trumps, yablon; **7** auction, authors, belotte, bezique, bolivia, canasta, colonel, control, cooncan, discard, finesse, misdeal, partner, pontoon, primera, primero *UK*, shuffle, signals, snooker, solomon, spinado, stayman, stopper, triumph; **8** canfield, conquian, contract, cribbage, declarer, director, imperial, klondike, mckenney, napoleon, oklahoma, overcall, patience, pinochle, redouble, response, rockaway, rollover, slapjack, straight, underbid, wildcard; **9** blackjack, blackwood *UK*, doubleton, lavinthal, sacrifice, singleton, solitaire; **10** convention, panguingue, tablanette, undertrick, vulnerable, wellington, Yarborough; **11** klabberjass, partnership; **12** distribution, intervention; **13** communication, concentration; PHRASES: **2, 3** no bid; **2-7** in-between; **3, 3** one eye, red dog; **3-3** boo-ray, fan-tan, mau-mau; **3, 4** cue bids, old maid; **3-4** set-back; **3, 4, 6** old man's bundle; **3, 5** gin rummy, low pitch; **3-5** ace-deuce; **3-6, 4** two-suited hand; **4, 2, 1, 4** four of a kind; **4, 2, 4** line of play; **4, 3** jump bid; **4, 4** face card, over ruff, side suit; **4, 4, 3** five card loo; **4, 4, 4** dead man's hand; **4, 5** draw poker, full house, open poker, over trick, part score, solo whist *UK*, stud poker, wild jacks; **4, 6** draw casino; **4, 7** five hundred; **4, 8** jump overcall; **4-8** semi-balanced; **5-2** seven-up; **5, 2, 1, 4** three of a kind; **5, 2, 4** third in hand; **5, 3** Irish loo, limit bid, sixty six; **5, 3, 3** catch the ten; **5, 3, 6** spite and malice; **5, 4** court card, forty five, grand slam, major suit, minor suit, small slam, spoil five; **5, 4, 5** grand slam force; **5, 5** joker pitch, pishe pasha, royal flush, under trick; **5, 6** crazy eights, match points, royal casino, spade casino; **5-6, 4** three-suited hand; **6, 2, 3** chemin de fer; **6, 2, 4** fourth in hand; **6, 3** thirty one; **6, 3-3** domino fan-tan; **6, 3, 6** around the corner, banker and broker; **6, 4** piquet pack, thirty five; **6, 5** boston whist, bridge whist, closed poker, double dummy, double rummy, German whist, humbug whist, racing demon, scotch whist; **6, 8** french pinochle; **7, 3** forcing bid, reverse bid; **7, 4** canasta deck, opening lead, picture card, playing card, Russian bank; **7, 5** auction pitch, bidding space, playing trick, running flush, swedish rummy; **7, 6** auction bridge; **7, 7** Chinese bezique, rubicon bezique; **7, 8** auction pinochle; **8, 3** slippery sam; **8, 4** balanced hand, biddable suit; **8, 5** straight poker, touching suits; **8, 6** baccarat banque, contract bridge; **9, 5** racehorse pitch; **9, 6** duplicate bridge, hollywood eights; **10, 3** preemptive bid; **10, 4** rebiddable suit; **11, 3** competitive bid, destructive bid; **12, 3** constructive bid, invitational bid.

cardinal **1** E, N, S, W; **2** HE; **3** Sin; **4** core; **5** basic, chief, prime; **6** number; **7** central, serious, virtues; **9** essential, important, principal; **11** fundamental; PHRASES: **4, 3** Hume key.

cardiovascular disease **4** clot; **6** angina, stroke; **7** dyspnea; **8** aneurysm, atheroma, carditis, coronary, embolism; **9** arteritis, phlebitis; **10** arrhythmia, infarction, thrombosis, vulvulitis; **11** hypotension, myocarditis, palpitation, tachycardia; **12** brachycardia, endocarditis, hypertension, pericarditis; PHRASES: **4, 5** weak heart; **5, 4** blood clot; **5-4** chest-pain; **5-5** chestspasm; **5, 6** heart attack; **5, 7** heart disease, heart failure, heart trouble; **5, 8** blood pressure; **5, 9** heart condition; **6-4** breast-pang; **6, 8** angina pectoris, mitral stenosis; **7, 6** cardiac arrest; **8, 5** athlete's heart, enlarged heart, varicose veins; **8, 6** valvular lesion; **8, 7** vascular disease; **9, 6** galloping rhythm.

care **5** worry; **6** repair, unease, upkeep; **7** anxiety, caution, concern, custody, support, trouble; **8** overhaul; **9** attention, provision, treatment; **10** precaution, protection; **11** carefulness *UK*, maintenance, supervision; **12** guardianship, watchfulness; PHRASES: **2, 9** be concerned; **2, 10** be interested; **4, 1, 7** feel a concern; **5, 7** child support.

career **3** job; **4** dash, race, rush; **5** hurry, speed; **7** calling; **8** vocation; **10** occupation, profession.

care for **4** like, love, mind, tend, want; **5** check, fancy *UK*, guard, nurse; **6** desire; **7** cherish, oversee; **8** chaperon; **9** safeguard, supervise; **10** appreciate; PHRASES: **2, 4, 2** be fond of; **3, 2** see to; **4, 2, 3, 2** keep an eye on; **4-3** baby-sit; **4, 3, 3** look out for; **4, 4, 2** keep tabs on, take care of; **4, 5** look after; **4, 6, 2** take charge of; **5, 4** watch over; **5, 5** stand guard; **6, 2** attend to.

carefree **6** blithe, cheery; **7** relaxed; **8** cheerful; **9** easygoing, unworried; **10** untroubled; **12** lighthearted; PHRASES: **5-2-5** happy-go-lucky.

careful **4** neat, nice, tidy, wary, wise; **5** alert, cagey, canny, chary, exact, faddy *UK*, fussy, ready; **6** caring, gentle, shrewd, tender; **7** finicky, guarded, heedful, mindful, orderly, perfect, politic, precise, prudent; **8** cautious, detailed, diligent, discreet, doubtful, gingerly, guarding, pedantic, prepared, reticent, sensible, thorough, vigilant, watchful, watching; **9** assiduous, attentive, judicious, observant, provident, sensitive, tentative; **10** fastidious, meticulous, particular, pernickety *UK*, protective, scrupulous, suspicious; **11** circumspect, painstaking, persnickety, punctilious, sympathetic; **12** anticipatory, conservative; **13** conscientious, perfectionist, unadventurous; PHRASES: **2, 5** on guard; **4, 5** wide awake; **4, 7-3** well thought-out.

careful (be careful) 4 heed, mind; **5** watch; **7** prepare; PHRASES: **3, 9** pay attention; **4, 2, 9** walk on eggshells; **5, 6** tread warily; **5, 9** tread carefully.

carefulness 4 care, heed; **5** sense; **6** wisdom; **7** caution; **8** judgment, prudence, scrutiny; **9** assiduity, attention, diligence, precision, suspicion, vigilance; **11** application; **12** surveillance; **13** concentration; **14** circumspection; PHRASES: **6, 5** common sense. *See also* **careful**

careless 3 lax; **4** rash; **5** dizzy, hasty, loose, slack; **6** amoral, casual, remiss, sloppy; **7** flighty, inexact, offhand; **8** cavalier, heedless, reckless, slapdash, slipshod, uncaring; **9** impetuous, imprecise, impulsive, negligent; **10** inaccurate, incautious, neglectful, unthinking; **11** inattentive, insensitive, precipitous, promiscuous, thoughtless, unconcerned; **12** disregarding; **13** inconsiderate, irresponsible, lackadaisical, unsympathetic; PHRASES: **3-2-4** hit-or-miss; **4-4** slam-bang; **5-2-5** happy-go-lucky; **5-3-4** devil-may-care; **7, 1, 5** without a worry.

caress 3 hug, pat; **5** touch; **6** cuddle, stroke; **7** embrace.

cargo 4 load, mail; **5** goods; **7** baggage, freight, luggage, payload; **8** contents, shipment; **11** consignment.

caricature 3 ape; **4** skit; **6** parody, satire, sendup, sketch; **7** cartoon, distort, drawing, lampoon, picture; **8** satirize, travesty; **10** distortion; **12** exaggeration, misrepresent.

caricaturist *See* **artist**

caring 6 tender.

caring person 5 carer, nurse; **6** doctor; PHRASES: **6, 6** social worker.

carnage 7 killing; **8** massacre; **9** bloodbath, bloodshed, slaughter.

carnal 4 lewd, sexy; **5** lusty; **6** erotic; **7** fleshly; **9** lecherous, lickerish; **10** libidinous; **12** concupiscent.

carnauba 3 wax.

carnival 4 gala; **6** bazaar; **8** festival.

carnivorous 10 omophagous; **11** creophagous; **13** cannibalistic; **14** ichthyophagous; **15** anthropophagous; PHRASES: **4-6** meat-eating; **5-6** flesh-eating.

carol 4 hymn, noel, sing; **6** chorus.

carom 6 bounce, cannon; **7** rebound; **9** billiards; PHRASES: **6, 9** French billiards.

carousel 4 drum, rack, ride; **6** holder; **8** magazine; **9** container; **10** receptacle, roundabout *UK*; PHRASES: **5-2-5** merry-go-round.

carp 3 bug, ide, nag; **4** beef, crab, fish, moan; **5** cavil, gripe, knock, whine; **6** grouse, hassle, niggle, object, pester; **7** grumble, quibble; **8** complain, derogate; **9** criticize; PHRASES: **2, 2** go on; **3-4** nit-pick; **4, 5** find fault, pick holes; **5, 5** split hairs.

carpenter 3 cog, cut, rip, saw; **4** bore, lath, post, sand, slat, trim; **5** board, drill, frame, joist, lathe, miter, panel, plane, plank, screw, shape, sheet, strut, tenon, truss; **6** carver, chippy, chisel, cooper, joiner, lumber, sawyer, timber, turner; **7** chippie, mortise, shingle; **8** crosscut, dovetail, ébéniste; **10** marqueteur, woodcarver, woodcutter; **11** wheelwright; **12** coachbuilder *UK*; **13** Formschneider, woodcraftsman; PHRASES: **3, 1, 4** fit a beam; **7-5** cabinet-maker; **9-5** furniture-maker.

carpenter's term 4 stud; **5** bevel, joint, joist, strut, tenon, truss; **7** cogging, framing, mortise; **8** studwork, trimming; **9** strutting; **11** dovetailing; PHRASES: **3, 5** lap joint; **4-4, 5** king-post truss; **4, 5** fish joint; **4, 5, 5** tusk tenon joint; **5-4, 5** queen-post truss; **5, 5** mitre joint, scarf joint; **6, 5** housed joint, timber joint; **7, 5** trimmed joist; **8, 5** flitched joint; **10, 5** birdsmouth joint.

carpet 3 mat, rug, wig; **4** coat, mass, moth, plot; **5** cover, layer, strew; **6** spread, swathe; **7** blanket, overlay; **8** covering, flooring; **9** carpeting; PHRASES: **5, 8** floor covering; **6, 5** ~ tiles.

carrageen 5, 4 Irish moss.

carriage 3 air, cab, gig; **4** gait, line, pose; **5** poise, trade; **6** stance; **7** bearing, haulage, posture; **8** attitude, carrying, delivery, presence, shipment; **10** conveyance, deportment; **11** comportment; **14** transportation.

carrier 3 bag *UK*; **5** mover; **6** carter, hauler; **7** airline, shipper, shopper *UK*; **8** exporter, importer; **11** transferrer, transporter; PHRASES: **4, 4** roof rack *UK Can*; **7, 4** luggage rack; **8, 3** shopping bag; **8, 5** shipping agent *UK*; **8, 7** delivery service.

carry 3 lug; **4** bear, cart, have, hold, keep, move, pass, take, tote; **5** agree, bring, relay, stock, store; **6** accept, clutch, convey, supply; **7** approve, conduct, contain, forward, include, involve, support, sustain, through; **8** transfer, transmit; **9** transport; **11** incorporate; PHRASES: **4, 2** pass on; **4, 2, 5** have in stock; **4, 3** vote for.

carry on 3 nag; **4** carp, keep, last, moan, rage, wage; **5** flirt; **6** witter *UK*; **7** conduct, execute, grumble, perform, persist; **8** complain, continue, practice; **9** persevere, prosecute, undertake; PHRASES: **2, 2** go on; **4, 2** keep at, keep on; **4, 5** keep going.

cart 3 lug, van; **4** boot, drag, draw, dray, haul, wain; **5** carry, dolly, heave, lorry *UK*, truck, wagon; **6** barrow *UK*; **7** pushcar, trolley *UK Can*, tumbrel; **8** handcart, pushcart; **10** handbarrow; **11** wheelbarrow; PHRASES: **8, 4** shopping ~.

carton 3 box; **4** pack; **6** sachet; **9** container; PHRASES: **9, 3** cardboard box.

cartoon 7 drawing, picture; **9** animation; **10** caricature; PHRASES: **5, 5** comic strip; **8, 5** animated movie.

cartridge 4 clip, unit; **5** blank, shell; **6** bullet, casing, holder, pickup; **8** cassette, magazine; **9** container.

cartwheel *See* **turn**

carve 3 cut; **4** etch, pare; **5** notch, slice; **7** engrave, whittle; **8** inscribe; PHRASES: **3, 2** cut up; **3, 2, 6** cut in slices.

carving 5 model; **6** figure, statue; **7** cutting, etching; **8** artifact; **9** engraving, sculpting, statuette; **10** fashioning.

cascade 4 drop, fall, flow, gush, pour; **5** chute, falls, force *UK*; **8** cataract; **9** waterfall.

case 3 abl, acc, bag, box, cot, dat, gen *UK*, job, nom, voc; **4** item, suit, task, test; **5** basis, cover, crate, event, issue; **6** basket, casing, dative, folder, holder, reason; **7** attaché, defense, example, lawsuit, problem, project, Wardian; **8** ablative, argu-ment, dispatch, dressing, genitive, incident, instance, locative, occasion, paradigm, suitcase, vocative; **9** briefcase, carrycase, container, rationale, situation; **10** accusative, assignment, commission, indictment, litigation, nominative; **12** circumstance, illustration; **13** justification; PHRASES: **5, 6** legal action.

casement 6 window.

cash 4 bill, coin, dosh *UK*, gelt, gold, jack, loot, note, pelf, swag; **5** brass, bread, dough, gravy, green, lolly *UK*, lucre, money; **6** boodle, change, mammon, moolah, silver, wampum; **7** coinage, coppers, readies *UK*, shekels; **8** currency; **9** spondulix; **10** greenstuff; PHRASES: **3, 5** the ready; **4, 2, 3, 4** root of all evil; **4, 3** palm oil; **4, 6** palm grease; **4, 10** dead presidents; **5, 5** ready money; **6, 5** filthy lucre; **7, 5** folding green, folding money.

cashew 6 acajou.

cashier 5 clerk, expel; **6** banker, bursar, teller; **7** dismiss; **8** official; **9** assistant, treasurer; PHRASES: **4, 3** boot out, drum out; **4, 5** bank clerk; **5, 7** court martial *UK*.

casing 3 box, pod; **4** bark, case, coat, hull, husk, peel, rind, skin; **5** chaff, crate, shell, shuck; **6** jacket, sheath, sleeve; **7** capsule, outside, tegumen; **8** carapace, cornhusk, covering, eggshell, exterior, nutshell; **10** integument.

casket 6 coffin. *See also* **box**

cassava 6 manioc.

cassette 4 tape; **9** cartridge, videotape.

cast 3 lob, set; **4** form, hurl, mold, molt, shed, toss; **5** breed, chuck, fling, found, heave, model, pitch, shape, sling, throw; **6** actors, chorus, create, slough, troupe; **7** company, players, produce; **8** ensemble; **10** characters, performers; PHRASES: **4, 4, 4** shed one's skin; **5, 2, 6** corps de ballet.

caste *See* **class**

castigate 5 scold; **6** rebuke; **8** chastise; PHRASES: **9** criticize, reprimand.

cast-iron 4 firm, sure; **5** fixed, rigid; **8** definite; **9** immutable; **10** guaranteed, inflexible, watertight; **12** unchangeable.

castor 6 beaver.

Castor and Pollux 6 Gemini; **8** Dioscuri.

castrate 3 fix; **4** geld, spay; **6** neuter; **9** sterilize; **10** emasculate.

casual 4 idle; 5 blasé; 6 chance; 7 offhand, relaxed; 8 familiar; 10 nonchalant.

cat 3 gib, kit, mog *UK*, rex, rig, tom; 4 boat, lion, lynx, manx, puma *UK*, puss; 5 cream, irman, kitty, moggy *UK*, pussy, queen, smoke, tabby, tiger; 6 bobcat, feline, havana, jaguar, kitten, litter, malkin *UK*, mouser, ocelot, ratter; 7 burglar, Burmese, cheetah, leopard, panther, Persian, scanner, Siamese, spotted, Turkish, wildcat; 8 pussycat; 9 grimalkin; 10 Abyssinian, chinchilla; 13 tortoiseshell; PHRASES: 3, 4 red self; 3, 5 red tabby; 3-5, 7 red-point Siamese; 3, 10 red Abyssinian; 4, 5 blue cream; 4, 7 blue Burmese; 5, 3 Devon rex; 5, 4 Maine coon; 5, 5 brown tabby; 5, 7 brown Burmese; 6, 5 silver tabby; 7, 3 Cornish rex, Maltese ~; 7, 4 British blue, Russian blue *UK*; 8, 3 Egyptian mau; 8, 4 mountain lion; 8, 5 chestnut brown; 9, 3 Himalayan ~.

cataclysm 7 debacle, tragedy; 8 calamity, disaster, upheaval; 11 catastrophe, devastation.

catalog 3 log; 4 file, list; 5 index, table; 6 detail, digest, litany, parade, record, series, string; 7 arrange, compile, include, itemize, listing; 8 assemble, classify, document, quantify, register, sequence; 9 directory, enumerate, gazetteer, inventory; 10 categorize, collection, compendium; PHRASES: 3, 3 set out; 4, 1, 4 make a list.

catalyst 5 agent; 6 enzyme; 9 influence, substrate; 11 accelerator.

cataract *See* **waterfall**

catastrophe 4 doom, ruin; 6 fiasco; 10 misfortune. *See also* **cataclysm**

catcall 3 boo, mew; 4 hiss, hoot, jeer, meow *UK*; 5 miaou, scorn, shout, taunt; 6 deride, insult; 7 mockery, whistle; 8 derision; 9 disparage, raspberry; PHRASES: 5, 5 Bronx cheer.

catch 3 bag, cop, get, hit, nab, net, pit, see; 4 bump, clip, crop, find, grab, hear, hold, hook, nick *UK*, snag, spot, take; 5 clasp, cling, grasp, hitch, knock, latch, seize, snare, snarl, stick; 6 arrest, clutch, detain, entrap, gather, notice, phrase, strike, tangle; 7 capture, ensnare, problem, receive; 8 contract, discover, drawback, entangle, fastener, obstacle, perceive, surprise; 9 apprehend, fastening; 10 difficulty, impediment, understand; PHRASES: 2, 4, 4 go down with *UK*; 3, 7, 2 get trapped in; 4, 2 pick up;

4, 2, 2 hold on to; 4, 4 bump into; 4, 4, 2 fall prey to, grab hold of; 4, 4, 4 come down with; 4, 6, 2 fall victim to; 4, 7 take captive, take hostage; 4, 8 take prisoner; 5, 3, 4 break out with; 6, 5, 2 become aware of; 6, 8 become infected.

catchword 3 saw, tag; 5 adage, jingo, maxim, moral, motto, quote; 6 byword, cliché, slogan; 7 proverb; 9 quotation, watchword; 11 catchphrase; PHRASES: 4, 4 buzz word; 4-4, 6 well-worn phrase; 5, 4 vogue word.

catechism 5 dogma, tenet; 6 mantra; 9 dialectic; 11 examination, questioning; 13 interrogation; PHRASES: 5, 4 party line.

categorical 4 firm; 8 definite, positive; 9 taxonomic; 11 taxonomical, unqualified; 13 unconditional; 14 classificatory, uncompromising; PHRASES: 5-3 clear-cut.

categorize 3 tag; 4 file, list, rank, rate, seed, sift, sort; 5 class, grade, group, index, label, place, sieve; 6 assort, codify, digest, divide, record, screen, select; 7 analyze, catalog *UK*, process, program; 8 classify, organize, register, stratify, tabulate; 9 catalogue *UK*, inventory; 10 pigeonhole, taxonomize; 11 alphabetize; PHRASES: 3, 2, 5 put in order; 4, 3 sift out, sort out.

category 3 set; 4 head, kind, rank, slot, sort, type; 5 class, genus, grade, group, level, niche, order, place; 6 family, status; 7 bracket, heading, section; 8 division, grouping, position, subclass, subgroup, suborder; 9 hierarchy; 10 department, pigeonhole; 11 compartment, subcategory, subdivision; 14 classification.

cater 5 serve; 6 outfit, supply; 7 furnish, gratify, provide; 11 accommodate; PHRASES: 4, 9 make provision.

caterer 4 chef, cook, host; 7 alewife, steward; 8 hotelier, landlady, landlord, licensee, publican, purveyor; 9 homemaker, housewife, innkeeper; 10 headwaiter, pastrycook; 11 hotelkeeper, housekeeper; 12 confectioner, restaurateur; PHRASES: 4, 4 mine host; 4, 7 hash slinger; 5, 7 hotel manager; 6, 6 maître d'hôtel.

catfish 8 wolffish.

cathartic 7 intense; 9 cleansing, emotional, excretory, expulsive, purgative, purifying, releasing; 10 liberating; 11 therapeutic.

Cathay 5 China.

Catholic 2 RC.

cathouse 7 brothel.

catkin 5 ament; PHRASES: **4-4** cat's-tail.

cat's-tail 6 catkin; PHRASES: **4, 4** reed mace.

cattle 4 cows, herd, kine, oxen; **5** Angus, Devon, Kerry, luing; **6** Brahma, dexter, Durham, Jersey, Sussex; **7** beefalo, Brahman, brangus, cattalo, criollo; **8** Alderney, Ayrshire *UK*, Galloway *UK*, Guernsey, Hereford, highland, Holstein, Limousin, longhorn; **9** Charolais, shorthorn, simmental; **11** marchigiana; **13** droughtmaster; PHRASES: **3, 4** Red Poll; **5, 5** Black Angus, brown Swiss, Brown Swiss, Welsh black; **5, 8** Texas longhorn; **5, 9** Santa Gertrudis; **6, 4** Murray gray; **7, 3** Lincoln red; **7, 4** Jamaica hope; **8, 5** Aberdeen Angus.

caucus 4 bloc; **5** union; **6** league; **7** faction; **8** alliance, assembly, conclave; **9** committee; **10** conference, convention.

caulk *See* **waterproof**

causal 5 basic; **6** primal; **7** central, crucial, genetic, pivotal, primary, radical, seminal, telling, weighty; **8** agential, creative, decisive, defended, germinal, maieutic, original, powerful; **9** causative, effective, effectual, elemental, embryonic, formative, impelling, inceptive, inspiring, intrinsic, inventive, primitive; **10** aboriginal, answerable, compelling, connecting, elementary, generative, initiatory, pressuring, primordial, productive, suggestive, underlying; **11** blameworthy, determinant, etiological, explanatory, fundamental, influential, interfering, intervening, responsible, rudimentary, significant; **12** contributing, contributory, foundational, instrumental; **13** inspirational; **14** intercessional, interventional; PHRASES: **2, 3, 6, 2** at the bottom of; **6, 3, 6** behind the scenes.

causality 4 fate; **5** karma; **7** destiny; **9** causation; **10** connection; **11** determinism; **13** causativeness, connectedness; **15** interconnection; PHRASES: **5, 3, 6** cause and effect.

causation 6 action; **9** causality; **10** connection; **12** relationship; **15** interconnection.

cause 3 let; **4** make, root; **5** basis, beget, begin, force, raise, spark, wreak; **6** author, create, derive, effect, father, invent, origin, prompt, reason, source; **7** grounds, produce, trigger; **8** creation, etiology, generate,

initiate, occasion; **9** causality, causation, cultivate, evocation, impulsion, instigate, invention, originate, propagate; **10** authorship, derivation, effectuate, foundation, generation, initiation, motivation, production, temptation; **11** attribution, cultivation, determinant, fomentation, inspiration, instigation, origination, precipitate, propagation, provocation, stimulation; **13** encouragement; PHRASES: **3, 3** set off; **4, 2** lead to; **4, 4, 2** give rise to; **4, 6** make happen; **5, 2, 4** bring to pass; **5, 3** bring off; **5, 4, 5** bring into being; **5, 5** bring about; **6, 2** result in.

causeless 7 unmeant; **8** uncaused; **9** unplanned; **10** groundless, undesigned, unintended; **11** inadvertent, unmotivated; **12** inexplicable; **13** unaccountable, unexplainable, unintentional; **14** unpremeditated.

caustic 4 acid; **6** acidic; **7** burning, cutting, mordant; **8** scathing; **9** corroding, corrosive, sarcastic; **10** astringent.

caution 4 care, heed, warn; **5** alert, doubt; **6** advise, caveat, notify, signal, wisdom; **7** warning; **8** admonish, forewarn, prudence, slowness, wariness; **9** alertness, attention, chariness, foresight, hesitance, hesitancy, reprimand, restraint, reticence, suspicion, ultimatum, vigilance; **10** admonition, discretion, hesitation, protection, providence, reluctance, skepticism; **11** carefulness *UK*, forethought, guardedness, heedfulness; **12** deliberation, notification, watchfulness; **13** attentiveness, consideration, judiciousness, tentativeness; **14** circumspection, thoughtfulness; PHRASES: **4, 6** give notice; **4, 9** risk avoidance; **7, 4** waiting game.

cautious 3 shy; **4** slow, wary; **5** alert, cagey, canny, chary, leery; **6** frugal, modest; **7** bashful, careful, guarded, heedful, mindful, nervous, politic, prudent, skeptic, thrifty; **8** discreet, doubtful, gingerly, hesitant, lukewarm, reticent, shirking, vigilant, watchful; **9** judicious, reluctant, secretive, shrinking, tentative, unzealous; **10** economical, restrained, suspicious, thoughtful; **11** circumspect, precautious; **12** anticipatory, conservative, experimental; **13** unadventurous, uncooperative; **14** unenthusiastic; PHRASES: **2, 3, 4, 4** on the safe side; **2, 4, 5** on one's guard; **4-7** half-hearted.

cautious (be cautious) 4 save; **5** doubt, hedge; **6** beware; **7** suspect; **8** hesitate; **9** economize, pussyfoot; **10** anticipate;

PHRASES: **4, 2, 3, 2** keep an eye on; **4, 2, 4** take it easy; **4, 2, 5** take no risks; **4, 3** look out; **4, 4** hang back, hold back, make sure, play safe, take care; **4, 4, 3** feel one's way; **4, 5** look twice; **4, 7** make certain; **5, 2, 3** count to ten; **5, 3, 4** count the cost; **5, 4, 4** hedge one's bets, watch one's step; **5, 5** think twice; **5, 7** cover oneself.

cautious person 7 doubter, killjoy, skeptic; **9** hesitator; **10** spoilsport.

cavalcade *See* **procession**

cavalier 7 offhand; **8** arrogant, careless; **13** inconsiderate; PHRASES: **4-6** high-handed.

cavalry 5 horse; **6** sabers; **7** charger; **8** destrier, warhorse, yeomanry; PHRASES: **5, 5** light horse; **5, 8** horse regiment, horse soldiers; **5, 9** horse artillery; **7, 6** mounted police, mounted rifles, mounted troops; **7, 8** mounted infantry.

cavalryman 5 rider, sowar, spahi *UK*, uhlan; **6** hussar, knight, lancer, yeoman; **7** Cossack, dragoon, trooper; **8** cameleer, cavalier, chivalry, horseman; **9** Ironsides *UK*; **10** cuirassier; PHRASES: **3-2-4** man-at-arms; **5-5** rough-rider; **5, 7** heavy dragoon, horse soldier, light dragoon; **7, 7** mounted soldier.

cavernous 4 vast; **5** empty; **6** gaping.

cavil *See* **quibble**

cavity 3 cup, gap, sac; **4** bowl, dent, foss, hole, nook, void; **5** cleft, crack, niche, space; **6** alcove, cranny, crater, dimple, hollow, recess, socket, trough; **7** fissure, opening.

CB 5 radio.

cease 3 die, end, jam; **4** drop, fold, halt, quit, stop; **5** stall, stick; **6** desist, finish; **8** abrogate, conclude; **9** disappear, terminate; PHRASES: **3, 2** let up; **3, 3** die off, run out; **3, 3, 2, 3** run out of gas; **3, 4** die away, die down, run down; **4, 2** draw up, fold up, give in, give up; **4, 2, 1, 3** call it a day; **4, 2, 1, 4** come to a halt, come to a stop; **4, 2, 1, 5** come to a close; **4, 2, 2, 3** come to an end; **4, 2, 5** call it quits; **4, 3** fade out, tail off; **4, 4** blow over, fade away, give over *UK*, shut down, stop dead; **4, 5** stop short; **5, 2, 1, 4** grind to a halt; **5, 3** break off, leave off, peter out; **5, 4** break down; **5, 6** admit defeat.

cease (cause to cease) 3 end, jam; **4** halt, hold, kill, sack, stay, stem, stop; **5** abort, annul, block, brake, catch, check,

scrap; **6** arrest, cancel, defeat, finish, freeze, hinder, murder, scotch, thwart; **7** dismiss, exhaust, scratch; **8** restrain; **9** checkmate, interrupt, stalemate, terminate; **10** disconnect, guillotine, relinquish; **11** discontinue; PHRASES: **3, 1, 4, 2** put a stop to; **3, 2** use up; **3, 2, 3, 2** put an end to; **3, 3** cut off, lay off, see off; **3, 3, 3, 2** put the lid on; **3, 4, 2** put paid to; **3, 5** cut short; **4, 1, 4** call a halt; **4, 2** hold up, pull up, shut up; **4, 3** call off, kill off; **4, 3, 4, 2** pull the plug on; **4, 4** shut down; **4, 9** make redundant; **5, 2, 2, 3** bring to an end; **5, 3** break off; **5, 4** close down; **6, 3** finish off, polish off; **7, 2** dispose of; **9, 2, 4** close/shut up shop.

cede *See* **yield**

ceiling *See* **limit**

celebrate 4 fete, hail, keep, laud, mark; **5** adore, exalt, extol, honor, party, revel; **6** junket, praise, revere; **7** acclaim, applaud, commend, dignify, glorify, magnify, observe, rejoice; **8** minister, remember, venerate; **9** merrymake, officiate; **10** felicitate, propitiate; **11** commemorate; PHRASES: **4, 1, 4, 4** have a good time; **4, 3** have fun; **4, 3, 4, 3** push the boat out *UK*; **4, 5** make merry.

celebration 2 do; **4** fair *UK*, fete, gala, mass, orgy, rage, rave; **5** beano, binge, feast, festa, party, revel; **6** bender, fiesta, gaiety, picnic, salute; **7** banquet, debauch, holiday, jollity, jubilee, revelry, service, Whoopee; **8** carnival, carousal, festival, function, jamboree, memorial, occasion; **9** beanfeast *UK*, festivity, merriment, rejoicing; **10** jubilation, observance, salutation, saturnalia; **11** celebrating, festivities, merrymaking, Oktoberfest, performance, quinceañera, remembrance; **12** conviviality; **13** commemoration, jollification; PHRASES: **4-3** blow-out; **5, 4** Mardi Gras; **7, 8** festive occasion.

celebrative 3 gay; **5** jolly, merry; **7** festive; **9** convivial, rejoicing; **11** celebratory.

celebrity 4 fame, name, star; **6** figure, renown; **9** notoriety, superstar; **10** prominence; **11** personality; **12** superstardom.

celerity *See* **speed**

celestial 4 holy; **5** godly, solar; **6** cosmic; **8** galactic, heavenly; **9** planetary, spiritual; **12** astronomical, otherworldly.

celestial equator 11 equinoctial.

celestial sphere 5 nadir; **6** zenith; **7** azimuth, equinox, horizon; **8** altitude, ecliptic, meridian, solstice; **11** declination; PHRASES: **4, 5** hour angle; **5, 9** right ascension; **6, 7** vernal equinox; **8, 7** autumnal equinox; **9, 5** celestial poles.

celibate **4** free, pure, sole; **5** unwed; **6** chaste, maiden, single, virgin; **7** unasked, unmated, unwooed; **8** maidenly, mateless, monastic, solitary, unwedded, virginal, wifeless; **9** abstinent, continent, misogamic, unmarried; **10** bachelorly, misandrous, misogynous, spinsterly, spouseless, unattached; **11** husbandless, independent, spinsterish, unpartnered; **12** bachelorlike, celibatarian, spinsterlike; **13** unconsummated; PHRASES: **2, 3, 5** on the shelf; **3-7** old-maidish; **4-10** self-restrained; **5-4** fancy-free.

celibate (be celibate) **4** bach; PHRASES: **3, 2, 3, 5** sit on the shelf; **4, 5** live alone; **4, 6** stay single.

cell (cells and cell parts) **3** DNA, dry, RNA, wet; **4** bone, fuel, germ, jail, mast, room, sect, stem, unit, wall; **5** basal, blood, cabal, group, guard, lymph, nerve, plasm, plate, solar, spore, swarm; **6** caucus, chitin, cilium, gamete, lignin, lockup, muscle, padded, plasma, prison; **7** cadmium, cellule, daniell, energid, faction, lamella, nucleus, pigment, plastid, somatic, vacuole, vesicle, voltaic; **8** bioplasm, cytosome, lysosome, membrane, mesosome, parietal, polysome, ribosome, selenium; **9** cellulose, centriole, chromatin, cisternum, coenocyte, corpuscle, cytoplasm, ectoplasm, endoplasm, eukaryote, flagellum, idioplasm, karyosome, microsome, nucleolus, organelle, reticulum, syncytium, tonoplast; **10** centrosome, hyaloplasm, karyoplasm, kinetosome, leucoplast, nucleosome, peroxisome, plasmosome, plastosome, prokaryote, protoplasm, protoplast, spherosome; **11** chloroplast, chromoplast, nucleoplasm, plasmalemma, plasmodesma, trophoplasm; **12** chondriosome, oxychromatin, reproductive; **13** basichromatin, chromatophore, mitochondrion, nucleopeptide, nucleoprotein, photoelectric; **15** heterochromatin; PHRASES: **5, 4** Golgi body; **5, 7** Golgi complex; **5, 9** Golgi apparatus; **7, 3** nuclear sap; **7, 4** central body, nuclear pore, nucleic acid; **7, 8** nuclear envelope, nuclear membrane.

cell division **7** meiosis, mitosis.

cellular **4** cell; **7** plasmic; **9** reticular, ribosomal, syncytial; **10** eukaryotic; **11** cytoplasmic, ectoplasmic, endoplasmic, prokaryotic; **12** protoplasmic; **13** mitochondrial.

cement **3** fix; **4** glue, join; **5** paste, stick; **7** fortify; **8** adhesive; **9** reinforce; **10** strengthen; PHRASES: **4, 2** prop up; **4, 8** make stronger; **5, 5** epoxy resin; **6, 8** fasten together.

cemetery **4** plot; **8** boneyard, catacomb, Golgotha; **9** graveyard, mausoleum; **10** churchyard, cinerarium, necropolis; **11** columbarium; PHRASES: **4, 4** God's acre; **6, 2, 4** garden of rest; **6, 6** burial ground.

censer **8** thurible.

censor **3** ban, cut, gag; **4** edit, kill, stop; **5** amend; **6** cancel, delete, remove, stifle; **7** control, repress; **8** prohibit, restrain, restrict, suppress; **9** expurgate, proscribe; **10** bowdlerize; PHRASES: **4, 1, 5** rate a movie; **4-6** blue-pencil; **5, 1, 1-6** issue a D-notice; **5, 3** black out, bleep out; **8, 1, 5** classify a movie.

censored **3** cut; **6** banned, secret; **7** amended, changed, deleted; **9** secretive, unsayable; **10** classified, expurgated, proscribed, restricted; **11** bowdlerized, restrictive, unprintable; **12** proscriptive; **13** unmentionable; PHRASES: **3-6** top-secret; **4-9** blue-pencilled *UK*; **7, 3** blacked out, bleeped out.

censure **3** rap; **4** rate, warn; **5** chide, fault, knock, scold, scorn, slate *UK*; **6** berate, carpet *UK*, earful, rebuke; **7** condemn, lecture, reprove, upbraid, wigging *UK*; **8** admonish, chastise, contempt, denounce, lambaste, reproach; **9** castigate, criticism, criticize, reprehend, reprimand; **11** deprecation, disapproval; **12** condemnation, denunciation; PHRASES: **3, 4** lay into; **4, 2, 4** take to task; **4, 2, 7** call to account; **4, 3** tell off, tick off *UK*; **4, 5** skin alive; **5, 4** black mark, dress down; **8-4** dressing-down.

census **4** poll; **5** count, tally; **6** survey; **12** registration.

centaur **8** horseman.

centenary *See* **anniversary**

center **3** eye, hub, nub; **4** axis, core, cost, mean, pith, root; **5** align, focus, heart, midst, pivot, place; **6** adjust, bottom, hotbed, inside, kernel, locate, marrow, median, middle, target; **7** address, balance, cluster, complex, examine, filling, fulcrum, nucleus; **8** backbone, building, converge, facility, focalize, interior, midpoint, position; **9** epicenter, interpose; **11** concentrate, headquarter, interpolate; **13** concentration; PHRASES: **4, 2** turn on; **4, 2, 1, 5** come to a point; **4, 2, 2** home in on, zero in on; **5, 2** focus on, pivot on; **5, 3** bull's eye; **5, 4, 5** bring into focus; **5, 5** focal point; **5, 6** happy medium; **6, 6** ~ ground, middle course, middle ground; **7, 5** halfway point, pivotal point; **7, 6** revolve around; **8, 2** converge on; **8, 6** breeding ground; **11, 2** concentrate on.

center of attraction 5 focus; **6** center; **8** cynosure; PHRASES: **5, 5** focal point.

central 3 key, mid; **4** main, mean; **5** axial, chief, civic, focal, inner, state, vital; **6** median, middle; **7** average, crucial, federal, midmost, nuclear, pivotal; **8** dominant, national; **9** essential, innermost, principal, umbilical; **11** centralized, fundamental, predominant, significant; PHRASES: **4, 9** most important.

Central American dish 4 taco; **5** nacho; **6** tamale; **7** burrito, tostada; **8** empanada, monteria, tortilla; **9** enchilada, guacamole; PHRASES: **4, 7** mole poblano, olla podrida; **5, 3, 5** chili con carne; **5, 4, 4** black bean soup; **10, 3** Montezuma pie.

centrality 6 import; **8** focusing; **9** centering; **10** centralism, centricity, confluence, focalizing, importance, uniqueness; **11** centralness, consequence, convergence, criticality, pinpointing; **12** focalization, significance; **13** concentration, concentricity; **14** centralization.

central reserve 6 median.

century See **period**

century plant 4 aloe.

ceramics 3 cup, jar, jug, mat, mug, pot, pug, urn; **4** bowl, clay, ewer, lens, tile, vase; **5** adobe, brick, china, crock, cruse UK, fired, glass, jolly, plate; **6** cement, firing, jigger, luting, mosaic, pipkin, saucer, tiling, vessel; **7** amphora, ampulla, crackle, faience, glazing, pitcher, pottery, pugging, redware, smoking, soaking, tessera, wedging; **8** blunging, bricking, clayware, concrete, crockery, fettling, figurine, grinding, ovenware, slipware, steaming, throwing; **9** agateware, chinaware, collaring, creamware, enameling, firebrick, glassware, ironstone, porcelain, screening, sgraffito, stoneware, whiteware; **10** basaltware, enamelware, lustreware, spongeware; **11** earthenware, overglazing; **12** underglazing; PHRASES: **2-6** de-airing; **3, 5** mud brick; **3-6** sun-drying; **4, 3** toby jug; **4, 3, 5** blue and white; **4, 5** bone china, fine china; **4, 7** lead crystal; **5, 5** terra cotta; **7, 4** biscuit ware, marbled ware; **7, 5** Tiffany glass; **8, 6** Portland cement.

ceramics (make ceramics) 3 dry, mix, pot, pug; **4** bake, cast, fire, gild, lute, mark, mold, seal, tile, turn; **5** brick, glass, glaze, grind, inlay, jolly, paint, shape, throw, wedge; **6** blunge, cement, enamel, fettle, filter, jigger, screen; **8** concrete, decorate, insulate, laminate, monogram; **9** devitrify, overglaze, pyroglaze; **10** underglaze; **11** crystallize; PHRASES: **2-3** de-air; **3-5** tin-glaze; **3-6** tin-enamel; **4, 1, 4** draw a kiln, roll a slab; **4-4** hand-turn.

ceramics (tools for ceramics) 3 rib; **4** kiln, oven; **5** dolly, stove, wheel; **6** jigger; **7** blunger, furnace, smelter; **8** limekiln; **9** converter, pyrometer; PHRASES: **3, 4** pug mill; **3, 7** ore roaster; **6, 4** mixing tank; **6, 5** filter cloth, filter press; **7, 5** potter's wheel.

cereal 3 cob, ear, oat, rye; **4** bran, corn, husk, oats, rice, sago; **5** chaff, durum, emmer, grain, grass, maize UK, straw, wheat; **6** barley, bulgur, méteil, millet; **7** burghul, corncob, frument, polenta, sorghum, spelled, stubble, tapioca; **8** semolina; **9** buckwheat; **10** barleycorn UK; PHRASES: **3, 2, 4** ear of corn; **7, 5** cracked wheat. See also **breakfast cereal**

cerebral 6 brainy; **7** logical; **8** highbrow, rational; **10** analytical UK; **12** intellectual.

ceremonial 4 pomp, rite; **5** grand, regal, state; **6** custom, formal, ritual, solemn; **7** stately; **8** ceremony, crowning, liturgic, majestic, official; **9** customary, dignified, formality, imperious, pageantry, triumphal; **10** procession; **11** ritualistic, sacramental.

ceremonial troops 9 Guardsman, housecarl UK, janissary, protector; PHRASES: **4, 5** Foot Guard, Life Guard; **5, 5** color guard, Horse Guard, Irish Guard, Scots Guard, Swiss Guard, Welsh Guard; **9, 5** Grenadier Guard; **10, 5** Coldstream Guard, Praetorian Guard.

ceremonious 6 polite; **7** courtly, pompous; **11** traditional. See also **ceremonious**

ceremony 4 fete, form, gala, mass, rite, show; **5** drill, scene; **6** office, parade, review, ritual, tattoo; **7** funeral, liturgy, ovation, pageant, routine, service, triumph, wedding; **8** function, practice; **9** formalism, formality, procedure, ritualism, spectacle;

10 ceremonial, coronation, graduation, initiation, observance, tournament; 11 celebration, Christening, convocation; 12 enthronement, inauguration; PHRASES: 3-6, 3 red-letter day; 3, 7 bar mitzvah; 4, 2, 7 rite of passage; 5, 4 march past.

cert *See* **certainty**

certain 3 one; 4 firm, real, safe, some, sure, true; 5 bound, clear, given, known; 6 actual, proved, secure; 7 assured, factual, obvious, precise, several; 8 absolute, accurate, definite, positive, reliable, selected, specific; 9 certified, confident, convinced, necessary, realistic, specified, undoubted, veracious; 10 dependable, documented, guaranteed, individual, particular, undeniable, unmistaken, verifiable; 11 ascertained, established, indubitable; 12 demonstrable, demonstrated, unmistakable; 13 authoritative, unmistakeable; 14 unquestionable; PHRASES: 1, 3 a few; 1, 6, 2 a number of; 1, 7, 2 a variety of; 4-7 self-evident, well-founded; 4-8 well-grounded; 5, 3, 6 tried and tested.

certain (be certain) 4 know; PHRASES: 4, 3, 4 know for sure; 4, 4 feel sure; 4, 5, 2 have faith in.

certain (make certain) 3 fix; 5 check, prove; 6 affirm, decide, ensure, evince, ground, secure, settle, verify; 7 certify, confirm, endorse, promise; 8 convince; 9 ascertain, determine, establish, guarantee; 11 demonstrate; 12 authenticate, substantiate; PHRASES: 3, 4 pin down; 4, 3 find out; 5, 2 clear up.

certainly 3 yes; 5 truly; 6 indeed; 8 honestly; 9 naturally; 12 emphatically; PHRASES: 2, 2, 5 be my guest; 2, 3, 5 by all means; 2, 4, 5, 2 no buts about it; 2, 5 go ahead, in truth; 2, 6 of course; 4, 8 help yourself; 6, 2, 3 honest to God; 7, 4, 3 nothing else but; 7, 5 without doubt; 7, 8 without question. *See also* **certain**

certainty 4 cert *UK*, fact, fate; 5 cinch, faith, proof, truth; 6 belief, surety, verity, winner; 7 reality; 8 accuracy, evidence, validity, veracity; 9 actuality, assurance, certitude, knowledge, necessity; 10 confidence, conviction, factuality; 13 inevitability; 14 indubitability; 15 indisputability; PHRASES: 4, 3 safe bet; 4-3-4, 4 open-and-shut case; 4, 4 dead cert *UK*; 4, 5 sure thing; 4, 8 fait accompli. *See also* **certain**

certainty (with certainty) 9 assured-ly; 10 stubbornly; 11 confidently, obstinately; 12 dogmatically.

certificate 2 ID; 4 deed; 5 title; 6 permit, rating, record, ticket; 7 charter, diploma, license; 8 document, warranty; 10 credential; 13 authorization, documentation, qualification.

certified *See* **official**

certify 5 cover, state; 6 attest, commit, insure, pledge, verify; 7 confirm, declare, endorse, promise; 12 authenticate.

cerumen 3 wax; 6 earwax.

cessation 3 end; 4 halt, stop; 5 cease, close, death, pause; 6 ending, expiry, finish; 7 ceasing, closing; 8 breakoff, stoppage, stopping; 9 annulment; 10 abrogation, desistance, expiration, withdrawal; 11 abandonment, termination; 12 cancellation; 14 discontinuance, relinquishment; 15 discontinuation.

cesspit 3 pit; 4 tank; 5 drain, sewer; 6 gutter.

cesspool 4 sink, sump.

cesura 4 rest; 5 pause; 6 hiatus, lacuna; 7 fermata.

Ceylon 3, 5 Sri Lanka.

chafe 3 rub, vex; 5 annoy; 6 abrade, bother, scrape; 7 provoke, scratch; 8 irritate.

chaff 4 josh, mock; 5 tease; 6 banter, joking; 7 teasing; 8 repartee; PHRASES: 4, 3, 2 make fun of.

chagrin 8 vexation; 10 irritation; 11 humiliation; 13 mortification; 14 disappointment.

chain 3 fob; 4 bind, bond, line, mail; 5 cable, group, links; 6 fetter, series; 7 manacle, shackle; 8 restrain, sequence; 9 restraint; 10 immobilize, procession, succession.

chair 3 pew, run; 4 head, lead, post, sofa; 5 bench, divan, sedan, stall, stool; 6 direct, leader, manage, settee, settle; 7 oversee, preside; 8 armchair, recliner; 9 highchair, president; 10 prolocutor; 11 chairperson; 12 chesterfield; 13 professorship; PHRASES: 3, 5 box ~; 4, 4 love seat; 4, 5 camp ~, cane ~, club ~, deck ~, easy ~, side ~, wing ~; 5-4, 5 panel-back ~, Queen-Anne ~, wheel-back ~; 5, 5 choir stall; 6-4, 5 ladder-back ~; 6, 6 barrel ~, carver ~, dining ~, lounge ~, Morris ~, Shaker ~, swivel ~; 6, 6 Boston rocker, chaise longue; 7, 5 folding ~, nursing ~, rocking ~, Windsor ~; 8, 5 bentwood ~, captain's ~, electric ~, Sheraton ~, straight ~; **9, 5** reclining ~.

chalk **4** draw, mark; **5** write; **6** crayon, doodle, sketch; **8** scribble.

chalky **3** dry; **4** fine, pale, soft; **5** ashen, dusty, white; **6** anemic, pallid; **7** crumbly, deathly, ghostly, powdery; **10** calcareous.

challenge **3** tax, vie; **4** call, dare, defy, risk, task, test; **5** argue, brave, taunt, trial; **6** insult, oppose, strain, threat; **7** contest, dispute, dissent, venture; **8** confront, question, struggle; PHRASES: **4, 2, 2** face up to; **6, 2** object to.

challenging **5** tough; **6** taxing; **7** defiant, testing; **8** exciting, impudent, insolent; **9** demanding, difficult, inspiring; **10** rebellious; **11** disobedient, interesting, stimulating.

chamber **4** cell, hall, room, slot; **5** privy, space, vault; **6** cavity, hollow; **9** boardroom; **11** compartment; PHRASES: **7, 4** meeting room; **8, 4** assembly room. *See also* **room**

chamberlain **7** manager, servant; **8** courtier, official; **9** attendant.

chamber pot **2** po; **5** jerry, potty.

champ **4** chew; **5** chomp, grind, munch; **6** victor, winner; **8** champion; **9** masticate; PHRASES: **5, 6** title holder.

champion **4** back; **5** champ; **6** backer, defend, victor, winner; **7** support; **8** advocate, defender; **9** supporter; **10** campaigner; PHRASES: **5, 3** fight for; **5, 6** title holder; **8, 3** campaign for.

championship **4** open; **5** title; **6** battle, finals; **7** contest; **9** challenge; **10** tournament; **11** competition.

chance **3** bet, hap, lot, try; **4** dice, fate, iffy, luck, odds, risk; **5** dicey, fluky, lucky, occur, risky, stake, wager; **6** befall, betide, casual, chancy, gamble, happen, hazard, option, random, tossup; **7** attempt, destiny, fortune, unlucky, venture; **8** accident, aleatory, fortuity, jeopardy, occasion, prospect; **9** aleatoric, fortunate, haphazard, speculate, uncertain, unplanned; **10** accidental, casualness, contingent, fortuitous, incidental, likelihood, randomness, stochastic, unexpected, unforeseen, unintended; **11** coincidence, contingency, opportunity, possibility, uncertainty, unfortunate; **12** adventitious, coincidental; **13** indeterminacy, serendipitous, unforeseeable, unpredictable; **14** indeterminable; **15** indetermination; PHRASES: **2, 3, 2, 1, 4** go out on a limb;

2, 6 so happen; **3, 2** pop up; **3-2-4** hit-or-miss; **3, 4, 4** try one's luck; **4, 1, 4** take a risk; **4, 2** crop up, risk it, turn up; **4, 3, 3** cast the die; **5-2-5-3** catch-as-catch-can; **5, 6** blind ~; **6, 6** random ~; **8, 6** sporting ~.

chance (by chance) **7** luckily; **8** casually, randomly; **9** unluckily; **11** fortunately, haphazardly; **12** accidentally, fortuitously, inexplicably, unexpectedly; **13** inadvertently, unaccountably, unfortunately, unpredictably; **14** coincidentally; **15** serendipitously, unintentionally; PHRASES: **2, 6** at random; **2, 8** by accident; **2, 11** by coincidence.

chance (calculation of chance) **8** gambling; **9** assurance, insurance; **10** aleatorics, bookmaking, statistics; **11** probability, speculation, stochastics; **12** underwriting; PHRASES: **4-6** risk-taking.

chance (up)on **3, 4** hit upon, run into; **3, 6** run across; **4, 4** bump into, come upon; **5, 4** light upon; **7, 4** blunder upon, stumble upon.

chancellor *See* **president**

change **3** mar, sou; **4** cash, coup, edit, fail, flux, mark, move, ruin, slip, swap, turn, vary, warp; **5** adapt, alter, amend, break, cause, coins, emend, evert, paisa, renew, reset, shift, spoil, trade; **6** adjust, affect, better, censor, detour, divert, doctor, impair, infect, invent, invert, kopeck, leaven, modify, mutate, reform, rehash, remold, repair, revamp, revert, revise, revive, revolt, silver, switch, weaken, worsen; **7** arrange, centime, commute, convert, coppers, decline, destroy, deviate, distort, ferment, improve, inflect, peanuts, pervert, piastre, process, qualify, remodel, renewal, reorder, replace, reshape, restore, restyle, reverse, revival, subvert, variety; **8** activate, discolor, exchange, innovate, modulate, mutation, relocate, reversal, revision, transfer; **9** allowance, amendment, deviation, diversify, diversion, diversity, fluctuate, influence, interpret, invention, inversion, leavening, modernize, rearrange, remolding, repairing, reshaping, restyling, transform, translate, transmute, vacillate, variation, variegate; **10** adaptation, adjustment, adulterate, alteration, ameliorate, betterment, bowdlerize, conversion, declension, degenerate, difference, distortion, emendation, inflection, innovation, modulation, mutability, perversion, redecorate, relocation, remodeling, reordering, reorganize, revolution, substitute, subversion, transition; **11** chickenfeed, contaminate, deteriorate, fluctuation, improvement, inconstancy, reformation, restoration, restructure, translation, variegation, vicissitude; **12** adulteration, amelioration, degeneration, fermentation, modification, redecoration, transference; **13** deterioration, inconsistency, metamorphosis, modernization, qualification, rearrangement, restructuring, revolutionize, transmutation; **14** reorganization, transformation; **15** diversification; **PHRASES: 1-4** U-turn; **3, 3, 4** wax and wane; **3, 6** get better, sea ~; **4, 3, 3, 4** blow hot and cold; **4, 3, 6** chop and ~, turn the corner; **4, 3, 7** ring the changes; **4, 4** mess with; **4-4** flip-flop; **4, 6, 4** turn upside down; **5-2** shake-up; **5, 6** loose ~, small ~; **6, 3** paltry sum; **6, 4** fiddle with, meddle with, tamper with; **6, 5** pocket money; **7, 3, 5** nickels and dimes; **8, 5** spending money.

changeable 4 soft; **5** fluid, giddy, loose, moody, rocky, shaky, worse; **6** fickle, fitful, labile, mobile, pliant, roving, shifty, supple, varied, wobbly; **7** diverse, erratic, fidgety, flighty, flowing, melting, mutable, plastic, protean, reverse, swaying, turning, unfixed, vagrant, variant, veering, wayward; **8** disloyal, flexible, floating, homeless, rambling, restless, rootless, shifting, unstable, unsteady, variable, wavering; **9** alterable, changeful, desultory, deviatory, different, ephemeral, irregular, mercurial, spasmodic, teetering, tottering, transient, uncertain, unsettled, versatile, vibrating, wandering, whimsical; **10** capricious, flickering, imbalanced, inconstant, indecisive, innovative, iridescent, irresolute, precarious, traitorous, transitory, unfaithful, unreliable, variegated; **11** alternating, fluctuating, impermanent, oscillating, vacillating; **12** ameliorative, inconsistent, innovational, transitional, undependable; **13** irresponsible, kaleidoscopic, reformational, revolutionary, temperamental, unpredictable; **14** featherbrained, impressionably; **15** vicissitudinous; **PHRASES: 2, 3, 3** on and off, to and fro; **3, 3, 2** off and on; **3, 4, 3, 4** now this now that; **3, 4, 3, 5** now here now there; **4, 3, 5** back and forth; **4-4** flip-flop; **4-8** ever-changing; **5-6** light-minded.

changeable (be changeable) 3 yaw;

4 back, flap, reel, rock, roll, sway, tack, turn, vary, veer, wave; **5** flash, pitch, shake, swing; **6** change, falter, gutter, teeter, totter, wobble; **7** flicker, flutter, shuttle, stagger, tremble, twinkle, vibrate, whiffle; **9** alternate, fluctuate, oscillate; **12** metamorphose; **PHRASES: 3, 3, 4** ebb and flow, wax and wane; **4, 2, 3, 4** wave in the wind.

changed 3 new; **6** varied; **7** altered, amended, emended, renewed, revised; **8** improved, modified, reformed, remolded, repaired, reshaped, restored, restyled; **9** different, qualified, remodeled, reordered; **10** modernized, rearranged; **11** degenerated, diversified, redecorated, reorganized, transformed; **12** deteriorated, restructured; **13** rehabilitated.

changeless 5 fixed; **7** eternal; **9** immutable, permanent; **10** consistent, unchanging; **11** everlasting, unalterable; **12** imperishable; **13** incorruptible; **14** indestructible.

change of mind 5 swing; **7** caprice; **10** conversion, fickleness; **11** vacillation; **12** whimsicality; **13** desultoriness; **14** capriciousness, tergiversation; **PHRASES: 4-4** flip-flop; **6, 2, 5** change of heart; **6, 2, 7** change of opinion.

changer 5 agent, yeast; **6** enzyme, leaven; **7** adapter; **8** catalyst, modifier; **9** activator, converter; **11** transformer; **12** kaleidoscope.

channel 3 bed, cut, way; **4** bore, dike, duct, exit, feed, gulf, head, lane, leat, path, pipe, side, tube; **5** aisle, alley, canal, chute, ditch, drain, flume, focus, force *UK*, gully, inlet, means, river, route, sewer, shoot, sound; **6** direct, groove, gutter, outlet, rapids, strait, stream, trench; **7** cascade, conduct, conduit, control, culvert, network, passage, station; **8** spillway, waterway; **9** frequency, midstream, sluiceway; **11** watercourse.

chant 4 hymn, sing, song, tune; **5** carol; **6** intone, mantra, recite, repeat; **8** vocalize.

chaos *See* **disorder**

chaotic *See* **disordered**

chapel *See* **worship (place of worship)**

chaperon 5 watch; **6** escort; **7** oversee; **8** overseer; **9** attendant, governess, supervise; **10** supervisor; **PHRASES: 4, 5** look after.

chaplain *See* **minister**

chapter 4 part; **5** phase, stage; **6** period; **7** episode, section, segment; **8** division, interval; **11** subdivision; **12** intermission.

char 4 burn, help, sear; 5 singe; 6 scorch; 9 carbonize, cauterize.

character 3 air; 4 aura, chap *UK*, code, role, rune, sign, sort, tone, type; 5 charm, honor; 6 appeal, fellow *UK*, letter, makeup, nature, oddity, person, spirit, symbol; 7 quality; 8 charisma, creature; 9 eccentric, integrity, rectitude; 10 atmosphere, hieroglyph, individual; 11 disposition, personality, temperament, uprightness; PHRASES: 5, 5 moral fiber.

characteristic 4 feel, mark, mold, odor, seal; 5 aroma, brand, point, quirk, savor, shape, smell, stamp, taste, token, touch, trait, trick, usual; 6 cachet, figure, flavor, marked, normal, quirky, unique; 7 curious, earmark, feature, natural, quality, routine, typical, unusual; 8 defining, habitual, hallmark, inherent, peculiar, personal, property, singular, specific, uncommon; 9 attribute, eccentric, idiomatic, mannerism, trademark; 10 individual, particular, remarkable; 11 distinctive, exceptional, peculiarity, singularity, symptomatic; 12 eccentricity, idiosyncrasy; 13 extraordinary, idiosyncratic; 14 discriminating, distinguishing, representative; PHRASES: 4, 2, 4 true to form; 4, 2, 5 like no other.

characterize 4 mark; 5 brand, label, stamp; 6 depict, inform, select, typify; 7 earmark, portray; 8 describe, identify, indicate, pinpoint; 9 delineate, demarcate, designate, exemplify, highlight, represent; 10 illustrate; 11 distinguish; 13 differentiate; PHRASES: 3, 4, 6, 2 put one's finger on; 3, 5 set apart; 4, 3 pick out; 5, 3 point out; 6, 3 single out.

characterless 4 dull; 5 bland, blank, plain, tepid; 6 boring, normal; 7 insipid, orderly; 8 faceless, soulless; 10 uninspired; 11 featureless, nondescript; 13 uninteresting.

character recognition 3 ICR, OCR; 4 MICR.

charade 4 fake, sham; 5 farce; 8 pretense, travesty.

charge 3 ask, con, fee, ion, tax; 4 care, cost, dash, duty, hand, levy, push, race, rate, rush, ward; 5 blame, exact, hurry, order, price, storm, tithe, trust; 6 accuse, allege, amount, assail, attack, burden, demand, hurtle, indict, inmate; 7 advance, arraign, assault, command, concern, custody, expense, patient, payment; 8 jailbird, prisoner, stampede; 9 electrify, offensive,

onslaught; 10 accusation, allegation, imputation, possession; 11 arraignment, exhortation, incriminate, instruction, safekeeping; 14 responsibility; PHRASES: 3, 3, 5, 2 lay the blame on; 4, 2 rush at.

chargeable 7 serious, taxable; 8 criminal, dutiable, rateable; 9 imputable; 10 actionable, declarable, deductible, indictable, punishable; PHRASES: 6, 2, 3 liable to tax.

charged 8 deferred, electric, exciting, magnetic; 9 emotional, polarized, thrilling; 10 electrical, electronic, mechanical; 11 stimulating; PHRASES: 6-2 souped-up.

charisma 2 it; 4 lure; 5 charm; 6 allure, appeal; 9 magnetism; 10 allurement, attraction; 11 captivation, fascination; PHRASES: 3, 6 sex appeal; 7, 4 winning ways.

charitable 6 giving; 7 helpful, lenient, liberal; 8 generous, gracious, tolerant; 9 accepting, bountiful, Christian, indulgent, unselfish; 10 altruistic, beneficent, benevolent, hospitable; 11 considerate, magnanimous; 13 philanthropic; PHRASES: 3-7 bighearted; 4-6 alms-giving, open-handed.

charitable (be charitable) 3 aid; 4 help; 7 benefit; 9 patronize; 14 philanthropize; PHRASES: 7, 3 provide aid.

charity 3 aid; 4 alms, fund, gift, help; 5 gifts, OXFAM; 6 relief; 8 altruism, donation, goodwill, handouts, humanity, kindness, sympathy; 9 offerings, patronage, tolerance; 10 assistance, compassion, generosity, liberality; 11 benefaction, benevolence, hospitality, magnanimity; 12 philanthropy, selflessness; 13 bountifulness, consideration, contributions, understanding, unselfishness; 14 charitableness; PHRASES: 3, 5 Red Cross; 3, 6 aid agency; 3-11 big-heartedness; 3, 12 aid organization; 4-3 hand-out; 4, 3, 8 Save the Children; 4, 5 good works; 4-6 alms-giving, fund-raiser; 6, 3 United Way; 6, 5 worthy cause; 6, 6 famine relief; 8, 6 disaster relief; 9, 4 Salvation Army; 9, 5 community chest; 10, 5 charitable trust.

charlatan 4 fake; 5 fraud, quack; 8 swindler.

Charles's Wain 6 Plough; PHRASES: 3, 6 Big Dipper.

charm 4 lure; 5 magic; 6 allure, amulet, appeal; 7 beguile, enchant, memento, trinket; 8 charisma, enthrall, entrance, keepsake, ornament, talisman; 9 accessory, captivate, enrapture, fascinate, hypnotize, magnetism, mesmerize; **10** attraction; **11** fascination.

charmer 4 hunk, stud, vamp; **5** Circe, flirt, Romeo, siren; **6** Adonis; **7** seducer; **8** Casanova, coquette, favorite, Lothario, smoothie; **9** enchanter, temptress; **10** fascinator, seductress; **11** enchantress; PHRASES: **3, 4** Don Juan; **3, 6** sex symbol; **4, 4** foxy lady, teen idol; **5, 6** femme fatale; **6, 3** ladies' man; **6, 6** smooth talker; **6, 8** smooth operator.

charming 7 amiable; **9** appealing; **10** attractive, delightful.

chart 3 map; **4** list, plan, plot; **5** graph, plane, table; **6** follow, record, schema, scheme; **7** diagram, outline; **9** horoscope; PHRASES: **3, 5** bar ~, pie ~; **4, 5** flow ~, flow sheet; **4, 7** Venn diagram; **6, 3** visual aid; **7, 5** scatter graph.

charter 4 deed, hire, rent; **5** grant, lease; **7** license; **8** contract; **9** agreement; **10** commission; PHRASES: **4, 2** take on.

chary *See* **wary**

chase 3 run; **4** beat, dash, etch, hark, hunt, race, rush, tail; **5** catch, drive, hound, hurry, stalk, track, trail, whoop; **6** battue, career, follow, halloo, hurtle, pursue, racing *UK*; **7** beating, hunting, pursuit, tallyho; **8** beagling, hounding; **12** steeplechase; PHRASES: **2, 5** go after; **3, 2** cry on; **3, 3, 3** hue and cry; **3, 4** fox hunt, run down; **3, 5** run after; **3, 7** hot pursuit; **4, 3** look for; **4, 4** boar hunt, ride down, stag hunt; **4, 5** give ~; **5, 5** blood sport; **6, 3** search for.

chasten 4 tame; **6** humble, punish, subdue; **7** censure; **8** chastise, restrain, suppress; **9** reprimand; **10** discipline.

chastise *See* **reprimand**

chastisement *See* **reprimand**

chastity 6 purity, virtue; **8** celibacy; **9** Encratism, innocence, virginity; **10** abstinence, continence, maidenhood.

chat 3 gab, gas, jaw, yak; **4** blab, blah, talk; **5** crack, prate; **6** babble, banter, confab, gabble, gibber, gossip, jabber, natter, tattle, waffle, witter *UK*; **7** blabber, chatter, chinwag, conflab, prattle; **8** backtalk, causerie, chitchat, converse, dialogue, exchange, repartee; **10** discussion; **12** conversation; **13** confabulation; PHRASES: **3-2-3** one-on-one; **4-1-4** tête-à-tête; **4, 3, 3** chew the fat; **4, 4** idle talk; **4, 6** idle gossip; **4, 9** talk privately; **5-2-**5 heart-to-heart; **5, 4** small talk, table talk; **6, 2** ramble on, rattle on; **6-6** tittle-tattle; **8, 4** fireside ~.

chatterer 6 gasbag, gasser, gossip; **7** windbag; **8** natterer.

chauffeur 5 valet; **6** driver; **8** motorist.

chauvinist *See* **bigot**

cheap 3 low; **4** base, bear, mean *UK*, poor, sale; **5** mingy, tacky, tight; **6** budget, cheapo, common, modest, scurvy, shoddy, stingy, tawdry, vulgar; **7** bargain, bearish, economy, miserly, nominal, reduced, slashed; **8** devalued, discount, economic, giveaway, grudging, inferior, markdown, moderate, sensible, shameful, slumping, uncostly; **9** brummagem, knockdown, niggardly, penurious, wholesale; **10** affordable, catchpenny, despicable, discounted, economical, manageable, reasonable; **11** competitive, depreciated, inexpensive, sacrificial, substandard, tightfisted, underpriced, unexpensive; **12** cheeseparing, concessional, contemptible, parsimonious; PHRASES: **1, 3, 6** à bon marché; **1, 4, 1, 5** a dime a dozen; **2, 3, 5** on the ~, on the house; **2, 4** on sale; **3, 1, 4** for a song; **3-4** cut-rate, low-cost, off-peak; **3-5** cut-price *UK*, low-price; **3-6** low-budget; **3, 7** for nothing; **4-3-3** five-and-ten; **4, 5** easy terms *UK*; **4-5** dime-store, dirt-cheap, half-price, saleprice; **4-6** down-market, rock-bottom; **5-4** penny-wise; **5-5** third-class, tight-arsed; **5-6** close-fisted; **5-8** money-grubbing, penny-pinching; **6, 4** marked down; **6-4** secondrate; **6, 4, 5** within one's means; **6-5** secondclass; **7, 2, 5** reduced to clear; **7-4** economysize; **7-5** bargain-price, economy-class, economy-price, slashed-price, touristclass; **7-8** bargain-basement; **9-5** knockdown-price; **10, 4** peppercorn rent.

cheap (become cheap) 3 sag; **4** fall; **5** drift, slump; **6** plunge; **7** decline, plummet; **10** depreciate.

cheapen 3 cut; **4** dump, trim; **5** lower, slash; **6** demean, unload; **7** degrade, devalue; **8** belittle, discount, undercut; **9** denigrate, sacrifice, undersell; **10** depreciate, undervalue; **11** undercharge; PHRASES: **4, 4** give away, mark down; **5, 4** knock down.

cheat 2 do; **3** con, gyp; **4** bilk, copy, crib, dupe, fake, rook, sham, spiv; **5** bluff, crimp, crook, faker, fraud, phony *UK*, poser, quack, rogue, shark, trick; **6** bilker, cowboy, fiddle, forger, gazump *UK*, gypper, humbug, phoney, poseur, ringer; **7** bluffer, cheater, cozener, deceive, defraud, diddler, magsman, shammer, shyster, swindle; **8** blackleg, chiseler, gazumper, imposter, swindler; **9** bamboozle, cardsharp, charlatan, defrauder, fraudster, pretender, quackster, trickster; **10** mountebank; **11** cardsharper, flimflammer, pettifogger; **12** impersonator; **13** counterfeiter, thimblerigger; PHRASES: **3, 3** con man, rip off; **3-5** twotimer; **3, 6** con artist; **4, 3, 5** cook the books; **4, 5** land shark; **5-5** mealy-mouth; **5, 6** bunco artist; **5-6** horse-trader; **5, 7** bunco steerer; **5-7** short-changer; **6, 4** smooth talk; **6-4** double-deal; **6-5** double-cross; **8, 3** flimflam man.

cheating 6 deceit; **9** chicanery, deceitful, deception, dishonest, duplicity; **10** dishonesty; **11** duplicitous; **12** unprincipled; PHRASES: **6-7** double-dealing.

check 3 dam, tab, try; **4** bill, curb, rein, stop, test; **5** audit, catch, delay, limit, plaid, prove, study, total, trial; **6** amount, charge, ensure, impede, tartan, verify; **7** account, certify, chequer, confirm, examine, inhibit, receipt, repress; **8** restrain, withhold; **9** constrain, establish, patchwork, restraint, safeguard, statement; **10** assessment, inspection; **11** examination; **13** investigation; PHRASES: **3, 3** try out; **4, 2** hold in, hold up; **4, 3** test out; **4, 4** make sure.

checked 5 check, plaid; **6** tartan; **7** patched, squared; **9** checkered, patterned.

cheek 3 lip; **4** face, gall, sass; **5** brass, crust, mouth, nerve, sauce; **6** retort; **7** provoke; **8** audacity, backtalk, boldness, chutzpah, rudeness; **9** brashness, impudence; **10** brazenness, effrontery; **12** impertinence; PHRASES: **6, 4** answer back.

cheeky 4 bold, pert, rude; **5** cocky, gally, nervy, sassy; **6** brassy, brazen, crusty, mouthy; **7** defiant; **8** impudent, insolent; **9** audacious; **11** impertinent, mischievous; **13** disrespectful; PHRASES: **4-4** wise-assd; **5-4** smart-assd; **5-6** smart-alecky.

cheer 2 ra; **4** clap, hail, spur, yell; **5** shout, whoop; **6** hooray, hurrah, praise, revive, uplift; **7** animate, applaud, enliven, gladden, hearten, lighten; **8** applause, brighten, clapping; **9** encourage; **10** exhilarate; PHRASES: **4, 2** buck up, perk up, spur on. *See also* **cheerfulness**

cheerful 2 up; **3** gay; **4** glad, high; **5** funny, happy, jolly, merry, perky, sunny; **6** bouncy, bright, cheery, chirpy, genial, jaunty, jovial, joyful, lively; **7** beaming, buoyant, chipper, gleeful, radiant, smiling; **8** animated, bouncing, carefree, grinning, laughing, sociable; **9** bonhomous, convivial, sparkling, vivacious; **10** optimistic; **11** exhilarated; **12** lighthearted; PHRASES: **3-6** fun-loving; **4-7** good-humored, good-natured; **4-8** high-spirited.

cheerful (be cheerful) 4 beam, grin; **5** enjoy, laugh, smile; **7** sparkle; PHRASES: **4, 3** have fun; **4, 3, 4, 2** grin and bear it.

cheerfulness 3 fun, joy; **5** cheer, mirth; **6** gaiety, levity; **7** jollity; **8** hilarity, laughter, optimism, vivacity; **9** animation, geniality, joviality, merriment; **10** exuberance; **11** merrymaking, sociability; **12** conviviality, exhilaration; PHRASES: **4, 5** good humor; **4, 7** high spirits. *See also* **cheerful**

cheerful person 6 smiler; **8** optimist; PHRASES: **3, 2, 8** ray of sunshine.

cheering 4 rosy; **5** sunny, wacky; **6** bright, golden; **7** amusing, hopeful, rousing; **8** positive, reviving; **9** diverting, favorable, promising, uplifting; **10** auspicious, heartening, propitious, reassuring; **11** encouraging; **12** entertaining; PHRASES: **5-7** heart-warming.

cheerless *See* **gloomy**

cheers 5 skoal; **6** prosit; **7** slàinte *UK*; PHRASES: **2, 2** to us; **3, 3** cin cin; **4-1-3** chug-a-lug; **4, 3, 5** down the hatch; **5, 2, 3** here's to you; **5, 6** here's health; **7, 2** bottoms up.

cheese 4 brie, curd, edam, feta, tome; **5** banon, brick, caboc, comté, danbo, derby, fetta, gouda, herve, leigh, molbo, murol, niolo, tamié; **6** asiago, bagnes, bresse, cachat, cantal, cendré, chèvre, dunlop, fourme, gapron, géromé, halumi, hramsa, leiden, morven, olivet, pourly, rollot, salers, samsoë, sbrinz, surati, tilsit, venaco; **7** bondard, brinzen, broccio, brocciu, brousse, brucciu, bryndza, cabécou, cheddar, crowdie, dauphin, fontina, gaperon, gjetöst, gruyère, jonchée, langres, levroux, Limburg, livarot, macquée, morbier, münster, nantais, picodon, quargel, ricotta, sapsago, stilton, vendôme; **8** auvergne, ayrshire, beaufort, bergkäse, boulette, chaource, cheshire, edelpilz, emmental, epoisses, manchego, parmesan, pecorino, pélardon, remoudou, scamorze, taleggio, vacherin, valençay; **9** appenzell, broodkaas, caithness, cambozola, camembert, chabichou, chevreton, emmenthal, excelsior, gammelöst, leicester, limburger, maroilles, mimolette, provolone, reblochon, roquefort, sovietski; **10** caerphilly, dolcelatte, gloucester, gorgonzola, lancashire, mascarpone, mozzarella, neufchâtel, pithiviers, saingorlon, stracchino; **11** coulommiers, katshkawalj, schabzieger, schlosskäse, weisslacker, wensleydale; **12** caciocavallo, soumaintrain; **14** trappistenkäse; PHRASES: **2, 7** la bouille; **3, 5** bel paese; **3, 7** red windsor; **3, 9** red leicester; **4-2-5** tête-de-moine; **4-3** demi-sel, mont-d'or; **4, 5** pavé d'auge; **4-5** port-salut; **4-7** pontl'évêque; **5, 2, 4** carré de l'est, coeur de bray; **5, 6** cream ~; **5-6** petit-suisse, saintpaulin; **5-8** saint-nectaire; **5-9** saint-florentin, saint-marcellin; **6-2-7** bouton-de-culotte; **6-3-4** selles-sur-cher; **6, 4** danish blue; **6-5** sainte-maure; **6, 6** farmer ~; **7, 2, 5** feuille de dreux; **7, 6** cottage ~; **7-7** brillatsavarin; **8, 4** Monterey Jack; **8, 6** American ~; **8-6** laguiole-aubrac.

cheesy *See* **tasteless**

chelonian 6 turtle; **8** terrapin, tortoise.

chemical 4 acid, alum, salt; **5** niter, oxide; **6** alkali; **7** amalgam, organic, polymer; **8** aldehyde, analytic; **9** elemental, inorganic, synthetic; **10** alchemical; **13** metallurgical; PHRASES: **7, 8** organic compound.

chemical element 3 tin; **4** gold, iron, lead, neon, zinc; **5** argon, boron, group, metal, radon, xenon; **6** barium, carbon, cerium, cesium, cobalt, copper, curium, erbium, helium, indium, iodine, nickel, osmium, oxygen, period, radium, silver, sodium, sulfur; **7** arsenic, bismuth, bromine, cadmium, calcium, element, fermium, gallium, hafnium, halogen, holmium, iridium, krypton, lithium, mercury, niobium, rhenium, rhodium, silicon, sulphur *UK*, terbium, thorium, thulium, uranium, wolfram, yttrium; **8** actinium, actinoid, aluminum, antimony, astatine, chlorine, chromium, europium, fluorine, francium, hydrogen, lutetium, nitrogen, nobelium, nonmetal, platinum, polonium, rubidium, samarium, scandium, selenium, tantalum, thallium, titanium, tungsten, vanadium; **9** americium, berkelium, beryllium, columbium, germanium, lanthanum, magnesium, manganese, metalloid, neodymium, neptunium, palladium, plutonium, potassium, ruthenium, semimetal, strontium, tellurium, ytterbium, zirconium; **10** chalconide,

dysprosium, gadolinium, lanthanoid, lawrencium, molybdenum, phosphorus, promethium, technetium; **11** californium, einsteinium, mendelevium; **12** praseodymium, protactinium; PHRASES: **4-5** rare-earth; **5, 3** inert gas, noble gas; **5, 5** heavy metal; **8, 5** periodic table.

chemical reaction 7 process, product, reagent; **10** ionization; **11** equilibrium; **14** neutralization, polymerization.

chemist 9 alchemist; **12** metallurgist.

chemistry 5 alloy, vibes; **7** alchemy, empathy, harmony, rapport; **8** analysis, chemurgy, sympathy; **9** synthesis; **10** attraction, metallurgy; **11** interaction; **13** understanding; **14** thermodynamics; **15** crystallography.

Chennai 6 Madras.

cherub 5 angel, cupid, putto; **8** amoretto.

chess 3 pin; **4** fork, king, mate, pawn, rook; **5** board, check, piece, queen; **6** bishop, castle, knight, square; **7** opening; **8** castling, chessman; **9** checkmate; PHRASES: **3, 4** end game.

chest 3 ark, box; **4** bust, ribs, tits; **5** boobs, bosom, pecks, torso, trunk; **6** breast, coffer, nipple; **8** knockers; PHRASES: **5, 4** upper body.

chew 3 eat; **4** bite, chaw, crop, gnaw, peck, rend, tear; **5** champ, chomp, crush, graze, grind, munch; **6** browse, crunch, nibble, squash; **7** pasture; **8** ruminate; **9** manducate *UK*, masticate.

chic 2 in; **4** posh; **5** jumpy, natty, ritzy, smart, style; **6** classy, dapper, glitzy, modish, spruce, swanky; **7** dashing, elegant, groomed, panache, soignée, stylish; **8** elegance; **10** attractive, classiness, modishness; **11** fashionable, stylishness; PHRASES: **4, 6-3** well turned-out *UK*; **4-7** well-dressed, well-groomed.

chicken 3 hen; **6** afraid, craven, scared; **7** fearful, gutless; **8** cowardly, hesitant; **9** reluctant; **10** frightened; **12** apprehensive; PHRASES: **4-7** lily-livered; **5-7** faint-hearted.

chicory 7 succory.

chief 4 boss, head, main; **5** ruler; **7** captain, leading, topmost; **8** foremost; **9** commander, principal.

chief justice 3 Jay (John); **4** Taft (William Howard); **5** Chase (Salmon Portland), Stone (Harlan Fiske), Taney (Roger

Brooke), Waite (Morrison Remick), White (Edward Douglass); **6** Burger (Warren Earl), Fuller (Melville Weston), Hughes (Charles Evans), Vinson (Frederick Moore), Warren (Earl); **8** Marshall (John), Rutledge (John); **9** Ellsworth (Oliver), Rehnquist (William Hubbs).

chigoe 6 jigger; PHRASES: **4, 4** sand flea.

child 3 boy, imp, kid, lad, son, tot; **4** babe, baby, brat, girl, lass, love, mite, teen; **5** bairn, issue, kiddy, minor, scion, spawn, sprog *UK*, youth; **6** infant, kiddie *UK*, laddie, lassie, moppet, nipper *UK*, peewee, poppet *UK*, result, rugrat; **7** darling, neonate, newborn, outcome, product, toddler; **8** creation, daughter, juvenile, nursling, suckling; **9** offspring, youngster; **10** adolescent; **14** whippersnapper; PHRASES: **4, 2, 4** babe in arms; **5-5** ankle-biter *UK*; **6, 2, 3** bundle of joy; **6, 5** little angel; **6, 6** little cherub, little monkey; **8, 4** bouncing baby.

childbearing 9 gestation, pregnancy; **10** childbirth, motherhood; **12** reproduction.

childbirth 5 labor; **6** Lamaze; **7** preemie, travail; **8** delivery; **9** Caesarian; **11** parturition; **12** accouchement, childbearing, contractions; PHRASES: **8-11, 7** estrogen-replacement therapy.

chill 3 fan, icy, nip, raw; **4** cold, cool, rest; **5** aloof, deter, gloom, nippy, parky *UK*, relax; **6** benumb, biting, chilly, formal, freeze, frigid, frosty, remote, wintry; **7** anxiety, depress, shudder; **8** coldness, coolness, detached, dispirit, exposure, freezing, frighten, glaciate, reserved, wariness; **9** aloofness, chilblain, chiliness, frostbite, nippiness, pneumonia; **10** depression, detachment, discourage, frostiness, remoteness, unfriendly, uninvolved; **11** hypothermia, indifferent, refrigerate; **12** apprehension, indifference, supercilious; **14** unfriendliness; PHRASES: **2, 4** be calm; **3, 2, 3** put on ice; **3, 4, 4, 2** put your feet up; **4, 1, 5** have a break; **4, 1, 6, 4** cast a shadow over; **4, 2, 4** take it easy; **4, 4** calm down; **5, 3** ~ out; **6, 2** loosen up; **6, 4** common cold, sudden fear.

chime 4 call, ding, peal, ring; **5** clang, sound; **6** strike; PHRASES: **4, 3** ring out; **4-4** ding-dong.

chimera *See* **fantasy**

chimney 3 lum *UK*; **4** flue; **5** stack; **6** funnel.

China 6 Cathay. *See also* **ceramics**

china clay 6 kaolin.

China rose 8 hibiscus.

Chinese cabbage 2-4 pe-tsai; **3-4** pakchoi.

Chinese dish 3, 3 dim sum, won ton; **3, 3, 4** egg foo yung; **3, 4** egg roll; **3, 4, 4** egg drop soup; **4-3** stir-fry; **4, 4** chop suey, chow mein; **4, 6** beef congee; **5, 4** fried rice; **5, 7** fried noodles, lemon chicken; **6, 4** Peking duck, spring roll; **6, 5** shrimp balls.

Chinese gooseberry 4, 5 kiwi fruit.

chinwag 4 chat, talk; **6** gossip, natter; **7** chatter; **8** converse.

chip 3 bit, hew; **4** flaw, mark, pare; **5** chunk, crumb, flake, notch, piece, token; **6** chisel, damage, marker, morsel, potato; **7** blemish, shaving, silicon, whittle; **8** fragment, splinter; **9** disfigure; **12** imperfection; PHRASES: **5, 3** break off; **5, 4** poker ~; **6, 4** potato ~; **6, 5** French fries; **7, 5** playing piece.

chipper 4 trim; **5** perky, smart; **6** bright, chirpy, dapper, frisky, lively, upbeat; **8** animated, cheerful; **9** energetic, exuberant, sprightly; PHRASES: **4-7** well-dressed; **4-8** high-spirited.

chippy 6 touchy; **9** carpenter; PHRASES: **4, 4** fish shop *UK*.

chit 4 bill; **5** tally; **7** account, receipt.

chivalrous 5 brave, civil, loyal, manly, noble; **6** heroic, polite; **7** courtly, gallant, valiant; **8** gracious, knightly, mannerly; **9** attentive, courteous; **11** considerate, magnanimous; PHRASES: **4-8** well-mannered.

chivalry 5 valor; **7** bravery, bushido, courage, heroics, loyalty, prowess; **8** civility, courtesy, kindness, nobility; **9** adventure, gallantry, gentility; **10** politeness; **11** courtliness, magnanimity; PHRASES: **4, 7** good manners; **7-2** derring-do.

chloride 7 muriate.

choice 4 best, fine, good, pick, rare; **5** group, prime, range; **6** option, select; **7** dilemma, special, variety; **8** adoption, choosing, election, superior, sympathy, tendency; **9** excellent, selection; **10** preference; **11** alternative, inclination, opportunity, possibility; **12** predilection; PHRASES: **2, 3** or set; **4-7** high-quality; **5, 4** blind date; **5, 8** tough decision.

choke 4 clog, weep; **5** block; **6** stifle; **7** congest; **8** obstruct, strangle, throttle; **9** suffocate; **10** asphyxiate; PHRASES: **4, 2** stop up, well up; **6, 2** freeze up.

choose 3 opt; **4** pick, take, want, wish; **5** elect, favor; **6** decide, desire, prefer, select; **9** determine; PHRASES: **2, 3** go for; **3, 3** see fit; **4, 3** vote for; **5, 3** plump for, point out; **6, 2** decide on; **6, 3** single out; **6-4** cherry-pick.

choosy *See* **particular**

chop 2 ax; **3** cut, hew, lop; **4** fell, food, hack; **5** sever, slash, slice, split.

chopper 2 ax; **5** tooth; **10** helicopter.

choppy *See* **rough**

chord 5 triad; **7** harmony; **8** arpeggio; PHRASES: **5, 5** major ~, minor ~.

chore 3 job; **4** bore, task; **6** errand; **7** routine; **10** assignment, imposition; **13** inconvenience; PHRASES: **3, 3** odd job; **4, 4** hard work.

chorus 4 sing; **5** canon, choir, round; **6** repeat; **7** refrain, reprize; **8** response; **10** repetition; PHRASES: **5, 2, 4** speak at once; **5, 2, 6** speak in unison; **5, 8** speak together.

chosen 2 A1; **3** pet; **4** pick; **5** drawn, elect, elite, fancy; **6** choice, picked, seeded, select, sorted *UK*; **7** adopted, elected, special; **8** favorite, pickings, returned, selected; **9** desirable, gleanings, preferred, recherché, selection; **10** preferable; PHRASES: **2, 11** by appointment; **3, 4** the best; **3, 5** the cream; **4, 3** God's own *UK*; **4-6** hand-picked; **5, 2, 2, 5** crème de la crème; **5, 6** first choice.

christen 4 name; **5** bless, debut; **6** launch; **7** baptize; **8** nickname; **10** inaugurate.

Christian 2 JW, RC; **6** Friend, Moonie, Mormon, Quaker; **7** Baptist, Hussite, Lollard, Puritan; **8** Anglican, Catholic, Huguenot, Lutheran, Wesleyan; **9** Adventist, Calvinist, Mennonite, Methodist, Unitarian; **10** conformist, evangelist, Protestant, revivalist; **11** communicant, Evangelical, Trinitarian; **12** Episcopalian, Presbyterian; **13** Nonconformist, televangelist; **14** fundamentalist; PHRASES: **3, 4** Wee Free *UK*; **3, 5** God squad *UK*; **4-5** born-again; **4, 6** holy roller; **5-6** Bible-basher *UK*; **5, 8** Roman Catholic; **5-8** Anglo-Catholic; **6-3, 5** Latter-Day Saint.

Christian rite 4 mass; **6** burial, chrism, ritual; **7** baptism, penance, unction; **8** ablution, asperges, exorcism, marriage, viaticum; **9** cleansing, Eucharist, immersion, sacrament; **10** confession, lustration, ordination, sprinkling; **11** christening; **12** confirmation, denunciation, propitiation, purification; **13** thurification; **15** excommunication; PHRASES: **4, 2, 3, 5** sign of the Cross; **4, 2, 5** kiss of peace; **4, 5** last rites; **4, 9** Holy Matrimony; **5, 9** first communion; **5, 10** seven sacraments; **6, 2, 2, 5** laying on of hands; **7, 4** nuptial Mass, Requiem Mass; **7, 7** extreme unction.

Christmas 4 noel, xmas, yule; **6** island; **8** yuletide.

chromosome 1 W, X, Y, Z; **3** DNA, RNA; **6** ploidy; **8** autosome, diploidy, haploidy; **10** polyploidy; PHRASES: **3, 10** sex ~; **4, 6** gene string; **7, 8** genetic material.

chronicle 3 log; **4** file, myth; **5** diary, notes, story; **6** annals, inform, legend, minute, record, relate, report; **7** account, archive, dossier, history, journal, logbook, memoirs, minutes, narrate, recount, summary; **8** describe, document, notebook, register; **9** biography, narration, narrative, recollect, recording, summarize, tradition; **11** description, documentary, information; **13** documentation; PHRASES: **3, 4** set down; **4, 1, 5** keep a diary; **4, 4** folk tale; **4, 4, 2** make note of; **4, 5** case notes, life story; **4, 5, 2** keep track of; **5, 4** write down.

chronicler 6 scribe; **7** diarist; **8** annalist, recorder; **9** historian; **15** historiographer.

chronology 4 date, hour, list; **6** annals, record; **7** account, history; **8** calendar; **9** chronicle, timetable; **10** summertime; **12** chronography; PHRASES: **2-4, 5** 12-hour clock, 24-hour clock; **3, 5, 4** the exact time; **5, 2, 6** order of events, train of events; **6, 6** carbon dating.

chronometry 2 UT; **4** date, hour; **8** calendar, horology; **10** summertime; **11** chronoscopy, clockmaking, timekeeping, watchmaking; **12** chronography; PHRASES: **2-4, 5** 12-hour clock, 24-hour clock; **4, 4** date line, time line, time zone; **5, 4** civil time, clock time, local time, solar time; **6, 8** Julian calendar; **8, 4** sidereal time; **9, 4** Universal Time.

chrysolite 7 olivine.

chuck 3 pat, tap; **4** hurl, quit, toss; **5** block, chock, clamp, fling, leave, pitch, throw, wedge; **6** resign, tickle; **7** discard; PHRASES: **3, 3, 2** get rid of; **3, 7** pat lightly; **4, 3** walk off, walk out; **5, 3** throw out; **5, 4** throw away; **7, 2** dispose of.

chuckle 5 laugh; **6** giggle; **7** chortle,

snicker, snigger *UK*; **8** laughter; **PHRASES: 5, 8** laugh inwardly; **6, 8** inward laughter.

chum *See* **friend**

chunk *See* **piece**

church 2 CE *UK*, CH *UK*, RC; **3** pew; **4** apse, dome, font, nave; **5** abbey, aisle, altar, choir, conch, crypt, spire, stall, tower; **6** chapel, chevet, clergy, flèche, podium, pulpit, temple, vestry; **7** chancel, lectern, minster, narthex; **8** basilica, cloister, crossing, sacristy, transept; **9** cathedral, Episcopal, sanctuary, triforium, vestibule; **10** ambulatory, blindstory, clerestory, presbytery, tabernacle; **12** confessional, denomination, meetinghouse; **PHRASES: 4, 6** amen corner, rood screen; **5, 5** choir stall; **6, 8** flying buttress; **7, 5** galilee porch; **7, 7** tribune gallery. *See also* **worship (place of worship)**

churchgoer *See* **worshipper**

churn 3 mix; **4** roil, whip; **5** shake; **7** agitate.

chute 5 force *UK*, shaft, slide; **6** sluice; **7** cascade, channel, descent, raceway; **8** cataract; **9** waterfall.

cigarette 3 fag *UK*; **4** weed; **5** smoke, snout; **PHRASES: 3-3** dog-end *UK*; **6, 4** coffin nail; **6, 5** cancer stick.

cinch 3 fix; **4** belt, bind; **5** girth, strap; **6** assure, breeze, doddle *UK*, insure, settle; **7** tighten; **8** restrain; **9** certainty, guarantee, restraint; **PHRASES: 4, 3** sure bet; **4, 5** sure thing; **4, 7** make certain; **4, 9** dead certainty; **5, 2, 4** piece of cake; **6, 4** child's play.

cinchona 5, 4 china bark; **8, 4** Peruvian bark.

cinema 4 nabe; **5** films *UK*; **6** movies, screen; **7** theater; **8** pictures *UK*; **9** directing; **13** screenwriting; **14** cinematography; **PHRASES: 3, 6** big screen; **6, 6** silver screen; **6, 8** motion pictures; **7, 5** picture house *UK*; **7, 6** picture palace *UK*.

cipher 4 code, zero; **6** nobody; **7** nothing, symbols; **9** nonentity; **10** encryption; **11** cryptograph; **PHRASES: 6, 7** secret message.

circle 1 O; **3** lap, orb, set; **4** ball, band, disc *UK*, disk *UK*, gang, hour, loop, lune, oval, ring; **5** ambit, chord, crowd, curve, cycle, group, orbit, round, wheel; **6** arctic, bypass, clique, detour, rotate, sphere, zodiac; **7** annulus, circuit, contain, ellipse, enclose, mandala, revolve; **8** encircle, epicycle, incircle, surround; **9** antarctic, circulate, racetrack; **10** annulation, racecourse,

roundabout; **14** circumambulate, circumnavigate; **PHRASES: 2, 5** go round *UK*; **4, 1, 4** take a turn; **4, 5** full cycle; **5, 4** round trip; **5, 6** skirt around; **7, 6** traffic ~.

circle (parts of a circle) 3 arc; **4** axis; **5** chord; **6** center, radius, sector; **7** segment, sextant; **8** crescent, diameter, quadrant; **13** circumference.

circuit 2 IC, OR; **3** AND, lap, LSI, NOR, NOT, XOR; **4** beat, chip, gate, gyre, loop, NAND, oval, path, ring, tour, trip, turn, VLSI; **5** ambit, cycle, orbit, round, route, track, trail; **6** bridge, circle, filter; **7** ellipse, journey, network, revolve; **8** circling, spinning, twirling, wheeling, whirling; **9** circuitry, microchip; **10** circumvent, revolution; **13** circumference; **14** circumambulate, circumnavigate; **PHRASES: 5, 4** logic gate; **5, 7** short ~.

circuitous 7 complex, devious, diffuse, oblique, winding; **8** indirect, tortuous, twisting; **9** deviating, excursive; **10** backhanded, convoluted, digressive, discursive, meandering, roundabout, tangential; **11** complicated; **12** periphrastic; **14** circumlocutory; **PHRASES: 3, 3, 5** off the point; **3, 3, 7** off the subject; **4-6** long-winded; **7, 6** traffic circle.

circuitous (be circuitous) 4 turn; **6** corner, ramble, wander; **7** deviate, digress, diverge, maunder, meander; **PHRASES: 1-4** U-turn.

circuitry 4 cell, tube; **5** anode, board, choke, diode, earth, valve, wires; **7** battery, breaker, cathode; **8** inductor, resistor, rheostat, terminal; **9** amplifier, capacitor, component, condenser, conductor, insulator, rectifier; **10** oscillator, transducer, transistor; **11** accumulator, electronics, motherboard, transformer; **13** semiconductor; **PHRASES: 7, 4** silicon chip; **7, 7** printed circuit.

circular 5 flier, ovate, ovoid, round, tract; **6** coiled, curved, cyclic, looped, radial, rotary, rotund, spiral; **7** annular, discoid, handout, helical, leaflet, orbital, rounded, spheric; **8** annulate, brochure, cyclical, elliptic, globular, gyratory, handbill, heliacal, pamphlet; **9** orbicular, spherical; **10** elliptical, spherelike, spheroidal; **13** advertisement; **PHRASES: 1-6** O-shaped; **3-6** egg-shaped; **4, 4** oval wavy; **4-6** ring-shaped; **5-6** wheel-shaped. *See also* **circuitous**

circular thing 4 band, belt, disc, disk

UK, dome, halo, hoop, ring, sash, tire; **5** crown, noose, orbit, plate, wheel; **6** anklet, choker, collar, corona, discus, girdle, saucer, wreath; **7** coronet, equator, horizon, rainbow; **8** bracelet, hairband, headband, neckband, necklace; **9** waistband, wristband; **10** cummerbund.

circulate 3 mix; **4** flow, move, pass; **5** issue; **6** mingle, spread, travel; **7** network, revolve; **8** interact; **9** broadcast, entertain, socialize; **10** distribute; **11** disseminate; PHRASES: **2, 8** be sociable; **4, 2** join in; **4, 3** give out, hand out, send out; **4, 5** make known; **4, 6** pass around.

circulation 4 flow; **5** sales; **6** motion, spread; **7** passage; **8** exchange, movement, rotation; **10** readership; **12** distribution, transmission; **13** dissemination.

circumlocution 6 ambage; **8** excursus, rambling; **9** conundrum, departure, deviation, equivoque, excursion, sidetrack, wandering; **10** digression, discursion, meandering; **11** aimlessness, irrelevance, obliqueness, periphrasis; **12** indirectness, tortuousness; **13** equivocalness, pointlessness; **14** circuitousness, convolutedness, roundaboutness; PHRASES: **4-10** long-windedness; **6, 4** double talk.

circumscribe See **limit**

circumspect 4 cagy, wary; **5** alert, chary, ready; **7** careful, guarded, prudent; **8** cautious, prepared, vigilant, watchful; **9** judicious; **10** scrupulous.

circumstance(s) 4 case; **5** basis, event, means, place, scene, setup, stand, state, terms; **6** factor, ground, layout, milieu, outfit, status; **7** climate, context, footing, picture, setting; **8** attitude, incident, instance, juncture, position, scenario, standing; **9** condition, happening, resources, situation, viewpoint; **10** atmosphere, background, conditions, occurrence, standpoint; **11** contingency, environment, eventuality; **12** surroundings; PHRASES: **3, 2, 3, 4** lay of the land, lie of the land; **3, 3, 4** ins and outs; **3, 4, 2, 2** the size of it; **3, 5** the score, the times; **3, 5, 7** the whole picture; **3, 6, 5** how things stand; **4, 4** ball game; **5, 2, 3** story so far; **5, 2, 4** state of play; **5, 2, 7** state of affairs; **6, 2, 4** kettle of fish; **6, 3** status quo.

circumstances (under the circumstances) 2 so; **4** thus; **11** accordingly; **12** consequently; PHRASES: **2, 2** as is UK; **2, 2, 2** as it is; **2, 2, 6** as it stands; **2, 2, 8** as it

happened; **2, 3, 5** in the event; **2, 4, 4** in that case; **2, 6, 5** as things stand; **2, 7, 5** as matters stand; **3, 2** and so; **4, 5, 2** that being so.

circumstantial 7 hearsay, implied; **8** indirect, inferred, presumed, relative, situated, variable; **9** anecdotal, secondary; **10** background, contextual, contingent, incidental; **11** atmospheric, conditional, conjectural, inferential, provisional, situational; **12** adventitious; **13** environmental.

circumstantiate 4 cite; **6** adduce, detail; **7** itemize, specify; **8** document, instance; **12** substantiate; **13** particularize; PHRASES: **2, 4, 6** go into detail; **5, 3** spell out.

circumvent See **avoid**

circus See **show**

circus performer 5 clown; **6** barker; **7** acrobat, juggler, tumbler; **9** gladiator, strongman; **10** ringmaster, ropewalker; **11** equilibrist, saltimbanco; **13** contortionist; PHRASES: **4-4, 6** high-wire artist; **4, 5** lion tamer; **4-5** fire-eater; **5, 3** stunt man; **5, 7** snake charmer; **5, 10** human cannonball; **7, 6** trapeze artist UK; **8, 5** bareback rider; **9, 6** tightrope walker.

cirque 3 cwm UK; **5** combe; **6** corrie UK, hollow, valley.

citation See **quotation**

cite See **quote**

citizen 5 voter; **8** national, resident; **10** inhabitant; PHRASES: **5, 8** legal resident.

citrine 5 topaz; **6** quartz.

city 2 EC UK, LA, NY, Ur; **3** NYC, Rio; **4** Bath, Rome, town; **5** Cairo, Miami, Paris, Tokyo, urban; **6** Ankara, Athens, Berlin, Boston, Dallas, Denver, hamlet, Lisbon, London, Madrid, Moscow, Prague, Quebec, Sydney, Vienna; **7** Atlanta, Beijing, Belfast, capital, Cardiff, Chicago, Detroit, Houston, Seattle, Toronto, village; **8** Ashgabat, Belgrade, Budapest, Calcutta, Carthage, Pretoria; **9** community, Edinburgh, Hollywood, Melbourne, municipal, Nashville; **10** metropolis, Pittsburgh, Washington; **11** conurbation, megalopolis; **12** metropolitan, municipality, Philadelphia; PHRASES: **2, 5** St Louis; **3, 2, 7** Rio de Janeiro; **3, 4** New York; **3, 5** Las Vegas; **3, 7** Los Angeles, New Orleans; **3, 9** San Francisco; **4, 4** Hong Kong; **5, 6** urban spread; **5, 7** state capital; **6, 4** county seat, Mexico C~.

city (part of city) 4 area, mart, slum,

ward, zone; **5** block, forum, plaza; **6** arcade, barrio, ghetto, hamlet, market, piazza, square, uptown; **7** midtown, quarter; **8** district, downtown, precinct; **10** metropolis, Tenderloin; **11** marketplace; PHRASES: **2-2, 4** no-go area; **4, 3** skid row; **4, 6** city center, high street, main street; **5, 4** inner city; **6, 6** market square; **6, 8** voting precinct; **7, 6** housing estate; **8, 4** blighted area, business zone, shopping area, shopping mall; **8, 6** shopping center; **11, 4** residential area.

civil **5** civic; **6** polite, public; **8** amicable, domestic, gracious, obliging; **9** courteous; **10** respectful; **11** considerate; **13** accommodating; PHRASES: **4-8** well-mannered.

civil engineer **2** CE; **8** surveyor; **10** contractor.

civil engineering **7** mapping; **8** planning; **9** surveying; **12** construction.

civil rights **4** King (Martin Luther, Jr.); **5** NAACP, Parks (Rosa); **6** Clarke (Septima), Garvey (Marcus), rights; **7** Jenkins (Esau); **8** freedoms, Robinson (Bernice); **9** Abernathy (Ralph), liberties; **10** privileges, Washingtom (Booker T.); PHRASES: **4, 6** free speech; **5, 5** Black Power; **5, 9** First Amendment; **7, 5** Freedom Rides; **7, 6** Freedom Summer; **10, 8** Birmingham Campaign.

Civil War **3** Reb; **4** gray; **5** Davis (Jefferson), Dixie, South, Union; **6** Athens (Battle of), Helena (Battle of), Rebels, Resaca (Battle of), Shiloh, Shiloh (Battle of); **7** Atlanta (Battle of), Federal, Kinston (Battle of), Lincoln (Abraham), Memphis (Battle of), Olustee (Battle of), Yankees; **8** Antietam (Battle of), Carthage (Battle of), grayback, Manassas, Manassas (Battle of), Piedmont (Battle of), Richmond (Battle of), Yorktown (Battle of); **9** Chantilly (Battle of), doughface, Galveston (Battle of), Nashville (Battle of), secession, Secession, Vicksburg, Vicksburg (Battle of); **10** Gettysburg, Gettysburg (Battle of), Kirksville (Battle of), nightrider, Perryville (Battle of), Petersburg (Siege of), Sharpsburg, Winchester (Battle of); **11** bushwhacker, Chattanooga (Battle of), Chickamauga (Battle of), Confederacy, Confederate, Springfield (Battle of); **12** carpetbagger; **13** Andersonville; **14** Fredericksburg; **16** Chancellorsville, Chancellorsville (Battle of); PHRASES: **3, 4** Rio Hill (Battle of); **3, 5** New Berne (Battle of), Pea Ridge (Battle of); **3, 6** New Market (Battle of); **3, 7** New Orleans (Battle of), Red Strings; **3, 7, 3, 6** War Between the States; **4, 3** Bull Run (First and Second); **4, 4** Fair Oaks, free soil; **4, 5** Bear River (Battle of), Five Forks (Battle of), Fort Henry (Battle of), Free State; **4, 6** Cold Harbor (Battle of), Fort Fisher (Battle of), Fort Sumter (Battle of), Port Hudson (Battle of); **4-6** post-bellum; **4, 7** Fort Stedman (Battle of); **4, 8** Fort Donelson (Battle of); **5, 3, 4** Stars and Bars; **5, 4** Billy Yank; **5, 4, 8** Seven Days Campaign; **5, 7** Bayou Fourche (Battle of); **5, 8** South Mountain (Battle of); **5, 10** Hill's Plantation (Battle of); **6, 3** Johnny Reb; **6, 5** Stones River (Battle of); **6, 6** Border States; **6, 10** Brice's Crossroads (Battle of); **7, 5** Hampton Roads (Battle of), Harper's Ferry (Battle of), Palmito Ranch (Battle of), Prairie Grove (Battle of), Wilson's Creek (Battle of); **7, 6** Enfield musket; **7, 7** buffalo soldier; **8, 4** Anaconda Plan, Arkansas Post (Battle of), Glorieta Pass (Battle of); **9, 5** Peachtree Creek (Battle of); **10, 5** Missionary Ridge; **12, 12** Emancipation Proclamation.

clad *See* **dressed**

claim **4** aver; **5** right; **6** allege, assert, charge, demand; **7** contend; **8** arrogate, maintain; **9** assertion; **10** accusation, allegation, contention; **11** appropriate, entitlement.

clamber *See* **climb**

clammy **3** wet; **4** damp, dank; **5** close, humid, moist, muggy, slimy; **6** sticky, sweaty.

clamor **3** bay, cry, din; **4** call, yell; **5** noise, shout; **6** appeal, demand, insist, scream, uproar; **7** request, screech; **8** shouting; **9** commotion; **10** hullabaloo; PHRASES: **3, 3** cry out.

clan **3** set; **4** band; **5** tribe; **6** clique, family; **7** coterie; **9** relations; **10** fraternity.

clang **4** bang, call, ring, toll; **5** clank, clink, sound; **6** jangle; **11** reverberate; PHRASES: **4-4** ding-dong.

clap **3** din, pat, tap; **4** bang, boom, slam, slap; **5** blast, burst, cheer, clang, clash, crash, stamp, storm; **6** deafen, hammer, rattle, thwack, wallop; **7** acclaim, applaud, clatter, explode, resound, thunder; **9** fulminate; **11** reverberate.

clapping **7** ovation, support; **8** applause; **11** acclamation; PHRASES: **5, 2, 8** round of applause; **8, 7** standing ovation. *See also* **clap**

claptrap *See* **nonsense**

clarify 4 open; **5** defog; **6** define, filter, purify, refine; **7** cleanse, explain, process, uncloud; **8** brighten, decipher, simplify; **9** elucidate, enlighten, explicate, interpret; **10** illuminate; **11** crystallize, demonstrate; **12** disambiguate; PHRASES: **4, 5** make clear; **4, 5, 2** shed light on; **5, 2** clear up; **5, 3** spell out; **5, 5, 2** throw light on.

clarity 5 focus; **6** purity; **8** accuracy, blatancy, exposure, lucidity; **9** clearness, coherence, exactness, limpidity, plainness, precision, sharpness, starkness, vividness; **10** brightness, brilliance, definition, directness, prominence, simplicity; **11** obviousness, pellucidity, perspicuity; **12** definiteness, distinctness, explicitness, transparency; **15** intelligibility, perspicuousness, unambiguousness.

clash 3 jar, row; **4** bang; **5** brush, clang, clank, crash, fight; **6** battle; **7** clatter, collide, quarrel; **8** argument, conflict, disagree, mismatch; **9** encounter; **10** contravene; **12** disagreement.

clasp 4 hold, hook; **5** catch, grasp; **6** clutch, popper *UK*; **8** fastener; PHRASES: **4, 3, 3** hook and eye; **9, 4** alligator clip.

class 1 U; **3** fix, ilk, set; **4** band, chic, head, kind, list, rank, slot, sort, tier, type; **5** brand, caste, flair, genre, genus, grade, group, label, level, niche, order, place, style, taste; **6** assign, branch, clique, course, league, lesson, period, status, subset; **7** arrange, bracket, catalog *UK*, coterie, heading, lecture, listing, panache, section, seminar, session, species, station, stratum; **8** category, classify, division, elegance, grouping, standing, subclass, subgroup, tutorial; **9** catalogue *UK*, designate; **10** background, categorize, department, discussion, distribute, pigeonhole, refinement, subsection; **11** compartment, subcategory, subdivision; **14** classification, sophistication; PHRASES: **8, 5** tutorial group.

class (be in a class of one's own) 5 excel, shine; PHRASES: **5, 3** stand out.

classic 5 model; **6** simple; **7** abiding, typical; **8** immortal, landmark, standard, timeless; **9** benchmark, memorable; **10** definitive, masterwork; **11** masterpiece; **13** unforgettable; **14** characteristic.

classical music 5 opera; **6** choral, sonata; **7** chamber; **8** madrigal, romantic, symphony; **10** minimalist, orchestral; **12** contrapuntal; **13** impressionist; PHRASES: **6-4** twelve-tone; **7, 8** musique concrète.

classification 3 set; **5** class, group; **6** triage; **7** grading, ranking, sorting; **8** category, division, grouping, ordering, taxonomy; **9** hierarchy; **10** cataloging; **11** arrangement, cataloguing *UK*; **12** organization; **14** categorization.

classify 3 fix; **4** rank, rate, sort, type; **5** brand, class, grade, group, index, label, order, place; **6** assign; **7** arrange, catalog *UK*, dispose; **8** organize, tabulate; **9** catalogue *UK*, designate; **10** categorize, distribute, pigeonhole.

classy *See* **elegant**

clatter 4 bang; **5** clang, clank, smash; **6** jangle, rattle.

clause *See* **section**

claw 4 hook, nail, tear; **5** graze, talon; **6** pierce, scrape; **7** scratch; **8** scrabble; **10** fingernail.

clay 3 mud; **4** dirt, marl, slip, soil, till; **5** adobe, argil, earth; **6** kaolin; **8** petuntse.

clean 3 dry, mop, new, rub; **4** beat, buff, comb, dewy, dust, iron, neat, nice, pure, swab, tidy, trim, wash, wipe; **5** bathe, black, blank, brush, clear, erase, flush, fresh, groom, natty, preen, purge, quite, scour, scrub, shave, shine, snowy, strip, sweep, valet, whisk, white, wring; **6** bleach, bright, dainty, dapper, decent, hoover, kosher, mangle, neaten, polish, purify, refine, scrape, simple, sponge, spruce, starch, vacuum, whiten, wholly; **7** aseptic, cleanly, cleanse, freshen, launder, orderly, perfect, shining, sterile, totally, unmixed, utterly; **8** entirely, hygienic, sanitary, spotless, thorough, unsoiled, virginal; **9** carbolize, disinfect, expurgate, holystone, sandblast, shipshape, sparkling, stainless, sterilize, undefiled, unmuddied, unstained, unsullied, untainted, untouched, whitewash, wholesome; **10** absolutely, altogether, antiseptic, completely, fastidious, immaculate, obliterate, pasteurize, salubrious, unpolluted; **11** untarnished; **13** decontaminate, unadulterated; **14** uncontaminated; PHRASES: **3, 2** mop up; **3, 3** rub out; **3-5** dry-clean; **4, 2** wash up, wipe up; **4, 3** muck out, wash off, wash out; **4, 3, 6** spit and polish; **4, 4** wash down; **4-4** dirt-free; **4-7** well-groomed; **5, 2** brush up, clear up, sweep up; **5, 2, 1, 5** fresh as a daisy; **5, 2, 1, 7** ~ as a whistle; **5, 2, 4**

white as snow; **5, 3** brush off, clear out, flush out; **5-3-4** spick-and-span; **6, 3** sponge off; **6-5** spring-clean *UK*; **7, 2** freshen up; **7-5** squeaky-clean.

cleaner 3 elp, wax; **4** char *UK*, crow, maid, soap, soda; **5** daily, dhobi *UK*, sweep, water; **6** barber, bleach, gargle, phenol, picker, polish, pumice; **7** buzzard *UK*, gleaner, servant, shampoo, swabber, sweeper, varnish, vulture, whiting; **8** abrasive, blacking, charlady *UK*, cleanser, domestic, graphite, purifier, scrubber, scullion; **9** bootblack, charwoman, deodorant, detergent, freshener, holystone, housemaid, launderer, laundress, mouthwash, scavenger, shoeblack *UK*, washerman, washwoman, whitewash; **10** antiseptic, beautician, dentifrice, dishwasher, laundryman, shoeshiner, soapflakes, toothpaste; **11** beachcomber, hairdresser, hearthstone, washerwoman; **12** disinfectant, housecleaner; PHRASES: **3, 3** Mrs Mop *UK*; **3, 9** air freshener; **4, 3, 5** soap and water; **4, 4** home help *UK*; **4, 5** cold cream, face cream; **4, 6** shoe polish, soap powder; **4, 9** room freshener; **6, 3** shower gel; **6, 4** baking soda, bubble bath; **6, 9** refuse collector; **7, 5** chimney sweep; **7, 6** washing powder *UK*; **8, 3** scouring pad; **8, 4** carbolic acid; **9, 3** shoeshine boy.

cleaning 5 enema; **6** airing; **7** asepsis, balneal, bathing, hygiene, lustral, purging; **8** aperient, dialysis, drainage, flushing, hygienic, laxative, refining, sanitary, sewerage; **9** bleaching, cleansing, delousing, detergent, purgative, purgatory; **10** antisepsis, filtration, freshening, fumigation, laundering, sanitation; **11** ablutionary, ventilation; **12** chlorination, disinfectant, disinfection, purification, purificatory, sanitization; **13** clarification, deodorization, distilllation, sterilization; **14** disinfestation, pasteurization; **15** decontamination; PHRASES: **3, 8** dry ~; **5, 7** stain removal; **6, 2** wiping up; **7-2** mopping-up; **7, 3** washing out. *See also* **housework**

cleanly 6 easily, simply; **7** quickly; **11** effectively, efficiently. *See also* **clean**

clear 3 lit, net, rid; **4** earn, fair, fine, free, gain, make, open, pure, rich, tidy, wipe; **5** empty, exact, filmy, light, lucid, lurid, naked, plain, sharp, sheer, showy, stark, sunny, vivid; **6** acquit, bright, direct, limpid, patent, settle, simple, strong, unclog; **7** absolve, blatant, certain, defined, evident, exposed, forgive, glaring, obvious, perfect, release, ringing, salient, unblock, vibrant, visible; **8** accurate, coherent, definite, disperse, distinct, explicit, flawless, pellucid, striking, sunshiny; **9** authorize, brilliant, cloudless, disappear, discharge, dissipate, evaporate, exculpate, exonerate, prominent, unclouded, uncovered, undoubted, vindicate; **10** apodeictic, diaphanous, noticeable, resounding, signposted, straighten, unhampered, unmissable; **11** outstanding, perspicuous, translucent, transparent, unambiguous, unblemished, uncluttered; **12** intelligible, unmistakable, unobstructed; **13** apprehensible; **14** comprehensible, understandable; **15** straightforward; PHRASES: **2, 4** on show; **2, 4, 6** in bold relief, in high relief; **2, 5** in focus; **2, 5, 2, 3** as ~ as day; **2, 7** on display; **3, 3, 2, 3** for all to see; **3-3-3** out-and-out; **3-7** see-through; **4, 2** tidy up *UK*; **4, 4** take home; **4-4** bell-like; **4-7** self-evident, well-defined; **4-10** high-definition; **5, 2** bring in, clean up; **5, 2, 3** plain to see; **5-3** clear-cut; **5, 4, 4** under one's nose; **7-5** crystal-clear.

cleave 3 cut, hew; **4** chop, gape, gash, link, nick, open, rend, rive, slit, slot, tear; **5** break, cling, crack, notch, sever, slash, split, stick; **6** adhere, breach, furrow, groove, incise, sunder; **7** embrace, rupture; PHRASES: **4, 2** hold on; **5, 4, 4** stick like glue.

clef 1 c, f, g; **3** key; **4** alto, bass; **5** tenor, viola; **6** treble; **7** soprano.

clemency *See* **mercy**

clergyman 3 Rev; **4** curé, dean, pope; **5** canon, cloth, elder, vicar; **6** bishop, cleric, curate, deacon, parson, pastor, priest, rector; **8** cardinal, chaplain, minister; **10** archbishop, archdeacon; **11** clergywoman; **12** ecclesiastic.

cleric *See* **priest**

clerk 6 cleric; **7** actuary; **8** official; **9** assistant; **12** receptionist; **13** administrator; PHRASES: **6, 6** office worker.

clever 4 glib, wily; **6** crafty; **7** cunning; **9** dexterous. *See also* **intelligent**

cleverness 3 wit; **5** flair, guile, skill; **6** acuity, brains, genius, talent, wisdom; **7** slyness; **8** aptitude, sagacity, subtlety, trickery; **9** acuteness, adeptness, alertness, canniness, dexterity, ingenuity, quickness, sharpness, smartness; **10** astuteness, braininess, brightness, brilliance, shrewdness; **12** incisiveness, intelligence; PHRASES: **4-10**

keen-wittedness; **5-10** quick-wittedness.

cliché **3** saw; **4** corn, line; **5** adage; **6** saying, slogan; **7** formula; **8** buzzword, chestnut, prosaism; **9** catchword, platitude.

click **4** snap, tick; **5** clack, clunk; **7** connect; PHRASES: **3, 2** get on; **3, 2, 3** hit it off; **4, 2** sink in; **4, 4, 5** fall into place; **4, 5** make sense; **6, 2** relate to; **6, 5** become clear.

cliffhanger **6** crisis; **10** tiebreaker; PHRASES: **4-5** nail-biter; **5-4** knife-edge.

climate **3** sun; **4** mood, rain; **5** sense; **7** feeling, weather; **8** ambiance; **9** situation, temperate; **10** atmosphere, conditions; **11** environment, temperature; **12** surroundings.

climate **(words describing climate)** **3** dry, hot; **4** arid, cold, cool; **5** humid, polar, rainy; **6** desert, tundra; **8** maritime, moderate, mountain, semiarid, subpolar, tropical; **9** semihumid, temperate; **10** equatorial; **11** continental, subtropical; **13** Mediterranean; PHRASES: **4, 6** rain forest.

climax **3** end; **4** acme, apex, peak; **5** close; **6** apogee, finish, height, orgasm, summit; **8** pinnacle; **9** culminate, highlight, terminate; PHRASES: **4, 5** high point.

climb **3** top; **4** hike, ramp, rise, shin, soar; **5** clear, mount, scale; **6** ascend, ascent, breast, hurdle, rocket; **7** clamber, upclimb, upswing; **8** escalade, escalate, increase, scrabble, scramble, surmount; **11** mountaineer; PHRASES: **2, 2** go up; **2, 4, 3, 3** go over the top; **3-6** sky-rocket; **5, 2** shoot up; **5, 3, 7** scale the heights; **6, 2** monkey up, shinny up.

climbing equipment **2** ax; **3** adz, map, nut, peg; **4** belt, bolt, bong, rope, RURP, skis, tape, tent; **5** boots UK, chalk, chock, knife, parka, piton, sling, spike, torch UK; **6** anchor, étrier UK, hammer, helmet, runner; **7** compass, goggles, harness, mittens, prodder, skyhook, stirrup; **8** ascender, backpack, crampons, extender, rucksack, snaplink; **9** bandoleer, descender, karabiner, microwire, screwgate; **10** flashlight, sunglasses; **11** snowglasses; **12** kletterschuh UK; PHRASES: **3, 2** ice ax; **3, 3** nut key; **4, 4** cow's tail, snap ring; **5, 5** belay brake; **5, 6** belay anchor.

climbing technique See **mountaineering terms**

clinch **3** hug; **4** hold, seal; **5** close; **6** cuddle, decide, settle; **7** embrace; PHRASES: **3, 2**

tie up; **4, 3** bear hug.

cling **3** hug; **4** grip, hold; **5** grasp, stick; **6** adhere, attach, clutch, retain; **8** maintain; PHRASES: **2, 9, 2** be dependent on; **3, 7** fit tightly; **4, 2** hang on, hold to, keep to; **4, 2, 2** hang on to; **5, 4** latch onto; **6, 2** depend on.

clinic **5** class; **7** meeting, seminar, surgery UK; **8** hospital, workshop; PHRASES: **6, 6** health center; **7, 6** private ~; **10, 4** consulting room.

clink **4** jail, stir; **5** chink, clank; **6** jangle, jingle, prison, tinkle.

clip **3** cut, fix, hit, lop, pin; **4** blow, crop, pare, trim; **5** clasp, piece, prune, quote, shave, shear, slide UK; **6** attach, fasten, secure, staple; **7** excerpt, extract, passage, shorten; **8** fastener; **9** cartridge, quotation; PHRASES: **3, 3** cut off; **5, 4** sound bite.

clique **3** set; **4** band, clan, club, gang, ring, sect; **6** circle; **7** coterie, faction; PHRASES: **2-5** in-crowd, in-group.

cliquish **6** closed, narrow; **8** clannish; **9** exclusive; PHRASES: **5-4** close-knit.

cloak **4** cape, cope, toga, wrap; **5** cappa, palla; **6** abolla, almuce, Batman, birrus, mantle, poncho, serape; **7** amictus, burnous, chlamys, jellaba, pallium, zimarra; **8** burnoose, mantelet; **9** djellabah; PHRASES: **4, 4** abbé cape; **4, 7** toga virilis; **5, 4** opera cape; **5, 5** cappa magna, opera ~; **6, 4** Oxford gown.

cloakroom See **restroom**

clobber **3** hit; **4** beat; **5** punch, thump; **6** outfit, strike.

clock **3** hit; **4** bash, belt, biff, dial, face, time; **5** alarm, meter, timer, watch, water; **6** strike, wallop; **7** clobber, control, sundial; **8** horologe; **9** clepsydra, hourglass, regulator, stopwatch, timepiece; **10** timekeeper, wristwatch; **11** chronometer, speedometer; PHRASES: **5, 5** alarm ~, ~ radio, water ~; **6, 5** analog ~, atomic ~, cuckoo ~, pocket watch; **7, 5** digital ~.

clockwork **6** device; **8** accuracy; **9** machinery, mechanism; **10** regularity, smoothness; **11** preciseness; **12** flawlessness.

clod See **lump**

clog See **block**

cloister **5** abbey; **6** arcade, closet, friary; **7** convent, nunnery, portico, retreat, seclude, shelter, walkway; **8** withdraw; **9** colonnade, monastery; **10** quadrangle.

close 3 bar, end, mum; 4 bolt, dear, dusk, fail, firm, fold, join, lock, mean, meet, near, nigh, plug, seal, shut, slam, warm, wrap; 5 block, cease, cheap, cover, dense, exact, handy, humid, latch, local, muggy, quiet, solid, tight, unite; 6 button, chummy, ending, fasten, finale, finish, loving, nearby, packed, secure, silent, sticky, stingy, stuffy, sultry; 7 airless, compact, connect, cramped, devoted, evening, fulfill, looming, miserly, padlock, precise, resolve, similar; 8 accurate, adjacent, attached, blockade, collapse, complete, conclude, confined, deadline, definite, faithful, familiar, friendly, grudging, imminent, intimate, obstruct, taciturn, upcoming; 9 cessation, culminate, foreclose, impending, niggardly, secretive, terminate; 10 completion, compressed, conclusion, denouement, oppressive, sweltering, ungenerous; 11 approaching, discontinue, forthcoming, neighboring, tightfisted; 12 parsimonious; 13 uncomfortable; 15 uncommunicative; PHRASES: 2, 2 do up; 2, 3, 2, 8 go out of business; 2, 3, 4, 6 in the near future; 2, 3, 7 on the horizon; 2, 4 at hand, go bust; 2, 4, 8 on your doorstep; 3, 2 zip up; 3, 2, 3, 3 end of the day; 3, 3, 3, 2 put the lid on; 4, 2 lock up, time up, wind up, wrap up; 4, 2, 2, 3 come to an end; 4, 3 last lap, seal off; 4, 3, 4, 2 pull the plug on; 4, 4 last ball, last call, last over, shut down, wind down; 4, 5 last night, last round, last stage; 4, 7 home stretch, last innings; 5, 2, 2, 3 bring to an end; 5, 7 cease trading; 5-8 penny-pinching; 6, 2 button up; 6, 4 batten down; 7, 4 closing time; 7, 6 closing stages; 9, 2, 4 close/shut up shop.

close (person who closes) 5 screw; 6 jailer, porter, sentry, warder; 7 doorman, janitor, turnkey; 8 sentinel; 9 caretaker *UK*, concierge; 10 doorkeeper, gatekeeper; PHRASES: 5, 8 night watchman.

closed 4 over, shut; 5 elite, ended; 6 barred, bolted, locked, sealed, secure, zipped; 7 bigoted, blocked, cliquey, decided, latched, limited, private, secured, settled; 8 airtight, buttoned, clannish, cliquish, fastened, unopened; 9 concluded, exclusive, padlocked; 10 impassable, impervious, intolerant, obstructed, prejudiced, restricted, terminated, waterproof, watertight; 11 impermeable, unnavigable; 12 impenetrable, inaccessible; PHRASES: 4, 2 shut up; 6, 2 zipped up; 6-6 closed-minded, narrow-minded, vacuum-packed; 7-5 burglar-proof; 8-2 buttoned-up *UK*.

closeness 7 empathy; 8 intimacy, vicinity; 9 immediacy, imminence, proximity; 10 attachment, confidence, friendship; 11 familiarity; 13 understanding. *See also* close

closet 6 secret; 7 confine, private, seclude; 8 cloister; 10 undeclared; 11 clandestine, unprofessed; PHRASES: 4, 2 shut up.

closing *See* final

closure 3 bar, end, let; 4 stop; 5 block, chock; 6 ending, finish; 7 barrier, closing, impasse; 8 blockade, blockage, collapse, deadlock, finality, shutdown, shutting, stoppage; 9 cessation, hindrance, occlusion, stalemate; 10 bankruptcy, completion, conclusion, congestion, resolution, standstill; 11 contraction, dissolution, foreclosure, fulfillment, obstruction, termination; 12 constipation, constriction; 13 impassability, inevitability, strangulation; 14 conclusiveness, discontinuance, impermeability, imperviousness; 15 impenetrability; PHRASES: 7, 3 sealing off; 8, 4 shutting down.

clot 3 set; 4 blob, lump, mass; 7 congeal, globule, thicken; 8 coalesce; 9 coagulate; 12 accumulation.

cloth 3 rag; 5 stuff, towel; 6 fabric, napkin. *See also* fabric

clothe 4 garb; 5 cloak, cover, dress; PHRASES: 3, 3 fit out.

clothes 3 aba, kit; 4 baju, cote, duds, garb, gear, haik, slop, togs, wear; 5 choli, cotta, dress, getup, jabot, jamah, mufti, pagne, pilch, weeds; 6 attire, bodice, halter, inseam, kabaya, magyar, outfit, vestee; 7 apparel, baggies, civvies, clobber *UK*, cuirass, cutaway, fashion, garment, jumpers, layette, leotard, maillot, pattern, raiment, regalia, rompers, singlet, tatters, threads, uniform, vesture, watteau, woolens, wrapper; 8 castoffs, clothing, coonskin, dalmatic, knitwear, neckline, overalls, parament, playwear, snowsuit, wardrobe, woollens, woollies; 9 coveralls, outerwear, sanbenito, stomacher, vestments, waistband; 10 cruisewear, dishabille, elasticize, formalwear, pantywaist, sportswear, waterproof; 11 combination, leisurewear, overgarment; PHRASES: 3, 4 dry wash; 4-1-3, 5 peek-a-boo waist; 4-2 step-in; 4, 3 tank top, tube top; 4-3 bias-cut; 4, 4 body suit, glad rags; 4-4 half-size; 4, 5 body linen; 4-9 full-fashioned; 5, 7 dress ~; **6, 4** Sunday best *UK*; **6, 5** formal dress; **6, 7** sports ~; **7, 6** peasant blouse; **7-6** shalwar-kameez; **7, 7** Chilkat blanket. *See also* **accessories, beachwear, cloak, coat, dress, footwear, glove, headgear, jacket, neckwear, nightwear, robe, shirt, skirt, suit, sweater, swimwear, trousers, tunic, underwear**

clothing (make clothing) 3 fit, sew; **4** fold, seam; **5** bewig, equip, pleat, style; **6** adjust, blouse, bushel, cobble, design, finish, gather, outfit, powder, stitch, tailor; **7** costume, measure, uniform; **8** accouter; PHRASES: **3, 3** fit out, rig out; **4, 2, 5** make to order; **6-4** custom-make, tailor-make.

cloud 3 dim, fog; **4** band, bank, belt, blur, dark, dull, gray, haze, mist, roll, scud, thin, veil, wisp; **5** anvil, break, gloom, sheet, swarm; **6** cirrus, darken, nimbus, shadow, throng; **7** confuse, cumulus, obscure, stratus; **8** overcast; **10** cloudiness, overshadow; **11** altocumulus, altostratus, thunderhead; **12** cirrocumulus, cirrostratus, cumulonimbus, nimbostratus, thundercloud; **13** stratocumulus; PHRASES: **4, 4** grow dark; **4, 5** dark ~, rain ~; **4, 7** make unclear; **5-4** mare's-tail; **5, 5** ~ cover, layer ~, mixed ~, storm ~, water ~; **6, 5** funnel ~, heaped ~; **7, 5** cottony ~; **8, 3** mackerel sky; **10, 3** buttermilk sky.

cloudiness 7 opacity; **9** confusion, dirtiness, muckiness; **11** imprecision, obfuscation. *See also* **cloudy**

cloudy 3 dim; **4** dark, dull, gray, hazy; **5** heavy, milky, misty, muddy, murky, vague; **6** dreich *UK*, gloomy, leaden, opaque; **7** cirrose, unclear; **8** confused, cumulous, overcast, stratous; **9** ambiguous, cirriform, imprecise, uncertain; **10** indistinct, unstrained; **11** overclouded; **12** nephological; PHRASES: **7, 2** churned up.

clout 3 hit; **4** blow, cuff, slap; **5** power, smack, thump, whack; **6** strike, weight; **9** authority, influence.

clove 5 piece; **7** portion, section, segment; **8** fragment.

clover 4 ease; **7** melilot; PHRASES: **4, 4** good life, high life.

clown 3 wag; **4** fool, jest, joke, zany; **5** buffo, cutup, joker, Punch, tease; **6** jester, motley; **7** buffoon, Pierrot; **8** Pasquino; **9** Columbine, Harlequin, Pantalone, Pantaloon, Pedrolino, prankster, slapstick; **10** Pulcinella, Scaramouch; **11** Punchinello; **12**

Polichinelle; PHRASES: **2, 5** be silly; **3-6** legpuller *UK*; **4, 3, 4** play the fool; **4, 3, 6** play for laughs; **4, 5** lark about *UK*, mess about *UK*; **4, 6** fool around, mess around; **5, 6** ~ around, horse around; **5-6** merry-andrew.

club 3 bat, hit; **4** bang, bash, beat, book, cosh *UK*, hand, iron, mace, maul, slug, wood; **5** baton, crown, disco, group, guild, lions, smash, stick, strip, union, wedge; **6** assail, attack, batter, casino, cudgel, league, strike, weapon; **7** concuss, sandbag, society; **8** alliance, bludgeon, sandwich; **9** blackjack, nightclub, truncheon; **10** fellowship, shillelagh; **11** association, discotheque; **12** organization; PHRASES: **3, 4, 3, 4** hit over the head; **5, 10** blunt instrument.

club moss 7 lycopod.

cluck 3 coo, tut; **4** flap, fuss; **5** clack; **6** cackle, squawk; **7** chuckle.

clue *See* **sign**

clump 4 mass, plod, tuft; **5** bunch, clomp, stomp, tramp; **7** clatter, cluster, thicket.

clumsy 4 rude; **5** bulky, gawky, hasty, inept, rusty, stiff, surly; **6** gauche, uneasy, wobbly; **7** awkward, boorish, gawkish, groping, hulking, inexact, uncouth, unhandy; **8** babbling, bumbling, bungling, careless, churlish, clownish, fumbling, gangling, lopsided, lubberly, slapdash, slipping, slovenly, tactless, ungainly, unsteady, unwieldy; **9** dribbling, graceless, haphazard, inelegant, lumbering, maladroit, negligent, ponderous, shambling, stumbling, tentative, uncertain, unrefined; **10** blundering, cumbersome, indiscreet, slatternly, stammering, stuttering, unadjusted, unbalanced, ungraceful; **11** unpracticed, unsteerable; **12** discourteous, experimental, unaccustomed, unhabituated, unmanageable; **13** uncoordinated; **14** butterfingered; PHRASES: **3, 2, 4** out of sync; **3, 2, 6** out of kilter; **3, 4** off form; **3, 4, 6** off one's stride, off one's timing; **3-5** topheavy; **3, 6** all thumbs; **3-6** ham-fisted, handed; **3-8** ill-mannered; **4-6** cack-handed *UK*; **5-6** heavy-footed, heavy-handed; **6, 2** losing it; **6, 4, 5** losing one's touch.

clumsy (be clumsy) 3 mar; **4** blow, boob, drop, fail, hulk, muff, pull, slop, trip; **5** bodge *UK*, botch, fluff, grope, spill, spoil; **6** bobble, bumble, bungle, foozle, fumble, impair, lumber, meddle, mishit; **7** blunder, dribble, galumph, stammer, stumble, stutter; **8** flounder, miscarry, misthrow, overstep; **9** overshoot, overthrow; PHRASES: **3, 2, 3, 3** get in the way; **3, 4** let fall; **3, 4, 4, 2, 2** put one's foot in it; **4, 1, 4, 2** make a hash of, make a mess of; **4, 1, 5** drop a brick; **4, 2** cock up, foul up, mess up; **4, 4** trip over; **5, 1, 4** catch a crab; **5, 2** balls up *UK*; **5, 2, 3, 4** score an own goal.

cluster 4 band, knot, mass, tuft; **5** bunch, crowd, group, swarm; **6** bundle, galaxy, gather, huddle, nebula; **7** collect; **8** assemble; **9** gathering; **10** collection; **13** constellation; PHRASES: **4, 6** star system; **4, 8** come together.

clutch 5 brood, clasp, cling, flock, grasp, seize.

clutter 4 fill, mess; **5** cover, strew; **6** litter; **8** disorder, encumber; **9** confusion; **10** untidiness.

CO 4 firm; **6** cobalt; **7** company; PHRASES: **4, 2** care of.

coach 5 teach, train, tutor; **7** prepare, teacher, trainer; **8** instruct; **10** instructor.

coal 4 coke; **5** ember, slack; **7** lignite; **9** briquette; **10** anthracite; PHRASES: **5, 7** black diamond.

coalesce *See* **merge**

coalfish 6 saithe.

coalition 4 bloc; **5** union; **6** caucus, league, merger; **8** alliance; **10** federation; **11** association, combination, confederacy, co-operative, partnership; **12** commonwealth; **13** confederation.

coarse 3 raw; **4** base, foul, racy, rude, sick; **5** basic, bawdy, crass, crude, gaudy, gross, jaggy, lumpy, nubby, pocky, rocky, rough, rutty, scaly, sharp, spiny, stiff, stony, tacky, tweed, warty; **6** bouclé, broken, craggy, gauche, gnarly, grainy, grated, hispid, jagged, knobby, knotty, nodose, pimply, pitted, pocked, ridged, rutted, scabby, smutty, snaggy, tawdry, tweedy, uneven, vulgar; **7** boorish, bristly, chapped, cracked, cragged, gnarled, knobbly *UK*, knotted, knurled, loutish, nodular, obscene, organic, scraggy, slubbed, snagged, studded, uncivil, uncouth, villous; **8** abrasive, furrowed, granular, gravelly, indecent, potholed, scabrous, scraggly, serrated, snaggled; **9** blistered, encrusted, inelegant, ironbound, rockbound, shattered *UK*, tasteless, unrefined, untreated; **10** corrugated, granulated, indelicate, pockmarked; **11** insensitive, unprocessed; PHRASES: **3-8** bad-mannered; **4-7** foul-mouthed; **5-5** rough-edged; **5-7** cross-grained, rough-grained; **6-5** deckle-edged; **6-7** coarse-grained.

coarsen 5 gnarl; **6** harden, season; **7** roughen, stiffen, thicken, toughen; PHRASES: **5, 2** rough up.

coast 3 bar, sea; **4** bank, sail, sand, spit; **5** beach, cliff, costa, drift, glide, shore, slide; **6** breeze, cruise, lagoon, strand; **7** pebbles, seaside, shingle; **8** sandbank, seaboard, seashore; **9** bicoastal, coastland, coastline, freewheel, peninsula, shoreline; PHRASES: **3, 4** sea wall; **3, 5** sea cliff; **3, 7** the Riviera; **4, 3** sand bar; **4, 4** sand dune; **5, 3, 3** Costa del Sol; **5, 5** Costa Brava; **7, 4** barrier reef; **7, 5** coastal plain; **9, 5** ironbound ~.

coastal 5 tidal; **7** neritic, seaside; **8** littoral, seashore; **10** intertidal.

coat 3 dip, fur, ice, mac *UK*, tan, top, wax; **4** bark, cake, daub, film, foil, gild, hide, leaf, mink, peel, pelt, scum, skin, wool; **5** bloom, cloak, cover, crust, cymar, dross, frost, glaze, japan, jelab, layer, loden, paint, plate, sheet, smear, stain; **6** afghan, anorak, banyan, batter, byrrus, capote, caraco, carpet, dolman, duster, enamel, facing, fascia, jacket, lamina, patina, polish, raglan, silver, spread, tabard, ulster, veneer; **7** Barbour™, blanket, blouson, broigne, coating, conceal, crombie, lacquer, lamella, manteau, overlay, paletot *UK*, parquet, pelisse, plaster, plating, sheathe, slicker, smother, surcoat, surtout, topcoat, varnish; **8** Burberry™, covering, creosote, mackinaw, membrane, midicoat, oilskins, overcoat, pellicle, raincoat, tailcoat; **9** balmacaan, gabardine, greatcoat, housecoat, inverness, redingote, undercoat, upholster, whitewash, wyliecoat; **10** douillette, fearnought, mackintosh *UK*; **11** dreadnought; **12** chesterfield, electroplate; PHRASES: **3, 4** box ~, pea ~; **4, 4** body ~, cape ~, dust ~; **5, 4** cholo ~, dress ~, frock ~, light ~, pilot ~, watch ~; **5-4** houri-coat; **6, 4** blouse ~, brunch ~, coolie ~, covert ~, duffel ~ *UK*, duffle ~, jigger ~, sports ~, trench ~; **6, 6** Prince Albert; **7, 4** British warm, swagger ~; **8, 4** mandarin ~; **9, 4** coachman's ~, teddybear ~. *See also* **clothes**

coated 5 caked, faced, lined; **6** dusted, glazed, plated; **7** covered, crusted, frosted, painted, smeared, treated; **8** battered, overlaid, sheathed, veneered; **9** encrusted, laminated, plastered; **10** overlapped; **11**

undercoated.

coating 3 wax; 4 cake, coat, film; 5 crust, glaze, icing, japan, layer, paint, plate, stain; 6 enamel, polish, veneer; 7 lacquer, outside, overlay, topping, varnish; 8 covering, creosote, frosting; 9 undercoat; 10 plastering; 11 copperplate; 12 electroplate; PHRASES: 4, 5 gold plate; 6, 5 silver plate.

coax 4 lure; 5 cable, charm, tempt; 6 cajole, entice; 7 beguile, blarney, flatter, wheedle; 8 inveigle, persuade; PHRASES: 5-4 sweet-talk.

cobble 4 mend, sett; 5 patch, paver, stone; 6 repair, stitch; 11 cobblestone; PHRASES: 5, 2 patch up; 6, 5 paving stone *UK*.

cocaine 1 C; 4 blow, snow.

cockeyed 4 awry; 5 askew, silly; 6 absurd, madcap, uneven; 7 crooked, foolish; 10 misaligned, ridiculous.

cockiness 5 swank; 7 bombast; 8 blatancy, pertness; 9 brashness, flagrancy, loftiness, perkiness; 10 brazenness, flashiness; 11 flamboyance, pompousness; 13 bumptiousness, obtrusiveness, shamelessness; 14 aggressiveness; PHRASES: 4, 3, 6 airs and graces; 4-10 self-confidence.

cocktail 3 mix; 4 brew; 5 blend; 6 mojito; 7 mélange, mixture, stinger; 8 mixology; 10 concoction; 11 combination.

cocktails 5 julep; 6 gimlet; 7 martini, sidecar, waldorf; 8 daiquiri, highball, nightcap, snowball; 9 alexander, applejack, manhattan, margarita, moonlight, moonshine, snakebite; 11 beachcomber, screwdriver; 13 knickerbocker; PHRASES: 3, 5 gin sling *UK*; 3, 7 rum collins, tom collins; 3-9 old-fashioned; 4, 4 pink lady, whiz bang; 4, 5 bee's knees, buck jones, mint julep; 4, 6 pina colada; 4, 7 john collins; 5, 4 bucks fizz, white lady; 5, 5 black maria, merry widow; 5, 6 black velvet *UK*; 6, 4 angel's kiss, bloody mary, horse's neck; 7, 6 prairie oyster; 7, 7 tequila sunrise; 8, 5 planter's punch; 9, 4 champagne buck; 9, 5 Singapore sling.

cocky 4 pert, smug; 5 brash, perky, saucy; 6 cheeky, swanky; 7 foppish, pompous; 8 affected, arrogant, boastful; 9 bumptious, conceited; 10 aggressive, flamboyant, overclever, swaggering; 11 pretentious; 12 supercilious; 13 overconfident; PHRASES: 3, 6, 2, 4 too clever by half; 4, 2, 7 full of oneself; 4, 3, 6 high and mighty; 4-7 high-falutin,

self-assured; 4-9 self-assertive, self-confident, self-satisfied.

cocoa bean 4 nibs; 5 cacao.

coconut 4 coir, head; 5 copra.

cocoon 4 case, wrap; 5 cover, shell; 6 bubble, sheath; 7 envelop, protect; 8 covering, insulate.

coda 3 end; 5 close; 6 ending, finale; 7 adjunct; 8 addendum, addition; 10 conclusion, postscript; 12 afterthought.

code 3 zip; 4 laws; 5 canon, morse, rules; 6 binary, cipher, enigma, policy, puzzle; 7 program; 8 language, protocol; 9 procedure, semaphore; 10 cryptogram, encryption; 11 cryptograph, regulations; 12 instructions.

coded 6 arcane, closed, secret, tagged; 7 labeled; 10 classified; 13 cryptographic.

coefficient *See* **number**

coelenterate 5 coral, hydra, polyp; 6 medusa; 9 jellyfish; PHRASES: 3, 7 sea anemone.

coerce 5 bully, drive, force, press; 6 compel; 10 intimidate; PHRASES: 6-3 strong-arm.

coercion 5 draft, force, order; 6 duress, hijack, threat; 7 bribery, command, forcing, slavery, torture; 8 bullying, pressure, violence; 9 blackmail, extortion, restraint, sanctions, terrorism; 10 bulldozing, compulsion, constraint, kidnapping; 11 bludgeoning, browbeating, enforcement; 12 conscription, intimidation, pressganging, steamrolling; PHRASES: 3, 5 big stick, the draft; 3-8 arm-twisting; 4-2 call-up; 4, 5 main force; 5, 5 brute force; 5, 7 force majeure; 6, 5 forced labor; 6-6 strong-arming; 8, 5 physical force.

coffee 4 bean, java; 5 decaf, latte, mocha; 6 filter; 7 instant; 8 espresso; 9 americano; 10 cappuccino, mochaccino; 11 Frappuccino; 13 decaffeinated; PHRASES: 4, 2, 4 café au lait; 4, 4 café noir; 4, 6 drip ~, iced ~; 5, 5 caffè latte; 5, 6 Greek ~, Irish ~; 6, 5 French press; 7, 6 Turkish ~.

coffer 3 ark, box; 4 safe; 5 chest; 6 casket; 8 moneybox; 9 strongbox; PHRASES: 4, 3 cash box; 8, 5 treasure chest.

coffin 4 bier, cist, kist; 6 casket; 11 sarcophagus.

cog 4 gear, part; 8 cogwheel; 9 component, mechanism.

cogent 5 lucid; 8 coherent, forceful; 10 convincing, persuasive.

cogitate *See* **think**

cohere 4 bind; 5 match, stick, tally; 6 adhere; 7 conform; 10 correspond; PHRASES: 4, 8 hang together, join together; 5, 8 stick together.

coherent 5 clear, lucid, sound; 7 logical; 8 rational, reasoned; 9 apodictic; 10 apodeictic, consistent, reasonable.

cohesive 5 close, dense, solid, tight; 6 sticky, united; 7 viscous; 8 coherent; 11 indivisible, inseparable; 12 inextricable; PHRASES: 4, 1, 6 like a limpet; 4, 2, 4 side by side; 4, 3 like ivy; 5, 2, 4 cheek by jowl.

cohort 4 army, unit; 5 troop; 6 legion; 8 regiment.

coiffure 2 do; 3 cut; 4 coif; 5 style; 6 hairdo; 7 haircut; 9 hairstyle.

coil 4 curl, kink, loop, turn, wind; 5 helix, twine, twirl, twist, whorl; 6 shimmy, spiral, spring, squirm; 7 meander, ringlet, wriggle; 8 curlicue, squiggle; 9 convolute, corkscrew, corrugate, intricacy; 11 screwthread.

coin 1 d, p; 3 bit, sou; 4 cent, dime, euro, fido, mint; 5 crown, disme, ducat, groat, penny, piece, pound, soldo; 6 bezant, copper, nickel, obolus, shekel, talent; 7 pistole; 8 denarius; PHRASES: 4, 5 half eagle; 5, 2, 5 piece of eight.

coincide 5 agree, match; 6 accord, concur; 10 correspond.

coincidence 4 link, luck; 5 fluke, quirk; 6 chance; 8 accident, casualty; 9 agreement; 11 concurrence, serendipity; 12 happenstance; 13 synchronicity; 14 correspondence; PHRASES: 5, 2, 4 twist of fate; 5, 5 lucky break.

col 3 dip, gap; 4 pass; 6 defile, saddle; 7 passage.

cold 1 C; 3 flu, icy, raw; 4 cool, dead, hoar, iced; 5 algid, aloof, bleak, chill, cough, fresh, frost, gelid, nippy, parky *UK*, polar, sharp, snowy, stony; 6 arctic, biting, bitter, breezy, chilly, formal, frappé, frigid, frosty, frozen, glazed, remote, severe, sleety, unkind, winter, wintry; 7 bracing, callous, chilled, cooling, coolish, distant, frosted, glacial, iciness, pinched, shivery, storage, subzero; 8 coldness, coolness, detached, freezing, perished *UK*, Siberian, uncaring, unheated; 9 aloofness, chiliness, formality, freshness, heartless, inclement, influenza, nippiness, perishing *UK*, snowbound, stoniness, unfeeling; 10 frostiness,

impersonal, inclemency, remoteness, unfriendly, unkindness, wintriness; 11 callousness, distantness, emotionless, hardhearted, indifferent, standoffish, unemotional; 12 indifference, pitilessness, ruthlessness; 13 impersonality, unfeelingness, unsympathetic; 14 unfriendliness; 15 emotionlessness, hardheartedness; PHRASES: 2, 3 on ice; 2, 3, 5 on the rocks; 3-4 icecold; 4, 2 iced up; 4, 2, 3, 5 ~ as the grave; 4, 2, 6 ~ as marble; 4, 4 ~ snap, ~ wave, head ~; 4, 4, 4 blue with ~; 4-5, 6 wind-chill factor; 4, 6 hard winter; 4-11 cold-heartedness; 5, 2, 3, 3 chill in the air; 5, 4, 4 stiff with ~; 5-6 frost-bitten; 6, 4 common ~; 6, 5 frozen solid.

cold (be cold) 6 freeze, quiver, shiver; 7 shudder, tremble; PHRASES: 5, 4, 4 stamp one's feet.

cold (become cold) 6 freeze; 7 congeal; PHRASES: 3, 2 ice up; 3, 4 ice over; 4, 3 cool off; 4, 4 cool down; 6, 4 freeze over.

cold (make cold) 3 fan; 5 chill; 6 benumb, freeze; 7 freshen; 8 glaciate; 9 ventilate; 11 refrigerate; PHRASES: 3-9 aircondition; 6-3 freeze-dry.

collaborate 4 ally; 5 unite; 6 assist; 7 collude, partner; 8 conspire; 9 cooperate; 10 fraternize; PHRASES: 4, 2 team up; 4, 4 join with, side with; 4, 6 join forces; 4, 8 pull together, work together; 4, 9 pool resources.

collaboration 8 alliance, teamwork; 11 association, cooperation, partnership.

collaborator 4 ally; 5 agent; 7 partner; 8 coworker, teammate; 9 associate, colleague; 13 coconspirator; PHRASES: 6, 5 double agent.

collapse 3 end; 4 fail, flop, fold, ruin; 6 attack, crisis; 7 crumple, failure, illness, subside; 8 dissolve, downfall, minimize; 9 breakdown; 11 disassemble; PHRASES: 3, 4 put away; 4, 2 cave in, fold up; 4, 3 give way; 4, 4 fall down; 5-2 crack-up; 5, 4 break down.

collar 3 dog, nab; 4 grab, ruff; 5 bring, catch, pinch, seize, shawl; 6 arrest, corner; PHRASES: 3, 5, 2 get ahold of.

collarbone 8 clavicle.

collation 4 meal; 5 snack; 6 buffet, spread; 8 ordering; 9 gathering; 10 assembling, collection; 12 organization.

collect 5 amass, hoard, store; 6 garner, gather; 8 assemble, squirrel; 9 stockpile; 10

accumulate.

collected 4 calm, cool; 5 piled; 6 heaped *UK*, massed, placid, poised, serene; 7 amassed, boarded, hoarded, stacked; 8 composed, together; 9 unruffled; 10 stockpiled; 11 accumulated; 13 imperturbable; PHRASES: 3, 8 put together.

collection 3 lot, set, zoo; 4 file, pool; 5 album, bunch, diary, group; 6 bundle, corpus, folder, museum, throng; 7 almanac, archive, exhibit, gallery, library, omnibus; 8 aquarium, archives, assembly, waxworks *UK*; 9 anthology, gathering, inventory, menagerie, portfolio, repertory, thesaurus; 10 assemblage, assortment, compendium, exhibition, repertoire, repository; 11 collectanea, compilation; 12 accumulation, encyclopedia; PHRASES: 3, 2, 6 bag of tricks; 3, 6 art museum, wax museum; 3, 7 art gallery; 8, 3 complete set.

collective 4 farm; 5 group, joint; 6 colony, mutual, shared, united; 7 commune, enclave, kibbutz; 8 combined, communal, security; 9 collegial; 11 cooperative; PHRASES: 2-2 co-op.

collector 6 reaper, taxman; 7 amasser, bailiff, gleaner, hoarder, rentier; 8 gatherer, receiver; 9 exciseman *UK*, harvester; 10 liquidator; 11 accumulator, beachcomber, confiscator, numismatist, philatelist; 12 sequestrator; PHRASES: 6, 7 excise officer; 7, 7 customs officer.

college *See* **educational institution**

collide 3 hit, ram; 4 bang, bash, bump, butt, foul, jolt, meet, tamp; 5 brunt, clash, crash, crump, fence, nudge, smash, whomp; 6 attack, careen, charge, crunch, hammer, hurtle, impact, strike; 7 concuss, percuss; 8 bulldoze, confront, converge, shoulder; 9 encounter; 12 sledgehammer; PHRASES: 2, 4 go into; 3, 4 run into, run over; 3, 4, 2 run foul of; 4, 2 pile up; 4, 4 plow into, slam into; 4-5 pile-drive; 5, 2 smash up; 5, 4 carom into; 5, 6 cross swords; 6, 4 cannon into, plough into *UK*.

collision 4 bump, jolt; 5 carom, clash, crash, nudge, shock, smash; 6 attack, cannon, charge, crunch, impact, pileup, scrape; 7 assault, bashing, beating, bulling, butting, licking, meeting, overlap, raining, ramming, rapping, smashup, tapping; 8 accident, conflict, drumming, flogging, friction, paddling, smashing, spanking, whipping; 9 encounter, hammering, pum-

meling, thrashing, thrusting *UK*, trouncing; 10 bulldozing, concussion, difficulty, percussion; 11 convergence; 12 disagreement; 13 confrontation; 15 sledgehammering; PHRASES: 4-2 head-on; 6, 3, 5 hammer and tongs.

colloquial 5 slang; 6 slangy, verbal; 7 obscene; 8 informal; 11 blasphemous, idiomatical; 12 scatological.

collude *See* **conspire**

Cologne 4 Köln.

colonist *See* **settler**

colonnade *See* **arcade**

colony 5 group; 7 cluster, outpost; 9 gathering, satellite; 10 collection, dependency, settlement; 11 association; 12 protectorate.

color 3 dye, hue, red, tan; 4 blue, coat, cyan, fade, flag, gild, lake, line, tint, tone, wash; 5 alter, blush, flush, green, imbue, paint, rouge, shade, stain, tinge; 6 affect, crayon, darken, enamel, ensign, filter, imbrue, indigo, mellow, modify, orange, redden, scheme, silver, violet, whiten, yellow; 7 blacken, lacquer, magenta, pigment, rainbow; 8 brighten, coloring, colorise, contrast, discolor, emblazon, tincture; 9 chromatic, colorwash, distemper, influence, secondary, variegate, whitewash; 10 achromatic, chromatism, coloration, illuminate, monochrome, supplement, watercolor; 11 iridescence; 12 chromaticism, pigmentation; PHRASES: 2, 3 go red; 3-3 tiedye; 4, 4 tone down. *See also* **colors**

Colorado 2 CO; 6 Denver (capital); 9 columbine (flower); PHRASES: 4, 7 lark bunting (bird); 7, 7, 10 Nothing without providence (motto); 8, 4, 6 C~ blue spruce (tree); 10, 5 Centennial State (nickname).

colored 4 dyed, fast, shot; 5 tinct, toned; 6 shaded, tinged, tinted; 7 painted, stained; 8 bleached, unfading; 9 chromatic, colorable, colorfast, colorific, colorised, pigmented, prismatic; 10 polychrome, tinctorial, variegated; 11 highlighted; 12 multicolored; 13 kaleidoscopic, polychromatic, spectroscopic, technicolored; PHRASES: 2, 11 in Technicolor™.

colorful 3 gay; 4 deep, rich, warm; 5 gaudy, vivid; 6 bright, florid, lively, strong, toning; 7 glowing, intense, uniform, unusual, vibrant; 8 emphatic, exciting, matching; 9 brilliant, multihued; 10 flamboyant, harmonious; 11 imaginative, interesting; 12

multicolored; PHRASES: 4, 2, 9 full of character.

colorless 3 dim; 4 drab, dull, gray, pale; 5 dingy, faded, faint, milky, mousy, washy; 6 dreary, fading, leaden, pallid; 7 hueless, neutral, prosaic, whitish; 8 bleached, toneless; 9 decolored, etiolated, uncolored, weathered, yellowish; 10 achromatic, discolored, lackluster, lustreless UK, monochrome, monotonous, uneventful; 11 overexposed, unpigmented; 12 underexposed; 13 uninteresting; PHRASES: 5-5 wishy-washy; 6, 3 washed out.

colors 3 aal, aba, jet, red; 4 blue, bois, bure, cuir, drab, gray, gris, hopi, iris, lake, lark, noir, onyx, opal, pied, pink; 5 brown, capri, chair, cream, cymar, delft, flesh, green, grège, jaspé, jaune, jewel, loden, maize UK, ombré, pêche, prune, shade, topaz, white; 6 acajou, alesan, basané, burnet, cendré, chroma, dorado, jasper, madder, matara, motley, orange, orchid, pastel, pirned, purple, rachel, raisin, silver, yellow, zircon; 7 anamite, ardoise, caldron UK, corbeau, filbert, grizzle, ingénue, jonquil, lacquer, mottled, nacarat, natural, neutral, pearled, platina, thistle, tilleul, tussore, violine; 8 absinthe, aurulent, bordeaux, burgundy, capucine, chaldera, châtaine, crevette, écarlate, grizzled, insignia, larkspur, pistache, shagreen, spectrum, standard; 9 harlequin, moonstone, parchment; 10 auricomous, polychrome, versicolor; 11 pomegranate; 12 multicolored; PHRASES: 3, 5 gun metal; 4-3-6 salt-and-pepper; 5, 2, 4 clair de lune; 5, 4 olive drab; 5, 5 solid color; 5-7 parti-colored; 6-2-5 mother-of-pearl; 6, 5 smoked pearl; 7, 5 primary color; 8, 5 tortoise shell; 9, 5 secondary color.

colossal 2 OS; 4 huge, vast; 5 giant; 7 immense, massive, titanic; 8 enormous, gigantic, oversize.

colostrum 8 foremilk.

colouring *See* **complexion**

column 3 row; 4 file, line, list, pole, post; 5 flute, piece, queue UK, shaft, spine, spire, stake; 6 convoy, impost, pillar; 7 article, capital, fluting, support; 8 abutment, buttress, diastyle, monolith, pedestal, pilaster; 9 cavalcade, colonnade, editorial, hexastyle, paragraph, peristyle, stylobate, vertebral; 10 procession; 11 entablature; 12 columniation, contribution, underpinning;

14 correspondence; PHRASES: 2-2 op-ed; 5, 5 Doric order, Ionic order; 6, 5 Tuscan order; 6, 8 flying buttress; 9, 5 Composite order; 9, 6 Salomonic ~; 10, 5 Corinthian order.

coma *See* **unconsciousness**

comb 4 rake; 6 search; 7 examine, explore, unsnarl; 8 untangle; 10 scrutinize; 11 disentangle; PHRASES: 3, 7 run through.

combat 3 war; 5 check, fight; 6 attack, battle, oppose, reduce, resist; 7 assault, besiege, contest, crusade, hitting, prevent, warfare; 8 conflict, fighting, sparring, struggle; 10 engagement; PHRASES: 4, 1, 8 wage a campaign; 5, 4 fight back; 6, 7 active service; 7, 3 declare war; 7, 3, 5 shatter the peace.

combatant 4 thug; 5 brave, enemy; 6 dueler, knight; 7 fighter, soldier, warrior; 8 opponent; 9 adversary, aggressor, swordsman, warmonger; 12 swashbuckler; PHRASES: 3-2-4 man-at-arms; 5, 7 storm trooper; 6, 3 bovver boy; 6-3, 3 strong-arm man; 8, 3 fighting man.

combative 7 hostile, warlike; 8 militant; 9 bellicose; 10 aggressive, pugnacious; 11 adversarial, belligerent; 12 antagonistic, militaristic.

combat sports 4 judo; 6 aikido, boxing, karate; 9 wrestling; PHRASES: 3, 4, 2 tae kwon do; 7, 3 martial art.

combination 3 mix; 4 code; 5 alloy, blend, union; 6 fusion, merger, mixing; 7 amalgam, mélange, mixture; 8 blending, cocktail, compound, grouping, infusion, marriage, mingling, pastiche, sequence; 9 combining, potpourri, synthesis; 10 concoction, confection; 11 arrangement, association, composition, conjunction, integration, unification; 12 amalgamation, assimilation; 13 incorporation; PHRASES: 7, 8 joining together.

combine 3 mix; 4 fuse, join, link, meld, pool; 5 blend, group, merge, share, unify, unite; 6 absorb, digest, dilute, infuse, mingle, reaper; 7 conjoin, connect, instill, network; 8 assemble, coalesce, compound, thresher; 9 aggregate, harmonize, harvester, integrate, syndicate; 10 amalgamate, assimilate, intertwine, synthesize; 11 association, consolidate, incorporate; PHRASES: 3, 8 fit together, mix together, put together; 4, 8 come together, grow together, join together, lump together; 5, 8 bring together; 7, 8 bracket together.

combined 5 joint; 6 mutual; 7 organic; 8 conjoint, embodied; 9 ingrained, saturated; 10 coalescent, collective. *See also* **combine**

combustible 8 burnable; 9 explosive, flammable, ignitable; 10 incendiary; 11 inflammable.

come 2 go; 4 fall; 5 occur, reach, touch; 6 appear, arrive, befall, derive, extend, happen, toward; 7 stretch; 8 approach; 9 originate; PHRASES: 3, 4 get here; 3, 6, 2 get nearer to; 4, 2 roll up, turn up; 4, 2, 2 ~ up to; 4, 4 ~ from, hail from, stem from; 4, 5 take place; 4, 6, 2 draw closer to; 4, 7 move towards *UK*.

comeback 5 reply; 6 retort, return; 7 revival; 8 recovery, response; 11 retaliation; 12 reappearance; 13 reinstatement.

come between 6 divide, sunder; 8 separate; 9 interfere, interpose; PHRASES: 3, 7 put asunder; 4, 5 keep apart, pull apart; 4, 7 step between; 5, 5 drive apart.

comedian *See* **humorist**

comedy 3 wit; 5 farce, humor; 6 joking, parody, satire, sitcom; 7 cartoon, jesting, lampoon; 8 burletta, clowning; 9 amusement, burlesque, funniness, slapstick; 11 tragicomedy; 13 entertainment; PHRASES: 3, 3, 5 cap and bells; 3, 6 low ~; 4, 6 dark ~, high ~; 5-2 stand-up; 5-2, 6 stand-up ~; 5, 4 comic muse; 5, 6 black ~, comic relief, light ~, light relief; 6, 2, 7 ~ of manners; 6, 5 French farce; 7, 5 bedroom farce; 8, 6 romantic ~; 9, 6 situation ~. *See also* **comic**

comely *See* **attractive**

come out 6 appear, emerge; 7 surface; 8 graduate; 11 materialize; PHRASES: 4, 2, 5 come to light; 4, 3 leak out, pass out.

comestible 6 edible.

comet 4 coma, Faye, tail; 5 Biela, Encke, Kopff; 6 Halley, Olbers, Tuttle; 7 Bennett, D'Arrest, Väisälä, Whipple; 8 Borrelly, Daylight, Kohoutek *UK*, Westphal; 9 Crommelin; 10 Schaumasse; PHRASES: 4, 5 Oort cloud; 4-6 Pons-Brooks; 4-8 Pons-Winnecke; 5, 4 Comas solà; 5-6 Arend-Roland; 5-10 Grigg-Skjellerup; 7-6 Stephan-Oterma; 7-7 Bronsen-Metcalf; 9-6 Giacobini-Zinner.

comfort 3 hug; 4 calm, ease, help, warm; 5 cheer, salve; 6 assure, coddle, cosset, cuddle, luxury, pacify, pamper, relief, soften, solace, soothe, succor; 7 appease, console, hearten, placate, refresh, relieve, support; 8

coziness, reassure, security; 9 alleviate; 10 prosperity, relaxation; 11 consolation, contentment, reassurance; 13 encouragement; PHRASES: 5, 2 cheer up; 5, 8, 2 offer sympathy to; 10, 4 sympathize with.

comfortable 4 cozy, easy, rich, snug, well; 5 comfy, happy, lucky; 6 secure; 7 relaxed, restful, wealthy; 8 affluent, relaxing, soothing; 9 contented; 10 prosperous; PHRASES: 2, 4 at ease; 4-3 well-off; 4-6 wellheeled.

comfy *See* **comfortable**

comic 3 wit; 5 clown, droll, funny, joker; 6 jester; 7 amusing, comical, standup; 8 comedian, farcical, humorist, humorous, magazine; 9 hilarious; 13 sidesplitting; PHRASES: 3-8 rib-tickling; 5, 3 funny man *UK*; 5, 4 ~ book; 5, 5 ~ opera, ~ strip, funny paper.

command 3 act, ban, law; 4 boss, bull, fiat, head, lead, post, rule, sign, sway, word; 5 canon, edict, grasp, order, pilot, power, steer, ukase; 6 behest, charge, compel, decree, demand, dictum, direct, govern, manage, ruling, signal; 7 captain, conduct, control, declare, dictate, mandate, oversee, preside, skipper; 8 dominate, dominion, guidance, instruct, navigate, proclaim, prohibit, shepherd; 9 authority, captaincy, direction, directive, expertise, interdict, knowledge, legislate, prescribe, pronounce, proscribe, supervise; 10 administer, domination, government, manipulate; 11 commandment, countermand, instruction; 12 proclamation; 13 pronouncement, understanding; PHRASES: 2, 2, 6 be in charge; 3, 2 say so; 3, 4, 3, 3 lay down the law; 4, 1, 6 pass a decree; 4, 4 call upon, hold sway; 5, 2, 3, 3 order of the day; 5, 5 legal order; 5, 6 papal decree; 6, 5 direct order; 8, 6 marching orders.

commandeer *See* **seize**

commander 7 admiral, general, premier; 9 brigadier *UK*, president; 10 chancellor, commandant; PHRASES: 3, 7 air marshal; 4, 2, 5 head of state; 5, 7 field marshal, fleet admiral, major general; 5, 8 prime minister; 5, 9 chief executive.

commandingly 7 grandly, regally; 10 powerfully; 11 imperiously, masterfully; 12 compellingly, imperatively, impressively, majestically; 13 dictatorially, domineeringly; 14 autocratically; 15 authoritatively; PHRASES: 2, 5 to order; 2, 7 as ordered, by command; **2, 8** as required; **4-8** high-handedly; **4-9** self-assuredly; **4, 10** with confidence; **4-11** self-confidently.

commemorate 4 keep, mark; **5** honor, toast; **6** hallow; **7** observe, perform; **8** jubilate, remember, sanctify, venerate; **9** celebrate, solemnize; **11** memorialize; PHRASES: **3, 4, 8** pay one's respects; **3, 7, 2** pay tribute to; **4, 3, 8** mark the occasion; **4, 4** keep holy; **5, 3, 4** honor the dead.

commemoration 7 holiday, jubilee, tribute; **8** honoring, memorial; **10** observance; **11** anniversary, remembrance; **13** solemnization; PHRASES: **8, 7** memorial service.

commence *See* **begin, open**

commence *See* **begin**

commend 4 laud; **5** extol; **6** commit, praise; **7** acclaim, applaud, approve, consign, entrust, suggest; **8** advocate, eulogize; **9** recommend; PHRASES: **5, 6, 2** speak highly of.

commendation 6 credit, praise; **7** tribute; **8** accolade, approval; **9** panegyric; **11** acclamation, approbation, recognition; **14** recommendation.

commensurate 5 equal; **8** adequate; **11** appropriate; **13** corresponding, proportionate.

comment 4 note; **5** aside, state; **6** remark; **7** mention, observe; **8** analysis, critique, judgment; **9** criticism, expansion, reference, statement; **10** commentary; **11** explanation, observation; **13** clarification; **14** interpretation.

commentator 6 critic; **7** analyst; **8** observer, reporter, reviewer.

commerce *See* **trade**

commercial 2 ad; **5** promo, trade; **6** advert *UK*; **7** preview, trailer; **8** business, economic, monetary; **9** financial; **10** industrial, marketable, mercantile, profitable; **11** moneymaking; **12** profitmaking; **13** advertisement; PHRASES: **3-6** for-profit; **8-7** business-related.

commission 3 cut, job; **4** duty, hire, task; **5** board, costs, group, order, power; **6** agency, assign, charge; **7** appoint, command, mission, payment, warrant; **8** contract, election; **9** authority, authorize, committee, directive; **10** assignment, delegation, deputation, percentage; **11** appointment, empowerment, instruction,

investiture; **12** installation; **14** administration, responsibility; PHRASES: **6, 5** formal order; **7, 5** working group.

commit 2 do; **4** bind, give; **5** place; **6** devote, oblige, pledge; **7** consign, earmark, entrust, execute, perform, promise, reserve; **8** dedicate, obligate; **9** designate; **10** perpetrate; PHRASES: **4, 4** hand over; **5, 3** carry out.

commitment 3 tie, vow; **4** bond, duty, oath, word; **6** charge, pledge; **7** loyalty, promise, warrant; **8** contract, covenant, devotion; **9** assurance, attention, guarantee; **10** allegiance, dedication, engagement, obligation; **12** faithfulness; **13** concentration, steadfastness; **14** responsibility; PHRASES: **4, 2, 5** word of honor; **4, 4** hard work.

committee 4 body, team; **5** board, group, panel; **7** cabinet, council; **10** commission, consortium; PHRASES: **7, 5** working group.

commodious *See* **spacious**

commodity 5 goods; **7** product, service.

common 4 park; **5** green, heath, joint, stock, usual; **6** mutual, normal, public, shared, vulgar; **7** average, regular, routine; **8** communal, everyday, frequent, ordinary, plebeian, standard; **9** universal, unrefined; **10** collective, ubiquitous, widespread; **11** commonplace, proletarian; PHRASES: **2, 3, 6** of the people; **2, 6, 5** of humble birth; **3-2-3-4** run-of-the-mill; **3-4** low-born; **3, 6, 4** the ~ good; **3-8** ill-mannered; **4, 5** open space; **6, 3 ~** era, ~ law; **6, 4 ~** cold, ~ time; **6-4** common-room; **6, 5 ~** sense; **6, 6 ~** ground, ~ market; **6, 8 ~** fraction; **6, 9 ~** knowledge; **7, 5** playing field.

common (in common) 7 jointly; **8** commonly, globally, together, unitedly; **10** communally; **12** collectively; **15** internationally, sympathetically.

commonplace 5 banal, stale, tired, trite, usual; **6** common, normal; **7** clichéd, humdrum, prosaic, routine; **8** everyday, familiar, ordinary, overused; **9** hackneyed; **10** overworked, uninspired, unoriginal; **11** predictable, stereotyped; **12** conventional; **13** platitudinous, stereotypical, unexceptional, unimaginative, uninteresting; PHRASES: **6, 7** garden variety.

common sense 4 nous *UK*; **5** savvy, sense; **7** realism; **8** judgment, prudence; **11** discernment; **12** practicality, sensibleness; **14** reasonableness; PHRASES: **4, 5** good sense; **4, 8** good judgment; **5, 5** horse sense;

5, 8 clear thinking, sound judgment; **6, 3** mother wit, native wit.

commotion 3 ado, din; **4** fray, fuss, riot, stir; **5** chaos, furor *UK*, noise; **6** bedlam, bother, bustle, clamor, fracas, furore *UK*, hoopla, hubbub, kickup, outcry, racket, ruckus, rumpus, tumult, uproar; **7** ferment, ruction, scuffle, trouble, turmoil; **8** brouhaha, disorder, outburst, upheaval; **9** confusion, lumberman, shemozzle; **10** hullabaloo; **11** disturbance; PHRASES: **2-2** todo; **4, 2, 6** spot of bother; **5-5** hurly-burly.

commune 7 connect, kibbutz; **8** converse; **9** community, empathize; **10** collective; **11** communicate, cooperative; PHRASES: **10, 4** collective farm.

communicable 8 catching; **10** contagious, infectious; **13** transmissible, transmittable.

communicate 3 fax; **4** call, join, link, mail, page, post, talk, tape, wire; **5** bleep, phone, radio, relay, share, speak, telex, video, watch, write; **6** convey, impart, inform, record, repeat, report, reveal, signal; **7** amplify, commune, connect, narrate, publish, receive, recount; **8** announce, converse, describe, telecast, televize, transfer, transmit; **9** advertise, broadcast, propagate, publicize, telegraph, telephone; **10** correspond; **11** disseminate; **12** interconnect; PHRASES: **2, 2, 5** be in touch; **2, 2, 7** be in contact; **3, 2, 5** get in touch; **3, 3** put out; **4, 2** call up, link up, pass on, tune in; **4, 5** make known; **4-6** tape-record; **4, 7** make contact; **5, 3, 4** break the news; **6, 2** listen in.

communication 3 fax; **4** wire; **5** cable, order, telex; **6** letter, notice, report, review; **7** account, contact, message; **8** briefing, bulletin, dispatch, exchange, telegram, transfer; **9** broadcast, cablegram, diffusion, narration, statement; **10** communiqué; **11** instruction, interaction, publication, Telemessage™; **12** announcement, consultation, notification, transmission; **13** dissemination; **14** teleconference; **15** videoconference; PHRASES: **1-4** e-mail; **5, 4** phone call; **10, 4** conference call.

communications 5 links, media, radio; **6** speech; **7** network, talking, writing; **9** signaling, transport; **10** television; **12** broadcasting; **14** correspondence, infrastructure, transportation; PHRASES: **3, 5** the press; **4, 5** data lines, mass media; **6, 6** postal system; **6, 8** public services.

communism 6 Maoism; **7** commune, kibbutz, kolkhoz, Marxism; **9** community, socialism; **10** Trotskyism; **11** communalism; **12** collectivism.

communist 3 red; **6** Maoist; **7** Marxist; **9** socialist; **10** collective, Trotskyist; **12** collectivist.

community 4 area; **5** group; **6** hamlet, people, public; **7** society, village; **10** population; **12** neighborhood; PHRASES: **9, 4** ~ care; **9, 5** ~ chest; **9, 6** ~ center.

commute 5 alter; **6** travel; **7** convert, shuttle; **8** exchange; **9** transform; **10** substitute.

compact 2 CD; **4** cram, deal, disk *UK*, firm, neat, poky *UK*, tiny; **5** bijou *UK*, dense, short, small, solid; **6** pocket; **7** bargain, concise, cramped, squeeze; **8** abridged, compress, condense, contract; **9** agreement, compacted, condensed; **10** compressed; **11** arrangement; PHRASES: **5, 8** press together.

companion 4 chum, mate; **5** buddy; **6** escort, fellow, friend; **7** comrade, partner; **8** chaperon, roommate; **9** associate, attendant, classmate, colleague; **12** acquaintance; PHRASES: **2-6** co-worker; **4, 6** best friend; **6, 8** fellow traveler.

companionship 7 company, society; **8** marriage; **9** community, mateyness; **10** fellowship, friendship; **11** association, camaraderie, comradeship, partnership; **12** cohabitation, togetherness; PHRASES: **6, 2, 5** esprit de corps.

company 2 co; **3** plc, set; **4** band, firm; **5** corps, crowd, group, house, party, troop, works; **6** ballet, circle, guests, troupe; **7** concern, coterie, friends, holding; **8** assembly, business, visitors; **9** gathering, syndicate; **10** companions, enterprise, friendship; **11** camaraderie, comradeship, corporation; **12** congregation; **13** companionship, establishment; PHRASES: **6, 2, 5** esprit de corps; **6, 7** public ~; **6, 11** public corporation; **7, 5** concert party *UK*, theater group; **7, 7** limited ~, private ~, theater ~, touring ~.

company (keep company with) 4 date; **6** escort, hobnob; **7** cohabit, partner; **8** befriend, frequent; **9** socialize; PHRASES: **2, 3, 4** go out with; **3, 4** run with; **4, 2** gang up, pair up, team up; **4, 3, 4** hang out with; **4, 4** live with, work with; **4, 6, 4** hang around with; **4, 8** club together, live together; **6, 4**

travel with; **7, 4** consort with; **9, 4** associate with.

company leader 3 CEO, VIP; **4** boss, head; **5** chair, chief, doyen; **6** bigwig, tycoon; **7** doyenne, kingpin, manager; **8** chairman, director, employer, oligarch, superior; **9** executive; **10** capitalist, chairwoman, controller; **11** chairperson; PHRASES: **3, 3** big gun, top dog; **3, 4** big shot; **3, 5** big wheel; **3, 6** big cheese; **4, 6** head honcho; **5, 6** board member.

comparable 4 like, near; **5** close, equal, exact, false; **7** related, similar; **8** faithful; **9** analogous, different, realistic; **10** artificial, equivalent, synonymous, tantamount; **11** approximate; **13** corresponding; PHRASES: **3, 4** the same.

comparably 7 vividly; **9** naturally; **11** eidetically, graphically, identically, imitatively; **13** homogeneously, realistically, symmetrically, synthetically; **14** alliteratively; **15** correspondingly; PHRASES: **2, 3, 4, 3** in the same way; **2, 3, 4, 4** at the same time; **4, 1, 10** like a photograph. *See also* **comparable**

compare 4 link; **5** equal, liken, match; **6** assess, equate, relate; **7** compete; **8** contrast, evaluate, parallel; **9** associate; PHRASES: **5, 2, 2** match up to; **7, 2** measure up.

comparison 4 link; **8** contrast, judgment, likeness; **9** appraisal; **10** assessment, evaluation, similarity; **11** association; **12** relationship.

compartment 3 bay, box, pew; **4** cage, cell, nook; **5** booth, cubby, niche, stall; **6** alcove, cranny, recess; **7** cubicle; **9** cubbyhole, inglenook.

compassion *See* **mercy**

compass point 1 E, N, S, W; **3** nor'; **4** east, west; **5** north, south; **6** sunset; **7** sunrise; **8** eastward, westward; **9** northeast, northward, northwest, southeast, southward, southwest; PHRASES: **4-5** half-point; **8, 5** cardinal point, magnetic North.

compatible 5 equal; **7** attuned, fitting, similar, uniform; **8** friendly, matching, parallel; **9** congruent, congruous; **10** coinciding, conforming, consistent, harmonious; **11** harmonizing; **12** synchronized; **13** companionable, corresponding; PHRASES: **4-6** like-minded, well-suited; **4-7** well-matched.

compatriot *See* **national**

compel 4 bind, make; **5** drive, force, impel, order, press; **6** coerce, demand, impose, induce, insist, oblige; **7** command, dictate, enforce, prevail, require, squeeze; **8** convince, pressure, regiment, restrain; **9** constrain; **10** discipline, pressurize; **11** necessitate; PHRASES: **3, 4** pin down, tie down; **3, 8, 2** put pressure on; **4, 2** lean on; **4, 4** hold back; **4, 4, 2** bear down on; **5, 2, 6** leave no choice, leave no option; **5, 4, 3** twist one's arm; **5, 8** apply pressure; **6, 1, 4** impose a duty; **6, 2** insist on.

compel (be compelled) 4 must; **6** should; PHRASES: **4, 2** have to; **4, 3, 2** have got to; **5, 2, 8** yield to pressure.

compelling 6 cogent, urgent; **8** coercive, exciting, forceful, forcible, gripping, hypnotic, mesmeric, powerful; **9** absorbing, insistent, inspiring, necessary; **10** attractive, bulldozing, compulsive, imperative, inevitable, oppressive, overriding, persuasive, undeniable; **11** bludgeoning, captivating, dictatorial, fascinating, influential, involuntary, unavoidable; **12** constraining, enthralling, irresistible; PHRASES: **2, 9** of necessity; **4-8** high-pressure; **6-3** strongarm. *See also* **compel**

compendium 5 album; **6** corpus, digest; **8** ephemera, excerpts, extracts, treasury; **9** anthology, clippings, scrapbook, selection; **10** collection, miscellany; **11** compilation.

compensate 3 pay; **4** mend; **5** atone, remit, repay; **6** offset, redeem, refund, remedy, reward, settle, square; **7** balance, expiate, rectify, redress, replace, requite, restore, satisfy; **9** indemnify, reimburse, restitute; **10** counteract, recompense, remunerate; **12** counterweigh; **14** counterbalance; PHRASES: **3, 3** pay off; **3, 3, 1** pay off a loan; **3, 4** pay back; **3, 4, 5** pay back taxes; **3, 5** pay costs; **3, 7** pay damages; **3, 12** pay compensation; **4, 2** even up; **4, 2, 3** make up for; **4, 4** give back, make good; **4, 6** make amends; **4, 6, 3** make amends for; **4, 11** make reparations; **6, 4** render good.

compensation 5 costs; **6** amends, ransom, refund, remedy, return, reward; **7** benefit, damages, payment, penalty, penance, redress; **8** recovery, requital, squaring; **9** amendment, atonement, expiation, indemnity, repayment, retrieval; **10** recompense, recoupment, redemption, remittance, reparation, settlement; **11** comeuppance, replacement, restitution, restoration, retaliation; **12** propitiation, remuneration, satisfaction; **13** consideration, rectification, reimbursement; **15** indemnification; PHRAS-ES: **3-3** pay-off; **4, 3, 3** quid pro quo; **5, 4** money back; **5, 5** blood money; **6, 4** making good, paying back; **6, 6** making amends; **6, 9** double indemnity, golden handshake, golden parachute; **10, 5** conscience money, redundancy money *UK*.

compete 3 vie; **5** equal, match, rival; **6** strive; **7** compare, contend, contest; **11** participate; PHRASES: **7, 2** measure up.

competence *See* **ability**

competent *See* **able**

competition 3 war; **4** race; **5** games *UK*, match, medal, title; **6** battle, record; **7** contest, rivalry; **8** struggle; **10** antagonism, opposition; PHRASES: **4, 5** gold medal; **5, 5** World Games; **6, 5** bronze medal, silver medal; **6, 6** beauty parade; **7, 5** Olympic Games; **8, 5** European Games.

competitive 4 good, keen *UK*; **5** cheap; **6** driven, modest, viable; **8** spirited; **9** ambitious, cutthroat, rivalrous; **10** aggressive, economical, reasonable; **11** adversarial, inexpensive; **12** bloodthirsty, cliffhanging; PHRASES: **3-3-3** dog-eat-dog; **3-4** low-cost; **4, 2** gung ho; **4-4** ding-dong; **4-6** well-fought; **5-3** close-run.

competitor 5 rival; **6** player; **7** entrant; **8** opponent; **9** contender; **10** challenger, contestant; **11** participant; **12** sportsperson.

compilation 3 set; **6** corpus; **7** edition, omnibus, roundup; **9** anthology, collation, compiling, composing, gathering; **10** assemblage, assembling, collecting, collection, compendium; **11** composition; **12** accumulation; PHRASES: **7, 8** drawing together.

compile 4 list; **5** amass, hoard; **6** gather, record, select; **7** collect, compose; **8** assemble, register; **10** accumulate; **11** anthologize, consolidate; PHRASES: **3, 4** set down; **3, 8** put together; **4, 2** draw up, pile up; **5, 8** bring together; **7, 8** collect together.

complacent 4 smug; **7** content; **9** contented, gratified, satisfied; **10** nonchalant; PHRASES: **4-9** self-righteous, self-satisfied.

complain 3 boo, nag; **4** carp, hiss, howl, jeer, moan, rant; **5** gripe, groan, knock, whine; **6** grouse, murmur, object, squawk, whinge *UK*; **7** catcall, grumble, nitpick, protest, whistle; **9** bellyache, criticize;

PHRASES: **3-3** tut-tut; **3, 6, 6** cry bloody murder; **4, 5** find fault; **4, 5, 2** pick holes in.

complaint 3 boo; **4** hiss, moan, snub, tort; **5** gripe; **6** grouse, injury, rebuke, rocket, whinge *UK*; **7** ailment, grumble, illness, protest, reproof, whistle; **8** disorder; **9** condition, criticism, grievance, injustice, objection, reprimand; **13** remonstration.

complement 3 add, set; **4** foil; **5** match, quota; **6** number; **7** balance; **8** complete, quantity; **9** allowance, harmonize; **10** supplement; **11** counterpart; **13** accompaniment; PHRASES: **2, 1, 4, 3** be a foil for; **3, 3** set off; **4, 2, 3** make up for; **5, 3** round out.

complete 2 do; **3** cap, end; **4** done, full, join, over, peak, pure; **5** ample, broad, close, crown, enact, ended, plain, plumb, total, uncut, unite, utter, whole; **6** climax, closed, effect, entire, finish, intact, mature, overdo, united; **7** achieve, compose, execute, fulfill, overall, perfect, perform, plenary, quorate *UK*, realize, succeed, through; **8** absolute, conclude, detailed, dispatch, finalize, finished, sweeping, thorough, unbroken; **9** completed, concluded, construct, culminate, discharge, effective, effectual, extensive, faultless, finalized, fulfilled, implement, inclusive, integrate, perfected, terminate, undivided, unlimited, wholesale; **10** accomplish, complement, consummate, exhaustive, terminated, unabridged, widespread; **11** unmitigated, unqualified; **12** accomplished, unexpurgated, unmitigating; **13** complementary, comprehensive, supplementary, thoroughgoing, unadulterated; PHRASES: **3-2** all-in; **3-3** all-out; **3-3-3** out-and-out; **3, 5** all there; **3-9** all-embracing, all-inclusive; **4, 1, 3** fill a gap; **4, 1, 4** fill a need; **4, 2** fill in, make up, wrap up; **4-2-3-4** dyed-in-the-wool; **4, 3** fill out; **4-3-6** root-and-branch; **4-5** full-blown, full-grown, full-scale; **4-7** full-fledged *UK*, wide-ranging; **4-9** self-contained; **4-10** self-sufficient; **5, 2** build up; **5, 2, 2, 3** bring to an end; **5, 3** carry out, round off; **5, 5** bring about, fully grown; **5, 7** carry through, fully fledged; **5, 8** piece together; **6, 3** polish off.

complete (be complete) 3 end; **5** close; **6** climax, finish; **9** culminate, terminate; PHRASES: **2, 4** be full; **3, 2, 3** say it all; **3, 4** run over; **4, 2, 1, 5** come to a close; **4, 2, 2, 3** come to an end; **4, 3** fill out; **5, 8** reach maturity; **5, 10** reach perfection.

completely 4 hook, line, lock, pips, rind;

5 clean, fully, plain, plumb, quite, stark, stock; **6** hollow, wholly; **7** finally, solidly; **8** outright; **9** downright; **10** altogether, throughout; **13** unambiguously, unequivocally; **15** unconditionally; PHRASES: **2, 3** in all; **2, 3, 6** on all counts; **2, 3, 8** in all respects; **2, 4** en bloc, in toto; **2, 5** en masse; **2, 5, 3** in every way; **3, 2, 3** all in all; **3-2-4** all-or-none; **3, 3, 3** all the way; **3, 3, 4** far and wide; **3, 4** all told; **3, 5** all round; **3, 6** all around; **4, 1, 2, 1** from A to Z; **4, 3, 2, 3** from end to end, from tip to toe, from top to toe; **4, 3, 2, 6** from top to bottom; **4, 3, 3** fore and aft, high and low; **4, 3, 3, 4** from far and near; **4, 3, 4** body and soul; **4, 3, 6** root and branch; **4, 4, 2, 4** from head to foot, from wall to wall; **4, 4, 2, 5** from stem to stern; **4, 4, 5** head over heels; **4, 5, 2, 4** from first to last; **5, 3, 3** warts and all; **5, 3, 4** heart and soul. *See also* **complete**

complex **4** real; **5** dense; **6** campus, center, finite, launch, phobia, thorny; **8** compound, facility, fixation, involved, neurosis; **9** composite, difficult, imaginary, intricate, multipart, multiplex, obsession, psychosis; **10** convoluted; **11** complicated; **12** labyrinthine, multifaceted, multifarious; PHRASES: **4-2** hang-up; **5, 7** Diana ~; **6, 7** father ~, mother ~, parent ~; **7, 7** Electra ~, Oedipus ~.

complexion **4** face, glow, skin, tone; **5** blush, flush; **6** aspect, nature, pallor; **8** coloring, features, paleness; **9** character, cosmetics, ruddiness; **10** appearance; PHRASES: **4-2** make-up; **4, 6** rosy cheeks; **6, 3** sickly hue; **7, 3** healthy hue; **7, 5** natural color.

compliance **7** respect; **8** docility; **9** agreement, obedience, passivity; **10** accordance, conformity, observance, submission; **11** amenability; **12** acquiescence.

compliant **6** docile; **7** passive, willing; **8** amenable, biddable, obedient; **9** agreeable, tractable; **10** conforming, submissive; **11** acquiescent, complaisant; **13** accommodating; PHRASES: **2, 10** in compliance; **5-4** sheep-like.

complicate **5** ravel; **6** jumble, muddle, tangle; **7** confuse, involve; **8** compound, entangle; **9** aggravate; PHRASES: **3, 2** mix up; **4, 3, 5** make bad worse.

complication *See* **difficulty**

compliment **5** paean; **6** admire, eulogy, praise; **7** bouquet, commend, flatter, tribute; **8** accolade, approval, eulogize, flattery;

9 panegyric; **10** panegyrize; **12** congratulate, felicitation; **14** congratulation; PHRASES: **3, 1, 10** pay a ~; **3, 2, 3, 4** pat on the back; **3, 7** wax lyrical; **3, 7, 2** pay tribute to; **4, 2, 2** hand it to; **4, 2, 6** word of praise; **4, 4** good word; **4, 5** good press, rave about; **4, 6** rave review; **6, 2** butter up; **7, 5** glowing terms; **9, 6** favorable review.

comply **4** copy, obey; **5** agree; **6** accede, follow, submit; **7** consent, imitate, observe, respect; **9** acquiesce; PHRASES: **2, 4, 3, 4** go with the flow; **2, 5, 4** go along with; **3, 2** fit in; **3, 3, 4** toe the line; **3, 4, 3, 4** run with the pack; **4, 2, 4** fall in with, keep in step, stay in line; **4, 3, 4** play the game; **5, 2** abide by; **5, 2, 3, 5** stick to the rules.

component **3** cog; **4** item, limb, link, part; **5** facet, organ, piece; **6** aspect, detail, factor, member, module; **7** element, feature, section; **8** integral; **9** elemental, segmental; **10** ingredient; **11** constituent; PHRASES: **4, 3, 6** part and parcel; **8, 4** integral part.

components **4** guts *UK*; **5** works; **7** innards, insides; **8** workings; **9** mechanism.

compose **4** join, make; **5** score, write; **6** create, invent; **7** arrange, compile, connect; **8** comprise, organize; **9** construct, fabricate; **10** constitute; PHRASES: **3, 3** set out; **3, 8** fit together, put together; **4, 2** make up.

composed **4** calm; **6** poised, serene; **7** equable; **8** arranged, tranquil; **9** collected, unruffled; **10** formulated; **11** unflappable; PHRASES: **4-9** self-possessed.

composer **4** Arne (Thomas), Bach (Johann Sebastian), Berg (Alban), Byrd (William), Cage (John), Ives (Charles E.), Kern (Jerome), Monk (Thelonious), Orff (Carl), Part (Arvo), Wolf (Hugo); PHRASES: **5** Arlen (Harold), Basie (Count), Bizet (Georges), Bloch (Ernest), Davis (Miles), Elgar (Sir Edward), Fauré (Gabriel), Glass (Philip), Grieg (Edvard), Handy (W. C.), Haydn (Joseph), Holst (Gustav), Liszt (Franz), Loewe (Frederick), Lully (Jean-Baptiste), Ravel (Maurice), Reich (Steve), Satie (Erik), Sousa (John Philip), Verdi (Giuseppe), Weber (Carl Maria von), Weill (Kurt); **6** author, Barber (Samuel), Bartók (Béla), Boulez (Pierre), Brahms (Johannes), Chopin (Frédéric François), Delius (Frederick), Dvořák (Antonín), Franck (César Auguste), Gounod (Charles François), Handel (George Frederick), Joplin (Scott), Kodály (Zoltán), Ligeti (György), Mahler (Gustav), Miller (Glenn), Mingus (Charlie), Morton (Jelly Roll), Mozart (Wolfgang Amadeus), Parker (Charlie), Porter (Cole), Tallis (Thomas), Wagner (Richard), Waller (Fats), Walton (Sir William), Webern (Anton), writer; **7** Babbitt (Milton), Bellini (Vincenzo), Berlioz (Hector), Borodin (Aleksander), Britten (Benjamin), Brubeck (Dave), Copland (Aaron), Corelli (Arcangelo), creator, Debussy (Claude), Delibes (Léo), Górecki (Henryk Mikolaj), Guthrie (Woody), Herbert (Victor), Janáček (Leoš), Martinů (Bohuslav), Menotti (Gian-Carlo), Milhaud (Darius), Poulenc (Francis), Puccini (Giacomo), Purcell (Henry), Rodgers (Richard), Rossini (Gioacchino), Salieri (Antonio), Schuman (William), Shankar (Ravi), Smetana (Bedřich), Strauss (Johann), Strauss (Richard), Thomson (Virgil), Vivaldi (Antonio); **8** Bruckner (Anton), Coltrane (John), Couperin (François), Gershwin (George), Honegger (Arthur), Kreisler (Fritz), Massenet (Jules), Messiaen (Olivier), musician, Paganini (Niccolò), Schubert (Franz), Schumann (Robert), Sessions (Roger), Sibelius (Jean), Sondheim (Stephen), Sullivan (Sir Arthur), Taverner (John), Telemann (Georg Philipp), Williams (John); **9** Beethoven (Ludwig van), Bernstein (Leonard), Buxtehude (Dietrich), Cherubini (Luigi), Donizetti (Gaetano), Ellington (Duke), Hildegard (of Bingen), Hindemith (Paul), MacDowell (Edward Alexander), Offenbach (Jacques), Prokofiev (Sergey), Scarlatti (Alessandro), Scarlatti (Domenico); **10** Boccherini (Luigi), Gottschalk (Louis Moreau), Monteverdi (Claudio), Mussorgsky (Modest), originator, Paderewski (Ignace Jan), Palestrina (Giovanni Pierluigi da), Rubinstein (Anton), Schoenberg (Arnold), Stravinsky (Igor); **11** Beiderbecke (Bix), Humperdinck (Engelbert), Leoncavallo (Ruggero), Mendelssohn (Felix), Tchaikovsky (Peter Ilyich); **12** Rachmaninoff (Sergey), Shostakovich (Dmitri); **5-5** Saint-Saëns (Camille), Villa-Lobos (Heitor); **5, 6** Lloyd Webber (Andrew); **6-8** Rimsky-Korsakov (Nikolay); **7, 8** Vaughan Williams (Ralph).

composite **6** fusion; **7** amalgam, complex, mixture; **8** compound, multiple; **9** multipart; **14** multifactorial.

composition **4** opus, work; **5** parts, piece; **6** makeup; **8** creation; **9** structure; **10** components; **11** arrangement, masterpiece; **12** constituents, constitution; **13** configuration; PHRASES: **4, 2, 3** work of art.

compound **3** mix; **5** alloy, blend; **6** hybrid; **7** amalgam, complex, mixture; **8** cocktail, multiple, solution; **9** composite, courtyard, enclosure, multipart; **10** quadrangle, settlement, suspension; **11** combination; **12** multifaceted, multifarious.

comprehend **4** know; **5** grasp; **7** include, involve, realize; **10** understand; **11** incorporate; PHRASES: **3, 2** add in; **5, 2** bring in; **6, 3** figure out.

comprehension **5** grasp; **7** ability, command; **9** knowledge; **10** conception, perception; **12** apprehension; **13** understanding.

comprehensive *See* **complete**

compress **3** cut, pad, wad; **4** clip, tamp; **6** précis, squash; **7** abridge, compact, shorten, squeeze; **8** condense, contract, poultice; **10** abbreviate; PHRASES: **3, 4** ice pack; **4, 8** cold ~.

comprise **5** cover; **6** embody; **7** contain, embrace, include, involve; **9** encompass; **11** incorporate; PHRASES: **7, 2** consist of.

compromise **4** cede, deal; **5** adapt, agree, yield; **6** adjust; **7** balance, bargain, concede, halfway; **9** agreement, cooperate; **10** adaptation, adjustment, concession; **11** accommodate, arrangement, cooperation; **13** accommodation; PHRASES: **2, 5** go Dutch; **3, 2, 3, 5** sit on the fence; **4, 1, 4** make a deal; **4, 3, 4** give and take; **4, 7** meet halfway; **5, 3** trade off; **5, 6** happy medium; **5, 7** modus vivendi; **6, 1, 7** strike a balance; **6, 3** middle way; **6, 6** middle course, middle ground; **7, 3** average out; **7, 7** meeting halfway; **7, 8** central position.

compulsion **4** need, urge; **5** craze, drive, force, mania; **6** desire, duress; **7** craving, impulse, passion; **8** coercion, paranoia, pressure; **9** addiction, monomania, necessity, obsession; **10** dipsomania, obligation, satyriasis; **11** megalomania, nymphomania; **14** compulsiveness; PHRASES: **1, 4** a must; **2, 6** no choice; **4, 7** zero options; **8, 7** anorexia nervosa.

compulsive person **6** addict, smoker; **8** anorexic; **9** alcoholic; **10** chocaholic, shoplifter, workaholic; **12** kleptomaniac, megalomaniac; PHRASES: **10, 4** compulsive liar.

compulsory 8 enforced, required; 9 essential, mandatory, necessary, requisite; 10 obligatory; 12 prerequisite.

compunction *See* regret

computation *See* calculation

computer 2 OS, PC; 3 bit, CPU, DVD, FPU, GUI, PDA, RAM, ROM, VDU *UK*; 4 byte, chip, disk *UK*, icon, port, worm; 5 cache, ERNIE, macro, modem, mouse, pixel; 6 abacus, bitmap, cookie, cursor, laptop, memory, screen, server, window; 7 browser, console, desktop, machine, monitor, network, palmtop, printer, program, readout, scanner; 8 database, diskette, emoticon, gigabyte, joystick, keyboard, kilobyte, megabyte, notebook, password, software, terminal; 9 directory, interface, mainframe, microchip, processor, simulator, wallpaper; 10 peripheral; 11 application, motherboard, screensaver, spreadsheet, workstation; 14 microprocessor, numbercruncher; PHRASES: 2-3 CD-ROM; 2, 6 CD burner, CD writer; 3, 5 log table; 4, 4 hard disk; 4, 5 disk drive; 4, 8 cash register; 4, 9 word processor; 5, 4 slide rule, smart card, sound card; 5, 6 touch screen; 5, 7 spell checker; 5, 8 ready reckoner *UK*; 6, 4 floppy disk; 6, 6 search engine; 6, 7 adding machine; 7, 5 Napier's bones; 7, 6 numeric keypad; 9, 6 operating system. *See also* computing

computer languages 1 c; 3 ada, apl, cpl, csl, ipl, rpg, vba; 4 java, lisp, logo, sgml; 5 algol, cobol, comal, coral, forth, pilot; 6 eulisp, jovial, pascal, prolog *UK*, snobol; 7 fortran, maclisp; 8 autocode; 9 assembler; PHRASES: 4, 5 word basic; 4, 6 ucsd pascal; 5, 5 quick basic; 6, 4 common lisp; 6, 5 visual basic.

computing 2 DP, IT; 3 bug, CAD, CAI, CAL, CAM, CAT, CBL, CIM, CMI, DOS *tm*, DTP, EDP, job, OCR; 4 data, file, goto, help, menu; 5 crash, field, input, login, logon, patch, virus; 6 access, backup, format, header, leader, logoff, logout, output, sector, sprite; 7 archive, ARPAnet, command, display, gateway, nesting, scanner, toolbox, wysiwyg; 8 download, downtime, function, protocol, robotics; 9 debugging, directory, interface; 11 computation, cybernetics, diagnostics, programming; 13 compatibility; 15 numbercrunching; PHRASES: 4, 4 band rate, baud rate; 4-4 flip-flop; 4, 6

hard return, soft return; 4, 10 data processing; 5, 10 batch processing; 6, 5 Trojan horse; 6, 6 random access; 7, 8 systems analysis; 8, 7 computer science.

comrade *See* friend

con 2 do; 4 dupe, lure, ploy, scam; 5 cheat, fraud; 6 entrap; 7 against, convict, deceive, defraud, mislead, swindle; 8 downside, hoodwink, jailbird, negative, prisoner; 9 objection; 12 disadvantage; PHRASES: 3, 3 ~ man, old lag *UK*, rip off; 3-3 rip-off; 3, 5 ~ trick *UK*; 4, 1, 4, 3 pull a fast one; 4, 2 take in; 10, 4 confidence game.

concave 3 dip, pit; 4 cave, cove, glen, gulf, hole, mine, vale; 5 abyss, combe, fosse, gorge, gully, inlet; 6 canyon, cavern, crater, dented, dished, hollow, pitted, quarry, ravine, sunken, trough, valley; 7 dimpled, pothole; 9 cavernous, depressed; 10 excavation; PHRASES: 3-6 cup-shaped; 4-6 bowl-shaped; 6, 2 curved in.

conceal 4 bury, hide, mask, veil; 5 cloak, cover, inter, stash; 6 censor, screen, shroud; 7 obscure, seclude, secrete; 8 disguise, suppress, withhold; 9 whitewash; 10 camouflage; PHRASES: 3, 2 sit on; 4, 1, 4, 4 draw a veil over; 4, 2 hush up, lock up, seal up, wall up, wrap up; 4, 3 keep mum; 4, 4 hide away, hold back; 4, 5 keep quiet; 4, 5, 5 keep under wraps; 5, 2 cover up; 5, 4 gloss over, paint over, paper over; 6, 2 bottle up.

concealed 6 covert, hooded, secret, unseen; 7 lurking, muffled, private; 8 skulking, stealthy; 9 invisible, smothered; 10 undercover, undetected; 11 underground, undisclosed; 13 incommunicado; PHRASES: 5, 5 under wraps; 6, 4 hidden away; 7, 3 blotted out. *See also* conceal

concealment 4 code; 6 ambush, hiding; 7 eclipse, privacy, secrecy, stealth; 8 disguise, intrigue; 9 obscurity, seclusion, secretion; 10 camouflage; 11 suppression; 12 cryptography; PHRASES: 5-2 cover-up.

concede 3 own; 4 cede; 5 admit, allow, grant, yield; 6 accept; 9 recognize, surrender; PHRASES: 4, 2 give up.

conceit 5 pride; 6 egoism, hubris, vanity; 7 egotism; 9 arrogance, insolence, vainglory; 10 narcissism, pretension; 11 affectation, haughtiness, superiority; 13 bigheadedness; PHRASES: 4-10 self-importance; 5, 5 false pride.

conceited 4 smug, vain; 5 proud; 6 brazen, snooty; **7** haughty, pompous; **8** affected, arrogant, insolent, snobbish, superior; **9** bigheaded, egotistic, strutting; **12** narcissistic, vainglorious; **13** condescending; PHRASES: **2, 4, 4, 5** on one's high horse; **4-2-3-3** nose-in-the-air; **4, 3, 6** high and mighty; **4-9** self-important, self-satisfied; **5-2** stuck-up; **5-5** purse-proud; **6-5** toffee-nosed *UK*.

conceivable 6 likely; **8** possible; **9** plausible; **10** believable, imaginable.

conceive 6 create, invent, regard; **7** imagine; **8** consider, envisage, envision, perceive; **9** visualize; PHRASES: **4, 2** look on, make up; **5, 2** dream up, think of, think up.

concentrate 5 focus, study, think; **6** purify, reduce; **7** collect, distill, essence, thicken; **8** assemble, condense, converge; **10** strengthen; **12** quintessence; PHRASES: **4, 2** home in; **4, 4** boil down; **4, 9, 2** give attention to; **5, 4, 4** apply one's mind.

concentration 4 zeal; **5** ardor, drive, focus, vigor; **6** energy; **7** potency; **8** devotion, strength; **9** attention, intensity; **10** absorption, commitment, dedication; **11** application; **12** condensation; **13** attentiveness; **15** crystallization.

concept *See* **idea**

conception 4 idea, view; **5** birth, grasp, start; **6** belief, cradle, notion, origin, outset, theory; **7** concept, infancy, thought; **8** babyhood; **9** beginning, formation; **10** perception; **12** commencement; **13** comprehension, understanding.

concern 4 care, firm, task; **5** touch, worry; **6** affair, affect, bother, matter; **7** anxiety, company, disturb, trouble; **8** business, disquiet; **10** enterprise; PHRASES: **2, 5, 5** be about; **2, 9, 4** be connected with; **4, 2, 2, 4** have to do with; **5, 2** refer to; **6, 2** relate to.

concerning *See* **about**

concert hall 5 salon, venue; PHRASES: **5, 5** opera house.

concertina 9 accordion; PHRASES: **7-3** squeeze-box.

concession 8 decrease, granting, yielding; **9** allowance, conceding, privilege; **10** indulgence; **12** dispensation, surrendering; **14** acknowledgment; PHRASES: **6, 3** giving way.

concise 4 curt; **5** brief, brisk, crisp, exact, pithy, short, terse; **6** abrupt; **7** brusque, clipped, compact, Spartan; **8** abridged, suc-

cinct; **9** condensed, shortened, truncated; **10** compressed, economical, elliptical; **11** abbreviated; **12** monosyllabic; PHRASES: **2, 1, 8** in a nutshell; **2, 3, 5** to the point; **5, 3, 5** short and sweet.

conclave *See* **meeting**

conclude 3 end; **4** halt; **5** close, infer; **6** assume, clinch, decide, deduce, finish, reckon, settle; **7** achieve, presume, resolve, suppose; **8** complete, construe; **9** determine, terminate; **10** accomplish; PHRASES: **4, 1, 4** call a halt; **4, 2** wind up, wrap up; **4, 3** work out; **5, 5** bring about; **6, 3** figure out, finish off.

conclusion 3 end; **4** peak; **5** close, death, finis; **6** climax, ending, finale, finish, payoff, result, upshot, windup; **8** decision, epilogue, solution; **9** deduction, inference; **10** assumption, completion, denouement, resolution; **11** culmination, supposition, termination; PHRASES: **3, 7** end product; **4, 3** last act; **4, 4** swan song; **4, 5** last words; **4, 6** last hurrah; **5, 5** final story; **5, 7** final chapter.

conclusive 4 sure; **5** final; **7** certain; **8** decisive, definite; **10** convincing; **11** categorical.

conclusively 2, 2, 5, 3 as it turns out; **2, 3, 3** in the end; **2, 10** in conclusion; **3, 4** for good; **3, 4, 3, 3** for good and all; **4, 3, 3, 3** once and for all; **5, 5** never again; **6, 8** beyond question. *See also* **conclusive**

concoct 3 mix; **4** brew, cook, make, plan, plot; **5** hatch; **6** create, devise, invent; **7** develop, prepare; **9** fabricate, formulate; PHRASES: **3, 2** gin up; **3, 8** put together; **4, 2** cook up; **6, 2** rustle up.

concomitant 7 adjunct, feature, related, symptom; **8** parallel, syndrome; **9** attendant, connected, corollary; **10** affiliated, associated, coexistent, concurrent, indication; **12** accompanying, simultaneous.

concord 4 pact; **5** peace, unity; **6** accord, treaty; **7** compact, harmony; **9** agreement; **10** settlement.

concourse 4 mass; **5** crowd, horde, rally; **6** muster, square, throng; **7** meeting; **8** assembly; **9** courtyard, forecourt, gathering, multitude; PHRASES: **4, 5** open space; **6, 5** public space.

concrete 5 solid; **6** actual; **7** certain; **8** definite, distinct, existing, material, specific, tangible; **10** particular.

concubine 7 hetaera; **8** mistress; **9** odalisque; **PHRASES: 4, 5** kept woman *UK*.

concur 5 agree; **6** accept, assent; **7** consent; **8** coincide, conspire; **9** acquiesce, harmonize; **11** synchronize; **PHRASES: 2, 2, 6** be in accord; **2, 5, 4** go along with; **3, 3, 2, 3** see eye to eye; **5, 2** agree to.

concurrent 8 parallel; **10** coexistent, coexisting, cohabiting, coincident, coinciding, concurring; **11** concomitant, correlative, synchronous; **12** contemporary, simultaneous; **15** contemporaneous.

condemn 4 damn, doom; **5** blame, curse, judge, slate *UK*; **6** punish, revile; **7** censure, convict, reprove; **8** denounce, reproach, sentence; **9** criticize, deprecate, disparage; **PHRASES: 4, 2, 3, 5** send to the devil; **8, 2, 5** sentence to death.

condensation 4 damp; **5** water; **7** cutting, wetness; **8** dampness, humidity; **9** reduction; **10** abridgment, shortening; **11** compression; **12** abbreviation; **13** concentration, summarization.

condense 4 pack; **6** reduce; **7** abridge, compact, shorten, squeeze; **8** compress; **9** summarize; **10** abbreviate; **11** concentrate.

condensed 3 cut; **5** caked, dense, thick; **6** edited, jelled, matted; **7** clotted, curdled, jelling, reduced, setting; **8** abridged, clotting, précised; **9** congealed, thickened; **10** abstracted, congealing, evaporated, solidified; **11** crystalline; **12** crystallized. *See also* **condense**

condescend 5 deign, stoop; **9** patronize; **PHRASES: 4, 4** talk down; **4, 4, 2** look down on; **5, 7** lower oneself; **6, 7** demean oneself; **6, 8** humble yourself.

condescension 7 disdain; **8** contempt, deigning, snobbery, stooping; **9** aloofness, arrogance, pomposity; **10** snootiness; **11** haughtiness.

condition 4 form, term; **5** order, rider, state, train; **6** clause, demand, repair; **7** ailment, disease, fitness, grounds, illness, prepare, proviso; **8** disorder, syndrome; **9** complaint, parameter, provision, requisite; **10** obligation; **11** acclimatize, requirement, reservation, restriction, stipulation; **12** precondition, prerequisite; **13** circumstances, qualification, specification; **PHRASES: 3, 4, 2** get used to; **3, 5** get ready; **4, 3, 3** sine qua non; **5, 2** shape up; **5, 5** small print; **6, 6** escape clause.

conditioning 6 reflex, taming; **8** training; **10** suggestion; **11** habituation; **13** reinforcement; **PHRASES: 6, 6** simple reflex; **8, 2** breaking in.

condolence 4 balm, keen, pity; **6** lament, regret, sorrow; **7** comfort, concern; **8** mourning, sympathy; **11** compunction, condolences, consolation; **13** commiseration.

condom 4 safe; **6** johnny, sheath; **12** prophylactic; **PHRASES: 6, 6** French letter *UK*.

condone 6 excuse, ignore, pardon; **7** forgive, justify; **8** overlook, tolerate; **9** disregard; **PHRASES: 3, 2, 2** let it go; **3, 4** let pass; **4, 1, 5, 3, 2** turn a blind eye to; **4, 2** wink at; **4, 4** pass over; **5, 4, 4, 2** close one's eyes to.

conduct 3 run, way; **4** lead, look, mien, mood, rule, show, tone; **5** carry, guide, pilot, steer, style, usher; **6** action, aspect, convey, direct, escort, handle, manage, manner, motion, output, record; **7** actions, bearing, control, fashion, gesture, history, manners, operate, oversee; **8** attitude, behavior, carriage, demeanor, handling, organize, shepherd, transmit; **9** accompany, supervise; **10** deportment, management, observance; **11** comportment; **12** organization; **14** administration; **PHRASES: 4, 2, 6** line of action; **4, 2, 8** mode of behavior; **4, 8** past behavior; **5, 3, 5** wield the baton; **5, 6** track record; **8, 7** personal bearing.

conductor 5 guard, guide, pilot, usher; **6** driver, escort, leader; **7** carrier, maestro; **8** director; **9** electrode; **PHRASES: 4, 6** band leader; **7, 8** musical director.

conduit *See* **channel**

cone 3 top; **4** horn, nose; **6** cornet *UK*, funnel; **7** trumpet; **PHRASES: 3-5** ice-cream; **8, 3** spinning top.

confectionery 3 gum; **4** rock *UK*; **5** candy, fudge, sweet *UK*; **6** bonbon, comfit, dragée, humbug, nougat, sweets, toffee; **7** candies, caramel, fondant, gumdrop, praline, sweetie *UK*, truffle; **8** licorice, lollipop, lollypop, marzipan, sweeties; **9** chocolate, jellybean, sweetmeat; **10** gobstopper *UK Can*, jawbreaker, peppermint; **11** marshmallow; **12** butterscotch; **PHRASES: 4, 9** milk chocolate; **5, 4** sweet shop; **5, 5** candy apple, candy store; **5, 7** dolly mixture; **5, 9** white chocolate; **6, 3** bubble gum; **6, 5** boiled sweet *UK*, cotton candy; **7, 3** chewing gum.

confederate 4 ally, join; **5** unite; **6** allied,

joined, united; **7** partner; **9** affiliate, associate, colleague; **10** affiliated, associated.

confederation 5 union; **6** league; **9** coalition; **11** association, confederacy.

confer 4 give; **5** award, grant; **6** bestow, debate, parley, powwow; **7** analyze, bargain, canvass, consult, discuss, present; **8** consider; **9** negotiate; PHRASES: **2, 4** go over; **3, 2, 7** sit in council; **3, 2, 9** sit in committee; **3-3** pow-wow; **3, 4, 8** sit down together; **4, 3** hash out; **4, 4** talk over; **5, 2** refer to; **6, 3** thrash out *UK Can*; **8, 5** exchange views; **10, 4** deliberate over.

conference 4 diet; **5** forum, synod, talks, union; **6** caucus, debate, huddle, parley, powwow, summit; **7** cabinet, council, meeting, seminar; **8** assembly, conclave, congress; **9** gathering, symposium; **10** colloquium, convention, discussion; **12** consultation; PHRASES: **4, 5** open forum; **5-2** teach-in; **5, 5** peace talks; **7, 2, 3** council of war; **8, 2, 5** exchange of views.

confess *See* **admit**

confess 5 admit; **6** affirm, assert; **7** declare, profess; **11** acknowledge; PHRASES: **3, 2** own up; **4, 5** make known.

confession 9 admission, assertion, statement; **10** concession, profession, revelation; **11** affirmation, declaration; **14** acknowledgment.

confidant 6 friend, sister; **7** brother; PHRASES: **4, 4** soul mate; **5, 3** alter ego.

confide 4 tell; **5** admit; **6** impart, reveal; **7** confess, divulge, whisper; **8** disclose, intimate, unburden; PHRASES: **3, 3, 4, 5** get off your chest; **4, 1, 6** tell a secret; **4, 3, 4** come out with; **4, 4, 5** open one's heart.

confident 4 bold, sure; **5** brave; **6** daring; **7** assured, certain; **8** fearless, positive, sanguine; **9** audacious, convinced, outspoken, unabashed; **10** courageous, determined, optimistic; PHRASES: **4, 2, 8** sure of yourself; **4-7** self-assured; **4-9** self-confident, self-possessed.

confidential 5 privy; **6** secret; **7** private; **8** personal; **10** classified, restricted; PHRASES: **2, 7** in private; **2, 10** in confidence; **3, 3, 6** off the record; **3, 6** top secret; **4-4** hush-hush; **5, 4** entre nous; **7, 3, 3, 2** between you and me.

confine 4 jail, keep; **5** limit; **6** detain, narrow; **8** imprison, restrain, restrict; **10** quarantine; PHRASES: **4, 2** lock up.

confinement (place of confinement) *See* **prison**

confining 6 narrow. *See also* **confine**

confirm 4 back; **5** check; **6** assure, attest, ratify, second, settle, verify; **7** approve, certify, endorse, fortify, support; **8** sanction, validate; **9** authorize, reinforce; **10** strengthen; **11** corroborate; **12** authenticate, substantiate; PHRASES: **4, 2** back up, firm up; **4, 3** bear out; **5, 2, 4, 4** stick to one's guns.

confirmation 5 proof; **6** second; **7** backing, grounds, support; **8** evidence, sanction; **9** assurance; **10** validation; **11** affirmation, attestation, endorsement; **12** ratification, verification; **13** authorization, certification, corroboration, determination, fortification, reinforcement; **14** authentication, substantiation; PHRASES: **7, 2** backing up.

confiscate 5 seize; **6** remove; **7** impound; **9** repossess, sequester; **10** commandeer; **11** appropriate; PHRASES: **4, 4** take away.

confiscation 7 removal, seizure; **10** divestment; **11** deprivation; **12** repossession; **13** appropriation, dispossession, expropriation, sequestration; **14** disinheritance.

conflagration *See* **fire**

conflict 3 row, war; **5** argue, clash, fight, scrap; **6** attack, battle, debate, enmity, fracas, strife, tussle; **7** discord, dispute, dissent, quarrel, rivalry, warfare; **8** argument, clashing, fighting, friction, skirmish, squabble, struggle; **9** encounter; **10** contention, difference, dissension, engagement, opposition; **12** disagreement; **13** confrontation, inconsistency; PHRASES: **2, 2, 4** be at odds; **2, 12** be incompatible; **3, 5** bad blood; **4, 1, 4** mano a mano.

conform 3 fit; **4** copy, meet, obey, suit; **5** adapt, agree, align, match, tally; **6** accord, adjust, comply, concur, follow, kowtow; **7** imitate, reflect; **8** coincide, parallel, resemble, typecast; **9** correlate, harmonize; **10** correspond, homogenize, stereotype; **11** accommodate, standardize; PHRASES: **2, 4** be like; **2, 4, 3, 4** go with the flow; **2, 10** be consistent; **3, 2, 4** tie in with; **3, 3, 4** toe the line; **3, 4, 2, 4** run true to form; **4, 2** fall in, line up; **4, 3, 4** play the game; **4, 4** look like; **4, 4, 4** fall into line; **4, 4, 5** know one's place; **4-7** mass-produce; **4, 8** hang together, hold together; **5, 2** match up; **5, 3, 5** serve the times; **5, 4** sound like; **6, 3, 5** follow the crowd; **6, 4** square with; **7, 2** ~ to, measure up.

conformist 6 formal, kosher, lapdog, parrot, proper, square, stodgy, stuffy; 7 copycat, correct, prudish, uptight; 8 follower, imitator, loyalist, obedient, orthodox, pedantic; 9 bourgeois; 11 traditional; 12 conservative, conventional; 13 unadventurous, unquestioning; 14 traditionalist; 15 conventionalist; PHRASES: 2-5, 3 do-right man; 3-3 yes-man; 3-7 law-abiding; 3-9 old-fashioned; 5-2-3-3 stick-in-the-mud; 6-5 strait-laced; 6, 8 Middle American; 7, 3 company man.

confound 4 stun; 5 amaze, floor, stump; 6 babble, baffle, muddle, puzzle; 7 confuse, flummox, mistake, mystify, perplex; 8 bewilder; PHRASES: 3, 2 mix up.

confront 4 defy, face, meet; 5 clash, rival; 6 breast, oppose, tackle; 7 contend, grapple, provoke; 8 threaten; 9 challenge, encounter; 10 antagonize; PHRASES: 3, 4 vie with; 3, 7 pit against, set against; 4, 2 take on; 4, 2, 2 face up to; 4, 4 deal with; 4, 4-2 meet head-on; 4, 6 join battle; 5, 7 match against; 6, 3 brazen out; 7, 4 compete with, contest with, grapple with.

confuse 4 blur, mess; 5 botch, cloud, muddy, stump, trick; 6 baffle, boggle, bungle, muddle, puzzle; 7 deceive, flummox, mistake, mystify, obscure, perplex; 8 befuddle, bewilder, confound, disorder; 9 bamboozle, bumfuzzle, challenge; 10 complicate; PHRASES: 3, 2 mix up; 4, 1, 4, 2 make a hash of; 4, 1, 4, 3, 2 make a pig's ear of UK; 4, 2 cock up, foul up; 5, 2 balls up UK, snarl up; 5, 3, 6 muddy the waters.

confused 6 senile; 7 bemused, chaotic, cryptic, jumbled, puzzled, tangled, worried; 8 puzzling; 9 difficult, enigmatic; 10 disorderly, incoherent, nonplussed; 11 discomposed, disoriented, embarrassed, floundering; 12 disconcerted, disorganized, muddleheaded, unmethodical, unsystematic; 13 disconcerting; 14 featherbrained, scatterbrained; PHRASES: 2, 1, 4 at a loss; 2, 1, 4, 3, 5 at a loss for words; 2, 1, 8 in a quandary; 2, 8 in disarray; 3, 2, 4, 5 out of one's depth; 3, 7, 2 not getting it; 5, 2 mixed up. *See also* **confuse**

confusion 4 mess; 5 chaos; 6 bedlam, hubbub, jumble, mayhem, muddle, racket, tumult, uproar; 7 ferment, inferno, mistake, shyness, turmoil; 8 disorder, madhouse, quandary, upheaval; 9 cacophony, commotion; 10 hullabaloo, perplexity; 11 pande-monium; 12 bewilderment, discomposure; 13 disconcertion, embarrassment; 14 disorientation; PHRASES: 3-2 mix-up; 3, 4, 3, 5 all hell let loose; 4-2 slip-up.

congeal *See* **set**

congenial *See* **agreeable**

congenital 6 inborn, inbred; 7 genetic; 8 habitual; 9 ingrained, inherited; 10 hereditary; 11 established.

congested 4 full; 6 choked, jammed, packed; 7 blocked, clogged, crammed, crowded, stuffed, teeming; 11 overcrowded, suffocating.

congestion 6 charge; 8 blockage, blocking, clogging, cramming, crowding; 10 bottleneck; 11 obstruction; 12 overcrowding.

conglomeration 9 composite, potpourri; 10 assortment, hodgepodge, hotchpotch UK; 12 accumulation.

congratulate 5 cheer, toast; 6 praise, reward; 7 applaud, commend; 10 compliment; 11 acknowledge; PHRASES: 3, 2, 3, 4 pat on the back; 3, 7, 2 pay tribute to; 5, 2 drink to.

congregation 4 host, mass; 5 crowd, flock; 6 throng; 9 gathering; 11 churchgoers, worshippers UK; 12 parishioners.

congress 7 council, meeting; 8 assembly; 10 conference, convention.

congruent 7 sharing, similar; 8 matching; 10 coincident, compatible, consistent, coordinate, harmonious, homologous; 11 coextensive, equidistant, equilateral, harmonizing; 13 corresponding.

conjecture 3 try; 5 guess, infer; 6 assume; 7 imagine, suppose, surmise; 8 estimate; 9 guesswork, inference, intuition, speculate, suspicion; 10 assumption, estimation; 11 guesstimate, speculation, supposition; PHRASES: 4, 2, 3, 4 shot in the dark; 4, 6 mere notion; 4, 11 pure speculation; 5, 5 rough guess; 5, 8 crude estimate; 5, 9 vague suspicion; 6, 4 shrewd idea.

conjoin *See* **link**

conjunction 5 union; 11 coincidence, combination, concurrence, unification.

conjure 5 charm, evoke, raise; 6 invoke, juggle, summon; PHRASES: 4, 1, 6 hold a séance; 4, 2 call up; 4, 3, 4 wake the dead; 6, 7 summon spirits; 7, 2 ~ up.

connect 3 fix, peg, pin, sew, tie, zip; 6 bind, bolt, bond, clip, glue, hook, join, knot, lace, lash, link, nail, snap, tack, tape, wire; **5** braid, click, graft, hinge, merge, plait, rivet, screw, stick, unite; **6** attach, bridge, buckle, button, couple, fasten, skewer, staple, stitch, zipper; **7** bandage, bracket, conjoin, entwine, network; **8** entangle; **9** associate; **10** interweave; **12** interconnect; PHRASES: **4, 2** hook up, link up.

Connecticut 2 CT; **8** Hartford (capital); PHRASES: **2, 3, 12, 5, 8** He who transplanted still sustains (motto); **7, 3** charter oak (tree); **8, 5** American robin (bird); **8, 6** mountain laurel (flower); **12, 5** Constitution State (nickname).

connection 3 col, tie; **4** arch, band, beam, bond, hoop, join, link, neck, stay, yoke; **5** brace, canal, chain, hinge, joint, nexus, ridge, steps, strut, union; **6** branch, copula, fetter, girder, hyphen, ladder, merger, stairs, zeugma; **7** bracket, isthmus, joining, linking, meeting, shackle; **8** adhesion, assembly, cohesion, coupling, junction, relation, stairway; **9** fastening; **11** association, conjunction, correlation, involvement; **12** entanglement, relationship; **15** interconnection; PHRASES: **8, 5** stepping stone.

connive *See* **plot**

connoisseur *See* **specialist**

conquer 3 win; **4** beat, take; **5** crush, quell, seize, storm; **6** defeat, maraud, master, subdue; **7** capture, prevail, subject; **8** overcome, suppress, surmount, vanquish; **9** overpower, overthrow, subjugate; PHRASES: **3, 3, 6, 2** get the better of; **4, 7, 2** take control of; **7, 4** triumph over.

conquest 3 win; **4** rout; **6** defeat; **7** success, triumph, victory; **8** takeover; **9** overthrow; **11** subjugation.

conscientious 7 careful, dutiful, upright; **8** thorough; **9** honorable; **10** meticulous; **11** painstaking, punctilious, responsible.

conscious 5 awake, aware; **8** sensible, sentient; **9** cognizant, sleepless; **10** considered, deliberate, determined; **11** intentional; PHRASES: **4, 5** wide awake.

conscript 5 draft; **6** enlist, enroll, novice, rookie; **7** recruit; PHRASES: **4, 2** call up; **4, 2, 4** call to arms.

conscription 5 draft; **9** enrolment *UK*; **10** enlistment; **11** recruitment; **12** mobilization; PHRASES: **8, 7** national service.

consecutive 4 next; **6** linear, serial; **7** on-going, ordinal, running; **8** repeated; **9** following; **10** sequential, succeeding, successive; **11** progressive; **13** chronological, uninterrupted; PHRASES: **2, 1, 6** in a series; **2, 3, 3** on the run; **2, 3, 4** on the trot; **2, 4** in turn; **2, 5** in order; **2, 10** in succession; **3, 5, 7** one after another; **6, 5** coming after; **7, 2** running on; **9, 2** following on.

consensus *See* **agreement**

consent 2 OK; **3** nod; **4** okay, sign, tick; **5** agree, allow, bless, check, leave, stamp; **6** accede, accept, accord, affirm, assent, attest, comply, concur, permit, ratify, second; **7** approve, certify, confirm, endorse, support; **8** accredit, approval, blessing, sanction; **9** acquiesce, agreement, authority, consensus, vouchsafe; **10** compliance, permission, underwrite; **11** affirmation, attestation, concurrence, endorsement, recognition; **12** acquiescence, authenticate, ratification; **13** authorization, certification; PHRASES: **2-5** go-ahead; **3-2** say-so; **3, 3** say aye; **3, 3, 4** say the word, tip the wink; **3, 4, 4** say hear hear; **4, 2** back up; **4, 3, 2-5** give the go-ahead; **5, 5** green light; **6, 5** rubber stamp.

consequence 5 value; **6** effect, import, moment, payoff, result, sequel, upshot; **7** concern, outcome, product; **9** aftermath, corollary, magnitude; **10** importance; **11** aftereffect; **12** significance; PHRASES: **3, 6** end result.

consequent 6 caused; **7** ensuing; **9** following, resultant, resulting *UK*; **10** subsequent; **13** consequential.

conservation 6 saving, upkeep; **7** ecology, storing; **10** management, protection; **11** maintenance, reservation, safekeeping; **12** preservation, safeguarding.

conservationist 5 green; **9** ecologist; **11** conservator.

conservative, Conservative 4 Tory; **7** careful, diehard; **8** cautious, moderate, rightist, stubborn; **9** hardliner, obstinate; **10** conformist, Republican; **11** reactionary, traditional; **12** conventional; **13** unprogressive; **14** fundamentalist, traditionalist; PHRASES: **2, 3, 5** on the right; **3-4** die-hard; **3-6** old-school; **3-9** old-fashioned; **4-2-3-4** dyed-in-the-wool; **4, 4** true blue *UK*; **4-5** hard-right; **5-2-3-3** stick-in-the-mud; **5-4** right-wing; **5-6** right-winger; **9, 6** obstinate person.

conservatory 5 porch; **8** hothouse; **10**

glasshouse *UK*, greenhouse; **13** conservatoire; PHRASES: **3, 6** art school; **5, 6** music school; **6, 2, 5** school of dance; **6, 4** garden room.

conserve **3** jam; **4** keep, save; **5** jelly, store; **7** protect; **8** preserve; **9** marmalade, safeguard; PHRASES: **2, 7, 4** be careful with; **3, 3** eke out.

consider **4** deem; **5** count, infer, judge, study, think; **6** deduce, ponder, reason, regard; **7** believe, observe, reflect, respect; **8** cogitate, ruminate; **10** deliberate; **11** contemplate; PHRASES: **4, 2, 4** bear in mind; **4, 4** chew over, mull over; **4, 4, 7** take into account; **4, 5** care about; **5, 2** weigh up *UK*; **5, 5** think about; **5, 7** think through.

consideration **3** TLC; **4** care, fact, item; **5** issue, point; **6** esteem, factor, matter, regard, weight; **7** concern, respect, thought; **8** courtesy, kindness, sympathy; **9** allowance, attention, substance; **10** compassion, importance, reflection, solicitude; **11** consequence, mindfulness, sensitivity; **12** deliberation, selflessness; **13** contemplation, understanding; **14** thoughtfulness; **15** considerateness; PHRASES: **6, 4** loving care.

considering **5** given; PHRASES: **2, 4, 2** in view of; **7, 2, 4** bearing in mind; **8, 3** allowing for.

consign **4** give, send; **6** banish, commit; **7** condemn, deliver, entrust; **8** dispatch, relegate, transfer; PHRASES: **3, 3, 2** get rid of; **4, 4** hand over.

consistency **4** feel; **6** makeup; **7** texture; **8** evenness; **9** constancy, runniness, thickness; **10** steadiness, uniformity; **11** reliability.

consistently **6** always, evenly; **8** reliably, steadily; **9** regularly; **10** constantly, dependably, invariably, repeatedly; **11** continually, unfailingly; **12** continuously, unswervingly; PHRASES: **4, 3, 4** over and over; **4, 3, 5** time and again; **4, 5, 4** time after time; **5, 3, 5** again and again; **5, 4** every time; **7, 4** without fail.

consist of **6** embody; **7** contain, embrace, include, involve; **8** comprise; **9** encompass; **11** incorporate; PHRASES: **2, 4, 2, 2** be made up of.

consolation *See* **comfort**

console **4** dash; **5** board, cheer, panel; **6** solace, soothe; **7** comfort, hearten, support; **8** controls, keyboard, reassure; **9** dashboard;

PHRASES: **7, 5** control panel.

consolidate **4** fuse, join; **5** merge, unite; **7** combine, confirm, enhance; **9** establish; **10** strengthen; PHRASES: **4, 2** firm up.

consort **4** band, wife; **5** group; **6** spouse; **7** partner; **8** ensemble; **9** associate, companion, orchestra.

conspicuous **5** overt, plain; **6** marked, patent; **7** blatant, evident, exposed, notable, obvious, visible; **8** distinct, striking; **9** prominent; **10** noticeable; **11** outstanding; PHRASES: **2, 3, 9** in the limelight; **2, 4** on show; **3-8** eye-catching; **4-7** well-defined; **5-3** clear-cut; **7, 7** clearly visible, plainly visible.

conspiracy *See* **plot**

conspire **3** spy; **4** plan, plot; **5** unite; **6** scheme; **7** collude, connive; **8** contrive; **11** collaborate; PHRASES: **4, 7** work against; **4, 8** work together.

constant **3** set; **4** even; **5** loyal; **6** stable, steady; **7** chronic, devoted, endless, lasting, nonstop, regular, staunch, uniform; **8** enduring, faithful, frequent, repeated, unbroken, unending; **9** ceaseless, continual, incessant, permanent, perpetual, recurrent, recurring, steadfast, unceasing, unvarying; **10** changeless, consistent, continuous, invariable, persistent, relentless, unchanging; **11** everlasting, trustworthy, unrelenting, unremitting; **12** interminable; PHRASES: **5, 2, 3, 2** going on and on.

Constantinople **8** Istanbul.

constellation **3** Ara, Leo; **4** Apus, Crux, Grus, Lynx, Lyra, Pavo, Vela; **5** Aries, Cetus, Draco, group, Hydra, Indus, Lepus, Libra, Lupus, Musca, Orion, Pyxis, Virgo; **6** Aquila, Auriga, Boötes, Cancer, Carina, Corvus, Crater, Cygnus, Dorado, Fornax, galaxy, Gemini, Hydrus, Octans, Pictor, Pisces, Puppis, Taurus, Tucana, Volans, zodiac; **7** Cepheus, cluster, Columba, Lacerta, pattern, Pegasus, Perseus, Phoenix, Polaris (North Star), Sagitta, Serpens, Sextans; **8** Aquarius, Equuleus, Eridanus, Hercules, Scorpius, Sculptor; **9** Andromeda, Centaurus, Delphinus, gathering, Monoceros, Ophiuchus; **10** Cassiopeia, Chamaeleon, collection, Triangulum; **11** arrangement, Capricornus, Sagittarius; **14** Camelopardalis; PHRASES: **3, 5** Leo Minor; **3, 6** Big Dipper; **4, 5** Ursa Major, Ursa Minor; **4, 9** Coma Berenices; **5, 5** Canis Major, Canis Minor; **5, 8** Canes Venatici; **6, 8** Corona Borealis; **6, 9** Corona Australis, Piscis Austrinus; **7, 7** stellar cluster; **8, 4** multiple star.

constituency 4 area, ward; **6** public, region, voters; **7** borough; **9** community; **10** electorate, population.

constituent 3 bit; **4** part, unit; **5** voter; **6** factor; **7** elector, element; **9** component; **10** ingredient; PHRASES: **9, 4** component part.

constitute 4 form; **5** found, total; **6** create; **7** compose, signify; **9** establish, institute, represent; PHRASES: **3, 2** set up; **3, 2, 2** add up to; **4, 2** make up; **6, 2** amount to.

constitution 4 bill; **6** health, makeup, nature; **7** charter, statute; **8** creation; **9** condition, formation, structure; **10** components, foundation; **11** composition, disposition; **12** constituents, organization; **13** establishment.

constrain 4 make; **5** limit; **6** coerce, compel, oblige; **7** confine; **8** pressure, restrain, restrict; PHRASES: **4, 4** hold back.

constraint *See* **restriction**

constrict 5 limit; **6** narrow, shrink; **7** control, tighten; **8** compress, contract, restrict; **9** constrain.

constriction 5 limit; **9** condition, narrowing, shrinking; **10** constraint, limitation, tightening; **11** compression, contraction, restriction.

construct 4 form, make; **5** build, erect, raise; **6** create; **7** compose, concoct, fashion; **8** assemble; **9** fabricate, structure; **10** hypothesis; PHRASES: **3, 2** get up, put up, set up; **3, 8** put together; **5, 8** piece together.

construction 4 dome, fort, hall, pile, spin, take, tomb; **5** folly, house, tower, works; **6** castle, chapel, church, palace, prefab, school, temple; **7** college, complex, derrick, edifice, mansion, masonry, meaning, pyramid, reading, theater; **8** assembly, building, cenotaph, Coliseum, creation, elevator, erection, fortress, hospital, monument, workings, ziggurat; **9** acropolis, brickwork, cathedral, Colosseum, construct, formation, mausoleum, stonework, structure, timbering; **10** habitation, production, skyscraper; **11** composition, explanation, foundations, manufacture; **13** establishment, understanding; **14** infrastructure, interpretation, prefabrication, superstructure; PHRASES: **3, 7** guy derrick; **4, 3, 7** lath and plaster; **5, 5** great house, tower

crane *UK*; **6, 3, 4** wattle and daub; **6, 3, 6** bricks and mortar; **6, 5** mobile crane, office block; **6, 8** office building; **7, 4** stately home *UK*; **7, 8** ancient monument *UK*.

constructive 6 useful; **7** helpful; **8** positive; **10** beneficial, productive.

construe 3 see; **4** read, take; **9** interpret; **10** understand.

consult 3 ask, see; **5** check, refer, visit; **6** access, confer, huddle, parley; **7** discuss; **9** negotiate; PHRASES: **4, 2** call in, call on, look up, talk to, turn to; **4, 2, 4, 5** have at one's elbow; **4, 4** meet with; **4, 5** swap ideas; **4, 6** seek advice; **5, 2** refer to; **5, 3** sound out; **5, 4** learn from; **6, 2** listen to; **7, 2** confide in; **7, 5** compare notes.

consultation 4 talk; **6** huddle, parley, powwow; **7** council, meeting, session; **8** dialogue, referral; **10** conference, discussion; **12** deliberation, negotiations; PHRASES: **4-1-4** tête-à-tête; **4, 8** open exchange; **7, 6** seeking advice; **8, 2, 5** exchange of views.

consume 3 eat, use; **4** burn; **5** chomp, drink, drown, munch, spend, swamp, waste; **6** devour, engulf, expend, gobble, guzzle, ingest; **7** deplete, destroy, envelop, exhaust, utilize; **8** squander; **9** overwhelm; **10** incinerate; PHRASES: **2, 7** go through; **3, 2** eat up, use up; **3, 4** put away; **3, 7** get through, run through; **4, 2** burn up, feed on; **4, 4** burn down; **5, 2, 3, 4** throw to the dogs; **5, 4** throw away; **6, 2** gobble up; **7, 2** swallow up.

consumer 4 user; **5** buyer; **6** punter *UK*; **7** shopper, spender; **8** customer; **9** clientele, purchaser; PHRASES: **3, 4** end user.

consummate 5 total, utter; **6** expert; **7** achieve, perfect, skilled; **8** absolute, complete, conclude, skillful, talented; **9** excellent; **10** accomplish; **12** accomplished; PHRASES: **3-3-3** out-and-out; **5, 3** carry out.

consumption 3 use; **6** eating; **7** feeding; **8** drinking, feasting, spending; **9** depletion, ingesting; **11** expenditure, utilization.

contact *See* **touch, communicate**

contact 5 write; **6** friend; **8** dealings, exchange; **10** connection; **11** communicate, interaction; **12** acquaintance; **13** communication; PHRASES: **3, 2, 5** get in touch; **4, 1, 4** drop a line; **4, 7** make ~.

contain 4 hold; **5** check, cover, limit; **6** harbor; **7** conceal, confine, control, delimit, enclose, include, inhibit, repress; **8** comprise, restrain, restrict, suppress, surround; **9** encompass; PHRASES: **3, 2** box up *UK*; **4, 2** take in; **4, 2, 5** keep in check, take on board; **4, 4** hold back.

container **3** bag, bin, box, can, cup, jar, keg, pot, tin *UK*, urn, vat; **4** bowl, case, cask, drum, sack, tank, vase; **5** caddy, chest, crate, creel, glass, jelly, store, trunk; **6** ashcan, barrel, basket, bottle, bucket, carton, casket, drawer, hamper, holder, punnet *UK*, vessel; **7** pillbox, pitcher; **8** billycan *UK*; **9** cartridge, reservoir; **10** depository, pigeonhole, receptacle, repository; PHRASES: **3, 3** jam jar *UK*; **3, 5** tea caddy; **5, 3** jerry can; **5, 4** jewel case; **6, 4** pencil case; **7, 3** biscuit tin *UK*, storage bin; **7, 4** storage tank; **9, 3** cardboard box.

contemplate **4** muse; **5** brood, think; **6** ponder; **7** reflect; **8** cogitate, consider, meditate; **10** deliberate; PHRASES: **4, 4** mull over; **5, 2** dwell on.

contemplation **5** study; **6** survey; **7** thought; **8** scrutiny; **10** inspection, meditation, reflection; **11** examination, observation; **12** deliberation; **13** consideration; PHRASES: **5-6** navel-gazing.

contemporary **4** peer; **5** class; **6** friend, latest, modern, sister; **7** brother, current, ongoing, present; **8** existing; **9** classmate, colleague; PHRASES: **2-4** up-to-date; **3, 2, 3, 4** one of the boys, one of the gang, one of the lads; **3, 2, 3, 5** one of the girls; **5, 2** class of; **7-3** present-day.

contempt **5** scorn; **6** hatred; **7** disdain, dislike; **8** derision, sneering; **10** disrespect; **11** disapproval, superiority; **12** scornfulness; **13** condescension, disparagement; PHRASES: **3, 7** low opinion.

contemptuous **4** cold, cool; **5** lofty; **6** snooty; **7** haughty; **8** arrogant, derisive, scornful, sneering, snobbish; **9** withering; **10** disdainful; **11** disparaging; **12** disapproving, supercilious; **13** condescending, disrespectful.

contend **3** bet, run, try, vie; **4** cope, race; **5** argue, enter, rival, state, wager; **6** allege, assert, battle, combat, insist, oppose, resist, strive, tackle, tussle; **7** attempt, compete, contest, declare, wrestle; **8** maintain, struggle; **9** challenge, withstand; PHRASES: **3, 2, 4** put up with; **3, 4** vie with; **4, 2** take on; **4, 4** deal with.

content **4** gist; **5** happy, theme; **6** matter, please, soothe; **7** gladden, pleased, satisfy; **9** contented, gratified, satisfied, substance; PHRASES: **4, 5** make happy; **7, 6** subject matter.

contentious **4** moot; **6** touchy; **7** hawkish, prickly, warlike, warring; **8** critical, divisive; **9** debatable, irritable; **10** aggressive, pugnacious; **11** provocative, quarrelsome; **13** argumentative, controversial; PHRASES: **2, 11** at loggerheads; **3-6** hot-button; **3-7** hot-blooded; **4-2-4** head-to-head.

contents **3** nub; **4** gist, meat; **5** parts; **6** makeup, matter; **7** essence; **8** elements, features, material; **9** structure, substance; **10** components; **11** composition, ingredients; **12** constituents, constitution, quintessence.

contest **4** bout, gala *UK*, game, hand, race; **5** argue, event, fight, match, query, round; **6** oppose; **7** dispute, matchup, session, tourney; **8** question; **9** challenge; **10** tournament; **11** competition.

continent **4** Asia, land; **5** India; **6** Africa, chaste, Europe; **7** America, Eurasia, Oceania, terrain; **8** landmass, mainland; **9** landscape; **10** Antarctica, restrained; **11** Australasia; **12** subcontinent; PHRASES: **3, 4** dry land; **5, 7** North America, South America.

contingent **5** group, party; **6** liable; **7** reliant; **8** legation; **9** committee, dependent, depending; **10** commission.

continual **6** steady; **7** endless, flowing, ongoing, running; **8** constant, frequent, repeated, unbroken, unending; **9** ceaseless, incessant, recurrent, sustained, unceasing, undivided; **10** continuing, continuous, persistent, repetitive; **11** everlasting, unrelenting, unremitting; **12** interminable; **13** inexhaustible, uninterrupted; **14** interconnected.

continually **6** always; **7** forever, nonstop; **9** eternally; PHRASES: **2, 3, 2** on and on; **3, 3, 4** all the time; **4, 2, 5** with no letup; **7, 7** without respite. *See also* **continual**

continuation **6** sequel; **8** addition; **9** extension; **11** installment, maintenance, persistence, progression; **12** perpetuation; PHRASES: **7, 3** drawing out.

continue **3** add, run; **4** flow, last, stay; **5** recur, renew; **6** cohere, endure, extend, linger, remain, repeat, resume, revive; **7** advance, connect, persist, proceed, prolong, reprize, restart, succeed, support, sustain; **8** maintain, preserve, progress; **10** perpetuate, supplement; PHRASES: **2, 2** go on; **3, 2** run on; **3, 3, 3** run and run; **3, 4** not stop; **4, 2** harp on, keep on, keep up; **4, 2, 7, 2** keep on keeping on; **4, 5** keep alive, keep going; **4, 8** make progress; **5, 2** carry on; **6, 7** follow through.

continuing 7 current, ongoing; **8** enduring, unending; **9** remaining.

continuous 5 solid; **6** smooth; **7** endless, nonstop, serried, uniform; **8** constant, seamless, unbroken, unending; **9** ceaseless, continual, incessant, perpetual, unceasing; **10** monotonous, unrelieved; **11** featureless, unremitting; **12** interminable; **13** uninterrupted; PHRASES: **3-3** one-hop; **5-6** neverending; **8, 7** straight through.

contort *See* **distort**

contour *See* **outline**

contract 3 get, tie, vow, wed; **4** bond, deal, hire, pact, sign; **5** catch, marry; **6** accord, commit, employ, engage, pledge, shrink, treaty; **7** bargain, shorten, tighten; **8** alliance, covenant; **9** agreement, betrothal, concordat, matrimony; **10** assignment, commission, engagement, obligation, settlement; **11** arrangement, partnership, transaction, undertaking; **13** understanding; PHRASES: **2, 9, 2** be afflicted by; **4, 2** sign up; **4, 4, 4** come down with; **4, 7** grow smaller; **5, 9** legal agreement; **6, 7** commit oneself; **6, 9** mutual agreement; **7, 4** suicide pact; **9, 3** exchanged vow.

contraction 3 tic; **5** cramp, crush, pinch, spasm; **6** précis, waning; **7** atrophy, elision, pursing, squeeze, wasting; **8** cramping, decrease, ellipsis, pinching, slimming *UK*, synopsis, trimming; **9** clenching, deflation, lessening, narrowing, puckering, reduction, shrinkage, shrinking, squeezing, tightness, wrinkling; **10** abridgment, convulsion, limitation, shortening, shriveling, tightening; **11** abridgment, compression, curtailment, restriction; **12** abbreviation, condensation, constriction; **13** concentration, strangulation; PHRASES: **4-2** cave-in; **6, 6** losing weight; **7-4** scaling-down; **7, 8** drawing together; **9, 2** puckering up.

contractor 4 doer, vise; **5** clamp, press; **6** corset, dealer, jobber, worker; **7** builder, crusher, grinder; **8** diplomat, operator, ratifier, servicer, squeezer, supplier; **9** architect, condenser, signatory; **10** astringent, compressor, covenanter, journeyman, negotiator, peacemaker, tourniquet; **11** constrictor; **12** entrepreneur, straitjacket; **13**

subcontractor; PHRASES: **2-6** co-signer; **3, 11** the undersigned; **6-5** treaty-maker; **7-6** wheeler-dealer; **10, 5** consenting party.

contractual 5 sworn; **6** agreed, signed; **7** nuptial; **8** arranged, assigned, conjugal, promised, ratified; **9** assenting, bilateral; **10** consensual, covenanted, negotiated; **11** matrimonial; **12** multilateral; **13** countersigned; PHRASES: **6, 2** agreed to.

contradict 4 deny; **6** cancel, oppose, refute; **7** dispute; **8** disprove; **9** challenge, undermine.

contradiction 6 denial; **7** paradox; **8** antinomy, conflict, negation, oxymoron, rebuttal; **9** challenge, dichotomy; **10** opposition, refutation; **11** disputation, mésalliance, misalliance; **12** disagreement, illogicality; **13** inconsistency.

contradictory 3 odd; **6** absurd; **8** contrary, opposing, opposite; **9** ambiguous, anomalous, misallied; **10** mismatched, oxymoronic; **11** conflicting, incongruous, maladjusted, paradoxical; **12** inconsistent; PHRASES: **2, 4** at odds.

contrary 3 con; **7** defiant, inverse, reverse, willful; **8** converse, opposing, opposite, perverse; **9** diametric, difficult, divergent, obstinate; **10** antithesis, rebellious; **11** conflicting, contrasting, disagreeing, disobedient; **12** antagonistic, incompatible, inconsistent; **13** contradictory, uncooperative; **14** irreconcilable.

contrast 3 gap; **5** weigh; **6** differ; **7** compare; **9** analogize, disparity, juxtapose; **10** difference; **11** distinction, distinguish; **13** dissimilarity; PHRASES: **5, 3** stand out.

contravene 5 break, flout; **6** breach; **7** disobey; **9** disregard.

contribute 4 give, help; **5** endow; **6** donate, supply; **7** provide; **9** subscribe; PHRASES: **3, 2** add to; **4, 1, 4, 2** play a part in; **4, 2** chip in; **4, 4** take part.

contribution 3 say; **4** gift, role; **5** input; **6** giving; **7** payment, subsidy; **8** donation; **9** influence; **11** involvement.

contributor 5 agent, aider, donor, giver; **6** backer, funder, helper; **7** abettor, sponsor; **8** supplier; **9** accessory; **10** benefactor; **11** underwriter.

contrition *See* **remorse**

contrivance 4 plan, plot, ruse; **6** device, gadget, scheme; **7** machine; **9** apparatus; **11** contraption.

contrive 4 plan, plot, ruse; 6 devise, manage, scheme; 7 arrange; 8 engineer; PHRASES: 5, 5 bring about; 5-6 stage-manage.

control 3 run; 4 curb, dial, knob, lead, rule; 5 brake, check, guide, lever; 6 adjust, button, direct, manage; 7 command, monitor, operate; 8 dominate, regulate, restrain; 9 dominance, restraint; 10 discipline, management, regulation; PHRASES: 3, 2, 7 out of ~; 4, 3, 5 wear the pants; 4, 3, 7 pull the strings; 4-7 self-control; 5, 7 birth ~; 7, 4 preside over.

controllable 9 malleable, tractable; 10 governable, manageable; PHRASES: 4-7 well-behaved; 4-9 well-regulated.

controversial *See* **contentious**

controversy 5 storm; 6 debate; 8 argument; 10 hullabaloo; 12 disagreement.

conundrum *See* **puzzle**

convalesce *See* **improve**

convalescence *See* **recuperation**

convene 5 rally; 6 muster, summon; 7 arrange, marshal; 8 assemble, mobilize, organize; PHRASES: 3, 2 set up; 4, 2 call up; 4, 8 call together.

convenience 2 WC; 3 aid, lav, loo *UK*; 4 ease, tool; 5 means; 6 profit, toilet; 7 amenity, benefit, fitness, utility; 8 bathroom, facility, lavatory, nearness; 9 appliance, closeness, expedient, handiness, propriety, usability; 10 adaptation, expedience, expediency, facilities, pragmatism, timeliness, usefulness; 11 application, contrivance, suitability; 12 advisability, desirability, practicality; 13 accessibility, accommodation, opportuneness; 14 auspiciousness, practicability, utilitarianism; PHRASES: 5, 4 right time; 11, 4 ~ food.

convenient 3 fit; 4 near; 5 close, handy; 6 nearby, timely, useful; 7 fitting, helpful, politic, prudent; 8 adjacent, suitable, workable; 9 befitting, opportune, pragmatic; PHRASES: 4-5 well-timed; 5, 2, 4 close at hand.

convenient (be convenient) 2 do; 4 suit, wash; 5 befit, serve; 7 benefit; 9 advantage; PHRASES: 3, 2, 5 not go amiss; 3, 3, 4 hit the spot; 4, 2, 5 come in handy; 4, 2, 6 come in useful; 4, 3, 4 fill the bill; 7, 3, 5 deliver the goods; 7, 7 produce results.

convention 4 form, norm, pact, rule; 5 habit, order, style, trend, vogue; 6 custom, method, system; 7 fashion, meeting, precept, routine; 8 assembly, congress, covenant, practice, standard; 9 agreement, gathering, orthodoxy, principle, tradition; 10 conference, stereotype; 11 institution; PHRASES: 3-8 get-together; 4, 5 done thing; 5, 2, 3, 3 order of the day; 5, 4 party line; 8, 4 received idea.

conventional 5 stock, usual; 6 common, normal; 7 mundane, regular, typical; 8 accepted, habitual, ordinary, orthodox, standard, straight; 9 customary; 10 conformist, mainstream, unoriginal; 11 commonplace, established, predictable, traditional; 12 conservative, standardized; 13 institutional, stereotypical, unadventurous; 14 quintessential; PHRASES: 5, 2, 4 comme il faut; 6-2-3-4 middle-of-the-road.

converge 4 join, meet; 5 close, pinch, taper, touch, unite; 6 funnel; 8 approach; 9 intersect; 10 congregate; PHRASES: 4, 4 draw near; 4, 8 come together; 5, 2 close in, close up; 5, 4 close with; 6, 3, 3 narrow the gap.

convergent 5 focal; 6 radial; 7 conical, focused, meeting, pointed, uniting; 8 focusing, tapering; 9 centering, narrowing, pyramidal, radiating; 10 concurrent, converging, tangential; 11 centripetal; PHRASES: 5-5 knock-kneed.

conversant *See* **familiar**

conversation 4 chat, talk; 6 natter, parley; 8 colloquy, dialogue, exchange; 9 discourse; 10 discussion; 11 intercourse; 12 pleasantries; 13 communication; PHRASES: 4-1-4 tête-à-tête; 5, 5 bandy words.

conversational 6 casual, chatty, spoken; 7 gossipy, relaxed; 8 familiar, informal, intimate, ordinary; 9 talkative; 10 colloquial, loquacious, unreserved, vernacular; 13 communicative.

conversationalist 6 gossip, talker; 7 speaker; 9 raconteur; 10 chatterbox, respondent; 11 interviewer; 12 interlocutor, interrogator; PHRASES: 5-8 cross-examiner.

converse 4 chat, talk; 5 speak; 6 natter, parley; 7 adverse, chatter, commune, counter, discuss, inverse, reverse; 8 contrary, opposing, opposite; 9 discourse; 10 antithesis; 11 communicate, confabulate; 12 antithetical; PHRASES: 4, 1, 4, 4 have a word with; 4, 3, 3 chew the fat; 4, 8 talk together; 8, 5 exchange words.

conversion 4 move; 5 shift; 6 change,

switch; **7** alchemy, melting; **8** exchange, mutation, transfer; **9** chemistry, reduction; **10** adaptation, alteration, changeover, converting, processing, renovation, transition; **11** bewitchment, dehydration, enchantment, translation; **12** fermentation, modification, substitution, transference; **13** metamorphosis, transposition; **14** reorganization, transformation; **15** crystallization, transfiguration; PHRASES: **8, 6** chemical change, physical change.

convert 5 adapt, alter; **6** change, induce, modify, switch; **7** recruit, remodel, traitor; **8** apostate, convince, defector, exchange, persuade, renegade, renovate, transfer, turncoat; **9** brainwash, influence, supporter, transform, transmute; **10** evangelize, substitute; **11** proselytize, transfigure; **12** indoctrinate, propagandize; **13** tergiversator; PHRASES: **2, 4** go over; **3, 3** new man; **3, 4** win over; **4, 4** talk into; **4, 5** talk round *UK*; **5, 5** bring round *UK*; **6, 4** change over; **7, 6** changed person.

convex 5 bowed, bulgy; **6** arched, curved, humped; **7** bulbous, bulging, curving, gibbous, rounded, swelled, swollen, vaulted; **8** swelling; **9** billowing, distended, prominent, tumescent; **10** protruding; PHRASES: **1-6** U-shaped; **5, 3** bowed out.

convey *See* **carry**

convey 4 bear, send, take; **5** carry; **7** express, suggest; **9** transport; **11** communicate; PHRASES: **3, 6** get across, put across.

convict 3 con; **5** felon, lifer; **6** detain, inmate, outlaw, reject; **7** condemn, villain; **8** criminal, imprison, offender, prisoner, sentence; **9** blacklist; **10** lawbreaker; **13** excommunicate; PHRASES: **3, 3** old lag *UK*; **3, 4** put away; **4, 4** send down *UK*; **4, 6** find guilty; **4, 7** find against; **5, 6** prove guilty; **8, 2, 5** sentence to death; **9, 6** pronounce guilty.

convicted 6 damned, guilty, liable; PHRASES: **2, 4** in hell; **6, 2, 4** frying in hell, having no case; **7, 1, 4** without a case. *See also* **convict**

conviction 4 bias, view; **5** faith, trust; **6** belief, fervor; **7** bigotry, opinion, passion, verdict; **8** judgment, outlawry, sentence; **9** assurance, certainty, certitude, dogmatism, orthodoxy, principle; **10** confidence, fanaticism, persuasion, punishment; **11** assuredness; **12** condemnation, imprisonment; PHRASES: **4-9** self-assurance; **4-10** self-confidence; **5, 2, 4, 4** price on one's head; **5, 3** black cap, death row; **5, 4** going down; **5, 8** death sentence; **6, 4** thumbs down; **6, 8** prison sentence; **9, 4** condemned cell *UK*.

convince *See* **persuade**

convinced 4 firm, sure; **6** biased, strong, swayed; **7** assured, bigoted, certain, earnest, induced, staunch; **8** cocksure, dogmatic, orthodox, partisan, positive, stubborn, trusting; **9** accepting, assertive, believing, committed, confident, converted, fanatical, obstinate, persuaded, satisfied; **10** influenced, undoubting, unswerving; **11** doctrinaire, opinionated; **13** overconfident, unquestioning; PHRASES: **3, 4** won over; **4-7** self-assured; **4-9** self-confident; **6-6** narrow-minded.

convincing 8 credible, lifelike; **9** authentic, plausible, realistic, undoubted; **10** believable, compelling, conclusive, persuasive, resounding; **11** substantial; **12** considerable.

convivial *See* **pleasant**

convolute 4 coil, curl, loop, roll, turn, wave, wind; **5** braid, snake, twine, twirl, twist, weave; **6** spiral, squirm, writhe; **7** distort, entwine, meander, wriggle; **8** squiggle; **9** corkscrew; PHRASES: **5, 3, 4** twist and turn; **5, 8** twist together, weave together.

convoy 4 band, line; **5** group, party; **7** caravan, company, cortege; **8** flotilla; **9** cavalcade, motorcade.

convulsion *See* **seizure**

convulsive 5 jerky, jolty, jumpy; **6** abrupt, fitful, sudden; **7** jarring, jolting, jumping, palsied, spastic, twitchy, violent; **8** orgasmic; **9** eclamptic, epileptic, irregular, spasmodic; **10** cataleptic, paroxysmic; **14** uncontrollable.

cook 3 fry; **4** bake, boil, chef, heat, stew, stir; **5** baker, baste, broil, brown, curry, devil, grill, poach, roast, sauté, scald, steam, stuff, toast; **6** blanch, braise, coddle, flambé, reheat, simmer; **7** caterer, griddle, parboil, prepare; **8** barbecue, scramble; **9** casserole, charbroil, microwave; PHRASES: **3-5** pan-broil, pot-roast; **4, 2** heat up; **4-3** deep-fry, stir-fry; **4, 4** head chef, sous chef; **4-5** spit-roast; **4, 7** warm through *UK*; **4, 9, 2** whip something up; **5-5, 4** short-order ~; **6, 4** commis chef *UK*, pastry chef; **7-3** shallow-fry; **8, 4** pressure ~; **8-5** charcoal-grill; **9, 4** celebrity chef.

cooker 4 chef, cook, spit; **5** broil, grill; **6**

burner, kettle; **7** griddle, toaster; **8** barbecue, hotplate; **9** microwave; PHRASES: **6**, **4** waffle iron; **8-5** sandwich-maker.

cookie 3 bun; **4** sort, type; **6** person; **7** biscuit; **9** character; **10** individual; **13** snickerdoodle.

cooking 6 baking, recipe; **7** cuisine, heaping; **8** catering *UK*; **10** gastronomy; PHRASES: **4**, **9** home economics; **4**, **10** food processing; **4**, **11** food preparation; **5**, **7** haute cuisine; **7**, **4** cookery book; **8**, **7** domestic science, nouvelle cuisine, pressure ~; **9**, **7** microwave ~.

cool 3 hip, icy, raw; **4** calm, cold, good; **5** abate, aloof, bleak, chill, fresh, muted, nifty, nippy, parky *UK*, snowy; **6** arctic, boreal, casual, chilly, colder, cooler, dampen, frigid, frosty, groovy, placid, serene, slushy, trendy; **7** coldish, distant, freshen, frosted, glacial, offhand, stylish, subzero; **8** composed, detached, freezing, Siberian, terrific, tranquil; **9** collected, excellent, fantastic, perishing *UK*, unruffled, wonderful; **10** impersonal, nonchalant, unfriendly, unsociable; **11** fashionable, magnificent, refrigerate, unemotional, unflappable, unperturbed; **12** inhospitable; **13** dispassionate, imperturbable, sophisticated; **14** unenthusiastic; PHRASES: **3**, **6** air cooler; **4-2** with-it; **4**, **3** ~ off; **4**, **4** ~ down, make cold; **4-4** snow-clad; **4-7** snow-covered; **5**, **4** below zero; **5-6** level-headed, stand-offish; **5-7** frost-covered; **6**, **4** dampen down; **6-7** fridge-freezer *UK*; **8**, **4** bitterly cold.

cooler 3 fan; **4** Esky *UK*; **6** fridge, icebox, prison, punkah; **7** chiller, coolant, freezer; **10** cryogenics; **11** refrigerant; **12** refrigerator; PHRASES: **3**, **3** ice bag; **3**, **4** ice pack; **3**, **5** ice house; **3**, **6** ice bucket; **3**, **7** ice machine; **3**, **11** air conditioner; **3**, **12** air conditioning; **4**, **3** cool bag *UK*, cool box *UK*; **4**, **6** deep freeze; **5**, **8** chill cupboard; **6**, **6** liquid oxygen; **6-7** fridge-freezer *UK*; **7**, **5** cooling tower; **7**, **7** chiller cabinet.

coolness 3 nip; **4** calm, cold; **5** chill, poise; **7** reserve; **8** coldness, distance; **9** assurance, composure, hostility; **10** detachment; **13** inhospitality; PHRASES: **4-9** self-assurance; **4-10** self-possession. *See also* **cool**

coop *See* **pen**

cooperate 4 help; **5** unite; **6** assist, concur, liaise, oblige; **7** support; **8** dovetail; **11** accommodate, collaborate; PHRASES: **4**, **1**, **4**

lend a hand; **4**, **2** join in; **4**, **3**, **4** play the game; **4**, **4** play ball; **4**, **4**, **6** pull one's weight; **4**, **6** join forces; **4**, **8** work together.

cooperation 3 aid; **4** help; **5** cabal, unity; **6** backup; **7** concord, harmony, support; **8** alliance, marriage, teamwork; **9** agreement; **10** assistance, conspiracy, federation; **11** association, confederacy, helpfulness; **12** counterpoint; **13** collaboration, confederation, orchestration; **15** cooperativeness, synchronization.

cooperation (in cooperation) 2, **6** in league, in tandem; **2**, **7** in cahoots, in concert; **2**, **9** in collusion; **2**, **11** in conjunction; **2**, **13** in collaboration.

cooperative 5 joint; **6** allied, common, mutual, shared, united; **7** company, helpful, willing; **8** obliging; **9** compliant, symbiotic; **10** collective, enterprise, harmonious, supportive, synergetic; **11** association, confederate, cooperating, synchronous, synergistic; **12** contributory, orchestrated, organization; **13** accommodating, collaborative, participatory; **14** conspiratorial; PHRASES: **2-2** co-op; **2**, **6** in league; **2**, **7** in harmony; **2**, **9** in agreement; **2**, **11** in association, in partnership; **3-3** two-way.

cooperator 4 ally; **6** fellow, helper; **7** partner; **8** quisling; **9** assistant; **11** conspirator; **12** collaborator; PHRASES: **2-6** co-worker.

coordinates 5 match; **7** arrange; **8** organize; **9** harmonize; **11** synchronize; PHRASES: **1-10** x-coordinate, y-coordinate, z-coordinate.

coordination 5 grace, skill; **9** dexterity, direction, logistics; **10** adroitness, management; **11** proficiency; **12** organization; **13** harmonization.

cope 6 handle, manage; **7** survive; PHRASES: **3**, **7** get through; **4**, **4** deal with.

copier 5 faker, mimic, press; **6** camera, forger, parrot; **7** copycat, copyist, painter, printer; **8** imitator, sketcher; **9** camcorder, Photostat™, stenciler; **10** bootlegger, duplicator, plagiarist; **11** photocopier, transcriber; **12** impersonator, photographer; **13** counterfeiter; PHRASES: **4**, **8** tape recorder; **5**, **7** laser printer, Xerox™ machine; **6**, **6** record pirate; **7**, **6** fashion victim *UK*; **8**, **7** computer printer.

copy 3 ape; **4** crib, fake, item, mime, mock, pony, sham, take, text, twin; **5** clone, dummy, forge, mimic, phony *UK*, print, Xerox™; **6** borrow, phoney, pirate; **7** bootleg, emulate, fashion, forgery, imitate, replica, stencil, version; **8** knockoff, likeness, pastiche, portrait, simulate; **9** duplicate, facsimile, imitation, photocopy, replicate, reproduce; **10** Mimeograph™, plagiarism, plagiarize, simulation, typescript; **11** counterfeit, duplication, impersonate, publication; **12** doppelgänger, reproduction; PHRASES: **2-6** re-create; **3-3** rip-off; **4-2** mock-up; **4, 4** ~ book, fair ~; **5, 4** laser ~, spare ~, Xerox™ ~; **5, 7** cover version; **6, 4** backup ~, carbon ~; **7, 4** bootleg ~, feature ~; **7, 5** working model; **8, 4** faithful ~.

cor anglais **7, 4** English horn.

cord **4** flex *UK*, lead, rope, sash; **5** cable, twine; **6** string, thread; PHRASES: **6, 4** spinal ~; **9, 4** emergency ~, umbilical ~.

cordial **4** warm; **5** toddy, tonic; **6** genial, jovial; **7** affable, amiable; **8** friendly, pleasant; **9** convivial; **12** affectionate.

cordon **4** line; **5** chain; **7** barrier; **8** obstacle; **9** barricade; **11** obstruction; **12** stringcourse.

core **3** hub, nub; **4** crux, gist, main, meat, plug, soul; **5** basic, basis, elite, heart, nexus, pivot; **6** basics, center, kernel, middle, sample, spirit, staple; **7** bedrock, central, essence, extract, keynote, kingpin, nucleus; **8** midpoint; **9** essential, principal, substance; **10** underlying; **11** cornerstone, fundamental; **12** fundamentals; PHRASES: **5, 5** focal point, grass roots; **5-6** nitty-gritty.

corn **3** rye; **4** oats, samp; **5** candy, grain, maize *UK*, wheat; **6** hominy, mealie; **10** corndodger; PHRASES: **4, 4** ~ meal; **4, 5** ~ dolly *UK*, ~ poppy, ~ syrup; **4, 8** ~ exchange *UK*; **5, 4** field ~.

corner **4** area, bend, spot, trap, turn; **5** angle, crook, curve, place; **7** turning *UK*; **8** confront, junction, locality, location, restrict, surround; PHRASES: **3, 4** pin down.

corn poppy **5, 5** field poppy; **8, 5** Flanders poppy *UK*.

corollary *See* **consequence**

corporal **6** bodily, carnal; **7** fleshly, somatic; **8** material, physical; **9** corporeal; **10** anatomical.

corporal punishment **3** hit, rap; **4** blow, cuff, slap; **5** clout, smack, spank; **6** caning, hiding, stripe, stroke; **7** beating, dusting, hitting, racking, torture; **8** birching, drubbing, flogging, slapping, smacking, spanking, striking, whipping; **9** bastinado, scourging, strappado, thrashing, trouncing; **12** flagellation; **13** horsewhipping; PHRASES: **4, 2, 3, 3** clip on the ear; **4, 2, 3, 5** slap on the wrist; **5, 6** third degree.

corporate **5** group, joint, trade; **6** merged, mutual, public, shared; **7** company, limited, private; **8** business, communal; **9** community; **10** commercial, privatized; **12** incorporated, nationalized.

corporation **3** Inc, Ltd *UK*; **4** firm; **5** group, house; **7** company, concern; **8** business; **12** conglomerate, organization; **13** establishment, multinational, transnational; PHRASES: **5, 11** close ~; **7, 7** limited company.

corps **4** body; **5** cadre, force, group, troop; **6** league; **7** company; **12** organization.

corpse **4** body; **5** mummy, stiff; **7** cadaver, carcass, remains; **8** fatality, skeleton; PHRASES: **4, 4** dead body.

correct **3** fix; **4** mark, true; **5** alter, amend, emend, exact, right, tweak, valid; **6** adjust, modify, proper, revise; **7** factual, genuine, improve, literal, precise, rectify; **8** accurate, approved, faithful, lifelike, standard, truthful, verbatim; **9** authentic, realistic; **10** legitimate; **11** appropriate; **12** naturalistic; PHRASES: **2, 3, 6** on the button; **3, 5** put right; **4-2** bang-on, spot-on *UK*; **4-2-3-6** true-to-the-letter; **4-2-4** true-to-life; **4, 3** sort out; **4, 5** dead right; **4-7** word-perfect; **4-8** high-fidelity; **5, 2, 4** comme il faut.

correctly **4** bang; **5** truly; **6** aright; **8** squarely. *See also* **correct**

correctness **5** truth; **7** realism; **8** accuracy, fidelity, validity, veracity; **9** precision, rectitude; **10** legitimacy, literalism, naturalism, perfection; **11** suitability, uprightness; **12** authenticity; **13** acceptability; PHRASES: **3, 6** the letter; **3, 7, 5** the literal truth; **4, 8** high fidelity; **9, 2, 4** attention to fact. *See also* **correct**

correlate **4** link; **5** align, equal, match, tally; **6** answer, relate; **7** balance, compare, connect; **8** parallel, resemble; **9** associate; **10** correspond; PHRASES: **4, 1, 8** draw a parallel; **8, 4** identify with.

correlation **4** link; **5** match, tally; **7** analogy, pattern; **8** allegory, analogue, parallel; **10** comparison, connection, proportion, similarity; **11** association, equivalence; **12** relationship, significance; **14** correspondence; **15** proportionality.

correspond 3 fax; **4** mail, post, wire; **5** agree, cable, marry, match, reply, tally, telex, write; **6** answer, relate; **7** imitate, reflect; **8** coincide, parallel; **9** telegraph; **11** communicate, reciprocate; PHRASES: **1-4** e-mail; **4, 1, 4** drop a line; **4, 1, 4, 2** drop a line to; **4, 1, 6, 2** send a letter to; **4, 1, 8** send a telegram; **4, 2, 5** keep in touch; **5, 2** match up; **8, 7** exchange letters.

correspondence 3 fax; **4** mail, memo, note, post *UK*; **5** match, tally; **6** letter, packet, parcel; **7** mailbag, mailbox, message, postbag *UK*; **8** aerogram, mailsack, postcard; **9** agreement; **10** congruence, connection, similarity; **11** association, correlation, equivalence, parallelism, resemblance; **13** communication; PHRASES: **1-4** e-mail; **3, 6** air letter; **7, 6** airmail letter; **10, 3** diplomatic bag.

correspondent 6 keypal, writer; **8** reporter; **9** columnist; **10** journalist; **11** contributor *UK*; PHRASES: **3, 3** pen pal; **3, 6** pen friend *UK*; **6, 6** letter writer.

corresponding 7 fitting; **8** agreeing, matching, parallel; **9** analogous; **10** conforming, equivalent; **11** correlative, symmetrical.

corrida 9 bullfight.

corridor 4 hall; **5** strip; **7** hallway, passage, walkway; **10** passageway; PHRASES: **3, 8** air ~; **6, 4** flight path; **6, 5** access strip.

corroborate *See* **validate**

corrosive 5 harsh; **6** biting, bitter; **7** acerbic, eroding; **8** scarring; **9** sarcastic; **11** destructive.

corrupt 4 bent *UK*, harm, ruin, soil, warp; **5** abuse, alter, bribe, shady, shame, spoil, taint; **6** amoral, damage, debase, defile, rotten, sinful, sleazy; **7** crooked, debauch, degrade, deprave, immoral, pervert, spoiled; **8** decadent, depraved; **9** debauched, dishonest, dissolute, unethical; **10** degenerate; **11** contaminate; PHRASES: **2, 3, 4** on the take; **4, 6** lead astray.

corruption 4 harm; **5** fraud; **6** sleaze; **7** bribery; **9** depravity; **10** debasement, dishonesty, immorality, perversion; **12** exploitation.

cosh *See* **hit**

cosmetic 5 outer, token; **7** surface; **10** or-

namental; **11** superficial; PHRASES: **4-4** skin-deep.

cosmetics 4 kohl, slap *UK*; **5** paint, rouge; **6** makeup, powder; **7** blusher, mascara, pancake; **8** eyeliner, lipstick; **9** blackface, concealer, facepaint, whiteface; **10** foundation; **11** greasepaint; PHRASES: **3, 5** war paint; **3, 6** eye makeup; **3-6** eye-shadow; **4, 6** nail polish; **4, 7** nail varnish *UK*; **7, 6** eyebrow pencil.

cosmic 4 huge, vast; **7** immense; **8** enormous, galactic; **9** planetary, universal; **12** interstellar; **13** intergalactic; **14** interplanetary.

cosmos *See* **universe**

cosset *See* **spoil**

cost 3 fee; **4** loss, rate; **5** costs, fetch, price, total; **6** amount, charge, damage, effort, outlay; **7** expense; **8** expenses; **9** detriment, outgoings *UK*, sacrifice, suffering; **11** expenditure; PHRASES: **4, 2** come to; **4, 2, 6** ~ of living; **5, 3** price tag; **6, 2** amount to; **6, 5** asking price; **8, 5** purchase price.

costly 4 dear; **5** steep; **6** pricey; **7** harmful; **8** damaging, precious, valuable; **9** expensive; **10** exorbitant, overpriced; **12** extortionate, unaffordable; PHRASES: **3-4** sky-high; **4-6** high-priced; **6, 6** highly priced.

costume 5 dress, habit, robes; **6** attire, cozzie *UK*, livery, outfit; **7** clothes, regalia, uniform; **8** ensemble; **9** vestments; **10** carmagnole; PHRASES: **3-2** get-up; **3-3** rig-out *UK*; **5, 5** fancy dress.

coterie *See* **clique**

cotton candy 10 fairyfloss *UK*; PHRASES: **4, 5** spun sugar.

couch 3 set; **4** sofa, word; **5** divan; **6** phrase, settee; **7** express, ottoman; **12** chesterfield; PHRASES: **3, 3** day bed; **5, 5** ~ grass, quack grass, quick grass; **6, 5** quitch grass, studio ~, twitch grass; **6, 6** chaise longue; **7, 5** Grecian ~.

council 4 body, diet; **5** board, court, group, panel, party, synod; **6** agency, soviet, summit; **7** cabinet, hearing, meeting, mission, session, sitting; **8** assembly, audience, conclave, congress, legation, tribunal; **9** committee, presidium, Sanhedrin; **10** commission, conference, convention, delegation, deputation, roundtable; **11** association, bureaucracy; PHRASES: **5, 7** Privy C~; **5, 9** elder statesmen; **5, 10** Royal Commission *UK*; **7, 2, 6** ~ of elders; **7, 7** ~ chamber;

8, 5 advisory board; **8, 7** Security C~.

counsel **3** aid; **4** help; **5** guide; **6** advice, advise; **7** propose, suggest, support, warning; **8** advocate, guidance; **9** direction, encourage, recommend; **10** guidelines.

count **3** sum; **4** deem, earl, hold, poll, view; **5** tally, total, weigh; **6** adding, amount, census, esteem, matter, reckon, regard; **7** compute, signify, telling; **8** consider, counting, nobleman, totaling; **9** calculate, inventory, numbering, reckoning; **10** accounting; **11** calculating, calculation, computation, stocktaking; PHRASES: **2, 9** be important; **3, 2** add up, tot up; **3, 5** sum total; **4, 1, 10** make a difference; **4, 4, 4** make your mark; **4, 5** head ~; **5, 2** ~ up; **6, 4** bottom line; **6-6** number-crunch; **7, 4** opinion poll.

countenance **4** back, face, phiz *UK*; **5** brook; **6** endure; **7** approve, condone, support; **8** features, tolerate; **10** appearance, expression; **11** physiognomy; PHRASES: **3, 2, 4** put up with; **4, 5** look allow; **5, 3** stand for.

counter **3** rev; **4** defy, deny, foil; **5** piece, rebut, token; **6** answer, appeal, marker, offset, oppose, refute, rejoin, resist, retort, thwart; **7** against, dispute, nullify, protest, worktop *UK*; **8** computer, opposite; **9** retaliate; **10** calculator, contradict, contrarily, counteract, invalidate, neutralize; **11** countermand; **12** counterblast, counterclaim, counterforce, counterorder; **13** counteraction, countercharge, counterstroke; **14** contraindicate; PHRASES: **2, 5, 2** in spite of; **2, 8** in contrast; **2, 10, 2** in opposition to; **4, 7** work surface; **6, 7** geiger ~; **7, 2** ~ to; **8, 2** contrary to.

counteract **4** cure, drag, foil, undo, veto; **5** annul, block, check, clash, cross, match, react, rebel; **6** cancel, hinder, lessen, negate, offset, oppose, recoil, reduce, resist, thwart; **7** compare, counter, inhibit, nullify, obviate, prevent, recover, repress, respond; **8** backfire, contrast, obstruct, polarize, prohibit, restrain, retrieve, suppress, traverse; **10** deactivate, deregulate, invalidate, neutralize; **11** countermine, demagnetize; **12** countercheck, counterpoise; **13** counterattack, decriminalize; **14** counterbalance; PHRASES: **2, 7** go against; **3, 2, 10** set in opposition; **3, 4** get back; **3, 7** act against; **3, 7, 2** run counter to; **4, 1, 3, 5** find a way round; **4, 4** kick back; **4, 7** work against; **5, 7** fight against, react against; **6, 3** cancel out; **6, 7** defend against; **8, 4** conflict with; **10, 3** compensate for.

counteraction **4** drag, kick; **6** recoil, remedy; **7** defense; **8** backlash, friction, kickback, negation, reaction; **9** antipathy, hostility, inhibitor, rebellion, restraint; **10** opposition, resistance; **11** countermove, intolerance, neutralizer, obstruction, retroaction; **12** cancellation, compensation, counterblast, countercharm, counterpoise, counterpunch, counterspell, deactivation, deregulation, interference, invalidâtion, repercussion; **13** counterattack, counterweight, recalcitrance; **14** counterbalance, countermeasure; **15** counterirritant, counterpressure; PHRASES: **6, 6** return action; **8, 5** opposing force; **8, 6** opposing action; **9, 6** boomerang effect.

counterfeit **4** copy, fake; **5** bogus, forge, phony *UK*; **6** forged, phoney; **7** bootleg, forgery, imitate; **9** fabricate, imitation; **12** reproduction.

counterfeit (money) **4** bill, copy, fake; **5** bogus, forge, phony *UK*; **6** forged, phoney; **7** bootleg, forgery; **9** fabricate, imitation; **12** reproduction; PHRASES: **3, 5** bad check, bad money, dud check; **5, 4** flash note; **5, 5** funny money; **6, 4** forged note; **6, 5** rubber check; **7, 7** clipped coinage.

countermand *See* **cancel**

counterpart **4** mate, twin; **5** clone, equal, other; **6** double, fellow, ringer, shadow; **9** colleague, companion; **10** equivalent, reflection, understudy; **12** doppelgänger; **13** correspondent; PHRASES: **4, 4** soul mate; **4-5** look-alike; **5, 3** alter ego, stunt man; **5, 4** other half; **5, 7** blood brother; **6, 4** better half, second self; **6, 5** living image; **7, 6** kindred spirit; **7, 7** another edition; **8, 5** spitting image; **8, 6** opposite number.

country **4** land; **5** power, realm, rural, state; **6** nation, people, rustic, voters; **7** grazing, kingdom, prairie; **8** agrarian, farmland, homeland, monarchy, pastures, populace, republic, woodland; **9** citizenry, democracy, greenbelt, oligarchy, provinces, residents, statehood; **10** fatherland, motherland, nationhood, population, superpower, wilderness; **11** countryseat, countryside, inhabitants, sovereignty; **12** dictatorship, principality; PHRASES: **4, 7** free ~; **6, 5** nation state; **7, 4** ~ club, ~ code *UK*; **7, 5** ~ house, ~ music; **7-5** country-dance; **7, 7** ~ cousins; **9, 5** sovereign state.

countryman **4** hick; **5** yokel; **6** farmer,

native, rustic; **7** bumpkin, bushman *UK*, crofter, paisano, peasant; **8** national, villager; **9** hillbilly, lowlander; **10** compatriot, highlander, inhabitant, provincial; **11** smallholder; **12** backwoodsman, countrywoman, frontiersman; PHRASES: **7**, **6** country cousin; **7**, **7** country bumpkin; **7-7** country-dweller.

county *See* **region**

coup **4** feat; **6** putsch; **7** triumph; **9** overthrow, rebellion; **10** revolution; **11** achievement; **14** accomplishment; PHRASES: **4**, **5** ~ d'état.

couple **3** duo; **4** dyad, join, link, pair, team; **5** blend, twins; **6** fasten; **7** combine, connect, twosome; PHRASES: **3**, **2**, **1**, **4** two of a kind; **3**, **4**, **2**, **1**, **3** two peas in a pod; **5**, **2**, **1**, **7** birds of a feather; **7**, **4** matched pair; **8**, **3** matching set.

coupling **4** join, link; **5** blend; **7** coupler, mixture, pairing; **9** connector; **10** connection; **11** combination; **13** juxtaposition.

courage **3** vim; **4** grit, guts *UK*; **5** balls, nerve, pluck, spunk, valor; **6** bottle *UK*, daring, mettle, spirit; **7** bravery; **8** audacity, backbone, valiance; **13** determination; **14** courageousness; PHRASES: **6**, **2**, **5** nerves of steel; **7-2** derring-do; **8**, **6** fighting spirit. *See also* **courageous**

courageous **4** bold; **5** brave, gutsy, hardy, tough; **6** ballsy, daring, heroic, plucky, spunky; **7** doughty, gallant, valiant; **8** fearless, intrepid, spirited, valorous; **9** audacious, undaunted; **10** undismayed, unshakable; **11** indomitable, unflinching, unshakeable, unshrinking; PHRASES: **4**, **2**, **1**, **4** bold as a lion; **4-7** lion-hearted; **5-7** stouthearted.

courier **3** rep; **5** agent, biker, guide; **7** carrier; **9** messenger; PHRASES: **7**, **3** holiday rep *UK*; **8**, **5** dispatch rider *UK*.

course **3** run, way; **4** flow, path, plan, pour, road; **5** class, flood, march, route, surge, track; **6** afters *UK*, career, choice, entrée, lesson, module, option, policy, series, stream; **7** current, dessert, ongoing, passage, program, pudding *UK*, starter, studies; **8** sequence, strategy; **9** appetizer, direction, procedure; **10** curriculum; **11** possibility, progression; PHRASES: **2**, **5** go ahead; **3**, **7** way forward; **4**, **6** golf ~, main ~, race ~; **5**, **2**, **4** march of time; **6**, **4** flight path; **6**, **6** onward ~; **7**, **6** lecture series; **8**, **6** obstacle ~, sandwich ~ *UK*; **9**, **6** refresher ~.

court **3** woo; **4** lure, risk, tout; **5** chase; **6** entice, invite, pursue; **7** circuit; **8** persuade; **9** encourage; PHRASES: **3**, **3** ask for; **3**, **5**, **2** pay ~ to; **4**, **5** clay ~, hard ~; **5**, **4** ~ card, ~ shoe *UK*; **5**, **5** grass ~; **5**, **8** ~ circular *UK*; **5**, **9** royal household; **6**, **5** tennis ~. *See also* **courtship, courtyard, law court**

courteous **4** fair, kind, mild, nice; **5** civil, sweet; **6** decent, genial, gentle, humble, kindly, polite, urbane; **7** affable, amiable, courtly, gallant, genteel, refined, tactful; **8** amenable, discreet, friendly, generous, graceful, gracious, obliging, sociable; **9** agreeable, welcoming; **10** benevolent, charitable, chivalrous, solicitous, thoughtful; **11** considerate; **13** accommodating; PHRASES: **3-5** old-world; **3-9** old-fashioned; **4-7** good-humored; **4-8** even-tempered, mild-mannered, well-mannered.

courtesy **3** bob, bow, nod; **4** bend, help, tact; **6** curtsy, kowtow, salaam; **7** amenity, charity, decency, manners, respect; **8** chivalry, civility, flattery, humility, kindness, kneeling, mildness, niceness; **9** blandness, deference, gallantry, gentility, genuflect, obeisance, reverence, suaveness, sweetness; **10** affability, amiability, discretion, generosity, gentleness, kindliness, politeness, smoothness, solicitude; **11** benevolence, courtliness, sociability, tactfulness; **12** friendliness, gracefulness, graciousness; **13** agreeableness, consideration, courteousness; **14** chivalrousness, solicitousness, thoughtfulness; PHRASES: **3**, **6**, **5** the common touch; **4**, **4** soft soap; **4**, **5** good humor, soft words; **4**, **6** mild manner, soft tongue; **4**, **7** good manners; **5**, **6** sweet tongue; **6**, **8** common ~; **8**, **6** noblesse oblige.

courtly *See* **courteous**

courtroom **3** bar; **4** dock; **5** bench; **8** woolsack; **10** courthouse; PHRASES: **3**, **6** law courts; **4**, **3** jury box; **5**, **4** mercy seat; **7**, **3** witness box *UK*; **7**, **5** witness stand; **8**, **3** judgment seat.

courtship **4** date, pass, suit; **6** dating, favors, wooing; **7** necking, petting, sighing; **8** advances, coquetry, courting, dallying, flirting, proposal, spooning; **9** addresses, dalliance, gallantry, proposing, smooching, smoodging *Aus and NZ*; **10** engagement, flattering, flirtation, lovemaking; **11** familiarity; **12** lollygagging, philandering, relationship; **15** flirtatiousness; PHRASES: **4**, **4** love suit; **4-4** love-play; **4-6** side-glance; **6**, **3**

making out, taking out; **6, 4** sheep's eyes; **7, 3** walking out; **7, 6** fooling around, getting pinned.

courtyard **4** quad, yard; **5** close *UK*, court, patio, plaza; **6** piazza, square; **9** enclosure; **10** quadrangle.

cousin **6** friend; **7** partner; **9** colleague, companion; **11** counterpart.

couturier **6** draper, glover, hatter, hosier, tailor; **7** furrier; **8** milliner; **9** costumier, outfitter; **10** dressmaker; **11** haberdasher; **PHRASES: 7, 8** costume designer, fashion designer.

cove *See* **bay**

covenant *See* **agreement**

cover **3** cap, lid, top; **4** bury, case, coat, dust, flap, hide, mask, pall, plug, wrap; **5** cloud, crown, crust, drape, guard, mulch, shell; **6** asylum, casing, encase, enfold, jacket, report, screen, sheath, shield, shroud, swathe, travel; **7** conceal, contain, defense, embrace, enclose, envelop, include, obscure, overlap, overlay, protect, sheathe, shelter, shutter, stopper, suffice, topsoil, version; **8** comprise, coverage, covering, disguise, ensconce, piecrust, scabbard, wrapping; **9** bedspread, fallboard, safeguard; **10** gravestone, protection, substitute; **11** concealment, incorporate, smokescreen, sneezeguard, superimpose; **PHRASES: 2, 7** go through; **3, 2** lay on; **3, 4** lay over; **3, 5** air ~; **4, 2** take in; **4, 4** deal with; **4, 7** pass through; **5, 2** ~ up; **5, 4** ~ girl, ~ note *UK*; **5, 6** loose covers; **6, 2** report on; **6, 5** ground ~, hiding place.

coveralls *See* **overalls**

covered **5** faced, tiled; **6** capped, corked, glazed, roofed, tented, topped; **7** bricked, painted, paneled, papered, stained; **8** enclosed, shielded, thatched; **9** protected, sheltered, varnished; **11** wallpapered, whitewashed; **PHRASES: 6, 2** roofed in; **7, 2** ~ up; **7, 4** ~ over.

covering **3** lid, top; **4** bark, coat, film, foil, leaf, peel, scum, skin; **5** bloom, cloak, cover, layer, plate, sheet, shell; **6** casing, facing, fascia, hiding, jacket, lamina, patina, paving, shroud, veneer; **7** blanket, coating, overlay, sheathe, topping, wrapper; **8** coverage, membrane, wrapping; **9** including, obscuring, overlying, screening, shielding; **10** blanketing, overlaying; **11** envelopment, overlapping; **12** superimposed;

13 incorporating, overshadowing; **15** superimposition.

covert **4** wood; **5** copse; **6** hidden, secret; **7** coppice, thicket; **9** concealed; **11** clandestine, underground, undergrowth.

cover up **4** bury, hide, mask; **7** conceal, obscure; **8** disguise, suppress; **9** whitewash; **PHRASES: 4, 2** hush up; **4, 5, 5** keep under wraps; **4, 6** keep secret; **5, 4** paper over.

covet *See* **want**

covetous **6** greedy; **7** envious, jealous; **10** avaricious; **11** acquisitive.

coward **3** rat; **4** baby, funk, weed, wimp; **5** mouse; **6** rabbit; **7** chicken, milksop; **8** deserter, poltroon; **9** jellyfish; **11** yellowbelly; **PHRASES: 3, 2, 6** bag of nerves; **6-3** fraidy-cat; **7-3** scaredy-cat *UK Can*; **7, 5** nervous wreck.

coward (be a coward) **4** flee; **5** cower, quail; **6** cringe, desert, shrink; **7** retreat, scuttle; **PHRASES: 2, 1, 4** do a bunk *UK*; **3, 3, 3** cut and run; **3, 4** run away; **3, 4, 4** get cold feet; **4, 3** back out; **4, 4** turn tail; **4, 4, 5** lose one's nerve; **4, 4, 6** lose one's bottle; **4, 7** lack courage; **7, 3** chicken out.

cowardly **3** shy, wet; **4** soft, weak; **5** cowed, timid; **6** afraid, craven, scared, yellow; **7** chicken, daunted, fearful, gutless, panicky, rattled; **8** chinless, cowering, timorous; **9** dastardly, defeatist, spineless; **10** frightened; **13** pusillanimous; **PHRASES: 4-5** weak-kneed; **4-7** lily-livered; **5-5** namby-pamby; **5-7** faint-hearted; **6-7** yellow-bellied; **7-7** chicken-hearted, chicken-livered.

cowboy **5** crook; **6** cowman; **7** cowhand, rancher; **8** herdsman, stockman; **PHRASES: 3-2-5** fly-by-night; **5, 8** dodgy operator *UK*.

cowpea **5-4, 3** black-eyed pea.

cowshed **3** pen; **4** barn, byre *UK*; **6** stable; **9** stockyard.

cowslip **5, 8** marsh marigold.

coy **3** shy; **4** prim; **5** timid; **6** demure, modest; **7** prudish; **8** reticent; **9** shrinking, withdrawn; **10** coquettish.

coyote **7, 4** prairie wolf.

cozy **4** snug, warm; **5** close; **7** cliquey; **8** clannish, familiar, friendly, intimate, pleasant; **9** expedient; **10** convenient; **11** comfortable; **PHRASES: 4-7** self-serving.

crack **1** c; **3** ace, cut, dig, gag, gap, hit, pop, rap, tap; **4** bang, bash, blow, bump, clap, dike, flaw, gash, gibe, hole, jest, joke, nick, quip, rend, rift, slap, slit, slot, snap, tear; **5** aside, break, chink, cleft, click, clunk, crash, ditch, fault, knock, plonk, smack, solve, split, whack; **6** breach, cavity, cleave, cranny, decode, defect, expert, fathom, fizzle, furrow, groove, remark, sizzle, trench; **7** clatter, crackle, crevice, decrypt, fissure, opening, orifice, rupture; **8** aperture, collapse, crevasse, decipher, fracture, incision, splinter, weakness; **9** crackling, wisecrack; **12** disintegrate, imperfection; PHRASES: **2-2** ha-ha; **2, 2, 6** go to pieces; **3, 3-3** rat tat-tat; **4, 2** lose it; **4, 3** work out; **4, 7** lose control; **5, 2** ~ up; **5, 4** break down; **5, 5** split apart; **6, 3** figure out; **8, 5** hairline ~.

cracked **4** daft, open, rent, slit, torn; **5** cleft, crazy, riven, split; **6** broken, cloven, crazed, gaping, stupid; **7** fissile, foolish; **8** fissured, furrowed, ruptured; **9** eccentric; **10** irrational, splintered.

cracking **4** fast, very; **5** rapid, swift; **7** furious; **9** extremely; **10** especially; **11** exceedingly.

crackle **3** pop; **4** snap; **5** crack; **6** crunch, sizzle.

Cracow **6** Krakau, Kraków.

cradle **4** hold; **5** clasp, frame; **6** cuddle; **7** embrace, support; **9** framework, structure; **12** underpinning.

craft **3** ark, art, jet, job; **4** boat, punt, ship; **5** barge, plane, skill, trade; **6** vessel; **7** mastery; **8** aircraft; **9** expertise; **10** handicraft, spacecraft; PHRASES: **7, 5** landing ~.

crafty **3** sly; **4** wily; **6** astute, shrewd, sneaky; **7** cunning, devious; **8** guileful; **9** underhand; **11** duplicitous; **12** manipulative; **13** untrustworthy.

cram **3** ram; **4** mass, pack, swot UK; **5** crowd, force, learn, shove, study, stuff; **6** review, revise UK; **7** compact, squeeze; **8** compress, memorize; **11** concentrate; PHRASES: **2, 4** go over; **3, 2** gen up UK, mug up UK; **3, 4** ram down; **4, 2** fill up, swot up UK.

cramp **4** pain; **5** limit, spasm; **6** hamper, twinge; **8** restrict; **9** constrain, constrict; **11** contraction; PHRASES: **7, 5** charley horse; **8, 4** shooting pain.

crane fly **5-8** daddy-longlegs.

crank See **turn**

crash **3** din, hit; **4** bang, bash, boom, bump, dive, fail, fold, roar, thud; **5** clang,

clash, crack, prang UK, smash, thump; **6** hurtle, pileup, racket, rumble, wallop; **7** clatter, collide, failure, resound, smashup, thunder; **8** accident, collapse, shutdown; **9** breakdown, collision; **10** bankruptcy; **11** liquidation; PHRASES: **2, 5** go broke, go under; **2, 5, 2** go belly up; **2, 8** go bankrupt; **3, 4** run into; **5, 3** ~ out UK, ~ pad, write off UK; **5, 4** smash into; **5, 6** ~ helmet; **5, 7** ~ barrier.

crass See **insensitive**

crave **3** ask, beg; **4** need, pray, want; **6** desire; **7** entreat, request; PHRASES: **4, 3** long for; **5, 3** yearn for.

craven See **cowardly**

crawl **4** edge, fawn, inch; **5** creep, skulk, slink, sneak; **6** grovel; **7** flatter, scuttle, slither, wriggle; **9** apologize; PHRASES: **3, 6, 3** eat humble pie; **4, 2** suck up.

crazy See **mad**

crazy **4** fond, keen; **5** silly; **6** unwise; **7** devoted, foolish; **9** senseless; **10** irrational, passionate; **12** enthusiastic.

creak **5** grate, groan; **6** scrape, screak, squeak; **7** screech.

cream **4** balm, best, mash, skim; **5** blend, elite, sauce; **6** finest, soften; **7** combine, unguent; **8** ointment; PHRASES: **3, 5** ice ~; **4, 2, 3, 5** pick of the bunch; **4, 5** cold ~, sour ~; **5, 2, 3, 4** ~ of the crop; **5, 3** ~ tea UK; **5, 4** ~ puff, ~ soda; **5, 5** heavy ~, light ~; **5, 6** ~ cheese; **5, 7** ~ cracker UK; **7, 5** clotted ~; **8, 5** whipping ~; **9, 5** vanishing ~; **10, 5** Devonshire ~.

crease **4** fold, line, tuck; **5** pleat; **6** furrow, gather, groove, pucker, rumple; **7** crinkle, crumple, scrunch, wrinkle; PHRASES: **5, 4** crow's foot.

create **4** coin, form, make; **5** build, cause, craft, found, start; **6** design, devise, invent; **7** compose, fashion, produce, realize; **8** complain, conceive, generate, initiate; **9** construct, establish, originate; PHRASES: **3, 2** set up; **3, 5** get going; **4, 1, 4** make a fuss; **4, 2, 1, 4** kick up a fuss; **4, 2, 1, 6** kick up a rumpus UK; **4, 4, 2** give rise to.

creation **4** dawn; **5** birth, world; **6** cosmos, design, making, nature, origin; **7** concept, genesis; **8** assembly, universe; **9** evolution, formation, invention; **10** conception, innovation, production; **11** fabrication, manufacture; **12** construction; **13** establishment; **15** materialization; PHRASES:

3-4, 6 big-bang theory.

creature 3 man; **5** beast, being, woman; **6** animal, insect, person; **7** critter; **8** organism; PHRASES: **6, 5** living being.

credential 7 diploma; **11** certificate, testimonial; **13** qualification; **14** recommendation.

credible 5 sound; **6** likely; **7** sincere; **8** probable, reliable; **9** plausible; **10** believable, convincing, dependable; **11** trustworthy.

credit 2 HP *UK*; **4** bill, debt, lend, loan, tick, VISA™; **5** faith, glory, grant, honor, tally, trust; **6** accept, belief, esteem, praise, thanks; **7** acclaim, believe, plastic, tribute; **8** mortgage, prestige, receipts; **9** overdraft, phonecard, recognize; **10** confidence, MasterCard™; **11** acknowledge, recognition; **14** acknowledgment; PHRASES: **3, 3** the red; **3, 5** the black; **3, 5-5** the never-never; **3, 7** pay tribute; **4, 2** rely on; **4, 2, 6** line of ~; **4, 5, 2** have faith in; **4, 6** give ~; **6, 4** charge card, ~ card, ~ hour; **6, 5** ~ limit; **6, 6** ~ rating, ~ status; **6, 7** charge account, ~ account, ~ control; **11, 4** installment plan.

credulous *See* **gullible**

creep 4 edge, inch; **5** crawl, skulk, slink, sneak, steal; **6** tiptoe; **7** slither.

crepitation 3 pop, rap, tap; **4** clap, plop, slap, snap; **5** click, clunk, crack, knock, plonk, plunk, smack; **6** rattle; **7** clatter; **8** sizzling, spitting, staccato; **10** effervesce; PHRASES: **3-3-3** rat-tat-tat.

crest 3 top; **4** apex, comb, peak, tuft; **5** crown; **6** blazon, emblem, growth, summit, symbol; **7** topknot; **8** heraldry; **9** cockscomb; PHRASES: **4, 2, 4** coat of arms.

crew 3 lot, man, men; **4** band, four, gang, pack, team, unit; **5** bunch, corps, crowd, eight, group, hands, squad; **7** company.

crib 4 copy; **5** cheat, steal; **6** borrow; **10** plagiarize.

crick 4 hurt, pain, pull; **5** cramp, spasm; **6** strain, wrench; **10** discomfort.

crime 3 DUI, DWI, sin; **4** rape, scam, tort; **5** fault, fraud, grift, guilt, theft, wrong; **6** felony, fiddle, malice, murder, racket; **7** assault, battery, bombing, bribery, forgery, larceny, misdeed, offense, robbery, slander, swindle; **8** burglary, homicide, nuisance, stalking, thieving, trespass; **9** embracery, extortion, parricide, vandalism, violation; **10** conspiracy, contraband, corruption, illegality, infraction, misconduct, misprision, negligence, wrongdoing; **11** criminality, crookedness, delinquency, fraudulency, lawbreaking, lawlessness, malfeasance, misdemeanor, misfeasance; **12** embezzlement, infringement, manslaughter, racketeering; **13** transgression; PHRASES: **3, 5** war ~; **3, 7** tax evasion; **4, 4** foul play; **4-6, 8** five-finger discount; **4, 7** high treason; **5, 6** black market; **5-6, 6** first-degree murder; **5, 7** grand larceny, petit larceny, petty larceny; **5-7** drunk-driving; **5, 7, 8** ~ against humanity; **5, 8** dirty dealings, sharp practice; **6, 2, 3, 5** breach of the peace; **6, 7** sexual assault; **6, 8** public nuisance; **7, 3, 7** assault and battery; **7, 5** capital ~; **7, 8** driveby shooting; **8, 6, 4** grievous bodily harm; **8, 7** criminal offense, indecent assault; **8, 8** indecent exposure; **8, 10** criminal negligence; **9, 4** statutory rape; **9, 5** organized ~; **10, 5** confidence trick, victimless ~; **11, 2, 7** obstruction of justice, trafficking in persons; **11, 12** involuntary manslaughter.

criminal 3 lag; **4** bent *UK*, hood; **5** crook, felon, shady, thief, wrong; **6** bandit, guilty, gunsel, killer, mugger, outlaw, rapist, robber, sinful, wicked; **7** bribing, burglar, convict, crooked, culprit, hoodlum, illegal, illicit, immoral, lawless, lowlife, Mafioso, mobster, ruffian, villain; **8** aberrant, assassin, culpable, gangster, hooligan, jailbird, murderer, offender, prisoner, reckless, thieving, unlawful; **9** felonious, miscreant, negligent, offensive, swindling, wrongdoer; **10** antisocial, delinquent, embezzling, fraudulent, iniquitous, lawbreaker, malefactor, outrageous, recidivist, scandalous; **11** blameworthy, disgraceful, lawbreaking; **12** extortionist, housebreaker, illegitimate; PHRASES: **3, 8** not straight; **4-8** wife-batterer; **5, 6** Mafia member; **5, 8** petty ~; **5-8** light-fingered; **6, 6** sexual abuser; **7, 3, 3** against the law.

criminal (be criminal) 3 rob; **5** cheat, fence, steal; **6** fiddle, pilfer, thieve; **7** defraud, smuggle, swindle; **8** embezzle, shoplift; **9** racketeer; PHRASES: **4, 3, 5** cook the books.

crimp 4 coif, curb, curl, fold; **5** frizz, pleat, press, ruche; **6** hamper, hinder, rumple; **7** crinkle, crumple, scrunch.

cringe 5 blush, wince; **6** flinch, recoil, shrink, squirm; PHRASES: **2, 11** be embarrassed; **3, 4** shy away.

crinkle 4 fold, line; 6 crease, pucker, ruffle, rumple; 7 crumple, wrinkle.

crisis 3 rub; 4 crux, head; 5 nexus, pinch; 6 crunch, divide; 8 calamity, disaster; 9 emergency, watershed; 10 crossroads; 11 catastrophe, predicament; PHRASES: 7, 5 turning point; 8, 4 eleventh hour; 8, 6 defining moment.

crisp 4 cold, cool, curt, hard; 5 blunt, brief, brisk, fresh, sharp, short, terse; 6 chilly, crusty, frosty, snappy; 7 bracing, brittle, brusque, crunchy; 8 decisive, incisive; 9 competent, efficient; 12 businesslike, invigorating; PHRASES: 6, 4 potato chip; 6, 5 potato ~ UK.

criterion See **standard**

critic 5 enemy, judge; 6 censor; 7 decrier; 8 opponent, reviewer; 9 appraiser, evaluator; 10 criticizer, denigrator; 11 commentator, faultfinder, pettifogger; PHRASES: 3-6 nit-picker.

critical 3 key; 5 acute, grave, vital; 7 abusive, crucial, pivotal, serious; 8 decisive, decrying, libelous; 9 dangerous, essential, important, maligning; 10 analytical UK, censorious, defamatory, derogatory, diagnostic, judgmental, nitpicking, slanderous; 11 denigrating, deprecatory, disparaging, significant, unfavorable; 12 denunciatory, disapproving, faultfinding, vituperative; 13 indispensable, unsympathetic; 15 uncomplimentary; PHRASES: 4-11 life-threatening.

criticism 3 rap; 4 flak, puff, slam; 5 blame, knock, movie, stick UK; 6 notice, report, review; 7 censure, comment, panning, slating; 8 analysis, brickbat, critique, diatribe, knocking, reproach; 9 hostility; 11 denigration, disapproval; 12 condemnation, denunciation; 13 disparagement; PHRASES: 3, 5 bad press; 3, 6 bad review; 4, 6 book review, film review, good review, rave review; 7, 3 hatchet job; 8, 6 critical review, negative review; 9, 6 favorable review.

criticize 3 pan, rap; 4 carp, lash, maul, puff, slam, slur; 5 abuse, blast, decry, fault, knock, libel, slate, smear, snipe; 6 assess, berate, defame, malign, rebuke, review, revile, vilify; 7 analyze, censure, condemn, deplore, dissect, nitpick, reprove, slander, traduce; 8 appraise, belittle, chastise, complain, critique, denounce, evaluate; 9 castigate, denigrate, deprecate, disparage, dispraise, reprimand; 10 depreciate, disapprove, vituperate; PHRASES: 3, 4 put down,

run down; 4, 2, 4 take to task; 4, 2, 6 pull to pieces, tear to shreds; 4, 3 slag off; 4, 5 find fault, tear apart; 4, 5, 2 pick holes in; 4, 5, 4 find fault with; 4, 8, 2 pass judgment on; 5, 2 snipe at; 5, 9 offer criticism; 7, 7 inveigh against.

croak 3 caw, cry; 4 call, moan, rasp; 5 grate, growl; 6 grouse, mutter, squawk; 7 grumble; 8 complain; 11 gutturalize.

crockery 4 bowl, dish, tray; 5 china, plate; 6 dishes, plates, salver, saucer, teaset; tureen; 7 charger, platter, pottery, ramekin, terrine; 8 dishware, utensils; 9 chinaware, glassware, porringer, tableware; 10 Tupperware™; 11 earthenware; PHRASES: 4, 4 soup bowl; 5, 4 gravy boat, jelly mold, salad bowl, sugar bowl; 6, 4 cereal bowl, finger bowl; 6, 7 dinner service UK.

crook 3 rod; 5 felon, staff, stick; 6 robber; 7 crosier; 8 criminal, offender.

crooked 4 awry, bent UK; 5 askew, shady; 6 squint, tilted, zigzag; 7 corrupt, illegal, illicit; 8 criminal, deformed, lopsided, unlawful; 9 dishonest, distorted, underhand; 12 unscrupulous; PHRASES: 3-6 off-center; 4-6 skew-whifff.

croon See **sing**

crop 3 cut, rye; 4 clip, corn, flax, kale, oats, okra, pare, peas, pick, rape, reap, rice, trim; 5 beans, maize UK, shave, shear, vetch, yield; 6 barley, clover, cotton, fescue, garner, gather, millet, swedes; 7 alfalfa, cabbage, collect, curtail, earlies, harvest, linseed, mangels, mustard, peanuts, shorten, sorghum, tobacco, turnips; 8 potatoes, ryegrass; 9 soyabeans; 10 groundnuts; PHRASES: 4, 4 cash ~, root ~; 5, 2 bring in; 5, 4 field peas, sugar beet; 5, 5 black beans, field beans, first early; 5, 8 early potatoes; 6, 4 cereal ~, fodder beet, fodder ~, fodder peas, fodder rape, spring oats, winter oats; 6, 5 second early, spring wheat, winter wheat; 6, 6 spring barley, winter barley; 7, 4 oilseed rape; 7, 8 Italian ryegrass.

cross 3 mix, vie; 4 ankh, foil, ford, mark, meet, sign, span; 5 angry, annoy; 6 bridge, convey, hybrid, impede, oppose, resist, snappy, thwart; 7 annoyed, calvary, overfly, overlap, peevish, traject, transit; 8 bestride, crucifix, navigate, obstruct, straddle, transfer, transmit, traverse; 9 frustrate, intersect, irritable, irritated, negotiate, translate, transport; 10 circumvent, crisscross; 11 interchange; 12 interconnect; PHRASES: 2, 6 go across; **2**, **7**, **5** St Andrew's ~, St George's ~; **2**, **8**, **5** St Anthony's ~; **3**, **6** cut across; **3-8** bad-tempered; **4**, **4** hand over, step over; **4**, **5** iron ~; **4**, **6** move across; **5**, **2**, **8** ~ of Lorraine; **5**, **3**, **7** ~ the Rubicon; **5**, **4** ~ over; **5**, **5** Greek ~, Kings C~, Latin ~, papal ~ *UK*; **5**, **6** carry across; **5-7** cross-country; **6**, **5** Celtic ~, George C~ *UK*; **7**, **5** Charing C~, Maltese ~; **8**, **5** northern ~, southern ~, Victoria C~; **9**, **5** Jerusalem ~.

cross-examine *See* **question**

crossing **4** ford, jump; **6** voyage; **7** flyover *UK*, passage; **8** junction, overpass; **9** thwarting; **10** crossroads; **12** intersection; **15** interconnecting; PHRASES: **4-4** leap-frog; **5**, **8** grade ~, level ~ *UK*; **6**, **5** border point. *See also* **pedestrian crossing**

crossroads **6** crisis, crunch; **7** Rubicon; **8** crossing, decision, junction, juncture, landmark; **10** cloverleaf, roundabout *UK*; **11** interchange; **12** intersection; PHRASES: **4**, **8** road junction; **5**, **2**, **2**, **6** point of no return; **5**, **5** match point; **6**, **2**, **5** moment of truth; **7**, **5** turning point; **7**, **6** traffic circle.

crosswalk **6** subway; **8** overpass; **9** underpass.

crouch **3** bow; **4** bend, duck; **5** crawl, creep, squat, stoop; **6** grovel, hunker; PHRASES: **6**, **4** hunker down.

crow **3** caw, cry, jim; **4** brag, call; **5** boast, gloat, swank; **6** hooded, squawk; **7** carrion, screech, swagger; PHRASES: **4**, **3** show off.

crowd **3** hum, jam, mob, set; **4** brim, buzz, cram, gang, herd, host, mass, mill, pack, pile, pour, rush, teem; **5** burst, crawl, crush, flock, flood, group, horde, press, serry, surge, swarm, sweep, troop; **6** circle, clique, gather, rabble, seethe, squash, stream, throng; **8** assemble, assembly, overflow; **9** gathering, multitude, overcrowd; **10** congregate; PHRASES: **3**, **3**, **4**, **4** all and then some; **3**, **3**, **6** the hoi polloi; **3**, **6** the masses; **5**, **4**, **4** swarm like ants; **5**, **4**, **5** swarm like flies; **5**, **7**, **3** every mother's son.

crowded **4** busy, full; **5** close, dense; **7** milling, overrun, teeming; **8** crawling, seething, swarming; **9** bristling, cluttered, congested; **10** overmanned; **11** overstaffed; **13** overpopulated; PHRASES: **2**, **5** en masse; **3-6** jam-packed; **4-7** high-density; **5-1-5** chock-a-block; **5**, **2**, **5** thick as flies. *See also* **crowd**

crown **2** ER; **3** cap, tip, top; **4** acme, apex,

head, king, peak; **5** adorn, crest, glory, prize, queen, ruler, tiara; **6** diadem, induct, invest, reward, trophy, wreath; **7** circlet, coronet, festoon, garland, laurels, monarch, royalty; **8** champion, enthrone, monarchy; **9** sovereign; PHRASES: **5**, **2**, **3**, **5** jewel in the ~.

crucial **3** key; **5** vital; **7** central, pivotal; **8** critical, decisive; **9** essential, important, necessary; **10** imperative; **11** fundamental.

crucible **3** pot, vat; **4** test; **5** trial; **6** hotbed, kettle, ordeal; **8** hothouse; **9** container; **10** receptacle; PHRASES: **6**, **4** ground zero; **7**, **2**, **4** baptism of fire; **7**, **3** melting pot; **7**, **6** forcing ground *UK*.

crucify **4** hang, kill, maul; **6** attack, punish, savage; **7** execute, torment; **9** victimize.

crude **3** raw; **4** racy, rude, sick; **5** basic, crass, gaudy, gross, loose, rough, tacky; **6** coarse, earthy, gauche, simple, smutty, tawdry, vulgar; **7** boorish, inexact, obscene, sketchy, uncouth; **8** indecent; **9** inelegant, makeshift, offensive, tasteless, unrefined, untreated; **10** inaccurate, indelicate, uncultured, unfinished, unpolished, unskillful; **11** approximate, insensitive, rudimentary, unprocessed; **15** unsophisticated; PHRASES: **4-7** foul-mouthed; **5-4** rough-hewn; **5-5** broad-brush.

cruel **4** hard, mean; **5** harsh, nasty; **6** animal, bloody, brutal, savage, unkind; **7** beastly, bestial, brutish, callous, heinous, hellish, inhuman, painful, satanic, vicious, violent; **8** barbaric, demoniac, devilish, fiendish, ghoulish, infernal, inhumane, pitiless, ruthless, sadistic, spiteful, subhuman, wounding; **9** atrocious, barbarous, ferocious, fiendlike, heartless, homicidal, malicious, merciless, monstrous, murderous, punishing, terrorful, torturous; **10** demoniacal, diabolical, vindictive; **12** bloodthirsty; **13** cannibalistic; PHRASES: **5-7** cruel-hearted.

cruelty **5** spite; **6** malice, sadism; **8** atrocity, ferocity, savagery, violence; **9** animality, barbarism, bloodlust, brutality, terrorism, vandalism; **10** bestiality, inhumanity; **11** cannibalism. *See also* **cruel**

cruise **4** boat, sail, skim, spin, tour, trip; **5** coast, glide; **6** travel, voyage; **7** journey; **8** vacation.

crumb **3** bit; **4** iota, spot; **5** flake, scrap, scurf, speck; **6** morsel, tidbit; **7** crumble, filings, smidgen; **8** dandruff, fragment; **11** smithereens.

crumble 4 chip; **5** crumb, crush, decay, flake, grind, pound, smash; **6** powder; **7** implode; **8** collapse, dissolve; **9** pulverize; **11** deteriorate; **12** disintegrate; PHRASES: **4, 2** cave in; **4, 4** fall down; **4, 5** fall apart.

crumbly 5 crisp, flaky, scaly; **6** scurfy; **7** brittle, fragile, friable, powdery; **8** crumbled; **9** crumbling.

crumpet 7 pikelet *UK*.

crunch 4 chew, crux; **5** champ, chomp, munch; **6** crisis; PHRASES: **6, 2, 5** moment of truth; **6, 4** ~ time.

crusade 5 cause, fight, lobby; **6** battle; **8** campaign, movement, struggle; PHRASES: **5, 8** apply yourself.

crush 4 beat, mash, pulp, swat; **5** break, crowd, pound, press, quash, quell, smash; **6** crease, crunch, liking, mangle, squash; **7** conquer, crumple, flatten, passion, scrunch, trample, wrinkle; **8** compress, stampede, vanquish; **9** humiliate, overwhelm, pulverize; **11** infatuation; PHRASES: **3, 4** mad dash; **4, 2** step on; **5, 2** break up, stamp on.

crust 3 top; **5** shell; **7** coating, outside; PHRASES: **5, 5** outer layer.

crux *See* **root**

cry 3 baa, bay, boo, low, mew, moo, sob, yap; **4** bark, bawl, bell, blub *UK*, bray, call, fret, gasp, hiss, hoot, howl, jeer, keen, meow *UK*, mewl, moan, ouch, pule, purr, roar, sigh, snap, wail, weep, yawl, yawp, yell, yelp, yowl; **5** bleat, bravo, cheer, croak, groan, growl, grunt, neigh, shout, snarl, snort, whine, whoop; **6** bellow, boohoo, clamor, crying, gibber, holler, hooray, hubbub, hurrah, lament, nicker, outcry, scream, shriek, snivel, squall, squawk, squeak, squeal, throat, uproar, whinny, yammer, yippee; **7** blubber, catcall, exclaim, grizzle *UK*, hosanna, screech, trumpet, ululate, whicker, whimper; **8** alleluia, outburst; **9** caterwaul, expletive; **10** hallelujah, hullabaloo, vociferate; **11** exclamation; **12** vociferation; PHRASES: **3, 2, 3, 4** bay at the moon; **3, 3** war ~; **3-3, 6** hip-hip hurrah; **3, 4, 4, 3** ~ your eyes out; **4, 3** call out, loud ~; **4, 5** shed tears; **5, 3** shout out; **6, 3** battle ~; **8, 3** rallying ~.

crying 5 awful, lousy, teary, weepy; **7** bawling, howling, keening, moaning, sighing, sobbing, tearful, ululant, wailing, weeping, whining; **8** blubbing *UK*, dread-ful, groaning, horrible, terrible; **9** desperate, sniveling, ululation; **10** blubbering, deplorable, lachrymose, whimpering; **11** lamentation; PHRASES: **2, 5** in tears.

cry out 3 cry; **4** bawl, call, howl, roar, yawl, yell, yowl; **5** shout; **6** bellow, demand, holler, scream, shriek, squall; **7** exclaim, explode, require; **9** caterwaul; **10** vociferate; PHRASES: **2, 2, 4, 2** be in need of; **3, 3** ask for; **4, 3** call for, call out; **5, 3** blast out, shout out; **5, 4, 6** crack one's throat; **6, 4, 5** strain one's lungs; **7, 3** thunder out.

crypt *See* **vault**

crystal 5 glass; **6** pickup, quartz, Stuart; **7** mineral; **9** structure, Waterford; **11** crystallite; **12** microcrystal; **15** crystallization, crystallography; PHRASES: **4, 7** lead ~, rock ~; **7, 4** ~ ball; **7, 6** C~ Palace *UK*.

CU 6 copper.

cub *See* **novice**

cubicle 5 booth, stall; **9** partition, workspace; **11** compartment.

cuckoo 5 weird; **6** shrike; **7** bizarre, strange, unusual; **9** eccentric; **14** unconventional; PHRASES: **6, 4** ~ spit; **6, 5** ~ clock.

cuddle 3 hug; **4** hold; **5** clasp; **6** clinch, nuzzle; **7** embrace.

cudgel *See* **hit**

cue 4 show, sign; **6** prompt, remind, signal; **8** indicate, reminder; **10** indication.

cuff 3 hit, rap; **4** slap; **6** buffet, fetter, strike; **7** manacle, shackle; **8** handcuff; **9** restraint.

cuisine 4 fare, food; **5** Cajun, Cuban, vegan; **6** Creole, fusion; **7** cookery, cooking, Mexican; **8** Jamaican, Southern, Suburban; **9** Quebecois; **10** California, gastronomy, Midwestern, vegetarian; PHRASES: **3-3** Tex-Mex; **3, 7** New England; **4, 4** fast food, soul food; **4-5** Euro-Asian; **6, 5** Puerto Rican.

cul-de-sac *See* **dead end**

culinary 3 raw, red; **4** done, food, rare; **5** burnt, fried; **6** beaten, boiled, cooked, ground, mensal, minced, stewed; **7** braised, browned, chopped, coddled, cookery, cooking, curried, deviled, dressed, grilled, poached, roasted, sautéed, steamed, stuffed, toasted; **8** mealtime, prandial, prepared; **9** barbecued, epicurean, scrambled, underdone; **10** overcooked; **11** gastronomic, undercooked; **12** postprandial; PHRASES: **1, 2, 4** à la mode; **1, 2, 5** à la carte; **2, 5** al dente; **2, 6** au gratin; **2, 7** au naturel; **3-8** pre-prandial; **4-2** made-up; **4-4** well-done; **4-5** deep-fried, oven-ready *UK*, stir-fried; **5, 2, 1, 5** burnt to a crisp; **5-2-4** ready-to-cook; **5-2-5** ready-to-serve; **5, 5** table d'hôte; **5-6** after-dinner.

cull 4 pick; 5 scrap; 6 choose, gather, reject, remove, second, select; 7 castoff, discard, harvest; PHRASES: **3, 3, 2** get rid of.

culminate *See* **end**

culmination 4 peak; 6 finale, height, zenith; 10 conclusion.

culpable *See* **guilty**

cult 3 fad; 4 sect; 5 craze, trend; 7 offbeat, unusual; 8 movement; 9 adoration; 10 veneration; 11 alternative; PHRASES: **9, 5** religious group.

cultivate 3 cut, dib *UK*, dig, hoe, lop, mow, pot, set, sow, top; 4 bale, farm, fork, grow, muck, plow *UK*, rake, reap, seed, tend, thin, till, turn, weed, work; 5 breed, debud, delve, drill, glean, graft, layer, mulch, plant, prune, spade, spray, stake, strim, train, water; 6 dibble, enrich, foster, harrow, manure, plough *UK*, refine, swathe, trench; 7 compost, develop, harvest, improve, nurture, promote, support; 8 deadhead, irrigate, rotavate *UK*, sprinkle; 9 broadcast, deblossom, enlighten, fertilize, pollinate, propagate; 10 transplant; PHRASES: **3, 2** pot on, put in, tie in; **3, 3** bed out; **3-5** top-dress; **4, 2** heel in, work on; **4, 3** thin out; **4, 4** turn over; **5, 3** plant out *UK*, prick out; **6, 2** puddle in; **6-3** double-dig; **7, 4** scatter seed.

culture 4 arts; 5 ethos, mores; 7 customs, society; 8 urbanity; 10 humanities, philosophy, refinement, traditions; 12 civilization; 14 sophistication; PHRASES: **4, 4** fine arts; **10, 4** performing arts.

cumulate 6 joined, united; 8 combined; 9 aggregate, confluent, connected, glomerate; 10 collective, convergent; 11 agglomerate; 12 conglomerate.

cunning 3 art, fly, sly; 4 arch, foxy, wily, wise; 5 acute, cagey, canny, craft, guile, knack, sharp, skill, smart; 6 acuity, artful, astute, clever, crafty, feline, shifty, shrewd, sneaky, subtle, tricky, urbane; 7 devious, elusive, knowing, sleight, slyness, stealth, vulpine; 8 artifice, foxiness, guileful, intrigue, planning, plotting, scheming, skillful, slippery, stealthy, trickery, wariness, wiliness; 9 beguiling, canniness, chicanery,

duplicity, ingenious, ingenuity, insidious, insincere, sharpness, smartness, sophistry; 10 artfulness, astuteness, cleverness, contriving, craftiness, intriguing, mystifying, serpentine, shiftiness, shrewdness, smoothness, sneakiness, trickiness; 11 beguilement, machination, maneuvering, resourceful; 12 intelligence, manipulating, manipulation, slipperiness, stealthiness; 13 Machiavellian; 14 gerrymandering, sophistication; 15 resourcefulness; PHRASES: **2, 2, 10** up to everything; **2, 5, 2** no flies on; **3, 6, 2, 4** too clever by half; **3, 6, 3** too clever for; **5, 8** sharp practice; **6-7** double-dealing; **6, 8** monkey business; **6-8** double-crossing.

cunning (be cunning) 3 con; 4 coax, hide, lurk, plan, plot, turn; 5 cheat, dodge, outdo, shift, skulk, trick, twist; 6 betray, outwit, scheme, tinker, wangle, waylay; 7 beguile, blarney, confuse, deceive, defraud, finesse, flatter, swindle, wheedle, wriggle; 8 conspire, contrive, flimflam, intrigue, maneuver, outsmart; 9 overreach; 10 circumvent; 11 gerrymander; PHRASES: **2, 3, 6** go one better; **3, 3, 4** put one over; **3, 3, 5** see the catch; **4, 1, 5, 2, 3** know a trick or two; **4, 2, 4, 4** live by one's wits; **5, 2, 7** match in cunning; **5-4** sweet-talk; **6-5** double-cross; **6, 5, 4** monkey about with.

cup 3 mug; 5 prize, stoup; 6 beaker, eggcup, goblet, teacup, trophy; 7 chalice, stirrup; 9 demitasse; PHRASES: **5, 3** Davis C~, fruit ~, World C~; **6, 3** coffee ~ *UK*; **8, 3** Americas C~.

cupola *See* **dome**

curate 5 mount, stage; 6 cleric, create, priest; 7 install; 8 minister; 12 ecclesiastic.

curb 5 check, limit; 7 control; 8 restrain; 9 restraint; 11 restriction; PHRASES: **4, 2** rein in; **4, 4** hold back.

curdle 3 gel; 4 clot, sour, turn; 7 congeal, thicken; 9 coagulate; PHRASES: **2, 3** go bad, go off *UK*; **2, 4** go sour.

cure 3 dry, set; 4 heal, salt; 5 close, nurse, smoke, treat; 6 doctor, physic, pickle, remedy, revive; 7 bandage, operate, restore, therapy; 8 antidote, detoxify, medicate, medicine, preserve; 9 alleviate, treatment; 10 medication; PHRASES: **4, 4** heal over, make well; **4, 8** knit together; **7, 2, 6** restore to health.

cured 6 better, healed, smoked; 7 healthy; 8 kippered; 12 convalescent; PHRASES: **2, 3, 4** on the mend; **2, 4, 2, 3** as good as new; **2,**

4, 5, 4 in one's right mind; **4, 2, 4, 4** back on one's feet; **4, 2, 6** back to normal; **4, 3** like new; **4, 3, 5** none the worse; **5, 3, 7** alive and kicking; **7, 5** oneself again.

curfew *See* **restriction**

curiosity **5** curio; **6** marvel, oddity, prying, rarity, wonder; **7** inquiry, novelty, probing; **8** interest, nosiness, snooping; **10** phenomenon, puzzlement; **11** curiousness, inquisition, questioning; **15** inquisitiveness; PHRASES: **4-9** soul-searching; **7, 5** strange thing; **9, 4** inquiring mind.

curious **3** odd; **4** keen, nosy; **5** nosey, weird; **6** prying; **7** bizarre, probing, strange, unusual; **8** peculiar, snooping; **9** inquiring; **10** interested, intriguing, remarkable; **11** adventurous, inquisitive, questioning, sightseeing; **13** inquisitorial; PHRASES: **4, 2, 5** keen to learn; **4, 4, 7** with ears burning; **7, 2, 4** wanting to know.

curious (be curious) **3** pry; **4** quiz; **5** snoop; **6** meddle; **7** inquire; **8** question, sightsee; **9** eavesdrop; **10** rubberneck; **11** interrogate; PHRASES: **4, 2, 4** want to know; **4, 3** seek out; **4, 4, 4, 2** poke one's nose in; **4, 6** nose around; **5, 2, 4, 4** prick up one's ears; **5, 3** sniff out; **6, 3** search for; **6-6** tittle-tattle; **7, 5** inquire after.

curl **4** bend, coil, eddy, lock, wave; **5** curve, swirl, twirl, twist, whorl; **6** spiral; **7** ringlet; PHRASES: **4, 4** spit ~.

currency **2** as; **3** ecu, kip, yen; **4** lira, mark, peag, pelf, peso, real; **5** dinar, franc, litas, pound, ruble *UK*, tical; **6** cowrie, dollar, escudo, florin, gulden, peseta, rouble; **7** centavo, drachma, guilder; **8** quetzale, shilling, sterling; **9** boliviano; PHRASES: **4, 4, 6** Hong Kong dollar; **4, 8** hard ~, soft ~; **5, 5** shell money; **5, 8** sound ~; **7, 8** decimal ~.

current **3** ebb; **4** flow, flux, tide, wake, wash; **5** draft, drift, river; **6** charge, course, direct, modern, recent, reflux, ripple, stream, vortex; **7** present, torrent, voltage; **8** backflow, backwash, capacity, electric, existing, undertow; **9** turbidity, whirlpool; **10** resistance, thermionic; **11** counterflow; **12** contemporary, crosscurrent, undercurrent; PHRASES: **2-2-4** up-to-date; **2, 8** in progress; **7-3** present-day.

curriculum **4** core; **6** course; **7** program; **8** syllabus; **10** prospectus.

curriculum vitae **6** résumé.

curse **3** hex; **4** bane, cuss, damn, jinx,

oath; **5** magic, spell, swear, trial; **6** blight, burden, hoodoo, ordeal, plague, voodoo; **7** afflict, epithet, malison, scourge, setback, torment, trouble; **8** swearing; **9** blaspheme, blasphemy, expletive, invective, obscenity, profanity, sacrilege, scatology, swearword, vulgarity; **10** affliction, execration, misfortune, scurrility; **11** imprecation, malediction, profanation; PHRASES: **3, 3, 5** eff and blind *UK*; **3, 3, 8** use bad language; **3, 4** bad word; **4, 3** evil eye; **4, 4** blue joke, cuss word; **4, 5** foul mouth, talk dirty; **4-6, 4** four-letter word; **4-8** foul-mouthing; **5, 3, 5** ~ and swear; **5, 4** dirty talk, dirty word; **6, 5** voodoo ~; **7, 4** tinker's damn.

cursory *See* **superficial**

curt **4** rude; **5** brief, brisk; **6** abrupt; **7** brusque.

curtail *See* **limit**

curtain **4** veil, wall; **5** blind, cloak, drape, shade; **6** bamboo, screen, shield, speech; **7** shutter; **9** partition; PHRASES: **4, 7** Iron C~; **6, 7** safety ~; **7, 4** ~ call.

curvature **3** arc; **4** arch, bend, warp; **5** curve, twist; **7** arching, bending, curving; **9** concavity, convexity, curliness; **10** sinuousity; **11** circularity, incurvature; **12** circularness; **14** curvilinearity.

curve **3** arc, bow; **4** arch, bend, coil, curl, hook, loop, turn; **5** helix, sweep, twine, twist; **6** camber, circle, detour, spiral, swerve; **7** entwine, evolute; **8** involute, logistic; **9** cruciform, curvature; **10** trajectory; PHRASES: **4, 5** sine ~.

curvy **4** wavy; **6** curved; **7** rounded; **10** curvaceous, undulating; **11** curvilinear.

cushion **3** pad; **5** guard; **6** lessen, pillow, shield, soften, stifle; **7** beanbag, bolster, protect, support; **8** headrest, mitigate, moderate.

cusp **3** end, nib, tip; **4** edge; **5** limit, point, verge; **6** border; **9** crossover.

cuspidor **8** spittoon.

custard **3** pie; **5** apple; **6** powder.

custodian **6** keeper, warden; **7** curator, janitor; **8** defender, guardian, upholder; **9** caretaker, concierge; PHRASES: **5, 8** night watchman.

custody **4** care; **6** arrest, charge; **7** keeping; **9** detention; **10** protection; **11** confinement, safekeeping; **12** imprisonment; **13** incarceration.

custom 3 rut, way; 4 cult, form, lore, norm, rite, wont; 5 craze, drill, habit, mores, trend, usage; 6 demand, groove, market, method, patron, policy, praxis, ritual, system; 7 fashion, pattern, routine; 8 business, ceremony, customer, folklore, goodwill, practice, religion; 9 patronage *UK*, procedure, tradition; 10 convention, observance; 11 institution; PHRASES: 3, 2, 5 the in thing; 4, 5 done thing; 5, 2, 6 order of things.

customary 5 usual; 6 normal, wonted; 7 general, orderly, regular, routine, typical; 8 everyday, expected, habitual, ordinary, standard; 9 regulated; 10 accustomed, methodical, regulation, systematic; 11 established, traditional; 12 conventional; 14 characteristic; PHRASES: 4-7 time-honored; 4-11 long-established.

customs *See* **tax**

cut 2 in, up; 3 mow, saw; 4 chop, drop, edit, fall, gash, hack, nick, open, slit, snip, stop, trim; 5 carve, drunk, graze, limit, mince, notch, prune, score, sever, share, shear, short, slash, slice, wound; 6 censor, excise, finish, incise, pierce, reduce, remove, scythe, string; 7 abridge, curtail, cutback, decline, engrave, opening, scratch, shorten; 8 condense, decrease, diminish, incision, kickback, lacerate, puncture, restrict, shortcut, withdraw, withhold; 9 expurgate, reduction; 10 abbreviate, commission, disconnect, percentage; 11 discontinue; PHRASES: 3, 3 ~ off; 3-3 off-cut, outcut; 3, 4 ~ back, ~ down; 3-4 cut-offs; 3, 5 ~ glass; 4, 3 crew ~; 4-3 half-cut *UK*, rake-off; 5, 2, 1, 4 bring to a halt; 5, 2, 2, 3 bring to an end; 5, 3 choke off; 5-3 power-cut; 6, 4 ground beef.

cute 5 quick, sharp, smart; 6 pretty, shrewd; 7 cunning; 8 charming; 9 appealing; 10 attractive, delightful.

cutpurse 10 pickpocket.

cut short 4 stop; 7 suspend; 9 interrupt, terminate; 11 discontinue; PHRASES: 3, 1, 6 cut a corner; 3, 6 cut across; 3, 7 cut through; 4, 1, 4 call a halt; 4, 2, 4, 4 stop in full flow; 5, 3 break off.

cutting 3 icy; 4 cold, keen; 5 scion, sharp, sprig; 6 biting, unkind; 7 acerbic, hurtful; 8 critical, offshoot, wounding.

cutting edge 3 top, van; 4 edge, fore, lead; 5 blade, front, limit; 8 frontier, vanguard; 9 forefront, frontline, sharpness; PHRASES: 5, 2, 6 point of action; 5, 3 sharp end; 5, 4 knife edge, razor edge, sharp edge; 5, 5 knife blade, razor blade; 5-5 avantgarde; 6, 4 razor's edge; 7, 4 leading edge.

CV 6 résumé; 10 horsepower; PHRASES: 6-6 cheval-vapeur.

cycle 2 go; 3 lap, run, set; 4 rota, turn; 5 orbit, phase, round, shift; 6 menses, period, return, season, series; 7 bicycle, circuit, routine; 8 rotation, sequence; 9 biorhythm; 10 revolution, succession; 11 progression; 12 menstruation; PHRASES: 4, 5 life ~; 5, 2, 4 wheel of life; 5, 4 alpha wave; 5, 5 daily round; 5, 6 alpha rhythm; 8, 5 oestrous ~ *UK*; 8, 6 circular return; 9, 5 menstrual ~; 9, 6 circadian rhythm; 10, 5 biological clock.

cyclic 5 daily; 6 annual, hourly, weekly, yearly; 7 diurnal, monthly, nightly, orbital, routine, tertian; 8 biannual, biennial, biweekly, circling, circular, cyclical, harmonic, oestrous *UK*, periodic, rhythmic, rotating, rotative, seasonal; 9 bimonthly, menstrual, perennial, quotidian, recurrent, revolving; 10 repetitive, rotational, semiannual, semiweekly; 11 biorhythmic, fortnightly, hebdomadary, semimonthly.

cyclist 5 biker, bikie *UK*; 6 rocker; 7 greaser; 9 bicyclist; 12 motorcyclist; PHRASES: 4, 5 bike rider, easy rider; 7, 7 bicycle courier; 9, 5 motocross racer.

cyclone *See* **storm**

cylinder 3 rod; 4 bole, drum, pipe, roll, rung, tank, tube; 5 cigar, stalk, trunk; 6 bottle, column, roller; 8 canister; 9 container; PHRASES: 7, 3 rolling pin.

Cymru 5 Wales.

cyst *See* **growth**

czar 4 Ivan; 5 Peter; 6 Alexis; 7 emperor; 8 Nicholas; 9 Alexander; PHRASES: 4, 3, 8 Ivan the Terrible; 5, 3, 5 Peter the Great; 5, 7 Boris Godunov.

D

D **3** God (Latin: Deus); **4** died; **5** penny; **8** daughter, diamonds; **PHRASES: 4, 7** five hundred.

DA **8, 6** American lawyer.

dab **3** bit, pat; **4** dash, daub, drop, spot; **5** apply, touch; **7** smidgen; **11** fingerprint.

dabble **3** dip; **6** paddle, splash; **7** immerse; **10** experiment; **PHRASES: 3, 4** dip into; **3, 4, 4** try your hand; **4, 2** play at.

dachshund **7, 3** sausage dog *UK*.

dactylogram **11** fingerprint.

dad *See* **father**

daddy-longlegs **10** harvestman; **5, 3** crane fly.

daffodil **4, 4** lent lily *UK*.

dagger **6** obelus; **7** obelisk; **8** stiletto.

Dahomey **5** Benin.

daily **7** diurnal, regular; **8** everyday; **9** circadian; **PHRASES: 3, 2, 3** day by day; **3-2-3** day-to-day; **3, 5, 3** day after day; **4, 3** each day; **5, 3** every day.

dale *See* **valley**

dally *See* **linger**

dam **4** boom, dike, stem, weir; **5** block; **6** impede; **7** barrage, barrier; **8** obstruct, restrict; **9** reservoir; **10** embankment; **11** obstruction; **PHRASES: 4, 3** arch ~; **5, 3** earth ~; **7, 3** gravity ~; **7, 8** control blockade; **8, 3** buttress ~.

damage **4** bill, cost, harm, hurt; **5** price, spoil, total; **6** amount, injure, injury; **10** impairment; **11** destruction; **PHRASES: 5, 2** smash up. *See also* **compensation**

damn **3** pan; **4** doom; **5** curse; **7** censure, condemn, consign; **8** denounce, lambaste; **9** imprecate, proscribe; **12** anathematize; **13** excommunicate.

damned **6** bloody, cursed, darned; **7** blasted, dratted *UK*, hellish; **8** accursed, damnable, devilish, diabolic, infernal; **9** execrable; **10** confounded; **PHRASES: 8-5** blankety-blank.

damningly **8** cursedly; **12** bewitchingly, execratively; **PHRASES: 2, 1, 5** as a curse.

damp **3** wet; **4** dank, weak; **5** humid, moist, soggy; **6** clammy, dampen; **7** insipid, moisten, wetness; **8** dampness, humidify, humidity, moisture; **10** clamminess; **11** indifferent; **14** unenthusiastic; **PHRASES: 4-7** half-hearted.

dampen *See* **moisten**

damper **4** mute; **7** control, muffler, stopper; **8** silencer, softener; **9** hindrance, regulator; **10** controller, impediment, inhibition; **11** obstruction; **14** discouragement.

damsel **4** girl; **6** maiden.

damselfish/damselfly **10** demoiselle.

dance **3** bop, cry, hop, jig; **4** ball, haka *UK*, hula, jerk, jive, jump, leap, prom, rave, reel, rock, skip, sway, turn; **5** bebop, blues, caper, cheer, conga, disco, fling, galop, gigue, limbo, mambo, polka, rumba, salsa, samba, stomp, tango, twist, valse, volta, waltz, whirl; **6** ballet, bolero, boogie, cancan, cavort, frolic, gambol, jiggle, Kabuki, minuet, prance, rapper, rotate, shimmy, valeta, wiggle; **7** beguine, bodypop, ceilidh, foxtrot, gavotte, hoedown, lambada, Lancers, mazurka, norteño, peabody, rollick, shindig, shuffle; **8** cakewalk, courante, fandango, flamenco, habanera, hornpipe, macarena, merengue, rigadoon, saraband, snowball; **9** allemande, cotillion, écossaize, farandole, jitterbug, pirouette, polonaise, quadrille, quickstep; **10** breakdance, Charleston, corroboree *UK*, masquerade, semiformal, strathspey *UK*, tarantella; **11**

choreograph, contredanse; **12** congratulate; PHRASES: **2, 7** St Bernard; **3-3** cha-cha; **3-3-3** cha-cha-cha; **3, 3, 5** the big apple; **3, 4** pas seul; **3-4** one-step, two-step; **3, 5** fan ~, tap ~, tea ~, toe ~, war ~; **3, 7** Gay Gordons; **4, 2** hoof it; **4, 2, 5** Duke of Perth; **4, 3** keel row; **4, 3, 4** rock and roll; **4, 4** hunt ball; **4-4** hula-hula; **4-4, 7** soft-shoe shuffle; **4, 5** barn ~, clog ~, folk ~, high kicks, last waltz, long sword, paso doble, Paul Jones *UK*, rain ~, sand ~, solo ~, step ~; **4, 7** line dancing, step dancing; **5, 1, 7** tread a measure; **5-2** knees-up *UK*; **5, 2, 8** Walls of Limerick; **5, 3** bunny hop, Irish jig, lindy hop; **5, 3, 6** Strip the Willow; **5, 4** bossa nova, conga line; **5-4** hitch-hike; **5, 5** belly ~, court ~, danse basse, devil ~, hokey cokey, sword ~, totem ~; **5-5** hokey-pokey; **5, 6** black bottom; **6-1-5** boomps-a-daisy; **6-2, 5** excuse-me ~; **6, 3-4** Boston two-step; **6, 4** Castle walk, turkey trot; **6, 5** morris ~, Palais Glide, ritual ~, sacred ~, social ~, square ~, trance ~; **7, 3-4** English one-step; **7, 4** charity ball, Lambeth Walk; **7, 5** Cossack ~, English waltz, maypole ~, Russian ~, sailor's ~; **7-5** country-dance; **7-7** hootchy-kootchy; **8, 3-4** military two-step; **8, 4** foursome reel, Scottish reel, Virginia reel; **8, 5** Highland fling, medieval ~, Viennese waltz; **9, 4** eightsome reel *UK*; **9, 5** courtship ~; **10, 5** hesitation waltz.

dance hall 5 disco; **8** ballroom; **11** discotheque; PHRASES: **6, 2, 5** palais de danse.

dancer 5 jiver; **6** geisha, hoofer, jumper; **7** danseur, waltzer; **8** bebopper, coryphée, danseuse, figurant, shuffler, stripper; **9** ballerina, figurante, jitterbug; **10** foxtrotter; **11** entertainer; **13** choreographer, Terpsichorean; PHRASES: **2-2, 6** go-go ~; **4-6** high-kicker; **5, 9** prima ballerina; **6, 4** geisha girl.

dancers 4, 5 Gene Kelly; **4, 8** Jack Buchanan.

dandle 3 jog, pet, rub; **4** rock; **5** dance; **6** bounce, caress, fondle, jiggle, pamper, stroke.

danger 4 risk, snag, trap; PHRASES: **0, 4, 3!** look out!; **5** peril, Pista!, Piste!; **6** ambush, crisis, hazard, menace, threat; **7** Achtung!, pitfall, urgency, venture; **8** jeopardy; **9** deathtrap, emergency, riskiness, treachery; **10** overdaring; **11** imperilment, predicament; **12** endangerment, perilousness, slipperiness, unsteadiness; **13** dangerousness, hazardousness, vulnerability; **14** precariousness; **15** treacherousness, venturesomeness; **4, 2, 1, 4** turn of a card; **4, 2, 3, 4** leap in the dark; **4, 2, 3, 5** spin of the wheel; **4, 2, 4** road to ruin; **4, 2, 5** jaws of death; **4, 4** near miss; **4, 5** near thing *UK*; **4, 7** dire straits; **5, 2, 3, 4** throw of the dice; **5, 2, 8** sword of Damocles; **5, 4** black spot; **5, 5** close shave, lion's mouth; **5, 7** risky venture; **6, 2, 5** shadow of death; **6, 4** razor's edge; **6, 6** narrow escape; **7, 4** dragon's lair; **7, 5** parlous state; **8, 5** perilous state, slippery slope; **8, 6** surprise attack.

danger (be in/face danger) 4 dare, defy, fall, risk; **5** slide; **6** gamble, hazard, totter, tumble; PHRASES: **2, 3, 2, 1, 4** go out on a limb; **3-3** hot-dog; **3, 3, 4, 2** run the risk of; **3, 3, 8** run the gauntlet; **3, 4** get lost; **4, 1, 5** ride a tiger, take a flier; **4, 1, 6** take a chance; **4, 2, 1, 6** hang by a thread; **4, 4, 4** play with fire; **4, 4, 5** dice with death; **4, 5, 4** come under fire, face heavy odds; **5, 2, 3, 4** swing in the wind; **5, 2, 4, 3** skate on thin ice; **5, 8** court disaster; **5, 10** tempt providence; **6, 2, 3, 4** teeter on the edge; **6, 4** wander away.

dangerous 5 dicey, dodgy *UK*, grave, hairy, nasty, risky; **6** chancy, clutch, deadly, sticky, tricky, unsafe; **7** crucial, harmful, ominous; **8** alarming, critical, grievous, menacing, perilous; **9** difficult, explosive, hazardous, poisonous, venturous; **10** foreboding, infectious, precarious; **11** frightening, radioactive, threatening, treacherous, venturesome; PHRASES: **2, 5** at stake; **2, 5, 5** at flash point; **4-11** life-threatening; **5, 4, 6** beset with perils.

danger signal 3 SOS; **4** bell, call, horn, ring, toot; **5** alarm, alert, flare, light, shout, siren; **6** alarum, beacon, Klaxon, mayday, tattoo, tocsin; **7** foghorn, gunshot; PHRASES: **3, 3** war cry; **3, 3, 3** hue and cry; **3, 4** car horn, red flag; **3, 5** red alert; **3, 6** fog signal; **4, 2, 3** hair on end; **4, 2, 4** beat of drum; **4, 5** fire alarm; **5, 4** alarm bell; **5, 5** fiery cross, rocks ahead; **5, 6** panic button; **5, 7** storm brewing; **6, 5** rising river; **7, 4** trumpet call, warning shot, warning sign; **7, 5** warning alarm, warning flare, warning light; **7, 6** ticking parcel; **8, 3** rallying cry, snarling dog; **8, 5** breakers ahead, distress flare, flashing light; **8, 6** distress signal.

Danish 4 blue, Dane, loaf; **5** bacon; **6** pastry.

dapper 4 neat, trim; **5** smart; **7** elegant; PHRASES: **4-7** well-dressed.

Dardan 6 Trojan.

Dardanelles 10 Hellespont.

dare 4 goad, risk, spur, urge; 5 taunt; 6 gamble; 7 provoke, venture; 9 challenge; 11 provocation; PHRASES: 2, 2, 4 be so bold; 3, 4, 3, 3 lay down the law; 4, 2 lord it; 4, 3, 4 have the guts; 4, 3, 5 have the cheek *UK*, have the nerve; 4, 3, 7 take the liberty; 4, 3, 8 have the audacity; 5, 2 queen it; 6, 2, 3 brazen it out.

daredevil 4 rash, wild; 6 madcap; 7 hothead; 8 reckless; 9 foolhardy, hotheaded; PHRASES: 4-3 show-off; 4-5 risk-taker.

daring 4 bold; 5 brave, nerve, risky; 6 unsafe; 7 bravery, courage; 8 audacity, boldness; 9 audacious, dangerous, hazardous; 10 courageous; 11 treacherous; 12 enterprising.

dark 3 dim; 4 deep, dusk, evil, grim, inky, murk; 5 black, bleak, brown, dingy, dusky, ebony, gloom, livid, murky, night, sable, shade, shady, smoky, swart, unlit; 6 cloudy, dismal, dreary, gloomy, leaden, opaque, pitchy, shaded, shadow, somber, spooky, stormy, wicked; 7 darkish, dimness, eclipse, melanic, obscure, ominous, shadows, shadowy, Stygian, sunless, swarthy; 8 blackout, brunette, darkness, funereal, melanous, moonless, mournful, overcast, sinister, starless; 9 blackness, cheerless, Cimmerian, lightless, nefarious, nighttime, nocturnal, obscurity, pigmented, tenebrous, unlighted; 10 achromatic, depressing, lightproof, melanistic, mysterious, umbrageous; 11 inscrutable, sunlessness, swarthiness, threatening; 12 underexposed; 13 unilluminated; PHRASES: 2, 3, 7, 3 of the deepest dye; 3-3 ill-lit; 3-5 jet-black; 5-4 pitch-dark; 5-5 pitch-black; 7, 5 Stygian gloom.

darken 3 dim, dip, fog; 4 veil; 5 cloud, cover, douse, hatch, shade, snuff; 6 deepen, shadow, shroud; 7 blacken, depress, eclipse, obscure, shutter; 9 adumbrate, blindfold, obfuscate; 10 overshadow, silhouette; 11 underexpose; PHRASES: 3, 2, 3, 5 put in the shade; 4, 1, 6, 4 cast a shadow over; 4, 2, 3, 4 keep in the dark; 5, 2 shade in; 5, 3 black out, snuff out; 5, 4 cloud over; 5-5 cross-hatch.

darkly 2, 3, 4 in the dark; 2, 3, 5 in the night, in the shade; 2, 5 by night; 2, 8 at midnight; 2, 9 at nightfall. *See also* **dark**

darling 3 pet; 4 dear, love; 6 lovely; 7 beloved, dearest; 8 adorable, favorite, gorgeous; 9 wonderful; 10 sweetheart; PHRASES: 4, 8 firm favorite.

darn 3 sew; 4 mend, very; 6 repair, stitch; 9 extremely; 13 exceptionally; 15 extraordinarily; PHRASES: 3, 2 sew up.

dart 3 run, zip; 4 barb, dash, rush, tear, whiz, zoom; 5 arrow, shaft, shoot, spear; 6 scurry, sprint; 7 harpoon, javelin, missile; 10 projectile.

dash 2 em, en; 3 bit, run, zip; 4 bolt, dart, drop, race, ruin, rush, slam, tear; 5 hurry, sling, smash, spoil, throw, trace; 6 career, hasten, hurtle, plunge, scurry, sprint, thwart; 7 destroy, scamper, scuttle, shatter, smidgen, soupçon; 8 confound; 9 frustrate; 10 disappoint.

dashing 4 bold, chic; 6 jaunty; 7 elegant, stylish; 8 debonair, spirited; 9 confident; 10 flamboyant; 11 fashionable.

data *See* **information**

date 3 age, day, era; 4 Ides, time, year; 5 epoch, Nones, point, tryst; 6 moment, period; 7 Calends, meeting; 8 birthday, calendar, juncture, occasion; 10 engagement, rendezvous; 11 anniversary, appointment, assignation; 12 chronologize; PHRASES: 1-3 D-day; 1-4 H-hour; 3-6, 3 red-letter day; 4, 3 name day; 4, 4 zero hour; 5, 2, 4 point in time; 5, 3 fixed day; 5, 4 blind ~; 6, 3 saint's day; 9, 3 appointed day.

dated 10 annalistic; 11 calendrical; 12 chronometric; 13 chronographic, chronological; PHRASES: 2, 4, 5 in date order.

dating 6 carbon; 11 radioactive, radiocarbon, radiometric; PHRASES: 4-4 tree-ring; 6-2 carbon-14; 7-4 uranium-lead.

daub 4 blot, slap, slop, spot; 5 smear, stain; 6 blotch, spread; 7 spatter, splotch.

daunt *See* **put off**

dawdle 3 lag; 4 plod; 5 dally, delay; 6 linger, loiter; PHRASES: 4, 5 hang about *UK*; 4, 6 hang around; 5, 4 waste time.

dawn 5 begin, birth, start; 6 advent, appear, emerge, origin; 7 genesis, lighten, morning, sunrise; 8 cockcrow, commence, daybreak, daylight; 9 beginning, emergence, inception, originate; 12 commencement; PHRASES: 5, 2, 4 crack of ~; 5, 4, 4 cross your mind; 5, 5 first light; 9, 4 unearthly hour.

day 3 age, era; **4** date, time; **5** epoch; **6** period; **7** daytime; **8** daylight; **10** generation; PHRASES: **3, 2, 3, 4** ~ of the week; **8, 3** calendar ~; **8, 5** daylight hours, sunlight hours.

daybreak, daylight *See* **dawn**

daydream 4 muse, wish; **5** dream; **6** desire, musing, trance; **7** fantasy, imagine, reverie; **8** escapism, fantasia, stargaze; **9** fantasize, sophistry; **10** woolgather *UK*; **11** contemplate, fantasizing, pensiveness; **13** contemplation, woolgathering; PHRASES: **2, 4, 2, 7** be lost in thought; **2, 5, 4** be miles away; **4, 5** pipe dream; **4, 7** deep thought; **5, 4, 5** stare into space; **5, 5** brown study; **7, 8** wishful thinking.

daylight 3 day; **4** dawn; **7** daytime, sunrise; **8** daybreak, sunshine; PHRASES: **5, 2, 3** light of day; **5, 2, 4** crack of dawn; **5, 5** first light.

daystar 3 sun; PHRASES: **7, 4** morning star.

daze 4 stun; **5** dream, shock; **6** stupor, trance; **7** astound; **8** astonish, daydream, surprise; PHRASES: **8, 5** confused state.

dazzle 4 daze; **5** amaze, blaze, blind, glare; **7** astound, confuse, impress; **8** astonish, bedazzle; **9** overwhelm; **10** brightness, brilliance, reflection.

dazzling 6 bright; **7** amazing, blazing, glaring; **8** alluring, luminous, stunning; **10** astounding, glittering, incredible.

dead 4 dull, gone, numb, over, past; **5** empty, ended, inert, kaput, quiet, relic, stiff, still; **6** boring, buried, corpse, deadly, former, fossil, killed, passed, silent; **7** cadaver, carcass, carrion, defunct, demised, extinct, remains; **8** benumbed, casualty, deceased, departed, fatality, inactive, lamented, lifeless, murdered, obsolete, skeleton; **9** exanimate, inanimate, massacred, stillborn; **10** breathless, posthumous; **11** slaughtered; PHRASES: **2, 3, 5** in the grave; **2, 4** no more; **2, 8, 5** in Abraham's bosom; **3, 2, 4, 5** out of this world; **3, 2, 4, 6** out of one's misery; **3, 4, 5** six feet under; **4, 2, 1, 4** ~ as a dodo; **4, 2, 1, 8** ~ as a doornail; **4, 2, 7** ~ on arrival (DOA); **4, 3** done for; **4, 3, 1, 6** gone for a burton; **4, 3, 4** ~ and gone; **4, 3, 5** food for worms; **4, 3, 6** ~ and buried; **4, 4** born ~, done with *UK*, long gone; **4, 8** dear departed, late lamented; **5, 2, 3** taken by God; **5, 4** loved ones, stone ~; **5, 7** under hatches; **6, 2** passed on; **6, 2, 3** called by God; **6, 2, 4** bereft of life; **6, 3, 4** behind the veil; **6, 3, 5** be-

yond the grave; **6, 4** passed away, passed over; **6, 6, 3** beyond mortal ken.

dead (person dealing with the dead) 7 coroner; **8** embalmer; **9** mortician; **10** undertaker; PHRASES: **7, 8** funeral director.

dead end 5 block; **7** impasse; **8** deadlock; **9** roadblock, stalemate; **10** standstill; PHRASES: **2, 7, 4** no through road *UK*; **3-2-3** cul-de-sac; **5, 5** blind alley.

dead heat 3 tie; **4** draw; **5** deuce; **9** stalemate; PHRASES: **3-3-4** nip-and-tuck; **4-3-4** neck-and-neck; **4, 4** lock step; **5, 6** photo finish; **5, 7** level pegging *UK*.

deadline 5 limit; **6** target; **7** urgency; **8** pressure; PHRASES: **4, 4** zero hour; **4, 5** time limit; **6, 4** cutoff date; **7, 4** closing date.

deadly 4 dead, dull, fell; **5** fatal, toxic; **6** boring, lethal, mortal; **7** capital, deathly, extreme, noxious, tedious; **8** terminal, tiresome; **9** incurable, malignant, murderous, perfectly, poisonous; **10** absolutely, asphyxiant, completely; **11** suffocating; **12** insalubrious, pathological; **13** uninteresting; PHRASES: **4-11** life-threatening; **5-8** death-bringing.

deaf 7 earless, stunned, unmoved; **8** deafened, heedless; **9** oblivious, unhearing, unmusical; **10** unaffected; **11** indifferent; **12** unresponsive; PHRASES: **4, 2, 7** hard of hearing; **4-4** tone-deaf; **5, 4** stone ~; **7-8** hearing-impaired; **9, 4** partially ~.

deaf (be deaf) 6 ignore; **7** unmoved; **10** impervious; PHRASES: **3-4** lip-read; **4, 1, 4, 3** turn a deaf ear; **4, 2, 7** hard of hearing; **4, 3** tune out; **4, 4, 7** lose one's hearing; **5, 4, 4** close one's ears.

deafening 4 loud; **7** booming; **8** piercing; **10** resounding, thunderous; PHRASES: **3-8** ear-piercing; **3-9** ear-splitting; **3-10** ear-shattering.

deafness 8 oblivion; **11** inattention; **12** indifference; **13** insensitivity; PHRASES: **4, 4** deaf ears; **4-6** deaf-mutism; **7, 4** hearing loss. *See also* **deaf**

deal 4 hawk, pact; **5** trade; **6** barter, matter, treaty; **7** compact; **8** allocate, bankroll, business, contract, covenant; **9** agreement, apportion, negotiate; **10** distribute; **11** transaction; PHRASES: **2, 8** do business; **4, 3** dole out.

dear 3 pet; **4** love; **5** fancy *UK*, loved, lovey *UK*, steep; **6** costly, poppet *UK*, pricey, prized, valued; **7** beloved, bullish, darling, dearest, gouging, soaring, sweetie; **8** climbing, precious; **9** cherished, expensive, treasured; **10** exorbitant, overpriced, sweetheart; **11** extravagant; **12** extortionate, inflationary, unreasonable; PHRASES: **2-6** up-market; **3, 2, 5** out of sight; **3-4** sky-high; **4-4** high-cost; **4-6** high-priced; **6, 4, 5** beyond one's means.

dear (be dear) 4, 1, 6 cost a bundle, cost a packet; **4, 1, 7** cost a fortune; **4, 3, 4** cost one dear; **4, 3, 5** cost the earth; **4, 4, 6** hurt one's pocket.

dearest *See* **loved one**

dearly 6 deeply; **7** greatly; **9** extremely, sincerely; **10** profoundly, usuriously; **11** exceedingly; PHRASES: **2, 5, 4** at great cost, at heavy cost; **2, 5, 7** at great expense. *See also* **dear**

dearth *See* **lack**

death 3 end; **4** exit, fate, loss, Mors, ruin; **5** decay, dying, sleep; **6** demise, expiry; **7** autopsy, decease, parting, passing, quietus, release; **8** collapse, downfall, fatality, necrosis, quietude, Thanatos; **9** departure; **10** expiration *UK*, extinction, postmortem; **12** obliteration, putrefaction; **13** mortification; **14** cadaverousness; PHRASES: **3, 2, 3, 4** end of the line; **3, 3, 5** the big sleep; **3, 4, 4** the last defer; **3, 4, 8** the Last Summoner; **3, 5** Big Chill; **3, 5, 6** the final thrill, the great divide; **3, 6** the beyond; **4, 2, 5** hand of ~, jaws of ~, King of D~; **4, 2, 7** King of Terrors; **4, 3** deep six; **4, 4** last gasp, swan song; **4, 4, 5** cold meat party; **4, 5** crib ~; **4-5** dead-house; **4, 6** Grim Reaper, last breath; **5, 2, 5** Angel of D~, dance of ~; **5, 4** Irish wake; **5, 5** brain ~; **5, 6** rigor mortis; **6, 2, 5** shades of ~, shadow of ~; **6-4** death's-head; **7, 4** eternal rest, memento mori, passing away.

deathless *See* **immortal**

deathly 3 wan; **4** deep, pale; **5** ashen, fatal, livid, stony; **6** deadly, pallid; **7** ghastly, ghostly, haggard; **9** deathlike, extremely, intensely *UK*; **10** cadaverous; **11** intensively; PHRASES: **6-4** corpse-like.

death sentence 4 doom; **5** knell; **7** hanging, quietus; **9** execution; **10** guillotine; **11** crucifixion; **13** electrocution; PHRASES: **3, 7** gas chamber; **5, 2, 4** crack of doom; **5, 3** death row; **5, 5** death house, death knell; **5, 7** death chamber; **6, 5** firing squad; **6, 9** lethal injection; **8, 5** electric chair.

debar *See* **exclude**

debase 4 snub, soil; **5** abase, lower, shame, sully, taint; **6** defile, demean, humble; **7** corrupt, deflate, degrade, tarnish; **8** disgrace, dishonor; **9** humiliate; **10** adulterate; PHRASES: **5, 4** Uriah Heep, water down; **5, 9** lower standards.

debasement 5 shame, taint; **7** tarnish; **8** disgrace, dishonor, ignominy, spoilage, sullying; **9** ruination; **10** corruption, defilement, tarnishing; **11** degradation, humiliation; **12** adulteration; **13** deterioration, disparagement.

debate 5 argue; **6** ponder, refute; **7** contend, contest, discuss, dispute, inquiry, oratory; **8** colloquy, consider, dialogue, litigate, polemics, question, rhetoric; **9** challenge, deduction, discourse, heuristic, logomachy, reasoning, sophistry, symposium; **10** contradict, deliberate, discussion, polemicize; **11** apologetics, contemplate, disputation, examination, hermeneutic, questioning; **12** conversation, deliberation, dialecticism; **13** interlocution *UK*, ratiocination; PHRASES: **5, 2** weigh up *UK*.

debilitate *See* **weaken**

debility *See* **weakness**

debit 4 debt; **6** charge, deduct; **8** subtract, withdraw; **9** deduction; **10** withdrawal; **11** subtraction; PHRASES: **4, 3** take out.

debonair *See* **suave**

debt 4 dues, duty; **5** bills, debit; **7** arrears; **10** obligation; **12** indebtedness; PHRASES: **3, 3** the red; **9, 5** something owing.

debt (be in debt) 3 owe; **8** overdraw; **9** overspend; **13** collateralize; PHRASES: **2, 2, 4** be in hock; **3, 4, 4** run into debt; **3, 5** owe money; **3, 8** pay interest.

debt (forgive a debt) 5, 3 write off.

debtor 6 drawee, loanee; **7** obligor, pledger, pledgor; **8** borrower, nonpayer; **9** defaulter, insolvent, mortgagor.

debut 8 entrance; **9** unveiling; **12** inauguration, introduction, presentation.

decade *See* **period**

decadent *See* **corrupt**

decamp *See* **run away**

decapitate 6 behead; **7** execute; **8** amputate, truncate; **10** guillotine.

decay 3 rot; **4** mold, rust, turn; **5** spoil, stale; **6** fester, mildew, perish *UK*, rankle; **7**

corrode, corrupt, crumble, decline, putrefy, rotting; **8** gangrene; **9** breakdown, corrosion, decompose, suppurate; **10** degenerate, rottenness; **12** putrefaction; **13** decomposition, deterioration; **14** disintegration; PHRASES: **2, 3** go bad, go off *UK*; **2, 4** go sour; **2, 5** go moldy, go stale; **4, 3** fall off.

decease *See* **death**

deceit 4 lies, wile; **5** guile; **7** treason; **8** artifice, sedition; **9** duplicity, treachery; **10** dishonesty, sneakiness; **11** fraudulence; **13** deceitfulness, faithlessness; PHRASES: **5, 4** Judas kiss; **5, 9** false pretenses.

deceitful 4 glib, wily; **5** dodgy *UK*, false, lying, phony *UK*; **6** crafty, phoney, shifty, sneaky, tricky; **7** conning, cunning, devious, fibbing, furtive; **8** cheating, guileful, slippery, specious, spurious; **9** collusive, contrived, deceiving, deceptive, dishonest, faithless, underhand; **10** contriving, fallacious, fraudulent, perfidious, treasonous; **11** calculating, duplicitous, forswearing, treacherous; **13** surreptitious, untrustworthy; PHRASES: **5-7** false-hearted; **6-7** double-dealing.

deceive 3 con; **4** blag *UK*, dupe, fool, hoax; **5** bluff, charm, cheat, dodge, elude, evade, sneak, spoof, trick; **6** betray, delude, diddle, entrap, fleece, outwit, scheme; **7** connive, cuckold, defraud, ensnare, mislead, swindle, swizzle; **8** contrive, embezzle, hoodwink, outsmart; **9** bamboozle, blindfold, dissemble; **10** manipulate, masquerade; **11** dissimulate, outmaneuver; PHRASES: **3, 2, 2, 3** put on an act; **3-4** two-time; **4, 1, 4, 3** pull a fast one; **4, 2** take in; **4, 2, 4, 4** have it both ways; **4, 3, 1, 4** take for a ride; **4, 4** play away *UK*; **5-4** sweet-talk; **6-4** double-deal; **6-5** double-cross.

deceiver 4 liar, Loki, Puck, sham; **5** bluff, cheat, duper, faker, fraud, phony *UK*, poser, pseud *UK*, quack, rogue; **6** hoaxer, kidder, phoney, poseur, ringer; **7** bluffer, guisard, seducer, spoofer; **8** beguiler, Casanova, imposter, swindler; **9** cardsharp, charlatan, fraudster, hypocrite, pretender, quackster, trickster; **10** bamboozler; **11** masquerader, quacksalver; **12** dissimulator, impersonator; PHRASES: **3, 2, 1, 5, 4** ass in a lion's skin; **3, 3** con man; **3, 4** Don Juan; **3, 6** con artist; **3-6** leg-puller; **4-7** four-flusher; **9, 5** practical joker.

deceiving *See* **deceitful**

deceleration 7 braking, slowing; **8**

checking, flagging; **10** slackening; **11** retardation; PHRASES: **6, 3** easing off.

decency 7 decorum, modesty; **8** civility; **9** integrity; **10** politeness; **11** uprightness; **12** decorousness; **14** respectability.

decent 4 clad, good; **5** moral, right; **6** demure, garbed, honest, proper; **7** clothed, correct, covered, dressed, sizable; **8** adequate, generous, suitable, virtuous; **9** wholesome; **10** reasonable; **11** respectable.

decentralization, 10 devolution; **12** localization; **14** federalization, reorganization; **15** deconcentration, regionalization.

decentralize 7 devolve; **8** disperse, localize; **10** depopulate, distribute, reorganize; **11** regionalize; **13** deconcentrate.

deception 3 con; **4** ruse, sham; **5** fraud, guile, lying; **6** deceit; **7** perjury; **8** cheating, trickery; **9** duplicity; **10** artfulness, dishonesty, subterfuge; **11** fraudulence, furtiveness; **13** deceitfulness, deceptiveness, dissimulation; **15** underhandedness; PHRASES: **6-7** double-dealing.

deceptive *See* **deceitful**

decide 6 choose, settle; **7** resolve; **8** conclude; **9** determine; PHRASES: **4, 1, 8** make a decision; **6, 2** settle on.

decided 4 firm, sure; **5** fixed; **7** certain, settled; **8** decisive, definite, emphatic, resolute; **10** determined, undisputed, unwavering; **11** categorical, indubitable, irrefutable, unequivocal; **12** indisputable; **13** unimpeachable; **14** unquestionable; **15** unchallengeable; PHRASES: **4-3-4** open-and-shut; **5-3** clear-cut.

decider 4 game; **5** match, trial; **7** contest, playoff.

decimate *See* **devastate**

decipher 4 read; **5** crack, solve; **6** decode; **7** decrypt, unravel; **8** unriddle, untangle; **9** demystify, interpret, translate; **10** unscramble; PHRASES: **4, 3, 3, 2** find the key to; **4, 5, 2** make sense of; **5, 1, 4** crack a code; **5, 3, 6** crack the cipher; **5, 8** piece together; **6, 1, 4** unlock a code; **6, 3** figure out, puzzle out.

decision 6 choice, result; **7** resolve, verdict; **8** firmness; **9** willpower; **10** conclusion; **13** determination, pronouncement.

decisive 3 key; **7** certain, pivotal; **8** critical, resolute; **10** conclusive, determined; **11** significant; PHRASES: **5-7** clear-sighted; **6-6** strong-minded.

deck 4 area; 5 adorn, cover, dress, floor, level, punch, thump; 6 bedeck, clothe, strike, tennis; 7 surface, wreathe; 8 decorate.

declare 4 aver; 5 state; 6 affirm, assert, insist; 7 profess; 8 proclaim; 9 pronounce.

decline 3 ebb; 4 drop, fall, flag, sink, wane, wilt; 5 decay, slump; 6 plunge, refuse, weaken, worsen; 7 sinking; 8 decrease, downturn, nosedive; 10 degenerate, depression; 11 deteriorate; PHRASES: 2, 2, 4 go to seed; 3, 3 beg off; 4, 2 pass up; 4, 3 fall off; 4, 4 turn down; 7-3 falling-off; 8, 3 leveling off, leveling out; 8, 5 downward curve, downward trend; 8, 6 downward spiral.

decode See **decipher**

decompose See **rot**

decomposed 5 fetid, moldy; 6 putrid, rotten; 7 decayed, spoiled; 8 perished *UK*; 9 putrefied.

decomposition See **decay**

deconstruct 5 parse; 6 divide; 7 analyze, devolve, disband, dissect, liquefy; 8 catalyze, disperse, dissolve, separate, simplify; 9 criticize, dismantle, dismember; 10 decompound, unscramble; PHRASES: 4, 2, 6 pull to pieces, take to pieces.

deconstruction 7 fission; 8 analysis, disunion, division; 9 breakdown, catalysis, dispersal; 10 demolition, devolution, dissection, hydrolysis; 11 atomization, destruction, dismantling, dissolution; 12 electrolysis, liquefaction; 13 dismemberment; 14 simplification.

decorate 4 deck, etch, mold; 5 adorn, array, award, color, crown, honor, paint; 6 bedeck, emboss, enrich, knight, spruce; 7 bedizen, bejewel, engrave, enhance, festoon, garland, garnish, wreathe; 8 beautify, emblazon, ornament; 9 embellish, embroider; PHRASES: 4, 3 deck out; 5, 2 fancy up.

decorated 4 dyed; 5 edged, inset; 6 beaded, carved, draped, framed, ornate, tinted; 7 incised, trimmed; 8 enameled, sequined, veneered; 9 bejeweled, encrusted. See also **decorate**

decoration 4 sash; 5 award, honor, medal; 6 border, doodad; 7 beading, carving, feature, festoon; 8 ornament; 9 adornment; 13 embellishment, ornamentation; 14 beautification.

decorative 4 gilt; 5 braid, fancy; 6 gilded, inlaid, ornate, pretty, rococo, scenic, worked; 7 baroque; 8 enhanced, enriched, frippery; 9 enhancing, patterned; 10 attractive, ornamental; 11 embellished, embroidered, picturesque; PHRASES: 3-10 nonfunctional; 6-6 pretty-pretty *UK*.

decorator 6 gilder; 7 jeweler, painter, smocker; 11 embroiderer, illustrator, pyrographer; PHRASES: 4, 5 lace maker; 6, 6 scroll worker.

decoy 4 lure, trap; 5 plant, snare, trick; 6 allure, entice, entrap; 7 ensnare, stoolie; 8 distract; 11 distraction; PHRASES: 3, 7 red herring; 4-2, 3 come-on man; 4-5, 5 wildgoose chase; 5, 5 false scent; 5, 6 fool's errand, smoke screen, stool pigeon.

decrease 3 cut, ebb; 4 drop, fade, fail, fall, loss, shed, thin, wane; 5 abate, decay; 6 easing, fading, lessen, reduce, shrink, weaken, wither; 7 cutback, decline, dimming, dwindle, leakage, shrivel, slacken, subside; 8 diminish, evanesce, fadeaway, rollback, slowdown; 9 abatement, attrition, corrosion, disappear, evaporate, lessening, reduction, shrinkage, withering; 10 depreciate, diminuendo, diminution, downsizing, limitation, shortening, slackening; 11 attenuation, contraction, curtailment, decrescendo, diminishing, evanescence, evaporation, extenuation, restriction, subtraction; 12 degeneration, depreciation, detumescence, enfeeblement; 13 deliquescence, disappearance; PHRASES: 2-8 de-escalate; 2-10 de-escalation; 3, 2 dry up; 3, 3 die out, run low; 3, 4 cut down, die away, die down, eat away, ebb away, run down; 4, 3 cast off, drop off, grow dim, tail off, thin out; 4-3 fade-out; 4, 3, 4 wear and tear; 4, 4 baby bust, cast away, come down, fade away, grow less, melt away, pass away, slow down, wear away; 4, 4, 5 fade from sight; 4, 7 grow smaller; 5, 3 level off, level out, peter out, taper off; 5, 4 drain away, waste away; 6, 3 bottom out; 6, 7 become extinct.

decreasingly 8 downward; 9 removably; 10 eradicably; 11 deductively; 13 diminishingly; PHRASES: 2, 7 in decline; 4, 2 less so; 4, 3, 4 down and down, less and less; 4, 4 even less.

decree 4 rule; 6 ruling; 7 command, dictate, verdict; 8 announce; 9 pronounce; 11 declaration; 12 announcement; 13 pronouncement.

decrepit 3 old; 4 weak; 5 frail; 6 feeble, infirm; 8 decaying; 9 crumbling; 11 dilapidated; PHRASES: 7, 5 falling apart.

decrescent 6 waning; 8 decadent; 9 corrosive, decayable, declinate, declining, reductive, shrinking; 10 declinable, decreasing, deductible, depressive, regressive; 11 depreciable; 12 debilitative, deflationary, deflationist, deliquescent, depreciative, depreciatory; 13 decompressive; PHRASES: 4-6 loss-making.

decry *See* **criticize**

dedicate 4 give; 6 bestow, commit, devote, donate, pledge; 10 consecrate, contribute; PHRASES: 3, 5 set aside.

deduce 5 infer; 6 assume, gather, reason; 7 presume, suppose; 8 conclude; PHRASES: 4, 3 work out; 6, 3 figure out.

deduction 7 removal; 8 judgment; 9 inference; 10 assumption, conclusion, withdrawal; 11 abstraction, presumption, subtraction; 12 contribution.

deductive *See* **logical**

deed 3 act, job; 4 feat, task, work; 5 crime, lease, stunt; 6 action, doings; 7 actions, affairs, charter; 8 dealings, document, endeavor; 9 operation; 10 proceeding, wrongdoing; 11 achievement, masterpiece, transaction, undertaking; 14 accomplishment; PHRASES: 4, 2, 4 coup de main; 4, 2, 5 coup de grâce, tour de force; 4, 4 foul play; 4, 5 beau geste, coup d'état; 4-6 chef-d'œuvre; 5, 3 overt act; 5, 4 title ~.

deem *See* **think**

deep 3 low; 4 bass; 5 depth; 6 gaping, hidden, innate, secret, sunken, untold; 7 lowness, vibrant, yawning; 8 inherent, plunging, profound, resonant; 9 cavernous, soundless, unplumbed; 10 bottomless, entrenched, fathomless, meaningful, mysterious, sepulchral, unfathomed; 11 inscrutable; 12 concentrated, multifaceted, multilayered, subconscious, subterranean, unfathomable; PHRASES: 2, 2, 4, 4 up to one's eyes; 2, 4, 2, 1, 4 as ~ as a well; 2, 4, 2, 4 as ~ as hell; 2, 4, 6 at rock bottom; 3, 2, 4, 5 out of one's depth.

deepen 4 dive, drop, fall, gape, grow, sink, yawn; 5 lower, plumb; 6 expand, extend, fathom, plunge, tunnel; 7 descend, immerse; 8 increase, submerge; 9 intensify, reinforce; 10 accumulate, strengthen;

PHRASES: 3, 3 dig out; 4, 2, 3, 6 sink to the bottom; 5, 3 scoop out; 5, 3, 4 heave the lead; 5, 3, 6 plumb the depths, reach the bottom; 5, 6 touch bottom; 6, 3 hollow out.

deeply 4 very; 7 greatly; PHRASES: 9 extremely, intensely *UK*, seriously. *See also* **deep**

deep-seated 7 earnest, extreme, intense, serious, sincere; 8 profound; 9 heartfelt; 4-6 deep-rooted.

deface *See* **spoil**

defaced 7 damaged, spoiled; 8 impaired; 10 disfigured.

defamation 4 slur; 5 libel, smear; 7 calumny, obloquy, slander; 10 backbiting, muckraking; 11 denigration, mudslinging; 12 vilification; PHRASES: 5, 8 smear campaign.

defamatory 5 catty, snide; 6 bitchy; 7 abusive, caustic; 8 damaging, libelous, venomous; 9 aspersive, injurious, insulting, offensive; 10 backbiting, blackening, calumnious, derogatory, scandalous, scurrilous, slanderous, tarnishing; 11 besmirching, deprecating, disparaging, insinuating, mudslinging; 12 calumniatory.

defame 5 libel, smear; 6 insult, malign, smirch, vilify; 7 besmear, blacken, slander, tarnish; 8 backbite, besmirch, dishonor, muckrake; 9 denigrate, deprecate, discredit, disparage; 10 calumniate; PHRASES: 3-5 badmouth; 4, 2, 3, 4 stab in the back; 4, 9, 2 cast aspersion on; 5, 3 sling mud, throw mud.

default 5 dodge, evade, lapse, shirk; 6 levant; 7 evasion; 9 avoidance; 10 defaulting, nonpayment; 13 nonappearance, nonattendance; PHRASES: 3, 5 let lapse; 4, 3 duck out.

defeat 4 beat, foil, lick, loss, rout; 5 crush, trump; 6 baffle, master, thrash, thwart; 7 beating, capture, conquer, oppress, retreat, reverse, setback, trounce; 8 collapse, confound, conquest, dominate, downfall, overcome, override, overstep, reversal, suppress, trashing, vanquish; 9 bamboozle, constrain, frustrate, overpower, overthrow, overwhelm, tyrannize, whitewash; 10 overshadow; 11 outdistance, subjugation; PHRASES: 4, 2, 7 lead in triumph; 4, 5 lost cause; 4, 7 lead captive; 4, 8 take prisoner; 5, 4 fatal move; 5, 5 tower above; 6, 4 losing move; 6, 6 narrow ~; 7, 4 prevail over, triumph over.

defeated 6 bested, licked, pipped; 8 outshone, outvoted, trounced; **9** outgunned, outplayed, outwitted; **10** outclassed, outmatched, subjugated; **13** outmaneuvered; PHRASES: **2, 3, 6, 4** on the losing team; **2, 7** in retreat; **3, 2, 3, 7** out of the running; **5, 3** wiped out; **7, 3** knocked out. *See also* **defeat**

defeated (be defeated) 4 lose; **7** retreat; **9** surrender; PHRASES: **4, 2, 1, 7** lose by a whisker; **4, 2, 4** come in last; **4, 5, 4** lose hands down; **6, 6** suffer defeat; **7, 6** concede defeat.

defeatist 5 loser; **8** fatalist, negative, resigned; **9** doomsayer, pessimist; **10** despondent, fatalistic; **11** pessimistic; PHRASES: **4-6** doom-monger.

defecate 4 foul, move, pass, soil, void; **5** expel, purge; **7** excrete; **8** evacuate; PHRASES: **2, 6, 5** be caught short; **5, 3, 6** empty the bowels.

defecation 4 flux; **5** purge; **6** motion; **8** diarrhea, movement, voidance; **9** catharsis, dysentery, excretion, purgation; **10** evacuation; **12** constipation; PHRASES: **3, 4** the runs; **5, 3-4** Aztec two-step; **5, 5** Delhi belly; **5, 8** bowel movement (BM); **7, 6** regular motion.

defect 4 flaw, kink, lack, mark, snag, tear; **5** crack, error, fault, quirk, stain, taint; **6** decamp, desert, foible, lacuna; **7** abscond, failing; **8** loophole, weakness; **9** shortfall; **10** deficiency, difficulty, limitation; **11** shortcoming; **12** disadvantage, imperfection; PHRASES: **4-2** hang-up; **4, 5** weak point; **4, 7** turn traitor; **5, 4** blind spot; **5, 5** loose screw; **6, 4** tragic flaw; **6, 5** change sides; **8, 4** Achilles' heel.

defective 4 weak; **6** broken, failed, faulty, feeble, flawed, marred, spoilt; **7** unsound; **8** inferior, shopworn; **9** blemished, imperfect; **10** inadequate, shopsoiled; **11** substandard, underweight; **14** malfunctioning; PHRASES: **2, 3, 5** on the blink; **3, 2, 5** out of order; **3, 7** not working.

defector 5 rebel; **7** convert, traitor; **8** apostate, renegade, turncoat.

defenceless *See* **unprotected**

defend 4 back, ward; **5** guard, watch; **6** police, secure, shield, uphold; **7** endorse, protect, support; **8** champion, preserve; **9** represent, safeguard; PHRASES: **5, 2, 3** stand up for.

defended 6 moated, walled; **7** armored,

secured; **8** ironclad; **9** accouterd, fortified, palisaded, panoplied, protected; **10** barricaded; **11** castellated; PHRASES: **4-4** mailclad; **5-5** heavy-armed; **5-6** armor-plated.

defender 5 guard; **6** backer, knight, minder *UK*, patron, warden; **7** bouncer, paladin, sponsor; **8** advocate, champion, guardian, upholder; **9** bodyguard, protector, supporter; PHRASES: **5, 6** white knight; **6, 6** knight errant; **8, 5** Guardian Angel.

defending 8 excusing, tutelary; **9** defensive, resisting; **10** challenged, protective; **11** extenuating, vindicating; PHRASES: **2, 3, 9** on the defensive; **2, 5** on guard.

defense 5 alibi, cover, guard, truth; **6** excuse, reason, safety, shield; **7** apology, grounds; **8** argument, firewall, fortress, rebuttal, security; **9** reasoning, rejoinder; **10** mitigation, palliation, protection, refutation, resistance, validation; **11** explanation, extenuation, safekeeping, vindication; **12** preservation, safeguarding; **13** corroboration, justification, qualification, recrimination; **15** counterargument; PHRASES: **3-2-3, 7** man-to-man ~; **3, 5, 4** the front four; **3, 9** the defensive; **4, 5** just cause; **4, 7** zone ~; **5, 7** legal ~; **7, 5** Chinese walls *UK*.

defensive 4 wary; **6** touchy; **7** armored, hostile; **8** cautious, watchful; **9** defending, resistant; **10** apologetic, protective; **11** distrustful.

defensive (be defensive) 4, 3, 1, 4 play for a draw.

defensiveness 7 shyness; **11** nervousness. *See also* **defensive**

defer 5 delay; **6** submit; **8** postpone; **10** reschedule; PHRASES: **2, 11** be deferential; **3, 2** bow to; **3, 3** put off; **3, 4** put back.

deference 3 awe; **6** esteem, homage, regard; **7** fawning, respect; **8** glibness, toadying; **9** kowtowing, obeisance, reverence; **10** admiration, compliance, sycophancy; **12** complaisance, ingratiation; **13** condescension; **14** obsequiousness, submissiveness; PHRASES: **8, 4, 3** touching one's cap; **8, 5** currying favor.

deferential 4 glib, oily, smug; **5** slimy; **6** bowing; **7** fulsome, nodding; **8** obeisant, reverent, unctuous; **9** compliant, courteous; **10** obsequious, respectful, submissive; **11** complaisant, sycophantic; **12** ingratiating; **13** condescending.

defer to 3 bow, nod; **5** kneel; **6** curtsy,

kowtow; **10** condescend; PHRASES: **3, 2, 2** lay it on; **3, 6** pay homage; **3, 8** pay respects; **4, 2** fawn on; **4, 4, 3** doff one's cap.

defiance **3** lip; **4** neck; **5** cheek, nerve, sauce; **6** bottle, daring; **7** bluster, bravado, bravura, courage; **8** audacity, backtalk, boldness, chutzpah, pertness, temerity; **9** arrogance, brashness, cockiness, impudence, insolence, nerviness; **10** brazenness, cheekiness, effrontery; **11** presumption; **12** belligerence, contrariness, impertinence, insurrection; **13** bumptiousness, shamelessness; **14** noncooperation, rebelliousness; **15** insubordination; PHRASES: **4, 4** back talk; **4, 5** bold front; **4-9** self-assurance; **5, 4** brave face, rebel yell; **9, 4** answering back; **10, 5** opposition rally.

defiant **4** bold; **5** brash, cocky, nervy, sassy, saucy; **6** brassy, brazen, cheeky, daring; **7** assured; **8** arrogant, impudent, insolent, militant; **9** assertive, audacious, bellicose, bumptious, obstinate, unabashed; **10** courageous, disdainful, rebellious; **11** belligerent, challenging, disobedient, impertinent, provocative; **12** antagonistic, contemptuous, recalcitrant; **13** insubordinate; PHRASES: **4, 2, 5** bold as brass; **4-7** self-assured; **5-6** stiff-necked.

defiantly **6** pertly; **10** derisively, recklessly, stubbornly; **11** insultingly, offensively, shamelessly; **12** emphatically; **14** presumptuously; PHRASES: **2, 1, 4** as a dare; **2, 3, 4, 2** in the face of; **2, 3, 5, 2** in the teeth of; **2, 4, 4** to one's face; **7, 5** without shame. *See also* **defiant**

deficiency **4** flaw, lack; **5** fault; **6** dearth, defect; **7** absence, deficit, failing, paucity; **8** scarcity, shortage, weakness; **9** shortfall; **10** faultiness, impairment, inadequacy; **11** shortcoming; **12** disadvantage, imperfection; **13** deterioration, insufficiency.

deficient **4** poor; **5** short; **6** faulty, flawed; **7** lacking; **9** defective; **10** inadequate; **13** underprovided, undersupplied; **14** unsatisfactory.

deficit *See* **shortfall**

defile **5** spoil, sully, taint; **6** debase; **7** corrupt, degrade, pollute, profane, tarnish, violate; **8** besmirch, dishonor; **9** desecrate; **11** contaminate.

define **4** name; **6** detail; **7** delimit, explain, outline, specify; **8** describe; **9** delineate, demarcate; **11** distinguish; **12** characterize; PHRASES: **4, 3** mark out.

definite **4** sure; **5** exact, fixed, known; **6** agreed, stated; **7** assured, certain, settled; **8** absolute, specific; **10** determined, recognized, undisputed, unshakable; **11** categorical, indubitable, unambiguous, unequivocal; **12** indisputable, unmistakable; **14** unquestionable; PHRASES: **3-2** set-on; **4-7** well-defined; **5-3** clear-cut.

definiteness **8** finality; **9** certainty; **10** conviction; **13** determination; **14** indubitability. *See also* **definite**

definition **5** focus; **7** clarity, meaning; **9** clearness, sharpness; **11** description, explanation; **12** distinctness; **14** classification.

definitive **4** best; **5** final; **7** classic, perfect; **8** absolute, decisive, ultimate; **10** conclusive; **13** authoritative.

deflate **5** quash; **6** humble, reduce, shrink, squash, subdue; **7** depress, devalue, flatten; **8** belittle, collapse, decrease, dispirit, puncture; **9** humiliate; **10** depreciate, disappoint; PHRASES: **2, 4** go down; **3, 3, 3, 3** let the air out; **3, 4** cut back, cut down, let down *UK*, put down.

deflation **8** collapse, decrease; **9** reduction, shrinking; **10** depression; **11** devaluation; **12** depreciation.

deflect **4** bend, stop; **5** avert, crush, repel; **6** glance; **7** diverge, prevent, refract; **8** diffract, disperse, redirect, ricochet; **9** sidetrack; PHRASES: **3, 2, 3, 3** nip in the bud; **4, 3** head off, ward off; **4, 4, 4** wean away from; **4, 5** turn aside.

deflection **4** bend; **5** parry; **6** glance, swerve; **7** defense, rebound; **8** ricochet; **9** diversion; **10** resistance.

deform **4** warp, weal, welt; **5** stain, twist, wheal *UK*; **6** buckle, damage, deface, impair; **7** blemish, distort, malform; **8** misshape, pockmark; **9** cicatrize, disfigure.

deformation **7** bending, rupture, sliding, torsion; **8** fracture; **9** corrosion; **10** distortion, elongation; **11** compression, instability.

deformed **5** bowed; **6** maimed, marked, pitted, ruined, warped; **7** buckled, crooked, damaged, defaced, twisted; **8** shrunken; **9** blemished, contorted, corrupted, distorted, imperfect, malformed, misshapen, mutilated; **10** disfigured; PHRASES: **3-4** ill-made.

deformity **4** mark, weal, welt; **5** stain, wheal *UK*; **7** blemish; **8** mutation; **10** defacement, distortion; **12** imperfection, irregularity, malformation; **13** disfigurement, misshapenness.

defraud **3** con, fix, gyp, rob; **4** dupe, fake, hoax, scam; **5** cheat, forge, screw, steal, sting *UK*, trick; **6** fiddle, fleece, juggle, pilfer; **7** deceive, falsify, swindle; **8** embezzle, flimflam, shoplift; **9** racketeer, whitewash; **10** adulterate; **11** counterfeit; PHRASES: **3, 3** rip off; **4, 9, 2** take advantage of; **5-6** shortchange.

defray **3** pay; **4** fund; **5** cover, stand, treat; **6** donate; **7** finance; **8** bankroll; **10** contribute; PHRASES: **3, 3, 5** pay the piper; **3, 3, 7** pay the freight; **4, 2, 3, 4** pick up the bill; **4, 3, 4** bear the cost, foot the bill, meet the cost; **5, 3, 4** stand the cost.

defunct **4** dead, gone; **7** expired, extinct, invalid; **8** deceased, obsolete, outdated; **9** redundant.

defy **5** flout; **6** oppose, resist; **7** affront, bluster, disobey, protest; **8** confront, outstare; **9** challenge, disregard, withstand; **10** contravene; PHRASES: **3, 2, 3, 4, 2** fly in the face of; **3, 3, 8** run the gauntlet; **3, 8, 2** bid defiance to; **4, 1, 5** cock a snook; **4, 4** crow over; **4, 4, 5** bare one's teeth, call one's bluff; **4, 8** have chutzpah; **5, 2, 2** stand up to.

degenerate **4** fall, sink, slip; **6** wicked, worsen; **7** corrupt, debased, immoral, relapse; **8** collapse, decadent; **9** debauched, perverted; **11** deteriorate.

degeneration **5** decay; **9** decadence, worsening; **13** deterioration; **14** disintegration.

degradation **4** ruin; **5** filth, shame; **6** infamy, misery; **7** poverty, squalor; **8** disgrace; **11** deprivation, humiliation; **12** dilapidation; **13** mortification.

degraded **6** shamed; **7** debased, demoted; **8** demeaned, downcast; **9** corrupted, depressed, disgraced, kowtowing; **10** decomposed, downgraded, humiliated; **11** deferential.

degree **4** rate; **5** depth, grade, level, pitch, point, range, scale, scope; **6** amount, extent, height; **7** caliber; **9** gradation, intensity, magnitude.

degree (to a degree) **4** very; **5** quite; **6** fairly, pretty, rather; **8** scarcely, slightly *UK*, somewhat; **9** extremely; PHRASES: **1, 3** a bit; **1, 6** a little; **2, 1, 3** in a way; **2, 1, 5, 6** to a great degree, to a small degree; **2, 1, 7** in a measure; **2, 4, 6** to some degree, to some extent; **2, 4, 7** in some measure; **4, 2** kind of, sort of.

degrees (by degrees) **6** slowly; **8** inchmeal; **9** gradually, piecemeal; **12** decreasingly, increasingly; **13** progressively; PHRASES: **1, 6, 2, 1, 4** a little at a time; **2, 6** by inches, by stages; **3, 2, 3** bit by bit; **4, 2, 4** drop by drop, inch by inch, step by step; **4, 3, 4** less and less, more and more; **6, 2, 6** little by little; **6, 3, 6** slowly but surely.

dehydrate **3** dry; **5** drain, parch; **8** vaporize; **9** anhydrate, desiccate, evaporate, exsiccate; **10** dehumidify; PHRASES: **3-3** air-dry; **6-3** freeze-dry.

deification **8** sainting; **9** adulation, elevation; **10** apotheosis, assumption, exaltation; **11** idolization, lionization; **12** angelization, canonization, divinization, enshrinement; **13** beatification, glorification, magnification, santification; **15** immortalization.

deify **5** bless, exalt; **7** adulate, beatify, elevate, glorify, idolize, magnify, worship; **8** angelize, canonize, divinize, enshrine, sanctify, venerate; **11** apotheosize, immortalize.

deity **3** god; **4** deva, devi, idol, mana *UK*, muse; **5** dryad, naiad, numen, nymph, satyr, totem, wakan; **6** daemon, fetish, genius, Nereid, pokunt, spirit, undine; **7** demigod, goddess, godhead, manitou; **8** divinity, immortal, tamanoas; PHRASES: **3, 9** the Olympians.

dejected *See* **unhappy**

dejection *See* **sadness**

Delaware **2** DE; **5** Dover (capital); PHRASES: **4, 3, 7** blue hen chicken (bird); **5, 5, 5, 6, 4, 3, 5** First State, Small Wonder, Blue Hen State (nickname); **5, 7** peach blossom (flower); **7, 3, 12** Liberty and Independence (motto); **7, 5** Diamond state (nickname); **8, 5** American holly (tree).

delay **3** lag; **4** halt, hold; **5** block, defer, pause, stall; **6** dawdle, detain, extend, hinder, holdup, impede, linger, retard; **7** adjourn, prolong; **8** deferral, hesitate, interval, obstruct, postpone, prorogue, protract, restrain, shelving, stoppage, withhold; **9** deferment, detention, hindrance, stonewall; **10** filibuster, moratorium, pigeonhole; **12** dilatoriness, intermission, interruption, postponement; **13** procrastinate; **15** procrastination; PHRASES: **3, 2, 3** put on ice; **3, 2, 4** put on hold; **3, 3** put off; **3, 4** buy time, put back, red tape, set back; **4, 2** hang on, hold on, hold up, slow up; **4, 3** spin out; **4, 3, 3** wait and see; **4, 3, 4** hold the line, play for time; **4, 3, 5** keep for later; **4, 4** gain time, hang back, hold back, hold over, slow down; **4, 4, 4** bide one's time; **5, 2** stand by; **5, 2, 2** sleep on it; **5-5** dilly-dally; **6, 1, 6** create a logjam; **6, 8** mañana attitude.

delay (with delay) 10 contrarily; **11** defensively, intrusively, unhelpfully, unwillingly; **12** dissuasively, preclusively, preventively, repressively; **13** obstructively, prohibitively, restrictively; **14** discouragingly; **15** counteractively, uncooperatively; PHRASES: **4, 4, 3** with much ado; **7, 4** without help.

delayed 4 late; **5** stuck, tardy; **6** behind; **7** checked, impeded, overdue; **8** dallying, dawdling, deferred, detained, hindered, retarded; **9** postponed; **10** hysteretic, tardigrade; **12** lollygagging; **15** shillyshallying; PHRASES: **5-8** dilly-dallying; **6, 2** caught up; **6, 8** behind schedule.

delectable 5 tasty; **8** adorable, charming, heavenly, luscious; **9** appealing, delicious; **10** appetizing, delightful; **13** mouthwatering.

delegate 5 agent, allot, clerk, elect, envoy, order; **6** assign, charge, consul, depute, deputy, invest, legate, Senate; **7** appoint, consign, devolve, empower, entrust, install, instate, nominee; **8** accredit, allocate, deputize, diplomat, emissary, minister, nominate, transfer; **9** appointee, authorize, councilor, designate, messenger, patronize; **10** ambassador, commission, inaugurate, negotiator; **11** Congressman; **12** commissioner, decentralize; **13** Congresswoman; **14** representative; **15** Parliamentarian; PHRASES: **3-5** job-share; **4, 3** farm out; **4, 4** hand over; **4, 4, 2** turn over to; **6, 3, 4** spread the load; **7, 6** cabinet member.

delegation 7 mission; **10** allocation, assignment, commission, deputation, deputizing, devolution, nomination; **11** appointment, devolvement, entrustment; **12** consignation; **13** authorization; PHRASES: **3, 7** job sharing; **6, 3** giving out; **7, 2** passing on; **7, 4** handing over.

delete *See* **erase**

deliberate 4 muse, wary; **5** study, think; **6** ponder, willed; **7** advised, careful, devised, planned, reflect, studied, weighed; **8** cautious, consider, designed, measured; **9**

conscious, contrived; **10** calculated, considered, controlled, meditative, methodical, preplanned; **11** intentional; **12** aforethought, premeditated; **14** preestablished; PHRASES: **3-2** put-up, set-up; **4, 4** mull over; **5, 2** weigh up *UK*; **5, 5** think about.

deliberation 4 care; **6** debate; **7** thought; **8** planning; **9** pondering; **10** discussion; **11** calculation, forethought; **13** consideration, premeditation; PHRASES: **8, 7** abstract thought.

delicacy 4 care, tact; **5** charm, grace, skill, treat; **6** dainty, luxury, tidbit; **7** frailty; **8** deftness, elegance, fineness, subtlety, weakness; **9** diplomacy, fragility, precision; **10** adroitness, flimsiness, refinement; **11** sensitivity, slenderness; **12** gracefulness; **13** consideration; **14** attractiveness, fastidiousness.

delicate 4 deft, fine, pale, soft, weak; **5** faint, frail; **6** adroit, dainty, flimsy, gentle, slight, subtle, tricky; **7** awkward, elegant, fragile, refined, slender; **8** finespun, graceful; **9** sensitive; **10** fastidious; **13** insubstantial, uncomfortable; PHRASES: **4-4** thin-spun; **4-5** fine-drawn.

delicious 5 tasty; **6** lovely; **8** luscious, pleasant; **9** enjoyable, wonderful; **10** appetizing, delectable, delightful.

delight 3 joy; **4** glee; **5** amuse, charm, enjoy; **6** please, relish, thrill; **7** gratify; **8** pleasure; **9** enjoyment, happiness; **10** appreciate; PHRASES: **5, 2** revel in.

delightful 6 lovely; **7** Elysian; **8** charming, gorgeous, heavenly, pleasant; **9** agreeable, marvelous; **10** enchanting, entrancing; **11** captivating; **12** enthrallling; PHRASES: **3, 2, 4, 5** out of this world.

delineate 6 define; **7** delimit, explain, outline, portray; **8** describe; **9** demarcate; PHRASES: **4, 3** mark out.

delinquent 5 felon; **8** aberrant, careless, criminal, reckless; **9** felonious, negligent, offending, wrongdoer; **10** antisocial, lawbreaker, neglectful; **13** irresponsible; PHRASES: **6, 5** guilty party.

delirious 3 hot; **6** elated; **7** excited, fevered; **8** ecstatic, feverish, rambling; **11** transported; **13** hallucinating; PHRASES: **6, 8** beside yourself.

delirium 5 fever; **6** fervor, frenzy; **7** ecstasy, elation; **8** euphoria; **9** confusion; **10** excitement; **12** restlessness; **13** hallucination.

deliver 4 free, give, save, send; 5 bring, carry, serve, untie; 6 acquit, convey, exempt, redeem, rescue, supply, unbind, unlock; 7 consign, furnish, present, produce, provide, recover, release, relieve, restore, salvage; 8 liberate, reprieve, retrieve, unburden, unfetter; 9 disburden, extricate, surrender, transport; 10 distribute, emancipate, relinquish; 11 disencumber; PHRASES: 3, 3 buy off, get off, get out, let off, let out; 3, 4 set free; 4, 2, 3, 4 save by the bell; 4, 2, 3, 6 come to the rescue; 4, 3 bail out; 4, 4 save from; 7, 4 declare free; 8, 4 dispense with.

deliverable 8 salvable, saveable; 9 rescuable; 10 extricable, redeemable; 11 salvageable; PHRASES: 3, 3, 7 fit for release.

deliverance 6 escape, ransom, relief, rescue, saving; 7 amnesty, freedom, release, respite, salvage; 8 delivery, recovery, reprieve; 9 acquittal, reprieval, retrieval, salvation; 10 extraction, liberation, redemption; 11 extrication, restoration; 12 dispensation, emancipation; 15 disencumberment; PHRASES: 3, 2, 5 day of grace; 3-3 let-off, let-out *UK*.

deliverer 6 savior; 7 rescuer; 8 redeemer; 9 liberator; 11 emancipator; PHRASES: 4-5 life-saver.

delivery 6 flight, manner, rescue, supply; 7 release, sending; 8 approach, transfer; 9 technique, transport *UK*; 10 conveyance, liberation; 11 deliverance; 12 distribution, presentation; 14 transportation.

delude 3 con; 4 dupe, fool; 5 cheat, trick; 7 deceive, mislead; 8 hoodwink; PHRASES: 4, 1, 4 spin a yarn; 4, 2 take in.

deluge 4 bury, soak; 5 drown, flood, spate, swamp; 7 cascade, overrun, torrent, upsurge; 8 downpour, inundate, overload; 9 avalanche, overwhelm, rainstorm; 10 cloudburst.

delusion 5 craze, mania; 6 frenzy, mirage, vision; 7 fallacy, fantasy, mistake, ravings; 8 delirium, hysteria, illusion, paranoia; 9 fetishism, misbelief, obsession; 10 aberration, compulsion; 12 hypochondria, onomatomania; 13 hallucination, misconception; 15 misapprehension; PHRASES: 4-9 self-deception; 5, 1, 4 folie à deux; 5, 10 false impression; 6, 5 trompe l'oeil; 7, 2, 4 sleight of hand; 8, 7 delirium tremens.

delve 3 dig; 4 hunt; 5 probe; 6 burrow, search, tunnel; 7 explore, rummage, scratch; 8 research, scrabble; 11 investigate; PHRASES: 4, 4 look into.

demand 3 ask, tax; 4 bill, levy, need, plea, want, writ; 5 claim, order, plead, query; 6 extort, impose, insist, notice, summon; 7 command, mandate, request, require, summons, warrant; 8 exaction, mittimus, petition, subpoena; 9 challenge, extortion, interdict, necessity, stipulate, ultimatum; 10 injunction; 11 necessitate, requirement, requisition; PHRASES: 3, 4 lay upon; 3, 4, 4, 4 put one's foot down; 4, 2, 7 writ of summons; 4, 3 call for; 4, 3, 4 beck and call; 5, 1, 7 issue a warrant; 5, 2 order up; 5, 3 press for; 5, 7 bleed someone, final warning; 6, 2 insist on; 7, 2, 6 warrant of arrest.

demanding 4 hard; 5 needy, tough; 6 taxing, trying; 7 arduous, exigent; 8 exacting, forcible, pressing; 9 difficult, extorting, extortive, insistent; 10 imperative, injunctive, persistent, threatened; 11 blackmailed, challenging, threatening; 12 blackmailing.

dematerialize 6 vanish; 9 disembody; 12 disincarnate, spiritualize; 13 immaterialize.

demented 4 wild; 5 crazy, manic; 7 frantic; 8 frenzied; 10 irrational.

demise 3 end; 4 ruin; 5 death; 6 expiry; 7 decease; 8 downfall; 10 expiration *UK*; 11 termination.

demo 4 show; 5 march; 6 sample; 7 display, example, protest; 8 specimen; 9 showpiece; 10 exhibition; 12 demonstrator, presentation; 13 demonstration; PHRASES: 7, 5 protest march, protest rally.

democracy 8 equality, republic; 9 consensus; 13 classlessness; 14 egalitarianism; PHRASES: 6, 8 social equality.

democrat 3 Dem; 4 Dino; 8 populist; 9 Dixiecrat; 10 republican; 11 egalitarian; PHRASES: 6, 8 social ~.

Democrat 3 FDR, JFK; 4 Gore (Al), Polk (James Knox); 5 Kerry (John); 6 Carter (Jimmy), donkey, Pierce (Franklin), Truman (Harry S.), Wilson (Woodrow); 7 Clinton (Bill), Dukakis (Michael), Edwards (John), Jackson (Andrew), Jackson (Jesse), Johnson (Lyndon), Kennedy (John F.), Kennedy (Ted); 8 Buchanan (James); 9 Cleveland (Grover), Jefferson (Thomas), Roosevelt (Franklin Delano); PHRASES: 3, 4 New Deal; 3, 5 Van Buren (Martin); 8-10 Democrat-Republican.

demoiselle 6 damsel; 9 damselfly; 10 damselfish.

demolish 3 eat, ram; 4 beat, bomb, fell, pulp, raze, ruin; 5 blast, blitz, crush, grind, level, scoff, shred, smash, trash, wreck; 6 batter, devour, ravage, thrash, topple; 7 atomize, bombard, butcher, consume, destroy, flatten, shatter, subvert, trounce; 8 bulldoze, disprove; 9 dismantle, overthrow, pulverize, slaughter; 10 annihilate; 11 steamroller; PHRASES: 3, 4 cut down, mow down; 4, 2 blow up; 4, 2, 3, 6 raze to the ground; 4, 2, 4 blow to bits, take to bits, tear to bits, tear to rags; 4, 2, 6 pick to pieces, pull to pieces, take to pieces, tear to pieces, tear to shreds; 4, 4 beat down, blow away, blow down, kick over, pull down, tear down; 4, 5 pull apart, take apart, tear apart; 4, 6, 4 turn upside down; 4, 7 rend asunder; 4, 9, 2 make mincemeat of; 5, 2 break up, smash up; 5, 2, 4 grind to dust; 5, 2, 6 crush to pieces; 5, 9 grind underfoot.

demolition See **destruction**

demonetize 6 debase; 7 devalue; 10 depreciate.

demonstrability 11 provability; 13 verifiability; 14 accountability, confirmability.

demonstrable 6 patent; 7 certain, evident, obvious; 8 apparent, definite, distinct, palpable, provable; 10 attestable, conclusive, undeniable, verifiable; 11 discernible, perceptible, perspicuous; 12 indisputable; 14 unquestionable; PHRASES: 4-7 self-evident; 5-3 clear-cut.

demonstrably 11 accountably, justifiably; 12 exegetically, indicatively. See also **demonstrable**

demonstrate 4 show; 5 lobby, march, prove, rally; 6 expose, parade, reveal; 7 display, exhibit, explain, expound, perform, protest; 8 brandish; 9 determine, establish, exemplify; PHRASES: 4, 3 roll out, show off; 4, 5 make plain; 4, 7 make evident.

demonstration 4 demo, expo, show; 5 march, proof, rally; 6 picket, sample, strike; 7 boycott, display, example, protest; 8 specimen; 9 showpiece; 10 exhibition, exposition; 11 explanation; 12 presentation; 13 manifestation; PHRASES: 3-2 sit-in; 4-2 work-in UK; 5-2 sleep-in.

demonstrative 4 open, warm; 5 frank, showy; 6 candid, flashy, loving; 8 dramatic, effusive, friendly; 9 emotional, expansive; 10 expressive, flamboyant, histrionic, theatrical; 12 affectionate, ostentatious; 13 exhibitionist.

demonstrativeness 6 candor; 9 dramatics, theatrics; 11 flamboyance, histrionics, ostentation; 12 emotionalism; 13 exhibitionism. See also **demonstrative**

demonstrator 5 tutor; 7 marcher, showman, teacher, trainer; 8 activist, lecturer, lobbyist; 9 announcer, exegetist, expositor, expounder, presenter UK, protester, supporter; 10 campaigner, instructor; 11 illustrator; PHRASES: 4-3 show-off.

demur See **object**

demure 3 coy, shy; 4 prim; 6 modest, sedate; 7 prudish; 8 decorous, reserved.

den 4 drey, lair, nest, sett; 5 aerie, haunt, study; 6 burrow, tunnel, warren; 7 retreat.

denial 7 dissent, refusal; 8 apostasy, negation, rebuttal; 9 disavowal, recusance, rejection; 10 abnegation, disclaimer, disownment, refutation, withdrawal; 11 confutation, recantation, repudiation; 12 denunciation, renunciation; 14 disaffirmation.

denigrate 5 abuse, libel; 6 defame, vilify; 7 degrade, slander; 8 belittle; 9 disparage; 10 stigmatize; PHRASES: 4, 5, 2 pour scorn on.

denizen See **inhabitant**

denote 4 mean; 5 imply; 6 convey; 7 express, signify; 9 represent, symbolize; PHRASES: 5, 2 refer to; 5, 3 stand for; 6, 2 allude to.

denouement See **ending**

denounce 5 blame; 6 accuse, charge, inform; 7 censure, condemn, deplore; 9 criticize, deprecate.

dense 4 dark, deep, firm, full; 5 bushy, close, heavy, solid, thick; 6 jammed, massed, packed; 7 clotted, compact, complex, crowded, intense, obscure, serried, styptic, teeming, viscous, weighty; 8 cohesive, involved, thickset; 9 condensed, congealed, difficult, thickened; 10 compressed, consistent, impervious, monolithic; 11 complicated, impermeable, indivisible, infrangible, inseparable, intensified; 12 constrictive, impenetrable; 14 incompressible; PHRASES: 3-6 jam-packed; 4-6 firm-packed, full-bodied; 5-1-5 chock-a-block; 5-4 close-knit; 5-5 close-woven; 5-6 close-packed; 5-7 thick-growing; 6, 2 packed in; 6-4 boiled-down.

dense (become dense) 3 set; 4 cake, clot; 5 crust; 6 cement, cohere, freeze, harden, ossify; 7 congeal, densify, petrify, thicken; 8 condense, solidify; 9 coagulate, fossilize; 10 gelatinize, inspissate; 11 consolidate, crystallize, precipitate; 12 conglomerate.

dense (make dense) 4 bind, cram, mass, pack; 7 compact, squeeze; 8 compress; 11 concentrate; PHRASES: 4, 2 firm up; 4, 7 load tightly; 7, 2 squeeze in.

density 5 depth; 7 opacity; 8 solidity; 9 closeness, heaviness, intensity, obscurity, thickness, tightness; 10 complexity, difficulty; 11 coagulation, compression, congealment, crowdedness; 15 impenetrability.

dent 3 dip, hit; 4 blow, bump, dint, hole, mark; 5 knock, stamp; 6 damage, dimple, hollow, indent, lessen, reduce; 7 blemish, impress, imprint; 8 diminish; 9 concavity, reduction; 10 depression, impression; 11 indentation.

dentistry 10 exodontics; 11 endodontics; 12 orthodontics, periodontics; 14 periodontology, prosthodontics; PHRASES: 4, 7 oral surgery; 4, 9 oral pathology; 6, 7 dental surgery.

Denver boot 4 lock; 11 immobilizer; PHRASES: 5, 5 wheel clamp *UK*.

deny 5 argue, block, forgo; 6 abjure, disown, forbid, naysay, negate, oppose, recant, refuse, refute, reject, repugn; 7 decline, disavow, dispute, gainsay, prevent; 8 abnegate, disallow, disclaim, forswear, renounce; 9 disaffirm, repudiate; 10 contradict, contravene, controvert; PHRASES: 4, 4 turn down; 5, 2, 3, 3 stand in the way.

deodorant 9 fumigator; 10 deodorizer, ventilator; 12 disinfectant; PHRASES: 3, 6 air filter; 3, 8 air purifier; 3, 9 air freshener; 4-10 anti-perspirant.

deodorize 5 scent; 7 cleanse, freshen, perfume, refresh; 8 fumigate; 9 aromatize, disinfect, fragrance.

depart 2 go; 3 die; 4 exit, flee, quit; 5 leave, sally, stray; 6 decamp, differ, escape, expire, perish, retire; 7 decease, deviate, digress, diverge, retreat, scarper *UK*, vamoose; 8 withdraw; 9 disappear; PHRASES: 2, 1, 6 do a runner; 2, 3 be off; 2, 3, 2 up and go;

3, 3 bow out, set off, set out; 3, 4 get away, run away; 3, 5 get along, set forth; 4, 2 pass on; 4, 3 head off, move off, pull out, push off; 4, 4 melt away, pass away, slip away, stay away, walk away; 4, 5 gang along, play hooky, take leave, trot along; 4, 6 make tracks, play truant; 5, 3 clear off *UK*, fling off, slink off, slope off *UK*, stamp off, start out, storm out; 6, 4, 4 ~ this life; 6, 5 toddle along.

departed 4 dead, gone, late; 7 defunct; 8 deceased, lifeless.

departing 4 last; 5 final; 7 leaving, parting, retreat; 10 withdrawal; 11 leavetaking, valedictory.

department 4 area; 5 realm; 6 branch, sector, sphere; 7 section; 8 division; 9 specialty; 10 speciality *UK*; 11 subdivision; 14 responsibility.

departure 4 exit; 6 change, egress, escape, exodus, flight; 7 getaway, leaving, parting; 9 deviation, elopement, migration, variation; 10 decampment, difference, digression, divergence, emigration, withdrawal; 11 abandonment, remigration; PHRASES: 5-6 leave-taking.

departure (place of departure) 4 dock, gate, port; 7 airport, station; 11 springboard; PHRASES: 3, 4 bus stop; 3, 7 bus station; 7-3, 5 jumping-off point; 7, 7 railway station; 8, 7 railroad station.

dependable *See* **reliable**

dependency 4 need; 5 habit; 6 colony; 7 adjunct; 8 reliance; 9 addiction, territory; 10 dependence; PHRASES: 9, 5 dependent state.

dependent 4 ward; 5 child, needy; 6 charge, junior, orphan; 7 needful, protégé, reliant, subject; 8 follower, helpless, parasite; 9 satellite, supported; 10 contingent; 11 conditional; PHRASES: 2, 3, 5, 2 at the mercy of; 2, 4, 2 in need of; 6, 2 hooked on; 6-2 hanger-on; 7, 2 reliant on, subject to.

deplorable 5 awful; 6 woeful; 7 pitiful; 8 terrible; 9 appalling, execrable; 10 lamentable; 11 disgraceful; 12 unacceptable.

deplore 3 rue; 6 bemoan, lament, regret; 7 censure, condemn; 9 criticize, deprecate; 10 disapprove; PHRASES: 2, 5 be sorry.

deploy 3 use; 5 adopt; 6 employ; 7 arrange, utilize; 8 position; 9 implement; PHRASES: 3, 2 set up; 3, 3 set out.

depopulate 5 clear; 6 remove; 8 depeople, desolate, evacuate, unpeople; 9 dispeople.

deport *See* **expel**

depose *See* **overthrow**

deposit 3 mud, put; 4 drop, silt; 5 layer, leave, place; 6 pledge, surety; 7 buildup, payment, residue; 8 security, sediment; 9 accretion, guarantee; 12 accumulation; PHRASES: 3, 2 pay in, put in; 3, 4 lay down, put down, set down; 3, 5 the black; 4, 2 pile up; 4, 2, 3, 5 stay in the black; 5, 2 build up; 5-4, 5 right-hand entry; 5, 6 leave behind.

deposition 7 buildup, ousting, removal, silting; 9 accretion, admission, overthrow, statement, testimony, unseating; 10 confession; 12 accumulation, dethronement; 13 sedimentation; PHRASES: 5, 9 sworn testimony.

depositor 5 saver; 7 hoarder; 8 creditor, investor.

depot 4 quay, yard; 5 wharf; 6 garage, siding; 8 entrepot; 9 warehouse.

deprecate 7 censure, condemn, deplore; 8 denounce; 9 denigrate.

depreciate 4 drop, fall; 6 lessen; 7 decline, deflate, devalue; 8 decrease; 9 denigrate, disparage; PHRASES: 3, 4 run down.

depreciation 4 drop, fall; 7 decline; 8 decrease; 9 reduction; 11 devaluation, downgrading.

depredation 6 attack; 7 pillage, plunder; 11 destruction; 12 despoliation.

depress 4 push; 5 lower, press; 6 dampen, sadden, squash; 8 dispirit; 10 demoralize, disappoint, discourage, dishearten; PHRASES: 4, 4, 5, 2 pour cold water on.

depressed 3 low, sad; 4 blue, down, glum, gray, sunk; 5 moody; 6 dreary, gloomy, moping, morose, pushed; 7 joyless, killjoy, rundown, unhappy; 8 dejected, downcast, listless, suicidal; 9 flattened, miserable, neglected; 10 despondent, dispirited, lackluster, lugubrious, melancholy, miseryguts, spoilsport; 11 atrabilious, melancholic; 12 disheartened; PHRASES: 2, 1, 5, 4 in a black hole; 2, 3, 6 in the depths; 2, 3, 8 in the doldrums; 3, 2, 5 out of sorts; 3, 7 wet blanket; 4, 2, 3, 5 down in the dumps; 4-5 long-faced.

depression 3 dip, pit; 4 cove, dent, gulf, hole, vale, well; 5 fosse, gloom, gully, inlet, slump; 6 apathy, cavern, cavity, crater, dimple, hollow, indent, misery, quarry, trench, trough; 7 decline, despair, lowness, malaise, sadness; 8 crevasse, downturn, glumness, lethargy; 9 concavity, dejection; 10 dreariness, gloominess, impression, melancholy; 11 despondency, indentation, joylessness, melancholia; 12 dejectedness; 13 cheerlessness; 14 dispiritedness; 15 downheartedness; PHRASES: 3, 5 the blues, the dumps; 3, 7 low spirits; 3, 8 the doldrums; 5, 7 black despair.

deprivation 4 lack; 6 denial; 7 deficit, poverty; 10 deficiency, withdrawal.

depth 4 drop, fall; 6 extent, wisdom; 7 gravity, sinkage; 8 deepness, distance, strength; 9 immersion, intensity; 10 complexity, profundity; 11 seriousness; 13 cavernousness; 14 bottomlessness, fathomlessness.

deputize 3 sub; 7 appoint, empower, entrust; 8 delegate, nominate; 9 authorize, designate; 10 commission, substitute; PHRASES: 4, 2 fill in; 5, 2 stand in.

deputy 4 aide; 5 agent, locum; 6 backup, helper, nuncio; 7 reserve; 8 delegate; 9 assistant, auxiliary, messenger, secretary, spokesman, supporter; 10 lieutenant, propraetor, substitute, understudy, viceregent; 11 replacement, spokeswoman; 12 spokesperson; 14 representative; PHRASES: 4-3 stop-gap; 4, 6 girl Friday, vice consul; 4, 7 vice admiral; 4, 8 vice chairman; 4, 9 vice president; 4, 10 vice chancellor; 5-2 stand-in; 5-4, 3 right-hand man; 6-2-7 second-in-command; 6, 3 number two; 6, 6 relief worker; 7, 3 twelfth man *UK*; 8, 5 éminence grise.

derange 5 shock, spoil, upset, wreck; 6 derail; 7 disturb, unhinge; 8 disorder, distress, unsettle; 9 unbalance; PHRASES: 5, 2, 3, 4 drive up the wall; 5, 3 drive mad; 5, 6 drive insane.

deranged 3 mad; 6 insane; 8 demented, neurotic, unhinged, unstable; 9 disturbed, psychotic; 10 disordered, unbalanced; 11 maladjusted; PHRASES: 3, 2, 5 out to lunch; 3, 4 off one's head; 4-2 hung-up; 6, 3, 4 around the bend.

derangement 6 muddle; 7 madness; 8 disorder, insanity; 11 disturbance, instability; 13 irrationality.

derelict *See* **dilapidated**

deride 4 mock; 5 knock, scoff, scorn; 6 debunk; 7 deflate, disdain, lampoon, pillary, snicker; **8** ridicule, satirize; **9** disparage; **10** pasquinade; PHRASES: **3, 4** put down; **4, 2** jeer at, send up; **4, 3, 2** poke fun at; **4, 3, 6** take the mickey *UK*; **5, 2** laugh at, scoff at; **7, 5** snigger about.

derider 5 joker, mimic; **8** satirist; **9** lampooner; **10** cartoonist, lampoonist; **12** caricaturist.

derision 4 joke; **5** scorn, spoof; **6** parody, satire, windup; **7** disdain, lampoon, mockery, pasquil; **8** ridicule, travesty; **9** burlesque; **10** caricature, disrespect, pasquinade; **13** disparagement; PHRASES: **4-2** send-up.

derisive 7 cynical, mocking; **8** farcical, sardonic, scathing, scornful; **9** satirical; **10** ridiculing.

derivative 6 copied, result; **7** derived; **8** offshoot; **9** byproduct *UK*, imitative; **10** unoriginal; **11** boilerplate; **12** plagiaristic; PHRASES: **3, 7** end product.

derive 3 get; **4** draw, gain, stem; **5** arise; **6** obtain, spring; **7** descend, receive; **9** originate.

derogatory *See* **disparaging**

descend 3 ebb; **4** dive, fall, sink; **5** crash, slope, slump, stoop; **6** abseil, alight, derive, plunge, rappel; **7** decline, subside; **8** decrease, dismount; **9** gravitate, originate; PHRASES: **3, 4** dip down, get down, run down; **4, 2** drop in, fall on, turn up; **4, 3** drop off, fall off; **4, 4** come down, drop away, fall away, fall down, move down, seep down, sink down; **4, 6** lose height; **5, 4** climb down *UK*, slide down; **5, 8** lower yourself; **6, 4** tumble down.

descendants *See* **future generation**

descending 4 down; **7** sliding; **8** downhill, downward, lowering, tumbling; **9** decurrent; **10** collapsing, descendent, tumbledown; **11** declivitous, downflowing, downrushing, downturning, submersible; PHRASES: **2, 3, 10** on the descendent. *See also* **descend**

descent 4 dive, drop, fall; **5** crash, tribe; **6** family, origin, plunge, tumble; **7** decline, lineage; **8** ancestry, comedown, downbend, downcome, downturn, lowering, pedigree; **9** downdraft, parentage; **10** background; **12** degeneration, depreciation; **13** deterioration; PHRASES: **8, 6** downward spiral.

describe 4 draw, limn; **5** paint, style; **6** define, depict, design, sketch; **7** explain, express, fashion, outline, picture, portray; **9** adumbrate, delineate, designate, pronounce, represent; **10** illustrate; **11** communicate; **12** characterize; PHRASES: **5, 1, 8** catch a likeness; **5, 2** refer to; **5, 3** rough out; **6, 3** sketch out.

description 4 kind, sort, type; **5** blurb, notes; **6** report; **7** account, details, picture, profile, summary; **8** portrait; **9** depiction, narrative, portrayal; **11** delineation, explanation, particulars; **13** specification; PHRASES: **4, 7** case history; **9, 6** character sketch *UK*.

descriptive 5 vivid; **7** eidetic, graphic; **8** colorful, detailed, eloquent, striking; **9** depictive, evocative, narrative, realistic, thrilling; **10** expositive, expository, expressive, suggestive; **11** elucidatory, explanatory, explicatory, imaginative, informative, picturesque; **12** illuminating, illustrative, interpretive *UK*; **15** impressionistic; PHRASES: **4-2-4** true-to-life; **4-4** real-life; **4-5** well-drawn.

desecrate 6 damage, defile, insult; **7** degrade, despoil, outrage, profane, violate; **9** vandalize; PHRASES: **3, 5, 2** lay waste to; **6, 9** commit sacrilege.

desecration 4 ruin; **6** damage; **9** sacrilege, vandalism, violation; **10** defilement; **12** despoliation.

desensitization 8 hypnosis, narcosis; **9** catalepsy, catatonia, paralysis; **10** anesthesia, quiescence, stagnation; **12** stupefaction; **13** narcotization.

desensitize 4 dope, drug, dull, numb; **6** deaden, freeze; **7** stupefy; **8** paralyze; **9** hypnotize, narcotize; **12** anaesthetize.

desert 4 dump, heat; **5** karoo, Karoo, leave, Negev, waste; **6** barren, Fezzan, maroon, Mojave, return, reward, Sahara; **7** abandon, forsake, scarper *UK*, Sonoran; **8** Colorado; **9** Patagonia, wasteland; **10** Chihuahuan, punishment, recompense, wilderness; **11** comeuppance; PHRASES: **2, 4** go AWOL; **3, 2-5** Rub al-Khali; **4, 3** take off, walk out; **4, 3, 2** walk out on; **4, 4** dust bowl, jump ship, salt flat, sand dune; **4, 6** Gobi D~, just reward, Thar D~; **5, 4, 3, 3** leave high and dry; **5, 5** Great Basin, sunny South; **5, 5, 6** Great Sandy D~; **5, 6** Death Valley, Namib D~; **5, 8, 6** Great Victoria D~; **6, 6** Gibson D~, Libyan D~, Mojave D~, Tanami D~; **7, 6** Garagum D~, Painted D~, Simpson D~, Sonoran D~; **7, 10** Qattara

Depression; **8, 6** Colorado D~; **10, 6** Chihuahuan D~, Patagonian D~.

deserted 5 empty; **7** ditched; **8** derelict, desolate, forsaken, solitary; **9** abandoned, discarded; **11** uninhabited; PHRASES: **4, 3** cast off.

deserter 4 AWOL; **6** jilter; **7** dropout, retiree, runaway, striker, traitor, yielder; **8** apostate, defector, fugitive, recanter, renegade, turncoat; **9** abdicator, abnegator, absconder, abstainer.

desertion 4 flit; **6** flight, hookey; **7** absence; **9** elopement; **10** absconding; **11** abandonment; PHRASES: **6, 5** French leave.

deserve 5 merit.

desiccate *See* **dry up**

design 3 aim, set; **4** form, goal, mode, mold, plan; **5** build, draft, frame, model, motif, shape, style; **6** create, devise, figure, intend, invent, layout, revise, scheme, sketch; **7** compose, drawing, outline, pattern; **8** strategy; **9** blueprint, construct, fabricate, intention; **10** appearance; **12** prefabricate; PHRASES: **4, 2** draw up; **4, 3** work out.

designate 4 call, term; **5** elect, label, title; **6** assign, choose, select; **7** entitle, specify; **8** allocate, delegate, indicate; PHRASES: **2, 2** to be; **2, 7** in waiting; **5, 3** point out.

desirability 6 allure, appeal, cachet; **10** attraction, expedience, popularity; **11** suitability; **12** advisability. *See also* **desirable**

desirable 6 proper, wanted *UK*, worthy; **7** desired, likable, popular, welcome; **8** enviable, inviting, laudable, likeable, required, suitable, tempting; **9** admirable, appealing, deserving, expedient; **10** acceptable, appetizing, attractive, convenient, profitable, worthwhile; **11** appropriate, meritorious; **12** advantageous, praiseworthy; PHRASES: **5-8** mouth-watering; **6-3** looked-for; **6, 5** sought after.

desire 3 ask, yen; **4** hope, itch, lust, miss, need, will, wish, zeal; **5** ardor, covet, crave, fancy *UK*, favor; **6** hunger, libido, pining, prefer, thirst, venery; **7** avidity, caprice, coition, craving, entreat, impulse, itching, leaning, longing, passion, request, require, welcome; **8** ambition, appetite, cupidity, fondness, penchant, voracity, weakness, yearning; **9** appetency, eagerness, eroticism, hankering, nostalgia, prurience; **10** aphrodisia, aspiration, erotomania, love-making, partiality, preference, wantonness; **11** amorousness, fascination, fornication, inclination, libertinage; **12** covetousness, homesickness, predilection; PHRASES: **2, 5, 3** be dying for; **3, 3** aim for; **3, 3, 3** cry out for; **3, 4, 6, 2** set one's sights on; **4, 2, 4** fire of love; **4, 3** ache for, hope for, itch for, long for, pant for, pine for, pray for, wish for; **4, 5** lust after; **5, 2** dream of; **5, 3** yearn for; **6, 2** aspire to; **6, 2, 4** flames of love; **6, 3** hunger for, thirst for; **6, 5** hanker after; **6, 9** carnal knowledge.

desire (cause desire) 4 draw, lure; **5** tempt; **6** allure; **7** attract; **9** stimulate, tantalize, titillate; PHRASES: **4, 2** turn on.

desire (object of desire) 3 aim; **4** goal, lure; **5** catch, ideal, prize; **6** appeal, trophy; **9** objective; **11** desideratum, requirement; PHRASES: **3, 5, 4** the brass ring; **3, 12** the unattainable; **9, 5** forbidden fruit.

desired 6 chosen, envied, needed, wanted *UK*; **7** coveted, popular; **8** enviable, required; **9** desirable, preferred, requested; PHRASES: **2, 6** in demand; **6, 3** longed for, wished for; **6-3** looked-for; **6, 5** sought after; **7, 3** yearned for.

desirer 5 hoper; **6** wanter, wisher; **7** coveter, devotee, fancier; **8** aspirant; **9** libertine.

desirous 4 avid, keen; **5** eager; **6** ardent, greedy, hoping, pining; **7** craving, envious, hopeful, wanting, wishful, wistful; **8** aspiring, covetous, yearning; **9** demanding, voracious; **10** insatiable, passionate; **11** acquisitive; PHRASES: **7, 2** partial to; **7, 3** itching for, longing for, wishing for.

desist 3 end; **4** stop; **5** cease; **7** abstain, forbear; **11** discontinue; PHRASES: **4, 2** give up; **7, 4** abstain from, refrain from.

desk 6 bureau, podium, pulpit; **7** lectern; **10** escritoire; PHRASES: **4-3, 4** roll-top ~; **4-4, 4** knee-hole ~; **5-3, 4** slant-top ~; **7, 4** reading ~, writing ~.

desolate 5 bleak; **6** dismal, gloomy; **7** austere, forlorn, unhappy; **8** deserted, forsaken, isolated; **9** abandoned, depressed, miserable; **10** depressing, forbidding; **12** inconsolable.

desolation 6 misery; **7** anguish, despair, sadness; **9** bleakness, emptiness, isolation; **10** barrenness; **11** dereliction, unhappiness.

despair 4 mope, sulk; **5** brood, gloom; **6** misery; **7** anguish, despond; **9** dejection; **10** depression, desolation; **11** despondency; **12**

hopelessness; **PHRASES: 3, 4, 6** hit (rock) bottom; **4, 2, 4** give up hope; **4, 5** lose heart; **5, 3, 6** plumb the depths.

desperado 6 bandit, outlaw; **7** villain; **8** criminal, gangster.

desperate 4 rash; **5** dying, eager, grave; **6** raring; **7** anxious, extreme, frantic, serious, worried; **8** bursting, careless, critical, hopeless, reckless; **9** dangerous, impatient, impulsive; **10** distracted, distressed; **11** threatening.

despoil *See* **rob**

despondent *See* **hopeless**

despot 6 tyrant; **8** autocrat, dictator, martinet; **9** oppressor; **13** authoritarian; **14** disciplinarian.

despotic 10 autocratic, oppressive, overmighty, repressive, tyrannical; **11** dictatorial, domineering; **PHRASES: 1, 3, 4, 7** a law unto oneself; **4-6** high-handed; **4-9** self-important; **5-6** power-hungry.

dessert 3 pie; **4** fool, tart; **5** betty, bombe, candy, crisp, icing, sweet *UK*; **6** afters *UK*, gateau, junket, mousse, sorbet, sundae, trifle; **7** baklava, brownie, cassata, cobbler, compote, custard, granita, parfait, pavlova *UK*, soufflé, tapioca; **8** clafouti, frosting, marquise, marzipan, meringue, pandowdy, semolina, streusel, syllabub, tiramisu; **9** charlotte, clafoutis, fruitcake, shortcake; **10** blancmange, cheesecake, pannacotta, zabaglione; **12** profiteroles; **PHRASES: 3, 5** ice cream; **4-1** Jell-o; **4-4** roly-poly; **5, 3** apple pie, fruit cup, water ice; **5, 5** brown betty, Brown Betty, fruit salad, peach melba; **5, 6** crème brûlée; **5, 6, 3** black bottom pie; **5, 7** bread pudding, crème caramel; **6, 4** sponge cake; **6, 5** banana split, cheese board; **6, 6** Danish pastry; **7, 4** spotted dick *UK*; **8, 3** banoffee pie *UK*; **8, 6** floating island; **9, 4** chocolate cake; **9, 5** charlotte russe. *See also* **pudding**

destination 3 aim, end; **4** goal, home, port; **5** bourn, depot, haven; **6** finish, harbor, target; **7** purpose; **8** terminal, terminus; **9** objective; **PHRASES: 3, 2, 3, 4** end of the line, end of the road; **3, 5** end point; **5, 2, 7** point of arrival; **5, 5** terra firma; **8, 3** journey's end; **8, 5** stopping place, terminal point.

destiny 3 lot; **4** call, fate, luck; **7** calling, fortune, purpose; **8** vocation; **9** intention; **10** providence.

destitute *See* **poor**

destroy 2 ax; **4** kill, raze, ruin, slay; **5** break, crush, drown, erase, level, quash, smash, spoil, wreck; **6** ablate, damage, delete, efface, injure, murder, quench, squash, stifle, subdue, uproot; **7** abolish, blanket, despoil, expunge, flatten, nullify, repress, scatter, silence, smother, subvert; **8** abrogate, decimate, demolish, destruct, dispatch, disperse, dissolve, massacre, spoliate, vaporize; **9** devastate, dissipate, eradicate, evaporate, extirpate, liquidate, pulverize, slaughter, suffocate, terminate; **10** annihilate, deracinate, extinguish, neutralize, obliterate; **11** exterminate; **PHRASES: 2, 3** do for; **2, 4, 4** do away with; **3, 3** rub out; **3, 4** put down; **4, 2** root up, tear up; **4, 3** blot out, blow out, wipe out; **4, 3, 3** wipe off the map; **4, 4** blow away; **5, 3** snuff out, stamp out, throw out; **7, 2** dispose of; **7, 3** scratch out.

destroy (be destroyed) 12 disintegrate; **PHRASES: 2, 2, 3** go to pot; **2, 2, 3, 4** go to the dogs, go to the wall; **2, 2, 3, 5** go on the rocks; **2, 2, 4, 3, 4** go to rack and ruin; **2, 2, 5** go to waste; **2, 2, 6** go to pieces; **2, 4** go west; **2, 5** go under; **2, 8** go downhill; **4, 2, 4** turn to dust; **4, 3, 4** bite the dust; **4-8** self-destruct; **5, 2** break up; **6, 4** tumble down; **7, 2** crumple up.

destroyed 4 bust, sunk; **5** kaput; **6** broken, dished, fallen, ground, pulped, undone; **8** bankrupt, shredded; **9** shattered *UK*, torpedoed; **11** dilapidated; **13** disintegrated; **PHRASES: 2, 3, 5** up the chute; **2, 5** in ruins; **2, 7** in tatters; **4, 3** done for; **4-3-3** down-and-out; **5, 3** wiped out. *See also* **destroy**

destroyer 5 death; **6** eraser, killer, rubber, slayer, vandal; **7** defacer, leveler, Luddite, ravager, scourge, spoiler, wrecker; **8** arsonist, assassin, murderer, nihilist, polluter, saboteur; **9** barbarian, berserker, despoiler; **10** demolisher, iconoclast, liquidator; **11** executioner; **12** exterminator, extinguisher; **14** destructionist; **15** annihilationist; **PHRASES: 3, 3** hit man; **3, 4, 2, 4** the hand of time; **3, 4, 6** the grim reaper; **5, 2, 5** Angel of Death, cause of death; **5, 6** time's scythe.

destruction 4 ruin; **5** havoc, wreck; **6** damage; **7** erasure, undoing; **8** ablation, deletion, sabotage, unmaking; **9** abolition, overthrow, silencing, vandalism; **10** demolition, denudation, extinction, spoliation; **11** abolishment, despoilment, devastation, elimination, liquidation, suffocation; **12** annihilation, obliteration; **13** extermination, nullification.

destructive **5** fatal; **6** deadly, lethal, mortal; **7** abusive, adverse, baneful, caustic, harmful, noxious, ruinous, vicious; **8** damaging; **9** cutthroat, injurious, insidious; **10** disastrous, incendiary, pernicious, subversive; **11** anarchistic, apocalyptic, cataclysmic, detrimental, devastating, disparaging, internecine; **12** annihilating, catastrophic; **PHRASES: 3-9** all-consuming.

destructively **11** corrosively, explosively, reductively; **12** depressingly, disturbingly, necrotically; **13** deleteriously; **PHRASES: 2, 1, 6** at a stroke; **4, 3, 4** with one blow; **4, 3, 6** root and branch. *See also* **destructive**

destructiveness **8** violence; **9** roughness, vandalism; **10** iconoclasm, negativity. *See also* **destructive**

desultory **6** casual, random; **7** aimless; **9** haphazard, unfocused.

detach *See* **separate**

detached **4** calm, cool; **5** aloof, apart; **6** remote, serene, steady; **7** distant, equable, pacific, removed, stoical; **8** composed, distinct, isolated, separate, tranquil, unbiased; **9** impassive, pragmatic, separated, temperate, unruffled; **10** equanimous, impersonal, restrained, uninvolved; **11** indifferent, undisturbed, unemotional, unperturbed; **12** disconnected; **13** disinterested, dispassionate, imperturbable, unimpassioned; **PHRASES: 4-6** cool-headed; **4-8** even-tempered; **4-9** self-possessed; **4-10** self-restrained; **5-6** level-headed.

detachment **4** unit; **5** group, party, posse; **6** aplomb, detail; **8** ataraxia, distance, patience, quietude, serenity, stoicism; **9** composure, isolation, placidity, severalty, severance; **10** dispassion, equanimity, moderation, separation, spartanism, temperance, uncoupling; **11** disinterest, extrication, objectivity, rationality, tranquility; **12** impartiality, indifference; **13** disengagement; **14** inexcitability; **15** disentanglement; **PHRASES: 4, 5** task force; **4-5** sang-froid; **4-9** self-restraint; **4-10** self-possession; **5, 2, 4** peace of mind; **5, 5** horse sense; **6, 5** common sense. *See also* **detached**

detail **4** list, part, unit; **5** group, party, point; **6** aspect, assign; **7** element, feature, itemize, specify; **8** allocate, delegate, describe; **9** conscript, designate; **10** detach-

ment; **13** particularize; **PHRASES: 4, 5** task force.

detailed **6** minute; **7** finicky, precise; **8** specific, thorough; **9** elaborate; **10** exhaustive, meticulous, particular, pernickety *UK*; **11** persnickety; **13** comprehensive; **PHRASES: 2, 5** in depth; **3-7** nit-picking.

detain **4** cage, hold, jail, keep, stop; **5** block, delay, guard, seize, store; **6** arrest, collar, hinder, impede, intern, kidnap, remand, retain; **7** besiege, capture, confine, contain, control, impound, protect; **8** blockade, imprison, preserve, restrain, sentence; **9** apprehend; **10** quarantine; **11** incarcerate; **PHRASES: 3, 2** run in; **3, 4** put away; **4, 2** haul in, hold in, hold up, keep in, lock in, lock up, slow up, wall in; **4, 2, 3, 5** send up the river; **4, 2, 4, 5** take to one's bosom; **4, 2, 6** send to prison; **4, 2, 7** keep in custody; **4, 4, 7** take into custody; **4, 7** take hostage; **4, 8** take prisoner; **5, 2** fence in; **6, 2** bottle up; **6, 3** starve out; **6, 4** refuse bail.

detained **6** inside; **7** captive; **8** besieged, enslaved, fogbound; **9** snowbound; **10** housebound, obstructed; **PHRASES: 2, 3, 3, 5** in the big house; **2, 3, 5** up the river; **2, 5** in bonds, in irons; **2, 6** on remand; **2, 7** in custody; **2, 9** in captivity, in detention; **4-2** shutin; **5, 4** doing time; **6, 4** behind bars. *See also* **detain**

detect **4** spot; **5** catch, sense; **6** notice, reveal, unveil; **7** ensnare, uncover, unearth; **8** disclose, discover, identify, perceive; **11** distinguish; **PHRASES: 3, 4, 2** get wind of; **4, 3** worm out; **4, 3, 4, 2** lift the veil on; **5, 2, 3, 3** catch in the act; **5, 2, 5** bring to light; **5, 3** smell out, sniff out; **5, 3, 5** spill the beans; **5, 3-6** catch red-handed; **5, 4** track down; **6, 3** ferret out.

detective **6** sleuth; **7** gumshoe; **11** sleuthhound; **12** investigator; **PHRASES: 7, 3** private eye.

detector **5** gauge, probe, radar, sonar; **6** sensor; **7** scanner; **9** indicator, polygraph.

detention **4** bird, time; **6** arrest, remand; **7** bondage, custody, durance, slavery, stretch; **8** porridge, sentence; **9** captivity, servitude; **10** immurement, internment, kidnapping, quarantine; **11** confinement, containment, impoundment, imprisoning; **12** imprisonment; **13** incarceration; **PHRASES: 5, 6** house arrest; **7, 2** keeping in, locking in, locking up; **7, 4** holding back.

deter **7** prevent, unnerve; **8** dissuade,

frighten, threaten; **9** terrorize; **10** discourage, intimidate; PHRASES: **3, 3** put off; **8, 3** frighten off.

detergent *See* **cleaner**

deteriorate 3 age; **4** fade, fail, fall, fray, sink, slip, wane, wilt; **5** droop, lapse, slide, slump; **6** perish *UK*, plunge, shrink, sicken, totter, weaken, wither, worsen; **7** crumble, decline, descend, shrivel, wrinkle; **8** collapse, decrease, diminish; **10** degenerate, depreciate, retrograde, retrogress; **12** disintegrate; PHRASES: **2, 2, 3** go to pot; **2, 2, 3, 4** go to the dogs; **2, 2, 4** go to seed; **2, 2, 4, 3, 4** go to rack and ruin; **2, 2, 6** go to pieces; **2, 8** go downhill; **3, 3, 5** hit the skids; **3, 7, 2** let oneself go; **4, 3** fall ill, fall off; **4, 4** slip back, slow down; **4, 6** lose ground; **4-8** self-destruct; **5, 4** break down.

deterioration 5 lapse, slump; **7** decline, descent, relapse, setback, tragedy; **8** decrease, downturn, twilight; **9** downtrend, recession, weakening, worsening; **10** depression, recidivism, regression; **11** backsliding; **12** deceleration, depreciation; **13** retrogression; **14** retrogradation, tergiversation; PHRASES: **3, 4, 2, 4** the road to hell; **4, 3, 3, 5** turn for the worse; **6, 6** losing ground; **7, 3** falling off; **7, 4** slowing down; **8, 4** primrose path.

determination 4 grit, will; **5** nerve; **6** aplomb, fixity; **7** purpose, resolve; **8** obduracy, tenacity; **9** fortitude, obstinacy, willpower; **10** doggedness, resolution, steeliness; **12** immovability, perseverance, stubbornness; **13** inflexibility, intransigence; PHRASES: **2, 10** no compromise; **4, 4** hard line, iron will; **4, 5** iron nerve; **6, 2, 5** nerves of steel; **7, 8** bulldog tenacity; **8, 2, 4** strength of mind.

determination (show determination) 7 persist, stiffen; **9** persevere; PHRASES: **3, 3, 2, 6** not bat an eyelid; **3, 4, 4, 4** put one's foot down; **3, 5** not budge; **5, 2, 3** stick it out; **5, 2, 4, 4** stick to one's guns; **5, 3** stand pat; **5, 4** stand firm, stick fast; **5, 4, 6** stand one's ground; **7, 3, 5** weather the storm.

determine 3 fix; **4** form, mold; **5** learn, limit, shape; **6** affect, decide, define, settle, verify; **7** clarify, resolve, uncover; **8** conclude, discover, finalize, regulate; **9** ascertain, establish, influence; PHRASES: **4, 1, 4, 2** have a hand in; **4, 3** find out; **4, 3, 5** turn the scale; **6, 3, 5** decide the issue.

determined 4 firm, sure; **6** dogged, grit-

ty, heroic, nerved, steely; **7** adamant, certain, doughty; **8** obdurate, resolute, stubborn; **9** obstinate, steadfast, tenacious; **10** purposeful, unwavering, unyielding; **11** indomitable; **13** imperturbable, indefatigable; PHRASES: **4-3** dead-set; **4-6** iron-nerved, iron-willed; **6-6** single-minded. *See also* **determine**

deterrence 9 deterrent, restraint; **10** deflection, dissuasion, prevention; **11** restriction; **12** disincentive, intimidation; **14** discouragement, disinclination; PHRASES: **4, 5** cold water.

detest *See* **hate**

detonate 6 ignite; **7** explode; PHRASES: **3, 3** set off; **4, 2** blow up; **5, 3** spark off.

detour 5 avoid; **6** ambage, bypass, zigzag; **7** deviate, digress, diverge, meander; **9** deviation, diversion, excursion; **10** divagation; **11** periphrasis; **12** circumlocute; **14** circumbendibus, circumlocution; PHRASES: **4, 3, 5** long way round *UK*; **5-7** short-circuit.

detract (from) 6 lessen, reduce, weaken; **8** belittle, diminish; **9** undermine; **10** depreciate; **11** underpraise; PHRASES: **3, 3, 3, 3, 2** let the air out of; **3, 4, 2, 4** cut down to size.

detraction 5 abuse; **7** calumny, slander; **9** aspersion, deduction, discredit, reduction; **10** diminution; **11** denigration, subtraction; **12** belittlement; **13** disparagement; PHRASES: **3, 6** two cheers; **5, 6** faint praise.

detriment 4 harm, loss; **6** damage, injury; **10** impairment; **12** disadvantage.

detrimental 6 deadly, mortal; **7** baneful, harmful, noxious; **8** damaging, negative; **9** corrosive, injurious, malignant, troublous; **10** corruptive, pernicious; **11** deleterious, destructive, distressing; **15** disadvantageous.

deuce *See* **tie**

devaluation 9 deflation, recession, reduction, weakening; **10** depression; **12** belittlement, depreciation; PHRASES: **4, 6** bear market; **5, 7** Dutch auction; **6, 6** buyers' market.

devalue 6 debase, lessen, reduce; **7** cheapen, degrade; **8** diminish; **9** devaluate; **10** undervalue; PHRASES: **5, 4** bring down.

devastate 3 gut; **4** nuke, raid, rape, raze, ruin, sack; **5** trash, wreck; **6** damage, denude, ravage; **7** despoil, destroy, pillage, plunder, ransack, violate; **8** confound, decimate, demolish, desolate; **9** defoliate, vandalize; **10** annihilate, depopulate, obliterate; PHRASES: **3, 4** run amok; **3, 5** lay waste; **5, 5** wreak havoc.

develop 4 brew, cure, farm, grow; **5** arise, breed, build, hatch, nurse, raise, ripen; **6** create, evolve, expand, extend, fledge, foster, happen, mature, mellow, pupate, result, temper; **7** acquire, advance, concoct, explain, expound, gestate, improve, nurture, process, prosper, upgrade, utilize; **8** incubate, progress, renovate; **9** cultivate, elaborate, refurbish; PHRASES: **2, 2** do up; **4, 2** come on, fill in, pick up, work up; **4, 3** work out; **4, 4, 5** come into being; **5, 2** build on, build up; **5, 2, 1, 4** bring to a head; **5, 2, 8** bring to fruition; **5, 3** flesh out.

developed 4 ripe; **5** adult, grown; **6** mature, mellow; **7** fledged, labored, matured, ripened; **8** advanced, blooming, expanded; **9** completed, elaborate, perfected; **11** established, overwrought; **14** industrialized; PHRASES: **4-4** deep-laid *UK*; **4-5** full-grown; **5, 7** fully fledged; **6, 2** worked up; **6, 7** highly wrought.

developer 5 buyer, maker; **6** brains; **7** creator; **8** designer, inventor; **10** contractor, speculator; PHRASES: **4, 9** land ~.

developing 5 afoot; **6** mooted; **7** brewing, cooking, planned, stewing; **8** emergent, evolving, hatching, maturing; **9** embryonic, impending; **10** incubating; **11** forthcoming; PHRASES: **2, 3, 5** on the anvil; **2, 3, 6** in the offing, on the stocks; **2, 8** in progress; **2, 11** in preparation; **5, 8** under training; **5, 9** being discussed.

development 5 event; **6** change, growth; **7** advance, brewing, nurture; **8** blooming, exposure, fruition, hatching, incident, increase, progress, training; **9** education, evolution, expansion, extension, flowering, gestation, happening; **10** incubation, maturation, occurrence, production; **11** advancement, cultivation, enhancement, enlargement, florescence, furtherance, improvement, manufacture.

developmental 5 fetal *UK*, pupal; **6** larval; **8** amniotic, evolving, germinal; **9** embryonic, germinant, ontogenic; **10** primordial; **11** germinating, germinative, progressive, rudimentary; **12** paedogenetic; PHRASES: **2, 3, 3** in the bud.

developmental biology 10 embryogeny, embryology; **11** germination; **12** blastulation, gastrulation, paedogenesis; **13** embryogenesis, metamorphosis.

deviant 7 unusual; **8** aberrant; **9** divergent, eccentric, irregular; **10** exorbitant, unexpected; **11** misdirected, nonstandard; **12** aberrational; **13** nonconformist; PHRASES: **3, 2, 5** out of orbit; **3-6** off-center.

deviate 3 yaw; **4** skew, tack, turn, vary; **5** curve, evade, stray; **6** depart, detour, differ, divert, swerve; **7** deflect, digress, diverge, meander; **10** divaricate; **12** circumlocute; PHRASES: **2, 3, 2, 1, 7** go off at a tangent; **4, 3** bear off; **4, 3, 5** bend the truth; **4, 4** move away; **4, 5** turn aside; **6, 3** branch out; **6, 4** depart from; **6, 9** change direction.

deviation 4 skew; **6** change, vagary; **7** anomaly, tangent, variant; **8** mutation; **9** aberrancy, curvature, departure, diversion, excursion, obliquity, variation; **10** aberration, deflection, digression, divagation, divergence, perversion; **11** abnormality, declination, indirection, obliqueness, unorthodoxy; **12** divarication, eccentricity, misdirection; **13** nonconformism.

device 4 bomb, logo, plan, ploy, ruse, tool; **5** badge, crest, means, trick; **6** design, emblem, gadget, method, scheme; **7** gimmick, machine, pattern; **8** artifice; **9** apparatus, appliance, mechanism, stratagem; **10** instrument; **11** contraption, contrivance.

devil 4 deil *UK*, Loki, Mara; **5** demon, fiend, Satan, Teukl; **6** afreet, Belial, diable, diablo, dybbuk; **7** Abaddon, Ahriman, diavolo, incubus, Lucifer, Shaitan; **8** Apollyon, Diabolus, Mephisto, succubus; **9** Archfiend, Beelzebub; **10** Antichrist; **14** Mephistopheles; PHRASES: **3, 4** Old Nick; **3, 4, 3** the Evil One; **3, 5** Old Harry, the Enemy; **3, 6** Old Hornie; **3, 6, 5** the Common Enemy; **3, 7** Old Clootie, The Tempter; **3, 8** Old Scratchy; **4, 2, 3, 5** Lord of the Flies; **5, 5** rebel angel; **6, 5** fallen angel.

devilish 4 evil; **6** damned, fallen; **7** abysmal, Avernal, demonic, hellish, satanic; **8** chthonic, demoniac, diabolic, fiendish, infernal; **9** chthonian, fiendlike; **10** diabolical, pandemonic; **12** subterranean; **15** Mephistophelean; PHRASES: **4-4** hell-born.

devious 3 sly; **4** wily; **5** shady; **6** artful, crafty, shifty, sneaky, tricky; **7** cunning, deviant, furtive, oblique, winding; **8** indirect, scheming, spurious, tortuous; **9** conniving, deceitful, deceptive, equivocal, underhand; **10** circuitous, distortive, meandering; **11** dissembling; **13** Machiavellian.

deviousness 5 guile; 7 cunning; 9 deception; 10 distortion; 11 indirection, periphrasis; 12 dissemblance, equivocation; 14 backhandedness, circumlocution; 15 underhandedness. *See also* **devious**

devote 4 give; 5 apply, offer; 6 assign; 8 dedicate.

devoted 4 fond, keen; 5 loyal; 6 ardent, caring, loving; 7 dutiful, fervent, staunch, zealous; 8 constant, faithful; 9 attentive, committed, dedicated, fanatical, steadfast; 12 affectionate, enthusiastic; PHRASES: 5-3-4 tried-and-true.

devotedly 4, 7 with loyalty. *See also* **devoted**

devotion 4 care, love, zeal; 5 piety; 6 fervor; 7 loyalty, support; 8 fondness, keenness *UK*; 9 affection; 10 admiration, attachment, commitment, dedication, devoutness, enthusiasm; 13 attentiveness; PHRASES: 9, 4 religious zeal.

devour 4 glut, gulp, wolf; 5 binge, gorge, scoff, stuff; 6 engulf, gobble, guzzle; 7 consume, destroy; 8 demolish, overcome.

devout 4 keen; 5 pious; 6 ardent, solemn; 7 devoted, dutiful, earnest, fervent, sincere, staunch, zealous; 8 reverent; 9 committed, dedicated, fanatical, religious, spiritual; 12 enthusiastic.

dexterity 5 skill; 6 acuity; 8 deftness; 9 handiness, ingenuity, quickness, sharpness; 10 adroitness; 11 legerdemain.

dexterous 4 deft; 5 acute, handy, sharp; 6 adroit, clever, nimble; 11 resourceful; PHRASES: 5-6 quick-witted; 6-8 nimble-fingered.

diadem *See* **crown**

diagnose 4 spot; 6 detect; 7 analyze; 8 identify; PHRASES: 4, 3 make out.

diagnosis 6 biopsy; 7 autopsy, finding, verdict; 8 analysis, judgment; 9 prognosis; 10 conclusion, postmortem; 11 diagnostics; 14 identification.

diagnostic 8 analytic; 10 analytical *UK*, indicative, prognostic; 11 pinpointing, symptomatic; 13 investigative; PHRASES: 7-7 problem-solving.

diagram 3 map; 4 plan, venn; 5 chart, graph, table; 6 figure, schema, scheme; 7 drawing; 9 indicator; 12 illustration.

diagrammatic 6 visual; 7 graphic; 8 analytic; 9 pictorial, schematic; 12 illustrative.

dial 4 call, disc *UK*, disk *UK*, face, knob, ring *UK*; 5 gauge, phone; 6 button, handle; 7 control; 9 indicator, telephone; PHRASES: 5, 2 phone up *UK*; 7, 5 control panel.

dialect 5 argot, idiom, lingo; 6 accent, brogue, patois, Strine, tongue; 7 Lallans; 8 Irishism, language, localism, parlance; 9 Anglicism, Briticism, Franglais, Gallicism, regionism, Teutonism; 10 Africanism, Scotticism, vernacular; 11 Americanism, Hibernicism; 13 provincialism, vernacularism; PHRASES: 6, 6 lingua franca; 7, 7 Estuary English.

dialectical 8 analytic, aporetic, elenctic; 9 heuristic; 10 apodeictic.

dialogue 8 exchange; 9 discourse, interview; 10 discussion; 11 interaction; 12 conversation; 13 interlocution *UK*; PHRASES: 8, 2, 5 exchange of ideas; 11, 4 information flow.

diaper 6 napkin.

diaphanous 5 gauzy, sheer; 8 delicate; 11 transparent; PHRASES: 3-7 see-through.

diary 6 memoir; 7 account, journal.

Diaspora 10 Dispersion.

diatribe 4 rant; 6 attack, tirade; 7 lecture; 8 harangue, outburst; 9 criticism; 12 denunciation.

dice 4 chop, cube, risk; 5 stake, wager; 6 chance, gamble, hazard; 7 venture; PHRASES: 3, 2 cut up.

dicker *See* **haggle**

dictate 3 say; 4 rule; 5 order, shape, speak, state, tenet; 6 decree; 7 command, control, precept; 8 standard; 9 determine, influence, principle; 10 injunction; 12 prescription; PHRASES: 3, 5 say aloud; 4, 3 read out; 4, 5 read aloud.

dictator *See* **tyrant**

dictatorship 4 rule; 5 junta, reign; 6 regime; 7 tyranny; 9 autocracy, despotism; 10 absolutism, government, leadership, militarism, repression; 15 totalitarianism; PHRASES: 4, 4 iron hand; 5, 2, 6 reign of terror; 8, 4 absolute rule.

diction 7 wording; 8 delivery, language, phrasing; 9 elocution; 10 expression; 11 enunciation, phraseology; 12 articulation; 13 pronunciation.

dictionary 5 gloss, lexis; 6 gradus *UK*; 7 almanac, lexicon; 8 glossary, wordbook; 9 directory, thesaurus; 10 vocabulary; 11 concordance; **12** encyclopedia, lexicography; PHRASES: **4, 3** who's who; **4, 4** word list; **6, 4** phrase book; **9, 4** reference book.

didactic **9** educative, pedagogic; **11** educational.

die **4** fail, pass, stop; **6** expire, perish; **7** decease, succumb; **8** flatline; **10** predecease; PHRASES: **2, 2, 4, 5** go up Salt River; **2, 2, 5** go to glory; **2, 3, 1, 6** go for a burton; **2, 4** go west; **2, 5, 2** go belly up; **3, 2** cop it, peg it; **3, 2, 3, 5** lie in the grave; **3, 3** peg out, pop off; **3, 3, 4** buy the farm, hop the twig; **3, 4, 5** pop one's clogs; **4, 2** kick it, pack in, pack up *UK*, pass on, quit it; **4, 2, 3, 3** curl up and ~; **4, 2, 3, 5** give up the ghost; **4, 2, 4** come to dust; **4, 2, 4, 4** turn up one's toes; **4, 2, 4, 5** cash in one's chips; **4, 2, 7** push up daisies; **4, 3** conk out, drop off, give out; **4, 3, 4** bite the dust; **4, 3, 5** quit the scene; **4, 3, 6** join the angels, kick the bucket; **4, 3, 8** join the majority; **4, 4** pass away; **4, 4, 3** meet one's end; **4, 4, 4** lose one's life, meet one's fate; **4, 4, 5** meet one's Maker; **4, 5, 5** meet Saint Peter; **4, 6** fall asleep; **5, 3, 3** cross the bar; **5, 3, 4** cross the Styx; **6, 4, 4** depart this life; **7, 4, 4** breathe one's last.

die (ways of dying) **7** release, suicide; **8** drowning; **10** euthanasia, starvation; PHRASES: **3-3, 5** old-age death; **5, 3** quiet end; **5, 7** happy release *UK*; **6, 5** sudden death, watery grave; **6, 7** mortal illness; **7, 3** welcome end; **7, 5** natural death, violent death; **8, 3** untimely end; **8, 7** terminal illness.

diehard **4** fogy; **10** conformist; **11** reactionary; **12** conservative, intransigent; **14** traditionalist.

diet **4** fare, food, menu; **6** intake, regime, starve; **7** council, regimen; **8** assembly, congress, slimming *UK*; **10** parliament, sustenance; **11** nourishment; PHRASES: **3, 4** cut down; **6-8** weight-watching; **7-8** calorie-counting.

dieter **6** faster; **7** slimmer *UK*, starver; **9** abstainer; PHRASES: **6, 7** weight watcher.

dietitian **9** dietician; **12** nutritionist; PHRASES: **7, 6** dietary expert; **9, 6** nutrition expert.

differ **4** vary; **5** argue; **7** quarrel, wrangle; **8** disagree; **9** fluctuate; PHRASES: **2, 2, 8** be at variance; **2, 6** be unlike; **2, 9** be different; **4, 3** fall out.

difference **3** gap; **4** loss; **5** debit; **6** change, excess, margin, profit; **7** balance,

deficit, discord, dispute, quarrel, surplus; **8** argument, contrast, variance; **9** deviation, disparity, diversity, variation; **10** divergence; **11** discrepancy, distinction, incongruity; **12** differential, disagreement; **13** inconsistency, nonconformity; **15** differentiation, incompatibility; PHRASES: **3, 3** bad fit; **3, 5** bad match; **5-4** carry-over.

different **3** odd; **5** alien; **6** unique, unlike; **7** altered, another, changed, diverse, strange, unequal, unusual, variant; **8** atypical, discrete, distinct, separate, uncommon; **9** deviating, differing, divergent; **10** discordant, discrepant, dissimilar, mismatched; **11** distinctive, incongruous; **12** incompatible, inconsistent; PHRASES: **4, 3, 3** like oil and water; **4, 5, 3, 3** like night and day; **5, 5** poles apart; **6, 5** worlds apart.

differential *See* **difference**

differentially **7** levelly; **9** regularly, routinely; **10** comparably, frequently, relatively; **11** extensively; **13** comparatively; **14** hierarchically, proportionally; PHRASES: **2, 10** by comparison.

differentiate **4** vary; **6** change, modify; **7** convert, discern, distort; **8** disguise, separate; **9** segregate; **10** camouflage; **11** distinguish; **12** discriminate; PHRASES: **3, 5** set apart; **4, 5** tell apart; **5, 5** split hairs; **6, 3** single out.

differentiation **9** disparity, diversity, variation; **10** difference, separation; **11** convolution, delineation, demarcation, discrepancy, distinction, integration; **12** differential; **14** discrimination; PHRASES: **4, 2, 6** rate of change.

differently **9** otherwise; **10** contrarily, unsuitably; PHRASES: **7, 3** another way. *See also* **different**

difficult **4** grim, hard; **5** heavy, steep, tough; **6** knotty, severe, tricky, trying; **7** arduous, complex, onerous, testing, unclear; **8** abstruse, baffling, critical, exacting, grueling, involved, puzzling, stubborn, toilsome; **9** ambiguous, demanding, enigmatic, Herculean, intricate, laborious, obstinate, punishing, recondite, strenuous; **10** convoluted, exhausting, impossible, oppressive, perplexing *UK*, sphinxlike; **11** challenging, complicated, inscrutable, problematic, troublesome; **12** backbreaking, recalcitrant, unmanageable; **13** impracticable; **14** unintelligible; PHRASES: **4, 4, 4** over one's head; **5, 2, 3** clear as mud; **6, 3** beyond one.

difficult (be difficult) 6 hassle, pester; PHRASES: 4, 8 pose problems; 7, 8 present problems.

difficult person 7 handful; 8 criminal; 10 delinquent, malcontent; 12 troublemaker; PHRASES: 3, 3, 3, 6 all one can manage; 4, 5 bête noire.

difficulty 4 snag; 6 hurdle; 7 problem; 8 obstacle, severity; 9 adversity, intricacy, obscurity; 10 complexity, impediment; 12 complication, disadvantage, technicality; PHRASES: 9, 5 stumbling block. *See also* **difficult**

difficulty (be in difficulty) 8 flounder, struggle; PHRASES: 2, 2, 3, 4 go to the wall; 2, 2, 4, 4, 3 be at one's wits' end; 2, 5 go under; 3, 4, 5 hit hard times; 3, 4, 7 run into trouble; 4, 2, 3, 5 walk on hot coals; 4, 3, 5 bear the brunt, feel the pinch; 4, 7 come unstuck; 4, 8 swim upstream; 5, 2, 4 tread on eggs; 6, 1, 3, 5 strike a bad patch.

difficulty (cause difficulties) 6 bother, hamper, hinder, puzzle; 7 confuse, disrupt, disturb, mystify, nonplus, perplex, perturb; 8 bewilder; 10 discommode; 13 inconvenience; PHRASES: 3, 2 box in; 3, 3 put out; 3, 4, 4, 2, 2 put one's foot in it; 4, 5 find fault; 5, 2, 3, 4 force to the wall.

diffident *See* **timid**

diffraction 7 bending, curving; 8 diaspora; 9 diffusion, diversion; 10 deflection, dispersion, reflection, refraction.

diffractive 7 diffuse; 8 diffused; 9 dispersed, reflected, refracted, scattered; 10 diffracted, refractile, refractive.

diffuse 4 epic; 5 prosy, wordy; 6 effuse, ornate, prolix, spread, strewn; 7 flowing, gushing, lengthy, profuse, scatter, verbose; 8 abundant, detailed, disperse, effusive, expanded, extended, prolific, rambling; 9 bombastic, circulate, dispersed, exuberant, redundant, scattered; 10 circulated, distribute, loquacious, pleonastic, protracted, rhetorical, voluminous; 11 disseminate, distributed, reiterative, superfluous, tautologous; 12 disseminated, magniloquent, tautological; 13 superabundant; 14 sesquipedalian; PHRASES: 4, 3 spun out; 4-5-3 long-drawn-out; 4-6 long-winded; 5-3 drawn-out; 5-4 loose-knit; 5-6 never-ending.

diffuse (be diffuse) 4 flow, gush; 5 orate; 6 dilate, expand, extend; 7 amplify; 8 overflow; 9 elaborate, reiterate; 11 tautologize; PHRASES: 3, 8 wax eloquent; 4, 1, 4, 4 spin a long tale; 4, 3 draw out, pour out, spin out; 6, 2 rabbit on, ramble on.

diffusely 8 minutely, sparsely; 12 infrequently, sporadically; PHRASES: 2, 5, 6 at great length; 2, 6 in detail; 2, 7 ad nauseam, in extenso; 4, 3, 5 here and there. *See also* **diffuse**

diffuseness 4 flow, gush; 7 oration; 8 effusion, pleonasm, rhetoric, richness, verbiage; 9 abundance, amplitude, diffusion, expansion, extension, logorrhea, loquacity, prolixity, tautology, verbosity; 10 exuberance, minuteness, redundancy, repetition; 11 copiousness, elaboration, superfluity; 12 dissertation; 13 diffusiveness, talkativeness; 14 productiveness, repetitiveness. *See also* **diffuse**

diffusion 4 flow; 9 dispersal; 10 dispersion; 11 circulation; 12 distribution, transmission; 13 dissemination.

dig 3 hoe, jab; 4 gibe, jeer, mine, plow *UK*, poke, prod, push, till, turn; 5 crack, nudge, shove, taunt; 6 burrow, insult, plough *UK*, tunnel; 8 excavate; PHRASES: 5, 2 break up; 6, 3 hollow out.

digest 4 book; 5 grasp; 6 absorb, résumé; 7 consume, journal, process, summary; 8 abstract, magazine; 10 abridgment, assimilate, periodical; 11 publication; 12 condensation; PHRASES: 4, 2 take in; 4, 2, 5 take on board; 5, 4 break down.

digger 5 borer, miner; 7 crawler, dredger, driller; 8 burrower, tunneler; 9 bulldozer, excavator, quarryman; 10 earthmover, prospector; 11 gravedigger; 13 archaeologist.

dignitary 3 VIP; 6 worthy; 7 notable; 8 luminary; 9 celebrity.

dignity (with dignity) 5 nobly; 7 gravely, soberly; 8 sedately, solemnly, worthily.

dig out 4 find, mine; 6 excise, exhume, expose, locate, quarry, reveal; 7 uncover, unearth; 8 discover, disinter, excavate; 9 disentomb, extricate; PHRASES: 5, 2, 5 bring to light; 6, 2 dredge up.

digress 6 depart, ramble; 7 deviate, diverge; 8 divagate; PHRASES: 2, 3, 2, 1, 7 go off at a tangent.

dike 3 dam; 4 bank, wall; 5 ditch, drain; 7 barrier, channel, conduit; 10 embankment; 11 watercourse.

dilapidated 3 old; 4 weak, worn; 5 frail, spent; 6 broken, frayed, infirm, rotten, ruined; 7 decayed, rickety, ruinous, rundown, tottery, unkempt, wrecked; 8 battered, decaying, decrepit, derelict, mildewed, unsteady, weakened, withered; 9 condemned, crumbling, destroyed, exhausted, neglected; 10 ramshackle, tumbledown; PHRASES: 2, 3, 4, 4 on its last legs; 2, 4, 3, 6 in bits and pieces; 2, 5 in ruins; 2, 7 in tatters; 2, 9 in disrepair; 3, 2, 5 out of order; 3, 2, 6 out of kilter; 3-5 dog-eared; 3, 5, 3, 4 the worse for wear; 4, 2, 1, 6 worn to a shadow; 4-2-4 down-at-heel; 4, 3 worn out; 4-3-3 down-and-out; 4, 4 laid bare; 4-4 well-worn; 4-5 moth-eaten, worm-eaten; 6-4 broken-down; 6, 6 beyond repair; 7-6 weather-beaten.

dilapidation 4 ruin; 5 decay; 7 erosion, neglect; 8 collapse, marasmus; 9 breakdown, corrosion, disrepair, moldiness, ruination, rustiness; 10 corruption, rottenness, weathering; 11 decrepitude, dereliction, destruction; 12 putrefaction; 13 decomposition; 14 disintegration; PHRASES: 4, 3, 4 moth and rust, rack and ruin, wear and tear.

dilate 4 open; 5 widen; 6 expand; 7 amplify, enlarge, expound; 8 increase; 9 expatiate; PHRASES: 5, 2 dwell on.

dilemma 6 crisis, puzzle; 7 impasse, problem; 8 quandary; 10 difficulty; 11 predicament; PHRASES: 3, 6 hot button; 4, 6 zero option; 5-2 catch-22 *UK*; 5, 4 third rail, tight spot; 7, 6 Hobson's choice.

diligence 8 industry; 11 persistence. *See also* **diligent**

diligent 7 careful; 8 sedulous, studious, thorough; 9 assiduous, attentive; 10 fastidious, meticulous; 11 industrious; 13 conscientious.

dilute 4 thin, weak; 6 reduce, temper, watery, weaken; 7 insipid, liquefy, thinned; 8 dissolve, mitigate, saturate; 9 attenuate, dissipate, evaporate; 10 adulterate, dissipated; PHRASES: 4, 3, 4, 3 take the edge off; 5, 4 water down; 7-4 watered-down.

dilution 7 potency; 8 banality, flatness, solution, strength, thinning, watering; 9 intensity, reduction, triteness, weakening; 10 jejuneness; 11 attenuation, dissipation, evaporation; 12 adulteration, liquefaction; 13 concentration, deliquescence; PHRASES: 5-9 wishy-washiness.

dim 3 dip, fog; 4 dark, drab, dull, fade, lour, matt, pale, wane, weak; 5 cloud, dingy, dusky, faded, faint, glaze, lower, misty, muted, shade, shady, smear, vague; 6 bleary, blurry, cloudy, darken, dulled, gloomy, shadow, shroud, stupid, twilit, waning; 7 blurred, clouded, darkish, diffuse, louring, obscure, shadowy, subdued, sunless, unclear; 8 overcast, semidark; 9 obfuscate, tenebrous; 10 indistinct, lackluster, lustreless *UK*; 11 crepuscular; PHRASES: 3-3 ill-lit; 4, 3 fade out; 4, 4 grow pale; 4-4 half-dark; 5, 4 cloud over.

dimension 5 facet, width; 6 aspect, factor, height, length; 7 breadth, element, feature; 11 measurement.

diminish 3 ebb; 4 fade; 6 lessen, reduce, shrink, weaken; 8 moderate; PHRASES: 4, 3 fade out; 4, 4 fade away; 4, 7 make smaller.

diminish, diminution *See* **decrease**

diminutive *See* **small**

dimly 2, 3, 8 in the gloaming, in the twilight. *See also* **dim**

dimming 9 shadowing; 10 blackening; 13 overshadowing.

dimness 4 dusk; 5 shade; 8 gloaming, penumbra, twilight; 9 stupidity; PHRASES: 5, 5 first light; 6, 2, 3, 4 waning of the moon; 7, 5 evening light, oblique light. *See also* **dim**

dimple *See* **hollow**

din 5 noise; 6 hammer, hubbub, racket, rumpus; 7 impress, instill; 9 inculcate; 10 hullabaloo; PHRASES: 4, 4 drum into.

diner 4 café; 5 guest; 6 bistro, patron; 7 canteen, dinette; 8 customer; 9 brasserie, cafeteria, refectory, trattoria; 10 restaurant; PHRASES: 4, 4 mess room; 6, 4 dining room.

dingy 4 drab, dull, worn; 5 dirty, grimy, tatty; 6 grubby, shabby, soiled; 7 squalid.

dinosaur 5 relic; 6 fossil; 7 monster, vestige; 8 Godzilla, hangover, leftover, mosasaur, sauropod; 9 hadrosaur, iguanodon, nothosaur, oviraptor, pterosaur, stegosaur, trachodon; 10 allosaurus, altispinax, ankylosaur, barosaurus, cotylosaur, dicynodont, diplodocus, dryosaurus, megalosaur, orthomerus, pelycosaur, plesiosaur, pteranodon, stegoceras, titanosaur; 11 anatosaurus, anchisaurus, apatosaurus, cetiosaurus, coelophysis, deinonychus, ichthyosaur, kritosaurus, monoclonius, polacanthus, pterodactyl, riojasaurus, saurolophus, scolosaurus, spinosaurus, stegosaurus, tarbo-saurus, triceratops, tyrannosaur; **12** ankylosaurus, brontosaurus, camptosaurus, ceratosaurus, chasmosaurus, deinocheirus, hylaeosaurus, kentrosaurus, lambeosaurus, megalosaurus, ornithomimus, ouranosaurus, plateosaurus, velociraptor; **13** brachiosaurus, compsognathus, corythosaurus, desmatosuchus, dilophosaurus, edmontosaurus, erythrosuchus, hypselosaurus, hypsilophodon, ichthyosaurus, lesothosaurus, panoplosaurus, pentaceratops, protoceratops, scelidosaurus, styracosaurus, tenontosaurus, tyrannosaurus; **14** cetiosauriscus, chasmatosaurus, euoplocephalus, massospondylus, psittacosaurus, thescelosaurus; **15** parasaurolophus, procheneosaurus.

dint 4 dent, mark; **5** spoil; **6** damage, hollow, indent; **7** blemish; **10** depression; **11** indentation.

Dioscuri 6, 3, 6 Castor and Pollux.

dip 4 drop, duck, dunk, fall, sink, soak; **5** bathe, rinse, slant, slope, steep; **6** hollow, plunge; **7** decline, descend, immerse, incline, plummet; **8** downturn, submerge, submerse; **9** concavity; **10** depression, pickpocket; **11** inclination.

diploma *See* **certificate**

diplomacy 4 tact; **5** skill; **8** subtlety; **9** mediation; **10** discretion; **11** negotiation; **12** peacekeeping; PHRASES: **6-5** savoir-faire.

diplomat 5 envoy; **6** consul; **7** attaché; **8** mediator; **9** counselor, tactician; **10** ambassador, negotiator; **11** peacekeeper; **14** representative; PHRASES: **2-7** go-between; **5, 7** civil servant.

diplomatic 4 wily; **5** suave; **6** subtle; **7** politic, tactful; **8** cautious, consular, delicate, discreet; **9** political, sensitive; **13** ambassadorial.

dire *See* **terrible**

direct 3 aim, set; **4** host, lead, rule, show, turn; **5** chair, emcee, exact, frank, guide, order, pilot, point, steer; **6** advise, candid, govern, honest, manage, toward; **7** channel, command, conduct, control, counsel, dictate, nonstop, oversee, precise, skipper; **8** absolute, instruct, navigate, regulate, shortest, signpost, straight, unbroken; **9** determine, downright, immediate, outspoken, unveering; **10** simplistic, unswerving; **11** straightway, superintend, undeviating, unmitigated; **13** uninterrupted, unpretentious;

14 unidirectional; **15** straightforward, unsophisticated; PHRASES: **2, 1, 8, 4** in a straight line; **2, 2, 6** be in charge; **2, 3, 4, 5** as the crow flies; **2-5** up-front; **3-3** one-way; **3, 5** put right; **3, 8** set straight; **4, 3, 3** lead the way, show the way; **4, 3, 4** take the helm; **4, 3, 5** hold the reins, rule the roost, take the chair, wear the crown, wear the pants; **4, 4** lead over, rule over; **4, 4, 4** hold sway over; **4, 6** give orders; **5, 3, 3** point the way; **5, 3, 4** crack the whip; **5, 3, 7** wield the scepter; **5, 6** steer toward; **5-6** plain-spoken; **6-6** single-minded; **6, 7** assume command; **7, 4** preside over; **8, 4** straight away.

direction 3 way; **4** goal, line, path, road; **5** focus, route, track; **6** course; **7** bearing, command, control; **8** guidance, piloting, position, steerage; **9** objective; **10** leadership, management, navigation; **11** instruction, supervision; **12** helmsmanship; **14** administration.

direction (in all directions) 6 around, uptown, upwind; **8** downtown, downwind, upstream; **10** downstream, everywhere; PHRASES: **2, 5, 4** on every side; **3, 5** all round; **5, 2, 3, 4** close to the wind; **5, 3** every way; **5, 3, 5** round and about; **5, 5, 3** every which way; **5-6** close-hauled.

direction (take a direction) 2 go; **3** aim; **4** bear, head, lead, tend, turn; **5** point, trend; **7** incline; **8** navigate; PHRASES: **3, 2** aim at, fix on; **3, 3** run for; **3, 4, 6, 2** set one's sights on; **4, 2, 3, 4** stay on the beam; **4, 3** head for, make for, sail for; **4, 6** hold steady; **4, 7** keep pointed; **5, 2** sight on; **5, 3** steer for; **6, 2, 3, 4** cleave to the line; **6, 4, 4** follow one's nose.

directional 4 back, east, west; **5** north, south; **6** arctic, boreal, radial, rotary; **7** angular, austral, eastern, guiding *UK*, kinetic, oblique, sinking, soaring, turning, western; **8** backward, downward, easterly, eastward, gyratory, mounting, northern, Oriental, refluent, rotatory, sideward, southern, steering, westerly, westward; **9** antarctic, eastbound, kinematic, kinesodic, northeast, northerly, northward, northwest, reflowing, reversing, southeast, southerly, southward, southwest, westbound; **10** circuitous, descending, gyrational, meridional, northbound, Occidental, regressive, rotational, southbound; **11** backflowing, centrifugal, centripetal, easternmost, hyperborean, oscillating, westernmost; **12** northeastern, northernmost, northwestern, southeastern, southernmost, southwestern; **13** northeasterly, northwesterly, retrogressive, southeasterly, southwesterly.

directions 4 tips; **6** orders; **8** commands, guidance; **9** direction; **10** guidelines; **11** information, instruction.

directly 4 soon; **6** openly, wholly; **7** nonstop, quickly; **8** promptly, speedily, squarely, straight; **10** completely, forthright; **13** unambiguously, unequivocally; **15** straightforward; PHRASES: **2, 1, 7** in a beeline; **2, 1, 8, 4** in a straight line; **2, 3, 4, 5** as the crow flies; **2, 3, 5, 5** on the right track; **2, 4** at once; **2, 4, 4** in line with; **2, 5, 7** in every respect; **4, 5** dead ahead; **5, 4** right away; **5-5** point-blank; **7, 5** without delay; **8, 2, 1, 3** straight as a dye; **8, 5** straight ahead; **8, 6** straight across. *See also* **direct**

directness 6 candor; **7** clarity, honesty; **8** fairness; **9** bluntness, plainness, sincerity; **12** truthfulness; **14** scrupulousness. *See also* **direct**

director 3 VIP; **4** boss, head; **5** chair, chief, guide; **6** leader, master; **7** captain, headman, manager, premier, skipper; **8** chairman, employer, governor, helmsman, lawgiver, lawmaker, overseer, superior; **9** executive, navigator, president, principal, steersman; **10** chancellor, controller, headmaster, instructor, legislator; **11** chairperson; **14** superintendent; PHRASES: **4, 2, 5** head of state; **6, 4** hidden hand; **8-7** governor-general.

directorship 7 command; **8** pilotage, steerage; **9** captaincy; **10** leadership, presidency; **11** premiership; **12** chairmanship, dictatorship; **13** steersmanship; PHRASES: **7, 7** supreme control.

directory *See* **list**

dirigible 7 airship.

dirt 3 ash, fur, goo, mud, pus, rot; **4** crud, dung, dust, flea, gunk, lees, loam, mess, mire, mold, mote, muck, rust, scum, slag, smut, soil, soot, spot; **5** decay, dregs, dross, earth, feces, filth, froth, grime, guano, gunge *UK*, mucus, scurf, slime, smear, stain, stool, trash, waste; **6** fungus, gossip, grouts, grunge, litter, manure, mildew, ordure, refuse, slough, sludge, smudge; **7** carrion, garbage, mullock *UK*, residue, rubbish, scandal; **8** quagmire, residuum, sediment; **9** droppings, excrement, feculence, scourings; **12** offscourings.

dirtiness 5 filth; **6** sleaze; **7** soiling, squalor; **9** pollution, purulence, turbidity; **10** squalidity; **11** insalubrity, suppuration. *See also* **dirty**

dirty 4 dull, foul, lewd, miry, oily, rude, soil; **5** black, dingy, dusty, fusty, grimy, messy, moldy, mucky *UK*, muddy, murky, slimy, smear, sooty, stain, sully, taint; **6** befoul, bemire, cloudy, defile, filthy, fouled, frowzy, greasy, grotty *UK*, grubby, matted, scummy, sleazy, slummy, smirch, smudge, soiled, sordid, turbid, unfair, unjust; **7** begrime, beslime, besmear, blacken, clogged, clotted, corrupt, crooked, defiled, draggle, immoral, obscene, pollute, profane, smudged, squalid, stained, sullied, tarnish, unclean, unkempt, unswept; **8** befouled, begrimed, besmirch, indecent, maculate, polluted, prurient, slovenly, sluttish, unhallow, unwashed; **9** bedraggle, besmeared, bespatter, desecrate, salacious, tarnished, uncleaned, unscoured; **10** bedraggled, besmirched, insanitary, lascivious, slatternly, unsanitary, unscrubbed; **11** contaminate, unburnished; **12** pornographic, unscrupulous; PHRASES: **4, 2** mess up.

dirty (be dirty) 5 addle, decay; **6** fester, mildew, molder, wallow; **7** mortify, putrefy; **8** gangrene; PHRASES: **2, 3** go bad, go off; **4, 2** foul up; **7, 4** collect dust.

dis 4 maul; **6** attack, insult, savage; **7** affront; **8** belittle; **9** criticize, deprecate, disparage; **10** disrespect.

disability 8 debility, handicap, weakness; **9** infirmity; **10** incapacity.

disable 6 disarm; **8** handicap, restrict; **10** deactivate, inactivate; **12** incapacitate; PHRASES: **3, 3, 2, 6** put out of action; **5, 3** knock out.

disaccustom 4, 4 wean from; **5, 1, 5** break a habit; **5, 3** throw off; **6, 3** slough off.

disadvantage 8 drawback, weakness; **9** hindrance; **10** difficulty; **11** shortcoming.

disagree 3 row; **4** vary; **5** argue, clash, demur, fight; **6** bicker, differ, object, oppose; **7** contend, deviate, dispute, dissent, diverge, quarrel, wrangle; **8** conflict, squabble; **9** altercate, challenge, criticize; **10** antagonize, contradict; **11** expostulate, remonstrate; PHRASES: **2, 2, 4** be at odds; **3, 4, 4** not play ball; **4, 3** fall out; **4, 5, 4** take issue with; **5, 2, 8** agree to ~; **5, 4, 4** break away from; **5, 5, 5** stand poles apart; **5, 6** cross swords; **5, 9** sever relations; **6, 2** object to; **6, 4** differ with.

disagreeable 4 rude; **5** nasty, surly; **6** crabby; **7** brusque, hostile; **8** contrary, inimical; **9** difficult, offensive; **10** dislikable, dissenting, unfriendly; **11** disagreeing, displeasing, distasteful, quarrelsome; **12** antipathetic; PHRASES: **3-8** bad-tempered.

disagreement 5 cavil, clash; **6** enmity, strife; **7** discord, dispute, dissent, quarrel, wrangle; **8** argument, conflict, division, friction, variance; **9** bickering, challenge, criticism, deviation, disaccord, disparity, hostility, objection, wrangling; **10** antagonism, contention, difference, disharmony, dissension, dissidence, dissonance, divergence, opposition, squabbling; **11** altercation, bellicosity, controversy, discordance, discrepancy, incongruity; **12** belligerence, divisiveness; **13** confrontation, contradiction, dissimilarity; **14** noncooperation, uncongeniality; **15** incompatibility; PHRASES: **4, 2, 4** bone to pick; **4, 5** sore point; **5, 5** casus belli; **7, 2, 3** theatre of war; **7-3** falling-out; **8, 5** ticklish issue.

disallow 3 bar; **4** deny, veto; **5** throw; **6** cancel, forbid, refuse, reject; **8** prohibit; **10** disapprove.

disappear 2 go; **3** die, dim, ebb, end; **4** blur, fade, hide, melt, wane; **5** cease; **6** darken, expire, perish, recede, vanish; **7** dwindle; **8** dissolve, evanesce, withdraw; **9** evaporate; **13** dematerialize; PHRASES: **4, 3** fade out; **4, 4** fade away, pass away; **5, 3** peter out; **6, 7** become extinct; **7, 4** dwindle away.

disappear (cause to disappear) 4 bury, hide; **5** erase, expel; **6** cancel, dispel, remove; **7** conceal, obscure; **8** disguise, disperse, vaporize; **9** disembody, dissipate, eliminate, liquidate; **10** annihilate, camouflage, obliterate; PHRASES: **3, 3** rub out; **4, 3** blot out, wipe out; **6, 4** spirit away.

disappearance 3 end; **4** exit, wane; **6** dearth, fading, flight; **7** erosion, melting, passing, paucity; **8** shortage; **9** cessation, departure, desertion, dispersal, dwindling, vanishing; **10** deficiency, dispersion, extinction, scattering, vanishment, withdrawal; **11** dissipation, dissolution, evanescence, evaporation; **12** invisibility, nonexistence, vaporization; **13** disembodiment, nonappearance; PHRASES: **4-3** fade-out.

disappeared 4 dead, gone, past; **6** ab-

sent; **7** extinct, missing; **8** eclipsed, obsolete, occulted; **9** concealed, disguised, dispersed, invisible; **10** dissipated; **11** camouflaged, nonexistent, obsolescent; PHRASES: **3, 2, 3, 7** out of the picture; **3, 2, 5** out of sight; **4, 2, 5** lost to sight; **4, 2, 6** gone to ground; **4, 3, 4** past and gone. *See also* **disappear**

disappearing 8 fleeting; **9** declining, departing, transient; **10** endangered, evanescent; **11** diminishing. *See also* **disappear**

disappoint 4 fail; **5** upset; **6** sadden, thwart; **9** frustrate, tantalize; **10** disenchant, dishearten, dissatisfy; **11** disillusion; PHRASES: **3, 4** let down; **4, 2, 7** fail to deliver; **4, 4, 5** dash one's hopes; **4, 5** fall short; **5, 2, 3, 5** leave in the lurch; **5, 2, 7** drive to despair; **5, 3, 6** burst the bubble; **5, 4, 5** crush one's hopes; **6, 4, 5** betray one's hopes, blight one's hopes, defeat one's hopes.

disappointed 3 sad; **4** fail; **5** upset; **6** balked, bilked, denied, foiled; **7** crushed, humbled; **8** defeated, dejected, hampered, hindered, rejected, saddened, thwarted; **9** chagrined; **10** confounded, frustrated, humiliated; **11** crestfallen, discouraged, disgruntled, stonewalled; **12** discontented, disenchanted, disheartened, dissatisfied; **13** disillusioned; PHRASES: **3, 4** let down; **3, 6** led astray.

disappointing 8 abortive, inferior; **10** inadequate; **12** insufficient, unacceptable, unfulfilling, unsatisfying, unsuccessful; **13** discontenting; **14** unsatisfactory; PHRASES: **3, 2, 2, 7** not up to scratch; **5, 3** below par; **6-4** second-best, second-rate; **7, 5** falling short. *See also* **disappoint**

disappointment 6 defeat, regret; **7** chagrin, failure, regrets, setback; **10** discontent; **11** displeasure, frustration; **13** inconvenience, mortification, noncompletion, tantalization; **14** discouragement, disenchantment, nonfulfillment; **15** disillusionment, dissatisfaction; PHRASES: **4, 11** vain expectation; **5, 5** false hopes.

disapproval 6 denial; **7** censure, dislike, protest, refusal; **8** disfavor, distaste; **9** objection; **10** discontent; **11** displeasure, indignation; **12** condemnation, unpopularity; **14** disapprobation, discontentment, disgruntlement; PHRASES: **6, 4** thumbs down.

disapproval (show disapproval) 3 boo, mob; **4** hiss, jeer; **5** frown, lynch, scowl, sneer, taunt; **6** clamor, deride, heckle; **7** catcall, protest; **8** ridicule; PHRASES: **3-3** tut-tut; **4, 8** slow handclap *UK*; **5, 3** throw mud; **5, 4** shout down; **5, 6** throw stones; **6-7** cotton-picking.

disapprove 6 object; **7** condemn, deplore, dislike; **8** denounce, disfavor, ridicule; **9** criticize; **14** discountenance; PHRASES: **4, 1, 3, 4, 2** take a dim view of; **4, 2, 8** hold in contempt; **4, 4** turn down; **4, 4, 2** look down on; **5, 2** frown on; **5, 3, 2** think ill of; **5, 4** shout down; **5, 6** throw stones.

disapproved 6 banned, barred, vetoed; **7** blacked, opposed; **8** excluded; **9** boycotted; **10** ostracized; **11** blackballed, blacklisted.

disapproving 5 harsh, stern; **8** critical, negative; **9** indignant, seditious; **10** censorious, displeased; **11** deprecatory, disgruntled, reproachful; **12** dissatisfied; **13** contradictive, insubordinate; **14** disapprobatory.

disapprovingly 2, 3, 4, 2 in the face of; **2, 10** in opposition. *See also* **disapproving**

disarm 5 charm; **6** defuse; **7** beguile, enchant; **10** deactivate, neutralize; PHRASES: **3, 4** win over; **4, 4** make safe.

disarrange 6 jumble, muddle; **7** confuse, derange, disturb; **8** dishevel, disorder; **11** disorganize; PHRASES: **3, 2** mix up; **4, 2** mess up.

disarranged 5 messy; **6** untidy; **7** jumbled, muddled; **8** confused, deranged; **10** disheveled, disordered; **12** disorganized; PHRASES: **5, 2** mixed up; **6, 2** messed up.

disarrangement 8 disorder; **9** confusion; **11** derangement; **15** disorganization.

disarray 4 mess; **5** alarm, chaos, panic; **6** dismay; **8** disorder, hysteria; **9** confusion; **10** untidiness.

disaster 4 ruin; **5** farce; **6** fiasco; **7** debacle, failure, tragedy; **8** shambles; **9** adversity; **11** catastrophe.

disastrous 6 doomed, tragic; **7** unlucky; **8** luckless, terrible; **10** calamitous; **11** devastating, unfortunate; **12** catastrophic, unsuccessful.

disbanded 8 demobbed; **9** dismissed, dissolved; **11** deactivated, demobilized.

disbandment 9 dismissal; **11** dissolution; **12** deactivation; **14** demobilization.

disbar 5 expel, strip; **6** banish, demote, depose, remove; **7** cashier, defrock, degrade, deplume, dismiss, exclude, suspend,

unfrock; **8** dethrone, displume, relegate; **9** discharge, rusticate; PHRASES: **4, 4** send down *UK*; **4, 10** kick downstairs; **5, 3** throw out.

disbelief 5 doubt; **7** dissent, dubiety; **8** distrust; **9** hesitancy, misgiving, suspicion; **10** hesitation, skepticism; **11** dubiousness, incredulity, reservation; **12** doubtfulness; **14** suspiciousness.

disbelief (cause disbelief) 5 amaze; **7** stagger; PHRASES: **4, 5** cast doubt.

disbelieve 4 deny; **5** doubt, scorn; **7** dispute, dissent, suspect; **8** distrust, hesitate, mistrust, question; **9** challenge, discredit; **10** apostasize; PHRASES: **4, 6, 5** have doubts about; **5, 1, 3** smell a rat; **5, 2** scoff at.

disbelieved 7 suspect; **9** suspected; **10** disputable, improbable, incredible, suspicious, unbelieved; **11** discredited; **12** questionable, unbelievable; PHRASES: **2-6** so-called; **3-7** far-fetched.

disbeliever 5 pagan; **6** mocker *UK*; **7** atheist, doubter, heathen, heretic, infidel, skeptic; **8** agnostic, apostate; **9** detractor, dissenter, dissident; **10** secularist, unbeliever; **11** materialist, nonbeliever, rationalist; **13** irreligionist, nonconformist; PHRASES: **4-7** free-thinker; **8, 6** doubting Thomas.

disbelieving 5 pagan; **7** dubious, heathen; **8** agnostic, doubtful, doubting, hesitant, scornful; **9** atheistic, heretical, skeptical, uncertain; **10** dissenting, unfaithful; **11** distrustful, incredulous, unbelieving.

discard 4 oust, shed; **5** ditch, eject, expel, scrap; **6** depose, reject; **7** abandon, dismiss; **8** jettison, renounce; PHRASES: **3, 3, 2** get rid of; **3, 5** set aside; **4, 2** give up; **4, 3** boot out, cast off, cast out, kick out; **5, 3** chuck out, sling out, throw out; **5, 4** throw away; **7, 2** dispose of; **8, 4** dispense with.

discern 3 see; **6** fathom, notice; **8** discover, perceive, separate; **10** understand; **11** distinguish; **12** discriminate; **13** differentiate; PHRASES: **2, 5, 2** be aware of; **4, 3** make out.

discerningly 8 urbanely; **9** elegantly; **10** tastefully; **11** judiciously, sensitively; **12** insightfully, perceptively; **15** sophisticatedly.

discharge 4 emit, flow, free, ooze; **5** clear, expel; **6** settle; **7** dismiss, excrete, release, satisfy, seepage; **8** ejection, emission, liberate; **9** excretion, expulsion, liquidate, secretion; **10** emancipate, liberation; **12** emancipation; PHRASES: **3, 2** let go; **3, 3** lay off, pay off; **3, 4** set free; **4, 3** send out; **7, 2, 4** relieve of duty.

disciple 7 devotee; **8** believer, follower, partisan; **9** supporter.

disciplinarian 6 despot, tyrant; **8** martinet, stickler; **13** authoritarian.

discipline 3 law; **5** order, teach, train; **6** punish; **7** chasten, correct, educate; **8** chastise, instruct, regulate; **9** authority, castigate; **10** punishment, regulation; **11** castigation; **12** chastisement; PHRASES: **3, 3, 5** law and order; **4, 2, 3** rule of law; **4-7** self-control; **4-9** self-restraint.

disciplined 7 orderly; **8** decorous, obedient, punished; **9** peaceable; **10** controlled; PHRASES: **3-7** law-abiding; **4-7** well-behaved, well-drilled; **4-9** well-organized; **4-10** self-controlled; **5, 7** under control.

disclaim *See* **deny**

disclose 4 leak; **5** admit; **6** denude, expose, reveal, unfold, unfurl, unmask, unveil, unwrap; **7** confess, divulge, uncloak, uncover, unearth; **8** disinter, manifest, unkennel, unshroud; **9** uncurtain; **11** acknowledge; PHRASES: **2, 6** go public; **3, 2** dig up; **3, 4** lay bare, lay open, let slip; **4, 3, 4** lift the veil; **4, 3, 5, 3** take the wraps off; **4, 3, 7** open the windows; **4, 5** make known; **5, 2, 5** bring to light; **5, 3, 3** break the wax; **5, 4** strip bare.

disclose (be disclosed) 6 appear, emerge; **9** transpire; PHRASES: **3, 3** get out; **4, 2, 5** come to light; **4, 3** come out, leak out; **4, 4** dawn upon; **5, 8** stand revealed; **6, 5** become known.

disclosed 7 obvious; **11** transparent. *See also* **disclose**

discloser 6 source; **7** exposer, peacher; **8** betrayer, informer, reporter, squealer, telltale; **9** confessor, informant; **10** discoverer, publicizer, researcher, tattletale; **11** broadcaster, stoolpigeon; **12** blabbermouth, investigator; PHRASES: **7-6** whistle-blower.

disclosure 4 leak; **6** exposé; **8** epiphany, exposure; **9** discovery, unveiling; **10** confession, denouement, resolution, revelation, uncovering; **11** anagnorisis; **13** manifestation.

discolor 4 fade; **5** color, stain; **6** darken; **7** tarnish.

discomfort 4 ache, pain; **5** worry; **7** anxiety; **8** distress, soreness; **10** irritation, tenderness, uneasiness; **13** embarrassment.

discompose 5 addle, upset; **6** hassle; **7** confuse, derange, disturb, perturb; **8** befuddle, unsettle; **9** discomfit, disorient; **10** disconcert; PHRASES: **3, 2, 5** tie in knots.

disconnect 5 break, sever; **6** detach, divide; **7** disjoin, unhinge; **8** disjoint, disunite, separate; **9** disengage, dislocate, dismember; **13** disarticulate; PHRASES: **3, 3** cut off.

disconnected 3, 2, 5 out of joint. *See also* **disconnect**

disconnectedly 8 brokenly; **12** disjointedly; PHRASES: **2, 4, 3, 6** by fits and starts; **2, 7** by catches. *See also* **disconnect**

disconnection 8 luxation, stoppage; **9** cessation, severance; **10** decoupling, detachment, separation; **11** dislocation; **12** interruption; **13** disengagement, dismemberment; **15** disarticulation, discontinuation.

disconsolate *See* **unhappy**

discontent 7 sadness; **10** gloominess; **11** displeasure, unhappiness; **14** disgruntlement; **15** dissatisfaction.

discontentedly 8 aversely; **11** reluctantly, resentfully, unwillingly; **14** contemptuously; PHRASES: **4, 10** with misgivings; **5, 6** under duress.

discontinue 3 end; **4** drop, halt, quit, stop; **5** cease; **6** finish; **7** suspend; **8** withdraw; **9** terminate; PHRASES: **3, 2, 3, 2** put an end to; **3, 3** cut off; **4, 2, 1, 3** call it a day; **4, 2, 2** pack it in; **4, 2, 5** call it quits; **5, 3** break off, leave off; **7, 4** refrain from.

discontinued 8 obsolete; **9** withdrawn; **10** superseded; **12** nonrecurrent, unobtainable; PHRASES: **3-2-4** out-of-date. *See also* **discontinue**

discontinuity 3 gap; **5** break; **6** cutoff, cutout; **9** confusion, jerkiness, roughness; **10** brokenness, choppiness, fitfulness, unevenness; **11** disjunction, incoherence; **12** irregularity; **13** disconnection, intermittence; **14** discontinuance, disjointedness; **15** discontinuation.

discontinuous 5 bitty, bumpy, jerky, jolty; **6** broken, choppy, dotted, fitful, patchy, random, uneven; **7** erratic, scrappy, snatchy; **8** confused, episodic, periodic, sporadic; **9** desultory, disunited, irregular, spasmodic; **10** disjointed, fragmented, incoherent, infrequent; **11** alternating, unconnected; **12** intermittent, nonrecurrent, unsuccessive; **13** noncontinuous; PHRASES: **2-3** on-off; **4-2** stop-go *UK.*

discontinuously 6 passim; PHRASES: **2, 4, 3, 6** in fits and starts; **2, 5, 3, 5** in dribs and drabs; **2, 7** by degrees; **2, 9** at intervals; **3, 3, 2** off and on; **3, 3, 4** now and then; **4, 2, 1, 5** once in a while; **4, 3, 5** here and there. *See also* **discontinuous**

discord 7 dispute; **8** argument, conflict, friction; **9** cacophony; **10** disharmony, dissonance; **11** discordance; **12** disagreement.

discordant 6 shrill; **7** defiant, jarring; **8** clashing; **9** different, dissident, dissonant, unmusical; **10** dissenting, frictional; **11** acrimonious, adversarial, cacophonous, challenging, conflicting, contentious, dissentient; **12** disputatious, inharmonious; PHRASES: **2, 4** at odds; **2, 5, 8** at cross purposes; **2, 8** at variance; **2, 10** in opposition; **4-2** head-on; **4, 2, 4** face to face.

discount 3 cut; **4** agio; **5** lower, slash; **6** deduct, ignore, rebate, reduce; **7** cheapen; **8** contango, decrease, markdown, overlook, subtract; **9** decrement, deduction, disregard, reduction; **10** concession *UK*, disbelieve; **13** backwardation *UK*; PHRASES: **3, 4** cut rate; **4, 3, 4** tare and tret; **4, 4** mark down, pass over; **5, 1, 6** allow a margin; **5, 1, 7** offer a bargain; **5, 3** knock off, money off, price cut, write off; **5, 4** knock down.

discount (at a discount) 4 sale; **5** cheap; **7** bargain, rebated, reduced; **8** shopworn; **10** shopsoiled; **11** promotional; PHRASES: **2, 3, 4** in the sale; **2, 3, 5** at cut price; **2, 4** on sale; **2, 4, 5** at half price; **2, 5** on offer; **2, 7, 5** on special offer; **3-4** cut-rate; **3-5** cut-price *UK*; **5, 3** below par; **6, 4** marked down; **7-8** bargain-basement.

discount (take a discount) 4, 3 rake off.

discourage 4 stop; **5** quiet; **6** dampen, deject, dismay, hinder, oppose, sadden; **7** depress, prevent; **8** dispirit, dissuade; **10** disappoint, disenchant, dishearten, extinguish; **11** disillusion; PHRASES: **4, 3, 4, 3** take the edge off.

discourse 6 debate, homily, sermon, speech; **7** address; **8** converse, dialogue, treatise; **10** discussion; **12** conversation, dissertation; **13** communication; PHRASES: **4, 1, 4** have a word *UK*; **7, 5** compare notes.

discourteous 4 curt, rude, tart; **5** blunt, harsh, nasty, sharp, short, sulky, surly, testy; **6** abrupt, biting, gauche, snappy, sullen, unkind; **7** abusive, acerbic, awkward, bearish, boorish, brusque, offhand, parvenu, peevish, uncivil, uncouth; **8** cavalier, impolite, insolent, inurbane, petulant, tactless; **9** barbarian, charmless, offhanded, tasteless, uncourtly, ungallant, unrefined; **10** disorderly, uncultured, unfriendly, ungracious, unmannerly, unpleasant, unpolished, unsociable; **11** acrimonious, insensitive, thoughtless; **12** disagreeable, unchivalrous, unsolicitous, vituperative; **13** disrespectful, inconsiderate; **15** uncomplimentary; PHRASES: **3-8** ill-mannered; **4-8** cold-shoulder; **5-7** sharp-tongued; **7, 5** nouveau riche.

discourteous (be discourteous) 4 ogle, snub; **5** abuse, stare; **6** ignore, insult; **7** affront, outrage; **9** interrupt; PHRASES: **3, 4** cut dead; **4, 2, 6** know no better; **4, 3, 4** show the door; **4, 4, 4, 2** turn one's back on; **4-8** cold-shoulder; **5, 7** cause offense; **5, 9** flout etiquette; **6, 5** behave badly; **6, 8** ruffle feelings.

discourteous act 4 jeer, snub; **5** abuse, frown, scowl; **6** insult, rebuff; PHRASES: **3, 8** bad language; **4, 4** sour look; **4, 7** rude gesture; **4, 8** cold shoulder; **5, 4** dirty joke; **5, 6** short answer.

discourteously 2, 1, 5, 4 in a sharp tone. *See also* **discourteous**

discourtesy 7 jeering, mockery; **8** acerbity, asperity, backtalk, defiance, derision, raillery, ridicule, rudeness, scoffing, tartness; **9** bluntness, insolence, petulance, rejoinder, sharpness, shortness, surliness; **10** disrespect, incivility, inurbanity, sullenness; **11** brusqueness, inattention; **12** impertinence, impoliteness, tactlessness, ungentleness, unpoliteness; **13** insensitivity, ungallantness; **14** unfriendliness, ungraciousness, unpleasantness; **15** thoughtlessness.

discover 4 espy, find; **5** learn, sight; **6** descry, detect, locate, notice; **7** discern, observe, realize, uncover, unearth; **8** identify, perceive; **9** ascertain, determine; PHRASES: **3, 2** dig up; **3, 4** hit upon; **3, 4, 2** set eyes on; **4, 4** come upon, meet with; **4, 6** come across; **5, 1, 7, 2** catch a glimpse of; **6, 4** happen upon; **7, 2** stumble on.

discover (be discovered) 4, 2 turn up; **4, 2, 5** come to light.

discoverable 9 heuristic; **10** detectable; **11** perceptible; **12** identifiable.

discovered 5 found; 7 exposed, located, spotted; 8 revealed, unmasked; 9 uncovered, unearthed.

discoverer 3 spy; 4 mole; 5 agent, scout; 6 dowser, finder; 7 creator, pioneer, spotter; 8 explorer, inventor, observer; 9 detective, innovator; 10 originator, pathfinder, prospector; 13 archaeologist; PHRASES: 7, 3 private eye.

discovery 4 find; 7 finding, glimpse; 8 location, sighting, spotting; 9 detection, invention; 10 unearthing; 11 observation; 12 breakthrough.

discredit 4 slur; 5 doubt, query, smear; 6 demean, insult; 7 suspect; 8 question; 9 humiliate; 10 disbelieve.

discreet 6 subtle; 7 careful, prudent, tactful; 8 cautious; 11 circumspect, understated, unobtrusive; 12 unnoticeable; 13 inconspicuous.

discrete *See* **separate**

discretion 4 will; 6 choice, option; 7 caution; 8 pleasure, prudence; 9 canniness; 11 carefulness.

discriminate 5 favor, judge; 6 choose, divide, prefer, select; 7 discern; 8 classify, separate; 9 demarcate; 10 categorize; 11 distinguish; 13 differentiate; PHRASES: 4, 2, 3, 4 lean to one side; 4, 3 pick out; 4, 3, 6 pick and choose; 4, 5 tell apart; 5, 5 split hairs.

discriminating 5 picky; 6 astute, choosy; 7 refined; 8 critical, pedantic; 9 judicious, selective; 10 cultivated, diagnostic, discerning, divisional, fastidious, meticulous, perceptive; 12 appreciative, differential; 13 perfectionist; PHRASES: 4-9 hairsplitting.

discrimination 4 bias; 5 taste; 6 acumen; 7 bigotry; 8 contrast, inequity; 9 appraisal, diagnosis, prejudice; 10 difference, perception, refinement, separation; 11 demarcation, discernment, distinction, intolerance, percipience, selectivity; 13 selectiveness; 15 differentiation; PHRASES: 4, 5 good taste; 11, 6 affirmative action.

discriminatory 6 ageist, biased, racist, sexist, unfair; 7 bigoted, elitist, fascist, insular, partial; 8 classist, dogmatic, partisan; 9 blinkered, jaundiced, parochial; 10 chauvinist, homophobic, intolerant, jingoistic, nepotistic, prejudiced, xenophobic; 11 inequitable, prejudicial; 12 chauvinistic, ethnocentric, preferential; 14 fundamentalist,

superpatriotic; PHRASES: 3-5 one-sided; 5-6 small-minded; 6-6 narrow-minded.

discuss 4 chat; 6 confer, debate, reason; 7 inquire, reflect; 8 consider, converse, logicize; 9 discourse; 10 deliberate; 11 logomachize, ratiocinate; PHRASES: 3, 6 bat around; 4, 3 hash out; 4, 4 chew over, talk over; 4, 5 chop logic; 4, 6 kick around; 5, 2 weigh up *UK*; 5, 3, 4 argue the toss; 6, 3 thrash out *UK Can*.

discussion 4 chat, moot, talk; 6 confab, debate, powwow, summit; 8 dialogue; 10 conference; 12 conversation; PHRASES: 4-5 argy-bargy *UK*; 8, 2, 5 exchange of views.

disdain 5 scorn, spurn; 7 despise; 8 contempt, derision; 9 aloofness, disparage, disregard, obstinacy, patronize; 10 condescend, touchiness; 13 condescension, disparagement; PHRASES: 4, 2, 4 lord it over; 4, 2, 8 hold in contempt; 4, 4 pull rank; 4, 4, 2 look down on; 5, 2, 4 queen it over; 5-10 stiff-neckedness.

disease 3 bug; 5 virus; 6 malady; 7 ailment, illness; 8 disorder, sickness, syndrome; 9 complaint, infection; PHRASES: 6, 7 social ~. *See also* **disorder, cardiovascular disease**

disease carrier 6 vector; 8 diffuser; 11 transmitter; 12 contaminator.

diseased 3 ill; 4 sick; 5 gouty, mangy; 6 aguish, ailing, anemic, morbid, poorly, rotten, sickly, spotty, tender, unwell; 7 febrile, fevered, leprous, painful, palsied, pyretic, rickety, rotting, sniffly, snuffly, swelled, swollen, throaty; 8 affected, allergic, feverish, infected, inflamed, leukemic, morbific, purulent, spavined, stricken, ulcerous, venereal; 9 bloodless, bronchial, cancerous, cankerous, delirious, festering, paralyzed, phthistic, rheumatic, shivering, ulcerated, unhealthy; 10 bronchitic, contagious, infectious, oncogenous, pathogenic, rheumatoid, tubercular, unhygienic; 11 consumptive, distempered, rheumaticky, tuberculous; 12 carcinogenic, contaminated, degenerative, insalubrious, pathological; 13 carcinomatoid, carninomatous, hydrocephalic, psychosomatic; 14 hydrocephalous.

disembowel 3 gut; 6 fillet; 7 embowel; 10 eviscerate, exenterate.

disengage 4 undo; 5 untie; 6 unlock; 8 uncouple, unfasten.

disengagement *See* **separation**

disentangle 4 free; 5 untie; 7 obviate, unravel, unsnarl; 8 liberate, uncouple, untangle; 9 disengage, extricate; 10 disinvolve, unscramble; 11 disencumber; PHRASES: 3, 4 cut free.

disentanglement 11 extrication; 12 unscrambling; 13 disburdenment, disengagement; 14 disinvolvement; 15 disencumberment. *See also* **disentangle**

disentitle 6 depose; 7 uncrown, unfrock; 8 dethrone; 10 disqualify; 11 expropriate; 12 disestablish.

disentitlement 7 deposal; 9 expulsion; 10 unfrocking; 11 deprivation; 12 dethronement; 13 dispossession, expropriation.

disesteem 8 disfavor, dishonor; 9 disregard, disrepute; 11 disapproval; 14 disapprobation, undervaluation; 15 underestimation.

disfavor 5 scorn; 7 disdain; 8 disgrace, distaste; 9 discredit, disrepute, obscurity; 11 disapproval, displeasure; 12 unpopularity.

disgorge 4 gush, puke, spew; 5 eject, empty, erupt, expel, spout, spurt; 6 squirt, stream; 7 outpour; 9 discharge.

disgorgement 8 bleeding, effusion, eruption, spilling; 9 detrusion, discharge, excretion, extrusion, obtrusion, secretion; 11 ejaculation. *See also* **disgorge**

disgrace 5 shame; 7 degrade, scandal; 8 ignominy; 9 discredit; 11 humiliation; PHRASES: 5, 5, 2 bring shame on.

disguise 3 fog; 4 hide, mask, veil; 5 bedim, befog, cloak, cloud, cover; 6 darken, encode, masque; 7 becloud, conceal, costume, eclipse, obscure; 9 diversion, obfuscate, obscuring; 10 camouflage, masquerade; 11 concealment, obscuration, occultation, smokescreen; PHRASES: 3, 7 red herring; 5, 3, 6 muddy the waters; 5, 5 false beard, false front; 5, 6 false colors; 8, 6 borrowed plumes.

disguised 4 fake, sham; 5 coded; 6 hidden, latent, masked, occult, veiled; 7 cloaked, cryptic, seeming; 8 codified; 9 anonymous, concealed, distorted, imitation, imitative, incognito, simulated; 10 dissembled; 11 camouflaged, embellished, embroidered, whitewashed; 12 dissimulated, masquerading; 14 unrecognizable.

disgust 5 repel, shock; 6 appall, hatred, offend, revolt, sicken; 7 repulse; 8 aversion, loathing, nauseate; 9 antipathy, repulsion, revulsion; 10 abhorrence, repugnance; PHRASES: 4, 4, 7 turn one's stomach.

dish 4 beau, bowl, meze, soup, stew, tapa; 5 balti, curry, grits, halva, plate, salad, satay, sushi, tacos; 6 cheese, course, entrée, fondue, halvah, kebabs, nachos, paella, potage, quiche, ragout, recipe, sambal, saucer, tagine, tamale; 7 ceviche, dessert, fajitas, falafel, goulash, pudding, starter, tempura; 8 burritos, couscous, frijoles, pirozkhi, teriyaki, yakitori; 9 appetizer, casserole, entremets, fricassee, jambalaya, specialty, succotash; 10 sauerkraut, tetrazzini; PHRASES: 3, 4 hot ~; 4, 2, 3, 3 ~ of the day, soup of the day; 4, 2, 4 plat du jour; 4-3 stir-fry; 4, 4 meat loaf, soul food; 4-4 musi-yaki; 4, 6 nasi goreng; 4, 8 eggs Benedict, hors d'oeuvres; 5, 2 serve up *UK*; 5, 4 Irish stew; 5, 5 chef's salad, mixed grill *UK*, patty shell, shish kebab; 7, 5 Waldorf salad; 7, 6 western omelet; 9, 5 congealed salad. *See also* **British dish, Chinese dish, fish dish, French dish, Greek dish, Indian dish, Italian dish, vegetarian dish, West Indian dish**

dishabille (in dishabille) 6 ragged; 7 raggedy, topless; 8 barefoot, tattered; 9 décolleté, strapless; 10 barelegged, threadbare; 12 underclothed, underdressed; PHRASES: 3, 2, 6 out at elbows; 3-3 low-cut; 3-3-8 off-the-shoulder; 3-6 low-necked; 4-6 bare-headed; 4-7 half-clothed, half-dressed.

dishearten *See* **discourage**

dishonest 4 fake; 5 false, lying; 6 amoral; 7 corrupt, devious, immoral; 8 cheating, shamming; 9 deceitful, insincere, swindling, underhand; 10 defrauding, fraudulent, mendacious, misleading; 11 duplicitous, treacherous; 12 disingenuous, hypocritical, unprincipled, unscrupulous; 13 impersonating; PHRASES: 3-5 two-faced.

dishonest (be dishonest) 3 con; 4 bilk, dupe; 5 cheat, sting, trick; 6 delude, fleece; 7 deceive, defraud, mislead, swindle; 8 embezzle; PHRASES: 4, 3, 5 cook the books; 6, 4, 5 betray one's trust.

dishonestly 5, 3, 7 under the counter. *See also* **dishonest**

dishonest person 4 liar; 5 cheat, crook, ganef, shark; 6 forger, outlaw; 7 blagger, diddler, fiddler, hoodlum, sharper; 8 criminal, gangster, swindler; 9 defrauder, embezzler, hypocrite, peculator, racketeer, trickster; **10** highbinder; **13** counterfeiter; **PHRASES: 3, 3** con man; **5-2, 3** stick-up man.

dishonesty 4 blag, scam; **5** cheat, dodge, fraud, graft, sting; **6** deceit, fiddle; **7** forgery, swindle; **8** cozenage, flimflam, trickery; **9** blackmail, duplicity, treachery; **10** corruption; **11** fraudulence; **12** embezzlement; **14** counterfeiting; **PHRASES: 3-3** rip-off; **3, 4** con game; **3, 5** con trick *UK*; **5, 4** shell game; **5, 8** shady business; **6, 8** tricky business; **10, 4** confidence game; **10, 5** confidence trick. *See also* **deceitful**

dishonor 4 slur; **5** shame, stain; **6** defame, infamy; **7** scandal; **8** disgrace, ignominy; **9** discredit, disrepute; **PHRASES: 5, 5, 2** bring shame on.

dishonorable 4 base; **5** lying, shady, venal; **6** rotten, sleazy, tricky, unjust; **7** corrupt, crooked, debased, devious, ignoble, immoral, vulpine; **8** depraved, scheming, shameful, slippery; **9** dastardly, dishonest, nefarious; **10** despicable, untruthful, villainous; **11** corruptible, disgraceful, ignominious; **12** contemptible, disingenuous, disreputable, hypocritical, unprincipled, unscrupulous; **13** discreditable, disrespectful; **15** unsportsmanlike; **PHRASES: 2, 2, 2, 4** up to no good; **2, 2, 9** up to something; **2, 3, 6** on the fiddle; **3, 7** not cricket; **4-3-7** good-for-nothing.

dishonorable (be dishonorable) 3 lie; **5** evade; **6** wangle; **7** falsify, finagle; **11** prevaricate; **PHRASES: 4, 3, 4** pass the buck; **4, 3, 5** bend the rules; **4, 5, 4** play dirty pool; **5, 3, 5** shift the blame; **5, 5** smell fishy; **7, 7** perjure oneself.

dishonorable person 3 cad; **5** crook, felon, fraud, Judas, knave, rogue; **6** rascal; **7** bounder, mobster, shyster, traitor, villain; **8** criminal, gangster, poltroon; **9** embezzler, racketeer, scoundrel; **10** lawbreaker; **PHRASES: 3, 3** con man; **3-5** two-timer; **4-3-7** good-for-nothing; **5, 2, 3, 5** snake in the grass; **5, 9** shady character; **6-6** double-dealer; **6-7** double-crosser.

disinclined *See* **reluctant**

disingenuous 5 lying, shady; **6** tricky; **7** crooked; **8** slippery; **9** deceitful, dishonest, insincere, wrangling; **10** untruthful; **11** duplicitous; **12** hypocritical.

disintegrate 3 rot; **4** rust; **5** decay, erode; **6** molder, perish *UK*; **7** corrode, corrupt, crumble, mortify, necrose, putrefy, shatter;

8 collapse, fragment, splinter; **9** decompose, granulate; **10** degenerate; **PHRASES: 4, 4** wear away; **4, 5** fall apart; **5, 4** waste away.

disintegration 7 breakup, erosion, rotting; **8** disorder, necrosis; **9** breakdown, corrosion, crumbling, moldering; **10** corruption; **11** derangement, dissolution; **12** degeneration, putrefaction; **13** decomposition, fragmentation; **PHRASES: 4, 3, 4** wear and tear.

disinter 6 exhume, expose, reveal; **7** uncover, unearth; **PHRASES: 3, 2** dig up; **5, 2, 5** bring to light.

disinterest 6 apathy; **9** disregard, unconcern; **11** impassivity, insouciance; **12** heedlessness, indifference, listlessness.

disinterested 4 cool; **7** neutral; **8** detached; **9** equitable, impartial, objective; **10** impersonal, nonaligned, uninvolved; **11** indifferent, nonpartisan; **12** unprejudiced; **13** dispassionate; **PHRASES: 4-6** fair-minded, open-minded.

disinterestedness 7 ataraxy; **8** ataraxia, distance, stoicism; **10** detachment, dispassion, neutrality; **11** disinterest, objectivity; **12** indifference, nonalignment; **14** noninvolvement. *See also* **disinterested**

dislike 4 hate, mind; **5** abhor; **6** detest, enmity, hatred, horror, loathe, resent; **7** despise, dissent, mislike; **8** aversion, disfavor, distaste, loathing; **9** animosity, antipathy, avoidance, disrelish *UK*, hostility, rejection, repulsion, revulsion; **10** abhorrence, antagonism, disapprove, discontent, repugnance, resentment; **11** detestation, disapproval, displeasure; **12** disaffection, disagreement; **14** disinclination; **15** dissatisfaction; **PHRASES: 2, 7, 3** no stomach for; **3, 4** ill will; **3, 5** bad blood, pet peeve; **3, 7** ill feeling; **4, 1, 3, 4, 2** take a dim view of; **4, 2, 2, 3** have it in for; **4, 3, 8** gall and wormwood; **4, 5** bete noire; **5, 2** frown on; **6, 2** object to, sicken at.

dislike (cause dislike) 3 jar; **4** jade; **5** annoy, grate, repel, shock, upset; **6** enrage, offend, revolt, sicken; **7** disgust; **8** nauseate; **9** displease; **10** antagonize; **PHRASES: 3, 2, 4, 6** get on one's nerves; **3, 3** put off; **3, 3, 5, 3** rub the wrong way.

dislike (sign of dislike) 5 frown, scowl; **6** nausea; **7** shyness; **10** queasiness, shuddering; **PHRASES: 4, 5** cold sweat.

disliked person 5 enemy; **9** loudmouth;

10 antagonist; PHRASES: **3, 4, 4** not one's type; **3-6** ill-wisher; **4, 5** bête noire; **5, 5** sworn enemy; **5-6** fault-finder; **7, 3, 5** persona non grata.

dislocate **5** upset; **7** disrupt, disturb; **8** disjoint, dislodge, disorder, displace; **9** interrupt.

dislodge **4** free; **6** remove; **8** displace; **9** extricate; PHRASES: **3, 3** get out.

dislodged **8** uprooted; **9** displaced, extracted; **10** disengaged, eliminated, extricated; **11** deracinated.

disloyal *See* **unfaithful**

dismal *See* **miserable**

dismantle **4** undo; **10** deactivate; **11** disassemble.

dismay **5** panic, shock; **6** sadden; **7** depress, perturb; **10** disappoint; **12** apprehension; **13** consternation; **14** disappointment.

dismiss **2** ax; **4** drop, fire, rout, sack; **5** expel; **6** dehire, dispel, reject, retire, shelve; **7** disband, disdain; **8** furlough; **9** discharge, disemploy; **10** demobilize; PHRASES: **3, 2** let go; **3, 3** lay off; **3, 3, 2, 7** put out to pasture; **4, 3** boot out, send off; **4, 3, 4** give the boot, give the hook, give the sack; **4, 4** send away, send home; **4, 6** give notice; **4, 7** send packing; **4, 9** make redundant *UK*; **5, 3** elbow out, write off; **6, 3** muster out; **7, 2, 4** relieve of duty; **7, 3** pension off.

dismiss (be dismissed) **3, 3, 4** get the bird; **4, 3** walk out.

dismissal **4** sack; **5** axing, catch, congé; **6** firing, notice; **7** release, removal, sacking; **8** demotion, furlough; **9** depluming, discharge, severance, stripping; **10** cashiering, defrocking, displuming, redundancy *UK Can*, unfrocking; **13** disfellowship; **15** excommunication; PHRASES: **3, 2** the ax; **3, 4** the boot, the gate, the sack; **4, 4** pink slip; **4, 5** one's cards; **6, 3** laying off.

dismissed **5** fired; **6** sacked; **10** discharged; PHRASES: **4, 3** laid off; **4, 9** made redundant; **5, 3, 4** given the boot, given the chop, given the sack; **5, 3, 5-2** given the heave-ho.

disobedience **6** mutiny, strike; **7** dissent, perfidy, refusal; **8** defiance; **9** challenge, contumacy, defection, desertion, disregard, rebellion; **10** disloyalty, dissension, indocility, opposition, orneriness, resistance, unruliness; **11** delinquency, dereliction, misbehavior, mutineering,

naughtiness, obstruction, restiveness, stroppiness *UK*, waywardness; **12** indiscipline, mutinousness, stubbornness; **13** faithlessness, fractiousness, noncompliance, nonconformity, nonobservance, recalcitrance, undutifulness, unreliability, unwillingness; **14** intractability, noncooperation, obstructionism, perfidiousness, rebelliousness, refractoriness, tergiversation, unfaithfulness; **15** insubordination, perfunctoriness, undependability; PHRASES: **6, 6** monkey shines, monkey tricks *UK*; **8, 7** grudging service.

disobedient **6** ornery, unruly; **7** defiant, lawless, naughty, restive, riotous, wayward; **8** criminal, disloyal, mutinous, opposing, recusant, restless, stubborn; **9** deserting, obstinate, undutiful, unwilling; **10** delinquent, disobeying, disorderly, dissenting, misbehaved, perfidious, rebellious, tumultuous; **11** intractable, lawbreaking, obstructive, uncomplying; **12** noncompliant, nonobservant, obstreperous, recalcitrant, unmanageable; **13** insubordinate, transgressing, uncooperative, undisciplined; **14** noncooperative, tergiversatory; PHRASES: **3, 2, 7** out of control; **5, 7** badly behaved; **6-6** bloody-minded *UK*; **8-6** mischief-making.

disobedient (be disobedient) **4** defy, riot; **6** defect, desert, oppose, strike; **7** disobey, dissent; **8** obstruct, trespass; **9** misbehave, vandalize; **10** transgress; **12** tergiversate; PHRASES: **2, 4** go AWOL; **4, 6** defy orders; **4, 8** make mischief; **5, 3, 3** break the law; **5, 9** flout authority; **6, 1, 5** commit a crime; **6, 3, 5** breach the peace.

disobediently *See also* **disobedient**

disobey **4** defy; **7** violate; **10** contravene; PHRASES: **5, 3, 5** break the rules.

disorder **3** ado; **4** fray, fuss, muss, riot, stir; **5** brawl, chaos, mêlée, snarl, upset; **6** affray, bedlam, bother, crease, dustup, jumble, mayhem, muddle, mutiny, putsch, revolt, ruckus, ruffle, rumple, rumpus, tousle, unrest; **7** ailment, anarchy, crumple, derange, discord, disrupt, illness, rioting, ruction, scatter, shuffle, turmoil; **8** disarray, dishevel, disperse, scramble, sedition, sickness, syndrome, uprising; **9** agitation, bedraggle, commotion, complaint, condition, confusion, obfuscate, rebellion; **10** disarrange, disharmony, disruption, donnybrook, fisticuffs, insurgency, roughhouse;

11 derangement, disjunction, disorganize, disturbance, lawlessness, pandemonium; **12** discomfiture, discomposure, insurrection; **14** disarrangement, disintegration, disorderliness; **15** disorganization; PHRASES: **2-2** to-do; **3, 2** mix up; **3, 4** mob rule; **3, 4, 3, 5** all hell let loose; **4, 2** mess up; **4, 2, 6** spot of bother; **4-3-3** free-for-all; **4, 5** coup d'état; **4-5** argy-bargy *UK*; **4, 6, 4** turn upside down; **5, 2** break up; **5-2** punch-up; **5, 3, 6** rough and tumble; **5-5** hurly-burly.

disorder (in disorder) **10** confusedly; **11** chaotically, erratically, haphazardly, irregularly; **12** sporadically; **13** spasmodically; PHRASES: **2, 4, 3, 6** by fits and starts; **2, 6** at random, by chance; **2, 8** in disarray; **2, 9** in confusion.

disorder (medical) **2** MS, TB; **3** flu; **4** AIDS, gout, lyme; **5** ebola, lupus, polio; **6** asthma, Crohn's, dengue, eczema, herpes, rabies; **7** cholera, leprosy, lumbago, malaria, rickets, rubella, scabies, tetanus, typhoid; **8** diabetes, Hodgkin's, impetigo, leukemia, pellagra, syphilis; **9** distemper, dystrophy, eclampsia, gonorrhea; **10** diphtheria; **11** Huntington's, kwashiorkor; **12** Legionnaire's; PHRASES: **4-4** beri-beri. *See also* **cardiovascular disease**

disordered **5** messy; **6** untidy; **7** chaotic, jumbled, muddled; **8** confused, deranged; **9** displaced, disrupted, misplaced; **10** disjointed, dislocated; **11** disarranged; **12** disorganized; PHRASES: **2, 8** in disarray; **3, 2, 5** out of joint, out of order, out of place; **5-5** topsy-turvy.

disorderliness *See* **disorder**

disorderly **4** wild; **5** messy, rowdy; **6** unruly; **7** chaotic, jumbled, lawless, muddled, riotous; **8** anarchic, confused, mutinous; **10** boisterous, disruptive, rampageous, rebellious; **11** disobedient; **12** contumacious, disorganized, obstreperous, unmanageable; **13** insubordinate, undisciplined; **14** uncontrollable; PHRASES: **3, 2, 7** out of control; **4-7** hell-raising; **5-5** topsy-turvy; **5-6** harum-scarum.

disorderly (be disorderly) **3** mob; **4** riot; **5** storm; **7** rampage, roister; PHRASES: **3, 2, 5** cut up rough; **3, 4** run amok, run riot, run wild; **5, 4** raise hell; **5, 6** horse around.

disown **6** reject; **8** disclaim, renounce.

disparage **3** dis; **4** mock; **5** decry, scorn; **6** attack, demean, deride, insult, slight; **7** affront, detract; **8** belittle, derogate, ridicule;

9 criticize, denigrate, deprecate; **10** depreciate, disrespect, understate, undervalue; PHRASES: **2, 4** do down *UK*; **3, 4** cry down, put down, run down; **4, 4** play down; **4, 5** sell short; **4, 5, 2** pour scorn on.

disparagement **5** scorn; **7** decrial; **8** derision; **9** criticism, slighting; **10** belittling, derogation, detraction; **11** denigration, deprecation; **12** belittlement, depreciation, vilification; PHRASES: **3-7** nit-picking; **5, 6** faint praise; **5-7** fault-finding; **7, 4** putting down.

disparager **6** critic; **7** decrier, knocker; **9** belittler, derogator, detractor; **11** depreciator; PHRASES: **7, 3** hatchet man.

disparaging **8** critical, derisive, negative, scornful; **9** offensive; **10** censorious, derogatory, detractory, pejorative, slanderous; **11** denigratory, deprecatory; **12** contemptuous, unflattering; **15** uncomplimentary; PHRASES: **3-7** nit-picking. *See also* **disparage**

disparate **3** odd; **6** unlike; **7** diverse, strange, unequal, unusual, variant; **8** distinct, unlikely; **9** different, equivocal, irregular, unrelated; **10** ambivalent, asymmetric, discrepant, dissimilar, immiscible, nonuniform; **11** contrasting, incongruent; **13** heterogeneous; **14** incommensurate.

disparity **3** gap; **8** variance; **9** asymmetry, diversity; **10** difference, divergence; **11** discrepancy; **12** incongruence, inconsonance, irregularity; **13** disproportion, dissimilarity, heterogeneity, inconsistency, nonuniformity.

dispassionate *See* **calm**

dispatch **4** kill, mail, post *UK*, slay; **6** murder; **7** destroy; **8** transmit; **9** slaughter; **11** assassinate; PHRASES: **3, 2, 5** put to death; **4, 3** send off, send out.

dispel **7** dismiss, scatter; **8** disperse; PHRASES: **5, 3** drive out *UK*; **5, 4** chase away.

dispense *See* **give out**

disperse **6** dispel, divide, sunder; **7** diffuse, disband, scatter; **8** diffract, dissolve, separate; **9** dislocate; PHRASES: **4, 4** melt away; **5, 2** break up, split up; **5, 5** drift apart.

disperse (be dispersed) **4** part; **5** stray; **6** spread; **7** scatter; **8** straggle; PHRASES: **4, 7** part company; **5, 2** break up, split up; **5, 3** drift off; **5, 5** drift apart; **6, 3** spread out.

dispersed **6** sparse; **7** diffuse; **8** sporadic; **9** displaced, scattered; **10** infrequent, widespread; PHRASES: **6, 5** dotted about.

dispersion 6 sowing; **7** seeding; **8** issuance, strewing; **9** diffusion, dispersal, spreading; **10** scattering; **11** circulation, propagation, publication, scatterment; **12** broadcasting, displacement, distribution; **13** dissemination.

Dispersion 8 Diaspora.

dispersive 9 diffusive; **10** scattering; **11** diffractive; **12** distributive; **13** disseminative.

dispirit 6 dampen, deject, dismay; **7** depress; **10** discourage; PHRASES: **4, 4** cast down.

dispirited 3 low, sad; **4** down; **10** despondent; **11** discouraged; **12** disheartened.

displace 4 move, oust; **5** expel, shift, shunt, upset; **6** depose, derail, unseat; **7** disrupt, disturb, succeed; **8** dislodge, relocate, supplant; **9** dislocate, supersede; **10** disarrange; **11** disorganize, translocate; PHRASES: **5, 3** lever out, smoke out, wring out; **5, 3, 2, 4** throw out of gear; **5, 3, 6** knock off course; **7, 3** squeeze out.

displaced person 5 exile, stray; **7** evacuee, outcast, refugee; **8** deportee; PHRASES: **4, 3, 2, 5** fish out of water; **8, 6** homeless person; **9, 6** stateless person.

displacement 7 removal, sinkage; **8** movement, overload, thinning; **9** expulsion, surcharge; **10** aberration, deflection, derailment, expression, relocation; **11** derangement, dislocation, dislodgment, disturbance, overloading, supplanting, translation; **12** perturbation, transference; **13** overweighting, translocation, transposition, transshipment; **14** disarrangement.

display 3 act; **4** expo, fair, show; **5** array, model, sport, strut, teach, vaunt; **6** expose, flaunt, parade, reveal; **7** exhibit, explain, panoply, perform, present, publish, release, showing; **8** brandish, carnival, ceremony, disclose, manifest; **9** spectacle; **10** collection, exhibition, exposition; **11** demonstrate; **12** presentation; **13** demonstration, retrospective; PHRASES: **3, 2** put on; **3, 3** set out; **3, 4** art show; **4, 1, 4, 2** make a show of; **4, 1, 7** hang a picture; **4, 3** show off; **4, 9, 2** draw attention to; **5, 3** point out; **6, 2, 4** expose to view.

displayer 5 emcee, flack, model; **6** barker; **7** peacock, showman; **8** flaunter, stripper; **9** exhibitor, mannequin, presenter UK,

publicist; **10** advertiser, impresario, publicizer; **12** demonstrator; **13** exhibitionist; PHRASES: **5, 5** press agent; **5, 7** stage manager.

displease 3 irk; **5** anger, annoy, peeve, repel, upset; **6** appall, enrage, offend, revolt, sicken; **7** disgust; **8** irritate, nauseate; **9** discomfit; **10** discomfort.

displeasure 5 anger; **9** annoyance; **10** discontent, irritation; **11** disapproval, unhappiness; **14** discontentment.

disport *See* **show off**

disposal 6 disuse; **7** cession, dumping UK, removal, sacking; **8** ejection, riddance, transfer; **9** clearance, desuetude, dismissal, excretion, releasing; **10** abrogation, discarding, liberation; **11** abandonment, dissolution, forswearing; **12** availability, dispensation, nonretention, renunciation; **13** disposability; **14** relinquishment; PHRASES: **8, 6** marching orders.

dispose 3 fix, set; **5** place; **6** decide, prompt, settle; **7** arrange, incline, resolve; **8** persuade, position; **9** determine, influence; PHRASES: **3, 3** set out.

disposed 5 ready; **6** gotten, liable, likely; **7** forgone, willing; **8** disowned, forsworn, inclined, prepared, released; **9** abandoned, discarded, liberated; **12** relinquished; PHRASES: **2, 1, 4** of a mind; **3, 3, 2** got rid of; **9, 4** dispensed with.

dispose of 2 ax; **3** bin UK; **4** cede, dump, free, kill, lift; **5** chuck, ditch, eject, enjoy, forgo, scrap, spare, waive; **6** abjure, assign, cancel, deploy, devour, disown, expend, maroon, murder, negate, recant, revoke, settle; **7** consume, control, destroy, discard, divorce, execute, possess, replace; **8** abrogate, dispatch, dissolve, disunite, forswear, jettison, renounce, transfer; **9** decontrol, determine, eliminate, supersede; **10** deregulate, derestrict, disinherit, impoverish, relinquish; **11** assassinate, disentangle, requisition; PHRASES: **2, 4, 4** do away with; **2, 7** do without, go through; **3, 2** let go, mop up, use up; **3, 2, 2** get by on; **3, 2, 6** set in motion; **3, 3** let out; **3, 3, 2** get rid of; **3, 4, 2** get shot of UK; **3, 7** get through; **4, 2** call in, give up, pass on; **4, 2, 4** make do with; **4, 3** cast off, cast out, sort out; **4, 3, 4** call the tune; **4, 3, 4, 2** make the most of; **4, 4** cast away, part with; **4, 4, 4** call into play; **4, 4, 5, 2** wash one's hands of; **4, 5** stop using; **4, 9** cast overboard; **5, 3** marry off, swear off, throw out; **5, 4** throw away; **6, 2** attend to, finish up; **6, 3** finish off; **6-3** eighty-six; **7, 4, 4** release one's hold; **8, 4** dispense with.

disposition *See* **nature**

disproportion 8 inequity; **9** disparity, imbalance; **10** inequality; **11** discrepancy; **13** inconsistency.

disproportionately 3 too; **6** overly, unduly; **11** excessively; **12** asymmetricly, unreasonably.

disprove *See* **refute**

dispute 3 row; **4** deny, fray; **5** argue, fight; **6** debate, oppugn; **7** contend, contest, quarrel, wrangle; **8** argument.

disqualify *See* **ban**

disquiet 5 upset, worry; **6** unrest; **7** anxiety, concern, disturb; **10** disconcert, uneasiness.

disregard 6 ignore, slight; **7** disdain; **8** contempt, discount, disgrace, dishonor, overlook, pejorate; **10** disrespect; **12** indifference; **13** underestimate; PHRASES: **3, 2, 9** pay no attention; **4, 1, 5, 3, 2** turn a blind eye to; **4, 2, 3, 3** drag in the mud.

disreputable 5 dodgy *UK*, seedy, shady; **7** devious; **8** infamous; **9** degrading, nefarious, notorious, underhand; **10** scandalous, suspicious; **11** disgraceful, ignominious; **12** dishonorable, questionable; PHRASES: **3, 2, 3, 5** not on the level.

disreputable person 3 cad; **5** rogue; **6** rascal; **7** bounder, lowlife; **8** scalawag *UK*; **9** scallywag, scoundrel; **10** blackguard; **11** undesirable; PHRASES: **3, 3** bad egg, bad lot *UK*; **3, 9** bad influence; **4, 2, 3, 4** talk of the town; **4-2-4** ne'er-do-well; **5, 3** alley cat; **5, 5** black sheep.

disrepute 5 shame; **6** infamy; **8** disgrace, dishonor; **9** disregard, notoriety; **10** opprobrium; **13** shamefastness; **14** shamefacedness; PHRASES: **3, 6** ill repute; **10, 4** shamefaced look.

disrepute (bring into disrepute) 5 shame; **8** dishonor; **9** discredit; PHRASES: **4, 4, 5** fall from favor, fall from grace; **5, 7** lower oneself; **6, 7** demean oneself; **7, 7** degrade oneself; **8, 7** disgrace oneself.

disrespect 3 dis; **6** infamy, insult; **7** affront, obloquy; **8** belittle, contempt, disfavor, disgrace, dishonor, ignominy, misprise; **9** denigrate, discredit, disesteem, disparage, disregard, disrepute, impu-

dence, insolence, perjorate, underrate; **10** defamation, opprobrium, scurrility; **11** degradation, irreverence; **12** impertinence, impoliteness; **13** obnoxiousness, underestimate; **15** disreputability; PHRASES: **3, 4** bad name, dim view; **3, 5** bad light; **3, 6** low esteem; **3-6** ill-repute; **4, 2, 7** lack of respect; **4, 2, 8** hold in contempt; **4, 5** hold cheap; **4, 7** poor opinion.

disrespect (show disrespect) 6 jostle; PHRASES: **5, 5** brush aside, elbow aside, shove aside; **6, 6** remain seated.

disrespect (sign of disrespect) 5 snook; **7** mooning; PHRASES: **1, 4** V sign; **4, 7** rude gesture.

disrespectful 4 pert, rude; **5** sassy, saucy; **6** brazen, cheeky; **7** forward, uncivil; **8** impolite, impudent, insolent; **10** irreverent, scurrilous, unmannered; **11** impertinent; **12** discourteous; **13** insubordinate, irreverential; PHRASES: **3-8** bad-mannered, ill-mannered; **6-5** brazen-faced.

disrupt 5 upset; **6** molest; **7** disturb, pervert; **8** disorder, sabotage, unsettle; **9** interfere, interrupt, intervene; PHRASES: **3, 3** put off, put out; **4, 2** mess up; **6, 4** tamper with.

disruption 5 upset; **8** disorder; **9** commotion, intrusion; **10** perversion; **11** disturbance, molestation; **12** interference, interruption, intervention; **13** inconvenience.

dissatisfaction 7 censure; **8** contempt; **9** rejection; **10** discontent; **11** deprecation, disapproval, displeasure, frustration, reprobation; **13** consternation; **14** disappointment, disapprobation, discontentment, disgruntlement; **15** disillusionment.

dissatisfied 7 sulking; **8** brooding *UK*, derisory, scornful; **9** disgusted; **10** discontent, displeased, frustrated, malcontent, pejorative; **11** disaffected, disgruntled, unapproving, unimpressed; **12** disappointed, disapproving, discontented, malcontented; **13** disillusioned; PHRASES: **8, 2** critical of.

dissatisfied (be dissatisfied) 3 boo; **4** carp, hiss, moan, sulk; **5** brood, cavil, gripe, scorn, slate, whine; **6** defame, deride, grouse, kvetch, rebuke, reject, resent, revile, vilify, whinge; **7** condemn, deplore, dislike, grumble, reprove; **8** belittle, complain, disfavor; **9** bellyache, criticize, deprecate, perjorate; **10** disapprove; PHRASES: **3-3** tut-tut; **3, 4** run down; **3, 5, 4, 2** not think much of; **4, 3** slag off; **4, 5, 2** pick holes in; **4, 5, 4** find fault with; **4, 7, 2** look askance at; **6, 2** object to; **7, 2** whistle at.

dissatisfy **5** peeve; **6** revolt; **7** disgust; **9** displease, frustrate; **10** disappoint, disgruntle; **11** disillusion; PHRASES: **3, 3** put out.

dissemble **3** act; **4** mask, veil; **5** cloak, feign; **7** conceal, deceive, pretend; **8** disguise; **10** camouflage; **11** dissimulate; PHRASES: **3, 2, 2, 3** put on an act; **4-3** playact.

dissension **7** discord; **8** conflict, fighting, friction; **9** bickering; **10** antagonism, disharmony, opposition, squabbling; **11** controversy, discordance; **12** disagreement; PHRASES: **3, 7** bad feeling.

dissent **3** war; **4** feud, spat, tiff, vary, veto; **5** brawl, clash, rebut, scrap, spurn; **6** differ, fracas, object, oppose, rebuff, refute, reject, revolt, secede, strife; **7** abstain, confute, discord, dispute, embargo, gainsay, nullify, protest, quarrel; **8** conflict, disagree, friction, rebuttal, squabble, variance; **9** interdict, objection, rebellion, recusance, repudiate, stonewall, withstand; **10** contradict, difference, dissidence, fisticuffs, infraction, opposition, refutation, renunciate; **11** altercation, confutation, contrariety, controversy, discordance, prohibition, repudiation, schismatize; **12** disagreement, interdiction, renunciation; **13** confrontation, contradiction, nonobservance, recalcitrance; **14** nonconcurrence; PHRASES: **3-2** set-to; **4, 2, 3, 5** kick in the teeth; **4, 3** walk out; **4, 5** make waves; **4, 7** vote against; **7, 6** express doubts; **8, 4** breaking away, contrary vote; **8, 7** withhold consent.

dissenter **4** scab; **5** rebel; **6** critic, misfit, outlaw, zealot; **7** caviler, fanatic, heckler, heretic, radical; **8** agitator, apostate, blackleg, disputer, mutineer, objector, opponent, outsider, partisan, recusant, renegade; **9** anarchist, dissident, insurgent, protester, quarreler; **10** iconoclast, malcontent, protestant, schismatic, separatist; **11** dissentient; **12** factionalist, troublemaker; **13** nonconformist, noncooperator, revolutionary, tergiversator; PHRASES: **3, 2, 1, 5, 4** ass in a lion's skin; **3, 3, 3** odd man out; **4, 3, 2, 5** fish out of water; **4-7** gate-crasher; **5, 5, 3** angry young man.

dissentience **6** strike; **8** sedition; **9** rebellion, secession; **10** disharmony, dissidence, separatism; **11** discordance,

unorthodoxy; **12** disaffection, disobedience, factionalism, sectarianism; **13** nonconformity; **14** noncooperation; **15** quarrelsomeness.

dissenting **7** arguing, denying, warlike; **8** contrary, divisive, opposing, opposite, partisan, recusant, refuting, revoking; **9** bellicose, breakaway, demurring, differing, dissident, heretical, rejecting, resistant, sectarian, seditious, skeptical; **10** discordant, intolerant, protesting, quarreling, rebellious, revocatory, schismatic, separatist; **11** adversarial, conflicting, confutative, contentious, disagreeing, repudiating; **12** cantankerous, contravening, disputatious, dissatisfied, interdictive, renunciative, renunciatory, secessionist; **13** contradictory, controversial, nonconformist; **14** prohibitionary; **15** confrontational; PHRASES: **2, 4** at odds.

dissertate **5** argue, orate; **6** define, survey; **7** descant, discuss, explain, expound; **8** annotate, perorate; **9** discourse, elucidate, sermonize; **10** commentate; **11** pontificate, proselytize; PHRASES: **2, 4** go into; **5, 5** speak about, write about; **7, 2** comment on; **7, 4** inquire into.

dissertation **5** essay, gloss, paper, study, tract; **6** homily, lesson, memoir, screed, sermon, survey, thesis; **7** comment, descant, inquiry, oration; **8** argument, critique, exegesis, harangue, tractate, treatise; **9** discourse, monograph; **10** commentary, discussion, exposition, peroration UK; **11** composition, explanation, lucubration; **12** disquisition; **14** interpretation.

dissertator **6** author, critic, editor, orator, writer; **7** exegete, speaker; **8** essayist, exponent, lecturer, reviewer; **9** expositor, expounder, proselyte; **10** glossarist, journalist, publicizer; **11** commentator, contributor UK, interpreter, pamphleteer; **12** propagandist, proselytizer.

dissident **5** rebel; **8** mutineer; **9** dissenter, insurgent, protester; **10** malcontent, rebellious, separatist, unorthodox; **13** nonconformist.

dissimilar **3** new; **5** novel; **6** unique, unlike; **7** diverse, unalike, unequal, unusual, various; **8** atypical, peculiar, peerless, singular; **9** different, disparate, divergent, matchless, nonpareil, unrelated, untypical; **10** asymmetric, discordant, discrepant, nonuniform; **11** contrasting, distinctive, incongruous, unidentical; **12** incomparable, unresembling; **13** contradictory; **14** incommensurate; **15** incommensurable; PHRASES: **1, 3, 3, 4** a far cry from; **3, 3** way off, way out; **3, 4, 2** far from it; **5, 5** poles apart; **7, 4** nothing like; **9, 4** something else.

dissimilar (be dissimilar) **6** differ; **7** deviate; **8** contrast; PHRASES: **6, 4** depart from.

dissimilarity **7** variety; **9** disparity, diversity, variation; **10** difference, unlikeness; **11** discrepancy; **12** multiformity; **13** dissimilitude, heterogeneity, nonuniformity; **14** extraneousness.

dissimilarly **7, 5** without equal. *See also* **dissimilar**

dissipate **5** waste; **6** dispel; **7** scatter; **8** disperse, dissolve, squander; **12** disintegrate; PHRASES: **5, 4** throw away; **7, 4** fritter away.

dissipated **7** immoral, riotous; **9** debauched, dispersed, dissolute, scattered; **10** degenerate, licentious, profligate; **11** intemperate; PHRASES: **4-6** fast-living, free-living, high-living.

dissipation **4** orgy; **8** carousal; **10** debauchery, degeneracy, profligacy, saturnalia, scattering; **12** intemperance; **13** dissoluteness; **14** licentiousness; PHRASES: **4, 6** fast living, free living, high living.

dissociate **6** detach; **7** divorce; **8** distance, separate; **10** disconnect; **12** disassociate.

dissociation **6** apathy; **7** divorce; **8** aversion, distance, division; **9** severance, shrinking; **10** abhorrence, abstention, alienation, averseness, detachment, hesitation, repugnance, separation; **12** indifference, lifelessness, unenthusiasm; **13** disconnection; **14** disassociation, nonassociation; PHRASES: **2, 7, 3** no stomach for; **4-11** halfheartedness.

dissolution **6** ending; **7** closure; **10** disbanding, suspension; **11** termination.

dissolve **4** melt, thaw, thin; **5** solve; **6** decoct, dispel, infuse, soften, unclot, vanish; **7** adjourn, disband, liquefy, resolve; **8** disperse; **9** disappear, dissipate, evaporate, lixiviate *UK*, percolate; **10** solubilize; **11** decoagulate; PHRASES: **5, 2** break up.

dissonance **3** row; **5** noise; **6** bedlam, clamor, hubbub, racket, tumult, uproar; **7** discord, jarring, turmoil; **8** conflict, flat-

ness, jangling; **9** cacophony, stridency; **10** disharmony, dissension, hullabaloo; **11** discordance, pandemonium; **12** caterwauling, disagreement, tunelessness; **15** unmelodiousness; PHRASES: **4, 7** cat's concert.

dissonant **5** harsh; **6** atonal, shrill; **7** jarring, rasping, raucous; **8** clashing, strident, tuneless; **9** unmusical; **10** discordant; **11** cacophonous; **12** inharmonious; **13** disharmonious.

dissuade **5** deter; **7** caution, confute, reprove; **10** discourage; **11** expostulate, remonstrate; PHRASES: **3, 3** put off; **4, 3, 2** talk out of.

dissuasion **7** caution, protest, reproof; **9** objection; **10** admonition, deterrence, opposition, persuasion, resistance; **12** remonstrance; **13** expostulation; **14** discouragement; PHRASES: **3, 5** red light; **6, 4** closed door.

dissuasive **7** damping; **8** contrary, monitory, opposing; **9** deterrent; **10** cautionary, inhibitive; **12** discouraging; **13** disheartening, expostulatory.

distance **3** gap; **4** void; **5** avoid, space; **6** detach; **7** expanse; **8** coldness, infinity, separate; **9** aloofness, deviation; **10** detachment, dissociate, divergence, remoteness, separation; **15** inaccessibility; PHRASES: **4, 4** move away; **4, 5** deep space; **5, 5** light years.

distant **3** far, yon; **4** cold, cool; **5** aloof, apart, faint; **6** distal, remote, yonder; **7** asunder, extreme, faraway, farther, further; **8** detached, farthest, furthest, isolated, outlying, reserved, secluded, ultimate; **9** separated, withdrawn; **10** antipodean, peripheral, tramontane, transpolar, unsociable; **11** farthermost, furthermost, godforsaken, hyperborean, transalpine, transmarine; **12** inaccessible, transmontane, transmundane, transoceanic, transpontine, ultramontane, ultramundane; **13** transatlantic; PHRASES: **3-2-3-3** out-of-the-way; **3, 2, 4, 5** out of this world; **3, 2, 5** out of reach, out of sight; **3-3** far-off; **3-5** far-flung; **4-5** long-range; **4-8** long-distance.

distant (be distant) **6** outlie; **8** outrange; **11** outdistance.

distant place **4** pole; **6** offing; **7** horizon, outback, outpost, Siberia, skyline; **8** Timbuktu; **9** antipodes, outskirts, periphery; PHRASES: **3, 2, 3, 7** end of the rainbow; **3, 4, 2, 6** the back of beyond; **3, 5, 4** the North Pole, the South Pole; **3, 5, 6** the Great Divide; **3, 6** the sticks; **3, 7** the boonies; **3, 9** the boondocks; **4, 2, 3, 5** ends of the earth; **4, 4** Pago Pago; **4, 7** back o'Bourke; **5, 5** outer space; **5, 8** Outer Mongolia; **6, 3** world's end; **9, 5** vanishing point.

distension *See* **swelling**

distill 4 cull; **5** glean; **6** garner, purify, refine; **7** extract; **8** condense; **11** concentrate.

distillation 7 epitome, essence, extract; **8** tincture; **9** summation; **10** embodiment, extraction, refinement; **11** concentrate, distillate; **12** condensation, purification; **13** concentration.

distinct 5 clear, exact; **6** patent; **7** evident, obvious; **8** apparent, definite, discrete, manifest, separate; **9** different, divergent; **10** individual, noticeable, uninvolved; **11** conspicuous, distinctive; PHRASES: **4-7** welldefined.

distinction 4 fame, mark, note; **5** award, honor, merit, trait, worth; **6** renown; **7** feature; **8** accolade, breeding, contrast, eminence, prestige; **9** otherness; **10** decoration, difference, importance, reputation; **11** discrepancy; **12** idiosyncrasy; **13** dissimilarity, particularity; **14** characteristic.

distinguish 3 see; **4** mark; **6** decide; **7** discern; **8** classify, perceive; **9** recognize; **12** characterize, discriminate; **13** differentiate; PHRASES: **3, 5** set apart; **4, 3** make out; **4, 5** tell apart; **4, 7** tell between; **6, 3** single out.

distort 4 bend, scar, skew, warp; **5** alter, screw, spoil, twist; **6** change, deform, garble, stress; **7** contort; **8** misshape, mutilate; **9** disfigure; **13** disproportion; PHRASES: **9, 4** interfere with.

distort (the truth) 3 lie; **4** fake; **5** forge; **7** concoct, deceive, falsify, pervert; **9** dissemble, embroider, fabricate, misinform, whitewash; **10** exaggerate; **11** misconceive; **12** misrepresent, propagandize; PHRASES: **4, 7** tell porkies; **5, 2** dress up; **5, 5** twist words; **7, 3, 5** stretch the truth.

distorted 4 bent; **5** askew; **6** unfair; **7** crooked, partial; **8** cockeyed, lopsided; **9** grotesque, malformed, misshapen, skewwhiff *UK*; **10** asymmetric, discordant, dissimilar, inaccurate, misleading, unbalanced; **11** incongruent; **12** asymmetrical; **14** unrecognizable; PHRASES: **3, 2, 5** out of shape; **3, 2, 6** out of kilter; **3, 2, 7** out of balance; **3, 2, 10** out of proportion; **3-5** onesided; **3-6** off-center, off-target. *See also*

distort

distortedly 9 evasively; **10** perversely, spuriously; **11** deceitfully; **12** perfidiously; **14** hypocritically.

distortion 4 bias, spin, warp; **5** twist; **6** buckle, strain, stress; **7** torsion; **8** skewness; **9** disparity, imbalance; **10** contortion, inequality; **11** crookedness, deformation, twistedness; **12** lopsidedness; **13** disfigurement, disproportion, dissimilarity, falsification.

distortion (of the truth) 3 lie; **6** hoopla, parody; **7** falsity, fiction, perfidy; **8** travesty; **9** deception, falsehood, mendacity; **10** perversion, propaganda; **11** fabrication; **12** exaggeration, whitewashing; **14** disinformation, misinformation; **15** misconstruction; PHRASES: **4, 3** pork pie *UK*; **4, 4** tall tale; **6, 5** poetic truth; **9, 5** selective facts.

distract 5 addle, amuse; **6** absorb, divert, engage; **7** confuse, disturb, engross; **8** befuddle; **9** entertain, sidetrack.

distracted 5 upset; **6** insane; **7** anxious, frantic, nervous; **8** agitated, diverted, neurotic; **11** preoccupied; PHRASES: **3, 4, 2** not with it; **5, 4** miles away; **6, 7** beside oneself.

distraction 5 hobby; **7** anxiety, pastime; **9** agitation, commotion, confusion, diversion; **10** disruption; **11** desperation, disturbance; **12** bewilderment, interference, interruption; **13** entertainment.

distress 4 ache, pain; **5** agony, angst, grief, trial, upset, worry; **6** bother, danger, misery, sorrow, stress; **7** afflict, anguish, disturb, torment, trouble; **8** hardship; **9** suffering; **10** difficulty, misfortune.

distressing 3 sad; **6** tragic; **7** painful; **8** grievous; **9** harrowing, upsetting; **10** depressing, lamentable; **13** heartbreaking.

distribute 4 deal; **5** issue; **6** deploy, spread, supply; **7** publish, scatter; **8** allocate, disperse; **9** circulate, propagate; **11** disseminate; PHRASES: **4, 3** deal out, mete out; **5, 3** share out *UK*.

distributed 4 sown; **6** issued, strewn; **8** diffused; **9** broadcast; **10** circulated, propagated; **12** disseminated.

distribution 6 supply; **7** sharing; **8** delivery, division; **9** allotment, dispersal, spreading; **10** allocation, scattering; **11** circulation; **13** dissemination; PHRASES: **6, 3** giving out.

district 4 area, ward, zone; **5** block; **6** barony, canton, fylker, region, sector; **7** borough, commune, eparchy, quarter; **8** locality, precinct, vicinity; **9** guberniya; **10** department, prefecture; **12** constituency; **13** arondissement.

District of Columbia 2 DC; **10** Washington (capital); PHRASES: **4, 6** wood thrush (bird); **7, 2, 3** Justice to all (motto); **7, 7** Nation's Capital (nickname); **8, 6, 4** American beauty rose (flower).

distrust 5 doubt; **7** suspect; **8** cynicism, mistrust, wariness; **9** chariness, misgiving, suspicion; **10** disbelieve; **14** solicitousness, suspiciousness; **15** mistrustfulness; PHRASES: **2, 4** be wary; **2, 10** be suspicious.

distrustful 4 wary; **5** chary; **7** cynical, nervous; **8** doubtful; **10** solicitous, suspicious; **11** misdoubtful, mistrustful; **12** disbelieving.

disturb 3 bug, irk, vex; **4** carp, move, stir; **5** alarm, scare, shake, shift, upset, worry; **6** harass, hassle, muddle, pester, rattle, ruffle, tamper; **7** agitate, concern, confuse, fluster, intrude, perturb, trouble; **8** disquiet, distress, irritate, unsettle; **9** discomfit, interrupt; **10** disconcert; PHRASES: **3, 3** put out; **4, 2** mess up.

disturbance 4 riot; **5** clash, furor UK; **6** fracas, furore UK, ruckus, rumpus, tumult, uproar; **7** trouble, turmoil; **8** brouhaha, disorder, disquiet, nuisance, outburst, upheaval; **9** agitation, bloodbath, commotion, confusion, intrusion; **10** disruption, roughhouse; **11** distraction; **12** discomfiture, discomposure, interruption, perturbation.

disturbed 6 fitful, uneasy; **7** anxious, nervous; **8** neurotic, paranoid, schizoid, unhinged, unstable; **9** psychotic; **10** disquieted, distraught, unbalanced; **11** discomposed, dissociated, traumatized; PHRASES: **2, 1, 5** in a tizzy.

disturbing 7 ominous; **8** alarming, muddling, worrying; **9** confusing, troubling, unnerving, vexatious; **10** bothersome, disruptive, irritating, unsettling; **11** disquieting, distressing; **13** disconcerting; PHRASES: **3-7** off-putting.

disunite 4 undo; **5** break, sever, split; **6** divide; **8** dissolve, separate.

disunity 7 discord, dispute, dissent; **8** conflict; **10** dissension, divergence; **12** disagreement; PHRASES: **2, 6, 6** no common ground; **4, 2, 5** lack of unity; **4, 2, 7** lack of

harmony; **5, 5** poles apart.

disuse 5 limbo; **7** dumping UK, neglect; **8** disposal, idleness; **9** desuetude, discharge, dismissal, rejection, scrapping; **10** discarding, inactivity, retirement; **11** abandonment, dereliction, resignation; **12** obsolescence, obsoleteness, unemployment; **14** superannuation UK.

disused 5 empty; **6** junked; **7** retired, rusting; **8** derelict, deserted, obsolete, scrapped; **9** abandoned, discarded, neglected; **10** jettisoned, mothballed, superseded, supplanted; **12** discontinued; **13** superannuated; **14** decommissioned; PHRASES: **2, 3, 5** on the shelf; **2, 5** in limbo; **3, 2, 3** out of use; **3, 2, 10** out of commission; **3, 4** run down; **3-9** old-fashioned; **4, 2** laid up, used up; **4, 3** worn out.

ditch 4 dike, drop; **5** drain, scrap; **6** trench; **7** channel, discard; **8** waterway; PHRASES: **3, 3, 2** get rid of; **5, 2, 4** split up with.

dithering 8 hesitant, wavering; **9** hesitancy; **10** indecisive; **11** uncertainty, vacillating; **14** indecisiveness; PHRASES: **6-9** shilly-shallying.

ditty 4 poem, song; **5** rhyme; **8** limerick; PHRASES: **7, 5** nursery rhyme.

dive 3 dip; **4** duck, fall, nose; **5** chute, crash, lunge, stoop, swoop; **6** plunge; **7** descent, plummet; **8** nosedive; **9** touchdown; **10** cannonball; PHRASES: **2, 4** go down; **4, 2** jump in; **4-4** free-fall.

diver 7 frogman, swimmer; **8** aquanaut; **10** snorkeller UK, submariner.

diverge 4 fork, part, vary; **5** splay, stray; **6** depart, differ, ramify, swerve, wander; **7** deviate, digress, radiate, scatter; **8** aberrate, conflict, disagree, disperse, separate; **9** bifurcate; **10** divaricate, relinquish; PHRASES: **2, 4** go away; **3, 3** fan out; **3, 4** get away, get free; **3, 4, 2** get shot of; **3, 5** cut loose, get loose; **4, 4** fall away, move away; **4, 6** cast adrift; **4, 7** free oneself, part company; **5, 4** break away; **6, 3** branch out.

divergence 7 breakup, parting; **8** conflict, splaying, variance; **9** branching, departure, deviation, radiation; **10** aberration, deflection, difference, divergency, separation; **11** contrariety, declination, diffraction, discrepancy; **12** crosscurrent, disagreement, divarication, ramification; **13** contradiction, fragmentation, nonconformity; **14** disintegration; PHRASES: **5-2**

split-up.

divergent 7 forking; 8 aberrant, contrary, opposing, ramiform, separate; 9 branching, dendritic, deviating, different, differing; 10 dendriform; 11 conflicting; 12 divaricating; 13 contradictory.

divers *See* **various**

diverse 6 fitful, sundry, uneven, varied; 7 erratic, unequal, various, varying; 8 assorted, distinct, manifold, sporadic, unstable, unsteady, variable; 9 checkered, different, disparate, haphazard, spasmodic, versatile; 10 changeable, dissimilar, inconstant, nonuniform, variegated; 11 contrasting, diversiform, exceptional, incongruous, omnifarious; 12 inconsistent; 13 heterogeneous, miscellaneous, unpredictable; PHRASES: 3, 2, 4 out of step; 3-6 all-around.

diversify 3 mix; 4 vary; 5 blend; 6 checkr, jumble, mutate; 7 deviate, diverge, shuffle; 8 contrast, intermix, scramble; 9 variegate; 11 intersperse; 13 differentiate; PHRASES: 4, 3, 7 ring the changes; 5, 2 shake up; 6, 3 branch out; 6, 4, 5 spread one's wings.

diversion 5 hobby; 6 change; 7 pastime; 9 departure; 10 alteration, digression; 11 distraction; 13 entertainment.

diversity 5 range; 7 mixture, variety; 8 contrast, disorder; 9 bumpiness, deviation, exception, variation; 10 assortment, difference, divergence, fitfulness, inequality, miscellany, raggedness, unevenness; 11 incongruity, instability, variability, variegation, variousness, versatility; 12 alterability, irregularity, multiplicity; 13 changeability, discontinuity, dissimilarity, haphazardness, heterogeneity, inconsistency, individuality, modifiability, nonconformity, nonuniformity; PHRASES: 3-3 one-off; 3, 3, 3 odd man out.

divert 4 pull; 5 amuse, avert, deter; 6 please, switch; 7 deflect, delight, disport, gladden, reroute; 8 dissuade, distract, redirect; 9 entertain, sidetrack; PHRASES: 4, 4 bowl wide, turn away; 4, 5 pull aside; 6, 6 change course.

divide 3 gap; 4 gulf, part, rift; 5 allot, chasm, divvy, halve, share, split; 6 bisect, sunder; 7 analyze, dissect, divorce, quarter, seclude, segment; 8 allocate, boundary, estrange, fragment, separate; 9 anatomize, apportion, factorize, partition, segregate; 10 distribute; 11 fractionate, fractionize; 12 sectionalize; 13 fractionalize; PHRASES: 3, 2

cut up; 4, 3 deal out, dole out; 4, 5 keep apart; 4, 7 come between; 5, 2 break up, carve up, split up; 5, 3 share out *UK*.

dividing line 6 border, divide, margin, radius; 7 equator; 8 bisector; 9 watershed; 10 borderline; 11 distinction.

divination 6 augury; 7 dowsing, insight; 8 forecast, geomancy, prophecy; 9 astrology, discovery, haruspicy, horoscope, horoscopy, logomancy, palmistry, pyromancy, pythonism, sortilege, theomancy; 10 astromancy, capnomancy, cartomancy, chiromancy, hieromancy, hydromancy, necromancy, numerology, ophiomancy, prediction; 11 bibliomancy, forecasting, foretelling, oneiromancy, premonition, psychomancy, sideromancy, soothsaying, speculation; 12 arithmomancy, clairvoyance, ichthyomancy, precognition, vaticination; 13 haruspication; 14 astrodiagnosis; PHRASES: 1, 5 I Ching; 3, 6 tea leaves; 4-7 palm-reading; 5, 5 birth chart, Tarot cards; 5-8 water-divining; 6, 5 second sight; 7, 4 crystal ball, dowsing rods; 7-6 crystal-gazing; 7-7 fortune-telling; 8, 4 divining rods.

divinatory 7 augural; 8 oracular; 9 prophetic, sibylline; 10 haruspical, predictive; 11 clairvoyant, predictable, premonitory; 12 clairaudient, precognitive; 13 clairsentient.

divine 4 holy; 5 dowse, godly, great, guess; 6 deduce, deific, intuit, lovely, sacred; 7 angelic, blessed, deistic, discern, foresee, godlike, perfect, predict, presume, sublime, supreme; 8 absolute, almighty, Christly, discover, forecast, foretell, graceful, hallowed, heavenly, immortal, infinite, majestic, numinous, oracular, perceive, pleasing, prophesy, seraphic, soothsay, theistic; 9 celestial, epiphanic, excellent, exquisite, incarnate, ineffable, messianic, religious, spiritual, unearthly, wonderful, Yahwistic; 10 Christlike, delightful, omnipotent, omniscient, sacrosanct, theocratic, ubiquitous, vaticinate; 11 omnipresent, theomorphic; 12 extramundane, immeasurable, providential, supernatural, supramundane, transcendent; 14 transcendental; PHRASES: 3-6 all-seeing; 3-7 all-knowing; 3-8 all-powerful; 4, 2, 5 full of grace; 4, 4 cast lots; 4, 5 read palms, read signs; 5-6 water-divine; 7-4 crystal-gaze.

divinely 2, 4, 4 by God's will; 3, 7 Deo volente. *See also* **divine**

diviner 4 seer; 5 augur, sibyl, vates; 6 auspex, dowser; 7 palmist, prophet, psychic; 8 haruspex; 9 geomancer, predictor, pythoness, pythonist; 10 astrologer, forecaster, foreteller, palmreader, pyromancer, soothsayer, theomancer; 11 astromancer, chiromancer, clairvoyant, hieromancer, necromancer; 12 clairaudient, icthyomancer, numerologist, oneiromancer, psychomancer, sideromancer; 13 clairsentient; PHRASES: 7, 5 crystal gazer; 7, 6 fortune teller.

divinity 5 deity; 7 godhead, godhood, godship, nirvana; 8 holiness, sanctity; 9 godliness, sublimity; 10 Brahmahood, Buddhahood, perfection, sacredness, sanctitude; 12 hallowedness, numinousness, spirituality; 13 sacrosanctity; PHRASES: 5, 2, 5 state of grace.

divisible 8 compound; 9 composite, dividable, separable; 10 detachable, isolatable; 13 commensurable; PHRASES: 2, 10 in proportion.

division 4 gulf, part, rift; 5 break, group, ratio, split; 6 border, branch, schism, sector; 7 discord, rupture, section, sharing; 8 boundary, category, disunion, dividend, fraction, grouping, quotient; 9 allotment, apartheid, partition, remainder, severance; 10 allocation, department, detachment, disharmony, dissection, proportion, separation, truncation; 11 compartment, demarcation, segregation, subdivision; 12 disagreement, distribution; 13 apportionment; 14 classification, discrimination; PHRASES: 7, 4 aliquot part.

divorce 4 part; 5 sever, split; 6 detach; 7 breakup, unmarry; 8 distance, separate; 9 annulment; 10 disconnect, dissociate, separation; PHRASES: 5, 2 break up, split up; 5, 3, 4 untie the knot; 5, 5 break apart; 5, 9 grass widowhood; 6, 2, 7 decree of nullity; 6, 4 broken home, decree nisi; 6, 8 broken marriage, decree absolute *UK*.

divorced 5 split; 8 deserted, detached; 9 abandoned, dissolved, estranged, separated; 11 unconnected; PHRASES: 6, 2 broken up; 6, 5 living apart.

divorced person 7 divorcé; 8 divorcée, divorcer; PHRASES: 5, 5 grass widow; 5, 7 grass widower.

divulge 4 hint, leak, tell, vent; 5 speak, utter; 6 inform, reveal; 7 confide, declare, publish; 8 announce, disclose; 9 broadcast, publicize, ventilate; 11 communicate; PHRASES: 3, 2 let on; 3, 3 let out; 3, 3, 2, 2 let one in on; 3, 4 let slip; 4, 3, 3 blow the lid off; 4, 3, 4 blow the gaff, come out with; 4, 4 give away; 4, 5 make known; 4, 6 talk turkey; 5, 3, 4 break the news.

divulgence 4 hint, leak; 6 avowal, exposé; 8 betrayal, giveaway; 9 admission, broadcast; 10 confession; 11 declaration; 12 announcement; 13 communication; PHRASES: 6, 8 queen's evidence, state's evidence.

dizzy 5 faint, giddy, shaky, silly, woozy; 7 flighty; 8 flippant; 9 frivolous; 11 lightheaded; 12 lighthearted.

do 3 act, con; 4 make, work; 5 cheat, party, solve, trick; 6 ensure, soirée; 7 achieve, defraud, execute, perform, prepare, swindle; 8 complete, function; 9 bamboozle, gathering, reception; 10 accomplish; PHRASES: 3-8 get-together; 5, 3 carry out.

docile *See* **submissive**

dock 3 cut; 4 crop, land, moor, quay, stop; 5 berth, wharf; 6 reduce; 7 mooring; 9 anchorage; PHRASES: 3, 2 tie up; 3, 3 cut off; 4, 2 come in.

docket 3 tag; 5 label; 6 agenda, marker, ticket; 7 declare, program, sticker; 8 calendar, disclose, identify, schedule.

doctor 3 ABD, doc, PhD *UK*, rub; 4 cure, dope, drug; 5 alter, amend, dress, locum, medic, nurse, quack, treat; 6 adjust, expert, extern, healer, intern, medico, modify, physic, rework; 7 falsify, massage, surgeon; 8 academic, houseman *UK*, medicate, resident, sawbones; 9 caregiver, clinician, physician; 10 administer, consultant *UK*, manipulate, pasteurize, specialist; 12 psychiatrist; 16 anesthesiologist; PHRASES: 2-3 ob-gyn; 4, 6 herb ~; 5, 6 house ~; 5, 7 trick cyclist *UK*; 5, 9 house physician; 6, 4 meddle with, tamper with; 6, 7 health officer; 7, 7 medical officer (MO); 8, 2 minister to.

doctrine 5 canon, dogma; 6 policy; 9 principle.

document 4 file, text; 5 bumph *UK*, essay, paper; 6 detail, record, report; 7 article, dossier; 9 statement; 10 manuscript; 11 certificate; PHRASES: 5, 4 write down; 5, 5 green paper, white paper; 6, 4 report card; 6, 6 compte rendu.

documentation 2 CV *UK*, ID; 4 chit, visa; 6 papers, permit, record, résumé, ticket;

7 receipt, records, voucher, warrant; **8** passport, warranty; **9** reference; **11** credentials, testimonial; **13** certification; PHRASES: **4, 7** case history; **8, 4** identity card; **10, 5** curriculum vitae *UK*.

dodder 4 reel; **5** quake, shake, waver; **6** quiver, teeter, totter, wobble; **7** stagger, tremble.

dodge 3 cut; **4** duck, move; **5** avoid, elude, evade, shirk; **8** sidestep; PHRASES: **3, 3, 2** get out of; **4, 4** move away.

doer 4 hand, hero; **5** actor, agent, mover; **6** artist, player, worker; **7** artisan, workman; **8** achiever, activist, criminal, director, evildoer, executor, militant, offender, operator; **9** committer, craftsman, executant, executive, operative, performer; **10** campaigner, controller, malefactor, undertaker; **11** perpetrator; **12** entrepreneur, practitioner; **13** administrator; PHRASES: **2-6** do-gooder, gogetter; **4, 3** whiz kid; **4, 4** live wire; **4-5** highflier; **4-7** self-starter; **5, 3** stunt man; **5, 3, 6** mover and shaker.

doff *See* **take off**

dog 3 box, cur, gun, pig, pug, pup, toy, vex; **4** chow, Fido, hunt, mutt, puli, tyke; **5** bitch, boxer, corgi, doggy, feist, hound, husky, pooch, puppy, spitz, stalk, track, trail, whelp; **6** anubis, badger, basset *UK*, beagle, borzoi, bother, briard, canine, collie, eskimo, follow, harass, hassle, kelpie, lapdog, Lassie, pariah, pester, plague, poodle, pursue, saluki, setter; **7** basenji, bulldog, griffon, harrier, lurcher, maltese, mastiff, mongrel, pointer, samoyed, sausage, Scottie, sheltie, sniffer, spaniel, terrier, tracker, trouble, whippet; **8** airedale, Airedale, Alsatian *UK*, cerberus, cockapoo, elkhound, foxhound, keeshond, Labrador, lakeland, papillon, Pekinese, Sealyham, sheepdog; **9** beleaguer, chihuahua, dachshund, dalmatian, deerhound, greyhound, Pekingese, retriever, schnauzer, staghound, wolfhound; **10** Bedlington, bloodhound, otterhound, pomeranian, Rottweiler *UK*, schipperke, weimaraner; **12** Newfoundland; **13** affenpinscher, Staffordshire; PHRASES: **2-3** pi-dog; **3-3** pye-dog; **3, 7** fox terrier; **4, 3** bird ~, dope ~, shih tzu; **4-3** shar-pei; **4, 3, 7** wire fox terrier; **4, 4** chow chow; **4, 4, 6** man's best friend; **4, 7** bull mastiff, bull terrier, Jack Russell, Skye terrier; **5, 4** Great Dane, Kerry blue, lhasa apso; **5, 7** cairn terrier, Saint Bernard; **5, 9** Irish wolfhound; **6, 5** Afghan hound, basset hound; **6, 7** Border terrier, cocker spaniel, dandie dinmont; **6, 8** German shepherd; **6, 9** golden retriever; **7, 3** service ~; **7, 3, 7** English toy spaniel; **7, 5** Finnish spitz, pharaoh hound; **7, 8** Alaskan malamute; **8, 4** Japanese chin; **8, 5** Siberian husky; **8, 7** springer spaniel; **8, 8** American foxhound; **9, 6** Hungarian vizsla; **9, 8** Norwegian elkhound.

dogged *See* **determined**

doggerel 5 ditty, rhyme, verse; **6** poetry; **7** garbage, prattle, rubbish; **8** limerick, nonsense; **9** gibberish.

dogmatic 4 deaf; **5** blind, fixed, rigid; **6** narrow; **7** bigoted; **8** obsessed, pedantic; **9** blinkered, fanatical, hidebound; **10** habituated, impervious, inflexible; **11** doctrinaire, opinionated; **12** conservative, intransigent, obscurantist; PHRASES: **4-4** hard-line; **4-7** hard-shelled.

Dog Star 6 Sirius.

doll 3 toy; **5** model; **6** figure, puppet; **8** figurine.

domain 4 area; **5** field; **6** sphere; **8** province.

dome 3 arc; **4** arch, hump; **5** mound, vault; **6** cupola; **7** ceiling, hillock, hummock, rotunda.

domestic 4 home; **5** house, local; **6** family, inland, native; **8** familial, internal, national; **9** household.

domesticated 3 pet; **4** bred, tame; **6** inbred, raised, reared; **7** trained; **8** purebred; **11** housebroken; **12** thoroughbred; PHRASES: **6, 2** broken in; **6-2** bought-in.

domicile *See* **home**

dominance *See* **domination**

dominant 4 main; **5** bossy, chief, major; **6** ruling; **7** central, leading; **8** foremost, imperial; **9** ascendant, assertive, officious, prevalent, principal; **10** dominating, overriding, prevailing, ubiquitous; **11** dictatorial, domineering, influential, magisterial, predominant; **12** monopolistic; **13** authoritarian, authoritative, multinational; PHRASES: **3-9** all-pervading; **4-7** wide-ranging.

dominate 4 boss, lead, rule; **5** bully, force, order; **6** direct, govern, ordain; **7** command, control, dictate, oppress; **8** bulldoze, domineer, overarch; **9** subjugate, tyrannize; **10** overshadow; PHRASES: **4, 3** play god; **4, 4** take over; **5, 4** tower over; **5, 5** tower above; **6, 7** assert oneself; **7, 2** dictate to; **7, 4** trample over.

dominating **10** conquering, oppressing, oppressive, repressive, tyrannical; **11** controlling, suppressive; **12** intimidating, overpowering.

domination **4** rule; **5** power; **7** command, control, mastery, tyranny; **8** conquest, dominion; **9** authority, supremacy; **10** ascendancy, conquering, government, oppression, repression; **11** suppression; **12** intimidation.

dominion **5** duchy, power, realm, state; **6** colony, domain, empire; **7** command, control, dukedom, earldom, kingdom, mandate; **8** province, statelet, toparchy; **9** archduchy, authority, dominance, sultanate, territory; **10** domination, Lebensraum, palatinate, principate; **11** archdukedom, chieftaincy, imperialism; **12** principality, protectorate; PHRASES: **3-2** say-so; **6, 5** buffer state; **6, 6** puppet regime; **9, 6** satellite nation.

don **6** assume; **8** nobleman, Spaniard; PHRASES: **3, 2** put on; **4, 2** pull on; **5, 2** throw on.

donate **4** give; **5** grant, offer, stand, treat; **6** bestow, defray; **7** provide, support; **8** bequeath; **9** volunteer; **10** contribute; PHRASES: **3, 3** pay for; **4, 4** give alms.

donation **4** gift; **5** grant, treat; **6** giving; **7** bequest, payment; **9** endowment; **10** bestowment, generosity, liberality; **12** contribution.

done See **complete**

donkey **3** ass; **4** moke, mule; **5** neddy UK; **6** Eeyore.

doodle **4** draw; **6** sketch; **7** drawing, picture; **8** scribble, squiggle.

doom **3** end, lot; **4** fate; **5** death; **6** kismet; **7** destiny, portion, tragedy, trouble; **8** disaster.

door **4** exit, flap, gate, open, trap; **5** entry, front; **6** access, egress; **7** ingress; **8** entrance.

dormant (be dormant) **4** rest, wilt; **5** exist, sleep; **6** wither; **7** survive; **8** vegetate; **9** hibernate, perennate; **10** overwinter.

dose **4** bout; **5** spell, treat; **6** amount, attack, dosage, period; **7** measure; **8** medicate, quantity; **10** experience; **12** prescription; PHRASES: **4, 2** ~ up.

doss **3** kip UK.

dosshouse **9** flophouse. See **flophouse**

dossier See **file**

dot **4** mark, spot; **5** fleck, point, speck; **6** blotch, pepper, pimple; **7** speckle; **8** sprinkle.

dotty **3** odd; **4** fond; **5** crazy; **6** absurd, doting; **7** foolish, strange; **8** besotted; **9** eccentric, illogical; **10** infatuated; **11** impractical, nonsensical; **13** idiosyncratic; **14** unconventional.

double **3** duo; **4** bend, copy, dual, duet, echo, fold, pair, twin; **5** biped, bipod, clone, duple; **6** cloned, copied, couple, duplex, expand, mirror, paired, repeat, second, tandem; **7** amplify, augment, biplane, bivalve, couplet, diptych, distich, doublet, magnify, twofold; **8** biathlon, geminate, multiply, repeated; **9** duplicate, geminated, replicate; **10** duplicated; **11** photocopied; **12** doppelgänger; PHRASES: **3, 5** two times; **3-5** two-piece; **3-6** two-hander, two-seater; **3-7** two-wheeler; **4, 2** fold up; **4, 4** bend over; **4-5** look-alike; **5-2** stand-in; **5, 3** alter ego; **5, 4** twice over; **8, 5** spitting image.

double-cross **3** con; **5** cheat, trick; **6** betray; **7** swindle; **8** betrayal; **9** deception; PHRASES: **3, 4** let down; **4, 3** sell out.

double-edged **6** ironic; **9** ambiguous; **10** ambivalent; **11** duplicitous; PHRASES: **3-5** two-faced; **3-6** two-timing; **5-4** Janus-like; **6-7** double-dealing.

double figures **5** dozen, teens; **9** dodecagon, fortnight, undecagon; **10** duodecimal, hendecagon; **11** hexadecimal, quindecagon UK, twelvemonth; **12** dodecahedron, quindecaplet; **13** hendecahedron, quindecennial; PHRASES: **4, 6** legs eleven; **6, 5** baker's dozen; **7, 3** Twelfth Day, twelfth man UK; **7, 5** Twelfth Night; **7, 6** monkey's cousin.

doubly **5** twice; **9** extremely, plicately; **10** flexuously; PHRASES: **2, 3** in two.

doubt **3** but; **4** moot; **5** guess, qualm, query; **6** aporia, debate, impugn; **7** confute, contest, dispute, dissent, dubiety, suspect; **8** distrust, hesitate, mistrust, question; **9** disbelief, misgiving, speculate, suspicion; **10** conjecture, disbelieve, hesitation; **11** reservation, uncertainty.

doubter **5** cynic; **7** skeptic; **8** agnostic; **9** pessimist; **11** nonbeliever; PHRASES: **8, 6** doubting Thomas.

dough See **cash**

doughty **5** brave, tough; **8** spirited; **10** determined; **11** indomitable.

dour **3** set; **4** sour; **5** stern; **6** severe; **8** resolute, stubborn; **10** determined, purposeful, unfriendly; PHRASES: **4-5** hard-faced.

douse **3** wet; **4** soak; **5** cover, snuff, souse; **6** drench, quench; **7** smother; **10** extinguish; PHRASES: **3, 3** put out.

dovetail **4** trim; **5** frame, miter, tenon; **7** mortise; **9** interlock; PHRASES: **3, 8** fit together; **4, 2** slot in.

dowdy *See* **plain**

down **3** bog, eat, low, sad; **4** beat, blue, fall, fuzz; **5** adown, along, drink, knock, round, shoot, south, under; **6** behind, defeat, guzzle, listed, losing, tabled, upside; **7** consume, swallow, through, unhappy; **8** dejected, downcast, downhill, downtown, downward, nosedown, overcome; **9** depressed, downgrade, miserable, nominated; **10** despondent, downstairs, downstream, downstreet, timetabled; **11** downhearted, inoperative, reductively; **12** decreasingly, oppressively, subversively; PHRASES: **2, 1, 3, 3** at a low ebb; **2, 3, 5** on the floor; **2, 3, 6** on the bottom, on the ground; **2, 4-4** at halfmast; **2, 4, 6** at rock bottom; **3, 2, 5** out of order; **3, 2, 6** out of action.

downbeat **4** dark; **5** bleak; **6** casual, gloomy; **7** relaxed; **8** informal, negative; **11** pessimistic; **13** unpretentious; PHRASES: **4-4** laid-back.

downcast *See* **sad**

downfall **3** end; **4** fall, ruin; **6** demise; **7** failure.

downplayed **7** diluted, reduced; **9** curtailed; **10** diminished, restrained; **11** disregarded, underplayed; PHRASES: **2-10** de-emphasized; **4, 5, 2** made light of; **5-4** pared-down, toned-down; **7-4** watered-down.

downplaying **8** dilution; **9** disregard; **10** constraint, moderation; **11** curtailment, deprecation; **12** diminishment, underplaying; PHRASES: **2-8** de-emphasis.

downthrow **5** upset; **7** overset; **8** leveling, overturn; **9** grounding, overthrow; **10** flattening, revolution, subversion; **13** precipitation; **14** defenestration.

downward *See* **descending**

doze *See* **nap**

drab **4** dull, gray; **5** dingy; **6** boring, dreary, gloomy, somber; **10** monotonous, unexciting; **13** uninteresting.

draft **4** brew, flow, plan, waft; **5** write; **6** breath, breeze, sketch; **7** current, mixture, outline, prepare, summary; **8** medicine; **10** concoction; PHRASES: **4, 2** draw up; **5, 4** rough copy; **6, 3** sketch out.

draftsman **6** drawer; **8** designer, sketcher.

drag **3** lag, lug, tow, tug; **4** draw, haul, puff, pull; **5** crawl, creep, heave, smoke, trail, trawl; **6** dawdle, dredge, linger, loiter; **7** draggle; **8** nuisance.

drain **3** sap; **5** ditch, sewer; **7** channel, conduit, consume, culvert, deplete, exhaust; **8** tailpipe; PHRASES: **3, 2** use up.

drainage **4** sink, sump; **5** ditch; **6** divide; **7** channel; **9** catchment, watershed; PHRASES: **3, 3** oil pan.

drama **4** agon, fuss, mask, mime, play; **5** farce, scene, stage; **6** action, cinema, comedy, crisis; **7** hamming, staging, theater, Thespis, tragedy; **8** Broadway, playland, stagedom; **9** commotion, dramatics, hysterics, repertory, spectacle, theatrics; **10** dramaturgy, excitement, stagecraft; **11** dramaticism, histrionics, performance, showmanship, theatricals; **13** theatricality; **14** sensationalism; PHRASES: **2-2** to-do; **3, 4, 3** the West End; **3, 6** the boards, the Fringe; **3, 10** the footlights; **4, 2, 7** coup de théâtre; **4, 3, 5** song and dance *UK*; **5, 3, 5** Sturm und Drang; **5, 4** stage show; **5, 7** Grand Guignol.

dramatic **5** stagy, vivid; **6** daring, staged, stagey; **7** enacted, intense, mimetic, musical; **8** affected, balletic, operatic, prompted, scripted, Thespian; **9** performed; **10** histrionic, improvised, noticeable, theatrical; **11** dramaturgic, sensational, spectacular; **12** considerable, melodramatic; **13** choreographic, protagonistic.

dramatist **4** Hugo (Victor); **5** Camus (Albert), Dumas (Alexandre), Eliot (T. S.), Havel (Václav), Synge (J. M.), Yeats (W. B.); **6** author, Coward (Sir Noel), Dryden (John), writer; **7** Anouilh (Jean), farceur, Ionesco (Eugène), Molière, Plautus (Titus Maccius); **8** Beaumont (Francis), comedian, farceuse, Schiller (Friedrich von), Stoppard (Sir Tom); **9** Aeschylus, Cervantes (Miguel de), Euripides, jokesmith, scenarist, Sophocles, tragedian; **10** dramatizer, dramaturge, librettist, playwright, Strindberg (August); **11** mimographer, scenarioist; **12** Aristophanes, Beaumarchais (Pierre Augustin Caron de), screenwriter, scriptwriter; **13** choreographer, melodramatist; PHRASES: **6, 2, 8** Cyrano de Bergerac (Savinien); **8, 2, 2, 5** Calderón de la Barca (Pedro); **9-6** Granville-Barker (Harley).

dramatize 3 act, ham; **4** star; **5** stage, write; **6** script; **7** feature, present, produce, release; **8** premiere, typecast; **9** embellish, overstate; **10** exaggerate; **13** melodramatize, theatricalize; **14** sensationalize; PHRASES: **3, 2** lay on, put on; **4, 2** blow up, play up.

drastic 4 dire; **6** severe; **7** extreme, radical; **8** sweeping.

draw 3 lug, tie, tow, tug; **4** drag, even, gain, haul, limn, lure, pull; **5** charm, draft, equal, heave, trace; **6** appeal, choose, depict, derive, doodle, elicit, entice, select, sketch; **7** attract, cartoon, extract, outline, portray, stencil; **8** deadlock, describe, standoff; **9** captivate, represent, stalemate, unsheathe; **10** allurement, attraction, enticement, illustrate, inducement; PHRASES: **4, 3** pull out; **4, 4** dead heat; **5, 2** bring in; **5, 6** crowd puller *UK*, photo finish; **6, 5** finish equal.

draw in 4 hook, suck; **5** sniff, snuff; **6** engage, inhale; **7** ensnare, involve, retract; **8** aspirate; **9** implicate; PHRASES: **4, 2** pull in, suck in.

drawing 5 comic, draft, graph, study; **6** design, doodle, sketch; **7** cartoon, diagram, limning, outline, picture, tracing; **8** doodling, drafting, graffiti, graffito, scribble, vignette; **9** animation, depiction, portrayal; **10** caricature; **11** delineation; **12** illustration; **13** draftsmanship; **14** representation; PHRASES: **3-3-3** pen-and-ink; **5-3-5** black-and-white; **9, 6** lightning sketch, thumbnail sketch.

drawl *See* **accent**

draw out 5 educe, evoke, glean, rouse; **6** arouse, deduce, derive, elicit, induce, obtain; **7** procure, prolong; **8** lengthen, protract; **9** stimulate; PHRASES: **5, 2, 5** bring to light; **5, 5** bring forth; **6, 2** summon up.

dread 4 fear; **5** alarm, panic, quail, shake; **6** blench, dismay, flinch, fright, horror, quiver, recoil, shiver, shrink, terror; **7** anxiety, shudder, tremble; **11** trepidation; PHRASES: **4, 4** draw back, turn pale; **4, 6** take fright; **6, 4** shrink from.

dreadful *See* **terrible**

dream 4 goal, hope, wish; **5** fancy, ideal; **6** desire, marvel, trance, vision; **7** fantasy, imagine, reverie; **8** ambition, daydream, delusion, envisage, envision, Morpheus; **9** fantasize, nightmare, visualize; **10** aspiration; **13** hallucination; PHRASES: **6, 2, 3, 3** castle in the air.

dreamland 2 Oz; **6** heaven, Narnia, Utopia; **7** Arcadia, Elysium, Erewhon, nirvana; **8** Atlantis, paradise; **9** Cockaigne, fairyland, Lyonnesse, Ruritania; **10** wonderland; PHRASES: **2-2, 4** la-la land; **2, 6** El Dorado; **5, 2, 3, 5** Isles of the Blest; **5-5, 4** never-never land; **5, 6** Happy Valley; **5-6, 4** cloud-cuckoo land; **6, 2, 4** Garden of Eden; **6-5** Middle-earth; **7-2** Shangri-la; **7, 6** Elysian Fields; **8, 4** promised land.

dreamy 5 vague; **6** superb; **7** faraway, pensive, wistful; **9** beautiful, fantastic, wonderful; **11** preoccupied.

dreary 4 dull, grim; **5** bleak; **6** boring, dismal; **7** tedious; **8** lifeless; **9** cheerless, miserable; **10** monotonous.

dregs 4 lees, silt; **7** deposit, residue; **8** sediment; **10** housedress.

dress 3 don, rig; **4** clad, garb, gown, robe, sack, sari, saya, wear; **5** adorn, array, cloak, cover, drape, frock, saree, shift, stola; **6** bedeck, clothe, enfold, enrobe, finery, jumper, mantua, muumuu, peplos, shroud, swathe; **7** apparel, clothes, envelop, garnish, gymslip *UK*, regalia, sarafan, sheathe, sultane, swaddle; **8** accouter, ballgown *UK*, chongsam, decorate, frippery, ornament, pinafore *UK*, sundress; **9** caparison, cheongsam, coatdress, maxidress, minidress, overdress, polonaise, trousseau; **10** shirtdress, shirtwaist; **11** habiliments, houppelande; **12** shirtwaister; PHRASES: **3, 3** fit out; **3, 4** tea gown; **4, 3** deck out; **4, 4** slip into; **4, 5** ball ~, cape ~, full ~, tent ~, tube ~; **5, 5** dance ~; **6, 4** dinner gown; **6, 5** cancan ~, dinner ~, sheath ~; **6, 6** salwar kameez; **6, 7** mother hubbard, Mother Hubbard; **7, 4** evening gown, Fortuny gown, hostess gown, wedding gown; **7, 5** boudoir ~, chemise frock, evening ~ *UK*, morning ~, wedding ~; **8, 5** backless ~, cocktail ~, mourning ~, pinafore ~, princess ~; **9, 5** maternity ~, strapless ~. *See also* **clothes**

dressage 4 gait; **5** habit, volte; **6** curvet, piaffe; **7** passage, renvers, travers; **8** caracole; **9** freestyle.

dressed 4 clad, shod; **5** robed; **6** booted *UK*, capped, draped, garbed, gloved, gowned, hatted, hooded, rigged, vested; **7**

arrayed, attired, cloaked, clothed, covered, frocked, habited, mantled; **8** bedecked, bewigged, bonneted, costumed, invested, liveried; **9** appareled, uniformed; **12** habilimented; PHRASES: **6, 3** decked out, kitted out *UK*.

dressed-up 4 chic; **5** natty, ritzy, smart; **6** dapper, glitzy, modish, soigné, spruce, togged; **7** bedight, groomed; **9** bedizened, uniformed; **11** fashionable; PHRASES: **1, 2, 4** à la mode; **2, 4, 7** in fine feather; **2, 5** in tails; **2, 6, 4** in Sunday best; **2, 6, 5** en grande tenue; **4, 6, 3** well turned out; **5, 3** black tie; **6, 2** dolled up, tarted up; **7, 2** gussied up, slicked up, spruced up; **7, 2, 4** dressed to kill.

dressily 6 chicly; **7** nattily, smartly; **8** modishly, snazzily; **9** elegantly, stylishly; **11** fashionably, glamorously; PHRASES: **2, 5** in vogue.

dress up 3 don; **5** array, dight, primp, prink; **6** bedeck, revamp; **7** bedizen; **8** beautify, disguise, titivate; **9** embellish; PHRASES: **2, 2** do up; **3, 2** rig out; **4, 2** doll up, tart up *UK*; **4, 3** deck out; **5, 2** gussy up; **5, 2, 4** dress to kill; **6, 2** spruce up.

dribble 4 drip, leak, ooze, seep; **5** drool; **6** drivel, slaver; **7** slobber, trickle; **8** salivate.

dried 3 dry; **4** sere; **5** corky; **7** parched, sapless, wizened; **8** scorched, weazened, withered; **9** juiceless, mummified, shriveled; **10** dehydrated, desiccated, exsiccated; PHRASES: **3, 2, 1, 4** dry as a bone; **3, 2, 1, 7** dry as a biscuit; **3, 2, 4** dry as dust; **3, 2, 9** dry as parchment; **4-3** bone-dry; **9-4** parchmentlike.

drier 3 mop; **4** swab; **5** towel; **6** mangle; **7** blotter, swabber, wringer; **9** absorbent, dehydrant, siccative, towelling; **10** dehydrator, desiccator, evaporator, exsiccator; **11** desiccative, exsiccative; **12** clotheshorse, dehumidifier.

drift 4 flow, gist, idea, waft; **5** coast, float, glide, point, sense; **7** meaning.

driftwood 5 waste; **6** jetsam, refuse; **7** flotsam; **8** wreckage.

drill 4 bore, fire; **5** coach, teach, train; **6** pierce, school; **8** exercise, instruct, practice, puncture, training; **9** penetrate; **10** discipline; **11** instruction, preparation.

drily 5 wryly; **6** aridly, subtly; **7** dustily *UK*, wittily; **9** thirstily, xerically; **10** humorously, ironically; **11** anhydrously.

drink 3 can, cup, lap, sip, sup; **4** brew, chug, down, dram, drop, glug, gulp, suck, swig, tope; **5** bevvy *UK*, booze, cuppa *UK*, draft, drain, glass, hooch, plonk, quaff, round, short *UK*, slurp, snort, souse, swill, toast, toddy; **6** bottle, fuddle, guzzle, imbibe, nectar, potate, potion, spirit, tipple; **7** alcohol, carouse, cordial, liqueur, snifter, swallow, wassail; **8** aperitif, beverage, cocktail, infusion, libation, mouthful, oblation, potation, schnapps; **9** decoction, sundowner; **10** concoction; **11** compotation; PHRASES: **3, 2** lap up; **3, 3, 3, 4** one for the road; **3, 4** put away; **3, 4, 6** cup that cheers; **3, 5** get drunk; **3-5** pub-crawl; **4, 2** soak up; **4-2-2** pick-me-up; **4, 2, 3, 3** hair of the dog; **4, 4** gulp down, wash down; **5, 1, 6** crack a bottle; **5, 2, 3, 4** ~ of the gods; **5, 3** quick one, short one, stiff one; **5, 4** knock back; **5, 4, 1, 4** ~ like a fish; **5, 4, 6** slake one's thirst; **6-8** thirst-quencher.

drink (provide drink) 4 wine; **5** nurse, water; **6** suckle; **8** irrigate; PHRASES: **3, 4, 1, 6** lay down a cellar.

drinkable 5 clean; **7** potable; **8** filtered; **10** distilled; PHRASES: **3, 2, 5** fit to drink.

drinker 4 lush, wino; **5** alkie, toper; **6** bibber, boozer, sipper; **7** alehead, guzzler, quaffer, swiller; **8** drunkard, pisshead *UK*; PHRASES: **5, 7** heavy ~, light ~; **6, 7** social ~.

drinking 6 toping, vinous; **7** boozing, drunken, gulping, lapping, nipping, sipping, soaking, sucking, supping; **8** bibulous, imbibing, potation, quaffing, swigging, swilling, tippling; **9** beeriness; **10** alcoholism, dipsomania, imbibition, vinousness; **11** drunkenness, sottishness; **12** bibulousness, intemperance; **13** dipsomaniacal; PHRASES: **3, 3, 5** off the wagon.

drinking bout 3 jag; **4** lush; **5** binge, blind, revel, spree; **6** bender; **11** bacchanalia; PHRASES: **3-5** pub-crawl; **4, 2, 8** orgy of drinking.

drink to 5 toast; **6** pledge, salute.

drip 4 drop, leak, ooze, pour, rain, seep, wimp; **6** patter, shower; **7** cascade, dribble, drizzle, droplet, trickle; **11** precipitate; PHRASES: **4, 4** flow down, pour down; **4, 4, 3, 4** rain cats and dogs.

drip-dry 3 air; **5** wring; **6** mangle; **9** evaporate; PHRASES: **4, 3, 2, 3** hang out to dry.

drive 4 disk *UK*, goad, push, urge; **5** force, guide, impel, motor, pilot, power, shove, steer; **6** appeal, coerce, compel, energy, propel, thrust; **7** operate, passion; **8** ambition, campaign, vitality; **9** chauffeur, transport; **10** enterprise, initiative, motivation; **13** determination; PHRASES: **3-2-3-2** get-up-and-go; **3, 2, 6** set in motion.

drivel *See* **nonsense**

drive out 3, 3, 2, 4 run out of town; **4, 3** drum out, hunt out, push out, rout out; **5, 3** chase out, force out, smoke out; **6, 3** freeze out.

driver 5 racer; **7** truckie *UK*; **8** helmsman, motorist; **9** chauffeur; **10** charioteer; **11** motocrosser; **12** motorcyclist.

driving 5 heavy; **7** dynamic, lashing, pouring; **8** forceful, powerful; **9** energetic; **10** motivating.

drizzle 4 rain, spit, spot; **6** shower; **7** trickle; PHRASES: **5, 4** light rain.

droll *See* **amusing**

drone 3 hum; **4** buzz, whir; **5** whine; **6** murmur.

droop 3 bow, sag; **4** fade, fail, flag, flop, sink, tire, wilt; **5** crash, slump; **6** slouch; **7** subside; **8** collapse, prolapse; PHRASES: **4, 2** cave in, fall in; **4, 3** give way, tire out, wear out; **5, 4** plump down, slump down; **5, 5** touch depth; **5, 6** touch bottom.

drop 3 cut, dip, sag; **4** bead, dive, drib, drip, dump, fall, seep, stop; **5** crash, ditch, gutta, pitch, slump, swoop; **6** plunge, shelve; **7** abandon, decline, descent, globule, plummet, release, skydive, trickle; **8** decrease, nosedive; **9** bellyflop, crashland, declivity, downswing, parachute, powerdive, precipice, reduction; **11** discontinue; PHRASES: **3, 2** let go; **3, 3** cut out; **3, 4** bow down, fly down, let fall; **4, 2** give up; **4, 4** fall down, nose dive *UK*; **4, 4, 2** come down on; **5, 3** leave out; **5, 4** light upon, throw down, touch down; **6, 4** alight upon, spiral down; **7, 2** descend on.

dropout 6 hippie; **7** beatnik; **13** nonconformist; PHRASES: **3, 3, 8** new age traveler.

dross *See* **rubbish**

drought *See* **lack**

drove *See* **throng**

drown 3 die; **4** hide, mask, sink, soak; **5** flood, swamp; **6** drench, engulf; **7** founder, obscure; **8** inundate, saturate, submerge; **9** overwhelm; PHRASES: **2, 5** go under.

drowsy *See* **sleepy**

drudge 4 plod, toil, work; **5** grind, labor; **6** menial, skivvy *UK*, worker.

drug 3 dex, fix, hit, kif, LSD, PCP, pot; **4** acid, bang, barb, coke, dexo, dope, dose, hash, hemp, junk, rock, scag, snow, weed; **5** candy, crack, dexie, ganja, grass, horse, joint, opium, roach, smack, snort, speed, stick, sulfa, tonic, upper; **6** curare, deaden, downer, elixir, emetic, heroin, opiate, orange, peyote, potion, reefer, sedate, spliff, Valium™; **7** anodyne, antacid, aspirin, cocaine, codeine, ecstasy, gungeon, hashish, insulin, muggles, panacea, placebo, pyrogen, steroid; **8** androgen, antidote, aperient, barbital, birdwood, cannabis, designer, diazepam, diuretic, dynamite, excitant, laxative, medicine, morphine, narcotic, relaxant, sedative; **9** albuterol, analeptic, analgesic, antiserum, antiviral, cathartic, coagulant, cortisone, demulcent, drugstore, febrifuge, fungicide, germicide, glyburide, humectant, inhibitor, marijuana, medicinal, mescaline, methadone, narcotics, narcotize, paregoric, purgative, soporific, speedball, stimulant, tamoxifen, temazepam, Thorazine, vermicide, vermifuge; **10** anesthetic, antibiotic, antiemetic, antifungal, antiseptic, antivenene, astringent, aureomycin, catholicon, depressant, hydragogue, intoxicant, medication, painkiller, palliative, penicillin, spermicide, taeniacide, thimerosal; **11** amphetamine, antifebrile *UK*, antimycotic, antipyretic, antitussive, bactericide, barbiturate, blockbuster, carminative, diaphoretic, expectorant, insecticide, neuroleptic, paracetamol, preparation, psychedelic, rubefacient, sulfonamide, vasodilator, vasopressor; **12** anaesthetize, anthelmintic, antihydrotic, antimalarial, antipruritic, antithrombin, decongestant, disinfectant, hallucinogen, parasiticide, pediculicide, prophylactic, somnifacient, streptomycin, tetracycline, tranquilizer; **13** abortifacient, acetaminophen, anticoagulant, antihistamine, antipsychotic, antispasmodic, premedication, sympatholytic; **14** anticonvulsant, antidepressant, antimetabolite, bronchodilator, pharmaceutical; **15** anticholinergic, counterirritant, sympathomimetic, vasoconstrictor; PHRASES: **3, 4** pep pill; **3, 9** MAO inhibitor; **4, 3** Mary Ann; **4-3** cure-all; **4, 4** Mary Jane; **4, 5** blue cheer, nose candy; **4, 6** Mary Warner; **4, 7** beta blocker; **5, 3** black tar, knock out; **5, 4** angel dust, dirty ~; **5, 5**

black stuff, brown sugar, dime's worth, truth serum, white stuff; **5, 6** black beauty, black gunion, green dragon; **5, 7** crack cocaine; **5, 8** magic mushroom; **6, 4** purple haze; **6, 5** purple heart *UK*; **6, 6** peanut butter, yellow jacket; **6, 8** yellow sunshine; **7, 3** Mexican mud; **7, 4** tootsie roll; **8, 4** Acapulco gold, sleeping pill; **8, 5** Jamaican ganga; **8, 7** anabolic steroid.

drug addict 2 DA; **4** head, hype, user; **5** freak, jones; **6** addict, junkie, scorer; **7** druggie, hophead, tripper; **8** acidhead, cokehead; **9** mainliner; PHRASES: **4, 5** dope fiend, scag jones.

drugged 4 high; **5** doped; **6** loaded, stoned, zonked; **7** sedated; **8** floating; **9** medicated; **10** insensible; **13** incapacitated; PHRASES: **6-3** spaced-out.

druggist 7 chemist *UK*; **8** pharmacy; **9** dispenser, drugstore; **10** apothecary, pharmacist, posologist; **14** pharmacologist.

drug pusher 5 narco, viper; **6** dealer, pusher; **7** peddler; PHRASES: **5, 3** candy man; **6, 3** reefer man.

drum 3 tap; **4** beat, boom, cask, thud; **5** bongo, pound, pulse, snare, throb, thrum, thump; **6** barrel, kettle, tattoo; **7** pulsate, timbale, tympano; **8** cylinder, tympanum; **9** container; **10** percussion; **11** reverberate; PHRASES: **3-3** tom-tom; **4, 1, 6** beat a tattoo; **4, 3, 5, 5** ~ and bugle corps; **8, 6** tumbling barrel.

drumming 4 beat, roll; **5** pulse; **6** tattoo; **7** beating, booming, rolling, tapping; **8** drumbeat, pounding, resonant, striking, thudding; **9** hammering, pulsation, throbbing, thrumming, vibration; **10** percussion; **11** palpitation, reverberant; **13** reverberation, reverberative.

drunk 3 cut, out; **4** gone, high, shot, wino; **5** beery, blind, boozy, dizzy, fried, giddy, happy, merry, muzzy, stiff, tight, tipsy, woozy, zonko; **6** bagged, blotto, bombed, boozer, canned, juiced, loaded, lushed, potted, ratted, soaked, soused, stewed, stinko, stoned, tiddly *UK*, toping, vinous, zonked; **7** bibbing, blasted, blitzed, boozing, bottled, drunken, ebriate, ebriose, flushed, fuddled, legless, maudlin, pickled, plotzed, screwed, sloshed, smashed, sottish, sozzled, squiffy *UK*, twisted, zonkers; **8** bibulous, ebriated, elevated, guzzling, swigging, swilling, tippling; **9** alcoholic, carousing, inebriate, paralytic, pixilated,

plastered, stupefied; **10** hiccupping, inebriated, staggering, wassailing; **11** dipsomaniac, intemperate, intoxicated; **13** dipsomaniacal; PHRASES: **3, 2** lit up; **3, 2, 1, 4** fou as a coot, fou as a wulk; **3, 2, 2** out of it; **3, 4** out cold; **3-4** pie-eyed; **3-5** rat-arsed *UK*, rat-faced, red-nosed; **3-6** gin-sodden; **3-7** pot-valiant; **4, 2, 3, 5** dead to the world; **4-3** half-cut *UK*; **4-4, 4** half-seas over; **4-5** well-oiled; **4-7** wine-bibbing; **4-10** well-lubricated; **5, 2, 1, 6** as a lord; **5, 2, 1, 5** ~ as a skunk; **5, 2, 1, 7** ~ as a fiddler; **5, 3** wiped out; **6, 2** tanked up; **6, 2, 1, 4** pissed as a newt; **6-4** glassy-eyed; **6, 5** plowed under; **8, 2** liquored up.

drunk (get drunk) 3 bib; **4** lush, soak, swig, tope; **5** booze, quaff, souse, swill; **6** fuddle, guzzle, tipple; **7** carouse, wassail; PHRASES: **2, 2, 1, 5** go on a spree; **2, 2, 1, 6** go on a bender; **3, 3, 6** hit the bottle; **3-5** pubcrawl; **4-1-3** chug-a-lug; **4, 2** tank up; **5, 1, 6** crack a bottle; **5, 4** drink deep, drink hard; **5, 4, 1, 3** knock back a few; **5, 4, 1, 4** drink like a fish; **6, 2** liquor up.

drunkard 3 sot; **4** soak, wino; **5** drunk, souse, toper; **6** bibber, boozer, maenad, soaker, sponge; **7** alehead, drinker, reveler, Silenus, swiller, tippler; **8** bacchant, carouser, wineskin; **9** alcoholic, bacchanal, inebriate; **11** dipsomaniac; PHRASES: **3-7** pub-crawler; **4-6** wine-bibber; **5, 2, 5** slave to drink; **5, 4** juice head; **5-6** froth-blower; **7, 4** thirsty soul.

drunkenly 7 tipsily; **11** crapulently, crapulously.

drunkenness 6 hiccup; **7** ebriety, reeling; **8** blackout; **9** dizziness, ebriosity, elevation, inebriety, tipsiness, wooziness; **10** excitation, hiccupping, insobriety, staggering, stammering, stuttering; **11** inebriation, stimulation; **12** befuddlement, exhilaration, intoxication; PHRASES: **5, 6** thick speech; **5, 7** Dutch courage; **5, 8** blind staggers; **6, 6** seeing double; **7, 6** drunken stupor, slurred speech.

dry 3 wry; **4** arid, dull, sere; **5** drain, droll, parch, plain, sober, towel; **6** boring, dreary, ironic, kipper, wither; **7** deadpan, gasping *UK*, laconic, parched, tedious, thirsty; **8** droughty, preserve, sardonic, teetotal, vaporize; **9** abstinent, anhydrate, anhydrous, dehydrate, desiccate, evaporate, exsiccate, sarcastic, shriveled, waterless; **10** abstemious, dehumidify, dehydrated, desiccated, uninspired; **11** emotionless, unemotional, unirrigated, unmoistened; **12** moistureless; **13** uninteresting; **14** prohibitionist; **PHRASES: 3, 2** mop up; **3, 2, 1, 4** ~ as a bone; **3-3** air-dry; **3, 4** rub down; **4-3** wind-dry; **4, 3, 3** high and ~; **5-3** smoke-dry; **6-2-4** matter-of-fact.

dryness 5 irony; **7** aridity, drought, sarcasm, siccity; **10** laconicism; **11** dehydration, desiccation; **14** understatement. *See also* **dry**

dry up 4 fail, wilt; **5** parch, wizen; **6** shrink, weazen, wither; **7** mummify, shrivel; **9** dehydrate, desiccate; **PHRASES: 3, 3** dry out, run out; **4, 2** shut up; **4, 3, 6** lose the thread; **4, 4** stop dead; **4, 9** stop midstream; **6, 4, 5** forget your lines.

dual *See* **double**

duality 4 dyad; **5** Janus; **7** dualism; **8** contrast; **9** ambiguity, dichotomy, duplexity; **10** doubleness, opposition; **11** ambivalence; **12** bilingualism; **13** ambidexterity; **PHRASES: 6, 3, 4** Jekyll and Hyde; **6, 4** double life; **6, 5** double agent; **6, 7** double meaning; **6-7** double-dealing; **6, 8** double entendre; **6-8** double-crossing; **6-9** double-sidedness.

dub *See* **call**

dubious 5 shady; **6** unsure; **7** suspect; **8** doubtful; **9** ambiguous, debatable, uncertain, undecided; **11** unconvinced; **12** questionable; **13** untrustworthy.

duck 3 bob, dip, nod; **4** bend; **5** avoid, dodge, elude, evade, lower, stoop; **6** bombay; **7** muscovy; **8** mandarin, sidestep; **9** harlequin, waterfowl; **10** circumvent.

duct *See* **channel**

dud 4 flop; **6** broken, fiasco; **7** failure, letdown, useless; **9** worthless; **11** ineffective; **14** disappointment; **PHRASES: 2, 4** no good.

due 4 owed; **5** owing; **6** credit, direct, merits, proper, thanks, unpaid; **7** fitting, payable, payment; **8** directly, expected, straight; **9** scheduled; **10** deservings, punishment; **11** anticipated, appropriate, comeuppance; **12** compensation; **14** acknowledgment; **PHRASES: 2, 7** in arrears; **4, 7** just deserts; **5, 3, 6** right and proper.

duel 5 clash, fight, joust; **6** battle, combat; **7** contest, tourney; **8** conflict, gunfight, struggle; **9** swordplay; **10** tournament; **PHRASES: 3-2-3** one-on-one; **4-2-4, 5** hand-to-hand fight.

dues 4 debt, levy, toll; **6** charge; **7** payment; **12** contribution, subscription.

dull 3 dim; **4** blur, dark, drab, gray, numb; **5** allay, bland, blunt, cloud, dingy, faded, foggy, misty, murky, muted; **6** boring, cloudy, dampen, deaden, dismal, dreary, gloomy, leaden, muffle, obtuse, reduce, somber; **7** assuage, humdrum, insipid, routine, tedious; **8** lifeless, overcast, sluggish, stultify; **10** lackluster, monotonous, unexciting, uninspired; **11** desensitize, featureless; **12** hebetudinous, unremarkable; **13** unimaginative, uninteresting; **PHRASES: 4-6** slow-witted *UK*; **4-7** mind-numbing.

dullness 4 murk; **5** gloom; **6** tedium; **8** hebetude, monotony; **9** obtundity; **10** cloudiness, insipidity; **13** impercipience *UK*. *See also* **dull**

dull sound 4 bump, plop, thud; **5** clunk, plonk, plunk, thump.

dumbfound 4 hush, mute, stun; **5** amaze; **6** deaden, muffle; **7** astound, stagger; **8** astonish, confound, gobsmack, surprise; **11** flabbergast.

dummy 4 copy, fake, form, mock; **5** model; **6** figure; **7** pretend, replica; **9** imitation, mannequin; **PHRASES: 3, 6** lay figure; **4-2** mock-up.

dump 3 put, tip *UK*; **4** mess; **5** hovel, leave, throw; **6** desert; **7** abandon, discard, eyesore, garbage; **8** junkyard, landfill; **9** scrapyard *UK*; **11** monstrosity; **PHRASES: 3, 3, 2** get rid of; **4, 3, 2** walk out on; **7, 2** dispose of; **7, 4** rubbish ~ *UK*.

dune 4 bank, hill, hump; **5** mound; **7** barchan *UK*; **8** sandbank.

dungeon *See* **prison**

dunk *See* **dip**

duo *See* **pair**

dupe 3 con, mug *UK*; **4** babe, fool, gull; **5** cheat, cinch, patsy, softy, trick; **6** monkey, pigeon, puppet, stooge, sucker, victim; **7** cuckold, deceive, schnook, swindle; **8** hoodwink, pushover; **9** plaything, schlemiel; **PHRASES: 4, 2** take in; **4, 2, 3, 5** babe in the woods; **4, 2, 4** babe in arms; **4, 3** cat's paw, fall guy; **4, 4** easy mark, fair game; **4, 5** soft touch; **4, 8** easy pickings; **5, 4** April fool; **6-5** double-cross; **7, 4** sitting duck; **8, 5** laughing stock *UK*.

duplicate 3 ape, fax; **4** copy, dupe; **5** clone, ditto, print, Xerox™; **6** copied, double, repeat; **7** imitate, replica, reprint, rubbing, xeroxed; **8** offprint; **9** facsimile, identical, imitation, photocopy, replicate, reprinted, reproduce; **10** impression, Mimeograph™, offprinted, photograph, replicated, reproduced, triplicate; **11** microcopied, photocopied, photostated, replacement, replication; **12** mimeographed, photographed, reproduction; **14** representation; PHRASES: **2, 5** do again; **6, 4** carbon copy.

duplicitous 3 sly; **5** false; **6** tricky; **9** deceitful, deceiving, deceptive, dishonest, equivocal; **10** backhanded, fraudulent, unfaithful; **11** dissembling, treacherous; PHRASES: **3-5** two-faced; **5-5** Janus-faced; **6-2-5** tongue-in-cheek; **6-6** double-minded; **6-7** double-dealing, double-tongued.

duplicity 5 craft; **6** deceit; **7** cunning, perfidy, slyness; **9** deception, falseness, hypocrisy, treachery; **10** dishonesty, disloyalty, doubleness, trickiness; **11** fraudulence, machination; **13** deceitfulness, equivocalness; PHRASES: **5, 4** Judas kiss; **6, 4** double life; **6, 6** double facade, forked tongue; **6-6** double-tongue; **6-7** double-dealing.

durable *See* **tough**

duration 4 span, term, time; **5** shift, space, spell, stint; **6** extent, length, period, tenure; **7** stretch, tenancy; **8** interval; **9** trimester; **12** intermission; PHRASES: **5, 4** fixed term.

duration (for the duration) 7 forever; PHRASES: **2, 3, 3** to the end; **2, 3, 6, 3** to the bitter end; **3, 4** for good; **3, 8** for evermore.

duress *See* **pressure**

dust 4 dirt, sand, soil, soot, wipe; **5** ashes, brush, clean, cover, earth, filth, grime; **6** dredge, powder; **7** scatter; **8** sprinkle; PHRASES: **4, 4** wipe down; **7, 10** Arizona cloudburst.

Dutch 3 cap, elm; **5** treat, uncle; **6** cheese; **7** auction, courage.

dutiful 5 loyal; **7** devoted, duteous, ethical, upright; **8** virtuous; **10** principled, respectful, scrupulous; **11** accountable, punctilious, responsible; **13** conscientious; PHRASES: **4-7** well-behaved.

dutifully 2, 3, 4, 2, 4 in the line of duty. *See also* **dutiful**

duty 3 due, job, tax; **4** levy, onus, task, toll; **5** death, point, stamp; **6** burden, charge, estate, impost; **7** calling, payment; **8** function; **9** liability; **10** assignment, conscience, imposition, obligation; **11** duteousness, dutifulness, undertaking, willingness; **13** answerability; **14** accountability, responsibility; **15** accountableness, responsibleness; PHRASES: **3, 5, 5** the right thing; **3, 6, 5** the proper thing; **4, 2, 4** call of ~; **5, 5** inner voice; **5, 10** moral imperative; **7, 4** bounden ~.

duty (be the duty of) 4 must; **5** befit; **6** become, should; **7** behoove; PHRASES: **3, 2, 3, 4, 2** lie at the door of; **4, 2** fall to; **4, 2, 3, 3, 2** fall to the lot of; **4, 4** rest with; **5, 2** ought to; **6, 2** belong to; **7, 4** devolve upon.

duty (do one's duty) 4 obey; PHRASES: **4, 2, 4, 4** stay at one's post; **5, 2, 7** think of England; **7, 4, 4** fulfill one's duty.

duty (impose a duty) 3 tie; **4** bind; **5** order; **6** decree, enjoin, expect, oblige; **7** command; **8** obligate; PHRASES: **4, 4** call upon; **6, 4** saddle with.

duty-bound 4 tied; **5** bound, sworn; **7** obliged, pledged, saddled; **8** beholden; **9** committed, obligated.

dwell 4 stay; **5** abide, lodge; **6** reside; **7** inhabit.

dwelling *See* **house**

dwindle *See* **decrease**

dye 4 tint, woad; **5** color, eosin, henna, rinse, stain; **6** bleach, madder; **7** aniline, crocein, mordant, pigment; **8** acridine, alizarin, colorant, coloring, dyestuff, fuchsine, mauveine, peroxide, xanthine; **9** rhodamine; **14** phthalocyanine; PHRASES: **6, 6** Tyrian purple.

dyed 7 colored; **8** bleached; PHRASES: **4-2-3-4** dyed-in-the-wool, dyed-in-the-yarn.

dyeing 5 batik; **8** coloring, printing, staining; PHRASES: **3-6** tie-dyeing.

dying 3 fey; **4** last; **5** final; **6** doomed, fading; **7** closing, deathly, failing; **8** expiring, moribund, slipping, ultimate; **9** condemned, deathlike, vanishing; **10** cadaverous; PHRASES: **2, 3, 4, 4** on its last legs; **2, 6, 4** at death's door; **2, 8** in extremis; **3, 4** far gone; **4, 3** done for; **4-4** half-dead; **5, 2, 1, 5** white as a sheet; **5, 4** about gone; **6, 4** fading fast; **7, 4** deathly pale.

dying day 8 deathbed, finality; **9** obsequies; **10** deathwatch; PHRASES: **4, 4** last gasp, last hour, swan song; **4, 5** last agony, last rites, last words; **4, 6** last breath; **5, 5** death scene, final words; **5, 6** death rattle, death throes, dying breath; **7, 4** passing bell.

dying person 5 goner; PHRASES: 4, 4 dead duck; 4, 6 dead pigeon; 8, 4 hopeless case.

dynamic 6 active, driven, lively; 7 drawing, kinetic, vibrant; 8 animated, forceful, spirited, vigorous; 9 energetic, impulsive, vivacious; 10 locomotive, percussive, propulsive; PHRASES: 2, 6 on stream; 3-6 pro-active; 4, 2, 4 full of life; 4-9 self-motivated.

dynamically 4, 8 with momentum. *See also* **dynamic**

dynamite *See* **blow up**

dynamo 5 motor; 7 turbine; 9 extrovert, generator; PHRASES: 2-6 go-getter; 4, 3 live one; 4, 4 live wire.

dynasty 3 era; 4 line, rule; 5 house, reign; 6 empire, family, period.

E

E 3 key; 4 note; 5 Spain; 7 eastern, Ecstasy; 8 oriental.

each 2 ea; 3 all, per; 5 every.

eager 4 avid, keen; 5 amped, ready; 6 prompt; 7 excited, fervent, psyched, willing, zealous; 9 fanatical, impatient; 10 alacritous; 12 enthusiastic; PHRASES: 4-2 gungho; 4, 2, 7 keen as mustard; 5, 3, 7 ready and willing; 6, 2, 2 raring to go; 7, 3, 4 willing and able.

eagerness 4 zeal; 5 ardor; 6 fervor; 8 alacrity, keenness, zealotry; 10 enthusiasm, excitement, fanaticism. *See also* **eager**

ear 3 lug *UK*; 4 heed, lobe; 5 knack, organ, shell; 6 talent; 7 auricle, earlobe, hearing, lughole *UK*, trumpet; 8 listener, tympanum; 9 attention; 11 cauliflower; PHRASES: 5-4 shell-like *UK*.

ear (parts) 5 anvil, incus, pinna; 6 hammer, stapes; 7 cochlea, eardrum, malleus, stirrup; 8 ossicles, tympanum; 9 labyrinth, vestibule; PHRASES: 10, 4 eustachian tube.

ear (problems with the ear) 7 earache, otalgia; 8 deafness, tinnitus; PHRASES: 4, 3 glue ear *UK*.

eared 8 auriform; 9 auricular; 10 auriculate.

earlier 4 past; 5 prior; 6 before, former; 8 formerly, previous; 10 beforehand, previously; PHRASES: 2, 7 in advance.

earliness 5 haste, hurry; 8 alacrity, dispatch; 10 expedition, promptness, timeliness; 11 promptitude, punctuality; PHRASES: 4, 2, 5 time to spare; 4, 5 head start.

early 2 am, ex; 3 now; 4 anon, bird, fast, soon; 5 first, hasty, prior, quick, ready; 6 prompt, speedy, timely; 7 betimes, closing, hurried, initial, primary, summary, warning; 8 advanced, directly, earliest, fore-hand, punctual, untimely; 9 forthwith, immediate, premature; 10 alacritous, beforehand; 11 expeditious; PHRASES: 2, 2, 5, 4 at an ~ time; 2, 3, 5, 5 in the small hours; 2, 3, 9 at the beginning; 2, 4 in time, on time; 2, 4, 4 in good time; 2, 7 in advance; 2, 8 on schedule; 5, 2, 4 ahead of time, crack of dawn; 5, 2, 4, 4 ahead of one's time; 5, 2, 7 ahead of oneself; 5, 2, 8 ahead of schedule; 5, 3, 7 ready and waiting; 5, 4 right away; 5, 5 first thing; 6, 4 before time; 6, 5 flying start; 7, 5 without delay.

early (be early) 5 hurry; 6 hasten; 7 preempt; 8 dispatch, expedite; 10 anticipate; PHRASES: 4, 3, 3 jump the gun; 4, 4 gain time.

early (too early) 8 previous; 9 antedated, overhasty, proleptic; 10 preemptive; 11 precipitate.

earn 3 get, net, win; 4 gain, make, rate; 5 clear, gross, merit; 6 secure; 7 deserve, produce, receive, warrant; PHRASES: 2, 4 be paid; 2, 6, 2 be worthy of; 4, 3 work for; 4, 4 take home; 5, 2 bring in.

earnest 4 deep; 5 eager, grave, sober; 6 intent, solemn, strong; 7 genuine, intense, serious, sincere; 8 resolute; 9 committed, dedicated, heartfelt; 10 determined, purposeful; 12 enthusiastic.

earnestly 5 truly; 6 really; 8 actually, honestly. *See also* **earnest**

earnings 3 fee, GNP, pay; 4 gain, gate, take, wage; 5 wages, yield; 6 income, profit, return, salary, spoils; 7 advance, alimony, annuity, makings, pension, returns, revenue, royalty, stipend, takings, tontine; 8 dividend, interest, palimony, pickings, proceeds, receipts, turnover, winnings; 9 gleanings; 11 maintenance; 12 remuneration; PHRASES: 3, 5 pay check; 3, 6 net return; 3, 7 net revenue; 3, 8 pay envelope; 4-2 take-in; **4-4, 3** take-home pay; **4, 5** gate money *UK*; **5, 5** privy purse; **5, 6** gross return; **5, 7** child support, gross revenue; **7, 6** private income.

ear shell 7 abalone.

earth 2 up; **3** mud, sod, wax; **4** clay, dirt, Gaia, loam, soil; **5** globe, Terra, world; **6** gravel, ground, mother; **7** surface, terrain, terrene, topsoil; **9** geosphere.

earthquake 5 focus, quake, seism, shake, shock; **6** tremor; **7** shaking; **8** upheaval; **9** epicenter, foreshock, trembling; **10** aftershock; **PHRASES: 7, 8** seismic activity.

earth science 7 geodesy, geology; **9** geography, hydrology, petrology, tectonics; **10** geoscience, glaciology, mineralogy; **11** planetology, volcanology; **12** geochemistry, paleontology, physiography; **13** geochronology, geomorphology.

earthy 4 rude; **5** basic, bawdy, crude, dirty, gross, loamy, muddy, rocky, rough, sandy, silty, stony; **6** clayey, coarse, pebbly, simple, vulgar; **7** raunchy; **8** gravelly; **13** unpretentious; **PHRASES: 2-8** no-nonsense.

earwax 7 cerumen.

ease 3 aid, nap, oil; **4** edge, help, lull, rest, slip, work; **5** break, clear, death, guide, leave, letup, pause, peace, quiet, relax, skill, sleep, slide, speed; **6** assist, catnap, grease, hasten, lessen, loosen, luxury, mellow, recess, reduce, repose, smooth, snooze, solace, soothe, subdue, temper, unclog, unwind, wealth; **7** advance, assuage, clarify, comfort, content, fluency, holiday *UK*, improve, interim, leisure, lighten, massage, mollify, nirvana, promote, relieve, respite, Sabbath, shuteye, slacken; **8** aptitude, breather, facility, furlough, idleness, interval, maneuver, mitigate, moderate, opulence, sedation, serenity, simplify, vacation; **9** abatement, affluence, alleviate, interpret, lubricate, remission, stillness; **10** facilitate, inactivity, mitigation, quiescence, relaxation, sabbatical, simplicity; **11** appeasement, consolation, contentment, refreshment, restfulness, tranquility; **12** intermission, painlessness; **14** effortlessness; **PHRASES: 3, 2, 5** bed of roses; **3, 3** day off; **3, 3, 6** oil the wheels; **3, 5** tea break *UK*; **4, 2** cool it; **4, 3** cool out, draw out, iron out, time off; **4, 3, 4, 4** load off one's mind; **4, 4** free time, tone down, turn down; **4, 5** hang

loose; **4-5** well-being; **4, 6** make better; **4, 7** bank holiday; **4, 8, 3** take pressure off; **5, 3** Lord's day; **5, 3, 5** peace and quiet; **5, 4** spare time; **5, 5** forty winks; **5, 6** sweet dreams; **6, 2** limber up, loosen up; **6, 3, 3** smooth the way; **6, 3, 4** soften the tone; **6, 4** simmer down, smooth over; **9, 5** breathing space *UK*.

ease (at ease) 4 easy, idle, lazy, slow, snug; **5** quiet, still; **6** casual; **7** content, easeful, relaxed, restful, resting; **8** carefree, leisured, peaceful, pillowed, relaxing, sluggish, tranquil; **9** cushioned, leisurely, quiescent, unhurried; **11** comfortable; **12** postprandial; **PHRASES: 2, 5** on leave; **2, 8** on furlough, on vacation; **2, 10** on sabbatical; **4-4** laid-back; **5-6** after-dinner.

easily 6 freely, simply; **7** clearly, handily, readily; **8** facilely, smoothly; **9** certainly; **10** definitely; **11** comfortably, undoubtedly; **12** effortlessly; **14** simplistically; **PHRASES: 2, 1, 4, 3** by a long way; **2, 1, 4, 4** by a long shot; **2, 1, 4, 5** by a long chalk *UK*; **2, 3** by far; **2, 5** no sweat; **2, 7** no problem; **4, 4, 4** just like that; **4, 7** like nothing; **4, 9** like clockwork; **5, 4** hands down; **7, 1, 5** without a hitch; **7, 3** without ado; **7, 5** without doubt.

easily (do easily) 5 coast; **9** freewheel; **PHRASES: 2, 2, 4, 7** be in one's element; **3, 2, 1, 4** win in a walk; **3, 2, 1, 6** win at a canter; **4, 2, 4** have it soft; **4, 4** sail home; **4, 5, 2** make light of; **4, 5, 4, 2** make short work of; **5, 4** coast home; **5, 7, 2** think nothing of; **6, 2** breeze in.

easily (go easily) 4 flow, roll, sail; **5** coast, glide, slide, sweep; **9** freewheel.

east 1 E; **6** exotic, orient.

Easter 4 Lent; **6** Island; **8** festival; **PHRASES: 6, 3** E~ egg; **6, 6** E~ basket.

easy 4 cool, game, glib; **5** clear, cushy, light, plain; **6** facile, simple, smooth; **8** downhill, informal, moderate, painless, tranquil; **9** leisurely, luxurious; **10** accessible, downstream, effortless, elementary, simplified, uninvolved; **11** comfortable, undemanding; **12** intelligible; **13** comprehensive, uncomplicated; **14** comprehensible; **15** straightforward; **PHRASES: 2, 5** no sweat; **2, 5, 7** in plain English; **2, 7** no problem, no trouble; **3, 3, 6** for the asking; **4, 4** dead ~; **4-4** laid-back; **4-5** easy-peasy *UK*; **4, 6** dead simple; **4-8** user-friendly; **6-4** stress-free; **6, 5** Mickey Mouse; **7, 2, 2** nothing to it; **7-4** trouble-free.

easy (make easy) 3 aid, oil; 4 ease, free, help; 5 allow, clear, gloss, loose, speed, unbar, unjam; 6 assist, enable, grease, hasten, permit, smooth, unclog; 7 advance, clarify, explain, forward, further, pioneer, promote, unblock; 8 expedite, simplify; 9 interpret, lubricate, translate, vulgarize; 10 facilitate, popularize; PHRASES: 4, 2 open up; 4, 3 iron out; 4, 3, 3 make way for, pave the way; 4, 3, 4, 2 open the door to; 4, 5 help along, make clear; 4, 6 make easier; 5, 3, 3 clear the way; 6, 3, 3 bridge the gap, smooth the way.

easy (take it easy) 3 nap; 4 doze, laze, loll, rest; 5 chill, couch, perch, relax, roost, sleep; 6 drowse, lounge, repose, snooze, sprawl, unbend, unwind; 7 recline; PHRASES: 2, 2, 3 go to bed; 2, 2, 5 go to sleep; 2, 2, 8 go on vacation; 3, 2 let up; 3, 4 bed down, kip down, lie back, lie down, sit back, sit down; 3, 4, 7 get some shuteye; 4, 1, 3 take a nap; 4, 1, 4 take a rest; 4, 1, 8 take a breather; 4, 2 cool it; 4, 2, 4 come to rest; 4, 2, 4, 4 rest on one's oars; 4, 4 slow down, take five; 4, 5, 5 have forty winks; 5, 3 slack off; 5, 4, 2 catch some Zs.

easygoing 4 calm; 5 blasé; 6 casual, docile, mellow, serene; 7 lenient, relaxed; 8 biddable, carefree, tolerant; 9 compliant, indulgent, tractable; 10 permissive, submissive; 11 acquiescent; PHRASES: 4-4 laidback; 4-8 even-tempered.

easy thing 3 pie; 4 ABCs, meat, ride, snap; 5 cinch, setup; 6 breeze, doddle UK, picnic, velvet; 8 pushover, sinecure, walkaway, walkover; PHRASES: 1, 8 a pleasure; 2-7 no-brainer; 3, 4, 4 the high road; 4, 4 dead cert UK, duck soup; 4, 5 kid's stuff, soft touch, sure thing; 4, 6 easy target, soft option UK; 5, 2, 4 piece of cake; 5, 4 clear road; 5, 5 clear coast; 5, 6 clear course, cushy number; 5, 7 plain sailing; 6, 4 child's play, smooth road; 6, 5 turkey shoot; 7, 4 sitting duck.

eat 3 sup, vex; 4 bite, bolt, chew, chop, crop, dine, fare, feed, gnaw, gulp, have, mess, nosh, peck, rend, sate, suck, tear, wolf; 5 annoy, binge, board, champ, chomp, drool, feast, gnash, gorge, graze, grind, lunch, mouth, munch, raven, scarf, scoff, slurp, snack, worry; 6 absorb, bother, browse, crunch, devour, digest, engulf, gobble, guzzle, ingest, nibble, plague, starve; 7 banquet, consume, engorge, partake, pasture, scrunch, subsist, swallow,

trouble; 8 ruminate; 9 breakfast, manducate UK, masticate; 10 gluttonize, gormandize; PHRASES: 3, 3 pig out; 3, 4 lay into, put away; 4, 1, 4 have a meal; 4, 2 chew up, prey on, snap up; 4, 3 dine out; 4, 3, 3 chew the cud; 4, 4, 7 fill one's stomach; 4, 5, 4, 2 make short work of; 5, 4, 5 clean one's plate; 5, 5 break bread; 5, 7 stuff oneself; 6, 2 shovel in; 6, 3 polish off.

eater 3 hog, pig; 4 wolf; 5 diner, hyena, vegan; 6 dieter, feeder, foodie, gannet, locust, messer, pecker, picker, taster, veggie; 7 boarder, bulimic, epicure, feaster, glutton, gobbler, gourmet, guzzler, luncher, nibbler, slimmer; 8 anorexic, bacchant, cannibal, consumer, devourer, gourmand, Lucullus, messmate, omnivore, partaker; 9 bacchanal, banqueter, carnivore, herbivore, picnicker; 10 vegetarian; 11 connoisseur, insectivore, trencherman; PHRASES: 3, 6 bon vivant; 6, 7 weight watcher.

eating (eating utensils and dishes) 4 bowl, dish, fork; 5 knife, ladle, plate, spoon; 8 teaspoon; 10 silverware, tablespoon; 12 dessertspoon; PHRASES: 4, 4 fish fork; 4, 5 fish knife, soup spoon; 4, 6 flat silver; 5, 4 salad fork; 5, 5 steak knife; 6, 4 fondue fork; 6, 5 butter knife; 7, 5 carving knife.

ebb 4 fade, fail, flow, ooze; 5 abate, drain; 6 recede, settle; 7 decline, retreat, subside; 8 diminish; 9 disappear, evaporate; PHRASES: 2, 3 go out; 3, 3 run off; 7, 4 falling tide.

Eboracum 4 York UK.

eccentric 3 nut, odd, rum; 4 card, case, kook, rare; 5 batty, crazy, freak, funny, kooky, queer, weird; 6 exotic, freaky, mutant, oddity, quirky, unique, weirdo; 7 bizarre, curious, deviant, monster, nutcase, oddball, offbeat, strange, unusual; 8 crackpot, doolally UK, freakish, headcase, original, peculiar, singular; 9 character, fruitcake, grotesque, monstrous, screwball; 10 basketcase, individual, irrational, outlandish, unorthodox; 11 exceptional; 13 extraordinary, idiosyncratic; 14 unconventional; PHRASES: 3, 2, 4, 5 out of this world; 3, 3 far out, odd bod, rum one, way out; 3-3 one-off; 3, 4 odd fish; 3, 6 odd fellow; 3, 8 odd customer; 5, 8 queer specimen.

ecclesiastic See **clergyman**

ecclesiastical court 5 Curia; 11 Inquisition; PHRASES: 4, 6 Holy Office; 5, 2, 6

Court of Arches.

echelon *See* **level**

echidna 5, 8 spiny anteater.

echinoderm 7 trepang; **8** asteroid, starfish; PHRASES: **3, 4** sea lily, sea star; **3, 6** sea urchin; **3, 7** sea biscuit; **3, 8** sea cucumber; **4, 6** sand dollar; **5-2-3** bêche-de-mer; **5-2-6** crown-of-thorns; **7, 4** brittle star, feather star.

echo 4 boom, copy; **6** parrot, repeat; **7** confirm, rebound, resound; **8** resonate, ricochet; **9** reiterate, resonance; **11** reverberate; **13** reverberation.

eclipse 4 hide; **5** cover, outdo; **6** darken; **7** conceal, obscure, surpass; **8** outshine; **10** overshadow.

economic 5 cheap; **6** fiscal, frugal, retail; **7** prudent, thrifty; **8** monetary; **9** budgetary, efficient, financial, lucrative, pecuniary, wholesale; **10** commercial, marketable, mercantile, profitable; **11** moneymaking; PHRASES: **4-9** cost-effective; **5-8** moneyspinning *UK*.

economist 5 buyer; **6** client, dealer, Jaycee, patron, seller, trader; **7** spender; **8** barterer, consumer, customer, employer, exporter, importer, merchant, supplier; **9** profiteer, purchaser; **11** businessman; **12** merchandiser.

economize 4 save; **6** ration; **7** protect; **8** retrench; **9** intervene; **10** monopolize; PHRASES: **3, 4** cut back, cut down; **4, 2** rein in; **6, 3, 4** scrimp and save; **7, 4, 4** tighten one's belt.

economy 5 cheap; **6** budget, family, saving, thrift; **7** bargain, cutback, reduced; **8** discount; **9** reduction; PHRASES: **3-4** lowcost; **5-8** penny-pinching.

ecosystem 5 biome, biota; **7** ecology, habitat; **11** environment.

ecstasy 3 joy; **4** high; **5** bliss, state; **6** frenzy, trance; **7** delight, elation, rapture.

ecstatic 4 high; **6** elated; **8** blissful, frenzied, thrilled; **9** delighted, overjoyed; **11** overexcited; PHRASES: **2, 1, 6** in a frenzy.

edge 3 hem, lip, rim; **4** bank, brim, curb, face, gimp, inch, line, pipe, side, trim; **5** beach, brink, coast, creep, flank, frame, frill, knife, limit, point, power, shore, sidle, skirt, verge; **6** border, bounds, flange, fringe, girdle, limits, margin, piping, strand, tiptoe; **7** acidity, control, enclose,

flounce, hemline, horizon, leading, seaside, selvage, skyline, valance, wayside; **8** approach, boundary, confines, decorate, encircle, frontier, furbelow, littoral, marginal, roadside, shoulder, sideline, surround, tideline, trailing, trimming; **9** advantage, coastline, extremity, harshness, perimeter, periphery, riverside, sharpness, shoreline, threshold, waterside; **10** bitterness, decoration, peripheral, waterfront; **11** superiority; **12** crenellation; **13** circumference; PHRASES: **4, 4, 3** pick one's way.

edible 4 good, rich; **5** candy, sweet, tasty; **6** dainty, savory; **7** dietary, eatable, feeding, moreish *UK*; **8** dietetic, esculent, slimming *UK*; **9** alimental, delicious, nutritive, palatable, succulent, wholesome; **10** alimentary, appetizing, comestible, consumable, digestible, nourishing, nutritious, sustaining; **11** nutritional, scrumptious; **13** mouthwatering; PHRASES: **6-7** finger-licking; **6-8** palate-tickling.

edifice 4 pile; **5** group; **7** mansion, network; **8** building; **9** structure; **11** association; **12** construction, organization.

edify *See* **enlighten**

Edinburgh 4, 6 Auld Reekie.

edit 3 run; **5** alter, amend; **6** change, manage, rehash, revise, rework; **7** control, correct, improve, oversee, rewrite; **9** rearrange; PHRASES: **4, 2** tidy up; **5, 4** check over.

editor 6 censor, cutter, dealer, tailor, trader; **7** alterer, amender, checker, reviser, swapper; **8** improver, reformer, replacer, restorer; **9** corrector, decorator, destroyer, innovator; **11** bowdlerizer, revisionist.

editorial 5 essay; **6** leader *UK*; **9** viewpoint; **11** perspective.

educable 3 apt; **5** quick, ready; **6** bright, clever, docile; **7** curious, pliable, willing; **9** malleable, motivated, receptive, teachable, trainable; **10** educatable, schoolable; **11** inquisitive, intelligent, susceptible; **12** autodidactic, instructable; **14** impressionable; PHRASES: **4-6** self-taught.

educate 4 form, mold, rear, tell; **5** brief, coach, drill, edify, equip, guide, prime, raise, shape, teach, train, tutor, verse; **6** advise, foster, ground, impart, inform, notify, refine, report, reveal, school; **7** advance, apprise, develop, divulge, improve, instill, nurture, prepare; **8** acquaint, civilize, disclose, instruct; **9** cultivate, encourage, enlighten, inculcate; **10** discipline, illuminate; **11** communicate; **12** indoctrinate; PHRASES: **3, 3** tip off; **5, 2** bring up.

educated 2 ed; **4** wise; **6** brainy, clever, swotty *UK*; **7** bookish, erudite, gnostic, learned, refined; **8** academic, cultured, highbrow, literary, literate, numerate, polished, studious, tasteful; **9** sagacious, scholarly; **10** cultivated, polymathic, scholastic; **12** accomplished, bibliophagic, intellectual; **13** contemplative, knowledgeable, sophisticated; PHRASES: **4-4** book-wise, well-read; **4-8** well-informed.

education 2 ed; **5** edbiz; **6** advice, course; **7** nurture, raising, rearing, tuition; **8** coaching, drilling, guidance, learning, pedagogy, progress, teaching, training, treatise, tutelage, tutoring; **9** schooling; **10** betterment, upbringing; **11** advancement, cultivation, edification, instruction, melioration, preparation; **12** amelioration, civilization, illumination; **13** acculturation, catechization, enlightenment; **14** indoctrination; PHRASES: **5, 9** basic ~; **12, 9** distributive ~.

educational 6 expert; **7** guiding *UK*, helpful, preachy; **8** academic, advisory, didactic, edifying, remedial; **9** bettering, educative, educatory, improving, revealing; **10** revelatory, scholastic; **11** informative, instructive, pedagogical, progressive; **12** enlightening, illuminating; **13** informational, instructional; PHRASES: **3-7** eye-opening.

educational institution 4 poly; **5** école; **6** lyceum; **7** academy, college, mesivta, yeshiva; **8** seminary; **9** institute, playgroup; **10** university; **11** polytechnic; **12** conservatory, kindergarten; PHRASES: **3, 4, 5** Phi Beta Kappa; **3, 4, 6** day care center; **3-4, 6** day-care center; **3, 7** art college, cow college, day nursery; **5, 7** drama college, early college; **6, 4** junior high, senior high *UK*; **6, 5** Talmud Torah; **6, 7** junior college; **6, 8** schola cantorum *UK*; **7, 5** student union; **8, 7** military academy, teachers college; **11, 6** alternative school. *See also* **school**

educator 3 B.Ed., don; **4** dean, guru; **5** coach, tutor; **6** docent, doctor, duenna, expert, fellow, intern, master, mentor, mullah, pundit, reader; **7** adviser, crammer *UK*, dominie, maestro, teacher, trainer; **8** academic, homilist, lecturer, mistress, preacher; **9** authority, governess, pedagogue, preceptor, principal, professor, schoolman *UK*; **10** chancellor, headmaster, instructor;

11 preceptress; **12** educationist *UK*, headmistress, schoolmaster; **14** schoolmistress; PHRASES: **4, 5** home tutor; **4, 7** form teacher, head teacher *UK*; **4, 10** vice chancellor; **7, 5** private tutor; **7, 7** student teacher.

e'er 2 ay; **3** aye; **4** ever; **6** always.

effect 3 end; **4** make; **5** drift, event, force, fruit, issue, power, sense; **6** action, create, impact, payoff, result, sequel, upshot, weight; **7** achieve, meaning, outcome, perform, product, realize, spinoff; **9** aftermath, byproduct *UK*, corollary, happening, influence; **10** completion, conclusion, denouement, impression; **11** achievement, consequence, culmination; **12** repercussion; PHRASES: **3, 6** end result, net result; **3, 7** end product; **5, 3** carry out; **5, 5** bring about.

effect (have a visible effect) 4 mark; **5** print; **7** imprint, inherit; PHRASES: **5, 1, 5** leave a trace; **5, 1, 9** leave a footprint; **7, 4** impress upon.

effect (show an effect) 3 act; **5** issue, react; **6** affect, happen; **7** achieve, produce; **8** complete, conclude; **9** culminate, terminate; **10** accomplish, counteract; **11** precipitate; PHRASES: **3, 2** end in; **3, 3** pay off; **4, 3** spin off; **6, 2** result in; **6, 4** impact upon.

effect (take effect) 5 arise, occur; **6** happen; **9** transpire; PHRASES: **3, 2** end up; **3, 3** pan out; **4, 2** crop up; **4, 2, 4** come to pass; **4, 3** come off, fall out, turn out, work out; **4, 4, 6** come into effect; **4, 5** come about, take place.

effect (with the effect of) 4 ergo; **5** hence; **9** naturally; **10** eventually; **11** accordingly, dependently, necessarily; **12** consequently, contingently, derivatively, subsequently; **15** consequentially; PHRASES: **2, 1, 6** as a result; **2, 1, 11** as a consequence; **2, 6** of course; **2, 11** in consequence; **3, 2** and so.

effective 4 real; **6** active, actual, direct, useful; **7** current, helpful; **8** forceful, fruitful, powerful, tactical, valuable; **9** effectual, efficient, executive, operative; **10** applicable, functional, productive, successful, worthwhile; **11** efficacious, influential, operational; **14** administrative; PHRASES: **2, 3, 3, 4** in all but name; **2, 5** de facto, in force; **2, 5, 2, 4** in point of fact; **2, 7** in reality; **2, 9** in operation.

effective (be effective) 2 do, go; **4** work; **6** answer; PHRASES: **3, 3** pay off; **3, 9** pay dividends; **4, 3** come off; **4, 3, 4** fill the bill; **4, 4, 1, 5** work like a charm; **4, 4, 5** work like magic; **4, 5** bear fruit; **4, 7** show results.

effectual *See* **effective**

effervescence 4 fizz, foam; **5** froth; **7** bubbles, sparkle; **8** vibrancy, vitality, vivacity; **9** animation.

effervescent 5 fizzy; **6** bouncy, bubbly, lively; **7** vibrant; **9** sparkling.

efficacious *See* **effective**

efficiency 5 speed; **8** efficacy; **9** adeptness, readiness; **10** competence; **11** proficiency; **12** productivity; **13** effectiveness.

efficient 9 effective; **10** economical, productive, proficient, timesaving; **11** inexpensive; PHRASES: **4-9** cost-effective, well-organized; **5-6** labor-saving.

effigy *See* **image**

effluent 5 spent, waste; **6** runoff, sewage; **7** seepage; **8** effusive, emission, expended, overflow; **9** discharge; **10** outpouring; PHRASES: **5, 5** bilge water.

effort 4 stab; **5** essay; **6** strain; **7** attempt; **8** exertion.

effrontery *See* **impudence**

effusive 4 flip, open; **5** frank, gushy, lippy; **6** candid, chatty, lavish, mouthy; **7** fulsome, gossipy, gushing, prating, profuse, yakking; **8** blabbing, sociable, tattling; **9** ebullient, expansive, prattling; **10** unreserved, vociferous; **11** extravagant; **12** unrestrained; **13** communicative, demonstrative; **14** conversational; PHRASES: **3, 5** all mouth; **3-7** big-mouthed.

egalitarian 4 fair, free, just; **5** equal; **9** classless, equitable, impartial; **10** democratic.

egg 1 O; **4** duck, nest, ovum, push, roll, spur, urge, yolk; **5** drive, ovule, shell; **6** gamete; **8** pressure; **9** encourage.

eggplant 9 aubergine.

eglantine 10 sweetbrier.

ego 4 self; **9** character; **11** personality; PHRASES: **4-5** self-image, self-worth.

egoism 3 ego; **6** vanity; **7** conceit, egotism; **10** narcissism; **11** egocentrism; **13** egocentricity; PHRASES: **3, 4** ego trip; **4-8** self-devotion; **4-10** self-absorption.

egoistic 4 vain; **8** bragging; **9** conceited, egotistic; **10** egocentric, egoistical; **11** egotistical; **12** narcissistic; PHRASES: **4-6** self-loving; **4-8** self-absorbed, self-centered; **5,**

2, 7 stuck on oneself.

Egyptian mythology 2 Nu, Ra; **3** Bes, Geb, Mut, Nun, Nut, Set, Shu; **4** Isis, Maat, Mont, Ptah, Seth; **5** Horus, Neheh, Thoth; **6** Anubis, Hathor, Osiris, Renpet, Tefnut, Upuaut; **7** Sekhmet; PHRASES: **4-2** Amon-ra.

eight 5 octad, octet; **6** eighth, octave, octavo; **7** octuple; PHRASES: **5, 4** Harry Tate; **6, 4** garden gate.

eighty 9 fourscore; **12** octogenarian.

either 2 or; **3** any; **4** both, each.

eject 4 emit, fire, oust, sack, spew; **5** evict, exile, expel, spout; **6** banish, bounce, cancel, censor, delete, deport, disbar, outlaw, remove, uproot; **7** defrock, discard, dismiss, suspend, unfrock; **8** disgorge; **9** discharge, eliminate, eradicate, expurgate, extradite; **10** bowdlerize, disqualify, expatriate, obliterate; **12** defenestrate; **13** excommunicate; PHRASES: **3, 3** rub out; **3, 3, 2** get rid of; **4, 3** blot out, boot out, cast out, edit out, kick out, pack off, take out; **4-6** blue-pencil; **4, 7** send packing; **4, 9** make redundant *UK*; **5, 3** cross out, drive out *UK*, force out, throw out; **6, 3** strike off, strike out, thrust out; **8, 4** dispense with.

ejection 5 exile; **6** firing; **7** removal, sacking; **8** deletion, eviction, riddance; **9** dismissal, expulsion; **10** banishment, censorship, disbarment, redundancy, suspension; **11** deportation, elimination, eradication, expurgation, extradition; **12** cancellation, expatriation, obliteration; **14** bowdlerization, defenestration; **15** excommunication; PHRASES: **3, 3, 1** the big E; **3, 4** the boot, the push, the sack; **3, 5** the elbow, the shove; **3, 5-2** the heave-ho; **8, 4** ~ seat; **8, 6** marching orders.

ejector 5 taker; **6** cuckoo, ouster; **7** bouncer, evictor; **8** expeller; **9** displacer; **10** substitute, superseder, supplanter; **12** dispossessor.

elaborate 4 rich; **6** detail, expand, ornate, soigné; **7** amplify, baroque, complex, develop, elegant, enlarge, explain; **8** artistic, detailed, finished, involved, polished; **9** embellish, intricate, sumptuous; **10** complicate, convoluted, decorative, ornamented; **11** complicated, extravagant; **12** ostentatious; **13** sophisticated; PHRASES: **2, 2** go on; **2, 4, 6** go into detail; **4, 2** work up; **4-6** well-turned; **4-7** well-groomed; **5, 2** build on; **5, 3** flesh out.

elapse *See* **pass**

elastic 4 cord, give; 5 tonic; 6 bouncy, coiled, expand, extend, flexed, giving, pliant, rubber, spring, sprung, supple; 7 coiling, ductile, flexing, mutable, plastic, pliable, rubbery, springy, stretch, tensile; 8 bouncing, extended, flexible, snapping, stretchy, tensible, variable, yielding; 9 adaptable, resilient; 10 changeable, extensible, rebounding; 11 distensible; PHRASES: 4-6 well-sprung.

elastic (be elastic) 4 flex, give, snap; 6 bounce, expand, extend, recoil, spring; 7 distend, rebound, stretch.

elastic (make elastic) 9 rubberize, vulcanize; 10 elasticate *UK*, elasticize, plasticize.

elasticity 4 flex, give, snap, tone; 5 tonus; 6 bounce, recoil, spring, strain; 7 pliancy, rebound, stretch, tension; 8 snapback, tonicity; 9 ductility, extension; 10 bounciness, distension, plasticity, pliability, resilience, stretching, suppleness; 11 flexibility, rubberiness, springiness; 12 stretchiness; 13 extensibility.

elastic thing 3 gum; 5 Lycra™; 6 baleen, condom, racket, spring; 7 spandex; 8 catapult; 9 slingshot, whalebone; 10 trampoline; 11 springboard; PHRASES: 4, 5 pogo stick; 6, 4 bungee rope, rubber ball, rubber band, tennis ball; 6, 5 diving board; 6, 6 bouncy castle *UK*; 7, 4 elastic band, jumping jack; 7, 6 stretch fabric.

elder *See* **leader**

elect 4 pick; 6 choose, chosen, future, return, select; 8 selected; 9 designate; 10 designated; PHRASES: 3, 3 opt for; 4, 3 vote for; 6, 2 decide on.

elected 5 voted; 6 chosen; 7 adopted, granted; 8 selected; 9 appointed, delegated, deputized, nominated; 10 authorized, designated; 11 accessional; 12 successional; PHRASES: 6, 3 picked out.

election 4 chad, poll, vote; 5 polls; 6 ballot, choice, ticket, voting; 7 polling, primary, returns; 8 hustings, stumping; 9 balloting, selection, unpledged; 11 appointment, designation; PHRASES: 5, 2 write in; 5-2 write-in; 5, 5 swing voter; 5, 6 split ticket; 6, 5 voting booth; 7, 3 polling day; 8, 6 straight ticket; 9, 6 butterfly ballot.

electioneering 10 canvassing; 11 campaigning; 12 doorstepping; PHRASES: 4-8 vote-catching.

elective 4 free; 6 voting; 8 optional; 9 electoral, selective, voluntary; 10 canvassing, volitional; 12 enfranchised; 13 discretionary, noncompulsory.

electorate 5 voter; 6 people, voters; 7 elector; 8 balloter; 9 taxpayers; 10 suffragist; 11 constituent, suffragette; PHRASES: 6, 6 voting public; 10, 5 registered voter.

electric 7 charged; 8 exciting, shocking, stirring; 9 absorbing, emotional, thrilling; 10 electrical, electronic; 11 captivating, stimulating; 12 electrifying, rechargeable; PHRASES: 4-2 plug-in; 5-6 power-driven; 5, 7 mains powered *UK*; 7-8 battery-operated.

electrical circuitry 4 cell, cord, flex, grid, lead, tube; 5 anode, cable, earth, pylon, valve; 6 copper, dynamo, ground, outlet, socket, switch; 7 battery, cathode, circuit, magneto, turbine; 9 capacitor, conductor, electrode, frequency, generator, induction, insulator, lightning, photocell; 10 conduction, resistance, transistor; 11 accumulator, capacitance, distributor, transformer; 12 nonconductor; 13 semiconductor; 14 superconductor; PHRASES: 3, 4 dry cell, wet cell; 4, 4 fuel cell, live wire; 5, 4 power cord, power line, power pack; 5, 5 power plant; 5, 6 power supply; 5, 7 short circuit; 6, 4 vacuum tube; 6, 7 closed circuit; 7-3, 4 cathode-ray tube; 7, 7 storage battery; 8, 3 electric eye, junction box; 8, 4 national grid *UK*; 8, 5 electric motor.

electrical instrument 7 ammeter; 9 voltmeter, wattmeter; 12 electrometer, galvanometer, oscilloscope; 13 potentiometer.

electric chair 3, 4 hot seat.

electrician 6 sparks.

electricity 4 bias, flux, live; 5 earth, juice, phase, power, pulse, shock; 6 charge, energy, ground, static; 7 current, neutral, voltage; 8 blackout, brownout, negative, positive; 9 frequency, induction, potential; 10 conduction, resistance; 11 capacitance, electrolyte, oscillation; 12 conductivity; 13 electrocution; 14 bioelectricity, electrostatics; 15 electrification; PHRASES: 5, 3 power cut, power outage; 6, 7 direct current.

electric light 4 bulb, dims, lamp; 6 beacon, pharos, sconce, winker; 8 headlamp, lamppost; 9 headlight, indicator *UK*, lightship, limelight, sidelight, spotlight, taillight; 10 Anglepoise™, floodlight, footlights, lighthouse, streetlamp; **11** searchlight, streetlight; PHRASES: **3, 4** fog lamp, sun lamp; **3, 5** fog light; **4, 5** neon light, rear light, stop light, wall light; **4-8** lamp-standard; **5, 3** green man *UK*; **5, 4** table lamp; **5, 5** brake light, klieg light, strip light; **5, 6** fairy lights *UK*; **6, 4** sodium lamp, sunray lamp; **6, 8** strobe lighting *UK*; **7, 4** ceiling rose *UK*; **7, 5** halogen light, parking light; **7, 6** Belisha beacon *UK*; **7, 7** traffic signals.

electric unit 1 A, C, F, V, W; **3** amp, ohm; **4** volt, watt; **5** farad; **6** ampere; **7** coulomb.

electrochemistry 2 pH; **4** cell; **5** anode; **7** battery, cathode, rusting; **11** electrolyte; **12** electrolysis, polarization; **14** electroplating; PHRASES: **3, 4** dry cell, wet cell; **4, 4** fuel cell, NIFE cell.

electrode 3 rod; **5** anode, probe; **7** cathode; **9** conductor.

electromagnetic radiation 3 UVA, UVB; **4** wave; **5** light, radar, radio; **6** photon; **8** infrared, spectrum; **9** radiation; **10** microwaves, television; **11** ultraviolet; PHRASES: **1-4** X-rays; **5, 4** gamma rays; **5, 5** radio waves; **7, 8** visible spectrum.

electronic 1 e; **6** online; **8** computer, cordless, electric, negative, onscreen, positive; **9** automated, automatic; **11** synthesized; **12** computerized; PHRASES: **2, 6** in series; **2, 8** in parallel; **4-4** high-tech; **5-5** solid-state.

electronics 2 TV; **3** ATM, fax; **5** modem, radio; **6** optics; **9** computing, microchip, telegraph, telephone; **10** automation, television; **12** microcircuit; **14** microprocessor; **15** computerization; PHRASES: **4, 10** data processing, word processing.

electron tube 2 TV; **3** CRT, VDU *UK*; **10** television.

elegance 4 chic, ease, flow; **5** class, grace, style, taste; **6** beauty, finish, polish, purity, rhythm; **7** aptness, balance, clarity, culture, decency, decorum, dignity, euphony, fluency, harmony, quality, suavity; **8** Atticism, civility, courtesy, delicacy, elegancy, felicity, flourish, fluidity, grandeur, neatness, ornament, symmetry, urbanity; **9** gentility, plainness, propriety, restraint, smartness, suaveness; **10** classicism, modishness, politeness, proportion, refinement, seemliness, simplicity; **11** distinction; **12** gracefulness, tastefulness; **14** sophistication; PHRASES: **3, 5** mot juste; **4, 7** good manners; **4, 8** good breeding; **5, 5** light touch; **6, 5** florid style; **8, 6** gracious living.

elegant 3 apt; **4** chic, easy, fine, good, neat, pure; **5** Attic, clear, fluid, lucid, plain, round, smart, suave; **6** classy, cogent, fluent, polite, simple, smooth, soigné; **7** classic, correct, courtly, fitting, gracile, natural, refined, stately, stylish; **8** artistic, Augustan, balanced, delicate, eloquent, finished, flawless, graceful, majestic, polished, readable, rhythmic, tasteful, tripping; **9** beautiful, classical, dignified, elaborate, exquisite, idiomatic, manicured, sensitive, unlabored; **10** artificial, Ciceronian, cultivated, euphonious, expressive, felicitous, harmonious, ornamented, restrained; **11** distinctive, mellifluous, symmetrical; **12** proportional; **13** distinguished, perspicacious, sophisticated; PHRASES: **4-6** well-turned; **4-7** well-dressed, well-groomed; **4-8** well-designed; **6, 3** neatly put; **6, 7** neatly wrought.

element 4 hint, part; **5** cause; **6** amount, factor; **7** feature, habitat, portion, section; **8** division, quantity; **9** component; **10** ingredient; **11** environment.

elemental 5 auric, basic, ceric, inert, iodic, osmic; **6** aurous, bromic, cerous, cupric, ferric, iodous, iridic, native, niobic, osmous, rhodic, uranic; **7** arsenic, bromous, chloric, chromic, cuprous, ferrous, fluoric, iridous, niobous, osmious, plumbic, primary, rhodous, scandic, selenic, silicic, stannic, thallic, titanic, uranous, vanadic; **8** argentic, arsenous, carbonic, chlorous, chromous, cobaltic, columbic, germanic, manganic, mercuric, metallic, molybdic, nickelic, platinic, plumbous *UK*, selenous, stannous, sulfuric, tantalic, telluric, thallous, titanous, tungstic, vanadous; **9** aluminous, antimonic, argentous, arsenious, bismuthic, cobaltous, essential, germanous, graphitic, manganous, mercurous, metalloid, molybdous, nickelous, platinous, selenious, sulfurous, tantalous, tellurous, tungstous; **10** antimonous, bismuthous, oxygenated, oxygenized, phosphoric, primordial, uncombined; **11** atmospheric, chlorinated, fluoridated, fluorinated, fundamental, hydrogenous, molybdenous, nitrogenous, phosphorous, rudimentary, transuranic; **14** meteorological.

elementary particle 2 xi; **3** eta, phi,

psi; **4** beta, kaon, muon, pion; **5** alpha, boson, gluon, meson, omega, quark, sigma, tauon; **6** baryon, hadron, lambda, lepton, photon, proton; **7** fermion, hyperon, neutron, nucleon, tachyon; **8** deuteron, electron, graviton, neutrino, positron; **9** antiquark, neutretto; **10** antiproton; **11** antineutron; **12** antielectron; PHRASES: **1, 5** K meson; **2, 5** pi meson.

elevate 4 lift; **5** exalt, hoist, raise; **6** uplift; **7** advance, further, improve, promote, upraise; PHRASES: **4, 2** lift up, move up.

elevation 6 height; **8** altitude; **9** promotion.

elevator 4 lift *UK*; **5** leven, yeast; **6** helium, raiser, spring; **8** conveyor, hydrogen; **9** escalator, funicular, lightener; **10** trampoline; **11** springboard; **12** fermentation; PHRASES: **3, 3** hot air, ski tow; **3, 4** ski lift; **4, 6** dumb waiter; **5, 4** chair lift; **7, 5** raising agent.

eleven 2 xi; **4** side, team.

Elia 4 Lamb *UK*.

elicit 4 draw; **5** cause, educe, evoke, glean; **6** induce, obtain, prompt; **7** extract, procure, produce, provoke; **8** occasion; PHRASES: **4, 2** call up; **4, 3** draw out, worm out; **5, 3** bring out; **5, 5** bring forth; **6, 2** summon up.

eligible 3 fit; **6** single; **8** entitled, suitable; **9** available, qualified, unmarried; **10** unattached; **11** appropriate.

eliminate 4 kill, pass; **5** expel, purge, waste; **6** cancel, delete, reject, remove; **7** abolish, destroy, dismiss, exclude, excrete, urinate; **8** defecate, dispense, jettison; **9** disregard, eradicate, expurgate, liquidate; **10** annihilate, obliterate; **11** exterminate; PHRASES: **2, 4, 4** do away with; **3, 3, 2** get rid of; **4, 3** wipe out; **5, 3** throw out.

elite 1 U; **3** SAS, top; **4** best, pick, plum; **5** cream, elect, prime, prize; **6** choice, chosen, flower, gentry, select; **7** Brahman, leading; **8** nobility; **9** exclusive, selective; **10** aristocrat; **11** aristocracy; PHRASES: **3, 3** jet set; **3, 6** the saints, top people; **3-6** top-drawer; **4, 2, 3, 5** pick of the bunch, salt of the earth; **4, 5** haut monde; **5, 2, 2, 5** crème de la crème; **5, 2, 3, 4** cream of the crop; **5, 5** upper class, upper crust; **5, 6** corps d'élite, crack troops; **6, 3** chosen few, select few; **6, 4** Valley Girl; **6, 6** chosen people, Sloane Ranger *UK*; **7, 6** Special Forces.

elixir 5 tonic; **6** potion; **8** medicine, solution, tincture; **11** preparation, restorative; PHRASES: **4-3** cure-all; **5, 3** snake oil.

elk 5 moose.

Ellice Islands 6 Tuvalu.

elongated 6 oblong; **8** extended; **9** prolonged; **10** elliptical, lengthened, protracted; PHRASES: **5-3** drawn-out; **9, 3** stretched out.

elope *See* **run away**

eloquence 7 fluency; **10** articulacy, expression; **14** articulateness, expressiveness, persuasiveness.

eloquent 6 fluent, moving; **8** powerful, stirring; **9** bombastic; **10** articulate, expressive, persuasive, rhetorical; **11** declamatory; **12** magniloquent; **13** grandiloquent; PHRASES: **4-6** well-spoken; **6-7** silver-tongued, smooth-talking.

else 3 new; **4** more; **5** other; **7** besides; **9** different, otherwise; **11** differently; **12** experimental; PHRASES: **2, 4** as well; **2, 8** in addition.

elucidate *See* **explain**

elude 4 flee, foil, hide, miss; **5** avoid, dodge, evade, stump; **6** baffle, escape, puzzle, thwart; **8** confound; PHRASES: **3, 3** lie low; **3, 3, 2** get rid of; **3, 4** get away; **4, 11** stay underground; **5, 3** shake off.

em 3 mut; **6** mutton.

emaciated 4 bony, lean, thin; **5** drawn, frail, gaunt; **6** peaked, skinny, wasted; **7** haggard, pinched, scraggy, scrawny, starved, tabetic, wizened; **8** anorexic, marasmic, shrunken, skeletal, starving, underfed, withered; **9** shriveled, tabescent; **10** cadaverous, wraithlike; **12** malnourished; PHRASES: **4, 2, 1, 4** thin as a lath; **4, 2, 1, 6** worn to a shadow; **4-3-5** skin-and-bones; **6-4** corpse-like, hollow-eyed, sunken-eyed; **6-7** hollow-cheeked; **7, 4** wasting away.

emaciation 5 tabes; **7** atrophy, frailty, wasting; **8** anorexia, boniness, leanness, marasmus, thinness; **9** gauntness; **10** skinniness, starvation; **12** malnutrition; PHRASES: **8, 7** anorexia nervosa.

emanate 4 come, emit, stem; **6** derive, spring; **7** radiate; **9** originate; PHRASES: **4, 3** give off, give out, send out.

emancipate *See* **liberate**

emancipation *See* **liberation**

emasculate *See* **weaken**

embargo 3 ban, bar; 4 shun; 6 impede, refuse; 7 boycott; 8 stoppage; 11 restriction.

embellish 5 adorn; 6 overdo; 7 enhance; 8 beautify, decorate, ornament; 9 elaborate, embroider; 10 aggrandize, exaggerate.

embellished 6 gilded; 7 glossed; 9 varnished; PHRASES: 7-2 dressed-up, touched-up. *See also* **embellish**

embellishment 9 adornment; 10 decoration, embroidery; 11 elaboration, enhancement, enlargement; 12 exaggeration; 13 ornamentation; 14 aggrandizement.

emblem *See* **symbol**

embodiment 6 symbol; 7 epitome, example; 10 expression; 11 incarnation; 12 quintessence; 14 representation; 15 personification.

embody 5 build; 7 compose, embrace, express, include, subsume; 8 comprise; 9 encompass, epitomize, exemplify, incarnate, personify, represent, structure, symbolize; 10 constitute; 11 incorporate; PHRASES: 4, 2 make up; 5, 3 stand for.

emboss *See* **stamp**

embrace 3 hug; 4 hold; 5 adopt, clasp; 6 accept, clinch, cuddle, embody, enfold; 7 contain, include, involve, squeeze, subsume, welcome; 8 comprise; 9 encompass; 10 assimilate; 11 incorporate; 12 encirclement; PHRASES: 4, 2 take on, take up.

embroider 3 sew; 4 trim; 6 stitch; 8 decorate; 9 elaborate, embellish, overstate; 10 exaggerate; PHRASES: 5-6 cross-stitch.

embryo 4 germ, seed; 6 kernel; 8 rudiment; 9 beginning.

embryonic 3 new, raw; 4 baby; 5 early, fetal *UK*, fresh, young; 6 infant; 7 budding, dawning, nascent, newborn; 8 emergent, germinal, inchoate; 9 unfledged; PHRASES: 2, 3, 3 in the bud.

emend *See* **alter**

Emerald Isle 7 Ireland.

emerge 3 jut; 4 dawn, show; 5 arise, begin, erupt, issue, occur, sally; 6 appear, arrive, effuse, egress, escape, spring, sprout; 7 debouch, develop, emanate, project, surface; 8 protrude; 9 germinate, originate, transpire; 11 materialize; PHRASES: 2, 4 be born; 4, 2 crop up, turn up; 4, 2, 2 come to be; 4, 2, 5 come to light; 4, 3 come out, leak out; 4, 4, 4 come into view; 4, 4, 5 come into being, come into sight; 5, 3 break out, burst out; 5, 5 break cover, break forth, burst forth, issue forth, sally forth; 6, 2 spring up.

emigrate 4 trek; 5 leave, 6 defect, deport, export, moving, travel; 7 dismiss, migrate; 8 evacuate, relocate; 10 expatriate, outmigrate; PHRASES: 4, 4 move away.

emigration 4 trek; 5 exile; 6 exodus, export, flight, moving, travel.

eminence *See* **distinction**

eminent 3 VIP; 6 famous; 7 exalted, primary, salient; 8 esteemed, glorious, renowned; 9 important, prominent, reputable; 10 celebrated, impressive; 11 distinctive, outstanding; 13 distinguished; PHRASES: 4-5 well-known.

eminently 4 very; 6 highly; 7 proudly; 8 signally; 9 extremely; 11 exceedingly, importantly, prominently; 12 impressively; 13 distinctively, exceptionally; PHRASES: 2, 4, 6 to one's credit.

emissary *See* **representative**

emission 7 fallout, release; 9 discharge, emanation, radiation, secretion; 10 absorption, emissivity, production; 13 radioactivity; PHRASES: 1-3, 8 X-ray spectrum; 4, 8 band spectrum, line spectrum; 7, 8 optical spectrum.

emit 4 fume, reek, send; 5 issue; 7 emanate, produce, radiate, release, secrete; 9 discharge; PHRASES: 4, 3 give off, give out.

emmet 3 ant.

emollient 4 balm; 5 salve; 6 lotion; 7 calming; 8 ointment, soothing; 9 calmative, placatory; 10 palliative; 11 moisturizer.

emolument *See* **payment**

emotion 3 ire, joy; 4 fire, hate, heat, love, mood, pang, zeal; 5 anger, ardor, mania, verve; 6 fervor; 7 ecstasy, feeling, passion, rapture; 8 attitude; 9 obsession, sentiment, vehemence; 10 excitement; PHRASES: 5, 2, 4 state of mind.

emotionalism 6 bathos; 9 nostalgia; 11 emotiveness, mawkishness, romanticism; 14 sentimentality.

emotive 6 moving; 8 poignant, touching; 9 affecting, emotional, heartfelt, sensitive; 11 impassioned; 12 overwhelming; 13 controversial.

empathize 4 pity; 10 sympathize, understand; 11 commiserate; PHRASES: 4, 3 feel for; 5, 3 bleed for; 6, 2 relate to; 6, 3 grieve for; 8, 4 identify with.

empathy *See* **understanding**

emperor *See* **ruler**

emphasis 3 vim; **4** bite, dash, fire, glow, tome, zest; **5** ardor, drive, force, gusto, oomph, power, punch, verve, vigor; **6** accent, acuity, energy, fervor, spirit, stress, warmth, weight; **7** feeling, italics, panache, passion, urgency; **8** asperity, boldness, keenness, priority, strength, vitality, vivacity; **9** intensity, iteration, poignancy, vehemence; **10** insistence, prominence; **11** reiteration, underlining; **12** accentuation, forcefulness; PHRASES: **6, 8** strong language.

emphasize 4 dash, glow, plug, roar, urge; **5** shout; **6** accent, bellow, insist, repeat, stress; **7** enhance, feature, thunder; **9** highlight, italicize, reiterate, spotlight, underline; **10** accentuate, underscore; PHRASES: **3, 2** rub in; **4, 2, 7** pull no punches; **4, 9, 2** call attention to; **5, 2** dwell on; **5, 3** point out; **5, 4** drive home, press home; **6, 4** hammer home; **7, 2** impress on.

emphatic 4 bold, firm, keen, sure, warm; **5** brisk, clear, fiery, meaty, peppy, pithy, sharp, vivid, zingy; **6** accusé, ardent, cogent, lively, marked, punchy, strong, urgent; **7** certain, cutting, dashing, earnest, fervent, glaring, glowing, graphic, mordant, obvious, piquant, pointed, ringing, zestful; **8** absolute, definite, dogmatic, eloquent, forceful, incisive, inspired, poignant, positive, powerful, spirited, stressed, vehement, vigorous; **9** energetic, insistent, trenchant, vivacious; **10** compelling, convincing, passionate, pronounced, resounding, underlined; **11** accentuated, affirmative, categorical, exaggerated, highlighted, impassioned, underscored, unequivocal; PHRASES: **2, 7** in italics; **8, 6** strongly worded.

empire *See* **territory**

employ 3 pay, use; **4** hire, post, work; **5** spend; **6** devote, engage, enlist, enroll, occupy, retain; **7** recruit, utilize; **8** exercise; **9** conscript; **10** commission, engagement, occupation; PHRASES: **3, 2, 3** put to use; **4, 2** take on; **4, 3, 2** make use of.

employed 4 busy, paid; **5** hired; **6** active; **7** engaged, working; **8** laboring; **9** mercenary; PHRASES: **2, 4** on duty.

employee 4 hand, help, scab; **5** staff; **6** worker; **7** servant; **9** operative, underling; **11** breadwinner; PHRASES: **5, 4** hired hand.

employer 4 boss, firm, user; **5** owner; **6** outfit; **7** company, manager; **8** business, director, overseer; **9** executive; **10** proprietor, supervisor; **12** organization; **13** establishment.

employment 3 job, pay, use; **4** hire, post, work; **5** berth, place, trade; **6** billet, employ, office; **7** service, station; **8** position; **10** engagement, livelihood, occupation, profession.

emporium 4 mall; **5** store; **6** arcade, bazaar, market; PHRASES: **6, 5** corner store, retail store; **7, 4** trading post; **7, 6** covered market, trading center; **8, 4** Aladdin's cave, shopping mall; **8, 6** shopping center; **10, 5** department store.

empower 3 arm; **4** vest; **5** allow, elect, endow, grant, rouse; **6** anoint, charge, enable, invest, permit, select; **7** animate, appoint, approve, charter, inspire, license; **8** accredit, coronate, delegate, deputize, embolden, energize, legalize, sanction; **9** authorize, electrify; **10** consecrate, strengthen; **12** legitimatize; PHRASES: **4, 2** plug in, turn on; **6, 2** switch on.

empress *See* **ruler**

emptiness 3 gap; **4** hole, husk, void; **5** blank, break, limbo, space; **6** lacuna, vacuum; **7** nothing, vacancy, vacuity; **8** bareness, futility, interval, voidness; **10** barrenness, desolation, hollowness; **11** aimlessness, nothingness; **12** intermission; **13** pointlessness, worthlessness; **15** meaninglessness, purposelessness; PHRASES: **5, 5** blank paper, blank slate, clean slate; **6, 4** tabula rasa.

empty (leave empty) 6 desert, vacate; **7** abandon, forsake; **8** evacuate; **10** depopulate.

empurple 6 bruise.

emulate 3 ape; **4** copy; **5** match, mimic, rival; **6** follow; **7** imitate; PHRASES: **5, 7, 2** model oneself on; **6, 3, 4** follow the herd; **6, 4** follow suit; **6, 4, 5** follow like sheep.

emulsion 3 mix; **5** blend, cream, paint; **7** colloid, gelatin, mixture; **9** collodion; **10** suspension; **11** combination.

enable 3 aid; **4** fund, plan; **5** allow, equip, float, staff; **6** assist, permit, supply; **7** empower, finance, furnish, prepare, sponsor, support; **8** contrive; **9** authorize, subsidize; **10** facilitate.

enact 4 pass, play; **6** decree, ratify; **7** endorse, perform, portray; **8** sanction; **9** represent; PHRASES: **3, 3** act out.

enamel 4 coat; **5** cover, glaze, paint; **6** veneer; **7** coating, lacquer, varnish.

enamored 3 mad; **4** fond; **6** crazed, doting, hooked, insane, loving; **7** amorous, charmed, devoted, fervent, gallant, smitten; **8** besotted, enslaved, ensnared, lovelorn, lovesick; **9** attracted, bewitched, enchanted, entranced, rapturous; **10** captivated, fascinated, infatuated; **11** languishing; **12** heartsmitten; PHRASES: **2, 4** in love; **3, 2** mad on; **4, 2** keen on *UK*, sold on; **5, 4** taken with.

encampment *See* **camp**

encase *See* **cover**

enceinte 8 pregnant.

enchant 5 charm; **6** allure, enamor; **7** attract, beguile, bewitch, delight; **8** enthrall, entrance; **9** captivate, enrapture, fascinate, hypnotize, mesmerize.

enchantment 5 charm, magic; **6** allure; **9** hypnotism; **10** attraction; **11** fascination.

encircle 4 ring; **5** flank, skirt; **6** circle, enfold, girdle; **7** embrace, enclose, envelop; **8** surround; **9** encompass; **12** circumscribe; PHRASES: **3, 2** hem in.

enclave 4 area; **5** class, group; **6** clique, region; **7** commune, reserve; **9** community, territory; **11** reservation.

enclose 3 add, pen; **4** bury, cage, coop, fold, jail, rail, ring, shut, wall; **5** close, fence, hedge; **6** append, attach, circle, corral, enfold, entomb, immure, insert, intern, kennel; **7** confine, impound, include; **8** cloister, encircle, imprison, surround; **9** encompass; **11** incarcerate; PHRASES: **3, 2** hem in, pen up; **4, 2** bang up, keep in, lock up, shut in, shut up, wall in; **4, 3** seal off; **4, 4** send down *UK*; **5, 2** close in, fence in; **6, 3** cordon off.

enclosed 3 enc; **6** indoor; **7** bounded; **8** monastic; **10** cloistered, conventual, intramural; **14** claustrophobic; PHRASES: **4-2** pent-up; **5-2** built-in; **6-2** hemmed-in, walled-in.

enclosure 3 can, pen, zoo; **4** cage, cell, coop, dike, fold, jail, moat, mole, nick, pale, park, quad, tomb, trap, wall, yard; **5** arena, clink, close *UK*, ditch, fence, field, fosse, grave, hedge, hutch, patio, pound; **6** cooler, corral, ghetto, harbor, insert, kennel, marina, paling, pigpen, pigsty *UK*, prison, trench; **7** barrier, borstal *UK*, confine, convent, dungeon, enclave, paddock, railing, reserve, slammer; **8** cloister, compound, hedgerow, palisade, precinct, stockade; **9** courtyard, monastery, oubliette, roadblock, sanctuary, sepulcher; **10** balustrade, quadrangle; **11** reformatory, reservation; PHRASES: **2-2** ha-ha; **3-2-3** culde-sac; **3, 3, 5** the big house; **4, 3** dead end; **5, 5** blind alley.

encompass *See* **include**

encore *See* **repeat**

encounter 4 face, meet; **7** contest, meeting; **8** argument, confront, skirmish; **10** engagement; **12** happenstance; **13** confrontation; PHRASES: **3, 4** run into; **4, 4** bump into, come upon; **4, 6** come across; **6, 7** chance meeting; **7, 4** contend with, grapple with.

encourage 3 aid; **4** help, lift, spur, urge; **5** boost, cheer, favor; **6** assist, assure, exhort, foster, incite, praise, prompt; **7** hearten, inspire, nurture, support; **8** embolden, inspirit, motivate, reassure; PHRASES: **3, 2** egg on; **4, 2** buoy up.

encouragement 3 aid; **4** help; **5** boost; **6** backup, praise; **7** backing, empathy, nurture, support; **9** animation, assurance; **10** assistance, incitement; **11** exhortation, inspiration; PHRASES: **5, 7** moral support; **7, 2** bucking up.

encouraging 7 hopeful; **8** positive. *See also* **encourage**

encumber 6 burden, hamper, hinder, impede; PHRASES: **3, 2, 3, 3** get in the way.

encumbrance 6 burden; **8** handicap, nuisance; **9** hindrance; **10** impediment.

end 3 aim, cap, tip, top; **4** back, base, coda, doom, edge, goal, halt, ruin, side, stop, stub, tail; **5** close, crown, death, finis, gable, limit, point; **6** border, bottom, climax, demise, design, finale, finish, object, reason, result, upshot; **7** decline, destroy, outcome, product, purpose, remnant; **8** boundary, complete, conclude, downfall, finalize, leftover, terminal, terminus; **9** culminate, extremity, intention, objective, remainder, tailpiece, terminate; **10** completion, conclusion, consummate, expiration *UK*, extinction; **11** consequence, culmination, dissolution, termination; **12** annihilation; PHRASES: **3, 1, 4, 2** put a stop to; **4, 2** wind up, wrap up; **4, 4** last gasp, last stop, wind down; **5, 3** leave off, round off; **6, 3** finish off.

endanger 4 loom, risk; 5 stake; 6 expose, gamble, hazard, menace; 7 imperil, venture; 8 threaten; 10 compromise, jeopardize.

endangered 4 rare; 6 scarce; 10 vulnerable; PHRASES: 2, 1, 3 in a jam; 2, 1, 4 in a bind; 2, 1, 5, 6 in a tight corner; 2, 3, 3 on the run; 2, 3, 3, 4 in the hot seat; 2, 3, 4 in the soup; 2, 3, 5 on the rocks; 2, 3, 5, 3 in the lion's den; 2, 3, 6, 4 on the razor's edge; 2, 4 at risk; 2, 4, 3 on thin ice; 2, 5 in peril; 2, 5, 3 on death row; 2, 6 in danger; 2, 8 in jeopardy; 5, 3 dying out; 5, 4 under fire; 5, 5 under siege. *See also* **endanger**

endear 7 commend; 9 insinuate, recommend; 10 ingratiate; PHRASES: 4, 9 make appealing.

endearment (term of endearment) 3 luv, pet; 4 baby, dear, doll, duck, lamb, love; 5 angel, chick, deary, lovey *UK*, petal; 6 cherub, poppet *UK*; 7 darling, sweetie; 8 flattery, lambkins, precious; 10 compliment, sweetheart; 11 chickabiddy *UK*; 12 blandishment; PHRASES: 5, 4 sweet talk; 5, 7 sweet nothing.

endeavor 3 bid, try; 5 foray; 6 effort, strive; 7 attempt, venture; 8 exertion; 10 enterprise; 11 undertaking; PHRASES: 2, 4, 6 do your utmost.

endemic *See* **widespread**

ending 2 PS *UK*; 3 end; 4 coda, last; 5 envoy, final; 6 climax, finale, finish, suffix, windup; 7 capping, closing; 8 appendix, crowning, epilogue, terminal, ultimate; 9 finishing; 10 completion, concluding, conclusion, conclusive, denouement, postscript; 11 culmination, termination; 12 consummation; PHRASES: 4, 3 last act; 4, 4 last word; 4, 5 last laugh; 4, 6 back matter; 5, 2, 3, 4 sting in the tail; 5, 4 punch line; 5, 7 final curtain; 7, 4 parting shot; 8, 4 Parthian shot.

endless 7 eternal, nonstop; 8 constant, infinite, unbroken, unending; 9 boundless, ceaseless, continual, limitless, perpetual, unceasing; 10 continuous, persistent; 11 everlasting; 12 interminable; 13 uninterrupted; PHRASES: 5-6 never-ending.

endorse 4 back; 5 favor; 6 ratify; 7 approve, support; 8 advocate, sanction; 9 recommend; 11 countersign; PHRASES: 9, 2 subscribe to.

endurance 4 grit, guts *UK*; 6 fixity; 7 stamina; 8 strength, survival, tenacity; 9 constancy, fortitude, stability, tolerance; 10 durability, permanence, perpetuity, resolution; 11 persistence; 12 perseverance; PHRASES: 7, 5 staying power.

endure 4 bear, hold, last, live, stay, wear; 5 brave, stand; 6 remain, suffer; 7 persist, prevail, stomach, survive, sustain, undergo; 8 tolerate; 9 persevere, withstand; 10 experience; PHRASES: 2, 2 go on; 2, 7 go through; 3, 2, 4 put up with; 3, 2, 7 see it through; 5, 2, 3 stick it out.

enduring 6 stable; 7 durable, eternal, lasting; 9 permanent, resilient; 10 persistent; 11 everlasting; 12 imperishable; 14 indestructible; PHRASES: 4-4 long-term.

enemy 3 foe; 5 rival; 7 nemesis; 8 opponent; 9 adversary, aggressor; 10 antagonist, competitor, opposition.

energetic 4 live; 5 brisk, peppy, zingy; 6 active, bouncy, driven, lively, motive, moving, punchy, robust; 7 arduous, dynamic, kinetic; 8 animated, bouncing, spirited, vigorous; 9 sprightly, vivacious; 12 enthusiastic; PHRASES: 4, 2, 5 full of beans; 7, 2 powered up.

energy 1 E; 2 go; 3 jet, pep, vim; 4 élan, head, heat, life, push, work, zest; 5 ardor, cause, drive, force, moxie, oomph, power, verve, vigor; 6 charge, fervor, frenzy, spirit, spring, thrust; 7 abandon, impetus; 8 ambition, buoyancy, dynamism, momentum, strength, vitality, vivacity; 9 animation, eagerness, perkiness, potential, vehemence; 10 enthusiasm, horsepower, initiative, liveliness; 11 electricity; 12 vigorousness; 13 vivaciousness; PHRASES: 3-2-3-2 get-up-and-go; 4, 7 high spirits, warm feeling.

enfold 3 hug; 4 wrap; 5 clasp; 6 enwrap, swathe; 7 embrace, enclose, entwine, envelop; 8 surround.

enforce 5 apply; 6 coerce, compel, impose, oblige; 7 require; 9 implement; PHRASES: 4, 10 make compulsory; 5, 3 carry out; 6, 2 insist on.

engage 4 hold, join, keep; 5 charm, fight; 6 absorb, battle, employ, occupy; 7 appoint, attract, connect, involve; 9 interlock; PHRASES: 3, 4, 5 fit into place; 4, 2 slot in, take on.

engaged 4 busy; 6 booked; 8 plighted, promised, reserved; 9 affianced, betrothed; 11 unavailable; PHRASES: 2, 3 in use; 4, 2 tied up; **6, 3** spoken for. *See also* **engage**

engagement 3 gig, job, rep, run; **4** date, post, tour; **5** clash, fight, stand, tryst, visit; **6** action, battle; **7** booking, meeting; **8** conflict, position, skirmish; **9** betrothal, encounter; **10** commitment, employment, rendezvous; **11** appointment, arrangement, assignation; PHRASES: **3-5, 5** one-night stand.

engaging *See* **attractive**

engender 5 beget, cause, spawn; **6** create; **7** produce; **8** generate; **9** propagate, stimulate; PHRASES: **4, 5, 2** give birth to; **5, 5** bring about.

engine 5 motor; **6** donkey; **7** machine; **9** generator, mechanism; PHRASES: **6, 6** Wankel ~; **8, 6** Stirling ~.

engine (engine part) 1 p; **3** cam, cog; **4** pump, seal, sump *UK*, tank; **5** crank, lever, light, shaft, valve; **6** dynamo, gasket, piston; **7** gearbox, gearing, turbine; **8** camshaft, cogwheel, cylinder, manifold, radiator; **10** crankshaft; **11** distributor; PHRASES: **3, 3** oil pan; **5, 4** spark plug.

engineer 2 CE, RE *UK*; **3** dig, lay, map; **4** haul, plan, plot; **5** blast, build, cause, drill, erect, hoist; **6** design, dredge, sapper, survey, tunnel, wangle; **7** concoct; **8** contrive, designer, excavate, surveyor; **9** architect, construct; **10** contractor, technician; **11** orchestrate; PHRASES: **3, 2** fix up; **5, 5** bring about.

engineering 3 CAD, CAE.

England 6 Albion; **7** Blighty; PHRASES: **4, 4** John Bull.

English flute 8 recorder.

English horn 3, 7 cor anglais.

engrave 3 cut; **4** bite, etch; **5** carve, chase, grave, print, score; **6** emboss, incise, scrape; **7** impress, scratch; **8** aquatint, inscribe.

engraving 5 block, image, plate, print; **6** design; **7** carving, chasing, etching, linocut, picture, woodcut; **8** aquatint; **9** mezzotint; **10** cerography, lithograph, typography, xylography; **11** copperplate, inscription, lignography, zincography; **12** chalcography, glyptography, reproduction.

engulf 5 swamp, whelm; **7** consume, immerse, swallow; **8** submerge, surround; **9** overwhelm.

enhance 5 exalt, raise; **8** heighten; **9** embellish.

enigma 5 poser; **6** puzzle, riddle; **7** dilemma, mystery, paradox, problem, stumper; **8** question; **9** conundrum; **11** brainteaser; PHRASES: **4, 7** mind boggler; **6, 7** knotty problem.

enjoin *See* **order**

enjoy 3 dig, eat, own; **4** bask, have, like, love; **5** adore, drink; **6** relish, wallow; **7** possess; **9** celebrate, luxuriate; **10** appreciate, experience, gormandize; PHRASES: **2, 7, 4** be blessed with; **4, 3** have fun; **4, 5** make merry; **4, 8, 2** take pleasure in; **5, 2** revel in; **7, 2** delight in; **7, 4** benefit from; **7, 7** indulge oneself.

enjoyment *See* **pleasure**

enlarge 3 add; **5** bloat, boost, breed, flare, raise, stuff, swell, widen; **6** deepen, dilate, expand, extend, fatten, sprawl, square; **7** amplify, augment, broaden, distend, elevate, enhance, inflate, magnify, prolong, stretch, thicken; **8** disperse, escalate, heighten, increase, lengthen, maximize, multiply; **9** duplicate, intensify; **10** aggrandize; PHRASES: **3, 2** add to; **3, 3** pad out; **4, 2** blow up, fill up, hike up, puff up, pump up; **5, 2** build up, plump up; **5, 3** flesh out; **6, 3** spread out.

enlarged thing 5 bulge, tumor; **6** bubble; **7** balloon; **8** swelling; **9** extension; **11** enlargement.

enlarger 4 pump; **7** dilator, padding; **8** extensor, inflator, stuffing; **9** augmenter.

enlighten 4 tell; **5** edify; **6** inform; **7** clarify, educate, explain; **8** instruct; **10** illustrate.

enlightened 4 wise; **5** aware, clear, lucid; **6** bright; **8** educated, informed, rational, tolerant; **9** brilliant, civilized, clarified; **10** reasonable; **11** illuminated, intelligent; **12** unprejudiced; **13** knowledgeable; PHRASES: **4-6** open-minded.

enlightenment 4 clue; **7** clarity, insight; **9** awareness, education, knowledge; **10** revelation; **11** elucidation, explanation, information, instruction; **12** illumination; **13** clarification, comprehension, understanding; PHRASES: **5-10** broad-mindedness; **7, 4** guiding star.

enlist 4 join, levy; **5** demob, draft; **6** enroll, muster; **7** procure, recruit, solicit; **8** mobilize, register; **9** conscript, volunteer; **10** commission; **11** matriculate; PHRASES: **4, 2**

join up, sign on, sign up.

enliven 4 stir, wake, whet; 5 cheer; 6 arouse, excite, thrill; 7 agitate, animate, disturb, quicken; 8 activate, brighten; 9 galvanize, stimulate, titillate; 10 invigorate; PHRASES: 3, 2 pep up; 4, 2 wake up; 5, 2 cheer up.

enmity 4 hate; 5 clash, spite, venom; 6 hatred, malice, rancor; 7 dislike, vitriol; 8 conflict, friction, loathing; 9 animosity, antipathy, hostility; 10 aggression, antagonism, contention, dissension, opposition, quarreling; 11 bellicosity, inimicality, malevolence; 12 belligerence; 14 unfriendliness; 15 incompatibility; PHRASES: 3, 4 ill will.

ennui *See* **boredom**

enough 5 ample, amply; 6 plenty; 8 abundant, adequate; 9 copiously, endlessly, plentiful, profusely, tolerably; 10 abundantly, acceptably, adequately, sufficient; 11 plenteously, plentifully; 12 interminably, prolifically, sufficiently; 13 inexhaustibly; 14 satisfactorily; PHRASES: 2, 3 ad lib, on tap; 2, 3, 4 on the nose, to the full; 2, 6 on demand; 2, 7 ad libitum.

enough (have enough) 6 afford; PHRASES: 3, 4, 4 eat one's fill; 5, 4, 4 drink one's fill.

enrapture *See* **entrance**

enrich 6 deepen; 7 enhance, improve; 10 supplement.

enroll 4 join; 5 admit, enter; 6 enlist, induct, invest, ordain, settle; 7 baptize, install; 8 christen, initiate, inscribe, register; PHRASES: 3, 4, 4, 4 put your name down; 4, 2 join up, sign on, sign up; 5, 3 enter for.

enrolment 7 baptism; 9 admission, induction; 10 acceptance, enlistment, initiation, membership, ordination; 11 christening, investiture; 12 installation, introduction, registration; 13 matriculation *UK*; PHRASES: 5-7 house-warming.

ensconce 4 hide; 6 screen; 7 conceal; 8 entrench; PHRASES: 4, 4 hide away.

ensemble 3 set; 4 band, suit; 5 group, joint; 6 outfit, troupe; 7 company, costume; 8 assembly; 9 aggregate; 10 collection, collective; 11 combination, cooperative, coordinates; 13 collaborative; PHRASES: 3-3 rig-out *UK*.

enshrine 6 hallow; 7 cherish, protect; 8 preserve, treasure.

ensign 4 flag; 5 badge; 6 banner, colors, emblem; 7 officer, pennant; 8 standard.

ensnare 4 trap; 5 catch; 6 enmesh, entoil, entrap; 7 embroil.

ensue 5 arise; 6 derive, follow, result; 7 proceed, succeed; PHRASES: 6, 2 follow on.

ensure 3 fix; 5 check, prove; 6 affirm, evince, ground, secure, settle, verify; 7 certify, confirm, endorse, promise, warrant; 9 ascertain, determine, establish, guarantee, safeguard; 11 demonstrate; 12 authenticate, substantiate; PHRASES: 3, 4 pin down; 4, 3 find out; 4, 7 make certain.

entangle 4 snag, trap; 5 catch, snare, twist; 6 enmesh, tangle; 10 intertwine; PHRASES: 5, 2 catch up, snarl up.

enter 3 key, log; 4 call, join, note, type; 5 board, input, visit, write; 6 appear, arrive, embark, enlist, enroll, insert, record, submit; 7 compete, contest; 8 register; 9 penetrate; 10 infiltrate; 11 participate; PHRASES: 2, 8 be admitted; 3, 2 get in, key in, pop in; 3, 4 put down; 3, 4, 2 set foot in; 3, 7, 2 let oneself in; 4, 2 call in, come in, come on, hand in, look in, sign in, sign up, walk on; 4, 2, 8 make an entrance; 4, 4 take part; 5, 2 check in, clock in, punch in; 5, 4 write down.

enterprise 2 go; 4 firm, push; 5 drive; 6 scheme; 7 company, program, project, venture; 8 activity, ambition, boldness, business, endeavor; 9 operation; 10 creativity, initiative; 11 corporation, originality, undertaking, willingness; 12 organization; 13 establishment, inventiveness; 15 resourcefulness; PHRASES: 3-2-3-2 get-up-and-go.

enterprising 4 bold, rash; 6 daring; 8 creative, intrepid, original; 9 ambitious, ingenious, inventive; 10 courageous, innovative, managerial, pioneering; 11 adventurous, imaginative, opportunist, progressive, resourceful, speculative, venturesome; 15 entrepreneurial; PHRASES: 2-5 go-ahead.

entertain 3 pun; 4 busk *UK*, feed, jest, joke, josh, quip; 5 amuse, cheer, clown, treat; 6 banter, divert, invite, ponder, regale, tickle; 8 consider, distract, interest; 9 wisecrack; 11 accommodate, contemplate; PHRASES: 4, 3, 4 wine and dine; 4, 7, 2 give thought to; 5, 4 think over; 5, 5 think about.

entertainer 2 DJ, MC; 3 act; 4 foil, host, mime, star; 5 actor, clown, comic, emcee, mimic; **6** artist, busker *UK*, dancer, diseur, rapper, singer, stooge, talent; **7** actress, artiste, compere *UK*, diseuse, goliard, juggler, popstar, reciter; **8** comedian, conjurer, conjuror *UK*, humorist, jongleur, magician, minstrel, musician, stripper; **9** hypnotist, performer, presenter *UK*; **10** comedienne, mindreader, monologist, mountebank, troubadour; **12** escapologist, impersonator, vaudevillian; **13** contortionist, impressionist, ventriloquist *UK*; **15** prestidigitator; PHRASES: **4, 6** drag artist; **5-2, 5** stand-up comic; **6, 3** chorus boy; **6, 4** chorus girl; **6, 6** escape artist, memory artist; **6, 8** street musician; **6, 9** street performer; **7, 6** trapeze artist *UK*, variety artist; **8, 3** straight man; **9, 5** burlesque queen.

entertaining **7** amusing; **8** charming; **9** diverting, enjoyable; **11** pleasurable.

entertainment **3** act, fun; **4** show; **5** farce; **6** acting, comedy, parody, satire, sitcom; **7** cabaret, cartoon, concert, lampoon, takeoff, theater; **9** amusement, burlesque, diversion, enjoyment, slapstick; **10** attraction, caricature, performing, production, recreation; **11** distraction, performance; PHRASES: **4-2** send-up; **4, 3** show biz; **4, 8** show business; **5-2** stand-up; **5, 5** comic strip.

enthusiasm **4** zeal; **5** craze, gusto, hobby, mania; **7** passion; **8** interest; **9** eagerness.

enthusiast *See* **fan**

entice **4** bait, draw, lure, trap; **5** bribe, tempt; **6** cajole, induce, invite, seduce; **7** attract.

enticement **4** bait, lure, trap; **5** bribe, decoy; **7** bribery; **9** incentive; **10** attraction, inducement, temptation; PHRASES: **4-2** come-on; **4, 6** loss leader; **7, 4** greased palm; **7, 5** special offer.

enticing *See* **tempting**

entire **4** full, pure; **5** total, uncut, utter, whole; **6** intact, united; **7** perfect, plenary, quorate *UK*; **8** absolute, adequate, compleat, complete, integral, thorough; **9** undivided, wholesale; **10** consummate, exhaustive, unabridged; **11** unmitigated, unqualified; **12** unexpurgated; **13** comprehensive, unabbreviated; PHRASES: **3-9** all-inclusive.

entirety **3** sum; **5** total, whole; **8** totality.

entitle **3** dub; **4** call, name; **5** allow, label, title; **6** enable, permit; **7** empower, license,

qualify, warrant; **8** sanction; **9** authorize, designate.

entitle (be entitled to) **4** earn; **5** claim; **6** expect; **7** deserve; PHRASES: **2, 6, 2** be worthy of.

entitlement **3** due; **4** duty; **5** claim, power, right, title; **9** privilege; **10** obligation; **11** expectation, prerogative.

entity **5** being, thing; **6** object; **7** article.

entomologist **8** apiarist; **9** beekeeper; **13** lepidopterist; **15** sericulturalist; PHRASES: **3, 6** bug hunter.

entourage **5** staff, train; **9** followers, following; **10** associates.

entrance **4** adit, door, gate, pass; **5** charm, entry, foyer, hatch, inlet, lobby, mouth, porch, rivet, stile; **6** access, portal, ticket; **7** archway, arrival, channel, conduit, delight, doorway, enchant, engross, ingress, opening, orifice, passage, portico, postern; **8** approach, enthrall, entryway, lychgate, tollgate, trapdoor, turnpike; **9** admission, captivate, enrapture, fascinate, mesmerize, spellbind, threshold, turnstile, vestibule; **10** admittance, appearance, propylaeum; **11** penetration; **12** infiltration; PHRASES: **3, 2** way in; **5-7** porte-cochere.

entrant **5** comer, guest; **6** caller, intake, player, runner; **7** arrival, incomer *UK*, settler, visitor; **8** audience, beginner, colonist, newcomer, visitant; **9** applicant, candidate, contender, debutante, immigrant; **10** competitor, contestant; **11** participant; PHRASES: **3, 4** new face.

entreat *See* **plead**

entrée **6** access; **7** starter; **8** entrance; **9** appetizer, induction; **10** admittance; **12** introduction; PHRASES: **4, 7** hors d'oeuvre; **5, 6** first course.

entrench **3** man; **4** root; **5** embed; **6** cement; **7** ingrain; **8** ensconce, garrison; **9** establish; PHRASES: **3, 2** dig in; **3, 3, 4** man the fort, man the guns; **3, 3, 6** man the breach; **3, 3, 8** man the defenses; **4, 1, 5** make a stand; **4, 3, 3** plug the gap, stop the gap; **5, 4** stand firm; **5, 5** stand ready.

entrepreneur **6** trader, worker; **7** manager; **8** director; **9** financier, operative, organizer; **10** impresario; **14** businessperson; PHRASES: **2-6** go-getter; **4-3** whiz-kid.

entresol **9** mezzanine.

entrust **5** trust; **6** assign; **7** commend, deliver; **8** delegate.

entry 2 go; **3** try; **4** item, note; **5** debut, input; **6** effort, entrée, import, minute, record; **7** account, attempt, ingoing; **8** incoming; **9** enrolment *UK*, induction, reception, statement; **10** enlistment, ingression, initiation, submission; **11** application; **12** introduction. *See also* **entrance**

enumerate 4 list, name, tell; **5** count, tally, total; **6** detail, number, reckon; **7** catalog *UK*, compute, itemize, measure, specify; **8** evaluate, quantify; **9** calculate, catalogue *UK*; PHRASES: **5, 3** spell out; **6, 2** reckon up.

enunciate 5 speak, state, utter, voice; **6** detail; **7** express; **9** pronounce; **10** articulate; PHRASES: **3, 7** put forward; **5, 3** spell out.

envelop 4 wrap; **5** cloak, cover; **6** encase, engulf, shroud, swathe; **7** enclose; **8** surround.

envious 5 green; **7** jealous, longing; **8** covetous, desirous, grudging, spiteful; **9** jaundiced, resentful; PHRASES: **5-4** green-eyed.

environment 4 base; **5** abode, earth, haunt, niche, range, scene, world; **6** domain, locale, milieu, nature; **7** element, habitat, hangout, setting, terrain; **8** ambiance *UK*, environs, locality, location, vicinity; **9** bailiwick, ecosystem, situation, territory; **10** atmosphere, background, conditions, upbringing; **12** neighborhood, surroundings; **13** circumstances; PHRASES: **3, 4, 4** own back yard; **4, 6** home ground; **7, 5** natural world; **8, 6** stamping ground.

environmental 5 green, local; **6** around; **10** ecological; **11** ecofriendly, surrounding, territorial; **12** neighborhood; **14** conservational; **15** conservationist, preservationist; PHRASES: **5-8** ozone-friendly.

envisage *See* **imagine**

envoy *See* **representative**

envy 5 covet, crave, greed, spite; **6** desire, grudge, resent; **8** begrudge, jealousy; **10** bitterness, resentment; PHRASES: **4, 3** long for; **4, 5** lust after; **6, 5** hanker after.

enzyme 5 lyase; **6** ligase, lipase, papain, pepsin, rennin; **7** amylase, gastrin, lactase, trypsin, zymogen; **8** diastase, lysozyme, protease; **9** apoenzyme, hydrolase, isomerase, peptidase, substrate; **10** holoenzyme; **11** proteolysis, transferase; **12** endonuclease, transaminase; **13** dehydrogenase; **14** oxidoreductase.

eolian *See* **aeolian**

epic 6 heroic; **7** classic; **8** marathon; **10** impressive; **12** extravaganza; PHRASES: **6, 5** period piece; **7, 5** costume drama *UK*.

epicure 6 foodie; **7** gourmet; **9** epicurean; **10** gastronome; **11** connoisseur; PHRASES: **3, 6** bon vivant.

epicurism 10 gastronomy; **11** gourmandism; **12** epicureanism; **15** connoisseurship.

epidemic 4 rash, wave; **5** craze, spate; **6** plague; **7** endemic, rampant, scourge; **8** increase, outbreak, sweeping; **9** contagion, prevalent; **10** widespread; PHRASES: **4-7** wide-ranging.

epilepsy 7, 8 falling sickness *UK*.

epilogue 4 coda; **6** speech; **9** monologue; **10** conclusion.

episode 4 bout, part; **5** event, scene; **6** affair, attack; **7** chapter, section; **8** incident, outbreak; **9** incidence; **10** occurrence; **11** installment.

epistle *See* **letter**

epitaph *See* **inscription**

epitome 5 model; **7** essence; **10** embodiment; **12** quintessence; **15** personification.

epitomize 4 mean; **5** model; **6** embody, typify; **7** signify; **9** exemplify, personify, represent, symbolize; **12** characterize.

epoch *See* **era**

equable 4 calm; **8** composed; **9** easygoing; **11** unflappable.

equal 3 par; **4** copy, even, fair, just, like, make, mate, meet, oppo, peer, same, tied, twin; **5** alike, drawn, Dutch, flush, level, match, quits; **6** equate, fellow, sister, square; **7** abreast, brother, coequal, compeer, comrade, equable, similar, uniform; **8** balanced, parallel; **9** congruent, equalized, equitable, identical; **10** correspond, equivalent, homologous, tantamount; **11** coextensive, counterpart, equidistant, equilateral, symmetrical; **12** commensurate; **13** correspondent, corresponding, proportionate; PHRASES: **2, 1, 3** on a par; **2, 4, 2** as good as; **2, 5, 7** on level pegging *UK*; **3-2-3** one-to-one; **3, 3, 3, 4** one and the same; **3-3-4** nip-and-tuck; **3, 3, 4** the same; **4-3** love-all; **4, 3, 4** much the same; **4-3-4** half-and-half, neck-and-neck; **4, 4** dead heat; **4-4** ding-dong; **4-5** even-sided; **5-5** fifty-fifty; **6, 7** evenly matched; **8, 6** opposite number.

equal (be equal) 3 tie; **4** draw; **5** equal,

match; **7** balance; **8** parallel; **9** stalemate; **11** equilibrate; PHRASES: **2, 5** go Dutch; **2, 6** go halves; **4, 2, 4** keep up with; **4, 2, 4, 4** keep in step with; **4, 4, 4** keep pace with; **4, 7, 4** keep abreast with; **5, 2, 4** stack up with; **5, 4** agree with, break even; **7, 2, 2** measure up to; **8, 4** coincide with; **10, 2** correspond to.

equality **3** par, tie; **4** draw; **5** deuce, quits; **6** parity; **7** balance, justice, sharing; **8** deadlock, equation, identity, symmetry; **9** democracy, stalemate; **10** coequality; **11** equivalence, parallelism; **12** impartiality; **13** equilibration; **14** correspondence, egalitarianism, equiponderance; PHRASES: **2, 3, 3, 2, 3** an eye for an eye; **4, 4** dead heat, tied game; **4, 5** even break, even money; **5, 6** equal rights, equal status; **5, 7** equal footing, level pegging *UK*; **5, 8** equal standing; **7, 2, 2** nothing in it. *See also* **equal**

equalize **3** fit; **4** even; **5** align, level, match; **6** adjust, equate, offset, smooth, square; **7** balance; **8** readjust; **10** compensate, coordinate, proportion; **11** accommodate, countervail, synchronize; **12** counterpoise; **14** counterbalance; PHRASES: **3, 3** set off; **4, 2** even up, line up; **4, 3** even out; **5, 2** level up, round up; **6, 1, 7** strike a balance; **6, 3** cancel out.

equally **2** so; **5** alike; **7** abreast; **8** likewise; **11** impartially; **12** reciprocally; PHRASES: **2, 1, 3** on a par; **2, 2, 4, 4** on an even keel; **2, 3, 4, 3** in the same way; **2, 3, 4, 5** by the same token; **2, 4, 2** as good as; **3, 3, 4** nip and tuck; **4, 3, 4** neck and neck; **4, 5** pari passu; **4, 6** even Steven; **5-5** fifty-fifty; **7, 4** without bias. *See also* **equal**

equate **4** link; **5** equal, liken; **7** compare, connect; **8** parallel; **9** associate, correlate.

equation **7** balance; **8** equality; **11** calculation, equivalence.

equilibrium **3** tie; **4** draw, stop; **5** deuce, poise; **6** stasis; **7** balance; **8** deadlock, evenness, symmetry; **9** equipoise, stability, stalemate; **10** proportion, standstill, steadiness; **11** homeostasis; **12** counterpoise; PHRASES: **3, 4** the same; **4, 4** even keel; **4, 5** even break, fair shake; **4, 10** hung parliament; **6, 3** status quo; **5, 5** stable state, steady state; **7, 2, 5** balance of power; **7, 2, 6** balance of terror; **7, 5** knotted score.

equine **5** horsy *UK*; **6** horsey; **7** mounted; **10** equestrian.

equip **3** arm, fit, man; **4** crew; **5** dress, endow, stock; **6** outfit, supply; **7** furnish, pre-

pare, provide; PHRASES: **3, 2** set up; **3, 3** fit out, kit out *UK*, rig out.

equipment **3** kit; **4** gear, tack; **5** dress, tools, wares; **6** outfit, tackle; **7** fixture, harness; **8** chattels, fittings *UK*, hardware, property, utensils; **9** apparatus, furniture, trappings; **11** impedimenta, merchandise; **12** accouterment, appointments; **13** paraphernalia.

equitably **6** stably; **7** equably, roundly; **8** squarely, steadily; **9** uniformly; **13** symmetrically; **14** democratically; PHRASES: **4, 7** with justice. *See also* **equally**

equivalence **6** analog, shadow, simile; **7** analogy; **8** analogue, equality, likeness, metaphor, sameness, synonymy; **9** agreement; **10** accordance, congruence, equivalent, reflection, similarity, synonymity, uniformity; **11** concordance, homogeneity, parallelism; **12** equipollence; **13** reciprocation; **14** correspondence, representation, synonymousness; PHRASES: **5, 8** equal exchange.

equivalent **4** like, peer, same, twin; **5** alike, equal; **7** similar, synonym; **8** agreeing, parallel; **9** accordant, analogous, congruent; **10** comparable, concordant, harmonious, reciprocal, reflective, synonymous; **11** counterpart, equipollent, homogeneous; **12** metaphorical; **13** correspondent, corresponding; **15** interchangeable *UK*; PHRASES: **2-4** in-kind; **3-3-3** tit-for-tat; **8, 6** opposite number.

equivocal **5** vague; **6** double, shifty; **7** evasive, oblique, unclear; **8** oracular; **9** ambiguous, confusing; **10** ambivalent, backhanded, homonymous, indefinite, misleading, roundabout; **11** amphibolous; **13** prevaricating; **14** circumlocutory; PHRASES: **3-5** two-edged; **6-7** double-tongued.

equivocalness **3** pun; **6** enigma, oracle, riddle; **7** evasion, parable, quibble, untruth; **8** newspeak, polysemy, wordplay; **9** ambiguity, conundrum, equivoque, quibbling, sophistry; **11** ambivalence, amphibology, contrariety, paronomasia, uncertainty; **12** equivocation, gobbledygook; **13** prevarication; **14** circumlocution; PHRASES: **4, 4, 5** play upon words; **5, 3** white lie; **6, 4** double talk, weasel word; **6, 7** double meaning; **6, 8** double entendre. *See also* **equivocal, equivocation**

equivocate **3** pun; **4** tack, trim; **5** avoid, delay, dodge, evade, fence, fudge, hedge; **6**

swerve, waffle, weasel; **7** deceive, mislead, quibble, shuffle; **8** postpone, sidestep; **9** dissemble, pussyfoot, stonewall, vacillate; **11** prevaricate; **12** shillyshally, tergiversate; **13** procrastinate; PHRASES: **2, 1, 1-4** do a U-turn; **3, 2, 3, 5** sit on the fence; **3, 4, 4** cut both ways, get cold feet; **4, 3** back out; **4, 4, 4** face both ways; **5, 4, 6** shift one's ground; **5, 5** shift gears, skirt round, think again, wheel about; **5, 6, 2, 2** think better of it; **6, 4** double talk; **6, 4, 4** change one's mind, change one's tune.

equivocation 4 whim; **7** caprice, dodging, fencing; **8** reversal, waffling; **9** deviation, obscurity, shuffling; **10** shiftiness, withdrawal; **11** obfuscation, vacillation, versatility; **12** backpedaling, irresolution, pussyfooting; **13** inconsistency, mystification; **14** tergiversation; **15** procrastination; PHRASES: **1-4** U-turn; **4-8** side-stepping; **5-4** about-face, volte-face; **6, 2, 4** change of mind; **6, 8** second thoughts. *See also* **equivocalness**

equivocator 3 rat; **4** jilt, scab; **5** flirt, Janus, Judas, toady; **6** ratter, weasel; **7** quitter, reneger, runaway, seceder, tattler, traitor; **8** apostate, betrayer, blackleg, coquette, defector, deserter, informer, quisling, recanter, recreant, renegade, squealer, telltale, turncoat; **10** backslider, recidivist, tattletale; **11** opportunist, stoolpigeon, weathercock; **12** collaborator; **13** tergiversator; PHRASES: **5, 2, 4** Vicar of Bray; **5, 6** stool pigeon; **5, 9** fifth columnist; **6-6** double-dealer.

ER 4 king (Latin: Edwardus Rex); **5** queen (Latin: Elizabeth Regina); **6** erbium; **7** monarch; **10** hesitation.

era 3 age, eon; **4** aeon *UK*, date, time; **5** epoch, years; **6** period.

eradicate *See* **eliminate**

erase 3 rub; **4** wipe; **5** scrub, steal; **6** cancel, delete, remove; **7** expunge; **9** eliminate; **10** obliterate; PHRASES: **3, 3** rub out; **4, 3** wipe out; **5, 3** cross out; **6, 3** strike out.

eraser 6 rubber *UK*; PHRASES: **10, 5** correction fluid.

erect 5 build, found, raise, rigid, stiff, upend; **6** create; **7** elevate, upright; **8** assemble, straight, vertical; **9** construct, establish; **13** perpendicular; PHRASES: **3, 2** put up, set up.

erection 4 pile; **7** edifice; **8** assembly, building, creation; **9** formation, structure;

12 construction.

Erin 7 Ireland.

Erinyes 6 Furies.

erne 3, 5 sea eagle.

erode 3 rot; **4** fray, skin, wear; **5** erase; **6** attrit; **7** corrode; PHRASES: **3, 4** eat away, eat into; **4, 4** wear away, wear down; **5, 4** grind down.

erotica 4 porn; **8** facetiae; **11** pornography; PHRASES: **4, 5** blue movie.

err 3 sin; **4** boob *UK*, fall, muff, slip; **5** cheat, lapse, stray; **6** bungle, mishit, offend, wander; **7** blunder, distort, stumble; **8** misjudge, misstate, trespass; **9** misbehave; **10** transgress; **11** misconstrue; **12** miscalculate, misinterpret; PHRASES: **2, 5** go wrong; **2, 6** go astray; **4, 2** slip up; **8, 7** disgrace oneself.

errancy 6 heresy; **8** deviancy; **10** heterodoxy, perversion, wrongdoing; **11** unorthodoxy.

errand *See* **task**

errant 5 rowdy; **6** erring, guilty, sinful; **7** deviant, naughty, roaming, wayward; **8** perverse; **9** heretical, perverted, wandering; **10** delinquent, unorthodox; **11** misbehaving.

erratic 6 fitful, uneven; **8** variable; **9** irregular; **10** changeable, unreliable; **12** inconsistent, intermittent; **13** unpredictable; PHRASES: **3, 3, 2** off and on.

erratically 5 oddly; **9** strangely; **13** eccentrically.

erroneous 5 false, loose, wrong; **6** faulty, flawed, untrue; **7** inexact, invalid; **8** mistaken, specious; **9** distorted, incorrect; **10** fallacious, inaccurate.

error 3 bug; **4** boob *UK*, bull, slip, typo; **5** fault, lapse; **6** mishap; **7** blunder, erratum, mistake; **8** misprint, misusage, omission, solecism; **9** oversight; **10** inaccuracy, spoonerism; **11** malapropism; **14** miscalculation; PHRASES: **3-3** boo-boo; **4-2** slip-up. *See also* **grammatical error**

Erse 6 Gaelic.

erudition 7 culture; **8** learning; **9** education, knowledge; **11** learnedness.

erupt 4 vent; **7** explode; PHRASES: **2, 3** go off; **2, 4** go bang; **3, 3, 4** hit the roof; **4, 1, 4** blow a fuse; **4, 2** blow up; **4, 4, 3** blow your top; **5, 2** flare up; **5, 3** break out; **5, 5** burst forth.

erupting 8 bursting, volcanic; 9 explosive, expulsive.

eruption 5 belch, blast, burst; 6 geyser; 7 upsurge; 8 emission, epidemic, fumarole, outbreak, outburst; 9 discharge, explosion.

Erzgebirge 3, 9 Ore Mountains; 6, 4 Krusné Hory.

escape 3 fly; 4 bolt, drip, exit, flee, flit UK, flow, leak, seep, skip, vent; 5 avoid, break, dodge, drain, elope, elude, evade, hooky, issue, spurt, trick; 6 decamp, depart, egress, exodus, flight, relief, vanish; 7 abscond, elusion, evasion, freedom, getaway, leakage, outflow, pastime, release, retreat, seepage, survive, truancy, vamoose; 8 breakout, emission, loophole, reprieve; 9 acquittal, avoidance, departure, disappear, diversion, elopement, jailbreak, vanishing; 10 decampment, withdrawal; 11 deliverance, distraction; 13 disappearance; PHRASES: 2, 1, 4 do a bunk UK; 2, 4 go AWOL; 3, 3 get off, run off; 3, 3, 3 cut and run; 3, 4 get away, get free, run away; 4, 2, 2, 3, 3 take it on the lam; 4, 2, 4, 5 take to one's heels; 4, 3, 3 duck and run; 4, 4 jump bail; 4, 4, 4 slip one's lead; 4, 4, 5 save one's bacon; 4, 4, 6 slip one's collar; 4, 5 play hooky; 4, 6 play truant, take flight; 5, 3 break out, shake off, skive off, sneak off; 5, 4 close call, steal away; 5, 4, 6 break one's chains; 6, 5 French leave; 6, 6 narrow ~, narrow squeak; 6, 7 scrape through.

escaper 5 fleer; 6 eloper, evader, truant; 7 escapee, Houdini, refugee, runaway; 8 escapist, fugitive, survivor; 12 escapologist; PHRASES: 4-7 jail-breaker.

eschew See avoid

escort 4 aide, lead, mind, take; 5 guard, guide, pilot, usher; 6 attend, convoy, minder UK, squire; 7 conduct, marshal, protect; 8 chaperon, shepherd; 9 accompany, attendant, bodyguard, chaperone, companion, protector.

esophagus 6 gullet.

esoteric See obscure

esotericism 6 gnosis; 7 alchemy, arcanum, mystery, secrecy; 8 Kabbalah; 9 esoterica, Kabbalism, obscurity, occultism; 11 Freemasonry.

ESP 8 divining, prophecy; 9 telepathy; 11 soothsaying; 12 clairvoyance; PHRASES: 4, 7 palm reading; 6, 5 second sight; 7, 6 psychic powers; 7-7 fortune-telling.

especial See unusual

essay 3 try; 5 paper; 6 strive, thesis; 7 article, attempt; 8 endeavor; 11 composition; 12 dissertation.

essence 3 nub, sap; 4 core, crux, gist, meat, pith, soul; 5 basis, focus, heart, pivot, stuff; 6 center, fabric, kernel, marrow, matter, medium, spirit; 7 epitome, extract, nucleus, perfume, subject; 8 backbone, gravamen, keystone, material, quiddity, tincture; 9 highlight, lifeblood, principle, structure, substance; 11 concentrate, cornerstone, distilllate; 12 quintessence; 13 concentration.

essential 3 key; 4 main, must; 5 basic, chief, vital; 6 needed; 7 central, crucial; 8 cardinal, critical; 9 elemental, extracted, important, intrinsic, mandatory, necessary, necessity, paramount, principal, requisite; 10 compulsory, imperative, obligatory; 11 fundamental, inalienable, requirement; 12 prerequisite; 13 indispensable; PHRASES: 2, 3, 7 of the essence; 4, 3, 3 sine qua non.

essentially 6 mostly, really; 7 broadly, largely; 9 primarily; 10 materially; 11 effectively; 13 substantially; PHRASES: 2, 1, 5, 6 to a large extent; 2, 3, 4 in the main; 2, 3, 5 by and large; 2, 5 in brief; 2, 6 in effect; 2, 7 in essence, in outline; 3, 2 per se; 3, 3, 4 for the most part; 4, 2, 4 more or less. See also essential

establish 5 found, prove, start; 6 create; 7 confirm; 9 ascertain, determine, institute; PHRASES: 3, 2 set up; 4, 3 find out.

established 1 E; 2 in; 3 Est; 4 done; 5 fixed; 6 modish, proven; 8 accepted, admitted, approved, official, received; 9 customary, practiced; 10 accredited, recognized, understood; 11 fashionable, traditional; 12 acknowledged, conventional; PHRASES: 2, 3, 4 in the mode; 2, 5 in vogue; 2, 7 de rigueur, in fashion; 4, 2 with it; 4-5 well-known; 4-7 time-honored. See also establish

establishment 4 firm; 7 company, concern; 8 business, creation, founding; 9 formation; 11 authorities, institution; PHRASES: 3, 6 the system; 6, 4, 2 powers that be; 7, 2 setting up.

estate 4 area, land, park, zone; 5 funds, goods, lands, manor, means, plant, state, stock, wares, worth; 6 assets, domain, income, legacy, status, wealth; 7 bequest, capital, effects, fortune; 8 contents, heirloom, holdings, parkland, property; **9** homestead, patrimony, portfolio, resources, substance, valuables; **10** plantation; **11** inheritance; **13** circumstances; PHRASES: **8, 4** business park.

esteem **5** value; **6** regard; **7** cherish, respect; **8** venerate; **10** admiration, appreciate; PHRASES: **4, 4** hold dear; **4, 6** high regard.

esteem(ed) *See* **respect(ed)**

esthetic *See* **aesthetic**

estimable *See* **admirable**

estimate **3** vet; **4** cost, deem, rate; **5** check, gauge, guess, infer, judge, price, quote, value; **6** assess, esteem, reckon, regard, survey; **7** costing, examine, inspect, surmise; **8** appraise, ballpark, consider, evaluate; **9** appraisal, calculate, valuation; **10** assessment, conjecture, evaluation; **11** approximate, calculation, guesstimate; **13** approximation; PHRASES: **4, 2** size up; **5, 2** weigh up *UK*; **8, 5** educated guess; **8, 6** ballpark figure.

estimation **4** mark, view; **5** favor; **6** belief, cachet, credit, esteem, regard; **7** opinion; **8** approval, eminence, estimate, judgment, prestige; **9** appraisal, reference; **10** assessment, evaluation, reputation; **11** approbation, credibility, distinction, guesstimate; **13** approximation; PHRASES: **6, 4** street cred; **8, 5** educated guess; **8, 6** ballpark figure.

estranged **5** apart; **7** distant, divided; **8** disloyal; **9** alienated, disunited, separated; **11** disaffected; PHRASES: **2, 3, 5** on bad terms; **2, 4** at odds.

estrogen **7** oestrin.

estrone **10** folliculin.

estrus **3** rut; **4** heat, must; **6** frenzy.

et cetera **2, 2** et al.; **3, 2, 2** and so on.

etch *See* **engrave**

eternal **7** ageless, endless, undying; **8** constant, enduring, immortal, infinite, timeless, unending; **9** ceaseless, continual, deathless, permanent, perpetual; **10** continuous, unchanging; **11** everlasting, never-ending, sempiternal; **12** imperishable, interminable; PHRASES: **4-5** open-ended.

eternalize **8** maintain, preserve; **10** perpetuate; **11** immortalize, memorialize.

eternally **7** forever; **8** evermore; PHRASES: **2, 3, 2** on and on; **2, 10** in perpetuity; **3, 3** for aye; **3, 4** for good; **3, 4, 3, 1, 3** for ever and a

day; **3, 4, 3, 3** for good and all; **3, 4, 3, 4** for ever and ever; **3, 5** for keeps; **3, 6** for always; **3, 8** for evermore; **4, 3, 2, 3** from age to age; **5, 7, 3** world without end.

eternity **2** ay; **3** aye; **4** ages, eons, ever; **7** forever; **8** infinity; **10** infinitude, permanence, perpetuity; **11** endlessness; **12** sempiternity; **15** everlastingness; PHRASES: **4, 3, 1, 3** ever and a day; **7, 5** donkey's years *UK*.

ethanol **7** alcohol.

ether **3** air, gas, sky; **6** heaven; **10** atmosphere.

ethereal **4** airy; **5** frail; **7** ghostly, shadowy; **8** delicate, spectral, waiflike; **9** unearthly; **12** otherworldly; **13** insubstantial.

ethical **4** fair, just, pure; **5** moral, right, sober; **6** chaste, decent, honest, proper; **7** dutiful, fitting, prudent, upright; **8** faithful, virginal, virtuous; **9** honorable, righteous, temperate; **10** charitable, principled; PHRASES: **4-10** self-controlled.

ethics **5** maxim, mores, rules; **6** morals, values; **7** beliefs, precept; **8** morality, scruples; **9** integrity, standards; **10** conscience, principles; PHRASES: **4, 2, 4** code of duty; **4, 2, 5** code of honor; **4, 2, 7** code of conduct; **5, 4** moral code; **9, 4** unwritten code.

Ethiopia **9** Abyssinia.

etiquette **4** code, form; **5** mores; **6** comity, custom; **7** conduct, decorum, manners; **8** protocol; **9** decencies, politesse, propriety, punctilio; **10** civilities, convention, elegancies, politeness; **11** formalities; PHRASES: **3, 4, 5** the done thing; **4, 4** good form; **4, 7** good manners; **5, 2, 7** rules of conduct; **6, 6** social graces; **6, 7** social conduct.

Euboea **6** Éνvoia; **9** Negropont.

Eucharist **4** Mass; **6** housel, supper; **9** Communion; PHRASES: **3, 4** Low Mass; **4, 4** High Mass; **4, 9** Holy Communion; **5, 5** Missa bassa; **5, 6** Lord's Supper, Missa brevis; **5, 8** Missa solemnis; **8, 2, 5** breaking of bread.

eulogy *See* **tribute**

Eumenides **6** Furies.

eunuch **5** capon; **8** castrate, castrato.

euphemisms **4** dang, darn, durn, gosh; **5** ruddy; **6** blamed, blazes, bloody, crikey, danged, darned, deuced, durned; **7** blasted, blessed, doggone, goldarn, jeepers; **8** goshdarn; **10** confounded, goshdarned; PHRASES: **3, 4** gee whiz, Sam Hill; **3-5** dad-blast; **3-6**

dad-blamed, dad-burned; **3-7** dad-blasted; **3, 10** gee whillikers; **4, 2** dang it!; **7-8** jeepers-creepers; **8-5** blankety-blank.

evacuate 5 empty, leave; **6** vacate; **7** abandon; PHRASES: **4, 3, 2** move out of; **4, 4** send away; **5, 4** clear from; **6, 4** remove from; **8, 4** withdraw from.

evacuation *See* **removal**

evade 4 duck, hide; **5** avoid, delay, dodge, elude, fence, fudge, hedge, parry, shirk, skirt, skulk, table; **6** escape, shelve, waffle; **7** deflect; **8** postpone, sidestep; **9** pussyfoot, stonewall; **10** equivocate; **11** prevaricate; **13** procrastinate; PHRASES: **2, 2, 3, 3** go on the lam; **4-3-2-4** hide-and-go-seek; **4, 4-3-4** play hide-and-seek; **5, 5** skirt round.

evaluate 4 rate; **5** gauge, judge, price, value, weigh; **6** assess, review; **8** appraise, consider, estimate; **9** calculate; PHRASES: **5, 2** weigh up *UK*.

evaluation 6 review; **7** costing; **8** estimate; **9** appraisal, valuation; **10** assessment, estimation; **11** calculation.

evaporate 4 fade; **6** vanish; **8** disperse, dissolve, vaporize; **9** disappear, dissipate; **10** volatilize; PHRASES: **3, 2** dry up; **4, 4** boil away, fade away, melt away.

evaporation 4 loss; **9** vanishing; **11** dehydration; **12** vaporization; **13** disappearance.

evasion 3 lie; **4** duck; **5** dodge, parry; **6** escape; **7** dodging, ducking, elusion, fencing, fudging, hedging, perjury, quibble, untruth; **8** shirking, skirting, skulking, trickery; **9** avoidance, deception, duplicity, obscurity, shuffling; **10** deflection, dishonesty, subterfuge; **11** evasiveness, obfuscation; **12** equivocation, stonewalling; **13** circumvention, dissimulation, mystification, prevarication; **14** disinformation; PHRASES: **3, 7** red herring; **4-3-2-4** hide-and-go-seek; **4-3-4** hide-and-seek; **4-5, 5** wild-goose chase; **5-2** cover-up; **6, 4** double talk; **7, 3, 5** fudging the issue. *See also* **evasive**

evasive 3 coy; **5** cagey, vague; **6** shifty; **7** dodging, elusive, fencing, oblique; **8** indirect, oracular, slippery; **9** ambiguous, deceitful, equivocal, shuffling; **10** misleading, roundabout; **11** amphibolous; **13** doubletalking, prevaricating; **14** circumlocutory.

even 3 e'en, yet; **4** dusk, flat, tied; **5** drawn, equal, level; **6** smooth, steady, sunset; **7** evening, regular, sundown, uniform; **8** balanced, constant, straight, twilight; **9** eurythmic, nightfall, unvarying; **10** consistent, unchanging; **13** unfluctuating; PHRASES: **2, 1, 3** on a par; **2, 3, 4, 4** at the same time; **2, 5, 7** on level pegging *UK*; **4, 2** just as; **4-6** even-steven.

evening 2 p.m.; **3** eve; **4** dark, dusk, even, late; **5** dusky; **6** soirée, sunset, vesper; **7** sundown, vespers; **8** darkfall, dogwatch, eventide, gloaming, twilight, vesperal; **9** benighted, nightfall, nocturnal, vesperine; **11** crepuscular; **12** postmeridian; PHRASES: **5, 2, 3** close of day; **5, 4** after dark; **8-2, 4** lighting-up time *UK*.

evening star 5 Venus; **7** Lucifer; **8** Hesperus; **10** Phosphorus; PHRASES: **7, 4** morning star.

evensong 7 vespers.

event 4 news; **5** rumor, story; **6** affair, gossip; **7** episode; **8** business, incident, occasion; **9** happening; **10** experience, occurrence; **11** proceedings; PHRASES: **6-2** goings-on; **6-7, 7** rubber-chicken circuit.

eventing 8 Burghley, dressage; **9** Badminton, Hickstead; PHRASES: **4, 7** show jumping; **5-7** cross-country.

eventual 4 last; **5** final; **7** ensuing; **8** ultimate; **10** subsequent.

eventuality *See* **possibility**

ever *See* **always**

everlasting 7 endless, eternal, forever, undying; **8** unending; **9** ceaseless, incessant, perennial, permanent, perpetual; **10** continuous, immortelle; **12** interminable; PHRASES: **5-6** never-ending; **7, 3** without end.

every *See* **each**

everyday 5 daily, plain, stock, usual; **6** common, normal; **7** average, general, routine, typical; **8** familiar, middling, ordinary, standard, straight; **9** household, quotidian; **11** commonplace; **12** unremarkable; **13** unexceptional; PHRASES: **3-2-3-4** run-of-the-mill; **6, 7** garden variety.

everyone 3 all; **4** each; **9** everybody; **10** everything; PHRASES: **3, 3, 3** one and all; **3, 3, 6** all and sundry; **3, 4, 3, 5** Tom Dick and Harry; **3, 5** all hands; **3, 5, 5** the whole world; **3, 5, 7** the whole shebang; **4, 2, 5** tout le monde *UK*; **4, 3, 5, 3** each and every one; **5, 3, 4** every man Jack; **5, 4, 3** every last one; **5, 7, 3** every mother's son; **5, 9** whole enchilada.

everything *See* **all**

everywhere 4 rife; 6 passim; 11 universally; 12 ubiquitously; PHRASES: 2, 3, 4, 5 to the four winds; 2, 3, 8 in all quarters; 3, 3, 4 far and wide; 3, 4 all over; 3, 4, 3, 5 all over the place; 3, 5, 4 the world over; 8, 3, 4 wherever you look.

evict 4 oust; 5 eject, expel; 6 remove, uproot; 7 deprive, unhouse; 8 dislodge, jettison; 9 repossess; 10 dispossess; 11 expropriate; PHRASES: 3, 3 put out; 4, 3 kick out, turn out; 4, 3, 2, 5 turn out of doors; 5, 3 throw out.

evidence 3 gen *UK*; 4 data, mark, seal, show, sign; 5 facts, proof, prove, trace; 6 evince, permit, record, report, signal, verify; 7 exhibit, grounds, hearsay, reasons, support; 8 premises; 9 admission, affidavit, documents, reference, statement, testimony; 10 confession, credential, deposition, indication, suggestion; 11 corroborate, declaration, demonstrate, information, testimonial; 12 confirmation, intelligence, substantiate, verification; 13 documentation; 14 recommendation, substantiation.

evidence (give evidence) 5 state, swear; 6 affirm, allege, assert, attest; 7 declare, testify, witness; PHRASES: 4, 7, 2 bear witness to.

evidence (person who gives evidence) 3 rat, spy; 4 mole, narc; 5 grass *UK*, snout; 6 dobber *UK*, lagger; 7 witness; 8 squealer, telltale; 9 attestant, defendant, informant, plaintiff; 10 eyewitness, supergrass *UK*, tattletale; PHRASES: 5, 6 stool pigeon.

evident 5 clear, plain; 6 marked, patent; 7 obvious, seeming, visible; 8 apparent, distinct, manifest, palpable; 9 prominent; 10 ostensible; 12 unmistakable; PHRASES: 2, 5, 4 it would seem; 2, 5, 8 in broad daylight; 2, 7 on display; 3, 3, 2, 3 for all to see.

evident (make evident) 4 show; 5 imply; 7 suggest; 8 indicate; 9 represent; PHRASES: 5, 3, 6 speak for itself.

evidential 6 direct, proved; 7 certain, factual; 8 attested, informed, pointing *UK*, recorded, relevant, reported, telltale, verified; 9 authentic, confirmed, empirical, probative, witnessed; 10 documented, indicative, tattletale; 11 documentary, significant; 13 corroborative, demonstrative; PHRASES: 5, 5 prima facie.

evil 3 bad, ill, sin; 4 foul, mean, vice, vile; 5 awful, lousy, nasty, wrong; 6 blight, cancer, canker, deadly, hoodoo, malice, odious, plague, rotten, sinful, unkind, voodoo, wicked; 7 badness, beastly, corrupt, defiled, demonic, hateful, immoral, scourge, ungodly, vicious; 8 blighted, criminal, depraved, deviltry, diabolic, dreadful, foulness, horrible, iniquity, meanness, mischief, sinister, terrible, vileness, wretched; 9 atrocious, demonical, depravity, improbity, injustice, malicious, malignant, malignity, nastiness, nefarious, obnoxious, offensive, revolting, wrongness; 10 corruption, defilement, deplorable, despicable, detestable, diabolical, disgusting, immorality, iniquitous, maleficent, malevolent, rottenness, wickedness; 11 beastliness, hatefulness, malediction, maleficence, malevolence, mischievous, noxiousness, viciousness; 12 contemptible, dreadfulness, horribleness, terribleness; 13 atrociousness, reprehensible; 15 mischievousness; PHRASES: 3, 4 ill will; 3, 5 bad karma.

evil (do evil) 3 hex; 4 doom, harm, hurt, jinx, kill; 5 abuse, curse, wound, wrong; 6 befoul, blight, damage, defile, harass, impair, injure, menace, molest, plague, poison; 7 afflict, condemn, corrupt, despoil, destroy, pervert, pollute, torment, trouble, violate; 8 aggrieve, distress, maltreat, mistreat, threaten; 9 persecute; PHRASES: 2, 5 do wrong; 5, 5 wreak havoc.

evince *See* **show**

eviscerate 3 gut; 5 shell; 10 disembowel.

evocative 6 moving; 8 exciting, forceful, haunting, poignant, redolent, striking; 9 thrilling; 10 suggestive; 11 reminiscent.

evolution 6 change, growth; 7 turning; 8 evolving, progress; 9 Darwinism, phylogeny; 10 Lamarckism, speciation; 11 advancement, development, improvement, progression.

ex 6 former, lapsed; 7 earlier, onetime; 8 sometime; 9 erstwhile; PHRASES: 3, 5 old flame.

exact 6 demand, extort, obtain, strict; 7 careful, correct, extract, precise; 8 accurate, faithful, thorough; 10 meticulous, particular.

exacting 5 tough; 7 onerous, testing; 8 rigorous, thorough; 9 extortive; 11 challenging; **12** extortionate.

exaggerate 3 ham; **4** fuss, hype; **5** labor; **6** overdo, strain, stress; **7** amplify, enhance, inflate, overact, stretch, varnish; **8** overkill, overplay, overrate, oversell; **9** aggravate, burlesque, embellish, embroider, intensify, overreact, overstate, overvalue; **10** caricature, exacerbate, overpraise, overstress; **11** hyperbolize, overenthuse; **12** overestimate; **13** overemphasize; **14** sensationalize; PHRASES: **2, 4, 3, 3** go over the top; **3, 2** lay on; **3, 2, 2** ham it up; **4, 3, 4** gild the lily; **5, 2** touch up; **7, 1, 5** stretch a point.

exaggerated 3 OTT *UK*; **4** camp, fake; **5** false; **6** puffed *UK*; **7** extreme; **8** parodied, spurious; **9** bombastic, deceptive, excessive, flattered, grandiose, overdrawn; **10** exorbitant, fabricated, histrionic, hyperbolic, inordinate, prodigious; **11** extravagant, overcolored, pretentious, superlative; **12** bullshitting, histrionical, melodramatic; **13** grandiloquent; PHRASES: **3-7** far-fetched; **4-3-3** over-the-top; **5-2** blown-up; **6-4-4** larger-than-life; **6, 5** purple patch *UK*. *See also* **exaggerate**

exaggeration 4 fuss, hype; **6** pother; **7** hamming, puffery, varnish; **8** ballyhoo, laboring, overkill, travesty; **9** burlesque, commotion, extremism, hyperbole, inflation, melodrama, overdoing, sensation, straining; **10** caricature, embroidery, excitement, inordinacy, overacting, overstress, stretching; **11** aggravation, enhancement, exorbitance, histrionics, superlative; **12** exacerbation, exaggerating, overemphasis, overexposure, overreaction; **13** amplification, embellishment, excessiveness, magnification, overstatement; **14** sensationalism; **15** intensification; PHRASES: **2-2** to-do; **8, 2** touching up.

exaggerator 4 brag, liar; **6** hector; **7** boaster, fanatic, windbag; **8** braggart, fanfaron; **9** blusterer; **10** panjandrum; **11** braggadocio, bullshitter; **14** sensationalist.

exalt 4 laud; **5** raise; **6** praise; **7** elevate, promote.

exaltation 3 joy; **6** praise; **7** acclaim, rapture; **9** adoration, adulation, happiness; **10** excitement; **11** acclamation; **12** exhilaration.

exalted 2 up; **4** high; **5** grand, lofty, noble; **7** deified, eminent, sublime, supreme; **8** glorious, lionized, upgraded; **9** beatified, canonized, prominent; **11** illustrious, super-lative; **12** apotheosized; PHRASES: **2, 4** on high; **4-5** high-flown; **4-7** high-ranking.

examination 3 GRE; **4** exam, GMAT, MCAT, PSAT™, test; **5** paper; **6** prelim; **7** checkup, midyear, pretest; **8** posttest, scrutiny; **10** assessment, inspection; **13** investigation; PHRASES: **3, 4** pop quiz; **4, 5** term paper; **4-5, 4** true-false test; **9, 4** placement test.

examine 3 try, vet; **4** scan, sift, test; **5** audit, grade, judge, study, weigh; **6** assess, review, survey, winnow; **7** analyze, inspect, observe; **8** appraise, consider, evaluate, question, research; **9** criticize; **10** scrutinize; **11** investigate; PHRASES: **4, 2** look at; **4, 4** look into; **5, 2** weigh up *UK*.

examiner 5 judge; **6** grader; **7** auditor; **8** assessor, surveyor; **9** inspector; **14** superintendent.

example 4 case; **5** model; **6** sample; **7** paragon, pattern; **8** instance, paradigm, specimen, standard; PHRASES: **4, 2, 5** case in point.

excavate 3 dig; **4** bore, bury, mine; **5** drill, gouge, inter, scoop, spade; **6** burrow, exhume, hollow, quarry, tunnel; **7** uncover, unearth; PHRASES: **3, 2** dig up; **3, 3** dig out; **5, 3** scoop out; **6, 3** hollow out.

excavator 3 JCB™; **4** pick; **5** miner, scoop, spoon; **6** digger, dredge, pickax, shovel; **7** dredger; **8** quarrier.

exceed 3 lap, top; **4** beat, race; **5** excel, outdo; **6** outbid, outrun; **7** outride, surpass; **8** outclass, outflank, outrival, outstrip, overtake, surmount; **9** outdistance; **11** transcend; PHRASES: **2, 4** go over; **2, 5** go above; **2, 6** go beyond; **4, 5** rise above; **4, 6** beat hollow; **5, 6** leave behind; **5, 8** leave standing.

excel 3 cap, top, win; **4** beat, best; **5** outdo, shine; **6** better, exceed; **7** eclipse, overtop, prevail, surpass, triumph; **8** outclass, outrival, outshine, outstrip; **9** transcend; **10** overshadow; **11** predominate; PHRASES: **5, 3** stand out.

excellent 2 A1; **3** ace; **4** rare, star; **5** adept, crack, major, upper; **6** banner, chosen, expert, marked, master, superb; **7** classic, eminent, skilled, sublime, supreme; **8** champion, fabulous, finished, masterly, polished, singular, skillful, splendid; **9** admirable, brilliant, competent, important, marvelous, prominent, qualified, topflight, wonderful; **10** consummate, proficient, tremendous; **11** exceptional, outstanding, prestigious, superlative; **12** professional; **13** distinguished; PHRASES: **2, 6** of choice; **4-2** bang-up; **4-4** blue-chip; **4, 7** cat's pajamas; **5, 4** honor roll; **5-4** first-rate; **5, 4, 1, 4** every inch a king; **5-5** first-class; **5, 7** honor society.

except 3 bar, but; **4** omit, save; **6** unless.

exception 7 anomaly; **8** omission; **9** allowance, departure, exclusion, exemption; **10** concession; **11** peculiarity; **12** irregularity; PHRASES: **3-3** one-off; **7, 4** special case.

exceptional 4 rare; **5** primo; **6** exotic, unique; **7** notable, special; **8** ageneric, esoteric; **9** brilliant, excellent; **10** inimitable, noteworthy, phenomenal, remarkable; **11** outstanding; **12** incomparable; **13** distinguished, extraordinary; PHRASES: **3, 2, 1, 4** one of a kind; **3, 3** way out; **3, 7** sui generis.

excerpt *See* **extract**

excess 3 mob; **4** glut, most; **5** crowd, extra, flood, spare, spate, waste; **6** deluge, plenty; **7** bonanza, surfeit, surplus, upsurge; **8** extremes, leftover, overflow, overkill, overload, plethora, richness; **9** abundance, avalanche, overspill, plenitude, profusion; **10** additional, exuberance, inundation, luxuriance, redundance, redundancy, saturation; **11** exorbitance, prodigality, superfluity, superfluous; **12** exaggeration, extravagance, immoderation, intemperance; **13** overabundance; **14** inordinateness, overindulgence, superabundance; **15** supersaturation; PHRASES: **3, 4** too many, too much; **5, 5** lion's share.

excessive 3 OTT *UK*, too; **4** full, high, left, over; **5** sated, undue; **6** cloyed, gorged, soaked; **7** bloated, cloying, crammed, extreme, flowing, gushing, profuse, replete, riotous, stuffed, surplus, teeming; **8** abundant, bursting, crawling, drenched, effusive, flooding, inflated, overdone, overfull, overmuch, satiated, swarming; **9** bristling, congested, luxuriant, plentiful, plethoric, redundant, saturated, sickening, streaming; **10** exorbitant, immoderate, inordinate, nauseating, overloaded, overpolite; **11** exaggerated, extravagant, intemperate, overflowing, overwhelmed, superfluous, unnecessary, unwarranted; **12** overburdened, overreaching, overwhelming, unreasonable, unrestrained; **13** overstretched, superabundant; **14** supersaturated; PHRASES: **3, 4** too many, too much; **3-5** all-fired; **4, 3,**

3 over the top; **4, 3, 4** over the moon; **8-3** uncalled-for.

excessive (be excessive) 2 OD, OJ; **4** cloy, cram, fill, flow, glut, sate, soak; **5** choke, flood, gorge, spoil, stuff; **6** abound, deluge, drench, engulf, lavish, overdo, stream; **7** congest, overact, overeat, satiate; **8** inundate, overdose, overflow, overjolt, overload, overplay, overstep, saturate; **9** luxuriate, outnumber, overdrink, overspend, overwhelm, suffocate, surcharge; **10** exaggerate, overburden, overcharge, overexpand; **11** overindulge, superabound; PHRASES: **2, 4, 3, 3** go over the top; **2, 9** go overboard; **3, 2, 2, 5** lay it on thick; **3, 4** run riot; **4, 2** pile up, roll in; **4, 2, 2** pile it on; **4, 2, 6** know no bounds; **4, 4** brim over, teem with; **5, 2, 3, 5** burst at the seams; **5, 4** swarm with; **6, 2** wallow in; **7, 4** bristle with; **8, 3, 4** overstep the mark.

excessively 3 too; **4** over, very; **6** overly; **7** greatly, loosely; **8** greedily, lavishly, markedly, overmuch, terribly, wantonly; **10** needlessly; **11** arbitrarily, intrusively; **12** flamboyantly, licentiously, outrageously, permissively, prodigiously, unreservedly; **13** exceptionally, incontinently; **14** hyperbolically, ostentatiously; **15** overindulgently; PHRASES: **2, 6** to excess; **4, 3, 5** over and above; **4, 7** with abandon; **6, 7** beyond measure; **7, 5** without stint; **7, 7** without control. *See also* **excessive**

exchange 4 chat, deal, mail, pawn, post, swap, talk; **5** trade, truck; **6** barter, change, ransom, retort, switch; **7** commute, convert, dealing, logroll, pawning, permute, replace, require, shuffle, shuttle, traffic; **8** argument, displace, repartee, swapping, transact; **9** alternate, cooperate, interplay, mutuality, negotiate, shuffling, switching, transpose; **10** compensate, conversion, discussion, logrolling, recompense, substitute; **11** altercation, alternation, commutation, cooperation, interchange, negotiation, permutation, reciprocate, reciprocity, replacement, retaliation, transaction; **12** compensation, conversation, substitution; **13** consideration, reciprocation, transposition; PHRASES: **3, 2, 4** pay in kind; **3, 3** fob off; **3, 3, 2, 3** eye for an eye; **3, 3, 3** tit for tat; **3-3, 7** two-way traffic; **3, 5, 3, 3** new lamps for old; **4, 3** palm off; **4, 3, 3** quid pro quo; **4, 3, 4** blow for blow, give and take; **4-3-5** back-and-forth; **5, 3** trade off; **5, 5, 4** bandy words with; **6, 4** answer back, switch over

UK; **6, 5** change money, change round *UK*; **6, 6** change places.

exchange (in exchange) 6 mutual; **8** mutually; **10** changeably, equivalent, reciprocal; **11** commutative, convertible, correlative, retaliatory; **12** compensatory, exchangeable, substitutive; **13** complementary, reciprocative, substitutable; **15** interchangeable *UK*; PHRASES: **2, 3, 3** to and fro; **2, 4** au pair, in kind; **2, 5** by turns; **2, 6** in return; **3-3** two-way; **3-3-3** tit-for-tat; **4, 3, 5** back and forth; **4, 5** turn about, vice versa.

exchange (person who exchanges) 6 banker; **10** pawnbroker; **11** stockbroker; **12** moneychanger; PHRASES: **2, 4** au pair; **4, 7** wife swapper.

exchange (person who is exchanged) 7 hostage; **10** changeling, substitute.

exchange (place of exchange) 4 bank; **6** Bourse, cambio, market, rialto; **7** Weschel; **8** pawnshop; **11** marketplace; PHRASES: **5, 2, 5** place of trade; **6, 2, 6** bureau de change.

exchangeable 9 tradeable; **10** commutable, negotiable, permutable, redeemable, returnable; **12** transferable; **13** substitutable.

excise 4 edit; **5** erase; **6** delete, remove; **7** expunge; **9** eliminate, expurgate; PHRASES: **3, 3** cut out.

excision 7 editing, erasure, removal; **8** deletion; **11** elimination, expurgation, extirpation; PHRASES: **7, 3** cutting out.

excitable *See* **nervous**

excite 5 rouse; **6** arouse, awaken, incite, jacked, thrill; **7** agitate, animate, enliven, enthuse, provoke; **8** energize, motivate; **9** electrify, stimulate; PHRASES: **4, 2** stir up, wind up.

excitement 6 unrest; **7** ferment, tension; **8** pleasure; **9** agitation, eagerness; **10** enthusiasm; **12** anticipation, exhilaration, restlessness.

exciting 6 tickly, tingly; **7** emotive, prickly; **8** electric, poignant, stirring, striking; **9** inspiring; **10** impressive; **11** sensational, titillating; **12** breathtaking, exhilarating; PHRASES: **4-7** hair-raising.

exclaim *See* **cry out**

exclamation 3 cry; **4** hoot, howl, yell; **5** shout; **6** outcry, scream, shriek; **9** expletive; **11** ejaculation; **12** interjection.

exclude 3 ban, bar; **4** deny, miss, omit, shun, snub, stop, veto; **5** debar, eject, expel, limit, scorn, spurn, taboo; **6** banish, except, excuse, exempt, forbid, ignore, refuse, reject, slight, stifle; **7** abandon, boycott, disdain, dismiss, embargo, isolate, preempt, prevent, seclude; **8** disallow, discount, preclude, prohibit, relegate, suppress; **9** blackball, blacklist, disregard, eliminate, forestall, ghettoize, interdict, ostracize, proscribe, segregate, sequester; **10** quarantine; **12** circumscribe, discriminate; **13** excommunicate; PHRASES: **3, 3** box off; **4, 2, 8** send to Coventry *UK*; **4, 2, 9** make an exception; **4, 3** keep out, miss out *UK*, rule out, shut out, vote out, wall off, warn off; **4, 4** pass over, vote down; **4, 5** deny entry; **4-8** cold-shoulder; **5, 2** laugh at, sniff at; **5, 3** brush off, count out, fence off, leave out; **6, 3** freeze out, screen off; **7, 3** curtain off.

excluded person 5 alien, exile; **6** outlaw, pariah; **7** outcast; **8** outsider; **9** nonmember; **10** interloper, trespasser; PHRASES: **3, 3, 3** odd man out.

excluding 3 bar; **4** save, sole; **5** close, elite; **6** choice, closed, except, narrow, racist, select, sexist, unique; **7** barring, cliquey, limited, outside, private, without; **8** clannish, cliquish, ignoring, omitting; **9** excepting, exclusive, exclusory, exemptive; **10** preclusive, preemptive, preventive, restricted, xenophobic; **11** prohibitive, restrictive; **12** exclusionary, interdictory; PHRASES: **3, 5** let alone; **3, 8** not counting; **5, 2** short of; **5, 4** apart from; **5-4** close-knit; **6, 3** except for; **7, 2** outside of.

exclusive 5 elite, whole; **6** classy, select; **7** private, special, stylish; **8** absolute, complete; **9** undivided; **10** restricted; **11** fashionable; PHRASES: **4-5** high-class.

exclusiveness 6 clique, luxury; **7** elitism; **8** elegance, monopoly, snobbery; **9** apartheid; **10** refinement, xenophobia; **11** exclusivity, selectivity; **13** selectiveness; **14** discrimination, sophistication; **15** restrictiveness; PHRASES: **5, 6** inner circle; **6, 4** closed shop. *See also* **exclusive**

excommunicate *See* **exclude**

excoriate 4 flay, pare, peel, skin; **5** strip; **6** attack, berate; **7** upbraid; **8** denounce; **9** criticize.

excrement 4 dirt, dung, urea; **5** feces, waste; **6** manure, ordure, refuse, sewage; **7** excreta; **8** effluent, sewerage; **9** exudation;

PHRASES: 5, 6 waste matter.

excrete 2 go; 4 emit, pass, weep; 5 eject, expel, exude; 7 extrude, secrete; 9 discharge, eliminate; PHRASES: 3, 1, 4 pay a call; 4, 3 give off; 7, 7 relieve oneself.

excretion 4 flow, flux; 8 effusion, ejection, emission; 9 discharge, emanation, expulsion, extrusion, exudation, secretion; 11 elimination.

excruciating 5 awful; 7 painful, tedious; 8 terrible; 9 agonizing; 10 irritating, unbearable; 11 infuriating, stultifying; 12 embarrassing.

exculpate *See* **free**

excursion 4 team, tour, trip; 5 group, jaunt, party; 6 detour, junket, outing; 9 departure, deviation; 10 digression, expedition.

excuse 5 alibi; 6 acquit, exempt, pardon; 7 absolve, condone, defense, evasion, forgive, pretext; 9 exculpate, exonerate; 11 vindication.

execute 2 do; 3 gas; 4 burn, flay, hang, kill, slay; 5 lynch, purge, shoot, stone; 6 behead, impale, murder; 7 achieve, butcher, crucify, fulfill, garrote, perform; 8 complete, dispatch, garrotte, lapidate, massacre, necklace *S Afr*, strangle; 9 decollate, dismember, implement, slaughter, undertake; 10 accomplish, completion, decapitate, guillotine; 11 electrocute; PHRASES: 3, 2, 5 put to death; 4, 2, 3, 5 burn at the stake, send to the chair; 5, 3 carry out; 6, 2 string up; 7, 4, 4 stretch one's neck.

execution 6 effect; 8 massacre; 9 deathblow, slaughter; 10 completion, guillotine; 11 performance; 13 electrocution; 14 accomplishment, implementation.

execution (instrument of execution) 2 ax; 3 gas; 4 rope; 5 block, cross, noose, stake; 6 bullet, gibbet, halter, maiden, poison; 7 gallows, garrote, hemlock; 8 garrotte, necklace *S Afr*, scaffold; 10 guillotine; PHRASES: 3, 3, 4 the hot seat; 3, 5 the chair; 3, 7 gas chamber; 5, 7 death chamber; 6, 5 firing squad; 6, 9 lethal injection; 8, 5 electric chair; 9, 3 headsman's axe.

executioner 5 axman; 7 hangman.

executive 6 select; 7 manager; 8 director, official, superior; 9 exclusive, expensive; 10 management, managerial; 12 policymaking; 13 administrator; 14 administrative; PHRASES: 4, 5 high class; 6, 7 senior manager; 8-6 decision-making.

executor 4 doer; 9 architect, initiator; 10 originator; PHRASES: 5, 5 prime mover.

exemplar *See* **ideal**

exemplify *See* **represent**

exempt 4 free; 5 freed, spare; 6 except, excuse, immune, pardon; 7 exclude, excused, release, relieve; 8 excepted, excluded, exempted, released, relieved, shielded; 9 discharge, nonliable, protected; 10 privileged; 12 unanswerable; PHRASES: 3, 2 let go; 3, 3 let off; 3, 3, 4 off the hook; 3, 5 set apart; 3, 7, 2 not subject to; 3, 11 not accountable, not responsible; 5, 3 leave out; 5, 8 grant immunity, grant impunity.

exemption 7 freedom, release; 8 immunity, impunity; 9 discharge, exception, exclusion, indemnity, privilege; 10 absolution; 12 dispensation, nonliability.

exercise 2 PE *UK*, PT *UK*; 3 jog, run, use; 4 move, step, swim, walk, yoga; 5 apply, cycle, drill, exert, games *UK*, races, sport, train; 6 effect, employ, rowing, sports; 7 cycling, jogging, prepare, running, stretch, walking; 8 aerobics, practice, swimming, training; 9 implement; 10 employment, eurythmics, gymnastics, isometrics; 11 application, preparation; 12 calisthenics; 13 weightlifting; 14 implementation; PHRASES: 3, 4, 6 put into effect; 4, 2 warm up; 4, 3 keep fit *UK*, work out; 4, 4 pump iron; 5, 3 carry out; 5, 3, 5 track and field; 6, 2 limber up.

exert 3 tug, use; 4 lift, pull, push, toil; 5 apply, drive, force, heave, labor, wield; 6 strain, stress; 7 attempt, squeeze, stretch, trouble; 8 campaign, endeavor, exercise, pressure, struggle.

exertion 3 ado; 4 push, toil; 5 drive, force, pains, power; 6 action, battle, effort, energy, hassle, strain, stress; 7 trouble; 8 campaign, endeavor, pressure, struggle; 11 application; PHRASES: 3, 4, 3 the hard way; 4, 3, 7 toil and trouble; 4, 4 hard work; 5, 2, 4, 4 sweat of one's brow; 5, 3, 4 might and main; 5, 6 elbow grease; 6, 5 muscle power; 6, 6 mighty effort.

exhalation 6 breath; 8 emission; 10 expiration.

exhale 6 expire; 7 respire; PHRASES: 4, 3 blow out; 7, 3 breathe out.

exhaust 3 use; 5 drain; 6 weaken; 7 consume, fatigue; PHRASES: 3, 2 use up; 4, 3 tire out, wear out.

exhausting *See* **tiring**

exhaustion *See* **tiredness**

exhibit 4 show; 6 expose, flaunt, parade, unveil; 7 display, showing; 8 showcase; 10 exhibition; PHRASES: 3, 2, 4 put on view; 4, 3 show off.

exhibition 3 zoo; 4 demo, expo, fair; 6 museum; 7 display, gallery, showing; 8 aquarium, carnival, showcase; 10 exposition; 12 presentation; 13 demonstration; PHRASES: 5, 4 trade fair.

exhibitionism 6 vanity; 7 egotism; 8 boasting; 9 flaunting, peacockry, strutting; 10 swaggering; 13 swashbuckling; PHRASES: 7-3 showing-off.

exhort 4 call, goad, prod, push, spur, urge; 5 press; 6 appeal; 8 pressure; 9 encourage.

exhortation 4 call, urge; 6 advice, appeal, urging; 7 counsel; 8 pressure; 10 incitement; 13 encouragement; PHRASES: 3, 4 pep talk; 3, 5 pep rally; 7, 4 clarion call, trumpet call; 8, 3 rallying cry.

exhume 6 unbury; 7 unearth; 8 disclose, disinter; PHRASES: 3, 2 dig up.

exigency *See* **need**

exigent 5 tough, vital; 6 taxing, urgent; 7 crucial, testing; 8 pressing; 9 demanding, important; 11 challenging.

exile 5 expel; 6 banish, deport, émigré; 7 refugee; 8 deportee; 9 expulsion, ostracism; 10 banishment, expatriate, separation; 11 deportation; PHRASES: 3, 5 tax ~ *UK*; 4, 4 send away.

exist 2 be; 4 last, live; 5 dwell, occur; 6 happen; 7 subsist, survive; PHRASES: 2, 5 be found.

existence 3 ens; 4 esse, life; 5 being; 6 entity; 7 reality; 8 presence; 9 actuality; 10 occurrence; 11 subsistence.

existence (bring into existence) 9 actualize.

existing 4 real; 5 being; 6 actual, extant, living; 7 current, present; 8 existent, manifest, tangible; 9 occurring, prevalent, remaining, surviving; 10 prevailing, subsistent; 11 substantial; PHRASES: 2, 5 in force; 2, 6 in effect.

exit 2 go; 3 die, out; 4 door, gate; 5 issue, leave; 6 depart, egress, escape, exodus, out-

let; 7 leaving, walkout; 8 breakout, emerging, emersion, eruption, issuance, withdraw; 9 departure, egression, emergence; 10 evacuation, withdrawal; PHRASES: 2, 3 go out; 3, 3 bow out, get out, pop out, way out; 4, 3 pass out, take off, walk off, walk out; 5-6 leave-taking.

exonerate *See* **clear**

exorbitant 4 dear; 8 inflated; 9 excessive; 10 ridiculous.

exotic 5 alien, novel; 7 foreign, unusual; 8 striking, tropical; 9 nonnative; 11 interesting; PHRASES: 4, 6 from abroad.

expand 3 wax; 4 boom, grow; 6 extend; 7 develop, enlarge; 8 increase; PHRASES: 4, 3 open out; 6, 3 spread out.

expanse 4 area, span; 6 region; 7 breadth, stretch.

expansionism 10 emigration; 11 colonialism, imperialism; 12 colonization; PHRASES: 6, 8 empire building.

expect 4 fear, hope, plan; 5 await, dread, guess, think; 6 assume, demand, intend, reckon; 7 believe, daresay, foresee, imagine, predict, presume, require, suppose; 8 envisage, envision, forecast, forewarn; 10 anticipate; 13 prognosticate; PHRASES: 3, 2 bet on; 3, 2, 6 see it coming; 4, 3 hope for, look for, wait for; 4, 5 look ahead; 4, 7, 2 look forward to; 5, 2 count on; 6, 2 insist on.

expectation 4 fear, hope; 5 dread, dream, faith, trust; 6 belief, desire; 7 anxiety, outlook, waiting; 8 ambition, forecast, prospect, reliance, suspense; 9 assurance, certainty, prognosis; 10 aspiration, assumption, confidence, conviction, expectance, expectancy, foreboding, likelihood, prediction; 11 hopefulness, possibility, presumption, probability; 12 anticipation, apprehension.

expected 3 due; 4 sure; 6 chosen, feared, future, likely; 7 awaited, certain, desired, dreaded; 8 apparent, foreseen, imminent, probable, promised; 9 impending, predicted; 10 designated; 11 anticipated, foreseeable, predictable, prospective; PHRASES: 2, 3, 5 in the cards; 4-7 long-awaited; 5, 3 hoped for.

expecting 4 keen, sure; 5 eager, ready; 6 gravid, hoping; 7 anxious, assured, certain, excited, hopeful, waiting, wanting; 8 desiring, dreading, pregnant, prepared, sanguine, vigilant, watchful; 9 confident, expectant, forearmed; **10** forewarned, prognostic; **11** unsurprised; **12** anticipatory, apprehensive; PHRASES: **2, 3, 4** in the club *UK*; **2, 3, 6, 3** in the family way; **2, 3, 7** on the lookout; **2, 4, 5** in high hopes; **2, 7** on standby; **2, 8** in suspense; **2, 11** in expectation, on tenterhooks; **4, 2, 4** full of hope; **4, 5** with child; **4, 5, 6** with bated breath.

expedient 5 means; **6** device, method, useful; **7** fitting, measure; **8** maneuver, suitable; **9** advisable, necessary, practical; **10** beneficial, convenient; **11** appropriate; **12** advantageous.

expedition 4 crew, team, trip; **5** group, party; **6** outing, voyage; **7** company, journey; **9** excursion.

expel 4 fire, oust, sack; **5** eject, evict, exile; **6** banish, deport; **7** dismiss; **9** discharge, extradite; PHRASES: **3, 3** put out; **4, 3** boot out, cast out, kick out, push out, toss out, turf out *UK*, turn out; **4, 3, 4, 4** give the bum's rush; **5, 3** chuck out, drive out *UK*, flush out, force out, heave out, throw out.

expellee 6 outlaw; **7** outcast, refugee; **8** deportee.

expend 3 buy, pay, use; **4** blow, shop; **5** apply, spend; **6** afford, invest; **7** consume, splurge, utilize; **8** disburse, purchase, squander; **9** disinvest, dissipate; PHRASES: **3, 2** use up; **3, 3** lay out, pay out; **4, 3** fork out; **4, 3, 4** meet the cost; **4, 4** fork over; **4, 5** sink money; **5, 2, 7** spare no expense; **5, 3** shell out; **5, 4, 6** empty one's pocket; **5, 5** incur costs; **6, 3** splash out; **7, 4** fritter away.

expendable 6 usable; **9** throwaway; **10** consumable, disposable; **11** dispensable, replaceable, superfluous, unessential; **12** nonessential.

expense 3 fee, tax; **4** cost, loss, rate, toll; **5** price; **6** amount, charge, outlay, tariff; **7** outflow, payment, premium; **8** overhead, purchase, spending; **9** outgoings *UK*, sacrifice; **10** investment; **11** expenditure; **12** disbursement; PHRASES: **4, 2, 6** cost of living; **5, 3** price tag.

expensive 4 dear; **5** steep; **6** classy, costly, lavish; **8** affluent; **9** exclusive, luxurious; PHRASES: **4-6** high-priced.

experience 4 face, feel; **5** event, skill; **7** episode, undergo; **8** incident, practice; **9** encounter, knowledge; **10** occurrence; **11** involvement; **13** understanding; PHRASES: **2, 7** go through; **4, 7** live through.

experienced 4 able; **5** tried; **6** expert; **7** skilled, trained, veteran; **8** seasoned, skillful; **9** practiced, qualified; **10** conversant, proficient; **11** specialized; **13** knowledgeable; PHRASES: **6, 2** versed in.

experiment 2 go; **3** bid, try; **4** risk, shot, stab, test; **5** assay, check, crack, essay, fling, guess, probe, prove, sound, trial, whack; **6** effort, feeler, gambit, sample; **7** analyze, examine, explore, inquire, inquiry, sounder, venture; **8** analysis, endeavor, research; **9** probation; **11** investigate; **13** investigation; PHRASES: **3, 2, 3, 4** put to the test; **3, 2, 5** put on trial; **3, 3** try out; **4, 3, 5** test the water; **4, 4** acid test; **5, 3** check out, sound out; **5, 3, 5** trial and error.

experimental 3 new; **4** test; **5** rough, trial; **6** trying; **7** testing, untried; **8** analytic, practice; **9** empirical, tentative; **10** innovative, scientific; **11** conjectural, exploratory, probational, provisional, speculative; **12** probationary; **13** experimenting, investigative; PHRASES: **5-5** avant-garde.

experimentation 6 trying; **7** testing; **8** research; **9** trialling *UK*; **11** examination, exploration, vivisection; **12** verification; **13** ascertainment, determination, investigation; PHRASES: **1, 3, 1** R and D.

experimentation (place of experimentation) 3 lab; **6** studio; **8** workshop; **10** laboratory.

experimenter 5 trier; **6** tester; **7** analyst, assayer, quester, striver; **8** inquirer, inventor; **9** innovator, scientist; **10** empiricist, researcher; **12** investigator; **14** vivisectionist; **15** experimentalist.

expert 3 don, pro; **4** buff, guru, whiz, wonk; **5** brain, champ, crack, doyen, guide, sharp, tried, wonky; **6** adroit, artist, boffin *UK*, genius, master, pundit, savant; **7** adviser, artisan, doyenne, egghead, fancier, maestro, scholar, skilled, teacher, trained, veteran; **8** champion, graduate, highbrow, polymath, seasoned, skillful, slyboots, virtuoso, warhorse; **9** authority, competent, craftsman, efficient, practiced, professor, qualified, scientist, shellback; **10** consultant, proficient, specialist; **11** cognoscente, connoisseur, craftswoman, experienced, specialized; **12** accomplished, intellectual, practitioner, professional, sophisticate; **13** businesswoman, knowledgeable; PHRASES: **2, 2** up on; **2, 4** au fait *Fr*; **2, 6** no novice; **3, 2, 3, 5** man of the world; **3, 3** old dog, sea dog; **3, 4** dab hand *UK*, old hand; **4, 3** whiz kid, wise guy; **5, 6** grand master, smart cookie; **5, 8** smart customer; **6, 2** versed in; **6, 5** clever clogs *UK*; **9, 3** practiced eye; **9, 4** practiced hand.

expert (be expert) 4 know; PHRASES: **4, 3, 5** know the ropes; **4, 4, 5** know one's stuff; **4, 4, 6** know one's onions; **4, 8** know backward.

expertly 4 ably, well; **8** masterly. *See also* **expert**

expire 3 die, end; **4** pass; **5** lapse; **6** elapse, finish, perish; **7** decease; **8** conclude; **9** terminate; PHRASES: **3, 3** die out, run out; **4, 2** pass on; **4, 2, 3, 5** give up the ghost; **4, 4** pass away; **7, 4, 4** breathe your last.

expiry 3 end; **5** death, dying; **6** demise, ending, finish; **7** passing.

explain 4 cite, tell; **5** brief, gloss, quote; **6** defend, depict, unfold; **7** clarify, expound, express, itemize, justify, support; **8** describe, indicate, instruct; **9** delineate, elucidate, enlighten, exemplify, explicate, vindicate; **10** illuminate, illustrate; PHRASES: **3, 2, 5, 5** put in plain words; **4, 5** make clear; **7, 3** account for.

explanation 3 key; **4** talk; **5** basis, cause, gloss, model; **6** excuse, motive, reason, sample, theory; **7** account, defense, details, example, grounds, premise, pretext; **8** briefing, exegesis; **9** depiction; **10** exposition, expounding; **11** delineation, description, elucidation, vindication; **12** illumination, illustration; **13** clarification, demonstration, enlightenment, justification; **15** exemplification, rationalization.

expletive *See* **swearword**

explicit 5 blunt, clear, frank, plain; **7** precise; **8** definite, specific.

explode 3 pop; **5** blast, burst, erupt; **6** negate; **7** nullify, shatter; **8** detonate, disprove, fragment, splinter; **9** discredit; **10** invalidate; **12** disintegrate; PHRASES: **2, 3** go off; **2, 9** go ballistic; **3, 3** set off; **3, 3, 3, 6** fly off the handle; **3, 3, 4** hit the roof; **3, 3, 7** hit the ceiling; **3, 4, 1, 4** fly into a rage; **4, 2** blow up; **5, 2** break up.

exploit 3 use; **4** deed, feat, milk; **5** abuse, drain, stunt; **6** misuse; **7** convert, develop, extract, reclaim, utilize; **8** activity; **9** adventure; **10** manipulate; **11** achievement; PHRASES: **3, 2, 3, 4** use to the full; **3, 2, 9** use to advantage; **3-3** ill-use; **4, 1, 4, 2** make a fool

of; **4, 1, 5, 2** make a patsy of; **4, 2** play on; **4, 2, 2** cash in on; **4, 3, 2** make hay of, make use of; **4, 3, 4, 2** make the most of; **4, 9, 2** take advantage of; **6, 2** profit by; **6, 3** heroic act; **10, 2** capitalize on.

explore 5 study; **6** search, survey, travel; **8** discover, sightsee; **11** investigate, reconnoiter; PHRASES: **3, 3, 6** see the sights; **4, 2** look at.

explosion 3 fit; **4** bang, leap; **5** blast, burst, flood; **7** upsurge; **8** eruption, outbreak, outburst, paroxysm; **10** detonation.

explosive 3 cap, RLG, TNT; **4** bang, bomb, fuse, mine; **6** abrupt, charge, napalm, powder, Semtex™, sudden, touchy; **7** cordite, grenade, lyddite, missile, priming *UK*, torpedo, warhead; **8** dynamite, melinite, staccato, unstable, volatile; **9** dangerous, fireworks, gelignite, gunpowder, hotheaded, saltpeter; **10** propellant; **13** nitroglycerin, unpredictable; **14** nitroglycerine *UK*; PHRASES: **5, 6** depth charge; **5-8** quick-tempered, short-tempered; **7, 8** Molotov cocktail.

exponent 3 fan; **5** index, power; **6** backer; **7** booster; **8** advocate, champion, promoter; **9** performer, proponent, supporter; **12** practitioner.

export 4 ship; **6** outlay, spread; **7** freight; **8** transfer; **9** outgoings *UK*; **10** distribute; **11** disseminate; PHRASES: **4, 2** pass on.

expose 4 bare; **6** reveal, unmask; **7** display, imperil, subject, uncover; **8** endanger; PHRASES: **3, 2, 6** put in danger; **3, 4** lay bare; **3, 4, 2** lay open to; **4, 2** open up; **5, 2, 5** bring to light.

exposed 3 out; **4** bare, nude, open; **6** peeled; **7** denuded, mooning, showing, topless, visible; **8** barefoot, debagged, divested, flashing, revealed, stripped, unveiled; **9** uncovered, unearthed; **11** unprotected; **12** barebreasted, pornographic; PHRASES: **1-5** X-rated; **3, 2, 3, 4** out in the open; **4, 4** laid bare; **4-4** wide-open.

exposition 4 fair, show; **7** account, display; **8** carnival, exegesis, showcase; **9** depiction; **10** discussion, exhibition, expounding; **11** delineation, description, elucidation, explanation; **12** illumination, illustration; **13** clarification, demonstration; **15** exemplification.

expository 8 critical; **9** editorial; **10** annotative, discursive, exegetical, glossarial;

12 illuminating, interpretive *UK*; **14** disquisitional.

expostulate 6 object; **7** protest, reprove; **8** disagree; **11** remonstrate.

exposure 7 contact; **8** dealings; **9** publicity, revealing, unveiling; **10** disclosure, experience, revelation; **12** acquaintance, introduction.

expound 7 develop, explain; **10** illustrate; PHRASES: **4, 5** talk about; **6, 2** expand on.

express 4 fast; **5** exact, rapid, state, utter, voice; **6** direct, prompt; **7** extract, nonstop, precise; **8** definite, explicit, specific; **10** articulate; **11** communicate; PHRASES: **5, 3** force out, press out; **7, 3** squeeze out.

expression 3 air; **4** face, look, term; **5** idiom; **6** phrase, saying; **7** example; **10** appearance, extraction; **11** countenance; **12** illustration; **13** communication, demonstration, manifestation; PHRASES: **4, 2, 6** turn of phrase; **7, 3** forcing out; **8, 3** pressing out; **9, 3** squeezing out.

expressive 5 vivid; **8** dramatic; **9** emotional, evocative, sensitive.

expulsion 5 exile; **7** removal; **8** ejection, eviction; **9** discharge, dismissal, exclusion, rejection; PHRASES: **3, 3, 5-2** the old heave-ho; **3, 4** the boot, the push; **3, 4, 4** the bum's rush; **3, 5** the chuck.

exquisite 6 moving, superb; **7** intense, perfect, refined; **8** delicate, flawless, gorgeous, poignant, touching; **9** beautiful, excellent, sensitive, wonderful; **10** attractive, delightful, discerning, fastidious; **12** excruciating; **14** discriminating.

extempore *See* **improvised**

extend 2 go; **3** run; **4** give, hold, span; **5** cover, delay, raise, range, reach, sweep, widen; **6** deepen, dilate, expand, spread; **7** broaden, develop, distend, enlarge, present, proffer, prolong, stretch; **8** continue, increase, lengthen, postpone, protract; PHRASES: **2, 2** go on; **3, 2** add to, run on; **3, 3** put off; **4, 3** drag out, draw out, hold out, pull out, spin out; **5, 2** carry on; **6, 3** spread out; **7, 3** stretch out.

extension 4 wing; **5** delay; **6** leeway; **8** addition, increase, overtime; **9** allowance, expansion; **10** broadening; **11** enlargement, lengthening; **12** conservatory, postponement; PHRASES: **4-2** lean-to; **10, 4** additional room.

extensive 3 big; **4** high, huge, long, vast, wide; **5** broad, large; **6** global; **7** general, massive; **8** infinite; **9** boundless, universal, worldwide; **10** unconfined, widespread; **12** unrestricted; PHRASES: **3-5** far-flung; **3-8** far-reaching; **3-9** all-embracing; **3-12** all-encompassing; **4-7** wide-ranging.

extensively 3 far; **4** much; **7** greatly; **9** lengthily; **10** everywhere; **11** expansively; **12** considerably; **13** significantly; **15** comprehensively; PHRASES: **2, 1, 5, 6** to a great extent, to a large extent; **2, 5, 7** in every quarter; **3, 3, 4** far and wide; **3, 4** all over; **3, 4, 3, 4** all over the shop *UK*; **3, 5, 4** the world over; **3, 6** all around; **4, 3, 3** high and low, near and far; **5, 3, 3** under the sun; **5, 5, 3** every which way; **6, 3, 3** inside and out. *See also* **extensive**

extent 4 area, size; **5** level, limit, range; **6** amount, degree; **8** boundary, coverage.

exterior 3 pod; **4** aura, face, hull, husk, look, mien, rind, skin; **5** crust, facet, front, outer, shell; **6** border, cortex, façade, facing, fringe, veneer; **7** coating, cuticle, outdoor, outline, outside, outward, surface; **8** covering, envelope, external; **9** cuticular, epidermis, periphery; **10** appearance, epidermoid, integument, peripheral; **11** exoskeleton, superficies; **12** integumental, surroundings; **13** circumference.

exterminate 4 kill; **5** erase, purge; **6** murder; **7** destroy; **8** decimate, exorcize, massacre; **9** eliminate, eradicate, liquidate, slaughter, terminate; **10** annihilate, deracinate, obliterate; **11** assassinate; PHRASES: **2, 4, 4** do away with; **3, 3** rub out; **3, 3, 2** get rid of; **4, 3** root out, take out, wipe out.

external 5 outer; **7** distant, foreign, outdoor, outside, outward, without; **8** exterior; **9** extrinsic; **10** peripheral; **11** superficial.

externalize 5 utter, voice; **6** convey, reveal; **7** express, project; PHRASES: **3, 3, 4, 5** get off your chest; **4, 5, 2** give voice to; **5, 3** bring out.

externally 7 visibly; **8** alfresco; **9** outwardly, seemingly; **10** apparently; PHRASES: **2, 3, 4** in the open; **2, 3, 4, 2** on the face of it; **2, 3, 4, 3** in the open air; **2, 3, 7** on the outside, on the surface; **2, 3, 8** on the exterior; **3, 2, 5** out of doors. *See also* **external**

extinct 4 dead, lost; **5** passé; **6** lapsed; **7** defunct, expired; **8** obsolete, vanished; **9** destroyed; PHRASES: **5, 3** wiped out.

extinct animal *See* **dinosaur, prehis-**

toric animal

extinct bird 3 moa; 4 dodo; 9 Aepyornis;
13 Archaeopteryx; PHRASES: 5, 3 great auk;
8, 4 elephant bird; 9, 6 passenger pigeon.
See also **dinosaur**

extinction 4 loss; 5 death; 8 oblivion; 11
destruction, elimination; 12 annihilation,
obliteration, obsolescence; 13 disappearance, extermination.

extinguish 3 end; 5 douse, snuff; 6
quench; 7 destroy, eclipse, obscure, smother; 8 outshine; 10 overshadow; PHRASES: 2,
4, 4 do away with; 4, 2 show up; 4, 3 stub
out; 4, 4 take away; 5, 3 snuff out.

extol *See* **praise**

extort 5 claim, exact, force, screw, wrest,
wring; 6 demand, wrench; 7 extract,
squeeze; 9 blackmail.

extortion 5 force, usury; 7 gouging,
swindle; 8 coercion, exaction, pressure; 9
blackmail, squeezing; PHRASES: 3-3 rip-off;
4-8 loan-sharking.

extra 3 new, odd, tip; 4 find, gain, more,
perk, plus; 5 above, added, bonus, fresh,
gimme, graft, spare, treat, ultra; 6 beyond,
luxury, second; 7 benefit, freebie, further,
oddment, surplus; 8 addition, giveaway,
gratuity, reserves, sundries, trimming; 9
byproduct *UK*, provision; 10 additional,
decorative, especially, ornamental, peripheral, perquisite, supplement; 11 auxiliaries,
superfluity, superfluous; 12 extravagance,
particularly; 13 exceptionally, reinforcement, supernumerary; 14 supererogatory;
PHRASES: 2, 3 on top; 2, 8 in addition; 3-2
add-on; 3, 2, 3, 4 bit on the side; 4, 3, 4 odds
and ends, odds and sods *UK*.

extra (extra person) 5 locum; 6 backup, relief; 9 auxiliary; 10 substitute; 13 reinforcement; PHRASES: 3, 5, 3 the other man; 5-
2 stand-in.

extract 3 get, win; 4 drag, fish, free, mine;
5 force, juice, press, quote, steep, wrest,
wring; 6 avulse, decoct, dredge, elixir,
evulse, extort, infuse, obtain, purify, refine,
remove, render, spirit, uproot; 7 distill, essence, excerpt, isolate, passage, squeeze,
unearth; 8 abstract, citation, clipping, condense, infusion, liberate, separate, withdraw; 9 decoction, disengage, eliminate,
eradicate, extricate, quotation, selection; 10
deracinate; 11 concentrate, distilllate; 12 es-
sentialize, quintessence; PHRASES: 3, 2 dig

up; 3, 3 dig out, get out, rip out; 4, 3 draw
out, fish out, grub out, haul out, pick out,
pull out, rake out, root out, take out, tear
out; 5, 3 cream off, pluck out, wrest out; 6,
3 winkle out *UK*, wrench out; 7, 3 wheedle
out *UK*.

extraction 3 tug; 4 line, pull; 5 birth; 6
family, mining, origin, wrench; 7 descent,
drawing, fishing, lineage, removal; 8 ancestry, avulsion, dredging, evulsion, heritage; 9 uprooting; 10 liberation, withdrawal;
11 abstraction, elimination, eradication, extrication; 12 deracination; 13 disengagement; PHRASES: 6, 3 taking out; 7, 3 drawing
out, pulling out.

extractor 4 pump; 5 press; 6 mangle,
reamer, siphon; 7 pipette, syringe, wringer;
8 squeezer; 9 aspirator, separator; PHRASES:
5, 5 apple corer; 6, 4 vacuum pump; 6, 6
cherry stoner.

extraneous 5 alien, apart, extra, minor,
other; 6 abroad, exotic; 7 distant, foreign,
outward, strange, trivial; 8 external, overseas, separate; 9 different, extrinsic, pointless, redundant, secondary, unrelated; 10
immaterial, incidental, irrelevant, outlandish, peripheral, pleonastic; 11 superficial,
superfluous, unconnected, unessential, unimportant, unnecessary; 12 adventitious,
disconnected, inapplicable, otherworldly;
13 inappropriate, insignificant; PHRASES: 3,
3, 7 off the subject; 6, 3, 5 beside the point.

extraneous (be extraneous) 6 ramble; 7 digress; PHRASES: 2, 3, 2, 1, 7 go off at
a tangent; 4, 3, 5 miss the point.

extraordinary 3 odd; 5 great; 7 special,
strange, unusual; 10 particular, remarkable,
unexpected; 11 astonishing, exceptional.

extravagance 5 extra, folly, spree, treat,
waste; 6 luxury; 7 splurge; 9 profusion; 10
indulgence, inordinacy, profligacy; 11 exorbitance, flamboyance, ostentation, prodigality, squandering; 12 improvidence,
intemperance, overspending; 14 overindulgence; PHRASES: 5, 2, 8 going to extremes; 5,
3, 3 going too far; 6, 2, 2 piling it on; 7, 4
running riot; 8, 5 spending spree; 9, 2 overdoing it. *See also* **extravagant**

extravagant 5 showy; 6 lavish, ornate; 7
profuse; 8 overdone, prodigal, wasteful; 9
elaborate, excessive, grandiose, unthrifty;
10 exorbitant, flamboyant, immoderate, inordinate, outrageous, overstated, profligate, thriftless, uneconomic; 11

exaggerated, intemperate, spendthrift; **12** ostentatious; PHRASES: **3, 5** OTT gaudy.

extravagant (be extravagant) 6 lavish, overdo; **9** overshoot, overspend; **11** overindulge; PHRASES: **2, 2, 8** go to extremes; **2, 3, 3** go too far; **3, 4** run riot; **4, 2, 2** pile it on; **8, 3, 4** overstep the mark.

extravaganza *See* **show**

extreme 3 end; **4** edge, pole; **5** acute, great, risky; **6** margin, severe, utmost; **7** intense, maximum, radical, zealous; **8** boundary, exciting, farthest, furthest, ultimate; **9** dangerous, excessive, fanatical, outermost, punishing, thrilling; **10** tremendous.

extremist 5 rebel; **7** fanatic, radical; **8** activist; **9** fanatical, terrorist; **13** revolutionary.

extremity 3 arm, leg; **4** edge, foot, hand, limb; **5** limit; **6** margin; **7** extreme; **8** boundary.

extricate 6 detach, remove; **7** extract; **11** disentangle; PHRASES: **3, 3** get out.

extrovert 6 social; **8** friendly, outgoing, sociable; **10** befriender, gregarious, socializer; PHRASES: **4, 4** live wire.

exudate 3 pee, wee; **5** sweat, tears, urine; **6** saliva; **7** spittle; **9** exudation, urination; **12** perspiration.

exude 4 leak, ooze, show; **7** display, radiate, release, secrete; **9** discharge; PHRASES: **4, 3** give off, give out.

eye 2 ee; **3** orb; **4** gaze, ogle; **5** optic, watch; **6** glance, peeper; **7** observe; **10** perception; **11** discernment; **12** appreciation; **14** discrimination, perceptiveness; PHRASES: **4, 2** gaze at, look at; **5, 2** stare at.

eye (parts) 3 rod; **4** cone, iris, lens; **5** fovea, orbit, pupil; **6** cornea, retina, sclera; **7** choroid, eyelash; **11** conjunctiva; PHRASES: **5, 4** blind spot; **5, 5** optic nerve.

eye (treatment for eye) 7 Braille, eyewash, glasses; **8** optician; **9** optometry; **10** spectacles; **13** ophthalmology; PHRASES: **3, 5** eye drops; **5, 3** glass eye, guide dog; **5, 5** white stick *UK*; **6, 3, 3** Seeing Eye dog; **7, 4** talking book.

eyeblack 7 mascara.

eyebright 8 euphrasy.

eyeglasses 5 specs; **10** spectacles.

eyehole 8 peephole.

eyepiece 6 ocular; **8** eyeglass.

eyesore 4 blot; **6** eyeful, horror; **7** blemish; **8** disgrace; **9** carbuncle; **11** monstrosity.

F

F 2 fa; **3** key; **4** note; **5** forte; **6** Fellow, female; **10** Fahrenheit.

fabric 3 fur, PVC, rag; **4** felt, lamé, silk, warp, weft, wool, work; **5** baize, build, cloth, crepe, denim, frame, gauze, linen, loden, nylon, print, rayon, satin, stuff, terry, tulle, tweed, twill, voile, weave; **6** alpaca, angora, basics, burlap, calico, canvas, carpet, chintz, cotton, damask, facing, fleece, jersey, madras, makeup, mohair, muslin, poplin, sateen, tiling, tissue, velour, velvet, vicuna, Wilton; **7** acrylic, brocade, chiffon, content, drapery, fishnet, flannel, gingham, hessian, leather, masonry, organdy, percale, roofing, sacking, spandex, taffeta, textile, texture, ticking, viscose, worsted; **8** cashmere, chambray, chenille, cladding, corduroy, cretonne, material, moleskin, moquette, pashmina, toweling; **9** astrakhan, Axminster, brickwork, carpeting, framework, gabardine, grosgrain, horsehair, lambswool, materials, polyester, sailcloth, shahtoosh, stonework, structure, substance, synthetic, tarpaulin; **10** broadcloth, foundation, seersucker, winceyette *UK*; **11** cheesecloth, composition, flannelette; **12** constitution; **14** superstructure; PHRASES: **4, 5** yard goods; **5, 2, 5** crêpe de Chine; **5, 4** camel hair; **5, 8** terry toweling; **6, 5** screen print.

fabricate 3 lie; **4** fake, form, make; **5** build, feign, hatch; **6** devise, invent; **7** concoct, imitate, produce; **8** assemble, contrive, engineer, simulate; **9** construct, formulate; **11** counterfeit, manufacture; PHRASES: **3, 8** put together; **4, 1, 4** spin a yarn; **4, 2** cook up, make up; **5, 2** dream up, trump up.

fabrication 3 fib, lie; **4** fake; **7** fiction, forgery; **8** assembly, building, creation; **9** falsehood, invention; **10** production; **11** counterfeit, manufacture; **12** construction.

fabulous 8 mythical; **9** legendary, marvelous; **10** fictitious, incredible.

facade 3 act; **4** face, fake, gild, mask, sham, show; **5** bluff, front, gloss; **7** seeming, varnish; **8** bluffing, disguise; **9** semblance, whitewash; **10** appearance, embroidery, masquerade, simulacrum; **11** fanfaronade, ostentation; **12** dissemblance; **13** deodorization, dissimulation, embellishment; PHRASES: **5, 2** touch up; **5, 3** false air; **5, 4** false show; **5, 5** false front, false light; **6-8** window-dressing; **8, 2** touching up.

face 3 air, mug, pan; **4** bold, clad, defy, dial, gall, look, meet, mien, mush, nose, phiz *UK*, play, puss, side, wall; **5** admit, fight, front, panel, pluck, revet; **6** accept, aspect, façade, kisser, parget, phizog *UK*, render, stucco, tackle, visage; **7** encrust, outside, plaster, profile, surface, towards; **8** audacity, boldness, confront, features, frontage, typeface; **9** challenge, encounter, impudence, insolence, wallpaper, whitewash; **10** appearance, effrontery, expression; **11** countenance; PHRASES: **2, 5, 2** be in front of; **3, 4** mug shot; **4, 4** cope with, deal with; **4, 6** look toward; **4, 7** play against; **5, 2, 5, 2** stand in front of; **6, 3** brazen out; **6, 4** analog dial; **7, 7** digital display.

face (make a face) 4 girn, leer, pout; **5** frown, scowl, snarl, sneer; **7** grimace.

face (part of face) 3 eye, jaw; **4** brow, chin, jowl, lips, nose; **5** beard, cheek, chops, mouth; **6** temple; **7** eyebrow, jawline; **8** forehead, mandible.

facet 4 face, part, side; **5** plane; **6** aspect, façade, factor; **7** feature, surface; **9** component.

facetious 5 droll, silly, witty; **7** playful; **8** flippant, humorous; **12** lighthearted; **13** inappropriate; PHRASES: 3-5 ill-timed; 3-6 ill-judged.

facile *See* **easy**

facile *See* **superficial**

facility 5 flair, skill; 6 talent; 7 feature, service; 8 capacity, resource; 9 advantage, provision; 10 capability.

facing *See* **opposite**

facsimile *See* **copy**

fact 3 act, gen *UK*; 4 case, deed, dirt, dope, info; 5 datum, event, point, scoop, score, truth; 6 detail, verity; 7 reality; 9 actuality, happening, statistic; 10 occurrence; PHRASES: 3, 5, 5 the whole story; 3, 6 the basics; 3, 7 the picture; 3, 9 the realities, the specifics; 3, 10 the essentials; 3, 12 the fundamentals; 4, 3, 5 nuts and bolts; 4, 8 fait accompli; 5, 4 what's what; 5, 5 brass tacks; 5-6 nitty-gritty.

faction 4 bloc, rift, sect, side; 5 group, party, split; 6 breach, circle, clique, schism, strife; 7 discord, rupture, section; 8 conflict, disunity, division, offshoot; 10 contention, disharmony, dissension; PHRASES: 8, 5 splinter group.

factor 2 ph, rh; 4 load, part, unit; 5 agent, cause, issue, power, thing; 6 aspect, broker, reason; 7 element, feature, quality, steward; 9 component, influence; 12 circumstance; 13 consideration.

factory *See* **plant**

factual 4 hard; 6 honest; 8 accurate, truthful; 9 authentic, objective, realistic; 10 verifiable; PHRASES: 4, 4 bona fide.

faculty 4 gift; 5 knack, power, sense, staff; 6 talent; 7 ability; 8 facility, function, teachers; 9 endowment; 10 capability, professors; PHRASES: 8, 4 teaching body; 8, 5 teaching staff.

fad *See* **fashion**

fade 3 die; 4 fail, flag, pale, tire, wane, wilt; 5 abate, droop, lower; 6 bleach, recede, weaken, wither; 7 decline, dwindle, lighten, shrivel; 8 decrease, diminish, languish; 9 disappear, evaporate; PHRASES: 3, 4 die away; 4, 3 ~ out, tail off; 4, 4 ~ away; 5, 3 taper off; 5, 4 waste away; 6, 5 become paler.

fading *See* **disappearing**

fag 4 tire; 5 chore *UK*; 9 cigarette *UK*.

fail 3 ail, die; 4 bomb, fade, fall, flag, flop, fold, lose, miss, poop, sink, stop, tire, wane; 5 crash, droop, fluff, flunk; 6 bungle, weaken; 7 blunder, decline, dwindle; 8 collapse, diminish, miscarry; 9 disappear; 10 disappoint; 11 discontinue, disillusion; PHRASES: 2, 2, 3, 4 go to the dogs, go to the wall; 2, 2, 3, 5 go on the blink, go on the rocks; 2, 3, 2, 8 go out of business; 2, 4 go bust, go down; 2, 4-6 go pear-shaped *UK*; 2, 5 go under; 2, 5, 2 go belly up; 2, 8 go bankrupt; 3, 4 let down, not pass; 3, 4, 3 not come off; 3, 4, 3, 5 not make the grade; 3, 7, 4 let someone down; 4, 1, 4, 2 make a hash of; 4, 1, 5 draw a blank; 4, 2 ball up, give up, pack up *UK*, slip up, wind up; 4, 2, 7 come to nothing; 4, 3 fink out; 4, 3, 4 bite the dust, miss the boat, miss the mark; 4, 4 fall flat, shut down; 4-4 nose-dive; 4, 5 fall short; 4, 7 stop working; 5, 2 balls up *UK*, close up, seize up; 5, 2, 1, 4 grind to a halt; 5, 3 bogue out; 5, 4 break down; 6, 3 fizzle out.

failed 3 dud; 4 weak; 5 empty, kaput; 6 ailing, closed, futile; 7 aborted, botched, bungled, failing, flunked, unlucky, useless; 8 abortive, bankrupt, bootless, bungling, hopeless, shutdown; 9 blundered, fruitless, stillborn; 10 blundering, disastrous, miscarried, profitless; 11 ineffective, ineffectual, miscarrying, unfortunate; 12 unproductive, unsuccessful; 13 inefficacious; PHRASES: 2, 3, 5 on the rocks; 6, 2 washed up.

failure 3 end; 4 fall, flop, halt, mess, miss, ruin; 5 botch, crash, error, stall; 6 ailing, bungle, defect, fiasco; 7 blunder, closure, debacle, decline, default, failing, letdown, mistake, neglect, seizure, setback; 8 bungling, collapse, comedown, disaster, downfall, futility, omission, shortage, shutdown, stalling, stoppage, weakness; 9 breakdown, shortfall; 10 bankruptcy, incapacity, insolvency, negligence, withdrawal; 11 catastrophe, fallibility, frustration, malfunction, miscarriage, nonfeasance, shortcoming; PHRASES: 2, 4 no luck; 3, 4 the pits; 4-2 slip-up; 4, 4 near miss; 4, 5 lost labor; 4, 7 vain attempt.

faint 3 dim, low; 4 dead, dull, hazy, pale, soft, weak; 5 bated, dizzy, faded, giddy, muted, piano, quiet, swoon, woozy; 6 damped, feeble, gentle, hoarse, hushed, slight, wobbly; 7 distant, muffled, shadowy, stifled, subdued, syncope, unclear; 8 collapse, unsteady; 9 inaudible, voiceless, whispered; 10 diminished, indistinct, pianissimo; 11 lightheaded; 13 imperceptible;

PHRASES: **3, 2, 7** out of earshot; **4, 3** pass out; **4, 4** fall down; **4-5** half-heard; **4, 5, 6** with bated breath; **5, 3** black out; **5, 4** sotto voce.

faint (sound faint, faint sound) 3 hum, low, pad; **4** fizz, hiss, moan, purr, roll, sigh, soft, weak; **5** croon, drone, sough, whine; **6** mumble, murmur, mutter, rustle, sizzle; **7** breathe, crackle, whisper; **9** susurrate, undertone; PHRASES: **4, 4, 5** drop one's voice.

fair 4 even, fete, fine, gala, game, good, just, pale, sale, show; **5** blond, clear, fayre *UK*, light, right, sunny; **6** bazaar, bright, decent, equity, flaxen, honest, lovely, pretty; **7** average; **8** adequate, balanced, festival, mediocre, moderate, ordinary, passable, pleasant, pleasing, unbiased; **9** beautiful, cloudless, equitable, favorable, honorable, impartial, objective; **10** acceptable, attractive, evenhanded, exhibition, exposition, reasonable; **13** dispassionate; PHRASES: **3-2-3-4** run-of-the-mill; **3-6** tow-headed; **4-6** open-minded; **4-7** good-looking; **6, 4** county ~.

fairly 5 quite *UK*; **6** rather; **8** properly, somewhat; **9** literally; **10** absolutely, completely, positively, reasonably; **11** practically; **12** legitimately. *See also* **fair**

fairness 7 justice; **8** equality; **11** objectivity; **12** impartiality. *See also* **fair**

fairy 3 elf, fay, imp; **4** peri, puck; **5** genie, jinni, nymph, pixie; **6** sprite; **7** brownie, gremlin; **9** hobgoblin; **10** leprechaun.

faith 5 trust; **7** loyalty; **8** devotion, reliance; **10** commitment, confidence, conviction, dedication; **12** faithfulness.

faithful 4 real, true; **5** close, exact, loyal; **6** trusty; **7** correct, devoted, staunch; **8** accurate, constant, reliable, truthful; **9** authentic, committed, dedicated, honorable, realistic; **10** believable, dependable; **11** trustworthy; PHRASES: **4, 2, 4** true to life; **4-4** true-blue.

faithless 5 false, shaky; **6** fickle, untrue; **7** atheist; **8** disloyal; **9** betraying, deceitful, deserting, dishonest, seditious; **10** inconstant, perfidious, rebellious, treasonous, unfaithful, unreliable; **11** disobedient, duplicitous, treacherous; **12** undependable; **13** untrustworthy; PHRASES: **3, 2, 2, 7** not to be trusted; **3-5** two-faced; **6-7** double-dealing; **6-8** double-crossing.

faithlessness 6 deceit; **7** falsity, perfidy, sellout, treason; **8** betrayal, sedition; **9** defection, desertion, duplicity, rebellion, treachery; **10** dishonesty, disloyalty, infidelity; **11** inconstancy, **12** disobedience; **13** unreliability; **14** tergiversation; **15** undependability; PHRASES: **1-4** U-turn; **3, 5** bad faith; **4, 2, 3, 4** stab in the back; **5, 4** Judas kiss; **5-4** volte-face; **6, 2, 5** breach of faith; **6, 2, 7** breach of promise; **6, 4** broken word; **6, 7** broken promise; **6-7** double-dealing; **6-8** double-crossing. *See also* **faithless**

fake 3 act, bum, cod; **4** copy, faux, junk, mock, sham; **5** bogus, dummy, false, feign, forge, fraud, junky, paste, phony *UK*, pseud *UK*, quack; **6** ersatz, forged, invent, phoney, pseudo, tinsel; **7** bootleg, falsify, forgery, garbage, pretend, replica, rubbish; **8** simulate; **9** charlatan, dissemble, fabricate, facsimile, imitation, imitative, replicate, reproduce, simulated; **10** artificial, simulation; **11** counterfeit; PHRASES: **4-2** mock-up.

fall 3 die, dip, end, sin; **4** dive, drop, flop, ruin, sink, trip; **5** close, crash, spill; **6** autumn, golden, plunge, rapids, reduce, season, sunset, tumble; **7** cascade, decline, descend, descent, dipping, equinox, failure, harvest, plummet, stumble; **8** autumnal, cataract, collapse, comedown, decrease, demotion, downfall, dropping, plunging, pratfall, swooping; **9** reduction, stumbling, waterfall; **10** Michaelmas, plummeting, titubation; **11** culmination, humiliation, overturning; PHRASES: **2, 4** go down; **2, 4, 4, 5** go head over heels; **4, 2, 3, 4** ~ of the leaf; **4, 3** back end; **4, 4** come down, trip over; **4, 4, 1, 5** drop like a stone; **5, 2, 5** point of Libra; **6, 6** Indian summer; **7, 4** harvest moon, harvest time *UK*, hunter's moon.

fallen 4 sunk; **6** soused, sunken; **8** downcast; **9** submerged; **10** downfallen, downthrown.

fallible 4 weak; **5** frail, human; **6** mortal; **9** imperfect.

falling 6 diving; **7** dipping, ducking, gliding, sinking, sliding; **8** coasting, dropping, flopping, plunging, skidding, slipping, spilling, stooping, swooping, toppling, tripping, tumbling; **9** declining, dwindling, lessening, sprawling, stumbling, subsiding; **10** decreasing, plummeting; **11** diminishing, precipitous; **13** deteriorating; PHRASES: **4-6** nose-diving.

falling star 6 meteor; **9** meteorite.

fallow 4 idle; **6** unused; **7** sterile; **8** inactive, unplowed, unseeded; **9** infertile, unplanted; **10** unploughed *UK*; **12** uncultivated, unproductive.

false **4** dawn, fake, sham, step; **5** alarm, bogus, phony *UK*, wrong; **6** copied, forged, phoney, untrue; **7** pretend, seeming; **8** delusive, mistaken, specious, spurious; **9** deceitful, deceiving, deceptive, dishonest, erroneous, imitation, incorrect, insincere, simulated, truthless, ungenuine; **10** artificial, fabricated, fallacious, fictitious, mendacious, misleading, untruthful; **11** counterfeit, dissembling, unveracious; **12** hypocritical; PHRASES: **3-2** put-on; **4-2** made-up.

false (be false) **3** lie; **4** mock; **5** trick; **6** betray, delude; **7** beguile, deceive, falsify, mislead; **8** misguide; **9** dissemble, misdirect, misinform; PHRASES: **3, 1, 5, 5** lay a false scent; **3, 4, 4** not ring true; **4, 4, 2, 4** have feet of clay; **4, 5** ring false; **4, 9** lack integrity; **6, 5** string along.

false alarm **4** hoax; **5** bogey, scare; **6** canard; PHRASES: **3, 2, 4** cry of wolf.

falsehood **3** fib, lie; **4** lies, myth, tale; **5** error, lying, story; **6** canard, deceit, sleaze; **7** fallacy, falsity, fiction, untruth; **8** delusion, unverity; **9** deception, imposture, invention, mendacity, unreality; **10** dishonesty, inveracity; **11** fabrication; **12** dissemblance, spuriousness; PHRASES: **4, 4** tall tale; **5, 4** fairy tale; **5, 5** fairy story *UK*.

false person **4** liar; **5** cheat, fraud, pseud *UK*; **6** hoaxer, humbug; **7** plotter, schemer, seducer, traitor; **8** betrayer, Casanova, imposter, informer, perjurer, Pharisee, saboteur, swindler; **9** charlatan, hypocrite, pretender; **13** counterfeiter; PHRASES: **3, 3** con man; **3, 4** Don Juan; **5-5** goody-goody; **5, 8** Judas Iscariot; **6, 5** double agent; **6-7** double-crosser; **8, 6** Benedict Arnold; **10, 3** confidence man.

false thing **4** bill; **6** mirage; **7** mockery; **13** hallucination; PHRASES: **3, 5** bum steer; **4-1-3-4** will-o'-the-wisp; **4-3, 4** nine-bob note *UK*; **5, 3** paste gem; **5, 4** fool's gold; **6, 5** Trojan horse; **6, 7** Hitler diaries; **11, 4** counterfeit note.

falsification **3** fix, lie; **4** fake, myth; **5** fable; **6** canard, faking, fiddle, legend; **7** fiction, figment, forgery, rigging, warping; **8** fiddling, garbling, juggling, slanting, twisting; **9** collusion, deception, doctoring, invention, misciting, straining, tampering; **10** alteration, concoction, distortion, falsifying, perversion; **11** fabrication; **12** manipulation; **13** confabulation; **14** counterfeiting; PHRASES: **3, 3, 1, 4** nod and a wink; **5-2** frame-up; **5, 8** sharp practice.

falsify **3** fix, lie, rig; **4** fake, warp; **5** alter, forge, frame, plant, slant, twist; **6** change, doctor, fiddle, garble, invent, wangle; **7** collude, concoct, distort, imagine, pervert, retouch; **8** misquote, misstate; **9** fabricate, misreport; **10** manipulate; **11** confabulate, counterfeit, mythologize; **12** misinterpret, misrepresent; PHRASES: **3, 4** cry wolf; **4, 3, 5** cook the books; **5, 2** trump up; **6, 4** tamper with.

falter **3** yaw; **4** back, fade, fail, flag, reel, rock, roll, sway, tack, trip, turn, veer, wane; **5** abate, lurch, pause, pitch, shake, swing, waver; **6** fumble, teeter, totter, weaken, wobble; **7** shuttle, stagger, stammer, stumble, stutter, tremble; **8** hesitate; **9** vacillate; PHRASES: **4, 2** trip up; **4, 3** tail off.

familiar **4** cozy, easy, free, near; **5** aware, banal, close, known, plain, stock, thick, trite, usual; **6** beaten, common, folksy, friend, homely, simple, wonted; **7** clichéd, current, haymish *Yiddish*, natural, regular, relaxed, trodden, typical; **8** everyday, favorite, frequent, friendly, habitual, informal, intimate, ordinary, personal; **9** customary, hackneyed, household, prevalent, recurring; **10** accustomed, acquainted, conversant, unaffected, unoriginal, widespread; **11** commonplace, established, traditional; **12** recognizable; **13** unexceptional; PHRASES: **2-2-4** up-to-date; **2, 4** au fait; **2, 4, 4** at ease with, at home with; **2, 8, 5** on intimate terms, on visiting terms; **3-2-3** arm-in-arm; **4, 2** used to; **4-2-4** hand-in-hand; **4-2-5** hand-in-glove; **4-4** well-worn; **4-5** well-known; **4-7** time-honored; **4-8** well-informed; **5, 2, 7** thick as thieves; **6, 7** garden variety; **9, 2** cognizant of.

familiarity **4** ease; **5** skill; **7** fluency; **8** affinity, devotion, firmness, intimacy, trueness; **9** constancy, expertise, homeyness, knowledge, triedness; **10** casualness, commitment, dedication, experience, friendship, simplicity; **11** devotedness, informality, staunchness; **12** acquaintance, friendliness; **13** steadfastness, understanding; **14** inseparability; PHRASES: **3, 6, 5** the common touch; **4-3** know-how. See also **familiar**

family 3 kin; 4 clan, kind, line, type; 5 blood, breed, class, folks, genus, group, tribe; 6 circle, people, strain; 7 dynasty, lineage, private, species, variety; 8 category, children, domestic, everyday, intimate, kinsfolk; 9 ancestors, community, household, relations *UK*, relatives; 11 descendants, domiciliary; PHRASES: 4, 3, 3 kith and kin; 5, 4 loved ones; 5, 6 first ~; 6, 4 ~ unit.

family of languages 5 Aryan, Bantu, Carib, Malay; 6 Baltic, Celtic, Fijian, Italic, Manchu, Tagula, Turkic; 7 African, Austric, Hamitic, Romance, Semitic, Tarapon; 8 Anatolic, Germanic, Hellenic, Mongolic, Slavonic, Teutonic, Turanian; 9 Anatolian, Dravidian, Sabellian, Tocharian; 10 Melanesian; 11 Micronesian; 12 Austronesian, Scandinavian; PHRASES: 4-6 Ural-Altaic, Zulu-Kaffir; 4-7 Afro-Asiatic, Indo-Iranian, Sino-Tibetan; 4-8 Indo-European, Indo-Germanic; 5-5 Finno-Ugric; 5-7 Assam-Burmese, Paleo-Asiatic; 5-8 Balto-Slavonic; 6-7 Hamito-Semitic.

famous (become famous) 3, 3, 9 hit the headlines; 4, 2, 2, 3, 3 make it to the top.

fan 4 blow, cool, fuel, waft, wave; 6 foamer, foment, hacker, incite; 7 agitate, provoke; 8 increase, railbird, vaulting; 9 encourage, percolate, stimulate; PHRASES: 4, 2 stir up. *See also* **fanatic**

fanatic 3 fan; 4 buff; 6 zealot; 7 devotee, extreme, radical; 8 addicted, crusader, follower; 9 extremist, fanatical, obsessive; 10 enthusiast, passionate; 14 fundamentalist.

fanciful 9 fantastic, imaginary, whimsical; 12 unbelievable.

fancy 3 fad; 4 hope, posh, whim; 5 craze, dream, hobby, mania, phase, shine, showy, think, trend; 6 assume, choice, desire, lavish, notion, ornate, relish, rococo, swanky, vagary; 7 believe, caprice, conjure, craving, fantasy, imagine, picture, reverie, suppose, upscale; 8 conceive, consider, daydream, illusion, pleasure, upmarket; 9 elaborate, expensive, intricate, visualize; 10 decorative, ornamental; 11 extravagant, infatuation; PHRASES: 6, 2, 3, 3 castle in the air; 6, 2, 5 castle in Spain.

fancy dress 3 rig, wig; 4 gear, gown, mask; 5 armor, beard, guise, plume, silks, tunic; 6 buskin, motley, outfit; 7 costume; 8 disguise; 10 camouflage, masquerade; 11 bedizenment, greasepaint; PHRASES: 3, 3, 5 cap and bells; 4-2 make-up.

fanfare 3 cry; 4 hymn, pomp, yell; 5 cheer, glory, shout; 6 hurrah, huzzah, praise, salute; 7 display, hosanna, ovation; 8 applause, ballyhoo, flourish; 10 hallelujah; 12 thanksgiving; 15 congratulations; PHRASES: 5, 6 three cheers; 7, 5 trumpet blast.

fanlike 7 deltoid, palmate, splayed; 12 spreadeagled; PHRASES: 5-6 delta-shaped.

fantasize 4 muse; 5 dream; 6 invent; 7 imagine, picture; 8 contrive, daydream, idealize; 9 poeticize, visualize; 10 rhapsodize; 11 romanticize; PHRASES: 7, 2 conjure up.

fantastic 5 great; 6 absurd, unreal; 7 bizarre, Laputan; 8 fanciful, quixotic; 9 grotesque, visionary, whimsical; 10 outlandish; 11 extravagant, impractical; 12 otherworldly, preposterous; PHRASES: 3, 5 all right; 4, 4 well done; 4-5 airy-fairy *UK*; 4, 8 Rube Goldberg; 5, 8 Heath Robinson *UK*.

fantasy 4 hope; 5 bogey, dream, error, fancy, ghost, image, vapor; 6 desire, mirage, shadow, vision, whimsy; 7 caprice, chimera, dimness, fiction, phantom, specter; 8 daydream, delusion, illusion; 9 nightmare, unreality; 10 apparition; 11 fabrication, imagination; 13 hallucination; PHRASES: 4, 5 pipe dream; 4, 7 Fata Morgana; 4-7 make-believe; 7, 6 wildest dreams.

far 4 much; 6 remote; 7 distant, faraway, greatly; 12 considerably; 13 significantly; PHRASES: 1, 3 a lot; 3, 3 ~ off; 3, 3, 4 ~ and wide; 3, 4 ~ away; 3-5 far-flung; 3, 6 ~ afield.

fare 2 do; 3 fee; 4 cope, cost, food, meal, menu; 5 payer, price, rider; 6 client, dishes, manage, tariff, ticket; 8 customer; 9 passenger; 10 provisions; PHRASES: 3, 2 get by, get on.

farewell 4 exit; 7 goodbye, leaving, send-off; 9 departure; PHRASES: 2, 6 au revoir; 3-3 bye-bye; 3, 11 auf Wiedersehen *UK*.

far-fetched *See* **unbelievable**

farm 3 dig, hoe, mow, sow; 4 fold, grow, plot, plow *UK*, rake, reap, stud, till, toft *UK*, turn, weed, work; 5 croft, dairy, delve, drill, glean, hutch, plant, raise, ranch, stall; 6 aviary, corral, estate, gather, grange *UK*, harrow, plough *UK*, rancho, spread, stable, swathe; 7 demesne, harvest, haybarn, holding, kibbutz, kolkhoz, piggery, station; 8 barnyard, hacienda, henhouse, irrigate, rotavate *UK*, steading *UK*; **9** cultivate, farmhouse, farmstead, fertilize, homestead, sharecrop; **10** plantation; **12** smallholding *UK*; PHRASES: **4, 3, 4** till the soil, work the land.

farmable **6** arable, fallow, farmed, grazed, plowed, tilled; **7** cropped, fertile; **8** fruitful, plowable, tillable; **10** cultivable, productive.

farmland **3** lea, row; **4** gate, mead, plot; **5** field, glebe, paddy, patch, piece, ridge, stake, strip; **6** arable, furrow, meadow, parcel, swathe; **7** acreage, paddock, pasture, seedbed, stubble, terrace, windrow; **8** clearing, hayfield, hedgerow, quickset *UK*, tramline; **9** cornfield, enclosure, grassland; **10** wheatfield; PHRASES: **4, 5** rice paddy.

farm tool **4** plow *UK*, race, rick; **5** baler, churn, crush, drill, mower, stook; **6** binder, feeder, harrow, midden, plough *UK*, ridger, scythe, shovel, sickle, tedder, topper, trough; **7** breaker, combine, drinker, feedbin, haycock, hayrack, hayrick *UK*, haywain, plasher, scubbin, sprayer, swather, tractor, trailer; **8** buckrake, haystack, muckfork; **9** deadstock, feedstore, harvester, irrigator, pitchfork, Rotavator™, subsoiler; **10** cultivator; **11** hedgecutter; **12** muckspreader; PHRASES: **3, 5** pea viner; **4, 4** flat roll; **4, 5** seed drill; **4, 6** bale sledge; **4, 7** bale carrier, bale wrapper, disc harrows, disk harrows; **5, 3** grain bin; **5, 5** flail mower; **6, 5** rotary mower, silage clamp; **7, 4** reaping hook; **9, 4** Cambridge roll.

farm worker **4** crew, hand; **5** groom; **6** cowboy, cowman, drover, gaucho, herder, ostler, pigman; **7** bailiff, cowgirl, cowhand, cowherd, farmboy, hostler, laborer, manager, plowman, puncher; **8** buckaroo, goatherd, gooseboy, herdsman, milkmaid, shepherd, stockman, swanherd, wrangler; **9** dairyhand, dairymaid, goosegirl, ploughman, stableboy, stableman, swineherd; **10** cowpuncher; **11** shepherdess, stockperson; PHRASES: **4, 4** farm hand; **6-6** bronco-buster.

far-reaching **9** extensive; PHRASES: **3-5** far-flung; **4-7** wide-ranging; **4-8** wide-reaching.

farsighted **10** presbyopic; **13** hypermetropic.

fashion **3** cut, fad, fit, hew, set, way; **4** cast, chic, form, look, make, mode, mold, rage, turn; **5** adapt, alter, build, carve, craze, forge, frame, model, round, shape, style,

taste, trend, usage, vogue; **6** chisel, create, custom, devise, figure, manner, method, sculpt, tailor; **7** pattern, produce; **8** approach, elegance; **9** construct, fabricate, formulate, technique, transform, vestiture; PHRASES: **2, 5** in thing; **3, 3** cut out; **3, 4** new look; **3, 5** rag trade; **3, 6** the latest; **4, 7** high ~; **5, 4, 5** knock into shape; **5, 5** Rodeo Drive; **5, 6** Fifth Avenue; **5, 7** haute couture; **6, 3** hammer out, Savile Row; **7, 3** dernier cri; **7, 6** Carnaby Street; **7, 8** Garment District; **8, 5** designer label.

fashionable **2** in; **3** hip; **4** chic, cool, posh; **5** smart, swish; **6** classy, dressy, groovy, modern, modish, snazzy, swanky, trendy; **7** crucial, stylish, voguish; **8** designer, tasteful; **9** glamorous, happening; **12** trendsetting; PHRASES: **1, 2, 4** à la mode; **2-2-3-6** up-to-the-minute; **2-2-4** up-to-date; **2, 5** in vogue; **3, 3, 4** all the rage; **4, 2** with it; **4-7** well-dressed, well-groomed.

fashion designer **5** sewer; **6** booter, cutter, draper, fitter, glover, hatter, hosier, mercer *UK*, sartor, souter, tailor; **7** cobbler, furrier, modiste *UK*; **8** clothier, costumer, finisher, milliner, stitcher; **9** bootmaker, busheller, costumier, couturier, outfitter, shoemaker; **10** cordwainer *UK*, dressmaker, seamstress; **11** haberdasher; **12** needleworker; **13** garmentworker; PHRASES: **3-5** dry-goods dealer; **6, 6** fabric dealer; **7-5** garment-maker; **7, 8** costume designer.

fashion model **5** model; **9** mannequin; **10** coathanger, supermodel; **12** clotheshorse; PHRASES: **6, 7** snappy dresser; **7, 5** fashion plate.

fast **3** far; **4** clem *UK*, diet, firm, food, Lent, slim, wild; **5** brief, brisk, fixed, fleet, hasty, quick, rapid, sharp, short, swift, tight; **6** abrupt, famish, firmly, flying, hunger, prompt, reduce, secure, speedy, stable, starve, steady, sudden, wanton, winged; **7** abstain, briskly, express, fixedly, hastily, hurried, quickly, Ramadan, rapidly, solidly, staunch, swiftly, tightly; **8** constant, faithful, fleeting, promptly, reckless, securely, speedily, steadily; **9** debauched, dissolute, immediate, immovable, momentary, steadfast; **10** abstention, abstinence, profligate, unwavering; **11** expeditious, immediately, irremovable, precipitous, tenaciously; **13** expeditiously; PHRASES: **2, 1, 4, 4** at a good pace; **2, 1, 5** in a flash; **2, 2, 1, 4** go on a diet; **2, 2, 4** in no time; **2, 3, 6** on the double; **2, 4** at once; **2, 4,**

6 at full stride; **2, 6** go hungry; **2, 7** go without, in advance; **4, 2, 3** live on air; **4, 4** keep Lent; **4-5** high-speed; **4, 6** half starve, lose weight; **4, 9** like lightning; **5-5** short-lived; **5, 8** count calories; **6, 6** hunger strike; **7, 4, 4** tighten one's belt; **7, 5** without delay.

fast (go fast) 3 fly, hie, run, zip; **4** dash, dive, flit, jump, leap, lope, race, rush, trot, wing, zing, zoom; **5** bound, chase, hurry, lunge, scoot, scour, shift, skirr, speed, swoop, vroom, whisk, whizz; **6** canter, careen, career, charge, gallop, hasten, hurtle, hustle, plunge, pounce, scorch, scurry, spring, streak; **7** scamper, scuttle; **8** expedite, stampede; **9** grayhound, skedaddle; **11** precipitate; PHRASES: **2, 3, 3** go all out; **2, 4, 4** go full tilt; **3, 1, 4, 2** get a move on; **3, 3, 3** cut and run; **3, 8** get cracking; **4, 2, 2** step on it; **4, 3** hare off, haul ass, shag ass; **4, 4** move fast; **4, 5** bowl along, tear along; **4, 6** burn rubber, make tracks; **6, 5** barrel along, rattle along; **7, 2** hotfoot it.

fast (make fast) 6 secure, steady; **7** fortify; **9** stabilize; **10** strengthen; PHRASES: **3, 2** fix to; **4, 4** nail down; **5, 4** screw down.

fast day 4 fast, Lent; **6** Friday; **7** Ramadan; PHRASES: **3, 2, 10** day of abstinence; **3, 6** Yom Kippur; **4, 3** fish day; **4, 6** Good Friday, jour maigre; **6, 3** Tishah b'Av; **8, 3** meatless day.

fasten 3 fix, tie; **4** clip, shut; **5** clasp, close; **6** attach, secure; PHRASES: **2, 2** do up; **3, 2** tie up.

fastening 3 bar, nut, peg, pin, tie, zip UK; **4** bolt, brad, clip, frog, grip, hasp, hook, lock, loop, nail, pale, pile, post, ring, spit, stud, tack; **5** brace, catch, clamp, clasp, cleat, cramp, dowel, hinge, latch, rivet, screw, slide, snaps, stake; **6** batten, braces UK, brooch, buckle, button, eyelet, fixing, garter, hatpin, popper UK, skewer, staple, stitch, tiepin UK, toggle, Velcro TM, zipper; **7** basting, bollard, closure, curlers, garters, hairpin, kingpin, padlock, pushpin, rollers; **8** barrette, cufflink, fastener, hairgrip UK, holdfast, linchpin, manacles, treenail; **9** attaching, bracelets, brochette, handcuffs, suspender, thumbtack; **10** buttonhole, suspenders; PHRASES: **3, 4** tie tack; **3, 5** tie clasp; **4, 3, 3** hook and eye, lock and key; **4, 4** dead bolt, Yale lock; **4, 8** snap fastener; **5, 3** bobby pin; **6, 3** cotter pin, safety pin, toggle pin; **6, 4** collar stud; **6, 5** safety catch UK, spring catch; **8, 3** straight pin; **11,** **4** combination lock.

fastidious 4 neat, nice, tidy; **5** exact, fussy, picky; **6** choosy, dainty; **7** careful, faddish, finicky, orderly, precise, refined; **8** delicate, pedantic, thorough; **9** assiduous, squeamish; **10** meticulous, particular, pernickety UK; **11** persnickety; **13** perfectionist.

fasting 4 diet, fast, thin; **5** empty, unfed; **6** hungry, Lenten; **7** ascetic, atrophy, austere, clemmed, dieting, Spartan, starved; **8** anorexia, anorexic, famished, ravenous, reducing, slimming UK, starving, underfed; **9** abstinent, austerity, famishing; **10** abstemious, abstinence; **13** Quadragesimal; PHRASES: **4, 7** lean cuisine; **4-7** half-starved; **5, 4** crash diet UK; **6, 4** Lenten fare, liquid diet; **6, 6** hunger strike; **6-8** weight-watching; **7, 4, 4** keeping one's fast; **10, 4** starvation diet.

fat 2 OS; **3** big, oil, wax; **4** flab, full, huge, lard, oily, rich, soap, suet, wide; **5** bonny, busty, buxom, cream, dumpy, ester, fatty, gross, heavy, hefty, hippy, large, obese, plump, podgy UK, pudge, pudgy, puffy, round, sebum, squab, stout, thick, tubby; **6** bosomy, butter, chubby, chunky, flabby, fleshy, grease, greasy, paunch, portly, rotund, tallow; **7** adipose, bloated, blubber, ceresin, lanolin, overfed, padding, paunchy, sizable, swelled, swollen, wealthy; **8** affluent, blubbery, enormous, potbelly; **9** cellulite, corpulent, distended, glyceride, margarine; **10** abdominous, buttermilk, insulation, overweight, prosperous; **11** endomorphic; PHRASES: **3-5** fat-arsed, top-heavy; **3-7** big-bellied, pot-bellied; **3-8** big-bottomed; **4-2-2** well-to-do; **4, 3** baby ~; **4-3** well-fed, well-off; **4-4** roly-poly; **4, 5** beer belly; **4-5** full-faced, moon-faced; **4, 6** soap powder; **4-7** full-bellied, full-bosomed, well-endowed; **4-11** well-upholstered UK; **5, 2, 3, 4** broad in the beam; **5, 4** spare tire; **5-5** round-faced; **6-5** chubby-faced; **6-7** chubby-cheeked, double-chinned.

fat (fat person) 5 blimp, fatso, fatty, hippo; **8** dumpling, Falstaff; **11** heavyweight; PHRASES: **3, 2, 4** tub of lard; **4-4** roly-poly.

fatal 5 grave; **6** deadly, lethal, mortal; **7** crucial, fateful, pivotal, ruinous, serious; **8** critical, decisive, terminal; **9** incurable; **10** disastrous; **11** destructive.

fate 3 end, lot; **4** doom, luck; **6** chance, kismet, result, upshot; **7** destiny, fortune, outcome; **8** doomsday; **10** apocalypse, providence; **11** consequence, eschatology; **15** Götterdämmerung; PHRASES: **3, 2, 3, 5** end of the world; **3, 2, 4** end of time; **3, 2, 8** Day of Judgment; **4, 8** last judgment; **5, 2, 4** crack of doom.

fate (meet one's fate) *See* **die**

fated 5 meant; **6** doomed; **8** destined; **10** inevitable; **11** inescapable, predestined, preordained; **13** predetermined.

fat hen 7 pigweed; PHRASES: **5-7** lamb's-quarter.

father 2 Fr, pa; **3** dad, get, pop, Rev; **4** papa, sire; **5** beget, daddy, padre, pappy, pater *UK*, spawn, taata, vicar; **6** advise, author, pastor, priest; **7** comfort, faither, founder, nurture, protect; **8** ancestor, engender, forebear, minister; **9** architect, initiator, patriarch, procreate; **10** forefather, originator, progenitor; **11** predecessor; **13** paterfamilias; PHRASES: **3, 3** old man; **4, 4, 2** take care of; **4, 5** look after.

fatherland 4 home; **8** homeland; **10** motherland; PHRASES: **3, 7** old country; **6, 4** native land; **6, 7** mother country.

fathom 5 gauge, grasp, plumb, probe, sound; **7** measure; **10** comprehend, understand; PHRASES: **4, 3** work out; **6, 3** figure out.

fatigue 3 fag, irk, tax, vex; **4** bore, jade, task, tire, wear, wind, work; **5** annoy, drain, faint, swoon, weary, whack; **6** bother, harass, strain, weaken; **7** boredom, exhaust, gasping, languor, overtax; **8** blackout, collapse, distress, dullness, enervate, exertion, fainting, lethargy, overload, overwork, weakness; **9** faintness, jadedness, lassitude, overdrive, prostrate, staleness, tiredness, weariness; **10** debilitate, drowsiness, enervation, exasperate, exhaustion, overburden, overstrain, sleepiness; **12** debilitation, languishment, listlessness, overexertion, palpitations; PHRASES: **2, 2** do in, do up; **3, 2, 5** put to sleep; **3, 3** fag out; **4, 2, 5** bore to tears, tire to death; **4, 3** burn out, tire out, wear out; **4, 9** hard breathing; **5, 2** knock up; **6, 2** double up; **6, 7** aching muscles; **9, 2** overdoing it.

fatigue (be fatigued) 3 nod; **4** blow, drop, fail, flag, gasp, pant, puff, sink, tire, yawn; **5** droop, faint, grunt, sleep, swoon; **6** drowse; **7** stagger, succumb; **8** collapse, languish, overwork; **9** overexert; PHRASES:

4, 1, 8 need a vacation; **4, 2** pack up; **5, 2** crack up; **5, 3** flake out; **6, 2** overdo it; **7, 7** breathe heavily.

fatigued 4 beat, dozy, dull, flat, pale, sore, weak, worn; **5** dopey, faint, spent, stale, stiff, tired, weary; **6** aching, bushed, drowsy, fagged *UK*, pooped, sleepy; **7** drained, haggard, languid, nodding, wayworn, wearied, whacked *UK Can*, yawning; **8** drooping, dropping, fainting, flagging, footsore, listless, strained, swooning, unrested, weakened; **9** enervated, exhausted, footweary, knackered *UK*, lethargic, overtired, prostrate, shattered *UK*; **10** languorous, overworked; **11** overwrought, unrefreshed; PHRASES: **3, 2** all in; **3, 2, 2** out of it; **3, 2, 4** fit to drop; **3-5** dog-tired, dog-weary; **3-6** jet-lagged; **4, 2** done in; **4, 2, 3, 5** dead to the world; **4, 3** done for, flat out, worn out; **4, 4** dead beat *UK*; **4-4** half-dead; **4, 5** dead tired; **4-5** half-awake; **4-6** half-asleep; **5, 3** tired out, wiped out; **5-4** heavy-eyed, tired-eyed; **5-6** heavy-lidded; **6, 2** washed up; **6, 3** burned out, fagged out, flaked out, sacked out; **6-4** hollow-eyed; **6-5** travel-weary; **7, 2** knocked up; **7, 3** clapped out; **8, 3** tuckered out.

fatten 3 pad; **4** feed; **5** plump, stuff; **7** coarsen, thicken; **9** upholster; PHRASES: **3, 2, 6** put on weight; **4, 2** feed up *UK*; **4, 3** fill out; **5, 2** build up.

fatuous 5 silly; **7** unaware; **10** complacent; **13** unintelligent.

faucet 1 C, H; **4** cold, plug; **5** bleed, drain, spout, valve; **6** outlet, spigot; **8** stopcock; PHRASES: **3, 3** run off.

fault 3 bug; **4** chip, flaw, mark, slip, tear, vice; **5** blame, crack, error, lapse; **6** burden, defect, foible; **7** blemish, blunder, censure, condemn, demerit, failing, frailty, mistake; **8** drawback, fracture, omission, question, weakness; **9** criticize, infirmity, liability, oversight; **10** deficiency, disloyalty, peccadillo; **11** culpability, shortcoming; **12** imperfection; PHRASES: **4-2** slip-up; **4, 4** weak spot; **4, 5, 4** find ~ with; **6, 3** mortal sin.

fault-finding 7 carping, fussing, nagging; **8** captious, caviling, crabbing, niggling, pedantry; **9** pestering, quibbling; **10** censorious, fastidious, henpecking; **12** overcritical, pettifoggery; **13** hypercritical, ultracritical; PHRASES: **3-7** nit-picking; **4-9** hair-splitting.

faultless 5 ideal; **7** correct, perfect; **8**

flawless, spotless; **9** blameless; **10** immaculate, impeccable; **14** irreproachable.

favor 3 aid; **4** back, boon, gift, help, like; **5** token; **6** assist, cachet, choose, errand, esteem, oblige, prefer, profit, regard; **7** advance, approve, benefit, further, present, promote, service, support, trinket; **8** approval, courtesy, increase, keepsake, kindness, sympathy; **9** encourage; **10** indulgence, partiality, preference; **11** approbation; PHRASES: **4, 4** good turn.

favorable 4 good, kind; **6** bright, useful; **7** helpful; **8** positive; **9** approving, opportune, promising; **10** auspicious, beneficial, convenient, flattering, optimistic, profitable, propitious; **11** encouraging, sympathetic; **12** advantageous, constructive; **13** complimentary; PHRASES: **2, 4, 4** on your side.

favorite 3 pet; **4** pick; **6** choice, chosen; **7** beloved, darling, favored; **10** preference.

favoritism 4 bias; **8** cronyism, nepotism; **9** prejudice; **10** partiality, preference; **12** partisanship; **14** discrimination; **15** preferentialism.

fawn 4 buff, deer; **5** beige, crawl, creep *UK*, tawny, toady; **6** grovel; **7** flatter, truckle; **8** bootlick; **9** handshake; **11** lickspittle; PHRASES: **3, 5, 2** pay court to; **4, 2** suck up; **4, 2, 2** make up to, play up to; **4, 3, 3, 2** lick the ass of; **4, 3, 4, 2** lick the feet of; **4, 3, 5, 2** lick the shoes of; **4-4** soft-soap; **4, 7, 4** worm oneself into; **5-4** brown-nose; **5, 5** curry favor; **6, 3, 5** polish the apple.

fear 3 awe; **4** funk; **5** alarm, dread, panic, quake, shake, start, worry; **6** cringe, dismay, fright, horror, nerves, phobia, qualms, shiver, shrink, terror, twitch, unease; **7** anxiety, concern, tension, tremble; **8** affright, aversion, disquiet; **9** agitation, awfulness, misgiving, scariness, trembling; **10** foreboding, horridness, uneasiness; **11** hatefulness, nervousness, trepidation; **12** apprehension, dreadfulness, palpitations, perturbation, terribleness, timorousness; **13** atrociousness, consternation, frightfulness, horrification; PHRASES: **2, 2, 4** be on edge; **2, 7** be nervous; **3, 5** the jumps; **3, 7** the jimjams, the jitters, the willies; **3, 12** the collywobbles; **4, 4** blue funk, cold feet; **4, 5** cold sweat; **4, 6** have qualms; **4, 7** have kittens; **5, 5** blind panic, goose bumps, goose flesh; **5, 6** stage fright; **6, 4** mortal ~, shrink from; **6, 6** unholy terror; **7, 7** sinking stomach; **8, 5** knocking knees; **10, 5** chattering teeth.

fearful 3 bad; **4** dire, edge; **5** awful, jumpy, nervy, scary, shaky, tense, timid; **6** afraid, scared, uneasy; **7** abysmal, alarmed, anxious, jittery, nervous, panicky, quaking, shaking, twitchy, uptight, worried; **8** agitated, dreadful, fearsome, horrible, horrific, strained, terrible, timorous; **9** appalling, atrocious, frightful, trembling, tremulous; **10** disquieted, distressed, frightened, horrendous, terrifying; **11** frightening; **12** apprehensive; PHRASES: **2, 4** on edge; **2, 11** on tenterhooks; **6, 6** highly strung.

fearless *See* **courageous**

fearsome 7 awesome; **8** alarming; **10** formidable, impressive, terrifying, tremendous; **11** frightening; PHRASES: **3-9** awe-inspiring.

feasible 2 on; **6** likely, viable; **7** helpful; **8** possible, workable; **9** practical, realistic; **10** achievable, attainable, reasonable; **11** practicable.

feast 2 do; **3** eat, joy; **4** dine, meal, orgy; **5** beano, gorge, party, treat; **6** buffet, devour, dinner, fiesta, gobble, junket, picnic, regale, repast, spread, thrash; **7** banquet, blowout, cookout, delight, holiday, indulge, partake; **8** barbecue, bunfight, clambake, festival, pleasure; **9** beanfeast *UK*, enjoyment, entertain, reception; **10** indulgence; **11** bacchanalia, celebration; PHRASES: **3, 3** pig out; **3, 5** tea party; **4-2** nosh-up *UK*; **4-2, 4** slap-up meal *UK*; **4, 3** holy day; **4, 9** fête champêtre; **5, 3** ~ day; **5, 4** Roman orgy; **5, 7** state banquet; **6, 3** saint's day; **6, 5** dinner dance, weenie roast, wiener roast; **6, 6** annual dinner, formal dinner; **7, 4** harvest home; **7, 6** feeding frenzy, harvest supper; **9, 6** Christmas dinner.

feat 3 act; **4** coup, deed; **5** stunt, trick; **7** exploit; **11** achievement; **14** accomplishment.

feather 4 barb, down; **5** plume, quill; **7** plumage.

feature 3 act; **4** item, mark, show, star; **5** piece, story, trait; **6** appear, figure, report; **7** article, contain, contour, include, perform, present, quality; **8** showcase; **9** attribute, highlight, introduce, lineament; **11** participate; **14** characteristic; PHRASES: **4, 1, 4** play a part; **4, 2** turn up; **4, 4** take part; **5, 3** bring out; **6, 7** facial ~.

featureless *See* **dull**

fecal 5 dungy; **8** feculent; **9** stercoral; **10** scatologic, stercorous; **11** excremental; **12**

scatological.

feces 3 poo *UK*; 4 dirt, dung, muck, pooh, poop; 5 ~ *UK*, guano, jakes, stool; 6 manure, motion, ordure; 9 droppings; 11 dingleberry; PHRASES: 2-2 ca-ca; 3-3 doo-doo, poo-poo; 3, 4 cow pats; 3, 5 cow chips, cow flops; 5, 4 night soil; 6, 4 number twos; 6, 8 sheep's currants; 7, 5 buffalo chips.

fecund 4 rich; 7 fertile; 8 creative, fruitful, prolific; 10 productive; 11 industrious.

federal 5 civic, state; 7 central; 8 national; 11 centralized.

federation 5 union; 8 alliance, grouping; 9 coalition; 11 association, combination, partnership; 12 amalgamation; 13 confederation.

fee 3 cut, pay, sub, sum; 4 cost, dues, fare, hire, rate, rent, toll; 5 extra; 6 charge, demand, rental, salary, tariff; 7 ceiling, corkage, payment, stipend; 9 surcharge; 10 commission, supplement; 12 subscription; PHRASES: 3-3 rip-off; 4-3 rake-off; 4, 4 flat fare, flat rate; 5, 6 cover charge; 7, 6 service charge.

feeble 4 thin, weak; 5 frail, shaky, small; 6 flimsy, meager, paltry, slight; 7 fragile; 8 delicate, pathetic, trifling; 9 enervated, spineless; 10 inadequate; 11 ineffectual; 12 unconvincing; 13 insubstantial; PHRASES: 4-7 half-hearted; 5-5 namby-pamby.

feed 4 dine, fete; 5 board, cater, feast, graze, nurse; 6 fatten, purvey, regale, suckle; 7 banquet, nourish, nurture, pasture, sustain, victual; 9 provision; PHRASES: 4, 3 cook for; 4, 3, 4 wine and dine; 4-4 drip-feed; 5-4 force-feed; 6, 2 fatten up; 6, 4 invite over; 6-4 breast-feed.

feel 3 air; 4 aura, bear, deem, know, mood; 5 sense, think, touch; 6 caress, fondle, handle, intuit, stroke, suffer; 7 believe, feeling, quality, realize, suspect, texture; 8 ambiance, consider, perceive; 9 character, sensation; 10 atmosphere, comprehend, experience, impression, manipulate, understand; PHRASES: 2, 2, 3, 7 be of the opinion; 2, 5, 2 be aware of; 4, 2, 8 know by instinct.

feel (someone or something that feels) 5 nerve; 6 finger; 7 antenna, epicure, neurone, whisker; 8 aesthete, tentacle; 9 epicurean, fingertip, proboscis, sensorium; PHRASES: 3-4 cry-baby; 3, 5 raw nerve; 5, 4 nerve cell; 5, 5 nerve fiber, sense organ; 5, 6 nerve center; 5-6 nerve-ending; 7, 6 nervous

system; 9, 6 shrinking violet.

feel for 4 pity; 9 empathize; 10 sympathize, understand; 11 commiserate; PHRASES: 2, 5, 2 be moved by; 2, 5, 3 be sorry for; 5, 3 bleed for; 6, 2 relate to; 6, 3 grieve for.

feeling 3 air; 4 aura, feel, idea, love, mood, pity, view; 5 aware, hunch, sense, touch; 6 belief, notion, regard; 7 concern, emotion, empathy, groping, knowing, opinion, quality, sensing; 8 ambiance, attitude, esthesia, instinct, reaction, response, sensible, sentient, stroking, sympathy, touching; 9 affection, awareness, character, conscious, intuition, knowledge, realizing, sensation, sensitive, sentiment, suspicion; 10 atmosphere, attachment, compassion, experience, impression, perception, perceptive, responsive; 11 sensibility, sensitivity, susceptible; 12 presentiment; 13 consciousness, understanding; 14 impressionable; PHRASES: 3, 8 gut reaction.

feeling (lack of feeling) 6 apathy; 8 dullness; 9 analgesia, paralysis; 10 anesthesia; 15 insensitiveness; PHRASES: 4, 2, 9 lack of awareness, lack of sensation.

feeling (with feeling) 4 warm; 6 ardent; 7 fervent, intense; 8 vehement; 9 affecting, rapturous; 10 ecstatical, hysterical, passionate; PHRASES: 7, 8 zealous touching.

feign *See* **pretend**

feint *See* **trick**

felicitous 3 apt; 5 lucky; 6 timely; 7 blessed, fitting; 8 apposite, suitable; 9 fortunate; 11 appropriate.

felicity 3 joy; 4 luck; 7 aptness; 8 pleasure; 9 happiness; 11 contentment, fittingness, suitability; 12 appositeness; 15 appropriateness.

fell 3 hew; 4 deck; 5 floor; 8 demolish; PHRASES: 3, 4 cut down; 4, 4 chop down; 5, 3 knock out; 5, 4 knock down.

fellow 3 boy, guy, man; 4 chap *UK*; 5 bloke *UK*; 6 member; 7 comrade, partner; 9 associate, colleague, companion; 10 researcher.

fellowship 4 club; 5 group; 6 accord; 7 college, concord, harmony, society; 8 clanship, sodality, sorority, sympathy; 9 agreement, communion, community, consensus, mutuality; 10 fraternity, friendship, solidarity; 11 affiliation, association, brotherhood, camaraderie, concordance, cooperative, freemasonry, partnership, sociability; 12

fraternalism, friendliness, togetherness; **13** companionship; **14** bipartisanship; **15** cooperativeness; PHRASES: **4, 6** team spirit; **6, 2, 5** esprit de corps; **9, 6** community spirit.

felon *See* **criminal**

female **1** F; **2** Ms; **3** Eve, gal, her, she; **4** girl, lady, lass, miss; **5** woman; **6** Amazon, damsel, lassie, maiden, matron, sheila *UK*; virago; **7** colleen, dowager, girlish, herself, lesbian, womanly; **8** feminine, grisette, ladylike, maidenly, matronly, womanish; **9** Amazonian, womanhood, womankind; **10** effeminate; PHRASES: **4, 3** fair sex; **5, 5** young woman; **6, 3** gentle sex, second sex; **6, 4** little girl.

female animal **3** cow, doe, ewe, hen, pen, sow; **4** gilt, hind, jill, mare; **5** bitch, filly, queen, vixen; **6** heifer; **7** lioness, tigress; **10** leopardess; PHRASES: **3-4** ewe-lamb, she-goat; **5, 4** nanny goat.

female title of address **2** Ms; **3** Mrs; **4** Dame, Frau, lady, Lady, lass, ma'am, marm, Miss; **5** Donna, goody, hinny, Madam; **6** lassie, madame, milady, missus, señora, sister; **7** signora; **8** Fraulein, goodwife *UK*, memsahib, mistress, señorita; **9** signorina; **12** mademoiselle; PHRASES: **2, 4, 4** my good lady; **2, 4, 5** my dear woman; **3, 8** her ladyship.

feminine *See* **female**

femur **9** thighbone.

fen *See* **marsh**

fence **3** hit, log, pen; **4** duel, gird, mine, moat, rail, wall; **5** block, dodge, evade, feint, glide, guard, hedge, lunge, march, parry, touch; **6** attack, clinch, hurdle, paling, screen, thrust; **7** barrier, confine, contest, enclose, pronate, railing, recover, riposte, trellis; **8** boundary, obstruct, palisade, restrict, supinate, surround; **9** barricade, disengage, enclosure, encompass, swordplay; **10** balustrade; **12** circumscribe; **13** counterattack; PHRASES: **3, 8** use footwork; **5-3-5** stake-and-rider; **5, 4** split rail; **6, 5** zigzag ~.

fencer **6** dueler; **7** épéeist; **8** foilsman.

fencing **5** kendo; **6** paling; **7** dueling; **8** badinage, palisade, parrying, raillery, repartee, wordplay; **9** swordplay.

fencing equipment **4** cane, épée, foil; **5** blade, guard, saber, sword.

fend off **5** deter, parry, repel; **6** resist; **7** deflect, repulse; **10** discourage; PHRASES: **3,**

3 put off; **4, 2, 3** keep at bay; **4, 3** beat off, head off, hold off, keep off, ward off; **5, 3** fight off, stave off.

fennel **7** mayweed.

feral *See* **wild**

ferment **4** turn; **5** yeast; **6** aerate, leaven.

fern **5** brake, cycad; **7** bracken, lycopod, osmunda; **8** calamite, clubmoss, lycopsid, staghorn; **9** equisetum, Filicinae, horsetail, quillwort; **10** cliffbrake, maidenhair, spleenwort, sporangium; **11** archegonium; PHRASES: **5, 6** hart's tongue.

ferocious **5** cruel; **6** brutal, fierce, heated, raging, strong; **7** extreme, intense, vicious, violent.

ferret *See* **hunt**

ferry *See* **transport**

fertile **3** fat; **4** lush, rich, rife; **6** fecund, paying; **7** booming, copious, pouring, profuse, teeming, verdant; **8** abundant, creative, fruitful, pregnant, prolific, thriving; **9** bounteous, bountiful, exuberant, inventive, lucrative, luxuriant, plenteous, plentiful, procreant, streaming; **10** generative, parturient, productive, profitable, prosperous; **11** flourishing, multiparous, procreative, propagatory, resourceful; **12** fructiferous, remunerative; PHRASES: **5-7** fruit-bearing.

fertile (be fertile) **4** bear, boom, teem; **5** bloom, swarm; **6** thrive; **7** blossom, burgeon, prosper; **8** conceive, flourish, fructify, multiply, mushroom, populate; **9** germinate; **11** proliferate; **12** overpopulate; PHRASES: **4, 5** give birth.

fertility **6** bounty, hotbed, plenty, wealth; **7** potency; **8** lushness, richness; **9** abundance, fecundity, plenitude, profusion; **10** cornucopia, exuberance, luxuriance; **12** fruitfulness; **14** productiveness; PHRASES: **4, 2, 6** horn of plenty; **4, 4** rich soil; **4, 5** rich earth; **4, 7** rich harvest; **5, 3** milch cow; **7, 6** nature's bounty.

fertility goddess **5** Ceres; **7** Demeter; PHRASES: **5, 6** Earth Mother; **5, 7** Earth Goddess; **6, 5** Mother earth.

fertility symbol **4** yoni; **6** lingam; **7** phallus; PHRASES: **7, 6** phallic symbol.

fertilize **4** feed, marl; **5** dress, mulch, plant, water; **6** enrich, manure; **7** compost, produce; **8** fructify, generate, irrigate; **9** fecundate, pollinate, procreate, propagate; **10** impregnate, inseminate; PHRASES: **3-5** top-dress; **5, 3, 6** green the desert.

fertilizer 4 dung, dust, lime, marl, muck, peat; **5** guano, mulch, prill, semen, sperm; **6** manure, potash, sewage, sludge, slurry; **7** bagmuck, compost, nitrate, sulfate; **8** bonemeal, dressing, effluent, enricher, fishmeal, nitrates; **9** limestone, phosphate, quicklime; **12** gonadotropin; PHRASES: **3, 8** top dressing; **4, 8** soil enricher; **5, 4** basic slag; **5, 6** green manure; **6, 4** foliar feed, slaked lime; **7, 4** potting soil; **7, 6** organic manure; **8, 5** ammonium salts.

fervent *See* **keen**

fervor 4 zeal; **7** passion; **9** eagerness; **10** dedication, enthusiasm.

fester 3 rot, run; **4** fret, gall, gnaw, rile, weep; **5** annoy, chafe; **6** rankle; **8** embitter, irritate; **9** aggravate, suppurate.

festive 3 fun; **4** gala; **5** happy, jolly, merry; **6** festal, jovial, joyful, joyous; **8** cheerful; **11** celebratory; **12** entertaining.

festivity 2 do; **4** gala; **5** event, party; **8** carnival, pleasure; **9** enjoyment, merriment, rejoicing; PHRASES: **4, 5** good cheer.

festoon 4 hang, swag; **5** adorn, chain, drape; **6** swathe; **7** garland; **8** decorate, ornament; **10** decoration.

fetch 3 get; **4** make; **5** bring, carry, raise; **6** obtain; PHRASES: **4, 3** sell for; **5, 4** bring back.

fete 4 fair, gala; **5** event, honor; **6** bazaar, fiesta, praise, salute; **7** holiday, jubilee, lionize; **8** carnival, festival, jamboree; **9** celebrate, entertain; **11** celebration, commemorate; **12** congratulate; PHRASES: **3, 8, 2** pay respects to.

fetter 3 tie; **4** bind, bond, yoke; **5** chain; **6** hamper; **7** shackle; **8** handcuff, restrain.

feud 3 row; **5** argue, fight; **7** dispute, quarrel; **8** argument; PHRASES: **3, 5** bad blood.

fever 6 fervor; **7** disease, illness, malaise, passion; **9** agitation, infection, vehemence; **10** excitement; **11** temperature.

few 4 dash, hint, rare, some; **6** couple, little, scarce; **7** handful, limited, smidgen, soupçon *Fr*, trickle; **8** uncommon; **10** scattering, sprinkling; **12** insufficient; PHRASES: **1, 6** a little; **2, 5, 6** in short supply; **3, 2, 3** one or two; **3, 2, 5** two or three; **3, 4** not many; **4, 2, 3, 6** thin on the ground; **6, 3** hardly any; **6, 4** almost none; **8, 3** precious ~, scarcely any; **8, 6** derisory amount.

fewer 4 less; **5** least; **7** minimal, minimum, reduced; **8** minority; **9** inquorate *UK*; **10** diminished; **11** diminishing.

fewness 4 lack; **6** dearth; **7** paucity; **8** exiguity, shortage, sparsity; **10** scantiness, sparseness; **11** undersupply; **15** underpopulation.

fey 8 fanciful; **9** unworldly, whimsical; **11** fantastical; **12** otherworldly.

fiat 5 edict, order; **6** decree; **7** command; **8** sanction; **10** permission; **13** authorization.

fib 3 lie; **7** untruth; **12** misrepresent; **13** falsification; PHRASES: **4, 4** tall tale; **4, 7** tell stories; **5, 3** white lie.

fiber 3 tow; **4** cane, coir, grit, jute, yarn; **5** grain, kapok, ramie, sisal, straw, stuff, twine; **6** denier, makeup, raffia, rattan, strand, string, thread, wicker; **7** matting; **8** backbone, filament, roughage, seagrass, strength; **9** character, fortitude, integrity; **10** fiberglass; **12** monofilament.

fibrous *See* **tough**

fickle 5 giddy; **7** erratic, flighty; **8** restless, unstable, variable; **9** faithless, frivolous, mercurial, whimsical; **10** adulterous, capricious, changeable, inconstant, indecisive, unfaithful, unreliable; **11** superficial, vacillating; **12** inconsistent; **13** irresponsible, temperamental, unpredictable; PHRASES: **7-7** feather-brained.

fiction 3 fib, lie; **4** myth, tale; **5** bogus, conte, fable, fancy, geste, novel, roman, story; **6** deceit, legend, sketch, utopia; **7** fabliau, fantasy, Märchen, novella, parable, romance, untruth, western; **8** dystopia, illusion, nonsense, nouvelle, vignette; **9** antinovel, falsehood, invention, mythology, narrative, potboiler; **10** literature, mythopoeia; **11** blockbuster, cliffhanger, fabrication, imagination; **13** Bildungsroman, Künstlerroman; PHRASES: **3-2** sci-fi; **3, 5** spy story; **4, 4** folk tale; **4, 5** epic novel, folk story, love story; **4-6** best-seller; **4, 7** pulp ~; **5, 0, 4** Mills & Boon; **5, 1, 4** roman à clef; **5, 1, 5** roman à thèse; **5, 4** fairy tale, urban myth; **5, 5** beast fable, crime story, ghost story, short story, whole cloth; **5, 6** roman fleuve; **5, 8** penny dreadful; **6, 5** horror story; **6, 6** bodice ripper, Gothic horror; **7, 7** science ~; **8, 7** creative writing; **9, 5** adventure story, detective story. *See also* **novel**

fictional 5 false; **6** unreal, untrue; **8** fabulous, illusory, imagined, mythical, romantic; **9** fantastic, imaginary, legendary; **10** fictitious; **11** allegorical; **12** mythological.

fictitious *See* **untrue**

fiddle 5 cello; **6** racket, string, tinker, violin; **7** deceive, twiddle. *See also* **fidget**

fiddling 5 fraud, petty; **6** fixing; **7** trivial; **8** cheating, trifling; **9** deception; **11** unimportant; **13** insignificant.

fidelity 7 loyalty; **11** reliability; **12** faithfulness; **13** dependability; **15** trustworthiness.

fidget 3 toy; **4** fret, play; **6** fiddle, jiggle, squirm, twitch; **7** shuffle; PHRASES: **4, 6** play around.

field 3 lea; **4** area, park, turf; **5** arena, pitch *UK*, topic; **6** domain, ground, meadow, return, sphere; **7** pasture, subject; **8** retrieve; **9** grassland; **10** discipline; PHRASES: **2, 5** go after; **4, 2** pick up; **4, 2, 4** line of work; **4, 4** deal with; **4, 4, 2** take care of; **4, 5** look after; **6, 6** sports ground *UK*.

field events 9 decathlon; **10** heptathlon, pentathlon; PHRASES: **4, 3** shot put; **4, 4** high jump, long jump; **4-5** pole-vault; **5, 4** broad jump; **6, 4** triple jump; **6, 5** discus throw, hammer throw; **6, 7** triple jumping; **7, 5** javelin throw.

field hockey 3 tie; **4** back, dead, fake, foul, goal, hold, knee, pads, pass, push, trip; **5** elbow, field, flick, scoop, slash, spear, stick; **6** assist, corner, goalie, helmet, indoor, screen, strike, stroke; **7** dribble, forward, offside, Olympic, striker; **8** fullback, halfback; **10** goalkeeper; PHRASES: **3, 2** hit in; **3-2** hit-in; **3-2-3** man-to-man, one-on-one; **4, 2** push in *UK*; **4-2** push-in; **4, 3** free hit; **4, 3, 4** face the ball, lose the ball; **4, 4** pass back, wing half; **4-4** drop-pass, passback; **4, 5** shin guard; **4, 6** push stroke; **4-7** drop-passing; **5, 6** flick stroke, scoop stroke; **6, 4** center half; **6, 7** center forward; **7, 4** penalty spot; **7, 6** penalty corner, penalty stroke; **8, 6** shooting circle, striking circle.

fieldwork *See* **research**

fiend 5 beast, brute; **7** monster, villain; PHRASES: **4, 6** evil person.

fierce 4 deep; **6** brutal, savage, severe, strong; **7** extreme, intense, violent; **8** powerful, profound; **9** ferocious, turbulent; **10** aggressive.

fiery 5 angry; **6** fierce, heated; **7** blazing, burning, flaming, furious; **10** blistering,

passionate, sweltering.

fiesta 5 feast; **7** holiday; **8** carnival, festival; **11** celebration.

fifteenth 13 quindecennial.

fifth 7 quinary.

fifty 1 L; **7** jubilee; PHRASES: **4-1** demi-C; **4, 7** half century.

fight 3 box, hit, jab, row, war; **4** bout, butt, duel, fray, meet, riot, slug, sock, spar, stun, tiff, tilt; **5** argue, blast, blows, brawl, brush, clash, fence, joust, match, melee, punch, scrap, scrum *UK*; **6** affray, assail, attack, battle, charge, combat, dustup, fracas, oppose, pummel, resist, rumpus, shindy, strike, tussle; **7** contest, dispute, grapple, ruction, scuffle, shindig, warfare, wrangle, wrestle; **8** argument, brouhaha, campaign, conflict, dogfight, scramble, shootout, showdown, skirmish, struggle; **9** bushwhack, collision, encounter, firefight, fistfight, horseplay, scrimmage, scrummage, theomachy *UK*; **10** engagement, fisticuffs, infighting, roughhouse; **11** competition, hostilities; **12** belligerency; PHRASES: **3-2** run-in, set-to; **3, 2, 1, 3** win by a TKO; **4, 2, 5** come to blows; **4, 3** wage war; **5-2** punchup *UK Can*; **5, 3, 4** enter the ring; **5, 3, 5** enter the lists; **5, 5** prize ~; **5, 9** leave senseless; **7, 6** pitched battle; **8, 5** exchange blows.

fighting 6 combat, unrest; **7** hostile, warfare; **8** violence; **9** hostility; **10** aggressive, pugnacious, rebellious; **11** belligerent.

fighting animal 4 cock; **8** gamecock; PHRASES: **3, 4, 7** pit bull terrier; **4, 3, 3** bear and dog; **6, 3, 3** badger and dog.

figure 3 map, sum; **4** body, cost, form, icon; **5** build, chart, digit, guess, prism, shape, table, think, total; **6** amount, appear, assume, number, person, reckon, square, symbol; **7** believe, decagon, diagram, diamond, feature, hexagon, imagine, lozenge, numeral, octagon, outline, picture, presume, pyramid, rhombus, stature, suppose; **8** consider, heptagon, hexagram, pentagon, quantity, rhomboid, tetragon, triangle; **9** celebrity, character, dignitary, personage, rectangle, statistic; **10** decahedron, individual, polyhedron, quadrangle; **11** participate; **12** illustration; **13** parallelogram, quadrilateral; PHRASES: **2, 8** be included; **4, 1, 4** play a part; **6, 2** ~ in; **7, 8** scalene triangle. *See also* **number**

filament *See* **thread**

filch *See* **steal**

file 3 row, rub; 4 case, keep, line, rasp, sand, sort; 5 march, queue *UK*, snake, store, trail, troop; 6 column, folder, funnel, indian, lineup, parade, record, report, scrape, single, sleeve, smooth, wallet; 7 dossier, heading, profile, summary; 8 billfold, organize; 9 organizer, sandpaper; 10 categorize, procession; 11 information; PHRASES: 3, 2, 6 put on record; 5, 5 emery board.

fill 3 jam, pad, ram, top, wad; 4 brim, bung, cram, lade, line, load, pack, plug, sate, seal, soak, stop, stow, tamp; 5 bloat, block, cover, drown, imbue, stock, stuff, swamp; 6 charge, drench, impart, occupy, supply; 7 fulfill, overrun, package, pervade, satiate, satisfy, suffuse; 8 permeate, saturate; 9 overwhelm, replenish; PHRASES: 6, 4 spread over; 7, 2 squeeze in.

filled 4 full; 5 flush, sated; 7 bloated, chocker *UK*, content, glutted, replete, stuffed, teeming; 8 crawling, satiated; 9 contented, satisfied; 11 overflowing; PHRASES: 2, 2, 4, 4, 2 up to one's neck in; 4, 2 full up, rich in; 4-7 well-stocked; 4-8 well-provided; 4-9 well-furnished; 4-11 well-provisioned; 5-1-5 chock-a-block; 5, 2, 5 ready to burst; 5-4 chock-full.

fillet 3 gut; 4 bone, list, skin; 5 clean, scale; 6 listel; 7 prepare.

filling 3 big; 4 bulk, down, foam, guts *UK*, rich; 5 heavy, kapok; 6 filler, inside, stodgy; 7 innards, packing, padding, wadding; 8 contents, dressing, feathers, quilting, stuffing; 9 packaging *UK*, Styrofoam; 10 satisfying; 11 polystyrene, substantial.

filling station 6 garage; 8 services; PHRASES: 3, 7 gas station; 4, 4 rest stop; 6, 7 petrol station *UK*; 7, 4 service area; 7, 7 service station.

film 3 cel; 4 cine, coat, reel, roll, scum, skim, skin, take, tape, veil; 5 glaze, layer, movie, sheet, spool, strip, video; 6 veneer; 7 capture, coating; 8 covering, membrane, Polaroid™; 9 cartridge.

filmy 4 airy; 5 light; 10 diaphanous; 11 translucent, transparent.

filter 3 tip; 4 leak, mesh, ooze, perk, pump, seep, sift, sort; 5 clean, press, sieve; 6 divide, purify, riddle, screen, sifter, strain, stream; 7 clarify, dribble, trickle; 8 colander, permeate, separate, strainer; 9 penetrate, percolate; 10 categorize; PHRASES: 4, 3 sort out.

filth, filthy *See* **dirt, dirtiness, dirty**

fin 5 blade, organ; 6 paddle; 7 flipper; 9 appendage, propeller; 10 projection, stabilizer; PHRASES: 6, 3 dorsal ~.

final 3 end; 4 game, last; 5 match, round; 6 ending; 7 capping, closing, decider; 8 absolute, crowning, decisive, eventual, terminal, ultimate; 9 finishing; 10 completing, concluding, conclusive, definitive; 11 culminating, irrevocable; 12 irreversible; PHRASES: 2, 3, 6 at the finish; 2, 4 at last; 2, 4, 4 at long last; 2, 5 to close; 2, 6 to finish; 2, 8 to conclude; 2, 10 in conclusion; 4, 3 last leg; 4, 4 over with.

finale 3 end; 4 coda; 5 envoy; 6 climax, ending, finish, suffix; 8 appendix, epilogue; 10 denouement, postscript; 11 catastrophe, culmination; PHRASES: 4, 3 last act; 5, 7 final curtain; 8, 5 crowning glory.

finance 4 back, fund, lend, loan; 5 endow, grant, money; 6 bestow, budget, donate; 7 advance, backing, banking, funding, pension, sponsor, support; 8 bankroll, business, commerce, maintain; 9 economics, patronize, subsidize; 10 accounting, investment, underwrite; PHRASES: 3, 2 set up; 3, 3 pay for; 3, 5, 4 put money into; 4, 2 chip in; 4, 3 bail out, bale out; 4, 4 tide over; 5, 2 pitch in; 5, 6 stock exchange; 5, 7 purse strings; 5, 8 stock exchange; 7, 3, 5 provide the means; 10, 2 contribute to.

financial 4 bear, bull; 6 fiscal; 8 business, economic, floating, monetary; 9 pecuniary; 10 commercial, devaluated, monetarist, numismatic; 11 depreciated; 12 deflationary, inflationary, reflationary; 15 disinflationary.

financial loss 4 cost; 5 debit; 6 losses; 7 deficit, expense, losings; 9 overdraft, shortfall; 10 bankruptcy, deficiency, insolvency; 11 expenditure; 12 overspending; PHRASES: 3, 4 cut rate; 4, 2, 8 loss of earnings; 4, 6 loss leader, poor return; 5, 2, 3, 4 going to the wall; 5, 5, 2 going belly up; 7, 2, 1, 4 running at a loss.

financial support 4 cash, loan; 5 dowry, funds, grant, money; 6 assets, credit, income, upkeep, wealth; 7 advance, alimony, backing, bursary, capital, charity, funding, pension, readies, revenue, stipend, subsidy, support; 8 bestowal, donation, finances, premises, property, receipts; 9 allowance, endowment, liquidity, overdraft, patronage, provision, substance; **10** fellowship, settlement, subvention, sustenance; **11** investments, maintenance, scholarship, sponsorship, subsistence, sustainment; **12** contribution; PHRASES: **4, 2, 6** line of credit; **4-3** hand-out; **4, 4** cash flow; **5-2-5** stock-in-trade; **5-2, 7** start-up capital; **5, 7** child support; **6, 3, 5** stocks and bonds; **6, 3, 6** stocks and shares; **6, 5** credit limit; **7, 7** working capital; **8, 3** economic aid, monetary aid; **9, 3** financial aid.

financier 6 backer, banker, bursar, coiner, dealer, forger, minter, purser, tycoon, usurer; **7** cambist, cashier, magnate, moneyer, sponsor; **8** investor, quaestor; **9** paymaster, supporter, treasurer; **10** capitalist; **11** moneylender, numismatist; **12** moneychanger; PHRASES: **4, 9** coin collector; **5, 3** money man; **8, 6** merchant banker *UK*.

finback 7 rorqual.

find 3 get, hit; **5** trace; **6** attain, detect, locate, obtain, regain, strike; **7** achieve, acquire, bargain, novelty, realize, recover, uncover, unearth; **8** discover, pinpoint, retrieve; **9** discovery, invention; **10** trouvaille, understand; **11** triangulate; PHRASES: **3, 2, 5** run to earth; **3, 4** hit upon, pin down; **3, 4, 5, 2** lay one's hands on; **3, 5, 2** get ahold of; **4, 2** turn up; **4, 2, 2** home in on, zero in on; **4, 6** come across; **5, 2** light on; **5, 4** track down; **6, 4** chance upon; **7, 2** stumble on; **8, 5** treasure trove.

find fault *See* **carp**

find out 4 hear, note, suss *UK*; **5** catch, learn; **6** detect, expose, notice, reveal, unmask; **7** observe, realize, uncover; **8** discover; **9** ascertain, determine; **10** understand; PHRASES: **3, 2** get it; **3, 3, 5** see the light; **3, 4, 2** get wind of; **5, 2** catch on.

fine 1 F; **2** A1, OK; **3** dry, end, tax; **4** calm, fair, good, keen, lacy, levy, mild, okay, thin, tiny, well; **5** brisk, clear, crisp, drier, faint, fresh, gauzy, light, roger, sharp, sheer, small, sunny, wispy; **6** bright, charge, dainty, finale, flimsy, milder, minute, papery, punish, refine, scanty, select, slight, subtle, superb; **7** forfeit, fragile, payment, penalty, refined, settled, skilled, slender, spidery, spindly, tenuous; **8** adequate, delicate, exiguous, filiform, finespun, gossamer, hairlike, penalize, pleasant, rainless, splendid, superior; **9** beautiful, cloudless, excellent, spindling; **10** acceptable, diaphanous, discerning, fastidious, punishment, sufficient, threadlike; **11** bacilliform, exceptional, filamentous, outstanding, translucent; **12** satisfactory; **13** insubstantial; **14** discriminating; PHRASES: **3, 5** all right; **4-5** fine-drawn, well-honed, wire-drawn; **4, 6** good enough; **5-4** first-rate, wafer-thin; **7-6** spindle-shaped.

fine (fine thing) 4 film, lace, lath, slat; **5** gauze, paper, wafer; **6** muslin, tissue; **8** gossamer.

finesse 4 tact; **5** flair, grace, poise, skill; **8** delicacy, subtlety; **9** assurance, diplomacy; **10** discretion.

finger 4 feel, name; **5** digit, index, piece, pinky, point, slice, touch, wedge; **7** portion, slither, smidgen; **8** identify; **9** extremity; **10** manipulate; PHRASES: **3, 4** toy with; **4, 3** pick out; **6, 2** inform on; **6, 3** single out; **6, 4** fiddle with; **11, 2** stoolpigeon on.

fingerprint 3 dab; **4** loop, mark, sign; **5** print, whorl; **7** pattern; **8** evidence; **11** dactylogram; **14** characteristic.

finicky *See* **fastidious**

finish 3 end, rub; **4** buff, dead, gild, gilt, ruin, stop; **5** cease, close, drain, empty, glaze, gloss, photo; **6** defeat, ending, finale, mirror, patina, polish; **7** blanket, deplete, destroy, exhaust, lacquer, quality, surface, texture, varnish; **8** complete, conclude, demolish; **9** cessation, devastate, terminate; **10** annihilate, appearance, completion, conclusion; **11** termination; PHRASES: **3, 2** use up; **4, 2** wrap up; **5, 3** clean out; **6, 3** polish off. *See also* **end**

finished 2 up; **4** dead, done, lost, over, past; **5** ended, fired, honed; **6** broken, buffed, closed, failed, gilded, planed, ruined, sacked; **7** elegant, glossed, perfect, refined, stopped, wrecked; **8** bankrupt, complete, polished, resolved; **9** adjourned, destroyed, redundant, varnished; **10** devastated; PHRASES: **2, 2, 3** at an end; **4, 3** done for; **4, 3, 4, 4** over and done with; **4, 4** shut down; **5, 2** wound up; **6, 2** broken up; **6-2** washed-up.

finite *See* **limited**

Finland 3 FIN; **5** Suomi.

fire 3 lob; **4** glow, pyre, sack; **5** ardor, arson, blast, blaze, flame, flare, forge, ingle, light, match, shoot, snipe, spark, torch, vesta, vigor; **6** arouse, beacon, embers, energy, excite, fervor, launch, spirit, strafe, volley; **7** animate, bonfire, brazier, cinders, dismiss, enliven, enthuse, furnace, inferno, inspire, lighter, lucifer, passion, smelter; **8** balefire, campfire, detonate, fireball, firebomb, ignition, wildfire; **9** discharge, firebrand, fireplace, firestorm, fireworks, fusillade, inglenook; **10** combustion, enthusiasm, excitement; **12** pyrotechnics; **13** conflagration; PHRASES: **3, 2** let go, pop at; **3, 2, 6** sea of flames; **3, 3** lay off, let fly, set off; **3, 5** the stake; **4, 3** pick off; **4, 3, 7** pull the trigger; **8, 7** towering inferno.

fire (false fire) 6 bolide; **7** firefly; **8** fireball; **9** corposant; **10** marshlight; PHRASES: **2, 5, 4** St Elmo's fire; **4-1-3-4** will-o'-the-wisp; **4-1-7** jack-o'-lantern; **4-4** glow-worm; **4, 9** ball lightning; **5, 6** ignis fatuus; **9, 3** lightning bug.

firearm 3 gat, Uzi; **4** Bren, Colt(r), Sten; **5** fusil, Lewis, Luger, Maxim, piece, rifle; **6** hagbut *UK*, limber, magnum, mortar, musket, pistol, zipgun; **7** battery, bazooka, carbine, Gatling, hackbut, handgun, shooter, shotgun; **8** arquebus, basilisk, culverin, falconet, firelock, haquebut, howitzer, petronel, pistolet, repeater, revolver, takedown; **9** automatic, broadside, carronade, chassepot, firepower, flintlock, harquebus, matchlock, needlegun; **10** peashooter, Winchester; **11** blunderbuss, Kalashnikov; **12** flamethrower, mitrailleuse, muzzleloader; **13** semiautomatic; PHRASES: **2-2** AK-47; **2, 3** BB gun; **3, 3** pop gun, vgo gun, zip gun; **3-3** pom-pom; **3, 6** Big Bertha; **3-7** six-shooter; **3-7, 3** sub-machine gun; **3, 8** gun carriage; **4, 3** bren gun, burp gun, punt gun, sten gun; **4-4, 3** anti-tank gun; **4-8, 3** anti-aircraft gun; **5, 3** Tommy gun, water gun; **5-3, 7** sawed-off shotgun; **5, 4** Brown Bess, wheel lock; **6-6** thirty-thirty; **7, 3** machine gun; **7-4** seventy-four; **7, 5** Enfield rifle, fowling piece; **8, 3** elephant gun, sporting gun; **8, 4** shooting iron; **8, 5** Kentucky rifle; **9, 5** repeating rifle. *See also* **weapons**

firearm (part of firearm) 4 bore, butt, lock; **5** sight; **6** breech, ramrod; **7** trigger; **8** gunstock.

fire lighter 7 firebug; **8** arsonist; **10** firebomber, incendiary, pyromaniac; PHRASES: **4, 6** fire raiser *UK*.

firing 4 fire, shot; **5** burst, salvo, shots, spray; **6** strafe, volley; **7** gunfire, gunnery, sniping; **8** musketry, shooting; **9** crossfire, fusillade; **13** sharpshooting.

firm 3 set; **4** hard, safe; **5** dense, fixed, rig-

id, solid; **6** harden, secure, stable, strong; **7** certain, compact, company, stiffen; **8** business, definite, resolved, solidify; **10** determined; **11** corporation, partnership; **13** multinational; PHRASES: **5, 4** press down.

firmament *See* **sky**

first 1 A, I; **3** 1st, key, top; **4** Adam, base, head, main; **5** ahead, basic, chief, front, major; **6** former; **7** firstly, initial, leading, primary; **8** earliest, foremost, formerly, original; **9** initially, paramount, primarily, principal, principle; **10** originally; **11** fundamental; PHRASES: **2, 1, 5** as a start; **2, 3, 5** in the ~ place; **2, 3, 6** at the outset; **2, 3, 9** in the beginning; **2, 5** in front; **2, 5, 4** to begin with, to start with; **2, 7** in advance; **3, 1, 4-3** for a kick-off; **3, 1, 5** for a start; **3, 8** for starters; **5, 2, 3** ~ of all; **5, 5** ~ thing.

first lady 4 Bush (Barbara), Bush (Laura), Ford (Elizabeth Bloomer); **5** Adams (Abigail), Nixon (Thelma Catherine Ryan); **6** Carter (Rosalynn), Reagan (Nancy), Truman (Bess); **7** Johnson (Claudia Alta Taylor), Kennedy (Jackie), Lincoln (Mary Todd), Madison (Dolley); **9** Roosevelt (Eleanor); **10** Eisenhower (Mamie), Washington (Martha Dandridge Custis).

fish 3 eel, gar, roe; **4** bass, dace, gill, goby, orfe, seek, spot; **5** angle, bream, catch, cisco, guppy, perch, probe, roach, scale, scout, seine, shoal, smelt, snook, trawl; **6** bowfin, burbot, darter, kipper, Pisces, plaice, redfin, salmon, sauger, school, search, shiner, sucker, tautog, tomcod; **7** beignet, bloater, crappie, croaker, dipnoan, kokanee, mooneye, pigfish, pompano, sculpin, solicit, sunfish, teleost, walleye; **8** bluegill, bocaccio, bullhead, cavefish, drumfish, fallfish, hornpout, menhaden, pickerel, spiracle, stonecat, sturgeon, tilefish, weakfish, wolffish; **9** blackfish, mummichog, operculum, placoderm, quillback, sablefish, surfperch, whitefish; **10** cyclostome, midshipman, muttonfish, placodermi, sheepshead, troutperch; **11** cyprinodont, muskellunge, pumpkinseed, stickleback; **12** elasmobranch, holocephalan, mouthbrooder; **14** Chondrichthyes; **15** crossopterygian; PHRASES: **3, 4** sea bass; **3-4** fly-fish; **3, 5** sea raven, sea robin, sea trout; **3, 6** dig around, mud minnow; **3, 7** red snapper, sea lamprey; **4, 1, 4** cast a line; **4, 3** sand dab, wolf eel; **4, 4** rock bass; **4, 5** lake trout, nose about *UK*; **4, 6** nose around; **5, 4** black bass, Dover sole; **5, 5** brook trout, white perch; **5, 6** Dolly Varden; **5, 7** black crappie, white crappie; **5, 8** chain pickerel, white sturgeon; **6, 4** archer ⁓, arctic char, silver hake, yellow jack; **6, 5** golden trout, yellow perch; **6-5, 8** shovel-nosed sturgeon; **6, 6** golden shiner; **7, 4** striped bass; **7, 5** miller's thumb, rainbow trout; **7-6** sailor's-choice; **7, 8** Spanish mackerel; **8, 4** redbelly dace; **8, 10** Colorado pikeminnow; **9, 4** labyrinth ⁓; **9, 5** cutthroat trout; **10, 4** largemouth bass, smallmouth bass. *See also* **freshwater fish, sea fish, game fish**

fish dish **3** lox, roe; **5** smoky; **6** caviar, kipper, scampi; **7** bloater; **8** kedgeree, quenelle, rollmops; **9** gravadlax *UK*; **12** taramasalata; PHRASES: **3, 6** red caviar; **4, 3, 5** fish and chips; **4, 4** fish cake; **4, 5** fish stick; **4, 6** fish finger; **4, 7** clam chowder; **5, 6** black caviar; **5, 7** fried catfish, Maine lobster; **6, 4** Bombay duck, smoked fish; **6, 6** Beluga caviar; **6, 7** finnan haddock; **7, 3** jellied eel; **7, 4** gefilte fish, poached fish; **7, 7** pickled herring; **8, 4** kippered fish; **8, 6** Arbroath smokey, lumpfish caviar.

fisher **6** angler, whaler; **7** fishman; **8** fishwife, piscator; **9** fisherman; **10** fisherfolk, fishmonger, trawlerman; PHRASES: **4, 6** fish farmer, fish seller.

fishery **7** piscary.

fishing animal **5** otter; **6** osprey; **10** kingfisher; PHRASES: **3, 5** sea otter; **4, 5** fish eagle; **5, 4** polar bear.

fishing gear **3** eye, fly, net, rod; **4** bend, cork, gaff, hook, lead, line, pole, reel, shot; **5** float, point, shank; **6** bobber, bobbin, forcep, sinker; **7** ferrule, harpoon, keepnet *UK*, trawler; **8** handgrip; **9** disgorger; PHRASES: **3, 3** fly rod, tip top; **3, 6** eel basket.

fish product **3** roe; **4** glue; **6** caviar; **8** fishmeal; **9** isinglass; PHRASES: **3-5, 3** cod-liver oil.

fishy **3** odd, rum; **5** dodgy *UK*, shady; **6** gadoid, shifty; **7** devious, dubious, percoid, piscine, strange; **8** doubtful, ichthyic, sharkish; **9** ichthyoid, irregular, pisciform, underhand; **10** suspicious; **11** piscatorial; **12** questionable.

fission **5** split; **6** schism; **8** division, scission; **10** separation, shattering; **11** atomization; PHRASES: **4, 8** atom smashing; **5, 8** chain reaction; **8, 2** breaking up.

fissure *See* **crack**

fist **3** paw, wad; **4** duke, hand, mitt; **5** bunch; **7** fistful, handful, knuckle.

fit **2** A1; **3** add, apt, fix; **4** able, fine, hale, jibe, size, suit, turn, well, **5** check, equip, match, mount, right, serve, shape, spasm, tally; **6** accord, attack, belong, hearty, modify, proper, robust, sporty, strong, supply, tailor; **7** capable, condign, fashion, fitting, healthy, install, measure, pertain, qualify, seizure; **8** adequate, athletic, outburst, paroxysm, suitable, vigorous; **9** appertain; **10** acceptable, convulsion, correspond, salubrious; **11** appropriate; PHRASES: **2, 3, 4** on top form; **2, 4, 5** in good shape; **2, 4, 6** in fine fettle; **2, 5** in shape; **3, 2** put in; **3, 3** let out; **4, 2** take in, take up; **4, 3, 4** fill the bill; **7, 4** provide with.

fitch, fitchew **7** polecat.

fitful **6** broken; **8** restless, sporadic; **9** disturbed, irregular.

fitness **5** vigor; **6** health; **8** strength; **10** capability; **11** suitability; **13** qualification; PHRASES: **4-5** well-being. *See also* **fit**

fitting **3** apt, fit; **5** right; **6** decent, proper; **7** correct, germane; **8** apposite, relevant, suitable; **9** belonging, expedient, pertinent; **10** pertaining; **11** appropriate; **12** appertaining; PHRASES: **2, 7** in keeping; **3, 3, 3** cut out for; **9, 3** qualified for.

five **1** V; **3** fin; **4** quin; **5** fiver, quint; **6** cinque *UK*, pentad; **7** quintet; **8** fivesome, quincunx.

fivefold **9** quintuple.

fix **2** do; **3** con, fit, hit, rig, set; **4** cook, dose, glue, hole, join, mend, mess, shot; **5** affix, agree, fraud, renew, setup, stick, sting, trick; **6** answer, attach, corner, fasten, fiddle, handle, locate, remedy, repair, report, secure, settle; **7** arrange, correct, dilemma, install, massage, prepare, resolve, restore, swindle; **8** organize, overhaul, position, quandary, renovate, schedule, solution; **9** establish, injection, publicize, refurbish; **10** manipulate, resolution; **11** predicament; PHRASES: **3, 2** set up; **3, 2, 6** put to rights; **4, 3** sort out; **4, 4, 2** take care of; **4, 5** make ready, make right; **5, 2** patch up; **5, 4** tight spot; **6, 2** rustle up.

fixation **5** mania, thing; **7** complex, passion; **8** neurosis, paranoia; **9** addiction, obsession; **11** fascination; **13** preoccupation; PHRASES: **4, 4** idée fixe.

fixed **3** set; **4** dyed, fast, flat; **5** rigid, sound; **6** agreed, imbued, preset, rooted, secure, soaked, stable, static, steady; **7** decided, staunch; **8** constant, immobile; **9** immovable, implanted, ingrained, permanent, permeated, steadfast; **10** inflexible, motionless, stationary, unchanging; **12** unchangeable; **13** predetermined; PHRASES: 4-2-3-4 dyed-in-the-wool; 4-3-4 hard-and-fast; 4-4 cast-iron, true-blue; 4-6 deep-rooted, deep-seated.

fixer 7 handler; **9** publicist; **10** journalist; PHRASES: 4, 6 spin doctor.

fixture 7 fitting; **9** accessory; **10** decoration.

fizz 4 foam; **5** froth; **6** bubble; **7** bubbles, sparkle; **10** effervesce; **13** effervescence.

fizzle 4 fail, fizz, hiss, spit; **6** sizzle; **7** sputter; **9** disappear; PHRASES: 4, 3 tail off; 4, 4 fade away; 5, 3 peter out.

flag 3 ebb, fly, pin, sag; **4** clip, fade, fail, jack, mark, note, pall, sink, tire, wane, warn, wave, wilt; **5** abate, droop, faint, hoist, label, slump, swoon, truck, weary, white; **6** banner, burgee, canton, colors, emblem, ensign, guidon, pennon, select, signal, sleeve, weaken; **7** bunting, decline, dwindle, labarum, pennant, stagger; **8** bannerol, bookmark, diminish, flagpole, gonfalon, identify, indicate, languish, masthead, signpost, standard, streamer, Tricolor, vexillum; **9** banderole, highlight, oriflamme; **10** bannerette; **11** swallowtail; PHRASES: 2, 7, 5 St Andrew's cross, St George's cross; 2, 8, 5 St Patrick's cross; 3, 5 Old Glory; 3, 6 red duster, Red Ensign; 4, 5 blue peter; 4, 6 Blue Ensign UK; 5, 3, 7 Stars and Stripes; 5, 4 Union Jack; 5, 5 Jolly Roger; 5, 6 King's Colour, White Ensign UK.

flagellate See **whip**

flagon See **bottle**

flagrant See **blatant**

flagship 3 top; **4** lead, star; **5** jewel, pearl, prize; **6** leader; **7** leading, warship; **10** battleship; PHRASES: 3-2-3 man-of-war; 7, 4 capital ship.

flail 3 hit; **4** beat, flap, flog, wave; **5** whirl; **6** batter, strike, thrash; **8** flounder.

flair 4 chic, feel, gift; **5** skill, style; **6** talent; **7** panache; **8** aptitude, elegance; **11** stylishness.

flak See **criticism**

flake 3 bit; **4** chip, peel; **5** fleck, patch,

scale; **6** sliver; **7** blister, crumble, shaving; **8** fragment; PHRASES: 4, 3 chip off, come off.

flamboyant 4 loud; **5** gaudy, lurid, showy; **6** flashy, glitzy, lavish, ornate; **7** flaunty, profuse; **8** colorful, overdone, splendid; **9** excessive, exuberant, grandiose; **10** exorbitant, inordinate, outrageous; **11** extravagant, intemperate, overstepped; **12** meretricious, ostentatious; **13** overindulgent, swashbuckling; PHRASES: 5-2 piled-on; 6-4-4 larger-than-life.

flame 4 burn, fire, glow; **5** blaze, flare, spark; PHRASES: 5, 2 light up.

flaming 3 lit; **5** afire, angry, fiery; **6** ablaze, alight, ardent, fierce, heated, stormy; **7** furious, intense, violent; **8** sparking, vehement; **10** flickering, passionate; PHRASES: 2, 4 on fire.

flammable 9 pyrogenic; **10** incendiary; **11** combustible, inflammable.

flank 4 edge, line, side; **5** skirt, verge; **6** border, fringe, margin.

flap 3 lap, tab, wag; **4** fold, fret, tail, wave; **5** flail, panic, shake, state; **6** dither, lappet; **7** fluster, flutter.

flare 4 bell, burn; **5** blaze, burst, flame, flash, splay, widen; **6** spread; **7** broaden, flicker.

flash 3 fly, set, zip; **4** burn, card, dash, line, race, rush, show, tick UK, wink, zoom; **5** blaze, burst, flame, flare, gleam, glint, jiffy, point, spark, speed, trice; **6** flaunt, minute, moment, report, second, streak, update; **7** display, exhibit, flicker, glimmer, glisten, glitter, instant, sparkle, twinkle; **8** bulletin, flourish, smelting; **9** explosion, flashbulb; **10** eliminator UK, photolysis; **12** announcement; **13** communication; PHRASES: 3-4 hot-shoe; 4, 3 show off; 4, 5 news ~.

flashlight 4 lamp; **5** light, torch UK; **8** penlight.

flashy 4 loud; **5** flash UK, gaudy, jazzy, showy, tacky; **6** bright, frilly, garish, glitzy, jaunty, rakish, snappy, snazzy, tawdry; **7** foppish, painted; **8** colorful, dazzling, tinselly; **9** bombastic, tasteless; **10** flamboyant, glittering; **11** extravagant; **12** meretricious, ostentatious; **13** exhibitionist.

flask See **bottle**

flat 4 bald, dead, dull, even; **5** fixed, flush, level, plain, plane, prone, stale, total, utter; **6** boring, double, dreary, smooth; **7** regular, surface, tedious, uniform; **8** absolute, complete, definite, emphatic, lifeless, thorough; **9** downright; **10** horizontal, invariable, monotonous, unexciting; **11** categorical, unequivocal, unqualified; **13** nonnegotiable, uninteresting; PHRASES: 3-3-3 out-and-out; 5-5 point-blank.

flat (flat thing) 3 bed; **4** disc, disk *UK*, slab, tray; **5** floor, layer, ledge, plain, plate, table; **6** pampas, saucer, steppe, tablet; **7** ceiling, horizon, pancake, plateau, platter, prairie, skyline, stratum, terrace; **8** flatfish, flatware, flounder, gridiron, platform; **9** esplanade, tableland; PHRASES: **7, 5** bedding plane, bowling green.

flatten 2 KO; **3** hew; **4** beat, chop, deck, dent, down, fell, raze, roll; **5** crush, floor, level; **6** ground, hollow, lumber, smooth, spread, squash; **7** trample; **8** compress, demolish, smoothen; PHRASES: **3, 4** cut down, mow down; **4, 2, 3, 6** raze to the ground; **4, 3** even out, roll out; **4, 4** chop down, dash down, pull down, tear down; **5, 4** knock down, knock over.

flattener 4 iron; **5** plane, press; **6** mangle, poleax *UK*, roller; **7** poleaxe; **8** flatiron; **9** bulldozer; **11** steamroller; PHRASES: **6, 6** garden roller; **7, 3** rolling pin; **7, 5** trouser press.

flatter 4 fawn; **5** charm, creep *UK*, toady; **6** cajole, praise; **7** adulate, wheedle; **8** blandish, bootlick, inveigle, overlaud; **9** brownnose; **10** compliment, overesteem, overpraise; **11** overcommend; **12** overestimate; PHRASES: **3, 2, 2** lay it on; **3, 2, 2, 5** lay it on thick; **4-4** soft-soap; **5-4** sweet-talk; **5-6** apple-polish; **6, 2** butter up, overdo it; **6, 4** smooth talk.

flattering 4 kind; **6** smarmy, smooth; **8** becoming, cheering, pleasing, praising, suitable, toadyish, unctuous; **9** adulatory, favorable, forgiving, insincere, laudatory; **10** gratifying, obsequious, satisfying; **11** pleasurable, sycophantic, sympathetic; **12** hypocritical, satisfactory; **13** complimentary.

flattery 4 hype, puff; **6** praise, urging; **7** coaxing, fawning, teasing; **8** advocacy, cajolery, toadyism; **9** adulation, hypocrisy, panegyric, wheedling; **10** compliment, enticement, incitement, invitation, sycophancy, temptation; **11** compliments, hagiography, insincerity; **12** blandishment, solicitation, unctuousness; **13** encouragement; PHRASES: **7, 5** honeyed words.

flatulent 5 gassy, windy; **6** turgid; **7** burping, pompous, verbose; **8** belching; **9** bombastic; **10** eructative; **11** pretentious; **13** grandiloquent.

flaunt *See* **show off**

flavor 3 air, MSG; **4** feel, herb, hint, lace, mark, salt, tang, tone, zest; **5** aroma, color, dress, gusto, imbue, sauce, savor, sense, smack, spice, taste, touch; **6** ginger, relish, season; **7** enhance, essence, extract, feeling, garnish, pervade; **8** additive, piquancy, richness, sourness; **9** condiment, flavoring, saltiness, seasoning, sweetness; **10** bitterness, suggestion; **11** distinguish; **12** characterize.

flavouring *See* **flavor**

flay 4 beat, flog, lash, whip; **6** thrash; **7** censure, condemn, pillory; **8** lambaste; **9** criticize.

fledgling 3 new; **4** tyro; **5** young; **6** novice; **7** learner, untried; **8** beginner, inexpert, neophyte; **13** inexperienced.

flee 3 fly, run; **4** bolt; **5** scram, split; **6** escape; **7** abscond, scamper, scarper *UK*, vamoose; **8** hightail; **9** skedaddle; **12** absquatulate; PHRASES: **3, 3** nip off, run off; **3, 4** cut away, run away; **4, 3** dash off, make off, rush off, skip off *UK*, take off; **4, 6** take flight.

fleece 3 con; **4** coat, wool; **5** shear; **7** swindle; **9** sheepskin.

fleet 4 navy; **6** armada, convoy; **8** flotilla; PHRASES: **4, 5** task force.

fleeting 4 fast; **5** brief; **7** melting, passing; **8** fugitive; **9** momentary, temporary, transient; **10** evanescent, transitory.

flesh 3 ham, kin; **4** beef, body, lamb, meat, pork, pulp, skin; **6** corpus, dermis, family, muscle, tissue; **7** details, reality, surface; **9** epidermis, pulpiness, relations *UK*, relatives, solidness, substance; **10** epithelium; **11** information, physicality; **12** corporeality; PHRASES: **4, 6** soft tissue; **5, 3, 5** ~ and blood; **5, 9** blood relatives.

fleshy 4 ripe; **5** plump; **6** carnal; **9** succulent. *See also* **fat**

flex 4 bend, move; **5** tense; **7** tighten; **8** activate, contract; PHRASES: **4, 2** warm up; **6, 2** loosen up.

flick 3 tap; **4** film, flip; **5** brush, graze, movie; **6** glance; **7** picture; PHRASES: **3, 6** big screen; **6, 6** silver screen.

flicker **4** flit, spit, wave; **5** blink, dance, flash, flick, ghost, glint, spark, trace, waver; **6** bicker, glance, gutter, quiver; **7** flutter, glimmer, shimmer, sparkle, spatter, sputter, twinkle; **8** splutter; **10** impression, suggestion.

flight **3** hop, lam; **4** trip; **6** escape, exodus, voyage; **7** evasion, getaway, journey; **8** breakout; **9** breakaway, departure.

flightless bird **3** emu; **4** kiwi, rhea; **6** ratite, takahe *UK*; **7** ostrich, penguin; **9** cassowary.

flight path **5** orbit; **6** skyway; **7** airlane; **10** trajectory; PHRASES: **3, 8** air corridor; **6, 4** flight lane.

flight recorder **5, 3** black box.

flimsy **4** poor, weak; **6** feeble, slight; **7** fragile; **8** delicate; **10** inadequate; **12** unconvincing; **13** insubstantial.

flinch *See* **recoil**

fling **3** lob; **4** hurl, toss; **5** pitch, throw; **6** affair; **7** romance; **11** involvement; **12** relationship; PHRASES: **4, 6** love affair.

flip **4** spin, toss; **5** flick, jokey; **6** casual, joking; **8** flippant, overturn; **10** dismissive; PHRASES: **2, 7** go berserk; **3, 3, 4** hit the roof; **4, 4** turn over; **4, 4, 3** ~ your lid.

flirt **3** toy; **4** flip, jerk, play, toss; **5** flick; **6** propel, seduce, trifle; PHRASES: **4, 2** lead on.

flit **3** fly; **4** dart, skim; **5** flash; **7** flutter.

float **4** hang, sail, soar, swim; **5** drift, glide, hover, offer; **7** promote, propose, suggest; PHRASES: **3, 7** put forward; **5, 5** tread water.

flock **3** mob, nye, set; **4** army, bevy, cast, herd, host, pack, tuft, wisp; **5** brood, charm, covey, drive, drove, group, shoal, siege, skein, swarm, troop, watch, wedge; **6** clutch, colony, flight, gaggle, gather, kennel, kettle, muster, school, stable, string; **7** cluster, collect, rookery; **8** assemble; **10** congregate.

flog **4** beat, lash, whip; **6** thrash; **7** scourge.

flood **4** bore, glut, gush, hail, pour, rush, tide, wave; **5** drown, spate, storm, surge, swamp; **6** deluge, engulf, excess, shower, stream, volley; **7** outflow, surplus, torrent; **8** downpour, inundate, overflow, saturate, submerge; **9** abundance, weltering; **10** inundation, outpouring, underwater; PHRASES: **5, 4** tidal wave.

flooded **5** awash; **6** afloat, dipped, ducked, dunked, washed; **7** drowned, whelmed; **8** immersed; **9** submersed; **11** waterlogged. *See also* **flood**

flood in **6** inflow, inrush; **7** inflood; **10** congregate; PHRASES: **4, 2** flow in, pack in, rush in; **7, 2** squeeze in.

floodlight **5** flood, light; **6** stream; **8** lighting; **9** irradiate, spotlight; **10** illuminate; **11** searchlight; **12** illumination; PHRASES: **5, 2** light up.

floor **4** base, deck, flat, stun; **5** amaze, flair, level, story, stump; **6** baffle, bottom, ground; **7** astound, flummox, stagger, stupefy, surface; **8** astonish, bewilder, confound; **11** flabbergast.

floor covering **3** mat, rug, wax; **4** lino *UK*; **5** tiles, vinyl; **6** carpet, runner, tiling; **7** bathmat, doormat, drugget, matting, parquet; **8** linoleum; **9** carpeting, dropcloth; **10** duckboards; **11** floorboards, groundsheet; PHRASES: **6, 5** ground cloth.

flop **3** dud, sag; **4** fail, fold; **5** close, crash, loser, slump; **6** fiasco; **7** failure, slacken; **8** collapse; PHRASES: **4, 4** dead loss, fall down.

flophouse **5** spike; **6** hostel; **7** shelter; **9** dosshouse *UK*; PHRASES: **5, 7** night shelter.

floral **6** bloomy, florid, ornate; **7** flowery; **8** floreate, floriate, flowered, fragrant; **9** floristic; **10** florescent; PHRASES: **6-4** flowerlike.

florid **3** red; **5** ruddy; **6** ornate; **7** baroque; **8** sanguine.

Florida **2** FL; **11** mockingbird (bird), Tallahassee (capital); PHRASES: **2, 3, 2, 5** In God we trust (motto); **5, 4** sabal palm (tree); **6, 7** orange blossom (flower); **8, 5** Sunshine State (nickname); **9, 5** Peninsula State (nickname).

flounder **3** dab; **4** flap; **5** delay, flail, fluke, lurch, waver; **6** dawdle, dither, falter, splash, thrash, wallow, welter; **7** stagger, stumble; **8** hesitate, struggle.

flourish **2** Fl; **4** boom, curl, grow, show, wave; **5** bloom, flash, shake, swing, vaunt, wield; **6** flaunt, thrive; **7** blossom, bravado, burgeon, display, fanfare, prosper, succeed, swagger, trumpet; **8** brandish, curlicue, emblazon, increase, ornament, proclaim; **10** decoration; **13** embellishment; PHRASES: **2, 4** do well; **4, 4** fare well; **5, 7** grand gesture.

flow **3** ebb, lap, run; **4** eddy, fall, flux, gush, ooze, pour, purl, race, roll, rush, seep, spew, tide, wash, weep, well, wind; **5** arise, bleed, braid, drain, drift, flood, flush, glide, issue, plash, slide, slosh, snake, spill, spout, surge, swamp, swash, sweat, swirl, trill, twirl, whirl; **6** babble, bubble, burble, course, emerge, engulf, gurgle, murmur, riffle, ripple, splash, spring, stream; **7** cascade, channel, current, dribble, emanate, fluency, fluxion, meander, overrun, torrent, trickle; **8** converge, inundate, movement, overflow, submerge; **9** fluxility, secretion; **10** hemorrhage; **11** suppuration; **12** menstruation.

flower 3 bud, lip; **4** cyme, posy; **5** ament, bloom, bract, calyx, glume, lemma, ovary, ovule, palea, petal, sepal, spike, spray, stock, style, tepal, umbel, whorl; **6** anther, carpel, catkin, corymb, floret, nectar, pistil, pollen, raceme, spadix, spathe, stamen, stigma, thrive, thyrse, wreath; **7** blossom, bouquet, corolla, develop, garland, nectary, nosegay, panicle, pedicel; **8** epicalyx, filament, flourish, floweret, peduncle, perianth, spikelet; **9** gynoecium, involucre, micropyle; **10** androecium, buttonhole *UK*, effloresce, receptacle; **11** boutonniere; PHRASES: **4, 2, 8** come to fruition; **4, 4, 5** come into bloom; **5, 5** daisy chain; **6, 4** ~ head, pollen tube. *See also* **plants and flowers, river**

flowering 4 acme, blow, peak; **5** bloom; **6** zenith; **8** anthesis, blooming, pinnacle; **9** unfolding; **10** blossoming, florescent; **11** florescence, flourishing; **12** efflorescent, inflorescent; PHRASES: **4, 5** high point.

flowery 5 fancy; **6** floral, florid, ornate; **7** baroque; **8** flowered; **9** elaborate, floriated; **10** ornamental; **11** embellished, extravagant.

flowing *See also* **fluid**

fluctuate *See* **vary**

flue 4 duct, pipe, tube, vent; **5** shaft; **6** outlet; **7** chimney.

fluent 4 easy; **6** smooth; **7** assured, flowing, voluble; **8** eloquent; **9** confident; **10** articulate; PHRASES: **6-6** smooth-spoken *UK*; **6-7** smooth-tongued.

fluff 3 pat; **4** fuzz, hair, lint, ruin; **5** botch, shake, spoil; **6** ruffle; PHRASES: **2, 5** do badly; **4, 1, 4, 2** make a mess of; **5, 2** ~ up, plump up.

fluffy 4 soft; **5** downy, foamy, furry, fuzzy, light; **6** bubbly, fleecy, frothy; **7** cottony, velvety; **8** feathery.

fluid 4 oozy; **5** drink, juicy, moist, runny, sappy, water; **6** fluent, liquid, liquor, melted, molten, smooth, sweaty, watery; **7** curving, elegant, flowing, fluidic, fluxile, rolling, sinuous; **8** beverage, flawless, flexible, graceful, shifting, solution, unbroken, unstable; **9** adaptable, fluxional, liquefied, liquiform, succulent; **10** adjustable, changeable, effortless, indefinite; **11** fluctuating, mellifluous, uncongealed; **12** condensation, unsolidified; **13** unpredictable.

fluid (make fluid) 5 blend; **7** liquate, liquefy; **8** emulsify, fluidify, fluidize, liquesce; **9** liquidize.

fluidity 4 flux; **5** grace; **7** agility, fluxure; **9** fluidness, fluxility, liquidity; **10** bloodiness, mutability, plasticity, rheuminess, volatility; **11** flexibility, fluctuation, instability, uncertainty, variability; **12** liquefaction; **13** changeability, liquidescence. *See also* **fluid**

fluke 4 lobe; **5** freak; **6** chance; **8** accident, flounder; **11** coincidence; PHRASES: **5, 5** lucky break; **6, 2, 4** stroke of luck.

flummox *See* **confuse**

flunk *See* **fail**

flurry 4 gust, wind; **5** burst, spell; **7** agitate, disturb, fluster, perturb; **8** outbreak; **10** disconcert.

flush 4 even, flat, glow, rich, true; **5** blush, clear, color, level, rinse, swill; **6** redden; **7** cleanse, redness; **8** rosiness; **9** ruddiness; PHRASES: **2, 3** go red; **2, 3, 5** in the money; **2, 5** in funds *UK*; **4, 3** wash out, well off; **4, 5** high color; **7, 2, 2** rolling in it.

flute *See* **groove**

flutter 4 beat, flap, wave; **6** flurry, quiver; **7** fluster, tremble; **9** agitation, confusion; **10** excitement.

flux 6 unrest; **8** fluidity; **10** mutability; **11** fluctuation, instability.

fly 3 jet, yaw; **4** bank, bolt, buzz, dart, dash, dive, flee, flit, land, loop, race, roll, rush, sail, soar, spin, tear, turn, wing, zoom; **5** climb, coast, glide, hover, hurry, pitch, split, stall; **6** cruise, escape, spiral; **7** descend, flutter; **8** hedgehop, maneuver *UK*; PHRASES: **3, 1, 4, 2** get a move on; **3, 3** run off; **3, 3, 4** ~ the coop; **3, 4** run away; **4, 2, 3, 3** take to the air; **4, 3** take off; **4, 3, 4** loop the loop; **4, 4** take wing; **4-4** nose-dive; **4, 6** take flight; **6, 4** barrel roll. *See also* **flying insect**

fly (artificial fly) 3 jig; 4 lure, plug; 5 spoon; 6 popper; 7 spinner, wagtail; 8 barspoon, streamer.

flying animal 3 bat, fly; 4 bird; 5 flier; 9 butterfly; PHRASES: 6, 3 flying fox; 6, 4 flying fish.

flying bomb 1-1 V-1.

flying insect 3 bee, fly; 4 gnat, wasp; 5 aphid, midge, mozzy; 6 cicada, hornet, locust, mayfly, sawfly, thrips; 7 antlion, blowfly, firefly, ladybug, monarch, peacock, ringlet, satyrid, skipper; 8 alderfly, blackfly, cranefly, greenfly, honeybee, horntail, horsefly, housefly, hoverfly UK, lacewing, ladybird UK, mosquito, snakefly, stonefly, whitefly, woodwasp; 9 anopheles, brimstone, bumblebee, butterfly, damselfly, dobsonfly, dragonfly, ichneumon; 10 bluebottle, drosophila, fritillary, hairstreak; 11 grasshopper, swallowtail; 13 tortoiseshell; PHRASES: 3, 3 bot fly, gad fly; 3, 7 red admiral; 4, 3 deer fly, sand fly; 4, 4 gall wasp; 4, 5 corn borer; 5, 3 crane fly, fruit fly, mason bee; 6, 3 caddis fly, robber fly, tsetse fly, warble fly; 6, 4 digger wasp, potter wasp, spider wasp; 7, 3 spanish fly; 7, 4 buffalo gnat, painted lady; 7, 4, 3 cabbage root fly UK; 7, 5 cabbage white UK; 8, 3 scorpion fly; 9, 3 carpenter bee, lightning bug; 10, 3 leafcutter bee UK. See also **insect, moth**

foam 4 fizz; 5 froth; 6 bubble, lather; 7 bubbles; 10 effervesce; PHRASES: 5, 2 froth up.

focal 3 key; 4 head, main; 5 chief; 7 central, crucial, pivotal, primary; 8 favorite; 9 cynosural, principal.

focus 3 aim, fix, hub, nub; 4 core, firm, head, meet, star; 5 chief, heart, pivot, taper; 6 center, direct, effort, radius, target; 7 clarify, concern, nucleus; 8 converge, cynosure, emphasis, focalize; 9 asymptote, attention, spotlight; 10 centralize, motivation; 11 application, centerpiece, concentrate, personality; 13 concentralize, concentration; PHRASES: 3, 6 key figure; 4, 2 home in, zero in; 4, 2, 3, 5 come to the point; 4, 8 come together, main interest; 5, 5 focal point; 5, 8 bring together; 7, 5 central point, meeting point; 8, 5 rallying point.

focused 5 based, basic, clear; 6 angled; 7 central, defined, founded, pointed; 8 thematic; 10 programmed; PHRASES: 7, 4 dealing with; 9, 4 concerned with.

fodder 3 hay; 4 feed, food; 6 silage; 9 feedstuff.

fog 3 fug; 4 daze, fret, haar UK, haze, mist, smog; 5 befog, brume, cloud, vapor; 6 bemist, enmist, fuddle, miasma, muddle, stupor, trance; 7 confuse, obscure, perplex, stupefy; 8 bewilder, enshroud, haziness; 9 confusion, fogginess, mistiness, murkiness, peasouper UK; 12 bewilderment, condensation; 13 precipitation; PHRASES: 3, 3 ice ~, sea ~; 3, 4 ~ bank, pea soup.

foggy 3 dim; 4 hazy; 5 misty, murky, thick, vague; 6 cloudy, opaque, smoggy; 7 fuddled, muddled, unclear; 8 confused, fogbound, nebulous, vaporous; 9 stupefied; 10 bewildered, enshrouded.

foible 5 fault, quirk; 8 weakness; 11 shortcoming; 12 idiosyncrasy.

foil See **prevent**

fold 3 lap, pen; 4 bend, coil, flex, furl, roll, turn; 5 close, layer, pleat, plica, quake, shake; 6 buckle, cleave, crease, double, strain; 7 crinkle, overlap, wrinkle; 8 buckling UK, collapse, doubling, flection; 9 plication; 10 acorrugate; PHRASES: 2, 2, 3, 4 go to the wall; 2, 3, 2, 8 go out of business; 2, 4 go bust; 2, 5 go under; 2, 8 go bankrupt; 3-3 dog-ear.

folded 4 bent; 6 creasy, flexed, plical, rolled, ruched; 7 creased, doubled, pleated, plicate; 8 bankrupt, crumpled, gathered; 10 corrugated; PHRASES: 3-5 dog-eared; 4, 4 bent over; 6, 2 rucked up, turned up; 6, 4 turned over; 6, 5 turned under; 7, 2 doubled up; 7, 4 doubled over.

folding 6 foldup, hinged; 7 camping, compact; 8 foldaway, portable; 9 traveling; 11 collapsible.

foliage 6 leaves, plants; 7 leafage, verdure; 8 greenery; 9 shrubbery; 10 vegetation; 11 undergrowth.

folios 2 ff.

folk 3 kin, men; 6 people, public; 7 general, popular, society; 8 everyone, informal; 10 population, vernacular, widespread; 11 traditional; 12 conventional.

folk music 6 ballad; 7 skiffle; 8 folksong; 9 bluegrass; PHRASES: 4, 4 folk rock; 7, 5 country music; 9, 5 hillbilly music.

follow 3 dog, see; 4 hunt, obey, tail, twig UK; 5 arise, chart, chase, enjoy, ensue, grasp, segue, spoor, stalk, track, trail; 6 admire, derive, pursue, result, shadow, sleuth, survey; **7** imitate, monitor, replace, respect, succeed, support; **8** supplant; **10** comprehend, understand; PHRASES: **2, 4, 2** be keen on *UK*; **2, 5** go along; **3, 3, 4** get the gist, get the idea; **4, 2** hang on, keep on, keep to, stay on; **4, 2, 3, 2** keep an eye on; **4, 2, 4** keep up with; **4, 4** take over; **4, 4, 3, 4** swim with the tide; **5, 2** abide by, catch on, check on, stick to; **5, 2, 2** latch on to; **5, 3** scent out, sniff out; **5, 4, 4** stick like glue; **5, 5** prowl after; **6, 2** adhere to, batten on, cotton on.

follower 3 fan; **4** tail; **6** school, shadow, suitor; **7** admirer *UK*, apostle, clinger, devotee, groupie; **8** adherent, disciple, parasite, partisan; **9** dependent, latecomer, proselyte, satellite, supporter, sycophant; PHRASES: **2-5** no-hoper; **4, 2, 3, 5** last in the field; **4-3** also-ran; **4, 3, 2** last man in; **4, 8** camp ~, poor relation; **6-2** hanger-on; **8, 4** clinging vine.

following 4 fans, next, post; **5** later; **7** ensuing, retinue; **9** attendant, resulting *UK*; **10** subsequent.

follow up 7 persist; **8** progress; **9** persevere; PHRASES: **4, 4, 3** push one's way; **5, 2** press on; **5, 4, 3** fight one's way, force one's way; **7, 5** contact again.

folly 5 error, gaffe; **6** idiocy, lunacy; **7** bloomer *UK*, blooper, blunder, conceit, foolery, inanity, madness, mistake; **8** daftness *UK*, insanity, rashness, senility; **9** absurdity, asininity, craziness, flippancy, frivolity, giddiness, ignorance, puerility, silliness, stupidity; **10** imbecility, imprudence, ineptitude, tomfoolery; **11** fatuousness, foolishness, misjudgment; **12** childishness, eccentricity, extravagance, heedlessness, indiscretion, recklessness; **13** foolhardiness, irrationality, ludicrousness, pointlessness, senselessness; **14** ridiculousness, unintelligence; **15** thoughtlessness; PHRASES: **5-10** empty-headedness.

fond 4 keen, weak; **6** caring, doting, liking; **7** partial; **8** attached, involved; **12** affectionate.

fondle *See* **massage**

fondness 4 love; **6** warmth; **7** empathy; **8** devotion, sympathy; **9** affection; **10** attachment, cordiality, partiality; **11** amicability, involvement; **12** friendliness; PHRASES: **4, 4** soft spot. *See also* **fond**

font 4 type, well; **5** basis, fount; **6** source, spring, supply; **8** fountain, typeface; **9** lettering; **10** wellspring; PHRASES: **4, 5** type style; **5, 6** water source.

food 3 bun, egg, ham, pap; **4** bran, cake, chop, chow, diet, eats, fare, grub, meat, nosh, rice, tack, tart, tuck *UK*; **5** bread, chain, cheer, chuck, manna, scoff; **6** amrita, fodder, health, Pablum™, snacks, staple, stodge *UK*, stores, tucker *UK*, viands; **7** aliment, biscuit, cuisine, edibles, goodies, nurture, pabulum, rations, tidbits, vittles; **8** ambrosia, dainties, eatables, luxuries, peckings, pemmican, supplies, victuals; **9** foodstuff, groceries, nutrients, nutriment, nutrition, provender; **10** delicacies, foodstuffs, provisions, sustenance; **11** comestibles, nourishment; **12** alimentation; PHRASES: **3, 2, 3, 4** fat of the land; **4, 7** care package, iron rations *UK*; **5, 2, 4** staff of life; **5, 4** whole ~; **5, 5** daily bread.

food content 3 fat, MSG, oil; **4** bulk, iron, salt; **5** fiber, sugar, water; **6** starch; **7** calcium, glucose, lactose, protein, sucrose; **8** additive, calories, coloring, fructose, minerals, roughage, vitamins; **9** flavoring, sweetener; **10** emulsifier; **11** cholesterol; **12** preservative; **13** carbohydrates; **14** polyunsaturate; PHRASES: **1, 6** E number *UK*; **5, 4** amino acid; **6, 8** flavor enhancer; **9, 4** saturated fats.

food provider 4 chef, cook; **5** baker; **6** farmer, grocer; **7** butcher, caterer, milkman, rancher; **9** fisherman; **10** fishmonger; **11** greengrocer; **12** confectioner, restaurateur.

food store 4 deli; **6** baker's, bakery, market; **7** grocer's *UK*; **8** butcher's *UK*; **9** megastore; **10** commissary, superstore; **11** fishmonger's *UK*, hypermarket, supermarket; **12** delicatessen, greengrocer's *UK*; PHRASES: **4, 4** food hall, tuck shop *UK*; **5, 4** sweet shop; **5, 5** candy store, fruit stall; **6-4, 5** health-food store; **7, 5** grocery store; **7, 6** covered market, farmers' market.

fool 3 ass, cod, con, git, kid, mug *UK*, nit, sap; **4** boob, clot, dolt, dope, dupe, jerk, prat, twit; **5** clown, dimbo, dumbo, dunce, idiot, ninny, trick, wally; **6** cretin, dimwit, dotard *UK*, nitwit, noodle, sucker; **7** asshole *UK*, buffoon, deceive, dessert, dingbat, halfwit, jackass, mislead, pillock *UK*, pinhead, skylark; **8** hoodwink, imbecile, meathead; **9** bamboozle, birdbrain, blockhead, simpleton; **10** nincompoop; PHRASES: **4, 2** take in; **4, 5** lark about *UK*; **4, 6** ~ around; **5, 6** horse around; **5, 7** right Charlie; **6, 6** monkey around.

foolish 3 mad; 4 daft, dull, rash, slow, wild; 5 barmy *UK*, crazy, inane, inept, nutty, potty *UK*, silly; 6 absurd, insane, senile, simple, stupid, unwise; 7 asinine, doltish, fatuous, idiotic, lunatic, moronic, puerile, risible; 8 anserine, childish, flippant, gormless *UK*, heedless, hellbent, ignorant, mindless, prodigal, reckless; 9 brainless, eccentric, foolhardy, frivolous, hotheaded, imbecilic, imprudent, laughable, ludicrous, pointless, senseless; 10 headstrong, incautious, irrational, ridiculous; 11 harebrained, inattentive, injudicious, nonsensical, thoughtless; 12 preposterous; 13 unintelligent; PHRASES: 3-6 dim-witted; 3-7 ill-advised; 3-10 ill-considered; 4-7 bird-brained; 5-3-4 devil-may-care; 5-6 empty-headed; 6-3 spaced-out; 7-4-4 couldn't-care-less.

foot 2 ft; 3 end, pad, paw, pes, rot, toe; 4 ball, base, heel, hoof, rule, sill, sole; 5 stand, tread, verse; 6 bottom, plinth; 7 measure; 8 pedestal, wainscot; 9 underside; 10 foundation, underneath.

football 3 AFC, MVP, NFC, NFL; 4 foul, game, kick, miss, pass; 5 draft, field, issue, NFPLA (National F~ League Players' Association), point, rugby, score; 6 direct, ground, handle, matter, nutmeg, rugger *UK*, soccer, tackle; 7 fouling, gridder, handoff, holding, kicking, kickoff, passing, pigskin, playoff, problem, reserve, rollout, runback, scoring; 8 crossbar, handling, midfield, pitchout, playbook, tackling; 9 backfield, noseguard, perimeter, touchback; 10 buttonhook, cornerback, linebacker, lineswoman, scoreboard; 11 flankerback, linesperson; PHRASES: 1, 9 I formation; 1-9 T-formation; 2, 5, 4 St. Louis Rams; 3, 3 end run; 3-3 red-dog; 3, 4 end zone, Pro Bowl; 3, 4, 5 New York KJets; 3, 4, 6 New York Giants; 3, 5, 8 San Diego Chargers; 3, 6 hot potato; 3-6 end-around; 3, 7, 6 New Orleans Saints; 3, 7, 8 New England Patriots; 3, 9, 5 San Francisco 49ers; 4, 2, 9 line of scrimmage; 4, 3 hand off; 4, 4 drop ball, goal line, goal post, Rose Bowl; 4, 5 taxi squad; 4-6, 4 play-action pass; 4, 7 zone defense; 4-7 flea-flicker; 4, 8 wide receiver; 4, 9 punt formation; 5, 3 split end, tight end; 5, 3, 7 Green Bay Packers; 5, 3, 10 Tampa Bay Buccaneers; 5, 4 first down, quick kick, squib kick, Sugar Bowl, Super Bowl, World Bowl; 5, 5 extra point, mouth guard; 5, 7 Dalls Cowboys, naked reverse;

5, 8 Miami Dolphins, touch ~; 6, 4 Cotton Bowl, onside kick, Orange Bowl, screen pass, strong side; 6-4 double-team, triple-team; 6, 4, 6 Kansas City Chiefs; 6-5 broken-field; 6, 6 coffin corner; 6, 7 Denver Broncos; 7, 4 forward pass, halfway line, running back, special team; 7, 5 Buffalo Bills, Chicago Bears, Detroit Lions; 7, 6 Houston Texans; 7, 7 Arizona Falcons, Atlanta Falcons, Oakland Raiders; 7, 8 Seattle Seahawks; 8-1 wishbone-T; 8, 4 inbounds line; 8, 8 Canadian ~, Carolina Panthers; 9, 6 Baltimore Ravens, Cleveland Browns, Tennessee Titans; 9, 7 Minnesota Vikings; 10, 7 Cincinnati Bengals; 10, 8 Pittsburgh Steelers, Washington Redskins; 12, 5 Indianapolis Colts; 12, 6 Philadelphia Eagles; 12, 7 Jacksonville Jaguars.

footballer 3 sub; 4 club, side, team; 5 coach, zebra; 6 goalie, rookie, umpire, winger; 7 captain, manager, referee, striker, sweeper, trainer; 8 defender, fullback, linesman, redshirt; 9 playmaker; 10 goalkeeper, substitute; PHRASES: 3-3 All-Pro; 3-8 All-American; 4-4, 4 side-line crew; 4, 5 back judge, free agent, head coach, line judge, side judge; 4, 8 head linesman; 5, 4 chain gang, draft pick; 5, 5 field judge; 6, 4 center back, center half; 6, 7 center forward; 8, 7 midfield striker; 9, 5 assistant coach.

football player 4 Camp (Walter Chauncey); 5 Brown (Jim), Shula (Don), White (Byron); 6 Grange (Red), Landry (Tom), Payton (Walter), Rockne (Knute Kenneth), Sayers (Gale), Thorpe (Jim), Unitas (Johnny); 7 Montana (Joe), Simpson (O. J.); 8 Bradshaw (Terry), Lombardi (Vince), Staubach (Roger); 9 Tarkenton (Fran).

foothold 4 base, grip; 7 toehold; 8 position, purchase.

footloose 4 free; 6 single; 10 unattached; 11 uncommitted; 12 unrestricted.

footsore 4 sore; 5 tired, weary; 6 aching; 9 exhausted.

footwear 2 DM; 3 dap; 4 boot, calk, clog, daps *UK*, geta, muil, mule, pump, shoe, skid, tabi *UK*, vamp, vibs, welt, zori; 5 plate, sabot, scuff, spike, stoga, stogy, suede, thong, upper, wader; 6 Arctic, bootee, brogan, brogue *UK*, bumper, buskin, calcei, caliga, calker, calkin, cawker, chopin, cothum, gaiter, galosh, golosh, jandal, loafer, mukluk, Oxford, panton, patten, rivlin, sandal, sannie, stogie, vamper, vibram, wedgie, wellie *UK*; **7** baboosh, bottine, casuals, caulker, chappal, chopine, creeper, crepida, flattie, galoche, ghillie, klompen, oxonian, peeptoe, rubbers, rullion, sabaton, shoepac, slipper, sneaker, trainer *UK*, wingtip; **8** Balmoral, calceate, footgear, gamashes, huarache, jackboot, larrigan, moccasin, overshoe, platform, plimsole, plimsoll *UK*, poulaine, sabotine, sandshoe *UK*, snowshoe, solleret, stiletto; **9** alpargata, brodequin, pantoffle, scarpetto, slingback, veldskoen *UK*; **10** clodhopper, espadrille, overgaiter, shankpiece, veldschoen; **11** wellingtons; PHRASES: **3, 4** gum boot, gum shoe, gym shoe *UK*, hip boot, hot shoe, ski boot, top boot; **3, 7** Doc Martens™; **4-2** lace-up, slip-on; **4-3** high-low, high-top; **4, 4** fell boot, flat shoe, high boot, high heel; **4-4** boot-hose, flip-flop; **4-5** rope-soled; **4, 7** Hush Puppies™ *UK*; **5, 4** ankle boot, brake shoe, court shoe *UK*, Cuban heel, dress shoe, Jesus boot, rugby boot, sling shoe, spike heel, thigh boot, track shoe, wedge heel; **6, 4** ballet shoe, canvas shoe, combat boot, cowboy boot, desert boot, hiking boot, riding boot, rubber boot, saddle shoe, tennis shoe; **6, 5** chukka boots, wooden shoes; **6-6** winkle-picker; **6-7** beetle-crusher; **7, 4** buckled shoe, dancing clog, fashion boot, hobnail boot, hunting boot, running shoe, Russian boot, walking boot, walking shoe; **7, 5** evening shoes; **7, 7** brothel creeper; **8, 4** athletic shoe, baseball boot, cavalier boot, elevator shoe, football boot, platform heel; **8, 5** elevator shoes; **8, 6** barefoot sandal, egyptian sandal; **9, 4** acrobatic shoe, spectator shoe; **10, 4** wellington boot *UK*. *See also* **clothes**

for **2** to; **3** cos, per, pro; PHRASES: **2, 5, 2** in favor of, in order to; **2, 7, 2** in support of; **2, 9, 2** in pursuance of; **4, 1, 4, 2** with a view to; **4, 2, 3, 2** with an eye to; **5, 2** aimed at.

forage **4** feed, food, hunt, seek; **5** foray, quest; **6** fodder, search, silage; **7** rummage; **8** scavenge; **11** exploration; PHRASES: **4, 3** look for; **6, 3** search for.

foray **4** raid; **6** sortie; **7** venture; **9** incursion; **10** expedition.

forbear *See* **refrain**

forbearing *See* **patient**

forbid **3** ban, bar; **4** deny, stop, veto; **5** block, taboo; **6** enjoin, hinder, outlaw, stifle; **7** embargo, inhibit, prevent; **8** disallow,

prohibit, suppress; **9** interdict, proscribe.

forbidden **7** illegal, illicit; PHRASES: **5, 3** ruled out. *See also* **forbid**

forbidding **5** harsh, stern; **6** dismal; **7** hostile, ominous; **8** menacing, sinister; **9** dangerous; **10** depressing, unfriendly, uninviting, unpleasant; **11** threatening; **13** unsympathetic.

force **1** F, G; **2** TA *UK*; **3** jam, RAF *UK*, ram, RUC *UK*; **4** army, flux, make, navy, push, take, unit; **5** bully, corps, draft, drive, exact, fleet, foist, might, power, press, prize, shove, squad, troop, vigor, wring; **6** coerce, compel, energy, extort, impose, legion, moment, strain, stress, torque, weight; **7** brigade, cogency, dragoon, impress, inflict, osmosis, platoon, potency, torsion; **8** bludgeon, browbeat, bulldoze, buoyancy, division, dynamism, friction, pressure, railroad, regiment, squadron, stampede, strength, threaten; **9** battalion, blackmail, conscript, constrain, influence, intensity, pressgang, viscosity; **10** commandeer, intimidate; **11** steamroller; PHRASES: **3, 8** use violence; **4, 2** call up; **5, 4** break down, break open; **6-3** strong-arm.

forceful **5** valid; **6** cogent, mighty, potent, strong; **7** dynamic, weighty; **8** powerful, vehement, vigorous; **9** energetic, strenuous; **10** compelling, convincing, persuasive; **11** influential.

forceps **6** pliers; **7** pincers; **8** tweezers.

forces *See* **armed forces**

forcible **5** armed; **7** violent; **8** forceful, powerful; **9** effective; **10** aggressive, compulsory, convincing, persuasive.

ford **5** cross; **7** passage; **8** crossing, shallows, traverse; **9** negotiate; PHRASES: **5, 4** cross over; **8, 5** stepping stone.

forearm *See* **prepare**

foreboding **4** fear; **7** feeling, ominous; **8** menacing, sinister; **9** intuition; **10** forbidding; **11** premonition, threatening; **12** presentiment.

forecast **3** tip; **4** warn; **5** guess; **6** herald; **7** predict, presage, project; **8** estimate, foretell, prophecy; **9** calculate, prognosis; **10** anticipate, prediction, projection; **15** prognostication.

forecaster **5** augur; **6** auspex, dowser; **7** analyst, diviner, gambler, palmist, prophet, tipster; **8** haruspex; **10** astrologer, consultant, palmreader, speculator, weatherman;

11 interpreter; 12 futurologist; 13 meteorologist; 14 prognosticator; PHRASES: 4-5 oddsmaker; 7, 5 crystal gazer; 7, 6 fortune teller; 7, 7 forward planner.

foreclose 3 ban; 5 exile; 7 exclude; PHRASES: 4, 3 shut out; 5, 3 close out.

forefront 3 van; 4 face, head, lead; 5 front; 8 forepart, frontage, vanguard; 10 foreground.

foreign 3 odd; 5 alien, gypsy, other; 6 exotic, remote; 7 distant, migrant, nomadic, roaming, strange, unknown; 8 barbaric, external, homeless, imported, overseas, rambling; 9 barbarian, deviating, different, stateless, traveling, unrelated, wandering; 10 extraneous, irrelative, irrelevant, outlandish, tramontane, unfamiliar; 11 continental, unconnected; 12 ultramontane; 13 transatlantic; PHRASES: 3-3 far-off.

foreign (be foreign) 4 roam; 6 ramble, travel, wander; 8 emigrate; 9 immigrate; PHRASES: 4, 2, 3, 4 live on the road.

forerun 5 found; 6 invent; 7 explore, pioneer; 8 discover, initiate, innovate; 9 influence; 10 inaugurate; 11 reconnoiter; PHRASES: 3, 1, 5 set a trend; 3, 3 map out; 4, 3, 3 pave the way; 4, 3, 5 lead the dance; 5, 1, 5 blaze a trail.

foresee 5 augur, scent; 6 divine, expect; 7 portend, predict, presage, presume, promise, suppose, surmise; 8 envisage, envision, forebode, forecast, foreknow, foretell, forewarn, prophesy; 9 forejudge; 10 anticipate, foreshadow.

foreseeable 4 near; 6 likely; 8 forecast, imminent, probable; 9 immediate, impending; 10 calculable, imaginable; 11 conceivable, predictable, prospective; 13 anticipatable; PHRASES: 5-4 short-term.

foreseen 7 awaited; 8 expected, foretold, promised; 9 predicted; 11 anticipated; PHRASES: 5, 3 hoped for; 6, 3 looked for.

foresight 7 caution, insight; 8 forecast, prophecy, prudence, sagacity; 9 foretaste, intuition, prevision, prognosis; 10 precaution, prediction, prescience; 11 expectation, forethought, premonition; 12 anticipation, clairvoyancy, precognition; 13 foreknowledge; 14 farsightedness; PHRASES: 6, 5 second sight.

forest 3 New; 4 bush, Dean, wood; 5 taiga, woods; 6 jungle; 8 forestry, woodland; 10 plantation, timberland; PHRASES: 4, 6 rain ~.

forester 6 logger, ranger, tapper; 7 tapster, woodman; 8 arborist, lumberer, verderer *UK*, woodsman; 9 timberman; 10 lumberjack, woodcutter, woodlander; 12 dendrologist; 14 silviculturist; 15 arboriculturist; PHRASES: 4, 6 tree farmer; 4, 7 tree surgeon.

forestry 9 woodcraft; 10 dendrology; 12 silviculture; 13 arboriculture; PHRASES: 4, 7 tree farming.

foretaste 4 hint; 5 taste, token; 6 herald, prolog *UK*, sample, taster *UK*; 7 example, insight, preface, prelude, prequel, presage, preview, trailer; 8 foreword, prologue; 9 precursor; 10 forerunner, indication, prediction, prerelease; 12 introduction.

forever 9 endlessly, eternally; 10 repeatedly; 11 continually, incessantly; 12 indefinitely, persistently; PHRASES: 2, 9 ad infinitum; 2, 10 in perpetuity; 3, 3, 4 for all time.

forewarn *See* **warn**

foreword *See* **preface**

forfeit 4 lose, loss; 7 penalty; 9 sacrifice, surrender; 10 forfeiture, punishment; 12 penalization; PHRASES: 2, 7 go without; 2, 8, 2 be deprived of, be stripped of; 3, 3 pay for; 3, 4 pay with; 4, 2 give up; 4, 4 part with.

forgather 4 ally, bond, join, meet, plot; 5 agree, bunch, group, unite; 6 concur, couple, gather, huddle; 7 cluster, partner; 8 assemble, conspire, federate; 9 associate, cooperate, harmonize; 10 congregate, fraternize, rendezvous; 11 collaborate, concentrate, confederate; PHRASES: 5, 6 rally around.

forge 4 copy, fake, form; 5 build, shape; 6 create, hearth; 7 falsify, fashion, furnace, imitate; 11 counterfeit.

forget 4 miss, omit; 6 ignore; 7 neglect, repress, unlearn; 8 overlook, suppress; 9 disregard; 11 disremember; PHRASES: 3, 6, 3 put behind you; 5, 3 block out; 5, 4 blank over; 5, 6 clean ~.

forget (be forgotten) 4, 4, 4 slip one's mind; 4, 4, 6 fade from memory.

forgetful 3 dry; 5 vague; 8 amnesiac; 10 insensible; 14 scatterbrained; PHRASES: 6-6 absent-minded.

forgetfulness 5 lethe; 7 amnesia; 8 oblivion; 10 forgetting, repression; 11 suppression; PHRASES: 4, 2, 6 loss of memory; 4,

4, 1, 5 mind like a sieve; **6, 3** memory gap; **6, 5** mental block. *See also* **forgetful**

forgivable 6 venial; 9 allowable, excusable; 10 defensible, pardonable; 11 justifiable; 14 understandable; PHRASES: 6, 7 easily excused.

forgive 4 pity; 5 favor, humor, spare; 6 excuse, exempt, forget, pardon, redeem, shrive; 7 absolve, concede; 8 reprieve; 9 disregard, exonerate, indemnify, reconcile; 10 conciliate; PHRASES: 2, 10 be reconciled; 3, 2, 2 let it go; 3, 2, 4 let it pass; 3, 3 let off; 4, 3, 4, 2 kiss and make up; 4, 3, 7 bury the hatchet; 4, 5 make peace; 5, 2, 4, 2 think no more of; 5, 5 shake hands; 5, 7 grant amnesty; 5, 8 grant immunity; 5, 10 grant absolution.

forgiveness 4 pity; 5 favor, grace, mercy; 6 lenity, pardon, shrift; 7 amnesty, sparing; 8 clemency, immunity, kindness, patience, reprieve, stoicism; 9 disregard, exemption, indemnity, remission, tolerance; 10 absolution, compassion, indulgence; 11 benevolence, exculpation, exoneration, forbearance, magnanimity, placability; 12 dispensation; 13 understanding; 14 reconciliation; PHRASES: 9, 2, 3 remission of sin.

forgiving 4 free, kind; 7 lenient, patient; 8 merciful, tolerant; 9 indulgent; 10 benevolent; 11 magnanimous, sympathetic; 12 conciliatory; 13 compassionate; PHRASES: 4-9 long-suffering. *See also* **forgive**

forgotten 4 gone, lost, past; 6 buried; 9 neglected; 10 overlooked; 11 disregarded, unmemorable; PHRASES: 3, 2, 4 out of mind; 3, 6 not missed; 6, 6 beyond recall; 7, 3 blotted out.

fork 1 Y; 3 fan; 4 prod, stem, tine; 5 cleft, delta, prong, split; 6 branch, divide; 7 diverge, furcula, trident; 8 division, furculum, junction, offshoot; 10 divergence; 11 bifurcation; PHRASES: 1-5 V-shape.

forlorn 3 sad; 4 lost; 6 lonely; 7 unhappy; 8 dejected, desolate; 9 abandoned, miserable, neglected; 10 despondent.

form 3 cut, hew, way; 4 blow, body, cast, coin, draw, grow, idea, kind, look, make, mint, mode, mold, turn, type, work; 5 arise, blank, build, carve, class, draft, forge, found, frame, knead, lines, model, order, paper, round, setup, shape, sheet, smith, stamp, start, state, style, table, throw, usage; 6 chisel, create, custom, design, figure, format, manner, method, nature, relief, ritual, sculpt, sketch, square, status, system; 7 anatomy, arrange, contour, develop, essence, express, fashion, forming, formula, gestalt, outline, pattern, produce, profile, shaping, variety, whittle; 8 creation, document, physique, practice; 9 composure, condition, construct, designing, establish, formality, formalize, formation, formulate, procedure, structure, substance; 10 appearance, morphology, nominalism, patterning, silhouette; 11 arrangement, composition, development, fabrication, materialize, systematize; 12 architecture, conformation, constitution, construction; 13 configuration, questionnaire; PHRASES: 3-2 get-up; 3, 3 cut out, lay out; 3, 5 pro forma; 4, 2 work up; 4-2 make-up; 4, 4, 5 come into being, lick into shape; 4, 5 take shape; 5, 4, 5 bring into being, knock into shape; 6, 3 hammer out.

form (on form) 3 fit; 4 able, hale; 6 hearty; 7 capable, healthy; 10 salubrious; PHRASES: 2, 3, 4 in the pink; 2, 4, 4 in good nick; 2, 4, 6 in fine fettle; 2, 4, 9 in good condition; 2, 5 in shape.

formal 3 dry, set; 4 prim; 5 exact, grave, proud, rigid, royal, smart, staid, stiff; 6 proper, ritual, sedate, solemn, strict, stuffy, trendy; 7 correct, elegant, orderly, pompous, precise, refined, routine, starchy, stately, stilted, stylish, weighty; 8 decorous, habitual, official, pedantic, precious, protocol, puristic, reserved, starched, stylized; 9 customary, dignified, formulary, litigious; 10 behavioral, ceremonial, fastidious, legalistic, methodical, meticulous, prescribed, procedural, recognized, scrupulous; 11 ceremonious, fashionable, formalistic, punctilious, ritualistic, traditional; 12 conventional; PHRASES: 2, 3, 4 by the book; 5-6 stiff-necked; 6-5 strait-laced.

formal (be formal) 6 comply; 7 conform; 9 solemnize; PHRASES: 3, 3, 4 toe the line; 4, 4, 2, 3, 2 mind one's p's and q's; 4, 4, 7 mind one's manners; 5, 2, 3, 5 stick to the rules; 5, 2, 8 stand on ceremony; 6, 8 follow protocol.

formalism 6 purism; 8 pedantry; 9 ritualism; 10 preciosity; 11 preciseness; 12 precisionism; 13 ceremonialism; 14 scrupulousness; 15 conventionalism, conventionality, punctiliousness; PHRASES: 4-10 over-refinement.

formality 4 form, pomp, rule; 5 habit, pride, state, style, trend; 6 custom, ritual; 7 conduct, decorum, dignity, fashion, gravity, reserve, routine; 8 behavior, ceremony, practice, protocol; 9 etiquette, procedure, propriety, solemness, solemnity, tradition; 10 convention, litigation, regulation; 11 requirement, stylization; 12 circumstance, correctitude; 15 conventionalism, conventionality; PHRASES: 3, 5, 2, 2 the thing to do; 3, 6 red carpet; 4, 3, 6 spit and polish; 5, 2 royal we. *See also* **formal**

formalize 5 enact, honor; 6 ratify; 7 stylize; 8 sanctify, validate; 9 celebrate, ritualize, solemnize; 15 conventionalize.

formal occasion 4 ball, fete, gala, rite, show; 5 dance, drill, march, scene; 6 parade, review, ritual, tattoo; 7 baptism, flyover, flypast, liturgy, pageant, routine, service, tableau, turnout, wedding; 8 ceremony, practice; 9 procedure, spectacle; 10 ceremonial, coronation, graduation, initiation, tournament; 11 celebration, christening, convocation; 12 confirmation, inauguration; PHRASES: 3-6, 3 red-letter day; 3, 7 bar mitzvah; 4, 2, 7 rite of passage; 4, 6, 4 Lord Mayor's show.

formation 5 shape; 7 pattern; 8 creation; 9 structure; 10 foundation; 11 arrangement, development; 12 construction; 13 configuration, establishment.

formative 5 solid; 6 formal, hearty; 7 generic, healthy, plastic, stylish; 8 concrete, creative, original; 10 expressive, productive, systematic; 11 conformable; 12 constructive, prototypical; 13 morphological.

former 2 ex; 3 old; 4 last, late, once, past; 5 first, prior; 6 bygone; 7 earlier, quondam, retired; 8 anterior, deceased, emeritus, previous, sometime; 9 erstwhile; PHRASES: 3-4 one-time.

formerly 4 once; 6 before; 7 earlier; PHRASES: 2, 3, 4 in the past; 2, 6 no longer; 2, 7, 5 in earlier times; 4, 4, 1, 4 once upon a time. *See also* **former**

formidable 5 tough; 7 arduous, awesome; 8 alarming, daunting, dreadful, fearsome; 9 difficult; 10 astounding, impressive, remarkable; 11 challenging, frightening, redoubtable; PHRASES: 3-9 awe-inspiring.

formless *See* **shapeless**

Formosa 6 Taiwan.

formula 4 plan; 6 cliché, method, phrase, recipe; 10 expression; 11 boilerplate, formulation; 12 prescription; PHRASES: 5, 6 stock phrase; 5, 8 modus operandi.

forsake 4 quit; 5 leave; 6 desert, disown; 7 abandon; 8 renounce; 9 sacrifice; 10 relinquish; PHRASES: 4, 2 give up.

forswear 4 deny; 5 swear; 6 abjure, disown, reject; 7 disavow; 8 disclaim, renounce; 10 contradict; PHRASES: 4, 2 give up.

fort 4 burg, gate, keep, moat, ward; 5 tower; 6 castle, donjon, laager, refuge, turret, zareba; 7 capitol, citadel, curtain, pillbox, postern, rampart; 8 barbican *UK*, bartizan, fastness, fortress, garrison, stockade; 9 acropolis, earthwork, fortalice, gatehouse; 10 blockhouse, drawbridge, portcullis, stronghold; 11 battlements; 13 fortification; PHRASES: 8, 5 Martello tower.

forth 2 on; 3 out; 4 away, from; 5 ahead, apart, hence; 6 onward; 7 forward, outward; 8 forwards, outwards; PHRASES: 4, 3, 4 into the open; 4, 3, 5 into the world.

forthright *See* **straightforward**

forthwith *See* **immediately**

fortification 4 wall; 5 scarp; 6 bailey, escarp, gabion, glacis, merlon, vallum; 7 bastion, bulwark, curtain, defense, ditches, outwork, parapet, ravelin; 8 abutment, barbette *UK*, buttress, casemate, loophole; 9 banquette, embrasure, gabionade; 10 protection; 11 buttressing, demibastion, emplacement; 12 counterscarp; 13 machicolation, reinforcement, strengthening; 15 circumvallation; PHRASES: 3, 11 gun emplacement; 4, 4 town wall; 8, 2 building up. *See also* **fort**

fortify 3 mix; 4 wall; 5 boost, brace; 6 defend, enrich, revive, secure; 7 bolster, enhance, improve, protect, refresh, support, sustain; 8 garrison; 9 reinforce; 10 invigorate, strengthen; 12 reinvigorate; PHRASES: 4, 1, 5, 2 give a boost to; 4, 8 make stronger; 5, 2 build up.

fortis 4 hard; 5 sharp.

fortitude 4 dash, élan, grit, guts *UK*; 5 moxie, pluck, spunk, steel; 6 aplomb, bottle *UK*, daring, mettle, spirit; 7 courage, stamina; 8 backbone, strength; 9 endurance; 10 resilience; 13 dauntlessness, determination; PHRASES: 4, 4 iron rock; 5, 2, 3 heart of oak; 5, 5 moral fiber; 5, 5, 3 stiff upper lip; 7, 5 gritted teeth, staying power.

fortunate 4 well; 5 blest, happy, lucky; 7 charmed.

fortune 3 lot, ton; 4 bomb UK, doom, fate, luck, mint, pile; 5 grand, karma, lakhs, money; 6 bundle, chance, crores, future, kismet, packet UK, riches, wealth; 7 destiny; 8 accident, billions, millions, opulence, treasure, zillions; 9 affluence, megabucks; 10 prosperity, providence; 11 loadsamoney; PHRASES: 2, 3, 3, 1, 3 an arm and a leg; 3, 5 big bucks; 4, 2, 5 wads of money; 4, 3 tidy sum; 4, 7 cool million; 5, 2, 5 scads of money; 6, 2, 5 stacks of money; 8, 2, 5 mountain of money.

fortune (good fortune) 5 break; PHRASES: 3, 2, 4 run of luck; 6, 2, 4 streak of luck, stroke of luck; 7, 4 charmed life.

forum 5 scene; 6 debate, medium; 7 meeting, setting; 10 conference, discussion, roundtable; 11 environment, opportunity.

forward 2 on; 4 bold, come, mail, post UK, send; 5 ahead, along, forth, pushy; 6 brazen, cheeky, direct, onward; 7 advance, forrard, further, onwards UK, promote; 8 advanced, dispatch, familiar, forceful, headlong, progress, redirect; 9 headfirst, reformist; 10 accelerate, forthright, frontwards UK; 11 progressive, uninhibited; 12 enterprising, overfriendly, presumptuous; PHRASES: 2-2-4 up-to-date; 2-5 go-ahead; 2-7 go-getting; 4, 2 pass on, send on; 4-7 self-assured.

fossil 3 oil; 4 cast, coal, mold, peat; 5 amber, relic; 7 hominid, mammoth, remains, remnant, vestige; 8 ammonite, dinosaur; 9 coprolite, petroleum, trilobite; 10 coelacanth, graptolite; 14 mineralization; PHRASES: 3-2-4 out-of-date.

fossilize 6 harden, ossify; 7 calcify, petrify; 8 solidify; 10 mineralize.

fossilized 9 preserved; 13 fossiliferous. *See also* **fossilize**

foul 3 wet; 4 evil, lewd, rank, soil, vile; 5 dirty, fetid, nasty, shady, snarl, sully, taint; 6 coarse, defile, filthy, rotten, soiled, stormy, vulgar; 7 crooked, ensnare, ensnarl, noisome, obscene, pollute, profane, tainted, unclean, uncouth; 8 criminal, dreadful, entangle, horrible, indecent, polluted, stinking; 9 dishonest, frightful, inclement, offensive, repellent, repulsive; 10 abominable, disgusting, unpleasant; 11 contaminate, distasteful, treacherous, unwholesome; 12 dishonorable; PHRASES: 4, 2 mess up; 4, 5 make dirty; 6, 2 tangle up.

found 4 base, cast; 5 build, forge, start; 6 create; 7 located; 8 detected, initiate; 9 establish, institute, locatable, originate, unearthed; 10 discovered, pinpointed; PHRASES: 3, 2 set up; 5, 4, 5 bring into being; 6, 4 pinned down; 7, 4 tracked down.

foundation 5 basis; 7 charity, grounds, society; 9 institute, substance; 10 groundwork; 11 institution; 12 underpinning; 13 establishment.

founder 4 fail, sink; 5 wreck; 6 author, plunge, wallow; 7 creator, misfire; 8 submerge; 9 initiator, organizer; 10 forefather, originator; PHRASES: 2, 4 go down; 4, 2, 5 come to grief; 4, 2, 7 come to nothing; 5, 4 break down.

Founding Fathers (Constitution) 3 Few (William); 4 King (Rufus), Read (George); 5 Blair (John), Broom (Jacob); 6 Blount (William), Butler (Pierce), Clymer (George), Dayton (Jonathan), Gilman (Nicholas), Gorham (Nathaniel), Morris (Robert), Wilson (James); 7 Baldwin (Abraham), Bassett (Richard), Bedford (Gunning, Jr.), Brearly (David), Carroll (Daniel), Johnson (William Samuel), Langdon (John), Madison (James, Jr.), McHenry (James), Mifflin (Thomas), Sherman (Roger), Spaight (Richard Dobbs); 8 Franklin (Benjamin), Hamilton (Alexander), Paterson (William), Pinckney (Charles Cotesworth), Rutledge (John); 9 Dickinson (John), Ingersoll (Jared); 10 Livingston (William), Washington (George), Williamson (Hugh); 11 Fitzsimmons (Thomas).

Founding Fathers (Declaration of Independence) 3 Lee (Francis Lightfoot), Lee (Richard Henry); 4 Hall (Lyman), Hart (John), Paca (William), Penn (HJohn), Read (George), Ross (George), Rush (Benjamin); 5 Adams (John), Adams (Samuel), Chase (Samuel), Clark (Abraham), Floyd (William), Gerry (Elbridge), Hewes (Joseph), Lewis (Francis), Lynch (Thomas, Jr.), Paine (Robert Treat), Smith (James), Stone (Thomas), Wythe (George); 6 Clymer (George), Ellery (William), Hooper (William), McKean (Thomas), Morris (Lewis), Morris (Robert), Morton (John), Nelson (Thomas,

Jr.), Rodney (Caesar), Taylor (George), Walton (George), Wilson (James); **7** Braxton (Carter), Carroll (Charles), Hancock (John), Heyward (Thomas, Jr.), Hopkins (Stephen), Sherman (Roger), Whipple (William), Wolcott (Oliver); **8** Bartlett (Josiah), Franklin (Benjamin), Gwinnett (Button), Harrison (Benjamin), Rutledge (Edward), Stockton (Richard), Thornton (Matthew), Williams (William); **9** Hopkinson (Francis), Jefferson (Thomas), Middleton (Arthur); **10** Huntington (Samuel), Livingston (Philip); **11** Witherspoon (John).

Founding Fathers (Others) 4 Burr (Aaron); **5** Henry (Patrick), Paine (Thomas); **6** Eustis (William), Revere (Paul); **7** Clinton (George), Lincoln (Levi); **8** Randolph (Edmund).

fount *See* **source**

fountain 3 jet; **5** cause, spout; **6** origin, source, spring; **7** cascade; **9** beginning; **12** fountainhead; PHRASES: **5, 7** water feature.

four 2 IV; **4** quad; **6** quatre, tetrad; **7** quartet.

foursome 5 group, winds; **7** quartet, seasons; **8** ensemble, quatrain, tetrapod; **9** quadrille, tetragram, tetralogy; **14** tetragrammaton.

fourth 7 quarter.

four times 8 fourfold; **9** quadruple, quarterly.

fowl 3 hen; **4** bird, duck; **5** goose, quail; **6** bantam, grouse, Houdan, pigeon, pullet, turkey; **7** chicken, Dorking; **8** pheasant, wildfowl, woodcock; **9** partridge, waterfowl; PHRASES: **4, 7** Rock Cornish; **5, 6, 3** Rhode Island Red; **6, 4** guinea ~; **8, 4** Plymouth Rock. *See also* **birds**

fox 3 con; **4** fool; **5** trick; **6** baffle, muddle, outwit, puzzle; **7** confuse, deceive, perplex. *See also* **animals**

fracas *See* **quarrel**

fraction 3 bit, mil; **4** half, part, some; **5** fifth, ninth, piece, share, sixth, tenth, third; **6** eighth, fourth, little, ration; **7** element, portion, quarter, section, segment, seventh, twelfth; **8** division, eleventh; **9** billionth, hundredth, millionth; **10** percentage, proportion, thousandth; **11** subdivision.

fractional 4 half, part, tiny; **5** small; **6** paltry, slight; **7** aliquot, decimal, partial, quarter, radical; **8** marginal; **9** minuscule,

sectional, segmental; **10** divisional, incomplete; **11** fragmentary; **12** proportional; **13** insignificant.

fracture 5 break, crack, pott's, split; **6** colles'; **7** fissure, rupture, shatter; **8** breakage, compound, hairline, splinter; **10** greenstick; **11** comminution, splintering.

fragile 4 weak; **5** crisp, frail, rigid; **6** flimsy, infirm, shoddy; **7** spindly; **8** delicate, unsteady; **10** vulnerable; **13** insubstantial.

fragment 3 bit, jot; **4** atom, chip, drop, iota, mote, part, whit; **5** break, crack, crumb, fleck, minim, piece, scrap, shard, shred, speck, split; **6** divide, filing, morsel, sliver, tittle; **7** crumble, destroy, minutia, portion, section, shatter, shaving, snippet; **8** particle, splinter; **12** disintegrate; PHRASES: **4, 2, 6** fall to pieces; **4, 5** fall apart; **5, 2** break up.

fragrance 4 balm, musk, odor; **5** aroma, attar, scent, smell, spice; **6** parfum; **7** bouquet, cologne, perfume; **9** balminess, fragrancy, muskiness, spiciness; PHRASES: **3, 2, 8** eau de toilette; **6, 5** toilet water.

fragrant 5 balmy, heady, musky, spicy; **6** floral, fruity; **7** flowery, odorous, pungent, scented; **8** aromatic, perfumed; **9** ambrosial; **11** camphorated; PHRASES: **5-8** sweet-smelling.

frail 4 puny, weak; **6** feeble, flimsy, infirm; **7** fragile, spindly; **8** delicate; **13** insubstantial.

frame 4 body, case, cold, edge, form, hull, plan, plot, trap; **5** build, mount, trick; **6** border, edging, entice, entrap; **7** enclose, lattice, setting; **8** physique, surround; PHRASES: **3, 2** fit up *UK*, set up. *See also* **framework**

framework 4 cage, plan, rack; **5** basis, cadre, frame, shell; **6** agenda; **7** charter, chassis, context, framing, lattice, outline, support, trellis; **8** bodywork, casement, scaffold, skeleton; **9** doorframe, structure; **10** background, cantilever; **11** latticework; **12** construction; PHRASES: **6, 4** window case.

franchise 5 grant, right; **6** permit; **7** charter, license; **8** contract, suffrage; **9** agreement, authorize; **13** authorization; PHRASES: **3, 4** the vote; **8, 3** contract out.

frangible 7 brittle, crumbly, fragile, friable.

frank 4 bold, free, open, true; **5** blunt, plain, stamp; **6** candid, honest; **7** defiant, sincere; **8** truthful; **9** guileless, honorable, outspoken, veracious; **10** aboveboard, forthright; **11** transparent, undesigning; **15** straightforward; PHRASES: **4-2-5** down-to-earth; **6-2-4** matter-of-fact.

frantic 4 wild; **6** hectic; **7** panicky; **8** agitated, feverish, frenetic, frenzied; **9** desperate; **10** hysterical; PHRASES: **6, 8** beside yourself.

fraternity 4 clan; **5** group, world; **7** network; **9** community; **10** friendship; **11** brotherhood, comradeship; **13** brotherliness; PHRASES: **6, 7** mutual support.

fraternize 3 mix; **4** date; **6** hobnob, mingle; **7** consort, network; **9** associate, socialize; PHRASES: **3, 2, 4** pal up with; **4, 2, 4** hook up with; **4, 3** hang out, have fun; **4, 6, 4** hang around with; **4, 7, 4** keep company with.

fraud 3 con, fix, gyp; **4** fake, hoax, ramp, scam, sell, sham, swiz *UK*; **5** cheat, dodge, phony *UK*, sting *UK*; **6** canard, deceit, diddle, fakery, faking, fiddle, hoaxer, phoney, racket, scheme, wangle; **7** falsity, forgery, swindle, swizzle; **8** cheating, flimflam, impostor, swindler, trickery; **9** charlatan, deception, fraudster, imitation, imposture; **10** dishonesty, mountebank; **11** counterfeit, crookedness, fraudulence; **12** adulteration, cardsharping; **14** counterfeiting, gerrymandering; PHRASES: **3-2** put-on; **3-2, 3** put-up job; **3-3** rip-off; **4, 4** foul play; **5-2** frame-up; **5, 3** snake oil; **6, 7** ballot rigging; **6-7** double-dealing; **7, 4** stacked deck; **7, 7** insider dealing *UK*, juggled figures; **9, 3** whitewash job; **10, 4** confidence game.

fraudulent 4 fake, sham; **5** false, pseud *UK*; **6** copied, forged, tricky, untrue; **7** cheated, crooked, illegal, illicit, pirated; **8** cheating, fiddling, swindled; **9** deceitful, deceptive, dishonest, falsified, imitation, infringed, piratical, swindling; **10** impostrous; **11** counterfeit, duplicitous, imposturous, plagiarized, underhanded, whitewashed; **12** blackmailing, unauthorized; **15** misappropriated.

fraudulent (be fraudulent) 3 con, fix, gyp; **4** bilk, burn, copy, fake, gull, hoax, load, pack, salt, scam, sell; **5** cheat, dodge, forge, screw, stack, sting, trick; **6** fiddle, fleece, juggle, nobble *UK*, wangle; **7** defraud, falsify, swindle, swizzle; **8** flimflam; **9** whitewash; **10** adulterate; **11** counterfeit; PHRASES: **2, 3, 2** do out of; **3, 2** put on; **3, 3** rip off; **4, 3, 4** load the dice; **4, 3, 5** cook the books, mark the cards; **5, 1, 4** force a card;

5, 1, 5 throw a fight; **5, 2** cheat on; **5, 2, 3, 5** leave in the lurch; **5, 3, 4** stack the deck; **5-6** short-change.

fraught 4 full; **5** laden, tense; **6** filled; **7** anxious, charged, nervous; **8** troubled; **12** apprehensive; PHRASES: **7, 4** weighed down.

fray 4 wear; **5** fight, ravel; **6** fracas, tatter; **7** dispute, quarrel, unravel; **8** argument; PHRASES: **4, 3** wear out.

freak 4 buff; **5** fiend, fluke, lover; **6** chance, oddity, rarity; **7** fanatic; **8** accident, surprise; **9** curiosity; **10** enthusiast; **12** happenstance; PHRASES: **3-3** one-off *UK*.

freckle 4 mark, mole, spot; **5** patch, speck; **6** blotch; **7** lentigo, speckle.

free 2 no; **3** f.o.b., lax, rid; **4** able, easy, just, open; **5** clear, freed, given, loose; **6** excuse, exempt, gratis, honest, immune, pardon, unpaid; **7** allowed, charity, deliver, escaped, liberal, neutral, release, unbound, welcome; **8** autarkic, buckshee *UK*, carefree, courtesy, excepted, floating, freeborn, giveaway, honorary, liberate, moderate, optional, relaxing, released, tolerant, unbiased, unburden, uncurbed; **9** autarchic, available, easygoing, exculpate, expansive, footloose, indulgent, irregular, liberated, permitted, unbridled, unchained, uncharged, unchecked, undecided, unimpeded, unmuzzled, voluntary; **10** authorized, autonomous, emancipate, franchised, gratuitous, nonaligned, permissive, privileged, unattached, unconfined, unfettered, ungoverned, unhindered, unoccupied, unsalaried, unshackled; **11** emancipated, independent, libertarian, noninvolved, nonpartisan, spontaneous, uninhibited, unregulated; **12** capitalistic, eleemosynary, enfranchised, uncontrolled, uninfluenced, unprejudiced, unregimented, unrestrained, unrestricted, unstructured; **13** complimentary, discretionary, unconstrained; **14** constitutional, unconventional; PHRASES: **2, 3, 5** on the house, on the loose; **2, 5** at large; **2, 7** at liberty; **3, 2** let go; **3, 3** let off; **3, 4** set ~; **3, 7** for nothing; **4, 2, 6** ~ of charge; **4-3-4** free-and-easy; **4-4** scot-free; **4-5** zero-rated; **4-6** open-minded, self-ruling; **4-9** self-governing; **4-10** self-determined, self-regulating; **4-11** self-determining; **5-3-5** grace-and-favor; **5, 4** given away; **5-5** cross-bench; **5-6** broadminded; **7, 1, 4** without a care; **7, 6** without charge.

freedom 4 ease; **5** leave; **6** candor, choice,

escape, laxity, leeway, margin, option; **7** abandon, liberty, license, release; **8** autonomy, immunity, latitude; **9** discharge, exception, exemption, frankness, privilege, seclusion, tolerance; **10** capitalism, discretion, indulgence, initiative, liberalism, liberation, neutrality, relaxation, toleration; **11** bohemianism, deliverance, forbearance, noncoercion, prerogative, sovereignty, unrestraint; **12** emancipation, freethinking, independence, irregularity, isolationism, nonalignment, nonliability, unconstraint; **13** inventiveness, nonconformity; **14** libertarianism, noninvolvement, permissiveness; **15** noninterference, nonintervention, nonintimidation; PHRASES: 1, 4, **4** a free hand; 3, 4, **4** own free will; 3, **6** own accord; 3, **8** own volition; 3, **10** gay liberation, own initiative; 4, **4** free port, free will, high seas; 4, **6** free speech; 4, **7** free thought; 4, **10** free expression; 6, **7** poetic license; 7, **5** laissez faire; 8, **7** artistic license. *See also* **free**

freehold 4 land; **5** right; **6** estate, tenure; **7** holding; **8** building, property; **9** occupancy, ownership.

freeloader 5 idler; **6** ligger *UK*; **7** slacker; **8** parasite; PHRASES: **6-2** hanger-on.

freely 4 free, lief; **5** alone; **6** easily; **10** generously; **12** unreservedly; PHRASES: 2, **4** at will; 7, **8** without stinting. *See also* **free**

free market 2 EU; **3** EEA *UK*, EEC, WTO; **4** ALCA, APEC, EFTA, GATT, LAIA, OPEC; **5** CAFTA, CEFTA, NAFTA; **7** CARICOM; **8** MERCOSUR; **10** capitalism, Euromarket; PHRASES: 4-4, **6** open-door policy; 4, **5** free trade; 6, **6** Common Market; 8, **5** European Union.

free thing 4 gift, pass, perk, ride; **7** charity, freebie, service; **8** Freefone™, Freepost™, giveaway, gratuity; **10** perquisite; PHRASES: 3, **6** 800 number; 4, **6** 0800 number; 5, 2, **4** labor of love; 9, **4** volunteer work.

freethinker *See* **individualist**

free-thinker 5 cynic, loner; **6** hippie; **7** atheist, skeptic; **8** Bohemian, humanist; **9** eccentric, libertine; **11** libertarian, nonbeliever, rationalist; **13** nonconformist; **14** latitudinarian; PHRASES: 4, **4** lone wolf.

free will 6 choice; **7** freedom, liberty; **8** autonomy; **10** discretion; **12** independence.

freeze 3 fix, ice, nip; **4** cool, halt, hold, stay, stop; **5** check, chill; **6** arrest, harden,

shelve; **7** congeal, control, embargo, glacier, stiffen, suspend; **8** mothball, preserve, restrict, solidify, stoppage; **10** immobilize, suspension; **11** refrigerate, restriction; **12** interruption; PHRASES: 3, **2** ice up; 3, **4** ice over; 4, **4** stop dead; 5, **3** black ice, break off.

freezing 3 icy; **4** cold; **5** frost, gelid, icing; **6** bitter, chilly, wintry; **7** glacial, halting, iciness, subzero; **8** gelidity; **9** frigidity; **10** suspending; PHRASES: 8, **4** absolute zero.

freight 4 load; **5** cargo, goods; **8** carriage, shipping; **9** transport *UK*; **10** conveyance; **11** consignment, merchandise; **14** transportation.

French dish 4 pâté; **5** aioli; **7** soufflé; **9** cassoulet, escargots, rillettes; **11** ratatouille; **13** bouillabaisse, chateaubriand; PHRASES: 3, 2, **3** coq au vin; 5, 2, **6** steak au poivre; 5, **4** frogs legs, onion soup; 5, **7** steak tartare; 5, **10** boeuf bourguignon; 6, **4** petits pois; 6, **7** crêpes suzette; 6, **8** quiche Lorraine; 7, **4** pressed duck.

French Sudan 4 Mali.

frenzied 7 frantic; **8** feverish; **9** emotional; **10** hysterical; **11** hyperactive, overexcited.

frenzy 3 fit; **4** fury, rage, rush; **5** anger, fever, state, whirl; **6** flurry, tumult; **7** passion, turmoil; **9** agitation.

frequency 4 rate; **5** cycle, hertz, pulse, speed; **9** assiduity, constancy, frequence, incidence; **10** continuity, incessancy, occurrence, prevalence, recurrence, regularity, repetition; **11** crowdedness, periodicity, persistence, sustainment; **12** frequentness. *See also* **frequent**

frequent 4 many; **5** haunt, often, visit; **6** common, cyclic, normal, steady; **7** crowded, nonstop, regular; **8** constant, cyclical, everyday, habitual, haunting, numerous, periodic, repeated; **9** assiduous, continual, incessant, patronize, prevalent, recurrent, recurring, sustained; **10** persistent, repetitive; **11** consecutive, repetitious; **13** multitudinous; PHRASES: 3-2-3-4 run-of-the-mill; 4, **2** shop at; 4, 3, **2** hang out at; 4, **6** hang around; 5, 4, **2** spend time at.

frequent (be frequent) 5 recur; **6** repeat; **7** prevail, reoccur; **8** continue; PHRASES: 2, **2** go on.

frequently 3 oft; **5** daily, often; **6** hourly; **7** usually; **9** generally, routinely; **10** oftentimes, ordinarily; **11** perpetually; **12** periodically, sustainingly; PHRASES: 2, 5, 2, 3 as often as not; 3, 2, 3, 3 day in day out; 3, 3, 4 all the time; 3, 3, 5 day and night; 3, 5, 3 day after day; 4, 1, 4 many a time; 4, 1, 4, 3, 3 many a time and oft; 4, 3, 4 ever and anon, over and over; 4, 3, 5 time and again; 4, 5, 4 time after time; 5, 3, 4 thick and fast; 5, 3, 5 again and again; 5, 4 every hour; 5, 6 every second; 7, 7 without ceasing. *See also* **frequent**

fresh 3 new; 4 airy, pert; 5 alert, clean, crisp, juicy, moist, novel, other, sappy, young; 6 active, breezy, bright, cheeky, lively, vernal; 7 renewed; 8 blooming, creative, original, pleasant, pristine, spotless, unmarked, vigorous, youthful; 9 different, energetic, inventive, unsullied, wholesome; 10 additional, immaculate, innovative, refreshing, springlike, unpolluted; 11 flourishing, replacement; PHRASES: 3, 4 pan fish; 4, 2, 5 full of beans; 5-3 brand-new; 8, 3 spanking new.

fresh start 6 change, remake; 7 renewal, revisal, revival; 8 redesign, updating; 9 upgrading; 10 alteration, rebuilding, renovation, repainting, supplement; 11 restoration, restructure; 12 regeneration, rejuvenation, resurrection; 13 modernization, refurbishment; 14 reconstruction, reorganization, revivification; PHRASES: 3, 4 new leaf, new look; 5, 5 clean slate; 6, 4 tabula rasa.

freshwater fish 3 gar; 4 bass, carp, char, chub, dace, pike, rudd, shad; 5 bleak, danio, loach, molly, perch, roach, tench, tetra, trout; 6 barbel, bowfin, burbot, minnow, salmon; 7 catfish, cichlid, crappie, gourami, gudgeon, lamprey, mudfish, piranha, tilapia, walleye; 8 bullhead, characin, goldfish, grayling, lungfish; 9 angelfish, killifish, pikeperch, swordtail, tigerfish, whitefish; 10 paddlefish; 11 muskellunge; PHRASES: 3, 6 top minnow; 4, 5 lake trout, Nile perch; 5, 4 zebra fish; 5, 5 brook trout; 6, 5 yellow perch; 7, 5 miller's thumb, rainbow trout; 8, 3 electric eel; 8, 4 northern pike; 8, 5 climbing perch. *See also* **fish, sea fish**

fret *See* **worry**

friable *See* **crumbly**

friction 3 rub; 4 drag, grip; 5 force; 6 strife; 7 chafing, contact, discord, erosion, gnawing, rasping, rubbing, tension; 8 abrasion, adhesion, brushing, conflict, frottage, purchase; 9 animosity, attrition, frication, hostility, roughness, viscosity; 10 affriction, antagonism, irritation, resistance; 12 disagreement.

friend 3 ami, bud, pal; 4 ally, chum, mate *UK*; 5 amigo, buddy, butty *UK*, crony; 6 fellow, helper; 7 comrade, contact, paisano, partner; 8 compadre, coworker, messmate, playmate, roommate, shipmate, sidekick, workmate; 9 associate, classmate, colleague, companion, supporter; 10 playfellow, schoolmate; 12 acquaintance, collaborator, schoolfellow *UK*; PHRASES: 4-6 well-wisher.

friend (famous friends) 5, 3, 7 Damon and Pythias; 6, 3, 6 Castor and Pollux.

friendliness *See* **amiability**

friendly 4 kind, open, warm; 5 close, matey *UK*, pally; 6 ardent, chummy, genial, hearty, kindly; 7 affable, amiable, cordial, helpful; 8 amicable, effusive, familiar, generous, gracious, intimate, outgoing, pleasant, sisterly, sociable; 9 agreeable, brotherly, comradely, congenial, courteous, favorable, fraternal, peaceable, receptive, simpatico, unhostile, welcoming; 10 beneficial, benevolent, compatible, friendlike, harmonious, hospitable, neighborly, responsive, supportive; 11 cooperative, sympathetic; 12 affectionate, approachable, confraternal; 13 companionable, demonstrative, philanthropic, understanding; PHRASES: 4-7 warm-hearted, well-meaning; 4-8 back-slapping, well-disposed, well-intended; 5-5 buddy-buddy, palsy-walsy.

friendship 4 bond, love; 5 amity; 6 regard, warmth; 7 ardency, concord, harmony, rapport, support; 8 alliance, bonhomie, courtesy, goodwill, kindness, sodality, sorority, sympathy, warmness; 9 closeness, geniality, mateyness, palliness, prejudice; 10 attachment, chumminess, cordiality, fellowship, fraternity, kindliness, partiality, sisterhood, solidarity; 11 amiableness, amicability, benevolence, brotherhood, camaraderie, comradeship, cooperation, familiarity, hospitality, sociability; 12 acquaintance, amicableness, friendliness, philanthropy, relationship, togetherness; 13 companionship, compatibility, confraternity, understanding; 14 fraternization, neighborliness; PHRASES: 4, 5 good terms; 4-11 warm-heartedness; 6, 7 fellow feeling *UK*.

friendship (expression of friend-

ship) 3 hug, pat; 4 kiss; 5 toast; 7 embrace; 9 handclasp, handshake; PHRASES: 4, 2, 3, 5 peck on the cheek; 4, 4 open arms; 7, 5 holding hands, rubbing noses.

friendship (seek the friendship of) 3 woo; 4 date, frat; 5 court; PHRASES: 2, 3, 4 go out with; 3, 5, 2 pay court to; 4, 2, 2 play up to, suck up to *UK*; 4, 3 take out; 5, 2, 2 shine up to; 6, 2, 2 cotton up to.

fright 4 fear, turn; 5 dread, scare, shock, start; 6 terror; 7 anxiety, seizure; 10 foreboding.

frighten 3 cow; 5 alarm, bully, daunt, panic, scare, shake, shock, upset, worry; 6 appall, dismay, fright, menace; 7 horrify, petrify, stagger, startle, terrify, unnerve; 8 affright, browbeat, bulldoze, distress, enervate; 9 terrorize; 10 intimidate; PHRASES: 5, 8 scare shitless.

frightened 4 frit; 5 upset; 6 afraid, aghast; 7 anxious, fearing, panicky; 8 affright, blanched; 11 demoralized; PHRASES: 4, 2, 1, 5 pale as a ghost; 4-8 fear-stricken; 5, 2, 1, 5 white as a sheet; 5-5 ashen-faced; 5-8 panic-stricken; 6, 2, 3, 4 rooted to the spot; 6, 4 deadly pale; 6, 5 scared stiff; 6-6 horror-struck, terror-struck. *See also* **frighten**

frightened person *See* **coward**

frightener 4 bane; 5 bogey, bully, ghost; 6 scarer; 7 bugbear, specter; 8 alarmist, bogeyman; 9 nightmare, terrorist; 11 scaremonger; PHRASES: 3, 5 pet peeve; 4, 5 bête noire; 4, 8 doom merchant.

frightening 4 dire, gall, grim; 5 awful, scary; 6 spooky; 7 awesome, fearful, ghastly, hideous, scaring; 8 alarming, daunting, dreadful, fearsome, horrible, horrific, menacing, shocking, terrible; 9 appalling, dismaying, frightful, startling, unnerving, upsetting; 10 enervating, formidable, horrendous, horrifying, petrifying, terrifying; 11 redoubtable; 12 intimidating; PHRASES: 4-7 hair-raising.

frigid 3 icy; 4 cold; 6 chilly, frosty; 7 distant; 8 freezing; 10 unfriendly; 11 standoffish.

frigid(ity) *See* **cold**

frill 5 extra, ruche; 6 luxury, ruffle; 7 flounce; 8 trimming; 10 decoration; 13 accompaniment; PHRASES: 3-2 add-on.

fringe 4 edge; 6 border, edging, tassel; 7 extreme, radical; 8 frontier, marginal, outlying, trimming; 9 extremist, perimeter, periphery; 10 peripheral; 14 unconventional; PHRASES: 3-5 far-flung.

frisk 4 play; 6 cavort, frolic, gambol, search; 7 examine, inspect; PHRASES: 3, 4 pat down; 4, 6 body search.

frivolous 4 idle; 5 perky, silly; 7 playful, shallow, trivial; 10 frolicsome; 12 lighthearted; 15 inconsequential.

Frobisher Bay 7 Iqaluit.

frock 6 invest, ordain.

frolic *See* **play**

from 2 ex; 3 off, out; 4 frae.

front 3 bow; 4 face, fore, head, lead, mask, prow; 5 cheek, cover, first, foyer, lobby, shore; 6 façade, marina, prefix, prolog; 7 forward, frontal, leading, obverse, preface, prelims; 8 anterior, anteroom, bowsprit, entrance, foredeck, foremost, forepart, foreword, frontage, fronting, overlook, prologue, seafront, vanguard; 9 beginning, forecourt, forefront, preceding, spearhead, vestibule; 10 appearance, brazenness, figurehead, forecastle, foreground, proscenium, waterfront; 11 antechamber; 12 battleground, frontispiece, introduction; 13 preliminaries; PHRASES: 4-7 full-frontal; 4, 8 main entrance; 5-5 avant-garde; 7, 2, 3 theatre of war; 7, 4 forward line; 7, 5 advance guard; 8, 4 entrance hall.

front (be in front) 4 ante, face, head, lead; 5 front; 6 prefix; 7 preface, prelude; 8 confront; 9 challenge, introduce, spearhead; PHRASES: 4, 3, 4 take the helm, take the lead.

front (in front) 5 ahead, first; 6 before; PHRASES: 2, 3, 4 in the lead, to the fore; 2, 3, 8 in the vanguard; 2, 5 up front; 2, 7 in advance; 7, 7 leading forward.

frontal 4 fore; 5 front; 7 forward; 8 anterior, forehead.

frontier *See* **border**

frost 3 ice; 4 cold, hoar, jack, rime; 5 chill; 7 iciness; 8 coolness; 9 frigidity; 10 frostiness, permafrost.

frosty 3 icy; 4 cold, cool; 6 chilly, frigid; 8 freezing; 10 unfriendly.

froth 4 fizz, foam, head; 6 bubble, lather, trivia; 7 bubbles; 9 frivolity; 10 triviality; 11 shallowness; 14 superficiality; PHRASES: 2, 6, 5 to become foamy; 6, 2 lather up.

frown 4 pout, snap; 5 glare, growl, lower, scowl, snarl; 6 glower; 7 grimace; PHRASES:

4, 1, 4 pull a face; **4, 4, 4** knit your brow; **8, 4** puckered brow.

frozen 4 cold; **5** solid, still; **8** freezing, immobile, unmoving; **10** motionless, stationary; PHRASES: **3-7** ice-covered; **4, 2** iced up.

frugal *See* **thrifty**

fruit 3 fig, hip, key, nut, pip, pit, pod; **4** crop, date, husk, kiwi, lime, meat, pear, peel, pepo, pith, plum, pome, pulp, rind, seed, skin, sloe; **5** apple, berry, drupe, flesh, grain, grape, guava, juice, lemon, maize *UK*, mango, melon, olive, ovary, papaw *UK*, peach, ripen, shell, shuck, stone, yield; **6** achene, banana, bounty, cherry, citron, citrus, damson, kernel, lichee, litchi, loquat, lychee, maypop, medlar, nutlet, orange, papaya, pawpaw, prunus, quince, result, reward, samara, tomato; **7** apricot, avocado, benefit, bramble, bullace, currant, genipap, kumquat, outcome, produce, product, results, rhubarb, satsuma; **8** bilberry, cucumber, dewberry, fructify, fruition, fruitlet, mandarin, maturing, mulberry, oleaster, tamarind; **9** blaeberry, cranberry, crowberry, greengage, nectarine, persimmon, pineapple, raspberry, sapodilla, tangerine; **10** blackberry, clementine, elderberry, gooseberry, grapefruit, loganberry, strawberry, watermelon; **11** consequence, huckleberry, pomegranate; **12** blackcurrant *UK*, whortleberry; PHRASES: **3, 6** end result; **3, 7** red currant; **4-2-3** coco-de-mer; **4, 5** bear ~, crab apple, star apple; **7, 5** passion ~; **9, 3** marmalade box. *See also* **pulse, vegetables**

fruit-eating 5 vegan; **9** frugivore; **10** fruitarian, vegetarian; **11** frugivorous.

fruitful 7 fertile; **8** abundant, creative, prolific; **9** abounding, inventive, plentiful; **10** productive, profitable; **11** resourceful.

fruitless *See* **unsuccessful**

fruit tree 6 cordon; **8** espalier, standard.

fruity 4 deep, rich, ripe, rude; **5** candy, sweet, tangy, zesty; **6** citric, citrus, fleshy, grapey, lemony, mellow, plummy, risqué; **7** citrine, citrous; **8** indecent, resonant; **9** succulent; **10** harmonious; **11** mellifluous.

frustrate 3 try, vex; **4** dash, foil, stop; **5** annoy, block, cross, upset; **6** bother, hinder, stymie, thwart; **7** disturb, prevent; **8** irritate, obstruct; **9** aggravate, infuriate; **10** discourage, exasperate.

fry *See* **cook**

fuchsine 7 magenta.

fuddle 4 dull, mess; **5** state; **6** dither, muddle; **7** confuse, stupefy; **8** bewilder.

fudge 5 alter, stall; **6** doctor, fiddle, waffle; **7** falsify, garbage, massage, rubbish; **8** nonsense, verbiage; **11** prevaricate; PHRASES: **5, 3, 5** evade the issue.

fuel 3 gas, oil, run; **4** coal, coke, derv *UK*, feed, fire, peat, wood, work; **5** drive, light, power, stoke; **6** charge, diesel, kindle, petrol *UK*; **7** cordite, gasohol, operate, promote; **8** charcoal, energize, firewood, gasoline, hydrogen, increase, recharge; **9** electrify, encourage, petroleum, stimulate; **10** invigorate; **11** electricity; PHRASES: **4, 2** fill up, fire up, plug in; **4, 2, 3, 3** step on the gas; **4, 3** peat bog; **4, 4** peat moss; **5, 5** solar power; **5, 8** white gasoline; **6, 6** energy source.

fug *See* **fog**

fugitive 5 brief, quick, short; **6** outlaw, runner, truant; **7** elusive, escaped, refugee, runaway; **8** deserter, fleeting; **9** absconder, transient.

fulcrum *See* **pivot**

fulfill 4 meet, obey; **5** match; **6** finish, follow, supply; **7** achieve, deliver, execute, justify, perform, provide, realize, satisfy, succeed, survive; **8** complete; **10** accomplish; PHRASES: **4, 3** bear out; **4, 4** make good; **4, 11** gain fulfillment; **5, 3** carry out; **5, 4** agree with; **5, 5** bring about; **6, 4** accord with, comply with; **6, 7** follow through; **7, 2** conform to.

fulfilled 5 happy, sated; **7** content, pleased; **8** rewarded; **9** completed, contented, satisfied.

fulfillment 3 joy; **7** nirvana, success; **8** serenity; **9** discharge, enjoyment, execution; **10** completion; **11** achievement, contentment, realization; **12** satisfaction; **13** gratification; **14** accomplishment, implementation; PHRASES: **5, 5** inner peace.

full 3 fat; **4** deep, rich; **5** ample, broad, flush, laden, plump, pudgy, round, sated, solid, tight; **6** chubby, filled, gorged, jammed, loaded, mellow, oozing, packed, plummy, rotund; **7** brimful, bulging, crammed, crowded, drowned, fraught, leaking, overrun, replete, rounded, stuffed, swamped; **8** brimming, bursting, complete, detailed, infested, occupied, refilled, resonant, satiated, sonorous, thorough; **9** congested, extensive, inclusive, satisfied, saturated; **10** harmonious, overfilled, overloaded; **11** mellifluous, overflowing, overwhelmed, replenished; **13** comprehensive; PHRASES: 3, 2, 4 fit to bust; 3, 5, 5 all seats taken; 3-6 jam-packed; 4, 2, 3, 4 ~ to the brim; 4, 2, 8 ~ to bursting; 4, 3 sold out; 4-4 cram-full *UK*, crop-full; 4-5 well-lined; 4-7 well-stocked; 5-1-5 chock-a-block; 5, 4 alive with, stiff with; 5-4 chock-full; 5, 5 fully laden; 5-5 heavy-laden; 5, 7 fully charged; 6, 2 filled up, topped up; 6, 5 jammed tight; 7, 2 rolling in; 7, 4 jumping with, running over, teeming with; 8, 4 seething with.

fullness 5 quota; **6** quorum; **7** maximum, satiety; **8** capacity, overflow; **9** abundance, plenitude, pregnancy, repletion; **10** saturation. *See also* **full**

fully 5 quite; **6** wholly; **7** forever, totally; **8** entirely; **10** absolutely, altogether, completely; PHRASES: 2, 2, 3, 4 up to the ears, up to the eyes, up to the neck; 2, 3, 3 to the end, to the max, to the top; 2, 3, 4 to the brim, to the core, to the full, to the hilt; 2, 3, 4, 3 to the last man; 2, 3, 4, 6 to the last breath; 2, 3, 5 to the heart, to the quick; 2, 3, 6, 3 to the bitter end; 3, 4 for good; 3, 4, 3, 3 for good and all; 3, 4, 4 and then some; 3, 7 the fixings; 4, 1, 9 with a vengeance; 4, 3, 3 over the top; 4, 5, 2 with knobs on; 5, 4 every inch, every whit.

fulminate *See* **rage**

fumble 4 mess, root; **5** error, grope; **6** muddle, search; **7** blunder, mistake, rummage; **8** scrabble; **9** mishandle; PHRASES: 5, 2 botch up; 6, 2 muddle up; 7, 3 botched job.

fume 4 odor, rage, reek, smog; **5** smell, smoke, stink, vapor; **6** miasma, seethe, stench; **7** bristle; **8** emission; PHRASES: 2, 5 be angry; 2, 7 be furious.

fun 3 joy; **4** buzz, cool, high, jest, kick, lark, play; **5** great, party, sport, treat, whizz; **6** heaven, thrill; **7** amusing, holiday, revelry; **8** exciting, paradise, pleasure, vacation; **9** amusement, diversion, enjoyable, enjoyment, merriment; **10** excitement; **11** celebration, merrymaking, pleasurable; **12** entertaining; **13** entertainment.

function 2 do, go; **3** act, job, map, run; **4** part, role, task, work; **5** event, party, serve; **6** affair, behave, soiree; **7** meeting, operate, perform, purpose, utility; **8** occasion; **9** gathering; **10** occupation.

functional 5 going, handy; **6** useful; **7** running, working; **9** efficient, operative, practical; **10** purposeful; **11** operational, serviceable.

fund 3 aid; **4** back, bank, cash; **5** means, money, purse, stock, store; **6** income, monies, source, supply, wealth; **7** account, backing, capital, credits, finance, payment, readies, reserve, revenue, sponsor, subsidy, support; **8** balances, finances, premises, property, receipts, reserves, treasure; **9** endowment, exchequer, liquidity, overdraft, provision, subsidize, substance; **10** collection, remittance; **11** investments, sponsorship, wherewithal; PHRASES: 4, 4 cash flow.

fundamental 5 basic, major, vital; **7** central, primary; **8** original, ultimate; **9** essential; **10** elementary.

funeral 3 end, sad, urn; **4** bier, cist, dark, fate, keen, obit, pall, taps, wake; **5** black, dirge, elegy, knell, rites, shell; **6** burial, casket, coffin, eulogy, hearse, lament, morgue, shroud, somber, wreath; **7** cortege, elegiac, epitaph, flowers, ossuary, requiem, service; **8** cenotaph, cinerary, exequies *UK*, funerary, funereal, lapidary, memorial, monument, mortuary, mournful, mourning, obituary; **9** cerecloth, cerements, cremation, crematory, footstone, hatchment, headstone, interment, lamenting, obsequies, tombstone; **10** catafalque, eulogistic, gravestone, procession; **11** crematorial, crematorium, inscription, lamentation; PHRASES: 3, 5 hic jacet; 3, 8 war memorial; 4, 2, 5 Rest in Peace (RIP); 4, 4 Dies Irae, here lies, last post *UK*; 4, 4, 5 cold meat party; 4, 5 dead march; 5-2-5 lying-in-state; 5, 7 grave clothes; 6, 7 burial service; 7, 4 ~ hymn, muffled drum, passing bell; 7, 5 ~ rites, winding sheet; 7, 6 ~ parlor; 8, 7 memorial service.

funeral (person at funeral) 4 mute; **6** keener, priest, sexton, weeper; **7** elegist, mourner; **8** eulogist, minister; **9** eulogizer; **10** pallbearer, undertaker.

funereal 6 somber; **7** elegiac; **9** obsequial; **10** sepulchral; **12** necrological; PHRASES: 2, 8 in memoriam; 4, 6 post mortem.

fungal 5 moldy, musty; **6** rotten, yeasty; **7** fungoid, fungous, mildewy; **8** blighted, cankered, mildewed; **9** fermented, fungiform; **11** mycological.

fungus 3 cap, cep, rot; **4** cèpe, conk, gill, mojo, mold, must, veil; **5** ascus, favus, hypha, morel, rusts, smuts, spore, stalk, stipe, tinea, volva, yeast; **6** agaric, blight, canker, lichen, mildew, pileus, thrush; **7** amanita, annulus, blewets, boletus, bracket, candida, lamella, mycosis, rhizoid, thallus, truffle; **8** ascocarp, basidium, conidium, Eumycota, hymenium, mushroom, mycelium, mycetoma, parasite, puffball, ringworm, sterigma; **9** ascospore, earthstar, mycobiont, psilocybe, stinkhorn, toadstool; **10** carpophore, champignon, haustorium, moniliasis, mycorrhiza, plasmodium, rhizomorph, saprophyte, sporophore; **11** ascomycetes, aspergillus, chanterelle, myxomycetes, penicillium; PHRASES: **3, 3** dry rot, ink cap, wet rot *UK*; **3, 6** cup ~, fly agaric, sac ~; **4, 2, 6** horn of plenty; **4, 3** inky cap; **4, 6** club ~, pore ~, rust ~, skin ~; **5, 3** death cap; **5, 3, 7** Dutch elm disease; **5, 4** dhobi itch, slime mold; **5, 6** flask ~, honey ~, jelly ~, tooth ~; **6, 4** Madura foot; **6, 8** meadow mushroom, oyster mushroom; **7, 4** farmer's lung; **7, 6** bracket ~; **7, 8** parasol mushroom; **8, 4** athlete's foot, fruiting body; **9, 6** beefsteak ~; **10, 5** destroying angel.

funnel 4 flue, pipe; **5** focus, guide; **6** direct; **7** channel, chimney, conduit; **10** smokestack; **11** concentrate.

funny 3 gag, odd, pun, rum; **4** jest, joke; **5** comic, droll, faint, giddy, weird, witty; **6** poorly, quaint, quirky, unwell; **7** amusing, comical, curious, offbeat, risible, strange, unusual, waggish *UK*; **8** humorous, nauseous, peculiar; **9** diverting, eccentric, facetious, hilarious, laughable, witticism; **10** hysterical, perplexing *UK*, uproarious; **12** entertaining; **14** unconventional; PHRASES: **3, 3** bon mot; **3-3-4** off-the-wall; **4-9** sidesplitting.

fur 4 coat, fuzz, hair, pelt; **6** fleece.

Furies 7 Erinyes; **9** Eumenides.

furious 3 mad; **5** angry, cross, irate, livid, manic, upset; **6** fuming; **7** enraged, frantic, violent; **8** feverish, vehement; **9** desperate, energetic, ferocious; **10** infuriated; PHRASES: **3-3** all-out; **4-2** full-on; **6, 4, 4** purple with rage; **6, 7** beside oneself; **7, 3** hopping mad.

furnace 4 kiln, oven; **6** boiler, heater; PHRASES: **5, 7** blast ~.

furnish *See* **supply**

furniture 4 sofa; **5** chest, divan, hutch, stall; **6** bureau, closet, lowboy; **7** cabinet, cassone, commode, dresser, effects, high-boy, shelves, tallboy *UK*, whatnot; **8** bookcase, fittings *UK*, painting, property, wardrobe; **9** bookshelf, davenport, equipment, sideboard; **10** canterbury *UK*, upholstery; **11** chinoiserie, furnishings; PHRASES: **4, 5** hope chest; **5, 2, 7** chest of drawers; **5, 7** china cabinet; **6, 5** trompe l'oeil; **6, 7** drinks cabinet *UK*, liquor cabinet, mirror cabinet; **8, 7** cocktail cabinet *UK*. *See also* **bed, cabinet, chair, couch, desk, stool, table**

furniture style 5 Tudor; **6** boulle, Empire, Gothic, modern, rococo, Shaker; **7** baroque, Bauhaus, Regency; **8** colonial, Georgian, Jacobean, Sheraton; **9** Victorian; **11** Biedermeier, chinoiserie, Chippendale, Elizabethan; **12** Scandinavian; PHRASES: **3, 7** Art Nouveau; **4, 11** Adam Hepplewhite; **5-4** Queen-Anne; **5, 5** Louis Seize; **5, 6** Louis Quinze; **5, 7** Early Federal; **5, 8** Early American, Louis Quatorze; **7, 3, 4** William and Mary; **7, 6** William Morris.

furor 4 hype; **6** frenzy, outcry, uproar; **7** protest; **8** ballyhoo, hysteria; **9** commotion; **10** excitement; **11** controversy.

furrow 3 cut, rut; **4** draw, etch, line, plow *UK*, rill; **5** ditch, flute, gully, score, track; **6** groove, gutter, plough *UK*, runnel, trench, trough; **7** channel, conduit, engrave, fissure, scratch, wrinkle; PHRASES: **5-5** wheeltrack.

further 3 aid; **4** else, grow, help, lift, more, push; **5** added, boost, extra, favor, force, raise, speed; **6** better, expand, extend, foster, hasten, prefer, spread; **7** advance, augment, broaden, conduce, develop, elevate, forward, improve, promote, propose, quicken, subvene, upgrade; **8** expedite, subserve; **9** advantage, auxiliary, modernize; **10** accelerate, additional, facilitate; **13** supplementary; PHRASES: **4, 2** step up; **4, 5** help along; **4, 5, 2** lend wings to; **5, 2** bring on; **10, 2** contribute to.

furthest 4 edge; **5** brink, verge; **6** border, margin, utmost; **7** extreme, farness, outpost; **8** boundary, frontier; **9** extremity, outermost, uttermost; **11** furthermost.

furtive *See* **secretive**

furuncle 4 boil.

fury 3 ire; **4** rage; **5** anger, wrath; **8** ferocity.

furze 5 gorse.

fuse 4 meld; **5** blend; **6** mingle; **7** combine; **8** coalesce.

fusion *See* **synthesis**

fuss **3** ado, row; **4** flap, fret, jerk, jump, rush, stew, tizz; **5** noise, scene, storm, tizzy, worry; **6** bother, bustle, dither, flurry, hassle, niggle; **7** bluster, concern, fluster, flutter, protest, trouble, twitter; **8** activity, argument, brouhaha, reaction; **9** commotion, complaint, kerfuffle *UK*; **10** excitement; **11** aggravation, controversy; PHRASES: **2-2** to-do; **3-3** tiz-woz; **3, 5** hop about; **4, 3, 5** song and dance *UK*; **4, 6** mill around; **5-2** carry-on *UK*.

futile **4** idle, vain; **6** barren, failed, wasted; **7** sterile, useless; **8** abortive, bootless, hopeless, wasteful; **9** fruitless, pointless, Sisyphean, thankless, worthless; **10** impossible, profitless, unavailing, unrewarded; **11** ineffective, ineffectual, purposeless, unrewarding; **12** unproductive, unprofitable, unsuccessful; PHRASES: **2-2** no-go; **2, 4** in vain; **3-5** ill-spent; **3, 10** not worthwhile; **4-7** time-wasting *UK*; **6-7** effort-wasting.

future **3** due; **4** fate, near, next, nigh, sure; **5** ahead, fated, later; **6** coming, mañana; **7** certain, destiny, outlook, pending, waiting; **8** destined, doomsday, eventual, imminent, oncoming, possible, probable, prospect, tomorrow, upcoming; **9** impending, potential, predicted; **11** anticipated, approaching, foreseeable, forthcoming, predictable, prospective, threatening; PHRASES: **2, 2** to be; **2-3-2** by-and-by; **2, 4** at hand, to come; **3, 2, 2** yet to be; **3, 10** the millennium; **4, 2, 4** near at hand; **5, 2, 4** close at hand; **5, 2, 5** what's in store; **6, 4** latter days; **6, 6** coming events; **8, 3** Judgment Day.

future (be in the future) **4** come, loom; **8** approach, overhang, threaten; PHRASES: **4, 4** draw near, draw nigh.

future (in the future) **4** anon, soon; **5** later; **7** someday; **8** tomorrow; **10** eventually, imminently, ultimately; PHRASES: **2, 3, 2** by and by; **2, 3, 6** in due course, in the offing, on the morrow; **2, 3, 7** on the horizon; **3, 4, 3** one fine day.

future generation **5** heirs; **7** progeny; **9** posterity; **10** inheritors, successors; **11** descendants.

fuzz **3** fur; **4** down, hair; **5** fluff.

fuzzy **3** dim; **4** hazy; **5** downy, filmy, foggy, furry, hairy, misty, vague, wooly; **6** bleary, blurry, fluffy, unsure, woolly; **7** bleared, blurred, shadowy, unclear; **8** nebulous, obscured; **9** ambiguous, uncertain, undefined, unfocused; **10** incoherent, indefinite, indistinct; PHRASES: **3-7** ill-defined; **3-10** low-definition.

G

G 3 key; 4 good, gram, note; 7 gravity; 8 thousand.

gab *See* **chat**

gabble 6 jabber, yabber; 7 blather, chatter, prattle.

gad about 6 schlep; 7 traipse; 9 gallivant, globetrot; PHRASES: 4, 6 swan around.

gadget 5 gizmo; 6 doodad, widget; 9 appliance; 11 contraption, thingamajig.

gadolinium 2 GA.

Gaelic 4 Erse.

gaffe 5 error; 6 howler; 7 bloomer *UK*, blunder, clanger *UK*, mistake; 8 solecism; PHRASES: 3-3 boo-boo; 4, 3 faux pas.

gaffer 4 tape.

gag 3 ban, tie; 4 bind, curb, joke, quip; 5 choke, crack, funny, heave, leash, retch; 6 collar, muzzle; 7 binding, silence; 8 prohibit, restrict, suppress; 9 interdict, restraint, witticism; 10 injunction; 11 prohibition, restriction; 12 interdiction, straitjacket; PHRASES: 3, 5 ~ order; 3-5 one-liner; 5, 5 court order.

gain 3 add, ROI, win; 4 earn, make, reap; 5 bunce, gravy; 6 attain, earner, extend, fruits, obtain, profit, return, reward, secure, spoils; 7 acquire, advance, benefit, collect, payback, plunder, procure, rakeoff, realize, takings; 8 addition, earnings, increase, multiply, trophies, windfall, winnings; 9 advantage; 11 acquisition, moneymaking, procurement; PHRASES: 3, 2 put on; 3, 5, 2 get ahold of; 3-6 ill-gotten; 4, 2 come by; 4, 2, 2 rake it in; 4, 3, 6 reap the fruits; 4, 5 make money; 5, 2 bring in, clean up; 5-8 money-grubbing; 6-6 profit-taking.

gainful 3 net; 4 paid; 5 gross; 6 paying; 7 earning; 9 lucrative, rewarding; 10 productive, profitable; 11 moneymaking; 12 advantageous, compensatory, profitmaking, remunerative; PHRASES: 5-8 money-spinning *UK*.

gainsay 4 deny; 6 refute; 7 dispute; 10 contradict.

gait 3 jog, run; 4 lope, pace, step, trot, walk; 5 march, strut; 6 canter, gallop, stride, waddle; 7 bearing, posture; 8 carriage; 9 goosestep; PHRASES: 3, 4 jog trot; 5, 5 quick march *UK*.

gal 4 girl.

gala 5 event, miner; 7 concert; 8 festival.

galaxy 4 disc, disk *UK*, halo; 6 nebula, quasar, spiral; 7 cluster, Seyfert; 8 assembly; 9 gathering, starburst; 10 collection; 12 congregation; 13 constellation; PHRASES: 4, 6 star system; 5, 3 Milky Way.

gale 5 storm; 6 squall; 7 tempest; 9 hurricane; PHRASES: 4, 4 high wind.

gall 3 vex; 4 bile, sore; 5 annoy, cheek, nerve; 6 enrage; 8 audacity, irritate; 10 bitterness, effrontery, resentment.

gallant 4 beau; 5 lover, swain; 7 admirer *UK*; 8 cicisbeo *UK*; 9 courteous; 10 chivalrous.

gallery 4 gods *UK*; 6 arcade; 7 balcony, portico, veranda; 8 galleria; 9 colonnade; PHRASES: 6, 7 ladies' ~ *UK*, public ~, rogues' ~; 8, 7 shooting ~.

galley 5 proof, slave; 6 bireme; 7 caboose, kitchen, trireme.

gallium 2 GA.

gallop 4 dash, trot; 6 barrel, canter, career, hurtle, sprint.

gallows 4 beam, bird; 5 humor; 6 gibbet; 8 scaffold; PHRASES: 7, 4 ~ tree.

galore 6 plenty; 7 aplenty; 9 abundance; PHRASES: 1, 4 a gogo; 2, 6 in spades.

galvanize 4 spur, zinc; 5 rouse; 9 stimulate; PHRASES: 3, 5 get going; 4, 2 fire up.

gam 3 pod; 6 school.

gambit 4 ploy, ruse; 6 opener; 8 maneuver; 9 stratagem.

gamble 3 bet; 4 back, draw, risk; 5 stake, wager; 6 chance; 7 flutter *UK*; 9 speculate; PHRASES: 3, 5, 2 put money on.

gambling 3 bet; 4 risk, Tote; 5 stake, wager; 6 chance, gaming, parlay, raffle; 7 betting, lottery, tombola *UK*, whipsaw; 8 croupier, roulette, vigorish; 9 crapshoot; 10 bookmaking, superfecta; 11 speculation, sweepstakes; PHRASES: 3, 4 pit boss; 4, 3 crap out, grab bag; 4, 6 high roller; 4-6 parimutuel; 5-1-4 chuck-a-luck; 5, 4 shell game, snake eyes.

game 2 go; 4 brag, keen, keno, lark, ludo *UK*, snap; 5 brave, cards, chess, craps, darts, derby, gutsy, match, poker, ready, rummy, shogi, whist; 6 bridge, Cluedo™, euchre, feisty, hearts, hurley, plucky, quoits, tipcat; 7 bezique, birling, camogie, canasta, contest, fixture *UK*, Frisbee™, ninepin, pachisi, pastime, pontoon *UK*, reversi, willing; 8 baccarat, checkers, cribbage, dominoes, mahjongg, Monopoly™, ninepins, Nintendo™, patience *UK*, pinochle, resolute, ringtoss, roulette, rounders, Scrabble™, skittles *UK*, spirited; 9 amusement, bagatelle, billiards, blackjack, diversion, paintball, solitaire; 10 backgammon, casablanca, determined, horseshoes, recreation, spillikins *UK*, tournament; 11 competition, tiddlywinks; PHRASES: 2, 3 up for; 2, 5 no trump; 3, 2, 3 tug of war; 3, 3, 5 cat and mouse; 3, 4 big ~, old maid, war ~; 3, 5 gin rummy; 4, 2, 3, 4 king of the hill; 4, 4 ball ~, card ~, word ~; 4-4-3 tick-tack-toe; 5-2-2 vingt-et-un; 5, 4 board ~, small ~, video ~; 5, 8 happy families; 5-9 shove-halfpenny *UK*; 6, 2, 3 chemin de fer; 6, 2, 3, 6 monkey in the middle; 6-3-6 follow-the-leader; 6, 4 arcade ~, deuces wild; 7, 3, 7 cowboys and Indians; 7, 8 Chinese checkers; 8-3 mumblety-peg; 8, 4 computer ~; 8, 6 contract bridge. *See also* **gamebird, sport**

gamebird 4 duck, teal; 5 capon, quail, snipe; 6 grouse, pigeon, turkey; 7 chicken, widgeon *UK*; 8 pheasant, woodcock; 9 partridge, ptarmigan; PHRASES: 6, 4 guinea fowl.

game fish 3 eel; 4 carp, chub, pike, rudd; 5 bream, perch, roach, skate, snook, tench, trout; 6 barbel, bonito, plaice, salmon, tarpon; 7 pollack, snapper, walleye; 8 bluefish, bonefish, grayling, mackerel, sailfish; 9 barracuda; 10 yellowtail; 11 muskellunge; PHRASES: 3, 5 sea trout; 4, 5 blue shark, lake trout; 4, 6 blue marlin, gray mullet; 5, 5 brook trout; 6, 3 conger eel; 6, 4 arctic char; 6, 5 yellow perch; 6, 6 silver salmon; 7, 4 channel bass, striped bass; 7, 5 rainbow trout; 7, 6 chinook salmon, Pacific salmon; 7, 8 Spanish mackerel; 8, 3, 4 European sea bass; 8, 4 northern pike; 8, 6 Atlantic salmon. *See also* **fish, freshwater fish, sea fish**

gamekeeper 6 keeper, warden; 7 handler, Mellors; PHRASES: 4, 6 game warden *UK*.

gammon 3 win; 4 tosh *UK*; 5 bacon; 7 rubbish; 8 nonsense.

gamut 5 range, scale, scope; 7 compass.

gander 4 look, peek; 5 dekko *UK*; 6 shufti *UK*; 12 Newfoundland.

gang 2 go; 3 mob; 4 band, crew, pack, ring, team; 5 Mafia, posse, squad, Triad *UK*; PHRASES: 4, 6 cosa nostra; 5, 3 heavy mob.

gangrene 3 rot; 5 decay; 6 fester; 7 putrefy; 9 decompose, infection; 12 putrefaction; 13 decomposition.

gangster 4 goon, hood; 6 hitman, yakuza, Yardie; 7 hoodlum, mafioso, mobster; PHRASES: 8, 6 contract killer.

gangway 4 road; 5 aisle; 7 walkway; 8 corridor; 10 passageway.

gannet *See* **glutton**

Ganymede 9 cupbearer; PHRASES: 4, 4 moon gaol. *See* **jail**

gap 4 hole, lull, pass, rift, slit; 5 break, chasm, crack, gorge, pause, space; 6 breach, canyon, hiatus, lacuna, ravine; 7 fissure, opening; 8 aperture, interval, mismatch; 9 disparity, interlude; 10 interstice; 12 intermission, interruption; PHRASES: 5, 3 trade ~ *UK*; 10, 3 generation ~; 11, 3 credibility ~.

gape 3 eye; 4 ogle, yawn; 10 rubberneck.

gaping 4 deep, huge, wide; 7 abysmal, yawning; 9 cavernous.

garage 4 shed; 6 lockup *UK*; 7 carport; PHRASES: 3, 7 gas station; 7, 7 service station.

garb 5 getup; 6 outfit, rigout; 7 apparel, costume.

garbage 3 tat *UK*; 4 bosh, gash, junk, scum, slam, tosh *UK*; 5 dross, hokum, hooey, slate *UK*, trash, tripe, waste; 6 bunkum, debris, drivel, jumble, litter, refuse, scraps; 7 baloney, dismiss, hogwash, rubbish *UK*, seconds, twaddle; 8 claptrap, nonsense, ridicule; 9 criticize, disparage; PHRASES: 4-4 pooh-pooh; 4, 5, 2 pick holes in.

garbage collector 6 binman *UK*; 7 dustman, junkman; PHRASES: 3-3-4, 3 rag-and-bone man; 6, 6 litter picker; 6, 7 street sweeper; 7, 3 dustbin man, garbage man.

garble 5 twist; 6 jumble, muddle; 7 confuse, corrupt, distort.

garden 3 bed; 4 Eden, roji; 5 arbor, bower, patch; 6 border, grotto, rosery; 7 gardens, hanging, kitchen, orchard, pergola, planter, potager *UK*, rockery, terrace, topiary; 8 parterre, vineyard; 9 allotment *UK*, arboretum, cultivate, landscape, shrubbery; 10 Gethsemane, Hesperides, zoological; PHRASES: 3, 6 bog ~; 4, 4 back yard; 4, 5 lawn party; 4, 6 beer ~, herb ~, knot ~, rock ~, roof ~, rose ~; 5, 4 truck farm; 5, 5 lemon grove, olive grove; 5, 6 civic ~, water ~; 6, 2, 4 ~ of rest; 6, 2, 6 common or ~ *UK*; 6, 3 window box; 6, 4 ~ city *UK*; 6, 5 ~ party, orange grove; 6, 6 alpine ~, flower ~, formal ~, ~ center, ~ suburb *UK*, market ~, sunken ~, winter ~; 6, 7 ~ variety; 7, 5 cabbage patch; 7, 6 cottage ~, hanging ~, kitchen ~; 8, 6 Japanese ~; 9, 6 botanical ~, vegetable ~.

gardener 6 grower, weeder; 7 planter; 14 horticulturist.

gardening 5 drill, graft, scion, stock, tilth; 6 offset, sowing, strain, sucker; 7 cutting, pruning, tilling, weeding; 8 cultivar, grafting, layering, planting, watering; 9 repotting; 10 composting, cultivator, winterkill; 11 aquiculture, deadheading, hydroponics, propagation; PHRASES: 4, 4 yard work; 4, 5 grow light; 4, 7 hard pruning; 5, 5 green thumb; 5, 7 grass catcher, green fingers; 6, 9 market ~ *UK*; 7, 2 potting on; 7, 3 bedding out; 7, 4 cutting back; 8, 3 pinching out, pricking out.

gardening tool 3 hoe; 4 fork, hose, rake, trug *UK*; 5 edger, spade, stake; 6 dibber, riddle, roller, scythe, shears, shovel, trowel; 8 clippers, Strimmer™; 9 lawnmower, Rotavator™, sprinkler; 11 wheelbarrow; PHRASES: 5, 3 Dutch hoe; 5, 7 hedge clipper, hedge trimmer; 6, 5 rotary mower; 8, 3 watering can.

gargantuan 4 huge, vast; 8 colossal, enormous; 11 Rabelaisian.

gargle 4 glug; 5 rinse; 6 bubble, burble, gurgle; 7 freshen; 9 disinfect; PHRASES: 4, 3 wash out.

gargoyle *See* **ornament**

garish 4 loud; 5 brash, gaudy, jazzy, showy; 6 flashy.

garland 3 lei; 4 swag; 6 anadem, wreath; 7 circlet, coronet, festoon.

garment 4 gown, robe, sari, togs, wrap; 5 burqa *UK*, cloak, habit, lapel, mufti, shift, stole, tunic, weeds; 6 attire, caftan *UK*, chador, closet, gusset, kaftan *UK*, kimono, lining, muumuu, outfit, poncho, sarong, sheath; 7 apparel, cagoule *UK*, catsuit, civvies, jellaba, raiment, uniform; 8 ensemble, neckline, negligée *UK*, overalls, pantsuit, peignoir, vestment, wardrobe; 9 coveralls, tracksuit, waistband; 10 shirtdress; 11 leisurewear; PHRASES: 6, 4 boiler suit *UK*.

garnet 3 red; 9 carbuncle, rhodolite; 11 spessartine.

garnish 7 enhance; 8 decorate; 9 embellish, garniture, trimmings; PHRASES: 4, 4 side dish.

garret 4 loft; 5 attic, gable; 9 penthouse.

garrulous 5 gassy; 6 prolix; 7 gushing, voluble; 9 talkative.

garter 7 bowyang; 9 suspender.

gas 3 air, jaw, yak; 4 chat, coal, fume, neon, wind; 5 argon, blast, calor, ether, ideal, sarin, tabun, vapor; 6 bunkum, butane, flatus, helium, miasma, natter, oxygen, waffle; 7 blather, bombast, chatter, chinwag, garbage, methane, perfect, propane, rubbish; 8 chlorine, claptrap, firedamp, hydrogen, nitrogen, nonsense, phosgene; 9 acetylene, poppycock; 10 asphyxiate; PHRASES: 2, 3 CS ~, VX ~; 3, 3 hot air; 4, 3 coal ~, rare ~, tear ~; 4, 3, 3 chew the fat; 5, 3 Calor ~, inert ~, marsh ~, nerve ~, noble ~; 5, 3, 3 North Sea ~; 6, 3 poison ~; 6, 6 liquid oxygen; 7, 3 mustard ~, natural ~; 7, 5 nitrous oxide; 8, 3 laughing ~; 10, 3 greenhouse ~.

gash 3 rip; 4 tear; 5 slash, wound; 8 incision; 10 laceration.

gasoline 3 gas, LRP *UK*; 4 fuel; 5 juice; 8 unleaded; PHRASES: 4, 4 four star.

gasp 4 huff, pant, puff; 6 wheeze.

gassy 4 fumy; **5** fizzy, smoky; **6** bubbly, chatty, steamy; **7** aerated, gaseous, gossipy, verbose, voluble; **8** vaporous; **9** garrulous, prattling, sparkling, talkative; **10** carbonated, chattering, loquacious; **12** effervescent; PHRASES: **4-6** long-winded.

gastronome 6 foodie; **7** epicure, gourmet; **8** gourmand; **11** connoisseur; PHRASES: **3, 6** bon vivant, bon viveur.

gastropod 4 slug; **5** conch, snail, whelk; **6** limpet; **7** abalone; **10** periwinkle; PHRASES: **3, 4** sea slug.

gate 4 door, lych; **5** crowd; **6** access, portal; **7** doorway, gateway, opening, postern, turnout; **8** audience, entrance, moongate; **9** turnstile, watergate; **10** attendance; PHRASES: **6, 4** Golden G~; **7, 4** kissing ~ UK; **8, 4** starting ~; **11, 4** Brandenburg G~.

gatepost 4 jamb; **7** upright; **8** doorpost; **9** scuncheon.

gather 4 crop, fold, reap, ruck, tuck; **5** amass, bunch, crimp, glean, pleat, ruche, shirr, smock; **6** garner, muster, pucker; **7** cluster, collect, harvest, marshal; **8** assemble; **10** congregate.

gathering 5 rally; **7** reunion; **8** assembly, jamboree; **9** symposium; **10** corroboree UK; **11** convocation; **12** congregation.

gauche 4 left; **6** callow, clumsy; **7** awkward; **8** tactless.

gaudy 4 loud; **5** lurid, showy, tacky; **6** brassy, flashy, garish, tawdry; **7** kitschy; **8** tinselly.

gauge 6 assess; **7** caliber, measure; **8** estimate, evaluate; **9** benchmark, criterion, indicator, yardstick.

gaunt 4 lean; **7** haggard, scrawny; **9** Lancaster UK.

gauze 5 tulle; **6** muslin; **7** chiffon, organdy; **8** dressing, gossamer, organdie; **11** cheesecloth.

gauzy 4 thin; **5** filmy, light; **8** delicate; **10** diaphanous; **11** transparent; PHRASES: **3-7** see-through.

gawky 6 clumsy; **8** gangling.

gaze 3 eye; **4** gawp, moon, pore; **5** stare; **6** goggle.

gear 3 kit; **4** mesh, togs; **5** stuff; **6** outfit, tackle, things; **7** clobber UK; **8** clothing; **9** apparatus, equipment; **10** derailleur, syncromesh; **13** paraphernalia; PHRASES: **4, 3, 6** rack and pinion; **5, 4** bevel ~; **7, 4** helical ~.

gelatine 3 gel; **8** collagen; **9** carrageen, isinglass.

gelatinous 5 gooey, gummy, gungy UK; **6** sticky, viscid; **7** viscous; **9** glutinous.

geld 4 spay; **6** neuter; **8** castrate; **9** sterilize.

gem 4 star; **8** gemstone, treasure. See also **jewel**

Gemini 5 Twins; **6** Castor, Pollux.

gemstone 4 jade, onyx, opal, rock, ruby, sard; **5** agate, beryl, jewel, stone, topaz; **6** garnet, zircon; **7** diamond, emerald; **8** amethyst, cabochon, sapphire; **9** carnelian, malachite, moonstone, turquoise; **10** aquamarine, bloodstone, chalcedony, serpentine, tourmaline; **11** chrysoprase; PHRASES: **5, 6** lapis lazuli.

gender See **sex**

genealogy 3 ilk, kin; **4** clan, line, race; **5** birth, blood, breed, stock, tribe; **6** family, strain; **7** descent, lineage; **8** ancestry, pedigree; **9** ancestors, forebears; **10** extraction; **11** descendants; PHRASES: **6, 4** family tree; **6, 7** family history.

general 3 Ike, Lee; **5** Grant, Monty, staff, synod, Wolfe; **6** Caesar, common, Custer, Franco, Patton, Pompey, strike; **7** blanket, overall; **8** assembly, catholic, eclectic, election, Hannibal, Napoleon, sweeping, synoptic; **9** Alexander, commander, customary, extensive, inclusive, panoramic, universal; **10** anesthetic, ecumenical, unspecific; **11** nonspecific; **12** heterogenous, nonexclusive, practitioner; **13** comprehensive; PHRASES: **3-7** all-purpose; **3-9** all-inclusive; **4-7** wide-ranging; **5-5** broad-based; **5-8** broad-spectrum; **6-3-5** across-the-board.

generality 5 axiom; **6** cliché, truism; **7** bromide; **8** banality, chestnut, overview; **9** platitude, vagueness; **13** inclusiveness; **14** generalization, simplification; PHRASES: **5, 4** broad view.

generally 6 mostly; **7** broadly, largely, loosely, usually; **8** normally UK; **13** approximately; PHRASES: **2, 1, 4** as a rule; **2, 3, 4** in the main; **2, 3, 5** by and large; **2, 7** in general; **3, 2, 3** all in all. See also **general**

general public 3 mob; **5** plebs; **6** masses, rabble; **8** populace; **9** multitude; PHRASES: **3, 6** hoi polloi, vox populi; **4, 3, 4** rank and file; **5, 5** grass roots; **5, 8** great unwashed; **6, 6** common people.

generate 4 sire; **5** beget, breed, cause,

spawn; **6** create, father; **7** produce; **8** engender; **9** propagate, stimulate.

generation 3 age, eon, era; **5** epoch, group, peers, phase; **6** making, period; **8** compeers, creation; **9** invention; **10** initiation, production; **11** origination; PHRASES: **3, 5** age group; **4, 5** peer group.

generator 4 sire; **5** maker; **6** author, dynamo, father; **7** creator, magneto; **8** begetter, producer; **9** initiator; **10** alternator, originator.

generosity 6 bounty; **8** kindness, largesse; **10** liberality; **11** hospitality, munificence. *See also* **generous**

generous 4 kind; **5** large; **6** lavish; **7** liberal; **8** handsome, princely; **9** bounteous, bountiful, plentiful; **10** beneficent, charitable, hospitable, munificent, unstinting; **11** magnanimous, substantial; PHRASES: **3-7** big-hearted; **4-6** open-handed.

generous person 5 angel, donor; **6** backer; **10** benefactor; **12** humanitarian; **14** philanthropist; PHRASES: **4, 9** good Samaritan, Lady Bountiful; **5, 5** Santa Claus; **5, 9** fairy godmother; **6, 9** Father Christmas.

genetic 4 gene; **5** genic; **6** inborn, innate, native; **7** genomic, natural; **8** dominant, inherent; **9** inherited, Mendelian, recessive; **10** hereditary; **11** chromosomal.

genetic material 3 DNA, RNA; **4** exon, gene; **5** codon; **6** allele, factor, genome, intron, operon; **10** transposon; PHRASES: **4, 8** gene mutation, gene sequence, gene splicing; **4, 10** gene complement; **7, 4** genetic code.

Geneva 4 Genf; **6** Genève; **9** Genfersee.

genial 5 matey *UK*; **6** jovial; **7** affable, amiable; **8** friendly, pleasant, sociable; **9** convivial.

genie 3 imp; **4** jinn; **5** djinn; **6** sprite; **8** Mazikeen.

genitals 4 yoni; **7** pudenda; **8** privates; PHRASES: **7, 5** private parts.

genius 6 marvel, talent; **7** maestro, prodigy; **8** brainbox *UK*, virtuoso; **10** mastermind; **11** inspiration; PHRASES: **5, 3** whizz kid.

genteel 5 civil; **6** polite, proper; **7** refined; PHRASES: **4-8** well-mannered.

gentle 4 kind, meek, mild, soft; **5** bland, quiet; **6** mellow, placid, smooth, tender; **7** clement, lenient; **8** delicate.

gentleman 2 Mr; **3** nob *UK*, Sir; **4** Herr, toff; **5** Senor; **6** aristo, Mister, Signor, squire; **7** grandee; **8** Monsieur, nobleman, smuggler.

gentry 5 elite; **11** aristocracy, squirearchy; PHRASES: **6, 6** landed ~.

gents 4, 4 men's room.

genuflect 3 bob, bow; **6** curtsy, kowtow; PHRASES: **3, 4, 8** tug one's forelock; **4, 3, 4** bend the knee.

genuine 4 echt, real; **5** pukka; **6** kosher; **7** sincere; **9** authentic; PHRASES: **4, 4** bona fide; **4-4** true-blue; **4, 5** real McCoy, real thing.

genus 4 sort, type; **5** class, genre.

geographic region 4 veld, zone; **5** plain, tract; **6** desert, region, steppe, tropic, tundra, upland; **7** equator, outback, prairie, tropics; **8** latitude, meridian, moorland, parallel, savannah; **9** grassland, longitude; **10** hinterland, subtropics, wilderness; PHRASES: **3, 4** the Line; **4, 6** rain forest; **5, 8** prime meridian; **5, 9** horse latitudes; **7, 7** roaring forties.

geologic time 3 eon, era; **5** epoch; **6** Eocene, period; **7** Miocene, Permian; **8** Cambrian, Cenozoic, Devonian, eonothem, Holocene, Jurassic, Mesozoic, Pliocene, Silurian, Tertiary, Triassic; **9** Oligocene, Paleocene, Paleozoic; **10** Cretaceous, Ordovician, Quaternary; **11** Pleistocene, Precambrian; **13** Carboniferous, Mississippian, Pennsylvanian; PHRASES: **3, 3** ice age.

geologist 9 geodesist; **10** geochemist, pedologist; **11** hydrologist, petrologist; **12** glaciologist, mineralogist; **13** physiographer, planetologist, stratigrapher, volcanologist; **14** paleontologist; **15** geochronologist, geomorphologist.

geometry 5 shape, solid; **6** figure; **7** fractal, section, segment; **8** symmetry; **13** configuration.

Georgia 2 GA; **7** Atlanta (capital); PHRASES: **4, 3** live oak (tree); **5, 5** Peach State (nickname); **5, 8** brown thrasher (bird); **6, 5, 6, 2, 5** Goober State, Empire of South (nickname); **6, 7, 3, 10** Wisdom, justice and moderation (motto); **8, 4** cherokee rose (flower).

geranium 10 cranesbill; **11** pelargonium.

germ 3 bud, bug; **4** root, seed; **5** cause, lurgy, spark, virus; **6** embryo, kernel, origin; **7** microbe, nucleus; **8** bacteria, rudiment; **9**

bacterium, beginning, contagion, infection; **13** microorganism.

German 1 D; **3** Von; **4** Hans, Herr.

germane *See* **relevant**

Germanic 5 Aryan; **8** Prussian, Teutonic; **9** Alemannic.

germanium 2 GE.

germinate 3 bud; **4** grow; **5** breed; **6** evolve, sprout; **7** burgeon, develop; **8** incubate, multiply; **9** propagate.

gesticulate 5 point; **8** indicate. *See also* **gesticulation**

gesticulation 4 sign, wave; **6** beckon, motion, salute, signal; **7** gesture; **8** movement.

gesture 3 nod, tap, tic; **4** mime, moue, wave, wink; **5** point, shrug; **6** beckon, motion, salute, signal, stroke, twitch; **7** grimace; **8** kinesics, movement, ticktack; **9** handshake, pantomime, raspberry; **13** gesticulation; PHRASES: **1, 4** V sign; **4, 1, 5** cock a snook; **4, 6** hand signal; **4, 8** body language, sign language; **8, 4** clenched fist.

get 4 gain, rile, twig *UK*; **5** annoy, grasp; **6** attain, obtain, secure; **7** acquire, procure, realize; **8** irritate; **10** understand.

get at 3 nag; **5** annoy; **9** criticize.

getaway *See* **escape**

get by 4 cope; **6** manage; **7** survive; PHRASES: **6, 7** muddle through.

get on 3 gel; **5** click; **6** thrive; **7** succeed; PHRASES: **2, 4** do well; **3, 2, 3** hit it off; **3, 5** get along.

get out 4 exit; **5** leave; **6** escape, remove; **7** extract, retreat; **8** evacuate, withdraw; **9** extricate; **11** disentangle.

gewgaw 6 bauble; **7** trinket; **10** knickknack.

geyser 3 jet; **5** spout; **6** gusher, spring.

Ghana 4, 5 Gold Coast.

ghastly 3 wan; **4** pale; **5** ashen, awful; **6** grisly, pallid; **7** hideous; **8** gruesome.

Ghent 4 Gand, Gent.

ghetto 4 slum; **6** barrio, favela; **7** quarter.

ghost 5 demon, dwarf, fairy, ghoul, jinni, manes, pixie, shade, spook, troll; **6** spirit, sprite, undead, wraith, zombie; **7** lemures, phantom, specter, Titania, vampire; **8** phantasm, presence, werewolf; **9** hobgoblin; **10** apparition, changeling, cluricaune, lepre-

chaun; **11** poltergeist; **13** manifestation; PHRASES: **4-1-3-4** will-o'-the-wisp.

ghostly 5 eerie; **6** creepy, spooky; **7** phantom, uncanny; **8** ethereal, spectral; **9** ghostlike; **12** supernatural.

GI 7 private, recruit, soldier.

giant 4 huge, ogre, vast; **5** great, jumbo, large, titan, whale; **7** Goliath, mammoth, massive, monster, whopper; **8** behemoth, colossal, colossus, elephant, enormous, gigantic; **9** Gargantua, humdinger, leviathan; **10** juggernaut *UK*; **14** Brobdingnagian; PHRASES: **4, 4** King Kong.

gibberish 3 rot; **6** drivel; **7** garbage, rubbish, twaddle; **8** claptrap.

gibe 4 jeer, joke, mock; **5** sneer, taunt, tease; **6** remark; **8** ridicule.

giddy 5 dizzy, shaky, silly, woozy; **6** scatty *UK Can*; **7** flighty; **8** unstable, unsteady, volatile; **9** frivolous, impulsive; **10** capricious; **14** scatterbrained; PHRASES: **3-7** off-balance; **5-6** light-headed.

gift 3 tip; **4** alms, boon, bung *UK*, help, perk; **5** award, bonus, flair, knack, manna, prize, skill, token; **6** talent; **7** ability, alimony, bequest, bonanza, cumshaw, douceur, fairing, freebie, handsel *UK*, present, pressie *UK*; **8** aptitude, donation, gratuity, offering, palimony, windfall; **9** baksheesh, lagniappe, pourboire, sweetener, Trinkgeld; **10** backhander *UK*, inducement, perquisite; **11** inheritance; **13** consideration; PHRASES: **2, 6, 7** ex gratia payment; **4-3** hand-out, rake-off; **4, 4** free ~; **4-5** whip-round *UK*; **4, 6** door opener; **6, 9** golden handshake; **8, 7** birthday present; **9, 3** Christmas box *UK*.

gifted 4 able; **6** bright; **7** skilled; **8** talented; **11** exceptional, intelligent; PHRASES: **2, 4, 5** of many parts.

gift of tongues 11 glossolalia.

gigantic 7 massive, titanic; **8** colossal, oversize; **10** gargantuan.

giggle 6 cackle, titter; **7** chortle, chuckle, snicker, snigger *UK*; PHRASES: **3-3** tee-hee.

gigolo 10 ladykiller; PHRASES: **4, 3** kept man *UK*; **6, 6** lounge lizard.

gilt 4 gold; **6** golden, ormolu; PHRASES: **4-6** gold-plated.

gimmick 4 ploy; **5** stunt, trick.

gin 4 trap; **5** rummy, sling; **6** palace; **7** genever; **8** Hollands *UK*; PHRASES: **7, 4** mother's ruin.

ginger 3 ale; 4 beer, snap, wine; 5 group; 10 gingerroot.

gingili 6 sesame.

gingiva 3 gum.

ginkgo 10, 4 maidenhair tree.

giraffe 10 camelopard.

girder 3 RSJ *UK*; 4 beam, spar; 5 joist; 6 rafter; 7 support; 9 crossbeam.

girdle 3 tie; 4 belt, sash; 6 corset; 8 encircle, surround; 10 cummerbund.

girl 2 Di; 3 gal, Pam, Sue, Val; 4 babe, doll, Kate, lass, miss; 5 Betty, quine *UK*; 6 damsel, maiden, sheila *UK*; 7 floozie; 8 Fraulein, senorita; 10 bobbysoxer; 12 mademoiselle; PHRASES: 2, 4 It ~ *UK*; 4, 6 ~ Friday; 5, 4 cover ~; 6, 4 chorus ~, flower ~, Gibson ~; 10, 4 continuity ~.

girlfriend 4 date, girl, moll; 5 bride, flame, lover; 6 escort; 7 fiancée, partner, squeeze; 8 mistress; 9 inamorata; 10 ladyfriend *UK*, sweetheart; PHRASES: 4, 5 kept woman *UK*; 5, 5 fancy woman.

girth 4 size, span; 5 width; 13 circumference.

gist 3 nub; 5 point; 6 kernel; 7 essence, meaning, nucleus; 9 substance.

give 4 cede, fund, gift, lend; 5 allot, award, endow, grant, leave, offer, share, treat, yield; 6 assign, bestow, confer, donate, impart, render, reward, tender; 7 consign, crumble, entrust, present, provide, shatter; 8 allocate, bequeath, collapse, covenant, dispense, fracture, transmit; 9 subscribe, vouchsafe; 10 contribute, elasticity; 11 flexibility; PHRASES: 4, 2 chip in, kick in *US and Aus*; 4, 3 deal out, dish out, dole out, fork out, ~ way, mete out; 4, 4 fork over, ~ away, hand over, make over, part with; 5, 3 shell out; 6, 4 lavish upon, shower upon.

give-and-take 9 mutuality; 11 cooperation, reciprocity; 13 collaboration.

give back 5 atone, repay; 6 redeem, refund, return; 7 replace, requite, restore; 9 reimburse.

give birth 3 cub, pup; 4 drop, foal, lamb; 5 beget, breed, calve, spawn, whelp; 6 farrow, kindle, kitten, litter; 9 procreate, reproduce.

give in 5 yield; 6 relent, submit; 7 concede; 9 surrender; 10 capitulate; PHRASES: 4,

2 cave in; 5, 2, 3, 5 throw in the towel; 5, 6 admit defeat.

give off 4 emit, fume, reek, spew; 5 exude, smoke, steam; 6 exhale; 7 radiate; 9 discharge.

give out 4 emit, fail; 5 allot, award, exude; 7 provide; 8 collapse, dispense, transmit; 9 discharge; 10 distribute; PHRASES: 4, 3 hand out, mete out; 5, 4 break down.

give up 4 cede, quit, stop; 7 abandon; 8 renounce; 9 sacrifice; 10 relinquish.

give way 3 sag; 5 yield; 6 buckle; 7 crumble; 8 collapse.

glacial 3 icy; 4 cold; 5 polar; 6 arctic; 7 subzero; 8 freezing; 10 unfriendly; PHRASES: 3-4 ice-cold.

glacier 4 floe, till; 5 drift, sérac, snout; 6 cirque, icecap; 7 erratic, iceberg, icefall, moraine; 8 crevasse; 9 meltwater; PHRASES: 3, 4 ice floe; 3, 5 ice field, ice sheet, ice shelf.

glad 4 fain; 5 eager, happy, ready; 7 pleased, willing; 8 grateful, prepared, thankful; PHRASES: 4, 4 ~ rags.

gladden 5 cheer, elate; 6 please; 7 delight, hearten.

gladiator 7 fighter, Samnite; 8 champion, Mirmillo, Thracian; 9 Retiarius, Spartacus.

glamorous 6 glitzy; 7 stylish; 8 alluring; PHRASES: 1-4 A-list; 3, 3 jet set; 9, 6 Beautiful People.

glamour 5 charm, glitz, style; 6 allure, appeal, beauty; 10 attraction, glitziness; 11 fascination; PHRASES: 4, 5 good looks.

glance 4 look, peek, peep, scan, skim; 5 flash, flick, glint; 6 browse, squint; 7 rebound, reflect; 8 ricochet; PHRASES: 4-4 once-over; 5, 1, 4 steal a look.

gland 6 thymus; 7 nectary, parotid, thyroid; 9 hydathode, laticifer; PHRASES: 6, 5 pineal ~; 7, 5 adrenal ~, eccrine ~, mammary ~; 8, 5 ductless ~, exocrine ~, lacrimal ~, prostate ~, salivary ~; 9, 5 endocrine ~, pituitary ~; 10, 5 suprarenal ~.

glare 4 lour; 5 frown, lower, scowl, sheen, shine, stare; 6 dazzle, glower; 7 glimmer, glitter, grimace, shimmer, smolder; 10 brightness, brilliance; PHRASES: 4, 7 look daggers; 5, 4 dirty look.

glaring 7 blatant, evident, obvious; 8 flagrant; 9 egregious; 11 conspicuous.

glass 4 pane; 5 flute, light, Pyrex™, Stein, storm, water; 6 beaker, bumper, cheval, cullet, goblet, jigger, noggin, rummer, silica, window; 7 chalice, crystal, cupping, Favrile, Lalique, pilsner, tankard, Tiffany, tumbler; 8 cannikin, murrhine, pannikin, schooner; 9 glassware, wineglass; 10 fiberglass, windowpane, windscreen *UK*, windshield; PHRASES: 3, 5 cut ~; 4, 5 lead ~, opal ~, pier ~; 4, 7 lead crystal, rock crystal; 5, 5 clear ~, crown ~, flint ~, plate ~; 6, 5 bottle ~, ground ~, quartz ~, safety ~, window ~; 6-5 bullet-proof; 6, 7 brandy balloon; 7, 5 crystal ~, frosted ~, looking ~, optical ~, stained ~; 8, 5 Venetian ~; 9, 5 champagne flute, laminated ~, toughened ~; 10, 5 magnifying ~.

glassblowing 4 lehr; 5 punty; 6 marver; PHRASES: 5, 4 glory hole; 9, 4 annealing oven.

glasses 5 specs; 6 shades; 7 goggles, monocle; 8 bifocals, sunspecs *UK*; 9 lorgnette; 10 sunglasses, varifocals; PHRASES: 4, 7 dark ~; 5-3 pince-nez; 5, 7 field ~, opera ~.

glasshouse 10 greenhouse.

glassy 5 blank, shiny; 6 glazed, glossy, smooth, vacant; 8 gleaming, lustrous, polished, slippery, vitreous; 9 varnished; 10 reflective; 11 crystalline, transparent.

glaze 4 coat, seal, slip; 5 cover, paint; 6 finish, polish, veneer; 7 coating, crackle, crazing, reflect, refract, varnish; 9 overglaze; 10 underglaze; 12 decalcomania; PHRASES: 4-5 salt-glaze; 5, 5 smear ~; 7, 5 fritted ~; 8, 5 eggshell ~.

gleam 3 ray; 4 beam, burn, glow, wink; 5 blink, flame, flare, flash, glare, glint, gloss, sheen, shine; 6 dazzle, glance, luster, patina, polish; 7 flicker, glimmer, glisten, glister, glitter, radiate, shimmer, sparkle, twinkle; 9 coruscate, fluoresce; 11 scintillate; 12 phosphoresce.

glee 3 joy; 4 song; 5 mirth; 7 triumph; 9 merriment; 10 jubilation.

glen 4 dale, dell, vale; 5 chine *UK*, gorge; 6 ravine, strath *UK*, valley.

glib 3 pat; 4 flip; 5 slick; 6 facile, fluent, smooth.

glide 3 fly; 4 roll, skid, slip, soar; 5 coast, drift, float, hover, skate, slide, wheel; 6 sashay; 7 slither; 9 freewheel; 10 hydroplane.

glider 10 microlight *UK*, paraglider; PHRASES: 4, 6 hang ~.

glimmer 4 glow; 5 gleam; 7 flicker, shimmer.

glimpse 4 hint, peek; 5 flash; 6 glance; 7 pointer; 8 sighting; 9 foretaste.

glint 4 wink; 5 flash, gleam; 7 sparkle, twinkle.

glisten 5 gleam, sheen, shine; 7 glimmer, glister, shimmer.

glitter 5 flash, gleam, glint, glitz, shine; 6 allure, dazzle, tinsel; 7 glamour, glimmer, glisten, glister, sequins, shimmer, sparkle, twinkle; 8 charisma, spangles; 10 glitterati.

glitzy 5 plush, ritzy; 6 flashy, swanky; 9 glamorous; PHRASES: 1-4 A-list.

gloat 4 crow; 5 exult, revel, smirk; 7 rejoice.

gloating 8 smugness; 10 exultation; 13 Schadenfreude.

globe 3 orb; 4 ball; 5 earth, world; 6 sphere; 7 rondure.

globetrotter 6 gapper; 7 tourist; 8 traveler; 9 jetsetter; 10 backpacker; PHRASES: 8, 5 frequent flyer.

globule 4 ball, bead, blob, drop; 6 bubble, gobbet.

gloom 4 murk; 6 shadow; 8 darkness, gloaming, twilight; 9 dejection, obscurity; 10 depression, melancholy.

gloomy 4 dark, glum; 5 murky; 6 dismal, dreary, morose, somber; 7 doleful, Stygian; 8 funereal, overcast; 9 cheerless, miserable, saturnine; 10 depressing, despondent; 11 melancholic, pessimistic; 12 disconsolate; PHRASES: 4, 2, 3, 5 down in the dumps.

glorification 6 praise; 7 worship; 9 adoration, elevation, extolment; 10 exaltation, veneration; 11 deification.

glorify 4 laud; 5 deify, exalt, extol; 6 praise; 7 lionize.

glorious 6 superb; 7 sublime; 8 splendid; 11 magnificent; PHRASES: 8, 7 G~ Twelfth *UK*.

glory 4 fame, halo; 5 kudos; 6 beauty, praise, wonder; 7 laurels, stardom, success, triumph; 8 grandeur, splendor; 10 brilliance, exaltation; 12 magnificence.

gloss 5 sheen, shine; 6 luster, patina, polish, veneer; 7 comment; 8 footnote; 10 annotation; 11 explanation.

glossary **7** catalog *UK*, lexicon; **9** catalogue *UK*, thesaurus; **10** dictionary, vocabulary.

glossy **5** shiny, silky, slick; **6** smooth; **8** lustrous; **9** burnished.

glove **4** mitt; **6** mitten; **8** gauntlet; PHRASES: **3, 5** kid ~; **6, 5** string ~.

glow **5** blush, flush, gleam, light; **6** embers; **7** smolder, sparkle; **8** radiance; **9** happiness, ruddiness; **10** brightness, brilliance, luminosity; **15** phosphorescence.

glowing **4** rosy, warm; **5** aglow, happy; **6** bright; **7** beaming, healthy, radiant, shining; **8** blooming, dazzling, gleaming, luminous, lustrous; **9** brilliant; **10** flattering; **12** appreciative, incandescent; **13** complimentary.

glue **3** gum; **4** bond, join, size; **5** paste, stick; **6** attach, cement, fasten; **8** adhesive; **9** superglue.

gluey **5** gooey, gummy, tacky; **6** sticky; **7** viscous; **10** gelatinous.

glum **3** low, sad; **4** blue; **6** gloomy, morose; **10** sepulchral; **11** crestfallen; PHRASES: **4, 2, 3, 5** down in the mouth.

glut **6** excess; **7** surfeit, surplus; **10** oversupply.

glutinous *See* **gluey**

glutinous *See* **sticky**

glutton **3** hog, pig; **4** wolf; **5** piggy; **6** foodie, gannet *UK*, locust, porker; **7** epicure, gourmet; **8** gourmand, Lucullus, omnivore; **9** cormorant, epicurean, wolverine; **10** gastronome; **11** trencherman; **13** trencherwoman; PHRASES: **3, 5** big eater; **3, 6** bon vivant; **6, 4** greedy guts *UK*.

gluttonous **6** greedy; **7** piggish; **8** edacious, esurient, ravenous; **9** rapacious, voracious; **10** insatiable, omnivorous; **11** gastronomic, intemperate, polyphagous; **13** overindulgent.

gluttony **5** greed; **6** excess; **7** edacity; **8** bingeing, hedonism, rapacity, voracity; **10** greediness, overeating, polyphagia; **11** hoggishness, piggishness, wolfishness; **12** edaciousness, intemperance, ravenousness; **13** concupiscence, insatiability, overindulging, rapaciousness, voraciousness; **14** overindulgence; PHRASES: **3, 8** big appetite; **4-10** self-indulgence.

gnarled **6** knotty, knurly; **7** crooked, knobbly *UK*, twisted.

gnash **4** grit; **5** grate, grind; **6** clench.

gnat **3** bug; **5** midge; **6** mossie *UK*; **8** blackfly, mosquito.

gnaw **4** fret; **5** erode, worry; **6** bother; **7** bedevil, concern, trouble; PHRASES: **3, 4, 2** eat away at.

gnome **3** elf; **5** pixie, troll; **6** banker, goblin, kobold, sprite; **7** brownie; **10** leprechaun; PHRASES: **5, 3** money man.

gnu **8** antelope; **10** wildebeest.

go **3** run, try, zip; **4** bash *UK*, shot, stab, zest; **5** drive, leave, oomph, scram, verve; **6** decamp, depart, energy, repair; **7** abscond, attempt, pizzazz, proceed, vamoose; **8** function; **9** skedaddle.

goad **3** rod; **4** prod, spur; **5** hound, stick; **6** badger, incite, needle; **7** provoke; **9** stimulate.

go after **5** chase, hound; **6** pursue, target.

goal **3** aim, end; **4** lure; **5** ideal, prize; **6** object, target; **7** mission, purpose; **8** ambition; **9** goalmouth, objective; **10** aspiration; **11** desideratum; PHRASES: **4, 5** holy grail.

go around **4** move, ride, spin, turn, walk; **5** orbit, twirl, twist; **6** bypass, circle, gyrate, rotate, spread, travel; **7** revolve; **8** transmit; **9** circulate.

go astray **3** err; **5** drift, stray; **6** wander; **7** deviate; **8** divagate, straggle; **10** transgress; PHRASES: **2, 3, 3, 5** go off the rails; **3, 4** get lost; **4, 4, 3** lose one's way.

goat **4** ibex; **5** billy, nanny; **6** angora; **7** chamois, kashmir; PHRASES: **8, 4** mountain ~.

goatsucker **8** nightjar.

go away **4** blow, walk; **5** scram; **6** begone, depart, vanish; **7** vamoose; **9** disappear, skedaddle; PHRASES: **3, 4** get lost; **4, 2** beat it *UK*; **4, 3** buzz off, push off; **5, 3** clear off *UK*, shove off.

go back **6** return, revert; **7** retreat, revisit; **9** backtrack; PHRASES: **4, 4** turn back; **6, 4** double back.

go backward **5** lapse; **6** return, revert; **7** regress, relapse, retreat, reverse; **9** roundtrip; **10** retrogress; PHRASES: **4, 4** fall back.

gobble **4** bolt, gulp, wolf; **5** binge, gorge, scoff; **6** devour, guzzle; **7** consume, overeat; **10** gluttonize, gormandize; **11** overindulge; PHRASES: **3, 2** use up.

go-between **5** proxy; **6** broker; **8** mediator; **9** middleman; **10** matchmaker.

goblet 3 cup; **7** chalice; **9** wineglass.

goblin 3 elf, fay, imp, orc; **4** trow *UK*; **5** dwarf, fairy, gnome, pixie, troll; **6** kobold, sprite; **7** brownie, gremlin; **9** hobgoblin; **10** cluricaune, leprechaun.

god (gods and goddesses) 2 Ra; **3** Fea, Ira, Tyr; **4** Amor, Ares, Eris, Eros, Hera, Juno, Kali, Kama, Mars, Odin, Rama, Siva, Zeus; **5** Cupid, Freya, Frigg, Horus, Hymen, Indra, Janus, Lares, Pluto, Venus, Wotan; **6** Apollo, Athena, Erinys, Furies, Hermes, Osiris, Saturn, Teleia, Vishnu, Vulcan; **7** Allecto, Astarte, Bacchus, Bellona, Jupiter, Krishna, Megaera, Mercury, Minerva, Nemesis, Neptune, Penates, Pronuba; **8** Dionysus, Morpheus, Posiedon; **9** Aphrodite, Eumenides, Kartikeya, Tisiphone; **10** Hephaistos.

God 3 Jah; **4** Lord, Soul; **5** Allah, Atman, Maker; **6** Adonai, Buddha, Elohim, Father, Yahweh; **7** Creator, Jehovah; **8** Almighty, demiurge, Trimurti; **9** Principle; **10** Paramatman, Providence; **11** Bodhisattva, Everlasting; PHRASES: **3, 5** Dai Nichi; **4, 2, 5** King of Kings, Lord of Lords; **4, 5** Holy Ghost; **4, 6** Holy Spirit; **4, 7** Holy Trinity; **5, 3, 5** Alpha and Omega; **5, 5** Ahura Mazda, First Cause, Prime Mover; **7, 5** Supreme Being; **8, 3** Almighty G~. *See also* **deity**

goddess *See* **deity**

godless 7 heathen, impious; **8** agnostic; **11** irreligious.

godly 4 holy; **5** pious; **6** divine; **7** eternal, godlike, saintly; **8** almighty, heavenly, immortal, infinite; **9** ineffable, religious, righteous; **10** omnipotent, omniscient, superhuman; **12** transcendent; PHRASES: **3-6** all-seeing; **3-7** all-knowing; **3-8** all-powerful.

godparent 6 gammer, gossip; **7** sponsor.

go forward 4 move, roll; **6** travel; **7** advance, proceed; **8** progress; PHRASES: **4, 7** make headway; **4, 8** make progress.

go-getter 4-5 high-flier; **4-7** self-starter; **5, 3** whizz kid.

goggle 4 gape, gawp, ogle; **5** stare; **10** rubberneck.

go halves 5 share; PHRASES: **2, 5** go Dutch.

go in 5 enter; PHRASES: **3, 4, 2** set foot in.

gold 2 Au; **3** sol; **4** gilt; **5** money; **6** ingots,

riches, trophy, wealth; **7** bullion, moidore, nuggets; **8** treasure; **9** doubloons; **10** sovereigns; PHRASES: **4, 4** ~ leaf, ~ rush; **4, 5** ~ brick, ~ plate; **4-6** gold-plated; **4, 8** ~ standard; **5, 4** fool's ~, white ~; **5, 5** first place, first prize; **6, 2, 5** pieces of eight; **6, 4** filled ~.

Gold Coast 5 Ghana.

golden 4 gilt; **5** elite, goose, ideal; **6** gilded, select, superb; **7** favored, special, utopian; **8** esteemed, favorite, superior; **9** excellent, promising, wonderful; **10** privileged; **12** paradisaical *UK*; PHRASES: **5-4** first-rate; **5-5** first-class; **6, 3** ~ age; **6, 4** G~ Gate, ~ rule; **6, 5** ~ eagle, ~ oldie, ~ syrup *UK*; **6, 6** G~ Fleece; **6, 7** ~ section; **6, 9** G~ Delicious, ~ handshake, ~ retriever.

golf club 3 cap, toe; **4** face, grip, head, heel, iron, neck, sole, wood; **5** baffy, cleek, hosel, shaft, spade, spoon, wedge; **6** driver, mashie, putter; **7** brassie, midiron, niblick; PHRASES: **7, 4** driving iron.

golfer 3 dub; **4** Berg (Patty); **5** Hagen (Walter), Hogan (Ben), Jones (Bobby), Snead (Sam), Woods (Tiger); **6** caddie, duffer, marker, Norman (Greg), Palmer (Arnold), Wright (Mickey); **7** Sarazen (Gene), Trevino (Lee); **8** linksman, Nicklaus (Jack), Zaharias (Babe Didrikson); **9** Sorenstam (Annika), Whitworth (Kathy); **10** forecaddie; PHRASES: **7, 6** scratch player.

Golgotha 7 Calvary.

golly 2 my; **3** wow; **4** gosh; **6** blimey *UK*, crikey; **7** heavens.

gone 4 away, dead, left; **5** spent; **6** absent; **8** consumed, deceased, depleted, finished; **11** disappeared; PHRASES: **2, 4** no more; **4, 2** used up; **5, 3** moved out; **6, 2** passed on; **6, 4** passed away.

goner 5 stiff; **6** corpse; **7** cadaver.

goo 4 goop, gunk, slop; **5** gunge *UK*, slime.

good 1 G; **2** OK; **3** ace, bon, fab; **4** boon, cool, fair, fine, nice, plum; **5** brill, cushy, dandy, great, moral, noble, pious, right, super, swell; **6** lovely, spiffy, superb, wicked, wizard; **7** corking *UK*, upright; **8** fabulous, pleasant, salutary, smashing *UK*, splendid, superior, talented, terrific, topnotch, virtuous; **9** admirable, advantage, agreeable, copacetic, enjoyable, excellent, exquisite, favorable, wholesome, wonderful; **10** auspicious, beneficial, delightful, excellence, impressive, proficient, profitable, propitious; **11** crackerjack *UK*, magnificent, respectable, superiority, trustworthy; **12** accomplished, advantageous, magnificence, praiseworthy, satisfactory; PHRASES: **1-2** A-OK; **3-4** top-hole *UK*; **4-5** high-class; **4, 7** ~ quality; **4-7** high-quality; **4, 9** ~ Samaritan; **5-4** first-rate, hunky-dory; **5-5** first-class; **6-4** heaven-sent.

good behavior **8** docility; **9** obedience; **10** compliance; **11** biddability, dutifulness, willingness; **12** tractability; PHRASES: **4, 7** good manners.

Good Book 5 Bible.

goodbye 3 bye; **4** ciao; **5** adieu, adios; **6** cheers *UK*; **7** cheerio *UK*; **8** farewell, sayonara; **9** goodnight; **11** arrivederci; PHRASES: **2, 4** so long; **2, 6** au revoir; **3, 3** see you; **3-3** bye-bye; **3, 3, 5** see you later; **3, 6** bon voyage; **3, 11** auf Wiedersehen *UK*.

good-for-nothing 3 bum; **7** shirker, wastrel; **8** layabout, parasite, scalawag *UK*; **9** scallywag; PHRASES: **4-2-4** ne'er-do-well.

good-looking 5 dishy; **6** comely, pretty; **8** handsome; **10** attractive, personable.

good luck *See* **luck**

good manners 6 polish; **7** decorum, manners; **8** breeding, civility, courtesy, protocol, urbanity; **9** etiquette, gentility, propriety; **10** refinement; **11** correctness; PHRASES: **4, 8** good breeding.

good-natured 6 genial, mellow; **7** affable, amiable; **8** friendly; **9** agreeable; PHRASES: **4-8** even-tempered.

goods 5 cargo, stock, wares; **7** freight; **8** chattels, property; **10** belongings; **11** merchandise.

good thing 3 gem, hit; **4** boon, find, plus; **5** beaut *US and Aus*, dandy, dilly, doozy, dream, favor, jewel, peach, prize, smash; **6** corker, killer, winner; **7** benefit, fortune, godsend; **8** blessing, knockout, treasure, windfall; **9** advantage, humdinger; **11** crackerjack *UK*, masterpiece; **12** lollapalooza, masterstroke; PHRASES: **4, 2, 5** tour de force; **4, 5** bees knees; **4-6** best-seller; **4-7** chef-d'oeuvre; **4, 8** cat's whiskers; **5, 3** smash hit.

goodwill 5 favor; **7** concern; **8** kindness; **10** generosity; **11** benevolence, cooperation, helpfulness, willingness; **12** friendliness; PHRASES: **13** collaboration.

goody-goody 4 prig, swot *UK*; **5, 3-5**

goody two-shoes; **8, 3** teacher's pet.

gooseberry 8 goosegog *UK*.

goose flesh 13 horripilation.

gore 4 stab; **5** blood, spear; **6** pierce; **9** bloodshed; PHRASES: **10, 4** Kensington ~.

gorge 3 gap; **4** glut, sate; **5** binge, gulch; **6** arroyo, canyon, defile, ravine; **7** overeat.

gorgeous 6 lovely, superb; **7** elegant; **8** splendid; **9** beautiful, sumptuous.

Gorgon 6 Medusa, Stheno; **7** Euryale.

gorse 4 whin; **5** broom, furze.

gory 6 bloody, grisly; **8** gruesome; **12** bloodthirsty.

gosh 2 my; **3** cor *UK*, gee, wow; **5** lawks *UK*; **6** blimey *UK*.

gossamer 5 gauzy, sheer; **6** flimsy; **7** cobwebs; **10** diaphanous.

gossip 4 chat, dirt; **5** rumor; **6** tattle; **7** chatter, chinwag, hearsay, lowdown, prattle, scandal; **8** informer, telltale; **10** scuttlebut, tattletale; **11** scuttlebutt; PHRASES: **4, 7** bull session; **6-6** tittle-tattle.

Gotham City 3, 4 New York.

Gothic 5 eerie; **6** creepy, gloomy, spooky; **9** grotesque; **12** melodramatic; PHRASES: **5, 6** black letter.

gouge 4 gash; **5** score; **6** chisel, groove, hollow, router.

gourmand 3 pig; **6** gannet *UK*; **7** glutton; **9** overeater; PHRASES: **4, 5** food lover; **6, 4** greedy guts *UK*. *See also* **gourmet**

gourmet 6 foodie; **7** epicure; **9** epicurean; **10** gastronome; **11** connoisseur.

govern 3 run; **4** head, lead, rule; **5** reign; **6** direct, manage, police; **7** command, control, dictate, oppress, oversee, preside; **8** dominate, regulate; **9** legislate; **10** administer; **12** administrate.

governance 3 raj; **4** grip, rule, sway; **5** reach, reign; **6** empery, empire, regime; **7** apparat, command, control, dynasty, mastery, regency, regimen; **8** autonomy, clutches, dominion, politics, regnancy; **9** beadledom, bumbledom, direction, dirigisme, supremacy; **10** ascendancy, domination, government, heteronomy, management, presidency, subjection, suzerainty; **11** bureaucracy, condominium, officialdom, sovereignty; **12** directorship, jurisdiction, overlordship; **14** administration; PHRASES: **3, 2, 6** rod of empire; **3, 5** the board; **3, 5, 6** the inner circle; **3, 6** the system; **3, 6, 4, 2** the powers that be; **3, 6, 5** the ruling class; **3, 7** Big Brother; **3, 11** the authorities; **4, 3** long arm; **4, 4** iron sway, whip hand; **5, 7** civil service; **8, 7** absolute command.

governing 5 regal, royal; **6** acting, kingly, lordly, regnal, ruling; **7** leading, queenly, regnant; **8** dynastic, imperial, majestic, princely, reigning; **9** dictating, sovereign; **10** commanding; **11** controlling, magisterial; PHRASES: **2, 3, 6** on the throne; **2, 5** in power; **2, 6** in charge.

governing body 4 diet; **5** board, brass, House; **6** bosses, quango *UK*, Senate; **7** cabinet, council; **8** assembly, Congress, managers; **9** committee, directors, employers, executive; **10** management, Oireachtas *UK*, Parliament; **11** directorate, legislature, Westminster; **14** administration; PHRASES: **3, 5** top brass; **4, 7** Dáil Éireann; **5, 2, 5** House of Lords, House of Peers; **5, 2, 7** House of Commons; **5, 5** Lower House, Upper House; **5, 7** Lower Chamber, Upper Chamber; **5, 8** Lords Temporal *UK*; **5, 9** Lords Spiritual *UK*; **6, 7** Seanad Éireann *UK*; **6, 9** select committee; **7, 4** Capitol Hill.

government 4 rule; **6** Maoism, Nazism, polity, regime; **7** anarchy, command, control, dynasty, Fascism, mandate, regency, statism, Titoism, tyranny; **8** autarchy, autonomy, demagogy, gynarchy, isocracy, kingship, legality, Leninism, monarchy, regnancy, thearchy; **9** authority, autocracy, communism, democracy, despotism, direction, executive, Fabianism *UK*, feudalism, feudality, gynocracy, hierarchy, mobocracy, oligarchy, pluralism, Poujadism *UK*, socialism, sovietism, theocracy, tribalism; **10** Bolshevism, duumvirate, federalism, heteronomy, hierocracy, leadership, management, matriarchy, ochlocracy, parliament, patriarchy, plutocracy; **11** aristocracy, bureaucracy, colonialism, demagoguery, gynecocracy, imperialism, interregnum, meritocracy, paternalism, physiocracy, quangocracy, squirearchy, stratocracy, supervision, syndicalism, technocracy, triumvirate; **12** collectivism, dictatorship, gerontocracy, independence, matriarchate, pantisocracy; **13** misgovernment, republicanism; **14** administration, egalitarianism, proletarianism; **15** ecclesiasticism, totalitarianism; PHRASES: **3, 3** mob law; **3, 3, 3, 4** one man one vote; **3, 4** mob

rule; **3, 6** vox populi; **4, 2, 3** rule of law; **4, 2, 6** rule of terror, rule of wealth; **4, 4** army rule, home rule; **4-4** self-rule; **4-10** self-government; **5, 4** papal rule, party rule; **5, 5** Black power; **5, 7** state control; **5, 9** guild socialism, White supremacy; **6, 5** police state; **7, 3** martial law; **7, 4** popular will; **7, 6** people's choice; **7-8** Marxism-Leninism; **8, 4** majority rule, minority rule.

governmental 4 Nazi; **5** civic, civil, Green, regal, royal, state; **6** feudal, Labour; **7** Fascist, federal, Liberal, Marxist, queenly; **8** imperial, Leninist, official, suzerain; **9** autarchic, Communist, executive, lawmaking, monarchal, political, Socialist, sovereign; **10** autocratic, autonomous, democratic, managerial, oligarchic, republican, senatorial, theocratic, tyrannical; **11** centralized, communistic, dictatorial, legislative, matriarchal, ministerial, monarchical, patriarchal, plutocratic, socialistic, territorial; **12** aristocratic, bureaucratic, Conservative, meritocratic, presidential, technocratic, totalitarian; **13** authoritarian, congressional, gubernatorial, parliamentary; **14** administrative, constitutional, jurisdictional, organizational.

governmental organization 4 city; **5** duchy, House, realm, state; **6** canton, colony, county, empire, nation, regime, Senate; **7** country, dukedom, kingdom, mandate; **8** Congress, district, dominion, judicial, province, republic; **9** executive, territory; **10** dependency, federation, palatinate; **11** legislative; **12** commonwealth, principality, protectorate; **13** confederation; PHRASES: **4, 6** land office; **4, 7** body politic; **5, 5** Lower House, Upper House; **5, 6** Foggy Bottom; **5, 7** Lower Chamber, Upper Chamber; **7, 3, 7, 7, 3, 10** Centers for Disease Control and Prevention; **7, 4** Capitol Hill; **7, 5, 10** Federal Trade Commission; **7, 8, 10** Federal Election Commission; **7, 8, 14** General Services Administration; **7, 10, 10** Nuclear Regulatory Commission; **8, 5, 9, 5** National Labor Relations Board; **8, 10, 2, 6** National Institutes of Health; **8, 14, 6, 5** National Transportation Safety Board; **10, 2, 3, 8** Department of the Interior; **10, 2, 6** Department of Energy; **10, 2, 6, 8** Department of Social Services; **10, 2, 7** Department of Defense; **10, 2, 7, 3, 5, 11** Department of Housing and Urban Development; **10, 2, 8, 8** Department of Homeland Security; **10, 2, 13, 10** Department of Environmental Protection; **10, 8** lieutenant governor.

governor **3** guv *UK*; **4** head; **5** chief, reeve, ruler, solon; **7** manager, premier; **8** director, lawgiver, lawmaker; **9** president, regulator, statesman; **10** chancellor, controller, legislator; **11** stateswoman; **13** administrator; **14** superintendent; PHRASES: **5, 8** prime minister.

gown *See* **dress**

gown *See* **dress**

GP **5** medic; **6** doctor; **9** clinician, physician; **12** practitioner; PHRASES: **6, 6** family doctor.

grab **4** grip, lift, nick *UK*, take; **5** grasp, seize, steal; **6** appeal, clutch, remove, snatch; **7** attract, impress; **9** influence.

grace **5** charm, honor, mercy; **6** beauty, Charis; **7** Charity, dignify, enhance; **8** decorate, elegance; **10** comeliness, kindliness, refinement.

graceful **5** agile, fluid; **6** nimble, poised, smooth, supple; **7** elegant, flowing, refined, stylish; **8** polished; **9** beautiful, dignified; **10** attractive; PHRASES: **4, 2, 3, 3** easy on the eye *UK*.

graceless **4** rude; **5** crude, dumpy, gawky; **6** clumsy, gauche, klutzy; **7** awkward, boorish, gawkish, uncouth; **8** bumbling, clownish, impolite, ungainly; **9** inelegant, maladroit, offensive; **10** cumbersome, ungraceful; **11** undignified; PHRASES: **3-6** ham-fisted; **3-8** ill-mannered; **4-6** cackhanded *UK*; **5-6** heavy-handed.

gracious **4** kind; **5** civil, plush; **6** humane, polite; **7** elegant, haughty, lenient, tactful; **8** merciful, superior; **9** courteous, luxurious; **10** charitable; **11** comfortable, patronizing; **13** compassionate, condescending; PHRASES: **4, 3, 6** high and mighty; **4-9** well-appointed.

gradation **3** peg; **4** line, mark; **5** notch, ratio, shade, shift, stage; **6** degree, nuance, remove; **7** ranking, shading; **9** valuation; **10** comparison, graduation, proportion; **11** calibration, measurement; **12** differential; **14** classification; **15** differentiation.

gradational **5** level, sized; **6** graded, scaled, sorted *UK*, valued, waning, waxing; **7** gradual, limited, regular; **8** frequent, measured, relative, standard, tapering; **9** extensive, graduated, portioned; **10** calibrated, classified, increasing; **11** comparative, diminishing, progressive; **12** differential, pro-

portional; **14** differentiated, proportionable; PHRASES: **2, 5** in scale; **4-7** slow-ranging; **4-8** slow-changing.

grade **4** mark, rank, sort; **5** class, order, score; **6** rating, status; **7** arrange, ranking; **8** classify, position, standing; **10** categorize, evaluation.

gradient *See* **slope**

gradual *See* **slow**

graduate **4** rank; **5** order; **7** advance, arrange; **8** classify, progress; **10** categorize; PHRASES: **2, 7** go forward *UK*; **4, 2** move on, move up; **4, 3** mark off; **6, 2** divide up; **7, 3** measure off.

graduation **4** line, mark, step, unit; **8** ceremony, division; **10** attainment, completion, salutatory, validation; **11** calibration, measurement; **13** matriculation *UK*, qualification; PHRASES: **5, 8** award ceremony; **7, 2** marking up; **7, 3** marking out, passing out *UK*; **10, 3** ~ day.

graffiti **6** doodle, scrawl; **7** drawing, writing; **8** scribble.

graft **4** join, slip; **5** embed, scion, slave; **6** attach, insert, splice; **7** implant; **10** transplant.

grain **3** bit, oat, rye; **4** corn, grit, mote, rice, seed, silk; **5** crumb, maize *UK*, piece, speck, wheat; **6** barley, cereal, kernel, millet; **7** granule, pattern, sorghum, texture; **8** delicacy, fineness, fragment, granulet, particle; **9** direction, filminess, roughness; **10** daintiness, graininess, grittiness, refinement, smoothness; **11** granulation.

grain (go against the grain) **6** rankle, rumple; **7** wrinkle; PHRASES: **3, 3, 5, 3** rub the wrong way.

grainy **5** sandy; **6** gritty, pebbly; **7** pebbled, shingly; **8** breccial, detrital, detrited, granular, gravelly, sabulose, sabulous, shingled; **10** arenaceous, arenarious, brecciated.

graminivorous **7** grazing; **8** browsing; **11** herbivorous.

grammar **4** case, mood, root, stem; **5** tense, voice; **6** gender, number; **7** parsing; **8** paradigm, sentence; **10** declension, inflection; **11** conjugation, punctuation; **12** accentuation, assimilation; **13** dissimilation; PHRASES: **8, 5** language rules; **8, 7** Standard English, systemic ~.

grammatical **5** right; **7** correct, regular; **8**

standard, systemic; **9** syntactic; **10** acceptable; PHRASES: **4-6** well-formed.

grammatical error 8 cacology, misusage, solecism; **9** barbarism, tautology; **11** anacoluthia, catachresis, misspelling; PHRASES: **4, 9** folk etymology; **5, 10** split infinitive; **6, 8** double negative.

grampus 6, 5 killer whale.

grand 4 duke, fine, good, posh, prix, slam, tour; **5** chief, major, piano, plush, ritzy; **6** canyon, famous, glitzy, lavish, siècle, swanky; **7** elegant, revered, stately, supreme; **8** glorious, imposing, majestic, splendid; **9** brilliant, elaborate, excellent, expensive, luxuriant, luxurious, memorable, respected, sumptuous; **10** celebrated, impressive; **11** illustrious, magnificent, spectacular, substantial; **12** ostentatious; **13** comprehensive, distinguished; PHRASES: **3-8** far-reaching; **3-9** all-inclusive, awe-inspiring; **3-12** all-encompassing; **4-5** well-known.

grandeur 5 glory; **6** luxury; **7** dignity, majesty; **8** elegance, opulence, splendor; **12** magnificence, resplendence. *See also* **grand**

grandfather 6 gramps; **7** grandad, grandpa; **8** granddad; **9** grandsire.

grandiloquence 7 bombast, fustian; **8** rhetoric; **9** pomposity, verbosity; **10** orotundity; **13** magniloquence.

grandiose 7 stately; **9** elaborate; **11** extravagant, pretentious.

grandmother 3 nan, Oma; **4** gran, nana; **5** nanny; **6** granny; **7** grandam, grandma.

grant 3 aid; **4** cede, gift, give, perk; **5** admit, allow, award, endow; **6** accord, afford, bestow, confer, donate, payoff, payola, permit, render; **7** bequest, bursary, concede, damages, funding, present, provide, stipend, subsidy, tribute; **8** bestowal, donation; **9** allowance, conferral, endowment, indemnity, patronize, privilege, provision, subsidize, sweetener; **10** assistance, bursarship, conferment, exhibition *UK*, fellowship, perquisite, subvention; **11** acknowledge, scholarship; **12** contribution, subscription.

granted 7 donated; **8** afforded, bestowed, rendered; **9** conferred, presented.

granule 5 crumb, grain; **6** morsel, pellet; **8** particle.

graph 4 axis, grid, plot; **5** chart, curve; **7** diagram, display; **9** histogram; **11** scattergram; PHRASES: **1-4** x-axis, y-axis, z-axis; **3, 5** bar chart, bar ~, pie chart.

grapple 4 cope, face, grab; **5** grasp, seize; **6** handle; **7** contend, wrestle; **8** struggle; PHRASES: **4, 4** deal with.

grasp 3 get; **4** grab, hold; **5** catch, clasp, reach, scope, seize, sense; **6** clutch, fathom, snatch; **7** command, control, grapple; **9** apprehend; **10** comprehend, possession, understand; **13** comprehension.

grass 3 awn, ley, rye; **4** cane, crab, culm, lawn, lyme, reed, rush; **5** beach, blade, cheat, couch, glume, haulm *UK*, roots *UK*, sedge, snake, spear, spire, sword; **6** bamboo, fescue, marram *UK*, pampas; **7** bulrush, esparto, pasture, Poaceae, prairie, timothy; **8** bluestem, spinifex; **9** Gramineae, marijuana; **10** greensward; **11** switchgrass; PHRASES: **4, 4** wild rice; **4, 5** gama ~, reed ~; **5, 5** beach ~, witch ~; **6, 5** ribbon ~; **7, 5** buffalo ~, pangola ~; **8, 9** Kentucky bluegrass.

grass (eat grass) 4 crop; **5** graze; **6** fodder, forage; **7** pasture; **8** ruminate; PHRASES: **4, 3, 3** chew the cud.

grassland 3 lea, ley; **4** lawn, mead, moor, park, turf, veld, wold; **5** campo, divot, downs *UK*, field, green, heath, llano, plain, range, sward; **6** common, meadow, pampas, steppe; **7** grazing, pasture, prairie, verdure; **8** campagna, downland, moorland, parkland, savannah; **9** champain, heathland *UK*, pasturage; **10** greensward.

grassy 4 lush; **5** green, reedy, rushy, sedgy, turfy; **6** swardy; **7** meadowy, verdant; **8** poaceous; **10** gramineous; **12** graminaceous; **13** graminiferous.

grate 3 rub, saw, vex; **4** file, grid, rasp; **5** annoy, chafe, croak, grind, peeve, shred; **6** abrade, bother, grille, nettle, scrape, screen; **7** lattice, provoke, scratch, trellis; **8** irritate; **9** aggravate, fireplace; **10** exasperate.

grateful 4 glad; **7** obliged, pleased; **8** beholden, indebted, thankful; **9** gratified, satisfied; **10** gratifying, satisfying; **12** appreciative; PHRASES: **2, 4, 4** in one's debt; **4, 7** much obliged; **5, 10** under obligation.

grateful (be grateful) 3 tip; **5** thank; **6** praise, reward; **7** applaud; **9** recognize; **10** appreciate; **11** acknowledge; PHRASES: **3, 5, 3** say thank you; **3, 7** pay tribute; **4, 1, 4** give a hand; **4, 6** give credit; **6, 1, 5** return a favor; **6, 6** render thanks; **7, 6** express thanks.

gratification *See* satisfaction

gratify *See* please

grating 5 harsh, rough; 8 strident; 10 discordant; 11 insensitive. *See also* **grate**

gratitude 6 thanks; 10 cognizance, obligation; 11 mindfulness; 12 appreciation, gratefulness, thankfulness.

gratuitous 4 free; 6 gratis, wanton; 11 unjustified, unnecessary, unwarranted; 13 complimentary; PHRASES: 2, 2, 6 at no charge; 2, 3, 5 on the house; 8-3 uncalled-for.

gratuity 3 fee, tip; 4 perk; 6 reward; 8 donation; 10 perquisite; 13 gratification; PHRASES: 7, 6 service charge.

grave 4 dire, grim, tomb; 5 crypt, mound, sober, vault, vital; 6 barrow, dakhma, dolmen, menhir, severe, shrine, solemn, somber, watery; 7 crucial, fateful, mastaba, ominous, pyramid, serious, tumulus, weighty; 8 cemetery, cenotaph, critical, cromlech, memorial, pantheon; 9 dangerous, graveyard, important, mausoleum, sepulcher, unsmiling; 10 forbidding, foreboding; PHRASES: 4, 3 deep six; 4, 4 long home; 4, 5 mass ~, open ~; 5, 2, 7 Tower of Silence; 5, 7 mummy chamber; 6, 3 plague pit; 6, 5 narrow house; 6, 7 burial chamber; 7, 4 beehive tomb.

gravity 1 G; 4 draw, pull; 7 dignity; 8 enormity, severity; 9 magnitude, solemnity; 10 importance, sedateness, somberness; 11 gravitation, seriousness; 12 significance; PHRASES: 1-5 G-force.

gravy 4 boat; 5 train.

gray 3 ash, dun, fox; 4 area, ashy; 5 ashen, friar, frost, mousy, slate, smoky, taupe; 6 greige, leaden, matter, pearly, pewter, steely, undyed; 7 chamois, grayish, neutral, silvery; 8 eminence, griseous, gunmetal, silvered; 9 canescent, cinereous; 10 fuliginous, unbleached; PHRASES: 4, 4 dove ~, mole ~; 5, 4 cadet ~, pearl ~; 5-7 mouse-colored; 6, 4 castor ~, silver ~; 6-4 dapple-gray, donkey-gray, powder-gray; 8-4 charcoal-gray; 10, 4 battleship ~.

gray-haired 3 old; 4 aged, hoar; 5 hoary; 7 elderly, graying, grizzly; 8 grizzled; PHRASES: 4-3-6 salt-and-pepper.

grayness 5 taupe; 6 greige, oyster; 9 grisaille; 10 canescence; 11 grayishness; PHRASES: 7, 4 neutral tint.

graze 3 eat, rub; 4 crop, feed, skim, skin; 5 brush, scuff, touch; 6 abrade, browse, forage, glance, lesion, nibble, scrape; 7 pasture, scratch; 8 abrasion, ruminate; PHRASES: 4, 3, 3 chew the cud.

grease 3 fat, oil; 4 lard; 5 smear; 6 monkey; 9 lubricate.

greasy *See* **oily**

great 3 ace, big; 4 huge, vast; 5 grand, large, lofty, major, noble, super, utter; 6 famous, groovy, heroic, mighty; 7 awesome, eminent, exalted, extreme, immense, intense, notable, serious, stately, weighty; 8 absolute, abundant, complete, critical, elevated, enormous, imposing, majestic, numerous, powerful, profound, skillful, splendid, talented, terrific; 9 boundless, downright, excellent, excessive, fantastic, important, momentous, wonderful; 10 celebrated, impressive, incredible, inordinate, prodigious, pronounced, remarkable, tremendous; 11 illustrious, magnificent, significant; 13 distinguished.

Great Britain 4 Brit; 6 Briton; 7 Britain; 9 Britannia, Briticism; 10 Britishism; PHRASES: 3, 7 the British; 3, 7, 5 the British Isles; 6, 7 United Kingdom; 7, 7 British bulldog.

greatness 4 size; 6 degree, extent, weight; 9 magnitude; 10 importance; 12 significance. *See also* **great**

Greece 5 Ellás; 6 Hellas.

greed 6 hunger; 7 avarice; 8 gluttony, voracity; 10 greediness; 11 materialism; 12 covetousness, ravenousness; 13 insatiability; 15 acquisitiveness.

greedy 6 grabby; 8 covetous, grasping, ravenous; 9 voracious; 10 avaricious, gluttonous, insatiable; 11 acquisitive; 13 materialistic; PHRASES: 2, 3, 4 on the make; 4-7 gold-digging; 5-8 money-grubbing.

greedy (be greedy) 4 bolt, cram, glut, gulp, wolf; 5 binge, gorge, snarf, stuff; 6 devour, gobble, guzzle; 7 engorge, overeat; 10 gluttonize, gormandize; 11 overindulge; PHRASES: 3, 3 pig out; 3, 4, 1, 5 eat like a horse; 4, 2, 2 tuck in to.

Greek 5 Attic, Doric, Ionic; 6 Aeolic, Ionian; 7 Achaean, Grecian, Hellene, Spartan; 8 Hellenic; 10 Corinthian.

Greek alphabet 2 mu, nu, pi, xi; 3 chi, eta, phi, psi, rho, tau; 4 beta, iota, zeta; 5 alpha, delta, gamma, kappa, omega, sigma, theta; **6** lambda; **7** epsilon, omicron, upsilon.

Greek and Roman mythology **3**
Eos, Pan, Sol; **4** Ajax, Ares, Dido, Eros, Hebe, Hera, Juno, Luna, Mars, Mors, Rhea, Styx, Zeus; **5** Atlas, Ceres, Circe, Cupid, Diana, Hades, Hydra, Jason, Lethe, Midas, Pluto, Venus, Vesta; **6** Adonis, Aeneas, Apollo, Athene, Aurora, Boreas, Charon, Cronos, Cybele, Faunus, Graces, Hecate, Helios, Hermes, Hestia, Hypnos, Plutus, Saturn, Satyrs, Scylla, Selene, Sirens, Somnus, Vulcan; **7** Artemis, Bacchus, Cyclops, Demeter, Gorgons, Jupiter, Mercury, Minerva, Nemesis, Neptune, Oedipus, Olympus, Orpheus, Pandora, Perseus, Romulus, Theseus, Ulysses; **8** Achilles, Cerberus, Charites, Daedalus, Dionysus, Heracles, Hercules, Minotaur, Odysseus, Poseidon, Thanatos; **9** Agamemnon, Aphrodite, Asclepius, Charybdis, Narcissus; **10** Hephaestus, Persephone, Polyphemus, Proserpine; **11** Aesculapius, Bellerophon; **PHRASES: 5, 2, 4** Helen of Troy.

Greek dish **4** meze; **5** kefta; **6** hummus; **7** baklava; **8** calamari, dolmades, moussaka, souvlaki, tzatziki *UK*; **12** taramasalata; **PHRASES: 5, 5** Greek salad.

green 4 bean, belt, card, jade, lawn, lime, mold, nile, vert; **5** apple, beret, leafy, lovat *UK*, olive, paris, rifle; **6** bottle, callow, dragon, gretna, kendal, monkey, pallid, pepper, plover, reseda, sylvan, turtle, unripe; **7** avocado, bowling, celadon, emerald, envious, fingers, Lincoln, verdant; **8** glaucous, inexpert, verditer, viridian; **9** verdigris, virescent; **10** aquamarine, celadonite, chartreuse, woodpecker; **11** viridescent; **PHRASES: 3-2-3** eau-de-nil; **3, 5** pea ~, sea ~; **4, 5** leaf ~, moss ~; **4-5** bice-green, blue-green, gray-green; **5, 5** kelly ~, terre verte; **6, 5** forest ~, parrot ~; **7, 5** hunter's ~; **9, 5** pistachio ~, turquoise ~.

green-eyed 7 envious, jealous; **8** covetous; **9** resentful; **PHRASES: 5, 4, 4** green with envy.

green-eyed monster 4 envy; **8** jealousy; **12** covetousness.

greenhorn *See* **novice**

green light 2 OK; **4** okay; **7** consent; **8** approval; **9** clearance; **10** permission; **PHRASES: 2-5** go-ahead; **3, 5** all clear; **5, 2, 8** stamp of approval; **6, 2** thumbs up.

greenness 7 naivete, verdure; **8** green-

ery, jealousy, verdancy, viridity; **9** evergreen, freshness, grassland, greenbelt, greenwood; **10** immaturity, virescence; **12** viridescence.

green politics 6 Greens; **7** ecology; **10** ecowarrior, Greenpeace; **15** conservationism, preservationism; **PHRASES: 5, 5** Green Party.

green thing 4 jade; **5** beryl, money; **6** patina; **7** emerald, olivine; **8** greenfly, greenlet; **9** greensand, malachite, verdigris; **10** aquamarine, greenfinch, greenheart, greenshank, greenstone; **11** chrysoprase; **PHRASES: 4, 7** verd antique; **6, 5, 3** little green men.

greet 3 hug; **4** fete, hail, kiss, meet, wave; **5** reply, smile; **6** accost, salute; **7** address, embrace, present, receive, squeeze, welcome, wreathe; **8** acquaint; **9** celebrate, introduce; **11** acknowledge; **PHRASES: 3, 4, 3** bid good day; **4, 1, 4** blow a kiss; **4, 1, 6** fire a salute; **4, 3** turn out; **5, 5** clasp hands, shake hands; **7, 2, 4** advance to meet; **7, 4, 4** squeeze one's hand.

greeting 2 hi, yo; **3** hug; **4** fete, hail, kiss, wave; **5** hello, smile; **6** parade, salute; **7** address, embrace, garland, obsequy, squeeze, welcome; **9** obeisance, reception; **10** salutation; **14** acknowledgment.

gregarious *See* **outgoing**

Gregorian 5 chant; **8** calendar; **9** telescope.

grid 3 net, web; **7** lattice, network; **8** gridiron.

grief *See* **sorrow**

grievance 5 wrong; **7** grumble, protest; **9** complaint, criticism, injustice, objection; **10** unfairness; **PHRASES: 3-9** ill-treatment.

grieve 3 cry, sob; **4** howl, hurt, moan, pain, pine, sigh, wail, weep; **5** mourn, upset; **6** lament, sadden, sorrow, suffer; **7** afflict, depress, ululate; **8** aggrieve, distress, languish; **PHRASES: 2, 10** be distressed; **3, 4, 5, 3** eat one's heart out.

grievous 5 awful, grave; **7** painful, serious; **8** critical, dreadful, shameful, terrible; **9** dangerous; **11** significant.

grill 4 cook; **5** brown, grate, press, probe, toast; **7** examine, frizzle, griddle; **8** barbecue, question; **10** rotisserie; **11** interrogate.

grim 3 bad, ill; **4** dire, dour, gray, ugly; **5** awful, bleak, stern; **6** dismal, gloomy, morose, severe, shoddy, unwell; **7** ghastly, serious; **8** gruesome, horrible, horrific, shocking; **9** appalling, cheerless; **10** depressing, forbidding, uninviting; **12** unattractive; PHRASES: **3-5** off-color.

grimace **4** girn, leer, moue, pout; **5** frown, scowl, snarl, sneer; **6** rictus, squint; **10** contortion; PHRASES: **4, 1, 4** pull a face; **4, 4** long face.

grin **4** beam; **5** laugh, smile, smirk; **7** chortle.

grind **4** file, fret, gall, mill, rasp, slog, toil, whet; **5** chafe, chore, flour, gnash, grate, mince *UK*, plane, pound; **6** abrade, polish, scrape, tedium; **7** routine, sharpen; **8** drudgery, irritate; **9** granulate, granulize, pulverize; PHRASES: **6, 4** ground beef.

grinder **4** mill; **6** mincer, mortar; **7** crusher, pounder; **10** pulverizer; PHRASES: **4, 7** meat ~.

grinding **6** filing; **7** chafing, galling, grating, rasping; **8** fretting, unending; **10** levigation, oppressive, relentless, screeching; **11** cacophonous; PHRASES: **5-6** never-ending.

grip **4** hold, rule, sway; **5** catch, clasp, cling, grasp, power, rivet, seize, stick; **6** adhere, clutch; **7** command, control, mastery, pervade, suffuse; **8** clutches, enthrall, transfix; **9** authority, awareness, fascinate, mesmerize, spellbind; **12** appreciation; **13** comprehension, understanding; PHRASES: **3, 4** the claw, the palm; **4, 2** hang on.

gripe **4** moan; **6** object; **7** grumble, protest; **8** complain; **9** complaint, grievance.

grippe **9** influenza.

grisly *See* **gruesome**

grit **4** sand; **5** gnash, grate, grind; **6** clench, debris, gravel; **7** bravery, breccia, courage, pebbles, shingle; **8** detritus, tenacity; **12** perseverance; **13** determination.

groan **4** carp, moan; **5** creak, grind, growl, grunt; **6** squeak, squeal; **7** grumble, screech, whimper; **8** complain; PHRASES: **3, 3** cry out.

groggy **4** slow; **5** tired; **6** bleary, sleepy; **8** unsteady.

groin **4** mole, spur; **5** jetty; **7** barrier, bulwark; **10** breakwater, projection.

groom **4** tidy; **5** clean, dress, preen, prime, prink, teach; **7** smarten; **9** stableboy; **10** bridegroom.

groove **3** rut; **4** line, slot; **5** canal, flute, glyph, gouge; **6** furrow, trough; **7** channel; **11** indentation.

grope **4** feel; **5** touch; **6** caress, fondle, fumble, molest; **8** flounder, scrabble; PHRASES: **4, 2** feel up; **4, 5** cast about.

gross **3** get, net; **4** earn, foul, make, rude, take, vile; **5** awful, crass, crude, heavy, major, nasty, obese, total, whole; **6** arrant, coarse, flabby, vulgar; **7** blatant, boorish, hideous, loutish, obvious, overall, receive, uncouth; **8** combined, unseemly; **9** abhorrent, aggregate, repellent, repugnant, revolting, sickening, tasteless, unrefined; **10** disgusting, nauseating, overweight, uncultured, unpolished; **15** unsophisticated; PHRASES: **5, 2** bring in.

grossness **10** incivility; **11** discourtesy, impropriety; PHRASES: **3, 4** bad form; **3, 7** bad manners; **3-8** ill-breeding. *See also* **gross**

grotesque **5** gross; **7** bizarre; **9** distorted, laughable, ludicrous, misshapen, monstrous; **10** outrageous, ridiculous; **11** incongruous.

ground **4** base, home, land, rule, soil; **5** arena, basis, coach, earth, field, floor, found, pitch *UK*, train, tutor; **6** common, middle, milled, minced; **7** crushed, gardens, justify, pounded, prepare, stadium, support, terrain; **8** instruct, pavilion, powdered; **9** landscape; **10** pulverized, topography; **12** substantiate; PHRASES: **3, 4** dry land; **5, 5** terra firma.

ground beef **9** mincemeat *UK*; PHRASES: **6, 4** ground meat, minced meat *UK*.

groundwork (do the groundwork) **4** plan, plot; **5** begin, draft, found; **6** sketch; **7** outline; **8** contrive, organize, research; **9** blueprint, establish; **10** prearrange, predispose; **12** predetermine; PHRASES: **3, 3, 4** sow the seed; **5-3** rough-hew.

group **3** bee, duo, set; **4** bale, band, bevy, bind, body, cell, clan, folk, gang, knot, pack, race, sect, sort, trio, unit; **5** batch, bunch, caste, clump, crowd, grade, octet, party, posse, tribe, troop, truss; **6** bundle, circle, clique, clutch, family, gather, ghetto, parcel, people, public, septet, sextet, troupe; **7** arrange, bracket, cluster, collect, company, convene, faction, package, quartet, quintet, society; **8** assemble, assembly, classify, ensemble, populace, sorority, taxonomy; **9** citizenry, community, orchestra; **10** Bloomsbury, categorize, collection, congregate, fraternity, generality; **11** brotherhood.

grouping 3 set; 4 type; 5 class; 8 category, indexing, taxonomy; 10 assemblage, cataloging, consortium, federation; 11 cataloguing *UK*, combination; 12 amalgamation, codification, pigeonholing; 13 confederation, specification; 14 categorization, classification. *See also* **group**

group of mammals 3 gam; 4 bevy, herd, pack; 5 drove, flock, pride, troop; 6 litter, school.

grouse 4 bird, game; 5 gripe, growl, peeve; 6 mutter.

grovel 3 beg; 4 fawn; 5 crawl, creep *UK*, kneel, plead, stoop; 6 cringe, crouch; PHRASES: 3, 3, 6 bow and scrape.

grow 3 bud, wax; 4 gain; 5 bloat, bloom, breed, bulge, flare, raise, swell, widen; 6 accrue, expand, extend, fatten, flower, mature, profit, spread, sprout, tumify, unfold; 7 amplify, augment, balloon, blossom, broaden, burgeon, develop, distend, enlarge, inflate, magnify, nurture, produce, stretch; 8 escalate, flourish, increase, lengthen, multiply, mushroom, snowball; 9 crescendo, cultivate, germinate, intensify, propagate, pullulate; 11 hypertrophy; PHRASES: 4, 3 fill out; 5, 2 shoot up; 6, 3 branch out.

growing 6 rising, upward, waxing; 7 brewing, budding, bulbous, fanning; 8 blooming, crescent, dilating, emergent, patulous, shooting, swelling, thriving; 9 branching, expanding, extending, flowering, sprawling, spreading, sprouting, tumescent; 10 blossoming, burgeoning, developing, increasing, turgescent; 11 flourishing, germinating, heightening, multiplying, mushrooming, pullulating, snowballing; 12 flabelliform.

growl 3 yap; 4 bark, carp, howl, roar, snap; 5 bitch, snarl; 6 bellow, grouch, grouse, mutter, rumble; 7 grumble; 8 complain.

grow light 4 dawn; 5 break; 7 lighten; 8 brighten.

grow old 3 age, rot; 4 fade, rust; 5 decay, spoil; 6 dodder, molder, wither; 7 crumble, decline; 9 decompose; 11 deteriorate; PHRASES: 4, 3 burn out; 4, 8 lose currency; 7, 4, 4 crumble into dust.

growth 3 bud; 4 crop, cyst, gain, lump; 5 edema, flare, fruit, polyp, swell, tumor; 6 cancer, dropsy, flower, nodule, profit, sprawl, spread, waxing; 7 advance, blossom, budding, bulging, harvest, produce, stretch; 8 addition, bloating, blooming, breeding, building, diastole, dilation, increase, progress, splaying, stuffing, swelling, thriving, tumidity, widening; 9 branching, carcinoma, crescendo, evolution, expansion, extension, fattening, flowering, inflation, outgrowth, puffiness, reflation, sprawling, spreading, sprouting, turgidity; 10 blossoming, broadening, burgeoning, dilatation, distention, escalation, maturation, tumescence, turgidness, vegetation; 11 development, enlargement, florescence, flourishing, germination, heightening, hypertrophy, progression, pullulation, swollenness, tumefaction, turgescence; 12 augmentation, intumescence, outspreading, ramification; 13 amplification, magnification; 14 aggrandizement, multiplication; 15 intensification, overdevelopment; PHRASES: 5-2 build-up.

grub 3 bug, dig; 4 feed, food, hunt; 5 larva; 6 burrow, ferret *UK*, forage, maggot, search; 7 rummage; 8 excavate, victuals; 10 sustenance; 11 caterpillar; PHRASES: 4, 2 pull up; 4, 3 root out.

grudge 4 envy, mind; 6 hatred, rancor, resent; 7 dislike; 8 begrudge; 9 animosity, antipathy, complaint; 10 bitterness, resentment; 11 malevolence; PHRASES: 4, 2, 4, 4 turn up one's nose.

gruesome 6 grisly, horrid, morbid; 7 ghastly, hideous, macabre.

gruff 5 angry, husky; 6 grumpy, hoarse; 7 brusque, rasping; 8 gravelly; 9 impatient; PHRASES: 3-8 bad-tempered.

grumble 4 moan; 5 gripe; 6 grouse, mutter, object, whinge *UK*; 7 protest; 8 complain; 9 bellyache, complaint, grievance, objection.

grumbler 5 grump; 6 grouch, moaner, whiner; 7 groaner, whinger *UK*; 8 agitator, objector; 10 bellyacher, complainer, malcontent; 12 troublemaker; PHRASES: 6-6 rabble-rouser.

grunt 6 mumble.

guarantee 3 IOU; 4 chit, word; 6 assure, ensure, insure, pledge, secure, surety; 7 certify, promise, voucher, warrant; 8 contract, security, warranty; 9 agreement, assurance, insurance; 10 underwrite; 11 undertaking; 13 certification; PHRASES: 4, 6 give surety, pawn ticket; 5, 3 vouch for *UK*; 5, 4, 3 stand bail for; **6, 2** attest to; **6, 3** answer for; **6, 7** commit oneself; **6, 9** accept liability; **10, 4** promissory note.

guaranteed 4 sure; **5** bound; **6** pawned, signed; **7** assured, certain, insured, pledged; **8** attested, definite, promised; **9** certified, committed, mortgaged, obligated, warranted; **10** contracted, covenanted, promissory; **12** underwritten; **13** authenticated; PHRASES: **2, 3, 3** in the bag; **2, 4** in hock; **4-4** cast-iron, fail-safe, sure-fire; **4-5** gilt-edged; **5, 8** under warranty.

guarantor 5 angel; **6** backer, patron; **7** insurer, pledger, sponsor; **9** supporter, warrantor; **11** underwriter.

guard 4 home, iron; **5** watch; **6** defend, patrol, secure, sentry, shield; **7** bouncer, defense, doorman, lookout, protect, provost; **8** garrison, national, security, sentinel, vanguard; **9** bodyguard, lifeguard, patrolman, pretorian, protector, rearguard, safeguard, vigilante; **10** praetorian, protection; PHRASES: **5, 4** watch over.

guard (on guard) 2, 8 by parrying; **3-6** low-inside; **3-7** low-outside; **4-6** high-inside; **4-7** high-outside; **4, 8** with footwork; **4, 9** with swordplay.

guardian 5 Argus, guard, nanny, nurse, tutor; **6** duenna, keeper, mentor, minder *UK*, patron, sentry, warden; **7** curator, doorman, janitor, lookout, sheriff, watcher; **8** Cerberus, chaperon, defender, garrison, sentinel, shepherd, upholder, vanguard, watchdog, watchman; **9** bodyguard, caregiver, caretaker, concierge, custodian, godparent, governess, patrolman, preserver, protector, vigilante; **10** benefactor; **11** conservator, surveillant; PHRASES: **4-6** baby-sitter; **5, 6** child minder *UK*.

guerrilla 5 rebel; **6** Maquis, raider; **7** cateran; **8** fedayeen, Frondeur, partisan; **9** insurgent, terrorist; **11** mosstrooper; **12** paramilitary; **13** revolutionary; PHRASES: **7, 7** freedom fighter.

guess 5 solve; **6** deduce, fathom; **7** predict, presume, suppose; **8** estimate; **9** deduction, speculate; **10** conjecture; **11** presumption, speculation, supposition; PHRASES: **4, 3** work out.

guesthouse *See* **hotel**

guidance 4 help; **6** advice; **7** control, support; **9** direction; **10** assistance, counseling, leadership, management; **11** supervision.

guide 3 dog; **4** beam, buoy, girl, helm, lead, rope, show; **5** canon, drive, ideal, maxim, pilot, point, radar, steer, teach, tenet, usher; **6** direct, escort, funnel, leader, manual, rudder, tiller; **7** channel, compass, conduct, example, foghorn, precept, teacher; **8** chaperon, cicerone, director, handbook, joystick, lodestar, shepherd, standard; **9** benchmark, condition, conductor, criterion, direction, influence, lightship, principle, supervise; **10** controller, lighthouse; **11** instruction; PHRASES: **4, 3, 4, 4** hard and fast rule.

guild *See* **club**

guile 7 cunning, slyness; **8** wiliness; **9** treachery; **10** astuteness.

guilt 5 blame, fault; **7** censure; **8** peccancy, reproach; **9** liability; **10** accusation, complicity, conscience, conviction; **11** compunction, criminality, culpability, delinquency, implication, inculpation; **13** indictability; **14** impeachability, responsibility; **15** blameworthiness, reproachfulness; PHRASES: **4, 5** one's fault.

guilt (signs of guilt) 5 blush, shame; **6** qualms, regret; **7** remorse; **9** penitence; **10** contrition; **13** embarrassment; PHRASES: **3, 5** red hands; **3, 10** bad conscience; **4, 2, 5** onus of guilt; **4-8** self-reproach; **5, 5** dirty hands; **5, 7** guilt complex; **6, 2, 5** burden of guilt; **6, 5** bloody hands.

guilty 4 evil; **5** sorry; **6** blamed, sinful, wicked; **7** ashamed, hangdog, peccant; **8** blushing, censured, criminal, culpable, shameful, sheepish, unlawful; **9** accusable, condemned, convicted, injurious, mortified, regretful; **10** abominable, censurable, chargeable, delinquent, implicated, inculpated, remorseful, shamefaced; **11** blameworthy, embarrassed, impeachable, inexcusable, mischievous, responsible; **12** reproachable, unforgivable, unpardonable; **13** objectionable, reprehensible, transgressive, unjustifiable; PHRASES: **2, 3, 5** in the wrong; **2, 5** at fault, to blame; **3-6** red-handed; **4, 2, 9** open to criticism; **6, 2, 3, 3** caught in the act; **6, 3-6** caught red-handed.

guilty person 5 felon; **7** convict, culprit; **8** criminal, jailbird, offender, prisoner; **9** reprobate, wrongdoer; **10** accomplice, delinquent, malefactor, recidivist; PHRASES: **3, 3** old lag; **6, 5** guilty party.

guise 4 form, mask, show; **5** dress, light, shape; **6** excuse, outfit; **7** costume, pretext;

8 disguise; **9** semblance; **10** appearance.

gulf 3 bay, col, cwm, gap; **4** cove, dell, hole, pass, rift, void; **5** abyss, bight, chasm, donga *UK*, flume, gorge, gulch, gully, inlet, kloof *UK*, sound; **6** canyon, clough, coulee, harbor, hollow, ravine, valley; **7** couloir; **8** crevasse; **10** separation.

gullet 3 maw; **4** craw, crop; **6** throat; **9** esophagus.

gullible 5 green, naive; **8** innocent, trusting; **9** credulous; **11** susceptible; **12** unsuspecting.

gully 3 gap, rut; **5** chasm, ditch, gorge; **6** furrow, ravine, valley; **7** channel, culvert.

gulp 4 slug, swig; **5** drink; **6** guzzle; **7** swallow; **8** mouthful; PHRASES: **4, 4** toss down.

gum 3 sap; **4** bond, glue; **5** affix, candy, kauri, latex, paste, resin, stick, sugar, sweet *UK*; **6** bubble, cement; **7** acaroid, exudate, gingiva; **8** adhesive; **9** secretion, superglue; PHRASES: **5, 5** epoxy resin.

gumption 5 nerve, pluck, sense; **6** mettle; **7** bravery, courage; **10** shrewdness; **12** practicality; PHRASES: **6, 5** common sense.

gunman 2 RA; **3** gun; **4** shot; **6** sniper; **8** rifleman; **10** gunslinger; **12** artilleryman; PHRASES: **3, 3** hit man.

gunner *See* **soldier**

guns *See* **firearm**

gurgle 3 coo; **4** crow; **5** slosh; **6** babble, bubble, burble, murmur, ripple, splash, warble.

guru 6 expert, leader, pundit; **9** authority, maharishi; PHRASES: **7, 5** leading light; **9, 5** spiritual guide.

gush 3 jet; **4** flow, ooze, pour, rush; **5** flood, spout, spurt, surge; **6** admire, babble, stream; **7** enthuse, flatter, prattle; PHRASES: **4, 5** hold forth.

gust 4 blow; **5** blast, burst, draft; **6** breeze, flurry, squall; **7** bluster; **8** eruption, outburst; **9** explosion, expulsion.

gut 4 gall, raze, sack; **5** belly, bowel, empty, ileum, nerve, pluck, strip; **7** innards, stamina, viscera; **8** audacity, duodenum, entrails; **9** fortitude, heartfelt; **10** disembowel, eviscerate; **11** instinctive; PHRASES: **4-4** knee-jerk.

gutter 4 drip, fade; **5** drain, sewer, waver; **6** groove, trench; **7** channel, flicker, sputter.

guy 4 chap *UK*, rope, wire; **5** bloke *UK*, tease; **6** fellow; **7** imitate.

guzzle 3 use; **4** gulp, swig, wolf; **5** stuff; **6** devour, gobble; **7** consume; PHRASES: **3, 2** use up; **4, 2** burn up.

gymnastic 5 agile, lithe; **6** active, sporty, supple; **8** athletic, rhythmic, sporting, vaulting; **9** acrobatic *UK*, balancing, energetic; **11** competitive; PHRASES: **3-6** all-around *UK*.

gymnastics 4 beam, hang, hold, jump, land, turn; **5** horse, rings, vault; **6** tumble; **7** balance, rebound; **8** aerobics; **9** exercises, pirouette; **10** acrobatics, difficulty, somersault; **11** springboard; **12** calisthenics; PHRASES: **4, 3** keep fit *UK*; **7, 4** balance beam; **8, 4** parallel bars.

gynecology 10 gyniatrics, obstetrics.

gyrate *See* **rotate**

H

H 6 hearts; 8 aspirate, hydrogen.

habit 3 bad, use; 4 bent, garb, wont; 5 dress, usage; 6 attire, custom, outfit, praxis; 7 apparel, complex, garment, leaning, pattern, problem, routine, uniform; 8 fixation, practice, tendency, weakness; 9 addiction, cacoethes, obsession, tradition; 10 compulsion, convention, dependency, inveteracy, regularity; 11 familiarity, inclination; PHRASES: 6, 2, 6 matter of course; 6, 6 second nature; 8, 6 habitual action.

habit (become a habit) 5 cling, stick; 6 adhere, obtain, settle; 7 prevail; PHRASES: 4, 2, 3 grow on one; 4, 4 take root; 4, 4, 3 come into use; 5, 2 catch on.

habit (have a habit) 5 haunt; 8 frequent; 9 habituate; PHRASES: 2, 2, 3 go in for; 4, 2 take up; 5, 4 never vary; 7, 7 observe routine.

habitat 3 pad; 4 digs *UK*, home; 5 abode, haunt, house, rooms, squat; 6 billet, locale; 7 lodging; 8 domicile, dwelling, quarters; 9 residence, territory; 10 habitation; 11 environment; 12 surroundings; 13 accommodation; PHRASES: 6, 8 living quarters; 8, 5 dwelling place, sleeping place.

habit-forming 8 clinging; 9 addictive, besetting, obsessive.

habitual 5 daily, usual; 6 annual, normal, weekly, wonted; 7 chronic, monthly, ongoing, regular, routine, typical; 8 everyday, expected, frequent, ordinary; 9 automatic, customary, quotidian; 10 accustomed, consistent, invariable, persistent; 11 predictable, traditional; 14 characteristic; PHRASES: 4-4 long-term.

habitually 2, 4, 6 in one's stride; 2, 5 as usual; 2, 5, 2, 5 by force of habit; 2, 6 as always, by custom; 2, 9 by tradition; 7, 8 without thinking. *See also* **habitual**

habituate 4 tame; 5 adapt, imbue, inure, teach, train; 6 adjust, harden, orient; 7 implant, ingraft; 8 accustom, practice; 9 brainwash, condition, orientate; 10 naturalize; 11 acclimatize, domesticate, familiarize; 12 indoctrinate; PHRASES: 3, 3, 4, 2 get the hang of; 3, 4, 2 get used to; 4, 2 take to, warm up; 4, 4, 4, 2 keep one's hand in; 4-6 case-harden; 5, 2 break in; 6, 8 become addicted; 8, 7 accustom oneself.

habituated 4 used; 5 given; 6 wedded; 7 chronic, devoted, trained; 8 addicted, constant, familiar, frequent, habitual, seasoned; 9 confirmed, dedicated, perpetual, practiced, recurrent; 10 conversant, inveterate; PHRASES: 2, 3, 5 in the habit; 2, 4 at home, au fait *Fr*; 6, 2 broken in.

habituation 4 rote; 6 reflex; 8 drilling, maturing, training; 9 hardening, inurement; 10 adaptation, adjustment; 11 association, orientation; 12 brainwashing, conditioning; 14 indoctrination, naturalization; 15 acclimatization, familiarization.

hack 3 cut; 4 chop, cope; 5 slash, slave; 6 drudge, flunky, handle, manage, scythe, writer; 7 succeed; 8 dogsbody *UK*, factotum, lacerate, reporter, stringer; 9 scribbler; 10 journalist; PHRASES: 4, 4 deal with.

hackbut 8 arquebus.

hackneyed *See* **trite**

Hades 6 shades.

hagbut 8 arquebus.

haggle 6 barter, hondle; 7 bargain, quibble, wrangle; 9 negotiate.

hagioscope 6 squint.

hail 4 call, rain, wave; 5 burst, flood, greet, storm; 6 affirm, beckon, salute, shower, signal, summon, volley; 7 acclaim, address, barrage, confirm, welcome; 8 greeting; 9

hailstorm; **10** salutation; **11** acknowledge; **PHRASES: 4, 2** call to, wave to; **4, 4** call over, flag down; **4, 5** hoar frost, rave about; **5, 2** speak to; **5, 3** glaze ice; **6, 5** glazed frost, silver frost *UK*; **8, 4** freezing rain.

Hail Mary 3, 5 Ave Maria.

hair 3 fur, gel, mop; **4** coat, fuzz, mane, pelt, wool; **5** beard, curls, dryer, locks, shirt, shock, slide, spray; **6** fleece; **7** lacquer, tresses, trigger; **8** follicle, mustache, restorer, whiskers; **9** burnsides; **PHRASES: 7, 4** curling iron.

hairdresser 6 barber, cutter; **8** coiffeur; **9** coiffeuse; **PHRASES: 4, 7** hair stylist.

hairdressing 3 cut, dye; **4** clip; **5** style; **6** barber, mousse; **7** restyle; **10** straighten, trichology; **PHRASES: 4, 3** hair gel; **4, 5** hair cream, hair spray; **7, 5** styling spray; **12, 3** colorstyling gel.

hairless 4 bald, thin; **6** shaved, shaven, smooth; **8** glabrous, receding, tonsured; **9** baldpated, beardless; **10** baldheaded *UK*, depilatory; **PHRASES: 4, 2, 1, 4** bald as a coot; **4, 2, 3** thin on top; **5-6** clean-shaven; **6-5** smooth-faced.

hairstyle 3 bob, bun, cut; **4** Afro, crop, perm; **5** bangs, braid, curls, frizz, plait, quiff *UK*, style; **6** braids, dreads, fringe *UK*, hairdo, mohawk, mullet; **7** beehive, bunches *UK*, chignon, cornrow, cowlick, mohican *UK*, pageboy, pigtail, ringlet, topknot; **8** bouffant, coiffure, ponytail, skinhead; **9** pompadour; **10** dreadlocks; **11** dundrearies; **PHRASES: 3, 4** big hair; **3-4** wet-look; **4, 3** buzz cut, crew cut, flat top; **4, 4** Eton crop *UK*, spit curl; **4, 5** rats' tails; **5, 3** brush cut, pixie cut, wedge cut; **6, 4** French roll; **6, 5** French pleat *UK*; **7, 3** layered cut; **9, 3** feathered cut; **9, 4** permanent wave.

hairy 5 bushy, curly, furry, fuzzy, risky, scary, wooly; **6** frizzy, lanate, shaggy, woolly; **7** bearded, hirsute, stubbly, unshorn; **8** perilous; **9** dangerous, hazardous; **10** flocculent.

halcyon 4 calm; **5** quiet, still; **6** serene; **7** idyllic; **8** heavenly, peaceful, tranquil; **10** kingfisher, untroubled.

hale *See* **healthy**

half 3 fly, mid; **4** fork; **5** cleft; **6** better, branch, center, cloven, forked, halved, middle, midway, moiety; **7** equator, halfway; **8** bisected, bisector, branched, diameter; **10** bifurcated, hemisphere, semicircle;

11 dichotomous, swallowtail; **PHRASES: 5, 3, 4** split two ways; **5, 6** great circle; **5, 7** fifty percent; **7, 2, 3** divided by two.

half (in half) 2, 3 in two; **2, 5** in twain; **2, 6** in halves; **4-3-4** half-and-half; **4, 3, 6** down the middle; **5-5** fifty-fifty.

half-baked 5 silly; **9** impulsive, unplanned; **10** idealistic; **11** impractical, unrealistic; **PHRASES: 3-10** ill-considered; **6-4** starry-eyed.

half-board 4-7 demi-pension.

half-hearted 8 lukewarm; **11** indifferent, perfunctory; **13** lackadaisical; **PHRASES: 14** unenthusiastic.

half-measure 7 stopgap; **9** makeshift, temporary; **6, 4** second best.

half-truth 6 canard; **9** deception; **10** misleading, propaganda; **12** equivocation; **PHRASES: 3, 5, 4** old wives' tale; **4, 2, 5** gate of ivory; **4-5** near-truth; **5, 3** white lie; **5, 5** false rumor; **5, 6** empty gossip; **7, 2, 4** factory of lies; **7, 5** partial truth; **9, 5** distorted truth.

hall 4 city, mess, town; **5** foyer, great, lobby, manor, music; **7** gallery, hallway, liberty, mansion, Tammany; **8** Carnegie, corridor, entrance, Festival; **9** vestibule; **10** passageway; **11** countryseat; **PHRASES: 6, 4** public room.

hallmark 4 logo, seal; **5** stamp, trait; **6** symbol; **7** feature, quality; **8** property; **9** trademark; **14** characteristic.

hallucination *See* **vision**

halo 4 aura; **5** crown, glory; **6** corona, nimbus; **7** aureole; **8** gloriole, radiance.

halt 4 stop; **5** break, cease, close, pause; **6** freeze; **10** standstill; **PHRASES: 4, 2, 2, 3** come to an end.

halve 3 cut; **4** fork; **5** share, slash, split; **6** bisect, branch, cleave, divide, ramify, reduce, sunder; **8** decrease, downsize, transect; **9** bifurcate; **11** dichotomize; **PHRASES: 3, 2, 3** cut in two; **3, 2, 4** cut in half; **4, 4** pare down; **5, 2** carve up, divvy up; **5, 2, 3** split in two; **5, 2, 4** split in half; **5, 3** share out; **5, 5-5** split fifty-fifty; **6, 2** divide up; **6, 2, 3** divide by two; **6, 2, 4** divide in half.

ham 5 actor, radio; **6** gammon; **7** amateur, overact; **10** exaggerate; **PHRASES: 3, 2, 2, 5** lay it on thick; **6, 2** overdo it.

hamadryad 4, 5 king cobra.

hamlet *See* **village**

hammer 3 hit; 4 beat, drum, nail, slam, whip; 5 drive, knock, paste, pound; 6 attack, batter, defeat, strike, thrash; 7 assault, malleus, trounce; 9 criticize, disparage, slaughter; PHRASES: 4, 4 walk over.

hamper 6 basket, hinder, impede; 7 pannier; 8 obstruct; PHRASES: 3-3 hog-tie; 4, 4 slow down; 6, 6 picnic basket.

hand 3 big, dab, old, paw; 4 clap, club, dead, deck, farm, fist, free, give, glad, hour, iron, lone, mitt, part, whip; 5 offer, share, sweep, upper; 6 charge, finger, minute, needle, scrawl, script, second, tender; 7 helping, ovation, pointer, writing; 8 dispense, handclap, scribble; 10 administer, distribute; 11 calligraphy, handwriting, involvement; 13 participation; PHRASES: 5, 2, 8 burst of applause, round of applause; 8, 7 standing ovation.

handcart 4 cart; 5 dolly; 6 barrow *UK*; 7 trolley *UK Can*; 8 pushcart; 10 handbarrow; 11 wheelbarrow; PHRASES: 3, 7 tea trolley; 4, 3 push car; 7, 4 baggage cart; 7, 6 coster's barrow; 7, 7 luggage trolley; 8, 4 shopping cart.

handcuff 5 chain, irons; 6 chains, fasten; 7 darbies *UK*, fetters, manacle, shackle.

handful 4 some, test; 5 trial; 7 problem; 8 nuisance; PHRASES: 1, 3 a few; 3, 2, 3 one or two; 3, 4 not many; 4, 4 hard work; 6, 3 hardly any.

hand in hand 3, 2, 3 arm in arm; 4, 2, 4 side by side; 4, 2, 5 hand in glove; 5, 2, 4 cheek by jowl.

handle 3 buy, run; 4 feel, grip, hold, move, name, sell; 5 title, touch; 6 finger, holder, import, manage; 7 conduct, control, operate; 8 nickname; 9 sobriquet, supervise; PHRASES: 4, 2 deal in; 4, 4 cope with, deal with; 4, 6, 2 take charge of; 5, 2 trade in.

handshake 7 embrace; PHRASES: 4, 4 open arms; 7, 5 holding hands, rubbing noses.

handsome 4 fair, fine; 6 Adonis, Apollo, comely; 9 beautiful; 10 attractive.

handy 4 near; 6 clever, nearby, usable, useful; 7 helpful, skilled; 8 skillful; 9 dexterous, practical; 10 convenient; PHRASES: 2, 4, 5 in easy reach; 6, 5 within reach.

hang 3 sag; 4 flop; 5 drape, droop, lynch, relax, trail; 6 dangle; 7 execute, suspend; PHRASES: 3, 2, 5 put to death; 4, 3 ~ out; 4, 4 ~ down; 4, 5 ~ loose; 4, 6 ~ around; 5, 3 chill out.

hanger 3 peg; 4 coat, hook, knob, nail; 5 crane; 6 braces *UK*, gibbet; 7 gallows, support; 9 suspender; 10 clothespin; 11 clothesline; 12 clotheshorse; PHRASES: 3, 4 hat rack; 7, 4 picture hook *UK*.

hanger-on 8 disciple, follower; 9 associate, proselyte, sycophant.

hanging 5 drape; 7 killing; 8 lynching, tapestry; 9 execution; PHRASES: 4, 7 wall ~.

hangover *See* **relic**

Hanguk 5, 5 South Korea.

hank 4 ball, coil, reel; 5 skein; 6 length.

Hansen's disease 7 leprosy.

haphazard 5 messy; 6 random; 7 chaotic, jumbled; 8 careless, slapdash; 9 arbitrary, irregular, unplanned; 11 unselective; 12 disorganized, unsystematic; 14 indiscriminate; PHRASES: 3-2-4 hit-or-miss; 3, 4, 3, 5 all over the place.

happen 5 arise, ensue, occur; 6 befall, betide, chance; 9 transpire; 11 materialize; PHRASES: 3, 2 end up, pop up; 3, 6 run across; 4, 2 crop up, turn up; 4, 2, 4 come to pass; 4, 3 fall out, turn out; 4, 5 come about, take place; 5, 4 light upon.

happiness 3 joy; 4 glee; 6 gaiety; 7 delight, rapture; 8 felicity, pleasure; 9 enjoyment, merriment; 11 contentment, delectation, enchantment; 12 exhilaration, intoxication; PHRASES: 4, 2, 5 joie de vivre *Fr*; 4, 7 high spirits. *See also* **happy**

happy 3 gay; 4 glad, hour; 5 event, merry; 6 blithe, cheery, jovial, joyful, joyous, medium; 7 content, gleeful, pleased, release; 8 blissful, cheerful, ecstatic, euphoric, gladsome; 9 contented, delighted, enchanted, fortunate, opportune, overjoyed; 10 captivated, enraptured, felicitous, prosperous; 11 intoxicated; 12 lighthearted; PHRASES: 2, 3, 2, 3, 5 on top of the world; 2, 4, 7 in high spirits; 2, 5, 4 on cloud nine; 2, 7, 6 in seventh heaven; 4, 2, 1, 4 high as a kite; 4, 2, 5 full of joy; 4, 3, 4 over the moon; 5, 2, 1, 7 ~ as a sandboy; 6-4 starry-eyed; 7, 2, 5 pleased as Punch, tickled to death; 7, 3 blissed out; 7, 4 tickled pink.

hara-kiri 7 seppuku.

harangue 4 rant; 6 berate, tirade; 7 address, lecture; 8 diatribe; 9 criticism, criticize.

harbor 4 dock, hide, hold, port; 5 wharf; 7

believe, cherish, conceal, protect, shelter; **9** anchorage, entertain; **10** waterfront; **11** dockominium; PHRASES: **4, 2, 4** bear in mind; **4, 6, 2** give refuge to.

hard 3 hat, pit; **4** bony, cash, copy, core, disk *UK*, fast, firm, iron, rock, sell; **5** chewy, court, cruel, harsh, horny, labor, lines, lumpy, nails, rigid, rocky, solid, steel, stiff, stone, stony, stuck, tough, woody; **6** cheese, crusty, fierce, flinty, fortis, glassy, gritty, hitter, lithic, marble, pebbly, severe, steely, strict, thorny, tricky; **7** arduous, awkward, complex, durable, feeling, fibrous, granite, gristly, intense, lithoid, osseous, painful, testing, violent; **8** corneous, granitic, gravelly, grueling, leathery, ligneous, rocklike, shoulder, standing, unsprung, vitreous; **9** demanding, difficult, intensely *UK*, laborious, sclerotic, strenuous, violently; **10** forcefully, hardboiled, petrifying, relentless; **11** challenging, crystalline, intractable, remorseless, troublesome, unbreakable; **12** indigestible; **13** cartilaginous, problematical; **14** uncompromising; PHRASES: **7-4** diamond-like.

hard (mentally) 4 firm; **5** tough; **6** brutal; **7** callous; **8** obdurate, pitiless, stubborn, ungiving; **9** difficult, heartless, obstinate, unbending; **10** hardboiled, inflexible, unyielding; **11** hardhearted, insensitive, unadaptable, unalterable, unmalleable; **12** intransigent; PHRASES: **4-8** case-hardened; **5, 2, 3, 5** tough as old boots; **5-7** stony-hearted, thick-skinned.

hard coal 10 anthracite.

harden 3 set; **4** bake, case, heat; **5** brace, crisp, inure, prove, shore, steel, tense; **6** anneal, freeze, season, tauten, temper; **7** congeal, fortify, stiffen, tighten, toughen; **8** buttress, hardboil, solidify; **9** coagulate, reinforce, stabilize, vulcanize; **10** strengthen; **11** consolidate, refrigerate; PHRASES: **4-5** heat-treat.

hardened 3 icy, set; **5** tough; **6** frozen; **7** armored, callous, cynical, proofed, steeled; **8** annealed, indurate, ossified, sunbaked, tempered; **9** calcified, calloused, fortified, petrified, vitrified; **10** fossilized, granulated, hardboiled; **12** crystallized; **13** unsentimental; PHRASES: **3-8** oil-tempered; **4-5** hard-edged; **4-6** hard-bitten; **4-7** heat-treated; **5-6** armor-plated; **6, 4** frozen over; **6, 5** frozen solid.

hardness 5 rigor; **6** temper; **7** backing,

density, tension, tensity; **8** hardcore, nodosity, rigidity, solidity, strength; **9** starching; **10** difficulty, nodularity, resistance, stiffening, toughening; **12** inelasticity; **13** inflexibility; **15** impenetrability, inextensibility; PHRASES: **4, 6** hard center. *See also* **hard**

hardness (mental hardness) 8 asperity, obduracy; **9** obstinacy; **12** immovability, unpliability; **13** inflexibility, intransigence; **14** intractability, unmalleability; **15** hardheartedness. *See also* **hard**

hardship 4 lack; **7** poverty; **9** adversity, privation; **11** destitution.

hard substance 3 oak, pit; **4** bone, corn, grit, horn, iron, nail, rock, teak, wood; **5** armor, board, brick, crust, flint, ivory, metal, spine, steel, stone; **6** callus, cement, hammer, marble, pebble, quartz, silica; **7** adamant, boulder, diamond, duramen *UK*, granite, gristle, toenail; **8** aluminum, backbone, concrete; **9** cartilage, heartwood, stoneware; **10** fingernail, jawbreaker; **13** ferroconcrete; PHRASES: **4, 4** cast iron; **5, 2, 3** heart of oak; **5, 4** brick wall, stone wall; **7, 4** wrought iron; **8, 5** concrete block.

hardtack 3, 7 sea biscuit; **5, 7** pilot biscuit, ship's biscuit *UK*.

hardware *See* **equipment**

harebell 8 bluebell.

harem 8 seraglio.

harlequin bug 7, 3 cabbage bug.

harm 4 hurt, maim; **5** wound; **6** damage, injure; **8** aggrieve; **9** detriment.

harmful 4 acid, dire, evil; **5** cruel, fatal, harsh, rough, snide, toxic; **6** bitchy, bloody, deadly, malign, unsafe; **7** adverse, baleful, baneful, hurtful, killing, malefic, miasmal, noisome, noxious, ruinous, violent, wasting; **8** accursed, damaging, devilish, dreadful, sinister, spiteful, venomous, virulent; **9** corrosive, dangerous, injurious, malicious, malignant, monstrous, poisonous, polluting, unhealthy; **10** calamitous, disastrous, infectious, intolerant, malevolent, pernicious, vindictive; **11** deleterious, destructive, detrimental, persecuting, prejudicial, radioactive, unwholesome; **12** bloodthirsty, degenerative, insalubrious; **13** contaminating; **15** disadvantageous; PHRASES: **3-8** illdisposed; **8-6** mischief-making.

harmfulness 3 ill; **4** ache, gall, harm, hurt, jinx, mojo, pain, pang, risk, ruin; **5** abuse, agony, angst, curse, libel, spell, spite, sting; **6** damage, danger, hoodoo, injury, malice, miasma, rancor, voodoo; **7** anguish, anxiety, cruelty, gremlin, slander, sorcery, tyranny; **8** calamity, disaster, mischief, toxicity, violence, wormwood; **9** adversity, detriment, hostility, malignity, pollution, virulence; **10** harassment, inhumanity, malignancy, oppression, subjection, witchcraft; **11** destruction, insalubrity, intolerance, malediction, malevolence, molestation, persecution, poltergeist; **12** maltreatment; PHRASES: **3, 4** bad omen, ill wind; **3, 4, 3** the evil eye; **3-9** ill-treatment; **4, 4** evil star; **5, 5** black magic, child abuse; **6, 4** voodoo doll; **6, 5** sexual abuse. *See also* **harmful**

harmless **4** safe; **5** bland; **8** innocent, nontoxic; **9** innocuous; **11** inoffensive, meaningless; **12** nonhazardous; PHRASES: **4-4** risk-free.

harmonic **5** lyric, tonal; **6** agogic, catchy, dulcet; **7** attuned, tuneful; **8** singable; **10** harmonious; **11** harmonizing, synchronous; PHRASES: **2, 4** in tune. *See also* **harmonious**

harmonica **5** glass; PHRASES: **5, 5** mouth organ.

harmonics **4** beat; **5** tempo; **6** figure, monody, phrase, rhythm, timing, unison; **7** cadence, passage; **8** continuo, melodics, phrasing, sequence, tonality; **9** homophony, monophony, polyphony, rhythmics; **10** musicology, resolution; **11** arrangement, fauxbourdon, heterophony, syncopation; **12** counterpoint; **13** harmonization, orchestration; **15** instrumentation; PHRASES: **5, 6** music theory; **5, 8** basso continuo, tonal sequence; **6, 4** ground bass; **7, 4** figured bass; **7, 7** perfect cadence; **8, 4** thorough bass.

harmonious **4** calm; **5** quiet, sweet; **6** choral, stable, steady; **7** affable, attuned, blended, chiming, cordial, echoing, melodic, monodic, musical, regular, rhyming, tuneful; **8** adjusted, agreeing, amicable, assonant, balanced, conjoint, euphonic, friendly, harmonic, matching, peaceful, pleasant; **9** agreeable, congenial, congruent, congruous, consonant, melodious, modulated, regulated, symphonic, unanimous; **10** coincident, concordant, enharmonic, euphonious, homophonic, modulating, monophonic, polyphonic, resonating, resounding, syncopated; **11** concomitant, coordinated, harmonizing,

mellifluous, symmetrical, synchronous; **12** alliterative, contrapuntal, orchestrated, synchronized; **13** corresponding.

harmoniously **2, 4** in sync, in tune; **2, 6** in accord, in chorus, in unison; **2, 7** en rapport *Fr*, in concert, in concord, in consent, in harmony. *See also* **harmonious**

harmonize **4** echo, tune; **5** agree, blend, match, merge, rhyme; **6** accord, adjust, attune; **7** balance, concert, conform, resolve, resound; **8** assonate, coincide, equalize, modulate, regulate; **10** alliterate, complement, coordinate, correspond, regularize; **11** equilibrate, orchestrate, standardize, synchronize; PHRASES: **2, 4** go with; **2, 8** be together; **4, 2** tune up; **4, 7** make conform, make uniform; **5, 2** chime in; **5, 4, 4** bring into line.

harmony **4** calm; **5** choir, peace, quiet, rhyme; **6** accord, chorus, melody, unison; **7** balance, concord, euphony; **8** quietude, symmetry, symphony; **9** agreement, assonance, coherence, homophony, quietness; **10** adjustment, congruence, consonance, modulation, regularity, resolution; **11** coincidence, conjunction, equilibrium, synchronism, tranquility; **12** alliteration, concomitance, coordination, counterpoint; **13** harmonization, orchestration; **14** euphoniousness; PHRASES: **5, 3, 5** peace and quiet.

harness **4** bind, yoke; **6** attach, employ; **7** channel, control, exploit, utilize; PHRASES: **3, 8** tie together; **5, 2** strap up.

harp **3** nag; **4** plug; **7** belabor; PHRASES: **2, 2, 2** go on at *UK*; **2, 2, 3, 2** go on and on; **2, 2, 5** go on about; **3, 4** din into; **3, 4, 3, 4** say over and over; **6, 4, 2** hammer away at.

harpsichord **7** cembalo; **12** clavicembalo.

harsh **4** loud; **5** bleak, cruel, stark, stern; **6** jangly, severe, strict, unkind; **7** austere, blaring, callous, raucous; **8** exacting, punitive; **10** discordant; **11** insensitive; **12** inhospitable; **13** unsympathetic.

hartshorn **3, 8** sal volatile.

harvest **3** mow; **4** crop, home, mite, moon, pick, reap; **5** mouse, yield; **6** garner, gather; **7** collect, produce; **8** fruitage, ingather; PHRASES: **5, 2** bring in.

harvestman **5-8** daddy-longlegs.

hash **4** chop, dice; **5** grind, mince; PHRASES: **3, 2** cut up; **6, 4** ground beef.

hassle **5** annoy; **6** bother, harass; **8** irritate;

9 annoyance; **10** irritation; **11** disturbance.

haste 4 dash, flap, fuss, spur, urge, whip; **5** drive, panic, speed, whirl; **6** bustle, fidget, flurry, hassle, hustle, scurry; **7** flutter, urgency; **8** alacrity, celerity, deadline, dispatch, lateness, pressure, rapidity, scramble, stampede, velocity; **9** agitation, briskness, hastening, impulsion, quickness, skedaddle, swiftness; **10** expedition, promptness; **11** hurriedness; **12** acceleration; **15** expeditiousness; PHRASES: **2, 4, 2, 4** no time to lose; **4, 3** rush job; **4-6, 4** last-minute rush; **4, 7, 4** race against time; **5-6** hurry-scurry; **6, 5** forced march; **7, 5** tearing hurry.

haste (make haste) 3 fly, run; **4** bolt, dash, race, rush, scat; **5** hurry, speed, spurt; **6** bustle, decamp, hasten, hustle, scurry, sprint; **7** scamper, scuttle; **9** skedaddle; **10** accelerate; PHRASES: **2, 4** be late, go fast; **2, 6** go faster; **3, 4, 4** run like hell; **3, 7** cut corners; **4, 2, 2** jump to it; **4, 2, 3, 4** pick up the pace; **4, 3** tear off; **4, 3, 3** jump the gun; **4, 4** move fast, zoom past; **4, 5, 4, 2** make short work of; **4, 8** rush headlong; **5, 2** catch up, speed up, whirl by; **5, 2, 4, 4** think on one's feet; **5, 2, 5** brook no delay.

hasten 4 flog, goad, lash, push, spur, urge, whip; **5** drive, impel, press; **6** hustle, incite, propel; **7** quicken; **8** dispatch, expedite, railroad, stampede; **11** precipitate.

hastily 3 p.d.q.; **4** ASAP, fast; **5** apace; **6** pronto; **7** hotfoot; **9** posthaste; PHRASES: **2, 1, 5** in a flash; **2, 5, 6** at short notice; **4, 1, 6** like a rocket; **4, 3, 5** with all haste; **4-4** pell-mell; **4, 7** with urgency; **5, 4** right away; **5, 8** under pressure; **6-7** helter-skelter; **7, 3, 5** against the clock; **7, 5** without delay; **7-5** lickety-split; **8, 4** straight away. See also **hasty**

hastiness 9 overhaste; **10** impatience, negligence; **11** impetuosity; **12** precipitance; PHRASES: **9, 2, 4** inability to wait. See also **hasty**

hasty 4 fast, rash; **5** brief, brisk, fleet, quick, rapid, swift; **6** ardent, driven, forced, presto, prompt, racing UK, rushed, speedy, urgent; **7** allegro, cursory, furious, hurried, running, rushing, shoving, violent; **8** careless, elbowing, feverish, fleeting, headlong, heedless, reckless, slapdash, speeding; **9** breakneck, haphazard, hastening, hotheaded, immediate, impatient, impetuous, impulsive, negligent; **10** boisterous, breathless, scampering, unprepared, unthinking; **11** expeditious, perfunctory, precipitant, precipitate, superficial, thoughtless; **12** unconsidered, uncontrolled; PHRASES: **2, 1, 4** in a rush; **2, 1, 5** in a hurry; **3-10** ill-considered; **4-6** last-minute; **4-7** hard-pressed; **5, 3, 5** rough and ready; **5-3-6** rough-and-tumble; **7, 3, 4** pressed for time.

hat 3 old; **5** brass, opera, stand, trick. See also **headgear**

hatch 4 mark, plan; **5** shade; **6** devise, emerge; **7** produce; **9** formulate, highlight, originate; **10** crisscross, crosshatch; PHRASES: **4, 2, 4** come up with; **4, 3** come out; **4, 5** give forth; **5, 4** break open.

hatchet 3 job, man.

hate 4 envy, gall; **5** abhor, avoid, curse, odium, scorn, spite, spurn, venom; **6** detest, enmity, grudge, hatred, loathe, malice, rancor, reject, revile, spleen, toward; **7** condemn, despise, disgust, dislike; **8** acrimony, aversion, denounce, disfavor, distaste, execrate, jealousy, loathing; **9** abominate, animosity, antipathy, disrelish UK, hostility, malignity, repulsion, revulsion, virulence; **10** abhorrence, antagonism, bitterness, disapprove, execration, repugnance, resentment; **11** abomination, detestation, disapproval, displeasure, malediction, malevolence; **12** disaffection, spitefulness; **14** disapprobation; PHRASES: **3, 4** ill will; **3, 5** bad blood; **3, 7** ill feeling; **4, 1, 6** bear a grudge; **4, 2, 2, 3** have it in for; **4, 2, 8** hold in contempt; **4, 4** spit upon; **4, 7** take against; **4, 8** hard feelings; **6, 2** object to, recoil at; **6, 4** shrink from; **7, 2** shudder at.

hate (cause hate) 4 sour; **5** grate, repel; **6** enrage, poison; **7** disgust, envenom, incense; **8** alienate, embitter, estrange, nauseate; **9** aggravate; **10** antagonize, exacerbate; PHRASES: **3, 10** sow dissension.

hated 4 vile; **5** alien, nasty; **6** horrid, odious; **7** baneful, beastly, foreign, hateful, loathed, scorned, spurned, unloved; **8** accursed, despised, detested, disliked, loveless, unvalued, unwanted; **9** abhorrent, condemned, execrable, invidious, loathsome, obnoxious, repelling, repugnant, repulsive, revolting, unlovable, unwelcome; **10** abominable, despicable, detestable, disgusting, nauseating, unlamented; **12** contemptible; PHRASES: **3, 2, 5** out of favor; **3, 4** not nice.

hated person 3 cad, foe, git; **4** bane, pest, scab; **5** devil, enemy; **6** Hitler, menace,

Stalin, tyrant; **7** dastard, heretic; **8** blackleg, criminal, murderer; **9** archenemy; PHRASES: **2, 4** Dr Fell; **5, 5** sworn enemy; **6, 5** public enemy; **7, 7** nobody's darling.

hated thing 5 death, filth; **6** injury, phobia; **7** bugbear, illness; **8** anathema; **11** abomination; PHRASES: **3, 4** pet hate *UK*; **3, 5** pet peeve; **4, 5** bête noire *Fr*; **6, 4** bitter pill.

hateful 4 sour; **5** sharp; **6** bitter, sullen; **7** beastly, envious, hostile, jealous, vicious; **8** spiteful, venomous, virulent; **9** loathsome, malicious, malignant, obnoxious, poisonous, rancorous, resentful; **10** despicable, malevolent, vindictive; **11** acrimonious; **12** contemptible, contemptuous, disreputable.

hatefully 3-9 ill-naturedly; **4, 5** with spite; **4, 6** with malice; **4, 8** with contempt; **4, 9** with hostility. *See also* **hateful**

hatefulness 9 discredit, disrepute; **10** alienation; **12** estrangement, unpopularity; **15** contemptibility; PHRASES: **3, 4** bad odor; **3, 5** bad books; **5, 5** black books. *See also* **hateful**

hater 5 bigot; **6** phobic, racist; **9** homophobe, xenophobe; **10** Anglophobe, misandrist, misogamist, misogynist; **11** Francophobe, misanthrope; **13** misanthropist; PHRASES: **4-6** anti-Semite.

hatred *See* **hate**

haul *See* **drag**

haunch 3 hip; **4** loin, side; **5** flank, thigh; **7** buttock; **11** hindquarter; PHRASES: **5, 3** upper leg.

haunch bone 5 ilium.

haunt 4 roam, walk; **5** prowl, worry; **6** bother; **7** disturb, hangout, inhabit, trouble; **8** frequent; **9** preoccupy; **10** rendezvous; PHRASES: **7, 5** meeting place; **8, 6** stamping ground.

hautboy 4 oboe.

haute couture 4, 7 high fashion.

have 3 eat, get, own; **4** bear, gain, give, hast, hath, hold, must, need, plan, take; **5** allow, boast, drink, enjoy, grasp, nurse; **6** devise, devour, endure, obtain, permit, should, suffer; **7** arrange, consume, develop, exhibit, partake, possess, produce, receive, require, undergo; **9** entertain; **10** experience; PHRASES: **2, 3, 4** be ill with *UK*; **2, 4, 2, 4** be laid up with; **2, 8, 2** be affected by; **2, 9, 4** be afflicted with; **4, 5, 2** give birth to; **5, 2** ought to; **5, 5** bring forth; **6, 2** engage

in; **6, 4** suffer from.

haven 4 dock, port; **6** harbor, refuge; **7** shelter; **9** anchorage, sanctuary; PHRASES: **4, 2, 4** port of call; **4, 5** safe place; **5, 2, 6** place of safety.

havoc 4 raid, rape; **5** blitz, chaos; **6** damage, desert, mayhem, rapine; **7** carnage, looting, pillage, raiding, turmoil; **8** disaster, disorder, shambles; **9** confusion, holocaust, wasteland; **10** despoiling, spoliation; **11** depredation, destruction, devastation; **14** slaughterhouse; PHRASES: **6, 5** laying waste; **7, 5** nuclear blast; **7, 6** nuclear winter; **8, 4** disaster area; **8, 5** scorched earth.

Hawaii 2 HI; **4** nene (bird); **8** Honolulu (capital); **9** candlenut (tree); PHRASES: **3, 4, 2, 3, 4, 2, 11, 2, 13** The life of the land is perpetuated in righteousness (motto); **5, 5** Aloha State (nickname); **8, 2, 7** Paradise of Pacific (nickname); **8, 12** hibiscus brackenridge (flower).

hawk *See* **sell**

hawkish *See* **aggressive**

hawk moth 6, 4 sphinx moth; **11, 4** hummingbird moth.

hawksbill turtle 8 hawkbill; **13** tortoiseshell.

hawthorn 3 haw, may; **9** mayflower; **10** whitethorn *UK*.

hay fever 10 pollinosis.

haywire 4 wild; **7** erratic, fuddled; **8** confused; **10** irrational; **13** nonfunctional; PHRASES: **2, 3, 5** on the blink; **3, 2, 5** out of order.

hazard 3 bet; **4** risk; **5** peril, wager; **6** chance, danger, gamble, menace, threat; **7** imperil, proffer, propose, suggest, venture; **8** endanger, obstacle; **9** deathtrap, speculate; **10** jeopardize; PHRASES: **3, 2, 4** put at risk; **3, 7** put forward; **4, 1, 6** take a chance; **6, 2** chance it.

haze 3 fog; **4** film, mist, smog; **5** cloud, smoke, steam, vapor; **6** darken, miasma; **9** peasouper *UK*; PHRASES: **3, 4** pea soup.

hazy 5 foggy, misty; **6** cloudy; **7** blurred, muddled, obscure, unclear; **8** confused; **10** indistinct.

head 2 go; **3** cap, nut, top, wit; **4** apex, boss, dome, lead, mind, move, pate, peak, rule; **5** bonce *UK*, brain, chief, crown, scone, sense, skull, spire, start, steer, visor; **6** brains, direct, header, height, leader, master, noggin, noodle, source, summit, travel; **7** advance, command, control, cranium, journey, pinhead, precede, proceed, topknot, topmast, topsail, treetop; **8** commence, masthead; **9** beginning, commander, intellect, president, supervise; **10** controller, leadership, promontory, supervisor, topgallant; **12** intelligence, introduction; PHRASES: **2, 2, 6** be in charge; **2, 5** be first; **2, 8** be foremost; **3, 2** aim at; **3, 3** set out; **4, 5** come first; **4, 6** gray matter; **4, 7, 4** have control over.

headache 4 bore, pain; **5** worry; **6** bother, megrim; **7** problem, trouble; **8** migraine, nuisance; **9** annoyance; **10** difficulty.

headdress 8 coiffure.

header 4 goal, pass, shot; **5** title; **6** legend, slogan; **7** caption, heading.

head for 2 go; **3** aim, set; **4** bear, lead, tend, turn; **5** point, trend, verge; **8** navigate; PHRASES: **3, 2** fix on; **3, 3** run for; **4, 3** make for, sail for.

headgear 3 cap, fez, hat, lid, net, rug, tam, wig; **4** agal, barb, coif, cowl, hood, kepi, tile, topi, veil; **5** ampyx, beret, boina, busby, crest, crown, derby, pagri, shako, snood, tiara, topee, toque, visor, vizor; **6** almuce, anadem, barret, beanie, beaver, bicorn, biggin, boater, bonnet, bowler, calash, capuce, chunni, cloche, cornet, corona, diadem, domino, earcap, fedora, fillet, helmet, hennin, lungee, mobcap, peruke, pileus, plumes, pugree, sunhat, titfer *UK*, topper, toupee, trilby, turban, wimple; **7** bandeau, bashlyk, basinet, biretta, brimmer, calotte, capuche, chapeau, chaplet, coxcomb, cuculla, curchef, dulband, dupatta, earmuff, flatcap, homburg, periwig, petasos, pillbox, puggree *UK*, stetson, tricorn, yashmak; **8** babushka, Balmoral, bandanna, bearskin, burgonet, bycocket, caputium, carcanet, chaperon, dormeuse, faldetta, hairband, headband, kaffiyeh, liripipe, mantilla, nightcap, pileolus, skullcap, somberro, tarboosh, toquette, trencher, tricorne, yarmulke; **9** balaclava, billicock, billycock, bourrelet, broadbrim, casquette, glengarry, hairpiece, headdress, headscarf, millinery, sou'wester, sunbonnet, sweatband; **10** berrettino, coverchief, fascinator, headsquare *UK*, liripipium; **11** deerstalker, mortarboard, southwester; **12** headkerchief; PHRASES: **3, 3** tin hat, top hat; **3-6, 3** ten-gallon hat; **3-8** tam-o'shanter; **4, 3** cape hat,

chip hat, chou hat, Eton cap, hard hat *UK*, high hat, rain hat, skid lid; **4-4** snap-brim; **4-4, 3** snap-brim hat; **4, 6** baby bonnet, pith helmet, poke bonnet; **5, 3** cloth cap *UK*, couch hat, crush hat, dandy hat, dunce cap, dutch cap, opera hat, straw hat; **5, 4** Alice band *UK*; **5-4, 3** sugar-loaf hat; **5, 6** crash helmet; **6, 3** alpine hat, beegum hat, bobble hat *UK*, cocked hat, coolie hat, cowboy hat, forage cap, jockey cap, Juliet cap, panama hat, safety hat, shovel hat, slouch hat; **6, 4** bumper brim; **6-4** couvre-chef, riding-hood; **6, 6** Easter bonnet *UK*, Quaker bonnet, scotch bonnet; **7, 3** angelus cap, bathing cap, bellboy cap, boudoir cap, chignon cap, cossack cap, jester's cap, picture hat, porkpie hat, service cap; **7, 4** wedding veil; **7-4, 3** cabbage-tree hat; **7, 6** cottage bonnet; **8, 3** alsatian bow, baseball cap, clerical hat, military cap, overseas cap, stocking cap, tyrolean hat; **8, 4** crusader hood, motoring veil; **9, 3** stovepipe hat; **10, 5** montgomery beret; **11, 3** continental hat. *See also* **clothes**

heading 5 route, title; **6** banner, course, header, legend, slogan; **7** bearing, caption; **8** headline; **9** direction; **10** trajectory.

headline 4 flag, head; **5** title; **6** banner, header, legend; **7** caption; **8** masthead; PHRASES: **2-4** by-line.

headlong 4 rash; **5** hasty; **6** diving, rashly; **7** hastily, hurried; **8** pitching, plunging, reckless; **9** headfirst, hurriedly, impetuous; **10** recklessly; **11** impetuously; PHRASES: **4, 4, 5** head over heels.

headphones 4 cans; **7** headset; **8** earpiece, receiver; **9** earphones.

headshrinker 12 psychiatrist.

headstrong *See* **obstinate**

headway *See* **progress**

heady 4 rash, rich; **6** strong; **7** pungent; **8** aromatic, exciting, reckless; **9** impetuous, imprudent, impulsive, thrilling; **11** stimulating; **12** exhilarating, invigorating.

heal 4 cure, mend; **5** nurse; **6** repair, settle; **7** rebuild, rectify, restore; **9** reconcile; PHRASES: **3, 5** set right; **4, 4** make well; **5, 2** patch up.

healer 3 doc, vet; **5** faith, Galen, hakim, leech, medic, nurse, quack; **6** doctor, medico, shaman, shrink; **7** dentist, masseur, oculist, surgeon; **8** alienist, masseuse, optician, sawbones; **9** dietician, herbalist, homeopath, hypnotist, osteopath, physician, therapist; **10** bonesetter *UK*, naturopath, pedicurist, podiatrist; **11** Aesculapius, chiropodist, Hippocrates; **12** chiropractor, nutritionist, psychiatrist, veterinarian; **13** acupuncturist, psychoanalyst, reflexologist; **14** aromatherapist; **15** psychotherapist; PHRASES: **5-2, 2, 5** layer-on of hands; **5, 6** horse doctor, witch doctor; **6, 6** flying doctor *UK*; **6, 7** dental surgeon; **8, 3** medicine man.

health 4 food, pink, rude, tone, trim; **5** bloom, salts, vigor; **6** center, energy, fettle, Hygeia; **7** fitness, visitor; **8** eupepsia, haleness, strength, vitality; **9** condition, longevity, soundness; **10** heartiness, robustness; **11** healthiness; **12** constitution, recuperation; **13** convalescence; PHRASES: **3-3, 9** tip-top condition; **4, 3, 3** ripe old age; **4, 4** long life; **4-5** well-being; **4, 6** rosy cheeks; **4, 9** good condition; **5, 6** apple cheeks; **5, 10** ruddy complexion.

health care 7 hygiene, medical; **8** physical, podiatry, referral; **9** chiropody, dietetics, midwifery, nutrition, prognosis; **11** inoculation, prophylaxis, vaccination; **12** fluoridation, immunization; PHRASES: **4-3** call-out; **4, 5** home visit; **4, 7** case history; **5-2** check-up; **6-2** follow-up; **6, 7** second opinion; **7, 7** medical history.

healthful 5 tonic; **7** bracing, healthy; **8** hygienic, salutary, sanitary; **9** wholesome; **10** beneficial, nourishing, nutritious, salubrious; **12** advantageous, invigorating; PHRASES: **4, 3, 3** good for one.

healthiness 3 vim; **4** zeal; **5** vigor, youth; **6** acuity, energy, health; **7** hygiene; **8** goodness, keenness, vitality; **9** vehemence; **10** compulsion, dedication, enthusiasm; PHRASES: **4-5** well-being; **4, 9** good condition; **8, 7** physical fitness. *See also* **healthy**

healthy 3 fit; **4** fine, hale, rosy, well; **5** bonny *UK*, cured, fresh, great, hardy, lusty, ruddy, sound; **6** healed, hearty, robust, strong, sturdy; **7** bracing, glowing; **8** blooming, bouncing, eupeptic, hygienic, salutary, sanitary, stalwart, thriving, vigorous; **9** energetic, healthful, strapping, wholesome; **10** beneficial, nourishing, nutritious, salubrious; **11** flourishing; **12** advantageous, convalescent, invigorating; PHRASES: **2, 3, 2, 3, 2** on the up and up; **2, 3, 4** in the pink, on the mend; **2, 3, 5** up and about; **2, 4, 4** in fine form, in good nick; **2, 4, 5** in good shape; **2, 4, 6** in fine fettle, in

good health; **2, 4, 9** in good condition, in peak condition; **3, 2, 1, 6** fit as a fiddle; **3, 3** not bad; **4, 2, 5** full of beans; **4, 2, 8** fair to middling; **4, 3, 3** good for you; **4, 3, 6** hale and hearty; **4-7** rosy-cheeked; **5, 2, 1, 4** sound as a bell; **5, 2, 1, 5** fresh as a daisy; **6, 2, 2, 2** strong as an ox; **6-6** health-giving; **7, 2, 6** picture of health; **8, 3** fighting fit.

healthy (be healthy) 5 bloom; **6** thrive; **8** flourish; PHRASES: **4, 3** keep fit *UK*; **4, 4** feel fine, feel well, keep well; **4, 5** look young.

healthy (get healthy) 4 mend; **7** recover; **10** convalesce, recuperate; PHRASES: **3, 4** get well; **6, 1, 3, 3** become a new man; **6, 2, 6** return to health; **6, 4** bounce back.

healthy (make healthy) 4 cure, heal; **5** treat; **6** revive; **7** restore; PHRASES: **4, 4** make well; **7, 2, 6** restore to health.

heap 4 mass, pile; **5** layer, mound, stack; **6** bundle; **8** mountain; PHRASES: **4, 2** pile up.

hear 3 bug, tap; **4** hark, heed, mind, tape; **5** catch, judge, learn, sound; **6** attend, gather, listen; **7** examine, hearken, monitor, receive, wiretap; **8** consider, overhear, perceive; **9** eavesdrop; **10** auscultate, understand; **11** concentrate; PHRASES: **2, 2, 5, 4** be in touch with; **2, 3, 9** on the grapevine; **3, 2, 4** get to know; **3, 2, 8** sit in judgment; **3, 4, 2** get wind of; **3, 4, 4, 4** pin back one's ears; **3, 9** pay attention; **4, 2** pick up, tune in; **4, 2, 3** lend an ear; **4, 3** find out, ~ out, make out; **4, 8, 3** have someone's ear; **5, 2, 4, 4** prick up one's ears; **7, 4** preside over.

hear (be heard) 4 echo; **5** carry, reach, sound; **7** resound; **8** transmit; **9** broadcast; **11** reverberate.

hear (something heard) 4 echo, talk; **5** noise, rumor, sound; **6** earful, gossip, report, speech; **7** hearsay; **8** doorbell, tinnitus; **9** grapevine; **12** conversation; **13** reverberation; PHRASES: **2, 3** on dit *Fr*; **4, 2, 4, 3** word in one's ear; **4, 2, 5** word of mouth; **5, 5** alarm clock, clock radio; **6-6** tittle-tattle; **6, 9** jungle telegraph; **7, 7** Chinese whisper; **7, 8** hearsay evidence; **9, 5** reflected sound.

hearable 4 loud, soft; **5** harsh; **6** echoic; **7** audible, echoing; **8** resonant, sonorous; **10** listenable; PHRASES: **3-9** ear-splitting; **4, 2, 3** easy on the ear; **4-9** easy-listening; **6, 7** within earshot.

heard 6 heeded; **7** audible; **8** distinct, hearable; **9** overheard.

hearer 7 auditor, monitor; 8 audience, listener; 9 hearkener; 10 audiophile; 12 congregation, eavesdropper; PHRASES: 2-2, 10 hi-fi enthusiast; 9, 6 telephone tapper.

hear hear 4 hist, oyez.

hearing 5 range, reach, trial; 7 earshot, inquiry; 8 audition, sounding; 9 acoustics, attention, listening; 10 audibility, musicality; 11 examination; 12 auscultation, radiophonics; 13 consideration, eavesdropping, investigation; PHRASES: 3, 4 all ears; 4, 3 good ear, poor ear; 5, 3 sharp ear; 7, 3 musical ear; 7, 5 perfect pitch; 8, 5 absolute pitch; 9, 2 listening in.

hearsay 5 rumor; 6 gossip; PHRASES: 4, 2, 5 word of mouth; 4, 4 idle talk; 6-6 tittle-tattle.

heart 4 core, guts UK, mind, mood, pith, pity, soul; 5 anima, pluck; 6 animus, marrow, nature, purple, sacred, spirit; 7 bravery, courage, emotion, feeling; 8 bleeding, kindness, sympathy; 9 affection, character, fortitude; 10 compassion, resolution, tenderness; 11 sensitivity, temperament; PHRASES: 5-6 nitty-gritty.

heart (at heart) 9 basically, radically; 13 fundamentally; PHRASES: 2, 3, 4 at the core; 2, 4 au fond Fr; 2, 6 at bottom; 2, 9 in substance.

heartburn 5 colic; 7 pyrosis; 9 dyspepsia; 11 indigestion; PHRASES: 4, 7 acid stomach.

heartless See callous

heartsease 5 pansy.

hearty 4 deep, warm; 6 genial, jovial, strong; 7 abiding, filling, sincere; 8 abundant, cheerful, emphatic, profound, vigorous; 9 plentiful, welcoming; 10 nourishing; 11 substantial; 12 enthusiastic, wholehearted.

heat 3 fug, red; 4 body, boil, burn, cold, cook, dead, fuel, warm, wave, zeal; 5 ardor, black, blood, blush, fever, flush, roast, steam, stove, sunny, sweat, total, white; 6 atomic, fervor, heater, latent, sizzle, warmth; 7 burning, emotion, freezer, furnace, hotness, inflame, passion, prickly, pyrexia, radiant, sizzler; 8 humidity, scorcher, tepidity, warmness; 9 humidness, intensity, microwave, tepidness; 10 calescence, combustion, excitement, steaminess, stuffiness, sweatiness, torridness; 11 overheating, temperature; 12 feverishness, inflammation, lukewarmness, perspiration,

refrigerator; 13 incandescence, refrigeration; PHRASES: 3, 5 hot flush, hot spell; 3, 7 hot weather; 3, 9 hot substance; 4, 2 warm up; 4, 5 warm spell; 4, 7 warm through UK, warm weather; 4, 11 high temperature, room temperature; 4-11 warm-bloodedness; 5, 5 flash point, sunny spell; 6, 6 Indian summer; 7, 5 boiling point, melting point.

heat (loss of heat) 7 chiling, cooling, cryonic; 8 freezing, unmelted; 9 cryogenic, freezable, insulated, resistant; 10 frigorific; 11 refrigerant; 12 refrigerated; PHRASES: 3-6 air-cooled; 3-11 air-conditioned; 4-5 heatproof; 5-6 quick-frozen, water-cooled; 6-5 freeze-dried.

heated 5 angry, baked, burnt, fiery, fired, lined; 6 boiled, lagged, molten, padded, singed; 7 excited, intense, roasted, toasted; 8 animated, frenzied, scorched; 9 centrally, defrosted, insulated; 10 passionate; 11 impassioned; PHRASES: 3-5 fur-lined, gas-fired UK, oil-fired UK; 4-5 coal-fired; 5, 4 burnt down; 6, 2 warmed up, worked up; 6-6 double-glazed; 6, 7 warmed through.

heater 3 fan, gas; 4 fire, iron; 5 duvet, parka, quilt, stove; 6 boiler, copper, deicer, geyser, hottie Aus and NZ, warmer; 7 blanket, furnace, lagging, Thermos™; 8 crucible, electric, overcoat, radiator; 9 comforter, hypocaust UK, immersion, Styrofoam; 10 antifreeze, convection, insulation, thermostat; 11 fomentation, polystyrene; PHRASES: 3-3, 4 hot-air vent; 3-5, 4 hot-water tank; 3-5, 5 hot-water pipes; 3-5, 6 hot-water bottle; 4, 5 long johns; 4-6 foot-warmer; 5, 4 steam iron; 5, 5 solar panel; 5, 6 space ~; 5, 7 solar heating; 6, 7 double glazing UK; 6, 8 winter woollies; 7, 3 warming pan; 7, 6 storage ~ UK; 7, 7 central heating, heating element; 8, 4 branding iron; 8, 6 ethylene glycol; 9, 4 soldering iron.

heat flow 9 radiation; 10 conduction, convection; PHRASES: 4, 8 heat capacity, heat exchange, heat transfer.

heather 4 ling; 5 erica, heath.

heat measurement 3 BTU (British thermal unit); 5 joule, scale, therm; 7 calorie, Celsius, Réaumur; 10 centigrade, Fahrenheit; 11 calorimeter, kilocalorie, temperature, thermograph, thermometer; PHRASES: 4, 4 heat unit; 6, 4 latent heat; 8, 4 specific heat; 9, 5 calorific value.

heave 3 lug; 4 drag, haul, pull, toss, yank;

5 chuck, fling, pitch, surge, swell, throb, throw; **9** palpitate; PHRASES: **4, 3, 4** rise and fall.

heaven 3 air, sky; **4** Zion; **5** bliss, ether; **6** cosmos, welkin; **7** ecstasy, Elysium, nirvana, Olympus, rapture; **8** empyrean, paradise, Valhalla; **9** dreamland, firmament; PHRASES: **3, 9** New Jerusalem; **4, 4** Holy City; **5, 2, 3, 4** Abode of the Gods; **5, 2, 3, 5** Isles of the Blest; **5, 4** cloud nine; **6, 2, 3** throne of God; **6, 5** Pearly Gates; **7, 2, 3** Kingdom of God; **7, 4** Kingdom come; **7, 6** Elysian fields; **9, 4** Celestial City.

heavenly 3 sky; **4** holy; **6** divine, lovely; **7** angelic, blessed, Elysian, saintly; **8** blissful, cherubic, empyreal, empyrean, ethereal, Olympian, seraphic, supernal; **9** angelical, celestial, fantastic, paradisic, spiritual, wonderful; **10** delightful, paradisiac, paradisial; **11** archangelic, paradisical; **12** paradisiacal; PHRASES: **2, 4** on high.

heavily 5 heavy; PHRASES: **4, 1, 5** like a horse; **4, 4** like lead; **4, 5, 6** with great weight. *See also* **heavy**

heaviness 4 beef, bulk, heft, lump, mass; **5** brawn; **6** weight; **7** obesity, tonnage; **8** poundage, solidity; **9** immensity, substance; **10** corpulence; **11** birthweight; PHRASES: **4, 6** body weight; **5, 4** solid body; **5, 6** extra weight. *See also* **heavy**

heavy 3 fat; **4** busy, deep, full, hard, lead, thug; **5** beefy, bulky, dense, grave, great, hefty, large, lumpy, massy, obese, solid, stout, thick, tight; **6** baddie, chunky, hectic, leaden, minder *UK*, opaque, packed, tiring; **7** arduous, compact, intense, lumpish, massive, onerous, serious, violent, viscous, weighed, weighty; **8** forceful, frenetic, hooligan, powerful, profound, weighing, weighted; **9** bodyguard, corpulent, crippling, demanding, difficult, important; **10** burdensome, depressing, oppressive, overweight; **11** substantial; **12** backbreaking; PHRASES: **3, 3** bad guy; **4, 1, 6, 2** with a weight of; **5-2** weigh-in; **5-3** weigh-out; **6, 6** having weight.

heavy (be heavy) 4 sink; **6** settle, wallow; **7** descend, founder; **8** outweigh; **9** gravitate; **11** overbalance; **12** counterpoise, counterweigh; PHRASES: **3, 2, 6** put on weight; **3, 3, 6** tip the scales; **3, 3, 7** tip the balance; **4, 3, 6** turn the scales; **5, 1, 3** weigh a ton; **5, 6** carry weight.

heavy (make heavy) 3 tax; **4** lade,

load; **6** burden, charge, cumber, hamper, hinder, saddle; **7** ballast, oppress, overtax; **8** encumber, handicap, overload; **10** overburden; PHRASES: **3, 5, 5** lie heavy upon; **5, 4** weigh down.

heavy hydrogen 9 deuterium.

heavy spar 7 barytes.

heavy water 9, 5 deuterium oxide.

hebdomadal 6 weekly.

Hebrew alphabet 2 he, pe; **3** mem, nun, sin, tav, vav, yod; **4** ayin, beth, kaph, koph *UK*, resh, sadi, shin, teth; **5** aleph, cheth *UK*, gimel, lamed, zayin; **6** daleth, samekh.

Hebrides 7, 5 Western Isles.

heckle 3 boo; **4** jeer; **9** interrupt; PHRASES: **4, 2** butt in.

hector *See* **bully**

hedge 4 ring; **5** evade, fence, stall, verge; **6** border, privet; **7** protect; **8** encircle, hedgerow; **9** windbreak; **11** prevaricate.

hedgehog 6 urchin.

hedonist *See* **pleasure-seeker**

heed 4 care, note; **6** follow, notice, regard; **7** observe; **9** attention; **11** mindfulness; **13** attentiveness; **6, 2** listen to.

heedless 4 hard, rash; **7** callous; **8** careless, reckless; **9** heartless, impassive, oblivious; **10** neglectful; **11** thoughtless; PHRASES: **4-7** hard-hearted; **5, 4** thick skin.

heel *See* **repair**

heel bone 9 calcaneus.

hefty 5 bulky, heavy, large; **6** robust; **7** awkward, weighty; **10** cumbersome; **11** substantial.

height 3 top; **4** acme, apex, fell, knap, lift, mesa, moor, peak, rise, wold; **5** climb, downs, pitch; **6** summit, uplift, zenith; **7** hilltop, incline, plateau, stature, uplands; **8** altitude, eminence, highness, moorland, pinnacle, tallness; **9** elevation, foothills, highlands, loftiness, sublimity, tableland; **10** escarpment, exaltation, prominence; **11** mountaintop; PHRASES: **6, 6** rising ground.

heir *See* **successor**

helicopter 7 chopper; **8** windmill; **9** eggbeater; **10** whirlybird.

heliotrope 10 bloodstone.

helix 4 coil; **6** double, spiral, spring; **7** helices, ringlet; **9** corkscrew.

hell 3 Dis, Hel; **4** pain, Styx; **5** abyss, agony, Hades, limbo, Sheol; **6** Erebus, misery; **7** Abaddon, Acheron, anguish, Avernus, Gehenna, inferno, torment, torture; **8** Tartarus; **9** damnation, nightmare, perdition, purgatory, suffering; **10** underworld; **11** netherworld; PHRASES: **3, 2, 7** pit of Acheron; **4, 2, 4** lake of fire; **5, 2, 3, 4** place of the dead; **5, 2, 5** realm of Pluto; **5, 5** lower world.

Hellespont 11 Dardanelles.

hello 2 hi; **4** ciao, hail; **5** howdy; **6** howzit; **7** bonjour *Fr*, morning; **10** salutation; **12** introduction; PHRASES: **4, 3** good day *UK*; **4, 7** good morning; **4, 9** good afternoon.

helm 5 wheel; **6** rudder, tiller; **7** command, control.

help 3 aid, SOS, use; **4** abet, desk, ease; **5** amend, avail, edify, favor, serve; **6** assist, better, mayday, profit, relief, rescue, succor; **7** advance, benefit, deliver, improve, promote, relieve, service, support; **8** function, tailwind; **9** advantage, alleviate; **10** ameliorate, assistance, facilitate, instrument; **11** improvement, springboard; PHRASES: **2, 2, 10** be of assistance; **2, 9** do something; **3-2** leg-up; **3, 3, 4** aid and abet; **4, 1, 4** lend a hand; **4, 2, 3, 3, 2** come to the aid of; **4, 4** fair wind; **5, 6** rally around; **7, 3** proffer aid; **7, 4** helping hand.

helper 3 aid; **4** aide, ally, mate; **5** aider, angel, gofer, hands, locum, staff; **6** backer, backup, deputy, patron, savior, second; **7** abettor, backing, enabler, partner, reserve, standby, stopgap, support; **8** adjutant, adjuvant, assister, coworker, employee, helpmate, helpmeet, henchman, sidekick; **9** assistant, attendant, auxiliary, colleague, supporter; **10** coadjutant, lieutenant, substitute, understudy; **11** facilitator, subordinate; **12** collaborator; **14** reinforcements; PHRASES: **3, 6** man Friday; **4-2-4** aide-de-camp; **4, 6** girl Friday; **4, 9** good Samaritan; **5-2** stand-in; **5-4, 3** right-hand man; **5, 6** locum tenens; **5, 9** fairy godmother; **6, 4** second line; **7, 3** twelfth man *UK*; **7, 4** helping hand; **7, 5** backing group.

helpful 4 kind; **5** handy; **6** useful; **8** gracious, obliging, positive, valuable; **9** conducive, effective, favorable, practical; **10** beneficial, benevolent, convenient, furthering, neighborly, supportive; **11** cooperative, informative, serviceable, utilitarian; **12** advantageous, constructive, contributory; **13** collaborative, philanthropic; PHRAS-

ES: **2, 3** of use.

helpful (be helpful) 5 avail, serve; **6** profit; **7** benefit; **9** advantage.

helpfully 10 profitably; PHRASES: **2, 3, 4** to the good; **2, 9** to advantage. *See also* **helpful**

helpfulness 4 care; **5** value; **7** benefit, concern, support, utility; **8** goodwill; **11** benevolence, cooperation; **13** collaboration, profitability. *See also* **helpful**

helping 6 ration; **7** portion, serving; **8** adjuvant, plateful; **9** selection; **12** facilitative, instrumental; PHRASES: **2, 4** of help; **2, 7** of service; **2, 10** of assistance. *See also* **help**

helplessness 7 infancy; **8** babyhood, weakness; **9** innocence; **10** dependence; **13** powerlessness, vulnerability; **15** defenselessness.

Helvetian 5 Swiss.

hem 4 edge; **7** shorten; **8** lengthen; PHRASES: **3, 2** sew up; **4, 2** turn up.

hematite 4, 6 iron glance.

hemimorphite 8 calamine.

hemorrhoids 5 piles.

hemp 6 Indian; **8** cannabis.

hen 3 run; **5** party; **7** harrier.

hence 5 later; **9** therefore; **10** henceforth; **12** consequently; PHRASES: **2, 6** in future; **3, 2** and so; **3, 4, 6** for this reason; **4, 3, 2** from now on; **4, 4, 4** from this time; **5, 3** that's why.

hen harrier 5, 4 marsh hawk; **5, 7** marsh harrier.

henna 8 camphire.

Heracles 8 Hercules.

herald 4 omen, sign; **5** crier; **6** signal; **7** courier, portent, presage; **8** announce, proclaim; **9** announcer, harbinger, messenger, precursor, prefigure, publicize; **10** Clarenceux *UK*, forerunner, foreshadow, proclaimer, pursuivant *UK*; PHRASES: **4, 2, 4** king of arms, Roll of Arms; **4, 3** give out; **4, 4** Lord Lyon; **4, 4, 2, 4** Lyon King of Arms; **4, 6** make public; **4, 7** Earl Marshal; **5, 5** Rouge Croix; **5, 6** Rouge Dragon; **7, 2, 4** College of Arms.

heraldic devices and terms 2 or; **3** bar, fur; **4** arms, base, bend, fret, lion, pale, pile, vair, vert, wavy; **5** azure, badge, barry, baton, bendy, chief, crest, cross, crown, eagle, field, flank, flory, fusil, gules, gyron, label, metal, molet, motto, party, rebus, sable; **6** argent, armory, billet, blazon, canton, charge, device, dexter, ermine, falcon, flanch, fleury, helmet, mullet, murrey, potent, shield, wreath; **7** annulet, bandeau, bearing, bordure, chaplet, chevron, coronet, gardant, garland, griffin, lozenge, martlet, passant, purpure, quarter, rampant, roundel, saltire, statant, trefoil, unicorn; **8** armorial, blazonry, couchant, crescent, impaling, mantling, ordinary, sinister; **9** embattled, engrailed, hatchment, quarterly, regardant; **10** cinquefoil, cockatrice, difference, emblazoned, emblematic, escutcheon, impalement, lambrequin, marshaling, portcullis, quartering, supporters; **11** achievement, dimidiation; **12** differencing; PHRASES: **3, 8** bar sinister; **4, 2, 4** coat of arms; **4, 7** lion rampant; **4, 8** bend sinister, lion couchant; **5-2-3** fleur-de-lis; **5, 4** Tudor rose; **5, 5** fesse point, honor point; **6, 5** spread eagle; **6, 6** animal charge, floral charge; **6, 7** planta genista; **7, 5** nombril point.

herbaceous 6 annual, border, exotic; **8** biennial; **9** ephemeral, epiphytic, perennial, succulent; **10** xerophytic; **11** saprophytic.

herbarium 5 flora; **6** herbal; **11** florilegium; PHRASES: **4, 4** seed bank; **6, 6** hortus siccus; **7, 6** botanic garden.

herb Christopher 9 baneberry.

herb Gerard 8 goutweed.

herbicidal 10 fungicidal, pesticidal; **12** insecticidal.

herbs and spices 3 bay, rue; **4** balm, dill, mace, mint, sage; **5** anise, basil, caper, chili, chive, clove, cumin, myrrh, tansy, thyme; **6** betony, borage, burnet, cassia, chives, cicely, fennel, garlic, ginger, hyssop, lovage, nutmeg, pepper, savory, sesame, sorrel; **7** aniseed, boneset, caraway, cayenne, chervil, comfrey, dittany, gentian, juniper, mustard, oregano, paprika, parsley, perilla, pimento, saffron, salsify, tabasco, vanilla, verbena; **8** allspice, angelica, camomile *UK*, cinnamon, feverfew, licorice, marjoram, rosemary, tarragon, turmeric, wormwood; **9** asafetida, chamomile *UK*, coriander, fenugreek, spearmint; **10** lemongrass, peppermint; **11** horseradish; PHRASES: **3, 4** bay leaf; **4, 2, 5** herb of grace; **5, 5** lemon thyme, mixed herbs; **5, 6** fines herbes *Fr*; **5, 7** lemon verbena; **6, 7** French mustard *UK*; **7, 5** bouquet garni *Fr*; **7, 7** English mustard.

Hercules 8 Heracles.

herd 3 mob, pod; **4** band, bevy, gang, mass, pack; **5** crowd, drive, drove, flock, group, guide, leash, pride, sheep, shoal, steer, swarm, troop, usher; **6** colony, corral, direct, funnel, kennel, litter, masses *UK*, school; **7** channel, cluster, marshal, rookery; **8** shepherd; PHRASES: **3, 6** hoi polloi; **4, 2** call in, whip in; **5, 2** round up; **5, 8** drive together; **6, 8** gather together.

here 3 now; **5** there, where; **8** anywhere; **9** somewhere; **10** everywhere; PHRASES: **2, 4, 4** at this time; **2, 4, 5** at this point.

hereafter 4 hell; **6** future, heaven; **7** nirvana; **8** hellfire, paradise; **9** damnation; **10** henceforth, underworld; **12** henceforward; PHRASES: **2, 6** in future; **4, 3, 2** from now on; **4, 4, 4** from this time; **5, 4** after this; **7, 4** kingdom come.

hereditary 6 family, inborn, inbred, innate; **7** genetic; **9** heritable, inherited; **11** traditional; **13** transmissible.

heresy 7 dissent; **9** deviation, sacrilege; **10** dissidence, heterodoxy, iconoclasm; **11** profanation, revisionism, unorthodoxy.

heretical 7 profane; **9** deviating, dissident, heterodox; **10** dissenting, unorthodox; **12** iconoclastic, sacrilegious; **14** unconventional.

hermit 5 loner; **7** ascetic, eremite, recluse, stylite; **8** marabout, solitary; **9** anchorite; **12** isolationist; PHRASES: **4, 4** lone wolf.

hern 5 heron.

hero 4 idol, star; **8** champion, superman; **9** conqueror; **11** protagonist; PHRASES: **4, 4** male lead; **7, 3** leading man; **7, 5** leading actor.

heroin 4 scag; **5** horse, smack; **11** diamorphine.

heroine 4 idol, star; **8** champion; **9** conqueror; **10** superwoman; **11** protagonist; PHRASES: **6, 4** female lead; **7, 4** leading lady; **7, 7** leading actress.

heroism 5 pluck, valor; **6** daring; **7** bravery, courage, prowess; **8** boldness, chivalry, virility; **9** gallantry, manliness; **10** pluckiness; **12** fearlessness, intrepidness, knightliness; PHRASES: **5, 5, 3** stiff upper lip.

heron 4 hern.

herpes 8 shingles; PHRASES: **4, 4** cold sore.

herpetologist 5, 7 snake charmer.

hesitant 3 shy; **5** timid; **7** groping; **8** cautious, dawdling, doubtful; **9** diffident, reluctant, tentative, uncertain, undecided, unwilling; **10** indecisive, irresolute; PHRASES: **4, 3, 3, 4** slow off the mark; **4-8** foot-dragging; **6-6** softly-softly *UK*.

hesitate 3 jib, lag, shy; **4** balk *UK*, drag, halt; **5** avoid, check, dally, delay, evade, hover, pause, waver; **6** dawdle, dither, falter, linger, loiter; **7** stumble; **9** vacillate; **10** equivocate; **11** prevaricate; PHRASES: **3, 2, 3, 5** sit on the fence; **4, 3, 3, 4** blow hot and cold; **4, 4** back away, hang back; **4, 4, 4** take one's time; **5, 4** waste time; **5, 5** think twice; **5-5** dilly-dally; **6-6** shilly-shally.

hesitation 2 er, um; **4** drag; **5** delay, pause, qualm; **6** holdup; **7** caution, scruple, setback; **9** detention, hesitancy; **10** hysteresis, indecision, reluctance; **11** uncertainty, vacillation; **14** disinclination; **15** procrastination; PHRASES: **4-8** foot-dragging. *See also* **hesitant, hesitate**

heterogeneous *See* **varied**

hew 2 ax; **3** cut; **4** chop, fell; **5** carve, model, shape; **6** cleave, sculpt; **7** fashion.

hex 4 jinx; **5** curse, spell; **6** voodoo, whammy; **8** pishogue *UK*; PHRASES: **4, 3** evil eye.

heyday *See* **prime**

HF 7 hafnium.

HG 7 mercury.

hiatus *See* **pause**

hibiscus 5, 4 China rose.

hidden 4 dark; **6** buried, covert, secret, unseen, veiled; **7** cryptic, obscure, unknown; **8** secreted, ulterior; **9** concealed, invisible; **10** indistinct, mysterious, mystifying; **11** camouflaged, clandestine; PHRASES: **3, 2, 5** out of sight.

hide 3 dim; **4** blur, bury, cowl, hood, lurk, mask, veil; **5** cloak, cloud, cover, creep, erase, skulk, slink; **6** screen, shroud; **7** conceal, eclipse, obscure, secrete; **8** disguise, inundate, submerge, suppress, withhold; **9** disappear; **10** camouflage, masquerade; PHRASES: **2, 11** go underground; **3, 3, 2, 5** put out of sight; **4, 2** hole up; **4, 3** blot out; **4, 4** hold back, keep back; **4, 4, 4** ~ from view; **4, 5** keep quiet, take cover; **4, 6** keep secret; **5, 2** cover up; **5, 3** black out, blank out.

hideous 4 ugly; **5** gross; **8** dreadful, gruesome, horrible; **9** contorted, graceless, grotesque, inelegant, repellent, repulsive, unsightly; **10** disgusting.

hideousness 9 deformity; **10** defacement, mutilation, repugnance; **13** disfigurement. *See also* **hideous**

hiding place 3 den; **4** hole, lair, nook, safe; **5** attic, cache, niche, stash; **6** asylum, cellar, closet, cranny, dugout, recess, refuge; **7** doormat, foxhole, hideout, shelter; **8** hideaway, mattress; **9** cubbyhole, sanctuary; PHRASES: **4, 4** bolt hole; **4, 5** bank vault, safe house; **4, 7** bomb shelter; **4-7** safe-deposit; **5, 2, 6** place of escape; **5-4** hidey-hole; **6, 4** hidden cave, hollow tree; **6, 7** secret passage.

hierarchical 6 graded, ranked, serial, tiered; **7** ordered; **9** taxonomic; **10** classified, sequential; **11** categorized, gradational, progressive; **12** alphabetical; PHRASES: **2, 5** in order.

hierarchy 5 order; **6** ladder, series; **7** grading, pyramid; **8** sequence; **9** gradation; **11** progression; PHRASES: **5, 2, 7** chain of command; **7, 5** pecking order; **9, 5** ascending order, numerical order.

hieroglyph 6 cipher, symbol; **7** picture; **8** ideogram; PHRASES: **10** pictograph.

higgledy-piggledy *See* **untidy**

high 3 day, hat, sky, tea; **4** airy, buzz, jump, kick, kite, lift, over, peak, seas, spot, tall, tech, tide, time, wire; **5** above, aloft, altar, boost, court, dizzy, giddy, happy, jinks, lofty, point, table, water; **6** aerial, Church, climax, comedy, flying, German, priest, rising, school, season, shrill, street, summit, thrill; **7** command, country, eminent, exalted, extreme, fashion, pitched, ranking, soaring, society, soprano, sublime, topping, treason, Wycombe; **8** aspiring, beetling, ecstatic, elevated, ethereal, falsetto, fidelity, holidays, mounting, overhead, piercing, pleasure, superior, supernal, towering, uplifted, upraised, upstairs; **9** ascending, explosive, important, prominent; **10** dominating, excitement, multistory, technology; **11** altitudinal, anticyclone, overhanging, overlooking, overtopping, penetrating, prohibitive, skyscraping, vertiginous; **12** altitudinous, astronomical, commissioner; **13** distinguished, extraordinary, overshadowing; **2, 2, 3, 5** up to the knees, up to the waist; **2, 3** on top; **2, 3, 3** in the air; **2, 6** in height, on stilts, on tiptoe; **2, 9** in elevation; **4-5** high-level; **5-6** cloud-capped; **5, 7** above average.

high (be high) 3 fly, top; **4** soar; **5** clear, tower; **6** aspire, beetle; **7** command, overtop; **8** bestride, dominate, overarch, overhang, overlook, surmount; **10** overshadow; PHRASES: **4, 4, 2** look down on; **5, 5** tower above.

highbrow 4 sage; **7** scholar; **8** academic, cultured; **9** scholarly; **11** philosopher; **12** intellectual.

higher 2 up; **5** upper; **6** taller; **7** highest, tallest, topmost, upwards; **8** skywards *UK*, superior; **9** uppermost; **10** vertically; **11** heavenwards *UK*; PHRASES: **7, 3, 3** nearest the top; **8, 2** straight up.

high fashion 5, 7 haute couture.

high-flown 8 affected; **9** grandiose; **11** pretentious; **13** grandiloquent.

highland 4 down, fell *UK*, mesa, wold; **5** dress, fling; **6** cattle, region, upland; **7** heights, hilltop, incline, plateau; **8** moorland; **9** acclivity, foothills, mountains, tableland; **10** escarpment.

highlight 4 acme, halo; **5** laser; **6** climax, corona, nimbus, stress; **7** aureole, rainbow, uplight; **8** gloriole, hologram, showcase, spectrum; **9** downlight, emphasize, underline; **10** holography, underscore; **11** chiaroscuro *It*; PHRASES: **3, 2, 7** son et lumière *Fr*; **4, 2** show up; **4, 3** best bit *UK*; **4, 4** high spot *UK*; **4-4** half-tone; **4, 5** high point; **4, 9, 2** draw attention to; **5, 2** focus on; **5, 2, 3, 4** icing on the cake; **5, 2, 5** bring to light; **5-3-5** black-and-white.

highly 4 very, well; **5** aloft; **6** vastly *UK*, warmly; **7** greatly; **9** decidedly, favorably; **10** graciously; **11** approvingly, exceedingly; PHRASES: **2, 4** on high; **2, 6** on stilts, on tiptoe. *See also* **high**

high thing 3 sky; **4** dome, loft, roof; **5** aerie, attic, ether, eyrie *UK*, steps, vault; **6** cupola, garret, heaven, ladder, stilts; **7** ceiling, mansard, topmast, tsunami; **8** cockloft *UK*, masthead; **9** exosphere, highchair, penthouse, viewpoint; **10** clerestory, mesosphere; **11** weathercock; **12** stratosphere, thermosphere; PHRASES: **3, 5** top floor; **4, 4** high tide; **4-4** high-rise; **4, 5** high heels, high water; **5, 4** crow's nest, tidal wave; **6, 4** spring tide; **7, 4** weather vane; **7, 5** vantage point; **8, 5** platform soles; **10, 4** topgallant mast.

highway 1 I; **4** road, spur; **6** bypass; **7** freeway; **8** Autobahn, motorway; **9** autoroute; **10** autostrada, expressway, interstate, intrastate; **12** superhighway.

hijack 5 seize, steal; **6** borrow; **7** capture, seizure, skyjack; **8** takeover; **10** commandeer, skyjacking; **11** appropriate; PHRASES: **4, 4** take over.

hike 4 trek, walk; **5** climb; **6** ramble.

hilarious *See* **funny**

hilarity 4 glee; **5** mirth; **8** laughter; **9** amusement, merriment.

hill 3 tor; **4** heap, loma, peak, pile, rise; **5** grade, knoll, mound, mount, scarp, slope; **6** pepino; **7** hillock, hummock, incline; **8** gradient, mountain; **9** razorback.

hilltop 3 top; **4** brow, peak; **5** crown; **6** summit; **8** pinnacle.

hind 4 back, rear; **8** hindmost, rearmost; **9** posterior.

hinder 4 curb, drag, foil, rear, stop; **5** block, check, choke, crimp, delay, deter, limit, queer, snafu, spike, stall, upset; **6** bother, damper, detain, hamper, hassle, heckle, hobble, impair, impede, meddle, oppose, resist, retard, scotch, stifle, stymie, thwart; **7** disable, inhibit, obviate, prevent, repress, snooker; **8** dissuade, encumber, obstruct, preclude, prohibit, restrain, restrict, suppress; **9** forestall, frustrate, intercept, interfere, interpose, interrupt, intervene, persecute, posterior, undermine; **10** counteract, discourage; **12** circumscribe, incapacitate; PHRASES: **3, 2** mix up; **3, 2, 3, 3** get in the way, nip in the bud; **4, 2** foul up; **4, 3, 2, 3, 3** stop one in the act; **4, 4** hold back; **4, 4, 5** clip one's wings; **4, 7** come between; **5, 2** louse up; **9, 4** interfere with.

hinderer 6 damper; **7** gremlin, heckler, impeder, killjoy, marplot, meddler; **8** intruder, saboteur; **9** hindrance, introvert; **10** filibuster, interferer, negativist, obstructer, spoilsport; **11** interrupter, poltergeist; **12** troublemaker; PHRASES: **3, 2, 3, 6** dog in the manger; **3, 7** wet blanket; **5, 2, 3, 5** snake in the grass; **5-6** party-pooper; **8-5** mischiefmaker.

hindmost 3 end; **4** back, last, rear, tail; **5** final; **7** endmost; **8** rearmost.

hindquarters 4 back, rear; PHRASES: **4, 4** hind legs, rear legs.

hindrance 3 let; **4** curb; **6** burden; **7** barrier, control, foiling, refusal; **8** friction, obstacle, sabotage; **9** detention, deterrent, hampering, obviation, restraint; **10** difficulty, dissuasion, impediment, injunction, limitation, opposition, prevention, repression, resistance; **11** encumbrance, frustration, obstruction, prohibition, restriction, retardation; **12** forestalling, interdiction, interference, interruption, intervention; **13** counteraction, interposition; **14** countermeasure, discouragement.

Hindu deities 3 Ahi, Ihi; **4** Agni, Bali, Devi, Diti, Kama, Soma, Vayu, Yama; **5** Aditi, Indra, Shiva, Surya; **6** Amrita, Brahma, Garuda, Kubera, Manasa, Varuna *UK*, Vishnu; **7** Ganesha, Hanuman, Jyestha, Lakshmi, Saranyu, Shitala, Sugriva; **8** Prithivi; **9** Amaravati, Sarasvati; **10** Gandharvas, Karttikeya, Visvakarma.

hinge 4 axis, crux; **5** joint, pivot; **6** center; **7** fulcrum.

hint 3 tip; **4** clue, dash, help; **5** hunch, imply, speck, tinge, touch, trace, whiff; **6** breath, signal; **7** element, inkling, mention, modicum, pointer, soupçon, suggest; **8** indicate, intimate; **9** deduction, induction, inference, insinuate, suspicion, undertone; **10** indication, intimation, suggestion; **11** insinuation; **PHRASES: 3-3** tip-off; **8, 4** telltale sign.

hip 4 bath, cool; **5** flask, joint; **6** pelvis, pocket, trendy; **7** current, stylish; **11** fashionable; **PHRASES: 2, 5** in vogue; **3, 3, 4** all the rage; **4-2** with-it.

hipbone 10, 4 innominate bone.

hippopotamus 5, 5 river horse.

hire 3 let; **4** rent; **5** lease; **6** employ, engage; **7** appoint, charter; **8** contract; **PHRASES: 4, 2** sign up, take on.

hirsute *See* **hairy**

Hispaniola 5 Haiti; **PHRASES: 5, 7** Santo Domingo.

hiss 3 boo; **4** fizz, hoot, hush, jeer, lisp; **5** shush, swish; **6** fizzle, murmur, rustle, sizzle, sneeze, splash, wheeze; **7** catcall, lisping, sputter, whisper, whistle; **8** ridicule, rustling, sibilate, splutter; **9** sibilance, susurrate; **10** assibilate, effervesce, sibilation; **11** susurration; **12** assibilation; **13** effervescence; **PHRASES: 5, 5** white noise; **5, 7** stage whisper.

hisser 5 goose, sigma, snake; **7** serpent; **8** sibilant; **PHRASES: 6, 1** letter s.

historian 8 recorder; **9** archivist; **10** biographer, epigrapher; **12** Egyptologist, paleographer; **13** archaeologist; **14** paleontologist; **15** historiographer.

historic 5 Roman, Saxon, Tudor; **6** famous, feudal, Gothic, heroic, Norman, primal; **7** ancient, antique, archaic, notable, Ottoman, Persian; **8** Colonial, Etruscan, Georgian, Hellenic, Jacobean, medieval; **9** ancestral, atavistic, Byzantine, classical, Edwardian, important, momentous, vestigial, Victorian; **10** aboriginal, antiquated, celebrated, diachronic, Hanoverian, monumental, primordial, remarkable, Romanesque; **11** Elizabethan, Hellenistic, prehistoric, Renaissance, significant; **12** antediluvian; **PHRASES: 6, 3, 5** before the Flood. *See also* **historical**

historical 3 old; **4** past; **5** dated, prior; **6** bygone, former; **12** epigraphical; **14** archaeological, paleographical.

historically 3 ago, yet; **4** once; **7** usually; **8** formerly, hitherto; **9** aforetime, generally, yesterday; **10** yesteryear; **12** aboriginally, primordially; **13** retroactively, traditionally; **14** diachronically; **15** prehistorically; **PHRASES: 1, 4, 4, 3** a long time ago; **2, 1, 4** as a rule; **2, 3** of old; **2, 3, 4** in the main; **2, 3, 5** by and large; **2, 4** of yore; **2, 4, 4, 2** in days gone by; **2, 5, 5** in olden times; **2, 7** in general, in history; **4, 3** long ago, over all; **4, 5** long since; **4, 9** with hindsight; **5, 3** until now.

historical period 11 Renaissance; **PHRASES: 3, 2, 6** Age of Reason; **4, 4** Dark Ages; **6, 3** heroic age; **6, 4** Middle Ages; **6, 6** ancien régime *Fr*; **9, 3** Classical Age.

historicism 8 archaism; **10** excavation, exhumation; **11** medievalism; **14** antiquarianism.

history 4 case, life, oral, past, saga; **5** diary, local, story; **6** annals, memoir, record, social; **7** account, ancient, Marxist, natural; **8** economic; **9** antiquity, chronicle, narration, political, religious; **10** yesteryear; **14** constitutional, historiography; **PHRASES: 3, 4** the past; **4, 5** life story; **5, 4** olden days, times past; **5, 4, 2** times gone by; **5, 5** olden times; **6, 4** bygone days.

histrionic 8 dramatic; **10** theatrical; **11** exaggerated; **12** melodramatic, unrestrained.

hit 3 bat, bop, box, cut, jab, man, off, osh, out, ram, rap, tan, win; **4** bang, bash, beat, belt, biff, blow, bonk, bump, cane, club, cuff, dash, deck, dent, dint, drub, dust, flay, flog, gain, gore, hide, hurt, kick, lash, lick, list, pelt, poke, shot, slam, slap, slog, slug, sock, stab, swat, welt, whip, whop; **5** birch, clout, flail, knock, lunge, paste, plunk, pound, punch, reach, smack, smash, smite, strap, swing, swipe, thump, whack; **6** affect, attain, batter, buffet, cudgel, damage, lather, paddle, parade, strike, stroke, thrash, thrust, thwack, wallop, winner; **7** achieve, afflict, belabor, clobber, collide, knifing, leather, passado, scourge, slipper, stoning, success, triumph, trounce; **8** bludgeon, knockout, lambaste; **9** bastinado, fustigate, horsewhip, sensation; **10** bayoneting, bestseller, flagellate; **11** blockbuster, swordthrust; PHRASES: **3, 1, 4** aim a blow; **3, 3, 6** cut and thrust *UK*; **3, 4** run into; **3, 4, 4** tan one's hide; **3, 8, 4** box someone's ears; **4, 1, 4** deal a blow; **4, 1, 6** give a hiding; **4, 2, 3, 5** slap on the wrist; **4, 4** bang into, bash into, bump into; **4, 5, 3, 3** clip round the ear; **4-6** home-thrust; **5, 4** crash into, knock cold, smash into; **6, 2** arrive at, strike at; **6, 6** market leader; **7, 4** collide with.

hitch **3** tie; **4** hook, join, lash, snag, yoke; **5** catch, clove, delay; **6** attach, couple, fasten, glitch, holdup, tether; **7** connect, harness, problem, rolling, trouble, weaver's; **8** drawback, loophole; **9** hindrance, hitchhike; **10** difficulty; PHRASES: **2, 5, 1, 4** be given a lift; **3, 4, 5, 3** put your thumb out; **4, 4** make fast; **5, 1, 4** thumb a ride.

hive **3** bee; **4** keep, save; **5** amass, hoard, store; **6** apiary, garner; **7** anthill; **8** squirrel, vespiary; **9** stockpile; **10** accumulate; **11** termitarium; PHRASES: **3, 4** put away; **3, 5** put aside; **5, 4** wasps' nest; **7, 6** termite colony.

hives **9** urticaria.

HMS **4** ship (Her/His Majesty's Ship).

HO **5** house; **7** holmium; PHRASES: **4, 6** Home Office *UK*.

hoard **4** heap, hide, mass, pile, save; **5** amass, cache, stash, stint, stock, store; **6** gather, scrimp, starve; **7** collect, reserve, secrete; **8** squirrel; **9** stockpile; **10** accumulate, collection; **12** accumulation; PHRASES: **4, 2** save up; **4, 4** hide away; **8-5** treasure-trove.

hoarder **5** miser, saver; **6** magpie; **7** niggard, Scrooge; **8** squirrel; **9** collector; **11** accumulator; PHRASES: **5-7** penny-pincher.

hoarse **3** dry, low; **5** gruff, husky, nasal, rough; **6** croaky; **7** cracked, rasping, raucous, throaty, unoiled; **8** gravelly, guttural, scratchy; **10** stertorous; **11** nonresonant.

hoarse (sound hoarse) **3** caw, hem, saw; **4** gasp, hawk, rasp; **5** belch, choke, clank, cough, croak, drone, grate, grind, grunt, snore, twang; **6** scrape; **7** scratch; **11** gutteralize; PHRASES: **5, 4, 6** clear one's throat.

hoarseness **7** scratch, stertor; **8** friction, nasality; **9** harshness, rustiness; PHRASES: **4, 2, 3, 6** frog in the throat; **5, 4** nasal tone; **7, 5** cracked voice, rasping sound. *See also* **hoarse**

hoax **3** con, rag; **4** dupe, game, joke, ruse, scam, sham; **5** bluff, fraud, prank, spoof, sport, trick; **6** humbug; **7** deceive, defraud, mislead, swindle; **9** deception; PHRASES: **3-2, 3** put-up job; **3-4** leg-pull *UK*; **3, 5** con trick *UK*; **4, 4, 3** pull one's leg; **5, 4** April fool; **9, 4** practical joke; **10, 4** confidence game.

hobble **3** hop; **4** limp; **6** totter; **7** shamble, shuffle, stagger, stumble.

hobby *See* **pastime**

hobgoblin *See* **goblin**

hobo *See* **traveler**

hock **4** pawn; **6** pledge; **7** deposit; **8** exchange.

hockey **3** ice, pad; **4** back, ball, deke, fake, foul, goal, hold, hook, IIHF (International Ice H~ Federation), knee, NWHL (National Women's H~ League), pads, pass, puck, push, rink, trip; **5** board, check, elbow, glove, rough, slash, stick; **6** assist, charge, faking, goalie, helmet, indoor, screen, strike, stroke; **7** drawing, forward, garbage, headman, hooking, offside, Olympic; **8** backhand, breakout, elbowing, enforcer, offsides, roughing, slashing, tripping; **9** backcheck, bodycheck, endboards, forecheck, highstick, interfere, pokecheck; **10** crosscheck, defenseman, goalkeeper, goaltender, sideboards, stickcheck; **11** backchecker, forechecker, goaltending; **12** highsticking, interference; **13** crosschecking, stickchecking; PHRASES: **3-2-3** man-to-man, one-on-one; **3-3** sin-bin; **3, 3, 4** ice the puck; **4, 1, 7** draw a penalty; **4, 3** butt end; **4-3** face-off, peel-off; **4, 3, 2** give and go; **4, 3, 4** rush the puck; **4, 4** dead puck, Lady Byng, pass back; **4-4** drop-pass, pass-back; **4, 6** goal crease, push stroke; **4-6** butt-ending; **4-7** drop-passing, puck-carrier; **5, 3** Allan Cup; **5, 3, 4** carry the puck, steal the puck; **5, 4** power play; **5, 5, 5** Hobey Baker Award;

5, 6 field ~, floor ~; **5-6** short-handed; **6, 4** center line, center spot, center zone; **7, 3** Stanley Cup; **7, 4** defense zone, garbage goal, neutral zone, offside pass; **7, 5** barrier board, neutral stick; **8, 3** Memorial Cup; **8, 3, 4** stealing the puck; **8, 4** backhand shot, breakout play; **9, 4** attacking zone.

hockey player 3 Orr (Bobby); **4** Howe (Gordie), Hull (Bobby); **7** Gretzky (Wayne), Lemieux (Mario), Richard (Joseph Henri Maurice "Rocket"); **8** Beliveau (Jean), Esposito (Phil).

hog 4 boar; **5** duroc.

hogwash *See* **nonsense**

hoist 4 lift, pull; **5** crane, erect, heave, raise, winch; **6** pulley; **8** elevator.

hold 3 fix, hug; **4** bind, deem, feel, grab, grip, have, keep, seat, stow, sway, wait; **5** carry, claim, clamp, clasp, close, forth, grasp, opine, power, seize, spell, store, think, tight, wedge; **6** attach, clench, clutch, cuddle, detain, enfold, fasten, occupy, reckon, regard, remand, retain, secure; **7** arrange, believe, conduct, confine, contain, control, convene, embrace, possess, presume, squeeze, storage, sustain; **8** assemble, comprise, consider, continue, imprison, maintain, restrain; **9** influence, storeroom; **11** accommodate, compartment, incarcerate; PHRASES: **4, 2** hang on, keep up, lock up, shut in, take in; **4, 3** draw out; **4, 5, 3** have space for; **5, 2** carry on, cling to; **5, 3** cargo bay; **6, 2** cleave to; **7, 5** storage space.

hold (on hold) 2, 1, 4, 6 on a back burner; **2, 3, 5** on the shelf; **2, 3, 5, 4** on the scrap heap; **2, 8** in abeyance; **3, 3, 6** off the agenda.

hold back 4 balk *UK*, hide, keep, save; **5** check, delay, demur, limit; **6** hamper, hinder, impede, retain, shelve, stifle; **7** conceal, contain, control, inhibit, repress, reserve; **8** hesitate, obstruct, postpone, restrain, suppress, withhold; **13** procrastinate; PHRASES: **3, 3** put off; **3, 4** sit back; **3, 5** sit tight; **4, 4** hang back, hang fire, keep back; **4, 4, 2** keep hold of; **4, 4, 4** drag one's feet; **5, 6** tread warily.

holding 4 bond, farm, land, plot; **5** asset, croft, field, share, small, stock; **7** acreage; **8** interest, property; **9** allotment; **10** investment.

hold out 4 give, last; **5** offer; **6** endure, extend, resist; **7** persist, present, proffer; **9** persevere, withstand; PHRASES: **4, 2** hang on; **4,**

2, 4 sink or swim; **4, 4** hold fast; **5, 2, 4, 4** stick to one's guns; **5, 4** stand fast, stand firm; **5, 4, 4** stick like glue; **5, 4, 6** stand your ground; **7, 3** stretch out.

hole 3 air, den, dip, eye, gap, key, pin, pit, rip; **4** blow, bolt, bore, cave, coal, dump, gash, gulf, knot, lair, mine, peep, pore, port, ream, sett, slot, slum, stab, tear, void, well; **5** abyss, black, break, chasm, crack, drill, error, fault, glory, hovel, lance, prick, probe, shaft, shoot, slash, stick, water; **6** burrow, button, cavern, cavity, defect, hollow, inject, outlet, pierce, pigpen, pigsty *UK*, trepan, tunnel, warren; **7** bayonet, eyehole, fissure, fleapit *UK*, opening, retreat, swallow, volcano; **8** aperture, excavate, permeate, puncture, watering, weakness; **9** honeycomb, mineshaft, penetrate, perforate; **10** excavation, nineteenth; **11** perforation; **13** inconsistency; PHRASES: **3, 7** run through; **4, 1, 9** sink a mineshaft; **6, 4, 4** pepper with shot.

holiday 4 bank *UK*, half, hols *UK*; **5** feast, legal, Roman; **6** fiesta, public; **7** busman's; **8** carnival, festival, vacation; **9** festivity; **10** sabbatical; **11** anniversary, celebration; PHRASES: **3, 3** day off; **4, 3** holy day; **5, 3** feast day; **6, 3** saint's day.

Holland 7 Batavia; **11** Netherlands.

hollow 3 dip, pit; **4** bowl, cave, dell, dent, vain; **5** empty, gouge, scoop; **6** cavity, dimple, futile, recess, sunken, vacant; **7** concave, echoing; **10** depression; **11** indentation.

holly 4 holm; PHRASES: **4, 3** holm oak.

hollyhock 4, 6 rose mallow.

Hollywood 10 Tinseltown.

holm 5 holly.

holm oak 4 ilex; **5** holly.

holy 3 day, Joe, See, war; **4** City, Land, Mary, rood, week, writ; **5** Bible, Ghost, Grail, water; **6** Father, Island, Office, Orders, roller, Spirit; **9** Communion, scripture, Sepulchre.

holy day 5 feast; **6** Lammas, Sunday; **7** holiday, Sabbath; **8** Epiphany, Saturday; **9** Candlemas, Martinmas; **10** Assumption, Michaelmas, Whitsunday; **12** Purification; PHRASES: **3, 2, 9** Day of Atonement; **3, 3** Yob Tom; **3, 5, 3** All Souls' Day; **3, 6** Yom Kippur; **3, 6, 3** All Saints' Day; **3, 7, 3** All Hallows' Day; **3, 9** Ash Wednesday; **4, 3** fast day, Lady Day; **4, 6** Good Friday, Palm

Sunday; **4, 7** Rosh Chodesh; **4, 8** Rosh Hashanah; **5, 3** Lord's Day; **5, 4** Mardi Gras; **6, 7** Shrove Tuesday, vernal equinox; **6, 8** Maundy Thursday, summer solstice, winter solstice; **7, 3** Pancake Day; **7, 5** Twelfth Night; **8, 7** autumnal equinox; **9, 3** Ascension Day.

Holy Island 11 Lindisfarne.

holy water 7 baptism; **9** immersion; **10** hydromancy; **11** christening.

homage 4 duty; **7** respect, service; **9** deference, reverence.

hombre 3 man.

home 3 run; **4** base, farm, loan, nest, rest, rule, town, unit; **5** abode, grown, guard, house, local, plate, range, truth, villa; **6** cradle, family, ground, hearth, mental, mobile, Office, remand, target; **7** address, habitat, harvest, hospice, nursing, stately; **8** counties, domestic, domicile, dwelling, eventide, fireside, homeland, homemade, homespun, interior, internal, national, quarters, straight; **9** apartment, children's, economics, homestead, homestyle, homewards *UK*, household, inglenook, residence, Secretary; **10** background, birthplace, fatherland, motherland; **11** environment, institution, residential; **13** establishment; PHRASES: **4, 2** zoom in; **4, 5, 4** ~ sweet ~; **5, 2, 5** place of birth; **6, 3, 4** hearth and ~; **6, 4** family unit, native land; **6, 6** family circle.

home (at home) 2 in; PHRASES: **2, 3, 8** on the premises; **2, 9** in residence.

homecoming *See* **return**

homespun *See* **plain**

homestead *See* **farm**

homework 5 study; **6** lesson; **8** exercise, research; **10** assignment, groundwork, schoolwork; **11** preparation; PHRASES: **7, 2** reading up.

homicide 6 murder; **7** killing; **8** genocide, regicide; **9** matricide, parricide, patricide, slaughter, uxoricide; **10** fratricide, sororicide; **11** infanticide, tyrannicide; **12** manslaughter; **13** assassination; PHRASES: **6, 9** ethnic cleansing.

homily *See* **lecture**

homogeneous 4 same; **5** equal; **6** stable; **7** regular, similar, uniform; **8** constant; **10** consistent; **12** standardized.

homosexual 3 gay; **4** drag; **7** lesbian,

Sapphic, tribade; **8** bisexual; **9** homophile; **11** transsexual; **12** transvestite.

hone 4 file, whet; **5** grind; **6** polish, refine; **7** enhance, improve, perfect, sharpen.

honest 4 fair, good, open, true; **5** frank, moral; **6** candid, decent, direct; **7** genuine, sincere, upright; **8** reliable, truthful; **9** authentic, heartfelt, honorable; **10** scrupulous; **11** responsible, trustworthy; **15** straightforward; PHRASES: **3-7** law-abiding.

honesty 5 honor, truth; **6** candor; **8** moonwort, morality, veracity; **9** integrity, rectitude, sincerity; **11** reliability; **12** authenticity. *See also* **honest**

honeycomb 9 reticulum.

honeyed 4 soft; **5** candy, sweet; **6** dulcet, sugary; **7** blarney, cloying, fawning, melodic; **8** pleasing, soothing; **9** melodious; **10** flattering, persuasive, saccharine; **11** mellifluous; **12** ingratiating; PHRASES: **4-7** softsoaping; **5-6** sugar-coated; **5-7** honeytongued, sweet-talking; **6-7** smoothtongued.

honeysuckle 8 woodbine.

honor 4 pips, star; **5** award, badge, order, pride, spurs, title, toast, value; **6** credit, degree, esteem, garter, knight, regard, renown, repute, revere; **7** decency, dignity, fulfill, glorify, lionize, respect, stripes, tribute; **8** nobility, venerate; **9** integrity, medallion, principle, rectitude, reverence; **10** admiration, compliment, decoration, reputation; **11** certificate, distinction, remembrance, uprightness; **12** commendation; **13** commemoration, righteousness; **14** scrupulousness; PHRASES: **3, 6, 2** pay homage to; **3, 7, 2** pay tribute to; **4, 4** gold star, good name; **4, 6** blue ribbon; **5, 2** stick to; **5, 3** carry out. *See also* **honors**

honorable 4 fair, good, just, open, true; **5** frank, loyal, moral, noble, overt, plain, right, sound; **6** candid, decent, direct, honest, square, trusty, worthy; **7** devoted, dutiful, ethical, sincere, upfront, upright; **8** constant, laudable, manifest, reliable, sporting, straight, truthful; **9** admirable, equitable, impartial, righteous, steadfast, veracious; **10** chivalrous, dependable, principled, scrupulous, upstanding; **11** gentlemanly, respectable, responsible, trustworthy, unambiguous; **12** praiseworthy; **13** conscientious, incorruptible, sportsmanlike; **15** straightforward; PHRASES: **2, 3, 5** on the level; **3-7** law-abiding; **4, 3, 6** fair and square; **4, 4** bona fide; **4-4** true-blue; **4-6** high-minded; **4-7** fair-dealing; **4-10** high-principled; **5, 5** above board; **5-6** plain-spoken; **8, 2** straight up.

honorable (be honorable) **4, 2, 3, 5** play by the rules; **4, 2, 4, 2, 2** tell it like it is; **4, 3** fear God; **4, 3, 5** tell the truth; **4, 4, 7** keep one's promise; **4, 5** keep faith; **4, 6** deal fairly; **5, 2, 3, 5** stick to the rules; **5, 3, 5** speak the truth; **5, 7** speak plainly; **5, 8** shoot straight.

honorary **5** token; **6** unpaid; **7** amateur, nominal, titular, unwaged *UK*; **8** symbolic; **9** voluntary; **10** unsalaried.

honors **4** gong *UK*; **5** award, favor, medal, prize; **6** battle, degree, ribbon; **8** accolade; **PHRASES: 3, 5** cum laude; **5, 3, 5** summa cum laude.

hooded crow **5-4** scald-crow.

hoodlum **4** thug; **6** vandal; **8** criminal, gangster; **10** lawbreaker.

hoodwink *See* **trick**

hoof **6** ungula.

hoofed mammal **2** ox; **3** cow, hog, pig; **4** deer, goat, suid; **5** bovid, camel, horse, llama, okapi, sheep, tapir; **6** bovine, cattle, cervid *UK*; **7** camelid, giraffe; **8** hyracoid, ruminant, ungulate; **9** dromedary; **10** camelopard, rhinoceros; **11** artiodactyl; **12** hippopotamus; **13** perissodactyl.

hook **3** eye, fix, peg; **4** boat, fish, meat, nail; **5** catch; **6** anchor, attach, button, fasten, hanger, secure, sickle; **8** fishhook.

hookah **6** kalian; **8** narghile; **PHRASES: 5, 4** water pipe; **6-6** hubble-bubble.

hooked **4** bent, keen; **5** bowed; **6** curved; **7** angular, curving, married; **8** aquiline, obsessed; **10** infatuated, passionate; **12** enthusiastic.

hooligan **4** thug; **7** hoodlum; **8** criminal, gangster; **10** lawbreaker.

hoop *See* **ring**

hoot **3** cry, gas *UK*; **4** beep, blow, honk, howl, riot, roar, toot; **5** blare, blast, laugh, shout, whoop; **6** scream; **PHRASES: 3, 3** cry out; **8, 5** laughing stock *UK*.

hop **3** leg; **4** jump, leap, skip, trip; **5** bound, dance, disco, party, stage; **6** flight, social, spring; **7** journey; **PHRASES: 4, 5** barn dance.

hope **3** ray; **4** goal, last, long, plan, pray, want, wish; **5** dream, faint, faith, trust,

yearn; **6** assume, chance, desire, expect; **7** believe, courage; **8** buoyancy, optimism, prospect; **9** potential; **10** anticipate, aspiration, confidence, likelihood; **11** expectation, hopefulness, possibility; **12** anticipation; **PHRASES: 4, 2** bank on, rely on; **4-6, 4** rose-tinted view; **4, 7** rest assured; **4, 7, 2** look forward to; **4, 7, 4** ~ against ~; **4, 9** feel confident; **5, 2** count on; **6, 4** bright side; **6, 6** silver lining; **7, 8** wishful thinking.

hope (lose hope) **5** doubt; **7** despair; **PHRASES: 4, 2** give up; **4, 5** lose heart; **5, 3** write off; **5, 3, 5, 2** think the worst of; **5, 10** think negatively.

hopeful **2** up; **4** rosy, sure; **6** hoping, likely, upbeat; **7** budding, bullish, buoyant, certain; **8** aspirant, cheerful, desirous, positive, sanguine; **9** applicant, candidate, confident, contender, embryonic, expectant, potential, promising; **10** auspicious, optimistic, propitious; **11** prospective; **12** anticipative; **PHRASES: 4, 2, 4** full of hope; **5-2** would-be; **6-4** starry-eyed.

hopeful (be hopeful) **4, 2** buck up; **4, 4, 5, 2** keep one's hopes up; **4, 5** take heart; **4, 7** keep smiling; **5, 2** cheer up; **5, 3, 3** never say die; **5, 4** touch wood.

hopefully **3, 5, 4** all being well; **4, 1, 3, 2, 4** with a bit of luck; **4, 3, 4** with any luck; **4, 4** with hope. *See also* **hopeful**

hopeless **3** bad, low; **5** bleak, inept; **6** broken, doomed, gloomy, morose; **7** forlorn, useless; **8** clueless, defeated, dejected, desolate, downcast, negative, pathetic, suicidal, unviable; **9** cheerless, defeatist, depressed, desperate, fruitless, incurable, miserable; **10** despairing, despondent, impervious, impossible, inoperable, unfeasible, unworkable; **11** comfortless, downhearted, impractical, incompetent, insuperable, irreparable, irrevocable, unreachable; **12** disconsolate, impenetrable, inaccessible, irredeemable, unachievable, unattainable; **13** irrecoverable; **14** insurmountable; **PHRASES: 2, 3, 8** in the doldrums; **2, 7** in despair; **4, 2, 3, 5** down at the mouth, down in the dumps; **7, 4** without hope.

hopelessly **4** very; **7** totally, utterly; **8** terribly; **10** completely; **PHRASES: 2, 7** in despair. *See also* **hopeless**

hopelessness **5** doubt, gloom; **6** misery; **7** despair; **8** cynicism, futility; **9** defeatism, dejection, inability, pessimism; **10** depression, ineptitude, melancholy, negativism, skepticism; **11** desperation, despondency; **12** incompetence; **13** impossibility, inoperability, unfeasibility, unworkability; **14** discouragement, impracticality, insuperability, unavailability; **15** impenetrability, inaccessibility, unattainability; PHRASES: **2, 4** no hope; **4, 2, 4** lack of hope, loss of hope; **4-5** self-doubt; **5, 3, 4** gloom and doom. *See also* **hopeless**

hopeless situation 6 downer; **7** letdown; **8** quandary; **11** predicament; **14** disappointment; PHRASES: **4, 5** lost cause; **5-2** catch-22; **5-3** write-off; **5, 7** bleak outlook; **6, 5** dashed hopes.

hoper 7 dreamer, hopeful, utopian, wannabe; **8** aspirant, idealist, optimist; **9** Pollyanna.

horde *See* **throng**

horehound 9 bugleweed.

horizontal 4 even, flat; **5** flush, level, lying, plane; **6** planar, smooth, supine; **7** tabular; **8** straight; **9** reclining, sprawling; PHRASES: **4, 2, 1, 7** flat as a pancake; **4, 2, 4, 4** flat on one's back.

horizontal (be horizontal) 3 lie; **6** grovel, sprawl; **7** recline; PHRASES: **2, 4, 4** on one's back; **6-5** spread-eagle.

horizontal (make horizontal) 3 lay; **4** even, fell, iron, raze; **5** flush, grade, level, plane, press; **6** smooth, spread; **7** flatten; **8** equalize, smoothen; **9** prostrate; PHRASES: **4, 2, 3, 6** raze to the ground; **4, 3** roll out; **4, 4** beat flat; **5, 3** level out; **5, 4** knock down, tread flat; **6, 3** smooth out; **6, 4** squash flat; **7, 4** trample down.

horizontal bar 5 swing, vault; **6** finish; **7** balance, landing; **8** straddle, upstarts; **9** handstand, pirouette; **10** somersault; PHRASES: **3, 5** guy wires; **4, 4** full turn; **8, 4** parallel bars; **8, 5** backward swing.

horizontality 10 accumbency, decumbency, recumbency; **11** prostration; **14** horizontalness. *See also* **horizontal**

horizontally 8 flatways; **10** lengthways, lengthwise; PHRASES: **2, 3, 4** on its side. *See also* **horizontal**

hormone 3 sex; **7** insulin, steroid; **8** androgen, dopamine, estrogen; **9** endocrine, pheromone, releasing; **11** ectohormone; **12** gonadotropic, gonadotropin, neurohormone; **13** catecholamine, prostaglandin; **14** corticosteroid, glucocorticoid; PHRASES: **8, 7** anabolic steroid.

horn 4 butt, tusk; **5** alarm, alert, bugle, point, siren; **6** antler, buzzer, hooter, Klaxon, rattle; **7** bleeper *UK*, trumpet, whistle; **10** bullroarer *UK*, projection.

horned viper 3 asp; PHRASES: **4, 5** sand viper.

horny 7 callous, lustful; **8** corneous.

horologically 2 a.m., p.m.; **6** o'clock; **14** annalistically; **15** chronologically; PHRASES: **2, 3, 5** by the clock; **2, 4, 4** at that hour, at that time, at this hour, at this time.

horology 11 clockmaking, watchmaking.

horoscope 4 star; **5** chart.

horrible 3 bad; **4** vile; **5** awful, nasty; **6** horrid; **7** ghastly, hideous; **8** dreadful, horrific, shocking, terrible; **9** appalling, atrocious, frightful, repulsive; **10** disgusting, horrendous; **11** unspeakable.

horrid *See* **horrible**

horrid 4 vile; **5** awful, nasty; **8** dreadful, horrific, shocking; **9** appalling, frightful; **10** disgusting.

horrific *See* **horrible**

horrify 5 shock; **6** appall, dismay, revolt, sicken; **7** depress, disgust, disturb, perplex.

horripilation 5, 5 goose flesh.

horror 4 fear; **5** shock; **6** dismay; **7** disgust; **9** revulsion.

hors d'oeuvre 4 pâté; **5** mezze, raita *UK*, snack; **6** canapé, entrée, hummus, samosa; **7** nibbles *UK*, starter; **8** crudités; **9** antipasto, appetizer; **11** smorgasbord; PHRASES: **3-2-4** vol-au-vent; **5, 6** first course; **6, 8** shrimp cocktail.

horse 2 GG; **3** bay, cob, dam, dun, nag, pad, sea; **4** Arab, cart, colt, dark, foal, gray, hack, hock, hoof, iron, jade, mane, mare, plug, pole, pony, post, roan, sire, stud, wild; **5** black, brass, croup, draft, filly, flank, laugh, light, mount, opera, pacer, pinto, river, sense, shank, shire, steed, stock, wheel, white; **6** ambler, Bayard, bronco, brumby *Aus*, cayuse, county, dobbin, Exmoor, guards, heroin, hunter, jennet, knight, marine, Morgan, nettle, saddle, Silver, sorrel, Trojan, Velvet, winged, wooden; **7** Arabian, charger, charley, courser, Criollo, fetlock, foreleg, gelding, hackney, liberty, mustang, palfrey, pastern, Pegasus, piebald, quarter, rocking, Sheltie, trading, Trigger, trotter, withers; **8** bangtail, Camargue, Champion, chestnut, Dartmoor, forelock, mackerel, mushroom, palomino, roadster, skewbald, stallion, warhorse, yearling; **9** Appaloosa, Connemara, Falabella, Houyhnhnm, packhorse, Percheron, quadruped, racehorse, Rosinante, workhorse; **10** Clydesdale, Hanoverian, horseflesh, Lippizaner; **11** Przewalski's; **12** hindquarters, thoroughbred; **PHRASES: 2, 5** Al Borak; **3-3** gee-gee *UK*, pad-nag; **3, 4** cow pony; **3, 6** New Forest; **4, 4** polo pony; **5, 2, 6** beast of burden; **5, 3** Welsh cob; **5, 4** Black Bess, brood mare *UK*; **5, 5** shire ~; **5, 6** Black Beauty; **5, 8** Welsh mountain; **6-4** dapple-gray; **7, 5** Arabian ~, Suffolk Punch; **8, 4** Shetland pony; **9, 3** Cleveland bay; **9, 7, 5** Tennessee Walking H~; **10, 4** strawberry roan.

horse bean 5, 4 broad bean.

horse mackerel 6 saurel.

horseman 3 vet; **5** groom, rider; **6** cowboy, drover, gaucho, hussar, jockey, knight, lancer, ostler; **7** breaker, centaur, Cossack, cowgirl, dragoon, eventer, farrier, loriner, Mountie, saddler, trainer; **8** buckaroo, cavalier, huntsman, jockette; **9** bookmaker, caballero, postilion; **10** blacksmith, cavalryman *UK*, equestrian, roughrider; **12** equestrienne; **13** steeplechaser; **PHRASES: 5, 6** horse doctor; **6, 3** stable boy *UK*; **6, 6** knight errant; **6-6** bronco-buster; **6, 7** racing steward.

horsemanship 6 manège, racing *UK*, riding; **8** dressage, eventing, gymkhana; **10** equitation; **11** horseracing; **13** equestrianism; **14** horsewomanship, steeplechasing; **PHRASES: 4, 6** high school; **4, 7** show jumping; **4, 8** pony trekking; **5-2-5** point-to-point; **5, 4** horse show; **5, 5** haute école *Fr*; **5, 6** horse riding; **8, 6** bareback riding; **9, 6** classical riding.

horseracing 3 bet, win; **4** flat, form, leap, meet, Oaks, odds, post, show, tote, turf; **5** Derby, entry, evens *UK*, jumps, place, price, silks, start; **6** double, exacta, fences, finish, jumper, maiden, ringer, runner, stayer, sticks; **7** betting, blinder, hurdler, hurdles, paddock, scratch, sleeper, weights; **8** favorite, handicap, outsider, perfecta, sprinter, trifecta, walkaway, walkover; **9** certainty, objection, pacemaker, Preakness, racetrack; **10** racecourse; **11** horseplayer, teletheater, totalisator *UK*; **12** Standardbred, steeplechase; **14** steeple-

chasing; **PHRASES: 2, 5** St Leger *UK*; **2-8** co-favorite; **3, 4** the Turf; **3, 5** the field; **3-5, 4** two-horse race; **4-2, 3** odds-on bet; **4-3** also-ran; **4-3, 3** each-way bet; **4, 4** dead heat, race card; **4, 5** dark horse, dirt track, sure thing; **4, 6** flat racing; **4-6** pari-mutuel; **4, 7** race meeting *UK*; **5, 2** weigh in; **5, 2, 5** sport of kings; **5-2-5** point-to-point; **5, 6** photo finish; **5, 7** mixed meeting; **5, 8** Grand National *UK*, joint favorite; **6, 4** Jockey Club, maiden race, racing form; **6, 5** racing track; **6, 6** hurdle racing; **6, 9** weight allowance; **7, 5** scratch sheet; **7, 8** English Classics; **8, 4** futurity race, National Hunt, weighing room; **8, 5** Kentucky Derby; **8, 6** starter's orders, training tracks *Aus*; **8, 7** antepost betting.

horse-riding terms 3 bit; **4** shoe, tack, whip; **5** reins; **6** bridle, livery, numnah, saddle, stable; **8** blinkers, farriery, grooming, noseband; **9** currycomb, neckstrap; **PHRASES: 4, 5** tail guard; **4, 6** side saddle; **5, 3** horse box; **5, 6** stock saddle *Aus*; **5-7** horse-trading; **6, 6** racing saddle, riding school; **7, 6** English saddle; **8, 6** American saddle.

horseshoe 3 arc; **4** bend, loop; **5** curve, token; **6** amulet, mascot; **8** crescent, talisman; **PHRASES: 5, 5** lucky charm.

horticultural 6 annual, cereal, exotic, floral, garden, herbal, sylvan; **7** botanic, flowery, nursery, vegetal; **8** arboreal, biennial, dendroid, tropical; **9** arborical, perennial, succulent, vegetable; **10** florescent, herbaceous, hydroponic, leguminous, ornamental, uniflorous, vegetative; **11** farinaceous, pomological, subtropical; **12** agricultural, aquicultural, efflorescent, multiflorous, vinicultural, viticultural; **13** floricultural, silvicultural; **14** arboricultural; **PHRASES: 2, 5** in bloom; **5, 4** truck farm; **6, 6** market garden.

horticulture 8 fruitage, pomology; **9** gardening; **11** agriculture, cultivation, hydroponics, pomiculture, propagation, viniculture, viticulture; **12** citriculture, floriculture, silviculture; **13** arboriculture; **PHRASES: 6, 9** market gardening *UK*.

horticulture (practise horticulture) 6 garden; **9** cultivate, landscape; **PHRASES: 4, 5** grow fruit; **4, 10** grow vegetables.

horticulturist 7 fruiter; **8** gardener, rosarian, seedsman *UK*, vigneron *Fr*; **9** plantsman, topiarist; **10** landscaper, nurseryman, orchardist, pomologist; **11** landscapist; **13**

viniculturist; **14** floriculturist; **15** arboriculturist; PHRASES: **3, 6** hop picker; **4, 6** rose grower; **5, 6** fruit farmer; **5-8** under-gardener; **6, 8** market gardener; **9, 6** vegetable grower.

hose 4 bath, lave *UK*, line, pipe, soak, tube, wash; **5** bathe, spray, water; **6** douche, garden, inject, shower, sluice, sponge, squirt; **7** syringe; **8** hosepipe *UK*; **9** stockings; PHRASES: **4, 4** wash down.

hospitable (be hospitable) 5 carve, greet, serve; **7** embrace, shelter, welcome; **9** entertain, introduce; PHRASES: **2, 3, 6** do the honors; **3, 2** ask in; **4, 2** take in; **4, 2, 5** take on board; **4, 4, 5, 2** open one's doors to; **4, 5** have round; **4, 7, 2** give shelter to; **5, 1, 4, 2** grant a visa to; **5, 2** allow in; **5, 5** clasp hands, shake hands.

hospital 1 H; **3** bed, CSH, ITU (intensive therapy unit), spa; **4** CASH, HOPE, MASH, ship, tent, ward; **5** baths, hydro; **6** asylum, clinic, mental, women's; **7** cottage, general, hospice, private, scanner, sickbay, sickbed, surgery; **8** sickroom, teaching; **9** ambulance, children's, infirmary, lazaretto, maternity, stretcher; **10** dispensary, polyclinic, respirator, sanatorium; PHRASES: **2, 7** CT scanner; **3, 5** NHS trust; **3-7** out-patient; **4, 4** iron lung, rest home; **4-4, 6** well-baby clinic; **4-5, 6** well-woman clinic; **5-3, 7** first-aid station; **5-5** lazar-house; **6, 3** ripple bed; **6, 4** oxygen tent; **6, 6** health center; **6, 7** kidney machine; **7, 4** medical mall, nursing home; **7, 6** medical center; **8, 6** prenatal clinic; **8, 7** dressing station *UK*; **9, 4** emergency room, isolation ward, operating room; **9, 5** operating table; **10, 4** consulting room.

hospitality 6 warmth; **7** welcome; **8** kindness; **10** generosity; **12** friendliness.

host 2 MC; **4** army, fete, hold, mass; **5** crowd, emcee, horde, swarm; **6** invite, regale, throng; **7** compère, present; **8** landlady, landlord; **9** announcer, entertain, introduce, multitude, presenter *UK*; **11** accommodate, entertainer; **12** congregation; PHRASES: **3, 2** lay on, put on.

hostel 3 inn; **5** hotel, motel; **6** refuge; **7** shelter; **9** dosshouse *UK*, flophouse; **10** guesthouse *UK*; PHRASES: **8, 5** boarding house.

hostile 3 icy; **4** acid, cold, cool, mean, sour, tart; **5** acrid, aloof, catty, harsh, nasty, sharp, snide, tense; **6** acidic, bitchy, biting, bitter, cussed; **7** acerbic, adverse, baneful, beastly, caustic, cutting, eristic, feuding, jealous, mordant, opposed, warlike, waspish; **8** brawling, contrary, fighting, inimical, piercing, spiteful, stinging, venomous, virulent; **9** bellicose, envenomed, malicious, poisonous, polemical, rancorous, resentful, sarcastic, splenetic, truculent, vitriolic; **10** aggressive, antisocial, malevolent, mordacious, pugnacious, unfriendly, unpleasant, vindictive; **11** acrimonious, belligerent, penetrating, provocative, unfavorable, unreceptive, unwelcoming; **12** antagonistic, antipathetic, inhospitable, intimidating; **13** unsympathetic; PHRASES: **2, 3** at war; **2, 6** in battle; **3-8** ill-disposed; **6-6** bloody-minded *UK*.

hot 3 air, dog, new, rod; **4** line, mild, seat, spot, warm; **5** angry, fiery, fresh, metal, money, muggy, spicy, stuff, tepid; **6** ardent, baking, fierce, heated, molten, pepper, piping, potato, spiced, spring, strong, sultry, torrid; **7** boiling, burning, candent, chambré, fervent, glowing, intense, peppery, piquant, pungent, searing, sweltry, thermal, warming; **8** lukewarm, roasting, scalding, sizzling, stifling, tropical, vehement; **9** calorific, emotional, excitable, scorching; **10** blistering, equatorial, oppressive, passionate, smoldering, sweltering; **11** calefacient, subtropical, suffocating; **12** incandescent; PHRASES: **2, 3, 4** on the boil; **3-3** red-hot; **5-3** white-hot.

hot (be or make hot) 3 fry, lag; **4** bake, boil, cook, glow, heat, melt, stew, thaw, warm, weld; **5** broil, deice, grill, parch, roast, scald, smelt, steam, toast; **6** braise, reheat, simmer, solder, wither; **7** defrost, parboil, shrivel; **8** insulate; PHRASES: **4, 2** heat up, warm up; **4, 4** melt down; **4, 7** heat through; **5, 4, 4** stamp one's feet; **6, 5** double glaze.

hotel 3 inn, pub *UK*; **5** local, lodge, motel; **6** boozer, hostel, tavern; **7** fleabag, pension *Fr*; **8** hostelry; **10** guesthouse *UK*; PHRASES: **1, 3, 1** B and B; **3, 3, 5** bed and board; **3, 3, 9** bed and breakfast; **4, 5** desk clerk; **5, 3** motor inn; **5, 3, 7** board and lodging; **5, 6** youth hostel; **7, 5** capsule ~, lodging house *UK*; **8, 4** American plan, European plan; **8, 5** boarding house, boutique ~.

hot place 4 Etna, Gobi, Hell, lava; **5** magma, sauna; **6** Africa, desert, geyser, hotbed, jungle, Sahara; **7** equator, inferno, sirocco, sunbelt, thermae, tropics, volcano; **8** hellfire, hothouse, Kalahari, Vesuvius; **9**

caldarium; **10** greenhouse, subtropics; **12** conservatory; **13** Mediterranean; PHRASES: **3-3, 7** hot-air current; **3, 4** hot spot, sun deck; **3, 5** sun porch; **3, 6** hot spring; **4, 6** Gulf Stream, rain forest; **4, 7** warm current; **5, 4** south wind; **5, 6** Death Valley; **6, 4** boiler room; **6, 5** Amazon Basin; **7, 4** Turkish bath.

hot seat 8, 5 electric chair.

hound 3 dog; **5** chase; **6** harass, pester, pursue; **8** foxhound; **9** deerhound, persecute, wolfhound; PHRASES: **6, 5** basset ~.

hour 4 rush, zero; **5** happy, lunch; **8** eleventh, sidereal, witching.

hourglass 6 figure; **9** sandglass; PHRASES: **3, 5** egg timer.

house 3 ice, pad, row; **4** clan, firm, flat *UK*, free, full, hold, home, keep, line, loft, open, safe, semi, town, wash; **5** abode, attic, bothy *UK*, cabin, coach, dower, guest, igloo, jacal, lodge, Lords, manor, opera, organ, party, plant, ranch, shack, stock, store, story, upper, villa, wendy, White; **6** arrest, bedsit *UK*, chalet, coffee, custom, duplex, family, grange *UK*, lights, martin, palace, public, retain, spider, studio; **7** address, areaway, charnel, chateau, chattel, Commons, company, contain, cottage, country, dynasty, fashion, forcing, halfway, issuing, lodging, mansion, meeting, picture, rooming, saltbox, shelter, simplex, sparrow, station, Trinity; **8** boarding, building, bungalow, business, clearing, counting, detached, discount, domicile, dwelling, hacienda, software, terraced; **9** accepting, Admiralty *UK*, apartment, community, farmhouse, homestead, household, penthouse, physician, rainspout, residence, timeshare; **10** disorderly, maisonette *UK*; **11** accommodate, corporation, partnership; **12** semidetached; **13** establishment; PHRASES: **2-3, 5** in-law suite; **3, 2** put up; **3-2-3-4** two-up-two-down; **3, 5** log cabin; **4-1-5** pied-à-terre *Fr*; **4, 2** take in; **4-2-4** back-to-back; **4, 3** Cape Cod; **4, 4** love nest; **4, 5** milk ~; **4-6** half-dugout; **4, 7, 2** give shelter to; **5, 5** storm sewer, tract ~; **5-5** split-level; **5, 7** ~ trailer; **6, 4** garden flat *UK*, granny flat, mobile home; **6, 8** dormer bungalow; **6, 9** duplex apartment, garden apartment, studio apartment; **7, 4** starter home, stately home *UK*; **7, 5** shotgun ~; **7, 6** Persian blinds; **8, 4** railroad flat; **8, 9** bachelor apartment; **9, 9** accessory apartment; **10, 9** efficiency apartment; **12, 4** manufactured home.

household 4 home; **5** house; **6** family; **8** domestic, everyday; **11** domiciliary; PHRASES: **6, 4** family unit; **6, 6** family circle.

householder 5 guest, owner; **6** lessee, lodger, roomer, tenant; **7** boarder, visitor; **8** flatmate *UK*, roommate; **9** addressee; **10** freeholder; **11** leaseholder; PHRASES: **5-8** owner-occupier; **6, 5** paying guest *UK*; **7, 6** sitting tenant *UK*.

housel 9 Eucharist.

house of ill repute 7 brothel.

housework 7 dusting, laundry, tidying, washing; **8** sweeping; **9** hoovering, polishing, scrubbing, vacuuming; PHRASES: **6-8** spring-cleaning; **7-2** washing-up *UK*; **8, 2** clearing up.

housing 4 case, home; **5** board, cover, frame; **6** casing; **7** lodging, shelter; **8** covering; **14** accommodations.

hover 3 fly; **4** hang, soar; **5** craft, drift, float, poise, tower; **6** linger, loiter; **8** levitate; PHRASES: **4, 4** loom over.

how 2 as, so; **4** like, thus; **6** anyhow, anyway; **7** anywise, however, somehow; **10** regardless; **11** nonetheless; **12** irregardless, nevertheless; PHRASES: **2, 3, 5, 2** on the lines of; **2, 4, 3** in what way; **2, 4, 5** by what means; **2, 4, 6** by what method, in what manner; **5, 1, 7** after a fashion; **5, 5, 5** along these lines; **7, 2, 5** somehow or other.

however 3 but, yet; **5** still; **6** howe'er, though; **9** howsoever; **10** conversely; **11** nonetheless; **12** nevertheless; PHRASES: **2, 3, 5, 4** on the other hand; **2, 5, 2, 4** in spite of this; **4, 5** then again.

howl 3 bay, cry; **4** wail, yowl; **6** scream, shriek.

HP 10 horsepower; PHRASES: **4, 8** hire purchase; **5, 9** hardy perennial *UK*.

Huang Hai 6, 3 Yellow Sea; **6, 5** Yellow River.

hub 4 boss, core; **5** focus, heart, pivot; **6** center, middle; **7** nucleus; PHRASES: **5, 5** focal point.

hubble-bubble 6 hookah.

hubbub *See* **noise**

hubby 7 husband.

huckleberry 9 blueberry; **12** whortleberry.

huddle 3 set; **4** bend, knot, mass, read, snap; **5** bunch, clump, cower, crowd, group, hunch; **6** crouch, jumble, nestle; **7** cluster, signals; PHRASES: **4, 2** curl up; **4, 4** line call; **4, 8** come together; **5, 5** quick count; **5, 8** crowd together; **6, 8** gather together; **7, 2** snuggle up.

hue 4 cast, kind, pale, sort, tint, tone, type, warm; **5** color, shade, tinge, value; **6** chroma, manner, patina; **7** variety; **8** darkness, dullness, softness, tincture; **9** intensity, mezzotint; **10** brilliance, luminosity, saturation; **12** chromaticity; **13** discoloration; PHRASES: **4-4** half-tone; **4-5** half-light; **5, 7** color quality.

huff 4 blow, gasp, mood, pant, puff, rant, sulk; **5** gripe; **6** temper, wheeze; **7** bluster, grumble; **8** complain; PHRASES: **3, 2, 5** fit of pique; **3, 4** bad mood.

hug 4 bear, hold; **5** clasp; **6** clinch, cuddle, enfold; **7** embrace, squeeze; PHRASES: **4, 5** hold close.

huge 4 vast; **5** giant; **7** amazing, awesome, massive; **8** enormous, gigantic; **10** incredible, phenomenal; PHRASES: **4-7** mind-blowing.

hulk 4 ogre; **5** frame, giant, shell, titan, wreck; **7** carcass, goliath; **8** colossus, skeleton.

hull 4 body, keel; **6** casing; **8** exterior; **9** underside.

hullabaloo See **noise**

hum 4 buzz, purr, whir; **5** drone, whine; **6** murmur; **7** vibrate; **9** bombinate *UK*, vibration.

human 5 being; **6** bionic, ethnic, mortal, nature, person, racial, rights, social; **7** hominid; **8** creature, hominoid, humanoid, interest, personal; **9** civilized, earthborn, resources, tellurian; **10** anthropoid, individual; **14** ethnographical; **15** anthropocentric, anthropological, anthropomorphic; PHRASES: **4, 7** Homo sapiens.

human (make human) 8 civilize, humanize.

humanity 5 mercy; **6** people; **7** charity; **8** kindness, sympathy; **9** humankind, mortality; **10** compassion; PHRASES: **5, 4** human race.

humankind 2 us; **3** man, men; **4** folk; **6** people; **7** hominid, mankind; **8** everyone, humanity; **9** everybody, mortality, ourselves, womankind; **10** earthlings; PHRASES: **3, 5** the quick, the world; **3, 6** the living; **4, 7** Homo sapiens; **5, 4** human race; **5, 6** human

beings; **5, 6, 4** every living soul.

humanly 8 feasibly, mortally, socially; **10** personally, physically, **12** individually; **13** realistically; **15** internationally; PHRASES: **2, 3** at all; **2, 3, 3** in any way; **2, 3, 5** by any means.

human nature 5 flesh; **7** frailty; **8** weakness; **9** mortality; **11** fallibility.

humanoid 5 robot; **6** cyborg; **7** android; **9** automaton; PHRASES: **6, 3** bionic man; **6, 5** bionic woman.

human resources 5 staff; **7** workers; **8** manpower; **9** personnel; PHRASES: **4, 2, 5** pool of labor; **4, 5** work force.

human society 5 caste, elite; **6** family, gentry, public; **7** commune, mankind; **8** humanity, nobility; **9** community, humankind; **11** aristocracy; PHRASES: **3-6, 6** one-parent family; **4, 5** beau monde, peer group; **4, 6** home circle; **4, 7** high society; **5, 5** upper class; **6, 3** social set; **6, 5** middle class, social class, social group; **6, 6** family circle, social circle; **7, 5** working class.

humble 3 shy; **4** mean, meek, poor; **5** abase, lower, lowly, shame; **6** debase, demean, modest, simple; **7** chasten, obscure, servile; **9** humiliate; **10** respectful, unassuming; **11** deferential, subservient, unimportant; **13** disadvantaged, unpretentious; **15** underprivileged; PHRASES: **3, 4** put down; **3, 5** not proud; **4-8** self-effacing; **5, 4, 1, 3** bring down a peg; **7, 4** without airs.

humblebee 9 bumblebee.

humbled 6 abject, dashed *UK*; **7** abashed, crushed, hangdog, rebuked, reduced, scorned; **8** debunked, defeated, deflated, degraded, dejected, sheepish; **9** chagrined; **10** diminished, shamefaced; **11** discomfited, embarrassed; **12** disconcerted; PHRASES: **2, 3, 4** in the dust; **2, 4, 5** on one's knees; **3, 4, 2, 4** cut down to size; **4, 3** laid low; **5, 4** bowed down; **6-8** broken-spirited; **7, 4** brought down, slapped down. *See also* **humble**

humble person 4 wimp; **5** mouse; **9** sycophant; PHRASES: **2, 7** no boaster; **5, 4** Uriah Heep; **9, 6** shrinking violet.

humbug 4 lies; **6** deceit; **7** garbage, rubbish; **8** claptrap, nonsense; **9** deception, gibberish, hypocrisy; **10** propaganda.

humdrum 4 dull; **6** boring; **7** routine; **8** everyday; **10** unexciting.

humid 3 wet; **4** damp, dank; **5** close,

heavy, moist, muggy; **6** clammy, steamy, sticky, sultry, sweaty; **8** tropical; **10** oppressive.

humidity 4 damp; **8** absolute, moisture, relative; **9** humidness; **10** saturation; **14** humidification; PHRASES: **3, 5** dew point. *See also* **humid**

humiliate 3 cut; **4** snub; **5** abash, crush, shame; **6** demean, humble, slight; **7** chasten, degrade, mortify; **8** disgrace, dishonor; **9** embarrass; **10** disconcert; PHRASES: **3, 4** put down; **3, 4, 2, 4** cut down to size; **3, 4, 4, 2, 2** rub one's nose in it; **4, 2** show up; **4, 3, 3, 4** make one eat dirt.

humiliate (be humiliated) 4, 4, 4 hang one's head, hide one's face; **4, 5** feel cheap, feel small; **4, 7** look foolish.

humiliation 5 shame; **7** chagrin; **8** comedown, disgrace, dishonor, ignominy; **9** deflation; **13** embarrassment, mortification; PHRASES: **4, 5** hurt pride; **7, 4** hangdog look; **7, 5** injured pride, wounded pride; **8, 7** offended dignity.

humility 7 modesty, shyness; **8** meekness; **10** humbleness; **12** unimportance; PHRASES: **4-10** self-effacement.

humility (with humility) 6 humbly, meekly.

humming 5 pongy *UK*; **6** smelly, stench, stinky *UK*; **7** whiffy *UK*; **7** buzzing, droning, purring, reeking, whining; **8** stinking, whirring; **9** murmuring, vibrating; **10** malodorous, stridulous; **11** bombination; PHRASES: **4-4** blah-blah; **4-8** foul-smelling.

hummingbird moth 4, 4 hawk moth.

humor 3 ill, wit; **5** sense, spoof; **6** cajole, comedy, cosset, joking, pacify, pamper, satire; **7** aqueous, flatter, gallows, indulge, jesting, placate; **8** hilarity, vitreous; **9** absurdity, cultivate, funniness, patronize, slapstick, wittiness; **10** comicality, condescend; **11** accommodate, comicalness; PHRASES: **2, 5, 4** go along with; **3, 5, 4** the funny side; **4, 2, 2** suck up to *UK*; **4-4** soft-soap; **5, 2, 3** sense of fun; **6, 2** butter up; **6, 5** string along.

humor (person who humors) 5 creep, toady; **9** flatterer, sycophant; **10** bootlicker.

humorist 3 wag, wit; **5** clown, comic, joker, tease; **6** jester, teaser; **7** buffoon, gagster, ironist, punster, standup; **8** comedian, satirist; **9** jokesmith, lampooner; **10** cartoonist; **11** entertainer, wisecracker; **12** car-

icaturist; **13** impressionist; PHRASES: **3, 6** gag writer; **5-2, 5** stand-up comic; **5-2, 8** stand-up comedian; **8, 3** straight man.

humorless 4 dour, dull, sour; **6** sullen; **7** serious, unfunny; **8** straight; **9** unamusing; PHRASES: **2-5** po-faced *UK*.

humorous 3 dry; **4** zany; **5** comic, corny, droll, funny, jokey, merry, pawky, smart, witty; **6** ironic, jocose, joking, quirky; **7** amusing, comical, jocular, teasing, waggish *UK*; **8** farcical, flippant; **9** facetious, hilarious, sarcastic, satirical, slapstick, whimsical; **11** Pythonesque *UK*; **12** entertaining; PHRASES: **5-6** quick-witted; **6-2-5** tongue-in-cheek.

humorous (be humorous) 3 kid, pun, rag, rib; **4** jest, joke, josh, mock, quip, twit; **5** amuse, clown, tease; **6** banter, divert, parody; **7** lampoon; **8** satirize; **9** entertain; **10** caricature; PHRASES: **4, 2** send up; **4, 3** take off; **4, 3, 2** make fun of, poke fun at; **4, 3, 4** play the fool; **4, 8, 3** pull someone's leg; **5, 1, 4** crack a joke.

humorousness 3 wit; **5** humor; **8** drollery; **9** flippancy. *See also* **humorous**

humors 8 choleric, sanguine; **10** phlegmatic; **11** melancholic.

hump *See* **bulge**

hunch 4 bend; **5** stoop; **6** crouch, huddle; **7** feeling; **9** intuition; **11** premonition; PHRASES: **3, 7** gut feeling; **4, 7** lean forward; **5, 5** sixth sense.

hundred 1 C; **2** ct; **3** cwt, ton; **5** gross; **6** monkey; **7** century, percent; **8** centuple; **9** centenary, centipede, centurion; **10** centennial, centennium, centesimal, centigrade, centimeter; **11** centenarian, hundredfold; **12** centuplicate; **13** hundredweight.

hunger 4 long, need, wish; **5** binge, crave, greed, yearn; **6** desire, famine, hanker, thirst; **7** bolting, craving, gorging, longing, passion; **8** appetite, feasting, gluttony, gobbling, guzzling; **9** emptiness; **10** famishment, hungriness, overeating, starvation; **11** deprivation, gourmandism; **12** malnutrition, ravenousness; **13** voraciousness; **14** malnourishment, overindulgence; PHRASES: **4, 2, 4** lack of food; **4, 8** food shortage.

hungry 4 avid, keen; **5** eager, empty; **6** driven, greedy; **7** parched, peckish *UK Can*, starved, thirsty; **8** desirous, famished, ravening, ravenous, starving; **9** ambitious, impatient, thrusting *UK*, voracious; PHRASES:

4-7 half-starved.

hungry (be hungry) 5 raven; 6 hunger, starve, thirst; 8 salivate; PHRASES: **4, 4, 4** lick one's lips.

hunt 3 bag, fox, net; 4 beat, drag, fish, fowl, hawk, hook, look, seek, trap; 5 angle, catch, chase, flush, hound, mouse, poach, quest, scout, shoot, stalk, track, trail, trawl, whale; 6 course, follow, forage, guddle *UK*, pursue, safari, search, shrimp; 7 ensnare, pursuit, rummage; 8 scavenge, treasure; 9 deerstalk, scavenger; 10 expedition; 11 reconnoiter; PHRASES: **3-4** fly-fish, ice-fish; **3, 5** lay traps; **4, 2** prey on, reel in; **4, 2, 6** ride to hounds; **4, 3** seek out; **4, 3, 3, 5** play cat and mouse; **4, 4, 3** cast one's net; **4, 5** root about *UK*; **5, 4** start game, track down; **6, 3, 5** follow the chase; **6, 6** ferret around.

hunted person 4 game, prey; 6 quarry, victim; 7 escapee; 8 criminal, deserter, fugitive; PHRASES: **4, 5** lost child; **7, 6** missing person.

hunter 3 gun; 4 deer, duck, hawk, head, lion, pack, shot; 5 Diana, hound, Orion, scout, tiger, white; 6 angler, beater, chaser, dogger *Aus*, falcon, fowler, gundog, hawker, killer, mouser, Nimrod, seeker, whaler; 7 Artemis, beagler, buffalo, forager, poacher, pursuer, stalker, tracker, trapper, trawler; 8 cannibal, falconer, foxhound, huntress, huntsman, marksman, piscator, predator, searcher, shrimper; 9 fisherman, oysterman, sportsman; 10 bloodhound, markswoman, otterhound, trawlerman, wildfowler; 11 deerstalker, sportswoman; 12 sportsperson; PHRASES: **3-4** big-game; **3-5** man-eater; **3-7** rat-catcher; **4, 2, 4** bird of prey; **4, 4** good shot; **4-7** bird-catcher, mole-catcher; **5, 2, 4** beast of prey; **6, 7** grouse shooter; **6, 9** rodent operative; **7-2** whipper-in; **8, 6** compleat angler.

hunting 3 cry, fox; 4 drag, horn, hunt, meet; 5 chase, chivy, decoy, earth, hound, knife, lodge, music, party, scent, shoot, stock; 6 baying, hunter, tongue, venery; 7 beating, Charley, culling, driving, fishing, gunning, killing, ratting, shotgun, whaling; 8 beagling, draghunt, foxhound, shooting, stalking, tracking, trapping; 9 draghound, ferreting, rabbiting *UK*; 10 ammunition, binoculars; 11 pigsticking, piscatorial, wildfowling; 12 bullfighting, deerstalking; PHRASES: **3, 4** fox hunt; **3-4** big-game; **3-8** dog-fighting; **4, 4** deer hunt, lawn meet,

stag hunt; **4, 6** open season; **4, 7** game license; **4-7** bear-baiting; **4, 8** game shooting, hare coursing; **4-8** mole-catching; **5-4** small-game; **5, 5** blood sport, field trial, rifle sling, scope sight; **5, 6** field sports; **5, 7** night lamping, otter ~; **5, 8** rough shooting *UK*; **6, 6** closed season *UK*, hunter trials; **6, 8** grouse shooting; **7, 4** opening meet; **7, 5** ~ rifle; **8-2** sighting-in; **8, 3** shooting box *UK*; **8, 5** shooting party *UK*, shooting stick, sporting rifle; **10, 5** ammunition round, telescopic sight.

hunting and fishing equipment 3 fly, gun; 4 bait, trap; 5 rifle; 7 dragnet, fishnet, keepnet *UK*, shotgun; PHRASES: **3, 3, 4** rod and line, rod and reel; **3, 3, 6** rod and tackle; **7, 3** casting rod, fishing net, fishing rod; **7, 4** fishing line, fishing pole; **7, 5** fowling piece, hunting rifle; **7, 6** fishing tackle.

hunting cry 4 whoa; 6 halloa, halloo, yoicks; 7 tallyho; PHRASES: **3, 2, 3, 5** cry of the chase; **3, 3, 3** hue and cry; **4, 6** view halloo.

hurdle 4 jump, leap, snag; 7 problem; 8 obstacle; 10 difficulty; PHRASES: **4, 4** jump over, leap over; **9, 5** stumbling block.

hurl 3 gag; 4 spew, toss; 5 fling, heave, retch, throw, vomit; 6 launch; PHRASES: **2, 4** be sick.

hurling 4 ball, boss, goal; 5 camán *Gael*, stick; 6 hurley, iomáin *Gael*, shinty; 7 sliotar *Gael*; 8 crossbar; 9 camanachd *Gael*; 11 association; PHRASES: **5, 6** Irish hockey; **8, 6** Scottish hockey.

hurly-burly *See* **commotion**

hurrah 6 huzzah.

hurricane 4 deck, gale, lamp; 5 storm; 7 cyclone, tempest, tornado, typhoon; 9 whirlwind; PHRASES: **8, 5** tropical storm.

hurry 3 cut, lam, run; 4 bolt, dash, flee, rush, skip; 5 haste, panic, scram, speed, split; 6 decamp, flurry, frenzy, hasten, hurtle, hustle; 7 quicken, scarper *UK*, urgency, vamoose; 8 hightail; 9 skedaddle; 10 accelerate; 12 absquatulate; PHRASES: **3, 3** nip off, run off; **3, 3, 3** cut and run; **3, 3, 4, 4** run for one's life; **3, 4** run away; **4, 1, 6** take a powder; **4, 2** beat it *UK*; **4, 2, 4, 5** take to one's heels; **4, 3** dash off, make off, rush off; **4, 4** move fast; **4, 6** take flight; **4, 8** time pressure; **5, 2** speed up; **6, 3** hasten off; **7, 4** scamper away.

hurt 3 cut, hit, jab, mar, rot, sap; 4 ache,

beat, bite, bump, burn, claw, dock, flog, fray, gash, gnaw, harm, kill, lame, maim, maul, pain, rack, ruin, rust, scar, sear, stab, tear; **5** blast, break, chafe, cramp, decay, erode, graze, pinch, pound, scald, shoot, slash, smart, spoil, stain, sting, throb, unman, upset, wince, wound; **6** batter, blight, bruise, censor, damage, deface, flinch, hamper, harrow, hinder, impair, impale, injure, injury, insult, mangle, martyr, misuse, offend, plague, punish, savage, scathe, scotch, sprain, squirm, strain, suffer, thrash, tingle, uglify, weaken, writhe; **7** agonize, blemish, contuse, corrode, crucify, curtail, damnify, deplete, disable, frazzle, injured, offense, scratch, torment, torture, trouble, unhappy, wounded; **8** castrate, distress, fracture, hobbling, lameness, maltreat, mischief, mutilate, offended, puncture, soreness, truncate, weakness; **9** crippling, decompose, disabling, disfigure, expurgate, hamstring, suffering, undermine, weakening; **10** bowdlerize, demoralize, dilapidate, discomfort, eviscerate, excruciate, exhaustion, mutilation, traumatize; **11** disablement, dislocation; **12** whortleberry; **13** injuriousness; **14** demoralization; PHRASES: **2, 4** be sore; **2, 7** be painful; **4, 3** wear out; **4, 3, 5** clip the wings; **4, 4** trim back; **5-5** asset-strip; **5, 7** cause offense; **6, 2, 4** reduce to rags; **6, 6** pulled muscle.

hurtle *See* **hurry**

husband 3 man; **4** mate; **5** hubby; **6** spouse; **7** consort, cuckold, partner; **8** Benedick, bigamist; **10** monogamist, polygamist; **12** househusband; PHRASES: **3, 3** old man; **5, 4** other half.

hush 2 sh; **4** mute, soft; **5** peace, quiet, shush, whist; **7** quieten *UK*, silence; **9** quietness, stillness; **11** tranquility *UK*; PHRASES: **2, 5** be quiet; **3, 1, 4** not a word; **3, 2** can it, dry up; **3, 3, 6** cut the cackle; **4, 2** shut up; **4, 4** pipe down; **4, 4, 6** hold your tongue; **5, 2, 3** knock it off; **5, 6** that's enough; **7, 4** quieten down *UK*.

husk *See* **shell**

hustle 4 push; **5** hurry, shove; **6** jostle, propel; **9** manhandle; PHRASES: **3, 1, 4, 2** get a move on; **3, 5** get going; **3, 8** get cracking; **5, 2** hurry up.

hut *See* **shelter**

huzzah 6 hurrah.

hyacinth 7 jacinth.

hybrid 3 cur, mix; **4** mule, rose; **5** cross, hinny, métis, tigon; **6** Creole, fusion, tiglon; **7** amalgam, mestizo, mixture, mongrel; **8** Eurasian, octaroon, tayberry; **10** clementine, loganberry; **11** boysenberry; PHRASES: **3, 3** cur dog; **4, 5** half blood *Offensive*; **4-5** half-breed *Offensive*; **5-5** cross-breed.

hydrargyrum 7 mercury.

hydrate 9 hydration; **10** hydrolysis; PHRASES: **7, 5** wetting agent.

hydraulic 11 hydrometric, hydroscopic, hydrostatic.

hydraulics 9 hydrology; **10** hydrometry; **12** hydrostatics; **13** hydrodynamics, hydrokinetics.

hydrochloric acid 8, 4 muriatic acid.

hydrography 9 hydrology; **10** hydraulics, hydrometry, hygrometry; **11** aquiculture, hydroponics; **12** hydrostatics; **13** hydrodynamics, hydrokinetics; **14** hydromechanics.

hydrologist 5, 7 water diviner.

hydrophobia 6 rabies.

hydrotherapeutics 10 hydropathy; **12** hydrotherapy; PHRASES: **5, 4** water cure; **6, 3, 6** taking the waters.

hygiene 7 asepsis; **8** immunity; **9** cleanness, hygienics, isolation, sterility; **10** antisepsis, asepticism, fumigation, protection, quarantine, sanatorium, sanitation; **11** cleanliness, inoculation, prophylaxis, vaccination; **12** chlorination, disinfection, immunization, prophylactic, purification, sanitariness, sanitization; **13** sterilization; **14** pasteurization; **15** decontamination; PHRASES: **6, 9** cordon sanitaire *Fr*.

hygienic 4 pure; **5** clean; **6** benign, immune; **7** aseptic, healthy, sterile; **8** harmless, remedial, salutary, sanative, sanitary; **9** healthful, immunized, innocuous, innoxious, protected, sanitized, wholesome; **10** antiseptic, beneficial, immunizing, inoculated, nourishing, nutritious, protective, refreshing, salubrious, sterilized, vaccinated, ventilated; **11** chlorinated, disinfected, pasteurized, restorative; **12** invulnerable, noninjurious, prophylactic; **13** noninfectious; PHRASES: **4-4** germ-free; **4-10** well-ventilated; **6-6** health-giving.

hygienic (make hygienic) 3 dry; **4** boil; **5** clean, drain; **6** aerate, purify; **7** cleanse, freshen, isolate; **8** conserve, fumigate, immunize, preserve, sanitate, sanitize; **9** disinfect, inoculate, sterilize, vaccinate, ventilate; **10** chlorinate, pasteurize, quarantine; **13** antisepticize, decontaminate.

hygienist 6 dental; **9** dietician; **10** sanitarian; **12** nutritionist; PHRASES: **5-3, 5** fresh-air fiend; **6, 9** health inspector; **7, 7** medical officer.

hymn 4 amen, laud, song; **5** carol, chant, extol, motet, paean, psalm, Vedic; **6** anthem, chorus, Gloria, hymnal, mantra, praise; **7** acclaim, cantata, Gradual, Homeric, Hosanna, hymnary, psalter, Rigveda, Sanctus; **8** Alleluia, antiphon, canticle, doxology, eulogize, psalmody, response, Samaveda; **9** celebrate, hymnology, plainsong; **10** Benedicite *UK*, Hallelujah, Magnificat, panegyrize, plainchant; **11** hymnography; PHRASES: **2, 4** Te Deum; **5-7** psalm-singing; **6, 4** gospel song; **6, 5** Gloria Patri; **6, 8** lesser doxology; **7, 8** greater doxology; **8, 3** Jubilate Deo; **9, 5** Ambrosian chant, Gregorian chant.

hyperbole *See* **exaggeration**

hypnotize 8 enthrall, entrance; **9** fascinate, mesmerize, spellbind.

hypocrisy 4 cant, sham, show; **5** guile; **6** bubble, deceit, fakery, humbug, veneer; **7** blarney, mockery, mummery, varnish; **8** artifice, delusion, disguise, flattery, oiliness, pretense, quackery, tokenism; **9** chicanery, deception, duplicity, falseness, mendacity; **10** camouflage, Pharisaism, sanctimony, Tartuffery, Tartuffism; **11** dissembling, insincerity, religiosity; **12** charlatanism, Pecksniffery, unctuousness; **13** artificiality, mountebankery; PHRASES: **3, 7** lip service; **3-9** two-facedness; **4, 4** soft soap; **4-6** playacting; **5, 4** false face, false show; **5-4** sweet-talk; **5, 5** false piety; **5, 7** empty gesture; **6-2-**

5 tongue-in-cheek; **6-7** double-dealing; **6, 8** double standard; **6-8** window-dressing; **7, 4** outward show; **8, 4** cupboard love *UK*; **9, 5** crocodile tears.

hypocrite 3 spy; **4** fake, sham; **5** bogus, fraud, phony *UK*; **6** phoney, pseudo; **8** apostate, pharisee, Tartuffe; **9** charlatan, Pecksniff, pretender; **10** dissembler; PHRASES: **5-5** goody-goody, mealy-mouth; **5, 6** false friend; **6-6** double-dealer; **6, 9** whited sepulchre *UK*.

hypocritical 4 fake, oily, sham; **5** bogus, empty, false, lying, phony *UK*; **6** faking, hollow, phoney, pseudo; **7** mocking; **8** delusive, feigning, unctuous; **9** deceitful, deceptive, dishonest, insincere, Pharisaic, pretended, religiose; **10** artificial, flattering, fraudulent, mendacious, pretending, Tartuffian, tokenistic; **11** counterfeit, dissembling, duplicitous; **12** disingenuous, meretricious, ostentatious, Pecksniffian; **13** dissimulating, sanctimonious; PHRASES: **2-6** so-called; **3-5** two-faced; **3-6** two-timing; **4-7** soft-soaping; **5-5** false-faced; **5-7** mealy-mouthed, sweet-talking; **6-4-4** holier-than-thou; **6-7** double-dealing.

hypocritical (be hypocritical) 4 cant, mock; **5** mouth; **6** delude; **7** conceal, deceive, flatter, pretend; **8** blandish, disguise; **10** camouflage; PHRASES: **3, 3, 7** pay lip service; **4-4** soft-soap; **4, 6** lack candor; **5-4** sweet-talk.

hypothesis testing 11 alternative; **12** significance; PHRASES: **3-6, 4** one-tailed test, two-tailed test; **4, 9** test statistic; **4, 10** null hypothesis; **8-2-3** goodness-of-fit.

hypothetical *See* **theoretical**

hysteria 5 panic; **6** frenzy; **7** emotion, madness; **9** hysterics.

I

I 2 me, us, we; 3 one (Roman numeral); 10 interstate; PHRASES: 1, 3, 1 I and I; 1, 6 I myself; 2, 6, 4 my humble self; 5, 5 yours truly; 6, 3 number one.

ice 4 berg, cool, floe, hail, rime, snow; 5 chill, frost, glaze, sleet, slush; 6 flurry, freeze, icicle; 7 glacier, snowman; 8 blizzard, diamonds, frosting, snowball, snowfall; 9 avalanche, hailstone, hailstorm, snowdrift, snowflake, snowstorm; 10 frostiness; PHRASES: 4, 5 Jack Frost; 5, 3 black ~, shore ~; 5-3 white-out; 5, 6 frost hollow; 6, 2 freeze up; 6, 4 frozen rain; 6, 5 freeze solid.

iceberg 4 berg, floe; 7 growler; PHRASES: 3, 3 sea ice; 3, 4 ice floe, ice pack; 4, 3 pack ice.

Iceland agate 8 obsidian.

ice-skate 4 jump, lift, loop, spin; 5 pairs *UK*, pivot, skate, twist; 6 figure, rocker; 7 lifting, lugeing; 9 pirouette; 3, 4 sit spin, toe jump; 4, 4 axel jump, axel lift, loop jump; 4-7 free-skating, pair-skating; 5, 4 camel spin, lasso lift, split jump, throw axel, twist lift; 5-5 catch-waist, short-track, speed-skate; 5, 6 death spiral; 5, 7 throw salchow; 6, 3 flying axl; 6, 4 change loop; 6-5 figure-skate, shadow-skate, sprint-skate; 7, 4 salchow jump; 9, 4 paragraph loop.

ichthyological 5 fishy, scaly; 8 squamous; 11 piscatorial; 13 piscicultural.

icing 5 glaze; 7 ganache, glazing; 8 freezing, frosting; 10 decoration; PHRASES: 8, 2 freezing up; 8, 4 freezing over.

icon 4 idol, sign, star; 5 image, model; 6 symbol; 7 picture; 8 likeness; 10 embodiment; 14 representation.

icy 5 aloof; 6 frosty, frozen; 7 distant, hostile, subzero; 8 freezing; 10 unfriendly; PHRASES: 3-4 ice-cold.

ID 6 papers; 8 identity, passport; 9 documents; 14 identification.

Idaho 2 ID; 5 Boise (capital); 7 syringa (flower); PHRASES: 3, 2, 2, 9 Let it be perpetual (motto); 3, 5 Gem State (nickname); 7, 5, 4 western white pine (tree); 8, 8 mountain bluebird (bird).

idea 3 aim; 4 gist, goal, plan; 5 fancy, imago; 6 belief, design, intent, notion, précis, scheme, theory; 7 concept, essence, feeling, ideatum, inkling, opinion, outlook, precept, premise, purpose, thought; 8 judgment, noumenon, proposal, solution, thinking; 9 construct, intention, intuition, objective, sentiment, viewpoint; 10 brainchild, brainstorm, conception, conjecture, estimation, hypothesis, impression, initiative, perception, reflection, suggestion; 11 inspiration, observation, supposition; 12 apprehension; 13 comprehension, understanding; 14 recommendation; PHRASES: 3, 8, 4 the Absolute I~; 4, 6 good wheeze; 5, 2, 4 point of view; 5, 4 brain wave *UK*; 6, 5 mental image; 6, 7 mental picture; 7, 4 quantum leap; 8, 4 Platonic I~.

idea (have an idea) 3 see; 5 grasp, infer; 6 deduce, intuit, invent; 7 realize, suppose, surmise; 8 conclude, perceive, theorize; 9 apprehend, speculate; 10 conjecture, understand; 11 hypothesize; PHRASES: 3, 4, 4, 4 pop into one's head; 4, 4 dawn upon; 5, 4, 4 cross one's mind; 6, 3 strike one; 7, 6 suggest itself; 8, 2 conceive of.

idea (person of ideas) 6 boffin, mentor; 7 creator, dreamer, egghead, thinker, Utopian; 8 idealist, inventor, romantic; 9 ideologue, theorizer, visionary; 10 ideologist; 11 philosopher; 12 theoretician.

ideal 4 best, icon; 5 dream, fancy, model, value; 6 belief, dreamy, Utopia, vision; 7 epitome, essence, example, fantasy, idyllic, paragon, pattern, perfect, supreme, Utopian; **8** exemplar, paradigm, romantic, standard, ultimate; **9** archetype, exemplary, fantastic, idealized, principle, prototype, visionary; **10** epitomical, idealistic, optimistic, stereotype; **11** ideological, impractical, sentimental, superlative; **12** archetypical, paradigmatic, prototypical, quintessence; **14** quintessential; PHRASES: **6, 2, 3, 3** castle in the air; **7, 8** wishful thinking.

idealism 4 zeal; **6** fervor; **7** naiveté, naivety *UK*; **8** ideality, optimism; **9** idealness, Platonism; **10** fanaticism, Kantianism, utopianism; **11** daydreaming, Hegelianism, romanticism; **12** idealization; **13** perfectionism, visionariness; **14** impracticality; PHRASES: **3, 2, 3, 3** pie in the sky; **3, 2, 3, 7** end of the rainbow; **3, 8** jam tomorrow; **3-9** Neo-Platonism; **4, 5** idle fancy; **7, 2, 3, 3** castles in the air; **7, 2, 5** castles in Spain; **7, 8** wishful thinking.

idealist 7 dreamer, fanatic; **8** crusader, optimist; **13** perfectionist. *See also* **idealistic**

idealistic 5 naive; **7** Kantian; **8** Hegelian, Platonic, romantic; **10** optimistic, principled, unwavering; **11** impractical, unrealistic; **14** uncompromising; PHRASES: **3-8** Neo-Platonic.

ideality 4 whim; **5** fancy, ideal, novel; **6** maggot, poetry, vagary, whimsy; **7** caprice, concept, fantasy, figment, romance; **8** daydream, quixotry; **9** absurdity, sciamachy, unreality; **10** conception, impression, projection; **12** extravaganza, idealization, shadowboxing; PHRASES: **3, 5** ego ideal; **4, 2, 5** play of fancy; **5, 4** fairy tale; **5-8** brain-creation; **6, 2, 5** flight of fancy; **6, 8** knight errantry; **7-7** crinkum-crankum; **9, 6** whimsical notion.

idealize 5 exalt; **8** venerate; **9** fetishize; **11** romanticize; PHRASES: **3, 2, 1, 8** put on a pedestal.

ideally 9 supremely; **10** preferably; **13** superlatively, theoretically *UK*; **14** hypothetically; PHRASES: **2, 1, 7, 5** in a perfect world; **2, 2, 3, 8** if at all possible; **2, 2, 5, 5** in an ideal world; **2, 6** in theory; **2, 8** if possible.

ideational 6 mental; **8** cerebral, creative, fanciful, imagined, inspired; **9** ingenious, inventive; **10** visualized; **11** imaginative; **12** intellectual; PHRASES: **2, 3, 5, 3** in the mind's eye; **2, 4, 4** in one's head.

identical 4 like, same; **5** equal; **8** matching; PHRASES: **4, 3, 4** just the same.

identically 4 ibid, like; **5** alike, ditto; **6** ibidem; **8** likewise; **11** analogously, congruently, imitatively; **12** equivalently, harmoniously, homogenously, repetitively, synonymously; **13** repetitiously, synchronously; **14** coincidentally, metaphorically, tautologically; **15** correspondingly; PHRASES: **2, 3, 4, 3** in the same way; **2, 9** in duplicate.

identifiably 12 indicatively, symbolically; **14** emblematically.

identification 5 trait; **7** empathy, rapport; **8** affinity, sympathy; **9** detection, diagnosis, discovery, documents; **10** indication; **11** association, classifying, designation, pinpointing, recognition; **12** denomination, verification; **13** corroboration, documentation; **14** authentication, categorization, classification, substantiation, superscription; **15** differentiation.

identification (means of identification) 1 X; **2** ID; **3** tag; **4** card, chip, chit, copy, ISBN (International Standard Book Number), logo, name, scar, seal, sign, visa; **5** badge, brand, label, plate, sigil, stamp, tally, title, token; **6** cachet, chitty, docket, emblem, fascia, marque, paraph, permit, signet, stigma, symbol, tattoo, ticket; **7** blemish, earmark, feature, imprint, quality, sticker, tessera; **8** colophon, hallmark, initials, logotype, masthead, monogram, passport, password, property; **9** autograph, birthmark, copyright, footprint, nameplate, signature, trademark, watchword, watermark; **10** letterhead, shibboleth, thumbprint; **11** certificate, credentials, fingerprint; **13** dactylography; **14** characteristic; PHRASES: **2-6** ex-libris; **3, 3** dog tag; **4, 2, 6** bill of lading; **4, 6** open sesame; **5, 4** brand name, caste mark, great seal, place card, privy seal, trade sign; **5, 5** brass plate; **7, 4** tavern's bush; **8, 4** business card; **8, 5** official stamp; **10, 4** strawberry mark.

identified 5 known, named; **6** marked, tagged, titled; **7** branded, indexed, labeled, scarred; **8** numbered, pictured, tattooed, verified; **9** cataloged, earmarked, imprinted, sigillary, signatory; **10** catalogued *UK*, classified, designated, hallmarked, recognized, referenced; **11** categorized, stigmatized, trademarked; **12** corroborated, photographed; **13** authenticated, characterized, fingerprinted, substantiated.

identify 4 etch, find, mark, name, note, scar, seal, tick; 5 brand, check, label, punch, stamp; 6 detect, docket, emboss, equate, number, record, relate, screen, tattoo, verify; 7 catalog *UK*, connect, earmark, engrave, impress, imprint, isolate, specify; 8 classify, diagnose, emblazon, hallmark, indicate, pinpoint, register; 9 ascertain, associate, catalogue *UK*, establish, recognize, reference, underline; 10 categorize, underscore; 11 corroborate, distinguish, fingerprint; 12 authenticate, characterize, substantiate; 13 differentiate; PHRASES: 3, 1, 4, 2 put a mark on; 4, 2 burn in; 4, 3 mark off, tick off; 4, 4, 2 keep tabs on.

identity 2 id; 3 ego; 4 name, self; 6 psyche; 7 oneself; 9 character; 10 uniqueness; 11 personality; 13 individuality; 15 distinctiveness; PHRASES: 5, 3 alter ego; 5, 4 inner self, other self, outer self; 6, 4 hidden self; 7, 4 outward self.

ideologically 12 archetypally; PHRASES: 2, 2, 5 so it seems; 2, 3, 4, 2 as one sees it; 2, 4, 7 in one's opinion.

ideology 4 view; 5 credo, creed, dogma, ethos; 6 belief, stance, tenets; 7 beliefs; 8 position; 9 manifesto, standards, viewpoint; 10 philosophy, prejudices.

idiom 5 style; 6 phrase, saying, speech; 7 dialect; 8 language; 10 expression, vernacular; PHRASES: 3, 6 set phrase; 4, 2, 6 turn of phrase.

idiosyncrasy 5 quirk; 6 foible; 9 mannerism; 11 peculiarity; 12 eccentricity; 14 characteristic.

idiot 3 nut; 4 fool, twit; 5 clown; 7 buffoon; 9 eccentric.

idle 4 laze, lazy, vain; 5 still, waste; 6 casual, futile, hollow; 7 workshy *UK*; 8 immobile, impotent, inactive, indolent, listless, slothful, sluggish; 9 frivolous, pointless, shiftless; 10 groundless, unoccupied; 11 ineffectual, inoperative, speculative; PHRASES: 2, 4 at rest; 3, 6 sit around; 4, 6 hang around, laze around, loaf around; 5, 4 while away; 7, 4 fritter away.

idleness 5 sloth; 6 apathy, phlegm, torpor; 7 inertia, languor; 8 dawdling, inaction, lethargy, slowness; 9 indolence; 11 impassivity; 15 procrastination. *See also* **idle**

idler *See* **slacker**

idol 3 god; 4 Baal, hero, icon, joss, star, yoni; 5 deity, image, pinup; 6 effigy, fetish,

lingam, maumet, statue; 8 megastar; 9 celebrity, obsession, sculpture, superstar; PHRASES: 6, 4 golden calf; 6, 5 graven image, poster child.

idolater 3 fan; 5 pagan; 7 admirer *UK*, cultist, devotee, fanatic, heathen; 8 idolizer, totemist, zoolater; 9 animatist, fetishist; 10 aficionada, aficionado, iconolater, necrolater, ophiolater, phallicist, worshipper *UK*; 11 bibliolater, dendrolater, zoomorphist; 13 ecclesiolater.

idolatrize 5 deify; 6 admire; 7 idolize, lionize; 9 fetishize; 10 heathenize; 11 apotheosize; PHRASES: 3, 2, 1, 8 put on a pedestal; 4-7 hero-worship.

idolatrous 4 cult; 7 cultish, heathen, Satanic, totemic; 9 animistic; 10 totemistic, zoolatrous, zoomorphic; 11 animatistic, fetishistic; 12 allotheistic, heliolatrous, iconolatrous, necrolatrous; 13 bibliolatrous, superstitious; 15 ecclesiolatrous.

idolatry 3 obi; 4 cult; 6 obiism; 7 animism, cultism, idolism, paganry; 8 devotion, paganism, Satanism, totemism, zoolatry; 9 adoration, adulation, animatism, diabolism, fetishism, heathenry, obsession, reverence; 10 admiration, allotheism, fanaticism, heathenism, veneration; 12 superstition.

if 5 doubt, rider; 7 proviso, unknown; 9 condition; 11 stipulation, uncertainty; 13 qualification; PHRASES: 8, 4 question mark.

ignis fatuus 4-1-3-4 will-o'-the-wisp.

ignite 4 stir; 5 light; 6 kindle; 7 inflame; PHRASES: 2, 2, 2, 6 go up in flames; 3, 1, 5, 2 put a match to; 3, 4, 2 set fire to; 3, 5, 2 set light to *UK*; 3, 6 set alight; 4, 2 stir up; 5, 2 flare up; 5, 4 catch fire; 5, 5 catch light.

ignoble *See* **dishonorable**

ignominy 5 shame; 6 infamy; 8 disgrace; 11 humiliation; 13 embarrassment.

ignorance 5 folly; 7 naiveté, naivety *UK*; 9 gaucherie, innocence, nescience, stupidity; 10 illiteracy; 11 unawareness, uncertainty; 12 backwardness, incognizance, inexperience; 13 insensibility, obliviousness, unfamiliarity; 14 nonrecognition, unintelligence; 15 incomprehension, unenlightenment; PHRASES: 5-10 emptyheadedness.

ignorant 3 dim; 4 dull, slow; 5 green, naive, thick; 6 gauche, simple, stupid; 7 awkward, unaware; 8 backward, clueless, innocent, nescient, untaught; **9** oblivious, unknowing, unskilled, untutored, unwitting; **10** illiterate, Philistine, uneducated, uninformed, unlettered, unschooled; **11** incognizant, misinformed, uninitiated, unscholarly; **12** uninstructed; **13** unenlightened; PHRASES: **2, 3, 4** in the dark; **3-4** low-brow; **3, 8** pig ~; **3-8** ill-informed; **4-6** slow-witted *UK*; **5-6** empty-headed.

ignorant (be ignorant) 3, 4, 1, 4 not have a clue.

ignorant (make ignorant) 7 mislead, mystify; **9** misinform; PHRASES: **4, 2, 3, 4** keep in the dark.

ignorant person 6 cowboy, humbug, layman, novice; **7** amateur, bluffer, bungler, dabbler; **9** charlatan, greenhorn; **10** dilettante, illiterate, Philistine; PHRASES: **3, 4** dim bulb; **4, 5** dumb cluck. *See also* **stupid person**

ignore 3 igg; **4** shun, snub; **5** avoid, blank, exile, flout; **6** rebuff, reject; **7** boycott, isolate, seclude; **8** discount, displace, overlook; **9** blackball, blacklist, disregard, ostracize, segregate, sequester; **10** quarantine; PHRASES: **3, 2, 4, 2** pay no heed to; **3, 4** cut dead; **4, 2, 6** keep in purdah; **4, 2, 8** send to Coventry *UK*; **4, 3** cast out, shut out, turn out; **4, 3, 4, 2** shut the door on; **4, 4** pass over; **4, 4, 4, 2** turn one's back on; **4, 7** look through; **4-8** cold-shoulder; **5, 4, 4, 2** close your eyes to; **6, 3** freeze out.

ill 3 bad; **4** evil, harm, pale, sick; **5** amiss, badly, cruel, faint, frail, harsh, shaky, unfit; **6** ailing, anemic, feeble, groggy, infirm, pallid, poorly, sickly, sinful, unkind, unwell, wasted, weakly, wicked; **7** cruelly, harmful, languid, ominous, trouble, unsound; **8** asthenic, decrepit, nauseous, shoddily, skeletal, unkindly, unsteady; **9** adversely, emaciated, harmfully, hostilely, ominously; **10** iniquitous, misfortune, unfriendly; **11** detrimental, unfavorable; **12** inadequately, inauspicious, unpleasantly, unpropitious; **13** detrimentally; **15** inappropriately; PHRASES: **2, 4, 6** in poor health; **3, 2, 5** out of sorts; **3-5** off-color; **4, 2** laid up; **4, 2, 1, 4** weak as a baby; **4, 2, 1, 5** weak as a child; **4, 2, 1, 6** weak as a kitten; **4, 2, 5** weak as water; **4-3-4** skin-and-bone; **5, 2, 1, 5** white as a sheet; **5, 3** below par *UK*; **5, 3, 7** under the weather.

illegal 5 wrong; **6** banned; **7** illicit; **8** criminal, unlawful, verboten; **9** dishonest, forbidden; **10** prohibited, proscribed, unlicensed; **12** illegitimate; **13** impermissible; PHRASES: **3-2-6** out-of-bounds; **7, 3, 3** against the law; **8, 2, 3** contrary to law.

illegal (do something illegal) 6 offend; PHRASES: **4, 3, 3** bend the law, defy the law; **5, 3, 3** break the law, twist the law; **6, 1, 5** commit a crime; **7, 3, 3** violate the law.

illegal (make illegal) 3 ban; **4** veto; **6** forbid, outlaw; **8** prohibit; **9** proscribe; **10** illegalize; **11** criminalize; **12** illegitimize.

illegality 3 ban; **5** crime; **6** felony; **7** offense; **9** violation; **10** infraction; **11** criminality, impropriety, misdemeanor; **12** illegitimacy, infringement, proscription; **13** contravention, transgression. *See also* **illegal**

illegitimate *See* **unlawful**

ill health 6 nerves; **7** allergy, catarrh, disease, frailty, illness; **8** debility, delicacy, neurosis, sickness, weakness; **9** diathesis, infirmity, morbidity, seediness; **10** sickliness, weakliness; **12** hypochondria; **13** indisposition, unhealthiness; PHRASES: **3, 6** bad health; **4, 6** poor health; **8, 6** delicate health.

illiberal 4 mean; **5** cheap, tight; **7** bigoted, miserly; **9** niggardly; **10** intolerant; **11** reactionary; **12** parsimonious; PHRASES: **6-6** narrow-minded.

illicit *See* **illegal**

illicit love 5 amour; **7** liaison; **8** adultery, intrigue; **9** cuckoldry; **10** cuckolding, infidelity; **11** concubinage; **14** unfaithfulness; PHRASES: **1, 3, 2, 3, 4** a bit on the side; **6, 1, 5** ménage à trois; **7, 8** eternal triangle; **9, 5** forbidden fruit.

Illinois 2 IL; **6** violet (flower); **8** cardinal (bird); **11** Springfield (capital); PHRASES: **4, 2, 7** Land of Lincoln (nickname); **5, 11, 8, 5** State sovereignty, national union (motto); **6, 3** native oak (tree); **7, 5** Prairie State (nickname).

ill-mannered *See* **rude**

ill-natured 9 irascible; **10** unpleasant; **12** disagreeable; PHRASES: **3-8** bad-tempered, ill-tempered.

illness 3 bug; **5** fever, virus; **6** malady, nausea, plague, stroke; **7** ailment, disease, malaise, seizure; **8** apoplexy, deathbed, debility, disorder, epidemic, sickness, syndrome, weakness; **9** complaint, condition, contagion, distemper, infection, infirmity;

10 affliction, visitation; **12** malnutrition; **13** indisposition; PHRASES: **3, 6** ill health. *See also* **disorder**

illogical 5 silly; **6** absurd, random; **7** invalid, labored, unsound; **8** perverse, specious, strained; **9** aleatoric, arbitrary, extrinsic, ludicrous, senseless, unfounded; **10** improbable, incidental, incoherent, irrational, unreasoned; **11** impractical, incongruous, nonsensical; **12** coincidental, inconsistent, unscientific; **13** contradictory; **14** irreconcilable; **15** incommensurable; PHRASES: **3-2-3-3** out-of-the-way; **3, 3, 7** off the subject; **3-7** far-fetched; **6, 3, 5** beside the point.

ill-treat 3 hit; **4** maul, rape, ruin, slap, stab, tear; **5** abuse, force, libel, spite, wound, wrong; **6** batter, bruise, defeat, harass, misuse, molest, savage, squash, strike; **7** crucify, destroy, oppress, outrage, slander, torment, torture, trample, violate; **8** aggrieve, distress, maltreat, mistreat; **9** persecute, tyrannize, victimize; **10** overburden; PHRASES: **3-3** ill-use; **4, 4** prey upon, walk over; **4, 4, 4, 2** wipe one's feet on; **5, 2** tread on.

illuminate 4 limn; **5** light; **6** illume; **7** clarify, explain, lighten; **8** brighten, illumine; **9** elucidate, irradiate; **10** illustrate.

illumination 5 light; **6** lights; **7** insight; **8** lighting; **10** brightness, brilliance; **11** explanation; **13** clarification, enlightenment.

illusion 4 idea; **5** dream, fancy, fetch, ghost, magic, spook, trick; **6** effect, mirage, spirit, vision, wraith; **7** chimera, fantasy, figment, phantom, specter; **8** artifice, daydream, delusion, phantasm, trickery; **9** deception, semblance; **10** appearance, impression, simulacrum; **12** doppelgänger; **13** hallucination, misconception; **14** phantasmagoria; **15** misapprehension; PHRASES: **4-1-3-4** will-o'-the-wisp; **4-1-7** jack-o'-lantern; **4, 5** pipe dream; **4, 7** fata morgana; **5, 6** ignis fatuus; **6, 2, 3, 3** castle in the air; **6, 2, 5** flight of fancy; **7, 2, 4** sleight of hand.

illusory 4 sham; **5** false, magic; **6** tricky, unreal; **7** magical; **8** conjured, delusory, fanciful, illusive, imagined; **9** deceptive, dreamlike, erroneous, fantastic, figmental, imaginary; **10** chimerical, misleading, phantasmic; **13** hallucinatory, insubstantial; PHRASES: **4-7** make-believe; **5-5** hocus-pocus, mumbo-jumbo; **7-2-4** sleight-of-hand.

illustration 6 figure; **7** diagram, drawing,

example, picture; **8** instance; **13** demonstration; **15** exemplification; PHRASES: **4, 2, 5** case in point.

image 3 air; **4** aura, bust, head, icon, idea, idol, view; **5** dummy, model, torso; **6** double, effigy, figure, notion, statue, symbol, vision; **7** concept, drawing, eidesis, picture, replica, waxwork; **8** figurine, hologram, likeness; **9** scarecrow, sculpture, semblance, statuette; **10** appearance, embodiment, impression, photograph, reflection, silhouette; **12** doppelgänger, illustration; **14** representation; PHRASES: **3, 6** Guy Fawkes; **6, 3** visual aid; **6, 4** carbon copy; **6, 5** graven ~, mirror ~; **8, 5** spitting ~.

imaginable 8 possible; **9** plausible, thinkable; **10** presumable, supposable; **11** conceivable.

imaginary 5 ideal; **6** fabled, unreal, untrue; **7** created, fancied, fantasy, fictive, pretend; **8** abstract, ethereal, fabulous, fanciful, illusive, illusory, imagined, invented, mythical, notional, vaporous; **9** contrived, dreamlike, fantastic, fictional, legendary, simulated; **10** chimerical, conceptual, fictitious, subjective; **11** nonexistent; **12** hypothetical, unhistorical; **13** insubstantial, suppositional; PHRASES: **3, 2, 4, 5** not of this world; **4-2** made-up; **4-7** make-believe.

imagination 4 mind; **5** dream; **6** mirage, vision, wraith; **7** chimera, fantasy, figment, phantom, specter; **8** artistry, daydream, dreaming, illusion, phantasm, thoughts; **9** invention, semblance; **10** apparition, creativity, imaginings, perception; **11** daydreaming, inspiration, originality; **13** inventiveness, visualization; **14** fantasticality, phantasmagoria; **15** objectification, resourcefulness; PHRASES: **3, 5, 3** the mind's eye; **4-1-3-4** will-o'-the-wisp; **4, 2** déjà vu; **4, 5** pipe dream; **4, 7** fata morgana; **4, 8** pink elephant; **5, 3** mind's eye; **5, 6** ignis fatuus; **6, 5** second sight; **7, 8** optical illusion.

imaginative 5 vivid; **6** clever, dreamy, fecund, lively, poetic; **7** eidetic, fertile, utopian; **8** artistic, creative, dreaming, inspired, original, romantic, skillful; **9** fantastic, fictional, ingenious, inventive, visionary; **10** idealistic, innovative, perceptive, productive; **11** exaggerated, resourceful, visualizing; **12** enterprising; **13** inspirational; PHRASES: **2, 1, 5, 5** in a brown study; **2, 1, 6** in a trance; **4-5** high-flown.

imaginatively 2, 3, 5, 3 in the mind's

eye. *See also* **imaginative**

imagine 3 see; **4** feel, scry *UK*; **5** dream, fancy, hatch, think; **6** create, devise, ideate, invent; **7** capture, concoct, foresee, picture, predict, pretend, reflect, suppose; **8** conceive, daydream, envisage, envision, idealize, perceive; **9** fabricate, fantasize, formulate, improvise, objectify, recapture, represent, visualize; **10** deliberate, excogitate; **11** hallucinate, romanticize; **13** conceptualize; PHRASES: **3, 6** see things; **4, 2** call up, make up; **4, 2, 4** call to mind; **4, 5** pipe dream; **4, 6** hear things; **4, 7** make believe; **5, 2** dream up, think of, think up; **6, 2** summon up; **7, 2** conjure up.

imaging 10 photometry; **12** spectrometry; **14** interferometry.

imbibe *See* **drink**

imbroglio 4 mess; **10** enmeshment; **12** complication, entanglement; **13** embarrassment.

imitate 3 ape; **4** copy, echo, mime, mock; **5** clone, mimic, spoof, Xerox™; **6** follow, mirror, parody, parrot, repeat; **7** emulate, reflect; **8** simulate, travesty; **9** burlesque, duplicate, Photostat™, replicate, reproduce; **10** camouflage, caricature, Mimeograph™; **11** counterfeit, impersonate; PHRASES: **3, 3** rip off; **4, 2** send up; **4, 3** take off; **7, 2, 2** pretend to be.

imitation 4 copy, echo, fake, mock, sham, skit; **5** canon, fugue, image; **6** copied, ersatz, forged, mirror, ormolu, parody, pseudo, sendup, tinsel; **7** copycat, mimesis, pretend, slavish, takeoff; **8** artifact; **9** emulation, facsimile, imposture, mirroring, simulated, synthetic; **10** artificial, impression, reflection, simulation; **11** counterfeit, plagiarized, replication, slavishness; **12** onomatopoeia, reproduction; **13** artificiality, impersonation; **14** representation; PHRASES: **3-3** rip-off; **3-4** man-made; **4-2** mock-up; **5, 4** fool's gold; **6, 6** German silver, nickel silver; **8, 5** cultured pearl; **9, 4** simulated wood; **9, 5** Britannia metal; **9, 6** synthetic rubber.

imitative 4 fake, mock, sham; **5** aping, apish, fugal, phony *UK*; **6** copied, echoic, forged, phoney; **7** clichéd, echoing, mimetic; **8** rubbishy; **9** emulating, parroting, synthetic, unnatural; **10** artificial, derivative, secondhand, unoriginal; **11** counterfeit, plagiarized; **12** onomatopoeic; PHRASES: **3-4** man-made; **6-4** parrot-like; **6-7** parrot-fashion *UK*.

imitatively 5 ditto, quasi; **8** verbatim; **9** literally, literatim, mockingly; PHRASES: **2, 3, 6** to the letter; **4, 3, 4** word for word; **6, 3, 6** letter for letter. *See also* **imitative**

imitator 3 ape; **5** actor, clone, mimic, sheep; **6** copier, double, parrot, poseur; **7** copycat; **8** disciple, follower; **9** charlatan; **11** illusionist; **12** impersonator; **13** impressionist, ventriloquist *UK*; PHRASES: **4-5** look-alike.

immaculate 4 pure, tidy; **5** clean; **7** perfect; **8** flawless, pristine, spotless; **9** faultless; PHRASES: **4, 3, 4** neat and tidy.

immaterial 4 airy; **6** unreal; **7** eternal, ghostly, psychic, shadowy; **8** ethereal, illusory, supernal; **9** celestial, imaginary, spiritual, unearthly, unworldly; **10** impalpable, intangible, irrelevant; **11** disembodied, incorporeal, nonmaterial, nonphysical, unimportant; **12** extramundane, metaphysical, otherworldly, transcendent; **13** disincarnated, insubstantial; **15** dematerializing, inconsequential; PHRASES: **2, 2, 10** of no importance; **2, 2, 11** of no consequence; **6, 3, 5** beside the point.

immature 3 raw; **4** naïf; **5** crude, fresh, green, naive, pupal, young; **6** callow, larval, maiden, novice, unborn, unripe, virgin; **7** amateur, awkward, babyish, budding, newborn, parvenu, puerile, ungrown, unready, upstart; **8** backward, childish, inchoate, innocent, juvenile, nonadult, retarded, unformed, unworked, virginal, youthful; **9** chrysalid, embryonic, infantile, premature, unfledged, unhatched, unwrought; **10** adolescent, amateurish, apprentice, precocious, unfinished, unmellowed, unprepared, unseasoned; **11** rudimentary, undeveloped, unfashioned; **13** inexperienced; PHRASES: **5, 2, 1, 3, 3** clean as a new pin; **5, 2, 1, 5** fresh as a daisy; **5, 2, 5** fresh as paint; **5-4** rough-hewn; **7, 5** nouveau riche.

immaturity 5 youth; **7** fatuity, infancy, naiveté, naivety *UK*, newness, rawness; **8** babyhood, dewiness; **9** childhood, crudeness, freshness, greenness, innocence, precocity, puerility, silliness, stupidity, virginity; **10** callowness, unripeness; **11** adolescence, awkwardness, prematurity, unreadiness; **12** childishness, inexperience; **13** ingenuousness, undevelopment; **14** incompleteness, unpreparedness.

immeasurable 4 huge, vast; **5** great; **6** myriad, untold; **7** endless, immense, massive; **8** colossal, enormous, infinite; **9** countless; **10** numberless, unnumbered; **11** inestimable, innumerable, uncountable; **12** astronomical, incalculable, transcendent, unfathomable; **14** indeterminable; PHRASES: **4-8** mind-boggling.

immeasurably 4 very; **12** considerably. *See also* **immeasurable**

immediacy 7 urgency; **8** exigency; **9** emergency; **10** directness; **11** promptitude; **13** instantaneity.

immediate 4 near; **5** close, quick, swift; **6** abrupt, direct, prompt, speedy, urgent; **7** instant; **8** pressing; **9** important, proximate; **13** instantaneous; PHRASES: **2-3-4** on-the-spot; **5-6** split-second.

immediately 3 now; **7** rapidly; **9** forthwith, presently, thereupon; **12** straightaway; PHRASES: **2, 3, 4** on the spot; **2, 4** at once; **2, 4, 2** as soon as; **2, 5, 2, 1, 5** as quick as a flash; **3, 6** the minute, the moment, the second; **3, 7** the instant; **5, 3** right now; **5, 4** right away; **7, 5** without delay. *See also* **immediate**

immerse 3 dip; **4** duck, dunk; **5** flood, inter, souse, steep; **6** drench, engage, occupy, plunge; **7** baptize, engross, immerge; **8** submerge, submerse.

immersed 4 deep; **8** absorbed, interred, occupied; **9** engrossed, submerged, submersed.

immersion 3 dip; **4** bath; **6** plunge; **7** baptism, bathing, ducking, dunking, rinsing *UK*, soaking; **8** steeping; **9** interment, obsession; **10** absorption, engagement, submersion; **11** submergence; **13** preoccupation.

immigrant 6 émigré; **7** migrant, refugee, settler; **8** colonist.

imminent 4 soon; **7** looming, pending; **8** expected; **9** impending; **11** forthcoming; PHRASES: **2, 3, 5** in the cards, in the stars; **2, 3, 6** in the offing, on the agenda; **2, 3, 7** on the horizon; **2, 3, 8** in the pipeline.

immobility *See* **stillness**

immobilize 3 jam; **4** halt, lock; **5** catch, lodge; **6** arrest, splint; **7** suspend; **8** restrain; **9** stalemate; PHRASES: **5, 2, 1, 4** bring to a halt.

immoderate *See* **excessive**

immodest *See* **boastful**

immoral 3 bad; **4** evil; **5** wrong; **6** amoral,

carnal, impure, sinful, vulgar, wicked; **7** corrupt, illegal, illicit, impious, obscene, profane; **8** criminal, decadent, degraded, depraved, devilish, immodest, indecent, infamous, perverse, shameful, unchaste, unlawful; **9** debauched, dishonest, dissolute, perverted, salacious, shameless, unethical; **10** degenerate, diabolical, dissipated, iniquitous, licentious, profligate, scandalous, unvirtuous; **11** blasphemous, disgraceful, irreligious; **12** dishonorable, sacrilegious, unprincipled, unscrupulous; PHRASES: **7, 2, 4** steeped in vice.

immoral (be sexually immoral) 4 lech; **5** cheat; **7** cuckold; **8** womanize; **9** fornicate, philander; PHRASES: **4, 3, 4, 3** have the hots for; **5, 6** sleep around; **6, 8** commit adultery.

immorality 3 sin; **4** evil, vice; **5** wrong; **8** iniquity; **9** amorality, decadence, depravity; **10** corruption, debauchery, wrongdoing; **11** criminality, delinquency, dissipation; PHRASES: **5, 9** moral turpitude. *See also* **immoral**

immoral man 4 pimp, rake, roué; **5** satyr; **6** gigolo, lecher, pander; **7** hustler, playboy; **8** Casanova, procurer, rakehell; **9** adulterer, debauchee, libertine, womanizer; **10** degenerate; **11** philanderer; PHRASES: **3, 4** Don Juan.

immoral woman 5 madam; **6** harlot; **7** Cyprian, trollop; **9** concubine, courtesan; **10** adulteress, prostitute; PHRASES: **4, 5** kept woman *UK*; **5, 5** loose woman; **7, 5** scarlet woman.

immortal 6 famous; **7** eternal, undying; **8** enduring; **9** memorable, perpetual; **11** everlasting, illustrious; **13** unforgettable; PHRASES: **4-5** well-known.

immovable 5 fixed, rigid; **6** secure, steady; **8** immobile, resolute, stubborn; **9** obstinate, unbending.

immune 4 safe; **5** proof; **6** exempt; **7** excused; **8** absolved, excepted; **9** protected, resistant, untouched; **10** impervious, inoculated, unaffected; **11** untouchable; **12** invulnerable; **13** insusceptible; PHRASES: **3, 6** not liable.

immunization 3 jab; **4** shot; **9** injection; **11** inoculation, vaccination; **12** safeguarding.

immure *See* **imprison**

immutability 10 permanence, perpetuity; **13** inevitability.

imp 3 elf; **5** demon, fairy, pixie, scamp; **6** goblin, rascal, sprite, urchin; **7** gremlin; **8** scalawag *UK*; **9** hobgoblin, scallywag; **11** rapscallion.

impact 3 hit; **4** blow, bump; **5** brunt, crash, force, power, shock, smash; **6** effect; **7** contact; **9** collision, influence; PHRASES: **3, 2** ram in, run in; **4, 2** cram in, pack in, push in *UK*; **5, 2** drive in, knock in, pound in, press in.

impair 3 mar; **4** harm, maul, rape; **5** botch, spoil, wreck; **6** blight, bungle, damage, meddle, ravage, tamper, tinker, weaken, worsen; **7** derange, destroy; **9** prejudice, pulverize, vandalize; **10** deactivate; **11** disorganize; PHRASES: **3, 3, 2, 6** put out of action; **3, 5** lay waste; **4, 2** cock up, mess up, muck up; **4, 4** fool with; **4, 5, 4** play havoc with; **5, 6, 4** screw around with; **6, 4** monkey with, trifle with.

impairment 4 loss; **5** waste; **6** damage, injury; **7** outrage; **8** sabotage, spoilage, spoiling; **9** contagion, detriment, infection, pollution, ruination, weakening; **10** debasement, deficiency, defilement, demolition; **11** derangement, destruction, devastation; **12** adulteration, exacerbation, intoxication; **13** contamination; **15** disorganization.

impart 4 tell; **6** convey, inform; **7** divulge; **11** communicate.

impartial 4 fair, just; **7** neutral; **8** balanced, detached, tolerant, unbiased; **9** objective; **10** equanimous, evenhanded, mugwumpish, nonaligned; **11** independent, nonpartisan; **12** unprejudiced; **13** disinterested, dispassionate, nonjudgmental; **14** indiscriminate; PHRASES: **4-6** open-minded; **5-6** broad-minded.

impartiality 7 balance, justice; **9** tolerance; **10** detachment, equanimity, mugwumpism, neutrality; **11** objectivity; **12** independence, nonalignment; PHRASES: **6, 3** middle way. *See also* **impartial**

impartial person 5 judge; **6** umpire; **7** referee; **9** moderator; **10** arbitrator.

impassable 6 closed; **7** blocked; **10** obstructed; **12** impenetrable.

impassive 5 aloof, blank; **6** stolid; **7** deadpan, unmoved; **8** indolent, listless, slothful, sluggish; **9** apathetic, lethargic; **10** phlegmatic; **11** emotionless, indifferent; **14** expressionless.

impassively 6 lazily; **7** deadpan; **9** languidly. *See also* **impassive**

impatience 5 haste, hurry; **7** anxiety; **8** edginess, keenness; **9** annoyance, eagerness; **10** irritation; **11** intolerance.

impatient 4 edgy, keen; **5** antsy, eager; **6** raring; **7** annoyed, anxious; **9** irritated; **10** intolerant; **11** exasperated; PHRASES: **2, 1, 5** in a hurry.

impeach *See* **accuse**

impeccable *See* **perfect**

impecunious *See* **poor**

impediment *See* **obstacle**

impel 3 jog, tug; **4** butt, goad, hurl, jerk, jolt, move, poke, prod, push, spur, urge; **5** drive, eject, elbow, expel, fling, force, heave, press, shove; **6** coerce, compel, incite, induce, joggle, jostle, propel, thrust, thwack, wrench; **7** actuate, animate, require, traject; **8** motivate; **9** frogmarch, galvanize; PHRASES: **3, 2, 6** set in motion; **4, 6** push around; **5, 2** drive on; **6, 8** import momentum.

impelling 6 moving; **7** driving, dynamic, pulsive; **9** impulsive, thrustful, thrusting *UK*.

impend 4 hang, loom; **5** hover; **6** menace; **8** approach, threaten; PHRASES: **2, 8** be imminent.

impending 6 coming, future; **8** imminent; **11** forthcoming; PHRASES: **2, 3, 4, 6** in the near future; **2, 3, 7** on the horizon; **2, 4** at hand. *See also* **impend**

impenetrable 5 dense, solid, thick; **10** impassable, unsolvable; **11** inscrutable; **12** unfathomable; **14** indecipherable; PHRASES: **7, 6** tightly packed.

impenitence 8 hardness, obduracy; **9** obstinacy; **11** callousness; **12** stubbornness; **13** nonrepentance; **14** hardheartedness, incorrigibility, remorselessness; PHRASES: **2, 5, 4** no going back; **2, 7** no regrets; **4-11** cold-heartedness; **5, 2, 5** heart of stone.

impenitent 4 hard; **6** brazen; **7** callous, defiant, unmoved; **8** hardened, obdurate; **9** heartless, obstinate, shameless, unashamed, unshriven; **10** indurative, regretless, unblushing, uncontrite, unredeemed, unreformed; **11** hardhearted, remorseless, unchastened, unrecanting, unrepentant; **12** incorrigible, irredeemable, unapologetic, unremorseful; **13** irreclaimable, unregenerated; **14** conscienceless; PHRASES: 4-2-3-4 dyed-in-the-wool; **6, 2, 3, 4** rotten to the core.

impenitent (be impenitent) 8 indurate; PHRASES: **4, 2, 7** feel no remorse; **4, 7** feel nothing; **5, 7** steel oneself; **6, 4, 5** harden one's heart.

imperative 5 bossy, vital; **6** urgent; **7** crucial; **8** priority; **9** essential, imperious, necessary, necessity; **10** commanding, obligation; **11** domineering, overbearing, requirement.

imperceptible 4 tiny; **5** faint, vague; **6** slight, subtle; **7** gradual, shadowy; **9** inaudible, invisible; **10** impalpable, indistinct, intangible; **12** undetectable, unnoticeable; **13** inconspicuous, indiscernible.

imperfect 3 bad, off; **4** poor, weak; **5** dodgy, leaky, shaky, stale, unfit; **6** broken, corked, faulty, flawed, marked, patchy, soiled, uneven, wobbly; **7** botched, bungled, chipped, cracked, damaged, rickety, stained, tainted, unsound; **8** fallible, inferior, overripe, peccable, shopworn, unsteady; **9** blemished, defective, deficient, irregular, scratched, unhealthy; **10** inadequate, incomplete, shopsoiled, vulnerable; **11** perfectible; **12** unacceptable; **13** dysfunctional; **14** unsatisfactory; PHRASES: **3, 2, 3, 4** not in the pink; **3-5** off-color; **3, 6** off stride; **4, 2, 5** good in parts; **4, 3, 3** good and bad; **4, 3, 5** past its prime; **4, 4, 7** less than perfect; **5, 3** below par; **5-4** third-rate; **5-5** third-class; **6-4** second-best, second-rate; **6-5** second-class.

imperfect (be imperfect) 4 fail, leak; **10** dissatisfy; PHRASES: **3, 4, 3, 5** not make the grade; **3, 4, 5** not hold water; **3, 4, 6** not pass muster; **4, 4, 2, 4** have feet of clay; **4, 5** fall short; **6, 7** scrape through.

imperfection 4 blot, flaw, lack; **5** botch, error, fault; **6** damage, defect; **7** blemish, failing, failure, frailty; **9** deformity, infirmity, shortfall; **10** deficiency, distortion, immaturity, inadequacy, limitation, peccadillo, unripeness; **11** cursoriness, fallibility, inferiority, peccability, shortcoming; **12** adulteration, carelessness, irregularity; **13** erroneousness, insufficiency, vulnerability; **14** perfectibility; **15** perfunctoriness; PHRASES: **5, 5** third class; **6, 4** second rate; **6, 5** second class; **7, 3** curate's egg *UK*; **8, 4** Achilles' heel. *See also* **imperfect**

imperfectly 6 almost, barely; **8** scarcely; PHRASES: **3, 3** all but; **3, 5** not quite; **5, 3** below par. *See also* **imperfect**

imperial 5 regal, royal; **8** majestic; **9** Caesarian; **10** commanding.

imperil *See* **endanger**

imperishable 6 stable; **7** durable, eternal; **8** enduring; **9** permanent, resilient; **11** everlasting; **14** indestructible.

impermanent 6 mortal; **7** fragile, passing; **9** ephemeral, temporary, throwaway, transient; **10** evanescent, nondurable, transitory; **13** biodegradable; PHRASES: **3-3** one-off; **6-3** single-use.

impermeable 5 solid; **8** hermetic; **9** nonporous, rainproof, resistant; **10** impassable, impervious, waterproof, watertight; **12** impenetrable.

impersonal 4 cold, cool, gray; **5** aloof; **6** frosty; **7** careful; **8** detached, faceless, measured, soulless; **9** anonymous, objective; **10** unfriendly; **11** featureless.

impersonate 3 ape; **4** copy; **5** mimic; **7** imitate; **8** satirize; **9** personate; PHRASES: **4, 2** pose as; **4, 3** pass off; **7, 2, 2** pretend to be; **10, 2** masquerade as.

impersonation 6 parody, sendup; **7** takeoff; **8** pretense; **9** imitation, imposture; **10** caricature, impression, masquerade; **11** personation.

impertinence *See* **impudence**

impertinent *See* **impudent**

imperturbable *See* **calm**

impervious 5 proof, rigid; **6** obtuse; **7** unaware; **8** obdurate; **9** unbending, unfeeling, unmovable; **10** unaffected, unwavering, watertight; **11** unreceptive; **12** invulnerable.

imperviousness 8 obduracy, solidity; **10** resistance; **11** obstruction; **13** impassability, impercipience *UK*; **14** impermeability; **15** impenetrability, invulnerability. *See also* **impervious**

impetuosity 11 spontaneity; **12** precipitance. *See also* **impetuous**

impetuous 4 rash; **5** hasty; **7** flighty; **8** reckless; **9** foolhardy, hotheaded, impulsive; **10** headstrong; **11** precipitous.

impetus 4 push; **5** force; **6** energy, thrust; **8** momentum, stimulus; **9** impulsion, incentive; **10** motivation; PHRASES: **7, 6** forward motion.

impious 3 bad; 6 damned, sinful, wicked; 7 godless, immoral, profane; 8 accursed, devilish, fiendish, infernal; 9 reprobate; 10 irreverent; 11 blasphemous, godforsaken, irreligious; 12 sacrilegious; 15 Mephistophelian.

implausibility 12 unlikelihood; 13 improbability; 15 questionability, unbelievability; PHRASES: 4, 4 tall tale. *See also* **implausible**

implausible 8 doubtful, unlikely; 9 fantastic; 10 improbable, incredible; 12 questionable, unbelievable; PHRASES: 3-7 farfetched.

implement 4 tool; 5 apply; 6 device, gadget; 7 execute, realize; 10 instrument; 11 contrivance; PHRASES: 5, 3 carry out.

implicate 4 link; 5 imply; 6 assume; 7 connect, involve, suggest; 9 associate; 11 incriminate; PHRASES: 4, 2 hint at; 5, 2 point to *UK*.

implication 4 hint, link, part; 6 result; 7 outcome; 8 innuendo; 9 inference; 10 connection, suggestion; 11 association, consequence, insinuation, involvement; 12 repercussion.

implied 5 tacit; 6 veiled; 7 oblique; 8 implicit, indirect, unspoken; 10 understood.

implore 3 beg; 4 pray; 5 plead.

imply 4 hint, mean; 6 allude, denote, entail; 7 connote, suggest; 8 indicate, intimate; 9 implicate, insinuate, symbolize; PHRASES: 4, 2 hint at; 5, 2 point to *UK*.

impolite 4 rude; 7 boorish; PHRASES: 3-8 bad-mannered, ill-mannered.

import 7 ingress, meaning, smuggle; 9 introduce; 10 importance; 11 consequence, importation; 12 introduction, significance; PHRASES: 5, 2 bring in, trade in.

importance 4 mark, note, pith, rank; 5 merit, power, value, worth; 6 degree, import, moment, rating, repute, status, weight; 7 account, gravity, primacy, urgency; 8 eminence, emphasis, prestige, priority, severity, standing; 9 greatness, influence, magnitude, solemnity, substance, supremacy; 10 insistence, notability, precedence, prominence, reputation, usefulness; 11 consequence, distinction, materiality, paramountcy, preeminence, seriousness, superiority, weightiness; 12 essentiality, memorability, significance; 13 momentousness; 14 noteworthiness, substantiality; PHRASES: 4, 8 high standing.

important 3 big, key, top; 4 main; 5 chief, first, grand, great, large, major, prime, vital; 6 solemn, staple, summit, urgent, worthy; 7 bedrock, capital, central, crucial, eminent, leading, notable, ominous, pivotal, primary, radical, serious, supreme, topmost; 8 cardinal, critical, distinct, foremost, historic, pregnant, relevant, required, superior, valuable; 9 essential, memorable, momentous, necessary, paramount, principal, prominent, trenchant, uppermost; 10 imperative, meaningful, overriding, overruling, remarkable; 11 fundamental, influential, significant; 12 considerable; 13 indispensable, irreplaceable; PHRASES: 2, 6 of weight; 2, 7 of concern; 2, 10 of importance; 2, 11 of consequence; 3-5 top-level; 4-3-5 life-and-death; 4-5 high-level; 4-7 high-ranking; 4-8 high-priority; 5, 5 grass roots; 5-7 earthshaking; 5-10 world-shattering.

important (be important) 5 count, weigh; 6 import, matter; 7 concern, signify; 9 influence; 11 predominate; PHRASES: 3, 1, 4 cut a dash; 3, 1, 6 cut a figure; 4, 2, 3 make it big; 4, 3, 4 take the lead; 4, 5 bulk large, come first, make waves; 4, 6 come before; 4, 8 have priority; 5, 6 carry weight; 7, 7 command respect.

important (make important) 5 exalt, honor, value; 6 esteem, regard, splash, stress; 7 enhance, enlarge, glorify, lionize, magnify, promote, respect; 8 headline, overrate; 9 advertise, celebrate, emphasize, highlight, publicize, underline; 10 exaggerate; 12 overestimate; PHRASES: 4, 4, 2 make much of; 4, 9 take seriously; 5, 2, 3, 4 bring to the fore.

importantly 12 preeminently; PHRASES: 2, 3, 4 in the main; 2, 5, 3 to crown all; 3, 10 par excellence; 5, 3 above all. *See also* **important**

important matter 4 news; 6 crisis; 8 landmark; 9 milestone; 10 memorandum; PHRASES: 2-3, 3, 3-3 be-all and end-all; 2, 4 no joke; 3, 3 big day; 3, 4 big deal, big news; 3, 5 key point; 3, 6 the crunch; 3-6, 3 red-letter day; 5, 6 grave affair; 7, 5 turning point.

importunate *See* **persistent**

importune *See* **bother**

impose 4 dump, levy; 5 exact, foist, force; 6 bother, burden, hassle, insist; 7 enforce, execute, impress, inflict, intrude; 9 overwhelm; PHRASES: 6, 2 insist on.

imposition 4 levy; 5 force; 6 bother, burden, hassle; 8 nuisance; 9 annoyance; 13 inconvenience.

impossibility 7 paradox; 9 absurdity, unreality; 12 illogicality, nonexistence, unlikelihood; 13 unfeasibility; 14 impracticality, unthinkability; 15 unimaginability; PHRASES: 4, 6, 2 what cannot be.

impossible 6 absurd; 7 awkward; 8 hopeless, unviable; 9 difficult, illogical; 10 incredible, irrational, ridiculous, unbearable, unfeasible, unworkable; 11 impractical, intolerable, irresoluble, paradoxical, unthinkable; 12 insufferable, irresolvable, unachievable, unattainable, unbelievable, unimaginable, unmanageable, unreasonable; 13 impracticable, inconceivable; 14 unquestionable; PHRASES: 3, 2 not on *UK*; 4-9 self-defeating.

impossible (be impossible) 3, 5, 1, 6 not stand a chance.

impossible (make impossible) 3 ban, bar; 4 deny; 5 block; 6 forbid, negate; 7 scupper; 8 prohibit; 9 disenable; PHRASES: 4, 3 rule out.

impossibly 9 extremely; 12 ridiculously. *See also* **impossible**

impostor 8 deceiver, imitator; 9 pretender; 12 impersonator.

impotent 4 beat, weak; 5 frail, tired; 6 feeble, senile, supine, unable, zonked; 7 drugged, swamped; 8 comatose, decrepit, fatigued, helpless, unnerved; 9 catatonic, etiolated, exhausted, incapable, paralyzed, powerless, prostrate, spineless; 11 debilitated, demoralized, incontinent, ineffective, ineffectual, unconscious, waterlogged; 13 incapacitated; PHRASES: 2, 4, 4 on one's back; 3, 2 all in; 3, 2, 3, 7 out of the running; 3, 2, 7 out of control; 4, 2 done in, used up; 4, 2, 6 hors de combat; 4, 3 worn out; 4, 4 dead beat *UK*; 5, 2 belly up; 5, 3 tired out; 5-7 shell-shocked; 7, 3 clapped out.

impotent (make impotent) 4 geld, spay; 5 unman, unsex; 6 neuter; 7 evirate, unnerve; 8 castrate, enervate; 9 sterilize; 10 devitalize, emasculate; 11 vasectomize.

impoverish 3 rob; 4 ruin; 5 strip; 6 beggar, fleece; 7 deplete, deprive; 8 bankrupt, diminish, disendow; 9 pauperize; 10 disinherit, dispossess.

impractical 8 unviable; 10 idealistic, unfeasible, unworkable; 11 unpractical, unrealistic; 12 unreasonable; PHRASES: 6-4 starry-eyed.

imprecation 4 oath; 6 insult; 7 cursing; 8 swearing; 9 blasphemy, expletive, profanity, swearword.

impresario 5 agent; 7 manager; 8 producer, promoter; 12 entrepreneur.

impress 4 move; 5 amaze; 6 affect, excite, stress; 9 emphasize, influence; PHRASES: 3, 4 din into; 4, 4 drum into; 5, 4 drive home.

impression 3 dip; 4 copy, dent, dint, hint, idea, mark, sway; 5 brand, clone, hunch, image, model, sense, stamp, vibes; 6 belief, dimple, effect, hollow, impact, notion, nuance, parody, sendup; 7 edition, feeling, impress, imprint, inkling, insight, persona, picture, replica, takeoff, thought, vestige; 8 likeness; 9 imitation, influence, intuition; 10 depression, intimation, reflection, suggestion; 12 undercurrent; 13 impersonation; 14 representation; PHRASES: 3, 8 gut reaction; 4, 5 face value; 4-5 look-alike; 5, 5 sixth sense; 6, 5 mirror image.

impressionable 7 pliable; 8 formable, gullible; 9 adaptable, complying, formative, receptive, sensitive; 10 vulnerable; 11 suggestible, susceptible; 12 nonresistive.

imprint 3 fix; 4 mark, name, seal, sign; 5 print, stamp; 6 effect, emblem, hollow; 7 impress; 8 hallmark; 9 establish; 10 impression, indication; 11 indentation, inscription; PHRASES: 4, 4 drum into; 5, 4 drive home.

imprison 3 jug; 4 jail; 6 detain, immure, intern; 7 confine, impound; 11 incarcerate; PHRASES: 3, 4 put away; 3, 6 put inside; 4, 2 lock up, send up; 4, 2, 3, 5 send up the river; 4, 4 lock away, send down *UK*; 4, 8 take prisoner; 5, 2, 3, 4 throw in the tank; 5, 4, 3, 3 throw away the key.

imprisoned 4 held; 5 bound; 6 buried, inside, jailed; 7 captive; 8 confined, detained, interned; 10 restrained; 12 incarcerated; PHRASES: 2, 3 on ice; 2, 3, 3, 5 in the big house; 2, 3, 4 in the nick; 2, 3, 5 up the river; 2, 3, 6 in the cooler; 2, 4 in stir; 2, 6 on remand; 2, 9 in captivity, in detention; 4, 2 shut in; 5, 4 doing time; 5, 4, 3, 3 under lock and key; 5, 6 under arrest; 6, 2 locked up; 6, 4 behind bars.

imprisonment 4 term, time; 7 custody, durance; 8 porridge; 9 captivity, detention; 10 immurement, internment; 11 confinement; **13** incarceration; PHRASES: **4, 4** jail term.

improbability 5 doubt; **7** dubiety; **11** dubiousness, uncertainty; **12** doubtfulness, unlikelihood, unlikeliness; **13** incredibility; **14** implausibility; **15** questionability; PHRASES: **3, 6** fat chance; **4, 4** long odds, long shot; **4, 5** pipe dream; **4, 6** slim chance; **5, 2, 1, 6** ghost of a chance; **5, 6** small chance; **6, 1, 6** hardly a chance; **6, 2, 3, 3** castle in the air; **7-2-3** million-to-one; **7, 6** outside chance.

improbable 7 dubious; **8** doubtful, unlikely; **9** dubitable, uncertain; **10** incredible; **11** implausible, unrealistic; **12** questionable, unbelievable, unconvincing; PHRASES: **3-7** far-fetched.

improbable (be improbable) 2, 6, 6 go beyond belief.

improbity 4 bias; **5** shame; **7** knavery; **8** baseness, disgrace, dishonor, trickery, venality, villainy; **9** chicanery, depravity, disrepute, hypocrisy, indecency, injustice, prejudice, turpitude; **10** corruption, debasement, dishonesty, immorality, partiality, wickedness; **11** contrivance, crookedness, deviousness, insincerity; **14** villainousness; PHRASES: **4, 4** foul play; **5, 5** dirty trick.

impromptu *See* **unprepared**

improper 4 rude; **5** crude, inapt, unfit, wrong; **6** coarse, vulgar; **7** boorish, crooked, illegal, illicit, uncouth; **8** churlish, criminal, indecent, shocking, unlawful, unseemly; **9** dishonest, offensive, tasteless, unfitting; **10** inadequate, indecorous, unbecoming, unsuitable; **11** incongruous, inopportune, unbefitting, undesirable; **12** unacceptable; **13** inappropriate, reprehensible; PHRASES: **3, 2, 5** out of place; **3, 3, 4, 5** not the done thing; **3, 4** not done.

impropriety 9 immodesty, indecency, indecorum, vulgarity; **10** indelicacy; **11** discourtesy; **12** unrefinement; PHRASES: **3, 5** bad taste. *See also* **improper**

improvable 7 curable; **10** corrigible, meliorable, reformable; **11** ameliorable, perfectible.

improve 4 cure, hype, mend, tidy, till, weed; **5** adorn, amend, clean, dress, learn, primp, prink, rally, renew, ripen, study, tweak; **6** better, enrich, evolve, foster, leaven, mature, mellow, neaten, polish, purify, redeem, refine, reform, repair, revive, up-

lift; **7** advance, correct, develop, elevate, enhance, forward, further, indulge, perfect, promote, prosper, recover, rectify, refresh, restore, succeed, upgrade; **8** beautify, civilize, decorate, graduate, increase, mitigate, ornament, palliate, progress, renovate, titivate; **9** alleviate, cultivate, elaborate, embellish, encourage, meliorate, modernize, refurbish, sublimate; **10** ameliorate, convalesce, recuperate, regenerate, straighten, supplement; **11** accommodate, rationalize, recondition, transfigure; **12** rehabilitate; PHRASES: **2, 2** do up; **3, 2** fix up; **3, 6** add frills, get better; **4, 1, 4, 4** help a lame duck; **4, 2** make up, perk up, pick up, tidy up *UK*, tone up, vamp up; **4, 3, 4** gild the lily; **4, 3, 4, 2** make the most of; **4, 7** make headway; **5, 2** build up, clean up, dress up, patch up, shape up, touch up; **5, 2, 2, 4** bring up to date; **5, 2, 8** bring to fruition; **6, 2** spruce up; **7, 2** freshen up, smarten up; **10, 3** straighten out.

improved 5 wiser; **6** better, edited; **7** amended, revised; **8** bettered, enhanced, enriched, reformed, repaired, restored, superior, upgraded; **9** developed, perfected, renovated, rewritten; **10** beautified, modernized; **11** transformed; PHRASES: **2, 3, 4** on the mend; **3, 3, 6, 3** all the better for; **5-5** value-added; **6, 3** better off.

improvement 4 cure; **5** rally; **6** polish, reform, remedy, repair, upturn; **7** advance, headway, renewal, revival, success, upgrade, upswing; **8** ornament, progress, recovery; **9** adornment, amendment, education, elevation, expansion, promotion, upgrading; **10** betterment, completion, conversion, correction, decoration, enrichment, graduation, mitigation, palliation, perfection, prosperity, redemption, refinement, renovation, titivation; **11** advancement, alleviation, development, elaboration, enhancement, furtherance, melioration, progression, reformation, refreshment, restoration; **12** amelioration, civilization, purification, recuperation, regeneration; **13** convalescence, embellishment, modernization, ornamentation, rectification, refurbishment, socialization; **14** beautification, reconditioning, rehabilitation, transformation; **15** rationalization, transfiguration; PHRASES: **3, 4** new leaf; **3, 6** sea change; **3, 10** new resolution; **4-4** facelift; **4, 8** kick upstairs; **4, 9** good influence; **5, 2, 3, 4** icing on the cake; **5, 5** final touch; **6,**

5 onward march; **6, 8** upward mobility; **9, 5** finishing touch.

improving 7 radical, utopian; **8** remedial; **9** reforming, reformist; **10** civilizing; **11** meliorative, progressive, reformative, reformatory, restorative; **12** ameliorative.

improvisation 7 cadenza, standup; **9** invention; **12** creativeness; **13** inventiveness; **15** extemporization, unpremeditation; PHRASES: **2-3** ad-lib.

improvise 3 jam, rig; **4** vamp; **5** blurt; **6** invent; **11** extemporize; PHRASES: **2-3** ad-lib; **3, 2** rig up *UK*; **4, 2** make up, wing it; **4, 2, 4** come up with; **4, 2, 4, 4** rely on your wits; **5, 2** think up; **5, 2, 4, 4** think on one's feet; **5, 8** knock together, throw together; **6, 8** cobble together.

improvised 7 offhand; **9** extempore, impromptu, makeshift, unplanned; **10** unarranged, unprepared; **11** extemporary, spontaneous, unmeditated, unrehearsed; **12** uncalculated; **14** extemporaneous, unpremeditated; PHRASES: **2, 3** ad hoc, ad lib; **3, 3, 4** off the cuff; **4-2-3-6** spur-of-the-moment; **4-6** jury-rigged; **5-2-5-3** catch-as-catch-can.

improviser 8 inventor; **12** extemporizer; **13** improvisatore; **14** improvisatrice; PHRASES: **2-6** ad-libber.

imprudent 4 rash; **7** foolish; **9** impulsive; **10** indiscreet; **13** irresponsible.

impudence 4 gall; **5** cheek, nerve; **8** audacity; **9** arrogance, flippancy, insolence; **10** disrespect, effrontery; **11** presumption; **12** impertinence. *See also* **impudent**

impudent 4 bold, pert, rude; **5** cocky, fresh; **6** brassy, brazen, cheeky, mouthy; **8** flippant, impolite, insolent; **9** shameless; **10** unblushing; **11** impertinent; **12** presumptuous; **13** disrespectful; PHRASES: **4, 2, 5** bold as brass; **6-5** brazen-faced.

impugn *See* **question**

impulse 3 yen; **4** beat, spur, tick, urge, whim, wish; **5** drive, nerve, pulse; **6** desire, motive; **8** instinct, stimulus; **9** pulsation; **10** compulsion.

impulsion 5 force, power; **6** thrust; **7** impetus; **8** dynamics, momentum, pressure; **10** motivation, propulsion; **11** inclination; PHRASES: **7, 5** driving force. *See also* **impulse**

impunity (with impunity) 6 freely; **12** unanswerably; **13** unaccountably; PHRASES: **4-4** duty-free.

impute 6 accuse, allege, assert, assign, credit; **8** accredit, complain; **9** attribute, implicate; PHRASES: **5, 2** chalk up.

in 3 hip; **4** amid; **6** around, inside, inward, modish, trendy, within; **7** arrived, batting, indoors, inwards, popular, stylish, voguish, wearing; **8** inwardly; **9** available; **11** fashionable; **15** parenthetically; PHRASES: **2, 3, 2** on the up; **2, 4** at home; **2, 5** ~ vogue; **2, 8** ~ brackets; **2, 11** ~ parenthesis; **3, 3** not out; **3, 3, 4** all the rage; **7-4** cutting-edge.

inaccessible 7 oblique, obscure; **8** abstruse, esoteric; **9** difficult; **11** unreachable; **14** unapproachable; PHRASES: **3-2-3-3** out-of-the-way; **4, 2, 4** hard to find.

inaccuracy 4 boob *UK*, flaw, slip; **5** error; **6** laxity; **7** blunder, mistake; **9** guesswork, looseness; **10** negligence; **11** imprecision, inexactness; **12** carelessness, inexactitude, mistakenness; **13** approximation, erroneousness, impreciseness, incorrectness; **14** generalization, miscalculation; PHRASES: **3, 2, 4** hit or miss; **4-2** slip-up.

inaccurate 3 out; **5** loose, vague, wrong; **7** inexact; **8** mistaken; **9** distorted, erroneous, illogical, imprecise, incorrect; **12** inconsistent; PHRASES: **3-3** way-out.

inaction 4 calm, lull, rest, stop; **5** delay, quiet; **6** apathy, nonuse, repose, torpor; **7** inertia, leisure; **8** abeyance, calmness, deadlock, dormancy, idleness, laziness, lethargy, sinecure; **9** avoidance, cowardice, defeatism, dithering, Fabianism *UK*, impotence, indolence, inertness, nonaction, paralysis, passivity, quietness, stalemate, stillness, torpidity; **10** abstention, immobility, inactivity, indecision, negligence, quiescence, redundancy, relaxation, stagnation, standstill, suspension, vegetation; **11** impassivity, tranquility; **12** indifference, slothfulness, sluggishness, unemployment; **13** insensibility, sedentariness; **14** indecisiveness; **15** inoperativeness, noninterference, nonintervention, procrastination; PHRASES: **3, 3** log jam; **4, 2, 3, 4** head in the sand; **4, 2, 4** time to kill; **4, 2, 4, 5** time on one's hands; **4, 2, 8** lack of progress; **4, 5** idle hours; **5, 3, 6** dolce far niente; **7, 5** laissez faire.

inactive 4 calm, dead, dull, idle, lazy; **5** inert, quiet, still; **6** Fabian, fallow, frozen, sleepy, static, torpid; **7** dormant, extinct, passive, relaxed, skiving; **8** becalmed, benumbed, immobile, impotent, indolent, leisured, lifeless, lounging, mooching, slothful, sluggish, stagnant, tranquil, unmoving; **9** apathetic, deskbound, impassive, inanimate, lethargic, negligent, nonactive, paralyzed, powerless, quiescent, redundant, sedentary, suspended; **10** abstaining, collecting, cunctative, deadlocked, insensible, motionless, neglectful, phlegmatic, stalemated, stationary, unemployed, unoccupied; **11** abstentious, indifferent, inoperative; **13** underemployed, unprogressive; **15** procrastinating; PHRASES: **2, 1, 10** at a standstill; **2, 4** at rest; **2, 8** in abeyance; **3, 2, 4** out of work; **3, 2, 5** out of order; **3, 2, 6** out of action; **4, 3** laid off; **4-3-3** wait-and-see; **4-4** half-dead, half-gone; **5-3** hands-off; **7-4** ostrich-like.

inactive (be inactive) **4** idle, laze, loaf; **5** cadge, drift, mooch, skive; **6** dawdle, lounge, slouch; **8** stagnate, vegetate; **13** procrastinate; PHRASES: **4, 4** hang fire, kill time; **4, 4, 5** kick one's heels; **4, 5** hang about *UK*; **5, 4** waste time.

inactive (make inactive) **4** dope, drug; **6** deaden, defuse, sedate; **7** disable, suspend; **9** dismantle, hypnotize, narcotize; **10** demobilize, extinguish, immobilize, inactivate, neutralize; **12** anaesthetize, incapacitate; PHRASES: **3, 2** lay up; **3, 3** lay off.

inadequacy **4** flaw, lack; **5** fault; **6** dearth, defect; **7** failing, failure, paucity; **8** scarcity, shortage; **9** shortfall; **10** deficiency, meagreness *UK*, scantiness, skimpiness; **11** shortcoming; **12** incompetence; **13** insufficiency.

inadequate **4** poor; **5** scant; **6** meager, scanty, scarce, skimpy; **7** lacking; **8** mediocre; **9** defective, deficient, imperfect, incapable, laughable; **11** incompetent, ineffective, ineffectual, inefficient, substandard; **12** insufficient; **14** unsatisfactory; PHRASES: **3, 2, 2, 7** not up to scratch; **6-4** second-rate.

inadmissible **6** banned, barred; **8** censored, excluded; **9** precluded; **10** disallowed, peripheral, prohibited; **12** unacceptable.

inalienable **8** absolute; **9** immutable; **10** inviolable, sacrosanct, undeniable; **12** indisputable, unassailable; **14** unquestionable.

inanimate **4** dead, dull; **5** inert; **7** extinct; **8** deceased, inactive, lifeless, listless; **9** apathetic, inorganic, insensate, lethargic,

nonliving; **10** insentient, spiritless.

inappropriate **5** inapt, wrong; **8** improper, tactless, unseemly, untimely; **9** incorrect, intrusive, misplaced, tasteless, unfitting; **10** inapposite, indecorous, unbecoming, unsuitable; **12** inapplicable; PHRASES: **3-5** ill-timed; **3-6** ill-chosen.

inappropriateness **10** inaptitude, incapacity, inelegance; **11** impropriety, incongruity, irrelevance; **12** inexpedience; **13** insensitivity, unsuitability; **15** inadmissibility, inapplicability, unacceptability. *See also* **inappropriate**

inarticulate **6** clumsy; **7** aphasic, garbled, lisping, mumbled, unclear; **8** babbling, mumbling, muttered, sibilant; **9** dysphasic, dysphemic, faltering, stumbling; **10** incoherent, indistinct, paraphasic, speechless, stammering, stuttering; **14** unintelligible; PHRASES: **6-4** tongue-tied.

inattention **6** apathy; **9** disregard, unconcern; **10** aberration, detachment, negligence; **11** abstraction, daydreaming, distraction, incuriosity; **12** indifference; **13** nonobservance, woolgathering; **15** inattentiveness; PHRASES: **4, 8** cold shoulder. *See also* **inattentive**

inattentive **4** dozy; **6** dreamy; **8** careless, detached, heedless, reckless; **9** apathetic, desultory, forgetful, impulsive, incurious, negligent, oblivious, unheeding, unmindful; **10** abstracted, distracted, unthinking; **11** daydreaming, indifferent, unconcerned, unobservant; **12** disregarding; **13** inconsiderate, woolgathering; PHRASES: **3, 2, 2** out of it; **6-6** absent-minded.

inattentive (be inattentive) **6** ignore; **8** daydream, overlook, stargaze; **9** disregard; **10** woolgather; PHRASES: **3, 2, 4, 2** pay no heed to; **3, 2, 9** pay no attention; **3, 3, 2, 4** put out of mind; **4, 2, 6, 2** take no notice of.

inattentive person **7** dreamer; **10** daydreamer *UK*; **12** scatterbrain, woolgatherer.

inaudible **4** soft; **5** faint, quiet, still; **6** silent; **9** noiseless, soundless; **13** imperceptible.

inaugural **5** first; **6** maiden; **7** initial, opening, primary; **8** germinal, inchoate, original; **9** inceptive, incipient; **10** inchoative; **11** instigative, instigatory; **12** foundational, inauguratory, introductory.

inaugurate **4** open; **5** begin, float, found, start; **6** create, induct, launch, unveil; **7** install, instate; **8** initiate, premiere; **9** auspicate, establish, instigate, institute, introduce; PHRASES: **3, 2** set up; **3, 2, 4** set on foot; **3, 2, 5** put in place; **3, 2, 6** set in motion; **3, 3, 5, 2** sow the seeds of; **3, 8** get underway; **4, 3, 4, 2** open the door to; **5, 2** start up, swear in.

inauguration **5** start; **6** launch; **7** opening; **9** inception, induction, unveiling; **10** foundation, inchoation, incipience, initiation; **11** embarkation, instigation, investiture; **12** installation, introduction; **13** establishment; PHRASES: **8, 2** swearing in.

inauspicious **5** hexed; **6** doomed, jinxed; **7** fateful, ominous, unlucky; **8** accursed, hoodooed, voodooed; **11** unfavorable, unpromising; **12** discouraging, unpropitious; PHRASES: **3-5** ill-fated; **3-6** ill-omened; **3-7** ill-starred.

incalculable **8** infinite; **9** countless, haphazard, uncertain; **11** innumerable; **13** multitudinous, unforeseeable, unpredictable; **14** indeterminable; PHRASES: **7, 6** without number.

incandescent *See* **glowing**

incapable **4** weak; **5** frail, inept; **6** feeble, unable; **8** helpless, inexpert; **9** powerless; **10** vulnerable.

incapacitate **4** harm, stun; **6** injure, weaken; **7** disable; **8** paralyze; **10** debilitate, immobilize; PHRASES: **3, 2** lay up.

incautious *See* **careless**

incendiary **6** burner; **8** activist, agitator, arsonist, stirring; **9** demagogue, flammable; **10** aggressive, firebomber, pyromaniac; **11** combustible, inflammable, provocative; **12** inflammatory, troublemaker; PHRASES: **4, 6** fire raiser *UK*; **6-7** rabble-rousing.

incense **4** joss, musk, otto, rile; **5** anger, annoy, attar, civet, myrrh, resin; **6** chypre, enrage; **7** camphor, perfume, vetiver; **8** olibanum; **9** ambergris, infuriate, patchouli, spikenard; **10** eucalyptus, exasperate, frangipani, sandalwood; **12** frankincense.

incentive **3** rod, sop; **4** goad, lure, prod, spur, whip; **5** nudge; **6** allure, carrot, fillip, motive; **8** stimulus; **9** magnetism, seduction; **10** allurement, attraction, enticement, inducement, motivation; **13** encouragement, seductiveness, tantalization; **14** attractiveness; PHRASES: **3, 5** big stick; **3, 6** sex appeal; **3, 8** jam tomorrow; **5, 2, 3, 4** crack of the whip; **5, 4** siren song; **6, 3, 5** carrot and stick; **7, 4** winning ways.

incident **5** clash, event, fight; **7** episode; **8** occasion, skirmish; **9** happening; **10** occurrence; **13** confrontation.

incinerate *See* **burn**

incise *See* **cut**

incision *See* **cut**

incisive **4** keen; **5** pithy, sharp; **6** biting; **7** acerbic, cutting, pointed; **9** trenchant; **10** insightful, perceptive; **11** penetrating; PHRASES: **5-5** razor-sharp.

incite **4** bait, goad, spur, whet; **5** anger, cause, rouse; **6** elicit, enrage, foment, madden; **7** inflame, provoke, trigger; **8** irritate, motivate; **9** aggravate, infuriate, instigate, stimulate; **10** exacerbate, exasperate; PHRASES: **3, 2** egg on.

inclination **4** bent, bias, mind, turn; **5** grade, pitch, slant; **6** choice; **7** feeling, incline, leaning; **8** fondness, gradient, penchant, tendency; **9** prejudice, readiness, steepness; **10** partiality, preference, proclivity, propensity; **11** disposition; **12** predilection; **14** predisposition.

incline **4** bias, fall, lean, rise, tilt; **5** grade, slant, slope; **6** ascent; **7** dispose; **8** gradient, persuade; **9** prejudice.

include **4** hold; **5** admit, allow, count, cover; **6** embody, number; **7** compose, contain, embrace, enclose, envelop, involve; **8** comprise, encircle; **9** encompass, integrate, recognize; **10** constitute; **11** accommodate, encapsulate, incorporate; PHRASES: **3, 2** add in; **4, 2** rope in, take in; **4, 4, 7** take into account; **4, 5, 3** find space for; **4, 7, 2** take account of; **5, 2** admit of, bring in; **5, 3** allow for; **7, 2** consist of.

include (be included) **5** merge; **6** belong; **11** participate; PHRASES: **2, 4, 2** be part of; **4, 2** make up; **4, 4** take part; **5, 4** enter into; **7, 2** pertain to; **9, 2** appertain to.

included **4** akin; **5** added; **6** joined, linked, listed; **7** allowed, related; **8** admitted, combined, eligible, inherent, interior, involved, recorded; **9** component, comprised, intrinsic, pertinent; **10** congeneric, integrated, pertaining; **11** appurtenant, congenerous, constituent, encompassed; PHRASES: **2, 3, 4** on the list; **4, 2** part of; **4, 3, 6, 2** part and parcel of; **5-2** built-in; **10, 4** classified with.

including **4** plus; **6** global; **7** blanket, general; **8** counting, covering, sweeping, umbrella; **9** expansive, extensive, inclusive, wholesale, worldwide; **10** comprising, containing; **12** encyclopedic, nonexclusive; **13** accommodating, comprehensive, incorporating, incorporative; PHRASES: **2, 4, 2** as well as; **3-2** all-in; **3-9** all-embracing, all-inclusive; **4, 2, 2** made up of; **6-3-5** across-the-board; **8, 2** composed of.

inclusion **7** package; **8** addition, capacity, coverage, presence; **9** admission, comprisal, enclosure, insertion; **10** admittance, annexation, attachment, complement, embodiment, membership; **11** composition, containment, eligibility, implication, integration, involvement; **12** constitution, encirclement, universality; **13** accommodation, admissibility, encapsulation, inclusiveness, incorporation, participation; PHRASES: **2, 9** no exception; **4-2** make-up; **4, 5** full quota; **4, 8** full coverage; **4, 10** full complement; **7, 4** package deal; **7, 8** blanket coverage.

inclusive **5** broad; **8** embodied; **12** encompassing; **13** comprehensive; PHRASES: **3-12** all-encompassing.

inclusively **3** etc.; **6** inside, within; **8** globally; **9** generally; **10** inherently; **11** pertinently, universally; **13** intrinsically; **15** comprehensively; PHRASES: **2, 3, 5** on all sides; **2, 4, 2** as well as; **2, 6** et cetera; **3, 2, 2** and so on; **3, 2, 5** and so forth; **4, 1, 2, 1** from A to Z; **5, 2, 5** alpha to omega; **5, 3, 5** above and below.

incoherent **7** garbled, jumbled, mumbled; **8** confused; **9** illogical; **10** disjointed; **12** inarticulate; **14** unintelligible.

income **3** pay; **4** fees; **5** grant, wages; **6** salary; **7** aliment, alimony, annuity, bursary, pension, profits, returns, revenue, takings; **8** earnings, palimony; **9** allowance, emolument; **10** bursarship, fellowship; **11** maintenance, scholarship; **12** remuneration; PHRASES: **5, 7** child support; **6, 5** pocket money; **8, 5** spending money.

incomplete **3** raw; **4** half; **5** begun, bitty *UK*, crude, rough, short; **6** broken, docked, flawed, lopped, maimed, manqué, marred, scanty, unripe; **7** armless, cropped, cursory, eyeless, halting, lacking, legless, mangled, needing, partial, scrappy, sketchy, unready, wanting; **8** abridged, careless, impaired, inchoate, limbless, omitting, unfilled; **9** curtailed, defective, deficient, embryonic, imperfect, makeshift, mutilated, neglected,

piecemeal, requiring, shortened, truncated, underdone, unrefined, untrained; **10** developing, inadequate, unequipped, unfinished, unpolished, unprepared, unthorough; **11** abbreviated, fragmentary, ineffective, ineffectual, interrupted, perfunctory, provisional, superficial, undercooked, undermanned, undeveloped; **12** insufficient; **13** insubstantial; **14** underdeveloped, unsatisfactory; PHRASES: **2, 3, 6** on the stocks; **2, 3, 8** in the pipeline; **2, 6** in embryo; **2, 11** in preparation; **3, 2** shy of; **3, 3, 5** not all there; **3-4** one-eyed; **3-5** one-armed; **3-6** one-legged; **4-4** half-done; **4-6** half-filled; **4, 7** left hanging; **4-7** half-hearted; **4-8** half-finished; **5, 3, 5** rough and ready; **5-4** rough-hewn; **5-5** jerry-built; **5-6** short-handed; **5-7** short-staffed.

incomplete (be incomplete) **4** lack, need, want; **5** draft; **7** exclude, neglect; PHRASES: **4, 5** fall short; **5, 2** skimp on; **5, 2, 3, 3** leave in the air; **5, 7** leave hanging; **5, 8** leave dangling.

incompletely **4** half; **5** minus; **6** partly, poorly; **7** without; **13** approximately, preliminarily; PHRASES: **2, 4** in part; **2, 6** by halves. *See also* **incomplete**

incompleteness **4** lack, need, want; **7** poverty; **10** deficiency, immaturity, impairment, inadequacy, negligence; **12** imperfection; **13** insufficiency; **14** ineffectuality, nonfulfillment, superficiality; PHRASES: **7, 5** falling short. *See also* **incomplete**

incomplete thing **4** part; **5** draft; **6** embryo, sketch; **8** fraction; **10** proportion.

incomprehensible *See* **unintelligible**

incongruous *See* **odd**

inconsiderate **6** unkind; **7** selfish; **8** careless, heedless, tactless, uncaring, ungenial; **9** pestering, unamiable, uncordial, unfeeling, unhelpful, unmindful; **10** neglectful, unfriendly, ungracious, unobliging; **11** disobliging, inattentive, insensitive, thoughtless, unchristian; **12** discourteous, inhospitable, unbenevolent, uncharitable, unresponsive, unthoughtful; **13** unsympathetic; **15** unaccommodating, unphilanthropic.

inconsistency **8** variance; **9** variation; **11** discrepancy; **12** irregularity; **13** changeability, contradiction, unreliability. *See also* **inconsistent**

inconsistent **7** erratic; **8** variable; **10**

changeable, unreliable; **11** conflicting, incongruous; **12** incompatible; **13** contradictory, unpredictable.

inconstancy **6** levity; **11** variability; **12** whimsicality. *See also* **inconstant**

inconstant **6** fickle; **7** varying; **8** disloyal, variable; **9** irregular; **10** capricious, changeable, unfaithful; **11** fluctuating; **13** unpredictable; PHRASES: **3-6** two-timing.

inconvenience **3** irk, vex; **4** harm, trap; **5** annoy, stump, wrong; **6** bother, burden, corner, hassle, hinder, pester; **7** disrupt, disturb, problem, snooker; **8** drawback, handicap, irritate, nuisance, obstacle, obstruct; **9** annoyance, embarrass, hindrance, incommode, wrongness; **10** difficulty, discomfort, discommode, disruption, impediment, inaptitude; **11** aggravation, disturbance; **12** disadvantage, inexpedience, inexpediency, unseemliness; **13** unsuitability; **14** inadvisability, undesirability; PHRASES: **3, 3** put out; **4, 6** poor timing. *See also* **inconvenient**

inconvenient **5** unapt, undue, unfit; **6** trying, vexing; **7** awkward, hulking, irksome, onerous, tedious; **8** annoying, improper, tiresome, untimely, untoward, unwieldy; **9** difficult, hindering, impolitic, lumbering, troubling, unfitting, unhelpful, vexatious, worrisome; **10** bothersome, burdensome, cumbersome, disrupting, disruptive, disturbing, irritating, malapropos, unsettling, unsuitable; **11** aggravating, inadvisable, inexpedient, injudicious, inopportune, problematic, troublesome, unadvisable, undesirable, unfortunate; **12** exasperating, inadmissible, incommodious, infelicitous; **13** discommodious, inappropriate, objectionable, uncommendable; **14** unprofessional; PHRASES: **3-5** ill-timed; **3-7** ill-planned; **3-9** ill-contrived; **3-10** ill-considered.

incorporate **5** merge; **7** combine, contain, feature, include; **9** integrate; **10** assimilate; PHRASES: **3, 2** add in, fit in.

incorrect **5** false, wrong; **6** untrue; **7** invalid; **8** improper, indecent, mistaken, unseemly; **9** erroneous, imprecise, offensive; **10** fallacious, inaccurate, indecorous, unsuitable, untruthful; **11** misinformed; **13** inappropriate; PHRASES: **2, 5** at fault; **3, 4** off base; **3-6** off-target; **4, 2, 3, 4** wide of the mark.

incorrectness **5** error, gaffe; **7** fallacy, mistake; **10** inaccuracy, invalidity; **11** im-

propriety; **13** unsuitability; PHRASES: **4, 3** faux pas. *See also* **incorrect**

incorruptible **4** just; **5** moral; **8** immortal, straight; **9** honorable; **10** principled, unchanging; **11** everlasting; **12** imperishable; **14** indestructible.

increase **3** bud, wax; **4** boom, gain, grow, rise, soar; **5** boost, breed, bulge, climb, mount, raise, surge, swell; **6** dilate, exceed, expand, extend, fatten, growth, profit, rocket, spiral, spread, sprout, thrive, unfold, upturn, waxing; **7** accrual, advance, amplify, augment, balloon, blossom, broaden, buildup, burgeon, develop, distend, enlarge, inflate, thicken, upsurge; **8** addition, dilation, doubling, escalate, multiply, mushroom, progress, snowball, trebling; **9** accretion, crescendo, elevation, expansion, extension, increment, intensify, intumesce, skyrocket; **10** accumulate, appreciate, enrichment, escalation, exaltation, redoubling, supplement; **11** advancement, aggravation, duplication, enhancement, enlargement, heightening, proliferate, propagation, protraction; **12** acceleration, accumulation, appreciation, augmentation, exacerbation, exaggeration, invigoration, prolongation, reproduction, triplication; **13** amplification, glorification, magnification, proliferation; **14** aggrandizement, multiplication; **15** intensification, quadruplication; PHRASES: **3, 3, 4** hit the roof; **4, 2, 1, 4** rise to a peak; **4, 2, 5** gain in value, rise in price; **4, 3** fill out, take off; **5, 2** flare up, shoot up; **5-2** build-up; **6, 2** spring up; **10, 6** convention bounce.

increased **5** hiked; **7** bloated, swelled, swollen; **8** enlarged, expanded, extended; **9** augmented, magnified; **10** heightened; **11** accelerated, intensified; **12** supplemented.

increasing **6** waxing; **7** growing; **8** crescent, prolific; **9** expanding, spreading; **10** cumulative, escalating; **11** progressing, progressive, snowballing; **12** augmentative; PHRASES: **2, 3, 2, 3, 2** on the up and up; **2, 3, 8** on the increase; **6, 3, 6** bigger and better.

incredible **6** superb; **7** amazing; **9** excellent; **10** improbable, prodigious, staggering, tremendous; **11** astonishing, implausible; **12** unbelievable; **13** extraordinary; PHRASES: **3-7** far-fetched.

incredulity **5** doubt; **6** denial, wonder; **9** amazement, disbelief, discredit, suspicion; **10** bafflement, perplexity, skepticism; **12**

astonishment, bewilderment.

incredulous **8** doubtful, doubting; **9** skeptical; **10** suspicious; **11** unbelieving, unconvinced; **12** disbelieving.

increment *See* **increase**

incumbent **7** binding, officer; **8** occupant, official; **9** appointee, mandatory; **10** compulsory, obligatory; **11** unavoidable; **12** officeholder.

incur **6** suffer; **7** sustain; **9** encounter; **10** experience; PHRASES: **4, 4** meet with.

incurable **4** lost; **5** fatal; **6** deadly; **7** undying; **8** hopeless, terminal; **9** permanent; **10** inoperable, inveterate; **11** irreparable, untreatable; **12** incorrigible, irredeemable, irremediable, irreversible; **13** irretrievable.

incurious **7** unmoved; **8** gullible; **9** apathetic, credulous; **11** indifferent; **12** uninterested; **13** unquestioning.

incursion **4** raid; **6** attack, sortie, spread; **8** invasion; **9** intrusion; **12** infiltration; PHRASES: **5, 4** night raid.

indecency **4** dirt, porn, smut; **5** filth; **6** bawdry; **7** erotica, Playboy; **8** lewdness, ribaldry; **9** bawdiness, crudeness, depravity, obscenity, prurience, voyeurism, vulgarity; **10** coarseness, corruption, defilement, filthiness, indelicacy; **11** impropriety, pornography; **13** offensiveness, salaciousness; **14** indecorousness, licentiousness; PHRASES: **5, 4** dirty joke, loose talk; **6, 8** double entendre.

indecent **4** blue, lewd, racy, sexy; **5** bawdy, crude, dirty; **6** coarse, erotic, filthy, fruity, impure, louche, ribald, risqué, smutty, vulgar; **7** naughty, obscene; **8** defiling, improper, prurient, scabrous, shocking; **9** depraving, offensive, salacious; **10** corrupting, indecorous, indelicate, licentious, lubricious, scrofulous, suggestive, uncensored, unquotable; **11** provocative, titillating, unprintable; **12** insalubrious, pornographic, scatological, unexpurgated; **13** inappropriate, unmentionable.

indecision **5** doubt; **7** dubiety; **8** wavering; **9** hesitancy; **10** hesitation; **11** uncertainty, vacillation; **12** equivocation, irresolution; **13** indeterminacy, pusillanimity. *See also* **indecisive**

indecisive **5** wooly; **6** woolly; **7** gutless, unclear; **8** cowardly, hesitant, sheepish, timorous, wavering; **9** spineless, tentative; **10** indefinite, irresolute; **11** vacillating; **12** inconclusive; **13** indeterminate; PHRASES: **2, 3, 5** in two minds *UK*.

indecorous **4** rude; **5** crude; **6** coarse, vulgar; **7** boorish, uncouth; **8** churlish, impolite, improper, unseemly; **9** barbarous, tasteless, unrefined; **10** indelicate; **11** undignified; **12** discourteous; **13** inappropriate; PHRASES: **2, 3, 5** in bad taste; **3-8** ill-mannered; **5, 10** infra dignitatem; **6, 3, 4** beyond the pale.

indecorum **8** solecism; **11** impropriety; **12** indiscretion; **13** offensiveness.

indeed **5** truly; **6** really; **8** actually; **9** certainly; **10** absolutely, definitely; **14** unquestionably; PHRASES: **2, 1, 6, 2, 4** as a matter of fact; **2, 2, 4** to be sure; **2, 4** in fact; **2, 5** in truth; **2, 5, 2, 4** if truth be told; **2, 6, 4** in actual fact; **2, 7** in reality; **7, 1, 5** without a doubt.

indefensible **4** weak; **5** shaky; **7** exposed, invalid; **9** untenable; **10** undefended, vulnerable; **11** inexcusable, unprotected; **12** unpardonable; **13** unsustainable.

indefinite **4** hazy; **5** vague, wooly; **6** woolly; **7** unclear, unfixed, unknown; **9** imprecise, uncertain, undecided, unlimited; **11** unspecified; **13** indeterminate.

indelible **4** fast; **5** fixed; **7** lasting; **8** enduring, stubborn; **9** permanent; **12** ineradicable; **13** unforgettable; PHRASES: **4-6** deep-rooted, deep-seated.

indemnify **3** pay; **5** cover, repay; **6** assure, insure, refund; **7** protect; **9** reimburse; **10** compensate, underwrite.

indemnity **5** cover; **7** payment; **8** security; **9** insurance; **10** protection, reparation; **12** compensation, remuneration; **13** reimbursement; PHRASES: **4, 9** life insurance.

indemonstrable **10** unprovable; **12** unverifiable; **13** unconfirmable, unpredictable.

indent **4** dent, nick, pink; **5** gouge, notch, scoop; **6** incise; **7** depress, serrate; PHRASES: **5, 2** stave in; **6, 3** hollow out.

indentation **6** dimple, groove, hollow; **8** incision, pockmark; **9** indention, indenture, serration; **10** depression. *See also* **indent**

independence **7** autarky, freedom, liberty; **8** autonomy; **9** authority; **10** liberation, neutrality; **11** objectivity; **12** bachelorhood, impartiality, nonalignment; **13** individualism, individuality, unilaterality; **15** enfranchisement; PHRASES: **2, 10** no allegiance; **3,**

3 own way; **3, 5, 5** the Magna Carta; **4, 4** home rule; **4-4** self-rule; **4-8** self-reliance; **4-10** self-government; **4-11** self-sufficiency; **6, 2, 7** Statue of Liberty; **7, 4** Liberty Bell.

independent 4 free; **7** neutral, wildcat; **8** anarchic, Bohemian, detached, humanist, maverick, unbiased, unwedded; **9** breakaway, footloose, freelance, impartial, liberated, objective, sovereign, unmarried; **10** autonomous, individual, nonaligned, unattached, unfettered, ungoverned; **11** nonpartisan, unsubjected; **12** freewheeling, uncontrolled, ungovernable, uninfluenced, unprejudiced; **13** dispassionate, nonconforming, nonconformist, rationalistic; **14** latitudinarian, unconventional; **15** individualistic; PHRASES: **4, 2, 1, 4** free as a bird; **4, 2, 3, 4** free as the wind; **4, 3, 3** one's own man; **4, 3, 4** one's own boss; **4, 3, 6** one's own master; **4-6** free-minded; **4-7** self-reliant; **4-8** free-spirited, free-thinking, self-employed; **4-9** self-contained, self-governing, self-motivated; **4-10** self-regulating, self-sufficient, self-supporting; **5-4** fancy-free.

independent (be independent) 4 roam; **5** drift, stray; **9** freelance; PHRASES: **3, 2, 6** ask no favors; **3, 3** opt out; **4, 2, 3, 6** call no man master; **4, 2, 7** stay in control; **4, 3** drop out; **4, 3, 5** buck the trend; **4, 7** suit oneself; **5, 3, 4** break the mold; **5, 3, 5** break the habit; **5, 4** break away, break step; **5, 5** stand alone; **6, 7** please oneself.

indescribable 5 great; **7** extreme, intense; **8** dramatic; **10** tremendous; **11** indefinable, unspeakable, unutterable; **13** inexpressible; **14** incommunicable.

indestructible 7 abiding, durable, eternal; **9** resistant; **11** everlasting, nonbreaking, unbreakable; **12** imperishable, shatterproof; PHRASES: **4-5** rock-solid.

indeterminacy 6 laxity; **9** ambiguity, broadness, obscurity; **10** generality, inaccuracy; **11** imprecision, incoherence. *See also* **indeterminate**

indeterminate 3 lax; **4** hazy; **5** faint, foggy, fuzzy, loose, misty, vague; **7** general, inexact, obscure, unclear, unknown; **8** unstated; **9** ambiguous, amorphous, equivocal, imprecise, uncertain, undefined; **10** inaccurate, incoherent, indefinite, indistinct; **13** unpredictable; PHRASES: **3-7** ill-defined.

index 3 key; **4** file, list, menu; **5** guide, table; **7** catalog *UK*; **8** contents, syllabus; **9**

catalogue *UK*, directory, indicator; **10** forefinger, indication; **11** discography, filmography, spreadsheet; **12** bibliography.

Indian 3 ink; **4** hemp; **5** ocean; **6** Mutiny, rubber, summer; **11** reservation.

Indiana 2 IN; **5** peony (flower); **8** cardinal (bird); **12** Indianapolis (capital); PHRASES: **3, 10, 2, 7** The crossroads of America (motto); **5, 4** tulip tree (tree); **7, 5** Hoosier State (nickname).

Indian dish 4 dahl, gobi, imli, puri; **5** bhaji, bhuna *UK*, curry, haldi, korma, kulfi, laddu, lassi, pilaf, pilau *UK*, rasam, tikka; **6** dansak, kulcha, madras, malaya, pakora *UK*, pathia, raitha, samosa; **7** biryani, dopiaza *UK*, mughlai, paratha; **8** chapatti, golgappa, jalfrezi, kashmiri, poppadom, tandoori, vindaloo; PHRASES: **3, 5** nan bread; **5, 3** keema nan; **5, 4** rogan josh; **5, 5** gulab jamun; **6, 3** bombay mix *UK*; **6, 4** masala dosa; **6, 7** butter chicken.

indicate 3 fix; **4** lead, show, wink; **5** flash, guide, imply, steer; **6** denote, evince, signal; **7** betoken, display, express, signify, suggest; **8** disclose, signpost; **9** determine; **11** demonstrate; PHRASES: **4, 2** hint at; **4, 5** make known; **5, 2** point at, point to *UK*; **5, 3** point out.

indication 4 clue, hint, sign, wake; **5** scent, spoor, track, trail; **6** signal; **7** pointer, symptom, warning; **9** footprint; **10** suggestion; PHRASES: **5, 5** vapor trail.

indicative 7 telling; **8** symbolic, telltale; **9** prophetic, revealing; **10** diagnostic, expressive, meaningful, semaphoric, signficant, suggestive, tattletale; **11** symptomatic; **12** interpretive *UK*, semiological; **13** demonstrative.

indicatively 2, 4, 5 by this token; **4, 10** with expression. *See also* **indicative**

indicator 3 arm; **4** buoy, dial, hand, star; **5** arrow, cairn, clock, gauge, index, meter, radar; **6** cursor, finger, needle, winker; **7** blinker, Catseye™, compass, display, pointer; **8** landmark, lodestar, milepost, odometer, signpost, tidemark, windsock; **9** barometer, benchmark, guidepost, milestone, watermark; **10** lighthouse, mileometer *UK*; **11** speedometer, thermometer, weathercock; PHRASES: **4, 6** wind sleeve; **5, 4** water line; **7, 4** weather vane.

indictment 7 censure, comment, summons; **9** criticism; **10** accusation; **11** arraignment, impeachment, prosecution; **12** condemnation, denunciation.

indifference 6 apathy, phlegm; **7** inertia; **8** ataraxia, lethargy; **9** avoidance, passivity, unconcern; **10** detachment, dispassion, inactivity, oscitation, uninterest; **11** disinterest, inappetence, inappetency, incuriosity, informality, insouciance, nonchalance; **12** inexactitude; **13** insensibility, insensitivity; **14** indifferentism, inexcitability, noninvolvement, superficiality; **15** meaninglessness, procrastination; PHRASES: **3, 5** the blahs; **7-5** laissez-faire. *See also* **indifferent**

indifferent 3 lax; **4** calm, cold, cool, lazy; **5** aloof, blasé, inert, messy, slack; **6** casual, frosty; **7** deadpan, inexact, passive, shallow, unaware, unmoved; **8** benumbed, carefree, comatose, detached, inactive, listless, lukewarm, slapdash, slipshod, uncaring; **9** apathetic, ataractic, impassive, incurious, lethargic, oblivious, offhanded, unfeeling, unruffled, untouched, withdrawn; **10** dispirited, impersonal, inappetent, incomplete, insensible, insouciant, nonchalant, phlegmatic, spiritless, unaffected, undesirous, uninvolved; **11** inexcitable, insensitive, passionless, perfunctory, pococurante, superficial, unconcerned, unconscious, unemotional, unimpressed, unsurprised; **12** noncommittal, uninterested, unresponsive, unscrupulous; **13** disinterested, dispassionate, lackadaisical, unexceptional, uninquisitive, unsympathetic; **14** unaffectionate; PHRASES: **2-2** so-so; **4, 2** dead to, deaf to, lost to; **4-4** laid-back; **4-5** easygoing; **4-7** cold-blooded, cold-hearted, half-hearted; **5, 2** blind to; **5-4** fancy-free; **5-7** thick-skinned; **6-2-4** matter-of-fact.

indifferent (be indifferent) 4 yawn; **7** dismiss; **8** oscitate; **9** disregard; PHRASES: **3, 4, 1, 3, 3** not give a fig for; **3, 4, 1, 4** not give a damn, not give a hoot, not turn a hair; **4, 3, 5, 3** look the other way; **4, 8** lose interest; **5, 3** shrug off; **5, 4, 4, 2** close one's eyes to; **6, 4, 5** harden one's heart.

indifferent (make indifferent) 4 bore, dull, numb; **5** blunt; **6** benumb, deaden; **11** desensitize.

indigence *See* **poverty**

indigenous *See* **native**

indigent *See* **poor**

indigestion 3 gas; **4** wind; **5** colic, cramp; **6** flatus, gripes, nausea; **7** acidity, cholera, colitis, pyrosis; **8** acidosis, diarrhea; **9** bellyache, dyspepsia, enteritis, gastritis, heartburn; **10** cardialgia, flatulence, gastralgia; **11** biliousness, stomachache; **12** collywobbles, constipation, hyperacidity; PHRASES: **3, 4** the runs; **3, 5** the trots; **4, 9** food poisoning; **5, 5** gyppy tummy *UK*; **5, 7** upset stomach; **6, 5** peptic ulcer; **6, 7** Crohn's disease; **7, 5** gastric ulcer.

indignant *See* **angry**

indignation *See* **anger**

indignity 5 shame; **7** chagrin; **8** disgrace, dishonor, ignominy; **11** degradation, humiliation; **13** embarrassment, mortification; PHRASES: **3, 2, 4, 4** egg on one's face; **4, 2, 4** loss of face.

indirect 4 mazy; **5** stray; **6** astray, zigzag; **7** bending, crooked, curving, devious, implied, oblique, snaking, veering, winding; **8** implicit, inferred, swerving, tortuous, twisting; **9** ancillary, deflected, secondary; **10** circuitous, deflective, incidental, meandering, roundabout, serpentine, subsidiary, unintended; **12** labyrinthine; **14** circumlocutory; PHRASES: **3-2-3-3** out-of-the-way; **3, 3, 4** off the mark; **3, 3, 7** off the fairway; **3, 6** off course, off target; **4, 2, 3, 4** wide of the mark.

indiscreet 8 careless, tactless, unsubtle; **9** garrulous, imprudent; **10** incautious, indelicate, unthinking; **11** injudicious; **12** undiplomatic.

indiscretion 7 misdeed; **8** nosiness; **10** imprudence, peccadillo; **11** impropriety; **12** carelessness, recklessness, tactlessness; **13** garrulousness, transgression; **14** indelicateness; **15** injudiciousness; PHRASES: **4, 2, 7** lack of caution.

indiscriminate 5 mixed; **6** motley, random; **7** blanket, jumbled, muddled; **8** assorted, catholic, confused; **9** arbitrary, haphazard, scrambled, wholesale; **10** disordered, uncritical, unselected; **11** unselective; **12** intermingled, undiscerning, unsystematic; **13** miscellaneous.

indiscriminateness 4 heap; **6** jumble, muddle; **7** mixture; **9** confusion; **10** generality; **12** inexactitude, universality. *See also* **indiscriminate**

indispensable 3 key; **5** vital; **6** needed; **7** crucial; **8** required; **9** essential, necessary; **10** imperative.

indisposition 7 illness, problem, refusal; **8** debility; **9** complaint, condition; **10** reluctance, resistance; **13** unwillingness; **14** disinclination.

indistinct 3 dim, low; **4** hazy, soft; **5** faint, misty, vague; **7** blurred, inexact, unclear; **9** imprecise, inaudible; **10** indefinite; **13** imperceptible, indeterminate.

individual 6 entity, person, unique; **7** private, special, unusual; **8** discrete, distinct, original, separate, singular; **9** character, exclusive, separable; **10** particular; **11** distinctive, personality; **13** idiosyncratic; **14** particularized; **15** individualistic; PHRASES: **5, 5** human being.

individualist 5 loner, rebel; **6** hermit; **7** ascetic, skeptic; **8** bohemian, maverick; **11** freethinker, independent; **12** isolationist; **13** nonconformist; PHRASES: **4, 4** lone wolf; **4, 6** free spirit.

individuality 11 personality; **12** eccentricity, independence. *See also* **individual**

indoctrinate 5 brief, coach, guide, prime, teach, train; **6** inform; **8** instill, instruct; **9** brainwash, inculcate; **11** proselytize.

indolence *See* **laziness**

indolent *See* **lazy**

indomitable 5 gutsy, tough; **6** plucky; **7** doughty, staunch; **8** resolute, unbeaten; **9** steadfast, undaunted; **10** invincible, undefeated, undeterred; **11** unconquered; **13** unconquerable; PHRASES: **4, 2, 3, 4** game to the last.

indoor 6 inside; **7** covered; **8** enclosed, interior, internal.

induce 4 bait, coax, lure; **5** bribe, bring, cause, charm, lobby, tease, tempt; **6** allure, entice, invite, patter, prompt, seduce; **7** attract, bewitch, flatter, produce, provoke, solicit; **8** convince, engender, generate, persuade; **9** encourage, stimulate; PHRASES: **4, 4** talk into; **5, 2** bring on; **5, 5** bring about.

inducement 6 carrot; **8** cajolery, stimulus; **9** incentive, magnetism, seduction, wheedling; **10** allurement, attraction, enticement, invitation, propaganda; **11** advertising, bewitchment, provocation; **12** blandishment, solicitation; **13** encouragement, seductiveness; **14** attractiveness, persuasiveness; PHRASES: **4, 4** hard sell. *See also* **induce**

induct 5 train; **7** educate, receive, welcome; **8** initiate, instruct; **9** introduce; **10** inaugurate; PHRASES: **5, 2** swear in.

indulge 5 spoil, treat; **6** cosset, pamper, pander.

indulgent 4 kind; **7** lenient; **8** generous, tolerant; **10** permissive.

industrial 4 work; **5** labor, trade; **6** manual, modern; **9** developed, nonmanual, technical; **10** commercial, mechanized; **13** manufacturing; **14** industrialized; PHRASES: **5-2** built-up.

industrialist 4 Duke (James Buchanan), Ford (Henry); **5** Frick (Henry Clay); **6** Cooper (Peter), Hammer (Armand), Hughes (Howard), Kaiser (Henry J.); **8** Carnegie (Andrew); **9** Arkwright (Sir Richard); **10** Guggenheim (Meyer), Vanderbilt (Cornelius); **11** Rockefeller (John D.), Rockefeller (John D., Jr.); PHRASES: **2, 4, 2, 7** du Pont de Nemours (Eleuthère Irénée).

industrial relations 5 labor; **6** strike; **7** lockout, pension; **8** unionism; **11** negotiation; **14** featherbedding; PHRASES: **2-4** go-slow; **3, 6, 4** the common rule; **4-2-4** work-to-rule *UK*; **4, 5** work force; **4, 10** line management; **5, 3** labor law; **5, 5** labor costs, labor force, labor union, trade union; **5, 7** works council *UK*; **6, 4** closed shop; **6, 5** casual labor; **6, 7** social charter; **7, 5** working hours; **7, 6** general strike.

industrious 4 busy; **6** active; **8** bustling, diligent, laboring, sedulous, slogging, studious, tireless; **9** assiduous, efficient, energetic, laborious, unwearied; **10** productive, unflagging, unsleeping, workaholic; **11** hardworking, persevering; **12** businesslike, professional; **13** conscientious, indefatigable; PHRASES: **5-6** never-tiring.

industry 5 trade; **8** activity, business, commerce; **9** diligence; **11** engineering; **13** manufacturing; **14** productiveness; PHRASES: **4, 4** hard work.

ineffective 4 vain; **6** failed, feeble, futile; **7** useless; **8** abortive; **9** fruitless; **11** ineffectual; **12** unproductive, unsuccessful; PHRASES: **4, 3, 4** null and void.

inefficient 3 lax; **5** inept; **8** wasteful; **10** inadequate; **11** incompetent, ineffectual, timewasting; **12** disorganized, uneconomical, unproductive.

inelegance 8 solecism; **9** gaucherie, roughness, vulgarity; **11** affectation; **15** overelaboration; PHRASES: **3, 5** bad taste; **4, 2, 7** lack of finesse. *See also* **inelegant**

inelegant 5 dowdy, dumpy, gawky, plain; 6 clumsy, coarse, common, frumpy, gauche, klutzy, vulgar, wooden; 7 awkward, labored, pompous, stilted, uncouth; 8 affected, unfluent, ungainly; 9 graceless, grotesque, maladroit, tasteless, unnatural, unstylish, vernacula; 10 artificial, solecistic, unpolished; 12 dysphemistic; 13 grandiloquent, overelaborate; 15 unsophisticated; PHRASES: 4-6 cack-handed *UK*; 5-6 heavy-handed.

inequality 4 odds, tilt; 6 camber, defect; 7 oddness; 8 addition, handicap, imparity, inequity, overload, shortage, skewness; 9 asymmetry, disparity, diversity, dizziness, imbalance, lightness, obliquity, roughness, shortfall, unbalance, variation; 10 deficiency, difference, distortion, patchiness, unevenness, unfairness, unlikeness; 11 discrepancy, inferiority, overbalance, subtraction, superiority, variability; 12 disadvantage, irregularity, lopsidedness; 13 disproportion, dissimilarity, heterogeneity, insufficience, insufficiency, nonuniformity, preponderance; 14 discrimination, disequilibrium; PHRASES: 3, 6 odd number; 6, 4 loaded dice; 7, 4 casting vote.

inert 4 dead, idle, lazy, limp, numb, slow; 5 slack, still; 6 fallow, latent, sleepy, static, stolid, torpid; 7 doltish, dormant, flaccid, languid, pacific, passive; 8 immobile, inactive, indolent, lifeless, peaceful, slothful, sluggish, stagnant; 9 apathetic, impassive, paralyzed, quiescent, unwarlike; 10 indecisive, irresolute, motionless, slumberous, stagnating, unreactive, vegetating; 11 hibernating, indifferent, unexcitable, unreceptive; 12 unaggressive, unresponsive.

inert (be inert) 3 lie; 4 doze, lurk; 5 sleep; 6 snooze; 7 slumber; 8 stagnate, vegetate; PHRASES: 3, 3 nod off; 3, 4 lie idle; 3, 5 lie doggo, lie still; 4, 4 hang fire; 4, 4, 6 hold one's breath; 4, 5, 5 have forty winks.

inert gas 4, 3 rare gas; 5, 3 noble gas.

inertly 2, 3 on ice; 2, 4 at rest, on hold; 2, 7 in reserve; 2, 8 in abeyance, in suspense. *See also* **inert**

inertness 5 sloth; 6 apathy, torpor; 7 inertia, languor, latency; 8 dormancy, inaction; 9 indolence, paralysis, passivity, stolidity, torpidity; 10 immobility, inactivity, quiescence *UK*, stagnation, vegetation; 11 hibernation, impassivity; 12 indifference, irresolution; 13 insensibility; 14 inex-

citability. *See also* **inert**

inevitability 4 doom, fate; 5 karma; 7 destiny, nemesis; 9 necessity; 11 fatefulness; 13 inexorability; 14 ineluctability, inescapability, inevasibleness, irrevocability, predestination, predictability, unavoidability; PHRASES: 3, 2, 3 act of God; 3, 5 vis major; 5, 7 force majeure.

inevitable 3 set; 4 sure; 5 fated, fixed; 6 doomed, karmic; 7 certain, fateful; 8 destined, ordained; 9 necessary; 10 determined, inevasible, inexorable, relentless; 11 foreseeable, ineluctable, inescapable, irrevocable, predestined, predictable, preordained, unavoidable; 13 predetermined, unpreventable; PHRASES: 2, 2, 8 to be expected.

inevitably 2, 3, 3 in the end; 7, 5 without doubt. *See also* **inevitable**

inexpedient 6 unwise; 8 untimely; 10 unsuitable; 11 impractical, inadvisable, injudicious, inopportune; 12 inconvenient; 13 inappropriate; PHRASES: 3-5 ill-timed.

inexpensive *See* **cheap**

inexperience 5 bluff; 7 naiveté, naivety *UK*; 8 quackery, sciolism; 9 greenness, innocence; 10 amateurism, immaturity; 12 charlatanism, dilettantism, inexpertness; 13 ingenuousness.

inexpert 5 inept; 6 clumsy; 9 unskilled, untrained; 13 inexperienced.

infallibility 7 loyalty; 8 accuracy, security, solidity; 9 stability; 10 exactitude, perfection; 11 reliability; 13 dependability; 14 predictability. *See also* **infallible**

infallible 4 firm, sure; 5 exact, solid, sound; 6 secure, stable, steady; 7 certain, correct, perfect, staunch; 8 accurate, flawless, reliable, unerring; 9 faultless, foolproof, unfailing; 10 unshakable, unwavering, watertight; 11 predictable, trustworthy, unshakeable; PHRASES: 4-4 fail-safe, sure-fire.

infamous 6 wicked; 9 loathsome, notorious; 10 abominable, iniquitous, villainous; 12 dishonorable, disreputable; PHRASES: 3-5 ill-famed; 3-7 ill-reputed.

infamy 5 shame; 7 outrage, scandal; 8 atrocity, disgrace; 9 disrepute, notoriety; 11 abomination; PHRASES: 3, 4 ill fame; 3, 6 ill repute.

infant 4 baby; 5 child; 7 newborn, toddler; PHRASES: 4, 2, 4 babe in arms.

infatuation 4 love; 5 craze; 7 passion; 9 obsession; 11 fascination.

infect 4 foul; 5 dirty, taint; 6 affect, blight, canker, debase, defile, poison; 7 afflict, corrupt, disease, envenom, inspire, pollute; 11 contaminate.

infection 3 bug; 4 germ; 5 fever, toxin, virus; 6 blight, miasma, sepsis, vector; 7 carrier, disease, illness; 8 bacteria, impurity, pathogen, toxicity; 9 bacterium, contagion, festering, poisoning, purulence; 10 corruption, pestilence; 13 contamination; 14 contagiousness, infectiousness. *See also* disorder

infectious 8 alluring, catching; 10 compelling, contagious; 11 captivating; 12 communicable, irresistible, transferable.

infer 4 hint; 5 imply; 6 assume, deduce, derive, gather, reason, reckon; 7 presume, suggest, suppose, surmise; 8 conclude; 9 insinuate; 11 extrapolate; PHRASES: 4, 3 work out; 6, 3 figure out.

inferior 3 bad; 4 naff, poor, ropy *UK*; 5 beast, cheap, least, loser, lower, minor; 6 crummy, deputy, faulty, flawed, flunky, junior, klutzy, lesser, lowest, menial, minion, rabble, ruined, second, shoddy, tawdry, vassal; 7 bungled, failure, lowlife, nowhere, private, servant, spoiled, subject, younger; 8 canaille, follower, henchman, hireling, mediocre, pathetic, retainer, sidekick, unworthy; 9 assistant, defective, dependent, imperfect, nonentity, satellite, secondary, subaltern, tributary, underling; 10 bottommost, subsidiary; 11 backbencher, incompetent, inefficient, subordinate, subservient, substandard; 14 unsatisfactory; PHRASES: 2-5 no-hoper; 3, 2, 2, 4 not up to much; 3, 2, 2, 5 not up to snuff; 3, 6 hoi polloi, the masses; 4-3 also-ran; 4, 5 poor third; 4, 6 poor second; 5, 3 small fry; 5, 4 badly made, small beer; 5-4 third-rate; 5, 7 lower classes; 5, 8 small potatoes; 6, 2, 3, 3 lowest of the low; 6-4 second-best, second-rate; 6-8 second-stringer; 7, 7 nothing special.

inferior (be inferior) 3 lag; 4 fail; 5 trail; PHRASES: 3, 4 not pass; 4, 4, 4 drag one's feet; 4, 5 fall below, fall short; 4, 5, 2 come short of; 4, 6 fall behind.

inferiority 4 blip, flaw; 5 fault; 6 bungle, defect, glitch, hiccup; 8 baseness, humility, weakness; 9 abasement, cheapness, lowliness, obscurity; 10 clumsiness, dependency, faultiness, humbleness, inadequacy, klutziness, mediocrity, shoddiness, tawdriness; 12 imperfection, incompetence, inefficiency, ordinariness, subservience, subsidiarity, unimportance; 13 secondariness, subordination; 14 insignificance, unskillfulness; PHRASES: 4, 4 back seat; 5, 5 lower class; 6, 6 second fiddle, second string; 10, 4 supporting role.

inferiorly 4 less; 5 below, under; 7 beneath; 9 minimally; PHRASES: 2, 1, 3, 3 at a low ebb; 2, 4, 6, 3 at one's lowest ebb; 4, 4 less than; 5, 2 short of; 5, 3 under par; 5, 3, 4 below the mark; 5, 8 below standard.

infertile 3 dry; 4 arid, bare; 5 bleak, empty, gaunt, stark, stony, waste; 6 barren, desert, eroded, fallow, gelded, sparse, spayed, wasted; 7 sterile; 8 celibate, desolate, impotent, infecund, neutered, stagnant, treeless, withered; 9 castrated, childless, fruitless, shriveled; 10 sterilized, unfruitful, unprolific; 12 uncultivated, unfertilized, unproductive, unprofitable, vasectomized; PHRASES: 3-5 low-yield.

infertile (be infertile) 4 fail; 5 abort; 8 miscarry, stagnate; PHRASES: 3, 2, 4 run to seed; 3, 6 lie fallow.

infertile (make infertile) 4 geld, spay; 5 unman; 6 neuter; 8 castrate; 9 sterilize; 10 emasculate; 11 vasectomize; PHRASES: 3, 3, 5 tie the tubes.

infertility 6 dearth, desert, famine; 7 aridity; 8 aridness, celibacy, dustbowl; 9 impotence, menopause, sterility, wasteland; 10 barrenness, desolation, fallowness, stagnation, wilderness; 11 defoliation, infecundity, miscarriage; 13 childlessness, deforestation, fruitlessness; 14 unfruitfulness, unproductivity; 15 desertification, unprofitability; PHRASES: 3, 5 low yield.

infest 4 fill; 5 drone, swarm; 6 blight, infect, invade, plague, riddle; 7 flyblow, overrun, pervade; 8 permeate; 9 overwhelm; 10 infiltrate, parasitize; 11 contaminate; PHRASES: 4, 4 teem with; 5, 4 crawl with, swarm with.

infestation 5 swarm; 6 influx, plague; 8 invasion; 9 incursion; 12 infiltration.

infiltrate 4 seep; 6 pierce; 7 intrude; 8 permeate, puncture; 9 insinuate, penetrate, percolate; 14 interpenetrate; PHRASES: 3, 4 eat into; 4, 2 bore in, slip in; 5, 2 creep in, slink in, sneak in; 5, 4 break into, creep into; 5, 7 break through; 6, 2 filter in.

infinite **4** huge, vast; **5** large; **7** endless, immense; **9** boundless, countless, limitless, recurring, unbounded, unlimited; **10** bottomless; **11** illimitable, inestimable; **12** immeasurable, interminable; PHRASES: **5-6** never-ending.

infinite (be infinite) **5** recur; **8** continue; **10** perpetuate; PHRASES: **2, 2, 3, 2** go on and on.

infinitely **8** markedly; **12** indefinitely; **13** substantially; PHRASES: **1, 5, 4** a great deal; **2, 1, 4, 3** by a long way UK; **2, 1, 4, 4** by a long shot; **2, 1, 4, 5** by a long chalk UK; **2, 8** to infinity; **2, 9** ad infinitum; **7, 3** without end. See also **infinite**

infinity **8** eternity; **9** immensity; **10** infinitude, perpetuity; **11** endlessness; **12** infiniteness; **13** boundlessness, limitlessness; **14** illimitability; **15** interminability; PHRASES: **10, 3** bottomless pit.

inflame **3** fan; **4** fuel; **5** anger; **6** arouse; **7** provoke; **8** increase; **9** aggravate, intensify; **10** exacerbate; PHRASES: **4, 2** stir up.

inflammable **7** igneous; **9** flammable, ignitable; **10** incendiary; **11** combustible.

inflammation **7** redness; **8** soreness, swelling; **10** irritation, tenderness.

inflatable **7** balloon; **10** expandable; PHRASES: **4-2** blow-up.

inflate **4** fill; **5** bloat, boost, raise, swell; **6** expand; **7** amplify, magnify; **8** escalate, increase; **9** overstate; **10** exaggerate; **12** overestimate; PHRASES: **2, 2** go up; **4, 2** blow up, puff up, pump up; **5, 2** drive up.

inflexibility **5** rigor; **8** rigidity; **9** dogmatism, obstinacy; **13** implacability, intransigence; **14** intractability. See also **inflexible**

inflexible **3** set; **4** firm, hard, taut; **5** fixed, harsh, rigid, stiff; **6** severe, strict; **7** adamant; **8** obdurate, resolute, stubborn; **9** hidebound, immovable, obstinate, pigheaded, unbending; **10** implacable, inexorable, unbendable, unyielding; **11** intractable, unrelenting; **12** intransigent, recalcitrant; **14** uncompromising.

inflow See **influx**

influence **3** run; **4** bias, grip, hold, lure, pull, push, rule, sway; **5** clout, color, force, guide, impel, might, power, tempt; **6** affect, appeal, change, compel, direct, effect, impact, induce, motive, prompt, thrust, weight; **7** ability, control, dispose, gravity, impress, impulse, inspire, pervade, potency, prevail, suggest; **8** dominate, guidance, leverage, motivate, overcome, override, persuade, pressure, stimulus, strength; **9** authority, brainwash, encourage, hypnotize, magnetism, mesmerize, prejudice; **10** attraction, importance, impression, manipulate, mightiness, monopolize, motivation, overmaster, persuasion, predispose, pressurize, prevalence; **11** inspiration, predominate; **12** potentiality, predominance, significance; **13** encouragement; PHRASES: **3, 3, 5** set the trend; **3, 4** win over; **3, 8, 2** put pressure on; **4, 1, 4, 4** have a hold over; **4, 2, 4, 5** have in one's power; **4, 3, 3, 4** hold all the aces; **4, 3, 3, 5** hold all the cards; **4, 3, 4, 4** hold the whip hand; **4, 3, 5** wear the pants; **4, 3, 8** wear the trousers UK; **4, 4** bear upon, take root, work upon UK; **4, 5** have clout, pull wires; **4, 7** pull strings; **5, 4** upper hand; **5, 5** carry clout; **5, 6** carry weight; **5, 7** reign supreme; **6, 8** vested interest; **7, 4** casting vote.

influenced **9** converted, persuaded; **11** brainwashed, evangelized; **12** proselytized.

influential **5** great; **6** causal, mighty, potent, ruling, strong; **7** guiding UK, leading, regnant; **8** decisive, dominant, forceful, powerful, reigning, superior; **9** educative, effective, effectual, important, prominent; **10** commanding, impressive, persuasive; **11** instructive, interfering, prestigious, significant; **12** contributory, instrumental; **13** authoritative; PHRASES: **2, 9** in authority; **5-7** earth-shaking; **5-10** world-shattering.

influentially **7** vitally; **8** docilely; **9** teasingly, tractably; **10** alluringly, charmingly, invitingly; **11** hortatively, hortatorily, momentously, pervasively, seductively, susceptibly; **12** bewitchingly, compellingly, convincingly, hypnotically, infectiously, irresistibly, suggestively, ubiquitously; **13** encouragingly, fascinatingly, insinuatingly, predominantly, provocatively, stimulatingly, tantalizingly; **15** inspirationally; PHRASES: **2, 4, 6** to good effect; **4, 5, 6** with great effect; **4, 9** with authority. See also **influential**

influential person **5** chair; **6** bigwig, doctor, lawyer, parent, priest; **7** manager, premier; **8** chairman, director, lobbyist, preacher; **9** president; **10** chairwoman; **11** manipulator; PHRASES: **3, 4** big shot; **3, 5** big noise, big wheel, top brass; **3, 6** big cheese; **4, 6** best friend; **5, 3** brass hat, queen bee; **5,**

8 prime minister; **9, 4** uncrowned king.

influenza 3 bug, flu; **4** cold; **5** virus; **6** grippe.

influx 5 entry, flood, inrun; **6** afflux, inflow, inrush, intake; **7** arrival, indraft; **8** indrawal, invasion; **9** affluxion, incursion, indrawing; **10** inflooding, inhalation; **12** introduction.

inform 3 rat; **4** blab, narc, nark *UK*, shop *UK*, sing, tell, warn; **5** alert, brief, grass *UK*, peach, teach; **6** advise, betray, delate, notify, report, snitch, squeal, tattle; **7** apprise, confide, educate, testify; **8** acquaint, denounce, disabuse, instruct; **9** enlighten, undeceive; **11** disillusion; **12** tergiversate; PHRASES: **3, 2, 3, 7** put in the picture; **3, 3** tip off; **3, 5** put right; **4, 2** clue up, fill in, tell on, wise up; **4, 5** tell tales; **4, 6** keep posted; **5, 2** sneak on *UK*; **5, 2-2-4** bring up-to-date; **5, 3** point out; **6, 2** report to; **11, 2** stoolpigeon up.

informal 4 open; **5** frank, plain; **6** candid, casual, dégagé; **7** natural, offhand, relaxed; **8** everyday, familiar, friendly, unstuffy; **9** easygoing, idiomatic; **10** colloquial, nonchalant, unaffected, unassuming, unbuttoned, unofficial, vernacular; **11** comfortable, spontaneous, unconfirmed, uninhibited; **12** unauthorized, unsanctioned; **13** nonconformist, unceremonious, unconstrained; **14** unconventional; PHRASES: **2, 4** at ease, at home; **2, 7** at leisure; **3, 2, 7** out of harness; **3-3-6** off-the-record; **4-3-4** free-and-easy; **4-8** free-speaking; **4-10** self-expressive; **5-6** plain-spoken.

informal (be informal) 5 relax; PHRASES: **2, 6** go native; **3, 4, 4, 4** let one's hair down; **4, 2, 3, 3** come as you are; **4, 2, 4** feel at home, take it easy; **4, 2, 7** feel at liberty; **4, 4** feel free.

informality 4 ease; **6** candor; **11** familiarity; **12** indifference; **13** nonconformity. *See also* **informal**

informally 3, 3, 6 off the record; **4, 6** with candor; **7, 8** without ceremony. *See also* **informal**

informant 3 rat, spy; **4** hack, mole, narc; **5** flack, grass *UK*, guide, sneak *UK*; **6** herald, snitch, source, teller; **7** adviser, tipster, witness; **8** dopester, informer, notifier, reporter, squealer, stringer; **9** anchorman, announcer, messenger, newshound, publicist, publisher, spokesman, testifier; **10** advertiser, eyewitness, journalist, mouthpiece, newscaster, newsreader *UK*, publicizer; **11** broadcaster, interpreter; **12** spokesperson; PHRASES: **4-4** tell-tale; **5, 6** stool pigeon; **5, 9** fifth columnist; **6, 5** inside agent; **6-7** strikebreaker; **7-6** whistle-blower.

information 3 gen *UK*; **4** data, info, news, word; **5** facts, skill; **6** report; **7** figures, tidings; **8** evidence, material; **9** knowledge, suspicion; **10** intimation, smattering, statistics; **12** acquaintance, intelligence; **13** communication; PHRASES: **3, 4** the know; **3-4** low-down; **4-3** know-how; **5, 3, 7** facts and figures.

information technology 2 IT; **8** database, viewdata *UK*; **9** computing; PHRASES: **4, 10** data processing, word processing.

informative 5 clear; **6** candid, useful; **7** gossipy, helpful; **8** edifying, explicit, monitory; **9** revealing, talkative; **10** expository, expressive, loquacious, suggesting; **11** educational, explanatory, informatory, insinuating, instructive; **12** enlightening, illuminating; **13** communicative, informational, instructional.

informed 5 aware; **6** posted, primed; **7** abreast, briefed, learned; **8** educated; **9** cognizant; **10** conversant; **11** enlightened; **13** knowledgeable; PHRASES: **2, 2** in on; **2-2-4** up-to-date; **2, 3, 4** in the know; **2, 3, 7** in the picture; **2, 4** au fait; **2, 5** in touch; **2, 7** au courant; **4-6** well-versed; **5, 2** clued up, wised up; **6, 2** genned up.

informed (be informed) 4 hear, know; **5** infer, learn; **7** realize; **8** discover, overhear; **10** understand; PHRASES: **3, 2, 4, 2** get to hear of; **3, 2, 4, 2** get wind of; **4, 2, 4** come to know.

infrequent *See* **rare**

infringe 5 break, cheat, flout; **6** breach, invade, pirate; **7** bootleg, disobey, violate; **8** overstep, trespass; **9** disregard; **10** contravene, transgress; PHRASES: **7, 2** impinge on, intrude on; **8, 2** encroach on; **9, 4** interfere with.

infuse 4 brew, fill, soak; **5** imbue, steep; **6** impart; **7** immerse, instill, pervade, suffuse; **8** permeate, saturate; **9** inculcate, introduce.

infusion 3 tea; **4** brew; **5** drink; **12** fermentation; **13** distilllation.

ingenious 5 nifty; **6** clever; **7** cunning; **8** inspired, original; **9** effective, inventive; **11** imaginative, resourceful.

ingenuity *See* **inventiveness**

ingenuous 4 open; 5 frank, lucid, naive; 6 candid, direct, honest, patent; 7 artless, obvious, sincere; 8 innocent, manifest; 9 guileless, unworldly; 11 unambiguous, undisguised; 13 inexperienced; 15 straightforward, unsophisticated; PHRASES: 4-7 openhearted.

ingest 3 eat, sip; 4 gulp, swig; 5 drink, slurp; 6 devour, engulf, gobble, imbibe; 7 consume, engorge, swallow; 11 ingurgitate; PHRASES: 3, 2 lap up; 4, 2 take in; 4, 4 gulp down, wolf down; 5, 2 drink up.

ingratiating *See* **sycophantic**

ingratitude 11 boorishness, selfishness; 13 thanklessness; 14 nonrecognition, unappreciation, ungraciousness, ungratefulness, unmannerliness, unthankfulness; 15 thoughtlessness; PHRASES: 4, 2, 9 lack of gratitude; 8, 6 grudging thanks; 9, 4 thankless task.

ingredient 4 item, part; 5 piece; 6 factor; 7 element, feature; 8 additive, contents; 9 component; 11 constituent; 12 appurtenance.

ingredient (for cooking) 3 oil; 4 eggs, ghee, herb, lard, salt, suet; 5 aspic, flour, spice, sugar, yeast; 6 balsam, butter, grease, pepper; 7 vinegar; 8 cornmeal, demerara *UK*, gelatine; 9 margarine, seasoning, wheatmeal *UK*; 10 cornstarch, wholewheat; PHRASES: 4-6, 5 self-rising flour; 5, 3 olive oil; 5, 5 icing sugar, plain flour *UK*; 6, 5 caster sugar *UK*; 6, 6 baking powder; 7, 4 cooking salt; 9, 3 sunflower oil, vegetable oil.

inhabit 4 rent, stay; 5 board, dwell, lease, lodge, squat; 6 occupy, people, reside, settle; 7 sojourn; 8 colonize, populate; PHRASES: 4, 2 live in; 5, 2 abide in, dwell in; 6, 2 reside in.

inhabitant 4 clan; 5 local, tribe; 6 colony, family, inmate, ménage, native, people, tenant; 7 citizen, commune, denizen, dweller, resider; 8 indigene *UK*, national, occupant, occupier, populace, resident; 9 citizenry, community, household, incumbent, indweller, inhabiter; 10 autochthon, population; 12 residentiary.

inhabitant (US inhabitants) 4 Okie, Yank; 5 Amish; 6 Badger, Latina, Yankee; 7 Buckeye, Hoosier; 8 American, mexicana; 9 Easterner, Jayhawker, Westerner; 10 Eastlander, Northerner, Westlander; 11 Ar-

kansawyer; 13 Knickerbocker, Mississippian; PHRASES: 2, 3 GI Joe; 2, 4 La Raza; 3, 4 Tar Heel; 3, 6 New Yorker; 3, 9 New Englander; 4-6 Afro-Latino; 4-8 Afro-American; 5, 3 Uncle Sam; 5, 8 Asian American; 5-8 Anglo-American; 6, 5 Basket Maker; 6, 6 Alaska Native; 6, 8 Indian American; 7, 8 African American, Mexican American; 8, 8 Hispanic American.

inhabited 3 let; 7 indwelt; 8 populous; 11 residential. *See also* **inhabit**

inhabiting 6 housed, living, lodged, roofed; 7 abiding, staying; 8 dwelling, resident, residing; 9 domiciled, sheltered; 11 residential; 12 residentiary; PHRASES: 2, 4 at home; 2, 9 in residence.

in hand 4 free, over; 5 extra, spare; 6 unused; 7 surplus; 9 available, remaining; 11 superfluous; PHRASES: 2, 4, 4 to play with; 2, 5 in store; 2, 7, 5 in working order; 3, 3, 3 fit for use; 4, 4 left over; 5, 3, 3 ready for use; 5, 7 under control.

inharmonious (be inharmonious) 3 jar; 5 clash, grate, thrum, whine; 6 jangle, scrape; PHRASES: 4, 3, 4 hurt the ears.

inherent 6 innate; 7 natural; 9 essential, intrinsic; 14 characteristic.

inherit *See* **receive**

inhibit 3 bar; 4 slow; 5 deter, stall; 6 hamper, hinder, impede, reduce; 7 prevent; 8 obstruct, restrain; 9 constrain; PHRASES: 4, 4 hold back.

inhibition 7 reserve, shyness; 8 obstacle; 9 hindrance, reticence; 10 negativism; 12 introversion; 13 embarrassment; PHRASES: 4-2 hang-up; 4-8 foot-dragging.

inhibitive 3 shy; 8 negative; 9 hindering; 10 forbidding; 11 embarrassed, obstructive; 12 conservative, introversive; PHRASES: 4-8 foot-dragging.

inhuman 5 cruel, eerie, weird; 6 brutal; 7 callous, strange, vicious; 8 inhumane; 9 merciless, unearthly, unfeeling; 11 insensitive; 12 otherworldly; PHRASES: 4-7 cold-blooded, cold-hearted.

inimical 4 cold; 7 adverse, hostile, opposed; 8 contrary; 10 unfriendly; 11 unfavorable, unwelcoming; PHRASES: 3-8 ill-disposed.

iniquity *See* **wickedness**

initial 5 early, first; 6 letter; 7 acronym, opening, primary; 8 monogram, original; 11

preliminary.

initiate 4 open; 5 admit, begin, start, teach; 6 induct; 8 instruct; 9 introduce, originate.

initiation 5 start; 6 launch; 7 opening; 9 admission, beginning, induction; 10 admittance; 11 instigation, instruction; 12 introduction.

initiative 4 edge, idea, lead, plan, wits; 6 scheme; 7 program; 8 proposal; 9 advantage; 10 creativity, enterprise; 13 inventiveness; 15 resourcefulness; PHRASES: 4, 8 pole position; 5, 4 upper hand.

inject 3 add; 5 bring, imbue, shoot; 6 infuse, insert, pierce; 7 implant, instill, perfuse; 9 inoculate, introduce, penetrate, transfuse, vaccinate; 10 impregnate; PHRASES: 4, 4 drip feed.

injection 3 jab *UK*; 4 dose, drip, shot; 7 booster, implant; 8 addition, infusion; 9 insertion, perfusion; 10 intubation; 11 inoculation, instillment, intradermal, intravenous, penetration, transdermal, transfusion, translumbar, vaccination; 12 implantation, impregnation, introduction; 13 instilllation, intramuscular; 14 intracutaneous.

injunction 3 ban; 5 order; 7 embargo; 8 sanction; 11 restriction.

injure 3 cut; 4 bite, bump, burn, tear; 5 graze, scald, wound, wrong; 6 bruise, damage, scrape, sprain; 7 scratch.

injured 4 hurt, torn; 5 gammy *UK*; 6 broken; 8 battered; 13 incapacitated. *See also* **injure**

injury 4 gash; 6 lesion, shiner, trauma; 7 mauling; 8 abrasion, fracture, puncture; 9 contusion; 10 laceration; PHRASES: 5, 3 black eye; 6, 4 bloody nose. *See also* **injure**

injustice 4 bias; 5 wrong; 6 ageism, racism, sexism; 7 bigotry; 8 inequity, mistrial, nepotism; 9 prejudice, racialism; 10 chauvinism, favoritism, homophobia, inequality, insularity, partiality, unfairness, xenophobia; 11 intolerance; 12 parochialism, partisanship, predilection, sectarianism; 14 discrimination, predisposition; PHRASES: 3, 7 not cricket; 3-9 one-sidedness; 4, 4 foul play.

inkling *See* **suspicion**

inlaid 5 inset, tiled; 6 boulle, mosaic; 8 enameled, veneered; 9 decorated; 10 ornamented; 11 marquetried, parquetried.

inland 6 inside, inward, within; 7 central, inlands, inshore, inwards, midland, upstate; 8 interior, internal; 9 centrally, heartland, upcountry; 10 hinterland, landlocked; 11 continental; PHRASES: 3, 7 the Midwest; 3, 8 the interior, the Midlands.

inlay 4 tile; 5 inset, piece; 6 enamel, mosaic; 7 pattern; 8 ornament; 9 enameling; 10 decoration.

inlet 3 bay; 4 cove, gulf, port; 5 bayou, bight, creek, delta, fiord, firth *UK*, fjord, fleet, mouth, sound; 6 harbor, outlet; 7 channel, estuary, straits; 9 backwater; 10 Hellespont; 11 Dardanelles; PHRASES: 3, 2, 3, 3 arm of the sea; 3, 2, 6 Bay of Bengal, Bay of Biscay; 4, 2, 6 Gulf of Alaska, Gulf of Guinea, Gulf of Mexico; 4, 2, 8 Gulf of Campeche, Kyle of Lochalsh; 5, 2, 5 Bight of Benin, Firth of Forth; 5, 5 tidal creek; 6, 2, 7 Strait of Messina; 6, 3 Hudson Bay; 7, 4 Persian Gulf; 7, 6 natural harbor; 8, 5 Plymouth Sound; 10, 3 Chesapeake Bay.

inmate 7 convict, patient; 8 internee, prisoner.

innate 6 inborn, native; 7 natural; 9 essential; 11 distinctive.

inner 4 deep; 6 hidden, inside, inward, middle, secret; 7 central, private; 8 interior, internal, intimate; 9 innermost.

innocence 6 purity, virtue; 7 naiveté, naivety *UK*, probity; 8 chastity, goodness, morality; 9 acquittal, ignorance, virginity, whiteness; 10 absolution, immaculacy, perfection, simplicity; 11 artlessness, exculpation, exoneration, gullibility, saintliness, uprightness; 12 incorruption, inexperience, virtuousness; 13 blamelessness, faultlessness, guiltlessness, impeccability, inculpability, ingenuousness, unworldliness; 15 inoffensiveness; PHRASES: 5, 2, 5 state of grace; 5, 5 clean hands; 5, 10 clear conscience; 6, 2, 5 purity of heart.

innocent 4 good, pure; 5 clean, naive, white; 6 chaste, simple; 7 angelic, cleared, playful, saintly, sinless, upright; 8 absolved, dovelike, gullible, harmless, ignorant, lamblike, pardoned, restored, spotless, unerring, unsoiled, virginal, virtuous; 9 acquitted, blameless, childlike, faultless, guiltless, incorrupt, ingenuous, innocuous, stainless, uncorrupt, undefiled, unknowing, unsullied, untainted, untouched, unworldly; 10 discharged, exculpated, exonerated, immaculate, impeccable, inculpable, unblamable; **11** inoffensive, unblemished, unconscious, uncorrupted; **12** prelapsarian, reproachless; **13** incorruptible, unblameworthy, uncorruptible, unintentional; **14** irreproachable; **15** irreprehensible, unsophisticated; PHRASES: **2, 3, 5** in the clear; **3, 6** not guilty; **4, 2, 5** pure of heart; **4, 4, 3** free from sin; **4, 5, 5** with clean hands; **5-5** goody-goody; **5, 9** above suspicion; **6-4-4** holier-than-thou.

innocent (be innocent) 4, 2, 4 mean no harm.

innocent (declare innocent) 5 clear; **6** acquit; **7** absolve; **9** exculpate, exonerate.

innocently 8 unawares; PHRASES: **2, 3, 9** in all innocence. *See also* **innocent**

innocent person 4 babe, dove, lamb; **5** angel, child, saint; **6** infant, virgin; **7** ingenue; **9** greenhorn; PHRASES: **4, 2, 4** babe in arms; **5-5** goody-goody; **8, 5** innocent party.

in order 2 OK; **4** neat, okay, tidy; **7** correct; **8** adequate; **9** organized, permitted, shipshape; **10** acceptable; **11** permissible; **12** satisfactory, sequentially; **13** consecutively; PHRASES: **2, 4** in line, in rank, in turn; **2, 8** in sequence; **3, 2, 1, 4** one at a time; **3, 2, 3** one by one; **3, 5** all right; **5-3-4** spick-and-span.

inordinate *See* **excessive**

inquest 2 p.m.; **5** probe; **6** review; **7** autopsy, inquiry; **8** necropsy; **10** exhumation, postmortem; **11** examination; **12** disinterment; **13** disentombment, investigation.

inquiring 6 prying; **7** curious, probing; **9** searching; **10** analytical *UK*, interested; **11** inquisitive, penetrating, questioning.

inquiry 4 quiz; **5** query; **6** review; **7** autopsy, request; **8** question; **10** postmortem; **11** examination; **13** interrogation, investigation.

inquisitive 6 prying; **7** curious; **8** prurient; **9** inquiring, intrusive, officious; **10** interested, meddlesome; **11** questioning.

inroad 8 invasion; **9** incursion, insertion, intrusion; **11** penetration; **12** encroachment, infiltration; PHRASES: **6, 5** forced entry.

insane 3 mad, odd; **4** bats, daft, loco, nuts, zany; **5** barmy *UK*, batty, crazy, dippy, dotty, funny, loopy, nutty, wacky, weird; **6** absurd, cuckoo, raving, screwy, stupid; **7** bananas, bonkers, cracked, dolally, foolish, lunatic; **8** crackers *UK*, demented, deranged, doolally *UK*, peculiar, unhinged; **9** disturbed, eccentric, ludicrous, senseless; **10** irrational, ridiculous, unbalanced; **11** certifiable, impractical, nonsensical; **12** unreasonable; PHRASES: **2, 4, 5** in left field; **3, 2, 1, 5, 4** mad as a march hare; **3, 2, 1, 6** mad as a hatter; **3, 2, 4, 4** out of one's tree; **3, 3, 4** off the side, off the wall; **3, 4, 4** off one's head, off one's nuts; **3, 4, 6** off one's rocker; **3, 4, 7** off one's trolley; **3, 6, 6** non compos mentis; **4, 2, 1, 5** daft as a brush; **5, 2, 3, 4** loose in the head; **5, 6, 3** stark raving mad; **5-7** crack-brained; **6, 3** raving mad; **6, 3, 4** around the bend; **7, 3** barking mad.

insane (become insane) 4 rave; **6** ramble; PHRASES: **2, 3** go ape, go mad *UK*; **2, 3, 4, 4** go off one's head; **3, 4** run amok; **4, 4, 4** lose one's wits; **4, 4, 7** lose one's marbles.

insane (make insane) 6 dement, madden; **7** confuse, derange, unhinge; **9** unbalance; PHRASES: **4, 4, 3, 4** send over the edge; **5, 2, 3, 4** drive up the wall.

insane person 3 nut; **4** loon; **5** booby, crank, dummy, idiot; **6** cretin, maniac, nutter *UK*; **7** lunatic, oddball; **8** crackpot, headcase, imbecile, neurotic; **9** fruitcake, obsessive, screwball.

insanity 5 folly; **6** idiocy, lunacy; **7** madness; **9** absurdity, battiness, craziness, nuttiness, stupidity; **10** aberration, crankiness; **11** derangement, incoherence; **12** eccentricity; **13** irrationality, senselessness; PHRASES: **4, 2, 3, 6** bats in the belfry; **5, 5** screw loose, slate loose.

inscribe 3 cut, pen; **4** etch, mark, note, sign; **5** carve, enter, write; **6** chisel, enroll, incise, record; **7** engrave, impress, imprint, scratch; **8** dedicate, register; **9** autograph; **10** consecrate, transcribe.

inscription 5 label; **6** legend; **7** caption, epitaph; **8** epigraph, graffiti; **9** autograph, corollary, engraving, lettering, signature; **10** dedication, impression.

inscrutable 6 arcane; **7** cryptic; **8** baffling; **9** ambiguous, enigmatic, recondite; **10** indefinite, mysterious, mystifying, unknowable; **12** impenetrable, inexplicable, unfathomable; **14** indecipherable, unintelligible; PHRASES: **5, 2, 3** clear as mud; **6-4** sphinx-like.

insect-eating mammal 7 echidna; **8** aardvark, anteater, pangolin; **9** pholidote; **11** insectivore; **13** tubulidentate; PHRASES: **3, 4** ant bear.

insectiform 7 phasmid; 8 dipluran, dipteran, insectan; 9 anopluran; 10 hemipteran, homopteran, mecopteran, thysanuran, zorapteran; 11 coleopteran, collembolan, dermapteran, mallophagan, neuropteran, orthopteran, plecopteran; 12 dictyopteran, heteropteran, hymenopteran, lepidopteran, megalopteran, trichopteran; 13 strepsipteran; 14 ephemeropteran; PHRASES: 6-4 insect-like.

insect noise 7 buzzing, droning, humming, whining; 11 bombination; 12 stridulation.

insects 3 ant, bug; 4 flea, grub, mite, pest, pupa, tick; 5 aphid, borer, emmet, imago, larva, louse; 6 bedbug, chigoe, earwig, jigger, locust, maggot, mantis; 7 beastie, chigger, cricket, katydid, pismire, stylops, termite; 8 firebrat, mealybug; 9 bumblebee, chrysalis, dobsonfly; 10 froghopper, phylloxera, silverfish, spittlebug, springtail, treehopper, webspinner; 11 backswimmer, bristletail, caterpillar; PHRASES: 2, 4 Io moth; 3, 6 lac insect; 3, 7 red admiral; 4, 3 army ant, fire ant, June bug, rose bug; 4, 4 luna moth, sand flea, wood tick; 4, 5 gall midge; 4, 6 June beetle, leaf hopper, leaf insect, pond skater, rose beetle, rose chafer; 4, 7 bush cricket, mole cricket; 5, 3 honey ant, sheep ked, stink bug, water bug; 5, 4 gypsy moth, yucca moth; 5, 6 plant hopper, stick insect; 5, 7 house cricket, water boatman, water strider, white admiral; 5, 8 water scorpion; 5, 11 tiger swallowtail; 6, 3 amazon ant, chinch bug, driver ant, shield bug, squash bug; 6, 4 cotton moth, woolly bear; 6-6 creepy-crawly; 6, 7 cotton stainer; 7, 4 harvest mite, leopard moth; 7, 4, 6 Mexican bean beetle; 7, 9 monarch butterfly; 8, 3 assassin bug; 8, 4 cecropia moth, imperial moth; 8, 5 mourning cloak; 9, 3 harlequin bug; 9-4, 6 seventeen-year locust; 10, 3 leafcutter ant; 10, 6 periodical cicada. *See also* **beetle, flying insect, louse, worm**

insecure 5 loose, shaky; 7 anxious, rickety; 8 unstable, unsteady; 9 uncertain, unguarded; 10 undefended, vulnerable; 11 unconfident, unprotected; PHRASES: 4-8 self-doubting.

insensibly 7 bluntly; 11 obliviously, somnolently, unfeelingly; 13 imperceptibly, insensitively, unconsciously.

insensitive 4 cold, dull, numb; 5 blasé, blunt, crass, cruel, thick, tough; 6 brutal, immune, obtuse, vulgar; 7 callous, selfish, unaware, unmoved; 8 hardened, tactless, uncaring; 9 apathetic, heartless, impassive, insensate, merciless, oblivious, obnoxious, unfeeling; 10 impervious, indelicate, indiscreet, insensible, unaffected; 11 inattentive, indifferent, thoughtless, unconscious, unemotional; 12 imperceptive, impercipient; 13 inconsiderate, unsusceptible, unsympathetic; PHRASES: 4-7 cold-blooded, coldhearted; 5-5 rhino-hided; 5-7 thick-skinned.

insensitive (render insensitive) 4 dope, drug, numb; 5 blunt, brain; 6 benumb, deaden, freeze; 7 concuss, stupefy; 8 paralyze; 9 hypnotize, narcotize; 11 desensitize; 12 anaesthetize; PHRASES: 5, 3 knock out; 5, 9 knock senseless.

insensitivity 10 anesthesia. *See also* **insensitive**

inseparable 5 close; 6 united; 7 devoted; 8 intimate; 11 indivisible; 12 indissoluble, inextricable.

insert 3 add; 4 hole; 5 embed, graft, inset, plant; 6 append, import, inject; 7 enclose, implant, include, pullout; 8 addition, intromit; 9 enclosure, insertion, insinuate, interject, introduce, introject; 10 interleave, supplement, transplant; 11 incorporate, intercalate, interpolate; PHRASES: 3, 2 pop in, put in, set in; 4, 2 drag in, drop in, slot in; 5, 2 bring in, place in, stick in.

inserted 6 inlaid; 7 infixed; 8 impacted; 13 parenthetical. *See also* **insert**

insertion 5 graft, inset; 6 import, insert; 7 pullout; 8 addition, embolism, grafting, infixion, planting; 9 embedment, enclosure, impaction, inclusion, intrusion; 10 impactment, supplement, transplant; 11 importation, insinuation, parenthesis, penetration; 12 implantation, infiltration, interjection, introduction, introjection, intromission; 13 incorporation, intercalation, interpolation; 15 transplantation.

inset 3 add, box; 5 cover, embed, frame, infix, inlay, mount; 6 encase, insert; 7 pullout, sheathe; 8 addition, dovetail, position; 9 ensheathe, inclusion, insertion; 10 supplement; 11 incorporate; 12 circumscribe; PHRASES: 3, 2 put in, set in.

inside 2 in; 4 core, home, jail; 5 heart, inner; 6 center, depths, indoor, inmost, inward, middle, prison, within; 7 indoors, private; 8 interior, internal, intimate; 9 innermost; 10 imprisoned; 12 confidential;

PHRASES: **2, 4** at home; **5, 4** doing time; **6, 2** banged up *UK*, locked up.

inside (keep inside) 4 hide, jail; **7** conceal, confine, contain; **8** imprison; **11** internalize; PHRASES: **6, 2** bottle up.

inside (the inside) 3 can, jug, pen; **4** nick, poky, quod *UK*, stir, tank; **5** clink; **6** bucket, chokey *UK*, cooler; **7** borstal *UK*, slammer, sneezer; **8** hoosegow; **10** glasshouse *UK*; PHRASES: **3, 3, 5** the big house; **3, 6** big school; **6, 6** little school.

insides 4 core, guts *UK*, pith, womb; **5** belly, heart, liver, tummy; **6** bowels, kernel, marrow, paunch; **7** abdomen, innards, jejunum, stomach, viscera; **8** contents, entrails; **10** intestines; PHRASES: **3, 6** the vitals; **5, 6** vital organs.

insight 5 hunch; **6** acumen, vision; **7** empathy, impulse; **8** sympathy; **9** awareness, intuition; **10** foreboding, impression, perception; **11** discernment, sensitivity; **13** comprehension, understanding; **14** perceptiveness.

insight (have insight) 9 empathize; **10** sympathize, understand.

insignia 3 bar, pip; **4** bays, logo, mace, sash, sign, star, wand; **5** badge, baton, crest, cross, crown, gavel, medal, motif, staff; **6** emblem, hackle, ribbon, stripe, throne, trophy, wreath; **7** chaplet, chevron, cockade, epaulet, garland, laurels, regalia, rosette, scepter; **8** brassard, markings; **10** decoration; **11** aiguillette; PHRASES: **4, 2, 9** mark of authority; **4, 4** hash mark; **4, 5** gold medal, Iron Cross; **4, 6** blue ribbon; **5, 2, 5** badge of merit, sword of state; **5, 2, 6** badge of office, Croix de Guerre, robes of office; **6, 3** silver cup; **6, 5** George Cross *UK*, silver plate, spread eagle; **7, 7** victory laurels; **8, 5** Victoria Cross (VC).

insignificance *See* **triviality**

insignificant *See* **trivial**

insignificantly 10 middlingly, ordinarily; **11** worthlessly; **13** unimportantly; **14** inconsiderably.

insincere *See* **dishonest**

insinuate 4 hint; **5** imply; **7** suggest, wheedle; **8** indicate, intimate; PHRASES: **4, 2** cozy up; **5, 5** curry favor.

insinuation *See* **suggestion**

insipid 4 dull, mild, tame, weak; **5** banal, bland, inane, plain, trite, vapid, wersh *Scot*;

6 boring, pallid, watery; **7** diluted, humdrum; **8** lifeless; **9** colorless, savorless, tasteless; **10** flavorless, lackluster; **11** featureless; **12** unappetizing; **13** characterless, uninteresting; PHRASES: **4-7** half-hearted; **5-5** wishy-washy; **7-4** watered-down.

insipidness 7 inanity, wanness; **8** banality, thinness, vapidity; **9** staleness; **10** feebleness, insipidity. *See also* **insipid**

insist 4 aver, hold, urge; **5** claim, press, swear; **6** adhere, assert, demand; **7** contend, enforce; **8** maintain; **9** stipulate; PHRASES: **3, 4, 2, 4** not give an inch; **3, 4, 4, 2** dig one's toes in; **3, 4, 4, 4** put one's foot down; **3, 5** not budge; **4, 3** stay put; **4, 4** hold fast; **5, 3** press for; **5, 4** stand fast, stand firm, stick fast.

insolence 3 lip; **5** cheek, sauce; **8** audacity; **9** impudence, vulgarity; **10** coarseness, disrespect, effrontery, incivility, misconduct, truculence; **11** boorishness, caddishness; **12** churlishness, impertinence; **13** offensiveness; PHRASES: **3, 7** bad manners; **3-8** ill-breeding. *See also* **insolent**

insolent 4 flip, pert, rude; **6** brazen, cheeky; **8** flippant, impudent, malapert; **9** bumptious; **10** precocious; **11** impertinent; **12** contumelious; **13** disrespectful.

insoluble 9 difficult, enigmatic, intricate; **10** insolvable; **11** irresoluble; **12** impenetrable, inexplicable, unfathomable; **14** indecipherable.

insolvency 4 debt, ruin; **5** slump; **8** collapse; **9** overdraft, recession; **10** bankruptcy, dependence, depression; **11** liquidation; **12** indebtedness; **13** dispossession; **14** disinheritance; PHRASES: **3, 5** bad times; **4-4, 6** cash-flow crisis; **4, 5** hard times; **4, 8** bare cupboard; **4-10** belt-tightening; **5, 5** empty purse; **5, 6** light pocket, queer street; **7, 2** Chapter 11.

insolvent 4 bust; **5** broke, short, skint *UK*; **6** broken, pushed, robbed, ruined; **7** fleeced, pinched, pressed; **8** bankrupt, indebted, strapped, stripped; **10** pauperized; **12** disinherited, dispossessed, impoverished; PHRASES: **2, 3, 3** in the red; **2, 3, 5** on the rocks; **2, 4** in debt, in hock; **2, 4, 6** on one's uppers; **2, 5, 6** in queer street; **2, 12** in receivership; **3-2-6** out-of-pocket; **4, 2** hard up; **4, 5** dead broke; **4-7** hard-pressed; **5, 2** belly up; **5-5** stone-broke, stony-broke *UK Can*; **7, 1, 4** without a bean, without a cent; **7, 3** cleaned out.

inspect 4 scan, view; 5 check, study; 6 peruse, review, survey; 7 examine, eyeball; 10 scrutinize; 11 reconnoiter; PHRASES: 4, 1, 6 take a gander.

inspiration 4 idea, muse, spur; 5 flash; 6 genius, vision; 7 insight; 8 afflatus, stimulus; 10 brainstorm, brilliance, creativity, motivation, revelation; 11 stimulation; 13 encouragement, inventiveness; PHRASES: 5, 4 brain wave *UK*.

inspire 4 move, stir; 5 rouse; 6 arouse; 7 animate, breathe, enliven, enthuse; 8 inspirit, motivate; 9 encourage, stimulate; 10 exhilarate.

install 3 fit, fix; 5 crown, mount; 6 enlist, enroll, induct, invest, launch, ordain; 7 appoint, connect, instate; 8 ensconce, enthrone, initiate; 9 auspicate, establish; 10 inaugurate; PHRASES: 3, 2 put in, set up; 4, 2 sign up.

installment 4 part; 7 chapter, episode, payment, portion, section, segment.

installment plan 2 HP *UK*; 6 credit; PHRASES: 8, 7 deferred payment.

instant 2 mo *UK*; 4 fast, tick *UK*; 5 flash, jiffy, rapid, swift, trice; 6 direct, minute, moment, prompt, second, sudden, urgent; 8 powdered, premixed, prepared, pressing; 9 immediate, precooked, twinkling; 12 microwavable, straightaway; 13 instantaneous; PHRASES: 1, 3 a sec; 2, 3, 4 on the spot; 2, 4 at once; 5, 6 split second.

instantly 4 ASAP; 9 posthaste; PHRASES: 2, 1, 5 in a flash, in a trice; 2, 2, 4 in no time; 5, 4 right away. *See also* **instant**

instead 12 additionally, equivalently; 13 alternatively, provisionally; PHRASES: 2, 2, 11 as an alternative; 2, 3, 5 in its place; 2, 4, 2 in lieu of; 2, 4, 5 in one's place, in one's shoes; 2, 4, 8 in loco parentis *L*; 2, 5 by proxy; 2, 5, 2 in favor of, in place of; 2, 6, 2 on behalf of; 2, 7 by default; 2, 7, 2 in default of; 3, 3 per pro; 4, 2, 5 faux de mieux.

instill 4 drip, pour; 6 impart, infuse, inject; 9 inculcate, introduce; PHRASES: 4, 4 drum into; 5, 4 drive into; 7, 4 impress upon.

instinct 4 gift, need, urge; 5 drive, flair, hunch, knack, sense; 6 nature, reflex, talent; 7 ability, feeling, impulse; 8 aptitude; 9 intuition; 10 compulsion, proclivity; 11 disposition; 12 constitution; 14 predisposition; PHRASES: 3, 8 gut reaction; 5, 5 sixth sense.

instinctive 6 inborn, innate, reflex; 7 natural; 8 inherent; 9 automatic, impulsive, intuitive, Pavlovian; 11 involuntary, spontaneous; 12 subconscious; PHRASES: 4-4 knee-jerk.

institute 5 found; 9 establish, introduce; 10 foundation; 11 association, institution; 12 organization; 13 establishment; PHRASES: 3, 2 set up; 5, 5 bring about.

institution 4 body; 6 custom, ritual; 7 society; 8 creation; 9 tradition; 10 convention, foundation; 11 association; 12 introduction, organization; 13 establishment.

instruct 4 tell; 5 coach, order, teach, train, tutor; 6 charge; 7 command, educate; PHRASES: 4, 6, 2 give orders to.

instruction(s) 5 order; 6 manual; 7 classes, command, lecture, lessons, tuition; 8 briefing, teaching, training; 9 direction, directive, education, guidebook.

instructor 5 coach, tutor; 6 mentor; 7 teacher, trainer; 8 lecturer.

instructorship 5 chair, staff; 7 faculty; 8 tutelage, tutorage; 9 tutorship; 10 fellowship, readership; 11 lectureship; 12 professorate; 13 professorhood, professorship, schoolmastery.

instrument 4 tool; 5 force, gizmo, means, organ; 6 agency, device, gadget, medium, method; 7 machine, utensil; 8 catalyst; 9 apparatus, equipment, expedient, implement, influence, mechanism; 11 contraption.

instrument (be an instrument) 2 do; 3 act; 4 help, work; 5 cause; 6 assist, effect; 7 achieve, advance, channel, mediate, operate, perform, promote, support; 8 expedite, function; 9 implement, influence, interpose; 12 intermediate; PHRASES: 4, 1, 4, 2 have a hand in; 4, 3 work for; 4, 7 pull strings; 5, 3 carry out; 5, 4, 6 bring into effect; 5, 7 carry through; 6, 2 pander to; 8, 2 minister to.

instrumental 4 able, alto, bass; 5 tenor; 6 active, choral, hymnal, treble, useful; 7 helpful, soprano; 8 baritone, dramatic, falsetto, involved, operatic, powerful; 9 advancing, assisting, conducive, effective, effectual, efficient, promoting, promotive; 10 applicable, employable, liturgical, orchestral, subsidiary, supportive; 11 efficacious, influential; 12 contributory.

instrumentality 3 use; 5 cause, clout, means, power; 6 agency, effect, medium; 7

ability, potency, service, utility; **8** adequacy, efficacy, function, occasion, pressure; **9** handiness, influence, mediation, operation; **10** automation, competence, efficiency, employment; **11** achievement, application, cooperation, opportunity, performance, sufficiency; **12** interference, intermediacy, intervention, practicality, significance, subservience; **13** functionality, mechanization; **14** responsibility, serviceability; **15** instrumentation. *See also* **instrumental**

instrumentally 2 by; **3** per, via; **4** with; **7** through; **8** manually; **12** mechanically; **13** automatically, significantly; **14** electronically; **15** technologically; PHRASES: **2, 3, 2** by way of; **2, 5, 2** by means of; **2, 6, 2** by virtue of; **4, 3, 3, 2** with the aid of; **6, 2** thanks to. *See also* **instrumental**

insubordinate (be insubordinate) 4 dare; **5** rebel, scorn, spurn, taunt; **6** ignore, insult, resist, slight; **7** disobey, dissent; **8** confront, threaten; **9** challenge, disregard; **11** demonstrate; PHRASES: **6, 4** answer back.

insubstantial 4 airy, thin, weak; **5** foamy, frail, light; **6** bubbly, dainty, flimsy, floaty, frothy, gentle, slight, tender, unreal; **7** buoyant, gaseous, sublime; **8** bubbling, cobwebby, delicate, ethereal, feathery, illusory, volatile; **9** imaginary; **10** irrelevant, unsinkable; **11** unsupported; **12** effervescent, levitational.

insufficiency 4 lack; **6** anemia, dearth, defect; **7** absence, deficit, failure, fasting, paucity; **8** pittance, scarcity, shortage, slippage, weakness; **9** austerity, parsimony, scantness, shortfall, unfitness; **10** asceticism, bankruptcy, deficiency, inadequacy, insolvency, meagreness *UK*, scantiness, stinginess; **11** inferiority; **12** imperfection, incompetence, inefficiency; **14** incompleteness, ineffectuality, nonfulfillment; PHRASES: **2, 6** no quorum; **3, 6** not enough; **4, 2, 3, 5** drop in the ocean; **4, 8** half measures; **4-10** belt-tightening; **5, 3, 5** bread and water; **6, 4** Lenten fare; **7, 4** Spartan fare; **7, 8** stopgap measures.

insufficient 3 low; **4** mean, poor, thin, weak; **5** cheap, faint, light, muted, quiet, scant, small, wersh *UK*; **6** faulty, flimsy, jejune, meager, scanty, scarce, slight, sparse, stingy; **7** diluted, distant, insipid, invalid, lacking, limited, miserly, shallow, sketchy, slender, wanting; **8** inferior, pathetic; **9** deficient, inaudible, incapable, invisible,

tasteless; **10** inadequate, incomplete, infrequent; **11** incompetent, substandard; **12** inconclusive, parsimonious, unacceptably, unconvincing; **13** disappointing, imperceptible, insubstantial; **14** unsatisfactory; PHRASES: **3, 2, 2, 5** not up to snuff; **3, 6** not enough, too little; **4-3-5** milk-and-water; **5, 3** below par; **5-5** wishy-washy; **5, 8** under strength.

insufficient (be insufficient) 4 fail, lack, need, want; **6** hinder; **8** restrict; **10** disappoint; PHRASES: **3, 3** run out; **4, 5** fall below, fall short.

insufficient (make insufficient) 5 drain, skimp, stint, waste; **6** impair, ration; **7** deplete, deprive, exhaust; **8** overcrop, overfish, overwork, squander; **9** overgraze; **10** impoverish, overextend; PHRASES: **3, 3, 4** ask too much.

insufficiently 2, 7 in default. *See also* **insufficient**

insulate 3 lag, pad, wad; **4** fill, line; **6** shield; **7** isolate, protect; **8** cloister; PHRASES: **3, 3** cut off.

insulation 6 lining; **7** filling, lagging, padding, wadding; **9** insulator, isolation; **10** dielectric, protection; **11** segregation; **12** nonconductor; **13** sequestration, soundproofing; PHRASES: **6, 7** double glazing *UK*.

insulator *See* **insulation**

insult 4 slur, snub; **5** abuse, scorn, snook, spurn, taunt; **6** offend, rebuff, revile, slight; **7** affront, offense, putdown; **8** brickbat, rudeness; **9** aspersion, criticism; PHRASES: **1, 4** V sign; **3, 2-2** the go-by; **3, 4** cut dead, put down; **4, 2, 3, 4** slap in the face; **4, 8** cold shoulder.

insulting 4 rude; **7** abusive, cutting; **8** insolent, snubbing, spurning, taunting, wounding; **9** offensive, rebuffing, repulsing, slighting; **10** backhanded, defamatory, pejorative; **11** impertinent, opprobrious; **12** contumacious, discourteous; PHRASES: **8-3** uncalled-for.

insurance 5 cover; **8** adjuster, coverage, security; **9** assurance, indemnity, safeguard; **10** precaution, protection; **15** indemnification; PHRASES: **4, 3** nest egg; **5, 7** major medical; **8, 4** assigned risk.

insure 5 cover; **6** assure; **7** protect; **9** indemnify; **10** underwrite.

insurgent 5 rebel; **8** mutineer, mutinous; **9** guerrilla; **10** rebellious; **13** revolutionary;

15 insurrectionary.

insurrection *See* **uprising**

intact *See* **complete**

intake 4 duct, gulp, pipe, suck, tube; **5** entry, inlet, slurp, sniff; **6** eating; **7** gulping, indraft, opening, sucking, suction, swallow; **8** aperture, drinking, indrawal, slurping, sniffing; **9** engulfing, ingestion; **10** engulfment, imbibition, inhalation, inhalement, swallowing; **11** consumption, engorgement, inspiration; **13** ingurgitation.

integral 4 full; **5** basic, vital, whole; **6** intact; **8** complete, unbroken; **9** component, essential, important, undivided; **10** integrated; **11** constituent, fundamental, indivisible, inseparable; **12** ineradicable; PHRASES: **5-2** built-in.

integrate 3 add, mix; **7** combine; **10** assimilate; **11** desegregate, incorporate; PHRASES: **3, 2** fit in; **3, 8** put together; **4, 2** join in, open up; **4, 4** take part; **4, 8** join together.

integrity *See* **honesty**

intellect 3 wit; **4** mind, suss *UK*; **5** brain; **7** faculty; **10** brainpower; **12** intelligence; **13** understanding.

intellect (lacking intellect) *See* **stupid**

intellect (lack intellect) 4, 2, 3 fail to see; **4, 3, 4** play the fool.

intellect (lack of intellect) *See* **stupidity**

intellectual 4 guru, sage; **5** brain; **6** genius, master, pundit, savant; **7** scholar, thinker; **8** academic, bookworm, brainbox *UK*, cerebral, highbrow, polymath; **9** intellect, scholarly; **10** illuminati; **11** academician, bibliophile, intelligent, littérateur, philosopher; **13** knowledgeable; PHRASES: **4, 3** wise man. *See also* **know-it-all**

intelligence 2 IQ, MI; **3** gen *UK*, KGB, wit; **4** mind, news, nous *UK*, wits; **5** brain, sense; **6** acumen, genius, humint, masint, reason, sigint; **7** reports; **8** aptitude, gumption; **9** intellect, mentality, smartness; **10** astuteness, brainpower, brightness, brilliance, cleverness; **11** information, inspiration, receptivity; **13** communication, comprehension, understanding; **15** intellectualism; PHRASES: **4, 5** good sense; **4, 6** gray matter; **5, 5** horse sense; **5-10** quick-wittedness; **6, 3** mother wit; **6, 4** bright idea; **6, 4, 5** little gray cells; **6, 5** common sense.

intelligence test 2, 4 IQ test; **4, 4** beta test; **4, 6, 4** Kent mental test; **5, 4** alpha test, Binet test; **7-4, 4** Babcock-Levy test.

intelligent 4 sage, wise; **5** acute, alert, canny, quick, sharp, smart; **6** astute, brainy, bright, clever, crafty, gifted, shrewd; **7** cunning, erudite, learned, logical; **8** cerebral, rational, sensible, skillful, smartass, talented; **9** brilliant, judicious, sagacious, scholarly; **10** farsighted, perceptive, reasonable, reflective, streetwise, thoughtful; **11** calculating; **12** intellectual; **13** knowledgeable, understanding; PHRASES: **2, 3, 4** on the ball; **3, 5** all there; **3, 6, 2, 4** too clever by half; **5-6** clear-headed, quick-witted, sharp-witted.

intelligent (be intelligent) 4 know; **5** shine; **11** scintillate; PHRASES: **3, 4, 4** use one's head; **4, 5, 4** know what's what.

intelligibility 5 sense; **9** certainty, coherence, precision, vividness; **11** unambiguity; **12** definiteness, scrutability, teachability; **13** explicability, penetrability, unambivalence. *See also* **intelligible**

intelligible 4 sane; **5** clear, lucid, plain; **7** audible, graphic, logical, precise, visible; **8** coherent, distinct, explicit, knowable, luminous, positive, striking, univocal; **9** scrutable, teachable, unblurred; **10** articulate, explicable, expressive, fathomable, meaningful, penetrable; **11** descriptive, explanatory, explicatory, informative, unambiguous, unequivocal; **12** illustrative, unambivalent, unmistakable; **13** apprehensible, interpretable; **14** comprehensible, understandable; PHRASES: **5-3** clear-cut.

intelligible (be intelligible) 8 register; **9** penetrate; PHRASES: **3, 2** add up; **3, 6** get across; **4, 2** dawn on, sink in; **4, 4, 4** open one's eyes; **4, 5** come alive, make sense; **5, 3, 6** speak for itself; **5, 7** speak volumes.

intelligibly 6 simply; PHRASES: **2, 5, 7** in plain English. *See also* **intelligible**

intend 3 aim; **4** mean, plan, will; **5** augur, cause, shall; **6** design, effect, entail, ponder; **7** foresee, involve, portend, presage, propose, purpose; **9** determine; **10** predestine; PHRASES: **2, 4, 2** be bent on; **2, 5, 2** be about to; **4, 2** mean to, plan to; **4, 2, 4** have in mind.

intended 5 meant; **6** fiancé; **7** fiancée, planned, willful; **8** designed, proposed, purposed; **9** betrothed, projected; **10** calculated, deliberate, determined, envisioned, purposeful, volitional; **11** anticipated, intentional; **12** aforethought, premeditated; **13** predetermined; PHRASES: **2, 7** on purpose; **4-2-2** wife-to-be; **7-2-2** husband-to-be.

intending 7 hopeful, seeking; **8** aspiring, disposed, hellbent, inclined, resolute; **9** ambitious, purposive; **11** prospective; **12** teleological; PHRASES: **2, 6** so minded; **2, 8** so inclined; **3, 2** out to; **4, 7, 2** with designs on; **5-2** would-be.

intense 4 deep; **6** severe, strong; **7** extreme; **8** forceful, powerful; **10** passionate; **11** penetrating; **12** concentrated.

intensity 5 depth, force, power; **6** extent, stress, weight; **7** cogency, measure, urgency; **8** emphasis, keenness, pressure, severity, strength; **9** greatness, intension; **10** trenchancy; **12** incisiveness; **13** concentration, determination.

intent 3 aim; **4** goal; **5** fixed; **6** target; **7** focused; **8** absorbed, directed, resolved; **9** intention, objective; **10** determined; **12** concentrated; PHRASES: **3, 2** set on; **4, 2** bent on; **9, 2** intending to.

intention 3 aim; **4** goal, plan; **6** intent, motive; **7** meaning, purpose; **9** objective; PHRASES: **2, 2, 5** ax to grind; **4, 3** mens rea; **8, 6** ulterior motive.

intentionality 7 resolve; **10** resolution; **13** determination, premeditation.

intentionally 9 knowingly, purposely, willfully, wittingly; **10** designedly, ruthlessly, tactically; **11** voluntarily; **12** deliberately, methodically, purposefully; **13** strategically; **14** systematically; PHRASES: **2, 4, 5** in cold blood; **2, 7** on purpose; **4, 11** with forethought.

inter *See* **bury**

interaction 5 blend; **7** contact; **8** dealings; **9** interface, relations; **11** cooperation; **13** collaboration, communication, compatibility, reciprocation; PHRASES: **6, 6** common ground.

intercession 9 mediation; **11** arbitration, negotiation; **12** intervention.

interchange 4 swap; **5** trade; **6** barter, retort, switch; **7** balance; **8** comeback, exchange, junction, requital, swapping; **9** bartering, interplay; **10** compromise, crossroads, substitute; **11** alternation, interaction, retaliation, transaction; **12** intersection, substitution; **13** counteraction, reciprocation; PHRASES: **2, 3, 3, 2, 3** an eye for an eye; **2, 6** tu quoque; **3, 3, 3** tit for tat;

4, 3, 3 quid pro quo; **4, 3, 4** blow for blow, give and take; **5, 3** trade off; **7, 2, 4** payment in kind.

intercommunicate 4 meet, talk; **6** cohere, liaise, relate; **7** contact, discuss, involve, network; **8** converse, entangle; **9** associate, interface; **11** communicate; PHRASES: **4, 2** pair up; **4, 2, 8** form an alliance; **5, 8** stick together.

interconnected 6 mutual; **8** opposite; **9** bilateral, symbiotic; **11** cooperative, interlinked; **12** interlocking, interrelated; **13** complementary; **14** interdependent; PHRASES: **3-3** two-way.

interconnection 7 sharing, synergy; **9** mutualism, mutuality, symbiosis; **10** complement; **11** cooperation, counterpart, partnership; **13** mutualization; **15** interdependence; PHRASES: **3, 7** one another; **4, 5** each other; **5, 3** alter ego; **8, 6** opposite number.

intercourse 3 sex; **5** trade; **6** coitus, nookie; **7** contact, traffic; **8** commerce, congress, dealings; **9** communion; **10** connection, copulation; **11** association, interaction; **13** communication; **14** correspondence; PHRASES: **5-5** rumpy-pumpy.

interdict 3 ban; **4** veto; **5** order; **6** forbid; **7** embargo; **8** prohibit; **11** prohibition; PHRASES: **5, 5** court order.

interest 3 APR; **4** draw, gain; **5** hobby, usury; **6** appeal, arouse, excite, profit; **7** attract, concern, pastime, pursuit; **8** activity; **9** advantage, attention, awareness, curiosity, fascinate, relevance; **10** importance, investment; **11** fascination; **12** significance; **13** attentiveness, concentration; PHRASES: **4, 4** bank rate; **5, 2, 5** pound of flesh; **5, 4, 3** catch your eye; **7, 7** leisure pursuit.

interesting *See* **stimulating**

interface 4 abut, edge, meet; **5** touch; **6** adjoin, border; **7** contact; **8** abutment, boundary, confront, interact; **9** adjacency, threshold; **10** contiguity; **11** battlefront; PHRASES: **4, 7** Iron Curtain; **5-5, 4** Mason-Dixon Line; **6, 2** border on; **6, 4** Berlin Wall; **6, 7** Bamboo Curtain; **6, 8** shared frontier; **7, 4** Maginot Line; **7, 5** meeting point; **8, 4** Hadrian's Wall; **9, 4** Siegfried Line.

interfere 3 pry; **5** delay; **6** affect, meddle; **7** disturb, inhibit, intrude; **8** restrict; **9** intervene; PHRASES: **3, 2, 3, 3** get in the way.

interference 4 hiss; **5** delay; **6** holdup,

static; **8** meddling, nosiness, obstacle, snooping; **9** hindrance, intrusion; **10** impediment; **11** interloping, obstruction; **12** intervention; PHRASES: **5, 5** white noise.

interim 5 break, pause; **6** acting; **8** interval; **9** interlude, temporary; **11** intervening, provisional; **12** intermission; PHRASES: **5-4** short-term.

interior 4 core, deep; **5** depth, heart, inner; **6** center, indoor, inland, inside, inward, mental; **7** central, endemic, subsoil; **8** domestic, enclosed, endoderm, homelike, internal, personal; **9** subcortex; **10** centrality, endodermal, inwardness, subjective, substratum; **11** internality, intravenous, nonexternal, subcortical, substrative; **12** subconscious, subcutaneous, undersurface.

interior (be interior) 8 underlie; PHRASES: **3, 6** lie within; **3, 7** lie beneath.

interlace *See* **interweave**

interlocutor *See* **speaker**

interloper 5 snoop; **7** meddler; **8** busybody, impostor, intruder; **10** trespasser; **11** gatecrasher; PHRASES: **4, 6** nosy parker *UK*.

intermediary 6 middle, midway; **8** mediator; **10** arbitrator, negotiator; **11** intercessor; **12** intermediate, transitional; PHRASES: **2-7** go-between, in-between.

intermediate *See* **middle**

interminable *See* **endless**

intermission 3 gap; **4** rest; **5** break, pause, space; **6** hiatus, lacuna, recess; **7** timeout; **8** breather; **9** interlude; **12** interruption; PHRASES: **3-2** let-up; **5, 3, 6** pause for breath; **5, 3, 7** pause for thought; **9, 5** breathing space *UK*.

intern 4 bury, jail; **5** medic; **6** detain, doctor, entomb, immure; **7** confine, trainee; **8** imprison; **11** incarcerate.

internal 4 core, homy; **5** civil, inner, local; **6** center, indoor, inside, inward, mental; **8** domestic, homelike, interior, national, personal; **9** conscious; **10** intramural, subjective; **11** nonexternal, solipsistic, unconscious; **12** subconscious; **14** psychoanalytic; PHRASES: **2-5** in-house.

internalization 2 id; **4** mind; **6** psyche, spirit; **7** privacy, secrecy; **8** selfhood, superego; **9** introvert, solipsism; **10** inwardness; **11** egocentrism; **12** introversion, subconscious, subjectivity; **13** secretiveness; **14** nonexternality.

internalize 4 hide; **5** adopt; **6** absorb, affect, assume; **7** conceal, confine, contain; **8** suppress; PHRASES: **4, 4** mull over; **6, 2** bottle up.

internalized 6 inmost, inward, secret; **7** private; **8** intimate, personal; **9** secretive; **10** egocentric; **11** introverted; PHRASES: **4-8** self-absorbed.

internally 6 inside, within; **11** inclusively; PHRASES: **2, 3, 4** to the brim, to the core.

internationalism 9 globalism; **12** universalism, universality; **15** cosmopolitanism; PHRASES: **6, 7** global outlook.

international language 5 koine; **9** Esperanto; **12** metalanguage; PHRASES: **6, 6** lingua franca.

Internet 3 bot, FAQ, FTP, ISP, URL; **4** HTML, http, MIME; **5** robot, Sysop, Yahoo™; **6** cookie, gopher, portal, router, Usenet; **7** browser, surfing, webcast, webzine; **8** bookmark, Netscape™, webspeak; **9** newsgroup; **10** cyberspace, netiquette; PHRASES: **3, 3** the Net, the Web; **3, 4** web page *UK*, web site *UK*; **4, 4** chat room, home page; **5, 4, 3** World Wide Web; **6, 6** search engine; **7, 8** service provider; **8, 5** bulletin board.

interpolate 6 insert; **7** include; **9** interject, interpose, interrupt; **11** incorporate, intercalate; PHRASES: **3, 2** cut in; **5, 2** throw in.

interpose 6 meddle; **9** intercede, interfere, interject, interrupt, intervene; **11** interpolate; PHRASES: **3, 2** cut in; **4, 2** butt in; **5, 2** throw in.

interpret 4 edit, read, take; **5** amend, emend, infer, judge, twist; **6** decode, deduce, define, reason; **7** analyze, clarify, explain, expound, unravel; **8** construe, decipher, simplify; **9** elucidate, exemplify, explicate, translate; **10** illuminate, illustrate, popularize, understand; **12** disambiguate; PHRASES: **4, 2, 4** take to mean; **4, 4** read into; **4, 5, 2** make sense of, shed light on; **5, 3** spell out; **5, 5, 2** throw light on; **6, 3** figure out.

interpretation 3 key; **4** clue; **5** light, twist; **6** answer; **7** insight, lection, meaning, opinion, reading, version; **8** analysis, decoding, exegesis, judgment, metaphor, solution; **9** amendment, eisegesis, rendering, rendition; **10** definition, emendation, epexegesis, exposition; **11** connotation, description, elucidation, explanation, explication, subaudition; **12** decipherment, illumination, illustration; **13** clarification, demonstration, enlightenment, understanding; **14** allegorization, deconstruction, simplification; **15** exemplification; PHRASES: **4, 8** code cracking.

interpretation (science of interpretation) 8 prophecy; **9** criticism, epigraphy, exegetics, semiology, tropology; **10** cryptology, divination, graphology, phrenology; **11** diagnostics, linguistics, paleography; **12** cryptography, hermeneutics, lexicography; **13** cryptanalysis; **14** symptomatology.

interpreted 7 cracked, decoded, defined, encoded, glossed; **8** rendered, unlocked; **9** clarified, explained; **10** deciphered, elucidated, simplified, translated; **11** illustrated, unscrambled.

interpreter 5 actor; **6** medium, reader; **7** decoder, definer, diviner, exegete, teacher; **8** exponent, linguist, musician; **9** clarifier, emendator, exegetist, explainer, expounder, performer, portrayer, scholiast; **10** euhemerist, explicator, paraphrast, simplifier, translator; **11** epigraphist, paraphraser, transcriber; **12** cryptanalyst, cryptologist, oneirocritic, paleographer; **13** cryptographer, lexicographer; PHRASES: **3-6** lip-reader.

interpretive 8 defining, exegetic; **9** exemplary; **10** definitive, exegetical, expositive, expository, insightful; **11** descriptive, elucidative, elucidatory, explanatory, explicative, explicatory, hermeneutic; **12** definitional, euhemeristic, illustrative, semiological; **13** demonstrative.

interrelate 4 twin; **5** share; **6** relate; **7** connect; **9** cooperate, correlate, interlink, interlock; **10** complement; **11** interdepend; **12** interconnect; **14** interassociate.

interrelated 6 mutual; **7** engaged, similar; **8** parallel, relative; **9** analogous; **10** associated, comparable, correlated, homologous, interwoven, reciprocal, relational; **11** interacting, interallied, interlinked, interlocked, intermeshed, intertwined; **12** commensurate, interchanged, interworking, proportional; **13** complementary, corresponding; **14** interconnected, interdependent; **15** interassociated; PHRASES: **5-8** cross-referred.

interrogate 4 quiz; **5** grill, probe; **7** debrief, examine, torture; **8** question; **9** cate-chize, interview; PHRASES: **5-4** witch-hunt; **5-7** cross-examine; **5-8** cross-question.

interrogation 8 grilling; **9** interview; **10** debriefing; **11** examination, questioning.

interrupt 4 stay, stop; **5** defer, delay, pause, table; **6** arrest, shelve; **7** adjourn, disrupt, disturb, suspend; **8** postpone; **9** interfere, interject, interpose, intersect, intervene; **10** disconnect; **11** discontinue, interpolate; PHRASES: **3, 2** cut in; **3, 2, 2** cut in on; **3, 3** put off; **3, 5** cut short; **4, 2** butt in, chip in, hold up; **5, 2** barge in, break up, chime in; **5, 3** break off.

interrupted 7 abeyant, dormant, pending; **8** withheld. *See also* **interrupt**

interruption 3 gap; **5** break, crack, delay, fault, pause, split; **6** breach; **7** fissure; **8** crevasse, dormancy, fracture, interval, stoppage; **9** deferment, interlude, intrusion; **10** disruption, moratorium, suspension; **11** adjournment, disturbance; **12** intermission, postponement; **13** disconnection; **14** discontinuance; **15** procrastination.

intersect *See* **cross**

intersection 4 fork, node; **5** joint; **6** carfax; **7** meeting; **8** crossing, gyratory *UK*, junction, juncture; **10** cloverleaf, connection, crossroads, roundabout *UK*; **11** interchange; PHRASES: **1-8** T-junction *UK*; **7, 6** traffic circle.

interstellar medium 6 nebula; **8** Coalsack; PHRASES: **2, 6** HI region; **3, 6** HII region; **4, 6** Crab nebula; **5, 6** Orion nebula; **6, 4** cosmic dust; **9, 6** Horsehead nebula.

interstice *See* **space**

intertwine *See* **interweave**

interval 3 gap; **4** leap, lull, rest, rift, rung, span, step, time; **5** blank, break, chord, gamut, letup, level, pause, shift, space, spell, stage, stair, stint; **6** hiatus, lacuna, leeway, margin, period, recess, remove; **7** caesura, interim, layover, passage, plateau, respite, spacing, stretch, timeout; **8** arpeggio, breather, diapason, diapente, distance, duration, headroom, juncture, meantime, stopover; **9** clearance, firebreak, freeboard, interlude, milestone; **10** interspace, separation; **11** diatessaron, interregnum; **12** acciaccatura, appoggiatura, intermission, interruption; **13** discontinuity, stepping-stone; PHRASES: **3, 5** tea break *UK*; **4, 3** time lag; **4, 4** time warp; **5, 3, 6** pause for breath; **5, 3, 7** pause for thought; **9, 5** breathing space *UK*.

intervene 5 arise; 6 befall, happen; 7 intrude, mediate; 9 arbitrate, intercede, interfere, interpose; PHRASES: 3, 8 get involved; 4, 2 butt in; 4, 2, 4 come to pass.

intervention 9 intrusion, mediation; 10 disruption; 11 disturbance; 12 intercession, interference, interjection, interruption; 13 interpolation; 14 intermediation.

interview 4 quiz, talk; 7 meeting; 8 analysis, audition, dialogue, question; 10 conference, discussion, roundtable; 11 examination, interrogate; 12 consultation, conversation; 13 consideration, interlocution *UK*, interrogation, investigation; PHRASES: 4, 2 talk to; 5-7 cross-examine; 8, 4 converse with.

interweave 3 sew, tat, web; 4 knit, knot, lace, link, spin; 5 braid, plait, twine, weave; 6 enlace, mingle, pleach; 7 crochet, entwine, macramé; 8 entangle, espalier, filigree; 9 interfuse, interlace, interline, interlink, interlock; 10 crisscross, interleave, intertwine, reticulate; 11 intermingle; 12 interconnect; 13 interdigitate; 14 interpenetrate; PHRASES: 4, 8 mesh together.

interweaving 6 lacing; 7 twining, weaving, webbing; 8 braiding, plaiting; 9 pleaching; 10 crisscross; 11 interlacing; 12 entanglement, intertexture, intertwining, reticulation; 13 interlacement; 14 intertwinement; 15 interdigitation.

interwoven 4 lacy; 5 laced, woven; 6 tweedy, twined, webbed; 7 braided, knitted, plaited; 8 pleached, wreathed; 10 crisscross, interlaced; 11 intertwined; 14 interdigitated.

intimacy 6 caring, warmth; 7 privacy; 9 affection, seclusion; 10 confidence, tenderness; 11 familiarity, informality; 13 understanding.

intimate 4 cozy, dear, hint, snug; 5 bosom, close, imply, infer; 6 allude, friend, inmost, inward, secret; 7 private, relaxed, special, suggest; 8 familiar, friendly, informal, personal, thorough; 9 cherished, innermost, insinuate, secretive; 10 confidante; 11 comfortable, inseparable, introverted; 12 confidential; PHRASES: 2-5 in-depth.

intimately 4 well; 5 fully; PHRASES: 3, 2, 3 arm in arm; 4, 2, 4 hand in hand; 4, 2, 5 hand in glove. *See also* **intimate**

intimation 4 hint; 5 rumor; 7 inkling; 8 allusion; 10 indication, suggestion; 11 insinu-ation.

intimidate 5 alarm, bully, daunt, scare; 6 coerce; 7 overawe, terrify; 8 browbeat, frighten, threaten; 9 terrorize; PHRASES: 3, 3 put off; 5, 4 stare down.

intimidation 6 cowing; 7 threats; 8 bullying, coercion, pressure; 9 extortion, hectoring, terrorism; 13 terrorization; 14 demoralization; PHRASES: 3, 2, 6 war of nerves; 5, 2, 6 reign of terror; 5, 2, 8 Sword of Damocles.

into 2 in, to; PHRASES: 3, 5 mad about; 4, 2 keen on *UK*; 5, 5 crazy about; 6, 2 hooked on; 8, 2 addicted to, obsessed by.

intolerance 4 bias; 6 racism; 7 bigotry; 9 apartheid, prejudice; 10 chauvinism, impatience; 12 intimidation; 13 victimization.

intolerant 6 biased, racist; 7 bigoted; 9 blinkered, impatient; 10 oppressive, prejudiced; 11 unforgiving; 12 chauvinistic; PHRASES: 6-6 narrow-minded.

intonation 4 lilt; 5 chant, pitch; 6 timbre; 7 cadence; 8 chanting, intoning; 10 inflection, invocation; 11 incantation.

intone 3 say; 4 sing; 5 chant, drone, utter; 7 declare; 8 intonate; 9 pronounce; 10 articulate.

intoxicant 4 dope, drug; 8 narcotic.

intoxicating 4 neat; 5 heady, proof; 6 potent, vinous; 7 elating, unmixed; 8 exciting, powerful, straight; 9 alcoholic, inebriant, overproof, spiritous, undiluted; 10 compulsive, enchanting, intoxicant; 11 fascinating, inebriating, inebriative, stimulating; 12 enthrallling, exhilarating, invigorating; 14 hallucinogenic.

intoxicating (be intoxicating) 6 fuddle; 7 stupefy; 8 befuddle; 9 inebriate, stimulate; 10 exhilarate.

intractable 6 knotty; 7 awkward, willful; 8 obdurate, stubborn; 9 difficult, obstinate; 10 headstrong; 11 problematic, troublesome.

intransigence 8 obduracy; 9 obstinacy; 10 doggedness, mulishness; 11 willfulness; 12 stubbornness; 13 inflexibility, pigheadedness; PHRASES: 4-4 self-will.

intransigent 5 bigot; 7 diehard; 8 dinosaur, obdurate, stubborn; 9 extremist, obstinate, unbending; 10 inflexible, unyielding; 11 intractable; 12 conservative; 14 uncompromising; PHRASES: 6-6 narrow-minded.

intrigue 4 plot; 5 charm; 6 scheme; 7 attract; 8 interest, plotting, trickery; 9 captivate, deception, fascinate, stratagem; 10 conspiracy; 11 maneuvering.

intrinsic 3 key; 4 core; 5 basic; 6 inborn, innate; 7 central, natural; 8 immanent, inherent; 9 essential, ingrained, innermost; 10 underlying; 11 fundamental, ontological, substantial; PHRASES: 4-6 deep-rooted, deep-seated.

introduce 4 host, lead; 5 begin, start; 6 enlist, enroll, invest, launch, ordain; 7 baptize, install, pioneer, present, propose; 8 acquaint, announce, commence, initiate, register; 9 establish; 10 inaugurate; 11 familiarize; PHRASES: 5, 2 bring in, usher in; 5, 8 bring together; 7, 4 preside over.

introduction 6 gambit, opener, primer, prolog UK, taster UK; 7 baptism, opening, preface, prelims, prelude, starter; 8 exordium, foreword, overture, preamble, prologue; 9 beginning, enrolment, induction; 10 enlistment, initiation, ordination; 11 instatement, institution, investiture; 12 frontispiece, inauguration, presentation, registration; 13 preliminaries; 14 naturalization; PHRASES: 4, 2, 7 rite of passage; 5, 6 front matter; 7, 4 opening line.

introductory 5 basic, first; 6 simple; 7 initial, opening; 8 proemial; 9 baptismal, prefatory, preludial; 10 initiative, precursory; 11 exploratory, preliminary, preparatory, prepositive; PHRASES: 5-5 entry-level.

introvert 3 shy; 5 loner, quiet, timid; 6 hermit; 7 recluse; 8 reserved, reticent; 9 reclusive, withdrawn.

intruder 6 raider; 7 burglar, invader, prowler, stalker; 8 picklock, squatter, stowaway; 10 interloper, trespasser; 11 gatecrasher; 12 housebreaker; PHRASES: 6, 2, 3, 4 cuckoo in the nest; 7, 3, 5 persona non grata.

intrusion 8 invasion; 10 imposition; 11 disturbance; 12 interference, interruption.

intrusive 8 invasive; 10 indiscreet; 11 insensitive, interfering.

intuit 4 feel; 5 sense; 7 discern; 8 perceive.

intuition 5 flash, hunch; 7 inkling, insight, surmise; 8 instinct; 9 suspicion; 10 perception; 11 sensitivity; 12 clairvoyance, presentiment; PHRASES: 5, 5 sixth sense.

intuitive 3 fey; 6 shrewd; 7 sensing; 8 inspired, untaught; 9 sensitive; 10 insightful, perceptive; 11 clairvoyant, instinctive, instinctual, spontaneous; 13 inspirational, perspicacious.

intuitive (be intuitive) 4 feel; 6 divine, intuit; PHRASES: 4, 4 just know; 6, 4, 5 follow one's hunch.

intuitively 12 subliminally, unthinkingly; 13 automatically, instinctively, spontaneously; 14 subconsciously.

intuitive person 4 seer; 5 carer, sibyl; 6 medium; 7 diviner, prophet; 11 clairvoyant.

inundate 5 drown, flood, swamp; 6 deluge; 7 besiege, immerse; 8 submerge; 9 overwhelm; 10 overburden; PHRASES: 4, 5 snow under.

inundation 3 sea; 4 wave; 5 flood; 6 deluge, shower, stream; 7 barrage; 8 blizzard.

inure 6 harden, season; 7 toughen; 8 accustom; 11 acclimatize.

invade 4 raid; 5 annex, storm; 6 ambush, attack, burgle, infest, irrupt, occupy; 7 besiege, conquer, overrun; 8 colonize, encroach, escalade, trespass; 9 gatecrash, interrupt; 10 parasitize; PHRASES: 4, 2 butt in; 5, 2 barge in, break in, burst in, storm in; 5, 3, 5 break and enter; 6, 2 muscle in.

invalid 4 null, sick, void; 6 ailing, faulty, infirm, untrue; 7 patient, unsound; 8 spurious, sufferer; 9 enfeebled, unfounded, untenable; 11 debilitated; 12 convalescent; 13 incapacitated, unenforceable, unsustainable; 14 valetudinarian; PHRASES: 4, 3, 4 null and void.

invariable 3 set; 8 constant; 10 inflexible, unchanging.

invasion 4 raid, rape; 5 foray; 6 attack; 7 ingress, pillage; 8 burglary, conquest; 9 incursion, irruption, offensive; 10 annexation, dragonnade, occupation; 11 overrunning, penetration, subjugation, trespassing; 12 infiltration; 13 housebreaking.

invasive 7 hostile, ingrown, martial; 8 imposing; 9 bellicose, incursive, inflowing, ingrowing, inpouring, inrushing, intrusive, irruptive; 10 aggressive, inflooding; 11 insensitive, interfering, penetrating, trespassing.

inveigh See **protest**

invent 4 coin, form; 5 hatch; 6 create, design, devise, herald; 7 concoct, develop, explore, fashion, pioneer, venture; 8 conceive, contrive, discover, endeavor, engineer, innovate; **9** fabricate, formulate, originate, undertake; **10** rediscover; PHRAS-ES: **3, 3, 5** sow the seeds; **3, 4** hit upon; **3, 4, 4** try one's hand, try one's luck; **3, 4, 8** try one's strength; **4, 1, 4, 2** have a stab at; **4, 1, 5, 2** take a crack at; **4, 2** cook up, make up; **4, 2, 4** come up with; **5, 2** dream up, think of, think up; **7, 2** conjure up.

invention 4 baby, idea, lies, sham; **6** design, device, gadget; **7** coinage, fantasy, fiction; **8** creation; **9** discovery, falsehood, formation, ingenuity; **10** brainchild, conception, creativity, experiment, innovation; **11** contraption, contrivance, development, fabrication, inspiration, originality, rediscovery; **14** innovativeness.

inventive 5 nifty; **6** clever, daring; **7** cunning; **8** creative, inspired, original; **9** effective, ingenious; **10** innovative; **11** imaginative, resourceful.

inventively 2, 5, 6 as never before. *See also* **inventive**

inventiveness 9 fertility, ingenuity; **10** creativity, initiative; **11** imagination, inspiration, originality. *See also* **inventive**

inventor 5 maker; **6** author; **7** creator; **8** designer; **9** architect; **10** discoverer, originator.

inventorially 9 tabularly; **11** numerically; **12** glossarially; **13** taxonomically; **14** alphabetically; PHRASES: **2, 5** in order; **2, 8** in sequence.

inventory 3 log; **4** list; **5** range, stock; **6** record, roster; **7** account, catalog *UK*; **8** cadastre, glossary, register; **9** catalogue *UK*.

inversely 8 backward; **10** conversely; **12** contrariwise; PHRASES: **2, 7** in reverse; **3, 4, 3** ass over tit; **4, 4, 5** head over heels; **4, 5** vice versa; **5-5** topsy-turvy; **6-4** upside-down.

inversion 5 upset; **6** upturn; **8** downturn, overturn, reversal; **9** capsizing, cartwheel, headstand, reversion; **10** antithesis, palindrome, somersault, transposal; **11** evagination, overturning; **12** counterpoint, invagination, retroversion; **13** transposition.

invert 5 spill, upend, upset; **6** upturn; **7** capsize, reverse; **8** overturn; **9** cartwheel, evaginate, retrovert; **10** somersault; PHRAS-ES: **4, 3, 6** turn the tables; **4, 4** turn over; **4-4** flip-flop; **4, 6** turn turtle; **4, 6, 3** turn inside out; **4, 6, 4** turn upside down; **5, 2, 4, 4** stand on one's head; **6, 4** double back.

invertebrate 4 slug, worm; **5** conch, coral, snail, squid; **6** limpet, sponge, urchin; **7** anemone, bivalve, mollusk, octopus, protist; **8** arachnid, barnacle, mesozoan, metazoan, parazoan, starfish; **9** centipede, earthworm, jellyfish, millipede, protozoan, spineless; **10** crustacean, cuttlefish; **11** insectiform; **12** hemichordate; **13** protochordate; **15** cephalochordate, pseudocoelomate; PHRASES: **4-4** worm-like; **4, 5** wood louse.

inverted 15 transpositional; PHRASES: **4-2-5** back-to-front; **4-4-5** head-over-heels; **4-5** arsy-versy *UK*; **5-5** topsy-turvy; **6-2** bottom-up; **6-3** inside-out; **6-4** upside-down. *See also* **invert**

invest 4 fund, risk, save; **5** endow, float; **6** devote, ordain, supply; **7** appoint, empower, finance, install, instate, license, provide; **9** establish; **10** capitalize, inaugurate; PHRASES: **3, 3** bid for; **4, 2, 7** deal in futures; **4, 3, 6** play the market.

investigate 5 probe, recce, study; **7** examine, explore, inspect; **8** consider, research; **10** scrutinize; **11** reconnoiter; PHRASES: **4, 4** look into; **4, 6** poke around; **5, 4** delve into.

investigation 5 probe, recce, study; **6** search; **7** enquiry *UK*, inquiry; **8** analysis, elenchus, research; **10** inspection; **11** examination, exploration; **12** deliberation; **13** introspection; **14** reconnaissance.

investigator *See* **detective**

investment 5 asset; **7** savings, venture; **11** instatement, investiture, speculation; **12** enthronement, installation; PHRASES: **8-2** swearing-in.

invigorate 5 boost, rouse; **6** excite, kindle, revive; **7** animate, enliven, fortify, freshen, hearten, inflame, inspire, quicken, refresh; **8** energize, revivify, vitalize; **9** electrify, galvanize, reanimate, stimulate; **10** exhilarate, intoxicate, rejuvenate, revitalize, strengthen; PHRASES: **3, 2** egg on, pep up; **3, 5, 4** put heart into; **4, 2** fire up; **4, 2, 3, 3** step on the gas; **4, 2, 3, 5** turn up the juice; **5, 2** cheer on, liven up *UK*, psych up.

invigorating 5 brisk, fresh; **7** bracing, healthy; **11** restorative. *See also* **invigorate**

invisibility 3 fog; **4** haze, mist; **7** absence, latency, privacy; **8** haziness, paleness; **9** faintness, fogginess, fuzziness, mistiness, obscurity; **11** concealment, nonpresence; **12** transparency; **13** disappearance, nonappearance; **15** undetectability; PHRASES: **3, 7** low profile; **4, 10** poor definition, poor visibility, zero visibility.

invisible 6 covert, hidden, latent, veiled; **7** lurking; **8** eclipsed, obscured; **9** concealed, disguised, imaginary, unseeable; **10** immaterial, impalpable, intangible, unobserved; **11** nonexistent, transparent, unwitnessed; **12** undetectable, unnoticeable; **13** imperceptible, inappreciable, indiscernible, insubstantial, unperceivable, unsubstantial; **14** unidentifiable, unrecognizable; PHRASES: **3, 2, 4** out of mind; **3, 2, 5** out of sight; **4, 3, 7** over the horizon.

invisible (become invisible) 3 dim; **4** blur, fade, hide, lurk; **6** vanish; **7** retreat; **9** disappear; PHRASES: **3, 3** lie low; **4, 1, 3, 7** keep a low profile; **4-3-2-4** hide-and-go-seek; **4, 4** fade away; **4, 4-3-4** play hide-and-seek; **6, 6** escape notice.

invisible (make invisible) 3 dim; **4** blur, bury, hide, mask, veil; **5** cloak, cover, erase; **6** delete, Tippex™; **7** conceal, eclipse, obscure; **8** disguise; PHRASES: **3, 3** rub out; **3, 3, 2, 5** put out of sight; **4, 4** hide away; **5, 3** black out, white out.

invisible (that which makes invisible) 3 fog; **4** haze, hide, mask, mist, veil; **5** blind, night, smoke; **6** chador, domino, eraser, purdah, screen, shroud, Tippex™; **7** curtain, eclipse, horizon, shutter, yashmak; **8** darkness, disguise; **9** partition, peasouper; **10** camouflage; **11** smokescreen; PHRASES: **4-4** hidy-hole; **5, 4** brick wall; **5, 6** muddy waters; **6, 5** hiding place.

invisibly 8 inwardly, secretly; **9** backstage; **10** internally, underneath; **12** indistinctly, unnoticeably; **13** imperceptibly, indiscernibly; **14** unidentifiably; PHRASES: **2, 3, 5, 4** on the blind side; **2, 6** in hiding; **2, 7** in private; **3, 2, 4** out of view; **3, 2, 5** out of sight; **5, 5** under cover; **6, 3, 6** behind the scenes.

invitation 4 lure; **5** offer; **7** bidding, request, summons; **9** challenge; **10** enticement, incitement, inducement, temptation; **11** provocation; **12** solicitation; **13** encouragement.

invite 3 ask, bid; **4** call; **5** offer; **6** incite, induce, summon; **7** attract, provoke, request, summons; **9** encourage; **10** invitation.

invocation 4 call; **6** prayer; **7** request; **8** entreaty, petition.

invoice 4 bill; **5** debit; **6** charge, demand; **7** account; **9** statement.

invoke 3 beg, use; **4** cite; **5** evoke, quote, refer; **6** appeal; **7** mention; PHRASES: **4, 2** call up; **4, 2, 4** call to mind; **4, 4** call upon.

involuntary 6 forced, reflex; **9** automatic, autonomic, impulsive, Pavlovian, reluctant, unwilling; **10** compulsory, mechanical, obligatory, unthinking; **11** spontaneous; **12** uncontrolled; **13** unintentional; PHRASES: **4-4** knee-jerk.

involve 4 grip, mean; **5** imply, rivet; **6** absorb, affect, engage, enmesh, entail, occupy; **7** concern, contain, embrace, embroil, engross, include, require; **8** comprise, entangle, interest; **9** encompass, implicate, preoccupy; **11** necessitate; PHRASES: **3, 2** mix up; **4, 2** draw in, take in; **7, 2** consist of.

involved 7 tangled; **11** complicated. *See also* **involve**

involvement 7 concern; **8** interest; **10** attachment, connection, enthusiasm; **11** association, engrossment; **12** contribution; **13** participation.

invulnerable 4 safe; **5** proof; **6** immune, secure, strong; **7** armored; **9** bombproof, fireproof, foolproof, panoplied; **10** childproof, defensible, invincible, unbeatable; **11** impregnable, indomitable, unbreakable, untouchable; **12** impenetrable, inexpugnable, shatterproof, unassailable; **13** unconquerable; **14** indestructible; **15** unchallengeable; PHRASES: **4-4** fail-safe; **5-4** steel-clad.

inward 5 inner; **7** ingoing; **8** entering, incoming, interior, internal; **9** inflowing, innermost; PHRASES: **6, 5** ~ bound.

inwardly 6 inside; **8** secretly, silently; **9** privately; **10** intimately; **11** secretively; **13** intrinsically; PHRASES: **2, 7** to oneself. *See also* **inward**

iota *See* **jot**

Iowa 2 IA; **3** oak (tree); PHRASES: **3, 6** Des Moines (capital); **3, 9, 2, 5, 3, 3, 6, 2, 4, 8** Our liberties we prize and our rights we will maintain (motto); **4, 4** wild rose (flower); **4, 5** Corn State (nickname); **7, 5** Hawkeye State (nickname); **7, 9** eastern goldfinch (bird).

IQ 6 brains; **7** faculty; **8** capacity; **9** intellect; **12** intelligence; PHRASES: **3, 4, 2** the same as (Latin: idem quod).

irascibility 4 bile, gall; **7** acidity, vinegar; **8** acerbity, acidness, asperity, meanness; **9** crossness, gruffness, huffiness, petulance, testiness; **10** crabbiness, crankiness, grumpiness, impatience, orneriness, sullenness, tetchiness, touchiness; **11** fretfulness, grouchiness, peevishness, prickliness, waspishness; **12** belligerence, churlishness, irritability, shrewishness; **13** fractiousness, querulousness; **15** contentiousness, quarrelsomeness; PHRASES: **3, 6** bad temper; **5, 4** short fuse; **5, 6** fiery temper, quick temper, short temper.

irascible *See* **irritable**

irate *See* **angry**

Ireland 4 Eire, Erin; **8** Hibernia, Irishism; **9** Irishness; PHRASES: **3, 3, 8** the Six Counties; **3, 5** the Irish, the North, the South; **3, 8** the Republic; **7, 4** Emerald Isle; **8, 7** Northern I~.

iridescent 5 moiré, shiny; **6** pearly; **7** opaline, rainbow, shining; **8** dazzling, gleaming, lustrous, nacreous, pavonine, shimmery; **9** chatoyant, prismatic, sparkling; **10** glistening, glittering, opalescent, shimmering; **13** kaleidoscopic; **15** semitransparent.

iris 3 eye; **7** rainbow; PHRASES: **5-2-3** fleur-de-lys; **7, 6** rainbow quartz.

Irish 3 sea; **4** moss, stew; **6** potato; **7** terrier, whiskey *UK*; **8** republic.

irk 3 bug, nag, vex; **4** gall, rile; **5** annoy, peeve; **6** bother, rankle; **7** bedevil; **8** irritate; **9** aggravate; **10** exasperate; PHRASES: **5, 4** raise Cain.

iron 3 pig; **4** cast, firm, hard, Mars; **5** ingot, press, steam, tough; **6** smooth, steely, strong; **7** curtain, filings, flatten, pyrites, wrought; **9** grappling, smoothing, soldering; **10** corrugated; PHRASES: **4, 3** even out; **4-4** rock-hard.

ironic 3 dry, odd; **6** biting; **7** caustic; **8** peculiar, poignant; **9** sarcastic, satirical; PHRASES: **11** incongruous, paradoxical.

iron-willed 7 adamant; **8** resolute; **9** steadfast, tenacious; **10** determined, purposeful, unyielding; **6-6** single-minded.

irony 6 satire; **7** dryness, sarcasm; **11** causticness, insincerity, sardonicism.

irrational 5 batty, crazy, silly; **6** absurd; **9** arbitrary, illogical, senseless; **11** implausible.

irregular 5 bumpy, jerky, rough, shaky; **6** broken, choppy, fitful, jagged, patchy, random, spotty, uneven, wobbly; **7** chaotic, crooked, diverse, erratic, halting, jerking, shaking, unequal, unusual, varying, veering; **8** abnormal, formless, improper, lopsided, lurching, periodic, restless, sporadic, unstable, unsteady, variable, wavering, wobbling; **9** careening, changeful, desultory, displaced, haphazard, misplaced, misshapen, shapeless, spasmodic, unregular; **10** asymmetric, capricious, changeable, disordered, disorderly, flickering, inconstant, infrequent, nonuniform, staggering, unbalanced, unorthodox, unrhythmic, unsuitable; **11** fluctuating, nonstandard, oscillating, oscillatory; **12** asymmetrical, inconsistent, intermittent, unacceptable, unmethodical, unrhythmical, unsystematic; **13** discontinuous, inappropriate, nonconforming, unpredictable, unsymmetrical; **14** nonsymmetrical, unconventional, unsystematical; PHRASES: **2, 3, 3** on and off; **2, 4, 3, 6** in fits and starts; **2-5-3-5** on-again-off-again; **3, 2, 4** out of line, out of step, out of tune; **3-2-4** hit-or-miss; **3, 2, 5** out of place; **3, 7** not cricket; **4-2** stop-go *UK*; **5-5** herky-jerky.

irregularity 4 bump, jerk; **5** lurch; **6** careen, change, wobble; **7** anomaly, bumping, caprice, flicker, misdeed, variety, veering; **8** disorder, loophole, wavering; **9** asymmetry, careening, diversity; **10** flickering, inequality, peccadillo, unsymmetry, wrongdoing; **11** abnormality, fluctuation, inconstancy, infrequency, instability, oscillation, variability; **12** indiscretion; **13** changeability, disconnection, discontinuity, disproportion, inconsistency, intermittence, nonuniformity; **15** discontinuation; PHRASES: **2, 5, 2, 6** no rhyme or reason; **4, 3, 6** fits and starts. *See also* **irregular**

irregularly 12 huggermugger; PHRASES: **2, 3, 3** on and off; **2, 4, 3, 6** by fits and starts; **2, 5, 3, 5** on again off again; **2, 6** at random; **2, 7** in turmoil; **3, 3, 4** now and then; **3, 4, 3, 5** all over the place; **4, 2, 1, 5** once in a while; **4, 3, 2** stop and go; **5-5** topsy-turvy, willy-nilly; **5, 5, 3** every which way; **5-6** harum-scarum; **6-7** helter-skelter. *See also* **irregular**

irrelevance 6 detail; **8** pleonasm; **10** redundancy, triviality; **11** superfluity; **12** technicality, unimportance; **13** immateriality, inconsequence, secondariness; **14** inessentiality, insignificance, superficiality; **PHRASES: 3, 7** red herring; **4, 5** side issue. *See also* **irrelevant**

irrelevant 5 inapt; **7** trivial; **9** pointless, redundant, unrelated; **10** extraneous, immaterial, inapposite, incidental, pleonastic; **11** inessential, superficial, superfluous, unconnected; **12** inapplicable; **13** inappropriate, insignificant; **PHRASES: 3, 4** off base; **6, 3, 5** beside the point.

irresistible 6 strong; **8** alluring, enticing, tempting; **9** appealing, desirable; **10** compelling; **12** overpowering, overwhelming; **14** uncontrollable.

irresolute 4 weak; **5** moody; **6** fickle, shifty, unsure; **7** evasive, fencing, fidgety, flighty, hedging, nervous, neutral, wayward; **8** disloyal, hesitant, lukewarm, restless, slippery, unsteady, volatile, wavering; **9** desultory, faltering, malleable, seesawing, uncertain, undecided, unsettled, whimsical; **10** ambivalent, capricious, hesitating, indecisive, traitorous, unresolved; **11** vacillating; **12** dishonorable, equivocating, noncommittal, undetermined; **13** pusillanimous; **14** impressionable; **15** procrastinating; **PHRASES: 2, 3, 5** in two minds *UK*; **3-3** cop-out; **5-5** wishy-washy; **5-6** light-headed, light-minded; **7, 4** hanging back.

irresolute (be irresolute) 4 flit; **5** dally, delay, drift, float, waver; **6** fidget, seesaw; **7** flitter; **8** hesitate; **9** vacillate; **12** shillyshally, tergiversate; **13** procrastinate; **PHRASES: 3, 2, 3, 5** sit on the fence; **3, 3** cop out, put off; **4, 3, 3, 4** blow hot and cold; **4, 3, 4** duck and dive; **4, 3, 6** chop and change; **5, 2, 8** leave in suspense; **5-5** dilly-dally; **6, 3, 5** change the rules; **6, 4, 4** change one's mind; **6-6** teeter-totter.

irresolutely *See also* **irresolute**

irresolution 4 whim; **7** caprice; **8** disquiet; **9** agitation, fidgeting, hesitancy; **10** disloyalty, erraticism, hesitation, indecision, infidelity, inquietude, volatility; **11** ambivalence, uncertainty, vacillation; **12** equivocation, whimsicality; **14** tergiversation. *See also* **irresolute**

irreverent 4 rude; **7** mocking; **8** derisive, impudent; **13** disrespectful.

irrigate 3 wet; **4** hose; **5** flood, water; **7** moisten.

irrigator 3 tap; **4** pipe, pump, well; **5** oasis;

7 conduit, hydrant, shadoof; **PHRASES: 7, 5** Persian wheel.

irritability 9 petulance; **12** irascibility; **PHRASES: 3, 6** bad temper. *See also* **irritable**

irritability (sign of irritability) 3 mow; **4** lour; **5** frown, glare, growl, lower, scowl, snarl; **6** glower; **7** grimace; **PHRASES: 5, 4** black look.

irritable 4 acid, sour; **5** angry, cross, gruff, huffy, riled, short, testy; **6** abrupt, bitter, crabby, cranky, grumpy, ornery, snappy, sullen, tetchy, touchy; **7** acerbic, annoyed, bearish, bilious, brusque, fretful, grouchy, nettled, peckish, peevish, peppery, prickly, uptight, waspish; **8** churlish, petulant, strained; **9** bellicose, crotchety, dyspeptic, fractious, impatient, irascible, querulous; **11** belligerent, contentious, quarrelsome; **12** cantankerous, disputatious; **13** argumentative, oversensitive, temperamental; **PHRASES: 3-7** hot-blooded, ill-humored, ill-natured; **3-8** bad-tempered, hot-tempered, ill-tempered; **4-6** high-strung; **4-7** thin-skinned; **5-8** quick-tempered, short-tempered.

irritable (be irritable) 4 fret; **5** argue; **7** dispute, quarrel; **PHRASES: 3, 2** fly at; **4, 2** snap at; **4, 4, 4, 3** snap one's head off; **4, 7** turn against.

irritant *See* **nuisance**

irritate 3 irk, rub, vex; **4** hurt, rile; **5** annoy, chafe, peeve, rouse, sting; **6** bother, madden, nettle, rankle; **7** envenom, inflame; **8** acerbate, embitter; **9** aggravate, infuriate; **10** dissatisfy, exacerbate, exasperate; **PHRASES: 3, 3, 5, 3** rub the wrong way; **4, 2** wind up.

irritated 5 angry, cross. *See also* **irritate**

irritation 4 itch, pain, pest, rash, sore; **5** anger; **6** bother; **8** irritant, nuisance, soreness; **9** annoyance, crossness, itchiness; **10** impatience; **11** aggravation, frustration, indignation; **12** exasperation, inflammation, irascibility.

island 3 ait *UK*, cay, key; **4** holm, inch, isle, reef; **5** atoll, islet; **6** skerry; **7** iceberg, sandbar; **8** landmass, sandbank; **11** archipelago; **PHRASES: 5, 6** coral ~; **6, 6** desert ~.

isle *See* **island**

isolate 6 detach; **7** divorce; **8** insulate, separate; **9** segregate, sequester; **10** quarantine; **PHRASES: 3, 3** cut off; **3, 5** set apart.

isolation 8 solitude; **9** seclusion; **10** detachment, loneliness, quarantine, remoteness, separation; **11** segregation; **13** sequestration; **15** inaccessibility.

isolation (in isolation) **4** away; **5** aloof, apart; **6** adrift; **10** abstractly, distinctly, externally; **11** selectively; **12** separatively; **13** distinctively, extrinsically; **14** diagnostically.

isotope **4** form; **7** element, nuclide; PHRASES: **4, 6** mass number; **6, 4** atomic mass; **6, 6** atomic number, atomic weight, proton number.

issue **3** son; **4** case, copy, flow, gush, make, rise, stem; **5** allot, arise, child, erupt, focus, heirs, point, topic, young; **6** affair, agenda, emerge, matter, result, spring, supply; **7** concern, deliver, dispute, edition, emanate, problem, proceed, progeny, publish, release, subject; **8** children, daughter, delivery, dispense, issuance, question; **9** circulate, offspring, originate, posterity, situation; **10** distribute, production; **11** circulation, descendants, disseminate, installment, publication; **12** distribution; PHRASES: **3, 3** put out; **4, 3** come out, deal out, give out, hand out, send out; **4, 5** come forth; **8, 2, 4** business on hand.

isthmus **4** neck, spit; **5** strip; **6** bridge; **9** peninsula.

Italian dish **5** pasta, pizza; **7** cannoli, lasagna, lasagne, risotto; **8** frittata, rigatoni, tiramisu; **9** antipasto, bolognese; **10** bruschetta, cannelloni, minestrone, zabaglione.

itch **3** yen; **4** ache, burn, long, wish; **5** crave, crawl, creep, yearn; **6** desire, hanker, tickle, tingle; **7** craving, longing, prickle, scratch; **8** appetite, irritate; **9** eagerness, hankering, itchiness, prickling; **10** irritation; PHRASES: **4, 3** pine for.

itchy **6** tickly, tingly; **7** prickly; **8** desirous, inflamed; **9** irritated; **13** uncomfortable.

item **3** bit, duo; **4** pair; **5** entry, piece, thing;

6 couple, detail, lovers; **7** article, element, twosome; **8** instance; **10** particular.

itemize **4** list; **5** index, tally; **6** detail, divide, record; **7** catalog *UK*, program, section, specify; **8** classify, document, register, schedule, tabulate; **9** catalogue *UK*, enumerate, subdivide; **10** schematize.

itemized **6** tabled; **7** charted, tabular; **8** thematic; **9** schematic. *See also* **itemize**

iterate **4** redo; **5** recap; **6** recite, relate, repeat, retell; **7** recount, restate; **8** rehearse; **9** emphasize, reiterate; **11** reemphasize; **12** recapitulate; PHRASES: **2, 4** go over; **3, 5** say again.

iterated **6** retold; PHRASES: **5-4** twice-told. *See also* **iterate**

iteration **5** recap; **6** résumé; **7** summary; **8** relating, relation; **9** rehearsal, repeating, retelling, tautology; **10** peroration *UK*, plagiarism, recounting, redundancy, repetition; **11** duplication, reiteration, restatement; **14** recapitulation.

itinerant **5** nomad; **6** roving; **7** nomadic, vagrant; **8** ambulant, drifting, rootless, traveler, wanderer; **9** migratory, traveling, wandering; **11** peripatetic; PHRASES: **6-6** fiddle-footed.

itinerary **5** route; **7** journey, program; **8** schedule; **9** timetable.

ivy **5** grape; **6** boston, league, poison; **7** creeper, weeping; **8** japanese; **9** evergreen.

Ivy League **4** Yale; **5** Brown; **7** Cornell, Harvard; **8** Columbia; **10** Phrinceton; PHRASES: **5, 7** King's College (Columbia); **6, 5** Little Ivies; **7, 2, 3, 6** College of New Jersey (Princeton); **7, 2, 5, 6** College of Rhode Island (Brown); **7, 2, 12** Academy of Philadelphia (University of Philadelphia); **9, 7** Dartmouth College; **10, 2, 12** University of Pennsylvania; **10, 6** Collegiate School (Yale).

J

J 4 jack; **5** curve, joule.

jab 4 poke, prod, stab; **5** nudge, punch.

jabber 3 gas, yak; **4** chat; **6** gabble; **7** chatter; **8** injector; **12** immunologist.

jabot 4 lace; **5** frill; **6** cravat.

jacinth 8 hyacinth.

jack 1 J; **2** AB *UK*; **3** boy, man, tar; **4** ball, card, flag, lift; **5** hoist, knave, raise, screw; **6** sailor; **7** jackass; **8** bootjack, jackboot, turnspit; **9** applejack, jackfruit; **10** jackrabbit, jackstones, lumberjack; PHRASES: 4-2-3-6 jack-of-all-trades; 4-3 jack-tar; **4, 3, 3** J~ the lad; **4, 3, 6** J~ the Ripper; **4, 4** ~ plug; **4, 5** J~ Frost, J~ Ketch, ~ plane; **4, 6** J~ Horner; **4, 7** J~ Russell; **4, 8** J~ Robinson; **5, 4** Union J~; **7, 4** jumping ~.

jackass 4 fool; **6** donkey; **10** kookaburra.

jackdaw 3 daw; **5** thief; **6** chough, Rheims.

jacket 2 DJ *UK*; **3** tux; **4** coat, peel, skin, vest; **5** cover, gilet *UK*, lapel, parka, shell, tails; **6** blazer, bolero, casing, jerkin, kagool, topper, tuxedo; **7** cagoule *UK*, doublet, spencer; **8** Mackinaw; **9** waistcoat *UK*; **10** bumfreezer *UK*; **11** dustwrapper, windbreaker, Windbreaker; **12** straitjacket; PHRASES: **3, 6** Mao ~, pea ~; **4, 5** dust cover, slip cover; **4, 6** bush ~, dust ~, Eton ~, flak ~, life ~; **5, 6** loden ~, Nehru ~, steam ~, water ~; **6, 6** bomber ~, combat ~, dinner ~ *UK*, donkey ~ *UK*, lumber ~, monkey ~, reefer ~ *UK*, riding ~, safari ~, sports ~, yellow ~, zouave ~; **7, 6** combing ~, hacking ~, hunting ~, leather ~, matinee ~, Norfolk ~, reefing ~, smoking ~; **8, 5** dressing saque; **8, 6** dressing ~, shooting ~.

jack in 4 quit; **5** chuck; **6** resign.

jackknife 4 dive, fold, pike.

jackpot 4 pool; **5** kitty, prize; **7** bonanza;

10 cornucopia.

jackstraws 10 spillikins *UK*.

jack up 4 hike; **5** boost, hoist, raise; **8** increase.

Jacob 4 Esau; **5** Isaac, sheep, staff; **6** Israel; **7** Rebekah; PHRASES: **4, 2, 7** mess of pottage; **6, 6** Jacob's ladder.

jade 3 nag; **4** hack, slag; **5** green, horse, hussy, screw, stone; **6** wanton; **8** nephrite. *See also* **horse**

jaded 4 dull; **5** bored, sated, tired, trite, weary; **8** fatigued; **9** apathetic, exhausted.

Jaffa 4 Yafo; **5** Joppa; **6** orange; PHRASES: **3, 4** Tel Aviv.

jag 3 jab; **4** bout; **5** binge, spree.

Jagannath 10 Juggernaut.

jagged 5 rough; **6** ragged, uneven; **7** crenate, dentate, raggedy; **8** serrated; **10** sawtoothed; **11** denticulate.

jaguar 3 car, Jag; **7** leopard, panther; PHRASES: **1-4** E-type.

jail 3 bin, can, jug, pen; **4** gaol *UK*, quod *UK*; **5** choky *UK*, clink, pokey; **6** chokey *UK*, commit, cooler, lockup, prison; **7** confine, Newgate; **8** Alcatraz, hoosegow, imprison; **9** Bridewell; **10** Marshalsea, roundhouse; **11** confinement, incarcerate; **12** penitentiary. *See also* **prison**

jailbird *See* **prisoner**

jailer 5 guard, screw; **6** keeper, warder *UK*; **7** alcaide, turnkey; **9** custodian.

Jakarta 7 Batavia.

jalopy 3 car; **4** heap; **5** buggy, crate, wreck; **6** banger *UK*; **10** boneshaker *UK*, rattletrap.

jam 4 bind, clog, lock, spot; **5** block, choke, crush, jelly, seize, snarl, stick, stuff, wedge; **7** congest, dilemma, traffic, trouble;

8 conserve, gridlock, preserve, tailback *UK*; **9** improvise; **10** congestion; **11** predicament; PHRASES: **3, 7** ~ session; **4-2** hold-up; **5-2** snarl-up *UK Can.*

Jamaica pepper 8 allspice.

jamb 7 upright; **8** doorpost; **9** scuncheon.

James 3 Jim; **4** John; **5** Jamie, Jemmy, Jimbo, Jimmy *UK*; **6** Seamus, Seumas; **7** Jacobus.

Jane 4 Sian; PHRASES: **4, 3** J~ Doe; **4, 4** J~ Eyre; **4, 5** J~ Shore; **4, 6** J~ Austen; **4, 7** J~ Seymour; **8, 4** Calamity J~.

jangle 5 clang, clash, clink; **6** rattle, tinkle; **7** clatter, quarrel, wrangle.

Janus 7 January; **11** duplicitous; PHRASES: **3-5** two-faced.

Japan 1 J; **2** No; **3** dan, noh, obi; **4** judo, zori; **5** haiku, Hondo, issei, Nihon, nisei, resin, Tokyo; **6** aikido, Honshu, kabuki, kaiten, karate, kimono, Kyushu, mikado, Nippon, sansei, sensei, Shinto, shogun, yakuza; **7** ikebana, jujitsu, lacquer, netsuke, origami, samurai, shellac, Shikoku, varnish; **8** bugeikan, Hokkaido; PHRASES: **6, 3** Rising Sun.

Japanese quince 8 japonica.

jar 3 can, din, jog, pot, saw; **4** jolt, pint, rasp; **5** clash, crash, crock, cruet, drone, grate, grind, jelly, knock, nudge, shock, thrum, whine; **6** jangle, pithos, scrape, vessel; **7** amphora, canopus, quarrel, tankard; **8** preserve; PHRASES: **3, 3** jam ~ *UK*; **5, 3** Mason ~; **6, 3** Kilner ~ *UK*, Leyden ~.

jargon 4 cant, jive; **5** argot, lingo, slang; **6** patter; **8** legalese, newspeak, parlance; **9** bafflegab, Europeak; **10** journalese; **11** officialese, Pentagonese, technospeak, terminology; **12** gobbledegook *UK*, gobbledygook, psychobabble, technobabble, telegraphese; PHRASES: **7, 6** Chinook ~.

jarring 5 harsh; **7** grating; **8** clashing; **9** dissonant; **10** discordant, mismatched; **12** caterwauling; PHRASES: **3, 2, 4** out of tune; **3-3** off-key.

Jason 8 Argonaut; PHRASES: **6, 6** Golden Fleece.

jaundice 7 icterus, yellows; **9** prejudice.

jaundiced 6 sallow, yellow; **7** cynical, envious; **10** prejudiced.

jaunt 4 swan, trip; **5** sally; **6** outing; **7** journey; **9** excursion.

jaunty 3 gay; **4** spry; **5** brisk, jolly; **6** lively, rakish; **7** chipper; **8** cheerful, debonair; **9** sprightly.

javelin 4 dart, pile; **5** lance, pilum, spear; **7** harpoon.

jaw 3 yak; **4** chap, chat, chin, jowl, talk, yack; **5** chaft, chaps, cheek, chide, chops, mouth, shark; **6** gossip, muzzle, natter; **7** chatter, jawbone, jawline; **8** gnathion, gnathite, mandible, overshot; **9** mouthpart, undershot; PHRASES: **5, 3** glass ~; **6-3** yakety-yak; **7, 3** lantern ~; **11, 3** prognathous ~.

jawbone 7 maxilla; **8** mandible; **12** premaxillary.

jay 1 J.

jazz 3 bop, pop; **4** blue, cool, folk, jive, punk, riff, scat, soul, trad *UK*; **5** bebop, blues, spice, stomp, swing; **6** boogie, doowop, fusion; **7** country, enliven, ragtime; **9** Dixieland; **10** mainstream, syncopated; **11** progressive, syncopation, traditional; **13** paraphernalia; PHRASES: **5-5** avant-garde; **6, 4** modern ~; **6-6** boogie-woogie.

jazzer, jazzman, jazz musician 3 cat; **6** Blakey (Art), Mingus (Charles), Simone (Nina); **7** Satchmo, sideman, swinger; **8** Calloway (Cab); **11** Beiderbecke (Bix); PHRASES: **4, 7** Dave Brubeck; **4, 8** John Coltrane; **4, 9** Duke Ellington; **4, 10** Ella Fitzgerald; **5, 4, 6** Jelly Roll Morton; **5, 5** Miles Davis; **5, 6** Glenn Miller, Tommy Dorsey; **5, 7** Benny Goodman, Sarah Vaughan; **5, 9** Dizzy Gillespie, Louis Armstrong; **6, 5** Bessie Smith, Lester Young; **6, 7** Billie Holiday; **6, 9** Django Reinhardt; **7, 6** Charlie Parker; **9, 4** Thelonius Monk.

jazz up 5 spice; **8** brighten, decorate.

jazzy 4 loud; **6** bright, garish, lively, snazzy; **10** syncopated.

JC 5, 6 Jesus Christ; **6, 6** Julius Caesar.

jealous 4 sour; **5** green, rival; **6** yellow; **7** envious, hostile, Othello; **8** covetous, insecure, vigilant, watchful; **9** invidious, jaundiced, resentful; **10** possessive, suspicious; **11** distrustful, mistrustful; PHRASES: **4-4** lynx-eyed; **5-4** green-eyed.

jealous (be jealous) 4 envy; **5** covet; **6** resent; PHRASES: **3, 4, 5, 3** eat one's heart out.

jealousy 4 envy; **7** rivalry; **8** jaundice; **9** heartburn, hostility, suspicion; PHRASES: **4, 6** sour grapes; **5, 2, 7** crime of passion; **7, 8**

eternal triangle; **9, 3** jaundiced eye. *See also* **jealous**

jeans 5 Levis™, pants; **6** chinos, denims; **8** trousers *UK*; **9** Wranglers™.

jeer 3 boo, dig, rag; **4** bawl, hiss, hoot, howl, jibe, mock, rail, twit; **5** flout, scoff, sneer, taunt; **6** deride, heckle; **7** barrack *UK*, catcall, exclaim, whistle; **8** ridicule; **9** raspberry; **PHRASES: 5, 4** shout down.

Jehovah *See* **God**

jejune 3 dry; **4** dull, poor, thin; **6** barren; **7** insipid; **12** unsatisfying; **13** insubstantial.

jelly 3 gel, jam; **4** agar, comb; **5** aspic, brawn, shape; **6** napalm; **8** conserve; **9** explosive, gelignite, isinglass; **10** blancmange, carragheen, chaudfroid; **PHRASES: 4-4** agar-agar; **5-4, 5** calf's-foot ~; **5, 5** royal ~; **9, 5** petroleum ~.

jellyfish 6 medusa; **7** acaleph; **8** acalepha; **10** scyphozoan; **12** coelenterate.

jenny 3 ass; **4** wren; **5** Janet; **8** spinster; **PHRASES: 5, 4** J~ Lind; **8, 5** spinning ~.

jeopardise *See* **endanger**

jeopardy *See* **danger**

jerk 3 bob, jig, jog, tic; **4** flip, hike, hoik, jolt, toss, yank, yerk; **5** flick, flirt, hitch, hoick, idiot, pluck, shake, spasm, start, surge, tweak; **PHRASES: 6** jiggle, joggle, snatch, twitch, wrench.

jerkin *See* **jacket**

Jerry *See* **German**

jerry-built *See* **poor quality**

jersey *See* **sweater**

jessamine 7 jasmine.

jest *See* **joke**

jester 4 fool; **5** clown, comic, Feste, joker, Patch, Wamba; **6** motley, Yorick; **7** buffoon, farceur, goliard; **8** comedian, humorist, merryman; **9** Rigoletto; **10** Touchstone; **PHRASES: 4, 5** Jack Point; **8, 5** (Lancelot) Gobbo.

jesting 3 fun; **5** funny, jokey; **6** joking; **7** kidding; **8** clowning, flippant, humorous; **9** slapstick; **12** lighthearted.

Jesus 3 HIS; **4** INRI; **6** Christ, Savior; **7** Messiah; **8** Emmanuel, Redeemer.

jet 5 black, plane, spirt *UK*, spout, spray, spurt; **6** douche, shower, squirt, stream; **8** fountain. *See also* **aircraft**

jettison *See* **discard**

jetty 4 mole, pier, quay; **5** black, wharf; **PHRASES: 7, 5** landing stage.

Jew 5 Hasid, Tubal; **6** Chasid, Essene, Hassid, Hebrew, Zealot; **7** Chassid, Falasha, Karaite, Marrano, Shylock; **8** Maccabee, Pharisee, Sadducee, Sephardi; **9** Ahasuerus, Ashkenazi, Israelite; **PHRASES: 9, 3** Wandering J~.

jewel 3 gem; **4** rock, star; **8** sparkler, treasure; **PHRASES: 8, 5** precious stone. *See also* **gemstone**

jewelry 3 pin; **4** drop, ouch, ring, stud; **5** badge, cameo, chain, clasp, crown, tiara; **6** amulet, anklet, armlet, bangle, bauble, brooch, choker, collet, diadem, gorget, hatpin, locket, signet, tiepin *UK*, torque; **7** coronet, earcuff, earring, necklet *UK*, pendant, sleeper, spangle, trinket; **8** baguette, bracelet, cufflink, intaglio, necklace, nosering; **9** medallion; **PHRASES: 3, 4** tie tack.

Jewish 6 Judaic; **7** Semitic, Yiddish.

Jezebel 4 Ahab.

jib 3 shy; **4** balk, balk *UK*, face, sail, stop; **5** demur; **6** refuse; **8** foresail, staysail.

jibe 3 dig, rag; **4** jeer, mock, rail, twit; **5** agree, chime, scoff, sneer, taunt, tease; **6** accord, deride; **8** ridicule; **10** correspond.

jiffy 2 mo *UK*; **3** bag, sec; **4** tick *UK*, wink; **6** minute, moment; **9** twinkling.

jig 3 hop; **4** jerk, leap, skip; **5** caper.

jiggle 3 bob, jig, jog; **4** bump, jerk, jump; **5** knock, nudge, shock; **6** bounce, hustle, jigget, joggle, jostle, jounce, judder, tremor, twitch; **7** shudder.

jilt *See* **reject**

jimmy 3 pee; **5** jemmy *UK*; **6** piddle; **7** crowbar; **PHRASES: 5, 6** J~ Riddle.

jimson weed 5, 5 thorn apple *UK*.

jingle 4 tune; **5** ditty, rhyme, verse; **6** tinkle; **8** clerihew, doggerel.

jinni 4 jinn; **5** genie.

jinx 3 hex; **5** curse; **6** kibosh, voodoo, whammy; **7** gremlin.

jitters *See* **nerves**

jittery *See* **nervous**

job 4 crib, duty, game, line, post, task, work; **5** berth, chore, craft, trade; **6** career, errand, metier, office, pensum, racket; **7** calling, mission, opening, project, vacancy; **8** business, capacity, function, position, sinecure, vocation; **9** situation *UK*; **10** assignment, commission, employment, livelihood, occupation, profession; **11** appointment, undertaking; **14** responsibility; PHRASES: **4, 2, 4** line of work; **4, 2, 8** line of business.

Job 8 patience; 9 comforter, hypocrite.

jockey 5 cheat, rider, trick; 6 jostle; 8 maneuver.

jocular 5 funny, jokey; 6 joking, jovial; 7 playful.

Joe 2, 3 GI J~; 3, 4 J~ Blow, J~ Soap *UK*; 3, 6 J~ Public *UK*; 4, 3 holy J~; 6, 3 sloppy J~.

jog 3 run; 4 trot; 5 nudge; 6 remind. *See also* **jar, jiggle, jolt**

join 3 tie, wed; 4 abut, ally, bond, fuse, glue, hook, knit, link, meet, weld; 5 enter, marry, merge, miter, unite; 6 accede, attach, cement, couple, enlist, enroll, fasten, solder, splice; 7 combine, connect, mortise; 8 coalesce, dovetail, federate, initiate; 9 affiliate, associate, subscribe; 10 amalgamate; 11 confederate, consolidate; PHRASES: **4, 2, 4** gang up with, line up with, team up with; **4, 6** ~ forces; **4, 8** band together, club together. *See also* **joint**

joined 6 allied, bonded, hinged, linked; 7 hitched, twinned; 9 connected; 10 affiliated, associated; PHRASES: **5, 8** fixed together.

joint 3 bar, lap; 4 bond, dive, fish, hasp, hook, join, knee, knot, link, node, seam, weld; 5 ankle, bevel, catch, clasp, hitch, miter, roast, scarf, tenon, wrist; 6 common, copula, global, hyphen, mutual, pooled, reefer, saddle, shared, splice, spliff, suture, united; 7 bracket, general, knuckle; 8 combined, communal, conjunct, dovetail, ecumenic, junction, together; 9 accessory, associate, communist, concerted, corporate, fastening, ginglymus, nightclub, partaking, socialist; 10 collective, ecumenical, empathetic, reciprocal; 11 communalist, communistic, conjunction, cooperative, interactive, socialistic, sympathetic; 12 collectivist, interrelated; 13 international, participating, participatory; PHRASES: **4, 3, 6** ball and socket; **5, 5** elbow hinge.

joint operation 6 merger; 7 commune, pooling; 8 takeover, teamwork; 9 coalition, community; 10 collective; 11 cooperation, cooperative, interaction; 12 coordination; PHRASES: **3-3** buy-out; **4, 6** mass action; **6, 5** united front; **6, 8** common endeavor; **7, 6**

joining forces; **7, 8** pulling together; **8, 6** combined effort; **9, 6** concerted action, concerted effort.

joint possession 4 park, pool; 5 kitty, share, store, union; 7 commune, kibbutz, kolkhoz, tontine; 8 alliance, dividend, dominion; 9 communism, community, democracy, socialism; 10 collective, commonweal, dependency, federation; 11 association, condominium, cooperative, partnership; 12 collectivism, commonwealth; 13 communization, confederation, copartnership, socialization; 15 communalization, nationalization; PHRASES: **4-7** timesharing; **6, 6** public domain; **6, 7** global village, profit sharing, public company, United Nations; **6, 11** public corporation; **8, 5** European Union.

joist 3 bar; 4 beam; 5 strut, truss; 7 sleeper.

joke 3 gag, kid, pun; 4 boob, fool, gibe, jape, jest, lark, quip, yarn; 5 caper, crack, laugh, prank, sally, trick; 6 howler, wheeze; 7 foolery, mistake, riposte, skylark; 8 chestnut, clowning, drollery; 9 wisecrack, witticism; 10 pleasantry, spoonerism; PHRASES: **3-4** leg-pull *UK*; **3-5** one-liner; **3, 8** old chestnut; **4, 4** tall tale; **5, 5** dirty story, funny story; **6-3, 5** shaggy-dog story; **6, 8** double entendre; **9, 4** practical ~.

joker *See* **jester**

jollity *See* **cheerfulness**

jolly 3 fun; 4 very; 5 happy; 6 hugely, jovial, really; 8 cheerful; 12 terrifically, tremendously.

jolt 3 jar, jig, jog; 4 bump, jerk, jump; 5 knock, nudge, shock, start, throb; 6 bounce, hustle, jigget, joggle, jostle, jounce, judder, shiver, tremor, twitch; 7 shudder.

josh *See* **tease**

jostle 3 jog; 4 bump, push; 5 barge, elbow, knock, nudge, shove; 6 bounce, hustle, jigget, joggle, jounce; 8 shoulder.

jot 3 bit; 4 iota, memo, note, whit; 5 grain, scrap, speck; 6 tittle.

journal 5 comic, daily, diary, organ, paper; 6 annual, review, serial, series, weekly; 7 daybook, gazette, monthly; 8 biweekly, magazine, pamphlet, seasonal; 9 newssheet *UK*, quarterly; 10 newsletter, periodical; 11 fortnightly, semimonthly; 12 newsmagazine. *See also* **magazine**

journalism 5 press, scoop; 6 banner, byline, column, leader, notice, report; 7 tabloid; **8** coverage, headline, screamer, streamer; **9** editorial, personals, reportage, reporting; **10** broadsheet, rapportage; **12** newspapering; PHRASES: **4, 6** Grub Street; **5-2** write-up; **5, 6** Fleet Street; **6, 2, 5** Street of Shame; **6, 5** gutter press, yellow press; **6, 6** advice column, fourth estate; **6, 8** banner headline; **7, 5** popular press, tabloid press.

journalist 2 ed; **3** cub, NUJ *UK*, sub; **4** hack; **6** critic, editor, journo *UK*, writer; **7** newsman; **8** hackette, reporter, stringer; **9** anchorman, columnist, muckraker, newshound, newswoman, spokesman; **10** freelancer, gatekeeper, newscaster, newsperson, newsreader *UK*; **12** anchorperson, newspaperman, sportscaster; **13** correspondent, scandalmonger; **14** newspaperwoman; PHRASES: **3, 8** cub reporter; **4, 6** copy editor, copy taster; **5, 4** agony aunt; **5, 5** press agent; **6, 6** leader writer; **6, 9** gossip columnist.

journey 2 go; **3** ply, run; **4** roam, rove, tour, trek, trip, walk; **5** foray, jaunt; **6** bummel, cruise, errand, outing, safari, travel, voyage, wander; **7** circuit, odyssey, passage, proceed; **8** crossing; **9** excursion, walkabout; **10** expedition.

joust 4 tilt; **6** combat; **7** tourney; **10** tournament.

jovial *See* **cheerful**

joy 5 dream, treat; **6** heaven, thrill; **7** delight, ecstasy, jollity, nirvana, rapture; **8** felicity, gladness; **9** happiness, transport; **10** exultation, jubilation; **11** enchantment; **12** intoxication; **13** schadenfreude.

joy (cause joy) 4 send; **5** charm, cheer; **6** please, thrill; **7** delight, enchant, gladden, rejoice; **8** enthrall; **9** captivate, enrapture, transport; **10** intoxicate.

joy (show joy) 4 beam, crow, grin, purr, sing; **5** cheer, gloat, laugh, smile; **6** giggle, guffaw; **7** chortle, chuckle, rejoice.

joyful 3 gay; **4** glad; **5** happy, merry; **6** blithe, elated, festal; **7** gleeful; **8** cheerful, exultant, exulting, jubilant; **9** delighted; **10** captivated, enraptured, triumphant; **11** intoxicated; PHRASES: **4-1-4** cock-a-hoop.

joyful person 5 raver; **7** groover, reveler; **10** merrymaker.

joyless 3 sad; **4** glum; **6** dismal, dreary, gloomy; **8** listless; **10** lugubrious.

joyous *See* **joyful**
jubilant *See* **joyful**

jubilation *See* **joy**

jubilee 8 festival; **9** festivity; **11** anniversary, celebration; **13** commemoration.

judder 4 jerk; **5** shake, shock; **7** vibrate.

judge 2 JP; **3** ref, try; **4** beak, cadi, deem, doom, find, hear, jury, rate, rule; **5** award, bench, Dredd, ephor, gauge, hakim, Minos, mufti, opine, panel, Paris, value; **6** acquit, assess, censor, critic, Daniel, decide, decree, dicast, expert, Gideon, hakeem, jurist, puisne, settle, syndic, tester, umpire, valuer; **7** adjudge, adviser, alcalde, approve, arbiter, censure, condemn, coroner, justice, preside, referee, Solomon; **8** assessor, conclude, estimate, evaluate, examiner, Jephthah, mediator, recorder, reporter, reviewer, surveyor, verderer *UK*; **9** appraiser, arbitrate, authority, counselor, criticize, determine, estimator, inspector, judiciary, justicier, ombudsman, pronounce, surrogate; **10** adjudicate, arbitrator, disapprove, justiciary, magistracy, magistrate; **11** adjudicator, commentator, connoisseur, justiceship; **12** Rhadamanthus; PHRASES: **2, 3** mi lud; **3, 2** sum up; **3, 2, 8** sit in judgment; **3, 4** his nibs, Roy Bean, the beak; **4, 5** your Honor; **4, 8** pass judgment, your Lordship; **5, 7** chief justice; **6, 1, 7** return a verdict; **7, 5** hanging ~; **9, 5** Recording Angel *UK*.

judgment day 8 Doomsday; **9** afterlife, hereafter; **10** millennium; PHRASES: **3, 2, 8** day of judgment; **4, 5** Last Trump; **4, 8** Last Judgment; **12, 3** resurrection day.

judgment, judgement 4 view, vote; **5** guess, sense, taste, value; **6** belief, choice, decree, notice, rating, remark, report, review, survey, wisdom; **7** censure, comment, hearing, opinion, surmise, verdict; **8** absolute, critique, estimate, sentence, umpirage; **9** appraisal, corollary, criticism, deduction, guesswork, inference, reasoning, selection, valuation; **10** assessment, conjecture, discretion, estimation, evaluation, inspection, plebiscite, referendum; **11** arbitration, calculation, comparative, discernment, sensibility, speculation; **12** adjudication, appreciation, dissertation; **13** consideration; **14** discrimination; **15** differentiation. *See also* **court**

judicial 5 jural; **6** curial; **8** critical, forensic, original, tribunal; **9** appellate, judicious; **10** judicative, judicatory, justiciary; **11** magisterial; **12** judicatorial, jurisdictive; **13** inquisitional, inquisitorial, Rhadamanthine; **14** jurisdictional; **15** jurisprudential.

judicious 4 fair, just, wise; **5** right; **6** shrewd; **7** careful, prudent; **8** accurate, critical, delicate, discreet, judicial, pedantic, tasteful, unbiased; **9** juridical, sensitive; **10** analytical *UK*, discerning, fastidious, insightful, judgmental, judicatory, meticulous, perceptive; **12** appreciative; **13** dispassionate; **14** discriminating.

judiciousness 4 feel; **5** flair, taste; **6** acumen, palate; **7** finesse, insight; **8** delicacy, judgment; **9** criticism, quibbling; **10** discretion, perception, refinement; **11** discernment, sensibility, sensitivity; **12** appreciation, dilettantism; **13** perfectionism; **14** discrimination; **15** connoisseurship. *See also* **judicious**

judo 3 dan, kyu, uka; **4** dojo; **7** judoist; **8** recorder; **PHRASES: 2-4** te-waza; **4-4** ashi-waza, nage-waza; **4, 6** tori judoka; **5, 4** black belt, brown belt; **5-4** koshi-waza, shime-waza, tachi-waza; **6-4** sutemi-waza.

jug 3 can, urn; **4** ewer, toby; **5** clink; **6** prison; **7** creamer, growler, pitcher, tankard; **9** blackjack, graybeard; **10** bellarmine.

juggernaut 9 Jagannath.

juggle 4 cook, fake; **5** trick; **7** conjure.

juice 3 oil, sap; **4** ghee, milk, soup, whey; **5** fluid, gravy, latex, sauce, stock, water; **6** liquor, petrol; **7** current, extract; **8** gasoline; **10** buttermilk.

juicy 5 meaty, milky, moist, runny, sappy; **6** fleshy, fruity, watery; **8** luscious, overripe; **9** succulent; **11** lactiferous.

jumble 3 mix; **5** chaos; **6** garble, lumber, mingle, ragbag; **7** confuse, farrago, mixture; **8** mishmash, scramble; **11** gallimaufry.

jumbled 4 awry; **5** amiss, askew; **7** chaotic, haywire, muddled, tangled; **8** cockeyed, confused; **9** scrambled; **PHRASES: 5-5** topsyturvy; **6-4** upside-down.

jump 3 gap, hop; **4** axel, gate, high, land, leap, long, lutz, omit, skip, step, wall; **5** bound, broad, caper, fence, start, vault, water; **6** bounce, double, flinch, hurdle, pounce, recoil, spring, triple; **7** salchow, upheave; **8** capriole, hurdling, leapfrog, overlook, scissors, straddle; **9** entrechat, saltation; **10** handspring, quersprung; **12** steeplechase; **14** steeplechasing; **PHRASES: 3-4** ski-jump; **4, 4** high ~, pole ~; **4-5** polevault; **5, 4** water ~; **6, 4** bungee ~, triple ~; **6,**

5 spread fence; **7, 4** Fosbury flop, western roll; **8, 4** parallel bars, scissors ~, standing ~; **8, 5** Beecher's Brook.

jumper 4 flea; **6** cicada, impala; **7** cricket, eventer; **8** kangaroo; **11** parachutist; **PHRASES: 3, 5** sky diver. *See also* **sweater**

jumpy 5 jerky; **6** abrupt, sudden; **7** anxious, erratic, jittery, nervous, worried; **8** unsteady.

junction 5 focus, joint, union; **6** Carfax, suture; **8** alliance; **9** spaghetti; **10** cloverleaf, crossroads, rendezvous; **11** decussation; **12** intersection.

jungle 4 maze, mess; **6** forest, jumble, muddle, tangle; **10** wilderness; **PHRASES: 4, 6** rain forest; **8, 6** tropical forest.

junior 5 lower; **6** novice; **7** trainee; **8** beginner, inferior; **9** underling; **11** subordinate; **PHRASES: 3-7** low-ranking.

junk 4 boat, tatt; **5** trash, waste; **6** jetsam, jumble *UK*, litter, refuse; **7** castoff, discard, flotsam, garbage, rubbish; **8** castoffs, jettison; **PHRASES: 4-1-4** bric-a-brac; **4, 4** ~ bond, ~ mail; **5, 8** white elephant.

junkie *See* **drug addict**

junta 4 band, gang; **5** cabal; **6** clique, regime; **7** council, faction; **9** committee; **10** government; **PHRASES: 7, 3** martial law; **8, 4** military rule.

jurisdiction 4 soke; **5** soken; **6** office; **7** mandate; **8** capacity, function, province, tribunal; **9** authority, bailiwick, bumbledom, mayoralty, portfolio; **10** cognisance *UK*, competence.

jurisprudence 3 law; **8** nomology.

jury 5 jurat, juror, panel; **6** assize, jurist; **7** foreman, inquest, juryman; **9** jurywoman; **PHRASES: 6, 4, 3** twelve just men; **7, 4** hanging ~.

just 3 due; **4** fair, only; **5** right; **6** barely, hardly, honest, lawful, merely, proper, simply, square; **7** exactly, fitting, merited; **8** deserved, suitable, unbiased; **9** equitable, impartial, objective; **10** legitimate; **PHRASES: 4-6** even-handed.

justice 5 judge, right; **6** equity; **7** coroner, Nemesis, provost; **8** fairness, recorder; **10** magistrate; **PHRASES: 7, 7** ~ Shallow, J~ Silence *Shakespeare*.

justification *See* **defense**

justify 5 alibi, align, argue, plead, prove, rebut; **6** defend, excuse, refute, rejoin, retort, soften, uphold; **7** explain, qualify, warrant; **8** champion, mitigate, palliate; **9** extenuate; **11** corroborate, demonstrate, recriminate; **12** substantiate; PHRASES: **4, 2, 3** find an out; **5, 2, 3** speak up for, stand up for, stick up for.

juvenile 5 child, minor, young, youth; **7** babyish, puerile, teenage; **8** childish, immature, teenager, youthful; **9** infantile, pubescent, youngster; **10** adolescent.

juxtapose 4 abut, butt, join; **5** touch; **6** adjoin, appose, border; **7** connect; **8** neighbor.

juxtaposed 4 near; **5** close; **6** joined; **7** linking, tangent; **8** abutting, adjacent, touching; **9** adjoining, bordering, connected; **10** connecting, contiguous, continuous, tangential; **11** coterminous; **12** conterminous.

juxtaposition 6 border; **7** abuttal *UK*, contact, joining; **8** abutment, frontier, junction, nearness, tangency, touching; **9** adjacency, bordering, closeness; **10** apposition, borderland, connection, contiguity, continuity; **14** contiguousness.

K

K 1 A, B, C, D, E, F, G; 4 kilo, king, knit; 6 kelvin; 8 thousand; 9 potassium.

K2 7 Dapsang; PHRASES: 6, 6 Godwin Austen.

kaleidoscope 3 set, web; 6 medley, series; 7 display, mixture; 14 phantasmagoria; PHRASES: 5, 2, 6 chain of events; 5, 8 chain reaction; 6, 6 domino effect; 7, 7 complex pattern; 8, 5 changing scene.

kaleidoscopic 6 motley; 7 dappled, rainbow, various; 8 variable; 9 chameleon; 10 changeable, multicolor, variegated; 11 varicolored; 12 multicolored, particolored; 13 polychromatic.

kalian 6 hookah.

kangaroo 4 joey; 6 boomer, jumper; 7 bounder, wallaby; 8 wallaroo; 9 notothere; 11 diprotodont; PHRASES: 3, 3 old man.

Kansas 2 KS; 6 Topeka (capital); 10 cottonwood (tree); PHRASES: 2, 3, 5, 7, 12 To the stars through difficulties (motto); 4, 6, 9 wild native sunflower (flower); 5, 5, 9, 5, 6, 3 Wheat State, Jayhawker State, Midway USA (nickname); 7, 6, 4 western meadow lark (bird); 9, 5 Sunflower State (nickname).

kaolin 5, 4 china clay; 9, 4 porcelain clay UK.

karate 3 Dan, Kyu; 4 dojo; 5 judge; 8 Shotokai, Shotokan, Shukokai; 10 arbitrator, timekeeper; 11 scorekeeper; 12 Kyokushinkai; PHRASES: 3-4 jun-zuki, kin-geri, maegeri; 4, 3 Wado Kyu; 4-3-3 soto-ude-uke, uchi-ude-uke; 4-4 yoko-geri; 5-3 jodan-uke; 5-4 gyaku-zuki; 5-5 gedan-barai; 7-4 mawashi-geri.

karma 4 aura, fate; 6 kismet; 7 destiny, feeling, fortune; 8 ambiance; 10 atmosphere, providence, vibrations.

keel 4 skeg; 6 bottom, carina; 9 underside; 11 centerboard.

keel over 4 fall, list; 5 faint, swoon; 7 capsize, founder; 8 overturn; 11 overbalance; PHRASES: 4, 3 pass out; 4, 4 heel over; 4, 6 turn turtle; 5, 3 black out.

keen 3 cry, sob; 4 acid, agog, avid, howl, wail; 5 acute, dirge, eager, elegy, greet, mourn, quick, ready, sharp; 6 ardent, astute, bemoan, bewail, biting, grieve, lament, shrewd, sorrow; 7 athirst, devoted, fervent, intense, zealous; 8 aspiring, diligent; 9 assiduous, dedicated, energetic, fanatical, sensitive; 10 discerning, passionate, perceptive; 11 penetrating; 12 enthusiastic.

keenness 4 wish, zeal, zest; 5 ardor; 6 acuity, desire, fervor; 7 avidity; 8 fervency; 9 assiduity, diligence, intensity; 10 enthusiasm. *See also* **keen**

keep 4 feed, fort, have, hold, mark, mind, obey, save, stet, stow, tend; 5 board, guard, stock, store, tower, watch; 6 castle, defend, donjon, living, pickle, remain, retain, secure; 7 bastion, citadel, conceal, confine, fulfill, lodging, nurture, observe, protect, reserve, support, sustain; 8 conserve, continue, maintain, preserve, withhold; 9 celebrate; 10 stronghold; 11 commemorate, maintenance; PHRASES: 4, 3 care for; 4, 5 look after; 5, 7 child support.

keep away 8 separate; PHRASES: 4, 3 keep off; 5, 3 space out, stand off; 5, 4 stand away, stand back; 5, 5 stand aloof; 5, 5, 2 steer clear of.

keep back 5 delay; 6 detain, retain, retard; 7 reserve; 8 withhold.

keeper 4 clip, ward; 5 guard; 6 gaoler UK, goalie, jailer, minder UK, warder UK; 7 curator, janitor; 8 armature, chaperon, guardian; 9 attendant, caretaker, castellan, chaperone, chatelain, custodian; **10** chatelaine, goalkeeper.

keep out 3 ban, bar; **7** exclude, prevent; **8** preclude, prohibit.

keepsake 5 token; **7** memento; **8** memorial, reminder, souvenir; **11** remembrance.

keep under 3 cow; **6** squash, subdue; **7** oppress, repress, squelch; **8** submerge; **9** subjugate.

keep up 5 equal, match; **8** continue, maintain, preserve; PHRASES: **4, 7** keep abreast.

keg *See* **barrel**

Kelvin 1 K.

ken 3 see; **4** know; **5** grasp, sight; **6** notice; **8** perceive; **9** knowledge; **10** perception, understand; **12** apprehension; **13** understanding.

Kentucky 2 KY; **3** Ken; **5** Derby; **8** cardinal (bird); **9** Frankfort (capital); PHRASES: **4, 5, 5** Blue Grass State (nickname); **5, 6** tulip poplar (tree); **6, 2, 5, 7, 2, 4** United we stand, divided we fall (motto); **6, 3** golden rod (flower).

kernel 3 nub, nut, pip; **4** core, germ, gist, seed; **5** copra, grain, heart; **7** essence, nucleus.

kerosene 8 paraffin; PHRASES: **8, 4** aviation fuel.

ketch 4 boat; **7** hangman; **11** executioner; PHRASES: **4, 5** Jack K~.

kettle 3 pot; **4** dixy, drum; **5** dixie *UK*; **6** boiler; **7** caldron.

key 3 ait *UK*, cay; **4** clef, clue, crib, holm, inch, lead, main, mode, note, raga, sign, yale; **5** basic, chief, gamut, gloss, ivory, major, minor, prime, prong, scale, table, vital, wedge; **6** answer, chroma, legend, locker, opener, series, spline, tuning; **7** caption, central, crucial, leading, pivotal, pointer; **8** critical, decisive, glossary, latchkey, passport, tonality; **9** essential, important, indicator, principal; **10** mixolydian, modulation; **11** fundamental, translation; **13** transposition; PHRASES: **3, 3** alt ~, ash ~, hot ~; **3, 4** ~ grip, K~ lime; **3, 5** ~ fruit, K~ Largo, ~ light, ~ money; **3, 9** ~ signature; **4, 3** door ~, pass ~; **5, 3** allen ~, shift ~; **5-7** passe-partout; **7, 3** control ~; **7, 4** Florida Keys; **8, 3** function ~, ignition ~, skeleton ~.

keyboard 4 keys; **6** manual, Qwerty; **7** console, ivories.

keyboard instrument 5 organ, piano; **6** spinet; **7** celesta, celeste, clavier, pianola; **8** calliope, carillon, melodeon, melodica; **9** accordion, dulcitone, harmonium, mellotron, virginals, Wurlitzer™; **10** clavichord, fortepiano, pianoforte; **11** harpsichord, synthesizer.

key fruit 6 samara.

keynote 4 core, gist, idea; **5** major, theme; **7** crucial, essence; **8** defining; **9** essential, important.

keystone 4 crux; **5** basis; PHRASES: **5, 9** quoin headstone.

Keystone (state) 2 PA; **4** Penn; **12** Pennsylvania.

Khmer Republic 8 Cambodia.

kick 3 fad, jag *UK*, pep, toe, zip; **4** boot, buzz, chip, clop, drub, hack, high, hoof, knee, pass, punt, quit, spur, stab, turn, zest, zing; **5** clump, flick, place, power, punch, stamp, stomp; **6** corner, recoil, return, thrill; **7** dribble, flutter, penalty, trample; **8** scissors; **9** garryowen; PHRASES: **2-3-5** up-and-under; **3, 3, 8** hit the crossbar; **3-5** toe-ender; **4, 4** drop ~, free ~, frog ~, goal ~; **4, 5** ~ pleat; **5, 4** place ~; **6, 4** corner ~ *UK*; **7, 4** penalty ~; **8, 4** scissors ~.

kickback 3 cut; **5** bribe; **6** payola, recoil, reward; **7** rebound; **9** sweetener; **10** backhander *UK*, inducement.

kick off 5 begin, start; **6** launch; **8** initiate; **10** inaugurate.

kick out 4 fire, oust, sack; **5** eject, evict; **7** dismiss; **9** discharge.

kid 3 rag, rib; **4** dupe, fool, goat, gull, hoax, joke, josh; **5** hocus, tease, trick; **6** humbug; **7** leather, pretend; **8** hoodwink; PHRASES: **3-4** leg-pull *UK*; **4, 2** have on *UK*, wind up *UK*. *See also* **child**

kidnap 5 crimp, steal; **6** abduct, dognap; **7** impress; **8** shanghai; PHRASES: **5, 3** carry off; **6, 4** spirit away.

kidney 4 kind, sort; **5** reins, renal; **6** mettle; **9** character; PHRASES: **6, 4** ~ bean; **6, 5** ~ stone.

kidney stone 8 nephrite.

kieselguhr 9 diatomite.

kif 9 marijuana.

kill 2 KO; **3** end, ice, off, top *UK*, zap; **4** burn, cull, frag, hang, kayo, slay, stab, stop, swat, veto; **5** croak, fordo, lynch, shoot, snuff, stiff, waste, whack; **6** behead, deaden, martyr, murder, poison, scotch, squash, stifle; **7** butcher, crucify, destroy, execute, garrote, scupper; **8** decimate, despatch, dispatch, dissolve, garrotte, immolate, massacre, strangle, suppress, throttle; **9** eliminate, euthanize, extirpate, liquidate, sacrifice, slaughter, terminate; **10** annihilate, extinguish; **11** exterminate; PHRASES: **2, 2** do in; **2, 3** do for; **2, 4, 4** do away with; **3, 2, 3, 3** nip in the bud; **3, 2, 5** put to sleep; **3, 3** cut off, rub out; **3, 3, 2** get rid of; **3, 4** cut down, gun down, put down; **3, 8, 4** end someone's life; **4, 3** bump off, wipe out; **4, 4** blow away; **4, 5** shed blood; **5, 3** knock out; **5, 4** shoot down.

killer 4 thug; **5** axman, ninja, shark; **6** slayer, Vandal; **7** butcher, hangman, soldier; **8** assassin, cannibal, filicide, homicide, murderer, predator, regicide; **9** barbarian, combatant, cutthroat, guerrilla, matricide, parricide, patricide, prolicide, terrorist, uxoricide; **10** fratricide, liquidator, sororicide, terminator; **11** executioner, infanticide, slaughterer; **12** exterminator; PHRASES: **3, 3** hit man; **3-5** man-eater; **4-6** head-hunter; **5, 3** hired gun.

killer whale 4 orca; **7** grampus.

killing 6 murder; **7** carnage, comical, slaying; **8** filicide, genocide, homicide, massacre, murderer, regicide, shooting, stabbing; **9** bloodshed, execution, hilarious, matricide, parricide, patricide, poisoning, prolicide, slaughter, uxoricide; **10** euthanasia, fratricide, liquidator, sororicide, terminator; **11** destruction, infanticide, termination; **12** manslaughter; PHRASES: **5-7** blood-letting.

killing (make a killing) 4, 1, 4 make a pile; **5, 2** clean up; **6, 2, 4** strike it rich.

killjoy 4 crab, prig; **5** priss, prude; **6** moaner; **7** puritan; **8** Jeremiah, sourpuss; **9** Cassandra; **10** curmudgeon, spoilsport; PHRASES: **3, 7** wet blanket; **5, 6** party pooper; **7, 5** stuffed shirt.

kilogram 1 k; **2** kg.

kilometer 2 km.

kin 3 sib; **4** clan, kind, kith, like; **5** folks, tribe; **6** family; **7** kindred, lineage, sibling; **8** relation; **9** relations, relatives; PHRASES: **4, 2, 3** next of ~.

kind 3 ilk, kin; **4** cast, fair, form, good, make, nice, race, sort, type; **5** brand, breed, class, genre, genus, group, model, moral, order, stamp, style; **6** benign, branch, family, gentle, goodly, honest, humane, kidney, kindly, manner, nature, phylum, strain, tender; **7** amiable, caliber, generic, helpful, lenient, species, variety; **8** category, friendly, generous, gracious, obliging, selfless, virtuous; **9** character, honorable, indulgent; **10** altruistic, beneficent, benevolent, charitable, thoughtful; **11** considerate, description, sympathetic; **13** understanding; PHRASES: **4-7** good-natured, warm-hearted, well-wishing; **6-7** tender-hearted.

kindle 4 fire, spur, wake; **5** light, rouse, spark, start, waken; **6** arouse, awaken, ignite, incite; **7** inflame, inspire, trigger; **9** stimulate; PHRASES: **3, 2, 4** set on fire; **3, 4, 2** set fire to; **3, 5** get going; **3, 5, 2** set light to *UK*; **5, 3** touch off.

kindness 4 care, help; **5** favor, grace; **6** virtue, warmth; **7** concern, honesty; **8** altruism, humanity, sympathy; **9** benignity, rectitude; **10** amiability, generosity; **11** beneficence, benevolence; **13** consideration; PHRASES: **4, 4** good turn, good will. *See also* **kind**

kindred 3 kin; **4** like, ties; **5** alike, blood, close; **6** allied, family; **7** kinship; **8** kinsfolk; **9** relations, relatives; **10** associated.

king 3 rex; **4** card, lord; **5** ruler; **6** prince; **7** monarch, pharaoh; **9** sovereign; PHRASES: **4, 5** ~ cobra, ~ prawn; **4, 6** ~ cotton; **4, 7** ~ penguin.

king cobra 9 hamadryad.

kingdom 4 Fife, land; **5** Judah, Lydia, Nepal, realm, state, Tonga; **6** Aragon, domain, Jordan, Mercia, nation, throne, Wessex; **7** Castile; **8** dominion, province; **9** Barataria.

kingfisher 7 halcyon.

kingly *See* **royal**

kingpin 7 headpin; PHRASES: **6, 3** swivel pin *UK*.

kings (biblical kings) 3 Asa, Evi, Hur; **4** Ahab, Ahaz, Amon, Bera, Elah, Hada, Jehu *UK*, Omri, Saul; **5** Balak, Basha, Cyrus, David, Eglon, Hiram, Hoham, Hosea, Jabin, Joash, Joram, Judah, Nabat, Nadab, Pekah, Piram, Reban, Zebar, Zimri; **6** Darius, Hoshea, Japhia, Josiah, Jothan, Lemuel, Sargon, Uzziah, Xerxes; **7** Ahaziah, Amaziah, Azariah, Jehoash, Jehoram, Menahem, Shallum, Solomon, Tryphon; **8** Hezekiah, Jehoahaz, Jeroboam, Manasseh, Pekahiah, Rehoboam, Zedekiah; **9** Jehoiakim, Zechariah; **10** Artaxerxes, Belshazzar, Jehoiachin, Jehosaphat, Salmanazar; **11** Melchizedek, Sennacherib; **14** Nebuchadnezzar.

kings (other kings) **3** Zog; **4** Fahd; **5** Louis, Midas, Priam; **6** Clovis, Farouk; **7** Ptolemy, Tarquin; **8** Baudouin, Leonidas, Menelaus; **9** Agamemnon, Wenceslas; **11** Charlemagne.

kingship **4** rule; **5** crown, power, reign; **8** monarchy; **9** authority, supremacy; **11** sovereignty.

kings of England and Britain **4** Cnut, Edwy, John, Knut, Lear, Offa; **5** Brute, Edgar, Edwin, Henry, James, Sweyn; **6** Alfred, Arthur, Canute, Eadred, Eadwig, Edward, George, Harold; **7** Charles, Richard, Stephen, William; **8** Ethelred; **9** Aethelred, Athelstan, Caratacus, Cymbeline, Ethelwulf; **10** Aethelwulf, Caractacus; PHRASES: **5, 9** Uther Pendragon; **6, 3, 5** Alfred the Great; **6, 8** Edmund Ironside, Harold Harefoot; **7, 5** William Rufus.

kings of Scotland **4** Aedh, Duff; **5** Colin, David, Edgar, Eocha, Girac, James; **6** Donald, Duncan, Robert; **7** Kenneth, Macbeth, Malcolm; **9** Alexander, Indolphus; **11** Constantine; PHRASES: **4, 7** John Balliol; **6, 3, 5** Robert the Bruce; **6, 4** Donald Bane; **7, 3, 4** William the Lion.

kink **4** bend, coil, curl, knot, wave; **5** crimp, crook, curve, frizz, knurl, twirl, twist; **6** tangle; **7** crinkle, wrinkle.

kinkajou **5** potto; PHRASES: **5, 4** honey bear.

kinky **3** odd; **4** bent, sexy, sick, wavy; **5** curly, pervy, saucy; **6** coiled; **7** buckled, crimped, crooked, deviant, naughty, strange; **9** perverted.

kip *See* **nap**

kismet *See* **fate**

kiss **3** paw, pet, rub; **4** buss, maul, neck, snog *UK*; **5** drool, goose, grope, smack, spoon; **6** bundle, caress, coddle, cosset, cuddle, dandle, enfold, fondle, nestle, nuzzle, smooch, stroke; **7** embosom, embrace, slobber, smacker, snuggle, squeeze; **8** lollygag, osculate; PHRASES: **4, 3** make out; **4, 3, 3** bill and coo; **4, 6** fool around; **4, 7** make

whoopee, play footsie; **6, 2** pucker up.

kit **3** rig, set; **4** gear, togs; **5** dress, stuff, tools; **6** attire, outfit, tackle, things; **7** clobber *UK*, clothes, costume, effects, uniform; **8** hardware; **9** apparatus, equipment; PHRASES: **3-2** get-up; **3-3** rig-out *UK*; **4-4** flat-pack.

kitchen **6** bakery, cellar, galley, larder, pantry; **7** buttery, caboose; **9** bakehouse *UK*, cookhouse; PHRASES: **5, 4** still room *UK*. *See also* **eating (eating utensils and dishes)**

kit out **5** equip.

kitsch **4** camp; **5** campy, tacky; **6** cheesy, trashy, vulgar; **7** chintzy; **9** tasteless; **10** artificial.

kitten **3** kit; **5** kitty; **7** catling.

knack *See* **ability**

knapsack **3** bag; **7** daypack; **8** backpack, rucksack; PHRASES: **8, 3** shoulder bag.

knead **3** rub; **4** mold, work; **7** massage; **10** manipulate.

knee **3** lap; **4** genu, hock.

kneecap **6** poleyn; **7** patella.

kneepan **7** patella.

knell **4** call, peal, ring, toll; **5** chime, sound; **7** ringing.

knickknack **3** toy; **5** curio; **6** doodad, gewgaw, trifle; **7** bibelot, trinket, whatnot; **8** ornament; **9** bagatelle; **11** thingumajig; PHRASES: **4-1-4** bric-a-brac.

knife **3** cut; **4** bolo, dirk, gash, kris, stab; **5** blade, kukri, skean, slash, spade, sword; **6** carver, kirpan *UK*, lancet, parang, skiver, slicer, switch, trench; **7** chopper, cleaver, cutlass, grinder, machete, poniard, scalpel; **8** bistoury, penknife, scimitar, stiletto; **9** drawknife, jackknife; **10** broadsword, misericord; **11** pocketknife, snickersnee, switchblade; PHRASES: **4, 5** bush ~, case ~, fish ~; **5-3** skean-dhu *UK*; **5, 5** bowie ~, bread ~ *UK*, clasp ~, craft ~, flick ~ *UK*, fruit ~, ~ pleat *UK*, steak ~; **6, 5** butter ~, pallet ~, sheath ~; **7, 5** carving ~, hunting ~, kitchen ~, pruning ~, Stanley ~ *tm*.

knight **2** KB *UK*, KG *UK*; **3** KBE *UK*; **5** noble; **7** samurai, templar, vavasor; **8** banneret, cavalier, crusader, horseman, vavasour; **9** chevalier; **10** equestrian; **11** hospitaller.

Knights of the Round Table **3** Kay; **4** Bors; **6** Gareth, Gawain, Modred; **7** Galahad, Geraint, Mordred, Tristan; **8** Bedivere, Lancelot, Percival, Tristram.

knit 3 tie; **4** bond, fuse, join, mesh, purl; **5** unite, weave; **6** fasten, stitch; **7** combine, crochet, entwine, wrinkle; **8** contract; **9** interlock; **10** intertwine, interweave.

knob 4 bump, dial, lump; **5** bulge; **6** button, handle; **8** doorknob, handhold; **10** protrusion; **12** protuberance.

knock 3 hit, jar, rap, tap; **4** bang, bash, beat, biff, blow, bonk, bump, clip, jolt, pink, slap; **5** pound, thump; **6** batter, buffet, hammer, patter, pummel, strike; **7** setback; **9** criticize, disparage; PHRASES: **3-1-3** rat-a-tat, rub-a-dub; **3-3** rat-tat; **6-6** pitter-patter.

knock down 3 cut; **4** fell; **5** floor; **7** flatten; **8** decrease, overturn; PHRASES: **6, 6** reduce topple.

knock off 3 nab; **4** kill, make, nick *UK*, stop, take; **5** break, filch, pinch, steal; **6** finish, murder; **7** produce; PHRASES: **4, 1, 5** take a break; **4, 5** down tools *UK*; **5, 3** clock off.

knock out 2 KO; **3** wow; **4** daze, kayo, stun, tire; **5** amaze; **6** defeat; **7** astound, exhaust, stupefy; **9** eliminate, overpower, overwhelm.

knot 3 bow; **4** bend, burr, knar, knur, loop, node; **5** gnarl, knurr *UK*; **6** nodule, sleave, tangle; **7** bowline; **10** sheepshank; PHRASES: **4, 3** cat's paw; **4, 4** love ~, reef ~, slip ~, wall ~ *UK*; **4, 5** half hitch; **5, 4** sheet bend, thumb ~; **6, 4** french ~, granny ~, square ~; **7, 4** carrick bend, Gordian ~; **8, 4** surgeon's ~, truelove ~; **10, 4** fisherman's ~, stevedore's ~.

knotty 4 hard; **5** tough; **6** thorny, tricky; **7** awkward, complex; **9** difficult; **11** complicated, problematic.

know 3 ken, see; **4** twig *UK*; **5** grasp, judge, savvy, sense; **6** accept, credit, master, retain; **7** believe, command, discern, realize; **8** conceive, identify, memorize, perceive; **9** apprehend, convinced, recognize; **10** appreciate, comprehend, understand; **11** distinguish; **12** discriminate; PHRASES: **3, 3, 4, 2** get the hang of; **4, 3, 5** ~ the ropes, ~ the score; **4, 4, 1, 4** ~ like a book; **5, 2** catch on.

knowing 8 eloquent, intended; **9** conscious; **10** deliberate, expressive, meaningful, perceptive; PHRASES: **11** calculating, intentional, significant.

know-it-all 4 nerd, swot *UK*, wonk; **6** boffin, smarty; **8** wiseacre; **4, 3** wise guy; **5,**

4 smart alec; **6, 4** clever dick; **6, 5** bright spark *UK*, clever clogs *UK*, smarty pants.

knowledge 3 ken; **4** info, lore; **5** grasp, savvy; **6** gnosis; **7** insight, knowing, mastery, science; **9** awareness, cognition, erudition, expertise, foresight, intuition; **10** cognisance *UK*, perception, smattering; **11** familiarity, learnedness, omniscience, realization; **12** acquaintance, apprehension, illumination; **13** comprehension, consciousness, enlightenment, understanding.

knowledgeable 3 hep, hip; **4** wise; **5** aware, nerdy, smart; **6** astute, brainy, clever, expert, gifted, primed, shrewd, sussed, swotty *UK*; **7** briefed, coached, erudite, knowing, learned, skilled, trained; **8** educated, informed, skillful, talented; **9** attentive, cognizant *UK*, competent, conscious, efficient, practiced, qualified, sagacious; **10** acquainted, omniscient, perceptive, polymathic, proficient, streetwise; **11** enlightened, experienced, intelligent; **12** accomplished; PHRASES: **2-2-4** up-to-date; **2, 2, 5** up to speed; **2, 3, 4** in the know; **2, 3, 7** in the picture; **2, 4** au fait; **2, 4, 4** at home with; **2, 5** in touch; **2, 7** au courant; **4, 2** with it; **4-4** well-read; **4-6** well-versed; **4-7** well-trained; **4-8** well-grounded, well-informed; **5, 2** clued up; **6, 2** genned up; **7-2** plugged-in; **10, 4** acquainted with, conversant with.

knowledgeable person 3 don; **4** sage; **6** boffin, expert, genius, pedant, savant(e); **7** egghead, scholar, teacher; **8** academic, brainbox *UK*, highbrow, smartass; **9** authority, scientist; **10** mastermind; **12** intellectual.

known 4 seen, true; **5** noted; **6** common, famous, proved, public; **7** certain; **8** explored, infamous, knowable, renowned, verified; **9** confessed, notorious, perceived; **10** celebrated, discovered, recognized.

knuckle under 3 bob, bow; **4** bend, duck, quit; **5** cower, kneel, stoop; **6** cringe, crouch, kowtow, submit; **9** acquiesce, surrender; **10** capitulate; PHRASES: **3, 3, 6** bow and scrape; **3, 4, 8** tug one's forelock; **4, 2** give in, give up; **4, 3, 4** bend the knee, lick the dust; **4, 4** back down; **5, 2** defer to; **5, 2, 3, 5** throw in the towel; **6, 7** demean oneself.

kookaburra 7 jackass; PHRASES: **8, 7** laughing jackass.

kosher 4 pure, real; **5** legit; **7** genuine; **8** approved; **10** legitimate.

kudos 4 fame; 5 glory, honor; 6 cachet, credit, praise, status; 7 tribute; 8 prestige, standing.

kumara 5, 6 sweet potato.

kumbaloi 5, 5 worry beads.

L

L **4** lake, left, live, loch *UK*; **5** fifty, large, Latin, liter, money, pound; **6** league, length; **7** learner, Liberal; **8** latitude.

LA **9** Louisiana; PHRASES: **3, 7** Los Angeles.

label **3** dub, tab, tag; **4** call, chit *UK*, flag, logo, mark, name, sign; **5** badge, brand, class, stamp; **6** chitty, define, docket, marker, ticket; **7** sticker; **8** classify, identify; **9** designate; **10** categorize, stereotype; **11** designation.

labor **3** job; **4** plod, task, toil, work; **5** chore, exert, hands; **6** effort, strain, strive; **7** agonize, efforts, grapple, stagger, workers, wrestle; **8** complain, delivery, endeavor, exertion, struggle; **9** employees, jobholder; **10** childbirth, drudgework, exaggerate; **11** confinement, malfunction; **12** contractions; **13** overemphasize; PHRASES: **2, 2** go on; **4, 2** play up; **4, 2, 2** keep at it; **4, 4** hard work; **4, 5** work force; **4, 8** drag yourself; **5, 2** dwell on, seize up; **5, 4** drive home, grind away; **5, 5** ~ force; **6, 5** giving birth, manual ~.

laboratory **3** lab; **6** studio; **8** workshop; PHRASES: **5, 4** think tank; **5, 7** field station; **7, 6** proving ground.

labored **5** fussy, harsh, heavy, stiff, weary; **6** clumsy, forced; **7** arduous, awkward, painful, stilted, studied; **8** strained; **9** contrived, difficult, elaborate, laborious, unnatural.

laborer **4** hand, peon; **5** kanak, navvy *UK*, prole; **6** casual, cottar *UK*, drudge, menial, worker; **7** brickie *UK*, pioneer, workman; **10** rouseabout *UK*, roustabout.

laborious **4** hard; **5** fussy, heavy, weary; **6** heroic, tiring, uphill; **7** arduous, killing, labored, painful; **8** crushing, detailed, fiddling, grueling, thorough, toilsome; **9** difficult, elaborate, Herculean, punishing, strenuous, wearisome; **10** burdensome, exhausting; **11** painstaking, troublesome, unremitting; **12** backbreaking; PHRASES: **3-7** nit-picking; **4-3** hard-won; **4-6** hard-fought.

laboriously **4** hard; **8** heartily, manually; **13** energetically; PHRASES: **2, 4** by hand; **2, 4, 6** to one's utmost; **3, 4, 3** the hard way; **5, 3, 4** tooth and nail; **6, 3, 5** hammer and tongs. *See also* **laborious**

labour, Labour **3** job, Lab; **4** help, plod, slog, task, toil, work; **5** birth, chore, exert, graft, grind, hands, pains, pangs, slave, sweat, trial; **6** corvée, effort, overdo, strain, strive, worker; **7** agonize, grapple, handful, stagger, travail, workers, wrestle; **8** complain, delivery, drudgery, endeavor, exertion, overplay, overwork, struggle; **9** employees; **10** childbirth, exaggerate, overstress; **11** backbreaker, confinement, malfunction, tribulation; **12** contractions; **13** overemphasize; PHRASES: **2, 3, 3** go all out; **4, 5** hard graft, tall order, work force; **5, 5** labor force; **6, 5** manual labor; **6, 8** uphill struggle.

Labours of Hercules **4, 2, 7** hind of Cryneia; **6, 2, 6** cattle of Geryon; **6, 4** Cretan bull, Nemean lion *UK*; **6, 7** Augean stables; **7, 5** Lernean hydra.

laburnum **6, 5** golden chain *UK*.

labyrinth **3** web; **4** maze; **7** network; **8** Daedalus; PHRASES: **8, 3** internal ear *UK*.

lace **3** net, tat, tie; **4** bash, beat, drub; **5** blend, braid, Cluny, orris, picot, plait, point, spike, thump, twine, weave; **6** bobbin, fasten, fillet, flavor, pillow, reseau, string; **7** Alençon, babiche, entwine, fishnet, guipure, Honiton, latchet, macramé, Malines, Mechlin, shoetie, tatting, torchon; **8** Brussels, dentelle, duchesse, filigree, openwork, rosaline; **9** Chantilly; **10** mignonette, Nottingham, shoestring; **12** Valenciennes.

Lacedaemonian 7 Spartan.

lacerate 3 cut, rip; 4 maim, maul, slit, tear; 5 gouge, graze, score, shred, slash, wound; 6 incise, injure, mangle, scrape; 7 scratch; 8 mutilate.

laceration 4 gash; 6 injure, injury; 8 abrasion, incision. *See also* **lacerate**

lachrymose 3 sad; 6 crying, dismal, moving, tragic; 7 tearful, unhappy; PHRASES: 2, 5 in tears; 6, 5 easily moved.

lack 3 lag; 4 lose, miss, need, void, want; 5 fault, minus; 6 dearth, famine; 7 absence, aplasia, deficit, drought, paucity, poverty, require; 8 scarcity, shortage, sparsity; 9 privation, shortfall, shortness; 10 deficiency, inadequacy, scantiness, scarceness; 11 deprivation, shortcoming; 13 insufficiency.

lackadaisical 3 lax; 4 lazy; 5 blasé; 6 casual; 7 languid, offhand, relaxed; 8 careless, indolent, lukewarm, uncaring; 9 apathetic; 10 nonchalant; 11 unconcerned; 14 unenthusiastic; PHRASES: 4-7 half-hearted.

lackey 4 help, page, tool; 5 boots *UK*, groom, toady, valet; 6 drudge, flunky, menial, minion, skivvy, stooge, vassal; 7 flunkey, footman, orderly, servant, spaniel; 8 dogsbody *UK*, domestic, factotum, follower, henchman, hireling, inferior, retainer, servitor; 9 assistant, attendant, subaltern, underling; 10 bootlicker, manservant; 11 subordinate; PHRASES: 4-3 cat's-paw; 6-2 hanger-on.

lacking 4 sans; 5 minus; 6 absent, bereft; 7 missing, wanting, without; 9 defective, deficient; 10 inadequate; 11 unavailable.

lacklustre *See* **dull**

laconic 7 Spartan. *See also* **concise**

lacquer *See* **coat, coating**

lacrosse 4 foul, goal; 5 glove, judge, point; 6 center, crosse, helmet; 7 offside, passing, pushing; 8 slashing, tripping; 9 faceguard; 10 baggataway; 12 bodychecking, interference; PHRASES: 4, 2, 4 loss of ball; 4, 4 free play, goal area *UK*, left wing, wing area; 4, 6 goal crease; 4, 8 free position; 5, 4 right wing; 5, 5 cover point *UK*; 5, 6 first attack; 5, 7 first defense; 6, 3, 4 facing the ball; 6, 4 center line, inside home; 6, 6 attack player; 7, 4 outside home, penalty play; 7, 5 penalty award; 7, 6 defense player.

lactate 4 milk; 5 nurse; 6 suckle; PHRASES:

6-4 breast-feed.

lactose 4, 5 milk sugar; 5, 2, 4 sugar of milk.

lacy 3 net; 4 fine; 8 delicate, filigree, lacelike.

lad 3 boy, guy, man; 5 bloke *UK*, fella, youth; 8 teenager; 9 youngster; PHRASES: 5, 3 young man *UK*.

ladder 5 scale, steps *UK*; 6 ratlin; 7 ratline; 9 companion, hierarchy, staircase; 10 stepladder; 12 companionway; PHRASES: 4, 6 loft ~, roof ~, rope ~, side ~; 5, 6 stern ~; 6, 6 aerial ~, Jacob's ~; 7, 6 folding ~, gangway ~, quarter ~; 9, 6 companion ~, extension ~.

ladle 4 bail; 5 scoop, spade, spoon; 6 dipper, shovel, trowel; 7 spatula.

lady 4 dame; 5 woman; 6 madame; 7 duchess, peeress; 8 baroness, countess; 11 gentlewoman, viscountess; PHRASES: 3, 4 bag ~, day ~, old ~, Our L~; 4, 4 ~ fern *UK*, L~ Muck *UK*; 4, 6 ~ chapel, ~ orchid; 4, 8 ~ mayoress; 4, 9 L~ Bountiful; 4, 10 L~ Windermere; 5, 4 first ~, naked ~, white ~, young ~ *UK*; 6, 4 dinner ~ *UK*; 7, 4 painted ~. *See also* **woman**

lady's finger 6 bhindi *UK*.

lag 4 drag; 5 delay, trail; 6 dawdle, loiter, retard; 7 convict; 8 jailbird, prisoner; PHRASES: 4, 4 hang back; 4, 4, 4 drag one's feet; 4, 6 fall behind; 5, 2, 3, 4 bring up the rear.

lagoon 3 bay; 4 cove, lake, loch *UK*, pond, pool; 5 creek, inlet, lough *UK*.

lair 3 den; 4 cave, drey, hole, holt *UK*, nest, sett; 5 aerie, earth *UK*, perch, roost, study; 6 burrow, covert, tunnel, warren; 7 anthill, beehive, hideout. *See also* **animal home**

lake 3 Tuz, Van; 4 Bear, Chad, Como, Conn, Derg, Erie, Eyre, Kivu, linn *UK*, llyn, loch *UK*, Mead, mere, Ohau, pond, pool, Tana, tarn; 5 Allen, broad *UK*, Celyn, flash, Garda, Gatun, Huron, Kyoga, Leane, lough *UK*, Neagh, Nyasa, Ogwen, Onega, oxbow, Sevan, Tahoe, Urmia, Volta; 6 Albert, Baikal, Brenig, Corrib, Edward, Geneva, George, Kariba, Ladoga, lagoon, Lugano, Malawi, Nakuru, Nasser, Placid, Rudolf, Saimaa, salina, Severn, Swilly, Texoma, Vänern, Wanaka, Zurich; 7 Avernus, Axolotl, Balaton, Balqash, Bolsena, Chapala, Francis, Iliamna, lakelet, Lucerne, Mälaren, Managua, Nipigon, Ontario, Quesnel, Turkana; 8 Attersee, Balkhash, Bodensee, Flathead, Kentucky, Maggiore,

Manitoba, Menteith, Michigan, Okanagan, Onondaga, Seminole, Shoshone, Superior, Tiberias, Titicaca, Victoria, Wakatipu, Winnipeg; **9** Athabasca, Champlain, Churchill, Constance, Esthwaite, Llangorse, Maracaibo, Neuchatel, Nicaragua, Nipissing, reservoir, Trasimeno, Winnebago; **10** Chautauqua, IJsselmeer, Miraflores, Mistassini, Okeechobee, Tanganyika, Windermere; **11** Yellowstone; **12** Memphremagog, Winnipegosis; **13** Pontchartrain, Winnipesaukee; PHRASES: **2, 4** St. John; **2, 5** St. Clair; **3-1-4** Tal-y-lynn; **3, 2, 7** Sea of Galilee; **3, 4** sea loch *UK*; **3, 5, 5** the Great Lakes; **4, 2, 3, 5** L~ of the Woods; **4, 3** Aral Sea, Dead Sea, Kara Kul; **4, 4** Loch Ness, salt ~; **4, 6** Loch Lomond; **4, 8** L~ District; **5, 3** Tonle Sap; **5-3** Issyk-Kul; **5, 4** Clear L~, oxbow ~; **5, 4, 4** Great Bear L~, Great Salt L~; **5, 5** Great Lakes; **5, 5, 4** Great Slave L~; **6, 3** inland sea, Salton Sea; **6, 4** Seneca L~; **6, 5** Finger Lakes; **6, 5, 4** Lesser Slave L~; **7, 2** Qinghai Hu; **7, 3** Caspian Sea; **8, 4** Reindeer L~, Victoria Nile; **9, 5** Ennerdale Water; **10, 4, 5** Bonneville Salt Flats.

lake dweller 5 laker; **10** lacustrian; PHRASES: **4, 7** pile builder, pile dweller.

lake dwelling 7 crannog, kampong; PHRASES: **4, 5** pile house; **5, 5** Cajun cabin, stilt house; **5, 7** stilt village; **8, 5** lakeside house.

lake herring 5 powan.

lamb 3 leg, rib; **4** baby, dupe, fool, loin; **6** breast; **7** lambkin, Persian, riblets; **8** innocent, shoulder, yearling; PHRASES: **4, 4** loin chop; **4, 5** fore shank, hind shank, neck slice; **5, 3** scrag end *UK*; **5, 4** chump chop; **6, 4** middle neck.

Lamb 4 Elia.

lament 3 cry, rue, woe; **4** howl, keen, moan, sigh, wail, weep; **5** groan, mourn; **6** bemoan, bewail, beweep, grieve, regret, threne; **7** deplore, elegize; **8** complain; **10** threnodize; PHRASES: **4, 4, 6** beat one's breast.

lamentable 4 dire; **5** awful, grave; **6** tragic, woeful; **7** pitiful; **8** wretched; **9** sorrowful; **10** deplorable, depressing; **11** distressing, regrettable, unfortunate.

lamentation 4 wake; **5** dirge, elegy, knell; **6** crying, sorrow; **7** keening, requiem, sobbing, wailing, weeping; **8** coronach *UK*; grieving, mourning, swansong, threnody; **9** complaint, lamenting, obsequies, plangen-

cy, ululation; **11** dolefulness, tearfulness, thanatopsis; **12** mournfulness, wretchedness; **13** sorrowfulness; PHRASES: **3, 5** sob story; **4, 2, 3** tale of woe; **4, 4** last post *UK*; swan song; **4, 5** last rites; **6, 5** widow's weeds. *See also* **lament**

laminate 5 inlay, layer, paint; **6** veneer; **7** Formica *tm*, lacquer.

lamp 5 pilot, torch; **7** cruisie, lantern; **10** flashlight; PHRASES: **3, 5** oil ~, sun ~; **3, 5** arc light; **4, 4** Davy ~, lava ~, tail ~; **5, 4** Aldis ~ *TM*, floor ~; **6, 4** Argand ~, quartz ~, safety ~, spirit ~; **8, 4** tungsten ~; **9, 4** hurricane ~; **10, 4** anglepoise ~ *TM*. *See also* **lantern, light**

lampoon 3 guy; **4** mock, skit; **5** spoof, squib; **6** parody, satire; **7** cartoon; **8** ridicule, satirize; **9** burlesque; **10** caricature, pasquinade; PHRASES: **4, 2** send up; **4, 3** take off.

lance 3 cut; **5** prick, spear; **6** pierce, weapon; **7** bayonet, javelin; PHRASES: **5, 4** slice into, slice open.

lancet arch 5 ogive; PHRASES: **6, 4** Gothic arch; **7, 4** pointed arch.

land 3 sod; **4** clay, dock, feod, feud, fief, marl, moor, plot, soil, turf; **5** beach, berth, debus *UK*, feoff, glebe, perch, realm; **6** alight, anchor, arrive, debark, domain, emerge, estate, ground, nation, parcel, realty, return, settle, unboat, unload; **7** acreage, demesne, deplane, detrain, holding, terrain, unhitch; **8** dismount, property; **9** discharge, disembark, territory; **10** disemplane; PHRASES: **3, 2** tie up; **3, 3** get off; **3, 7** run aground; **4, 4** come home, ~ bank, ~ crab, ~ girl *UK*, ~ line; **4, 6** drop anchor, ~ bridge, step ashore; **5, 4** touch down.

landform 3 cwm; **4** hill; **5** basin, fjord, gorge, plain, scarp; **6** arrête, canyon, cirque, ravine, shield, valley; **7** plateau; **8** mountain; PHRASES: **4, 6** rift valley; **5, 5** flood plain; **6, 5** valley floor; **7, 5** coastal plain; **7, 6** glacial valley, hanging valley; **7, 7** natural feature, surface feature.

landing 4 pier, quay; **5** beach, berth, solar, wharf; **7** docking, mooring; **8** halfpace, landfall; **9** disember, touchdown; **10** splashdown; **11** debarkation; **13** disembarkment; **14** disembarkation; PHRASES: **7, 5** ~ stage; **7, 6** ~ ground; **7, 7** pancake ~.

landlord 5 owner; **7** manager; **8** hotelier, licensee; **9** landowner; **10** landholder, proprietor; PHRASES: **8-5** property-owner.

landmark 4 sign; **5** sight; **6** marker; **8** signpost; **9** benchmark, milestone, momentous; **10** attraction, innovation, innovative, revolution; **12** breakthrough; **13** revolutionary.

land rail 9 corncrake.

landscape 4 form, land, site; **5** model, scene, shape; **6** design; **7** drawing, picture, scenery, setting; **8** backdrop, painting; **9** situation; **10** background, watercolor; **11** countryside; **13** circumstances; PHRASES: **3, 8** oil painting.

landslide 5 creep, glide, lahar, slide, slump; **7** mudflow; **9** avalanche, earthflow; **12** overwhelming; PHRASES: **4, 4** rock fall; **6, 4** debris flow; **7, 4** plastic flow.

langouste 5, 7 spiny lobster.

language 2 Wu; **3** Ibo, Ido, Kwa, Min, Twi; **4** Ainu, Akan, cant, Erse, Igbo, Manx, Norn, Pali, Thai, Tupi, Urdu, Zulu; **5** argot, Aztec, Bantu, Basic, Carib, Czech, Doric, Dutch, Fante, Fanti, Farsi, Greek, Hindi, idiom, Irish, Karen, Khmer, Latin, lingo, Malay, Maori, Norse, Oriya, Oscan, Saxon, Scots, Shona, Tamil, Uzbek, Welsh, Xhosa, Yakut; **6** Altaic, Arabic, Basque, Basuto, Berber, Bihari, Breton, Creole, Danish, French, Gaelic, German, Gullah, Hebrew, Herero, Ionian, jargon, Kalmyk, Korean, Ladino, Pahari, Pashto, pidgin, Polish, Pushtu, Romany, Shelta, Sindhi, Slovak, speech, Strine, Telugu, tongue, Tswana, Turkic, Ugrian, Yoruba; **7** Amharic, Aramaic, Avestan, Bengali, Burmese, Catalan, Chinese, Chinook, Choctaw, Cornish, English, Finnish, Flemish, Frisian, Guarani, Iranian, Italian, Kalmuck, Kurdish, Latvian, Lettish, Marathi, Nahuatl, Nynorsk, Punjabi, Quechua, Russian, Semitic, Slovene, Sorbian, Spanish, Swahili, Swedish, Tagalog, Turkish, Yiddish; **8** Akkadian, Assamese, Cherokee, Gujarati, idiolect, Japanese, Javanese, Kashmiri, Mandarin, Romansch, Rumanian, Sanskrit; **9** Afrikaans, Bulgarian, Cantonese, Franglais, Hungarian, Icelandic, Norwegian, Sinhalese, Ukrainian; **10** Algonquian, Hindustani, Lithuanian, Portuguese, Rajasthani, vernacular, Vietnamese; PHRASES: **4, 8** body ~, dead ~, sign ~; **5-5** Anglo-Saxon, Serbo-Croat; **5, 8** first ~, tonal ~; **6, 5** Tatarm Ugric; **6, 8** formal ~, second ~; **7, 8** machine ~, natural ~.

languish 4 fail, flag, pine, sink; **6** grieve, suffer, teeter, weaken; **7** decline; PHRASES: **4, 3** long for; **4, 4** fade away, pine away.

langur 4, 6 leaf monkey.

lantern 4 glim, link; **5** brand, torch; **6** sconce; **8** flambeau; **9** flashlamp; **10** flashlight, nightlight; PHRASES: **4, 7** dark ~, horn ~; **5, 7** magic ~, storm ~; **6, 7** friar's ~, turnip ~; **7, 7** Chinese ~, pumpkin ~; **8, 7** Japanese ~. See also **lamp, light**

lanthanide 4, 5 rare earth.

Laois 4 Leix; PHRASES: **6, 6** Queen's County.

lap 3 leg; **4** part, tour; **5** drink, round, slurp, stage; **6** circle; **7** circuit, section, segment; PHRASES: **3, 2** ~ up; **4, 2** lick up.

lapse 3 end; **4** drop, fail, fall, slip; **5** break, delay, drift, error, pause, space; **6** falter, tumble; **7** blunder, decline, descend, failure, mistake; **8** interval; **12** intermission; PHRASES: **4, 2** give up; **4, 2, 2, 3** come to an end; **4, 3** tail off; **5, 3** trail off.

lapwing 5 pewit; **6** peewit, plover; PHRASES: **5, 6** green plover.

larboard 4 port.

large 1 L.; **2** OS, XL; **3** big; **4** high, huge, mega, tall, vast, wide; **5** ample, baggy, broad, bulky, giant, great, gross, hefty, jumbo, roomy, stout; **6** goodly, mighty; **7** immense, mammoth, monster, outsize, sizable, skookum; **8** colossal, enormous, generous, gigantic, sizeable, spacious, thumping, whacking, whopping; **9** extensive, ginormous, humongous, strapping; **10** commodious, gargantuan, monumental, prodigious, tremendous, voluminous; **11** substantial; **12** astronomical; **13** Brobdignagian; PHRASES: **4-4** king-size; **4-5** good-sized; **5-4** giant-size; **6-4** family-size, record-size; **7-4** economy-size.

largeness 4 size; **5** width; **6** volume; **7** breadth; **8** enormity; **9** amplitude, immensity; **14** substantiality. See also **large**

large number 1 C, D, K, M; **4** raft, slew, slue; **5** fermi; **6** googol; **7** billion, jillion, million, umpteen, zillion; **8** infinity, milliard UK, trillion; **9** decillion, nonillion, octillion, squillion UK; **10** googolplex, septillion, sextillion; **11** centrillion, quadrillion, quintillion, undecillion; **12** duodecillion, sexdecillion, tredecillion, vigintillion; **13** octodecillion, quindecillion; **14** novemdecillion; **15** septendecillion.

largest part 4 bulk, gist, mass; **7** summary; **8** majority; PHRASES: **4, 4** best part, main body, main part; **4, 8** vast majority; **5, 5** lion's share.

lark 3 fun; **4** game, jape, joke; **5** caper, laugh, pipit, prank; **6** giggle; **7** mudlark *UK*, skylark; **9** adventure.

larva 3 bot; **4** bott, grub, nest, pupa, zoea; **5** imago, naiad, nidus, nymph, redia, zoaea; **6** caddis, chigoe, cocoon, jigger, looper, maggot, porina; **7** antlion, bagworm, chigger, cutworm, planula, veliger; **8** glowworm, mealworm, silkworm, wireworm; **9** bloodworm, chrysalis, doodlebug, screwworm; **10** miracidium, spiderling; **11** caterpillar; **13** leatherjacket *UK*, metamorphosis; PHRASES: **4, 4** army worm; **6, 4** caddis worm, woolly bear; **9, 4** witchetty grub *UK*.

larynx 5, 3 voice box.

lascivious *See* **lecherous**

lash 3 cat, fix, lam, tie; **4** beat, belt, bind, cane, flay, flog, knot, rope, whip; **5** birch, hitch, knout, quirt, strap, thong; **6** attach, batter, buffet, couple, fasten, larrup, secure, splice, swinge, switch, tether, thrash; **7** connect, leather, scourge; **9** horsewhip; PHRASES: **3-1-4-5** cat-o'-nine-tails; **3, 8, 4** tan someone's hide; **5, 3** rope's end.

lashings *See* **lots**

lass *See* **girl**

last 1 Z; **3** end, zed, zee; **4** rear, stay; **5** abide, anvil, dying, final; **6** bottom, endure, extend, latest, latter, remain, utmost; **7** closing, extreme, outlast, outlive, persist, survive; **8** continue, eventual, rearmost, terminal, ultimate; **10** concluding, conclusive; PHRASES: **4, 2** hang on; **4, 2, 2, 5** hang on in there; **4, 3** hold out; **4, 3, 6** stay the course; **4, 4** ~ name, ~ post *UK*; **4, 5** ~ rites, ~ stand, ~ straw, ~ thing *UK*; **4, 6** ~ supper; **4, 7** ~ trumpet; **4, 9** ~ judgement; **5, 2** carry on.

lasting 4 fast, firm; **5** fixed; **6** secure, stable; **7** abiding, chronic, durable, endless, eternal; **8** constant, enduring, lifelong; **9** continual, evergreen, indelible, perpetual; **10** continuing, continuous, immemorial, persistent, persisting; **11** everlasting, horological; PHRASES: **4-4** long-term; **4-5** long-lived; **4-7** long-lasting, time-honored; **4-8** long-standing.

last word 4 amen; **5** envoi; **9** ultimatum.

late 2 ex; **4** dead, slow; **5** later, tardy; **6** former, recent, unpaid; **7** belated, delayed,

overdue, unready; **8** dilatory, lamented, sluggish; **9** postdated; **10** behindhand, unprepared, unpunctual; **14** parachronistic; PHRASES: **2, 3, 4, 6** at the last minute; **2, 4** at last; **3, 2, 4** not on time; **4, 2** hung up; **4, 3, 4** none too soon; **5, 2, 4** never on time; **6, 4** behind time; **6, 8** behind schedule.

latecomer 5 idler; **7** delayer, laggard; **8** slowpoke, slugabed *UK*, sluggard; **9** slowcoach; PHRASES: **4, 5** late riser; **4, 7** late bloomer, slow learner, slow starter; **4, 9** late developer.

latency 5 sleep; **8** abeyance, dormancy; **9** anonymity, passivity, sublimity; **10** inactivity, quiescence *UK*, virtuality; **11** aestivation *UK*, hibernation, possibility; **12** potentiality. *See also* **latent**

lateness 3 lag; **5** delay; **7** lagging; **11** retardation; **13** unpunctuality. *See also* **late**

latent 5 inert; **7** dormant, passive, virtual; **8** inactive, possible, sleeping; **9** potential, quiescent, submerged; **10** archetypal, subliminal, underlying; **11** aestivating, clandestine, delitescent, hibernating, undeveloped; **12** subconscious; **14** unacknowledged.

later 5 after; **6** future; **7** distant; **8** upcoming; **10** subsequent; PHRASES: **2, 1, 5** in a while; **2, 3, 6** in due course, in the future; **2, 4** in time; **5, 1, 5** after a while.

lateral 4 side; **8** adjacent, creative; **9** inventive; **10** horizontal, unorthodox; PHRASES: **7, 8** ~ thinking.

laterally 6 askant; **7** oblique; **8** edgeways *UK*, sideways, sidewise; **9** alongside, crossways, obliquely, sidewards; PHRASES: **2, 3, 4** on the side, to one side, to the side.

lather 4 foam, soap, suds; **5** froth, panic; **6** dither, pother; **7** anxiety, bubbles; **8** soapsuds; **9** agitation; PHRASES: **4, 2** soap up; **6, 2** ~ up.

Latin 1 L.; **7** Italian; **8** Hispanic, Spaniard; PHRASES: **5, 5** L~ cross; **5, 7** L~ America, L~ quarter.

Latin phrases 4 fiat, lege, stet, veni, vici, vidi; **5** brute, circa, fecit, spero; **7** peccavi; **8** emeritus; **9** excelsior; **12** perseverando; PHRASES: **1, 6** a priori; **2, 2** et tu, in re; **2, 3** ad hoc, ad lib, ad rem; **2, 3, 2, 4** de die in diem; **2, 4** ad usum, in situ, in toto, in vivo; **2, 4, 5** ex post facto; **2, 4, 7** in vino veritas; **2, 4, 8** in loco parentis; **2, 5** ad finem, de facto, et grege, in vitro; **2, 6** ut prosim; **2, 6, 5** ne fronti crede; **2, 7** ad interim, ad literam, ad nauseam, ex officio; **2, 8** ex cathedra, in extremis, in memoriam; **2, 9** ad infinitum, de profundis; **3, 2, 4** hic et nunc; **3, 3** pro tem; **3, 4** cui bono?, per diem, pro rege, sub rosa, una voce; **3, 4, 7** pro bono publico; **3, 5** dum spiro, mea culpa, pro forma; **3, 6** dei gratia, pro patria, sub judice, vox populi; **3, 6, 6** non compos mentis; **3, 7** deo gratias; **3, 8** non sequitur, pax vobiscum; **3, 11** nil desperandum; **4, 3** fiat lux, sine die; **4, 3, 3** sine qua non; **4, 4** bona fide, nota bene; **4, 5** vice versa; **4, 6** anno domini, loco citato, post mortem; **4, 8** ante meridiem, post meridiem; **5, 2, 4** animo et fide; **5, 3** alter ego; **5, 3, 4** jacta est alea; **5, 4** inter alia; **5, 5** prima facie, terra firma; **5, 6** locus standi; **5, 6, 4** omnia vincit amor; **5, 8** modus operandi; **5, 10** infra dignitatem; **6, 3** status quo; **6, 5** gloria patri, tempus fugit; **6, 6** caveat emptor, compos mentis; **6, 7** corpus delicti, vincit veritas; **6, 8** editio princeps; **7, 3, 5** persona non grata; **7, 5** festina lente, servabo fidem; **7, 7** ceteris paribus; **7, 8** fortuna sequatur; **8, 2, 5** fortiter et recte.

latitude 1 L; **4** play, room; **5** scope, slack; **6** leeway; **7** breadth, freedom, liberty, license; **8** parallel; **9** amplitude, roominess; **11** flexibility; **12** spaciousness; PHRASES: **4, 4** free hand, free play, free rein; **9, 5** breathing space *UK*.

latter *See* **last**

latter-day *See* **modern**

Latter-day Saint 6 Mormon.

lattice 3 web; **4** mesh; **5** frame; **6** matrix; **9** framework.

Latvian 4 Lett; **7** Lettish.

laud *See* **praise**

laugh 3 fun, yuk; **4** boff, hoot, howl, jeer, mock, roar; **5** scorn, tehee, whoop; **6** cackle, deride, giggle, guffaw, nicker, scream, titter; **7** chortle, chuckle, screech, snicker, snigger; **10** cachinnate; PHRASES: **2-2** ha-ha, he-he, ho-ho; **4, 1, 3** blow a gut; **4, 2, 3, 6** roll in the aisles; **4, 4, 6** slap one's thighs; **4, 5** fall about *UK*; **5, 4, 5** split one's sides; **5, 5** ~ lines.

laughable 5 comic, funny, silly; **6** absurd; **7** amusing, fatuous, idiotic, risible; **8** derisory, humorous; **9** hilarious, ludicrous; **10** ridiculous; **12** preposterous; PHRASES: **4-9** side-splitting. *See also* **funny**

laughing gas 7, 5 nitrous oxide.

laughing jackass 10 kookaburra.

laughing stock 4 butt, dupe, foil; **5** patsy; **6** stooge; PHRASES: **4, 3** fall guy; **4, 5** Aunt Sally *UK*; **6, 2, 3** figure of fun *UK*; **8, 3** straight man.

laughter 4 fits; **5** laugh, mirth; **6** giggle, titter; **7** chortle, snicker, snigger; **8** giggling, hilarity; **9** hysterics, tittering; **11** cachination, convulsions; PHRASES: **3, 7** the giggles.

launce 4, 3 sand eel.

launch 4 cast, fire, hurl; **5** begin, fling, float, pitch, start, throw; **7** present, release; **8** catapult, initiate; **9** instigate, institute, introduce; **12** introduction, presentation; PHRASES: **4, 3, 4, 3** lift off take off; **5, 3** blast off.

laundry 4 wash; **7** washing; PHRASES: **5, 5** dirty linen; **5, 7** dirty clothes.

lavatory 2 WC *UK*; **3** bog, can, loo *UK*; **4** dike, head, john, room; **5** dunny *UK*, Elsan *TM*, gents *UK*, jakes, khazi *UK*, privy; **6** ladies *UK*, toilet, urinal; **7** latrine; **8** basement, bathroom, facility, outhouse, Portaloo *TM*, restroom, washroom; **9** backhouse, cloakroom *UK*; **10** facilities, thunderbox *UK*; **11** convenience; PHRASES: **4, 4** rest room *UK*; **5, 6** earth closet *UK*; **6, 4** ladies' room, powder room; **6, 4, 4** little boys' room; **6, 5, 4** little girls' room; **7, 7** comfort station.

lavender water 5 scent; **7** perfume; PHRASES: **3, 2, 7** eau de Cologne; **4, 5** rose water.

lavish 4 heap, load, pour; **5** cover; **7** copious, smother; **8** abundant, prolific, wasteful; **9** excessive, plentiful, sumptuous; **10** profligate; **11** extravagant; **12** unrestrained.

law 3 act; **4** rule, tort; **5** axiom, bylaw, edict, model, order, tenet; **6** decree, dictum, police, thesis; **7** charter, natural, pandect, precept, premise, statute, theorem; **8** equation; **9** criterion, Decalogue, directive, ordinance, prescript, principle, statement; **10** hypothesis, litigation, Pentateuch, regulation; **11** institution, legislation, Procrustean, proposition; **12** codification, constitution; PHRASES: **3, 2, 3, 3** ~ of the air, ~ of the sea; **3, 2, 3, 4** ~ of the land; **3, 2, 7** ~ of nations; **3, 2, 8** ~ of commerce, ~ of contract; **3, 3, 6** ~ and equity; **3, 3, 7** lex non scripta; **3, 7** jus gentium (Roman Law), lex scripta; **3, 8** jus naturale (Roman Law); **3, 9** jus canonicum; **3, 10** lex mercatoria; **3, 12** Ten Commandments; **4, 2, 3** body of ~; **4, 2,**

6 laws of motion; **4, 3, 2, 3, 3** long arm of the ~; **5, 3** canon ~, civil ~, lynch ~, Salic ~; **5, 4** civil code, legal code, penal code; **5, 5** Magna Carta; **6, 3** Boyle's ~, common ~, equity ~; **6, 5** corpus juris; **6, 6** Twelve Tables; **7, 3** Murphy's ~, natural ~, private ~, statute ~, written ~; **7, 4** statute book; **8, 2, 5** equation of state; **8, 3** business ~, codified ~, criminal ~, Gresham's ~; **8, 5** standing order; **9, 3** unwritten ~; **10, 3** commercial ~, Parkinson's ~; **10, 4** Napoleonic code.

law-abiding 4 good; **6** decent, honest; **7** upright; **8** licensed, obedient, virtuous; **9** competent, honorable, righteous; **10** authorized, upstanding.

lawbreaker *See* **criminal**

law court 4 banc, moot; **5** court; **6** Temple; **7** assizes *UK*, chamber, circuit, sidebar; **8** sessions, tribunal; **9** counselor; PHRASES: **3, 5** the bench; **3, 6** Old Bailey; **4, 2** hand up; **4, 4** jury duty; **4, 5** FISA court, High Court, open court; **4-6, 4** blue-ribbon jury; **5, 2, 3** court of law; **5, 2, 5** House of Lords; **5, 2, 6** court of claims, court of equity *UK*, court of record; **5, 2, 7** Court of Appeals, court of inquiry, court of justice, court of session, Court of Session *UK*; **5, 5** civil court, court watch, crown court *UK*, King's Bench, trial court, World Court, youth court *UK*; **5, 6** trial lawyer; **5, 7** court martial *UK*; **5, 8** court reporter, petty sessions *UK*; **6, 5** county court, family court, feudal court, police court, Queen's Bench; **7, 5** divorce court, General Court, probate court, sheriff court, summary court, Supreme Court; **7, 8** closing argument, quarter sessions *UK*; **8, 5** coroner's court, criminal court, district court, domestic court, juvenile court, kangaroo court, manorial court; **9, 5** appellate court, children's court; **9, 7** associate justice, mandatory minimum; **12, 13** confidential communication; **13, 5, 2, 7** International Court of Justice.

lawless 4 wild; **6** random; **7** chaotic, riotous, violent; **8** anarchic, mutinous; **9** insurgent, seditious; **10** antinomian, licentious, rebellious; **12** ungovernable; **13** undisciplined.

lawlessness 4 riot; **5** chaos; **6** mutiny, revolt; **7** anarchy, rioting; **8** disorder, nihilism, outlawry, sedition, upheaval, uprising; **9** amorality, rebellion, rowdiness, vandalism; **10** arrogation, insurgence, revolution, ruffianism, unruliness, usurpation; **11** hooliganism, laddishness, vigilantism; **12** disobedience; **13** antinomianism; **14** boisterousness, disruptiveness, rebelliousness; PHRASES: **3, 3** mob law; **4, 4** gang rule; **4, 5** coup d'état; **5, 3** lynch law; **5, 4** crime wave; **8, 5** kangaroo court.

lawmaker 2 MP; **4** Coke; **5** Draco, judge, Moses, Solon; **6** censor; **7** Solomon, Spartan; **8** lawgiver; **10** legislator; PHRASES: **3, 4** Law Lord.

lawn bowling 4 bias, dead, draw, fast, jack, lawn, live, skip, slow; **5** block, fours, front, green, pairs *UK*, third; **6** aiming, firing, leader, marker, second, smooth, umpire; **7** backest, running, singles, triples; **8** backhand, forehand, measurer, reaching; **9** wrestling; **10** controlled; PHRASES: **3-7** runthrough; **4-2** yard-on; **4-4** jack-high; **4-6** draw-weight; **5-2-1-4** three-on-a-side; **5, 5** fours match, pairs match; **5-5** crown-green, level-green; **6-7** follow-through.

law officer 2 DA, JP; **5** judge, mayor; **6** beadle; **7** bailiff, sheriff; **8** official, summoner; **9** apparitor, policeman; **10** macebearer; **11** patrolwoman, policewoman; PHRASES: **4, 7** city manager; **5, 2, 3, 5** clerk of the court; **5, 7** court officer; **5, 8** Crown Attorney *Canada*, judge advocate; **6, 7** police officer; **7, 6** process server; **7, 7** provost general.

lawyer 2 DA, D.J., JA, JD, JJ, P.A., WS; **3** ABA, bar, D.C.L., law, LL.B., LL.D., LL.M.; **4** atty., Hand (Learned), Root (Elihu), silk; **5** brief *UK*, Bryan (William Jennings), clerk, Field (David Dudley), judge, Nader (Ralph), pupil; **6** Darrow (Clarence), jurist, Laskin (Bora), legist, notary; **7** counsel, Grotius (Hugo), learned; **8** advocate, attorney, defender, Lockwood (Belva Ann), recorder; **9** barrister *UK Can*, counselor, solicitor *UK*, Stanfield (Robert Lorne); **10** Haliburton (Thomas Chandler), magistrate, prosecutor; **11** pettifogger; **12** jurisconsult; **15** constructionist; PHRASES: **3, 5** law clerk; **4, 4** Pros. Atty.; **4, 10** vice chancellor; **5, 5** legal eagle; **5, 6** legal beagle; **5, 7** King's Counsel, legal adviser; **5, 8** judge advocate; **6, 7** Queen's counsel, Queen's Counsel; **6, 8** public defender; **8, 2, 3** attorney at law; **8-2-3** attorney-at-law; **8, 7** assigned counsel; **9, 6** ambulance chaser, jailhouse ~; **10, 10** mitigation specialist; **11, 7** independent counsel; **11, 8** prosecuting attorney; **12, 6** Philadelphia ~.

lax 4 wide; **5** loose, slack; **6** droopy, excess, impure, sloppy, unruly, wanton; **8** careless; **9** abandoned, unbridled; **10** immoderate, licentious, permissive; **11** incontinent, intemperate, uninhibited; PHRASES: **4-3-3** free-for-all.

lay 3 air, bed, bet, put, set; **4** aria, drop, rest, song; **5** apply, chant, place, stake, wager; **6** ballad, gamble, impose, repose; **7** deposit; PHRASES: **3, 4** put down; **3, 6** ~ reader; **3, 7** ~ brother.

layabout *See* **slacker**

layer 3 bed, hen, lap, lay, ply; **4** band, belt, coat, deck, face, flap, fold, line, lode, seam, tier, vein, zone; **5** cover, level, plate, pleat, strip, table; **6** course, lining, spread, veneer; **7** bedding, overlap, overlay, section, shingle, stratum, topcoat, topsoil; **8** division, laminate, sandwich, stratify, underlay; **9** overlayer, thickness, undercoat; **10** substratum, underlayer; **11** interlining; **12** superstratum; PHRASES: **3, 4** lay down; **7, 2, 6** arrange in layers.

layered 8 foliated, laminate, terraced; **9** laminated; **10** multistage, stratified, stratiform; **12** straticulate; PHRASES: **3-3** two-ply; **3-6** two-tiered; **3-7** two-storied; **5-3** three-ply; **5-6** three-tiered; **5-7** three-storied; **6-6** double-decker.

layered thing 5 onion; **7** Formica™, plywood; **8** coalmine, laminate, sandwich; **10** atmosphere; PHRASES: **4, 2, 6** nest of tables; **4, 8** club sandwich; **5, 4** layer cake; **6, 5** safety glass; **6-6** double-decker; **7, 4** Russian doll *UK*; **8, 4** shingled roof; **9, 4** laminated wood; **9, 5** clapboard house, laminated glass.

layman 4 laic; **7** secular.

lay off *See* **dismiss**

lay waste 3 gut; **4** kill, loot, nuke, raid, rape, raze, ruin, sack; **5** strip, trash, waste; **6** damage, denude, murder, ravage; **7** despoil, destroy, pillage, plunder, ransack, violate; **8** deforest, demolish, desolate, sabotage; **9** defoliate, devastate, vandalize; **10** depopulate, obliterate; PHRASES: **4, 3** wipe out; **5, 4** strip bare; **5, 5** wreak havoc.

lazar 5 leper.

lazaretto 5, 4 glory hole.

laze 4 bask, idle, loaf; **5** relax; **6** lounge; PHRASES: **3, 6** lie around; **4, 6** ~ around, loaf around; **6, 6** lounge around.

laziness 5 sloth; **6** apathy; **7** languor; **8** lethargy; **9** indolence; **10** inactivity. *See also* **lazy**

lazy 3 lax; **4** dull, idle, slow; **5** slack, tardy; **6** torpid; **7** laggard, languid, loafing, lolling, workshy *UK*; **8** dawdling, dilatory, indolent, listless, slothful, sluggish; **9** apathetic, lethargic, parasitic; **10** languorous; **15** procrastinating; PHRASES: **4, 4** bone idle.

leach 9 percolate.

lead 3 run; **4** head, rank, rope, star; **5** chain, front, leash; **6** direct, manage, Saturn, string, tether; **7** captain; **9** spearhead; PHRASES: **4, 5** come first, rank first.

leaden 4 dark, dull, flat, grim, slow; **5** ashen, heavy; **6** dreary, steely; **7** labored, weighty; **8** lifeless, sluggish; **9** ponderous; **10** monotonous.

leader 2 CO; **4** Duce, guru, head, king, whip; **5** chief, elder, emcee, judge, Mahdi, mayor, pasha, queen, rajah, ruler, sheik, trace; **6** bailie *UK*, consul, cowboy, despot, drover, Führer, priest, Senate, tyrant; **7** bailiff, captain, emperor, empress, headman, justice, manager, marshal, Messiah, monarch, officer, pioneer, premier, sheriff, supremo *UK*, viceroy; **8** agitator, autocrat, choragus, dictator, director, fugleman, governor, herdsman, mandarin, mayoress *UK*, minister, official, shepherd, superior, suzerain, teamster; **9** authority, ayatollah, chieftain, conductor, constable, demagogue, dignitary, executive, maharajah, pacemaker, patrician, potentate, precentor, president, proconsul, protector, secretary, sovereign, spearhead; **10** bellwether, chancellor, coryphaeus, magistrate, mystagogue, pacesetter, pathfinder, ringleader, ringmaster; **11** cheerleader, condottiere, Congressman, functionary, quarterback, symposiarch, toastmaster, trailblazer; **12** commissioner; **14** representative; PHRASES: **3, 3** top man; **4, 2, 5** head of state; **4, 5** drum major; **4, 6** high priest; **4, 7** team captain; **4, 10** Your Excellency; **5, 2, 5** chief of state; **5, 3** point man; **5, 4** chief whip *UK*; **5, 5** prime mover; **5, 6** floor ~, point person; **5, 8** prime minister; **5, 9** chief executive; **5, 10** chief magistrate; **6-6** rabble-rouser.

leadership 3 top; **4** rule, spot, sway; **5** power; **7** command, control; **8** dominion, headship, hegemony, imperium, kingship, lordship; **9** authority, captaincy; **10** management, mastership, presidency; **11** generalship, premiership, sovereignty; **12** directorship, jurisdiction; **13** authorization.

leading 5 first; PHRASES: **7, 3** ~ dog *UK*, ~ man; **7, 4** ~ edge, ~ note; **7, 5** ~ light, ~ reins; **7, 7** ~ article *UK*; **7, 8** ~ question.

leading article 6 leader *UK*.

lead monoxide 8 litharge.

lead poisoning 9 saturnism.

leaf 1 P; **4** page, vein; **5** bract, frond, petal, sepal, spine, stoma; **6** lamina, ligule, needle; **7** cladode, foliage, leaflet, petiole, stipule, tendril; **8** greenery, palisade, phyllode; **9** bracteole, cotyledon, involucre, leafstalk, megaphyll, mesophyll; **10** abscission, microphyll; **11** phylloclade.

leaf beet 5 chard.

leaf monkey 6 langur.

leaf type 5 lobed, ovate; **6** entire, linear, simple; **7** cordate, crenate, dentate, hastate, palmate, peltate, pinnate, serrate, sessile, stalked, toothed; **8** compound; **9** bipinnate, orbicular, sagittate, unstalked; **10** lanceolate, trifoliate.

league *See* **association**

leak 4 drip, emit, gush, ooze, seep, weep; **5** drool, exude, issue, leach, spurt, sweat; **6** drivel, effuse, emerge, exhale, filter, reveal, strain; **7** divulge, dribble, emanate, excrete, exudate, secrete, slobber, trickle; **8** filtrate, perspire, salivate; **9** discharge, lixiviate *UK*, percolate; **10** exfiltrate; **11** extravasate; PHRASES: **4, 3** flow out, ooze out, seep out; **4, 5** lose water.

leakage 4 loss; **6** oozing; **7** outflow, seepage, weeping; **8** dripping, effusion, emission, leaching; **9** dribbling, filtering, straining, trickling; **10** filtration; **11** lixiviation, percolation; **12** exfiltration; **13** extravasation.

leaky 4 oozy; **5** runny; **6** porous; **7** weeping; **9** excretory, exudative, permeable; **12** transudative.

lean 3 tip; **4** bend, thin, tilt, trip; **6** meager, skinny, topple, tumble; **7** capsize, incline, scrawny; **8** desolate.

leap 4 loup *UK*, skip; **6** spring.

leaping 7 hopping, jumping, saltant; **8** bouncing, bounding, prancing, skipping *UK*, vaulting; **9** saltatory, spiraling, springing; **11** saltatorial; **12** skyrocketing.

learn 3 ace, con; **4** cram, read, swot *UK*; **5** grasp, study, train; **6** peruse, retain; **7** acquire, realize; **8** discover, memorize, remember, research; **9** apprehend, ascertain, determine; **10** assimilate, comprehend, understand; **11** contemplate; PHRASES: **3, 2** rub up; **3, 3, 4, 2** get the hang of; **4, 2, 2** bone up on, read up on; **4, 3** find out; **5, 2** brush up; **5, 2, 5** ~ by heart; **6, 2** polish up; **6, 5, 2** become aware of; **6, 7** attend classes; **7, 3, 4** broaden the mind.

learned 4 deep, wise; **6** brainy, expert; **7** bookish, erudite, skilled; **8** academic, cultured, educated, highbrow, informed, lettered, literate, profound, studious; **9** sagacious, scholarly; **11** enlightened, intelligent; **12** accomplished, intellectual; **13** knowledgeable; PHRASES: **4-4** well-read; **4-6** well-versed.

learnedness 4 nous; **5** savvy; **8** literacy; **9** erudition, polymathy; **11** scholarship; **15** intellectuality. *See also* **learned**

learner 1 L *UK*; **4** swot *UK*, tiro; **5** pupil; **6** alumna, novice, rookie; **7** alumnus, egghead, recruit, scholar, student, trainee; **8** beginner, bookworm, freshman, graduate, initiate, neophyte; **9** classmate, schoolboy, sophomore, undergrad; **10** apprentice, autodidact, researcher, schoolgirl; **11** abecedarian; **12** postgraduate; **13** undergraduate; PHRASES: **5-6** sixth-former.

learning 4 lore; **5** study; **6** review, wisdom; **7** conning, culture, letters, mastery, perusal, reading; **8** cramming, literacy, numeracy, practice, sagacity, swotting, teaching; **9** brainwork, education, erudition, knowledge, polymathy, schooling; **10** absorption, cleverness, experience; **11** attainments, bookishness, cultivation, instruction, omniscience, proficiency, scholarship; **12** acquirements, booklearning, civilization, intelligence; **13** autodidactism, contemplation, craftsmanship; **15** accomplishments.

lease *See* **rent**

leash *See* **lead**

least 4 last, less; **7** minimum; **8** minority, smallest.

leather 3 kid, tan; **4** beat, buff, calf, hide, roan; **5** mocha, nappa, suede; **6** Nubuck, oxhide, shammy, skiver, thrash, wallop; **7** chamois, doeskin, morocco, rawhide, saffian; **8** buckskin, capeskin, cheverel, cordovan, cordwain, deerskin, goatskin, marocain, maroquin, shagreen; **11** whitleather; PHRASES: 3, 4 box calf; 6, 7 Russia ~.

leatherhead 9 friarbird.

leave 4 omit, quit, will; 5 break; 6 except, maroon, reject, sickie; 7 abandon, deposit, discard, exclude, holiday *UK*; 8 bequeath, furlough, vacation; 10 permission, sabbatical; PHRASES: 3, 3 day off; 4, 3 cast off, time off; 4, 4 cast away; 4, 5 sick ~; 5, 5 shore ~; 6, 5 French ~; 9, 5 maternity ~.

leavening 4 barm; 5 yeast; 6 enzyme, leaven, yeasty; 7 enzymic, ferment, raising, zymotic; 9 diastasic, seasoning; 10 enlivening, fermenting; 12 fermentation, fermentative; PHRASES: 4-6, 5 self-rising flour; 4-7 self-raising; 6, 6 baking powder; 7, 5 raising agent.

lecherous 3 hot; 4 lewd, sexy, wild; 5 horny, randy; 6 amoral, carnal, rakish; 7 fleshly, goatish, lustful, Paphian, priapic, rampant, rutting, ruttish, vicious; 8 depraved; 9 debauched, dissolute, libertine, lickerish, oversexed; 10 adulterous, dissipated, lascivious, libidinous, licentious, profligate, unfaithful, voluptuous; 11 incontinent; 12 concupiscent; 14 whoremongering; PHRASES: 3-3 sex-mad; 3-5 sex-crazy; 5-3 woman-mad; 5-5 woman-crazy; 6, 2 turned on.

lecture 3 nag; 4 talk; 5 class; 6 berate, homily, lesson, preach, rebuke, rocket, sermon, speech, tirade; 7 address, declaim, expound, seminar, wigging *UK*; 8 admonish, diatribe, harangue, scolding; 9 castigate, discourse, reprimand, sermonize; 10 discussion, telecourse; 11 pontificate; 12 presentation; PHRASES: 5, 4 chalk talk; 7-2 talking-to; 7-3 telling-off *UK*; 8-4 dressing-down.

ledge 4 rack, sill; 5 niche, ridge, shelf; 7 outcrop; 8 foothold.

ledger 4 book; 6 record; 8 register; PHRASES: 6, 4 record book; 7, 4 account book.

lee *See* **shelter**

leer 3 eye; 4 ogle; 5 smirk, sneer, stare; 7 grimace; PHRASES: 4, 3 evil eye.

leeway *See* **scope**

left 1 L; 4 port; 5 louie, verso; 7 liberal; 8 larboard, leftwing, sinister; 9 abandoned, discarded, socialist; PHRASES: 4, 4 ~ bank, ~ wing; 4-4 left-face.

left (be left) 4 rest, stay; 6 remain, result; 7 subsist, survive; PHRASES: 8 continue.

left-handed 8 southpaw; 9 sinistral; 15 dextrosinistral.

left-winger 7 leftist; 9 communist, reformist, socialist; 11 progressive.

leg 3 lap; 4 base, foot, limb, part, pole, step; 5 phase, stage, stand; 6 member; 7 foreleg, support; 9 extremity; PHRASES: 4, 3 hind ~.

legacy 5 dower; 7 bequest; 8 heirloom, heritage; 9 patrimony; 10 birthright; 11 inheritance.

legal 4 just; 5 jural, legit, licit, right, valid; 6 lawful, proper; 8 judicial, juristic, licensed, official; 9 allowable, legalized, mandatory, permitted, statutory, warranted; 10 authorized, compulsory, injunctive, legitimate, obligatory, procedural, regulatory, sanctioned; 11 legitimized, permissible; 12 prescriptive; 13 legitimatized; 14 administrative, decriminalized, jurisdictional.

legal (make legal) *See* **legalize**

legalistic 9 litigious, quibbling; 11 contentious; 12 disputatious.

legality 5 right; 7 justice; 8 legalism, validity; 10 legitimacy. *See also* **legal**

legalization 7 license, warrant; 8 sanction; 9 authority; 10 permission; 13 authorization; 14 legitimization.

legalize 5 allow; 6 permit, ratify; 7 license, warrant; 8 sanction, validate; 9 authorize; 10 legitimize; 13 decriminalize.

legally 9 judgingly; 14 jurisprudently; PHRASES: 2, 3 by law; 2, 4 de jure; 2, 5 by right, in court; 6, 3, 3 within the law; 6, 3, 5 before the bench; 9, 2, 3 according to law. *See also* **legal**

legal process 4 bail, stay, writ; 5 order; 6 arrest, surety; 7 summons, warrant; 8 citation, mandamus, security, subpoena; 9 committal, detention, restraint; 10 certiorari, injunction; 11 proceedings, questioning; 12 apprehension, jurisdiction, recognisance *UK*; PHRASES: 3, 2, 3, 3 arm of the law; 3, 7 due process; 4, 5 nisi prius; 5, 9 legal procedure; 6, 6 habeas corpus; 6, 7 search warrant.

legal terms 5 chose; 6 domain, entail, seisin, tenure; 7 demesne; 8 dominium *UK*, jointure, messuage, mortmain, movables, tenement; 9 remainder, reversion; 10 immovables, limitation, personalty, preemption; **12** hereditament, prescription; **PHRASES: 3, 4** fee tail; **3, 6** fee simple; **3, 10** uti possidetis *UK*; **4, 4** dead hand; **5, 2, 6** chose in action.

legate *See* **representative**

legend **4** code, epic, myth, saga, tale, yarn; **5** fable, story; **7** caption; **9** corollary, tradition; **PHRASES: 3, 5, 4** old wives' tale. *See also* **Arthurian legend**

legendary being *See* **mythical or imaginary being**

legible **5** clear; **8** readable; **12** decipherable, intelligible; **14** understandable.

legion *See* **multitude**

legislate **4** pass, vest, vote; **5** enact, order; **6** affirm, codify, decree, ordain, ratify; **7** confirm, endorse; **9** establish, formalize.

legislation **3** law; **5** rules; **8** enacting, nomology; **9** enactment, lawgiving, lawmaking; **10** regulation, validation; **11** affirmation, legislature; **12** codification, confirmation, prescription, ratification; **14** legislatorship.

legislative **8** decretal; **9** lawgiving, lawmaking; **10** nomothetic; **11** nomological; **13** legislational, legislatorial; **15** jurisprudential.

legislative body **6** Cortes, Majlis, quorum, senate; **7** senatus; **8** division, Storting; **9** Bundesrat, Bundestag, Folketing *UK*; **10** government, parliament; **11** legislature; **PHRASES: 4, 7** Dáil Éireann; **6, 7** Seanad Éireann *UK*, States General; **7, 6** Supreme Soviet.

legislature *See* **governing body**

legitimate **4** real, true; **5** legal, legit, licit, pukka; **6** kosher, lawful, proper; **7** allowed, genuine; **8** approved, licensed, rightful; **9** allowable, authentic, permitted, statutory; **10** admissible, authorized, recognized, sanctioned; **11** permissible; **14** constitutional.

leguaan **6** iguana.

legwear **4** hose, sock; **5** spats; **6** anklet, garter, nylons, tights; **7** argyles, gaiters, hosiery, puttees; **9** fleshings, pantyhose, stockings, suspender; **10** legwarmers; **13** spatterdashes; **PHRASES: 3, 5** ski socks; **4-3** hold-ups; **4-4** half-hose; **4, 5** crew socks; **4-5** knee-highs; **4, 9** silk stockings; **5-4** trunkhose; **5, 5** ankle socks, bobby socks, sweat socks; **5-5** thigh-highs; **5, 9** lisle stockings,

sheer stockings; **6, 9** seamed stockings; **7, 6** fishnet tights *UK*.

leisure **4** ease, rest; **5** break, peace, quiet; **6** relief, repose; **7** freedom, holiday *UK*, liberty, respite; **8** idleness, sinecure, vacation; **10** inactivity, recreation, relaxation; **11** convenience, opportunity; **12** recreational; **PHRASES: 2, 5** no hurry; **4, 2, 4** time to kill; **4, 2, 4, 5** time on one's hands; **4, 4** free time; **4, 7** idle moments; **5, 3, 5** peace and quiet; **5, 3, 6** dolce far niente; **5, 4** ample time, spare time; **9, 5** breathing space *UK*.

leisure (at leisure) **5** fired; **6** sacked; **7** jobless, relaxed, resting, retired; **8** inactive, leisured; **9** available, dismissed, redundant; **10** discharged, disengaged, unemployed, unoccupied; **11** unhurriedly; **12** conveniently; **PHRASES: 2, 3, 6** in due course; **2, 4** at ease; **2, 4, 3, 4** in one's own time; **2, 4, 5, 4** in one's spare time; **2, 5** on leave; **2, 5, 4** at loose ends; **2, 8** on furlough, on vacation; **2, 10** in retirement, on sabbatical; **3, 2, 4** out of work; **3, 4** off duty; **4, 3** laid off.

leisure (have leisure) **4** rest; **6** repose, resign, retire; **PHRASES: 4, 1, 5** take a break; **4, 1, 8** take a vacation; **4, 2, 4** give up work; **4, 4, 3** find time for, take time out; **4, 5** take leave.

leisurely **4** easy, free, idle, slow; **6** casual, gentle, sedate; **7** languid, relaxed; **8** leisured; **9** reposeful, unhurried; **10** effortless, langourous; **11** comfortable; **PHRASES: 2, 4, 3, 4** in one's own time; **2, 4, 5, 4** in one's spare time; **2, 4, 7** at one's leisure.

lemon **6** reamer; **10** lemongrass; **PHRASES: 5, 4** ~ balm, ~ drop, ~ fish, ~ sole; **5, 6** ~ cheese, ~ squash; **5, 7** ~ verbena; **5, 8** ~ geranium.

lend **3** sub; **4** give, loan; **5** grant; **6** credit; **7** advance; **11** accommodate; **PHRASES: 5, 6** allow credit; **8, 5** practice usury.

lender **3** dun, IMF (International Monetary Fund); **4** bank, VISA; **5** uncle; **6** banker, loaner, usurer; **7** pledgee, Shylock; **8** creditor; **9** financier, mortgagee; **10** pawnbroker; **11** moneybroker, moneylender; **12** extortionist; **PHRASES: 3, 4** pop shop *UK*; **4-2-5** mont-de-piété; **4, 4** hock shop *UK*; **4, 5** loan shark; **4, 7** bank manager *UK*, loan officer; **4, 9** debt collector; **5, 4** World Bank; **6, 5** credit union; **6, 7** credit company; **7, 7** finance company; **8, 4** European Bank; **8, 6** mortgage holder; **8, 7** American Express *TM*, building society, friendly society *UK*, mortgage company.

lending 5 grant, usury; 6 giving; 7 advance, hocking, loaning, popping; 9 advancing; 11 advancement, pawnbroking; 12 moneylending; 13 accommodation; PHRASES: 4-8 loan-sharking.

length 4 foot, inch, knot, mile, span, yard; 5 meter, reach; 6 extent, height, parsec; 7 footage, measure, mileage, stretch, yardage; 8 distance, duration, infinity, longness, tallness; 9 extension, longitude, prolixity; 10 elongation; 11 endlessness, lengthening, lengthiness, protraction; 12 prolongation; 14 protractedness; 15 interminability; PHRASES: 4-10 long-windedness; 5-4 light-year.

lengthen 4 draw, drop; 6 expand, extend, uncoil, unfold, unfurl, unroll; 7 enlarge, produce, prolong, stretch; 8 continue, elongate, increase, protract; PHRASES: 3, 4 let down; 4, 3 drag out, draw out, spin out; 6, 3 string out.

lengthy *See* **long**

leniency 3 sop; 4 pity; 5 favor, leave, mercy; 6 laxity, lenity, pardon; 7 amnesty, charity, quarter; 8 clemency, humanity, humoring, lenience, patience, softness, spoiling; 9 allowance, tolerance; 10 compassion, concession, indulgence, moderation, permission, toleration; 11 benevolence, forbearance, forgiveness, magnanimity; 13 consideration, gratification; PHRASES: 3, 6 kid gloves; 5, 4 light hand, light rein; 6, 5 velvet glove; 7, 5 laissez faire. *See also* **lenient**

lenient 3 lax; 4 easy, kind, mild, soft; 6 gentle, humane, kindly, tender; 7 clement, patient, pitying; 8 generous, gracious, merciful, moderate, spoiling, tolerant; 9 accepting, forgiving, indulgent; 10 benevolent, charitable, forbearing, permissive, reasonable; 11 considerate, magnanimous; 13 accommodating, compassionate; PHRASES: 3-5 kid-glove; 4-3-3-4 live-and-let-live; 4-5 easy-going; 4-9 long-suffering.

lenient (be lenient) 4 pity; 5 allow, favor, humor, spare; 6 forget, oblige, pardon, permit; 7 concede, forbear, forgive, gratify, indulge; 8 moderate, tolerate; PHRASES: 2, 4, 2 go easy on; 3, 3, 3, 4 let off the hook; 4, 1, 4 bend a rule; 4, 1, 5, 4 keep a light rein; 4, 4 bear with; 4, 4, 7 pull one's punches; 5, 3, 3 spare the rod; 5, 7 grant amnesty, treat lightly; 7, 1, 5 stretch a point.

leniently 4, 1, 5, 4 with a light hand, with a light rein; 4, 3, 6 with kid gloves; 4, 8 with kindness. *See also* **lenient**

lenient person 3 wet; 7 liberal; 14 latitudinarian, philanthropist; PHRASES: 3, 5 old softy.

Leningrad 9 Petrograd; PHRASES: 5, 10 Saint Petersburg.

lens 5 focus, prism; 8 eyeglass, eyepiece; 9 condenser, objective; 10 pentaprism; PHRASES: 4, 3 ~ cap; 4, 4 ~ hood, zoom ~; 4, 5 ~ cover, ~ mount; 4-5, 4 long-focus ~, wide-angle ~; 5, 4 macro ~, shift ~, short zoom, toric ~; 5, 6 focal length; 6, 4 camera ~, coated ~, convex ~, mirror ~, reflex ~; 7, 4 bloomed ~, concave ~, contact ~, fisheye ~; 8, 4 biconvex ~, compound ~, standard ~; 9, 4 spherical ~, telephoto ~, telephoto zoom, ultrawide ~; 11, 4 cylindrical ~.

lentigo 7 freckle.

leopard 7 panther.

Léopoldville 8 Kinshasa.

leper 5 lazar.

leprosy 7, 7 Hansen's disease.

Lesbos 6 Lésvos; 8 Mytilene.

Lesotho 10 Basutoland.

less 5 minus; 9 excluding; PHRASES: 3, 2, 4, 2 not as much of; 4, 4 take away.

lessen 3 cut, dim, ebb; 4 dull, ease, fade, flag, leak, wane, wear; 5 abate, allay, blunt, drain, erode, lower, slash; 6 deaden, dilute, reduce, shrink, soften, temper, weaken; 7 assuage, decline, deplete, dwindle, exhaust, subside; 8 decrease, diminish, minimize, moderate, palliate; 9 alleviate, attenuate, evaporate; 10 depreciate, hemorrhage, impoverish; 11 deteriorate; PHRASES: 3, 2 let up; 4, 3 drop off, ease off, fade out, tail off; 4, 4 seep away, tone down, wear away; 5, 3 taper off; 5, 4 waste away; 7, 4 dribble away.

lesson 4 text; 5 class, moral; 6 period; 7 example, reading, seminar, warning; 8 tutorial.

let 4 hire, rent; 5 allow, grant, lease; 6 enable, hinder, permit; 7 charter, entitle, indulge, license, warrant; 8 obstacle, obstruct, sanction, validate; 9 authorize; 10 impediment, legitimize.

let down *See* **lower, disappoint**

lethal 5 fatal, toxic; 6 deadly, mortal; 7

baneful, deathly, killing, noxious; **8** suicidal, terminal, virulent; **9** homicidal, incurable, malignant, murderous, poisonous; **12** bloodthirsty; PHRASES: 4-11 life-threatening; **5-7** death-dealing.

let out 3 jet; **4** blow, emit, fume, ooze, puff, reek, spew; **5** bleed, drool, egest, eruct, erupt, scent, smoke, spout, spurt, steam, sweat; **6** exhale, expire, faucet, slaver, squirt, stream; **7** breathe, debouch, detrude, dribble, excrete, exhaust, extrude, obtrude, outpour, perfume, radiate, respire, secrete, slobber, sputter, urinate; **8** defecate, disgorge, perspire, splutter, vaporize; **9** discharge, ejaculate, suppurate; **10** disembogue; **11** extravasate; PHRASES: **4, 2, 3, 3** turn on the tap; **4, 4, 2** give vent to; **4, 5** cast forth, send forth.

letter 3 wen; **4** mail, note, ogam, post, rune, sign, type; **5** Kanji, ogham, print, thorn; **6** leaser, Nagari, Pinyin, symbol, uncial; **7** acronym, anagram, capital, digraph, epistle, initial, message, missive, writing; **8** acrostic, grapheme, ideogram, inscribe, monogram, postcard; **9** character, cuneiform, dominical, ideograph, lettering, majuscule, minuscule, pictogram; **10** communiqué, Devanagari, encyclical, hieroglyph, lexigraphy, pictograph; **13** anagrammatism, communication; PHRASES: **3, 6** air ~; **4, 6** dead ~, form ~, love ~, open ~; **5-4, 6** lower-case ~, upper-case ~; **5, 6** black ~, chain ~; **6, 3** ~ box; **6-3** poison-pen; **6, 4** ~ bomb, ~ card *UK*; **6, 6** French ~ *UK*; **7, 6** begging ~ *UK*, scarlet ~; **8, 6** covering ~. *See also* **Greek alphabet, Hebrew alphabet**

level 1 A, O; **3** row; **4** deck, even, fell, iron, rank, raze, roll, step, tier; **5** class, floor, flush, grade, layer, ledge, plane, press, shelf, stage, story; **6** smooth, spread; **7** echelon, flatten, landing, terrace; **8** equalize.

lever 4 lift; **5** hoist, prize; **6** wrench; **7** crowbar; **9** corkscrew; **11** screwdriver.

leviathan *See* **giant**

levy 3 tax; **4** duty, fine, toll; **5** tithe; **6** charge, excise, impose, impost, muster, octroi *UK*, ransom, tariff; **7** collect, customs, militia, penalty, scutage, tribute; **8** exaction, mobilize; **9** blackmail, conscript; **10** imposition.

lexicon 5 lexis; **8** glossary, idiolect, language; **10** dictionary, vocabulary; PHRASES: **4, 4** word list; **10, 4** vocabulary list.

liability 4 jinx; **6** burden, charge; **7** problem; **9** millstone; **10** obligation; **12** disadvantage; **14** accountability, responsibility.

liable 5 given, prone; **6** likely; **7** subject, triable; **8** disposed, inclined; **9** accusable; **10** actionable, answerable, cognisable *UK*; **11** accountable, predisposed, responsible.

liaison *See* **link**

liar 5 phony *UK*, Satan; **6** fibber, phoney, yarner; **7** Ananias, fibster; **8** fabulist, palterer, perjurer, romancer; **9** falsifier; **10** fabricator; **11** bullshitter, equivocator, mythomaniac, pseudologue, storyteller; **12** prevaricator, propagandist, pseudologist; PHRASES: **4-7** yarn-spinner; **5, 7** false witness; **6, 2, 4** Father of Lies.

libel 5 smear, sully; **6** defame, malign, vilify; **7** slander, tarnish; **10** defamation; **11** denigration; **12** vilification.

liberal 1 L; **3** Lib; **4** free, Whig; **6** giving, lavish; **7** profuse, radical; **8** generous, handsome, princely, tolerant, unbiased; **9** bounteous, bountiful; **10** beneficent, forbearing, hospitable, munificent, ungrudging, unstinting; **11** enlightened, progressive; PHRASES: **4-6** open-handed, open-minded; **5-6** broad-minded.

liberality 6 excess, laxity; **7** abandon, charity, laxness, license; **9** tolerance; **10** generosity, unruliness, wantonness; **11** abandonment, libertinism; **12** immoderation, incontinence, intemperance; **14** licentiousness, permissiveness; **15** uninhibitedness; PHRASES: **5, 5** blank check; **5, 7** carte blanche; **7, 4** Liberty Hall.

liberate 4 bail, free, save; **5** demob, loose, steal, untie; **6** acquit, except, excuse, exempt, loosen, pardon, parole, redeem, rescue, unbind, unbolt, uncage, unhand, unknot, unlock; **7** absolve, deliver, disband, dismiss, manumit, release, relieve, unchain, unleash, unloose; **8** reprieve, unbridle, unburden, unfetter, unloosen; **9** decontrol, discharge, disengage, extricate, unshackle; **10** demobilize, deregulate, emancipate, liberalize; **11** disencumber, enfranchise; PHRASES: **3, 2** let go; **3, 2, 4** let go free; **3, 3** let out; **3, 3, 4** let off the hook; **3, 4** set free; **3, 5** let loose; **4, 3, 3, 2** give the run of; **4, 4** send home; **4, 5** cast loose, give scope.

liberated 4 free; **5** loose; **7** unbound; **9** absolving; **10** exemptible, liberating, redemptive; **11** independent; PHRASES: **2, 6** on parole; **3, 2, 4** out on bail; **4-4** scot-free. *See also* **liberate**

liberated man 3, 3 new man; **4, 8** male feminist; **9, 3** sensitive man.

liberated woman 6 sister; **8** feminist; **10** superwoman; **11** suffragette; **12** working-woman; PHRASES: **3, 5** new woman; **3, 6** bra burner; **6, 5** career woman, modern woman; **6, 6** women's libber; **7, 4** working wife.

liberation 4 bail; **6** escape, parole, relief, rescue; **7** freedom, freeing, loosing *UK*, release; **8** delivery, immunity, impunity, reprieve, riddance; **9** absolving, acquittal, decontrol, discharge, dismissal, exemption, pardoning, quitclaim, quittance, salvation, unbinding, unhanding, unloosing; **10** absolution, disbanding, redemption, relaxation, unbridling, unchaining, unknotting, unleashing; **11** acquittance, deliverance, extrication, forgiveness, manumission, unburdening, unfettering, unshackling; **12** deregulation, emancipation; **13** disengagement, exemptibility; **14** demobilization, liberalization; **15** disencumberment; PHRASES: **6, 7** mental freedom; **7, 4** setting free.

liberator 6 savior; **7** Bolivar, escapee, parolee, rescuer; **8** absolver, redeemer; **9** deliverer; **10** manumitter; **11** emancipator.

libertine 3 cad; **4** buck, rake, slag, stud; **6** gigolo; **7** bounder; **8** Casanova, Lovelace, stallion; **11** philanderer; **12** heartbreaker; PHRASES: **3, 2, 3, 5** man of the world; **3, 4** Don Juan; **4, 3** rent boy *UK*; **4, 10** male prostitute; **6, 3** ladies' man; **7, 3** worldly man.

liberty 4 bail; **5** leave, sauce, scope; **6** choice, option; **7** freedom, license, release; **9** franchise, impudence; **10** discretion; **12** impertinence, independence; PHRASES: **3, 2, 7** cap of ~; **7, 4** hall *UK*, ~ ship; **7, 5** ~ horse *UK*; **7, 6** ~ bodice *UK*, L~ Island.

libido 4 Eros; **8** Thanatos; **9** eroticism; PHRASES: **3, 8** sex instinct; **4, 8** life instinct; **5, 4** death wish; **5, 5** vital force; **5, 8** death instinct; **6, 5** motive force, sexual drive.

library 8 Bodleian *UK*; PHRASES: **4, 7** film ~; **6, 7** mobile ~ *UK*; **7, 7** lending ~.

license 4 pass; **5** leave; **6** patent, permit, poetic; **7** charter, driving, freedom, liberty, special; **8** aegrotat *UK*; **9** franchise, privilege; **10** debauchery, permission, profligacy; **11** certificate, dissipation; **12** intemperance; PHRASES: **5, 2, 7** leave of ab-

sence; **6, 7** poetic ~; **7, 7** artist's ~.

license 3 let; **5** allow, grant; **6** enable, permit; **7** entitle, warrant; **8** sanction, validate; **9** authorize; **10** legitimize.

licentious *See* **immoral**

lichen 4 root; **6** archil, crotal, orchil; **7** crottle, isidium, rhizine; **8** epiphyte, podetium, soredium; **9** mycobiont, symbiosis; **10** phycobiont; **11** lichenology; **12** lichenometry; **13** lichenologist; PHRASES: **3, 4** oak moss; **4, 5** rock tripe; **7, 4** Spanish moss; **7, 6** foliose ~; **8, 4** reindeer moss; **9, 6** fruticose ~.

lid 3 cap, hat, top; **4** bung, cork, flap, plug; **5** cover, crust, limit; **7** shutter, stopper.

lie 3 fib; **4** bull, flam, rest, yarn; **5** fable, lying, porky *UK*, story; **6** deceit, delude, parody; **7** concoct, deceive, distort, falsify, fantasy, fiction, perjure, recline, untruth, whopper; **8** flimflam, travesty; **9** burlesque, dissemble, fabricate, falsehood, poppycock; **10** propaganda, taradiddle; **11** fabrication, romanticize; **12** fictionalize; **13** incredibility; **14** implausibility; **15** unbelievability; PHRASES: **4, 4** tall tale; **4, 5** fish story, tall story *UK*; **5, 4** fairy tale; **6, 2, 7** breach of promise; **6-3, 5** shaggy-dog story; **6, 7** broken promise; **9, 3** barefaced ~ *UK*, shameless ~; **9, 4** traveler's tale; **10, 4** fisherman's yarn. *See also* **lying**

Liepaja 5 Libau; **6** Libava.

life 3 bio, zoe; **4** biog, brio, esse, vita; **5** being; **6** energy, entity, ginger, living, nature, person, spirit; **8** existing, survivor, vitality, vivacity, wildlife; **9** animation, assurance, biography, existence, humankind, sensation, sentience, symbiosis; **10** expectancy, individual, liveliness; **11** sensibility, subsistence; **12** vitalization, vivification; **13** sprightliness; PHRASES: **4, 4** ~ belt, ~ buoy, ~ form, ~ peer, ~ raft, ~ span, real ~; **4, 5** élan vital, ~ cycle, ~ force, ~ style; **4, 6** ~ guards, ~ jacket, ~ member; **4, 7** ~ history, ~ science; **4, 9** ~ assurance *UK*, ~ insurance, ~ preserver; **4, 10** ~ expectancy; **5, 4** plant ~, shelf ~, still ~; **5, 5** vital flame, vital force, vital spark; **6, 4** living soul; **6, 5** living being; **6, 7** animal spirits; **7, 4** private ~ *UK*.

life after death 6 heaven; **8** paradise; **11** immortality; **13** deathlessness; PHRASES: **3, 4, 5** the next world; **3, 9** the afterlife, the hereafter; **4, 11** life everlasting; **7, 4** eternal rest.

life cycle 5 birth, death, youth; **6** heaven; **7** Lazarus, revival; **8** biometry, eternity, lifetime, paradise, survival; **9** adulthood, afterlife, childhood, longevity; **11** adolescence, immortality, reanimation, renaissance; **12** resurrection; **13** reincarnation, survivability; **14** revivification; PHRASES: 3, 3 old age; 3, 5 new birth; 5, 4, 2, 3 seven ages of man; 6, 3 middle age; 8, 4 allotted days, allotted span.

lifeless 4 dead, dull; **5** inert; **7** tedious; **8** listless, unmoving; **10** unexciting; **11** unconscious; **12** unresponsive; **13** uninteresting.

lifelike 5 exact, vivid; **6** living; **7** eidetic, graphic, natural; **8** faithful, speaking; **9** breathing, realistic, veracious; **10** unmistaken; **11** verisimilar; **12** naturalistic, photographic; **14** representative; PHRASES: 4-2-4 true-to-life, true-to-type; 4-2-5 true-to-scale; 4-2-6 true-to-nature.

life requirements 3 air; **4** food; **5** bread, heart, manna, water; **6** artery, oxygen; **9** lifeblood; **10** sustenance; **11** nourishment, subsistence; PHRASES: 5, 2, 4 staff of life; 5, 3 vital air; 5, 5 daily bread; 6, 2, 4 breath of life; 6, 5 heart's blood.

life science 6 botany; **7** anatomy, biology, bionics, ecology, zoology; **8** algology, biometry, bryology, cytology, genetics, pomology, taxonomy, virology; **9** bionomics, evolution, fungology, histology, phytology; **10** bioecology, biophysics, dendrology, embryology, enzymology, exobiology, immunology, morphology, physiology; **11** biogenetics, cryobiology, cybernetics, paleobotany, phytography, systematics, xenobiology; **12** astrobiology, bacteriology, biochemistry, epidemiology, ethnobiology, gnotobiotics, microbiology, neuroscience, paleontology, parasitology, phytobiology, phytoecology, radiobiology, sociobiology; **13** biotechnology, endocrinology; **14** electrobiology, phytochemistry; PHRASES: 4, 7 cell biology; 5, 7 space biology; 6, 7 marine biology; 7, 7 natural history, natural science.

life scientist 7 cladist; **8** botanist; **9** anatomist, biologist, Darwinist, ecologist, zoologist; **10** biochemist, biometrist, cytologist, geneticist, naturalist, taxonomist, virologist; **11** histologist; **12** biophysicist, embryologist, evolutionist, immunologist, morphologist, physiologist; **13** cryobiologist; **14** bacteriologist, ethnobiologist, microbiologist, paleontologist, parasitologist, sociobiologist; **15** endocrinologist; PHRASES: 3-9 neo-Darwinist; 4, 9 cell biologist; 5, 9 space biologist; 6, 9 marine biologist.

life story 7 history, memoirs; **9** biography; **13** autobiography.

lift 3 aid; **4** copy, heft, hump; **5** boost, davit, elate, filch, heave, hoist, raise, steal, vault, winch; **6** uplift; **7** elevate, enhance, improve, upswing; **8** buoyancy; **9** escalator, funicular, promotion, upgrading; **10** plagiarize; PHRASES: 3-2 leg-up; 3, 3 ski tow; 3, 4 ski ~; 5, 3 cable car; 5, 4 chair ~; 6, 5 sursum corda; 11, 4 paternoster ~. *See also* **lifter**

lifter 4 crab, jack; **5** crane, hoist, jeers, lever, thief, winch; **6** tackle; **7** capstan, derrick, dredger; **8** elevator, forklift, purchase, windlass; **9** jackscrew; **10** trampoline; **11** springboard; PHRASES: 4, 3, 6 rope and pulley; 4-6 luff-tackle; 4, 7 jeer capstan; 5, 3, 6 block and tackle; 6, 5 gantry crane.

ligature 3 tie; **4** bond, cord, line, link, rope; **5** union; **6** string; **7** linkage; **10** connection.

light 2 UV; **3** eye, lux, ray; **4** airy, beam, bulb, fair, fire, glow, lamp, land, pale; **5** blond, faded, flare, flash, glare, gleam, glint, gloss, laser, match, pasty, sheen, shine, spark, taper, torch, white; **6** albino, bright, candle, dazzle, flaxen, ignite, kindle, luster, pallid, pastel, photon, strobe, subtle, window; **7** amusing, clarity, flicker, glister, glitter, lantern, lighten, lucency, shimmer, shining, spangle, sparkle, sunbeam, trivial, twinkle, unheavy, whitish; **8** bedazzle, bleached, brighten, casement, daylight, dazzling, flambeau, flippant, gaslight, gossamer, headlamp, illumine, lightish, luminous, radiance, splendor, sunlight, sunshine; **9** colorless, disembark, flyweight, headlight, highlight, irradiate, limelight, moonlight, moonshine, peroxided, radiation, reversing, rushlight, spotlight, starlight, vividness; **10** brightness, brilliance, earthshine, effulgence, flashlight, floodlight, illuminate, luminosity, refulgence, visibility, weightless; **11** candescence, candlelight, coruscation, imponderous, lightweight, overexposed, searchlight, underweight, unweighable; **12** bantamweight, fluorescence, illumination, imponderable, luminescence, luminousness, resplendence, welterweight; **13** featherweight, incandescence, scintillation; **15** phosphorescence; PHRASES: **3, 4, 2** set fire to; **3, 5** arc ~, red ~; **3, 6** set alight; **3-6** low-weight, tow-headed; **4, 2** turn on; **4, 5** neon ~; **5, 2, 1, 5** ~ as a fairy; **5, 2, 1, 7** ~ as a feather; **5, 2, 3** ~ as air; **5, 2, 4, 4** ~ on one's feet; **5, 3** ~ ray; **5, 4** ~ show, ~ wave; **5-4** light-year; **5, 5** brake ~, first ~, green ~, inner ~, klieg ~, ~ meter, ~ music, ~ opera, ~ touch, pilot ~, strip ~; **5-7** cream-colored, light-colored; **5-8** light-fingered; **5, 9** ~ fantastic; **6, 2** switch on; **6, 5** bengal ~, strobe ~; **7-4-3** lighter-than-air; **7, 5** guiding ~, leading ~, traffic ~; **7, 8** visible spectrum; **8, 5** coherent ~, courtesy ~, electric ~, infrared ~; **8, 6** northern lights; **9, 5** Eddystone ~. *See also* **lights**

light color 5 cream, ivory; **6** pallor; **8** fairness, paleness; **9** blondness, lightness, pastiness; **13** colorlessness; PHRASES: **3-5** off-white; **4, 5** pale color; **6, 5** pastel color.

light emission 5 umbra; **6** shadow; **8** penumbra; **9** luminance; **11** illuminance; **12** fluorescence, illumination, luminescence; **13** incandescence; **15** bioluminescence, phosphorescence; PHRASES: **3, 2, 5** ray of light; **5, 4** light beam; **6, 2, 5** pencil of light; **8, 4** luminous flux.

lighten 4 buoy, ease, work; **5** empty, fluff, raise, untax; **6** aerate, gasify, leaven, unlade, unload, uplift; **7** ferment, relieve, upraise; **8** jettison, unburden, unsaddle, vaporize; **9** alleviate, disburden, unballast; **10** volatilize; **11** disencumber; PHRASES: **3-4** off-load; **4, 2** buoy up, hold up; **4, 6** lose weight; **6, 6** reduce weight; **7, 4** ~ ship.

lighter 3 cap, log; **4** dung, fuse, punk, turf, wick, wood; **5** brand, flint, match, paler, spark, spill, spunk, taper, torch, vesta; **6** faggot, tinder; **7** lucifer; **8** brighter, charcoal, firebomb, firewood, kindling, matchbox; **9** brushwood, detonator, explosive, firebrand, scintilla, tinderbox; **10** flashlight, touchpaper *UK*; **11** firelighter *UK*; PHRASES: **4, 3** Yule log; **4, 4** fire ship; **5, 4** spark plug; **6, 5** safety match; **7, 5** burning glass; **8, 6** ignition system; **10, 3** percussion cap; **10, 4** incendiary bomb.

light meter 9 bolometer; **10** photometer, radiometer; **11** colorimeter, polarimeter; **14** interferometer.

lightness 6 levity, pallor, rarity; **8** buoyancy, delicacy; **9** downiness, joviality, pastiness, sparkling; **10** levitating, levitation,

triviality, volatility; **11** ethereality, portability; **12** floatability, unimportance, vaporization; **13** effervescence; **15** imponderability.

lightning 5 levin; **6** éclair; **8** wildfire; **11** fulmination, thunderbolt; PHRASES: **4, 9** ball ~, fork ~, heat ~; **5, 9** chain ~, sheet ~; **6, 9** forked ~ *UK*.

lights 5 lungs, offal; **11** houselights; PHRASES: **5, 6** fairy ~ *UK*, polar ~; **6, 6** bright ~; **6, 8** aurora borealis; **6, 9** aurora australis; **7, 6** ancient ~ *UK*; **8, 6** northern ~, southern ~.

light thing 3 air; **4** cork, down, dust, foam, fuzz, mote, oose *UK*; **5** ether, float, fluff, froth, spume, straw; **6** bubble, cobweb, helium, mousse, sponge; **7** balloon, feather, soufflé; **8** gossamer; **9** snowflake; **11** thistledown; PHRASES: **3, 3** hot air; **3, 4** mae west; **4, 4** life belt, life buoy; **4, 6** life jacket; **4, 9** life preserver.

light up 4 beam, burn, glow, wink; **5** blaze, blink, flame, flare, flash, glare, gleam, glint, shine, spark; **6** glance; **7** flicker, glimmer, glisten, glitter, radiate, spangle, sparkle, twinkle; **8** iridesce; **9** coruscate, fluoresce; **10** incandesce; **11** scintillate; **12** phosphoresce; PHRASES: **5, 2** flare up.

lightweight 4 pawn; **7** trivial; **9** frivolous; **11** unimportant; **13** insubstantial; **15** inconsequential; PHRASES: **5, 3** small fry; **6, 3** little guy, little man.

likable 4 good, kind; **5** civil, sunny; **6** bright, genial, kindly, lovely, polite; **7** admired, affable, amiable, amusing, cordial, favored, lovable, popular; **8** adorable, alluring, amicable, engaging, friendly, intimate, pleasing, tempting; **9** appealing, congenial, courteous, easygoing, endearing; **10** attractive, chivalrous, compatible; **11** appreciated, captivating, fascinating, infatuating, titillating; **12** affectionate; PHRASES: **4-5** easy-going; **4-7** good-natured; **4-8** well-mannered.

like 3 dig, woo; **4** love, want; **5** adore, chase, court, enjoy, equal, fancy *UK*, prize, savor, yearn; **6** admire, desire, esteem, fellow, pursue, relish; **7** cherish, similar; **8** treasure; **9** identical; **10** appreciate, compatible; PHRASES: **2, 7, 2** be devoted to; **3, 5** run after; **4, 1, 5, 2** have a crush on, take a fancy to; **4, 2** take to; **4, 3** care for; **4, 3, 7** wish for oneself; **4, 4** hold dear; **4, 5** lust after; **5, 3, 5, 2** think the world of; **6, 5** hanker after; **7, 2**

delight in; **10, 4** sympathize with.

likely **3** apt; **5** prone; **6** liable; **7** tending; **8** apparent, expected, presumed, probable, suitable; **9** plausible, undoubted; **10** ostensible, predictive, presumable; **11** anticipated, indubitable, predictable, presumptive, prospective; **14** unquestionable; PHRASES: **2, 3, 3** in the air; **2, 3, 4** in the wind; **2, 3, 5** in the cards.

liking **3** fad; **4** love, whim, wish; **5** craze, crush, fancy *UK*, hobby, mania, phase, shine, taste, trend; **6** choice, desire, loving, relish, whimsy; **7** caprice, craving, empathy, feeling, leaning, longing, passion, tending, willing, wishing; **8** affinity, appetite, approval, devotion, fondness, intimacy, penchant, pleasure, sympathy, weakness, yearning; **9** adoration, affection, hankering, prejudice, selection; **10** admiration, allurement, attachment, attraction, friendship, partiality, preference, tenderness; **11** fascination, inclination, infatuation, predisposal; **12** friendliness, predilection; PHRASES: **4, 4** soft spot.

lilac **5** mauve; **7** syringa; PHRASES: **5-3** goat's-rue.

limb **4** spur; **5** bough; **6** branch, member; **9** appendage, extremity.

limit **3** ban, cap, end, rim, tie, tip, top; **4** bind, curb, cusp, drag, edge, goal, pale, peak, pole, term, veto; **5** allot, ambit, bound, brake, check, limes, march, point, range, stint, verge; **6** border, censor, define, demark, extent, freeze, fringe, hamper, hinder, patent, ration, summit, tether, zenith; **7** ceiling, compass, confine, contain, control, curtail, embargo, enclose, exclude, extreme, inhibit, measure, qualify, repress, specify; **8** boundary, deadline, frontier, mitigate, moderate, prohibit, restrain, restrict, terminus; **9** constrain, copyright, demarcate, determine, extremity, parameter, perimeter, periphery, proscribe, threshold, trimester; **10** monopolize; **12** circumscribe; PHRASES: **3, 1, 4, 2** put a stop to; **4, 2** hold in, rein in; **4, 3** mark out; **4, 3, 4, 2** draw the line at; **4, 4** hold back; **4, 8** last frontier; **5, 5** lower ~, speed ~, upper ~; **6, 2** bottle up.

limitation **3** bar; **4** curb, flaw; **5** check, limit; **6** damper, defect; **7** barrier, control, failing; **9** exclusion, restraint; **10** constraint, definition, inhibition, mitigation, moderation; **11** containment, demarcation, restriction, shortcoming; **12** proscription; **15**

circumscription.

limited **3** set; **5** fixed, small, tight; **6** finite, frozen, little, meager, narrow, scanty, slight, sparse; **7** cramped, slender; **8** confined, definite, patented; **9** curtailed, exclusive, hidebound; **10** inhibiting, repressive, restricted; **11** copyrighted, determinate, prohibitive, proscripted, restrictive; PHRASES: **2, 5** in check; **3-4** one-note; **4, 4** held back; **5, 6** under curfew; **5, 7** under control; **5, 9** under restraint.

limiting factor **3** ban, lot; **4** curb, dose, drag, veto; **5** brake, check, quota, trust; **6** bottom, cartel, curfew, extent, patent, tariff; **7** ceiling, embargo, measure; **8** monopoly; **9** allotment, copyright, hindrance, rationing, stricture, threshold; **10** censorship, repression; **11** curtailment, prohibition; **13** specification; PHRASES: **2-2, 4** no-go area; **3-5, 4** low-water mark; **4-5, 4** high-water mark; **4-7** self-control; **4-9** self-restraint; **5, 6** price freeze; **6, 4** closed shop.

limner *See* **painter**

limp **6** floppy, hobble, wilted, wobble; **7** flaccid, shamble, shuffle, stagger; **8** drooping, lifeless.

limpid **5** clear, lucid; **10** diaphanous; **11** translucent, transparent; **14** understandable; PHRASES: **3-7** see-through; **5, 2, 3** clear as day; **7, 5** crystal clear.

linctus **4** wash; **6** douche, gargle, undine; **7** eyebath; **9** mouthwash.

Lindisfarne **4, 6** Holy Island.

line **2** ry; **3** arc, bar, guy, ray, row, tag, tie; **4** back, band, bast, clew, coat, cord, edge, face, file, lace, land, lead, rope, tape, wait, wire; **5** braid, cable, chord, curve, fiber, front, grade, panel, plait, queue *UK*, serif, slope, stock, thong, train, twine, withe; **6** binder, border, hawser, logjam, picket, radius, raffia, stitch, string, tendon, thread; **7** backlog, bandage, binding, contour, descent, dynasty, lashing, lineage, mooring, painter, ribband, ripcord, tangent, towline, towrope; **8** altitude, bisector, bootlace, boundary, diagonal, diameter, geodesic, gradient, insulate, lifeline, ligament, ligature, pedigree, shoelace, slipknot, tailback *UK*, whipcord; **9** asymptote, bloodline, curvature, direction, frontline, genealogy, interface, interline, linearity, perimeter, undercoat, wallpaper; **10** drawstring, soundproof, tourniquet; **11** orientation, transversal; **13** circumference, perpendicular; PHRASES: **3, 2, 4** get in ~; **3, 4** guy wire, ley ~; **4, 2** fall in, ~ up; **4, 2, 4** wait in ~; **4, 2, 6** ~ of flight; **4, 4** base ~, chow ~, date ~, fall ~, main ~, snow ~, tree ~; **4, 4, 4** wait your turn; **4-6, 4** Oder-Neisse ~; **4, 7** ~ abreast; **5, 2, 4** stand in ~; **5, 4** guest rope, party ~, plumb ~, power ~, punch ~, story ~, water ~; **5-5, 4** Mason-Dixon ~; **6, 4** bottom ~, branch ~, family tree, firing ~, ledger ~, timber ~; **7, 4** Maginot ~; **8, 4** assembly ~, parallel ~, Plimsoll ~, straight ~; **9, 4** Siegfried ~, umbilical cord; **10, 4** Hindenburg ~, production ~. *See also* **verse**

line (in a line) **2,** 1, 3 in a row; **2,** 1, 9 in a crocodile; **2, 4** in file; **2, 6, 4** in Indian file, in single file; **3, 2, 3** end to end; **4, 2, 4** nose to tail; **6, 2, 6** bumper to bumper.

lineage **4** race; **5** tribe; **7** descent; **8** ancestry, pedigree; PHRASES: **6, 4** family tree.

linear **4** flat, skew; **6** angled, lineal, normal; **7** angular, oblique, pointed, slanted, sloping, upright; **8** parallel, straight, vertical; **9** collinear, divergent; **10** asymptotic, convergent, horizontal, orthogonal, tangential; **11** equidistant, equilateral, rectilinear; **12** intersecting, orthographic; **13** perpendicular; PHRASES: **2, 2, 5** at an angle; **8-5** straight-edged, straight-lined.

line of argument **4** case; **5** claim, issue, point, topic; **6** stance, thesis; **7** grounds, opinion, premise, pretext; **8** evidence, position; **9** assertion, postulate, rationale, reasoning, statement, testimony; **10** contention, hypothesis; **11** affirmation, attestation, proposition.

line up **4** file, line; **5** queue; **6** parade; **9** promenade; PHRASES: **3, 2, 4** get in line; **4, 1, 5** form a queue *UK*; **4, 2** draw up, fall in; **4, 4** file past; **4, 4, 5** fall into place, find one's level; **5, 2** queue up *UK*; **5, 2, 4** stand in line; **5, 4** march past.

ling **7** heather.

linger **3** lag; **4** hang; **5** dally, delay, dwell, hover, tarry; **6** dawdle, endure, loiter; **7** persist; **8** straggle; PHRASES: **5-5** dilly-dally; **6-6** shilly-shally.

lingerie *See* **underwear**

lingo *See* **language**

lingua **6** tongue.

linguist **4** poet; **5** namer; **6** author, writer; **7** exegete; **8** polyglot; **9** bilingual, clarifier, expositor, logophile, namechild, namegiver, neologist, phonetist; **10** christener, clas-

sicist, grammarian, orthoepist, translator; **11** epigraphist, etymologist, geolinguist, interpreter, nomenclator, philologist, phonemicist, phonetician, phonologist, phrasemaker, semanticist; **12** dialectician, glossologist, lexicologist, morphologist, multilingual, orthographer, paleographer, phrasemonger; **13** epigrammatist, lexicographer, linguistician, proverbialist, semasiologist, sociolinguist, structuralist, terminologist; **14** dialectologist, grammatologist, onomasiologist, psycholinguist.

linguistics, linguistic terms **6** common, etymon, formal, slangy, syntax; **7** grammar, lingual, meaning; **8** analytic, informal, literary, morpheme, orthoepy, phonemic, phonetic, polyglot, semantic, standard; **9** bilingual, dialectal, etymology, idiomatic, jargonish, onomastic, orthoepic, paleology, philology, phonemics, phonetics, phonology, semanteme, semantics, syntactic, Vernerian; **10** colloquial, derivative, diachronic, glossology, graphemics, lexicology, morphology, onomastics, structural, stylistics, synchronic, syntactics, vernacular; **11** comparative, descriptive, grammatical, paleography, phonography, semasiology; **12** bilingualism, dialectology, etymological, journalistic, lexicography, multilingual, nomenclature, orthographic, paleological, philological, phonological, polyglottism, sprachgefühl *Ger*; **13** geolinguistic, glossological, glottological, lexicographic, lexicological, morphological, pronunciation, structuralism; **14** conversational, geolinguistics, morphophonemic, paleographical, semasiological; **15** dialectological, lexicographical, morphophonemics, morphophonology, sociolinguistic; PHRASES: **4, 9** folk etymology. *See also* **grammar, part of speech, syntax**

liniment *See* **ointment**

lining **6** facing; **7** backing, coating; **10** insulation; **11** interfacing, interlining; **12** undercoating.

link **3** fit, pin, sew, tie, wed; **4** bind, bolt, clip, cuff, drag, fuse, gird, glue, grip, join, knot, lash, lock, nail, span, tape, weld, wrap, yoke; **5** affix, annex, braid, clamp, clasp, hitch, leash, rivet, screw, stick, truss, twist, weave; **6** attach, bridge, buckle, cement, clinch, couple, engage, fasten, fetter, prefix, solder, splice, staple, stitch, suffix, suture, swathe, tether, thread; **7** conjoin, connect, contact, entwine, harness, liaison, missing, network, shackle, swaddle; **8** dovetail, handcuff, straddle; **9** interlace; **10** connection; **11** communicate, concatenate; **12** interconnect, relationship.

linoleum 8 oilcloth, waxcloth *UK*.

linseed 8 flaxseed.

lion 3 Leo; **4** Elsa; **5** celeb, Simba; **9** celebrity, personage; PHRASES: **6, 4** Nemean ~ *UK*; **8, 4** mountain ~.

lip 3 rim; **4** brim, edge; **5** brink, cheek; **8** attitude, rudeness; **9** impudence; **12** impertinence.

Lipari Islands 7, 7 Aeolian Islands.

lipid 3 fat, oil, wax; **6** sterol; **7** steroid, terpene; **8** cephalin, lecithin; **10** glycolipid; **11** cerebroside, cholesterol, lipoprotein, phosphatide; **12** phospholipid, sphingolipid; **13** sphingomyelin; PHRASES: **4, 4** bile acid.

liquefy 3 run; **4** free, melt, thaw, undo; **5** blend, loose; **6** detach, loosen, unglue, unpeel; **7** unstick; **8** emulsify, fluidify, fluidize, separate; **9** liquidize.

liqueur 4 saké, saki; **5** anise, anram; **6** cassis, kümmel, mêliss, qetsch, scubac, strega; **7** alcamas, allasch, baileys, curaçao, escubac, ratafia, sambuca; **8** absinthe, advocaat, anisette, drambuie, persicot, prunelle; **9** arquebuse, cointreau, framboise, guignolet, mirabelle; **10** chartreuse, maraschino; **11** benedictine, trappistine; PHRASES: **4, 2, 4** brou de noix; **5, 2, 5** crème de cacao; **5, 2, 6** crème de menthe; **5, 7** grand marnier; **6, 3** triple sec; **6, 6** cherry brandy *UK*; **8, 7** southern comfort.

liquid *See* **fluid**

liquidity 6 assets; **8** fluidity; **9** fluidness, resources; **10** liquidness, wateriness; PHRASES: **6, 6** liquid assets.

liquor *See* **alcoholic drink**

lissome 5 agile, light, lithe, quick; **6** lively, nimble, supple, svelte; **7** willowy; **8** flexible.

list 3 tip; **4** bill, cant, edge, file, hark, note, poll, roll, rota *UK*, tilt; **5** chart, class, enter, index, items, panel, slant, slate, slope, stock, table, tally; **6** agenda, border, census, record, roster, scroll, series, tariff; **7** catalog *UK*, credits, diarize, hearken, invoice, itemize, listing, payroll, program, waybill; **8** cadastre, classify, register, registry, schedule, syllabus, synopsis, tabulate, transfer; **9** blacklist, catalogue *UK*, checklist, chronicle, directory, enumerate, inventory, itinerary, repertory, shortlist, timetable *UK*; **10** categorize, compendium, curriculum, pigeonhole, prospectus; **11** enumeration, itemization; PHRASES: **3, 4** hit ~, put down, set down; **4-2** line-up; **4, 4** back ~, book ~, cast ~, sick ~; **5, 4** black ~, check ~, civil ~, entry ~, short ~, write down; **6, 4** active ~ *UK*, honors ~; **7, 4** mailing ~, waiting ~; **9, 4** electoral roll *UK*.

listed 5 filed, noted; **7** charted, entered, indexed; **8** itemized, recorded; **9** cataloged, scheduled, tabulated, taxonomic; **10** catalogued *UK*, enumerated, programmed, registered, timetabled *UK*; **11** inventoried; **14** classificatory.

listen 3 ear; **4** hark, hear, heed; **6** attend.

listing 8 taxonomy; **10** cataloging, tabulation; **11** cataloguing *UK*, enumeration, itemization; **12** registration; **14** classification. *See also* **list**

lit 5 drunk, light; **6** alight, bright, landed, sunlit; **7** firelit, lamplit, moonlit, spotlit, starlit; **8** flashlit, floodlit, torchlit; **9** candlelit, lightened; **10** brightened; **11** highlighted, illuminated.

litany 4 list; **6** series; **7** catalog *UK*, listing, prayers, recital; **9** catalogue *UK*, petitions, responses; **11** invocations.

liter 1 L.

literal 4 true; **7** textual; **8** verbatim; **10** denotative; PHRASES: **4, 2, 3, 6** true to the letter; **4-3-4** word-for-word; **7, 3, 5** chapter and verse.

literally 3 sic; **8** verbatim; **10** rigorously; **12** legitimately, pedantically; PHRASES: **2, 3, 4** by the book; **2, 3, 6** to the letter; **4, 3, 4** word for word; **6, 3, 6** letter for letter.

literary 6 formal; **7** erudite, learned, written; **8** critical, decadent, lettered, polished, romantic; **9** classical, realistic, scholarly; **10** futuristic, humanistic, postmodern; **12** belletristic, interpretive *UK*, intertextual, metaphysical, naturalistic, surrealistic; PHRASES: **4-4** well-read.

literary person 8 educator; **9** Leavisite; **10** belletrist; **13** deconstructor, structuralist; PHRASES: **3, 2, 7** man of letters; **3, 6** New Critic; **3, 7** the clerisy; **4, 8** book reviewer; **5, 2, 7** woman of letters; **8, 6** literary critic; **8, 7** literary scholar.

literate 7 donnish, erudite, worldly; **8** academic, cultured, educated, highbrow, numerate, pedantic, schooled; **9** scholarly; **10** cultivated; **12** intellectual, semiliterate; **13** overqualified, sophisticated; PHRASES: **4-8** well-educated.

literature 4 lore; **5** bumph *UK*, prose, verse; **7** culture, fiction, letters, writing; **8** brochure, learning; **9** erudition; **12** civilization; PHRASES: **3, 4** the arts; **3, 8** the classics; **3, 10** the humanities; **4, 10** folk ~, oral ~; **6-7** belles-lettres.

lithify 6 cement; **7** petrify; **9** fossilize; **10** mineralize; **11** consolidate, crystallize.

lithium oxide 6 lithia.

litigant 4 suer; **5** party; **6** suitor; **7** accused, accuser, libelee, pursuer; **8** claimant, informer, libelant, objector; **9** appellant, defendant, litigator, plaintiff; **10** intervener, petitioner, prosecutor, respondent; PHRASES: **4-1-5** John-a-Nokes; **4-1-6** John-a-Stiles; **4, 3** John Doe; **5, 2, 1, 4** party to a suit; **6, 8** common informer; **7, 6** accused person.

litigate 3 sue, try; **4** cite; **5** argue, claim, plead; **6** accuse, charge, indict, summon; **7** arraign, impeach, implead, request; **8** advocate, petition; **9** prosecute; PHRASES: **3, 2, 5** put on trial; **4, 1, 4** file a suit; **4, 1, 5** file a brief, file a claim; **4, 1, 7** seek a verdict; **4, 2** have up *UK*; **4, 2, 5** take to court; **4, 7** seek justice; **4, 8** call evidence; **5, 1, 7** bring a lawsuit; **5, 2, 3, 3** bring to the bar; **5, 2, 5** bring to trial; **5, 2, 7** bring to justice; **5, 6, 2** serve notice on; **5, 7** brief counsel, press charges; **6, 2, 3** appeal to law; **6, 7** prefer charges; **7, 1, 5** prepare a brief.

litigation 4 case, plea, suit, writ; **5** cause, claim, issue, trial; **6** action, charge; **7** contest, dispute, justice, lawsuit, quarrel, request, summons, verdict; **8** averment, demurrer, petition, pleading, sentence; **9** affidavit, assertion, judgement, objection; **10** accusation, punishment; **11** affirmation, arraignment, impeachment, prosecution; **12** counterclaim, jurisdiction; **13** litigiousness; **15** quarrelsomeness; PHRASES: **4, 2, 3** suit at law; **4, 4** test case; **5, 4** legal case; **5, 5** legal issue; **5, 6** legal action, legal remedy; **5, 7** legal dispute, legal process.

litter 3 tip; **4** bier, dump, hash, heap, mess, slum; **5** brood, dooly (East Indies), sedan, trash, young; **6** jumble *UK*, lumber, midden, muddle, pallet, pickle, pigpen, pigsty *UK*, tonjon (Sri Lanka); **7** clutter, garbage, jainpan, norimon, rubbish *UK*, scatter; **8** mishmash, muncheel, shambles; **9** palanquin, stretcher; **10** disarrange, hodgepodge.

little 3 wee; **4** baby, cozy, fine, less, mini, poky, puny, snug, thin, tiny; **5** bijou *UK*, bitsy, dinky, dumpy, dwarf, elfin, handy, least, model, petty, pygmy, runty, scant, short, small, squat, teeny, weeny; **6** atomic, bantam, dainty, meager, minute, paltry, petite, pocket, scanty, shrunk, skimpy, slight, tiddly *UK*, titchy *UK*; **7** amoebic, compact, cramped, dwarfed, limited, minimal, scraggy, scrawny, scrubby, stunted, tenuous, trivial, weensie, wizened; **8** amoeboid, dwarfish, exiguous, germinal, granular, littlest, microbic, piddling, pindling, portable, shrunken, smallish, trifling, twelvemo; **9** bacterial, duodecimo, embryonic, incipient, invisible, microbial, miniature, minuscule, molecular, protozoan, shriveled, subatomic, undersize; **10** contracted, diminutive, impalpable, inadequate, intangible, negligible, restricted, rudimental, undersized; **11** animalcular, corpuscular, Lilliputian, microcosmic, microscopic, rudimentary, unimportant; **12** imponderable, miniaturized, subminiature; **13** imperceptible, inappreciable, indiscernible, infinitesimal, insignificant; **14** inconsiderable; PHRASES: **3-5** one-horse; **4-4** knee-high, pint-size; **4-5** itsy-bitsy, itty-bitty, pint-sized; **4-6** vest-pocket; **5-5** small-scale, teeny-weeny; **6-3-4** nickel-and-dime; **6, 4** L~ John *UK*; **6-4** pocket-size.

littleness 8 exiguity; **9** undersize; **10** micrometer, microscope, microscopy; **11** micrography, portability; **12** invisibility; **13** impalpability, intangibility; **15** imponderability, miniaturization; PHRASES: **5, 5** small scale. *See also* **little**

little person 3 elf, tot; **4** chit, mite, runt, slip, snip, wisp; **5** banty, dwarf, fairy, gnome, midge, mouse, squit *UK*, titch *UK*; **6** bantam, hobbit, minnow, peewee, shorty, shrimp, sprite, squirt; **7** brownie, manikin, tiddler *UK*; **8** Alberich, halfling, munchkin, Nibelung, weakling; **9** Pinocchio, pipsqueak; **10** fingerling, homunculus, leprechaun, Thumbelina; **11** lightweight, Lilliputian; **13** featherweight; PHRASES: **3-1-2-5** Hop-o'-my-thumb; **3, 5** Tom Thumb; **4-4** half-pint; **5, 3** small fry; **5, 5** short stuff.

little piece 3 bit, jot; **4** drop, iota, mote; **5** crumb, fleck, minim, scrap, speck; **6** filing, morsel, sliver, tittle; **7** droplet, minutia, shaving, snippet; **8** fragment.

little space 4 hole; 5 pinch; 9 cubbyhole, dollhouse; 10 pigeonhole; PHRASES: 5, 4 tight spot; 5, 7 tight squeeze.

little thing 3 dot, ion, toy; 4 atom, baby, cell, chip, doll, germ, mini, muon, seed; 5 grain, meson, model, monad, pixel, point, quark, virus; 6 amoeba, parton, proton, puppet; 7 euglena, granule, microbe, neutron, nucleus, pinhead; 8 bacillus, electron, microdot, molecule, neutrino, particle, pinpoint, plankton, twelvemo, zoospore; 9 bacterium, corpuscle, duodecimo, microchip, microcosm, microfilm, miniature, protozoan; 10 animalcule, microfiche, microphyte; 13 microorganism; 15 microphotograph; PHRASES: 5, 2, 4 grain of sand; 6, 7 pocket edition; 7, 4 mustard seed, silicon chip; 7, 7 Elzevir edition; 9, 6 thumbnail sketch.

live 2 be; 4 last; 5 dwell, exist, liven; 6 endure, revive; 7 breathe, cohabit, persist, quicken, respire, subsist, survive; 8 continue; PHRASES: 2, 5 be alive; 4, 2 come to; 4, 2, 4 come to life; 4, 3 hang out; 4, 3, 5 walk the earth; 4, 5 have being; 4, 6 come around, draw breath; 4, 7 come through; 5, 2 carry on; 5, 2, 4 shack up with; 5, 5 cheat death.

livelihood 3 job; 4 wage, work; 5 means; 6 income, living; 10 occupation; PHRASES: 5, 2, 7 means of support; 5, 3, 6 bread and butter; 5, 5 daily bread.

liveliness 5 vigor; 6 energy, spirit; 7 sparkle; 8 dynamism, vivacity; PHRASES: 3-2-3-2 get-up-and-go; 4, 2, 5 joie de vivre. *See also* **lively**

lively 4 pert, spry; 5 alert, brisk, perky, vital; 6 active, breezy, cheery, chirpy, frisky, vivace; 7 allegro, chipper, dynamic, gingery; 8 animated, spirited, vigorous; 9 ebullient, energetic, sprightly, vivacious; 10 allegretto.

liver 10 liverwurst; PHRASES: 5, 5 ~ fluke, ~ salts *UK*.

livery 5 dress; 6 colors; 7 costume, uniform; 8 insignia; 9 vestments; PHRASES: 6, 6 racing colors.

livestock 3 cow, ewe, hen, hog, kid, pig, ram, sow, teg, tup; 4 boar, bull, calf, cock, duck, fowl, gilt, goat, hogg *UK*, lamb; 5 capon, chick, drake, goose, layer, poult, sheep, steer, stirk *UK*, stock, store, swine; 6 barrow, beasts, boiler, cattle, cutter, gander, heifer, hogget *UK*, milker, piglet,

porker, pullet, weaner, wether; 7 baconer *UK*, broiler, bullock, chicken, fatling, gosling, poultry, roaster, rooster; 8 duckling, fatstock, yearling; PHRASES: 3, 3 dry cow; 4, 4 bull beef, veal calf; 4-5, 3 free-range hen; 5, 3 milch cow, nurse cow; 5, 4 billy goat, nanny goat; 5, 6 store cattle; 6, 3 barren cow, laying hen; 6, 4 barley beef; 7, 3 battery hen, suckler cow; 7, 4 suckler beef.

livid 4 blue, pale; 5 angry, white; 6 purple; 7 bruised, enraged, furious; PHRASES: 5, 3, 4 black and blue.

living 4 keep, live; 5 alive, biont, vital; 6 animal, biotic, viable; 7 animate, current, natural, organic; 8 advowson, benefice, sentient; 10 inhabiting, livelihood; PHRASES: 5, 5 daily bread; 6, 4 ~ room, ~ wage; 6, 5 ~ death. *See also* **livelihood**

living matter 4 cell, gene; 6 tissue; 8 bioplasm, bioplast, organism; 10 protoplasm; 13 macromolecule; PHRASES: 6, 6 living tissue.

living world 5 biota; 6 nature; 9 biosphere, ecosphere; PHRASES: 5, 3, 5 flora and fauna; 7, 5 natural world.

lizard 6 Sauria; 7 saurian; 8 scincoid; 10 Lacertilia; 11 lacertilian; 14 rhynocephalian; PHRASES: 6, 6 lounge ~; 7, 6 legless ~. *See also* **reptiles**

load 3 arm; 4 bend, cock, lade; 5 cargo, prime; 6 burden, charge, hamper, hinder, lading, saddle, strain, stress; 7 ballast, busload, carload, freight, payload, stowage, tension, tonnage; 8 boatload, encumber, overload, shipment; 9 trainload, truckload; 10 overburden; 11 compression; 13 containerload.

loaded 4 full; 5 laden, lined; 6 biased, packed, padded; 7 crammed, holding, stuffed; 8 brimming, squeezed, weighted; 9 overladen; 10 burdensome, containing, overloaded; 12 overweighted; PHRASES: 5-1-5 chock-a-block; 5-4 chock-full; 6, 2 topped up. *See also* **load, wealthy**

loaf 3 bap *UK*, bun, cob, pan; 4 farl *UK*, head, idle, laze, roll; 5 bagel, braid, brain, crêpe *UK*, scone, wafer; 6 cookie, lounge, muffin, waffle; 7 bannock, bloomer *UK*, brioche, cracker, crumpet, oatcake, pancake, pikelet *UK*, popover, teacake; 8 baguette, flapjack; 9 croissant, farmhouse; 10 battercake, crispbread, shortbread; PHRASES: 3, 4 pan ~ *UK*; 4, 4 barm cake, milk ~; 4, 5 drop scone *UK*; 4, 7 soda biscuit, soda cracker; **5, 3** split tin *UK*; **5, 5** bread stick; **5, 7** water biscuit; **6, 4** bridge roll *UK*; **6, 5** French bread, French stick *UK*; **7, 3** currant bun; **7, 4** cottage ~ *UK*; **7, 6** English muffin; **9, 4** breakfast roll.

loan 3 IOU, sub; 4 debt, lend; 6 credit; 7 advance, imprest, lending; 8 guaranty, leverage, mortgage; 9 borrowing, debenture, overdraft; 10 remortgage; PHRASES: 4, 4 bank ~; 4-5 lend-lease; 4, 7 debt capital, ~ capital; 4, 9 ~ repayment; 6, 8 second mortgage; 7, 4 secured ~, student ~; 8, 4 business ~, personal ~; 9, 4 unsecured ~; 10, 4 collateral ~, guaranteed ~; 11, 4 installment ~.

loathe *See* **hate**

loathing *See* **hate**

lob 3 bat, hit; 4 ball, hurl, toss; 5 fling, knock, pitch, throw, whack; 6 strike.

lobby 5 foyer; 6 atrium; 8 petition; 9 vestibule; PHRASES: 4, 7 sway opinion; 5, 4, 4 press your case; 5, 8 apply pressure; 6, 5 ginger group; 8, 4 entrance hall; 8, 5 campaign group, interest group, pressure group; 9, 4 reception area.

lobe *See* **part**

lobster 4 cock; 7 decapod; 8 crawfish, crayfish, tomalley; 9 langouste; PHRASES: 7, 3 ~ pot; 7, 4 ~ moth; 7, 7 ~ newburg.

local 4 time; 5 color; 6 native, nearby; 7 gossipy, insular, limited; 8 confined, diocesan, domestic, downtown, familiar, neighbor; 9 localized, parochial; 10 anesthetic, provincial; 11 neighboring; PHRASES: 4-4 next-door.

locale *See* **location**

locality 4 area, beat, turf, walk; 5 haunt, manor, orbit, patch, place, round; 6 locale; 7 circuit; 8 confines, environs, precinct, purlieus, vicinage, vicinity; 10 approaches, foreground; 12 neighborhood, surroundings; PHRASES: 4, 2, 3, 5 neck of the woods; 4, 4 back yard; 8, 6 stamping ground.

locate 3 fix, put; 4 base, post, site, spot; 5 place, plant, stick; 6 billet; 7 emplace, install, quarter, situate, station; 8 ensconce, pinpoint, position; 9 establish; PHRASES: 3, 2 set up; 3, 2, 5 put in place.

located 3 set; 7 settled. *See also* **locate**

location 3 dot; 4 base, beat, hole, post, seat, site, spot, turf; 5 field, haunt, manor, parts, patch, pitch, place, point; 6 locale; 7 address, habitat, setting, station; 8 bearings,

environs, locality, position, postcode; 9 situation, territory; 11 coordinates, declination, environment, whereabouts; 12 surroundings; PHRASES: 3, 4 zip code, ZIP code; 3, 9 map reference; 4, 2, 3, 5 neck of the woods; 4, 9 grid reference; 6, 7 postal address; 6, 8 postal district.

locational 8 geodetic, situated, surveyed; 10 geographic, positional; 12 geographical, navigational; 13 topographical; 14 cartographical.

lock 3 bar, jam; 4 bolt, hasp, ward; 5 clasp, latch, quiff *UK*, stick, tress; 6 clinch, secure, strand; 7 cowlick, padlock, ragbolt, ringlet; 8 curlicue, deadbolt, fastener; PHRASES: 4, 4 dead bolt, make fast, snap ~, yale ~; 5, 4 Chubb ~, stock ~, vapor ~, wheel ~; 6, 4 spring ~; 10, 4 percussion ~; 11, 4 combination ~.

locomotive 4 loco; 5 train; 6 diesel, engine, jigger, puffer, tanker; 7 chuffer, shunter, steamer, wildcat; PHRASES: 4, 4 choo choo, puff puff; 4, 5 iron horse; 5, 5 tank engine; 5, 5 chuff chuff; 5, 6 light engine; 5, 10 steam ~; 6-8 diesel-electric *UK*; 8, 6 shunting engine; 9, 6 jerkwater engine.

locomotive part 4 tank; 6 boiler, funnel, piston, tender; 7 firebox, sandbox; 8 motorcar; 9 footplate *UK*; 10 pantograph; PHRASES: 4, 4 side tank; 4, 4, 6 dead man's handle; 6, 4 saddle tank; 8, 4 traction unit.

locust 6 acacia.

lodge 3 inn; 4 live, stay; 5 board, cabin, catch, embed, hotel, motel, stick; 6 billet, chalet, resort; 7 cottage, implant, quarter; 11 accommodate; PHRASES: 2, 1, 6 be a lodger; 3, 2 put up; 3, 2, 5 fix in place; 4, 8 take lodgings; 5, 5 small house; 7, 5 hunting ~.

lofty 4 high, tall; 5 grand, noble; 6 lordly; 7 soaring; 8 arrogant, elevated, superior, towering; 9 admirable; 10 disdainful; 12 supercilious; 13 distinguished; PHRASES: 4-9 high-ceilinged.

log 4 note; 5 chart, notes; 6 record; 7 journal, logbook, minutes; PHRASES: 4, 1, 4, 2 make a note of; 4, 4 note down.

logarithm 3 log; 4 base; 8 mantissa; 13 antilogarithm; 14 characteristic; PHRASES: 3, 6 log tables; 6, 9 common ~; 9, 6 ~ tables.

logic 6 acumen; 7 insight; 8 instinct; 9 deduction, induction, intuition, rationale, reasoning; 10 dialectics; 11 inspiration; 13 argumentation.

logical 4 true; 5 sound, valid; 6 stated; 7 claimed, correct; 8 affirmed, asserted, attested, complete, converse, elenctic, proposed, rational; 9 deductive, empirical, heuristic, inductive, necessary; 10 compatible, consistent, contingent, equivalent, postulated, reasonable, sufficient; 11 conditional, inferential; 12 hypothetical; 13 propositional.

loiter 4 lurk, wait; 5 amble, dally, drift, skulk; 6 linger, stroll, wander; PHRASES: 4, 6 hang around.

loll 3 lie, sag; 4 flop; 5 droop; 6 dangle, lounge, slouch, sprawl; PHRASES: 3, 4 lie back; 4, 4 hang down.

Lombard 9 Langobard, Longobard.

lone 4, 4 ~ hand, ~ wolf.

lonely 4 lone, lorn; 5 alone; 6 banned, exiled, single; 7 avoided, blanked, forlorn, shunned; 8 banished, celibate, confined, deserted, desolate, isolated, lonesome, solitary; 9 concealed, separated; 10 friendless, ostracized; 11 godforsaken; PHRASES: 2, 4, 3 on one's own, on one's tod; 2, 6 in purdah; 3, 2, 5 out of place; 4-2-4 stay-at-home; 4, 2, 8 sent to Coventry; 4-10 cold-shouldered; 6-3 frozen-out.

loner 6 hermit; 7 ascetic, eremite, recluse, stylite; 8 marabout, solitary; 9 anchorite; 12 isolationist, seclusionist; PHRASES: 4, 4 lone wolf; 4, 5 only child.

long 1 L; 3 far; 4 high, itch, lust, pine, tall; 5 crave, yearn; 6 boring, desire, hanker, hunger, thirst; 7 endless, lengthy, tedious, verbose; 8 extended, overlong, vacation; 9 extensive, prolonged, stretched, sustained; 10 lengthened, parliament, protracted, straggling, unabridged; 11 sesquipedal; 12 interminable, outstretched, polysyllabic; 14 sesquipedalian; PHRASES: 1, 4, 4 a mile ~; 2, 4, 2, 4, 3 as ~ as one's arm; 3-8 far-reaching; 4, 3 ~ arm, ~ hop UK, ~ tom, spun out; 4, 4 ~ face, ~ haul, ~ jump, ~ shot, ~ suit; 4, 5 L~ Beach, ~ jenny UK, ~ johns; 4-5-3 long-drawn-out; 4, 6 L~ Island; 4-6 full-length, knee-length, long-winded; 4, 7 ~ weekend; 4, 10 L~ Parliament; 5-3 drawn-out; 5-6 ankle-length, waist-length; 6-3 strung-out; 6, 8 summer vacation; 7, 3 dragged out, without end; 8-6 shoulder-length; 9, 3 stretched out.

long duration 3 age, eon; 4 ages, days, eons, olam; 5 years, yonks UK; 8 lifetime; 10 millennium; 11 generations; PHRASES: 2, 3 an age; 2, 8 an eternity; 4, 8 life sentence; 4, 10 time immemorial; 5, 2, 3 years on end; 5, 2, 7 month of Sundays; 7, 5 donkey's years UK.

longing See **desire**

longitude 8 meridian.

longitudinally 5 along; 7 endways, endwise; 8 linearly, longways, longwise; 10 lengthways, lengthwise; PHRASES: 2, 1, 4 in a line; 2, 6 in tandem; 2, 6, 4 in single file.

long-lasting 5 fixed; 6 stable; 7 durable, lasting; 8 constant, enduring; 9 indelible, permanent; PHRASES: 10 perdurable.

long-suffering 7 patient; 8 resigned, tolerant; 9 forgiving; 13 accommodating.

long-winded 5 wordy; 6 prolix; 7 lengthy, verbose; 8 cumbrous, rambling; 9 expansive, garrulous, ponderous; 10 circuitous, discursive, loquacious; 12 interminable; 13 grandiloquent; 14 sesquipedelian; PHRASES: 4-5-3 long-drawn-out; 6-8 throat-clearing.

long-windedness 7 bombast; 9 pomposity, turgidity, verbosity; PHRASES: 14 grandiloquence. See also **long-winded**

look 1 V; 2 lo; 3 air, eye; 4 gape, gawk, gawp, gaze, leer, ogle, peek, peep; 5 dekko UK, focus, glare, scowl, stare; 6 aspect, gander, glance, glower, goggle, regard, shufty, squint; 7 glimpse, grimace; 8 butcher's UK; 3, 2 eye up; 4, 3 evil eye; 4, 5 coup d'oeil; 4, 7 ~ askance, ~ daggers; 5, 1, 6 steal a glance; 5, 4 black ~, dirty ~; 5, 4, 4, 2 feast one's eyes on; 6, 3 roving eye; 6, 4 sheep's eyes; 7, 4 melting ~; 8, 4 sidelong ~, sideways ~.

look ahead 5 augur; 6 divine; 7 foresee, predict, presage; 8 foretell, prophesy; 11 haruspicate; PHRASES: 4, 3 hope for; 4, 3, 6 read tea leaves; 4, 5 cast bones.

look-alike 4 copy, pair, spit, twin; 5 clone, match; 6 cloned, double, paired, ringer; 7 replica; 8 matching, portrait; 9 duplicate, facsimile, homophyly; 10 reflection; 11 counterpart, homophyllic; 12 doppelgänger; PHRASES: 3, 2, 1, 4 two of a kind; 3, 4, 2, 1, 3 two peas in a pod; 4, 4 dead spit UK; 4, 5 very image; 4, 6 dead ringer; 5, 3 alter ego; 5, 4 other self; 6, 5 living image; 7, 2 picture of; 7, 4 Siamese twin; 8, 5 spitting image.

look back 6 relive, review; 7 regress, reprize; 8 archaize, remember; 9 flashback, nostalgia, reminisce; **11** remembrance, reminiscing; **12** reminiscence; **14** antiquarianize; PHRASES: **4, 2** déjà vu; **4, 2, 3, 4** live in the past; **4, 4** hark back; **6, 2, 3, 4** return to the past.

look out! **4** cave!, fore!; **6** beware!; **7** careful!; PHRASES: **4, 3, 3** mind the gap!; **4, 4, 4** mind your step!; **5, 2** watch it!; **5, 3** watch out!.

loom **4** soar; **5** tower; **6** emerge, impend, menace; **8** forebode, jacquard, threaten; **10** intimidate; PHRASES: **4, 3** bode ill.

loop **4** coil, hoop, ring, wind; **5** twist; **7** circlet, entwine; **8** encircle.

loose **3** lax; **4** fast, free; **5** baggy, broad, rough, slack; **6** impure, sloppy, untied, wanton, wobbly; **7** general, immoral, inexact, movable, rickety, unbound; **8** detached, insecure, unchaste, unsteady; **9** dissolute, imprecise, shapeless; **10** indefinite, profligate, unattached; **11** promiscuous; PHRASES: **2, 5** at large; **5, 3** ~ end; **5, 5** ~ cover; **5, 6** ~ change; **7, 4** hanging free.

loose woman **4** goer, slag; **5** hussy, nymph; **7** nymphet; PHRASES: **5, 6** femme fatale.

loot **3** rob; **4** cash, dosh *UK*, swag; **5** booty, money; **6** assets, burgle, spoils, wealth; **7** pillage, plunder, ransack.

lop **3** cut; **4** chop, crop, hack; **5** sever; **6** deduct, reduce, remove; **8** amputate, discount, subtract; PHRASES: **3, 3** cut off; **4, 3** chop off, take off; **5, 3** slice off.

lope **4** gait, move, pace, step, walk, yomp *UK*; **5** tread; **6** lollop, stride.

loquacious *See* **talkative**

lord **2** ld; **3** God, nob *UK*; **4** duke, earl, peer; **5** chief, count, laird *UK*, liege, noble, thane; **6** aristo, Father, master, squire; **7** grandee; **8** nobleman, overlord, suzerain, viscount; **9** patrician; **10** aristocrat, earldorman; **11** chamberlain; PHRASES: **4, 2, 3, 5** ~ of the manor; **4, 3-3** L~ Haw-haw; **4, 3, 6** ~ and master; **4, 4** L~ Muck *UK*; **4, 5** L~ Byron, L~ Elgin, L~ Mayor *UK*; **4, 7** L~ Provost *UK*; **4, 8** L~ Advocate *UK*; **4, 9** L~ Protector; **4, 10** L~ Chancellor, L~ Lieutenant *UK*; **4, 11** L~ Chamberlain *UK*; **5, 8** Lords Temporal *UK*; **5, 9** Lords Spiritual *UK*.

Lord of the Flies **9** Beelzebub.

lore **6** wisdom; **9** knowledge, teachings, tradition; **10** experience.

Los Angeles **2** LA.

lose **4** diet, drop, fail, fast, miss, slim, tank; **5** avoid, dodge, elude, evade; **6** escape, forget, mislay, outrun; **7** forfeit; **8** misplace, outstrip, subtract; **9** sacrifice; **10** relinquish; PHRASES: **3, 7, 2** say goodbye to; **4, 2, 1, 7** ~ by a whisker; **4, 2, 4, 3** look in vain for; **4, 7** kiss goodbye; **5, 3** shake off; **5, 6** leave behind.

lose color **3** run; **4** fade, pale, peak; **6** blanch, bleach, whiten; PHRASES: **4, 4** turn pale.

lose one's money **2, 2, 3** go to pot; **2, 2, 3, 4** go to the wall; **2, 4** go bust; **2, 5** go broke; **2, 5, 2** go belly up; **2, 6** go busted; **2, 8** go bankrupt; **4, 2, 4, 5** fall on hard times; **4, 10** lose everything.

loser **3** dud; **4** dupe, flop, prey; **5** lemon; **6** reject, victim, waster; **7** bungler, failure, washout; **8** bankrupt, underdog; **9** defaulter, scapegoat; **10** flounderer, nonstarter, squanderer, wallflower; **11** incompetent, overspender; **13** underachiever; PHRASES: **2-4** no-good; **2-5** no-hoper *UK*; **3-4** has-been; **4-2-4** ne'er-do-well; **4, 3** fall guy, lame dog; **4-3** also-ran; **4-3-3** down-and-out; **4-3-7** good-for-nothing; **4, 4** lame duck, lost soul; **6-2** runner-up; **6-5** second-rater.

loss **4** cost, toll; **5** death, debit; **6** defeat, denial, losing, outage, ullage; **7** apocope, deficit, dieting, elision, expense, failure, fasting, forfeit, penalty, reverse, robbery, setback, wastage; **8** anorexia, decrease, omission, reversal, riddance, slimming *UK*; **9** decrement, detriment, mislaying, overdraft, perdition, privation, sacrifice, shortfall, stripping; **10** bankruptcy, divestment, extinction, forfeiture, insolvency, misplacing; **11** bereavement, deprivation, expenditure, nonrecovery, subtraction; **12** disadvantage; **13** dispossession, expropriation; **14** disentitlement, nonrestoration.

loss (at a loss) **6** astray; **8** confused; **10** astonished, bewildered, dumbstruck, gobsmacked, prodigally, wastefully; **11** deficiently, disoriented, floundering; **14** insufficiently, unsuccessfully; PHRASES: **2, 1, 3, 4** at a cut rate; **2, 1, 3, 5** at a cut price; **2, 3, 3** in the red; **3, 2, 3** all at sea; **3, 2, 4, 5** out of one's depth; **3, 2, 5** out of place; **3, 6** of course; **4, 2, 7** lost in thought; **4, 2, 9** lost in amazement.

loss (make a financial loss) **8** overdraw; **9** overspend; PHRASES: **2, 2, 3, 4** go to the wall; **2, 4** go bust; **2, 5** go broke; **2, 5, 2** go belly up; **3, 1, 7** run a deficit; **3, 2, 1, 4** run at a loss; **4, 5** fall short, lose money; **5, 6** incur losses.

lost 4 gone, rapt; **5** shorn, spent; **6** adrift, astray, bereft, damned, fallen, ruined, wasted; **7** extinct, lacking, mislaid, missing; **8** depleted, hopeless, immersed, stripped, vanished; **9** engrossed, forgotten, misplaced; **10** squandered; **12** incorrigible, irredeemable; **13** irreclaimable, irrecoverable, irretrievable; PHRASES: **4, 2, 3, 5** gone by the board; **6, 8** beyond recovery.

lot 3 bid, due, hap, mob, set; **4** area, crew, doom, fate, gang, host, load, many, much, plot; **5** batch, crowd, group, horde; **6** bundle, chance, clique, parcel, plight, wealth; **7** destiny, fortune; **9** abundance, condition, profusion, situation; **10** collection; **11** consignment; PHRASES: **1, 4, 4** a good deal; **1, 5, 4** a great deal. *See also* **lots**

lotion *See* **ointment**

lots 4 many, pots, slew, slue, tons, wads; **5** heaps *UK*, loads, miles *UK*, piles, reams, scads; **6** masses *UK*, oceans, oodles, plenty, scores, stacks; **7** slather; **8** hundreds, lashings *UK*, millions; **9** mountains, shedloads, thousands.

lottery 4 draw, luck, risk; **5** bingo, lotto; **6** chance, gamble, raffle; **7** fortune; **11** sweepstakes.

loud 4 deep, full; **5** brash, gaudy, lusty, noisy, rowdy, vocal; **6** brassy, crying, flashy, shrill; **7** blaring, booming, braying, clamant, dinning, echoing, pealing, rackety, ringing, yelling; **8** carrying, crashing, piercing, plangent, powerful, rattling, resonant, shouting, sonorous, strepent, strident, swelling, whooping; **9** bellowing, clamorous, crescendo, deafening, screaming; **10** boisterous, clangorous, discordant, resounding, stentorian, thundering, thunderous, uproarious, vociferous; **11** cacophonous, loudmouthed, multisonous, rumbustious; **12** caterwauling, obstreperous, ostentatious, rambunctious; PHRASES: **3-7** big-mouthed, ear-rending; **3-9** ear-splitting; **4-8** full-throated, high-sounding; **7-7** trumpet-tongued.

loud (be loud) 3 cry, din; **4** bang, boom, bray, call, clap, howl, peal, ring, roar, slam, stun, yell, yowl; **5** blare, blast, bugle, burst, clang, clash, crash, drill, knock, laugh, shout, skirl, snore, sound, speak, stamp, storm, swell; **6** bellow, deafen, hammer, rattle, scream, shriek, shrill, squawk; **7** catcall, clatter, explode, rampage, resound, thunder, trumpet, ululate, whistle; **8** detonate; **9** caterwaul, fulminate; **10** cachinnate, vociferate; **11** reverberate; PHRASES: **4, 3, 3** fill the air; **4, 3, 4** wake the dead; **4, 3, 4, 3** blow the roof off; **5, 2** speak up; **5, 3, 4** raise the roof, split the ears; **5, 3, 6** awake the echoes; **5, 4** raise Cain; **6, 4, 5** strain one's voice; **7, 3, 5** shatter the peace.

loudly 1 F; **2** FF; **5** forte, tutti; **7** lustily, noisily; **9** crescendo; **10** disorderly, fortissimo; PHRASES: **2, 4, 3** in full cry; **2, 4, 5** at full pitch; **2, 4, 6** on full volume; **4, 5** full blast; **4, 6** full chorus. *See also* **loud**

loud noise 3 bel; **4** bang, boom, bray, call, clap, fire, honk, peal, roll, slam, toot; **5** alarm, bells, blare, blast, blitz, burst, clang, forte, noise, siren, storm, surge, swell, tutti; **6** chimes, rattle, report, retort, rumble, volume; **7** clangor, decibel, fanfare, gunfire, hissing, snoring, stridor, surging, thunder; **8** diapason, flourish, laughter, sonority; **9** artillery, cacophony, crescendo, explosion, plangency, resonance, stridency; **10** brassiness, dissonance, fortissimo, shrillness, sibilation; **11** bombardment, campanology, ostentation, thunderclap; **12** cachinnation, extravagance, sonorousness; **13** reverberation; **14** stertorousness.

loud person 6 Hermes; **7** Stentor; **8** braggart; **9** Boanerges, loudmouth; PHRASES: **3, 6** hog caller; **4, 5** town crier; **5, 6** opera singer; **5, 8** drill sergeant.

loudspeaker 6 action, Tannoy *UK*, woofer; **7** tweeter; **8** bullhorn; **9** megaphone. *See also* **loud person**

lough 4 lake.

Louisiana 2 LA; **8** magnolia (flower); PHRASES: **4, 7** bald cypress (tree); **5, 5** Baton Rouge (capital); **5, 7, 10** Union, justice, confidence (motto); **7, 5** Pelican State (nickname); **7, 5, 7** eastern brown pelican (bird).

lounge 3 lie; **4** flop, idle, laze, loaf, loll, rest; **5** relax; **6** lollop *UK*, parlor, saloon, slouch; **7** recline; PHRASES: **6, 4** living room, ~ suit *UK*; **6, 6** ~ lizard.

louse 3 nit; **4** chat, crab; **6** cootie, isopod, psylla; **7** psyllid; **9** booklouse; PHRASES: **3, 3** sow bug; **4, 5** wood ~. *See also* **insects**

lousy 4 mean; **5** awful; **6** rotten, stupid; **7**

abysmal, useless; **8** dreadful; **9** miserable, worthless; PHRASES: **6-4** second-rate.

lout **3** oaf, yob *UK*; **4** boor, slob, thug; **5** ocker *UK*, rowdy, tough, yahoo, yobbo *UK*; **7** bruiser, gorilla, hoodlum, ruffian; **8** hooligan; **9** roughneck; PHRASES: **5, 3** bully boy.

loutish **4** rude, wild; **5** crude, rough, rowdy; **6** coarse, oafish; **7** boorish, uncouth, yobbish; **8** impolite, thuggish; PHRASES: **3-4** ill-bred; **3-8** ill-mannered.

lovability **5** charm; **6** appeal, beauty, charms; **8** coquetry; **10** allurement, amiability, endearment, likability; **11** adorability, enchantment, lovableness; **12** agreeability, desirability; PHRASES: **3, 6** sex appeal; **7, 4** winning ways. *See also* **lovable**

lovable **4** sexy; **5** sweet; **6** cuddly, divine, lovely; **7** angelic, likable, popular, winning, winsome; **8** adorable, alluring, charming, engaging, graceful, huggable, kissable, lovesome, pleasing, seraphic, tempting; **9** appealing, beautiful, beguiling, congenial, desirable, endearing, seductive; **10** attractive, caressable, compatible, cuddlesome, enchanting, intriguing, loveworthy; **11** captivating, flirtatious, interesting.

love **1** O, X; **3** lou, nil; **4** Amor, Eros, Kama, like, lust, mush, pash; **5** adore, Agape, ardor, crush, Cupid, fancy *UK*, Freya, lovey *UK*, prize, shine, value, Venus; **6** admire, desire, esteem, fervor, liking, regard, relish, revere; **7** Astarte, charity, cherish, ecstasy, egotism, idolize, loyalty, respect, worship; **8** devotion, fondness, idolatry, treasure; **9** adoration, affection, Aphrodite, sentiment, transport; **10** admiration, appreciate, attachment, attraction, friendship, narcissism, patriotism, popularity; **11** bewitchment, enchantment, fascination, idolization; **12** uxoriousness; **13** compatibility, understanding; PHRASES: **2, 3** go for; **2, 5, 5** be crazy about; **4, 1, 5, 2** have a crush on, take a fancy to, take a shine to; **4, 1, 6, 2** take a liking to; **4, 2** dote on, take to, warm to; **4, 3** care for, fall for, feel for, long for; **4, 4** calf ~ *UK*, free ~, hold dear, ~ game *UK*, ~ knot, ~ life, ~ nest, ~ seat; **4, 4, 2** make much of; **4, 5** ~ apple, ~ child, ~ match; **4, 6** ~ affair, ~ letter, ~ potion; **4, 7** hero worship; **4, 8, 2** take pleasure in; **5, 4** puppy ~; **6, 7** fellow feeling *UK*; **6, 9** mutual affection; **7, 2** delight in; **7, 4** courtly ~; **7, 6** popular regard; **8, 4** cupboard ~ *UK*, maternal ~, parental ~,

paternal ~, Platonic ~; **9, 4** brotherly ~, Christian ~, spiritual ~. *See also* **loved one**

love (expressions of love) **3** hug, nip, pat; **4** buss, kiss, ogle, peck, poke, wink; **5** clasp, goose, grope, pinch, smack; **6** caress, cuddle, fondle, nibble, nuzzle, stroke, tickle; **7** embrace, footsie, groping, hugging, kissing, necking, petting, smacker, squeeze; **8** bundling, cuddling, flattery, fondling, lovebite, nuzzling, spooning, tickling; **9** caressing, embracing, smooching, smoodging, snuggling, squeezing; **10** enfoldment, osculation; **13** blandishments; PHRASES: **4, 3** bear hug; **4, 3, 6** slap and tickle; **4, 4** fond look; **4, 5** soft words; **5, 4** sweet talk; **5, 8** sweet nothings; **6, 4** French kiss, sheep's eyes; **6, 5** loving words; **7, 5** honeyeyed words.

love (in love) **6** bitten, caught, hooked; **7** smitten; **8** besotted; PHRASES: **3, 2** set on; **3, 5** mad about; **4, 2** fond of, gone on, keen on *UK*, sold on; **4, 5** nuts about, wild about; **5, 2** stuck on, sweet on; **5, 4** taken with; **5, 5** crazy about; **6, 2** wedded to; **8, 2** attached to, enamored of; **10, 4** infatuated with.

love (make love) **4** ball, mate; **6** couple; **7** cohabit; **8** copulate; **9** fornicate; PHRASES: **4, 4, 3, 4** have one's way with; **5, 4** sleep with; **5, 6** sleep around; **5, 8** sleep together.

loveability *See* **lovability**

loveable *See* **lovable**

love affair **5** amour, fling; **6** affair; **7** liaison, romance; **8** adultery, espousal, intrigue; **9** amourette, betrothal, cuckoldry, seduction; **10** engagement, flirtation, infidelity; **12** entanglement, relationship; **14** unfaithfulness; PHRASES: **3, 3, 3, 5** the old old story; **5-5** hanky-panky; **6, 1, 5** ménage à trois; **7, 8** eternal triangle; **9, 5** forbidden fruit.

love apple **6** tomato.

lovebird **10** budgerigar.

loved one **2** jo; **3** hon, pet; **4** babe, baby, dear, doll, duck, hero, idol, lamb, love; **5** angel, chick, deary, ducky, honey, lover, lovey *UK*, sugar; **6** cherub, cookie, cosset, future, poppet *UK*, sweets; **7** beloved, darling, dearest, heroine, petkins, sweetie; **8** favorite, gorgeous, intended, lambkins, mistress, precious, snookums, sweeting; **9** betrothed, sweetkins, valentine; **10** honeybunch, preference, sweetheart; **11** chickabiddy *UK*; PHRASES: **4, 4** baby doll, soul mate, true love; **4-4, 3** blue-eyed boy; **4, 5** dear heart, kept woman *UK*; **4-6, 3** fair-haired boy; **4-7** well-beloved; **5-2-2** bride-to-be; **5, 2, 4, 3** apple of one's eye; **5, 2, 4, 4** light of one's life; **5, 5** honey child; **6, 7** dearly beloved; **7, 3** sweetie pie; **7, 4** matinée idol; **8, 3** teacher's pet.

love-in-idleness 5 pansy.

lovely 6 pretty; **7** perfect; **8** gorgeous, pleasant; **9** agreeable, beautiful, wonderful; **10** attractive, delightful; PHRASES: **4-7** good-looking.

love nest 5 bower, harem; **6** zenana; **7** boudoir; **8** seraglio; **9** gynaeceum; PHRASES: **5, 2, 5** bower of bliss; **6, 3** bridal bed; **6, 5** bridal suite; **6, 8** woman's quarters; **7, 7** nuptial chamber; **9, 5** honeymoon suite.

lover 2 jo; **3** fan; **4** beau, bird, date, gill, girl, lass, vamp, wolf; **5** catch, fella, flame, flirt, Romeo, sheik, swain, wooer; **6** adorer, escort, fiancé, fiancé(e), gigolo, lecher, masher, squire, steady, suitor; **7** admirer *UK*, amorist, captive, fiancée, gallant, goddess, groupie, pursuer, seducer; **8** Casanova, cavalier, conquest, coquette, Dulcinea, follower, Lothario, mistress, paramour; **9** Amaryllis, boyfriend, dreamboat, inamorata, libertine, temptress, womanizer; **10** aficionado, girlfriend, sweetheart; **11** philanderer, teenybopper; **12** heartbreaker; PHRASES: **3, 4** Don Juan; **3, 5, 5** the other woman; **4-6** gold-digger, lady-killer; **4-9** hero-worshiper; **5, 3** dream man, young man *UK*; **5, 4** blind date, dream girl; **5, 5** heart throb, sugar daddy; **5, 6** femme fatale, skirt chaser, sweet potato, woman chaser; **6, 3** ladies' man. *See also* **loved one**

lovers 9 lovebirds; **11** turtledoves; PHRASES: **4, 3, 7** Hero and Leander; **4, 5** soul mates; **5, 3, 5** Paris and Helen; **5, 3, 6** Romeo and Juliet; **7, 3, 5** Daphnis and Chloe.

loving 4 fond, kind; **5** loyal; **6** tender; **7** amative, amorous, devoted; **8** amicable, attached, faithful, friendly, motherly, paternal, platonic, uxorious; **9** agapistic, brotherly, Christian, fraternal, patriotic; **10** charitable; **11** sentimental, sympathetic; **12** affectionate; **13** demonstrative.

lovingness 7 emotion, feeling; **9** sentiment; **11** romanticism; **12** lovelornness, lovesickness; **14** sentimentality, susceptibility; PHRASES: **6, 7** tender feeling. *See also* **loving**

low 1 B; **3** moo, sad; **4** base, bass, blue,

down, mean, soft; **5** basal, below, cheap, crude, dwarf, lowly, neath, prone, quiet, short, small, squat, under; **6** humble, little, scanty, scarce, skimpy, smutty, sparse, stumpy, subway, sunken, supine, vulgar; **7** abysmal, beneath, ignoble, lowered, shallow, stooped, stunted; **8** couchant, crouched, downward, dwarfish, inferior, profound, stooping; **9** contralto, crouching, décolleté, depressed, flattened, prostrate, reclining, recumbent, underfoot; **10** dispirited, downstairs, underneath; **11** underground; PHRASES: **3, 4** ~ blow, ~ down, ~ mass, ~ tech, ~ tide; **3, 6** ~ church, ~ comedy; **3, 7** ~ profile; **3, 9** ~ countries; ~ frequency; **4, 3** laid ~; **4, 4** knee high; **5, 4** ankle high; **6-5** single-story. *See also* **low-voiced**

lowbrow 7 popular; **10** philistine; **11** undemanding; PHRASES: **4-6** mass-market.

lower 3 cow, dim, dip; **4** drop, vail; **5** abase, abate, frown, glare, gloom, scowl; **6** bottom, darken, debase, demean, demote, lowest, nether, reduce, worsen; **7** deflate, degrade, depress, devalue, flatten; **8** decrease, inferior, relegate; **9** subdorsal, subjacent, submental, subscript, underlaid, undermost; **10** bottommost, condescend, hypodermic, subclavian, subcranial, subglottal, suborbital, underlying; **11** deteriorate, hypogastric, infracostal, subaxillary, subcortical, subscapular; **12** subabdominal, subauricular, subcutaneous; PHRASES: **3, 3** lay low; **3, 4** lay down, let down, put down, set down; **4, 4** take down; **5, 4** knock down, knock flat, knock over; **6, 4** squash flat.

lowest point 3 ebb; **5** nadir; PHRASES: **3, 4** ebb tide, low tide; **3, 5** low water; **4, 4** neap tide.

lowland 3 lea; **4** flat, inch, mead, moor, vale, veld; **5** campo, field, flats, heath, level, llano, plain, range, weald; **6** campos, hollow, meadow, pampas, polder, steppe, strath *UK*, valley; **7** hillock, hummock, prairie, savanna; **8** moorland, piedmont; **9** foothills, grassland, subalpine, submerged; **10** depression, submontane; PHRASES: **2, 3, 5** at sea level; **3, 6** the plains; **5, 3, 5** below sea level; **5, 5** flood plain; **5, 6** water meadow *UK*; **6, 4** bottom land, grouse moor; **8, 5** alluvial plain.

lowly 3 low; **4** base, mean, poor; **5** plain, small; **6** common, humble; **7** obscure; **8** ordinary, plebeian; PHRASES: **3-2-3-4** run-of-the-mill; **3-4** low-born, low-bred; **7-5** working-class.

lowness 8 lowering; 9 reclining; 10 coarseness, flattening, recumbency; 11 inferiority, prostration; 13 subordination. *See also* **low**

low thing 4 base, foot; 5 flats, floor; 6 bottom, cellar; 7 bedrock, subbase, subsoil; 8 basement, bungalow, flatties *UK*, subfloor, subgrade, underlay; 9 dachshund, subcortex, submucosa, subscript, underbody, underfelt *UK*, underpart, underside, undersoil; 10 subjacency, substratum, underbelly, underneath; 11 décolletage, hypolimnion; 12 undersurface; 13 undercarriage; PHRASES: 3-3, 8 low-cut neckline; 3-4 mid-rise; 3, 5 low heels; 6, 7 nether regions.

low-voiced 3 low; 5 faint, husky, muted; 6 hoarse; 7 cracked, muffled; 8 breaking, croaking, mumbling; 9 inaudible, murmuring, muttering, whispered; 10 whispering.

loyal 4 leal *UK*, true; 5 sworn; 6 docile, trusty; 7 devoted, staunch, willing; 8 amenable, constant, faithful, obedient; 9 compliant, dedicated, patriotic, steadfast, tractable; 10 dependable, respectful, submissive; 11 deferential, reverential, sycophantic; PHRASES: 4-4 true-blue.

loyalty 6 comity, fealty; 7 service; 8 devotion, fidelity; 9 adherence, constancy; 10 allegiance, patriotism; PHRASES: 4, 5 good faith. *See also* **loyal**

lozenge 7 rhombus.

LP 4 disc, disk *UK*; PHRASES: 6, 5 Labour Party.

LR 10 lawrencium.

LSD 4 acid, drug (lysergic acid diethyamide); 5 sugar.

LT 5 light; 10 Lieutenant.

LTD 7 limited.

LU 8 lutetium.

lubricant 3 oil, wax; 4 lard, soap, spit; 5 mucus, oleum; 6 butter, grease, saliva, tallow; 7 beeswax, spittle, synovia; 8 glycerin, graphite, lenitive, mucilage, plumbago, silicone, soothing; 9 emollient; 10 lubricator; 11 lubricating, lubricative, lubricatory; 12 antifriction; 13 lubricational; PHRASES: 4, 6 cart grease; 5, 3 motor oil; 5, 4 black lead; 11, 3 lubricating oil.

lubricate 3 oil, wax; 6 grease, lather; 7 lubrify; 11 glycerinate, glycerinize, glycero-

late, lubricitate.

lubrication 4 lube; 6 oiling; 8 greasing; 9 sleekness, slickness; 10 smoothness; 11 nonfriction; 12 slipperiness.

lubricator 6 oilcan; PHRASES: 6, 3 grease gun.

lucent *See* **luminous**

lucerne 7 alfalfa.

lucid 4 sane; 5 clear, sober; 6 limpid; 7 shining; 8 luminous, rational; 10 articulate; 11 luminescent, translucent; PHRASES: 4-6 well-spoken; 5-6 clear-headed; 6, 6 compos mentis; 6-7 silver-tongued, smooth-tongued.

luck 3 hap, lot; 4 cass, fate; 5 break, favor, fluke; 6 amulet, chance; 7 bonanza, destiny, fortune, godsend, potluck, success; 8 talisman, windfall; 9 adversity, blessings; 10 misfortune, providence; 11 ominousness, serendipity, unluckiness; 14 auspiciousness; PHRASES: 1, 4, 4 a good hand; 3, 2, 4 run of ~; 3, 4 bad ~ *UK*, ill ~, ill wind; 3, 7 ill fortune; 4, 2, 3, 4 ~ of the draw; 4, 4 evil star, good ~, hard ~, lady ~; 4, 7 good fortune; 5, 2, 7 wheel of fortune; 5, 4 blind ~, lucky shot, tough ~; 5, 5 Midas touch; 5, 6 lucky strike; 6, 2, 4 stroke of ~; 6, 3 chance hit; 6, 3, 6 slings and arrows; 6, 4 rotten ~; 7, 4 halcyon days; 7, 6 winning streak.

lucky 3 apt; 5 fluky, happy; 6 chance, timely; 7 blessed, charmed; 9 fortunate, opportune; 10 accidental, auspicious, fortuitous, propitious, successful; 12 providential; 13 serendipitous; PHRASES: 4, 3 grab bag; 5, 5 ~ charm; 5, 6 ~ mascot, ~ streak; 6-4 heaven-sent.

ludicrous 4 daft, zany; 5 droll, inane, nutty; 6 absurd; 7 asinine, bizarre, comical, fatuous, foolish, idiotic, risible; 8 bathetic, farcical; 9 eccentric, laughable, senseless, whimsical; 10 ridiculous; 12 preposterous.

lug 3 tow, tug; 4 bear, drag, draw, haul, hump, pull, tote; 5 carry; 6 schlep; 9 manhandle, transport.

luggage 3 kit; 4 bags, gear; 5 cases, traps, trunk; 6 things; 7 baggage, dunnage; 8 suitcase; 10 belongings; 11 impedimenta; 13 paraphernalia; PHRASES: 3, 3, 7 bag and baggage.

lugubrious *See* **mournful**

lull 4 calm; 5 pause, quiet; 6 soothe; 7 quieten *UK*, silence; 8 reassure; 9 stillness; PHRASES: 6, 4 settle down.

lumber 4 land, logs, plod; 5 clump; 6 burden, hobble, impose, planks, trudge; 7 scalage, shamble; 8 encumber, stumpage; 10 lumberyard; PHRASES: 5, 4 weigh down.

luminance 1 L.

luminous 3 lit; 5 aglow, lucid, vivid; 6 bright, lucent; 7 glowing, lambent, radiant, shining; 8 dazzling, gleaming, lustrous; 9 brilliant; 11 fluorescent, resplendent; 12 incandescent; 13 scintillating; 14 phosphoresecnt.

lump 3 wad; 4 cake, clod, clot, curd, hunk, mass, rock, slab, wart; 5 block, chunk, clump, stone; 6 endure, growth, nugget; 8 coagulum, tolerate; 9 aggregate; 10 concretion; 12 conglomerate, protuberance.

lunar 5, 4 ~ year; 5, 5 ~ month; 5, 6 ~ module; 5, 7 ~ eclipse.

lunatic See **mad, mad person**

lunge 4 dive, grab, leap, stab; 5 swing, swipe; 6 attack, spring, thrust.

lurch 4 list, reel, rock, sway, tilt; 5 pitch; 6 totter; 7 stagger, stumble.

lure 4 bait, coax; 5 charm, decoy, siren, snare, tempt; 6 allure, entice, seduce; 7 ensnare; 8 enthrall; 9 captivate, fascinate, hypnotize, mesmerize, tantalize; PHRASES: 4, 2 draw in, lead on; 5, 4 siren song.

lurid 4 loud; 5 gaudy, juicy, vivid; 6 bright, garish; 8 colorful, explicit, shocking; 11 sensational.

luscious 5 candy, juicy, moist, sweet; 9 delicious, succulent.

lush 3 fat; 4 rich, rife; 5 fresh, plush; 6 fecund; 7 booming, fertile, verdant; 8 abundant, prolific, thriving; 9 alcoholic, bountiful, exuberant, luxuriant, plenteous, plentiful; 10 productive, prosperous; 11 flourishing.

lust 5 ardor; 6 libido; 7 lechery, passion; 9 carnality, randiness, sexuality; 10 satyriasis; 11 nymphomania; 13 concupiscence, lecherousness; 14 libidinousness; PHRASES: 3, 4 the hots; 3, 5 hot pants; 6, 4 sexual urge; 6, 6 carnal desire, sexual desire; 6, 8 sexual appetite.

lustful 3 hot; 4 sexy; 5 horny, randy; 9 fanciable UK, lecherous, seductive; 10 lascivious, libidinous; 11 provocative, titillating; 12 concupiscent; PHRASES: 3, 3 hot for.

lustrous 5 glacé, shiny; 6 glassy, glossy, haloed, pearly; 8 gleaming, polished, shimmery; 9 burnished, pearlized; 10 glistening, iridescent, opalescent, shimmering.

Luxembourg 1 L.

luxuriant 4 lush, rank, rich, rife; 5 dense, thick; 6 fecund, jungly; 7 fertile, profuse, rampant, riotous, teeming, verdant; 8 abundant, prolific, thriving; 9 exuberant, overgrown, plenteous, plentiful.

luxuriate 4 bask; 5 revel; 6 wallow; 7 delight, indulge.

luxurious 4 posh; 5 grand, plush, ritzy, swish; 6 classy, costly; 7 opulent; 8 decadent, palatial, splendid; 9 epicurean, sumptuous; 10 hedonistic; 11 comfortable, extravagant, magnificent; PHRASES: 2, 4 de luxe; 4-9 self-indulgent.

luxury 4 ease; 5 extra, frill, plush, ritzy, treat; 7 comfort; 8 opulence; 10 indulgence, refinement; 12 extravagance, magnificence; 13 sumptuousness; PHRASES: 3, 2, 6 lap of ~; 4, 2, 6 life of Reilly; 5, 4 dolce vita.

Lviv 4 Lvov, Lwów; 7 Lemberg.

lycopod 4, 4 club moss.

lying 5 doggo, libel, prone; 6 shifty, supine; 7 evasive, fibbery, fibbing, perfidy, perjury, slander; 8 couchant, sprawled; 9 accumbent, ambiguous, decumbent, prostrate, reclining, recumbent, romancing, sprawling; 10 defamation, mendacious, mythomania, perfidious, procumbent, pseudology, untruthful; 11 fabrication, forswearing; 12 equivocating, flimflamming, spreadeagled, storytelling; 13 falsification; 14 mendaciousness, propagandizing; PHRASES: 4, 3 flat out; 4, 4 face down.

lynx 6 bobcat; 7 caracal.

lyric 6 poetic; 7 melodic, musical, tuneful; 8 inspired, romantic; 9 emotional; 10 expressive, harmonious.

lyssa 6 rabies.

M

M 4 male, mass, mega-, mile; **5** meter; **6** minute; **7** million; **8** Monsieur, motorway *UK*.

MA 6 mother; PHRASES: **6, 2, 4** Master of Arts.

macabre *See* **gruesome**

macadamia 10, 3 Queensland nut.

machination 8 intrigue; **11** demagoguery, obfuscation; **12** manipulation.

machine 3 car, fax, gin; **4** loom, tool, unit; **5** gizmo, robot; **6** device, dynamo, engine, shaper; **7** grinder, turbine; **8** aircraft, computer; **9** apparatus, appliance, automaton, clockwork, dynamotor, generator, machinery, mechanism, motorbike, wheelwork; **10** instrument, motorcycle; **11** contraption, contrivance; PHRASES: **4, 7** slot ~; **6, 6** Wankel engine; **6, 7** adding ~, kidney ~, sewing ~; **7, 3** ~ gun; **7, 4** ~ part, ~ shop, ~ tool; **7, 7** milling ~, vending ~, washing ~.

machine part 3 cam, rod; **4** axle, belt, bush, gear, head; **5** crank, motor, shaft, wheel; **6** clutch, pulley; **7** bearing, journal; **8** coupling; **9** component, gearwheel; **10** hairspring, mainspring; PHRASES: **4, 3, 5** nuts and bolts; **4, 7** ball bearing; **6, 7** roller bearing.

machine tool 3 saw; **5** drill, lathe; **6** planer, shaper; **7** grinder; PHRASES: **4, 3** band saw; **6, 5** engine lathe, turret lathe; **6, 7** boring machine; **7, 5** capstan lathe; **7, 7** milling machine; **8, 3** circular saw; **8, 7** drilling machine; **10, 4** multipoint tool.

machinist 6 driver, fitter, minder *UK*; **7** artisan; **8** engineer, mechanic, operator; **9** craftsman, mechanist, operative; **10** technician; **11** mechanician *UK*; PHRASES: **4-4** tool-user; **6, 6** manual worker; **7-6** machineminder.

macho 5 manly; **6** virile; **9** masculine;

PHRASES: **3-7** red-blooded.

macho man 4 jock, stud; **7** caveman; **9** muscleman; PHRASES: **2-3** he-man.

mackerel 4 scad; **9** scombroid; PHRASES: **5, 8** horse ~; **8, 3** ~ sky; **8, 5** ~ shark; **8, 6** ~ breeze.

mackerel shark 9 porbeagle.

maculation 4 spot; **5** fleck, speck; **6** blotch, macula, splash; **7** freckle, speckle; **8** dappling, mottling; **9** birthmark, brindling, freckling, speckling, stippling; **10** spottiness; **11** blotchiness; PHRASES: **10, 4** strawberry mark.

mad 3 ape; **5** angry, crazy, rabid; **7** furious. *See also* **insane**

mad cow disease 3 BSE.

madden 5 anger; **6** dement, enrage; **7** unhinge; **9** infuriate, unbalance; PHRASES: **5, 2, 3, 4** drive up the wall; **5, 3** drive mad *UK*; **5, 5** drive crazy.

made 5 built, fecit; **6** molded, styled, turned; **7** modeled; **8** composed, produced, tailored; **9** fashioned; **11** constructed; PHRASES: **3-2** set-up.

madness *See* **insanity**

Madras 7 Chennai; PHRASES: **5, 4** Tamil Nadu.

maelstrom *See* **tumult**

maestro *See* **genius**

Mafia 3 mob; **4** capo; **7** camorra; **9** godfather.

magazine 3 mag, rag; **4** clip, Lady, Time, zine; **5** Cosmo, store, Vogue; **6** glossy, Tatler, weekly; **7** arsenal, Esquire, fanzine, Fortune, Harper's, monthly, Playboy; **8** clipping, Newsweek; **9** clipsheet; **10** newsweekly, periodical; **12** Cosmopolitan; PHRASES: **3, 6** New Yorker; **4, 5** back issue;

4, 6 Utne Reader; **4, 8** news ~; **6, 4** Vanity Fair; **6, 5** Mother Jones; **6, 8** girlie ~; **8, 7** Atlantic Monthly; **8, 10** National Geographic.

magenta 7 fuchsin.

magic 3 art; **7** conjury, sorcery; **8** illusion, wizardry; **10** witchcraft; **11** enchantment, legerdemain; PHRASES: **5, 3** ~ eye *UK*; **5, 5** ~ charm, ~ spell, ~ trick; **5, 6** ~ carpet, ~ circle; **5, 8** ~ mushroom. *See also* **magical**

magical 6 occult; **9** beguiling, enchanted; **10** bewitching, enchanting, entrancing; **11** captivating, necromantic; **12** spellbinding, supernatural, thaumaturgic.

magician 4 whiz; **7** Houdini; **8** conjuror *UK*; **9** performer; **11** entertainer, illusionist; PHRASES: **6, 6** escape artist. *See also* **witch, wizard**

magistrate 2 JP; **4** beak, cadi, doge; **5** judge, jurat, reeve; **6** aedile, archon, bailie *UK*, censor, consul, syndic; **7** bailiff, podesta, praetor, prefect; **8** quaestor; **9** landdrost, proconsul; **10** propraetor.

magnanimity 8 altruism, fairness; **10** generosity; **11** benevolence; **12** generousness.

magnanimous 4 kind; **6** kindly; **8** generous; **9** bountiful; **10** benevolent, charitable; **13** philanthropic.

magnate 3 VIP; **5** baron, mogul, nabob; **6** tycoon; PHRASES: **3, 4** big shot; **3, 6** big cheese.

magnet 4 coil; **5** focus; **7** ferrite; **8** solenoid; **9** loadstone, lodestone, magnetite; **13** electromagnet; PHRASES: **3, 6** bar ~, pot ~; **4, 6** coil ~; **9, 6** permanent ~.

magnetic 7 dynamic; **10** attractive; **11** charismatic; **13** gravitational; PHRASES: **8, 3** ~ ink; **8, 4** ~ card, ~ disk, ~ flux, ~ pole, ~ tape; **8, 5** ~ field, ~ north; **8, 7** ~ compass; **11, 4** geomagnetic pole.

magnetism 2 it, od; **4** pull; **5** gauss, tesla; **7** maxwell; **8** charisma; **10** attraction; PHRASES: **7, 5** drawing power, pulling power *UK*.

magnificence 5 glory; **7** majesty; **8** grandeur, opulence, splendor; **12** resplendence. *See also* **magnificent**

magnificent 4 fine; **5** grand, noble, regal, royal; **6** lavish, lordly, superb; **7** awesome, opulent; **8** fabulous, glorious, gorgeous, imposing, majestic, splendid, stunning, wondrous; **9** excellent, marvelous, sumptuous; **10** impressive, prodigious, stupendous;

11 resplendent; **12** breathtaking; PHRASES: **3-9** awe-inspiring.

magnify 5 boost; **7** enlarge, greaten; **8** heighten, increase; **10** exaggerate; PHRASES: **4, 2** blow up.

magnitude 4 size; **6** amount, degree, extent, weight; **8** enormity; **9** greatness; **10** importance; **11** consequence; **12** significance.

magot 7, 3 Barbary ape.

magpie lark 6 peewee.

maid 4 amah, char; **5** bonne *UK*; **6** drudge, skivvy, tweeny; **7** abigail, servant; **8** domestic, milkmaid; **9** housemaid; **10** parlormaid; **11** chambermaid, kitchenmaid; **12** scullerymaid; PHRASES: **4, 2, 3, 4** ~ of all work *UK*; **5, 4** lady's ~.

maiden 1 M; **4** girl, maid, miss; **5** unwed; **6** single, virgin; **7** initial; **8** spinster; **9** inaugural; PHRASES: **4, 6** iron ~; **6, 4** ~ name, ~ over *UK*; **6, 6** ~ flight, ~ voyage.

maidenhair 6 ginkgo; PHRASES: **10, 4** ~ fern, ~ tree.

mail 3 fax; **4** post *UK*, send, spam; **5** armor, email, nixie, telex; **6** letter, mailer; **7** address, airmail, express; **8** indicium, maildrop; **9** readdress; **10** mailperson, registered; **14** correspondence; PHRASES: **3, 4** air ~, fan ~, sea ~; **3-7** air-express; **4, 4** bulk ~, ~ drop, ~ shot, ~ slot, note card; **4, 5** ~ order; **4-6, 6** dead-letter office; **5, 4** chain ~, snail ~; **5, 5** rural route; **5, 8** poste restante; **6, 4** postal card; **6, 5, 5** postal money order; **6, 7** postal service; **7, 4** metered ~; surface ~; **7, 5** postage meter; **7, 6** sorting office *UK*; **7, 7** mailing address; **7, 8** express delivery, general delivery, special delivery; **8, 4** overseas ~; **8-6, 6** returned-letter office; **8, 8** recorded delivery; **9, 4** certified ~, forwarded ~; **10, 4** electronic ~, registered ~; **13, 4** international ~.

mailbag 7 postbag *UK*; **8** mailsack.

maim 4 hurt, lame; **5** wound; **6** injure; **7** disable; **8** mutilate; **9** disfigure.

main 3 sea; **4** foam, head; **5** brine, briny, chief, major, ocean, prime; **7** central, leading, primary; **8** foremost; **9** principal; **10** overriding; **11** predominant; PHRASES: **4, 4** ring ~ *UK*; **5, 4** water ~; **7, 4** Spanish ~.

Maine 2 ME; **7** Augusta (capital); **9** chickadee (bird); PHRASES: **1, 4** I lead (motto); **4, 5** Pine Tree State (nickname); **5, 4** white pine (tree); **5, 4, 4, 3, 6** white pine cone and tassel (flower).

maintain 3 say; **4** aver, avow, keep; **5** argue, claim, state; **6** allege, assert, insist, uphold; **7** protest, sustain; **8** continue, preserve; PHRASES: **2, 2** go on; **4, 2** keep on, keep up; **5, 2** carry on.

maintenance 4 care; **6** repair, upkeep; **7** alimony, support; **9** allowance, provision, servicing.

majestic 5 regal, royal; **6** solemn; **7** stately.

majesty 2 HM, SM; **4** pomp; **8** grandeur, maestoso; **11** sovereignty.

major 3 key; **4** main; **5** chief, grave; **7** crucial, serious, weighty; **8** foremost; **9** important; **11** significant, substantial.

majority 4 mass, more, most; **7** greater; **8** eighteen; **9** adulthood; PHRASES: **4, 4, 4** more than half; **5, 5** lion's share; **7, 4** greater part.

make 4 earn, form; **5** amass, build, erect, force, forge; **6** coerce, compel, create; **7** compile, compose, concoct, fashion, prepare, produce; **8** assemble; **9** construct, fabricate, structure; PHRASES: **3, 2** set up; **3, 8** put together; **4, 2** ~ up; **5, 8** piece together.

makeshift 7 stopgap; **9** temporary; **10** improvised; PHRASES: **2, 3** ad hoc; **4-2** make-do.

make up 3 fix; **4** form; **5** hatch, paint; **6** devise, invent, powder, redden; **7** compose, concoct, prepare; **8** complete; **9** construct, fabricate; **10** constitute; PHRASES: **2, 3** ad lib; **4, 2** tart up *UK*.

make-up 8 warpaint; **11** composition, greasepaint; **12** constitution. *See also* **cosmetics**

making *See* **creation**

malady *See* **sickness**

malaise 6 unease; **7** anxiety, disease, illness; **8** disorder, disquiet, sickness; **9** condition; **10** discontent; **15** dissatisfaction.

malaria 8 paludism; PHRASES: **5, 5** marsh fever, swamp fever.

male 1 M; **2** he, Mr; **3** boy, dom, Esq, guv *UK*, guy, him, lad, man, ram, Sir, son, Sri; **4** Adam, babu, boyo, chap *UK*, cock, cove, dude, gent, Jock *UK*, Lord; **5** blade, bloke *UK*, Jimmy *UK*, joker, macho, manly, sahib, señor, swain, youth; **6** father, fellow, gaffer *UK*, geezer, guvnor *UK*, Johnny, master, mister, senhor, signor, squire; **7** chappie *UK*, esquire, himself, laddish *UK*, rooster; **8** monsieur; **9** gentleman, masculine; PHRASES: **3, 3** gay dog; **4-4, 3** blue-eyed boy; **5, 4** young buck, young Turk; **6, 3** little boy.

male animal 2 ox; **3** dog, hog, ram, tup; **4** boar, buck, bull, colt, hart, jack, lion, stag, stud; **5** steer, tiger; **7** bullock, gelding; **8** stallion; PHRASES: **3, 3** tom cat; **5, 4** billy goat.

male bird 3 cob; **4** cock; **5** capon, drake; **6** gander; **7** gobbler, peacock, rooster; **8** cockerel; **9** blackcock, heathcock; **11** chanticleer; PHRASES: **3, 6** tom turkey; **4-5** cock-robin; **4-7** cock-sparrow; **5-4** bubby-jock; **6, 4** guinea cock.

malediction 3 hex; **4** jinx; **5** curse, spell; **7** malison; **8** anathema; **9** damnation; **11** imprecation; PHRASES: **3, 6** ill wishes; **6, 5** voodoo spell.

malefactor 3 yob *UK*; **4** crim *UK*, hood, lout, thug; **5** bully, crook, felon, Judas, rogue, snake, viper, yobbo; **6** abuser, baddie, gunman, killer, mugger, outlaw, racist, rapist, sadist, sinner, tyrant, vandal; **7** butcher, hoodlum, mobster, traitor, villain; **8** assassin, betrayer, bullyboy, criminal, evildoer, gangster, hooligan, larrikin *UK*, murderer, offender, torturer; **9** cutthroat, desperado, miscreant, phansigar, roughneck, terrorist, wrongdoer; **10** blackguard, lawbreaker, malfeasant; PHRASES: **3, 3** bad egg, bad lot *UK*, con man, hit man; **4-7** back-stabber; **4, 8** mass murderer; **6, 6** serial killer; **6-7** double-crosser; **7, 3** hatchet man; **8, 6** contract killer.

malevolence 4 evil, hate; **5** spite; **6** enmity, hatred, malice; **7** cruelty; **8** deviltry, loathing, misandry, misogyny; **9** animosity, hostility, malignity; **10** antagonism, malignance; **11** maleficence, misanthropy; PHRASES: **3, 4** bad will, ill will; **3, 5** bad blood; **4, 6** evil intent. *See also* **malevolent**

malevolent 3 bad; **4** evil, mean; **5** nasty; **6** malign, racist, wicked; **7** baleful, hateful, malefic; **8** menacing; **9** malicious, malignant; **10** pernicious, tyrannical; **11** persecuting; PHRASES: **4-6** evil-minded; **7, 4** meaning harm.

malfunction 4 fail, stop; **5** break, crash, error, fault, seize, stall; **6** glitch; **7** misfire; **8** overheat; PHRASES: **2, 5** go wrong; **3, 4** not work; **4, 3** conk out; **4, 5** lose power; **4, 7** stop running; **5, 2** seize up.

Mali 3 RMM; PHRASES: **6, 5** French Sudan.

malice *See* **malevolence**

malicious 5 catty, cruel, snide; **6** bitchy. *See also* **malevolent**

malign 6 defame, vilify; **7** harmful; **8** negative; **9** criticize, denigrate, disparage.

malinger 5 dodge, shirk; PHRASES: **4, 6** play truant; **5, 3, 4** swing the lead.

malleable 4 soft; **5** bendy *UK*; **6** supple; **7** pliable; **8** biddable, flexible; **9** compliant; **11** acquiescent, manipulable; **14** impressionable.

malt 4, 7 ~ extract *UK*, ~ whiskey.

maltreat *See* **hurt**

mammal 7 primate; **8** Mammalia; **9** marsupial, monotreme; **13** monotrematous; PHRASES: **4-7** warm-blooded; **5, 2, 7** study of mammals. *See also* **animal**

mammalian characteristic 3 dug, fur, pap; **4** hair, milk, teat, wool; **5** mamma, spine, udder; **6** nipple, pelage; **8** mammilla; PHRASES: **5, 5** scent gland, sweat gland; **7, 5** mammary gland; **9, 5** sebaceous gland.

man 1 M; **2** he; **3** cat, dad, dog, dom, don, Esq, guv *UK*, guy, him, men, pop, Sir, son, Sri; **4** Adam, babu, boyo, chap *UK*, crew, gent, homo, male, mate *UK*, pawn; **5** bloke *UK*, piece, sahib, señor, staff, uncle; **6** father, fellow, godson, guvnor *UK*, hombre, Johnny, master, mister, nephew, patron, people, senhor, signor; **7** brother, esquire, husband, junkman, padrino, servant, widower; **8** monsieur; **9** godfather, graybeard, patriarch; **11** grandfather; **12** househusband; PHRASES: **3, 2, 3, 5** ~ of the world; **3, 3** con ~, hit ~, old boy, old git, old ~; **3-3-4, 3** rag-and-bone ~; **3, 5, 4** the human race; **3, 6** M~ Friday, old buffer, old codger, old duffer, old geezer; **4, 2, 3** Isle of M~; **4, 3** best ~; **5, 3** fancy ~, front ~, inner ~, straw ~; **6, 3** anchor ~, family ~, ladies' ~, muffin ~; **7, 3** hatchet ~, leading ~; **8, 3** medicine ~, Piltdown ~, straight ~; **11, 3** Neanderthal ~. *See also* **chess, boy's names**

manacle 4 iron; **5** chain; **6** fetter, hamper, hinder, impede; **7** shackle; **9** constrain.

manage 3 run; **4** cope, lead, rule; **5** nurse; **6** direct, govern, handle, police; **7** conduct, control, oversee, proctor, succeed; **8** maneuver, minister, organize, regulate; **9** influence, supervise; **10** administer, invigilate, manipulate; **11** orchestrate, superintend; PHRASES: **4, 3, 5** hold the reins; **4, 4, 2** take care of; **4, 5** keep order, look after; **5, 4** watch over.

manageable 5 handy; **6** doable, viable, wieldy; **8** feasible, possible; **9** adaptable; **10** achievable; **11** practicable; **12** controllable; **13** untroublesome; PHRASES: **4, 2, 3** easy to use; **4-8** user-friendly.

management 4 care, tact; **5** power, reins, skill; **6** agency, charge, policy, regime; **7** cabinet, conduct, control, regimen, running; **8** handling, managing, ministry; **9** authority, direction, economics, husbandry; **10** governance, government, regulation; **11** bureaucracy, housewifery, maintenance, maneuvering, proctorship, secretariat, stewardship, supervision; **12** housekeeping, manipulation, organization; **13** orchestration; **14** administration, responsibility; PHRASES: **3-10** man-management; **8-6** decision-making.

manager 3 CEO; **4** boss, exec, head, jefe, whip; **5** chief; **7** foreman, proctor, steward; **8** director, overseer; **9** caretaker, executive; **10** controller, manageress, supervisor; **13** administrator; **14** superintendent; PHRASES: **4, 7** bank ~ *UK*, farm ~, line ~ *UK*; **5, 4** chief whip *UK*, party whip; **5, 7** store ~.

Mandarin 7 satsuma; **8** official; **10** bureaucrat; PHRASES: **5, 7** civil servant; **6, 7** public servant; **8, 4** M~ duck; **8, 6** M~ collar.

mandate 5 order; **6** assign, decree, tenure; **7** command; **8** instruct; **9** authority, authorize, directive; **10** permission; **13** authorization; PHRASES: **4, 2, 6** term of office.

mandible 7 jawbone.

mandrake 3, 5 May apple.

mane 4 hair; **5** crest.

maneuver 4 move, plan, plot, ploy, push, ruse, wile; **5** dodge, drive, pilot, steer, trick; **6** castle, gambit, handle, jockey, manage, scheme, tactic, wangle, zigzag; **7** control; **8** contrive, engineer, exercise, navigate; **9** stratagem; **10** subterfuge; **11** gerrymander, machination.

mangle 4 mash; **5** crush, smash, twist; **7** contort.

manhandle *See* **shove**

mania 3 fad; **5** craze; **7** complex, passion; **8** fixation; **9** agromania, fetishism, obsession, pyromania; **10** dipsomania; **11** fascination, kleptomania, megalomania, nymphomania; **12** onomatomania.

manic 4 wild; **6** raving; **7** berserk, frantic;

8 demented, frenetic, frenzied; **9** delirious; **10** hysterical.

manifest 4 show; **5** clear, overt, plain; **6** appear, arrant, evince, marked, patent, public, reveal; **7** blatant, certain, evident, glaring, notable, obvious, salient, uncover, visible; **8** apparent, declared, disclose, flagrant, infamous, palpable; **9** disclosed, inventory, prominent, uncovered; **10** noticeable, pronounced; **11** accentuated, conspicuous, highlighted, unconcealed, undisguised; **12** identifiable, ostentatious, recognizable, unmistakable; **13** incontestable; PHRASES: **2, 3, 7** on the surface; **2, 4, 4** in full view; **3, 3, 2, 3** for all to see; **3-8** eye-catching; **4-7** self-evident; **5, 2, 8** clear as daylight; **5-7** stark-staring.

manifestation 4 omen, show, sign; **5** proof, token; **6** avatar, signal; **7** display, symptom; **8** epiphany, evidence, syndrome; **9** highlight, occultism, promotion, publicity; **10** apparition, appearance, disclosure, exhibition, exposition, expression, indication, revelation, uncovering; **11** incarnation; **14** representation; **15** materialization, personification.

manifestly 2, 3, 4 in the open; **2, 3, 4, 2, 2** on the face of it; **2, 4, 5** in open court; **2, 5, 8** in broad daylight; **3, 2, 3, 4** out in the open. *See also* **manifest**

manifesto 6 policy; **7** program; **11** declaration; **12** proclamation.

manifold *See* **various**

manikin 3 guy *UK*; **4** doll; **5** model, robot; **6** puppet; **7** snowman; **9** automaton, scarecrow; **10** marionette; PHRASES: **7, 5** tailor's dummy.

Manila hemp 5 abaca.

manipulate 3 rub, use; **4** cook, spin, work; **5** knead, tempt; **6** doctor, fiddle, handle, juggle; **7** control, falsify, massage, mislead; **8** maneuver; **10** substitute; **11** gerrymander; PHRASES: **3, 2, 2** put up to; **3, 3, 4** aid and abet; **4, 2** play on; **5, 8** exert pressure; **6, 4** tamper with; **7, 2** operate on.

manipulator 7 masseur; **8** masseuse, operator; **9** intriguer, osteopath; **10** maneuverer; **12** chiropractor; PHRASES: **4-6** spin-doctor; **6, 6** puppet master.

manner 3 way; **4** kind, sort, type; **5** style; **6** method; **7** bearing, conduct; **8** behavior, demeanor; PHRASES: **11** comportment.

mannerly *See* **well-behaved**

manners 7 culture; **8** breeding, elegance, protocol; **9** etiquette, formality; **10** convention, refinement; **11** correctness; **14** sophistication; **6-5** savoir-faire.

man-of-war bird 7, 4 frigate bird.

manor 4 hall; **5** patch, villa; **6** estate; **8** district.

mansion 4 seat; **5** house; **6** castle, palace; **7** chateau.

mantle 4 duty, role; **5** layer; **8** function, position; **14** responsibility. *See also* **cloak**

manual 5 guide; **8** handbook; **9** guidebook; **11** enchiridion; **12** instructions; PHRASES: **3-2** how-to; **4, 2, 4** hand to hand; **4-8** hand-operated; **5-8** touch-operated.

manually 2, 4 by hand. *See also* **manual**

manufacture 4 make; **5** build; **6** create, making; **7** concoct, process; **8** assembly, building, engineer; **10** processing; **11** development, fabrication; **12** construction; PHRASES: **4, 10** mass production; **5, 8** heavy industry, light industry.

manufactured 8 handmade, homemade, homespun; **9** synthetic; **10** artificial; PHRASES: **3-4** man-made; **4-8** mass-produced; **6-4** tailor-made; **6-5** custom-built; **7-4** machine-made. *See also* **manufacture**

manuscript 4 copy, text; **6** script; **8** document.

many 1 C, D, K, L, M; **4** lots, tons; **5** heaps, loads, piles; **6** masses *UK*; **7** umpteen; **8** hundreds, majority, manifold, millions, numerous; **9** countless, thousands; PHRASES: **1, 3** a lot; **3, 1, 3** not a few.

map 2 OS; **4** plan, plat; **5** atlas, chart, globe; **6** layout; **7** diagram, explore; **8** describe; **9** cartogram, mapmaking; **10** projection; **11** cartography; PHRASES: **1, 2, 1** A to Z; **4, 3** road ~, star ~; **4, 4** town plan; **4, 5** flow chart; **5, 4** floor plan; **5, 5** world atlas; **6, 3** relief ~, sketch ~, street ~; **6, 4** ground plan; **8, 3** treasure ~; **9, 3** political ~.

maple 4 acer.

maquis 7 thicket; **8** garrigue; **10** resistance; **11** underground.

mar 4 flaw; **5** spoil; **6** blight, deface, impair; **7** blemish, distort.

march 4 file, hike, pace, slog, step, trek, walk, yomp *UK*; **5** rally, stamp, stomp, strut, tramp, troop; **6** parade, picket, stride, trudge; **7** process, protest; **8** progress; **9** goosestep; **13** demonstration; PHRASES: **4, 5**

slow ~; **5, 4** M~ hare, ~ past; **5, 5** quick ~ *UK*; **6, 5** forced ~.

margin 3 gap, rim; **4** curb, edge, side; **5** bound, bourn, brink, verge; **6** border, fringe, leeway; **8** boundary, latitude, littoral; **9** periphery; **10** difference; PHRASES: **6, 6** profit ~.

marijuana 3 hay, kef, kif, pot, tea; **4** dope, hash, hemp, herb, leaf; **5** bhang, dagga *UK*, ganja, grass, skunk; **6** spliff; **7** hashish; **9** skunkweed; **10** sinsemilla; PHRASES: **4, 4** mary jane; **5, 5** wacky backy.

marine 2 RM *UK*; **5** jolly; **11** leatherneck. *See also* **sailor**

marjoram 7 oregano; PHRASES: **5, 8** sweet ~.

mark 1 M; **2** DM, MB, NB; **3** dot, ink, see; **4** blot, dash, dent, heed, line, logo, nick, note, scar, smut, star, tick, weal *UK*, welt; **5** badge, brand, caret, colon, comma, label, point, score, scuff, smear, speck, stain, tally, trait, watch, wheal *UK*; **6** accent, bruise, crease, hyphen, macron, notice, period, stigma, streak, tattoo, umlaut; **7** blemish, cedilla, feature, lentigo, observe, scratch, splodge *UK*, splotch; **8** asterisk, cicatrix, dieresis *UK*, hallmark, insignia; **9** diacritic, diaeresis *UK*, watermark; **10** apostrophe; **14** characteristic; PHRASES: **3, 5, 4** low water ~; **4, 4** hash ~, kite ~, pock ~; **4, 5, 4** high water ~; **5, 3** bull's eye; **5, 4** bench ~, black ~; **8, 4** question ~; **9, 4** quotation ~; **11, 4** punctuation ~.

marked 5 clear, plain; **6** dented, doomed, pitted, signal; **7** decided, flecked, glaring, labeled, obvious, scabrid, scarred, spotted, stained; **8** distinct, manifest, scabrous, striking; **9** blemished; **10** noticeable, pronounced.

marker 4 sign; **6** symbol; **7** pointer; **9** indicator; **10** indication.

market 2 EC, EU; **4** fair, mart, sell, shop, souk; **5** agora, forum, store; **6** bazaar, peddle; **7** auction, promote, traffic; **8** carnival, exchange; **10** Smithfield; **11** marketplace; **12** Billingsgate; PHRASES: **4, 6** fish ~, flea ~, meat ~, open ~; **4, 8** corn exchange *UK*; **5, 3** wheat pit; **5, 4** horse fair, truck farm; **5, 6** black ~, money ~, share ~, stock ~; **6, 4** ~ town; **6, 5** ~ cross, ~ price, ~ value; **6, 6** buyer's ~, common ~, Covent Garden, Fulton Street, ~ garden, street ~; **6, 8** ~ research; **7, 4** auction room; **7, 6** farmers' ~, Orchard Street, seller's ~; **8, 6** shopping center; **9, 4** Petticoat Lane; **10, 4** Portobello Road.

marmot 7, 3 prairie dog.

marquetry 6 boulle; **8** intarsia; PHRASES: **4, 5** wood inlay.

marriage 5 match, union; **6** bigamy, bridal; **7** exogamy, marital, nuptial, trigamy, wedding, wedlock; **8** alliance, endogamy, levirate, monogamy, polygamy, polygyny, shivaree, wifehood; **9** matrimony, polyandry; **11** conjugality, deuterogamy, husbandhood, matrimonial, mesalliance, misalliance; **13** intermarriage, miscegenation; PHRASES: **3, 5** one flesh; **4, 7** holy wedlock; **4, 9** holy matrimony; **5, 3, 4** tying the knot; **5, 8** civil ~, mixed ~; **6, 5** wedded bliss; **7, 5** married state; **8, 3** ~ bed; **8, 5** conjugal bliss; **8, 6** ~ bureau *UK*.

marriageable 6 nubile; **7** engaged; **8** eligible, plighted, promised; **9** affianced, betrothed; PHRASES: **2, 3** of age.

marriage settlement 3 dot; **5** dower, dowry; **7** aliment, alimony, portion; **8** palimony; **9** allotment; **11** maintenance; PHRASES: **5, 5** bride price; **5, 7** child support; **8, 7** marriage portion.

married 1 M; **3** one; **6** hooked, joined, paired, united, wedded; **7** coupled, hitched, spliced; **8** espoused, newlywed; **9** partnered; **12** honeymooning; PHRASES: **2, 3, 3** Mr and Mrs; **3, 2, 4** vir et uxor; **3, 3, 4** man and wife; **3, 5** one flesh; **3, 5, 6** the happy couple; **3, 6, 4** the bridal pair; **5, 3, 4** Darby and Joan; **7, 6** ~ couple.

married man *See* **husband**

married woman *See* **wife**

marrow 4 core, soul; **5** heart; **6** spirit; **7** essence.

marry 3 wed; **4** join; **5** elope, rewed, unite; **6** couple; **7** betroth, espouse, remarry; **8** afiance, mismarry; **10** intermarry; **11** miscegenate; PHRASES: **3, 1, 2** say "I do"; **3, 3, 4** tie the knot; **3, 4** run away; **3, 7** get hitched, get spliced *UK*; **4, 2, 3, 5** lead to the altar; **4, 3, 6** take the plunge; **6, 3** become one; **6, 4, 5** plight one's troth; **6, 6** commit bigamy.

marsh 3 bog, fen, mud, wet; **4** carr *UK*, fern, flat, mire, moor, ooze, quag, sudd; **5** bayou, delta, playa, swamp; **6** morass, salina, slough, sludge; **7** fenland *UK*, mudhole, saltpan; **8** quagmire, wetlands; **9** marshland, quicksand, swampland; PHRASES: **3, 4** mud flat; **3, 10** the Everglades; **4, 3** peat bog; **4, 4** salt flat; **4, 5** salt ~; **5, 3** ~ gas, ~ hen; **5, 4** ~

hawk; **5, 5** flood plain, ~ fever; **5, 6** ~ mallow, ~ orchid; **5, 7** ~ harrier; **5, 8** ~ marigold.

marshal 5 order; **6** deputy; **7** arrange, officer; **8** assemble, position; PHRASES: **3, 7** law officer.

marsh mallow 4, 6 rose mallow.

marsh marigold 7 cowslip; PHRASES: **3, 5** May blobs.

marshy 4 oozy; **5** boggy, fenny, muddy, soggy; **6** sludgy, slushy, swampy; **8** squelchy; **11** waterlogged.

marsupial 3 roo; **5** bilby, koala, quoll, yapok; **6** cuscus, kowari, numbat *UK*, possum, wombat; **7** dasyure, dibbler, dunnart, opossum, potoroo *UK*, wallaby; **8** kangaroo, wallaroo; **9** bandicoot, phalanger, thylacine.

martial 5 armed, brave, naval; **7** warlike; **8** militant; **9** bellicose, combative, mercenary, soldierly; **10** pugilistic; **11** belligerent; **12** gladiatorial.

martial art 4 judo; **5** kendo; **6** aikido, boxing, karate; **8** capoeira; PHRASES: **2, 3** ba gua; **2-5** ju-jitsu; **3, 3** t'ai chi; **3, 3, 5** t'ai chi chuan; **3, 4-2** tae kwon-do; **4, 2** kung fu; **4-6** kick-boxing.

martyr 5 Alban; **6** suttee; **7** Stephen; **9** Catherine, Sebastian.

marvel 4 gape, gasp, gawk, gawp; **5** sight, stare; **6** wonder; **7** miracle; **9** sensation, spectacle; **10** phenomenon; PHRASES: **3, 2, 1, 8** one in a thousand; **3, 4, 4** rub one's eyes; **3-6** eye-opener; **5, 9** quite something; **6, 2** goggle at.

marvelous 3 fab; **7** amazing, awesome; **8** fabulous, splendid, wondrous; **9** fantastic, ineffable, wonderful; **10** astounding, miraculous, remarkable, stupendous, surprising; **11** astonishing, magnificent.

Maryland 2 MD *UK*; **9** Annapolis (capital); PHRASES: **3, 4, 5** Old Line State (nickname); **5, 3** white oak (tree); **5-4, 5** black-eyed Susan (flower); **5, 5, 7, 5** Manly deeds womanly words (motto); **9, 6** baltimore oriole (bird).

mascara 8 eyeblack.

masculine 4 male; **5** macho, manly; **6** boyish, virile; **7** mannish.

masculinity 8 machismo, virility; **11** laddishness.

mash *See* **squash**

mask 4 hide, veil; **5** cloak, cover, vizor; **6** domino, façade, screen, veneer, vizard; **7** conceal, varnish; **8** disguise; **9** dissemble, whitewash; **10** camouflage, masquerade; PHRASES: **3, 4** gas ~; **4, 4** life ~; **5, 2** dress up, touch up; **5, 4** death ~; **6, 4** oxygen ~; **6-8** window-dressing; **8, 4** stocking ~.

masonry 4 tile; **5** brick, grout, slate, stone; **6** ashlar, cement, gravel, header, marble, mortar, pavior; **7** granite; **9** brickwork, limestone, sandstone, stonework; **11** bricklaying, freemasonry; PHRASES: **5, 5** terra cotta; **6, 5** breeze block; **8, 6** Portland cement.

mass 1 M; **3** gob, wad; **4** body, bulk, cake, clod, clot, dune, glob, gobs, heap, hill, hunk, lump, pile, size; **5** block, chunk, clump, drift, group, knoll, missa, mound, stack, wodge *UK*; **6** bundle, dollop, weight; **7** density, hillock, requiem; **8** assemble, majority, mountain, sandbank, sediment; **9** snowdrift; **10** embankment; PHRASES: **6, 2, 4** center of ~; **8, 7** relative density, specific gravity.

Massachusetts 2 MA; **4** Mass; **6** Boston (capital); **9** mayflower (flower); PHRASES: **2, 3, 5, 2, 4, 5, 3, 5, 4, 5, 7** By the sword we seek peace, but peace only under liberty (motto); **3, 3, 5** (Old) Bay State (nickname); **5-6, 9** black-capped chickadee (bird); **8, 3** American elm (tree).

massacre 4 kill, slay; **6** murder, pogrom; **7** butcher, carnage; **8** genocide; **9** bloodbath, slaughter.

massage 3 pet, rub; **4** work; **5** knead; **6** caress, facial, fondle, pummel, stroke; **7** Jacuzzi *tm*, rolfing, rubdown, Shiatsu; **8** kneading, stroking; **10** manipulate; **11** reflexology; **12** massotherapy; **13** physiotherapy *UK Can*; PHRASES: **3, 4** rub down; **4, 3** iron out; **6, 7** facial ~; **8, 7** physical therapy.

masseur 8 masseuse; **10** beautician; **14** massotherapist.

massive 4 huge; **5** bulky, heavy, solid; **7** immense, weighty; **8** colossal, enormous, gigantic.

mass media 5 media, press, radio; **9** magazines; **10** newspapers, television; **11** telecasting; **12** broadcasting, cablecasting; **13** communication; PHRASES: **5-6** cable-vision; **5, 10** cable television.

mass, parts of 5 credo, kyrie; **6** gloria; **7** sanctus; **10** benedictus; PHRASES: **5, 3** agnus dei; **5, 7** kyrie eleison.

master 2 MA; **3** ace, dan, old, sir; **4** boss, guru, head, lead, lord; **5** bwana, crush, elder, laird, learn, liege, owner, sahib, tutor; **6** defeat, expert, govern, manage, mentor, squire, subdue; **7** command, conquer, control, husband, maestro, skipper, teacher; **8** dominate, nobleman, original, overcome, overlord, overseer, seigneur, vanquish; **9** landowner, overpower, patriarch; **10** aristocrat, proprietor; **PHRASES: 3, 2, 3, 5** man of the house; **4, 2, 3, 5** lord of the manor; **4, 3, 6** lord and ~; **4, 6** past ~; **5, 4** liege lord; **5, 6** grand ~; **6, 3** ~ key; **6, 4** ~ copy, ~ race; **6, 6** harbor ~; **6, 7** ~ bedroom, ~ builder; **8, 6** question ~ *UK*.

masterful 6 lordly; **8** coercive; **9** imperious, magistral; **10** commanding, dominating; **11** controlling, dictatorial, domineering, magisterial, overbearing; **13** authoritarian, authoritative. *See also* **masterly**

masterly 3 ace; **4** deft; **5** adept, crack; **6** adroit, expert; **7** skilled; **8** peerless, skillful, virtuoso; **9** brilliant, excellent; **10** consummate, proficient; **12** accomplished; **PHRASES: 5-4** first-rate.

mastermind 4 plan; **5** brain; **6** brains, devise; **7** oversee; **8** engineer, organize; **9** architect, organizer; **10** instigator.

masterpiece 3 hit; **4** coup, feat; **5** jewel, trump; **6** beauty; **7** classic; **9** fireworks; **10** brilliance, perfection; **11** collectible; **12** masterstroke; **PHRASES: 4, 2, 3** work of art; **4, 2, 5** tour de force; **4-6** best-seller; **4-7** chef-d'oeuvre; **5, 2, 2, 5** crème de la crème; **5, 4** objet d'art; **6, 2, 6** stroke of genius; **6, 4** magnum opus.

masterstroke 4 coup; **9** brainwave; **11** inspiration; **PHRASES: 4, 2, 5** tour de force; **6, 4** bright idea.

masthead 4 flag.

masturbation 7 onanism; **PHRASES: 4-5** self-abuse.

mat 3 rug; **4** knot; **5** doily; **6** carpet, tangle; **7** bathmat, coaster, doormat, entwine; **10** intertwine; **PHRASES: 5, 3** place ~, table ~ *UK*.

match 3 fit, tie; **4** bout, game, meet, pair, twin; **5** agree, equal, final, fusee, light, tally, vesta; **6** double, rubber; **7** conform, contest, fixture *UK*, lucifer, playoff, striker; **8** friendly, marriage; **9** semifinal; **10** coordinate, correspond; **11** competition, counter-

part; **12** quarterfinal; **13** international; **PHRASES: 4, 5** love ~, slow ~, test ~ *UK*; **4-5** look-alike; **6, 5** safety ~; **8, 5** slanging ~ *UK*.

matchmaker 6 broker; **8** shadchan *Yiddish*; **PHRASES: 2-7** go-between; **6, 6** dating agency *UK*; **6, 7** dating service; **8, 6** computer dating, marriage broker, marriage bureau *UK*; **8, 7** marriage adviser.

mate 3 Eve; **4** oppo, wife; **6** spouse; **7** consort, husband, partner; **8** roommate, teammate; **9** bedfellow, classmate; **PHRASES: 4, 4** soul ~; **5, 4** first ~; **6, 4** second ~; **7, 4** running ~.

material 4 real; **5** solid; **6** bodily, carnal, fabric; **7** earthly, fleshly, natural, sensual, somatic, worldly; **8** clinical, concrete, corporal, embodied, palpable, physical, tangible; **9** corporeal, empirical, incarnate, objective, substance; **11** substantial; **14** spatiotemporal; **PHRASES: 2, 3, 5** in the flesh; **2, 5, 3, 5** of flesh and blood. *See also* **materials**

materialist 7 chemist, Marxist, realist; **8** consumer; **9** collector, physicist, scientist; **10** capitalist; **12** geophysicist.

materialize 5 arise, reify; **6** appear, become, emerge, evolve, unfold; **7** realize, surface; **9** actualize; **10** factualize; **PHRASES: 2, 4** be born; **4, 5** come about, take shape.

materials 3 fur, net, oil, ore, rep; **4** calf, clay, coal, felt, food, fuel, hemp, hide, lace, lamé, lawn, meat, mull, roan, rope, sand, silk, skin, vair, wood, wool; **5** abaca, adobe, baize, board, cloth, crape, crash, denim, epoxy, fiber, fitch, gauze, genet, glass, grist, gunny, kapok, laine, latex, linen, lisle, lurex, means, metal, moire, ninon, nylon, orlon, piqué, plush, print, rayon, satin, scrim, serge, sisal, stave, stick, stock, straw, stuff, suede, surah, tammy, toile, tulle, tweed, twill, union, voile; **6** alpaca, angora, armure, bengal, berber, burlap, burnet, byssus, calico, camlet, canvas, castor, catgut, chintz, chrome, coburg, cotton, crepon, cubica, damask, diaper, dimity, domett, dowlas, ermine, fabric, faille, fodder, frieze, gurrah, gypsum, kersey, lampas, lumber, madras, matter, melton, merino, mohair, mulmul, muslin, napery, oxford, pongee, poplin, ribbon, rubber, samite, sateen, saxony, shoddy, staple, tartan, Teflon™, thatch, timber, tinsel, tissue, tricot, tussah, tusseh, vellum, velure, velvet, vicuna, wincey *UK*, woolen *UK*; **7** acrylic, alamode, bagging, batiste, batting, bunting, cambric, caracal, caracul, challis, chamois, cheviot, chiffon, cowhide, curbing, delaine, doeskin, dornick, drabbet *UK*, drugget, durance, duvetyn, esparto, fishnet, fitchew, flannel, Formica™, foulard, fustian, galatea, gingham, grogram, guipure, hessian, holland, jaconet, kashmir, kidskin, leather, leghorn, mineral, miniver, morocco, nankeen, netting, oilskin, organdy, organza, ottoman, paisley, paragon, percale, pighide, pigskin, plastic, plywood, polymer, raccoon, rawhide, sacking, saffian, satinet, suiting, taffeta, textile, ticking, tiffany, tussore, uranium, velours, viscose, viyella, webbing, woollen, worsted; **8** armozeen, armozine, barathea, barracan, baudekin, bobbinet, buckskin, calfskin, capeskin, cashmere, chambray, chenille, corduroy, coteline, cretonne, elements, eolienne, florence, goathide, goatskin, gossamer, homespun, kolinsky, lambskin, lustrine, marabout, marcella, marocain, moleskin, moquette, muslinet, musquash, nainsook, oilcloth, organdie, sarcenet, sarsenet, sealskin, shagreen, shantung, shirting, tapestry, tarlatan, tarletan, toilinet, toweling, whipcord, zibeline; **9** astrakhan, bengaline, bombazine, brocatell, calamanco, celluloid, cellulose, charmeuse, cottonade, crepoline, crinoline, curbstone, farandine, gabardine, georgette, grenadine, grosgrain, haircloth, horsehair, horsehide, huckaback, longcloth, lustering, Naugahyde, organzine, parchment, patchwork, petersham, petroleum, polyamide, polyester, polythene *UK*, resources, sackcloth, satinette, sharkskin, sheephide, sheepskin, snakeskin, stockinet, Styrofoam, substance, swansdown, tarpaulin, velveteen, worcester; **10** anthracite, balbriggan, barleycorn *UK*, broadcloth, circassian, components, essentials, fiberglass, horsecloth, mousseline, seersucker, toilinette, winceyette *UK*; **11** cheesecloth, dreadnought, everlasting, flannelette, leatherette, marquisette, overcoating, polystyrene; **12** constituents, fluorocarbon, polyethylene, polyurethane; **13** petrochemical, polypropylene, thermoplastic; PHRASES: **3-2-3, 5** end-to-end cloth; **3, 4** jap silk, pig iron, raw silk; **3, 5** box cloth, wax cloth; **3, 6** cut velvet, fur fabric, the basics; **3-6, 6** sea-island cotton; **3, 7** hop sacking; **3, 9** raw ~; **3, 10** the essentials; **4, 2, 4** peau de soie; **4, 2, 5** drap de berry; **4, 3** fake fur; **4, 4** hard coal, pure

silk, shot silk, soft coal, wild silk; **4, 5** bark cloth, book linen, sail cloth; **4, 6** aida canvas, book muslin; **4, 7** napa leather; **5, 2, 3, 4** fruit of the loom; **5, 2, 4** toile de jouy; **5, 3** crude oil, metal ore; **5, 4** china clay, china silk; **5, 5** dress linen, grass cloth, Irish linen, pilot cloth, terry cloth; **5, 6** Irish poplin, panne velvet; **6, 4** angola yarn, berlin wool, bouclé yarn; **6, 4, 5** camel's hair cloth; **6, 5** bomber cloth, canton crepe, canton linen, carbon fiber, cotton crepe, diaper cloth, harris tweed, scotch plaid, sponge cloth, waffle cloth; **6, 6** cotton velvet, croisé velvet, double damask, glazed chintz; **6, 7** cotton flannel, cotton worsted, patent leather; **6-7** linsey-woolsey; **7, 3** natural gas; **7, 4** arabian lace, brushed wool, potter's clay; **7, 5** brushed rayon, caracul cloth, cavalry twill *UK*, crinkle cloth, slipper satin, viscose rayon; **7, 6** crushed velvet; **7, 8** ostrich feathers, turkish toweling; **8, 4** duchesse lace, shetland wool; **8, 5** brittany cloth, casement cloth; **8, 6** algerian stripe, american cotton, egyptian cotton, jacquard fabric; **8, 7** shirting flannel; **9, 5** broadtail cloth, honeycomb cloth, shepherd's plaid, synthetic resin; **9, 6** parachute fabric; **10, 4** bituminous coal; **10, 5** embroidery linen, tattersall check, tattersall plaid.

material world 6 nature, weight; **7** density, gravity; **8** solidity; **9** existence; **10** corporeity; **11** corporality, materiality, palpability, tangibility; **12** concreteness, corporeality; **14** substantiality; PHRASES: **4, 2, 6** laws of nature; **4, 5** real world; **8, 5** physical being, physical world; **9, 5** empirical world.

mathematical 8 analytic, integral; **9** algebraic, geometric; **10** analytical *UK*; **11** algebraical, algorithmic, geometrical, logarithmic, statistical, topological; **12** arithmetical, differential; **15** trigonometrical.

mathematical terms 3 sum; **4** bill, toll; **5** image, limit, range, score, tally, total, whole; **6** amount, domain, factor; **7** mapping, operand, product; **8** argument, codomain, function, operator, quantity, residual, totaling; **9** aggregate, remainder, summation; **10** arithmetic, difference, functional; **11** calculation, composition, computation; **14** transformation; PHRASES: **4, 4** plus sign; **4, 8** beta function, step function; **5, 4** equal sign, minus sign; **5, 6, 8** least common multiple; **5, 6, 11** least common denominator; **5, 8** gamma function; **6-2** adding-up; **6,**

6 double digits; **6, 7** common divisor; **7, 4** radical sign; **7, 8** inverse function, logical operator; **8-2** counting-up; **8, 4** division sign, integral sign; **8, 6, 7** greatest common divisor; **9, 7** repeating decimal; **10, 5** inflection point; **11, 4** implication sign; **11, 6** significant digits.

mathematician 7 actuary; **8** geometer; **9** geodesist; **10** accountant, algebraist; **12** geometrician, psephologist, statistician; **13** arithmetician; PHRASES: **4-6** book-keeper.

mathematics 4 math, sums *UK*; **5** maths *UK*; **7** algebra, figures, numbers; **8** addition, calculus, counting, division, equation, figuring, geometry, mathlete, numeracy; **9** algorithm, inversion, logarithm, numbering, reckoning, reduction; **10** arithmetic, involution, numeration, statistics; **11** calculation, computation, convolution, enumeration, integration, measurement, permutation, precalculus, subtraction; **12** trigonometry; **14** multiplication, transformation; **15** differentiation; PHRASES: **3, 11** new ~; **4, 11** pure ~.

matinée 5, 4 early show; **7, 4** ~ coat *UK*, ~ idol.

matriarchy 8 gynarchy; **9** gynocracy.

matrimonial 6 bridal, wifely; **7** marital, nuptial, spousal, wedding; **8** conjugal, marriage; **9** connubial, husbandly.

matrimony *See* **marriage**

matrix 3 row; **4** mold; **5** array, order; **6** column; **7** pattern; PHRASES: **4, 6** null ~; **6, 6** square ~; **8, 6** diagonal ~, identity ~.

matter 3 ion, pus; **4** atom, body, mass; **5** cells, earth, flesh, issue, meson, monad, quark, stuff, thing, topic; **6** affair, corpus, fabric, factor, phlegm, photon, plasma, proton; **7** concern, element, isotope, mineral, neutron, nucleon, nucleus, quantum, subject; **8** business, electron, material, molecule; **9** materials, situation, substance; **10** protoplasm; **11** materiality; PHRASES: **3, 4, 8** the four elements; **3, 5-6** the nitty-gritty; **4, 1, 10** make a difference; **4, 2, 5** unit of being; **4, 3, 5** nuts and bolts; **4, 6** back ~, gray ~; **5, 3, 5** flesh and blood; **5, 6** front ~, prime ~, white ~; **5, 9** first principle, solid substance; **7, 6** organic ~, subject ~; **8, 5** building block; **8, 7** chemical element, physical element.

mature 4 aged, grow, ripe; **5** adult, grown, ready, ripen; **6** flower, mellow; **7** develop, rounded; **8** seasoned; **11** responsible; PHRAS-ES: **2, 4, 5** in full bloom; **2, 5** in bloom; **4, 2** grow up; **4, 2, 3** come of age; **4, 2, 8** come to maturity; **4-5** full-grown; **5-2** grown-up; **5, 5** fully grown; **5, 7** fully fledged, reach manhood.

maturity 3 age; **5** bloom; **7** manhood; **9** adulthood, womanhood; PHRASES: **6-2-3** coming-of-age. *See also* **mature**

maul *See* **attack**

maverick *See* **nonconformist**

mavis 6 thrush; **8** throstle.

maxim 3 law, mot *UK*, saw; **4** rule; **5** adage, axiom, gnome, moral, motto, order, truth; **6** byword, cliché, dictum, mantra, saying, slogan, truism; **7** bromide, epigram, epithet, formula, precept, proverb; **8** aphorism, apothegm, epigraph; **9** principle, watchword, witticism; **11** catchphrase; PHRASES: **3, 8** old chestnut; **5, 2, 6** words of wisdom; **5, 6** stock phrase; **9, 6** hackneyed phrase.

maximum 4 most; **5** limit; **6** utmost; **7** ceiling, highest; **8** greatest; PHRASES: **3, 6** top figure; **5, 5** upper limit; **8, 6** greatest extent.

May 3, 3 M~ day; **3, 5** M~ apple, M~ queen; **3, 6** M~ beetle; **3, 7** M~ blossom.

maybe *See* **perhaps**

may tree 8 hawthorn.

maze 3 web; **4** mess; **6** jumble, muddle, warren; **7** network; **9** confusion, intricacy, labyrinth.

MB 6 doctor; **8** millibar.

MC 5 emcee; **7** compere *UK*; PHRASES: **8, 5** Military Cross.

MD 6 doctor; PHRASES: **5, 4** right hand (French: main droite).

ME 6, 4 Middle East.

meadow mouse 4 vole.

meadow saffron 6, 6 autumn crocus.

meager 5 small; **6** slight, sparse; **10** inadequate; **12** insufficient.

meal 3 tea; **4** bran, corn, fare, feed, meat; **5** flour, grain, grist, grits, lunch, snack; **6** brunch, buffet, dinner, farina, groats, picnic, repast, supper, tiffin; **7** takeout; **8** luncheon; **9** breakfast, collation, elevenses; **11** refreshment; PHRASES: **2, 6** TV dinner; **3, 3, 3** tea for two; **3-4, 4** sit-down ~; **3, 5** bag lunch, box lunch; **4, 2, 3** bite to eat; **4, 3** fish fry, high tea *UK*; **4, 3, 4** surf and turf; **4-5** blue-plate, pack-lunch; **4, 6** fork supper; **5, 3**

cream tea *UK*; **5, 4** light ~; **5, 5** light lunch; **5, 6** shore dinner; **5-6, 4** three-course ~; **6, 4** square ~; **6, 5** family style, Sunday lunch; **6, 6** finger buffet *UK*; **7, 4** evening ~; **7-4** covered-dish; **9, 3** afternoon tea; **9, 5** austerity lunch.

meal (have a meal) 3 sup; **4** dine, mess; **5** board, feast, graze, lunch, snack; **6** picnic; **7** banquet, partake; **9** breakfast; PHRASES: **3, 3** eat out; **4, 3** dine out; **5, 4, 4** break one's fast; **5, 5** break bread.

mealy 6 floury; **7** crumbly; **11** farinaceous; **12** furfuraceous.

mean 4 near, tell; **5** close, imply; **6** denote, intend; **7** average, betoken, connote, purport, signify, suggest; **8** indicate, midpoint; **9** designate, represent, symbolize; PHRASES: **3, 2** get at; **3, 2, 2** add up to; **3, 2, 3** try to say; **3, 2, 5, 5** say in other words; **3, 6** get across; **3, 7, 3** put another way; **4, 2** hint at; **4, 2, 4** have in mind; **4, 4, 2** boil down to; **5, 2** drive at; **5, 3** stand for.

meander 4 roam, wind; **5** amble, snake; **6** ramble, wander, zigzag; PHRASES: **5, 3, 4** twist and turn.

meaning 4 gist, idea, pith; **5** drift, force, sense, tenor, value; **6** effect, import, matter, spirit; **7** bearing, essence, latency, message, purport; **8** coloring; **9** etymology, intention, reference, relevance, semantics, semiology, semiotics, substance; **10** definition, denotation, derivation; **11** connotation, equivalence, explanation, implication; **13** signification; **14** interpretation, meaningfulness; **15** intelligibility; PHRASES: **3, 3, 9** sum and substance; **4, 3, 5** nuts and bolts; **4, 8** idea conveyed; **4, 9** deep structure; **5-6** nitty-gritty; **7, 6** subject matter; **7, 8** message conveyed; **8, 4** semantic flow; **8, 7** semantic content.

meaningful 7 implied, pointed, special, telling; **8** allusive, eloquent, explicit, implicit, inferred, symbolic, telltale; **9** evocative, important; **10** denotative, expressive, figurative, indicating, indicative, monosemous, polysemous, purporting, suggestive, tattletale; **11** affirmative, allegorical, connotative, perspicuous, significant, unambiguous; **14** comprehensible.

meaningless 4 null; **5** banal, empty, inane, trite; **6** futile, hollow, trashy; **7** fatuous, foolish, invalid, trivial, vacuous; **9** hackneyed, illegible, illogical, pointless, senseless, sophistic; **11** ineffective, ineffectual,

unimportant; **13** platitudinous; **14** unintelligible.

meaninglessness 7 inanity, nullity, vacuity; **8** nonsense; **9** absurdity, amphigory, sophistry; **10** invalidity; **11** incoherence, irrelevance; **12** illegibility, illogicality, unimportance; **14** ineffectuality, insignificance. *See also* **meaningless**

means 3 way; **4** dint, mode, tool; **5** money, organ, power, skill, steps, tools; **6** agency, choice, course, device, manner, medium, method, remedy, resort; **7** ability, finance, process, vehicle; **8** facility, measures, recourse, resource; **9** appliance, expedient, knowledge, resources, technique; **10** capability, facilities, instrument, technology; **11** contrivance; PHRASES: **2, 3, 7** ad hoc measure; **2, 4, 2** by dint of; **2, 4, 2, 5** by hook or crook; **3, 2, 6** bag of tricks; **3, 11** the wherewithal; **4-3** know-how; **4, 3, 5** ways and ~; **5, 2, 3, 5** tools of the trade.

meant 7 implied, planned; **8** designed, destined, intended; **10** deliberate; **11** predestined.

measles 7 rubeola; **8** morbilli.

measurable 9 estimable, gaugeable, meterable; **10** assessable, calculable, computable, fathomable; **12** determinable, quantifiable.

measure 3 peg; **4** cost, mark, rank, rate, size, time; **5** assay, count, dance, gauge, grade, meter, order, plumb, probe, scale, score, sound, value, weigh; **6** assess, fathom, reckon, survey; **7** compare, compute; **8** appraise, estimate, evaluate, quantify; **9** admeasure, calculate, calibrate, criterion, determine; **10** proportion; **11** triangulate; **13** differentiate; PHRASES: **4, 2** size up; **4, 3** mark off, pace off. *See also* **dance**

measured 4 even, slow; **6** steady; **7** guarded, regular, stately, studied, uniform; **8** moderate, rhythmic; **9** dignified; **10** deliberate, rhythmical. *See also* **measure**

measurement 3 day, tot; **4** dose, hour, size, unit, week, year; **5** depth, month; **6** decade, height, metage, minute, radius, second, sizing; **7** breadth, century, geodesy, reading; **8** diameter, distance, lifetime; **9** appraisal, geodetics, metrology, valuation; **10** assessment, biometrics, estimation, evaluation, millennium, topography; **11** calculation, cartography, craniometry, mensuration; **12** oceanography; **13** approximation, triangulation; **14** quantification.

See also **weights and measures**

measure out 5 allot; 9 apportion; PHRAS-ES: 4, 3 dole out, mete out; 5, 3 share out, weigh out.

measurer 6 valuer; 7 actuary; 8 assessor, surveyor, valuator; 9 appraiser, estimator; 10 quantifier, timekeeper.

measuring instrument 3 log; 4 lead, line, rule; 5 chain, gauge, meter, ruler, scale; 6 needle, octant; 7 humidor, pointer, sextant, vernier; 8 calipers, dipstick, dividers, quadrant, udometer *UK*; 9 astrolabe, hydrostat, kymograph, milestone, Nilometer, yardstick; 10 hydrograph, hygrograph, hygrometer, hygroscope, protractor, vibrograph, vibroscope; 11 pluviometer, seismograph, seismometer, seismoscope; 12 oscillograph, oscillometer, oscilloscope, psychrometer; PHRASES: 1-6 T-square; 3, 6 set square, try square; 4, 4 foot rule, load line; 4, 5 rain gauge; 4, 7 echo sounder, tape measure; 5, 4 plumb line, steel rule; 6, 5 feeler gauge; 7, 5 Gunter's chain; 9, 3 measuring rod; 9, 5 graduated scale; 10, 5 calibrated scale.

measuring system 2 SI; 4 troy; 6 metric; 8 imperial; 11 avoirdupois.

meat 3 cut, ham; 4 beef, chop, duck, game, gist, goat, hare, lamb, loin, pâté, pith, pork, spam, veal; 5 bacon, brawn, flesh, fryer, goose, joint, liver, mince, offal, steak, tripe; 6 cutlet, faggot, flitch, gammon, grouse, haslet, kidney, mutton, oxtail, pigeon, rabbit, saddle, salami, tongue, turkey; 7 biltong, bologna, chicken, fatback, flanken, poultry, sirloin, venison; 8 braciola, chilidog, drumette, embutido, escalope, noisette, pastrami, pheasant, woodcock; 9 entrecote, middlings, partridge; 10 headcheese, liverwurst, sweetbread, tenderloin; 11 slumgullion; 12 chitterlings; 14 Braunschweiger; PHRASES: 3, 3 rib eye; 3, 4 red ~; 3, 5 top round; 4, 3 corn dog; 4, 4 side ~; 4, 5 cube steak; 4, 6 ~ locker; 4, 8 pig's trotters; 5, 3 daisy ham, lamb's fry; 5, 4 pope's nose, short ribs, white ~; 5, 5 shell steak, skirt steak, strip steak, Swiss steak; 6, 4 ground beef, ground ~, minced ~ *UK*; 6, 5 bottom round; 7, 4 boiling ~, chipped beef; 7, 5 buffalo wings; 7-5, 5 chicken-fried steak; 8, 4 luncheon ~; 8, 5 Canadian bacon; 9, 5 Delmonico steak, Salisbury steak.

meat dish 3 pie; 4 hash, stew; 5 broil, daube, grill, joint, kebab, pasty, roast; 6 burger, haggis; 7 goulash, rissole, sausage; 9 carbonade, casserole, fricassée, hamburger, meatballs; 10 beefburger; PHRASES: 3, 5 pot roast; 5, 5 mixed grill *UK*.

meat-eating 9 omophagic; 11 carnivorous; 13 cannibalistic; PHRASES: 5-6 flesheating.

meat substitute 3 soy, TVP; 4 soya, tofu; 5 Quorn *tm*; PHRASES: 4, 4 bean curd.

mecca 3 hub; 5 focus; 6 center, magnet; PHRASES: 5, 5 focal point.

mechanical 7 powered, robotic; 8 habitual; 9 automated, automatic, hydraulic, motorized; 10 electronic, mechanized; 12 computerized; PHRASES: 5-6 power-driven.

mechanism *See* **device**

MED 6 medium; 7 medical; 13 Mediterranean.

medal 3, 5 Air M~; 4, 5 Navy Cross; 5, 2, 5 M~ of Honor; 5, 3, 5 M~ for Merit; 6, 2, 5 Legion of Merit; 6, 4 Bronze Star, Silver Star; 6, 5 George Cross *UK*, Purple Heart; 8, 5 Airforce Cross, Military Cross, Victoria Cross; 11, 7 Meritorious Service; 12, 5, 2, 7 Presidential M~ of Freedom; 13, 7, 5 Distinguished Service Cross.

meddle 3 pry; 5 touch; 6 fiddle, pester, tamper, tinker; 7 intrude; 9 importune, interfere, interpose, interrupt, intervene; PHRASES: 4, 2 butt in; 4, 4, 4, 2 poke one's nose in.

meddler 3 pry, spy; 4 mole; 5 snoop; 6 gossip, voyeur; 7 stirrer *UK*; 8 busybody, quidnunc; 9 intriguer; 10 interferer; 12 troublemaker; 13 scandalmonger; PHRASES: 4, 3 Paul Pry; 4-4, 6 back-seat driver; 4, 6 nosy parker *UK*; 4-6 fuss-budget; 6-7 tittle-tattler.

meddlesome *See* **meddling**

meddling 4 nosy; 6 prying, snoopy; 7 gossipy; 9 intrusive, officious; 10 intriguing, meddlesome; 11 interfering, troublesome.

media *See* **mass media**

median 3 par; 4 mean; 6 medial, mesial; 7 average; PHRASES: 5, 6 happy medium; 6, 4 golden mean.

mediate 5 judge; 6 pacify, umpire; 7 bargain, referee; 8 moderate; 9 arbitrate, intercede, interfere, intervene, negotiate, officiate, reconcile; 10 compromise, conciliate; 12 intermediate; PHRASES: 2, 1, 2-7 be a go-between; 4, 2 step in; 4-3-4 give-and-take; **5, 2, 3, 5** bring to the table; **5, 8** bring together; **9, 5** negotiate peace.

mediation 9 diplomacy; **10** moderation; **11** arbitration, negotiation; **12** conciliation, intercession, intervention, pacification; **13** statesmanship; **15** troubleshooting.

mediator 4 ACAS *UK*, dove; **5** judge; **6** umpire; **7** arbiter, liaison, referee; **8** appeaser, diplomat, pacifier, Pandarus; **9** counselor, middleman, moderator, statesman; **10** arbitrator, matchmaker, negotiator, peacemaker; **11** conciliator, intercessor; **12** intermediary; **14** troubleshooter; PHRASES: **2-7** go-between; **5, 5** third party; **8, 6** marriage broker.

medical 6 iatric; **7** cardiac; **8** clinical, forensic, orthotic; **9** geriatric, obstetric, pediatric; **10** allopathic, anaplastic, orthopedic, urological, veterinary; **11** Hippocratic, homeopathic, obstetrical, osteopathic; **12** homoeopathic, neurological, pathological; **13** genitourinary, gynecological; **14** dermatological; **15** epidemiological.

medical art 7 healing; **8** ayurveda, medicine, practice; **9** allopathy; **11** acupuncture, homoeopathy *UK*; **12** therapeutics; PHRASES: **3, 2, 7** art of healing; **4, 2, 7** gift of healing; **4, 8** folk medicine; **5, 7** faith healing; **6, 2, 2, 5** laying on of hands; **6, 4** nature cure; **7, 5** healing touch.

medical assistance 4 cure; **6** remedy; **7** surgery, therapy; **8** medicine; **9** treatment; PHRASES: **5, 3** first aid.

medical covering 4 cast; **7** bandage, plaster; **8** dressing; **9** bandaging; **11** Elastoplast™; PHRASES: **4-3** Band-Aid *tm*; **7, 4** plaster cast.

medical fields 3 ENT; **7** anatomy, urology; **8** eugenics, oncology, serology; **9** andrology, audiology, histology, necrology, neurology, osteology, pathology, radiology; **10** cardiology, embryology, geriatrics, gynecology, hematology, immunology, morphology, nephrology, obstetrics, pediatrics, proctology, psychology; **11** dermatology, gerontology, orthopedics, radiography; **12** epidemiology, pharmacology, rheumatology, therapeutics, traumatology; **13** endocrinology, ophthalmology; **14** anesthesiology; PHRASES: **4, 8** arts medicine.

medical specialist 7 surgeon; **9** clinician, urologist; **10** consultant, oncologist, specialist, virologist; **11** anesthetist, neurol-

ogist, orthopedist, pathologist, radiologist; **12** cardiologist, embryologist, geriatrician, gynecologist, hematologist, immunologist, neurosurgeon, obstetrician, pediatrician, toxicologist; **13** dermatologist, diagnostician, gerontologist; **14** bacteriologist, epidemiologist, radiotherapist, rheumatologist; **15** endocrinologist, ophthalmologist; PHRASES: **5, 7** brain surgeon, heart surgeon; **7, 7** general surgeon, plastic surgeon; **7, 8** medical examiner.

medicament *See* **medicine**

medicine 3 jab; **4** balm, dose, drip, drug, herb, pill, shot; **5** bolus, draft; **6** balsam, elixir, physic, potion, powder, remedy, tablet; **7** capsule, linctus, lozenge, mixture, placebo, shiatsu; **8** curative, infusion, Medicare, pastille; **9** herbalism, injection, treatment; **10** homeopathy, medicament, medication, osteopathy; **11** acupressure, acupuncture, preparation, reflexology; **12** aromatherapy, chiropractic, prescription; **13** pharmacopoeia; **14** pharmaceutical; PHRASES: **2-3** ob-gyn; **5, 7** faith healing; **5, 8** group practice; **6, 4** health care; **6, 6** herbal remedy; **7, 4** generic drug; **7, 8** general practice, private ~; **8, 3** ~ man; **8, 5** ~ chest; **8, 6** ~ bottle; **8, 7** ~ cabinet; **8, 8** boutique ~; **9, 8** defensive ~; **10, 8** socialized ~; **11, 4** Hippocratic oath.

medicine (practise medicine) 4 cure, heal, scan, tend; **5** nurse, refer, treat; **6** attend, doctor, inject, screen; **7** consult, examine, relieve, restore; **8** diagnose, immunize; **9** inoculate, prescribe, vaccinate; **10** administer; PHRASES: **1-3** X-ray; **4, 3** care for; **4, 5** look after; **8, 2** minister to.

medieval 6 feudal; **9** primitive; **13** unenlightened; PHRASES: **3-2-4** out-of-date; **3-9** old-fashioned.

mediocre 4 gray, okay; **5** banal; **7** alright, average, prosaic; **8** adequate, lukewarm, middling, moderate, ordinary, passable; **11** indifferent, uninspiring; **12** unremarkable; **13** unexceptional; PHRASES: **2-2** so-so; **2, 5, 6** no great shakes; **3-2-3-4** run-of-the-mill; **3, 3** not bad; **3, 5** all right; **4, 2, 8** fair to middling; **4-4** così-così *It*; **4, 5** beta minus; **4-7** half-measure; **5, 2, 5, 2** comme ci comme ça *Fr*; **6, 4** second best; **6, 8** second division; **7, 7** nothing special.

mediocre (be mediocre) 3, 2 get by.

mediocrity 8 adequacy; **12** indifference, mediocreness. *See also* **mediocre**

meditate *See* contemplate

meditation *See* thought

medium 3 mid; 4 mean; 6 center, medial, median, mesiad, mesial, method, middle, midway; 7 average, balance, central, halfway, midterm; 8 balanced, middling, midpoint; 10 instrument, middlemost; 11 clairvoyant; 12 intermediary, intermediate, spiritualist *UK*; PHRASES: 5, 6 happy ~, juste milieu; 6-2-3-4 middle-of-the-road; 6, 4 golden mean; 7-4 average-size.

medusa 9 jellyfish.

meek 4 mild, weak; 5 cowed, quiet, timid; 6 docile, gentle, humble; 7 fearful; 9 compliant.

meerschaum 3, 4 sea foam.

meet 3 hit, rub; 4 face, fill, hunt, join, kiss; 5 brush, elbow, graze, greet, shave; 6 glance, muster, scrape, tackle; 7 convene, fulfill, meeting, satisfy; 8 assemble, confront, converge, suitable; 9 encounter, interface; 10 congregate, foregather, rendezvous; PHRASES: 3, 4 run into; 4, 2, 2 come up to; 4, 4 bump into, come upon; 4, 4, 7 come into contact; 5, 4 knock into; 7, 2, 2 measure up to; 7, 4 collide with.

meeting 4 date, demo, diet, meet; 5 brush, forum, graze, races, rally, synod, touch, tryst, visit; 6 indaba, social, soirée, summit; 7 contact, council, reunion, session; 8 assembly, audience, conclave, congress; 9 encounter, gathering, interface, interview, reception, symposium; 10 conference, convention, engagement, rendezvous; 11 appointment, assignation; 12 congregation; 13 confrontation; PHRASES: 2, 4 at home; 3-3 pow-wow; 3-8 get-together; 4-1-4 tête-à-tête; 5, 2, 6 round of visits; 5, 4 blind date; 5, 7 class reunion, dirty weekend; 6, 4 social call; 6, 5 social round; 6, 7 annual ~, coffee morning *UK*, family reunion; 6, 9 social gathering; 7, 5 ~ place; 8, 4 courtesy call; 8, 5 official visit.

megalomaniac *See* despot, despotic

melancholy 3 low, sad; 4 down; 6 sorrow; 7 sadness; 9 dejection, miserable; 11 downhearted, unhappiness; PHRASES: 3, 5 the blues.

Melba 5, 5 M~ sauce, M~ toast, peach M~.

mellow 4 aged, full, rich, ripe, soft, warm; 5 relax, ripen; 6 genial, mature, smooth, soften; 7 develop, improve; 8 tolerant; 9 easygoing; 12 approachable; PHRASES: 4, 2 ease up; 4, 4 calm down; 4-7 good-humored; 4-8 full-flavored; 6, 4 settle down.

melodious 4 soft; 5 sweet; 6 catchy, smooth; 7 chiming, lilting, lyrical, melodic, musical, Orphean, silvery, tuneful; 8 singable, tripping; 10 euphonious, harmonious; 11 mellifluent, mellifluous; PHRASES: 5-8 sweet-sounding.

melody 3 air; 4 aria, line, riff, song, tune; 5 canto, chime, motif, theme; 6 monody, strain; 7 descant, refrain; 9 leitmotif, leitmotiv; PHRASES: 5, 4 theme song; 6, 6 cantus firmus; 7, 4 melodic line; 7, 6 popular ~; 8, 6 Broadway ~; 9, 4 signature tune.

melt 4 fuse, thaw; 5 smelt; 6 render, soften; 7 clarify, defrost, liquefy; 8 unfreeze; 10 deliquesce; PHRASES: 4, 4 ~ down.

member 1 M; 2 MP; 3 arm, leg, MBE *UK*; 4 beam, limb, part, wing; 5 strut; 6 fellow; 7 brother, element, insider; 9 associate, colleague, component; 10 cardholder; PHRASES: 3, 2, 2 one of us; 4, 6 life ~, team ~; 6, 2, 5 ~ of staff; 6, 5 ~ state; 7, 6 charter ~.

membrane *See* skin

memento 5 relic, token; 6 trophy; 8 keepsake, reminder, souvenir; PHRASES: 4, 5 love token.

memo *See* memorandum

memoir 5 essay; 6 report, thesis; 7 account, article, history; 9 biography, chronicle.

memorable 5 socko; 8 haunting, mnemonic; 9 indelible, nostalgic; 10 remembered; 11 reminiscent, unforgotten; 13 unforgettable.

memorandum 3 IOU; 4 chit, memo, note; 6 minute; 7 message; 8 reminder.

memorial 7 funeral; 8 monument; 9 mausoleum, tombstone; 10 gravestone; 11 remembrance; 13 commemoration, commemorative.

memorize 5 learn; 6 retain; 8 remember; PHRASES: 3, 2, 4, 4 fix in one's mind; 5, 2, 4 learn by rote; 5, 2, 5 learn by heart; 6, 2, 6 commit to memory.

memory 3 RAM, ROM; 4 bank, DRAM; 5 cache, EAROM *UK*, store, trace; 6 buffer, engram, recall; 7 storage; 8 database, register; 9 Mnemosyne, nostalgia; 10 reputation, scratchpad; 11 recognition, remembering, remembrance; 12 memorization, recollection, reminiscence; **14** identification; PHRASES: 2-3 CD-ROM; **4, 4** data bank; **4, 6** good ~; **5, 3** mind's eye; **5, 6** total recall; **8, 2, 5** learning by heart; **8, 6** computer ~.

menace 5 peril; **6** danger, hazard, threat; **8** endanger, jeopardy, threaten; **10** jeopardize.

menacing 4 dark, ugly; **5** scary; **7** looming, ominous; **8** alarming; **10** foreboding; **11** frightening, threatening; **12** intimidating.

mend 3 fix, sew; **4** darn, heal; **5** amend, patch; **6** repair; **7** improve, recover, restore; **9** transform; **10** recuperate; PHRASES: **3, 4** get well; **3, 5** put right; **5, 2** patch up.

mendicant 6 beggar.

menial 5 basic, lowly; **6** boring; **7** tedious; **9** unskilled.

menopause 6, 2, 4 change of life.

menses 12 menstruation.

menstruate 5 bleed; PHRASES: **4, 2** come on.

menstruation 4 flow; **6** menses, period; **7** courses; **9** monthlies; PHRASES: **3, 5** the curse; **3, 5, 2, 3** the Curse of Eve; **4, 2, 3, 5** time of the month; **9, 4** menstrual flow.

mensuration 9 metrology, telemetry.

mental 5 crazy; **7** phrenic; **8** cerebral, thinking; **9** deductive, intuitive; **10** conceptual; **11** instinctive; **12** intellectual; **13** psychological; PHRASES: **6, 3** ~ age; **6, 5** ~ block; **6, 7** ~ cruelty.

mental breakdown 6 crisis; **8** hysteria; **10** brainstorm, depression; **11** melancholia; PHRASES: **5-2** crack-up; **5, 5** shell shock.

mental deterioration 3 GPI *UK*; **6** rabies; **7** seizure; **8** dementia, epilepsy, paroxysm; **9** confusion; **11** hydrophobia; PHRASES: **3-3, 7** mad-cow disease; **5, 3** grand mal, petit mal; **5, 6** brain damage; **6, 8** senile dementia; **9, 3** epileptic fit.

mental hospital *See* **psychiatric hospital**

mentally ill 4 sick; **6** schizo; **8** neurotic, paranoid, schizoid; **9** certified, depressed, disturbed, psychotic; **12** psychopathic; **13** schizophrenic.

mention 4 name; **5** quote, raise, refer; **6** allude, broach; **8** allusion, citation; **9** reference; PHRASES: **5, 2** touch on.

mercenary 6 greedy; **7** soldier; **8** covetous; **10** avaricious; **11** legionnaire; PHRASES:

3, 2, 3 dog of war *UK*; **7, 7** freedom fighter.

merchandise 4 line, load; **5** cargo, goods, range, stock, store, wares; **6** staple; **7** article, freight, product; **8** durables, saleable, sundries, supplies; **9** commodity; **11** perishables; PHRASES: **3, 5** dry goods; **4, 5** shop goods; **4, 6** loss leader; **4-6** best-seller; **5-2-5** stock-in-trade; **5, 5** white goods; **8, 5** consumer goods; **10, 5** perishable goods.

merchant 5 buyer; **6** broker, dealer, mercer *UK*, monger, seller, trader; **7** Antonio, magnate; **8** exporter, importer, retailer *UK*; **9** middleman; **10** speculator, wholesaler; **11** businessman; **12** entrepreneur, merchandiser; PHRASES: **8, 4** ~ bank, ~ navy, ~ ship; **8, 6** ~ marine.

merciful 4 kind; **7** clement, lenient; **8** tolerant; **9** forgiving, indulgent; **10** benevolent, forbearing; **11** magnanimous; **13** compassionate, unreproachful.

merciless 5 cruel; **8** pitiless, ruthless; **9** heartless; PHRASES: **4-7** hard-hearted.

mercurial 6 active, lively; **9** impulsive; **10** changeable; **13** unpredictable.

mercury 2 Hg; **5** azoth; **11** quicksilver.

mercy 4 pity; **5** favor, grace; **6** pardon, relief; **7** quarter; **8** clemency, leniency, reprieve; **9** acquittal; **10** compassion; **11** forgiveness; PHRASES: **5, 4** ~ seat; **5, 7** ~ killing, ~ mission; **6, 6** second chance; **7, 3** letting off.

mercy (ask for mercy) 3, 3, 4 ask for pity; **3, 3, 5** beg for mercy; **4, 2, 4, 5** fall on one's knees.

mercy (show mercy) 5 relax, spare; **6** pardon, relent, soften, unbend; **7** absolve, forbear, forgive; **8** reprieve; PHRASES: **2, 4, 2** go easy on; **2, 7, 4** be patient with; **3, 2, 3, 4, 2** not be too hard on; **4, 10** show compassion; **5, 1, 6** grant a pardon; **6, 2, 7** accept an apology.

mere 5 scant, sheer; **6** meager, paltry, simple; **8** ordinary. *See also* **lake**

merge 4 fuse, join, link, meld; **5** blend, unite; **6** mingle; **7** combine; **8** coalesce; **9** integrate; **10** amalgamate; **11** consolidate; PHRASES: **3, 2, 4** tie up with; **4, 2, 4** hook up with.

merit 4 earn; **5** value, worth; **7** deserve, qualify, warrant.

meritorious 6 worthy; **9** deserving; PHRASES: **11** commendable.

merriment *See* **cheerfulness**

merry *See* **cheerful**

merry-go-round 8 carousel; 10 roundabout *UK*.

mesh 3 net, web; 6 engage, enmesh; 7 netting, network, webbing; 9 interlock; 12 interconnect; PHRASES: 3, 8 fit together.

mesmerise *See* **hypnotize**

mesquite 5, 6 honey locust; 5, 8 honey ~.

mess 4 glop, gunk, hash, meal; 5 botch, chaos; 6 bollix, fiasco, untidy; 7 clutter, failure, farrago; 8 horlicks, shambles; PHRASES: 4-2 cock-up; 4, 2, 7 ~ of pottage; 4, 3 ~ kit; 4, 4 ~ hall; 4, 6 ~ jacket; 5-2 balls-up *UK*, screw-up.

message 3 SOS; 4 bull, memo, news, note, wire, word; 5 cable, drift, email, moral, telex; 6 errand, letter, signal, thrust; 7 meaning, missive; 8 bulletin, despatch, dispatch, telegram; 10 communiqué; 13 communication.

messenger 4 Iris; 6 Hermes; 7 courier, mailman, Mercury, postman; PHRASES: 4, 7 Pony Express; 5, 4 Royal Mail; 6, 9 winged ~; 7, 6 carrier pigeon.

MET 11 meteorology.

metal 2 Ag, Al, Au, Fe, Pb, Sn; 3 tin; 4 foil, gold, iron, lead, zinc; 6 barium, cobalt, copper, nickel, silver, sodium; 7 bismuth, cadmium, calcium, iridium, lithium, mercury, uranium, wolfram; 8 aluminum, antimony, chromium, europium, platinum, titanium, tungsten; 9 magnesium, manganese, potassium, strontium, zirconium; PHRASES: 7, 5 Babbitt ~.

metamorphose 4 melt; 5 alter; 6 change, mutate; 9 transform, translate, transmute; 11 transfigure.

metaphor 5 image; 6 symbol; 8 allegory.

meteor 5 comet; 6 bolide, Leonid; 7 Geminid, Perseid, radiant, tektite; 8 aerolite, fireball, siderite; 9 chondrite, meteorite, meteoroid; 10 achondrite, Quadrantid, siderolite; 14 micrometeorite; PHRASES: 4, 9 iron meteorite; 5, 9 stony meteorite; 6, 6 ~ shower; 7, 4 falling star; 8, 4 shooting star.

meteorologic 8 climatic, synoptic; 9 elemental; 14 meteorological.

meteorologist 10 weatherman; 11 aerographer; 12 weatherwoman; 13 climatologist.

meter 5 count, gauge; 7 ammeter, measure; 8 odometer; 9 altimeter, barometer, pedometer, voltmeter; 10 hydrometer, micrometer, mileometer *UK*, photometer, tachometer, theodolite; 11 calorimeter, chronometer, speedometer, thermometer, voltammeter; 12 oscilloscope, spectrometer; 15 thermobarometer; PHRASES: 3, 5 gas ~; 3, 7 rev counter *UK*; 4, 5 wind gauge; 5, 5 water ~; 5, 8 chart recorder; 6, 7 Geiger counter; 8, 5 pressure gauge.

meter 4 beat, foot, iamb, peon; 5 ionic; 6 accent, dactyl, rhythm, stress; 7 anapest, caesura, dimeter, distich, measure, metrics, numbers, prosody, pyrrhic, spondee, trochee; 8 dieresis *UK*, emphasis, quantity, scansion, trimeter; 9 anacrusis, catalexis, diaeresis *UK*, hexameter, octameter; 10 heptameter, pentameter, tetrameter; 12 accentuation, counterpoint; PHRASES: 5, 5 duple ~; 6, 5 triple ~; 6, 6 sprung rhythm; 6, 7 heroic couplet; 8, 4 metrical unit.

methanol 4, 6 wood spirit; 4, 7 wood alcohol.

method 4 mode, plan; 6 course, custom, manner, system, tactic; 7 pattern, routine; 8 approach; 9 structure, technique; 10 discipline; 12 coordination, organization.

methodical 4 neat, tidy; 7 orderly, regular; 9 efficient, organized; 10 deliberate, scientific; 12 businesslike, systematical; PHRASES: 2, 3, 4 by the book.

methylated spirits 5 metho *UK*, meths *UK*.

meticulous 5 exact, fussy; 6 strict; 7 careful, precise; 8 diligent, rigorous, thorough; 9 assiduous, laborious; 10 fastidious, methodical, particular, scrupulous; 11 painstaking; 13 conscientious; PHRASES: 4, 2 just so.

metrical 2 SI; 6 iambic, linear, metric; 7 scanned; 8 dactylic, imperial, measured, mensural, rhythmic, scanning, spondaic, trochaic; 9 anapestic; 10 rhythmical; 12 quantitative.

mettle *See* **courage**

mew *See* **animal cry**

Mexican dish 4 mole, taco; 5 salsa, tamal; 6 posole; 7 burrito, tostado; 8 tortilla; 9 enchilada, guacamole; 10 quesadilla; 11 chilaquiles; PHRASES: 4, 2, 5 pico de gallo; 6, 9 huevos rancheros; 7, 5 refried beans.

mezzanine 8 entresol.

MF 10 millifarad; PHRASES: **5, 4** quite loud; **5, 5** mezzo forte.

MI 8 motorway *UK*.

miasma 4 damp, fume, reek, smog; **5** smoke; **6** biogas; **7** malaria; **8** firedamp, mephitis.

miasmic 4 fumy; **6** foetid, fuming; **7** miasmal; **8** mephitic; **9** miasmatic.

Michaelmas 10, 4 M~ term *UK*; **10, 5** M~ daisy.

Michigan 2 MI; **5** robin (bird); **7** Lansing (capital); PHRASES: **2, 3, 4, 1, 8, 9, 4, 5, 3** If you seek a pleasant peninsula, look about you (motto); **5, 4** white pine (tree); **5, 5, 5** Great Lakes State (nickname); **5, 7** apple blossom (flower); **9, 5, 5, 10** Wolverine State, Water Wonderland (nickname).

Mickey 6, 4 M~ Finn; **6, 5** M~ Mouse.

microbe 4 germ; **5** virus; **6** amoeba; **8** bacillus; **9** bacterium, protozoan; **13** microorganism.

microscopic 4 tiny; **5** small, teeny; **6** atomic, minute; **9** invisible; **10** impalpable, intangible; **13** imperceptible, indiscernible, infinitesimal; PHRASES: **5-5** teeny-weeny.

midday *See* **noon**

middle 1 C; **3** hub, mid; **4** core; **5** focus, heart, midst, waist; **6** center, kernel, medial, median, mesial, midway; **7** central, halfway, midriff; **8** midpoint; **9** epicenter; **10** middlemost; **11** equidistant; **12** intermediate, transitional; PHRASES: **5, 3** bull's eye; **6-2-3-4** middle-of-the-road; **6, 4** ~ ages, M~ East, ~ name; **6, 6** ~ school.

middle age 3, 5, 2, 4 the prime of life; **4, 5** one's prime; **5, 5** riper years; **6, 4** middle life; **6, 5** middle years; **7, 6** midlife crisis.

middle-aged 8 matronly; **14** fortysomething; **15** thirtysomething; PHRASES: **2, 6, 5** of mature years; **2, 6, 7** no spring chicken; **2, 7** no chicken; **4, 2, 3, 5** long in the tooth.

middle class 2 C1 *UK*, C2 *UK*; **6** Pooter, suburb; **7** Babbitt; **8** commuter, suburban, suburbia; **9** Babbittry, bourgeois; **11** bourgeoisie, suburbanite; **12** professional; **14** respectability; PHRASES: **4, 3, 4** Dick and Jane; **4, 6** Main Street; **4, 8** Home Counties; **5, 4** small town; **6, 7** Middle America, middle manager; **7, 6** bedroom suburb, skilled worker; **8, 4** commuter belt *UK*; **8, 5** merchant class.

middleman 4 pimp; **5** agent; **6** broker, medium, umpire; **7** linkman *UK*, referee; **8** mediator; **9** counselor, messenger, moderator, ombudsman; **10** arbitrator, mouthpiece, negotiator; **11** distributor, intercessor; **12** intermediary, spokesperson; PHRASES: **2-7** go-between; **3-2-3-6** pig-in-the-middle; **5, 5** third party.

middling 4 fair; **7** average; **8** mediocre; **15** undistinguished; PHRASES: **2-2** so-so; **3-2-3-4** run-of-the-mill.

midline 7 equator, midriff; **8** diameter; **9** waistline; PHRASES: **3-7** mid-section.

midnight 3 OAM *UK*; PHRASES: **3, 4, 2, 5** the dead of night; **3, 8, 4** the witching hour; **8, 3** ~ sun; **8, 4** ~ blue.

mien 4 look; **6** manner; **7** bearing; **10** appearance, expression.

might 5 force, power, valor; **8** capacity, strength.

mighty *See* **great**

migrant *See* **itinerant**

migrate *See* **travel**

migratory *See* **traveling**

mild 4 flat, kind, meek, soft, warm, weak; **5** balmy, bland; **6** gentle, slight; **7** clement, insipid, trivial; **8** pleasant, trifling; **9** easygoing, tasteless, temperate; **11** unimportant; **13** insignificant.

mile 3, 4 air ~; **5, 4** Roman ~; **7, 4** statute ~, Swedish ~; **8, 4** nautical ~; **9, 4** admiralty ~.

milestone 4 sign; **6** marker, record; **8** landmark, signpost; **9** highlight; **11** achievement; PHRASES: **4, 5** high point.

miliaria 4, 4 heat rash; **7, 4** prickly heat.

militant 7 hawkish, warlike, warring; **8** activist; **9** bellicose, combative, offensive; **10** aggressive; **11** belligerent; **12** militaristic, warmongering; PHRASES: **2, 2, 4** up in arms; **2, 3, 7** on the warpath; **2, 3, 9** on the offensive; **5-8** saber-rattling.

militarist 4 hawk; **5** sepoy; **6** Gurkha, pirate, raider, robber; **7** samurai; **8** crusader, marauder, militant; **9** auxiliary, buccaneer, centurion, conqueror, hardliner, mercenary, plunderer, privateer, warmonger; **10** adventurer, chauvinist, freelancer; **11** imperialist; **12** conquistador, expansionist; PHRASES: **2, 11** Dr Strangelove.

military 2 PX, RE *UK*, RN *UK*, SS, TA *UK*; **3** SAS *UK*; **4** army, navy, SEAL; **5** naval; **6** armory; **7** marines, martial, militia, service, veteran, warlike; **8** militant, regulars, reserves; **9** bellicose, combative, defensive, mercenary, offensive, soldierly, strategic; **10** aggressive; **11** belligerent, operational, soldierlike; **12** gladiatorial, paramilitary; PHRASES: **3, 5** air force; **3, 8** the services *UK*; **4-2** gung-ho; **4, 5** Home Guard *UK*; **4, 6** land forces *UK*; **6, 4** active duty; **6, 6** ground forces; **6, 7** Senior Service *UK*; **7, 6** special forces; **8, 6** ~ forces, ~ honors, ~ police; **8, 7** ~ academy, national defense; **9, 4** volunteer army; **9, 6** mercenary forces; **11, 4** Territorial Army *UK*.

military aircraft 5 AWACS, scout; **6** bomber; **7** fighter, trainer; **8** warplane; **11** interceptor; PHRASES: **3, 5** spy plane; **5, 6** heavy bomber, light bomber; **5, 7** night fighter, troop carrier; **7, 6** stealth bomber; **7-6** fighter-bomber; **7, 7** barrage balloon; **9, 5** transport plane. *See also* **aircraft**

military leader 3 Cid (El), Lee (Robert E.); **4** Díaz (Porfirio); **5** Craig (Sir James Henry); **6** Dumont (Gabriel), Nelson (Horatio), Powell (Colin), Stuart (James Ewell Brown Jeb), Taylor (Zachary); **7** admiral, general, Jackson (Andrew), Jackson (Thomas Jonathan Stonewall), Sherman (William Tecumseh), warlord; **8** Sheridan (Philip Henry); **9** commander, Kitchener (Horatio Herbert), MacArthur (Douglas); **10** commandant, Kosciuszko (Thaddeus), Rochambeau, Washington (George); **11** Schwarzkopf (Norman); **13** generalissimo; PHRASES: **3, 3, 3** the Old Man; **3, 7** air marshal; **5, 3** brass hat; **5, 7** field marshal, fleet admiral; **6, 3-4** Chiang Kai-shek; **8, 7** military officer.

military rank 2 AB *UK*, CO; **3** NCO; **5** major; **6** ensign, gunner; **7** admiral, captain, colonel, general, private; **8** corporal, corpsman, sergeant; **9** brigadier *UK*, commander, commodore, subaltern; **10** bombardier, lieutenant, midshipman; **11** aircraftman *UK*; **13** aircraftwoman *UK*, sublieutenant *UK*; PHRASES: **3, 4, 7** air vice marshal; **3, 5, 7** air chief marshal *UK*; **3, 7** air marshal; **3, 8** top sergeant; **3, 9** air commodore *UK*; **4, 6** able rating *UK*, able seaman; **4, 7** bird colonel, flag officer, rear admiral, vice admiral; **4-7** vice-admiral; **4, 9** wing commander; **5, 2, 5** chief of staff; **5, 6, 8** chief master sergeant; **5, 7** field marshal, fleet admiral, group captain, major general, petty officer, pilot officer *UK*; **5, 8** lance corporal, staff sergeant; **5, 9** corps commander; **5, 10** first lieutenant, lance bombardier; **6, 5, 5, 7** master chief petty officer, senior chief petty officer; **6, 6, 8** senior master sergeant; **6, 7** flying officer *UK*, seaman recruit; **6, 7, 8** master gunnery sergeant; **6, 8** flight sergeant *UK*, master sergeant; **6, 10** seaman apprentice; **7, 2, 3, 3, 5** General of the Air Force; **7, 2, 3, 4** General of the Army; **7, 2, 3, 6** General of the Armies; **7, 5, 5** private first class; **7, 7** warrant officer; **7, 8** gunnery sergeant; **7, 8, 5** command sergeant major; **8, 5** sergeant major; **8, 5, 5** sergeant first class; **8, 6** squadron leader *UK*; **8, 7** adjutant general; **9, 7** brigadier general; **9, 8** technical sergeant; **10, 2, 3, 6, 5** Commandant of the Marine Corps; **10, 6, 5** lieutenant junior grade. *See also* **officer**

military unit 2 KP, MP, TA *UK*; **4** file, MASH, rank, wing; **5** fleet, group, squad, troop; **6** column, detail, flight, outfit; **7** battery, brigade, company, platoon, section; **8** division, regiment, squadron; **9** battalion; **10** detachment; PHRASES: **1-4** A-team; **3, 5** Air Corps; **3, 7** aid station; **3, 8** air division; **4, 5** army corps, drum corps, task force; **5, 5** bugle corps, nurse corps; **6, 5** battle group; **6, 7** supply service; **6, 9** signal battalion; **7, 4** support unit; **7, 5** medical corps, reserve fleet, support fleet; **7, 8** armored division; **8, 4** commando unit; **8, 6** military police; **9, 5** auxiliary fleet.

milk 3 sap, UHT; **5** cream, pinta; **7** exploit; **9** beestings, colostrum; PHRASES: **3, 2, 3, 4** top of the ~; **3, 4** ice ~; **4, 2, 8** ~ of magnesia; **4, 3** ~ bar *UK*, ~ run; **4, 4** cow's ~, skim ~ *UK*; **4-4, 4** long-life ~; **4, 5** ~ fever, ~ float *UK*, ~ round *UK*, ~ shake, ~ stout *UK*, ~ tooth; **4, 7** ~ pudding *UK*; **4, 9** ~ chocolate; **5, 4** dried ~, fresh ~, goat's ~; **5, 5** milky drink; **6, 4** breast ~, camel's ~, malted ~; **7, 4** mother's ~, skimmed ~; **8, 4** powdered ~; **9, 4** chocolate ~, condensed ~; **10, 4** evaporated ~; **11, 4** homogenized ~, pasteurized ~, semiskimmed ~.

milky 6 cloudy, lactic, opaque.

mill 5 crowd, crush, grind, plant, pound, quern, works; **6** kibble, throng; **7** factory, grinder; PHRASES: **5, 4** stamp ~, strip ~ *UK*, water ~; **6, 4** coffee ~, pepper ~.

million 1 M.

millions *See* **many**

millstone 10 grindstone, quernstone.

mime 3 ape; **5** mimic; **6** parody; **7** express; **8** satirize; **9** represent; **10** caricature; PHRAS-

ES: 3, 3 act out.

mimic **4** mock; **6** mirror; **7** imitate; **8** imitator, parodist; **11** impersonate; **12** caricaturist, impersonator; **13** impressionist.

mince **4** hash; **5** shred; **7** crumble; **PHRASES: 3, 2** cut up; **4, 2** chop up.

mind **4** care, heed, wits; **5** guard, watch; **6** brains, object, psyche; **7** scholar, thinker; **9** intellect, intention; **11** inclination; **12** intellectual; **13** consciousness; **PHRASES: 4, 5** look after; **5, 6** tread warily; **5, 9** tread carefully.

mine **3** dig, pit; **4** fund; **5** store; **6** quarry, source; **7** extract; **8** coalmine, colliery, excavate; **9** coalfield; **10** excavation, repository; **PHRASES: 3, 3** dig out; **4, 4** gold ~; **5, 4** strip ~.

mineral *See* **rocks and minerals**

mingle *See* **mix**

minimum **3** jot; **4** iota; **5** least; **6** lowest; **7** tiniest; **8** minutest, smallest; **PHRASES: 4, 7** bare ~; **8, 6** smallest amount.

minion **5** crony *UK*; **8** follower; **9** assistant, underling; **11** subordinate; **PHRASES: 6-2** hanger-on.

minister **4** help, tend; **5** nurse, padre, treat, vicar; **6** cleric, divine, parson, pastor, priest, rector; **8** chaplain, preacher; **9** clergyman, secretary; **PHRASES: 4, 3** care for; **4, 5** look after; **6, 2** attend to.

ministry **6** agency, bureau, office; **10** department; **12** organization.

Minnesota **2** MN; **PHRASES: 2, 4** St. Paul (capital); **4, 2, 3, 5** Star of the North (motto); **4, 3, 5, 4, 7** pink and white lady slipper (flower); **5, 4, 5** North Star State (nickname); **6, 4** common loon (bird), Norway pine (tree); **6, 5, 5, 3, 6, 5** Gopher State, Bread and Butter State (nickname).

minor **5** child, small, youth; **6** junior, lesser, slight; **7** trivial; **8** inferior, juvenile, teenager; **9** secondary; **10** adolescent, negligible; **15** inconsequential.

minor planet **8** asteroid.

minstrel *See* **musician**

mint **4, 5** ~ julep, ~ sauce *UK*.

minus **4** less; **7** without; **8** negative, subtract; **PHRASES: 4, 4** take away.

minute **2** mo *UK*; **3** wee; **4** tiny; **5** small; **6** little, moment; **9** miniature, minuscule; **11** microscopic; **13** infinitesimal; **PHRASES: 6, 4**

~ hand; **6, 5** ~ steak.

miracle *See* **wonder**

mirage **8** illusion; **13** hallucination; **PHRASES: 4, 7** fata morgana; **5, 2, 3, 5** trick of the light.

mirror **4** copy; **5** glass; **6** cheval; **7** imitate, reflect; **9** reproduce; **PHRASES: 4-4, 6** rearview ~; **4, 6** wing ~ *UK*; **6, 5** ~ image; **6, 6** ~ finish; **6, 7** ~ writing; **6, 8** ~ symmetry.

mirth **3** fun; **5** humor; **7** jollity; **8** hilarity, laughter.

misanthrope **5** cynic; **6** egoist; **7** egotist; **8** solitary; **9** homophobe, xenophobe; **10** misogynist; **13** misanthropist; **PHRASES: 3-5** man-hater; **5-5** woman-hater, world-hater; **7-5** mankind-hater.

misanthropic **4** mean; **7** baleful, cynical, hateful; **8** egoistic; **10** antisocial, malevolent, misandrous, unsociable; **11** egotistical; **PHRASES: 3-6** man-hating; **5-6** woman-hating.

misapplication *See* **misuse**

misappropriate *See* **steal**

miscarry **5** abort; **7** misfire; **8** backfire; **PHRASES: 2, 2, 2, 5** go up in smoke; **2, 4** go awry; **2, 5** go amiss, go wrong; **3, 4, 3** not come off; **4, 2, 5** come to grief; **4, 2, 7** come to nothing; **5, 1, 6** prove a fiasco.

miscellaneous *See* **various**

miscellany **5** babel; **6** circus, medley, motley, muddle, ragbag; **7** farrago, mixture, variety; **8** oddments, sundries; **9** anthology, menagerie, potpourri, thesaurus; **10** assortment, collection, hodgepodge, hotchpotch *UK*; **11** gallimaufry, miscellanea, smorgasbord; **PHRASES: 3, 3** job lot; **3, 5** all sorts; **4, 3** grab bag; **4, 3, 4** bits and bobs, odds and ends, odds and sods *UK*; **4, 3, 6** bits and pieces; **5, 2, 5** Tower of Babel; **5, 3** mixed bag, mixed lot; **6, 4** motley crew; **7, 4** variety show.

mischief **4** harm; **5** larks; **6** capers, damage, injury, pranks, tricks; **7** roguery; **8** deviltry; **9** devilment; **11** misbehavior, shenanigans; **PHRASES: 6, 8** monkey business.

mischief maker **3** elf, imp; **4** Puck; **6** rascal; **7** gremlin.

mischievous **6** impish, unruly; **7** naughty, puckish, roguish; **8** rascally; **11** disobedient, misbehaving, troublesome; **12** incorrigible; **PHRASES: 7, 2** playing up.

miscreant 8 criminal; **9** scoundrel, wrongdoer; **12** troublemaker; PHRASES: 8-5 mischief-maker.

misdemeanour *See* transgression

miser 6 meanie *UK*; **7** hoarder, niggard, Scrooge; **8** tightwad; **9** skinflint; **10** cheapskate, pinchpenny; PHRASES: 5-7 pennypincher.

miserable 3 low, sad; **4** blue, dark, down, drab, dull, glum, grim, mean, poor; **5** bleak; **6** abject, dismal, dreary, gloomy, morose, woeful; **7** doleful, forlorn, tearful, ululant, unhappy; **8** dejected, desolate, dolorous, funereal, mournful, wretched; **9** cheerless, depressed, sorrowful, woebegone; **10** depressing, melancholy; **11** downhearted, languishing; **12** heavyhearted, inconsolable; PHRASES: 3, 2 cut up; 5-8 grief-stricken; 6-7 broken-hearted.

misery 3 woe; **4** hell, pain; **5** gloom, grief; **7** anguish, despair, poverty, sadness; **8** distress; **10** affliction, depression, heartbreak; **11** despondency, unhappiness.

misfit 5 alien, freak; **6** weirdo; **7** beatnik, oddball; **8** outsider; **9** eccentric; **13** individualist, nonconformist.

misfortune 3 ill; **4** blow; **7** problem, reverse, setback, tragedy, trouble; **8** accident, calamity, disaster; **9** adversity; **10** affliction; **14** disappointment.

misgovern 7 misrule; **8** mistreat; **9** mismanage.

misguided 7 foolish; **8** gullible, mistaken.

mishandle *See* misuse

mishap 8 accident; **10** misfortune; **12** misadventure.

mishit 4 clip, hook, miss, nick; **5** error.

misjudge 4 miss; **7** misread, mistake, mistime; **8** overrate, prejudge; **9** overvalue, underrate; **10** undervalue; **11** misconstrue; **12** misinterpret, overestimate; **13** misunderstand, underestimate; PHRASES: 3, 5 get wrong.

mislay *See* lose

mislead 4 dupe, fool; **5** cheat, trick; **6** delude; **7** deceive, mystify; **8** hoodwink; **9** bamboozle, misdirect, misinform, obfuscate; PHRASES: 4, 6 lead astray.

misplace 4 lose; **6** mislay; PHRASES: 4, 5, 2 lose track of.

misrepresent 3 fib, lie; **5** color, frame, fudge, libel, slant, twist; **6** defame, parody; **7** distort, falsify, pervert, slander; **8** misquote, misstate; **9** embroider, obfuscate, whitewash; **10** camouflage, caricature, exaggerate; **13** overemphasize; PHRASES: 4, 3, 4 gild the lily.

misrepresentation 3 fib, lie; **5** libel; **6** parody; **7** slander; **8** travesty; **9** burlesque, falsehood; **10** caricature, distortion, perversion; **12** exaggeration, misquotation, misstatement, overemphasis; **13** falsification; PHRASES: 3, 8 bad likeness; 5, 5 false light; 9, 5 distorted image.

miss 4 fail, girl, lack, lass, want; **5** crave; **6** desire, maiden; **7** colleen; **8** Fräulein, senorita; **12** mademoiselle; PHRASES: 3, 3, 3 cry out for; 4, 3 long for; 4, 4 M~ Otis.

missile 3 SAM, SSM; **4** ball, bolt, dart, ICBM, Scud, shot, slug; **5** arrow, shaft, shell, spear, stone; **6** bullet, Exocet *tm*, mortar, pellet, rocket, weapon; **7** grenade, harpoon, javelin, Patriot, Polaris, torpedo, Trident; **8** brickbat, Pershing; **9** boomerang, Minuteman, slingshot; **10** cannonball, projectile, Sidewinder; PHRASES: 1-1 V-1, V-2; 6, 7 Cruise ~, guided ~.

missing 5 minus, short; **6** absent; **7** deleted, lacking, omitted, wanting; **8** excluded; **9** deficient; PHRASES: 4, 3 left out; 5, 4 taken away.

mission 2 op; **3** job; **4** duty, task; **5** quest; **6** charge, errand; **7** crusade, embassy; **8** legation, vocation; **10** assignment; **11** chancellery.

Mississippi 2 MS; **7** Jackson (capital); **8** magnolia (flower), magnolia (tree); **11** mockingbird (bird); PHRASES: 2, 6, 3, 4 By valour and arms (motto); 8, 5 Magnolia State (nickname).

missive *See* letter

Missouri 2 MO; **8** bluebird (bird), hawthorn (flower); PHRASES: 3, 7, 2, 3, 6, 5, 2, 3, 7, 3 The welfare of the people shall be the supreme law (motto); 4, 2, 5 Show Me State (nickname); 9, 4 Jefferson City (capital); 9, 7 flowering dogwood (tree).

misspelling 4 typo; **5** error; **7** literal.

mist 3 fog; **4** blur, haar *UK*, haze, murk; **5** smoke, vapor; PHRASES: 4, 4 heat haze; 6, 4 Scotch ~; 8, 4 mountain ~.

mistake 4 boob *UK*, gaff, muff, slip, typo; **5** error, fault, fluff, gaffe, lapse; **6** bobble, howler; **7** bloomer *UK*, blooper, blunder, clanger *UK*, erratum, literal *UK*; **8** misprint; **9** oversight; **10** inaccuracy; **11** malapropism, misjudgment; **13** misconception; **14** miscalculation; **15** misapprehension; PHRASES: **3-3** boo-boo; **4-2** cock-up; **4, 3** faux pas; **4, 9** dog's breakfast; **5-2** balls-up *UK*; **5, 4** false move; **5, 7** wrong turning.

mistake (make a mistake) 3 err; **4** goof, omit, slip; **6** bungle, mishit; **7** blunder; **8** misjudge, misprint, misquote, misspeak, misspell, overlook; **10** caricature; **11** misconstrue; **12** miscalculate, misinterpret, mispronounce; PHRASES: **3, 4, 4, 2, 2** put one's foot in it; **4, 1, 7** drop a clanger; **4, 2** cock up, foul up, slip up; **5, 2** balls up *UK*, louse up.

mistaken 3 off, out; **5** false, wrong; **7** deluded, unsound; **9** erroneous, incorrect; **10** fallacious, inaccurate; PHRASES: **2, 5** in error; **3, 3, 3, 4** way off the mark; **3-4** offbeam; **3, 5** all wrong; **4, 2, 3, 4** wide of the mark.

mister *See* **Mr**

mistimed 8 untimely; **9** premature; **11** inopportune; **13** inappropriate.

mistiness 3 fog; **4** rain; **5** cloud; **7** drizzle; PHRASES: **6, 4** Scotch mist.

mistreat 4 harm, hurt; **5** abuse; **6** damage, defile, injure, molest; **7** pervert, pollute, violate; **8** maltreat.

mistress 3 Mrs; **4** dame, lady, wife; **5** lover, madam, owner; **6** matron; **7** dowager; **8** paramour; **9** concubine, courtesan, inamorata, matriarch; PHRASES: **4, 2, 3, 5** lady of the house.

mistrust *See* **distrust**

misuse 5 abuse, force, fraud, waste; **6** batter, damage, defile, injure, injury, molest, strain; **7** battery, defraud, distort, exploit, fritter, misrule, overtax, overuse, pervert, pollute, profane, violate; **8** maltreat, misapply, mistreat, overfish, overwork, solecism, squander; **9** barbarism, desecrate, manhandle, misdirect, mismanage, overgraze, pollution, violation; **10** defilement, distortion, peculation, perversion, prostitute; **11** desecration, expropriate, malapropism, malpractice, mishandling, molestation, overfishing, overgrazing, profanation; **12** embezzlement, exploitation, extravagance, maltreatment, manipulation, misdirection, mistreatment,

prostitution; **13** maladminister, misemployment, mismanagement; **14** misapplication; PHRASES: **3, 3** bad use; **3-3** ill-use; **3-5** illtreat; **3, 7** use wrongly; **3-9** ill-treatment; **4, 9, 2** take advantage of; **5, 6** knock around.

misused *See* **misuse**

mite 3 bit; **5** child; PHRASES: **4, 4** dust ~, itch ~; **6, 4** little ~, spider ~, widow's ~; **7, 4** harvest ~.

miter 5, 3 ~ box; **5, 5** ~ block, ~ joint; **5, 6** ~ square.

mitigate 5 allay; **6** lessen, reduce, soften, temper; **7** commute, justify, qualify, relieve; **8** diminish, moderate; **9** alleviate, extenuate; **10** ameliorate; PHRASES: **4, 3, 4, 3** take the edge off.

mitt *See* **hand**

mix 4 brew, fuse, lace, stir; **5** admix, alloy, blend, churn, color, cross, imbue, merge, shake, spike, tinge, water; **6** debase, dilute, doctor, infuse, jumble, mingle, temper, weaken; **7** agitate, combine, fortify, instill, mixture, suffuse; **8** compound, intermix, sprinkle; **9** commingle, harmonize, hybridize, integrate, interlace; **10** adulterate, amalgamate, crossbreed, interbreed, interleave, interweave, mongrelize; **11** contaminate, intermingle, intersperse; PHRASES: **3, 2** ~ up, pep up; **3, 3, 5** ~ and match; **4, 8** lump together; **5, 4** water down; **5-5** cross-breed; **5-9** cross-fertilize; **6, 2** muddle up. *See also* **mix up**

mixed 4 shot; **5** fused; **6** dilute, hybrid, merged, motley, patchy, shaken, tinged; **7** alloyed, blended, chaotic, crossed, diluted, jumbled, mingled, mongrel, mottled, stirred, tangled; **8** combined, confused, eclectic, shuffled, tempered, unsorted; **9** colloidal, composite, dissolved, entangled, interbred, pervasive, scrambled; **10** harmonized, integrated, interfaith, interlaced, interwoven, variegated; **11** adulterated, amalgamated, interracial, intertwined, multiracial; **12** intermarried, intermingled, interspersed, miscegenetic; **13** heterogeneous, miscellaneous, multicultural; PHRASES: **2, 5, 5** of ~ blood; **3, 2, 5** out of order; **4-3-4** half-and-half; **5-2** mixed-up; **5, 3** ~ bag; **5-4** cross-bred; **5, 5** ~ grill *UK*; **5-5** fifty-fifty; **5, 7** ~ doubles; **5, 8** ~ blessing, ~ marriage, ~ metaphor; **7-4** watered-down.

mixed drink 3 kir; **5** mixer, negus, Pimms *tm*; **6** posset *UK*; **7** sangria; **8** cocktail, spritzer; PHRASES: **3-3** red-eye; **3, 3, 2**

gin and It; **3, 3, 3** rum and pep; **3, 3, 4** rum and Coke; **3, 3, 5** gin and tonic, rum and black; **3, 4** kir rose; **3, 5** gin sling *UK*; **4, 3** pink gin *UK*; **5, 3, 5** vodka and tonic; **5, 4** Bucks fizz; **6, 3, 4** brandy and soda; **6, 9** brandy Alexander; **7, 3** whiskey mac; **7, 3, 4** whiskey and soda; **7, 4** whiskey sour.

mixed race 4-5 half-breed *Offensive.*

mixed thing *See* **mixture**

mixed-up 5 snafu; **7** jumbled, muddled; **8** confused, mistaken; **9** scrambled; **10** confounded; PHRASES: **6-2** fouled-up, fucked-up, messed-up, mucked-up; **7-2** screwed-up.

mixer 4 chef, cook, soda; **5** baker, churn, spoon, tonic, whisk, witch; **6** beater, shaker; **7** blender, chemist, stirrer *UK*; **8** lemonade; **9** bartender, scrambler, socialite; **10** liquidizer; PHRASES: **4, 9** food processor; **6, 3** ginger ale; **6, 5** wooden spoon *UK*; **7, 3** melting pot; **8, 6** cocktail shaker.

mixture 3 mix; **4** hash, soup, stew; **5** alloy, blend, brass, broth, chaos, combo, gumbo, paste, punch, union; **6** bronze, fusion, jumble, medley, mixing, potion, ragbag; **7** amalgam, collage, colloid, harmony, linctus, mélange, variety; **8** allogamy, blending, cocktail, compound, dilution, infusion, mingling, mishmash, pastiche, scramble, solution; **9** admixture, confusion, contagion, infection, macedoine, pasticcio, patchwork, pervasion, pollution, potpourri, selection, suffusion, synthesis; **10** assemblage, assortment, collection, commixture, concoction, confection, hodgepodge, hotchpotch *UK*, miscellany, patchiness, permeation, salmagundi, saturation, suspension; **11** combination, composition, eclecticism, gallimaufry, integration, transfusion; **12** adulteration, amalgamation, entanglement, infiltration; **13** contamination, instilllation, interbreeding, intermarriage, intermingling, miscegenation; PHRASES: **3-2** fry-up *UK*; **5, 5** cough syrup; **5-8** crossbreeding; **6, 3, 6** bubble and squeak; **6, 4** Mickey Finn, witch's brew.

mix up 5 blend; **6** mingle, muddle; **7** concoct, confuse, embroil, mistake, prepare, shuffle; **8** bewilder, confound, entangle, scramble; PHRASES: **4, 2** cock up, foul up, mess up. *See also* **mix**

mix-up 4 mess; **5** error, snafu; **6** muddle; **7** mistake; **9** confusion, imbroglio; PHRASES: **4-2** cock-up, foul-up, fuck-up; **4, 3** pig's ear;

5-2 balls-up *UK*, screw-up.

MO 5, 5 money order; **5, 8** modus operandi; **7, 7** Medical Officer.

moan 4 beef, howl, keen, sigh, wail; **5** gripe; **6** lament, whinge *UK*; **7** keening; **9** complaint, ululation; **11** lamentation.

mob 4 crew, gang, mass, rout; **5** crowd, horde, plebs, swarm; **6** masses *UK*, rabble, throng; **7** besiege; **8** canaille; PHRASES: **3, 6** hoi polloi; **4-4** riff-raff.

mobile 5 fluid, going; **6** active, fluent, flying, motile; **7** movable, nomadic; **8** ambulant, portable, shifting; **9** traveling, wandering; **10** automotive, locomotive; **11** peripatetic; PHRASES: **4, 5** cell phone; **6, 4** ~ home; **6, 5** ~ phone *UK*.

mobile home 4 tent; **5** tepee; **6** camper, wigwam; **7** caravan *UK*, trailer; **8** pavilion; **9** campervan *UK*, houseboat.

mock 3 ape, dig, rag; **4** fake, hiss, hoot, howl, jeer, jibe, rail, sham; **5** chaff, dummy, false, mimic, paste, scoff, scorn, sneer, spoof, taunt; **6** deride, ersatz; **7** lampoon, pillory; **8** ridicule, satirize; **9** imitation, simulated, synthetic; **10** artificial; **12** reproduction.

mockery 4 joke, mime; **5** aping, scorn, spoof; **6** parody, satire; **7** cartoon, jeering, lampoon, mimicry, sarcasm, takeoff; **8** scoffing; **10** caricature; **12** derisiveness; **13** impersonation; PHRASES: **3-4** put-down; **4-2** send-up; **4-4** piss-take *UK*.

mocking 6 ironic; **7** jeering; **8** derisive, laughing, sardonic, scornful, sneering; **9** insulting, sarcastic; **10** disdainful; **12** contemptuous.

mode 3 way; **5** major, means, minor, style, vogue; **6** Dorian, Ionian, Lydian, method; **7** Aeolian, fashion; **8** Phrygian; **9** technique.

model 1 T; **3** toy; **4** cast, copy, doll, mold; **5** carve, dummy, ideal, poser, shape; **6** figure, sculpt; **7** classic, epitome, example, paragon; **8** figurine, original, paradigm; **9** archetype, mannequin, prototype; PHRASES: **4-2** mock-up; **4, 5** male ~, test ~; **4, 6** test design; **7, 5** clothes horse, fashion ~, working ~.

moderate 4 cool, curb, ease, fair, hush, just, lull, mild; **5** allay, blunt, chair, check, judge, limit, quiet, relax, still; **6** adjust, center, dampen, deaden, disarm, gentle, lessen, medium, modest, pacify, reduce, relent, settle, soften, soothe, steady, subdue, temper, umpire, weaken; **7** average, chasten, control, cushion, equable, liberal, lighten, limited, mediate, mollify, preside, quieten, referee, relieve; **8** balanced, composed, decrease, diminish, harmless, measured, middling, mitigate, modulate, passable, rational, regulate, restrain, restrict, sensible, tempered, tolerant; **9** alleviate, arbitrate, constrain, judicious, peaceable, temperate; **10** compromise, controlled, nonviolent, reasonable, restrained; **12** unremarkable; **13** unexceptional; PHRASES: 2-2 so-so; **4, 2, 8** fair to middling; **4, 3, 4, 3** take the edge off; **4, 3, 5** take the chair; **4, 4** play down, tone down; **4-5** soft-pedal; **4-6** blue-pencil; **6, 4** smooth over; **6, 6** within bounds, within limits, within reason.

moderately 5 quite; **6** fairly, pretty, rather; **7** equably; **8** somewhat; **10** reasonably; PHRASES: **2, 1, 6** to a degree; **2, 4, 5** at half speed; **2, 4, 6** to some extent; **2, 10** in moderation; **4, 10** with moderation. *See also* **moderate**

moderation 5 check, letup; **6** easing; **7** calming, control; **8** calmness, coolness, decrease, fairness, mildness, prudence, sobriety; **9** abatement, composure, lessening, reduction, restraint; **10** adjustment, compromise, equanimity, mitigation, modulation, neutrality, regulation, relaxation, steadiness, temperance; **11** alleviation, assuagement; **12** impartiality, moderateness; **14** reasonableness; PHRASES: **3, 7** due measure; **4, 3, 4** give and take; **4-7** self-control; **4-9** self-restraint; **5, 6** happy medium; **6, 3** middle way; **7, 2, 6** nothing in excess; **7, 5** halfway house.

moderator 5 brake, judge; **6** buffer, damper, downer, umpire; **7** anodyne, arbiter, bromide, killjoy, referee; **8** lenitive, mediator, nightcap, pacifier, sedative; **9** analgesic, mollifier, restraint; **10** arbitrator, controller, painkiller, palliative, peacemaker; **11** alleviative, chairperson; **12** tranquilizer; PHRASES: **3, 7** wet blanket; **4, 5** rose water; **5, 8** shock absorber; **11, 4** restraining hand.

modern 2 AD; **3** hip, mod, new; **6** latest, recent; **7** current, present; **11** progressive; **12** contemporary; PHRASES: **6-3** latter-day; **7-3** present-day.

modest 3 coy, shy; **4** meek, poor; **6** chaste, decent, demure, humble, seemly; **8** decorous, discreet, maidenly, moderate, reserved; **9** diffident; **10** unaspiring, unassuming, unboastful; **11** unobtrusive; **12** unimpressive; **13** unpretentious; **14** unostentatious; PHRASES: **4-8** self-effacing.

modesty 8 humility. *See also* **modest**

modification 6 change; **9** softening, variation; **10** adaptation, adjustment, alteration, mitigation, modulation, palliation, regulation; **11** improvement; **12** coordination; **13** qualification; **14** reconciliation.

modify 4 vary; **5** adapt, alter, color; **6** adjust, attune, change, soften, temper; **7** improve, qualify; **8** mitigate, moderate, modulate, palliate, regulate; **9** extenuate, reconcile; **10** coordinate; PHRASES: **4, 4** tone down.

modish *See* **fashionable**

modular 6 atomic, fitted, joined, linked; **8** cellular, integral; **9** molecular; PHRASES: **5-2** built-in.

modulation 5 swing; **6** accent, change; **9** variation; **10** adjustment, alteration, inflection, intonation.

module *See* **unit**

moist 3 wet; **4** damp, dank; **5** close, humid, rainy, soggy, tacky; **6** clammy, sodden, sticky; **7** dampish, wettish.

moisten 3 wet; **4** damp; **5** bedew; **6** dampen; **8** humidify; PHRASES: **3, 5** add water.

moisture 3 dew, wet; **4** rain; **5** fluid, humor, spray, water; **7** wetness; **8** dampness; **9** moistness; **10** wateriness; **11** humectation; **12** condensation.

moke 6 donkey.

mola 7 sunfish.

mold 3 die, fur; **4** cast, form, must, soil; **5** earth, forge, model, shape; **6** create, fungus, mildew, sculpt; **7** fashion, pattern; **9** construct.

molder 3 rot; **7** ferment, putrefy; **9** decompose; **10** deliquesce.

mole *See* **spy**

molecule *See* **particle**

molest 5 abuse, annoy; **6** attack, bother, harass, pester; **7** assault, torment; **8** mistreat; PHRASES: **4, 2** feel up.

mollify *See* **pacify**

mollusk 4 clam, slug, tusk; **5** bulla, conch, drull, drupe, gaper, murex, ormer *UK*, polyp, sepia, shell, snail, solen, squid,

Venus, whelk; **6** chiton, cockle, cowrie, cuttle, limpet, mussel, oyster, quahog, tellin, teredo, triton, winkle; **7** abalone, bivalve, octopus, pandora, piddock, scallop; **8** argonaut, nautilus, shipworm; **9** lampshell; **10** cuttlefish, nudibranch; PHRASES: **3, 4** sea hare, sea slug; **3, 5** ark shell, sea lemon; **3, 9** sea butterfly; **4, 5** cone shell, wing shell; **5, 5** auger shell, razor shell; **6, 5** turban shell; **7, 5** trumpet shell; **8, 4** pelican's foot.

Moluccas 6 Maluku; PHRASES: **5, 7** Spice Islands.

mom 2 ma; **6** mother.

moment 5 flash; **6** import, minute, second, weight; **7** instant; **9** substance; **10** importance; **12** significance; PHRASES: **5, 6** split second.

momentous *See* **important**

momentum 3 run; **4** flow, flux, rush; **5** drift, trend; **6** action, career, course, flight, onrush, stream, travel; **7** current, impetus, traffic; **8** activity; **9** actuation, agitation, transport; **10** motivation, propulsion; **12** mobilization; **14** transportation; PHRASES: **4, 2, 7** flow of traffic.

monarch *See* **ruler**

monastic 7 monkish, nunnish; **8** monachal, priestly; **9** religious; PHRASES: **4, 4, 1, 4** live like a monk; **4, 4, 1, 6** live like a hermit; **8, 5** ~ order. *See also* **monk**

monetary 6 coined, fiscal, issued, minted; **7** decimal, nummary, stamped; **8** devalued, floating, nummular; **9** budgetary, fiduciary, financial, pecuniary, withdrawn; **10** numismatic; **11** demonetized, depreciated; **12** deflationary, inflationary; PHRASES: **4-5** gold-based.

money 1 d, l, p, s; **2** as; **3** bit, bob, IOU, pie, PIN, sol, sou, wad; **4** anna, bill, bond, buck, call, cash, cent, coin, dime, doit, dosh *UK*, gate, gold, hoot, jack, mail, mite, note, obol, pice, pony, quid, real, tael; **5** angel, belga, brass, bread, broad, check, conto, crown, daric, dough, draft, ducat, eagle, fiver, groat, liard, livre, lolly *UK*, louis, lucre, mohur, noble, order, pence, pengo, penny, pound, rhino, scudo, soldo, stuff, sugar, sycee, unite; **6** aureus, baubee, bawbee *UK*, bezant, bundle, copper, coupon, cowrie, décime, doblon, dollar, florin, guinea, kopeck, mammon, monies, monkey, moolah, nickel, packet, pocket, riches,

sequin, siller, silver, specie, stater, stiver, supply, talent, tanner, tenner, tester, teston, thaler, wampum; **7** bullion, carolus, centavo, coinage, jacobus, milreis, moidore, pistole, plastic, quarter, readies *UK*, sawbuck, smacker, testoon; **8** assignat, banknote, currency, denarius, doubloon, farthing, johannes, kreutzer, maravedi, napoleon, picayune, sesterce, sixpence, zillions; **9** debenture, dupondius, Eurocheck, greenback, halfpenny, megabucks, pistareen, rixdollar, sovereign; **10** Asiadollar, Eurodollar, greenbacks, sestertium, threepence; **11** spondulicks *UK*; PHRASES: **1-4** C-note; **3, 4** one cent, two bits; **3, 5** big bucks, big ~, hot ~, key ~, new ~, ten cents; **3-6, 4** one-dollar bill, ten-dollar bill; **3-6, 5** two-dollar piece; **4, 2, 5** pots of ~; **4, 3** tidy sum; **4, 4** four bits; **4-4** five-spot; **4, 4, 6** Hong Kong dollar; **4, 5** easy ~, five cents, head ~, hush ~, long bread, long green, seed ~, ship ~ *UK*, tall ~; **4-5** rose-noble; **4-6** half-dollar; **4-6, 4** five-dollar bill; **4, 8** mill sixpence; **5, 2, 7** ~ of account; **5, 3** louis d'or; **5, 5** blood ~, fifty cents, ~ order, paper ~, prize ~, ready ~; **5, 6** king's ransom, legal tender, ~ market; **5-6, 4** fifty-dollar bill; **5, 8** pound sterling; **6-4, 5** twenty-five cents; **6, 5** danger ~, filthy lucre, maundy ~, postal order *UK*; **6, 6** silver dollar; **7, 4** premium bond; **7, 5** caution ~ *UK*, folding ~; **8, 4** monetary unit; **8, 5** precious metal; **9, 6** traveler's cheque; **10, 3** threepenny bit *UK*; **10, 4** promissory note; **10, 5** conscience ~. *See also* **currency**

moneylender *See* **lender**

moneymaking *See* **profitable**

money received 3 GST, tax, VAT *UK*; **4** dues, duty, gain, rent, take; **5** bonus, rates, taxes; **6** tariff; **7** credits, customs, premium, profits, returns, revenue, royalty, takings; **8** interest, proceeds, receipts, turnover; **9** incomings, royalties; PHRASES: **3, 7** net profits; **3, 8** net receipts; **4, 5** gate money *UK*; **5, 3** sales tax; **5-5, 3** value-added tax; **5, 7** gross profits, sales revenue; **5, 8** gross receipts; **6, 3** direct tax; **6, 4** import levy; **7, 4** capital gain; **8, 3** indirect tax, property tax.

money store 3 box; **4** safe; **5** chest, purse; **6** coffer, pocket, wallet; **7** handbag; **8** billfold, mattress, moneybag, moneybox, stocking; **9** strongbox; **10** depository, pocketbook, strongroom; PHRASES: **4, 3** cash box; **4, 4** Fort Knox, wall safe; **4-7** safe-deposit; **5, 4** money belt, piggy bank; **8, 5** treasure chest.

moneywort 8, 6 creeping Jennie.

mongrel 3 cur, dog; 5 hound; 10 crossbreed; PHRASES: 3-3 pye-dog.

monitor 3 VDU *UK*; 4 CCTV; 5 study, track, watch; 6 lizard, record, screen; 7 examine, observe, prefect; 8 detector, observer, watchdog; PHRASES: 4, 1, 5, 2 keep a watch on; 4, 2, 3, 2 keep an eye on; 4, 5, 2 keep track of.

monk 5 abbot, bonze, fakir, friar, prior; 6 abbess, Austin, bhikku, hermit, novice, palmer; 7 ascetic, brother, caloyer, Cluniac, dervish, pilgrim, stylite; 8 cenobite *UK*, monastic, talapoin, Trappist; 9 anchorite, bhikkunis, Celestine, Cellarist, coenobite, Dominican, mendicant, pillarist, postulant; 10 Bernardine, Carthusian, Cistercian; 11 Augustinian, Benedictine; PHRASES: 2-3 bosan; 3, 8 lay disciple; 8, 6 reverend father. *See also* **nun**

monkey 3 ape; 4 mona *UK*, saki, titi; 5 Diana, patas; 6 baboon, gibbon, grivet, howler, langur, rhesus, tamper, tinker, uakari, vervet; 7 colobus, Hanuman, macaque, tamarin; 8 capuchin, mandrill, mangabey, marmoset, talapoin, wanderoo; 11 douroucouli; PHRASES: 3, 5, 6 new world ~, old world ~; 5, 6 green ~; 6, 3 ~ nut *UK*; 6, 4 ~ suit; 6, 5 ~ bread; 6, 6 grease ~, howler ~, ~ jacket, ~ orchid *UK*, ~ tricks *UK*, ~ wrench, spider ~, woolly ~; 6-6 monkey-puzzle; 6, 8 ~ business; 8, 6 squirrel ~; 9, 6 proboscis ~.

monkey bread 6 baobab.

monkey nut 6 peanut.

monkey-puzzle 5, 4 Chile pine.

monkfish 9 goosefish; PHRASES: 5, 5 angel shark.

monogram 4 logo, mark, seal, sign; 5 stamp; 6 signet; 7 initial; 8 identify, initials.

monograph 4 book; 5 essay, paper; 6 thesis; 7 article.

monopolize 3 hog; 6 corner; 7 engross; 8 dominate.

monotonous 4 drab, dull, gray, same; 5 stale; 6 boring; 7 clichéd, droning, humdrum, mundane, routine, tedious, uniform; 8 habitual, monotone; 9 hackneyed; 10 changeless, invariable; 11 repetitious; PHRASES: 6-6 cliché-ridden.

monotony 3 rut; 6 groove, tedium; 7 boredom, droning, routine; 8 drabness, dullness, grayness, sameness; 9 staleness, treadmill; 10 repetition; 11 humdrumness, tediousness.

monster 4 huge, ogre; 5 beast, brute, fiend, giant; 6 biggie; 7 whopper; 8 behemoth, enormous, gigantic; 9 leviathan, monstrous.

monstrous 4 evil, huge, ugly; 5 giant; 7 hideous, immoral, monster; 8 enormous, gigantic, gruesome, horrible, horrific; 9 atrocious, grotesque; 10 outrageous.

Montana 2 MT; 6 Helena (capital); 10 bitterroot (flower); PHRASES: 3, 3, 7, 4, 2, 7, 9, 7, 5 Big Sky Country, Land of Shining mountains, Bonanza State (nickname); 4, 3, 6 Gold and Silver (motto); 7, 10 western meadowlark (bird); 8, 5 Treasure State (nickname); 9, 4 ponderosa pine (tree).

month 2 Ab; 3 May; 4 Adar, Elul, July, June, Rabi; 5 April, Iyyar, March, Nisan, Rajab, Safar, Sivan, Tebet; 6 August, Hesvan, Jumada, Kislev, Nivose, Shaban, Tishri; 7 Floreal, January, October, Ramadan, Shawwal, Thammuz, Ventose; 8 Brumaire, December, February, Frimaire, Germinal, Messidor, Muharram, November, Pluviose, Prairial; 9 Fructidor, September, Thermidor; 11 Vendemiaire.

monument 4 bust, slab, tomb; 5 cairn, mound; 6 barrow, column, dolmen, menhir, pillar, plaque, shrine, statue, tablet; 7 obelisk, pyramid; 8 cromlech, megalith, memorial, monolith; 9 mausoleum, tombstone; 10 gravestone; PHRASES: 3, 8 war memorial; 7, 4 victory arch; 7, 8 ancient ~ *UK*; 8, 4 memorial arch.

mood 4 tone, vein; 5 humor, tenor; 6 fettle, morale, temper; 7 spirits; 8 attitude; 10 imperative, indicative, infinitive; 11 disposition, subjunctive, temperament.

moon 4 Luna, mare, mope; 5 Diana, phase, rille; 6 crater, mascon, Selene, waning, waxing; 8 crescent, daydream; 9 moonlight, satellite; PHRASES: 3, 2, 3, 4 man in the ~; 3, 4 new ~, old ~; 4, 4 blue ~, full ~, half ~; 4, 7 last quarter; 5, 2, 5 queen of night; 5, 5 lunar month; 5, 7 first quarter, lunar eclipse; 6, 4 horned ~; 7, 4 gibbous ~, harvest ~, hunter's ~; 8, 4 crescent ~. *See also* **satellite**

moonwort 7 honesty.

moor 4 dock, land; 5 downs *UK*, heath; 7 Othello; PHRASES: 3, 2 tie up; 5, 7 North African.

mop *See* **wipe**

moral 3 saw; 4 fair, good, just, pure; 5 adage, clean, godly, maxim, motto, noble, pious, point, right; 6 decent, honest, lesson, proper, saying; 7 epigram, ethical, message, upright; 8 apothegm, straight, virtuous; 9 honorable, righteous; 10 principled, scrupulous, upstanding; PHRASES: 4-6 highminded.

moralist 4 prig; 5 prude; 6 censor; 7 puritan; 8 watchdog; PHRASES: 3, 6 Mrs Grundy; 5, 9 Watch Committee.

moralistic 2 pi; 4 prim, smug; 5 pious, stern; 6 severe; 7 prudish, puritan; 8 censored, edifying, priggish; 9 pietistic, shockable, squeamish, Victorian; 10 censorious, expurgated, moralizing, overmodest; 11 bowdlerized, euphemistic; 12 overdelicate; 13 sanctimonious; PHRASES: 4-9 self-righteous; 5-7 mealy-mouthed; 6-4-4 holierthan-thou; 6-5 strait-laced; 6-6 narrowminded.

morality 5 honor, mores, right; 6 ethics, ideals, morals, virtue; 7 beliefs, decency, honesty, justice, manners, probity; 8 scruples; 9 integrity, propriety, rectitude, standards; 10 conscience, principles. *See also* **moral**

moralize 6 preach; 7 lecture; 8 harangue; 9 sermonize; PHRASES: 2, 2, 5 go on about; 4, 5 hold forth.

morals *See* **ethics**

moral support 4 help; 5 favor; 6 succor; 7 backing, empathy; 8 advocacy, approval, sympathy; 10 assistance, friendship, protection; 11 endorsement; 12 championship, intercession; 13 collaboration, corroboration, encouragement.

morass *See* **quagmire**

morbid 4 dark; 5 moody; 6 gloomy, morose; 7 macabre; 8 gruesome, perverse, sinister; 11 melancholic.

morbilli 7 measles.

more 3 piu; 4 else, over, plus; 5 extra; 6 longer; 10 additional.

morgue 8 mortuary.

moribund *See* **dying**

Mormon 6-3, 5 Latter-day Saint.

morning 2 AM; 4 dawn, dewy, morn; 5 early, fresh, matin, prime, sunup, terce; 6 Aurora, matins; 7 dawning, sunrise; 8 cockcrow, daybreak, daylight, forenoon; 12 ant-

emeridian; PHRASES: 3, 4 ack emma; 4, 6 dawn chorus; 5, 2, 3 break of day; 5, 2, 4 crack of dawn; 5, 5 first light; 7, 4 ~ coat *UK*, ~ star, ~ suit; 7, 5 ~ dress, ~ glory, ~ light, ~ watch *UK*; 7-5 morning-fresh; 7, 8 ~ sickness.

morning star 7 daystar.

morose *See* **miserable**

morph *See* **transform**

morsel 5 crumb, scrap; 6 tidbit.

mortal 4 soul; 5 fatal, grave, great, human; 6 deadly, finite, lethal, person, severe; 7 earthly, extreme, serious, worldly; 8 terminal; 9 corporeal; 10 individual; PHRASES: 5, 5 human being.

mortgage 6 wadset; PHRASES: 4, 4 home loan *UK*; 7, 3 Freddie Mac; 10-4, 8 adjustable-rate ~.

mortician 10 undertaker.

mortification *See* **shame**

mortuary 6 morgue.

mosaic 5 inlay; 7 montage, tessera; 8 tessella.

mosquito 4 gnat; PHRASES: 8, 3 ~ net; 8, 4 ~ boat *UK*, ~ hawk.

moss 4 seta; 5 layer; 6 lichen; 7 rhizoid; 8 bryology, sphagnum; 9 bryophyte, liverwort; 10 bryologist; PHRASES: 3, 4 bog ~, oak ~; 4, 4 hair ~, long ~ *UK*, ~ pink, ~ rose, peat ~, tree ~, wall ~, wood ~; 4, 6 ~ stitch; 5, 4 Irish ~; 8, 4 reindeer ~.

most 4 very; 5 truly; 6 highly, really; 9 extremely; PHRASES: 1, 4, 6 a good number; 1, 5, 6 a large amount; 3, 8 the majority; 6, 3 nearly all; 6, 8 nearly everyone.

moth 5 eggar, egger; 6 burnet, lackey, lappet; 7 bagworm, emerald, emperor; 8 cecropia; 9 clearwing, woodborer; PHRASES: 2, 4 io ~; 3, 4 wax ~; 4, 4 goat ~, hawk ~, luna ~, puss ~; 5, 4 gypsy ~, owlet ~, swift ~, tiger ~; 5-4 brown-tail; 6, 4 cactus ~, tineid ~; 6-4, 4 death's-head ~; 7, 4 cabbage ~, clothes ~, codling ~, noctuid ~, pyralid ~, tussock ~; 8, 4 hercules ~, peppered ~; 9, 4 geometrid ~, saturniid ~, underwing ~.

mothball 5 delay; 8 postpone; 12 decommission; PHRASES: 3, 2, 3 put on ice; 3, 5 put aside; 4, 2 shut up; 4, 4 pack away.

mother 2 ma; 3 mam *UK*, mom, mum *UK*; 4 mama; 5 mamma, mammy, mommy, mummy *UK*, queen; 6 bearer, cosset, mither; PHRASES: **6, 3** ~ wit, soccer mom; **6, 4** ~ lode, ~ ship; **6, 5** ~ earth, ~ goose; **6, 6** foster ~, ~ church, ~ nature, ~ tongue, single ~; **6, 7** ~ country, M~ Courage, M~ Hubbard, M~ Machree, M~ Shipton; **6, 8** ~ superior; **8, 6** reverend ~.

mother-of-pearl 5 nacre.

motif 4 idea; **5** image, shape, theme, topic; **6** design; **7** keynote, pattern, subject; **10** decoration.

motion 6 signal; **7** gesture, kinesis; **8** dynamics, kinetics, mobility, motility, movement, proposal; **9** migration, perpetual; **10** kinematics, locomotion; **13** perambulation; PHRASES: **4, 2, 6** laws of ~; **4, 6** slow ~; **5, 3, 6** early day ~ UK; **7, 6** kinetic energy. See also moving

motionless 5 fixed, still, stuck; **6** frozen, poised, static, steady; **8** balanced, becalmed, immobile, inactive, stagnant, standing, unmoving, windless; **9** immovable, paralyzed, petrified, sedentary, unmovable; **10** spellbound, stationary, transfixed; PHRASES: **2, 6** at anchor; **5, 2, 5** still as death; **5-5** stock-still; **6, 2, 3, 4** rooted to the spot.

motionless (be motionless) 3 sit; **4** halt, land, rest, stay, stop, wait; **5** abide, cease, check, pause, perch, sleep, stand, tarry; **6** alight, freeze, remain, settle; **7** slumber; **8** stagnate, vegetate; PHRASES: **3, 4** die down, not stir; **3, 5** not budge, sit tight; **4, 2, 1, 4** come to a halt; **4, 2, 4** come to rest; **4, 3** stay put; **4, 5** keep quiet, keep still, stop short; **5, 4** stand fast, stand firm, stick fast; **5, 5** stand still; **6, 6** remain seated.

motionlessness 4 coma, halt, lock, stop; **5** pause, poise, stand, truce; **6** freeze, stasis, torpor, trance; **7** balance, inertia, languor, latency; **8** abeyance, deadlock, dormancy, fixation, gridlock, inaction, numbness, stoppage; **9** catalepsy, catatonia, cessation, inertness, passivity, stability, stagnancy, stalemate, stiffness, stillness; **10** deadliness, immobility, inactivity, stagnation, standstill, steadiness, suspension, vegetation; **11** deathliness, equilibrium; PHRASES: **4, 3** jake leg; **4, 4** dead stop, full stop.

motion toward 7 advance, headway, ingress; **8** approach, progress; **9** evolution; **11** progression.

motivate 4 coax, jolt, lead, move, pull, spur; **5** begin, cause, evoke, impel, prick, rally, rouse, start; **6** advise, arouse, cajole, enlist, excite, exhort, hustle, induce, prompt; **7** animate, attract, dispose, flatter, impress, incline, inspire, provoke, recruit; **8** advocate, blandish, convince, energize, initiate, interest, intrigue, persuade; **9** captivate, challenge, electrify, encourage, fascinate, galvanize, influence, instigate, stimulate, tantalize; PHRASES: **3, 1, 5** set a trend; **3, 2, 6** set in motion; **3, 3, 4** set the pace; **4, 2** spur on, turn on; **4, 4** talk into; **4, 5** call forth; **5, 2** bring on, cheer on, drive on; **5, 3, 4** sugar the pill; **5, 3, 7** sound the trumpet; **5-4** sweet-talk; **5, 4, 5** carry one's point; **6, 2** appeal to; **7, 3, 4** sweeten the pill.

motivated 4 keen; **5** eager, moved, urged; **6** caused, coaxed, goaded, roused; **7** devoted, enticed, incited, induced, prodded, seduced, whipped; **8** animated, exhorted, impelled, inflamed, inspired, prompted, provoked; **9** bewitched, committed, energized, flattered, persuaded, pressured; **10** challenged, encouraged, galvanized, hypnotized, influenced, mesmerized, spellbound, stimulated; **11** electrified; PHRASES: **4-9** self-motivated; **5, 2** egged on; **7, 2** spurred on.

motivated (be motivated) 6 submit; **7** concede, succumb; PHRASES: **4, 3** fall for; **4, 3, 4** feel the urge, heed the call; **5, 3, 3** catch the bug.

motivational 7 kinetic, rousing, teasing; **8** alluring, charming, hypnotic, inciting, inviting, magnetic, mesmeric, tempting; **9** incentive, provoking; **10** attractive, bewitching, compelling, convincing, energizing, motivating, persuasive, suggestive; **11** challenging, encouraging, fascinating, galvanizing, influencing, influential, instigating, instigative, provocative, stimulating, tantalizing; **12** electrifying, inflammatory, irresistible, spellbinding.

motivator 5 agent, mover; **6** coaxer, orator; **7** abettor, adviser, lobbyer, manager, planner, tempter; **8** activist, agitator, inspirer, lobbyist, preacher, prompter, Rasputin, salesman, Svengali; **9** counselor, demagogue, firebrand, flatterer, hypnotist, influence, persuader, publicist, temptress; **10** advertiser, hypnotizer, instigator, politician, ringleader, seductress; **11** manipulator, rhetorician, seditionist, trendsetter; **12** propagandist, troublemaker; PHRASES: **5, 3, 7** aider and abettor; **5, 5** press agent, prime mover; **5, 6** femme fatale; **6, 6** moving spirit;

6-6 rabble-rouser; **8, 5** pressure group.

motive **3** aim; **4** call, duty, goal, hope; **5** angle, cause, ideal; **6** design, desire, excuse, object, reason; **7** grounds, impetus, impulse, kinetic, pretext, purpose; **8** ambition, lodestar, vocation; **9** brainwave, direction, intention, objective, rationale, reasoning; **10** aspiration, compulsion, conscience, mainspring, motivation; **11** inspiration, stimulation; **13** justification; PHRASES: **5, 2, 4, 2** words to live by; **6, 4** bright idea; **7, 4** guiding star; **7, 5** driving force, guiding light; **7, 8** driving ambition; **8, 6** ulterior ~; **8, 7** personal reasons.

motiveless **6** casual, chance, random; **7** aimless; **9** arbitrary, unplanned; **10** accidental, fortuitous, incidental, irrational, unintended; **11** purposeless, unmotivated; **12** coincidental; **13** serendipitous, unaccountable.

motley *See* **assorted**

motor **5** drive; **6** dynamo, engine; **8** motorcar; **9** generator; PHRASES: **5, 7** ~ scooter, ~ vehicle; **8, 5** outboard ~.

motorcycle **4** bike; **5** moped; **7** scooter; **9** motorbike; **11** combination; **12** motorscooter.

motorcycle racing **2** TT; **9** motocross, superbike; **10** scrambling; PHRASES: **4, 2, 3, 2** Isle of Man TT; **4, 2, 3, 4** Race of the Year; **4-5, 6** dirt-track racing; **5, 2** Dutch TT; **5, 4** Grand Prix; **5, 4, 2, 4** Grand Prix (GP) race; **5, 5** rally cross; **5, 5, 4** Macau Grand Prix; **7, 5** sidecar class; **9, 4** motorbike race; **9, 5** unlimited class; **10, 4** motorcycle race; **10, 5** motorcycle class.

motoring *See* **driving**

motor racing **2** FI, GP; **3** WRC; **4** NHRA, race, SCCA; **6** NASCAR; **7** karting, raceway; **8** rallying; **9** autocross, Champcars, racetrack; **10** Daytona500; PHRASES: **2, 4** Le Mans; **2-7** Go-Karting *tm*; **3-3, 4** hot-rod race; **4, 4** drag race, road race; **4, 5** hill climb; **4, 6** auto racing, drag racing, road racing; **5-3, 4** stock-car race; **5, 4, 4** Grand Prix race; **5, 5** motor rally; **5, 5, 5** Monte Carlo rally; **5, 6** Busch Series; **6, 6** banger racing; **6, 7** racing circuit; **7, 3** Formula One, Formula Two; **7, 5** Formula Three; **7, 6** IndyCar racing; **8, 6** speedway racing.

motor-racing terms **3** lap, pit; **4** bend, grid, oval; **5** Armco™, setup, start, track; **6** corner; **7** chicane, circuit, gearing, hacking, hairpin, jetting, restart, skidpan *UK*, wheelie; **8** spoiling, straight; **9** funneling; **10** scrambling; **11** carburation; **13** slipstreaming; PHRASES: **1-4** S-bend *UK*; **1-5, 7** G-force loading; **1-6** T-boning; **3, 4** pit lane, pit stop, pit wall; **4-3** over-rev, spin-out; **4, 4** fuel stop; **4-4, 4** left-hand kink; **4, 5** parc fermé; **4-5** down-force; **4-6** left-hander; **4, 7** long circuit, road circuit, tire stagger; **4, 8** pole position; **5, 3** mixed set; **5-4, 4** right-hand kink; **5-6** right-hander; **5, 7** short circuit; **6, 3** flying lap; **6-4** clutch-slip; **6, 7** banked circuit, safety barrier; **6, 9** ground clearance; **7, 3** hooking off, peeling off, sliding off; **8, 3** spinning out; **8, 4** hoicking back, starting grid; **8, 7** mountain circuit; **9, 4** checkered flag.

motorway **7** highway.

mottled **5** dusty, tabby; **6** dotted, pocked, spotty; **7** dappled, macular, spotted; **8** brindled, freckled, maculate, peppered, speckled; **9** speckledy; PHRASES: **3-7** fly-spotted; **4-3-6** salt-and-pepper.

mouldy *See* **stale**

moult *See* **shed**

mound *See* **mass**

mount **4** back; **5** board, horse, mound, steed; **6** ascend, embark; **8** bestride, increase; **10** bestraddle; PHRASES: **3, 2** get on, hop in, set up; **3, 6** hop aboard; **4, 2** jump in; **5, 2** climb on. *See also* **mountain**

mountain **2** K2, mt; **3** alp, ben *UK*, Ida, kop, tor; **4** berg, brae, Cook, crag, dune, Etna, fell *UK*, Fuji, heap, hill, hump, knob, Ossa, peak, pike, pile, scar, spur, tump; **5** Athos, Atlas, bluff, butte, chain, cliff, climb, crest, devil, downs, Eiger, Horeb, Kenya, knoll, kopje *UK*, Logan, motte, mound, mount, range, ridge, Sinai; **6** Ararat, Averno, Bonete, Carmel, Egmont, Elbrus, Hermon, Lhotse, massif, Pelion, saddle, sierra, summit; **7** Brocken, drumlin, Everest, heights, Helicon, hillock, hilltop, hummock, Olympus, Palomar, Skiddaw, Snowdon, volcano; **8** foothill, Jungfrau, McKinley, pinnacle, Rushmore; **9** Annapurna, highlands, inselberg, Kosciusko, monticule, Parnassus, precipice, steepness; **10** Chimborazo, cordillera, Hellvellyn, Matterhorn; **11** Kilimanjaro, mountaintop; **12** Kanchenjunga; **14** mountaineering; PHRASES: **3, 5** Ben Nevis; **4, 4** sand dune; **4-4, 4** snow-clad peak; **4, 5** Mont Blanc; **5, 4**

Pikes Peak; **5, 5** Great Gable; **5, 6** Mount Wilson; **5-6, 4** cloud-capped peak; **5, 7** Mount Whitney; **5, 8** Table M~; **5, 9** roche moutonnée; **6, 6** Godwin Austen; **7, 4** Scafell Pike, Wheeler Peak; **8, 3** ~ ash, ~ cat, ~ dew; **8, 4** ~ goat, ~ lion; **8, 5** ~ range. *See also* **mountain range**

mountain ash 5 rowan.

mountain building 7 orogeny; **10** orogenesis.

mountaineering terms 3 aid, jam; **4** camp, edge, frig, solo, yeti; **5** belay, cheat, clean, climb, guide, route, smear, swing; **6** abseil, ascend, bridge, garden, porter, prusik *UK*, rappel; **7** aneroid, belayed, Bigfoot, bivouac, camming, chimney, cleated, climber, deadman, descend, goggles, gullied, layaway, pendule, reverse, soloing, upclimb; **8** alpinism, alpinist, ascender, belaying, cleaning, climbing, cragsman *UK*, glissade, polished, scramble, terraced, traverse, Tyrolean; **9** boldering, crevassed, gardening, hexentric, prusiking, Sasquatch, upclimber; **10** bouldering, glissading, laybacking, scrambling; **11** outcropping, overhanging; PHRASES: **2-2** yo-yo; **3, 4** top rope; **3, 5** air route; **3, 8** aid climbing *UK*; **4-2** boot-ax; **4, 3** rope off; **4-3** step-cut; **4, 4** base camp; **4-4** heel-hook; **4, 5** bolt route; **4-5** rock-climb; **4, 7** fell walking, rock climber; **4-7** step-cutting; **4, 8** free climbing, hill climbing, rock climbing; **5, 1, 4** scale a peak; **5-5** front-point; **5, 7** belay braking; **5, 8** clean climbing; **5-8** front-pointing; **6, 5** Sherpa guide; **7, 2, 6** descend en rappel; **7, 4** advance camp; **7, 5** classic route; **7, 7** Brocken Spectre; **7, 8** balance climbing; **8-5** mountain-climb; **8-7** mountain-dweller; **10, 5** artificial route.

mountain laurel 6, 4 calico bush.

mountain lion 4 puma.

mountainous 4 high, huge; **5** giant, hilly, lofty, rocky, steep; **6** alpine, Andean, craggy, upland; **7** highest, rolling, soaring, topmost, topping; **8** alpigene, elevated, enormous, gigantic, highland, hillocky, hummocky, mounting, Olympian, orogenic, towering; **9** ascending, Himalayan, subalpine; **10** alpestrine, monumental, mountained, orogenetic, undulating; **11** monticulous, precipitous; **12** altitudinous; PHRASES: **4-4** snow-clad; **4-6** snow-capped; **4-8** hill-dwelling; **5-6** cloud-capped.

mountain range 2 os; **3** col; **4** Alps, bank, comb, Jura, kame, spur; **5** Andes, arête, bench, chain, chine, crest, esker, Ghats, ridge, spine, Urals; **6** divide, massif, Ortles, Ozarks, Pamirs, saddle, sierra, Vosges; **7** hogback, moraine, Rockies; **8** Caucasus, Pennines, Pyrenees; **9** Apennines, Catskills, Dolomites, Himalayas, Snowdonia, watershed; **10** Cairngorms, cordillera, saddleback; **11** Carpathians; PHRASES: **4, 4** hog's back; **4, 9** Blue Mountains, Harz Mountains; **5, 6** Great Divide; **5, 9** Atlas Mountains, Rocky Mountains, Smoky Mountains; **6, 6** Sierra Nevada; **6, 7** Massif Central; **7, 5** Cascade Range.

mountain sheep 7 bighorn.

mountain sickness 4 puna.

mountebank 5 cheat, fraud; **8** deceiver; **9** charlatan, trickster.

mounting *See* **rising**

mourn *See* **grieve**

mournful 3 sad; **4** blue, down, glum; **6** dismal, gloomy, pining, woeful; **7** doleful, forlorn, tearful, ululant, unhappy; **8** dejected, desolate, dolorous, funereal, mourning, plangent, wretched; **9** depressed, miserable, plaintive, sorrowful, threnodic, woebegone; **10** lugubrious, melancholy; **11** heartbroken, languishing; **12** disconsolate, heavyhearted, inconsolable; PHRASES: **5-8** grief-stricken; **6-7** broken-hearted.

mouse deer 10 chevrotain.

mouth 3 gob *UK*, yap; **4** trap; **6** kisser.

mouthful 4 bite, dish; **5** bolus, candy, piece, slice, sweet; **6** afters *UK*, course, entrée, gobbet, morsel, nibble, remove, sliver, tidbit; **7** dessert, helping, portion, pudding *UK*, seconds, serving, starter; **9** appetizer, entremets; PHRASES: **4-4** side-dish; **4, 6** fish course, main course; **4, 7** hors d'oeuvre; **5, 6** first course; **6, 7** second helping.

movable 6 mobile; **7** mutable; **8** portable, variable; **10** adjustable, changeable, detachable; **11** impermanent; **12** transferable; **13** transportable.

move 2 go; **3** ebb, tug; **4** back, draw, flow, haul, pull, push, rise, rush, send, sink, soar, spin, stir, wane; **5** budge, climb, drift, drive, impel, mount, nudge, shift, shove, steps, throw, upset, whirl; **6** affect, ascend, change, convey, effort, evolve, gather, gyrate, hustle, plunge, propel, rotate, stream; **7** actuate, advance, descend, develop, deviate, proceed, propose, regress, scatter, subside; **8** dislodge, dispatch, disperse, displace, mobilize, motivate, progress, relocate, transfer; **9** oscillate, transport, transpose; **10** retrogress; PHRASES: **4, 2** back up; **4, 4, 3** pick one's way; **4, 5** keep going; **4, 7** wade through; **6, 3** gather way; **6, 5** change place; **6, 8** change position; **6, 9** change direction.

move apart 3 fan; **4** part; **6** deploy, spread; **9** outspread; PHRASES: **3, 3** fan out; **6, 3** spread out.

move forward 4 bunt, butt; **5** drive, shunt, sweep; **6** hustle; **7** advance; PHRASES: **4, 2** move on; **5, 4, 6** drive like leaves; **5, 6, 3** sweep before one.

movement 3 tic; **4** step, tide, trio, wave; **5** largo, rondo, taxis, trend; **6** action, dadism, minuet, motion, presto, twitch; **7** allegro, andante, crusade, gesture, kinesis, scherzo; **8** activity, Chartism, diaspora, diastole, futurism, maneuver; **9** andantino, communism, larghetto, modernism, socialism; **10** allegretto; **11** communalism; **12** collectivism; **13** ecumenicalism, expressionism, impressionism; PHRASES: **6, 8** Oxford M~.

move round 3 lap; **5** orbit; **6** circle; **9** circulate; **14** circumambulate, circumnavigate.

move sideways 5 avoid, sidle; **7** deviate; **8** sidestep; PHRASES: **4, 5** step aside.

move slowly 4 chug, drip, ease, idle, inch, laze, limp, ooze, plod; **5** amble, crawl, creep, mince, mooch, mosey, scuff; **6** hirple _UK_, hobble, stroll, toddle, totter, trudge, wobble; **7** dogtrot, saunter, shamble, shuffle, stagger, traipse, trickle; PHRASES: **2, 2, 1, 6, 4** go at a snail's pace; **2, 4** go slow; **3, 4** peg away _UK_; **3-4** jog-trot; **4, 2, 4** take it easy.

movie 2 ET; **3** set; **4** take; **5** flick, image, shoot, video; **6** record; **7** picture; **9** Bollywood, Hollywood; PHRASES: **3, 6** big screen; **6, 6** silver screen; **6, 7** motion picture, moving picture; **7, 5** bromide paper.

moving 3 sad; **5** astir, going, motor; **6** active, fluent, flying, mobile, motile, motive, riding; **7** driving, erratic, flowing, movable, nomadic, passing, runaway, running, rushing, walking; **8** agitated, ambulant, bustling, drifting, fleeting, marching, motional, poignant, restless, shifting, stirring, touching; **9** emotional, impelling, mercurial, scurrying, streaming, traveling,

wandering; **10** automotive, locomotive, propellant, propelling, relocating; **11** distressing, peripatetic; **12** motivational, transitional; PHRASES: **2, 3, 2** on the go; **2, 3, 3** on the hop, on the run; **2, 3, 4** on the move, on the road, on the wing; **2, 3, 5** on the march, up and about; **2, 5** en route; **2, 6** in motion; **2, 7** in transit; **4-9** self-propelled; **5, 3** under way; **5, 4** under sail; **6, 6** having motion.

mow _See_ **cut**

MP 7, 5 melting point; **8, 6** Military Police.

MPG 5, 3, 6 miles per gallon.

MPH 5, 3, 4 miles per hour.

Mr 3 sir, sri; **4** babu, Herr; **5** sahib, senor; **6** Master, Messrs; **7** effendi; **8** monsieur.

Mrs. 2 Fr; **3** Mme; **8** Mistress.

MS 10 manuscript; **11** millisecond.

MT 8 Mountain.

much 4 glut, lots, many, more, most, tons; **5** ample, great, heaps _UK_, loads, often, piles, scads; **6** masses _UK_, muckle _UK_, myriad, oodles, plenty; **7** copious, greatly; **8** abundant; **9** plentiful; **11** exceedingly; PHRASES: **1, 3, 2** a lot of.

mucilaginous 4 gory; **5** gluey; **6** mucous; **9** glutinous.

muck _See_ **dirt**

mucky _See_ **dirty**

mucus 3 pus; **4** clot, glue, gore, size; **5** glair, grume; **6** gluten, matter, phlegm; **7** albumen, pituita; **8** mucilage.

mud 4 clay, daub, dirt, mire, muck, ooze, silt, slob, slop; **5** adobe, clart, slime, slush, swill; **6** sludge; **8** sediment; **10** mudskipper, mudslinger; PHRASES: **3, 3** ~ hen, ~ map, ~ pie; **3, 4** ~ bath, ~ flat; **3, 5** ~ puppy; **3, 6** ~ turtle.

muddle 4 mess; **5** chaos; **6** baffle, jumble, puzzle, tangle; **7** clutter, confuse, nonplus, perplex, stupefy; **8** bewilder, confound, disarray, disorder, shambles, upheaval; **9** bamboozle, commotion, confusion; **10** disarrange; **11** disentangle, disorganize; **15** disorganization; PHRASES: **3, 2** mix up; **3-2** mix-up; **4, 2** mess up.

muddled 4 awry; **5** amiss, askew; **7** chaotic, haywire, jumbled, tangled; **8** cockeyed, confused; **9** scrambled; **12** labyrinthine; PHRASES: **4, 4, 5** head over heels; **4-5** arsy-versy _UK_; **5-5** topsy-turvy; **6-4** upside-down.

muddy 4 drab, miry, oozy; 5 boggy, dingy, dirty, mucky, murky, silty; 6 clarty *UK*, filthy, grubby, marshy, quaggy, slabby, sloppy, sludgy, slushy, sodden, turbid; 7 squishy; 8 squelchy; 11 sedimentary, waterlogged.

muff 4 drop, miss; 5 botch; 6 bungle, fumble, mishit; 9 mishandle; PHRASES: 4, 2 mess up. *See also* **accessories**

muffle 3 jam; 4 mute; 5 drown; 6 baffle, deaden; 7 silence; 8 insulate; 10 soundproof; PHRASES: 3, 8 use earplugs; 5, 3 drown out.

muffled 4 flat; 5 heavy, muted; 6 damped, dulled; 7 stifled; 8 deadened, silenced; 9 smothered; 10 soundproof; 11 nonresonant.

mug 3 rob; 4 face; 6 ambush, attack, phizog *UK*; 7 assault; 8 features; 11 countenance; PHRASES: 4, 2 hold up.

muggy *See* **humid**

mulch 5 cover, dress; 6 leaves; 7 protect; 8 covering, insulate; 10 insulation, protection; PHRASES: 3, 5 top dress; 7, 6 organic matter.

multiple 4 many; 7 several, various; 8 compound, manifold, numerous.

multiplication 3 GCF, HCF, lcm; 4 cube, surd; 5 power; 6 factor, square; 7 product; 8 breeding, doubling, exponent, multiple, tripling; 9 factorial; 10 multiplier; 11 submultiple; 12 multiplicand; 13 factorization, proliferation; 14 exponentiation; PHRASES: 4, 4 cube root; 4, 4, 6 root mean square; 5, 6 prime factor; 6, 4 square root.

multiplicity 7 polygon, variety; 8 infinity, polygamy, polygyny; 9 diversity, multitude, pluralism, polyandry; 10 polyhedron, polytheism; 12 multiformity, numerousness; 13 compositeness, countlessness, multifoldness; 14 innumerability; 15 multilateralism.

multiply 5 breed; 6 expand; 7 burgeon; 8 increase, mushroom, recreate, snowball; 9 propagate, reproduce; 11 proliferate.

multipurpose vehicle 6, 5 people mover; 6, 7 people carrier *UK*.

multitude 3 mob; 4 army, host, lots, many, wads; 5 crowd, horde, scads; 6 dozens, scores, throng; 7 legions, myriads, umpteen; 8 billions, hundreds, jillions, millions, plethora, zillions; 9 thousands, trillions; PHRASES: 1, 3 a lot; 3, 5 big bucks; 4, 2, 9 tens of thousands; 4, 3 tidy sum; 5, 1, 3 quite a few; 5, 6 great number, large amount; 5, 7 large numbers.

multitudinous 6 legion; 8 manifold, multiple, numerous; 9 multifold; 12 multifarious, multitudinal.

mum 2 sh; 5 quiet; 6 silent.

Mumbai 6 Bombay.

mumble 4 mump, sigh, slur; 5 mouth; 6 murmur, mutter; 7 whisper.

munch *See* **chew**

mundane *See* **ordinary**

municipal building 9 firehouse; 10 courthouse; PHRASES: 4, 4 city hall, town hall; 4, 7 fire station; 6, 7 police station; 6, 8 county building; 8, 7 precinct station; 9, 6 community center.

muntjac 7, 4 barking deer *UK*.

murder 3 gas; 4 bomb, burn, kill, rope, stab; 5 brain, burke, choke, drown, knife, lance, saber, shoot, smite, spear, waste; 6 pistol, poison, poleax *UK*, stifle, strike; 7 bayonet, garrote, hanging, knifing, murther, poleaxe, sandbag, smother, wasting; 8 drowning, garrotte, homicide, shooting, strangle, thuggery; 9 eliminate, garroting, poisoning, suffocate; 10 asphyxiate, garrotting; 11 assassinate, electrocute, suffocation; 12 asphyxiation, manslaughter; 13 assassination, strangulation; PHRASES: 2, 2 do in; 2, 3 do for; 2, 4, 4 do away with; 3, 3 rub out; 3, 4 gun down; 3, 7 run through; 4, 2 wall up; 4, 2, 5 beat to death; 4, 3 bump off, pick off, take out; 4, 3, 1, 4 take for a ride; 4, 5 burn alive, bury alive; 4, 6 gang ~, mass ~; 5, 2, 7 crime of passion; 5, 4 shoot down; 5, 10 blunt instrument; 6, 4, 4 ~ most foul; 6, 6 commit ~, ~ weapon; 7, 6 capital ~, classic ~; 8, 6 contract ~; 8, 7 unlawful killing.

murderer 4 Cain, thug; 5 bravo; 6 bomber, gunman, killer, psycho; 7 ruffian; 8 assassin, gangster, homicide, poisoner, regicide, whodunit; 9 cutthroat, desperado, garrotter, matricide, murderess, parricide, patricide, strangler, terrorist, uxoricide, whodunnit; 10 fratricide, psychopath, sororicide; 11 infanticide, tyrannicide; PHRASES: 2, 8 ax ~; 3, 3 hit man; 4, 8 mass ~; 5, 3 hired gun; 5, 6 hired killer; 5, 8 hired assassin; 6, 6 serial killer; 7, 3 hatchet man; 8, 6 contract killer; 9, 6 homicidal maniac.

murderous 4 gory; 5 cruel; 6 bloody, brutal, savage; 8 suicidal; 9 genocidal, homicidal; 10 sanguinary; 11 destructive, ensanguined, internecine; **12** bloodthirsty, pathological, psychopathic, slaughterous; **13** cannibalistic; PHRASES: **3-6** man-eating, red-handed; **4-7** cold-blooded, head-hunting; **5-7** blood-stained, death-dealing; **7-5** trigger-happy.

muriate **8** chloride.

murk **3** fog; **4** blur, film, fret, haar *UK*, haze, mist, smog, veil; **5** smoke, steam, vapor; **6** miasma, muslin; **7** tarnish; **8** cataract, distance, drabness, dullness, grayness, haziness; **9** dinginess, filminess, fogginess, fuzziness, mistiness, murkiness, obscurity, peasouper, sandstorm, vagueness; **10** bleariness, blurriness, cloudiness, exhalation, opaqueness, remoteness; **12** condensation; **14** indistinctness; PHRASES: **3, 4** sea mist; **3, 10** low definition, low visibility; **4, 5** fret vapor, poor sight, soft focus; **4, 10** poor visibility.

murky **4** dark, hazy, pale, weak; **5** blear, dusty, faint, filmy, foggy, fuzzy, milky, misty, muted, muzzy, smoky, thick, vague, white; **6** bleary, blurry, cloudy, feeble, opaque, remote, smoggy, smoked, steamy, veiled; **7** bleared, blurred, distant, dubious, frosted, miasmal, miasmic, obscure, shadowy, stygian, suspect, unclear; **8** diffused, nebulous, obscured; **10** indistinct, suspicious; **12** questionable; PHRASES: **3-7** ill-defined; **3-10** low-definition; **4-5** smog-laden, soft-focus; **5, 2, 3** clear as mud; **5-5** smoke-laden; **5-6** smoke-filled; **7, 2** steamed up.

murmur **3** hum, lap; **4** blow, buzz, fizz, flow, hiss, moan, plop, purl, purr, sigh, whir; **5** chink, clink, clunk, croon, plash, plunk, sough, swish; **6** babble, burble, gurgle, mutter, patter, ripple, rustle, sizzle, splash, squash, squish, swoosh, tinkle, wheeze; **7** breathe, crackle, droning, sputter, whining, whisper; **8** mumbling, splutter; **9** undertone; **11** susurration.

Murphy's Law **4, 3** Sod's law.

murther **6** murder.

muscle **4** beef, thew; **5** brawn, clout, power, psoas, sinew, teres; **6** biceps, flexor, rectus, soleus, tendon; **7** agonist, deltoid, erector, gluteus, iliacus, levator, rotator, triceps; **8** abductor, adductor, detrusor, elevator, extensor, gracilis, masseter, opponent, pectoral, peroneal, pronator, rhomboid, scalenus, splenius, strength; **9** beefiness, depressor, influence, obturator, sartorius, sphincter, supinator, trapezius; **10** antago-

nist, buccinator, latissimus, quadriceps, robustness, temporalis; **11** constrictor, intercostal, muscularity, stringiness; **13** gastrocnemius.

muscleman **4** hulk, hunk; **5** Atlas, bully, giant, heavy, Rambo, Titan; **6** Amazon, Samson, Tarzan *UK*; **7** bouncer, bruiser, Goliath; **8** beefcake, bullyboy, Hercules, meathead, Superman; **9** superhero; **11** bodybuilder; PHRASES: **2-3** he-man; **2, 8** Mr Universe; **5, 2, 8** tower of strength; **5, 3** tough guy; **6-3, 3** strong-arm man; **6, 3, 5** Batman and Robin; **7-3** chucker-out; **7, 7** Captain America; **8, 4** mythical hero.

muse **4** Clio; **5** Erato, query, think; **6** ponder, Thalia, Urania, wonder; **7** Euterpe, suspect; **8** Calliope, meditate, question; **9** Melpomene, speculate; **10** conjecture, Polyhymnia; **11** inspiration, Terpsichore.

mush **3** pap; **4** mash, slop; **5** paste, purée, slush; **10** sugariness; **14** sentimentalism, sentimentality.

mushroom **7** burgeon; **8** flourish, multiply; **9** germinate, toadstool; **10** champignon; **11** proliferate; PHRASES: **4, 8** wild ~; **5, 4** fairy ring; **5, 8** field ~, magic ~; **6, 2** spring up; **6, 8** button ~; **8, 5** ~ cloud.

music **4** song, tune; **6** melody; **7** harmony; **11** composition.

music (piece of music) **3** air; **4** duet, hymn, Lied, mass, solo, song, trio; **5** canon, carol, chant, étude, fugue, march, motet, nonet, octet, opera, psalm, rondo, round, suite; **6** anthem, aubade, ballad, chorus, entrée, septet, sextet, shanty, sonata; **7** arietta, ballade, cantata, canzone, chanson, chantey, chorale, fanfare, fantasy, lullaby, prelude, quartet, quintet, requiem, romance, scherzo, toccata; **8** berceuse, canticle, cavatina, chaconne, concerto, coronach *UK*, entr'acte, fantasia, madrigal, movement, nocturne, operetta, oratorio, overture, partitia, rhapsody, ricercar, serenade, sinfonia, sonatina, symphony; **9** bagatelle, capriccio, impromptu, interlude, polonaise, spiritual; **10** barcarolle, canzonetta, concertino, humoresque, intermezzo; **11** passacaglia; **12** divertimento; PHRASES: **8, 6** concerto grosso.

music (type of music) **3** AOR, emo, pop, rag, rap; **4** jazz, jive, pogo *UK*, punk, rave, rock, soul; **5** bebop, disco, house, indie, opera, ragga, swing; **6** ballet, cumbia, garage, gospel, jungle, melody, motown, nortec, reggae, techno, zydeco; **7** ambient, country, cowpunk, harmony, hymnody, norteño, ragtime, skiffle; **8** highlife, psalmody, ranchera; **9** bluegrass, crossover, hymnology, plainsong, spiritual, warehouse; **10** barbershop, musicality, rockabilly; **11** barrelhouse, tunefulness; **12** musicianship; **13** melodiousness; PHRASES: **3-3** doo-wop, hip-hop; **3, 4** big beat; **3, 5** bel canto; **4-3** trip-hop; **4, 3, 4** rock and roll; **4, 4** jazz funk; **4, 5** acid house; **4, 9** easy listening; **5, 4** dance hall; **5, 5** heavy metal, plain chant; **6, 3, 5** rhythm and blues; **6, 5** church music; **6-6** boogie-woogie; **7, 5** chamber music; **8, 4** township jazz; **8, 5** elevator music; **9, 5** classical music. *See also* **music (piece of music), world music**

musical **4** Cats, Gigi, Hair, Mame, show; **5** Blitz *UK*, Evita; **6** dulcet, Grease, Kismet, Oliver; **7** Cabaret, melodic, tuneful; **8** Godspell, operetta, Showboat, virtuoso; **9** Brigadoon; **10** harmonious, musicianly; **11** musicophile; **12** philharmonic; PHRASES: **2, 4, 4** My Fair Lady; **4, 3, 5** Guys and Dolls; **5, 2, 5** Sound of Music; **5, 3** Mamma Mia; **5, 5** Hello Dolly; **5-6** music-loving; **6, 4, 4** Flower Drum Song.

musical arrangement **5** score; **7** version; **10** adaptation; **12** choreography; **13** orchestration; **14** interpretation; **15** instrumentation.

musical cry **4** solo, song; **5** chant, yodel; **6** chorus.

musical group **3** duo; **4** band, trio; **5** nonet, octet; **6** septet, sextet; **7** quartet, quintet; **8** ensemble, songfest; **9** orchestra; **11** sinfonietta; PHRASES: **3-3, 4** one-man band; **3, 5** pop group *UK*; **4, 4** glee club, jazz band, pipe band *UK*, punk band, rock band; **5, 4** brass band, steel band; **6, 4** string band; **6, 7** string quartet; **7, 4** mounted band, ragtime band; **7, 5** chamber group, skiffle group; **8, 4** marching band, military band.

musical instrument **2** ud, yü; **3** bin, kit, lur, oud, saz, shô, tar, uti; **4** bata, biwa, ch'in, drum, fife, fuye, gong, harp, horn, kena, khen, koto, lira, lute, lyra, lyre, mvet, oboe, outi, pipe, rote, ruan, sona, urua, vina, viol, whip, zobo; **5** auloi, banjo, bells, bhaya, brass, bugle, bumpa, cello, chang, chime, clave, cobza, cornu, crwth, dauli, dhola, dobro, fidel, fidla, flute, gaita, gajdy, guiro, gusle, huruk, kakko, kanun, kazoo, kerar, mbila, ngoma, nguru, okedo, organ,

piano, qanun, quena, raspa, rebab, rebec, saron, shawm, sheng, sitar, tabla, tabor, taiko, tibia, tiple, tudum, tumyr, tupan, viola, zurla, zurna; **6** alboka, arghul, bagana, biniou, carnyx, chakay, cornet, curtal, darbuk, fandur, fiddle, fujara, gekkin, gender, gongue, guitar, hummel, kenong, kissar, koboro, lirica, lirone, lituus, lontar, maraca, mayuri, moropi, nakers, naqara, ntenga, ombgwe, pommer, racket *UK*, ramkie, rattle, santir, shaing, shaker, shanai, shield, shofar, sopile, spinet, spoons, sralay, surnaj, switch, syrinx, txistu, valiha, vielle, violin, yangum, zither; **7** adenkum, alphorn, anklung, atumpan, bagpipe, baryton, bassoon, beatbox, bodhran, bonnang, buccina, buisine, bumbass, celeste, changko, cittern, cornett, cowbell, crotals, cymbals, diplice, dugdugi, enzenze, fithele, gadulka, gittern, ingungu, isigubu, kachapi, kalungu, kamanje, kantele, kemanak, kithara, komungo, machete, mandola, maracas, marimba, masenqo, migyaun, mokugyo, murumbu, musette, obukano, ocarina, octavin, orphica, pandora, panpipe, pianino, pibcorn, piccolo, piffaro, quinton, reshoto, rinchik, sackbut, salpinx, samisen, sampler, santoor, sarangi, sarinda, saxhorn, saxtuba, serpent, shiwaya, sistrum, sordine, sordone, spagane, strings, tambura, terbang, theorbo, tiktiri, timpani, trumpet, tsuzumi, ujusini, ukulele, vihuela, violone, whistle, zummara; **8** alghaita, altohorn, autoharp *UK*, bandoura, bombarde, bouzouki, calliope, carillon, cimbalom, cipactli, clappers, clarinet, clavicor, courtaut, crecelle, crumhorn, dulcimer, dvoynice, handbell, hawkbell, kayakeum, khumbgwe, langleik, langspil, mandolin, melodeon, melodica, mirliton, mridanga, oliphant, ottavino, penorcon, pochette, psaltery, putorino, recorder, sonajero, sringara, surbahar, talambas, tarabuka, tarogato, timbales, triangle, trombone, violetta, virginal, woodwind, yangchin, zampogna; **9** accordion, aerophone, arpanetta, balalaika, bandurria, banjolele, bassonore, bombardon, castanets, chalumeau, componium, cornemuse, cornopean, daibyoshi, darabukke, djunadjan, dudelsack, dvojachka, euphonium, flageolet, flexatone, hackbrett, harmonica, harmonium, hydraulis, idiophone, kelontong, könighorn, launeddas, mandobass, mandolone, orpharion, rommelpot, saxophone, sequencer, tallharpa, totombito, Wurlitzer *TM*, xylophone, xylorimba; **10** bassanello, bicitrabin, chengcheng, chitarrone, clavichord, claviorgan, colascione, contrabass, didgeridoo, flugelhorn, geigenwerk, kettledrum, lithophone, mandocello, mellophone, moshupiane, ophicleide, percussion, ranasringa, saxotromba, shakuhachi, sousaphone, spitzharfe, symphonium, tambourine, teponaztli, tlapiztali; **11** chordophone, harpsichord, heckelphone, nickelodeon, nyckelharpa, paimensarvi, panhuéhuetl, synthesizer, violoncello; **12** glockenspiel, kanteleharpe, mandolinetto, rauschpfeife, sarrusophone; **13** contrabassoon, hardangerfele, heckelclarina, schrillpfeife; **14** clavicytherium, tlapanhuéhuetl, triccaballacca; PHRASES: **2-3, 7** hi-hat cymbals; **3-3** tam-tam, tom-tom; **3, 4** bow harp, box lyre, yun ngao; **3-4** saw-thai; **3, 6** cog rattle; **3, 7** cor anglais, tin whistle; **4, 3** drum set, hula ipu; **4, 4** bass drum, bass horn, bowl lyre, buzz disk, claw bell, gong drum, Jew's harp, side drum, slit drum; **4, 5** pien ch'ing, wood block; **4-5** tuba-dupré; **4-6** bull-roarer; **4, 7** bell cittern; **5, 2, 5** viola da gamba; **5, 3** chime bar; **5, 4** angle harp, conga drum, crook horn, picco pipe; **5, 5** bible regal, bongo drums, grand piano, hurdy gurdy, mouth organ, thumb piano, tsuri daiko; **5, 6** angel chimes, board zither, saron demong, spike fiddle, viola d'amore; **5, 7** gansa gambang, gansa jongkok; **5-7** diplokithara; **5, 8** slide trombone, viola bastarda; **6, 4** barrel drum, basset horn, double bass, french horn; **6, 5** barrel organ, fipple flute, sleigh bells, uchiwa daiko; **6-5** guitar-banjo; **6, 7** double bassoon; **7, 4** aeolian harp, bivalve bell, bladder pipe, clapper bell, English horn, gambang kaya; **7-4** theorbo-lute; **7, 5** peacock sitar, tippoo's tiger, tubular bells, whistle flute; **7, 7** cithara anglica; **7, 8** turkish crescent; **8, 6** clarinet d'amore, jingling johnny; **9, 4** savernake horn; **9, 6** classical guitar.

musical notation **3** bar; **4** clef, line, rest; **5** brace, breve, chart, minim, notes, paper, pause, score, space, staff, stave; **6** quaver, script; **7** measure, solfege, symbols; **8** crotchet UK, interval; **9** semibreve, signature, solfeggio; **10** characters, semiquaver; **11** solmization; **14** demisemiquaver UK; PHRASES: **3, 4** cut time; **3, 9** key signature; **4, 4** alto clef, bass clef, half note, half rest; **4, 9** time signature; **5, 3-2** tonic sol-fa; **5, 4** tenor clef, whole note, whole rest; **5, 5** sheet music; **5-6, 4** sixty-fourth note; **6, 4** eighth note, eighth rest, ledger line, treble clef; **7, 4** musical note, quarter note, quarter rest; **8, 5** compound meter; **9, 4** sixteenth note, sixteenth rest.

musical note **4** flat, tone, turn; **5** chord, fifth, gamut, grace, ninth, pitch, scale, shake, sharp, sixth, third, tonic, triad, trill; **6** fourth, manual, octave, pickup, second; **7** cadenza, ivories, keynote, mediant, mordent, natural, partial, seventh, tremolo, vibrato; **8** arpeggio, diapason, dominant, harmonic, interval, keyboard, ornament, overtone, semitone, subtonic; **10** accidental, submediant, supertonic, tetrachord; **11** diatessaron, fundamental, subdominant; **12** acciaccatura, appoggiatura; PHRASES: **4, 4** half note, half step; **5, 4** crush note, grace note, whole step; **5, 5** black notes, pedal point, white notes; **5, 8** major interval; **6, 4** double flat; **6, 5** broken chord, common chord, double sharp; **7, 4** leading note, leading tone, quarter step; **7, 5** primary chord; **7, 8** musical interval; **8, 4** neighbor note; **8, 5** tertiary chord; **9, 5** secondary chord; **11, 4** fundamental note.

musician **2** MD UK; **3** cat; **4** bard; **6** busker UK, oboist, player, scorer, singer; **7** artiste, bassist, cellist, drummer, flutist, harpist, jazzman, maestro, pianist, popster, soloist, swinger, violist; **8** arranger, bluesman, composer, flautist, funkster, lyricist, minstrel, organist, psalmist, songster, virtuoso, vocalist; **9** balladeer, conductor, guitarist, performer, timpanist, tunesmith, violinist; **10** bandleader, bandmaster, bassoonist, librettist, repetiteur, songwriter, syncopator, trombonist, troubadour; **11** clarinetist, saxophonist; **12** clarinettist, orchestrator; **13** concertmaster, kappelmeister; **15** concertmistress, instrumentalist; PHRASES: **3, 4** pop star; **4, 6** lead singer; **5, 5** prima donna; **5, 6** choir master, music master; **5, 7** music teacher; **6, 8** street ~; **7, 8** musical director.

music making **7** jamming, playing; **9** composing; **11** composition, performance; **13** improvisation, orchestration; **15** instrumentation.

musing **7** pensive, reverie; **8** absorbed, daydream, thinking; **10** cogitation, meditation, reflection, reflective, thoughtful; **11** speculative; **12** deliberation; **13** consideration, contemplation, contemplative.

musk See **perfume**

musk mallow 8 abelmosk.

Muslim 9 Mussulman; 10 Mohammedan, Muhammadan.

must 3 mun *UK*; 4 maun *UK*, mote, stum.

mustard 7, 3 ~ gas, ~ oil; 7, 4 ~ bath; 7, 7 ~ plaster.

muster 6 gather; 7 collect, meeting; 8 assembly, congress; 9 gathering; 10 congregate; 12 congregation; PHRASES: 3, 8 get together; 6, 8 gather together.

mutant 7 altered; 9 distorted, malformed, misshapen; 11 transformed.

mutate, mutation *See* **change**

mutation *See* **change**

mute 5 quiet; 6 dampen, damper, deaden, muffle, soften, stifle; 7 muffler, quieten *UK*, silence; 8 silencer; PHRASES: 4, 4 damp down.

muted 1 P; 2 PP; 3 low; 4 soft; 5 piano, quiet; 6 gentle, hushed; 7 distant, subdued, unclear; 9 whispered; 10 indistinct, pianissimo; 13 imperceptible.

mutilate *See* **maim**

mutineer *See* **rebel**

mutinous 9 guerrilla, insurgent, seditious, terrorist; 10 rebellious, treasonous; 13 insubordinate, revolutionary; 20 counterrevolutionary.

mutiny *See* **rebellion**

mutual 5 joint; 6 common, shared; 7 related; 8 communal, conjoint; 10 reciprocal; 12 reciprocated.

mutuality 7 sharing, synergy; 8 repartee, tradeoff; 9 interplay, symbiosis; 10 concession, networking; 11 cooperation, correlation, interaction, reciprocity, retaliation; 12 compensation; PHRASES: 3-3, 7 two-way traffic; 4-3-4 give-and-take.

muzzle *See* **silence**

myopia *See* **short-sightedness**

myopic *See* **nearsighted**

myriad 7 billion, hundred, million, zillion; 8 thousand, trillion; PHRASES: 1, 7, 3, 3 a hundred and one; 1, 8, 3, 3 a thousand and one.

mysterious 4 dark, deep; 6 arcane, hidden, mystic, occult, secret; 7 cryptic, gnostic, oblique, unknown; 8 abstruse, esoteric, puzzling, symbolic; 9 anonymous, concealed, confusing, disguised, enigmatic, incognito, secretive; 10 figurative, mystifying, perplexing *UK*, unknowable, unresolved; 11 allegorical, bewildering, camouflaged, clandestine, inscrutable, Kabbalistic *UK*.

mysterious (make mysterious) 4 code; 6 cipher, encode; 8 encipher; 9 obfuscate.

mystery 6 enigma, puzzle, riddle, secret; 7 secrecy; 8 darkness, mystique, thriller, whodunit; 9 conundrum; PHRASES: 7, 4 ~ play, ~ tour *UK*.

mystic 6 medium, shaman, wizard; 7 magical; 8 mystical, sorcerer; 9 spiritual; 10 mysterious; 12 spiritualist *UK*, supernatural.

mysticism 6 oracle, secret; 7 mystery; 8 darkness, Kabbalah; 9 occultism, symbolism; 11 esotericism.

mystify 5 stump; 6 baffle, puzzle; 7 confuse, perplex; 8 bewilder; 9 bamboozle.

myth 5 fable; 6 legend; 8 folklore. *See also* **Egyptian mythology, Greek and Roman mythology, Norse mythology**

mythical 6 fabled; 8 fabulous; 9 fictional, imaginary, legendary, storybook; 10 fictitious; 12 mythological; PHRASES: 4-2 made-up.

mythical or imaginary being 3 elf, nix, orc, roc; 4 faun, jinn, ogre, puck, yeti; 5 demon, dwarf, fairy, fiend, genie, ghost, ghoul, giant, gnome, golem, harpy, jotun, lamia, nymph, pixie, preta, satyr, siren, sylph, troll; 6 afreet, amazon, azazel, bunyip *UK*, daemon, dragon, dybbuk, Fafnir, furies, goblin, hobbit, kelpie, kobold, kraken, ravana, Sinbad, sphinx, sprite, undine, wyvern, zombie; 7 banshee, Bigfoot, brownie, centaur, chimera, cyclops, gremlin, Grendel, griffin, incubus, Lorelei, mermaid, phoenix, unicorn, vampire; 8 barghest, basilisk, behemoth, minotaur, succubus, werewolf; 9 firedrake, hobgoblin, manticore, nibelungs, Sasquatch; 10 cockatrice, hippogriff, leprechaun, salamander; 11 amphisbaena, hippocampus, poltergeist; 12 Scheherezade; PHRASES: 3, 3, 6 Rip van Winkle; 4, 4 Baba Yaga; 4, 4, 7 Loch Ness monster; 4, 5 Pied Piper; 5, 3 Queen Mab; 5, 4 Robin Hood *UK*; 5, 5 Santa Claus; 5, 10 Robin Goodfellow; 6, 9 Father Christmas.

Mytilene 6 Lesbos.

N

N 2 en; 3 née; 4 name; 5 north; 8 nitrogen.

NA 6 sodium; PHRASES: 3, 9 not available; 3, 10 not applicable; 5, 6 North Africa.

nab 4 bust, nail; 5 catch, pinch, seize; 6 arrest, collar, nobble *UK*; 7 capture; 9 apprehend.

nacre 6-2-5 mother-of-pearl.

nadir 4 base; 5 dregs, floor; 6 bottom, depths, trough; 7 minimum; 8 baseline; 10 depression; PHRASES: 4, 4 zero hour; 4, 6 rock bottom; 6, 5 crisis point, lowest point.

nag 3 irk, vex; 4 carp, gnaw, moan; 5 bully, horse, hound, scold; 6 badger, berate, bother, chivvy, harass, hassle, pester, plague; 7 grumble, upbraid; 8 harangue, irritate. *See also* **horse**

nagor 8 reedbuck.

nail 3 pin; 4 brad, claw, tack; 5 clout, spike, sprig, talon; 7 hobnail, toenail; PHRASES: 4, 4 ~ file; 4, 6 ~ enamel *UK*, ~ polish; 4, 7 ~ varnish *UK*; 8, 4 tenpenny ~; 9, 4 finishing ~, fourpenny ~; 10, 4 eightpenny ~; 11, 4 twelvepenny ~.

naive 3 DIY, shy; 4 naïf, open, wild; 5 blunt, frank, green, plain, young; 6 callow, candid, honest, modest, native, savage, simple, vulgar; 7 artless, literal, natural, prosaic, sincere, uncouth; 8 Arcadian, backward, clueless, gullible, homespun, ignorant, immature, innocent, trusting, truthful, unguided, untaught, unversed; 9 childlike, confiding, credulous, guileless, ingenuous, outspoken, primitive, unadorned, unlearned, unmusical, unrefined, unskilled, unstudied, untutored, unworldly, veracious; 10 inartistic, Philistine, unaffected, unassuming, uncultured, uneducated, unpolished, unreserved; 11 spontaneous, transparent, uncivilized, uncontrived, undesigning, undisguised, uninhibited, unini-

tiated, unvarnished; 12 inarticulate, prelapsarian, unartificial, unpretending, unscientific, unsuspecting, unsuspicious; 13 inexperienced, uncomplicated, unconstrained, undissembling, unpretentious, unprogressive; 15 straightforward, unsophisticated; PHRASES: 4-4 home-made; 4-6 free-spoken, self-taught; 4, 9 born yesterday; 6-7 single-hearted; 7, 2, 5 knowing no wrong; 7, 2, 6 knowing no better; 7, 3 without art.

naive person 4 clod, dolt, dupe, fool, hick, lamb; 5 child, ninny, stick, yokel, youth; 6 novice, rustic, savage, sucker; 7 bumpkin, Candide, hayseed, ingenue; 8 beginner, innocent; 9 greenhorn, hillbilly, simpleton; 10 Philistine, provincial; PHRASES: 4, 2, 4 babe in arms; 4, 5 pure heart; 5, 2, 6 child of nature; 5, 3 plain man; 5, 6 noble savage; 6, 4 simple soul; 6, 7 candid speaker; 7, 6 country cousin; 7, 7 country bumpkin.

naiveté 5 truth, youth; 6 candor; 7 crudity, honesty, modesty, probity; 8 veracity; 9 barbarism, childhood, credulity, ignorance, innocence, nescience, sincerity, vulgarity; 10 immaturity, simplicity; 11 gullibility; 12 imperfection, inexperience, Philistinism; PHRASES: 4, 2, 9 days of innocence; 5, 4 salad days; 6, 3 golden age. *See also* **naive**

naked 4 bald, bare, nude; 5 plain, stark; 6 unclad; 7 denuded, exposed; 8 explicit, indecent, starkers *UK*, stripped, unveiled; 9 revealing, unadorned, unclothed, uncovered; 11 unvarnished; PHRASES: 2, 3, 3 in the raw; 2, 3, 4 in the buff, in the nude; 2, 3, 5 in the nuddy; 2, 3, 10 in the altogether; 4, 7, 2 with nothing on.

naked ladies 6, 6 autumn crocus.

namby-pamby 4 soft; 6 feeble; 8 pathetic; 9 spineless; 11 ineffectual.

name 1 N; 3 dub; 4 call, noun, term; 5 alias, clepe, label, nomen, quote, title; 6 eponym, handle, repute; 7 agnomen, allonym, appoint, baptize, entitle, epithet, mention, moniker, nametag, surname, toponym; 8 christen, cognomen, forename, hallmark, markings, monicker, namesake, nickname, nominate, password, tautonym; 9 autograph, celebrity, designate, praenomen, pseudonym, signature, sobriquet, trademark; 10 diminutive, matronymic, patronymic, reputation; 11 appellation, appellative, proprietary; PHRASES: 3, 2, 5 nom de plume; 3, 2, 6 nom de guerre; 3, 4 pen ~, pet ~; 4, 3 ~ day; 4, 4 full ~, last ~; 5, 4 brand ~, false ~, first ~, given ~, place ~, stage ~, trade ~; 6, 4 family ~, maiden ~, middle ~, proper noun, second ~ *UK*; 7, 4 assumed ~, married ~; 9, 4 baptismal ~, Christian ~, household ~, technical term. *See also* **boy's names, girl's names**

nameless 4 anon; 7 unknown, unnamed; 9 anonymous; 12 unidentified.

namely 2 e.g., i.e., sc; 3 viz *UK*; 4 scil.; 8 scilicet; 9 videlicet; PHRASES: 2, 3 to wit; 4, 2, 2, 3 that is to say.

nanny 5 state; 6 minder *UK*; 9 caregiver; PHRASES: 2, 4 au pair; 5, 6 child minder *UK*. *See also* **grandmother**

Nansen 6, 6 N~ bottle; 6, 8 N~ passport.

nap 3 kip *UK*, nod, nub, pit; 4 doze, knub, pile, pock, shag; 5 sleep; 6 catnap, fibers, siesta, snooze; 7 slumber, threads; 11 indentation; 12 protuberance; PHRASES: 5, 5 forty winks.

Napoleon 3 Nap, pig; 6 brandy, cognac; 8 Corsican; 9 Bonaparte; PHRASES: 6, 8 Little Corporal.

narc 5 decoy, grass *UK*; 8 informer; 10 supergrass *UK*; PHRASES: 5, 6 stool pigeon.

nard 9 spikenard.

narghile 6 hookah.

nark *See* **narc**

narrate *See* **recount**

narration 7 telling; 9 unfolding; 10 recitation, recounting; 11 description. *See also* **narrative**

narrative 4 epic, myth, plot, saga, soap, tale, yarn; 5 conte, diary, drama, essay, fable, story; 6 annals, ballad, legend, record, serial, simile; 7 account, faction, fantasy, fiction, history, journal, parable, subplot; 8 allegory, anecdote, metaphor, scenario; 9 chronicle, docudrama, narration, reportage, storyline; 10 travelogue; 11 documentary; 12 reminiscence; PHRASES: 4, 4 folk tale, tall tale; 4, 5 soap opera; 5, 4 fairy tale; 9, 4 ~ poem; 10, 4 cautionary tale.

narrow 4 draw, pent, thin; 5 close, cramp, limit, pinch, taper, tight; 6 strait; 7 confine, cramped, limited, pinched, slender, stretch, tighten; 8 clinging, compress, confined, contract, converge, restrict, straiten; 9 attenuate, constrict; 10 compressed, contracted, restricted, straitened; 11 constricted; 12 circumscribe, incommodious; 13 circumscribed; PHRASES: 4-2 pent-up; 5-7 close-fitting; 6, 4 ~ boat *UK*, ~ seas; 6, 5 ~ gauge; 6-7 figure-hugging *UK*.

narrowing 5 taper; 6 funnel; 8 stenosis, tapering; 9 shrinking, stricture; 10 bottleneck; PHRASES: 11 attenuation, contraction, convergence.

narrow-leaved 8 isthmian; 10 catarrhine; 11 leptorrhine; 13 leptocephalic, leptophyllous, stenopetalous, stenophyllous; 14 angustifoliate; 15 angustirostrate.

narrowly 6 barely, hardly, nearly; PHRASES: 2, 1, 5-7 by a hair's-breadth; 2, 1, 7 by a whisker; 4, 4 only just. *See also* **narrow**

narrow-minded 5 petty; 7 insular; 8 dogmatic; 9 blinkered, fanatical, parochial; 10 intolerant; 14 fundamentalist; PHRASES: 5-6 small-minded.

narrowness 10 limitation, straitness; 11 confinement, restriction; 12 constriction; 14 circumspection. *See also* **narrow**

narrow place 4 ford, pass, slip, spit; 5 chink, crack, ditch, gully, ridge; 6 bridge, defile, ravine, strait, tunnel; 7 channel, isthmus, narrows, passage, straits; 8 corridor; 9 peninsula; 10 bottleneck; PHRASES: 5, 3 small gap; 5, 7 tight squeeze; 8, 5 confined space.

narrow thing 3 rod; 4 band, cone, hair, line, neck, peak, pipe, tube, wire, wisp; 5 point, spire, stick, strip, taper, waist, wedge; 6 strand, streak, stripe, thread; 7 fingers, spindle; 8 filament, splinter; PHRASES: 5, 4 knife edge; 6, 4 razor's edge; 6, 5 narrow gauge, single track.

naseberry 9 sapodilla.

nashi 5, 4 Asian pear.

nastiness 5 spite; 6 malice; 7 cruelty; 11 malevolence. *See also* **nasty**

nasty 4 base, vile; 5 lowly, petty, ribby, small, yucky; 6 horrid, odious, shabby, sordid, trying, unkind; 7 beastly, hateful, hurtful, irksome, painful, squalid; 8 annoying, disliked, horrible, spiteful, unsavory; 9 invidious, loathsome, offensive, repulsive, revolting, sickening, unwelcome; 10 despicable, discordant, disgusting, nauseating, uninviting, unpleasant, unpleasing; 11 displeasing, distasteful, rebarbative, unpalatable; 12 disagreeable, discomfiting, unacceptable, unharmonious; 13 uncomfortable; PHRASES: 5-6 small-minded.

nasty person 3 cad, git, oaf; 4 boor, lout, pain, pest; 5 beast; 6 meanie; 7 fighter, shitbag; 8 hooligan, nuisance, wrangler; 9 aggressor, quarreler; 12 troublemaker; PHRASES: 4, 2, 3, 3 pain in the ass; 4, 2, 3, 4 pain in the neck; 8-5 mischief-maker.

nasty woman 3 bag, cow, nag; 5 witch.

nation 4 land, race; 5 demos, realm, state, tribe; 6 empire, people, polity; 7 country, kingdom; 8 republic; 9 democracy, statehood; 10 fatherland, federation, motherland; 12 commonwealth, dictatorship; 13 confederation; PHRASES: 4, 5 city state; 4, 7 body politic; 5, 5 civil state; 5, 7 civil society; 6, 5 ~ state; 7, 3 melting pot; 7, 5 welfare state; 9, 5 socialist state; 9, 6 political entity; 10, 5 democratic state, republican state. *See also* **country**

national 5 civic, civil, state; 6 public, social, tribal; 7 citizen, federal, general, subject; 8 communal, domestic, internal, societal; 9 patriotic, sovereign; 10 compatriot, countryman, jingoistic, republican; 12 chauvinistic, countrywoman, governmental; 13 nationalistic; PHRASES: 6, 7 fellow citizen; 8, 4 ~ debt, ~ grid *UK*; 8, 5 N~ Front, N~ Trust *UK*; 8, 6 ~ anthem; 8, 7 N~ gallery, ~ service.

nationalism 6 racism; 8 jingoism; 10 chauvinism, patriotism, xenophobia; 12 isolationism; 13 protectionism.

nationalist 6 racist; 7 patriot; 8 jingoist; 9 xenophobe; 11 colonialist; 12 isolationist; 13 protectionist.

national monument 5 Tonto; 6 Navajo; 7 Wupatki; 8 Cabrillo, Chamizal, Colorado, Coronado, Dinosaur, Ocmulgee, Tuzigoot; 9 Aniakchak, Bandelier, Homestead, Hovenweep, Parashant, Pinnacles, Pipestone; 10 Chiricahua, Petroglyph; PHRASES: 2, 4 De Soto; 2, 5 El Morro; 2, 7 El Malpais; 3, 7 USS Arizona; 4, 3, 6, 4 John Day Fossil Beds; 4, 4 Laya Beds; 4, 5 Fort Union, Muir Woods; 4, 6 Fort Sumter, Gila Cliffs, Pipe Spring; 4, 6, 4 Buck Island Reef; 4, 6, 5 Casa Grande Ruins; 4, 7 Fort Clatsop, Fort McHenry, Fort Moultri, Fort Pulaski, Fort Stanwix; 4, 8 Fort Caroline, Fort Matanzas, John Ericsson; 4, 9 Fort Frederica; 4, 11 Cape Krusenstern; 5, 4 Jewel Cave; 5, 4, 5 Great Sand Dunes; 5, 4, 6 Organ Pipe Cactus; 5, 5 Aztec Ruins, Yucca House; 5, 6 Cedar Breaks, David Berger, Ellis Island; 5, 6, 4 Agate Fossil Beds; 5, 7 Catle Clinton, Grand Portage; 5, 8 Mount Rushmore; 6, 2 Flight 93; 6, 2, 6 Canyon de Chelly; 6, 2, 7 Statue of Liberty; 6, 5 Devils Tower, Fossil Nutte, George Mason, Oregon Caves, Scotts Bluff; 6, 6 Effigy Mounds, Walnut Canyon; 6, 6, 7 Sunset Crater Volcano; 6, 8 Devils Postpile, Wright Brothers; 6, 9 Thomas Jefferson; 7, 2, 3, 4 Craters of the Moon; 7, 4 Federal Hall, Hohokam Pima, Russell Cave; 7, 5 General Grant, Poverty Point; 7, 6 Rainbow Bridge; 7, 6, 8 Salinas Pueblo Missions; 7, 7 Capulin Volcano, Lincoln Boyhood, Natural Bridges; 7, 8 Lincoln Memorial, Vietnam Veterans; 8, 2, 3, 6 Castillo de San Marcos; 8, 4 Arkansas Post, Oklahoma City; 8, 5, 8 Alibates Flint Quarries; 8, 6, 4 Hagerman Fossil Beds; 8, 6, 9 Franklin Delano Roosevelt; 8, 10 Minidoka Internment, Thaddeus Kosciuszko; 9, 5 Arlington House, Johnstown Flood; 9, 6 Governors Island, Montezuma Castle; 10, 4 Timpanogos Cave; 10, 6, 4 Florissant Fossil Beds; 10, 8 Washington Monument.

national park 6 Acadia, Arches, Denali, Katmai, Lassen; 7 Glacier, Olympic, Redwood, Saquaro, Sequoia; 8 Badlands, Biscayne, Catoctin, Congaree; 9 Anacostia, Haleakala, Voyageurs; 10 Everglades, Shenandoah; 11 Canyonlands, Yellowstone; PHRASES: 3, 4 Big Bend; 3, 7 Hot Springs; 3, 8 Dry Tortugas; 4, 4 Wind Cave; 4, 5 Lake Clark, Mesa Verde; 4, 6 Isle Royale; 5, 2, 3, 6 Gates of the Arctic; 5, 5 Grand Teton, Great Basin; 5, 5, 9 Great Smoky Mountains; 5, 6 Bryce Canyon, Death Valley, Grand Canyon, Kenai Fjords, Kings Canyon, Kobuk Valley, Mount Ranier; 5, 6, 2, 3, 8 Black Canyon of the Gunnison; 5, 8 North Cascades, Rocky Mountain; 5, 8, 10 Adams National Historical; 6, 4 Crater Lake, Joshua Tree; 6, 7 Virgin Islands; 6, 9

Hawaii Volcanoes; **7, 3** Glacier Bay; **7, 4** Capitol Reef, Mammoth Cave; **7, 7** Channel Islands; **8, 2, 5** Wrangell St. Elias; **8, 6** Cuyahoga Valley; **8, 7** Carlsbad Caverns; **8, 8** American Memorial; **8, 9** Theodore Roosevelt; **9, 6** Petrified Forest; **9, 9** Guadalupe Mountains.

national preserve 6 Denali, Katmai, Mojave; **8** Timucuan; PHRASES: **3, 6, 9** New Jersey Pinelands; **3, 7** Big Cypress, Big Thicket; **4, 2, 5** City of Rocks; **4, 5** Lake Clark; **5, 2, 3, 6** Gates of the Arctic; **6, 4, 6** Bering Land Bridge; **6, 5, 6** Little River Canyon; **7, 3** Glacier Bay; **8, 2, 5** Wrangell St. Elias; **9, 7** Tallgrass Prairie.

native 5 local, urban; **6** ethnic, inborn, rustic, tribal; **7** citizen, genuine; **8** indigene *UK*, national, original, suburban; **9** aborigine, belonging; **10** aboriginal, countryman, indigenous, inhabitant, provincial; **12** countrywoman, metropolitan; **13** autochthonous; PHRASES: **6, 3** ~ son; **6, 4** ~ land; **6, 6** ~ oyster.

Native American 4 Gall, Ross; **5** Brant, Uncas; **6** Indian, Joseph, Philip, Quanah; **7** Cochise, Pontiac, Samoset, Sequoya, Squanto; **8** Geronimo, Hiawatha, Powhatan, Tecumseh; **9** Mankiller, Manuelito, Massasoit, Metacomet; **10** Amerindian, Pocahontas; **11** McGillivray; PHRASES: **3, 5** Red Cloud; **4, 5** Dull Knife; **5, 4** Black Hawk; **5, 5** Crazy Horse; **5, 6** Black Kettle; **6, 6** Plains Indian; **7, 4** Sitting Bull; **8, 6** American Indian.

Native Americans (South and Central America) 4 Cuna, Inca; **5** Indio, Olmec, Otomi, Taino; **6** Arawak, Aymara, Galibi, Jivaro, Lumbee; **7** Chibcha, Fuegian, Mochica, Vinland, Zapotec; **8** Garifuna, Yanamami; **9** Chichimec; **10** Araucanian; PHRASES: **6, 6** Tohono O'Odham; **7, 4** Mushuau Innu.

Native American terms 5 canoe, igloo, kayak, parka, tepee, totem; **6** anorak, mukluk, powwow, sachem, wampum, wigwam, wikiup; **7** kachina, manitou, mestiza, papoose, wickiup; **8** berdache, inukshuk, moccasin, pemmican, potlatch, sagamore, tomahawk; **9** longhouse; **12** kinnikinnick; PHRASES: **3, 5** sun dance; **4, 4** band list; **4-4-1-4** high-muck-a-muck; **5, 4** peace pipe, scalp lock; **5, 5** snake dance, sweat lodge; **7** button blanket; **8, 5** medicine dance, medicine woman; **8, 6** medicine person.

Native American tribe 3 Fox, Oto, Ute; **4** Cree, Crow, Dene, Hopi, Maya, Pima, Pomo, Sauk, Tewa, Tiwa, Yuma, Zuni; **5** Aztec, Caddo, Carib, Creek, Haida, Huron, Kansa, Karok, Kiowa, Lipan, Mayan, Miwok, Omaha, Osage, Ponca, Ponka, Sioux, Teton, Yaqui, Yurok; **6** Apache, Dakota, Digger, Mandan, Micmac, Mi'kmaq, Mixtec, Mohave, Navajo, Nootka, Oglala, Ojibwa, Oneida, Ottawa, Paiute, Papago, Pawnee, Pequot, Salish, Santee, Seneca, Shasta, Yakama; **7** Abenaki, Anasazi, Arapaho, Arikara, Catawba, Chinook, Choctaw, Chumash, Hidatsa, Klamath, Kutenai, Mahican, Mohegan, Montauk, Palouse, Shawnee, Shuswap, Tlingit, Wichita, Wyandot; **8** Arawakan, Cahuilla, Cherokee, Cheyenne, Comanche, Delaware, Flathead, Hopewell, Hunkpapa, Illinois, Iroquois, Kickapoo, Kwakiutl, Malecite, Maricopa, Mikasuki, Mogollon, Muskogee, Okanagan, Onondaga, Sahaptin, Seminole, Shoshone; **9** Algonquin, Blackfoot, Chickasaw, Chipewyan, Havasupai, Iroquoian, Jicarilla, Kaskaskia, Menominee, Mescalero, Suquamish, Tsimshian, Tuscarora, Wampanoag, Wappinger, Winnebago; **10** Assiniboin, Miniconjou, Montagnais, Potawatomi; **11** Narraganset; **12** Massachusett; **13** Susquehannock; PHRASES: **3, 5** Nez Percé; **3, 7** Six Nations; **5, 5** Bella Coola; **5, 6** Coast Salish, Kiowa Apache; **5, 7** Mound Builder; **8, 6** Interior Salish, Northern Paiute, Southern Paiute.

native land 4 home; **6** cradle, patria; **8** homeland; **9** Vaterland; **10** birthplace, fatherland, motherland; PHRASES: **3, 3, 7** the old country; **4, 6** home ground; **4, 7** God's country; **6, 4** native soil; **6, 7** mother country; **7, 2, 6** country of origin.

natrium 6 sodium.

natter *See* **chat**

natural 3 raw; **4** easy, fool, open, pure; **5** blunt, frank; **6** candid, direct, expert, gifted, honest, innate; **7** artless, organic, sincere; **8** talented, unforced, untaught; **9** guileless, ingenuous, simpleton, veracious, wholesome; **10** biological, forthright, unaffected, unassuming, unfeigning; **11** instinctive, spontaneous, unprocessed; **12** illegitimate; **13** unpretentious; **15** straightforward, unsophisticated; PHRASES: **5-8** plain-speaking; **6-7** simple-hearted.

naturalize 7 Russify; **9** Anglicize, Frenchify, Germanize, Indianize; **10** Africanize, assimilate, westernize; **11** Americanize, Europeanize, orientalize.

nature 3 cut, hue, set; **4** body, cast, face, look, mien, mold, mood, trim, turn, type; **5** biota, breed, build, humor, shape, stamp, trait; **6** aspect, fettle, figure, health, make-up, stance, strain, stripe, temper; **7** anatomy, essence, fitness, outlook, pattern, posture, quality; **8** attitude, demeanor, elements, features, ontology, outdoors, physique, property, quiddity, suchness, thusness, wildlife; **9** attribute, biosphere, character, condition, ecosphere, ecosystem, ectomorph, endomorph, lineament, mesomorph, soundness; **10** appearance, complexion, expression, innateness; **11** composition, disposition, environment, materiality, personality, physiognomy, temperament; **12** constitution; **14** substantiality; PHRASES: **3-2** get-up; **5, 3, 5** flora and fauna; **9, 6** essential ~.

naughty 3 bad; **4** blue, racy, rude; **5** broad, crude, dirty, girly, saucy, spicy; **6** impish, remiss, ribald, risqué, smutty, unruly, wicked; **7** puckish, raunchy, roguish, selfish, wayward, willful; **8** contrary, impolite, improper, indecent, perverse; **9** obnoxious, salacious; **10** suggestive, ungracious; **11** disobedient, misbehaving, mischievous, titillating, troublesome; **12** discourteous, incorrigible; **13** inconsiderate; PHRASES: **1-5** X-rated; **3-4** ill-bred; **3-8** bad-mannered, ill-mannered; **7, 2** playing up.

nausea 7 disgust; **8** sickness, vomiting; **10** queasiness, repugnance.

nauseous 4 sick; **6** queasy, unwell; **7** bilious; **9** nauseated, repellent, repulsive, revolting, sickening; **10** disgusting.

nautical 4 able; **5** naval, salty; **6** afloat, marine, plying, yawing; **7** aquatic, buoyant, rolling, sailing, tossing; **8** coasting, ferrying, floating, launched, maritime, natatory, pitching, sailorly, seaborne, steaming, swimming; **9** amphibian, seafaring, seaworthy, wallowing; **10** amphibious, waterborne; PHRASES: **2, 3** at sea, by sea; **2, 3, 4** at the helm; **2, 3, 4, 4** on the high seas; **2, 3, 5** at the wheel; **2, 3, 6** on the bridge; **2, 4** on deck; **2, 5** on board; **3-5** sea-going; **4, 3, 5** over the water; **4-6** able-bodied; **5, 3** under way; **5, 4** under sail; **5, 5** under steam; **5-5** ocean-going; **5, 6** under canvas; **6, 3, 4** before the

mast; **6-4** seaman-like.

nautical person *See* **sailor**

naval person 4 swab, Wave, Wran *UK*, Wren; **5** limey; **6** rating, sailor, Seabee, seaman; **7** admiral, captain, mariner, swabbie; **8** detailer; **9** buccaneer, commander, commodore; **10** bluejacket, lieutenant, midshipman, submariner; **14** coastguardsman; PHRASES: **3-10** sub-lieutenant; **4, 3** navy man; **4, 4** wavy navy; **4, 6** able rating *UK*, able seaman; **4, 7** vice admiral; **4-7** rear-admiral; **5, 3** cabin boy; **5, 6** naval airman; **5, 7** naval officer, petty officer; **5, 7, 7** chief warrant officer; **5, 9** naval reservist; **6, 3** powder boy; **6, 6** powder monkey; **7, 3** pressed man; **8, 6** ordinary rating, ordinary seaman. *See also* **admiral, captain**

naval unit 5 fleet; **6** argosy, armada, convoy; **8** flotilla, squadron; PHRASES: **5, 3, 3** Fleet Air Arm *UK*; **6, 5** battle group, little ships.

navel 8 omphalos; **9** umbilicus.

navelwort 9 pennywort.

navigate 4 crew, plot, sail, tack, veer, wear; **5** chart, pilot, steer; **6** direct; **7** captain, skipper; **8** traverse; PHRASES: **7, 8** control maneuver.

navigation 3 log; **4** buoy, card, helm, lead, line; **5** chart, radar, sonar, wheel; **6** needle, pharos, rudder, tiller; **7** boating *UK*, compass, sailing, sextant; **8** bearings, binnacle, pilotage, piloting, plotting, quadrant, steering; **9** ephemeris, lightship, pilotship; **10** lighthouse, seamanship; **11** chronometer, gyrocompass; **12** astrocompass, helmsmanship; **15** astronavigation; PHRASES: **3, 4** sea mark; **4, 4** lead line; **4, 9** dead reckoning; **5, 2, 3, 3** rules of the sea; **5, 3** ship's log; towed log; **5, 6** decca system, loran system; **5, 7** plain sailing, plane sailing, ship's compass; **7, 3** sailing aid; **7, 4** compass card; **7, 6** Transit system; **7, 7** angular measure, compass reading; **8, 3** steering oar; **8, 6** magnetic needle; **8, 7** magnetic compass, nautical almanac, parallel sailing; **9, 3** submerged log; **9, 5** Admiralty chart; **12, 3** navigational aid.

navigator 5 guide, pilot; **7** skipper; **9** autopilot; PHRASES: **5, 6** route finder.

navy 2 RN *UK*; **3** RCN *Can*, USN; **5** fleet; **6** armada; **8** flotilla; **9** admiralty; PHRASES: **3, 5** sea power; **3, 5** fleet arm; **5, 4** Royal N~ *UK*; **5, 7** naval service; **5, 8** naval armament; **6, 5** wooden walls; **6, 7** senior service *UK*, silent service; **8, 4** merchant ~ *UK*; **8, 5** mothball fleet; **8, 6** merchant marine.

Nazi 2 SA, SS; **4** Hess; **6** Hitler; **9** gauleiter *UK*; **10** brownshirt; **12** stormtrooper.

NB 7 niobium; PHRASES: **2, 4** no ball *UK*; **4, 4** note well (Latin: nota bene).

NC 2, 6 no charge.

NE 4 neon; **9** northeast; PHRASES: **3, 7** new edition.

near 2 by; **3** hot; **4** home, mean, next, nigh, warm; **5** about, cheap, close, handy, local, tight; **6** around, closer, nearby, stingy; **7** closely, closest, inshore, locally, looming, miserly, vicinal, wayside; **8** adjacent, approach, converge, imminent, intimate, proximal, roadside, touching; **9** adjoining, available, hereabout, immediate, niggardly, proximate; **10** accessible, contiguous, convenient, convergent, converging, hereabouts *UK*; **11** approaching, approximate, forthcoming, inseparable, neighboring, thereabouts; **13** approximating; PHRASES: **2, 1, 5-7** by a hair's-breadth; **2, 1, 7** by a whisker; **2, 3, 4** on the spot; **2, 3, 5, 2** on the brink of, on the verge of; **2, 3, 8** in the vicinity; **2, 4** at hand, to hand; **2, 5, 5** at close range; **2, 5, 8** at close quarters; **3-2-4** get-at-able; **3, 3** not far; **4, 2** hard by, move up; **4, 2, 4** ~ at hand; **4-2-4** hand-in-hand, side-by-side; **4-3-4** neck-and-neck; **4, 4** come ~, draw ~, draw nigh; **4-4** next-door; **4, 5** move close; **5, 2** close by, close up, verge on; **5, 2, 4** close at hand; **5-2-4** cheek-by-jowl; **5-2-5** elbow-to-elbow; **5-3** close-run; **5, 7** level pegging *UK*; **6-2-6** bumper-to-bumper; **6, 3, 5** around and about; **6, 4** within call; **6, 5** within range, within reach, within sight; **6, 7** within earshot, within hearing; **7, 2** verging on; **9, 2** bordering on.

nearby 5 close, local, ready; **8** adjacent, touching; **9** available; **10** accessible; **11** neighboring; PHRASES: **2, 3, 8** in the vicinity; **2, 4** at hand; **4, 2** next to; **4-4** next-door; **5, 2** close by; **6, 5** within reach; **9, 2** bordering on.

nearly 6 almost; **7** roughly; **9** virtually; **11** approximate, practically; PHRASES: **2, 4, 2** as good as; **2, 5, 7** in round numbers; **3, 3** all but; **3, 5** not quite; **4, 2, 4** more or less; **4-4** well-nigh; **4, 5** just about; **4, 6** near enough.

nearness 7 appulse, perigee; **8** approach, intimacy, juncture, vicinity; **9** adjacency, closeness, handiness, immediacy, proximity; **10** perihelion; **11** conjunction, conve-

nience, convergence, propinquity; **12** availability; **13** accessibility, approximation, juxtaposition; **14** inseparability; PHRASES: **9, 6** collision course.

near place 5 front; **8** confines, environs, locality, precinct, purlieus, vicinage, vicinity; **10** approaches, foreground; **12** neighborhood, surroundings; PHRASES: **8, 4** ringside seat.

nearsighted 6 myopic, owlish; **7** bigoted; **9** parochial; **10** prejudiced; PHRASES: **6-6** narrow-minded.

neat 2 ox; **3** cow; **4** deft, tidy, trim; **5** clean, dinky, smart, uncut; **6** adroit, clever, dapper, pretty, spruce; **7** compact, precise, unmixed; **8** accurate, skillful, straight; **9** shipshape, undiluted, unwatered.

Nebraska 2 NE; **7** Lincoln (capital); **9** goldenrod (flower); **10** cottonwood (tree); PHRASES: **4, 8, 5** Tree Planters' State (nickname); **7, 10** western meadowlark (bird); **8, 6, 3, 3** Equality before the law (motto); **10, 5** Cornhusker State (nickname).

nebulous *See* **unclear**

necessary 4 cash; **5** money, vital; **6** needed, urgent; **7** certain; **8** required; **9** essential, mandatory, requisite; **10** imperative, inevitable, obligatory; **11** fundamental; **13** indispensable.

necessitate 4 need, want; **5** cause, order; **6** compel, demand, entail, indent, oblige; **7** dictate, earmark, involve, request, require, reserve; **9** constrain, stipulate; **11** requisition; PHRASES: **3, 5** set aside; **4, 2, 5, 3** send an order for; **4, 3** call for; **6, 1, 4** create a need; **6, 9** render necessary.

necessitous 4 bust, poor; **5** broke, needy, skint *UK*, stony; **6** hungry; **7** craving, lacking, needing, pinched; **8** bankrupt, brassick, deprived, starving; **9** destitute, penniless; **13** disadvantaged; PHRASES: **2, 3, 9** on the breadline; **2, 4** in hock, in need, in want; **2, 7, 5** at poverty level; **4, 5** dead broke, flat broke; **7, 1, 5** without a penny; **7, 3** longing for; **7, 3, 5** feeling the pinch; **8, 2** deprived of.

necessity 4 must, need, want; **7** urgency; **9** essential, necessary, requisite; **10** imperative; **11** desideratum, fundamental, requirement; **12** precondition, prerequisite.

neck 1 V; **3** col, pet; **4** kiss, nape, snog *UK*; **5** cheek, nerve, scrag; **6** cervix, cuddle, scruff, smooch, strait; **7** isthmus; **8** canoodle; **10** bottleneck, turtleneck; PHRASES: **4, 4** boat ~, crew ~, swan ~; **5, 4** brass ~ *UK*; scoop ~; **6, 4** turtle ~.

necklace **4** band; **5** chain; **6** choker, string; **7** necklet *UK*.

neckwear **3** boa, fur, tie; **4** ruff; **5** amice, ascot, fichu, jabot, stock, stole; **6** choker, collar, cravat, dickey *UK*, guimpe, rabato, tucker; **7** bavolet, betsies, muffler, necktie, tallith; **8** bandanna, carcanet, kerchief, neckband, necklace; **9** comforter, neckcloth, neckpiece *UK*; **10** chemisette; **11** neckerchief; PHRASES: **3, 3** bow tie; **3, 6** dog collar; **4-2-4** four-in-hand; **4, 3** wing tie; **4, 6** cape collar, Eton collar, high collar, wing collar; **5-2, 6** stand-up collar; **5, 3** dicky bow *UK*; **5, 3, 6** Peter Pan collar; **5, 6** shawl collar, stiff collar; **6, 3** string tie; **6, 6** bertha collar; **7, 3** eclipse tie, Windsor tie; **7, 6** Vandyke collar; **8, 6** clerical collar, Mandarin collar, starched collar. *See also* **clothes**

need **3** gap; **4** call, debt, lack, want; **5** claim, input, pinch; **6** crisis, demand, desire, intake, lacuna, penury; **7** craving, poverty, urgency; **8** exigency, hardship, occasion, shortage, slippage; **9** breadline, emergency, indigence, necessity, neediness, privation, shortfall, vitalness; **10** obligation; **11** consumption, destitution, predicament, requirement; **12** desirability, essentiality; **13** insufficiency; PHRASES: **3, 2** run on; **3, 2, 3, 6** gap in the market; **4, 3** call for; **5, 6** Queer Street; **7, 3** balance due; **7, 4** poverty trap *UK*; **7, 5** poverty level; **7, 6** sellers' market; **8, 6** consumer demand.

needed **3** due; **5** vital; **6** urgent; **8** pressing; **9** essential, necessary; **10** imperative; **13** indispensable; PHRASES: **4, 3, 3** sine qua non.

needle **3** irk, vex; **4** bait, goad, hand, hype, prod; **5** annoy, pique, prick, spike, sting, taunt, tease; **6** bodkin, harass, marker, stylus; **7** pointer; **8** irritate; **10** hypodermic; PHRASES: **3, 6** dip ~, ice ~; **4, 6** pine ~; **7, 6** darning ~; **8, 6** electric ~, magnetic ~.

needy **4** poor; **7** needful; **8** indigent; **9** destitute; **11** impecunious, necessitous; **12** impoverished; PHRASES: **4, 2** hard up; **7-8** poverty-stricken. *See also* **poor**

negate **4** deny, veto; **6** cancel, refuse, reject; **7** decline, disavow; **8** abnegate, disallow, prohibit; **10** invalidate; PHRASES: **3, 2** say no.

negation **2** no; **3** nay, nix; **6** denial; **8** negative, rebuttal; **9** defeatism, naysaying, pessimism; **10** abnegation, negativism, negativity; **11** despondence, despondency; **12** negativeness; **13** contradiction; **15** counterargument.

negative **2** no; **3** nay, nix, non, not, yin; **4** anti, nein, nope, nyet, veto; **5** minus, never; **6** gloomy; **7** defiant, nowhere; **8** agnostic, contrary, doubtful, recusant; **9** defeatist; **10** abjuratory, abrogative, despondent, dismissive, dissenting, revocatory; **11** deprecative, dissentient, obstructive, pessimistic, repudiative; **12** dissociative, renunciative, renunciatory; **13** contradictive, contradictory, uncooperative.

negative (be negative) **4** deny, veto; **6** disown, naysay, negate, refuse, reject; **7** decline, disavow, disobey; **8** abnegate, disallow, disclaim, prohibit; **9** repudiate; **10** disbelieve, invalidate, renunciate; PHRASES: **3, 2** say no; **5, 4, 4** shake one's head; **6, 2, 6** refuse to accept; **6, 7** refuse consent.

neglect **4** fail, omit; **6** forget, ignore; **8** overlook; **9** disregard; **10** negligence; PHRASES: **3, 4** not heed; **3, 4, 3** not care for; **4, 1, 5, 3, 2** turn a blind eye to; **4, 2, 6, 2** take no notice of; **5, 4-4** leave half-done; **5, 6** leave undone.

neglectful *See* **negligent**

negligence **8** oblivion; **9** disregard, unconcern; **11** dereliction, inattention, insouciance, nonchalance; **12** indiscretion. *See also* **negligent**

negligent **3** lax; **5** slack; **6** remiss, sloppy; **8** careless, heedless, slipshod, uncaring; **9** forgetful, oblivious, unmindful; **10** insouciant, neglectful, nonchalant; **11** inattentive, thoughtless, unconcerned; **12** disregardful.

negligently **9** cursorily; PHRASES: **3, 3, 3** any old way. *See also* **negligent**

negligent person **4** slob; **5** idler; **6** sloven; **7** shirker; **14** procrastinator.

negotiable **8** feasible, workable; **9** debatable, practical, pragmatic, provisory; **11** practicable, provisional; **12** conciliatory, exchangeable; **13** concessionary.

negotiate **4** deal; **5** trade; **6** barter, confer, haggle, parley, powwow, settle; **7** bargain, discuss, mediate, wrangle; **8** exchange; **9** arbitrate, cooperate, stipulate; **10** compromise, conciliate, deliberate; **11** communicate; PHRASES: **2, 8** do business; **3-3** jaw-jaw *UK*; **4, 1, 4** make a deal; **4, 1, 6** hold a summit; **4, 2, 5** come to terms; **4, 5** hold talks, make terms; **4, 6** seek accord; **4, 9** make overtures; **4, 11** make concessions; **5, 3** trade off; **8, 5** exchange views.

negotiation 4 deal; **5** trade; **6** powwow, treaty; **7** bargain, dealing; **8** exchange, haggling, tradeoff; **9** bartering, diplomacy, mediation, wrangling; **10** bargaining, compromise; **11** arbitration, discussions; **12** compromising, conciliation, negotiations; **13** communication; PHRASES: **4-5** argy-bargy *UK*; **6-6** treaty-making.

negotiator 4 ACAS *UK*, link; **6** broker, lawyer; **8** diplomat, mediator; **9** middleman, solicitor; **10** ambassador, arbitrator, matchmaker, peacemaker; **11** intercessor, stockbroker; **12** intermediary; PHRASES: **2-7** go-between.

neigh 4 bray; **5** hinny; **6** nicker, whinny; **7** whicker.

neighbor 5 touch; **8** onlooker; **9** bystander.

neighborhood 4 area; **5** local, manor, patch; **6** ghetto; **8** district, environs, locality, precinct, vicinity; **9** closeness; **12** surroundings.

neighboring 5 local; **6** nearby; **9** adjoining, bordering; **11** surrounding.

nemesis 4 doom, fate; **7** alastor, avenger; **8** revenger; **9** vengeance; **10** punishment, retaliator, vindicator; **11** retribution.

neon 2 Ne.

nephrite 6, 5 kidney stone.

nepotism *See* **favoritism**

nerve 3 lip; **4** axon, face, gall, neck; **5** cheek; **6** bottle *UK*, daring; **8** abducens, afferent, audacity, temerity; PHRASES: **5, 3** ~ gas; **5, 4** ~ cell; **5, 5** ~ fiber, optic ~; **5, 6** ~ center; **5, 7** ~ impulse; **6, 2, 5** nerves of steel; **6, 4** spinal cord; **6, 5** radial ~; **7, 5** cranial ~.

nerves 6 abdabs, shakes, vapors; **7** anxiety, habdabs *UK*, jitters, willies; **11** butterflies; **12** collywobbles; PHRASES: **6-7** heebie-jeebies. *See also* **agitation**

nervous 4 edgy; **5** jumpy, nervy *UK*, tense, timid; **6** scared, uneasy; **7** anxious, fearful, fidgety, twitchy, worried; **8** agitated, neurotic, restless, skittish, timorous; **9** excitable; **10** frightened; **12** apprehensive; PHRASES: **2, 4** on edge; **2, 11** on tenterhooks; **6, 6** highly strung *UK*; **6, 7** having kittens.

nervous disorder 2 MS; **3** CJD, tic; **5** palsy, polio, spasm; **6** chorea, tremor, twitch; **7** atrophy, paresis, seizure; **8** diplegia, epilepsy, numbness, sciatica; **9** neuralgia, paralysis; **10** hemiplegia, myasthenia, neurilemma, paraplegia; **11** tetraplegia; **12** quadriplegia; **13** insensibility, poliomyelitis; PHRASES: **2, 6, 5** St Vitus's dance; **3, 10** tic douloureux; **5, 3** grand mal, petit mal; **5, 6** spina bifida; **7, 7** general paresis; **7, 8** falling sickness *UK*; **8, 5** cerebral palsy.

nervy *See* **nervous**

nest 3 den, lek, mew; **4** lair, peck; **5** aerie, brood, bunch, eyrie *UK*, hatch, perch, preen, roost; **6** covert, hotbed, nestle, nidify; **7** hideout, nestbox, rookery; **8** hatchery, snuggery; **9** birdhouse; **12** nidification; PHRASES: **4, 3** bird box; **4, 4** ~ site; **4, 8** ~ building; **6, 4** settle down.

nestle 3 lie; **5** place; **6** huddle, nuzzle, settle, soften; **7** cushion, shelter; PHRASES: **4, 2** cozy up; **6, 2** cuddle up.

net 3 web; **4** lace, mesh, neat, trap; **5** catch, seine, snare, trawl, tulle; **6** entrap; **7** lattice, network, trammel, webbing; **8** openwork; PHRASES: **4, 3** gill ~; **5, 3** drift ~, pound ~, shark ~, stake ~; **6, 3** safety ~, tunnel ~; **8, 3** mosquito ~.

nether 4 back, hind, rear; **5** after; **6** hinder.

Netherlands 7 Holland; **9** Nederland.

Netherlands Guiana 7 Surinam.

nettle *See* **irritate**

nettle rash 9 urticaria.

network 3 LAN, net, WAN, web; **4** grid, maze, mesh, node, rete, ring, star; **5** JANET (Joint Academic Network); **6** BITNET, cobweb, plexus, server; **7** Arpanet (Advanced Research Projects Agency Network), Euronet, gateway, lattice, SOSENET (Social Security Network), Telenet, trellis; **8** Ethernet; **9** labyrinth; **10** crisscross; **11** teleworking; **12** multitasking; **13** telecommuting; **15** Internetworking; PHRASES: **3, 3, 7** old boy ~; **4, 6** file server; **4, 9** bush telegraph; **5, 4** grape vine.

neurosis 6 phobia; **7** anxiety; **8** hysteria; **9** breakdown, deviation, psychosis; **10** depression; **11** melancholia, neuroticism; **12** hypochondria; **13** pathoneurosis; **14** psychoneurosis; PHRASES: **5, 5** shell shock; **6, 7** battle fatigue; **6, 8** combat ~, flight reaction, fright ~; **6, 9** mental breakdown; **7, 8** anxiety ~, anxiety reaction.

neurotic 7 anxious, lunatic, nervous; **8** deranged, escapist, obsessed, paranoid, schizoid, unstable; **9** disturbed, neuropath, psychotic, sociopath; **10** cyclothyme, psychopath; **11** schizothyme; **14** psychoneurotic; PHRASES: **4, 11** dual personality.

neutral 4 pale, safe; **5** bland; **6** pastel; **7** anodyne, insipid; **8** balanced, harmless, lukewarm, moderate, unallied, unbiased; **9** impartial, innocuous, unaligned; **10** compromise, uninvolved; **11** independent, inoffensive, nondescript; **12** unprejudiced; **15** unexceptionable; PHRASES: **3-7** non-aligned; **3-8** non-partisan; **4-6** open-minded.

Nevada 2 NV; **9** sagebrush (flower); **16** mountainbluebird (bird); PHRASES: **6, 4** Carson City (capital); **6, 4, 4** single leaf pine (tree); **6-4, 5** Battle-Born State (nickname); **6, 5** Silver State (nickname); **9, 5** Sagebrush State (nickname); **11, 4** bristlecone pine (tree).

never 4 nary, ne'er; PHRASES: **2, 6** no sirree!; **3, 2, 1, 4, 4** not by a long shot!; **3, 2, 1, 4, 5** not by a long chalk!; **3, 4, 2, 6** you must be joking!; **3, 6** fat chance!, God forbid!; **4, 2, 4, 4** over my dead body!; **6, 2** forget it!; **8, 3** anything but!.

nevertheless 3 yet; **6** withal; **7** however; PHRASES: **3, 3, 4** all the same; **4, 2** even so.

nevus 4 mole.

new 1 N; **2** in; **4** mint, pure; **5** blank, clean, first, fresh, novel; **6** latest, modern, recent, trendy, virgin; **7** current, faddish, topical; **8** advanced, gimmicky, original, unbeaten, unopened, unreaped, untapped, untilled; **9** inventive, neophytic, unhandled, unplucked, untouched, untrodden; **10** futuristic, innovative, neological, newfangled, postmodern, ungathered; **11** modernistic, neologistic, replacement, ultramodern, undeveloped, unexploited, unharvested; **12** contemporary; **13** neologistical, revolutionary; PHRASES: **2-2-4** up-to-date; **2, 4, 9** in mint condition; **3, 3, 3, 5** hot off the press; **4, 2-2-4** bang up-to-date; **4, 3** just out; **4-5** oven-fresh; **5-2-3-3** state-of-the-art; **5, 3** brand ~. *See also* **new thing**

new (make new) 5 alter, renew; **6** change, remake, revise, revive, update; **7** rebuild, refresh, repaint, restore, upgrade, yuppify; **8** gentrify, redesign, renovate, revivify, trendify; **9** modernize, refurbish, resurrect; **10** regenerate, rejuvenate, reorganize, supplement; **11** reconstruct, restructure; PHRASES: **2, 2** do up; **3, 2** add on; **5, 2** touch up; **5, 2, 2, 4** bring up to date; **7, 2**

freshen up.

new arrival *See* **newcomer**

new beginning 3, 4 new leaf, new page, new tack; **3, 7** new chapter; **3, 9** new departure; **5, 5** fresh start; **5, 6** fresh fields; **8, 3** pastures new.

Newcastle disease 4, 4 fowl pest.

newcomer 4 baby, tyro; **5** alien, exile; **6** émigré, novice, rookie; **7** amateur, fresher *UK*, incomer *UK*, parvenu, refugee, settler, upstart; **8** beginner, emigrant, freshman, neophyte; **9** debutante, fledgling, foreigner, greenhorn, immigrant, latecomer; **10** expatriate, tenderfoot; **12** Gastarbeiter; PHRASES: **3, 4** new face; **3, 5** new broom *UK*; **3, 6** new member; **3, 7** new recruit, raw recruit; **5, 4** novus homo; **5, 6** guest worker; **7, 5** nouveau riche; **8, 7** economic migrant; **9, 6** displaced person (DP).

New England state 2 CT, MA, ME, NH, RI *UK*, VT; **4** Mass.

New Hampshire 2 NH; **7** Concord (capital); PHRASES: **4, 4, 2, 3** Live free or die (motto); **5, 4** birch tree (tree); **6, 5** purple finch (bird), purple lilac (flower); **7, 5** Granite State (nickname).

New Jersey 2 NJ; **7** Trenton (capital); PHRASES: **3, 3** red oak (tree); **6, 5** Garden State (nickname); **6, 6, 6** common meadow violet (flower); **7, 3, 10** Liberty and Prosperity (motto); **7, 9** eastern goldfinch (bird).

New Mexico 2 NM; **10** roadrunner (bird); PHRASES: **2, 5, 2, 2, 4** It grows as it goes (motto); **4, 2, 11** Land of Enchantment (nickname); **5, 2** Santa Fe (capital); **5, 4** pinon pine (tree); **5, 6** yucca flower (flower).

newness 6 purity; **7** neology, novelty, recency; **8** currency; **9** gimmickry, invention, modernism, modernity, neologism, neophilia, virginity; **10** innovation, topicality; **11** originality, unknownness; **13** unfamiliarity; **15** contemporaneity; PHRASES: **4, 9** mint condition. *See also* **new**

news 4 dope, info, item, word; **5** event, facts, griff, rumor, scoop, story; **6** agency, column, exposé, gossip, leader, report, update, vendor; **7** feature, tidings; **8** bulletin, newscast, newsreel; **9** editorial, exclusive; **10** conference, journalism, sportscast; **11** documentary, information; **12** intelligence, notification; PHRASES: **4, 4** hard ~; **4, 5** ~ flash; **4, 10** ~ conference; **5, 7** press release; **5, 10** press conference, print journalism; **6,**

6 Fourth Estate; **7, 7** current affairs; **8, 4** breaking ~, straight ~.

newspaper **3** rag; **4** post; **5** daily, extra, paper, sheet, Times *UK*; **7** copyboy, deskman, edition, gazette, journal, tabloid; **8** giveaway, Guardian *UK*, national; **9** freesheet *UK*, shirttail, Telegraph *UK*; **10** broadsheet, copyreader, deskperson, feuilleton, newsletter, supplement; PHRASES: **3, 4, 5** New York Times; **3, 4, 5, 4** New York Daily News; **3, 5** USA Today; **3, 7** the heavies; **3, 7, 5** Los Angeles Times; **4, 4** city desk, city room; **4, 5** late extra; **4, 6** city editor; **4, 6, 7** Wall Street Journal; **4, 7** late edition; **5, 5** daily paper, local paper; **5, 7** early edition, extra edition; **5, 10** color supplement, trade supplement; **5, 11** press association; **6, 5** Sunday paper, weekly paper; **6, 7** Herald Tribune, sports edition; **6, 7, 4** Dallas Morning News; **7, 5** evening paper, morning paper, quality daily; **7, 7** Chicago Tribune, special edition; **8, 5** national paper; **10, 4** Washington Post; **10, 5** provincial paper; **12, 8** Philadelphia Inquirer.

newspaperman, newspaperwoman *See* **journalist**

newsroom **4, 4** copy desk, news desk; **5, 4** press room; **5, 6** press office; **6, 4** sports desk.

newsworthy **5** newsy; **8** headline; **9** important; **11** significant; PHRASES: **5-4** front-page.

New Testament **2** NT. *See also* **Bible**

new thing **5** trend; **7** gimmick, novelty; **9** discovery, neologism; **10** innovation; PHRASES: **3, 4** New Deal, new look, new math, new moon, new town, new wave, New Year, New York; **3, 5** new broom *UK*, new penny, new world; **3, 6** New Forest; **3, 7** new wrinkle.

Newton **1** N.

New York **2** NY; **4** rose (flower); **6** Albany (capital), Gotham, Harlem, Queens; **8** bluebird (bird), Brooklyn, Richmond; **9** Chinatown, Manhattan; PHRASES: **3, 3, 5** the Big Apple; **3, 5** the Bronx; **3, 6** the Bowery; **4, 4** East Side, West Side; **4, 6** Ever Upward (motto), Wall Street; **5, 5** sugar maple (tree); **5, 6** Times Square; **5, 7** Hell's Kitchen; **6, 5** Empire State (nickname), Little Italy; **7, 3, 4** Greater New York; **7, 4** Central Park; **9, 5** Excelsior State (nickname).

next **4** near; **5** later; **6** latter; **9** following,

proximate; **10** subsequent.

NI **6** nickel; PHRASES: **8, 7** Northern Ireland.

nib *See* **tip**

nibble **3** nip; **4** bite, chew, gnaw, peck; **5** crumb, speck; **6** morsel, tidbit.

nice **5** exact, fussy; **6** honest; **7** finicky, refined; **8** accurate, delicate, engaging; **10** fastidious, particular, scrupulous. *See also* **pleasant**

niche *See* **slot**

nick **3** cut; **4** chip, dent, gash; **5** notch; **7** scratch; **8** incision. *See also* **defraud**

nickel **2** Ni.

nickel silver **8** pakthong; PHRASES: **6, 6** German silver.

nickname **3** Hub; **5** alias; **7** agnomen, epithet, moniker; **8** Beantown, cognomen; **9** sobriquet; **10** soubriquet; PHRASES: **2-2** La-La; **4, 4** Down East; **6, 5** Empire State.

Nicosia **7** Lefkosa; **8** Levkosia.

nifty **4** good, neat; **5** handy, natty, quick, smart; **6** clever, useful; **8** skillful; **9** effective, ingenious; **10** attractive, convenient; PHRASES: **4-8** well-designed.

niggard *See* **miser**

niggle **3** nag; **4** carp; **5** annoy, cavil, doubt; **6** bother, twinge; **7** anxiety, concern, grumble, nitpick, trouble; **8** irritate; **9** complaint, criticism, criticize, grievance, misgiving, objection.

night **3** eve; **4** dark; **7** bedtime; **8** darkness, darktime; **9** blackness, blindness, nightclub, nightlife; PHRASES: **5, 3** ~ owl; **5, 4** ~ time; **5, 5** first ~, ~ nurse, ~ shift, ~ watch; **5, 6** ~ school; **5, 10** ~ depository.

night blindness **10** nyctalopia.

nightdress *See* **nightwear**

night flier **3** bat, owl.

nighthawk **7** bullbat; PHRASES: **8, 4** mosquito hawk.

nightingale **6** bulbul; **8** Florence, Philomel; PHRASES: **5, 4** Jenny Lind.

nightjar **10** goatsucker.

nightmare **5** dream; **6** vision; **7** incubus; **8** dreadful, terrible; **9** traumatic; **11** frightening; **13** hallucination; PHRASES: **3, 5** bad dream.

nightwear **3** PJs; **4** robe; **7** bedgown, nightie, pajamas; **8** bedsocks, negligée *UK*, nightcap; **9** nightgown, sleepwear; **10** nightdress *UK*, nightshirt; **12** nightclothes; PHRASES: **3, 6** bed jacket; **4, 4, 7** baby doll pajamas; **8, 4** sleeping suit. *See also* **clothes**

nil **1** O; **3** zip; **4** duck, love, none, zero; **5** zilch; **6** naught; **7** nothing.

nimble **3** fit; **4** deft, spry; **5** agile, alert, fleet, light, lithe, quick; **6** lissom *UK*, supple; **7** lissome; **9** acrobatic *UK*, sprightly.

nine **2** IX; **5** muses, niner, ninth, nonet; **6** ennead, nonary, novena; **7** nonagon, nonuple; **8** enneadic, enneagon, ninefold, nonuplet, novenary; **9** nonagonal; **10** enneagonal; **11** enneahedral, enneahedron; **12** nonagenarian; PHRASES: **4-4, 6** nine-days wonder; **4, 7** ~ tailors; **4, 8** ~ worthies.

niobite **9** columbite.

nip **3** pop, tot; **4** bite, dart, dash, peck; **5** hurry, pinch, tweak; **6** nibble, scurry, splash.

niton **5** radon.

nitrogen **1** N; **5** azote.

nitroglycerin **4** soup.

nitrous oxide **8, 3** laughing gas.

NM **9** nanometer; PHRASES: **8, 4** nautical mile.

no **3** nae, nay, nix, non; **4** nein, nope, nyet; **5** never; **10** impossible; PHRASES: **1, 5, 3** I think not!; **1, 6** I object; **2, 3** ~ way; **2, 9** au contraire; **3, 2** not so; **3, 2, 3** not at all; **3, 3, 3, 5** not for the world; **3, 4, 2** far from it; **3, 6** not likely; **4, 4** like hell; **5, 2, 3** count me out; **7, 5** nothing doing; **9, 3** certainly not; **10, 3** absolutely not.

NO **6** number; **8** nobelium; PHRASES: **3, 3** not out; **5, 7** naval officer.

nob *See* **noble**

Nobel Prize **3** Dam (Henrik), Paz (Octavio); **4** Bohr (Niels), Böll (Heinrich), Buck (Pearl S.), Gide (André), Hull (Cordell), King (Martin Luther, Jr.), Koch (Robert), Mann (Thomas), Root (Elihu), Tutu (Desmond); PHRASES: **5** Annan (Kofi), Begin (Menachem), Camus (Albert), Chain (Sir Ernst Boris), Cohen (Stanley), Crick (Francis H. C.), Curie (Marie), Curie (Pierre), Doisy (Edward Adelbert), Ebadi (Shirin), Elion (Gertrude Belle), Eliot (T. S.), Fermi (Enrico), Grass (Günter), Hesse (Hermann), Krebs (Sir Hans), Lewis (Sinclair), Luria (Salvador), Nobel (Alfred), Ochoa (Severo), Peres (Shimon), Rabin (Yitzhak), Raman (Sir Chandrasekhara),

Sadat (Anwar al-), Yeats (W. B.); **6** Addams (Jane), Arafat (Yasir), Bellow (Saul), Brandt (Willy), Briand (Aristide), Bunche (Ralph), Dunant (Jean Henri), Florey (Sir Howard Walter), France (Anatole), Heaney (Seamus), Milosz (Czeslaw), Nansen (Fridtjof), Neruda (Pablo), O'Neill (Eugene), Pavlov (Ivan), Planck (Max), Ramsay (Sir William), Sanger (Frederick), Singer (Isaac Bashevis), Tagore (Rabindranath), Teresa (of Calcutta) (Mother), Wałęsa (Lech), Watson (James D.), Wiesel (Elie), Wigner (Eugene Paul), Wilson (Woodrow); **7** Banting (Sir Frederick Grant), Beckett (Samuel), Behring (Emil von), Bergson (Henri), Borlaug (Norman), Brodsky (Joseph), Canetti (Elias), Coetzee (J. M.), Compton (Arthur Holly), Ehrlich (Paul), Eijkman (Christiaan), Feynman (Richard), Fleming (Sir Alexander), Hodgkin (Dorothy Mary), Kipling (Rudyard), Kuznets (Simon), Mahfouz (Naguib), Mandela (Nelson), Marconi (Guglielmo), Medawar (Sir Peter), Naipaul (V. S.), Pauling (Linus), Pearson (Lester), Russell (Bertrand), Soyinka (Wole), Walcott (Derek); **8** Asturias (Miguel Ángel), Blumberg (Baruch S.), Einstein (Albert), Faulkner (William), Friedman (Milton), Gordimer (Nadine), Kawabata (Yasunari), Kornberg (Arthur), Leontief (Wassily), Marshall (George), Morrison (Toni), Roentgen (Wilhelm Conrad), Sakharov (Andrei), Williams (Jody); **9** Bourgeois (Léon Victor), Churchill (Sir Winston), Gorbachev (Mikhail), Hemingway (Ernest), Hitchings (George Herbert), Kissinger (Henry), Pasternak (Boris), Roosevelt (Theodore), Steinbeck (John), Tinbergen (Jan); **10** McClintock (Barbara), Pirandello (Luigi), Rutherford (Ernest), Schweitzer (Albert); **11** Landsteiner (Karl); **12** Hammarskjöld (Dag), Solzhenitsyn (Aleksandr); **2, 5** de Klerk (F. W.); **2, 9** Ōe Kenzaburō; **4, 3, 3, 3** Aung San Suu Kyi (Daw); **4-4** Gell-Mann (Murray); **4, 6** Sato Eisaku; **4-10** Levi-Montalcini (Rita); **5, 7** Arias Sánchez (Oscar); **6-5** Joliot-Curie (Frédéric), Joliot-Curie (Irène); **6, 6** García Robles (Alfonso); **6, 7** García Márquez (Gabriel).

noble **3** nob *UK*; **4** duke, earl, gent, lady, lord, peer, toff *UK*; **5** baron, count, ducal, thane; **6** decent, gentle, knight, lordly, savage, titled; **7** baronet, duchess, grandee, marquis; **8** baroness, baronial, countess, ennobled, highborn, ladylike, margrave, marquess, marquise, optimate, princely, virtuous, viscount; **9** blueblood, gentleman, honorable, patrician; **10** aristocrat, chivalrous, margravine; **11** gentlemanly, gentlewoman, magnanimous, marchioness, viscountess; **12** thoroughbred; PHRASES: **2, 4, 6** of good family; **3-6** top-drawer; **4, 4** Lady Muck *UK*, life peer, Lord Muck *UK*; **4-4** well-bred; **4-5** high-class; **4-7** blueblooded; **5, 3** ~ art, ~ gas; **5, 4** grand duke; **5, 5** upper class; **5, 6** crown prince.

noble (make noble) 6 knight; **7** ennoble; PHRASES: **4, 8** kick upstairs.

nobleman, noblewoman *See* **noble**

nobody 4 none; **7** parvenu, unknown, upstart; PHRASES: **2-3** no-one; **3, 1, 4** not a soul; **3, 1, 6, 5** not a living thing; **3, 3** not one.

nocturnal 4 dark; **5** dusky; **7** nightly; **8** twilight; **9** benighted, vesperine; **11** crepuscular; PHRASES: **5-4** night-time.

nod 3 bob, bow, dip; **4** move, sign; **6** jiggle, signal; **7** gesture; **10** permission; **11** affirmation.

node 4 bump, join, lump; **5** bulge, point; **8** swelling; **10** connection; **12** intersection, protuberance; PHRASES: **7, 5** meeting point.

noise 3 din, hum, row; **4** bang, bong, coil, fuss, ping, roar; **5** babel, blare, boing, clang, clash, clink, sound; **6** bedlam, clamor, hubbub, racket, scream, shreik, tumult, uproar; **7** clangor, clatter, screech, shindig, turmoil, yowling; **9** cacophony; **10** hullabaloo; **11** pandemonium; **12** caterwauling; PHRASES: **3, 3, 3** hue and cry.

noisome *See* **foul**

noisy *See* **loud**

no longer 2 ex; **4** past. *See also* **no more**

nominal 5 small, token; **7** minimal, titular; **8** supposed, trifling; **10** ostensible; **13** insignificant; PHRASES: **2, 4, 4** in name only; **2-6** so-called.

nominate 4 name; **5** elect; **6** choose, select, submit; **7** appoint, propose, suggest; **9** designate; PHRASES: **3, 7** put forward.

nomination 6 choice; **7** nominee; **8** proposal; **9** candidate, selection; **10** submission, suggestion; **11** appointment; **14** recommendation.

nomogram 4 abac.

no more 2 ex; **4** dead, past; **5** ended, kaput; **7** defunct, extinct; **8** finished, obsolete, vanished; **9** destroyed; **11** annihilated, obliterated; PHRASES: **3, 4** all over; **4, 2, 1, 4** dead as a dodo; **4, 3** died out; **4, 3, 4** dead and gone; **5, 3** wiped out; **6, 4** passed away.

nonacceptance 3 ban, bar; **4** veto; **7** boycott, refusal; **8** shunning; **9** ostracism, rejection; **12** blackballing, blacklisting; **15** circumscription; PHRASES: **3, 5** red light; **4, 8** cold shoulder; **6, 4** thumbs down; **8, 4** negative veto.

nonalcoholic 4 soft; **11** unfermented; PHRASES: **4, 5** cold drink; **7-4** alcohol-free.

nonchalance *See* **indifference**

nonchalant *See* **casual**

noncommittal 5 cagey, close, vague; **7** evasive; **8** clamlike, discreet; **9** secretive; **13** uninformative; **15** uncommunicative; PHRASES: **5-5** poker-faced; **5-6** tight-lipped; **8-2** buttoned-up *UK*.

noncompliance 6 mutiny; **7** treason; **9** defection, desertion, treachery; **10** disloyalty, disrespect, dissidence; **12** disobedience, mutinousness; **13** nonconformity; **15** insubordination.

nonconductor 9 insulator; **10** dielectric, insulation.

nonconforming 3 odd; **5** nutty, wacky, weird; **6** freaky, unique; **7** bizarre, heretic; **8** distinct, freakish, maverick, peculiar, singular; **9** different, eccentric, heterodox; **10** individual, outlandish, rebellious, unorthodox; **11** contrasting, incongruous; **12** incompatible, inconsistent; **13** idiosyncratic, unconformable; **14** unconventional.

nonconformism *See* **nonconformity**

nonconformist 4 hobo; **5** crank, gypsy, nomad, rebel, tramp; **6** hippie, misfit, outlaw, weirdo; **7** beatnik, defiant, dropout, Jacobin, radical, vagrant; **8** anarchic, Bohemian, contrary, Frondeur, humanist, maverick, opponent, outsider, recusant, renegade, traveler; **9** anarchist, atheistic, breakaway, dissident, eccentric, heretical, heterodox; **10** dissenting, malcontent, protestant, rebellious, schismatic, unorthodox; **11** dissentient, freethinker, independent, rationalist, uncompliant; **12** contumacious, deviationist, iconoclastic, nonbelieving, nonconformer, recalcitrant, schismatical, unsubmissive; **13** individualist, nonconforming, revolutionary; **14** latitudinarian, unconventional; PHRASES: **3, 3, 3** odd man out; **3-3, 8** New-Age traveler; **3, 4** bag lady; **4, 3, 2, 5** fish out of water; **4, 6** free spirit; **6, 5** flower child; **6, 8** enfant terrible.

nonconformity 6 heresy, schism; **8** contrast; **9** anarchism, disaccord, disparity, diversity, hippiedom, rebellion; **10** difference, heterodoxy, iconoclasm, uniqueness; **11** Bohemianism, incongruity, peculiarity, revisionism, singularity, unorthodoxy; **12** deviationism, disagreement, distinctness, eccentricity, freakishness, idiosyncrasy, unconformity; **13** inconsistency, individuality; **14** nonconformance; **15** incompatibility; PHRASES: **4, 6** Free Church *UK*.

none 1 O; **3** nil, zip; **4** duck, love, zero; **5** zilch; **6** naught; **7** nothing.

nonentity 4 pawn, scum, wimp, zero; **5** creep, squit *UK*, trash; **6** cipher, nobody, puppet, squirt, stooge; **7** nothing, servant, trifler, unknown; **8** fribbler, inferior, unperson; **9** anonymity, nonperson, pipsqueak, smatterer, underling; **10** Cinderella, commonalty, figurehead, instrument, mediocrity; **11** beachcomber, lightweight, subordinate; **13** understrapper *UK*; PHRASES: **3, 2, 5** man of straw; **4, 5, 5** poor White trash; **4, 7** slum hustler; **4, 8** poor relation; **5, 3** small fry; **5, 4** small beer, small game; **5, 6** small change; **5, 8** small potatoes; **6, 6** second fiddle; **6, 7** silent partner.

nonexistence 5 blank; **6** vacuum; **7** nullity, unbeing, vacuity; **8** nonbeing; **9** emptiness, nonentity, unreality; **11** ethereality, nothingness; **12** nonhappening, subjectivity; **13** immateriality, impalpability, intangibility, nonoccurrence; **14** incorporeality, nonsubsistence.

nonexistent 4 null, void; **5** blank, empty, minus; **6** absent, devoid, vacant; **7** missing, vacuous; **8** negative; **9** imaginary; **10** unexisting; PHRASES: **4, 3, 4** null and void.

nonfiction 4 life, real, true; **5** diary, essay, study; **6** annals, homily, letter, memoir, record, report, résumé, review, thesis; **7** anatomy, apology, factual, history, journal, memoirs, polemic, profile; **8** critique, obituary, treatise; **9** biography, chronicle, criticism, discourse, reference; **10** commentary, journalism, travelogue; **11** confessions, documentary, hagiography; **12** dissertation; **13** autobiography; **14** historiography; PHRASES: **4, 5** life story; **6, 7** travel writing; **8, 7** personal account.

nonfulfillment 4 lack; **5** delay; **7** failure, neglect; **8** deadlock, omission; **9** oversight, shortfall, stalemate; **10** immaturity, scantiness, skimpiness, sloppiness; **11** scrappiness, sketchiness; **12** imperfection; **13** desultoriness; **14** incompleteness, superficiality; **15** perfunctoriness, procrastination; PHRASES: **3, 8** non sequitur; **4, 8** half measures; **5, 4** loose ends; **5, 5** rough edges; **7, 4** missing link.

nonhuman 4 dumb; **5** brute; **6** animal; **7** mineral; **9** inanimate, inorganic, vegetable; **10** irrational, vegetative; **11** instinctive, instinctual; PHRASES: **7, 6** without reason.

nonmaterial 4 airy; **5** other; **6** higher, unreal; **7** eternal, ghostly, psychic, shadowy; **8** bodiless, ethereal, heavenly, illusory, supernal; **9** celestial, imaginary, perpetual, psychical, religious, spiritual, unearthly, unfleshly, unworldly; **10** immaterial, impalpable, intangible, unembodied, unphysical; **11** disembodied, incorporate, incorporeal, nonphysical; **12** extramundane, imponderable, metaphysical, otherworldly, transcendent, transmundane; **13** disincarnated, immaterialist, insubstantial; **14** dematerialized; **15** dematerializing, immaterialistic; PHRASES: **7, 4** without body, without mass.

nonmaterial world 4 hell; **5** Hades; **6** heaven; **7** Elysium, Olympus; **8** eternity, Valhalla; **9** afterlife, hereafter; **10** perpetuity, underworld; PHRASES: **4, 5, 5** life after death; **5, 5** lower world, other place, other world; **6, 5** nether world; **6, 7** nether regions; **7, 4** eternal life; **8, 7** heavenly kingdom.

nonsense 3 rot; **4** blah, bosh, bull, bunk, hoke, tosh *UK*; **5** Babel, balls, bilge, Greek, hokum, hooey, trash, tripe; **6** babble, bunkum, drivel, gammon, humbug, piffle; **7** baloney, bombast, eyewash, garbage, hogwash, rubbish, twaddle; **8** claptrap, cobblers *UK*, doggerel, flimflam, tommyrot; **9** absurdity, amphigory, gibberish, moonshine, poppycock, rigmarole; **10** balderdash, humbuggery; **11** glossolalia; **12** gobbledegook *UK*, gobbledygook, psychobabble; **13** senselessness; PHRASES: **5, 4** empty talk; **6, 4** double talk; **8, 5** ~ verse.

nonsensical 3 mad; **5** comic, crazy, droll, funny, merry, silly; **6** absurd; **7** asinine, fatuous, foolish, idiotic, jocular, waggish; **8** anserine, fanciful, farcical, humorous, piffling; **9** laughable, ludicrous, senseless; **10** ridiculous; **11** imaginative, meaningless; **12** preposterous.

nonspecific 5 broad, loose; **7** blanket, dragnet, inexact; **8** sweeping; **9** imprecise; PHRASES: **5-3** catch-all.

noon 1 M, N; **6** midday; **7** noonday; **8** meridian, noontide, noontime; PHRASES: **4, 4** high ~; **5, 5** eight bells; **6, 2, 3, 3** middle of the day.

noose 3 con; **4** loop, rope, trap; **5** lasso, snare, trick; **6** halter; PHRASES: **5, 4** booby trap.

Norfolk 7, 6 N~ island, N~ jacket; **7, 7** N~ terrier *UK*.

norm *See* **standard**

normal 3 par; **4** sane; **5** sober, usual; **6** ritual; **7** lasting, natural, regular, routine, typical; **8** expected, habitual, ordinary, orthodox, standard; **9** customary, permanent, traditive; **11** commonplace, stereotyped, traditional; **12** conventional, traditionary, unsurprising; **13** perpendicular, unexceptional; PHRASES: **2, 9** in character; **3-4** old-line; **3-5** old-world; **3-9** old-fashioned; **4-7** time-honored.

Norse mythology 3 Ask, Eir, Hel, Sif, Tyr; **4** Frey, Idun, Loki, Odin, Thor, Ymir; **5** Aegir, Bragi, Embla, Frigg, Hödur, Norns; **6** Asgard, Balder, Freyja; **7** Alfheim, Forseti, Gungnir, Heimdal, Midgard; **8** Ragnarok, Sleipnir, Valhalla; **9** Valkyries; **10** Yggdrasil.

North Carolina 2 NC *UK*; **7** dogwood (flower), Raleigh (capital); **8** cardinal (bird); PHRASES: **2, 2, 6, 4, 2, 4** To be rather than to seem (motto); **3, 4, 5** Tar Heal State (nickname); **3, 5, 5** Old North State (nickname); **4, 4, 4** long leaf pine (tree).

North Dakota 2 ND; **7** Bismark (capital); PHRASES: **4, 7, 4** wild prairie rose (flower); **5, 6, 5** Peace Garden State (nickname); **7, 3, 5, 3, 3, 7, 3, 3, 11** Liberty and union now and forever, one and inseparable (motto); **7, 10** western meadowlark (bird); **8, 3** American elm (tree); **11, 5, 10, 5** Flickertail State, Roughrider State (nickname).

northern lights 6, 8 aurora borealis.

north, northern 1 N.

north of Paris 4 nord.

nose 3 pry; **4** beak, conk *UK*; **5** sneak *UK*, snoop, snout, watch; **6** muzzle; **9** proboscis; PHRASES: **4, 6** poke around.

nosh 3 eat; **4** food, tuck *UK*; **5** champ, munch, snack; **7** consume, goodies, rations; PHRASES: **3, 2** eat up.

nostrum 4 plan; **6** remedy, scheme; **7** program; **8** solution; PHRASES: **3, 4** big idea.

notability 3 VIP; **6** import, weight; **7** notable; **8** somebody; **9** celebrity, dignitary, personage, relevance; **10** importance; **11** personality; **12** significance; PHRASES: **6, 6** famous person, public figure.

notable 2 A1; **3** VIP; **6** august, signal; **7** eminent, exalted, leading, ranking, seismic; **8** eventful, imposing, powerful, sterling, stirring, superior; **9** dignified, egregious, excellent, memorable, prominent, topflight; **10** commanding, formidable, impressive, monumental, newsworthy, noteworthy, remarkable, shattering; **11** conspicuous, influential, outstanding, prestigious; **12** breathtaking; **13** distinguished, unforgettable; PHRASES: **2, 4** of mark; **3-3** top-ten; **3-4** top-rank; **4-5** gold-medal; **4-7** high-ranking; **5-4** first-rate, front-page; **5-6** epoch-making; **5-7** earth-shaking; **5-10** world-shattering; **6-5** bronze-medal, silver-medal.

notary *See* **lawyer**

notation *See* **musical notation**

not bad 2 OK; **3** oke *UK*; **4** fair, nice, okay; **5** fresh, sound; **6** decent, median; **7** average; **8** adequate, mediocre, middling, ordinary, passable, standard; **9** tolerable, unspoiled; **10** sufficient; **11** indifferent, respectable; **12** satisfactory; **15** unexceptionable, unobjectionable; PHRASES: **2-2** so-so; **2, 2, 3, 4** up to the mark; **2, 2, 5** up to snuff; **2, 4, 9** in fair condition, in good condition; **3-3-2** yes-and-no; **3, 5** all right; **4, 2, 8** fair to middling; **4-4** okey-doke; **4, 6** good enough; **5-5** fifty-fifty; **6-2-3-4** middle-of-the-road; **6, 4** pretty good.

notch 3 cog, cut; **4** dent, gash, hack, kerf, nick, nock, pink, slit; **5** cleft, gouge, score, split, tooth; **6** crenel, groove, incise, indent; **7** serrate; **8** incision, incisure; **9** crenation, crenature, crenelate, serration; **11** crenulation, indentation, serrulation.

notched 3 cut; **4** slit; **5** jaggy, split; **6** cogged, jagged, notchy, pinked, uneven, zigzag; **7** crenate, dentate, sawlike, toothed; **8** crenated, indented, serrated; **9** incisural, scalloped, serriform, zigzagged; PHRASES: **3-7** saw-toothed.

notch up 3 win; **4** gain; **5** score; **7** achieve; **10** accomplish; PHRASES: **3, 2** add to.

NOT circuit 7 negator; **8** inverter.

note 1 A, B, C, D, E, F, G, N; **2** do, fa *UK*, la, me, mi, PS *UK*, re, so, te, ti, ut; **3** doh, fah *UK*, jot, lah, ray, soh, sol; **4** bill, flat, memo, tone; **5** breve, minim, pitch, sharp, tonic; **6** advice, demand, excuse, letter, quaver *UK*, record; **7** keynote, mediant, natural; **8** annotate, crotchet *UK*, dominant, footnote, harmonic, overtone, remember, semitone; **9** auxiliary, semibreve; **10** accidental, semiquaver; **14** demisemiquaver *UK*; PHRASES: **4, 4** bank ~ *UK*, blue ~, half ~, half step; **5, 4** cover ~ *UK*, grace ~, whole ~; **5-6, 4** sixty-fourth ~; **6, 4** eighth ~; **7, 4** leading ~, passing ~, quarter ~; **8, 4** currency ~, treasury ~; **9, 4** sixteenth ~; **10, 4** promissory ~. *See also* **notes**

note (take note of) 4 mark; **5** watch; **6** minute; **7** examine, observe; **8** register; PHRASES: **4, 2, 3, 2** keep an eye on; **4, 5** stay alert; **4, 7** miss nothing; **5, 2, 4, 4** prick up one's ears; **5, 7** guard against.

notes 3 wad; **4** roll; **6** record, report; **7** dossier, minutes, summary, writing; **8** jottings; **9** doodlings; **10** adversaria, marginalia; **11** annotations; PHRASES: **6, 5** margin ~, school ~. *See also* **music (piece of music)**

notes (makes notes) 4 sing; **7** compose.

not even 5 empty, rough.

nothing 1 O; **3** nix, zip; **4** nada, none, void, zero; **5** aught, nihil, zilch; **6** naught, nichts, nobody, vacuum; **7** vacancy; **9** emptiness; PHRASES: **2-3** no-one; **3, 1, 3** not a bit, not a jot, not a one; **3, 1, 4** not a hint, not a lick, not a mite, not a soul, not a whit; **3, 1, 5** not a scrap, not a trace; **3, 1, 7** not a sausage, not a smidgen; **3, 2, 4** not an iota; **3, 3** not any, sod all; **4, 3** damn all; **5, 2** sweet FA *UK*; **5, 5, 5** sweet Fanny Adams; **6, 3** bugger all.

nothingness 3 nil; **4** love, nowt *UK*, void, zero; **5** space, zilch; **6** naught, nought; **7** nothing, nullity; **8** nihility, nonbeing; **9** blankness, emptiness; **12** nonexistence; PHRASES: **2, 4, 5** no such thing; **5, 5, 5** sweet Fanny Adams; **7, 2, 3** nothing at all; **7, 2, 5** nothing on earth; **7, 8** nothing whatever.

notice 1 D; **2** ad, NB; **3** see; **4** bill, heed, mark, obit; **5** banns, blurb, watch; **6** caveat, descry, poster, review; **7** discern, examine,

observe, placard, warning; **8** circular, obituary, register; **9** attention; **10** cognisance *UK*; PHRASES: **4, 7** miss nothing.

notify 4 warn; **5** alert; **6** advise, inform, report.

notion 4 idea, urge, view, whim; **5** fancy; **6** belief; **7** concept, impulse; **8** instinct; **10** conception.

notional 5 ideal; **8** abstract, academic, esoteric; **9** visionary; **10** conceptual; **11** conjectural, ideological, impractical, speculative, theoretical; **12** hypothetical, metaphysical; **13** philosophical.

not known 2 NK.

notoriety *See* **disrepute**

notwithstanding 6 anyhow; **7** despite; **9** excluding; **11** nonetheless; **12** nevertheless; PHRASES: **2, 5, 2** in spite of; **3, 3, 4** all the same; **5, 4** aside from; **7, 5** setting aside.

nought 1 O; **3** nil, zip; **4** duck, love, none, zero; **5** zilch; **7** nothing.

nourish *See* **nurture**

nourishment *See* **food**

nous *See* **wisdom**

novel 3 Kim, new; **4** Emma; **5** fresh, story; **6** Pamela, unique; **7** novella, offbeat, Rebecca, Ulysses, unusual; **8** Clarissa, personal, thriller, whodunit; **9** different, Kidnapped, novelette, Pendennis, unmatched, whodunnit; **10** individual, inimitable, Kenilworth, Persuasion; **11** Middlemarch; **12** incomparable, transcendent, unparalleled; **13** Bildungsroman, revolutionary, unprecedented; PHRASES: **3, 2, 1, 4** one of a kind; **3, 2, 5** out of reach; **3-3** one-off; **3, 3, 4** one and only; **3, 3, 5** War and Peace; **3, 5** Tom Jones; **3-6** pot-boiler; **3, 7** sui generis; **4, 2, 3, 5** Mill on the Floss; **4, 4** Jane Eyre; **4, 5** dime ~; **5-5** avant-garde; **6, 4** Vanity Fair; **6, 5** campus ~, erotic ~, Gothic ~, social ~, thesis ~; **6-6** bodice-ripper; **7, 2** unheard of; **7, 5** fantasy ~, graphic ~, nouveau roman *Fr*, problem ~; **8, 5** regional ~; **9, 5** cyberpunk ~; **10, 5** epistolary ~, historical ~, picaresque ~. *See also* **fiction**

novelist *See* **writer, poet**

novice 1 L; **3** cub; **4** colt, tyro; **7** learner, recruit, trainee; **8** beginner, initiate, neophyte, newcomer; **9** greenhorn; **10** apprentice, tenderfoot.

now 9 currently, instantly, presently; **11** immediately; **12** straightaway; PHRASES: **2,**

3, 6 at the moment; **2, 3, 7** at the present; **2, 4** at once; **2, 4, 4** at this time; **5, 4** right away.

noxious *See* **poisonous**

NP 9 neptunium; PHRASES: **3, 8** net proceeds; **3, 9** new paragraph; **8, 4** national park.

NS 10 nanosecond; PHRASES: **4, 4** near side.

NT 2, 6 no trumps; **3, 9** New Testament; **8, 5** National Trust *UK*.

nuclear 7 nucleal, nucleic; **8** nucleary, nucleate, reaction; **9** nucleolar, threshold; **10** nucleolate; **11** uninucleate; **13** multinucleate; PHRASES: **4, 6** cold fusion; **4-8** atomsmashing; **5, 8** chain reaction; **6, 6** atomic energy; **6, 8** fusion reaction; **7, 4** ~ bomb, ~ fuel; **7, 5** ~ power; **7, 6** ~ energy, ~ family, ~ fusion, ~ winter; **7, 7** fission product, ~ fission, ~ physics, ~ reactor; **7, 8** fission reaction; **8, 4** critical mass.

nucleus 3 hub, nub; **4** core; **5** focus, heart, inner, midst, pivot; **6** inside, kernel, marrow; **7** nuclear, pivotal; **8** interior, keystone, lynchpin; **9** heartland; PHRASES: **5-3** bull's-eye; **5, 5** focal point.

nude 4 bare; **5** naked, plain; **8** starkers *UK*; **9** unclothed; PHRASES: **2, 3, 3** in the raw; **2, 3, 4** in the buff; **2, 3, 10** in the altogether; **6-6** skinny-dipper. *See also* **naked**

nude person 4 nude; **6** nudist, peeler; **7** adamite, exposer, flasher; **8** disrober, naturist, streaker, stripper; **9** ecdysiast; **11** stripteaser; **12** gymnosophist; **13** exhibitionist; PHRASES: **4, 5** nude model; **4, 8** male stripper; **5-1-4** strip-o-gram; **5, 4** naked lady; **6, 6** exotic dancer; **6-6** skinny-dipper; **7, 6** topless dancer; **7, 8** topless waitress.

nudge *See* **push**

nugget *See* **piece**

nuisance 3 imp; **4** bane, bind *UK*, bore, drag, pest; **5** aggro *UK*, trial; **6** blight, bother, gadfly, hassle, ordeal, plague; **7** bugbear, trouble; **8** bullying, irritant; **9** annoyance; **10** harassment, irritation; **11** aggravation; **13** victimization; PHRASES: **4, 2, 6** spot of bother; **6, 2** seeing to.

null 4 gone, void; **7** lacking, missing, useless; **8** annulled, vanished; **9** abrogated, nullified, suspended, worthless; **10** superseded; **11** nonexistent; PHRASES: **2, 6, 3** no longer law; **4, 3, 4** ~ and void.

numb 4 dead, stun; **5** blunt, dazed; **6** asleep, deaden, freeze, frozen, torpid; **7** stunned, torpefy; **9** senseless, unfeeling; **12** anaesthetize.

number 1 C, D, E, I, K, L, M, N, V, X; **2** no, pi; **3** add, air, mob; **4** drug, list, lots, many, poll, real, sign, song, tell, tune; **5** count, digit, gauge, group, opium, piece, prime, spate, tally; **6** amount, binary, cipher, factor, figure, opiate, reckon, symbol; **7** cocaine, decimal, integer, measure, numeral, several; **8** abscissa, constant, numerate, plethora, quantify, quantity, quantize, variable; **9** bazillion, calculate, enumerate, inventory, multitude; **10** anesthetic, centillion, painkiller; **11** coefficient; PHRASES: **3, 2** sum up, tot up; **3, 6** box ~, odd ~; **4, 3** dope out, tick off; **4, 5** take stock; **4, 6** back ~, even ~, mach ~; **5, 2** count up, notch up; **5, 5** count hands, count heads; **5, 6** index ~, magic ~, prime ~, whole ~, wrong ~; **5, 7** Roman numeral; **6, 3** figure out; **6, 6** atomic ~, binary ~, finite ~, golden ~, random ~, serial ~; **6, 7** Arabic numeral; **7, 6** complex ~, decimal system, ordinal ~, perfect ~; **8, 6** cardinal ~, compound ~, concrete ~, infinite ~, negative ~, opposite ~, positive ~; **9, 6** accession ~, algebraic ~, composite ~, telephone ~.

numberless 6 myriad, untold; **7** endless; **8** infinite; **9** boundless, countless, limitless, uncounted; **10** unnumbered; **11** innumerable, measureless, uncountable; **12** immeasurable, incalculable; **13** inexhaustible; PHRASES: **2, 3, 2** no end of; **6, 7** beyond measure; **7, 3** without end; **7, 5** without limit.

numbers 3 nos.

numbness 6 stupor; **8** idleness, slowness; **10** anesthesia, inactivity, stagnation; **12** sluggishness; **13** insensibility.

numeral *See* **number**

numerous 1 C, D, L, M; **4** lots, many, tons; **5** heaps, loads, piles; **6** divers; **7** aplenty, umpteen; **8** hundreds, infinite, manifold, millions, multiple; **9** countless, thousands; **11** innumerable; **12** multifarious; **13** multitudinous; PHRASES: **1, 3** a lot; **1, 4, 3** a good few; **3, 1, 3** not a few.

nun 5 Clare; **6** abbess, novice, sister, vestal; **7** Beguine; **8** minoress, prioress; **9** postulant; PHRASES: **4, 5** Poor Clare; **6, 8** mother superior; **8, 6** reverend mother.

nuptial *See* **matrimonial**

nurse 3 SEN *UK*, SRN *UK*; **4** amah, tend; **5** nanny, treat; **6** attend, Cavell, harbor, matron, sister, tender; **7** midwife; **9** nursemaid; **11** probationer; PHRASES: **2, 4** au pair; **3, 5** day ~; **4, 3** care for; **4, 4, 1, 4** lady with a lamp; **4, 5** head ~, home ~, look after; **4, 6** ward sister *UK*; **5, 2, 5** angel of mercy; **5, 5** night ~, staff ~ *UK*; **5, 6** night sister; **6, 5** charge ~, school ~; **6, 7** health visitor; **7, 5** cutting horse, private ~, special ~, student ~, trainee ~; **7, 6** theatre sister *UK*; **7, 7** nursing officer; **8, 5** district ~ *UK*, Enrolled N~, visiting ~; **8, 9, 5** licensed practical ~; **9, 5** practical ~; **10, 5** registered ~; **10, 9** physician's assistant.

nursery 5 frame; **6** cloche, hotbed; **7** planter; **8** hothouse, orangery; **9** coolhouse, flowerpot, preschool; **10** glasshouse *UK*, greenhouse, jardinière, polytunnel, propagator; **12** conservatory, kindergarten; PHRASES: **3, 4, 6** day care center; **4, 3** grow bag; **4, 4** seed tray; **4, 5** cold frame; **6, 4** garden shed; **6, 6** infant school *UK*; **7, 3** forcing bed; **7, 4** compost heap *UK*, potting shed *UK*; **7, 5** forcing house, ~ rhyme; **7, 6** ~ school, ~ slopes, ~ stakes; **11, 2-2** babysitting co-op.

nurture 4 farm, feed, rear, tend; **5** breed, cater, nurse, raise, stock; **6** purvey, suckle; **7** aliment, nourish, promote, rearing, sustain; **8** incubate, maintain; **9** cultivate, provision; **10** upbringing; PHRASES: **4, 5** look after; **4, 6** grow plants; **6, 2** fatten up; **6-4** breast-feed.

nut 3 cob, fan, haw; **4** bean, buff, cola, head; **5** acorn, areca, betel, freak, hazel, pecan; **6** addict, almond, Brazil, cashew, conker, maniac, peanut, pignut, walnut; **7** filbert, lunatic, nutcase, praline; **8** chestnut, headcase; **9** chincapin, fruitcake, groundnut, macadamia, pistachio; PHRASES: **4, 3** wing ~; **5, 8** water chestnut; **7, 6** English walnut; **9, 3** butterfly ~. *See also* **head, mad person**

nuts *See* **mad**

NY 3, 4 New York.

nyctalopia 4, 9 moon blindness; **5, 9** night blindness.

nyctitropism 5 sleep.

nye 3 eye; **4** nide.

nymph 4 Echo, girl, lass, pupa; **5** Doris, dryad, houri, larva, naiad, oread, sylph; **6** Daphne, insect, nereid, sprite, Syrinx, Thetis, undine; **7** Calypso, Galatea, mermaid, oceanid, Sabrina; **8** Arethusa; **9** hamadryad.

NZ 3, 7 New Zealand.

O

O 3 nil, old; **4** blob, call, duck, ring, zero; **5** ocean, order, Oscar; **6** octavo, office, Orient, oxygen; **7** October; **8** ordinary; PHRASES: **5, 5** blood group.

oaf 3 yob *UK*; **4** boor, lout, slob, thug; **5** churl, clown, ocker *UK*, rowdy, tough, yahoo, yobbo *UK*; **7** bruiser, bumpkin, gorilla, hoodlum, ruffian; **8** hooligan; **9** blockhead, roughneck; **10** clodhopper; PHRASES: **5, 3** bully boy.

oafish 4 dumb, rude, wild; **5** crude, rough, rowdy; **6** clumsy, coarse, stupid; **7** awkward, boorish, loutish, uncouth, yobbish; **8** cloddish, clownish, impolite, thuggish; **10** boneheaded; **11** clodhopping; PHRASES: **3-4** ill-bred; **3-8** ill-mannered.

oasis *See* **retreat**

oath 3 vow; **4** damn, dang, drat, word; **5** balls, blast, curse, damme; **6** pledge; **7** promise; **9** affidavit, assurance, damnation, expletive, guarantee, tarnation; **10** adjuration; **11** affirmation; PHRASES: **1-4** the f-word; **3, 3** bad word; **4, 2, 5** word of honor; **4, 2, 6** ~ of office; **4, 4** rude word; **4-6, 4** four-letter word; **5, 4** Bible ~; **5, 9** sworn statement, sworn testimony; **7, 4** naughty word.

obdurate 7 callous; **8** stubborn; **9** obstinate; **10** inflexible; **11** hardhearted.

obedience 4 duty; **7** pliance; **8** docility, goodness, meekness, softness, tameness, yielding; **9** deference, passivity, readiness, servility; **10** compliance, conformity, inactivity, observance, submission; **11** dutifulness, passiveness, slavishness, willingness; **12** acquiescence, complaisance, malleability, subservience, tractability; **13** nonresistance; **14** obsequiousness, submissiveness; PHRASES: **7, 2, 3, 3** abiding by the law.

obedient 4 good, meek, soft, tame; **5** ready; **6** docile, pliant; **7** duteous, dutiful, passive, servile, slavish, trained, willing; **8** amenable, biddable, resigned, yielding; **9** compliant, complying, malleable, observant, tractable; **10** conforming, manageable, obsequious, regimented, submissive, submitting; **11** acquiescent, complaisant, deferential, disciplined, subservient, unresisting; **12** nonresisting; PHRASES: **2, 4, 7** at one's command; **2, 4, 8** at one's disposal, at one's pleasure; **3-7** law-abiding; **4-7** well-behaved, well-trained; **5-4** sheep-like; **5, 4, 5** under one's thumb; **5, 7** under control.

obedient person 5 gofer, slave; **7** servant, soldier; **8** loyalist; **10** conformist; **14** traditionalist; PHRASES: **8, 3** teacher's pet.

obeisance 3 bow; **6** curtsy, homage, kowtow, salaam; **7** obsequy, respect, worship; **8** courtesy, humility, kneeling; **9** groveling, reverence; **11** prostration; **12** genuflection.

obeisance (show obeisance to) 3 bow; **4** bend; **5** kneel, stoop; **6** curtsy, grovel, kowtow, salaam, scrape; **7** worship; **9** genuflect; PHRASES: **3, 6** pay homage; **3, 7** pay tribute; **4, 3, 5** keep the faith; **5, 6** offer homage.

obelisk 6 dagger.

obelus 6 column, dagger, needle, pillar; **8** monument.

obey 4 heed, mind; **5** defer, serve, yield; **6** assent, comply, submit; **7** conform, consent, perform; **8** minister; **9** acquiesce, discharge; PHRASES: **2, 5, 4** go along with; **3, 3, 4** toe the line; **4, 2, 4** stay in line; **4, 4** wait upon; **4, 4, 2, 3, 2** mind one's p's and q's; **4, 6** ~ orders; **5, 2** defer to, yield to; **6, 3, 4** follow the book; **6, 4** comply with; **6, 6** follow orders.

object 4 balk, body, defy, deny, goal, item, kick, moan; **5** belie, demur, fight, gripe, rebut, thing; **6** assail, attack, combat, defend, entity, gadget, grouse, impugn, negate, oppugn, person, refute, target; **7** article, counter, dispute, dissent, gainsay, protest, purpose; **8** artifact, complain, disagree, litigate; **9** challenge, commodity, criticize, deprecate, recipient, retaliate, something, thingummy; **10** contradict, contravene, controvert; **11** expostulate, remonstrate, thingumabob, thingumajig; PHRASES: **3, 2, 6** beg to differ; **4, 1, 4** make a fuss; **4, 9** take exception; **5, 3** speak out; **5-3-4** what's-its-name; **5, 10** raise objections; **8, 6** tangible ~; **9, 6** inanimate ~.

objection **4** fuss; **5** demur; **6** clamor, denial; **7** dissent, protest, refusal; **8** argument, defiance, demurral, rebuttal; **9** challenge, complaint, rejection; **10** dissidence, impugnment, refutation; **11** controversy, disputation, impugnation; **12** disagreement; **13** contradiction, contravention, controversion, expostulation, remonstration.

objectionable **4** mean, rude; **6** crabby, unkind; **7** awkward, beastly, boorish, crabbed, uncivil, uncouth; **8** impolite; **9** bellicose, obnoxious, unwelcome; **10** aggressive, quarreling, ungracious, unpleasant; **11** impertinent, quarrelsome; **12** cantankerous, discourteous, unattractive, unchivalrous; **13** discomforting; PHRASES: **6-6** bloody-minded *UK*.

objective **3** aim, end; **4** butt, case, goal, mark, prey; **5** crown, dream, Mecca, prize; **6** object, quarry, target, trophy, vision, wreath; **7** laurels, neutral; **11** destination; **13** disinterested; PHRASES: **3, 2, 4** end in view; **4, 5** Holy Grail; **5-3** bull's-eye; **6, 4** target area; **6, 6** heart's desire; **7, 4** winning post *UK*; **8, 4** Promised Land; **8, 5** lifelong dream; **9, 4** finishing line, finishing tape.

obligation **3** IOU, tie; **4** duty, task; **6** burden, charge; **10** commitment, compulsion, constraint; **12** indebtedness; **14** responsibility.

obligatory **7** binding; **9** mandatory; **10** compulsory, imperative, peremptory; **11** categorical, inescapable, unavoidable; **13** unconditional; PHRASES: **2, 7** de rigueur; **9, 2** incumbent on.

oblige **3** tie; **4** bind; **5** force, humor, order, serve; **6** commit, compel, decree, engage, enjoin, expect, pledge; **7** command, gratify, indulge, require; **8** obligate; **9** constrain; **11** accommodate; PHRASES: **2, 7, 1, 5** do someone a favor.

obliged **4** tied; **5** bound, sworn; **7** engaged, pledged, saddled; **8** beholden, grateful, indebted; **9** committed, obligated; **12** appreciative; PHRASES: **4-5** duty-bound.

obliging **4** kind; **7** affable, willing; **8** amenable, friendly; **9** agreeable, compliant; **11** complaisant, considerate, cooperative; **13** accommodating.

oblique **4** skew; **5** askew, atilt, hilly, slash, slide, steep; **6** across, angled, biased, dogleg, hinted, skewed, sloped, stroke, thwart, tilted, veiled, zigzag; **7** askance, bending, beveled, crooked, implied, leaning, listing, pitched, slanted, sloping, solidus, tangent, tilting, turning, twisted, virgule; **8** diagonal, inclined, indirect, rhomboid, slanting; **9** deflected, deviating, distorted, divergent, inclining, skewwhiff *UK*, zigzagged; **10** antigoglin, catawampus, convoluted, deflective, digressive, insinuated, meandering, separatrix, tangential, transverse; **13** inclinational; PHRASES: **3, 6** off course, off target; **5-8** cater-cornered, kitty-cornered.

oblique line **5** slash, slide; **6** dogleg, stroke; **7** oblique, solidus, virgule; **8** diagonal, rhomboid; **10** separatrix; PHRASES: **5, 2, 4** Tower of Pisa; **6, 5** rakish angle; **7, 4** beveled edge; **7, 5** hairpin curve, oblique angle.

obliquely **5** askew, atilt; **6** across, zigzag; **7** askance; **8** sideways; **9** crosswise; **10** diagonally; **12** transversely; PHRASES: **2, 2, 5** at an angle; **2, 3, 4** on the bias, on the tilt; **2, 3, 5** on the slant, on the slope; **2, 3, 8** on the diagonal. *See also* **oblique**

obliqueness **3** tip; **4** bank, bend, bias, cant, list, ramp, tilt, turn, veer; **5** grade, pitch, slant, slide, slope, twist; **6** camber, swerve, zigzag; **7** tangent; **8** diagonal; **9** curvature, deviation, obliquity; **10** deflection, digression, divergence, meandering; **11** convolution, inclination, indirection. *See also* **oblique**

obliterate **4** blot, bury, raze; **5** annul, cover, drown, erase, purge, scrub; **6** cancel, censor, deface, delete, efface, remove; **7** conceal, destroy, expunge; **8** abrogate, demolish, submerge, vaporize; **9** eliminate, eradicate, extirpate, liquidate; **10** annihilate; **11** exterminate; PHRASES: **3, 3** rub off, rub out; **4, 2, 3, 6** burn to the ground; **4, 3** blot out, edit out, rule out, take out, wash off, wash out, wipe off, wipe out; **4-6** blue-pencil; **5, 2** cover up; **5, 2, 5** leave no trace; **5, 3** black out, brush off, cross out, score out, white out; **5, 4** paint over, write over; **5, 7** cross through, score through; **6, 3** sponge out, strike out; **6, 7** strike through; **7, 3** scratch out; **7, 7** scratch through; **8, 3** scribble out.

obliteration 6 burial; **7** amnesty, editing, erasing, erasure, removal, silence; **8** deletion, oblivion; **9** annulment, cessation, interment; **10** abrogation, censorship, defacement, demolition, effacement, expunction; **11** concealment, destruction, elimination, eradication, extirpation, liquidation; **12** annihilation, cancellation, illegibility, overprinting; **13** extermination; PHRASES: **4, 6** blue pencil.

oblivion 4 coma, void; **5** Lethe, limbo; **6** stupor, trance; **7** ecstasy, nirvana, rapture; **8** ataraxia, ecstasis, hypnosis, narcosis; **9** catatonia, obscurity; **10** absorption, detachment, withdrawal; **11** nothingness; **12** nonexistence; **13** insensibility, introspection, obliviousness, senselessness; **14** abstractedness; **15** unconsciousness.

oblivious 4 deaf; **5** blind; **7** unaware; **8** absorbed, detached, ecstatic, hypnotic; **9** catatonic, rapturous, senseless, wandering, withdrawn; **10** abstracted, distracted, insensible; **11** preoccupied, unconscious; **13** introspective; **14** depersonalized; PHRASES: **3, 2, 5** out to lunch; **4, 2, 3, 6** head in the clouds; **5, 4** miles away; **6-3** spaced-out; **6-4** trancelike.

oblong 7 ellipse; **9** rectangle.

obnoxious 4 base, foul, vile; **5** nasty; **6** horrid, odious, sordid, trying, unkind; **7** beastly, hateful, hurtful, squalid; **8** annoying, horrible, spiteful, unsavory; **9** loathsome, offensive, repugnant, repulsive, revolting, sickening; **10** despicable, disgusting, nauseating; **11** displeasing, distasteful; **12** disagreeable, unacceptable.

oboe 7 hautboy.

obscene 4 blue, lewd, rude, vile; **5** adult, dirty, gross; **6** filthy, ribald, risque, risqué, smutty; **8** indecent, prurient, scabrous, shocking; **9** atrocious, loathsome, salacious; **10** lascivious, licentious, outrageous, scandalous; **12** pornographic, scatological; PHRASES: **1-5** X-rated; **4, 3, 7** near the knuckle; **4-4** hard-core.

obscenity 4 porn, smut; **7** outrage; **8** atrocity, lewdness, ribaldry, rudeness; **9** indecency, prurience, scatology; **10** smuttiness; **11** pornography; **13** salaciousness; **14** lasciviousness, licentiousness; PHRASES: **5, 4** dirty book, dirty joke; **5, 5** dirty movie; **5, 8** dirty magazine.

obscure 3 dim; **4** blur, code, deep, hard, hide, mean, poor, veil, wrap; **5** blear, cloud, cover, foggy, fuzzy, lowly, muddy, murky, vague; **6** arcane, cipher, cloudy, darken, gnomic, humble, measly, muddle, opaque, paltry, shabby; **7** complex, conceal, confuse, crabbed, cryptic, diffuse, disturb, eclipse, envelop, gnostic, inexact, muddled, pitiful, unclear, unknown; **8** abstract, abstruse, allusive, confound, confused, disguise, esoteric, hermetic, indirect, involved, obsidian, pathetic, pitiable, profound, puzzling, tortuous, wretched; **9** ambiguous, amorphous, Cimmerian, difficult, enigmatic, equivocal, imprecise, miserable, neglected, obfuscate, powerless, recondite, shapeless, uncertain; **10** complicate, convoluted, elliptical, indefinite, indistinct, mysterious, overlooked, overshadow, perplexing *UK*; **11** disregarded, inscrutable, kabbalistic, obfuscatory; **12** contemptible, impenetrable, impoverished, unrecognized; **14** unintelligible; PHRASES: **2, 5, 2, 3** as clear as mud; **2-7** no-account.

obscurity 5 depth; **6** enigma, muddle; **7** opacity, secrecy; **8** darkness, ellipsis, oblivion; **9** ambiguity, anonymity, confusion, jibberish; **10** complexity, difficulty, profundity; **11** abstraction, convolution, imprecision, inexactness, obfuscation, obscuration, uncertainty; **12** gobbledygook; **14** inscrutability. *See also* **obscure**

obsequious *See* **sycophantic**

observance 4 duty; **6** caring, custom, notice, regard, ritual; **7** heeding, keeping, loyalty, respect; **8** accuracy, ceremony, fidelity; **9** attention, diligence, following, obedience, vigilance; **10** accordance, attachment, compliance, conformity, regularity; **11** recognition, reliability; **13** dependability.

observant 5 alert, aware, exact, sharp; **6** devout; **7** careful, dutiful, heeding, literal; **8** accurate, constant, diligent, faithful, obedient, pedantic, punctual, reliable, watchful; **9** attentive, compliant, regarding, religious; **10** conforming, dependable, fastidious, meticulous, scrupulous; **11** responsible; **13** conscientious.

observation 4 note, scan; 5 recce, study; 6 prying, remark, spying, survey; 7 comment, opinion, peering, perusal; 8 scanning, scrutiny, watching; 9 discovery, espionage, voyeurism; 10 compliance, inspection, revelation; 11 examination, supervision; 12 surveillance, watchfulness; 13 investigation; 14 reconnaissance; PHRASES: 1-3 I-spy; 4-3 look-see; 4-4 once-over.

observatory 3 RGO; 4 dome; 5 tower; 6 orrery; 10 watchtower; 11 observation, planetarium, planisphere; PHRASES: 5, 4 crow's nest; 7, 4 Jodrell Bank.

observe 2 NB; 3 say, see, spy; 4 espy, heed, keep, look, mark, note, spot; 5 study, watch; 6 behold, follow, notice, regard, remark; 7 comment, examine, witness; 9 recognize; 11 acknowledge; PHRASES: 4, 2 look at; 5, 2 abide by, cling to, stick to; 6, 2 adhere to, attend to; 6, 4 comply with; 7, 2 conform to.

observer 4 seer; 5 gaper, gazer, guard, prier, scout; 6 gawper, looker, peerer, sentry, starer, viewer, voyeur; 7 janitor, lookout, monitor, proctor, scanner, seeress, spotter, tourist, watcher, witness; 8 audience, beholder, onlooker, overseer, sentinel, watchdog, watchman; 9 bystander, caretaker, inspector, patrolman, scrutator, sightseer, spectator, stargazer, vigilante, visionary; 10 eyewitness, scrutineer, supervisor; 11 birdwatcher, clairvoyant, invigilator, scrutinizer; 12 rubbernecker; PHRASES: 4, 6 nosy parker UK; 5, 7 train spotter; 5, 8 night watchman; 6-2 looker-on; 7, 3 peeping Tom; 7, 5 crystal gazer; 8, 3 security man.

obsession 5 mania; 7 passion; 8 fixation; 11 fascination; 13 preoccupation.

obsolete 4 dead, past; 5 ended, kaput, passé; 7 antique, archaic, defunct, extinct, outworn; 8 finished, outdated, outmoded, vanished; 9 abandoned, destroyed; 10 antiquated; 11 annihilated, obliterated; PHRASES: 3-2-4 out-of-date.

obstacle 3 bar, bug, dam, jam, let, rub; 4 drag, flat, flaw, snag, stay, wall; 5 block, botch, catch, check, delay, ditch, fence, hitch; 6 arrest, cockup UK, glitch, hazard, hiccup, hurdle, mishap, strike; 7 barrier, embargo, impasse, lockout, problem, trouble; 8 accident, blockade, blockage, deadlock, drawback, sabotage, stoppage, tollgate; 9 breakdown, deterrent, roadblock, stalemate, turnstile; 10 bottleneck,

contraflow UK, difficulty, filibuster, impairment, impediment; 11 bureaucracy, contretemps, malfunction, obstruction, prohibition, regulations; 12 intervention; 13 inconvenience; PHRASES: 2-2 no-no; 2-2, 4 no-go area; 3-2 mix-up; 3, 3 log jam; 3, 4 red tape; 3, 5, 7 not plain sailing; 4-2 foul-up, hang-up; 4, 2, 6 spot of bother; 4, 4 flat tire; 5-2 Catch-22, screw-up; 6, 4 picket line; 7, 3 traffic jam; 7, 6 vicious circle; 9, 4 Sisyphean task; 9, 5 stumbling block, technical hitch.

obstetrics 4 caul; 5 fetus, fetus UK, labor, stork; 6 embryo, waters; 7 midwife, travail; 8 childbed, delivery, epidural, placenta, tocology; 9 Caesarian, midwifery; 10 afterbirth, childbirth, gynecology, unigravida; 11 confinement; 12 accouchement, contractions, gynecologist, multigravida, obstetrician, primigravida; 13 amniocentesis; PHRASES: 3, 2, 6 bag of waters; 5-2 lying-in; 5, 5 birth pangs UK, labor pains; 6-2-2 mother-to-be; 7, 8 forceps delivery; 8, 3 amniotic sac; 8, 5 amniotic fluid, pregnant woman; 9, 4 umbilical cord; 10, 4 gooseberry bush.

obstinacy 8 obduracy, rigidity; 9 contumacy; 10 adamantine, indocility, perversity, resistance; 11 pertinacity; 12 disobedience, inelasticity; 13 inflexibility, intransigence, recalcitrance; 14 intractability; 15 incorrigibility; PHRASES: 4, 2, 4, 3 mind of one's own; 4-4 self-will; 5, 4 stiff neck. See also obstinate

obstinate 4 dour, firm, hard; 5 rigid, stiff, tough; 6 cussed, dogged, entêté, mulish; 7 awkward UK, callous, froward, starchy, willful; 8 hardline, obdurate, stubborn; 9 pigheaded, tenacious, unbending; 10 headstrong, inflexible, refractory, unyielding; 11 intractable, traditional, unmalleable; 12 conservative, intransigent, pertinacious, recalcitrant; 14 uncompromising; PHRASES: 3-2-3-6 dog-in-the-manger; 3-4 die-hard; 4-6 bull-headed, self-willed; 6-6 bloody-minded UK; 8, 2, 1, 4 stubborn as a mule; 8, 4 standing firm.

obstinate (be obstinate) 6 ignore, insist; 7 persist; 9 dogmatize, persevere; PHRASES: 3, 2, 4, 4 dig in one's toes; 3, 2, 4, 5 dig in one's heels; 3, 5 not budge, sit tight; 4, 3 stay put; 5, 2, 4, 4 stick to one's guns; 5, 2, 6 brook no denial; 5, 4 stand firm.

obstinate person 3 dry; 4 mule; 5 bigot, blimp; **6** pedant, stayer, zealot; **7** fanatic; **8** rigorist, stickler; **9** dogmatist, hardliner; **10** persecutor; **11** reactionary; **12** conservative, obscurantist; PHRASES: **3, 2, 3, 6** dog in the manger; **3, 4** old fogy; **3-4** die-hard; **4-3** hard-ass; **4-4** hard-head, hard-nose; **4-7** last-ditcher; **5-2-3-3** stick-in-the-mud; **6-5** bitterender; **7, 5** Colonel Blimp.

obstruct **4** stop; **5** block; **6** hamper, hinder, impede, thwart; **9** barricade, frustrate; **10** complicate; PHRASES: **4, 2** hold up.

obstruction **3** dam, jam; **8** blockage, obstacle, stoppage; **9** barricade; **10** bottleneck; PHRASES: **9, 5** stumbling block.

obtain *See* **get**

obtrude **3** pry; **6** extend, impose, meddle, thrust; **9** interfere; PHRASES: **4, 3** push out; **5, 3** stick out.

obtrusive **6** garish; **7** blatant, forward; **9** intruding, prominent; **10** meddlesome; **11** conspicuous, interfering; **12** unmistakable.

obtuse **11** insensitive; **12** imperceptive; PHRASES: **4-6** dull-witted.

obverse **4** face, side; **5** front, heads, other; **7** visible; **8** anterior, opposing, opposite; **10** complement, equivalent; **11** counterpart; **13** complementary; PHRASES: **7-6** forward-facing; **8, 6** opposite number.

obvious **4** open; **5** clear, lucid, overt, plain; **6** patent; **7** blatant, evident, glaring, salient, visible; **8** apparent, flagrant, manifest, palpable; **10** pronounced, undeniable; **11** transparent, unambiguous, undisguised; PHRASES: **4-7** self-evident.

occasion **2** do; **3** day; **4** call, date, fete, time; **5** cause, party; **6** chance, entail, reason; **11** celebration, opportunity.

occasional **6** casual; **7** interim, passing; **8** sporadic; **9** temporary; **10** ceremonial, infrequent; **11** provisional; **12** intermittent; PHRASES: **3, 3** pro tem; **4-4** part-time.

occlude **4** seal, shut; **5** block, close; PHRASES: **3, 3** cut off, cut out; **4, 2** stop up; **4, 3** shut off; **5, 3** block off, close off.

occult **3** ESP; **4** code, hide, veil, yoga; **5** cloak, magic, runic; **6** arcane, covert, darken, encode, enigma, latent, secret, voodoo, yogism; **7** alchemy, animism, arcanum, cryptic, eclipse, encoded, mystery, obscure, occlude, secrecy, sorcery, telergy, ufology; **8** anagogic, eeriness, esoteric, hermetic, Kabbalah, prophecy, psychics, psychism, symbolic; **9** anagogics, astrology, enigmatic, esoterica, esoterics, hermetics, hermetism, hypnotism, Kabbalism, mediumism, mesmerism, mysticism, shamanism, spiritism, symbolics, symbolism, telepathy, theosophy, voodooism; **10** automatism, divination, levitation, mysterious, paranormal, phrenology, witchcraft; **11** esotericism, hermeticism, Kabbalistic *UK*, metaphysics, psychosophy, Rosicrucian, supernature, supernormal, supranature, telekinesis, telesthesia; **12** hyperphysics, metapsychism, numinousness, psychography, psychorrhagy, pyramidology, spiritualism, spirituality, supernatural, supranatural; **13** anthroposophy *UK*, autohypnotism, dematerialize, immaterialize, mystification, preternatural, psychokinesis, reincarnation, superhumanity, superphysical, supersensible, teleportation, unearthliness, unworldliness; **14** miraculousness, mysteriousness, parapsychology, poltergeistism, Rosicrucianism; **15** otherworldliness, supernaturalism, supernaturality, supernormalness, supranaturalism; PHRASES: **3, 10** the paranormal; **3, 12** the supernatural; **4, 7** mind reading; **5, 5** ghost dance; **5, 7** faith healing, table tapping; **6, 5** astral plane, spirit world; **6, 7** spirit rapping, spirit writing; **7, 7** fortune telling.

occult influence **5** charm, curse, magic, stars; **6** heaven, voodoo; **7** sorcery; **9** astrology, horoscope, hypnotism, mesmerism; **10** witchcraft; **11** malevolence; PHRASES: **5, 5** magic spell; **6, 9** malign influence.

occultist **4** yogi; **5** adept, druid, fakir; **6** medium, mystic; **7** houngan, mahatma, psychic; **8** druidess, ecstatic, esoteric, exorcist, psychist; **9** alchemist, exorcizer, hypnotist, Kabbalist, spiritist, ufologist, unspeller; **10** automatist, mystagogue, psychicist; **11** ghostbuster, panpsychist, psychometer, Rosicrucian, telekinetic, telepathist, telesthetic, theosophist; **12** metapsychist, phrenologist, spiritualist *UK*; **13** metaphysician, metaphysicist, psychometrist; **14** psychographist, pyramidologist; **15** anthroposophist, supernaturalist; PHRASES: **4, 6** fork bender, mind reader; **5, 6** faith healer, table tapper; **6, 6** spirit rapper; **7, 6** thought reader.

occupant **6** inmate, tenant; **7** denizen; **8** resident, squatter; **9** incumbent; **10** inhabitant.

occupation 3 job; 4 line, post, rule, task, work; 5 craft, field, skill, trade; 6 career, living, metier, tenure; 7 pursuit, seizure, tenancy; 8 activity, business, conquest, position, vocation; 9 avocation, diversion, residency, situation *UK*; 10 annexation, employment, livelihood, oppression, possession, profession, subjection.

occupy 4 busy, hold, live, rent, stay; 5 dwell, lease, lodge, squat, visit; 6 absorb, engage, people, reside, settle; 7 engross, inhabit, involve, sojourn; 8 colonize, populate.

occur 2 be; 3 are; 4 fall; 5 arise, recur; 6 appear, betide, happen; 7 perform; 8 reappear.

occurrence 4 case, hour; 5 event, point, stage; 6 moment; 7 episode; 8 incident, instance, juncture, occasion; 9 happening, milestone; 11 conjuncture, opportunity.

ocean 3 sea; 4 blue, deep, main; 5 waves; 7 Pacific; 8 Atlantic; PHRASES: 6, 5 Arctic O~, Indian O~; 8, 5 Southern O~; 9, 5 Antarctic O~. *See also* **sea**

OCT 6 octave, octavo; 7 October.

octahedrite 7 anatase.

octave 5 octet; 6 eighth.

octopus 6 spider; 9 devilfish.

ocular 8 eyeglass, eyepiece.

OD 8 overdose; 9 overdrawn; PHRASES: 5, 3 right eye (Latin: oculus dexter); 7, 8 outside diameter.

odd 3 rum *UK*; 4 left, lone; 5 droll, queer, weird; 6 impair, quirky, single, uneven; 7 bizarre, erratic, offbeat, strange, unusual; 8 peculiar, singular; 9 anomalous, different, eccentric, irregular; 10 asymmetric, individual, irrational, mismatched, unbalanced; 11 incongruous, paradoxical, superfluous.

oddball *See* **odd person**

oddity 5 freak, quirk, twist; 6 foible, rarity; 7 oddness; 8 original; 9 character, curiosity, eccentric; 10 phenomenon, quirkiness; 11 bizarreness, peculiarity, strangeness; 12 idiosyncrasy.

odd person *See* **eccentric**

odds (at odds) 2, 2, 4 up in arms; 2, 5 at issue; 2, 5, 8 at cross purposes; 2, 7, 5 at daggers drawn; 2, 8 at variance; 2, 13 in confrontation; 4, 2, 4 face to face.

ode *See* **poem**

odometer 10 mileometer *UK*.

odontalgia 9 toothache.

odor 2 BO; 3 air; 4 nose, waft; 5 aroma, savor, scent, smell, smoke, stink, vapor, whiff; 6 breath, stench; 7 bouquet, perfume; 8 pungency; 9 emanation, fragrance, redolence; 10 exhalation, fruitiness, odorimetry, smelliness, suggestion; 11 aromaticity, odorousness, olfactology; 12 olfactometry, olfactronics; 13 olfactologist.

odorless 5 clean, fresh; 8 noseless; 9 fumigated, inodorous, scentless, smokeless, unscented; 10 deodorized, unperfumed, ventilated; 11 disinfected; PHRASES: 2, 3, 5, 3 in the fresh air; 4-4 odor-free; 5-4 smellless, smoke-free; 6, 2 upwind of; 9-4 fragrance-free.

odorous 5 heady, herby, olent, spicy; 6 smelly, whiffy *UK*; 7 noisome, noxious, pungent, scented; 8 aromatic, fragrant, perfumed, redolent, savorous, smelling, stinking; 9 emanative; 10 olfactible, pheromonal; 11 odoriferous.

Odysseus 7 Ulysses.

odyssey 4 trek; 7 crusade, journey; 10 pilgrimage, wanderings.

off 3 bad; 4 away, gone, high; 5 start, wrong; 6 absent; 7 inexact; 10 inaccurate; PHRASES: 3, 3 ~ key; 3, 4 ~ line; 3, 5 ~ color; 3, 6 ~ limits, ~ season.

offal 4 gore, guts *UK*; 5 brawn, elder, heart, liver, melts, tripe; 6 brains, kidney, lights, oxtail, tongue; 7 cowheel, garbage, giblets, innards, rubbish; 8 trotters; 9 leftovers; 10 sweetbread; 12 chitterlings; PHRASES: 2, 5 ox cheek; 2, 6 ox tongue; 4, 3 pig's fry; 4, 4 Bath chap, pig's feet, pig's head; 4, 5 cow's udder; 4, 8 pig's knuckles; 5, 4 calf's head, thick seam; 5, 5 calf's liver, lamb's liver; 7, 4 variety meat; 7, 5 chicken liver.

off-color 3 ill; 4 sick; 5 unfit; 6 risqué, unwell; 8 improper; 10 indecorous, indiscreet, suggestive.

offend 3 sin, vex; 4 bait, fret, goad, huff, hurt, miff, rile; 5 annoy, chafe, pique, sting, taunt, tease, wound; 6 arouse, bother, grieve, harass, insult, needle, nettle, pester, rankle, ruffle, slight; 7 affront, incense, inflame, outrage, provoke, torment; 8 aggrieve, irritate, pinprick; 9 aggravate; 10 antagonize, exasperate; PHRASES: 3, 2, 4, 6 get on one's nerves; 4, 2 stir up, work up; 5, 2, 4, 4 stick in one's craw; 5, 3, 3 break the law.

offended (be offended) 4 mind; PHRASES: 3, 4, 1, 4 not take a joke; 4, 4 feel hurt; 4, 5 feel pique, take amiss; 4, 7 take offense, take umbrage.

offender *See* **criminal**

offending 3 bad; 4 bent; 5 shady; 6 guilty, wicked; 7 corrupt, crooked, heinous, sinning; 8 criminal, culpable; 9 breaching, dishonest, felonious, nefarious, violating; 10 fraudulent, infringing, villainous; 11 encroaching, trespassing; 13 transgressing; PHRASES: 8, 3, 3 breaking the law.

offense 3 sin; 4 huff, hurt, miff; 5 crime, wrong; 6 attack, insult, slight; 7 affront, dudgeon, umbrage; 9 exception, hostility, indignity; 11 provocation; 13 transgression; PHRASES: 3, 3, 2, 1, 4 red rag to a bull; 3, 5 raw nerve; 4, 5 last straw, sore point; 4, 7 high dudgeon.

offensive 3 bad; 4 blue, foul, push, raid, rank, rude, ugly, vile; 5 dirty, nasty; 6 attack, filthy, putrid, sortie; 7 abusive, assault, hostile, noisome, obscene, profane, uncivil; 8 impolite, invasion, invasive; 9 incursion, insulting, obnoxious, onslaught, repellent, repulsive, revolting, unsightly; 10 aggressive, derogatory, disgusting, indelicate, scandalous, scurrilous, unpleasant; 11 provocative, threatening; 12 disagreeable; 13 disrespectful, objectionable; 15 unparliamentary; PHRASES: 5-5 Anglo-Saxon.

offer 3 bid, ONO; 4 bait, goad, lure, spur; 5 bribe; 6 donate, extend, induce, submit, tender; 7 advance, auction, bargain, freebie, present, proffer, propose, suggest; 8 approach, dedicate, persuade, proposal; 9 advertise, subscribe, volunteer; 10 consecrate, contribute, invitation; 11 proposition; PHRASES: 3, 2, 3, 4 put up for sale; 3, 2, 3, 6 put on the market; 3, 6 lay before; 7, 5 special ~.

offering 4 alms, dole, gift; 5 manna, tithe; 6 appeal, bounty; 7 benefit, incense, largess, present; 8 donation, donative, giveaway, hecatomb, largesse, oblation; 9 expiation, martyrdom, offertory, sacrifice; 10 collection, dedication; 11 appeasement; 12 conciliation, consecration, contribution, propitiation, subscription; PHRASES: 4, 3 flag day, food aid, Live Aid, mite box; 4-3 hand-out; 4, 4 free meal; 4, 5 food stamp; 4, 6 food parcel, meal ticket; 4-9 self-sacrifice;

4-10 self-immolation; 5, 8 burnt ~, peace ~, thank ~; 6, 4 widow's mite; 6, 5 Maundy money *UK*, Peter's pence; 6, 8 Easter ~, votive ~; 7, 4 charity game; 7, 5 benefit match; 11, 4 sacrificial lamb.

offhand 6 casual; 8 informal; 9 easygoing, impromptu; 10 improvised, nonchalant; 11 indifferent, spontaneous, unrehearsed; 14 extemporaneous.

office 3 den, job; 4 duty, mail, post, rite, room, sext; 5 lauds, nones, prime; 6 agency, bureau, matins; 8 compline, evensong, function, ministry, position, sinecure; 9 portfolio; 10 department; PHRASES: 3, 6 box ~, War O~; 4, 6 holy ~, Home O~ *UK*, Oval O~, post ~; 5, 6 crown ~; 6, 4 bucket shop; 6, 6 divine ~, patent ~; 7, 6 Foreign O~; 8, 6 register ~ *UK*.

office assistant 2 PA *UK*; 4 peon; 5 clerk, gofer; 6 runner; 7 courier; 8 dogsbody, employee; 9 assistant, messenger, secretary; PHRASES: 3, 4 tea lady *UK*; 3, 6 man Friday; 4, 4 copy aide; 4, 6 girl Friday; 5-4, 3 right-hand man; 5, 6 staff member; 6, 3 errand boy, office boy; 6, 6 office worker.

officer 2 CO, DI, LT, OC, PO, SM, WO; 3 Col, cop, Gen, NCO; 4 bosn, Brig, Capt, CIGS, mate; 5 bosun, chair; 6 purser; 7 captain, general; 8 adjutant, chairman; 9 centurion, constable, executive, policeman, secretary, subaltern, treasurer; 11 functionary; PHRASES: 5, 3 brass hat; 6-6 office-bearer, office-holder; 6, 7 action ~. *See also* **military rank**

officer commanding 2 OC.

official 2 MP; 3 ref; 4 peer; 5 clerk, envoy, legal, mayor; 6 aedile, consul, deputy, formal, public, scorer, umpire, vizier; 7 marshal, monitor, officer, praetor, prefect, senator, servant, steward; 8 alderman, approved, delegate, Eurocrat, licensed, mandarin, minister, quaestor; 9 certified, councilor, counselor, intendant, jobsworth *UK*, proconsul, secretary; 10 accredited, ambassador, Areopagite, authorized, bureaucrat, councilman, magistrate, Sanhedrist; 11 apparatchik, backbencher, Congressman, functionary; 12 commissioner, governmental; 13 administrator; 14 representative, Representative, undersecretary; 15 Parliamentarian; PHRASES: 3, 3 tin god; 4-2-6 Jack-in-office; 4, 7 city manager, fire marshal, shop steward; 5, 6 grand vizier; 5, 7 civil servant; 5, 9 first secretary; 6,

7 public servant, school prefect; **6, 8** junior minister; **7, 2, 5** officer of state; **7, 5** special envoy; **7, 8** cabinet minister.

official language 2 RP; **8** legalese; PHRASES: **3, 7** BBC English; **6, 7** Oxford English *UK*, Queen's English; **8, 5** standard usage.

official residence 4 hall, pile; **5** lodge, manse, villa; **6** castle, estate, grange *UK*, palace; **7** château, deanery, embassy, mansion, rectory; **8** Balmoral, Chequers, vicarage; **9** consulate, parsonage; **11** chancellery; PHRASES: **2, 7, 6** 10 Downing Street; **5, 5** manor house, White House; **7, 4** stately home *UK*; **7, 5** Mansion House *UK*; **7, 6** Windsor Castle; **9, 4** ancestral hall.

officiate 5 chair; **6** direct; **7** control, oversee, preside, proctor; **8** minister; **10** invigilate.

officious 4 nosy; **5** bossy, pushy; **8** meddling; **9** bumptious, intrusive, tampering; **10** meddlesome; **11** busybodying, dictatorial, domineering, importunate, interfering, overbearing, overzealous; PHRASES: **4-9** self-important.

off-putting 8 daunting; **9** offensive, repellent, repulsive, upsetting; **10** disgusting, disturbing, forbidding; **11** distasteful; **13** disconcerting.

of French 2 de, du.

offset 7 balance; **9** equalizer; **10** counteract; **12** counterpoise, counterweigh; **14** counterbalance; PHRASES: **4, 2, 3** make up for.

offshoot 4 limb, slip; **5** scion, shoot, sprig; **6** branch, member, runner, sucker; **7** adjunct, cutting, tendril; **9** appendage, by-product *UK*, outgrowth; **10** derivative, descendant, subsidiary; **12** ramification.

offspring 3 boy, son; **4** girl, seed; **5** brood, child, issue, spawn; **6** litter; **7** progeny; **8** children, daughter. *See also* **child**

ogive 6, 4 lancet arch.

ogre 5 fiend, giant, troll; **6** tyrant; **7** monster.

Ohio 2 OH; **7** buckeye (tree); **8** cardinal (bird), Columbus (capital); PHRASES: **3, 9** red carnation (flower); **4, 3, 3, 6, 3, 8** With God all things are possible (motto); **7, 5** Buckeye State (nickname).

oil 3 wax; **4** balm, derv *UK*, ease, soap; **5** attar, bribe, crude, ester, lipid, meths *UK*,

oleum; **6** anoint, diesel, grease, lather, oilcan, petrol *UK*, smooth; **7** camphor, essence, lubrify, moisten, naphtha; **8** cracking, gasoline, kerosene, macassar, oilfield, paraffin, refining; **9** hardening, lubricate, petroleum; **10** oleaginize; **13** fractionation; PHRASES: **3, 3** gas ~, nut ~, ~ rig; **3, 4** ~ cake, ~ drum, ~ rape, ~ well; **3, 5** ~ paint, ~ shale, ~ slick; **3-5, 3** cod-liver ~; **3, 6** ~ beetle, ~ tanker; **3, 7** gas station; **3, 8** ~ painting, ~ platform, ~ refinery, ~ reserves; **4, 3** coal ~, corn ~, hair ~, palm ~; **5, 3** benne ~, crude ~, olive ~, sperm ~, whale ~; **5, 3, 3** North Sea ~; **6, 3** castor ~, diesel ~, peanut ~; **6, 4** petrol pump *UK*; **6, 6** octane number; **7, 3** Alaskan ~, coconut ~, linseed ~, mineral ~; **7, 6** nodding donkey; **7, 7** filling station; **8, 3** midnight ~, offshore rig; **8, 4** aviation fuel; **8, 6** unleaded petrol; **9, 3** essential ~, sassafras ~, vegetable ~; **11, 3** camphorated ~.

oilcloth 8 linoleum.

oily 3 fat; **4** rich, waxy; **5** fatty, lardy, milky, oleic, sleek, slick, soapy, suety; **6** creamy, creepy, fleshy, greasy, mucoid, smarmy, smooth; **7** adipose, buttery, butyric, cereous, pinguid, tallowy; **8** blubbery, slippery, slithery, toadying, unctuous; **9** sebaceous, unguinous; **10** obsequious, oleaginous, paraffinic; **11** butyraceous, saponaceous.

ointment 3 oil, rub; **4** balm, nard; **5** cream, paint, salve, syrup; **6** balsam, chrism, lotion, pomade; **7** eyewash, lanolin, unction, unguent; **8** inunctum, lenitive, liniment, macassar, poultice; **9** collyrium, demulcent, emollient, inunction *UK*, spikenard, unguentum; **10** abirritant; **11** arquebusade, embrocation, fomentation; **12** brilliantine; PHRASES: **8, 5** soothing syrup.

Oklahoma 2 OK; **6** redbud (tree); **9** mistletoe (flower); PHRASES: **6, 5** Sooner State (nickname); **6, 8, 3, 6** Labour conquers all things (motto); **7-6, 10** scissor-tailed flycatcher (bird); **8, 4** O~ City (capital).

OK, okay 3 oke *UK*, vet; **4** fair, fine, good; **5** agree, right; **6** agreed, kosher; **7** approve; **8** sanction; PHRASES: **4-4** okey-doke.

okra 5 gumbo.

OL 4, 3 left eye (Latin: oculus laevus).

old 1 O; **2** ex; **4** aged, gray, late, past, ripe, used, worn; **5** dated, elder, hoary, musty, stale; **6** adamic, former, mature, mellow, prewar, rooted, senile, senior; **7** ancient, antique, archaic, classic, elderly, veteran, vintage; **8** decrepit, grizzled, historic, outdated, outmoded, timeworn; **9** ancestral, classical, crumbling, doddering, moldering, senescent, venerable; **10** antiquated, archaistic, historical, immemorial, Methuselah, secondhand; **11** antiquarian, established, patriarchal, traditional; **12** antediluvian; PHRASES: **2, 3, 2, 3, 5** as ~ as the hills; **2, 3, 2, 4** as ~ as Adam, as ~ as time; **2, 4** of yore, ye olde; **2, 8, 5** of advanced years; **3, 3** ~ boy, ~ hat, ~ man; **3-3** age-old; **3, 4** O~ Bill UK, ~ girl, ~ gold, ~ hand, ~ lady, ~ maid, O~ Nick; **3, 5** ~ style; **3, 6** O~ Bailey, ~ school; **3, 7** ~ country, the elderly; **3, 9** O~ Testament; **3-9** old-fashioned; **4, 2** past it; **4, 3, 4** over the hill; **4-5** moth-eaten; **4-6** grayhaired, olde-worlde UK; **4-7** time-honored; **4, 11** long established; **5-6** white-haired; **7, 2** getting on.

old age 7 anility, decline, frailty; **8** grayness, maturity, senility; **9** hoariness, infirmity, longevity, seniority; **10** anecdotage, mellowness, senescence; **11** decrepitude, elderliness; **13** venerableness; PHRASES: **4, 3, 3** ripe old age; **5, 3** third age; **6, 5** golden years; **8, 4** allotted span; **8, 5** advanced years; **10, 3** retirement age.

old article 2 ye.

old boy 2 OB; **7** alumnus.

old city 2 Ur; **4** Troy.

Old English 2 OE.

old-fashioned 3 out; **4** trad UK; **5** dated, passé, stale; **6** square; **7** defunct, disused; **8** obsolete, outdated, outgrown; **9** discarded, primitive; **10** antiquated; **13** unfashionable; **3-2-4** out-of-date; **3, 3** old hat.

old girl 2 OG; **6** alumna.

Old Harry 5 Satan.

old lady 2 ma; **3** mom, mum UK; **4** gram; **6** mother. See also **mother**

old man 2 pa; **3** pop; **6** father. See also **father**

Old Nick 5 Satan.

old person 3 OAP UK; **5** adult, doyen, elder, oldie; **6** dotard UK, Nestor, senior; **7** crumbly, oldster, retiree, veteran, wrinkly; **8** ancestor, dodderer, forebear, Tithonus; **9** geriatric, graybeard, pensioner; **10** Methuselah; **11** centenarian, grandparent; **12** nonagenarian, octogenarian, sexagenarian; **14** septuagenarian; PHRASES: **2, 6, 7** no spring chicken; **3, 3, 9** old age pensioner; **3, 4** old

fogy; **4, 7** Gray Panther; **5-2** grown-up; **5, 3, 4** Darby and Joan; **6, 4** Father Time; **6, 5** golden oldie; **6, 7** senior citizen; **7, 6** retired person.

Old Testament 2 OT. See also **Bible**

old thing 5 relic; **6** fossil; **7** antique; **8** archaism, artifact, dinosaur, heirloom; **10** Stonehenge, Victoriana; PHRASES: **4, 3, 7** Dead Sea Scrolls; **5, 2, 3, 4** relic of the past, thing of the past; **6, 5** museum piece; **6, 8** listed building UK; **7, 8** ancient monument UK.

oleander 7 rosebay.

olefine 6 alkene.

olive 5, 3 ~ oil; **5, 4** ~ drab; **5, 5** ~ brown, ~ crown, ~ green; **5, 6** ~ branch.

Oliver 4 Noll; PHRASES: **6, 3, 6** Roland and O~; **6, 5** O~ Hardy, O~ Twist; **6, 8** O~ Cromwell; **6, 9** O~ Goldsmith.

olivine 10 chrysolite.

Olympian 3 Eos, Pan; **4** Ares, Eros, Hebe, Hera, Juno, Mars, Zeus; **5** Ceres, Cupid, Diana, Hades, Pluto, Venus, Vesta; **6** Apollo, Athene, Aurora, Helios, Hermes, Plutus, Vulcan; **7** Artemis, Bacchus, Demeter, Jupiter, Mercury, Minerva, Neptune; **8** Dionysus, Poseidon; **9** Aphrodite; **10** Hephaestus; PHRASES: **5, 3** Greek god, Roman god.

omen 4 sign, type; **6** augury, herald; **7** auspice, caution, portent, presage, symptom, warning; **8** syndrome; **9** foretoken, harbinger, messenger, precursor; **10** forerunner, indication, prognostic; **11** forewarning, ominousness; **13** prefigurement; **15** prognostication; PHRASES: **4, 2, 3, 5** sign of the times.

ominous 3 bad; **4** dire, evil; **7** baleful, fateful; **8** alarming, menacing, sinister; **10** foreboding, portentous; **11** threatening.

omission 3 gap; **4** lack, loss, miss, need, void, want; **5** break; **6** lacuna, ullage; **7** apocope, arrears, default, deficit, elision, failure, neglect; **8** breakage, ellipsis, interval, slippage; **9** oversight, shortfall; **10** aphaeresis, apostrophe, deficiency; **11** defalcation; **12** intermission; **13** insufficiency; PHRASES: **5, 5** screw loose; **7, 4** missing link.

omit 3 cut; **4** drop, miss, skip; **5** elide; **7** scratch; **8** overlook; PHRASES: **4, 3** miss out UK.

omnibus See **compilation**

omnipresence 7 company, society; **8**

ubiquity, visiting; **9** diffusion, pervasion; **10** appearance, attendance, permeation; **11** association, frequenting; **13** accompaniment, companionship, diffusiveness, participation, pervasiveness; **14** ubiquitousness; PHRASES: **3-8** all-presence.

on 2 at, re; **3** leg; **4** over; PHRASES: **2, 3** ~ dit *UK*, ~ key; **2, 4** ~ line.

once 4 when; **5** after; **8** formerly; **10** previously; PHRASES: **1, 4, 4, 3** a long time ago; **2, 4, 2** as soon as; **3, 6** the minute; **4, 4, 3** some time ago.

one 1 a, I; **2** an; **3** ace, ane; **4** atom, item, lone, mono, only, self, sole, solo, soul, unit; **5** first, monad, point, unity; **6** atomic, entity, module, person, single; **7** article, integer, monadic, persona, primary; **8** solitary; **9** singleton; **10** individual.

one (become one) 4 fuse, join; **5** blend, merge, unify, unite; **6** cohere; **7** combine; **9** integrate.

one (French) 2 un; **3** une.

one (German) 3 ein; **4** eine, eins; **5** einer, eines.

one (Scots) 3 ane.

oneness 5 union, unity; **8** solidity; **9** coherence, integrity, wholeness; **10** solidarity; **11** integrality; **13** undividedness; **14** indivisibility; **15** indissolubility. *See also* **one**

one o'clock 3 IAM, NNE.

onerous 4 hard; **5** heavy, stiff; **6** severe, taxing, tiring, uphill; **7** arduous, tedious, wearing, weighty; **8** exacting; **9** demanding, difficult, laborious, punishing, strenuous, troublous; **10** burdensome, formidable, oppressive; **11** troublesome; PHRASES: **4-8** back-breaking.

one's 2 IS.

ongoing 6 moving, onward; **7** current, pending; **8** enduring, unbroken; **9** profluent; **10** continuing, continuous, developing, inexorable, proceeding; **11** outstanding; **12** irreversible; PHRASES: **2, 8** in progress; **3-4** non-stop; **5, 3** under way.

only 3 but; **4** just, lone, mere, sole; **6** except, merely, simply, single.

onset *See* **start**

onslaught *See* **attack**

onus *See* **responsibility**

onward 2 on; **5** ahead; **7** forward; **8** forwards, headlong.

oodles *See* **plenty**

oomph *See* **energy**

ooze 4 leak, seep; **5** drool, exude, leach; **7** dribble, radiate, trickle; PHRASES: **2, 4, 2** be full of; **4, 2** reek of; **8, 4** overflow with.

OP 4 opus, work; **10** outpatient; PHRASES: **5, 6** other people; **8, 6** opposite prompt.

opacity *See* **opaqueness**

opaque 4 dark, dull, hazy; **5** black, blank, dense, dirty, filmy, foggy, fuzzy, milky, muddy, murky, solid, thick; **6** cloudy, coated; **7** covered; **10** impervious, lightproof, windowless; **11** impermeable; **12** impenetrable; **14** nontranslucent, nontransparent; PHRASES: **5-5** light-tight.

opaque (make opaque) 3 dim; **4** coat; **5** cloud, cover, frost, muddy, smoke; **6** darken, screen; **7** obscure, thicken; **9** devitrify, obfuscate; PHRASES: **4, 2** stir up.

opaqueness 7 density, dimness, opacity; **8** solidity; **9** mirroring, turbidity; **10** reflection; **11** obfuscation; **14** impermeability; **15** impenetrability. *See also* **opaque**

opaque thing 3 fog; **4** film, haze, mist; **5** blind, cloud, smoke, steam; **6** drapes, screen; **7** curtain, leucoma, leukoma, shutter; **8** blizzard; **9** peasouper, sandstorm; **11** smokescreen; PHRASES: **4, 5** dust storm; **5, 4** brick wall; **5, 5** muddy water; **6, 5** ground glass; **7, 5** frosted glass.

open 3 air, out; **4** airy, ajar, bare, bold, free, hewn, show, tear, torn, undo; **5** agape, begin, blunt, clear, crack, erupt, frank, naive, naked, overt, plain, split, start, unbar; **6** access, brazen, breach, broach, broken, candid, cleave, daring, expose, extend, gaping, honest, public, reveal, spread, unbolt, uncork, unfold, unlock, unseal, unstop, unveil, unwrap, vacant; **7** artless, cracked, defiant, exposed, rupture, sincere, unblock, unclose, uncover, unlatch, visible; **8** breached, disclose, emphatic, explicit, fracture, immodest, impudent, ruptured, truthful, unclosed, unfasten, unfolded; **9** barefaced, downright, flaunting, fractured, ingenuous, outspoken, shameless, uncovered, unwrapped, veracious; **10** forthright, unreserved; **12** unrestricted; **15** straightforward; PHRASES: **3, 3, 5, 4** cut the first turf; **3, 3, 6** cut the ribbon; **3-3-6** off-the-record; **4, 3** ~ day; **4, 4** ~ book; **4, 5** ~ house; **4, 6** ~ letter; ~ market, ~ prison *UK*, ~ sesame; **4, 7** ~ verdict *UK*; **4, 10** O~ University *UK*; **5-6** plain-spoken; **5-8** plain-speaking; **6-2-3** honest-to-God; **7, 4** declare ~; **7-5** crystal-clear.

open-air 7 outdoor, outside; **8** alfresco; PHRASES: **3-2-4** out-of-door; **3-2-5** out-of-doors.

opener 2 ax; **3** awl, bit, key, pin, saw; **4** pick; **5** auger, drill, knife, lance, miner, probe, punch; **6** bodkin, digger, lancet, needle, pickax, reamer, trepan, warder; **7** bayonet, doorman, Pandora, passkey, plumber, surgeon; **8** password, picklock, trephine, tunneler; **9** carpenter, corkscrew, excavator, locksmith; PHRASES: **3, 4** key card; **3-6** tin-opener *UK*; **4, 6** open sesame; **4, 7** wine steward; **5, 3, 3** brace and bit; **5, 4** smart card; **6, 3** master key; **6-6** bottle-opener; **7, 5** leather punch; **8, 3** skeleton key.

opening 3 cut, gap; **4** adit, bore, door, duct, flaw, flue, gate, hole, pass, port, rent, slit, slot, tear, vent; **5** break, chasm, chink, cleft, crack, entry, fault, mouth, onset, space, split, start; **6** breach, cavity, hollow, outlet, portal, window; **7** crevice, fissure, manhole, orifice, passage, rupture; **8** aperture, crevasse, fracture, interval, loophole, overture, peephole, piercing, pricking, puncture; **9** beginning; **10** passageway; **11** perforation; **12** intermission; PHRASES: **4, 5** open space; **8, 5** hairline crack.

openly 8 outright; PHRASES: **2, 3, 4** in the open; **2, 5, 5** in plain words. *See also* **open**

openness 5 truth; **6** candor; **7** honesty, naiveté, naivety *UK*; **8** glasnost, lucidity; **9** sincerity; **11** obviousness; **12** apparentness, indiscretion; **13** guilelessness; PHRASES: **2, 5, 6** no holds barred; **4-3-4, 4** open-and-shut case; **4, 5** home truth; **4, 7** full details; **5, 5** plain words; **5, 8** plain speech; **5, 8** plain speaking; **6, 5** simple truth. *See also* **open**

open space 4 yard; **5** beach, court, glade, stage; **6** desert, meadow; **8** clearing; PHRASES: **4, 3** open sea; **4, 7** open country.

opera 3 ENO *UK*, hat, Met, ROH *UK*; **4** Aida, aria, Lulu; **5** Faust, Norma, Orfeo, Tosca; **6** Figaro, Oberon, Onegin, Otello; **7** Fidelio, musical, Nabucco, prelude, Tristan; **8** Idomineo, libretto, operetta, overture, Parsifal, sinfonia, surtitle, Turandot; **9** leitmotiv, Lohengrin, pasticcio, Singspiel; **10** intermezzo, recitative; **12** Sprechgesang; PHRASES: **3, 4** The Ring; **3, 5** bel canto; **3, 6** Don Carlos; **3, 8** Don Giovanni; **4, 5** soap ~; **5, 5** comic ~, grand ~, horse ~, light ~, Magic Flute, music drama, ~ buf-

fa, ~ cloak, ~ house, ~ seria; **5, 6** opéra bouffe; **5, 7** opéra comique, ~ glasses; **5, 9** Madam Butterfly, ~ semiseria.

opera hat 5 gibus.

operate 2 go; **3** act, run, use; **4** work; **6** employ, handle, manage; **7** actuate, conduct, perform; **8** activate, function; PHRASES: **4, 4** tick over *UK*; **4, 6** take effect.

operation 2 op; **3** job, use; **4** play, task, work; **5** doing, force, power; **6** action, agency, course, motion, result; **7** formula, measure, process, running, surgery, working; **8** business, campaign, exercise, function, movement; **9** execution, procedure, treatment; **11** performance, undertaking; **14** implementation; PHRASES: **6, 2, 6** course of action.

operational 5 going; **6** active, usable; **7** running, working; **9** operating; **10** functional; **11** functioning; PHRASES: **2, 3** in use; **2, 3, 5** up and doing, up and going; **2, 3, 6, 4** on the active list; **2, 4** in play; **2, 7, 5** in running order, in working order; **2, 9** in operation.

operative 3 key; **4** hand; **5** agent, armed, valid; **6** worker; **7** crucial, laborer, working; **8** critical, relevant, workable; **9** effective, effectual, efficient, important, machinist; **11** efficacious, established, influential, significant; PHRASES: **2, 5** in force; **6, 5** having teeth; **8, 2** switched on *UK*; **9, 6** unskilled worker.

operator 5 actor, agent; **6** dealer, driver, trader, worker; **7** handler, manager; **8** director, employee, liveware, mechanic; **9** conductor, executive, performer; **10** controller, programmer, speculator, technician; **11** telephonist *UK*; **13** administrator.

opinion 4 idea, mind, view; **5** angle, guess, sense; **6** belief, notion, stance, thesis; **7** feeling, outlook; **8** attitude, position; **9** judgement, viewpoint; **10** contention, conviction, estimation, persuasion, standpoint; **11** perspective; PHRASES: **3, 2, 8** way of thinking; **5, 2, 4** point of view.

opinion (be of the opinion) 4 deem; **5** fancy, guess, opine, think; **6** assume, esteem, regard; **7** imagine, presume, suppose, surmise, suspect; **8** consider; **10** understand; PHRASES: **4, 2, 4** have in mind.

opinionated 6 biased, closed; **7** bigoted; **8** cocksure, dogmatic; **9** assertive, fanatical; **10** inflexible, intolerant; PHRASES: **6-6** narrow-minded.

opinionatedness 4 bias; 7 bigotry; 8 rigorism, zealotry; 9 blindness, dogmatism, ignorance, obsession, prejudice; 10 fanaticism; 11 intolerance; 12 illiberality, obscurantism; 14 opiniativeness; PHRASES: 4, 4 idée fixe *Fr*; 5, 4 blind side; 6, 4 closed mind; 6, 7 ruling passion.

opinionated person 5 bigot; 6 zealot; 7 fanatic; 8 believer, partisan; 9 dogmatist; 10 positivist; 11 doctrinaire; 13 exhibitionist; PHRASES: 3, 4 old fogy; 4-3 show-off; 5-2-3-3 stick-in-the-mud.

opium 5, 3 ~ den; 5, 4 ~ wars; 5, 5 ~ poppy.

opponent 3 foe; 4 anti; 5 enemy, rival; 9 adversary, combatant; 10 antagonist, challenger.

opponents 2 EN *UK*, ES, NE, NW, SE, SW, WN, WS.

opportune 3 apt, fit; 5 happy, lucky; 7 apropos, fitting; 8 suitable; 9 befitting, favorable, fortunate; 10 auspicious, convenient, propitious, seasonable; 11 appropriate; 12 providential.

opportunity 3 job; 4 luck, room; 5 break, scope; 6 chance; 7 opening, toehold, vacancy; 8 foothold, occasion, position; 9 certainty, elbowroom; 10 likelihood; 11 possibility, probability; PHRASES: 3, 2, 3, 4 toe in the door; 4, 2 odds on; 4-2 look-in; 4, 3 safe bet; 4, 4 good luck, good odds, open door; 4, 5 sure thing; 4, 6 good chance, only chance; 5, 2, 4 piece of luck; 5, 3 clear run; 5, 4 brass ring; 5, 5 lucky break; 5, 6 happy chance; 6, 2, 4 stroke of luck; 8, 5 stepping stone.

oppose 4 buck, face, feud; 5 clash, fight, rebut; 6 differ, object, resist; 7 collide, dissent, protest, quarrel; 8 conflict, traverse; 9 challenge; PHRASES: 3, 7 act against; 4, 3, 4 fall out with; 5, 7 fight against, stand against; 6, 7 strive against; 7, 7 protest against.

opposed to 1 v; 4 agin, anti; 6 versus; 7 against, despite; PHRASES: 2, 3, 4, 2 in the face of; 2, 5, 2 in spite of; 2, 8, 2 in contrast to; 2, 8, 4 at variance with, in conflict with; 2, 10, 2 in opposition to; 7, 2 counter to; 8, 2 contrary to.

opposer 4 anti; 5 rebel; 7 heckler, radical; 8 agitator, litigant, naysayer, objector, resister; 9 defendant, disputant, dissenter, dissident, gainsayer, plaintiff, protester; 10 negativist; 11 dissentient, obstructive, reac-

tionary; 12 conservative, filibusterer, intransigent; 13 oppositionist, revolutionary; 14 obstructionist; 20 counterrevolutionary; PHRASES: 3-4 die-hard; 4-7 last-ditcher; 6-5 bitter-ender.

opposing 3 con; 4 anti; 5 rival; 6 facing; 7 adverse, defiant, hostile; 8 fighting, inimical, opposite; 9 competing, different, objecting, resistant; 11 challenging, contentious; 12 antagonistic, antipathetic, disapproving; 15 confrontational; PHRASES: 4, 1, 4 mano a mano.

opposite 5 other; 6 facing; 7 inverse, obverse, opposed, reverse; 8 contrary, contrast, converse, inverted, oncoming, opposing, reversed; 9 antipodal, diametric, polarized; 10 antithesis, antithetic; 11 confronting, contrasting, diametrical; 12 antithetical, contrariwise, oppositional; 14 contrapositive; PHRASES: 2, 5, 2 in front of; 4-2-4 face-to-face; 5, 4 other side; 5, 5 poles apart; 5, 10 polar opposition; 8, 4 opposing side, ~ pole, ~ side; 8, 6 ~ number.

opposition 4 hate; 6 enmity, hatred; 7 balking, dislike, faction, refusal, rivalry; 8 argument, aversion, conflict, defiance, minority, turndown; 9 animosity, antipathy, hindrance, hostility, rejection, renitency; 10 antagonism, contention, filibuster, repugnance, repugnancy, resistance; 11 competitors, disapproval, inimicality, obstruction; 12 disagreement; 13 confrontation, counteraction, recalcitrance, unhelpfulness; 14 disapprobation, noncooperation, unfriendliness; PHRASES: 3, 5 the enemy; 3-6 all-comers; 5, 4 other side, other team; 5-7 cross-benches; 8, 4 opposite camp; 8, 5 opposing force, opposing party.

oppress 5 bully, crush, hound; 6 hector; 8 browbeat, suppress; 9 persecute, victimize; PHRASES: 4, 4 hold down; 5, 4 grind down; 7, 2 trample on.

oppressive 5 close, cruel, harsh, heavy, humid, muggy; 6 brutal, sultry; 7 airless, binding, violent; 8 despotic, forceful, stifling; 9 enforcing, hubristic, tyrannous; 10 autocratic, bulldozing, tyrannical; 11 bludgeoning, dictatorial, domineering, overbearing, overweening, restraining, steamroller, suffocating; 12 constraining; PHRASES: 4-6 iron-fisted; 6-3 strong-arm.

opprobrium 5 scorn, shame; 8 contempt, disgrace, ignominy; 9 criticism; 11 humiliation; 12 condemnation; 13 embarrassment.

opt *See* **choose**

optical 5 optic; 6 visual.

optical device 4 lens; 5 prism; 6 mirror; 7 glasses, grating; 8 bifocals; 10 reflection, refraction, spectacles, sunglasses; 11 diffraction; 12 refractivity; PHRASES: 4-4, 6 rear-view mirror; 4, 6 hand mirror, wing mirror *UK*; 4, 7 dark glasses; 5, 4 light pipe; 5, 5 light guide; 5, 6 plane mirror; 6, 6 convex mirror; 6, 7 silver coating; 7, 5 optical fiber; 7, 6 concave mirror, shaving mirror; 8, 7 aluminum coating; 10, 4 achromatic lens; 10, 5 refractive index. *See also* **lens**

optical instrument 6 camera; 7 sextant; 9 periscope, telescope; 10 binoculars, microscope, photometer, resolution, theodolite; 12 spectrometer; 13 magnification; 14 interferometer; PHRASES: 5, 2, 4 field of view; 5, 2, 5 depth of field, depth of focus; 5, 4 field stop; 5, 7 field glasses, opera glasses; 8, 4 aperture stop; 10, 5 magnifying power.

optimism 8 buoyancy; 9 assurance, sunniness; 10 brightness, confidence, enthusiasm, positivity, sanguinity; 11 hopefulness; 12 cheerfulness, positiveness.

optimist 8 idealist, promoter; 10 panjandrum; 11 exaggerator; 12 megalomaniac; PHRASES: 5, 7 young hopeful.

optimistic 4 rosy; 6 bubbly, upbeat; 7 buoyant, hopeful; 8 cheerful, positive, sanguine.

option *See* **choice**

opulence 4 ease; 6 bounty, luxury, plenty; 7 comfort; 9 abundance, fleshpots, profusion; 10 cornucopia; 11 superfluity; PHRASES: 3, 2, 3, 4 fat of the land; 3, 4, 4 the good life; 4, 2, 5 life of Riley; 4, 5 good times; 4, 6 easy street. *See also* **opulent**

opulent 4 lush, posh, rich; 5 plush, ritzy; 6 costly, gilded, glitzy, lavish, plushy, swanky; 7 moneyed, wealthy; 8 abundant, palatial, splendid; 9 expensive, luxurious, sumptuous; 10 glittering; PHRASES: 2, 4 de luxe; 4-2 slap-up *UK*; 5-5 first-class.

opus *See* **composition**

or 2 au; 4 gold; 6 yellow; 13 alternatively.

oracle 4 sage, seer; 5 sibyl, witch; 6 medium, Pythia, warner; 7 prophet, warlock; 8 doomster *UK*, sorcerer; 9 Cassandra, occultist, pythoness, visionary; 10 prediction, prophetess, revelation, soothsayer; 11 clair-

voyant, doomwatcher, Nostradamus, telepathist, vaticinator; PHRASES: 4, 8 doom merchant; 5, 2, 5 Witch of Endor; 7, 2, 4 prophet of doom; 7, 6 Delphic ~, Pythian ~; 9, 5 Sibylline books.

oral 4 said; 5 parol; 6 spoken, verbal; 9 unwritten; 11 nuncupative; PHRASES: 4, 4 viva voce.

orange 2 or; 3 tan; 4 sand; 5 agent, amber, flame, henna, navel, ocher *UK*, ochre *UK*, osage, peach; 6 bitter, brassy, bronze, ginger, golden, Titian; 7 apricot, blossom, carroty, coppery, pumpkin, saffron, satsuma, seville; 8 carotene, goldfish, mandarin, marigold, ochreous; 9 marmalade, nectarine, sunflower, tangerine; 10 clementine; PHRASES: 3-4 old-gold; 3, 6 raw sienna; 5, 5 terra cotta; 5, 6 blood ~; 5-7 flame-colored; 6, 4 ~ peel; 6, 5 ~ juice, ~ pekoe; 6, 6 ~ squash *UK*; 6, 8 ~ hawkweed; 7, 7 tequila sunrise.

orate 5 speak; 6 preach; 7 declaim, lecture; PHRASES: 4, 1, 6 make a speech; 4, 3, 5 take the floor; 4, 5 hold forth.

oration *See* **speech**

orator *See* **speaker**

oratory 7 ranting; 8 rhetoric; 9 eloquence; 11 declamation; 12 speechifying; 13 magniloquence; 14 grandiloquence; PHRASES: 3-8 tub-thumping; 4, 2, 3, 3 gift of the gab; 4, 3 soap box; 6, 8 public speaking.

orb 3 eye; 4 ball; 5 globe, round; 6 circle, sphere; 7 eyeball.

orbit 3 lap; 4 beat, gyre, loop, spin, tour, turn, walk; 5 ambit, cycle, nadir, wheel; 6 circle, rotate, rounds, spiral, zenith; 7 circuit, eclipse, revolve, transit; 8 aphelion, redshift, rotation; 9 blueshift, circulate, reddening, twinkling; 10 perihelion, precession, revolution, trajectory; 11 inclination, occultation; 12 eccentricity; 13 scintillation; PHRASES: 1-4 U-turn; 2, 5 go about; 2, 6 go around; 3, 6 eye socket; 4, 4, 6 come full circle; 4, 6 full circle; 5, 4 round trip; 5, 4, 4 chase one's tail; 7, 6 orbital period.

orbital 6 bypass, rotary; 7 beltway, oblique, turning; 8 indirect, rotatory; 9 ambagious, deviating; 10 circuitous, meandering, roundabout; 11 circulatory; 13 circumambient, revolutionary; 14 circumlocutory; 15 circumnavigable; PHRASES: 4, 4 ring road *UK*; 7, 6 traffic circle.

orbital motion 4 coil, gyre; 5 helix, orbit; **6** gyring, spiral; **7** ellipse, turning; **8** circling, orbiting, rotation, rounding, wheeling; **9** spiraling; **10** revolution; **11** circularity, circulation; **13** circumflexion; **14** circumambiance; **15** circummigration.

orbiting body 3 sun; **4** moon, star; **6** planet; **7** Sputnik; **8** asteroid; **9** planetoid, satellite, spaceship; **12** planetesimal.

orchestra 3 duo; **4** band, trio; **5** group, nonet, octet; **6** septet, sextet; **7** quartet, quintet; **8** ensemble; PHRASES: **7, 5** chamber group.

orchestrate 5 score; **7** arrange; **8** melodize, organize; **9** accompany, harmonize, syncopate; **10** symphonize.

orchestration 7 scoring; **8** planning; **10** adaptation; **11** arrangement, composition, preplanning; **12** choreography, organization; **13** improvisation, transposition; **15** instrumentation.

ordain 4 call, rule; **5** elect, enact, frock, order, state; **6** anoint, decree, enjoin, invest, select; **7** appoint, command; **8** nominate; **9** authorize, legislate, pronounce; **10** consecrate, predestine; **12** predetermine; PHRASES: **3, 4** lay down, set down; **4, 2** read in; **4, 3, 4** take the veil; **4, 3, 5** wear the cloth.

ordeal *See* **trial**

order 2 OM, PO; **3** DSO; **4** fiat, form, hest, list, rank, rule, sort, tell, vary; **5** align, array, Attic, class, edict, grade, index, Ionic, money, setup, ukase; **6** adjust, degree, demand, diktat, direct, enjoin, firman, layout, manage, ordain, scheme, system, Tuscan; **7** arrange, catalog *UK*, command, compose, dictate, dispose, marshal, pattern, program, request; **8** approach, classify, instruct, organize, schedule, tidiness; **9** catalogue *UK*, composite, directive, Dominican, formalism, formation, normalize, prescribe, structure; **10** Corinthian, Franciscan, fraternity, injunction, lawfulness, possession, uniformity; **11** affiliation, alphabetize, arrangement, Benedictine, composition, disposition, standardize, supervision; **12** denomination, distribution, organization; **13** formalization; **14** prioritization; PHRASES: **3, 2** set up; **3, 3** lay out; **3, 2** line up; **4, 5** mail ~, word ~; **5, 2, 3, 4** O~ of the Bath *UK*; **5, 2, 5** O~ of Merit *UK*; **5-3, 5** apple-pie ~; **5, 5** loose ~, money ~, short ~; **6, 5** Orange O~, postal ~ *UK*; **7, 5** banker's ~, pecking ~; **8, 5** enclosed ~, standing ~; **9, 5** numerical ~.

ordered 4 bade, neat, told; **6** formal,

ranked, sorted *UK*; **7** arrayed, indexed, regular, uniform; **8** accurate, arranged, balanced, composed, disposed, ordained, straight; **9** commanded, organized, schematic; **10** classified, formalized, methodical, meticulous, scientific, structured, systematic; **11** formalistic, punctilious, symmetrical; **12** alphabetized, businesslike, hierarchical; PHRASES: **4-9** well-organized.

orderliness 3 law; **4** rule; **5** order; **6** custom; **7** balance, routine; **9** constance, constancy, normality, tradition; **10** continuity, regularity, regulation, uniformity; **11** consistency; **14** continuousness; PHRASES: **4, 4** good nick, good trim; **4, 6** fine fettle; **4, 9** good condition; **5, 2, 5** state of order; **5-3, 5** apple-pie order; **7, 7** Bristol fashion. *See also* **orderly**

orderly 4 even, flat, neat, tidy, trim; **5** clean, dinky, kempt, legal, level, sleek, slick, smart; **6** batman, dapper, normal, smooth, spruce, steady; **7** cleaner, correct, groomed, regular, routine, typical, uniform; **8** balanced, constant, metrical, ordinary, straight; **9** attendant, continual, customary, shipshape; **10** consistent, methodical, systematic; PHRASES: **4, 2** just so; **4, 2, 1, 6** neat as a button; **4, 3, 4** neat and tidy; **4-4** well-kept; **4-5, 3** well-cared for; **4-7** well-groomed; **5-3-4** spick-and-span; **8, 6** hospital porter; **9, 2, 3** according to law; **9, 2, 4** according to rule.

orders 4, 6 holy ~; **5, 6** major ~, minor ~; **6, 6** sealed ~; **8, 6** marching ~.

ordinary 4 base, dull; **5** plain, usual; **6** common, homely, median, modest, normal, simple, vulgar, wonted; **7** average, humdrum, mundane, prosaic, routine, typical; **8** bearable, everyday, habitual, homespun, mediocre, middling, moderate, passable, plebeian, standard, unheroic; **9** customary, primitive, quotidian, tolerable; **10** accustomed, mainstream, pedestrian, prevailing, uncultured; **11** commonplace; **12** conventional, unremarkable; **13** unexceptional, unpretentious; **15** undistinguished, unsophisticated; PHRASES: **2-2** so-so; **3-1** non-U *UK*; **3-2-3-4** run-of-the-mill; **4, 2, 1, 8** much of a muchness; **5, 7** plain vanilla; **6-2-3-4** middle-of-the-road; **8, 6** ~ rating, ~ seaman, ~ shares.

ordnance 4 arms, guns; **7** weapons; **8** weaponry; **9** artillery.

ordure *See* **excrement**

ore 4 lode, vein; 6 gangue, placer; 7 deposit; 9 lodestuff.

Oregon 2 OR; 5 Salem (capital); PHRASES: 3, 5, 4, 3, 3, 5 She flies with her own wings (motto); 6, 5 Beaver State (nickname), oregon grape (flower); 7, 3 douglas fir (tree); 7, 10 western meadowlark (bird).

organ 3 ear, eye; 4 lung, nose, skin, womb; 5 gland, heart, liver, paper, penis, regal; 6 spleen, tongue, uterus; 7 gazette, journal; 8 calliope, magazine, pancreas; 9 harmonium, newspaper; 10 periodical; PHRASES: 4, 5 pipe ~, reed ~; 5, 5 house ~, mouth ~, sense ~, vocal ~; 6, 5 barrel ~; 7, 5 Hammond ~; 8, 5 electric ~; 9, 5 portative ~.

organic 5 vital; 6 formal; 7 natural; 8 coherent, inherent; 9 organized; 10 anatomical, biological, organismal, systematic; 11 fundamental; 13 morphological, organological; 14 constitutional.

organism 4 body, germ; 5 being, monad, phage, plant, virus; 6 aerobe, animal, coccus, entity, fossil, virion, viroid; 7 microbe, plasmid, protist; 8 anaerobe, bacillus, creature, provirus; 9 bacterium, eukaryote, spirillum; 10 animalcule, individual, microphyte, mycoplasma, prokaryote, retrovirus, rickettsia; 13 bacteriophage, microorganism; PHRASES: 6, 5 living being, living thing.

organization 2 UN; 3 CIA, UNO; 4 body, club, firm; 5 group, setup, union; 6 agency, method, system; 7 combine, company, running, society; 8 alliance, business, charting, planning; 10 consortium, federation, management; 11 arrangement, association, corporation, structuring; 12 coordination; 13 confederation, methodization, routinization; 15 rationalization, standardization, systematization.

organize 3 run; 4 plan, tidy; 5 order, shape; 6 codify, direct, manage; 7 arrange, control, dispose, marshal; 8 assemble, classify, engineer, regulate; 9 methodize, normalize; 10 categorize, centralize, coordinate, schematize; 11 choreograph, orchestrate, rationalize, standardize, systematize; PHRASES: 3, 2 see to, set up; 3, 2, 5 put in order; 3, 8 put together; 5, 5 bring about.

organized 4 neat, tidy; 7 planned; 8 together; 9 concerted; 10 methodical, structured, systematic; 11 prearranged.

orient 1 E; 4 east; 5 adapt, align, steer; 6 adjust, direct; 11 accommodate; PHRASES: 4, 3, 3 take the sun; 5, 4, 6 check one's course.

orientation 3 map; 5 gauge; 7 azimuth, compass, degrees; 8 bearings, signpost; 9 alignment; 10 adaptation, adjustment; 11 collimation, rangefinder; 13 accommodation; PHRASES: 5, 4 rhumb line; 6, 4 lubber line; 7, 4 compass card, compass rose; 8, 6 tracking device; 9, 6 direction finder (D/F).

orifice *See* **opening**

origan 8 marjoram.

origin *See* **source**

original 2 it; 3 new; 4 mold; 5 first, fresh, model, novel, pilot, risky; 6 chancy, daring, master, modern, source, unique; 7 pattern, seminal, strange; 8 creative, paradigm, reckless; 9 archetype, autograph, blueprint, firsthand, holograph, invention, inventive, modernist, precedent, prototype, signature; 10 archetypal, innovative, manuscript, pioneering, prototypal, unfamiliar, unimitated; 11 imaginative, venturesome; 12 enterprising, experimental; PHRASES: 3, 3, 3, 4 the one and only; 3, 4, 5 the real McCoy, the real thing; 3, 4, 7 the real article; 4, 4 test case; 5-5 avant-garde; 5, 7 first edition.

originality 4 risk; 6 daring; 7 novelty; 8 creation; 9 beginning, modernism; 10 creativity, initiation, innovation, precedence; 11 genuineness, imagination; 12 authenticity, creativeness, eccentricity, idiosyncrasy, independence, nonimitation; 13 dissimilarity, individuality, unfamiliarity; 15 experimentation. *See also* **original**

originate 5 begin, start; 6 create, design, devise, invent, patent; 7 imagine, pioneer; 8 conceive, generate, initiate, innovate; 9 auspicate, blueprint, copyright, trademark; PHRASES: 5, 2 dream up.

originator 3 God; 5 maker; 6 source; 7 creator, deviser; 8 composer, designer, inventor; 9 architect, initiator, innovator; PHRASES: 3, 7 the Creator; 5, 5 prime mover; 8, 6 creative writer.

orison 6 prayer.

ornament 4 deck, gild, rant, rave, ring, sing, trim; 5 adorn, boast, color, grace, grace (note), trill, trope; 6 enrich, frills, simile; 7 carving, enhance, épergne, festoon, garnish, overlay; 8 beautify, cynosure, decorate, euphuism, euphuize, flourish, gargoyle, metaphor, overload, rhetoric, trimming; **9** adornment, arabesque, assonance, elaborate, embellish, embroider, euphemism, euphemize, overstate; **10** decoration, embroidery, figurehead, floridness, hyperbaton, preciosity; **11** arrangement, floweriness, masterpiece; **12** alliteration, preciousness; **13** embellishment, ornamentation, overelaborate; **14** figurativeness; PHRASES: **3, 4, 5** use long words; **4, 3, 4** gild the lily; **5, 8** house fluffing; **6, 2, 6** figure of speech; **6, 8** purple passages; **7, 2, 6** flowers of speech; **7, 7** picture molding.

ornamental **4** gilt; **5** fancy, showy; **6** gilded, ornate, pretty, rococo; **7** baroque; **9** garnished, patterned; **10** decorative; **11** picturesque; PHRASES: **3-10** non-functional; **6-6** pretty-pretty *UK*.

ornamentation **8** trimming; **9** adornment; **10** decoration, garnishing; **11** enhancement; **13** embellishment; **14** beautification.

ornate **4** loud, rich; **5** fancy, fussy, lofty, showy, stiff, tumid; **6** brassy, flashy, florid, frothy, gilded, turgid; **7** adorned, colored, diffuse, flowery, fustian, orotund, pompous, ranting, ringing, singing, stately, stilted, swelled, swollen, trimmed; **8** affected, eloquent, inflated, Latinate, pedantic, precious, resonant, sonorous, tortuous; **9** bombastic, decorated, elaborate, garnished, grandiose, luxuriant, ponderous; **10** beautified, convoluted, decorative, euphuistic, figurative, flamboyant, hyperbolic, Johnsonian, oratorical, ornamental, ornamented, overloaded, overstated, rhetorical; **11** declamatory, embellished, euphemistic, exaggerated, extravagant, highfalutin, pretentious; **12** alliterative, antithetical, magniloquent, meretricious, metaphorical, ostentatious; **13** grandiloquent; **14** circumlocutory, sesquipedalian; PHRASES: **4-5** high-flown; **4-6** high-flying, long-worded; **4-7** high-pitched; **4-8** high-sounding; **6, 9** richly decorated.

ornithological **5** avian; **11** avicultural; PHRASES: **4-8** bird-watching.

ornithologist **6** birder, ringer; **7** fancier; **8** twitcher *UK*; **11** birdwatcher; **12** aviculturist; PHRASES: **6, 7** pigeon fancier.

ornithology **4** hide; **6** aviary; **7** nestbox, ringing; **8** birdcage, dovecote, hatchery, swannery; **9** birdhouse; **10** aviculture; **11** birdbanding, columbarium, reservation; **12** birdwatching; PHRASES: **4, 7** bird reserve; **4, 9** bird sanctuary; **6, 4** pigeon loft.

orotund **4** loud; **5** clear, wordy; **6** strong; **7** pompous, ringing, verbose; **9** bombastic; **10** stentorian; **13** grandiloquent.

orphan **4** ward; **5** Annie, dogie; **9** foundling; PHRASES: **6, 5** Oliver Twist.

orthodox *See* **conventional**

OS **6** osmium; **7** outside, outsize; **11** outstanding.

Oscar **1** O; **5** Wilde; PHRASES: **7, 5** Academy Award.

oscillate **4** spin, sway, vary; **5** swing, whirl; **6** gyrate, nutate, rotate, seesaw, teeter, wigwag, zigzag; **7** shuttle; **8** leapfrog; **9** alternate, fluctuate, pendulate; **11** reciprocate; PHRASES: **2-2-4** va-et-vien *Fr*; **3, 3, 4** ebb and flow, wax and wane; **4, 2, 3, 3** move to and fro; **4, 3, 2** come and go; **4, 3, 4** back and fill; **4, 3, 6** pass and repass; **5, 3, 4** hitch and hike; **6-6** teeter-totter.

oscillation **4** spin; **5** swing, whirl; **6** seesaw, wigwag, zigzag; **8** gyration, leapfrog, nutation; **9** agitation, frequency, libration, vibration; **11** alternation, fluctuation, pendulation, periodicity, shuttlecock; **13** reciprocation; PHRASES: **3, 3, 4** ebb and flow; **3, 3, 5** ups and downs; **4, 3, 4** boom and bust; **4, 3, 6** flux and reflux; **5, 3, 3** night and day; **5, 3, 6** toing and froing; **5, 6** lunar motion; **6, 3, 5** coming and going; **6-6** teeter-totter, wibble-wobble; **7, 7** shuttle service; **8, 6** harmonic motion, pendular motion.

osier **4** redd; **5** withy; **6** sallow, willow.

osprey **4, 4** fish hawk; **4, 5** fish eagle.

ostensible **7** seeming; **8** apparent, illusory, specious; **9** deceptive, dreamlike, imaginary, professed, visionary; **10** chimerical; **11** superficial; **13** hallucinatory.

ostentation **4** pomp, show; **5** éclat, swank; **6** parade, splash; **7** display; **11** flamboyance. *See also* **ostentatious**

ostentatious **4** fine, loud; **5** flash *UK*, gaudy, grand, showy; **6** flashy, florid, plumed, swanky; **7** crested; **9** flaunting; **10** flamboyant; **11** extravagant, fashionable.

ostentatious (be ostentatious) **5** strut, swank; **7** swagger; PHRASES: **4, 3** show off.

ostler **5** groom; **7** hostler, marshal.

ostracism **5** exile; **7** banning; **8** outlawry; **9** exclusion, exilement, outlawing, seclusion; **10** banishment, fugitation; **11** deportation, extradition, rustication; **12** blackballing, expatriation, proscription, repatriation; **14** transportation; PHRASES: **3, 4, 8** the cold shoulder; **3, 8** the brushoff.

ostracize 3 ban, cut; **4** snub; **5** exile, spurn; **6** banish, deport, outlaw; **7** exclude, seclude; **8** fugitate, prohibit; **9** blackball, extradite, proscribe, rusticate, transport; **10** expatriate, repatriate; PHRASES: **4, 2, 8** send to Coventry; **4, 4** send away; **5, 3** brush off.

ostracize 4 Eden; **5** bliss; **6** utopia; **7** Arcadia, Elysium, nirvana; PHRASES: **5, 4** cloud nine; **7-2** Shangri-la; **7, 6** seventh heaven.

ostrich 4 rhea.

OT 8 overtime; PHRASES: **3, 9** Old Testament.

otalgia 7 earache.

other 3 new; **4** more; **5** extra, fresh; **10** additional.

otiose 6 futile.

otology 3 ENT; **6** aurist, otitis; **7** earache, otalgia; **9** audiology, auriscope, otologist; **10** audiometer; **11** audiologist; **13** labyrinthitis; **14** otolaryngology; PHRASES: **3, 3** ear wax; **3, 5** ear drops.

oubliette *See* **prison**

ounce 2 oz; PHRASES: **4, 7** snow leopard.

oust 5 exile, expel; PHRASES: **3, 3, 2** get rid of; **5, 3** drive out *UK*, throw out.

out 3 aus, bad, uit; **4** away, gone, hors, york *UK*; **5** wrong; **6** absent, bowled, caught, yorked; **7** inexact, skittle, stumped; **8** blooming, skittled; **9** flowering; **10** inaccurate.

out and out 5 sheer, total, utter; **6** arrant; **8** absolute, complete, outright, thorough.

outback *See* **wilderness**

outbreak 4 rash; **5** blaze, flood, onset, spate, start; **6** flurry, plague; **7** upsurge; **8** epidemic, eruption, outburst; **9** beginning, explosion.

outburst 3 fit; **4** gush, gust, rant; **5** blaze, flood, furor *UK*, spate, storm; **6** access, flurry, furore *UK*, tirade, volley; **7** boutade, passion, tantrum, torrent, upsurge; **8** diatribe, eruption, harangue, outbreak, paroxysm; **9** explosion, fusillade; PHRASES: **5, 3** hissy fit.

outcast 5 exile, leper; **6** pariah; **7** flotsam,

Ishmael; **8** expelled; **9** abandoned; **11** untouchable; PHRASES: **7, 3, 5** persona non grata.

outclassed 6 beaten, bested, ruined; **7** humbled, worsted; **8** defeated, outshone, trounced; **10** humiliated; PHRASES: **3, 1, 5, 2** not a patch on.

outcome 3 end, tie; **4** draw; **5** event; **6** defeat, effect, result, sequel, upshot; **7** victory; **11** consequence.

outcry 3 cry, din, row; **4** howl, roar; **5** alarm, clash, crash, shout, whoop; **6** bedlam, clamor, hubbub, racket, rumpus, scream, shriek, tumult, uproar; **7** banging, bawling, clatter, hooting, protest, roaring, turmoil, yelling; **8** ballyhoo, chanting, shouting, slamming, stamping, stramash *UK*; **9** noisiness, objection, screaming, shemozzle, ululation; **10** hullabaloo; **11** pandemonium; **12** vociferation; PHRASES: **3, 4, 3, 5** all hell let loose; **4, 3** song and dance; **9, 3** deafening row.

outdated *See* **antiquated**

outdo 3 cap, top; **4** beat, crow; **5** trump, worst; **6** outbid, outrun, outwit, picnic; **7** outjump, outleap, outpace, outplay, outrace, outrank, outride, outstep, surpass; **8** outmarch, outrange, outreach, outshine, outstare, outstrip; **10** outperform; **11** outdistance, outmaneuver; PHRASES: **3, 3, 6, 2** get the better of; **7, 4** triumph over.

outdoor 7 outside; **8** alfresco; PHRASES: **4-3** open-air; **5-3** fresh-air.

outer 3 top; **6** visual; **7** outward, surface, visible; **8** exterior, external, mirrored; **9** mirroring, reflected; **10** reflecting; **11** superficial.

outfit 3 kit, rig; **4** band, crew, firm, gang, garb, gear, suit, team, togs; **5** bunch, dress, equip, group; **6** attire, supply; **7** clothes, company, costume, furnish, provide; **8** ensemble; **12** organization.

outflow 3 jet; **4** gush, well; **5** flood, spill, sweat, waste; **6** efflux, gusher, spring, stream; **7** exhaust, gushing, outfall, outflux, outpour; **8** effusion, emission, fountain, sweating, voidance; **9** defluxion, discharge, effluence, effluxion, emanation, excretion, exudation, secretion, streaming, waterfall; **10** hemorrhage, inundation, outflowing, outpouring; **11** diaphoresis, evaporation; **12** perspiration, transudation; PHRASES: **5, 4** runny nose; **7, 4** running sore; **9, 4** streaming eyes.

outgoer 4 goer; 5 exile; 6 émigré, leaver; 7 migrant, settler; 8 colonist, departer, emigrant, expellee; 10 expatriate, outmigrant; PHRASES: 10, 3 remittance man *UK.*

outgoing 4 open; 5 going; 6 chatty, social; 7 arising, emanant, issuing, leaving; 8 emergent, emerging, erupting, eruptive, outbound, sociable, volcanic; 9 departing, egressive, emanating, emanative, explosive, expulsive, extrovert, surfacing, talkative, transient; 10 emigratory, gregarious; 11 forthcoming; PHRASES: 7-5 outward-bound.

out in Amsterdam, etc 3 uit.

outing 4 trip; 5 jaunt, visit; 9 excursion; PHRASES: 3, 4 day trip.

out in Germany 3 aus.

outlandish *See* **unusual**

outlaw 3 ban, bar; 4 hood, veto; 5 exile; 6 bandit, banish; 7 brigand, embargo; 8 criminal, fugitive, prohibit, vagabond; 9 proscribe; PHRASES: 3, 3 Rob Roy; 5, 4 Robin Hood *UK.*

outlay 3 sum; 4 cost; 5 spend; 6 expend; 7 expense; 8 disburse, spending; 11 expenditure; PHRASES: 3, 3 lay out, pay out.

outlet 3 tap; 4 anus, exit, hole, pore, shop, vent, weir; 5 chute, drain, flume, spout, store; 6 egress, faucet, gutter, market, sluice, socket; 7 conduit, estuary, opening, orifice, outfall, release, ventage; 8 blowhole, gargoyle, overflow, spiracle, venthole; 9 downspout, drainpipe, floodgate.

outline 4 edge, etch, limn, note, plan; 5 bones, chart, curve, draft, frame, graph, haiku, maxim, model, notes, proof, rough, shape, trace; 6 depict, digest, emblem, layout, précis, relief, résumé, revise, sample, sketch, survey; 7 abridge, cartoon, contour, diagram, elision, engrave, epigram, epitome, etching, limning, pattern, picture, portray, profile, project, pruning, summary, syncope, tracing; 8 abstract, aphorism, brochure, clerihew, condense, contract, revision, skeleton, syllabus, synopsis; 9 apheresis, blueprint, delineate, depiction, engraving, epitomize, monostich, portrayal, prototype, reduction, represent, roughcast, summarize, synopsize; 10 abbreviate, abridgment, compendium, diminution, essentials, illustrate, projection, prospectus, shortening, silhouette, truncation; 11

abridgement, compression, contraction, delineation; 12 abbreviation, condensation, illustration; 14 representation; PHRASES: 3, 3 lay out; 4, 4 boil down; 4, 5 bare bones; 4, 10 bare essentials; 5, 3 block out, rough out; 5, 5 first draft; 5, 6 stick figure; 5, 7 pilot program; 6, 3 sketch out; 6, 4 ground plan; 6, 6 random sample, single aspect; 6, 7 potted version, simple picture; 7, 4 contour line, revised copy; 9, 6 thumbnail sketch.

outlook 4 view; 5 vista; 6 future; 8 attitude, panorama, position, prospect; 9 viewpoint; PHRASES: 4, 2, 4 time to come; 4, 5 time ahead; 5, 2, 4 point of view.

outmoded *See* **old-fashioned**

out-of-doors 6 abroad; 7 outside; 8 alfresco; PHRASES: 2, 3, 3 in the sun; 2, 3, 4 in the open; 2, 3, 4, 3 in the open air; 2, 5, 3 en plein air; 5, 3, 4, 3 under the open sky.

out of order 2 US; 6 broken, faulty, unfair; 9 defective; 11 unwarranted; 12 unacceptable, unreasonable; 13 unserviceable, unwarrantable; 14 malfunctioning; PHRASES: 2, 3, 5 on the blink, on the fritz; 3, 2, 7 out of service; 6, 3 conked out; 6-4 broken-down; 8, 3 uncalled for.

out of sorts 3 ill; 4 sick; 6 poorly, unwell; PHRASES: 3, 5 off color; 5, 3, 7 under the weather.

output 5 yield; 6 return; 7 harvest, product.

outrage 4 fury, rage; 5 anger, shock, wrath; 6 enrage, offend; 7 affront, disgust, incense, violate; 8 atrocity, enormity; 9 desecrate, infuriate, violation; 10 scandalize; 11 abomination, indignation.

outrageous 3 OTT *UK*; 4 bold; 5 gross; 6 absurd; 8 dreadful, shocking; 9 appalling, atrocious, ludicrous, monstrous, offensive, shameless, startling; 10 flamboyant, ridiculous, scandalous; 11 disgraceful, distressing, extravagant; 12 preposterous; 13 reprehensible.

outright 5 clear, fully, total, utter; 6 direct, openly; 7 frankly, obvious, totally; 8 absolute, complete, entirely; 10 absolutely, completely; 11 immediately, transparent; 12 forthrightly, straightaway, unreservedly; 13 unequivocally; PHRASES: 2, 4 at once; 3-3-3 out-and-out; 5, 4 right away.

outset 4 dawn; 5 birth, debut, onset, start; 6 launch; 7 dawning, opening; 9 inception; 10 initiation; 12 commencement; PHRASES:

3, 3 day one; **6, 3** square one.

outside 4 open; **6** beyond; **7** outback, outdoor, outland, outward; **8** alfresco, external, outlying; **9** outermost; **10** extramural, hinterland; **11** outwardness; PHRASES: **3, 2, 5** out of doors; **3, 4** the open; **4, 3** open air; **4-3** open-air.

outside broadcast 2 OB.

outsider 2 ET; **4** waif; **5** alien, exile, expat, leper, stray, trash; **6** bandit, orphan, outlaw, pariah, reject; **7** evacuee, flotsam, Martian, outcast, refugee; **8** deportee, outcaste, prisoner, stranger, vagabond; **9** auslander, foreigner, foundling, outlander; **10** expatriate, tramontane; **11** untouchable; **12** ultramontane; PHRASES: **3, 4, 4** man from Mars; **4, 5, 5** poor white trash; **5, 7** space invader; **6, 5, 3** little green man; **9, 6** displaced person (DP), stateless person.

outsiders 6 aliens, others; **9** strangers; **10** foreigners; PHRASES: **3-7** non-members.

outsize 2 OS; **4** huge, vast; **5** giant; **8** gigantic; **9** capacious; **10** voluminous.

outskirts 4 edge; **6** fringe; **7** borders, suburbs; **9** periphery.

outspoken 4 curt; **5** bluff, frank; **6** abrupt, candid, direct; **15** straightforward; PHRASES: **5-6** plain-spoken.

outstanding 2 A1; **3** ace, due; **4** rare, star, tall; **5** adept, major, owing; **6** banner, choice, expert, superb, unpaid; **7** classic, eminent, jutting, supreme; **8** champion, finished, masterly, singular; **9** brilliant, excellent, prominent, topflight, unsettled; **10** consummate; **11** prestigious; **12** accomplished; **13** distinguished, extraordinary; PHRASES: **2, 6** in relief; **4-4** blue-chip; **5-4** first-rate; **5-5** first-class.

outstrip See **outdo**

outward 5 outer; **6** facial; **7** assumed, surface; **8** external; **9** displayed, projected; **11** superficial.

outweigh 10 outbalance UK; **11** overbalance.

outworn See **obsolete**

ouzel 9 blackbird.

oven 3 aga; **4** kiln, oast; **5** range, stove; **6** cooker UK; **7** furnace; **9** microwave.

over 2 on, re; **3** o'er; **4** atop, dead, done, gone, ower; **5** above, again, along, ended, extra; **6** across, bygone, maiden; **7** extinct; **8** covering, finished, superior; **9** completed,

exhausted; **13** irrecoverable; PHRASES: **3, 5** six balls; **4, 2, 1, 4** dead as a dodo; **4, 3, 4** dead and gone, gone for good; **4, 3, 4, 4** ~ and done with; **4, 3, 6** dead and buried; **6, 4** upside down.

overact 3 ham; **4** rant, roar; **7** upstage; **8** overplay; **9** barnstorm, improvise; **13** melodramatize; PHRASES: **2-3** ad-lib; **3, 2, 2** ham it up; **3-5, 5** out-Herod Herod; **4, 2** milk it; **4, 3, 4** play the fool; **5, 3, 4** steal the show.

overacting 7 hamming, puffery; **8** ballyhoo, travesty; **9** burlesque, melodrama; **10** caricature; **11** histrionics.

overall 4 main; **5** chief, total; **6** global, mainly, mostly, wholly; **7** general, largely; **8** complete; **9** generally, inclusive; PHRASES: **2, 1, 5** as a whole; **2, 3, 4** in the main; **2, 3, 4, 3** in the long run; **2, 3, 5** on the whole; **2, 7** in general, on average, on balance; **3, 2, 3** all in all; **3, 3, 4, 4** for the most part.

overalls 5 smock; **6** denims; **8** fatigues; **9** dungarees.

overambitious 4 rash; **8** arrogant; **9** excessive, hubristic; **10** overloaded; **12** overextended; **13** overconfident; **14** overoptimistic; PHRASES: **6, 5** snowed under.

overcast 4 dull; **6** cloudy, dismal; **7** louring; **9** glowering.

overcharge 2 do; **3** con; **4** burn, clip, skin, soak; **5** bleed, gouge, screw, sting; **6** extort, fleece; **7** inflate, swindle; **8** oversell; **9** overprice, profiteer, surcharge; PHRASES: **3, 3** rip off; **3, 3, 4** ask too much; **4, 2** hold up, mark up; **4, 4** sell dear; **4-4** rack-rent.

overcharger 5 shark; **6** usurer; **7** Shylock; **12** extortionist; PHRASES: **3, 3** con man; **3-3, 6** rip-off artist; **4, 5** loan shark; **4-6** rackrenter.

overcome 3 win; **4** beat, best, kill; **6** beaten, bested, defeat, master; **7** conquer, prevail; **8** convince, surmount, vanquish; **9** overwhelm, persevere, subjugate; **10** speechless; **11** overwhelmed; PHRASES: **4, 1, 3, 5** find a way round; **4, 2, 4, 4** land on one's feet; **4, 2, 6** turn up trumps; **4, 2, 7** come up smiling; **4, 3, 4** stem the tide, turn out well; **6, 7** muddle through; **7, 3, 5** weather the storm.

overconfident 4 smug, vain; **8** arrogant; **10** complacent; PHRASES: **4-9** self-satisfied.

overcrowd 3 jam; **4** pack; **5** swamp; **6** infest; **7** congest, overman, overrun; **9** outnumber, overstaff, overwhelm; **12** overpopulate; PHRASES: **4, 5** snow under.

overdo 4 burn, char, stew; **5** spoil; **8** overcook, overplay; **9** overstate; **10** exaggerate; **13** overemphasize.

overdoing it 2 OD, OJ; **3** fat, OTT *UK*; **6** burden, excess; **7** hamming, obesity, satiety; **8** bellyful, gluttony, overdose, overjolt, overload; **9** fattiness; **10** overacting, overeating, overpraise, overweight; **11** drunkenness, engorgement, overfeeding, overmeasure, overpayment, overworking, sufficiency; **12** effusiveness, immoderation, intemperance, overactivity, overdrinking, overoptimism; **13** officiousness, overextension; **14** overestimation, overindulgence, overpoliteness; PHRASES: **3, 3, 4** one too many; **3, 4** red tape; **4, 4, 6** more than enough; **4, 5** last straw.

overdose 2 OD.

overdraft 3 red; **4** bill, debt, loan, tick; **5** tally; **8** mortgage; PHRASES: **7, 5** account score.

overdrawn 2 OD; PHRASES: **2, 3, 3** in the red.

overdue *See* **late**

overeat *See* **overindulge**

overemphasise *See* **exaggerate**

overflow 5 extra, flood; **6** excess, runoff; **7** surfeit, surplus; PHRASES: **3, 4** run over; **4, 3** pour out; **4, 4** brim over; **5, 4** spill over.

overhang 5 ledge; **6** extend; **7** outcrop, project; **9** extension; **10** projection; **11** outcropping; PHRASES: **3, 3** jut out; **4, 4** hang over.

overhaul 5 outdo, refit; **6** repair; **7** service, surpass; **8** overtake, renovate; **9** refurbish; **13** refurbishment.

overhead 5 above; **8** upstairs; PHRASES: **2, 3, 3** in the air; **5, 4, 4** above your head; **8, 5** directly above.

overhead 6 oncost *UK*; PHRASES: **5, 5** fixed costs; **8, 5** indirect costs.

overhead covering 4 dome, roof, tarp, tent; **5** tepee, tiles; **6** awning, canopy, canvas, cupola, slates, thatch, wigwam; **7** ceiling, marquee, rafters, roofing, rooftop; **8** ciborium, housetop, overhead, shingles; **9** tarpaulin; PHRASES: **3, 3** big top; **7, 7** ceiling plaster; **8, 4** overhead beam; **8, 7** mosquito netting.

overindulge 3 hog, pig; **5** binge, feast,

gorge, waste; **6** guzzle, overdo; **7** carouse, debauch, surfeit; **8** squander; **9** dissipate; **11** gourmandize; PHRASES: **2, 2, 1, 6** go on a bender; **3, 3** pig out; **3, 4, 4** sow one's wild oats; **5, 4** stuff one's face.

overindulgence 5 greed; **6** excess; **7** abandon; **8** gluttony; **9** addiction, overdoing, uncontrol; **10** crapulence, inordinacy, overeating; **11** drunkenness, prodigality, unrestraint; **12** extravagance, immoderation, incontinence, indiscipline, intemperance; **13** concupiscence, gourmandizing. *See also* **overindulgent**

overindulgent 5 drunk; **6** greedy; **8** addicted, prodigal, wasteful; **9** abandoned, crapulent, excessive; **10** gluttonous, immoderate, inordinate; **11** extravagant, incontinent, intemperate; **12** concupiscent, uncontrolled, unrestrained; **13** gourmandizing, undisciplined; PHRASES: **3-11** ill-disciplined.

overlap 4 edge, join, meet; **5** cover, touch; **7** overlay, overlie; **8** coincide; **9** intersect; **10** connection, correspond, similarity; **12** intersection; **14** correspondence; PHRASES: **4, 8** come together; **6, 5** partly cover; **6, 6** common ground.

overlay *See* **cover**

overlie 3 jut, lap; **4** span; **6** bridge; **7** overlap, shingle; **8** overarch, overhang; **9** imbricate; **10** overshadow; PHRASES: **3, 4** lie over.

overload 3 tax; **6** burden, excess, strain; **7** surplus; **8** overkill, overwork; **10** overburden; PHRASES: **5, 4** weigh down.

overlook 4 miss, omit; **6** excuse, forget, ignore; **7** condone, neglect; **9** disregard; PHRASES: **4, 1, 5, 3** turn a blind eye; **4, 4** pass over.

overmaster 4 beat, best; **5** trump; **6** master; **7** outplay; **8** outclass, outflank, outpoint, overcome, override, overturn; **9** overpower, overthrow; **11** outmaneuver; PHRASES: **5, 1, 5** carry a point, score a point.

overmuch 6 excess; **7** extreme, overage, surplus; **9** excessive; **11** excessively, superfluity; **13** unnecessarily; PHRASES: **3, 4** too much; **4, 4** very much.

overpower 2 KO; **4** beat, kill, lame, maim, numb, wind; **5** choke; **6** benumb, deaden, disarm, hobble, muzzle, nobble *UK*, stifle; **7** deflate, garrote, silence, smother; **8** garrotte, overcome, paralyze, strangle, throttle; **9** hamstring, overthrow, prostrate, suffocate; PHRASES: **3, 2** tie up; **3, 3, 2, 6** put out of action; **3, 4, 3, 4** tie hand and foot; **4, 4** bowl over; **5, 3** knock out; **5, 4** knock down, power down.

overrule **6** cancel, master, refuse; **8** domineer, override; PHRASES: **4, 4** pull rank; **4, 7** rule against.

overrun **5** beset; **7** flooded, plagued, teeming; **8** brimming, flooding, infested, invasive, swarming; **9** intrusive, inundated, overgrown; **10** overspread; **11** encroaching, overflowing, trespassing.

overseas **6** abroad; **7** foreign; **8** external; **11** ultramarine.

oversee **3** run; **4** boss; **5** chair; **6** direct, handle, manage, umpire; **7** control, inspect, preside; **9** supervise; **10** administer; **11** superintend.

overseer **4** boss; **5** chief; **6** gaffer *UK*, guvnor *UK*, honcho; **7** captain, foreman; **8** governor; **10** chargehand, controller, supercargo, supervisor; **14** superintendent.

oversensitive **5** jumpy, nervy; **6** touchy; **9** irascible, irritable; **13** temperamental; PHRASES: **4-7** thin-skinned; **6, 6** highly strung.

oversensitive person **5** mouse; **8** neurotic; **9** jitterbug; PHRASES: **6, 2, 6** bundle of nerves; **9, 5** sensitive plant; **9, 6** shrinking violet.

oversight **4** slip; **7** control, mistake; **8** omission; **10** management, overseeing; **11** supervision; **14** administration.

overspend **5** spend; **7** overpay; **8** overdraw; PHRASES: **5, 5, 4** throw money away; **6, 3, 2** splash out on.

overstate **5** color; **7** inflate, magnify; **9** dramatize, embellish, embroider; **10** exaggerate; **13** overemphasize.

overt **4** open; **5** clear, plain; **6** patent; **7** blatant, evident, glaring, obvious, visible; **8** apparent, flagrant, manifest, palpable; **11** transparent, unambiguous, undisguised.

overtake **3** hit; **4** pass; **6** assail, engulf, strike; **8** overhaul; PHRASES: **2, 4** go past; **2, 6** go beyond; **5, 4** sweep over; **5, 6** leave behind.

overthrow **4** oust; **5** upset, usurp; **6** depose, remove, topple; **7** conquer, oppress, overset, subvert; **8** demolish, dethrone, overturn, suppress; PHRASES: **4, 4** cast down.

overtime **2** OT. *See also* **time**

overture **5** intro, offer, start; **6** Egmont; **7** Leonora, opening, prelude; **8** Coriolan, Hebrides; **9** beginning; **11** proposition; **12** introduction; PHRASES: **7, 4** Fingal's Cave.

overturn **3** tip; **5** quash, upset; **6** cancel, repeal, revoke, topple; **7** capsize, rescind, reverse; **11** countermand.

overview **6** survey; **7** summary; PHRASES: **5-3, 4** bird's-eye view; **8, 4** ballpark view.

overwhelm **2** KO; **4** beat, bury, daze, rout; **5** crush, flood, floor, shake, swamp; **6** assail, dazzle, deluge, engulf; **7** conquer, impress, oppress, smother; **8** inundate, overcome, submerge, vanquish; **9** dumbfound, overpower; PHRASES: **4, 5** snow under.

overwrought **5** tense; **8** strained, stressed; **9** emotional; **10** distraught.

ovolo **5** thumb; PHRASES: **7, 5** quarter round.

owed **3** due; **6** unpaid; **7** payable; **9** unsettled; **10** chargeable, redeemable; **11** outstanding; PHRASES: **2, 7** in arrears; **6, 2** coming to.

owl **4** bubo; **6** Bunter, hooter, strich; PHRASES: **4, 3** barn ~, fish ~ *UK*; **5, 3** eagle ~, snowy ~, tawny ~; **6, 3** horned ~, little ~; **7, 3** screech ~; **9, 3** burrowing ~.

own **4** have; **5** share; **7** possess.

ownership **5** title; **6** rights, tenure; **10** possession; **14** proprietorship.

ox **4** bull; **5** steer; **7** bullock.

oxeye **5** daisy.

Oxford Group **5, 10** Moral Rearmament.

Oxford Movement **8** Puseyism; **13** Tractarianism.

oxpecker **8** tickbird; PHRASES: **10, 4** rhinoceros bird.

oyster **5, 6** pearl ~; **6, 3** ~ bed; **6, 4** ~ bush, ~ crab, ~ pink; **6, 5** ~ plant; **7, 6** prairie ~; **9, 6** vegetable ~.

P

P 3 per; **4** page, pawn, pint, soft (Italian: piano); **5** after (Latin: post), pages, pedal, penny; **7** parking; PHRASES: **4, 7** four hundred (medieval Roman numeral).

PA 3, 5 per annum.

pace 4 clip, lick, rate, step, trot, walk; **5** amble, march, pound, speed, tempo, tread; **6** patrol, stride; **8** footstep.

pacemaker 5 pacer; **10** pacesetter.

pachyderm 10 rhinoceros; **11** subungulate; **12** hippopotamus, proboscidean; PHRASES: **5, 5** river horse.

pachydermatous 11 elephantine, elephantoid, subungulate; **12** proboscidean, rhinocerotic; PHRASES: **5-7** thick-skinned.

pacific 5 balmy; **6** irenic; **7** clement, lenient; **8** irenical, merciful, moderate, peaceful, soothing; **9** agreeable, forgiving; **11** mediatorial; **13** accommodating.

pacification 4 lull; **5** demob, truce; **6** ahimsa, treaty; **7** détente, entente, irenics; **9** agreement, armistice, cessation, mediation, pacifying; **10** adjustment, compromise, convention, disbanding, moderation, moratorium, satyagraha; **11** appeasement, arbitration, disarmament, nonviolence, peacemaking; **12** conciliation, propitiation; **13** accommodation, mollification, rapprochement, reconcilement, understanding; **14** demobilization, reconciliation.

pacificatory 5 happy; **6** irenic; **7** calming, content; **8** dovelike, friendly, irenical, lenitive, pacified, soothing; **9** appeasing, disarming, emollient, mediatory, pacifying, placatory, satisfied; **10** negotiated, pacifiable, satisfying; **11** peacemaking; **12** conciliatory, propitiatory; PHRASES: **5-6** peace-loving.

pacifist 4 dove; **6** Quaker; **7** conchie UK, neutral; **8** civilian, mediator, pacifier, peacenik; **10** negotiator, peacemaker; **11** peacekeeper, peacemonger; **12** intermediary, noncombatant; **14** nonbelligerent; PHRASES: **3, 6** CND member; **5-4, 6** draft-card burner; **5, 5** draft exile; **5-5** peace-lover; **5, 6** draft dodger, draft evader; **5, 9** draft protester, peace protester; **5, 10** peace negotiator; **6, 5** Sabine women; **7, 8** passive resister.

pacify 4 calm, cure, ease, heal; **5** allay, quell; **6** adjust, disarm, govern, police, soothe, subdue; **7** appease, assuage, compose, content, control, mediate, mollify, placate, restore, satisfy; **9** alleviate, harmonize, reconcile; **10** conciliate, discipline, propitiate; **11** accommodate, tranquilize; PHRASES: **3, 4** win over; **4, 3** cool off; **4, 3, 4, 4** hold out one's hand; **4, 3, 5** keep the peace; **4, 4** calm down, cool down, make well; **4, 5** give terms, keep order, make happy, make peace; **5, 1, 5** grant a truce; **5, 3, 6** douse the flames; **5, 8** bring together; **7, 5** restore order, restore peace; **7, 7** restore harmony.

pack 3 bag, can, pot, ram, tin UK; **4** cage, cram, fill, film, herd, load, stow, tamp, wrap; **5** cover, crate, crowd, flock, store, stuff, troop; **6** bearer, bottle, bundle, cocoon, entomb, kitbag UK, sheath, squash, throng; **7** blister, carrier, enclose, package, pannier, reserve, shelter, squeeze; **8** backpack, compress, envelope, knapsack, rucksack, surround; **9** packhorse, saddlebag; **12** containerize; PHRASES: **3, 2** box up UK; **3, 4** ice ~, rat ~; **4, 3** ~ ice; **4, 4** cold ~, face ~; **4, 5** ~ drill UK; **4, 6** ~ animal; **5, 2** crate up; **5, 4** power ~; **7, 4** blister ~.

packed 4 full; **6** filled; **7** crammed, crowded, heaving UK; **8** bursting; **11** overflowing; PHRASES: **3-6** jam-packed; **5-1-5** chock-a-block; **5-4** chock-full.

packet 4 boat, file, pack, ship; 5 cover; 6 bundle, folder, jacket, parcel, sachet, sheath, wallet; 7 package, steamer, wrapper; 8 billfold, document, envelope; 9 container, packaging *UK*.

packing *See* **stuffing**

pact 6 treaty; 7 compact; 8 alliance; 9 agreement; PHRASES: 6, 4 Warsaw P~.

pad 3 paw, wad; 4 fill, line, pack, step; 5 block *UK*, creep, sneak, steal, stuff; 6 jotter *UK*, tablet, tiptoe; 7 cushion, padding, wadding; 8 compress, stuffing; PHRASES: 3, 5 leg guard; 4, 3 hard ~, lily ~; 5, 9 elbow protector; 6, 3 launch ~; 7, 3 scratch ~; 8, 3 shoulder ~.

padding 6 bustle; 7 bombast, cushion, falsies, wadding; 8 stuffing.

paddle 3 oar, row; 5 blade, scull, sweep; 6 propel.

page 1 P; 4 call, leaf; 5 folio, recto, sheet, verso; 6 summon; 7 bellboy, bellhop, Buttons, pageboy.

pageant 6 parade; 7 tableau; 10 exhibition; 11 performance.

paid 2 PD; 5 hired, waged; 7 cleared, earning, prepaid, settled; 8 salaried; 10 discharged, liquidated; 12 professional; PHRASES: 2, 3, 5 in the black; 3, 2, 3, 3 out of the red; 3, 2, 4 out of debt; 4-4 debt-free; 4-7 wage-earning; 5, 7 owing nothing. *See also* **pay**

pain 3 gyp; 4 ache, hell, hurt, pang, stab; 5 agony, colic, cramp, dolor, pangs, prick, spasm, sting, throb; 6 aching, misery, ordeal, stitch, throes, twinge; 7 anguish, malaise, myalgia, passion, torment, torture; 8 distress, nuisance, pinprick, smarting, soreness; 9 martyrdom, neuralgia, purgatory, suffering, throbbing; 10 affliction, convulsion, discomfort, irritation, punishment, tenderness; 11 hurtfulness, lancination, painfulness; 12 inflammation; PHRASES: 4, 2, 5 hell on earth; 4, 3, 7 pins and needles; 4, 4 sore spot; 5, 3, 5 aches and pains.

pain (express pain) 3 cry, sob; 4 gasp, howl, moan, wail, yell, yelp, yowl; 5 groan; 6 scream, shriek, squawk, squeal; 7 screech, whimper.

pain (feel pain) 4 ache, hurt; 5 chafe, smart, wince; 6 flinch, squirm, suffer, twitch, writhe; 7 agonize; PHRASES: 4, 3, 6 bite the bullet.

pain (inflicting pain) 5 cruel; 6 brutal; 7 hurtful, hurting, painful; 8 sadistic; 9 torturing; 10 tormenting.

pain (inflict pain) 3 cut, hit, jab, nip; 4 beat, bite, bump, burn, claw, flog, gash, hurt, maul, pain, rack, stab, tear; 5 graze, knife, pinch, prick, scald, shoot, slash, smash, sting, tweak, wound, wring; 6 batter, bloody, bruise, harrow, impale, injure, mangle, martyr, punish, savage, scrape, sprain, thrash; 7 contuse, crucify, scratch, torment, torture; 8 convulse, fracture, puncture; 10 excruciate, traumatize; PHRASES: 3, 2, 3, 5 cut to the quick; 3, 7 run through; 4, 2 beat up; 4, 5 draw blood; 5, 1, 3, 5 touch a raw nerve; 5, 2 carve up.

pain (in pain) 3 raw; 4 hurt, sore; 6 aching, pained; 7 hurting, wincing; 8 agonized, bleeding, martyred, tortured, writhing; 9 afflicted, anguished, blistered, convulsed, suffering, tormented; 10 distressed; 11 traumatized; PHRASES: 2, 5 in agony; 5-3-4 black-and-blue; 6, 3, 4 aching all over.

painful 3 raw; 4 sore; 5 acute; 6 aching, biting, tender; 7 burning, chronic, extreme, gnawing, hurting, racking, searing; 8 cramping, grinding, gripping, pounding, scalding, shooting, smarting, stabbing, stinging, tingling; 9 agonizing, exquisite, harrowing, miserable, splitting, throbbing, traumatic; 10 unbearable; 11 distressing, intolerable, lancinating, purgatorial; 12 excruciating; 13 uncomfortable.

painful (be painful) 4 ache, bite, burn, gnaw, grip, hurt, sear, stab; 5 cramp, grind, pound, shoot, smart, sting, throb; 6 tingle.

painful condition 5 colic, grips, ulcer; 6 angina, cramps, hernia, megrim; 7 earache, lumbago, myalgia, pyrosis, rupture; 8 backache, headache, migraine, sciatica; 9 arthritis, bellyache, dyspepsia, heartburn, neuralgia, toothache, tummyache; 10 afterpains, laryngitis, rheumatism; 11 indigestion, stomachache; 12 dysmenorrhea; PHRASES: 3-4 gut-ache; 4, 6 sore throat; 4, 8 sick headache; 5, 2, 3, 4 crick in the neck; 5, 5 labor pains; 5, 7 upset stomach; 6, 8 angina pectoris.

pain relief 9 analgesia.

pain-relieving 7 numbing; 8 sedative, soothing; 9 analgesia; 10 anesthetic.

paint 3 dye, hue, oil; 4 coat, daub, draw, etch, form, matt, plan, plot, tint, tone, wash;

5 brush, color, draft, gloss, shade, shape, trace; **6** design, enamel, medium, primer, raddle, sketch; **7** acrylic, gouache, outline, picture, scumble, tempera; **8** colorise, describe, eggshell, emulsion; **9** overpaint, undercoat, whitewash; **10** caricature, illuminate, illustrate, underpaint; **11** watercolors; PHRASES: **3, 5** oil ~, war ~; **5, 2** touch up; **5, 3** block out, rough out; **5, 4** color wash; **5, 5** gloss ~; **5, 7** basic palette; **6, 3** sketch out; **6, 5** poster ~; **7, 6** acrylic paints, colored crayon, colored pencil; **8, 7** expanded palette, standard palette.

painter **3** Ray (Man); **4** Bell (Vanessa), Cole (Thomas), Dali (Salvador), Doré (Gustave), Dufy (Raoul), Dyck (Sir Anthony van), Eyck (Jan van), Goya (Francisco de), Gris (Juan), Hals (Frans), Hunt (Holman), John (Augustus), Kent (Rockwell), Klee (Paul), Lear (Edward), Luks (George Benjamin), Marc (Franz), Miró (Joan), West (Benjamin), Wood (Grant); PHRASES: **5** Abbey (Edwin Austin), Avery (Milton Clark), Bacon (Francis), Beuys (Joseph), Blake (William), Bosch (Hieronymus), Corot (Jean-Baptiste), Davis (Stuart), Degas (Edgar), Dürer (Albrecht), Ensor (James Sydney), Ernst (Max), fauve, Gorky (Arshile), Grosz (George), Henri (Robert), Hirst (Damien), Homer (Winslow), Johns (Jasper), Kahlo (Frida), Klimt (Gustav), Kline (Franz), Koons (Jeff), Léger (Fernand), Lippi (Fra Filippo), Manet (Édouard), Marin (John), Marsh (Reginald), Monet (Claude), Morse (Samuel F. B.), Moses (Grandma), Munch (Edvard), Peale (Charles Willson), Redon (Odilon), Riley (Bridget), Sloan (John), Sully (Thomas), Weber (Max), Wyeth (Andrew), Wyeth (N. C.); **6** Albers (Josef), artist, Benton (Thomas Hart), Braque (Georges), Calder (Alexander), Catlin (George), Church (Frederick Edwin), Copley (John Singleton), dauber, Davies (Arthur B.), Demuth (Charles), Derain (André), Durand (Asher B.), Eakins (Thomas), Escher (M. C.), French (Daniel Chester), Giotto, Guardi (Francesco), Haring (Keith), Hassam (Childe), Hopper (Edward), Ingres (Jean-Auguste), LeWitt (Sol), Millet (Jean-François), Morris (William), Newman (Barnett), Orozco (José Clemente), Renoir (Auguste), Rivera (Diego), Rivers (Larry), Romney (George), Rothko (Mark), Rubens (Peter Paul), Seurat (Georges), Sisley (Al-

fred), Stella (Frank), Stuart (Gilbert), Stubbs (George), Tamayo (Rufino), Tanguy (Yves), Titian, Turner (J. M. W.), Vasari (Giorgio), Warhol (Andy), Weyden (Rogier van der); **7** Allston (Washington), Audubon (John James), Bellini (Jacopo), Bellows (George Wesley), Bingham (George Caleb), Bonnard (Pierre), Boucher (François), Cassatt (Mary), Cézanne (Paul), Chagall (Marc), Chardin (Jean Baptiste), Chirico (Giorgio de), Christo, Courbet (Gustave), Cranach (Lucas, the Elder), Daumier (Honoré), Duchamp (Marcel), Gauguin (Paul), Hartley (Marsden), Hockney (David), Hofmann (Hans), Hogarth (William), Hokusai, Holbein (Hans, the Elder), Holbein (Hans, the Younger), Krasner (Lee), Martini (Simone), Matisse (Henri), Millais (Sir John Everett), Morisot (Berthe), Murillo (Barolomé Esteban), O'Keefe (Georgia), Parrish (Maxfield), Picasso (Pablo), Pollock (Jackson), Poussin (Nicolas), Rackham (Arthur), Raphael, Sargent (John Singer), Schiele (Egon), Sheeler (Charles), Tiepolo (Giovanni Battista), Utrillo (Maurice), Vermeer (Jan), Watteau (Jean-Antoine); **8** Brueghel (Jan), Brueghel (Pieter), colorist, Daubigny (Charles-François), Glackens (William), Hilliard (Nicholas), Magritte (René), Malevich (Kasimir), Mantegna (Andrea), Masaccio, Mondrian (Piet), Piranesi (Giovanni Battista), Pissarro (Camille), Pontormo (Jacopo da), Reynolds (Joshua), Rossetti (Dante Gabriel), Rousseau (Henri), Veronese (Paolo), Vlaminck (Maurice de), Vuillard (Édouard), Whistler (James McNeill); **9** Beardsley (Aubrey), Bierstadt (Albert), Canaletto (Antonio), Constable (John), Correggio, decorator, Delacroix (Eugène), Donatello, Feininger (Lyonel Charles Adrian), Fragonard (Jean Honoré), Friedrich (Caspar David), Géricault (Théodore), Giorgione, Kandinsky (Wassily), Kokoschka (Oskar), paysagist, Remington (Frederic), Siqueiros (David Alfaro), Velázquez (Diego); **10** Botticelli (Sandro), Caravaggio (Michelangelo Merisi da), chromatist, Fiorentino (Rosso), Giacometti (Alberto), Modigliani (Amedeo), Motherwell (Robert), Tintoretto; **11** aquarellist, Covarrubias (Miguel), Gentileschi (Artemisia), Prendergast (Maurice Brazil); **12** Anuszkiewicz (Richard), Gainsborough (Thomas), Lichtenstein (Roy), Michelangelo, Parmigianino, Rauschenberg (Robert); **13** expressionist, Frankenthaler (Helen), impressionist, watercolorist; **2, 4** La Tour (Georges de); **2, 5** El Greco, La Farge (John); **2, 7** de Kooning (Willem); **3, 4** van Gogh (Vincent); **3, 6** old master; **3, 7** oil ~; **3, 8** Fra Angelico; **4, 7** icon ~, sign ~; **5-5** Burne-Jones (Sir Edward); **5, 7** mural ~, scene ~; **5-7** easelpainter; **6, 2, 7** Pietro da Cortona; **6, 3, 5** Andrea del Sarto; **6-4** Moholy-Nagy (László); **6, 6** modern master; **6, 7** action ~, Sunday ~; **7, 6** graphic artist; **8, 2** "Bronzino, il"; **8, 2, 5** Leonardo da Vinci; **8, 7** portrait ~; **8-7** Toulouse-Lautrec (Henri de). *See also* **artist**

painting 3 oil; **4** daub, head, icon, nude, view, wash; **5** mural, pietà, scene, water; **6** canvas, fresco, maestà, pastel; **7** acrylic, daubing, diptych, gouache, impasto, profile, reredos, retable, tempera, tinting, vanitas, washing; **8** coloring, exterior, interior, nativity, nocturne, panorama, pastoral, portrait, prospect, seascape, skyscape, triptych; **9** aquarelle, encaustic, grisaille, landscape, miniature, townscape; **10** altarpiece, cloudscape, colorising, monochrome, nightpiece, polychrome, riverscape, watercolor; **11** composition, crucifixion; **12** annunciation, illumination, overpainting; **13** underpainting; PHRASES: **3, 8** oil ~; **4, 8** cave ~, sign ~, wall ~; **4, 9** fête champêtre; **5-3, 4** bird's-eye view; **5-4** still-life; **5, 8** easel ~, genre ~, scene ~; **6, 5** profil perdu; **6, 8** action ~, battle ~, finger ~, marine ~; **7, 8** cabinet ~.

pair 2 PR; **3** duo, two; **4** dyad, link, mate, span, team, twin, yoke; **5** brace, match, twain; **6** couple; **7** bracket, twosome; **9** matchmake; PHRASES: **4, 3** ~ off; **6, 2** couple up; **6, 4** pigeon ~; **6-7** double-harness.

pak-choi 7, 7 Chinese cabbage.

pal *See* **friend**

palace 5 court; **6** Louvre; **7** mansion, Schloss, Trianon, Vatican; **8** Alhambra, Escorail, Escurial, seraglio; **9** Tuileries; **10** Versailles; PHRASES: **3, 6** gin ~ *UK*; **4, 5** Sans Souci; **5, 6** Pitti P~; **6, 6** Elysee P~; **7, 6** Crystal P~ *UK*, Lambeth P~, Lateran P~, picture ~ *UK*, Topkapi P~; **8, 5** Holyrood House; **8, 6** Blenheim P~.

palatable 5 tasty; **6** edible; **8** passable, pleasant; **9** agreeable, toothsome; **10** acceptable, appetizing; **12** satisfactory.

palatial 5 grand; **6** lavish; **8** splendid; **9** luxurious; **10** impressive.

palaver 4 chat, fuss, talk; **6** bother, gossip; **7** chatter, trouble; **8** chitchat, nuisance.

pale 3 dim, wan; **4** ashy, fair, post, thin, weak; **5** ashen, drawn, faint, fence, light, livid, pasty, stake, waxen, white; **6** blanch, bleach, feeble, limits, pallid, pastel, sallow, whiten; **7** blanche, ghastly, ghostly, haggard, kingdom; **9** bloodless, enclosure; PHRASES: **5, 2, 1, 5** white as a sheet.

paleness 6 anemia, pallor; **8** albinism; **9** albinoism, pallidity. *See also* **pale**

paleoanthropology 9 epigraphy; **10** Egyptology, Sumerology; **11** Assyriology; **14** paleoethnology.

paleology 9 epigraphy; **10** Egyptology, Sumerology; **11** archaeology, Assyriology.

pall 4 fade, wall; **5** cloud, gloom, sheet; **6** shroud, wither; **7** blanket, despair, sadness; **8** diminish; **10** depression, melancholy; PHRASES: **2, 4** go sour.

palliative *See* **soothing**

pallid *See* **pale**

palm 4 hand, hide; **5** award, crown, prize; **6** laurel, trophy, wreath; **7** success, triumph, victory; **8** accolade; PHRASES: **4, 3** ~ oil; **4, 4** ~ wine *UK*; **4, 5** P~ Beach, ~ sugar; **4, 6** P~ Sunday.

palmistry 10 chiromancy.

palpable 4 real; **5** gross, plain, solid; **7** evident; **8** concrete, manifest, material, tangible; **9** touchable; **10** detectable; **11** discernible, perceivable, perceptible, substantial.

paltry 4 mean; **5** cheap; **7** trivial; **8** trifling, wretched; **9** miserable, worthless; **10** despicable; **12** contemptible.

pamper *See* **spoil**

pan 3 pot, wok; **5** slate *UK*; **6** berate, deride; **7** dishpan, skillet; **8** saucepan; **9** criticize, disparage; PHRASES: **4, 3** tube ~; **6, 3** frying ~; **7, 3** broiler ~; **10, 3** springform ~.

pancake 8 flapjack, slapjack.

Pancake Day 6, 7 Shrove Tuesday.

pander 5 serve; **6** comply, squire; **9** matchmake; PHRASES: **3, 5** run after; **4, 2** wait on; **5, 3** cater for; **5, 3, 5** fetch and carry; **6, 3** stooge for.

panel 4 jury, pane, team; **5** board, group, piece, plate, sheet; **7** council.

pangolin 8 anteater; PHRASES: **5, 8** scaly anteater.

panic 4 bolt, flap; 5 alarm, grass, scare; 6 frenzy, terror; 8 hysteria, stampede; PHRAS-ES: **5, 6** ~ button, ~ buying; **5, 8** ~ stations *UK.*

panoply *See* **display**

panorama 6 survey; 8 overview, synopsis; 10 conspectus; PHRASES: **5, 4** world view.

pansy 10 heartsease; PHRASES: **4-2-8** love-in-idleness.

pant 4 blow, gasp, puff; 5 crave, snort, yearn; 6 hanker, wheeze.

panther 3 cat; 6 cougar, jaguar; 7 leopard; 8 Bagheera; PHRASES: **4, 7** Pink P~.

panties 5 pants *UK*, tanga, thong; 6 briefs, shorts, smalls, undies; 7 drawers; 8 bloomers, culottes; 9 underwear; 10 underpants; 14 knickerbockers, unmentionables; PHRASES: **6, 6** bikini briefs; **10, 7** Directoire drawers.

pantihose 6 tights *UK*; 9 pantyhose.

panting 6 winded; 10 breathless; 14 breathlessness; PHRASES: **3, 2, 6** out of breath; **5, 2, 6** short of breath; **6-6** broken-winded. *See also* **pant**

pants 4 bags *UK*; 5 bucks, chaps, cords, jeans, Levi's, trews; 6 bracae, braies, breeks *UK*, chinos, denims, flares, khakis, moggan, shorts, slacks; 7 bavette, cutoffs, joggers, pistols, shalwar; 8 breeches, britches, chausses, culottes, dungaree, fatigues, flannels, hipsters *UK*, jodhpurs, leggings *UK*, overalls, striders, trousers *UK*; 9 bluejeans, buckskins, chivarras, churidars, dungarees, shaksheer, shintiyan; 10 calzoneras, drainpipes, lederhosen, pantaloons, pinstripes, salopettes *UK*, sweatpants; 12 galligaskins, smallclothes, trouserettes; 14 knickerbockers; PHRASES: **3-3** peg-top *UK*; **3-3-5** bib-and-brace; **3, 5** gym ~, hot ~, ski ~; **3-7** hip-huggers; **4-2** warm-up; **4, 5** blue jeans, long ~, plus fours; **4-5, 5** high-water ~; **4-7** bell-bottoms; **4, 8** knee breeches, long trousers; **5, 5** Capri ~, cargo ~, harem ~, short ~; **5, 6** short shorts; **5, 7** pedal pushers; **5-8** trunk-breeches; **6, 4** Oxford bags *UK*; **6, 5** gaucho ~, riding ~; **6, 8** pegged trousers, riding breeches; **7, 5** palazzo ~, stirrup ~; **7, 6** Bermuda shorts, cycling shorts; **8, 5** toreador ~. *See also* **trousers**

paper 2 FT *UK*, MS; 3 rag, Sun; 4 bond, card, leaf, pulp, ream, roll; 5 daily, essay, organ, quire, sheet, Times; 6 manila, thesis;

7 journal; 8 banknote, document, foolscap, mulberry, nautilus; 9 cardboard, cartridge, newspaper, newsprint, notepaper, wallpaper; 10 cellophane, pasteboard, stationery; 11 certificate; PHRASES: **2, 5** A4 ~; **3, 5** art ~ *UK*, rag ~, wax ~; **4, 5** rice ~; **5, 5** Bible ~, brown ~, crepe ~, flock ~, graph ~, green ~, India ~, music ~ *UK*, order ~ *UK*, ~ chase, ~ money, ~ tiger, waxed ~; **6, 5** ballot ~ *UK*, carbon ~, cotton ~, filter ~, glossy ~, tissue ~, toilet ~, typing ~; **6-5** papier-mâché; **7, 5** Bristol board, tracing ~, writing ~; **8, 5** blotting ~, computer ~, imperial ~, lavatory ~, wrapping ~; **9, 5** cartridge ~ *UK*, cellulose fiber, cigarette ~, laminated ~; **10, 5** calendered ~, commercial ~, waterproof ~; **12, 5** construction ~. *See also* **newspaper**

paperback *See* **book**

paper measures 4 bale, copy, demy, post, pott, ream; 5 atlas, brief, crown, draft, quire, royal; 6 bundle, casing, medium; 7 emperor; 8 elephant, foolscap, imperial; 9 cartridge, colombier; 11 antiquarian; PHRAS-ES: **3, 3** bag cap; **4, 3** kent cap; **5, 3** haven cap; **5, 4** large post, music demy; **5, 5** grand eagle, super royal; **6, 4** double demy, double post; **6, 5, 4** double large post; **6, 8** double elephant; **7, 4** pinched post; **8, 3** imperial cap.

paper money 3 IOU; 4 bill, bond, note *UK*; 5 check, draft, order, scrip; 6 coupon; 7 warrant; 8 assignat, banknote; 9 debenture, Eurocheck; 11 certificate, shinplaster; PHRASES: **4, 2, 4** note of hand; **4, 2, 8** bill of exchange; **4, 5** fiat money, giro check; **4, 6, 4** zero coupon bond; **5, 5** money order; **6, 2, 6** letter of credit; **6, 4** bearer bond; **6, 5** postal order *UK*; **7, 4** premium bond; **8, 4** treasury note; **8, 5** cashier's check; **9, 4** corporate bond; **9, 5** certified check; **9, 6** traveler's cheque; **10, 4** promissory note; **10, 5** commercial paper; **11, 4** convertible bond.

papery 3 dry; 4 thin; 5 frail; 6 flimsy; 8 delicate; 10 diaphanous; PHRASES: **5-4** paper-thin.

par 4 tied; 5 drawn, equal, level, quits, value; 7 average; 8 sameness, standard; 10 deadlocked, excellence, stalemated; PHRAS-ES: **3-3-4** nip-and-tuck; **4-3-4** half-and-half, neck-and-neck; **4-4** dead-heat; **5-5** fifty-fifty; **5-7** level-pegging.

parade 3 air; 4 gala, show; 5 march, strut; 6 flaunt; 7 display, pageant; 9 cavalcade, pageantry, promenade *UK*, spectacle;

paraffin 6 alkane; 8 kerosene.

paragon 3 ace; 4 diva, star; 6 expert, genius, victor, winner; 7 prodigy; 8 champion, laureate, superman, virtuoso; 9 celebrity, nonpareil, superstar; 10 mastermind, specialist, superwoman; 11 prizewinner; PHRASES: 3, 3 the biz; 3, 4 the most; 3-6 cupholder; 3, 8 the greatest; 4, 3 whiz kid; 4-5 high-flier; 4, 8 poet laureate; 5, 4 first lady; 5, 5 prima donna; 5-6 chart-topper, world-beater; 6, 3 number one, numero uno; 6, 5 wonder woman; 6-6 record-holder; 6, 7 record breaker.

paragraph 4 item, part; 5 piece, story; 6 clause; 7 article, passage, section; 10 subsection.

parallel 5 equal, match; 6 mirror; 7 abreast; 8 analogue, coextend; 9 alongside, collimate; 10 collateral, concentric; 11 coextensive, equidistant; 12 nondivergent; 13 nonconvergent; PHRASES: 3, 7 run abreast; 3, 8 lie ~, run ~; 4, 2, 4 side by side.

parallelogram 5 rhomb; 7 rhombus; 13 quadrilateral; 14 parallelepiped.

paralysis 5 cramp, palsy; 8 deadness, diplegia, numbness, shutdown, stoppage; 10 hemiplegia, immobility, paraplegia; 12 quadriplegia.

paralyze 4 halt, lame, numb, stop, stun; 6 deaden, freeze; 7 disable; 8 transfix; 10 immobilize; 12 incapacitate; PHRASES: 3, 3, 2, 6 put out of action.

paramedic 5 carer, nurse; 7 dresser, midwife, orderly; 9 dietician, hygienist; 10 podiatrist; 11 anesthetist, paramedical; 12 ambulanceman, nutritionist, radiographer; 15 physiotherapist; PHRASES: 4, 7 ward orderly; 4, 9 care attendant UK; 5, 4 crash team; 6, 9 dental auxiliary, dental hygienist, speech therapist; 9-6 stretcher-bearer.

parameter 4 mean, mode; 5 range; 6 median, spread; 7 average; 9 variation, weighting UK; 10 covariance, dispersion, percentile; 14 characteristic; PHRASES: 4, 5 mean error; 4, 9 mean deviation; 7, 5 average value, typical value; 8, 4 weighted mean; 8, 5 expected value, probable error, standard error; 9, 4 geometric mean; 10, 4 arithmetic mean; 10, 5 confidence level UK.

paramilitary See **guerrilla**

paramount See **supreme**

parapsychological 6 astral, occult; 7 animist, phantom, psychic, psychic(al); 9 animistic, spiritual; 10 telepathic; 11 clairvoyant; 12 extrasensory, precognitive, spiritualist UK, supernatural; 13 psychokinetic, supersensible; 14 spiritualistic.

parapsychology 9 telepathy; 12 clairvoyance, precognition; 13 psychokinesis; PHRASES: 7, 8 psychic research.

paraselene 4, 4 mock moon.

parasite 3 bot, bug, nit; 4 conk, flea, lice, mite, pest, tick; 5 drone, fluke, leech, louse, toady; 6 insect, lackey; 7 giardia, pinworm, sponger; 8 helminth, hookworm, nematode, tapeworm; 9 entamoeba, mistletoe, piroplasm, protozoan, scrounger; 10 freeloader, leishmania, toxoplasma; 11 bloodsucker, trypanosome; PHRASES: 4, 4 sand flea; 4, 5 fish louse; 5, 5 blood fluke, liver fluke, whale louse; 6, 4 guinea worm.

parasitic 4 lazy; 6 biting; 8 sponging; 9 dependent; 10 scrounging; 11 freeloading; 12 bloodsucking; 13 opportunistic.

parcel 3 box; 4 pack, plot, wrap; 5 piece, tract; 6 bundle, carton, packet; 7 package, portion, section; PHRASES: 4, 2 wrap up.

parch 3 dry; 4 wilt; 5 wizen; 6 weazen, wither; 7 mummify, shrivel; 8 preserve.

pardon 5 relax, sorry, spare; 6 acquit, relent, unbend; 7 absolve, amnesty, forbear, forgive; 8 reprieve; 9 acquittal; 11 exculpation; PHRASES: 3, 3 let off.

pare 3 cut; 4 clip, peel, skin, trim; 5 shave, strip; PHRASES: 3, 4 cut back; 4, 2 tidy up.

parenthood 9 maternity, parentage, paternity.

parhelion 6 sundog; PHRASES: 4, 3 mock sun.

parish 4 area, cure; PHRASES: 6, 4 ~ pump UK; 6, 5 ~ clerk; 6, 7 ~ council UK; 6, 8 ~ register UK.

Parisian (a Parisian) 2 un; 3 une.

Parisian (of the Parisian) 2 de, du; 3 des.

parity 3 par, tie; 4 draw; 5 deuce, quits; 6 stasis; 8 deadlock, equality; 9 levelness, stalemate; 10 congruence; PHRASES: 4, 4 dead heat.

park 1 P; 6 tarmac; 8 minipark; PHRASES: 4, 4 game ~, Hyde P~; 5, 4 theme ~; 6, 4 forest ~ UK, pocket ~, safari ~; 7, 4 country ~ UK, science ~; 7, 6 parking garage; 8, 4 business

~, national ~; **9, 4** amusement ~.

parley 4 talk; **6** confer; **7** discuss, meeting; **9** negotiate; **10** conference, deliberate, discussion; **12** consultation, negotiations.

parliament 1 P; **4** Dail, diet, Duma, parl, Rump; **5** Lords; **6** Cortes, Majlis; **7** Commons; **8** Congress, Stormont; **9** Bundestag; **11** legislature, Westminster; PHRASES: **3, 5** Lok Sabha; **4, 10** Long P~.

parody 5 twist; **6** satire; **7** distort, imitate, lampoon, pervert; **8** satirize, travesty; **9** burlesque, imitation; **10** caricature, distortion, perversion; **12** misrepresent; PHRASES: **4, 9** pale imitation.

parole 4 bail; **8** liberate; **10** liberation.

paroxysm 3 fit; **5** spasm; **6** attack, frenzy; **7** seizure; **8** outburst; **9** explosion; **10** convulsion, outpouring.

parrot 3 kea; **4** copy, echo, lory, poll; **5** macaw, polly *UK*; **6** repeat; **7** imitate; **8** cockatoo, lovebird, parakeet.

parrot fever 11 psittacosis.

parry 4 turn; **5** avert, avoid, fence; **7** counter, deflect, repulse, riposte; PHRASES: **4, 3** fend off, hold off, keep off, ward off; **5, 3** fight off, stave off; **5, 4** throw back.

parsimonious 4 mean *UK*, near; **5** cheap, close, mingy, tight; **6** stingy; **7** miserly; **8** grudging; **9** niggardly, penurious, scrimping; **10** ungenerous; **11** tightfisted; **12** cheeseparing; PHRASES: **5-4** penny-wise, tight-assd; **5-6** close-fisted; **5-8** money-grubbing, penny-pinching.

parsimonious (be parsimonious) 6 scrimp; **9** economize; PHRASES: **4, 4, 4** make ends meet; **6, 3, 4** scrape and save.

parsimony 6 thrift; **9** frugality; PHRASES: **5-8** penny-pinching. *See also* **parsimonious**

parson *See* **clergyman**

part 2 PT; **3** arc, bit; **4** area, half, limb, lobe, role, ward; **5** break, class, curve, genus, group, quota, sever, share, split, tenth, third, tithe, whack; **6** bisect, county, depart, divide, eighth, factor, family, moiety, parish, phylum, region, sector; **7** aliquot, balance, dissect, divisor, element, faction, portion, quarter, section, segment, species, surplus; **8** aliquant, category, district, dividend, division, fraction, fragment, majority, minority, particle, quotient, separate, subclass, subgenus, subgroup; **9** apportion, community, dismantle, partition, remainder, subdivide, subfamily; **10** department, hemisphere, percentage, proportion, semicircle, subspecies; **11** compartment, installment, subcategory, subdivision; **12** sectionalize; PHRASES: **3, 2** cut up; **3, 8** bid farewell; **4, 7** ~ company; **5, 2** break up.

partake 3 eat; **4** dine; **5** drink, share, taste; **7** consume; **10** contribute; **11** participate; PHRASES: **4, 1, 4** play a part; **4, 4** take part.

partial 4 fond, keen, part; **5** bitty, diced, wispy; **6** atomic, biased, brashy, broken, ground, minced, skewed, sliced, unfair; **7** aliquot, armless, crumbly, divided, legless, scrappy, slanted; **8** headless, limbless, partisan, shredded; **9** elemental, imperfect, molecular, partitive, piecemeal, sectional, segmental; **10** fractional, fragmented, inadequate, incomplete, prejudiced, unfinished; **11** fragmentary; **12** departmental, insufficient, proportional; **13** compartmental, proportionate; PHRASES: **2, 4** in bits; **2, 6** in pieces; **2, 11** in smithereens; **3, 5** not whole; **3-5** one-sided; **4, 4, 7** with bits missing; **4-8** half-finished.

partiality 4 bias, love; **5** fancy, favor; **6** liking, relish; **8** weakness; **9** prejudice; **10** favoritism; **14** discrimination; PHRASES: **4, 4** soft spot. *See also* **partial**

partially 8 somewhat; PHRASES: **2, 1, 6** to a degree; **2, 4** in part; **2, 4, 6** to some extent; **2, 4, 7** in some measure. *See also* **partial**

participant 4 ally; **5** party; **6** member, sharer; **7** partner; **8** flatmate *UK*, partaker, roommate; **9** accessory, associate, colleague, communard, communist, copartner, socialist; **10** accomplice, empathizer, kibbutznik; **11** confederate, shareholder, stockholder, sympathizer; **12** collaborator, participator, sharecropper; PHRASES: **2-6** co-tenant; **5, 5** joint owner; **5, 6** party member, share farmer, union member; **6, 6** fellow tenant; **7, 6** commune member; **9, 6** apartment sharer.

participate 4 play; **5** enter, share; **7** compete, contend, partake; PHRASES: **4, 2** join in; **4, 4** take part.

participation 4 duty, role; **7** empathy, sharing; **8** function, sympathy; **9** character, inclusion, mutualism, partaking; **10** complicity, engagement, fellowship, membership; **11** affiliation, association, cooperation, involvement; **12** contribution; **13** collaboration, companionship; **14** responsibility; **PHRASES: 6, 7** fellow feeling *UK*; **6, 8** shared feelings; **8, 6** sympathy strike.

particle 3 bit, dot, ion; **4** atom, cell, iota, seed; **5** grain, monad, pixel, point, speck; **6** parton; **7** granule, nucleus, pinhead, quantum; **8** fragment, microdot, molecule, pinpoint; **9** corpuscle. *See also* **elementary particle**

particular 3 fog, pet; **4** fact, item, nice, prim, smog; **5** exact, fixed, fussy, named, picky, point; **6** choosy, dainty, detail, marked, single, unique; **7** certain, express, faddish, feature, finical, finicky, notable, precise, special; **8** definite, detailed, discrete, explicit, peculiar, specific; **9** exclusive; **10** fastidious, meticulous; **11** distinctive, painstaking, punctilious; **12** identifiable.

parting 5 adieu, congé, leave; **6** spread; **7** epitaph, fanning, goodbye, sendoff; **8** division, farewell, nightcap, obituary, splaying, viaticum; **9** dismissal, goodnight; **10** deployment, separation; **11** leavetaking, valediction, valedictory; **13** centrifugence; **PHRASES: 3, 3, 3, 4** one for the road; **4, 4** last post *UK*; **4, 5** last words; **4, 9** last handshake; **5-2-6** deoch-an-doruis; **6, 9** golden handshake; **7, 3** stirrup cup; **7, 4** ~ shot; **7, 7** funeral oration; **8, 5** drifting apart; **8, 7** farewell address; **9, 3** spreading out.

partisan 2 ax; **3** fan; **4** pike; **5** spear; **6** biased; **7** bigoted, devotee, partial; **8** adherent, champion, clannish, cliquish; **9** exclusive, factional, sectarian, sectional, supporter; **PHRASES: 3-5** one-sided.

partition 5 panel; **6** divide, screen; **7** divider; **8** division, separate; **10** separation; **PHRASES: 4, 3** wall off; **5, 3** fence off; **7, 5** sliding doors; **8, 4** dividing wall.

partly 4 half; **5** quasi; **8** slightly *UK*, somewhat; **9** gradually, partially, piecemeal, scrappily; **10** moderately; **12** fractionally, inadequately, incompletely; **14** proportionally; **15** proportionately; **PHRASES: 1, 3** a bit; **1, 6** a little; **1, 6, 2, 1, 4** a little at a time; **2, 1, 6** to a degree; **2, 4** in part; **2, 4, 3, 6** by fits and starts; **2, 4, 6** to some extent; **2, 4, 7** in some measure; **2, 5, 3, 5** in dribs and drabs; **2, 6** in detail; **2, 7** by degrees; **3, 2, 3** bit by bit; **3, 4** pro rata; **4, 2, 4** drop by drop, part by part; **4, 3, 4** half and half, part for part; **6, 2, 6** little by little.

partner 1 E, N, S, W; **4** ally, date, mate, oppo, pard, twin, wife; **5** buddy, lover; **6** escort, hubbie, spouse; **7** consort, husband; **8** workmate; **9** accompany, associate, boyfriend, cohabitee, colleague, companion; **10** cohabitant, girlfriend; **PHRASES: 2-6** coworker; **4-2, 5** live-in lover; **5, 4** other half; **6-3, 4** common-law wife; **6-3, 6** common-law spouse; **6, 4** better half; **6, 6** fellow worker.

partnership 4 pool; **5** kitty, share, stock, store, union; **6** common; **7** tontine; **8** alliance, coagency, marriage; **10** federalism; **11** association; **12** collegialism, comanagement; **13** confederation, copartnership; **14** cochairmanship; **PHRASES: 2-9** co-ownership; **6-7** profit-sharing.

part of garment 3 arm, bib, fly, top, zip *UK*; **4** cuff, flap, fold, gore, neck, trim, yoke; **5** bosom, lapel, pleat, train; **6** bodice, button, collar, crotch, edging, gusset, peplum, pocket, sleeve, Velcro *TM*, zipper; **7** armhole, corsage, hemline, opening, placket; **8** codpiece; **9** garniture, stomacher, waistline; **PHRASES: 4-2** turn-up *UK*; **4, 3, 3** hook and eye; **4-4** coat-tail *UK*; **4, 5** kick pleat; **4, 6** long sleeve, puff sleeve; **5-5** shirtfront; **5, 6** patch pocket, short sleeve; **6, 6** dolmen sleeve, raglan sleeve; **7, 4** trouser cuff.

part of speech 4 noun, verb; **5** affix, infix, modal; **6** adverb, copula, dative, object, plural, prefix, suffix; **7** adjunct, article, pronoun, subject; **8** ablative, genitive, modifier, particle, preterit, vocative; **9** adjective, formative, intensive, predicate, preterite *UK*, qualifier; **10** accusative, complement, determiner, diminutive, indicative, infinitive, nominative, participle, prenominal; **11** conditional, conjunction, preposition, subjunctive, substantive; **12** augmentative, interjection, intransitive; **PHRASES: 4, 10** past participle; **6, 4** common noun, proper noun; **6, 6** direct object; **7, 4** phrasal verb; **8, 6** indirect object; **8, 7** definite article; **9, 4** reflexive verb; **10, 4** collective noun, transitive verb.

party 2 do; **3** ANC, BBQ, bop, hop, man, mob, set; **4** ball, band, bash, bloc, body, camp, cell, crew, gala, gang, line, orgy, rave, sect, team, unit, wall, wing; **5** beano, bunch, cabal, cadre, dance, debut, disco, event, feast, group, guild, junta, squad; **6** barbie, caucus, circle, clique, kegger, masque, quango *UK*, search, shindy, smoker, soirée, troupe; **7** banquet, blowout, ceilidh, company, faction, funfest, gabfest, hoedown, shindig; **8** alliance, barbecue, jamboree, movement, musicale, wingding; **9** beanfeast *UK*, committee, festivity, gathering, reception; **10** federation, masquerade; **11** association, cornhusking, discotheque, partnership; **12** presentation; **13** entertainment; **PHRASES: 2, 4** at home; **3, 5** hen ~ *UK*, tea ~; **3-8** get-together; **4, 3** open day; **4, 4** hunt ball; **4, 5** barn dance, lawn ~, open house, stag ~; **4, 6** baby shower; **4-7** barn-raising; **4, 9** fête champêtre; **5-2** knees-up *UK*; **5, 5** block ~, Green ~, house ~, third ~; **5-5, 5** fancy-dress ~; **5-7** house-raising, house-warming; **5, 8** ~ politics; **6, 3** coming out; **6, 4** masked ball; **6, 5** bottle ~ *UK*, dinner ~ *UK*, drinks ~ *UK*, firing ~ *UK*, garden ~, Labour ~, square dance, supper ~, wienie roast; **6, 6** coffee klatch; **7, 5** costume ~, Liberal ~, wedding ~, weekend ~, working ~; **7, 6** potluck dinner; **8, 5** bachelor ~, birthday ~, cocktail ~, surprise ~, tailgate ~; **9, 5** Communist ~; **10, 5** Democratic ~, Republican ~; **12, 5** bachelorette ~.

pass 2 go, OK; **3** col, die, end, fly, gap; **4** drag, emit, flow, gate, neck, okay, omit; **5** allow, cross, notch, skirt, throw; **6** defile, elapse, exceed, expire, finish, Khyber, permit, ticket; **7** approve, Brenner, pathway, qualify, Simplon, succeed; **8** continue, graduate, overhaul, overtake, passport; **9** disappear, intervene; **11** predicament, proposition; **PHRASES: 2, 7** St Bernard; **3, 2** fly by; **3, 3** die out, run out; **3, 3, 6** run its course; **3, 4** get past; **3, 7** get through; **4, 2** drag on, hand on, ~ by, roll by, roll on; **4, 3, 5** make the grade; **4, 4** ~ away; **4, 7** move through, ~ through; **5, 2** flash by; **5, 2, 3, 4** leave on one side; **5, 7** shoot through *UK*; **6, 7** become extinct; **7, 2, 4** sleight of hand.

passable 2 OK; **3** fit; **4** fair; **6** decent, enough; **8** adequate, suitable; **9** competent, tolerable; **10** sufficient; **11** appropriate; **12** satisfactory; **PHRASES: 2, 2, 3, 4** up to the mark; **3, 3** not bad; **3, 5** all right.

passage 4 beat, duct, fare, hall, lane, part, path, trip; **5** aisle, alley, entry, piece, quote, route; **6** arcade, bridge, flight, voyage; **7** archway, channel, episode, excerpt, extract, ingress, journey, osmosis, passing, portion, section, transit; **8** corridor, crossing, entrance, movement, progress, traverse; **9** quotation; **10** endosmosis, permeation, traversing; **11** penetration, percolation, transfusion; **12** infiltration,

intervention, transcursion, transduction, transference, transmission, transudation; **13** perambulation; **PHRASES: 4, 7** back ~ *UK*. *See also* **passageway**

passage of time *See* passing of time

passageway 3 gap, way; **4** adit, arch, duct, exit, flue, gate, hose, pass, pipe, tube, vein, vent; **5** aisle, colon, drain, gorge, porch, sewer, stoma; **6** artery, defile, dormer, funnel, portal, subway *UK*, throat, tunnel, ureter, window; **7** chimney, conduit, doorway, foxhole, gallery, gangway, hallway, manhole, passage, postern, transom, walkway; **8** corridor, entrance, molehole, pipeline, skylight, windpipe; **9** breezeway, esophagus, mousehole, smokehole, underpass; **10** intestines, rabbithole, smokestack; **12** chimneystack; **PHRASES: 3, 4** air walk; **4, 5** anal canal; **5, 4** sperm duct; **10, 5** alimentary canal.

passenger *See* traveler

passing 4 loss; **5** brief, death, dying, hasty, quick, rapid, short; **6** demise, expiry, moving; **7** cursory, hurried; **8** crossing, elapsing, fleeting; **9** ephemeral, transient, vanishing; **10** acceptable, expiration *UK*, overtaking, proceeding, traversing; **11** transducing, transilient; **12** ratification, transferring; **PHRASES: 5-5** short-lived; **7, 4** ~ bell, ~ note, ~ shot.

passion 3 fad, ire, yen; **4** fire, fury, heat, love, lust, rage, zeal; **5** anger, ardor, mania, wrath; **6** desire, fervor, hunger; **8** appetite; **10** enthusiasm; **PHRASES: 2, 4** St John; **2, 7** St Matthew; **7, 4** P~ play, P~ week; **7, 5** ~ fruit; **7, 6** P~ Sunday.

passionate 3 OTT *UK*; **4** keen; **5** fiery, manic; **6** ardent, heated, loving, raging, raving, torrid, touchy; **7** devoted, envious, fervent, intense, jealous, zealous, zestful; **8** ecstatic, effusive, inflamed, inspired, obsessed, seething, spirited, unstable, vehement, vigorous, volatile; **9** committed, emotional, excitable, fanatical, hotheaded, impetuous, mercurial, rapturous; **10** hysterical; **11** impassioned; **12** enthusiastic, melodramatic; **13** temperamental; **PHRASES: 4-3-3** over-the-top; **4-7** warm-blooded.

passive 5 inert; **8** inactive; **9** reflexive; **11** unreceptive.

Passover 5 Pasch; **6** Pesach.

passport 2 ID; **4** pass, visa; **6** papers, permit; **9** clearance; **13** documentation; **PHRAS-**

ES: 4, 7 safe conduct; **7, 6** laissez passer; **9, 6** clearance papers.

past 2 ex; **3** ago, eld, old; **4** gone, over; **5** early, elder, ended, olden, passé; **6** bygone, lapsed, lately, primal; **7** ancient, defunct, earlier, expired, extinct, history; **8** finished, formerly, historic, obsolete, primeval, recently, yestreen; **9** aforetime, antiquity, primitive, yesterday; **10** historical, prehistory, yesteryear; **11** prehistoric, retroactive; **12** protohistory; **13** prehistorical, protohistoric; **PHRASES: 2, 4** no more; **2, 5, 4, 2** in times gone by; **3, 3** old hat; **3-4** has-been; **3, 5** old story; **4, 2, 1, 4** dead as a dodo; **4, 3, 2, 4** time out of mind; **4, 3, 4** dead and gone; **4, 3, 4, 4** over and done with; **4, 3, 6** dead and buried; **4, 10** time immemorial; **5, 4** olden days; **6, 3** golden age; **6, 5** former times; **7, 5** ancient times; **10, 4** yesterday's news.

past (in the past) 1, 5, 3 a while ago; **2, 3** of old; **2, 4, 2, 4** in days of yore; **3, 5, 3** the other day; **4, 3** ages ago, long ago; **4, 4, 1, 4** once upon a time; **4, 4, 3** some time ago; **4, 5** long since.

past (thing of the past) 4 fogy, ruin; **5** fogey, relic; **6** barrow, dolmen, eolith, menhir, relict, tholos; **7** antique, pyramid, remains; **8** artifact, cromlech, dinosaur, megalith, monument, survival, vestiges, ziggurat; **9** arrowhead, earthwork, microlith, remainder; **10** Stonehenge; **PHRASES: 6, 5** museum piece; **6, 7** burial chamber; **7, 4** ancient ruin; **7, 5** ancient flint; **7, 8** ancient monument **UK**; **8, 5** standing stone(s).

pasta 4 pipe; **5** dough, penne; **6** bigoli, ditali, noodle, risoni, rotini; **7** capelli, fusilli, lasagna, lasagne **UK**, lumache, noodles, pastina, ravioli, rotelle; **8** bucatini, ditalini, ditaloni, farfalle, fettucce, fidelini, gramigna, linguine, macaroni, rigatoni, stelline, taglioni, trenette; **9** agnolotti, annellini, manicotti, spaghetti, tuffoloni; **10** cannelloni, conchiglie, cravattine, farfalline, fettuccine, tagliolini, tortellini, tortelloni, vermicelli; **11** cappelletti, orecchiette, pappardelle, spaghettini, spaghettone, tagliatelle, tortiglioni; **PHRASES: 6, 1, 5** paglia e fieno.

paste 3 gum; **4** glue, pâté, pulp, size; **5** glair, glaze, punch, stick; **6** batter, filler, slurry, spread; **8** adhesive, emulsion, marzipan; **10** rhinestone, simulation.

pastern 6, 4 fetter bone.

pastime 4 game; **5** hobby, sport; **8** activity, sideline; **9** amusement, diversion; **10** recreation; **13** entertainment.

pastor *See* **minister**

pastry 4 cake, flan; **5** choux, flaky, fleur, pasty **UK**; **6** phyllo; **10** shortcrust; **PHRASES: 4, 4** puff tart; **4, 5, 6** suet crust ~; **5, 4, 6** rough puff ~; **6, 6** cheese ~, Danish ~; **7, 6** Genoese ~.

pasty 3 wan; **4** pale; **5** ashen; **6** pallid; **PHRASES: 7, 5** Cornish ~ **UK**.

pat 3 tap; **4** mold, work; **5** knead, shape, touch; **6** caress, smooth, stroke; **7** massage; **8** fluently; **9** perfectly; **10** impeccably; **11** faultlessly; **PHRASES: 2, 5** by heart.

patch 3 bed, bit, lot; **4** area, darn, mark, mend, plot, spot, time, vamp; **5** cover, phase, place, speck, spell, stain, tract; **6** blotch, cobble, period, repair, smudge, solder, tinker; **7** speckle; **PHRASES: 3, 2** sew up; **5, 4** ~ test; **5, 6** ~ pocket.

patchwork *See* **mixture**

pate *See* **head**

patella 7 kneecap, kneepan.

patent 5 clear, right; **7** blatant, charter, obvious; **8** flagrant; **9** barefaced, copyright.

pater *See* **father**

paterfamilias 4 head; **6** father; **7** headman; **11** paternalist.

path 3 rut, way; **4** berm, lane, road; **5** track, trail; **6** bridle, bypath **UK**, flight, groove, towing; **7** calling, footway, passage, pathway, towpath; **8** footpath, pavement **UK**, sidewalk; **9** direction, racetrack; **10** racecourse; **PHRASES: 3, 4** sea lane, sea ~; **5, 4** flare ~, glide ~; **6, 4** bridle ~; **6, 5** hiking trail, racing track; **7, 4** bicycle ~; **8, 4** primrose ~, shipping lane.

pathetic 3 sad; **4** poor; **5** sorry; **6** feeble, moving, paltry, woeful; **7** piteous, pitiful; **8** pitiable, poignant, touching, wretched; **9** miserable, plaintive; **10** deplorable, despicable, inadequate; **12** contemptible.

pathfinder 5 guide, scout; **6** leader; **7** pioneer; **11** trailblazer.

pathological 5 viral; **6** morbid; **7** extreme, medical; **8** allergic, clinical, systemic; **10** compulsive, diagnostic, scientific; **11** unreasoning; **12** uncontrolled, unreasonable; **13** immunological.

pathology 7 therapy; **8** etiology, nosology; **9** diagnosis, prognosis; **12** bacteriology, epidemiology, parasitology.

pathos 7 anguish, despair, sadness, tragedy; 9 bleakness.

patience 8 stoicism; 9 composure, disregard, endurance, tolerance; 10 indulgence; 11 forbearance, overlooking.

patient 4 calm, case; 5 stoic; 6 client; 7 invalid; 8 resigned, tolerant; 9 unhurried; 10 forbearing, persistent; PHRASES: 2-7 in-patient; 3-7 out-patient; 4, 6 sick person; 4-9 long-suffering; 7, 8 P~ Griselda; 8, 4 terminal case.

patois 4 cant; 5 argot, idiom, slang; 6 jargon, patter; 7 dialect; 8 language; 10 vernacular.

patriarch 4 head; 6 bishop, father, leader; 7 headman, prelate; 10 archbishop; 13 paterfamilias; PHRASES: 4, 2, 6 head of family.

patrician *See* **noble**

patriotism 7 loyalty; 8 jingoism; 10 xenophobia; 11 nationalism; 12 partisanship.

patrol 4 beat, tour, unit; 5 guard, round, squad, troop, watch; 7 circuit; 10 detachment; 13 perambulation; PHRASES: 4, 3, 6 make the rounds.

patrol wagon 5, 5 paddy wagon; 6, 5 police wagon.

patron 5 angel; 6 backer, client; 7 shopper, sponsor; 8 advocate, champion, customer; 9 supporter; 10 benefactor.

patronage 5 aegis, trade; 6 client; 7 backing, support; 8 abetment, advocacy, auspices, customer, tutelage; 9 clientele, fosterage, seconding; 11 countenance, sponsorship; 12 championship; 13 encouragement, subsidization; PHRASES: 6, 4 client base; 8, 6 consumer demand.

patter 3 tap; 4 beat, cant, drum, rant; 5 slang; 6 jabber, jargon, patois, rhythm, speech; 7 prattle; PHRASES: 6, 2 rattle on; 6-6 pitter-patter.

pattern 4 form, lace, mold, norm, plan; 5 array, check, draft, guide, model, motif; 6 Argyle, design, detail, diaper, format, mosaic, scheme, system; 7 example, molding, Paisley, program, stencil, tracery; 8 appliqué, exemplar, filigree, lacework, ornament, paradigm, smocking, tapestry, template; 9 benchmark, blueprint, guideline, patchwork, pinstripe, pokerwork *UK*, structure, tattooing; 10 decoration; 11 herringbone; PHRASES: 4, 5 dog's tooth; 6, 5

hound's tooth; 6, 7 willow ~.

patty 3 pie; 4 cake; 5 pasty *UK*; 6 burger, pastry; 7 rissole.

paunch *See* **stomach**

pauper 3 bum; 5 lazar, tramp; 6 beggar; 7 vagrant; 8 bankrupt, indigent, squatter; 9 insolvent, mendicant; PHRASES: 3, 4 bag lady; 4-3-3 down-and-out; 4-7 slum-dweller; 4, 8 poor relation; 6, 5 church mouse; 8, 6 homeless person.

pause 3 gap, nap; 4 lull, rest, stay, stop; 5 break, delay, letup, relax, sleep, space, truce; 6 hiatus, lacuna, recess; 7 adjourn, caesura, fermata, holiday *UK*, interim, leisure, respite, suspend; 8 breather, interval, vacation; 9 armistice, ceasefire, interlude, interrupt; 10 moratorium, suspension; 12 intermission, interruption; PHRASES: 3, 2 let up; 3, 3 day off; 3, 4 lay over; 4, 1, 5 have a break, take a break; 4, 1, 8 take a breather; 4, 2 hold up; 4, 3 cool off, time off, time out; 4, 4 hang fire, hold back, stop over, take five; 5, 4 cease fire; 6, 6 closed season; 7, 4 leisure time; 7, 6 interim period; 9, 5 breathing space *UK*.

pavement 8 sidewalk.

paving 3 tar; 4 flag, sett; 6 cement, cobble, gravel, Tarmac *tm*; 7 asphalt, macadam; 8 blacktop, concrete, pavement, sidewalk; 9 chippings, flagstone, surfacing; 11 cobblestone; PHRASES: 4, 7 road surface; 5, 6 crazy ~ *UK*; 8, 5 stepping stone; 8, 6 Portland cement.

paw 3 pet; 4 fist, hand, maul, mitt; 6 fondle, molest, stroke.

pawn 1 P; 3 pop; 4 dupe, gage, hock, tool; 5 piece; 6 pledge, puppet, stooge; 7 hostage; 8 mortgage.

pay 3 fee, tip; 4 foot, give, meet, perk, wage; 5 bonus, bribe, honor, remit, repay, spend, stand, wages; 6 barter, expend, income, payoff, payout, redeem, reward, salary; 7 advance, alimony, annuity, bursary, credits, payroll, pension, profits, requite, returns, revenue, royalty, stipend, takings; 8 disburse, dividend, earnings, gratuity, proceeds, receipts, winnings; 9 allowance, discharge, emolument, indemnify, restitute, retaliate, severance, subscribe; 10 commission, compensate, honorarium, perquisite, remunerate; 11 maintenance, scholarship; 12 remuneration; PHRASES: 2, 6, 7 ex gratia payment; 3, 2, 4 ~ in kind; 3, 2, 5

~ on sight; **3, 2, 6** ~ on demand; **3, 3** lay out, ~ bed *UK*; **3, 4** ~ back, ~ cash, ~ dirt, ~ slip, put down; **3, 5** ~ check, pin money; **3, 6** ~ dearly; **3, 8** ~ envelope; **4, 2** ante up; **4, 3** back ~, fork out, sick ~; **4, 4** fork over; **4-4, 3** take-home ~; **4, 6** come across, make amends; **5, 2** cough up, stump up *UK*; **5, 3** shell out; **5, 4, 6** empty one's pocket; **5, 7** child support; **6, 2** settle up; **6, 3, 4** grease the palm; **6, 5** golden hello, pocket money; **6, 7** fringe benefit; **6, 9** golden handcuffs, golden handshake, golden parachute; **9, 3** severance ~; **10, 3** redundancy ~.

pay (be unable to pay) 4 fail, sink; **5** break, crash; **8** collapse; PHRASES: **2, 2, 3, 4** go to the wall; **2, 4** go bust; **2, 5, 2** go belly up; **2, 8** go bankrupt; **4, 2** wind up; **4, 4, 7** fall into arrears.

pay (not pay) 4 bilk; **5** welsh; **6** decamp, divert, levant; **7** abscond, default, defraud, swindle; **8** embezzle; **9** defalcate, sequester; PHRASES: **5, 5** evade taxes.

payable 3 due; **4** owed; **5** owing; **10** redeemable, refundable, remittable.

pay back 5 repay; **6** refund, return; **7** requite, restore, revenge; **9** indemnify, reimburse, restitute, retaliate; **10** compensate, recompense; PHRASES: **3, 4** get even; **6, 3, 5** settle the score; **6, 8** settle accounts.

payer 6 bursar, purser; **7** cashier; **9** paymaster, treasurer.

payment 3 COD, fee; **4** ante, cost, giro, rent; **5** bonus, money, price, tithe; **6** appeal, charge, EFTPOS, outlay, paying, payoff, payout, reward, salary; **7** deposit, earnest, guerdon, handsel *UK*, plastic, premium, receipt, release, tribute; **8** defrayal, dividend, donation, offering; **9** clearance, defraying, discharge, emolument, quittance; **10** collection, defrayment, remittance, settlement; **11** acquittance, expenditure, installment, liquidation, receivables; **12** compensation, contribution, disbursement, remuneration, satisfaction, subscription; PHRASES: **4, 2, 8** cash on delivery; **4-5** whip-round *UK*; **4, 7** cash ~, down ~; **4, 10** full settlement; **6, 5** direct debit; **7, 2, 4** ~ in kind, receipt in full; **7, 7** advance ~, overdue ~, partial ~; **8, 5** standing order.

pay off 4 meet; **5** clear, honor; **6** redeem, settle; **7** satisfy; **9** discharge, liquidate; PHRASES: **3, 2** pay up; **3, 2, 4** pay in full; **5, 1, 4** honor a bill; **6, 2, 7** settle an account.

pay one's way 2, 5 go Dutch; **3, 1, 5** buy a round; **3, 4, 5** pay one's share; **5, 1, 5** stand a round; **5, 8** share expenses.

PB 4 lead.

PC 7 percent; **8** postcard; PHRASES: **5, 4** petty cash.

pea 5, 3 sweet ~. *See also* **pulse**

peace 3 pax; **4** dove, lamb, rest; **5** amity, demob, Irene, order, quiet, truce; **6** ahimsa, Eirene, pardon, repose; **7** amnesty, calumet, concord, harmony, irenics, silence; **8** pacifism, serenity; **9** armistice, peacetime, stillness; **10** friendship, neutrality, quiescence; **11** coexistence, disarmament, forgiveness, nonviolence, peacemaking, restfulness, tranquility; **12** indifference, nonalignment, pacification, peacefulness; **13** nonaggression, noninvolvment, peaceableness; **14** demobilization; **15** nonintervention; PHRASES: **3, 6** Pax Romana; **3, 9** Pax Americana; **3, 10** Pax Britannica; **5, 2, 4** ~ of mind; **5, 3, 5** ~ and quiet; **5, 4** ~ camp *UK*, ~ pipe, ~ sign, white flag; **5, 5** P~ Corps, ~ talks; **5, 6** civvy street *UK*, olive branch, ~ treaty; **5, 8** ~ offering; **5, 9** ~ agreement; **5, 10** armed neutrality; **6, 5** broken arrow, golden times.

peace (make peace) 5 agree; **6** disarm, pacify; **7** mediate; **9** surrender; **10** compromise, demobilize, plowshares; **12** demilitarize; PHRASES: **3, 3, 4** ban the bomb; **3, 3, 5** sue for peace; **3, 4, 4, 4** lay down one's arms; **3, 5** cry quits; **4, 1, 4** make a deal; **4, 2** cool it; **4, 2, 5** call it quits; **4, 3, 4, 2** kiss and make up; **4, 3, 7** bury the hatchet; **4, 7** make friends, meet halfway; **5, 2, 2** break it up; **5, 2, 6** agree to differ; **5, 2, 8** agree to disagree; **5, 5** shake hands; **7, 3, 5** sheathe the sword.

peaceful 4 calm, mild; **5** palmy, quiet, still; **6** golden, irenic, piping, prewar, serene; **7** amiable, halcyon, liberal, neutral, pacific, passive, postwar, unarmed; **8** civilian, dovelike, friendly, harmless, innocent, pacifist, tolerant, tranquil; **9** agreeable, bloodless, peaceable, peacetime, placatory, quiescent, unwarlike; **10** antebellum, harmonious, nonaligned, nonviolent, postbellum, submissive, submitting, unmilitant, unmilitary; **11** inoffensive, peacemaking, unresisting; **12** conciliatory, noncombatant, unaggressive; **13** nonaggressive, uncompetitive, uncontentious.

peacemaker *See* **negotiator**

peace offering 5 mercy; **6** pardon; **7** amnesty, calumet, wergild; **8** clemency, irenicon *UK*, leniency; **9** atonement; **10**

reparation; **11** forgiveness, restitution; **12** compensation, friendliness; PHRASES: **4, 2, 5** dove of peace, flag of truce; **4, 3, 5** plea for peace; **4, 5** easy terms *UK*, fair offer; **4, 6** full pardon; **5, 4** peace pipe, white flag; **5, 5** blood money; **5, 6** olive branch; **5, 8** peace overture.

peace pipe 7 calumet.

peach 3 wow; **5** pearl; **6** beauty; **7** cracker *UK*; **9** humdinger.

peak 3 ben *UK*, cap, tip, top, tor *UK*; **4** acme, apex, crag, knap; **5** crest, droop; **6** summit, zenith; **8** languish, mountain, pinnacle, protrude; **9** culminate. *See also* **mountain**

peal 4 call, clap, ring, toll; **5** chime, clang; **8** carillon, handbell.

peanut 6 goober; **9** groundnut; PHRASES: **6, 3** monkey nut *UK*.

pear 4 Bosc; **8** Bartlett, bergamot; PHRASES: **6, 4** Seckel ~; **7, 4** anchovy ~, avocado ~, prickly ~; **8, 4** Williams ~ *UK*; **9, 4** alligator ~; **10, 4** conference ~.

pearly 7 shining; **8** gleaming, lustrous; **10** iridescent; **11** translucent.

peasant 6 farmer, rustic; **7** crofter, laborer; **10** farmworker, provincial; PHRASES: **4, 4** farm hand; **7-7** country-dweller.

pebble *See* **stone**

peccadillo *See* **sin**

peck 3 dig, eat, jab; **4** bite, blow, kiss, poke; **5** brush; **6** caress, nibble, stroke; **8** osculate.

peculiar 3 odd, own, rum; **5** droll, funny, queer, weird; **6** proper; **7** bizarre, erratic, offbeat, special, strange, unusual; **8** distinct, especial, singular, specific; **9** anomalous, different, eccentric, exclusive, irregular; **10** irrational, unbalanced; **11** appropriate, paradoxical; **14** characteristic.

pedagogue *See* **teacher**

pedal 4 ride; **5** cycle, drive, guide, lever, steer; **6** device, propel; **7** control, operate, treadle.

pedant 7 scholar, sophist; **9** nitpicker; **10** obfuscator; **11** doctrinaire; **12** hairsplitter, theoretician.

pedantic 5 fussy, legal, rigid; **6** cogent, lawful, severe, strict; **7** weighty; **8** exacting, forceful, rigorous; **9** quibbling; **10** legitimate, meticulous; PHRASES: **3-7** nit-picking; **4-9** hair-splitting; **7-6** literal-minded.

peddle 4 hawk, hype, sell, tout, vend; **6** market, retail; **7** espouse, promote.

peddler 6 bagman, hawker, pedlar *UK*, seller, sutler, tinker; **7** chapman, junkman; **8** huckster, traveler; **10** colporteur; **12** costermonger *UK*; PHRASES: **3-3-4, 3** rag-and-bone man; **5-4** cheap-jack; **5-6** stall-keeper; **6, 3** barrow boy *UK*; **6, 6** market trader, street seller, street vendor.

pedestal 4 base, dais; **5** stand; **6** plinth; **8** platform.

pedestrian 4 dull; **5** hiker; **6** ambler, walker; **7** rambler, strider; **8** ordinary; **10** uninspired; **13** unimaginative.

pedigree 5 noble; **7** history, lineage; **8** ancestry, purebred; **10** derivation; **12** aristocratic, thoroughbred; PHRASES: **4-7** full-blooded.

peek *See* **glance**

peel 4 bark, molt, rind, shed, skin; **5** flake, scale, scalp, shell, strip; **6** scrape, slough; **7** undress; **8** exuviate; **9** excoriate, exfoliate; **10** desquamate; **11** decorticate; PHRASES: **4, 3** cast off, pick off; **4, 8** lose feathers; **5, 3** flake off, scale off, throw off.

peep 4 look, peek, peer, word; **5** cheep, chirp, noise, tweet; **6** glance, squeak; **7** chirrup, glimpse, twitter; PHRASES: **5, 1, 4** sneak a look, steal a look.

peepul 2, 4 bo tree.

peer 3 pry, spy; **4** duke, earl, gaze, lady, look, lord, peek, peep; **5** baron, equal, noble, snoop, stare, study; **6** regard, squint; **7** baronet, duchess, marquis; **8** baroness, countess, marquess, viscount; **10** aristocrat; **11** marchioness, viscountess.

peevish *See* **irritable**

peewee 6, 4 magpie lark.

peewit 7 lapwing.

peg 3 fix, leg, nog, pin, tee, tot; **4** clip, nail; **5** cleat, piton, spile, thole; **6** spigot; **8** Margaret.

pelt 3 fur; **4** coat, hair, hide, pour, skin; **6** assail, attack, strafe; **7** assault, bombard, cascade; PHRASES: **6, 4** bucket down *UK*.

pen 3 Bic *TM*, nib, run, sty; **4** biro, cage, coop, fold, poet, swan; **5** hutch, plume, quill, write; **6** author, corral, kennel, pigpen, pigsty *UK*, prison, scribe, writer; **7** compose, confine, paddock; **8** scribble; **9** ballpoint, enclosure; PHRASES: **3, 3** ~ pal; **3, 4** ~ name; **3, 6** ~ friend; **4-3** felt-tip; **8, 3**

fountain ~; **9, 3** cartridge ~.

penal *See* **punitive**

penalize 3 fix; **4** fine, gate; **6** avenge, ground, punish, settle; **7** condemn; **8** handicap, sentence; **9** retaliate; **10** discipline; PHRASES: **4, 4, 2** come down on; **4, 4, 4, 2** come down hard on; **5, 2, 4** bring to book; **5, 3, 4, 2** throw the book at; **6, 1, 7** impose a penalty; **6, 4** settle with.

penalty 4 fine; **5** costs, price; **6** hansel *UK*, ransom; **7** damages, forfeit, handsel *UK*, payment, penance; **8** sanction, sentence; **9** liability; **10** obligation, punishment, sentencing; **11** restitution, restoration; **12** compensation, condemnation.

penance 7 seppuku, suicide; **8** sentence; **9** atonement, purgation; **10** asceticism, punishment, reparation; **11** prostration; **12** flagellation, purification; **13** mortification; PHRASES: **4, 2, 2** felo de se; **4-4** hara-kiri; **4-10** self-discipline, self-punishment; **6-7** breast-beating.

penance (do penance) 5 atone; **6** repent; PHRASES: **4, 1, 4, 5** wear a hair shirt; **4, 4, 6** beat one's breast; **4, 6** make amends; **4, 9** wear sackcloth; **6, 7** punish oneself; **7, 7** scourge oneself.

penchant *See* **liking**

pencil 4 draw, mark; **5** color, write.

pending 4 till; **5** until; **6** during; **8** awaiting, expected, imminent; **9** impending, undecided; **10** incomplete, throughout, unresolved; **11** approaching.

pendulous 5 loose; **7** hanging; **8** drooping, swinging, wavering; **9** uncertain, undecided; **11** overhanging, uncommitted, vacillating.

pendulum 3 bob; **7** pendant; **9** metronome; **10** oscillator.

penetrate 3 cut; **4** bite, bore; **5** enter, imbue, probe, touch; **6** impale; **8** permeate; **10** infiltrate.

penetrating 5 acute; **7** osmotic; **8** piercing; **10** permeating; **11** intervening, percolating; **12** infiltrating, transudating.

penetration 6 access, acumen, breach; **7** insight; **8** entrance, invasion; **9** diffusion, incursion; **10** astuteness, dispersion, perception, permeation, saturation, shrewdness; **11** discernment; **12** infiltration, infringement, intelligence; **13** comprehension, dissemination, understanding.

peninsula 4 bill, cape, head, hook, mull, neck, spit, spur; **5** point; **6** tongue; **7** isthmus; **8** foreland, headland, sandspit; **10** chersonese, projection, promontory; PHRASES: **4, 2, 4, 4** Cape of Good Hope; **4, 2, 7** Hook of Holland; **4, 4** Cape Horn; **5, 2, 4** point of land; **8, 4** Portland Bill.

penis 3 rod; **4** knob, tool; **5** organ, peter, prick; **6** member, pecker, weapon; **7** chopper, phallus; PHRASES: **4, 6** John Thomas *UK*.

penitence 5 guilt, pangs, shame; **6** qualms, regret; **7** apology, regrets, remorse; **8** scruples; **9** apologies; **10** confession, contrition, conversion, regretting, repentance; **11** compunction, recantation, reformation; PHRASES: **3, 10** bad conscience; **4, 5** hair shirt; **4-8** self-reproach; **4-9** soul-searching; **4-10** self-accusation; **5, 8** guilt feelings; **6, 2, 5** change of heart; **6, 7** abject apology, humble apology; **8, 7** grudging apology. *See also* **penitent**

penitent 5 sorry; **6** guilty, rueful; **7** ashamed; **8** contrite, reformed, shameful; **9** confessed, converted, lamenting, reclaimed, regretful, remorsing, repentant, repenting, sorrowful; **10** apologetic, confessing, regenerate, regretting, remorseful, shamefaced; **12** compunctious; PHRASES: **4, 2, 7** full of regrets, full of remorse; **4-5** born-again; **4-8** self-accusing; **4-10** self-condemning; **4-11** self-reproachful.

penitent (be penitent) 6 recant, reform, regret, repent; **7** confess; **9** apologize; PHRASES: **2, 7** do penance; **3, 3, 3** rue the day; **3, 3, 5** see the light; **4, 1, 5, 5** make a fresh start; **4, 6** feel guilty; **4, 7** feel remorse; **5, 4, 6** learn one's lesson; **5, 5** think again; **5, 6, 2** think better of; **7, 4, 4** confess one's sins.

penitent person 7 ascetic; **8** magdalen *UK*, penitent; **9** confessor; **10** flagellant; PHRASES: **8, 3** prodigal son; **8, 6** contrite sinner.

penniless *See* **poor**

pennon *See* **flag**

Pennsylvania 2 PA; **7** hemlock (tree); **10** Harrisburg (capital); PHRASES: **6, 6** ruffed grouse (bird); **6, 7, 3, 12** Virtue, Liberty and Independence (motto); **8, 5** Keystone State (nickname); **8, 6** mountain laurel (flower).

penny 1 D, P; **4** cent; **5** pence; PHRASES: **3, 5** new ~; **5, 5** ~ black *UK*; **5, 6** ~ arcade; **5, 7** ~ whistle.

penny-pinching *See* **parsimonious**

pennywort 9 navelwort.

pensioner 3 OAP *UK*. *See also* **old person**

pensive *See* **thoughtful**

people 3 kin, men; **4** bods, clan, folk, ones, race, some; **5** demos, plebs, tribe; **6** family, nation, public, settle; **7** inhabit, society; **8** humanity, populace, populate; **9** humankind, plebeians; **10** commonalty, population; **11** bourgeoisie, proletariat; PHRASES: **3, 6** the masses; **3-6** hoi-polloi; **3, 6, 6** the common ~; **3, 7** the commons; **4-4** have-nots; **5-5** grass-roots; **5, 6** lower orders; **5, 8** great unwashed; **6, 4** vulgar herd; **7, 7** working classes.

pep *See* **energy**

pepper 5 spray; **6** infuse, shower; **7** scatter, speckle; **8** sprinkle; **9** interfuse, interlace; **10** interleave; **11** intersperse.

per 2 by; **4** each; **7** through.

perceive 3 see; **4** feel, hear; **5** grasp, sense; **6** descry, divine, intuit, notice, remark; **7** discern, observe, realize; **9** apprehend, recognize; **10** understand; **11** distinguish.

percentage 4 part, take; **5** ratio; **6** profit; **7** section; **8** fraction; **10** commission, proportion.

perception 4 view; **5** angle, grasp, sense; **6** notice, remark, seeing; **7** feeling, insight; **9** awareness, intuition; **10** astuteness, divination, shrewdness; **11** discernment, observation, realization, recognition; **12** appreciation, apprehension, perspicacity; **13** consciousness, understanding.

perceptive 4 deep, keen; **5** acute, aware, canny, sharp; **6** clever, shrewd; **7** refined; **8** delicate, profound; **9** sensitive; **10** discerning, fastidious, insightful, meticulous, responsive.

perch 3 rod, sit; **4** bass, fish, pole, rest; **5** roost; **6** alight, branch, settle.

perchance 7 perhaps; **8** possibly; PHRASES: **2, 2, 3, 2** as it may be; **2, 2, 3, 6** as it may chance, as it may happen; **2, 3, 4, 3, 2** as the case may be; **2, 3, 5** in any event; **3, 3, 3, 5** for all one knows; **8, 7** whatever happens.

percolate 4 ooze, seep, soak; **5** leach; **6** filter, strain; **8** permeate; **10** infiltrate.

percussion 7 beating, hitting; **8** drumming, striking.

perdition *See* **hell**

peremptory *See* **authoritative**

perennial 8 constant; **9** perpetual, recurrent, returning; **10** persistent.

perfect 2 A1; **3** set, top; **4** best, full, pure, ripe, trim, true; **5** crown, exact, final, godly, ideal, model, ready, ripen, sound, tight, total, utter, whole; **6** define, detail, entire, expert, finish, intact, mature, polish, refine, square, superb, unhurt; **7** achieve, classic, correct, execute, fulfill, improve, matured, pattern, precise, realize, rectify, ripened, saintly, sinless, skilled, sublime, supreme, unmixed; **8** absolute, accurate, airtight, Augustan, champion, complete, dazzling, finished, flawless, innocent, masterly, peerless, pinpoint, polished, skillful, spotless, standard, unbroken, unflawed, unmarked, unmarred; **9** blameless, brilliant, classical, completed, elaborate, excellent, exemplary, faultless, fulfilled, guiltless, impeccant, perfected, seaworthy, unalloyed, undamaged, unequaled, unmatched, unrivaled, unscarred, unscathed, unspoiled, unspotted, unstained, untainted; **10** accomplish, ameliorate, archetypal, consummate, immaculate, impeccable, infallible, proficient, scatheless, watertight; **11** unblemished, unscratched; **12** indefectible, transcendent, undiminished; **13** particularize, unimpeachable, unsurpassable; **14** irreproachable, uncontaminated; PHRASES: **1-2** A-OK; **2, 3, 4** in the pink; **4, 2** just so, spot on *UK*; **4, 3, 5** safe and sound; **4, 5** just right; **5, 2, 1, 4** sound as a bell; **5, 2, 4** right as rain; **5, 3** carry out; **6-3** number-one; **7, 7** present ~.

perfection 3 top; **4** acme, peak; **5** model, skill; **6** finish, polish, purity, summit, zenith; **7** essence, extreme, mastery, paragon, pattern; **8** accuracy, capstone, maturity, pinnacle, standard, ultimate; **9** archetype, expertise, innocence, sainthood; **10** brilliance, completion, excellence, immaculacy, impeccancy; **11** masterpiece, perfectness, proficiency, superiority; **12** consummation, correctitude, quintessence; **13** guiltlessness, impeccability, infallibility, transcendence; PHRASES: **2, 4, 5** ne plus ultra; **3, 3, 2, 3** ten out of ten; **3, 5** the ideal; **4, 4** last word; **4-7** chef-d'oeuvre; **4, 9** mint condition. *See also* **perfect**

perfectionist 5 fussy, picky; **6** choosy, expert, master, pedant, purist; **7** maestro, precise; **8** exacting, pedantic, stickler; **9** demanding, quibbling; **10** fastidious, meticulous, particular, scrupulous; **11** punctilious; PHRASES: **4-9** hair-splitting.

perfectly 8 verbatim; **9** literally; PHRASES: **2, 1, 4** to a turn; **2, 3, 6** to the letter; **2, 10** to perfection; **4, 3, 4** word for word. *See also* **perfect**

perfidious 8 disloyal; **10** traitorous, unfaithful; **11** treacherous.

perfidy 5 lying; **6** deceit; **8** betrayal; **9** duplicity, treachery; **10** dishonesty, disloyalty.

perforation *See* **hole**

perform 2 do; **3** act; **4** meet, play, sing; **5** enact; **6** acquit, recite, render; **7** achieve, execute, fulfill, pretend, satisfy, suffice; **8** practice; **9** discharge; **10** accomplish; PHRASES: **5, 3** carry out.

performance 3 gig; **4** bill, play, prom, show, turn; **5** debut, usage; **6** custom; **7** benefit, concert, jamming, matinée, preview, reading, recital, routine; **8** practice, premiere; **9** acquittal, discharge, execution, procedure; **10** convention, exhibition, hootenanny, production, recitation; **11** composition, fulfillment, sufficiency; **12** presentation, satisfaction; **13** improvisation, orchestration.

performer 4 mime; **5** actor, mimic; **6** player; **7** actress; **12** impersonator; PHRASES: **4, 6** drag artist, mime artist.

perfume 4 musk, odor; **5** aroma, cense, scent, smell, spray; **6** embalm; **7** cologne, essence, thurify; **9** aromatize, deodorant, fragrance; **10** aftershave.

perfunctory 6 casual; **7** offhand; **9** desultory; **11** indifferent, superficial; **13** lackadaisical.

perhaps 5 haply, maybe; **6** happen, mayhap; **8** possibly; **9** perchance.

peril *See* **danger**

perimeter *See* **boundary**

period 3 age, day, eon, era, fit; **4** date, olam, span, term, time; **5** break, class, epoch, pause, space, spell, while; **6** decade; **7** century, stretch; **8** breather, interval, timespan; **9** trimester; **12** intermission, menstruation; PHRASES: **4, 4** full stop *UK*. *See also* **historical period**

period (for short periods) 8 fitfully; **11** irregularly; **12** occasionally; PHRASES: **2,** **3, 3** on and off; **2, 3, 5** at odd times; **2, 4, 3, 6** by fits and starts; **2, 8** on occasion; **3, 3, 2** off and on; **3, 3, 4** now and then; **3, 3, 5** now and again.

period (for specified periods) 5 daily; **6** hourly, weekly, yearly; **7** monthly; **8** annually; **9** quarterly; **10** biannually, biennially; **14** quinquennially.

periodic 5 daily; **6** annual, cyclic, fitful, hourly, weekly, yearly; **7** journal, monthly, regular; **8** biannual, biennial, bulletin, magazine, seasonal, sporadic; **9** irregular, iterative, recurrent, returning; **10** millennial, newsletter, periodical, repetitive; **12** intermittent, quinquennial; **13** discontinuous.

periodical 3 mag, rag; **5** daily; **6** annual, cyclic, weekly, yearly; **7** journal, monthly, regular; **8** biannual, biennial, bulletin, magazine, seasonal; **9** iterative, millenary, recurrent, returning; **10** millennial, newsletter, repetitive; **11** repetitious; **12** quinquennial; PHRASES: **7, 7** learned journal; **8, 7** academic journal. *See also* **magazine**

periodical (be periodical) 5 recur; **6** repeat, return; **7** iterate; **8** reappear; **9** reiterate; PHRASES: **4, 6, 5** come around again.

period of activity 2 go; **4** bout, term, tour, turn; **5** phase, shift, spell, stint, watch, whack; **6** inning, tenure; **7** innings, session; **8** halftime, overtime, semester, sentence; **9** trimester; PHRASES: **3-4** man-hour; **4, 2, 4** tour of duty; **4, 2, 6** term of office; **4, 5** work shift; **6, 4** fiscal year, school term; **7, 3** working day; **8, 4** academic year.

peripatetic *See* **itinerant**

peripheral 3 MTU, VDU *UK*; **4** disk *UK*, port, wand; **5** minor, modem, mouse, outer; **6** floppy, fringe, lesser, reader; **7** console, monitor, plotter, printer, scanner, tonepad, vocoder; **8** cassette, diskette, joystick, keyboard, marginal, outlying, printout, terminal; **9** bordering, cartridge, digitizer, secondary; **10** incidental, minifloppy, subsidiary, Winchester; **11** microfloppy, unimportant; **12** minidiskette; **13** microdiskette; PHRASES: **2-3** CD-ROM; **3-3, 7** ink-jet printer; **3-4, 6** bar-code reader; **4, 4** disk pack, hard disk; **4, 5** card punch, tape punch; **4, 6** data tablet, disk reader, flat screen; **4, 7** band printer, drum printer, line printer; **4, 8** tape streamer; **5, 3** light pen; **5, 7** color printer, laser printer; **6, 4** floppy disk; **6, 7** impact printer, matrix printer, serial printer.

periphery 6 border, fringe; **7** outline; **9**

outskirts; **12** surroundings; **13** circumference.

perish *See* **die**
perished *See* **cold**
perishing *See* **cold**
perjure *See* **lie**
perky **4** pert; **6** jaunty, lively; **8** cheerful; **9** energetic; PHRASES: **4-7** self-assured; **4-9** self-confident, self-important.
perlemoen **7** abalone.

permanence **5** relic; **6** fixity; **8** abidance, eternity, finality, rigidity, solidity, survival; **9** constancy, endurance, stability; **10** continuity, durability, immobility, permanency, perpetuity; **11** conservancy, continuance, immortality, persistence, reliability, subsistence; **12** conservation, entrenchment, immutability, perseverance, preservation; **13** dependability, establishment; **15** imperishability; PHRASES: **2, 6** no change; **3, 6, 3** the status quo. *See also* **permanent**

permanent **4** firm; **5** fixed, rigid, solid; **6** stable, static, steady; **7** abiding, durable, eternal, lasting, undying; **8** constant, enduring, immobile, immortal, reliable, rocklike, standing, unfading; **9** ceaseless, conserved, continual, deathless, evergreen, immovable, immutable, incessant, indelible, perennial, perpetual, preserved, steadfast, surviving, sustained, unceasing, unfailing; **10** changeless, continuing, continuous, dependable, entrenched, invariable, inviolable, persistent, persisting, stationary, subsisting, unchanging; **11** established, everlasting, persevering, sempiternal, unalterable, unbreakable, unremitting; **12** imperishable, longstanding, unchangeable; **13** incorruptible; **14** indestructible; PHRASES: **4, 2, 4** here to stay, same as ever; **4, 3, 4** here for good; **4-6** rock-steady; **4-7** long-lasting; **4-9** well-preserved; **4-11** well-established; **5, 8** still standing.

permanent (be permanent) **4** last, stay; **5** abide; **6** endure; **7** outlive, persist, subsist, survive; **8** continue; **9** persevere; PHRASES: **3, 2** set in; **4, 2, 4** come to stay; **4, 4** take root; **4, 7** last forever; **5, 3** stand pat; **5, 4** stand fast, stand firm; **5, 4, 6** stand one's ground; **6, 2, 4** remain at rest; **6, 2, 5** refuse to budge; **6, 3, 4** remain the same; **6, 6** resist change.

permanent (make permanent) **3** fix; **4** keep; **7** sustain; **8** conserve, continue,

finalize, preserve; **9** establish, stabilize; **10** immobilize, perpetuate; **11** immortalize.

permanently **6** always; **7** forever; PHRASES: **2, 1, 10** at a standstill; **2, 2** as is *UK*; **2, 3, 5** at all times; **2, 4** as ever; **2, 5** as usual; **2, 5, 3** in statu quo; **2, 6** as before; **3, 4** for good; **3, 4, 3, 3** for good and all; **3, 4, 3, 4** for ever and ever; **4, 3, 3, 3** once and for all; **5, 3, 4** still the same. *See also* **permanent**

permeate **4** fill, leak, seep; **5** flood; **6** filter, infuse; **7** pervade; **9** penetrate.

permission **3** law; **4** visa; **5** leave; **6** avowal, permit, rights; **7** consent, freedom, license, mandate, warrant; **8** approval, blessing, easiness, evidence, legality, leniency, sanction; **9** authority, clearance, endowment, equipment, exemption, reference, testimony, tolerance; **10** concession, connivance, credential, enablement, indulgence, investment, toleration, validation; **11** approbation, benevolence, declaration, empowerment, endorsement; **12** acquiescence, confirmation, dispensation, ratification; **13** authorization, corroboration, justification; **14** permissiveness; PHRASES: **3, 2** the OK; **3-2** say-so; **3, 2-5** the go-ahead; **3, 2, 8** nod of approval; **3, 3** the nod; **3, 3, 5** the all clear; **3, 4, 6** the Open Sesame; **3, 5, 4** the magic word; **3, 5, 5** the green light; **3, 6, 2** the thumbs up; **4, 4** free hand; **5, 5** blank check, green light; **5, 7** carte blanche.

permissive **3** lax; **5** loose; **7** lenient, liberal; **8** allowing, tolerant; **9** indulgent.

permit **3** let; **4** chit, mark, pass, seal, sign, visa; **5** allow, bless, clear, cross, grant, leave, stamp; **6** docket, enable, exempt, parole, patent, ratify, ticket, verify, waiver; **7** approve, charter, confirm, connive, consent, diploma, empower, endorse, entitle, license, release, voucher, warrant; **8** legalize, passport, sanction, tolerate, validate, warranty; **9** acquiesce, authorize, clearance, exemption; **10** compromise, facilitate, imprimatur, legitimize, permission; **11** certificate, corroborate, countenance, endorsement, entitlement; **12** dispensation; **13** decriminalize; **14** recommendation; PHRASES: **3, 3, 2** say yes to; **4, 3, 2-5** give the go-ahead; **4, 5** give leave, make legal; **4, 6** work ~; **4-7, 4** safe-conduct pass; **4, 8** make possible; **4, 10** give permission; **4, 11** make concessions; **5, 4** green card; **5, 6** nihil obstat; **5, 8** grant immunity; **6, 5** rubber stamp;

7, 6 laissez passer, letters patent; **7, 7** driving license, fishing license.

permitted 5 legal, legit, licit; **6** lawful, passed, patent; **7** allowed; **8** approved, licensed; **9** chartered, legalized, warranted; **10** acceptable, authorized, legitimate, sanctioned, worthwhile; **13** unconditional; **14** decriminalized; PHRASES: **5, 5** above board; **7, 7** without strings.

pernicious 4 evil; **5** fatal; **6** deadly, malign, wicked; **7** harmful; **9** insidious, malicious; **10** malevolent; **11** destructive.

peroration *See* **speech**

peroxide *See* **bleach**

perpendicular 5 erect, plumb, sheer; **6** normal, square; **7** upright; **8** vertical; **10** orthogonal; **11** rectangular; PHRASES: **5-6** right-angled.

perpetual 7 lasting; **8** unending; **10** continuous; **11** everlasting; **13** uninterrupted.

perpetuate 8 maintain, preserve; **10** eternalize; **11** immortalize, memorialize.

perplex 4 beat, faze; **5** floor, stump, worry; **6** baffle, bemuse, fuddle, gravel, puzzle, tangle; **7** confuse, flummox, mystify, nonplus; **8** befuddle, bewilder, confound; **9** bamboozle, dumbfound; **10** disconcert.

perplexity 9 blankness, confusion; **10** bafflement, puzzlement; **12** bewilderment; **13** mystification; **15** incomprehension.

persecute 5 bully; **6** harass, plague; **7** oppress, torture.

persecution 6 hassle; **7** complex, pursuit, torment, torture, tyranny; **8** vexation; **9** suffering; **10** harassment, irritation, oppression, subjection; **12** intimidation, maltreatment; **14** discrimination.

perseverance 7 stamina; **8** patience, plodding, tenacity; **9** assiduity, fortitude, obstinacy; **10** doggedness, insistence, resolution; **11** persistence, pertinacity; **12** stubbornness; **13** determination.

persevere 4 plod, plug, slog; **5** labor, stick; **6** insist, repeat; **7** iterate, persist; **8** continue; **9** reiterate; PHRASES: **3, 2, 7** die in harness; **3, 3, 3, 5** try and try again; **3, 4** peg away *UK*; **4, 2** work at; **4, 2, 2** keep at it; **4, 2, 6** keep on trying; **4, 2, 7, 2** keep on keeping on; **4, 4, 3, 3** work one's ass off; **5, 2, 3** stick it out; **6, 4, 2** hammer away at.

persevering 6 dogged; **7** patient, staunch; **8** diligent, enduring, faithful, plod-

ding, resolute, sedulous, stubborn; **9** assiduous, obstinate, strenuous, surviving, tenacious; **10** determined, persistent; **11** industrious; PHRASES: **6, 4** trying hard; **7, 2, 5** hanging in there; **8, 4** slogging away.

Persian 3 cat; **4** Gulf, lamb; **5** melon; **6** blinds, carpet, empire; **9** greyhound.

persimmon 6, 5 sharon fruit *UK*.

persist 5 labor, press; **6** endure; **7** stiffen, survive; **8** continue; **9** persevere; PHRASES: **3, 4** die hard; **3, 8** die fighting; **4, 2** hang in; **4, 3** hold out; **4, 3, 4, 2** grin and bear it; **4, 5** keep going; **5, 2** carry on; **5, 2, 3** stick it out; **5, 2, 3, 5** fight to the death; **5, 3, 3** never say die; **5, 4** stand firm; **5, 7** never despair; **5, 9** never surrender; **7, 2** soldier on.

persistent 6 dogged, steady; **7** endless, patient; **8** constant, resolute, stubborn, tireless, untiring; **9** assiduous, continual, demanding, incessant, insistent, obstinate, overeager, tenacious, unceasing; **10** continuous, relentless, unflagging; **11** importunate, persevering, unrelenting; **12** intransigent; **13** indefatigable, uninterrupted; PHRASES: **3-4** non-stop.

persnickety 5 fussy; **7** finicky, precise; **8** detailed, exacting; **9** demanding; **10** meticulous; **11** painstaking.

person 1 I; **3** bod, boy, guy, joe, man, one, sod, VIP; **4** baby, body, cast, chap *UK*, girl, hand, head, nose, soul, star, suit, type, unit; **5** adult, being, celeb, child, human, party, woman; **6** mortal; **7** Adamite *UK*, element, someone; **8** creature, customer, everyman, favorite, somebody, teenager; **9** celebrity, character, earthling, personage, personnel, tellurian; **10** adolescent, everywoman, individual; PHRASES: **2, 3, 2** so and so; **3, 2, 3, 6** man in the street; **3, 3** the man, top dog; **3, 4** Joe Blow, Joe Soap *UK*; **3, 5, 3** the naked ape; **3, 5, 6** the noble animal; **4, 3** John Doe; **4, 5** God's image; **5, 3, 5** flesh and blood; **5, 5** human being; **6, 2, 4** ~ of note; **6, 3** common man; **6, 4** living soul.

person (in person) 4 live; **6** bodily, really; **7** solidly; **8** actually; **10** materially, personally; PHRASES: **2, 3, 5** in the flesh; **2, 9** in existence.

personable 4 rosy, tidy, trim; **6** peachy; **7** elegant; **8** blooming, charming, tasteful; **9** agreeable, appealing; **10** attractive, enchanting.

personage *See* **VIP**

personal 3 own; 5 inner; 7 private; 8 intimate.

personal assistant 2 PA *UK*.

personal attack 4 rape, slur; 5 abuse, libel, smear; 7 calumny, censure, decrial, mugging, slander; 9 aspersion, criticism, injustice; 10 defamation, revilement; 11 denigration; 12 denunciation, vilification; 13 disparagement; PHRASES: 4, 2, 3, 4 stab in the back; 4, 4 date rape, foul play; 5, 7 armed robbery; 6, 6 verbal attack; 8, 6 physical attack; 8, 7 indecent assault.

personal attendant 5 nanny, nurse, tutor; 6 barber, batman, driver; 7 masseur; 8 chaperon, henchman, masseuse; 9 bodyguard, chauffeur, companion, governess, nursemaid; 10 confidante; 11 hairdresser; PHRASES: 2, 4 au pair; 8, 7 personal servant.

personality 3 ego, VIP; 4 self, star; 5 anima, celeb; 6 nature, psyche; 7 grandee, persona; 8 charisma, identity; 9 celebrity, character, dignitary; 11 temperament; PHRASES: 4-2 make-up.

personality type 7 syntone, syntony; 8 ambivert, choleric, sanguine; 9 ectomorph, endomorph, extrovert, introvert, mesomorph; 10 ectomorphy, endomorphy, mesomorphy, phlegmatic; 11 ambiversion, ingoingness, melancholic; 12 ectomorphism, endomorphism, extroversion, introversion, mesomorphism, outgoingness; 15 extrovertedness, introvertedness.

personalized 7 bespoke; 14 individualized; PHRASES: 3-3 one-off; 4-2-7 made-to-measure *UK*; 6-5 custom-built.

personify 6 embody; 8 humanize; 9 epitomize, exemplify, incarnate; 11 personalize; 12 characterize; PHRASES: 5, 5 bring alive.

personnel 3 men; 4 band, cast, crew, gang, team; 5 cadre, hands, labor, squad, staff, women; 7 company, nucleus, payroll, workers; 8 manpower; 9 employees; 10 complement, workpeople; 11 proletariat; 12 organization; PHRASES: 4, 5 work force; 5, 4 labor pool; 5, 5 labor force; 5, 9 human resources; 6, 5 casual labor; 7, 7 working classes; 10, 6 contingent worker.

perspective 4 size, view; 5 depth, ratio, scale, scene, vista; 7 lookout, outlook; 8 prospect; 9 viewpoint; 10 perception, proportion, standpoint.

perspiration *See* **sweat**

perspire *See* **sweat**

persuade 4 coax, move, save, sway, urge; 5 cause, force, impel, lobby; 6 advise, cajole, coerce, compel, engage, enlist, induce, insist, pacify, preach, prompt, revive; 7 appease, convert, counsel, dispose, incline, procure, wheedle; 8 blandish, browbeat, convince, motivate, pressure; 9 brainwash, influence, instigate; 10 conciliate, evangelize, intimidate; 11 proselytize; 12 indoctrinate; PHRASES: 3, 2, 2, 5 lay it on thick; 3, 2, 4, 6 get in one's corner; 3, 4 win over; 4, 2, 5 take by storm; 4, 4 push into, talk into, wear down; 4, 5 talk round *UK*; 5, 2, 4, 4 bring to one's side; 5-4 sweet-talk; 5, 4, 5 carry one's point; 7, 4 prevail upon.

persuade (be persuaded) 3 buy; 5 agree, yield; 6 submit; 7 believe, concede, consent, succumb; PHRASES: 4, 2 give up; 4, 3 fall for; 4, 3, 4 feel the urge, hear the call; 5, 3, 3 catch the bug.

persuader 6 coaxer, orator; 7 pleader; 8 advocate, promoter, salesman, wheedler; 9 publicist; 10 advertiser, publicizer; 11 rhetorician; 12 propagandist; PHRASES: 2, 3 ad man, PR man; 4, 6 spin doctor; 4-7 flak-catcher, vote-catcher *UK*; 4-8 vote-snatcher; 9, 5 publicity agent.

persuasion 4 sect, side; 5 clout, creed, faith, group, party; 6 belief, patter; 7 faction; 8 lobbying, pressure; 9 influence, prompting; 10 evangelism, inducement, insistence, philosophy, preference, revivalism; 11 inclination; 12 brainwashing, salesmanship; 13 proselytizing; 14 evangelization, indoctrination, persuasiveness; 15 proselytization; PHRASES: 5, 2, 4 point of view; 5, 4 sales talk; 5, 5 sales pitch.

persuasive 4 glib; 5 slick; 6 cogent; 7 rousing, telling, winning; 8 alluring, charming, credible, didactic, eloquent, exciting, forceful, hypnotic, inducing, inviting, magnetic, mesmeric, tempting; 9 addictive, directive, effective, hortatory, incentive, inflaming, plausible; 10 attractive, bewitching, compelling, convincing, impressive, motivating, protreptic; 11 challenging, charismatic, encouraging, fascinating, influential, provocative, stimulating, tantalizing; 12 irresistible; PHRASES: 6-7 smooth-talking.

pert 5 perky; 6 breezy, lively; 8 flippant, impudent.

pertinacious *See* **resolute**

pertinent *See* **relevant**

perturb *See* **worry**

pertussis 8, 5 whooping cough.

peruse *See* **read**

Peruvian bark 8 cinchona.

pervasive 7 general; **9** extensive, prevalent, universal; **11** inescapable.

perverse 4 awry; **7** wayward; **8** aberrant, abnormal, contrary, stubborn; **9** obstinate; **10** disruptive; **11** disobedient; **12** cantankerous.

perversion 4 ruin; **5** abuse; **6** misuse; **8** impurity; **9** abasement, addiction, barbarism, decadence, depravity, vitiation; **10** cheapening, coarsening, corruption, debasement, degeneracy, distortion, immorality, impureness, indulgence, subversion; **11** deformation, degradation, depravation, devaluation, drunkenness, promiscuity; **12** degeneration, intoxication, prostitution; **13** brutalization, vulgarization; **14** degenerateness, dehumanization.

pervert 4 ruin, warp; **5** abase, abuse, lower, twist; **6** debase, deform, misuse; **7** cheapen, coarsen, corrupt, debauch, degrade, deprave, devalue, deviant, distort, subvert, vitiate; **8** denature, misteach; **9** barbarize, brainwash, brutalize, vulgarize; **10** dehumanize, prostitute; **11** detribalize; **12** denaturalize, propagandize; **13** denationalize; PHRASES: **3, 8** sex criminal; **5, 7** treat cruelly.

pessimism 5 doubt, gloom; **8** cynicism, distrust, nihilism; **9** suspicion; **10** negativity; **12** hopelessness.

pessimist 5 cynic; **6** grouch, misery, moaner; **7** grouser, killjoy; **8** alarmist, fatalist, Jeremiah, sourpuss; **9** defeatist, detractor, doomsayer, minimizer; **10** doommonger, spoilsport; PHRASES: **3, 7** wet blanket.

pessimistic 6 gloomy; **7** anxious; **8** dreading, hopeless, negative, resigned; **10** fatalistic.

pest 3 bug, nit, oaf; **4** boor, lout; **5** beast; **6** cootie, vermin; **8** hooligan, nuisance, parasite; **11** bloodsucker; **12** troublemaker. *See also* **insects**

pestilence *See* **plague**

pestilent 5 fatal; **6** deadly, killer, lethal; **7** irksome; **8** annoying, infected, polluted, virulent; **10** bothersome, irritating; **12** contaminated; PHRASES: **3-6** bug-ridden; **6-6** plague-ridden.

pet 3 cat, dog; **4** bate, hump, miff, neck, rage, snog *UK*, spat, tiff; **5** dumps; **6** caress, cosset, fondle, rabbit, smooch; **7** darling, hamster, umbrage; **8** canoodle, favorite, goldfish, tortoise.

petite *See* **short, small**

petition *See* **request**

pet peeve 6 phobia; **7** bugbear; **8** anathema; **11** abomination; PHRASES: **4, 5** bête noire.

petrify 3 fix; **5** alarm, scare; **6** harden, ossify; **7** terrify; **8** frighten, solidify; **9** fossilize; PHRASES: **4, 4, 4** fill with fear.

petrol 8 gasoline.

pettiness 10 triviality; **11** irrelevance; **12** pettifoggery; **13** inconsequence; **14** insignificance. *See also* **petty**

petty 4 mean; **5** minor, small; **6** little, narrow, paltry, stingy; **7** trivial; **8** childish, grudging, niggling; PHRASES: **4-6** meanminded; **5, 4** ~ cash, ~ jury; **5-6** small-minded; **5, 7** ~ larceny, ~ officer; **6-6** narrowminded.

pew *See* **bench**

pewit 7 lapwing.

peyote 6 mescal.

PG 4 page; PHRASES: **6, 5** paying guest *UK*.

PH 10 philosophy; PHRASES: **6, 6** public health.

phantasm *See* **ghost**

phantom *See* **ghost**

pharmacist 3 MPS; **7** chemist *UK*; **8** druggist; **9** dispenser.

phase 4 form, part, time; **5** patch, shape, spell, stage, state; **6** aspect, period; **7** episode; **9** condition.

phenomenon 4 fact; **6** genius, marvel, wonder; **7** miracle, prodigy; **8** incident; **9** happening, spectacle; **10** experience, occurrence; **11** singularity; PHRASES: **4, 3** whiz kid; **6, 4** bright star; **6, 8** enfant terrible.

philanthropic 4 kind; **5** civic; **6** aiding, humane, kindly; **7** liberal; **8** generous, gracious; **9** reforming, visionary; **10** altruistic, beneficent, benevolent, charitable, idealistic, munificent; **11** communistic, enlightened, socialistic, utilitarian; **12** eleemosynary, humanitarian; **13** compassionate; **15** philanthropical; PHRASES: **3-6**

aid-giving; **3-7** big-hearted; **4-6** alms-giving; **4-7** kind-hearted *UK*; **5-7** large-hearted; **6-8** public-spirited.

philanthropist **3** Fry (Elizabeth); **4** Kroc (Joan), Rice (William Marsh), Shaw (Run Run); **5** aider, Allen (Paul), Coles (Arthur), Cosby (Bill), Gates (Bill), Getty (Paul), Kavli (Fred), Mayer (Robert), Soros (George); **6** Drexel (Anthony J.), helper, Kirsch (Steve), Loomis (Alfred Lee), Raikes (Robert), Turner (Ted), Yarrow (Sir Alfred); **7** almoner, Barnado (Thomas John), Barnett (Samuel Augustus), Cadbury (George), Fischel (Harry), Hopkins (Johns), utopian; **8** altruist, assister, Carnegie (Andrew), Franklin (Benjamin), Harkness (Edward), idealist, Rowntree (Joseph), succorer; **9** Annenberg (Walter), MacArthur (John D.), Samaritan, visionary, volunteer, Whitworth (Joseph); **10** befriender, benefactor, Benthamite, Gulbenkian (Calouste), ideologist, missionary, Vanderbilt (Cornelius); **11** Rockefeller (John D.), utilitarian, Wilberforce (William); **12** benefactress, humanitarian; **PHRASES: 2-6** do-gooder; **3, 6** aid worker; **4, 6** kind person; **4, 8** good neighbor; **4, 9** Good Samaritan; **6, 6** social worker; **7, 4** helping hand; **7, 6** charity worker, mission worker; welfare worker; **9, 6** voluntary worker.

philanthropy **5** amity; **7** charity; **8** altruism, goodwill, humanity; **9** patronage; **10** compassion, generosity; **11** benevolence.

philistine **4** boor; **9** barbarian, untutored, vulgarian; **10** uncultured, uninformed; **15** unsophisticated.

Philomel **11** nightingale.

philosopher **4** Ayer, Hume, Kant, Mill, sage, Zeno; **5** asker, Bacon, Comte, cynic, Hegel, Locke, Occam, Plato, stoic; **6** Hobbes, seeker, Thales; **7** analyst, Bentham, Bergson, dreamer, Emerson, Russell, sophist, Spinoza, thinker; **8** academic, Berkeley, Diogenes, idealist, inquirer, logician, moralist, searcher, Socrates, surmiser, theorist; **9** Aristotle, Descartes, ideologue, syllogist, theorizer, visionary; **10** researcher, speculator; **11** cosmologist, hypothesist; **12** dialectician, doctrinarian, hypothecator, hypothesizer, investigator, theoretician; **13** metaphysician. *See also* **philosophy**

philosophical **4** cool; **7** logical, stoical; **8** detached, resigned, tolerant; **9** objective; **10** analytical *UK*, thoughtful.

philosophical term **5** axiom, sense; **6** thesis; **7** analogy, gestalt, paradox; **8** function, identity, modality, negation, noumenon, operator; **9** bivalence, deduction, dichotomy, inference, necessity, postulate, reference, subaltern, syllogism, synthesis, tautology; **10** antecedent, antithesis, hypothesis, imperative, quantifier, sensibilia; **11** conditional, conjunction, disjunction, equivalence, probability; **13** biconditional; **14** counterexample, counterfactual; **PHRASES: 3, 8** non sequitur; **5, 3** Hume's Law; **5, 4** major term, minor term, sense data; **5, 5** truth table, truth value; **5, 8** salva veritate, truth function, value judgment; **5, 9** truth condition; **7, 5** Ockham's razor; **8, 1, 6** argument a priori; **9, 3** Leibnitz's Law; **9, 4** assertion sign; **9, 5** necessary truth; **10, 5** contingent truth.

philosophize **3** ask; **4** muse, seek; **5** brood, dream, query, study; **6** ponder, search, survey, wonder; **7** analyze, examine, explore, inquire, observe, reflect, suppose, surmise; **8** cogitate, consider, idealize, question, research, ruminate; **9** challenge, postulate, speculate, visualize; **10** conjecture, deliberate, excogitate, introspect, scrutinize; **11** contemplate, hypothesize, internalize, investigate, ratiocinate; **13** conceptualize; **15** intellectualize.

philosophy **4** idea, view; **5** axiom, canon, Cynic, dogma, maxim, stoic, Sufic, tenet; **6** monist, mystic, notion, Taoist, thesis; **7** concept, deistic, Eleatic, feeling, Fregean, Hobbist, Kantian, Marxist, opinion, outlook, precept, premise, realist, Senecan, Thomist, thought, utopian; **8** agnostic, anarchic, aphorism, attitude, Baconian, Buddhist, Cyrenaic, doctrine, egoistic, esthetic, Hegelian, judgment, nihilist, pacifist, Platonic, Socratic, theistic, vitalist; **9** animistic, assertion, atomistic, Averroist, Berkelian, Cartesian, Chomskyan, communist, Confucian, dualistic, emotivist, epicurean, Euclidian, Keynesian, Lucretian, pluralist, postulate, principle, reasoning, sentiment, skeptical, socialist, solipsist, statement, viewpoint; **10** altruistic, assumption, Benthamite, Bergsonian, capitalist, conclusion, conjecture, dynamistic, empiricist, fatalistic, hedonistic, humanistic, hypothesis, idealistic, monetarist, nominalist, positivist, Pyrrhonist, relativist; **11** Augustinian, axiological, behaviorist, Democritean, determinist, Empedoclean, explanation,

Heraclitean, Leibnitzian, materialist, mechanistic, nationalist, Nietzschean, objectivist, pantheistic, peripatetic, physicalist, proposition, Protagorean, Pythagorean, rationalist, sophistical, speculation, supposition, syndicalist, utilitarian; **12** Aristotelian, collectivist, essentialist, euhemeristic, isolationist, naturalistic, reductionist, Schellingian; **13** compatibilist, contextualist, descriptivist, eudaemonistic, functionalist, justification, phenomenalist; **14** existentialist, Kierkegaardian, presupposition, subjectivistic; **15** conceptualistic, individualistic, instrumentalist, rationalization, Wittgensteinian; PHRASES: 3-9 Neo-Platonist; **5, 2, 4** point of view; **5-7** quasi-realist.

philosophy (branches of philosophy) 5 logic; **6** ethics; **8** axiology, ontology, theology; **9** casuistry, cosmology, esthetics, semantics, semiotics, teleology; **10** deontology, gnosiology, metaethics; **11** metaphysics; **12** epistemology, ontotheology; **13** phenomenology; PHRASES: **5, 5** modal logic; **5, 6** legal ethics; **5, 10** moral philosophy; **6, 5** formal logic; **7, 5** deontic logic; **7, 6** medical ethics; **7, 7** quantum physics.

phlegm 5 mucus, rheum; **7** catarrh; **8** calmness; **9** composure; PHRASES: **4-10** self-possession.

phobia *See* **fear**

phone 3 TEL; **4** bell *UK*, call, dial, ring *UK*; **6** blower *UK*, mobile; **8** intercom; PHRASES: **4, 5** cell ~.

phonetic 5 nasal, tonal, tonic; **6** phonic, twangy, voiced; **7** pitched, throaty; **8** accented, aspirate, guttural, stressed; **9** aspirated, voiceless; **10** unaccented, unstressed.

phosphorus 1 P.

photograph 3 pan, pic, vid; **4** film, shot, snap, take; **5** focus, image, movie, photo, pinup, print, shoot, slide, still, video; **6** expose, reduce; **7** develop, enlarge, picture, process, project; **8** hologram, monotone, Photofit, portrait, snapshot; **10** photomural, radiograph; **11** shadowgraph; **12** photomontage, transparency; **13** daguerreotype; PHRASES: **1-3** X-ray; **4, 2** blow up, zoom in; **4, 3** zoom out; **4, 4** long shot, stop down; **4-4** half-tone; **5-2** close-up; **5, 5** color photo; **10, 5** ~ album.

photographic 9 pictorial, realistic; **10** photogenic; **14** photosensitive; PHRASES: **6-3** camera-shy.

phrase 3 PHR, tag; **4** call, term, tune, word; **6** clause, cliché, sennet, slogan; **7** formula; **8** apodosis, flourish, protasis, sentence; **10** expression; **11** collocation.

phrasemonger *See* **rhetorician**

physical 6 bodily, carnal, earthy, manual, mortal; **7** fleshly, mundane, natural, worldly; **8** corporal, material, tangible, temporal; **9** corporeal.

physical exercise *See* **exercise**

physical training 2 PE *UK*, PT *UK*.

physician *See* **doctor**

physiognomy 4 face; **8** features; **10** appearance; **15** characteristics.

piano 1 P; **4** soft; **5** grand, quiet; **6** softly; **7** quietly, upright; **8** Steinway; **9** Bechstein; **10** pianoforte; PHRASES: **6, 5** player ~, square ~, street ~, stride ~; **7, 5** cottage ~; **9, 5** honkytonk ~.

pichiciego 9 armadillo.

pick 4 best, chip, cull, pass, sift, skim, tool; **5** cream, elite, glean, pluck; **6** choose, detail, flower, gather, pickax, scrape, select, winnow; **7** appoint, approve, earmark, excerpt, isolate, propose, reserve; **8** abstract, delegate, identify, nominate, plectrum, separate; **9** designate, highlight, preselect, recommend; **10** commission; **11** anthologize, distinguish; **12** discriminate; PHRASES: **3, 5** set apart, set aside; **4, 3, 3, 5** skim off the cream; **4, 3, 6** ~ and choose; **4, 4** mark down; **4-4** hand-pick; **6, 3** single out.

picket 3 peg, rod; **4** post; **5** fence, stake; **6** strike; **7** enclose, lookout, protest, striker; **8** restrain, sentinel; **9** boycotter, protester; **11** demonstrate; PHRASES: **5, 4** fence post.

pickings *See* **earnings**

pickle 4 bind; **6** plight; **8** quandary; **10** difficulty; PHRASES: **11** predicament. *See also* **preserve**

pick-me-up *See* **refreshment**

pickpocket 3 dip; **8** cutpurse.

picnic 5 cinch; **6** doddle *UK*; **7** nothing; **8** walkaway, walkover; PHRASES: **5, 2, 4** piece of cake. *See also* **meal**

pictorial 6 iconic, linear, mosaic, visual; **7** graphic, optical, tabular; **9** geometric, realistic; **10** atmosphere; **11** illusionist; **12** calligraphic, diagrammatic, photographic, pictographic.

picture 3 oil, pic; **4** card, copy, daub, icon,

snap, wash; **5** comic, draft, house, image, mural, plate, print, study; **6** canvas, doodle, fresco, mosaic, palace, poster, sketch, window; **7** cartoon, collage, diagram, drawing, impasto, molding, montage, outline, tableau, tracing, woodcut, writing; **8** aquatint, frottage, graffito, likeness, painting, postcard, scribble, tapestry, vignette; **9** animation, aquarelle, encaustic, engraving, grisaille, miniature, visualize; **10** altarpiece, caricature, photoprint, silhouette; **11** delineation, masterpiece; **12** illumination, illustration, photogravure, photomontage, reproduction; **14** representation; PHRASES: **3, 6** old master; **4, 2, 3** work of art; **5, 5** color print; **5-5** block-print; **5, 7** brass rubbing; **7, 3** ~ hat; **7, 8** ~ postcard.

picturesque 5 vivid; **6** pretty, scenic; **8** charming; **9** pictorial; **10** attractive; **12** pictographic; PHRASES: **9-3** chocolate-box.

pie 4 tart; **5** pasty *UK*; **6** potpie; PHRASES: **3, 3** mud ~; **3, 4** ~ dish; **4, 3** pork ~ *UK*; **5, 3** mince ~; **6, 3** humble ~; **7, 3** cottage ~ *UK*, custard ~, shoofly ~; **9, 3** shepherd's ~.

piece 3 bit, cut, gun, man, rag, sod, tag; **4** band, bite, bolt, chip, chop, clod, coil, dose, drop, heap, hunk, line, lump, mass, part, roll, slab, snip, tump, turf, unit, wisp; **5** block, chunk, class, crumb, crust, divot, flake, goods, patch, queue *UK*, scale, scrap, shard, sherd, shred, slice, speck, steak, strip, wedge, wodge *UK*; **6** branch, collop, cutlet, dollop, finger, gobbet, length, morsel, nugget, offcut, parcel, rasher, sector, sliver, streak, string, stripe, swatch; **7** faction, helping, measure, portion, section, segment, smidgen, smidgin, snippet, tranche; **8** addition, category, division, fraction, fragment, potsherd, splinter; **9** allotment, crocodile, insertion; **10** department; **11** subdivision; **13** interpolation. *See also* **chess**

piecemeal 9 gradually, haphazard; **10** disjointed, separately; **11** fragmentary; **12** disconnected, disorganized; PHRASES: **1, 3, 2, 1, 4** a bit at a time; **2, 7** by degrees; **3, 2, 1, 4** one at a time; **3, 2, 3** bit by bit, one by one; **5, 2, 5** piece by piece.

piece of eight 4 peso; PHRASES: **7** piastre.

pie-eyed *See* **drunk**

pierce 3 jag *UK*, tap; **4** bore, gore, spit, stab; **5** lance, probe, punch, spear, spike, stick, sting; **6** faucet, impale, riddle, skewer; **8** puncture; **9** penetrate, perforate.

piercing 3 raw; **4** cold, keen, loud; **5** acute, sharp; **6** bitter, shrewd, wintry; **7** intense; **8** freezing; **9** searching; **10** perceptive; **11** penetrating; **12** earsplitting.

piety 6 virtue; **8** devotion, smugness; **9** hypocrisy, piousness; **10** devoutness, moralizing; **13** religiousness.

piffle *See* **nonsense**

pig 3 hog, sow; **4** boar, runt; **5** duroc; **6** pigpen, pigsty *UK*, porker; **8** Napoleon, pietrain, Snowball, Squealer; PHRASES: **3, 2, 1, 4** ~ in a poke; **5, 5** large white; **6, 5** Poland China; **7, 5** Chester White, Pigling Bland.

pigeon 4 dove; **5** homer, squab; **6** culver; **7** fantail; PHRASES: **7, 6** carrier ~.

pigeonhole 3 box; **4** slot; **5** class, label, shelf; **8** category, classify; **9** cubbyhole; **10** categorize; **11** compartment; **14** classification.

pigment 3 dye; **4** tint, wash, woad; **5** glaze, grain, ocher *UK*, ochre *UK*, paint, stain, umber; **6** enamel, indigo, madder; **7** aniline, flavone, lacquer, mordant, varnish; **8** carotene, colorant, coloring, dyestuff, fixative, flavonol; **9** bilirubin, cochineal, colorwash, distemper, flavonoid, whitewash; **10** biliverdin, carotenoid, hemoglobin, phycobilin; **11** anthocyanin, chlorophyll, fucoxanthin, phytochrome, xanthophyll; **13** colorfastness; PHRASES: **5, 3** India ink.

pigweed 3, 3 fat hen *UK*.

pile 3 nap, pot, wad; **4** hall, heap, hill, mass, pier, post, shag; **5** amass, clump, mound, plush, stack, stock, tower; **6** bundle, carpet, castle, column, packet *UK*, palace, pillar; **7** edifice, fortune, killing, mansion, support; **8** assemble, building, quantity; **10** accumulate, foundation.

pilfer *See* **steal**

Pilgrims 5 Alden (John); **7** Clifton (Richard), Fortune; **8** Allerton (Mary), Brewster (William); **9** Mayflower, Speedwell; **12** Congregation, Provincetown; PHRASES: **4, 3** Cape Cod; **6, 5** Hudson River; **7, 7** Pilgrim Fathers; **8, 6** Plymouth Colony; **9, 7** Mayflower Compact.

pill 3 gel; **6** cachet, dragee, dragée, powder, tablet, troche; **7** capsule, lozenge; **8** pastille.

pillage *See* **plunder**

pillar 4 herm, pier, pile, pole, post; **5** shaft; **6** column; **7** telemon, upright; **8** caryatid, pilaster.

pillory *See* **ridicule**

pillow *See* **cushion**

pilot 3 fly; **4** test; **5** drive, flyer, guide, movie, steer, trial; **6** airman, flyboy, sample; **7** aviator; **8** aeronaut, helmsman, navigate; **9** navigator, steersman; **10** pilothouse; PHRASES: **5, 4** ~ bird, ~ film, ~ fish, ~ lamp; **5, 5** ~ cloth, ~ light, ~ plant, ~ study, ~ whale; **5, 6** ~ engine; **5, 7** ~ balloon, ~ biscuit, ~ officer *UK*.

pilot whale 9 blackfish.

pimento 8 allspice.

pimple 3 zit; **4** acne, boil, bubo, spot; **6** hickey; **7** blemish, pustule; **8** swelling; **9** blackhead, carbuncle, whitehead.

pin 3 fix, leg, peg; **5** badge, dowel, pivot, rivet, spike, thole; **6** brooch, fasten; **7** kingpin, trinket; **8** ornament; **9** accessory, thumbtack; PHRASES: **3, 4** ~ curl, ~ rail, ~ tuck; **3, 5** ~ joint, ~ money; **3, 6** ~ wrench; **5, 3** bobby ~, drift ~, panel ~, shear ~, stick ~, wrest ~, wrist ~; **6, 3** cotter ~, firing ~, safety ~; **7, 3** gudgeon ~, rolling ~, scatter ~.

pinch 3 bit, nip; **4** dash, take; **5** grasp, press, steal, taste, touch, tweak; **7** soupçon, squeeze; PHRASES: **4, 3, 4** make off with.

pine 4 ache, long, sigh; **5** yearn; **6** hunger; **7** conifer, decline; **8** languish; PHRASES: **4, 4** ~ cone; **4, 6** ~ marten *UK*, ~ needle; **5, 4** Scots ~.

ping *See* **sound**

pink 4 puce, rose, rosy; **5** blush, coral, knock; **6** salmon, shrimp; **8** dianthus; **9** raspberry; PHRASES: **4, 3** ~ gin *UK*; **4, 4** baby ~, ~ slip; **4, 5** ~ noise; **4, 9** ~ elephants; **5, 4** flesh ~, shell ~; **7, 4** hunter's ~; **8, 4** shocking ~.

pinnacle *See* **summit**

pioneer 4 head, lead; **5** found, guide, pilot; **6** invent; **7** explore; **8** discover, initiate, innovate; **9** influence, spearhead; **10** inaugurate, popularize, trailblaze; **11** reconnoiter, trailblazer; **12** frontiersman; PHRASES: **3, 3** map out; **4, 2** open up; **4, 3, 3** lead the way; **5, 1, 5** blaze a trail; **5, 3, 3** break the ice; **5, 3, 6** break new ground; **5-6** trend-setter.

pious 2 St; **5** moral; **6** devout; **7** saintly; **8** reverent, virtuous; **10** godfearing; **13** sanctimonious.

pip 3 nut, pit; **4** beat, beep, ding, peep, ping, seed, spot; **5** bleep, stone; **6** defeat, kernel; PHRASES: **3, 2, 3, 4** ~ to the post *UK*.

pipe 3 jet; **4** duct, flue, oboe, reed, tube; **5** briar *UK*, flute, hooka; **6** hookah; **7** calumet, chanter, chillum, piccolo, whistle; **8** narghile; **9** downspout; **10** meerschaum; **12** churchwarden; PHRASES: **4, 4** clay ~; **4, 5** ~ dream, ~ major *UK*, ~ organ; **4, 7** ~ cleaner; **5, 4** peace ~, pitch ~, waste ~; **7, 4** corncob ~, exhaust ~; **9, 4** rainwater ~.

piping 4 high; **5** pipes; **6** edging, shrill, tubing; **8** fringing, piercing, plumbing, trimming; **11** penetrating; PHRASES: **4-7** high-pitched.

pipit 7 titlark.

piquancy 4 bite, kick, tang, zest; **5** aroma, sting; **6** acuity, flavor; **8** asperity, pungency; **9** poignancy; **11** penetration. *See also* **piquant**

piquant 3 hot; **4** gamy, racy, sour, tart; **5** cured, herby, minty, salty, sharp, smoky, spicy, tangy; **6** biting, bitter, savory, smoked, soused, spiced, strong; **7** peppery, pickled, pungent; **8** aromatic, kippered, seasoned, stinging; **9** flavorful; **10** appetizing; PHRASES: **6, 8** highly flavored, highly seasoned.

pique 5 anger, annoy, upset; **6** arouse, bother, offend, temper; **7** attract; **8** interest, intrigue, irritate, stimulate; **10** resentment; PHRASES: **3, 4** ill will.

piracy 6 faking; **7** copying; **8** stealing; **9** plundering; **11** bootlegging; **14** counterfeiting.

pirate 3 Pew; **4** copy, fake, Hook, Kidd, Smee; **5** Flint, rover, steal; **6** hijack, Morgan; **7** bootleg, corsair, plunder; **8** hijacker; **9** buccaneer; **10** adventurer, Blackbeard, plagiarize; **11** counterfeit; **12** swashbuckler; PHRASES: **4, 4, 6** Long John Silver.

piscary 7 fishery, fishing.

pit 3 pip; **4** dent, dump, hole, mess, mine, pock, well; **5** ditch, fight, nadir; **6** bottom, crater, depths, hollow, kernel, oppose, pigpen, pigsty *UK*, quarry; **8** colliery; **10** depression; **11** indentation; PHRASES: **3, 7** set against; **4, 4** coal mine.

pitch 3 key, shy, tar; **4** apex, hurl, reel, rock, roll, swag, sway, tilt, toss; **5** angle, field, labor, lurch, spiel, swing, throw; **6** careen, dither, encamp, falter, plunge, stress, teeter, timbre, totter, waggle, wallop, wallow, welter, wobble; **7** bitumen, blunder, concert, flounce, founder, perfect, stagger, stumble; **8** absolute, flounder, struggle; **10** inflection, intonation; **13** pronunciation.

pitcher 3 jug; **6** carafe; **8** decanter.

pitchfork 4 fork, lift, push, toss, turn; **5** drive, force; **6** propel, thrust.

piteous *See* **pathetic**

pith *See* **essence**

pith helmet 4 topi; **5** topee.

pitiful 3 sad; **6** moving; **7** piteous, ruthful; **8** grievous, pathetic, pitiable, touching; **9** affecting; **11** distressing; PHRASES: **4-7** self-pitying, tear-jerking; **5, 3, 7** sorry for oneself; **5-7** heart-rending; **5-8** heart-breaking; **8, 4** arousing pity.

pitiless 4 cold, hard; **5** cruel, harsh, tough; **6** brutal, flinty, severe; **7** callous, unmoved; **8** barbaric, hardened, obdurate, ruthless, sadistic, soulless, uncaring, vengeful; **9** barbarous, heartless, impassive, unfeeling, unpitying; **10** revengeful, vindictive; **11** remorseless, unforgiving; **12** unremorseful, unresponsive; **13** unsympathetic; **14** unsympathizing; PHRASES: **4-7** cold-blooded, cold-hearted, hard-hearted; **5-7** stony-hearted; **7, 8** without feelings.

pity 6 caring; **7** charity, empathy, feeling, support; **8** humanity, kindness, sympathy; **9** empathize; **10** compassion, condolence, gentleness, sympathize, tenderness, understand; **11** benevolence, commiserate; **12** mercifulness; **13** commiseration, understanding; PHRASES: **4, 3** feel for; **4, 5** soft heart, warm heart; **4, 5, 3** feel sorry for; **4-11** soft-heartedness, warm-heartedness; **6, 5** tender heart; **6, 7** fellow feeling *UK*; **9, 4** empathize with; **10, 4** sympathize with.

pity (excite pity) 4 melt, move, thaw; **5** reach, touch; **6** affect, disarm, grieve, soften; PHRASES: **4, 2, 5** move to tears; **4, 3, 5** melt the heart.

pitying 4 kind, soft; **5** human; **6** caring, gentle, humane, tender; **7** clement, lenient; **8** generous, gracious, merciful, yielding; **9** condolent, consoling, forgiving; **10** benevolent, charitable, comforting, forbearant; **11** sympathetic; **12** sympathizing; **13** commiserating, commiserative, compassionate, understanding; PHRASES: **4-7** kind-hearted, soft-hearted, warm-hearted; **6-7** tender-hearted.

pivot 3 pin; **4** axis, pole; **5** hinge, point; **6** hingle, pintle, rotate, swivel; **7** fulcrum, gudgeon, oarlock, radiant, rowlock *UK*,

support; **8** trunnion.

pixie *See* **fairy**

PL 5 place; PHRASES: **4, 8** Poet Laureate; **8, 4** Plimsoll line.

place 2 PL; **3** bed, job, lay, pad, put, set; **4** area, home, lieu, pose, post, site, spot; **5** locus, lodge, niche, point, scene, stead; **6** locale, locate, region; **7** install, setting, situate; **8** location, position; **9** apartment; **11** whereabouts; PHRASES: **5, 4** ~ card, ~ kick, ~ name; **7, 5** decimal ~, resting ~.

place (take the place of) 5 usurp; **7** replace; **8** displace, supplant; **9** supersede; **10** substitute.

placid 4 calm; **7** equable; **9** easygoing; **13** imperturbable; PHRASES: **4-8** even-tempered.

placing 6 fixing, siting; **7** posting; **8** fixation, locating, settling; **9** placement, situating; **10** stationing; **11** emplacement; **12** installation; **13** establishment.

plagiarism 4 fake; **7** copying, lifting; **8** cheating, cribbing, pastiche; **9** imitating.

plagiarist 5 cheat, fraud, thief; **6** pirate; **7** copyist; **8** deceiver, imitator; **9** purloiner; **10** bootlegger.

plagiarize 4 copy, crib, lift; **5** cheat; **6** pirate; **7** bootleg, imitate.

plague 4 bane, pest; **7** disease, scourge; **8** epidemic, pandemic; **9** contagion, infection; **10** pestilence; PHRASES: **5, 5** Black Death; **7, 6** bubonic ~; **9, 6** pneumonic ~.

plaid *See* **checked**

plain 4 bald, drab, veld; **5** blunt, campo, clear, dowdy, frank, overt, sober, stark; **6** candid, direct, dreary, frumpy, homely, pampas, simple, steppe; **7** artless, austere, obvious, prairie; **8** definite, explicit, flatland, homespun, ordinary, prairies, savannah; **9** chocolate, dignified, grassland, tableland, unadorned; **10** restrained; **11** unambiguous; **12** unattractive; **13** distinguished, perspicacious; **15** straightforward, unprepossessing; PHRASES: **4-2-5** down-to-earth; **5-3** clear-cut; **5, 5** ~ flour *UK*; **5, 7** ~ clothes, ~ sailing.

plaint 4 plea; **6** action, charge; **9** complaint; **10** accusation.

plaintiff *See* **accuser**

plait *See* **braid**

plan 3 aim, map; **4** hint, idea, plot; **5** chart,

draft, frame, order; **6** agenda, budget, design, expect, intend, motion, notice, scheme; **7** almanac, arrange, foresee, predict, prepare, preview, program, project, propose, resolve, suggest, warning; **8** approach, contrive, envisage, envision, forecast, organize, planning, proposal, schedule, strategy; **9** amendment, brainwave, calculate, intention, invention, itinerary, methodize, timetable *UK*; **10** brainchild, brainstorm, intimation, prearrange, prospectus, resolution, suggestion; **11** proposition, publication, rationalize, systematize; **12** announcement, predetermine; PHRASES: 5, 2, 3, 3 order of the day.

plane **3** bus, jet, MIG *UK*; **4** even, kite, tool, tree; **5** glide, jumbo, level, shape; **6** chisel, router, shaver, smooth; **7** fighter; **8** aircraft. *See also* **aircraft**

planet **4** Mars; **5** Earth, Pluto, Venus; **6** albedo, aurora, Saturn, syzygy, Uranus; **7** Jupiter, Mercury, Neptune; **8** asteroid; **9** planetoid; **10** opposition; **11** conjunction, earthgrazer; **13** magnetosphere; PHRASES: 3, 5, 5 Van Allen belts; 5, 6 giant ~, major ~, minor ~; 6, 6 Jovian ~; 8, 4 asteroid belt; 8, 6 inferior ~, superior ~; 9, 4 wandering star.

planetary probe **6** lander, Venera, Viking; **7** Mariner, orbiter, Pioneer, Voyager *UK*.

planetoid **8** asteroid.

planned **5** meant; **7** orderly; **8** designed, intended, prepared, rational, tactical; **9** contrived, organized, schematic, strategic; **10** deliberate, methodical, systematic; **11** intentional; **12** premeditated; PHRASES: 2, 3, 6 on the stocks; 2, 5 in draft, in proof; 5, 2 drawn up; 5, 10 under discussion; 6, 3 worked out.

planner **5** cabal; **6** boffin, brains, framer; **7** deviser, founder, hatcher, manager, plotter, schemer; **8** designer, diplomat, inventor, promoter, proposer; **9** architect, contriver, intrigant *UK*, intriguer, organizer, projector, statesman, tactician; **10** maneuverer, mastermind, originator, politician, strategist; **11** conspirator, Machiavelli; **12** systematizer; PHRASES: 2-6 go-getter; 2-7 ax-grinder; 4-4, 3 back-room boy; 4-7 plot-spinner, town-planner; 7-6 wheeler-dealer; 7, 7 systems analyst.

plant **3** bud, imp, spy; **4** bush, herb, tree, vine, weed, wort; **5** graft, liana, shrub, works; **6** annual, armory, cactus, cereal, es-

cape, exotic, flower, insert, twiner; **7** aquatic, climber, engraft, factory, implant, ingraft, potherb, sapling; **8** biennial, epiphyte, parasite, seedling; **9** ephemeral, establish, evergreen, machinery, perennial, succulent, vegetable, xerophyte; **10** hydrophyte, transplant, wildflower; **11** maquiladora; **12** installation; PHRASES: 3, 3 bed out; 3, 5 air ~; 4, 5 food ~; 5-2 frame-up; 5, 5 green ~, house ~, woody ~; 5, 9 woody perennial; 6, 5 potted ~; 8, 5 hothouse ~, vascular ~; 9, 4 medicinal herb; 9, 5 medicinal ~; 10, 4 industrial unit; 10, 5 herbaceous ~. *See also* **plants and flowers**

plantation **4** farm; **5** manor; **9** farmstead, homestead. *See* **farm**

planter *See* **pot**

plant part **4** stem; **5** blade, float, frond, stipe, theca; **6** branch, lamina, starch, stigma, thread; **7** eyespot, rhizoid, thallus; **8** carotene, epitheca, frustule, hapteron, holdfast, pyrenoid; **9** branchlet, hypotheca, paramylum, protonema; **11** chlorophyll, fucoxanthin, phycocyanin, xanthophyll; **13** blepharoplast, phycoerythrin; PHRASES: 3, 7 air bladder; 4, 5 food store; 5, 7 algal pigment.

plants and flowers **3** abe, hop, ivy, rye; **4** dock, fern, flag, flax, geum, hemp, iris, jute, lily, pink, pita, rape, reed, rice, rose, rush, sage, tare, tule, upas, woad; **5** agave, ajuga, aster, avens, brier, bugle, camas, canna, cycad, daisy, henna, hosta, inula, jalap, kudzu, linum, lotus, lupin *UK*, oxeye, oxlip, pansy, peony, phlox, poppy, sedge, sedum, senna, sisal, tulip, viola; **6** allium, alsike, balsam, bellis, bluets, borage, bryony, cactus, caltha, cleome *UK*, clover, cobaea, coleus, cosmea, cosmos, cotton, cowpea, crocus, dahlia, darnel, fescue, hyssop, iberis *UK*, ipecac, lupine, madder, malope, medick, millet, nepeta, nettle, orchid, petrea, peyote, rattan, reseda, salvia, spurge, spurry, squill, sundew, teasel, thrift, twitch, violet, yarrow, zinnia; **7** aconite, alfalfa, alkanet, althaea, alyssum, anchusa, anemone, arugula, aruncus, astilbe, begonia, bistort, boneset, bracken, bugbane, bugloss, bulrush, burdock, campion, catawba, catmint, celosia, clarkia, cowbane, cowslip, dogbane, figwort, freesia, fuchsia, gazania, gentian, ginseng, gladdon, guarana, hemlock, henbane, honesty, ipomoea, jonquil, kingcup, liatris, linaria, liriope, lobelia, lunaria, lychnis, lythrum, milfoil, mimulus, monarda, mullein, nemesia, nigella *UK*, opuntia, papaver, papyrus, petunia, pigweed, pinesap, pinweed, primula, puccoon, raggedy, ragweed, ragwort, redroot, roselle, saguaro, sanicle, spurrey, stachys, statice, tagetes *UK*, tarweed, thistle, timothy, tobacco, trefoil, ursinia, verbena, vervain; **8** acanthus, achillea, aconitum, ageratum, agrimony, alumroot, arctotis, asphodel, auricula, bartonia, bedstraw, bellwort, bergamot, bergenia, bindweed, bluebell, boltonia, brunnera, camomile *UK*, catbrier, charlock, cleavers, clematis, crowfoot, cyclamen, daffodil, dianthus, dicentra, dropwort, echinops, eelgrass, eremurus, erigeron, eryngium, eucharis, feverfew, fleabane, fleawort *UK*, foxglove, fumitory, geranium, gloxinia, goutweed, harebell, hawkweed, helenium, henequen, heuchera, hibiscus, honewort, hornwort, hyacinth, ironweed, knapweed, knotweed, larkspur, lathyrus, lauatera, limonium, locoweed, lungwort, macleaya, marigold, mariposa, milkweed, milkwort, moonseed, myosotis, phacelia, physalis, plantain, plumbago, pokeweed, polypody, primrose, prunella, reedmace, roseroot, sainfoin, saltwort, samphire, scabiosa, scabious, shamrock, sidalcea, snowdrop, soapwort, solidago, stokesia, tiarella, tickseed, toadflax, trillium, trollius, tuberose, valerian, venidium, veronica, viscaria, wisteria, woodbine, woodrush, wormwood; **9** amaryllis, anaphalis, anthurium, aquilegia *UK*, arrowhead, arrowroot, astrantia, baneberry, birthroot, bloodroot, bluecurls, bluegrass, breadroot, broomrape, bryophyte, buckwheat, buttercup, calendula, campanula, candytuft, carnation, celandine, centaurea, chamomile *UK*, chickweed, cineraria, cocklebur, cocksfoot, collinsia, coltsfoot, columbine, cordgrass, coreopsis, corydalis, cymbidium, dandelion, dictamnus, digitalis, doronicum, echinacea, edelweiss, eglantine, epimedium, euphorbia, eyebright, germander, gladiolus, glasswort, goldenrod, goosefoot, groundnut, groundsel, heliopsis, hellebore, hollyhock, horsemint, horsetail, horseweed, houseleek, houstonia, impatiens, jaborandi, jewelweed, kniphofia *UK*, ligularia, malcolmia, matthiola, miterwort, molucella, moneywort, monkshood, moschatel, narcissus, navelwort, nemophila, nicotiana, oenothera, patchouli, pennywort, penstemon, pimpernel, pinedrops, polygonum, portulaca, put-

tyroot, pyrethrum, quillwort, rodgersia, rosinweed, rudbeckia, safflower, saponaria, saxifrage, snakeroot, speedwell, spikenard, stickseed, stickweed, stonecrop, sunflower, toothwort, tormentil, twinberry, verbascum, waterleaf, witchweed, woundwort; **10** acrolinium, agapanthus, agrostemma, alchemilla, amaranthus, aspidistra, barrenwort, beechdrops, belladonna, bellflower, bitterroot, bunchberry, butterwort, carpetweed, catananche, cimicifuga, cinquefoil, citronella, cliffbreak, cloudberry, coneflower, corncockle, cornflower, cortaderia, cranesbill, cuckoopint, delphinium, dragonroot, foamflower, fritillary, gaillardia, gayfeather, goatsbeard, goldenseal, goldthread, goosegrass, granadilla, greenbrier, gypsophila, helianthus, heliotrope, helleborus, jimsonweed, limnanthes, lysimachia, marguerite, masterwort, matricaria, meconopsis, mignonette, montbretia, moonflower, nasturtium, nipplewort, omphalodes, pennyroyal, periwinkle, platycodon, polemonium, polyanthus, potentilla, pulmonaria, ranunculus, sarracenia, snapdragon, sneezeweed, sneezewort, spiderwort, spleenwort, stitchwort, thalictrum, thunbergia, tropaeolum, turtlehead, twinflower, wallflower, watercress; **11** antirrhinum, bittersweet, bladderwort, calceolaria, camphorweed, centranthus, cheiranthus, convolvulus, crinkleroot, filipendula, gillyflower, helleborine *UK*, honeysuckle, horseradish, huckleberry, incarvillea, ipecacuanha, loosestrife, meadowsweet, physostegia, polygonatum, pontentilla, salmonberry, schizanthus *UK*, strawflower, thimbleweed, welwitschia *UK*, wintergreen, xeranthemum; **12** alstroemeria, callistephus, eschscholzia *UK*, helichrysumm, heliotropium, hemerocallis, kinnikinnick, monkeyflower, pasqueflower, pickerelweed, salpiglossis, schizostylis, thimbleberry, tradescantia; **13** chrysanthemum, dimorphotheca, passionflower, ranunculaceae; **14** partridgeberry; **PHRASES: 2, 5, 4** St John's Wort; **3-3, 4** joe-pye weed; **3-3, 5** red-hot poker; **3, 3, 6** old man cactus; **3-3, 8** mad-dog skullcap; **3, 4** bee balm, day lily, dog rose; **3, 4, 5** old man's beard; **3, 5** gum plant, ice plant, May apple, sea holly *UK*, sun plant, wax plant; **3, 6** big betony, dog violet *UK*, hog peanut, red clover, sea rocket; **3, 7** cow parsley *UK*, may blossom, sow thistle; **3, 8** fig marigold, pot marigold, red valerian *UK*, sea lavender; **4-2-1-4** love-in-a-mist; **4, 2, 3, 5** star of the veldt; **4-2-3-5** jack-by-the-hedge *UK*; **4, 2, 3, 6** lily of the valley; **4-2-3-6** jack-in-the-pulpit, lily-of-the-valley; **4, 2, 5** rose of China; **4, 2, 6** rose of heaven, rose of Sharon; **4, 2, 7** rose of Jericho; **4, 2, 9** Star of Bethlehem; **4-3** frogbit; **4, 4** arum lily, blue flag, cat's tail, fawn lily, fire pink, lady fern *UK*, lily turf, male fern, moss pink, rock rose, sand lily, seed fern, self heal, toad lily; **4, 4, 4** baby blue eyes; **4-4, 4** blue-eyed mary, blue-eyed Mary; **4, 4, 6** poor man's orchid; **4, 5** corn poppy, herb paris, musk plant, owl's claws, snow plant; **4-5** wake-robin; **4, 5, 6** dog's tooth violet; **4, 6** blue cohosh, busy lizzie, foam flower, herb robert, owl's clover, rose mallow, wild ginger, wild indigo, wood betony, wood sorrel; **4, 7** bull thistle, sand verbena, wood anemone; **4, 8** wild geranium; **5-2-3** touch-me-not; **5, 2, 7** bells of Ireland; **5, 3** goat's rue, sweet pea; **5-3** queencup; **5, 3, 3, 3** youth and old age; **5-3-6** lords-and-ladies *UK*; **5, 4** arrow arum, grass tree, lamb's ears *UK*, mare's tail, royal fern, stone mint, sweet flag, water lily; **5, 4, 4** bird's nest fern; **5-4, 5** black-eyed susan, black-eyed Susan; **5, 4, 6** bird's nest orchid; **5-4, 6** organ-pipe cactus; **5, 5** china aster, couch grass, death camas, dyer's broom, lady's smock, opium poppy, oxeye daisy, plume poppy, quack grass, sweet briar, thorn apple *UK*, Welsh poppy *UK*; **5, 6** Adam's needle, baby's breath, beard tongue, black cohosh, caper spurge, dwarf cornel, floss flower, globe flower, green dragon, horse nettle, lady's mantle *UK*, marsh mallow, satin flower, white clover; **5, 7** globe thistle, horse gentian, lady's slipper, skunk cabbage, sweet alyssum, sweet william, venus flytrap; **5-7** fool's-parsley; **5, 8** bear's breeches, grape hyacinth, marsh marigold; **5, 8, 9** Rocky Mountain columbine; **5, 9** black raspberry, white snakeroot; **5, 10** black nightshade, water chinquapin, woody nightshade; **6, 2, 2, 4** flower of an hour; **6-2-3** forget-me-not; **6, 3** aaron's rod, Aaron's rod, devil's fig, ground ivy, meadow rue, poison ivy, poison oak; **6-3, 5** castor-oil plant; **6, 4** amazon lily, Canada lily, cupid's dart, damask rose, golden club, ground pine, Indian hemp, Indian pink, Indian pipe, kaffir lily, lenten rose, rugosa rose, shield fern, snake's head *UK*, willow herb; **6-4-2** Johnny-jump-up; **6, 5** canary grass, golden aster, ground elder, London pride *UK*, marram grass, pampas grass,

ragged robin, rubber plant, shasta daisy, shrimp plant, spider plant, stokes' aster; **6, 6** annual mallow, autumn crocus, ground cherry, Jacob's ladder, ladino clover, meadow beauty, spring beauty, yellow rattle; **6, 7** Canada thistle, cherry blossom, garlic mustard *UK*, Indian tobacco, meadow saffron, orange blossom, winter aconite; **6, 8** French marigold, Robin's plantain, winter purslane; **6, 9** Seneca snakeroot; **6, 10** golden Alexanders, Indian paintbrush; **6, 11** pearly everlasting; **7, 3** bishop's hat; **7, 4** African lily, bishop's weed, blazing star, burning bush, foxtail lily, leopard lily, prickly pear, walking fern; **7, 5** African daisy, century plant, compass plant, morning glory, orchard grass, pitcher plant, prickly poppy, quaking grass, virgin's bower; **7, 6** African violet, balloon flower, blanket flower, calypso orchid, carrion flower, fringed orchis, painted tongue, prairie mallow, slipper flower, slipper orchid; **7, 7** Chinese lantern, fringed gentian, trumpet creeper; **7-7** prince's-feather; **7, 8** African marigold, evening primrose, fringed polygala; **7, 11** trumpet honeysuckle; **8, 3** kangaroo paw *UK*; **8, 4** leopard's bane, peruvian lily, shooting star, solomon's seal; **8, 5** bleeding heart, creeping jenny, elephant grass, townhall clock *UK*, virginia stock; **8, 6** cardinal flower, creeping Jennie; **8, 7** Japanese anemone, trailing arbutus, Virginia cowslip; **9, 3** traveler's joy; **9, 4** avalanche lily, butterfly weed, cathedral bell, Christmas fern, christmas rose; **9, 9** Jerusalem artichoke; **10, 4** belladonna lily, blackberry lily, canterbury bell, maidenhair fern; **10, 5** michaelmas daisy, Michaelmas daisy, turpentine plant.

plant science 6 botany; **8** algology, bryology, forestry, mycology, pomology; **9** phycology, phytology; **10** dendrology, palynology; **11** agrobiology, ethnobotany, lichenology, paleobotany, phytography, pteridology; **12** horticulture, phytogenesis, silviculture; **13** arboriculture; **14** phytochemistry, phytogeography, phytopathology, phytosociology; **16** paleoethnobotany; PHRASES: **4, 9** crop husbandry; **5, 7** plant anatomy, plant ecology; **5, 8** plant cytology, plant taxonomy; **5, 9** plant geography, plant pathology; **5, 10** plant physiology; **6, 8** pollen analysis.

plant scientist 8 botanist; **9** herbalist; **10** algologist, bryologist, mycologist, naturalist, pomologist; **11** phycologist, phytologist; **12** dendrologist, phytochemist, phytographer; **13** agrobiologist, ethnobotanist, lichenologist, paleobotanist, pteridologist; **15** phytogeneticist, phytogeographer; PHRASES: **5, 6** plant hunter.

plaster 4 cake, daub; **5** gesso, grout, secco, smeer; **6** fresco, gypsum, render, screed, stucco. *See also* **surgical dressing**

plastered *See* **drunk**

plastic 3 PVC; **4** soft; **5** bendy *UK*; **6** pliant; **7** ductile, plaible; **8** bakelite, bendable, flexible, melamine, moldable, yielding; **9** malleable, polythene *UK*; **12** polyethylene; PHRASES: **4, 4** bank card; **6, 4** credit card.

plastic surgery 8 facelift; **11** liposuction; PHRASES: **3, 3, 4** nip and tuck; **4, 3** boob job, nose job; **6, 9** breast reduction; **8, 7** cosmetic surgery.

plastron 11 breastplate.

plate 4 butt, coat, gild; **5** armor, cover, panel; **6** lamina, trophy; **7** denture, platter, surface; **12** illustration; PHRASES: **1, 5** L ~, T ~; **4, 5** gold ~, home ~; **5, 5** armor ~, swash ~, trade ~; **6, 5** nickel ~, number ~ *UK*, silver ~, wobble ~; **7, 5** fashion ~, futtock ~, license ~. *See also* **crockery**

plateau 4 hill; **5** level, phase, stage; **6** period, upland; **8** highland.

platelayer 8 trackman.

platform 5 stage, stand; **6** podium, policy; **7** program; **8** proposal; **9** manifesto.

plating 5 armor; **6** luster; **7** coating, gilding; **8** cladding; **14** electroplating; PHRASES: **5, 5** armor plate; **5, 6** metal casing, outer casing; **6-7** silver-plating.

platitude 6 cliché; **7** boredom, inanity; **8** banality, dullness; **9** plainness, triteness; **10** insipidity; **11** commonplace.

platonic 8 friendly; **9** nonsexual, spiritual; **11** nonphysical; **13** companionable.

platoon 4 team; **5** squad; **6** legion; **10** detachment; **11** subdivision.

platter *See* **crockery**

plausibility 10 likelihood; **11** credibility, possibility, probability; **13** acceptability, believability; **14** conceivability, reasonableness.

plausible *See* **believable**

play 3 act, bat, bet, bid, cut, fun, jam, MND, run; **4** call, cast, deal, draw, game, Lear, mime, move, pass, riff, rock, ruff, show, skip, skit, soap, text, trap; **5** drama, farce, lines, match, piece, raise, stack, sweep, swing, throw; **6** biopic, castle, cavort, comedy, depict, frolic, fumble, gamble, gambol, Hamlet, Kabuki, keeper, Kyogen, masque, pocket, render, script, serial, shadow, sketch, stroke; **7** bootleg, charade, compete, cutback, finesse, handoff, leisure, Macbeth, misdeal, perform, playlet, pretend, reverse, rollout, shuffle, tragedy, trilogy, vehicle; **8** dialogue, dumbshow, duodrama, duologue, entr'acte, libretto, pastoral, scenario, teleplay; **9** burlesque, docudrama, happening, improvise, interlude, interpret, melodrama, monodrama, monologue, Mousetrap, pantomime, swordplay, tetralogy; **10** antimasque, intermezzo, recreation, screenplay, sociodrama; **11** psychodrama; **12** harlequinade, Oberammergau, rockumentary; **13** improvisation; **14** divertissement; PHRASES: **2, 3, 4** up the ante; **2, 4** No ~; **3-3, 4** one-man show; **3-5, 4** one-woman show; **3-6** two-hander; **4, 2** join in; **4, 2, 3** ~ by ear; **4, 2, 5** book of words; **4, 5** soap opera; **4, 6** fool around; **5, 2, 4** slice of life; **5, 4** radio ~, stage ~; **5, 5** Greek drama, verse drama; **5, 7** Grand Guignol; **6, 2** strike up; **6, 4** double bill, fiddle with, prompt book; **6, 5** closet drama, heroic drama, poetic drama; **7, 4** miracle ~, mummers' ~, mystery ~, passion ~, problem ~, running game; **7-6** curtain-lifter, curtain-raiser; **8, 4** morality ~.

play down 4 pare; **6** dilute, reduce; **7** curtail; **8** diminish, downplay, moderate, restrain; **9** constrain, deprecate, disregard, underplay; PHRASES: **2-9** de-emphasize; **4, 4** pare down, tone down; **4, 5, 2** make light of; **5, 3** shrug off; **5, 4** water down.

player 1 E, N, S, W; **4** back, half, mime, prop, wing; **5** actor; **6** batter, bowler, goalie, hooker, keeper, mummer, stereo, winger; **7** actress, batsman, fielder, flanker, flyhalf, forward, jukebox, pitcher, striker, sweeper; **8** fullback, halfback, thespian, wingback; **10** goalkeeper; **11** participant, quarterback; **12** threequarter; PHRASES: **5-3, 4** stand-off half. *See also* **musician**

playfellow *See* **friend**

playful 5 jokey; **6** bouncy, frisky, lively; **7** teasing; **12** lighthearted; PHRASES: **4, 2, 3** full of fun; **4, 2, 4** full of life; **4-7** good-humored, good-natured.

playhouse 3 den; 5 venue; 6 studio; 7 theater; 10 auditorium; PHRASES: 4, 5 tree house; 5, 5 Wendy house *UK*.

playing card 1 X; 3 ace; 4 club, jack, king; 5 deuce, heart, joker, knave, queen, spade; 7 diamond; 8 wildcard; PHRASES: 4, 4 face card; 5, 4 court card; 7, 4 picture card.

playwright *See* dramatist

plea 3 cry; 4 suit; 5 cause, claim; 6 answer, excuse, plaint; 7 apology, defense, request; 8 argument, entreaty, pleading; 10 invocation; 11 explanation, vindication; 13 consideration, justification; 15 rationalization.

plead 3 ask, beg; 4 pray; 5 argue, claim; 6 answer, defend; 7 canvass, entreat, explain, implore, justify, request; 8 persuade; 9 apologize, vindicate; 11 rationalize; PHRASES: 7, 4 prevail upon.

plead for 7 support; 8 champion; 9 vindicate; PHRASES: 5, 1, 5, 3 break a lance for; 5, 3 argue for, fight for.

pleasant 3 fun; 4 cozy, good, kind, lush, nice, snug, soft, warm; 5 cushy, fresh, juicy, sweet; 6 divine, dulcet, genial, kindly, lovely, polite, silken, smooth, subtle; 7 affable, amiable, cordial, easeful, Elysian, genteel, helpful, idyllic, likable, lovable, restful, sublime, welcome; 8 blissful, charming, fragrant, friendly, generous, heavenly, inviting, luscious, obliging, pleasing, relaxing, soothing, tasteful; 9 agreeable, ambrosial, appealing, congenial, convivial, delicious, enjoyable, exquisite, luxuriant, luxurious, melodious, palatable, seductive, succulent, sumptuous, welcoming; 10 acceptable, attractive, comforting, cuddlesome, delectable, delightful, euphonious, gratifying, hospitable, refreshing, satisfying, voluptuous; 11 comfortable, mellifluous, pleasurable, scrumptious, titillating; 12 paradisiacal; 13 mouthwatering; PHRASES: 2, 4 de luxe; 2, 4, 5 to one's taste; 2, 4, 6 to one's liking; 3, 2, 4, 5 out of this world; 5-7 heart-warming; 5-8 sweet-smelling.

please 4 suit; 5 amuse, charm, cheer, humor; 6 divert, oblige; 7 content, delight, flatter, fulfill, gladden, gratify, indulge, satisfy; 9 entertain.

pleased 4 glad; 5 happy; 6 elated; 7 chuffed *UK*, content; 8 grateful, thankful, thrilled; 9 contented, delighted, gratified, overjoyed, satisfied; PHRASES: 2, 5, 4 on cloud nine; 2, 7, 6 in seventh heaven; 4, 3, 4 over the moon; 7, 2, 5 ~ as Punch; 7, 4 tickled pink.

pleasing *See* pleasant

pleasure 3 fun; 4 ease, will, zest; 5 bliss, taste; 6 liking, luxury, orgasm; 7 comfort, delight; 8 euphoria, felicity, hedonism; 9 amusement, carnality, diversion, enjoyment, eroticism, fragrance, happiness, sweetness, tastiness; 10 indulgence, loveliness, profligacy, sensualism; 11 contentment, dissipation, titillation; 12 conviviality, epicureanism, satisfaction, sensuousness; 13 entertainment, gourmandizing, gratification; 14 voluptuousness; PHRASES: 4-5 well-being; 4-10 self-indulgence.

pleasure (feel pleasure) 4 bask, purr; 5 enjoy; 6 climax, nestle, relish, wallow; 7 snuggle, splurge; 9 luxuriate; 10 gormandize; PHRASES: 3, 1, 4, 3, 2 get a kick out of; 4, 1, 4 have a ball; 4, 3 have fun; 4, 4 feel good; 4, 5 make merry; 4, 8, 2 take pleasure in; 5, 2 revel in; 5, 3, 4, 3 paint the town red; 5, 7 enjoy oneself; 6, 7 please oneself; 7, 2 delight in; 7, 4, 4 feather one's nest; 7, 7 indulge oneself.

pleasure (give pleasure) 3 hug, pet; 4 sate; 5 amuse, charm, cheer, treat; 6 arouse, cuddle, excite, fondle, please, regale, soothe, thrill, tickle; 7 comfort, delight, gladden, gratify, indulge, satiate, satisfy; 9 entertain, stimulate, titillate; PHRASES: 4, 3, 4 gild the pill, wine and dine; 5, 3, 4 sugar the pill; 5, 4 agree with; 6, 4 tickle pink *UK*; 7, 3, 4 sweeten the pill; 8, 4, 3 brighten one's day.

pleasure-loving 7 gourmet, sensual; 8 gourmand; 9 epicurean; 10 hedonistic, voluptuous; PHRASES: 3-6 fun-loving; 4-9 self-indulgent; 8-7 pleasure-seeking.

pleasure-loving person 8 hedonist; 9 epicurean; PHRASES: 10 voluptuary.

pleasure-seeker 4 rake, roué; 7 epicure, gourmet, playboy, seducer, swinger; 8 gourmand, hedonist, mistress, sybarite; 9 courtesan, epicurean, jetsetter, libertine; 10 degenerate, seductress, sensualist, voluptuary; 11 connoisseur, philanderer; 3, 6 bon viveur; 4-4, 4 good-time girl; 5, 2, 4 fille de joie; 5-5 lotus-eater.

pleat 4 ruck, tuck; 5 braid, crimp, plait, ruche, shirr; 6 crease, furrow, gather, pucker, ripple, ruffle, rumple; 7 crinkle, crumple, flounce, wrinkle; **8** inverted; **9** corrugate; **11** corrugation; PHRASES: **3, 5** box ~; **4, 2** tuck up; **4, 5** kick ~; **5, 5** knife ~ *UK*; **6, 5** french ~; **9, 5** accordion ~.

plebeian 3 low; **4** hick, pleb, serf; **5** cheap, churl, prole, tacky, yokel; **6** common, plebby, rustic, vulgar; **7** bumpkin, peasant, villein; **8** everyman, ordinary; **9** bourgeois, hillbilly, titleless, underling; **10** husbandman, provincial; **11** proletarian; PHRASES: **2, 6** Mr Nobody; **3-2-3-6** man-in-the-street; **3, 6** Joe Public *UK*; **4, 4** John Bull; **5, 3** Essex man *UK*; **6, 3** common man, little man; **6, 6** normal person; **7, 3** regular guy; **7, 6** country cousin; **7, 7** country bumpkin; **8, 5** ordinary bloke.

pledge *See* **promise**

plentiful 3 fat; **4** lush, rank, rich; **5** ample, great; **6** lavish; **7** copious, endless, fertile, liberal, opulent, profuse, riotous; **8** abundant, affluent, generous, prodigal, prolific; **9** bountiful, luxuriant, plenteous, redundant, unsparing, wholesale; **10** bottomless, unmeasured; **11** extravagant, luxuriating, overflowing, superfluous; **13** inexhaustible, superabundant; PHRASES: **4, 4, 6** more than enough; **4-6** open-handed; **7, 5** without stint.

plenty 3 fat, lot; **4** glut, lots, orgy, riot; **5** feast, flood, heaps *UK*, loads, piles, spate; **6** excess, foison, galore, luxury, oodles, riches, shower, stream, wealth; **7** banquet, bonanza, surplus; **8** fullness, lashings *UK*, lushness, richness; **9** abundance, affluence, amplitude, fecundity, fertility, fleshpots, plenitude, profusion; **10** cornucopia, luxuriance, outpouring; **11** copiousness, prodigality, prolificacy, superfluity; **12** extravagance, productivity, prolificness; **13** plenteousness, plentifulness, proliferation; **14** productiveness, superabundance; PHRASES: **1, 3** a lot; **3, 2, 4** fat of the land; **3, 4** boo koos, too much; **4, 2, 6** horn of ~; **4, 3, 5** milk and honey; **4, 4** rich vein; **4, 4, 6** more than enough; **4, 8** food mountain; **6, 4** bumper crop; **7, 6** endless supply; **7, 7** vintage harvest; **8, 5** groaning board.

plenty (time of plenty) 5 prime, youth; **6** heyday, summer; **7** holiday; **8** vacation; PHRASES: **3, 2, 8** age of Aquarius; **4, 5** easy times, good times; **5, 4** palmy days, salad days; **6, 3** golden age; **6, 4** golden days; **7, 4** halcyon days; **8, 5** Saturnia regna; **9, 6** honeymoon period.

pliable 6 docile; **8** yielding; **9** compliant.

See also **pliant**

pliant 4 waxy; **5** lithe, pasty; **6** doughy, giving, limber, lissom, supple; **7** ductile, elastic, flexile, lissome, melting, plastic, pliable, springy, willowy; **8** athletic, bendable, flexible, moldable, tractile, yielding; **9** acrobatic *UK*, adaptable, extensile, lithesome, malleable, shapeable, tractable; **10** extendible, extensible; **11** impressible, stretchable; PHRASES: **5-4** putty-like; **5-6** loose-limbed; **6-7** double-jointed.

plight 3 fix, jam; **4** hole; **5** pinch; **6** corner, crisis, pickle, pledge; **7** betroth, dilemma, trouble; **8** exigency, quandary; **9** emergency; **11** predicament; PHRASES: **5-2** catch-22; **6, 4** pretty pass.

plop *See* **plunk**

plot 3 bed, lot, map, web; **4** brew, game, land, plan, ploy, trap, yard; **5** block, cabal, claim, frame, hatch, patch, story, tract; **6** garden, racket, scheme; **7** acreage, collude, concoct, connive, ensnare, holding, latency, program, secrecy, section; **8** conspire, intrigue, maneuver; **9** allotment *UK*, collusion, enclosure, machinate, undermine; **10** conspiracy, manipulate; **11** countermine, counterplot, machination, wirepulling; **12** manipulation; PHRASES: **3-2** fit-up *UK*, put-up; **3-2, 3** put-up job; **3, 2, 8** web of intrigue; **4, 5** pull wires; **4, 7** pull strings, work against; **5-2** frame-up; **5, 3, 4** wheel and deal; **6, 2, 4** parcel of land; **6, 3** inside job; **6, 4** secret plan; **6, 7** string pulling; **6, 9** secret influence; **7, 7** insider dealing *UK*, insider trading.

plotter 7 schemer; **8** saboteur; **9** conspirer, intrigant *UK*, intriguer; **10** machinator, subversive; **11** conspirator, fraternizer; **12** collaborator; PHRASES: **3, 6** Guy Fawkes; **5, 9** fifth columnist; **6, 8** fellow traveler; **8, 4** security risk.

plover 7 lapwing.

plow 4 till, work; **9** cultivate; PHRASES: **4, 4** turn over.

ploy 4 plan, ruse; **5** trick; **8** maneuver, strategy.

pluck 3 tug; **4** pick, pull, take, yank; **5** grasp, plunk, strum, twang, tweak; **6** gather, remove, uproot; **7** bravery, collect, courage, harvest, resolve; **9** fortitude; **13** determination; PHRASES: **4, 3** pull out.

plucky *See* **brave**

plug 2 ad; **3** dam; **4** bung, fuse, puff, push,

stop, tamp; **5** block; **6** dimmer, outlet, socket, switch; **7** promote, stopper; **9** interface, promotion, publicity; **11** termination; PHRASES: **4, 2** stop up; **4, 6** trip switch; **7, 6** dimming switch; **7, 7** circuit breaker.

plum 5 award, bonus, prune; **6** choice, damson, reward, trophy; **8** windfall; **9** covetable, desirable; **10** profitable; **11** prestigious. *See also* **fruit**

plumage 4 down, ruff, vane; **5** alula, crest, frill, plume, quill, remex; **6** covert, rachis; **7** barbule, feather, primary, pteryla, rectrix, tectrix; **8** apterium, barbicel, feathers, plumulae; **9** eiderdown, filoplume, secondary; **10** aftershaft; PHRASES: **4, 7** tail feather, wing feather; **4, 8** down feathers; **5-4** swan's-down; **6, 7** flight feather; **7, 4** bastard wing; **7, 7** contour feather.

plumb 4 bang, face, know, slap, true; **5** grasp, right; **6** fathom, suffer; **7** exactly, undergo, upright; **8** vertical; **9** precisely; **10** comprehend, experience, understand; **13** perpendicular.

plump 3 fat; **4** drop, fall, flop; **6** chubby; **10** overweight; PHRASES: **4, 4** flop down, plop down.

plunder 3 rob; **4** loot, raid, rape, sack; **5** booty, foray; **6** forage, ravage, ravish, spoils; **7** despoil, pillage, ransack; **8** freeboot, spoliate; **9** depredate; **11** depredation; PHRASES: **3, 1, 5** rob a grave; **4, 3, 7** loot and pillage; **4, 4** prey upon.

plunderer 6 bandit, raider, rapist, sacker; **7** brigand, corsair, ravager, spoiler, wrecker; **8** marauder, pillager, ravisher; **9** buccaneer, despoiler, privateer, ransacker; **10** Blackbeard, depredator, freebooter; **11** mosstrooper; PHRASES: **4, 7** Jean Lafitte; **4-8** body-snatcher; **5-6** grave-robber, slave-raider.

plunge 4 dive, drop, fall, jump, leap, push, rush, sink; **5** force, lurch, pitch, throw; **6** thrust; **7** plummet; PHRASES: **4-4** nose-dive.

plunk 3 put; **4** dump, plop; **5** place; PHRASES: **3, 4** put down, set down. *See also* **wine**

plural 3 few; **4** many, more, most, some; **7** certain, several; **8** majority, multiple, numerous; **9** nonsingle; **13** multitudinous; PHRASES: **2, 3, 6** in the ~; **3, 8** not singular; **4, 4, 3** more than one; **4, 2** upwards of.

pluralist 8 polyglot, polymath; **10** polygamist, polytheist; **15** multilateralist; PHRAS-

ES: **3-7** all-rounder *UK*; **11, 3** Renaissance man.

pluralize 5 clone; **7** plurify; **8** increase, multiply; **9** propagate, replicate; **11** proliferate.

plus 4 boon; **5** bonus; **7** benefit; **8** positive; **9** advantage, desirable, favorable; **12** advantageous; PHRASES: **2, 4, 2** as well as; **2, 8, 2** in addition to; **3, 4** and more, and over; **3, 5** and above; **4, 5** ~ point *UK*; **5, 2** added to; **5, 4** along with; **8, 4** together with.

plush 4 lush, rich; **6** lavish; **9** expensive, luxurious.

plutocrat 8 merchant; **10** capitalist; **11** millionaire; PHRASES: **3, 3** fat cat.

plutonic 7 abyssal.

plutonium 2 PU.

ply 3 use; **4** load, pile, tier, work; **5** apply, hound, layer; **6** badger, employ, harass, pursue, strand, supply; **7** bombard, provide, utilize; **8** practice; **9** overwhelm, thickness.

Plymouth 8, 3 P~ hoe; **8, 4** P~ rock; **8, 6** P~ colony.

PM 7 pipemma; **9** afternoon (Latin: post meridiem); **10** postmortem; PHRASES: **5, 8** Prime Minister.

PO 4, 6 Post Office; **5, 7** petty officer; **6, 5** postal order *UK*.

poach 4 boil; **5** steal, steam; **6** braise, pilfer, rustle, simmer, thieve; **7** plunder.

pocket 3 bag; **4** sack, take; **5** pouch, small, steal; **7** concise, reduced, snaffle *UK*; **8** abridged; **11** appropriate, compartment.

pod *See* **shell**

poem 3 lay, ode; **4** alba, epic, epos, hymn, saga, song; **5** cento, dirge, elegy, epode, haiku, idyll, lyric, psalm, rhyme, tanka, verse; **6** aubade, ballad, monody, rondel, satire, sonnet; **7** ballade, bucolic, chanson, eclogue, epigram, georgic, rondeau, roundel, sestina, tenzone, triolet, virelay; **8** clerihew, encomium, limerick, madrigal, palinode, pastoral, reverdie, threnody; **9** complaint, dithyramb, roundelay, vilanelle; **12** epithalamium, prothalamion; PHRASES: **5, 7** verse epistle; **6, 3** choric ode; **6, 8** sonnet sequence; **7, 3** Sapphic ode; **7, 4** elegiac ~; **7, 5** nursery rhyme; **7, 6** English sonnet, Italian sonnet; **8, 3** Horatian ode, Pindaric ode; **8, 5** pastoral elegy; **9, 4** narrative ~; **10, 4** troubadour ~.

poem (part of poem) 3 fit; **4** book,

foot, line; **5** canto, envoi, epode, octet, stave, verse; **6** burden, chorus, octave, septet, sestet, stanza, strain, tercet; **7** couplet, distich, measure, refrain, strophe, triplet; **8** quatrain, tristich; **9** hemistich, hexastich, monostich, octastich; **10** heptastich, pentastich, tetrastich; **11** antistrophe; PHRASES: **4, 4** half line; **5, 9** verse paragraph; **6, 7** closed couplet; **7, 7** rhyming couplet.

poet 2 AE; **3** Gay, Key (Francis Scott); PHRASES: **4** Abse, bard, Dove (Rita), Dyer, Gray, Gunn, Hood, Hugo, Lear, Nash (Ogden), Ovid, Owen, Pope, Rumi (Jalal ad-Din Muhammad Din ar-); **5** Aiken (Conrad), Auden, Basho, Benét (Stephen Vincent), Blake, Bogan (Louise), Burns, Byron, Carew, Cinna, Clare, Crane (Hart), Dante, Dante, Donne, Eliot, Frost, Gower, Hardy (Thomas), Heine, Homer, Keats, Lorca, Lucan, Martí (José), Moore (Marianne), Morre, Noyes, odist, Plath, Pound, Prior, Riley (James Whitcomb), Rilke, Scott (Sir Walter), Smith (Stevie), Tasso, Yeats, Young; **6** Arnold, Austin, Barnes, Belloc, Bishop (Elizabeth), Brontë (Emily), Brooke, Brooks (Gwendolyn), Butler, Carman (Bliss), Ciardi (John), Clough, Cowper, Crabbe, Cullen (Countee), Dowson, Dryden, Dunbar, Éluard (Paul), Gibran (Khalil), Goethe, Graves, Heaney (Seamus), Hesiod, Horace, Hughes, Jonson, Kilmer (Joyce), Kunitz (Stanley), Larkin (Philip), Lowell, lyrist, McCrae (John), Millay (Edna St. Vincent), Milton, Motion, Neruda (Pablo), Ossian, Pindar, Pinsky (Robert), Ransom (John Crowe), rhymer, Sappho, Sexton (Anne), Sidney, Thomas, Valéry (Paul), Villon, Virgil, Waller, Warren (Robert Penn); **7** Alcaeus, Ariosto, Bridges, Brodsky (Joseph), Caedmon, Campion, Chapman, Chaucer, Collins, elegist, Emerson, Flecker, Herbert, Herrick, Hopkins, Housman, Jarrell (Randall), Johnson, Juvenal, Kipling (Rudyard), Larking, Martial, Marvell, Masters (Edgar Lee), Newbolt, Pushkin, Rimbaud (Arthur), Roberts (Sir Charles George Douglas), Roethke (Theodore), Ronsard, Sassoon, Shelley, Sitwell, Southey, Spender, Spenser, Statius, Stevens, Whitman; **8** Anacreon, Berryman (John), Betjeman, Browning, Campbell, Catullus, Crémazie (Octave), cummings, Firdawsi, Ginsberg (Allen), Langland, Lovelace, lyricist, MacLeish (Archibald), Mallarmé, minstrel,

Petrarch, Robinson (Edwin Arlington), Rossetti, Sandburg (Carl), Schiller (Friedrich von), Suckling, Tennyson, Thompson, Verlaine, Wheatley (Phillis), Whittier (John Greenleaf); **9** Akhmatova (Anna), Coleridge, Dickinson (Emily), Doolittle (Hilda), Goldsmith, Lamartine, Lermontov (Mikhail Yuryevich), Lucretius, Masefield, Pasternak (Boris), Quasimodo, rhymester, sonneteer, Stevenson, Swinburne, Tranherne, troubador, versifier, wordsmith; **10** Baudelaire, Bradstreet (Anne), Chatterton, Fitzgerald (Edward), Longfellow, MacDiarmid (Hugh), Mandelstam (Osip Yemilyevich), Mickiewicz (Adam), Propertius, Wordsworth; **11** Apollinaire (Guillaume), Minnesinger, Shakespeare (William), Yevtushenko (Yevgeny Aleksandrovich); **13** Meistersinger; **2, 2** Li Bo; **2, 2, 4** de la Mare; **3, 5** Van Doren (Mark); **3-5** Day-Lewis (Cecil); **4, 7** Omar Khayyam; **4, 8** ~ laureate; **6, 4, 3, 2** Camões (Luís (Vaz) de); **8, 2, 2, 5** Calderón de la Barca (Pedro); **8, 2, 6** Chrétien de Troyes.

poetic 7 elegiac, lyrical; **8** metrical, rhythmic; PHRASES: **6, 7** ~ justice, ~ license.

poetry 4 epos, song; **5** poesy, rhyme, verse; **7** ditties, jingles, numbers, poetics; **8** balladry, doggerel; **10** macaronics; **13** versification; PHRASES: **3, 6** dub ~ *UK*, rap ~; **4, 2, 7** vers de société; **4, 5** lame verse; **4, 6** epic ~, folk ~; **5, 5** light verse, runic verse; **5, 6** comic ~, lyric ~; **6, 6** erotic ~, heroic ~; **7, 6** elegiac ~; **8, 6** concrete ~, didactic ~, dramatic ~, pastoral ~; **9, 6** narrative ~.

poignant *See* **moving**

point 1 E, N, S, W; **3** dot, end, tip, use; **4** cusp, goal, idea, path, plan, spot, tine, west; **5** fesse, issue, limit, locus, prong, spike, spine, sting, value, worth, yield; **6** design, intent, moment, object, outlet, period, sample, vertex; **7** instant, meaning, purpose; **8** indicate, juncture, location, midpoint, occasion, position; **9** intention, objective; PHRASES: **3, 5** dew ~, dry ~, set ~; **4, 5** game ~, high ~, trig ~; **5, 5** cover ~ *UK*, fixed ~, flash ~, focal ~, match ~, petit ~; **6, 5** strong ~; **7, 5** boiling ~, brownie ~, compass ~, decimal ~, diamond ~, melting ~, turning ~, vantage ~; **8, 5** breaking ~, critical ~, fiducial ~, freezing ~, pressure ~, variable ~; **9, 5** reference ~, vanishing ~; **10, 5** saturation ~, stationary ~, suspension ~.

pointer 3 tip; **4** cane, hand, hint, pole; **5**

baton, stick; **6** advice, cursor, needle; **9** indicator; **10** suggestion.

point in time 5 point; **6** moment; **7** instant; **8** juncture, occasion.

pointless 6 futile; **7** useless; **9** senseless, worthless; PHRASES: **11** meaningless.

point-to-point 12 steeplechase.

poise 6 polish; **7** balance; **8** calmness; **9** sangfroid; **10** confidence; **11** insouciance, nonchalance.

poison 4 drug; **5** spoil, taint, toxin, venom; **6** infect; **7** arsenic, bespoil, cyanide, hemlock, pollute; **8** besmirch, Paraquat, ratsbane, rotenone, warfarin; **9** pollutant; **10** adulterate, carcinogen, intoxicate, strychnine, weedkiller; **11** contaminant, contaminate, insecticide; PHRASES: **3, 6** rat ~; **6, 8** carbon monoxide; **7, 4** prussic acid; **7, 5** exhaust fumes.

poisoning 8 toxicity; **9** contagion, infection, pollution; **12** venomousness; **13** poisonousness.

poisonous 4 evil; **5** fatal, nasty, toxic; **6** deadly, lethal, wicked; **7** hostile, noxious, vicious; **8** mephitic, spiteful, venomous; **9** malicious; **10** malevolent; **12** pestilential, vituperative; PHRASES: **3-11** ill-intentioned.

poke 3 jab, jut; **4** prod, push, root, stab; **6** browse, extend, thrust; **7** project, rummage; **8** protrude; PHRASES: **5, 3** stick out.

poker hands 5 flush; **8** straight; PHRASES: **3, 4** one pair; **3, 5** two pairs; **4, 2, 1, 4** four of a kind; **4, 5** full house; **5, 2, 1, 4** three of a kind; **5, 5** royal flush; **8, 5** straight flush.

pole 1 N, S; **3** rod; **4** post; **5** caber, perch, shaft, sprit, staff, stake; **6** Arctic; PHRASES: **7, 4** barber's ~; **8, 4** magnetic ~; **9, 4** celestial ~.

polecat 5 fitch; **7** fitchew, foumart; PHRASES: **4, 6** foul marten.

polemic 4 bold, plea; **6** speech; **8** argument, diatribe; **9** discourse, outspoken; **11** impassioned; **13** controversial; **14** uncompromising.

police 2 MP; **3** APB, ATF, CIA, DEA, FBI, NIJ; **4** Earp (Wyatt), Feeb, LAPD, NYPD, Peel (Robert), SFPD, SWAT; **5** bobby, state; **6** shamus; **7** control, marshal, sheriff; **8** bluecoat, Interpol, Mounties, regulate, stakeout; **11** gendarmerie; **12** constabulary; PHRASES: **3, 3** the law; **3, 4** the pigs; **3, 4, 2, 4** the boys in blue; **3, 4, 4, 4** the thin blue

line; **3, 5** the force; **3, 6** air ~; **3-6, 8** all-points bulletin; **4, 2, 4** boys in blue *UK*; **4, 6** park ranger; **5, 4** squad room; **5, 5** Amber alert; **5, 6** shore patrol; **5, 7** state trooper; **6, 5** ~ force; **7, 5** station house; **7, 6** airport ~, Highway Patrol, Transit P~; **7, 7** Customs Service; **8, 4** Scotland Yard *UK*; **8, 6** military ~.

police officer 3 cop; **4** bull, busy, dick, flic, plod; **5** bizzy *UK*, bobby *UK*, posse, super, watch; **6** copper *UK*, peeler, rozzer *UK*; **7** Mountie; **8** sergeant; **9** constable, detective, inspector, patrolman, policeman; **10** lieutenant; **12** commissioner; **14** superintendent; PHRASES: **3, 4** fly dick; **3-8** law-enforcer; **4, 8** desk sergeant; **5, 2, 6** chief of police; **5, 9** chief constable *UK*, posse comitatus; **6, 4** Smokey Bear; **7, 3** traffic cop; **7, 7** provost marshal.

policy 5 plank, slate, steps; **6** course, system, ticket; **7** actions, formula, mandate, tactics; **8** approach, doctrine, measures, platform, scenario, strategy; **9** diplomacy, foresight, manifesto, procedure; **10** prospectus; **11** forethought; **13** statesmanship; PHRASES: **4, 2, 6** plan of action; **5, 4** party line; **6, 2, 6** course of action; **7, 4** working plan.

polish 3 oil, rub, wax; **4** buff, sand; **5** dress, glaze, gloss, shine; **6** enamel, facing, grease, oilcan, patina, refine, smooth; **7** burnish, varnish; **9** lubricant; **10** lubricator; PHRASES: **3, 6** car ~; **4, 6** shoe ~; **5, 6** elbow grease, floor ~; **6, 3** grease gun; **6, 6** French ~, silver ~; **9, 6** furniture ~.

polished 4 oily; **5** glacé, oiled, shiny, slick, soapy, waxed; **6** glassy, glazed, glossy, greasy, skiddy; **7** buttery, greased, refined; **8** enameled, gleaming, slippery, slithery; **9** burnished, lacquered, perfected, varnished; **10** lubricated, lubricious, reflective; PHRASES: **6-4** mirror-like.

polite 5 civil; **7** elegant, refined; **8** cultured, gracious, polished; **13** sophisticated; PHRASES: **4-4** well-bred; **4-8** well-mannered.

political 3 red; **5** green; **7** leftist, liberal, popular, radical; **8** partisan; **9** factional, sectarian, sectional; **10** affiliated, associated, bipartisan, particular, separatist; **11** communistic, independent, nonpartisan, politicized, socialistic; **13** nationalistic; PHRASES: **4-4** left-wing, true-blue; **5-4** right-wing; **5-6** party-minded; **6-2-3-4** middle-of-the-road.

political family 4 Bush, Taft; **5** Adams; **7** Kennedy; **8** Harrison; **9** Roosevelt; PHRAS-

ES: **2, 7** La Follete.

political party 2 NF *UK*; **3** ANC, Con *UK*, GOP, Lab *UK*, Lib *UK*, PCP, SNP *UK*, UUP; **4** bloc, bund, SDLP *UK*; **5** Azapo, Baath, cadre, Nazis, Whigs; **6** cartel, Greens, Labour, Tories; **7** Falange; **8** Congress, Fascists, Jacobins, Liberals, Marxists, Radicals; **9** Carbonari; **10** Bolsheviks, Communists, Ecologists, Falangists, Girondists, Kuomintang, Mensheviks, Separatist, Socialists, Solidarity; **11** Blackshirts, Brownshirts, Trotskyists; **12** Nationalists; **13** International; PHRASES: **2, 5** Al Fatah; **3, 3** Mau Mau; **3, 6** New Labour *UK*; **4, 4** Fine Gael, Sinn Féin, Sinn Féin (Northern Ireland); **4, 5** Whig Party; **4, 5, 7** John Birch Society; **4-7** Know-Nothing; **4, 9** Bloc Québécois; **5, 2** Fatah, Al; **5, 3, 5** Grand Old Party; **5, 5** Green Party, Khmer Rouge, Plaid Cymru *UK*; **5, 9** Parti Québécois; **6, 4** Fianna Fáil; **6, 5** Labour Party, Reform Party; **6, 6** Muslim League, Social Credit; **6, 7** Fabian Society; **6, 8, 5** Ulster Unionist Party; **6, 10, 3, 6, 5** Social Democratic and Labour Party *UK*; **7, 4** Tammany Hall; **7, 5** Liberal Party, People's Party *Austria*, popular front; **7, 8, 8** African National Congress; **7, 14, 13** Partido Revolucionario Institucional; **8, 5** National Front, National Party, Populist Party; **9, 5** Communist Party, Greenback Party, Socialist Party; **10, 5** Democratic Party, Federalist Party, Republican Party; **10, 8, 5** Democratic Unionist Party; **11, 5** Libertarian Party, Progressive Party.

politician 2 MP *UK*; **3** dry, pol, Red, wet; **4** Nazi, peer, Trot *UK*, whip; **5** lefty; **6** commie, leftie, Senate; **7** comrade, fascist, leftist, liberal, Marxist, radical; **8** activist, centrist, democrat, diplomat, loyalist, minister, moderate, politico, populist, revolter, rightist, stalwart; **9** anarchist, canvasser, communist, ecologist, secretary, sectarian, socialist; **11** backbencher, Congressman, independent, nationalist, reactionary, syndicalist; **12** backgrounder, majoritarian; **14** Representative, undersecretary; **15** Parliamentarian; PHRASES: **3-4** neo-Nazi; **4, 4** life peer; **4-5** hard-liner; **4-6** left-winger; **4, 12** flag conservative; **5, 4** chief whip *UK*, party whip; **5, 6** party member, party worker; **5-6** right-winger; **5, 7** floor manager, party manager; **5, 8** party chairman; **6, 6** access broker; **6-6** smooth-talker; **6, 8** junior minister; **7, 3** advance man; **7, 5** advance woman; **7, 6** advance person, cabinet member; **7, 8** cabinet minister; **8, 4** majority whip, minority whip; **8, 6** majority leader, minority leader; **8, 12** resident commissioner.

politics 5 views; **6** policy, theory; **7** beliefs, bossism, Bushism; **8** opinions; **9** Bushistan; **10** boondoggle, government, principles; PHRASES: **3, 3** big lie; **4, 3** burn bag; **5, 5** brain trust; **5, 6** bully pulpit; **5-6** brass-collar; **6-4** boiler-room.

poll 4 head; **5** count; **6** ballot, parrot; **8** election; PHRASES: **3, 4** red ~; **4, 4** deed ~ *UK*, MORI ~; **5, 4** straw ~; **6, 4** Gallup ~; **7, 4** opinion ~.

pollen basket 9 corbicula.

pollinosis 3, 5 hay fever.

polliwog 7 tadpole.

pollute 6 damage, infect, infest, poison; **7** corrupt, pervert, violate; **10** adulterate, demoralize; **11** contaminate.

pollution 5 stain; **6** miasma; **7** fallout; **9** effluence.

poltergeist *See* **ghost**

polygon 5 rhomb; **6** oblong, square; **7** decagon, diamond, hexagon, lozenge, nonagon, octagon, rhombus; **8** heptagon, hexagram, pentacle, pentagon, polyline, tetragon, triangle; **9** pentagram, pentangle, rectangle, trapezium; **10** quadrangle; **13** parallelogram.

polygonal 6 square; **7** rhombic; **8** rhomboid; **9** hexagonal, octagonal, trapezoid; **10** heptagonal, pentagonal, rhomboidal, tetragonal, triangular; **11** rectangular; **12** multiangular; **13** quadrilateral; PHRASES: **5-6** wedge-shaped; **7-6** diamond-shaped.

polygraph 6 tester; **8** detector, recorder; PHRASES: **3, 8** lie detector.

polyhedron 4 cube; **5** prism, wedge; **6** cuboid; **7** frustum, pyramid; **8** prismoid; **10** hexahedron, octahedron, prismatoid; **11** icosahedron, pentahedron, tetrahedron; **12** dodecahedron, rhombohedron; **14** parallelepiped; PHRASES: **8, 5** Platonic solid.

polymer 3 PVC; **4** PTFE, uPVC, **5** chain, nylon, resin; **6** Teflon™; **7** monomer, Perspex™, plastic; **8** Bakelite™; **9** copolymer, polyester, polythene *UK*, Styrofoam, vulcanite; **10** Plexiglass™, stabilizer; **11** homopolymer, plasticizer, polystyrene; **12** polyethylene, polyurethane; **13** macromolecule, polycarbonate, polypropylene.

polyp *See* **growth**

pomelo 8 shaddock; 10 grapefruit.

pomp 5 pride, state; 6 parade; 7 majesty; 9 formality, pageantry, solemnity, stiffness; 11 starchiness; 12 circumstance.

pomposity 7 bombast; 9 turgidity; 10 stuffiness; 13 pontification; 14 grandiloquence; PHRASES: 4-10 self-importance.

pompous 5 windy; 6 stuffy, turgid; 9 bombastic; 13 grandiloquent, pontificating; PHRASES: 4-5-3 long-drawn-out; 4-9 self-important.

poncho *See* **cloak**

ponder 4 muse; 5 brood, think; 6 deduce; 7 reflect; 8 cogitate, consider, meditate, ruminate; 9 speculate; 10 deliberate.

ponderous 5 heavy; 6 clumsy, taxing; 7 onerous, weighty; 8 cumbrous, pressing, unwieldy; 10 burdensome, cumbersome, oppressive; PHRASES: 3-5 top-heavy; 5-6 heavy-handed.

pontiff *See* **pope**

pontifical 5 papal; 7 pompous; 8 prelatic; 9 episcopal, grandiose; 10 portentous; 13 pontificating; PHRASES: 4-9 self-important.

pony 3 cob; 6 garron; 7 express, sheltie; 8 galloway, Shetland; PHRASES: 4, 4 dell ~, fell ~, polo ~; 4, 8 ~ trekking; 5, 4 Welsh ~; 6, 4 riding ~.

pool 4 band, fund, lake, pond, tarn, team; 5 kitty, share; 6 puddle; 7 combine; 8 assemble; 10 collection, collective, consortium; PHRASES: 8, 4 swimming ~.

poor 3 bad, ill, low, off, sad; 4 duff, foul, mean, pair, puir, rank, sore; 5 cheap, dirty, fetid, gungy *UK*, gunky, lousy, mangy, manky, moldy, needy, stale, tatty, yucky; 6 abject, coarse, crummy, filthy, grotty *UK*, grubby, grungy, measly, morbid, patchy, rotten, shabby, shoddy, sleazo, sleazy, sordid, stinky, vulgar, woeful; 7 corrupt, decayed, lowpaid, pitiful, scratch, scruffy, scrungy, squalid, tainted, unsound, wanting; 8 affected, decaying, deprived, diseased, grievous, improper, indecent, indigent, infected, pitiable, shameful, shocking, sleazoid, unworthy, wretched; 9 destitute, insolvent, makeshift, miserable, moneyless, penniless, penurious, underpaid, worthless; 10 deplorable, despicable, lamentable, melancholy, straitened; 11 disgraceful, impecunious, necessitous, substandard, underfunded, undeserving; 12 contemptible, disreputable, impoverished, irremediable; 13 discreditable, reprehensible, underfinanced; 15 underprivileged; PHRASES: 2, 3, 4 on the dole; 2, 3, 9 on the breadline *UK*; 2, 4 in need; 2, 7 on welfare; 2, 8 in distress; 3, 4-4 the have-nots; 3, 5 the needy; 3, 5, 7 the lower classes; 3, 8 the deprived; 4, 2 hard up; 4, 2, 3 ~ as Job; 4-2-5 hand-to-mouth; 4, 2, 7 ~ as Lazarus; 4-7 poor-quality; 5, 3 badly off; 5, 5 Third World; 5-5 jerry-built *UK*; 7-8 poverty-stricken; 10, 3 unprovided for.

poor (be poor) 4 lack, need, want; 5 pinch; 6 starve; PHRASES: 2, 2, 7 go on welfare; 3, 3, 4, 5 beg for one's bread; 4, 2 sign on; 4, 3, 5 feel the pinch; 5, 7 pinch pennies; 7, 1, 6 scratch a living; 7, 4, 4 tighten one's belt.

poor health 6 anemia, waning; 7 burnout, failure, fatigue, frailty, vertigo; 8 anorexia, asthenia, caducity, deafness, debility, flagging, lameness, paleness, senility, thinness; 9 blindness, deflation, depletion, dizziness, faintness, giddiness, infirmity, shakiness, tiredness, weariness; 10 enervation, exhaustion, sickliness, weakliness; 11 decrepitude, dissipation; 14 impoverishment; PHRASES: 4, 2, 8 loss of strength; 8, 5 weakened state; 8, 7 anorexia nervosa.

poorly 3 ill; 4 sick; 6 ailing, unwell.

poor person 3 bum, Job; 4 hobo; 5 lazar, tramp; 6 beggar, pauper; 7 Lazarus, vagrant; 8 bankrupt, indigent, squatter; 9 insolvent, mendicant; 10 Cinderella, Franciscan, freeloader; PHRASES: 3, 4 bag lady; 3-6 rag-picker; 4-3-3 down-and-out; 4, 5 Grey Friar *UK*, Poor Clare; 4-7 slum-dweller; 4, 8 poor relation; 5, 6 needy person; 6, 3 broken man; 6, 8 ghetto resident; 8, 6 homeless person; 9, 5 mendicant friar.

poor quality 6 flimsy, kitsch, shoddy; 7 badness; 9 cheapness, vulgarity; 10 shabbiness, shoddiness; 13 worthlessness; PHRASES: 3, 5 bad taste; 5-5 jerry-built; 5-6 jerry-rigged.

poor sight 3 tic; 4 cast; 6 myopia, squint; 7 walleye, winking; 8 blinking *UK*, diplopia; 9 amblyopia, daltonism, esotropia, exotropia, eyestrain, nystagmus; 10 bleariness, nyctalopia, ophthalmia, presbyopia, protanopia, strabismus, tritanopia; 11 astigmatism, hemeralopia, nictitation, retinopathy; 12 deuteranopia, heterotropia, ophthalmitis, purblindness; **13** hypermetropia; **14** colorblindness, conjunctivitis; PHRASES: **3, 4** red eyes; **3, 5** far sight; **3, 9** day blindness; **3-9** red-blindness; **3-11** far-sightedness; **4, 3** pink eye; **4, 5** long sight, near sight; **4-9** sand-blindness; **4-11** long-sightedness, near-sightedness; **5-3** cross-eye; **5, 5** short sight; **5, 9** night blindness; **6, 6** double vision, tunnel vision; **7, 5** failing sight; **8, 6** detached retina, impaired vision; **9, 3** wandering eye.

pop 2 pa; **3** dad; **4** bang, hock, pawn, shop; **5** burst; **6** father, pledge; PHRASES: **3, 3** ~ art.

pope 3 Leo; **4** John, Paul, Pius; **5** Caius, Conon, Donus, Felix, Lando, Linus, Soter, Urban; **6** Adrian, Agatho, Eugene, Fabian, Julius, Lucius, Marcus, Martin, Sixtus, Victor; **7** Anterus, Clement, Damasus, Gregory, Hyginus, Marinus, Paschal, Pontian, pontiff, Romanus, Sergius, Stephen, Zosimus; **8** Agapetus, Anicetus, Benedict, Boniface, Eusebius, Formosus, Gelasius, Hilarius, Honorius, Innocent, Liberius, Pelagius, Sabianus, Siricius, Theodore, Vigilius, Vitalian; **9** Adeodatus, Alexander, Anacletus, Callixtus, Celestine, Cornelius, Dionysius, Eleuterus, Eutychian, Evaristus, Hormisdas, Marcellus, Miltiades, Severinus, Silverius, Silvester, Sisinnius, Symmachus, Zacharias; **10** Anastasius, Simplicius, Valentinus, Zephyrinus; **11** Christopher, Constantine, Marcellinus, Telesphorus; PHRASES: **4, 4** John Paul; **4, 6** Holy Father; **6, 2, 4** bishop of Rome.

poppet *See* **dear**

poppycock *See* **nonsense**

popular 2 in; **3** hot, pop; **4** mass; **5** dined, feted, liked; **7** beloved, lowbrow, welcome; **11** entertained, proletarian; PHRASES: **4-6** mass-market; **4-7** best-selling, ever-welcome; **5, 3, 5** wined and dined; **5-7** chart-topping; **6-5** sought-after.

popular music 3 AOR, hit, pop, rap, ska; **4** rock, rock (and roll), soul; **5** grebo, house, indie, ragga; **6** charts, fusion, garage, grunge, jungle, reggae, techno, trance; **7** ambient, britpop, electro, Karaoke; **8** hardcore; **9** dancehall; **10** ragamuffin; PHRASES: **3-3** hip-hop; **3, 4** New Wave, pop song; **3, 5** pop music; **3, 6** top twenty; **4, 1, 4** drum 'n' bass, rock 'n' roll; **4-3** trip-hop; **4, 4** acid rock, folk rock, hard rock, prog rock, punk rock, soft rock; **4-4** jazz-funk; **4, 5** acid house, hard house, soft

metal; **4, 9** easy listening; **5, 4** torch song; **5, 5** death metal, heavy metal, house music; **6, 1, 5** rhythm 'n' blues (R and B); **6, 4** thrash punk; **6, 5** thrash metal; **7, 3** gangsta rap; **7, 4** country rock.

porbeagle 8, 5 mackerel shark.

porcelain *See* **pottery and porcelain**

porcelain clay 6 kaolin.

porcupine grass 8 spinifex.

pore 4 hole; **5** stoma; **7** opening; **8** aperture.

pork 3 ham; **7** pigmeat.

pork cut 3 leg; **4** hand, hock, loin, side; **5** belly, blade; **7** trotter; **8** shoulder; **10** tenderloin; PHRASES: **3, 6** leg fillet; **5, 3** spare rib.

porous 5 leaky; **6** spongy; **9** absorbent, permeable.

porous thing 5 grate, sieve; **6** filter, grille, screen, sponge, teabag; **7** lattice; **8** colander; **9** honeycomb; PHRASES: **5, 9** nylon stockings; **8, 3** mosquito net.

port 1 L; **2** PT; **3** Ayr, Rio, Rye; **4** Acre, Aden, Cobh, Cork, Deal, Hull, left, Oban, Oran, Tyre, Wick; **5** Brest, Cadiz, Dover, genoa, Haifa, haven, Hythe, Ostia, Sidon, Tampa; **6** Boston, Bregen, Bremen, Calais, Canton, Danzig, Dieppe, harbor, Hobart, Ostend, Recife, Smyrna, Tacoma, Venice; **7** Antwerp, Bristol, Grimsby, Harwich, Mombasa, Palermo, Rangoon, Rapallo, Seattle, Swansea, Tangier, Trieste, Tripoli; **8** Bordeaux, Calcutta, entrepôt, Flushing, Greenock, Holyhead, larboard, Murmansk, Nagasaki, Newhaven, Penzance, Plymouth, Ramsgate, Sandwich, Shanghai, Yokohama; **9** anchorage, Archangel, Fishguard, Fleetwood, Fremantle, Gateshead, Gravesend, Newcastle, Rotterdam, Sheerness, Stranraer, Trondheim; **10** Portsmouth; **11** Southampton, Trincomalee.

portent 4 omen, sign; **6** marvel, wonder; **7** miracle, presage, prodigy, warning; **10** indication, phenomenon.

portfolio 3 set; **4** case; **5** group, range; **6** folder; **9** selection; **10** collection.

portion 3 gob, lot; **4** dole, dose, hunk, load, mass, pack, part, plot; **5** batch, bunch, chunk, piece, quota, ratio, share, slice, stint, whack; **6** dollop, dosage, packet, parcel, quorum, ration; **7** helping, measure, quantum; **8** dividend, fraction, majority, minority, pittance; **9** allotment, allowance;

10 allocation, proportion; PHRASES: **4, 5** fair share; **5, 2, 3, 3** piece of the pie; **5, 2, 3, 4** slice of the cake; **5, 2, 4** strip of land.

portrait 5 pinup; **8** abstract, beefcake, Photofit *tm*; **9** landscape; **10** cheesecake, cloudscape, photomural, silhouette; **12** photomontage; **14** photobiography; PHRASES: **3, 4** mug shot; **4, 4** long shot; **5-2** close-up; **5-4** still-life; **5, 5** split image; **5, 10** group photograph; **6, 4** action shot, medium shot; **6, 7** rogues' gallery; **6, 8** action sequence; **8, 5** multiple image.

pose 5 bluff, model, place, swank; **6** assume, baffle, stance; **7** posture, pretend; PHRASES: **4, 3** play act, show off.

posh 7 elegant, genteel; **8** upmarket; **9** expensive, luxurious; **11** fashionable; **12** aristocratic *UK*; PHRASES: **4-2-2** well-to-do *UK*; **5-5** upper-class *UK*.

position 3 job, lay, lie, put; **4** base, pose, post, rank, site, slot, spot; **5** class, grade, level, order, place, stand; **6** degree, office, rating, stance, status; **7** arrange, echelon, ranking, situate; **8** category, foothold, location; **13** subordination; **14** classification; PHRASES: **3, 2** set up.

position (of authority) 8 headship; **9** consulate, judgeship, mayoralty; **10** magistracy, prefecture, presidency; **11** premiership, secretariat; **12** chairmanship, directorship, governorship, proconsulate; **13** inspectorship; **15** superintendency; PHRASES: **4, 6** high office; **6, 2, 5** office of power; **6, 4** police rank; **7, 4** cabinet seat, federal post; **8, 4** military rank; **10, 4** government post.

positive 2 ay, ja, OK; **3** aye, oui, POS, yes; **4** plus, sure; **5** print; **6** upbeat; **7** certain; **8** definite; **12** constructive.

posse 4 band, gang; **5** group, party.

possess 3 buy, hog, own; **4** have, hold, keep, rent; **5** claim, enjoy, squat; **6** corner, occupy; **7** command, engross; **9** forestall; **10** monopolize; PHRASES: **3, 2** tie up; **4, 2, 4, 5** have in one's grasp; **4, 3, 7** keep for oneself; **4, 4** move into; **4, 4, 3** call one's own; **6, 3, 6** corner the market.

possessed 3 had; **4** held; **5** owned; **9** bedeviled, bewitched, exclusive; PHRASES: **2, 3, 4** in the bank; **2, 4** on hand; **2, 4, 5** in one's hands; **2, 4, 8** at one's disposal; **2, 5** in store; **3-6** hag-ridden.

possession 4 gear, grip, hold; **5** claim, goods, grasp, lease, stuff, title; **6** colony, estate, owning, taking, tenure, things; **7** baggage, chattel, control, custody, effects, heirdom, holding, luggage, tenancy; **8** claiming, dominion, freehold, heirship, heritage, lordship, monopoly, property, sublease, tenantry; **9** enjoyment, furniture, leasehold, occupancy, occupying, ownership, patrimony, retention, squatting, trappings; **10** belongings, dependency, landowning, occupation, plantation, possessing; **11** accessories, engrossment, impedimenta, inheritance, landholding, sovereignty, squatterism; **12** forestalment, protectorate; **13** accouterments, appropriating, appropriation, appurtenances, landownership, paraphernalia, possessorship, temporalities; **14** monopolization, proprietorship; PHRASES: **3, 3, 7** bag and baggage; **4, 2, 3, 4** bird in the hand; **4, 6** land tenure; **5, 5** legal claim; **6, 6** landed estate; **8, 5** original title; **8, 6** property rights; **8, 7** personal effects.

possessive 4 mean; **6** greedy; **7** jealous, selfish; **8** covetous, grasping; **11** controlling, domineering, tightfisted; **14** overprotective.

possessor 5 buyer, owner, taker; **6** holder, lessee, lodger, tenant; **8** landlord, occupant, occupier, resident, squatter; **9** landowner, mortgagee, purchaser; **10** proprietor; **11** householder, leaseholder, monopolizer; PHRASES: **5-8** owner-occupier; **7, 6** sitting tenant *UK*; **8, 5** property owner.

possibility 4 case, odds; **6** chance; **7** ability, outcome, promise; **8** capacity, facility, prospect; **9** potential, viability; **10** likelihood, virtuality; **11** contingency, credibility, eventuality, feasibility, operability, opportunity; **12** availability, plausibility, potentiality; **13** accessibility, admissibility; **14** conceivability, practicability; **15** approachability. *See also* **possible**

possible 3 apt; **4** able; **6** doable, likely, viable; **7** capable, tenable; **8** credible, feasible, flexible, operable, workable; **9** available, potential, practical, reachable, thinkable; **10** accessible, achievable, admissible, attainable, believable, imaginable, realizable, reasonable; **11** conceivable, performable, practicable; **12** approachable.

possible (make possible) 4 hope; **5** allow; **6** enable, gamble, permit; **7** empower; PHRASES: **4, 1, 6** take a chance; **5, 3, 3, 3**

clear the way for.

possibly 5 haply, maybe; 7 perhaps; 9 perchance; 12 peradventure; PHRASES: 2, 3, 3, 6 on the off chance; 2, 3, 5 by any means; 2, 6 by chance; 2, 8 if possible; 3, 3, 3, 5 for all one knows.

post 3 Cod, job; 4 goal, jamb, mail, pole, rail; 5 chair, newel, stake, stilt; 6 column, marker, pillar; 7 bollard, command, forward; 8 position; 11 observation; PHRASES: 4, 4 last ~ UK, ~ road, ~ town; 4, 6 ~ chaise, ~ office; 4, 8 ~ meridiem; 6, 4 finger ~ UK, inland ~; 6, 7 postal service; 7, 4 staging ~ UK, trading ~, winning ~ UK; 8, 4 hitching ~; 9, 4 listening ~.

postal worker 6 sorter; 7 courier, mailman, postman; 9 mailwoman, messenger, postwoman UK; 10 postmaster; 12 postmistress; PHRASES: 4, 7 mail carrier; 6, 7 letter carrier.

postcard 4 card, note; 6 letter; 7 message.

poster 4 bill; 5 print; 6 notice; 7 artwork, picture, placard; 10 photograph; 12 announcement, reproduction; 13 advertisement.

posterior 4 hind, next, rear; 5 later; 6 latter; 9 following; 10 subsequent.

postmark 4 date, mark; 5 frank, stamp; PHRASES: 4, 5 date stamp; 6, 5 rubber stamp.

postpone 4 balk UK, halt; 5 block, defer, delay, demur, stall, table; 6 extend, hinder, remand, shelve; 7 adjourn, prolong, suspend; 8 hesitate, mothball, obstruct, prorogue, protract; 13 procrastinate.

postponement 5 delay; 8 shelving; 9 deferment, extension; 10 filibuster; 11 adjournment, prorogation, protraction; 12 prolongation, stonewalling; 15 procrastination.

postulate 5 claim, guess; 6 assume, choose, select; 7 propose, suggest; 8 nominate; 11 hypothesize; PHRASES: 3, 7 put forward.

posture 4 pose; 6 stance; 7 bearing; 8 attitude, position.

pot 3 cup, jar, jug, mug, pan, urn, wok; 4 bowl, ewer, olla, ruin, vase; 5 crock, cruse UK, kitty, plant, potty; 6 boiler, cheese, jamjar, kettle, liquor, pepper, pipkin, teapot, vessel; 7 amphora, ampulla, brazier, caldron, chamber, lobster, melting, pitcher, planter, roaster, skillet, steamer; 8 cannabis, honeypot, saucepan; 9 cafetière, cas-

serole, coffeepot, container, marijuana; 10 percolator; PHRASES: 3, 3 tea urn; 3, 4 ~ shot; 3, 5 ~ roast; 3, 6 jug kettle; 4, 3 cake tin; 4, 3, 4 pots and pans; 4, 5 bain marie; 4, 6 fish kettle; 5, 3 bread tin, plant ~; 6, 3 coffee urn, flower ~, frying pan; 6, 5 coffee maker; 6, 6 double boiler; 7, 3 chamber ~, cooking ~, storage jar, warming pan; 8, 3 roasting tin.

potable 9 drinkable.

potassium nitrate 5 niter; 9 saltpeter.

potato 3 yam; 4 chip, spud; 5 tater; 6 murphy UK, tattie; PHRASES: 3, 6 hot ~; 4, 6 seed ~; 5, 6 sweet ~, white ~; 6, 3 French fry; 6, 4 ~ chip; 6, 5 ~ crisp UK; 6, 6 ~ beetle, ~ blight.

potent 4 firm; 5 clear, great; 6 cogent, fervid, fierce, marked, mighty, severe, urgent; 7 drastic, extreme, fervent, intense, staunch, telling, weighty; 8 distinct, forceful, powerful, pressing, puissant, superior, vehement; 9 Draconian, effective, trenchant; 10 compelling, convincing, formidable, persuasive; 11 redoubtable; 12 overpowering, overwhelming, unmistakable; 13 thoroughgoing; PHRASES: 4-7 high-powered.

potential 4 hope, omen; 6 future; 7 ability, dormant, virtual; 8 auspices, capacity, eventual, possible; 9 promising; 10 capability; 11 prospective, undeveloped; 13 possibilities; PHRASES: 4, 4 good omen; 4, 9 good prospects; 6, 9 bright prospects.

pothole 3 dip, pit, rut; 4 cave, hole; 5 fault; 6 cavern; 8 catacomb; 10 depression.

potter 5 firer; 6 glazer, turner; 8 ceramist; 9 enamelist; 10 pyroglazer; PHRASES: 4, 7 tile painter; 5, 7 china painter; 5, 9 china decorator; 8, 7 majolica painter.

pottery and porcelain 3 Bow; 4 Ault, Ming, Tang; 5 Delft, Derby, Imari, Spode; 6 bisque, Bretby, Canton, Minton, molded, Parian, Ruskin, Sevres; 7 Belleek, biscuit, Bristol, Chelsea, Doulton, faience, Italian, Meissen, redware, satsuma; 8 caneware, Caughley, chaffers, Coalport, fairings, maiolica, majolica, Nantgarw, Plymouth, Salopian, slipware, Wedgwood; 9 crackling, creamware, Davenport, Linthorpe, Liverpool, Lowestoft, Moorcroft, pearlware, prattware, stoneware, Worcester; 10 lustreware, martinware, Pilkington, polychrome, Rockingham; 11 Capodimonte, earthenware; 13 Staffordshire; PHRASES: 3, 4 New Hall; 4, 3 toby jug; 4-3-4 pate-sur-pate;

4, 3, 5 blue and white; **4, 5** hard paste, soft paste; **4-6** salt-glazed; **5, 4** agate ware, china clay; **5, 5** china stone *UK*, stone china, terra cotta; **5, 6** black basalt; **6, 4** Canton ware; **6, 7** willow pattern; **7, 4** famille rose, famille vert, Longton Hall; **7, 8** asiatic pheasant; **8, 4** Nagasaki ware; **8, 7** Cambrian pottery.

potty *See* **foolish**

pouch 3 bag; **5** purse; **6** pocket; PHRASES: **5, 3** money bag; **5, 4** fanny pack.

poultry 3 leg; **4** fowl, game, wing; **6** breast, grouse; **8** pheasant, wishbone; **9** drumstick, partridge; PHRASES: **4, 4** dark meat; **5, 4** white meat; **7, 4** parson's nose.

pounce 4 dive, jump, leap; **5** bound, swoop; **6** ambush, attack, spring, tackle; PHRASES: **5, 4** seize upon.

pound 3 hit; **4** beat, mash; **5** crush, grind, pulse, throb, thump; **6** batter, bruise, hammer, strike; **7** pulsate; **9** pulverize. *See also* **British money**

pour 4 flow, gush, lash, rain, rush, teem; **5** swarm; **6** decant, drench, stream; **8** dispense, transfer; **9** discharge; PHRASES: **5, 3** spill out; **5, 4** sheet down *UK*.

pout 4 mope, sulk; **5** frown, scowl; **6** glower, grouch, pucker; PHRASES: **5, 4, 4** purse one's lips.

poverty 3 woe; **4** lack, need, want; **5** decay; **6** blight, misery, penury; **7** lowness, squalor; **8** distress, hardship, meanness, poorness; **9** breadline, dirtiness, indigence, lousiness, necessity, neediness, pauperism, privation, recession; **10** abjectness, bankruptcy, depression, grottiness, grubbiness, shabbiness, sleaziness, sordidness; **11** deprivation, destitution, pitifulness, scruffiness, squalidness; **12** difficulties, unworthiness, wretchedness; **13** impecuniosity, pennilessness; **14** impoverishment; **15** disreputability, impecuniousness, necessitousness; PHRASES: **4, 2, 3, 4** wolf at the door; **4, 7** dire straits, Lady P~; **4, 9** dire necessity, mere existence; **6, 5** narrow means; **7, 4** ~ line, ~ trap *UK*; **7, 5** slender means; **8, 6** negative equity.

powan 4, 7 lake herring.

powder 3 ash; **4** dust, lint, sand, smog, smut, soot, talc; **5** flour, fluff, grind, rouge, smuts; **6** dredge, pounce; **7** crumble, fallout, flowers, kittens, pussies, sawdust, scatter; **8** attritus, sprinkle; **9** cosmetics, gunpowder, pulverize; **13** efflorescence; PHRASES: **4, 4**

coal dust; **4, 6** face ~; **5, 6** black ~, chili ~, curry ~, tooth ~; **6, 3** ~ keg; **6, 4** ~ blue, ~ burn, ~ horn, ~ puff, ~ room; **6, 5** ~ flask; **6, 6** baking ~, ~ monkey, talcum ~; **6, 7** ~ compact *UK*; **7, 2, 6** flowers of sulfur; **7, 6** custard ~ *UK*, washing ~ *UK*; **9, 6** bleaching ~.

powderiness 5 bloom; **9** dustiness; **10** chalkiness, flouriness; **12** pulverulence; **13** efflorescence.

powdery 5 dirty, dusty, sooty; **6** chalky; **9** chalklike, pulverous, scobicula, scobiform; **10** calcareous, flocculent; **11** pulverulent; PHRASES: **4-7** dust-covered.

power 3 log; **4** cube, mana *UK*, root, surd, sway; **5** drive, force, might, oomph; **6** accent, effort, energy, factor, muscle; **7** ability, antilog, cogency, control, gravity, potency, sorcery, stamina; **8** charisma, emphasis, energize, exponent, hegemony, manpower, mantissa, politics, strength, validity, virility; **9** authority, electrify, endurance, greatness, influence, logarithm, overdrive, puissance *UK*; **10** ascendancy, governance, government, mightiness, persuasion, prevalence, witchcraft; **11** gravitation, omnipotence, sovereignty, superiority; **12** forcefulness, powerfulness, predominance; **13** antilogarithm; PHRASES: **4, 4** cube root; **4, 6** high ground; **5, 3** ~ cut, right arm; **5, 4** ~ dive, ~ line, ~ pack, right hand; **5, 5** brute force, magic ~, ~ drill, ~ lunch, ~ plant; **5, 6** ~ vacuum; **5, 7** ~ failure, ~ station *UK*; **5, 8** brute strength, ~ dressing, ~ steering; **6, 2, 7** weight of numbers; **6, 4** square root; **6, 6** square weight; **7, 4** special gift; **7, 5** driving force, special ~, staying ~; **7, 6** vantage ground *UK*.

power (give power) 3 arm; **5** drive, endow, power; **6** charge, enable; **7** animate, empower; **8** energize; **9** authorize, electrify, magnetize; **10** strengthen; **13** transistorize; PHRASES: **4, 2** plug in, soup up, turn on; **4, 2, 2** step on it; **4, 2, 3, 3** step on the gas; **6, 2** charge up, switch on.

powerful 3 fit; **4** able, lean, wiry; **5** burly, great, hardy, rough; **6** brawny, brutal, cogent, gifted, mighty, potent, raging, robust, sinewy, strong, virile; **7** capable, endowed, intense, stringy, vicious, violent, virtual; **8** adequate, almighty, athletic, bullying, enduring, forceful, forcible, muscular, possible, puissant, stalwart, superior, talented, untiring; **9** competent, effective, effectual, efficient, empowered, hegemonic, potential, prevalent, qualified, resilient, sovereign, strapping, tenacious; **10** compelling, compulsive, omnipotent, prevailing, proficient, unflagging; **11** charismatic, efficacious, influential, predominant; **12** irresistible; **13** authoritative, indefatigable; **15** plenipotentiary.

powerless **3** dud; **4** duff, weak; **5** empty, frail, inept, kaput, unfit; **6** broken, feeble, unable; **7** deposed, illegal, invalid, useless; **8** buggered, helpless, impotent, inexpert; **9** incapable, suspended, worthless; **10** mothballed, unemployed, unworkable, vulnerable; **11** deactivated, incompetent, ineffective, ineffectual, inefficient, inoperative, invalidated, unqualified; **12** disqualified, unauthorized; **13** disfranchised, inefficacious; PHRASES: **2, 8** in abeyance; **3, 2, 5** out of order; **3, 2, 6** out of action; **3, 4** not able; **4, 2** laid up; **4, 3, 4** null and void; **4-3-7** good-for-nothing; **6-2** fucked-up; **6, 4** broken down; **8, 3** switched off.

powerlessness **7** frailty; **8** futility; **9** fragility, impotence, inability, inutility, sterility, vasectomy; **10** barrenness, incapacity, ineptitude; **11** decrepitude, disarmament; **12** incapability, incompetence, inefficiency, invalidation; **13** sterilization; **14** ineffectuality, neutralization; **15** ineffectiveness. *See also* **powerless**

powerless person **5** patsy; **7** invalid, schnook; **8** pushover, weakling; **10** figurehead; **13** hermaphrodite; PHRASES: **3, 2, 5** man of straw; **4-2** shut-in; **4, 4** easy mark, easy meat *UK*; **6, 4** broken reed; **7, 4** titular head.

power plant **7** turbine; **9** generator; **10** powerhouse; PHRASES: **5, 10** power generation, power production; **10, 5** generating plant.

power source **4** cell; **7** battery; **11** accumulator; PHRASES: **3, 4** dry cell, wet cell; **3, 7** dry battery; **4, 4** fuel cell; **5, 4** solar cell; **5, 5** solar panel; **5, 6** solar energy; **5, 7** solar battery; **7, 4** primary cell; **7, 7** battery charger, storage battery; **8, 7** alkaline battery; **9, 4** secondary cell.

PP **4** purl; **5** pages; **10** phosphorus; PHRASES: **2, 6, 2** on behalf of (Latin: per procurationem); **4, 7** very quietly (Italian: pianissimo).

practicable *See* **feasible**

practical **5** sound; **6** manual, usable, useful; **7** applied, logical, useable, working; **8** rational, sensible, workable; **9** automated, automatic, expedient, operating, operative, pragmatic, realistic, servicing; **10** electronic, functional, mechanical, pushbutton, reasonable; **11** functioning, operational, serviceable, utilitarian; **12** businesslike, computerized; PHRASES: **2-6** no-frills; **2, 7, 5** in working order; **2-8** no-nonsense; **4-2-5** down-to-earth; **4-6** hard-headed; **4-8** hand-operated; **5-6** level-headed; **6-2-4** matter-of-fact; **7-7** general-purpose.

practice **3** way; **5** habit; **6** custom, system; **8** exercise, training; **9** rehearsal, tradition; **10** repetition; **11** preparation.

practice **7** perform, prepare; **8** exercise, rehearse; PHRASES: **2, 7** go through; **3, 7** run through; **5, 3** carry out.

pragmatic *See* **practical**

prairie **5** plain; **6** pampas, steppe; **7** savanna; **9** grassland; PHRASES: **7, 3** ~ dog; **7, 4** ~ soil, ~ wolf; **7, 6** ~ oyster, ~ turnip; **7, 8** ~ schooner.

prairie dog **6** marmot.

prairie wolf **6** coyote.

praise **4** hype, laud; **5** boost, deify, exalt, extol, glory, honor; **7** acclaim, adulate, commend, flatter, glorify, idolize, lionize, magnify, trumpet, worship; **8** eulogize, flattery, idolatry; **9** adulation, extolment, laudation; **10** apotheosis, compliment, exaltation, overpraise, panegyrize; **11** apotheosize, compliments, deification, lionization; **12** congratulate, overestimate; **13** glorification; **14** overestimation; PHRASES: **3, 7** wax lyrical; **4, 2** puff up; **4, 7** hero worship.

praiser **8** eulogist, extoller, laudator; **9** commender, eulogizer; **10** panegyrist.

praiseworthy **6** worthy; **8** laudable; **9** admirable, deserving, estimable; **10** creditable; **11** commendable, meritorious; **13** unimpeachable; PHRASES: **4-9** well-deserving.

pram *See* **buggy**

prang *See* **crash**

prank *See* **trick**

prattle **5** prate; **6** drivel, gibber, jabber; **7** chatter; **8** nonsense.

pray **5** chant; **6** incant, invoke, rogate; **7** beseech, implore, request; **8** petition; **9** impetrate; **10** supplicate; PHRASES: **3, 3, 6** say 'Our Father'; **3, 5** say grace; **5, 1, 6** offer a prayer; **6, 3, 6** recite the rosary.

prayer 2 om; 3 Ave, Pax; 5 alenu, Credo, grace, motzi; 6 litany, mantra, norito, orison, rosary, vigils; 7 Angelus, benison, berakah, collect, dharani, eulogia, gayatri, geullah, meeting, nishmat, request; 8 blessing, devotion, epidesis, nembutsu, petition, rogation, suffrage; 9 anamnesis, intention; 10 allocution, invocation; 11 benediction, impetration, Paternoster; 12 comprecation, intercession, supplication; PHRASES: 3, 5 Ave Maria, kol nidre; 3, 5, 6 the Lord's P~; 3, 6 Our Father; 4, 4 Hail Mary; 4, 8 Nunc Dimittis; 5, 3 Agnus Dei; 5, 7 Kyrie Eleison; 6, 3 ~ mat, ~ rug; 6, 4 ~ book; 6, 5 ~ beads, ~ shawl, ~ wheel, Sursum Corda; 7, 6 bidding ~.

prayer book *See* **religious manual**

preach 4 rant; 7 baptize, convert, crusade, Judaize, lecture; 8 convince, Islamize, moralize; 9 preachify, sermonize; 10 evangelize; 11 proselytize; 12 Christianize; PHRASES: 5, 2, 7 speak in tongues; 5, 4 Bible bash; 6, 3, 4 spread the Word.

preamble *See* **introduction**

precarious 4 iffy; 5 dicey, dodgy *UK*, hairy, nasty, risky; 6 chancy, snaggy, sticky, tricky; 7 ominous, serious; 8 perilous; 9 dangerous, difficult, hazardous, uncertain; 11 threatening.

precaution *See* **protection**

precede 4 head, lead; 5 front, guide, pilot; 6 settle; 7 explore, forerun, outrank, predate, preempt; 8 antecede, antedate, discover, indicate; 9 spearhead; 10 anticipate, foreshadow; PHRASES: 2, 6 go before; 3, 5, 2 get ahead of; 4, 2 head up; 4, 3, 3 show the way; 4, 6 come before; 5, 2, 3, 4 stand at the head; 5, 3, 3 point the way; 5, 5 scout ahead.

precedence 8 priority; 9 preceding; 10 precession, preemption; 11 antecedence, antecedency, anteriority; 12 anteposition; PHRASES: 5, 6 going before.

precedent 4 lead; 5 model; 7 example, formula, pattern; 8 paradigm, standard; 9 criterion, prototype, yardstick; 10 antecedent, forerunner.

preceding 5 first; 7 earlier, leading; 8 anterior, earliest, previous; 9 precedent; 10 antecedent, preemptive; 12 precessional.

precept 3 act, law; 4 code, form, norm, rule, text, writ; 5 canon, guide, maxim, moral, order, tenet; 6 advice, charge, custom, decree, recipe, remedy, rubric; 7 arti-

cle, command, example, formula, mandate, mission, receipt, statute, warning, warrant; 8 decretal, judgment, practice, rescript; 9 direction, enactment, formulary, guideline, judgement, ordinance, precedent, prescript, principle; 10 admonition, commission, convention, injunction, regulation; 11 commandment, instruction, legislation; 12 constitution, prescription, technicality; PHRASES: 3, 2, 5 set of rules; 3, 6, 6 the Twelve Tables; 4, 2, 3 body of law; 4, 2, 6 rule of custom; 5, 3 canon law; 5, 4 moral rule, party line, penal code; 5, 6 party ticket; 5, 9 moral guideline; 6, 3 common law; 6, 4 golden rule; 6, 5 corpus juris; 7, 4 leading case; 9, 3 unwritten law.

precinct *See* **district**

precious 6 costly, pricey; 9 treasured; 12 profiteering; PHRASES: 4, 8 rare valuable.

precious metal 2 Ag, Au, or; 4 gold; 6 silver; 8 platinum.

precipice *See* **rock face**

precipitate 4 rash; 5 cause, hasty, rapid, swift; 6 abrupt, hasten, sudden; 7 hurried; 8 reckless; 9 impetuous, impulsive; 10 unexpected, unforeseen; PHRASES: 5, 2 bring on.

precipitation 3 dew; 4 hail, rain, snow; 5 flood, sleet, spate; 6 deluge, flurry, shower; 7 drizzle, rushing, wetness; 8 downpour, hurrying, raindrop, rainfall, snowfall; 9 hailstone, hastening, raininess, rainstorm, rainwater, snowflake; 10 cloudburst, pluviosity; 11 hydrometeor; PHRASES: 3, 7 ice crystal; 4, 3 rain day.

precipitous 4 high; 5 sheer, steep; 8 vertical.

precise 4 just; 5 exact; 8 accurate, specific; 10 particular.

preclude 7 exclude, preempt, prevent; 9 forestall.

precognition 3 ESP; 9 telepathy; 10 divination; 11 premonition; 12 clairvoyance, presentiment; PHRASES: 5, 5 sixth sense; 6, 5 second sight.

precognitive 10 divinatory, telepathic, unmediated; 11 presentient; 12 extrasensory; PHRASES: 1, 6 a priori.

precursor 5 crier, guide, pilot, scout; 6 herald, leader; 7 pioneer; 8 ancestor, explorer, forebear, foregoer, inventor, vanguard; 9 announcer, harbinger, innovator, messenger; 10 discoverer, forerunner, pathfinder; 11 frontrunner, trailblazer, trendsetter; 12

frontiersman; **13** groundbreaker; **PHRASES: 4, 6** lead runner; **5-5** avant-garde; **5-7** avant-gardist; **8, 6** founding father.

precursory 5 basic; **7** initial; **8** colonial, proemial; **9** ancestral, baptismal, inaugural, preceding, prefatory; **10** aboriginal, elementary, indigenous, initiatory, precursive; **11** exploratory, prefatorial, preliminary; **12** introductory.

predecessor 6 eldest, senior; **8** ancestor, forebear; **9** firstborn, prototype; **10** antecedent, forefather, foremother, forerunner, originator.

predetermination 3 lot; **4** doom, fate, will; **5** karma; **6** decree, kismet; **7** destiny; **13** preordination; **14** foreordination, predestination.

predetermine 4 doom; **6** decree, intend; **7** appoint, destine; **9** preordain; **10** foreordain, predestine; **12** predestinate.

predetermined 5 fated; **8** ordained; **PHRASES: 2, 3, 5** in the cards; **3-3-5** cut-and-dried. *See also* **predetermine**

predicament 3 fix, jam; **4** bind, hole, mess, spot; **5** pinch, snafu, snarl; **6** clutch, hobble, muddle, pickle, plight, scrape, tangle; **7** dilemma, problem, squeeze, trouble; **9** situation; **12** difficulties; **PHRASES: 2-3, 9** no-win situation; **3, 2, 1, 4** pig in a poke; **3-2-3-2** how-do-you-do; **3, 5** hot water; **4, 4** fine mess; **5-2** catch-22 *UK*, snarl-up; **5, 5** cleft stick *UK*; **6, 4** tricky spot; **6, 6** pretty pickle; **6, 9** tricky situation.

predict 4 bode, hint, warn; **5** augur, guess, lower, think; **6** assume, herald, menace, notify, reckon, reveal, typify; **7** believe, betoken, forerun, foresee, portend, presage, presume, promise, signify, suggest; **8** announce, estimate, forebode, forecast, foreshow, foretell, forewarn, indicate, prophesy, threaten; **9** advertise, calculate, foretoken, harbinger, prefigure, represent, speculate; **10** foreshadow, vaticinate; **11** guesstimate; **13** prognosticate; **PHRASES: 3, 4** bid fair; **4, 2** bank on; **4, 3, 5** hold out hopes; **4, 3, 7** take for granted; **4, 4** give hope; **4, 5** look black; **4, 6** come before, give notice; **4, 7** give warning, look ominous; **5, 2** cheer up, count on, point to, usher in; **5, 4** augur well; **7, 3** bargain for.

predictable 4 sure; **5** plain, usual; **6** common, likely; **7** certain; **8** expected, ordinary, possible, probable; **9** customary, potential; **11** foreseeable; **12** unsurprising; **15** straight-forward; **PHRASES: 3-2-3-4** run-of-the-mill.

predicting 5 vatic; **6** mantic; **7** fatidic; **8** monitory, oracular, sibyllic; **9** heralding, prescient, prophetic, sibylline; **10** cautionary, foreboding, foreseeing, indicative, precursory, predictive, signifying; **11** apocalyptic, clairvoyant, foretelling, forewarning, prefiguring, premonitory, presentient, symptomatic; **PHRASES: 7-4** weather-wise; **7-7** fortune-telling.

prediction 5 hunch; **7** feeling, fortune, pointer, portent, presage; **8** forecast, prophecy, prospect; **9** foresight, horoscope, prognosis; **10** apocalypse, divination, foreboding, foreseeing, indication, revelation; **11** expectation, forecasting, foretelling, forewarning, premonition; **12** presentiment; **13** prefiguration, prefigurement; **15** prognostication.

predictive 9 expectant, intuitive, prescient, prophetic; **10** anticipant, farsighted, prognostic, telepathic; **11** clairvoyant, long-sighted, prospective, statistical; **12** anticipatory, precognitive.

predictor 4 seer; **5** augur; **6** oracle; **7** diviner, prophet; **9** geomancer; **10** astrologer, forecaster, prophetess, soothsayer; **PHRASES: 7, 5** crystal gazer; **7, 6** fortune teller.

predilection *See* **liking**

predisposition *See* **tendency**

predominate *See* **prevail**

preen *See* **groom**

preface 5 proem; **6** opener, prolog *UK*; **7** opening, prelims, prelude; **8** apéritif, foreword, overture, preamble, prologue; **9** appetizer, introduce; **12** frontispiece, introduction; **13** preliminaries; **PHRASES: 4, 7** hors d'oeuvre; **5, 6** front matter; **7-6** curtain-raiser.

prefer 4 bend, lean, tend, turn, want; **5** fancy *UK*, favor; **6** choose, intend, select, toward; **7** approve, incline; **PHRASES: 4, 1, 10** have a preference; **4, 4** like best; **4, 6** like better; **4, 7** lean towards; **5, 2, 4** might as well; **5, 2, 5** might do worse; **5, 3** think fit; **5, 4** would like; **5, 6** would rather.

preference 4 bias; **5** fancy, favor, taste; **6** choice, liking; **7** leaning; **8** tendency; **9** prejudice; **10** favoritism, partiality; **11** inclination; **12** desirability, predilection; **13** preferability.

prefix and suffix 1 a-, e-, -o, -s, -y; **2** ab-, -ac, ad-, -ad, -al, an-, -an, -ar, be-, bi-, by-

, co-, -cy, de-, di-, -ed, -ee, em-, en-, -en, eo-, -er, -et, eu-, ex-, -fy, -ia, -ic, -id, -ie, in-, -in, -ly, Mc-, -mo, ob-, -ol, -on, oo-, -or, re-, -th, un-, ur-, -yl; **3** -ade, -age, ana-, -ana, -ane, -ant, apo-, -ard, -art, -ary, -ase, -ate, azo-, bio-, cis-, com-, dia-, dis-, -dom, duo-, dys-, eco-, -eer, -ein, -eme, -ene, -ent, epi-, -ery, -ese, -ess, -est, -eth, exa-, exo-, -fer, -fic, -fid, for-, -ful, -gen, geo-, -gon, -ial, -ian, -ics, -ide, -ile, -ine, -ing, -ion, -ish, -ism, iso-, -ist, -ite, -ium, -ive, -ize, -kin, -let, -log, Mac-, mal-, mid-, mis-, myo-, neo-, -nik, non-, -ode, -oid, -ole, -oma, -ome, -one, -ont, oro-, -ory, -ose, oto-, -ous, out-, ovi-, ovo-, oxy-, pan-, -ped, per-, -pod, pre-, pro-, pyo-, sex-, shm-, sub-, sur-, sym-, syn-, ter-, tri-, -ule, uni-, -ure, uro-, zoo-; **4** -able, acro-, aero-, Afro-, -agog, agro-, algo-, allo-, alto-, ambi-, -ance, ante-, anti-, aqua-, aqui-, arch-, -arch, atmo-, -ator, atto-, auri-, auto-, baro-, baso-, bryo-, caco-, -cade, -carp, cata-, -cele, -cene, cent-, -cide, cine-, -coel, -crat, -cyte, cyto-, deca-, deci-, demi-, -derm, ecto-, -emia, endo-, -eous, equi-, -etic, -ette, Euro-, eury-, -fold, fore-, -form, -fuge, gamo-, -gamy, -gate, -gene, giga-, gono-, -gony, -gram, -gyne, gyno-, gyro-, halo-, heli-, hemi-, hemo-, hexa-, holo-, homo-, -hood, hypo-, -ible, ideo-, idio-, indo-, Indo-, iodo-, -itis, keto-, kilo-, -less, levo-, -like, -ling, lipo-, -lite, -lith, logo-, -logy, lyso-, -lyte, -lyze, mast-, maxi-, mega-, meno-, -ment, -mere, mero-, meso-, meta-, meth-, mini-, mono-, -most, muco-, myco-, myxo-, nano-, naso-, -ness, -nomy, nona-, noso-, octo-, oleo-, omni-, onco-, onto-, -onym, -opia, -opsy, opto-, -osis, -otic, over-, para-, -para, pari-, -path, pedi-, pedo-, peri-, peta-, -phil, pico-, pleo-, poly-, post-, pyro-, rheo-, ribo-, schm-, -sect, self-, semi-, sero-, -ship, Sino-, -some, -stat, step-, -ster, taxo-, -taxy, tele-, telo-, tera-, theo-, thio-, -tion, -tome, -tomy, topo-, toxi-, -trix, -tron, -tude, uber-, uran-, -urgy, -uria, vago-, vaso-, veno-, vini-, viro-, -ward, -ways, -wide, -wise, xeno-, xero-, xylo-, -zoic, -zoon, zygo-, zymo-; **5** -acean, aceto-, adeno-, adipo-, affix, -algia, -amine, amino-, amphi-, amylo-, andro-, -andry, anemo-, angio-, Anglo-, aniso-, archi-, -arium, astro-, -athon, -ation, -ative, audio-, batho-, bathy-, benzo-, -biont, -blast, brady-, -caine, calci-, carbo-, carpo-, centi-, chemo-, chiro-, chole-, -chore, -chory, clado-, -cline, clino-, coeno-, collo-, colpo-, copro-, cosmo-, -cracy, cross-, cupro-, cy-

ano-, cyber-, cyclo-, cysto-, denti-, deoxy-, derma-, -derma, desmo-, diplo-, disco-, dorso-, -drome, eroto-, -esque, ethno-, extra-, femto-, ferri-, ferro-, fibro-, flavo-, Gallo-, -genic, gluco-, glyco-, grand-, -graph, great-, Greco-, hagio-, haplo-, hecto-, helio-, -hemia, hepta-, hiero-, histo-, homeo-, hyalo-, hydro-, hyeto-, hygro-, hyper-, hypno-, hypso-, -iasis, -iatry, -ician, icono-, infra-, inter-, intra-, intro-, irido-, Italo-, Judeo-, karyo-, labio-, lacto-, -latry, -lepsy, lepto-, leuko-, ligni-, ligno-, litho-, -logue, -lysis, macro-, mammo-, -mancy, -mania, matri-, melli-, -meter, metro-, -metry, micro-, milli-, -morph, multi-, -mycin, myelo-, narco-, -nasty, necro-, nepho-, neuro-, nitro-, nocti-, oculo-, -odont, oligo-, -ology, -onymy, -opsis, ortho-, osteo-, paleo-, panto-, patho-, -pathy, patri-, -penia, penta-, -petal, petro-, -phage, phago-, -phagy, -phane, -phany, pheno-, -phile, philo-, -phobe, -phone, phono-, -phony, -phore, photo-, phyco-, -phyll, phylo-, -phyte, phyto-, picro-, piezo-, pisci-, plano-, -plasm, -plast, -ploid, proto-, ptero-, pycno-, pyelo-, quasi-, quino-, radio-, retro-, rhino-, rhizo-, rhodo-, -rrhea, Russo-, sapro-, sarco-, scato-, -scope, septi-, socio-, somni-, -sophy, -speak, -sperm, spiro-, sporo-, stann-, stato-, steno-, -stomy, stylo-, sulfa-, super-, supra-, tachy-, tauto-, -taxis, teleo-, tetra-, thyro-, trans-, tropo-, -tropy, turbo-, ultra-, under-, urino-, -urous, vario-, vermi-, visco-, vitri-, -wards, yocto-, yotta-, zepto-, zetta-; **6** -aceous, actino-, adreno-, -agogue, -aholic, allelo-, arthro-, Austro-, biblio-, -biosis, blasto-, brachy-, cardio-, centro-, chalco-, chloro-, -chrome, chromo-, chrono-, chryso-, circum-, -clinal, -clinic, -coccus, -colous, concho-, contra-, cranio-, crypto-, dendro-, dextro-, dodeca-, dynamo-, echino-, -ectomy, entero-, entomo-, -escent, -ferous, fluoro-, Franco-, gameto-, gastro-, -genous, geront-, Graeco-, grapho-, -graphy, -hedron, helico-, hemato-, hepato-, hetero-, -iatric, immuno-, kerato-, kineto-, lepido-, -lithic, lympho-, malaco-, mangan-, megalo-, -megaly, melano-, mercur-, -merous, -metric, -mobile, -monger, morpho-, -mycete, nemato-, nephro-, nucleo-, odonto-, organo-, -parous, -phagia, -phasia, -philia, phlebo-, -phobia, -phobic, phreno-, phyllo-, physio-, plagio-, -plasia, plasmo-, -plasty, platin-, -plegia, pleuro-, pneumo-, preter-, procto-, proteo-, pseudo-, psycho-, quadra-, quadri-

, retino-, schizo-, sclero-, seismo-, seleno-, sesqui-, sidero-, silici-, somato-, spermo-, -spermy, spheno-, sphero-, steato-, stereo-, sterno-, techno-, terato-, thermo-, -thermy, -thymia, toxico-, tricho-, tropho-, -trophy, -tropic, -valent, varico-, ventro-, -vorous, xantho-, yester-, -zygous; **7** -androus, archaeo-, arterio-, brachio-, broncho-, carboxy-, carcino-, -centric, cephalo-, -cephaly, cerebro-, chondro-, cortico-, counter-, dactylo-, dermato-, deutero-, -dromous, electro-, -enchyma, erythro-, -escence, -facient, -faction, -florous, -foliate, galacto-, galvano-, -genesis, -grapher, hendeca-, Hiberno-, Hispano-, hystero-, -iatrics, ichthyo-, -kinesis, laryngo-, magneto-, mechano-, -meister, meningo-, metallo-, -metrics, musculo-, -odontia, ornitho-, -phagous, -phorous, phospho-, -phrenia, pinnati-, -plastic, -poiesis, -poietic, preface, psychro-, -pterous, quinque-, -rrhagia, spectro-, sphygmo-, strepto-, synchro-, -thermic, thoraco-, thrombo-, tracheo-, -trophic, -tropous; **8** anthropo-, bacterio-, -cephalic, chromato-, -fication, -gnathous, pancreat-, pharmaco-, pharyngo-, -phoresis, pneumato-, saccharo-, spermato-, thaumato-; **9** -cephalous, crystallo-, -dermatous, encephalo-, ophthalmo-, prefixion, prothesis; **11** prefixation.

pregnancy 6 import; **7** meaning; **8** prenatal; **9** condition *UK*, gestation, gravidity; **10** gravidness, importance; **11** confinement; **12** significance; PHRASES: **5-2** lying-in; **8, 6** prenatal period.

pregnant 6 broody, gravid, preggy; **7** pivotal; **8** breeding, enceinte, preggers *UK*, prenatal; **9** expecting, perinatal; **10** fecundated, fertilized, meaningful; **11** impregnated; PHRASES: **2, 3, 4** in the club *UK*; **2, 3, 5** up the spout; **2, 3, 6, 3** in the family way; **4, 5** with child; **5, 4** heavy with; **6, 3, 3** eating for two; **9, 1, 3** expecting a baby.

prehistoric 5 early; **7** ancient; **8** outmoded, primeval; **9** primitive; **10** antiquated; **12** antediluvian; PHRASES: **3-2-4** out-of-date; **3-9** old-fashioned.

prehistoric age 4, 3 Iron Age; **5, 3** Stone Age; **6, 3** Bronze Age; **9, 6** Neolithic period.

prehistoric animal 8 ammonite, dinosaur, eohippus, mastodon, rutiodon, smilodon; **9** trilobite; **10** allosaurus, euparkeria, mesohippus, pliohippus; **11** aphaneramma, mandasuchus, merychippus; **12** ticinosuchus; **13** pterodactylus, scleromochlus; **14** baluchitherium; PHRASES: **4, 4** dire wolf; **5, 5** giant sloth; **6, 7** woolly mammoth.

prehistoric people 7 caveman, hominid; **8** humanoid; **10** protohuman; **15** Pithecanthropus; PHRASES: **3-3** ape-man; **3-6, 3** Cro-Magnon man; **4, 3** Java man; **4-3, 3** Iron-Age man; **4, 7** cave dweller, Homo erectus, Homo sapiens; **5, 3** early man; **5-3, 3** Stone-Age man; **6, 3** Peking man; **6-3, 3** Bronze-Age man; **9, 3** primitive man; **10, 3** Heidelberg man; **11, 3** Neanderthal man.

prehistoric tool 4, 6 iron sickle; **5, 6** flint chisel; **6, 2** bronze ax; **6, 4-2** pebble hand-ax.

prejudge 4 bias, warp; **9** forejudge, prejudice; **10** precondemn; PHRASES: **5, 4, 4** close one's mind.

prejudgment 8 fixation; **9** obsession; **13** preconception; **14** presupposition; PHRASES: **4, 4** idée fixe; **4, 4, 2** mind made up; **5, 4** fixed idea, parti pris.

prejudice 4 bias; **6** ageism, sexism; **7** bigotry; **8** contempt, inequity, jaundice, snobbery; **9** pettiness; **10** chauvinism, homophobia, insularism, narrowness, unfairness; **11** intolerance, prejudgment; **12** heterosexism, parochialism, partisanship; **14** discrimination; PHRASES: **3, 7** not cricket; **3-9** one-sidedness; **4, 4** foul play; **5, 9** white supremacy; **5-10** small-mindedness; **6, 9** racial ~.

prejudiced 6 ageist, biased, sexist, unfair; **7** bigoted; **8** dogmatic, partisan, snobbish; **9** despising, fanatical, parochial; **10** chauvinist, homophobic, intolerant, jingoistic, xenophobic; **11** inequitable; **12** chauvinistic, contemptuous, ethnocentric, undemocratic; **14** fundamentalist, preferentially; PHRASES: **4-7** anti-Semitic; **5-9** class-conscious; **6-6** narrow-minded.

preliminary 5 first, pilot; **7** initial, opening; **9** beginning; **10** groundwork; **12** introduction, introductory; PHRASES: **5, 5** first round.

prelims 13 preliminaries; PHRASES: **5, 6** front matter.

prelude *See* **introduction**

premature 5 early, hasty; **7** forward; **8** forehand; **9** impetuous, overhasty, prophetic; **10** beforehand, precocious, preemptive, prevenient; **11** expectative, foresighted, precipitate, precipitous, preparatory; **12** anticipative, anticipatory; **13** precipitative; PHRASES: **3, 4** too soon; **3, 5** too early; **4-5** half-baked; **4-6** half-cocked; **5, 2, 4, 4** ahead of one's time.

prematurity 5 haste; **9** foresight, hastiness, precocity; **10** preemption; **11** expectation, impetuosity, preparation, prevenience; **12** anticipation, precipitance; **13** prematureness; **14** precociousness; PHRASES: **5, 8** early maturity.

premeditate 3 fix; **4** plan; **5** frame; **6** preset; **7** arrange; **8** contrive; **10** prearrange, preconcert; **11** preconceive; PHRASES: **3, 2** set up; **4, 3, 4** load the dice; **4, 10** plan beforehand; **5, 10** agree beforehand.

premeditation 4 plan, plot; **6** agenda; **7** project, resolve; **9** intention; **11** forethought, preparation; **14** prearrangement; **15** predeliberation; PHRASES: **3-2, 3** put-up job; **4-3-4, 4** open-and-shut case; **5-2** frameup; **5, 2, 3, 3** order of the day; **5, 4** parti pris; **5, 5** order paper *UK*; **6, 4** closed book, closed mind, packed jury; **6, 6** agreed result; **6, 7** primed witness.

premier 2 PM; **4** best; **5** first; **7** leading; **8** foremost; **9** president; PHRASES: **4, 2, 5** head of state; **5, 8** first minister, prime minister.

premiere 4 main; **5** debut; **6** launch; **7** opening; **9** flotation, launching, principal, unveiling; **12** presentation; PHRASES: **5, 4** first time; **5, 5** first night; **5, 10** first appearance; **6, 3** coming out; **6, 6** maiden speech *UK*, maiden voyage; **7, 4** curtain rise; **7-6** curtain-raiser; **7, 8** opening ceremony.

premise 5 axiom; **6** assume, defend, excuse; **7** explain, justify; **8** theorize; **9** postulate; **12** philosophize.

premium 3 top; **4** best, perk; **5** bonus; **6** finest, reward; **7** payment, quality; **10** percentage; PHRASES: **5-5** first-class.

premonition 4 omen; **6** augury; **10** divination, foreboding; **11** forewarning; **12** presentiment.

preoccupation 5 worry; **7** anxiety, concern; **8** fixation; **9** obsession.

preoccupied 7 anxious, worried; **9** elsewhere; **11** inattentive; PHRASES: **4, 2, 7** lost in thought.

preoccupy *See* **worry**

preordain 4 doom, fate; **6** ordain; **7** destine; **10** predestine; **12** predetermine.

preparation 4 plan; **5** basis, draft, frame,

pilot, rough, steps, store, study, trial; **6** sketch, tuning; **7** cocking, loading, outline, priming *UK*, savings; **8** homework, measures, planning, practice, reserves, scaffold; **9** blueprint, discovery, flotation, foresight, framework, launching, preparing, promotion, prototype, rehearsal, spadework; **10** experiment, foundation, groundwork, innovation, pioneering, prewriting; **11** arrangement, development, exploration, forethought, scaffolding; **12** anticipation, arrangements, breakthrough, consultation, inauguration, mobilization, organization; **13** preliminaries, premeditation; **14** prearrangement; **15** preconsultation; PHRASES: **2, 3, 6** on the stocks; **2, 4** in hand; **2, 9** in readiness; **2, 12** in anticipation; **4, 3** nest egg; **5, 3** trial run, under way; **5, 5** first draft; **5, 6** rough sketch; **5, 7** pilot program; **5-7** avant-gardism; **5, 9** dress rehearsal; **6, 6** bottom drawer; **7, 5** getting ready; **8, 5** original model; **11, 4** preliminary step, preparatory work.

preparatory 5 basic; **7** guiding *UK*, leading, stopgap; **8** founding, piloting; **9** makeshift, preparing; **10** elementary, innovative, innovatory, pioneering; **11** discovering, exploratory, preliminary, preparative, provisional; **12** foundational, introductory, trailblazing; **13** developmental, precautionary; **14** reconnoitering; **15** preprofessional; PHRASES: **5-5** avant-garde; **6-8** groundbreaking.

prepare 3 fix; **4** book, cock, stow, tune, wind; **5** alert, array, crank, focus, order, prime, study, train; **6** adjust, engage, expect; **7** arrange, forearm, foresee, pioneer, preempt, prevent, reserve; **8** assemble, exercise, forewarn, mobilize, practice, rehearse; **9** forestall, introduce; **10** anticipate, commission; **11** precipitate; PHRASES: **2, 2, 4** be on call; **2, 6** go before; **3, 2** rev up, tee up; **3, 5** get ready; **3, 8** put together; **4, 2** gear up, suit up, tune up, warm up, wind up; **4, 2, 2** lead up to; **4, 2, 4, 5** gird up one's loins; **4, 3, 3** lead the way, pave the way, show the way; **4, 3, 6** heat the boiler; **4, 4, 7** flex one's muscles; **4, 5** make ready, take steps; **4, 7** make contact; **5, 2** crank up, stand by, stoke up; **5, 3, 5** clear the decks; **5, 4** count down; **5, 5** stand ready; **5, 7** brace oneself, catch napping, ready oneself; **6, 2** limber up; **7, 3, 5** shuffle the cards; **8, 4** shoulder arms.

prepared 3 set; **4** fast; **5** alert, armed, ready, tuned; **6** primed, rigged, warned; **7**

briefed, dressed, groomed, readied, saddled, trained, tutored, waiting; **8** equipped, vigilant; **9** accouterd, forearmed, furnished, mobilized, organized, practiced, precooked, qualified; **10** forewarned, instructed; **11** convenience, experienced, unsurprised; PHRASES: **2, 3, 5** at the ready; **2, 3, 6** in the saddle; **2, 4** on call; **2, 4, 5** on one's marks; **2, 7** in harness, on standby; **2, 8** in practice; **2, 9** in readiness; **3, 3** all set; **3-3-4** off-the-rack; **4-9** well-appointed, well-rehearsed; **5, 2** keyed up; **5, 2, 2** ready to go; **5-2-3** ready-to-eat; **5, 2, 3, 5** armed to the teeth; **5-2-4** ready-to-wear; **5, 9** fully furnished; **6, 2, 2** raring to go; **6, 3** rigged out; **7, 2** psyched up; **8, 2** standing by.

prepared (be prepared) **4** save; **6** expect, insure; **7** forearm; **10** anticipate; PHRASES: **4, 3** look for, wait for; **5, 7** guard against; **5, 8** hoard supplies; **7, 3** prepare for.

preparedness **4** peak; **7** fitness, puberty; **8** maturity, nubility, ripeness; **9** readiness; **10** mellowness; PHRASES: **3, 9** top condition; **5, 9** prime condition.

preparer **4** cook; **5** coach, paver, sower, tutor; **6** brewer, farmer, fitter, grower, loader, packer; **7** paviour *UK*, pioneer, planter, plowman, teacher, trainer; **8** equipper, provider; **9** ploughman *UK*, stevedore; **10** cultivator; **11** drillmaster, provisioner, torchbearer, trailblazer; **15** agriculturalist; PHRASES: **5, 8** drill sergeant; **6-7** bridgebuilder.

preponderance **4** many, mass; **6** weight; **8** majority; **9** dominance, multitude; **10** prevalence; **11** superiority; **12** predominance.

prepossessing **8** alluring, pleasant; **10** attractive; PHRASES: **4-7** good-looking, nice-looking.

preposterous *See* **outrageous**

prerogative **5** claim, right, title; **6** demand; **9** authority, privilege; **10** birthright; **13** primogeniture.

presage *See* **predict**

prescribe **5** order; **6** advise, impose; **7** propose, suggest; **8** advocate; **9** recommend, stipulate; PHRASES: **3, 4** set down.

prescription **4** dose; **6** course, decree, ruling; **7** essence, formula; **9** excipient, galenical; **10** antagonist, confection; **11** prerogative; PHRASES: **6, 9** active principle; **9, 4** effective dose.

presence **5** being, poise; **7** reality, specter; **8** ontology, solidity, thusness; **9** actuality, closeness, existence; **10** attendance; **11** materiality; **12** manifestness, materialness; **13** manifestation; PHRASES: **4-10** self-confidence.

present **3** now; **4** gift, real, show, wrap; **5** flash, issue, solid, today, treat; **6** actual, expose, extant, launch, modern, reveal, screen; **7** current, display, exhibit, instant, outline, publish, realize, release, topical; **8** disclose, existent, existing, giftwrap, manifest, material, prettify, spectral; **9** attending, diffusive, highlight, pervading, pervasive, suffusing, suffusive; **10** everywhere, permeating, permeative, silhouette, ubiquitous; **11** fashionable, omnipresent, penetrating; **12** contemporary; **15** contemporaneous; PHRASES: **2-2-4** up-to-date; **2, 4, 4** of this date; **2, 5** in being, of today; **2, 6, 4** of today's date; **2, 7** in fashion; **3-4** all-over; **3, 7** put forward; **3-9** all-pervasive; **4, 2-2-4** bang up-to-date; **5, 2** point up; **5, 3** point out.

present (at present) **3** now; **5** today; **7** tonight; **8** nowadays; **9** presently; PHRASES: **2, 4, 4** at this time; **2, 4, 6** at this moment; **4, 3** just now; **5, 3** right now; **5, 4** these days.

present (be present) **2** be; **4** fill, live, soak; **5** exist, imbue, occur; **6** appear; **7** breathe, diffuse, overrun, pervade, suffuse; **8** permeate, saturate, solidify; **9** modernize, overswarm, penetrate; **10** impregnate, infiltrate; **11** materialize; PHRASES: **2, 5** be there; **3, 7** run through; **4, 3, 3, 3** live for the day; **4, 3, 5** live for today; **5, 2, 5** leave no space; **5, 4** carpe diem; **6, 7** filter through.

present (for the present) **9** meanwhile; **11** temporarily; **13** provisionally; PHRASES: **2, 3, 7** in the interim; **2, 3, 8** in the meantime; **3, 1, 5** for a while; **3, 3, 4** not for long; **3, 3, 4, 5** for the time being; **3, 3, 5** for the nonce; **3, 3, 6** for the moment; **3, 3, 8** for the occasion.

present (someone present) **6** patron, viewer; **7** habitué, haunter, regular, visitor, watcher, witness; **8** attendee, attender, audience, beholder, observer, onlooker; **9** bystander, spectator; **10** cinemagoer, eyewitness, frequenter; **11** participant, theatergoer; PHRASES: **6-2** looker-on, passer-by; **7, 8** regular customer.

presenter **9** announcer.

presently **4** soon; **7** shortly; PHRASES: **2, 1, 5** in a while; **2, 1, 5, 4** in a short time; **6, 4** before long. *See also* **present (at present)**

preservation 3 UHT; 6 curing, drying, saving, thrift, upkeep; 7 boiling, canning, ecology, economy, hygiene, packing, service, smoking, storage, support, tinning; 8 freezing, painting, pickling, valeting; 9 cleansing, embalming, frugality, packaging *UK*, provision, retention, salvation, servicing, taxidermy; 10 Greenpeace, insulation, marination, permanence, processing, protection, quarantine, redemption, varnishing; 11 conservancy, dehydration, deliverance, desiccation, irradiation, maintenance, reservation, safekeeping, selfishness; 12 conservation, continuation, perpetuation, prolongation; 13 mummification, refrigeration, sterilization, waterproofing; PHRASES: 3-6 sun-drying; 4, 7 cold storage; 4, 8 game preserve; 4-8 deep-freezing; 4, 9 bird sanctuary, heat retention; 5, 8 green movement; 6-6 freeze-drying; 6, 7 nature reserve; 6, 9 animal sanctuary, cordon sanitaire; 9, 4 protected area.

preservationist 5 green; 6 canner, ranger, savior, tinner; 7 bottler, rescuer; 8 embalmer, forester; 9 deliverer, ecologist, lifeguard, mummifier; 11 conservator; 15 conservationist; PHRASES: 4-5 life-saver.

preservative 3 can, ice, jar, tin; 4 salt; 5 amber, aspic, brine, spice; 6 bottle, pickle; 7 alcohol, camphor, plastic, varnish; 8 creosote, marinade, mothball; 12 formaldehyde, refrigerator; PHRASES: 6, 5 vacuum flask.

preserve 3 can, dry, fix, hug, jam, pot, tin *UK*; 4 cure, feed, hide, hold, keep, salt, save, tend; 5 grasp, guard, jelly, nurse, paint, smoke, souse, spare, store, stuff; 6 bottle, defend, embalm, foster, freeze, garage, kipper, mother, pickle, raisin, rescue, retain, season, supply, uphold; 7 bolster, cherish, chutney, currant, deliver, mummify, process, prolong, protect, provide, reserve, service, shelter, sultana, support, sustain, varnish; 8 conserve, continue, creosote, finalize, maintain, marinate, treasure, withhold; 9 dehydrate, irradiate, marmalade, provision, safeguard, stabilize, warehouse, whitewash; 10 perpetuate, waterproof; 11 immortalize, refrigerate, reservation; PHRASES: 3-3 sun-dry; 4, 2 keep up, prop up, save up; 4, 2, 3 keep on ice; 4, 4 keep safe; 4, 5 keep alive, keep fresh, keep going, look after; 4, 5, 5 keep under cover; 5, 2 shore up; 5, 5 dried fruit; 6, 2 bottle up;

6-3 freeze-dry.

preserved 4 iced, kept, safe; 5 alive, cured, dried, fresh, saved, whole; 6 canned, corned, frozen, intact, potted, salted, smoked, soused, stored, tinned *UK*; 7 bottled, perfect, pickled, stuffed; 8 embalmed; 9 cherished, conserved, marinated, mummified, protected, treasured, undecayed; 10 dehydrated, desiccated, mothballed; PHRASES: 2, 3 on ice; 2, 3, 7 in the freezer; 3-5 sun-dried; 4-4 well-kept; 4-9 well-preserved; 6-5 freeze-dried.

preserved thing 3 jam; 5 jelly, mummy; 6 canned, fossil, relish; 7 pickles; 8 conserve; 9 marmalade, preserves; PHRASES: 4-4, 4 long-life food, long-life milk; 5, 4 dried food, dried milk; 6, 4 canned food, frozen food, tinned food; 6-5, 4 freeze-dried food; 6, 8 listed building *UK*; 7, 6 stuffed animal; 9, 4 processed food; 10, 4 dehydrated food.

preserver 3 can, ice, jar, pot, tin; 4 salt, silo; 5 amber, aspic, brine, charm, Dewar, paint, spice; 6 amulet, bottle, fridge, mascot, pectin, pickle; 7 alcohol, camphor, cannery, freezer, plastic, Thermos™, varnish; 8 creosote, lifeline, marinade, mothball, talisman; 9 incubator, whitewash; 10 respirator; 12 formaldehyde, preservative, refrigerator; PHRASES: 3, 3 air bag; 3, 4 gas mask; 4, 4 iron lung, life belt, seat belt; 4-4, 5 good-luck charm; 4, 6 life jacket; 6, 4 safety belt; 6, 5 vacuum flask; 6, 6 rescue device, safety device; 8, 5 bottling plant.

president 1 P; 3 FDR, Ike, JFK, LBJ; 4 Bush (George), Bush (George W.), Ford (Gerald R.), Polk (James Knox), Taft (William Howard), veep; 5 Adams (John), Adams (John Quincy), chair, Grant (Ulysses S.), Hayes (Rutherford B.), Nixon (Richard), POTUS, Tyler (John); 6 Arthur (Chester A.), Carter (Jimmy), Hoover (Herbert), leader, Monroe (James), Pierce (Franklin), Reagan (Ronald), Taylor (Zachary), Truman (Harry S.), Wilson (Woodrow); 7 Clinton (Bill), Harding (Warren G.), Jackson (Andrew), Johnson (Andrew), Johnson (Lyndon B.), Kennedy (John F.), Lincoln (Abraham), Madison (James), premier; 8 Buchanan (James), chairman, Coolidge (Calvin), director, Fillmore (Millard), Garfield (James A.), Harrison (Benjamin), Harrison (William Henry), McKinley (William); 9 Cleveland (Grover), Jefferson (Thomas), moderator, Roosevelt (Franklin D.), Roosevelt (Theodore); 10 chancellor,

Eisenhower (Dwight D.), Washington (George); **14** superintendent; PHRASES: **3, 5** Van Buren (Martin); **4, 4** West Wing; **5, 6** First Family.

press 3 dab, hit, jab, nip, pot, tug; **4** blow, bump, goad, iron, kick, poke, prod, pull, push, slap, urge; **5** brush, crowd, crush, knock, media, nudge, pinch, punch, smash, surge, tweak; **6** mangle, strike, throng, tickle, twitch; **7** flatten, Reuters; **8** tabloids; **10** broadsheet, newspapers; PHRASES: **3, 5** fly ~; **4, 5** stop ~ *UK*; **4, 7** news service, wire service; **4, 8** snap fastener; **5, 3** ~ box; **5, 4** ~ gang; **5, 5** drill ~, ~ agent; **5, 6** Fleet Street, ~ agency; **5, 7** ~ gallery, ~ release; **5, 10** ~ conference; **6, 5** filter ~, gutter ~, racket ~; **8, 5** printing ~; **9, 5** hydraulic ~; **10, 5** Associated P~.

pressgang *See* **force**

pressing *See* **urgent**

press on 4 push, rise; **5** climb; PHRASES: **2, 5** go ahead; **4, 2** keep on, push on; **4, 6** gain ground, gain height, rise higher; **4, 7** make strides; **5, 2** drive on; **5, 5** forge ahead; **5, 6** cover ground; **5, 7** press forward; **6, 3** gather way.

pressure 1 F; **3** bar; **4** load; **5** force; **6** duress, strain, stress, threat, thrust; **8** coercion; **10** compulsion, constraint; **11** compression; PHRASES: **5, 8** blood ~, cabin ~, fluid ~; **7, 8** osmotic ~; **8, 4** ~ suit; **8, 5** ~ gauge, ~ group, ~ point; **8, 6** ~ cooker.

prestige 5 honor, kudos, merit, style; **6** desert; **7** dignity; **10** augustness, reputation; PHRASES: **4-5** high-flier.

prestigious 6 august, mighty; **7** stylish; **9** dignified; **10** commanding, impressive; PHRASES: **4-6** high-flying; **4-7** high-falutin.

presume 6 assume; **7** suppose.

presumption 4 gall; **5** nerve; **6** belief; **8** audacity; **9** impudence; **10** assumption, conjecture; **11** supposition; **12** impertinence; **14** presupposition.

presumptuous 4 bold, rash, rude; **5** pushy; **8** arrogant, impolite, improper, insolent; **9** audacious, presuming, shameless; **12** overfamiliar; **13** disrespectful, inappropriate, overconfident.

presumptuousness 12 impertinence; **14** licentiousness; **15** overfamiliarity. *See also* **presumptuous**

pretend 3 act; **4** fake, play, pose, sham, show; **5** bluff, evade, feign, feint, shift; **6** af-

fect, assume, delude, gammon, humbug; **7** conceal, deceive, imitate, posture, shuffle; **8** simulate; **9** dissemble, represent, whitewash; **11** dissimulate, impersonate; **12** attitudinize; PHRASES: **3, 2** put on; **4, 1, 4** play a part; **4, 1, 4, 2** make a show of; **4, 2** pose as; **4, 2, 2** make as if; **4-3** play-act; **4, 4** make like; **4-4** soft-soap; **4, 6** play possum; **5-4** sweet-talk.

pretender 5 actor, poser, swank; **6** humbug, poseur; **7** bluffer, ironist; **8** claimant, deceiver, Tartuffe; **9** charlatan, hypocrite; **13** attitudinizer, exhibitionist; PHRASES: **4-3** show-off; **5, 5** drama queen *UK*.

pretending 6 acting, posing; **7** seeming; **8** apparent, bluffing, feigning, romantic; **9** affecting, posturing; **10** hyperbolic, ostensible; **11** dissembling, exaggerated, pretentious; **12** masquerading, romanticized; **13** dissimulating; **14** attitudinizing; PHRASES: **2-6** so-called; **3-2** put-on; **4-6** play-acting.

pretense 4 pose, sham, show; **5** bluff, feint, shift; **6** acting, excuse, gammon, posing; **7** charade, evasion, fiction, posture, pretext; **8** cheating, feigning, flimflam, flummery, tokenism; **9** ambiguity, deception, hyperbole, imitation, imposture; **10** hollowness, humbuggery, pretending, pretension, subterfuge; **11** affectation, ambivalence, concealment, insincerity, unfrankness; **12** apparentness, exaggeration, speciousness, uncandidness; **13** artificiality, dissimulation, dramatization, impersonation, ostensibility, overstatement; **14** attitudinizing, overestimation, representation; **15** romanticization; PHRASES: **4-6** play-acting; **4-7** make-believe; **6, 7** poetic license; **7-6** jiggery-pokery.

pretension 4 airs; **6** posing; **9** posturing; **11** affectation.

pretentious 5 false, phony *UK*, showy; **6** hollow, phoney, posing; **8** affected, bluffing, unctuous; **9** deceptive, insincere, unnatural; **10** artificial, pretending, tokenistic; **12** hypocritical, meretricious; **13** sanctimonious; PHRASES: **5-6** artsy-fartsy; **5-7** artsy-craftsy, mealy-mouthed.

pretentiousness 7 falsity, posture; **8** artifice, bluffing; **9** euphemism; PHRASES: **4-6** play-acting. *See also* **pretentious**

pretty 5 quite; **6** fairly, rather; **8** handsome; **9** appealing, beautiful; **10** attractive, moderately, reasonably; PHRASES: **4-7** good-looking.

prevail 3 run, win; 4 rule; 5 force, reign; 6 compel, master, obtain, subdue; 7 control; 8 dominate, outweigh, overbear, overcome, override; 9 fascinate, hypnotize, mesmerize, subjugate, tyrannize; 11 predominate; 12 preponderate; PHRASES: 2, 2 be in.

prevailing 6 common, public; 7 popular; 8 accepted, communal, dominant; 9 community, prevalent; 10 widespread; 11 predominant; 12 unrestricted; 13 predominating.

prevalent 6 common; 7 rampant; 8 dominant; 10 ubiquitous, widespread; 11 predominant.

prevent 4 foil, stop; 5 avert, avoid; 6 thwart.

preview 4 omen; 6 taster UK; 7 trailer, warning; 9 foretaste; 11 premonition.

previous See **former**

prey 4 game, grab; 6 quarry, victim; 7 escapee, oppress; 8 criminal, deserter, fugitive; PHRASES: 4, 2 feed on; 4, 5 lost child; 7, 6 missing person.

price 2 PR; 3 fee; 4 cost, rate, toll; 5 value; 6 amount, assess, bounty, charge, figure, tariff; 7 valuate; 8 appraise, dearness, estimate, evaluate; 9 cheapness, quotation; 10 commission; 11 consequence; 12 intervention; 14 discrimination; PHRASES: 3, 5 bid ~, cut ~; 4, 5 cost ~, list ~, sale ~; 5, 3 ~ cut, ~ tag, ~ war; 5, 4 ~ list, ~ ring UK; 5, 5 bride ~, fixed ~, offer ~, ~ range; 5, 7 ~ control; 6, 5 asking ~, market ~, quoted ~, retail ~; 7, 5 factory ~, reserve ~, selling ~; 8, 5 discount ~, standard ~, starting ~ UK.

priced 5 rated, worth; 6 valued; 8 assessed; PHRASES: 6, 2 valued at.

priceless 5 comic, funny; 6 costly; 7 amusing; 9 hilarious; 10 invaluable; 11 inestimable; 12 incalculable; PHRASES: 6, 5 beyond price.

prick 3 jab; 4 hole, stab; 6 pierce; 7 pinhole; 8 puncture; 9 perforate; 11 perforation.

prickle 4 barb, itch; 5 prick, quill, spike, spine, sting, thorn; 6 tickle; 8 irritate, tingling; 10 irritation.

prickly 5 cross, itchy, rough, sharp, spiky, spiny; 6 barbed, briary, spiked, tingly; 7 awkward, brambly, bristly, peevish; 8 delicate, scratchy, ticklish, tingling; 9 irascible, irritable; 11 contentious, problematic; PHRASES: 7, 3 ~ ash; 7, 4 ~ heat, ~ pear; 7, 5

~ poppy.

prickly heat 8 miliaria.

pride 4 pick; 5 boast, honor, lions; 6 hubris, spirit; 7 courage; 8 favorite; 9 arrogance, proudness; 12 pridefulness; PHRASES: 4, 2, 3, 5 pick of the bunch; 4-6 self-esteem, self-regard; 4-7 self-respect; 4-10 self-confidence, self-importance; 5, 2, 3, 5 jewel in the crown; 5, 2, 5 ~ of place; 5, 3, 3 ~ and joy; 5, 6 amour propre; 6, 2, 5 source of ~.

pride (feel pride) 5 boast; PHRASES: 3, 7 hug oneself; 4, 5, 2 take pride in; 5, 4, 5 swell with pride; 5, 7 preen oneself; 7, 7 flatter oneself.

priest 1 p; 2 PR; 3 Eli, Rev; 4 abbé, curé, dean, guru, imam, lama, Levi, papa, pope, qadi; 5 augur, canon, elder, hakam, Kalif, kohen, padre, rabbi, rishi, vicar; 6 bishop, cantor, cleric, curate, Dastur, deacon, divine, father, flamen, Gosain, hazzan, Levite, maftir, maggid, mukdam, mullah, parson, pastor, pastor(ess), pundit, rector, scribe, sexton, sheikh, verger; 7 acolyte, almoner, Brahman, darshan, houngan, mamaloi, muezzin, papaloi, pontiff, prelate, primate, qasisha; 8 cardinal, chaplain, diocesan, haruspex, hierarch, koheleth, minister, mujtahid, ordinand, poonghie, purohita, Reverend; 9 ayatollah, churchman, clergyman, confessor, deaconess, monsignor, pastoress, patriarch, precentor, priestess, succentor, suffragan, thurifer; 10 archbishop, dhammaduta, hierophant, ministress; 11 clergywoman, ecclesiarch; 12 churchwarden, ecclesiastic; PHRASES: 3-2 zen-ji; 3, 2, 3, 5 man of the cloth; 3, 5 Sky Pilot; 4, 3 Holy Joe; 4, 5 Arch Druid; 4, 6 high ~; 4, 8 Arch Druidess; 5, 4 Dalai Lama, Grand Lama; 5, 5 chief rabbi; 5, 6 witch doctor; 7, 4 Panchen Lama; 8, 7 pontifex maximus.

priesthood 3 see; 6 abbacy, curacy, papacy, parish; 7 deanery, diocese, popedom, primacy; 8 deaconry, deanship, election, province; 9 bishopdom, bishopric, induction, pastorage, pastorate, prelature, rabbinate, rectorate, vicariate, vicarship; 10 Brahmanism, Brahminism, chaplaincy, conferment, deaconship, episcopate, hierocracy, nomination, ordainment, ordination, pastorship, preferment, priestship, rectorship; 11 appointment, archdiocese, clericalism, institution, investiture, pontificate; 12

cardinalship, chaplainship; **13** sacerdotalism; **15** ecclesiasticism; PHRASES: **3, 5** the cloth; **3, 6** the Church, the clergy; **3, 8** the ministry; **4, 6** holy orders; **8, 4** pastoral care.

priestly **5** papal; **7** druidic; **8** churchly, clerical, diocesan, hieratic, ordained, pastoral, prelatic, rabbinic; **9** canonical, episcopal, parochial; **10** hieratical, pontifical, sacerdotal; **11** hierocratic, ministerial; **12** ecclesiastic, hierophantic, presbyterial; **14** ecclesiastical.

priestly dwelling **5** manse; **6** ashram, friary, priory; **7** convent, deanery, nunnery, rectory, retreat, Vatican; **8** cloister, lamasery, vicarage; **9** hermitage, monastery, parsonage; **10** presbytery; **12** archdeaconry, chapterhouse; PHRASES: **7, 6** bishop's palace, Lambeth Palace.

prim **4** tidy; **5** fussy, stiff; **6** formal, prissy, proper; **7** orderly, precise, prudish, starchy; **9** dignified; **10** meticulous, moralistic; **11** puritanical; PHRASES: **6-5** strait-laced.

primacy **9** bishopric, dominance; **10** importance, prevalence; **11** preeminence; **12** predominance; **13** archbishopric.

primal **5** early; **7** ancient, central, glacial; **8** Cenozoic, Mesozoic, primeval; **9** embryonic, Neolithic, primitive; **10** Mesolithic, preglacial, primordial; **11** fundamental, Paleolithic, prehistoric; **12** antediluvian, Chalcolithic, prelapsarian; PHRASES: **4-3** Iron-Age; **5-3** Stone-Age; **6-3** Bronze-Age.

primary **5** chief, elder, first; **6** senior; **7** leading, supreme; **8** foremost, headmost, original, superior; **10** preeminent.

primate **4** apes; **6** bishop, pongid, simian; **7** hominid, monkeys, pongids, simious; **8** hominids, official, Pongidae, Primates; **9** Hominidae, primatial, prosimian; **10** anthropoid, prosimians; **11** anthropoids, primatology; PHRASES: **3, 5, 7** New World monkeys, Old World monkeys; **5, 2, 8** study of primates; **10, 4** anthropoid apes.

prime **4** main, peak; **5** first; **6** heyday, primal, zenith; **7** educate, eminent, prepare; **8** earliest, original, pinnacle, primeval, pristine, valuable; **9** primitive; **10** aboriginal, primordial; PHRASES: **5, 4** ~ cost, ~ rate, ~ time; **5, 5** ~ mover; **5, 6** ~ number; **5, 8** ~ meridian, ~ minister.

prime minister **4** Bute, Eden, Grey, King (Mackenzie), Peel, Pitt; **5** Atlee, Blair, Clark (Joe), Derby, heath, Heath (Ted),

Major, North; **6** Attlee (Clement), Borden (Sir Robert), Martin (Paul), Pelham, Turner (John Napier), Wilson; **7** Asquith, Baldwin, Balfour, Bennett (Richard Bedford), Canning, Chatham, Grafton, Laurier (Sir Wilfrid), Meighen (Arthur), premier, Russell, Trudeau (Pierre), Walpole; **8** Aberdeen, Campbell (Kim), Chrétien (Jean), Disraeli, Goderich, Mulroney (Brian), Perceval, Portland, Rosebery, Thatcher; **9** Addington, Callaghan, Churchill, Gladstone, Grenville, Liverpool, Macmillan, Melbourne, Newcastle, Salisbury, Shelburne; **10** chancellor, Devonshire, Palmerston, Rockingham, Wellington, Wilmington; **11** Chamberlain, Diefenbaker (John George); PHRASES: **2, 7** St. Laurent (Louis); **5, 3** Boanr Law; **5, 6** Lloyd George; **6, 9** Ramsay MacDonald; **7-4** Douglas-Home.

Prime Mover **3** God; **4** sire; **5** deity, Maker; **6** author, father, Father, mother, parent; **7** founder; **8** ancestor, begetter, inspirer, inventor, producer; **9** motivator; **10** instigator, originator, progenitor, propagator; PHRASES: **3, 5** the Deity; **3, 7** the Creator; **4, 8** only begetter; **6, 6** primum mobile; **6, 7** Divine Creator; **7, 5** Supreme Being.

primeval **6** fossil; **7** ancient, antique, archaic; **8** original; **9** primitive; **11** prehistoric.

primitive **5** basic, crude; **6** primal, simple; **7** ancient, archaic, nascent; **8** original, primeval; **9** embryonic; **10** aboriginal, primordial; **11** prehistoric; **13** uncomplicated; **15** unsophisticated.

primordial *See* **primal**

Prince of Darkness **5** Satan.

principal **3** key, top; **4** arch, head, lead, main, star; **5** basic, chief, focal, major, vital; **6** leader, staple; **7** capital, central, crucial, leading, primary, provost, supreme; **8** critical, dominant, foremost; **9** essential, paramount; **10** chancellor, overriding; **11** fundamental, predominant.

principle **4** code, rule; **5** basis, cause, tenet, value; **6** belief, notion, origin, source, theory; **7** concept; **8** attitude, standard; **10** wellspring.

principled *See* **honorable**

print **4** copy, mark, type; **5** clone, stamp, trace; **7** edition, impress, imprint, replica, reprint; **8** offprint; **9** duplicate, facsimile, footprint, photocopy; **11** fingerprint, publication; PHRASES: **3, 7** new edition; **6-5**

screen-print; **7, 7** revised edition.

printing 4 text; **5** words; **7** edition, wording, writing; **8** capitals; **9** lettering; **10** impression, production; **11** letterpress, lithography; **12** reproduction; PHRASES: **5, 3** print run; **5, 4** upper case.

prior 2 ex; **4** last, late; **5** abbot, above, elder, first; **6** before, eldest, former, primal, senior; **7** earlier, forward, leading; **8** advanced, foremost, previous; **9** aforesaid, erstwhile, foregoing, forenamed; **10** aforenamed; **14** aforementioned; **15** beforementioned; PHRASES: **3-4** one-time; **5-9** abovementioned.

priority 4 line; **5** front; **7** primacy, urgency; **8** dominion, vanguard; **9** forefront, privilege, seniority, supremacy; **10** importance, precedence, preference; **11** antecedence, anteriority, preeminence, prerogative, superiority; **12** preexistence, previousness; PHRASES: **3, 4** the lead; **4, 8** pole position; **5, 2, 3, 5** front of the queue; **5, 2, 5** pride of place; **5, 5** first place; **5, 7** first concern; **5, 8** front position.

prison 3 can, jug; **4** bird, brig, cage, cell, gaol *UK*, jail, nick *UK*, quod *UK*, stir; **5** bring, clink, Gulag, pound, vault; **6** bucket, chokey *UK*, cooler, lockup; **7** borstal *UK*, dungeon, slammer; **8** Alcatraz, compound, Dartmoor, lockdown, stockade; **9** Auschwitz, Broadmoor, jailhouse, oubliette; **10** Buchenwald, glasshouse *UK*, guardhouse; **11** reformatory; **12** penitentiary; PHRASES: **4, 4** city jail, Sing Sing; **5, 4** drunk tank, labor camp; **6, 4** county jail, ~ camp, ~ farm; **6, 6** Devil's Island, ~ colony, reform school; **7, 5** halfway house; **7, 6** debtor's ~, federal ~; **8, 6** approved school *UK*, military ~, Wormwood Scrubs; **9, 4** community home, detention home; **9, 6** detention center; **12, 8** correctional facility, disciplinary barracks.

prison cell 6 icebox; **7** bullpen, flowery; **8** birdcage, solitary; PHRASES: **3, 4** the hole; **4, 4** jail cell; **5, 3** death row; **5, 4** death cell.

prisoner 3 con, lag, POW; **5** lifer, zebra; **6** inmate; **7** captive, convict, hostage; **8** detainee, internee, jailbird, yardbird; PHRASES: **3, 3** old lag *UK*; **4, 7** rock crusher; **5-4, 6** chain-gang member; **10, 3** government man.

prison officer 5 horse, screw; **6** jailer, keeper, warden, warder *UK*; **7** turnkey; **9** custodian; PHRASES: **3, 3** the Man; **6, 5** prison guard; **6, 8** prison governor.

prison sentence 3 BOT, lag; **4** bird, life, time; **7** fistful, handful, stretch; **8** porridge, vacation; PHRASES: **3, 4** the book; **4, 7** five fingers.

pristine 6 virgin; **7** perfect; **8** original, primeval; **9** faultless, unspoiled, untouched; **10** immaculate.

privacy 3 den; **4** bath, lair; **5** study; **6** toilet; **7** bedroom, boudoir, convent, library, nunnery, retreat, sanctum, secrecy; **8** bathroom; **9** monastery, seclusion; **10** lighthouse; **11** mountaintop; PHRASES: **5, 5** ivory tower; **6, 5** closed order; **6, 6** desert island; **7, 4** private club; **7, 6** private garden.

private 2 GI; **3** own; **5** Tommy; **6** covert, hidden, inward, masked, ranker *UK*, secret, veiled; **7** covered, obscure; **8** internal, intimate, obscured, personal, screened; **9** backstage, concealed, detective, disguised, recondite, secretary; **10** enterprise, obstructed; **11** camouflaged, clandestine; PHRASES: **2, 6** in camera, in secret; **2, 7** in ~; **5, 5** under wraps; **6, 3, 6** behind the scenes; **7, 3** blacked out, ~ bar, ~ eye; **7, 4** ~ bill *UK*, ~ life *UK*; **7, 5** ~ parts; **7, 6** ~ income, ~ school, ~ sector; **7, 7** ~ company, ~ patient *UK*, ~ soldier; **7, 8** ~ practice *UK*, ~ property.

privilege 3 joy; **5** favor, honor, treat; **7** benefit, freedom, license; **8** pleasure; **9** advantage; **11** opportunity; **12** dispensation.

privy 2, 3, 4 in the know; **5, 2** aware of, party to; **7, 2** sharing in. *See also* **toilet**

Privy 5, 4 P~ Seal; **5, 5** P~ Purse *UK*; **5, 7** P~ Chamber, P~ Council.

prize 3 cup, pot; **4** Emmy, palm; **5** award, crown, kitty, lever, medal, money, Oscar, plate, purse, value; **6** esteem, regard, shield, trophy; **7** jackpot, Whiting; **11** certificate; PHRASES: **4, 5** cash ~; **4, 6** Blue Riband, blue ribbon; **5, 4** force open, ~ ring; **5, 5** booby ~, Nobel P~, ~ money; **6-2, 5** runner-up ~; **6, 4** kewpie doll; **6, 5** second ~, wooden spoon *UK*; **7, 5** Academy Award; **8, 3** America's Cup; **8, 4, 5** National Book Award; **8, 5** Bancroft P~, Faulkner Award, Pulitzer P~.

pro 3 for; PHRASES: **2, 5, 2** in favor of; **2, 7, 2** in support of; **3, 3** all for. *See also* **professional**

probability 4 odds; **6** chance; **7** outlook; **8** forecast, prospect; **9** certainty, liability, prognosis, proneness; **10** liableness, likelihood, likeliness, prediction; **11** expectation, presumption; **12** anticipation; **13** impossibility; **14** predictability; PHRASES: **3, 2, 8** law of averages.

probable 3 apt; **5** prone; **6** liable, likely; **7** evident, tending; **8** apparent, drifting, expected, presumed; **9** undoubted; **10** ostensible, predictive, presumable; **11** anticipated, indubitable, predictable, presumptive, prospective; **14** unquestionable; PHRASES: **2, 3, 5** in the cards; **2, 3, 7** in the running; **5, 2, 6** bound to happen.

probable (be probable) 6 impend; **7** promise; PHRASES: **4, 3, 2, 6** lead one to expect; **4, 6** seem likely.

probably 6 likely; **7** readily; **9** doubtless; **10** apparently, expectedly, ostensibly *UK*, presumably; **11** indubitably, predictably; **13** prejudicially, tendentiously; **14** unquestionably; PHRASES: **2, 2, 8** to be expected; **2, 3, 10** in all likelihood; **2, 5** as usual; **2, 6, 2, 3** as likely as not; **2, 7** on average; **2, 8** as expected; **2, 12** in anticipation; **3, 2, 3** ten to one; **4, 6** most likely.

probation 4 test; **5** trial; **6** tryout; **8** audition; **15** experimentation.

probe 5 delve; **6** review; **7** inquire, inquiry; **8** analysis, research; **11** examination, investigate; **13** investigation; PHRASES: **4, 4** look into.

probity 5 honor, truth; **6** candor, equity, ethics, morals, repute; **7** decency, honesty, justice, loyalty; **8** chivalry, devotion, fairness, fidelity, goodness, morality, openness, scruples, trueness, veracity; **9** constancy, frankness, integrity, nobleness, plainness, sincerity, soundness; **10** candidness, conscience, principles, trustiness; **11** carefulness, reliability, uprightness; **12** faithfulness, impartiality, truthfulness; **13** dependability, honorableness, steadfastness; **14** fastidiousness, meticulousness, respectability, scrupulousness; **15** trustworthiness; PHRASES: **4, 5** bona fides, good faith; **4, 6** high ideals; **4, 9** good character; **4, 10** high principles; **4-10** high-mindedness; **5, 2, 4** sense of duty; **5, 5** clean hands, moral fiber.

problem 3 sum; **4** crux, hole, knot, maze, snag, spot, stew; **5** fault, nodus, poser, worry; **6** enigma, niggle *UK Can*, puzzle, tangle, teaser; **7** anxiety, dilemma, nonplus; **8** headache, quandary; **9** conundrum, imbroglio; **10** perplexity; PHRASES: **3, 2, 5** can of worms; **4, 3, 2, 5** hard nut to crack; **5-6** brain-teaser; **5-7** brain-twister; **5, 8** vexed question; **6, 7** knotty ~, thorny ~; **7, 4** Gordian knot.

problematic 4 moot; **5** hairy, tough; **6** knotty, mooted, sticky, thorny, tricky; **7** complex, crabbed, cramped, crucial, curious, garbled, jumbled, obscure, unclear; **8** abstruse, baffling, confused, delicate, esoteric, exacting, involved, puzzling, riddling, ticklish; **9** confusing, debatable, demanding, difficult, enigmatic, illegible, intricate, quizzical, recondite, scrambled, technical, troubling, undecided; **10** challenged, convoluted, mysterious, pernickety *UK*, perplexing *UK*, questioned; **11** challenging, complicated, interesting, jawbreaking, obfuscating, persnickety, specialized; **12** impenetrable, labyrinthine; **14** indecipherable, unintelligible.

procedure 2 MO; **3** way; **5** drill, order, rules; **6** method, policy, system; **7** routine; **8** practice, protocol; **9** beadledom, etiquette, operation; **10** conformism, conformity; **11** bureaucracy; **12** conservatism; **14** traditionalism; **15** conventionalism, conventionality; PHRASES: **3, 4** red tape; **3, 6** old school; **5, 6** usual policy; **5, 8** modus operandi; **6, 8** common practice.

proceed 2 go; **4** head, lead, move, pass, roll, wend; **5** weave; **6** patrol, travel, voyage; **7** advance, journey; **8** progress; **9** circulate; PHRASES: **4, 2** pass on; **4, 3, 7** join the traffic; **4, 5** move along.

process 4 sort; **5** march, treat; **6** follow, method, system; **7** convert; **9** operation, procedure, refluxing, transform; **10** adsorption, filtration, separation, succession; **13** distilllation, precipitation; **14** chromatography, saponification; **15** crystallization.

procession 4 file, line; **5** march, queue *UK*, train; **6** column, convoy, parade, series, stream; **7** caravan, cortege, cortège, pageant; **8** gridlock, sequence, tailback *UK*; **9** cavalcade, crocodile *UK*, motorcade, promenade; PHRASES: **5, 4** march past; **6, 6** steady stream; **7, 3** traffic jam.

processor 2 CU; **3** ALU, CPU; **14** microprocessor; PHRASES: **4, 2-9** math co-processor.

proclaim 3 cry; **5** blast, blaze, shout; **6** blazon, herald, notify, scream; **7** declaim, declare, publish, thunder, trumpet; **8** announce; **9** pronounce; PHRASES: **4, 3, 3, 4** beat the big drum; **5, 1, 5** pitch a bitch; **5, 3,**

4 raise the roof; **5, 4** raise hell; **5, 6** blaze abroad.

proclamation 5 edict; **6** decree; **9** assertion; **11** declaration; **12** announcement.

procrastinate *See* **put off**

procrastinating 4 lazy; **6** remiss; **8** delaying, sluggish; **9** negligent; **10** neglectful, postponing.

prod 3 dig, jab; **4** push, stir, urge; **5** elbow, nudge; **6** prompt; **7** provoke; **9** stimulate.

prodigious 4 huge, vast; **7** copious, unusual; **8** abnormal, gigantic; **10** phenomenal; **11** exceptional; **13** extraordinary.

prodigy 4 star; **6** genius, wonder; **9** sensation; **10** phenomenon.

produce 2 do; **3** bud, egg, fur, sew, sow; **4** baby, bear, cast, coin, crop, eggs, farm, find, form, gain, give, grow, hide, knit, make, meat, milk, mill, mine, mint, mold, plan, rear, seed, show, sire, skin, spin, teem; **5** beget, breed, build, carve, cause, child, china, cloth, craft, cream, erect, forge, found, frame, fruit, goods, hatch, paint, raise, shape, spawn, stage, stalk, train, wares, weave, write, yield, young; **6** author, butter, cheese, chisel, create, design, devise, direct, effect, evolve, fabric, father, flower, income, invent, mother, output, profit, quarry, return, reveal, sculpt, supply, unfold; **7** achieve, arrange, blossom, combine, compose, concoct, develop, execute, exploit, extract, fashion, freight, furnish, harvest, imagine, machine, perform, present, process, provide, revenue, uncover, vintage; **8** assemble, conceive, discover, dividend, engender, engineer, generate, increase, innovate, interest, multiply, organize; **9** commodity, construct, cultivate, customize, establish, fabricate, formulate, germinate, implement, institute, offspring, originate, propagate, pullulate, reproduce, structure; **10** accomplish, constitute, synthesize; **11** manufacture, merchandise; **12** prefabricate; PHRASES: **3, 2** get up, run up, set up; **3, 2, 6** set in motion; **3, 8** put together; **4, 2** make up; **4, 3** bash out *UK*, take out, turn out; **4, 5** give birth; **4, 5, 2** give birth to; **4-7** mass-produce; **5, 2** bring up, dream up, think of, think up; **5, 3** bring out, carry out, churn out, knock out; **5, 4, 5** bring into being; **5, 5** bring about, brown goods *UK*, white goods; **5, 8** dairy products, plant products, young creature; **6-5** custom-build; **6, 8** animal products, cobble together.

produced 4 born, bred, made, sown; **5** grown; **6** raised, reared; **7** created, devised, hatched; **8** begotten, boughten, educated, handmade, homespun, imagined, invented; **9** processed, synthetic; **10** artificial, discovered; **12** manufactured; PHRASES: **3-4** man-made; **4-4** home-made; **4-8** mass-produced; **5-4** ready-made; **6, 3** worked out; **6-4** tailor-made; **6-5** custom-built; **7, 2** thought of; **7-2** dreamed-up; **7-4** factory-made, machine-made; **9-5** craftsman-built.

producer 2 MC, SM; **3** God; **4** poet; **5** agent, angel, emcee, maker, miner, movie; **6** artist, auteur, author, backer, farmer, father, grower, mother, Nature, parent, patron, worker, writer; **7** artisan, builder, creator, founder, grazier *UK*, laborer, manager, painter, planner, planter, rancher, showman; **8** begetter, choragus, composer, designer, director, engineer, gardener, inventor, musician, promoter, sculptor; **9** architect, artificer, costumier, craftsman, developer, dramatist, exhibitor, innovator, plantsman, regisseur; **10** contractor, costumière, cultivator, discoverer, fabricator, impresario, instigator, originator, playbroker, playwright, prospector, ringmaster; **11** businessman, constructor, craftswoman, craftworker, establisher, plantswoman; **12** entrepreneur, manufacturer, stockbreeder; **13** businesswoman, choreographer, industrialist; PHRASES: **4, 8** film director, film ~; **5, 5** prime mover; **5, 6** sheep farmer; **5, 7** press officer, stage manager; **5-7** actor-manager; **5, 8** stage director; **6, 5** ticket agent; **6, 6** Mother Nature; **7, 6** charter member; **7, 8** costume designer; **8, 6** creative artist, founding father; **8, 7** business manager; **9-5** programme-maker.

product 4 item, slag; **5** issue, thing, waste, yield; **6** effect, object, output, result; **7** article, essence, extract, fallout, outcome, spinoff, turnout; **8** artifact, compound, creation, creature, leavings, offshoot; **9** byproduct *UK*, commodity, decoction; **10** concoction, confection; **11** consequence, manufacture; PHRASES: **3-7** end-product; **5, 7** waste ~; **8, 7** finished article.

production 3 art, try; **4** film, play, show; **5** doing, movie, skill; **6** ballet, cinema, design, effort, making, output; **7** attempt, brewing, casting, concert, forming, molding, musical, preview, project, revival, shaping, staging, turnout, writing; **8** audition, blocking, creation, endeavor, mounting, painting, planning; **9** direction, discovery, enactment, execution, handiwork, invention, producing, rehearsal, sculpture, spectacle, structure; **10** authorship, cogitation, conception, concoction, enterprise, fermenting, innovation, technology, throughput; **11** achievement, composition, formulation, inspiration, originality, origination, performance, preparation, undertaking, walkthrough, workmanship; **12** musicianship, organization, presentation, productivity; **13** craftsmanship; **14** accomplishment, productiveness; PHRASES: **2, 7** TV program; **3-7** run-through; **4-2-5** mise-en-scène; **4-7** read-through; **5, 7** radio program; **5, 9** dress rehearsal; **5, 10** stage management; **6, 7** motion picture; **8, 4** literary work, original work; **8, 7** creative impulse.

productive 4 rich; **6** fecund, paying; **7** fertile, robotic; **8** creative, fruitful, original, prolific; **9** automated, developed, formative, inventive, lucrative; **10** developing, industrial, innovative, mechanized, profitable, structural, worthwhile; **12** agricultural, computerized, constructive, remunerative; **13** architectonic, manufacturing, nonindustrial; **14** industrialized, postindustrial, underdeveloped; PHRASES: **3-4** lowtech; **3-10** low-technology; **4-4** high-tech; **4-8** high-yielding; **4-10** high-technology; **8-7** interest-bearing.

productiveness 4 boom, glut; **8** menarche; **10** prosperity; **11** fecundation, pollination, procreation, propagation, superfluity; **12** menstruation, productivity, reproduction; **13** fertilization; **14** fructification, superabundance; **15** imaginativeness, resourcefulness; PHRASES: **4, 4** baby boom, wine lake; **4, 5, 4** high birth rate; **4, 10** mass production; **6, 8** butter mountain; **7, 7** booming economy; **8, 4** economic boom; **8, 6** economic upturn.

productivity 6 effort, output; **7** turnout; **8** endeavor; **10** efficiency, throughput.

profess 5 admit, claim, state; **6** affirm; **7** confess, declare; **8** announce, maintain, proclaim; **11** acknowledge; PHRASES: **3, 2** own up.

profession *See* **job**

professional 3 pro; **4** guru; **5** doyen; **6** expert, pundit, savant; **9** authority, efficient; **10** industrial, specialist, vocational; **12** occupational; PHRASES: **5, 6** white collar.

professor 4 prof; **5** chair; PHRASES: **6, 9** regius ~ *UK*.

proffer *See* **offer**

proficiency 4 gift; **6** talent; **7** ability; **9** expertise; **10** competence, efficiency; **11** versatility; **14** accomplishment. *See also* **proficient**

proficient 4 deft; **5** handy; **6** adroit, expert, gifted, wicked; **7** skilled; **8** masterly, skillful, talented; **9** competent, dexterous, efficient, masterful, versatile; **12** accomplished.

profile 4 form; **7** contour, outline, relievo, rilievo, summary; **9** elevation, lineament; **10** embossment, projection, silhouette; **11** delineation, description; PHRASES: **3, 6** low relief; **3-6** bas-relief; **4, 6** high relief; **4-7** alto-relievo; **5, 7** basso relievo *It*, mezzo relievo *It*.

profit 3 net, use; **4** boot, gain, good; **5** clear, gains, gravy, gross, value; **6** boodle, return, reward, wealth; **7** benefit, killing, mileage, plunder, prosper, returns, takings; **8** earnings, gettings, interest, proceeds, receipts, windfall, winnings; **9** advantage, allowance, dividends, emolument; **10** commission, honorarium, percentage, prosperity; PHRASES: **4, 1, 7** make a fortune; **4, 1, 8** earn a dividend; **4, 2, 2** cash in on, rake it in; **4, 2, 6** turn to ~; **4-3** rake-off; **4, 8** draw interest; **5, 2** clean up; **5, 3, 4** break the bank; **5, 6** clear ~; **5, 7** gross profits; **6, 4** bottom line; **7, 5** capital gains; **10, 2** capitalize on.

profitable 4 good; **5** risky; **6** paying; **7** gainful; **8** economic, edifying, fruitful, salutary, valuable; **9** lucrative, priceless, rewarding; **10** beneficial, commercial, invaluable, productive, worthwhile; **11** moneymaking, speculative; **12** advantageous, profitmaking, remunerative; PHRASES: **2, 4, 9** to one's advantage; **3, 6** for profit; **5, 1, 4** worth a mint; **5, 1, 7** worth a million.

profitable (be profitable) 3 pay; **5** avail, gross, yield; **6** accrue; **7** benefit, produce; PHRASES: **3, 1, 8** pay a dividend; **3, 4** pay well; **3, 8** pay interest; **4, 1, 6** show a profit; **4, 2** roll in; **4, 5** make money; **5, 1, 6** yield a return.

profiteer 5 abuse, crook; **7** exploit; **8** swindler; **9** embezzler, racketeer; PHRASES: **3, 3** con man.

profligate 6 wicked; **7** immoral; **8** decadent, reckless, wasteful; **9** dissolute, shameless; **10** licentious; **11** spendthrift, squandering.

profound **4** dark, deep, sage, wise; **5** acute, great; **6** clever; **7** complex, earnest, erudite, intense, learned, sincere, weighty; **8** abstruse, thorough; **9** extensive, heartfelt, scholarly; **10** discerning, exhaustive, insightful, mysterious, perceptive, percipient; **12** unfathomable; **13** comprehensive, knowledgeable, perspicacious; PHRASES: **2-5** in-depth; **2, 6** in detail.

profundity **5** depth; **6** acuity, wisdom; **7** insight; **8** sagacity; **10** astuteness; **11** discernment, penetration; **12** perspicacity, profoundness; **13** understanding.

profuse **4** rich; **6** lavish; **7** copious, fulsome, gushing, liberal; **8** abundant, effusive, prolific, wasteful; **9** bounteous; **11** extravagant.

profusion **4** glut; **6** excess, wealth; **7** surplus; **8** plethora; **9** abundance; **10** cornucopia.

progenitor See **predecessor**

progeny **3** kid; **4** baby; **5** brood, child, issue, spawn, sprog, young; **6** litter, nipper; **9** offspring.

prognosis **8** forecast, scenario; **9** diagnosis; **10** prediction, projection.

prognosticate See **predict**

prognostication See **prediction**

program **4** book, list, plan, show; **5** train; **6** agenda, course, series, system; **7** arrange, listing; **8** brochure, schedule, synopsis; **9** brainwash, broadcast, condition, timetable; **10** production; **12** transmission.

progress **4** pass; **6** evolve, travel; **7** advance, develop, headway, proceed, recover; **8** continue, movement, traverse; **9** promotion; **10** preferment, recuperate; **11** advancement, improvement.

progression **5** chain; **6** series, string; **7** advance; **8** movement, sequence; **9** evolution; **10** succession; **11** advancement, development.

progressive **3** new; **4** left; **6** modern; **7** dynamic, ongoing, radical; **8** advanced; **9** reforming, reformist; **10** continuing, continuous, escalating, increasing, innovative; **11** enlightened; **12** enterprising; PHRASES: **2-5** go-ahead; **7-7** forward-looking; **7-8** forward-thinking.

prohibit **3** ban, bar; **4** curb, stop, veto; **5** block *UK*, brake, taboo; **6** outlaw; **7** abolish, embargo, prevent; **8** disallow; **9** interdict.

prohibition **3** ban, bar; **4** tabu, veto; **5** taboo; **7** embargo; **9** interdict, outlawing; **11** forbiddance; **12** interdiction, proscription; PHRASES: **3, 5** dry state; **3, 6** dry county.

project **3** jut; **4** cast, hurl, plan, toss; **5** fling, hover, throw; **6** beetle, intend, scheme; **7** overlie, predict, program, venture; **8** estimate, forecast, overhang, proposal, protrude; **10** assignment, enterprise; **11** undertaking; PHRASES: **4, 4** hang over; **5, 3, 4** stick out over.

projectile **7** missile; **8** ejective; **9** ballistic, explosive, expulsive; **10** jaculatory, trajectile.

projecting object **4** nose, pier; **5** gable; **7** balcony; **8** buttress; **10** cantilever; **11** mantelpiece; PHRASES: **3, 4** hat brim; **6, 5** diving board.

projection **4** cape, mole, ness, peak, pier, spit; **5** cliff, jetty, ledge, point, shelf; **6** island; **7** balcony, outcrop, overlie; **8** foothill, forecast, headland, mountain, overhang; **9** peninsula; **10** breakwater, prediction, promontory; **12** protuberance; **13** fortification; PHRASES: **10, 4** projecting part.

proletarian **7** people's, popular; **10** grassroots *UK*; PHRASES: **4-6** blue-collar; **7-5** working-class.

proliferate **4** boom, brim, flow, riot, teem; **5** swarm; **6** shower, stream; **7** prosper; **8** multiply, mushroom, overflow, populate; **9** exuberate, luxuriate; **11** superabound; PHRASES: **5, 4** crawl with; **7, 4** bristle with.

prolific See **fruitful**

prolix See **wordy**

prologue See **introduction**

prolong See **extend**

prominence **4** knob, mark; **5** clout, glory, kudos; **6** cachet, esteem, repute; **7** primacy; **8** eminence, position, prestige, salience; **9** outgrowth; **10** importance; **11** distinction, exaltedness; **12** protuberance; **14** impressiveness.

prominent **3** big; **5** noted; **7** eminent; **8** standout; **9** important; **10** noticeable; **11** outstanding, protuberant; PHRASES: **7, 3** jutting out.

promiscuity **6** mixing, muddle, venery; **7** whoring; **8** harlotry, priapism, wenching;

9 decadence, depravity, lubricity, seduction; **10** debauchery, satyriasis, unchastity, wantonness, womanizing; **11** defloration, fornication, libertinism, nymphomania, whorishness; **12** incontinence; **13** salaciousness; **14** lasciviousness, licentiousness, permissiveness; PHRASES: **4, 4** free love; **4, 6** easy virtue; **4, 8** wife swapping.

promiscuous 5 loose; **6** wanton; **7** immoral; **10** licentious; **11** uninhibited; **12** philandering, unrestrained.

promise 3 IOU, vow; **4** bond, deed, oath, seal, word; **5** swear; **6** affirm, assure, pledge; **7** compact, confirm, endorse, warrant; **8** contract, covenant, warranty; **9** affidavit, assurance, authority, betrothal, guarantee, handshake, insurance, intention, potential, undertake; **10** commitment, engagement, obligation; **11** affirmation, undertaking; **12** recognizance; PHRASES: **4, 2, 5** debt of honor, word of honor; **5, 2, 2** shake on it; **5, 2, 4** swear on oath; **5, 4, 5** cross one's heart; **5, 6** stand surety; **6, 4, 5** pledge one's honor, plight one's troth; **6, 7** commit oneself, solemn ~; **8, 2, 4** exchange of vows.

promise (someone promised) 6 fiancé; **7** fiancée; **9** affianced, betrothed; PHRASES: **3, 8** the intended; **5-2-2** bride-to-be; **5, 3** lucky man.

promised 5 bound, sworn; **6** votive; **7** assured, engaged, pledged; **9** betrothed, committed, professed; **10** adjuratory; **11** affirmative, testimonial; PHRASES: **2, 4** on oath; **2, 4, 4** on one's word; **6, 3** spoken for.

promised land 6 Canaan, Elysia, Goshen, Heaven, Israel, Utopia; **7** Erewhon; **8** Sangreal, Valhalla; PHRASES: **2, 6** El Dorado; **3, 2, 3, 7** end of the rainbow; **3, 2, 4** pot of gold; **3, 10** the millennium; **4, 2, 7** land of promise; **4, 5** Holy Grail; **7-2** Shangri-la; **7, 4** eternal life; **7, 5** eternal youth; **7, 6** Elysian Fields; **8, 2, 5** Fountain of Youth.

promising 4 able; **6** gifted; **7** capable, hopeful; **8** talented; **10** auspicious.

promontory *See* **cape**

promote 3 aid; **4** hype, puff; **5** chair, crown, deify, exalt, raise; **6** foster, market, peddle; **7** advance, beatify, elevate, enhance, lionize; **8** canonize, enshrine, heighten, shoulder; **9** publicize, sublimate; **11** apotheosize; PHRASES: **4, 1, 4** give a lift; **4, 2** perk up.

promotion 4 deal, help, hype, plug, rise;

5 offer; **6** backup; **7** backing, support, upgrade; **9** elevation, marketing, publicity; **11** advancement, advertising, endorsement, sponsorship, stimulation; **13** encouragement.

prompt 4 goad, prod, urge; **5** quick, rapid, swift; **6** incite, induce, speedy, timely; **7** provoke, trigger; **8** occasion, punctual, reminder, stimulus; **9** encourage, stimulate; PHRASES: **2, 4** on time; **3, 3** set off; **4-7** aide-mémoire; **5, 5** bring about; **7, 5** without delay.

promptness 5 speed; **8** alacrity, rapidity, velocity; **11** punctuality, timekeeping. *See also* **prompt**

promulgate *See* **proclaim**

prone 4 flat; **6** liable, likely; **8** disposed, inclined; **10** horizontal; **11** predisposed; PHRASES: **4, 3** flat out; **4, 4** face down.

prong *See* **point**

pronounce 3 say; **4** rule; **5** order, sound, state, utter, voice; **6** assert, decree, ordain; **7** express; **8** announce, proclaim, vocalize.

pronounced 4 oral, said; **6** marked, strong; **7** decided, evident, notable, obvious; **8** definite, distinct, striking; **9** prominent; **10** noticeable; **11** conspicuous; **12** unmistakable.

pronouncement 6 decree; **7** verdict; **9** assertion, statement; **11** declaration; **12** announcement, proclamation.

pronunciation 6 accent; **9** elocution; **10** intonation; **11** enunciation; **12** articulation.

proof 3 Q.E.D.; **4** test; **5** trial; **6** method; **7** proving, support; **8** evidence; **9** certainty, procedure, steadfast, testimony; **10** estimation, evaluation, settlement; **11** affirmation, attestation, testimonial; **12** confirmation, illustration, invulnerable, ratification, verification; **13** ascertainment, clarification, corroboration, demonstration, determination; **14** substantiation.

prop *See* **support**

propaganda 2 PR; **8** agitprop; **9** promotion, publicity; **11** advertising; **12** brainwashing; **14** indoctrination, pamphleteering; PHRASES: **4, 7** hard selling; **4-9** self-promotion.

propagandist 6 orator, writer; **7** slanted, sophist, speaker; **8** essayist, partisan, satirist; **9** apologist, distorted, extremist, polemical, publicist; **10** mouthpiece, polemicist; **12** manipulative; PHRASES: **3-5** one-sided; **4, 6** spin doctor.

propagate 3 bud, sow; **4** crop, rear, seed, sire; **5** beget, breed, graft, hatch, plant, raise, spawn; **6** father; **7** produce; **8** engender, generate, incubate; **9** cultivate, fecundate, fertilize, pollinate, procreate; **10** impregnate, inseminate, transplant; PHRASES: **3, 3** bed out; **5, 2** bring up; **5, 2, 3, 4** carry on the line; **5, 4, 5** bring into being.

propagation 2 AI, DI; **3** AID, AIH, IVF, sex; **4** GIFT; **5** birth; **7** coition, genesis; **8** breeding, eugenics, fruition, hatching, natality, nativity, spawning; **9** flowering, gestation, pregnancy; **10** biogenesis, childbirth, conception, copulation, generation, incubation; **11** abiogenesis, autogenesis, fecundation, florescence, germination, parturition, pollination, procreation; **12** impregnation, insemination; **13** efflorescence, fertilization; **14** fructification; **15** parthenogenesis; PHRASES: **4-4, 4** test-tube baby; **5, 2, 4** facts of life; **5, 4** birth rate; **5, 5** happy event; **6, 5** virgin birth.

propagator 3 box; **4** tray; **6** cloche; **8** diffuser, spreader; **11** broadcaster, transmitter; **12** communicator; PHRASES: **4, 4** seed tray.

propel 3 row; **4** cast, kick, move, pole, push, send, spur; **5** chuck, drive, impel, pedal, pitch, shove, sling, throw, wheel; **6** launch, thrust; **7** project, traject, treadle; **8** jaculate; PHRASES: **4, 4** toss urge.

propellant 3 jet; **5** steam; **6** charge, emetic, energy, thrust; **7** ejector, emitter, volcano; **8** aperient, laxative, radiator, tailwind; **9** detonator, explosive, purgative; PHRASES: **7, 5** driving force; **8, 4** ejection seat; **9, 4** following wind; **9, 6** explosive device.

propeller 3 fan, oar; **4** prop; **5** blade, lever, pedal, rotor, screw, turbo, wheel; **6** driver, piston; **7** booster, turbine; **8** impeller, thruster, windmill; **9** propulsor; **10** propellant; PHRASES: **4, 6** twin screws; **5, 9** screw ~; **6, 5** paddle wheel.

propensity *See* **tendency**

proper 1 U; **3** apt, due, fit, own; **4** fine, prim, real; **5** pukka, right; **6** decent, formal, kosher, polite, seemly; **7** correct, fitting, genuine, refined, regular; **8** accepted, decorous, ladylike, suitable; **9** authentic, befitting, excellent; **10** acceptable, legitimate; **11** established, gentlemanly, respectable; **12** satisfactory; PHRASES: **4-4** well-made; **5-5** upper-class.

property 3 fee, feu *UK*, lot; **4** farm, feud, fief, flat *UK*, land, plot, toft *UK*; **5** acres, claim, goods, house, lands, manor, ranch, right, title, tract, villa; **6** castle, chalet, common, domain, estate, living, parcel, patent, realty, socage; **7** acreage, burgage, cottage, fiefdom, grounds, holding, mansion, quality, receipt; **8** allodium, appanage, benefice, building, bungalow, chattels, copyhold *UK*, dominion, freehold, hacienda, praedium, tenement; **9** allotment, apartment, copyright, feudality, homestead, leasehold, penthouse, seigneury, territory; **10** belongings, birthright, dependency, plantation, possession, villeinage; **11** villeinhold; **12** frankalmoign, smallholding *UK*; **14** characteristic; PHRASES: **4-4** rent-roll; **4, 6** free socage, real estate; **4, 8** real ~ *UK*; **5, 5** crown lands; **5, 6** legal estate; **6, 4** common land; **6, 6** landed estate; **6, 8** common ~, landed ~, public ~.

property holder 5 owner; **6** holder, lessee, tenant; **7** realtor; **8** investor; **9** developer, landowner; **10** freeholder, speculator; **11** householder, leaseholder, shareholder, stockholder; PHRASES: **3, 2, 3, 5** man of the house; **3, 2, 8** man of property; **4, 2, 3, 5** lord of the manor; **4, 6, 5** real estate agent; **4-6, 5** real-estate agent; **7, 6** sitting tenant *UK*; **8, 5** property owner.

prophesy 5 dowse; **6** divine, gamble, intuit; **7** foresee, predict; **8** forecast, foretell, soothsay; **10** vaticinate; PHRASES: **4, 8** tell fortunes.

prophetic 9 visionary; **10** farsighted, predictive; **11** foretelling, forewarning.

prophylactic 3 BCG; **6** gargle, iodine, poison; **7** hygiene, quinine, vaccine; **8** carbolic, cleanser, fluoride, fumigant; **9** germicide, isolation, mouthwash; **10** antisepsis, antiseptic, dentifrice, preventive, quarantine, sanitation, toothpaste; **11** bactericide, inoculation, insecticide, prophylaxis, vaccination; **12** disinfectant, disinfection, immunization, preventative; **13** contraception, Mercurochrome *tm*, sterilization; PHRASES: **3, 7** MMR vaccine; **5, 4** boric acid; **5, 6** tooth powder; **6, 7** triple vaccine; **6, 9** cordon sanitaire; **7, 4** boracic acid.

prophylaxis 7 hygiene; **8** fumigant; **9** germicide, isolation; **10** antisepsis, preventive, quarantine, sanitation; **11** bactericide, inoculation, insecticide, vaccination; **12** disinfectant, disinfection, immunization;

13 contraception, sterilization.

proponent 8 advocate, exponent, follower; **9** supporter; **11** protagonist.

proportion 5 ratio; **6** modify, rhythm; **7** balance; **8** equalize, quotient, symmetry; **10** percentage; **12** relationship.

proportionate (be proportionate to) 3 fit; **5** liken, match, tally; **6** accord, equate; **7** balance, compare; **8** equalize, interact, parallel; **9** correlate, interlink, interlock, interplay, interwork; **10** correspond, proportion, symmetrize; **12** interconnect; **14** interassociate, interpenetrate.

proposal *See* **offer**

propose 3 aim; **4** mean, plan; **5** offer; **6** advise, intend; **7** suggest; **9** recommend; **11** proposition; PHRASES: **4, 2, 4** have in mind.

propound 4 hint, moot, move, urge; **5** argue, offer; **6** advise, allude, submit; **7** advance, outline, propose, request, suggest; **8** motivate, persuade; **9** adumbrate, influence; PHRASES: **3, 2, 3, 6** put on the agenda; **3, 5** put forth; **3, 7** put forward; **5, 1, 4** plead a case; **5, 3, 2, 4** throw out an idea; **7, 1, 6** propose a motion; **7, 2, 3** venture to say.

propriety 7 aptness, decency, decorum, modesty; **10** politeness; **11** correctness, suitability; **14** respectability; **15** appropriateness; PHRASES: **4, 7** good manners.

propulsion 4 bunt, butt, kick, push; **5** drive, shove, shunt; **6** motive, thrust; **7** impetus, pulsion; **8** momentum; **9** impulsion; **10** jaculation, propelment.

propulsive 7 driving, pulsive, pushing, shoving; **10** propellant, propelling, propulsory.

prosaic 4 dull; **5** banal, plain; **6** simple; **7** humdrum, mundane; **8** everyday, ordinary; **15** straightforward; PHRASES: **3-2-3-4** run-of-the-mill; **6-2-4** matter-of-fact.

proscribe *See* **ban**

prospect 4 hope, plan, view; **5** study; **6** design, desire; **7** explore, project, pursuit, purview; **8** ambition, proposal; **10** aspiration, enterprise; **11** undertaking; PHRASES: **6, 3** search for.

prosper 4 grow; **5** bloom; **6** arrive, flower, profit, thrive; **7** achieve, advance, blossom, succeed; **8** flourish, progress; **10** accomplish; PHRASES: **2, 3** go far; **2, 4** do well; **2, 7, 2, 2** be rolling in it; **3, 2, 4** get on well; **3, 2, 6** lie on velvet; **3, 3, 3, 4** hit the big time; **3, 4** win fame; **3, 5** get going, win glory; **4, 1, 7** make a fortune; **4, 2** make it; **4, 2, 4** have it made, rise to fame; **4, 2, 6** live in clover; **4, 4** fare well, make good; **4, 4, 7** line one's pockets, make one's fortune; **4, 5** make money; **6, 2, 4** strike it rich; **6, 2, 5** strike it lucky; **7, 4, 4** feather one's nest.

prosperity 4 boom, ease, fame, weal; **5** glory; **6** clover, heyday, luxury, plenty, riches, wealth; **7** comfort, fortune, success, welfare; **8** felicity, prestige, security, thriving; **9** affluence, blessings, fleshpots, happiness; **11** blessedness; **14** prosperousness; PHRASES: **3, 2, 3, 4** fat of the land; **3, 2, 5** bed of roses; **3, 2, 6** lap of luxury; **3, 4, 4** the good life; **4, 2, 4** life of ease; **4, 2, 5** life of Riley; **4, 3, 5** milk and honey; **4, 3, 7** fame and fortune; **4-5** well-being; **4, 6** bull market, Easy Street; **5, 2, 3, 3** place in the sun; **5, 4** palmy days, salad days; **6, 2, 6** living in clover; **6, 3** golden age; **7, 4** halcyon days; **7, 5** roaring trade; **7, 7** booming economy; **9, 6** honeymoon period.

prosperous 3 fat; **4** cozy, rich, rosy; **5** balmy, happy, lucky, palmy; **6** famous, golden, rising; **7** blessed, booming, bullish, halcyon, opulent, wealthy; **8** affluent, blissful, thriving; **9** cloudless, favorable, fortunate, luxurious, promising; **10** auspicious, felicitous, propitious, prospering, successful; **11** comfortable, flourishing; **12** profiteering; PHRASES: **2, 2, 3, 5** up in the world; **2, 3, 2, 3, 2** on the up and up *UK*; **2, 3, 4** on the make; **2, 3, 5** in the money; **2-3-6** up-and-coming; **2, 4** at ease, in luck; **2, 4, 6** on Easy Street; **2, 5** in bliss; **2, 6** in clover, on velvet; **4-2-2** well-to-do; **4, 2, 3, 3** high on the hog; **4-3** well-off; **4-6** well-heeled; **5, 4** doing well; **7, 2, 2** rolling in it; **8, 6** upwardly mobile; **11, 3** comfortably off.

prosperous person 3 VIP; **7** success; PHRASES: **4-4, 3** self-made man; **5, 3** lucky dog; **5, 5** lucky devil; **7, 5** nouveau riche. *See also* **wealthy people**

prostitute 3 tom; **4** hook, pimp; **6** gigolo, harlot, hustle, pander; **7** devalue, procure, solicit; **9** courtesan, importune, mercenary; **10** streetwalk; PHRASES: **3-6** sex-worker; **4, 2, 3, 5** lady of the night; **4, 3** rent boy *UK*; **4, 4** call girl; **5, 2, 4** fille de joie.

prostitution 4 vice; **7** pimping; **8** harlotry, whoredom; **9** pandering, procuring; **10** soliciting; **11** degradation, importuning; **13** streetwalking; PHRASES: **3, 4** the game; **4, 5**

vice squad; **4, 8** curb crawling; **5, 5, 5** white slave trade; **7, 3** selling out; **7, 5** harlot's trade; **7-7** brothel-keeping.

prostrate 4 flat; **5** level, prone; **7** drained; **9** desperate, exhausted, powerless; **10** horizontal; PHRASES: **2, 1, 3, 3** at a low ebb; **4, 4** face down.

prostration 7 worship; **9** adoration; **14** incapacitation. *See also* **prostrate**

protect 3 arm, lag; **4** hide, keep, mind, save, tend, ward, wrap; **5** armor, cloak, cover, earth, flank, guard, hoard, house, nurse, shade, spare, store; **6** assure, buffer, cocoon, convoy, defend, enfold, escort, foster, garage, harbor, insure, mother, patrol, police, rescue, screen, secure, shield, shroud; **7** cherish, conceal, cushion, deliver, embrace, enclose, envelop, fortify, monitor, promise, retreat, shelter, support, warrant; **8** champion, chaperon, conserve, ensconce, entrench, garrison, immunize, imprison, insulate, preserve, sanitate, sanitize, shepherd, treasure; **9** disinfect, guarantee, indemnify, inoculate, patronize, safeguard, vaccinate, warehouse; **10** chlorinate, fluoridate, fluorinate, pasteurize, strengthen, weatherize; PHRASES: **4, 2, 3, 2** keep an eye on; **4, 2, 7** keep in custody; **4, 3** care for, hide out; **4, 4** hide away, keep safe, lock away, make safe; **4, 5** look after; **4, 6, 2** take charge of; **4, 7** make certain, ride shotgun; **5, 2** fence in; **5, 2, 3** stand up for; **5, 3** vouch for *UK*; **5, 4** watch over; **5, 5** fence round, mount guard; **5-5** armor-plate; **5, 6** grant asylum; **6, 9** afford sanctuary.

protected 5 bound, boxed, robed; **6** crated, exempt, hidden, hooded, immune, masked, secret, veiled; **7** cloaked, encased, swathed, wrapped *UK*; **8** bandaged, enclosed, obscured, packaged, screened, sheathed, shielded, shrouded; **9** concealed, disguised; **10** enshrouded; **11** camouflaged; PHRASES: **6, 2** walled up; **6-2** walled-in.

protection 3 aid; **4** BUPA, care, moat, ward; **5** aegis, armor, cover, ditch, guard, haven, store; **6** anchor, asylum, buffer, convoy, escort, permit, refuge, safety, screen, shield, surety, weapon; **7** bastion, bulwark, cushion, custody, defense, keeping, panoply, shelter, support; **8** auspices, defenses, immunity, mainstay, Medicare, palisade, security, stockade, tutelage, umbrella, wardship; **9** deterrent, insurance, isolation, patronage, provision, safeguard, sanctuary,

seclusion, surrogacy; **10** collateral, precaution, quarantine; **11** breastplate, inoculation, prophylaxis, safekeeping, segregation, sponsorship, vaccination; **12** guardianship, immunization, protectorate, surveillance; **13** contraception, custodianship; **14** impregnability; **15** invulnerability; PHRASES: **4, 3** nest egg; **4, 5** Blue Cross, safe hands, safe house; **4, 7** good offices, safe conduct; **4, 9** fire insurance, life assurance *UK*, life insurance; **5, 2, 8** tower of strength; **5, 5** armor plate; **5, 6** sheet anchor, trade tariff; **6, 9** cordon sanitaire, health insurance; **7, 5** burglar alarm, welfare state; **7, 7** savings account; **8, 3** fatherly eye; **8, 5** security check; **8, 6** security system; **8, 7** homeless shelter, positive vetting *UK*.

protective clothing 3 bib, box; **5** apron, visor; **6** gloves, helmet; **7** goggles; **8** dustcoat, overalls; **9** coveralls, gauntlets; PHRASES: **3, 4** gas mask; **4, 3** shin pad; **4, 4** body belt; **4, 5** head guard; **4, 6** flak jacket; **4, 7** body padding; **5, 6** crash helmet; **8, 3** shoulder pad; **10, 4** protective belt; **11, 4** bulletproof vest.

protective covering 4 mail; **5** armor, blind, doily, shade, topee, visor; **6** awning, brolly *UK*, screen, shades, shield; **7** Formica *tm*, housing, lagging, parasol; **8** eyeshade, placemat, sunshade, umbrella; **9** lampshade, slipcover, sunscreen; **10** fiberglass, insulation, sunglasses, tablecloth, upholstery; **11** bumbershoot; **12** antimacassar; PHRASES: **3, 3** sun hat; **4, 4** life belt; **4, 6** life jacket, pith helmet; **4, 7** fire curtain; **5, 5** chair cover, watch glass; **6, 6** suntan lotion; **7, 5** cushion cover; **8, 5** Venetian blind; **9, 5** furniture cover. *See also* **protective clothing**

protector 2 PC; **3** cop, WPC *UK*; **5** Argus, bobby, guard, mammy, nanny, nurse, tutor, watch; **6** copper, duenna, keeper, mentor, minder *UK*, patrol, patron, picket, police, ranger, sentry, sitter, warden, warder; **7** bouncer, curator, doorman, fireman, lookout, militia, sheriff, watcher; **8** Cerberus, champion, chaperon, defender, forester, garrison, guardian, sentinel, shepherd, vanguard, watchdog, watchman; **9** bodyguard, companion, custodian, detective, governess, lifeguard, nursemaid, patrolman, patroness, policeman, preserver, vigilante; **10** benefactor, gamekeeper, goalkeeper; **11** conservator, firefighter, firewatcher, policewoman, protectress, surveillant, Territorial; **12** benefactress, wicketkeeper; PHRASES: **4, 5** Home Guard *UK*; **4-5** life-saver; **4, 6** park keeper *UK*; **4-6** baby-sitter; **4, 7** fire fighter; **5, 3** guard dog; **5, 4** liege lord; **5, 5** armed guard, coast guard; **5, 6** white knight; **5-6** child-minder; **5, 8** night watchman; **5, 9** fairy godmother; **6, 3** police dog; **6-3, 3** strong-arm man; **6, 4** feudal lord; **6, 5** patron saint; **6, 7** police officer, Secret Service; **6, 8** police sergeant; **6, 9** police constable *UK*; **7, 3** private eye, sniffer dog *UK*; **7, 7** weekend warrior; **7, 8** customs official; **8, 3** tutelary god; **8, 5** guardian angel, security guard; **8, 6** Guardian Angels, security forces; **11, 4** Territorial Army *UK*. *See also* **protective clothing, protective cover**

protein 5 mucin, prion; **6** casein, fibrin, gluten; **7** albumen, albumin, gelatin, histone, insulin, keratin; **8** collagen, globulin, protomer; **9** myoglobin; **10** interferon; **11** hemoprotein, lipoprotein, mucoprotein; **12** flavoprotein, glycoprotein, proteoglycan; **13** nucleoprotein, peptidoglycan, scleroprotein; **14** denaturization, immunoglobulin, metalloprotein, phosphoprotein, sclerotization; PHRASES: **5-5** alpha-helix; **6, 4** biuret test; **7, 7** fibrous ~; **10, 5** prosthetic group.

protest 2 no; **3** nay; **4** beef, defy, demo, deny, kick, rail, warn; **5** anger, march, rally; **6** clamor, denial, mutiny, object, occupy, oppose, outcry, parade, picket, resist, strike; **7** agitate, boycott, detract, disavow, disobey, dissent, gainsay, inveigh, warning; **8** complain, defiance, disagree, disclaim, negation, renounce; **9** challenge, complaint, deprecate, disavowal, fulminate, hostility, intercede, objection, recusance, repudiate; **10** contradict, contravene, counteract, disapprove, disclaimer, discontent, gainsaying, negativity, nonpayment, opposition, refutation; **11** demonstrate, deprecation, disapproval, expostulate, repudiation; **12** disagreement, disobedience, intercession, protestation, renunciation; **13** contradiction, contravention, counteraction, expostulation, noncompliance, recalcitrance; **14** disapprobation, noncooperation, refractoriness; **15** dissatisfaction; PHRASES: **3, 2** say no, sit in; **5, 1, 3-2** stage a sit-in; **5, 1, 4** stage a demo; **5, 3** march for; **5, 3, 7** speak out against.

protester 4 scab; **5** rebel; **6** critic, hippie, moaner, picket, ranter, whiner; **7** dropout,

grouser, marcher, striker, whinger *UK*; **8** agitator, blackleg, grumbler, objector, picketer, recusant, reformer; **9** detractor, dissenter, dissident, sectarian; **10** bellyacher, campaigner, complainer, ecowarrior, malcontent, nonstriker, protestant, separatist, suffragist; **11** dissentient, suffragette; **12** demonstrator, recalcitrant, troublemaker; **13** nonconformist; PHRASES: **3-7** tub-thumper *UK*; **6, 6** women's libber; **6-6** rabble-rouser; **7, 6** moaning Minnie; **8, 5** minority voice; **8-5** mischief-maker.

protesting 4 anti; **5** angry; **6** booing; **7** bolshie, defiant, denying, hissing, hostile, jeering; **8** contrary, critical, negating, negative, opposing, recusant; **9** clamorous, objecting; **10** discontent, dissenting, malcontent, protestant, refractory, repudiated; **11** challenging, deprecatory, disobedient; **12** disapproving, discontented, dissatisfied, noncompliant, recalcitrant, unconsenting; **13** contradictive, counteractive, nonconformist; **14** noncooperative; PHRASES: **6-6** bloody-minded *UK*.

protocol 5 rules; **9** etiquette, procedure; **11** conventions.

prototype 3 die, jig; **4** cast, form, mold; **5** blank, dummy, frame, model, pilot, punch, stamp; **6** format, matrix; **7** example, formula, pattern, stencil; **8** paradigm, template; **9** blueprint.

prototypical 5 dummy, model; **7** generic; **8** designer, original; **9** exemplary; **12** paradigmatic; PHRASES: **3-3-3** off-the-peg *UK*; **3-3-4** off-the-rack; **5-4** ready-made; **6-4** tailor-made; **6-5** custom-built.

protozoan 6 Volvox; **7** amoebic, Ciliata, Giardia; **8** amoeboid, Protozoa, Sporozoa; **9** Gregarine, protozoic, protozoon, Sarcodina, sporozoan; **10** flagellate; **11** trichomonad, trypanosome; **13** Chlamydomonas, mastigophoran; **15** protozoological.

protract 5 delay; **6** extend; **7** prolong; **8** lengthen.

protracted 7 endless, eternal, lasting, nonstop, undying; **8** enduring, extended, unending; **9** perpetual, prolonged, unceasing, unfailing, unvarying; **10** lengthened, persistent; **11** everlasting, unrelenting, unremitting, unstoppable; **12** interminable; **13** inexhaustible; PHRASES: **4, 2, 5** with no letup; **5, 3** drawn out; **7, 7** without respite.

protrude 3 jut, pop; **4** pout; **5** bulge, swell; **7** project; **8** overhang; PHRASES: **2, 11**

be conspicuous; **3, 3** jut out; **4, 3** poke out; **5, 3** stand out, stick out; **5, 4, 3** catch one's eye.

protrusion 3 lip; 4 lump; 5 bulge; 6 flange; 7 outcrop, overlap; 8 overhang; 9 extension; 10 projection.

protuberance 4 beak, brow, bump, conk, face, knob, lump, nose; 5 bugle, snoot, snout, trunk; 6 hooter; 7 antenna; 8 forehead, swelling; 9 proboscis, schnozzle; 10 protrusion.

protuberant 5 beaky *UK*, bumpy, proud; 6 beaked; 8 swelling; 10 protrudent.

proud 4 haut, vain; 5 cocky, erect, flush, noble; 6 snooty, superb; 7 haughty; 8 arrogant, egoistic, prideful, snobbish, spirited; 9 conceited, honorable, hubristic; 10 courageous; 12 supercilious; 13 proudspirited; PHRASES: 4-6 high-hatted; 4-8 high-spirited; 4-9 self-confident, self-esteeming, self-important, self-regarding; 5-2 stuck-up; 5, 2, 1, 7 ~ as a peacock; 5-5 hoity-toity, house-proud; 6-4-4 holier-than-thou; 7, 2, 5 pleased as Punch.

proud (be proud) 7 presume; PHRASES: 3, 2, 4 put on airs; 4, 5, 2 take pride in; 5, 2 exult in, glory in; 5, 2, 8 stand up straight; 5, 5 stand erect; 6, 2, 5 refuse to stoop.

proud person 4 snob; 5 crach, swank; 6 bigwig, egoist; 7 bighead, boaster, bragger, paragon, parvenu, peacock; 8 braggart, swankpot; 9 blusterer, swaggerer, swellhead; 10 aristocrat, toffeenose; PHRASES: 3, 4 his nibs; 4, 2, 3, 4 cock of the walk; 4, 2, 8 Lord of Creation; 4, 4 Lord Muck *UK*; 4, 6 vain person; 4, 9 true gentleman; 5, 5 prima donna; 6, 4 grande dame; 7, 4 swelled head.

prove 3 fix, try; 4 rise, show, test; 6 affirm, attest, clinch, evince, ratify, settle, verify; 7 certify, clarify, confirm, endorse, justify, support, sustain, witness; 8 evidence, validate; 9 ascertain, determine, establish; 10 illustrate; 11 corroborate, countersign, demonstrate; 12 authenticate, substantiate; 15 circumstantiate; PHRASES: 4, 2 back up; 4, 3 bear out; 5, 2 clear up.

proven 5 shown, tried; 7 settled; 8 affirmed, attested, ratified, relevant, verified; 9 confirmed, justified, probative, probatory; 10 determined, evidential; 11 ascertained; 12 corroborated, demonstrated; 13 corroborative, substantiated; PHRASES: 5, 3 borne out; 5, 3, 6 tried and tested.

proverb 3 saw; 5 adage, gnome; PHRASES:

5, 6 maxim byword.

proverbial 5 banal, pithy, stock, trite, witty; 6 gnomic; 7 clichéd; 8 oracular; 9 axiomatic, enigmatic, hackneyed; 10 aphoristic, moralistic, moralizing, perceptive, preceptive; 11 commonplace, sententious, stereotyped; 12 epigrammatic; 13 platitudinous.

provide 4 find, give, lend; 5 allow, bring, cater, endow, equip, serve; 6 afford, supply; 7 arrange, furnish; 8 generate, maintain; PHRASES: 3, 2 lay on; 4, 2 dish up.

provident 4 wise; 6 frugal; 7 careful, prudent, sparing, thrifty; 8 cautious; 11 foresighted; PHRASES: 4-8 well-prepared.

provider 4 bawd, pimp; 5 baker, donor, giver; 6 bursar, butler, feeder, grocer, lender, pander, purser, sutler, waiter; 7 butcher, milkman, steward, vintner; 8 creditor, panderer, procurer, retailer *UK*, supplier, waitress; 9 drysalter, middleman, poulterer *UK*, treasurer, victualer; 10 commissary, fishmonger, shopkeeper, wholesaler; 11 greengrocer, moneylender, storekeeper; 13 quartermaster; PHRASES: 3, 5 wet nurse; 4, 8 ship chandler, wine merchant.

province *See* **area**

province (Canadian) 6 Quebec; 7 Alberta, Nunavut, Ontario; 8 Manitoba; 12 Newfoundland, Saskatchewan; PHRASES: 3, 9 New Brunswick; 4, 6 Nova Scotia; 5, 6 Lower Canada, Upper Canada; 5, 9 Yukon Territory; 6, 6, 6 Prince Edward Island; 7, 8 British Columbia; 9, 11 Northwest Territories.

provincial 5 local; 6 county, simple; 8 district, outmoded, regional; 9 parochial; 13 unfashionable; 15 unsophisticated; PHRASES: 4, 6 Main Street; 5-4 small-town.

provision 3 arm, man; 4 coal, feed, find, fuel, give, keep, lend; 5 cater, endow, equip, offer, serve, staff, stock; 6 afford, bunker, clothe, forage, outfit, pander, purvey, ration, refill, source, stores, supply; 7 deliver, economy, feeding, furnish, helping, lending, measure, portion, prepare, procure, produce, product, provide, rations, service, subsidy, support, victual; 8 catering *UK*, clothing, delivery, increase, maintain, pipeline, reserves, supplies; 9 budgeting, equipment, equipping, logistics, pandering, procuring, providing, purveying, stockpile, supplying; 10 assistance, distribute, furnishing, outfitting, precaution, purveyance, subvention, victualing; **11** accommodate, maintenance, preparation; **12** commissariat, conservation; **13** accommodation, entertainment, reinforcement, replenishment; PHRASES: **3, 3** fit out, kit out; **3, 3, 5** bed and board; **3, 3, 9** bed and breakfast; **3, 5** get ready; **4, 3** dish out; **4-3** hand-out; **4, 4** cash flow; **4, 5** hand round, make ready; **5, 2** bring in, serve up *UK*, stock up, truck in; **5, 3, 7** board and lodging; **5, 7** child support; **6, 4** supply line; **7, 3** fitting out.

provisional 7 interim; **9** makeshift, temporary; **11** conditional; PHRASES: **5-4** shortterm.

provisions 4 food, grub, nosh; **7** rations; **8** eatables, victuals; **9** groceries, provender; **10** drinkables, foodstuffs, sustenance; **11** comestibles; PHRASES: **1, 7** K rations; **4, 7** food rations, iron rations *UK*; **4-7** self-service.

provocative 8 alluring, enticing; **9** provoking, seductive; **10** incendiary, suggestive; **11** challenging, encouraging, stimulating; **12** inflammatory.

provoke *See* **incite**

provost 4 head; **6** leader; **8** director; **9** principal; **10** chancellor.

prowess 5 skill; **7** ability, bravery; **9** dexterity, expertise; **10** competence.

proximity *See* **nearness**

proxy *See* **substitution**

proxy (by proxy) 2 PP; **3** for; **10** indirectly; **11** imitatively; **13** ministerially; **14** diplomatically; PHRASES: **2, 6, 2** in behalf of; **2, 9, 2** in imitation of; **3, 7** pro persona; **4, 1, 8** like a diplomat.

prude 4 prig; **6** censor; **9** Victorian; PHRASES: **3, 6** Mrs Grundy; **4, 10** Mary Whitehouse; **5, 8** moral guardian; **5, 9** Watch Committee.

prudence 4 care, plan; **6** wisdom; **7** caution, insight; **8** sagacity; **10** precaution, providence; **11** forethought, preparation; **12** anticipation, perspicacity; **13** premeditation; **14** circumspection. *See also* **prudent**

prudent 4 wise; **7** careful; **8** cautious; **9** provident; **10** farsighted; **11** longsighted.

prudery 7 reserve; **8** primness; **10** prissiness, puritanism, stuffiness; **11** prudishness.

prune *See* **cut**

prying 4 nosy; **6** gossip, snoopy; **7** gossipy; **8** meddling, nosiness, prurient, snooping; **9** curiosity, officious, prurience, voyeurism; **10** meddlesome; **13** officiousness, rubbernecking; PHRASES: **6-6** tittle-tattle; **6, 9** morbid curiosity.

PS 10 postscript.

pseudocarp 5, 5 false fruit.

psittacosis 6, 5 parrot fever.

psyche 2 id; **3** ego; **4** mind, self, soul; **5** anima; **6** animus, pneuma; **7** persona; **8** superego; **10** subliminal; **11** coconscious, personality, unconscious; **12** preconscious, subconscious; **13** foreconscious; PHRASES: **3, 5** ego ideal; **5, 5** inner child; **7, 4** ethical self; **9, 4** conscious mind, conscious self, primitive self; **10, 4** subliminal self; **11, 4** unconscious mind.

psychiatric hospital 3 bin; **6** Bedlam; **8** madhouse; PHRASES: **5, 7** acorn academy, screw factory; **6, 4** mental home, padded cell; **6, 8** mental hospital *UK*; **7, 6** lunatic asylum; **7, 8** special hospital; **11, 4** psychiatric unit, psychiatric ward.

psychiatric treatment 2 TA; **3** ECT, EST, SAT; **8** analysis, modeling; **9** catharsis, leucotomy, leukotomy; **10** abreaction, counseling, stereotaxy; **11** biofeedback, logotherapy, psychodrama; **12** autohypnosis, cingulectomy, cocounseling, conditioning, electroshock, hypnotherapy, narcotherapy; **13** amygdalectomy, bioenergetics, narcoanalysis, narcohypnosis, psychosurgery, psychotherapy, suggestionism; **14** autosuggestion, psychoanalysis; **15** desensitization, electronarcosis, psychocatharsis; PHRASES: **3, 5** the couch; **3, 7** sex therapy; **3, 8** ego analysis; **4, 4** mind cure; **4, 7** play therapy; **4-7** role-playing; **4-8** self-hypnosis; **5, 7** drama therapy, shock therapy, sleep therapy; **5, 8** Arica movement, group dynamics; **5, 9** shock treatment; **6, 7** family therapy, primal therapy, scream therapy; **7, 7** Gestalt therapy, radical therapy, reality therapy, release therapy; **8, 5** marathon group; **8, 7** aversion therapy, behavior therapy, conjoint therapy, feminist therapy, Rogerian therapy; **9, 5** encounter group; **11, 4** psychiatric care.

psychiatrist 6 shrink; **7** analyst; **8** alienist; **9** counselor; **12** headshrinker; **13** psychoanalyst; **14** dramatherapist, hypnotherapist, narcotherapist; **15** psychotherapist; PHRASES: **3, 2, 5, 5** men in white coats; **3**, **6** mad doctor; **4**, **6** head doctor; **5**, **7** trick cyclist *UK*. *See also* **psychologist**

psychic **4** seer; **5** augur, sibyl, vates; **6** auspex, cosmic, medium, mental, occult, oracle; **7** diviner, magical, prophet; **8** haruspex, telergic; **9** psychical, pythoness; **10** astrologer, palmreader, panpsychic, soothsayer, telepathic; **11** clairvoyant, mediumistic, metapsychic, telekinetic, telesthetic, unconscious; **12** clairaudient, extrasensory, radiesthetic, subconscious, theosophical; **13** clairsentient, hyperphysical, metapsychical, psychokinetic, psychological, psychosensory, transphysical; **14** psychosophical, scientological, spiritualistic, transcendental; PHRASES: **4**, **5** wise woman; **7**, **5** crystal gazer; **7**, **6** fortune teller.

psychic phenomenon **3** ESP; **4** aura, maya, OOBE; **5** Ouija™; **6** dhyana, seance, trance; **7** dharana, samadhi, sitting; **8** hypnosis, illusion; **9** bioplasma, ectoplasm, ectoplasy, effluvium, emanation; **10** planchette, protoplasm; **11** biofeedback, premonition; **13** hallucination, synchronicity; PHRASES: **4**, **2** déjà vu; **4**, **6** crop circle, yoga trance; **5**, **9** alien encounter; **6-7** spiritraising; **6**, **9** cosmic vibration; **8**, **6** hypnotic trance; **10**, **5** telepathic dream.

psychic power *See* **sixth sense**

psychological **6** mental; **8** personal; **9** emotional, spiritual; **11** instinctive, psychiatric, psychogenic; **12** psychometric, psychosexual, psychosocial; **13** psychogenetic, psychosomatic; **14** psychophysical; **15** psychogeriatric *UK*, psychotechnical; PHRASES: **2**, **3**, **4** in the mind.

psychological disorder **8** neurosis; **9** psychosis; PHRASES: **6**, **8** mental disorder *UK*; **7**, **8** nervous disorder.

psychologically disturbed **7** nervous; **8** neurotic, paranoid, schizoid; **9** disturbed, emotional, psychotic; **11** dissociated, sociopathic, traumatized; **12** disconnected, psychopathic; **15** hypochondriacal.

psychologist **4** Jung; **5** Adler, Freud, James, Janrt, Klein, Lacan, Laing, Lange, Reich; **6** Horney, Pavlov, Piaget, Watson; **7** analyst, Skinner; **9** clinician, counselor, therapist; **11** psychologue; **12** psychiatrist; **13** psychoanalyst, psychochemist, psychographer; **14** dramatherapist, hypnotherapist, narcotherapist; **15** psychobiologist,

psychophysicist, psychotherapist.

psychology **6** nature; **7** gestalt, mindset; **8** thinking; **9** mentality; **11** behaviorism; PHRASES: **13**, **10** introspective ~.

PT **4** part, pint, port; **8** platinum.

PU **9** plutonium.

public **4** open; **5** overt, trail; **6** common, masses, rabble; **7** blatant, general; **8** communal, populace; **9** customers, multitude, municipal, prominent, published; **12** governmental, unrestricted; PHRASES: **3**, **6** hoi polloi, vox populi; **5**, **5** grass roots; **5-5** state-owned; **6**, **3** ~ bar *UK*; **6**, **5** ~ enemy, ~ house; **6**, **6** common people, ~ school, ~ sector; **6**, **7** ~ company, ~ gallery, ~ holiday, ~ opinion, ~ servant, ~ service; **6**, **8** ~ footpath, ~ nuisance, ~ speaking; **6**, **9** ~ ownership *UK*, ~ relations; **6**, **11** ~ corporation.

public (make public) **3** air; **5** bruit, radio, relay, rumor; **6** expose, gossip, inform, retail, reveal, spread; **7** diffuse, divulge, mention, release; **8** disclose, telecast, televize, transmit; **9** broadcast, cablecast, circulate, propagate, ventilate; **10** narrowcast, promulgate; **11** communicate, disseminate; PHRASES: **2**, **6** go public; **3**, **1**, **4** fly a kite; **3**, **2**, **5** let it be known; **3**, **3** get out, put out; **3**, **5** put about; **4**, **3** give out; **4**, **3**, **5** tell the world; **4**, **5** hawk about, make known, pass round, talk about; **5**, **2** bring up; **5**, **5** bandy about; **5**, **6** bruit abroad; **6**, **3**, **4** spread the word; **6**, **6** spread abroad.

publication **4** book; **5** edict, novel, organ, rumor, ukase; **6** decree, gossip, report, sermon, speech, Tannoy™; **7** hearsay, journal, library; **8** bulletin, bullhorn, cookbook, hardback, magazine, textbook; **9** broadcast, guidebook, manifesto, paperback, statement, thesaurus; **10** communiqué, dictionary, disclosure, divulgence, encyclical, newsletter, periodical, publishing; **11** bookselling, circulation, declaration, divulgation, loudspeaker, ventilation; **12** announcement, broadcasting, notification, proclamation, promulgation; **13** dissemination, pronouncement; **14** pronunciamento; PHRASES: **4**, **6** book review; **4-6** best-seller; **5**, **4** trade book; **5**, **7** trial balloon; **6**, **4** sports book; **6-5**, **4** coffee-table book; **6**, **6** public notice; **8**, **6** official notice; **9**, **4** children's book, reference book. *See also* **fiction, novel**

public holiday **7** Kwanzaa; **9** Navaratri; PHRASES: **3**, **5**, **3** New Year's Day; **4**, **6** Good

Friday (Canada); **5-4, 8, 3** Saint-Jean Baptiste Day (Québec); **5, 7** Civic Holiday (Canada); **6, 3** Boxing Day (Canada), Canada Day (Canada), Labour Day; **6, 6** Easter Monday (Canada), Easter Sunday; **6, 6, 4, 3** Martin Luther King Day; **7, 3** Nunavut Day; **8, 3** Columbus Day, Memorial Day, Veterans Day, Victoria Day (Canada); **8, 8** Lincoln's Birthday; **9, 3** Christmas Day, Discovery Day (Canada); **10, 3** President's Day; **11, 3** Remembrance Day (Canada); **11, 8** Washington's Birthday; **12, 3** Independence Day, Thanksgiving Day.

publicity **2** ad, PR *UK*; **4** fame, hype, puff; **5** blurb, promo; **6** airing, infamy, pulpit, renown; **7** display, rostrum, soapbox; **8** ballyhoo, coverage, currency, exposure, flackery, hustings, openness, platform; **9** limelight, notoriety, photocall, promotion, spotlight; **10** conference, exhibition, famousness, propaganda, publicness; **11** advertising, circulation, ostentation, showmanship; **12** exaggeration; **13** manifestation; **14** sensationalism; PHRASES: **3, 7** top billing; **4, 2, 6** name in lights; **4, 10** news conference; **5, 4** media hype; **5-4, 6** threering circus; **5, 5** media blitz, media event; **5, 6** press office; **5, 7** press release; **5, 10** press conference; **6, 5** public forum, staged event; **6-8** window-dressing; **6, 9** common knowledge, public knowledge; **8, 4** medicine show.

publicize **4** bill, hype, plug, puff, push, sell, tout; **5** boost, extol, shill; **6** splash; **7** feature, glorify, placard, promote, request; **8** announce, ballyhoo, headline, overrate, pinpoint, proclaim; **9** advertise, celebrate, emphasize, highlight, spotlight; **11** pamphleteer; **12** propagandize; PHRASES: **4, 4, 2** make much of; **4, 5** post bills, rave about; **5, 2** build up; **5, 3, 5** blitz the media; **9, 3** advertise for.

publicizer **3** PRO; **4** tout; **5** crier, flack, shill; **6** barker, herald; **7** spieler; **8** notifier, promoter; **9** announcer, messenger, publicist; **10** advertiser, copywriter, proclaimer; **11** pamphleteer, sandwichman; **12** propagandist; PHRASES: **2, 3** PR man; **2, 5** PR woman; **2, 6** PR person; **4, 6** bill poster, spin doctor; **4, 7** bill sticker; **5, 5** press agent; **5-5** image-maker; **5, 6** blurb writer; **9, 5** publicity agent.

publicly **2, 3, 4** in the open; **2, 3, 6, 3** in the public eye; **2, 3, 9** in the limelight; **2, 4, 4** in full view; **2, 5** on stage; **3, 3, 2, 3** for all to see; **3, 5** out front; **4, 4, 5** with open doors. *See also* **public**

public servant **10** politician; PHRASES: **5, 7** civil servant; **6, 8** public official.

public speaker, public speaking **4** rant; **6** orator, ranter, reader; **7** address, blarney, oratory, ranting; **8** lecturer, preacher, rhetoric, sermoner; **9** declaimer, demagogue, expositor, expounder, pulpiteer, sermonist, spokesman; **10** discourser, sermonizer; **11** declamation, rhetorician, spokeswoman; **12** pontificator, speechifying, spokesperson, vituperation; PHRASES: **3-7** tub-thumper *UK*; **5, 6** stump orator; **6-5** speech-maker; **6-6** rabble-rouser; **7, 6** soapbox orator.

public spirit **6** civism; **9** communism, reformism, socialism; **10** Benthamism; **11** citizenship; **14** utilitarianism; **15** humanitarianism; PHRASES: **4, 11** good citizenship.

publish **3** set, sub; **4** edit; **5** cover, issue, print, scoop, write; **6** report; **7** typeset; **8** copyedit; **9** circulate, serialize, syndicate; **10** distribute; **11** circularize; PHRASES: **3, 3** put out; **4-4** copy-edit; **5, 1, 5** break a story; **5, 2** write up; **5, 3** bring out.

publish (be published) **6** spread; **9** circulate; PHRASES: **3, 6** get around; **4, 3** come out; **4, 5** buzz about, pass round; **6, 6** spread abroad.

published **4** open; **5** aired; **6** public; **7** current, exposed, printed; **8** declared, revealed; **9** announced, broadcast, disclosed, televized; **10** proclaimed, ventilated; **11** circulating, distributed; **12** circularized, communicated, disseminated; PHRASES: **2, 3, 3** in the air, on the air; **2, 3, 4** in the news, in the open; **2, 5** in print; **2, 11** in circulation; **4, 6** made public; **6, 6** spread around.

publisher **6** editor, issuer; **8** producer; **10** originator; **12** commissioner. *See also* **publishing (person in publishing)**

publishing (person in publishing) **4** comp; **5** agent; **6** author, editor, writer; **7** printer; **8** novelist; **9** librarian; **10** bookbinder, bookperson, bookseller, compositor, copyeditor, typesetter; **11** ghostwriter, proofreader; PHRASES: **4, 6** desk editor *UK*; **4, 9** book publisher; **6-2-5** editor-in-chief; **6** fiction editor; **8, 5** literary agent; **8, 6** managing editor; **9, 6** reference editor.

pucker *See* **wrinkle**

pudding 5 sweet *UK*; 6 afters *UK*; 7 college, dessert; PHRASES: 4, 7 eve's ~, milk ~ *UK*, plum ~, rice ~ *UK*, suet ~ *UK*; 5, 7 black ~, blood ~, hasty ~, pease ~ *UK*, white ~ *UK*; 6, 7 Indian ~, summer ~ *UK*; 7, 7 cabinet ~, steamed ~. *See also* **dessert**

puddle 4 pool, wade; 5 slick; 6 paddle, splash, splosh *UK*.

puff 4 blow, gasp, gust, pant, waft, wisp; 5 blurb, cloud, draft; 6 billow, breath, exhale, flurry, praise, wheeze; 7 breathe, current; 9 publicity; 14 recommendation.

puffer 8 blowfish; 9 globefish, swellfish.

puggree 6 turban.

pugnacious *See* **aggressive**

puke *See* **vomit**

pukka *See* **proper**

pull 3 jig, lug, tow, tug; 4 drag, draw, flip, hale, haul, jerk, jolt, knob, warp, yank, yerk; 5 draft, flick, heave, hitch, kedge, pluck, trail, train, trawl, trice, tweak; 6 handle, joggle, rowing, snatch, strain, twitch, wrench; 7 attract, through; 9 magnetism, magnetize, spellbind; 10 attraction; PHRASES: 3, 2, 3 tug of war.

pulp 3 gel, jam, pap; 4 agar, curd, fool, mush, pith; 5 aspic, crush, dough, jelly, lurid, paste, purée, syrup; 6 junket, mousse, squash, stodge *UK*; 7 gelatin, pudding, treacle; 9 liquidize; 11 sensational; 12 bonnyclabber; PHRASES: 4, 7 ~ fiction.

pulpit 4 dais; 5 stand; 6 church, clergy, podium; 7 lectern; PHRASES: 7, 4 reading desk.

pulpy 5 mushy, soggy, soupy; 6 creamy, doughy, flabby, spongy, stodgy; 7 squashy, starchy; 10 amylaceous.

pulsatilla 12 pasqueflower.

pulse 3 pea; 4 bean, beat; 5 carob, pound, throb; 6 legume, lentil, rhythm; 7 alfalfa, calabar, haricot, pulsate, soybean; 8 garbanzo, pounding; 9 mangetout *UK*, palpitate, pulsation; PHRASES: 3, 4 wax bean; 4, 3 snow pea; 4, 4 lima bean, mung bean, soya bean *UK*; 5, 3 chick pea, split pea, sugar pea; 5, 4 aduki bean, azuki bean, black bean, broad bean, dwarf bean, green bean, petit pois, pinto bean; 5-4, 3 black-eyed pea; 5-4, 4 black-eyed bean *UK*; 6, 3 desert pea *UK*, pigeon pea; 6, 4 adzuki bean, butter bean, castor bean, french bean, kidney bean, runner bean *UK*, string bean; 7, 6 scarlet runner; 9, 3 marrowfat pea. *See also*

fruit, vegetables

pulverize 4 bray, sift; 5 crush, grate, grind, shard, shred; 6 pestle, powder; 7 atomize; 8 fragment, levigate; 9 brecciate, comminute, granulate, micronize, triturate; 12 contriturate, disintegrate; PHRASES: 5, 2, 4 grind to dust; 6, 2, 6 reduce to powder.

pulverizer 4 mill; 5 quern; 6 masher, muller, pestle, roller; 7 crusher, grinder, pounder; 8 atomizer; 9 bulldozer, kominuter, levigator, millstone; 10 comminutor, grindstone, quernstone, triturator; 11 steamroller; PHRASES: 4, 7 rock crusher; 4, 9 food processor; 6, 3, 6 pestle and mortar; 6, 4 pepper mill; 6, 7 coffee grinder.

puma 8, 4 mountain lion.

pummel *See* **beat**

pump 4 shoe; 5 drive, force, heart; 6 piston, ticker; 7 bellows; 8 question; 10 compressor; 11 interrogate; PHRASES: 3, 4 air ~; 4, 4 heat ~; 5-8 cross-question; 6, 4 parish ~ *UK*, rotary ~, vacuum ~; 7, 4 bicycle ~, stirrup ~, stomach ~, suction ~; 8, 4 gasoline ~.

pun 4 joke, quip; 6 banter; 9 witticism; PHRASES: 3, 3 bon mot; 4, 4, 5 play with words; 6, 8 double entendre.

punch 2 KO; 3 die, hit, jab; 4 biff, chop, fist, hook, left, slug, sock; 5 cross, right, thump, whack; 6 pummel; PHRASES: 3, 5 key ~; 4, 5 bell ~, card ~, milk ~ *UK*; 6, 5 center ~, rabbit ~; 7, 5 Suffolk ~; 8, 5 planter's ~.

punctilious 6 polite, seemly; 7 correct; 9 assiduous, courteous; 10 fastidious, meticulous, scrupulous; 11 painstaking.

punctuate 3 dot; 4 dash; 5 break, cross; 6 accent, indent, stress; 7 obelize; 8 asterisk; 9 emphasize, hyphenate, interrupt, italicize, underline; 10 abbreviate, underscore; 12 parenthesize.

punctuation 4 dash, fist, hand, star, stop; 5 blank, break, breve, caret, colon, comma, hacek, index, pause, point, query, tilde; 6 accent, braces *UK*, dagger, hyphen, macron, obelus, period, quotes, stroke, umlaut; 7 cedilla, solidus, virgule; 8 asterisk, asterism, brackets, dieresis *UK*, ellipsis; 9 diacritic, indention, paragraph, semicolon; 10 apostrophe, circumflex; 11 interrobang, parentheses, underlining; PHRASES: 2, 4 em rule, en rule; 4, 4 full stop *UK*; 5, 4 swung dash; 5, 5 vowel point; 5, 6 acute accent, grave accent; 6, 5 turned comma; 6, 6 double quotes, single quotes; 6, 8 square brackets; **8, 4** omission mark, printing mark, question mark; **8, 5** inverted comma *UK*; **9, 4** quotation mark, reference mark; **11, 4** diacritical mark, ~ mark.

puncture 4 hole, ruin, stab; **5** erode, prick, wound; **6** lesion, pierce; **7** deflate, destroy, pinhole; **9** perforate, undermine; **11** perforation; PHRASES: **5, 2** stick in.

pungency 3 wit; **4** bite; **5** force; **7** acidity. *See also* **pungent**

pungent 3 hot; **4** acid, racy, salt; **5** acrid, pithy, sharp, spicy, tangy; **6** bitter; **7** caustic, mordant, piquant, pointed.

punish 3 ban, tan; **4** beat, cane, duck, fine, flog, gate, hurt, jail; **5** chide, exile, expel, mulct, scold, shame, visit; **6** amerce, banish, demote, deport, ground, impose, intern, outlaw, picket, rebuke, strafe *UK*; **7** afflict, cashier, chasten, correct, degrade, deprive, forfeit, inflict, pillory, reprove, suspend, unfrock; **8** admonish, chastise, imprison, keelhaul, masthead; **9** blackball, castigate, downgrade, ostracize, persecute, proscribe, reprimand, transport, victimize; **10** confiscate, discipline; **11** incarcerate, sequestrate; PHRASES: **3, 3, 7** tar and feather; **3, 4** put away; **4, 2** keep in, lock up; **4, 2, 1, 7** toss in a blanket; **4, 2, 4** take to task; **4, 2, 8** send to Coventry; **4, 3** drum out, tell off; **4, 4** bind over, dust down *UK*, send down *UK*, take away; **4, 4, 4, 3** have one's head for; **5, 2, 3, 5** smack on the wrist; **5, 4** dress down; **6-5** spread-eagle; **7, 4** inflict pain.

punish (be punished) 5 swing; PHRASES: **3, 3, 5** die the death; **4, 3, 3** kick the air, take the rap; **4, 3, 5** face the music; **4, 4, 3** hold one's hand out; **5, 2** catch it; **5, 3, 2** smart for it; **5, 3, 6** stand the racket.

punished 5 caned, fined, gated; **6** beaten; **8** executed, grounded, tortured; **10** castigated, imprisoned; **11** disciplined; PHRASES: **2, 11** in confinement.

punisher 5 caner, judge; **6** tyrant; **7** avenger, flogger, hangman, lyncher, whipper; **8** assassin, headsman, murderer, revenger, scourger, torturer; **9** chastener, chastiser, corrector, garrotter, sentencer; **10** castigator, inquisitor, justiciary, magistrate, persecutor, retaliator, vindicator; **11** bowstringer, discipliner, executioner, flagellator *UK*; PHRASES: **3, 3** hit man; **4, 5** Jack Ketch; **4, 11** high executioner; **5-6** witch-hunter; **7, 3** hatchet man; **7, 5** hanging judge.

punishing 4 hard; **6** taxing; **7** arduous, painful; **8** grueling; **9** demanding, laborious, strenuous, torturous; **10** exhausting; PHRASES: **4-8** back-breaking.

punishment 3 rod; **4** belt, cane, club, cosh *UK*, fine, lash, whip; **5** birch, chain, exile, Gulag, irons, knout, lines, mulct, quirt, ruler, shame, stick, strap, tawse, thong; **6** cudgel, ferule, fining, gating, lesson, rebuke, stocks, switch; **7** banning, bilboes, chiding, cowhide, deodand, ducking, escheat, example, fetters, forfeit, galleys, pillory, reproof, sandbag, scourge; **8** demotion, drubbing, scolding, sentence; **9** degrading, detention, expulsion, grounding, horsewhip, ostracism, outlawing, reprimand; **10** admonition, amercement, banishment, chastening, correction, discipline, forfeiture, internment, suspension, unfrocking; **11** castigation, confinement, deportation, deprivation, downgrading, keelhauling, persecution; **12** blackballing, chastisement, confiscation, imprisonment, penalization, proscription; **13** expropriation, incarceration, sequestration, victimization; **14** transportation; PHRASES: **3-1-4-5** cat-o'-nine-tails; **4, 2, 7** debt to society; **4, 4** high jump; **4, 5** hard labor; **5, 4** chain gang, court fine, labor camp; **5, 6** house arrest, penal colony; **5, 9** penal servitude; **6, 8** prison sentence; **7, 3** kicking ass, telling off; **7, 4** dusting down *UK*; **7, 5** ducking stool; **8-4** dressing-down.

punishment (instrument of punishment) 3 cat, rod; **4** belt, cane, cell, club, cosh *UK*, jail, lash, whip; **5** birch, chain, irons, knout, quirt, ruler, stick, strap, tawse, thong; **6** corner, cudgel, ferule, prison, rattan, stocks, switch; **7** bilboes, cowhide, fetters, pillory, sandbag, scourge, sjambok (S Afr); **9** hairbrush, horsewhip; PHRASES: **3-1-4-5** cat-o'-nine-tails; **3, 5** big stick; **5, 3** rope's end; **5-3** birch-rod; **5, 5** cutty stool; **6, 4** rubber hose; **6, 5** prison house; **7, 5** bicycle chain, cucking stool, ducking stool; **8, 4** whipping post.

punitive 5 penal; **7** capital; **8** corporal, punitory *UK*; **9** punishing; **10** admonitory, corrective, penalizing, revengeful, vindictive; **11** castigatory, instructive, penological, retaliatory, retributive; **12** correctional, disciplinary.

punk 4 poor; **5** cheap, nasty; **8** inferior; PHRASES: **6, 4** second rate.

punt 3 bet; 4 kick; 6 gamble.

puny *See* **feeble**

pup 4 bear, brat; 7 deliver; PHRASES: 4-2-3 know-it-all; 4, 5 give birth; 5, 5 smart aleck. *See also* **young animal**

pupil 1 L; 4 ward; 5 apple, tutee; 7 boarder, eyeball, learner, protégé, scholar, student; 8 disciple, follower; 9 schoolboy; 10 apprentice, catechumen, schoolgirl.

puppet 4 doll, pawn, tool; 5 dummy; 6 lackey, lapdog; 10 instrument, marionette; PHRASES: 4, 6 hand ~; 5, 6 glove ~ *UK*.

purchase 3 buy, get; 4 bull, find, grip, stag; 5 bribe, order; 6 afford, barter, buyout, corner, obtain; 7 acquire, bargain, engross, procure; 8 foothold, leverage, shopping, takeover, teleshop; 9 speculate; 10 monopolize; 11 acquisition.

purchaser 4 bull, stag; 5 buyer, taker; 6 bidder, briber, client, emptor, patron, vendee; 7 haggler, hoarder, offerer, shopper, spender; 8 acceptor, consumer, customer, investor, ransomer, redeemer; 9 bargainer, clientele, consignee, preemptor; 10 speculator, transferee; 11 teleshopper; PHRASES: 5-5 share-buyer; 5, 8 loyal customer; 7, 6 bargain hunter, highest bidder; 7, 8 regular customer. *See also* **currency, money**

pure 3 coy, shy; 4 cold, neat; 5 blank, clean, clear, godly, pious, snowy, white; 6 chaste, frigid, modest, undyed, vestal, virgin; 7 bashful, cleanly, perfect, refined, saintly, sexless, sinless; 8 blushing, celibate, cleansed, complete, innocent, maidenly, Platonic, purebred, purified, spotless, unfallen, unspiced, unspoilt, untinged, unwedded, virginal, virtuous; 9 clarified, continent, faultless, pedigreed, religious, righteous, stainless, temperate, uncolored, undefiled, undiluted, unmuddied, unsullied, untainted, untouched; 10 immaculate, sanctified, sublimated, unflavored, unpolluted, unseasoned; 11 unblemished, unfortified, unmedicated, untarnished; 12 thoroughbred, unfragranced; 13 unadulterated; 14 uncontaminated; PHRASES: 4, 4 free from.

pure (be pure) 4, 4, 1, 3 live like a nun; 4, 4, 1, 4 live like a monk; 4, 6 live purely.

purebred 8 pedigree; 12 thoroughbred.

pure person 3 nun; 4 maid, monk; 5 angel, saint; 6 maiden, Quaker, vestal, virgin, wowser (Aus and NZ); 7 paragon, Puritan; 8 celibate, Lancelot, spinster; 9 Encratite; PHRASES: 3, 4 old maid; 3, 6, 4 the Virgin Mary; 3, 7 Sir Galahad; 5, 7 virgo intacta; 6, 6 vestal virgin. *See also* **virtuous person**

purgative 5 enema, purge; 6 douche, emetic, ipecac; 7 antacid, cascara; 8 aperient, diuretic, evacuant, laxative, licorice, nauseant; 9 cathartic, digestive; 11 carminative, expectorant, ipecacuanha; PHRASES: 4, 2, 8 milk of magnesia; 4, 5 dill water; 5, 4 senna pods; 5, 5 Epsom salts; 6, 3 castor oil; 6, 5 health salts *UK*; 9, 5 ~ agent.

purge 5 clean; 6 emetic, excuse, pardon, remove, sluice; 7 absolve, cleanse, forgive, removal; 8 laxative; 9 cathartic, eliminate, eradicate, exonerate, expulsion, purgative; 11 elimination, eradication; PHRASES: 4, 3 wash out; 5, 3 flush out.

purification 6 airing; 7 purging, washing; 8 Asperges, cleaning, dialysis, flushing, riddance; 9 cleansing, clearance, delousing, expulsion, purgation; 10 antisepsis, fumigation, lustration, sanitation; 11 elimination, ventilation; 12 disinfection; 13 deodorization, sterilization; 14 disinfestation; 15 decontamination; PHRASES: 7, 3 washing out.

purified 4 nice; 5 clean, fresh, halal, shiny, snowy, white; 6 bright, dainty, kosher; 7 aseptic, cleaned, shining, sterile; 8 cleansed, polished, scrubbed; 10 antiseptic, deodorized, sterilized; 11 disinfected; PHRASES: 4-5 snow-white; 5, 2, 1, 5 fresh as a daisy; 5-3-4 spick-and-span; 8, 5 ritually clean.

purifier 4 soap, soda; 5 water; 6 filter, gargle, lotion; 7 cleaner, shampoo; 8 cleanser, strainer; 9 deodorant, detergent, mouthwash; 10 dentifrice, soapflakes, toothpaste; 12 disinfectant; PHRASES: 3, 5 hot water; 3, 9 air freshener; 4, 3, 5 soap and water; 4, 5 cold cream, hand cream; 5, 6 water filter; 7-2, 6 washing-up liquid; 7, 4 washing soda; 7, 6 washing powder *UK*; 8, 4 carbolic acid; 9, 5 cleansing agent, cleansing cream, vanishing cream.

purify 3 air, fan; 4 lave *UK*, rack, scum, sift, skim, wash; 5 clean, clear, drain, flush, leach, purge, sieve; 6 censor, decant, decoke *UK*, desalt, filter, refine, strain, winnow; 7 clarify, cleanse, dialyze, distill, elevate, freshen; 8 depurate, fumigate, lixivate, lustrate, sanitate, sanitize; 9 deodorize, despumate, disinfect, eliminate, elutriate, expurgate, lixiviate *UK*, percolate, sterilize, sublimate, ventilate; **10** bowdlerize, chlorinate, desalinate, desalinize, edulcorate, pasteurize; **11** catheterize, decarbonize; **13** antisepticize, decontaminate; PHRASES: **4, 3** edit out, sort out, wash out, weed out; **4, 4, 5, 2** wash one's hands of; **4, 5** wash clean, wipe clean; **4-6** blue-pencil; **5, 2** clean up; **5, 3** clean out, flush out; **6, 7** ~ oneself.

purity 5 faith, honor, piety; **6** morals, virtue; **7** clarity, coyness, decency, honesty, modesty, prudery, pudency; **8** chastity, delicacy, holiness, morality, primness, pureness, sanctity; **9** cleanness, clearness, euphemism, freshness, godliness, Grundyism, innocence, integrity, propriety, rectitude, virginity; **10** censorship, immaculacy, perfection, Puritanism, sanctimony, simplicity; **11** cleanliness, expurgation, prudishness, sinlessness; **12** flawlessness, priggishness, spotlessness; **13** faultlessness, righteousness, stainlessness; PHRASES: **4, 5** good taste, pure heart; **4-10** high-mindedness; **5, 6** moral ~; **5, 7** false modesty; **5, 9** moral rectitude; **9, 6** Victorian values.

purl 4 edge, flow, trim; **5** frill; **6** babble, border, fringe, gurgle, murmur, ripple, thread; PHRASES: **4, 6** gold thread.

purloin *See* **steal**

purple 4 beet, plum, puce; **5** lilac, mauve; **6** damson, indigo, maroon, ornate, purply, violet; **7** fuchsia, heather, magenta, purpled, purpure; **8** amaranth, amethyst, eggplant, foxglove, lavender, mulberry, nobility, purplish; **9** gallinule; **10** heliotrope, violaceous; **11** amaranthine, amethystine, hyacinthine; PHRASES: **5, 6** Parma violet, regal ~, royal ~, Thalo ~; **6-3** purplered; **6-4** purple-blue; **6, 5** ~ heart *UK*, ~ medic, ~ patch *UK*; **6, 6** cobalt violet, methyl violet, Tyrian ~; **6, 7** ~ emperor; **7, 5** funeral color; **7, 6** bishop's ~, bishop's violet, gentian violet, Windsor violet; **8, 6** imperial ~.

purple medic 7 alfalfa.

purple thing 4 beet, plum; **5** lilac, pansy; **6** damson, violet; **7** heather; **8** amethyst, clematis, eggplant, foxglove, hyacinth, lavender; **10** heliotrope; **12** rhododendron; PHRASES: **6, 4** purple haze; **6, 5** Purple Heart, purple heart *UK*; **6, 6** purple martin; **6, 7** purple emperor, purple grackle; **6, 9** purple gallinule.

purport 3 aim; **4** mean, plan; **5** claim,

sense; **6** allege, assert, design, intend; **7** contend, meaning, profess, purpose; **9** intention; **10** importance; **11** implication; **12** significance.

purpose 3 aim, end; **4** goal; **5** point; **6** design, object, reason, target; **7** meaning; **8** function; **9** objective; **12** significance.

purposeless 5 empty; **7** aimless, useless; **9** illogical, pointless, senseless; **10** irrational; **11** meaningless; **12** unreasonable.

purposive 5 aimed; **6** aiming; **7** planned; **8** designed, proposed, reasoned, targeted; **9** schematic, targeting; **10** functional, meaningful, reasonable; **11** functioning, intentional, significant; **12** teleological; PHRASES: **4-8** goal-directed, well-reasoned.

purr 3 hum; **4** buzz, whir; **6** rumble; **7** vibrate; **9** vibration. *See also* **animal cry**

purse 3 bag; **4** fisc; **6** crease, pucker, wallet; **7** handbag *UK*, sporran; **8** billfold; PHRASES: **3, 5** sea ~; **4, 5** long ~ *UK*; **5, 5** privy ~; **8, 5** mermaid's ~.

pursue 3 dog; **4** seek; **5** chase, chevy *UK*, chivy, harry; **6** follow, harass, search, shadow; **7** oppress; **9** persecute; PHRASES: **2, 5** go after; **3, 3** dig for; **4, 3** fish for, hunt for, look for, send for; **4, 5, 3** cast about for; **6, 3** search for.

pursuer 6 dogger, shadow, sleuth; **7** quester; **8** searcher; **10** researcher.

pursuing 8 pursuant; PHRASES: **2, 3, 5** on the trail; **2, 3, 7** in hot pursuit; **2, 4, 3** in full cry; **2, 4, 4** on one's tail; **2, 4, 5** on one's scent; **2, 5, 2** in quest of; **4, 5** sent after. *See also* **pursue**

pursuit 3 APB; **4** beat, hunt, race; **5** chase, drive, hobby, quest; **6** battue, search; **7** casting, chasing, dogging, dragnet, gunning, hunting, manhunt, seeking, tailing, tallyho; **8** activity, business, hounding, interest, pursuing, shooting, spooring, stalking, tracking, trailing; **9** execution, following, pursuance, shadowing; **11** McCarthyism, persecution, persistence, prosecution; **12** effectuation, perseverance, steeplechase; PHRASES: **5-4** witch-hunt; **5, 5** paper chase.

purulent 5 pussy; **7** running; **9** festering, mattering; **11** suppurative.

purvey 4 sell, tell; **6** gossip, spread, supply, tattle; **7** furnish, provide, whisper; PHRASES: **4, 2** deal in.

pus 5 gleet, ichor; **6** matter, sanies; **7** mucopus, pustule, running, seropus, weeping;

8 rankling; **9** discharge, festering, mattering, purulence, pussiness; **10** leukorrhea; **11** suppuration.

push 3 jam, ply, ram; **4** edge, plug, sell, tout, urge; **5** barge, boost, drive, heave, impel, nudge, press, shove; **6** attack, effort, hustle, jostle, thrust; **7** advance, assault, obtrude, promote; **8** ambition, railroad, shoulder; **9** offensive, pitchfork; **10** propulsion; PHRASES: **4, 6** ~ button, send flying; **4, 8** send headlong; **5, 4, 3** elbow one's way; **6, 7** assert oneself.

pusher 7 hustler; **10** connection, propellant; PHRASES: **2-6** go-getter; **4, 6** drug dealer; **4, 7** drug peddler.

pushover *See* **dupe**

pusillanimous *See* **timid**

puss 3 mug; **4** face, phiz *UK*; **6** phizog *UK. See also* **cat**

pussyfoot 5 creep, ghost, steal, waver; **6** tiptoe, wander; **8** hesitate; **11** prevaricate; **13** procrastinate.

put 3 add, lay, pop, set; **4** bung *UK*, dump, lean, park, stow; **5** leave, offer, place, plant, plunk, stick; **6** assign, impose, submit, tender; **7** deposit, present, situate; **8** allocate, position; PHRASES: **3, 4** lay down, set down.

put in a container 3 can, pot, tin; **4** cage, pack, wrap; **5** cover, store; **6** bottle, bundle, cocoon, entomb, garage, sheath, stable; **7** enclose, package, reserve, shelter; **8** envelope, surround; **12** containerize; PHRASES: **3, 2** box up *UK*; **4, 2** pour in; **5, 2** crate up.

put off 5 dally, daunt, defer, delay, deter, repel, scare, stall; **6** shelve; **7** adjourn, disgust, disturb; **8** dissuade, distract, postpone; **9** disaffect, indispose; **10** discourage, disincline, intimidate, reschedule; **13** procrastinate; PHRASES: **3, 7** set against; **4, 7** turn against; **6, 6** render averse.

put out 5 anger, angry, annoy, cross, douse, eject, issue; **6** bother, offend, quench; **7** annoyed, publish, release, trouble; **8** irritate, offended; **9** displease, irritated; **10** displeased, extinguish; **13** inconvenience; PHRASES: **6, 2** impose on.

putrefaction 5 decay; **8** necrosis; **10** rottenness; **13** mortification.

putrefy 3 rot; **4** turn; **5** decay, spoil; **9** decompose; **11** deteriorate; PHRASES: **2, 3** go bad, go off *UK*.

putrid 3 off; **4** gamy, high, sour; **6** rancid, rotten; **7** rotting, tainted; **8** decaying; **10** decomposed, putrescent.

put right 3 fix; **4** cure, mend, redo; **6** reform, repair; **7** rectify, redress; PHRASES: **3, 5** set right; **4, 3** sort out; **5, 1, 5** right a wrong; **10, 3** compensate for.

putt *See* **knock**

putting together 7 collage, montage; **8** assembly, erection; **10** assemblage, connection; **11** fabrication, manufacture; **12** construction; PHRASES: **7, 8** fitting together; **8, 4** assembly line; **10, 4** production line.

put together 4 join, make; **5** erect, unite; **7** combine, compile, compose, connect; **9** colligate, construct, fabricate; **11** manufacture; PHRASES: **3, 8** fit together.

puzzle 4 beat, code, faze; **5** floor, stump, think; **6** baffle, bemuse, cipher, enigma, gravel, jigsaw, ponder, riddle, secret; **7** chinese, confuse, flummox, mystery, mystify, nonplus, paradox, problem; **8** bewilder, confound; **9** bamboozle, challenge, conundrum, crossword, dumbfound; **10** disconcert; PHRASES: **6-6** monkey-puzzle.

pyre *See* **fire**

pyrosis 9 heartburn.

Pyrrhic victory 7, 7 Cadmean victory.

Q

Q 5 quart, queen; **8** question.

QC 4 silk; **6** lawyer; PHRASES: **6, 7** Queen's Counsel; **7, 7** quality control.

QT 5 quart, quiet.

quack 4 fake, sham; **6** doctor; **8** imposter; **9** charlatan, pretender; **10** mountebank.

quadrilateral 6 oblong, square; **7** rhombus; **8** quadrate, tetragon; **9** rectangle, trapezium, trapezoid; **10** foursquare, quadrangle; **11** rectangular, tetrahedral, tetrahedron; **13** parallelogram; PHRASES: **4-5** four-sided.

quadruple 6 expand; **7** augment, magnify; **8** multiply, quadrate; **13** quadruplicate; PHRASES: **8, 2, 4** multiply by four.

quaff 3 sup; **5** drink; **6** imbibe; **7** carouse, swallow.

quagmire 3 bog, fen, mud; **4** mess, mire, ooze, quag; **5** marsh, slime, swamp; **6** morass, muddle, slough, sludge, wallow; **7** dilemma, mudhole, trouble; **9** imbroglio, marshland, quicksand, swampland; **11** predicament.

quahog 4-5 hard-shell; **4-5, 4** hard-shell clam; **5, 4** round clam.

quail 4 bevy; **5** cower, quake, waver; **6** blanch, blench, cringe, falter, flinch, shrink; **7** tremble.

quaint 3 odd; **4** twee; **7** curious, strange; **8** fanciful; **9** whimsical; **11** picturesque; PHRASES: **3-5** old-world; **3-9** old-fashioned; **4-6** olde-worlde *UK.*

quake 5 cower, quail, shake; **6** quaver, quiver, shiver, tremor; **7** shudder, tremble; **10** earthquake; PHRASES: **7, 4** seismic wave.

qualification 5 rider, skill; **6** degree, talent; **7** ability, aptness, diploma, dueness, fitness, proviso, quality; **8** ableness, adequacy, aptitude, efficacy; **9** attribute, condition, criterion, equipment, propriety, readiness, relevance, tempering; **10** capability, competence, credential, efficiency, experience, fittedness, limitation, suitedness, worthiness; **11** capableness, certificate, eligibility, entitlement, meritedness, proficiency, requirement, reservation, restriction, stipulation, sufficiency, suitability; **12** appositeness, deservedness, modification, potentiality, preparedness, prerequisite, suitableness; **13** acceptability, applicability, qualifiedness; **14** characteristic; **15** appropriateness; PHRASES: **4, 3, 3** sine qua non. *See also* **degree, diploma**

qualified 3 apt, fit; **4** able; **5** ready; **6** expert, fitted, gifted, seeded, suited, versed, worthy; **7** capable, endowed, fitting, limited, merited, skilled, trained; **8** accepted, deserved, eligible, enrolled, equipped, licensed, modified, prepared, skillful, suitable, talented, tempered; **9** certified, competent, efficient, masterful, nominated, practiced; **10** acceptable, accredited, authorized, contingent, proficient, recognized, registered; **11** appropriate, experienced; **12** businesslike, professional; PHRASES: **3, 3, 3** cut out for; **4, 4** bona fide; **4-7** well-adapted; **5, 3, 6** tried and tested; **5-6** short-listed; **5-9** board-certified.

qualified person 3 ace; **6** boffin, doctor, expert; **7** adviser; **8** graduate, virtuoso; **9** professor; **10** consultant, specialist, technician; **11** connoisseur; **12** postgraduate, professional; PHRASES: **3, 4** old hand; **7, 6** skilled worker.

qualify 4 pass; **5** allow, endow, equip, limit, train; **6** enable, invest, lessen, modify, permit, reduce, soften, temper; **7** certify, empower, entitle, license, succeed; **8** moderate, restrict; **9** authorize; PHRASES: **2, 2, 3, 7** be in the running; **2, 8** be eligible, be licensed, be suitable; **2, 9** be certified, be nominated; **3, 7** get through; **4, 3, 5** make the grade.

quality 5 class, grade, level, merit, trait; **7** caliber, feature; **8** eminence, property, standard; **9** attribute; **10** excellence; **11** distinction, superiority; **14** characteristic.

qualm 4 fear, pang; **5** doubt; **7** remorse, scruple; **9** misgiving; **10** contrition; **11** compunction.

quandary *See* **dilemma**

quantify 3 add, fix; **4** pack, rate, size, tell; **5** allot, count, limit, piece, share, weigh; **6** divide, extend, number, parcel, ration, reckon, reduce; **7** compute, measure, portion; **8** allocate, decrease, increase, quantize, subtract; **9** apportion, calculate, enumerate; PHRASES: **3, 1, 6, 2** put a figure on.

quantity 4 area, body, bulk, mass, pack, pile, ream, size; **5** depth, space, width; **6** amount, extent, height, length, matter, number, volume, weight; **7** breadth, gravity, measure; **8** altitude, capacity, deepness, thinness, weighing; **9** amplitude, dimension, heaviness, lightness, magnitude, measuring, multitude, substance, thickness; **11** measurement, proportions.

quarantine 4 hold; **6** detain, intern; **7** confine, isolate, seclude; **8** imprison, separate; **9** isolation, seclusion; **11** confinement; PHRASES: **3, 5** set apart; **4, 2** lock up.

quarantine flag 6, 4 yellow flag, yellow jack.

quarrel 3 nag, row; **4** bolt, duel, feud, spat, tiff; **5** aggro *UK*, argue, arrow, brawl, clash, fight, issue, melee, scrap, stick; **6** bicker, bother, fracas, insult, offend, strife; **7** dispute, dissent, grumble, problem, ruction, scuffle, wrangle; **8** argument, conflict, disagree, squabble, vendetta; **9** complaint, grievance; **10** fisticuffs; **11** altercation, disturbance; **12** chastisement, disagreement; PHRASES: **3-2** run-in, set-to; **4, 1, 4** have a tiff; **4, 2, 4** bone to pick; **4, 2, 6** spot of bother; **4, 3** fall out; **5, 6, 4** cross swords with; **7-3** falling-out.

quarry 3 pit; **4** game, mine, prey; **5** prize; **6** object, victim.

quarter 1 E, N, S, W; **4** area, part, pity, term, zone; **5** crack, house, lodge, mercy, slice; **6** barrio, billet, divide, fourth, region, sector; **7** section; **8** district, division, locality, quadrant, quartier *UK*, quartile; **9** subdi-

vide, trimester; **11** accommodate; **12** neighborhood; PHRASES: **3, 2** cut up; **3, 6** one fourth; **4, 1, 3, 3** find a bed for; **4, 7** last ~; **5, 2** split up; **5, 7** empty ~, first ~, Latin ~; **6, 4** fourth part; **7, 3** ~ day *UK*; **7, 4** ~ note, ~ tone; **7, 5** ~ horse; **7, 8** ~ sessions *UK*.

quartet 3 for; **4** fore, four; **6** tetrad; **8** foursome.

quash 5 annul, quell; **6** cancel, repeal, subdue; **7** nullify, suspend; **8** abrogate, suppress; PHRASES: **4, 4, 3, 4** make null and void.

quaver 4 note; **5** quake, shake, trill; **6** quiver, warble, wobble; **7** shudder, tremble, vibrate.

queasy 3 ill; **4** sick; **6** uneasy; **7** dubious, seasick; **8** doubtful, nauseous; **9** troubling; **10** indisposed; **13** uncomfortable.

queen 1 Q, R; **2** ER, HM; **3** Mab; **4** Anne, Bess, Dido, icon, Maam, Mary, star; **5** begun, Helen, ideal, model, nance, pansy, ranee, ruler, Sheba; **6** Hecuba, regina; **7** doyenne, Eleanor, empress, epitome, essence, monarch, sultana; **8** Adelaide, Boadicea, Caroline, Gertrude, Hermione; **9** Alexandra, Cleopatra, Guinevere, Hippolyta, Nefertiti, sovereign; PHRASES: **5, 2, 2, 5** crème de la crème; **5, 3** ~ bee; **5, 4** ~ post; **5, 5** prima donna, ~ olive; **5, 6** ~ mother, ~ regent; **5, 7** ~ consort, ~ dowager; **5, 10** Marie Antoinette; **7, 4** crowned head; **7, 5** African Q~.

Queensland nut 9 macadamia.

queer 3 odd; **4** sick; **5** dizzy, faint, fishy, funny, woozy; **6** cranky, groggy, queasy, unwell; **7** bizarre, curious, strange, unusual; **8** atypical, nauseous, peculiar; **9** eccentric; **10** surprizing, unexpected; **13** idiosyncratic; **14** unconventional; PHRASES: **5, 4** ~ fish *UK*.

quell 5 allay, crush, quash; **6** subdue; **7** assuage, mollify; **8** mitigate, suppress; **9** alleviate; PHRASES: **3, 4** put down.

quench 4 sate; **5** douse, slake; **6** reduce, stifle; **7** satiate, smother; **10** extinguish; PHRASES: **3, 3** put out.

query *See* **question**

quest 4 goal, hunt; **5** Grail; **6** search, voyage; **7** journey, odyssey, pursuit, venture; **10** expedition, pilgrimage.

question 3 ask, pry, try; **4** hear, hunt, mark, plea, poll, quiz, scan, seek, test, time; **5** check, doubt, grill, issue, plead, point, probe, query, quest, study; **6** appeal, demand, direct, impugn, master, matter, pursue, puzzle, review, search, survey, wonder; **7** analyze, canvass, debrief, dispute, entreat, examine, inquire, inquiry, inspect, leading, problem, request, subject; **8** distrust, entreaty, indirect, mistrust, research; **9** catechize, challenge, confusion, interview, objection; **10** difficulty, hesitation, introspect, rhetorical, scrutinize; **11** interrogate, investigate, proposition, reservation, uncertainty; **12** interpellate; **13** interrogation; PHRASES: **4, 3, 6, 2** pick the brains of; **4, 4** look into; **4-4** fact-find; **4, 5, 2** cast doubt on; **4-6** soul-search; **5, 2, 5** point at issue; **5, 3** sound out; **5-7** cross-examine; **6, 3** search out; **8, 4** ~ mark.

question (person questioned) 7 suspect, witness; **8** examinee; **9** candidate, defendant, plaintiff; **11** interviewee; PHRASES: **4, 4, 5** talk show guest.

questionable 4 moot, wild; **5** dodgy UK, risky, shady; **6** chancy; **7** dubious; **8** arguable, disputed, doubtful, fanciful, spurious, unlikely; **9** ambiguous, debatable, deceitful, deceptive, equivocal, uncertain; **10** borderline, disputable, improbable, incredible, suspicious, unreliable; **11** exceptional, implausible, problematic; **12** unbelievable, unverifiable; **13** controversial, extraordinary, untrustworthy; PHRASES: **2, 5** at issue, in doubt; **2, 8** in question; **3, 4, 2, 2, 4** too good to be true; **4, 2, 5** open to doubt; **4, 2, 6** open to debate; **4, 2, 7** hard to believe, hard to swallow; **4, 2, 8** open to question; **5, 10** under discussion; **6, 6** beyond belief.

questioner 5 asker; **6** lawyer, prober, seeker, tester; **7** analyst, coroner, doubter, skeptic, student; **8** agnostic, examiner, inquirer, pollster, reviewer, surveyor; **9** barrister UK Can, canvasser, detective, detractor, dissenter, inspector, scientist; **10** inquisitor, journalist, researcher, scrutineer; **11** interviewer, philosopher; **12** experimenter, interlocutor, interrogator, investigator; **13** interpellator; PHRASES: **4, 4, 4** talk show host; **4, 6** quiz master; **5-8** cross-examiner; **8, 6** doubting Thomas.

questioning 4 nosy, poll; **5** probe, quest, study; **6** prying, review, search, survey; **7** curious, inquest, inquiry, probing, pumping; **8** analysis, analytic, argument, doubting, elenctic, grilling, pleading, querying, questing, research, scrutiny; **9** challenge, examining, inquiring, quizzical, searching,

wondering; **10** inspection, requesting; **11** exploratory, inquisition, inquisitive, researching; **12** interpellant; **13** inquisitorial, interrogation, interrogative, introspective, investigation, investigative; **14** interpellation; PHRASES: **3, 5, 6** the third degree; **4-7** fact-finding; **6, 8** market research.

question mark 5 query.

questionnaire 4 form, poll, quiz, test, viva; **5** trial; **6** census, survey; **7** hearing; **8** audition; **9** catechism, checklist, interview; **11** examination; PHRASES: **4, 11** oral examination; **8-4** question-time; **8, 5** question paper.

queue 3 row; **4** file, line, wait; **5** train; **6** column, logjam, parade; **7** backlog; **8** tailback UK; **9** promenade; PHRASES: **3, 2, 4** get in line; **4, 2** fall in, line up; **4, 2, 4** wait in line; **4, 4, 4** wait your turn; **5, 2, 4** stand in line; **5, 4** march past.

quibble 4 carp; **5** cavil, hedge; **6** palter; **7** nitpick, shuffle; **8** complain, pettifog, quiddity; **9** objection, pussyfoot; **10** equivocate, filibuster; **11** prevaricate; **12** equivocation; PHRASES: **3, 3, 8** beg the question; **5, 3, 5** avoid the issue; **5, 5** bandy words, split hairs.

quibbling 7 hedging; **8** captious, caviling, subtlety; **9** equivocal, paltering, shuffling; **12** captiousness, equivocating, oversubtlety, pettifoggery, pettifogging, pussyfooting; **13** prevaricating, prevarication; PHRASES: **3-7** nit-picking; **4-9** hairsplitting; **7-6** jiggery-pokery.

quick 4 deft, fast, live, spry; **5** agile, alert, alive, brief, fleet, hasty, nifty, nippy UK, rapid, sharp, short, smart, swift; **6** abrupt, adroit, astute, bright, clever, lively, living, nimble, presto, prompt, shrewd, snappy, speedy, sudden; **7** cursory, hurried, instant, passing; **8** fleeting; **9** breakneck, immediate, momentary, sprightly, transient; **11** intelligent; PHRASES: **2, 3, 4** on the ball; **5, 3, 3, 4** ~ off the mark; **5-4** steel-trap; **5-6** quick-witted, sharp-witted; **5-8** quick-thinking.

quickly 4 fast; **5** apace; **6** presto; PHRASES: **2, 4** at once; **4-3-7** hell-for-leather; **4, 4** chop chop; **7, 5** without delay. See also **quick**

quickness 5 speed; **8** rapidity. See also **quick, quickness of mind**

quickness of mind 8 alacrity; **10** brightness, liveliness; **12** intelligence; PHRASES: **5, 2, 7** speed of thought; **5-10**

quick-wittedness; **6, 7** mental agility; **6, 9** mental quickness.

quicksilver 7 mercury.

quick-wittedness 5 flair; **6** acuity, acumen; **8** alacrity; **9** sharpness; **10** brightness, liveliness; **6, 7** mental agility.

quid 4 plug; **7** tobacco.

quiescence 4 rest; **7** inertia, latency; **8** dormancy; **10** inactivity, stagnation. *See also* **quiescent**

quiescent 4 calm, cool; **5** inert, quiet, still, stoic; **6** gentle, hushed, latent, placid, serene, silent, sleepy, smooth, stolid; **7** dormant, halcyon, pacific, restful, resting, unmoved; **8** composed, inactive, leisured, lifeless, peaceful, reposing, sluggish, tranquil, unmoving; **9** impassive, reposeful, soundless, unhurried, unruffled; **10** insensible, motionless, unagitated, unstirring, untroubled; **11** inexcitable, sequestered, undisturbed, unperturbed; **13** contemplative, imperturbable; PHRASES: **2, 4** at rest; **4, 2, 1, 4, 4** calm as a mill pond; **4, 2, 1, 8** cool as a cucumber; **4-5** easy-going; **5, 2, 5** quiet as death.

quiet 1 P; **2** PP, QT, SH; **3** low, mum; **4** calm, dead, easy, hush, soft; **5** muted, peace, still; **6** docile, modest, serene, silent, simple, subtle; **7** halcyon, private, relaxed, restful, silence, subdued; **8** discreet, intimate, peaceful, pleasant, quietude, relaxing, tranquil; **9** inaudible, leisurely, noiseless, soundless, stillness; **10** restrained, unofficial, untroubled; **11** tranquility, understated, undisturbed, unobtrusive; **12** confidential; **13** uncomplicated, uninterrupted; **15** straightforward; PHRASES: **3-3-6** off-the-record; **5, 3, 5** peace and ~; **6-4** hassle-free; **7-4** trouble-free.

quiet (keep quiet) 6 falter; **7** stammer, stutter; PHRASES: **3, 3, 5** use few words; **4, 4, 7** keep one's counsel; **4, 6** keep shtoom; **5, 4, 5** spare one's words; **6, 2, 7** refuse to comment.

quietly 1 P; **2** PP, SH; PHRASES: **2, 3, 2** on the QT.

quill 4 barb; **5** plume, spike, spine; **7** feather.

quintessence 4 soul; **5** heart, ideal; **6** elixir, flower, spirit; **7** epitome, essence, extract; **9** archetype, entelechy; **10** embodiment; **11** concentrate, distilllate,

incarnation; **13** distilllation; **15** personification.

quintessential 5 ideal, model; **6** unique; **7** classic, organic, typical; **8** peerless, singular; **9** essential, exemplary; **10** archetypal, consummate, structural; **12** archetypical, prototypical; **14** constitutional.

quintet 1 V; **4** five; **5** Trout.

quip *See* **joke**

quirk 4 kink, whim; **5** trait; **6** foible, notion, oddity; **7** conceit, feature; **8** crotchet; **9** mannerism; **12** eccentricity, idiosyncrasy; PHRASES: **4-2** hang-up.

quirky *See* **eccentric**

quit 4 flit, stop; **5** cease, elope, leave; **6** decamp, desert, escape, remove, resign, vacate, vanish; **7** abandon, abscond, debouch, suspend; **8** emigrate, relocate, renounce; **9** disappear; **10** expatriate, relinquish; PHRASES: **2, 6** up sticks; **4, 2** give up; **4, 2, 5** call it quits; **4, 3** walk out; **4, 4** slip away, take wing; **4, 6** give notice; **5, 3** march out; **5, 3, 4** leave the nest; **5, 3, 7** leave the country; **5, 4** break camp, leave home; **5, 4, 4** sling one's hook; **6, 4** strike camp; **7, 4** refrain from.

quite 4 very; **7** totally, utterly; **8** entirely; **10** completely.

quits 4 even; **5** level; **6** square.

quitter 5 loser; **6** coward; **7** dropout, failure; **8** deserter, fatalist; **9** defeatist, pessimist; PHRASES: **3-2-5** fly-by-night.

quiver *See* **tremble**

quiz 4 pump, test; **5** grill; **8** question; **11** interrogate.

quizzical 7 curious, puzzled; **9** perplexed, surprised; **11** questioning.

quod *See* **prison**

quota *See* **share**

quotation 3 bid, tag; **4** cite, line; **5** price; **6** gobbet, tender; **7** excerpt, extract, passage; **8** allusion, citation, estimate; **9** reference, soundbite.

quotation mark 5 quote; PHRASES: **8, 5** inverted comma.

quote 3 bid; **4** cite, copy, list, name; **5** price; **6** adduce, tender; **7** itemize, mention, specify; **8** estimate, instance; **9** enumerate. *See also* **quotation**

quotient 5 share; **6** amount; **7** measure; **10** percentage, proportion.

R

R **3** ray, run; **4** King (Latin: Rex), rook; **5** queen (Latin: Regina), right, river, Royal; **6** eighty (Medieval Roman numeral), radius, street (French: rue); **7** railway *UK Can*, reverse; **8** railroad.

RA **6** artist, radium; PHRASES: **5, 7** Royal Academy *UK*.

rabbit 3 doe; **4** buck, muff; **5** bunny, coney *UK*; **6** novice; **10** cottontail, jackrabbit; PHRASES: **4, 6** Brer ~, rock ~; **5, 6** Peter ~, Welsh ~; **6, 6** angora ~; **7, 4** Belgian hare.

rabble *See* **mob**

rabid 3 ill; **4** sick; **6** ardent; **7** extreme, fervent, intense, radical, violent, zealous; **8** diseased, infected; **9** fanatical; **14** uncompromising.

rabies 5 lyssa; **7** madness; **11** hydrophobia.

race 2 TT; **3** fly, jet, lap, run, vie, zip; **4** belt, dart, dash, heat, line, mile, Oaks, rush; **5** Aryan, Asian, color, Derby, event, fight, hurry, Negro, rally, relay, speed, tribe, White; **6** battle, ethnic, gallop, Indian, Latino, nation, origin, people, sprint; **7** classic, compete, contest, rivalry; **8** marathon, National *UK*, scramble, speedway, struggle; **9** Amerasian, autocross, Caucasian, motocross, roughride; **10** accelerate, Amerindian, Melanesian, Polynesian, rallycross *UK*; **11** Cesarewitch, competition; **12** Australasian, steeplechase; PHRASES: **2, 4** go fast; **2, 5** St Leger *UK*; **3-3-5, 4** egg-and-spoon ~; **3, 4** rat ~; **4, 4** arms ~, boat ~, drag ~, flat ~, sack ~; **5-2-5** point-to-point; **5, 4** mixed ~, motor ~, relay ~, stock ~; **5-6, 4** three-legged ~; **5, 8** Grand National *UK*; **6, 4** master ~; **6, 5** ethnic group; **6, 6** ethnic origin; **8, 4** obstacle ~.

racehorse 4 Arab; **5** Arkle, filly; **6** chaser, maiden, stayer; **12** thoroughbred; PHRASES: **3, 3** Red Rum.

racer 6 runner; **7** athlete, entrant; **8** sprinter; **9** contender; **10** competitor.

racetrack 6 Calder (FL), Laurel (MD); **7** Pimlico (MD); **8** Aqueduct (NY), Saratoga (NY); **9** Keeneland (KY); **11** Thistledown (OH); PHRASES: **3, 3** Del Mar (CA); **4, 4, 4** Lone Star Park (TX); **4, 7** Fair Grounds (LA); **5, 4** Ellis Park (KY); **5, 5** Santa Anita (CA); **6, 4, 6** Golden Gate Fields (CA); **7, 4** Belmont Park (NY), Oaklawn Park (AR), Turfway Park (KY); **8, 4** Monmouth Park (NJ); **9, 4** Arlington Park (IL), Hollywood Park (CA); **9, 5** Churchill Downs (KY); **10, 4** Gulfstream Park (FL).

racism 4 bias; **7** bigotry; **9** apartheid, prejudice, racialism *UK*; **10** xenophobia; **11** intolerance, segregation; **14** discrimination; PHRASES: **5, 9** color prejudice.

racist 6 phobic; **7** bigoted; **9** racialist *UK*; **10** prejudiced, xenophobic; **11** Anglophobic; **12** chauvinistic, Francophobic; **14** discriminatory; PHRASES: **4-7** anti-Semitic; **4-8** anti-American *UK*, anti-Semitism.

rack 3 bin; **4** deck, keep, pack, pain, rock, roof, stow; **5** beset, cloud, drier, dryer, floor, frame, layer, level, shake, shelf, stack, stand, store, story, toast, wreck, wrest, wring; **6** damage, holder, plague, shelve, strain; **7** afflict, agonize, disturb, support, torment, torture; **8** shelving; **9** devastate, framework; **11** scaffolding; PHRASES: **4, 5, 4** play havoc with.

racket 3 bat, con, din, row; **4** ramp, scam; **5** dodge, fraud, noise; **6** clamor, fiddle, fracas, hubbub, tumult, uproar; **9** commotion, shakedown; **11** pandemonium; PHRASES: **3-3** rip-off.

racy *See* **indecent**

RAD 7 radical; **8** radiator.

radar 4 echo, scan; 6 sensor, target; 7 display, locater; 8 detector; 10 radarscope; PHRASES: 5, 4 ~ beam; 5, 5 fixed array, pulse ~; 5, 6 ~ screen; 5, 8 ~ guidance, ~ tracking; 5, 9 ~ astronomy, ~ indicator; 5, 10 ~ navigation; 7, 5 primary ~, weather ~; 8, 5 military ~; 8, 6 locating system, position finder; 9, 5 secondary ~.

radial 7 outward; 8 circular, radiated; 9 outspread; 11 centrifugal.

radiance 3 joy; 4 glow; 5 light; 7 sparkle; 8 vivacity; 9 happiness; 10 brightness, brilliance, luminosity; PHRASES: 4, 2, 5 joie de vivre. *See also* **glow**

radiant 5 happy, sunny; 6 bright; 7 beaming, glowing, healthy, shining; 8 dazzling, luminous; 9 brilliant. *See also* **glowing**

radiate 3 ray; 4 emit; 5 exude, issue, strew; 6 spread; 7 diffuse, diverge, emanate, release, scatter; 8 disperse, eradiate; 9 circulate, discharge, irradiate; PHRASES: 4, 3 give off, give out; 4, 4 brim with, glow with; 5, 4 burst with; 6, 3 branch out, spread out; 7, 4 bristle with; 8, 4 overflow with.

radiating 5 rayed; 6 radial, spoked; 7 radiant, radiate; 8 gleaming.

radiation 3 ray; 4 glow; 5 spoke; 6 energy, radius; 7 fallout; 8 radiance; 9 diffusion, emanation, pollution; 10 dispersion, scattering; 13 contamination, radioactivity.

radiation belt 5, 5 ozone layer.

radiation detector 6, 7 Geiger counter; 8, 7 particle counter.

radiator *See* **heater**

radical 3 RAD, red; 4 amyl, root; 5 amide, basic, ester; 6 innate, methyl, severe; 7 drastic, extreme, leftist, organic; 8 complete, profound, sweeping, thorough; 9 essential, extremist, reformist, socialist; 10 structural; 11 fundamental, progressive; 13 comprehensive, revolutionary, thoroughgoing; PHRASES: 3-8 far-reaching; 4-4 left-wing; 4-6 deep-seated.

radio 2 a.f., AM, FM, LW *UK*, MW, SW; 3 NPR, UHF, VHF; 4 band; 5 bleep, pager, tuner; 6 signal, stereo, tuning; 7 booster, carrier, speaker, trannie *UK*, Walkman *TM*; 8 receiver, sideband, waveband, wireless; 9 amplifier, bandwidth, broadcast, modulator; 10 microwaves, modulation, radiopager, transistor; 11 demodulator, loudspeaker; 12 demodulation; PHRASES: 2, 5 CB ~; 3, 5 car ~; 4, 3 boom box; 4, 4 call sign, long

wave; 4, 7 call letters, cat's whisker, tone control; 5, 3 ~ car, ~ set; 5, 4 ~ beam, ~ link, ~ mast, ~ wave, short wave; 5, 5 clock ~, local ~, ~ tower; 5, 6 ~ signal; 5, 7 ~ channel, ~ station, relay station, World Service; 5, 8 ~ spectrum; 5, 9 ~ frequency, ~ telescope; 5, 10 phase modulation; 6, 4 medium wave, mobile unit; 6, 5 pirate ~; 6-6 walkie-talkie; 6, 7 ghetto blaster; 7, 3 crystal set; 7, 5 battery ~; 7, 7 booster station; 8, 5 portable ~; 8, 6 personal stereo; 9, 5 satellite ~; 10, 5 commercial ~.

radio (radio reception) 3 hum; 4 hiss; 5 drift, noise; 6 fading, static; 8 crawling, creeping; 9 reception; 10 distortion; 12 atmospherics, interference; PHRASES: 5, 4 cross talk; 5, 5 white noise.

radioactivity 5 decay; 6 energy; 7 fallout; 8 activity, emission; 9 radiation, radiology; 11 radiography; 12 radioisotope, radionuclide, radiotherapy; PHRASES: 1-4 X-rays; 4, 4 beta rays, mean life; 4-4 half-life; 4, 5 beta decay; 4, 7 beta emitter; 4, 8 beta particle; 5, 4 alpha rays, gamma rays; 5, 5 alpha decay; 5, 7 alpha emitter; 5, 8 alpha particle, decay constant; 6, 4 cosmic rays; 6, 7 parent nuclide; 8, 4 absorbed dose; 8, 7 daughter nuclide, daughter product.

radium 2 Ra.

radon 2 Rd; 5 niton.

raffia *See* **straw**

raffle 4 draw; 5 award, offer; 6 donate; 7 lottery, present, tombola *UK*; 11 sweepstakes; PHRASES: 4, 4 give away.

raft 5 range; 6 bundle, number; 7 tranche; 9 portfolio.

rag 3 rib; 4 bait, mock, wisp; 5 daily, paper, scrap, shred, taunt, tease; 6 tatter, thread; 7 tabloid; 9 newspaper; PHRASES: 3-3 red-top *UK*; 4, 3, 2 make fun of, poke fun at; 4, 5 call names.

rage 3 fad, ire; 4 boil, burn, fret, fume, fury, lour, rail, rant, rave, snap, stew; 5 anger, chafe, erupt, fight, frown, glare, growl, lower, scowl, smoke, snarl, storm, trend, wrath; 6 frenzy, glower, seethe, simmer, sizzle, temper; 7 bluster, explode, quarrel, rampage, smolder, thunder; 9 fulminate; 11 indignation; PHRASES: 2, 7 go berserk; 3, 3 see red; 3, 3, 4 hit the roof; 4, 2 lose it; 4, 3, 4 rant and rave; 4, 4, 3 blow your top; 4, 4, 5 blow your stack; 4, 7 look daggers; 5, 4 raise Cain, raise hell; 7, 4 breathe fire.

ragged 4 torn; 5 rough, tatty; 6 frayed, jagged, ripped, rugged, shabby, uneven; 8 tattered; 9 irregular; 10 threadbare; 14 tatterdemalion.

raging 6 strong; 7 furious, intense, rampant; 8 powerful.

raid 3 rob; 4 bust, loot; 5 blitz, foray; 6 attack, invade, maraud, razzia, sortie; 7 assault, mission, pillage, plunder; 9 incursion; PHRASES: 3-4 ram-raid *UK*.

rail 3 bar, tie; 4 bird, frog, kick; 5 fence, gauge, rails, track; 6 attack, berate, buffer, metals, object, points, switch; 7 ballast, barrier, condemn, inveigh, protest, railing, roadbed, sleeper, support; 8 banister, complain, denounce, handrail, harangue; 9 criticize, crossover, fishplate, fulminate, turntable; 10 vociferate; PHRASES: 3, 2, 5 end of steel; 4, 2 kick up; 4, 5 fish joint; 5, 5 broad gauge; 5, 6 catch points *UK*; 6, 5 narrow gauge; 8, 5 standard gauge; 9, 3 permanent way *UK*.

railing *See* **fence**

railroad 2 el, RY; 4 line, stop; 5 metro, rails, track; 6 boxcar, dinkey, points, siding, signal, subway, switch, tracks; 7 cutting, handcar, hotshot, roadbed, sleeper, station, tramcar *UK*, tramway, trestle, turnout, whistle; 8 crosstie, elevated, junction, metritis, monorail, platform, terminus, trackage, tramline; 9 sidetrack, streetcar, turntable; 10 embankment, switchback, yardmaster; PHRASES: 3, 2, 3, 4 end of the line; 3, 7 way station; 4, 3 club car, tank car; 4, 4 main line; 4, 5 last spike; 5, 3 cable car; 5, 4 trunk line; 5-7, 6 rapid-transit system (RTS); 5, 8 grade crossing, level crossing *UK*; 6, 3 signal box; 6, 4 branch line, feeder line; 6, 5 signal tower; 7, 3 gondola car; 7, 4 section gang, section hand; 8, 5 standard gauge; 9, 4 emergency cord. *See* **force**

railroad worker 5 guard; 6 porter; 7 fireman; 8 engineer, motorman, trackman; 9 conductor, inspector, lengthman, pointsman, signalman; 10 platelayer, railwayman; 13 stationmaster; PHRASES: 5, 6 gandy dancer; 6, 6 engine driver; 7, 7 station manager *UK*.

railway 2 el; 3 tie; 4 tram, tube *UK*; 5 gauge, route; 6 switch; 7 station, telpher; 8 elevated, railroad; 9 funicular, sidetrack; 11 underground *UK*; PHRASES: 3, 7 cog ~; 4, 7 rack ~ *UK Can*; 5, 7 cable ~ *UK*, horse ~, light ~ *UK*; 5, 8 grade crossing; 6, 5 signal

tower; 6, 7 scenic ~, street ~; 7, 4 ~ line; 8, 7 electric ~, elevated ~, inclined ~ *UK*.

rain 1 R; 4 drum, fall, hail, pelt, pour, smir *UK*, spit, spot, teem; 5 flood, plash, spate; 6 bucket *UK*, deluge, flurry, lavish, mizzle, patter, shadow, shower, stream, volley; 7 barrage, bombard, drizzle, spatter, torrent, trickle; 8 downfall, downpour, plethora, pourdown, rainfall, splatter; 9 overwhelm, raindrops, rainstorm, rainwater; 10 cloudburst; 11 gullywasher, precipitate; 13 precipitation; PHRASES: 4, 4 come down, fine ~, pelt down, piss down *UK*; 4, 4, 3, 4 ~ cats and dogs; 4, 5 ~ check, ~ gauge; 4, 8 frog strangle; 4, 9 toad strangler; 5, 4 light ~; 5, 6 light shower; 5, 7 April showers; 6, 4 bucket down *UK*, Scotch mist; 6, 7 steady drizzle; 7, 4 driving ~; 8, 6 thundery shower; 10, 4 persistent ~, torrential ~.

rainbow 3 arc, bow; 4 arch, iris; 6 fogbow; 8 colorful, spectral, spectrum; 10 variegated; 12 multicolored; 13 kaleidoscopic, polychromatic.

rain gauge 8 udometer *UK*; 11 pluviometer.

rainless 3 hot; 4 fair, fine; 5 sunny; 8 pleasant; 9 cloudless; PHRASES: 3, 4 set fair.

rainy 3 wet; 4 damp; 5 heavy; 7 driving, drizzly, pelting, pluvial, pouring, raining, showery; 8 blinding, drumming; 9 drizzling, inclement, streaming; 10 persistent, torrential; PHRASES: 7, 4 pissing down.

raise 2 up; 3 end; 4 grow, heft, hike, lift, luff, moot, rear; 5 amass, boost, breed, build, cause, erect, exalt, heave, heist, hoick, hoist, lever, mount, nurse, rouse, waken; 6 better, broach, create, elicit, excite, foster, induce, muster, obtain, uphold, uplift; 7 advance, augment, canvass, develop, educate, elevate, enhance, improve, inflate, mention, nurture, payrise, present, procure, produce, provoke, solicit, support, upgrade, upheave, uphoist, upraise, upthrow; 8 conclude, heighten, increase, levitate, shoulder; 9 construct, cultivate, introduce, stimulate, terminate; 11 precipitate; PHRASES: 3, 2 put up, set up; 3, 7 put forward; 4, 2 buoy up, help up, hold up, jack up, lift up, move up, perk up, prop up; 4, 5 look after; 5, 2 bring in, bring up, ~ up, stick up; 6, 2 result in; 6, 8 scrape together.

raising 5 heave, hoist; 6 ascent, upcast, uplift; 7 lifting, rearing, upthrow; 8 erection, upheaval, upthrust; 9 attollent, elevation, upbuoying, uplifting, uprearing; **10** escalation, levitation, uptrending; **11** antigravity, sublevation; PHRASES: **7, 2** picking up.

rake 3 rip; **4** comb, lech, roué, scan; **5** scour, sweep; **6** gather, lecher, strafe; **7** collect, scratch; **8** Casanova, enfilade, Lothario; **9** libertine, reprobate, womanizer; **10** ladykiller, profligate; **11** philanderer; PHRASES: **3, 4** Don Juan.

rakish 6 breezy, dapper, jaunty, louche; **7** dashing, raffish, stylish; **8** debonair; **9** dissolute; **10** profligate.

rally 3 run; **4** demo; **5** march, tease, unite; **6** banter, caucus, gather, revive; **7** collect, improve, meeting, protest, recover, regroup, reunite, revival, support; **8** assemble, assembly, comeback, recovery; **9** encourage, gathering, motocross, reconvene; **10** convention, reassemble, recuperate, resurgence; **11** improvement; **13** demonstration; **14** revitalization; PHRASES: **3-2** sit-in; **3, 6** get better; **4, 1, 8** make a comeback; **4, 2** perk up, pick up; **4, 6** join forces; **4, 7** mass meeting, pull through; **4, 8** call together, come together; **5, 4** motor race; **5-5** Paris-Dakar; **5, 8** bring together; **7, 7** protest meeting.

ram 3 bat, cue, hit, jam; **4** bump, cram, pack, peen, push, slam, tamp; **5** force, pound, punch, stuff; **6** hammer, mallet, monkey, pusher, rammer, ramrod, shover, sledge, strike, tamper, tapper; **7** knocker, puncher; **8** compress; **9** bulldozer; **10** hammerhead; **11** hammerstone; **12** sledgehammer; PHRASES: **4, 6** pile driver; **4, 7** door knocker; **5, 4** crash into; **6, 5** hockey stick; **6, 6** tennis racket; **6-6** carpet-beater; **7, 4** collide with, tamping iron; **8, 3** baseball bat, billiard cue, rounders bat; **9, 3** battering ~.

ramble 4 hike, roam, trek, walk; **5** amble, drift; **6** stroll, wander; **7** blather, blether UK, digress, saunter, traipse; **11** perambulate; PHRASES: **2, 2** go on; **2, 3, 1, 4** go for a walk; **2, 3, 2, 1, 7** go off at a tangent; **6, 2** rabbit on UK, ~ on, rattle on, witter on UK.

rambler 4 rose; **5** hiker, rover; **7** drifter; **8** traveler, vagabond, wanderer.

rambling 5 wordy; **6** prolix, shaggy; **7** tedious; **8** confused, trailing; **9** sprawling; **10** digressive, discursive, incoherent, straggling; **15** inconsequential; PHRASES: **4-6** long-winded; **6, 3** spread out.

ramp 4 bump, hump, rise; **5** grade, ridge,

slope; **7** incline, upgrade; **8** gradient; PHRASES: **5, 4** speed bump; **6, 5** rumble strip.

rampage *See* **riot**

rampart 4 wall; **6** vallum; **7** bastion, parapet; **9** earthwork; **10** breastwork; **13** fortification.

ramshackle 7 rickety, ruinous, unsound; **8** derelict, unstable; **9** makeshift; **10** tumbledown; **11** dilapidated; PHRASES: **3-4** rundown.

ranch *See* **farm**

rancour *See* **acrimony**

random 4 iffy; **5** dicey, fluky, risky; **6** casual, chance, chancy; **9** aleatoric, arbitrary, haphazard, noncausal, uncertain, unplanned; **10** accidental, contingent, fortuitous, incidental, stochastic, unexpected, unforeseen; **12** adventitious, coincidental, incalculable, unsystematic; **13** epiphenomenal, serendipitous, unforeseeable, unintentional, unpredictable; **14** indeterminable, indiscriminate; PHRASES: **3-2-4** hit-or-miss; **3, 3, 4** hit and miss; **4-2-4** sink-or-swim; **5-2-5-3** catch-as-catch-can.

range 2 go; **3** Aga *TM*, run; **4** area, band, kind, sort, span; **5** array, chain, field, gamut, grasp, limit, reach, ridge, scale, scope, stove, sweep; **6** bounds, choice, extend, extent, radius, series, sphere; **7** breadth, compass, stretch, variety; **8** coverage, spectrum; **9** alternate, fluctuate, oscillate, selection, vacillate; **10** assortment, collection, cordillera. *See also* **mountain range**

ranging 9 traveling; **10** unconfined, unfettered, untethered; **12** maneuverable; PHRASES: **4-5** free-range; **6, 4, 4** having full play; **7, 6** ~ freely.

rank 3 bad; **4** bald, foul, rate, sort, type; **5** caste, class, fetid, grade, level, order, place, sheer, title, total, utter, value; **6** coarse, estate, fecund, foetid, putrid, rancid, smelly, sphere, status; **7** arrange, blatant, echelon, footing, grading, pungent, rampant, ranking, reeking, station; **8** absolute, abundant, category, classify, complete, organize, position, standing, stinking, vigorous; **9** authority, downright, exuberant, hierarchy, luxuriant, overgrown; **10** categorize, leadership, precedence; **11** flourishing, generalship, unmitigated; **12** circumstance, overabundant; PHRASES: **5, 9** power structure; **6, 4** social ~; **8, 4** military ~. *See also* **military rank**

ranked 5 rated; 7 classed, leading, ordered; 9 preceding; 10 classified, hierarchic; 12 hierarchical; 13 authoritative; 14 ecclesiastical; PHRASES: 5, 6 given status.

rankle 3 irk; 4 gnaw; 6 fester; 8 irritate; PHRASES: 3, 2 eat up.

ransack 3 rob; 4 loot, sack; 5 rifle; 6 search; 7 pillage, plunder, rummage.

ransom 3 sum; 5 money; 6 redeem; 7 payment; PHRASES: 3, 2 pay up; 3, 4 buy back, set free; 6, 1, 4 strike a deal.

rant 3 gag, jaw, pun; 4 blah, fume, gush, joke, quip, rage, rave; 5 drool, prate, shout, spiel, spout, vapor; 6 babble, drivel, gabble, garble, gibber, jabber, seethe, tirade, waffle, yammer; 7 blarney, blather, bluster, bombast, flatter, prattle, romance, thunder, twaddle; 8 harangue, outburst; 9 fulminate, sermonize; 10 rhapsodize; 11 histrionics; PHRASES: 2, 2 go on; 5, 5 crack jokes; 7-3 yackety-yak.

rap 3 hit, tap; 4 blow; 5 crack, knock, smack; 6 rebuke, strike, thwack; 8 reproach; 9 criticism, reprimand; PHRASES: 6-7 tongue-lashing.

rapacious 4 avid; 6 greedy; 7 harmful, vicious; 8 grasping; 9 dangerous, voracious; 10 aggressive, avaricious; 11 destructive.

rape 5 abuse, force; 6 ravish; 7 outrage, violate; PHRASES: 3-4, 4 oil-seed ~; 9, 4 interfere with.

rapid 4 deft, fast, spry; 5 agile, alert, brief, fleet, hasty, nifty, nippy UK, quick, short, smart, swift; 6 abrupt, adroit, lively, nimble, presto, prompt, snappy, speedy, sudden; 7 cursory, hurried, instant, passing; 8 fleeting, meteoric; 9 immediate, momentary, sprightly, transient.

rapid motion 5 speed; 8 rapidity, velocity.

rapport See **relationship**

rapt 5 happy; 6 joyful; 7 content, gripped; 8 absorbed, blissful; 9 delighted, engrossed; 10 captivated, fascinated.

rare 3 few, odd; 4 thin; 6 bloody, scarce, superb, unique; 7 curious, unusual; 8 precious, singular, sporadic, superior, uncommon, uncooked; 9 scattered, underdone; 10 infrequent, occasional; 11 exceptional, outstanding; 12 intermittent; PHRASES: 3-3 one-off UK.

rare earth 10 lanthanide.

rarefied 3 cut; 4 weak; 6 dilute; 7 complex, diluted, obscure, refined, thinned, watered; 8 abstruse, dilatant, dilating, dilative, esoteric, expanded, extended, highbrow, thinning; 9 attenuate, dilatable, exclusive, expanding, expansive, extending, extensive, recondite; 10 attenuated; 11 adulterated; 12 dilatational, etherealized; 13 rarefactional; PHRASES: 7-3 thinned-out; 7-4 watered-down.

rarely 6 hardly, seldom; PHRASES: 3, 5 not often; 4, 2, 1, 4, 4 once in a blue moon; 4, 2, 1, 8 once in a lifetime; 6, 2, 4 seldom if ever; 6, 4 hardly ever. See also **rare**

rarity 3 gem; 4 find; 6 oddity; 7 paucity; 8 rareness, scarcity, shortage; 9 curiosity; 11 infrequency, singularity; 13 intermittence; 14 sporadicalness; PHRASES: 3-3 one-off UK; 7, 6 unusual object; 10, 4 collector's item. See also **rare**

rascal 3 imp; 4 limb; 5 devil, rogue, scamp; 6 monkey, pickle, wretch; 8 scalawag UK; 9 scallywag.

rash 4 bold, wave, wild; 5 brash, flood, flush, hasty, hives, spate, spots; 6 daring, madcap, series, string, sudden, unwary; 7 foolish, pimples; 8 careless, epidemic, eruption, flippant, headlong, heedless, outbreak, reaction, reckless, slapdash; 9 audacious, breakneck, daredevil, desperate, foolhardy, frivolous, hotheaded, impatient, impetuous, imprudent, impulsive, itchiness, negligent, overhasty; 10 capricious, incautious, indiscreet, irritation, regardless; 11 adventurous, harebrained, improvident, inattentive, injudicious, overzealous, precipitant, precipitate, precipitous, thoughtless; 12 inflammation; 13 inconsiderate, irresponsible, overambitious, overconfident, uncircumspect; PHRASES: 2-2-3 do-or-die; 3-3-4 hit-and-miss; 3-7 ill-advised; 3-10 ill-considered; 4, 2 gung ho; 4, 4 heat ~; 5-2-5 happy-go-lucky; 5-3-4 devil-may-care; 5-7 death-defying; 6, 3, 2 asking for it; 6, 4 diaper ~; 6-6 danger-loving; 7-4-4 couldn't-care-less; 7-5 trigger-happy.

rash (be rash) 6 gamble; PHRASES: 3, 3, 2 ask for it; 3, 3, 7 ask for trouble; 4, 3, 3 bell the cat; 4, 3, 5 ride the tiger; 4, 4 rush into; 4, 4, 4 play with fire; 4, 4, 5 drop one's guard; 4, 5 take risks; 5, 6 court danger; 5, 10 tempt providence; 6, 4, 3 chance one's arm.

rash move 4 risk; 6 gamble; PHRASES: 4, 2, 3, 4 leap in the dark; 8, 4 needless risk; 9,

4 dangerous game.

rashness 5 folly, haste; **6** daring, levity; **8** audacity, temerity; **9** flippancy, frivolity, overhaste; **10** impatience, imprudence, negligence; **11** daredevilry, desperation, impetuosity, inattention, presumption; **12** brinkmanship, excitability, improvidence, indiscretion, precipitance, precipitancy; **14** overconfidence, overenthusiasm; **15** inconsideration; PHRASES: **4, 2, 7** lack of caution; **7, 4, 4** playing with fire. *See also* **rash**

rash person 6 madcap; **7** gambler, hothead; **8** brinkman, hooligan; **9** daredevil, desperado, eccentric; **10** adventurer; PHRASES: **4, 3** wild boy.

rasp 3 rub; **4** bark; **5** chafe, grate, grind, growl; **6** scrape; **7** grating, rubbing; **8** grinding, scraping. *See also* **tool**

rate 3 fee; **4** cost, pace, rank, toll; **5** assay, grade, level, price, ratio, scale, speed, tempo, value; **6** amount, assess, charge, degree, esteem, figure, regard, tariff; **7** measure, valuate; **8** appraise, evaluate, quotient, velocity; **9** frequency; **10** percentage, proportion; PHRASES: **4, 4** bank ~, base ~, poor ~ *UK*; **5, 4** basic ~, birth ~, death ~, piece ~, prime ~; **8, 4** exchange ~, mortgage ~; **9, 4** mortality ~.

ratel 6 badger; PHRASES: **5, 6** honey badger.

rather 4 very; **5** quite *UK*; **6** pretty, sooner; **7** instead; **8** slightly *UK*, somewhat; **9** extremely; **10** noticeably, preferably; **12** considerably; **13** significantly; PHRASES: **2, 10** by preference.

ratify 4 back, sign; **7** approve, confirm, consent, endorse, initial; **8** inscribe, sanction; **9** authorize, autograph, undersign; **11** countersign; PHRASES: **2, 6** be behind.

rating 4 hand; **5** grade, score; **7** ranking; **10** assessment, evaluation.

ratio 4 part; **5** share; **7** decimal, percent; **8** fraction, quotient, relation; **9** numerator; **10** percentage, proportion; **11** denominator; **12** relationship; PHRASES: **6, 8** common fraction, proper fraction, simple fraction, vulgar fraction; **7, 8** decimal fraction; **8, 6** relative amount.

ration 5 limit, quota, share; **7** control, portion; **8** regulate, restrict; **9** allotment, allowance; PHRASES: **1, 6** C ~; **4, 6** iron ~.

rational 4 fair, sane, wise; **5** lucid, sound; **6** cogent, normal, stable, steady; **7** logical; **8** analytic, balanced, coherent, reasoned, sensible, unbiased; **9** deductive, impartial, inductive, judicious, objective, plausible, practical, pragmatic, realistic; **10** analytical *UK*, reasonable; **11** inferential, intelligent, justifiable; **12** intelligible, unprejudiced; **13** philosophical, ratiocinative, rationalistic; **14** commonsensical, discriminating; PHRASES: **2-8** no-nonsense; **4-2-5** down-to-earth; **4-7-3** well-thought-out; **4-8** well-balanced, well-reasoned; **5-6** clear-headed, level-headed; **6-2-4** matter-of-fact; **7, 4** without bias.

rationale 5 basis; **9** reasoning; **10** foundation, motivation; **13** justification.

rationality 4 wits; **5** logic; **6** reason, wisdom; **8** judgment, lucidity; **9** coherence; **10** equanimity, shrewdness; **12** intelligence; **15** intelligibility; PHRASES: **4, 5** good sense; **6, 5** common sense. *See also* **rational**

rationalize 4 read, show, tune; **5** grasp, infer, level, solve; **6** adjust, answer, deduce, define, excuse, fathom, follow, reason, reduce, reform, unfold; **7** clarify, compute, enhance, explain, expound, improve, justify, realize, resolve, unravel; **8** construe, downsize, evaluate, logicize, organize; **9** apprehend, calculate, economize, elucidate, exemplify, explicate, interpret, syllogize, vindicate; **10** comprehend, illuminate, illustrate, logicalize, streamline, understand, unscramble; **11** demonstrate, restructure, systematize; **12** philosophize; **15** intellectualize; PHRASES: **4, 2, 4** take it that, take to mean; **4, 3** work out; **4, 4** slim down; **4, 5** make clear; **4, 7** make excuses; **5, 2** clear up; **5, 3** spell out, think out; **5, 4** scale down; **5, 7** think through; **6, 3** figure out; **7, 3** account for; **10, 3** straighten out.

rattle 4 bang, chug, faze; **5** clack, crash, knock, shake, shock, throw; **6** babble, jangle, racket; **7** chatter, clatter, disturb, fluster, maracas, perturb, sputter, ticking, unnerve; **8** clicking, knocking, unsettle; **9** castanets, commotion; **10** disconcert; PHRASES: **3, 2** rev up; **3, 3** put off; **7-7** clitter-clatter.

rattling 4 fast; **5** brisk, pacey *UK*; **6** lively, speedy; **7** ticking; **8** clicking, knocking; **10** chattering, clattering, sputtering; PHRASES: **4-6** fast-moving; **5-4** quick-fire *UK Can*, rapid-fire.

ratty 5 messy, seedy, tatty; **6** crabby, shabby; **7** unkempt; **9** irascible, irritable; PHRASES: **3-8** bad-tempered; **5-8** short-tempered.

ravage *See* **devastate**

rave **4** bash, fume, rage, rant; **5** event, party; **6** praise; **7** enthuse, revelry; **9** festivity, fulminate; PHRASES: **2, 2, 5** go on about; **4, 5** hold forth.

ravel *See* **tangle**

raven **4** bolt, gulp, wolf; **5** ravin, scoff; **6** corbie *UK*, gobble; PHRASES: **4, 4** gulp down, wolf down; **6, 2** gobble up.

ravine *See* **valley**

ravish **7** delight; **8** overcome; **9** overpower, overwhelm, transport.

raw **3** icy, new, red; **4** blue, cold, pink, rare, rude, sore; **5** angry, basic, bleak, crude, fresh, green, harsh, naive, vivid; **6** bitter, bloody, brutal, callow, chilly, coarse, direct, gauche, grazed, primal, simple, tender, unripe; **7** artless, awkward, intense, natural, painful, untried; **8** bleeding, freezing, gullible, immature, inexpert, inflamed, innocent, uncooked, untested, visceral; **9** atavistic, authentic, credulous, inclement, ingenuous, perishing *UK*, primitive, sensitive, underdone, unrefined, unskilled, untrained, untreated; **10** unseasoned; **11** unprocessed; **13** inexperienced; **15** unsophisticated; PHRASES: **2-5-6** no-holds-barred; **3-9** gut-wrenching.

raw material **3** ore; **4** clay, marl, slip; **5** adobe, argil, flint; **6** engobe, gypsum, kaolin, silica; **8** feldspar, petuntse; **9** pegmatite; PHRASES: **3, 4** fat clay; **4, 3** bone ash; **4, 4** ball clay, lean clay, pipe clay; **5, 4** china clay; **5, 5** china stone *UK*; **5, 7** flint pebbles; **7, 4** potter's clay, primary clay; **7, 5** Cornish stone, potter's earth; **9, 4** porcelain clay *UK*, secondary clay; **10, 4** calcareous clay, refractory clay.

ray **2** re; **3** bar; **4** beam, beta; **5** gleam, light, manta, shaft, skate; **6** streak; **7** sunbeam; PHRASES: **5, 3** alpha ~, gamma ~; **7, 3** cathode ~; **8, 3** electric ~.

raze *See* **destroy**

RB **8** rubidium.

RC **3, 5** Red Cross; **5, 8** Roman Catholic; **7, 5** Reserve Corps.

RD **4** road; PHRASES: **5, 8** Royal Dragoons.

RE **5** about, again; **10** concerning.

reach **2** go; **3** get, hit, run; **4** find, grab, make, move, span, sway; **5** carry, catch, fetch, grasp, lunge, orbit, range, scope, touch; **6** access, affect, arrive, attain, extend, extent, fumble, spread; **7** achieve, contact, stretch; **8** discover, outreach; **9** influence; **10** accomplish, outstretch; **11** communicate; PHRASES: **3, 1, 7, 2** get a message to; **3, 2, 5, 4** get in touch with; **3, 4** hit upon; **3, 4, 2** get hold of; **3, 5** get there; **3, 7, 2** get through to; **4, 2** come to, lead to, make it; **4, 2, 4** come to rest; **4, 7, 4** make contact with; **5, 2** speak to; **5, 4** light upon, pitch upon; **6, 2** impact on; **6, 3, 4** breast the tape, finish the race; **6, 4** strike upon; **7, 4** connect with.

reach (out of reach) **8** secluded; **9** forbidden; **11** unreachable; PHRASES: **3-2-6** out-of-bounds; **3, 3** cut off; **3, 4** far away.

react **4** echo; **5** alter, reply; **6** answer, change, rebuff, recoil, rejoin, retort, return, shrink; **7** counter, grimace, respond, shudder; **8** catalyze, converse, exchange; **11** interchange, interlocute, reverberate; **12** recalcitrate; PHRASES: **4, 4** kick back; **6, 4** bounce back.

reaction **4** echo; **5** reply; **6** answer, rebuff, recoil, reflex, reflux, return; **8** antiphon, backlash, blowback, comeback, feedback, kickback, response; **9** reception; **10** antithesis, bounceback, responsory; **11** antistrophe, retroaction; **12** repercussion; **13** reverberation; **14** recalcitration.

reactionary **4** scab; **5** bigot; **7** bigoted, diehard; **8** blackleg, dinosaur, medieval, outdated; **9** extremist, illiberal; **10** intolerant, monarchist *UK*, nonstriker; **11** prehistoric, unreceptive; **12** conservative, intransigent, unreasonable; **14** traditionalist; **20** counterrevolutionary; PHRASES: **3-9** old-fashioned; **5-4** right-wing; **5-6** right-winger; **5, 7** White Russian; **6-7** strikebreaker; **8-7** backward-looking.

read **3** con; **4** scan, show; **5** study; **6** browse, decode, devour, peruse, record; **7** examine; **8** construe, decipher, indicate, register; **9** interpret; **10** scrutinize; PHRASES: **4, 4** pore over.

readiness **4** ease; **5** skill; **8** alacrity; **10** enthusiasm; **11** inclination; PHRASES: **6, 8** battle stations. *See also* **ready**

readjust **6** modify, settle; **7** realign, rectify; **9** calibrate, rearrange; **11** accommodate.

ready **3** apt, set; **4** cash, game, glad, keen; **5** acute, brass, dough, eager, equip, money, prime, prone, quick, swift; **6** astute, prompt, speedy, timely; **7** arrange, prepare, willing; **8** arranged, complete, disposed, equipped, flexible, inclined, organize, prepared, punctual; **9** attentive, immediate, organized; **10** alacritous, discerning, perceptive; **11** expeditious; PHRASES: **2, 3, 5, 2** on the brink of, on the point of, on the verge of; **3, 3** all set, fit out, lay out; **4, 5** just about; **4-5** wide-awake; **4, 5, 3** make plans for; **5, 2** about to, close to; **6, 2** geared up, liable to, likely to; **6, 2, 2** raring to go; **8, 2** standing by.

ready-made 7 instant; **9** precooked, processed; **11** convenience, predigested; **13** prefabricated; PHRASES: **3-3-4** off-the-rack; **3-3-5** cut-and-dried; **4-5** oven-ready *UK*; **5, 2, 3** ready to use; **5-2-4** ready-to-cook, ready-to-wear; **5-2-5** ready-to-serve; **5-5** ready-mixed; **5-6** ready-formed; **5-9** ready-furnished.

real 4 true; **5** frank, known, solid, valid; **6** actual, honest; **7** factual, genuine, sincere; **8** concrete, existent, existing, material, original, physical, positive, provable, tangible, truthful; **9** authentic, corporeal, empirical, heartfelt, occurring, unfeigned, veritable; **10** historical, phenomenal, unaffected, undeniable; **11** entelechial, substantial, substantive; **12** indisputable; **14** unquestionable; PHRASES: **2, 5** de facto; **3, 4** for ~; **4, 3** ~ ale *UK*; **4, 4** bona fide, ~ life; **4-5** well-known; **4, 6** ~ estate, ~ number, ~ tennis; **6-2-3** honest-to-God.

real (be real) 5 exist, occur; **6** happen; PHRASES: **4, 5** loom large.

real (make real) 5 reify; **7** realize; **9** actualize, visualize; **10** factualize; **11** materialize.

realisable 6 doable, likely, viable; **8** feasible, possible, probable; **9** plausible, reachable, realistic; **10** achievable, attainable; **11** practicable.

realism 6 sanity; **8** saneness; **10** naturalism, pragmatism; **11** documentary, naturalness; **12** authenticity, practicality; **13** veraciousness; **14** verisimilitude; PHRASES: **4, 2, 5** ring of truth; **4, 2, 7** look of reality; **4, 4** real life, true look; **4, 5** true sound; **5, 2, 4** slice of life; **5-10** level-headedness; **6, 5** common sense; **6, 6** cinema vérité.

realist 4 doer; **5** stoic; **7** radical; **8** humanist; **12** experimenter.

realistic 4 true; **7** eidetic, genuine, graphic, natural; **8** accurate, credible, faithful, lifelike, rational, sensible, truthful; **9** authentic, practical, pragmatic; **10** convincing, expressive, reasonable; **11** picturesque;

12 naturalistic, photographic; **14** representative; **15** impressionistic; PHRASES: **2-8** nononsense; **4-2-4** true-to-life; **4-2-5** down-to-earth; **4-4** real-life; **5-6** level-headed; **6-2-4** matter-of-fact.

reality 4 fact, life; **5** thing, truth; **6** basics, crunch, matter; **7** realism; **8** presence, solidity, validity, veracity; **9** actuality, certainty, entelechy, existence, facticity, necessity, substance; **10** experience, factuality, occurrence; **11** genuineness, historicity, materiality, tangibility; **12** authenticity, corporeality, fundamentals, practicality; **13** substantivity; **14** substantiality; PHRASES: **3, 4, 3, 3** the here and now; **3, 4, 5** the real world; **3, 8** the everyday; **4, 6** home truths; **6, 2, 4** matter of fact; **6, 2, 4, 3** things as they are.

realize 2 do; **3** get, see; **5** grasp, infer, reach; **6** attain, deduce, fathom, gather, intuit, invent; **7** achieve, execute, fulfill, premise, suppose, surmise; **8** complete, conclude, perceive, remember, theorize; **9** apprehend, originate, recognize, speculate; **10** accomplish, appreciate, comprehend, conjecture, consummate, understand; **11** hypothesize, PHRASES: **3, 3** hit one; **4, 2** take in; **4, 6** make happen; **5, 2, 8** bring to fruition; **5, 3** carry out; **6, 3** strike one; **6, 9** become conscious.

really 4 very; **5** truly; **6** indeed, surely; **8** actually; **9** basically, certainly, genuinely, sincerely; **10** especially, inherently, manifestly, positively, thoroughly, truthfully; **11** essentially, exceedingly, necessarily; **12** demonstrably; **13** categorically, existentially, fundamentally; PHRASES: **2, 1, 6, 2, 4** as a matter of fact; **2, 2, 7** as it happens; **2, 3, 10** in all likelihood; **2, 4** in fact; **2, 5** de facto, in truth; **2, 5, 2, 4** if truth be told, in point of fact; **2, 6** in effect; **2, 6, 4** in actual fact; **2, 7** in reality; **2, 8** in practice; **2, 9** in actuality; **4, 5** ipso facto.

realm 4 area, land; **5** range, scope; **6** domain, empire, sphere; **7** kingdom; **8** dominion, monarchy.

ream *See* **quantity**

reap 4 earn, gain, pick; **6** garner, gather, obtain, secure; **7** acquire, collect, harvest.

reappear 5 recur; **6** repeat, return; **9** resurface; PHRASES: **2-6** re-emerge *UK*; **4, 4** come back; **4, 5** come again.

reappearance 6 repeat, return; **7** reissue, revival; **8** comeback; **10** recurrence, repetition; **11** reemergence; **12** resurrection; **13** reincarnation, republication; PHRASES: **4, 2** déjà vu; **6, 6** second coming; **6, 7** second showing.

rear 3 aft, ass, bum *UK*, end; **4** anal, anus, back, butt, coda, heel, hind, last, rump, tail, tend, tush, wake; **5** after, fanny, lower, raise, stern, trail, train, upend, verso; **6** behind, bottom, caudal, cheeks, dorsal, latter, lumbar, mizzen, sitter, suffix, uprise; **7** educate, hunkers, keister, nurture, pigtail, postern; **8** appendix, backside, backward, buttocks, colophon, derriere, endpiece, epilogue, haunches, hindmost, rearward; **9** aftermost, afterpart, afterword, backstage, continued, cultivate, fundament, posterior, sternmost, tailpiece; **10** afterpiece, background, hindmost, hinterland, mizzenmast, postscript, supplement; **12** afterthought, continuation, hindquarters, supplemental; **13** afterquarters; PHRASES: **2, 3, 3** at the end; **2, 3, 10** in the background; **3-4** sit-upon; **3, 6** end matter; **4, 3** back end, care for, tail end; **4, 4** back door, poop deck, ~ mast; **4, 4, 2** take care of; **4, 5** look after; **4, 6** back matter; **4, 7** back passage *UK*; **5, 2** bring up; **5, 4** lower back, watch over; **5-5** rusty-dusty; **6, 3, 6** behind the scenes; **6, 6** lumbar region.

rear (be in the rear) 5 trail; **6** follow; PHRASES: **2, 4** be last; **2, 6** be behind; **3, 5** tag along; **3, 6** lag behind; **4, 6** drop behind; **5, 2, 3, 4** bring up the rear; **6, 2, 3, 4** follow in the wake.

rearrange 4 move; **5** delay; **6** adjust, change; **7** adjourn, realign, regroup, reorder; **8** postpone, readjust, relocate, simplify; **9** reshuffle; **10** reorganize, reschedule, streamline; **11** restructure; PHRASES: **3, 3** put off; **4, 6** move around; **5, 2** shake up; **6, 3, 4** change the date.

rearrangement 6 change; **7** anagram; **8** movement; **10** reposition; **11** transferral *UK*.

reason 3 aim, end, key, wit; **4** goal, idea, mind, wits; **5** argue, basis, cause, infer, judge, logic, sense, solve, think; **6** answer, brains, debate, deduce, excuse, ground, induce, motive, object, sanity, senses, wisdom; **7** analyze, discuss, dispute, grounds, pretext, purpose, thought; **8** conclude, judgment, occasion, perceive, persuade, saneness; **9** faculties, influence, intellect, intention, judgement, rationale; **10** general-ize, logicalize, motivation, perception, synthesize, understand; **11** explanation, opportunity, ratiocinate, rationality, rationalize; **12** intelligence; **13** comprehension, justification, understanding; PHRASES: **3, 3** the why; **4, 3** work out; **4, 4** talk over; **4, 7** talk through; **5, 2, 6** power of ~; **5, 4** right mind; **5, 4, 4** apply your mind; **6, 3** figure out; **6, 5** raison d'être.

reasonable 4 fair, sane, wise; **5** cheap, sound; **7** logical; **8** moderate, passable, rational, sensible; **9** equitable, judicious, practical, realistic, tolerable; **10** acceptable, affordable, economical, evenhanded, sufficient; **11** housebroken, inexpensive, intelligent; **12** satisfactory; PHRASES: **3, 3** not bad; **3, 5** all right; **4, 6** good enough; **5, 4** quite good; **5-6** level-headed.

reasonably 5 quite; **6** rather; **8** somewhat; **10** relatively; PHRASES: **2, 3, 2, 8** as far as possible; **4, 6** well enough; **6, 6** within bounds. *See also* **reasonable**

reasoner 7 thinker; **8** academic, logician; **9** apologist, syllogist; **11** philosopher, rationalist; **12** dialectician, intellectual.

reasoning 4 sane, wise; **5** logic, rigor, truth; **7** logical, premise, thought; **8** analysis, argument, converse, rational, sensible, thinking; **9** deduction, induction, inference, rationale, reckoning, syllogism; **10** conclusion, perceptive; **11** calculation, intelligent, rationalism, rationality; **12** intellectual, verification; **13** knowledgeable, philosophical, ratiocination, rationalizing, understanding; **14** interpretation; **15** rationalization; PHRASES: **1, 6** a priori; **1, 10** a posteriori.

reassemble 4 mend; **6** rejoin, repair; **7** collect, rebuild, restore, reunite; **9** reconvene; **10** congregate; **11** reconstruct; PHRASES: **3, 4, 8** get back together, put back together; **4, 5** meet again.

rebel 3 Red; **4** Cade, defy; **5** fight, pinko; **6** commie, Contra, leftie, mutiny, oppose, resist, revolt; **7** agitate, dissent, heretic, protest, radical, seceder; **8** agitator, campaign, maverick, mutineer, objector, renegade, revolter; **9** dissenter, dissident, insurgent, protester; **10** Bolshevist, campaigner, iconoclast, Trotskyist; **12** secessionist; **13** nonconformist, revolutionary, revolutionist; **15** insurrectionist; PHRASES: **4, 2** rise up, take on; **4, 2, 4** take up arms; **4-7** sans-culotte; **7, 7** freedom fighter.

rebellion 6 mutiny, revolt, rising; **8** sedition, upheaval, uprising; **9** agitation, terrorism; **10** insurgence, revolution; **12** insurrection; **13** nonconformity; **15** insubordination.

rebellious **5** armed; **6** unruly; **7** defiant; **8** contrary, disloyal, militant, mutinous, stubborn; **9** fractious, seditious; **10** refractory; **11** disobedient, treacherous; **12** iconoclastic, recalcitrant, unmanageable; **13** insubordinate, nonconformist, revolutionary; **14** uncontrollable.

rebirth **6** return; **7** renewal, revival; **10** renascence, resurgence, revolution; **11** reawakening, reformation, renaissance, restoration; **12** regeneration, rejuvenation; **14** revitalization; PHRASES: **2-9** re-education *UK*; **3, 9** new beginning.

rebound **5** rally; **6** recoil; **7** recover; **8** ricochet; PHRASES: **6, 4** bounce back, spring back.

rebuff **4** snub; **6** denial, refuse, reject, slight; **7** refusal, repulse; **9** rejection.

rebuild, rebuilt *See* **reform**

rebuke **5** chide, scold; **6** rebuff, retort; **7** censure, lecture, reproof, reprove; **8** admonish, reproach, scolding; **9** criticism, criticize, reprimand; **10** admonition; PHRASES: **4, 1, 7-2** give a talking-to *UK*; **4, 2, 3, 5** slap on the wrist; **4, 2, 4** take to task; **4, 3** tell off; **4, 4** call down; **7-3** telling-off *UK*; **8, 5** crushing reply.

rebut **4** defy, deny; **5** belie, cross, demur, doubt; **6** appeal, impugn, object, refute, rejoin, retort; **7** confute, contest, counter, dissent, gainsay, protest, reverse; **8** contrary, disagree, disprove, obstruct, opposite, question; **9** challenge, deprecate, disaffirm; **10** contradict, contravene, controvert, invalidate; PHRASES: **4, 5, 4** take issue with; **5, 2, 2** stand up to; **6, 8** refuse credence; **7, 6** express doubts.

rebuttal **6** appeal, denial, retort; **7** counter; **8** crossing, defiance, demurral, disproof, negation; **9** challenge, objection, rejoinder, retortion; **10** antithesis, contesting, countering, disproving, gainsaying, refutation; **11** confutation, deprecation, impugnation, obstruction, questioning; **12** contrariness, disagreement, doubtfulness; **13** contradiction, contravention; **14** disaffirmation; PHRASES: **4, 6** flat denial; **5-6** crossappeal; **8, 6** emphatic denial.

recall **5** evoke; **6** cancel, remind, repeal,

revoke; **7** rescind; **8** abrogate, callback, remember; **9** recollect, reminisce; **11** countermand; PHRASES: **4, 4** take back; **7, 2** conjure up.

recant **4** deny, turn; **5** crawl, unsay; **6** abjure, cringe, negate, recall, refute, renege, repent, revoke; **7** convert, disavow, rescind, retract; **8** abrogate, disclaim, forswear, renounce, withdraw; **9** apologize, backpedal, repudiate; **10** apostasize; PHRASES: **2, 4, 2** go back on; **3, 4** eat crow; **3, 4, 3** eat one's hat; **3, 4, 5** eat one's words; **3, 6, 3** eat humble pie; **4, 4** back down, take back; **5, 3** swear off; **6, 4, 5** recall one's words.

recantation **6** denial, recall; **7** apology; **8** apostasy, negation, revoking; **9** disavowal; **10** abjuration, abrogation, disclaimer, retraction, revocation, withdrawal; **11** forswearing, repudiation; **12** renunciation, retractation; PHRASES: **6, 3** humble pie; **6, 4** eating crow; **6, 4, 5** eating one's words.

recap **6** review; **7** outline, summary; **9** summarize; **11** restatement; PHRASES: **2, 4** go over; **3, 2** sum up; **3, 7** run through; **7, 2** summing up.

recapture **5** evoke; **6** recall, regain, retake; **7** reclaim; **9** recollect, repossess; PHRASES: **4, 4** take back; **6, 2** summon up.

recede **3** ebb; **4** fade, wane; **5** lapse; **7** decline, regress, relapse, retract, retreat; **8** withdraw; **9** disappear.

receipt **4** bill, chit *UK*, note, slip, stub; **7** voucher; **8** delivery; **9** receiving, reception, unloading; **10** acceptance; **11** counterfoil; **15** acknowledgement; PHRASES: **5, 2, 8** proof of purchase.

receive **3** get, net; **4** earn, gain, have, hear, host, meet, take; **5** admit, catch, clear, fence, grasp, greet, gross, sense; **6** accept, accrue, credit, gather, obtain, pocket, secure; **7** acquire, baptize, collect, confirm, convert, inherit, welcome; **8** christen; **9** entertain; **11** acknowledge; PHRASES: **4, 2** come by, pick up, take in, take up; **4, 2, 3** come in for; **4, 2, 4, 5** fall to one's share; **4, 4** come into, take home, take over; **4, 4, 5, 2** open one's doors to; **4, 5** have round *UK*; **4, 7** make welcome; **4, 8, 2** take delivery of; **5, 2** bring in, usher in; **6, 2** accede to; **7, 2** succeed to; **7, 2, 4** advance to meet.

receive (something received) **3** pay; **4** gift, perk; **5** bonus, prize, token; **6** income, salary, trophy; **7** alimony, annuity, bursary, credits, pension, profits, returns, revenue, stipend, takings, tontine, tribute; **8** dividend, earnings, palimony, proceeds, receipts, winnings; **9** allowance; **10** commission, fellowship, perquisite; **11** maintenance, scholarship; **12** compensation; PHRASES: **3, 4** the gate; **3, 5** pin money; **3-6, 5** ill-gotten gains; **3, 8** net receipts; **4-4, 3** take-home pay; **4, 5** gate money *UK*; **5, 7** child support; **5, 8** gross receipts, money received; **6, 5** pocket money; **6, 7** fringe benefit.

receiver 3 set; **4** dish; **5** donee, fence; **6** aerial *UK*; **7** antenna, catcher, grantee, headset; **9** earphones; **10** headphones; PHRASES: **5, 8** radar ~, radio ~. *See also* **recipient**

receiving 4 paid; **5** given; **6** legacy, taking; **7** awarded, bequest, getting; **8** allotted, heirloom, heirship, heritage, rewarded, salaried; **9** acceptant, accepting, patrimony, pensioned, reception, receptive, recipient; **10** acceptance, bequeathal, birthright, collecting, collection, recipience, succession; **11** acquisition, compensated, inheritance; **12** hereditament, receivership; **13** collectorship, primogeniture; PHRASES: **4-7** wage-earning; **9-3** pensioned-off.

recent 3 hot, mod, new; **4** late; **5** fresh; **6** modern; **7** current; **12** contemporary; PHRASES: **7-3** present-day.

receptacle 3 bag, bin; **4** bowl, tray; **5** depot, store, torus; **6** drawer, holder, hopper, vessel; **8** magazine, receiver; **9** container; **10** repository. *See also* **container**

reception 2 do; **4** bash; **5** aloha, debut, hello, lobby, party, sound; **6** signal, soirée; **7** baptism, clarity, picture, receipt, welcome; **8** delivery, function, greeting, reaction, response; **9** admission, admitting, gathering, handshake, receiving, treatment, unloading, welcoming; **10** acceptance, admittance, initiation; **11** christening, hospitality; **12** confirmation, entertaining; PHRASES: **3-6** red-carpet; **3-8** get-together; **5, 7** hero's welcome; **6, 4** living area, living room; **6, 5** drinks party *UK*; **7, 4** drawing room, sitting room; **8, 5** cocktail party; **9, 4** ~ room, triumphal arch.

receptive 4 open; **5** alert, quick, sharp; **6** bright, clever; **8** amenable, friendly, inviting, reactive; **9** recipient, sensitive, welcoming; **10** accessible, hospitable, interested, invitatory, perceptive, responsive, susceptive; **11** sympathetic; **12** approachable; PHRASES: **4-6** open-minded; **8-7** generous-hearted.

recess 3 bay, ebb; **4** apse, cove, nook, rest; **5** bower, break, niche; **6** alcove, cavity, closet, corner, cranny, hollow, rabbet; **7** cubicle, respite; **8** interval; **9** embrasure; **12** intermission.

recession 5 slump; **6** hollow; **7** decline, retreat; **8** collapse, downturn; **9** deflation, inflation; **10** depression, stagnation, withdrawal; **11** stagflation; **12** disinflation; PHRASES: **8, 5** boom/bust cycle.

recipient 4 butt, heir; **5** buyer, donee, fence, payee, taker; **6** beggar, earner, getter, hearer, holder, lessee, reader, victim, viewer, winner; **7** grantee, heritor, scholar, trustee; **8** accepter, acceptor, acquirer, allottee, audience, beholder, customer, endorsee, licensee, listener, obtainer, procurer, receiver, sufferer; **9** addressee, annuitant, consignee, dependent, inheritor, pensioner, purchaser, scapegoat, spectator; **10** panhandler; **11** beneficiary, prizewinner; **12** exhibitioner *UK*; **13** valedictorian; PHRASES: **3, 3, 9** old age pensioner (OAP); **4, 6** wage earner; **6, 2, 7** object of charity; **7, 4** charity case.

reciprocal 5 equal, joint; **6** common, mutual, seesaw, shared; **7** changed, swapped; **8** bartered, communal, reacting, requited, tradeoff; **9** alternate, balancing, exchanged, recoiling; **10** requitable; **11** alternating, alternative, interacting, retaliatory; **12** compensatory, compromising, exchangeable, interchanged, interplaying; **13** counteracting, counteractive, reciprocating, reciprocative, reciprocatory; **15** interchangeable *UK*; PHRASES: **3-3-3** eye-for-eye, tit-for-tat; **4-3-4** blow-for-blow, give-and-take; **6-6** teeter-totter.

reciprocate 4 mesh, swap; **5** react, repay, reply, share, trade; **6** barter, change, recoil, retort, return, seesaw; **7** balance, counter, requite, respond; **8** exchange, interact; **9** alternate, interplay, retaliate; **10** compensate, compromise, counteract; **11** interchange, interrelate; **13** counterchange, counterstrike; PHRASES: **3, 2, 4** pay in kind; **3, 3** aid and abet; **4, 2, 6** give in return; **4, 2, 8** give in exchange; **4, 3, 3** give tit for tat; **4, 3, 4** give and take; **4, 4** give back; **4, 4, 3, 4** give blow for blow; **4, 5** take turns; **4, 7** lend oneself; **5, 3** trade off; **6-6** teeter-totter.

recital *See* **performance**

recite 4 list; **7** declaim, itemize, narrate,

perform; **8** rehearse; **9** enumerate; **11** regurgitate; PHRASES: **4, 3** reel off; **5, 8** speak publicly.

reckless *See* **rash**

reckon 4 deem, rate; **5** count, judge, think, total; **6** regard; **7** believe, imagine, suppose; **8** consider; **9** calculate; PHRASES: **3, 2** add up, tot up.

recluse *See* **hermit**

recognition 3 tip; **5** bonus; **6** credit, praise, reward, thanks; **7** credits, respect, tribute; **8** applause, gratuity; **9** admission, awareness, detection, gratitude; **10** acceptance, concession, perception; **11** testimonial; **12** appreciation, establishing; **13** understanding; **14** acknowledgment, distinguishing, identification; **15** acknowledgement, differentiation; PHRASES: **2-4** by-line; **4, 2, 6** vote of thanks; **4, 5** gold watch; **5, 2, 8** round of applause; **5-3, 4** thank-you card; **5-3, 6** thank-you letter; **5, 8** thank offering; **6, 9** golden handshake; **7, 4** parting gift; **7, 7** leaving present; **10, 4** retirement gift.

recognizable 7 defined; **8** definite, distinct, familiar, knowable; **10** detectable, noticeable; **11** perceptible; **12** decipherable, identifiable, unmistakable; **15** distinguishable; PHRASES: **4-7** well-defined; **8, 3** standing out.

recognize 3 ken, own, see; **4** know, spot; **5** admit, agree, grant, value; **6** accept, credit, descry, detect; **7** ascribe, cherish, concede, discern, realize; **8** conceive, diagnose, identify, perceive; **9** attribute; **10** appreciate, comprehend, understand; **11** acknowledge, distinguish; PHRASES: **2, 5, 2** be aware of; **2, 8, 3** be grateful for, be thankful for; **2, 8, 4** be familiar with; **3, 2, 1, 6** see at a glance; **4, 3** make out.

recoil 4 balk, echo; **5** dodge, quail, react, start, wince; **6** cannon, cringe, flinch, mirror, reflex, reflux, return, revert, shrink, uncoil; **7** rebound, reflect, resound, retreat, shudder; **8** backfire, backlash, ricochet, withdraw; **9** boomerang, oscillate, refluence, resonance, reversion, shrinking; **10** elasticity, hesitation, resilience, withdrawal; **12** repercussion; **13** reverberation; PHRASES: **3, 4** shy away; **4, 4** back away, draw back, jump back, kick back; **5, 4** bound back, swing back; **6, 4** bounce back, spring back.

recollect *See* **remember**

recommend 4 plug, puff, urge; **5** refer; **6** advise, enjoin, exhort; **7** approve, command, commend, counsel, endorse, promote, propose, suggest, support; **8** advocate.

recommendation 4 plug; **6** advice; **7** command, counsel, support; **8** approval, blessing, proposal, sanction; **9** reference; **10** credential, suggestion; **11** endorsement, testimonial; **12** commendation; **13** encouragement; PHRASES: **4, 4** good word.

recompense 3 pay; **5** atone, repay; **6** return, reward; **7** appease, damages, payment, requite; **8** equalize; **9** indemnify, quittance, reimburse, repayment; **10** compensate, propitiate, remunerate, reparation; **11** restitution; **12** compensation, remuneration; **13** reimbursement; PHRASES: **4, 2, 3** make up for; **4, 6** make amends.

reconcile *See* **settle**

recondite *See* **obscure**

reconnaissance 6 survey; **8** scouting; **10** inspection; **11** exploration; **13** investigation.

reconnoiter 5 scout; **6** search, survey; **7** explore; **8** scouting; **11** exploration, investigate; **13** investigation; **14** reconnaissance.

reconsider 4 redo; **6** review; **7** reflect, rethink; **8** reassess; PHRASES: **2, 4, 4** go back over; **2-7** re-examine *UK*; **2-8** re-evaluate *UK*; **4, 2, 4** stop in time; **4, 3, 5** stop and think; **5, 5** think again; **5, 6, 2** think better of.

reconstitute 5 alter; **6** change, modify, revise; **7** rebuild; **10** reorganize; **11** reconstruct; PHRASES: **2-4** re-form; **5, 5** build again.

record 2 CD, EP, LP; **3** log; **4** best, bill, card, copy, disc, disk *UK*, file, film, form, high, item, list, memo, note, stub, tape, vita; **5** album, check, diary, entry, index, input, movie, print, table, tally, video, vinyl; **6** annals, detail, docket, enroll, jotter *UK*, ledger, memoir, papers, recite, relate, report, résumé, return, single, sketch, tablet, verify; **7** account, archive, catalog *UK*, cutting, dossier, empanel, Hansard, history, invoice, journal, logbook, minutes, narrate, notepad, picture, profile, receipt, recount, voucher; **8** archives, calendar, cashbook, cassette, database, document, inscribe, minidisk, notebook, obituary, portrait, register, reminder, rollbook, snapshot, tabulate; **9** biography, cartulary, catalogue *UK*, checkbook, chronicle, directory, documents, inventory, microcard, microfilm, narrative, photocopy, portfolio, recording, represent, scrapbook, statement, videodisc, videotape; **10** background, microfiche, photograph, reputation, scoreboard, scoresheet *UK*, transcript; **11** counterfoil, memorabilia; **12** transactions; **13** autobiography, documentation; **14** correspondence, representation; PHRASES: **3, 2, 6** put on ~; **3, 5** top score; **4, 1, 4** keep a note, make a note; **4, 1, 9** make a recording; **4, 2** pick up; **4, 4** jury list, note down; **4, 5** take notes; **4-6** tape-record; **4, 7** case history, keep details; **4, 11** keep information, past performance; **5, 4** check stub, write down; **5, 6** track ~, world ~; **5, 7** press cutting; **6-3, 6** income-tax return; **6, 4** report card; **6, 6** annual report, police ~, school report; **7, 4** waiting list; **7, 6** company report; **8, 4** personal best, personal file; **8, 6** criminal ~; **8, 7** personal history.

record book 3 log; **4** card, disk *UK*, roll, tape; **5** album, diary, index, table; **6** jotter *UK*, ledger, tablet; **7** catalog *UK*, journal, logbook, notepad; **8** calendar, cashbook, database, notebook, register, registry, rollbook; **9** cartulary, catalogue *UK*, checkbook, directory, microcard, microfilm, scrapbook; **10** microfiche, scratchpad; PHRASES: **4, 3** memo pad; **4, 10** data processing; **5, 4** index card; **6, 4** minute book; **7, 4** account book, address book; **8, 4** computer tape, magnetic tape; **11, 4** commonplace book.

recorder 4 tape, wire; **5** clerk; **6** artist, flight, notary, scribe, typist, writer; **7** diarist, newsman; **8** annalist, engraver, reporter; **9** archivist, cameraman, columnist, draftsman, historian, registrar, secretary; **10** accountant, amanuensis, biographer, chronicler, journalist, keyboarder, petitioner, timekeeper; **11** antiquarian, incremental, scorekeeper; **12** photographer, receptionist, stenographer; **13** archaeologist; **14** autobiographer; PHRASES: **4-6** book-keeper; **6, 5** filing clerk; **6-6** record-keeper; **7, 5** English flute.

recording 2 CD, EP, LP; **3** vid; **4** copy, disc, disk *UK*, film, tape; **5** movie, video; **6** record, single; **7** footage; **8** cassette, minidisc, pressing; **9** camcorder, videodisc; **10** soundtrack; PHRASES: **4, 9** tape ~; **5, 4** video game, video tape; **5, 5** video nasty *UK*; **5, 8** audio cassette, video cassette *UK*; **8, 4** cassette tape, magnetic tape.

recording instrument 3 bug; **5** gauge; **6** camera; **7** wiretap; **8** recorder; **9** camcorder, stopwatch; **10** dictaphone; **11** photocopier, seismograph, speedometer; PHRASES: **4, 7** tape machine; **4, 8** cash register, tape recorder; **5, 3** black box; **5, 6** video camera; **6, 8** flight recorder.

recount 4 tell; **5** cover, evoke; **6** detail, recite, record, relate, repeat, report, retell, review; **7** imagine, narrate, testify; **8** describe, rehearse; **9** chronicle, dramatize, reminisce; **10** correspond; **11** communicate, mythologize, romanticize; **12** characterize, fictionalize, recapitulate; PHRASES: **4, 1, 4** spin a yarn, tell a tale; **4, 1, 5** tell a story; **4, 2, 7** give an account; **4, 6** keep posted; **5, 2, 4** bring to life; **6, 1, 6** submit a report.

recover 4 heal, mend, rest, save; **5** claim, rally; **6** recoup, regain, repose, rescue, revive; **7** improve, salvage, survive; **8** reawaken, retrieve; **9** recapture, repossess; **10** convalesce, recuperate; PHRASES: **3, 4** get back, get well; **3, 6** get better; **4, 2** pick up; **4, 3** cool off; **4, 7** pull through; **4, 8** make progress; **6, 4** bounce back.

recovery 4 rest; **5** rally; **6** repose, rescue, upturn; **7** renewal, revival; **8** comeback; **9** regaining, retrieval, salvation; **10** reclaiming, recoupment, resurgence; **11** improvement, recapturing, reclamation; **12** recuperation, repossession; **14** revitalization.

recreation 4 play; **5** hobby, sport; **7** leisure, pastime; **8** activity, exercise; **9** amusement.

recreational 3 fun; **7** amusing, leisure; **8** relaxing; **9** enjoyable, frivolous, leisurely; **11** competitive; **12** entertaining; PHRASES: **5, 4** spare time.

recrimination 5 blame; **8** reproach; **10** accusation, allegation.

recruit 2 GI; **4** hire, tyro; **5** cadet, draft, Tommy; **6** employ, engage, enlist, enroll, novice, rookie; **7** convert, draftee, trainee; **8** beginner, employee, mobilize, newcomer; **9** conscript, greenhorn, volunteer; **10** apprentice; PHRASES: **4, 2** sign up, take on; **5, 2** round up.

rectify 3 fix; **4** cure, edit, mend; **5** alter, amend, emend, patch; **6** adjust, recast, redact, reform, remedy, remold, repair, retell, review, revise; **7** correct, redraft, redress, remodel, resolve, rewrite; **8** copyedit, recreate; **9** proofread, refashion; **10** regularize, reorganize, straighten, streamline; **11** rationalize; PHRASES: **3, 5** put right, set right; **4, 3** sort out; **4, 4** make good; **4-4** copy-edit, fine-tune; **4, 5** make clear; **4-6** blue-pencil; **6, 6** remove errors; **10, 3** compensate for, straighten out.

rector 4 dean, head; **5** vicar; **6** cleric, parson, priest; **8** director, minister; **9** principal; **10** chancellor.

recuperate 4 heal, mend; **5** claim; **6** recoup, regain, rescue; **7** improve, reclaim, recover, salvage; **8** retrieve; **9** recapture, repossess; **10** convalesce; PHRASES: **3, 4** get back, get well; **3, 6** get better; **4, 7** pull through.

recuperation 4 cure; **5** rally; **6** easing, relief, remedy, rescue, upturn; **7** closing, healing, mending, salvage; **8** rallying, recovery; **9** recapture, regaining, retrieval; **11** improvement, reclamation, restoration; **12** repossession; **13** convalescence; **14** rehabilitation; PHRASES: **1, 3, 1** R and R; **6, 2, 6** return to health, return to normal; **7, 2** perking up; **7, 4** healing over; **7, 6** getting better; **8, 4** scabbing over.

recur 6 repeat, return; **7** persist, relapse; **8** reappear; PHRASES: **4, 4** come back; **4, 5** come again; **6, 5** happen again.

recurrent 7 chronic, nonstop, regular; **8** constant, cyclical, frequent, haunting, periodic, repeated; **9** ceaseless, continual, incessant, recurring, returning, spasmodic; **10** continuing, continuous, persistent, ubiquitous; **11** reappearing, reoccurring, unremitting; **12** intermittent.

red 3 raw; **4** lake, left, pink, rose, rosy, ruby, sore; **5** angry, blood, coral, gules, henna, lefty, river, rouge, ruddy; **6** cerise, cherry, claret, florid, garnet, Maoist, maroon, ruddle, rufous, russet, salmon, tender; **7** ashamed, carmine, crimson, fuchsia, leftist, magenta, Marxist, oxblood, reddish, roseate, scarlet, vermeil; **8** alizarin, cinnabar, cramoisy, cyclamen; **9** carnation, carnelian, cochineal, Communist, rufescent, Socialist, solferino, vermilion; **10** rosaniline; **11** winecolored; **13** revolutionary; PHRASES: **3, 3** ~ rag, R~ Sea; **3, 4** old rose, ~ cent, ~ flag, ~ heat, ~ lead, ~ meat, ~ tape; **3, 5** ~ brick, ~ cedar, ~ cross, ~ dwarf, ~ ocher, R~ River, ~ shift; **3, 6** ~ carpet, ~ duster, ~ ensign, ~ pepper, ~ setter *UK*; **3, 7** ~ admiral, ~ her-

ring; **3, 8** ~ squirrel; **4, 3** tile ~; **4-3** rose-red; **4-4** rose-pink; **4-7** rust-colored; **5, 3** poppy ~, Thalo ~; **5-3** brick-red, flame-red; **5-7** flesh-colored, peach-colored; **6, 3** Indian ~, tomato ~, Turkey ~; **6-3** purple-red; **6-4** orange-pink; **7, 3** cadmium ~, Windsor ~; **7, 5** dragon's blood; **7, 7** cadmium scarlet; **8, 3** brownish ~, cardinal ~, lipstick ~, venetian ~; **8-3** beetroot-red; **9, 3** castilian ~, pillarbox ~.

red (red thing) 4 beet, dawn, fire, gore, Mars, plum, port, rose, ruby, rust; **5** blood, brick, flame, peach, peony, poppy; **6** cherry, claret, garnet, sunset, tomato; **7** redhead, redwing, redwood; **8** burgundy, cardinal, fireglow, geranium, mulberry; **9** carnation, carnelian, gingernob, pillarbox, raspberry; **10** strawberry; PHRASES: **3, 3** red bug, red fox; **3, 4** red card, red deer, red hair, red meat, red wine; **3, 5** red dwarf, red giant, red light; **3, 5, 4** red blood cell; **3, 6** red cheeks, red clover, red grouse, red pepper, red planet, red salmon; **3, 7** red admiral, red currant, red snapper; **3, 8** red squirrel; **4, 5** fire truck, high color; **4, 6** fire engine, rosy cheeks; **5, 6** apple cheeks; **5, 9** robin redbreast; **6-3** carrot-top; **6, 4** cherry lips; **6, 6** danger signal; **10, 4** strawberry mark.

redden 4 glow; **5** blush, color, flush, rouge; **6** mantle, raddle, rubefy, ruddle; **7** crimson; **9** rubricate; **11** incarnadine; PHRASES: **5, 2** color up.

redeem 4 cash, free; **7** convert, deliver, redress, release, restore; **8** exchange, liberate; **10** emancipate; PHRASES: **4, 2** cash in; **4, 2, 3** make up for; **4, 6, 3** make amends for; **5, 2** trade in; **10, 3** compensate for.

redemption 3 use; **6** rescue; **7** release; **8** exchange, recovery; **9** salvation; **10** conversion, liberation, renovation; **11** improvement; **12** emancipation; PHRASES: **5-2** trade-in.

red-faced 4 rosy; **5** fiery, ruddy; **6** blowzy, florid, hectic, rouged; **7** fevered, flushed, glowing; **8** blooming, blushing, feverish, flushing, reddened, rubicund, sanguine, sunburnt; **9** rubescent, sunburned; PHRASES: **3, 2, 1, 7** red as a lobster; **3, 2, 1, 8** red as a beetroot; **3-3** red-hot; **3-7** red-cheeked; **4-7** rosy-cheeked.

red-haired 5 sandy; **6** auburn, Titian; **7** carroty; **8** chestnut; PHRASES: **6-6** gingerhaired.

Red Indian *See* **Native American**

red mullet 8 goatfish; 9 surmullet.

redness 4 glow; 5 bloom, blush, flush; 6 warmth; 8 rosiness; 9 reddening; 10 irritation, rubescence, rufescence; 11 painfulness, rubefacient, rubefaction, rubicundity; 12 inflammation; PHRASES: 3, 4 red rash; 3, 5 red color; 3, 10 red complexion; 4, 5 high color; 6, 5 hectic flush; 7, 5 scarlet fever. *See also* **red**

redolent 7 scented; 8 aromatic, fragrant; 9 evocative; 10 indicative, suggestive; 11 reminiscent.

redress *See* **recompense**

reduce 3 cut, lop; 4 damp, diet, dock, ease, pare, slim, thin, trim, weed; 5 lower, prune, slash; 6 demote, lessen, rarefy, shrink; 7 degrade; 8 condense, decimate, decrease, diminish, downsize, moderate, relegate, underman; 9 downgrade, downscale, eliminate; 10 slenderize, understaff; 11 rationalize; PHRASES: 2, 2, 1, 4 go on a diet; 3, 4 cut back, cut down; 4, 3 thin out, weed out; 4, 4 pare down, slim down, trim down; 4, 6 lose weight; 5, 4 bring down, drive down, scale down.

reduced 4 worn; 5 cheap, minus, short; 6 docked, eroded, lopped; 7 bargain, chopped, severed; 8 abridged, beheaded, corroded, devalued, headless, lessened, limbless, tailless; 9 condensed, curtailed, decimated, decreased, mutilated, shortened; 10 diminished, discounted; 11 abbreviated, decapitated; PHRASES: 2, 4 on sale; 3-4 cut-rate; 3-5 cut-price *UK*, low-price.

reduction 4 drop; 6 saving; 8 decrease, discount; 9 lessening.

redundancy *See* **unemployment**

redundant 7 disused, surplus; 8 outmoded, unneeded; 11 superfluous.

reedbuck 5 nagor.

reek *See* **smell**

reel 4 coil, roll, spin, sway, turn, wind; 5 dance, lurch, round, spool, swirl, twirl, wheel, whirl; 6 bobbin, roller, totter, winder, wobble; 7 revolve, spindle, stagger, stumble; 8 cylinder; 9 pirouette; 10 whirlabout; PHRASES: 2, 5, 3, 5 go round and round; 3, 4 rat race; 5, 5 dizzy round.

ref 7 referee; 9 reference.

refashion *See* **reform**

refer 4 mean; 5 check; 6 belong, denote; 7 concern, consult, examine, mention, signi-

fy, suggest; 8 indicate; 9 insinuate; PHRASES: 4, 2 look up, send to, turn to; 4, 5 talk about; 5, 2 apply to, bring up; 6, 2 direct to, relate to; 7, 2 consign to.

referee 5 judge; 6 umpire; 7 arbiter; 11 adjudicator.

reference 5 locus; 7 mention; 8 allusion, citation, location, position; 9 situation; 10 indication, suggestion; 11 endorsement, orientation, testimonial; 12 commendation; 14 recommendation.

reference book 3 map; 4 ABCs, dict, plan; 5 atlas, chart, Fodor, index; 6 manual; 7 almanac, catalog *UK*; 8 Baedeker, Bradshaw, handbook, Michelin, roadbook, yearbook; 9 catalogue *UK*, directory, ephemeris, gazetteer, guidebook, itinerary, thesaurus, timetable; 10 dictionary, travelogue; 12 encyclopedia; 13 encyclopaedia; PHRASES: 1-1 A-Z; 4, 3 road map; 4, 5 vade mecum; 5, 3 route map; 5, 4 phone book; 6, 5 Yellow Pages *UK*; 8, 7 nautical almanac.

referendum 4 poll, vote; 6 ballot, survey; 10 plebiscite.

refill *See* **replenish**

refine 4 hone; 5 treat; 6 filter, polish, purify; 7 distill, enhance, improve, perfect, process, upgrade; 9 cultivate; PHRASES: 4, 6 make better; 7, 2 sharpen up.

refined 1 U; 4 chic, pure; 5 sharp, suave; 6 astute, classy, raised, shrewd, soigné, subtle, urbane; 7 elegant, genteel, stylish, treated; 8 advanced, artistic, cleansed, critical, cultured, delicate, educated, esthetic, filtered, graceful, gracious, ladylike, nurtured, polished, purified, sensible, superior, tasteful; 9 civilized, courteous, developed, dignified, distingué, judicious, processed, sensitive; 10 cultivated, discerning, distillled, fastidious, insightful, perceptive; 11 experienced, gentlemanly; 12 appreciative, cosmopolitan; 13 distinguished, sophisticated; 14 discriminating; PHRASES: 4-4 wellbred; 4-6 well-spoken; 4-8 well-finished, well-mannered.

refined person 4 gent; 8 aesthete; 9 gentleman; 10 dilettante; 11 connoisseur, gentlewoman; PHRASES: 3, 2, 5 man of taste; 5, 2, 5 woman of taste.

refinement 5 class, style, taste, tweak; 6 acumen, detail; 7 culture, finesse, insight, suavity; 8 breeding, civility, delicacy, elegance, judgment, maturity, subtlety, urbanity; **9** education; **10** alteration, background, extraction, perception, separation; **11** cultivation, discernment, enhancement, improvement, sensibility, sensitivity, sublimation; **12** condensation, modification, purification, vaporization; **13** distillation; **14** discrimination, perceptiveness, sophistication; **15** connoisseurship; PHRASES: 4-6 fine-tuning; **5, 6** minor change; **6-5** savoir-faire.

reflect 4 echo, muse; **5** think; **6** mirror, ponder, wonder; **7** suspect; **8** cogitate, consider, meditate, question, ruminate; **9** speculate; **10** conjecture.

reflection 4 echo, sign; **5** image; **6** musing, signal; **7** thought; **8** evidence, likeness, thinking; **10** expression, meditation, rumination, suggestion; **11** replication; **12** deliberation, reproduction; **13** consideration, contemplation, manifestation; **14** representation; PHRASES: **6, 5** mirror image.

reflector 5 glass; **6** mirror; **7** Catseye *TM*; **8** speculum; PHRASES: **4, 3** cat's eye; **4-4, 6** rear-view mirror; **4, 5** pier glass; **4, 6** hand mirror, wing mirror *UK*; **6, 5** cheval glass; **7, 5** looking glass; **7, 6** shaving mirror.

reflex 7 impulse; **8** instinct, reaction, response.

reform 4 mend; **5** alter, amend; **6** adjust, change, recast, revamp; **7** convert, correct, rebuild, reclaim, rectify, reshape; **8** renovate; **9** refashion, transform, transmute; **10** alteration, regenerate; **11** improvement; **12** rehabilitate; **14** reorganization, transformation; PHRASES: **2, 8** go straight; **4, 4, 4** mend one's ways.

reformatory 4 jail; **6** prison; **7** borstal *UK*; **11** institution; PHRASES: **6, 4** secure unit *UK*; **6, 6** reform school; **8, 4** juvenile home; **9, 6** detention center.

reformer 3 Fry, Red; **4** Knox; **6** Calvin, Fabian, Ghandi, Luther; **7** Hussite, liberal, Lollard, Marxist, radical, Utopian; **8** activist, agitator, chiliast, crusader, feminist, humanist, idealist, improver, Leveller, moderate, peacenik; **9** Beveridge, communist, ecologist, extremist, meliorist, reformist, socialist, visionary; **10** antiracist *UK*, campaigner, ecowarrior, gradualist, Protestant, suffragist; **11** antifascist *UK*, egalitarian, millenarian, progressive, reorganizer, suffragette; **13** perfectionist, progressivist, revolutionary; **14** integrationist, philanthropist, progressionist, prohibition-

ist, Prohibitionist; **15** assimilationist; PHRASES: **3, 6** CND member, New Dealer; **5, 8** peace advocate; **6, 6** social worker.

refractory 6 unruly; **7** restive, wayward; **8** contrary, indocile, perverse, stubborn; **9** arbitrary, crotchety, irascible, obstinate; **10** headstrong, rebellious; **11** disobedient, intractable; **12** contumacious, incorrigible, noncompliant, recalcitrant, ungovernable, unmanageable; **13** irrepressible, unpersuadable; **14** uncontrollable; PHRASES: 4-7 hardmouthed; **5-6** stiff-necked; **5-7** crossgrained.

refrain 4 idle, song, tune; **5** avoid, cease, defer, delay, theme; **6** chorus, desist, eschew, retard, strain; **7** abstain, forbear, repress; **8** renounce; **13** procrastinate; PHRASES: **3, 4** sit back; **4, 2** pass up; **4, 4** hold back; **5, 3** leave off; **5, 5** avoid doing.

refresh 3 air, fan; **4** cool, ease, feed, tidy; **5** brace, cheer, chill, clean, renew, shade; **6** aerate, dispel, repair, revive; **7** animate, enliven, fortify, freshen, recruit, relieve, restore; **8** energize, recharge, recreate, renovate, vitalize; **9** reanimate, stimulate, ventilate; **10** exhilarate, invigorate, rejuvenate, revitalize, strengthen; **11** refrigerate, resuscitate; **12** reinvigorate; PHRASES: **3, 2** pep up; **3-9** air-condition; **4, 2** tidy up; **4, 3** cool off; **4, 4** cool down; **4, 7** open windows; **5, 2** clean up; **5, 4** allow rest; **6, 2** spruce up; **7, 2** freshen up.

refresher 3 air, fee, nap; **4** food, lull, rest, wash; **5** break, drink, leave, tonic; **6** breeze, oxygen, recess, repose, review, shower, update; **7** holiday, reviver; **8** reminder, revision, vacation; **9** stimulant; **11** restorative; PHRASES: **4, 3, 5, 2** wash and brush up; **4, 6** cold shower, cool breeze; **6, 2, 3** breath of air; **6, 2, 5** change of scene; **6, 2, 6** breath of oxygen.

refreshing 4 cold, cool; **5** fresh, tonic; **7** bracing, cooling; **8** reviving; **9** relieving, uplifting; **10** comforting, energizing, fortifying, recreative; **11** restorative, stimulating; **12** exhilarating, invigorating, recreational, revitalizing; **13** inspirational; PHRASES: 6-9 thirst-quenching.

refreshment 4 ease, food, rest; **5** drink, shade, snack, tonic; **6** drinks, relief, repair, repose, snacks; **7** nibbles *UK*, renewal, revival; **8** aeration, breather, coolness, recovery, tidiness; **9** animation, cleanness, elevenses, freshness, nutriment, nutrition, refection, stimulant; **10** appetizers, recreation, renovation, sustenance; **11** cleanliness, nourishment, reanimation, recruitment, respiration, restoration, stimulation, ventilation; **12** exhilaration, invigoration, recuperation, rejuvenation, vitalization; **13** refrigeration, resuscitation; **14** reinvigoration, revitalization; PHRASES: **1, 3, 1** R and R; **3, 3, 3, 4** one for the road; **4-2-2** pick-me-up; **4, 3, 5** food and drink; **4, 8** hors d'oeuvres; **5, 3** quick one; **6, 5** finger foods; **10, 2** freshening up; **10, 4** nineteenth hole.

refrigerator 4 Esky *UK*; **6** fridge; **7** freezer; PHRASES: **3, 4** ice pack; **3, 6** ice bucket; **4, 3** cool box *UK*; **4-6** deep-freeze; **5, 8** chill cupboard; **6-7** fridge-freezer *UK*; **7, 7** chilled counter.

refuge 3 ark, bed, lap, pit; **4** cell, fort, hole, home, keep, prop, rock, wall, ward; **5** cache, haven, tower; **6** asylum, bunker, burrow, dugout, harbor, hearth, pillar, resort, temple, trench; **7** bastion, bedroom, bulwark, chamber, citadel, foxhole, hideout, nunnery, parapet, privacy, rampart, retreat, sanctum, sanctum (sanctorum), shelter, support; **8** buttress, cloister, fastness, fortress, mainstay, recourse; **9** acropolis, crosswalk, cubbyhole, hermitage, monastery, sanctuary; **10** battlement, blockhouse, protection, stronghold; **13** fortification; PHRASES: **3-4, 7** air-raid shelter; **4, 2, 4** Rock of Ages; **4, 2, 6** holy of holies; **4, 2, 9** Rock of Gibraltar; **4, 4** bolt hole, funk hole *UK*; **4-4** hidy-hole; **4, 5** safe house, safe place; **4, 6** last resort, safe harbor; **4, 7** bomb shelter; **5, 2, 6** place of safety; **5, 2, 8** tower of strength; **5-4** hidey-hole; **5, 5** ivory tower; **6, 4** priest hole, safety zone; **6, 5** hiding place; **7, 5** private space; **7, 6** traffic island; **7, 7** fallout shelter; **7, 8** pelican crossing *UK*; **8, 7** Anderson shelter *UK*, concrete shelter.

refund 5 repay; **9** reimburse, repayment; **10** compensate; **12** compensation; **13** reimbursement; PHRASES: **3, 4** pay back; **4, 4** give back; **5, 4** money back.

refurbish 5 refit, renew; **6** change, reform, repair, revamp; **7** improve, remodel, repaint, repaper, restore, retouch, upgrade, yuppify; **8** gentrify, overhaul, renovate, trendify; **9** modernize, refashion; **10** redecorate; **11** recondition; PHRASES: **2, 2** do up; **3, 2** fix up; **4, 4** make over; **5, 2** touch up; **6, 2** spruce up; **7, 2** freshen up, smarten up.

refusal 2 no; **3** nay; **4** snub, won't; **5** shan't; **6** denial, rebuff, strike; **7** default, lockout, repulse; **8** negation, rebuttal; **9** rejection, repulsion; **10** nonpayment, resistance; **11** denigration, repudiation; **13** nonacceptance, noncompliance, recalcitrance, unwillingness; **14** noncooperation, nonwillingness; PHRASES: **3, 5** red light; **5-4** knock-back *UK*; **6, 4** thumbs down; **8, 6** negative answer.

refuse 3 ash, jib; **4** bits, bran, deny, dirt, duck, dump, junk, muck, peel, scum, slag, snub; **5** avoid, bilge, chaff, demur, drain, dross, elude, fight, husks, offal, repel, scrap, shirk, tares, trash, waste; **6** cinder, crumbs *UK*, debris, flinch, leaves, litter, lumber, negate, object, oppose, rebuff, recoil, reject, resist, retain, scoria, scraps, strike; **7** carrion, castoff, clinker, compost, decline, default, dustbin *UK*, garbage, mullock *UK*, neglect, protest, repulse, rubbish, stubble, wastage; **8** cesspool, complain, dustheap, landfill, leavings, shavings, spoilage; **9** denigrate, leftovers, repudiate, scourings, sweepings, throwaway; **10** contradict, disapprove, disposable, wastepaper; **12** offscourings; PHRASES: **2, 2, 6** go on strike; **3, 2** jib at, say no; **4, 2** balk at, pass up; **4, 3, 4** odds and ends; **4, 3, 5** rags and bones; **4, 3, 6** bits and pieces; **4, 4** back away, slag heap, turn away, turn down; **4-4** cast-offs; **4, 4, 7** make one's excuses; **5, 4** trash dump; **6, 3 ~** tip; **6, 4** banana skin *UK*, orange peel, septic tank, shrink from; **7, 3** garbage can; **7, 4** compost heap *UK*, rubbish dump *UK*, rubbish heap *UK*.

refuser 4 scab; **6** truant; **7** striker; **8** blackleg, deserter; **9** abstainer, dissident, gainsayer, refusenik; **10** teetotaler; PHRASES: **3, 6** tax evader; **5, 6** draft dodger.

refutable 4 weak; **6** faulty, flawed; **7** unsound; **9** unfounded; **10** confutable, defeasible, groundless; **11** disprovable; **12** inconclusive; **13** objectionable.

refutation 6 denial, rebuff; **7** refusal; **8** disproof, negation; **9** disavowal, dismissal, rejection; **10** disclaimer, retraction; **11** confutation, repudiation; **13** contradiction.

refute 5 annul, belie, crush, floor, quash, rebut; **6** defeat, expose, forbid, negate, outwit, squash; **7** confute, contest, counter, deflate, destroy, dismiss, explode, nullify, silence; **8** abrogate, confound, demolish, disallow, disprove, outsmart, overturn; **9**

challenge, discredit, overthrow, repudiate, undermine; **10** contradict, disconfirm, invalidate; PHRASES: **4, 2** show up; **5, 4** argue down, knock down, shout down; **7, 2** dispose of.

REG 7 regular; **8** regiment, register; **9** registrar.

regard 3 eye; **4** deem, heed, look, scan, view; **5** count, judge, think, value, watch; **6** esteem, notice, revere, survey; **7** concern, observe, respect; **8** consider, estimate; **13** consideration.

regarding 2 re; PHRASES: **2, 2** as to.

regardless 6 anyhow, anyway; **12** nevertheless; PHRASES: **2, 6, 4** no matter what.

regards 7 devoirs; **8** respects; **9** greetings; **11** compliments, salutations; PHRASES: **4, 6** good wishes.

regent 5 proxy; **9** protector; **10** substitute; **11** replacement.

regime 4 rule; **6** system; **7** command, regimen, routine; **9** treatment; **10** government, management; **14** administration.

regiment 4 file; **5** order, troop; **7** arrange, brigade, oppress; **8** organize, regulate, squadron, suppress; **9** battalion; PHRASES: **8, 4** military unit.

region 4 area, belt, land, zone; **5** clime, islet, place, realm, shire UK, space, state; **6** canton, county, ground, island, sector; **7** borough, section, terrain; **8** district, landmass, locality, province; **9** continent, peninsula, territory; **12** constituency; PHRASES: **10, 4** geographic unit.

region (US regions) 5 Coast, Dixie, SoCal, South; **6** Acadia, Ozarks; **7** Midwest; **8** Acadiana, Cascadia, Piedmont; **9** Carolinas, Dixieland, Northeast; **10** Appalachia, Yankeeland; PHRASES: **3-2-3** Ark-La-Tex; **3, 4** Far West, Sun Belt; **3-5** Tri-State; **3, 7** New England; **3-8** Mid-Atlantic; **4, 3** Cape Cod; **4, 4** Corn Belt, Rust Belt, Wild West; **4, 5** Deep South, East Coast, Gulf Coast, West Coast; **4, 7** Four Corners; **5, 4** Bible Belt, Grain Belt, Jello Belt; **5, 5** Great Basin, Great Lakes, North Shore; **5, 6** Great Plains; **6, 4** Middle West; **6, 6** Border States; **7, 5** Pacific Coast; **7, 6** Silicon Valley; **7, 7** Central America; **7, 8** Eastern Seaboard; **7, 9** Pacific Northwest; **8, 5** Cherokee Strip; **10, 6** Shenandoah Valley; **11, 5** Mississippi Delta.

regional 4 area; **5** areal, local, zonal; **6** county; **7** eastern, insular, lowland, spatial, western; **8** district, highland, meridian, northern, Oriental, southern, tropical; **10** antipodean, geographic, Occidental, peninsular, provincial; **11** continental, latitudinal, subtropical, territorial, topographic; **12** geographical, longitudinal.

regions of Britain 4 Fens; **6** Broads; **7** Borders, Marches UK; **8** Midlands; PHRASES: **3, 5** the North, the South; **3, 9** the Highlands; **4, 7** West Country; **4, 8** Home Counties; **5, 2, 7** north of Watford.

regions of the world 6 Orient; **8** Occident; **9** Antipodes; PHRASES: **3, 4** Far East; **3, 5** New World, Old World; **4, 5** down under; **5, 5** Third World; **6, 4** Middle East; **9, 5** developed world.

register 1 R; **3** log; **4** book, join, list, poll, roll, rota UK, show, till; **5** enter, index, panel, range, reach, score, tally, touch; **6** census, convey, docket, enlist, enroll, record, reveal, roster, scroll; **7** catalog UK, display, empanel, express, itemize, measure, payroll, realize, reserve; **8** cadastre, calendar, disclose, indicate, schedule, tabulate, transmit; **9** catalogue UK, chronicle, inventory; **10** understand; **11** matriculate; PHRASES: **2, 4** go into; **3, 2** put in; **3, 4, 4, 4** put your name down; **4, 2** sign on, sign up; **4, 3, 5** tick off names; **4, 7** keep details; **5, 2** notch up; **5, 5** enter names.

registrar 5 clerk; **6** bursar; **8** recorder; **10** consultant UK, specialist; **13** administrator; PHRASES: **6-6** record-keeper; **6, 8** public official.

registration 3 REG; **5** entry; **6** filing; **7** booking, listing, writing; **8** accounts, indexing, printing, registry; **9** engraving, enlisting, enrolment UK, epigraphy, recording; **10** cataloging, enlistment, inscribing; **11** accountancy, bookkeeping, cataloguing UK, chronicling, empanelment, registering, reservation; PHRASES: **5, 9** class enrolment UK; **6, 5** double entry; **6-7** record-keeping; **6, 9** course enrolment UK, school enrolment UK; **7, 2** signing on, signing up.

regress 5 lapse; **6** return, revert; **7** decline, relapse, retreat; **9** backslide, retrocede, retroflex; **10** degenerate, recidivate, retrograde, retrogress; PHRASES: **2, 4** go back; **4, 3** fall off; **4, 4** fall back, move back, slip back; **4, 6** lose ground; **4, 7** lose headway.

regressive 8 reactive; **9** atavistic, recessive, reflexive, relapsing, returning, reverting; **10** recidivist, recidivous, retrograde, retroverse; **11** backsliding, reactionary, restitutive, restitutory, retroactive, reversional; **12** compensatory, degenerating, recidivistic, reversionary; **13** deteriorating, retrospective; PHRASES: **5, 4** going back.

regret 3 rue; **5** qualm; **6** bemoan, lament, repent, sorrow; **7** deplore, remorse, scruple; **10** reluctance, repentance; **11** compunction.

regular 3 set; **4** even, flat; **5** daily, fixed, level, tidal, timed, usual; **6** annual, common, hourly, normal, phased, phasic, serial, smooth, stable, steady, weekly, yearly; **7** monthly, mundane, ordered, orderly, phaseal, routine, soldier, ticking, uniform; **8** accepted, constant, expected, frequent, habitual, measured, ordinary, periodic, reliable, repeated, rhythmic, squaddie *UK*, standard, swinging, unvaried; **9** alternate, automated, clockwork, combatant, customary, invariant, pulsatile, pulsating, pulsatory, recurrent, recurring, repeating, returning, revolving, symmetric, throbbing, unaltered, unchanged, unvarying; **10** automotive, changeless, conforming, consistent, homogenous, invariable, isochronal, methodical, metronomic, monotonous, periodical, reciprocal, regimented, repetitive, rhythmical, serialized, systematic, tantamount, unchanging, undulating, unvariable; **11** alternating, alternative, equipollent, featureless, homeostatic, homogeneous, isochronous, legionnaire, oscillating, oscillatory, predictable, repetitious, symmetrical, undeviating; **12** commensurate, conventional, standardized, unchangeable; **13** correspondent, proportionate, undiversified; PHRASES: **2-3-3** to-and-fro; **4-5** even-sided; **4-7** well-ordered.

regular (be regular) 3 hum, ply; **4** sway, tick; **5** drone, pulse, recur, swing, throb; **6** repeat, typify; **7** commute, conform, holiday, iterate, persist, pulsate, reoccur, shuttle, succeed; **8** intermit, undulate, vacation; **9** alternate, oscillate; **11** reciprocate; PHRASES: **2, 4, 3, 5** go back and forth; **3, 3, 4** ebb and flow, toe the line; **4, 1, 2** have a go; **4, 1, 5** work a shift; **4, 3, 2** come and go; **4, 4** beat time; **5, 3, 4** swing and sway.

regular (make regular) 3 set; **4** rule, time; **5** level, order; **6** adjust, steady; **7** balance, flatten; **8** regulate; **9** normalize, serialize; **10** regularize; **11** rationalize, systematize; PHRASES: **4, 4** make even; **4, 7**

make uniform; **5, 3** level out; **6, 5, 4** impose order upon; **7, 3** flatten out.

regularity 4 beat, tick; **5** swing, tempo, throb; **6** return, rhythm, timing; **7** measure, pattern, phasing, routine; **8** monotony, sameness, symmetry; **9** constancy, frequency, invariant, pulsation, treadmill; **10** automation, conformity, precession, recurrence, repetition, undulation, uniformity; **11** alternation, conformance, consistency, equilibrium, homeostasis, homogeneity, oscillation, periodicity, reciprocity; **13** invariability, regimentation, serialization; **14** predictability; **15** standardization; PHRASES: **3, 3, 4** ebb and flow; **4, 3, 5** same old story, same old thing; **4, 4** even pace; **4, 10** mass production; **5, 4** tidal flow; **5, 5** daily round; **5, 7** daily routine. *See also* **regular**

regularly 4 days; **5** daily, often; **6** always, nights; **8** evenings, mornings; **10** afternoons; PHRASES: **2, 1, 3** in a rut; **2, 1, 5** on a level; **2, 1, 6** in a groove; **2, 3, 3** to and fro; **2, 3, 4** up and down; **2, 5** by turns, in phase; **2, 6, 5** at stated times; **4, 4, 2, 4** from side to side; **4, 9** like clockwork. *See also* **regular**

regular thing 4 beat, fall, tide; **5** comet, meter, pulse, tempo; **6** autumn, rhythm, serial, spring, summer, winter; **7** holiday; **8** calendar, drumbeat, pendulum, vacation; **9** breathing, heartbeat, metronome, pulsebeat; PHRASES: **3, 3, 5** day and night; **3, 4** ebb tide; **3, 8** Old Faithful; **4, 4** leap year, neap tide; **4, 7** bank holiday; **5, 3, 5** death and taxes; **6, 2, 3, 4** months of the year; **6, 4** spring tide; **6, 7** summer holiday; **6, 8** annual vacation; **7, 5** Halley's Comet; **7, 7** shuttle service; **8, 4** incoming tide.

regulate 3 set; **4** rule, time; **5** guide, order; **6** adjust, direct, govern, handle, manage, steady; **7** balance, control, dictate, flatten; **8** legalize, organize; **9** normalize, serialize, supervise; **10** regularize; **11** rationalize, standardize, synchronize, systematize; PHRASES: **5, 4, 4** bring into line.

regulation 4 rule; **7** control; **9** directive, guideline, parameter; **10** adaptation, adjustment, alteration, management; **11** instruction.

regulator 5 valve; **6** device; **7** manager; **8** watchdog; **9** mechanism; **10** controller, supervisor.

rehabilitate 7 recover, restore; **10** assimilate; **11** acclimatize; PHRASES: **2-7** re-educate *UK*.

rehearsal 5 block, model, study, train, trial; 6 sample, sketch, tryout *UK*; 7 hearing; 8 audition, practice; 11 preparation; PHRASES: 3, 3 dry run; 3-7 run-through; 4-2 mock-up; 4, 4 road test; 4, 6 test flight; 5, 3 dummy run *UK*, pilot run, trial run; 5, 5 rough draft; 5, 7 trial balloon; 5, 9 dress ~; 8, 3 practice run.

rehearse 5 draft, study, train; 6 recite, repeat, review, sample, sketch; 7 prepare; 8 memorize, practice, simulate; PHRASES: 2, 4 go over; 3, 2 mug up *UK*; 3, 3 try out; 4, 7 read through, walk through.

reign 4 lead, rule, sway; 6 govern; 7 control; 9 supremacy; 11 sovereignty; PHRASES: 4, 4 hold sway.

reimburse *See* **repay**

reinforce 5 armor, boost; 7 bolster, fortify, support; 8 buttress, underpin; 9 emphasize, highlight, underline; 10 strengthen; PHRASES: 3, 5, 2 add force to; 4, 2 beef up; 5, 2 shore up.

reinstate *See* **restore**

reiterate 6 repeat, stress; 7 restate; 9 reinforce; PHRASES: 2, 4 go over.

reject 3 ban, bar, nix; 4 deny, flop, jilt, snub, veto; 5 loser, repel, spurn; 6 ignore, rebuff, refuse, return, slight; 7 boycott, decline, discard, exclude, failure, repulse; 8 deselect, disallow, prohibit; 9 blackball, blacklist, disregard, eliminate, ostracize; 10 wallflower; PHRASES: 2-5 no-hoper; 3, 2, 2 say no to; 4, 3, 4, 2 draw the line at; 4, 4 pass over, send back, turn down; 4, 5 lost cause; 4, 7 vote against; 4, 8 cold shoulder; 5, 2 break up, split up; 5, 3 throw out; 6, 5 faulty goods.

rejected 5 nixed; 6 denied, vetoed; 7 crossed, disused, negated, refused, refuted, snubbed; 8 annulled, appealed, canceled, declined, disowned, excluded, rebutted, recanted, repealed, returned, reversed, unchosen, unusable, unwanted; 9 contested, disavowed, discarded, dismissed, disobeyed, disproved, nullified, redundant, renounced, rescinded, retracted; 10 challenged, deprecated, disallowed, disclaimed, ineligible, obstructed, prohibited, questioned, repudiated, unaccepted, unrequited, unselected, unsuitable; 11 contravened, disbelieved, invalidated, nonaccepted, nonobserved, unqualified; 12 relinquished, unacceptable; 13 countermanded, crossappealed; PHRASES: 3, 2, 7, 2 not be thought of; 3, 8 not accepted; 4, 3 cast out; 4, 4 sent back; 6, 4 thrown away, turned down.

rejection 4 kick, snub, veto; 5 spurn; 6 denial, rebuff, slight; 7 atheism, boycott, refusal, repulse; 8 apostasy, ejection, negative, unbelief; 9 avoidance, declining, disavowal, disbelief, dismissal, exception, exclusion, exemption, expulsion, nonbelief, recusance, recusancy; 10 disclaimer, disownment, refutation; 11 agnosticism, disapproval, elimination, nonapproval, prohibition, repudiation; 12 blackballing, denunciation, disallowance, disclamation, disobedience, dissociation, invalidation, renunciation; 13 nonacceptance, nonobservance; 14 disassociation, nonassociation; PHRASES: 4, 8 cold shoulder; 4, 9 cold reception; 5-3 brush-off; 7, 2, 6 refusal of belief.

rejoice 4 rave; 5 cheer, exult, feast, glory, revel; 7 banquet, carouse, delight, roister, triumph; 8 jubilate; 9 celebrate; PHRASES: 4, 1, 4 have a ball; 4, 1, 5-2 have a knees-up; 4, 3, 3 leap for joy; 4, 5 make merry; 4, 7 make whoopee; 5, 1, 5 throw a party, 5, 2, 2 whoop it up; 5, 3, 4, 3 paint the town red.

rejoicing 3 joy; 4 high, rave; 5 beano, feast, gaudy, happy, jolly, merry, party, revel; 6 cheery, joyful; 7 banquet, delight, holiday, jollity, jubilee, ovation, triumph; 8 applause, cheering, ecstatic, euphoric, exultant, festival, glorious, jubilant, reveling; 9 festivity, happiness, jolliness, merriment; 10 applauding, exultation, joyfulness, jubilation, mafficking *UK*, roistering, triumphant; 11 anniversary, celebrating, celebration, celebratory, festivities, merrymaking; 13 jollification; PHRASES: 4, 6 flag waving; 5, 3 feast day, field day, great day; 6, 5 street party; 7, 3 special day; 8, 7 standing ovation.

rejoin *See* **reply**

relapse 6 revert; 7 decline; 9 reversion; 10 degenerate; 11 deteriorate; 12 degeneration; 13 deterioration.

relate 3 fit, tie; 4 link, tell; 5 apply, match, touch; 6 affect, couple, liaise, report; 7 bracket, connect, pertain, recount; 8 contrast, interest; 9 appertain, associate, empathize, juxtapose, reconcile; 10 correspond, understand; PHRASES: 4, 1, 7, 2 have a bearing on; 4, 2, 2, 4 have to do with; 4, 4 bear upon, deal with, link with; **5, 2** apply to, refer to; **5, 2, 4, 4** bring to bear upon; **5, 4** touch upon; **5-5** cross-refer; **6, 2** answer to, belong to, sketch in; **6, 4** liaise with; **7, 2** pertain to.

related 4 tied; **5** added, bound; **6** agnate, allied, bonded, joined, linked, merged, paired, wedded; **7** cognate, germane, kindred, spliced, twinned; **8** apposite, attached, combined, involved, relevant; **9** connected, pertinent; **10** affiliated, associated, correlated, implicated; **11** accompanied, consanguine; **12** interrelated; **14** consanguineous, interconnected; PHRASES: **4, 2** akin to; **4, 2, 4** tied up with.

relation 2 ma, pa; **3** kin, mom, mum *UK*, nan, pop, sib, sis; **4** aunt, gran, tale; **5** niece, uncle; **6** cousin, family, father, granny, mother, nephew, report, sister; **7** account, affairs, brother, contact, grandad, kindred; **8** dealings; **9** relatives; **11** grandfather, grandmother, interaction; **12** associations; **13** relationships; PHRASES: **4, 3, 3** kith and kin; **6, 7** family members.

relationship 3 tie; **4** bond, link; **5** ratio; **6** merger; **7** adjunct, analogy, bearing, kinship, liaison, linkage, rapport; **8** addition, affinity, alliance, appendix, homology, parallel, relation; **9** agreement, mutuality, reference, relevance; **10** attachment, comparison, connection, friendship, pertinence, similarity; **11** affiliation, association, combination, correlation, germaneness, implication, involvement, partnership, propinquity; **12** appositeness; **13** accompaniment, connectedness, consanguinity, understanding; **14** correspondence; **15** interconnection; PHRASES: **3-2** tie-up; **5-9** cross-reference.

relative *See* **relation**

relax 3 nap; **4** calm, doze, ease, laze, loll, rest; **5** lower, sleep; **6** drowse, lessen, loosen, lounge, reduce, repose, snooze, unwind; **7** recline, slacken; **8** decrease, diminish, mitigate; **10** deregulate; PHRASES: **3, 2** let go, let up; **3, 2, 2** let up on; **3, 3** let out; **3, 4** lie down, lie idle, sit back; **3, 4, 4, 2** put your feet up; **4, 1, 5** have a break; **4, 2, 4** take it easy; **4, 4** calm down, kill time, slow down; **5, 3** chill out; **6, 2** loosen up; **6, 4** settle down; **7, 2** lighten up.

relaxed 4 calm, cool, cozy, idle, lazy; **5** quiet, slack; **6** casual, floppy, gentle; **7** content, easeful, lenient, resting; **8** carefree, painfree, peaceful, tranquil; **9** easygoing,

eudemonic, leisurely, unhurried; **10** nonchalant, unstressed, untroubled; **11** comfortable, troublefree, undisturbed, unperturbed; **12** derestricted; PHRASES: **2, 4** at ease; **4-4** laid-back; **6-4** hassle-free, stress-free.

relay 6 convey, spread; **8** transmit; **11** communicate; PHRASES: **4, 2** pass on.

release 4 drop, free, undo; **5** death, issue, spare, untie; **6** acquit, parole, unhand, unlock; **7** deliver, dismiss, manumit, publish, quietus, unloose; **8** delivery, disclose, liberate; **9** discharge; **10** emancipate; **12** announcement; PHRASES: **3, 2** let go; **3, 4** set free.

relent *See* **give in**

relentless 7 endless; **8** pitiless, ruthless; **9** ceaseless, merciless; **10** persistent; **11** remorseless, unremitting.

relevance 6 weight; **7** bearing; **10** importance; **11** application, consequence, irrelevance; **12** significance; **13** applicability.

relevant 3 apt; **5** valid; **6** useful; **7** germane, related; **8** apposite, apropros, touching; **9** connected, pertinent; **11** appropriate; PHRASES: **2, 3, 5** to the point; **2, 8** of interest.

reliable 4 good, safe, true; **5** loyal, solid, sound; **6** honest, steady; **7** certain, staunch; **8** constant, faithful, truthful; **9** steadfast, unfailing; **10** dependable; **11** trustworthy.

reliant *See* **dependent**

relic 4 ruin; **5** fogou; **6** barrow, dolmen, eolith, fossil, menhir, relict, scroll; **7** antique, memento, neolith, relique, remains, remnant, vestige; **8** archaism, artifact, cromlech, epigraph, hangover, heirloom, leftover, megalith, monolith, souvenir; **9** aftermath, antiquity, earthwork, microlith, remainder, throwback; **10** manuscript, Victoriana; **11** aftereffect, inscription, memorabilia; PHRASES: **4, 3, 7** Dead Sea Scrolls; **4, 5** Pipe rolls; **4, 8** cave painting; **5, 2** flint ax; **5, 4** flint tool; **6, 5** burial mound, museum piece; **7, 8** ancient monument *UK*.

relief 3 aid; **4** alms, help, lull, rest; **5** break, cameo; **6** repose; **7** carving, charity, comfort, outdoor, outline, profile, release, respite, support; **8** intaglio, reprieve; **9** assistant, auxiliary; **10** assistance, embossment, liberation, painkiller, relaxation; **11** alleviation, reassurance; **13** reinforcement; **14** reinforcements; PHRASES: **3, 6** low ~; **4, 6** high ~.

relief-carving 4 boss; 5 cameo, glyph, medal; 6 relief; 7 chasing, rilievo; 8 anaglyph, intaglio; 9 embossing, engraving, medallion; 10 embossment, stiacciato; 11 anaglyptics; 15 anaglyptography; PHRASES: 3, 6 low relief; 3-6 bas-relief; 4, 6 half relief, high relief; 4, 7 alto relievo; 5, 7 basso rilievo, mezzo rilievo; 8, 7 intaglio rilievo.

relieve 4 calm, ease, fire, free, sack; 5 abate, allay, quiet, relax; 6 lessen, pacify, reduce, sedate, soften, solace, soothe, temper; 7 appease, assuage, comfort, console, dismiss, lighten, mollify, refresh, release, replace, restore; 8 diminish, liberate, mitigate, moderate, palliate, reassure; 9 alleviate, discharge, reinforce; 11 tranquilize; 12 anaesthetize; PHRASES: 3, 2 let go; 4, 3, 5, 2 take the place of; 4, 4, 3 take over for; 4, 4, 4 take over from; 5, 2, 3 stand in for; 5, 3 cover for; 5-3, 3 pinch-hit for; 10, 3 substitute for.

relieved 5 cured, eased; 6 calmed; 7 pleased, relaxed, sedated, soothed; 8 appeased, assuaged, consoled, restored, thankful; 9 comforted, mollified, reassured, refreshed.

religion 3 Bon, obi, Zen; 4 cult, sect; 5 Bahai, canon, credo, creed, dogma, faith, Islam, order; 6 Babism, belief, branch, church, ethics, morals, school, Shinto, Taoism, voodoo; 7 Bahaism, chapter, faction, Jainism, Judaism, Lamaism, outlook, Sikhism; 8 attitude, Buddhism, doctrine, Hinduism, Humanism, movement, paganism; 9 Calvinism, catechism, manifesto, Methodism, Mormonism, pantheism, principle; 10 conviction, persuasion, philosophy; 11 Anglicanism, Arminianism, Catholicism, perspective, Scientology; 12 Christianity, denomination, spiritualism, superstition, Unitarianism; 13 Mohammedanism, Protestantism; 14 fundamentalism; PHRASES: 3, 2, 4 way of life; 5, 2, 4 point of view; 5, 4 moral code; 6, 6 belief system; 8, 2, 5 articles of faith; 9, 4 Salvation Army.

religionist 5 bigot, ghazi; 6 tyrant, zealot; 7 fanatic; 8 crusader, preacher; 9 formalist, precisian, pulpiteer; 10 evangelist, iconoclast, missionary, persecutor, sermonizer; 11 bibliolater, inerrantist, Sabbatarian; 12 salvationist; 13 televangelist; 14 fundamentalist; PHRASES: 2, 10 TV evangelist; 3, 5 god squad; 5-6 Bible-basher UK, witch-hunter.

religious 2 pi; 4 holy, pure; 5 godly, loyal, pious; 6 ardent, church, devout, humble, mystic, sacred, solemn, strict; 7 ascetic, bigoted, canting UK, churchy, devoted, dutiful, fervent, preachy, saintly, zealous; 8 cherubic, faithful, militant, monastic, orthodox, reliable, reverent, seraphic, thorough, unctuous; 9 believing, crusading, dedicated, fanatical, observant, Pharisaic, prayerful, prostrate, spiritual; 10 anchoretic, devotional, missionary, practicing, theopathic, worshipful; 11 churchgoing, consecrated, evangelical, formalistic, reverential, ritualistic, theological; 12 otherworldly, transcendent; 13 conscientious, sanctimonious; 14 fundamentalist; PHRASES: 3-7 God-fearing; 4-9 self-righteous; 4-11 self-sacrificing; 5-7 Bible-bashing; 6-4-4 holier-than-thou; 6-6 priest-ridden UK; 7, 3, 5 holding the faith.

religious book *See* **religious manual, religious text**

religious festival 4 Holi, Lent, Noel; 5 Agape, Delia, feast, Purim; 6 Advent, Baraim, Divali, Easter, fiesta, Pesach, taanit; 7 Beltane, Carneia, Dasehra, Ramadan, Samhain, Sukkoth, Whitsun; 8 Agrionia, Apaturia, Carnival, Dionysia, encaenia UK, festival, Floralia, Hanukkah, Muharram, Nativity, Passover, Yuletide; 9 Christmas, festivity, Hallowe'en, Zulhijyah; 10 Eastertide, Lupercalia, Panathenea, Saturnalia; 11 Anthesteria; 12 Thesmophoria; PHRASES: 3-2-4 Eid-ul-Adha, Eid-ul-Fitr; 4, 2, 2 Fast of Av; 4, 5 love feast; 5, 2, 5 Feast of Weeks; 5-4 Durga-puja; 7, 3, 4 Chinese New Year; 7, 8 Harvest Festival.

religious leader 1 R; 4 dean, guru, imam, lama, pope; 5 rabbi; 6 bishop, priest; 7 pontiff, provost; 8 cardinal; 9 ayatollah; 10 archbishop; PHRASES: 4, 6 high priest.

religious manual 5 canon, farse; 6 mahzor, missal, rubric, siddur; 7 machzor, menaion, ordinal; 8 breviary, Virginal; 10 lectionary, pontifical; PHRASES: 4, 2, 5 book of hours; 4, 4 mass book; 6, 4 church book, prayer book.

religious orders 6 Minims; 7 Servite; 8 Salesian, Templars, Theatine, Trappist, Ursuline; 9 Barnabite, Capuchins, Carmelite, Dominican; 10 Brigittine, Carthusian, Cistercian, Franciscan, Jeronymite, visitation; 11 Augustinian, Benedictine, Camaldolese, Sylvestrine, Trinitarian, Visitandine; 12 Hospitallers; PHRASES: 4, 6 Poor Clares.

religious person 5 fakir, hajji, sadhu, saint; **6** martyr, mystic, palmer, votary; **7** acolyte, bhikshu, convert, devotee, holyman, pietist, pilgrim; **8** believer, disciple, marabout, neophyte, sannyasi; **9** religious; **10** catechumen, worshipper; **11** bodhisattva, charismatic; PHRASES: **3, 2, 6** man of prayer; **3, 8** the faithful; **4, 5** real saint; **5, 2, 3** child of God.

religious text 2 AV, NT, OT; **4** Veda; **5** Agama, Bahir, Bible, canon, Koran, Quran, Sunna, sutra, Torah; **6** Avesta, Dhamma, Gemara, Granth, Hadith, Jataka, Nikaya, Pitaka, Purana, shruti, smriti, Talmud, Targum; **7** Apadana, Avadana, Gospels, Masorah, Mishnah, Nihongi, Rigveda, shastra; **8** Aranyaka, Epistles, Samaveda; **9** Apocrypha, Dipavamsa, Mahavastu, scripture, Theravada, Tripitaka UK, Upanishad, Yajurveda; **10** Dhammapada, Septuagint, Yengishiki; **11** Atharvaveda; PHRASES: **3-2** Lun-yu; **3, 4** the Book, the Word; **3, 4, 4** the Good Book; **3, 7, 5** New English Bible; **3, 9** New Testament, Old Testament; **4, 2, 3** word of God; **4, 2, 3, 4** Book of the Dead; **4, 2, 6** Book of Mormon; **4, 4, 5** Good News Bible; **4, 5** Holy Bible, Pali Canon; **4, 5, 5** King James' Bible; **4-6** Zend-Avesta; **6, 5** Geneva Bible, Gideon Bible; **7, 7** Revised Version; **8-4** Bhagavad-Gita; **8, 5** Breeches Bible; **8, 7** Synoptic Gospels; **9, 5** Jerusalem Bible.

relinquish 4 cede, doff, drop, junk, kick, lose, shed; **5** avoid, forgo, loose, scrap, shred, waive, yield; **6** assign, divest, recant, resign, slough; **7** abandon, abstain, discard, forfeit, release; **8** abdicate, abnegate, forswear, jettison, renounce, transfer, unclench; **9** repudiate, surrender; **11** disaccustom; **12** tergiversate; PHRASES: **3, 2, 2** let go by, let go of; **3, 3, 2** get rid of; **4, 2** give up, tear up; **4, 3** cast off; **4, 4** hand over; **4, 4, 4** quit one's hold; **5, 3** swear off, write off; **5, 4** throw away; **5, 4, 2** leave hold of; **6, 2** forget it; **6, 3** slough off; **6, 4, 4** change one's mind, loosen one's grip.

relish 4 like; **5** enjoy, savor; **7** delight, elation; **8** pleasure; **9** enjoyment; PHRASES: **7, 2** delight in. *See also* **preserved thing**

reluctant 4 wary; **5** loath, sulky; **6** averse; **7** opposed; **8** cautious, hesitant; **9** atheistic, resistant, skeptical, unwilling; **10** dissenting, indisposed, protesting; **11** disinclined; **14** unenthusiastic.

reluctant person 6 sulker; **7** atheist, dropout, shirker, skeptic; **8** objector, resister; **9** abstainer, dissenter, dissident, protester; **11** nonactivist, nonbeliever; **14** procrastinator.

remain 4 stay, wait; **5** abide; **6** endure, linger; **7** persist; **8** continue; PHRASES: **2, 2** go on; **4, 2** keep on, stay on; **4, 3** stay put; **4, 4** mark time; **4, 5** hang about UK; **4, 6** hang around, stay behind; **5, 5** tread water.

remainder 4 bits, body, butt, husk, plug, rest, rump, stub, wake; **5** ashes, bones, chunk, piece, relic, roach, ruins, shard, shell, stump, torso, trace, track, trail, trunk; **6** corpse, crumbs UK, debris, dottle, effect, fossil, memory, record, relict, result, scraps; **7** balance, cadaver, carcass, frustum, rejects, remains, remnant, residue, seconds, vestige; **8** leavings, reminder, remnants, skeleton, souvenir, survival, vestiges, wreckage; **9** afterglow, footprint, fragments, leftovers, sweepings; **11** aftereffect, fingerprint, memorabilia, remembrance; PHRASES: **3, 3** fag end; **4, 3** butt end; **4, 4** dead body; **5, 3** scrag end UK; **5, 4** what's left; **5, 5** empty shell; **6, 6** tribal memory; **9, 3** cigarette end; **9, 4** cigarette butt.

remaining 4 left; **5** spare; **6** bereft, excess, extant, orphan; **7** lasting, resting, widowed; **8** enduring, orphaned, rejected, residual; **9** abandoned, deposited, discarded, lingering, residuary, resultant, surviving, vestigial; **10** hereditary; **11** outstanding, patrimonial, sedimentary, superfluous; **12** precipitated; PHRASES: **4-3** cast-off; **4, 4** left over; **4, 6** left behind.

remains *See* **remainder**

remark 3 say; **4** note, quip, shot; **5** aside, crack, sally, state; **6** notice; **7** comment, mention, observe.

remarkable 3 fab; **4** rare; **6** exotic, unique; **7** amazing, awesome, bizarre, curious, strange; **8** fabulous, original, peculiar, singular, splendid, uncommon, wondrous; **9** eccentric, fantastic, ineffable, marvelous, wonderful; **10** astounding, miraculous, mysterious, outlandish, stupendous, surprising; **11** astonishing, exceptional, magnificent; PHRASES: **3-3** far-out, way-out.

remedial 5 tonic; **6** curing, emetic, peptic; **7** anodyne, healing, helpful, purging; **8** balsamic, curative, dietetic, hygienic, hypnotic, laxative, lenitive, narcotic, panacean, sanitary, soothing, specific, vomitory; **9** analeptic, analgesic, antidotal, cathartic, cleansing, demulcent, digestive, educative, emollient, medicinal, nutritive, paregoric, sovereign, theriacal; **10** alimentary, anesthetic, antiseptic, beneficial, corrective, febrifugal, insensible, palliative, preventive, salubrious; **11** antipyretic, nutritional, restorative, stimulative, therapeutic; **12** disinfectant, preventative, prophylactic, salutiferous; **13** counteracting, counteractive; PHRASES: **5, 3** first aid; **6-6** health-giving.

remedy 3 aid, fix; **4** cure, ease, heal, help, mend; **5** solve, tonic, treat; **6** amends, answer, elixir, recipe, relief, soothe, succor; **7** correct, demulce, formula, improve, mixture, nostrum, panacea, redress, relieve, resolve, restore, therapy; **8** antidote, medicine, palliate, recovery, solution, specific; **9** alleviate, amendment, atonement, expiation, moderator, remedying, treatment; **10** catholicon, correction, corrective, medication, neutralize, resolution; **11** alleviation, preparation, restitution; **12** prescription, recuperation; PHRASES: **3, 5** put right; **4, 1, 4** work a cure; **4, 3** sort out; **4-3** cure-all, heal-all; **4, 4** deal with; **4, 4, 2** take care of; **4, 6** make better; **6, 5** elixir vitae; **6, 8** patent medicine.

remember 5 evoke, learn; **6** recall, relive, retain, review; **7** reflect, regress, reprize, retrace; **8** archaize, consider, identify, memorize; **9** recapture, recognize, recollect, reminisce; PHRASES: **4, 2** call up; **4, 2, 4** bear in mind, call to mind, keep in mind; **4, 3, 3** have off pat *UK*; **4, 4** hark back, look back; **4, 4, 7** take into account; **4, 5** know again; **5, 2** think of; **5, 2, 4** bring to mind; **5, 4** think back; **6, 2** dredge up, summon up; **6, 2, 6** commit to memory; **7, 2** conjure up.

remembrance 6 memory; **7** tribute; **8** memorial, rosemary; **9** flashback, nostalgia, recalling, reviewing; **11** celebration; **12** recollection, reminiscence; **13** commemoration; PHRASES: **4, 2** déjà vu; **7, 4** harking back.

remind 3 nag; **5** haunt, recap; **6** prompt, repeat, retell, review; **12** recapitulate; PHRASES: **2, 11** be reminiscent; **3, 2, 5** run by again; **3, 4, 6** jog one's memory, jog your memory; **4, 1, 4** make a note, ring a bell; **4, 3, 4** take you back; **4, 4** hark back; **5, 2** brush up; **5, 2, 4** bring to mind; **5, 4** bring back; **6, 1, 5** strike a chord; **6, 7** ~ oneself.

reminder 3 cue; **4** memo, note; **5** album, recap, token; **6** notice, prompt, record; **7** memento; **8** calendar, keepsake, mnemonic, prompter, souvenir; **9** scrapbook; **10** knickknack, memorandum; **11** remembrance; PHRASES: **4-7** aide-mémoire; **10, 5** photograph album.

reminiscence *See* **remembrance**

remiss *See* **careless**

remit 3 pay; **4** send; **5** refer; **6** lessen, settle, submit; **7** concern, forward, slacken; **8** decrease, diminish, dispatch; PHRASES: **4, 2** pass on.

remnant *See* **remainder**

remonstrate 5 argue; **6** object, oppose; **7** protest; **8** complain.

remora 10 suckerfish; **11** sharksucker.

remorse 5 guilt, shame; **6** qualms, regret, sorrow; **9** penitence; **10** contrition, repentance; **11** compunction; **13** embarrassment; PHRASES: **4-8** self-reproach.

remote 3 far; **4** lone; **5** aloof; **7** distant, faraway, obscure; **8** isolated, lonesome, outlying, secluded, unlikely; **9** withdrawn; **10** irrelevant; **11** godforsaken; **12** inaccessible; PHRASES: **3-3** cut-off; **3, 3, 3** off the map; **3, 3, 7** dim and distant; **5-2-4** unget-at-able.

remote place 5 booay, bundu *UK*; **7** outback; **8** backveld; **9** backwater, backwoods; **10** backblocks *UK*, hinterland; PHRASES: **3, 6** the sticks; **4, 2, 6** back of beyond; **4, 7** back country.

removal 7 erasure, purging, voiding; **8** clearage, clearing, deletion, drainage, draining, ejection, emptying, voidance; **9** canceling, catharsis, clearance, deduction, depletion, exclusion, purgation, unfouling, uprooting; **10** amputation, evacuation, exhaustion, extraction, withdrawal; **11** abstraction, elimination, eradication, extrication, subtraction; **12** confiscation, displacement; PHRASES: **5-9** asset-stripping; **6, 4** taking away; **7, 2** pulling up; **7, 3** ripping out, tearing out; **8, 3** plucking out, scouring out.

remove 3 cut, lop; **4** clip, dock, flay, move, oust, pare, peel, skin; **5** eject, evict, exile, expel, flake, pluck, prune, shear, shift, strip; **6** banish, deduct, delete, denude, deport, depose, detach, unseat, uproot; **7** curtail, detract, extract, retreat; **8** amputate, displace, distance, subtract; **9** eliminate, eradicate, extricate; **10** confiscate, decapitate, disconnect; PHRASES: **2, 4, 4** do away with; **3, 3** cut off, rip out; **3, 3, 2** get rid of; **4, 2** pull up; **4, 3** draw out, pull out, root out, rule out, take off, take out, tear out; **4, 4** take away; **5, 3** pluck out, strip off *UK.*

remunerate 3 pay, tip; **4** wage; **5** bribe, repay; **6** reward; **9** reimburse; **10** compensate, distribute, recompense; PHRASES: **3, 3** pay off; **3, 10** pay commission; **4, 3** dish out, dole out; **6, 4, 4** tickle one's palm; **7, 3, 3** sweeten the pot.

remuneration 3 fee, pay, tip; **4** perk, wage; **5** bonus, bribe, wages; **6** income, payoff, return, reward, salary; **7** payment, pension, stipend; **8** earnings, expenses, retainer; **9** emolument, incentive; **10** commission, enticement, honorarium, inducement, perquisite; **12** compensation; **13** reimbursement; PHRASES: **6, 9** golden handshake; **10, 3** redundancy pay.

renaissance 7 rebirth, revival; **8** recovery; **10** resurgence; **11** reanimation, reawakening; **12** regeneration, resurrection; **13** reincarnation; **14** revitalization, revivification; PHRASES: **3, 5** new start; **3, 9** new beginning.

rend *See* **tear**

render 4 give, make; **5** cause, judge, yield; **6** afford, decide, decree, depict, purify, reduce, submit, supply; **7** declare, deliver, execute, extract, perform, portray, provide; **8** condense; **9** represent, translate; **10** adjudicate; **11** concentrate; PHRASES: **4, 4** boil down, hand over, melt down; **4, 9** make available; **5, 2, 6** cause to become.

rendezvous 4 date, meet, site; **5** tryst; **6** gather, muster, resort; **7** hangout, meeting, station; **8** assemble, location; **10** congregate, engagement; **11** appointment, assignation; PHRASES: **3, 8** get together; **4, 7** make contact; **4, 8** come together; **7, 5** meeting place, meeting point; **8, 5** assembly point.

renew 4 mend; **5** rerun; **6** change, recall, rehash, reheat, remake, repair, repeat, replay, resume, revamp, revise, revive, update; **7** freshen, rebuild, recycle, refresh, reissue, repaint, reprint, restart, restore, upgrade; **8** recharge, redesign, rekindle, renovate; **9** modernize, refurbish, reinstate, replenish, reprocess, resurrect, revitalize; **10** recommence, regenerate, rejuvenate, revitalize; **11** recondition, reconstruct, reintroduce; PHRASES: **2-2** re-up; **4, 2** warm up; **4, 4** come

back, make good, play back; **5, 1, 8** stage a comeback; **5, 5** begin again, start again; **5, 6** start afresh; **6, 2** return to.

renewable energy 7 biomass; **8** biofuels, windmill; **9** biodiesel; PHRASES: **4, 4** wind pump; **4, 5** wave power *UK*, wind power; **4, 7** wind turbine; **4, 9** wind generator; **5, 4** water mill; **5, 5** solar power, tidal power; **5, 6** solar energy, tidal energy; **5, 7** solar battery, water turbine.

renounce 4 deny, quit; **5** annul, demit, demur, forgo; **6** abjure, cancel, desert, recant, reject, repeal, revoke; **7** abandon, abstain, disavow, forsake, nullify, rescind, retract; **8** abdicate, abrogate, forebear, forswear; **9** repudiate, surrender; **10** apostasize, invalidate, relinquish; **11** countermand; **12** tergiversate; PHRASES: **2, 1, 1-4** do a U-turn; **2, 7** go without; **3, 4, 3** eat one's hat; **3, 4, 5** eat one's words; **4, 2** give up; **4, 4** hand over, take back; **5, 3** swear off; **6, 4, 4** change one's mind.

renovate *See* **renew**

renown 4 fame; **6** repute; **9** celebrity, notoriety; **10** popularity, prominence, reputation; **11** distinction, recognition.

renowned 3 VIP; **4** sung; **6** fabled, famous; **7** popular; **9** legendary, prominent; **10** celebrated, recognized; **11** established, illustrious; **13** distinguished; PHRASES: **4-5** well-known.

rent 3 fee, let, rip; **4** cost, gash, hire, hole, slit, tear, tore, torn; **5** cleft, crack, lease, slash, split; **6** charge, divide, rental; **7** charter, fissure, payment; PHRASES: **4, 3** hire out, lend out, ~ out; **4, 6** hire charge; **4, 7** ~ payment; **6, 4** ground ~ *UK*, market ~; **8, 4** economic ~; **10, 4** peppercorn ~.

renunciation 6 denial, repeal; **7** refusal; **9** annulment, disavowal, disowning, rejection, surrender; **10** abdication, abjuration, abrogation, refutation, retraction, revocation; **11** abandonment, countermand, forswearing, recantation, repudiation, rescindment; **12** cancellation, invalidation, renouncement, retractation; **13** nullification; **14** relinquishment; PHRASES: **8-3** swearing-off.

repair 2 go; **3** fix, sew, tie; **4** bind, darn, edit, fill, heel, join, line, mend, plug, seal, sole, stop, tune; **5** amend, caulk, clout, cover, emend, leave, patch, refit, right, visit; **6** adjust, cobble, fixing, reface, reline, remedy, resole, soling, splice, thatch, tuning; **7**

binding, correct, darning, editing, healing, heeling, mending, plaster, recover, rectify, renewal, repairs, restore, retread, service; **8** cobbling, maintain, overhaul, patching, resoling, splicing; **9** amendment, insertion, resurface, servicing; **10** adjustment, correction, emendation, reactivate, reassemble, renovation, reparation; **11** cannibalize, maintenance, overhauling, restoration, resurfacing *UK*, reupholster; **12** reactivation, reassembling; **13** rectification, reinforcement, reintegration; **14** beautification, reconditioning, redintegration; PHRASES: **2-2-8** do-it-yourself (DIY); **3, 2, 5** put in order; **3, 4, 8** put back together; **3, 5** put right; **4, 1, 3** stop a gap; **4, 1, 4** plug a hole; **4, 2** bind up, fill in, plug up; **4-2** tune-up; **4, 2, 3, 6** fill in the cracks, pick up the pieces; **4-3** Band-Aid; **4, 4** make good; **4-4** face-lift; **5, 2** patch up; **5, 4** paper over; **5, 8** piece together; **10, 3** straighten out.

repairer 5 curer, DIYer, fixer; **6** darner, doctor, editor, healer, mender, salvor, tailor, tinker; **7** amender, cobbler, painter, patcher, plumber, surgeon; **8** engineer, handyman, mechanic, reformer, restorer, salvager; **9** decorator, emendator, hypnotist, osteopath, rebuilder, rectifier, reformist, renovator, repairman, subeditor *UK*; **10** bonesetter *UK*, copyeditor, seamstress; **11** electrician, proofreader, refurbisher; **12** chiropractor, psychiatrist; **13** psychoanalyst; **15** psychotherapist; PHRASES: **2-2-10** do-it-yourselfer; **3, 8** art restorer; **4-8** shoe-repairer; **5, 6** faith healer; **5-7** knife-grinder; **7, 7** plastic surgeon.

reparation 6 amends; **7** apology, damages; **9** atonement, expiation, indemnity; **10** recompense; **11** appeasement, restitution; **12** compensation, propitiation; **13** reimbursement; **14** reconciliation.

reparation (make reparation) 5 atone; **6** pacify; **7** appease, expiate; **9** apologize; **10** conciliate, propitiate; PHRASES: **4, 6** make amends.

repast 4 meal; **5** feast; **6** buffet; **7** banquet.

repay 6 refund, return, settle; **7** compose, restore; **9** indemnify, reimburse, retaliate; **10** compensate, recompense; PHRASES: **3, 4** pay back; **5, 3** atone for.

repeal *See* **cancel**

repeat 3 bis; **4** copy, echo, redo; **5** ditto, extra, mimic, recap, rerun; **6** double, encore, mirror, parrot, recite, rehash, remake,

replay, retell; **7** imitate, iterate, reissue, reprint, reprize, restate; **8** offprint, practice, redouble, rehearse; **9** duplicate, reiterate, replaying, replicate, reproduce, reshowing; **10** plagiarize, recurrence, repetition; **11** duplication, reduplicate, reiteration, replication; **12** reappearance; PHRASES: **2, 1, 6** do a ~; **2, 4** go over; **2, 5** do again; **3, 5** say again; **3, 7** new edition; **4, 5** show again; **6, 5** return match; **6, 7** second helping; **7, 4** curtain call.

repeated 6 echoed, redone, remade; **7** doubled; **8** constant, frequent, mirrored; **9** continual, imitative, recurrent, recurring, redoubled; **10** duplicated, parrotlike, repetitive, replicated, reproduced; **11** plagiarized; **12** reduplicated.

repeatedly 5 often; **10** frequently, resonantly; **11** continually, incessantly, insistently, recurrently; **12** monotonously, persistently, repetitively, rhythmically; **13** reiteratively, repetitiously; PHRASES: **2, 7** ad nauseam; **2, 9** in duplicate; **2, 10** in triplicate; **3, 2, 3, 3** day in day out; **3, 5, 3** day after day; **4, 2, 4, 3** year in year out; **4, 3, 4** over and over; **4, 3, 5** time and again; **4, 5, 4** many times over, time after time, year after year; **5, 3, 5** again and again.

repeated word 5 rhyme; **6** cliché, slogan, truism; **8** anaphora; **9** assonance, catchword; **10** epistrophe; **11** catchphrase, reiteration, restatement; PHRASES: **4, 4** buzz word.

repel 3 cut, jar; **4** snub; **5** annoy, deter, grate, shock, spurn, upset; **6** enrage, offend, rebuff, refuse, reject, resist, revolt, sicken, slight; **7** disgust, prevent, repulse, torment; **8** nauseate; **9** displease; **10** antagonize, disincline, scandalize; PHRASES: **4, 2, 3** keep at bay; **4, 3** fend off, hold off, ward off; **4, 3, 4, 4** make you feel sick; **4, 4** keep away, turn back; **4-8** cold-shoulder; **5, 3** brush off, chase off; **5, 4** drive away, drive back.

repent 5 atone; **6** recant, reform, regret; **9** apologize; PHRASES: **2, 5** be sorry; **2, 8** be penitent; **2, 10** be remorseful; **3, 11** ask forgiveness; **4, 6** feel sorrow.

repercussion 6 effect, impact, result, upshot; **7** outcome; **8** backlash; **9** aftermath, causality, corollary, influence; **11** consequence, implication; **12** ramification; **13** reverberation; PHRASES: **5-2, 6** knock-on effect *UK*; **5, 3, 6** cause and effect; **5, 8** chain reaction; **6, 6** domino theory; **8, 6** snowball effect.

repertory 5 range, stock; 6 series; 7 company, staging, theater; 9 selection; 10 production, repertoire; 11 performance; PHRASES: 7, 5 theater group.

repetition 4 echo; 5 ditto; 6 reecho, repeat; 7 copying, recital, reprize; 8 anaphora, doubling, practice; 9 echolalia, imitation, rehearsal, repeating; 10 epistrophe, plagiarism, practicing, recurrence, redoubling; 11 duplication, reiteration, replication; 12 reappearance, reproduction; 13 reduplication, reverberation; PHRASES: 5, 5 doing again.

repetitious 4 dull; 5 wordy; 6 boring, dreary, otiose, prolix; 7 echoing, harping, tedious; 8 doubling, tiresome; 9 iterative, redundant, reiterant, repeating; 10 monotonous, pedestrian, pleonastic, redoubling, repetitive; 11 duplicative, reiterative; 12 repetitional, reproductive, tautological; 14 recapitulative; PHRASES: 2-7 re-echoing; 5-2-1-6 stuck-in-a-groove.

repetitive *See* **repetitious**

replace 4 oust, swap; 5 eject, evict, exile, expel, trade, usurp; 6 banish, change, deport, depose, return, switch, unseat; 7 restore; 8 dethrone, exchange, supplant; 9 overthrow, reinstate, replenish, restitute, supersede; 10 substitute; 11 interchange; PHRASES: 3, 4 put back; 3, 7 use instead; 4, 3, 5, 2 take the place of.

replacement 5 proxy; 6 deputy; 7 removal, reserve; 8 ejection, eviction, takeover, transfer; 9 expulsion, overthrow, surrogate, unseating; 10 deposition, relocation, substitute, understudy; 11 alternative, restoration; 12 substitution; 13 supplantation; PHRASES: 5-2 stand-in.

replay *See* **repeat**

replenish 4 fill; 6 refill, refuel, reload; 7 refresh, replace, restock; 8 resupply; 9 reinforce, revictual; 10 revitalize; PHRASES: 3, 2 top up *UK*; 4, 2 fill up, make up; 4, 4 make good; 5, 2 stock up.

replete *See* **full**

repletion 4 glut; 7 satiety, surfeit; 8 fullness.

replica 4 copy; 5 clone, model, print; 6 double; 9 duplicate, facsimile, imitation, photocopy; 11 duplication; 12 reproduction; PHRASES: 4-2 mock-up; 6, 4 carbon copy.

reply 5 react; 6 answer, refute, rejoin, retort; 7 account, confute, counter, respond, riposte; 8 comeback, feedback, reaction, response; 9 rejoinder, retortion; 10 refutation; 11 confutation; PHRASES: 4, 4, 4 come back with; 6, 4 answer back.

report 3 pop, say; 4 bang, boom, echo, shot, tale, tell; 5 break, cover, crack, crash, issue, noise, scoop, state, story, write; 6 arrive, convey, inform, relate; 7 account, narrate, publish, recount, testify, version; 8 describe, disclose, dispatch, document, register, transmit; 9 appraisal, broadcast, chronicle, circulate, explosion, freelance, interview, narrative, publicize, statement, syndicate, testimony; 11 description; PHRASES: 4, 2 show up, turn up; 4, 2, 7 give an account; 4, 5 loud noise; 4, 7 give details; 5, 2 check in; 7, 8 present yourself.

reporter 3 cub; 6 legman; 8 newshawk, pressman, stringer; 9 columnist, newshound; 10 journalist; 13 correspondent.

reporting 5 scoop; 7 legwork, spoiler; 8 coverage; 9 exclusive, informing, reportage; 10 journalism, muckraking; 11 newscasting; 12 doorstepping, doorstopping, newspapering; 13 sportscasting; PHRASES: 4, 8 live coverage; 4, 9 news gathering, news ~.

repose 3 lie; 4 calm, ease, hush, lull, rest; 5 death, peace, quiet, relax, sleep, still; 6 lounge, satori; 7 leisure, nirvana, recline, silence, slumber; 8 ataraxia, calmness, doldrums, quietism, quietude, serenity; 9 composure, placidity, quietness, stillness; 10 inactivity, placidness, quiescence, quiescency, relaxation; 11 restfulness, tranquility; 12 peacefulness, windlessness; 13 contemplation, insensibility; PHRASES: 3, 1, 6, 2, 3 not a breath of air; 3, 4 lie down; 3, 4, 4, 2 put your feet up; 4, 2, 4 take it easy; 4, 4 dead calm; 5, 9 horse latitudes; 6, 6 silken ~; 7, 3 stretch out; 7, 4 eternal rest; 7, 8 nothing stirring.

repository 4 mine; 5 store; 6 origin, source; 8 fountain; 9 container; 10 receptacle, storehouse; PHRASES: 7, 4 storage area.

represent 3 aid; 4 copy, draw, film, help, mean, show, snap; 5 catch, evoke, image, movie, print, shoot; 6 denote, depict, embody, mirror, record, render, rotate, typify; 7 capture, enlarge, imitate, mediate, portray, present, process, project, realize, reflect, signify; 8 generate, manifest, register, resemble; 9 construct, delineate, duplicate, epitomize, exemplify, incarnate, negotiate, personate, personify, reproduce, symbolize, transform, translate; **10** photograph, understudy; **11** impersonate; **12** characterize; PHRASES: **2, 1, 6, 2** be a symbol of; **3, 3** act for; **5, 2** stand in; **5, 2, 3** stand in for; **5, 3** speak for, stand for; **10, 2** correspond to; **10, 3** substitute for.

representation 4 copy, sign, type; **5** image, runes, Xerox *tm*; **6** double, sketch, symbol; **7** account, drawing, epitome, outline, picture, realism, replica, tracing, version, writing; **8** advocacy, argument, exemplar, likeness, notation, portrait; **9** complaint, depiction, duplicate, evocation, facsimile, imitation, photocopy, pictogram, portrayal, rendering, semblance, statement; **10** delegation, embodiment, figuration, impression, indication, lithograph, reflection, similarity, submission; **11** delineation, description, incarnation, presentment, realization; **12** doppelgänger, illustration, presentation, quintessence, typification; **13** demonstration, hieroglyphics, impersonation, manifestation, symbolization; **14** interpretation; **15** exemplification, personification; PHRASES: **4-5** look-alike; **4, 6** dead ringer; **5, 8** exact likeness; **6, 5** mirror image; **8, 5** spitting image.

representative 3 rep; **5** agent, envoy, proxy; **6** agency, deputy, herald, legate, sample; **7** adviser, attaché, example, pleader, typical; **8** attorney, delegate, diplomat, emissary, specimen, symbolic; **9** counselor, evocative, messenger, ombudsman, publicist, spokesman; **10** accountant, ambassador, archetypal, consultant, expressive, mouthpiece, peacemaker, substitute; **11** descriptive, propitiator, replacement, spokeswoman; **12** commissioner, illustrative, spokesperson; **13** demonstrative; **14** characteristic; PHRASES: **5-2** stand-in; **5, 3** sales rep *UK*; **5, 5** press agent; **5-7** cross-section.

representative body 5 forum, panel; **6** quorum, Senate; **7** council, embassy, mission; **8** conclave, Congress, legation, workshop; **9** committee, consulate; **10** conference, convention, delegation, Parliament, roundtable; PHRASES: **4, 7** city council, town council, town meeting; **5, 2, 8** board of aldermen; **5, 10** trade delegation; **6, 7** county council, parish council *UK*; **7, 5** working party; **7, 7** foreign service; **8, 4** official body; **10, 5** aldermanic board, diplomatic corps, diplomatic staff; **11, 4** negotiating body.

repress *See* **suppress**

reprieve *See* **pardon**

reprimand 3 rap; **4** rate; **5** blame, chide, scold; **6** berate, carpet *UK*, punish, rebuke, rocket; **7** censure, lecture, reproof, reprove, warning; **8** admonish, chastise, reproach, scolding; **9** castigate, criticism, criticize; **10** accusation, discipline, punishment; **12** admonishment; PHRASES: **4, 2, 3, 5** slap on the wrist; **4, 3** tell off, tick off *UK*; **7-2** talking-to; **7-3** telling-off *UK*, ticking-off *UK*; **8-4** dressing-down.

reprint 4 copy; **7** edition, reissue; **9** republish.

reprisal *See* **retaliation**

reproach *See* **reprimand**

reproduce 4 copy, echo; **5** breed, clone, mimic, print, Xerox *TM*; **6** repeat; **7** imitate, produce, reprint; **9** duplicate, photocopy, procreate, replicate; **11** counterfeit; PHRASES: **2-6** re-create; **4, 1, 4, 2** make a copy of; **4, 3** bash off, bash out *UK*, turn out; **4, 5** give birth; **4-7** mass-produce; **4, 8** have children; **5, 3** churn out, print off; **7, 5** produce young.

reproduction 3 oil, PMS; **4** copy, fake, film, plan, sham; **5** chart, clone, draft, graph, movie, phony *UK*, print, video, Xerox *TM*; **6** phoney, sketch; **7** artwork, cartoon, copying, diagram, drawing, etching, picture, rebirth, renewal, revival, tracing; **8** breeding, graphics, painting, Photofit *TM*, portrait, printing, spawning; **9** blueprint, collotype, engraving, Identikit *TM*, imitation, photocopy; **10** caricature, lithograph, photograph, publishing, renovation, repetition, resurgence, watercolor; **11** calligraphy, duplication, portraiture, reanimation, replication, restoration; **12** illumination, illustration, palingenesis, photocopying, regeneration, resurrection; **13** proliferation, reduplication, reincarnation, resuscitation; **14** multiplication, reconstruction; PHRASES: **6, 4** carbon copy.

reproductive 6 broody, gravid, penile, sexual, vulvar; **7** genetic, genital, ovarian, phallic, scrotal, seminal, vaginal; **8** bisexual, breeding, cervical, clitoral, enceinte, germinal, preggers *UK*, pregnant, prenatal; **9** expectant, expecting, obstetric, oviparous, perinatal, postnatal, procreant, puerperal, spermatic, unisexual; **10** fecundated, fertilized, generative, parturient, viviparous; **11** impregnated, originative, procreative, propagative; **14** multiplicative; **15**

parthenogenetic.

reproof *See* **criticism**

reprove *See* **criticize**

reptiles 3 asp, boa; 4 croc; 5 adder, agama, anole, cobra, gecko, krait, mamba, racer, skink, snake, swift, tokay, viper; 6 caiman, cayman, gavial, goanna, iguana, leguan, lizard, moloch, mugger, python, taipan, turtle, zaltys; 7 gharial, perenty, rattler, tuatara; 8 anaconda, basilisk, matamata, moccasin, perentie, ringhals, scincoid, slowworm, terrapin, tortoise; 9 alligator, blindworm, boomslang *UK*, chameleon, crocodile, galliwasp; 10 bushmaster, chuckwalla, copperhead, massasauga, racerunner, sidewinder; 11 amphisbaena, constrictor, cottonmouth, diamondback, rattlesnake; PHRASES: 3-2-5 fer-de-lance; 3, 5 pit viper, rat snake, sea snake; 3, 6 box turtle, mud turtle; 4, 5 bull snake, king snake, milk snake, puff adder, tree snake *UK*, vine snake, wart snake, whip snake; 4, 6 pond turtle, sand lizard *UK*, worm lizard; 4, 7 Gila monster; 5, 5 black snake, coral snake, glass snake, grass snake, green snake, water snake; 5, 6 green turtle; 5, 8 giant tortoise, water moccasin; 6, 5 flying snake, gaboon viper, garter snake, horned viper, ribbon snake, smooth snake *UK*; 6, 6 flying lizard, horned lizard, Komodo dragon; 7, 5 hognose snake; 7, 6 bearded lizard, frilled lizard, monitor lizard, painted turtle; 8, 5 mangrove snake, ringneck snake, russell's viper; 8, 6 snapping turtle; 9, 6 hawksbill turtle.

reptilian 4 cold; 5 scaly, stony; 6 apodal; 7 inhuman, reptant, saurian; 8 creeping, ophidian, squamous; 9 chelonian, reptiloid, snakelike; 10 lizardlike, serpentine, slithering, turtlelike, unfriendly; 11 crocodilian, emotionless, lacertilian, reptilelike, reptiliform; 14 poikilothermic; PHRASES: 4-7 cold-blooded.

republic *See* **state**

republican 12 antiroyalist; 14 antimonarchist; PHRASES: 3-8 pro-republic.

Republican 3 GOP; 4 Bush (George), Bush (George W.), Dole (Bob), Dole (Elizabeth), Ford (Gerald R.), Rice (Condoleezza), Taft (William Howard), Whig; 5 Grant (Ulysses S.), Hayes (Rutherford B.), Nixon (Richard); 6 Arthur (Chester A.), Cheney (Dick), Hoover (Herbert), Powell (Colin), Quayle (Dan), Reagan (Ronald); 7 Harding (Warren G.), Lincoln (Abraham); 8 Coolidge (Calvin), elephant, Garfield (James), Gingrich (Newt), Guiliani (Rudy), Harrison (Benjamin), McKinley (William), Rumsfeld (Donald); 9 Roosevelt (Theodore); 10 Eisenhower (Dwight D.); 14 Schwarzenegger (Arnold); PHRASES: 5-7 trust-busting.

repudiate *See* **deny**

repugnance 4 hate; 6 hatred; 7 disgust; 9 revulsion.

repugnant *See* **disgusting**

repulse 3 cut; 4 snub; 5 deter, repel, spurn; 6 appall, rebuff, reject, resist, revolt, sicken; 7 disgust, refusal; 8 ejection, nauseate, spurning; 9 dismissal, expulsion, rejection; PHRASES: 4, 2, 3 keep at bay; 4, 3 hold off, ward off; 4, 4 hold back, push away, turn away; 4, 8 cold shoulder; 5, 3 fight off, gross out; 5-3 brush-off; 5, 4 drive away, drive back, force away, force back.

repulsion 6 nausea, recoil; 7 disgust, dislike; 8 loathing, ugliness; 9 repelling, revulsion; 10 abhorrence, repellence, repellency, repugnance; 11 antigravity, disaffinity; 12 diamagnetism, polarization; 13 repulsiveness; PHRASES: 6, 9 mutual ~; 9, 5 repulsive force.

repulsive 4 foul, ugly, vile; 5 gross; 7 hideous, noisome, obscene; 8 horrible; 9 abhorrent, appalling, loathsome, obnoxious, offensive, repellent, repugnant, revolting, sickening; 10 disgusting, nauseating; 11 distasteful; 12 antipathetic; 13 objectionable; PHRASES: 3-7 off-putting; 7-7 stomach-turning.

reputable 5 sound; 6 decent, fabled, famous, honest; 7 eminent, honored, popular, upright; 8 approved, emeritus, reliable, renowned; 9 honorable, respected; 10 creditable, dependable; 11 respectable, trustworthy; 12 creditworthy; 13 distinguished; PHRASES: 2, 4, 4 in good odor; 2, 4, 6 of good repute; 2, 4, 8 of good standing; 2, 5 in favor; 2, 6 of repute; 4-7-2 well-thought-of; 5, 5 above board; 6, 7, 2 highly thought of; 6, 8 highly regarded.

reputation 4 aura, name, odor, tone; 5 savor; 6 regard, repute, status; 8 standing; 9 character, emanation; PHRASES: 3, 4 bad odor; 4, 4 good odor.

repute 5 trust; 7 probity; 8 prestige, standing; 10 confidence, reputation; 11 reliability.

reputed 6 fabled; 7 alleged; 8 apparent, believed, presumed, supposed; PHRASES: 2, 3, 5, 4 as the story goes; 2, 4, 3 so they say.

request 3 ask, beg, bid, bug, cry, woo; 4 call, coax, hawk, pray, tout, urge, want, wish; 5 apply, claim, court, favor, order; 6 accost, adjure, appeal, asking, cajole, desire, hustle, incant, insist, invite, invoke, motion, pester, prayer, urging, wooing; 7 begging, beseech, entreat, implore, propose, require, solicit, suggest, urgency; 8 approach, courting, entreaty, persuade, petition, pressure, proposal; 9 accosting, imploring, pestering; 10 adjuration, beseeching, insistence, invitation, invocation, persuasion, soliciting, suggestion, supplicate; 11 application, importunity, incantation, proposition, requirement; 12 counterclaim, solicitation, supplication; PHRASES: 3, 1, 5 ask a favor; 3, 2, 5 cri du coeur; 3, 3 ask for; 3, 3, 8 pop the question; 3, 5 ask leave, beg leave; 3, 10 ask permission, beg permission; 4, 3 call for, pray for; 5, 3 apply for; 5-5 round-robin; 6, 4 living will; 6, 8 solemn entreaty.

requester 5 asker, lover; 6 seeker, suitor; 7 hustler; 8 appealer, borrower, claimant, customer, inquirer, lobbyist; 9 appellant, applicant, candidate, canvasser, solicitor, suppliant; 10 petitioner, questioner, supplicant; 11 blackmailer; 12 extortionist; 15 counterclaimant; PHRASES: 4-6 fund-raiser.

require 4 lack, make, need, want; 5 force; 6 compel, demand, entail, expect, oblige; 7 command, involve; 11 necessitate; PHRASES: 2, 7 be without; 3, 4 not have; 4, 3 call for; 4, 3, 4, 3 feel the need for; 4, 4, 2 have need of; 5, 2, 4, 2 stand in need of.

required 5 vital; 6 absent, booked, needed, wanted UK; 7 desired, lacking, missing, needful, ordered; 8 demanded, reserved; 9 earmarked, essential, mandatory, necessary, requested, requisite; 10 compulsory, obligatory; 12 prerequisite; 13 indispensable; PHRASES: 2, 4 on call; 2, 5 on order; 2, 6 in demand; 6, 3 called for.

requirement 4 must, need; 5 order; 6 indent; 7 command, proviso, request; 8 standard; 9 condition, essential, necessary, necessity, provision, requisite, ultimatum; 10 constraint, injunction, obligation; 11 desideratum, necessaries, necessities, requisition, stipulation; 12 precondition,

prerequisite; 13 specification; PHRASES: 1, 4 a must; 4, 3, 3 sine qua non; 4, 10 bare essentials; 5, 10 prior conditions; 8, 4 shopping list.

requisite *See* **necessary**

requisition 5 seize; 6 demand; 7 request, summons; 10 commandeer; 11 application, appropriate; PHRASES: 4, 3 call for; 4, 4 take over; 5, 3 apply for.

rescind 5 annul; 6 cancel, repeal; 8 overturn, withdraw.

rescue 4 free, save; 6 saving; 7 deliver, release, salvage; 8 liberate; 9 salvation; 10 liberation; PHRASES: 3, 2 let go; 3, 4 set free; 4, 2, 3, 6 come to the ~.

rescuer 6 savior; 8 champion, redeemer; 9 deliverer, liberator.

research 3 dig; 4 plan, plot, seek; 5 draft, study; 6 sketch; 7 examine, explore; 8 analysis, contrive, document; 9 blueprint, enquiries UK, fieldwork; 11 examination, exploration, investigate; 13 investigation; PHRASES: 4, 4 look into; 4-7 fact-finding; 4, 9 make enquiries UK; 5, 4 delve into.

resemblance *See* **similarity**

resemble 4 echo; 5 agree, evoke, favor, match, tally; 6 accord, mirror; 7 compare, reflect, suggest; 8 coincide, parallel; 10 correspond; PHRASES: 2, 4 be like; 2, 7, 2 be similar to; 3, 3, 2, 4, 2 put one in mind of; 4, 2, 4 call to mind; 4, 4 look like, seem like; 4, 5 take after; 5, 2 savor of, smack of; 5, 2, 4 bring to mind.

resent 4 feel, hate, mind; 6 suffer; 7 dislike; 8 begrudge; PHRASES: 4, 1, 6 bear a grudge; 4, 5 take amiss; 4, 6 bear malice, feel piqued; 4, 6, 5 feel bitter about; 4, 7 take offense; 4, 9 feel aggrieved; 4, 9, 2 take exception to; 5, 5 smart under; 6, 2 object to.

resentful 4 acid, hurt, sore; 5 angry, moody, riled, sharp, stung, vexed; 6 bitter, pained, peeved, piqued, shirty; 7 acerbic, annoyed, bileful, bilious, caustic, envious, jealous, nettled, stroppy UK; 8 grudging, insulted, offended, provoked, smarting, spiteful, virulent; 9 acidulous, affronted, aggrieved, impatient, indignant, irritated, malicious, splenetic; 10 aggravated, displeased, embittered; 11 acrimonious, exasperated, reproachful; 12 disapproving, discontented; PHRASES: 2, 1, 3 in a pet; 2, 2, 4 up in arms; 3-3 put-out; 3, 6 not amused; 3-7 ill-humored; 6-2 worked-up; 7-2 wrought-up.

resentment 4 acid, bile, envy, gall; 5 anger, pique; 6 grudge, hatred, malice, rancor, spleen; 7 acidity, dislike, offense, umbrage; 8 acrimony, asperity, jealousy, rankling, soreness, vexation; 9 animosity, annoyance, antipathy; 10 bitterness, discontent, irritation; 11 aggravation, disapproval, displeasure, peevishness; 12 exasperation; 13 acidulousness, resentfulness; 14 disapprobation; 15 dissatisfaction; PHRASES: 3, 5 ill humor; 3, 8 ill feelings; 4, 2, 4 bone to pick; 4, 4 slow burn; 4, 8 hard feelings; 5-7 heartburning.

reservation 6 refuge; 7 booking, proviso; 8 distance; 9 aloofness, condition, corollary, sanctuary; 10 hesitation, reluctance; 11 stipulation; 12 registration; 13 unwillingness; PHRASES: 4, 4 game park; 4, 7 game reserve *UK*; 6, 7 nature reserve; 8, 6 wildlife refuge; 8, 9 wildlife sanctuary; 9, 4 protected area.

reserve 4 book, keep, save; 5 cache, extra, hoard, locum, order, spare, stash, stock, store; 6 retain, supply; 7 modesty, shyness, storage; 8 coldness, coolness, fallback, preserve, withhold; 9 aloofness, quietness, restraint, reticence, stockpile; 10 constraint, diffidence, reluctance, substitute; 11 replacement, subduedness; 12 backwardness; 15 standoffishness; PHRASES: 3, 2, 3, 4 put to one side; 3, 5 set aside; 4, 4 hold back, keep back, salt away; 5, 1, 7 leave a deposit; 5-2 stand-in; 9, 6 emergency supply.

reserved 3 shy; 4 cold, cool, kept; 5 aloof, quiet, taken; 6 booked, modest, unseen; 7 distant, engaged, ordered, subdued, unheard; 8 backward, detached, discreet, retained, reticent, retiring, snobbish; 9 diffident, earmarked, inhibited, reluctant, withdrawn; 10 restrained, unassuming, unfriendly; 11 constrained, introverted, standoffish, untouchable; 13 unforthcoming; 14 unapproachable; 15 uncommunicative; PHRASES: 3, 5 set aside; 3-7 low-profile; 4, 2, 7 held in reserve; 4, 4 kept back.

reserved space 4 room, seat; 5 berth, place; 7 seating, storage, stowage; 8 berthage, capacity; 13 accommodation; PHRASES: 7, 5 parking space, storage space; 7, 8 seating capacity; 8, 4 standing room.

reserves 4 cash; 5 funds, hoard, money, stash, store; 6 assets, backup, monies, stocks, stores; 7 capital, reserve, standby; 8

supplies; 9 resources, safeguard; 11 investments; 14 reinforcements; PHRASES: 4, 3 nest egg; 11, 4 contingency fund.

reservist *See* **soldier**

reservoir 4 lake, pool, tank; 5 basin; PHRASES: 10, 4 artificial lake.

reside 4 live, stay; 5 dwell, lodge; 6 occupy; 7 inhabit; PHRASES: 2, 1, 7, 2 be a feature of; 2, 1, 8, 2 be a resident of; 2, 6, 2 be vested in; 2, 7, 2 be located in, be present in; 2, 8, 2 be inherent in; 3, 6 lie within; 4, 2 live in; 4, 4, 4 have your home; 5, 2 exist in; 6, 2 belong to; 9, 2 appertain to.

residence 3 pad; 4 gaff, home, seat; 5 abode, house; 6 number; 7 habitat; 8 district, domicile, dwelling, location, postcode; 9 apartment, occupancy; 10 habitation; 11 inhabitance, whereabouts; PHRASES: 2, 5, 5 no fixed abode (NFA); 3, 4 ZIP code.

residence (take up residence) 4 camp, nest, room; 5 board, crash, lodge, perch, roost; 6 burrow, encamp, nestle, stable; 7 bivouac, quarter; PHRASES: 4, 2 move in; 4, 2, 4, 3 hang up one's hat; 4, 4 doss down; 4, 4, 7 park one's carcass; 4, 6 drop anchor; 5, 4, 4 pitch one's tent.

resident 2 in; 6 tenant; 7 citizen, denizen, dweller, settled; 8 colonial, dwelling, occupant, occupier, residing; 9 colonized, domiciled, immigrant, occupying; 10 inhabitant; 11 householder, naturalized, residential; PHRASES: 2, 3, 4 on the spot; 2, 3, 8 on the premises; 2, 4 at home; 2-5 in-house; 2, 9 in residence; 2, 10 in occupation; 4-2 live-in; 6, 2 living in.

residue 4 bran, dirt, junk, lees, peel, rest, scum, silt, skin, slag; 5 ashes, bilge, chaff, dregs, dross, husks, loess, scurf, trash, waste; 6 crumbs *UK*, excess, jumble, litter, lumber, powder, refuse, scoria, scraps, sewage, slough, sludge; 7 cinders, deposit, filings, garbage, grounds, moraine, offcuts, rejects, remains, rubbish, sawdust, stubble; 8 alluvium, castoffs, combings, dandruff, detritus, filtrate, heeltaps, leavings, oddments, peelings, remnants, residual, residuum, sediment, shavings; 9 clippings, excrement, leftovers, remainder, scourings, scrapings, skimmings, sweepings, trimmings; 11 precipitate; 12 offscourings; PHRASES: 4, 3, 4 bits and bobs, odds and ends; 4, 3, 6 bits and pieces.

resign 4 drop, quit; 5 chuck, forgo, leave; 6 depart, desert, retire, vacate; 7 abandon; 8

abdicate, withdraw; **9** surrender; **10** relinquish, renunciate; PHRASES: **3, 2, 2** let go of; **4, 2** give up; **4, 2, 2** jack it in; **4, 2, 4, 3** give up your job; **4, 2, 5** call it quits; **4, 3** walk out; **4, 4** quit work, step down; **4, 6** give notice; **5, 2, 3, 5** throw in the towel; **5, 4** stand down; **5, 4, 4** leave one's post; **5, 5** stand aside.

resignation **6** notice; **10** acceptance, submission; **11** forbearance; **12** acquiescence, notification; **14** acknowledgment.

resigned **5** stoic; **7** passive, stoical; **8** sanguine; **9** accepting; **10** fatalistic, forbearing, phlegmatic, reconciled, submissive; **11** acquiescent, indifferent; PHRASES: **4-9** long-suffering.

resilience **6** bounce, reflex, spirit; **8** buoyancy, strength; **9** endurance; **10** elasticity, pliability, resistance; **11** flexibility, springiness; **12** adaptability, cheerfulness; PHRASES: **6, 2, 4** return to base. *See also* **resilient**

resilient **5** hardy, tough; **6** bouncy, robust, strong, sturdy, supple; **7** buoyant, durable, elastic, pliable; **8** flexible, spirited; **9** reflexive, resistant; **13** irrepressible.

resin **3** gum, tar; **4** balm, tolu; **5** amber, japan, pitch, rosin; **6** dammar, mastic, resina; **7** asphalt, bitumen, gamboge, varnish; **8** resinoid; PHRASES: **5, 3** kauri gum.

resinous **5** gummy, tacky, tarry; **6** pitchy, rosiny, sticky; **7** viscous; **8** japanned; **9** asphaltic, varnished; **10** bituminous.

resist **4** defy, last; **5** avoid, fight, repel; **6** attack, battle, endure, harden, hinder, oppose, rebuff, refuse, strike; **7** abstain, contest, dissent, forbear, protest, refrain, repulse, stiffen, survive, toughen, weather; **8** confront, obstruct, struggle; **9** challenge, deprecate, withstand; **13** counterattack; PHRASES: **2, 5, 7** be proof against; **3, 2, 7, 2** not be tempted by; **4, 1, 5** make a stand; **4, 2, 3** keep at bay; **4, 3** come out, hold off, walk out; **4, 4** keep from; **5, 4** fight back, stand firm; **5, 7** stand against; **6, 2** object to; **7, 4** contend with.

resistance **1** R; **5** fight, stand; **6** battle, rebuff, strike; **7** dissent, protest, refusal, repulse, walkout; **8** capacity, conflict, defiance, fighting, immunity, struggle; **9** challenge, endurance, impedance, objection, reactance, renitency, repulsion; **10** inductance, opposition, reluctance, repellence; **11** capacitance, conductance, deprecation, resistivity; **12** conductivity, negativeness; **13** confrontation, unwillingness; **14** noncooperation; PHRASES: **5, 5** brave front.

resistant **4** anti; **5** hardy, proof, tough; **6** strong, sturdy; **7** defiant, opposed, unbowed; **8** hardcore, negative, opposing, refusing, renitent, striking; **9** objecting, rebuffing, reluctant, repellent, repelling, repulsing, resilient, resisting, unquelled, unsubdued, unwilling; **10** challenged, dissenting, impervious, invincible, protesting, unaffected, unbeatable, undefeated; **11** bulletproof, challenging, deprecating, deprecative, obstructive, reactionary; **12** unsubmissive, withstanding; **13** uncooperative; **14** noncooperative; PHRASES: **4, 3, 7** dead set against; **4-5** hard-nosed, hard-shell; **4-6** hard-headed.

resister **7** opposer, refuser; **8** defender, opponent, pacifist, repeller; **9** abstainer, anarchist, forbearer, hardliner, refrainer, refusenik, terrorist; **11** reactionary; **12** conservative; **13** revolutionary; **14** traditionalist; PHRASES: **3-4** die-hard; **4-4** hardhead; **5-2-3-3** stick-in-the-mud; **7, 7** freedom fighter.

resistor **5** choke; **7** winding; **8** inductor, rheostat; **9** capacitor, condenser, regulator; **10** controller; **13** potentiometer; PHRASES: **4, 9** mica capacitor; **9, 4** induction coil.

resolute **3** set; **4** firm; **6** dogged, intent, manful, plucky; **7** decided, earnest, serious, staunch; **8** decisive, definite, obsessed, resolved, stubborn; **9** obstinate, purposive, resilient, steadfast, tenacious; **10** courageous, deliberate, determined, headstrong, persistent, purposeful, unbendable, unwavering, unyielding; **11** persevering; **12** concentrated, stouthearted; PHRASES: **3, 4** set upon; **4, 4** bent upon; **4-4** hell-bent; **6, 4** intent upon; **6-6** single-minded.

resolution **3** end, vow; **4** oath; **6** answer, decree, ending, motion, pledge, ruling, upshot; **7** outcome, promise, purpose, resolve; **8** aperture, decision, firmness, solution, tenacity; **9** intention; **10** conclusion, doggedness, settlement; **11** decidedness, declaration; **12** conciliation, decisiveness, perseverance, resoluteness; **13** determination, steadfastness; **14** purposefulness; PHRASES: **5, 2, 4** field of view; **5, 7** fixed resolve.

resolve **3** fix; **4** seal, will; **5** agree, solve;

6 answer, decide, design, engage, intend, settle; **7** project, promise, purpose; **8** conclude, firmness, tenacity; **9** determine, obstinacy, sternness, terminate, undertake; **10** doggedness, resolution; **11** premeditate; **12** obdurateness, predetermine, stubbornness; **13** determination, inflexibility, steadfastness; **14** unyieldingness; **15** hardheartedness; PHRASES: **3, 2, 3, 2** put an end to; **4, 1, 8** make a decision; **4, 2** mean to; **4, 3** sort out, work out; **6, 4** really mean.

resonance **4** echo, hint, tone; **6** timbre; **7** buzzing, humming, meaning, quality; **8** whirring; **9** character, vibration; **10** hollowness, importance, rebounding, recurrence, reflection, resonation, resounding, suggestion; **11** oscillation; **12** reminiscence, significance; **13** reverberation; PHRASES: **2-4** re-echo; **9, 4** lingering note.

resonant **4** deep, rich; **6** echoic, hollow; **7** booming, buzzing, echoing, humming, reboant, ringing; **8** carrying, whirring; **9** evocative, important, lingering, pulsating, vibrating; **10** indicative, meaningful, persistent, persisting, rebounding, resonating, resounding, stentorian; **11** reminiscent, significant; **13** reverberating, reverberative; PHRASES: **2-7** re-echoing.

resonate **3** hum; **4** boom, buzz, call, echo, ring, whir *UK*; **5** recur; **7** rebound, resound, vibrate; **11** reverberate; PHRASES: **2-4** re-echo *UK*.

resonator **5, 3** sound box; **8, 5** sounding board; **10, 5** sustaining pedal.

resort (to) **2** go; **3** spa, use; **4** help, Hove, Nice; **5** haunt, hydro, Split; **6** choice, employ, option; **7** Clacton, seaside; **8** Biarritz, recourse, Southend; **9** Blackpool; **11** alternative, possibility, Scarborough; PHRASES: **4, 2** draw on, rely on, turn to; **4, 2, 2** give in to; **4, 3** head for; **4, 3, 2** make use of; **4, 4, 2** fall back on; **4, 8, 2** have recourse to; **5, 3** leave for; **5, 8, 2** avail yourself of; **6, 2** impose on; **6, 2, 6** course of action; **6-5-4** Weston-super-Mare; **6, 7** betake oneself; **7, 2** presume on; **7, 4** tourist town.

resound **4** beat, boom, call, drum, echo, ring; **5** pound, pulse, rhyme, throb, thrum; **6** hammer; **7** pulsate, vibrate; **8** resonate; **9** oscillate; **10** alliterate; **11** reverberate; PHRASES: **2-4** re-echo *UK*.

resource **4** lode, mine, pipe, seam, vein, well; **5** fount, means, shaft, store; **6** gusher, quarry, source, spring, strike, supply; **7** bo-

nanza, coalbed, reserve, working; **8** coalface, coalmine, colliery, deposits, fountain, gasfield, oilfield, stringer; **9** coalfield, discovery; PHRASES: **3, 4** oil well; **4, 4** gold mine, pipe vein, rich vein; **4, 7** coal deposit; **7, 7** mineral deposit, natural deposit; **7, 8** natural ~.

respect **3** way; **5** favor, honor, point, prize, sense, value; **6** accept, admire, detail, esteem, follow, manner, matter, regard, repute, revere; **7** cherish; **8** approval, prestige, relation, treasure, venerate; **9** attention, authority, deference, recognize, reverence; **10** admiration, appreciate, particular, veneration; **11** approbation, recognition; **12** appreciation; **13** consideration; **14** characteristic; PHRASES: **3, 5, 2** set store by; **3, 9, 2** pay attention to; **4, 2, 2** look up to; **4, 4** hold dear, rank high; **4, 7** good opinion, high opinion; **4, 8** high standing; **5, 1, 3, 2** think a lot of; **5, 2** abide by; **5, 4, 2** think well of; **5, 6, 2** think highly of; **6, 4** comply with; **6, 6** regard highly.

respect (mark of respect) **3** bob, bow, nod; **4** bend; **6** curtsy, kowtow, salaam, salute, scrape; **7** bending; **8** kneeling, stooping; **9** obeisance; **11** inclination, prostration; **12** genuflection; PHRASES: **7, 3, 3** kissing the hem; **7, 3, 4** bending the knee.

respect (show respect) **4** heed, obey; **8** consider; **11** acknowledge; PHRASES: **2, 3, 6** do the honors; **3, 4, 8** pay one's respects; **3, 7** pay respect; **3, 7, 2** pay tribute to; **5, 2** defer to; **6, 7, 2** accord respect to.

respectable **4** fair, good; **6** decent, proper, worthy; **7** upright; **8** adequate, laudable, suitable; **9** estimable, reputable, venerable; **10** acceptable, reasonable; **12** praiseworthy, satisfactory; PHRASES: **4-7-2** well-thought-of; **6, 8** highly regarded.

respected **8** reliable; **9** venerable; **11** prestigious; **13** authoritative, distinguished; PHRASES: **4-7** time-honored; **4, 7, 2** well thought of; **6, 7, 2** highly thought of; **6, 8** highly regarded. *See also* **respect**

respectful **6** humble, polite; **7** dutiful, fawning, servile; **8** gracious, obeisant, reverent; **9** attentive, compliant, courteous, honorific, kowtowing, regardful; **10** obsequious, submissive, submitting; **11** bootlicking, ceremonious, considerate, deferential, reverential; **12** appreciative, ingratiating.

respiratory disease **3** flu; **4** cold; **5**

cough, croup; **6** asthma, coryza; **7** catarrh; **8** pleurisy, rhinitis; **9** emphysema, influenza, pertussis, pneumonia, silicosis, sinusitis; **10** asbestosis, bronchitis, diphtheria, laryngitis, tracheitis; **11** anthracosis, consumption, pharyngitis, rhinorrhoea, tonsillitis; **12** tuberculosis (TB); **14** pneumoconiosis; PHRASES: **4, 3** glue ear *UK*; **4, 4** head cold; **4, 6** lung cancer, sore throat; **5, 4** black lung, runny nose; **6, 4** common cold; **6, 8** cystic fibrosis; **7, 5** smoker's cough; **7, 8** swollen adenoids; **8, 4** watering eyes; **8, 5** whooping cough.

respire **6** exhale, expire, inhale; **7** breathe, inspire; PHRASES: **4, 7** take breaths; **7, 2** breathe in; **7, 3** breathe out.

respite **4** lull; **5** break, delay; **6** hiatus, relief; **8** interval, reprieve; **11** adjournment; **12** intermission; PHRASES: **9, 5** breathing space *UK*.

respond **3** act; **5** react, reply; **6** answer, rebuff, recoil, rejoin, retort, return; **7** counter, riposte; **9** retaliate; **10** counteract, understand; PHRASES: **3, 2** act on; **4, 6** take action; **6, 4** answer back.

response **5** reply; **6** answer, effect, rebuff, recoil, reflex, retort; **7** retreat, riposte; **8** comeback, reaction; **9** rejoinder; **11** retroaction; **12** repercussion; PHRASES: **4-4** fallback.

responsibility **3** job; **4** baby, buck, duty, onus, role, task; **5** blame, guilt, trust; **6** burden, charge, office, pigeon; **8** function; **9** liability; **10** leadership, management, obligation; **11** culpability; **14** accountability.

responsible **6** guilty, liable; **8** culpable, poserful; **9** executive, important; **10** answerable; **11** accountable, blameworthy; PHRASES: **8-6** decision-making.

responsive *See* **receptive**

rest **3** bed, lay, lie, nap, put; **4** crib, lean, rack, sofa; **5** break, chair, couch, frame, place, relax, sleep, stand; **6** catnap, cradle, excess, holder, pillow, repose, saddle, siesta, snooze, uphold; **7** balance, bolster, ottoman, residue, respite, springs, support, surplus; **8** breather, footrest, headrest, mattress, remnants; **9** cessation, davenport, footstool, leftovers, remainder; **10** recreation, relaxation; PHRASES: **3, 4, 4, 2** put your feet up; **4, 1, 5** have a break, take a break; **4, 2, 4** take it easy; **4, 3** time out; **4, 4** back ~; **4, 5** easy chair; **8, 5** shooting stick.

restaurant **4** cafe, mess; **5** diner; **6** bistro, eatery; **7** beanery, canteen, takeout; **9** brasserie; **11** rathskeller; **12** luncheonette; PHRASES: **3, 3** raw bar; **3, 4** key club, tea room; **4, 5** hash house; **5, 3** snack bar; **5-3** brown-bag, table-hop; **6, 4** supper club; **6, 7** dinner theater.

resting place **3** bed; **4** home, jail, tomb; **5** grave, haven, hotel, motel; **6** billet, heaven, pillow, prison, refuge; **7** bivouac, hammock, lodging, shelter; **8** cemetery, hospital, paradise, quarters; **9** graveyard, mausoleum; PHRASES: **4, 4** last rest; **6, 4** prison cell; **6, 6** burial ground; **7, 4** nursing home; **7, 5** bedroom couch; **8, 3** journey's end; **10, 4** retirement home.

restitution **6** amends, return; **9** repayment; **10** recompense; **11** restoration; **12** compensation; **13** reimbursement, reinstatement.

restless **4** edgy; **5** giddy, itchy, jumpy; **7** excited, fevered, fidgety, fussing, nervous, panting, restive, twitchy, unquiet, wakeful; **8** agitated, feverish, fluttery; **9** flustered, impatient; **10** breathless, fluttering, unpeaceful; PHRASES: **2, 1, 4** in a flap, in a spin; **2, 4** on edge; **3, 2, 1, 4** all of a tizz; **3, 2, 1, 7** all of a flutter; **3, 3, 8** hot and bothered.

restlessness **4** fret; **5** fever; **6** nerves, unease, unrest; **7** hopping, itching, unquiet; **8** dawdling, disquiet, edginess, fiddling, insomnia, pruritus; **9** agitation, itchiness, jactation, pottering, puttering; **10** impatience, wanderlust; **11** aimlessness, formication, inattention, jactitation; **12** excitability, watchfulness; **13** desultoriness, sleeplessness; PHRASES: **3, 7** the fidgets; **5, 4** itchy feet; **7, 8** aimless activity. *See also* **restless**

restoration **6** amends, ransom, recall, repair, rescue, return; **7** redress, renewal, revival, salvage; **8** reaction, recovery, reprisal, transfer; **9** atonement, provision, recycling, retrieval, returning, salvation; **10** rebuilding, redemption, reerection, remodeling, renovation, reparation, replanting, resumption; **11** deliverance, reclamation, recruitment, reformation, relaunching, reparations, replacement, restitution, retaliation; **12** compensation, readjustment, reconversion, refashioning, reinvestment, repatriation, reprocessing, retrocession; **13** reforestation, refurbishment, reinforcement, reinstallment, reinstatement, reinstitution, reorientation, replenishment, reprogramming, strengthening; **14** recommencement, reconstitution, reconstruction, rehabilitation, reinstallation, reintroduction, reorganization; **15** reafforestation, re-establishment; **18** counterreformation; PHRASES: **3, 3** gut job; **3, 9** new beginning; **6, 2, 6** return to normal; **6, 4** taking back; **7, 4** putting back; **7, 5** finding again.

restorative 7 healing; **8** curative, remedial, reviving, sanative, soothing; **9** analeptic, medicated, medicinal, uplifting; **10** redemptive, reparative; **12** invigorating, recuperative.

restore 3 fix; **4** free, redo, save, stet, undo; **5** atone, clean, rally, rehab, renew, valet; **6** ransom, recall, redeem, reform, remake, repair, rescue, resume, return, revive, unmake; **7** deliver, rebuild, reclaim, recover, recycle, reerect, refound, release, replace, replant, restart, restock, salvage, service; **8** liberate, overhaul, reforest, relaunch, renovate, reorient, retrieve; **9** reappoint, reconvene, reconvert, refurbish, reinforce, reinstall, reinstate, replenish, reprocess, restitute, retaliate, retrocede; **10** compensate, reafforest *UK*, reassemble, recommence, reorganize, repatriate, revalidate, strengthen; **11** recondition, reconstruct, re-establish, reformulate, reinstitute, reintegrate, reintroduce, reprogramme; **12** reconstitute, redintegrate, rehabilitate; PHRASES: **2, 2** do up; **3, 2** fix up; **3, 4** pay back, put back; **4, 4** give back, hand back; **5, 2** cough up, touch up, yield up; **5, 4** bring back; **6, 4** change back.

restore (be restored) 5 rally; **6** resume, revive; **7** recover, survive; **8** reappear, reawaken; **10** convalesce, recuperate; PHRASES: **3, 2** get up; **3, 4** get over, get well; **3, 6** get better; **4, 1, 8** make a comeback; **4, 2** come to, pick up; **4, 3, 2, 2** snap out of it; **4, 3, 6** turn the corner; **4, 4, 2, 4** come back to life; **4, 4, 3, 4** rise from the dead; **4, 5** live again; **4, 6** come around; **4, 7** live through, pull through; **5, 3** sleep off; **5, 5** cheat death; **6, 2, 6** return to normal; **6, 4** bounce back; **7, 3, 5** weather the storm.

restrain 3 ban, bar, dam, tie; **4** bind, curb, drag, jail, keep, rein, rope, slow, stem, stop, veto; **5** allot, brake, chain, check, clamp, cramp, crush, deter, leash, limit, quash, quell, smash; **6** anchor, censor, coerce, damper, detain, fetter, hinder, impede, muzzle, patrol, police, punish, retard, stifle, subdue, tether; **7** confine, contain, control,

curtail, exclude, inhibit, oppress, prevent, repress, shackle, smother, squeeze, squelch; **8** handcuff, imprison, localize, pressure, prohibit, regulate, restrict, retrench, suppress, throttle; **9** blackball, constrain, constrict, copyright, demarcate, forestall, interdict, stipulate; **10** decelerate, discipline; **12** circumscribe, straitjacket; PHRASES: **3, 1, 4, 2** put a stop to; **3, 1, 6, 2** put a damper on; **3, 2** box in, hem in, sit on; **3, 3, 3, 2** put the lid on; **3, 4** put away; **4, 2** lock up; **4, 2, 5** keep in check; **4, 3** keep out, rope out; **4, 3, 4** draw the line; **4, 4** hold back, hold down, pull back, vote down; **4, 5** keep order; **5, 3** black out; **5, 4** close down, crack down; **5, 4, 2** clamp down on; **6, 1, 4** impose a fine; **6, 2** bottle up.

restrained 4 calm, pale, soft; **5** muted, sober; **6** steady, subtle; **7** guarded, subdues; **8** discreet, moderate, reserved, reticent; **10** controlled; **11** unemotional; **13** nonaggressive; **15** undemonstrative; PHRASES: **4-9** self-possessed.

restrainer *See* **restraint**

restraint 3 ban, bar, bit, gag, tie; **4** belt, bolt, bond, boot, curb, cuts, diet, drag, fine, hasp, knot, lead, lock, rein, rope, veto, yoke; **5** bonds, brake, catch, chain, check, clamp, clasp, cramp, cuffs, irons, latch, leash, limit, reins; **6** anchor, arrest, bridle, chains, circle, collar, corset, damper, duress, fetter, girdle, hobble, muzzle, stocks, tether; **7** bilboes, ceiling, command, control, fetters, harness, padlock, penalty, pillory, shackle, squeeze, subdual; **8** coercion, coolness, crushing, doorstop, governor, manacles, obstacle, pressure, quashing, quelling, severity, shackles, slowness, smashing, stifling, stopping, trammels; **9** allotment, authority, blackball, bracelets, captivity, composure, copyright, crackdown, detention, handcuffs, hindrance, interdict; **10** attachment, censorship, constraint, discipline, impediment, injunction, limitation, moderation, prevention, punishment, repression, smothering, squelching, strictness, throttling; **11** confinement, curtailment, demarcation, exclusivity, limitations, prohibition, requirement, restriction, retardation, stipulation, suppressant, suppression; **12** constriction, deceleration, imprisonment, retrenchment, straitjacket; **13** qualification; **15** circumscription; PHRASES: **1-6** D-notice *UK*; **2-2, 4** no-go area; **3-6, 4** off-limits area;

4, 3, 5 ball and chain; **4-7** self-control; **4-10** self-discipline, self-possession; **5, 5** speed limit, wheel clamp; **5, 7** apron strings; **5, 9** legal ~; **6, 4** Denver boot; **6, 7** strict control; **7, 4** slowing down; **7, 6** charmed circle; **9, 5** stumbling block; **9, 6** exclusive rights; **10, 4** restricted area.

restrict 3 ban, end, pen, tie; **4** bind, curb, veto; **5** brake, chain, check, limit, stint; **6** censor, define, demark, freeze, hamper, hinder, ration, tether; **7** confine, contain, control, curtail, embargo, enclose, inhibit, measure, qualify, repress, specify; **8** downzone, mitigate, moderate, prohibit, restrain; **9** constrain, copyright, demarcate, determine, proscribe; **10** monopolize; **12** circumscribe; PHRASES: **4, 2** hold in, rein in; **4, 4** hold back.

restricted 5 elite; **6** choice, secret, select; **7** limited, private; **9** delimited, regulated; **10** classified, controlled, privileged; **11** constrained; **12** confidential; **13** circumscribed; PHRASES: **3-6** top-secret.

restriction 3 bar; **4** curb; **5** check, limit; **6** curfew, damper; **7** barrier, control; **8** deadline; **9** exclusion, restraint; **10** constraint, definition, inhibition, limitation, mitigation, moderation; **11** containment, demarcation; **12** constriction, proscription; **15** circumscription.

restroom 2 WC; **3** loo *UK*; **6** toilet; **8** lavatory; PHRASES: **6, 4** powder room.

result 3 end, sum; **4** flow, mark, rise, stem; **5** arise, cause, ensue, grade, issue, score, tally, total; **6** answer, effect, follow, spring, upshot; **7** develop, emanate, outcome, product; **8** equation, findings, occasion, solution; **9** remainder; **10** conclusion, difference; **11** calculation, consequence; PHRASES: **2, 6, 2** be caused by; **3, 6** end ~; **4, 2** lead to; **4, 3** turn out.

resume 6 return; **8** continue, reoccupy; **10** recommence; PHRASES: **2, 4** go back; **5, 5** start again.

résumé 2 CV *UK*; **4** vita; **6** précis, review; **7** outline, rundown, summary; **10** compendium; PHRASES: **10, 5** curriculum vitae *UK*.

resurrection *See* **revival**

resuscitate *See* **revive**

retail 4 sell, tell; **7** narrate, recount.

retailer 4 shop; **5** baker, store; **6** dealer, grocer, mercer *UK*, monger, seller, tailor, trader, vendor; **7** butcher, florist; **8** merchant, milliner, regrater; **9** middleman, newsagent, tradesman; **10** fishmonger, groceryman, ironmonger, shopkeeper *UK*, wholesaler; **11** distributor, greengrocer, haberdasher, provisioner, storekeeper, tobacconist; PHRASES: **4, 6** shoe seller; **5, 5** store owner; **6, 6** retail outlet.

retain 3 gum, hug; **4** glue, grab, grip, hold, keep, lock, save; **5** clamp, clasp, grasp, gripe, paste, seize; **6** adhere, clench, clinch, clutch, cuddle, employ, recall, staple; **7** embrace, grapple, squeeze; **8** compress, maintain, preserve, remember, strangle, throttle; **9** recollect; **10** buttonhole; **11** agglutinate; PHRASES: **4, 2, 2** hang on to, hold on to; **4, 2, 4** keep in mind; **4, 4, 2** keep hold of; **4, 5** hold tight.

retained 4 fast, held, kept; **5** bound, glued, saved, stuck; **6** gummed, penned, pinned; **7** clasped, grasped, gripped, refused, stapled; **8** clutched, detained, employed, pinioned, withheld; **9** contained, preserved, strangled; **10** imprisoned, remembered; **13** circumscribed; PHRASES: **4, 2** held in, kept in; **5, 4** stuck firm; **6, 2** fenced in, walled in.

retaliate 3 cap; **5** parry, react, repay, repel; **6** answer, avenge, punish, recoil, recoup, resist, retort, return; **7** counter, redress, repulse, requite, revenge, riposte; **9** boomerang; **11** reciprocate; **13** countercharge; PHRASES: **2, 5** be quits; **3, 3** pay off; **3, 4** get even, hit back, pay back; **3, 4, 2** get back at; **3, 4, 3, 4** get your own back *UK*; **3, 7** get revenge; **4, 3, 3, 3** give tit for tat; **4, 3, 4** give and take; **4, 3, 5** even the score; **4, 4** come back, kick back, make good; **5, 2** round on; **5, 4** fight back, shoot back; **6, 1, 5** settle a score; **6, 4** answer back, strike back; **6, 7** avenge oneself.

retaliation 6 desert, retort, talion; **7** counter, deserts, dueness, justice, Nemesis, payback, redress, revenge, riposte; **8** backlash, comeback, reprisal; **9** boomerang, rejoinder, repayment, vengeance; **10** punishment, reparation; **11** comeuppance, countermine, counterplot, retribution; **12** counterblast, counterpunch; **13** counteraction, counterstroke, reciprocation; PHRASES: **3, 3, 3** tit for tat; **4, 3, 3** quid pro quo; **4, 3, 4** blow for blow *UK*, like for like; **4, 7** just deserts, just revenge.

retard *See* **delay**

retch *See* **vomit**

retention 3 hug; 4 grip, hold, lock; 5 clamp, clasp, grasp; 6 clench, clinch, clutch, cuddle, memory; 7 custody, embrace, footing, holding, keeping, seizure, squeeze, toehold; 8 adhesion, foothold, grabbing UK, handhold, headlock, tenacity; 9 recalling, retaining, viscidity; 10 hammerlock, memorizing, prehension, retainment, stickiness; 11 compression, maintenance, persistence, remembering, withholding; 12 prehensility, preservation, recollection, stranglehold; 13 tenaciousness; PHRASES: 4, 2, 4 grip of iron; 4, 2, 5 grip of steel; 4, 3 bear hug; 4, 4 firm hold, iron grip; 4, 6 full nelson, half nelson; 5, 4 death grip, tight grip; 8, 4 vicelike grip.

retentive 4 firm; 5 gluey, gooey, gummy; 6 spongy, sticky; 7 clogged, costive; 8 adhesive, clasping, clinging, cohesive, gluelike, grasping, gripping, vicelike; 9 absorbent, retaining, tenacious; 10 prehensile, strangling, throttling; 11 constipated, restraining; 12 indissoluble, parsimonious; PHRASES: 5-6 tight-fisted.

rethink 6 revise; 10 reconsider; 11 changearound UK; 13 consideration; 15 reconsideration; PHRASES: 2, 2, 5-4 do an about-face; 5-4 about-face, volte-face; 6, 2, 4 change of mind; 6, 2, 5 change of heart; 6, 4 change tack; 6, 4, 4 change your mind; 6, 6 change course; 6, 8 second thoughts; 6, 9 change direction.

reticence 7 modesty, reserve, shyness, silence; 9 quietness, restraint; 10 discretion; 11 bashfulness.

reticent See **reserved**

reticule 3 bag; 5 purse; 7 handbag; 9 container.

retire 3 ebb; 6 depart, repair, resign; 7 retreat; 8 withdraw; PHRASES: 2, 2, 3 go to bed; 4, 4 step down.

retired 2 ex; 3 OAP UK; 4 AARP, abed; 6 former; 9 pensioned; 13 superannuated.

retirement 3 IRA; 7 leaving, retreat; 9 departure, seclusion; 10 withdrawal; 13 sequestration; 14 superannuation UK.

retiring 3 shy; 6 modest; 8 reserved; 9 reclusive; 11 unassertive.

retort See **reply**

retract 4 deny; 6 recant; 7 rescind, sheathe; 8 withdraw; 9 apologize, backtrack; PHRASES: 4, 2 draw in, pull in; 4, 4 draw back, pull back, take back.

retreat 3 den, ebb; 4 back, flee, lair; 5 haven, leave, oasis, study; 6 escape, flight, recede, recess, recoil, refuge, resign, retire; 7 hospice, pullout, shelter; 8 fallback, hideaway, pullback, reculade, withdraw; 9 departure, disengage, resigning, sanctuary; 10 evacuation, retirement, withdrawal; 11 resignation; 13 disengagement; PHRASES: 3, 4 run away, run back; 4, 3 back out, give way, pull out; 4, 4 back away, back down, draw back, fall back, move away, move back, pull back; 4, 4, 1, 6 back into a corner; 4, 6 fall behind, give ground; 5, 4 stand back; 6, 4 motion from; 7, 5 halfway house.

retribution 4 doom; 7 deserts, justice, Nemesis, payback, revenge; 8 doomsday, judgment, reprisal, requital; 9 reckoning, repayment, vengeance; 11 comeuppance, retaliation; PHRASES: 3, 2, 8 day of judgment; 3, 2, 9 day of reckoning; 4, 2, 3 hell to pay; 4, 3 what for; 4, 6 meet reward; 4, 7 just deserts; 4, 11 just ~; 6, 7 divine justice, poetic justice.

retrieve See **recover**

retrograde 8 backward, rearward; 9 declining, reversing, worsening; 10 regressive; 13 deteriorating.

retrospect 6 review, survey; 7 history, memoirs, reprize; 8 anecdote; 9 flashback, hindsight; 11 remembrance; 12 recollection, reminiscence; 13 autobiography, retrospective; 15 reconsideration; PHRASES: 4, 2 déjà vu; 7, 4 looking back.

retrospective 4 show; 5 retro; 7 display, showing; 8 showcase; 9 backdated, nostalgic, reviewing, surveying; 10 diachronic, exhibition, exposition, reflective, retrograde; 11 remembering, reminiscing, retroactive, traditional; 12 conservative, presentation; 13 demonstration, reconsidering; PHRASES: 2, 4, 5 ex post facto; 7, 4 looking back; 8-7 backward-looking.

return 3 net, ret; 4 gain; 5 cycle, repay, round, swing, yield; 6 profit, recoil, refund, resume, revert; 7 arrival, benefit, rebirth, rebound, recycle, regress, relapse, renewal, replace, reprize, requite, restore, revenue, revisit, revival, shuttle; 8 comeback, earnings, proceeds; 9 extradite, reappoint, recursion, recycling, reimburse, reinstate, roundtrip; 10 homecoming, recurrence, reenthrone, reentrance, repatriate; 11 reestablish, renaissance, restoration; 12 reappearance, rehabilitate, remuneration, reoccurrence, repatriation; **13** reincarnation; PHRASES: **2, 4** go back; **2, 5** go again; **2-5** re-entry *UK*; **3, 4** pay back; **4, 3, 2** come and go; **4, 3, 4** give and take; **4, 4** come back, give back, kick back, send back, take back; **5, 4** round trip, swing back, trace back; **5, 6** swing around; **6, 4** coming back; **9, 6** roundtrip ticket.

reuse **7** reclaim, recycle, salvage; **9** reprocess.

reused product **10** blackboard, palimpsest; PHRASES: **4, 3** used car; **4, 7** milk bottles; **9, 4** reclaimed land.

rev **4** race, roar, turn; **5** cycle; **6** scream; **8** rotation; **10** revolution.

REV **7** revenue; **8** Reverend; **10** revolution.

reveal **4** bare, cite, show, tell, vent; **5** quote, solve; **6** adduce, betray, decode, evince, expose, inform, invent, unfold, unfurl, unmask, unroll, unveil, unwrap; **7** develop, divulge, enhance, explain, express, extract, mention, produce, promote, publish, uncover, unearth; **8** decipher, disclose, discover, evidence, indicate, manifest, proclaim; **9** advertise, emphasize, formulate, highlight, interpret, publicize, spotlight; **10** accentuate, illuminate; **11** communicate; PHRASES: **3, 4** lay bare, lay open, let slip; **4, 2** open up; **4, 3** drag out, draw out, show off, trot out; **4, 3, 4** come out with; **4, 4** give away; **4, 5** draw forth, make known, make plain; **4, 6** make public; **4, 7** make obvious; **4, 9, 2** draw attention to; **5, 2** bring up, point up; **5, 2, 5** bring to light; **5, 2, 6** bring to notice; **5, 3** bring out, point out; **5, 3, 5** spill the beans; **5, 4** throw open; **5, 4, 6** throw into relief; **5, 5** bring forth; **5, 5, 2** throw light on.

revel **4** bask; **5** enjoy, party; **7** delight; **8** carnival; **9** celebrate, luxuriate, socialize; **11** celebration, festivities, merrymaking; PHRASES: **4, 3** have fun; **4, 5** make merry.

revelation **4** leak; **5** shock; **6** exposé; **8** exposure, surprise; **9** admission; **10** disclosure; PHRASES: **3, 6** eye opener.

revenge **6** avenge; **7** payback, requite; **8** reprisal, requital; **9** retaliate, vengeance; **10** punishment; **11** retaliation, retribution; PHRASES: **3, 4** get back; **3, 4, 3, 4** get your own back *UK*; **4, 3, 5** even the score; **6, 7** poetic justice.

revenue **4** gain; **5** bonus; **6** income, return; **7** credits, premium, profits, returns, takings; **8** earnings, interest, proceeds, re-

ceipts, turnover; **9** incomings, royalties.

reverberate **4** beat, boom, call, echo, ring; **5** pulse, throb; **7** resound, vibrate; **8** resonate; PHRASES: **2-4** re-echo *UK*.

reverberation **4** beat, boom, call, echo, ring; **5** noise, pulse, sound, throb; **6** rhythm; **8** drumming; **9** assonance, hammering, pulsation, resonance, throbbing, vibration; **11** oscillation; **12** alliteration.

revere **5** adore, deify, honor; **6** admire; **7** cherish, idolize, lionize, respect, worship; **8** venerate; **9** reverence; **10** idolatrize; **11** apotheosize; PHRASES: **2, 2, 3, 2** be in awe of; **3, 2, 1, 8** put on a pedestal; **4, 2, 2** look up to; **4-7** hero-worship; **5, 3, 5, 2** think the world of.

reverent **6** devout; **7** adoring; **8** admiring, deifying; **9** adulatory, awestruck, idolizing, wondering; **10** venerative, worshipful; **11** awestricken, reverential, worshipping; **12** venerational; PHRASES: **2, 3** in awe; **4-11** hero-worshipping.

reverie **4** wish; **5** dream; **6** desire, musing, trance; **7** romance; **8** daydream, delirium, escapism, fantasia, stardust; **9** sophistry; **11** abstraction, romanticism; **12** sleepwalking, somnambulism, subjectivism; **13** contemplation, insensibility; **14** abstractedness, autosuggestion; PHRASES: **4, 2, 3, 6** head in the clouds; **4, 5** pipe dream; **5, 5** brown study; **6, 5** golden dream; **6-8** window-shopping; **7, 8** wishful thinking.

reversal **3** ebb; **4** blow, snag; **5** hitch; **6** backup, denial, reflux; **7** backing, problem, reverse, setback, treason; **8** apostasy, palinody, reneging, voidance; **9** cassation, disavowal, inversion, refluence, reversing, reversion; **10** abjuration, abnegation, abrogation, difficulty, disownment, misfortune, repentance, retraction, revocation, turnaround *UK*; **11** forswearing, recantation, repudiation; **12** backpedaling, backtracking, disclamation, renunciation; **13** regurgitation; **14** tergiversation; PHRASES: **1-4** U-turn; **4, 2, 3, 4** turn of the tide; **5-4** about-face, about-turn *UK*, volte-face; **6, 8** second thoughts; **7, 2** backing up.

reverse **3** ebb; **4** back, blow, rear, snag, swap, turn, undo; **5** annul, hitch, quash, unsay, waver; **6** abjure, betray, change, desert, disown, invert, recant, recede, recoil, renege, repeal, repent, retire, return, revert, revoke, revolt, switch; **7** disavow, inverse, problem, regress, relapse, reorder, retract, retreat, setback; **8** abnegate, abrogate, archaize, backfire, contrary, converse, crawfish, disclaim, forswear, opposite, overturn, renounce, reversal, withdraw; **9** backslide, backtrack, boomerang, rearrange, repudiate, roundtrip, transpose, vacillate; **10** antithesis, apostasize, counteract, difficulty, equivocate, invalidate, misfortune, recidivate, retrogress, underneath; **11** regurgitate; **12** countermarch, tergiversate; PHRASES: **1, 4** B side; **2, 1, 1-4** do a U-turn; **2, 2, 5-4** do an about-face; **2, 4** go back; **2, 4, 7** go into ~; **2, 8** go backward; **4, 2** back up; **4, 3** back off; **4, 4** back away, back down, flip side, slip back, turn back; **4, 5** back trail, back water, turn about; **4-5** back-pedal; **4, 6** turn around; **4, 8** move backward; **5, 4** other side; **5, 8** drive backward; **6, 4** double back; **8, 4** opposite side.

reverse (in reverse) 11 withershins; **13** anticlockwise; **16** counterclockwise; PHRASES: **1, 7** à rebours; **7, 3, 5** against the grain.

reversed 6 reflex; **7** counter; **8** backward; **9** backwards; **16** counterclockwise; PHRASES: **4-2-5** back-to-front; **5, 3** wrong way; **5, 3, 5** wrong way round; **6-3** inside-out; **6-4** upside-down; **6, 6** turned around.

reversion 5 lapse; **6** recoil, return; **7** atavism, decline, relapse, retreat; **8** apostasy, backfire, backlash, reaction, reversal, ricochet; **9** recession; **10** recidivism, regression, repentance, retirement, retraction, turnaround *UK*, withdrawal; **11** backsliding, recantation, retroaction; **12** degeneration, retroflexion, retroversion; **13** counteraction, deterioration, retrogression, retrospection *UK*; **17** counterrevolution; **18** counterreformation; PHRASES: **1-4** U-turn; **5, 4** going back; **5-4** about-face, volte-face; **5, 5-4** right about-face; **7, 4** backing down, looking back, turning back; **7, 8** turning backward.

revert 4 pass; **5** lapse; **6** return; **7** regress, relapse, revisit; **8** reoffend; **9** backslide; **10** degenerate; PHRASES: **2, 4** go back; **4, 4** slip back.

review 4 crit; **6** muster, notice, parade, repeat, report, survey, tattoo; **7** account, summary; **8** analysis, critique, magazine; **9** appraisal; **10** assessment, procession; PHRASES: **5-2** write-up; **5-4** march-past; **6, 4** report card.

revile 5 abuse, scorn; **6** insult; **7** censure, condemn.

revise 4 edit; **5** amend, emend; **6** repair; **7** correct, improve, restore, rewrite; **8** copyedit; **9** proofread.

revision 6 change, review; **9** amendment; **10** adjustment, alteration, correction; **11** improvement; **12** modification; **15** reconsideration.

revival 4 boom; **5** rally; **6** waking; **7** rebirth, renewal; **8** comeback, recovery; **9** turnabout; **10** evangelism, prosperity, recurrence, regeneracy, resumption, resurgence, revivalism, turnaround; **11** reanimation, reawakening, recruitment, refreshment, renaissance, respiration, restoration, stimulation; **12** palingenesis, reactivation, reappearance, regeneration, rejuvenation, resurrection, revivescence; **13** reinforcement, resuscitation; **14** rehabilitation, rejuvenescence, revitalization, revivification; PHRASES: **3, 4** new hope, new life; **6, 2** coming to; **6, 6** Indian summer, second chance, second spring; **8, 5** bringing round *UK*; **8, 7** economic miracle.

revive 4 redo, save; **5** boost, renew, stage; **6** awaken, repeat, resume; **7** develop, enliven, freshen, perform, recover, recruit, refresh, reprize, restage, restart, restore; **8** flourish, reawaken, rekindle, revivify; **9** reanimate, reinforce, resurrect, stimulate; **10** invigorate, recuperate, regenerate, rejuvenate, revitalize; **11** resuscitate; **12** reinvigorate; PHRASES: **4, 2** come to, perk up, pick up, wake up; **4, 5** show again; **4, 6** come around; **5, 5** bring round *UK*; **6, 2, 4** recall to life.

revoke 4 deny; **5** annul; **6** cancel, negate, recant, repeal; **7** disavow, rescind, retract; **8** abnegate, abrogate, disclaim, withdraw; **9** repudiate; **10** apostasize, invalidate.

revolt 4 riot; **5** rebel, repel; **6** mutiny, sicken; **7** disgust, horrify, repulse; **8** nauseate, upheaval, uprising; **9** rebellion; **10** insurgency, revolution; **12** insurrection; PHRASES: **3, 3** put off; **4, 2** rise up; **4, 3** turn off; **4, 4, 7** turn your stomach; **6, 7** defend oneself.

revolution 3 war; **4** coup, riot, spin, turn; **5** cycle, orbit; **6** change, circle, mutiny, putsch, reform, revolt, schism; **8** gyration, rotation, sedition, upheaval, uprising; **9** breakaway, rebellion, secession, terrorism; **10** alteration, conversion, innovation, insurgence, insurgency, resistance; **11** development; **12** insurrection, mutinousness; **13** modernization; **14** rebelliousness, transformation; PHRASES: **4, 5** coup d'état; **4-9** sansculottism; **5, 3** civil war.

revolve *See* **rotate**

reward 3 pay; **4** gift, meed; **5** award, bonus, favor, honor, prize, repay, thank, title; **6** bounty, credit, honors, praise, return, thanks; **7** acclaim, bouquet, deserts, guerdon, justice, payment, peerage *UK*, present, satisfy, tribute; **8** decorate; **9** gratitude, incentive, recognize, repayment; **10** compensate, decoration, recompense, remunerate; **11** acclamation, acknowledge, recognition; **12** compensation, remuneration, satisfaction; **14** acknowledgment; PHRASES: **3, 2, 3, 4** pat on the back; **3, 4, 6** New Year Honors; **3, 6** due credit; **3, 7** pay tribute; **3, 11** due recognition; **3, 12** job satisfaction; **4, 7** just deserts; **8, 5** honorary title; **8, 6** Birthday Honors, honorary degree.

rewarding 6 paying; **7** gainful; **8** pleasing; **9** lucrative; **10** fulfilling, gratifying, profitable, satisfying, worthwhile; **11** moneymaking; **12** advantageous, remunerative.

RH 6 rhesus; **7** rhodium; PHRASES: **5, 4** right hand; **5, 8** Royal Highness.

rhea 7 ostrich.

rhetoric 5 idiom, style; **6** speech; **7** bombast, fustian, oratory; **8** language; **9** loftiness, pomposity; **10** expression, orotundity, vocabulary; **12** speechifying, speechmaking; **13** magniloquence; **14** grandiloquence; PHRASES: **6, 8** public speaking.

rhetorician 6 orator, purist; **7** speaker, stylist; **8** euphuist; **9** demagogue, wordsmith; **10** classicist, politician; **12** phrasemonger; PHRASES: **4-7** word-spinner.

rheumatism 3 RSI; **4** gout; **7** lumbago, myalgia; **8** bursitis; **9** arthritis; **10** fibrositis, rheumatics *UK*; **14** osteoarthritis; PHRASES: **6, 5** tennis elbow; **6, 6** pulled muscle; **6, 8** frozen shoulder *UK*; **7, 4** slipped disk; **9, 5** rheumatic fever; **10, 4** housemaid's knee.

rheumy 5 pussy; **6** serous; **7** humoral, phlegmy, sanious, weeping; **8** chylific, ichorous, purulent, tearlike; **9** lachrymal; **10** suppurated; **11** suppurating, suppurative; **12** chylifactive, chylifactory, lachrymatory.

Rhine 4 Rijn; **5** Rhein.

Rhode Island 2 RI *UK*; **4** Hope (motto); **6** violet (flower); **10** Providence (capital); PHRASES: **3, 5** red maple (tree); **5, 5** Ocean State (nickname); **5, 6, 3** Rhode Island red (bird); **6, 5** Little Rhody (nickname).

rhombus 5 rhomb; **7** diamond, lozenge; **8** rhomboid; **13** parallelogram.

rhyme 4 poem; **5** verse; **6** jingle; **7** couplet, rhyming; **8** limerick, quatrain; **9** assonance; **10** consonance; PHRASES: **3, 5** end ~, eye ~; **4, 5** half ~, near ~, tail ~; **5, 6** ~ scheme; **6, 5** broken ~, double ~, single ~; **7, 5** initial ~, nursery ~; **8, 5** feminine ~, internal ~; **9, 5** masculine ~.

rhythm 4 beat, pace, time; **5** meter, pulse, tempo; **6** timing; **7** cadence, measure, pattern; **8** drumbeat, sequence; **9** heartbeat; **10** regularity; **11** progression, syncopation.

rib 3 kid, rag; **4** beam, josh, mock, spar; **5** costa, spine, spoke, strut, tease; PHRASES: **4, 2** have on *UK*; **4, 3, 2** make fun of; **5, 2** laugh at.

ribald 4 blue, lewd, rude; **5** bawdy, crude, funny; **6** coarse, earthy, filthy, risqué, smutty, vulgar; **7** immoral, obscene; **8** humorous, indecent; **9** barbarous; **10** suggestive, unquotable; **11** provocative, Rabelaisian, unprintable; **12** scatological; **13** unmentionable; PHRASES: **2, 3, 5** in bad taste.

ribbon 3 tie; **4** band, tape; **5** award, honor, strip; **6** length; **7** stretch; **8** trimming; **10** decoration.

rich 4 deep, fine, full, lush; **5** fatty, heavy, plush, sweet, vivid; **6** costly, creamy, ironic, loaded, ornate, strong; **7** amusing, buttery, cloying, fertile, intense, moneyed, opulent, stuffed, wealthy; **8** abundant, affluent, annoying, dripping, fruitful, gorgeous, powerful, precious, prolific, resonant, splendid, unlikely, valuable; **9** abounding, calorific, expensive, luxuriant, plentiful, unhealthy; **10** irritating, productive, prosperous, ridiculous; **12** indigestible; PHRASES: **4-2-2** well-to-do; **4-3** well-off; **4-5** well-fixed; **4-6** full-bodied, well-heeled; **7, 2, 2** rolling in it.

rich (be rich) 3, 2, 1, 8 sit on a goldmine; **4, 2, 2** rake it in; **4, 2, 5** roll in money; **4, 3, 2, 4** turn all to gold; **4, 4, 6** drip with wealth; **4, 5, 2, 4** have money to burn; **5, 2, 5** stink of money; **6, 2, 6** wallow in riches; **7, 7** command capital.

rich (get rich) 4 gain; **7** inherit, prosper; PHRASES: **3, 3, 5** win the pools; **3, 3, 7** hit the jackpot, win the lottery; **4, 1, 4** make a mint, make a pile; **4, 1, 6** make a bundle; **4, 1, 7** make a fortune; **4, 2** make it; **4, 2, 2** rake it in; **4, 4, 5** come into money; **4, 4, 6** line one's pocket; **4, 4, 7** make one's fortune; **4, 5** make money, mint money, spin money; **5, 2**

clean up; **6, 2, 4** strike it rich; **7, 4, 4** feather one's nest.

rich (the rich) *See* **wealthy people**

riches 6 assets, wealth; **8** reserves; **9** materials, resources, treasures; **11** possessions; PHRASES: **3, 9** raw materials.

ricochet 4 echo; **6** recoil; **7** rebound, reflect; **10** reflection; **13** reverberation; PHRASES: **6, 3** bounce off, glance off.

rid 4 free; **5** clear, purge; **6** divest; **8** liberate; PHRASES: **2, 4, 4** do away with; **3, 3, 2** get ~ of; **8, 4** dispense with.

riddle 4 pelt, poke, sift; **5** power, sieve; **6** damage, enigma, pepper, pierce, puzzle, screen, strafe; **7** mystery, problem; **8** puncture, question, separate; **9** conundrum, perforate; **11** brainteaser; PHRASES: **4, 4, 2, 4** pump full of lead.

ride 2 go; **4** hunt, jump, race, trip, trot; **5** curry, cycle, drive, groom, jaunt, mount, train; **6** canter, gallop, jockey, outing, saddle, travel; **7** journey; **12** steeplechase; PHRASES: **4, 2** rely on, rest on; **4, 3** muck out; **4, 4-6** ~ side-saddle; **4, 8** ~ bareback; **5, 2** break in; **6, 2** center on, depend on.

ridge 3 rim; **4** edge, fold; **5** crest, point; **6** crease; **7** crinkle, crumple, wrinkle; **9** elevation.

ridicule 3 guy, pan, rag; **4** jeer, mock, skit; **5** irony, roast, scoff, scorn, sneer, snort, squib, taunt, tease; **6** deride, parody, satire; **7** despise, imitate, lampoon, mockery, pillory, sarcasm, takeoff; **8** denounce, derision, satirize; **9** burlesque, humiliate, imitation; **10** caricature, pasquinade; **13** impersonation; PHRASES: **3, 4, 1, 3** not give a fig; **4, 1, 5** cock a snook; **4, 1, 9** blow a raspberry; **4, 2** send up; **4, 3, 2** take off; **4, 3, 2** make fun of, poke fun at; **4, 4, 3** pull one's leg; **5, 3, 2, 5** laugh out of court.

ridiculous 3 rum; **4** daft, zany; **5** comic, droll, funny, nutty, silly, wacky, witty; **6** absurd; **7** asinine, bizarre, comical, fatuous, foolish, risible; **8** clownish, derisory, farcical, humorous; **9** burlesque, eccentric, hilarious, laughable, ludicrous, priceless, slapstick; **10** incredible, knockabout, outlandish, outrageous; **11** nonsensical, Pythonesque *UK*; **12** preposterous, unreasonable; PHRASES: **3-7** far-fetched; **3-8** rib-tickling; **4-9** side-splitting; **5, 2-2** funny ha-ha.

rife 4 full; **5** laden; **6** common, loaded; **7** endemic; **8** bursting; **9** abounding, extensive,

prevalent; **10** widespread.

riffle 3 mix; **4** scan, skim; **5** flick; **6** glance, peruse, ripple, ruffle; **7** perusal, roughen, rummage, shuffle; **8** undulate; **9** randomise; PHRASES: **3, 2** mix up; **5, 7** flick through; **6, 2** glance at, jumble up.

rifle *See* **ransack**

rift 4 hole; **5** crack, split; **7** crevice, fissure, quarrel; **8** conflict; **10** difference; **12** disagreement.

rig 3 fit, fix; **6** invent; **7** arrange, derrick, falsify, prepare; **8** assemble, engineer, platform; **9** improvise; **10** manipulate; PHRASES: **3, 2** fix up, set up; **3, 3** oil ~; **4, 2** mock up. *See also* **clothes**

right 1 R; **2** RT, so; **3** apt, due, fit, fix; **4** best, fair, fine, hale, just, mend, true, very, well; **5** amend, aptly, claim, equal, exact, moral, plumb, Ralph, truth; **6** decent, desert, direct, remedy, repair, righty, square, suited; **7** correct, exactly, factual, fitting, healthy, honesty, justice, precise, rectify, redress, restore, station, totally, upright, utterly; **8** accurate, directly, entirely, fairness, goodness, morality, straight, suitable, suitably, unbiased; **9** correctly, desirable, equitable, faultless, honorable, intensely *UK*, perfectly, precisely, privilege, righteous, veracious; **10** absolutely, acceptable, acceptably, accurately, birthright, completely, dedication, deservedly, permission, reasonable, reasonably; **11** appropriate, entitlement, respectable; **12** satisfactory, unprejudiced; **13** appropriately, justification; **14** sanctification; PHRASES: **2, 2, 6, 2** as it should be; **2, 5** in shape; **4, 2** dead on; **4-2** spot-on *UK*; **4, 4** very well; **4-6** evenhanded; **5, 4** ~ wing; **5, 5** ~ angle; **5, 8** ~ reverend.

right (in the right) 3 due; **8** deserved, entitled, rightful; **9** excusable, justified; **10** forgivable; **11** justifiable; **13** unimpeachable; **15** unchallengeable.

righteous 4 good, just; **5** moral; **6** decent, honest; **7** upright; **8** virtuous; **9** blameless, honorable; **11** respectable.

righteousness 6 virtue; **7** decency, honesty, probity; **8** morality; PHRASES: **9** godliness, integrity, rectitude. *See also* **righteous**

right-hand 4 main; **5** right; **7** trusted; **8** reliable; **9** important, principal, rightward, starboard.

right-handed 7 dextral; PHRASES: 12 dextrorotary.

right-minded 4 sane; 5 sober; 6 decent; 8 sporting; 13 sportsmanlike; 3-7 law-abiding; 7, 5 squeaky clean.

rightness 5 truth; 8 accuracy; 9 precision, rectitude; 11 suitability. *See also* **right**

right of entry 4 pass, visa; 5 trade; 6 access, permit, ticket; 8 passport; 9 admission, importing; 10 admittance, permission; 11 immigration, importation; 12 expansionism; PHRASES: 3-11 non-restriction; 4, 4 free port; 4-4, 6 open-door policy; 4, 5 free trade; 4, 6 free market; 7, 6 foreign influx.

rigid *See* **inflexible**

rigmarole 4 fuss; 6 bother, excuse, hassle, ritual; 7 account, palaver; 8 business, verbiage; 11 explanation.

rigor 8 hardship, rigidity, severity; 9 adversity, dogmatism, precision; 10 difficulty, exactitude, stiffening; 11 consistency; 13 intransigence; PHRASES: 5, 6 ~ mortis. *See also* **rigorous**

rigorous 4 hard; 5 exact, harsh; 6 severe; 7 precise; 8 thorough; 9 demanding, laborious; 10 meticulous; 11 painstaking.

rile *See* **anger**

rim *See* **edge**

rime *See* **frost**

rind 4 coat, husk, peel, skin; 5 crust.

ring 1 O; 3 lap, mob; 4 band, bend, echo, gang, gird, halo, hoop, loop, peal, ping, team, toot; 5 blare, chime, chink, clang, clink, curve, flank, group, guard, knell, round, skirt, sound, twang; 6 burner, cartel, circle, girdle, jangle, jingle, keeper, tootle, vortex; 7 compass, enclose, resound; 8 carillon, encircle, resonate, surround; 9 encompass, extension, retaining, semblance; 10 appearance, circumvent, engagement, impression; 11 reverberate; 12 organization; 13 circummigrate; 14 circumambulate, circumnavigate, tintinnabulate; PHRASES: 2-4 re-echo *UK*; 3-4 ear-ring; 4, 2, 3, 3 ~ in the ear; 4, 3 ~ out; 4, 4 seal ~; 4-4 ding-dong; 5, 4 fairy ~, phone call *UK*, price ~ *UK*, prize ~; 6, 4 annual ~, growth ~, piston ~, signet ~; 7, 4 wedding ~; 8, 4 eternity ~, teething ~; 9, 4 telephone call *UK*.

ringing 3 pip; 4 loud, peal, ping, toll; 5 blare, brass, chime, chink, clang, clink, knell; 6 jingle, tinkle, tucket; 7 chiming, clangor, fanfare, pealing, pinging, tolling; 8 carillon, clanging, flourish, jingling, sounding, tinkling; 10 resounding; 11 campanology; 13 tintinnabular; PHRASES: 4-1-4 ting-a-ling; 4-4 ding-dong, ring-ring; 4-7 bell-ringing; 8, 5 sounding brass.

ringroad 6 bypass, detour; 7 beltway, orbital; 12 péripherique; PHRASES: 3, 6, 3 the pretty way; 4, 3, 5 long way round; 6, 5 scenic route; 7, 5 tourist route; 7, 6 traffic circle; 10, 3 roundabout way.

rinse 3 dip, dye; 4 tint, wash; 5 bathe, clean; 6 bleach, sluice; 8 colorant, solution.

riot 3 row; 4 demo, fray, orgy; 5 brawl, furor *UK*, melee; 6 clamor, fracas, furore *UK*, hubbub, mayhem, tumult, uproar; 7 anarchy, rampage, turmoil; 9 commotion; 11 disturbance, pandemonium; PHRASES: 3, 4 run amok, run ~.

riotous 3 mad; 4 wild; 5 noisy, rowdy; 6 unruly; 7 raucous; 8 anarchic; 9 hilarious, screaming; 10 boisterous, disruptive, rebellious, uproarious; 12 rambunctious; 13 side-splitting; PHRASES: 2, 3, 7 on the rampage.

rip *See* **tear**

ripe 3 apt, off; 4 sour; 5 grown, ready; 6 mature, strong; 7 pungent; 8 disposed, suitable; PHRASES: 5, 5 fully grown; 6, 3 crying out; 6-8 strong-smelling.

riposte *See* **reply**

ripple 4 flow, wave; 5 swell; 7 current, wrinkle; 8 undulate; 10 undulation; PHRASES: 4, 3, 4 rise and fall.

rise 4 bank, grow, hill, peak, rear, riot, soar; 5 arise, begin, climb, grade, knoll, mound, mount, rebel, slope, start, tower; 6 appear, ascend, ascent, awaken, emerge, growth, mutiny, revolt, rocket, spread, uprear, uprise, upturn; 7 advance, augment, hillock, incline, upsurge, upswing; 8 escalate, gradient, increase, levitate, progress; 9 acclivity, culminate, elevation, expansion, originate, promotion; 10 escalation; 11 development, enlargement, improvement; 12 amelioration, augmentation; 15 intensification; PHRASES: 2, 2 go up; 3, 2 get up; 3, 2, 4, 4 get to your feet; 3, 3, 2, 3 get out of bed; 3, 6 get higher; 4, 2 rear up, ~ up; 5, 2 shoot up, stand up; 5, 2, 6 stand on tiptoe.

rising 4 riot; 5 light; 6 mutiny, revolt; 7 bullish, buoyant, growing, lifting, rampant, rearing, soaring, upgoing, zooming; 8 airborne, anabatic, climbing, floating, mounting, upcoming, uprising; **9** ascendant, ascentive, expanding, rebellion, rocketing; **10** escalating, increasing, insurgence, revolution; **11** ascensional; **12** insurrection; PHRASES: **2, 3, 2, 3, 2** on the up and up.

risk 4 dare, defy; **5** peril, stake; **6** chance, danger, expose, gamble, hazard, menace, threat; **7** attempt, imperil, venture; **8** endanger, jeopardy; **9** speculate; **10** jeopardize; **11** consequence, possibility, probability.

rite 4 mass, muda, puja; **5** habit, usage; **6** custom, praise, prayer, ritual; **7** praying, routine, service; **8** astiamnu, blessing, ceremony, chalukah, oblation, offering, petition, potlatch, practice; **9** adoration, asvamedha, formality, laudation, penitence, procedure, sacrament, sacrifice, tradition; **10** almsgiving, confession, convention, exaltation, veneration; **11** benediction, celebration; **12** supplication, thanksgiving; PHRASES: **4-7** hymn-singing; **5-7** psalm-singing.

ritual 4 duty, form, mass, rite; **5** drill, habit, order, usage, usual; **6** custom, formal, normal, office, praxis; **7** formula, liturgy, routine, service, worship; **8** ceremony, expected, habitual, practice, protocol, schedule; **9** customary, formality, formulary, ordinance, procedure, sacrament, smartness, solemnity, tradition; **10** ceremonial, convention, observance, procedural; **11** ceremonious, correctness, institution, predictable, sacramental, traditional; **12** conventional; PHRASES: **5, 2, 7** order of worship; **6, 8** ~ practice; **10, 4** prescribed form.

rival 3 foe, top; **4** beat, peer; **5** enemy, equal, match, outdo; **6** exceed, oppose; **7** contest, surpass; **8** confront, opponent, opposing, outshine, resemble; **9** adversary, challenge, competing, contender; **10** antagonist, challenger, competitor, contending, equivalent; **11** challenging, conflicting, counterpart; PHRASES: **2, 2, 7** go up against; **2, 3, 5, 2** be the equal of; **2, 7** be against; **2, 7, 2** be similar to; **3, 5, 3** the other man; **3, 5, 5** the other woman; **5, 2, 4** ~ in love; **7, 4** compare with, compete with.

river 1 R; **2** Ob', Po; **3** Aar, Bug, cut, Don, Fox, Inn, Red, run; **4** Aire, Amur, Arno, Avon, Bear, beck *UK*, burn *UK*, Ebro, Elbe, fork, gill, Iowa, Isar, kill, Kura, Lena, Main, Milk, Nile, Oder, Ohio, Oise, Ouse, Oxus, rill, Rock, Ruhr, Saar, sike *UK*, Styx, Tyne, Ural, Vaal, wadi, Yalu; **5** bayou, Boi-

se, bourn, Boyne, brook, canal, Cedar, Clyde, Congo, Coosa, creek, crick, Douro, Dvina, Forth, Hugli, Indus, James, Liard, Loire, Marne, Meuse, Negro, Niger, Osage, Peace, Pecos, Pelly, Rhine, Rhône, Rogue, Saône, Seine, Snake, Somme, Tagus, Tiber, Tweed, Volga, Volta, Weser, Xingu, Yukon; **6** Albany, Amazon, arroyo, branch, Brazos, Danube, Donets, feeder, Finlay, flower, Fraser, Gambia, Ganges, Hudson, Iguaçu, Itchen, Jhelum, Jordan, Mamoré, Mekong, Mersey, Mobile, Mohawk, Morava, Murray, Nelson, Orange, Ottawa, Paraná, Platte, Powder, rillet, runnel, Sabine, Salmon, Saluda, Santee, Severn, stream, Sutlej, Thames, Tigris, Ubangi, Wabash, Yamuna, Yellow; **7** Alabama, Bighorn, Charles, Darling, Dnieper, freshet, Garonne, Genesee, Gironde, Guaporé, Kanawha, Limpopo, Madeira, Madison, Marañón, Moselle, Niagara, Orinoco, Orontes, Potomac, rivulet, Roanoke, Salinas, Salween, Schelte, Senegal, Shannon, Spokane, Ucayali, Uruguay, Vistula, Yangtze, Yenisey, Zambezi; **8** affluent, Arkansas, brooklet, Canadian, Cheyenne, Cimarron, Colorado, Columbia, Cuyahoga, Delaware, Dniester, Dordogne, effluent, Flathead, Flinders, Gallatin, Godavari, Illinois, Kennebec, Kentucky, Kootenay, Mahoning, Missouri, Ocmulgee, Okavango, Ouachita, Paraguay, Putumayo, Savannah, Suwannee, waterway; **9** Allegheny, anabranch, Aroostook, Athabasca, billabong *UK*, Churchill, confluent, Deschutes, Euphrates, Guadalupe, Irrawaddy, Kaskaskia, Kissimmee, Kuskokwim, Mackenzie, Magdalena, Menominee, Merrimack, Minnesota, Naugatuck, Pilcomayo, Porcupine, Qu'Appelle, streamlet, Tennessee, tributary; **10** Appomattox, confluence, Coppermine, Cumberland, Housatonic, millstream, Republican, Sacramento, Willamette; **11** Assiniboine, Brahmaputra, Connecticut, Mississippi, Monongahela, Montmorency, Susquehanna, watercourse, Yellowstone; **12** Apalachicola, distributary, Guadalquivir, Murrumbidgee, Rappahannock, Saskatchewan; **13** Chattahoochee; PHRASES: **2, 4** St. John; **2, 5** St. Johns, St. Marys, Xi Jiang; **2-6** Ob'-Irtysh; **2, 7** St. Francis; **2, 8** St Lawrence, St. Lawrence; **3, 3, 5** Old Man R~; **3, 4** San Juan; **3, 5** Amu Darya, Big Sioux, Han Jiang, New R~, Red R~; **3, 6** Des Moines, Eau Claire, Rio Grande; **3, 6, 6** Old Father

Thames; **3, 7** San Jacinto, San Joaquin; **4, 4** Blue Nile, Cape Fear; **4, 5** Gila R~, Göta Canal; **4, 6** Chao Phraya; **5, 2** Huang He; **5, 2-4** Shatt al-Arab; **5, 4** Smoky Hill, White Nile; **5, 5** Chang Jiang, R~ Plate; **5, 7** Belle Fourche; **5, 12** North Saskatchewan, South Saskatchewan; **6, 7** Little Bighorn; **6, 8** Little Missouri; **7, 5** Klamath R~.

rivet 3 pin; **4** bolt, hold, nail; **6** fasten; **8** enthrall, entrance, fastener, interest; **9** fascinate, mesmerize.

RM 5, 4 Royal Mail *UK*; **5, 7** Royal Marines *UK*.

RN 5 radon; PHRASES: **5, 4** Royal Navy.

RO 3, 3 run out; **6, 6** record office.

road 1 A *UK*, B *UK*, I, M *UK*; **3** row, way; **4** exit, lane, mews *UK*, path, pavé, wynd; **5** alley, byway, close, court, drive, route, track; **6** artery, avenue, bypass, camber, circus, feeder, filter, pedway, street; **7** beltway, bikeway, chicane, flyover *UK*, freeway, highway, parkway, roadway, terrace; **8** alleyway, Autobahn, causeway, clearway *UK*, crescent, driveway, junction, motorway *UK*, neckdown, overpass, ringroad, roadwork, shoulder, shunpike, turnpike; **9** autopista, autoroute, boulevard, crossroad, crosswalk, underpass; **10** autostrada, cloverleaf, crossroads, expressway, interstate, roundabout, throughway, turnaround; **11** carriageway *UK*, interchange; **12** intersection, superhighway, thoroughfare; PHRASES: **3-2-3** cul-de-sac; **3, 3** rat run *UK*; **3-3, 6** one-way street; **4, 3** curb cut, dead end; **4, 4** beef ~, dirt ~, exit ramp, farm ~, high ~, main ~, post ~, rest area, side ~, skid ~, toll ~; **4, 5** farm track, taxi stand; **4, 6** high street, main street, side street, toll bridge; **4, 8** soft shoulder; **5, 2** belly up; **5, 4** local ~, major ~, plank ~, royal ~ *UK*, rural ~, trunk ~ *UK*; **5, 5** blind alley; **5, 7** King's highway *UK*, state highway; **5, 8** urban clearway; **5, 10** grade separation; **6, 4** access ~, gravel ~; **6, 5** median strip, single track; **6, 6** safety island; **6, 7** Queen's highway; **7, 4** carpool lane, country ~, hairpin bend *UK*, highway ramp, private ~, service ~; **7, 6** neutral ground, traffic circle; **7, 7** divided highway; **8, 4** arterial ~, corduroy ~; **9, 4** secondary ~.

roadrunner 9, 4 chaparral cock.

road surface 4 curb, tile; **5** brick, stone; **6** causey, cement, Tarmac *TM*; **7** asphalt, bitumen, surface; **8** blacktop, concrete; **9**

curbstone, flagstone; **10** Tarmacadam *TM*; **11** cobblestone; PHRASES: **4, 5** road metal; **6, 5** paving stone *UK*.

roast *See* **bake**

rob 3 mug; **4** copy, loot, nick *UK*, prig, sack; **5** filch, heist, pinch, poach, steal, swipe; **6** burgle, fiddle, fleece, hijack, hustle, nobble *UK*, pilfer, pirate, rustle, snatch, snitch, thieve; **7** carjack, despoil, pillage, plunder, skyjack, snaffle *UK*; **8** shoplift; **10** burglarize, housebreak, pickpocket, plagiarize; **11** appropriate; PHRASES: **3-4** ram-raid *UK*; **5, 1, 4** crack a safe; **5, 3** knock off; **5, 3, 4** sneak off with; **5, 7, 2** stick someone up.

robber 5 thief; **6** bandit, dacoit, mugger, pirate, riever; **7** brigand, burglar, footpad, rustler; **10** highwayman.

robbery 5 heist, theft; **6** piracy, rapine; **7** mugging; **11** depredation; PHRASES: **4-2** hold-up; **5-2** stick-up; **8, 7** daylight ~.

robe 3 alb; **4** gown, izar; **5** burka, burqa *UK*, choga, drape, habit, ihram, kanga; **6** caftan *UK*, chadar, chador, chiton, dolman, jubbah, kaftan *UK*, kimono, kirtle, kittel; **7** cassock, chimere, chrisom, chuddar, jellaba, soutane; **8** bathrobe, colobium, djellaba, himation, peignoir, surplice; PHRASES: **4-2-7** robe-de-chambre; **8, 4** clerical ~, dressing gown, lounging ~. *See also* **clothes**

Robin Goodfellow 4 puck.

robust *See* **healthy**

rock 3 bob, gem, Gib, ice, nod, ore, wag; **4** crag, lump, reel, roll, stun, sway, wave; **5** dance, field, lurch, pitch, shake, shock, stone, swing, upset, waver; **6** bounce, careen, dangle, pebble, pillar, totter, tumble, waddle, waggle; **7** astound, boulder, disturb, flutter, mineral, stagger; **8** lopolith, mainstay, monolith, stalwart, swinging, xenolith; **9** batholith, flaunting, laccolith, undulancy; **10** undulation; **11** brandishing, flourishing; PHRASES: **3, 2, 3, 4** bob up and down; **4, 1, 4** rock' n' roll; **4, 4** ~ cake *UK*, ~ salt; **4, 6** ~ bottom, ~ garden, ~ steady; **4, 8** ~ climbing; **4, 9** ~ formation; **5, 2, 8** tower of strength; **7, 4** igneous ~; **11, 4** metamorphic ~, sedimentary ~. *See also* **rocks and minerals**

rockery plants 4 geum; **5** aster, draba, dryas, mazus, phlox, sedum; **6** acaena, arabis, erinus, iberis *UK*, onosma, oxalis, silene *UK*, thrift; **7** alyssum, armeria, astilbe, gentian, lewisia, linnaea, lychnis, mimulus, morisia, pigroot, pleione, ramonda, raoulia, shortia; **8** achillea, arenaria, dianthus, erigeron, erysimum, fleabane, gentiana, geranium, gromwell, haberlea, hepatica, origanum, sandwort, snowbell, uvularia; **9** anacyclus, androsace, aubrietia, bloodroot, campanula, candytuft, cerastium, edelweiss, houseleek, hypericum, penstemon, polygonum, saponaria, saxifraga, saxifrage, stonecrop, verbascum; **10** aethionema, antennaria, bellflower, cyananthus, lysimachia, pulsatilla, soldanella, throatwort; **11** dodecatheon, helichrysum, sanguinaria, sempervivum, vancouveria, waldsteinia; **12** helianthemum, leontopodium, lithospermum, sisyrinchium; **PHRASES: 2, 5, 4** St John's wort; **3, 4** sea pink; **3, 7, 4** New Zealand burr; **4-2-6** snow-in-summer; **4, 3** cat's ear; **4, 4** rock rose; **4, 5** rock cress; **4, 6** twin flower; **4, 7** moss campion, rock jasmine, rock mullein; **4, 8** rock soapwort; **4, 10** rock cinquefoil; **6-3, 6** inside-out flower; **6, 4** alpine geum; **6, 5** donkey plant; **6, 6** alpine yarrow, monkey flower, pasque flower; **6, 8** summer starwort; **7, 4** rockery pink; **7, 5** whitlow grass; **8, 4** shooting star; **8, 5** creeping jenny, mountain avens.

rocket 3 fly; **4** soar, whiz, zoom; **5** speed; **6** engine, hurtle; **7** warhead; **PHRASES: 5, 2** shoot up.

rocketry 4 burn; **5** Delta, flyby, orbit; **6** apogee, Ariane, engine, thrust; **7** booster, docking, payload, perigee; **8** launcher; **9** injection, insertion; **10** propellant, rendezvous, splashdown, trajectory; **11** retrorocket; **PHRASES: 2-5** re-entry; **4, 7** hard landing, soft landing; **5, 4** solid fuel; **5, 5** earth orbit; **6, 1** Saturn V; **6, 4** liquid fuel; **6, 7** launch vehicle; **6, 8** escape velocity; **7, 5** parking orbit; **8, 5** transfer orbit.

rock face 3 rib; **4** cave, crag, firn, hold, knob, neve, nose, peak, prow, ramp, roof, slab, wall; **5** arête, block, bulge, cliff, crack, flake, gully, ledge, niche, pitch, ridge, scoop, sérac, spike; **6** corner, glacis, groove, pillar, rimaye, stance, summit; **7** bollard, chimney, couloir, glacier, outcrop, terrace; **8** buttress, capstone, crevasse, foothold, overhang, pinnacle; **9** gritstone; **10** chockstone; **11** bergschrund, mantelshelf, mountaintop; **12** amphitheater; **PHRASES: 1-6** V-groove; **3, 5** air point; **5, 4** knife edge; **6, 4** pocket hold; **6, 5** fixing point; **7, 6** shallow groove; **8, 4** polished hold.

rocks and minerals 4 gold, mica, opal, ruby, talc; **5** agate, beryl, borax, emery, flint, shale, shard, skarn, topaz, trona; **6** acmite, albite, arkose, augite, barite, basalt, copper, dacite, dunite, gabbro, galena, garnet, gneiss, gypsum, halite, haüyne, humite, illite, levyne, minium, norite, nosean, pelite, pyrite, pyrope, quartz, rutile, salite, schist, schorl, silica, silver, sphene, spinel, urtite, zircon; **7** alnoite, altaite, alunite, anatase, apatite, arsenic, axinite, azurite, barytes, bauxite, biotite, bismuth, bornite, breccia, brucite, calcite, calomel, celsian, citrine, coesite, cuprite, diamond, diorite, emerald, epidote, felsite, foyaite, gahnite, gedrite, granite, gummite, helvite, hessite, hopeite, huntite, ijolite, jadeite, kainite, kernite, kyanite, leucite, lignite, mellite, mullite, olivine, orthite, raspite, realgar, sparite, syenite, sylvite, thorite, thulite, zeolite, zincite, zoisite; **8** aegirine, allanite, alunogen, analcime, analcite, andesine, andorite, ankerite, antimony, arcanite, augelite, autunite, basanite, bixbyite, bloedite, boehmite, boracite, braggite, braunite, bravoite, bronzite, brookite, calamine, chiolite, chlorite, chromite, cinnabar, corundum, crocoite, cryolite, cubanite, datolite, diallage, diaspore, digenite, diopside, dioptase, dolerite, dolomite, eclogite, enargite, epsomite, essexite, eulytite, euxenite, fayalite, feldspar, fluorite, gibbsite, goethite, graphite, hanksite, hawaiite, hematite, hyacinth, idocrase, ilmenite, iodyrite, jarosite, lazurite, limonite, litharge, marshite, meionite, melanite, melilite, melinite, mesolite, miersite, mimetite, monazite, monetite, mylonite, nephrite, orpiment, parisite, peridote, perthite, petalite, platinum, porphyry, prehnite, psammite, pyribole, pyroxene, rhyolite, rocksalt, sanidine, sapphire, sellaite, siderite, smectite, sodalite, stannite, steatite, stibnite, stilbite, stolsite, struvite, titanite, tonalite, trachyte, varisite, vaterite, wehrlite, wurtzite, xenotime; **9** acanthite, almandine, aluminite, amphibole, andradite, anglesite, anhydrite, anorthite, aragonite, argentite, atacamite, benitoite, brimstone, bromyrite, bunsenite, bytownite, carnalite, carnotite, celestite, cerussite, chabazite, chinaclay, cobaltite, columbite, copiapite, cotunnite, covellite, danburite, derbylite, diatomite, enstatite, erythrite, eucairite, euclasite, eudialite, ferberite, fibrolite, fluorspar, gehlenite, goslarite, granulite, graywacke, grossular, grunerite, harmotome, hercynite, herderite, hornstone, kaolinite, kieserite, lanarkite, lawsonite, leucitite, limestone, lodestone, magnesite, magnetite, malachite, malignite, manganite, marcasite, margarite, marialite, mendipite, microlite, migmatite, millerite, mispickel, monzonite, mordenite, mugearite, muscovite, nantokite, natrolite, nepheline, niccolite, oldhamite, olivenite, pectolite, penninite, percylite, periclase, phenakite, phonolite, pigeonite, pistacite, pollucite, powellite, proustite, pulaskite, quartzite, rhodonite, sandstone, scapolite, scheelite, scolecite, scorodite, smalltite, soapstone, spodumene, strengite, sylvanite, tachylite, tantalite, tapiolite, theralite, tholeiite, tremolite, tridymite, turquoise, uraninite, vivianite, wagnerite, wavellite, willemite, witherite, wulfenite, zeunerite; **10** actinolite, åkermanite, alabandite, andalusite, ankaramite, arsenolite, borolonite, bournonite, bronzitite, cacoxenite, caledonite, cancrinite, cervantite, chalcedony, chalcocite, chloritoid, chrysolite, claudetite, clintonite, colemanite, connellite, coquimbite, cordierite, douglasite, dyscrasite, emplectite, empressite, epidiorite, forsterite, ganomalite, garnierite, gaylussite, geikielite, glauberite, glauconite, greenstone, hambergite, heulandite, hornblende, huebnerite, ignimbrite, jamesonite, kimberlite, lanthanite, laumontite, laurionite, lepidolite, lherzolite, limburgite, mascagnite, matlockite, meerschaum, melilitite, melteigite, microcline, mirabilite, moissanite, newberyite, oligoclase, orthoclase, paragonite, pekovskite, peridotite, perthosite, phlogopite, phosgenite, piemontite, polybasite, pyralspite, pyrochlore, pyrolusite, pyrrhotite, rhyodacite, richterite, riebeckite, safflorite, samarskite, sapphirine, serpentine, shonkinite, sperrylite, sphalerite, staurolite, stercorite, stishovite, teschenite, thenardite, thomsonite, thorianite, torbernite, tourmaline, travertine, troegerite, ullmannite, ulvóspinel, vanadinite, vitrophyre, websterite, whewellite, wolframite, zincblende; **11** allemontite, amblygonite, anorthosite, apophyllite, baddeleyite, bertrandite, beryllonite, brochantite, calcarenite, calcilutite, calcirudite, carbonatite, carborundum *UK*; cassiterite, cerargyrite, charnockite, chiastolite, chloanthite, chondrodite, chrysoberyl, chrysocolla, clinochlore, daubreelite, eglestonite, ferroaugite, franklinite, glaucophane, greenockite, harzburgite, hastingsite, hausmannite, hypersthene, katophorite, leadhillite, loellingite, manganosite, melanterite, molybdenite, montroydite, nephelinite, nordmarkite, penfieldite, pentlandite, phillipsite, pitchblende, plagioclase, psilomelane, pumpellyite, pyrargyrite, pyrochroite, radiolarite, sillimanite, smithsonite, spessartite, titanaugite, triphyllite, valentinite, vermiculite, vesuvianite, villiaumite, zinnwaldite; **12** anorthoclase, arsenopyrite, bismuthinite, boulangerite, calcisiltite, chalcanthite, chalcopyrite, clinoptolite, clinozoisite, cristobalite, eddingtonite, feldspathoid, fergussonite, fluorapatite, grossularite, hedenbergite, hemimorphite, luxullianite, metacinnabar, monticellite, pyromorphite, pyrophyllite, rhodocrosite, senarmontite, skutterudite, strontianite, syenodiorite, terlinguaite, tetrahedrite, thomsenolite, trachybasalt, wollastonite; **13** anthophyllite, breithauptite, clinopyroxene, cummingtonite, jacupirangite, kaliophyllite, lepidocrocite, litchfieldite, orthopyroxene, quartzarenite, rhodochrosite, stilpnomelane, thermonatrite, uncompahgrite; **14** cryolithionite, hydromagnesite, lechatelierite, lithiophyllite, orthoquartzite, pseudobrookite, rammelsbergite, trachyandesite, xanthophyllite; **15** montmorillonite, pseudotachylite, stibiotantalite; PHRASES: **4, 4** blue john *UK*; **4, 7** rock crystal; **4, 8** clay minerals; **5, 6** lapis lazuli; **6, 5** cobalt bloom; **7, 4** iceland spar.

rocky 4 hard; **5** lumpy, shaky, stone, stony, tough; **6** flinty, gritty, lithic, marble, pebbly, trying, wobbly; **7** granite, lithoid, quaking, unsound; **8** gravelly, insecure, troubled, unstable, unsteady, wavering; **9** difficult, lapideous, strenuous, uncertain; **10** inconstant; PHRASES: **3, 4** not easy; **4-4** rock-hard; **4-6** rock-strewn.

rod 3 bar, gat, gun; **4** cane, pole, wand; **5** baton, dowel, perch, shaft, staff, stick; **6** pistol, switch; **7** pointer; PHRASES: **3, 3** con ~, fly ~, hot ~, tie ~; **5, 3** Black R~, drain ~, stair ~; **6, 3** aaron's ~, piston ~; **7, 3** control ~, dowsing ~, fishing ~, welding ~; **8, 3** divining ~; **9, 3** lightning ~; **10, 3** connecting ~.

roger 2 OK; **3** yes; **4** fine, okay; **5** great.

rogue 3 cad, cur; **4** rake; **6** rascal; **7** bounder; **8** poltroon, scalawag *UK*; **9** reprobate, scallywag, scoundrel; **10** blackguard; **11** undesirable; PHRASES: **3, 3** bad egg, bad lot *UK*; **3, 9** bad influence; **4-2-4** ne'er-do-well; **4, 8** ugly customer; **5, 5** black sheep.

roguish **6** impish, wicked; **7** naughty, wayward; **8** cheating, criminal; **9** deceitful, dishonest, malicious; **11** mischievous; **12** unscrupulous; PHRASES: **6-7** double-dealing.

roister **4** brag; **5** boast, drink, gloat, party, revel; **7** swagger; **9** celebrate; PHRASES: **4, 3** show off; **4, 5** make merry.

role **4** feed, fool, hero, lead, part; **5** cameo, heavy; **6** chorus, feeder, person; **7** buffoon, heroine, ingenue, Pierrot, support, villain; **8** antihero, function, position, vignette; **9** character, Columbine, Harlequin, Pantaloon, personage, soubrette; **10** antagonist, confidante, Scaramouch, stereotype; **11** protagonist; **13** deuteragonist, supernumerary; PHRASES: **3, 3** bad guy; **3, 4** bit part; **4-2** walk-on; **4-2, 4** walk-on part; **4, 4** lead ~; **4, 8** love interest; **5, 4** chief part, juicy part, minor ~, stock part, title part, title ~; **5, 5** merry widow, stage drunk; **5, 6** comic relief, Greek chorus; **5, 7** stage villain; **5, 8** jeune première, stage Irishman; **5, 9** miles gloriosus, stock character; **7, 4** leading ~, walking part; **7, 7** central casting, injured husband; **8, 3** straight man; **8, 4** breeches part, juvenile lead, speaking part, starring ~; **9, 3** principal boy *UK*; **9, 4** pantomime dame, principal girl; **10, 4** supporting ~.

roll **3** bap *UK*; **4** bolt, bowl, fold, furl, move, pipe, reel, spin, tube, turn, wind, yarn; **5** crank, screw, spool, trill, troll, twist; **6** muster, rotate, rumble, scroll; **7** revolve, trundle; **8** cylinder, undulate; PHRASES: **3, 4** egg ~; **4, 4** turn over; **4, 6** turn around; **5, 4** court ~ *UK*, dandy ~, music ~ *UK*, piano ~, Swiss ~ *UK*; **6, 4** barrel ~, bridge ~ *UK*, spring ~; **6, 6** scroll wamble; **7, 4** forward ~, sausage ~ *UK*, victory ~ *UK*, western ~.

roller **4** wave; **5** swell; **6** curler; **7** breaker; **8** whitecap.

rolling stock **3** car, van; **5** coupé *UK*, truck, wagon; **7** caboose, gondola, Pullman, railcar, sleeper; **8** carriage *UK*, roomette; **9** couchette, hoppercar, mailcoach; **12** freightliner; PHRASES: **3, 3** dog box; **3-6** low-loader *UK*; **4, 3** mail van; **4, 5** tank wagon; **5, 3** wagon lit; **6, 3** dining car, guard's van *UK*, parlor car; **7, 3** baggage car, freight car, luggage van; **8, 3** sleeping car; **10, 3** restaurant car *UK*; **11, 3** observation car.

ROM **5** Roman; PHRASES: **4-4, 6** read-only memory.

roman **5** plain; **7** ancient, upright; **8** straight; **9** classical.

Roman **2** RC; PHRASES: **5, 3** R~ law; **5, 4** R~ arch, R~ mile, R~ nose; **5, 6** R~ candle, R~ collar, R~ empire; **5, 7** R~ holiday; **5, 8** R~ calendar, R~ Catholic, R~ numerals. *See also* **Greek and Roman mythology**

romance **3** sex, woo; **4** date, gush, love, moon, romp, tale, yarn; **5** amour, ardor, court, fling, novel, story, swoon; **6** affair, allure, desire, weepie; **7** fantasy, feeling, fiction, liaison, passion; **8** daydream, intrigue; **9** adventure, amourette, eroticism, exoticism, fantasize, narrative, nostalgia, seduction, sensation; **10** enthusiasm, excitement, flirtation, tearjerker; **11** amorousness, association, fascination, involvement, romanticize; **12** entanglement, relationship; PHRASES: **3, 5, 2** pay court to; **4, 1, 5, 4** have a fling with; **4, 3, 4** step out with; **4, 4** tall tale; **4, 5** love story; **4, 6** love affair; **4, 7** tell stories; **5, 4** fairy tale.

romantic **6** dreamy, loving, tender; **7** adoring, amorous; **8** quixotic; **10** idealistic, passionate; **11** impractical; PHRASES: **6-4** starry-eyed.

romp **3** win; **4** sail, whiz; **5** caper, cinch, coast, frisk, steam; **6** cavort, cruise, frolic, gambol, prance; **7** chiller; **8** scramble, thriller, walkaway, walkover; PHRASES: **3-5, 4** one-horse race; **4-6** page-turner; **5, 2, 4** piece of cake; **5, 6** horse around.

roof **3** lid, top; **4** ceil, dome, rack, tile; **5** eaves, gable; **6** thatch; PHRASES: **3, 4** hip ~; **6, 4** hipped ~, saucer dome; **7, 4** gambrel ~, mansard ~, pitched ~; **8, 4** geodesic dome; **10, 4** imbricated ~, pendentive dome. *See also* **overhead covering**

roofed **5** domed; **6** hipped, topped; **7** covered, pitched, vaulted; **8** enclosed.

room **2** WC; **3** bog, den, lav, loo *UK*; **4** hall, loft, snug, span; **5** attic, berth, foyer, lobby, patio, porch, salon, scope, space, study, swing; **6** bunker, cellar, chance, extent, galley, garage, garret, gazebo, hangar, larder, leeway, lounge, margin, office, pantry, parlor, piazza, seaway, skybox, studio, toilet, volume; **7** balcony, bedroom, boudoir, canteen, carport, chamber, dinette, gallery, kitchen, landing, library, mudroom, nursery, passage, portico, seating, smoking, storage, stowage, sunroom, veranda, waiting, windage; **8** airspace, anteroom, basement, bathroom, berthage, capacity, corridor, hatcheck, headroom, homeroom, latitude, lavatory, occasion, orangery, outhouse, playroom, restroom, scullery, snuggery, solarium, wareroom, washroom, workroom; **9** amplitude, apartment, belvedere, boathouse, cafeteria, checkroom, clearance, cloakroom *UK*, clubhouse, dormitory, lunchroom, mezzanine, salesroom, storeroom, vestibule; **10** bedchamber, cafetorium, glasshouse *UK*, greenhouse, restaurant; **11** combination, compartment, kitchenette, opportunity, possibility, subbasement, temperature, withdrawing; **12** conservatory; **14** accommodations; PHRASES: **3, 4** box ~, sun ~; **3, 5** sun porch; **3, 6** sun lounge *UK*; **4-2** lean-to, walk-in; **4, 4** back ~, best ~, coal hole, game ~, junk ~, men's ~, mess ~, pump ~ *UK*, rest ~ *UK*; **4, 5** coat check; **4, 7** back kitchen; **5, 4** elbow ~, front ~, glory hole, squad ~, still ~ *UK*, study hall; **5, 6** water closet; **6, 4** common ~, dining hall, dining ~, engine ~, family ~, garden ~, living ~, lumber ~, powder ~, robing ~, rumpus ~, shower ~; **6, 5** summer house; **6, 7** dining kitchen; **7, 4** baggage ~, drawing ~, laundry ~, sitting ~, smoking ~, utility ~, waiting ~; **7, 5** baggage check; **7, 7** comfort station; **8, 4** dressing ~, entrance hall, sleeping ~, smallest ~; **9, 4** breakfast ~, reception ~; **10, 4** consulting ~, operations ~, projection ~, recreation ~.

roomy *See* **spacious**

roost *See* **settle**

root 3 dig, nub; **4** clap, core, corm, crux, grub, nose, stem, yell; **5** basis, canal, cause, cheer, delve, heart, radix, rifle, shout, theme, tuber; **6** bottom, burrow, forage, mallee, nodule, origin, rootle *UK*, search, source; **7** applaud, essence, radical, radicle, rhizoid, rhizome, rootlet, rummage, taproot; **8** calyptra; **9** rootstock; **10** derivation, foundation, rhizomorph; PHRASES: **4, 3** ~ cap; **4, 4** club ~, cube ~, prop ~, ~ beer, ~ crop, ~ hair; **4, 5** ~ tuber; **4, 6** ~ cellar, ~ nodule; **5, 4** stilt ~; **6, 4** aerial ~, square ~; **7, 4** fibrous ~, lateral ~; **8, 4** buttress ~.

rootless 6 roving; **7** nomadic; **8** drifting, homeless; **9** itinerant, traveling; **11** peripatetic; **12** freewheeling; **15** disenfranchised.

rope 3 tie; **4** cord, lash, lead, line; **5** cable,

twine; **6** attach, fasten, secure.

rorqual 6 finner; **7** finback.

rose 4 pink; **5** brier; **7** rambler; **9** eglantine; PHRASES: **3, 4** dog ~, tea ~; **4, 2, 4** bois de ~; **5, 4** Tudor ~; **6, 4** damask ~; **7, 4** cabbage ~; **8, 4** rambling ~.

rosebay 8 oleander.

rosebay willow herb 8 fireweed.

rose mallow 9 hollyhock; PHRASES: **5, 6** marsh mallow.

rose of Sharon 7 althaea; PHRASES: **6, 5** Aaron's beard.

rosette 4 rose; **5** badge, prize, shape; **6** design; **8** ornament; **10** decoration.

rose window 6 ribbon, rosace *UK*; **7** rosette; PHRASES: **5, 6** wheel window.

rosy 4 pink; **5** happy, ruddy; **7** flushed, glowing, healthy, hopeful, pinkish, reddish, roseate; **8** blushing; **9** favorable, promising; **10** auspicious, idealistic, optimistic, successful; **11** encouraging, unrealistic. *See also* **rose**

rot 4 mold; **5** decay; **6** fester, infect, mildew, perish *UK*; **7** crumble, garbage, pollute, putrefy, rubbish, twaddle; **8** claptrap, nonsense; **9** corrosion, decompose, poppycock; **10** balderdash, corruption; **11** contaminate; **12** disintegrate, putrefaction; **13** decomposition, deterioration; PHRASES: **2, 3** go off *UK*; **3, 3** dry ~, wet ~ *UK*; **4, 3** foot ~, soft ~; **5, 3** black ~, brown ~; **5, 4** break down.

rotate 4 gyre, spin, swap, turn; **5** hinge, orbit, pivot, swing, twirl, waltz, wheel, whirl; **6** circle, gyrate, switch, swivel; **7** circuit, replace, revolve; **8** exchange; **9** alternate, circulate, pirouette; **11** circumvolve, interchange; **12** circumnutate, circumvolute; PHRASES: **2, 5** go round *UK*; **4, 5** take turns.

rotation 4 revs, spin; **5** cycle, orbit; **7** turning, vertigo; **8** gyration, orbiting, sequence, volution; **9** dizziness, giddiness, revolving, switching, variation; **10** circuition, revolution; **11** alternation, circulation, interchange, replacement, revolutions, turbination; **13** circumference; **14** circumnutation, circumrotation, circumvolution; PHRASES: **4, 6** full circle; **5, 6** axial motion; **7, 6** angular motion, orbital motion; **8, 6** spinning motion.

rotator 3 cog, fan, top; **4** disc, disk *UK*,

gear, gyro, prop, spit; **5** drill, rotor, screw, spool, wheel, whisk; **6** bobbin, charka, winder; **7** capstan, spindle, turbine; **8** airscrew, autogyro, cogwheel, impeller, turnspit, windmill; **9** eggbeater, gyroplane, gyroscope, propeller, treadmill, turntable; **10** centrifuge; **11** gyrocompass; **14** gyrostabilizer; **15** ultracentrifuge; PHRASES: **3, 3** peg top; **3, 5** egg whisk; **4, 4** worm gear; **4-5** spin-dryer; **4, 9** food processor; **6, 4** floppy disk; **6, 5** rotary drill; **7, 3** humming top *UK*, rolling pin; **7, 4** compact disk; **8, 3** circular saw, spinning top; **8, 5** spinning jenny; **9, 3** extractor fan *UK*; **9, 4** revolving door.

rote **5** habit; **7** routine; **8** rotation; **10** repetition; **12** memorization.

rotten **3** bad, off; **4** foul, gone, high, poor, poxy *UK*, rank, sour; **5** fetid, moldy, nasty, venal; **6** addled, foetid, putrid, rancid, septic, unkind; **7** carious, corrupt, crooked, decayed, immoral, spoiled, tainted, useless; **8** decadent, dreadful, hopeless, terrible; **9** dishonest, festering, frightful; **10** unpleasant, villainous; **12** dishonorable.

rotter *See* **scoundrel**

rouge **6** redden; **8** beautify; **9** highlight. *See also* **cosmetics**

rough **3** ill; **4** hazy, rude, wild; **5** bumpy, bushy, crude, draft, fuzzy, gruff, hairy, harsh, hilly, lumpy, noisy, rocky, rowdy, seedy, tough, vague, wooly; **6** brutal, choppy, coarse, craggy, grainy, gritty, hodden *UK*, jagged, poorly, ragged, ribbed, ripply, rugged, rugose, shaggy, sickly, sketch, stormy, trying, tweedy, uneven, unwell, woolly; **7** boorish, bristly, brusque, cartoon, chafing, crinkly *UK*, crumply, diamond, fibrous, galling, grained, grating, inequal, inexact, jarring, outline, passage, raggedy, rasping, raucous, rippled, ruffled, sketchy, squally, summary, tangled, twilled, unhappy, violent, wrinkly; **8** crinkled, crumpled, forceful, forcible, fretting, granular, grinding, homespun, impolite, muricate, physical, rippling, scabrous, textured, unsifted, unsmooth, wrinkled; **9** difficult, estimated, imprecise, irregular, roughcast, roughened, turbulent, unrefined; **10** aggressive, boisterous, corrugated, discordant, granulated, impassable, uncultured, undulatory, unpleasant, unpolished; **11** approximate, challenging, distressing, tempestuous, unnavigable; **12** impenetrable, uncultivated; **13** uncomfortable; PHRASES: **3, 2, 5** out of

sorts; **4-2** mock-up; **5-3-5** rough-and-ready; **5-4** rough-hewn; **5-5** heavy-going, rough-going; **5-6** heavy-handed; **6-5** coarse-woven; **6-7** coarse-grained, linsey-woolsey.

roughcast **6** facing; **7** coating; **8** cladding, slapdash; **9** rendering; **10** pebbledash *UK*; **11** plasterwork, spatterdash *UK*.

roughen **4** fold, hack, kink, knot, mill, stud; **5** break, crack, gnarl, grate, notch; **6** crease, emboss, furrow, indent, ruffle, rumple, tangle, tousle; **7** coarsen, crenate, crinkle, crumple, engrail, pothole, serrate, wrinkle; **9** corrugate, granulate, roughcast, sandpaper; PHRASES: **5-3** rough-hew.

rough ground **3** rut; **5** crack; **6** canyon, furrow, sierra; **8** mountain; **10** overgrowth, sheeptrack; **11** undergrowth; PHRASES: **4, 4** dirt road; **4, 5** dirt track; **5, 4** rough road; **6, 6** broken ground; **8, 4** potholed road.

rough idea **5** draft, rough; **8** rudiment; **9** crudeness, vagueness; **11** cursoriness, sketchiness; **13** shapelessness; **14** incompleteness; **15** approximateness; PHRASES: **4-2** mock-up; **5, 4** rough copy; **5, 7** rough working; **10, 5** unfinished piece.

roughly **5** about; **6** around. *See also* **rough**

roughness **5** force, power; **8** severity, violence; **9** ambiguity, brutality; **10** turbulence; **11** astringency, discordance, imprecision; **12** irregularity. *See also* **rough**

rough thing **3** awn; **4** acne, barb, burr, file, kink, knot, scab, shag; **5** beard, braid, plaid, scale, thorn, tweed; **6** bouclé, goatee, grater; **7** bristle, pigtail, prickle, stubble, thistle; **8** corduroy, homespun, mustache, ponytail, splinter, whiskers; **9** horsehair, nailbrush, roughcast, sackcloth, sandpaper, washboard; **10** dreadlocks, glasspaper, handlebars; **11** muttonchops; PHRASES: **5, 4** steel wool; **5, 5** emery board, emery paper, emery wheel, goose bumps, goose flesh, scrub brush; **5, 7** goose pimples; **6, 4** barbed wire, matted hair; **6-7** linsey-woolsey; **7, 4** notched wood; **7, 5** chapped hands; **8, 7** designer stubble; **9, 5** scrubbing brush; **10, 4** corrugated iron.

round **1** C, O; **3** lap; **4** ring; **5** about, ambit, conic, orbit, ovoid; **6** around, change, circle, convex, groove, rotund; **7** bulbous, bullets, chukker, circuit, conical, gibbous, globose, globous, spheric, tubular; **8** globular, madrigal; **9** clockwise, orbicular, perfected, quodlibet, spherical; **10** ammunition, revolution, roundtable, spherelike; **11** approximate, cylindrical; **13** hemispherical *UK*; PHRASES: **2, 1, 6** in a circle; **2, 3, 5** on all sides; **2, 3, 8** in the vicinity; **2, 7** in circles; **3-6** egg-shaped; **4, 4** part song; **4, 5** milk ~ *UK*; **5, 4** ~ shot, ~ trip; **5, 5** daily ~, ~ about, ~ dance, ~ robin.

round (make round) 4 ball, roll, turn; **6** smooth; PHRASES: **4, 2** ball up, coil up, roll up; **4, 3** fill out; **5, 3** round off, round out; **7, 3** balloon out.

roundabout 4 ride; **7** oblique, winding; **8** carousel, indirect; **9** ambiguous; **10** attraction, circuitous, meandering; PHRASES: **5-2-5** merry-go-round; **7, 6** traffic circle.

rounded 3 fat; **4** wavy; **5** curvy, obese, plump, podgy, stout, tubby; **6** chubby, fleshy, mature, portly; **7** paunchy, shapely, sinuous; **8** complete; **9** corpulent, spherical; **10** curvaceous, overweight, undulatory; PHRASES: **3-7** pot-bellied; **4-6** pear-shaped.

roundness 9 convexity, globosity, rotundity; **10** sphericity; **11** circularity, globularity; **12** orbicularity; **14** cylindricality. *See also* **round, rounded**

round thing 3 egg, orb, pea; **4** ball, bead, bulb, drop, pill; **5** globe, orbit; **6** bubble, circle, marble, pellet, sphere; **7** balloon, circuit, dewdrop, droplet, globule; **8** spheroid; **10** hemisphere.

roundtrip 6, 4 return home; **6, 6** return ticket; **8, 7** homeward journey.

roundup 4 hunt; **5** recap, rodeo; **6** review; **7** capture, herding, rundown, summary; **8** assembly; PHRASES: **7, 2** summing up.

rouse *See* **stir**

rout 2 KO; **4** beat, drub, lick, riot, whip; **5** break, crush; **6** defeat, flight, hubbub, thrash, tumult; **7** beating, destroy, flatten, pasting, retreat, trounce; **8** collapse, disarray, disorder, massacre, stampede; **9** landslide, overpower, overthrow, overwhelm, surrender, thrashing, whitewash; PHRASES: **4, 3** wipe out; **4, 7** send packing.

route 3 run, way; **4** adit, beat, door, hall, lane, line, move, path, road, send, step; **5** aisle, drive, guide, march, means, orbit, track, trail; **6** access, artery, bypass, course, detour, direct, flight, ladder, method; **7** channel, circuit, doorway, gangway, hallway, passage, pathway; **8** approach, corridor, entrance, shortcut, transmit; **9**

direction, gangplank, itinerary, staircase, vestibule; **10** stepladder, trajectory; **13** circumference; PHRASES: **3, 2** way in; **3, 3** way out; **3, 4** sea lane, sea path; **3, 7** way through; **4, 2, 7** line of advance, line of retreat; **4, 4** back door, side door; **4, 8** side entrance; **5, 2, 3** right of way; **5, 2, 6** means of access; **6, 4** flight lane, garden path; **6, 5** beaten track; **6, 8** direct approach; **7, 4** traffic lane.

routine 4 dull; **5** habit, usual; **6** custom, normal, tedium; **7** humdrum, tedious; **8** dullness, everyday, monotony, practice, sequence, standard; **9** customary, procedure; **10** dreariness, monotonous, repetitive; **11** mundaneness.

rove 4 roam; **5** range, stray; **6** ramble, travel, wander; **7** excurse, journey, meander; **8** divagate, straggle; **9** pererrate.

roving 6 fickle; **7** erratic, nomadic, roaming; **8** rambling; **9** traveling, wandering; **10** capricious; **12** inconsistent.

row 3 cox, din; **4** file, line, punt, rank, tier; **5** argue, chain, fight, noise, queue *UK*, scull, slide, steer, strip, swing; **6** clamor, finish, paddle, propel, racket, ruckus, rumpus, square, strike, string, stroke; **7** balance, dispute, feather, quarrel, recover, wrangle; **8** argument, disagree, disorder, maneuver; **9** commotion; **11** controversy, disturbance; **12** disagreement; PHRASES: **3, 5** run level; **4, 2, 3** lift an oar; **4, 3** Skid R~, tone ~; **5, 1, 4** catch a crab; **5, 1, 5** cover a blade; **5, 3** death ~; **5, 3, 5** clear the water.

rowan 8, 3 mountain ash.

rowdy 4 loud; **5** noisy; **6** unruly; **7** raucous; **10** disorderly.

row house 4, 5 town house; **8, 5** terraced house *UK*.

rowing terms 3 oar; **4** loom, seat; **5** blade, catch, coxed, fours, notch, pairs *UK*, scull, skiff, sweep; **6** button, collar, dinghy, diving, double, eights, finish, handle, racing *UK*, sculls, single, stroke, swivel, thwart; **7** balance, gunwale, oarlock, regatta, rowboat, rowlock *UK*, squared; **8** balanced, finished, paddling, recovery, sculling, squaring, striking, tholepin; **9** balancing, outrigger, quadruple, stretcher; **10** feathering, recovering; **12** coxswainless; **15** intercollegiate; PHRASES: **3, 4** bow side; **3, 4, 4** the boat race; **3, 8** spade oar, spoon oar; **5, 4** blade slip; **5, 5** coxed fours, coxed pairs; **6, 4** rowing race, sprint race, stroke side; **6, 6** double sculls, single sculls; **6, 8** double sculling; **7, 4** sliding seat; **7-4, 4** Harvard-Yale race; **8, 1, 4** catching a crab; **8, 6** American stroke; **9, 6** quadruple sculls.

royal **5** grand, noble, regal; **6** kingly; **7** queenly, stately; **8** imperial, majestic, splendid; **9** excellent; **11** extravagant, magnificent; PHRASES: **5, 4** ~ blue, R~ Navy, ~ pair, ~ road *UK*; **5, 5** rhyme ~, ~ flush, ~ icing *UK*, ~ jelly; **5, 6** ~ assent, ~ prince, ~ purple, ~ tennis; **5, 7** R~ Academy *UK*, R~ Marines *UK*, ~ warrant *UK*; **5, 8** ~ highness, ~ standard *UK*; **5, 9** R~ Engineers, ~ Worcester; **5, 10** ~ commission; **6, 5** battle ~; **8, 5** princess ~.

RP **5, 4** reply paid; **6, 9** Regius Professor.

RR **5-5** Rolls-Royce; **5, 8** Right Reverend.

rub **3** dry, pat, wax; **4** buff, gall, hurt, sand, wipe; **5** brush, chafe, clean, curry, dress, knead, scour, scrub, shine; **6** caress, polish, scrape, smooth, stroke; **7** burnish, furbish, massage, squeeze; **8** abrasion, irritate, levigate, obstacle; **9** currycomb, sandblast, sandpaper; **10** irritation; **11** predicament; PHRASES: **3, 2** ~ up *UK*.

rubber **5** latex; **6** condom, eraser; **7** elastic, guayule; **8** neoprene; **9** elastomer, vulcanite; **10** caoutchouc; PHRASES: **3, 7** gum elastic; **4, 6** cold ~, foam ~, hard ~; **5, 6** crepe ~, crude ~, India ~; **5-6** gutta-percha; **6, 4** ~ band, ~ tree; **6, 5** ~ check, ~ goods *UK*, ~ plant, ~ stamp; **6, 6** sponge ~.

rubbish **7** garbage.

rubbish collector **7** junkman.

ruck **4** fold, heap, mass, pile; **6** crease, gather, rumple; **7** crumple, wrinkle; **12** accumulation.

ruction *See* **quarrel**

ruddy **3** red; **4** rosy, warm; **6** florid; **7** flushed; **8** blushing; **10** sanguinary; **11** sanguineous.

rude **3** raw; **4** foul; **5** bawdy, bluff, brash, crude, plain, rough, sassy; **6** cheeky, coarse, simple, vulgar; **7** boorish, obscene, uncivil, uncouth; **8** derisive, impolite, indecent, insolent; **9** barefaced, insulting, offensive, primitive; **10** unmannerly; **12** contemptuous, discourteous, inhospitable; **13** disrespectful; PHRASES: **3-8** bad-mannered, ill-mannered; **4-7** foul-mouthed.

rude (be rude) **4** dare; **7** presume; PHRASES: **4, 2, 8** hold in contempt; **4, 3, 5** have the cheek, have the nerve; **4, 3, 8** have the audacity; **6, 4, 5** forget one's place.

rudeness **5** cheek; **7** offense; **8** backtalk, contempt, derision, ridicule; **9** impudence, insolence, obscenity, vulgarity; **10** disrespect, simplicity; **11** discourtesy; **12** impertinence. *See also* **rude**

rudiment **3** bud, egg; **4** base, bulb, germ, pupa, root, seed, stem; **5** basis, fetus *UK*, larva, radix, sperm, spore, stock, tuber; **6** basics, cocoon, embryo, etymon; **7** bedrock, element, nucleus, radical, taproot; **9** chrysalis, principle, rootstock, spadework; **10** beginnings, foundation, groundwork, hypothesis; **11** preparation; **12** fundamentals; PHRASES: **3, 5-6** the nitty-gritty; **3, 8** raw material; **4, 3, 5** nuts and bolts; **5, 4** first step; **5, 5** first thing; **5, 9** first principle; **8, 6** building blocks.

rudimentary **5** basic; **6** simple; **7** primary; **8** immature; **10** elementary, rudimental; **11** fundamental, undeveloped.

rudiments **6** basics; **8** elements; **9** spadework; **10** beginnings, essentials, groundwork, principles; **11** preparation; **12** fundamentals; PHRASES: **4, 5** bare bones; **5, 10** first principles.

rue *See* **regret**

ruffian *See* **thug**

ruffle **5** annoy, upset; **6** rumple, tousle; **7** disrupt, disturb, perturb; **8** distress.

rug **3** mat; **5** cover, throw; **6** carpet; **7** blanket; **9** bedspread, sheepskin; PHRASES: **3, 3** car ~; **6, 3** hearth ~. *See* **wig**

rugby **2** RU *UK*; **3** run, try; **4** kick, maul, pass, ruck; **5** catch, cover, scrum, shove; **6** pileup, tackle; **7** defense, dropout, heeling, kickoff, looping, offside, passing, penalty, rebound, running; **8** dummying, fielding, tackling, tripping; **9** formation; **10** possession; **12** interception; PHRASES: **3-2** put-in *UK*; **4-3** line-out *UK*; **4, 4** drop kick, free kick; **4, 5** fair catch; **4-5** kick-ahead; **4, 6** high tackle; **5-2** knock-on; **5, 4** place kick, touch down; **5, 5** loose scrum, tight scrum; **5, 7** cover defense; **5-7** close-passing, throw-forward; **7, 3** penalty try; **7, 4** dropped goal, penalty goal, penalty kick; **9, 4** clearance kick; **10, 4** conversion goal.

rugby player **4** lock, prop; **6** hooker, jumper; **7** blocker, flanker, forward; **8** attacker, defender, fullback, halfback; PHRASES: **3, 6** try scorer; **4, 3** back row *UK*; **4, 7** prop forward; **4-7** ball-carrier; **5, 3** front row; **5-3, 4** stand-off half; **5, 4** scrum half

UK; **5, 7** loose forward; **6, 3** second row; **7, 6** support player.

rugged **5** hardy, harsh, rocky, rough, tough; **6** craggy, jagged, robust, strong, sturdy, uneven; **7** testing; **8** chiseled, furrowed; **9** demanding, difficult, resilient, weathered; PHRASES: **4-5** well-built; **6-8** strong-featured.

ruin **2** KO; **3** end, mar, rot; **4** blow, dish, doom, fall, hulk, loss, sink, undo; **5** abort, break, crash, death, decay, floor, knell, ruins, shell, smash, spoil, trash, waste, wrack, wreck; **6** damage, debris, deface, defeat, hobble, impair; **7** bedevil, breakup, clobber, debacle, decline, destroy, failure, flatten, remains, scupper, sinking, smashup, torpedo, trounce; **8** calamity, collapse, demolish, disaster, doomsday, downfall, meltdown, mutilate, shambles, upheaval, Waterloo, wreckage; **9** breakdown, cataclysm, devastate, hamstring, perdition, ruination, shipwreck; **10** apocalypse, bankruptcy, insolvency; **11** catastrophe, destruction, devastation, spifflicate *UK*; **12** dilapidation; **13** deterioration; **14** disintegration; PHRASES: **3, 5** cut short; **4, 2** mess up; **4, 3, 4** rack and ~; **4, 5, 4, 2** make short work of; **4, 9, 2** make mincemeat of; **5-2** break-up, crackup; **5, 3** knock out; **5-3** write-off; **5, 4** fatal blow, total loss; **5, 5** death knell; **5, 7** utter failure; **5, 8** China syndrome; **6, 2, 6** reduce to rubble; **8, 5** knockout punch, slippery slope.

rule **3** act, law, run; **4** deem, fiat, find, lead; **5** bylaw, canon, edict, judge, order, phase, power, reign, ruler, tenet, ukase; **6** decide, decree, direct, govern, manage, occupy, ordain, regime, ruling, settle; **7** control, declare, mandate, resolve, setting, statute; **8** colonize, covenant, regulate; **9** determine, directive, enactment, establish, ordinance, prescribe, principle, pronounce; **10** adjudicate, government, imperative, injunction, leadership, management, regulation; **11** commandment, instruction; **12** administrate, prescription; **13** parallelogram; **14** administration; PHRASES: **3, 4** lay down; **3, 4, 3, 3** lay down the law; **4, 4** foot ~, home ~; **4, 5, 4** have power over; **5, 4** chain ~, slide ~; **6, 4** ground ~; **7, 4** preside over; **8, 5** standing order.

rule (be the rule) **7** prevail; **11** predominate; PHRASES: **4, 4** hold sway.

rule (type of rule) *See* **government**

ruler **4** czar, Duce *It*, king, tsar; **5** queen; **6** captor, despot, Führer *Ger*, Hitler, leader, satrap, shogun, tyrant; **7** emperor, empress, monarch, tsarina, warlord; **8** autocrat, dictator, martinet, tsaritsa *UK*; **9** gauleiter *UK*, oppressor, potentate, regulator, sovereign; PHRASES: **3, 3** tin god; **3, 7** Big Brother; **4, 2, 5** head of state; **4-2-6** jack-in-office *UK*; **5, 4** slide rule; **5, 6** petty tyrant; **7, 4** crowned head.

ruling **5** chief, edict; **6** decree; **7** supreme, verdict; **8** decision, dominant, judgment, powerful, reigning; **9** governing, masterful, presiding, sovereign; **10** commanding; **11** controlling, declaration, influential; **13** authoritative.

rum **3** odd.

rumble **4** roar, roll; **5** crash, growl; **7** grumble, thunder.

ruminate **4** chew, crop; **5** graze; **6** browse, ponder; **7** pasture, reflect; PHRASES: **4, 4** chew over; **5, 4** think over.

rumor **3** say; **4** tale, talk; **5** claim; **6** allege, gossip, report; **7** believe, opinion; **9** speculate; **10** allegation; **11** speculation.

rumple *See* **wrinkle**

rumpus *See* **disturbance**

run **1** R; **2** go; **3** fly, jog, pen; **4** blur, bolt, cage, cast, coop, dart, dash, drip, flee, flow, gush, lane, last, lead, list, lope, move, pass, path, quit, race, ride, rule, rush, seep, slop, snag, trip; **5** chain, cycle, drain, elope, enter, flood, hurry, leave, reach, route, scoot, score, spate, spill, throw, track, train, trial, visit; **6** charge, course, decamp, depart, desert, direct, escape, extend, govern, handle, happen, manage, mingle, outing, retire, scurry, series, sprint, stream, string; **7** abscond, compete, contend, control, operate, paddock, persist, proceed, process, retreat, scamper, scuttle, stretch, trickle; **8** continue, duration, function, inundate, organize, overflow, progress, sequence, withdraw; **9** enclosure, excursion; **10** administer, disembogue, manipulate, succession; **11** participate; **12** administrate; PHRASES: **2, 2** go by, go on; **2, 2, 5** be in power; **2, 2, 6** be in charge; **2, 3** be off; **3, 3** dry ~, hen ~, ski ~; **4, 2** keep on, pass by; **4, 3** home ~, make off, milk ~, mole ~ *UK*, pour out; **4, 4** take part; **4, 5** move along; **4, 7** move forward, part company; **5, 2** carry on; **5, 3** dummy ~ *UK*.

run away **2** go; **3** fly, run; **4** bolt, flee,

quit, scat; **5** elope, leave, scoot; **6** decamp, depart, desert, escape, retire; **7** abscond, retreat, scarper *UK*; **8** withdraw; PHRASES: **2, 3** be off; **2, 4** go AWOL; **3, 3** run off; **3, 3, 2** run for it; **4, 1, 7** beat a retreat; **4, 2, 4, 5** take to one's heels; **4, 3** make off; **4, 3, 5** slip the cable; **4, 4** jump bail; **4, 6** make tracks, play truant, take flight; **4, 7** part company; **5, 3** clear off *UK*, slink off; **5, 4** break away, steal away; **5, 7** shoot through *UK*.

runaway 3 hit; **7** escapee; **8** absentee, fugitive; **9** absconder; **11** bestselling; **12** blockbusting.

rune *See* **character**

rung 3 peg; **4** step; **5** level, notch, stage.

runner 3 Coe (Sebastian, Lord); **5** gofer, Lewis (Carl), Nurmi (Paavo), Owens (Jesse), racer; **6** Devers (Gail), Jenner (Bruce), jogger, Thorpe (Jim); **7** Ashford (Evelyn), courier, entrant, Johnson (Michael), Rudolph (Wilma Glodean); **8** sprinter, Zaharias (Babe Didrikson); **9** Bannister (Sir Roger), candidate, contender, messenger, Samuelson (Joan Benoit); **10** competitor; **11** participant; PHRASES: **8, 6** Griffith Joyner (Florence).

running 8 seriatim; **9** operation; **10** management, overseeing; **11** controlling; **12** organization, successively; **13** consecutively; **14** administration; PHRASES: **2, 1, 3** in a row; **2, 3, 4** on the trot *UK*; **2, 10** in succession; **7, 4** ~ head, ~ mate; **7, 5** ~ board, ~ light; **7, 6** ~ stitch; **7, 7** ~ repairs, ~ rigging.

run out 2 RO; **3** end, jet; **4** gush, pour, slop, spew; **5** drain, flood, spill, spout, spurt, surge, vomit; **6** expire, finish; **7** outflow, outpour; **8** inundate, overflow; **10** disembogue; PHRASES: **4, 2, 2, 3** come to an end; **4, 3** blow out, flow out, gush out, pour out, spew out, well out; **4, 4** slop over; **5, 3** drain out, flood out, spout out, spurt out; **5, 4** spill over.

rupture *See* **split**

rural 6 rustic; **7** bucolic, country; **8** cornpone, downhome, pastoral; **11** countrified; PHRASES: **4-5** just-folks.

rural dweller 5 yokel; **6** rustic; **7** hayseed; **10** countryman; PHRASES: **7, 7** country bumpkin.

ruse 4 move, ploy, scam; **5** dodge, trick; **6** device, gambit, tactic; **8** artifice, maneuver; **9** stratagem.

rush 3 fly, run; **4** bolt, dart, dash, flow, gush, hare, pour, race, reed, scud, tear, zoom; **5** hurry, speed, surge; **6** bustle, career, charge, gallop, hasten, hurtle, sprint, streak, stream; **7** scamper; **8** expedite, stampede; **11** pandemonium; PHRASES: **4-4** hightail.

Russian 4 Igor, Ivan, Yuri; **5** Boris; **7** Russky; **8** Vladimir; **9** Muscovite; PHRASES: **7, 5** R~ salad *UK*; **7, 8** R~ dressing, R~ roulette.

rust 5 erode; **7** corrode, erosion, oxidize, tarnish; **9** corrosion, oxidation; **10** corruption; **13** decomposition.

rustic *See* **rural**

rustle 5 swish; **6** crunch; **7** crackle, whisper.

rut *See* **furrow**

ruthless *See* **cruel**

RV 7, 7 Revised Version; **8, 5** rateable value.

S

S **2** Mr (Italian: signor), on (French: sur); **3** soh; **5** seven (medieval Roman numeral), south; **6** school, second, spades, sulfur; **7** sulphur *UK*; **8** shilling.

SA **7** undated (Latin: sine anno); PHRASES: **3, 6** sex appeal; **5, 6** South Africa; **5, 7** South America; **9, 4** Salvation Army.

sabotage **4** ruin; **5** spoil, wreck; **7** destroy, disrupt; **9** undermine, vandalize; **10** disruption; **11** destruction.

sac **3** bag, pod; **4** case, sack; **5** pouch.

sack **3** bag, bed; **4** fire, loot, pack, poke, wine; **5** gunny, pouch; **6** depose, ravage; **7** despoil, dismiss, pillage, plunder, ransack; **9** devastate, discharge, dismissal; **10** redundancy; PHRASES: **3, 2** the ax; **3, 3** lay off; **3, 4** the boot, the chop, the push; **3, 5** the elbow; **3, 5-2** the heave-ho; **3, 6** the bullet; **4, 6** give notice; **5, 3** throw out.

sacking *See* **dismissal**

sacrament *See* **rite**

sacred **4** holy; **5** blest; **7** blessed, revered; **8** hallowed; **10** sacrosanct, sanctified; **11** consecrated.

sacred music **4** hymn, mass; **5** motet, psalm; **6** anthem, gospel; **7** cantata, chorale, hymnody, introit, passion, requiem; **8** canticle, doxology, oratorio, psalmody; **9** hymnology, offertory, spiritual; **11** recessional; PHRASES: **4, 4** hymn tune; **5, 9** negro spiritual; **6, 5** church music, gospel music; **6, 7** church parable; **7, 4** Requiem Mass; **10, 5** liturgical music.

sacred object **3** ark, pyx; **4** icon, rood; **5** bugia, cross, cruet, pietà, relic, totem; **6** candle, censer, fetish; **7** bambino, chalice, chaplet, incense, menorah, mezuzah, scrobis, tallith, urceole; **8** asperger, asterisk, beadroll, chrismal, ciborium, crucifix, Sangreal, tefillin, thurible, veronica; **9** incenso-

ry, prayermat; **10** monstrance, osculatory, phylactery, tabernacle; **11** aspergillum, ostensorium, prayerwheel; **12** eucharistial; PHRASES: **2, 4** Bo tree; **4, 5** holy cross, Holy Grail, holy water; **5, 4** totem pole; **5, 5** black stone, vigil light; **5, 7** Torah scrolls; **6, 4** Banyan tree; **6, 5** prayer shawl, rosary beads; **6, 6** votive candle; **6-6** aronhakodesh; **7, 4** sacring bell, sanctus bell; **7, 6** paschal candle. *See also* **talisman**

sacred text *See* **religious text**

sacrifice **4** burn, cost, lose, loss, toll; **5** forgo, price; **6** martyr; **7** abandon, crucify, expense, forfeit, penalty; **8** immolate, oblation, offering; **9** martyrdom, surrender; **10** forfeiture, immolation; **11** abandonment, crucifixion; **12** renunciation; **14** relinquishment; PHRASES: **3, 2** let go; **4, 2** give up.

sad **3** low; **4** blue, down; **6** gloomy, moving, pining, somber, woeful; **7** doleful, forlorn, tearful, ululant, unhappy; **8** dejected, desolate, dolorous, downcast, funereal, mournful, mourning, poignant, saddened, wretched; **9** cheerless, depressed, miserable, sorrowful, tormented, woebegone; **10** depressing, despondent, distressed, melancholy, sadhearted; **11** crestfallen, distressing, downhearted, heartbroken, languishing; **12** disconsolate, disheartened, heavyhearted, inconsolable; **13** heartbreaking; PHRASES: **3, 2** cut up; **5-8** grief-stricken; **6-7** broken-hearted.

saddlebill **6** jabiru.

sadistic *See* **cruel**

sadly **4** alas; **9** unluckily; **11** regrettably; **13** unfortunately; PHRASES: **4, 1, 3, 5** with a sad heart. *See also* **sad**

sadness **3** woe; **5** blues, gloom; **6** misery, pathos, sorrow; **9** dejection, heartache; **10** depression, desolation, melancholy; **11** despondency. *See also* **sad**

sad person 6 downer, wretch; 8 sufferer; 10 languisher; PHRASES: 4, 6 poor wretch.

safe 4 good, held, snug, sure, tame; 5 clear, peter, sound, vault, whole; 6 benign, edible, intact, secure, spared, unhurt; 7 anodyne, assured, careful, certain, covered, eatable, guarded, insured, lockbox, potable, prudent; 8 cautious, defended, harmless, hygienic, innocent, nontoxic, reliable, screened, shielded, unharmed; 9 drinkable, immunized, innocuous, preserved, protected, sheltered, strongbox, undamaged, unexposed, uninjured, unscathed, untouched, warranted; 10 dependable, garrisoned, guaranteed, imprisoned, inoculated, nonviolent, patronized, salubrious, unmolested, unpolluted, vaccinated; 11 disinfected, trustworthy, unhazardous; 12 nonflammable, unthreatened; 13 unthreatening; PHRASES: 2, 3, 5 in one piece, in the clear; 2, 4, 5 in ~ hands; 3, 2, 5, 3 out of harm's way; 3, 2, 6 out of danger; 3, 5 all right; 4, 2, 6 ~ as houses *UK*; 4, 3, 3 home and dry; 4, 3, 5 home and hosed, ~ and sound; 4, 4 home free, wall ~; 4-4 risk-free; 4, 5 bank vault; 4-7, 3 safe-deposit box; 5, 3, 4 alive and well; 5, 4, 3, 3 under lock and key; 5, 5 above water, under guard; 5, 10 night depository; 6, 4 behind bars.

safeguard 5 check, guard, nurse; 6 buffer, bumper, defend, fender, screen, shield, survey, uphold; 7 bulwark, defense, inspect, proctor, protect, rampart; 8 maintain, preserve; 9 chaperone; 10 invigilate, precaution, protection; PHRASES: 4, 3 care for; 4-3 baby-sit; 4, 5 look after; 5, 4 watch over; 6, 2 attend to; 6, 3 safety net; 6, 6 safety device; 6, 7 safety measure.

safety 6 refuge, rescue; 7 shelter; 8 immunity, Medicaid, Medicare, security, warranty; 9 assurance, avoidance, certainty, guarantee, sanctuary; 10 confidence, protection; 11 deliverance; 12 harmlessness; 14 impregnability; 15 invulnerability; PHRASES: 3, 5 all clear; 4, 5 safe place, wide berth; 4-5 well-being; 4, 6 home ground, sure ground; 4, 8 safe distance; 5, 2, 8 sense of security; 5, 5 coast clear, nanny state *UK*; terra firma; 6, 2, 7 ~ in numbers; 6, 6 escape clause; 7, 5 welfare state.

safety device 3 bar, key; 4 bolt, fuse, lead, lock, mail, mask, mole, rope; 5 alarm, armor, brake, earth, extra, groin, kedge, pilot, plank, reins, spare; 6 anchor, drogue, fetter; 7 ballast, grapnel, killick, railing, stopper; 8 deadlock, earmuffs, lifeboat, lifeline; 9 deterrent, guardrail, lightship, parachute, preserver, safeguard; 10 breakwater, cowcatcher, embankment, lighthouse, protection, respirator; 11 precautions; PHRASES: 3, 3 air bag; 3, 4 gas mask, Mae West, sea wall; 3, 5 ear plugs; 4, 3 jury rig; 4, 4 dead bolt, fire door, fire wall, jury mast, life belt, life buoy, life raft, life vest, seat belt; 4, 4, 6 dead man's handle; 4-4, 6 fail-safe system; 4, 5 fire alarm; 4, 6 fire escape, life jacket; 4, 7 fire blanket; 5, 4 chain mail, spare part *UK*; 5, 5 smoke alarm, water wings; 5, 6 crash helmet, sheet anchor; 5, 7 crash barrier, crush barrier *UK*; 6, 3 safety net, safety pin; 6, 4 oxygen tent, safety belt, safety lock; 6, 5 escape hatch, safety catch *UK*, safety chain, safety match, safety razor, safety valve; 6, 6 rubber dinghy, safety helmet; 6, 7 police barrier, safety goggles, safety harness; 7, 5 burglar alarm; 7, 7 circuit breaker; 8, 3 buoyancy aid; 8, 4 breeches buoy, ejection seat; 8, 6 football helmet; 9, 3 lightning rod; 9, 4 grappling iron; 9, 6 sprinkler system; 11, 3 bulletproof car; 11, 4 bulletproof vest.

saffron 9 safflower; PHRASES: 6, 6 autumn crocus.

sag 3 dip; 4 flag, flop, sink, swag, wilt; 5 bulge, droop, slump; 7 crumple, decline, subside.

sagacity *See* **wisdom**

sage 4 guru, herb, mage *UK*; 5 elder, Solon, tutor; 6 astute, boffin, clever, expert, genius, mentor, Nestor, pundit, savant, shrewd; 7 adviser, egghead, erudite, learned, Solomon, teacher; 8 academic, highbrow, Socrates; 9 authority, counselor, sagacious, statesman; 10 consultant, discerning, perceptive; 11 intelligent; 12 intellectual; PHRASES: 4-2-3 know-it-all; 4, 3 wise guy, wise man; 7, 4 nobody's fool.

said 4 oral; 5 quoth; 6 spoken; 7 alleged, assumed, reputed; 8 supposed; 9 aforesaid; 14 aforementioned.

sail 3 fly, jib, lug, rig, run, yaw; 4 beat, crab, crew, draw, flow, gybe, heel, kite, land, list, luff, moor, race, ride, scud, slew, slue, tack, veer, warp, wear; 5 drift, fetch, float, Genoa, glide, hitch, plane, royal, sheet, steer; 6 canvas, course, cruise, embark, jigger, lateen, mizzen, voyage; 7 captain, skipper, spanker; **8** clubhaul, gaffsail *UK*, headsail, mainsail, navigate, staysail, studding; **9** moonraker, spinnaker; **10** topgallant; PHRASES: **2, 5** go about; **3, 3, 4** run for port; **3, 4** set ~; **4, 1, 4** back a ~, furl a ~, reef a ~, roll a ~; **4, 3** cast off, hike out; **4-3-3, 4** fore-and-aft ~.

sailboat **3** hoy *UK*; **4** bark, brig, dhow, junk, proa, yawl; **5** dandy, kedge, ketch, nobby, prahu, sloop, smack, xebec, yacht; **6** barque *UK*, bawley, carvel, cutter, dinghy, lugger; **7** caravel, clipper, dromond, felucca, galleon, pinnace, polacca; **8** bilander, crumster, keelboat, schooner; **9** catamaran; **10** barkentine, brigantine, windjammer; PHRASES: **3-7** tea-clipper; **5-6** three-master; **6-6** square-rigger; **7, 5** fishing smack. *See also* **ship**

sailboat (parts of a sailboat) **3** bow, guy, jib, rig; **4** beam, boom, clew, deck, flag, gaff, hank, helm, hull, keel, lift, mast, prow, rope, sail, spar, stem, vang, warp, yard; **5** bilge, bitts, block, cleat, Genoa, sheet, sprit, stern, wheel; **6** burgee, drogue, ensign, gasket, gimbal, hawser, pulpit, rudder, sheave, shroud, spring, tackle, tiller, uphaul; **7** ballast, battens, cockpit, halyard, lanyard, lugsail, outhaul, painter, pennant, pushpit, quarter, ratline, rigging, transom, trysail; **8** backstay, bulkhead, bulwarks, deckhead, downhaul, fairlead, foresail, forestay, gaffsail *UK*, headsail, lifeline, mainmast, mainsail, purchase, staysail; **9** afterpart, amidships, gooseneck, leeboards, sidelight, spinnaker; **10** mizzenmast, rudderpost; **11** centerboard, chainplates, daggerboard; **12** companionway; PHRASES: **3, 4** aft mast, fin keel, GRP hull; **4, 3** gaff rig, jury rig; **4-3-3, 4** fore-and-aft sail; **4, 4** bolt rope, boom vang, claw ring; **4, 5** reef point; **5, 4** shock cord; **5-4** cross-tree; **5, 5** sheet winch; **5-6, 4** loose-footed sail; **6, 3** gunter rig; **6, 4** breast line, molded hull; **6, 5** bosun's chair, snatch block; **6, 6** barber hauler; **6, 7** coffee grinder; **7, 3** Marconi rig; **7, 4** forward mast, heaving line, mooring line; **7, 5** jamming cleat, kicking strap; **8, 3** Bermudan rig; **8, 7** standing rigging; **10, 4** Cunningham hole.

sailfish **7, 5** basking shark.

sailor **2** AB *UK*, O.S., RN *UK*; **3** tar; **4** crew, Jack, Noah, salt; **5** Anson, Drake, middy, pilot, rower; **6** hearty, marine, Nelson, pirate, Popeye, punter *UK*, rating *UK*, reefer, seaman, Sinbad, sitter, stroke, whal-

er; **7** admiral, captain, crewman, mariner, matelot, oarsman, sculler, skipper; **8** argonaut, coxswain, deckhand, helmsman, leadsman, seafarer, shipmate, waterman, wheelman; **9** boatswain, buccaneer, commodore, fisherman, navigator, privateer, steersman, yachtsman; **10** foretopman, Hornblower, midshipman, windsurfer; **11** boardsurfer; **13** quartermaster; **14** coastguardsman; **15** circumnavigator; PHRASES: **3, 3** sea dog; **3, 4** old salt, sea lord; **4-6** bluejacket; **5, 3** cabin boy; **5, 6** ship's master; **5, 7** naval officer, ship's steward; **6, 3** number one, number six, number two; **6, 4** bosun's mate.

saint **1** S; **2** ST; **3** Cyr, nun; **4** Bees, Chad, Elmo, Eloi, Hugh, John, Jude, Lucy, Luke, Malo, Mark, monk, Odyl, Olaf, Paul; **5** Agnes, Aidan, Alban, Alvis, Asaph, Basil, Elvis, fakir, Giles, Hilda, James, Kevin, Kilda, Leger, Linus, Mungo, Peter, Roche, Ronan, Roque, sadhu, Simon, Vitus; **6** Agatha, Alexis, Andrew, Anselm, Audrey, friend, George, Helena, helper, Hilary, Jerome, Joseph, Loyola, Martha, Martin, martyr, Monica, mystic, Ninian, Oswald, Patron, priest, Simeon, Teresa, Thecia, Thomas, Tobias, Ursula; **7** acolyte, Ambrose, Anthony, Barbara, Bernard, Brandan, Brendan, Bridget, Cecilia, Clement, Columba, convert, devotee, Francis, holyman, Leonard, Madonna, Matthew, Michael, Pancras, Patrick, pilgrim, Quentin, Regulus, rescuer, Rosalie, Severus, Stephen, Swithin, Theresa, Vincent, Walstan, Wilfred, William; **8** altruist, Barnabas, believer, Benedict, Boniface, canonize, Crispian, Cuthbert, disciple, Eualalie, Gertrude, hallowed, Ignatius, Lawrence, marabout, Margaret, neophyte, Nicholas, Veronica, Winifred; **9** Augustine, Catharine, Genevieve, hagiology, Kentigern, Latterday, Sebastian, Valentine; **10** catechumen, Crispinian, Stanislaus; **11** Bartholomew, bodhissatva, charismatic, Christopher; **14** philanthropist; PHRASES: **3, 4** Our Lady; **3, 6** the Virgin; **4, 8** good neighbor; **4, 9** Good Samaritan; **5, 6** white knight; **6, 5** patron ~; **8, 4** redeemed soul.

saintpaulia **7, 6** African violet.

Saint Petersburg **9** Leningrad, Petrograd.

salad **4** slaw; **5** cress; **6** celery, endive, pepper, radish, rocket *UK*, sorrel, tomato; **7** alfalfa, chicory *UK*, lettuce; **8** capsicum, coleslaw, cucumber, dressing, scallion; **9** macedoine, radicchio; **10** watercress; PHRASES: **4, 5** side ~; **4, 6** bean sprout; **5, 5** chef's ~, fruit ~, green onion, green ~, mixed ~; **5, 6** sweet pepper; **5, 7** ~ niçoise; **6, 5** Caesar ~, potato ~, tossed ~; **6, 6** cherry tomato; **7, 5** Russian ~ *UK*, Waldorf ~.

salary 3 fee, pay; **4** hire, wage; **5** screw, wages; **7** stipend; **8** earnings; **10** emoluments; **12** compensation, remuneration.

sale 4 deal, fair, mart, roup; **5** trade; **6** bazaar, vendue; **7** auction, selling, vending; **9** clearance, retailing; **11** transaction; PHRASES: **3, 4, 4** car boot ~ *UK*; **3, 7** art auction; **4, 2, 4** ~ of work *UK*; **4-3** sell-out; **4, 4** fire ~; **5-3** close-out; **5-3-3** bring-and-buy; **5, 4** white ~; **5, 7** Dutch auction; **6, 4** garage ~, jumble ~ *UK*; **7, 3** selling off; **7, 4** rummage ~; **9, 4** clearance ~; **10, 4** secondhand ~.

salesman 3 rep; **5** agent, Loman; **8** pitchman, traveler; **9** salesgirl; **10** salesclerk, saleswoman, shopwalker; **11** pitchperson, salesperson; **14** representative; PHRASES: **4, 4** shop girl; **4, 9** shop assistant *UK*; **5, 5** sales force; **6, 2, 3, 4** knight of the road.

salesmanship 5 pitch, spiel; **6** patter; **7** service; PHRASES: **4, 4** hard sell, soft sell; **5, 4** sales talk; **5, 6** sales patter; **5, 10** sales conference.

saliva 4 foam, spit; **5** cough, drool, froth, mucus, rheum; **6** drivel, phlegm, slaver, sputum; **7** catarrh, dribble, slabber *UK*, slobber, spittle; **8** coughing, ptyalism, spitting; **10** salivation; **11** sialorrhoea; **13** expectoration; PHRASES: **8, 5** salivary gland.

sallow 3 wan; **4** pale; **5** ashen; **6** pallid, sickly, yellow; **7** bilious; **9** jaundiced, yellowish; PHRASES: **6-3** washed-out.

sally 3 mot *UK*; **4** dash, jest, push, quip, raid, rush; **5** foray, Sarah; **6** attack, charge, sortie, strike, thrust; **8** breakout; **9** incursion, offensive, witticism; **12** breakthrough; PHRASES: **2, 3** go out; **2, 5** go forth; **3, 3** set out; **5-3** break-out; **7, 3** venture out; **7, 5** venture forth.

Sally 5, 4 S~ Army *UK*, S~ Lunn.

salmon 3 lox; **4** char, chum, coho, kelt *UK*, parr, pink; **5** smolt; **6** alevin, grilse; **7** Chinook, gravlax, kokanee, quinnat, redfish, sockeye; **9** blackfish, gravadlax *UK*; PHRASES: **4, 6, 6** Nova Scotia ~.

salon 6 soiree; **7** meeting; **9** gathering; **10** barbershop, rendezvous; **12** hairdresser's;

PHRASES: **4, 5** hair ~; **6, 5** beauty ~ *UK*.

saloon 3 bar, inn, pub *UK*; **6** lounge.

salt 2 AB *UK*, O.S.; **3** sal; **4** alum, saut; **7** hydrate; **9** anhydride, dihydrate; **10** trihydrate; **11** decahydrate, hemihydrate, hexahydrate, monohydrate, nonahydrate, octahydrate; **12** heptahydrate, pentahydrate; **13** dodecahydrate, quadrihydrate, sesquihydrate, undecahydrate; PHRASES: **4, 4** acid ~, bath ~, ~ cake, ~ flat, ~ lake, ~ lick, ~ pork; **4, 5** ~ marsh; **5, 4** basic ~; **6, 4** double ~; **9, 4** anhydrous ~. *See also* **salty**

salts 4, 5 bath ~; **5, 5** Epsom ~, liver ~ *UK*; **6, 5** health ~ *UK*; **8, 5** smelling ~.

saltwort 4 kali *UK*; **9** glasswort.

salty 4 salt; **5** briny; **6** saline, salted; **8** brackish.

salubrious 6 decent; **7** healthy; **8** hygienic; **9** wholesome; **11** respectable.

salutary *See* **beneficial**

salutation *See* **salute**

salute 3 mob, nod; **4** fete, hail, wave; **5** chair, cheer, flags, greet, salvo, toast; **6** praise, salaam, signal, tattoo, waving; **7** address, applaud, banners, bonfire, bunting, fanfare, flyover, flypast, garland, gesture, lionize, tribute, triumph, welcome; **8** drumroll, greeting; **9** fireworks, streamers; **10** salutation; **11** acknowledge, decorations, fanfaronade; **13** illuminations; **14** acknowledgment; PHRASES: **4, 1, 5** fire a salvo; **4, 1, 6** beat a tattoo, fire a ~; **4, 2, 7** sign of respect; **4, 3, 5** hang out the flags, turn out the guard; **4, 3, 8** blow the trumpets; **4, 4, 2** make much of; **4, 4, 7** deck with flowers; **5-4** march-past; **6, 4** ticker tape; **7, 4** present arms; **8, 4** dressing ship.

salvage *See* **save**

salve 4 balm, calm; **6** balsam, lotion, soothe; **7** appease, comfort, mollify; **8** liniment, ointment.

same 2 DO, ID; **3** one; **4** even, idem, like; **5** alike, equal, solid; **6** agreed, merged, united; **7** merging, similar, uniform; **8** absorbed, constant, matching, repeated, selfsame, verbatim; **9** coalesced, identical, redundant, unchanged, unvarying; **10** coalescent, consistent, equivalent, homoousian, invariable, isotrophic, repetitive, tautologic, unaffected; **11** assimilated, homogeneous, repetitious; **12** tautological; **14** consubstantial; PHRASES: **2, 4, 3** of that ilk; **3, 3** all one; **3, 3, 3, 4** one and the ~; **3, 4, 2, 1, 3** two peas in a pod; **5, 2, 1, 7** birds of a feather.

same (be the same) 5 agree, match, merge, quote, tally; **6** answer, repeat, shadow; **7** imitate, reflect; **8** coalesce, coincide; **9** harmonize; **10** correspond; **11** interchange, reciprocate; PHRASES: **2, 9** be identical; **4, 5** look alike.

same (make the same) *See* **standardize**

sameness 4 idem; **5** unity; **8** equality, mergence, monotony, verbatim; **9** agreement, homoousia, isotrophy, tautology; **10** redundancy, regularity, repetition, similarity, similitude, solidarity, uniformity; **11** coalescence, consistency, equivalence, resemblance; **12** assimilation; PHRASES: **2, 10** no difference. *See also* **same**

samphire 9 glasswort.

sample 3 bit, sip, try; **4** test; **5** dummy, pilot, taste; **6** browse, swatch, tester; **7** example, pattern, preview, snippet, trailer; **8** specimen; **9** foretaste.

sanatorium 3 san, spa; **6** clinic; **7** hospice, sickbay, thermae; **8** hospital, sickroom; **9** infirmary; PHRASES: **3, 7** hot springs; **6, 3** health spa; **6, 4** health farm; **6, 6** health resort.

sanctimonious 2 pi; **4** smug; **5** pious; **8** priggish, unctuous; **10** moralizing; **12** hypocritical; PHRASES: **6-4-4** holier-than-thou.

sanction 3 ban; **4** fine; **5** allow, leave; **6** permit; **7** approve, boycott, consent, embargo, license, penalty, warrant; **9** authorize, deterrent; **10** permission, punishment; **13** authorization.

sanctuary 3 den; **4** naos; **5** haven, oasis; **6** adytum, asylum, harbor, refuge, shrine, temple; **7** sanctum, shelter; **8** preserve; **10** tabernacle.

sanctum 3 den; **5** altar, study; **6** refuge, shrine, temple; **7** retreat; **8** hideaway; PHRASES: **4, 2, 6** holy of holies.

sand 3 rub; **4** grit, silt; **5** beach, shore; **6** bunker, gravel, polish, powder, scrape, smooth, strand; **8** sandbank; **9** sandpaper, shoreline; **10** sandcastle; PHRASES: **3, 4** rub down; ~ bar, ~ eel; **4, 4** ~ dune, ~ flea, ~ trap, ~ wasp; **4, 5** ~ viper, ~ wedge, ~ yacht *UK*; **4, 6** ~ hopper, ~ lizard *UK*, ~ martin *UK*.

sand eel 6 launce; PHRASES: **4, 5** sand lance.

Sandhurst 3 RMA *UK*.

sandpaper 3 rub; **4** file, sand; **6** polish, scrape, smooth; **10** glasspaper; PHRASES: **3, 4** rub down; **5, 5** emery paper.

sandwich 3 BLT, sub; **4** cake, cram, hero, roll, wrap; **5** butty *UK*, po'boy, snack; **6** burger, course, hoagie, insert, panini, sarnie *UK*, toasty *UK*; **7** bologna, grinder; **9** hamburger, submarine; **10** muffuletta; **12** cheeseburger; PHRASES: **2-3** po-boy; **3, 2** fit in; **3, 3** Big Mac™, hot dog; **4, 2** pack in, slot in; **4-3** poor-boy; **4-5, 8** open-faced ~; **4, 8** club ~; **5-4, 8** loose-meat ~; **5, 8** Cuban ~; **6, 2** squash in; **6, 4** oyster loaf, shrimp loaf; **6-6** double-decker; **6, 8** finger ~, Reuben ~; **7, 2** squeeze in; **7, 8** Dagwood ~, toasted ~, western ~; **8, 3** ~ man; **8, 5** ~ board.

sane 4 wise; **5** lucid, sober, sound; **6** normal, stable; **7** healthy; **8** rational, sensible, together; **10** reasonable; **14** commonsensical; PHRASES: **2, 4, 5, 4** in one's right mind; **2, 5, 4** of sound mind; **3, 5** all there; **4-8** well-balanced; **5, 2, 3, 4** right in the head; **6, 6** compos mentis; **8, 5** mentally sound.

sanguine 7 hopeful; **8** cheerful, positive; **9** confident; **10** optimistic.

sanitary *See* **hygienic**

sanity 5 sense; **6** reason, wisdom; **8** judgment, lucidity, saneness, sobriety; **9** normality, soundness, stability; **11** rationality; **13** understanding; **14** reasonableness; PHRASES: **4, 4** mens sana; **5, 4** sound mind; **6, 5** common sense; **6, 6** mental health; **8, 4** balanced mind; **9, 2, 4** soundness of mind.

Santa Claus 5, 7 Kriss Kringle; **6, 9** Father Christmas.

sap 3 mug; **4** dope, mine, nerd; **5** juice, latex, resin; **6** sucker, trench; **8** enervate, entrench.

sapient *See* **wise**

sapling 4 tree; **5** scion, youth; **6** sprout; **8** juvenile, plantlet, seedling, teenager; **9** youngster; **10** adolescent.

sapodilla 6 sapota; **9** naseberry.

sapper(s) 2 RE *UK*.

Sarah 3 Sal; **5** Sally.

sarcasm 5 irony; **7** mockery; **8** acerbity, cynicism, derision.

sarcastic 3 dry; **4** acid; **5** sarky *UK*; **6** biting, ironic; **7** mocking; **8** derisive, sardonic, scornful, sneering; **9** satirical; **12** contemptuous; PHRASES: **7, 4** jerring tart.

sardonic *See* mocking

sash 3 obi; 4 band, belt, zone; 6 girdle; 7 baldric; 8 cincture; 10 cummerbund; PHRASES: 4, 4 ~ cord; 4, 6 ~ window.

Satan 5 devil, enemy; 7 Lucifer; 9 adversary; PHRASES: 3, 4 Old Nick; 3, 5 Old Harry.

satchel 3 bag; 9 haversack; PHRASES: 6, 3 school bag; 8, 3 shoulder bag.

satellite 2 Io; 3 Pan; 4 Leda, moon, Puck, Rhea; 5 Ariel, Astra™, Atlas, Carme, Dione, Elara, Janus, Metis, Mimas, Naiad, Thebe, Titan; 6 Ananke, Bianca, Charon, colony, Comsat™, Deimos, Europa, Helene, Joliet, Nereid, Oberon, Phobos, Phoebe, planet, Portia, Sinope, Tethys, Triton; 7 Belinda, Calypso, Despina, Galatea, groupie, Hilalia, Iapetus, Miranda, Ophelia, orbiter, Pandora, Proteus, Sputnik, Telesto, Telstar™, Titania, Umbriel; 8 Adrastea, Amalthea, asteroid, Callisto, Cordelia, Cressida, Eutelsat™, follower, Ganymede, henchman, Hyperion, Intelsat™, Lysithea, Pasiphae, Rosalind, Thalassa; 9 dependent, Desdemona, Enceladus, entourage, Marcopole™; 10 dependency, Epimetheus, Prometheus; 12 protectorate; PHRASES: 3, 9 spy ~; 6-2 hanger-on; 9, 2 ~ TV.

satiate *See* satisfy

satire 4 skit; 5 spoof, squib; 6 parody; 7 lampoon, mockery, pasquil; 8 raillery, travesty; 9 burlesque, pasuinade; 10 caricature; PHRASES: 4-2 send-up; 4-3 take-off.

satirical 5 spoof; 6 ironic; 7 mocking; 8 humorous, sardonic; 9 sarcastic; 10 irreverent; PHRASES: 6-2-5 tongue-in-cheek.

satirist 3 wag, wit; 5 comic, joker; 8 humorist; 9 lampooner, satirizer.

satirize 4 mock; 6 deride, parody; 7 lampoon; 8 ridicule; 10 caricature; PHRASES: 4, 2 send up; 4, 3 take off.

satisfaction 3 joy; 4 ease; 5 pride, taste; 6 liking; 7 comfort, content, delight, redress, satiety, success; 8 approval, pleasure, serenity, smugness; 9 agreement, enjoyment, happiness, repayment, satiation; 10 equanimity, indulgence, recompense, reparation, settlement; 11 achievement, complacency, contentment, fulfillment; 12 compensation, consummation, thankfulness; 13 contentedness, gratification; PHRASES: 3, 4, 4 job well done; 4, 4 good work; 5, 2, 4 peace of mind.

satisfactory 2 OK; 4 fair; 6 enough; 7 fitting; 8 adequate, passable, pleasing, suitable; 9 agreeable, sufficing, tolerable; 10 acceptable, reasonable, sufficient, worthwhile; 11 permissible; PHRASES: 2-2 so-so; 3, 3 not bad; 3, 5 all right; 4, 6 good enough.

satisfied 4 full, safe, smug; 5 happy, sated; 6 secure, serene; 7 content, pleased; 8 satiated, thankful; 9 contented, fulfilled, gratified; 10 complacent; 11 comfortable, undemanding; 13 uncomplaining; PHRASES: 4, 2 full up.

satisfied (be satisfied) 4 purr; PHRASES: 7, 2 delight in.

satisfy 3 fit; 4 fill, glut, meet, sate, suit; 5 slake; 6 answer, assure, pacify, please, quench; 7 appease, assuage, content, fulfill, gratify, indulge, mollify, placate, satiate; 8 convince, persuade, reassure; 9 discharge; PHRASES: 3, 4 win over; 6, 4 comply with.

satisfying 5 ample; 8 adequate; 9 agreeable, enjoyable, rewarding; 10 comforting, nourishing, sufficient, sustaining; 11 substantial. *See also* satisfy

saturate 4 soak; 5 douse, flood, steep; 6 drench; 8 inundate, overload; 9 overwhelm; 10 oversupply; PHRASES: 3, 7 wet through.

sauce 3 dip, lip; 4 gall, roux; 5 aioli, cheek, cream, gravy, nerve, pesto, raita *UK*, salsa, stock; 6 catsup, coulis, fondue, tahini; 7 ketchup, tabasco, velouté, vinegar; 8 béchamel, dressing, marinade, rudeness; 9 guacamole, insolence; 10 applesauce, chaudfroid, mayonnaise, mousseline; 11 hollandaise, horseradish, insouciance, vinaigrette; 12 impertinence, taramasalata; PHRASES: 3, 5 soy ~; 4, 5 hard ~, mint ~ *UK*; 4-5 demi-glace; 5, 5 bread ~ *UK*, brown ~, chili ~, onion ~, salad cream *UK*, satay ~, white ~; 5, 7 ~ suprême; 5, 8 salad dressing; 5, 9 ~ espagnole; 6, 5 cheese ~, tartar ~, tomato ~; 6, 7 tomato ketchup; 6, 8 French dressing; 7, 5 Tabasco ~; 7, 8 Russian dressing; 8, 5 barbecue ~, béchamel ~, milanese ~; 9, 5 béarnaise ~, bolognese ~, cranberry ~; 10, 5 bordelaise ~.

saucer *See* crockery

sauciness 3 lip; 4 gall; 5 brass, cheek, nerve; 8 pertness; 9 impudence; 10 disrespect; 12 impertinence.

saucy 4 rude; 5 sassy, smart; 6 cheeky *UK*; 8 impudent; 11 impertinent.

saunter 4 idle, laze, walk; 5 amble, crawl,

creep, mince, mosey, paseo; **6** dander, hobble, ramble, stroll, toddle, wander; **7** meander, shamble, traipse, trickle; **9** promenade; PHRASES: **6, 5** toddle along; **7, 5** shuffle along.

saurian 6 lizard.

sausage 5 frank, wurst; **6** banger *UK*, haggis, polony *UK*, salami, weenie, wiener, wienie; **7** boloney, chorizo, saveloy *UK*; **8** cervelat; **9** andouille, Bratwurst, chipolata *UK*, pepperoni; **10** Knackwurst, liverwurst, mortadella; **11** frankfurter, sausagemeat *UK*, Wienerwurst; PHRASES: **4, 7** beef ~, pork ~; **5, 7** black pudding, blood pudding, blood ~; **6, 7** garlic ~ *UK*, Vienna ~; **7, 3** ~ dog *UK*; **7, 4** ~ roll *UK*; **7, 7** bologna ~; **8, 7** cocktail ~.

sausage dog 9 dachshund.

savage 3 mug; **4** maul, thug, wild; **5** brute, feral, harsh; **6** attack, fierce, severe; **7** destroy, drastic, ruffian, vicious, violent; **8** ruthless; **9** brutalize, criticize, ferocious, stringent; **12** unrestrained; **14** undomesticated; PHRASES: **4, 5** tear apart.

savanna *See* **grassland**

save 3 bar, but, rid; **4** bank, free, keep, stop; **5** amass, avert, avoid, hoard, salve, spare; **6** except, rescue, revive, scrape, scrimp; **7** collect, deliver, prevent, reclaim, recover, release, reserve, salvage; **8** liberate, preclude, reprieve, retrench, retrieve; **9** economize, excluding; **10** accumulate, emancipate; **11** resuscitate; PHRASES: **3, 4** cut back, cut down, put away, set free; **3, 5** cut costs, put aside, set aside; **3, 7** cut corners; **4, 3** bail out; **4, 4** hold back, keep back, salt away; **4, 5, 4** keep costs down; **5, 4** apart from; **7, 4, 4** tighten one's belt.

saver 6 magpie; **7** hoarder; **8** gatherer, investor, scrimper, squirrel; **9** collector; **10** economizer.

saving *See* **economy**

savor 4 tang; **5** aroma, enjoy, smell, taste; **6** flavor, relish; **7** cherish; **10** appreciate; PHRASES: **7, 2** delight in.

savory 5 salty, spicy, tasty; **7** piquant, pungent; **8** pleasant; **9** delicious, palatable, wholesome; **10** acceptable, appetizing, flavorsome; **11** respectable.

saw 3 cut; **4** chop, eyed; **5** adage, axiom, maxim, motto, sever, slice; **6** divide, saying; **7** compass, proverb, watched, whipsaw; **8** aphorism, circular, crosscut,

flooring, observed; PHRASES: **3, 3** rip ~; **4, 3** back ~, band ~, buzz ~, fret ~; **5, 3** chain ~, crown ~, tenon ~; **6, 3** coping ~, scroll ~; **7, 3** keyhole ~. *See also* **see**

sawhorse 4 buck.

say 2 as, eg; **3** cry; **4** aver, tell, view; **5** about, input, mouth, opine, speak, state, utter, voice; **6** around, convey, impart, reveal; **7** declare, display, exclaim, express, opinion, roughly; **8** disclose, indicate; **9** pronounce, verbalize; **10** articulate, pennyworth *UK*; **13** approximately; PHRASES: **2, 1, 5** at a guess; **4, 2, 4** give or take; **4, 4** give away; **5, 2, 6** right of speech; **5, 5** round about.

scabrous 5 flaky, mangy, rough, scaly.

scaffold 5 frame, noose, shell; **6** gibbet, halter; **7** gallows, support; **8** platform; **9** framework.

scald 4 boil, burn, heat, sear, warm; **5** singe, steam; **6** simmer; **7** blister; **9** autoclave, sterilize.

scale 1 A, B, C, D, E, F; **3** fur, key; **4** band, pare, peel, scab, shin, size, skin, tier; **5** climb, crust, flake, gamut, level, mount, piece, plate, range, ratio, scope, scurf, shave, strip; **6** amount, ascend, degree, extent, plaque, scales, tartar; **7** balance, deposit, measure, ranking; **8** covering, sequence; **9** dimension, exfoliate, gradation, hierarchy, magnitude, steelyard; **10** ballasting, calibrator, delaminate, desquamate, makeweight; **11** calibration, measurement, progression, weighbridge *UK*; **12** counterpoise; **14** counterbalance; PHRASES: **2, 2** go up; **4, 2, 6** pair of scales; **4, 3** peel off; **4, 5** drum ~; **5, 5** major ~, minor ~, modal ~; **5, 7** Roman balance; **6-4, 5** twelve-tone ~; **6, 5** barrel ~, spring ~ *UK*; **6, 7** spiral balance, spring balance *UK*; **7, 2** clamber up; **7, 5** melodic ~, torsion ~; **7, 6** kitchen scales; **8, 5** bathroom ~, diatonic ~, harmonic ~, platform ~; **8, 7** weighing machine; **9, 5** chromatic ~; **10, 5** enharmonic ~.

scaly anteater 8 pangolin.

scam 3 con; **4** ramp; **5** dodge, fraud, sting *UK*; **6** fiddle, racket; **7** swindle; **9** shakedown; PHRASES: **3-3** rip-off.

scamp 3 imp; **4** limb; **5** devil, rogue; **6** monkey, pickle, rascal, wretch; **8** scalawag *UK*; **9** scallywag.

scan 4 look, skim; **5** image; **7** examine, inspect, perusal; **9** visualize; **10** inspection, photograph, scrutinize; **11** examination; PHRASES: **1-3** X-ray; **2, 4** CT ~; **3, 4** CAT ~, MRI ~, PET ~; **4, 4** pore over; **6, 2** glance at; **6, 4** glance over.

scandal **4** talk; **5** rumor, shame; **6** gossip; **7** outrage; **8** disgrace, dishonor; **11** humiliation; PHRASES: **6-6** tittle-tattle.

scant **3** few; **5** stint; **6** little, meager, measly, scanty, scarce, slight, sparse; **7** limited; **10** inadequate, negligible; **12** insufficient; PHRASES: **4, 2, 3, 6** thin on the ground.

scapegoat **5** blame; **6** accuse, stooge, victim; **7** accused, condemn, culprit; **8** reproach; **11** incriminate.

scar **3** zit; **4** burn, hurt, mark, scab, spot, weal *UK*, welt; **5** score, stain, trace, wheal *UK*, wound; **6** affect, damage, effect, legacy, pimple, scrape, trauma; **7** blemish, scratch; **8** cicatrix, mutilate, pockmark; **9** devastate, disfigure; **10** mutilation, traumatize; **11** aftereffect.

scarce **3** few, off, out; **4** rare; **5** scant, short; **6** meager, sparse; **7** limited, unusual; **8** uncommon; **10** inadequate, infrequent, occasional, threatened; **11** nonexistent, unavailable; **12** insufficient, unobtainable, unprocurable; PHRASES: **2, 1, 7** at a premium; **2, 5, 6** in short supply; **3, 2, 5** out of print, out of stock; **3, 2, 6** out of season; **3, 3, 4** off the menu; **3, 3, 6** off the market; **4, 2, 3** hard to get; **4, 2, 3, 6** thin on the ground; **4, 3** sold out.

scarcity **3** ebb; **4** lack, need, want; **6** dearth, famine, rarity, scurvy; **7** absence, drought, paucity, poverty, rickets; **8** beriberi, decrease, leanness, pellagra, shortage; **10** diminution, inadequacy, scarceness, starvation; **11** deprivation, infertility, infrequency, shallowness; **12** malnutrition, uncommonness; **13** insufficiency; PHRASES: **3, 5** low water; **3, 6** oil crisis, the shorts; **4, 6** bear market; **4, 8** bare cupboard; **5, 4, 5** seven lean years; **5, 6** short supply; **6, 4** meager diet; **6, 6** energy crisis; **7, 2, 5** nothing to spare; **7, 6** sellers' market.

scare **3** cow; **4** fear; **5** alarm, bully, daunt, panic, shake, shock; **6** appall, dismay, fright, menace; **7** horrify, petrify, stagger, startle, terrify, unnerve; **8** affright, browbeat, distress, enervate, frighten; **9** terrorize; **10** intimidate.

scarecrow **3** guy *UK*; **6** effigy, figure; **9** mannequin.

scared **4** frit; **5** cowed; **6** afraid, aghast; **8** affright, blanched; **9** horrified, petrified, terrified; **10** frightened, terrorized; **11** demoralized, intimidated; PHRASES: **4, 2, 1, 5** pale as a ghost; **4-8** fear-stricken; **5, 2, 1, 5** white as a sheet; **5-5** ashen-faced; **5-8** panic-stricken; **6, 4** deadly pale; **6, 5** ~ stiff; **6-6** horror-struck, terror-struck.

scarlet **3** red; **7** carmine, crimson; **9** vermilion; PHRASES: **4, 7** Will S~; **7, 3** ~ hat; **7, 5** ~ fever, ~ woman; **7, 6** ~ letter, ~ runner.

scarper *See* **run away**

scary **4** dire, grim; **5** awful; **6** spooky; **7** awesome, fearful, ghastly, hideous; **8** alarming, daunting, dreadful, fearsome, horrible, horrific, menacing, shocking, terrible; **9** appalling, dismaying, frightful, startling, unnerving; **10** enervating, formidable, horrendous, horrifying, petrifying, terrifying; **11** frightening; **12** intimidating; PHRASES: **4-7** hair-raising.

scat *See* **run away**

scathing *See* **scornful**

scatter **3** dot, pin, sow; **4** flee, toss; **5** fling, strew, throw; **6** spread; **7** diagram, shatter; **8** disperse, sprinkle, squander; **9** broadcast; **10** distribute; **11** disseminate; PHRASES: **3, 4** fly away; **3, 5** dot about, fly apart; **4, 6** take flight; **5, 2** break up; **5, 3** space out; **6, 3** spread out, string out.

scavenge **4** hunt, sift; **6** forage, search; **7** rummage.

scenario *See* **situation**

scene **3** act; **4** area, fuss, item, part, site, spot, view; **5** arena, field, piece, place, sight, vista; **6** finale, number, prolog *UK*, sketch, speech; **7** episode, extract, outlook, passage, picture, section, setting, tableau; **8** backdrop, division, entr'acte, epilogue, location, outburst, panorama, prologue, prospect; **9** commotion, interlude, landscape, spectacle; **10** background, denouement, exhibition, intermezzo; **11** catastrophe; PHRASES: **2-2** to-do; **3, 5** set piece, sex ~; **4, 5** love ~; **5-2** carry-on *UK*; **5, 7** final curtain; **6, 5** battle ~; **7, 5** opening ~; **7-6** curtain-lifter, curtain-raiser; **8, 5** exposure ~.

scenery **3** set; **4** flat, view; **5** decor, vista; **7** outlook, setting, staging; **8** backdrop, panorama; **9** backcloth, cyclorama, landscape; **10** background; **11** countryside; **12** surroundings.

scent **3** air; **4** feel, hint, odor; **5** aroma, imbue, sense, smell, sniff, spoor, tinge, trace, track, trail, whiff; **6** detect, expect, infuse; **7** bouquet, cologne, foresee, perfume, predict, suffuse; **8** foretell, perceive; **9** fragrance, pheromone; **10** aftershave, indication, suggestion; PHRASES: **3, 2, 7** eau de cologne; **3, 2, 8** eau de toilette; **4, 2** pick up; **5, 5** ~ gland; **6, 5** toilet water.

schedule **4** form, list, plan, rota *UK*, slot, time; **6** agenda; **7** arrange, diarize, program; **8** calendar, organize; **9** timetable *UK*.

scheme **4** idea, plan, plot, ploy, ruse; **5** chart, order; **6** design, devise, format, method, policy, schema, system, wangle; **7** connive, diagram, graphic, outline, pattern, program; **8** conspire, contrive, intrigue, proposal; **9** calculate, machinate, schematic, stratagem, structure; **10** conspiracy; **11** arrangement; **12** organization; **14** representation.

scheming *See* **cunning**

schism *See* **split**

scholar **2** BA, MA; **5** pupil; **6** alumna; **7** alumnus, student; **8** academic, graduate; **9** schoolboy; PHRASES: **6, 7** Rhodes ~.

scholarship **5** grant, study; **7** bursary, subsidy; **8** learning, research; **9** allowance, erudition, knowledge; **11** studentship.

school **3** LSE *UK*, SCH; **4** coed, Eton; **5** coach, drill, group, lycée *Fr*, shoal, Slade, Stowe, teach, train, tutor; **6** busing, dayhop, Harrow, Oundle, Repton, Schule *Ger*, scuola *It*; **7** academy, coterie, crammer *UK*, educate, escuela *Sp*, Lancing, prepare, Roedean *UK*; **8** approved, boarding, Downside, flunkout, instruct, seatwork, seminary; **9** finishing, nongraded, preschool, secondary, Tonbridge; **10** Ampleforth, chautauqua, discipline, homeschool, sisterhood, sophomoric, Stonyhurst, Winchester; **11** brotherhood, Marlborough; **12** Charterhouse, conservatory, homeschooler, kindergarten; **13** comprehensive *UK*; **15** prekindergarten; PHRASES: **3, 4** key club; **3, 6** day ~, law ~; **3-6** all-choice; **4, 6** dame ~ *UK*, film ~, high ~, play ~, prep ~; **4, 9** open classroom; **5, 2, 8** place of learning; **5, 3** flunk out; **5, 4** study hall; **5, 6** Bible ~, choir ~, faith ~ *UK*, first ~ *UK*, grade ~, lower ~ *UK*, music ~, night ~, state ~, trade ~, upper ~ *UK*; **5-10** grant-maintained; **6, 4** senior high *UK*; **6-5** direct-grant; **6, 6** ballet ~, church ~, design ~, infant ~ *UK*, junior ~ *UK*, magnet ~, middle ~, public ~, riding ~,

summer ~, Sunday ~; **6, 8** schola cantorum *UK*; **7, 6** convent ~, driving ~, grammar ~, library ~, medical ~, nursery ~, primary ~, private ~, special ~; **7, 8** service learning; **8, 6** boarding ~, business ~, extended ~, graduate ~, training ~; **8, 7** military academy; **8, 8** practice teaching; **8, 9** guidance counselor; **9, 6** finishing ~, parochial ~, secondary ~; **13, 6** baccalaureate sermon.

school book **4** crib; **5** atlas; **6** manual, primer, reader; **7** grammar, lexicon; **8** copybook, database, handbook, notebook, textbook, workbook; **9** thesaurus; **10** dictionary, literature, scratchpad; **11** abecedarium, publication; **12** bibliography, encyclopedia; PHRASES: **4, 4** prep book; **4, 7** text edition; **5, 4** rough book; **6, 4** answer book; **7, 4** grammar book; **8, 4** exercise book.

school of thought **4** Yoga; **5** deism, Nyaya; **6** ahimsa, egoism, holism, Humism, monism, Sufism, Taoism, theism; **7** animism, atomism, dualism, Hobbism, Marxism, mimamsa, outlook, realism, Sankhya, Thomism; **8** altruism, attitude, Buddhism, cynicism, doctrine, dynamism, fatalism, hedonism, humanism, idealism, ideology, Lokayata, nihilism, Sartrism, stoicism, vitalism; **9** anarchism, apriorism, Averroism, communism, emotivism, hylozoism, mechanism, mentalism, modernism, mysticism, pantheism, Platonism, pluralism, socialism, solipsism, Vaisesika, viewpoint; **10** Benthamism, Bergsonism, capitalism, Eleaticism, empiricism, euhemerism, Gnosticism, Kantianism, monetarism, naturalism, nominalism, philosophy, positivism, pragmatism, relativism, satyagraha, skepticism, Utopianism; **11** agnosticism, behaviorism, determinism, estheticism, eudaemonism, Hegelianism, Manichaeism, materialism, nationalism, objectivism, panpsychism, physicalism, rationalism, Socraticism, syndicalism, Vijnanavada; **12** Berkelianism, Cartesianism, collectivism, Confucianism, epicureanism, essentialism, hylomorphism, intuitionism, isolationism, Keynesianism, reductionism, subjectivism; **13** conceptualism, contextualism, descriptivism, functionalism, individualism, phenomenalism, scholasticism, structuralism; **14** existentialism, Nietzscheanism, Pythagoreanism, sensationalism, utilitarianism; **15** Aristotelianism, instrumentalism; PHRASES: **3-6, 6** boo-hurrah theory; **3, 8** Zen Buddhism; **3-9** Neo-Platonism; **4, 6**

game theory; **4-7** anti-realism; **5, 6** chaos theory; **5-7** quasi-realism; **6, 6** Vienna circle; **9, 6** Frankfurt School.

schoolroom **4** hall; **6** campus; **7** library; **8** formroom, sickroom, workshop; **9** classroom, dormitory, gymnasium, staffroom; **10** auditorium, laboratory, playground, sanatorium, schoolyard; **11** schoolhouse; PHRASES: **3, 4** art room; **4, 2, 9** hall of residence; **5, 4** music room; **6, 4** common room, dining room; **6, 5** sports field; **7, 4** lecture hall; **7, 5** playing field; **8, 4** assembly hall; **8, 5** sorority house; **10, 5** fraternity house.

science **2** SC; **5** ology, skill; **7** biology, physics; **8** learning; **9** astronomy, chemistry, knowledge, mechanics; **10** discipline, geophysics, nucleonics, technology; **11** scholarship; **12** biochemistry; **14** thermodynamics; PHRASES: **4, 7** life ~; **6, 7** social ~; **7, 7** applied ~, natural ~, ~ fiction; **8, 7** domestic ~, physical ~.

scientist **3** Dam (Henrik), Dow (Herbert Henry), Ohm (Georg); **4** Bohr (Niels), Davy (Sir Humphry), Mach (Ernst); **5** Avery (Oswald), Chain (Sir Ernst Boris), Crick (Francis H. C.), Curie (Marie), Curie (Pierre), Doisy (Edward Adelbert), Elion (Gertrude Belle), Fermi (Enrico), Gamow (George), Hertz (Heinrich), Krebs (Sir Hans), Nobel (Alfred), Sabin (Albert), Volta (Alessandro); **6** Bunsen (Robert Wilhelm), Dalton (John), Nernst (Walther), Planck (Max), Sanger (Frederick), Watson (James D.), Wigner (Eugene Paul); **7** Compton (Arthur Holly), Dawkins (Richard), Faraday (Michael), Feynman (Richard), Fleming (Sir Alexander), Galileo, Goddard (Robert), Hawking (Stephen), Hodgkin (Dorothy Mary), Meitner (Lise), Pauling (Linus), Scheele (Carl Wilhelm), Szilard (Leo); PHRASES: **8** Avogadro (Amedeo), Einstein (Albert), Foucault (Jean-Bernard Léon), Franklin (Rosalind Elsie), Roentgen (Wilhelm Conrad), Sakharov (Andrei), Smithson (James); **9** Arrhenius (Svante August), Atanasoff (John V.), Baekeland (Leo), Bernoulli (Daniel), Berzelius (Jöns Jakob), Heaviside (Oliver), Hitchings (George Herbert), Lavoisier (Antoine Laurent), Priestley (Joseph); **10** McClintock (Barbara), Mendeleyev (Dmitry Ivanovich), Rutherford (Ernest), Torricelli (Evangelista); **11** Oppenheimer (J. Robert); **3, 5** Van Allen (James); **4-4** Gell-Mann (Murray); **4-10** Levi-Montalcini (Rita); **6-5** Joliot-Curie (Frédéric), Joliot-Curie (Irène).

scintillate **5** charm, flash, gleam, glint, shine; **6** dazzle; **7** glitter, sparkle; **9** fascinate.

scion **3** son; **4** heir; **5** child, graft, shoot; **7** cutting, implant; **9** offspring; **10** descendant; **12** implantation.

scoff **3** boo, dig, eat, rag; **4** bawl, gird, hiss, hoot, howl, jeer, jibe, mock, rail, twit; **5** fleer, flout, scorn, sneer, taunt; **6** deride; **8** ridicule.

scold **3** jaw, nag, wig UK; **4** rate; **5** chide, slate UK; **6** berate, rebuke; **7** censure, lecture, reprove, upbraid; **8** admonish, chastise, reproach; **9** criticize, reprimand; PHRASES: **4, 1, 7-2** give a talking-to UK; **4, 2, 4** take to task; **4, 3** tell off.

scoop **3** dig; **4** lift; **5** raise; **6** dipper, exposé, hollow, scrape, shovel; **8** excavate; **9** exclusive; **10** revelation; PHRASES: **4, 2** pick up; **4, 5** news story; **6, 2** gather up. See also **eating (eating utensils and dishes**

scope **4** play, room, span; **5** ambit, berth, range, reach, remit UK, space; **6** bounds, choice, extent, leeway, margin; **7** compass, freedom, purview; **8** capacity, latitude, leverage; **9** clearance, elbowroom, telescope; **10** Lebensraum, microscope; **11** flexibility, opportunity, possibility; **12** oscilloscope; **14** maneuvrability; PHRASES: **4, 5** free range, wide berth, wide range.

scorch See **burn**

score **3** bye, cut, get, net, one, run, six, try, two; **4** duck, etch, four, gain, goal, make, mark, nick, pair, wide; **5** carve, count, extra, fifty, grade, notch, point, slash, slice, tally, three, total; **6** attain, groove, nelson, record, result, scrape, twenty; **7** achieve, century, scratch; **8** boundary; **9** overthrow; PHRASES: **2-4** noball; **3, 2** tot up; **3, 3** leg bye UK; **3, 4** cut into; **4, 1, 5** keep a tally; **4, 4** king pair; **4, 5** keep count, keep ~; **5, 2** chalk up, notch up.

scorer See **composer**

scorn **4** hate, mock; **5** abuse, rebel, spurn, taunt, usurp; **6** defame, deride, ignore, insult, oppose, rebuff, refuse, reject, resist, revile, slight; **7** asperse, despise, disdain, disobey, dissent, mockery; **8** belittle, confront, contempt, derision, disagree, ridicule, sneering, threaten; **9** challenge, denigrate, disparage, disregard; **10** blackening, debasement, defilement, depreciate, disrespect, revilement, scurrility, tarnishing, trivialize; **11** degradation; **12** scornfulness, vilification; **13** disparagement; PHRASES: **3, 4** run down; **4, 2, 8** hold in contempt; **4, 4** turn down; **4, 4, 2** look down on; **4, 5, 2** pour ~ on; **4, 8, 3** show contempt for; **5, 2** scoff at, sneer at; **6, 4** answer back.

scornful 7 mocking; **8** derisive, scathing, scoffing, sneering; **9** sarcastic; **10** disdainful, ridiculing; **11** disparaging; **12** contemptuous, contumelious; **13** disrespectful.

Scot 3 Ian, Mac; **4** Celt, Gael, Jock *UK*, Knox, Pict; **5** Angus, laird.

Scotch 7 whiskey; PHRASES: **6, 3** S~ egg; **6, 4** S~ mist, S~ snap, S~ tape; **6, 5** S~ broth *UK*; **6, 7** S~ pancake *UK*, S~ terrier.

Scotsman 3 mon. *See also* **Scot**

scoundrel 3 cad, cur, dog, rat, SOB; **4** heel; **5** cheat, hound, knave, louse, rogue, skunk, swine; **6** rascal, rotter, wretch; **7** dastard, stinker, villain; **8** swindler; **9** reprobate; **10** blackguard.

scour 3 rub; **4** comb, hunt, wash; **5** clean, scrub; **6** polish, search.

scourge 3 cat; **4** bane, beat, flog, lash, whip; **5** birch, curse, knout, quirt, strap; **6** plague, thrash; **10** affliction.

scout 3 cub, spy; **4** hunt, mole, seek; **5** guide, recce, rover, watch; **6** queen's, search, survey; **7** explore, lookout, venture; **8** emissary; **9** detective; **10** pathfinder; **11** investigate, reconnoiter; PHRASES: **3, 3** spy out; **3, 5** air ~, boy ~, sea ~; **4, 3** look for; **4, 3, 3** look out for; **4, 5** girl ~; **4, 6** cast around, look around, nose around; **5, 3** check out; **6, 3** search for; **6, 5** queen's ~, talent ~; **10, 5** undercover agent.

scowl 5 frown, glare; **6** glower; **7** grimace; PHRASES: **4, 7** look daggers.

scrabble 3 dig; **4** claw, pick; **5** grope; **6** clutch, fumble, rootle *UK*, scrape; **7** rummage, scratch.

scramble 3 mix; **4** hike, rush; **5** climb, crawl; **6** ascent, jostle, jumble, muddle; **7** clamber, confuse, scuttle; **8** scrabble, stampede, struggle; **9** commotion; PHRASES: **3, 2** mix up.

scrap 3 bin *UK*, bit, jot, rag, row; **4** bout, dump, iota, junk, spar, whit, wisp; **5** brawl, crumb, ditch, fight, piece, shred, trash, waste; **6** fracas, morsel, offcut, refuse, tussle; **7** discard, dispute, garbage, oddment,

quarrel, remnant, scratch, scuffle, snippet; **8** conflict, fragment, jettison, particle; **12** disagreement.

scrape 3 cut, fix, jam, rub; **4** bark, mark, rasp, skin; **5** chafe, clash, grate, graze, scour, scrub, scuff; **6** abrade, pickle, plight; **7** problem, scratch; **8** abrasion; **11** predicament.

scratch 3 cut, rub; **4** drop, itch, mark, nick, omit; **5** ditch, erase, grate, graze, leave, score, scrap, scrub, scuff, sheet, video; **6** abrade, cancel, delete, forget, scrape; **7** abandon; **8** abrasion, together, withdraw; PHRASES: **3, 3** bow out; **4, 3** drop out, pull out; **5, 3** leave out; **7, 3** ~ pad; **7, 4** ~ test.

scrawl *See* **scribble**

scream 2 ow; **3** cry; **4** bawl, hoot, ouch, riot, yell, yelp; **5** groan, laugh, shout, whine; **6** bellow, shriek, squall, squawk, squeal; **7** screech, whimper.

screech 3 cry; **4** yelp; **6** scream, shriek, squeal.

screen 3 air, VDU *UK*, vet; **4** hide, mask, show, sift, test, veil; **5** blind, check, cloak, cover, guard, panel, shade, visor; **6** assess, awning, buffer, canopy, divide, select, shield; **7** barrier, conceal, curtain, display, divider, examine, inspect, monitor, project, protect, shelter, shutter; **8** diagnose, separate, transmit; **9** broadcast, partition; **10** camouflage, television; **11** investigate; PHRASES: **3, 2, 3** put on air *UK*; **3, 6** big ~; **4, 3** mark off, weed out; **4, 6** fire ~, rood ~; **5, 3** check out; **5, 6** small ~, smoke ~; **6, 6** silver ~; **8, 6** computer ~.

screw 3 fix; **4** bolt, coil, fold, spin, turn, wind; **5** miser, twist; **6** attach, crunch, fasten, furrow, jailer, rotate, salary, secure, warder *UK*; **7** contort, crinkle, crumple, distort, scrunch, wrinkle; PHRASES: **3, 5** lug ~; **4, 5** grub ~ *UK*; **8, 5** Phillips ~.

scribble 3 jot; **4** draw; **5** write; **6** design, doodle, scrawl; **7** jotting, writing; **8** squiggle; **9** lettering; **11** handwriting; PHRASES: **4, 3** dash off.

scrimmage 4 fray; **5** brawl, drill, fight, scrum *UK*; **6** battle, tussle; **7** scuffle; **8** exercise, practice, skirmish, struggle; PHRASES: **8, 4** practice play.

script 4 hand, text; **5** words; **7** cursive, writing; **8** dialogue, libretto; **10** screenplay; **11** calligraphy, handwriting.

Scripture 7 oracles; PHRASES: **4, 4** Holy

Writ; **4, 9** Holy S~. *See also* **religious text**

scrofula 6 struma; PHRASES: **5, 4** king's evil *UK*.

scroll 4 roll; **8** document; **9** parchment; **10** manuscript; **11** certificate.

scrooge *See* **miser**

scrounge 3 beg; **5** cadge, mooch; **6** borrow, forage, search, sponge; **7** rummage, solicit; **8** scavenge.

scrub 3 rub; **5** brush, clean, erase, scour, scrap; **6** delete, polish; **7** abolish, scratch, thicket; **11** undergrowth.

scruffy 4 worn; **5** messy; **6** grubby, ragged, shabby, shoddy, untidy; **7** raggedy, unkempt; **8** tattered; **10** disheveled; **12** disreputable.

scrum 3 jam; **4** fray, maul, ruck; **5** crush, press; **6** huddle, jostle, tussle; **7** scuffle, squeeze; **8** struggle; **9** scrimmage, scrummage; PHRASES: **4-3-3** free-for-all.

scrutinize 4 heed; **5** study; **6** search, survey; **7** analyze, dissect, examine, inspect; PHRASES: **3, 4** fix upon; **3-4** nit-pick; **4, 4** pore over.

scud 3 fly; **4** rush, sail; **5** speed, sweep.

scuff 3 rub; **5** graze; **6** scrape; **7** scratch; **8** abrasion; PHRASES: **4, 4** wear away.

scuffle 4 fray; **5** brawl, fight, scrap; **6** fracas; **7** wrestle; PHRASES: **4, 2, 5** come to blows; **5-2** punch-up *UK Can*; **8, 5** exchange blows.

scull 3 oar, row; **5** blade, canoe, sweep; **6** paddle, propel.

sculpt 3 cut; **4** cast, chip, form, mold; **5** carve, model, shape; **6** chisel; **7** fashion, whittle; **9** sculpture.

sculpted 6 carved, molded; **7** modeled; **8** embossed, engraved, repoussé; **10** sculptured.

sculptor 3 Arp; **4** Caro, Gabo, Gill; **5** Moore, Rodin; **6** Canova, carver, caster, chaser, etcher, molder, Pisano; **7** Bernini, Duchamp, Epstein, Gormley, modeler, Phidias; **8** Brancusi, Daedalus, engraver, figurist, Hepworth, Landseer, lapidary, statuary; **9** Bartholdi, Donatello, Pygmalion; **10** Giacometti, Praxiteles; **12** assemblagist, Michelangelo; PHRASES: **5-6** stonecarver; **10, 5** monumental mason.

sculptor's materials 3 wax; **5** burin, drill, point, punch; **6** bronze, chisel, mallet, marble, solder, stucco; **7** granite, plaster, spatula; **8** armature; **10** Plasticine™; PHRASES: **4, 6** claw chisel; **5, 5** terra cotta; **7, 5** cutting torch, welding torch; **8, 4** modeling clay, modeling tool; **8, 6** Parthian marble; **9, 3** sculptor's wax; **9, 4** soldering iron.

sculpture 4 bust, cast, head, herm; **5** cameo, group, medal, model, torso; **6** bronze, effigy, figure, marble, mobile, relief, statue; **7** carving, casting, chasing, etching, molding, stabile, telemon, waxwork; **8** atlantes, caryatid, figurine, figuring, intaglio, maquette, modeling, monument, pointing *UK*, statuary; **9** embossing, engraving, medallion, scrimshaw, statuette, whittling; **10** assemblage, petroglyph; **11** anaglyptics, environment, sculpturing, woodcarving; **12** ceroplastics, installation, stonecutting; PHRASES: **3, 8** wax modeling; **4-6** cire-perdue; **4, 7** sand casting; **4-7** bone-carving, rock-carving; **4, 9** clay ~, wire ~; **5, 3** earth art; **5-4** ready-made; **5, 5** terra cotta; **5, 6** found object, objet trouvé; **7, 3** plastic art; **7, 4** plaster cast; **7, 7** plaster casting.

scurf 4 coat; **5** crust, scale; **6** dander, flakes; **7** deposit; **8** dandruff; **12** encrustation.

scurry *See* **dash**

scuttle 4 dart, dash, ruin, rush; **5** spoil; **6** scurry, stymie, thwart; **7** destroy, scamper.

scythe 3 cut; **4** hack; **5** slice, sweep; PHRASES: **3, 4** cut down.

SE 8 selenium; **9** southeast; PHRASES: **5, 8** stock exchange; **6, 8** London district.

sea 1 S; **3** Med; **4** Aral, deep, foam, main, mare, tide, wave; **5** brine, briny *UK*, Ionia, ocean; **6** Aegean, Baltic, depths, Euxine, marine; **7** Andaman, aquatic, Arabian, Barents, benthos, Caspian, Galilee, oceanic; **8** Adriatic, Ligurian, maritime, nautical; **9** Caribbean; **13** Mediterranean; PHRASES: **3, 2, 4** S~ of Azov, S~ Of Azov; **3, 2, 5** S~ of Japan; **3, 2, 7** S~ of Marmara, S~ of Okhotsk; **3, 2, 8** S~ of Tiberias; **3, 3** Red S~, ~ bed; **3, 4** ~ lane, the blue, the deep; **3, 5** the briny, the drink; **4, 3** Aral S~, Dead S~, Kara S~; **4, 4** high seas; **4, 4, 3** deep blue ~; **4, 5** blue water, salt water; **4, 5, 3** East China S~; **5, 3** Banda S~, Black S~, Ceram S~, Coral S~, Irish S~, North S~, White S~; **5, 4** ocean blue, seven seas; **5, 5** ocean floor; **5, 5, 3** South China S~; **5, 6** ocean depths; **6, 3** Aegean S~, Baltic S~, Bering S~, Flores S~,

Ionian S~, Laptev S~, Yellow S~; **7, 3** Andaman S~, Arabian S~, Barents S~; **7, 4** herring pond; **7, 6** Mariana Trench; **8, 3** Adriatic S~, Labrador S~; **8, 4** shipping lane; **9, 3** Caribbean S~; **10, 3** Tyrrhenian S~; **13, 3** Mediterranean S~; **14, 3** Bellingshausen S~.

sea biscuit 8 hardtack.

sea eagle 4 erne.

sea fish 3 cod, dab, ray; **4** dory, hake, hoki, ling, opah, sild, sole, tope, tuna; **5** brill, coley *UK*, grunt, manta, porgy, saury, shark, skate, sprat, squid, tunny; **6** beluga, blenny, bonito, gunnel, marlin, mullet, plaice, puffer, remora, saithe, shrimp, tarpon, turbot, weever, wrasse; **7** alewife, anchovy, batfish, dogfish, eelpout, garfish, garpike, grouper, gurnard, haddock, hagfish, halibut, herring, hogfish, icefish, oarfish, octopus, pollack, pomfret *UK*, pompano, ratfish, sardine, sawfish, sculpin, snapper, sunfish, whiting; **8** albacore, bluefish, bonefish, brisling, brotulid, calamari, chimaera, coalfish, dragonet, filefish, flatfish, flathead *UK*, flounder, frogfish, kingfish, mackerel, monkfish, moonfish, pilchard, pipefish, sailfish, skipjack, stingray, toadfish; **9** barracuda, bristling, clingfish, globefish, goosefish, grenadier, latimeria, pearlfish, porbeagle, selachian, stargazer, stonefish, swordfish, threadfin, trunkfish, whitebait, wreckfish; **10** anglerfish, coelacanth, cornetfish, damselfish, dragonfish, lumpsucker, mudskipper, needlefish, ribbonfish, silverside, yellowtail; **11** hatchetfish, surgeonfish, triggerfish; PHRASES: **3, 4** sea bass; **3, 5** sea bream, sea horse, sea perch, sea robin, sea trout; **3, 6** red mullet, red salmon; **4, 4** john dory, wolf fish; **4-4** mahi-mahi; **4, 5** blue shark; **4, 6** blue marlin, gray mullet, pink salmon, rock salmon *UK*; **5, 3** devil ray, moray eel; **5, 4** Dover sole, lemon sole, pilot fish, stone bass; **5, 5** ghost shark, nurse shark, tiger shark, whale shark, white shark; **6, 3** conger eel, murray cod; **6, 4** Bombay duck, flying fish, guitar fish, parrot fish; **6, 5** goblin shark; **6, 6** silver salmon; **7, 4** channel bass, lantern fish, moorish idol; **7, 5** basking shark, requiem shark; **7, 6** chinook salmon, Pacific salmon, sockeye salmon; **8, 3** electric ray; **8, 4** scorpion fish; **8, 5** mackerel shark, thresher shark; **8, 6** Atlantic salmon; **9, 4** porcupine fish, saltwater fish, yellowfin tuna; **9, 5** greenland shark; **10, 5** hammerhead shark.

See also **fish, freshwater fish**

seafront 4 prom *UK*; **5** beach, coast, shore; **6** marina, strand; **8** seashore; **9** boardwalk, esplanade, promenade, shoreline; **10** waterfront.

sea god 5 Dylan, siren; **6** merman, Nereid, Nereus, Thetis, Triton, undine, Varuna *UK*; **7** Calypso, mermaid, Neptune, Oceanid, Oceanus; **8** Poseidon; **10** Amphitrite; PHRASES: **3, 5** sea nymph; **3, 7** sea serpent; **5, 6** water spirit, water sprite.

seal 3 fob; **4** bull, cork, plug, shut, stop; **5** block, caulk, close, stamp, wafer; **6** cachet, fasten, gasket, signet, walrus, washer; **7** impress; PHRASES: **3, 4** sea lion; **4, 4** gray ~, harp ~; **8, 4** elephant ~; **9, 4** crabeater ~.

seam 4 join, vein; **5** joint, layer, ridge; **7** closure, stratum.

seaman *See* **sailor**

sear *See* **burn**

search 4 comb, hunt, seek; **5** quest, rifle; **7** examine, pursuit; **11** examination, exploration; PHRASES: **4, 3** look for.

seashell 3 sun, tun; **4** clam, cone, harp, lima; **5** auger, chank, conch, drill, drupe, gaper, miter, ormer *UK*, tulip, venus, whelk; **6** bonnet, cockle, cowrie, helmet, limpet, lucine, mussel, nerite, nutmeg, oyster, quahog, tellin, triton, turban, volute, winkle; **7** abalone, junonia, piddock, scallop, sundial; **8** nautilus, pheasant; **9** telescope; **10** delphinula, marginella; PHRASES: **3-3-6** cup-and-saucer; **3, 5** ark shell, ear shell, sea snail; **4-2-4** coat-of-mail; **5, 3** lion's paw, noble pen, turk's cup; **5, 4** angel wing, bursa frog, giant clam, spiny vase, Venus clam, wedge clam; **5, 5** murex olive; **5, 6** pearl oyster, tiger cowrie; **5, 8** paper nautilus; **6, 5** spider conch; **6, 6** thorny oyster.

seaside 5 beach, coast, shore, spike; **7** coastal; **8** littoral, seafront, seashore, tideline; **9** shoreline, waterside; **10** waterfront.

season 4 cure, fall, Lent, salt, term, time; **5** curry, inure, smoke, souse, spell, spice; **6** Advent, anneal, autumn *UK*, Easter, flavor, harden, kipper, mature, pepper, period, pickle, soccer, spring, summer, temper, winter; **7** toughen, Whitsun; **8** accustom, interval, marinate; **9** acclimate, trimester; **10** discipline, springtime; **11** acclimatize; **12** intermission; PHRASES: **3, 6** dry ~, off ~; **4, 2,** 4 time of year; **4, 6** deer ~, duck ~, high ~, open ~; **5, 6** rainy ~, silly ~; **6, 6** closed ~, grouse ~; **7, 6** cricket ~, fishing ~, hunting ~, tourist ~; **8, 6** baseball ~, football ~, pheasant ~, shooting ~.

seasonable 6 seemly, timely; **7** fitting, welcome; **8** suitable; **9** opportune; **10** convenient; **11** appropriate; **12** providential; PHRASES: **4-5** well-timed.

seasonal 4 fall; **6** casual, cyclic, spring, summer, winter, wintry; **7** limited, summery; **8** autumnal, cyclical, periodic, sporadic; **9** recurrent, temporary, unsettled; **10** changeable, solstitial, springlike; **11** equinoctial; **12** intermittent; **13** deteriorating.

seasoned 6 expert, inured, salted, spiced, tested; **7** curried, matured, veteran; **8** flavored, hardened; **9** toughened, weathered; **10** accustomed; **11** experienced; PHRASES: **2, 4** au fait; **4, 2, 2** well up in; **6, 2** versed in.

seasoning 4 salt, zest, zing; **5** chive, curry, onion, sauce; **6** flavor, garlic, Madras, pepper, pickle, relish; **7** chutney, garnish, gherkin, ketchup, Tabasco tm; **8** additive, dressing, marinade; **9** condiment, flavoring; **10** mayonnaise, peppercorn, piccalilli; **11** vinaigrette; PHRASES: **3, 4** sea salt; **3, 5** soy sauce; **4, 5** mint sauce UK; **4, 6** dill pickle; **5, 6** black pepper, curry powder, white pepper; **5, 8** salad dressing; **6, 4** garlic salt; **6, 8** French dressing; **7, 5** pickled onion. See also **herbs and spices, sauce**

seat 2 HQ; **3** bum, pew, see, set, sit; **4** back, base, hold, home, rear, rump, sofa; **5** bench, nates, perch, place, siege, squab, stall, stool; **6** bottom, center, dickey, heinie, saddle, settle, throne, window; **7** capital, contain, cushion, hassock, install, pillion, station; **8** backside, bleacher, buttocks, derriere, marginal, woolsack; **9** banquette, epicenter, fundament; **10** foundation, misericord; **11** accommodate, countryseat; **12** headquarters; PHRASES: **3, 4** hot ~, sit down; **4, 4** love ~, safe ~ UK; **5, 4** mercy ~; **6, 4** bucket ~, county ~, rumble ~; **7, 4** ejector ~ UK, sliding ~; **7, 6** control center; **8, 4** ejection ~, ringside ~. See also **chair, couch, stool**

seat of feelings 4 guts UK, soul; **5** bones, bosom, heart; **6** spirit; PHRASES: **4, 2, 4, 5** core of one's being; **6, 6** secret places; **7, 8** deepest feelings.

seaweed 4 agar, kelp, tang; **5** laver, wrack; **10** carragheen; **12** bladderwrack.

SEC 6 second; **7** section; **9** secondary, secretary.

secede See **withdraw**

secession See **withdrawal**

seclude 6 remove; **7** isolate; **8** separate, withdraw; **9** segregate; PHRASES: **4, 4** keep away; **4, 5** keep apart; **5, 3** split off.

secluded 5 quiet; **6** hidden, remote; **7** private, unknown; **8** deserted, desolate, isolated, screened; **9** sheltered, unvisited; **10** cloistered, unexplored; **11** sequestered, uninhabited; PHRASES: **3-2-3-3** out-of-the-way.

seclusion See **shelter**

second 1 S; **3** sec; **4** abet, back, help, next, post, send, wink; **5** flash, jiffy, trice; **6** assign, attach, latter, minute, moment, reject, uphold; **7** another, endorse, instant, support; **8** transfer; **9** following, subscribe; **10** additional, subsequent, succeeding; **11** secondarily; PHRASES: **2, 3** mo: aid; **2, 4** be with; **2, 5, 4** go along with; **4, 2** back up; **5, 4** agree with; **6, 4** ~ hand, ~ mate, ~ name UK, ~ wind; **6, 5** ~ floor, ~ place, ~ sight; **6, 6** ~ coming, ~ cousin, ~ fiddle, ~ growth, ~ nature, ~ string; **6, 8** ~ thoughts.

secondary 5 minor; **6** lesser; **7** derived; **8** inferior; **9** ancillary, processes, resultant, resulting UK, tributary; **10** consequent, derivative, incidental, peripheral, subsidiary; **11** subordinate, unimportant; **13** consequential; PHRASES: **3-5** low-level; **9, 5** ~ color; **9, 6** ~ picket, ~ school, ~ stress.

secondhand 4 used; **10** indirectly; **12** circuitously; PHRASES: **4-2-4** hand-me-down; **6, 3** nearly new.

second-rate See **inadequate**

secrecy 6 secret; **7** mystery, privacy, silence, stealth; **8** blackout; **9** confidant; **10** censorship, confidence; **11** concealment, suppression; **15** misinformation; PHRASES: **5-2** cover-up; **6, 6** sealed orders; **6, 7** closed session; **7, 2, 6** meeting in camera; **7, 7** private meeting.

secret 5 privy; **6** closed, closet, covert, enigma, hidden, riddle, sealed, untold; **7** furtive, mystery, private; **8** censored, intimate, isolated, secluded, stealthy, unspoken; **9** underhand; **10** classified, confidence, restricted, suppressed, undercover, undivulged, unrevealed; **11** clandestine, underground, undisclosed; **12** confidential, unidentified; **13** surreptitious; PHRASES: **3-3-6** off-the-record; **3-6** top-secret; **4-3-6** hole-

and-corner *UK*; **4-4** hush-hush; **5-3-6** cloak-and-dagger; **5, 6** state ~; **6, 5** ~ agent; **6, 6** ~ police; **6, 7** ~ service, ~ society.

secret (in secret) 8 secretly; **9** incognito, privately; **11** anonymously; **14** confidentially; PHRASES: **2, 1, 7** in a whisper; **2, 2, 9** in an undertone; **2, 6** in camera; **2, 10** in confidence; **3, 3, 6** off the record; **3, 4** sub rosa; **3, 4, 4, 4** for your ears only; **5, 4** entre nous, sotto voce.

secret (keep secret) 3 ban; **4** hide, seal; **6** censor; **7** conceal; **8** classify, restrict, suppress, withhold; PHRASES: **3, 2, 2, 7** let go no further; **3, 3, 3, 2** put the lid on; **3, 7, 1, 4** not breathe a word; **4, 2** clam up, hush up; **4, 2, 7** keep to oneself; **4, 3** keep mum; **4, 4** keep back, keep dark; **4, 4, 7** keep one's counsel; **4, 5** keep close; **4, 5, 5** keep under wraps; **5, 2** cover up; **5, 3** black out.

secretary 2 PA *UK*; **3** sec; **4** temp; **5** clerk; **6** typist; **13** administrator; PHRASES: **4, 9** home ~; **6, 9** office assistant, social ~; **8, 6** clerical worker.

secrete 3 cry; **4** emit, hide, ooze, stow, void, weep; **5** eject, exude, stash, sweat; **6** secern, squirt; **7** conceal, emanate, excrete, lactate, produce, release; **8** liberate, perspire, salivate, transude; **9** discharge, lacrimate; PHRASES: **4, 2** give up; **4, 3** give off; **4, 4** hide away; **8, 4** squirrel away.

secretion 3 gum; **4** bile, gall, milk, musk, ooze; **5** latex, mucus, resin, rheum, sebum, semen, sweat, tears; **6** crying, nectar, phlegm, saliva, sputum, tannin; **7** chalone, hormone, release, weeping; **8** ejection, emission, honeydew, sweating, voidance; **9** colostrum, discharge, emanation, excretion, exudation, guttation, lactation, pheromone; **10** salivation, secernment; **11** ectohormone, lacrimation; **12** perspiration, transudation; PHRASES: **5, 9** plant ~; **7, 5** gastric juice, seminal fluid; **9, 5** digestive juice; **10, 5** pancreatic juice.

secretive 3 sly; **5** cagey, close; **6** covert, secret, shifty, silent, sneaky; **7** furtive, guarded, private; **8** cautious, reserved, reticent, stealthy; **9** enigmatic, underhand; **10** mysterious, undercover; **11** clandestine, kabbalistic; **13** surreptitious; **14** conspiratorial; PHRASES: **5-3-6** cloak-and-dagger.

secretiveness 3 CIA, KGB, MI5 *UK*, MI6 *UK*, spy; **4** mole, plot; **5** cabal; **6** omertà; **7** stealth; **8** intrigue; **9** espionage; **10** conspiracy; PHRASES: **6, 5** double agent, secret

agent; **6, 7** Secret Service; **10, 5** undercover agent. *See also* **secretive**

sect 4 camp, cult; **5** group, party; **6** clique; **7** faction; **8** movement; **12** denomination; PHRASES: **9, 5** religious group.

section 3 act; **4** part, unit; **5** piece, scene, slice, split; **6** clause, divide, gather, sector; **7** article, chapter, passage, platoon, portion, segment; **8** division, fragment; **9** Caesarian, component, gathering, partition; **11** installment, subdivision; PHRASES: **5, 7** conic ~; **6, 2** divide up.

sector 3 arm; **4** area, belt, part, zone; **5** field; **6** branch, sphere; **7** quarter, section; **8** category, district, division; **12** neighborhood.

secure 3 bag, bar, fix, get, pin, tie, win; **4** bind, bolt, fast, hook, knot, lace, land, lash, lock, moor, nail, rope, safe, seal, snug, sure, tack, take, trap; **5** belay, chain, cinch, close, guard, latch, sound, strap, tight, wedge; **6** anchor, assure, attach, cement, clench, clinch, closed, cocoon, defend, ensure, fasten, immune, insure, locked, obtain, patrol, police, shield, stable, staple, steady; **7** acquire, assured, capture, certify, fortify, procure, protect, shelter, support, tighten; **8** fastened, position, reliable, safekeep, shielded, together; **9** confident, deterrent, guarantee, indemnify, protected, safeguard, sheltered; **10** dependable, protective, underwrite; **11** impregnable, safeguarded; **12** invulnerable; PHRASES: **3, 4, 5, 2** get your hands on; **3, 5, 2** get ahold of; **4, 2** lock up; **4, 2, 6** safe as houses *UK*; **4, 2, 8** sure of yourself; **4, 3, 5** safe and sound; **4, 4** lock away, make fast, make safe; **4, 5** keep order; **4-7** self-assured; **4, 8** give security; **4-9** self-confident; **6, 2** locked up; **6, 4** locked away.

security 3 IOU; **4** bond, chit; **5** haven; **6** refuge, safety, surety; **7** defense, premium, retreat, voucher; **8** contract, warranty; **9** guarantee, indemnity, insurance, sanctuary; **10** collateral, confidence, protection; **11** precautions, reassurance, safekeeping; **12** underwriting; PHRASES: **4-5** well-being; **4, 6** pawn ticket; **4-9** self-assurance; **4-10** self-confidence; **6, 8** safety measures; **10, 4** promissory note.

sedan 3 car.

sedate 4 calm, cool, dope, drug, slow; **5** staid; **6** pacify, placid, serene, steady; **7** quieten, relaxed, soother; **8** composed, decorous, tranquil; **9** leisurely, unhurried; **11** tranquilize; **12** anaesthetize; PHRASES: **3, 5** put under; **5, 3** knock out.

sedative 6 downer; **7** calming; **8** hypnotic, narcotic, relaxing, soothing; **9** calmative, soporific; **10** depressant; **11** barbiturate, neuroleptic; **12** tranquilizer.

sedentary 4 bent, desk, dull, idle, tame; **5** inert; **6** seated; **7** hunched, languid, passive, sessile, sitting; **8** inactive, indolent, sleeping, sluggish, stooping; **9** apathetic, bedridden, deskbound; **10** chairbound, housebound, languorous, phlegmatic, slumbering, unemployed, vegetating.

sedentary person 8 sluggard; PHRASES: **4-2** shut-in; **5-2-3-3** stick-in-the-mud; **5, 6** couch potato; **7, 4** antenna head.

sediment 3 mud; **4** clay, ooze, rock, sand, silt; **5** delta, dregs, loess, stone; **6** chesil, gravel; **7** bedrock, boulder, deposit, grounds, pebbles, remains, residue, shingle; **8** granules.

sedimentary rock 3 bed; **7** bedding, breccia, stratum; PHRASES: **7, 4** clastic rock; **10, 4** nonclastic rock, stratified rock.

sedition 4 riot; **6** revolt; **7** treason; **9** treachery; **10** incitement, subversion; **12** insurrection.

seditionist 3 spy; **5** Provo UK; **6** rioter; **7** Luddite, traitor; **8** nihilist, partisan, quisling, revolter, saboteur; **9** anarchist, extremist, guerrilla, insurgent, terrorist; **10** counterspy, subversive, Weatherman; **11** conspirator, infiltrator, Provisional, seditionary; **12** collaborator; **13** revolutionary, tergiversator; **15** insurrectionist; PHRASES: **3, 6** Guy Fawkes; **4, 5** John Brown; **5, 9** fifth columnist, urban guerrilla; **7, 7** freedom fighter.

seditious 5 loyal; **8** disloyal, mutinous; **10** rebellious, subversive; **11** treasonable; PHRASES: **2, 2, 4** up in arms.

seduce 4 coax, lure, pull, rape; **5** abuse, force, tempt, wrong; **6** allure, entice, induce, ravish; **7** attract, violate, wheedle; **8** deflower, inveigle, persuade; **9** influence; PHRASES: **4, 4** talk into; **4, 4, 3, 4** have one's way with; **4, 6** lead astray; **4, 9, 2** take advantage of; **8, 5** sexually abuse; **8, 7** sexually assault; **9, 4** interfere with.

see 1 V; **2** lo; **3** get, spy, vid; **4** date, espy, look, meet, note, spot, twig UK, vide, view; **5** check, grasp, sight, visit, watch; **6** behold,

descry, ensure, escort, notice, regard; **7** consult, discern, foresee, glimpse, imagine, observe, picture, predict, realize, through, witness; **8** discover, envisage, envision, perceive, sightsee, spectate; **9** accompany, ascertain, establish, guarantee, recognize; **10** appreciate, comprehend, rubberneck, understand; **11** distinguish, investigate; PHRASES: **2, 3, 4** go out with; **2, 4** go with; **3, 1, 5, 2** pay a visit to; **3, 3, 5** get the drift; **3, 3, 7** get the message; **3, 4, 2** lay eyes on, set eyes on; **3, 4, 4** use one's eyes; **4, 2** call on, look at; **4, 2, 4** chew it over, mull it over; **4, 3** find out, make out, pick out; **4, 4** look into, make sure; **4, 4, 2** clap eyes on; **4, 7** make certain; **5, 1, 7, 2** catch a glimpse of; **5, 2** catch on, refer to; **5, 2, 2** weigh it up; **5, 2, 4** think it over; **5, 5, 2** catch sight of; **6, 2** attend to; **7, 2, 2** reflect on it; **8, 2** consider it.

seed 3 pea, pip, pit, sow; **4** germ; **5** grain, hilum, ovule, plant, semen, shoot, spore, start, stone, testa; **6** embryo, kernel, source; **7** funicle, hayseed, linseed, nucleus, plumule, radicle, scatter, seedpod; **8** birdseed, flaxseed, rapeseed, seedcase, seedling; **9** acrospire, beginning, broadcast, cotyledon, endosperm, micropyle; **10** coleoptile, coleorhiza, cottonseed; **11** germination; PHRASES: **4, 4** ~ coat, ~ leaf; **4, 5** ~ stalk; **4, 7** ~ capsule; **6, 5** bamboo shoot; **7, 3, 5** mustard and cress UK; **8, 5** starting point.

seedy 3 ill, wan; **4** pale, ropy UK, sick; **5** dingy, dodgy UK, seamy, tacky, tatty; **6** poorly, shabby, sickly, sleazy, sordid, unwell; **7** squalid; PHRASES: **3-5** dog-eared; **4-2-4** down-at-heel; **4-5** moth-eaten.

seeing 2 as; **4** eyed; **5** aware, since; **7** glaring, looking, popeyed, sighted, staring; **8** noticing, vigilant, watchful, watching; **9** observant, visionary; **10** discerning, perceptive; **11** considering, imaginative; **13** perspicacious; PHRASES: **2, 3, 7** on the lookout; **2, 4, 2** in view of; **3-6** far-seeing; **3-7** far-sighted; **4-4** hawk-eyed, lynx-eyed; **5-4** Argus-eyed, clear-eyed, eagle-eyed, sharpeyed; **5-7** clear-sighted; **6-4** gimlet-eyed, goggle-eyed; **7, 2, 4** bearing in mind.

seek 6 pursue; **7** request; PHRASES: **2, 5** go after; **3, 3** ask for; **6, 3** search for, strive for; **7, 5** enquire about UK.

seem See **appear**

seemly 3 apt, fit; **5** right; **6** decent, modest; **8** decorous, suitable; **11** appropriate.

seep 3 cry, pee, wee; **4** drip, leak, ooze,

soak, spit, weep; **5** bleed, drool, exude, leach, sweat; **6** escape; **7** dribble, slobber, trickle, urinate; **8** perspire, salivate; **9** percolate; PHRASES: **4, 5** pass water, shed tears.

seepage 5 waste; **7** leakage, outflow; **8** draining; **9** discharge; **10** permeation; **11** percolation; PHRASES: **3, 3** wet rot *UK*; **6, 4** rising damp. *See also* **seep**

seethe 4 boil, foam, fume, rage, teem; **5** churn, froth, swarm; **6** bubble.

segment *See* **part**

segregate 4 shun, snub; **6** detach, divide, remove, slight; **7** boycott, isolate, seclude; **8** separate; **9** ghettoize, ostracize, sequester; **10** quarantine; PHRASES: **3, 5** set apart, set aside; **4, 5** keep apart; **4-8** cold-shoulder; **8, 3** separate out.

segregation 7 boycott; **9** apartheid, exclusion, isolation, ostracism, seclusion; **10** preclusion, separation; **13** ghettoization, sequestration; **14** discrimination; PHRASES: **7, 5** setting apart.

seize 3 bag, cly, nab, nap, nim, pot; **4** claw, grab, grip, hend, raid, take; **5** cleek; **6** arrest, attach, collar, hijack, tackle; **7** capture, impound, possess; **8** distrain, distress; **9** apprehend; **10** commandeer, confiscate; **11** appropriate, requisition, sequestrate *UK*.

seizure 3 fit; **5** ictus, spasm; **6** arrest, attack; **7** capture; **8** apoplexy, paroxysm, takeover; **9** disseizin, distraint; **10** annexation, attachment, convulsion, occupation; **12** confiscation; **13** sequestration.

select 3 opt; **4** pick, sort; **5** adopt, coopt, elect, elite, judge; **6** accept, choice, choose, decide, medley, prefer; **7** cliquey, discern, limited, mixture; **9** determine, excellent, exclusive; **10** collection, handpicked, miscellany, privileged, restricted; **11** distinguish; **12** discriminate; **13** differentiate; PHRASES: **2, 3** go for; **3, 3** opt for; **3-7** top-quality; **4, 1, 6** make a choice; **4, 2** take up; **4, 3** pick out; **5, 3** plump for; **5-4** first-rate; **5-5** first-class; **6, 2** decide on, settle on.

selection 3 nap; **4** list, pick; **5** elite, range; **6** choice; **7** variety; **8** adoption, choosing, cooption, decision, excerpts, judgment; **9** anthology, gleanings, shortlist; **10** assortment, discretion, nomination; **11** appointment, designation; **13** determination; **14** discrimination, fastidiousness; PHRASES: **4, 4** free will; **5, 2, 6** range of choice; **7, 2, 6** freedom of choice; **7, 3** picking out; **8, 2, 5** embarras du choix *Fr.*

selective 5 picky; **6** choosy; **7** finicky; **8** choosing, deciding, decisive, eclectic, favoring, optional; **10** discerning, particular; **12** discretional, preferential; **14** discriminating; PHRASES: **1, 2, 5** à la carte.

self 2 id; **3** ego, sel; **4** auto; **6** nature, person, psyche; **8** identity; **9** character; PHRASES: **11** personality.

self-absorbed 4 smug, vain; **7** selfish; **9** egotistic; **12** narcissistic; **4-6** self-loving; **4-7** self-devoted; **4-8** self-centered, self-obsessed; **4-11** self-worshipping.

self-assured 5 bossy; **6** lordly, poised; **8** composed, positive; **9** assertive; **10** commanding; **11** controlling, domineering; **13** authoritative; PHRASES: **4-6** high-handed.

self-confident *See* **self-assured**

self-conscious 3 shy; **4** edgy; **5** tense, timid; **6** gauche, modest, uneasy; **7** awkward, bashful, nervous; **8** blushing, retiring, timorous; **9** diffident, inhibited; **11** embarrassed; PHRASES: **3, 2, 4** ill at ease.

self-conscious (be self-conscious) 5 blush, flush; **6** squirm; **7** crimson, stammer; PHRASES: **3, 2, 5** die of shame; **4, 3** turn red; **4, 5** feel shame; **5, 2** color up.

self-contained *See* **independent**

self-defense 4 judo, Mace™; **6** boxing, karate; **7** whistle; **8** security; **12** surveillance; PHRASES: **4, 5** rape alarm; **5, 3** guard dog; **7, 4** martial arts; **7, 5** burglar alarm; **8, 5** personal alarm. *See also* **martial art**

self-esteem 3 ego; **5** pride; **6** morale; **7** dignity; **9** assurance; **10** confidence; PHRASES: **4-6** self-regard; **4-7** self-respect; **5, 6** amour propre.

self-evident *See* **obvious**

self-indulgence 6 luxury; **8** hedonism; **9** carnality; **10** sensuality, sybaritism; **12** epicureanism, intemperance; **14** overindulgence, voluptuousness; PHRASES: **8-7** pleasure-seeking.

self-indulgent 6 carnal; **7** sensual; **9** epicurean, sybaritic; **10** hedonistic, voluptuous; PHRASES: **4-10** self-gratifying; **8-5** pleasure-bound; **8-7** pleasure-seeking.

self-indulgent person 5 toper; **6** egoist; **7** epicure, glutton, gourmet; **8** gourmand, hedonist, sybarite; **9** debauchee; **10** narcissist, sensualist, voluptuary; PHRASES: **3, 6** bon vivant; **4-5** fast-liver, free-liver, high-liver; **8-6** pleasure-seeker.

self-interest 6 egoism; 7 egotism; 9 solipsism; 11 selfishness; 13 egocentricism; 14 egoisticalness; 15 egotisticalness; PHRASES: **2-3** me-ism; **4-8** self-centered.

self-interested 11 solipsistic; PHRASES: **4-6** self-styled. *See also* **selfish**

selfish 4 mean; 5 venal; 6 greedy, stingy; 7 envious, jealous, miserly, worldly; 8 covetous, egoistic; 9 ambitious, egotistic, mercenary, niggardly; 10 avaricious, egocentric, possessive, ungenerous; 11 acquisitive, egotistical; 12 monopolistic, parsimonious, uncharitable; 13 materialistic, opportunistic; 15 individualistic; PHRASES: **2, 3, 4** on the make; **4-6** mean-minded; **4-7** cold-hearted, self-pitying, self-seeking, self-serving; **4-8** mean-spirited, self-centered; **4-9** self-concerned, self-indulgent, self-regarding; **4-10** self-interested; **5-8** money-grubbing.

selfishness 4 envy; 5 greed; 6 egoism; 7 avarice, egotism; 8 ambition, jealousy; 9 careerism, parsimony; 10 littleness; 11 egocentrism, materialism, mundaneness, opportunism; 13 egocentricity, individualism; PHRASES: **4-4** self-pity; **4-6** self-regard; **4-7** self-concern, self-seeking, self-serving; **4-8** self-interest, self-pleasing; **4-10** self-indulgence; **8, 4** personal aims; **8, 7** personal desires. *See also* **selfish**

selfish person 3 hog; 6 egoist; 7 egotist; 9 egomaniac; 10 monopolist, narcissist; 11 opportunist; 12 snollygoster; PHRASES: **3, 2, 3, 6** dog in the manger; **4, 3** road hog; **4-6** self-seeker, self-server; **4-7** self-pleaser; **5-7** money-grubber.

selfless *See* **unselfish**

self-reliant 6 dogged; 8 intrepid, resolute, unafraid; 9 confident, steadfast, tenacious, unfearing; 10 determined; 11 persevering; PHRASES: **4-7** self-assured.

self-respect *See* **self-esteem**

self-restrained 3 dry, shy; 4 cool, pure; 5 plain, quiet, sober, stiff, vegan; 6 chaste, formal, frugal, Lenten, modest, strict; 7 ascetic, costive, dieting, fasting, sparing, spartan, uptight; 8 celibate, moderate, reserved, stinting, teetotal, tempered; 9 abstinent, continent, inhibited, puritanic, repressed *UK*, temperate, ultracool; 10 abstaining, abstemious, economical, forbearing, inhibiting, prohibited, refraining,

repressive, restrained, restricted, vegetarian; 11 embarrassed, puritanical, restrictive; 12 embarrassing, introversive, parsimonious, relinquished, renunciative; PHRASES: **2, 3, 5** on the wagon; **4-7** self-denying; **4-9** anal-retentive; **4-10** self-controlled, self-sufficient; **4-11** self-disciplined; **6-5** straitlaced.

self-restraint 4 diet, fast; 6 purity; 7 ascesis, dieting, economy, fasting, modesty, reserve, shyness; 8 celibacy, chastity, eschewal, sobriety, veganism; 9 avoidance, formality, frugality, parsimony, plainness, quietness, restraint, soberness, stiffness; 10 abstaining, abstention, abstinence, asceticism, constraint, continence, discipline, inhibition, moderation, puritanism, repression, spartanism, temperance; 11 forbearance, prohibition, Rechabitism, refrainment, restriction, teetotalism; 12 introversion, renunciation; 13 embarrassment, temperateness, vegetarianism; 14 abstemiousness, relinquishment, Weightwatchers; PHRASES: **4, 3** fish day; **4-6** self-denial; **4-7** self-control, self-mastery; **4-10** self-abnegation, self-discipline; **4-11** self-sufficiency; **5, 6** plain living; **5, 10** total abstinence; **6, 4** Lenten fare, simple life.

self-righteous 2 pi; 4 prim, smug; 5 grave, pious; 7 genteel; 8 affected, priggish; 9 shockable, squeamish; 10 censorious; 11 puritanical; 13 sanctimonious; PHRASES: **3, 4, 2, 2, 4** too good to be true; **5-7** mealy-mouthed; **6-4-4** holier-than-thou; **6-6** narrow-minded.

self-satisfied 4 smug; 9 contented; 10 complacent; PHRASES: **4-7** self-assured; **4-9** self-contented; **4-10** self-sufficient.

self-sufficiency *See* **independence**

sell 2 go; 4 deal, dump, flog *UK*, gain, hawk, lose, plug, push, shop, tout, vend; 5 carry, offer, shift *UK*, stock, trade; 6 barter, convey, encash *UK*, handle, market, peddle, reduce, resell, retail, unload; 7 auction, canvass, promote, realize, solicit; 8 exchange, transfer, undercut; 9 advertise, remainder, wholesale; 11 merchandise; PHRASES: **2, 7** be popular; **2, 7, 2** be snapped up; **3, 2, 3, 4** put up for sale; **3, 2, 4** put on sale; **4, 2** deal in; **5, 2, 6** bring to market; **5, 3, 4** offer for sale; **5, 4, 2** knock down to; **5, 5** clear stock; **7, 2** dispose of, traffic in; **7, 3** auction off.

seller 4 bear; 6 dealer, hawker, trader,

vendor; **7** peddler; **8** merchant, purveyor, retailer *UK*, supplier; **9** consignor; **10** auctioneer, shopkeeper *UK*, trafficker, transferor, wholesaler; **11** storekeeper. *See also* **storekeeper**

selling 4 deal, sale; **5** sales, trade; **6** barter, export, retail, simony; **7** auction, dealing, hawking, trading, traffic, vending; **8** disposal, exchange, monopoly, peddling, transfer; **9** marketing, oligopoly, promotion, retailing, vendition, wholesale; **10** auctioning, canvassing, conveyance, soliciting; **11** trafficking, transaction; **12** distribution; **13** advertisement, merchandising; PHRASES: **4, 2, 6** sale of office; **5, 8** sales coverage; **7, 4** private sale; **9, 4** exclusive sale.

semblance 3 air; **5** shred, trace; **6** façade; **7** measure, modicum; **8** fragment; **10** appearance, impression; **11** resemblance.

semen 4 jism, seed; **5** sperm, spunk; **9** ejaculate; PHRASES: **9, 5** spermatic fluid.

semiliquid 3 goo; **4** glop, guck, gunk; **5** gunge *UK*, paste, slime; **6** sticky, viscid; **7** colloid, viscous; **8** emulsion, emulsoid; **9** semifluid; **10** incrassate, inspissate.

seminar 4 talk; **5** class; **7** meeting, session; **8** tutorial; **10** conference, discussion, roundtable.

senate *See* **governing body**

send 4 cast, emit, fire, hurl, lead, mail, post *UK*, seal, ship, show; **5** drive, fling, frank, guide, refer, relay, remit, shoot, stamp, throw; **6** convey, direct, launch, propel; **7** address, conduct, consign, deliver, express, forward, project; **8** dispatch, redirect, transmit; **9** broadcast, readdress; **11** disseminate; PHRASES: **4, 3** give off, pack off, ~ off, ~ out, shoo off; **5, 3** shake off.

send up 3 ape, lob, sky; **4** loft, mock; **5** boost, mimic, raise, swell; **6** flight, parody, propel; **7** augment, elevate, lampoon; **8** escalate, heighten, increase, ridicule, satirize; **9** burlesque; **10** caricature; **11** impersonate; PHRASES: **4, 2** blow up, bump up, puff up; **4, 3, 2** make fun of; **4, 8, 3** take somebody off.

senile 7 failing; **8** confused; **9** forgetful; **11** disoriented; PHRASES: **6-6** absent-minded.

senior 4 AARP, boss, head, high, over; **5** above, chief, elder, major, older; **6** eldest, higher, leader, oldest; **7** citizen, leading, manager, primary, service; **8** director, superior; **10** management; **11** aircraftman *UK*; PHRASES: **3, 6** big sister; **3, 7** big brother; **4-2** high-up *UK*; **4-5** high-grade; **4-7** high-ranking; **5-4** first-born; **5, 7** elder sibling; **6-2** higher-up; **6, 7** ~ citizen.

senior citizen 3 OAP *UK*.

sensation 3 ESP, hit; **4** buzz, fuss, stir; **5** sense, sight, smell, taste, touch; **6** marvel, ruckus, rumpus, sensum, thrill, uproar, wonder; **7** emotion, feeling, hearing, miracle; **8** reaction, response; **9** agitation, awareness, commotion, sentience, sentiment, spectacle, telepathy; **10** excitement, experience, impression, perception, phenomenon; **11** receptivity; **12** clairvoyance; **13** consciousness, receptiveness; **14** responsiveness; PHRASES: **2-2** to-do.

sensational 5 lurid, tacky; **6** garish, kitsch; **7** amazing, feeling, graphic, radiant; **8** dazzling, dramatic, exciting, gorgeous, shocking, stunning; **9** emotional, thrilling, wonderful; **10** scandalous; **11** exaggerated; **12** melodramatic; PHRASES: **5-6** shock-horror.

sense 3 end, nub, see, wit; **4** feel, gist, hear, idea, itch, know, mood, nous *UK*, view; **5** drift, guess, infer, logic, point, react, smell, taste, touch; **6** brains, detect, intuit, notice, reason, tickle, tingle, wisdom; **7** discern, essence, feeling, meaning, opinion, prickle, purpose, realize, respond, suspect; **8** function, identify, perceive, sagacity; **9** advantage, awareness, consensus, intellect, recognize, sensation, substance, viewpoint; **10** denotation, experience, impression, perception; **11** connotation, distinguish, horripilate, implication; **12** appreciation, intelligence, significance; **13** consciousness, signification; PHRASES: **2, 5** be aware; **2, 5, 2** be aware of; **4, 1, 7** have a feeling; **4, 2** pick up; **4, 2, 4, 5** feel in your bones; **4, 8** good judgment; **6, 5** common ~.

senseless 4 numb; **5** silly; **6** absurd, futile, stupid; **7** foolish, idiotic; **8** comatose, deadened, mindless; **9** pointless; **10** ridiculous; **11** meaningless, unconscious.

sensible 4 sane, wise; **5** aware; **6** shrewd; **7** feeling, mindful, prudent; **8** rational, sentient, workable; **9** cognizant, conscious, judicious, practical, pragmatic, sagacious, sensitive; **10** functional, percipient, reasonable; **11** serviceable, utilitarian; PHRASES: **2, 3, 7** in the picture; **2-8** no-nonsense; **5, 2** alive to, aware of, clued up *UK*; **5-6** level-headed; **8, 2** switched on *UK*.

sensitive 4 fond, warm; 5 aware, exact; 6 caring, secret, sloppy, sticky, subtle, tender, touchy, tricky; 7 awkward, complex, cordial, feeling, maudlin, mawkish, precise, tearful; 8 allergic, amicable, bathetic, delicate, friendly, overcome, profound, romantic, sentient; 9 difficult, emotional, irritable, nostalgic, receptive, searching; 10 affectable, classified, empathetic, perceptive, responsive, restricted, thoughtful, vulnerable; 11 considerate, impressible, overwhelmed, overwrought, penetrating, problematic, sentimental, suggestible, susceptible, sympathetic; 12 confidential, embarrassing; 13 compassionate, overemotional, understanding; 14 hypersensitive, impressionable; PHRASES: 3, 6 top secret; 4-4 hush-hush; 4-7 soft-hearted, thinskinned, warm-hearted; 6, 4 easily hurt; 6, 5 easily upset, finely tuned; 6, 6 highly strung; 6-7 tender-hearted.

sensitivity 4 pity; 6 warmth; 7 empathy, feeling; 8 accuracy, delicacy, feelings, response, sympathy; 9 awareness, precision; 10 compassion, kindliness, tenderness, touchiness; 11 calibration, prickliness, receptivity, sensibility; 12 ticklishness; 13 affectability, commiseration, hyperesthesia, sensitiveness, understanding, vulnerability; 14 impressibility, responsiveness, sentimentality, suggestibility, susceptibility, thoughtfulness; PHRASES: 4, 4 thin skin; 5, 8 finer feelings.

sensor 4 beam; 5 radar; 6 device; 10 instrument.

sensual 6 bodily, carnal, erotic, sexual; 7 fleshly, sensory; 8 physical; 9 corporeal.

sentence 3 lag; 4 bird, life, term, time; 6 decree, punish, ruling; 7 condemn, fistful, handful, stretch, verdict; 8 judgment, penalize, porridge; 10 punishment; 12 condemnation; PHRASES: 4, 2, 6 send to prison; 4, 4 send down UK; 4, 8, 2 pass judgment on; 6, 4 prison term.

sentiment 4 corn, gush; 7 emotion, feeling; 8 attitude, reaction, response; 11 mawkishness, romanticism; 14 sentimentality.

sentry See **guard**

separate 3 cut, hew, rip, run, saw; 4 bite, chip, chop, free, gash, hack, open, part, rend, rive, slit, tear, torn, undo; 5 apart, break, crack, expel, loose, sever, splay, split, untie, unzip; 6 cleave, detach, divide, halved, remove, secede, single, sunder, unbind, unhook, unlace, unlock, unmake, unpick, untied, wrench; 7 disband, disjoin, divided, divorce, isolate, release, removed, rupture, scatter, severed, shatter, unhitch, unlatch, unravel, unstick, unstuck; 8 anarchic, detached, discrete, dismount, disperse, displace, dissolve, distinct, disunite, dividing, divorced, fracture, isolated, lacerate, liberate, loosened, released, ruptured, solitary, splinter, unbutton, uncouple, unfasten, unfetter, unloosed, unstitch, unstring, unzipped, withdraw; 9 bipartite, disengage, dislocate, dismantle, dispersed, disunited, liberated, quartered, segregate, unrelated; 10 autonomous, disconnect, disjointed, dislocated, dissociate, fieldstrip, individual, segregated, subdivided, unattached, unfettered; 11 anarchistic, dichotomous, disassemble, disentangle, disjunctive, dismembered, dissociated, independent, interrupted, partitioned, unconnected; 12 disassociate, disconnected, disemboweled, disintegrate, multipartite, unaffiliated; 13 disaffiliated, discontinuous, nonconforming; 14 nonassimilated; PHRASES: 3, 7 cut through; 4, 2 blow up, cave in; 4, 5 come apart, fall apart, keep apart, take apart, tear apart; 4, 6 come undone; 4, 7 come unstuck, part company; 5, 2 break up, carve up, split up; 5, 2, 3 break in two; 5, 3 split off.

separately 5 alone; PHRASES: 2, 5, 3 on their own; 3, 2, 1, 4 one at a time; 3, 2, 3 one by one. *See also* **separate**

separation 4 rift; 5 exile, split; 6 purdah, schism, spread; 7 boycott, divorce, fission, freeing, goodbye, loosing UK, parting, retreat, undoing, untying; 8 analysis, breakage, disunion, disunity, division, farewell, solitude; 9 apartheid, blacklist, breakdown, departure, desertion, deviation, dispersal, exclusion, expulsion, isolation, loosening, ostracism, partition, rejection, seclusion, severance, splitting, spreading; 10 banishment, detachment, dispersion, disruption, dissection, divergence, impediment, liberating, loneliness, quarantine, resolution, scattering, separating, shattering, uncoupling, unraveling, withdrawal; 11 concealment, deportation, disjunction, disjuncture, dislocation, dissolution, divorcement, extrication, segregation, unbuttoning, unfastening, unthreading; 12 estrangement, separability, solitariness; 13 Balkanization, decomposition, disconnection, discontinuity, disengagement, fragmentation; **14** disintegration; PHRASES: **5-2** break-up, split-up; **5-6** leave-taking; **6, 5** living apart, moving apart, taking apart; **7, 5** growing apart; **7, 7** nuclear fission.

separator 4 dash; **5** comma, sieve, slash, wedge; **6** border, filter, hyphen, period, screen, umlaut; **7** barrier, caesura, divider, solidus; **8** dieresis *UK*, strainer; **9** diaeresis *UK*, extractor, interface, partition; **10** centrifuge; PHRASES: **4, 4** full stop; **8, 4** dividing line, dividing wall.

sepiolite 10 meerschaum.

seppuku 4-4 hara-kiri.

sepulchral 3 sad; **6** dismal, somber; **8** funereal; **10** melancholy.

sepulchre *See* **vault**

sequel 3 end; **4** coda; **6** effect, payoff, result, series, upshot; **7** autopsy, outcome; **8** epilogue, postlude; **9** aftermath, afterword; **10** conclusion, denouement, postmortem, postscript; **11** consequence, development; **12** continuation; PHRASES: **3, 6** net result; **6-2** follow-on, follow-up.

sequence 3 run; **5** chain, cycle, order; **6** series, string, system; **9** following, structure; **10** procession, succession; **11** arrangement, progression; **13** serialization; **14** categorization, classification; **15** consecutiveness.

sequential 6 serial; **7** ensuing, ongoing; **9** following, resultant, resulting *UK*; **10** consequent, continuous, sequacious, subsequent, succeeding, successive; **11** consecutive, progressive; **12** successional; **13** chronological; PHRASES: **2, 5** in order; **2, 8** in sequence.

sequester 5 seize; **7** impound, isolate; **8** separate; **9** segregate; **10** confiscate; **11** appropriate, requisition; PHRASES: **3, 3** cut off; **3, 5** set apart.

serenade 4 sing; **5** court, croon; **6** divert; **9** entertain.

serene 4 calm, cool; **5** quiet, still; **6** mellow, placid; **7** equable; **8** composed, peaceful, tranquil; **9** unruffled; **11** unflustered; PHRASES: **4-4** laid-back.

serenity 5 poise; **6** repose; **8** quietude; **9** composure; **10** equanimity; **11** contentment, disinterest, insouciance, tranquility; **14** inexcitability; PHRASES: **5, 2, 4** peace of mind. *See also* **serene**

serial *See* **sequential**

series 3 run, SER; **4** line; **5** chain, cycle, train; **6** course, rubber, string; **8** rotation, sequence; **10** succession; **11** alternation, progression.

serious 4 deep, dull, grim; **5** acute, grand, grave, heavy, lofty, major, quiet, sober, solid, staid, stern, vital; **6** honest, sedate, severe, solemn, somber; **7** crucial, decided, earnest, genuine, intense, sincere, sublime, weighty; **8** critical, elevated, majestic, powerful, profound, resolute, worrying; **9** dangerous, humorless, important, momentous, unsmiling; **10** determined, impressive, meaningful, thoughtful; **11** fundamental, significant; **12** considerable, magniloquent; **13** grandiloquent; PHRASES: **4-11** life-threatening; **7-6** serious-minded.

seriousness 6 weight; **7** earnest, gravity, honesty, urgency; **8** grandeur; **9** attention, elevation, eloquence, sincerity, solemnity, sublimity; **10** importance, prominence; **12** significance; **13** determination, magniloquence; **14** grandiloquence. *See also* **serious**

serious person 7 egghead; **8** highbrow; **10** sobersides; **11** heavyweight; **12** intellectual.

sermon *See* **lecture**

serpent *See* **snake**

servant 3 boy, man; **4** amah *China*, ayah, char, cook, girl, help, maid; **5** groom, nanny, nurse, valet; **6** butler, driver, drudge, flunky, lackey, menial, minion, nannie, skivvy, slavey, worker; **7** bailiff, cleaner, footman, laborer, orderly, steward; **8** domestic, employee, factotum, follower, gardener, handmaid, handyman, henchman, hireling, inferior, liegeman, retainer, servitor; **9** assistant, attendant, charwoman, chauffeur, gentleman, housemaid, nursemaid, stableboy, stableman, subaltern, underling; **10** dishwasher, handmaiden, manservant, parlormaid; **11** chamberlain, chambermaid, housekeeper, maidservant, subordinate; PHRASES: **2, 4** au pair; **3, 3** Mrs Mop *UK*; **3-3, 3** odd-job man; **4-2, 7** maid-in-waiting; **4-2-7** lady-in-waiting, lord-in-waiting; **4, 4** farm hand; **4, 6** paid helper; **5, 2, 7** femme de chambre; **5, 3** house boy; **5, 4** daily help, hired hand, hired help, lady's maid; **5-4** major-domo; **5, 7** house steward; **7, 4** kitchen maid, laundry maid, ~ girl; **8, 4** cleaning lady; **8, 5** cleaning woman; **8, 6** domestic drudge; **10, 7** indentured ~.

serve 2 do; **3** ace, aid; **4** char, help, obey, tend, wait, work; **5** ladle, spoon; **6** assist, attend, behave, follow, oblige, supply; **7** operate, perform, provide, receive; **8** function; **9** accompany; **10** distribute; PHRASES: **2, 3** do for; **4, 2** dish up, live in, wait on; **4, 2, 5** wait at table *UK*; **4, 3** care for, dole out, give out, hand out, work for; **4, 4** wait upon; **4, 4, 2** take care of; **4, 5** hand round *UK*, look after; **5, 3** cater for; **6, 2** pander to; **6, 4** attend upon; **8, 2** minister to; **10, 2** administer to.

service 2 RN *UK*; **3** ace, aid, let, RAF *UK*, use; **4** deal, help, mass, rite, tune; **5** check, force, refit; **6** matins, repair, retune, ritual; **7** amenity, benefit, examine, package; **8** ceremony, evensong, facility, overhaul; **9** advantage, provision, sacrament; **10** assistance, observance; **11** examination, maintenance; PHRASES: **3, 7** lip ~, tea ~; **4-2** tune-up; **4, 4** good turn; **4-4** once-over; **4, 7** room ~; **4, 9** Holy Communion; **5, 7** civil ~; **6, 7** active ~, dinner ~ *UK*, divine ~, public ~, secret ~, senior ~ *UK*, silver ~; **7, 4** ~ area, ~ road; **7, 6** ~ charge, ~ module; **7, 7** foreign ~, ~ station; **7, 8** ~ industry, ~ national.

serviceberry 8 shadbush; **9** Juneberry, shadberry.

servile 6 abject, menial, pliant, supple; **7** fawning, slavish; **8** toadying; **9** compliant, dependent, groveling; **10** obsequious, submissive; **11** deferential, subservient, sycophantic.

serving 5 quota; **6** aiding, menial, ration, unfree; **7** helping, portion, servile, subject, working; **8** obedient, plateful; **9** attendant, attending; **10** allocation; **11** ministering; PHRASES: **2, 3, 5** on the staff; **2, 3, 7** on the payroll; **2, 5** in bonds; **2, 7** in service, in slavery; **2, 9** in captivity, in servitude; **2, 10** in employment.

servitude 7 bondage, serfdom, slavery; **9** vassalage; **10** dependence, dependency, subjection; **11** enslavement, subjugation; **13** subordination.

sesame 3 til; **7** gingili.

session 2 go; **4** bout, term, turn, year; **5** phase, shift, spell, stint, watch, whack; **6** period, tenure; **7** hearing, innings, meeting, quarter, sitting; **8** assembly, semester; **9** gathering, trimester; **10** conference; PHRASES: **8, 4** academic year.

set 3 dry, fit, fix, gel, lay, lot, put; **4** clot,

firm, gang, hard, laid, nail, park, rest, ring, tune; **5** align, array, class, crowd, embed, field, fixed, group, movie, place, plonk, plunk, ready, rigid, smart, solid, stand, stick, suite, union, usual; **6** adjust, agreed, circle, clique, decide, freeze, frozen, harden, jelled, locate, normal, primed; **7** appoint, arrange, bigoted, blinded, closure, point, arrange, bigoted, blinded, closure, congeal, deposit, ordered, program, regular, scenery, setting, situate, thicken; **8** arranged, backdrop, blimpish, dogmatic, hardline, location, obsessed, pedantic, position, prepared, regulate, resolute, resolved, solidify, solution, stubborn; **9** blinkered, calibrate, coagulate, congealed, customary, establish, fanatical, hidebound, obstinate, organized, permanent, unbending; **10** collection, complement, determined, habituated, hardheaded, impervious, inflexible, unyielding; **11** arrangement, combination, established, opinionated, permutation, prearranged, reactionary, synchronize, traditional, unteachable; **12** conservative, conventional, intersection, obscurantist; PHRASES: **2, 4** go hard *UK*; **3, 3** jet ~; **3, 5** ~ point; **3, 6** ~ square; **4, 3** film ~ *UK*, love ~, null ~; **4-7** hard-shelled; **5, 3** empty ~, stage ~; **6, 3** finite ~; **6, 4** become hard; **7, 3** crystal ~, ordered ~; **8, 3** infinite ~.

setback 4 blow, cost, snag; **5** delay, hitch, upset; **6** hiccup, holdup; **7** backset; **8** obstacle, reversal, rollback; **9** hindrance, throwback; **10** impediment; **11** obstruction; PHRASES: **9, 5** stumbling block.

set free *See* **liberate**

set in motion 3 tug; **4** draw, haul, move, pull, push, send; **5** begin, cause, drive, impel, nudge, shove, start, throw; **6** convey, gather, hustle, propel; **7** actuate, scatter, trigger; **8** activate, dispatch, disperse, displace, initiate, mobilize, motivate, transfer; **9** transport, transpose; PHRASES: **3, 2** set up; **3, 3** set off; **4-5** kick-start; **5, 3** start off.

set out 2 go; **3** aim; **4** plan, show; **5** begin, board, embus *UK*, issue, leave, mount, start; **6** define, depart, design, detail, embark, emerge, intend, unmoor; **7** arrange, display, emplane, enplane, entrain, exhibit, explain, outline, present, specify; **8** commence, describe; **9** determine, elaborate; **10** illustrate; PHRASES: **2, 3** be off; **2, 6** go aboard; **3, 2** hop on; **3, 3** get off, lay out, set off; **3, 3, 4** hit the road; **3, 4** set sail; **3, 5** put forth, set forth; **3, 5, 3** get under way; **4, 2**

jump on; **4, 2, 7, 2** give an account of; **4, 3** cast off, head off, move off, push off, take off; **5, 3** march off, start off, start out; **5, 4** march away; **5, 5** issue forth, sally forth; **5, 6** weigh anchor; **6, 3** strike out; **6, 4** spread sail; **6, 6** spread canvas.

setter 1 I; **2** me; **3** dog; PHRASES: **3, 6** red ~ *UK*; **5, 6** Irish ~; **7, 6** English ~.

setting *See* scene

settle 3 lie, pay; **4** drop, fall, foot, land, mend, move, nest, sink, stay; **5** board, clear, crash, dwell, lodge, perch, relax, roost, squat; **6** alight, burrow, charge, defray, encamp, locate, nestle, people, remain, square, stable; **7** descend, inhabit, invoice, pioneer, quarter, resolve; **8** colonize, domicile, populate, relocate, trespass; **9** discharge, immigrate, reconcile; PHRASES: **2, 2, 3, 6** go to the bottom; **3, 2** pay up; **3, 2, 5** set up house; **3, 4, 5** put down roots; **4, 2** move in, stay at, stay on; **4, 2, 4** come to rest; **4, 4** calm down, slow down; **4, 5** move house; **5, 2** clear up, patch up; **6, 2** reside in, square up; **8, 7** ensconce oneself; **10, 3** straighten out.

settlement 4 town; **6** colony, hamlet, suburb; **7** commune, exurbia, payment, suburbs, village; **8** clearing, decision, defrayal, suburbia, township; **9** agreement, clearance, community, outskirts; **10** completion, conclusion, resolution; **11** arrangement, expenditure; **12** disbursement, municipality, neighborhood; **13** reimbursement; PHRASES: **3, 4** new town; **3-5, 4** one-horse town; **4, 4** boom town, tank town; **5, 4** ghost town, small town; **6, 4** county seat, market town, shanty town; **7, 6** bedroom suburb; **11, 4** stockbroker belt.

settler 7 incomer *UK*, migrant, pilgrim, pioneer, planter; **8** colonial, colonist; **9** colonizer, immigrant, precursor; PHRASES: **5, 7** early ~.

set to music 5 score; **8** melodize; **9** accompany, harmonize, syncopate; **10** symphonize; **11** orchestrate.

seven 4 week; **6** heptad, septet; **8** heptadic, heptagon, septuple; **9** septenary, septuplet, sevenfold; **10** heptagonal, heptameter, Heptateuch, heptatonic, septennial; **11** heptahedral, heptahedron, heptangular; **12** septuplicate; **14** septuagenarian; PHRASES: **3, 7** one seventh; **4, 2, 6** God's in heaven; **5, 4** ~ days; **5, 6, 4** ~ deadly sins.

seven deadly sins 4 envy, lust; **5** an-

ger, pride, sloth; **8** gluttony; **12** covetousness.

seven virtues 4 hope, love; **5** faith; **7** justice; **8** prudence; **9** fortitude; **10** temperance.

sever 3 cut, hew, rip, saw; **4** bite, chip, chop, gash, hack, part, rend, rive, slit, snap, tear, undo; **5** break, crack, slash, slice, smash, split, untie, unzip; **6** cleave, detach, dispel, remove, sunder; **7** disband, divorce, release, rupture, shatter, unclasp, unhitch, unravel; **8** amputate, disperse, displace, dissolve, disunite, fracture, liberate, separate, splinter, unbutton, uncouple, unfasten, unfetter; **9** disengage; **10** disconnect; **11** disassemble, disentangle; **12** disintegrate; PHRASES: **3, 3** cut off, lop off; **4, 3** chop off; **5, 2** break up, carve up; **5, 3** shear off, slice off.

severe 4 dour, firm, grim, hard; **5** acute, awful, bossy, cruel, exact, grave, harsh, plain, rigid, stark, stern, tough; **6** brutal, formal, mortal, rugged, simple, sparse, strict; **7** austere, bigoted, callous, Fascist, serious, spartan; **8** coercive, critical, despotic, exacting, inhumane, orthodox, pedantic, pitiless, rigorous, ruthless, stubborn, terrible; **9** censorious, dangerous, difficult, Draconian, inclement, merciless, obstinate, stringent, unadorned, unbending, unsmiling, unsparing; **10** autocratic, censorious, dominating, fastidious, inflexible, intolerant, meticulous, oppressive, regimented, relentless, repressive, tyrannical; **11** dictatorial, disciplined, domineering, fundamental, hardhearted, overbearing, undecorated, unforgiving; **12** exploitative, militaristic, totalitarian, uncharitable, undemocratic; **13** authoritarian, inquisitorial, unembellished; **14** fundamentalist, uncompromising; PHRASES: **4, 2, 5** hard as nails.

severity 5 power, rigor; **7** bigotry, cruelty, gravity, outrage; **8** asperity, bareness, bullying, pedantry, rigidity; **9** austerity, authority, brutality, clampdown, formality, obstinacy, orthodoxy, restraint; **10** difficulty, discipline, inclemency, inhumanity, simplicity, stringency; **11** intolerance; **13** inflexibility, regimentation; **14** fundamentalism; PHRASES: **2, 10** no compromise; **4, 4** firm hand; **5, 2, 5** pound of flesh; **5, 4** tight rein, tight ship; **6, 2, 3, 3** letter of the law; **6, 4** strong hand; **7, 3** martial law. *See also* **severe**

sew 3 hem; 4 darn, seam, tack; 5 baste; 6 stitch; 9 embroider.

sewer 4 sink, sump; 5 drain; 6 gutter, needle, tailor; 7 cesspit, culvert; 8 cesspool; PHRASES: 4, 5 open drain; 6, 4 septic tank.

sex 1 F, M; 4 oats; 6 gender, mating; 7 bonking, coition, pairing, wedlock; 8 coupling, intimacy, screwing; 10 copulation, femininity; 11 fornication, intercourse, masculinity, procreation, propagation; 12 consummation, reproduction; PHRASES: 5-5 rumpy-pumpy.

sex (have sex) 4 bonk; 5 knock, shaft; 8 copulate; PHRASES: 2, 2 do it; 5, 3 knock off.

sex appeal 2 IT, SA.

sex offender 6 rapist, sadist; 7 flasher, pervert; 8 pederast; 12 pornographer; PHRASES: 3, 5 sex fiend; 3, 8 sex criminal; 5, 6 child abuser.

sexual desire *See* **lust**

sexual immorality 4 lust; 6 laxity, libido, venery; 7 lechery, whoring; 8 harlotry, priapism, sexiness, wenching; 9 amorality, carnality, decadence, depravity, eroticism, immodesty, lightness, lubricity, seduction, sexuality; 10 debauchery, degeneracy, profligacy, satyriasis, unchastity, wantonness, womanizing; 11 defloration, dissipation, fleshliness, fornication, libertinism, nymphomania, promiscuity, whorishness; 12 incontinence; 13 concupiscence, dissoluteness, lecherousness, lickerishness, salaciousness, shamelessness; 14 lasciviousness, licentiousness; PHRASES: 3, 5 the flesh; 3, 7 bed hopping; 4, 4 free love; 4, 6 easy virtue; 4, 8 wife swapping; 5, 6 loose morals; 6, 3 roving eye; 6, 7 sexual license; 7, 6 fooling around.

shabby 4 mean; 5 cheap; 6 ragged, unjust, untidy; 7 raggedy, scruffy; 8 tattered; 12 contemptible, dishonorable; 13 inconsiderate; PHRASES: 4, 3 worn out.

shackle *See* **manacle**

shaddock 6 pomelo.

shade 3 hue, lid; 4 dark, dash, hide, hint, hood, mask, tint, tone, veil; 5 blind, color, cover, gloom, hatch, tinge, touch, trace; 6 awning, canopy, darken, screen, shadow, shield, shroud; 7 conceal, curtain, dimness, eclipse, flicker, parasol, protect, shelter; 8 blackout, darkness, eyeshade, shutters, sunshade; 9 blindfold; 10 gloominess, suggestion, sunglasses; PHRASES: 3, 3 sun hat; 3,

5 sun visor; 4, 2 fill in; 4, 3 blot out; 4, 7 dark glasses; 5, 2 block in, color in; 5, 3 block out; 5, 8 beach umbrella; 6, 3 little bit; 6, 5 roller blind, smoked glass; 7, 5 festoon blind; 8, 5 Venetian blind.

shades *See* **sunglasses**

shadow 4 dark, dusk, form, hint, tail; 5 chase, frame, ghost, gloom, shade, shape, stalk, touch, trace, track, trail; 6 darken, double, figure, follow, pursue, relief, sleuth, spirit, wraith; 7 contour, eclipse, flicker, observe, outline, phantom, profile, pursuer, specter, stalker, tracker; 8 darkness, follower, sidekick; 9 framework; 10 apparition, gloominess, silhouette, suggestion; 12 doppelgänger; PHRASES: 2, 5 go after; 4, 3 blot out; 5, 3 alter ego; 5, 4 other self; 7, 3 private eye.

shady 3 dim; 4 cool, dark, dull, hazy, matt; 5 dirty, dusty, filmy, fishy, foggy, fuzzy, grimy, milky, misty, muddy, murky, smoky, vague; 6 cloudy, misted, shaded, shifty, smoked, turbid; 7 blurred, clouded, crooked, dappled, devious, dubious, frosted, muddied, obscure, opaline, shadowy, suspect; 9 dishonest, sheltered, underhand; 10 lustreless *UK*, obfuscated, semiopaque, suspicious; 12 disreputable, questionable; PHRASES: 2, 3, 5 in the shade; 3, 2, 3, 3 out of the sun; 5, 3, 5 under the trees; 7, 2 steamed up.

shaft 3 air; 4 adit, butt; 5 drive; 6 escape; 9 propeller.

shaggy 5 bushy, hairy; 7 unkempt; 8 unshaven; 10 disheveled.

shake 3 jig, jog, mix, wag; 4 beat, jerk, jolt, rock, stir, sway, wave; 5 alarm, blend, lurch, quake, throb, twirl, upset, wield; 6 dodder, falter, fidget, flaunt, jigger, jiggle, joggle, judder, quaver, quiver, shiver, squirm, thrill, tremor, twitch, waggle, wiggle, wobble; 7 agitate, disturb, pulsate, shivers, shudder, tremble, twitter, unnerve, vibrate, wriggle; 8 brandish, distress, flourish, unsettle; 9 palpitate, vellicate, vibration; PHRASES: 4, 7 cold shivers; 5, 4, 1, 4 ~ like a leaf.

shaky *See* **unstable**

shallow 3 low; 4 flat, thin; 5 light, petty, reefy, shoal, silly; 6 narrow, shoaly, slight; 7 surface, trivial; 11 superficial, unnavigable; 13 insubstantial; PHRASES: 3, 4 not deep; 3-11 one-dimensional; 4-4 knee-deep; 5-4 ankle-deep, waist-deep.

shallow person 6 nobody; 9 nonentity; 10 mediocrity; 11 lightweight; PHRASES: 3, 2, 5 man of straw.

shallow thing 3 bar; 4 bank, film, flat, ford, pool, reef, skin; 5 flats, graze, shelf, shoal, swamp; 6 puddle, shoals, veneer; 7 cuticle, mudbank, scratch, shallow; 8 abrasion, pinprick, sandbank, shallows, wetlands; 9 epidermis; PHRASES: 3, 4 low tide, mud flat; 3, 5 low water; 4, 3 sand bar; 5, 4 coral reef; 5, 5 tidal flats; 7, 3 shallow cut; 7, 5 shallow water.

sham 3 act, con; 4 fake, mock; 5 bogus, fraud; 7 charade, pretend; 8 impostor, pretense; 9 charlatan, deception, imitation; PHRASES: 3, 2, 2 put it on.

shame 4 pity; 5 abash, stain; 6 defame, defile, demean, infamy, qualms, regret, stigma; 7 chagrin, degrade, mortify, remorse; 8 disgrace, dishonor, ignominy; 9 desecrate, discredit, embarrass, humiliate, indignity; 10 contrition; 11 degradation, humiliation; 13 embarrassment, mortification; 14 disappointment; PHRASES: 2, 4 be rude; 3, 2, 3, 5 put in the shade; 4, 1, 4, 2 make a fool of; 5, 5, 2 bring ~ on; 5, 7 lower oneself.

shank 3 bar, rod; 4 stem; 5 shaft, trunk.

shape 3 arc, bow, box, cut, hew, orb; 4 arch, ball, bend, bulb, cast, coil, cone, cube, curl, dome, form, hoop, loop, make, mold, oval, ring, star, sway, turn; 5 build, carve, cause, cross, curve, forge, frame, globe, heart, helix, model, raise, round, style, unify; 6 affect, chisel, circle, create, dogleg, evolve, figure, kidney, nature, oblong, sculpt, smooth, sphere, spiral, square, tailor; 7 circlet, compose, contour, diamond, fashion, lozenge, outline, polygon, produce, profile, pyramid, rhombus, whittle; 8 crescent, cylinder, identity, pentagon, rhomboid, spheroid, teardrop, tetragon, triangle; 9 character, construct, determine, elaborate, fabricate, formulate, horseshoe, influence, rectangle, structure, trapezium, trapezoid; 10 appearance, hemisphere, manipulate, quadrangle, semicircle, silhouette; 11 manufacture, tetrahedron; 12 dodecahedron; 13 parallelogram, quadrilateral; PHRASES: 6, 3 hammer out; 6, 5 figure eight.

shapeless 3 raw; 4 hazy; 5 baggy, fluid, fuzzy, misty, uncut, vague; 6 blobby, unhewn; 7 amoebic, blurred, obscure, unclear; 8 formless, shadowed, unformed, unlicked, unshaped; 9 amorphous, undefined; 10 incomplete, indefinite, unfinished; 11 featureless, undeveloped; 12 unstructured; 14 underdeveloped; PHRASES: 3-7 ill-defined; 5-7 loose-fitting.

shapeless thing 4 blob; 6 amoeba; 9 jellyfish; PHRASES: 3, 6 old pillow; 4, 5 sack dress; 6, 7 sloppy sweater.

share 3 bit, cut, lot; 4 deal, part; 5 allot, divvy, piece, quota, split, stake; 6 assign, divide, impart, ration, reveal; 7 portion, segment; 8 allocate, disclose; 9 allowance, apportion, communize, cooperate, socialize; 10 allocation, contribute, distribute; 11 communalize, communicate, nationalize, participate; 16 internationalize; PHRASES: 2, 5 go Dutch; 2, 6 go halves; 3, 8, 2, 2 let somebody in on; 4, 2 join in; 4, 3 dole out, give out; 5, 2 carve up; 6, 2 divide up; 6, 3 parcel out; 7, 2 partake of; 7, 7 involve oneself.

shared 4 same; 5 joint; 6 common, mutual; 7 blended; 8 combined, communal; 9 permeated; 10 collective, compatible, dovetailed; 11 cooperative; 12 intermediary.

sharon fruit 9 persimmon.

sharp 4 acid, hard, keen, loud, sour, tart; 5 acrid, acute, alert, angry, clear, conic, cross, harsh, honed, quick, smart, spiky, spiny, tangy, terse, wedgy UK; 6 abrupt, astute, biting, bitter, clever, jagged, pointy, severe, shrill, snappy, strong, sudden, thorny, unkind, urgent; 7 bristly, brusque, caustic, conical, cutting, exactly, hastate, intense, pointed, precise, prickly, pungent, tapered; 8 acicular, ascerbic, critical, cultrate, definite, distinct, ensiform, fusiform, incisive, piercing, promptly, sagittal, snappish, strident, tapering; 9 aciculate, acuminate, mucronate, precisely, pyramidal, sagittate, sarcastic, sharpened, spearlike, swordlike, unblunted; 10 accusatory, fastigiate, lanceolate, perceptive, punctually; 11 intelligent; PHRASES: 2, 3, 3 on the dot; 2, 3, 4 on the ball; 2, 5 in focus; 4-5 keen-edged; 4-7 high-pitched, well-defined; 5-3 clearcut; 5-5 knife-edged, razor-edged; 5-6 quick-witted.

sharpen 4 barb, edge, file, hone, spur, whet; 5 grind, notch, point, strap, strop, taper; 6 polish, refine; 7 improve, perfect, serrate; 8 oilstone; 9 sandpaper; PHRASES: 5, 2 brush up.

sharpener 4 file, hone; 5 emery, steel, strap, strop; 8 oilstone; 9 sandpaper, whetstone; 10 glasspaper, grindstone; 11 Carborundum *tm*; PHRASES: 5, 5 emery board, emery paper; 5, 9 knife ~; 6, 9 pencil ~.

sharpness 4 bite, zest, zing; 5 anger; 6 acuity; 7 acidity, clarity; 8 contrast, pungency, severity; 9 dentition, intensity, serration, spinosity; 10 definition; 11 acumination, mucronation; 12 intelligence, perspicacity; 13 denticulation. *See also* **sharp**

sharp point 4 cusp, dent, tine; 5 notch, point, prong, sting; 6 vertex; PHRASES: 3-4 saw-edge; 5, 4 knife edge, razor edge, sharp edge; 5, 5 knife point, sword point; 6, 4 jagged edge; 6, 5 pencil point; 7, 4 cutting edge.

sharp thing 2 ax; 3 adz, awl, awn, cog, nib, pin, saw; 4 adze, barb, bill, burr, claw, comb, crag, dirk, épée, foil, fork, gaff, goad, hair, hook, horn, kris, nail, peak, pick, pike, prod, rake, spit, tack, tuck; 5 ankus *UK*, arête, arrow, auger, beard, bilbo, blade, borer, brier, burin, drill, fleam, fluke, jerid, knife, kukri, lance, panga, plane, prick, quill, razor, rowel, saber, share, skean, spade, spear, spine, spire, sting, sword, talon, thorn, wedge, yucca; 6 antler, bodkin, broach, cactus, chisel, colter, cutter, dagger, flèche, gimlet, glaive, harrow, hatpin, lancet, needle, nettle, parang, pickax, poleax *UK*, pruner, rapier, scythe, shears, shovel, sickle, skewer, staple, stylet, stylus, summit, Toledo, trowel; 7 assegai, bayonet, bramble, bristle, caltrop, chopper, coulter, cutlass, dudgeon, gisarme, halberd, harpoon, hatchet, icepick, javelin, machete, matchet, mattock, nippers, poleaxe, poniard, prickle, pushpin, pyramid, quarrel, ratchet, scraper, spicule, steeple, sticker, thistle; 8 barbwire, billhook, claymore, clippers, cockspur, falchion, hedgehog, mustache, partisan, scimitar, scissors, sprocket, stiletto, tomahawk, yataghan; 9 arrowhead, drawknife, pitchfork, plowshare, porcupine, secateurs *UK*, spearhead, thumbtack, toothpick; 10 broadsword, fingernail, misericord, perforator, pigsticker, projection, spokeshave *UK*, swordstick; 11 ploughshare *UK*, snickersnee, switchblade; 12 marlinespike; PHRASES: 4-4 fish-hook; 4, 6 pine needle; 5-3 sgian-dhu *UK*; 5, 5 bowie knife, naked steel, razor blade, short sword; 5-6 Adam's-

needle; 6-2 battle-ax; 6-2-5 cheval-de-frise; 6, 4 barbed wire; 6, 5 broken glass; 7, 7 Spanish bayonet; 8, 6 knitting needle.

shatter 5 blast, break, crush, smash, wreck; 7 destroy; 8 demolish, fragment, splinter.

shave 3 cut; 4 clip, flay, pare, peel, skin, trim; 5 pluck, scalp, shear; 6 fleece; 7 deplume, tonsure; 8 depilate, exuviate; 9 excoriate, exfoliate; 10 desquamate; PHRASES: 3, 3 cut off.

shaving 4 chip; 5 flake, shred; 6 sliver; 8 splinter.

shawl *See* **wrap**

sheaf 3 wad; 5 clump; 6 bundle; 7 cluster.

sheath *See* **cover**

shed 3 hut; 4 barn, byre *UK*, cast, emit, lose, molt; 5 cabin, hovel, scale; 6 flayed, molted, recede, shaven, slough; 7 project, radiate, scalped, skinned; 8 disperse; PHRASES: 3, 3, 2 get rid of; 4-2 lean-to; 4, 3 cast off; 6, 3 slough off.

sheen *See* **shine**

sheep 3 ewe, ram; 4 Down, lamb, lonk, mule, soay; 5 cardy *UK*, chios, Jacob, lleyn, morfe, texel, wooly; 6 awassi, masham, merino, Romney, woolly; 7 cheviot, copycat, gotland, jumbuck *UK*, karakul, lacaune, lemming, Lincoln, Suffolk; 8 Cotswold, follower, herdwick, longmynd, polwarth, Portland, Shetland, woolskin; 9 Hampshire, Hebridean, longwools, montadale, oldenberg, Swaledale *UK*, Teeswater; 10 conformist, Corriedale, Shropshire; 11 Wensleydale; 14 traditionalist; PHRASES: 3, 3 yes man; 4, 6 poll Dorset; 4, 7 Manx loghtan; 5, 4 rough fell; 5, 8 Welsh mountain; 6, 4 Dorset horn, Exmoor horn; 6, 5 Romney Marsh; 9, 4 Wiltshire horn.

sheer 4 fine, pure; 5 bluff, filmy, gauzy, steep, total, utter; 6 abrupt; 8 absolute, complete, vertical; 9 unalloyed; 10 diaphanous; 11 precipitous, translucent, transparent, unmitigated, vertiginous; 13 perpendicular, unadulterated; PHRASES: 3-7 see-through.

sheet 4 area, dope, leaf, mass, page, pane, slip; 5 cover, folio, layer, piece; 7 balance, expanse; PHRASES: 3, 5 fly ~; 4, 5 time ~, work ~; 5, 3 ~ ice; 5, 4 ~ bend; 5, 5 ~ metal, ~ music; 5, 6 ~ anchor; 5, 9 ~ lightning; 6, 5 charge ~ *UK*; 7, 5 thunder ~, winding ~.

shelf 4 sill, step; 5 layer, ledge, ridge; 9 bookshelf; 10 projection; 11 mantelpiece;

PHRASES: 4, 5 rock ~.

shell 3 pod; **4** bomb, hull, husk; **5** armor, frame; **6** bullet, casing; **7** grenade, outside; **8** carapace. *See also* **seashell, shellfish**

shellfish 4 clam, crab; **5** prawn, snail, whelk; **6** cockle, mussel, oyster, shrimp, winkle; **7** abalone, crawdad, geoduck, lobster, mollusk, scallop, seafood; **8** crawfish, crayfish, escargot; **9** bluepoint, écrevisse, kingprawn, langouste; **10** crustacean; **11** langoustine; **PHRASES: 4, 4** rock crab; **4, 6** sand dollar; **5, 4** pismo clam, razor clam; **5, 7** spiny lobster; **6, 3, 5** Dublin Bay prawn *UK*; **9, 4** Dungeness crab.

shelter 3 cot, den, hut, lee; **4** camp, dock, dump, hide, hole, lair, port, quay, rest, roof, shed, tent; **5** booth, bothy *UK*, cache, cover, haven, hedge, hovel, hutch, joint, shack, shade, squat; **6** asylum, awning, bunker, cosset, covert, defend, harbor, huddle, marina, pigpen, pigsty *UK*, refuge, screen, shanty, shield; **7** hideout, housing, lodging, protect, retreat, secrecy; **8** blackout, eyeshade, hideaway, kiphouse, outhouse, stockade, sunshade; **9** dosshouse *UK*, flophouse, sanctuary, windbreak; **10** blockhouse, protection; **11** concealment, smokescreen; **14** accommodations; **PHRASES: 3-4, 7** air-raid ~; **4, 2** take in; **4-2** lean-to; **4, 5** safe haven, safe house, take cover; **4, 6** take refuge; **4, 6, 2** give refuge to; **6, 5** hiding place; **7, 7** fallout ~; **8, 7** Anderson ~ *UK*.

shield 5 armor, guard; **6** buffer, defend; **7** defense, protect, shelter; **9** safeguard; **10** protection.

shift 4 lift, move, ruse, tour, turn, vary, veer; **5** alter, budge, clean, erase, hurry, linen, shirt, spell, split, stint, swing, watch; **6** change, loosen, modify, period, remove; **7** chemise, nightie; **8** transfer; **9** expedient; **10** alteration; **12** modification, transference; **PHRASES: 3, 1, 4, 2** get a move on; **3, 5** day ~, red ~; **3, 6** get moving; **4, 2** buck up; **4, 5** back ~, blue ~; **5, 2** hurry up; **5, 5** night ~.

shifty 5 false; **7** devious, evasive, hedging; **8** slippery; **PHRASES: 9** deceitful, underhand.

shilly-shally *See* **dawdle**

shinbone 5 tibia.

shindig *See* **party**

shine 3 wax; **4** buff, burn, glow; **5** blaze, clear, excel, flash, glare, gleam, gloss, sheen; **6** dazzle, luster, patina, polish; **7** burnish, flicker, glimmer, glisten, glitter, light-en, radiate, shimmer, sparkle, twinkle; **8** brighten; **PHRASES: 2, 4** do well; **2, 4, 2** be good at; **2, 7, 2** be skilled at; **3, 1, 5, 2** put a ~ on; **4, 1, 4, 3** have a gift for; **4, 2** buff up; **5, 3** stand out.

shingles 6 herpes.

shiny 6 glossy; **8** gleaming, glittery, polished.

ship 2 SS; **3** ark, cog, HMS *UK*, tug *UK Can*, USS; **4** Argo, boat, dory, grab, punt, raft, saic, snow; **5** barge, canoe, coble *UK*, ferry, funny, kayak, liner, shell, skiff, tramp, umiak; **6** bireme, caique, dogger, galley, hooker, hopper, launch, lorcha, packet, randan, sampan, sealer, slaver, tanker, tender, whaler; **7** bumboat, carrack, coaster, collier, coracle, corsair, currach, dredger, drifter, gabbart, gondola, jangada, pinnace, piragua, polacre, rowboat, sculler, steamer, tartane, towboat, trawler, trireme, tugboat, warship; **8** budgerow, cockboat, dahabiya, foldboat, gallivat, lifeboat, outboard, showboat; **9** bucentaur, freighter, lightship, motorboat, motorship, outrigger, speedboat, steamboat, steamship, storeship, submarine; **10** quadrireme; **11** cockleshell, penteconter, quinquereme *UK*; **PHRASES: 3-3** dug-out; **3-4** fly-boat; **3-6** mudhopper; **4-4** long-boat, mail-ship; **5, 3** Noah's ark; **5, 4** house boat; **5-4** cargo-boat, jolly-boat, river-boat, slave-ship; **5-5** train-ferry; **5, 6** pilot vessel; **5-7** cabin-cruiser, stern-wheeler; **5, 9** ocean greyhound; **6, 4** picket boat, rowing boat *UK*; **6-4** banana-boat, paddle-boat, pirate-ship, prison-ship, viking-ship; **6, 6** escort vessel; **6, 7** paddle wheeler; **7-4** fishing-boat; **7, 7** channel steamer; **8, 4** hospital ~, merchant ~, pleasure boat; **8, 6** floating palace. *See also* **sailing boat, warship**

shipshape *See* **in order**

shirk 4 duck, shun; **5** avoid, dodge, evade, skive *UK*; **8** malinger; **10** scrimshank *UK*; **PHRASES: 3, 3** cop out; **3, 3, 2** get out of; **4, 3, 4** pass the buck; **4, 5** gold brick; **7, 3, 2** wriggle out of.

shirt 1 T; **3** top; **4** sark; **5** choli, smock; **6** blouse, camisa, camise, dickey, huipil, shimmy; **7** blouson, bustier, casaque, dashiki; **9** blousette, garibaldi, guayabera, overshirt; **10** overblouse, shirtwaist; **PHRASES: 1-5** T-shirt; **3, 5** tee ~; **4, 5** body ~, coat ~, hair ~, polo ~; **5, 5** bosom ~, Brown S~, dress ~; **5, 6** middy blouse; **6, 5** boiled ~, office ~, sports ~; **6, 6** balkan blouse; **7, 5** chukker ~, evening ~, stuffed ~; **8, 5** pullover ~. *See also* **clothes**

shiver *See* **shake**

shock 3 jar; **4** blow, jolt, jump, mane, mass, stun, turn; **5** alarm, facer, start, upset; **6** appall, fright, horror, offend, thatch, trauma; **7** astound, disturb, horrify, outrage, provoke, stagger; **8** astonish, distress, frighten, numbness, surprise; **9** amazement, bombshell, devastate, disbelief, surprisal; **10** scandalize, traumatize; **11** devastation, disturbance, flabbergast, thunderbolt; **12** astonishment; PHRASES: **3-6** eye-opener; **4, 2, 3, 5** kick in the teeth; **4, 4, 3, 4** bolt from the blue; **4, 5** take aback; **5, 2** shake up; **5, 3, 3** knock for six *UK*.

shocking *See* **outrageous**

shoddy 3 low; **4** base, mean, poky, poor; **5** cheap, gaudy, lousy, mangy, tacky, tatty; **6** crummy, paltry, rotten, scummy, shabby, sloppy, tawdry, trashy, unkind; **7** chintzy, scruffy, useless; **8** careless, inferior, shopworn, slapdash, twopenny, unbought, unwanted; **9** dishonest, unsalable, valueless, worthless; **10** shopsoiled, unsaleable; **11** disgraceful, substandard; **12** unmarketable; **13** inconsiderate; PHRASES: **3, 2, 7** out of fashion; **3-3** tin-pot, two-bit; **3-5** low-grade; **3-7** low-quality; **5-5** jerry-built *UK*; **6-4** second-rate.

shoe *See* **footwear**

shoot 3 aim, bud, gun, hit, jet, run, zip; **4** cast, cull, dart, dash, drop, fell, film, fire, gush, hunt, kill, plug, race, snap, stem, take, whiz, zoom; **5** blast, burst, drive, flush, force, movie, poach, point, score, snipe, speed, spurt, stalk, track, trail, waste; **6** appear, branch, direct, pistol, sprout, squirt, strike, volley; **7** bombard, capture, develop, explode; **8** detonate, retrieve; **9** cannonade, discharge, outgrowth, slaughter; **10** photograph; PHRASES: **3, 2** aim at; **3, 3** let fly, let off *UK*; **3, 4** gun down; **3, 6** new growth; **4, 1, 6** fire a volley; **4, 2** fire at; **4, 3** fire off, hunt for, leaf bud, send off; **4, 3, 7** pull the trigger; **4, 4** blow away, open fire; **4-5** deer-stalk; **5, 4** bring down; **5, 6** sight quarry; **6, 3, 5** follow the scent; **7, 4** produce buds.

shooter 3 gun; **4** shot; **6** gunman, gunner, sniper; **7** deadeye; **8** marksman, rifleman; **9** cannoneer, musketeer, pistoleer *UK*; **10** carabineer, markswoman; **11** trapshooter;

PHRASES: **4, 4** dead shot, good shot; **5, 4** crack shot; **6, 7** target ~; **9, 3** artillery man.

shooting 4 fire; **5** skeet; **6** culled, firing, killed, murder; **7** archery, gunfire, gunnery, hunting, killing, slaying; **8** homicide, musketry, shelling, stalking, tracking; **9** artillery, execution, toxophily; **10** ballistics; **11** bombardment; **12** trapshooting; **13** assassination; PHRASES: **5, 8** skeet ~; **6-4** single-shot.

shop 3 buy; **4** mail, swap; **5** spend, store, union, works; **6** arcade, bazaar, browse, expend; **7** factory, require, takeout; **8** carryout, purchase, teleshop, workshop; **9** drugstore; PHRASES: **3, 3, 3, 5** mom and pop store; **4, 7** ~ steward; **4, 9** ~ assistant *UK*; **5, 5** sales clerk; **6, 4** bucket ~ *UK*, closed ~, coffee ~; **6-4** window-shop; **7, 4** betting ~ *UK*, machine ~, talking ~ *UK*; **8, 5** shopping spree. *See also* **food store**

shoplift *See* **steal**

shore 4 beam, prop; **5** beach, coast; **6** strand; **7** seaside, support; **8** littoral, seaboard, seashore; **9** coastline, shoreline; **10** oceanfront; PHRASES: **5, 5** ~ leave; **5, 6** ~ patrol.

short 3 cut, low; **4** curt, rude, snub, tiny; **5** amiss, brief, brisk, dumpy, gruff, minus, needy, quick, rapid, sharp, small, squat, terse; **6** abrupt, curtly, little, petite, scanty, scarce, skimpy, snappy, stocky, stubby, stumpy; **7** briefly, brusque, circuit, concise, lacking, measure, missing, passing, sharply, shortly, snifter, stunted, summary, tersely, wanting; **8** abruptly, fleeting, succinct, suddenly, synoptic, thickset; **9** concisely, condensed, deficient, midstream, retroussé, transient, unreached; **10** diminutive, inadequate, incomplete, succinctly, undersized, unfinished, unfriendly; **11** compendious, unfulfilled; **12** insufficient; PHRASES: **2, 1, 4** in a word; **2, 1, 8** in a nutshell; **2, 3, 5** to the point; **2, 5** in brief, in ~; **3-5** pug-nosed; **4-4** half-done; **4-5** snub-nosed; **5, 3, 5** ~ and sweet; **5, 4** ~ fuse, ~ head *UK*, ~ list, ~ odds *UK*, ~ stop; **5, 5** ~ story, ~ straw; **5, 6** ~ shrift.

shortage *See* **lack**

shortcoming 4 flaw; **5** fault; **6** defect; **7** blemish, default, failing, failure; **8** diminish, weakness; **10** deficiency, inadequacy, limitation; **11** defalcation, inferiority; **12** imperfection.

short distance 2 em, en, ft, yd; **3** ace; **4**

inch, step; **5** brink, verge; **7** bowshot, earshot, gunshot; **8** shortcut; **10** millimeter; **13** fingerbreadth; PHRASES: **2, 8** no distance; **4, 4** near miss; **4, 5** near thing *UK*; **5, 3** short way; **5, 5** close range; **5, 6** photo finish; **5-7** hair's-breadth; **5, 8** close quarters; **6, 3** little way; **6, 5** stone's throw; **6, 6** narrow squeak; **7, 5** finger's width; **7-7** finger's-breadth.

shorten 2 ax; **3** bob, cut, lop, mow; **4** clip, crop, dock, edit, poll, reap, trim; **5** elide, prune, shave, shear, skimp, slash, stunt; **6** behead, digest, reduce; **7** abridge, curtail; **8** abstract, compress, condense, retrench, truncate; **9** capsulize, epitomize, summarize, synopsize, telescope; **10** abbreviate, decapitate; **11** encapsulate, foreshorten; PHRASES: **3, 2** sum up; **3, 3** cut off; **3, 4** cut back, cut down; **3, 5** cut short; **4, 2** take up, turn up; **4, 4** boil down.

shortened version 6 digest, precis, résumé; **7** capsule, epitome, outline, summary; **8** abstract, ellipsis, synopsis; **10** abridgment, compendium, conspectus; **12** abbreviation.

shortfall 3 gap; **4** lack, loss, need, want; **5** debit; **6** dearth, famine; **7** arrears, deficit; **8** scarcity, shortage; **11** cursoriness, discrepancy, requirement; **13** insufficiency, noncompletion; **14** incompleteness; PHRASES: **15** perfunctoriness.

short-lived *See* **brief**

shortly 4 soon; **2, 1, 5** in a while; **2, 1, 6** in a minute, in a moment; **6, 4** before long. *See also* **short**

shortness 5 speed; **7** brevity; **8** rapidity; **9** concision; **10** transience; PHRASES: **11** discourtesy. *See also* **short**

short person *See* **little person**

short-sightedness 4 bias; **6** myopia; **7** bigotry; **9** prejudice; **11** intolerance.

short thing 6 shorts; **8** February, shortcut; **9** miniskirt, shorthand; PHRASES: **3-3, 6** one-hit wonder; **4, 3** crew cut; **4-4, 6** nine-days wonder; **5, 2, 3, 3** flash in the pan.

short time 1 T; **2** mo *UK*; **3** min *UK*, sec; **4** tick; **6** moment; **7** instant.

shot 2 go; **3** jab *UK*, lob, nip, tot, try; **4** bang, bash *UK*, dram, lead, putt, slug, snap, stab, turn, view; **5** blast, crack, drink, drive, glass, photo, round, salvo, scene; **6** bullet, jigger, report, shells, stroke, tattoo, volley; **7** attempt, booster, bowshot, gunfire, gunshot, measure, pellets, picture, potshot,

snifter; **8** buckshot, ejection, sequence, shooting, snapshot; **9** cannonade, discharge, explosion, fusillade, injection, stoneshot; **10** ammunition, cannonball, detonation, photograph; **11** bombardment, inoculation, vaccination; PHRASES: **3, 4** big ~; **4, 4** drop ~, foul ~, jump ~, long ~, mail ~; **6-4** direct-mail; **7, 4** parting ~, passing ~; **8, 4** approach ~, Parthian ~.

shoulder 4 bear; **5** carry; **6** accept, assume; PHRASES: **4, 2** take on.

shoulder blade 7 scapula.

shout 3 cry; **4** bark, bawl, boom, bray, call, hoot, howl, roar, yell, yowl; **5** blare, whoop; **6** bellow, scream, shriek, shrill, squawk; **7** catcall, exclaim, screech, thunder, trumpet, ululate, whistle; **9** caterwaul; **10** cachinnate; PHRASES: **4, 3** call out.

shove 4 jolt, move, push, slap, toss; **5** heave, throw; **6** hustle, jostle, propel, thrust; **9** manhandle.

shovel 3 dig; **4** heap, move, rake, tool; **5** ladle, scoop, spade, spoon; **6** dredge, pickax, trowel; **7** dredger, shadoof; **8** excavate; **9** toothpick; PHRASES: **7, 5** Persian wheel.

show 3 act; **4** bare, bill, fair, fete, film, gala, mask, mime, open, play; **5** event, flash, floor, guide, image, light, march, movie, opera, point, prove, revue, rodeo, scene, sport, steer, stunt, teach, trial, usher; **6** appear, ballet, circus, direct, evince, expose, façade, flaunt, mirror, parade, reveal, review, tattoo, unmask; **7** cabaret, concert, confirm, display, exhibit, explain, Follies, lecture, musical, pageant, perform, persona, present, program, reflect, showing, surface, tableau, uncover, viewing; **8** carnival, disclose, flourish, indicate, manifest, peepshow, puppetry, sideshow; **9** accompany, advertise, establish, fireworks, highlight, promenade, screening, spectacle, spotlight; **10** appearance, exhibition, expression, fantoccini, illuminate, illustrate, striptease, tournament, vaudeville; **11** demonstrate, performance; **12** extravaganza, illustration, presentation; **13** demonstration, entertainment, manifestation; PHRASES: **2, 4** TV ~; **3, 2, 4** put on view; **3, 2, 7** son et lumière; **3, 3, 3** the Big Top; **3, 4** ice ~, sex ~, the ring; **4, 3, 5** song and dance; **4, 4** dumb ~, game ~, live ~, quiz ~, road ~, talk ~; **4-5, 6** late-night review; **4, 6** flea circus; **4, 8** ~ business; **5, 3** point out, spell out, stand out, stick out; **5, 3, 3** catch the eye; **5, 4** floor ~, laser ~, light ~, magic ~, music hall, panel ~, radio ~, raree ~, slide ~, stage ~, strip ~, trade ~; **5-6** stage-manage; **6, 4** county ~ *UK*, flower ~, puppet ~, shadow play; **6-5** window-dress; **7, 4** fashion ~, variety ~; **7, 6** tableau vivant; **8, 4** minstrel ~; **9, 4** burlesque ~, repertory ~; **9, 6** traveling circus; **10, 4** marionette ~, vaudeville ~.

show business 5 films; **6** movies; **7** theater, variety; **8** Broadway; **9** burlesque, Hollywood; **10** striptease, television, vaudeville; **13** entertainment; PHRASES: **3, 3, 3** the big top; **3-3-8** off-off-Broadway; **3, 5** the stage; **3, 6** the boards; **3-8** off-Broadway; **4, 3** show biz, West End; **4, 3, 5** song and dance; **5, 3** straw hat; **5, 4** music hall.

shower 4 pour, rain, spit, wash; **5** burst, flood, rinse, spray, storm; **6** deluge; **7** bombard, cascade; **8** downpour, inundate; **9** overwhelm; **10** cloudburst; PHRASES: **4, 4** pour down; **7, 2** freshen up.

show off 4 brag, pose; **5** boast, flash, strut, swank; **6** flaunt, parade, prance; **7** display, exhibit, peacock, swagger, upstage; **8** flourish; **9** promenade; PHRASES: **3, 2, 4** put on airs; **3, 4, 3, 4** fly your own kite *UK*; **4, 3** talk big; **4, 3, 6** talk for effect; **5, 7** preen oneself.

showpiece 5 curio, dummy, focus, model, pride; **6** sample; **7** antique, example, exhibit; **8** specimen; **10** attraction; **11** centerpiece, collectible, masterpiece; PHRASES: **4-2** mock-up; **5, 2, 3, 5** jewel in the crown; **5, 2, 8** piece of evidence; **5, 3, 3** pride and joy; **6, 5** museum piece.

showplace 4 bill, hall, sign; **5** label, scene; **6** museum, poster; **7** dumpbin *UK*, gallery, placard; **8** citation, pegboard, showcase, showroom; **9** billboard; **10** auditorium; **13** advertisement; PHRASES: **5, 6** store window; **6, 5** notice board; **7, 4** display case; **7, 7** display cabinet; **8, 5** bulletin board; **8, 6** sandwich boards; **10, 4** exhibition hall.

showy 5 brash, gaudy, jazzy, lucid, stark, vivid; **6** flashy, garish, glitzy, visual, vulgar; **8** dramatic, splendid, striking; **9** brilliant, prominent, shameless, tasteless; **10** attractive, impressive, remarkable; **11** highlighted, illuminated, magnificent, outstanding, pretentious, spectacular, spotlighted; **12** ostentatious; **13** demonstrative; PHRASES: **3-8** eye-catching; **4-7** high-profile.

shred 3 bit; **5** grate, piece, scrap, slice, strip; **6** sliver; PHRASES: **3, 2** cut up, rip up; **4, 2** tear up.

shriek 3 cry; **4** call, pipe, yell, yelp; **5** creak, shout; **6** screak, scream, squeak, squeal; **7** catcall, screech, whistle; PHRASES: **4-7** wolf-whistle.

shrill 4 high; **5** acute, harsh, reedy, sharp, tinny; **6** creaky, piping; **7** jarring, squeaky; **8** bleeping, creaking, piercing, strident; **9** squeaking, whistling; **11** penetrating; PHRASES: **3-8** ear-piercing; **4-7** high-pitched.

shrill (be shrill) 4 pipe; **5** creak; **6** scream, shriek, squeak, squeal; **7** catcall, screech, whistle; PHRASES: **4, 7** wolf whistle.

shrine 4 naos, tomb, tope; **5** Bayon, cella, grave, Kaaba, marae *UK*, Mecca, Mitla, stupa; **6** Abydos, Bethel, chapel, dagoba, Kumbum; **7** Avebury, Benares, Chorten, sanctum, Sarnath; **8** Butsuden, cromlech, Fujiyama, Gangotri, memorial, monument; **9** Badrinath, Bethlehem, Jerusalem, Myoskinji, reliquary, sacrarium, sanctuary; **10** Abhayagiri, Stonehenge, tabernacle; PHRASES: **3-3** Zem-Zem; **4, 2, 6** holy of holies; **4, 5** holy place, Shwe Dagon; **4, 6** Blue Mosque; **5, 3** Mount Tai; **5, 4** Adam's Peak, Ayers Rock, Mount Omei; **5, 5** Tashi Lumpo; **5, 6** River Ganges, River Kistna; **5, 7** River Narbada; **5, 8** River Godavari; **6, 3** Angkor Wat; **6, 5** sacred place; **7, 4** Wailing Wall.

shrink 3 cut, ebb, jib; **4** clip, dock, drop, fade, fall, file, pare, sear, slim, thin, trim; **5** avoid, cower, cramp, crush, grind, limit, pinch, press, prune, shave, shear, slash, stunt, waste; **6** cringe, doctor, flinch, grovel, lessen, narrow, recoil, reduce, wither; **7** abridge, analyst, compact, curtail, decline, deflate, dwindle, flatten, shorten, shrivel, squeeze, tighten; **8** belittle, compress, condense, contract, decrease, diminish, emaciate, minimize, restrict, retrench, strangle, withdraw; **9** constrict, counselor, disappear, economize, telescope, therapist; **10** abbreviate; **11** concentrate, miniaturize; **12** circumscribe, psychiatrist; **13** psychoanalyst; PHRASES: **3, 2** dry up; **3, 4** shy away; **4, 3** back off; **4, 4** back away, draw back, fall back, pull back; **5, 4** waste away; **6, 4** ~ away, ~ back; **7, 4** whittle away.

shrink back 3 jib, shy; **5** avoid, cower; **6** cringe, flinch, grovel, recoil, shrink; **7** retreat; **8** withdraw; PHRASES: **3, 4** shy away; **4,**

3 back off; **4, 4** back away, draw back, fall back, pull back; **6, 4** shrink away.

shrinking **6** waning; **7** pursing, searing, styptic, wasting; **8** cramping, crushing, limiting, pinching, reducing, slimming *UK*, stunting, thinning; **9** gathering, lessening, narrowing, puckering, tabescent; **10** astringent, collapsing, decreasing, emaciating, shortening, shriveling, strangling, tightening; **11** compressive, contracting, restricting; **12** constricting, constringent, deflationary; **15** circumscriptive.

shrivel *See* **shrink**

shroud *See* **covering**

shrub **4** bush, tree; **5** plant; PHRASES: **9, 5** flowering ~.

shudder *See* **shake**

shuffle **6** hobble, lumber; **7** reorder, rummage, scuffle, shamble, trundle; **9** rearrange; PHRASES: **3, 2** mix up; **6, 2** jumble up, muddle up.

shun **5** avoid, evade, exile, spurn; **6** disbar, eschew, ignore; **7** forbear; **9** blackball, blacklist, ostracize; PHRASES: **4-8** cold-shoulder.

shunt **3** hit; **4** jolt, move, push; **5** crash, prang *UK*, shift, shove, smash; **6** propel, thrust; **8** accident; **9** collision; PHRASES: **4, 4** bump into; **7, 4** collide with.

shush! **1** P; **2** PP; **3** tsk!; **4** hist!, tush!; **5** whist!; **6** wheesh!, whisht!.

shut **5** close; **6** fasten, secure; PHRASES: **4, 2** push to *UK*; **4, 4** ~ down; **5, 2** close up; **5, 4** close down.

shy **3** coy, jib, lob, mum; **4** funk, hurl, wary; **5** blink, chuck, demur, mousy, quiet, shier, start, throw, timid; **6** afraid, blench, flinch, humble, modest, refuse, shiest, shrink, shtoom *UK*, silent, sullen; **7** bashful, fearful, nervous, overshy, passive, retreat; **8** blushing, cautious, reserved, reticent, retiring, taciturn, timorous; **9** diffident, inhibited, mouselike, reluctant, shrinking, withdrawn; **10** antisocial, frightened, stammering, unsociable; **11** embarrassed, introverted, unassertive, unimportant; **12** apprehensive, inarticulate; **13** pusillanimous, unforthcoming; **15** incommunicable, uncommunicative; PHRASES: **4-8** self-effacing; **4-9** self-conscious; **5, 3** fight ~; **6, 2, 7** afraid of company, unsure of oneself.

shy (be shy) **4** hide; **5** blush; **6** flinch, shrink; **8** withdraw.

shy person **4** clam; **5** mouse; **7** doormat; **8** coquette, Trappist; **10** wallflower; PHRASES: **2, 6** no orator.

sibilant **1** S; **6** wheezy; **7** hissing, squashy; **8** swishing; **9** asthmatic, whistling; **12** effervescent.

sick **3** bad, ill, pay; **4** pale, vile; **5** bored, dizzy, dying, green, peaky *UK Can*, queer, seedy; **6** ailing, crummy, excuse, groggy, grotty *UK*, peaked, pining, poorly, queasy, seized, unwell; **7** bilious, bizarre, chronic, chunder *UK*, serious; **8** comatose, confined, critical, drooping, feverish, flagging, gruesome, headachy, moribund, nauseous, terminal; **9** bedridden, collapsed, greensick, incurable, invalided, nauseated, prostrate, revolting, sickening, squeamish, tasteless; **10** indisposed, inoperable, nauseating; **11** languishing, quarantined; **12** hospitalized; PHRASES: **2, 1, 3, 3** in a bad way; **2, 2, 4** up to here; **2, 3** in bed, in ICU; **2, 3, 5** in bad taste; **2, 3, 6** in bad health; **2, 4, 5** in poor shape; **2, 4, 6** in poor health; **2, 4, 9** in poor condition; **2, 8** in hospital; **2, 9, 4** in intensive care; **3, 2** fed up, had it; **3, 2, 5** out of sorts; **3, 2, 6** out of kilter; **3, 4** not well; **3-5** off-color; **4, 2** laid up, shut in; **4, 2, 5** ~ to death; **4, 3, 5** ~ and tired; **4, 4** ~ list; **4, 5** ~ leave; **5, 3** below par *UK*, taken ill; **5, 3, 7** under the weather; **8, 3** mortally ill.

sicken **3** ail; **4** drop, fail, flag, peak, pine, sink; **5** droop, faint, repel, shock, vomit; **6** appall, revolt, suffer, weaken; **7** disgust, repulse; **8** collapse, languish, nauseate; **11** deteriorate; PHRASES: **4, 3** feel ill; **4, 4** make sick; **4, 4, 7** turn your stomach.

sickening **4** vile; **6** emetic, trying; **7** galling; **8** annoying, horrible, shocking, terrible; **9** appalling, maddening, purgative, repellent, repulsive, revolting; **10** disgusting, irritating, nauseating; **11** infuriating; **13** disappointing; PHRASES: **7-8** stomach-churning.

sickle **4** hook; **9** grasshook.

sickly **3** ill; **4** pale, weak; **6** unwell; **7** cloying, mawkish; **9** unhealthy; **10** disgusting, saccharine; **11** sentimental, suffocating; **12** overpowering; PHRASES: **6-5** sickly-sweet.

sickness **3** bug; **5** serum, virus; **6** anemia, malady, nausea, waning; **7** burnout, disease, fatigue, frailty, illness, vertigo; **8** anorexia, asthenia, caducity, debility, disorder, flagging, lameness, paleness, senility, sweating, thinness, vomiting; **9** condition, deflation, depletion, dizziness, faintness, giddiness, infection, infirmity, radiation, shakiness, tiredness, weariness; **10** enervation, exhaustion, queasiness, sickliness, weakliness; **11** biliousness, decrepitude, dissipation; PHRASES: **3, 6** bad health, ill health; **4, 8** milk ~; **6, 8** motion ~; **7, 8** falling ~ *UK*, morning ~; **8, 2** throwing up.

sick person 4 case; **5** crock; **6** addict; **7** bleeder, invalid, patient; **8** diabetic, sufferer, weakling; **9** alcoholic, arthritic, asthmatic, dyspeptic, insomniac, neuropath; **10** bronchitic, hemiplegic, malingerer, paraplegic; **11** consumptive, hemophiliac; **12** quadriplegic; **13** hypochondriac; **14** valetudinarian; PHRASES: **2-7** in-patient; **3-7** outpatient; **4-2** shut-in; **4, 6** drug addict; **7, 7** chronic invalid; **8, 4** hospital case; **8, 6** disabled person; **8, 7** hospital patient; **9, 4** stretcher case.

side 1 L, R; **2** on; **3** leg, off; **4** area, bank, camp, club, edge, face, gang, left, part, port, ribs, spin, team, wall, zone; **5** cheek, facet, flank, group, plane, right, spear, squad, sunny, trait; **6** aspect, border, dexter, facing, fringe, margin, prompt, region, siding, temple; **7** feature, lateral, leeward, oblique, offside, profile, quality, quarter, section, segment, surface; **8** boundary, flanking, hillside, sidelong, sinister, skirting, snobbery, windward; **9** bilateral, elevation, periphery, starboard; **10** collateral, laterality, sideboards, trilateral; **12** multifaceted; **13** quadrilateral; **14** characteristic; PHRASES: **3, 4** air ~, far ~, lee ~, off ~; **3-5** two-sided; **4-2** line-up; **4, 2, 3, 4** ~ of the face; **4, 4** flip ~, left hand, near ~, ~ door, ~ view; **4-5** many-sided; **4, 8** ~ entrance, ~ whiskers; **4, 9** ~ elevation; **5, 4** right hand, spear ~; **7, 4** distaff ~.

side-dish 5 salad, sauce; **6** drinks; **8** dressing; **10** condiments, vegetables.

sidestep 3 gee, haw, jib, shy; **4** duck, side; **5** avert, avoid, dodge, evade, sidle, skirt; **6** bypass; **7** deviate, passage; **9** sidetrack; PHRASES: **2, 3** go off; **3, 3** fly off, shy off; **4, 3, 3** make way for; **4, 4** turn away; **4, 5** turn aside; **5, 5, 2** steer clear of.

sidewalk 8 footpath.

sideways 5 askew; **7** askance, oblique; **8** indirect, sidelong, slanting; PHRASES: **2, 3, 4** to one side.

side with 4 back; **7** embrace, endorse, espouse, support; PHRASES: **4, 3, 3** come out for; **5, 3, 7** cross the Rubicon; **6, 7** commit oneself; **8, 4** conspire with.

sidle 4 edge, inch; **5** creep, snake; **7** slither.

siesta *See* **rest**

sift *See* **filter**

sigh 4 long, moan, pine, want; **5** groan, yearn; **6** exhale, hanker, lament; **7** breathe; **9** complaint; **10** exhalation; PHRASES: **5, 1, 4** heave a ~.

sight 3 see; **4** spot, view; **5** scene; **6** notice, vision; **7** picture; **8** eyesight, prospect; **9** spectacle; PHRASES: **5, 5, 2** catch ~ of.

sign 1 X; **3** cue, key, sun; **4** clue, code, flag, hint, hire, lead, logo, mark, mojo, omen, pain, rune; **5** badge, brand, cross, fever, image, piste, scent, sigla, token, trace, track, trail; **6** banner, cipher, emblem, employ, engage, letter, manual, marker, motion, nausea, notice, plaque, poster, retain, signal, symbol, traces; **7** endorse, imprint, inkling, mandala, meaning, nametag, placard, portent, symptom, warning; **8** contract, crescent, evidence, hallmark, hoarding *UK*, insignia, language, password, signpost, swastika, syndrome, talisman; **9** authorize, autograph, billboard, dizziness, footprint, indicator, signature, trademark; **10** hieroglyph, indication, prediction, shibboleth; **11** connotation, countersign, fingerprint, gesticulate, premonition; **13** hieroglyphics, signification; **14** representation; PHRASES: **4, 4** high ~, plus ~, road ~, sure ~; **5, 4** equal ~, minus ~; **5, 5** fiery cross; **5, 6** magic symbol; **6, 3, 6** hammer and sickle; **6, 4** danger ~, secret ~; **6, 6** sacred symbol; **7, 4** highway ~, protest ~, warning ~, weather ~; **8, 4** division ~, motorway ~, telltale ~; **8, 6** rallying symbol; **9, 6** political symbol, religious symbol; **11, 4** directional ~, identifying ~. *See also* **signal, zodiac**

signal 3 cry, cue, dot, nod, SOS; **4** bell, call, dash, gong, hail, hint, honk, horn, mark, pips, sign, warn, wave; **5** alarm, alert, bleep, flare, imply, knell, light, shout, siren, timer; **6** alarum, beacon, beckon, herald, hooter, inform, motion, rocket, summon, wigwag; **7** bleeper *UK*, command, declare, foghorn, gesture, message, pointer, portend, publish, suggest, warning, whistle; **8** announce, balefire, doorbell, indicate *UK*, intimate, proclaim; **9** indicator *UK*, semaphore, signaling, stopwatch; **10**

heliograph, indication; **11** communicate, gesticulate; **13** manifestation; PHRASES: **3, 5** car alarm; **4, 3, 4** beat the drum, call for help; **4, 5** stop light, Very light; **4, 6** time switch *UK*, Very pistol; **5, 4** Morse code, watch fire; **5, 5** alarm clock, amber light, green light; **5, 6** smoke ~; **6, 3** minute gun; **6, 4** beacon fire, church bell, dinner gong, Lutine bell, wigwag flag; **6, 5** police siren; **6, 6** timing device; **7, 4** Angelus bell, sacring bell; **7, 5** burglar alarm, passing knell, traffic light; **7, 6** Belisha beacon *UK*; **8, 3** starter's gun, starting gun; **9, 6** telegraph ~. *See also* **danger signal**

signature *See* **name**

significance **4** pith; **5** drift, point, sense, trend, worth; **6** impact, import, moment, weight; **7** meaning, purport; **8** tendency; **9** magnitude, substance; **10** importance; **11** connotation, consequence, implication, seriousness.

significant **3** big; **5** hefty, large, major, meaty, pithy; **7** knowing, meaning, pointed, serious, sizable, weighty; **9** important, momentous; **10** expressive, meaningful, noteworthy, suggestive; **11** substantial; **12** considerable; **13** consequential; PHRASES: **2, 6** of moment.

signify **4** mean, show; **5** imply; **6** blazon, denote, reveal, signal, typify; **7** bespeak, betoken, connote, suggest; **8** disclose, indicate, intimate; **9** emphasize, highlight, represent, signalize, symbolize; **10** symptomize; **12** characterize; PHRASES: **2, 1, 4, 2** be a sign of; **4, 2** hint at; **4, 3, 5, 2** bear the stamp of; **4, 7, 2** bear witness to; **5, 2** smack of, smell of; **5, 3** stand for; **7, 2** witness to.

silence **2** sh; **3** gag; **4** calm, curb, hush, lull, mute, rest, stop; **5** drown, peace, quash, quell, quiet, shush, still; **6** muffle, muzzle, stifle, subdue; **7** aphonia, privacy, quieten *UK*, reserve, smother; **8** dumbness, muteness, quietude, softness, suppress; **9** clampdown, closeness, faintness, mutedness, quietness, reticence, solemnity, stillness; **10** discretion, laryngitis, quiescence, solemnness; **11** suppression, taciturnity; **12** inaudibility, wordlessness; **13** noiselessness, soundlessness, voicelessness; **14** speechlessness; **15** confidentiality; PHRASES: **3, 1, 5** not a sound; **3, 1, 6** not a squeak; **3, 2** can it; **3, 2, 3, 2** put an end to; **3, 3, 3, 2** put the lid on; **4, 2** shut up; **4, 4** play down; **4-5** soft-

pedal; **4, 7** dead ~; **7, 4** deathly hush.

silencer **4** cork, mute; **6** damper, filter; **7** sordino; **8** earplugs; **13** soundproofing; PHRASES: **4, 5** soft pedal; **6-7** double-glazing.

silent **3** mum; **4** calm, dumb, mute, soft; **5** aloof, awful, faint, muted, quiet, still, tacit; **6** hushed, solemn, stilly; **7** aphasic, aphonic; **8** peaceful, reserved, reticent, taciturn, unspoken, unvoiced, wordless; **9** deathlike, inaudible, noiseless, quiescent, soundless, unsounded, unuttered, voiceless, withdrawn; **10** soundproof, speechless, tongueless, understood, unsociable; **11** dumbfounded; **15** uncommunicative; PHRASES: **5, 2, 1, 4** quiet as a lamb; **5, 2, 1, 5** quiet as a mouse; **5-6** tight-lipped; **6, 2, 3, 4** ~ as the tomb; **6-4** tongue-tied; **7, 2** clammed up.

silent speech **7** Ameslan, gesture, signing; **9** semaphore, signaling; **13** gesticulation; PHRASES: **4, 8** body language, sign language; **10, 4** meaningful look.

silhouette **4** line; **5** shape; **6** shadow; **7** outline, profile.

silliness, silly *See* **stupid, stupidity**

silt **3** mud; **6** sludge; **7** deposit; **8** sediment.

silver **2** Ag; **4** Luna; **6** argent; **8** argentum.

similar **4** akin, like, near, same; **5** alike, close, quasi; **6** allied; **7** related, rhyming, uniform; **8** assonant, favoring, matching, parallel; **9** analogous, connected, following, homonymic, identical; **10** comparable, connatural, duplicated, equivalent, homophonic, resembling, synonymous; **11** approximate, homogeneous, homographic, homoiousian, symmetrical, synchronous; **12** alliterative, coincidental; **13** approximating, commensurable, corresponding; PHRASES: **2, 1, 5** of a piece; **3, 6** not unlike; **4, 2, 1, 8** much of a muchness; **4, 3, 4** much the same.

similar (be similar) *See* **resemble**

similarity **5** aping, match; **6** parity, simile; **7** analogy, copying, homonym, kinship, parable, seeming; **8** affinity, allegory, equality, homonymy, metaphor, parallel, suchlike, synonymy; **9** agreement, homograph, homophone, imitation, mimicking, portrayal, semblance; **10** accordance, comparison, conformity, connection, homoiousia, simulation, similitude, uniformity; **11** coincidence, duplication, equivalence, homogeneity, parallelism, resemblance; **12**

assimilation, relationship; **13** approximation, comparability, synchronicity; **14** correspondence; **15** proportionality; PHRASES:
3, 5, 2 the like(s) of; **4, 8** good likeness, near
likeness; **5, 8** close likeness; **6, 8** family
likeness. *See also* **similar**

similitude *See* **similarity**

simmer **4** boil, cook; **6** bubble, fester,
rumble, seethe.

simper **5** smirk, sneer; **7** grimace; PHRAS-
ES: **4, 4** smug look.

simple **3** dry, one; **4** bald, bare, easy, herb,
homy, meek, mere, neat, pure; **5** basic,
clean, clear, green, lowly, lucid, naive, naked, plain, sheer, sober, spare, stark, usual,
utter; **6** boring, chaste, common, direct, entire, homely, humble, limpid, modest, severe, single, stodgy, stupid; **7** artless,
ascetic, austere, classic, decoded, humdrum, legible, minimal, mundane, obvious,
popular, prosaic, regular, serious, Spartan,
tedious, uncoded, unfancy, unfussy, unified, uniform, unmixed; **8** backward, clinical, distinct, everyday, exoteric, explicit,
homespun, ordinary, pellucid, readable,
workaday; **9** apodictic, downright, elemental, explained, guileless, ingenuous, intrinsic, quotidian, unadorned, unalloyed,
unblended, undefiled, unevasive, unmin-
gled, unraveled, unworldly; **10** apodeictic,
articulate, effortless, elementary, forthright, monolithic, restrained, simplified,
unaffected, unassuming, uncombined, undramatic, unemphatic, uninflated, uninspired, uninvolved, unpoetical, vernacular;
11 commonplace, fundamental, homogeneous, indivisible, interpreted, irreducible,
perspicuous, popularized, transparent, uncluttered, undemanding, unelaborate; **12**
decipherable, disentangled, intelligible,
uncompounded; **13** unadulterated, uncomplicated, unimaginative, unintelligent, unpretentious, unsensational; **14**
comprehensible, unostentatious; **15**
straightforward, unsophisticated; PHRASES:
2, 5, 2, 3 as clear as day; **2, 6** no frills; **2, 6, 2,
3** as ~ as pie; **3, 2, 1, 5** all of a piece; **4, 2, 4**
easy to read; **4-2-5** down-to-earth; **4, 2, 6**
easy to follow; **4, 3, 6** pure and ~; **4-7** self-
evident; **4-11** self-explanatory; **5-3** clear-
cut; **6-2-4** matter-of-fact; **6, 7** garden variety; **7, 3** nothing but; **7-4** trouble-free; **7-5**
crystal-clear.

simple machine **5** lever, screw, wedge;
6 pulley; PHRASES: **4, 5** gear drive; **5, 3, 4**
wheel and axle; **5, 3, 6** block and tackle; **8, 5**
inclined plane; **9, 5** hydraulic press.

simplicity **4** ease; **5** idiom, prose; **6** candor, purity; **7** ascesis, bedrock, boredom,
clarity, dryness, essence, modesty, naiveté,
naivety *UK*, oneness; **8** baldness, bareness,
chastity, decoding, easiness, facility, glibness, humility, lucidity, meekness, neatness, severity; **9** austerity, cleanness,
clearness, homeyness, innocence, limpidity, lowliness, nakedness, plainness, precision, restraint, soberness, spareness,
starkness, usualness; **10** articulacy, asceticism, commonness, directness, facileness,
homeliness, humbleness, legibility, minimalism, simpleness, stodginess, uniformity, vernacular; **11** artlessness, austereness,
cleanliness, explanation, homogeneity,
mundaneness, obviousness, pellucidity,
perspicuity, preciseness, readability, seriousness, tediousness, unadornment, un-
fanciness, unfussiness; **12** absoluteness,
clinicalness, distinctness, explicitness, ordinariness, transparency; **13** amplification,
downrightness, guilelessness, ingenuousness, uninvolvement; **14** articulateness, effortlessness, forthrightness, indivisibility,
interpretation, popularization, simplification, superficiality, unaffectedness, unas-
sumingness; **15** decipherability,
intelligibility, unambiguousness, unelabo-
rateness; PHRASES: **5, 5** plain prose, plain
words; **5, 6** plain speech; **5, 7** plain English.

simplify **5** unify; **7** abridge, clarify, explain, shorten, unravel; **9** elucidate, explicate, interpret, predigest; **10** articulate,
facilitate, popularize, streamline, unscramble; **12** recapitulate; PHRASES: **3, 2, 5, 5** put in
plain words.

simply **4** just, only; **6** baldly, easily, humbly, meekly, merely, openly, purely, solely;
7 bluntly, cleanly, clearly, crudely, frankly,
naively, plainly, starkly; **8** candidly, directly, modestly; **9** artlessly, austerely, basically, minimally, naturally, obviously,
unfussily; **10** absolutely, innocently, undeniably; **11** guilelessly, ingenuously, prosai-
cally; **12** intelligibly, unassumingly; **13**
unelaborately; **14** undramatically, unquestionably; **15** unpretentiously; PHRASES: **2, 5,
5** in basic terms, in plain words.

simulate **3** ape; **4** copy, fake, sham; **5**
feign, mimic; **7** imitate, pretend, suggest; **9**
replicate, reproduce; PHRASES: **3, 2** put on.

simulated 4 aped, fake, mock, sham; PHRASES: 5 cyber-, false, phony *UK*; 6 copied, ersatz, mocked, phoney, pseudo; 7 pretend, virtual; 8 cultured, imitated, mimicked, spurious; 9 duplicate, imitation, imitative, synthetic; 10 artificial, duplicated, fabricated, replicated; 11 counterfeit.

simultaneous 6 coeval; 7 twinned; 9 coeternal, immediate; 10 coexistent, coexisting, coincident, coinciding, concurrent; 11 concomitant; 12 accompanying, coincidental, contemporary, synchronized; 13 instantaneous; 15 contemporaneous; PHRASES: 2, 3, 4, 3 of the same age; 2, 3, 4, 4 of the same year; 4-4 real-time.

sin 3 err, rob; 4 envy, evil, fall, lust, slip, tort, vice; 5 anger, crime, error, fault, lapse, pride, sloth, steal, wrong; 6 delict, felony, injury, kidnap, murder; 7 blunder, failure, impiety, misdeed, mistake, offense, outrage, sinning; 8 atrocity, enormity, gluttony, iniquity, misdoing, trespass; 9 blasphemy, depravity, injustice, sacrilege, turpitude; 10 debauchery, illegality, immorality, indulgence, misconduct, negligence, peccadillo, sinfulness, transgress, wickedness, wrongdoing; 11 assassinate, desecration, impropriety, malpractice, misbehavior, misdemeanor, naughtiness, profaneness, ungodliness; 12 covetousness, indiscretion; 13 transgression; PHRASES: 2, 2, 3, 3 go to the bad; 2, 2, 3, 4 go to the dogs; 2, 3, 6 be led astray; 2, 5 do wrong; 2, 6 go astray; 3, 2, 8 ~ of omission; 4, 3 faux pas; 4, 4, 5 fall from grace; 6, 3 deadly ~, mortal ~, venial ~; 6, 4 wicked deed; 7, 3 capital ~; 8, 3 original ~.

since 2 as; 3 ago, sin; 4 sith, syne, then; 5 later, while; 7 because; 9 meanwhile; 12 subsequently; PHRASES: 2, 3, 8 in the meantime; 5, 4 given that; 6, 2 seeing as.

sincere *See* **honest**

sinew 5 brawn, power, vigor; 8 strength; 11 muscularity.

sinful 3 bad; 4 evil; 6 deadly, errant, mortal, wicked; 7 corrupt, heinous, illegal, immoral, naughty, sinning; 8 aberrant, criminal, devilish; 9 murderous; 10 iniquitous; 11 trespassing; 13 transgressing.

sing 3 caw, coo, hum; 4 buzz, crow, honk, hoot, lilt, oink, peep, pipe, pule, purr, talk, whir; 5 carol, chant, cheep, chirp, chirr, clack, cluck, croon, flute, quack, trill, tweet, yodel; 6 cackle, chorus, gaggle, gobble, incant, intone, quaver, squawk, warble; 7 chatter, chirrup, chitter, chuckle, confess, descant, screech, twitter, vibrate, whistle; 8 resonate, serenade, vocalize; 9 harmonize; 11 reverberate, stoolpigeon; PHRASES: 3, 2 let on, own up; 4, 3 belt out; 4, 3, 4, 4 give the game away; 4, 4, 1, 4 ~ like a bird; 4, 5 come clean; 4, 8 ~ together; 5, 3, 5 spill the beans; 5, 4, 4 break into song.

singer 3 car; 4 alto, bard, bass, Bing, bird, Cher, diva, Ella, Lind, swan, wait; 5 Dylan, Elvis, hazan, Melba, Patti, siren, tenor, voice; 6 belter *UK*, Callas, canary, cantor, Caruso, chazan, Dawson, treble; 7 chanter, crooner, Domingo, gleeman, Robeson, Sinatra, soloist, soprano, warbler; 8 baritone, Carreras, castrato, falsetto, songster, vocalist; 9 balladeer, Chaliapin, chanteuse, chorister, Pavarotti, soubrette, succentor; 10 cantatrice, gleemaiden, songstress; 11 comprimario; PHRASES: 4, 6 lead ~; 4, 8 lead vocalist; 5, 6 torch ~; 7, 8 backing vocalist.

single 1 I, S; 3 one, run; 4 free, lone, only, sole, solo, song, unit; 5 alone, loner, track, unwed, widow; 6 chaste, record, thread, ticket; 7 release, widowed, widower; 8 bachelor, celibate, definite, distinct, divorced, divorcee *UK*, separate, solitary, specific, spinster, unwedded; 9 separated, singleton, unmarried; 10 particular, unattached; PHRASES: 2, 3, 3 on its own; 5, 5 light cream; 6, 4 maiden aunt, ~ bond, ~ file; 6, 5 ~ entry.

single-minded 3 set; 4 firm; 5 fixed, stern; 7 callous; 8 obdurate, resolute, stubborn, tireless; 9 committed, dedicated, obstinate; 10 determined, inflexible, unswerving, unwavering; 14 uncompromising; PHRASES: 4-4 hell-bent.

single out 6 choose, detach, select, target; 7 earmark, isolate; 8 identify, separate; 11 distinguish; 13 differentiate; PHRASES: 3, 5 set apart; 4, 2 pick on; 4, 3 pick out, pull out.

single person 4 bach, maid; 5 widow; 6 maiden, virgin; 7 divorcé, widower; 8 bachelor, debutant, divorcée, spinster; 9 exhusband; 10 misandrist, misogamist, misogynist; PHRASES: 3, 4 old maid; 5, 4 femme sole; 6, 3 single man; 6, 4 maiden aunt, maiden lady; 6, 6 single parent; 8, 4 bachelor girl; 9, 3 unmarried man; 9, 5 unmarried woman; 9, 6 unmarried mother.

sing out 4 yell; 5 chant, shout, yodel; 6

chorus; PHRASES: **4, 2** pipe up; **4, 3** belt out, call out; **5, 2** speak up; **5, 3** speak out.

singular 1 S; 3 odd, one; 6 unique; 7 curious, special, unusual; 8 distinct; 10 individual, particular, remarkable, unrepeated; 11 outstanding; 13 extraordinary; PHRASES: **3-3** one-off; **3, 3, 4** one and only; **5, 3, 4** first and last.

sinister 1 L; 4 evil, left, port; 5 black, shady; 6 louche, spooky; 7 baleful, ominous; 8 menacing; 9 insidious; 11 threatening; 12 inauspicious, unpropitious.

sink 3 bog, den, dig, dip, ebb, sag, tip; 4 bore, bowl, drop, dump, fall, flag, mine, slum, sump; 5 basin, drain, drill, lapse, sewer, slump, swamp; 6 cloaca, gutter, invest, midden, pigpen, pigsty *UK*, septic, settle, slough, worsen; 7 cesspit, cistern, compose, decline, descend, founder, immerse, scupper, scuttle, subside; 8 abattoir *UK*, cesspool, cuspidor, dunghill, landfill, shambles, soakaway *UK*, spittoon, submerge, tenement; 9 gravitate, washbasin; 10 quarantine; 11 deteriorate; PHRASES: **2, 4** go down; **2, 5** go under; **2, 8** go downward; **2, 9** be submerged; **4, 4** coal hole; **4, 5** hand basin; **6, 4** refuse dump, septic tank; **6, 7** Augean stables; **7, 4** kitchen ~; **8, 5** draining board.

sip *See* **drink**

siren 5 alarm, alert; 7 Lorelei, mermaid, warning; 9 temptress.

Sirius 6 Sothis; 8 Canicula; PHRASES: **3, 4** Dog Star.

sister 3 nun, sib, sis; 5 Minim, nurse.

sit 3 lie; 4 rest; 5 couch, hunch, perch, squat, stoop; 6 crouch; 7 convene, recline; 8 assemble, supinate; 9 prostrate; PHRASES: **2, 2, 7** be in session; **2, 6** be placed, be seated; **2, 8** be situated; **2, 10** be positioned; **4, 1, 3** take a pew; **4, 1, 4** take a seat; **4, 7** park oneself, seat oneself.

sitcom 4 MASH, Soap; 5 Maude; 6 Cheers; 7 Frasier, Friends; 8 Seinfeld, Simpsons; 10 Jeffersons; PHRASES: **1, 4, 4** I Love Lucy; **3, 2, 3, 6** All in the Family; **4, 3, 5** Will and Grace; **4, 5** Full House; **4, 8, 4** Andy Griffith Show; **6, 5** Golden Girls; **6, 6** Hogan's Heroes; **6, 7** Three's Company; **7, 3, 3** Sanford and Son; **7, 4, 8** Married With Children; **7, 11** Beverly Hillbillies.

site *See* **place**

sitting 7 hearing, meeting, session; PHRAS-ES: **5, 7** board meeting; **7, 4** S~ Bull, ~ duck, ~ room; **7, 6** ~ target *UK*, ~ tenant *UK*; **8, 7** business meeting; **10, 5** discussion group.

situate 3 fix, put, set; 4 post, site; 5 place, stand; 6 deploy, direct, locate; 7 install, station; 8 position; 9 establish, orientate; PHRASES: **3, 2** set up.

situate (be situated) 2 be; 3 lie, sit; 4 rest; 5 stand; PHRASES: **2, 7** be located.

situation 4 seat, side, site, spot; 5 place, point, scene, setup, state, venue; 6 aspect, locale, office; 7 scenery, setting; 8 altitude, bearings, frontage, latitude, locality, location, position, scenario; 9 condition, direction, geography, longitude; 10 topography; 11 orientation; 13 circumstances; PHRASES: **5, 2, 7** state of affairs; **6, 3** status quo.

six 2 VI; 5 hexad; 6 sextet, sixain *UK*; 7 hexadic, hexagon, hexapod, sextile, sixfold; 8 hexagram, sextuple; 9 hexachord, hexagonal, hexameter, Hexateuch, hexatonic, sexennial, sextuplet; 10 hexahedral, hexahedron, hexangular, sexagenary, sexpartite, threescore; 11 hexadecimal; 12 sexagenarian, sextuplicate; PHRASES: **3-6** six-footer; **3-7** six-shooter; **4-1-5** half-a-dozen; **5, 3** Jimmy Hix; **5, 4** sixth form *UK*, sixth part; **5, 5** sixth sense; **7, 5** Captain Hicks.

sixth sense 3 ESP; 5 hunch; 7 feeling, feyness, insight; 9 foresight, intuition, telepathy; 11 premonition, psychometry, telekinesis; 12 clairvoyance, precognition; 13 clairaudience, metapsychosis; 14 clairsentience; PHRASES: **3, 7** psi faculty; **5, 3** third eye; **5, 5** inner sense; **6, 5** second sight.

size 1 L, M, S; 2 OS, XL; 4 area, bulk, glue, mass, room; 5 depth, gauge, girth, limit, range, reach, scale, scope, space, value, width; 6 amount, burden, cubage, degree, dosage, extent, height, length, radius, spread, volume, weight; 7 azimuth, breadth, caliber, content, expanse, measure, stowage, tankage, tonnage; 8 abscissa, altitude, capacity, coverage, cubature, diameter, distance, latitude, ordinate, quantity; 9 amplitude, dimension, dimension(s), extension, longitude, magnitude, scantling; 10 proportion, proportion(s); 11 coordinates, declination, measurement, measurement(s); 12 displacement; 13 accommodation, circumference.

skeletal 4 bony, thin; 5 gaunt; 6 osteal, skinny, wasted; 7 osseous; 8 ossified; 9 emaciated, ossicular; 10 ossiferous; 14 undernourished.

skeleton 4 bone, horn, plan; **5** basic, bones, frame; **6** sketch, tendon; **7** carcass, keratin, minimal, minimum, ossicle, outline; **8** carapace, ligament; **9** cartilage, essential, framework, osteocyte; **10** osteoblast, osteoclast; **11** exoskeleton, preliminary; **12** chondroblast, endoskeleton, ossification; **13** chrondroblast; PHRASES: **4, 5** bare bones; **5, 8** axial ~.

skeptical 6 unsure; **7** cynical, dubious; **8** agnostic, doubtful, doubting, guessing; **9** uncertain; **10** hesitating, Pyrrhonist, scientific, suspicious; **11** conjectural, distrustful, incredulous, questioning, unconvinced; **12** disbelieving.

sketch 3 act; **4** draw, plan, skit; **5** draft, rough, scene; **7** drawing, outline; **9** delineate; PHRASES: **4-2** mock-up; **5, 2** block in; **5, 3** rough out; **5, 4** rough copy; **5, 5** rough draft; **5, 7** first attempt.

skew *See* **slant**

skewer 4 spit; **5** spear, spike; **6** impale, needle, pierce; **9** brochette.

skid 4 slew *UK*, slip, slue; **5** glide, slide; **7** slither; PHRASES: **4-5** jack-knife.

skiing 3 jet, ski; **4** boot, bump, jump, lift, poma, tuck, wall; **5** brake, ledge, loipe, mogul, piste, ridge, slope, slush; **6** aerial, anorak, basket, bubble, bucket, button, edging, gaiter, gloves, Schuss, weldel; **7** Abfahrt, binding, couloir, goggles, sidecut, skisuit, touring; **8** biathlon, christie, climbing, descente, Langlauf, motorway *UK*, porridge, sideslip, sidestep, snowplow, stemming, telemark, tramline, windslab; **9** avalement, cornering, funicular, gunbarrel, parablock, Steilhang, télésiège, washboard; **10** abonnement, Sesselbahn, sunglasses, traversing; **11** christiania, compression, herringbone, sidecutting, snowplowing, telemarking, unweighting; **12** birdsnesting, Luftseilbahn, sideslipping, sidestepping, téléphérique *UK*; **13** somersaulting; PHRASES: **1-3** I-ski; **1-3, 4** T-bar lift; **2-3** RS-ski; **3, 2, 4** ski du Fond; **3, 3** ski run, ski tow; **3-3** ski-tow; **3, 4** jet turn, ski jump, ski lift, ski pole; **3, 5** ski pants, ski slope, ski stick, toe piece; **3-5, 6** off-piste ~; **3, 6** ski jacket; **3-7** hot-dogging, ski-jumping; **4, 3** blue run; **4, 4** drag lift, jump turn, kick turn, star turn *UK*, stem turn, step turn; **4-4** fall-line; **4, 5** pole plant; **4, 8** stem christie; **4-11** down-unweighting; **5, 3** black run, cable car, green run; **5, 4** cabin lift, chair lift; **5, 5** bunny slope; **5, 6** bunny slopes, mogul ~; **5-6** speed-skiing, stunt-skiing; **6, 4** carved turn, hockey stop, powder snow; **6, 5** marked trail; **6, 6** alpine ~, nordic ~; **6, 8** uphill christie; **7, 4** gondola lift; **7, 5** moguled piste; **7, 8** reverse snowplow; **8, 3** straight run; **8, 4** pressure turn, rotation turn, scissors turn, snowplow turn; **8, 5** parallel swing; **8, 6** mountain ~, snowplow wedeln; **9, 6** acrobatic ~, freestyle ~; **10, 5** artificial slope; **11, 4** compression turn.

skill 3 art, use; **4** ease, grip, nous, tact; **5** craft, dodge, flair, forte, grace, knack, major, style, touch, trick; **6** finish, métier, talent; **7** ability, address, control, cunning, faculty, finesse, fluency, gimmick, mastery, prowess, tactics; **8** aptitude, artistry, capacity, deftness, delicacy, elegance, facility, goodness, neatness, sagacity, strength, wizardry; **9** adeptness, dexterity, execution, expertise, handiness, ingenuity, knowledge, sharpness, specialty, stratagem, technique; **10** adroitness, attainment, brilliance, capability, cleverness, competence, craftiness, discretion, efficiency, excellence, experience, expertness, mastership, perfection, specialism, speciality *UK*, suppleness, virtuosity; **11** acquirement, contrivance, flexibility, proficiency, versatility; **12** adaptability, exploitation, skillfulness; **13** ambidexterity, craftsmanship, dexterousness; **14** accomplishment, amphibiousness, discrimination, sophistication; **15** professionalism, resourcefulness; PHRASES: **5, 4** major suit; **5, 7** major subject; **6, 4** strong suit; **6, 5** clever hands, common sense, strong point; **6-5** savoirfaire; **7, 6** worldly wisdom.

skilled person 3 ace, dan; **4** diva, sage, seed, star; **5** adept; **6** expert, genius, master, wizard; **7** acrobat, athlete, dabster *UK*, gymnast, maestro, paragon, prodigy; **8** champion, exceller, graduate, handyman, musician, virtuoso; **9** craftsman; **10** mastermind; **11** craftswoman, prizewinner, titleholder; **12** intellectual; PHRASES: **2-2-10** do-it-yourselfer; **3-3** All-Pro; **3, 4** dab hand *UK*, top seed; **3-6** cup-holder; **3-7** all-rounder *UK*; **3-8** All-American; **4, 2, 3, 6** jack of all trades; **4, 4** dead shot; **4, 6** past master, star player; **4, 8** gold medalist; **5, 4** black belt, crack shot, white hope; **5, 5** prima donna; **5, 6** first fiddle; **5-6** first-string; **5, 8** world champion; **5, 9** prima ballerina; **6, 4** cordon bleu; **6, 8** bronze medalist, silver medalist; **7, 8** Olympic champion; **8, 6** lettered player; **11, 3** Renaissance man.

skillful 2 A1; **3** ace, apt; **4** able, deft, feat, good, neat, wise; **5** adept, agile, crack, handy, quick, ready, slick, smart, sound; **6** adroit, clever, crafty, expert, gifted, nimble, shrewd, superb, wizard; **7** cunning, natural, perfect, politic, skilled, stylish; **8** artistic, finished, flexible, masterly, panurgic, talented, topnotch; **9** adaptable, competent, dexterous, efficient, excellent, ingenious, masterful, practiced, sagacious, topflight, versatile; **10** diplomatic, proficient, scientific; **11** competitive, industrious, intelligent, magisterial, resourceful; **12** accomplished, ambidextrous, professional; **13** knowledgeable, statesmanlike; PHRASES: **3-5** top-level; **4, 2** good at; **4-5** many-sided; **4-6** sure-footed; **5-4** first-rate; **5-6** quick-witted; **5-8** green-fingered; **6-8** nimble-fingered; **6, 9** highly qualified.

skillful (be skillful) 5 excel, shine; **7** exploit; **12** discriminate; PHRASES: **2, 4** do well; **3, 6** get around; **3, 10** use skillfully; **4, 1, 4, 3** have a gift for; **4, 2, 4, 4** live by one's wits; **4, 5, 4** know what's what; **4, 9, 2** take advantage of; **6, 2** profit by.

skillfully 4 well; **10** swimmingly; PHRASES: **2, 4, 6** in one's stride; **4, 1, 6** like a master; **4, 1, 7** like a machine; **4, 2, 6** like an expert. *See also* **skillful**

skim 3 fly; **4** scan, soar; **5** float, glide; **6** browse; PHRASES: **5-4** speed-read; **6, 2** glance at.

skin 3 fur; **4** coat, fell, film, flay, hull, husk, pare, peel, pelt, rind; **5** crust, graze, scuff; **6** casing, cortex, scrape, sheath, tissue, veneer; **7** coating, cuticle; **8** covering, friction, membrane; **9** epidermis, excoriate; **10** desquamate; **11** exoskeleton; PHRASES: **4, 4** ~ game, ~ test; **4, 5** ~ diver, ~ flick, ~ graft; **4, 6** ~ diving.

skin disease 4 acne, cyst, itch, mole, rash, spot, wart, yaws; **5** hives, lupus, mange; **6** cowpox, eczema, herpes, macula, pimple, tetter; **7** blemish, blister, freckle, leprosy, prurigo, pustule, scabies, serpigo, variola, verruca; **8** albinism, eruption, erythema, impetigo, melanoma, miliaria, pockmark, pruritis, ringworm, shingles, smallpox, swelling, vitiligo; **9** birthmark, blackhead, frambesia, urticaria; **10** chickenpox, dermatitis, erysipelas, leucoderma,

leukoderma; **11** formication; PHRASES: **2, 8, 4** St Anthony's fire *UK*; **4, 4** heat rash; **4, 6** skin cancer, skin lesion; **5, 4** dhobi itch; **6, 4** nettle rash; **6, 6** herpes zoster; **7, 4** prickly heat; **8, 4** athlete's foot.

skinflint *See* **miser**

skinny *See* **thin**

skip 4 jump, leap, miss, omit; **5** caper, dance, frisk; **6** bypass, gambol, ignore, tittup; **8** overlook.

skirmish *See* **battle**

skirt 3 hug; **4** abut, duck, edge, kilt, line, maxi, midi, mini, tutu; **5** avoid, evade, lungi; **6** adjoin, border, bypass, circle, dirndl, kirtle, lungee, sarong; **7** filibeg *UK*; **8** basquine, neighbor, philibeg *UK*; **9** balayeuse, crinoline, overdress, overskirt; **10** fustanella, microskirt, wraparound; PHRASES: **1-4, 5** A-line ~; **2-2, 5** ra-ra ~ *UK*; **2, 6** go around; **4, 4** edge past, pass over, skim over; **4-4** lava-lava; **4, 5** full ~, hoop ~, slit ~; **5, 4** skate over *UK*; **5, 5** gored ~, grass ~, tight ~; **6, 5** ballet ~, empire ~, flared ~, hobble ~, pencil ~, sports ~, tennis ~; **7, 5** divided ~, evening ~, pleated ~; **8, 5** hawaiian ~, straight ~. *See also* **clothes**

skittish 4 edgy, wary; **5** jumpy; **6** frisky, lively, uneasy; **7** nervous, playful.

sky 4 blue; **5** azure, space, vault; **6** clouds, heaven, welkin; **7** heavens; **9** firmament; **10** atmosphere.

skyscraper 5 tower; PHRASES: **4-4** highrise; **5, 5** tower block *UK*.

slab 4 hunk, lump; **5** block, chunk, piece.

slack 3 lax; **4** idle, lazy, limp; **5** baggy, loose, shirk, skive; **6** casual, droopy, floppy, remiss, sloppy; **7** offhand; **8** careless, dilatory, malinger, slapdash, slovenly; **9** negligent; **13** lackadaisical.

slacken 4 ease, slow; **5** abate, loose, relax, remit; **6** lessen, loosen, reduce, weaken; **7** release, subside; **8** diminish, moderate; PHRASES: **3, 4** die down.

slacker 5 idler; **6** loafer, skiver *UK*; **7** laggard, lounger, shirker; **8** layabout; **10** freeloader, malinger, timewaster; **12** scrimshanker; PHRASES: **4, 5** gold brick; **4-7** lead-swinger; **5, 6** couch potato; **5-7** clockwatcher.

slackness 6 laxity; **10** negligence; **11** inattention. *See also* **slack**

slam *See* **criticize**

slander 4 slur; 5 smear; 6 insult, malign, slight; 7 calumny; 10 defamation; 13 disparagement.

slang 4 cant; 5 argot; 6 jargon; 7 dialect; 10 vernacular; 13 colloquialism; PHRASES: 3, 5 dog Latin, pig Latin; 4, 5 back ~; 5, 4 ~ term, ~ word; 7, 5 rhyming ~.

slant 3 tip; 4 bank, bias, cant, lean, list, skew, tilt; 5 angle, grade, pitch, slope, twist; 7 distort, incline; 8 attitude, diagonal, gradient; 9 viewpoint; 11 perspective; PHRASES: 5, 2, 4 point of view.

slap 3 hit; 4 blow, cuff; 5 clout, smack, spank, swipe.

slapdash 5 hasty, messy; 6 clumsy; 7 hurried; 8 careless.

slapstick 5 farce, humor; 6 comedy; 8 clowning; 9 burlesque; 10 knockabout; PHRASES: 7, 3 custard pie.

slash 3 cut, rip; 4 drop, gash, hack, slit, tear; 5 lower, slice; 6 reduce; 8 decrease; 10 laceration.

slattern 4 slag, slob; 6 sloven; 9 litterbug; PHRASES: 6, 4 litter lout *UK*.

slaughter 3 war; 4 beat, burn, duel, kill, nuke, rout, slay; 5 crush, purge; 6 battle, battue, defeat, hammer, murder, noyade, pogrom, poleax *UK*, ravage, scorch, thrash; 7 butcher, carnage, destroy, killing, poleaxe, trounce; 8 butchery, decimate, demolish, genocide, massacre; 9 bloodbath, ethnocide, holocaust, liquidate, overwhelm; 10 annihilate, decimation; 11 destruction, exterminate, liquidation; 12 annihilation; 13 extermination; PHRASES: 3, 2, 6 cut to pieces; 3, 2, 7 cut to ribbons; 3, 4 cut down, gun down, mow down; 3, 9 the Holocaust; 4, 3 wipe out; 4, 6 mass murder; 5, 4 shoot down; 5, 7 Roman holiday; 5, 8 Final Solution; 6, 9 ethnic cleansing; 8, 7 Sicilian Vespers.

slaughterhouse 8 abattoir, shambles; 12 packinghouse.

slave 4 serf; 5 Aesop, helot, Topsy; 6 drudge, thrall, vassal; 7 bondman, captive; 8 bondmaid, bondsman; 9 Androcles, bondwoman, Spartacus; 11 bondservant; PHRASES: 5, 3 ~ ant; 5, 4 ~ ship; 5-4 slave-girl; 5, 5 ~ coast, ~ state, ~ trade; 5, 6 acorn squash, ~ driver; 5, 8 ~ cylinder *UK*; 6, 5 galley ~.

slay *See* **kill**

sleazy 5 seedy; 6 grubby, sordid; 7 corrupt, immoral, squalid; 9 dishonest.

sled 4 drag, dray, luge, pung; 5 scoot; 6 hammer, jumper, sleigh, troika, weasel; 7 bobsled, dogsled; 8 toboggan; 9 Skimobile, snowboard; 10 bombardier, snowmobile; PHRASES: 3-3 Ski-Doo, Sno-Cat; 3-5 cattrain *Canada*.

sledge *See* **sled**

sleek *See* **smooth**

sleep 2 ZZ; 3 kip *UK*, nap; 4 coma, doss *UK*, doze, rest, yawn; 5 death; 6 catnap, drowse, repose, siesta, snooze, stupor, trance; 7 sandman, shuteye, slumber; 8 dormancy, doziness, hypnosis, Morpheus, oblivion; 9 aestivate *UK*, catalepsy, dreamland, heaviness, hibernate, oscitancy; 10 drowsiness, sleepiness, somnolence; 11 aestivation *UK*, hibernation; 12 nyctitropism; 13 insensibility; 15 unconsciousness; PHRASES: 2, 6 be asleep; 3, 3 nod off; 3-4 bye-byes *UK*; 3, 4, 4, 4 get one's head down; 3, 7 lie dormant; 4, 1, 3 take a nap; 4, 1, 3-4 have a lie-down *UK*; 4, 2, 3 land of Nod; 4, 5, 5 have forty winks *UK*; 5, 4, 1, 3 ~ like a log; 5, 5 forty winks, heavy ~, light ~.

sleeper 3 tie; 5 dozer; 7 drowser; 8 dormouse; 9 slumberer; 10 hibernator, sleepyhead; PHRASES: 3, 3, 6 Rip van Winkle; 3-4 lie-abed; 5, 6 Weary Willie; 8, 6 Sleeping Beauty.

sleepless 5 alert, ready; 6 active; 7 wakeful; 8 restless, vigilant; 9 attentive, disturbed; 10 unsleeping.

sleepy 4 dopy, dozy, dull, slow; 5 doped, dopey, fuzzy, quiet, tired, woozy; 6 boring, dozing, drowsy, torpid; 7 dormant, drugged, resting, sedated, yawning; 8 comatose, dreaming, inactive, peaceful, sluggish; 9 lethargic, somnolent, soporific; 10 hypnotized, insensible, narcotized, slumberous; 11 aestivating, hibernating, unconscious; 13 anaesthetized; PHRASES: 3, 4 out cold; 5-4 heavy-eyed.

sleeve 3 arm; 5 cover; 6 jacket, sheath; 7 armhole, wrapper; 8 envelope; PHRASES: 4, 5 dust cover; 4, 6 dust jacket; 5, 5 outer cover; 5, 6 gigot ~; 6, 6 bishop ~, dolman ~, Raglan ~; 7, 6 balloon ~, batwing ~, slashed ~; 10, 5 protective cover.

sleight of hand 5 bosey, curve, magic, skill; 6 googly *UK*; 7 cunning, wrong'un *UK*; 8 illusion, jugglery, juggling, trickery;

9 conjuring *UK*, curveball, dexterity; **10** adroitness, subterfuge, thimblerig; **11** conjuration, legerdemain; **13** ventriloquism; PHRASES: **5-4, 5** three-card trick *UK*; **5, 5** mumbo jumbo; **5-5** hocus-pocus.

slender *See* **slim**

sleuth **3** dog, spy; **4** tail; **5** snoop, stalk, track; **6** follow, pursue, shadow; **9** detective; **11** investigate; **12** investigator; PHRASES: **4, 3, 5** look for clues; **4, 4** hunt down; **4, 4, 6** look into things; **5, 4** track down; **5, 6, 3** check things out; **7, 3** private eye; **8, 6** Sherlock Holmes.

slice **3** cut; **4** chip, disc *UK*, disk *UK*, lath, pane, part, slab, slat, tile; **5** carve, flake, flock, panel, piece, plank, scale, scurf, shard, share, slate, wafer, wedge; **6** collop, divide, paring, plaque, rasher, sliver, squama, tablet; **7** floccus, portion, segment, serving, shaving; **8** dandruff, splinter; **10** percentage; PHRASES: **3, 2** cut up.

slick **4** glib; **5** shiny; **6** facile, glassy, glossy, smooth; **7** shallow; **8** polished, slippery; **9** efficient; **11** superficial; **12** professional; **13** untrustworthy.

slide **3** dip; **4** drop, fall, hill, list, skid, skim, slip, tilt; **5** coast, glide, skate, slope, swing, valve; **6** wobble; **7** incline, slidder, sliding, slither; **8** decrease, diminish, fastener, glissade, sideslip, slippage, toboggan, trombone; **9** acclivity, declivity, glissando, oscillate, precipice; **11** inclination; PHRASES: **2, 4** go down; **2, 7** be oblique; **5, 4** sheer drop, ~ rule; **5, 6** ~ guitar.

slight **4** slim, slur, snub, thin; **5** minor, scorn, small, smear; **6** feeble, insult, offend, rebuff; **7** affront, slender, trivial; **8** delicate; **11** unimportant; **13** insignificant.

slim **4** diet, lean, poor, thin, trim, wiry; **5** faint; **6** reduce, remote, slight, svelte; **7** slender; **8** unlikely; **10** slenderize; PHRASES: **2, 2, 1, 4** go on a diet; **4, 6** lose weight; **5, 4, 6** watch your weight.

slime **3** goo; **4** glop, gook, guck, gunk; **5** gunge *UK*, mucus, paste.

slimy **4** oily, oozy; **5** fluid, muddy, runny, snaky; **6** greasy, mucous, sludgy; **7** fawning; **8** slippery, toadying, unctuous; **10** obsequious, oleaginous; **12** ingratiating.

sling **3** lob; **4** hang, toss; **5** drape, fling, throw; **6** dangle; **7** suspend.

slip **3** err, sag; **4** chit *UK*, fall, flit, form, muff, skid, step, trip; **5** boner, creep, dress,

drift, error, gaffe, glide, lapse, skate, slide, slink, slope, sneak, steal; **6** docket, ticket, tumble; **7** blunder, fielder, mistake, skidder; slither, stumble; **8** glissade, omission, sideslip; **9** landslide, oversight, petticoat; **10** underskirt; PHRASES: **4-2** slip-up; **4, 3** faux pas; **4, 4** exit ramp; **4, 4, 7** lose your balance, lose your footing; **4, 5** ~ gauge; **4, 6** ~ stitch; **8, 4** Freudian ~.

slip back **3** ebb; **4** drop, fall, slip; **5** lapse; **6** return, revert; **7** decline, descend, relapse; PHRASES: **5, 4** slide back.

slipper **3** ski; **4** mule; **6** runner; **8** moccasin, toboggan; **9** pantoufle; PHRASES: **5, 4** house shoe.

slippery **3** fat, icy, lax; **4** free, oily, rich, waxy; **5** dodgy *UK*, fatty, fluid, lardy, loose, oleic, runny, slack, sleek, slick, slidy, slimy, soapy, suety; **6** crafty, glassy, greasy, liquid, mucoid, shifty, skiddy, slippy *UK*, smooth, sneaky, undone, watery; **7** adipose, buttery, crumbly, devious, friable, pinguid, relaxed, running, sliding, tallowy; **8** blubbery, nonstick, slithery, unctuous; **9** dishonest, sebaceous, streaming, unctional, unguinous; **10** lardaceous, oleaginous; **11** butyraceous, pinguescent, saponaceous; **12** pinguidinous; **13** untrustworthy; **14** unconsolidated.

slipshod **3** lax; **5** slack; **6** casual, remiss, sloppy; **7** hurried, offhand; **8** careless, heedless, slapdash, slovenly; **9** haphazard, negligent; **11** thoughtless; **12** disorganized; **13** lackadaisical.

slit **3** cut; **4** gash, nick, slot, tear; **5** slash; **7** opening.

sliver *See* **slice**

slog **4** drag, hike, plod, toil, trek, work; **5** grind, labor, trail, tramp; **6** effort, strain, trudge.

slope **3** tip; **4** drop, fall, hill, lean, ramp, rise, tack, tilt; **5** angle, grade, pitch, ridge, sheer, slant, sweep; **7** incline; **8** gradient.

sloppy *See* **slipshod**

slot **3** fit, gap; **4** hole, slip, slit, time; **5** niche, slide, space; **6** groove, insert, locate, period, window; **7** channel, opening; **8** aperture, position; **10** pigeonhole.

sloth *See* **laziness**

slouch **5** droop, idler, slump, stoop; **6** loafer, lounge, sprawl; **7** shirker, slacker; **10** freeloader.

slough 4 cast, molt, shed; 6 ecdyse; 8 exuviate; 10 desquamate.

slow 4 dull, late, poky, stem; 5 brake, largo, lento, tardy; 6 adagio, clumsy, gentle, poking, reduce, stupid; 7 ambling, andante, gradual, halting, languid, lengthy, limping, painful, relaxed, slacken, walking; 8 cautious, crawling, creeping, dawdling, dilatory, dragging, flagging, hobbling, indolent, measured, moderate, plodding, sluggish, waddling; 9 faltering, laborious, larghetto, leisurely, lingering, lumbering, reluctant, shambling, shuffling, slouching, strolling, tentative, tottering, unhurried; 10 decelerate, deliberate, languorous, protracted, sauntering, staggering; PHRASES: 4, 4 ~ burn, ~ time *UK*; 4, 5 ~ march; 4-5 easy-paced, slow-paced; 4, 6 ~ motion; 4-6 long-winded, slow-footed, slow-moving; 4-7 slow-running; 4, 8 ~ handclap *UK*; 4-9 time-consuming; 5-3 drawn-out; 5-4 snail-like; 5-5 snail-paced.

slow creature 4 slug; 5 sloth, snail; 8 tortoise; PHRASES: 6-6 creepy-crawly.

slow down 4 curb, reef, slow, stay; 5 brake, check, delay, relax; 6 arrest, detain, hinder, impede, retard; 7 regress, reverse; 8 moderate, obstruct; 10 decelerate; PHRASES: 3, 2 let up; 3, 4 set back; 4, 2 hold up, rein in, slow up; 4, 3 ease off; 4, 3, 5 clip the wings; 4, 4 draw rein, hold back, keep back; 4, 5 back water, lose speed; 4-5 back-pedal; 4, 6 lose ground; 4, 8 lose momentum; 6, 5 reduce speed; 7, 3 slacken off; 7, 4 shorten sail; 8, 4 throttle down.

slowly 4 idly, slow; 6 easily, lazily; 9 patiently; 13 circumspectly; PHRASES: 2, 1, 6, 4 at a snail's pace; 2, 7 by degrees; 3, 2, 3 bit by bit; 4, 2, 4 inch by inch, step by step; 6, 2, 6 little by little. *See also* **slow**

slow motion 3 jog; 4 limp, pace, plod, rack, trot, walk; 5 amble, crawl, creep; 6 dawdle, hobble, slouch, stroll, trudge, waddle; 7 dogtrot, piaffer, saunter, shamble, shuffle; 8 creeping, dragging, slowness; 9 lumbering, pottering; PHRASES: 3, 4 jog trot, low gear; 6, 4 snail's pace; 6-4 single-foot; 7, 5 mincing steps; 9, 4 leisurely gait, tortoise's pace.

slowness 3 jog; 4 limp, plod, trot, walk; 5 amble, crawl, sloth; 6 dawdle, hobble, slouch, stroll, trudge, waddle; 7 inertia, languor, piaffer, saunter, shamble, shuffle; 8 creeping, dragging, laziness, lethargy, pa-

tience; 9 Fabianism *UK*, indolence, inertness, lentitude, lumbering, pottering, restraint, slackness; 10 gradualism; 12 deliberation; 14 circumspection, methodicalness, meticulousness; PHRASES: 2, 5 no hurry; 4, 2, 5 lack of haste, time to spare; 7, 4 wasting time; 7, 5 festina lente. *See also* **slow**

slow person 4 slug; 5 drone, idler, sloth, snail; 6 dawdle; 7 dawdler, laggard, plodder, slacker; 8 lingerer, loiterer, sloucher, slowpoke, sluggard, tortoise; 9 slowcoach; 10 sleepyhead; 14 procrastinator; PHRASES: 4-3 goof-off; 4, 5 gold brick; 4, 7 slow starter; 4-7 foot-dragger; 5-2-3-3 stick-in-the-mud.

slowworm 9 blindworm.

sludge *See* **mud**

slug 3 hit; 4 blow, down, gulp, shot; 5 punch, shell, thump; 6 bullet, pellet, strike; 7 swallow; 9 cartridge.

sluggish 4 slow; 8 inactive, listless, slothful; 9 lethargic.

sluice 4 hose, race, wash; 5 clean, drain, flush, rinse; 6 gutter; 7 channel, conduit.

slumber 3 nap; 4 doze, rest; 5 sleep; 6 drowse, torpor; 7 inertia; 10 inactivity.

slump 4 fall, sink; 5 crash; 6 tumble; 7 decline, plummet; 8 collapse, decrease; 9 recession.

slur 5 blend, smear, speak, stain; 6 demean, insult, slight; 7 overlap, overrun; 8 besmirch, disgrace; PHRASES: 3, 8 run together.

sly 3 fly; 4 arch, foxy, wary, wily, wise; 5 acute, cagey, canny, nifty, pawky, sharp, slick, slier, smart; 6 artful, astute, clever, covert, crafty, feline, secret, shifty, shrewd, sliest, sneaky, subtle, tricky, urbane; 7 crooked, cunning, devious, evasive, furtive, knavish, knowing, tricksy, vulpine; 8 cautious, guileful, planning, plotting, rascally, reserved, reticent, scheming, skillful, slippery, stealthy, tactical; 9 beguiling, deceitful, dishonest, equivocal, ingenious, insidious, insincere, inventive, sophistic(al), underhand; 10 conspiring, contriving, flattering, intriguing, perfidious, practicing, serpentine; 11 calculating, clandestine, experienced, imaginative, intelligent, resourceful, strategical, temporizing, timeserving; 12 disingenuous, hypocritical; 13 knowledgeable, Machiavellian, sophisticated, surreptitious.

smack 3 hit; 4 bite, blow, cuff, slap, tang, wham; 5 clout, imply, savor, spank, taste, whack; 6 flavor, heroin; 7 suggest; PHRASES: 2, 11, 2 be reminiscent of; 4, 2 hint at; 4, 4 look like; 5, 4 sound like; 6, 2 remind of.

small 3 fry, wee; 4 baby, mini, poky *UK*, tiny; 5 minor, petty, tight; 6 lesser, little, meager, minute, paltry, petite, slight; 7 trivial; 8 trifling; 9 miniature, minuscule; 10 diminutive, negligible, undersized; 11 unimportant; 13 infinitesimal, insignificant; PHRASES: 5, 4 ~ arms, ~ beer, ~ slam, ~ talk; 5, 5 ~ hours; 5, 6 ~ change; 5, 9 ~ intestine.

small (become smaller) 4 diet, knit, slim, thin; 5 waste, wizen; 6 huddle, lessen, narrow, pucker, reduce, shrink, wither; 7 deflate, implode, shorten, shrivel, tighten, wrinkle; 8 collapse, condense, contract, decrease, emaciate; 9 telescope; 11 concentrate; PHRASES: 4, 2 curl up, draw in, fall in, fold up, roll up; 4, 2, 4, 1, 4 roll up into a ball; 4, 4 boil down; 5, 3 wane level off; 4, 6 lose weight; 5, 2 close up; 5, 4 waste away; 5, 8 crowd together; 6, 2 pucker up; 6, 3 bottom out; 7, 2 shrivel up.

smaller (make smaller) 3 cut, jam; 4 clip, cram, dock, draw, file, hush, knit, sear, slim, thin, trim, tuck; 5 clamp, cramp, crush, grind, limit, lower, pinch, press, prune, purse, shave, shear, slash, smock, stunt, waste; 6 clench, dilute, gather, lessen, narrow, precis, pucker, reduce, retard, scrape, shrink, weaken; 7 abridge, compact, curtail, deflate, degrade, depress, flatten, implode, quieten, shorten, shrivel, squeeze, tighten, whittle, wrinkle; 8 belittle, collapse, compress, condense, contract, decrease, downsize, emaciate, enfeeble, minimize, mitigate, restrict, retrench, strangle; 9 alleviate, constrict, downgrade, economize, extenuate, preshrink, Sanforize™, telescope; 10 abbreviate, constringe, debilitate, decelerate, impoverish, undervalue; 11 concentrate, miniaturize, rationalize, strangulate; 12 circumscribe; 13 underestimate; PHRASES: 3, 4 cut back, cut down, run down; 4, 2 draw in, roll up, take in; 4, 2, 4, 1, 4 roll up into a ball; 4, 3 thin out, weed out; 4, 4 boil down, pare down, play down, roll back, slow down, turn down; 4, 6 lose weight; 4, 8 draw together; 5, 2 close up; 5, 4 scale down, water down; 6, 2 pucker up; 6, 5 reduce speed; 7, 4 whittle away.

smallholding *See* **farm**

smallpox 7 variola; 8 alastrim.

small thing 3 elf, few, ion, tad, tot; 4 atom, drib, mite, runt, whit; 5 grain, pigmy, pinky, skosh, trace; 6 bantam, denier, insect, minnow, minute, pinkie, shrimp, tittle; 7 handful, modicum, smidgen, smidgin, soupcon, tiddler *UK*; 8 pittance; 9 miniature, scintilla; 10 centesimal; PHRASES: 4-4 half-pint.

smart 3 hip; 4 burn, chic, hurt, neat, rude, tidy; 5 brisk, chafe, money, natty, prick, quick, rapid, ritzy, sharp, sting, throb; 6 brainy, bright, clever, dapper, glitzy, lively, speedy, swanky, tingle, trendy; 7 dashing, elegant, prickle, stylish, voguish; 8 insolent, vigorous; 9 energetic, facetious, glamorous, sarcastic; 11 fashionable, impertinent, intelligent; 13 disrespectful; PHRASES: 4-6-3 well-turned-out *UK*; 4-7 well-dressed, well-groomed; 5, 3 ~ set; 5, 4 ~ card; 5, 5 ~ aleck.

smash 4 bang, blow, chop, kick; 5 break, crash, punch; 6 crunch, pileup, volley; 7 shatter; 8 accident; 9 collision.

smashing *See* **wonderful**

smear 4 blot, coat, daub, mark, slur, wipe; 5 cover, stain, sully; 6 blotch, insult, slight, smudge, spread; 7 affront, slander, tarnish; 8 besmirch, disgrace; 9 discredit.

smell 4 feel, nose, odor, pong *UK*, reek; 5 aroma, scent, sense, smack, sniff, snuff, stink, taste, whiff *UK*; 6 inhale, stench; 7 bouquet, breathe, perfume, sniffle, snuffle, suggest, suspect; 9 fragrance; PHRASES: 2, 8, 2 be redolent of; 3, 1, 5, 2 get a whiff of; 3, 4, 2 get wind of; 4, 3 nose out; 5, 2 ~ at, sniff at; 5, 3 ~ out, sniff out; 6, 3, 5 follow the scent; 6, 4, 4 follow one's nose.

smell (sense of smell) 4 beak, conk, nose; 5 herbs, naris, sniff, snoot, snout; 6 hooter, nosing, spices; 7 nostril, smeller, sniffle; 8 smelling, sniffing, snuffler; 9 olfaction, proboscis, schnozzle; 10 bloodhound, inhalation; PHRASES: 4, 4 good nose, keen nose; 5, 6 nasal cavity; 7, 3 sniffer dog *UK*; 8, 5 smelling salts; 8, 6 smelling bottle; 9, 5 olfactory nerve.

smell (unpleasant smell) 4 dung; 5 decay, sewer, skunk, sweat, urine; 6 flatus, garlic, sewage; 7 ammonia, armpits, cesspit, latrine, polecat, stinker; 8 cesspool, stinkard; 9 asafetida, dogbreath, excrement, halitosis, rancidity, stinkhorn; **10** corruption; **11** putrescence; **12** putrefaction; **13** decomposition; PHRASES: **3, 6** bad breath; **3, 9** air pollution; **4, 4** body odor (BO), sour milk; **5, 4** billy goat; **5-4** stink-bomb; **6, 3** rotten egg; **6, 6** strong cheese; **6, 7** boiled cabbage; **7, 5** exhaust fumes; **7, 7** sulphur dioxide; **8, 7** hydrogen sulfide; **9, 5** cigarette smoke.

smelt **4** cast, flux, melt; **5** found; **7** liquefy.

smile **4** beam, crow, grin, leer, purr, sing; **5** laugh, smirk, sneer; **6** giggle, guffaw; **7** chortle, chuckle, rejoice.

smirk **4** grin, leer; **5** sneer; **6** simper.

smite *See* **hit**

smoke **3** cig, fag *UK*; **4** burn, cure, drag, draw, pipe, puff, smog, tree; **5** bogue, fumes; **6** biogas, inhale; **7** smolder; **8** firedamp; **9** chokedamp; PHRASES: **2, 2, 4** be on fire; **5, 4** ~ bomb; **5-5** chain-smoke; **5, 6** ~ screen.

smoky **4** gray, hazy; **5** foggy, misty, murky; **6** cloudy, opaque, smoggy, steamy; **7** smoking; **8** steaming, vaporing; PHRASES: **5-6** smoke-filled.

smolder **4** burn, fume, glow, lurk; **5** smoke; **6** fester, glower, linger, rumble, seethe; **7** persist.

smooth **3** cut, mow, oil, rub, wax; **4** bald, buff, calm, coat, comb, easy, even, fine, flat, glib, iron, oily, pave, rake, roll, sand, soft, waxy; **5** allay, charm, clean, downy, emery, flush, furry, glacé, glaze, gloss, level, paint, plane, plush, press, satin, shave, shine, shiny, silky, sleek, slick, slimy, still, suave, toady, wooly; **6** butter, carded, combed, creepy, finish, fleecy, flossy, fluffy, glassy, glossy, grease, greasy, harrow, mangle, pacify, plushy, polish, satiny, silken, smarmy, soothe, starch, Tarmac *tm*, urbane, velvet, woolly; **7** appease, assuage, brushed, burnish, cottony, flatten, flowing, groomed, launder, overlay, planish, refined, shorten, unravel, unrough, varnish, velvety; **8** calender, charming, feathery, glabrous, hairless, levigate, lustrous, mitigate, slippery, slithery, smoothed, smoothen, uncrease, unctuous; **9** alleviate, Astroturf™, efficient, lubricate, peachlike, sandpaper, satinlike, smoothing; **10** ameliorate, effortless, flocculent, horizontal, persuasive, streamline, velvetlike; **11** streamlined, sycophantic; **12** frictionless, ingratiating; **13** nonfrictional, sophisticat-

ed; PHRASES: **3, 4** rub down; **3-5** hot-press; **4, 3** iron out; **4, 4** file down; **4-5** fine-woven; **5, 4** slick down; **5-5** close-woven; **5-6** cleanshaven; **6, 3** ~ out; **6, 4** ~ down; **6-6** smoothhaired; **6-7** silver-tongued, smooth-skinned; **7, 4** flatten down, plaster down.

smoother **4** card, comb, file, iron, rake; **5** brush, plane, press, waxer; **6** buffer, harrow, mangle, roller, sander, trowel; **7** chamois, wringer; **8** flatiron, nailfile; **9** bulldozer, burnisher, drawknife, flattener, hairbrush, sandpaper; **10** glasspaper, spokeshave *UK*; **11** steamroller; PHRASES: **3, 5** hot press; **5, 5** emery board, emery paper; **5, 8** floor polisher; **6, 6** garden roller; **7, 3** rolling pin; **7, 5** tailor's goose, trouser press; **9, 4** smoothing iron.

smooth-mannered **4** glib; **5** sleek, slick, suave; **6** creepy, smarmy, urbane; **8** unctuous; **11** sycophantic; **12** ingratiating; **13** sophisticated; PHRASES: **4-8** well-mannered; **6-6** smooth-spoken *UK*.

smoothness **4** calm, ease, help; **5** charm, shine; **6** finish, luster; **7** freedom; **8** serenity; **9** lubricity; **10** assistance, efficiency, levigation, plushiness, quiescence, regularity, uniformity; **11** flocculence, lubrication, velvetiness; **12** peacefulness; **13** horizontality; PHRASES: **4, 2, 9** lack of hindrance; **4, 4** dead calm. *See also* **smooth**

smooth over **4** calm, ease; **5** allay, charm, toady; **6** defuse, pacify, soothe; **7** appease, assuage, resolve; **8** mitigate; **9** alleviate; **10** ameliorate, ingratiate; PHRASES: **4, 2, 2** suck up to *UK*; **4, 3** iron out, sort out; **5, 2** clear up; **6, 3** smooth out.

smooth thing **3** ice; **4** down, hair, lawn, silk; **5** chute, glass, ivory, plain, satin, slide; **6** desert, marble, mirror, paving, Tarmac *tm*, velour, velvet; **7** asphalt, slipway; **8** mahogany, millpond; **9** alabaster, Astroturf *tm*, flagstone, velveteen; PHRASES: **3, 4** ice rink *UK*; **4, 4** bald head; **4, 5** calm water, dead water; **5-4** swan's-down; **5, 5** dance floor; **5, 6** baby's bottom, plumb wicket; **6, 5** tennis court; **7, 5** bowling alley, bowling green; **8, 4** billiard ball; **8, 5** billiard table; **10, 4** artificial turf.

smother **5** choke; **6** stifle; **7** oppress, repress; **8** restrain, suppress; **9** overpower, overwhelm, suffocate; **10** asphyxiate.

smudge **4** blot, blur, mark; **5** smear, stain; **6** blotch, smirch; **7** distort, splodge *UK*.

smut **4** dirt, soot; **5** filth, grime; **6** smudge;

7 erotica; **9** obscenity; **11** pornography.

SN 3 tin.

snack 4 bite, gorp, nuts, tapa; **5** butty *UK*, chips, fries, taste; **6** brunch, canapé, olives; **7** nibbles *UK*, peanuts, rarebit; **8** pretzels, sandwich, twiglets™; **11** refreshment; PHRASES: **4, 4** snow cone; **4, 5** pork rinds; **6, 4** salted nuts; **6, 5** potato chips; **6, 6** cheese straws.

snaffle *See* **steal**

snag 3 rip; **4** halt, stop, tear; **5** catch, hitch; **6** holdup, hurdle; **7** impasse, pitfall, problem; **8** deadlock, drawback, obstacle, stoppage; **9** annoyance, hindrance, stalemate; **10** difficulty, standstill; **11** aggravation, obstruction; **12** complication; **13** inconvenience; PHRASES: **2-2, 4** no-go area; **3-2-3** cul-de-sac; **3, 3** log jam; **4, 3** dead end; **5, 4** blank wall; **5, 5** blind alley.

snake 3 Kaa; **4** bend, naga, turn, wind; **5** cheat, hydra, Judas, sneak *UK*, twist, viper; **7** meander, Ophidia, serpent, traitor, twister; **8** betrayer, ophidian, turncoat; **9** Serpentes; **10** cockatrice; PHRASES: **6-7** double-crosser. *See also* **reptiles**

snaky 5 bendy *UK*, windy *UK*; **7** anguine, coiling, sinuous, winding; **8** twisting, viperish; **9** colubrine, zigzagged; **10** meandering, serpentine; **11** colubriform; **12** serpentiform.

snap 3 nip; **4** bark, bite, yell; **5** break, crack, shout; **6** retort, sudden; **7** instant; **9** impulsive; **11** spontaneous; PHRASES: **4, 3** give way.

snap fastener 6 popper.

snappy 4 chic, curt, fast; **5** brisk, hasty, quick, rapid, sharp, smart; **6** lively, speedy; **7** elegant, stylish; **9** irritable; **11** fashionable, stimulating; PHRASES: **2, 3, 5** to the point; **3-8** bad-tempered; **5-8** short-tempered.

snare 3 fly, gin, jig, nab, net, pit, web; **4** bait, hook, lime, lure, mesh, mine, nick, plug, trap, trip; **5** catch, decoy, lasso, noose; **6** ambush, cobweb, divert, entrap, hijack, kidnap, tangle, waylay; **7** capture, dragnet, ensnare, ensnarl, flytrap, pitfall; **8** birdlime, deadfall, entangle, flypaper, shanghai, tripwire; **9** deathtrap, diversion, hijacking, mousetrap; **10** kidnapping; **11** shanghaiing; PHRASES: **4, 2** hook in, trip up; **4, 4** lime twig, mole trap, trap door; **4-4** fish-hook; **5, 3** pound net; **5, 4** booby trap; **6, 3** spring gun.

snarl *See* **growl**

snatch 4 grab, nick *UK*, take; **5** filch, grasp, pinch, seize, steal.

snazzy *See* **flashy**

sneak 4 slip, tell; **5** creep, slink, steal, thief; **6** tiptoe; **7** preview.

sneer at *See* **scorn**

sneeze 5 sniff, snort; **7** sniffle, snuffle; **8** splutter.

snicker 4 bray, mock; **5** laugh, neigh, smirk, sneer, snort; **6** deride, whinny; **7** snuffle.

snide 4 mean; **9** malicious, sarcastic; **10** unpleasant.

sniff 5 scent, smell, snort; **6** breath, inhale; **7** breathe, lungful, snuffle.

snip 3 cut; **4** nick *UK*, trim; **5** shear, slice.

snitch 3 rob; **4** tell; **5** sneak *UK*, steal, swipe; **6** pilfer; **7** tattler; **8** informer, telltale; **10** tattletale; PHRASES: **4, 5** tell tales.

snivel 3 cry, sob; **4** weep; **5** sniff; **7** whimper.

snooker 4 balk, dash, foil, stop; **5** frame; **6** colors, hinder, stymie, thwart; **8** obstruct; **9** frustrate, stringing; **10** circumvent; PHRASES: **1, 4** D area; **3, 4** cue ball, red ball, the spot; **3, 4, 2** put paid to *UK*; **3, 6** top pocket; **4, 4** balk line, balk spot, blue ball, free ball, pink ball; **5, 4** black ball, brown ball, green ball, white ball; **6, 4** center spot, yellow ball; **6, 6** bottom pocket, center pocket; **7, 1, 4** potting a ball; **7, 4** pyramid spot.

snoop 3 spy; **5** sneak; **7** meddler; **8** intruder; **12** eavesdropper; PHRASES: **4, 6** poke around.

snooty 4 posh; **6** select; **8** snobbish; **9** exclusive; **12** supercilious; **13** condescending; PHRASES: **4, 3, 6** high and mighty; **5-5** hoity-toity.

snooze *See* **nap**

snout 4 nose; **6** muzzle; **9** proboscis.

snow 4 melt, thaw; **5** crack, frost, sleet, slush; **6** flurry, freeze; **7** cocaine, meltage, snowman; **8** blizzard, snowball, snowfall, whiteout; **9** avalanche, hailstone, meltwater, snowdrift, snowflake, snowstorm, spindrift; PHRASES: **3, 4** ice over, wet ~; **4, 3** ~ bed; **4, 5** ~ cover, S~ Queen; **4, 6** ~ shower; **6, 2, 4** mantle of ~; **6, 4** driven ~; **7, 2, 4** blanket of ~; **7, 4** powdery ~.

snowball *See* **increase**

snow leopard 5 ounce.

snub 6 ignore, rebuff, rebuke, slight; 9 rejection; 12 coldshoulder.

snuff 4 kill; 5 douse; 7 abolish, destroy; 9 eliminate; 10 extinguish; PHRASES: 3, 3 put out; 4, 3 blow out.

snug 4 cozy, warm; 5 close, tight; 6 homely; 11 comfortable; PHRASES: 4-7 well-fitting; 5-7 close-fitting.

so 3 sic; 4 ergo, thus; 5 argal, hence; 7 thereby; 9 therefore.

soak 3 wet; 5 steep; 6 drench, infuse; 7 immerse; 8 marinate, saturate.

soaking 4 soak; 5 souse; 6 drench, soaked, sodden; 7 ducking, dunking, soakage, sopping, sousing; 8 drenched, drowning, flooding, leaching, wringing; 9 drenching, immersion, saturated; 10 imbruement, inundation, permeation, saturation, submersion; 11 lixiviation, percolation, waterlogged; PHRASES: 3, 7 wet through; 4, 1, 7, 3 like a drowned rat; 6, 2, 3, 4 soaked to the skin; 7, 3 ~ wet, sopping wet; 8, 3 wringing wet.

soap 4 suds, wash; 5 amole; 6 lather, serial, series; 7 bubbles, castile, cleanse, program, shampoo; 8 cleanser, metallic, sanitize, soapsuds; 9 detergent, disinfect, sterilize; PHRASES: 3, 4 Joe S~ *UK*; 4, 4 soft ~, wash down; 4, 5 ~ opera; 4, 6 ~ powder; 5, 4 sugar ~ *UK*; 6, 4 saddle ~, toilet ~; 7, 6 washing powder *UK*.

soapberry 10 chinaberry.

soapstone 8 steatite.

soar 3 fly; 4 rise; 5 arise, climb, mount, wheel; 6 ascend, circle, rocket; 8 escalate; 9 skyrocket; PHRASES: 2, 3-4 go sky-high; 5, 2 shoot up.

sob 3 cry; 4 bawl, blub *UK*, fret, gasp, howl, keen, mewl, moan, pule, sigh, wail, weep; 5 groan, story, stuff, whine; 6 lament, sister, snivel, yammer; 7 blubber, sniffle, ululate, whimper; PHRASES: 4, 5 shed tears.

sober 3 dry; 4 calm, drab, dull; 5 grave, plain, sound, staid; 6 dreary, sedate, severe, solemn, somber, steady, strict; 7 serious, subdued; 8 cautious, composed, moderate, rational, sensible, teetotal, teetotal (TT); 9 abstinent, dignified, judicious, temperate, unexcited, unfuddled, unruffled; 10 abstemious, restrained, thoughtful; 11 nondrinking; 13 unintoxicated; 14 prohibitionist;

PHRASES: 2, 3, 5 on the wagon; 3, 5 off drink; 3-8 tea-drinking; 5, 2, 1, 5 ~ as a judge; 5-4, 5 stone-cold ~; 5-6 clear-headed, level-headed.

sober person 9 abstainer, nonaddict, Rechabite *UK*; 10 nondrinker, teetotaler; 12 nonalcoholic; 14 prohibitionist; PHRASES: 3, 4, 2, 4 the Band of Hope; 3, 7 tea- drinker; 5-7 water-drinker; 6, 7 social drinker; 8, 7 moderate drinker.

sobriety 4 calm; 7 gravity; 9 soberness, solemnity, staidness; 10 abstinence, moderation, sedateness, somberness, temperance; 11 seriousness, teetotalism; 14 abstemiousness, thoughtfulness; PHRASES: 2, 8 no hangover; 3, 8 tea- drinking; 5, 2, 8 state of ~; 5, 4 clear head; 5-8 water-drinking; 5-10 clearheadedness; 9, 5 unfuddled brain.

sobriquet *See* **nickname**

so-called *See* **supposed**

soccer 2 FA *UK*; 3 net; 4 FIFA, foul, game, goal, head, kick, miss, pass, push, save, stab, trap, trip; 5 flick, match, parry, pitch, point, score, shoot; 6 handle, onside, strike, tackle; 7 fouling, heading, kicking, kickoff, offside, passing, penalty, playoff, pushing, reserve, scoring, smother; 8 crossbar, dribbled, foosball, handball, handling, indirect, midfield, parrying, shinpads, shooting, striking, tackling, trapping; 9 advantage, dribbling, perimeter, touchline; 10 scoreboard; PHRASES: 3-3 one-two; 3-4, 3 six-yard box *UK*; 4, 4 back pass, free kick, goal area *UK*, goal kick, goal line, goal post, left half, wall pass *UK*, wing half; 5-2 throw-in; 5, 3 World Cup; 5, 4 right half; 6, 4 corner area, corner flag, corner kick *UK*, inside left; 6, 5 inside right; 6, 6 center circle; 7, 4 halfway line, outside left, penalty area, penalty spot; 7, 5 outside right; 8, 3 European Cup; 8, 6 Football League; 11, 8 Association Football. *See* **football**

sociability 5 cheer; 6 gaiety, warmth; 7 jollity, revelry, sharing; 8 civility, fratting, intimacy; 9 communion, enjoyment, festivity, geniality, joviality, merriment, partaking, sociality; 10 affability, amiability, consorting, cordiality, hobnobbing, membership; 11 affiliation, amicability, association, Bohemianism, cooperation, familiarity, hospitality, intercourse, merrymaking, relaxedness; 12 congeniality, consociation, conversation, conviviality; 13 communication, compatibility, hospitability, participation; **14** fraternization, inter-communion. *See also* **sociable**

sociable 4 easy, kind, open, warm; **5** civic, civil, jolly, matey *UK*, merry, pally, witty; **6** clubby, common, genial, hearty, jovial, lively, public, social, urbane; **7** affable, amiable, amusing, cordial, relaxed, smiling; **8** amicable, Bohemian, charming, cheerful, clubbish, communal, friendly, gracious, inviting, outgoing, pleasant; **9** convivial, courteous, extrovert, welcoming; **10** collective, gregarious, hospitable, neighborly; **11** charismatic; **12** affectionate; **13** communicative, companionable; PHRASES: **4, 2, 7** fond of company; **4-3-4** free-and-easy; **4-5** easy-going; **4, 7** good company; **5-6** party-minded; **6-6** social-minded.

sociable (be sociable) 3 hug, mix; **4** host; **5** share, toast; **6** invite, mingle, pledge; **7** embrace, preside, welcome; **8** freeload, interact; **9** circulate, entertain, volunteer; **11** participate; PHRASES: **2, 2, 1, 5** go on a spree; **2, 3** go out; **2, 3, 2, 3, 4** go out on the town; **2, 3, 6** do the honors; **2, 5** go Dutch; **2, 8** go clubbing, go partying; **3, 4** mix with; **3, 5** get about; **3, 8** get together; **4, 2** join in; **4, 3** dine out; **4, 4, 5** keep open house; **4-5** gate-crash; **5, 1, 5** throw a party; **5, 2** drink to; **5, 3, 4, 3** paint the town red; **6, 4** mingle with; **7, 4** consort with; **9, 4** associate with.

social 2 do; **4** work; **5** group, party; **6** common, public, shared; **7** climber, science, studies, welfare; **8** communal, security, services, societal; **9** community, gathering, secretary; **10** collective; PHRASES: **3-8** get-together.

social activity 5 hobby; **6** mixing; **7** pastime, pursuit, venture; **8** interest, mingling; **10** enterprise, occupation; **11** interaction, sociability, undertaking; **12** volunteering, volunteerism; **13** participation.

social animal 3 ant, ape, bee; **4** bird, lion, rook, wasp; **6** marmot; **7** dolphin, termite.

social assistance 4 dole; **6** relief; **7** aliment, alimony, benefit, pension, welfare; **10** protection; **11** maintenance; PHRASES: **3, 7** the welfare; **4, 9** life insurance; **5, 7** child benefit *UK*, child support, state pension; **5, 9** child allowance, state insurance; **6, 6** family credit *UK*; **6, 7** family benefit *UK*, income support *UK*, widow's pension; **6, 8** social security, social services; **6, 9** family allowance, health insurance; **7, 5** welfare

state; **7, 7** company pension, housing benefit; **7, 8** welfare services; **8, 7** sickness benefit *UK*.

social class 3 set; **4** band, rank, tier; **5** caste, grade, group, level, order; **6** clique, league, rating, sphere; **7** coterie, station, stratum; **8** position, standing; PHRASES: **6, 6** social status; **7, 5** pecking order.

social gathering 2 do; **3** bee; **4** bash, gala; **5** beano, party; **6** fiesta, shindy, social, soirée, thrash; **7** blowout, reunion, shindig; **8** bunfight, festival, function; **9** beanfeast *UK*, festivity, reception; **11** celebration; **13** conversazione; PHRASES: **2, 4** at home; **3, 5** hen party *UK*; **3-8** get-together; **4, 5** stag party; **5-7** house-warming.

social insect 3 ant, bee; **4** army, hive, king, wasp; **5** caste, drone, emmet, honey, queen, swarm; **6** apiary, plague, worker; **7** antheap, anthill, beehive, beeswax, pismire, soldier, termite; **8** honeybee, vespiary; **11** termitarium; **12** reproductive; PHRASES: **3, 3** red ant; **4, 3** army ant; **5, 3** queen bee, white ant; **5, 4** wasps' nest; **6, 6** yellow jacket; **7, 3** soldier ant; **7, 6** termite colony.

socialize 3 mix; **4** rage, rave; **5** party; **6** employ, gather, mingle, reform; **7** commute, contact, produce; **8** civilize, interact, organize, urbanize; **9** entertain; **11** communicate, intermingle, participate; **13** industrialize; PHRASES: **2, 3** go out; **3, 3** get out; **4, 2** join in; **4, 3** hang out; **4, 4, 2, 4** live side by side; **4, 5** make merry; **4, 6** meet people; **4, 8** work together.

society 3 SOC; **4** clan, club, folk, race; **5** class, elite, group, guild, stock, tribe, union; **6** circle, family, league, nation, people, strain; **7** culture; **8** humanity, ruralism, urbanism; **9** community, institute; **10** population; **11** association, homogeneity, nationality; **12** civilization, collectivity, organization, urbanization; PHRASES: **3, 5** the world; **3, 5, 5** the upper crust; **3, 5, 7** the upper classes; **3, 6** the public; **3, 6, 5** the social order; **3, 8** the populace; **3, 10** the population; **4, 7** high ~; **6, 7** polite ~; **8, 7** consumer ~.

sock 3 hit; **5** punch, thump, whack; PHRASES: **4, 4** crew ~. *See also* **clothes**

socket 4 hole, plug; **6** hollow, outlet; **7** opening; PHRASES: **5, 5** power point *UK*.

soda 8 lemonade; **10** gingerbeer.

sodium 2 NA; 7 natrium.

soft 1 P; 2 PP; 3 dim, lax, low, top, wet; 4 limp, weak; 5 faint, fluid, lithe, loose, muted, piano, quiet, silky, slack, soppy, touch; 6 drippy, feeble, flabby, flimsy, floppy, fluffy, gentle, limber, smooth, spongy, sprung, subtle, supple, tender; 7 ductile, elastic, flaccid, flowing, landing, lenient, pliable, relaxed, rubbery, springy, squashy, tensile, velvety, willowy; 8 bendable, diffused, flexible, nonrigid, pathetic, pleasant, softened, unstrung, yielding; 9 easygoing, forgiving, indulgent, malleable, melodious, sensitive, softening, spineless; 10 pianissimo, unstarched; 11 furnishings, mellifluous, sentimental, undemanding, unstiffened; 13 overindulgent; PHRASES: 4, 4 ~ line, ~ porn, ~ sell, ~ soap, ~ spot; 4, 5 ~ drink, ~ fruit *UK*, ~ goods; 4, 6 ~ option *UK*; 4-7 soft-hearted.

soft drink 3 pop; 4 Coke *tm*, cola, fizz, maté, soda; 5 cider, julep, mixer, water; 6 squash; 7 cordial, Perrier™, sherbet; 8 lemonade, refresco; 9 orangeade; 12 sarasparilla; PHRASES: 3, 7 eau potable; 4, 4 club soda, root beer; 4-4 Coca-Cola *tm*; 4, 5 soda water; 4, 8 soda fountain; 5, 3 black cow; 5, 4 cream soda, Pepsi Cola *tm*; 5, 5 apple juice, fizzy drink *UK*, fruit juice, tonic water; 6, 3 ginger ale; 6, 4 ginger beer, Virgin Mary; 6, 5 barley water *UK*, bitter lemon *UK*, orange juice, spring water, tomato juice; 6-8 thirst-quencher; 7, 4 coconut milk; 7, 5 mineral water; 8, 5 drinking water; 9, 5 pineapple juice, sparkling water, vegetable juice; 9, 9 chocolate phosphate; 10, 5 grapefruit juice.

soften 3 oil, pad, sag, wax; 4 bend, chew, flop, mash, melt, mold, pulp, thaw, whip; 5 allay, fluff, knead, plump, relax, ripen, shape, steep; 6 drench, grease, lessen, loosen, mature, mellow, reduce, spring, squash, temper, unbend; 7 assuage, cushion, impress, liquefy, massage, mollify, slacken; 8 diminish, macerate, marinate, mitigate, moderate, unstring; 9 alleviate, lubricate, masticate, overripen, pulverize, tenderize, unstiffen; 10 featherbed; PHRASES: 4, 4 tone down; 4, 7 make pliable; 5, 2 fluff up, plump up, shake up; 6, 2 ~ up; 6, 3 smooth out.

soft-hearted 3 lax; 4 easy, kind, mild; 6 gentle, mellow, tender; 7 lenient, relaxed; 8 delicate; 11 complaisant, sympathetic; 13 compassionate; PHRASES: 4-4 laid-back; 4-5 easy-going; 4-7 kind-hearted *UK*, warm-hearted; 6-7 tender-hearted.

softness 4 give; 7 pliancy; 8 lenience; 9 ductility, softening, springing; 10 elasticity, flaccidity, plasticity, pliability; 11 bendability, flexibility, nonrigidity; 12 malleability, tractability; 13 extendibility, extensibility; 14 impressibility; PHRASES: 9-2 softening-up. *See also* **soft**

soft option 8 walkaway.

soft thing 3 bog, fur, mud, pad, wax; 4 down, foam, fuzz, hair, puff, pulp, silk, snow, soap, sofa, wool; 5 dough, duvet, fluff, kapok, marsh, paste, plush, putty, satin; 6 breeze, butter, cotton, fleece, mousse, pillow, velvet, zephyr; 7 cushion, feather, padding, wadding; 8 armchair; 9 comforter, eiderdown, snowflake, velveteen; 10 Plasticine™, upholstery; 11 thistledown; PHRASES: 4, 5 easy chair, play dough; 4-7 foam-filling; 5-4 swan's-down; 7, 3 feather bed; 8, 4 modeling clay.

software 3 CP/M *tm*, DOS *tm*, OS/2 *tm*; 4 pipe, UNIX *tm*; 5 MSDOS (Microsoft DOS) *tm*; 6 driver, filter, parser; 7 package, program; 8 analyzer, compiler, language; 9 shareware; 11 interpreter; PHRASES: 9, 6 operating system (OS).

soil 3 mar, mud; 4 clay, dirt, dust, foul, land, loam, sand, silt; 5 dirty, earth, muddy, spoil, stain, sully; 6 gravel, ground, podzol; 7 country, pedocal, subsoil, topsoil; 8 alluvium, pedalfer, regolith; 9 territory; 11 contaminate; PHRASES: 1, 7 A horizon, B horizon, C horizon; 3, 5 get dirty; 4, 7 ~ erosion, ~ horizon, ~ profile, ~ texture; 4, 9 ~ structure.

sojourn *See* **stay**

solace *See* **comfort**

solar 5 power; PHRASES: 5, 4 ~ myth, ~ wind, ~ year; 5, 5 ~ flare, ~ month, ~ panel; 5, 6 ~ plexus, ~ system; 5, 7 ~ eclipse, ~ furnace, ~ heating.

sold 7 popular; PHRASES: 2, 6 in demand; 4, 3 ~ out; 6, 3 called for; 6-5 sought-after.

solder *See* **join**

soldier 2 GI, SM; 3 ant, man, NCO; 4 hero, kern, para; 5 Anzac, brave, plebe, poilu, Tommy; 6 ensign, gunner, marine, rookie, sapper, sniper, worker; 7 draftee, fighter, gallant, hoplite, officer, private, recruit, redcoat, regular, reserve, shooter, trooper, velites *UK*, warrior; 8 corporal, crusader, doughboy, fencible, returned, sergeant, squaddie *UK*; 9 combatant, conscript, effective, guardsman, Guardsman, irregular, reservist, supporter, volunteer, workhorse; **10** campaigner, militiaman, serviceman, skirmisher; **11** Guardmember, guardswoman, Territorial; **12** guardsperson, servicewoman, sharpshooter; PHRASES: 3-2-4 man-at-arms; **3, 7** old ~, tin ~; **4, 3** army man; **4, 7** foot ~; **4, 9** Home Guardsman; **5, 5** honor guard; **5, 6** Tommy Atkins; **5-6** bashi-bazouk, franc-tireur; **5, 10** drill instructor; **6-6** colors-bearer; **6, 7** common ~, tribal warrior; **7, 3** pressed man; **7, 5** provost guard, Section Eight; **7, 6** kitchen police; **7, 7** private ~, unknown ~, weekend warrior; **8, 3** enlisted man, fighting man, military man; **8-6** standard-bearer. *See also* **soldiers**

soldier (former soldier) 3 vet; **7** veteran; **9** legionary; **11** legionnaire; PHRASES: 2-**10** ex-serviceman *UK*; **2-12** ex-servicewoman *UK*; **3, 7** old soldier, old trooper; **3, 10** old campaigner.

soldier (historical soldier) 5 miner; **6** archer, bowman, lancer; **7** pikeman; **8** fusilier, rifleman, spearman; **9** cannoneer, grenadier, musketeer, pistoleer *UK*; **10** arbalester, carabineer, halberdier; **11** arquebusier, crossbowman; **12** matchlockman.

soldiers 3 GIs, men; **4** unit; **5** paras, squad; **7** militia, platoon, reserve; **8** regiment.

sole 3 one; **4** lone, only, rare; **6** single, unique; **8** nonesuch, peerless, singular; **9** matchless, nonpareil, unequaled; **10** inimitable; **12** incomparable; PHRASES: 3-3 one-off *UK*.

solecism 4 slip; **5** error, gaffe; **6** howler; **7** bloomer *UK*, blunder, mistake; **9** vulgarism, wellerism; **10** clumsiness, dysphemism, spoonerism; **11** malapropism; PHRASES: 4, 3 faux pas; **8, 4** Freudian slip.

solemn 3 sad; **4** dour, firm, glum, grim, holy; **5** grave, sober, staid, stern; **6** formal, ritual, sacred, sedate, severe, somber, sullen; **7** deadpan, earnest, intense, pensive, serious, sincere; **8** frowning, official; **9** humorless, unsmiling; **10** ceremonial, lugubrious, thoughtful; PHRASES: 4-5 long-faced; **5, 2, 1, 5** sober as a judge; **5-5** poker-faced, stony-faced; **8-5** straight-faced.

solemnity 5 gloom; **7** gravity; **8** gravitas, severity; PHRASES: 2, 4 no joke; **4, 4** long face; **8, 4** straight face. *See also* **solemn**

solicit 3 ask, beg, bum, tap; **4** busk, seek; **5** cadge, crave, lobby, mooch; **6** accost, appeal, bother, hustle, pester, sponge; **7** beseech, canvass, implore, request; **8** freeload, petition, scrounge; **9** importune, panhandle; PHRASES: 3, 3 ask for; **4, 3, 4, 4** hold out one's hand; **5, 3** plead for; **5, 4** plead with; **6, 2, 6** launch an appeal; **8, 3** petition for.

solicitation 5 OXFAM; **6** appeal, bazaar; **7** begging, bumming, busking, cadging, canvass; **8** mooching, sponging, telethon; **9** appealing, bothering, pestering; **10** canvassing, mendicancy, scrounging; **11** freeloading, panhandling; PHRASES: 3, 5 the touch; **4-3** Band-Aid *tm*; **4-7** fund-raising; **5, 6** chain letter; **6, 3** United Way; **7, 4** benefit game, charity ball; **7, 5** charity funds, charity match; **7, 6** charity appeal; **7, 7** benefit concert.

solicitor *See* **lawyer**

solicitous 4 kind; **6** caring; **7** anxious, gallant, mindful, worried; **9** attentive, concerned, courteous, indulgent; **10** protective; **11** considerate.

solicitude 4 care; **5** worry; **6** unease; **7** anxiety, concern; **8** courtesy, kindness, spoiling; **9** gallantry; **10** attendance, indulgence, protection; **12** apprehension; **13** attentiveness, consideration; **14** solicitousness.

solid 4 cube, firm, hard, item, pure, real; **5** dense, sound, thing, total; **6** closed, dilute, entity, figure, frozen, gelled, liquid, melted, molten, object, robust, rugged, sealed, secure, sphere, stable, strong, sturdy; **7** article, blocked, compact, gaseous, general, genuine, popular, pyramid, refined, unmixed; **8** artifact, concrete, disperse, emulsoid, eutectic, filtered, reliable, unbroken, vaporous; **9** compacted, condensed, lyophilic, lyophobic, saturated, unanimous, universal; **10** consistent, continuous, dependable, distilled, evaporated, stabilized, unyielding, widespread; **11** colligative, hydrophilic, hydrophobic, icosahedron, substantial, tetrahedron, thixotropic, trustworthy, unsaturated; **12** concentrated, destabilized, dodecahedron, precipitated; **13** unadulterated; **14** supersaturated; PHRASES: 4-4 rock-hard; **4-5** rock-solid; **5-6** level-headed.

solid body 3 pit; **4** bone, burl, cake, clay, clod, clot, curd, knot, lump, mass, node, rock, wall; **5** block, chunk, clump, earth, solid, stone; **6** cement, forest, nodule, nugget; **7** cluster, crystal, deposit, embolus, gristle, hardpan, nucleus, ossicle, thicket; **8** coagulum, concrete, hardcore, obstacle, sediment, thrombus; **9** aggregate, cartilage; **10** concretion, thrombosis; **11** precipitate; **12** conglomerate; PHRASES: **5, 4** blood clot, solid mass.

solidification 9 sclerosis; **10** glaciation; **11** granulation; **12** ossification, petrifaction; **13** calcification, fossilization, vitrification, vulcanization; **14** lapidification; **15** atherosclerosis, crystallization. *See also* **solidify**

solidify 3 gel, set; **4** firm, jell, melt; **5** candy, steel; **6** dilute, filter, freeze, harden, ossify, refine, temper; **7** calcify, congeal, distill, liquefy, petrify, stiffen, thicken, vitrify; **8** condense, disperse, dissolve, emulsify, glaciate, saturate, separate, vaporize; **9** coagulate, evaporate, fossilize, granulate, stabilize; **10** flocculate; **11** concentrate, crystallize, destabilize, fractionate, precipitate; **13** supersaturate; PHRASES: **2, 4** go hard *UK*; **5-7** steam-distill; **6-7** vacuum-distill; **11, 3** crystallize out.

solidus 5 slant, slash; **6** stroke; **7** oblique, virgule; **10** separatrix; PHRASES: **8, 4** shilling mark.

soliloquy 5 aside; **6** monody, speech; **7** oration, ravings; **8** monology; **9** monodrama, monologue; **10** apostrophe; **11** declamation; PHRASES: **3-3, 4** one-man show; **3-5, 4** one-woman show.

solitary 4 lone, sole, solo; **5** alone, aloof; **6** lonely, remote, single; **7** private; **8** desolate, isolated, retiring, secluded, unsocial; **9** reclusive; **10** antisocial, friendless, individual, unsociable; **11** independent, introverted, standoffish; **12** unfrequented; **13** unaccompanied; PHRASES: **3-2-3-3** out-of-the-way; **4-9** self-contained; **4-10** self-sufficient.

solitary place 3 den; **4** cell; **5** study; **6** Podunk; **7** hideout, retreat, sanctum; **8** cloister; **9** backwater, sanctuary; PHRASES: **4, 2, 6** back of beyond; **4, 4** hick town; **4, 7** back o'Bourke; **5, 5** ivory tower; **6, 5** hiding place; **6, 6** desert island, secret garden; **7, 8** private quarters; **9, 4** jerkwater town; **11, 4** godforsaken hole, sequestered nook.

solo 4 lone; **5** alone; **6** single, singly; **7** unaided; **9** unabetted; **10** unassisted, unescorted; **11** independent, unsupported; **12** unchaperoned; **13** unaccompanied; PHRASES: **2, 4, 3** on one's own, on your own; **2, 8**

by yourself; **3-3** one-man; **3-5** one-woman; **6-6** single-handed.

soloist 4 solo, star; **6** artist, singer; **7** artiste; **8** musician, virtuoso, vocalist; **9** monologue, soliloquy; **10** monologist; **11** soliloquist; PHRASES: **3-3, 4** one-man band, one-man show; **3-5, 4** one-woman show; **4, 6** solo effort.

soluble 8 solvable; **10** answerable, fathomable, resolvable; **11** dissolvable; **12** decipherable, deliquescent.

solution 3 key, lye, mix; **4** flux, plan; **5** blend, issue; **6** answer, apozem, liquid, reason, remedy, result, upshot; **7** measure, mixture, outcome; **8** antidote, cocktail, decoding, emulsion, infusion, lixivium, resource; **9** decoction, discovery, resolving; **10** conclusion, denouement, resolution, suspension; **11** contrivance, explanation; **12** unscrambling; **14** interpretation; PHRASES: **3, 3** way out; **7, 3** sorting out, working out; **8, 2** clearing up.

solve 3 sum; **4** plan; **5** crack, score, total; **6** answer, decode, equate, reason, remedy; **7** explain, measure, resolve, unravel; **8** conclude, contrive, decipher, discover; **9** elucidate, interpret; **10** unscramble; **11** disentangle; PHRASES: **4, 3** sort out, work out; **5, 2** clear up.

solvency 6 credit, wealth; **7** comfort; **8** solidity; **9** affluence, soundness, substance; **12** independence; PHRASES: **4-11** self-sufficiency.

solvent 4 flux, rich; **5** flush, solid, sound; **7** diluent, thinner, wealthy; **8** alkahest; **9** dissolver, liquefier, menstruum, resolvent; **10** dissolvent, hydragogue, resolutive; **12** creditworthy, liquefacient; **13** anticoagulant; PHRASES: **2, 3, 5** in the black, in the money; **2, 4** in cash; **2, 5** in funds *UK*; **2, 6** in clover, in credit; **3, 2, 4** out of debt; **3, 8** all straight; **4, 3, 2** good for it; **10, 5** dissolving agent.

somber 3 sad; **4** dark, dull; **5** dingy, muted; **6** gloomy, solemn; **8** funereal; **9** depressed; **10** depressing, melancholy.

some 5 about; **6** around; **7** certain, roughly, several; **8** selected, specific; **10** particular; **13** approximately; PHRASES: **1, 3** a few; **1, 6** a little; **1, 6, 2** a number of; **1, 8, 2** a quantity of; **4, 2, 4** more or less.

somebody 4 name; **6** bigwig; **7** someone; **9** celebrity, superstar.

somersault 4 flip; 6 tumble; 9 cartwheel; PHRASES: 4, 4 flip over, turn over; 4-4 flip-flop; 7, 4 forward roll.

sometime 6 former; 7 onetime, someday; 8 previous; PHRASES: 2, 3, 6 in the future; 2, 4, 4 at some time; 2, 4, 5 at some point; 3, 3 one day.

sometimes 5 often; 12 infrequently, occasionally, sporadically; 14 intermittently; PHRASES: 2, 3, 3 on and off; 2, 5 at times; 2, 8 on occasion; 3, 3, 4 now and then; 3, 3, 5 now and again; 4, 2, 1, 5 once in a while; 4, 4, 2, 4 from time to time; 5, 2, 5 every so often; 5, 3, 3, 4 every now and then.

son See **child**

song 3 air, coo, cry, lay; 4 aria, call, folk, glee, hymn, lied, lilt, part, solo, swan, tune; 5 carol, chant, ditty, lyric, piece, prick, psalm, round, theme, torch, yodel; 6 anthem, aubade, ballad, chorus, cooing, jingle, melody, number, patter, shanty, strain, warble; 7 calypso, cantide, chanson, chantey, chirrup, chorale, lullaby, refrain; 8 berceuse, birdsong, cavatina, folksong, madrigal, serenade, warbling; 9 roundelay, spiritual; 10 barcarolle, plainchant; 11 composition; PHRASES: 4, 4 love ~, part ~; 5, 4 torch ~; 6, 4 cradle ~, mating call, mating ~; 7, 4 popular ~; 7, 5 nursery rhyme; 8, 6 national anthem; 9, 5 Christmas carol.

songbird 3 tit; 4 chat, crow, lark, rook, wren; 5 finch, mavis, pipit, raven; 6 bulbul, canary, linnet, magpie, oriole, shrike, siskin, thrush, whydah; 7 babbler UK, bluetit UK, bunting, jackdaw, ortolan, skylark, sparrow, sunbird, swallow, tanager, wagtail, warbler; 8 accentor UK, avadavat, blackcap, bluebird, cardinal, hawfinch, redstart, reedling, starling, titmouse, whinchat, woodchat, woodlark; 9 bullfinch, chaffinch, chickadee, goldcrest UK, goldfinch, passerine, stonechat; 10 flycatcher, greenfinch, meadowlark, weaverbird; 11 butcherbird, gnatcatcher, mockingbird, nightingale, wallcreeper, whitethroat; 12 yellowhammer; PHRASES: 4, 3 coal tit; 4, 6 song thrush; 4-6, 3 long-tailed tit; 4, 7 pied wagtail, reed warbler, snow bunting; 5, 3 great tit; 5, 5 zebra finch; 5, 7 hedge sparrow UK, house sparrow; 6, 4 hooded crow; 6, 6 mistle thrush; 7, 3 bearded tit UK; 7, 4 carrion crow; 7, 7 Darwin's finches; 8, 4 perching bird; 9, 6 Baltimore oriole. See also **birds**

sonnet See **poem**

soon 4 anon; 5 later; 7 quickly, rapidly, shortly; 8 directly, suddenly; 9 presently; 10 imminently; PHRASES: 2, 1, 5 in a while; 2, 1, 5, 4 in a short time; 2, 1, 5, 5 in a short while; 2, 1, 6, 5 in a little while; 2, 3, 2 by and by; 2, 3, 4, 2, 1, 3 at the drop of a hat; 2, 4, 2, 2, 4 in next to no time; 2, 5, 6 at short notice; 6, 4 before long; 7, 6 without notice.

soot See **dust**

soothe 4 calm, ease, lull; 5 relax; 6 lessen, pacify, reduce; 7 appease, assuage, mollify, quieten UK, relieve; 8 palliate; 9 alleviate; 11 tranquilize.

soothing 4 calm, dead, soft; 5 bland, quiet, still; 6 easing, gentle, smooth; 7 anodyne, calming, restful; 8 balsamic, hypnotic, lenitive, mesmeric, narcotic, peaceful, relaxing, sedative; 9 analgesic, assuaging, demulcent, disarming, emollient, quiescent, relieving, soporific; 10 comforting, mollifying; 11 alleviative, lubricating, nonirritant; 12 pacificatory; PHRASES: 4-7 pain-killing.

sophism 4 blag, bosh, quip, ruse, scam; 5 cavil, dodge, hokum, hooey, quirk, trick; 6 bunkum, scheme; 7 baloney, fallacy, hogwash, paradox, quibble, shuffle, sleight; 8 antilogy UK, solecism; 9 stratagem; 10 paralogism, propaganda; 11 contrivance; 14 disinformation, misinformation; 15 pseudosyllogism; PHRASES: 3, 7 red herring; 3, 8 non sequitur; 6, 8 flawed argument.

sophist 4 liar; 5 faker, quack; 6 Jesuit; 7 casuist, caviler, charmer, schemer, shyster, waffler; 8 quibbler, solecist; 9 charlatan, demagogue, hypocrite, sophister UK, trickster; 10 mountebank, paralogist; 11 equivocator, pettifogger, pussyfooter; 12 philosophist, prevaricator, propagandist; 13 sophisticator; PHRASES: 3, 3 con man; 3-6 nit-picker; 4-8 hair-splitter; 5-6 sweet-talker; 5-7 logic-chopper.

sophistic 5 empty; 6 faulty, flawed, subtle; 7 dubious, invalid, unsound; 8 baseless, circular, illusory, jesuitic, specious, spurious, tortuous; 9 casuistic, casuistic(al), contrived, distorted, equivocal, erroneous, illogical, unfounded, untenable; 10 fallacious, fictitious, groundless, irrational, misapplied, misleading, rhetorical, solecistic; 11 misinformed, paradoxical, sophistical, superficial; 12 inconsistent, paralogistic, unreasonable; 13 contradictory; **15** inconsequential; PHRASES: **5-8** logic-chopping.

sophisticate 4 mold; **5** tutor; **6** school; **7** educate; **8** aesthete; **9** socialite; **11** acculturate, cognoscente, connoisseur, trendsetter.

sophistry 7 sophism; **8** jesuitry; **9** casuistry, moonshine; **10** dishonesty, distortion, invalidity, subterfuge; **11** circularity, fraudulence, unsoundness; **12** equivocation, illogicality, philosophism, speciousness; **13** illogicalness, inconsistency, irrationality, untenableness; **14** fallaciousness, misapplication; PHRASES: **4, 8** mere rhetoric; **5, 5** empty words; **5-8** logic-chopping; **6, 5** faulty logic.

sophistry (practise sophistry) 3 rig; **4** gild, mask, warp; **5** fudge, gloss, slant, twist; **6** juggle, scheme, strain; **7** distort, falsify, mislead, mystify; **8** contrive, disguise, misapply, misquote; **9** embroider, machinate, misinform, obfuscate, whitewash; **10** camouflage, manipulate; **11** misconstrue; **12** misrepresent, propagandize; PHRASES: **4, 3, 5** sway the crowd; **4, 5** chop logic; **5, 2** dress up.

soporific 4 dull; **5** opium, poppy; **6** boring, opiate, turgid; **7** calming, endless, tedious; **8** hypnotic, morphine, narcotic, nepenthe, nightcap, sedative; **10** anesthetic, monotonous; **11** barbiturate; **12** interminable, somnifacient; PHRASES: **5-8** sleep-inducing; **8, 4** sleeping pill.

soppy 3 wet; **4** soft; **6** slushy, soaked; **7** mawkish; **11** sentimental.

soprano 4 diva, high; **6** shrill, singer; **7** soaring; **8** piercing, vocalist; **9** chanteuse; PHRASES: **4-7** high-pitched.

sorcery *See* **witchcraft**

sordid *See* **sleazy**

sore 3 mad, raw; **4** boil, spot; **5** angry, cross, itchy, upset, wound; **6** aching, bitter, lesion, peeved, tender; **7** abscess, annoyed, awkward, blister, nettled, painful; **8** allergic, annoying, eruption, inflamed, offended, smarting, stinging, ticklish, tingling; **9** aggrieved, difficult, infection, resentful, sensitive; **10** irritating, sensitized; **11** contentious; **12** embarrassing; **13** controversial, uncomfortable; PHRASES: **6, 4** canker ~.

soreness 4 ache, hurt, pain; **5** agony; **6** aching; **7** allergy, redness; **8** distress, tingling; **10** discomfort. *See also* **sore**

sorrow 3 cry, woe; **4** pain, wail, weep; **5** agony, bleed, dolor, grief, mourn; **6** grieve, lament, misery, regret, soothe; **7** anguish, comfort, console, sadness, torment; **8** distress, mourning; **9** heartache, suffering; **10** desolation, heartbreak; **11** commiserate, unhappiness; **12** languishment, wretchedness; **13** sorrowfulness; **14** disappointment, sadheartedness; **15** downheartedness; PHRASES: **3, 4, 8** pay one's respects; **4, 3** weep for; **4, 4** weep with; **5, 4, 6** share one's ~; **5, 5** share grief; **5, 7** offer comfort; **6, 3** grieve for.

sorry 3 sad; **7** forlorn, pitiful; **8** pathetic, wretched; **9** miserable, regretful, repentant; **10** apologetic, remorseful.

sort 3 ilk; **4** kind, rank, rate, soul, type; **5** align, breed, class, genre, genus, grade, group, index, order, place, range; **6** assort, codify, divide, kidney, nature, person; **7** analyze, arrange, species, variety; **8** category, classify, organize, separate, tabulate; **9** character, subdivide; **10** categorize, individual; PHRASES: **4, 3** ~ out; **11, 4** personality type.

sortie 4 trip; **5** foray, jaunt; **6** attack, inroad, outing; **7** journey; **8** maneuver; **9** excursion, incursion.

SOS 5 alarm, alert, flare; **6** signal; PHRASES: **3, 3, 4** cry for help; **4, 3, 4** call for help; **4, 3, 5** save our souls; **8, 6** distress signal.

SO-SO 4 fair; **7** average; **8** mediocre; **11** indifferent; **12** unremarkable.

soul 5 blues, depth; **6** gospel, person, psyche, spirit; **7** essence, passion; **10** atmosphere, individual; **11** personality; **13** consciousness; PHRASES: **1, 0, 1** R & B; **4, 5** ~ music.

sound 3 baa, bay, boo, bow, caw, coo, cry, din, ear, fit, hum, lip, mew, moo, off, out, pip, pop, tap, yap; **4** bang, bark, bawl, beat, beep, blow, bong, bonk, boom, bray, bump, buzz, call, chug, clap, clop, ding, echo, firm, gasp, good, hale, hard, head, hiss, hole, honk, hoot, howl, look, meow, moan, oink, peal, peep, pick, ping, plop, purl, purr, rasp, ring, roar, seem, sigh, slam, thud, tick, ting, toll, toot, wail, wave, well, wham, whir, whiz, woof, yell, yelp; **5** bleat, bleep, check, cheep, chime, chink, chirp, clang, clank, clash, click, clink, cluck, clunk, crack, crash, creak, croak, drone, fjord, groan, growl, grunt, inlet, knell, mixer, music, neigh, noise, pluck, plunk, pound, quack, shout, slurp, smash, snarl, splat, strum, swish, throb, thrum, thump, trill, twang, tweet, valid, whine, whole, whoop; **6** appear, babble, bellow, better, burble, crunch, effect, fiddle, giggle, gurgle, intact, jangle, jingle, murmur, mutter, normal, patter, rattle, robust, rumble, rustle, scream, secure, severe, shriek, signal, sizzle, splash, squawk, squeak, squeal, squish, strait, strong, sturdy, swoosh, thwack, tinkle, titter, tongue, tootle, warble, wheeze, whinny, whoosh; **7** barrier, catcall, channel, chatter, chirrup, chortle, chuckle, clatter, crackle, declare, explode, express, healthy, perfect, screech, snicker, sniffle, snigger *UK*, squelch, thunder, trumpet, twitter, whimper, whisper, whistle; **8** announce, complete, proclaim, reliable, rigorous, sensible, splutter, thorough, ticktock; **9** advertise, broadcast, caterwaul, recovered, resonance, undamaged, vibration; **10** audibility, infrasound, ultrasound, watertight; **11** unblemished, vichysoisse; **12** encyclopedic, inaudibility, unassailable; **13** comprehensive, reverberation, thoroughgoing; PHRASES: **2, 3** go off; **2, 4, 6** in fine fettle, in good health; **3, 4** pea soup; **4-1-4** ding-a-ling; **4-1-6-3** cock-a-doodle-doo; **4, 3** ring out; **4, 3, 6** hale and hearty; **4-4** clip-clop, ding-dong; **4-6** able-bodied; **4-7** wide-ranging; **5, 4** sonic boom; **5, 5** white noise; **5, 8** fully restored; **6-6** double-tongue, pitter-patter, triple-tongue; **7-3** ratatat-tat *UK*.

sounding **5** sonar; PHRASES: **4, 8** echo ~; **5, 8** depth ~.

sound maker **2** PA; **3** amp; **4** bell, gong, horn, mike; **5** alarm, bugle, lungs, siren, voice; **6** buzzer, hooter, Klaxon, larynx, rattle; **7** speaker, trumpet, whistle; **9** amplifier, megaphone; **10** bullroarer *UK*, microphone; **11** loudspeaker; PHRASES: **3, 7** ear trumpet; **4, 3** boom box; **4, 5** good lungs, loud pedal; **4, 6** iron throat; **4-6** loud-hailer; **4, 7** door knocker; **5, 2, 5** lungs of brass; **5, 3** voice box; **5, 4** brass horn; **5, 6** vocal chords; **6, 7** ghetto blaster; **7, 3** hearing aid; **10, 5** stentorian voice.

soundness **5** depth, range; **6** health, safety; **7** breadth, fitness; **8** accuracy, security, strength; **11** reliability; **13** dependability; **15** unassailability. *See also* **sound**

soundproof **3** pad; **4** line, seal; **5** lined; **6** padded, sealed; **8** insulate; **9** insulated; **12** impenetrable.

sound quality **4** bass, bias, echo; **5** level,

phase, range; **6** reverb, treble; **9** reception; **12** equalization; **13** listenability; PHRASES: **4, 7** tone control; **10, 5** monophonic sound.

soup **4** stew; **5** broth, gravy, gruel, gumbo, purée, schav, slops, stock; **6** bisque, potage; **7** borscht, chowder, oatmeal; **8** bouillon, consommé, gazpacho, julienne, porridge; **10** minestrone; **11** vichysoisse; **12** mulligatawny; **13** bouillabaisse; PHRASES: **3-4, 4** ham-bone ~; **4-1-6** cock-a-leekie; **4, 7** clam chowder; **5, 4** clear ~; **5-4, 4** bird's-nest ~; **6, 4** oxtail ~; **6, 5** Scotch broth *UK*; **7, 4** chicken ~; **7, 6** lobster bisque; **9, 4, 7** Manhattan clam chowder.

soupçon **4** hint; **5** speck, touch; **6** morsel; **7** modicum.

sour **3** bad, dry, off; **4** acid, harm, mash, rank, ruin, tart, turn; **5** acrid, fetid, green, sharp, spoil, taint, tangy; **6** acidic, bitter, curdle, damage, molder, rancid, unripe; **7** acerbic, acidify, crabbed, curdled, ferment, hostile, sharpen; **8** embitter, vinegary; **9** acidulous, crotchety, irritable, resentful; **10** unfriendly, unpleasant; **12** disagreeable; PHRASES: **2, 3** go bad, go off *UK*; **2, 5** go moldy; **3-8** bad-tempered; **4, 5** ~ cream; **4, 6** ~ grapes; **5, 3** taste bad; **5, 4** taste foul.

source **3** bud, egg, rat; **4** find, font, fund, germ, home, mine, narc, nest, root, seed, well, womb; **5** basis, cause, fount, grass *UK*, snout *UK*, trace, track; **6** cradle, embryo, hotbed, locate, obtain, origin, quarry, snitch, spring, supply; **7** channel, nucleus, nursery, seedbed; **8** fountain, hatchery, hothouse, informer, resource, squealer, supplier, wellhead; **9** authority, beginning, genitalia, grapevine, incubator, informant, upwelling; **10** birthplace, derivation, foundation, greenhouse, headwaters, mainspring, propagator, protoplasm, provenance, wellspring; **12** fountainhead, spokesperson; PHRASES: **4, 2, 5** fons et origo; **4, 3** grow bag; **5, 4** track down; **5, 6** stool pigeon; **7, 6** growing medium, natural spring; **8, 5** starting place; **8, 6** breeding ground; **10, 4** primordial soup.

source of energy **3** gas, oil; **4** coal; **5** motor; **6** dynamo, heater; **7** magneto, turbine; **8** windmill; **9** generator, waterfall; **10** alternator, commutator, oscillator, powerhouse; **12** turbocharger; PHRASES: **4, 4** wind farm; **4, 5** wave power *UK*, wind power; **4, 9** heat exchanger; **5, 4** solar cell; **5, 5** power plant, solar panel, solar power, tidal power, water wheel; **5, 6** solar energy; **5, 7** power station *UK*, solar battery, tidal barrage; **6, 4** fossil fuel; **7, 3** natural gas; **7, 4** nuclear fuel; **7, 5** nuclear power; **10, 5** geothermal power.

source of information **6** source; **7** channel, Reuters; **8** quarters; **9** authority, grapevine; PHRASES: **4, 6** news agency; **4, 7** wire service; **4, 9** news syndicate; **5, 6** press office; **5, 7** press service; **10, 5** Associated Press.

sourness **4** tang; **5** spite; **7** acidity; **8** acerbity, acrimony; **9** hostility; **10** resentment, subacidity; **11** astringency; PHRASES: **4, 5** sour taste; **5, 9** sharp flavoring. *See also* **sour**

sour thing **4** lime, sloe; **5** aloes, lemon; **7** bitters, vinegar; **8** wormwood; **11** vinaigrette; PHRASES: **3, 4** dry wine; **4, 3** sloe gin; **4, 3, 8** gall and wormwood; **4, 4** acid rain, sour milk, sour wine; **4, 5** crab apple, sour cream; **5, 5** green apple; **6, 4** acetic acid; **6, 5** soured cream; **7, 4** whiskey sour; **8, 4** tartaric acid.

souse *See* **soak**

south **1** S.

South Africa **2** SA, ZA; **6** Azania; PHRASES: **7, 6** rainbow nation.

South Carolina **2** SC; **8** Columbia (capital); PHRASES: **5, 8, 8** South Carolina palmetto (tree); **6, 9** yellow jessamine (flower); **8, 2, 4, 3, 9, 9, 3, 5, 1, 7, 1, 4** Prepared in mind and resources and While I breathe I hope (motto); **8, 4** Caroline wren (bird); **8, 5** Palmetto State (nickname).

South Dakota **2** SD; **6** pasque (flower), Pierre (capital); PHRASES: **5, 3, 3, 6, 4** Under God the people rule (motto); **5, 5, 6** black hills spruce (tree); **5, 8, 5** Mount Rushmore State (nickname); **6, 5** Coyote State, (nickname); **7, 4-6, 8** chinese ring-necked pheasant (bird).

southern **1** S.

Southern Cross **4** Crux.

south of France, south of Paris **3** sud.

souvenir *See* **memento**

sovereign **2** ER, GR; **3** Rex; **4** czar, free, khan, king, rani, shah, tsar; **5** Mogul, nabob, pound, queen, rajah, ruler; **6** Caesar, caliph, Kaiser, mikado, prince, Regina *UK*, sultan; **7** emperor, empress, monarch, Pharaoh, supreme, tsarina; **8** absolute, domi-nant, Kaiserin, peerless, princess, superior; **9** ascendant, excellent, maharajah, matchless, potentate; **10** autonomous; **11** independent, outstanding, predominant; PHRASES: **3, 8** His Highness; **4, 7** Your Majesty; **4-9** self-governing; **4-11** self-determining; **5, 4** Dalai Lama; **5, 5** Great Mogul; **5, 6** crown prince, queen mother, queen regent; **5, 8** crown princess; **6, 2, 5** Prince of Wales; **6, 4** divine king; **6, 6** prince regent; **7, 4** crowned head; **8, 7** absolute monarch.

sow **4** cast, seed; **5** fling, plant, strew; **6** foster, litter, spread; **7** scatter; **8** disperse, initiate; **9** propagate; **10** distribute; **11** disseminate; PHRASES: **5, 6** throw around; **7, 6** scatter around.

sow thistle **4** puha; **7** rauriki; PHRASES: **4, 7** milk thistle.

spa **5** sauna; **9** whirlpool; **10** sanatorium; PHRASES: **6, 3** health ~; **6, 4** health farm, plunge pool; **6, 6** health resort; **7, 4** Turkish bath.

space **3** bay, gap; **4** area, hole, omit, part, play, plot, rank, room, seat, size, time, void, wait; **5** angle, array, blank, break, clear, crack, depth, empty, lapse, order, pause, place, scope, swing, tract, width; **6** cosmos, extent, galaxy, height, inside, lacuna, leeway, length, margin, period, radius, seaway, vacuum, volume, window; **7** breadth, expanse, freedom, headway, heavens, legroom, liberty, measure, opening, outside, surface, windage; **8** airspace, altitude, aperture, autonomy, capacity, diameter, exterior, headroom, interior, interval, latitude, organize, platform, position, separate, universe; **9** amplitude, character, clearance, dimension, elbowroom, expansion, extension, hypercube, thickness; **10** dimensions, hyperspace, interspace, interstice, Lebensraum, proportion; **11** coordinates, hypersphere, opportunity, proportions; **12** intermission; **13** circumference; PHRASES: **1-5** n-space; **3, 3** lay out, set out; **3, 4** sea room; **3, 5** set apart; **4, 2, 5** room to spare; **4, 2, 8** room to maneuver; **4, 3, 8** room for maneuver; **4, 4** make room, mark time; **4, 5** deep ~, free ~, keep apart, move apart; **5, 2** break up; **5, 3** ~ age; **5-4** spacetime; **5, 5** outer ~; **5, 6** solar system, ~ heater; **5, 7** ~ capsule, ~ shuttle, ~ station; **5, 8** S~ Invaders; **6, 3** spread out; **6, 5** living ~; **7, 3** measure out; **7, 5** turning ~; **8, 5** enclosed ~; **9, 5** breathing ~ *UK*, Cartesian ~, Euclidean ~.

spacecraft 3 bus, LEM, Mir, pod; 4 ship; 5 cabin, grain, rover, stage; 6 Apollo, lander, module, rocket, Salyut, shroud, Skylab; 7 footpad, orbiter, shuttle; 8 Atlantis, Columbia, spacelab, thruster; 9 Discovery, retropack, satellite, spaceship; 10 Challenger; 12 biosatellite; PHRASES: 3, 9 496 Discovery; 4, 4 nose cone; 5, 4 solar cell; 5, 5 space probe; 5, 6 lunar module, space rocket; 5, 7 space capsule, space shuttle, space station; 5, 8 space platform; 5, 10 space laboratory; 6, 6 plasma engine, rocket engine; 6, 7 launch vehicle; 6, 9 drogue parachute; 7, 6 booster rocket, command module.

spaceman 9 astronaut, cosmonaut; 10 spacewoman; 14 astronavigator; PHRASES: 5, 8 space traveler; 6, 3 rocket man; 6, 5 rocket pilot.

spaceship 3 UFO; PHRASES: 5, 5 alien craft; 5, 6 lunar module; 5, 7 space capsule, space shuttle; 6, 6 flying saucer.

space travel 3 ESA (European Space Agency); 4 NASA (National Aeronautics and Space Administration); 5 Soyuz; 6 Apollo, Vostok *UK*; 8 spaceman; 9 astronaut, cosmonaut, spacesuit, spacewalk; 10 spacewoman; 11 spaceflight; 12 microgravity; 14 weightlessness; PHRASES: 4, 4 free fall, moon base; 5, 3 space age; 5, 4 lunar base, space port; 5, 6 space helmet; 6, 6 manned flight.

spacious 4 airy, deep, high, long, open, vast, wide; 5 ample, broad, great, large, lofty, roomy; 7 immense; 8 enormous, extended, generous, outsized, sizeable; 9 capacious, cavernous, expansive, oversized; 10 commodious, voluminous; 13 amplitudinous.

spade *See* **shovel**

spades 1 S.

span 4 area, link, time; 5 cover, cross, limit, width; 6 bridge, extent, length, period; 8 bestride, distance, duration, straddle, traverse; PHRASES: 5, 4 reach over; 6, 4 extend over.

spangle 4 bead, star, stud; 5 shine; 6 bauble, pepper, sequin; 7 glisten, glitter, sparkle, twinkle; 8 sprinkle.

spar 3 arm, box, rod; 4 boom, mast, pole; 5 argue, fence, fight, scrap; 6 bicker; 7 dispute, scuffle; 8 squabble; PHRASES: 8, 5 exchange blows.

spare 3 dup; 4 lean, over, save, thin; 5

gaunt, other, stint; 6 pardon; 7 angular, reserve, slender; 9 duplicate.

sparing 6 frugal, meager, sparse; 7 careful, limited, thrifty; 10 economical, restricted; 12 parsimonious.

spark 3 arc; 4 beau, fire, glow, spur, zest; 5 blade, dandy, flash, glint; 6 create, ignite, incite, kindle; 7 animate, flicker, glimmer, inspire, produce, sparkle, trigger; 8 catalyst, generate, initiate, stimulus; 9 incentive; 11 inspiration, transmitter; PHRASES: 3, 3 set off; 5, 3 ~ gap; 5, 4 ~ coil, ~ plug.

sparkle 4 life; 5 gusto, shine; 6 energy, fizzle; 7 glisten, glitter; 8 vivacity; 10 enthusiasm; 11 scintillate; 13 effervescence.

sparkling 5 fizzy, witty; 6 bubbly; 7 aerated, vibrant; 9 brilliant, vivacious; 10 carbonated, iridescent; 12 effervescent. *See also* **sparkle**

sparrowgrass 9 asparagus.

sparse 4 airy, bare, fine, rare, thin, void; 5 empty, light, scant, spare, windy, wispy; 6 flimsy, little, meager, measly, scanty, scarce, slight, spongy, vacuum; 7 buoyant, gaseous, minimal, scrubby, tenuous, vacuous; 8 delicate, ethereal, exiguous, sporadic, uncommon, vaporous; 9 dispersed, niggardly, scattered, sprinkled, uncompact; 10 immaterial, infrequent, occasional; 11 incorporeal, undermanned, volatilized; 12 compressible, intermittent, uncompressed, understaffed; 13 insubstantial, volatilisable; 14 underpopulated; PHRASES: 3-7 low-density; 4, 2, 3, 6 thin on the ground; 10 near extinction; 6, 3 strung out; 6-3 spread-out; 6, 3, 4 seldom met with; 6, 4 seldom seen; 6, 5 dotted about; 6, 6 widely spaced.

sparse (make sparse) 3 cut; 4 thin; 5 empty, water; 6 dilate, dilute, expand, extend, gasify, rarefy, weaken; 7 exhaust; 8 vaporize; 9 attenuate; 10 adulterate, volatilize; 11 etherealize; PHRASES: 4, 3 pump out, thin out; 5, 4 water down; 6, 8 reduce pressure.

sparseness 6 rarity; 7 tenuity, vacuity; 8 buoyancy, delicacy, scarcity; 10 volatility; 11 ethereality; 12 volatileness; 13 immateriality; 14 incorporeality; 15 compressibility; PHRASES: 3, 8 low pressure; 4, 2, 8 lack of solidity; 4, 2, 9 lack of substance; 7, 8 reduced pressure. *See also* **sparse**

spasm 3 fit, tic; 4 grip, jerk, jump, pang; 5 cramp; 6 access, attack, climax, frenzy, orgasm, rictus, ripple, stroke, throes, tremor, twinge, twitch; **7** megrims, seizure, shudder; **8** apoplexy, epilepsy, paroxysm, staggers; **9** catalepsy, eclampsia, tarantism; **10** convulsion; **11** contraction, ejaculation, vellication; PHRASES: **3, 5** the jerks; **7, 3** nervous tic; **7, 8** falling sickness *UK*.

spat *See* **quarrel**

spatial 4 flat; **5** cubic, plane, solid, space; **6** cosmic, planar, radial; **7** regular, spacial, surface; **8** coplanar; **9** distorted, irregular; **10** asymmetric, volumetric; **11** dimensional, superficial, symmetrical; **12** asymmetrical, proportional, stereoscopic; **14** spatiotemporal; PHRASES: **3-11** two-dimensional; **5-4** space-time.

spatter *See* **sprinkle**

spawn 3 lay, roe; **4** seed; **5** breed, brood, hatch, issue, young; **6** create; **7** deposit, produce, progeny; **8** generate, initiate; **9** frogspawn *UK*, offspring, procreate, reproduce; PHRASES: **4, 4** fish eggs; **4, 5** give birth.

speak 3 gas, say, yak; **4** aver, chat, cite, talk, tell; **5** quote, reply, rhyme, state, utter, voice; **6** affirm, allege, answer, assert, convey, impart, natter, phrase, preach, recite, relate; **7** address, chatter, declare, exclaim, express, lecture, mention, respond; **8** disclose, proclaim, vocalize; **9** ejaculate, enunciate, formulate, interject, interrupt, pronounce, verbalize; **10** articulate, vociferate; **11** communicate; PHRASES: **2, 6, 2** be fluent in; **3, 4, 5** put into words; **4, 1, 4** give a talk; **4, 1, 7** give a lecture; **4, 5, 3** find words for; **4, 9, 2** call attention to; **5, 1, 8** ~ a language; **5, 2** refer to; **5, 3** blurt out; **6, 2** allude to; **8, 2** converse in.

speaker 3 rep; **5** sayer; **6** chorus, gossip, orator, ranter, talker; **7** debater, oratrix, reciter, utterer; **8** advocate, bigmouth, delegate, gossiper, lecturer, mediator, narrator, panelist *UK*, prattler, preacher, salesman; **9** announcer, chatterer, converser, demagogue, haranguer, presenter *UK*, raconteur, spokesman; **10** monologist, saleswoman, sermonizer; **11** broadcaster, rhetorician, salesperson, soliloquist, speechifier, spokeswoman; **12** blabbermouth, communicator, interlocutor, intermediary, soliloquizer, spokesperson; **14** representative; PHRASES: **3-7** tub-thumper *UK*; **6-5** speechmaker; **6, 6** smooth talker; **6, 7** public ~; **7, 6** soapbox orator.

speak in a particular way 3 coo, sob;

4 bark, crow, gasp, pant, pipe, sigh, snap, wail, yelp; **5** chant, drawl, flute, growl, snarl, whine; **6** cackle, mumble, murmur, mutter, squeak, warble; **7** breathe, whisper; **8** sibilate; PHRASES: **4, 3** sing out.

speaking 6 fluent, speech; **7** talking, voluble; **8** dialogue, language, monoglot, polyglot; **9** bilingual, discourse, outspoken, talkative; **10** Anglophone, articulate, loquacious, trilingual, unilingual; **11** monolingual; **12** multilingual; **13** communication.

speak loudly 3 cry; **4** bawl, boom, roar, yell; **5** blare, shout; **6** scream, shriek; **7** exclaim, screech, thunder, trumpet; PHRASES: **5, 2** speak up.

speak softly 4 sigh; **6** mumble, murmur, mutter; **7** whisper; PHRASES: **4, 4, 5** drop one's voice; **5, 5** sound faint; **5, 5, 4** speak sotto voce; **5, 7** stage whisper.

speak to 4 rail, rant; **5** orate, scold; **6** invoke; **7** address, contact, discuss, examine, lecture, mention, reprove; **8** approach, consider, harangue, perorate; **9** discourse, reprimand, sermonize, speechify; **10** discipline; **12** apostrophize; PHRASES: **2, 4** go into; **3, 2, 5, 4** get in touch with; **3-5** tubthump; **4, 1, 4, 4** have a word with; **4, 2** talk to; **4, 3** tell off, tick off *UK*; **4, 3, 5** take the floor; **4, 4** deal with, talk with; **4, 5** hold forth; **6, 2** appeal to, preach to; **7, 1, 6** deliver a speech.

speak with difficulty 4 hiss, lisp, sign; **6** babble; **7** gesture, stammer, stutter; **11** gesticulate; PHRASES: **3, 4, 8** use sign language; **4, 4, 5** lose one's voice; **4, 4, 6** lose one's tongue.

spear 4 stab; **5** spike; **6** impale, pierce. *See also* **weapons**

special 2 SP; **3** one; **6** single, unique; **7** express, feature, precise, unusual; **8** delivery, distinct, especial, original, pleading, separate, singular, specific, superior; **9** different, intrinsic, privilege; **10** assessment, individual, particular, respective; **11** distinctive, exceptional; **13** extraordinary; **14** quintessential; **15** individualistic; PHRASES: **3, 6** the unique; **3, 8** the specific; **3, 10** the individual, the particular; **4, 2, 3, 3** dish of the day; **5, 7** chef's ~; **7, 4** ~ case, ~ sort *UK*; **7, 6** ~ branch, ~ school; **7, 7** ~ effects, ~ license.

specialist 4 buff, whiz; **5** doyen; **6** boffin *UK*, expert, master; **7** scholar; **9** authority; **10** aficionada, aficionado, consultant, enthusiast, technician; **11** connoisseur; **12** professional.

specialization **3** bag; **4** area, baby, line; **5** craft, field, major, scene, thing, trade; **6** change, school, sphere; **7** pursuit, subject; **8** mutation, vocation; **9** evolution, selection; **10** adaptation; **13** concentration, transmutation; PHRASES: **3, 2, 3** cup of tea; **3, 7** pet subject; **5, 2, 4** claim to fame; **7, 5** special study; **7, 7** special subject; **7, 8** special interest; **8, 2** focusing in; **9, 4** narrowing down.

specialize **5** focus, study; **6** follow, pursue; **11** concentrate; PHRASES: **2, 2, 3** go in for; **5, 2** major in.

specialized **6** expert; **7** focused; **8** specific; **9** dedicated, scholarly, technical; **10** particular, specialist; **12** professional; **13** authoritative, knowledgeable.

specially **7** exactly; **10** personally; **12** specifically; PHRASES: **2, 2, 8** to be specific; **2, 5** to order; **2, 10** in particular. *See also* **special**

special skill **4** gift; **5** forte, skill; **6** genius, métier, talent; **8** aptitude; **9** expertise; PHRASES: **6, 5** strong point.

specialty **4** area, line; **5** field, forte; **6** domain, sphere; **7** subject; **10** department, specialism, uniqueness; **11** originality, specialness, specificity; **13** differentness, individuality, particularity; **15** differentiation, distinctiveness; PHRASES: **4, 2, 9** area of expertise; **8, 7** specific quality.

species *See* **class**

specific *See* **particular**

specification **4** plan; **5** check, order; **6** bounds, design; **7** control, mandate, pattern; **8** bounding; **9** condition; **10** conditions, definition, limitation; **11** arrangement, confinement, demarcation, description, measurement, requirement, restriction; **12** delimitation, prescription, proscription; **13** determination, qualification; **15** circumscription.

specifications **5** specs; **7** details; **8** minutiae; **10** conditions, essentials; **11** particulars; **12** fundamentals; **14** qualifications; PHRASES: **3, 3, 4** ins and outs; **4, 3, 5** nuts and bolts; **4, 5** fine print; **5-6** nitty-gritty; **9, 5** essential facts.

specify **3** fix, set; **4** bind, cite, give, list, name; **5** agree, check, frame, limit, order, quote, state; **6** assign, define, depict, detail, oblige; **7** confine, control, delimit, itemize,

measure, mention, qualify, require, reserve, signify; **8** describe, identify, indicate, instruct, quantify, restrain, restrict; **9** delineate, demarcate, designate, determine, enumerate, postulate, prescribe, proscribe, stipulate; **10** denominate; **12** circumscribe; **13** particularize; PHRASES: **3, 4** lay down, pin down; **4, 5** name names; **5, 2** point to; **5, 3** spell out; **5, 5** state terms; **6, 2** insist on.

specious **5** false; **6** hollow; **8** baseless; **9** erroneous; **10** inaccurate.

speck **3** dab, dot; **4** blob, iota, spot; **5** crumb, fleck, scrap; **7** speckle, stipple; **8** fragment, particle.

spectacle **4** show; **5** event, ghost, scene, sight; **6** marvel, mirage, parade, vision, wonder; **7** display, miracle, pageant, prodigy, seeming; **8** hologram, pretense; **9** emanation; **10** apparition, exhibition, phenomenon, revelation; **11** performance; **13** demonstration, hallucination.

spectacles **5** specs; **7** glasses, goggles; **10** eyeglasses; PHRASES: **3-5** gig-lamps.

spectacular **4** show; **6** mighty; **7** amazing, display, special; **8** fabulous, stunning; **9** fantastic; **10** impressive, remarkable; **11** performance; **12** extravaganza.

specter **5** ghost, spook; **6** danger, menace, shadow, spirit, threat; **7** phantom; **10** apparition; **11** possibility.

spectral *See* **ghostly**

spectrum *See* **range**

speculate **4** bear, bull, risk, stag; **5** guess; **6** gamble, hazard, invest, ponder, reason, wonder; **7** operate, suppose, surmise, venture; **8** cogitate, consider, estimate, prospect; **10** conjecture, deliberate; **11** contemplate, hypothesize; PHRASES: **2, 4** go bust; **3, 3, 6** rig the market; **4, 1, 6** take a chance; **4, 2, 7** deal in futures; **4, 5** take risks; **7, 2** reflect on.

speculation **5** rumor; **6** gossip, theory; **7** hearsay, opinion; **8** gambling; **9** guesswork; **10** assumption, conjecture, estimation, investment; **11** supposition; PHRASES: **7, 7** insider dealing *UK*, insider trading.

speculative **5** dicey, risky, rough; **6** chancy, dreamy, musing; **8** abstract, academic, fanciful, notional, pondered, profound; **9** dangerous, inventive, pondering, projected, tentative, uncertain; **10** conceptual, meditative; **11** approximate, conjectural, exploratory, provisional, theoretical;

12 deliberative, hypothetical; **13** introspective, suppositional, unpredictable; PHRASES: **2, 1, 5, 5** in a brown study; **5, 4** miles away.

speculator 8 investor; **10** adventurer; **11** opportunist; **12** entrepreneur; PHRASES: **4-5** risk-taker; **7, 6** fortune hunter; **7-6** wheeler-dealer.

speech 3 rap; **4** cant, chat, code, talk; **5** idiom, lingo, proem, slang, spiel, vocal, voice, words; **6** accent, direct, earful, eulogy, homily, jargon, langue, parole, patois, patter, prolog *UK*, rabbit, sermon, spoken, tirade, tongue, voiced; **7** address, chatter, chinwag *UK*, curtain, dialect, lecture, lingual, obloquy, oration, reading, recital, talking, uttered, yakking; **8** Checkers, colloquy, dialogue, diatribe, encomium, foreword, harangue, idiolect, indirect, language, mouthful, newspeak, parlance, preamble, prologue, reported, speaking; **9** broadcast, discourse, invective, monologue, obsequies, panegyric, soliloquy, vocalized; **10** enunciated, linguistic, peroration *UK*, pronounced, vernacular, vocabulary; **11** articulated, declaration, exhortation, valedictory; **12** conversation, dissertation, gobbledygook, psychobabble, technobabble; **13** communication, computerspeak; PHRASES: **4, 2, 6** vote of thanks; **4, 6** free ~; **6, 6** mother tongue, native tongue, Queen's ~ *UK*, vulgar tongue; **6, 8** living language, spoken language; **7-3** yakkety-yak; **7, 8** private language; **8, 5** speaking voice; **8, 7** farewell address, farewell oration; **11, 7** valedictory address.

speech (mode of speech) 4 burr, tone; **5** drawl, pitch, trill, twang, voice; **6** accent, brogue, stress, timbre; **7** cacoepy, lisping, stammer, stridor, stutter; **8** emphasis, nasality; **10** inflection, intonation, modulation; **13** pronunciation; PHRASES: **4, 2, 5** tone of voice; **5, 6** broad accent; **5, 7** voice quality; **6, 6** native accent, speech defect; **7, 6** foreign accent; **8, 5** suburban whine; **8, 6** regional accent.

speech (power of speech) 4 blah; **5** style; **7** blarney, fluency; **8** verbiage; **9** eloquence, logorrhea, loquacity, prolixity, verbosity, wordiness; **10** articulacy, orotundity, volubility; **11** glossolalia; **13** magniloquence, talkativeness; **14** articulateness, grandiloquence, repetitiveness; PHRASES: **3, 4, 5** way with words; **4, 2, 3, 3** gift of the gab; **4, 5** word power; **4, 10** rich vocabulary; **4-10** long-windedness; **6, 7** purple passage *UK*;

6, 8 verbal diarrhea; **7, 6** flowery speech.

speech defect 7 aphasia, lisping, stammer, stutter; **8** babbling; **9** dysphasia, dysphemia, lallation; **10** paraphasia, sibilation, stammering, stuttering.

speechless 3 mum; **4** agog, dumb, mute; **6** amazed, choked, gagged, shtoom *UK*, silent; **8** reticent, silenced, taciturn, wordless; **9** astounded; **10** astonished, dumbstruck, gobsmacked *UK*; **11** dumbfounded; **12** inarticulate; **13** flabbergasted, thunderstruck; PHRASES: **6, 4** struck dumb; **6-4** tongue-tied.

speechmaker 6 orator, ranter, reader; **7** speaker; **8** lecturer, preacher; **9** declaimer, demagogue, expositor, pulpiteer, raconteur; **10** sermonizer; **11** rhetorician; **12** communicator, pontificator, spokesperson; PHRASES: **3-7** tub-thumper *UK*; **6-6** rabble-rouser.

speed 3 bat, fly, hie, log, mph, nip, par, rpm, run, zip; **4** bolt, dash, drug, flit, fret, fume, hare, knot, lope, pace, race, rate, rush, scud, trap, wing, zoom; **5** chase, gauge, haste, hurry, limit, scoot, scour, skirr, spurt, tempo, whirl, whisk, whizz; **6** bustle, careen, career, fidget, flurry, hasten, hurtle, hustle, pickup, racing *UK*, scurry, sprint, streak; **7** agility, driving, scamper, scuttle; **8** airspeed, alacrity, celerity, dispatch, expedite, fastness, momentum, odometer, rapidity, rashness, speeding, velocity; **9** barreling, briskness, fleetness, hastiness, quickness, scorching, swiftness; **10** accelerate, anemometer, cyclometer, expedition, mileometer *UK*, nimbleness, promptness, speediness, tachometer; **11** amphetamine, groundspeed, precipitate, promptitude, speedometer; **13** accelerometer, instantaneity, precipitation; **15** expeditiousness; PHRASES: **4, 4** full lick, full pelt, full sail, good clip; **4, 5** bowl along *UK*, full ~, wind gauge; **4, 6** blue streak, burn rubber, fast motion, full career, Mach number; **5, 2, 4** press of sail; **5, 2, 5** ~ of light, ~ of sound; **5, 3, 4** drive too fast, miles per hour; **5, 4** quick pace, radar trap, ~ trap; **5, 5** sonic ~, sweep along; **5, 7** sound barrier; **6, 4** snappy pace; **6, 5** rattle along; **6, 6** making tracks; **7, 5** maximum ~, thunder along; **7, 6** burning rubber; **8, 4** rattling pace, spanking rate; **9, 5** breakneck ~, dangerous ~, lightning ~; **10, 5** hypersonic ~, supersonic ~, ultrasonic ~.

speedometer 5 clock, gauge; **6** speedo *UK*; **8** recorder.

speedy *See* **quick**

spell **3** fit, hex; **4** bout, jinx, mean, rune, term, time, turn; **5** bring, chant, charm, curse, imply, shift, stint, wanga, weird; **6** allure, denote, period, thrall, whammy; **7** abraxas, connote, glamour, philter *UK*, philtre *UK*, predict, presage, session, signify, stretch, suggest; **8** indicate; **9** evocation, influence, interlude, pentagram, trimester; **10** attraction, invocation; **11** abracadabra, bewitchment, conjuration, conjurement, enchantment, fascination, glossolalia, incantation, paternoster; PHRASES: **3, 2** end in; **3, 2, 2** add up to; **3, 3, 3** fee faw fum; **4, 2** lead to; **4, 3** evil eye; **4, 5** love charm; **4, 6** love potion, open sesame, time period; **5, 3** write out; **5, 5** bring about, hocus pocus, magic ~, magic words, mumbo jumbo; **6, 2** result in; **7, 2, 4** stretch of time.

spend **3** pay, use; **4** fill, idle, kill, pass; **5** apply, waste; **6** devote, employ, expend, finish, occupy; **7** consume, exhaust, fritter, splurge; **8** squander; PHRASES: **3, 2** use up; **3, 3** lay out, pay out; **3, 7** run through; **5, 4** throw away, while away.

spender **5** buyer; **7** shopper; **8** investor; **9** purchaser.

spendthrift **6** waster; **7** spender, wastrel; **8** prodigal, reckless, wasteful; **10** profligate, shopaholic, squanderer; **11** extravagant, improvident; PHRASES: **3, 7** big spender; **6, 2, 7** living on capital; **8, 3** prodigal son.

spent **4** done, over; **5** tired; **9** shattered *UK*; PHRASES: **4-3** worn-out; **6-3** washed-out. *See also* **spend**

sperm **4** cell, seed; **5** semen; **6** gamete; **9** ejaculate; **11** spermatozoa; **12** spermatozoon.

sperm whale **8** cachalot.

spew *See* **disgorge**

sphalerite **6** blende; PHRASES: **4, 6** zinc blende.

sphere **3** egg, orb, pea; **4** area, ball, bead, bulb, drop, line, pale, pill; **5** ambit, arena, field, forte, globe, orbit, range, realm, scope, topic; **6** branch, bubble, circle, course, domain, marble, métier, pellet, pigeon; **7** balloon, compass, concern, globule, subject, theater; **8** business, interest, province, spheroid; **9** bailiwick, specialty, territory; **10** department, discipline, speciality *UK*; **12** jurisdiction; PHRASES: **4, 2, 8** area of interest; **5, 2, 7** field of inquiry.

sphere of influence **4** turf; **5** ambit, orbit; **9** bailiwick, territory; PHRASES: **4, 2, 9** area of influence.

spherical **4** oval; **5** ovoid, round, toric; **6** oblate, rotund; **7** conical, prolate; **8** circular, disclike, globular, toroidal; **9** orbicular; **10** parabaloid(al), spheroidal; **11** cylindrical, ellipsoidal, hyperboloid(al); PHRASES: **3-6** rod-shaped; **4-6** cone-shaped, disk-shaped; **6-6** sphere-shaped.

spice **4** lace; **5** color; **6** flavor, season; **7** enhance, enliven; **8** additive, interest; **9** flavoring, seasoning; **10** excitement; PHRASES: **5, 2** liven up *UK*; **6, 2** ginger up.

spicebush **8** benjamin.

spicy **3** hot; **6** spiced; **7** curried, peppery, piquant.

spiel **4** talk; **5** pitch; **6** patter, speech; **7** lecture, prattle.

spigot **3** end, peg, tip; **4** bung, cork, plug; **5** point, spike; **7** stopper; **10** projection.

spike **4** barb, dash; **5** point, quash, spear, spine, thorn; **6** impale, pierce, skewer, thwart; **8** confound; **9** frustrate.

spiky **5** awned, sharp, spiny; **6** barbed, briery, hispid, jagged, pricky, stingy, thorny; **7** brambly, bristly, pointed, prickly, spinose, spinous, thistly; **8** pricking, starlike, stellate, stinging; **9** acanthoid, acanthous, bristling, hobnailed, stellular; PHRASES: **4-6** star-shaped; **4-7** star-pointed.

spill **4** drip, fall, leak, roll, slop, trip; **5** drool; **6** escape, tumble; **7** dribble, trickle; **8** overflow, spillage; **9** discharge.

spin **3** run; **4** bias, trip, turn; **5** angle, braid, drive, jaunt, plait, slant, swirl, twirl, twist, whirl; **6** gyrate, outing, rotate, swivel; **7** extrude, revolve, twiddle; **8** attitude, gyration, rotation; **9** viewpoint; **10** complexion, revolution; **11** perspective; PHRASES: **5, 2, 4** point of view.

spindle **3** bar, leg, rod; **4** axle, pole; **5** shaft; **7** support; **8** baluster, vertical.

spinner **3** web; **4** silk; **6** cobweb, cocoon, spider, turner; **7** gyrator, rotator, whirler; **8** silkworm; **9** spinneret, whirligig; PHRASES: **4, 5** silk gland; **7, 3** spider's web.

spinning **7** twining; **8** braiding, circling, extruder, orbiting, plaiting, rotating, twirling, twisting, whirling; **9** extrusion, spiraling; **10** spinerette; **12** intertwining; **13** interbraiding; PHRASES: **8, 3** ~ top; **8, 4** ~

mule; **8, 5** ~ jenny, ~ wheel.

spiny anteater 7 echidna.

spiny lobster 9 langouste; PHRASES: **4, 7** rock lobster.

spiral 3 fly; 4 coil, rise, soar; 5 helix, screw; 6 ascend; 7 descend; 8 escalate, increase.

spire 3 tip, top; 5 point, spike; 8 pinnacle.

spirit 2 go, id; 3 air, chi, ego, elf, gin, imp; 4 core, dash, elan, guts *UK*, life, mind, mood, ouzo, peri, soul, will; 5 anima, atman, demon, devil, geist, ghast, ghost, ghoul, heart, hooch, level, spook, steal, vodka; 6 abduct, animus, kidnap, liquor, mettle, nature, pneuma, psyche, remove, temper; 7 courage, essence, feeling, outlook, phantom, specter, varnish, whiskey; 8 attitude, chutzpah, kamarupa, strength, superego, surgical, tendency; 9 character, fortitude; 10 apparition, atmosphere, turpentine; 11 disposition, personality, temperament; 13 determination; PHRASES: **3, 11** the unconscious; **3, 12** the subconscious; **4, 5** life force; **4, 6** Holy S~, team ~, wood ~; **5, 3** third eye, whisk off; **5, 4** bliss body, inner mind, inner self, vital body; **5, 5** inner being, moral fiber; **5, 6** proof ~; **5, 7** linga sharira; **6, 3** ~ gum; **6, 4** astral body, causal body, karmic body, mental body, ~ lamp, subtle body; **6, 5** ~ level *UK*; **7, 4** Buddhic body; **8, 2, 4** strength of mind; **9, 4** spiritual body.

spirits 3 gin, rum; 4 arak, marc, mood, ouzo; 5 choum, vodka; 6 boukha, brandy, chicha, cognac, grappa, kirsch, mescal, metaxa, pastis, pernod, pulque; 7 akvavit, aquavit, bacardi, boukhra, bourbon, schnaps, tequila, whiskey, whiskey *UK*; 8 armagnac, calvados, falernum, feelings, schnapps; 9 slivovitz; 11 aguardiente; PHRASES: **3, 7** rye whiskey; **5, 2, 4** frame of mind, state of mind; **6, 5** mental state; **9, 5** emotional state.

spiritual 3 fey; 4 airy, holy; 5 alien, eerie, fairy, weird; 6 astral, creepy, divine, mental, sacred, spooky; 7 ghostly, phantom, saintly, shadowy, strange, uncanny, wraithy; 8 eldritch, ethereal, heavenly, internal, mystical, platonic, spectral; 9 elemental, emotional, religious, unearthly, unworldly; 10 immaterial, intangible, phantasmal, phantasmic, ufological, unembodied, unphysical, wraithlike; 11 disembodied, incorporeal, nonmaterial,

nonphysical; 12 extramundane, otherworldly, supramundane, transmundane; 13 insubstantial, psychological, temperamental.

spiritual world 3 ESP; 4 hell, Styx; 5 ghost, Hades, Sheol, souls; 6 ghosts, heaven, saints, spirit; 7 animism, phantom, spirits; 8 paradise, phantoms; 9 afterlife, animatism, hereafter; 10 underworld; 12 spiritualism; 15 supernaturalism; PHRASES: **3, 5, 4** the other side; **3, 5, 7** the lower regions; **3, 6** the occult, the shades; **4, 5** next world; **5, 2, 5** halls of death; **5, 2, 7** world of spirits; **5, 2, 8** meads of asphodel; **5, 5** sixth sense; **6, 4** astral body, mythic hell; **6, 5** astral plane, nether world, spirit world, unseen world; **6, 6** mythic heaven; **6, 7** nether regions; **7, 5** Stygian shore; **7, 6** Elysian fields; **8, 5** Abraham's bosom.

spit 3 pop, rod; 4 hawk, hiss, rain; 5 drool, expel, spear, spike, spurt, utter; 6 impale, mizzle, mutter, saliva, shower, sizzle, skewer, sputum; 7 dribble, drizzle, spatter, spittle, sputter; 8 splutter; 9 brochette; 10 rotisserie; 11 expectorate.

spittle *See* **saliva**

spittoon 8 cuspidor.

splash 3 wet; 4 dash, flap, plop, slap, slop, wade; 5 spray; 6 wallow; 7 spatter; 8 splatter.

splay 4 bend, open; 5 angle, bevel, slant, slope, twist; 6 spread; 7 distort, incline, splayed; 9 outspread; PHRASES: **6, 3** spread out; **6, 4** spread wide.

spleen 4 bile; 5 anger, pique, spite; 6 malice, rancor, temper; 8 sourpuss; 9 annoyance; 10 bitterness, crosspatch, grumpiness, irritation, moroseness, sullenness; 11 biliousness, crabbedness, malevolence; PHRASES: **3, 6** ill temper; **4, 6** sour grapes.

splendid *See* **magnificent**

splendor 5 glory; 6 marvel, wonder; 7 miracle, triumph; 8 grandeur; 10 brilliance; 12 magnificence.

splenetic 5 harsh; 6 bitter, crabby, grumpy, morose, sullen; 7 bilious, crabbed, peevish, waspish; 8 spiteful; 9 fractious, irritable, rancorous, sarcastic; PHRASES: **3-8** bad-tempered.

splice 3 wed; 4 join, link, seam; 5 joint, marry, merge, unite; 10 connection, intertwine, interweave.

splint 4 bind; 5 strap; 6 secure; 7 bandage; 10 immobilize.

splinter *See* **fragment**

split 2 go; 3 cut, gap, rip, run; 4 blow, gash, hole, rend, rent, rift, slit, slot, tear; 5 break, burst, chasm, cleft, crack, leave, shift; 6 breach, cleave, depart, divide, offcut, schism, second; 7 breakup, cutting, fissure, opening, ripping, rupture, section, tearing; 8 cleavage, cracking, decision, division, incision, scission, separate; 9 partition, resection, splitting; 10 abscission, amputation, castration, difference, divergence, infinitive, laceration, separation; 11 curtailment, personality; 12 decapitation, disagreement, retrenchment; PHRASES: 4, 3 head off; 4, 5 come apart; 5, 1, 4, 2 cause a rift in.

splotch 4 blot, mark, spot; 5 stain; 6 blotch, pimple; 7 blemish, splodge *UK*.

splurge 4 bout, orgy, show; 5 binge, spend, spoil, spree, treat, waste; 6 parade, wallow; 7 display, fritter, indulge; 8 squander; 10 exhibition; 13 demonstration.

spoil 3 mar, pet, rot; 4 dish, harm, hurt, ruin; 5 queer, taint; 6 blight, coddle, cosset, damage, deface, impair, pamper, ravage; 7 corrupt, indulge, protect, shelter, vitiate; 8 maltreat, mutilate; 9 disfigure; 11 mollycoddle.

spoils 4 gain, haul, head, loot, swag; 5 booty, prize, scalp; 6 profit, reward; 7 pillage, plunder; 8 earnings, pickings, winnings; PHRASES: 6, 2, 3 ~ of war; 8, 4 shrunken head.

spoilsport *See* **killjoy**

spoke 3 bar, rib, rod; 4 rung, step; 5 shaft, strut; 8 foothold.

spoken language 4 talk; 5 argot, idiom, slang; 6 jargon, langue, lingua, parole, patois, speech, tongue; 7 vulgate; 8 parlance, vocalism; 9 vulgarism; 10 vernacular; 11 phraseology; 13 colloquialism, vernacularism; PHRASES: 6, 6 common speech, vulgar tongue; 6, 8 living language; 7, 8 natural language; 8, 6 informal speech; 9, 6 idiomatic speech.

spoken letter 5 nasal, phone, pitch, vowel; 6 labial, liquid, sonant, stress; 7 digraph, phoneme, spirant; 8 aspirate, grapheme, guttural, sibilant, syllable; 9 consonant, diphthong, fricative, phonogram, polyphone; 10 inflection, labionasal; 11 labiodental; PHRASES: 6, 5 speech sound;

6, 9 voiced consonant; 7, 4 glottal stop.

sponge 3 bag, mop, rub, use; 4 bath, cake, down, swab, user, wash, wipe; 5 clean, cloth, idler; 6 cadger; 7 blotter, Parazoa, sponger; 8 parasite, parazoan, Porifera; 9 absorbent, adsorbent, poriferan, scrounger; 10 freeloader, parasitize; PHRASES: 4, 2 feed on; 4, 3 live off; 4, 3, 2 make use of; 4, 6 bath ~; 6, 2 fatten on, ~ on; 6-2 hanger-on; 8, 5 blotting paper.

sponger 4 user; 5 idler, leech; 6 cadger, gigolo, sponge; 8 barnacle, deadbeat, parasite; 9 scrounger; 10 freeloader; PHRASES: 6-2 hanger-on.

spongy 4 soft; 5 moist, soggy; 6 porous, sodden; 7 elastic, osmotic, springy, squishy; 8 flexible; 9 absorbent, malleable, permeable; 10 penetrable.

sponsor 4 back, fund; 6 backer, patron; 7 support; 8 champion, promoter; 9 guarantor, subsidize.

spontaneity 4 idea; 5 flash, hunch; 6 reflex; 7 freedom, impulse; 8 instinct, surprise; 9 impromptu, intuition; 11 inspiration; 13 improvisation; 14 extemporaneity; 15 extemporization; PHRASES: 4, 8 snap decision; 5, 2, 8 spurt of activity; 5, 7 blind impulse; 6, 7 sudden thought; 7, 2 winging it; 9, 6 automatic reflex. *See also* **spontaneous**

spontaneous 4 free, rash, snap; 6 sudden; 7 artless, natural, willing; 8 kneejerk, unforced, untaught; 9 automatic, emotional, impetuous, impromptu, impulsive, intuitive, unguarded, unplanned, unstudied, voluntary; 10 improvised, incautious, unprompted, unprovoked; 11 instinctive, involuntary, uncontrived, unmotivated, unrehearsed; 12 extemporized, unstructured; 13 unconstrained; 14 extemporaneous; PHRASES: 2, 3 ad hoc, ad lib; 2, 3, 4 on the spot; 3-3-4 off-the-cuff; 4-2-3-6 spur-of-the-moment; 7, 2 winging it.

spontaneously 2, 3, 4, 2, 1, 3 at the drop of a hat; 4, 1, 4 like a shot.

spoof 4 fool, hoax, skit; 5 bluff, prank, trick; 6 parody, satire; 7 deceive; 8 satirize; 9 burlesque, deception; 10 caricature.

spook 3 spy; 4 mole; 5 alarm, ghost, shock, snoop; 6 sleuth, wraith; 7 agitate, phantom, specter, startle; 8 surprise; 10 apparition; PHRASES: 6, 5 double agent.

spool *See* **reel**

spoor *See* **track**

sporadic *See* **irregular**

spore 6 pollen; 7 sporule; 9 bacterium; 10 microspore; 13 microorganism; PHRASES: 6, 5 pollen grain.

sport 2 RU *UK*; 3 bat, cue, don, pad, set, tee; 4 ball, bout, club, game, golf, judo, juke, meet, polo, pool, puck, shot, sumo, wear; 5 bowls *UK*, event, fives *UK*, kendo, match, model, round, rugby; 6 aikido, boules, boxing, discus, hockey *UK*, jayvee, joking, karate, league, mallet, pelota, racket, rowing, shinty, skiing, slalom, soccer, sprint, squash, tennis, tryout, wicket; 7 angling, archery, bobsled, bowling, contest, cricket, croquet, curling, display, exhibit, fencing, hurling, javelin, jujitsu, kabaddi *UK*, karting, netball, snooker, teasing, varsity; 8 baseball, biathlon, canoeing, coursing, division, falconry, football, gymkhana, handball, hurdling, inbounds, kickball, knockout, korfball *UK*, lacrosse, langlauf, marathon, petanque, shooting, softball, speedway, swimming, toboggan; 9 badminton, decathlon, motocross, skydiving, stoopball, triathlon, wrestling; 10 basketball, foxhunting, gymnastics, heptathlon, kickboxing, multisport, skysurfing, spelunking, tournament, volleyball; 11 basejumping, bearbaiting, bobsledding, bullbaiting, parachuting, penthathlon, shuttlecock, tobogganing; 12 bullfighting, canyoneering, cockfighting, invitational, orienteering, snowboarding, steeplechase, wakeboarding; 13 equestrianism, skateboarding; 14 mountaineering; PHRASES: 2-2, 3 go-to guy; 2-4, 7 in-line skating; 2, 6 XC skiing; 3, 4 jai alai, ski jump; 3, 4, 2 tae kwon do; 3, 6 ice hockey *UK*; 3, 7 ice dancing, ice skating; 4, 2 kung fu; 4-2-4 play-by-play; 4, 3 shot put, show off; 4, 4 high jump, long jump; 4-4 ping-pong; 4, 4, 4 Eton wall game; 4, 5 pole vault; 4, 6 ball player, drag racing, flat racing, real tennis; 4, 7 hang gliding, lawn bowling; 5-2-5 point-to-point; 5, 3, 5 track and field; 5, 4 relay race, water polo; 5, 5 Rugby Union; 5, 6 blood sports, field hockey, horse racing, motor racing, Rugby League, table tennis, water skiing; 5, 7 caber tossing, speed skating; 5-7 cross-country; 5, 8 ~ climbing; 5, 9 stunt bicycling; 6, 4 street luge, triple jump; 6, 5 hammer throw; 6, 6 alpine skiing, Nordic skiing; 6-6 triple-header; 6, 7 bungee jumping, figure skating, junior varsity, weight lifting; 7, 4 bannock ball, martial arts; 7, 6 fooling around, instant replay; 8, 4 disabled list; 8, 6 mountain biking; 9, 6 greyhound racing; 10, 4 grandstand play; 10, 5 Australian Rules. *See also* **game**

sporting 4 fair; 6 decent, honest, sporty; 8 athletic, generous, sportive; 9 acrobatic *UK*, agonistic, gymnastic, honorable; 10 evenhanded; 11 competitive.

sporting dog 6 gundog; 7 pointer; 8 Labrador; 9 retriever; PHRASES: 5, 6 Irish setter; 6, 9 golden retriever; 7, 3 hunting dog; 7, 6 English setter; 7, 8 English springer; 8, 7 Brittany spaniel.

sporting error 4 miss, wide; 6 miscue, mishit; PHRASES: 2-4 no-ball; 3, 4 own goal *UK*; 3, 6 hit wicket; 6, 5 double fault; 7, 5 dropped catch.

sporting hit 3 cut, hit, jab; 4 bunt, hook, left, pull; 5 drive, punch, slice, swing; 8 backhand, haymaker; 9 bolopunch; 10 backhander, backstroke, sidewinder; PHRASES: 4, 3 home run; 4, 4 body blow; 4, 5 line drive; 4, 7 Long Melford; 5-3, 4 roundarm blow, short-arm blow; 5, 5 round house; 5, 8 right uppercut; 8, 4 straight left; 8, 5 knockout punch, straight drive.

sportsground 4 ring; 5 alley, arena, court, field, green, links, pitch, track, venue; 6 course, ground; 7 stadium.

sportsman 6 player; 7 athlete; 8 defender, opponent; 9 contender; 10 challenger, competitor; 11 sportswoman; PHRASES: 4, 6 team member; 6, 4 sporty type.

spot 2 ad; 3 bit, dot, hot, see, spy, tad, wen, zit; 4 blot, boil, crud, dash, flaw, high, leaf, mark, mess, plug, scar, site, soft, weal, welt; 5 black, blind, dirty, fleck, place, point, smear, speck, stain, sully, touch, wheal *UK*; 6 advert *UK*, beauty, blotch, corner, defect, detect, notice, pepper, pimple, plight, smudge, stigma; 7 blemish, discern, pustule, setting, smidgen, soupçon, spatter, speckle, tarnish, trouble; 8 identify, location, perceive, pockmark, position, quandary; 9 blackhead, carbuncle, promotion, recognize, situation, whitehead; 10 commercial, difficulty, distortion; 11 predicament; 12 imperfection; 13 advertisement, disfigurement; PHRASES: 4, 3 pick out; 5, 1, 7, 2 catch a glimpse of; 5, 5, 2 catch sight of; 7, 4 blocked pore.

spotless 4 pure; 5 blank, clean; 7 perfect, unmixed; 8 flawless, gleaming, innocent, pristine, unsoiled, virginal; **9** faultless, stainless, undefiled, unmuddied, unstained, unsullied, untainted, untouched, wholesome; **10** immaculate, impeccable, unpolluted; **11** unblemished, untarnished; **13** unadulterated; **14** irreproachable, uncontaminated; PHRASES: **5, 2, 1, 3, 3** clean as a new pin; **5-3-4** spick-and-span; **7-5** squeakyclean.

spotlight 4 fuss; **5** focus; **8** interest; **9** attention, highlight, limelight, underline; PHRASES: **5, 2** point up.

spotted 6 dotted, marked; **7** dappled, flecked, mottled; **8** speckled, stippled; **9** patterned.

spotty *See* **blotchy**

spouse 4 wife; **5** bride, groom; **7** husband, partner; **8** affinity, espoused, espouser, helpmate, helpmeet; **10** bridegroom; PHRASES: **2, 5** GI bride; **3, 5** war bride; **4, 2, 3** next of kin; **4, 4** soul mate; **4, 8** one's promised; **4, 9** one's betrothed; **5, 4** other half; **6, 4** better half; **8, 5** blushing bride; **8, 7** marriage partner.

spout 3 jet; **4** pipe, talk, tube; **5** spray, spurt, utter; **6** column, nozzle, outlet, stream; **8** fountain; **9** discharge; **11** pontificate.

sprain 4 pull, rick *UK*; **5** twist; **6** injure, strain.

sprat 8 brisling.

sprawl 3 lie; **4** loll, mass; **5** cover, slump, trail; **6** lounge, ramble, slouch, spread; **7** stretch; **8** collapse, diaspora, straggle; **9** extension; **10** emigration; PHRASES: **5, 6** urban ~; **6, 3** spread out; **6, 4** extend over; **7, 3** stretch out; **7, 4** stretch over; **10, 5** population drift.

spray 3 jet; **4** dose, gush, mist, posy, spew, stem; **5** cover, sprig, spurt; **6** drench, squirt; **7** aerosol, bouquet, scatter; **8** atomizer, fountain; **10** buttonhole *UK*; **11** boutonniere; PHRASES: **5, 3** ~ can.

spread 4 boom, daub, farm, gush, jump, last, leap, meal, pâté, push, rise, span; **5** allot, apply, array, binge, boost, climb, feast, marge *UK*, paste, place, ranch, range, reach, smear, strew, surge, sweep, swell, widen; **6** butter, choice, divide, estate, expand, extend, extent, spiral, sprawl, supper, unfold, unfurl, unroll, uprush, upturn; **7** banquet, blowout, broaden, compass, diffuse, diverge, expanse, holding, persist,

publish, radiate, scatter, station, stretch, takeoff, upsurge, upswing, variety; **8** continue, coverage, disperse, division, increase, multiply, mushroom, swelling; **9** allotment, broadcast, circulate, crescendo, diffusion, propagate, selection; **10** assortment, distribute, plantation, promulgate; **11** disseminate, proliferate; **12** distribution, intumescence; PHRASES: **2, 2** go on; **3, 2** put on; **3, 3** lay out, put out; **4, 3** give out, open out; **5, 2** carry on; **5, 3** share out *UK*; **6, 3** smooth out; **6, 5** upward curve, upward trend.

spree 4 orgy, trip; **5** binge, break, fling, jaunt; **6** outing; **7** splurge; **9** excursion; **12** extravaganza.

sprightly 4 spry; **6** active, lively; **9** energetic.

spring 3 bob, jet; **4** coil, give, gush, jump, leap, lock, roll, skip, tide, well; **5** bound, brook, fever, fount, helix, juicy, onion, sappy, spout, vault, young; **6** bounce, Easter, pounce, season, source, spiral, stream, vernal; **7** balance, budtime, chicken, flowery, Maytime, upshoot; **8** fountain, mattress, movement, seedtime; **9** bedspring, upwelling; **10** Eastertide, elasticity, hairspring, mainspring, springlike, springtide, springtime; **11** flexibility, springiness; PHRASES: **3, 2** pop up; **3, 3** May Day; **3, 6** box ~; **4, 6** coil ~, leaf ~; **5, 2** start up; **5, 6** first cuckoo, water source; **5, 8** shock absorber; **6, 4** ~ tide; **6, 6** spiral ~, vernal season, volute ~; **6, 7** vernal equinox; **6, 8** launch yourself; **7, 4** blossom time.

springtime *See* **spring**

spring up 3 jet; **4** gush, play; **5** arise, dance, spout, spurt; **6** appear, arrive, emerge, upleap; **7** develop, explode, surface, upshoot, upstart; **8** fountain, mushroom, upspring; PHRASES: **3, 2** bob up, fly up, pop up; **4, 2** blow up, crop up, jump up, leap up; **4, 3** flow out; **5, 2** float up, shoot up, start up, vault up; **5, 5** burst forth.

sprinkle 3 dot; **4** dash, dust, hose, mist, slop, spot, stud; **5** clash, cover, flour, shake, slosh, speck, spray, strew; **6** dabble, dredge, hosing, litter, paddle, pepper, powder, shower, sparge, splash; **7** asperge, atomize, dusting, freckle, scatter, slobber, smatter, smidgen, spatter, speckle; **8** affusion, splatter, spraying; **9** aspersion, bespatter, peppering; **10** scattering, sprinkling; **11** intersperse; PHRASES: **5, 4** shake over.

sprinkled 6 dotted, dusted; **7** spotted,

sprayed, studded; **8** freckled, peppered, powdered, speckled; **9** smattered, spattered; **10** splattered.

sprinkler 4 hose, mist, rose; **5** spray; **6** filter, nozzle, sparge; **7** aerosol, sparger, sprayer, waterer; **8** atomizer, diffuser; **9** irrigator, vaporizer; **10** showerhead; **11** aspergillum; PHRASES: **5, 3** spray can; **5, 6** water pistol; **5, 7** speed sprayer; **6, 3** squirt gun; **8, 3** watering can; **9, 4** ~ head.

sprinkling 3 bit; **4** dash; **5** pinch, shake, touch; **7** dotting, dusting, smidgen; **8** spotting, spraying, sprinkle, studding; **9** freckling, peppering, powdering, speckling; **10** scattering, smattering, spattering; **11** splattering; **12** circumfusion.

sprint 3 run; **4** dash, race; **5** burst, hurry; **6** gallop.

sprite 3 elf; **5** dryad, fairy, nymph.

sprout 3 bud; **4** grow, leaf; **5** shoot; **6** appear, emerge, spring; **7** develop; PHRASES: **3, 2** pop up.

spruce 4 neat, tidy, trim; **5** natty, smart; **6** dapper; **7** conifer, elegant, orderly; PHRASES: **4-7** well-groomed; **5-3-4** spick-and-span.

spun 4 silk, yarn; **5** sugar; **6** twined; **7** braided, plaited, twirled, twisted, whirled; **8** extruded; **10** extrudable.

spun sugar 6, 5 cotton candy.

spur 4 barb, edge, limb, rush, urge; **5** point, ridge, shoot, speed, spike, spine; **6** branch, hasten, incite, motive, prompt, saddle; **8** offshoot, stimulus; **9** encourage, incentive, outgrowth, stimulate; **10** incitement, projection; **11** provocation; **12** mountainside; PHRASES: **5, 2** speed up.

spurious 4 fake, sham; **5** bogus, false, phony *UK*; **6** forged, hollow, humbug, phoney, unreal; **8** quackish, specious; **9** casuistic, charlatan, imitation, sophistic, ungenuine; **10** apocryphal, artificial, factitious, impostrous; **11** counterfeit, imposturous, inauthentic, unauthentic; **12** illegitimate; **13** counterfeited; **14** charlatanistic.

spuriousness 6 humbug; **7** forgery; **8** quackery, quackism; **9** casuistry, imposture, Jesuitism, sophistry; **10** humbuggery; **11** charlatanry; **12** charlatanism, illegitimacy; **13** artificiality, mountebankery; **14** counterfeiting, unauthenticity. *See also* **spurious**

spurn *See* **reject**

spurt 3 jet; **4** gush, rush; **5** burst, erupt, spout, spray, surge, swell; **6** squirt; **8** increase.

sputter 3 pop; **4** gasp, spit; **5** snort; **6** sizzle; **7** crackle, stammer; **8** splutter.

spy 3 pry; **4** mole; **5** agent, plant, recce, scout; **8** emissary; **11** infiltrator.

squabble *See* **quarrel**

squad 3 set; **4** bevy, crew, gang, team; **5** force, group, posse, troop; **7** company; **8** squadron; PHRASES: **4, 5** vice ~; **5, 5** fraud ~ *UK*; **6, 5** firing ~, flying ~, snatch ~.

squalid 3 low; **4** foul; **5** dirty, fetid, nasty, seedy; **6** filthy, sleazy, sordid; **9** repulsive.

squalor 4 dirt, smog; **5** filth, grime, gunge *UK*, smoke; **6** miasma; **8** foulness, meanness, mephitis; **9** dirtiness, nastiness, pollution, seediness; **10** immorality, shabbiness, sleaziness, sordidness; **11** degradation, uncleanliness; **13** uncleanliness; **14** unpleasantness.

squander 5 waste; **7** fritter; **9** overspend.

square 1 S, T; **3** fit, pay; **4** fair, fogy, form, just, word; **5** agree, align, bevel, check, miter, place, plaza, shape, tally, times; **6** accord, adjust, concur, fairly, honest, justly, openly, parade, piazza, settle; **7** balance, bracket, diehard, ethical, fogyish, genuine, realign, sharpen, upright; **8** directly, honestly, straight, tetragon; **9** discharge, harmonize, rectangle; **10** conformist, quadrangle, straighten, tetragonal; **11** marketplace, reactionary, rectangular; **12** conservative, intransigent, quadrangular; **13** parallelogram; **14** traditionalist; PHRASES: **2, 5, 6** at right angles; **3, 3** pay off; **3, 6** set ~; **3, 8** set straight; **4, 2** even up; **4-2-3-4** dyed-in-the-wool; **4, 4** file down, open area; **4-5** four-sided; **4-5, 6** four-sided figure; **5-2-3-3** stick-in-the-mud; **5, 5** clear level; **5-5** fuddy-duddy; **5-6** right-angled; **6, 3** ~ off; **6, 4** ~ meal, ~ root; **6, 5** ~ dance; **7, 5** stuffed shirt.

squash 3 jam, ram; **4** cram, mash, mush, pack, pulp, stop; **5** board, crowd, crush, force, pound, press, purée, quash, quell, wedge; **6** squish; **7** conquer, flatten, squeeze; **8** compress, overcome, racquets, suppress, telltale; **10** annihilate, congestion; PHRASES: **4, 4** back wall; **6, 5** ~ court; **6, 7** ~ rackets *UK*; **7, 4** service line; **7, 5** doubles court.

squat 3 sit; **5** beefy, burly, dumpy, fubby,

fubsy *UK*, heavy, hefty, lumpy, meaty, short; **6** brawny, chunky, crouch, hunker, square, stocky, stubby, stumpy; **7** hulking, lumpish; **8** thickset.

squawk 3 cry; **4** call, wail; **5** whine; **6** shriek, squeal; **7** protest, screech; **8** complain; **9** complaint.

squeal 3 cry; **4** howl, yell, yelp; **6** betray, inform, shriek; **7** screech; **8** denounce; PHRASES: **4, 2** tell on; **5, 2** sneak on *UK*.

squeamish 4 sick; **5** fussy, woozy; **6** queasy; **7** prudish; **8** delicate, nauseous; **10** fastidious, particular, scrupulous; **11** puritanical.

squeeze 3 hug, jam; **4** cram, grip; **5** clasp, crowd, crush, expel, grasp, pinch, press, wring; **6** clutch, cuddle, enfold, harass, squash; **7** embrace, extract, oppress; **8** compress; **9** constrict; **10** pressurize; PHRASES: **3, 2** fit in; **3, 8, 2** put pressure on; **4, 2** slot in; **5, 3** drive out *UK*.

squeeze-box 9 accordion; **10** concertina.

squelch 4 suck; **5** crush, quash; **6** scotch, splash, splosh *UK*, squash, squish; **7** flatten, silence, trample; **8** suppress.

squint 4 look, peek, peep, peer; **5** askew; **6** glance, tilted, uneven; **7** crooked, glimpse; **8** lopsided, unevenly; **9** crookedly; **10** hagioscope, lopsidedly, strabismus; PHRASES: **3, 7** off balance; **5, 4** quick look; **6, 4, 4** narrow your eyes.

squinting 8 walleyed; **10** strabismic; **11** nystigmatic; PHRASES: **4-4** boss-eyed *UK*.

squire 4 lord; **5** owner; **7** steward; **8** landlord, retainer; **9** attendant, landowner; **10** proprietor.

squirm 4 turn; **5** twist; **6** fidget, writhe; **7** wriggle.

squirrel 5 hoard, saver, store; **6** magpie; **7** collect, hoarder; **9** collector; **10** accumulate; **11** accumulator.

squirt 3 jet; **4** gush; **5** shoot, spray, spurt; **6** stream; **8** fountain.

Sri Lanka 6 Ceylon.

ST 5 Saint; **6** stanza; **7** statute; PHRASES: **6, 4** Summer Time.

stab 2 go; **3** cut, try; **4** ache, bash *UK*, gore, pain, pang, shot; **5** crack, gouge, guess, knife, lance, lunge, prick, slash, spear, stick, wound; **6** effort, impale, pierce, thrust, twinge; **7** attempt, bayonet, feeling;

9 sensation; PHRASES: **3, 4** cut down; **3, 7** run through; **6, 2** thrust at.

stability 3 rut; **4** calm, flow, rest; **5** quiet, trend; **6** fixity, stasis; **7** balance, routine; **8** equality, firmness, quietude, solidity, strength; **9** constancy, fixedness, hardening, soundness, stiffness; **10** durability, immobility, permanence, rootedness, secureness, steadiness, stiffening; **11** consistency, equilibrium, homeostasis, reliability; **12** immovability, immutability; **13** deathlessness, inflexibility, invariability, stabilization, steadfastness; **14** changelessness, immobilization; **15** irreversibility, unchangeability; PHRASES: **6, 5** steady state; **7, 2** firming up.

stabilizer 3 fin; **4** beam, keel, prop; **5** joist; **7** aileron, airfoil, ballast, spoiler, support; **8** aerofoil *UK*, buttress; **9** crossbeam; **11** centerboard; **13** counterweight; **14** counterbalance; PHRASES: **4, 4** wing flap.

stable 3 pen, sty; **4** barn, calm, even, fast, firm, gang, hard, held, shed, sure, team; **5** equal, fixed, group, pound, quiet, rigid, solid, sound, stall, stiff; **6** frozen, lineup, secure, static, steady, string, strong; **7** aground, durable, equable, restful, settled; **8** balanced, constant, enduring, immobile, reliable, rocklike, stabling; **9** collected, committed, deathless, evergreen, immovable, immutable, indelible, perennial, permanent, perpetual, steadfast, unvarying; **10** changeless, consistent, continuing, dependable, inflexible, invariable, unchanging, unshakable, unwavering; **11** established, homeostatic, inalterable, irrevocable, predictable, symmetrical; **12** imperishable, incommutable, indefeasible, indisputable, indissoluble, ineradicable, invulnerable, irreversible, unchangeable; **13** equiponderant; **14** indestructible, intransmutable; PHRASES: **2, 4** at rest; **2, 6** at anchor; **4-7** long-lasting, well-founded; **4-8** longstanding; **4-10** self-regulating; **5, 4** stuck fast; **5-6** level-headed; **6, 2, 1, 4** steady as a rock; **6, 2, 6** riding at anchor; **6, 3** ~ lad; **6, 4** ~ door *UK*; **7, 2, 5** written in stone.

stable (be stable) 4 hold, rest, stay; **5** stand; **6** adhere, harden; **7** stiffen; **9** stabilize; PHRASES: **3, 2** set in; **4, 2** hold up; **4, 3** stay put; **4, 4** take root; **4, 4, 7** keep one's balance; **5, 4** stand firm, stick fast; **6, 2** settle in; **6, 4** settle down, strike root; **6, 5** remain fixed; **7, 4** quieten down *UK*.

stable (make stable) 3 fix, set, tie; 4 bind, root; 5 erect, found, print, stamp; 6 ensure, freeze, ratify, secure, steady; 7 balance, confirm, engrave, quieten, support; 8 buttress, entrench, equalize, transfix, validate; 9 establish, stabilize; 10 stereotype; PHRASES: 3, 2 set up; 4, 2 firm up; 4, 4 make fast, make sure; 4, 6 keep stable; 6, 4 batten down, fasten down; 7, 4 quieten down *UK*.

stable person 6 square; 8 straight; 9 Victorian; PHRASES: 1, 3, 2, 3, 4 a man of his word; 4, 2, 9 Rock of Gibraltar; 5, 2, 8 tower of strength; 5, 3, 4 Darby and Joan; 6, 2, 7 pillar of society.

stable thing 4 rock; 5 tower; 6 pillar; 7 bedrock, fixture, pyramid; 8 constant, mountain; 9 engraving; 10 invariable; 11 cornerstone; PHRASES: 2, 12 US Constitution; 3, 4, 2, 6 the Bill of Rights; 3, 12 Ten Commandments; 4, 5 fast color; 4, 7 firm fixture; 4, 10 firm foundation; 5, 7 solid footing; 6, 6 Twelve Tables; 7, 4 granite rock; 9, 3 indelible ink; 9, 6 perpetual motion; 10, 4 Justinian's Code.

stack 4 flue, heap, load, mass, pile; 5 amass, mound; 7 chimney; 8 mountain; 10 smokestack.

stadium 4 bowl, ring; 5 arena, field, pitch *UK*; 6 ground; 7 Wembley; 8 gridiron; 9 Astroturf *tm*; 10 scoreboard.

staff 3 man, rod, run; 4 body, cane, pole, team, wand, work; 5 baton, force, nurse, stave, stick; 6 staves; 7 college, control, officer, operate, workers; 8 corporal, sergeant; 9 employees, entourage, personnel, supervise; 11 association; 12 organization; PHRASES: 4, 5 work force; 5, 9 human resources.

stag 4 buck, deer, male; 5 royal; 7 brocket; 8 imperial; PHRASES: 3-7 ten-pointer; 4, 5 ~ party; 4, 6 ~ beetle.

stage 2 do; 3 act, lap, leg, pit; 4 dais, door, grid, heat, left, play, show, step, time, trap; 5 above, apron, arena, below, board, flies, phase, point, right, round, stand, wings; 6 bridge, effect, fright, period, podium; 7 manager, perform, present, rostrum, soapbox, theater, upstage, whisper; 8 gridiron, juncture, platform, scaffold; 9 backstage, bandstand, direction, downstage, forestage, greenroom, orchestra, playhouse, sounddesk; 10 frontstage, lightboard, proscenium; 11 switchboard; PHRASES: 3, 2 put on; 3, 5 fly floor; 3, 6 the boards; 3, 7 fly gallery;

4, 5 slip ~; 5, 1 ~ L, ~ R; 5, 3 scene bay; 5, 4 scene dock, ~ door, ~ left; 5, 5 apron ~, ~ right, wagon ~; 6, 5 center ~, thrust ~; 7, 5 segment ~; 8, 4 dressing room; 9, 3 orchestra pit; 9, 5 revolving ~; 10, 4 proscenium arch; 10, 5 proscenium ~.

stagehand 5 usher; 6 flyman; 7 callboy, doorman, dresser; 8 prompter; 9 machinist, usherette *UK*; 11 electrician; PHRASES: 4-2, 6 make-up artist; 5, 3 sound man; 5, 7 scene painter, scene shifter; 5, 10 stage technician; 8, 3 lighting man; 9-6 programme-seller.

stage lighting 3 arc, gel; 4 gobo, iris, spot; 5 flood, foots; 6 lights, medium, strobe; 7 battens, gelatin; 8 Varilite™; 9 diaphragm, limelight, projector, spotlight; 10 floodlight, footlights, lightboard, sciopticon; 11 houselights, stroboscope; PHRASES: 3, 5 arc light; 4, 9 iris diaphragm; 5, 5 bunch light, color wheel, klieg light; 5, 6 color filter; 8, 4 lighting desk, lighting plot; 8, 5 lighting board; 9, 4 following spot.

stage requisite 4 prop; 6 closet; 7 costume; 8 handprop, property, wardrobe; 9 blackface, whiteface; 11 greasepaint; PHRASES: 4-2 make-up; 5, 4 clown face; 5, 8 stage property; 6, 3 spirit gum.

stage set 3 leg, set; 4 drop, flat, tabs, wing; 5 cloth, decor, drape, gauze, scene, scrim; 6 batten, border, teaser; 7 curtain, flipper, hanging, scenery, setting, wingcut; 8 backdrop; 9 backcloth, cyclorama, tormentor; 12 transparency; PHRASES: 3, 3 box set; 4-2-5 mise-en-scène; 4, 5 drop scene, side scene; 4, 7 drop curtain, fire curtain; 5, 7 house curtain, stage setting; 6, 7 safety curtain.

stagger 4 reel, rock, roll, step, stun, sway, toss, vary; 5 amaze, lurch, pitch, shake, shock, swing; 6 careen, falter, plunge, rotate, teeter, totter, tumble, wallow, welter, wobble, zigzag; 7 astound, flounce, stumble; 8 astonish, confound, flounder, surprise, volution; 9 alternate; PHRASES: 4, 2, 8 take by surprise; 4, 10 walk unsteadily; 5, 3 space out; 6, 3 spread out.

stagnant *See* **inactive**

stagnate 3 rot; 4 idle; 5 decay; 6 fester; 7 decline; 8 languish, vegetate; 11 deteriorate; PHRASES: 2, 3 go bad, go off *UK*; 2, 4 be idle; 2, 5 go stale; 2, 6 go rancid; 2, 7 do nothing; 2, 8 be inactive; 3, 6 sit around; 4, 2, 1, 4 come to a halt; 5, 2, 1, 4 grind to a halt; 5, 5 stand still.

stagnation 6 torpor; 7 inertia; 8 inaction; 10 immobility, inactivity; 12 sluggishness.

staid *See* **serious**

stain 3 dye; 4 blot, mark, slur, soil, spot, tint; 5 color, sully, taint, tinge; 6 debase, stigma; 7 blemish, pigment, tarnish; 8 discolor, disgrace, dishonor; 12 imperfection.

stair 4 rung, step; 5 tread; 8 stairway; 9 staircase; PHRASES: 6, 2, 5 flight of steps.

stairs 5 stair, steps *UK*; 6 perron; 8 stairway; 9 escalator, staircase; 10 stepladder; PHRASES: 3, 2, 5 set of steps; 4, 6 fire escape; 6, 2, 5 flight of steps; 6, 2, 6 flight of ~; 7, 5 landing stage; 9, 3 companion way.

stake 3 bet; 4 ante, pale, pole, post, risk; 5 claim, prize, purse, share, wager; 6 gamble, hazard, picket; 7 concern, venture; 8 palisade, winnings; 10 investment; 11 involvement.

stale 3 off, old; 4 dull, flat, rank, sour; 5 banal, decay, fusty, hoary, moldy, musty, trite, urine; 6 dreary, rotten, spoilt; 7 insipid; 8 mildewed, overused; 9 hackneyed, neglected; 10 unoriginal.

stalk 4 stem, twig; 5 shoot, track, trail, trunk; 6 branch, follow, pursue, shadow.

stall 3 box, pen, run, sty, zoo; 4 barn, byre *UK*, cage, coop, fold, halt, shed, shop, stop; 5 block, booth, check, defer, delay, hedge, kiosk, pause, pound, stand, store; 6 arcade, arrest, aviary, barrow *UK*, dither, freeze, impede, kennel, pigpen, pigsty *UK*, shelve, stable; 7 battery, cattery, counter, cowshed, cubicle, quibble, suspend; 8 aquarium, birdcage, boutique, cowhouse, dovecote, fishtank, henhouse, hesitate, loosebox *UK*, obstruct, postpone, pushcart; 9 birdhouse, menagerie, newsstand, stonewall, temporize, vacillate; 10 equivocate; 11 compartment, prevaricate; PHRASES: 3, 3 cut out, put off, sea zoo; 4, 3, 3, 4 blow hot and cold; 4, 3, 4 play for time; 4, 4 hold over, shut down; 5, 3 peter out; 5, 6 store window; 6, 4 marine park, pigeon loft; 6, 7 window display; 7, 4 chicken coop; 7, 7 vending machine.

stalwart 4 bold; 5 brave; 6 brawny, daring, strong, sturdy; 8 athletic, fearless, muscular, resolute, vigorous; 9 committed; 10 courageous, determined.

stamina 4 grit, guts *UK*; 5 moxie, pluck, vigor; 6 bottle, energy; 7 courage; 8 backbone, gameness, strength; 9 endurance, fortitude, gutsiness, hardiness; 10 doggedness, resilience, resistance, sturdiness; 12 perseverance; 13 determination; PHRASES: 4, 4 true grit; 7, 5 staying power; 7, 7 bulldog courage.

stammer *See* **stutter**

stamp 3 die, fix; 4 beat, cast, form, kind, make, mark, mill, mint, mold, plod, seal, sort, tool, type; 5 brand, chase, crush, label, pound, print, stomp; 6 emboss, squash, trudge; 7 earmark, engrave, impress, imprint, postage, quality, trample, variety; 8 hallmark, inscribe; 9 character, philately, signature, trademark; 10 collecting, impression; 11 endorsement; 14 characteristic, identification; PHRASES: 4, 5 date ~, duty ~; 5, 5 penny black *UK*; 6, 5 rubber ~; 7, 5 trading ~.

stamp collecting 9 philately.

stampede *See* **rush**

stance 4 view; 5 stand; 7 bearing, posture; 8 attitude, position; 10 deportment, standpoint.

stand 3 put, set; 4 base, bear, bier, dais, halt, hold, last, park, rack, rear, rest, rise, stay, stop, take, tent; 5 abide, arise, booth, brook, erect, exist, frame, hoist, kiosk, mount, pause, place, plonk, plunk, raise, shelf, stage, stall; 6 endure, holder, locate, podium, policy, remain, stance, suffer, tripod, trivet; 7 bracket, counter, deposit, opinion, outlook, persist, prevail, rostrum, situate, stomach, support, survive, sustain; 8 attitude, continue, pedestal, platform, position, tolerate, umbrella; 9 viewpoint, withstand; 10 standpoint, standstill; PHRASES: 2, 2, 4, 4 be on your feet; 3, 2 get up, put up; 3, 2, 4 put up with; 3, 2, 4, 4 get to your feet; 3, 5 hat ~; 3-5, 5 one-night ~; 3, 7 set upright; 4, 4 cope with; 4, 5 hall ~; 5, 2 ~ up, stick up; 5, 2, 4 point of view; 5, 3 ~ for, ~ pat; 5, 5 music ~; 6, 8 remain standing.

standard 3 par, set; 4 flag, jack, mean, norm, rank, test, type; 5 basic, canon, check, level, model, stock, usual; 6 banner, colors, degree, emblem, ensign, normal, scales; 7 average, balance, measure, pattern, pennant, regular, typical; 8 accepted, everyday, ordinary, orthodox, paradigm, streamer; 9 benchmark, criterion, customary, guideline, prototype, universal, yardstick; 10 prevailing, touchstone; 11 requirement, traditional, weighbridge *UK*; 13 specification; PHRASES: 4, 2, 5 rule of thumb; **4, 8** gold ~; **5, 4** floor lamp; **5, 8** royal ~ *UK*; **6, 8** double ~, silver ~; **8, 7** weighing machine.

standard-bearer *See* **leader**

standardize **4** join, pair, twin; **5** align, clone, level, liken, merge, order, phase, unify, unite; **6** divide, equate, smooth; **7** balance, flatten; **8** allocate, automate, coalesce, equalize, parallel, regiment, regulate; **9** harmonize, normalize; **10** assimilate, distribute, generalize, homogenize, proportion, regularize, stereotype, symmetrize, synthesize; **11** synchronize, systematize; **15** consubstantiate, conventionalize; PHRASES: **4, 2** even up; **4, 3** even out; **4-7** mass-produce; **5, 3** share out; **6, 3** smooth out; **7, 3** average out.

standby **4** late; **5** spare; **6** backup, deputy, double; **7** reserve; **8** fallback; **10** substitute; **11** replacement; PHRASES: **4-6** last-minute; **5-2** stand-in.

stand for **4** back, bear, mean, show, take; **5** abide, brook, stand; **6** accept, denote, endure, suffer; **7** endorse, promote, replace, signify, sponsor, stomach, support; **8** advocate, champion, indicate, tolerate; **9** exemplify, represent, symbolize, withstand; **11** emblematize; PHRASES: **2, 2, 5, 2** be in favor of; **3, 2, 4** put up with; **3, 3** act for; **4, 2** pass as; **4, 3** pass for; **5, 2, 3** stand in for; **10, 3** substitute for.

stand-in *See* **replacement**

stapes **7, 4** stirrup bone.

staple **3** pin; **4** clip, main, nail, tack; **5** affix, chief; **6** attach, fasten, secure; **7** primary; **8** fastener; **9** essential, principal.

star **3** dog, orb, pip, sun; **4** dark, film, icon, nova, pole, Ross, Vega, wars, Wolf; **5** Cygni, Deneb, dwarf, excel, fixed, flare, giant, grass, movie, north, radio, Rigel, shell, shine, Sirus, Spica; **6** Adhara, Altair, binary, Castor, Crucis, double, galaxy, Kruger, Luyten, nebula, Pollux, pulsar, quasar, Shaula, Sirius, sphere, stream, system, Vesper; **7** Antares, blazing, Canopus, Capella, chamber, evening, falling, feather, feature, Lalande, Lucifer, morning, neutron, Procyon, Regulus, succeed, thistle; **8** Achernar, Arcturus, Barnard's, Centauri, Hesperus, Kapteyn's, luminary, multiple, sapphire, shooting, showcase; **9** Aldebaran, Bellatrix, celebrity, exploding, Fomalhaut, pulsating, supernova, superstar; **10** Betelgeuse, connection; **11** personality; PHRASES:

2, 4 do well; **3, 3, 4** top the bill; **3, 4** Tau ceti; **3, 5** red giant; **4, 3, 4** head the cast, play the lead, take the lead; **4, 4** dark ~; **5, 3** stand out; **5, 3, 4** steal the show; **5, 4** black hole, dwarf ~, fixed ~, giant ~, white hole; **5, 5** brown dwarf, white dwarf; **5, 8** Alpha centauri; **6, 4** binary ~; **7, 4** Epsilon indi, evening ~, morning ~, neutron ~; **7, 7** Epsilon eridani; **7, 8** Proxima centauri; **8, 4** heavenly body, nebulous ~, variable ~; **9, 4** celestial body; **11, 4** circumpolar ~.

stare **4** gape, gaze, ogle; **5** glare.

stark **4** bare; **5** bleak, blunt, fully, plain, sheer, utter; **6** barren, simple, wholly; **7** austere, utterly; **8** absolute, complete, desolate, entirely; **9** downright; **10** completely; **11** unambiguous; **13** unadulterated.

starry **5** shiny; **6** bright; **7** shining, sparkly; **8** glittery, lustrous, spangled; **9** brilliant, sparkling, twinkling; **10** starbright; PHRASES: **4-7** star-studded; **4-8** star-spangled.

start **4** dawn, edge, jerk, jolt, jump, lead, open, plus, turn; **5** begin, birth, debut, float, found, leave, onset, shock; **6** ascent, broach, create, depart, father, flinch, fright, launch, outset, recoil, shrink, tackle, twitch; **7** arrival, liftoff, opening, pioneer, startle, takeoff; **8** blastoff, boarding, commence, initiate, surprise; **9** advantage, beginning, establish, inception, institute; **10** embarkment, foundation, inaugurate, initiation, initiative; **11** embarkation, emplanement, enplanement, entrainment; **12** commencement; PHRASES: **2, 2, 4, 3** be on your way; **2, 3** be off; **2, 5** go ahead; **3, 2** set to, set up; **3, 2, 6** set in motion; **3, 3** set off, set out, tee off; **3, 4** set sail; **3, 5** get going; **3, 6** get moving; **3, 7** get weaving; **3, 8** get cracking, get underway; **4, 2** dive in, fall to, fire up, turn to; **4, 3** kick off, take off; **4, 3, 6** take the plunge; **4, 4** fire away, head into, zero hour; **4, 5** bump ~, head ~; **5, 2** pitch in; **5, 3** blast off, ~ off, ~ out; **5, 4** blast away; **5, 5** sally forth; **6, 2** embark on, switch on; **6, 3** bundle off; **6, 4** plunge into; **6, 5** flying ~.

start again **6** reform; PHRASES: **5, 4** start anew; **5, 5** begin again; **5, 6** start afresh; **5, 7** renew oneself.

starter *See* **hors d'oeuvre**

star thistle **7** caltrop.

starting point **4** base; **5** basis, start; **6** origin; **7** kickoff, opening; **8** blastoff; **9** beginning; **10** foundation, initiative; PHRASES: **4-3** jump-off; **4, 4** zero hour; **5, 3** bully off; **5, 5**

false start; **6, 3** square one; **6, 5** flying start; **8, 4** starting gate, starting grid, starting line, starting post; **8, 5** starting block; **8, 6** starting pistol.

startle *See* **surprise**

startling *See* **surprising**

starvation *See* **hunger**

state 3 fit, Län, lot, say, way; **4** aver, avow, form, hold, land, Land, mess, mode, pomp, rank, role, show, soke, tone; **5** argue, chaos, claim, class, duchy, glory, guise, imply, light, order, phase, place, prove, realm, royal, shape, stamp, style, trend, utter; **6** affirm, aspect, assert, attest, canton, colony, county, denote, empire, estate, evince, fettle, formal, manner, nation, oblast, public, region, repair, riding, status; **7** betoken, country, declare, dignity, dukedom, enclave, eparchy, exclave, express, fashion, footing, kingdom, majesty, mandate, posture, propose, ranking, signify, stately, suggest, testify, turmoil; **8** category, ceremony, disarray, disorder, district, division, dominion, grandeur, imperial, indicate, maintain, majestic, modality, national, official, position, precinct, province, republic, splendor, standing; **9** archduchy, bailiwick, bishopric, condition, confusion, democracy, establish, lifestyle, municipal, postulate, situation, statewide, structure, territory; **10** appearance, ceremonial, complexion, dependency, electorate, federation, government, palatinate, superpower; **11** archdiocese, demonstrate, département, hypothesize; **12** commonwealth, constituency, magnificence, principality, protectorate; **13** archbishopric, circumstances, confederation; PHRASES: **4, 2, 4** walk of life; **4-5** city-state; **7, 2, 4** station in life. *See also* **state (US states)**

state (US states) 2 AK, AL, AR, AZ, CA, CO, CT, DC, DE, FL, GA, HI, IA, ID, IL, IN, KS, KY, LA, MA, MD, ME, MI, MN, MO, MS, MT, NC, ND, NE, NH, NJ, NM, NV, NY, OH, OK, OR, PA, RI, SC, SD, TN, TX, UT, VA, VT, WA, WI, WV, WY; **3** Cal; **4** Conn, Iowa, Mass, Ohio, Utah; **5** Idaho, Maine, Texas; **6** Alaska, Hawaii, Kansas, Nevada, Oregon; **7** Alabama, Arizona, Florida, Georgia, Indiana, Montana, Vermont, Wyoming; **8** Arkansas, Colorado, Delaware, Illinois, Kentucky, Maryland, Michigan, Missouri, Nebraska, Oklahoma, Virginia; **9** Louisiana, Minnesota, Tennessee, Wisconsin; **10** California, Washington; **11** Connecticut, Mississippi; **12** Pennsylvania; **13** Massachusetts; PHRASES: **3, 4** New York; **3, 6** New Jersey, New Mexico; **3, 9** New Hampshire; **4, 8** West Virginia; **5, 6** North Dakota, Rhode Island, South Dakota; **5, 8** North Carolina, South Carolina.

stated 4 read; **6** avowed; **7** alleged, averred, uttered; **8** admitted, affirmed, asserted, attested, avouched, declared, released; **9** announced, confessed, disclosed, professed, submitted; **10** enunciated, proclaimed, pronounced; **11** annunciated, asseverated.

stateliness 4 pomp; **5** glory; **7** dignity, hauteur, majesty; **8** grandeur, nobility, splendor; **9** formality; **12** magnificence; **13** condescension; PHRASES: **5, 7** proud bearing. *See also* **stately**

stately 5 grand, grave, lofty, noble, regal, royal; **6** august, kingly, lordly, sedate, solemn, somber, worthy; **7** pompous, queenly; **8** elevated, gracious, imperial, imposing, majestic, princely, splendid; **9** dignified, imperious, venerable; **10** statuesque; **11** magisterial; **12** aristocratic; **13** authoritative, condescending, distinguished; PHRASES: **4-3-6** high-and-mighty; **4-5** high-nosed; **4-6** high-handed, high-minded.

statement 4 bill, word; **5** creed, maxim, stand; **6** avowal, dictum, record, report, saying, speech, stance, thesis; **7** account, comment, invoice, receipt, waybill; **8** manifest, position; **9** assertion, manifesto, testimony, utterance; **10** conclusion, profession, submission; **11** declaration, enunciation, predication, proposition, supposition, testimonial; **12** announcement, annunciation, proclamation; **13** pronouncement; PHRASES: **3-2** say-so; **4, 5** ipse dixit; **4, 9** bank ~; **6, 4** report card; **6, 5** compte rendu; **7, 4** account paid; **7, 7** account settled; **7, 8** account rendered; **8, 4** prepared text; **8, 5** position paper.

state of affairs 5 setup; **7** picture, setting; **8** position; **9** condition, situation; PHRASES: **3, 2, 2** how it is; **3, 3, 2, 3** the lay of the land, the lie of the land; **3, 3, 6, 3** the way things are; **3, 4, 2, 2** the size of it; **3, 6, 5** how things stand; **5, 2, 4** state of play; **5, 3, 2** where it's at.

state of mind 4 mood, vein; **5** humor; **6** fettle, morale, temper; **7** spirits; **8** attitude, feelings; **9** mentality; **11** disposition, temperamert; PHRASES: **3, 5** bad humor; **3, 7** bad spirits, low spirits; **4, 5** good humor; **4, 6** fine fettle; **4, 7** good spirits, high spirits; **5, 2, 4** frame of mind.

static **5** inert, still; **8** constant, standing; **9** unvarying; **10** invariable, motionless, stationary, unchanging; **11** electricity; **12** interference.

station **4** base, post, rank; **5** class, depot, level, place; **6** status; **7** situate; **8** position, terminus.

stationary *See* **motionless**

statistical **9** actuarial; **13** psephological.

statistics **4** data; **5** facts, stats; **6** tables, values; **7** figures, indexes, numbers; **8** averages; **10** psephology; **11** information; **12** measurements; PHRASES: **5, 10** vital ~.

stature **4** rank; **5** build; **6** figure, height, status; **8** physique, standing; **10** importance, prominence.

status **4** rank, type; **5** class, grade, level, stage; **6** repute, symbol; **7** station; **8** category, eminence, position, prestige, standing; **9** condition; **10** importance, prominence, reputation; **12** significance; PHRASES: **6, 3** quo.

staunch **4** curb, halt, stem, stop; **5** loyal; **8** faithful, reliable; **9** steadfast; **10** dependable.

stave **3** bar; **4** band, lath, rung, slat, step; **5** board, plank, tread, verse; **6** stanza; **7** couplet, section, triplet; **10** crosspiece.

stay **3** tie; **4** bide, last, prop, rest, stop, wait; **5** abide, brace, dwell, lodge, tarry, visit; **6** endure, linger, remain; **7** bolster, persist, sojourn; **8** continue, restrain; PHRASES: **2, 2** go on; **4, 2** keep on, ~ on; **4, 3** ~ put; **4, 4** mark time; **4, 5** hang about *UK*; **4, 6** hang around, ~ behind; **5, 5** tread water.

stay near **3** dog, hug; **4** tail; **5** skirt; **6** follow, shadow; **7** embrace; **8** tailgate; PHRASES: **2, 4** go with; **3, 2, 3, 4, 2** sit on the tail of; **4, 5** hang about *UK*; **4, 5, 2** keep close to; **4, 6** hang around; **5, 2** cling to, stick to; **5, 4** hover over.

steadfast **4** firm; **5** loyal; **7** devoted; **8** constant, enduring, faithful, intrepid, resolute; **9** committed, confident, dedicated, tenacious; **10** dependable, determined, persistent; **11** persevering, trustworthy.

steady **3** fix; **4** calm, cool, even, firm; **5** fixed, solid, sound; **6** secure, stable, sturdy;

7 regular, renewed, staunch, support, uniform; **8** balanced, composed, constant, iterated, reliable, repeated, unbroken, untiring, vigilant; **9** ceaseless, collected, continual, immovable, perpetual, sleepless, stabilize, unceasing, unfailing, unruffled, unvarying, unwearied; **10** continuous, dependable, reiterated, relentless, strengthen, unchanging, undrooping, unflagging, unsleeping, unwavering; **11** unexcitable, unfaltering, unremitting; **12** unchangeable; **13** indefatigable; PHRASES: **4-8** self-mastered; **4-9** self-possessed; **4-10** self-controlled, self-restrained; **5-6** never-ending.

steak **9** tournedos; PHRASES: **1-4, 5** T-bone ~; **4, 5** rump ~; **6, 5** fillet ~, minute ~, tartar ~; **7, 5** sirloin ~.

steal **3** mug, rob; **4** copy, fake, hook, lift, nick *UK*, prig, slip, snip *UK*, take, whip *UK*; **5** boost, creep, filch, heist, pinch, poach, slink, slope *UK*, sneak, swipe; **6** borrow, burgle, fiddle, hijack, hustle, nobble *UK*, parody, pilfer, pocket, sample, snatch, snitch, thieve, tiptoe; **7** bargain, bootleg, carjack, imitate, purloin, skyjack, snaffle *UK*; **8** embezzle, giveaway, scrounge, shoplift; **10** burglarize, housebreak, pickpocket, plagiarize; **11** appropriate, expropriate; **14** misappropriate; PHRASES: **3-4** hotwire, joy-ride, ram-raid *UK*; **4, 3** good buy; **4, 3, 4** make off with, walk off with; **4, 4** good deal; **5, 3** knock off; **5, 7, 2** stick someone up.

stealing *See* **theft**

stealthy **6** covert; **7** catlike, cunning, furtive; **9** invisible; **12** huggermugger; **13** surreptitious; **14** conspiratorial; PHRASES: **2, 3, 2** on the q.t.; **2, 3, 3** on the sly; **2, 3, 4, 4** by the back door; **2, 3, 5** on the quiet; **2, 7** in secrecy; **4-3-6** hole-and-corner *UK*; **5, 3, 7** under the counter.

steam **3** fog; **4** haze, mist; **5** cloud, vapor; **12** condensation.

steamy **4** blue, damp; **5** humid, misty, muggy; **6** erotic, sticky; **7** sensual; PHRASES: **3, 3, 6** hot and sticky; **6, 2** fogged up.

steatite **9** soapstone.

steed *See* **horse**

steel **5** blade, brace, metal, sword; **6** harden; **7** fortify, toughen; **10** strengthen; PHRASES: **4, 5** cold ~; **5, 4** ~ band, ~ blue, ~ gray, ~ wool.

steep **4** dear, soak; **5** brine, imbue, sharp,

sheer, stand; **6** abrupt, drench, infuse, inject, pickle, seethe, sudden; **7** extreme, immerse, suffuse; **8** macerate, marinate, permeate, saturate, submerge, vertical; **9** excessive, expensive; **10** exorbitant, impregnate, infiltrate; **11** precipitous; **12** extortionate, unreasonable.

steeple 4 pile; **5** spire, tower; **6** belfry, flèche, pagoda, turret; **7** minaret; **8** barbican *UK*, windmill, ziggurat; **9** campanile; **10** lighthouse, watchtower; PHRASES: **4, 5** bell tower.

steeplechase 7 hurdles; **8** footrace; **9** horserace; PHRASES: **5-2-5** point-to-point; **5, 4** track race; **5, 5** track event.

steer 4 lead; **5** drive, guide, pilot, point; **6** direct; **7** conduct, control; **8** maneuver, navigate.

stem 4 axil, axis, bulb, corm, curb, halt, node, pith, seta, slow, stop, twig; **5** check, scion, shaft, shank, shoot, spray, stalk, stipe, stock, trunk, tuber, xylem; **6** branch, caudex, caulid, caulis, cortex, hinder, lessen, phloem, rachis, reduce, runner, sprout, stanch, stolon, sucker; **7** cambium, curtail, funicle, medulla, pedicel, petiole, plumule, rhizome, staunch, tendril; **8** decrease, offshoot, peduncle, rachilla *UK*, restrict; **9** epidermis, internode, leafstalk, rootstock; PHRASES: **3, 3** cut off; **4, 4** hold back; **4, 5** seed stalk, ~ tuber; **4, 6** ~ tissue; **6, 5** flower stalk; **8, 6** vascular bundle; **11, 4** underground ~.

stench 3 fug, gas, hum *UK*; **4** fust, niff *UK*, pong *UK*, reek; **5** fetor, stink, whiff *UK*; **6** miasma; **7** malodor; **8** mephitis; **9** effluvium, fetidness, fustiness, mustiness, staleness; **10** exhalation, frowziness, osmidrosis, smelliness, sweatiness; **11** frowstiness; **14** malodorousness; PHRASES: **3, 4** bad odor; **4, 5** foul smell; **10, 4** disgusting odor; **10, 5** unpleasant smell.

stencil 4 draw, work; **5** adorn, apply, guide, motif, paint, plate, trace; **6** border, cutout, design; **7** pattern; **8** decorate, ornament, template; **9** lettering.

step 4 jump, leap, move, pace, rest, rung, walk; **5** level, march, phase, riser, round, scale, spoke, spurt, stage, stair, stave, tread; **6** action, period, rundle, stride, string; **7** measure; **8** doorstep, footrest, footstep, movement; **9** kickstool, stepstool; **11** bridgeboard.

steppe *See* **prairie**

sterile 4 bare, dull; **5** banal; **6** barren; **8** desolate; **9** fruitless, infertile; **10** antiseptic, sterilized, unfruitful; **11** disinfected; **12** unproductive; **13** unimaginative; PHRASES: **4-4** germ-free.

sterility 10 antisepsis, desolation; **11** infertility; **12** disinfection; **15** decontamination. *See also* **sterile**

sterilize 3 dry; **4** boil, geld, spay; **5** drain; **6** aerate, bleach, neuter, purify; **7** cleanse, freshen, isolate; **8** castrate, conserve, fumigate, immunize, preserve, sanitize; **9** disinfect, inoculate, vaccinate, ventilate; **10** chlorinate, pasteurize, quarantine; **13** antisepticize, decontaminate; PHRASES: **4, 4-4** make germ-free; **5, 10** clean thoroughly.

sterling 4 real; **5** pound; **6** silver; **7** genuine; **9** authentic, excellent; **11** exceptional.

stern 4 dour, grim; **5** harsh; **6** severe, strict; **7** austere, serious; **10** forbidding, formidable; **13** unsympathetic. *See also* **sailing boat (parts of a sailing boat)**

sternum 10 breastbone.

stew 3 fix; **4** flap, fret, fuss; **5** poach, state, tizzy, worry; **6** braise, lather, simmer; **7** parboil, trouble; **9** casserole; PHRASES: **2, 5** be upset; **2, 8** be agitated, be troubled; **4, 6** boil slowly, cook slowly; **8, 4** mulligan ~; **9, 4** Brunswick ~.

stibium 8 antimony.

stick 3 bat, fix, gum, hug, jab, lay, put, rod, set, ski; **4** bond, cane, fuse, glue, gore, grip, join, lute, poke, pole, push, stab, twig, weld; **5** affix, baton, clamp, clasp, grasp, paste, place, plonk, plunk, shove, spear, spike, staff, unite; **6** adhere, around, attach, branch, cancer, cement, clench, clinch, clutch, fasten, pierce, solder, staple, switch, thrust; **7** control, deposit, embrace, grapple, walking; **8** cocktail, shooting, together; **9** penetrate; **11** agglutinate; PHRASES: **3, 2** gum up; **3, 5** big ~; **3, 7** run through; **4, 5** joss ~, pogo ~; **5, 2** cling on; **5, 5** white ~ *UK*; **5, 6** ~ insect; **6, 5** French ~ *UK*; **7, 5** swagger ~, swizzle ~.

sticker *See* **label**

sticky 3 hot; **5** close, gluey, gooey, gummy, humid, muggy, pasty, tacky, tight; **6** clammy, steamy, sultry, tricky, wicket; **7** awkward; **8** adhesive, delicate; **9** difficult, glutinous, sensitive; **10** oppressive; **11** complicated; PHRASES: **6, 3** ~ end.

stiff 4 firm, sore; **5** aloof, harsh, rigid,

tough; **6** aching, corpse, formal, robust, severe, strong, stuffy, tender; **7** arduous, cadaver, drastic, intense, painful, pompous, testing; **8** exacting, powerful, vigorous; **9** arthritic, excessive, stringent, unbending; **10** inflexible; **11** standoffish.

stiffen 5 brace; **6** harden; **7** congeal, thicken, toughen; **8** solidify; **9** reinforce; **10** strengthen.

stiffness 5 power, vigor; **8** rigidity, severity, strength; **9** extremity, formality, intensity, pomposity; **10** difficulty, stringency; **13** inflexibility. *See also* **stiff**

stifle *See* **smother**

stigma *See* **shame**

still 3 but, yet; **4** calm, even, hush; **5** check, doggo, inert, quiet; **6** hushed, placid, silent, soothe, static, though; **7** airless, alembic, assuage, however, placate, resting; **8** becalmed, immobile, inactive, snapshot, tranquil, windless; **9** currently; **10** motionless, photograph; **12** nevertheless.

stillness 4 calm, hush, lull; **6** fixity, stasis; **7** silence; **8** doldrums; **10** immobility; **11** tranquility; PHRASES: **5, 9** horse latitudes. *See also* **still**

stilt 4 pole, post; **6** column, pillar; **7** support.

stimulant 5 tonic, upper; **10** intoxicant; **11** restorative, stimulating; PHRASES: **3, 4** pep pill; **4-2-2** pick-me-up.

stimulate 4 fuel, plan, spur, whet; **5** evoke, rouse, speed, tempt; **6** arouse, awaken, elicit, excite, foment, hasten, incite, induce, kindle, manage, prompt; **7** inspire, procure, promote, provoke, quicken; **8** contrive, engineer, increase, motivate; **9** encourage, influence, intensify; **10** accelerate, invigorate; **11** precipitate; PHRASES: **3, 3** set off; **4, 2** fire up; **4, 3** draw out; **5, 2** speed up; **5, 3** bring out, spark off; **7, 3** trigger off.

stimulating 4 arch; **5** tonic; **6** emetic, lively; **7** purging, rousing; **8** anabolic, aperient, diuretic, exciting, hidrotic, laxative, poignant, spirited; **9** analeptic, cathartic, enhancing, inspiring, medicinal, purgative, sudorific; **10** astringent, choleretic, energizing, intriguing, motivating, refreshing, uricosumic; **11** diaphoretic, encouraging, expectorant, interesting, natriuretic, provocative, psychedelic, restorative, rubefacient, titillating; **12** invigorating; **13** abortifacient; **14** hallucinogenic; **15** sympathomimetic.

stimulation 4 spur, zest; **6** prompt, spirit; **8** archness, stimulus; **9** harshness, incentive, poignancy, roughness; **10** liveliness, motivation; **11** inspiration, titillation; **13** encouragement.

stimulus 3 pay, sop, tip; **4** bait, buzz, cash, gift, goad, itch, kick, lure, perk, prod, rise, spur; **5** bonus, bribe, charm, money, prick, raise, spell, throb, tonic, wages; **6** carrot, fillip, profit, salary, thrill, tickle, tingle; **7** freebie, frisson, impetus, payment, prickle; **8** benefits, donation, flattery, gratuity, kickback; **9** baksheesh, incentive, stimulant; **10** fluttering, gooseflesh, heightener, incitement, inducement, motivation; **11** formication, provocation, stimulation, titillation; **13** horripilation; PHRASES: **3, 6** the creeps; **3, 7** the shivers; **3, 8** pay increase; **4-2** come-on, turn-on; **4-3** hand-out; **4, 3, 7** pins and needles; **4, 4** sore spot; **4, 5** hush money; **4, 6** loss leader, pork barrel; **5, 4** slush fund; **5-4** sweet-talk; **5, 7** goose pimples; **5, 10** added attraction; **6, 3, 5** carrot and stick; **6, 5** golden apple; **6, 6** spoils system; **6-7** heebie-jeebies; **7, 5** limited offer, special offer; **8, 5** tempting offer; **9, 6** political favors.

sting *See* **smart**

stink 2 BO; **3** hum *UK*; **4** fuss, niff *UK*, pong *UK*, reek; **5** smell, whiff *UK*; **6** rumpus, stench, uproar; **7** scandal; **8** brouhaha; **9** commotion; PHRASES: **3, 3** let fly, let off; **5, 3** ~ out; **5, 4** break wind; **5, 8** smell horrible; **8, 5** horrible smell; **10, 4** unpleasant odor.

stinking 4 foul, olid, rank; **5** fetid, fuggy, fusty, gassy, musty, niffy *UK*, pongy *UK*, stale; **6** frowzy, putrid, rotten, smelly, stinky *UK*, sweaty, whiffy *UK*; **7** frowsty, humming *UK*, miasmal, miasmic, noisome, reeking; **8** mephitic, unwashed; **9** offensive, sulfurous; **10** ammoniacal, graveolent *UK*, malodorous; **11** unwholesome; **12** asphyxiating, overpowering, unventilated; PHRASES: **4-8** evil-smelling, foul-smelling.

stint *See* **spell**

stipulate *See* **specify**

stipulation *See* **condition**

stir 3 ado, can, mix; **4** beat, fold, fuss, move, whip; **5** blend, budge, cause, rouse, roust, shift, swirl, upset, whisk; **6** arouse, awaken, bustle, excite, hubbub, incite, revive, uproar; **7** agitate, disturb, inspire, provoke, trouble; **8** motivate; **9** commotion, stimulate; **10** hullabaloo; **11** disturbance; PHRASES: **2-2** to-do; **3, 2** get up; **3, 3, 3** hue and cry; **3, 5** get going; **4, 2** fire up, ~ up, wake up; **4, 2, 4** call to mind; **5, 4** bring back. *See also* **prison**

stirrup **4** loop, ring; **5** strap; **6** stapes; PHRASES: **4, 7** foot support; **7, 3** ~ cup; **7, 4** ~ bone, ~ pump.

stitch **3** sew; **4** darn, lock, moss, slip, tack, tent; **5** baste, cable, chain, close, satin; **6** garter, suture; **7** blanket, running; **8** stocking; **10** buttonhole; PHRASES: **3, 2** sew up; **6, 2** ~ up.

stock **4** farm, hogs, keep, pigs, sell; **5** carry, hoard, sheep, stash, store; **6** cattle, common, horses, normal, supply; **7** capital, provide, reserve, routine, typical; **8** ordinary, standard; **9** livestock, stockpile; **10** collection; **11** certificate; **12** accumulation; PHRASES: **3-2-3-4** run-of-the-mill; **4, 1, 6, 2** have a supply of; **4, 2** deal in; **4, 7** farm animals; **4, 9** have available; **5, 3** ~ car; **5, 5** joint ~; **5, 6** ~ market; **5, 8** ~ exchange; **6, 5** common ~; **7, 5** rolling ~; **8, 4** bouillon cube; **8, 5** laughing ~; **8, 7** domestic animals; **9, 5** preferred ~.

stockade **3** pen; **4** fort; **5** fence; **7** barrier; **8** palisade; **9** enclosure.

stockbroker **4** bear, bull; **6** backer, banker, bidder, broker, trader; **8** investor; **9** financier, plutocrat; **10** capitalist, speculator; PHRASES: **5-6** stock-jobber; **6, 5** market maker.

stock exchange, stock market **2** SE; **3** CAC, DAX; **4** FTSE; **5** issue; **6** bourse, change, market, Rialto; **7** Footsie *UK*, trading; **8** exchange; **9** dividends; PHRASES: **3, 3** the Dow; **3, 4** Big Bang, the City; **3, 5** bid price; **4, 4, 5** Hang Seng Index; **4, 6** bear market, bull market, Wall Street; **5, 4** share shop *UK*; **5, 5** issue price; **5, 6** money market, stock market, Third Market; **6, 3, 5** Nikkei Dow Index; **6, 4** bucket shop; **9, 6** commodity market, financial market.

stocky **5** beefy, bulky, burly, heavy, hefty, hulky, lumpy, lusty, meaty, solid, squat, stout; **6** brawny, chunky, square, sturdy; **7** hulking, lumpish; **8** heavyset, thickset; **9** lumbering, strapping; **11** elephantine; PHRASES: **4-5** well-built; **7, 5** heavily built.

stodgy **4** dull; **5** heavy; **6** turgid; **7** filling, starchy; **10** unexciting; **12** indigestible; **13** uninteresting.

Stoic **4** Zeno; **6** Seneca.

stoical **4** calm, cool; **5** quiet, sober; **6** placid, serene; **7** equable, passive, patient; **8** composed, moderate, resigned, sanguine; **9** temperate; **10** phlegmatic, restrained; **11** indifferent, unemotional; **13** dispassionate, imperturbable, philosophical.

stoicism **6** phlegm; **8** coldness, patience; **9** endurance, fortitude; **10** sanguinity; **11** resignation; **12** indifference; **13** impassiveness.

stoke **4** fuel; **9** encourage, intensify; **10** strengthen; PHRASES: **4, 2** stir up.

stole *See* **wrap**

stolen **3** hot; **4** bent; **6** nicked; **7** filched, looting, pinched, raiding; **8** foraging, hijacked, pilfered, poaching, ravaging, smuggled, thieving, thievish; **9** hijacking, kidnapped, larcenous, marauding, pillaging, predatory, purloined; **10** brigandish, contraband, kidnapping, piratelike, plundering, plunderous, predacious, skyjacking, spoliatory; **11** burglarious; **12** buccaneering, kleptomaniac, privateering; PHRASES: **3, 3, 2, 6** too hot to handle; **3-6** ill-gotten; **5, 6** black market; **5-7** grave-robbing; **5-8** light-fingered; **6-8** sticky-fingered.

stolen goods **4** haul, loot, swag, take; **5** booty, graft, prize, steal; **6** boodle, spoils; **7** pillage, plunder; **8** pickings; **9** gleanings, stealings; **10** contraband; PHRASES: **3-3** ripoff; **3, 5** hot goods; **3-6, 5** ill-gotten gains; **3, 8** hot property; **4, 8** rich pickings; **6, 2, 3** spoils of war; **6, 2, 6** spoils of office.

stomach **3** gut, pot, tum *UK*; **5** belly, tummy; **6** paunch; **7** abdomen, beergut, midriff; **8** potbelly; **11** breadbasket; PHRASES: **3, 6** bay window; **5, 4** spare tire.

stomach ache **5** colic, grips, ulcer; **7** pyrosis; **9** bellyache, dyspepsia, heartburn; **11** indigestion; PHRASES: **3-4** gut-ache; **5, 4** tummy ache; **6, 5** hunger pains.

stone **3** gem, shy; **4** flag, hone, lava, lime, onyx, opal, pelt, ragg, rock, ruby, sard, slab, tuff; **5** agate, beryl, chalk, chert, chuck, drupe, flint, humit, jewel, menah, metal, mocha, paste, quern, quoin, quoit, scree, shale, slate, sling, stane, stela, stele, topaz, Wyman; **6** ashlar, basalt, bezoar, cobble, coping, dolmen, fossil, gibber, gneiss, gravel, Jagger, jasper, marble, menhir, metate, nugget, oamaru, pebble, pumice, sarden, sarsen, scarab, schist; **7** adamant, asteria, Avebury, boulder, breccia, girasol(e), granite, hyacine, hyalite, olivine, parpent, peridot, Purbeck, putamen, sarsden, shingle, smaragd, tektite, telamon; **8** aerolite, aerolith, amethyst, asteroid, baguette, cabochon, calculus, cinnamon, cromlech, endocarp, imposing, lapidate, megalith, monolith, nephrite, omphalos, onychite, parpoint, precious, sapphire, sardonyx, stepping, tonalite; **9** alabaster, cairngorm, carnelian, cholelith, chondrite, cornelian, crossette, curbstone, dichroite, gannister, hessonite, hoarstone, limestone, malachite, paleolith, quartzite, sandstone, soapstone, tombstone, trilithon, turquoise, ventifact; **10** aragonites, chalcedony, draconites, foundation, hornblende, rhinestone; **11** peristalith; **12** conglomerate; PHRASES: **4, 5** Bath ~ *UK*; **5, 2, 5** ~ of Scone; **6, 5** coping ~, kidney ~, paving ~ *UK*; **7, 5** Blarney ~, Cornish ~, pudding ~, Rosetta ~; **8, 5** Portland ~.

stony **5** broke, rocky; **6** flinty, pebbly; **7** shingly; **8** pitiless; **9** penniless, unfeeling; **10** unyielding; **11** impecunious; **12** impoverished; **13** unsympathetic; PHRASES: **4-6** rock-strewn.

stool **5** cutty *UK*; **8** footrest; **9** faldstool; PHRASES: **3, 5** bar ~; **5, 5** piano ~ *UK*; **7, 5** cucking ~, ducking ~, milking ~ *UK*.

stoolpigeon **4** narc; **5** sneak; **6** snitch; **7** traitor; **8** informer; **9** bluegrass.

stoop **4** bend; **5** deign; **9** patronize; **10** condescend; PHRASES: **4, 4** bend down, bend over; **4, 7** lean forward; **6, 8** debase yourself.

stop **3** ban, bar, cap, dam, dot, end; **4** bung, clog, cork, foil, halt, quit, rest, stem, whoa; **5** avast, avert, black, block, break, cease, check, choke, comma, deter, erase, hitch, pause, point *UK*; **6** defeat, freeze, glitch, harbor, hinder, holdup, impede, period, strike, tampon; **7** adjourn, airport, bandage, closure, cloture, layover, occlude, prevent, sojourn, staunch; **8** blockade, blockage, deadlock, prohibit, shutdown, standoff, stopover, strangle, terminal, terminus, throttle; **9** breakdown, checkmate, closedown, frustrate, interrupt, stalemate; **10** standstill; **11** discontinue, resignation; **12** interruption; PHRASES: **2, 4** be over; **3, 3** log

jam; **3, 4** bus ~; **4, 1, 5** take a break; **4, 2** bung up *UK*, plug up; **4, 2, 2, 3** come to an end; **3** ~ off; **5, 2** block up; **5, 2, 1, 4** bring to a halt; **5, 2, 1, 5** bring to a close; **5, 2, 2, 3** bring to an end; **5, 3** block off, break off, peter out; **7, 7** railway station; **8, 3** breaking off; **8, 7** railroad station.

stopover **4** dock, halt, stop; **5** berth, pause, stage; **6** billet, stable; **7** shelter; PHRASES: **3, 4** dry dock; **4, 2, 1, 5** port in a storm; **4-3** stop-off.

stoppage **6** freeze, strike; **7** barrier, embargo, walkout; **8** blockage, obstacle, slowdown; **9** deduction; **10** moratorium; **11** obstruction; PHRASES: **4, 2, 4** work to rule; **4, 8** hire purchase, work ~; **7, 6** wildcat strike; **7, 7** reduced payment; **8, 7** deferred payment; **11, 4** installment plan.

stopped **4** full; **5** still; **6** bunged, capped, choked, closed, corked, dammed, halted, jammed, packed; **7** blocked, clogged, costive, crashed, plugged, stuffed; **8** bandaged, immobile, occluded; **9** congested, staunched; **10** impassable, motionless, obstructed, stationary; **11** constipated, constricted; **12** impenetrable; PHRASES: **2, 1, 10** at a standstill; **3, 2, 5** out of order; **3, 2, 10** out of commission; **3, 6** not moving; **3, 7** not working; **4-3** worn-out; **5, 2, 3, 5** given up the ghost; **6, 2** backed up, bunged up, choked up, packed up *UK*; **7, 2** blocked up, clogged up, ~ up, stuffed up.

stopper **3** cap, lid, peg, pin, tap, top, wad; **4** bung, clot, cork, plug, seal, stop; **5** choke, cover, valve, wedge; **6** damper, faucet, piston, spigot, tampon; **7** bandage, closure, embolus, infarct, tampion, wadding; **8** covering, stopcock, stuffing, thrombus; **10** tourniquet; PHRASES: **4, 6** trip switch; **5, 4** blood clot; **6, 6** cutout switch.

stopping place **4** halt, port, stop; **6** harbor; **7** airport, station; **8** cabstand, terminal, terminus; PHRASES: **3-2** lay-by; **3, 4** bus stop; **3, 7** bus station, gas station; **3, 8** air terminal; **4, 2, 4** port of call; **4, 4** taxi rank; **4, 7** tube station; **5, 7** train station; **5, 8** ferry terminal; **7, 4** railway halt, request stop *UK*, waiting room; **7, 7** railway station, service station; **8, 7** railroad station.

stop using **3** ban; **4** doff, drop, dump, junk, stop; **5** cease, ditch, eject, leave, scrap; **6** cancel, disuse, freeze, slough; **7** discard, replace, suspend; **8** abrogate, jettison, mothball, withdraw; **9** dismantle, stockpile, supersede; **10** relinquish, substitute; **11** deteriorate; **12** decommission; PHRASES: **3, 2** lay up; **3, 4** lie idle; **3, 5** lay aside, put aside, set aside; **3, 6** lie fallow; **4, 2** give up, hang up; **4, 3** cast off, take off, turn off; **4, 4** pack away, sock away; **4, 4, 4** have done with; **4, 5** take apart; **5, 3** leave off, write off; **5, 4** store away, throw away; **5, 9** throw overboard; **8, 4** squirrel away.

stop work 4 fire, sack; **6** resign, retire; **7** dismiss; **9** discharge; PHRASES: **2, 9** be dismissed; **3, 3** lay off, pay off; **3, 3, 2, 5** put out to grass; **4, 2, 2** hang it up; **4, 4** quit work; **4, 9** make redundant; **7, 3** pension off.

stop working 4 fail; **5** break, close; **6** resign, retire, strike; **8** collapse; PHRASES: **2, 2, 6** go on strike; **2, 3, 2, 8** go out of business; **2, 5, 2** go belly up; **2, 8** go bankrupt; **4, 1, 6** call a strike; **4, 2** pack up, wind up; **4, 3** walk out; **4, 4** shut down, stop work; **5, 1, 6** stage a strike; **5, 2** seize up; **5, 4** break down, close down, stand down; **5, 7** cease trading; **9, 2, 4** close/shut up shop.

storage 3 box, tip; **4** bank, barn, dock, dump, hive, hold, loft, room, safe, shed, silo, sump, tank, till; **5** attic, chest, depot, drain, shelf, space, trunk, vault, wharf; **6** armory, bunker, bureau, cellar, coffer, device, drawer, fridge, garage, garner, hangar, heater, holder, icebox, larder, memory, morgue, pantry, quiver, silage, stable; **7** arsenal, baggage, battery, boxroom *UK*, buttery, cabinet, chamber, cistern, freezer, garbage, granary, gunroom, hayloft, holdall *UK*, loading, packing, storing, stowage, stowing; **8** basement, bottling, capacity, carryall, cesspool, cupboard, ensilage, entrepôt, landfill, magazine, moneybag, moneybox, mortuary, stabling, suitcase, treasury, woodshed; **9** container, exchequer, garnering, gasholder, gasometer, gathering, honeycomb, reservoir, stockroom, storeroom, storeship, strongbox, warehouse; **10** deepfreeze, depository, protection, receptacle, storehouse, strongroom; **11** portmanteau, warehousing; **12** accumulation, conservation, preservation, refrigerator; **13** accommodation; PHRASES: **3, 3** oil pan; **3, 7** dry battery, gas station; **4, 4** data bank; **4, 5** arms depot, gold vault; **4, 6** wine cellar; **4-7** safe-deposit; **5, 2, 7** chest of drawers; **5, 4** blood bank, night safe, sperm bank, still room *UK*, trash dump; **5, 5** water tower; **5, 6** money drawer; **5, 10** night depository; **6, 4** petrol tank, refuse dump, septic tank; **6, 5** sewage works, silver vault, weapon store; **6-7** fridge-freezer *UK*; **7, 4** packing case *UK*, putting away, rubbish dump *UK*, ~ area, tidying away; **7, 5** ~ space; **7, 7** filling station, ~ battery; **7, 8** ~ capacity; **8, 4** gasoline pump; **8, 5** cupboard space, treasure house.

store 3 bag; **4** bank, bury, crop, file, fill, firm, fuel, fund, heap, hide, hive, hold, keep, load, mall, mart, mass, pack, pick, pile, pool, reap, save, stow; **5** amass, board, cache, depot, glean, hoard, house, kiosk, kitty, leave, share, stack, stock; **6** amount, assets, bagful, bottle, bundle, bunker, garage, garner, gather, invest, market, outlet, packet, pickle, refill, refuel, retain, stable, supply; **7** augment, backlog, buildup, capital, charity, chemist *UK*, conceal, concern, deposit, harvest, haycock, hayrick *UK*, holding, husband, nursery, provide, reserve, savings, secrete, vintage; **8** bakeshop, bookshop *UK*, boutique, conserve, emporium, haystack, increase, mothball, pharmacy, preserve, property, quantity, reserves, showroom, takeaway, treasure; **9** bookstore, bucketful, economize, megastore, newsstand, provision, replenish, reservoir, retailer's, salesroom, stockpile, stockroom, storeroom, trousseau, warehouse; **10** accumulate, collection, depository, dispensary, investment, repository, superstore; **11** communalize, hypermarket, merchandise, supercenter, supermarket; **12** accumulation, hairdresser's *UK* establishment; PHRASES: **3, 2** lay by, lay in, lay up, put by, top up *UK*; **3, 2, 7** put in storage; **3, 3, 3, 5** mom and pop ~; **3, 4** lay away, put away, sex shop; **3, 5** put aside, set aside; **3-5, 6** ice-cream parlor; **4, 2** fill up, fold up, pile up, roll up, save up, take in, take on; **4, 2, 2** hang on to; **4, 3** nest egg; **4-3** bulk-buy; **4-3-4, 4** fish-and-chip shop; **4-3-5** cash-and-carry; **4, 4** fish shop, junk shop, keep back, pack away, salt away, sock away, stow away, tuck shop *UK*, wine lake; **4-4** duty-free; **4, 5** hair salon; **4, 6** flea market, post office; **4, 8** food mountain; **5, 2** build up, stock up; **5-2-5** stock-in-trade; **5, 3** panic buy; **5, 4** stash away; **5, 5** candy ~, chain ~; **5-7** drive-through; **6, 4** corner shop *UK*; **6, 5** anchor ~, hiding place, liquor ~, retail ~; **6, 6** beauty parlor, bottom drawer, garden center, retail outlet; **6, 8** buried treasure, butter mountain; **7, 4** reserve fund; **7, 5** general ~, trading house, variety ~; **7, 8** bargain basement; **8, 4** squirrel away; **8, 5** discount ~; **9, 5** community chest; **10, 5** concession stand, department ~; **11, 5** consignment ~, convenience ~, refreshment stand. *See also* **shop**

storekeeper **5** baker; **6** bowyer, cutler *UK*, draper, grocer, hatter, hosier; **7** butcher, florist, furrier, glazier; **8** chandler, clothier, druggist, gunsmith, jeweller, milliner, perfumer; **9** fruiterer *UK*, newsagent, stationer; **10** fishmonger, ironmonger, newsdealer, victualler; **11** chocolatier, greengrocer, tobacconist; **12** cheesemonger *UK*, confectioner, costermonger *UK*.

storm **4** fume, gale, hail, rage, rain; **5** stalk, stamp, stomp; **6** squall; **7** bluster, cyclone, flounce, monsoon, tempest, thunder, tornado, typhoon; **8** blizzard, downpour, eruption, outbreak, outburst; **9** explosion, hurricane, lightning, rainstorm, snowstorm; **10** overmaster, trashmover; **12** chunkfloater, thunderstorm; PHRASES: **3, 2** set in; **3, 5** ice ~; **4, 1, 4** blow a gale; **4, 1, 9** blow a hurricane; **4, 2, 5** take by ~; **4, 3, 4** rant and rave; **5-2** flare-up; **5, 4** ~ cone *UK*; **5, 6** ~ petrel; **5, 7** ~ lantern, ~ warning; **5, 9** Idaho rainstorm; **8, 4, 7** lighterd knot floater; **8, 5** tropical ~.

stormy **4** foul, ugly, wild; **5** dirty, fiery, rainy, rough, windy; **6** raging; **7** squally, violent; **8** blustery, cyclonic, frenzied, thundery, vehement, volatile; **9** inclement, turbulent, unsettled; **10** passionate; **11** tempestuous.

story **5** floor, level; **7** landing, section; **8** division.

story **4** epic, saga, tale, yarn; **5** fable; **6** legend, report; **7** account, episode, fiction; **8** anecdote; **9** chronicle, narration, narrative.

stout **4** firm; **5** brave, heavy, plump, solid, tough; **6** strong, sturdy; **8** resolute, stalwart, thickset; **10** determined; **11** substantial.

stove **3** Aga™, hob *UK*; **4** oven; **7** cooktop; **9** cookstove; PHRASES: **3, 4** fan oven; **4, 6** base burner; **5, 4** Dutch oven; **7, 5** kitchen range; **8, 5** potbelly ~.

strabismus **6** squint.

straddle **4** link, span; **7** include, overlap; **8** bestride; PHRASES: **2, 7** be astride.

strafe **5** blitz, shell; **6** attack; **7** bombard; **8** shelling; **11** bombardment; PHRASES: **3, 6** air attack; **4, 2** fire at; **6, 6** aerial attack.

straggle **3** lag; **5** stray, trail; **6** extend,

sprawl, spread; PHRASES: **3, 6** lag behind; **4, 6** fall behind; **5, 6** trail behind; **6, 3** spread out.

straight **4** even, fair, neat, open, pure, tidy, true; **5** blunt, erect, frank, level, plain, plumb, right, rigid, sober; **6** candid, direct, honest, linear, square, unbent; **7** orderly, running, unmixed, upright; **8** arranged, directly, orthodox, truthful, uncurled, vertical; **9** instantly, organized, shipshape, undiluted; **10** aboveboard, forthright, horizontal, successive, vertically; **11** consecutive, immediately, rectilinear, respectable, traditional, trustworthy; **12** conservative, conventional, heterosexual, horizontally, straightaway, straightened, unswervingly; **13** perpendicular, unadulterated, uninterrupted; **15** straightforward; PHRASES: **2, 1, 3** in a row; **2, 1, 4** in a line; **2, 2, 5** as it comes; **2, 3, 4** on the beam; **2, 3, 4, 5** as the crow flies; **2, 4** at once, in line; **2, 5** in order; **2-5** up-front; **3-7** law-abiding; **4, 1, 2, 1** from A to B; **5, 4** right away; **6, 3** sorted out; **7, 5** without delay; **7, 8** without stopping; **8, 3** ~ bat, ~ man, ~ off; **8, 4** ~ face; **8, 5** ~ fight *UK*.

straighten **4** tidy; **5** align, level, order; **6** adjust, neaten, unbend, uncoil, uncurl, unfold, unfurl, unroll; **7** arrange, flatten, unravel, untwist; **8** organize, untangle; **10** unscramble; **11** disentangle; PHRASES: **3, 8** set straight; **4, 2** tidy up *UK*; **4, 3** comb out, iron out; **4, 5** make level; **4, 8** make straight; **6, 3** smooth out; **6, 4** smooth down; **7, 3** flatten out; **10, 2** ~ up; **10, 3** ~ out.

straightforward **4** easy, open; **5** basic, clear, frank, plain; **6** candid, direct, facile, honest, simple; **7** sincere; **8** straight; **9** guileless, ingenuous, outspoken; **10** forthright; **11** undemanding; **13** uncomplicated; PHRASES: **2-5** up-front; **4-7** open-hearted; **5-3** clearcut.

straight line **3** row; **7** beeline; **9** colonnade; **13** perpendicular; PHRASES: **5, 4** plumb line; **8, 4** unbroken line, vertical line; **9, 5** ascending order; **10, 4** horizontal line; **10, 5** descending order.

straight person **8** moderate; **12** conservative, heterosexual; PHRASES: **7, 2, 5** nonuser of drugs; **8-7** straight-shooter.

strain **3** tax; **4** fear, form, hurt, kind, pain, pull, sift, sort, type; **5** angst, crick, drain, force, labor, sieve, twist, worry; **6** burden, damage, effort, filter, injure, injury, sprain, stress, strive, trauma, wrench; **7** anxiety, overtax, species, stretch, tension, torment, variety; **8** endeavor, exertion, overload, pressure, separate, sourness, struggle; **10** bitterness, overburden, subspecies; **PHRASES: 3, 4** try hard; **5, 8** exert yourself; **7, 7** nervous tension.

strait 4 spit; **5** canal, chink, crack, ditch, gully, sound; **6** ravine, tunnel; **7** channel, isthmus, narrows, passage, straits; **8** corridor; **9** peninsula; **10** bottleneck.

strand 4 curl, lock, trap, wire, wisp; **5** fiber, tress; **6** aspect, maroon, string, thread; **7** abandon, element, feature; **8** filament; **9** component; **11** constituent; **PHRASES: 3, 3** cut off.

strange 3 new, odd; **5** alien, funny, novel, weird; **6** exotic, quaint; **7** bizarre, curious, foreign, oddball, unknown, unusual; **8** abnormal, peculiar, puzzling; **9** different, eccentric, enigmatic; **10** mysterious, outlandish, perplexing *UK*, remarkable, surprizing, unexpected, unfamiliar; **11** astonishing; **12** inexplicable; **13** extraordinary.

strangle 5 choke; **6** stifle; **7** garrote, inhibit, repress, smother; **8** garrotte *UK*, suppress, throttle; **10** asphyxiate; **11** strangulate.

strap 4 band, belt, lash; **5** leash, strip; **6** buckle, fasten, secure; **9** fastening, watchband.

stratagem 3 art, con, lie, net, pit, web; **4** game, move, plan, plot, ploy, ruse, scam, sham, trap, wile; **5** blind, catch, cheat, ditch, dodge, feint, fraud, shift, trick; **6** ambush, device, excuse, resort, scheme, tactic; **7** evasion, pitfall, pretext, swindle, tactics, wrinkle; **8** artifice, flimflam, maneuver, resource, strategy; **9** deception, expedient; **10** subterfuge; **11** contrivance, machination; **PHRASES: 3, 2, 6** bag of tricks, box of tricks, web of deceit; **3, 2, 7** web of cunning; **3, 3** old trick; **3, 7** red herring; **5, 3** white lie; **5, 4** Greek gift; **5, 6** smoke screen; **5, 7** trial balloon; **6, 5** Trojan horse; **6, 6** ballon d'essai; **8, 4** Parthian shot; **8-5** stalking-horse; **9, 5** political trick; **10, 5** confidence trick.

strategy *See* **tactic**

stratum *See* **layer**

straw 3 hay; **5** chaff, grass; **6** raffia; **7** stubble; **PHRASES: 4, 5** last ~; **5, 3** ~ man; **5, 4** ~ poll; **5, 5** short ~; **6, 5** cheese ~.

stray 4 lost; **5** drift; **7** vagrant; **8** homeless; **9** abandoned, wandering; **PHRASES: 2, 6** go astray; **3, 4** get lost; **6, 3** wander off.

streak 3 fly, run; **4** band, line, mark, roll, side, vein, whiz, zoom; **5** flash, fleck, stain, strip, trait; **6** stripe; **7** element, stretch.

stream 3 jet; **4** beck *UK*, flow, gush; **5** flood, river, spill, spurt; **7** barrage, cascade, rivulet, torrent; **9** onslaught; **11** watercourse.

streamer 4 flag; **6** banner, ribbon; **7** bunting; **10** decoration.

street 2 ST; **3** Ave, way; **4** gate, lane, mews *UK*, road; **5** alley, close, drive, paseo; **6** avenue, Strand; **7** highway; **8** crescent; **PHRASES: 4, 6** Cato S~, high ~, Wall S~; **5, 6** Broad S~, Queer S~; **6, 4** ~ Arab, ~ cred; **6, 5** ~ value; **6, 6** Oxford S~; **6, 7** ~ theater; **7, 6** Downing S~, Watling S~.

streetcar 7, 3 trolley car.

street trader 6 coster, sutler; **10** vivandiere; **12** costermonger *UK*; **PHRASES: 5-6** stall-holder, stall-keeper; **6, 3** barrow boy *UK*; **6, 6** market trader, street seller, street vendor.

strength 4 gift, grit, guts *UK*; **5** asset, brawn, depth, force, forte, might, nerve, pluck, power, spunk, thews, vigor; **6** biceps, métier, muscle, sinews; **7** bravery, courage, potency, stamina, triceps; **8** backbone, capacity, dilution, firmness, laterals, tenacity, virility; **9** beefiness, burliness, endurance, greatness, intensity, manliness, pectorals, stability, toughness; **10** aggression, durability, protection, resilience, resistance, resolution; **11** athleticism, bellicosity, muscularity, musculature, superiority; **12** effectuality; **13** assertiveness, concentration, determination, effectiveness, fortification, invincibility, inviolability, steadfastness, survivability; **14** aggressiveness, impregnability; **15** impenetrability, invulnerability, resourcefulness, unassailability; **PHRASES: 5, 5** brute force; **5, 8** brute ~; **6, 4** strong suit; **6, 5** strong point; **7, 5** staying power; **7, 8** tensile ~; **8, 5** physical force.

strengthen 3 pad, tan; **5** boost, brace, stuff; **6** anneal, deepen, harden, revive, stress, temper; **7** animate, confirm, enliven, fortify, protect, quicken, refresh, stiffen, support, sustain, toughen; **8** buttress, energize, entrench, revivify; **9** emphasize, intensify, mercerize, reinforce, underline, vulcanize; **10** invigorate, underscore; **12** reinvigorate; PHRASES: **4, 2** beef up, prop up, soup up, tune up; **4, 5, 2** lend force to; **4-6** case-harden; **5, 2** build up.

strengthened 5 armed, stout, tough; **6** braced; **7** durable, revived; **8** restored; **9** fortified, resistant, toughened; **10** buttressed, protective, reinforced; **11** substantial; PHRASES: **2, 1, 4, 7** on a firm footing; **4-5** well-armed, well-built; **4-7** hard-wearing; **4-9** well-protected; **5-4** heavy-duty.

strengthening 5 tonic; **7** revival; **8** reviving; **9** hardening, restoring, tempering; **10** fortifying, protecting, refreshing, stiffening, toughening; **11** refreshment, reinforcing, restoration, revivifying; **12** convalescing, invigorating, invigoration; **13** convalescence, reinforcement; **14** revivification.

strenuous 4 hard; **6** active, taxing; **7** arduous; **8** spirited, tireless; **9** demanding, energetic; **10** determined, exhausting.

stress 5 shock, worry; **6** accent, hassle, nerves, strain, trauma, weight; **7** anxiety, tension, urgency; **8** conflict, emphasis, hysteria, pressure; **9** emphasize, highlight, hysterics, underline; **10** accentuate, importance, psychalgia, traumatism, underscore; **11** ambivalence, frustration; **14** decompensation; PHRASES: **3, 8, 2** lay emphasis on; **5, 2** point up; **5, 6** panic attack; **5, 8** shock reaction; **6, 5** mental shock; **6, 6** mental ~; **6, 8** ~ reaction; **7, 3** nervous tic; **7, 5** anxiety state; **9, 6** emotional strain.

stretch 3 run; **4** area, give, time; **5** spell, stint, sweep, widen; **6** bounce, expand, extend, period, spread, spring, unfold; **7** broaden, enlarge, expanse, section; **8** elongate; **10** elasticity.

stretched 4 busy; **6** pushed; **7** fraught; **8** strained; **10** lengthened; **12** outstretched, overextended.

stricken *See* **afflicted**

strict 4 firm; **5** exact, harsh, stern; **6** narrow, severe; **7** precise; **8** accurate; **9** stringent; **10** meticulous.

strict person 3 dry; **4** hawk; **5** bully; **6** despot, pedant, purist; **7** puritan, Spartan; **8** autocrat, dictator, martinet, stickler; **9** hardliner, oppressor; **10** bureaucrat, inquisitor, militarist, persecutor, taskmaster; **11** bloodsucker; **12** taskmistress; **13** authoritarian; **14** disciplinarian; PHRASES: **3, 7** Big Brother; **4, 6** hard master; **5, 5** Dutch uncle; **5, 6** petty

tyrant, slave driver; **7, 5** hanging judge; **8, 5** sergeant major.

stride 4 gait, pace, step, walk; **5** tread; **7** advance, headway; **8** progress; **11** development, improvement.

strident 4 loud; **5** noisy, vocal; **6** baying, brassy, brazen, shrill, twangy; **7** blaring, braying, grating, howling, jarring, raucous, squawky, ululant; **8** forceful, metallic, piercing; **9** clamorous, dissonant, squawking, unmusical; **10** discordant, persuasive, stridulous, vociferous; **11** cacophonous, penetrating, unmelodious; **12** inharmonious; PHRASES: **3-9** ear-splitting.

strident (be strident) 3 jar; **4** bray, howl, rasp, wail, yawl, yawp, yell, yelp; **5** blare, blast, clash, grate, grind, skirl; **6** jangle, squawk; **7** discord, ululate; PHRASES: **4, 3, 4** lift the roof; **5, 2, 4, 4** grate on one's ears; **5, 4, 4** split one's ears.

strife *See* **trouble**

strike 3 hit, lam, mug, ram, rap, tap; **4** bash, beat, belt, butt, cuff, dash, kick, knap, lash, maul, poke, push, raid, sock; **5** clock, clout, flail, foray, knock, punch, reach, smack, swipe, thump; **6** assail, attack, attain, delete, effect, hammer, picket, savage, wallop; **7** achieve, arrange, assault, boycott, clobber, lockout, uncover, unearth, walkout; **8** discover, register, slowdown; **9** incursion; **13** demonstration; PHRASES: **2, 3** go for; **3, 2** set on; **3-2** sit-in; **3, 3** lay low; **3, 3, 2** let fly at; **3, 4** hit upon, lay into, run into; **3-4** sit-down; **3, 6** air ~; **4, 1, 2, 2** have a go at; **4, 2** beat up, come to, dawn on, fall on, turn up; **4-2** work-in *UK*; **4, 2, 4** come to mind, work to rule; **4, 3** come out *UK*, kick ass, walk out; **4, 4** bump into, fall upon, lace into, sail into, stop work, tear into; **4, 5** down tools *UK*; **4, 8** work stoppage; **5, 1, 4** fetch a blow; **5, 2** light on, occur to, round on; **5, 4** bring down, close with, crash into, knock down, pitch into, smash into; **5, 4, 4** cross your mind; **6, 2** arrive at; **6, 2, 6** launch an attack; **6, 3** ~ oil; **6, 4** chance upon, happen upon, pounce upon, ~ gold; **7, 4** collide with, grapple with; **7, 6** general ~, stumble across, wildcat ~; **8, 6** sympathy ~; **9, 6** lightning ~.

strike dumb 3 gag; **4** hush; **6** deaden, muffle; **7** silence; **8** gobsmack, suppress; **9** dumbfound; PHRASES: **3, 5** cut short; **4, 2, 2** hang up on; **5, 4** shout down; **6, 2, 7** reduce to silence.

striking 4 bold, loud, neat, pure; **5** heady,

sharp, spicy, stark; **6** biting, bright, daring, marked; **7** glaring, mordant, piquant, pungent, salient, unusual; **8** dazzling, handsome, stunning; **9** arresting, beautiful, brilliant, prominent, undiluted; **10** attractive, noticeable, remarkable; **11** conspicuous, outstanding; **12** concentrated, intoxicating; PHRASES: **3-8** eye-catching; **4-7** good-looking; **6-7** strong-tasting; **6-8** strong-smelling.

string 1 E, G; **3** row, run, tie; **4** band, cord, line, rope; **5** chain, twine; **6** course, series, thread; **8** filament, sequence, variable; **10** succession; PHRASES: **6, 4** ~ bean; **6, 7** ~ quartet; **6, 9** ~ orchestra.

stringent *See* **severe**

stringy 5 chewy, tough; **6** sinewy; **7** fibrous.

strip 3 bar, bit, rid; **4** band, bare, belt, doff, lath, peel, shed, skin, slip, tape, zone; **5** shred; **6** denude, divest, ribbon, sliver, streak, stripe, unwrap; **7** deprive, disrobe, isthmus, plunder, undress; PHRASES: **4, 3** peel off; **4, 4** take away; **5, 3** ~ off *UK*; **5, 4** ~ show; **5, 5** comic ~, ~ poker; **5, 7** ~ cartoon *UK*.

striped 5 jaspé, lined, paned; **6** banded, barred, marbly, stripy *UK*, veined; **7** marbled, paneled, striate; **8** streaked; **10** reticulate.

striping 3 bar; **4** band, line; **5** crack, craze, stria; **6** streak, stripe; **7** crackle; **8** marbling; **9** striation; **11** streakiness; **12** reticulation.

stroke 3 cut, hit, pat, rap, rub; **4** blow, edge, hook, lash; **5** block, drive, glide, knock, snick, sweep, thump, whack; **6** caress, fondle, glance; **12** stonewalling; PHRASES: **2, 5** on drive; **3, 5** leg glide, off drive; **3, 6** leg glance; **9, 6** defensive ~.

stroll *See* **saunter**

stroller 5 buggy; **6** pusher; **9** pushchair *UK*; **12** perambulator *UK*; PHRASES: **4, 8** baby carriage.

strong 3 fit, hot; **4** bold, deep, firm, keen, loud, neat, pure; **5** beefy, burly, clear, eager, great, hardy, heady, lusty, manly, sharp, solid, sound, spicy, stark, stout, tough; **6** ardent, biting, brawny, bright, feisty, fierce, potent, robust, sinewy, sturdy, virile; **7** durable, fervent, glaring, healthy, intense, mordant, piquant, pungent, staunch, zealous; **8** athletic, dazzling, muscular, powerful, stalwart, striking, vigorous; **9** amazonian, brilliant, dedicated, effective, fanatical, Herculean, resilient, strapping, undiluted; **10** compelling, convincing, formidable, passionate, persuasive; **12** concentrated, intoxicating; PHRASES: **3-7** red-blooded; **4-5** well-built; **4-6** deep-seated; **4-7** hard-wearing; **5-3** clearcut; **5-4** heavy-duty.

strong (be strong) 5 rally; **6** revive; **7** recover; **8** outmatch; **9** overpower, overwhelm; **10** convalesce, overmaster; PHRASES: **3, 6** not weaken; **4, 1, 5** pack a punch; **4, 2** bear up, hold up; **4, 2, 5** come in force; **4, 3** hold out; **4, 4, 2, 5** have what it takes; **4, 4, 5** gird one's loins; **5, 3, 3** never say die; **7, 8** possess strength.

strong in spirit 4 firm, keen; **5** acute, brave, eager, tough; **6** plucky; **7** warlike, zealous; **8** resolute; **9** assertive, bellicose, dedicated, energetic, resilient, steadfast, tenacious; **10** aggressive, courageous, determined, unyielding; **11** resourceful; **12** enthusiastic; PHRASES: **4-9** self-assertive; **5-7** stout-hearted.

strong-willed 3 icy; **4** grim, hard, iron; **5** stern, stony; **6** steely; **7** adamant; **8** pitiless, ruthless, stubborn; **9** merciless, obstinate, unbending, unfeeling; **10** implacable, inexorable, inflexible, relentless, unyielding; **12** intransigent; **14** uncompromising; PHRASES: **4, 2, 4** hard as iron; **4-4** cast-iron, rock-hard; **4-6** iron-willed; **5, 2, 5** tough as steel; **6-6** strong-minded.

structural 5 basic; **8** physical; **9** essential, important; **10** mechanical, underlying; **11** fundamental, operational; **14** organizational.

structural element 3 rib, RSJ *UK*, tie; **4** arch, beam, bolt, boom, dome, idea, pier, shoe, spar, weld; **5** frame, joist, model, rivet, shell, strut, tower, truss, vault; **6** column, flange, girder, pillar, system, theory; **7** bearing, concept; **8** abutment, argument, buttress, stringer; **9** deduction, elevation, framework, structure; **10** cantilever; **11** elaboration; **12** construction; PHRASES: **1-4** H-beam, I-beam, T-beam; **3, 10** pin connection, web connection; **4, 10** seat connection; **5, 5** space frame; **5, 6** plate girder; **7, 5** bearing plate; **8, 4** geodesic dome; **8, 5** skeletal frame; **8, 6** vertical member.

structure 3 dam, ORD; **4** form, plan, road; **5** pylon, shape; **6** anomer, bridge, design, epimer, invent, isomer, makeup, runway, tunnel; **7** arrange, edifice, formula, pattern, prepare, railway *UK Can*; **8** assembly, building, bulkhead, erection, organize, racemate, railroad; **9** anomerism, chirality, configure, construct, epimerism, formation, inversion, isomerism, tectonics, tunneling; **10** constitute, embankment, resolution; **11** arrangement, composition, polarimetry; **12** architecture, constitution, construction, organization, racemization; **13** configuration; **14** architectonics; **15** stereochemistry.

structured 5 tight; **6** bossed, fitted, formal, formed, molded, ribbed, shaped; **7** crowned, defined, fascial, planned; **8** abutting, arcuated, arranged, corniced, designed, embossed, geodesic, scrolled; **9** cuneiform, decorated, organized, parabolic, reentrant, regulated, segmental; **10** controlled, ornamental, ornamented, pendentive, rusticated, triglyphic; **11** articulated, coordinated, fenestrated; **12** intersecting, systematized; **13** ferrovitreous; PHRASES: **4-7** well-defined; **4-7-3** well-thought-out.

struggle 3 try; **4** toil; **5** brawl, fight, labor; **6** effort, strain, strive, thrash, tussle, writhe; **7** contend, grapple, scuffle, wrestle, wriggle; **8** exertion, skirmish.

strum 3 jam; **4** play; **5** thrum, twang; **9** improvise.

strut 3 rod; **4** walk; **5** brace, march; **6** girder, parade, prance; **7** support, swagger; **10** crosspiece.

stub 3 end, hit; **4** bang, bash, bump; **5** knock, stump; **7** remains, remnant; **11** counterfoil.

stubble 5 beard, stems; **6** debris, growth, refuse, stalks; **7** rubbish; **8** mustache, whiskers.

stubborn 6 dogged, mulish; **7** bolshie *UK*, callous, willful; **8** obdurate, stalwart, ungiving; **9** difficult, immovable, immutable, obstinate, pigheaded, tenacious, unbending; **10** determined, inflexible, persistent, unyielding; **11** hardhearted, intractable, persevering, unalterable; **12** intransigent; PHRASES: **4-6** hard-boiled; **4-8** case-hardened *UK*; **5-7** stony-hearted, thick-skinned; **6-6** single-minded.

stuck 5 fixed; **6** caught, jammed, wedged; **7** baffled, puzzled, trapped; **9** mystified.

stud 3 dot; **4** boss, knob; **5** rivet; **6** fasten,

pepper; **7** scatter, speckle; **8** decorate, sprinkle.

student 1 L; **3** Nus; **4** coed, grad, swot *UK*; **5** aggie, medic, pupil, sizar *UK*, tutee; **6** alumna, reader, rushee; **7** alumnus, fresher *UK*, learner, scholar; **8** commoner, disciple, freshman, wrangler; **9** sophomore, undergrad; **10** apprentice; **12** exhibitioner *UK*, salutatorian; **13** upperclassman; PHRASES: **5, 8** first classman.

studied See **deliberate**

studio 7 academy, atelier, pottery; **8** workroom, workshop; **9** workplace; **12** conservatory.

studious 7 bookish, careful, serious; **8** diligent; **9** assiduous, scholarly; **10** reflective, thoughtful; **11** industrious, painstaking.

study 3 con, den; **4** case, cram, read, swot *UK*, time; **5** brown, field, grasp, learn, paper, pilot, probe; **6** motion, nature, report, review, revise *UK*, search, survey; **7** analyze, classes, examine, explore, inquiry, lessons; **8** analysis, consider, discover, feedback, findings, homework, learning, research, revision *UK*, scrutiny, training; **9** acarology, education; **10** beekeeping, entomology, experiment, schoolwork, scrutinize; **11** arachnology, conclusions, examination, feasibility, investigate, scholarship, sericulture; **13** consideration, investigation; PHRASES: **3, 2** mug up *UK*; **4, 2** bone up, swot up *UK*, take in; **4, 3** find out; **4, 4** look into; **5, 4** delve into; **8, 5** research paper.

study of life 6 botany; **7** biology, zoology; **8** genetics; **9** sociology; **10** humanities; **12** anthropology; PHRASES: **4, 8** life sciences.

study of mankind See **anthropology**

stuff 3 jam, kit, pad, ram, rep; **4** cram, fill, gear, junk, load, mess, pack, stow; **5** cloth; **6** fabric, insert, matter, tackle, things; **7** effects, objects, squeeze; **8** articles, material, packages, property; **9** equipment, materials, substance; **10** belongings; **11** possessions; **13** paraphernalia; PHRASES: **3, 2** top up *UK*; **3, 5** hot ~, sob ~ *UK*; **3, 8** raw material; **4, 2** fill up, pack in, pour in; **4, 3, 6** bits and pieces; **4, 5** kids' ~; **5, 5** rough ~; **7, 2** squeeze in; **8, 7** personal effects.

stuffing 6 filler, lining; **7** filling, packing, padding, wadding; **11** interlining.

stuffy 3 hot; **4** warm; **5** stale; **6** formal, smelly; **7** airless, pompous; **9** congested; **12** conventional; PHRASES: **3-9** old-fashioned; **6-5** strait-laced; **7, 2** blocked up, clogged up, stuffed up.

stultify 4 bore, dull, numb; **5** block; **6** deaden; **7** preempt; **8** belittle, ridicule; **9** humiliate; PHRASES: **6, 3** cancel out; **6, 7** render useless.

stumble 4 find, roll, slip, sway, trip; **5** lurch; **6** falter, mishap, totter; **7** blunder, mistake, stagger, stammer; **8** discover, hesitate; **10** hesitation; PHRASES: **3, 3, 3** hem and haw; **4-2** slip-up; **4, 3, 5** stop and start; **5, 4** false step; **6, 2** happen on.

stump 3 end; **4** base, butt, stob, stub; **6** baffle, puzzle; **7** mystify, nonplus, perplex, remains.

stumpy See **squat**

stun 4 daze, numb; **5** amaze, shock, upset; **8** astonish, paralyze; **9** dumbfound; PHRASES: **5, 3** knock out.

stunt 3 act; **4** deed, feat, show; **6** arrest, impede; **7** exploit, inhibit; **8** restrict.

stupefaction 3 awe; **6** wonder; **8** surprise; **9** amazement, confusion; **10** bemusement, perplexity; **12** astonishment, befuddlement, bewilderment.

stupefy 4 stun; **5** amaze; **7** astound, confuse, perplex, stagger; **8** astonish, befuddle, bewilder, surprise.

stupid 3 dim; **4** daft, dull, rash, slow; **5** dense, inane, silly, thick; **6** absurd, futile, obtuse, simple, unwise, vacant; **7** asinine, doltish, fatuous, foolish, idiotic, moronic, puerile, trivial, vacuous, witless; **8** backward, demented, heedless, mindless, reckless; **9** brainless, cretinous, foolhardy, imbecilic, imprudent, laughable, ludicrous, senseless; **10** irrational, ridiculous; **11** blockheaded, injudicious, nonsensical, thickheaded, thoughtless; **13** irresponsible, unintelligent; PHRASES: **2, 7, 4** of unsound mind; **3, 3, 5** not all there; **3-6** dim-witted; **3-7** ill-advised; **4-6** dull-witted.

stupidity 5 folly; **6** idiocy; **7** inanity, vacancy, vacuity; **8** futility, hebetude, unreason; **9** absurdity, puerility, stolidity; **10** imbecility, triviality; **13** irrationality. See also **stupid**

stupid person 3 ass, bob, daw, git, jay, lob, log, nit, oaf, sap, sot; **4** berk UK, bozo, burk UK, calf, clod, clot, coot, dick, dolt,

dork, fool, geck, goat, goof, goon, goop, gouk, gowk UK, gull, gump, jerk, mutt, nana, nerd, nerk, nong UK, nurd, poop, prat, tony, twit, warb, zany; **5** bobby, booby, chump, clown, clunk, cuddy, cully UK, dimbo, divvy, dumbo, dummy, dunce, dweeb, galah, goose, idiot, neddy UK, ninny, noddy, ocker UK, prune, quack, schmo, snipe, sumph, waldo, wally; **6** bampot, boodle, buffer, cretin, cuckoo, dimwit, donkey, duffer, dumdum, ignaro, lummox, nidget, nincum, nitwit, noodle, numpty, scogan, sucker, thicko, turnip, zombie; **7** airhead, buffoon, charlie UK, dizzard, gubbins UK, jackass, juggins UK, muggins UK, natural, palooka, pillock UK, pinhead, plonker UK, schmuck, scoggin; **8** Baeotian, clodpoll, crackpot, dipstick, dumbbell, flathead UK, gobshite UK, imbecile, lunkhead, meathead, omadhaun, softhead, wiseacre, woodcock; **9** blockhead, doddypoll, gothamite, ignoramus, jobernowl, schlemihl, simpleton, thickhead; **10** analphabet, dunderhead, loggerhead, muttonhead, nincompoop, thimblewit, woodenhead; **12** shatterbrain; PHRASES: **2-2** yo-yo; **3-3** nignog; **3-4** pot-head; **3-5** pea-brain, tom-noddy; **4-3** half-wit, want-wit; **4-4** moon-calf; **7-4** leather-head.

stupor 4 daze; **5** dream, shock; **6** torpor, trance; **8** lethargy, numbness; **9** inertness.

sturdy 5 tough; **6** robust, strong; **7** durable; **8** decisive, powerful, resolute; **9** strenuous; **10** determined; PHRASES: **4-4** well-made; **4-5** well-built; **4-7** hard-wearing.

stutter 6 falter; **7** stammer, stumble; **8** hesitate; **10** impediment.

style 3 cut, dub, put, ton, way; **4** call, chic, form, kind, mode, mold, name, sort, term, tone, type, vein, word; **5** adapt, charm, class, couch, flair, frame, grace, idiom, label, shape, state, tenor; **6** design, graver, luxury, manner, method, phrase, polish, strain, tailor, wealth; **7** bravura, comfort, entitle, express, fashion, panache, pattern, present, quality, variety; **8** approach, elegance, grandeur, nickname, opulence; **9** character, formulate, mannerism, overwrite, smartness, specialty, technique; **10** lavishness, speciality UK; **11** affectation, peculiarity, stylishness; **12** extravagance, idiosyncrasy.

styled 3 put; **5** baggy, laced, natty, smart; **6** casual, curled, darted, dressy, folded, hemmed, permed, ruched, rucked, slinky, sloppy, snazzy, sporty, tucked, unisex, worded; **7** bespoke *UK*, bloused, classic, phrased, planned, pleated, stylish, trimmed; **8** arranged, bouffant, designed, designer, gathered, gusseted, informal, matching, tailored; **9** expressed, sartorial, skintight; PHRASES: **1-4** A-line; **3-2** zip-up; **3-3-4** off-the-rack; **3-5** one-piece, two-piece; **4, 2** pull- on; **4-2** step-in; **4-2-5** made-to-order; **4-2-7** made-to-measure *UK*; **4-3** well-cut; **4-7** long-sleeved; **5-2-4** ready-to-wear; **5-4** ready-made; **5-6** store-bought; **5-7** short-sleeved; **5, 9** fully fashioned; **6-4** custom-made, Empire-line, tailor-made; **6-7** button-through *UK*; **6-8** double-breasted, single-breasted; **8-2** buttoned-up *UK*; **8-4** princess-line.

stylish **4** chic; **5** smart; **6** classy, modish, trendy; **7** elegant, voguish; **8** graceful, polished, tasteful; **11** fashionable; **13** sophisticated.

stylishness **4** chic, élan; **5** charm, flair, grace, style; **7** panache; **8** elegance; PHRASES: **4, 5** good taste; **7, 5** perfect touch. *See also* **stylish**

stylist **6** orator, purist; **7** classic; **8** colorist, euphuist; **9** wordsmith; **10** classicist; **11** rhetorician; **12** phrasemonger; PHRASES: **4, 6** fine writer; **4-7** word-spinner; **7, 6** stylish writer; **9, 6** classical author.

stylus **5** style; **6** needle.

stymie **5** block; **6** hinder, thwart; **7** impasse, prevent; **8** confound, deadlock; **9** stalemate; **10** standstill; PHRASES: **4, 3** dead end.

suave **4** glib; **5** sleek; **6** creepy, smarmy, urbane; **7** elegant, refined; **8** charming, debonair, unctuous; **11** sycophantic; **13** sophisticated.

SUB **9** submarine; **12** subscription; PHRASES: **4, 6** copy editor.

subconscious **6** hidden; **7** blocked; **9** inhibited, intuitive, repressed *UK*; **10** controlled, restrained, subliminal, suppressed; **11** coconscious, involuntary, unconscious; **13** unintentional.

subdivision *See* **division**

subdue **4** calm; **6** defeat, pacify, soothe; **7** conquer, control, mollify; **8** restrain, suppress, vanquish; **9** overpower, subjugate.

subject **2** PE *UK*, PT *UK*, RE *UK*, RI *UK*; **4** area, arts, gist, tame, text; **5** field, focus,

issue, liege, lower, point, realm, study, theme, topic, tutor; **6** branch, civics, course, domain, employ, feudal, humble, junior, matter, module, sphere, subdue, thesis, unfree, vassal; **7** captive, citizen, exploit, faculty, meaning, servile, serving; **8** browbeat, business, colonize, employed, enslaved, inferior, language, obedient, province, question, railroad, regiment, syllabus, tutorial; **9** dependent, enslaving, henpecked, humiliate, indenture, specialty, subjected, subjugate, substance, symbiotic, timetable; **10** apprentice, browbeaten, compulsory, curriculum, department, discipline, employable, humanities, indentured, speciality *UK*, subjecting, subjugated, substitute; **11** apprenticed, involuntary, subordinate, subservient; **12** disfranchise; **14** disenfranchise; PHRASES: **2, 6** in chains; **2, 7** in bondage, in harness; **2, 9** in captivity; **3, 9** sex education; **4, 2, 4, 5** have at one's mercy; **4, 4** hold down, keep down, walk over; **4, 10** core curriculum; **5, 2, 4** bring to heel; **5, 4, 5** under one's thumb; **7, 3** brought low; **7, 7** general studies *UK*; **9, 2** answering to.

subject (be subject to) **4** obey; **5** serve; **6** grovel; PHRASES: **3, 6, 2** pay homage to; **3, 7, 2** owe loyalty to, pay tribute to; **4, 1, 6** lose a battle; **4, 2** wait on; **4, 4, 6** lose one's rights; **4, 4, 7** lose one's freedom; **6, 1, 5** become a slave; **6, 1, 7** become a hostage; **6, 2** depend on.

subjection **6** defeat, employ; **7** bondage, peonage, serfdom, service, slavery; **8** thraldom *UK*, tutelage, wardship; **9** captivity, feudalism, juniority, obedience, servility, servitude, symbiosis, thralldom, vassalage; **10** allegiance, constraint, dependence, dependency, domination, employment, oppression, villeinage; **11** enslavement, inferiority, subjugation, subordinacy; **12** overpowering, subservience; **13** indentureship, subordination; **14** apprenticeship; PHRASES: **5, 7** white slavery.

subjective **6** biased, skewed; **7** selfish, slanted; **8** personal; **10** individual, particular, prejudiced; **11** egotistical, independent, solipsistic; **13** idiosyncratic; **15** individualistic; PHRASES: **3-5** one-sided; **4-8** self-centered.

subjugate *See* **conquer**

sublimate **6** direct; **7** channel, reroute; **8** redirect, transfer.

sublime **6** superb; **8** splendid; **9** excellent,

inspiring, marvelous, uplifting; **13** inspirational.

submerge 3 dip; **4** duck, hide, sink; **6** plunge, stifle; **7** conceal, immerse; **8** suppress.

submission 3 bow; **4** idea, plan; **5** offer; **6** apathy, assent, curtsy, homage, kowtow, tender; **7** cession, consent; **8** agreeing, fatalism, humility, kneeling, lethargy, proposal, resigned, tameness, yielding; **9** deference, groveling, masochism, obedience, obeisance, passivity, servitude, surrender; **10** abdication, compliance, concession, inactivity, submitting, succumbing, suggestion, supineness; **11** abandonment, appeasement, passiveness, prostration, resignation, slavishness; **12** acquiescence, capitulation, genuflection, subservience; **13** collaboration, nonresistance; **14** relinquishment, submissiveness; PHRASES: 3-3 cop-out; **3, 5, 4** the white flag; **4-3** sell-out; **5, 2, 3, 5** peace at any price; **6, 2** caving in; **6, 3** giving way; **6, 7** abject loyalty.

submissive 4 meek; **5** timid; **6** docile; **7** dutiful, passive; **8** obedient, resigned; **9** compliant, tractable; **10** unassuming; **11** acquiescent, deferential, intimidated, subservient; **13** accommodating, disinterested, uncomplaining.

submit 3 buy; **4** cede, obey; **5** abide, allow, crawl, defer, grant, leave, offer, yield; **6** accept, assent, comply, grovel, ignore, relent, resign, retire; **7** appease, concede, condone, consent, retreat; **8** abdicate, overlook, withdraw; **9** acquiesce, disregard, pussyfoot, surrender; **10** capitulate, relinquish; PHRASES: 2, 5, 4 go along with; **2, 8** be defeated, be inactive; **3, 2** bow to; **3, 3** cop out; **3, 3, 5** sue for peace; **3, 4** eat dirt; **3, 4, 4, 4** lay down one's arms; **3, 5** cry uncle; **3, 6, 3** eat humble pie; **4, 2** cool it, give in, give up; **4, 2, 1, 3** call it a day; **4, 2, 4, 5** draw in one's horns, hold up one's hands; **4, 3** give way, pull out, sell out; **4, 3, 3** make way for; **4, 5** keep quiet, sing small, step aside; **4, 7** face reality; **4, 8** stop fighting; **5, 2, 3, 5** throw in the towel; **5, 3, 4** yield the palm; **5, 4** stand down; **5, 6** admit defeat; **6, 6** strike colors; **6, 7** resign oneself; **7, 5** knuckle under; **11, 4** collaborate with.

subordinate 3 fag *UK*; **4** aide, tool; **5** gofer, grunt, lower, minor; **6** helper, humble, junior, lackey, lesser, minion, stooge; **7** flunkey, learner, lowlife, servant, student,

subject; **8** criminal, employee, inferior, sidekick; **9** ancillary, assistant, attendant, auxiliary, conscript, dependent, outranked, secondary, secretary, subaltern, sycophant, tributary, underling; **10** apprentice, subsidiary, substitute; **11** subservient, untouchable; PHRASES: 4, 9 less important; 5-4, 3 right-hand man; **5, 6** staff member; **6-5** second-class; **6, 6** second fiddle; **6-8** second-division.

subordination 8 demotion; **9** reduction; **10** relegation; **11** inferiority; **12** subservience; PHRASES: 2, 8 no priority; 4, 5 last place; **5, 5** lower merit; **6, 5** little worth, second class, second place; **6, 6** second eleven; **6, 8** second division.

subscribe 6 pledge; **7** condone, promise, support; **10** contribute; PHRASES: 4, 2 give to; 5, 4 agree with; **7, 2** approve of.

subscription *See* **payment**

subsequent 7 ensuing; **9** following; **10** consequent, succeeding, successive.

subservient 5 under; **6** abject; **8** obedient; **10** obsequious, submissive; **11** deferential; PHRASES: 2, 4, 5 on one's knees; **2, 6, 4** on bended knee; **4, 3, 2, 4** with hat in hand; **4, 5, 6** with bated breath.

subside 4 drop, sink, wane; **6** lessen; **7** dwindle; **8** collapse, decrease, diminish; PHRASES: 4, 2 cave in; **4, 4** fall down.

subsidiary 5 lower; **6** branch, junior, lesser; **7** company; **8** division; **9** ancillary, auxiliary, secondary; **10** additional; **11** subordinate; **12** contributory; **13** supplementary.

subsidy 3 aid; **4** loan; **5** dowry, grant; **6** credit; **7** advance, backing, bursary, funding, stipend, support; **8** bestowal, donation; **9** allowance, endowment; **10** fellowship, settlement, subvention; **11** scholarship, sponsorship; **12** contribution; **13** appropriation, subsidization.

subsist 4 live; **5** exist; **7** survive; PHRASES: 4, 4, 4 make ends meet; **4, 5** keep going.

substance 4 body, core; **5** stuff; **6** import, matter; **7** essence; **8** material, property; **9** affluence; **10** ingredient.

substandard *See* **inferior**

substantiate *See* **validate**

substantive 5 basic; **6** decent; **7** central; **8** separate; **9** essential, practical; **10** applicable, autonomous, elementary, functional, individual; **11** fundamental, independent, respectable, significant, substantial, utilitarian; **12** considerable.

substitute **4** swap; **5** locum, proxy; **6** acting, deputy, foster, regent, second, switch, symbol; **7** analogy, bandage, doublet, relieve, remount, replace, reserve, standby, stopgap, synonym; **8** metaphor; **9** alternate, makeshift, pacemaker, sacrifice, surrogate, temporary; **10** additional, equivalent, ghostwrite, prosthesis, soundalike, transplant, understudy; **11** alternative, benchwarmer, provisional, replacement, succedaneum; **12** substitutive; **14** representation, substitutional; PHRASES: **3, 3** act for; **3, 7** use instead; **4, 2** back up, fill in; **4, 2, 3** fill in for; **4-5** look-alike; **5-2** stand-in; **5, 2, 3** stand in for; **5, 3** cover for; **5-8** guilt-offering; **6, 3** appear for; **7, 4** replace with; **8, 3** deputize for.

substitute (be a substitute) **4** oust; **5** cover; **6** foster; **7** imitate, relieve, replace, succeed; **8** deputize, displace, supplant; **9** represent, supersede; **10** ghostwrite, understudy; PHRASES: **3, 3** act for; **4, 2** fill in; **4, 3, 3** take the rap; **4, 3, 4** hold the fort; **4, 3, 5** take the blame; **4, 3, 5, 2** take the place of; **4, 4** take over; **5, 2** stand in; **5, 2, 5** serve as proxy; **5, 3** cover for, pinch hit; **6, 3** double for.

substituted **7** changed, swapped; **8** replaced, switched; **9** deputized, exchanged; **10** superseded, supplanted; **11** compensated.

substitute person **3** sub; **5** agent, locum, patsy, proxy; **6** depute, deputy, double, relief, ringer, supply; **7** reserve; **8** impostor; **9** alternate, reservist, scapegoat, successor, surrogate; **10** changeling, soundalike, supplanter, understudy; **11** ghostwriter, replacement; **12** Doppelgänger; **14** representative; PHRASES: **4-2** fill-in; **4, 3** fall guy, step dad, step mom; **4-5** look-alike; **4, 6** body double, step family, step father, step mother; **5-2** stand-in; **5, 3** stunt man; **5, 6** locum tenens, pinch hitter; **6, 6** father figure, foster parent, mother figure; **7, 3** twelfth man *UK*; **8, 3** whipping boy; **9, 6** surrogate mother.

substitute thing **6** symbol; **7** analogy, bandage, doublet, remount, synonym; **8** metaphor; **9** pacemaker, sacrifice; **10** prosthesis, transplant; **11** Elastoplast *UK*, succedaneum; **14** representation; PHRASES: **4-3**

Band-Aid *tm*; **5-8** guilt-offering; **8, 7** sticking plaster *UK*; **10, 4** artificial limb.

substitution **4** swap; **5** locum, proxy; **6** backup, change, double, relief, switch; **7** reserve, shuffle, stopgap; **8** deputing, exchange; **9** alternate, expedient, expiation, surrogacy, surrogate; **10** changeover, compromise, deputizing, equivalent, stepfather, stepmother, substitute, understudy; **11** alternation, alternative, commutation, equivalence, ghostwriter, replacement, supplanting, surrogation; **12** compensation, supersession; **13** vicariousness; **14** representation; PHRASES: **3, 5** pis aller; **4-2** fill-in; **4, 3, 3** quid pro quo; **5-2** stand-in; **5, 2, 8** power of attorney; **5, 3** stunt man; **5, 7** modus vivendi; **6, 4** second best; **9, 6** surrogate mother.

substructure **3** mat; **4** fill, pile, raft, slab; **7** caisson, footing; **8** backfill; **9** cofferdam; **10** foundation; **11** foundations; **12** underpinning.

subsume **4** list; **5** count, enter; **7** include; **8** consider; **11** incorporate; PHRASES: **3, 2** add to, put in; **5, 4** class with, count with; **6, 4** number with; **6, 5** reckon among.

subterfuge **3** con; **4** blag, ploy, quip, ruse, scam; **5** cavil, dodge, quirk, trick; **6** scheme; **7** quibble, shuffle; **8** artifice, maneuver; **9** deception, duplicity, stratagem; **10** propaganda; **11** contrivance, machination; **14** misinformation.

subterranean *See* **underground**

subtle **3** sly; **4** fine, thin; **5** faint; **6** artful, clever, crafty, pastel, shrewd, slight, tricky; **7** cunning, devious, elegant, elusive, refined; **8** delicate, indirect, tasteful; **9** sensitive; **10** fastidious, negligible, perceptive, restrained; **11** experienced, intelligent, understated; **13** imperceptible; **14** discriminating.

subtlety **4** tact; **6** detail, nicety, nuance; **7** finesse; **8** delicacy, elegance; **9** intricacy, restraint; **10** refinement, subtleness; **11** discernment, sensitivity; **14** discrimination; PHRASES: **4, 5** fine point, good taste. *See also* **subtle**

subtract **3** cut; **4** cull, omit, pick, thin, void, weed; **5** allow, drain, eject, empty, erase, erode, expel, shift; **6** cancel, censor, deduct, delete, except, garble, offset, remove, unload, uproot; **7** abridge, corrode, detract, devalue, exclude, extract, relieve; **8** abstract, condense, decimate, decrease, diminish, discount, mutilate, withdraw; **9** alleviate, eliminate, eradicate, expurgate, extirpate; **10** abbreviate, bowdlerize, obliterate; **11** precipitate; PHRASES: **3, 3** rip out, rub out, set off; **3, 6** cut prices; **4, 2, 9** make an exception; **4, 3** draw off, pick out, pull out, root out, take off, take out, thin out; **4, 4** file down, take away, take from; **4-4** handpick; **5, 3** cross out, hoick out, leave out, throw out; **7, 4** detract from.

subtracted item 3 cut; **4** loss; **6** rebate, refund; **7** cutback, forfeit, minuend; **8** clawback *UK*, discount, drawback; **9** allowance, decrement, remission, sacrifice, shortfall; **10** limitation, subtrahend; **11** restriction; PHRASES: **4-3** rake-off; **5, 3** price cut; **5, 8** thing deducted.

subtraction 3 cut; **5** debit, minus; **6** fixing, offset, relief; **7** cutting, docking, editing, erasure, erosion, lopping, minuend, removal; **8** altering, chopping, decrease, deletion, discount, ejection, excision; **9** beheading, corrosion, deduction, exception, exclusion, expulsion, severance, shrinkage; **10** abridgment, amputation, castration, decimation, detraction, difference, diminution, extraction, mutilation, shortening, subtrahend, withdrawal; **11** abstraction, alleviation, curtailment, devaluation, discounting, elimination, eradication, expurgation, extirpation; **12** abbreviation, circumcision, condensation, decapitation, emasculation, obliteration, retrenchment; **13** precipitation, sedimentation; **14** bowdlerization; PHRASES: **4, 3, 4** wear and tear; **5, 7** price cutting; **6, 4** taking away; **7, 3** cutting off, rubbing out; **7, 4** cutting back; **8, 3** striking out.

suburb 4 area; **5** exurb; **7** exurbia, purlieu; **8** district, environs, faubourg, subtopia *UK*, suburbia; **9** greenbelt, outskirts; **11** conurbation, development; PHRASES: **5-2, 4** built-up area; **6, 6** garden ~ *UK*; **7, 6** bedroom ~; **8, 4** commuter belt *UK*; **9, 6** dormitory ~ *UK*; **11, 4** stockbroker belt.

subversion 4 plot; **5** cabal; **6** mutiny, spying; **7** anarchy, faction, treason; **8** agitprop, intrigue, sabotage, sedition; **9** agitation, espionage, rebellion, terrorism; **10** conspiracy; **12** infiltration, insurrection; **13** seditiousness; **14** subversiveness; **15** destabilization; PHRASES: **4, 7** high treason; **4-7** lese-majesty; **5, 6** fifth column; **5, 9** fifth columnism; **6, 7** secret society.

subversive 7 traitor; **8** anarchic, mutineer, mutinous, quisling; **9** breakaway, dissident, factional, insurgent, seditious; **10** anarchical, rebellious, schismatic, traitorous, treasonous; **11** treasonable; **12** collaborator; **13** destabilizing, insubordinate, revolutionary; **14** conspiratorial, insurrectional; **15** insurrectionary; PHRASES: **2, 9** in rebellion.

subvert 6 topple; **7** disrupt; **8** sabotage; **9** overthrow, undermine; **11** destabilize; PHRASES: **5, 4** bring down.

succeed 3 win; **4** work; **5** ensue, usurp; **6** assume, follow, result, thrive; **7** achieve, inherit, prosper, relieve, replace, triumph; **8** flourish, overtake, supplant; **9** supersede, supervene; **10** accomplish, substitute; **11** consecutive; PHRASES: **2, 4** do well, go well; **3, 2** run on; **3, 2, 3, 3** get to the top; **3, 3, 6** hit the target; **3, 5** get ahead; **4, 2** make it; **4, 3** come off, work out; **4, 3, 4** take the helm, turn out well; **4, 4** come into, come next, make good, take over; **4, 5** bear fruit, come after; **5, 2, 3, 4** bring up the rear; **5, 3, 6** climb the ladder; **6, 2** accede to; **6, 3, 6** assume the mantle; **6, 4** result from; **6, 6** assume office.

succeeding 4 last, late, near, next; **5** close, every, later; **6** future, latest, latter, second; **7** another, ensuing, ordered; **8** arranged, pursuant; **9** alternate, following, impending, proximate; **10** consequent, sequential, subsequent, successive; **11** consecutive; **12** successional; PHRASES: **5, 5** every other; **5, 6** every second.

success 3 hit, win; **4** coup, fame, feat, luck, name, star; **5** smash; **6** luxury, plenty, riches, wealth, winner; **7** fortune, killing, mastery, stardom, triumph, victory; **8** thriving; **9** affluence, celebrity, happiness, sensation; **10** ascendancy, attainment, famousness, prosperity; **11** achievement, celebration, realization; **12** breakthrough; **14** accomplishment, successfulness; PHRASES: **3, 2, 4** run of luck; **3, 3** big hit; **3, 3, 4** the big time; **4, 2, 2, 6** name up in lights; **4, 3, 7** fame and fortune; **5, 2, 3, 3** flash in the pan; **5, 2, 7** place in history; **5, 3** smash hit; **5, 5** lucky break; **5, 6** happy ending, lucky stroke; **7, 5** ~ story; **7, 7** howling ~, roaring ~, runaway ~; **9, 4** beginner's luck.

successful 4 rich; **5** lucky; **6** famous, renown, rising; **7** booming, certain, wealthy, winning; **8** crowning, fruitful, masterly, positive, surefire, thriving; **9** effective, favorable, fortunate, lucrative; **10** productive, profitable, prosperous, succeeding; **11** efficacious, flourishing; PHRASES: **2, 3, 2, 3, 2** on the up and up *UK*; **2-3-6** up-and-coming; **4-3** well-off; **4, 3, 3** home and dry; **4, 4** home free; **4-4** best-ever; **4-6** sure-footed; **4-7** best-selling; **5-7** chart-topping, never-failing; **7, 6** sitting pretty.

successful (be successful) 4 pass; **5** click; **6** arrive, effect, flower, thrive; **7** achieve, advance, blossom, compass, prosper, qualify, succeed; **8** flourish, graduate, progress; **10** accomplish; PHRASES: **2, 4** do well, go over; **2, 5, 4** go great guns; **3, 2** get on; **3, 2, 3** hit it off; **3, 3, 4** hit the mark; **3, 3, 6** top the charts; **3, 3, 7** hit the jackpot; **3, 4, 5** win one's spurs; **3, 5** get ahead, get lucky, get there; **4, 2** make it; **4, 2, 3** pull it off; **4, 3** pull off; **4, 3, 5** make the grade; **4, 3, 6** reap the fruits; **4, 4** make good; **4, 5** make money; **4, 7** show results, work wonders; **4, 8** work miracles; **5, 3** bring off, carry off; **5, 3, 4** break the bank.

successful person 3 hit, MVP, VIP, wow; **4** hero, star; **5** comer; **6** corker, winner; **7** heroine, starlet, success; **8** achiever, graduate, superman; **9** celebrity, rainmaker; **10** superwoman; **13** valedictorian; PHRASES: **3, 2, 3, 4** man of the year; **3, 2, 3, 5** man of the match, top of the class; **3, 4** the tops; **4, 2, 3, 4** talk of the town; **4, 3** whiz kid; **4-4, 3** self-made man; **4, 5** high flyer; **5, 2, 2, 5** crème de la crème; **5-5** first-rater; **6, 3** number one; **6, 4** rising star; **6, 7** record breaker; **8, 6** surefire winner.

successful thing 2 KO; **3** hit, six, try, wow; **4** goal; **5** homer, score; **9** checkmate; **11** blockbuster; **12** championship; PHRASES: **3, 5** hat trick; **3-6, 3** box-office hit; **4, 2, 3** hole in one; **4, 3** home run; **4-3** sell-out; **4, 4** good move, good shot; **4-6** best-seller; **4, 7** rave reviews; **5-3** bull's-eye; **5, 4** grand slam; **5-6** chart-topper; **6, 3** number one; **9, 5** touchdown (TD)ace.

succession 3 run; **4** flow, flux, line, list, rota, turn, wake; **5** chain, cycle, order, queue, suite, train; **6** course, series, string; **7** process, retinue; **8** progress, sequence, tailback *UK*; **9** entourage, following, hierarchy; **10** procession; **11** arrangement, progression, subsequence; **12** continuation; **14** successiveness; PHRASES: **7, 4** Buggins turn; **7, 5** pecking order; **7, 6** forward motion; **7, 8** forward movement.

succession (in succession) 7 run-

ning; **12** successively; **13** consecutively; PHRASES: **2, 1, 3** in a row; **2, 3, 4** on the trot; **2, 4** in line; **2, 5** in order; **2, 8** in sequence; **3, 5, 7** one after another.

successor 4 heir; **7** heiress, legatee; **8** newcomer; **9** inheritor, recipient; **10** descendant, substitute; **11** beneficiary, replacement; PHRASES: **3, 3** new boy; **3, 5** new blood, new broom *UK*; **3, 7** new arrival; **4, 2, 4** next in line; **4, 3, 2** next man in; **4, 8** heir apparent; **4, 11** heir presumptive; **5, 5** fresh blood.

succinct *See* **concise**

succor 3 aid; **4** help; **6** relief, rescue; **7** comfort, relieve, rescuer, support; **10** assistance, benefactor.

succory 7 chicory.

succulent 5 juicy, moist; **6** tender; **8** luscious; **9** delicious.

succumb 3 bow, die, sag; **4** bear, bend, drop, tire, wilt; **5** crawl, faint, kneel, stoop, toady, yield; **6** accede, cringe, crouch, curtsy, depart, digest, endure, expire, grovel, kowtow, perish, submit, suffer; **7** stomach; **8** collapse; **9** apologize, surrender; **10** capitulate; PHRASES: **3, 2, 4** put up with; **3, 3, 6** bow and scrape; **3, 4** eat crow, eat dirt; **3, 6, 3** eat humble pie; **4, 2** cave in, give in, lump it, take it; **4, 2, 2, 3, 4** take it on the chin; **4, 2, 4, 5** keep in one's place; **4, 3, 3** kiss the rod; **4, 3, 4** lick the dust; **4, 3, 4, 2** grin and bear it; **4, 3, 6** bite the bullet; **4, 4** pass away; **5-4** brown-nose; **7, 3, 4** swallow the pill; **7, 5** knuckle under.

suck 3 cup, lap, tap; **4** bear, draw, milk, pull, pump; **5** bleed, carry, drain, drink, empty, force, shell, slurp, smell, sweep, taste; **6** broach, detect, imbibe, inhale, siphon, suckle, vacuum; **7** extract, inspire, pipette; **8** aspirate, mouthful, withdraw; **10** disembowel, eviscerate; PHRASES: **4, 2** pull on; **4, 3** draw off, pump out, ~ out, take out; **6, 3** siphon off.

suckerfish 6 remora.

suction 4 drag, draw, pull; **5** force; **8** pressure.

sudden 4 snap; **5** clean, hasty, quick, rapid, sharp, swift; **6** abrupt, speedy; **8** fleeting, headlong, meteoric; **9** impulsive, overnight; **10** unexpected; **11** precipitous; PHRASES: **3, 2, 1, 6** all of a ~; **3, 2, 3, 4** out of the blue; **7, 7** without warning.

sue 3 beg; **8** litigate, petition; **9** prosecute.

suffer 4 bear, hurt; 5 stand; 6 endure; 7 agonize, undergo; 8 tolerate; 10 experience.

suffering 3 raw, woe; 4 pain, sore; 5 agony, grief; 6 aching, misery, sorrow; 7 anguish, hurting, torment, torture, wincing; 8 bleeding, distress, martyred, tortured, writhing; 9 afflicted, blistered, tormented; 10 affliction, distressed; 11 traumatized; PHRASES: 2, 5 in agony; 5-3-4 black-and-blue.

suffice 2 do; 4 fill, meet, pass, sate, suit, wash, work; 5 gorge, reach, serve, stand; 6 answer, quench, refill, settle; 7 content, fulfill, overeat, qualify, satiate, satisfy, support; 9 replenish; PHRASES: 2, 10 be sufficient; 3, 2 get by; 4, 2 fill up; 4, 3, 4 fill the bill; 4, 3, 5 make the grade; 4, 6 pass muster; 5, 2, 2 stand up to; 5, 3 carry out; 5, 8 prove adequate; 5, 10 prove acceptable; 7, 2, 2 measure up to; 7, 3 provide for.

sufficiency 4 pass; 6 assets, enough, plenty, quorum; 7 autarky, content, minimum, satiety; 8 adequacy, bellyful; 9 abundance, repletion; 10 competence, completion; 11 contentment, fulfillment, requirement; 12 satisfaction; 13 acceptability; PHRASES: 4, 5 pass marks; 4, 7 bare minimum, full measure; 5, 6 right amount; 5, 9 right qualities; 6, 2, 3, 2 enough to get by; 6, 2, 4, 2 enough to live on; 6, 4 living wage; 8, 6 adequate amount, adequate income, required number.

sufficient 5 ample, equal; 6 enough, plenty; 7 fitting; 8 abundant, adequate, complete, measured, suitable; 9 competent, makeshift, necessary, sufficing; 10 acceptable, contenting, satisfying; 11 appropriate, provisional; 12 commensurate, satisfactory; PHRASES: 2, 2, 3, 4 up to the mark; 2, 2, 5 up to snuff; 3, 3, 4 not too much; 3, 3, 6 not too little; 3-9 all-sufficing; 4-2-5 hand-to-mouth; 4, 5 just right; 4-10 self-sufficient; 5, 2 equal to.

sugar 3 LSD, pet; 4 baby, love, milk, palm, spun, wood; 5 money; 6 barley, caster, invert; 7 darling, dearest, improve, sucrose, sweeten, sweetie UK; 8 disguise, precious, titivate; 10 saccharose, sugarhouse, sweetheart; PHRASES: 4, 4 make over; 4, 5 corn ~, loaf ~ UK; 5, 2 dress up; 5, 4 ~ beet, ~ cane; 5, 5 brown ~, fruit ~, grape ~, icing ~, maple ~, ~ candy UK, ~ daddy; 5, 8 ~ diabetes UK; 10, 5 granulated ~; 13, 5 confectioners' ~.

suggest 4 hint; 5 evoke, imply; 6 advise, remind; 7 propose; 8 indicate, intimate; 9 insinuate, recommend; PHRASES: 3, 7 put forward; 4, 2, 4 call to mind; 4, 4 warm over; 7, 2 conjure up.

suggestible 4 soft; 6 docile; 7 willing; 8 gullible; 9 adaptable, compliant, credulous, malleable, receptive, tractable; 11 impressible, susceptible; 14 impressionable; PHRASES: 6, 3 easily led.

suggestion 3 air, jot, tip; 4 aura, dash, hint, idea, iota, plan, sign; 5 offer, shade, smack, taint, taste, tinge, touch, trace; 6 advice; 7 counsel, inkling, smidgen, soupçon, thought, warning; 8 innuendo, proposal; 9 evocation, prompting, suspicion, tempering; 10 indication, intimation, smattering, sprinkling, submission; 11 implication, insinuation, proposition; 14 recommendation.

suggestive 4 lewd; 6 risqué; 8 improper, indecent, redolent; 9 evocative; 10 indelicate; 11 reminiscent.

suicide 3 gas; 5 death; 6 suttee; 7 madness, seppuku; 8 kamikaze, rashness; 10 perversity; 11 parasuicide; 12 recklessness; PHRASES: 3, 5, 7 die Roman fashion; 4, 2, 2 felo de se; 4, 2, 4, 5 fall on one's sword; 4, 4 hara-kiri; 4, 4, 3, 4 take one's own life; 4, 7 mass ~; 4-9 self-slaughter; 4-10 self-immolation; 4-11 self-destruction; 5, 4, 6 slash one's wrists; 7, 4 ~ pact.

suit 3 fit; 5 befit, clubs, dress, heart, match, spade; 6 become, hearts, spades, tuxedo, tweeds, wooing; 7 catsuit, diamond, enhance, flatter; 8 diamonds, ensemble, pantsuit; 9 cassimere, chemiloon, courtship, coveralls, harmonize, paternity, separates, spacesuit, tracksuit; 11 coordinates; PHRASES: 1-4 G-suit; 2, 4 go with; 2, 7 be fitting; 3-2-3 all-in-one; 3, 4 jog ~, Mao ~, sun ~, wet ~; 3-5, 4 one-piece ~, two-piece ~; 4, 2 show up; 4, 3 twin set; 4-3-4 soup-and-fish; 4, 4 jump ~, long ~, zoot ~; 5, 3 black tie, white tie; 5, 4 agree with, dress ~, major ~, minor ~, shell ~ UK, slack ~, tweed ~; 5-5 three-piece; 6, 4 boiler ~ UK, dinner ~, flying ~, lounge ~ UK, monkey ~, safari ~, sailor ~; 6, 5 riding habit; 7, 2 conform to; 7, 4 bathing ~, jogging ~, leisure ~, trouser ~ UK; 8, 4 birthday ~, business ~, pressure ~, tailored ~; 9, 4 pinstripe ~; 10, 4 camouflage ~, dressmaker ~. See also **clothes**

suitability 7 aptness, fitness; 9 relevance,

relevancy, rightness; **10** pertinence; **11** correctness, fittingness; **15** appropriateness.

suitable 3 apt, fit; **4** meet; **5** right; **6** proper, seemly; **7** fitting; **8** apposite, relevant; **9** pertinent; **11** appropriate.

suite *See* **set**

Sukkoth 11 Tabernacles.

sulfur 1 S.

sulk 4 fret, huff, moan, mood, mope, pout; **5** brood, strop *UK*, whine; **6** temper, whinge *UK*; **7** grumble; PHRASES: **2, 2, 1, 4** be in a huff, be in a mood; **2, 2, 1, 5** be in a strop *UK*; **3, 4** bad mood; **3, 6** bad temper.

sullen 4 blue, dark, dour, dull, glum, gray, grim, mopy, sour; **5** angry, black, moody, stern, sulky, surly, whiny; **6** cloudy, dismal, gloomy, grumpy, leaden, morose, somber; **7** grouchy, hostile, pouting, serious; **8** brooding *UK*, dejected, overcast; **9** cheerless, depressed, glowering, saturnine; **10** melancholy; **11** atrabilious, melancholic; PHRASES: **3-7** ill-humored, ill-natured; **3-8** bad-tempered.

sullen (be sullen) 4 fret, moan, mope, pout, sulk; **5** brood, whine; **6** whinge; PHRASES: **4, 1, 4, 4** have a long face; **4, 4, 3** hang one's lip.

sullenness 4 huff; **7** moaning, pouting, sighing; **9** dejection, hostility, petulance; **10** melancholy, resentment; **11** mumpishness; **12** grumpishness; **13** unsociability; PHRASES: **3, 4** the hump; **3, 5** ill humor, the blues, the sulks; **3, 6** bad temper, ill nature; **4, 2, 3, 5** down in the dumps; **4, 2, 4** lack of talk. *See also* **sullen**

sullen person 4 bear; **5** grump, witch; **6** grouch, sulker, whiner; **7** grouser, hothead, whinger *UK*; **8** grumbler, sorehead; **10** bellyacher, crosspatch.

sully *See* **taint**

sulphuric acid 7 vitriol; PHRASES: **3, 2, 7** oil of vitriol.

sultry 3 hot; **5** humid, muggy.

sum 5 total; **6** amount, corpus, figure, system; **7** complex; **8** addition, ensemble, entirety, quantity, totality; **9** aggregate, summation; **11** calculation, computation; PHRASES: **3, 2, 5** ~ of money; **4, 3** lump ~; **5, 3** round ~; **8, 6** ballpark figure.

summarily 7 crisply; **12** despotically, straightaway, tyrannically; **13** dictatorially; PHRASES: **2, 4** at once; **5, 4** right away; **7, 5**

without delay. *See also* **summary**

summariness 7 brevity; **8** laconism; **10** laconicism. *See also* **summary**

summarize 3 pot; **5** recap; **6** digest, precis, précis, reduce, resume, review, sketch; **7** abridge, outline, shorten; **8** abstract, condense, contract, truncate; **9** epitomize, synopsize; **10** abbreviate; **11** encapsulate; **12** recapitulate; **13** epigrammatize; PHRASES: **2, 4** go over; **3, 2** sum up; **3, 5** cut short; **3, 7** run through; **4, 1, 6** make a résumé; **4, 4** boil down; **6, 3** sketch out.

summarizer 6 cutter, editor; **8** abridger; **9** shortener; **10** epitomizer; **11** abbreviator; PHRASES: **6, 6** precis writer.

summary 2 CV *UK*; **4** curt, gist; **5** brief, cameo, drift, hasty, pithy, rapid, recap, short, swift, terse; **6** abrupt, aperçu, digest, exposé, legend, precis, précis, résumé, review, rushed, sketch, sudden, survey; **7** brusque, capsule, caption, compact, concise, epitome, heading, instant, laconic, outline, pointed, rundown; **8** abridged, abstract, ellipsis, overview, subtitle, succinct, synopsis, vignette; **9** arbitrary, condensed, immediate, summation; **10** abridgment, compendium, conspectus, extraction, indication, peremptory; **11** abridgement, compendious, irreducible, precipitate, precipitous; **12** abbreviation, condensation, epigrammatic; **13** instantaneous; **14** epigrammatical, recapitulation; PHRASES: **3-2** sum-up; **4-2** wrap-up; **4, 8** word portrait; **5-3, 4** bird's-eye view; **5, 3, 5** short and sweet; **9, 6** thumbnail sketch.

summer 3 sun; **4** heat, time; **5** adder, prime; **6** warmth; **7** summery, Whitsun; **8** aestival *UK*, solstice, sunshine, vacation; **9** haymaking, midsummer; **10** summertide, summertime; **11** aestivation *UK*, Whitsuntide; PHRASES: **2, 7, 6** St Martin's ~ *UK*; **3, 4** dog days; **3, 5** hot spell; **4, 4** best time, heat wave; **4-4** heat-haze; **4, 5** best years; **4, 6** high ~; **4, 7** warm weather; **6, 3** golden age; **6, 6** Indian ~, ~ school; **6, 7** ~ holiday, ~ pudding *UK*; **6, 8** ~ solstice; **7, 4** flaming June, halcyon days; **7, 6** growing season; **9, 3** Midsummer Day.

summit 3 sky, tip, top; **4** acme, apex, brow, cusp, peak, pole; **5** crest, crown, limit, pitch, point, ridge, talks; **6** apogee, climax, heaven, height, tiptop, vertex, zenith; **7** Everest, heavens, hilltop, maximum, meeting; **8** meridian, pinnacle; **9** exosphere, extremity; **10** conference; **11** culmination, mountaintop; PHRASES: **3, 2, 3, 5** top of the world; **3, 4** new high, Nob Hill; **3, 7** the heights; **4, 3** very top; **4, 6** high ground; **5, 2, 3, 4** crest of the wave; **5, 4** cloud nine; **5, 6** lofty ground; **6, 4** record high; **6, 7** ~ meeting; **7, 5** highest point; **7, 6** seventh heaven.

summon 4 call, find; **5** rally, rouse; **6** gather, muster; **7** convene; **8** activate; PHRASES: **4, 3** call for, send for.

summons 4 call, writ; **5** order; **7** command, warrant; **8** citation, subpoena; **9** directive.

sumptuous 6 costly, lavish; **7** opulent; **8** splendid.

sun 3 Sol, UVA, UVB; **4** disc, disk *UK*, halo, heat, star; **6** corona, facula, Helios, suntan; **7** daystar, drought, sizzler, sunburn, sunspot; **8** filament, heatwave, Hyperion, scorcher, sunlight, sunshine; **9** anthelion, parhelion, sunstroke; **10** prominence, sunbathing, suntanning; **11** photosphere; **12** chromosphere; PHRASES: **2-4, 5** 11-year cycle; **3, 4** ~ bear, ~ deck, S~ King, ~ lamp; **3, 5** dry spell, ~ blind *UK*, ~ block, ~ porch; **3, 10** ~ worshipper; **4, 3** blue sky; **5, 3** clear sky; **5, 5** solar cycle, solar flare, solar power; **5, 7** solar eclipse; **5, 8** solar activity, solar spectrum; **5, 9** solar radiation; **6, 3** active ~; **6, 6** Indian summer, suntan lotion; **6, 9** direct radiation; **7, 5** barrier cream *UK*, sunspot cycle; **8, 3** midnight ~; **8, 6** parhelic circle; **9, 3** cloudless sky.

sunbeam *See* **ray**

sunder *See* **separate**

sundry *See* **various**

sunfish 4 mola.

sunglasses 6 shades; **8** sunspecs *UK*; PHRASES: **4, 7** dark glasses.

sunken 5 gaunt, lower; **6** hollow; **7** pinched, settled; **8** immersed, recessed; **9** submerged; **10** cadaverous, underwater; PHRASES: **4-3** deep-set.

sunny 3 hot; **4** fair, fine, warm; **5** clear, happy, jolly, light; **6** bright, cheery, genial, sunlit; **7** affable, beaming, cordial, smiling; **8** cheerful, daylight, luminous, pleasant, positive, sunshiny; **9** brilliant, cloudless, unclouded; **10** optimistic; **12** lighthearted; PHRASES: **4-7** good-natured; **5, 2, 3** light as day; **6, 3, 6** bright and breezy *UK*.

sunrise 4 dawn, morn; **5** sunup; **7** morning; **8** daybreak, daylight, moonrise; PHRAS-

ES: **4-4** star-rise; **5, 2, 3** break of day; **5, 2, 4** crack of dawn; **5, 5** first light.

Suomi 7 Finland.

sup *See* **drink**

super 2 A1; **3** ace, fab; **4** arch, mega, tops; **5** extra, great, ideal; **8** fabulous, terrific; PHRASES: **3-3** tip-top; **6-2** walker-on.

superb 8 fabulous, splendid; **9** excellent, wonderful; **11** outstanding.

superficial 3 low; **4** flat, glib, idle, thin; **5** brief, empty, hasty, light, outer, petty, phony *UK*, quick, rapid, silly, trite; **6** casual, facile, flimsy, hollow, paltry, phoney, slight; **7** cursory, foolish, outward, passing, seeming, shallow, sketchy, surface, trivial; **8** apparent, exterior, external, feigning, trifling; **9** epidermal, frivolous, insincere, posturing; **10** artificial, simplistic; **11** lightweight, meaningless, unimportant; **13** insignificant; **15** inconsequential; PHRASES: **2, 3, 7** on the surface; **3-11** one-dimensional; **4-4** skin-deep.

superfluity 4 glut, perk; **5** bonus, extra, flood, frill, spare; **6** excess, luxury, margin, trifle; **7** balance, overlap, satiety, surfeit, surplus; **8** overkill, overplus, parasite, pleonasm, plethora; **9** accessory, expletive, inflation, inutility, lagniappe, leftovers, remainder, tautology; **10** inactivity, indulgence, oversupply, perquisite, redundancy, surplusage; **11** diffuseness, duplication, excrescence, overmanning, uselessness; **12** nonessential; **13** luxuriousness, overabundance; **14** overemployment, supererogation; **15** overfulfillment, superfluousness; PHRASES: **5, 2, 4** money to burn; **5, 4** spare cash, spare tire; **5, 5** fifth wheel, spare wheel *UK*; **6, 3** luxury car; **6, 4** luxury flat; **6, 5** luxury hotel.

superfluous 5 extra, spare; **6** excess, luxury, otiose; **7** diffuse, surplus; **8** leftover, needless, rambling, residual, unneeded; **9** excessive, redundant, remaining; **10** circuitous, gratuitous, overmanned, pleonastic; **11** overstaffed, tautologous, unessential, unnecessary; **12** nonessential, overemployed, tautological; **14** supererogatory.

superior 3 VIP; **4** arch, boss, fine, head, imam, king, more, over, pope; **5** above, ahead, aloof, chief, elder, finer, lofty, mayor, rabbi, ruler, sheik, super, upper; **6** better, bigger, bigwig, bishop, choice, expert, gaffer *UK*, higher, larger, leader, longer, master, senior, snooty, sultan; **7** capping, captain, emperor, foreman, general, grander, greater, haughty, leading, loftier, manager, notable, pompous, premier, prophet; **8** advanced, arrogant, cardinal, director, enhanced, favorite, fugleman, governor, improved, snobbish; **9** ascendant, commander, eclipsing, exceeding, excellent, exclusive, executive, imperious, nonpareil, preferred, president, principal; **10** archbishop, disdainful, headmaster, supervisor, surpassing; **11** exceptional, outclassing, outstanding, overtopping, patronizing, untouchable; **12** aristocratic, headmistress, supercilious; **13** condescending; **14** superintendent; PHRASES: **1, 3, 5** a cut above; **2, 3** Mr Big; **2, 3, 9** in the ascendant; **3-2** one-up; **3, 3** big gun, top dog; **3, 3, 6** the big cheese; **3, 3, 9** the big enchilada; **3, 4, 3** the main man; **3, 5** big noise, cut above; **3, 6** big cheese; **3-6** top-drawer; **3-7** top-quality; **3, 9** big enchilada; **4, 2, 3, 4** cock of the walk; **4, 3** head boy; **4, 3, 6** high and mighty; **4-5** high-class; **4, 6** head honcho; **4, 7** best quality; **4-9** self-important; **5-2** stuck-up; **5, 3** brass hat; **5-5** first-class; **5, 7** above average; **5, 8** prime minister; **6-2** higher-up; **6-7** better-quality; **7, 5** streets ahead.

superior (be superior) **3** cap, top, win; **4** beat, best, lick, pass, peak; **5** excel, trump; **6** batter, better, climax, defeat, exceed, hammer, thrash; **7** clobber, eclipse, overtop, prevail, surpass, triumph, trounce; **8** overcome, overjump, overleap, overlook, overplay, override, overstep; **9** culminate, overtrump, transcend; **10** extinguish, overshadow; **11** outdistance, predominate; PHRASES: **2, 3, 6** go one better; **3, 2, 3** cap it all; **3, 3, 3** win the cup; **3, 3, 5** win the prize; **3, 3, 6, 2** get the better of; **3, 5, 2** get ahead of; **3, 5, 6** run rings around; **4, 3, 3, 4** hold all the aces; **4, 3, 3, 5** hold all the cards; **4, 3, 4** bear the palm; **4, 3, 5** wear the crown; **4, 3, 6** beat the record; **4, 5** rise above; **5, 3, 3** carry the day; **5, 3, 4** steal the show; **5, 3, 7** reach new heights; **5, 5** tower above; **7, 2** improve on.

superiority **3** say; **4** lead, pull; **5** clout, power, right; **6** renown; **7** control, disdain, primacy, quality, success; **8** altitude, eminence, leverage, majority, prestige, priority; **9** advantage, arrogance, authority, dominance, influence, pomposity, privilege, seniority, sublimity, supremacy; **10** ascendancy, ascendency, domination, excellence, perfection, precedence, prepo-

tence, prepotency, prominence, virtuosity; **11** haughtiness, paramountcy, preeminence, prerogative; **12** predominance; **13** condescension, effectiveness, inimitability, predomination, preponderance, transcendence, transcendency; **15** incomparability; PHRASES: **4, 7** high caliber; **4-10** self-importance; **5, 2, 5** pride of place; **5, 4** upper hand; **5, 5** first place. See also **superior**

superior person **3** ace; **4** star, whiz; **6** genius, wonder; **7** paragon, prodigy; **8** champion, nonesuch, superman, virtuoso; **9** superstar; **10** superwoman, topnotcher, übermensch; PHRASES: **3, 4, 7** the cat's pajamas; **4, 2, 3, 5** pick of the bunch; **4, 3** whiz kid; **4, 5** high flyer; **4, 8** high achiever; **5, 2, 2, 5** crème de la crème; **5-5** first-rater; **6, 3** number one, numero uno.

superlative **9** excellent, unmatched; **10** unbeatable; **11** untouchable.

supernatural **3** elf, fay, imp; **5** eerie, fairy, genie, jinni, magic, pixie, weird; **6** mystic, spooky, sprite; **7** banshee, bizarre, brownie, ghostly, psychic, uncanny; **8** mystical; **9** ghostlike, unearthly, unnatural; **10** paranormal; **11** poltergeist; **13** preternatural; PHRASES: **5-7** other-worldly; **5, 9** fairy godmother.

supernumerary **5** extra, spare; **7** surplus; **9** ancillary, auxiliary, excessive; **10** substitute; **11** superfluous.

supersede See **succeed**

superstition (ill omens) **3** owl; **5** raven; PHRASES: **4, 2, 3, 4** bird of ill omen; **6, 6** broken mirror; **7, 4** spilled salt; **7, 7** peacock feather; **9, 6** gathering clouds.

superstructure **4** idea; **5** frame; **6** system; **7** concept; **8** argument; **9** elevation, structure; **12** construction.

supervise See **oversee**

supervisor See **manager**

supine **4** flat; **7** passive; **8** inactive, listless; **9** apathetic, lethargic, prostrate; **10** horizontal.

supple **5** agile, lithe; **6** mobile, pliant; **7** elastic, plastic, pliable, sinuous; **8** bendable; PHRASES: **6-7** double-jointed.

supplement **3** add; **5** annex, extra, rider; **6** append, extend, insert, sequel; **7** adjunct, augment, codicil, enhance, improve, section; **8** addendum, addition, appendix, increase; **9** accompany, appendage, extension, increment, insertion; **10** attachment, complement, postscript; **11** enhancement; PHRASES: **3-2** add-on; **4, 3** fill out; **6-2** follow-up; **6, 5** muscle candy.

supplementary 5 added, extra; **9** accessory, ancillary, auxiliary; **10** additional, subsidiary; **11** subservient; **12** accompanying, supplemental; **13** complementary; PHRASES: **2, 4** on call; **2, 4, 7** at one's service; **3-2** add-on, top-up *UK*.

supplier 6 dealer, seller, trader; **8** merchant, provider, purveyor; **10** contractor.

supplies 4 food; **5** goods, stock; **6** stores; **8** articles, material; **9** equipment, machinery, materials, munitions, purchases, resources; **10** ammunition, deliveries, provisions; **11** necessities; PHRASES: **3, 8** raw material; **4, 3, 5** nuts and bolts; **5, 8** basic ~, vital ~.

supply 3 tap; **4** deal, fund, give, sell; **5** bring, equip, hoard, range, stock, store, trade; **6** amount, outfit, plenty, source, stream; **7** deliver, furnish, present, provide, reserve; **8** pipeline, quantity, resource, scarcity; **9** abundance, provision; **10** allocation, collection, contribute, cornucopia, distribute, repertoire; PHRASES: **4, 9** make available; **5, 3** milch cow; **6, 8** broken pipeline; **8, 4** artesian well; **8, 6** constant ~.

support 3 aid; **4** abet, abut, back, base, bear, buoy, care, ease, help, hold, join, keep, lift, post, prop, stay, take, tend, wall; **5** adopt, boost, brace, carry, favor, frame, funds, honor, joist, nurse, proof, prove, rally, shore, stand, treat, truss; **6** advice, assist, column, crutch, defend, doctor, embank, follow, foster, pillar, praise, prayer, ratify, relief, remedy, rescue, revive, second, succor, uphold, upkeep, verify; **7** backing, benefit, bolster, bracket, bulwark, comfort, commend, confirm, counsel, defense, endorse, espouse, finance, forward, funding, further, hearten, offices, propose, rampart, recruit, relieve, restore, service, sponsor, sustain, trestle, warrant; **8** abutment, advocate, buttress, champion, guidance, kindness, maintain, ministry, scaffold, tolerate, underpin, validate; **9** alleviate, cooperate, encourage, establish, framework, intercede, patronage, promotion, provision, recommend, reinforce, stanchion, subsidize, undergird; **10** assistance, foundation, livelihood, strengthen, sustenance, underframe, underwrite, validation; **11** benediction, collaborate, corroborate, deliverance, en-

dorsement, furtherance, maintenance, sponsorship; **12** authenticate, confirmation, intercession, ministration, ratification, substantiate, underpinning, verification; **13** corroboration, encouragement, reinforcement, strengthening; **14** authentication, substantiation; PHRASES: **2, 2, 5, 2** be in favor of; **2, 5, 3** be there for; **3, 1, 11** lay a cornerstone; **4, 2** back up, buoy up, hold up, keep up, prop up; **4, 3** bear out, care for, fend for; **4, 4** good deed, good turn, make good, wish well; **4, 4, 2** take care of; **4, 5** look after; **4, 7** bear witness, good offices; **5, 2** cheer on, shore up, stand by; **5, 2, 3** speak up for, stand up for, stick up for; **5, 3** vouch for *UK*; **5, 3, 5** swell the ranks; **5, 4, 2** speak well of; **5, 6** stand behind *UK*; **5, 7** child ~, moral ~; **6, 2** adhere to; **7, 2** approve of; **7, 3** provide for; **8, 2** minister to; **10, 3** substitute for.

supportable 6 viable; **7** average; **8** bearable, passable, workable; **9** endurable, tolerable; **10** acceptable, defensible, manageable, sufferable; **11** justifiable, sustainable; **12** maintainable; PHRASES: **2-2** so-so; **3, 3** not bad.

supported 6 backed; **7** assured; **8** attested, endorsed, ratified, seconded, verified; **9** certified, confirmed, fortified, validated; **10** buttressed, reinforced; **11** established, unretracted; **12** corroborated; **13** authenticated, substantiated, unretractable.

supporter 3 fan; **4** aide, ally, base, beam, pier, pile, post, prop, stem, wall; **5** angel, brace, carer, shaft, shelf, stand, table; **6** backer, backup, column, friend, girder, helper, lintel, patron, pillar, rafter, struct, tripod; **7** acolyte, admirer *UK*, bedrock, bracket, bulwark, chassis, comfort, devotee, fulcrum, rampart, sponsor, transom; **8** abutment, adherent, advocate, backbone, basement, buttress, caryatid, champion, crossbar, defender, disciple, exponent, follower, guardian, helpmate, helpmeet, keystone, mainstay, mounting, neighbor, pilaster, promoter, proposer, seconder, sidekick, skeleton, succorer, underlay, upholder; **9** assistant, attendant, auxiliary, colleague, financier, framework, guarantor, protector, sustainer; **10** balustrade, benefactor, cooperator, embankment, enthusiast, foundation, groundwork, maintainer *UK*, substitute, underframe; **11** cornerstone, mantelpiece, scaffolding, sympathizer, underwriter; **12** collaborator, corroborator, substructure, underpinning; **13** undercarriage; PHRASES: **4-6** fund-raiser, well-wisher; **4, 8** good neighbor; **4, 9** good Samaritan; **5, 2, 8** tower of strength; **5-7** spear-carrier; **5, 9** fairy godmother; **6, 2, 4** friend in deed; **6, 8** fellow traveler, Social Security, Social Services; **7, 4** helping hand; **8, 5** guardian angel; **8, 6** friendly critic.

support financially 4 back, fund, keep; **5** grant; **7** finance, pension, sponsor; **8** bankroll, maintain; **9** patronize, subsidize; **10** contribute, underwrite; PHRASES: **3, 3** pay for; **7, 3** provide for.

supporting 3 for, pro; **6** backup; **7** backing; **9** ancillary, assistant, associate, auxiliary, secondary; **10** advocating, subsidiary, supportive; **11** championing; **12** accompanying, recommending; **13** supplementary; PHRASES: **2, 5** in favor.

supporting garment 3 bra; **6** corset, girdle; **9** brassiere, jockstrap; PHRASES: **8, 4** athletic belt.

supporting part 4 base, beam, pier, pile, post, prop, ribs, stem, wall; **5** brace, frame, shaft, shelf, spine, stand, strut, table; **6** column, girder, lintel, pillar, rafter, tripod; **7** bedrock, bracket, bulwark, chassis, fulcrum, rampart, support, transom; **8** abutment, backbone, basement, buttress, caryatid, crossbar, keystone, mainstay, mounting, pedestal, pilaster, skeleton, underlay; **9** crossbeam, framework, worktable; **10** balustrade, embankment, foundation, groundwork, underframe; **11** cornerstone, mantelpiece, scaffolding; **12** substructure, underpinning; **13** undercarriage; PHRASES: **1-5** A-frame; **4, 4** king post; **5, 5** music stand; **6, 8** flying buttress; **9, 4** retaining wall; **10, 5** foundation stone.

supportive 4 kind; **5** basal, loyal; **6** caring, ground, kindly; **7** helpful, tending; **8** guardian, patronal; **9** ancillary, attending, auxiliary, favorable, fostering, nurturing, retaining, succoring, upholding; **10** advocatory, benevolent, comforting, discipular, empathetic, heartening, ministrant, reassuring, subsidiary, substitute, supporting, sustaining; **11** cooperative, encouraging, maintaining, ministering, stipendiary *UK*, sympathetic; **12** contributory, foundational, ministrative, preferential; **13** collaborative, compassionate, corroborative, understanding; **14** intercessional; PHRASES: **4-8** well-disposed; **6-8** morale-boosting.

suppose 3 let; **4** plan, take; **5** draft,

dream, fancy, guess, infer, opine, posit, think; **6** affirm, assert, assume, deduce, divine, expect, gamble, gather, intuit, reason, reckon, sketch; **7** believe, imagine, outline, premise, presume, pretend, surmise, suspect; **8** conceive, conclude, consider, theorize; **9** postulate, predicate, speculate; **10** conjecture, presuppose, presurmize, understand; **11** guesstimate, hypothesize; PHRASES: **3, 4** lay down; **3, 4, 4, 4** get into one's head; **4, 1, 10** form a hypothesis; **4, 2** take it; **4, 3** dare say; **4, 3, 7** take for granted; **6, 1, 5** hazard a guess; **7, 2 ~** so; **8, 7** persuade oneself.

supposed 4 held, said; **5** given, quasi, taken; **6** fabled, mooted, unreal, untrue; **7** alleged, assumed, deduced, fancied, granted, guessed, reputed, rumored, thought, titular, topical; **8** abstract, assented, believed, fanciful, imagined, inferred, invented, premised, presumed, proposed, putative, surmised; **9** assumable, fictional, imaginary, pretended, purported, suggested; **10** imaginable, ostensible, postulated, presumable, supposable, surmisable, understood; **11** conjectured, suppositive, theoretical; **12** hypothesized, hypothetical; PHRASES: **1, 6** a priori; **2-6** so-called; **3, 4** not real; **4-2** made-up; **5, 2, 4** taken as read; **5, 3, 7** taken for granted.

supposedly 8 possibly; **9** evidently, seemingly; **10** apparently; **13** conjecturally, speculatively; PHRASES: **2, 1, 5** at a guess; **2, 2, 2, 4** so it is said; **2, 2, 4** as it were; **2, 3, 8** by all accounts; **2, 4, 3** so they say; **2, 5, 3, 2** as rumor has it; **2, 5, 4** it would seem; **2, 6** in theory; **2, 9** ex hypothesi. *See also* **supposed**

supposing 2 if; **3** say; **6** though; **7** imagine, suppose; **8** although, assuming; PHRASES: **2, 2** as if; **2, 3, 5, 4** in the event that; **2, 6** as though; **4, 2** even if, what if; **4, 3** let's say; **4, 6** let's assume; **8, 4** assuming that.

supposition 4 clue, data, hint, idea; **5** datum, fancy, guess, hunch, model, offer, stand, topic; **6** belief, notion, theory, thesis; **7** conceit, inkling, opinion, premise, surmise, theorem, thought; **8** argument, attitude, evidence, ideality, instinct, position, pretense, proposal, thinking; **9** condition, deduction, guesswork, induction, inference, intuition, postulate, suspicion; **10** assumption, conclusion, conditions, conjecture, hypothesis, intimation, pretending, standpoint, submission, suggestion; **11** affectation, explanation, orientation, possibility, postulation, presumption, probability, proposition, speculation, stipulation; **13** supposability; **14** presupposition, suggestiveness; PHRASES: **3, 4, 2** the idea of; **4, 3, 3** sine qua non; **5, 2, 4** point of view; **7, 8** lateral thinking.

suppositional 4 moot; **7** hinting; **8** academic, allusive, armchair, guessing, notional, putative, surmised; **9** intuitive, supposing; **10** assumptive, gratuitous, suggestive, unverified; **11** conjectural, postulatory, presumptive, speculative, stimulating, suppositive, theoretical; **12** hypothetical, suppositious; **13** guesstimating, propositional; PHRASES: **4, 2, 3, 4** hard to pin down; **4-3** blue-sky.

suppress 4 bury, curb, hide, kill, stem; **5** abuse, block, check, crush, quash, quell; **6** censor, coerce, defeat, extort, harass, muffle, squash, stifle, subdue; **7** conceal, conquer, contain, control, destroy, enslave, execute, exploit, misrule, oppress, repress, silence, smother, squelch, subject, torment, torture; **8** dominate, overcome, overturn, restrain, restrict, withhold; **9** expurgate, misgovern, mishandle, overpower, overwhelm, persecute, subjugate, terrorize, tyrannize, victimize; PHRASES: **3, 2** sit on; **3, 3, 3, 2** put the lid on; **3, 4** put down; **3, 5, 5** use brute force; **4, 2** hush up; **4, 2, 5** keep in check; **4, 2, 7** pull no punches; **4, 4** hold back, hunt down, walk over; **4, 5** shed blood; **4, 6** keep inside; **5, 2** cover up, stamp on, tread on; **5, 3** block out, snuff out; **5, 4, 2** clamp down on; **5, 5** treat rough; **5, 5, 4** tread under foot; **6, 2** bottle up.

suppression 5 wraps; **6** defeat, hiding, Nazism; **7** control, Fascism, torture, tyranny; **8** atrocity, coercion, conquest, jackboot; **9** autocracy, clampdown, despotism, dominance, execution, extortion, overthrow, restraint, silencing, squashing, Stalinism; **10** absolutism, censorship, harassment, inhibition, militarism, oppression, Rachmanism *UK*, repression, subjection; **11** concealment, containment, destruction, expurgation, inquisition, persecution, restriction, subjugation, withholding; **12** dictatorship, exploitation, overpowering; **13** victimization; **15** totalitarianism; PHRASES: **4, 2, 7** veil of secrecy; **4, 4** blue laws, iron hand, iron rule; **5-2** cover-up; **5, 5** brute force, naked force; **6, 4** mailed fist; **8, 3** snuffing out.

supreme 3 top; **4** best; **5** being, chief,

court, first, great; **6** utmost; **7** extreme, highest, topmost; **8** absolute, dominant, greatest, peerless, ultimate; **9** commander, matchless, nonpareil, paramount, principal, sacrifice, sovereign, unmatched, unrivaled, uppermost; **10** consummate, unbeatable; **11** superlative, untouchable; **12** incomparable.

supremely 4 very; **6** really; **7** totally, utterly; **8** uniquely; **9** perfectly; **10** completely, enormously, inimitably, invincibly, singularly; **11** unmatchably; **12** incomparably, particularly, tremendously; **13** unsurpassably, unsurpassedly; PHRASES: **2, 1, 7, 3** in a perfect way; **2, 3** by far; **2, 3, 4** at the peak; **2, 3, 5** on the crest; **2, 3, 6** at the zenith; **2, 5, 3** to crown all; **3, 2, 4, 5** out of this world; **3, 3, 4** all the more, far and away; **3, 4** the most; **3, 10** par excellence; **4, 4** even more; **4, 4, 4** more than ever; **5, 2, 3** first of all; **5, 3** above all; **5, 4** still more; **5, 8** nulli secundus; **6, 2, 4** second to none. *See also* **supreme**

surcharge 5 extra, price; **10** supplement; PHRASES: **4, 2** tack on; **5, 6** extra charge; **6, 5** hidden extra.

sure 3 yes; **4** safe; **5** bound, clear, fixed; **6** indeed; **7** assured, certain; **8** absolute, definite, positive, reliable; **9** confident; **10** protective, verifiable; **11** impregnable, indubitable; **12** indisputable, invulnerable; **13** incontestable; **14** unquestionable; PHRASES: **2, 6** of course; **3, 4** for ~; **4, 3, 5** safe and sound.

surety *See* **guarantee**

surface 3 tar, top; **4** area, back, coat, face, pave, side, skim, skin; **5** cover, front, noise, plane, plate, shell; **6** appear, ascend, bottom, cement, cobble, emerge, extent, façade, facing, gravel, lamina, Tarmac *tm*; **7** coating, outward, overlay, seeming, shallow, tension; **8** apparent, blacktop, concrete, exterior, external, flatness, interior, reappear; **9** concavity, convexity, curvature, resurface, structure; **10** macadamize, sphericity; **11** superficial; PHRASES: **2, 2** go up; **3, 2** pop up; **3, 5** top layer; **4, 2** come up, show up, turn up; **4, 2, 5** come to light; **4, 3** come out; **5, 2** float up; **6, 5** become known.

surfeit *See* **excess**

surge 4 flow, gush, pour, rush; **5** heave; **10** outpouring.

surgeon 6 doctor; **9** physician; **10** specialist; **12** neurosurgeon.

surgery 2 op; 5 graft; 6 premed, suture; 7 cupping, drawing, filling, section; 8 bleeding, bridging, crowning, dialysis, division, excision, grafting, incision, lobotomy, podiatry, sedation, stopping; 9 chiropody, colostomy, induction, operation, perfusion, resection, vasectomy; 10 amputation, anesthesia, extracting, laparotomy, mastectomy, phlebotomy, prosthesis, transplant; 11 acupuncture, advancement, prosthetics, rhinoplasty, transfusion, venesection; 12 electrolysis, hysterectomy, neurosurgery, trephination; 13 cauterization, premedication, psychosurgery, tonsillectomy; 14 appendicectomy; 15 transplantation; PHRASES: 4, 5 skin graft; 5, 5 renal graft; 5, 7 brain ~, heart ~, laser ~, major ~, minor ~; 5-7 blood-letting; 6, 7 bypass ~, dental ~; 7, 5 corneal graft; 7, 7 cardiac ~, general ~, keyhole ~, plastic ~; 8, 7 cosmetic ~.

surgery (practise surgery) 4 prep; 6 divide, excise, incise, induce, sedate, suture; 7 dialyze, operate, perfuse; 8 amputate, maintain; 9 transfuse; 10 transplant; 12 anaesthetize.

surgical dressing 4 cast, lint, roll, swab, tent; 5 gauze, patch, sling; 6 splint, tampon; 7 bandage, pessary, plaster, pledget; 8 compress, dressing, poultice; 9 cataplasm, traumatic; 10 tourniquet; 11 application, Elastoplast™, fingerstall, fomentation, suppository; PHRASES: 4-3 Band-Aid; 4, 7 corn plaster UK; 5, 7 court plaster UK; 7, 2, 5 plaster of Paris; 7, 7 mustard plaster; 8, 7 sticking plaster UK.

surmise 5 guess, infer; 6 deduce, gather; 8 construe; 9 deduction, guesswork, inference; 10 assumption, conclusion.

surmount 5 clear, climb, scale; 6 ascend; 7 conquer, prevail; 8 overcome.

surname 8 cognomen; PHRASES: 4, 4 last name; 6, 4 family name, second name UK.

surpass 5 outdo; 6 better, exceed; 8 outshine.

surpassing 6 better, higher, outbid; 7 greater, outdone; 8 overlong, superior; 9 overtaken; 10 outclassed, surmounted; 11 exceptional, outstanding, transcended; 12 overextended; 13 outmaneuvered; PHRASES: 2, 3, 4 in the lead; 3, 2, 2 one up on.

surplus 3 net, odd; 4 glut, over, owed; 5 bonus, extra, spare; 6 excess, extras, otiose, spares, unused; 7 outcast, overage, surfeit,

unspent; 8 dividend, leftover, overflow, overload, pleonasm, plethora, residual, unwanted; 9 abundance, excessive, leftovers, redundant, remainder, remaining, unexpired; 10 additional, overgrowth, overloaded, oversupply, pleonastic, redundancy, unconsumed; 11 outstanding, superfluity, superfluous, unnecessary; 12 overabundant; 13 overabundance, superabundant; 14 superabundance; PHRASES: 2, 3, 5 on the shelf; 2, 5 to spare; 3, 6 not needed; 5, 9 still remaining; 6, 4 passed over; 7, 4 carried over.

surprise 4 daze, jolt, stun; 5 alarm, amaze, shock; 6 ambush, baffle, wonder; 7 astound, disrupt, disturb, shocker, stagger, startle; 8 astonish, discover, frighten; 9 amazement, bombshell, disbelief, dumbfound, interrupt; 10 disclosure, disconcert, revelation; 11 flabbergast, unreadiness; 12 astonishment; 13 improbability; 14 miscalculation, unexpectedness, unpreparedness; PHRASES: 4, 2, 7 lack of warning; 4, 2, 8 take by ~; 4, 4 bowl over, come upon; 4, 4, 3, 4 bolt from the blue; 4, 5 take aback; 4, 8 take unawares; 5, 2, 2 burst in on; 5, 3 catch out; 5, 3, 3 knock for six UK; 5, 3, 5 catch off guard; 5, 3-6 catch red-handed; 5, 7 catch napping; 5, 8 catch unawares; 6, 2 spring on; 7, 2 intrude on.

surprised 7 trapped, unaware; 9 stupefied; 10 unprepared; 12 unsuspecting. *See also* **surprise**

surprising 3 odd; 6 freaky, sudden; 7 amazing, unusual; 8 abnormal, freakish, peculiar, shocking; 9 startling; 10 astounding, remarkable, staggering, unexpected, unforeseen; 11 astonishing, unannounced, unpredicted; 12 overwhelming, unbelievable; 13 extraordinary, serendipitous, unanticipated, unprecedented, unpredictable; PHRASES: 4, 2, 9 full of surprises.

surprisingly 8 unawares; PHRASES: 2, 2, 8 to my surprise; 2, 2, 9 to my amazement; 3, 2, 3, 4 out of the blue; 3, 5 off guard; 7, 7 without warning. *See also* **surprising**

surprising thing 5 treat, twist; 6 wonder; 8 reversal, windfall; 10 revelation; 11 serendipity; PHRASES: 3-6 eye-opener; 3, 10 the unexpected, the unforeseen; 7, 5 special treat; 10, 4 unexpected gift.

surrender 5 yield; 10 relinquish, submission; 12 capitulation, renunciation; PHRASES: 4, 2 give in, give up; 4, 4 hand over; 5, 6 admit defeat.

surrogate 5 proxy; 6 backup, deputy; 10 substitute, understudy; 11 replacement; PHRASES: 5-2 stand-in; 6, 5 father image; 6, 6 father figure, mother figure; 6, 9 mother ~, parent ~.

surround 3 rim; 4 edge, ring; 5 bound, frame, mount; 6 border, circle, edging, encase, enfold, girdle, mantle, outlie; 7 besiege, contain, enclose, envelop, environ, outline, setting; 8 encircle; 9 encompass; 12 circumscribe; PHRASES: 2, 5 go round *UK*; 3, 2 hem in; 3, 5, 2 lay siege to; 3, 6 lie around; 4, 2 keep in.

surrounded 6 girded; 7 wrapped *UK*; 8 enclosed, enfolded; 9 encircled, enveloped; 10 roundabout; 11 encompassed; 13 circumambient, circumscribed; PHRASES: 2, 3, 5 on all sides; 5, 3, 5 round and about; 6-2 hemmed-in; 7, 6 traffic circle.

surrounding 4 near; 5 close; 6 around, nearby; 8 adjacent, outlying, suburban; 9 adjoining, immediate, proximate; 10 background, contiguous, perimetric, peripheral; 11 neighboring; 12 neighborhood; 13 environmental.

surroundings 4 area; 5 arena, scene, stage; 6 locale, milieu, suburb; 7 context, habitat, scenery, setting; 8 backdrop, confines, environs, location, outposts, vicinity; 9 greenbelt, outskirts, perimeter, periphery, precincts, situation, surrounds; 10 background; 11 environment; 12 neighborhood; 13 circumstances.

surveillance *See* **observation**

survey 4 plot; 5 chart, study; 6 assess, peruse, regard, review; 7 analyze, examine, inquiry, inspect, measure; 8 analysis, consider, scrutiny; 9 appraisal; 10 assessment, evaluation, inspection; 11 examination; 13 investigation; PHRASES: 3, 3 map out.

survival 5 being; 9 endurance, existence.

survive 4 last, live, stay; 6 endure, escape, retire; 7 outlast, outlive, persist, subsist; 8 continue; 9 withstand; PHRASES: 2, 2 go on; 4, 2 live on; 4, 3, 5 bear the brunt; 4, 4 turn back; 4, 4, 2 fall back on; 4, 5 stay alive; 4, 7 live through; 5, 2 carry on; 6, 7 scrape through.

surviving spouse 5 relic, widow; 7 dowager, widower; 8 survivor, widowman; PHRASES: 3, 5 war widow; 4, 5 golf widow; 5, 5 grass widow, merry widow, widow

woman; 5, 6 queen mother; 5, 7 grass widower; 7, 5 dowager queen; 8, 5 baseball widow.

susceptibility 7 allergy; 8 delicacy, exposure, feelings; 9 liability; 10 sensuality; 11 sensibility, sensitivity; 12 irritability; 13 hyperesthesia, vulnerability; 14 predisposition; 15 oversensitivity; PHRASES: 4, 4 thin skin; 4, 10 soft underbelly; 9, 2, 4 threshold of pain. *See also* **susceptible**

susceptible 4 open, weak; 5 jumpy, prone; 6 carnal, docile, liable, tender, tetchy, touchy; 7 excited, prickly, stirred, subject; 8 agitated, allergic, amenable, delicate, disposed, esthetic, gullible, inclined, sensuous, swayable, thrilled, ticklish; 9 epicurean, excitable, irritable, irritated, receptive, sensitive; 10 perceptive, responsive, vulnerable; 11 defenseless, hyperactive, overexcited, predisposed, suggestible; 13 oversensitive, temperamental; 14 impressionable; PHRASES: 2, 4 at risk; 3-7 hot-blooded; 4-7 thin-skinned, warm-blooded.

suspect 4 iffy; 5 dodgy *UK*, doubt, fishy, scent, shady; 7 dubious; 8 mistrust; 10 suspicious.

suspend 4 halt, hang, hold, quit, stay, stop; 5 check, defer, delay, drape, droop, swing, trail; 6 append, dangle, fasten, shelve; 7 adjourn; 8 overhang, postpone; 9 interrupt; PHRASES: 3, 2 put up; 3, 2, 3 put on ice; 3, 2, 4 put on hold; 3, 3 put off; 3, 4 put back; 4, 2 hang up, hook up; 4, 4 hang down, push back; 4, 5 hang glide; 5, 3 break off; 5, 4 swing from; 6, 2 string up; 6, 4 bungee jump.

suspended 4 hung; 6 banned, barred; 7 hanging, pendent, pending, pensile, sagging; 8 dangling, deferred, excluded, floating, hovering, swinging; 9 abrogated, adjourned, pendulous, postponed, powerless; 10 proscribed, suspensive; 11 deactivated, overhanging, suspendible; 13 uninfluential; PHRASES: 2, 2, 3, 3 up in the air; 2, 3 on ice; 2, 3, 3 in the air; 2, 3, 4, 6 on the back burner; 2, 4 on hold; 2, 7 in reserve; 2, 8 in abeyance; 3, 3 put off; 4, 4 held over; 6, 2 strung up *UK*; 8, 3 switched off.

suspended object 5 braid, swing; 6 fringe, icicle, tassel; 7 curtain, earring, hammock, pendant, picture, pigtail, trapeze; 8 pendulum, ponytail; 10 chandelier; PHRASES: 4, 4 bell rope; 4-4 coat-tail *UK*; 5,

3 plumb bob; **7, 6** hanging object; **9, 6** suspended cymbal.

suspender 6 garter.

suspense 5 doubt; **7** anxiety, tension; **9** confusion; **10** excitement, expectancy, insecurity; **11** expectation, uncertainty; **12** anticipation, apprehension.

suspension 3 sag; **4** hang; **5** check, delay, drape, droop, pause, swing; **6** dangle, holdup; **7** hanging; **8** dangling, deferral, pendency; **9** deferment; **11** pensileness; **12** interruption, postponement; **13** pendulousness; **14** suspendibility, suspensiveness.

suspicion 4 clue, hint, idea; **5** doubt, hunch, tinge, touch, trace; **6** denial, notion; **7** atheism, caution, feeling, inkling, smidgen, soupçon, thought; **8** distrust, mistrust, question, wariness; **9** disbelief, misgiving, rejection; **10** conjecture, skepticism, suggestion; **11** agnosticism, incredulity; **12** apprehension; **14** suspiciousness.

suspicious 4 wary; **5** shady; **6** shifty; **7** dubious, suspect; **8** doubtful; **11** distrustful, mistrustful; **12** apprehensive.

sustain 4 bear, feed, keep, take; **5** brook, incur, stand; **6** coddle, cosset, endure, mother, pamper, suffer, uphold; **7** nourish, nurture, prolong, protect, support, undergo, weather; **8** continue, contract, maintain, protract, tolerate; **9** encounter, withstand; **10** experience, sympathize; PHRASES: **3, 2, 4** put up with; **4, 2** hold up, keep up, prop up; **4, 4** meet with; **4, 5** keep going; **5, 2** carry on; **7, 3** provide for.

sustenance 4 care, food, fuel, keep; **5** manna; **6** living, upkeep; **7** edibles, nurture, rations, support; **8** sympathy, victuals; **9** mothering, nutrition, provision; **10** livelihood, provisions, sustention; **11** maintenance, nourishment, subsistence, sustainment, wherewithal; **12** sustentation; PHRASES: **5, 5** daily bread; **5, 7** child support.

suture 3 sew; **4** join, seal, seam; **5** close, joint; **6** stitch; **7** closure; **8** junction; PHRASES: **3, 2** sew up; **6, 2** stitch up.

swab 3 pad; **4** lint, wash, wipe; **5** clean, cloth, gauze; **7** cleanse, moisten.

swaddle *See* **wrap**

swag 4 haul, loot; **5** booty, chain, drape; **6** spoils; **7** curtain, drapery, festoon, garland, hanging, plunder.

swagger 5 strut, sweep; **6** parade, prance;

7 bluster, conceit, flounce; **9** arrogance.

swaggering 4 smug; **8** arrogant, boastful, bragging, vaunting; PHRASES: **4-9** self-important, self-satisfied.

swain 5 lover; **7** admirer *UK*; **9** boyfriend; PHRASES: **5, 3** young man *UK*.

swallow 3 eat, nip, sip; **4** down, gulp, hide; **6** accept, credit, engulf, ingest, recant; **7** believe, consume, destroy, repress, retract; **8** suppress; PHRASES: **3, 4, 5** eat one's words; **4, 4** back down, hold back, take back, take over; **6, 2** gobble up. *See also* **songbird**

swamp 3 bog, fen; **4** mire; **5** drown, flood, marsh; **6** deluge, engulf, muskeg; **7** pocosin, swamper, wetland; **8** inundate, overload; **9** overwhelm; PHRASES: **4, 5** snow under; **5, 5** ~ buggy.

swamp fever 7 malaria.

swan 4 idle, laze, loaf; **5** drift, float; **6** maiden, wander; PHRASES: **4, 4** ~ dive, ~ neck, ~ song.

swank 4 brag, show; **5** boast, strut; **6** parade; **7** boaster, bragger, display, swagger; **9** swaggerer; **11** affectation, ostentation; **13** exhibitionism, exhibitionist; PHRASES: **4, 3** show off; **4-3** show-off.

swap *See* **exchange**

swarm 3 fly; **4** bevy, mass, rise, teem; **5** cloud, crowd, flock, group, horde, hover; **6** circle, flight, throng; **7** bristle; PHRASES: **2, 4** be full.

swarthy 4 dark; **8** leathery; PHRASES: **7-6** weather-beaten.

swastika 6 fylfot.

swathe 4 band, bind, wrap; **5** cloak, cover, drape, strip; **6** enfold, ribbon, shroud; **7** bandage, entwine, envelop.

sway 4 bend, bias, lean, rock, tilt, veer; **5** power, slant, swing, waver; **6** affect; **7** command, control; **8** persuade; **9** authority, influence, oscillate.

swear 3 vow; **4** avow, cuss, rail; **5** curse, shout; **6** attest, depose, pledge; **7** promise; PHRASES: **3, 3, 5** eff and blind *UK*.

swearword 4 oath; **5** curse; **9** expletive, obscenity, profanity, scatology, vulgarism; **10** coprolalia; **12** billingsgate; PHRASES: **3, 1-4** the f-word; **3, 4** bad word; **3, 8** bad language, low language; **4, 4** rude word; **4-6, 4** four-letter word; **4, 8** blue language; **5, 4** taboo word; **5-5** Anglo-Saxon; **6, 8** vulgar language; **7, 4** naughty word; **7, 8** obscene language.

sweat 2 BO; **4** drip, fret, glow, wilt; **5** dread, exude, panic, steam, sudor, worry; **7** exudate, swelter; **8** perspire, sudation, sweating; **9** exudation, sudoresis; **10** perspiring; **11** diaphoresis; **12** perspiration; PHRASES: **2, 6** be afraid; **2, 7** be anxious; **2, 8** be agitated; **2, 9** be concerned; **4, 5** cold ~; **5, 2, 5** beads of ~; **5, 4** ~ suit; **5, 5** ~ gland, ~ shirt; **6, 5** honest ~.

sweater 3 top; **4** knit; **5** gansy, wooly; **6** cardie *UK*, fleece, gansey *UK*, jersey, jumper *UK*, woolly; **7** twinset *UK*; **8** cardigan, chandail, Guernsey, pullover, slipover; **10** sweatshirt, turtleneck; PHRASES: **1-4** V-neck; **3, 7** ski ~; **4-2** slip-on; **4, 4** Fair Isle; **4-4** crew-neck, polo-neck, roll-neck; **4, 4, 7** hand- knit ~; **4, 6** mock turtle; **4, 7** Aran ~; **6, 3** sloppy joe; **6, 7** Siwash ~; **7, 7** knitted ~; **8, 7** cashmere ~, Cowichan ~. *See also* **clothes**

sweaty 3 hot, wet; **4** damp, dank, warm; **5** close, humid, moist, muggy; **6** clammy, soaked, sticky, sultry; **7** boiling, glowing, sudoric, wilting; **8** drenched, dripping, sudatory, sweating; **9** sudorific; **10** perspiring; **11** diaphoretic; PHRASES: **3, 4, 5** wet with sweat; **6, 2, 5** bathed in sweat.

sweep 3 arc, bow, fly; **4** arch, bend, draw, grab, move, race, span, zoom; **5** brush, carry, curve, range, scope, seize, speed, swing; **6** extent, raffle; **7** lottery, stretch; **11** sweepstakes; PHRASES: **4, 2** tidy up; **5, 2** clean up.

sweeping 5 broad; **7** blanket, general; **9** extensive; **11** generalized; **13** comprehensive; **14** indiscriminate; PHRASES: **3-8** far-reaching.

sweet 4 cute, iced, kind, pure; **5** fresh, tooth; **6** caring, dulcet, gentle, glazed, kindly, sickly, smooth, sugary, syrupy, tender; **7** amiable, candied, caramel, cloying, dessert, fondant, frosted, honeyed, lovable, melodic, musical, odorous, scented, sugared, sweetie, treacly *UK*, tuneful; **8** adorable, charming, engaging, fragrant, friendly, lollipop *UK*, lollypop, marzipan, nectared, obliging, perfumed, pleasant, pleasing, sweetish; **9** agreeable, ambrosial, appealing, enjoyable, melodious, rewarding, sweetened, sweetmeat, wholesome; **10** attractive, confection, delightful, gratifying, harmonious, nectareous, saccharine, satisfying, thoughtful; **11** bittersweet, considerate, mellifluous, pleasurable, sentimental, sympathetic; **12** crystallized; **13** accommodating; PHRASES: **4, 2, 3, 3** easy on the ear; **4-7** good-natured, soft-hearted; **5, 2, 1, 3** ~ as a nut; **5, 3** ~ pea; **5-3-4** sweet-and-sour; **5, 4** ~ corn, ~ shop; **5, 5** candy store, ~ basil; **5, 6** ~ pepper, ~ potato; **5-6** sugar-coated; **5, 7** ~ william; **5, 8** ~ chestnut *UK*; **5-8** sweet-smelling, sweet-tempered; **6, 5** boiled ~ *UK*; **6-5** sickly-sweet.

sweetbrier 9 eglantine.

sweet clover 7 melilot.

sweet drink 4 mead; **5** cocoa, punch; **7** cordial, liqueur, sherbet; **8** gluhwein *UK*, horchata, lemonade, muscatel; **9** orangeade, Sauternes; PHRASES: **3, 5** egg cream, hot toddy; **3-5, 4** ice-cream soda; **3, 9** hot chocolate; **4-4** Coca-Cola™; **4, 5** soft drink; **5, 3** fruit cup, juice box; **5, 4** cream soda, sweet wine; **5, 5** fruit crush, fruit juice; **5, 6** fruit squash; **6, 4** mulled wine, spiced wine; **7, 4** dessert wine.

sweeten 3 ice; **4** mull; **5** candy, frost, glaze, honey, sugar; **6** better, pacify, soothe; **7** appease, augment, enhance, improve, mollify; **8** heighten; **9** intensify; **11** crystallize; PHRASES: **3, 5, 2** add sugar to; **4, 7** make sweeter; **5, 3, 4** sugar the pill; **5-4** sugar-coat; **6, 2** soften up; **7, 3, 4** ~ the pill.

sweetener 3 jam; **5** bribe, fruit, honey, jelly, sugar, syrup; **6** carrot, nectar; **7** glucose, lactose, sucrose, treacle *UK*; **8** ambrosia, conserve, dextrose, fructose, glycerin, honeydew, molasses, preserve; **9** aspartame, cyclamate, honeycomb, marmalade; **10** backhander *UK*, delicacies, inducement, Nutrasweet *tm*, saccharine, sweetening, sweetmeats; PHRASES: **4, 5** beet sugar, cane sugar; **5, 4** sugar loaf, sugar lump; **5, 5** brown sugar, glacé fruit, icing sugar, maple syrup; **5, 9** sweet substance; **6, 5** caster sugar *UK*, clover honey; **7, 5** candied fruit, refined sugar; **8, 5** demerara sugar, powdered sugar; **9, 5** unrefined sugar; **10, 5** granulated sugar.

sweet flag 7 calamus.

sweet gum 6 copalm; PHRASES: **3, 3** red gum.

sweetheart *See* **loved one**

sweetness 5 candy, charm; **6** appeal, purity; **7** cloying, harmony, perfume; **9** fragrance; **10** amiability, attraction; **11** adorability, benevolence; **12** saccharinity;

13 consideration; PHRASES: **5, 5** sweet smell, sweet tooth. *See also* **sweet**

sweet potato 6 batata, kumara *UK*.

swell 3 fop; **4** grow, wave; **5** bulge, dandy, surge; **6** billow, roller; **7** breaker, enhance, enlarge, improve, inflate; **8** increase; **10** undulation; **12** clotheshorse; PHRASES: **4, 2** puff up; **4, 3** puff out.

swelling 4 boil, bump, cyst, weal *UK*, welt; **5** bulge, tumor, wheal *UK*; **6** bunion, growth; **7** abscess, blister; **9** chilblain, extension, puffiness; **10** distension; **11** engorgement, enlargement; **12** inflammation, protuberance.

swerve 3 yaw; **4** roll, skid, veer; **5** break, drift, pitch, shift, swing; **6** leeway; **7** deviate, diverge; **8** crabwalk, sideslip, sidestep; PHRASES: **3, 5** leg break; **4, 3** veer off; **4, 7** turn sharply; **5, 4** swing over; **6, 9** change direction.

swift 4 fast; **5** agile, early, fleet, hasty, nifty, quick, rapid, round, smart, zippy; **6** flying, nimble, prompt, racing *UK*, snappy, speedy, sudden, volant, winged; **7** darting, dashing, express, hurried, pelting, runaway, running; **8** charging, electric, flashing, headlong, hurrying, hurtling, hustling, meteoric, rattling, spanking, speeding, whirling, whizzing; **9** barreling, breakneck, cantering, galloping, immediate, scorching; **10** alacritous, hypersonic, supersonic, ultrasonic; **11** expeditious, precipitate, precipitous, streamlined, tempestuous; **13** instantaneous; PHRASES: **2-2** go-go; **3-2** ton-up *UK*; **3-3** all-out; **3-9** jet-propelled; **4, 1, 4** like a bird; **4, 2, 5** like an eagle; **4-3** flat-out; **4-4** wide-open; **4-5** high-speed; **4-6** high-geared, wing-footed; **4-7** hair-trigger; **4-8** high-velocity; **5, 2, 1, 4** quick as a wink; **5, 2, 1, 5** quick as a flash; **5, 2, 3, 4** quick as the wind, quick on the draw; **5, 2, 4** fleet of foot; **5-4** rapid-fire; **5-6** eagle-winged, light-footed, quick-footed, swift-moving; **6-2** hopped-up, hotted-up, souped-up; **6-5** double-quick *UK*; **6-6** nimble-footed.

swift animal 3 doe, fox; **4** deer, hare; **5** eagle, racer, swift; **7** cheetah, courser, gazelle, ostrich, swallow; **8** antelope, galloper; **9** greyhound, racehorse; **10** roadrunner; **12** thoroughbred; PHRASES: **3, 3, 2, 4** bat out of hell; **6, 6** scared rabbit.

swiftly 3 p.d.q.; **4** ASAP; **5** amain, apace; **6** presto, pronto; **7** allegro; **8** headlong; **9** posthaste; **11** accelerando, prestissimo;

PHRASES: **2, 1, 4, 2, 5** at a rate of knots *UK*; **2, 2, 4** in no time; **2, 3, 6** on the double; **2, 4, 4** at full tilt, in full sail, in high gear; **2, 4, 5** at full blast, at full speed; **2, 4, 6** in full gallop; **2, 4, 8** at full throttle; **2, 6-4** in double-time; **2, 6, 5** on eagle's wings; **3, 3** all out; **4, 3** flat out; **4, 3, 7** hell for leather; **4, 4, 3, 4** with whip and spur; **4, 5, 5** full speed ahead; **5-8** quick-wittedly; **6, 1, 5** ventre à terre; **6-5** double-quick *UK*; **6, 7** helter- skelter; **7-5** lickety-split. *See also* **swift**

swift person 4 Iris, Jehu *UK*; **5** Ariel, racer; **6** Hermes, runner; **7** courier, courser, harrier, hustler, Mercury, speeder; **8** scorcher, sprinter; **9** messenger; PHRASES: **4-6** hell-driver; **5, 5** speed demon, speed freak; **5, 6** speed maniac; **6, 6** racing driver.

swift thing 3 jet; **4** gale, race; **5** arrow; **6** bullet, rocket; **7** clipper, express, missile, tempest, torrent; **9** hurricane, lightning, speedboat, telegraph, telephone; **10** cannonball; **11** electricity; PHRASES: **3, 6** jet flight; **4, 3** race car; **4, 7** pony express; **5, 5** quick march *UK*; **5, 6** magic carpet; **5, 7** quick retreat; **6, 3** sports car; **6, 5** double march, forced march; **7, 5** express train; **9, 5** lightning flash.

swig *See* **drink**

swill 3 hog; **4** mash, swab, swig, wash; **5** bilge, clean, quaff, rinse, slops, slosh; **6** guzzle, scraps, sewage, slough, sluice, wallow; **7** hogwash; **8** drainage, pigswill *UK*, sewerage; **9** dishwater; **10** ditchwater *UK*; PHRASES: **3, 4** pig food; **3-6** hog-wallow; **4, 3** wash out; **4, 4** wash down; **5, 4** knock back; **5, 5** bilge water, dirty water; **8, 5** stagnant water.

swim 3 bob; **4** reel, spin, sway; **5** bathe, float, whirl; **7** snorkel; PHRASES: **2, 3, 1, 3** go for a dip; **2, 8** go swimming; **3-6** dog-paddle; **4, 5, 5** ~ under water; **5, 5** tread water.

swimmer 5 Spitz (Mark); **6** Ederle (Gertrude Caroline), Thorpe (Ian); **9** lifeguard; **10** snorkeller *UK*; PHRASES: **3, 5** Van Dyken (Amy); **4-5** life-saver, skin-diver; **5-5** scuba-diver; **7, 7** subaqua ~. *See also* **fish, aquatic animal**

swimming 3 fin, lap; **4** duck, frog, pike, swim, tuck, turn, whip; **5** crawl, entry, fancy, float, plain, relay, wedge; **6** double, indoor, inward, medley, paddle, stroke, wading; **7** bathing, bobbing, buoyant, dolphin, flipper, floated, flutter, outdoor, reverse, snorkel, subaqua, swallow, trudgen, variety; **8** backward, buoyancy, fishtail, floating, natation, natatory, paddling, platform, recovery, survival, twisting; **9** butterfly, crossover, freestyle, handstand, kickboard; **10** backstroke, natational, sidestroke, snorkeling, underwater; **11** competitive, springboard; **12** breaststroke, flutterboard, recreational, synchronized; PHRASES: **3-5** one-piece, two-piece; **3, 6** dog paddle; **3-6** dog-paddle; **4, 5** back crawl; **4, 6** skin diving; **5, 4** shark bait; **5, 5** front crawl, relay event; **5-6** short-course; **5-8** doggy-paddling, drown-proofing; **6-3** double-arm; **6, 4** medley race; **7-4** Olympic-size(d); **8, 5** treading water; **9, 5** freestyle event; **10, 5** Australian crawl.

swimming pool 4 lido *UK*, pond, pool; **5** baths *UK*, beach, river; **10** natatorium; PHRASES: **4, 4** wave pool; **6, 4** heated pool, plunge pool, wading pool; **7, 4** leisure pool; **8, 4** swimming bath *UK*, swimming hole, swimming lake; **8, 5** swimming baths *UK*, swimming beach.

swimming technique 4 kick; **6** up-kick; **8** downkick; PHRASES: **3, 6** arm stroke; **4, 4** frog kick, whip kick; **5, 4** wedge kick; **6, 7** double overarm, single overarm; **7, 4** dolphin kick, flutter kick; **7, 6** trudgen stroke; **8, 4** fishtail kick, scissors kick; **9, 4** crossover kick.

swimwear 4 togs; **5** tanga; **6** bikini, trunks; **7** bathers *UK*, goggles, tankini; **8** monokini, swimsuit; PHRASES: **7, 3** bathing cap; **7, 4** bathing suit; **7, 6** bathing trunks; **7, 7** bathing costume *UK*; **8, 6** swimming trunks; **8, 7** swimming costume *UK. See also* **beachwear, clothes**

swindle 3 con; **4** dupe, hoax; **5** cheat, fraud, trick; **12** embezzlement; PHRASES: **6-5** double-cross.

swing 4 blow, hang, reel, rock, slap, sway, veer; **5** pivot, smack, swipe, thump; **6** dangle, manage, rotate, swerve; **7** arrange; **9** fluctuate; **10** accomplish; PHRASES: **4, 4** hang down.

swipe 3 dig, hit; **4** blow, slap; **5** smack, steal, swing; **6** pilfer, strike; **7** putdown; PHRASES: **4, 3** lash out; **4, 3, 4** make off with.

swirl 3 mix; **4** eddy, moil, roil, roll, spin, stir; **5** churn, gurge, surge, twirl, whirl; **6** grovel, seethe, tumble, wallow, welter; **8** flounder; **9** whirlpool; PHRASES: **4, 5, 2** roll about in; **4, 6** mill around.

swish 4 hiss, posh; **5** smart; **6** classy, rus-

tle, whoosh; **7** whisper, whistle; **8** upmarket; **11** fashionable.

Swiss 7 Switzer; **9** Helvetian; PHRASES: **5, 4** S~ roll *UK*; **5, 5** S~ chard, S~ guard; **5, 6** S~ cheese, S~ muslin.

switch 4 cane; **5** birch; **6** change, points; **7** convert, replace; **8** exchange; PHRASES: **5, 6** light ~; **6, 6** rocker ~ *UK*, toggle ~.

switchback 4 bend, turn; **5** twist; **6** corner, zigzag; **7** hairpin; PHRASES: **3, 6** big dipper *UK*.

Switzerland 2 CH *UK*; **6** Suisse; **7** Schweiz; **8** Svizzera.

swoon 5 faint; **8** blackout; **15** unconsciousness; PHRASES: **4, 3** pass out; **5, 3** black out.

sword 4 dirk, foil; **5** saber, skean; **6** dagger, glaive, poleax *UK*, rapier; **7** bayonet, cutlass, machete, poleaxe *UK Can*; **8** battle-ax, claymore, falchion, scimitar, stiletto, tomahawk; **10** broadsword, swordstick; PHRASES: **5, 5** bowie knife.

swordfish 9 broadbill.

sword lily 9 gladiolus.

sycophancy 7 bobbing, ducking, fawning; **8** crawling, cringing, flattery, sponging, toadying, toadyism; **9** groveling, obeisance, servility, truckling; **10** abjectness, parasitism; **11** bootlicking, brownnosing, footlicking, handshaking, prostration, timeserving; **12** ingratiation; **13** mealymouthing; **14** backscratching, obsequiousness; PHRASES: **3-7** ass-licking; **4-7** soft-soaping; **5-9** apple-polishing; **7, 2** sucking up.

sycophant 4 dupe, peon, serf, suck, tool; **5** creep *UK*, helot, slave, toady; **6** fawner, jackal, lackie, lapdog, minion, poodle, puppet, stooge; **7** brownie, crawler *UK*, doormat, obligor, spaniel; **8** assentor, courtier, creature, groveler, kowtower, lickspit, smoothie; **9** flatterer, footstool, toadeater; **10** bootlicker, brownnoser, instrument, timeserver; **11** lickspittle; **13** backscratcher *UK*; PHRASES: **3, 3** yes man; **3-5** yea-sayer; **3-6** ass-licker; **4, 3** cat's paw; **4, 6** amen corner; **5, 4** Uriah Heep; **5-4** brown-nose; **5-5** mealy-mouth; **6-2** hanger-on; **8, 5** creeping Jesus; **8, 7** faithful servant.

sycophantic 4 oily; **5** bowed, slimy, soapy; **6** bowing, creepy, smarmy; **7** fawning, hangdog, servile, whining; **8** beggarly, cowering, crawling, creeping *UK*, cringing, obeisant, scraping, sneaking, sponging, stooping, toadying, toadyish, unctuous; **9** groveling, kowtowing, leechlike, parasitic, prostrate, sniveling, truckling; **10** flattering, obsequious; **11** bootlicking, footlicking, freeloading, handshaking; **12** ingratiating; **13** overattentive; **14** backscratching; PHRASES: **2, 4, 5** on one's knees; **2, 6, 4** on bended knee; **3-7** ass-licking; **4-4** make-nice; **4-7** soft-soaping, timeserving; **5-6** brown-nosing; **5-7** mealymouthed; **5-9** apple-polishing.

sycophantic (be sycophantic) 4 fawn; **5** crawl, creep, toady; **8** bootlick; **11** backscratch; PHRASES: **3-4** ass-lick; **4, 2** fawn on; **5-4** brown-nose.

sylph *See* **nymph**

symbol 4 ankh, clef, flag, icon, lion, logo, mace, mark, rose, rune, sign, star; **5** badge, caret, colon, crest, crown, eagle, image, tilde, token, totem; **6** cachet, cipher, emblem, letter, obelus; **7** cedilla, mandala, mezuzah, thistle; **8** asterisk, daffodil, ideogram, metaphor, pentacle, shamrock, swastika, talisman; **9** semicolon; **10** hieroglyph, pictograph; PHRASES: **1, 4** V sign; **4, 2, 5** flag of truce; **5, 4** peace pipe, peace sign, white flag; **5, 6** olive branch; **6, 5** broken arrow.

symbolism 4 hint; **5** image, imago; **6** symbol; **7** imagery, meaning; **8** allegory; **9** archetype, evocation, iconology, ritualism, semiology, semiotics, signaling, symbology; **11** iconography, implication; **12** significance; **13** symbolization; **14** representation, symptomatology; PHRASES: **6, 6** mother symbol; **7, 6** phallic symbol; **9, 6** fertility symbol, universal symbol; **10, 5** archetypal image.

symmetrical 4 even; **5** equal; **7** regular, uniform; **8** balanced, chiastic, rhythmic; **9** congruent, isosceles, symmetric; **10** coordinate, harmonious, reciprocal; **11** bisymmetric(al), equilateral, interacting; **12** proportional, proportioned; **13** correlational, correspondent, corresponding, proportionate; **14** enantiomorphic, interdependent; **15** counterbalanced; PHRASES: **4-5** even-sided; **4-8** well-balanced.

symmetry 5 order, poise, rhyme; **7** balance, harmony; **8** chiasmus, equality, evenness, tidiness; **9** congruity, equipoise; **10** congruence, proportion, regularity, uniformity; **11** correlation, equilibrium, interaction, parallelism, reciprocity; **13**

interrelation, reciprocation; **14** coordinateness, correspondence, counterbalance; **15** interdependence, proportionality, symmetricalness; PHRASES: **4, 5** even sides; **7, 2, 4** balance of form.

sympathetic 4 kind; **6** kindly; **7** amiable, likable; **8** friendly; **9** agreeable, approving, concerned, congenial; **10** supportive; **13** compassionate, understanding; PHRASES: **2, 6** in accord; **2, 9** in agreement; **4-8** well-disposed.

sympathy 4 pity; **7** empathy, support; **8** approval, kindness; **9** agreement; **10** compassion; **11** condolences; **13** commiseration, consideration, understanding.

symposium *See* **conference**

symptom 4 ague, lump, pain, rash, sign, sore; **5** chill, cough, fever, spasm, spots, tumor; **6** growth, nausea, shakes; **7** blister, fatigue, malaise, pimples, pyrexia, shivers; **8** bleeding, collapse, delirium, diarrhea, fainting, headache, migraine, numbness, swelling, syndrome, vomiting, weakness; **9** breakdown, calenture, carcinoma, discharge, dizziness, indicator, paralysis, stiffness; **10** congestion, depression, hoarseness, indication, queasiness; **11** hyperthermy, hypotension, hypothermia, prostration, temperature; **12** feverishness, hyperpyrexia, hypertension, hyperthermia, inflammation; **13** insensibility; **15** unconsciousness; PHRASES: **4, 2, 8** lack of appetite; **4, 6** sore throat; **4, 11** high temperature; **5, 2, 6** waves of nausea; **6, 4** weight loss; **6, 7** queasy stomach; **7, 4** warning sign.

synagogue 4 shul; **6** temple.

synchronism 4 sync; **11** coincidence, concurrence, conjunction, isochronism; **12** simultaneity; **15** contemporaneity, synchronization; PHRASES: **2-10** co-occurrence; **3-4** lip-sync.

synchronize 4 sync; **5** match; **6** chorus; **9** harmonize; **10** coordinate; **11** orchestrate; PHRASES: **4, 2, 4** keep in step, keep in time, stay in time; **4, 3, 4, 4** keep the same beat; **4, 4, 4** keep pace with; **5, 2, 4, 4** march in lock step; **5, 4, 4** bring into line.

synchronized 5 timed; **6** phased; **7** matched; **10** harmonized, isochronal; **11** co-ordinated, isochronous, synchronous; **13** corresponding; PHRASES: **2, 3, 4** on the beat; **2, 4** in line, in step, in sync, in time; **2, 4, 4** in lock step.

syncopate 3 jam; 4 play, riff, rock; 5 shift, swing; 6 accent, modify, stress.

syndrome 7 disease, pattern; 8 disorder; 9 condition.

synopsis *See* **summary**

syntax 6 clause; 8 ellipsis, syndeton; 9 agreement, asyndeton, gradation, hypotaxis, parataxis; 10 apposition, attraction, construing; 11 arrangement, attributive, composition; PHRASES: 4, 5 word order.

synthesis 5 blend, union; 6 fusion, making; 7 mixture; 8 creation; 9 byproduct *UK*, synthetic; 10 production; 11 combination, manufacture; 12 amalgamation, biosynthesis; 13 biotechnology.

synthesize 4 fuse, join, make; 5 blend; 6 create; 7 analyze, combine, degrade, produce; 9 integrate; 10 amalgamate; 11 manufacture.

synthetic 4 fake, faux, mock, sham; 5 bogus, dummy, false, phony *UK*, quasi; 6 ersatz, phoney, pseudo; 7 plastic, pretend; 8 specious, spurious; 9 imitation, insincere, simulated; 10 artificial, separative; 11 counterfeit, synthesized; PHRASES: 2-6 so-called; 3-2 put-on; 3-4 man-made.

syrup 5 sauce; 7 treacle *UK*; 8 molasses; PHRASES: 5, 5 maple ~; 6, 5 golden ~ *UK*.

syrupy 5 candy, soppy, sweet, thick; 6 sickly, sugary; 7 cloying, honeyed, mawkish, treacly *UK*, viscous; 9 schmaltzy; 11 sentimental.

system 5 logic; 6 method, scheme; 7 routine; 9 procedure, structure, technique; 10 regularity; 11 arrangement, orderliness; 14 classification.

systematize 4 rank, sift, sort; 5 class, grade, group, index, order, place; 6 codify; 7 arrange, catalog *UK*; 8 classify, organize, position, regulate, tabulate; 9 catalogue *UK*, methodize; 10 categorize, pigeonhole, prioritize; 11 rationalize, standardize; PHRASES: 3, 2, 5 put in order; 4, 3 sort out.

T

T 2 te; 3 tee, ton; 5 model, shirt, tonne; 8 junction; 9 Testament; 11 Territorial.

TA 6 thanks; 8 tantalum; PHRASES: 11, 4 Territorial Army *UK*.

tab *See* **tag**

tabernacle 3 box; 4 case; 5 chest; 6 coffer, sukkah; 7 cabinet; 9 container.

Tabernacles 7 Sukkoth.

table 4 diet, fare, file, food, list, menu, move, rota, slab; 5 bench, board, enter, graph, index, stall, stand; 6 bureau, podium, record, submit, teapoy; 7 catalog *UK*, counter, diagram, dresser, propose, suggest; 8 contents, database, duchesse, register, schedule, syllabus, tabletop, tabouret; 9 catalogue *UK*, davenport, provision; 10 roundtable, secretaire; 11 discography, filmography, spreadsheet; 12 bibliography; PHRASES: 3, 5 end ~, tea ~; 3, 7 put forward; 4, 4 book list; 4-4, 5 drop-leaf ~; 4, 5 bird ~ *UK*, card ~, high ~, life ~, pier ~, pool ~, sand ~, side ~, tide ~, work ~; 4, 7 card catalog; 5, 2, 8 ~ of contents; 5, 3 T~ Bay; 5, 4 ~ salt *UK*, ~ talk, ~ wine; 5, 5 chart ~, steam ~, ~ d'hote, ~ money, water ~; 5, 6 ~ napkin, ~ tennis; 5, 7 ~ lectern, ~ license, ~ rapping; 5, 8 T~ Mountain; 6, 5 coffee ~, dining ~, gaming ~, league ~ *UK*, picnic ~, vanity ~; 6, 6 filing system; 7, 4 reading list; 7, 5 bedside ~, console ~, gateleg ~, kitchen ~, library ~, trestle ~, writing ~; 8, 5 credence ~, dressing ~, pedestal ~, pembroke ~, periodic ~; 8, 7 computer listing; 9, 4 reference list; 9, 5 operating ~, refectory ~; 10, 5 occasional ~.

table bird 5 quail, snipe; 6 grouse, pigeon, turkey; 8 pheasant, woodcock; 9 partridge; PHRASES: 4, 4 game bird, game fowl; 6, 4 guinea fowl; 8, 4 domestic fowl.

tablet 3 bar, tab; 4 cake, drop, pill, sign, slab; 5 brick, chunk, panel, piece, slate, stone; 6 caplet, pellet, plaque; 7 capsule, lozenge; 8 memorial, pastille.

taboo 3 ban, bar; 6 banned, barred, forbid; 8 anathema, prohibit; 9 forbidden, offensive, proscribe; 10 prohibited, proscribed; 11 distasteful, prohibition, restriction, unthinkable; 13 unmentionable; PHRASES: 2-2 no-no; 2-2, 4 no-go area; 3, 3 non dit; 3-6 off-limits.

taciturn 3 mum, shy; 5 aloof, quiet; 6 shtoom *UK*, silent, sullen; 7 distant; 8 reserved, reticent; 9 diffident, withdrawn; 10 antisocial, unsociable; 11 introverted; 13 unforthcoming; 15 uncommunicative; PHRASES: 4-9 self-contained; 5-6 tight-lipped.

tack 3 fix, hem, leg, pin, sew, yaw; 4 bind, gybe, nail, plan, stud, veer; 5 angle, baste, rivet; 6 attach, cobble, course, fasten, method, policy, staple, stitch, swerve, tactic, zigzag; 8 approach, saddlery, strategy; 9 direction, technique; PHRASES: 6, 4 riding gear; 6, 6 change course.

tackle 3 guy, kit, rig, try; 4 face, gear, grab, halt, hold, rope, stay, stop; 5 begin, block, chain, grasp, seize, throw, tools; 6 accost, attack, collar, gamble, garnet, outfit, sheets, shroud; 7 attempt, bowline, cordage, halyard, harness, lanyard, ratline, rigging, venture, wrestle; 8 confront; 9 apparatus, challenge, equipment, speculate, trappings, undertake; 10 implements; 13 confrontation; PHRASES: 3, 2, 5, 4 get to grips with; 3, 4, 2 get down to; 3, 4, 4 try one's luck; 4, 1, 6 take a chance; 4, 2 take on; 4, 4 clew line, deal with; 5, 2 speak to; 5, 4 bring down; 6, 2 engage in; 6, 4 embark upon.

tactful 8 delicate, discreet; 9 sensitive; 10 diplomatic, thoughtful.

tactic **4** deed, game, line, move, plan, ploy; **5** delay, shift, skill, trick; **6** course, gambit, method, policy, scheme; **7** cunning, devices, program; **8** approach, campaign, maneuver, planning, politics, strategy; **9** advantage, diplomacy, jockeying, logistics, maneuvers, procedure, stratagem; **10** governance, seamanship; **11** contrivance, generalship, lifemanship, maneuvering, opportunism, outflanking, realpolitik; **12** brinkmanship, gamesmanship; **13** statesmanship; PHRASES: **3-9** one-upmanship; **4, 4** game plan; **5, 2, 3, 4** rules of the game; **5, 4** party line; **6, 4** little game; **7, 3, 4** playing for time; **8, 3, 4** stalling for time.

tactless *See* **insensitive**

tadpole **8** polliwog.

tag **3** tab, tig *UK*; **4** chip, code, mark; **5** aglet, label, quote; **6** append, attach, cliché, device, docket, follow, marker, phrase, saying, ticket; **7** epithet, sticker; **8** identify; **9** quotation; **10** identifier.

tail **3** dog, end, fan, tip; **4** butt, coat, coda, dock, lees, rear, scut; **5** brush, chase, dregs, stalk, track, trail, train; **6** follow, pursue, shadow; **7** pursuer, stalker, tracker; **8** colophon, follower, tailcoat; **9** appendage; PHRASES: **3, 3** bin end, fag end; **4, 3** ~ end; **4, 4** coat ~; **5, 3** scrag end *UK*; **6, 3** bitter end; **6, 6** bottom dollar.

tailor **3** cut, fit; **4** make, mold; **5** adapt, alter, shape, style; **6** cutter, design, modify, sartor; **7** convert, costume, fashion; **8** accouter; **9** couturier, customize, outfitter; **11** personalize; PHRASES: **3, 3** fit out, rig out; **4, 2, 7** make to measure; **6-4** custom-make; **6-5** custom-build; **7, 6** bespoke ~.

tailpiece **3** end; **4** coda; **6** finale, finial; PHRASES: **3, 5** end piece.

taint **3** mar; **4** blot, foul, ruin, scar, slur, soil, spot; **5** dirty, smear, spoil, stain, sully, tinge, touch, trace; **6** defect, infect, poison, stigma; **7** blacken, blemish, corrupt, pollute, tarnish; **8** besmirch, tincture; **11** contaminate. *See also* **spoil**

Taiwan **7** Formosa.

take **3** bag, bum, buy, get, net, rob, use, win; **4** bear, book, cart, deem, draw, feel, gain, grab, haul, have, hire, hold, hook, lead, need, nick *UK*, rape, read, rent, root, shot, show, trap, view, work; **5** abide, adopt, angle, annex, apart, bring, brook, carry, catch, ferry, fetch, filch, grasp, gross, guide, house, learn, lease, merge, mooch, scene, seize, squat, stand, steal, stick, study, usher, usurp, yield; **6** accept, assume, choose, convey, deduce, deduct, demand, derive, employ, endure, engage, escort, expend, hijack, income, indent, manage, obtain, occupy, pilfer, pocket, ponder, ravish, regard, remove, secure, select, snatch, subdue, suffer; **7** acquire, believe, capture, conduct, conquer, consume, contain, discuss, earmark, examine, extract, inherit, opinion, overrun, possess, presume, procure, profits, purloin, receive, require, reserve, returns, revenue, subject, succeed, support, swallow, takings, undergo, violate; **8** colonize, consider, deflower, earnings, overcome, perceive, proceeds, purchase, receipts, scrounge, sequence, shoulder, subtract, tolerate, transfer; **9** accompany, eliminate, interpret, subjugate, transport, undertake, withstand; **10** confiscate, experience, impression, plagiarize, understand; **11** accommodate, appropriate, communalize, nationalize, requisition; **14** interpretation; PHRASES: **3, 3** buy out, pay for; **3, 4, 2** get hold of; **3, 4, 5, 2** lay one's hands on; **4, 2** hold up, look at; **4, 4, 2** grab hold of; **5, 2, 2** catch on to; **5, 2, 4** point of view; **5, 4** swarm over; **5, 4, 2** catch hold of; **5, 5** seize power; **6, 9** assume ownership.

take away **3** cop, cut, dig, dip, fix, lop, mug, nab, rob, tap; **4** bail, clip, dish, dock, doff, dupe, flay, fool, fork, geld, grab, help, hold, kill, loot, milk, mine, move, nick, pare, peel, raid, sack, side, skin, spay, take, trap; **5** erase, flake, heist, ladle, minus, pinch, pluck, prune, scoop, sever, shear, shift, shunt, spade, spoon, steal, strip, unman; **6** abduct, arrest, befool, behead, borrow, bucket, deduct, delete, denude, detach, divest, excise, extort, fleece, hijack, kidnap, outwit, pilfer, pirate, remove, shovel, snatch, thieve, unload, uproot; **7** capture, curtail, deceive, despoil, detract, enslave, ensnare, extract, imitate, pillage, plunder, purloin, retreat, shorten, skyjack, swindle, uncover; **8** amputate, caponize, castrate, dislodge, displace, distance, embezzle, outsmart, relegate, relocate, shanghai, shoplift, subtract, withdraw; **9** apprehend, blackmail, eliminate, eradicate, extricate, manhandle; **10** circumcise, commandeer, confiscate, decapitate, disconnect, dispossess, emasculate, manipulate, plagiarize; **11** disencumber, sequestrate *UK*; PHRASES: **2,**

3, 2 do out of; **3, 2** run in; **3, 3** rip off, rub out; **3, 3, 4** run off with; **3, 4, 4** run away with; **3, 5** lay aside, set aside; **4, 1, 4, 2** make a fool of; **4, 3** blot out, cart off, take off, take out; **4, 3, 1, 4** take for a ride; **4, 4** cart away; **4, 4, 7** take into custody; **4, 7** take captive; **5, 3** carry off; **5, 4** carry away, shake down.

take back 3 tax; **4** levy, swap; **5** annex, evict, seize; **6** divest, recall, recant, recoup, redeem, refund, regain, remind, retake, return, revoke; **7** deprive, disavow, impound, overtax, reclaim, recover, restore, retract; **8** disclaim, distrain, exchange, reaccept, reassume, renounce, retrieve, withdraw; **9** apologize, backpedal, backtrack, foreclose, recapture, reinstate, repossess, sequester, transport; **10** confiscate, disinherit, dispossess; **11** expropriate; PHRASES: **3, 3, 2, 4, 2** put you in mind of; **3, 4, 5** eat your words; **3, 4, 6** jog your memory; **3, 6, 3** eat humble pie; **4, 1, 4** ring a bell; **4, 3, 5, 2** make you think of; **5, 2** trade in.

take off 2 go; **3** ape, fly, tip; **4** boom, copy, doff, drop, kite, lift, take, tilt, zoom; **5** alter, bloom, leave, mimic, minus, plane, scoot, scrub, spire, strip, unman; **6** ascend, cancel, depart, launch, parody, remove, rocket, thrive; **7** abolish, discard, imitate, prosper, scarper UK, succeed, suspend, uncover; **8** flourish, satirize; **9** disappear, skedaddle, skyrocket; **10** caricature, circumcise; **11** discontinue, impersonate; PHRASES: **2, 4, 4** do away with; **3, 3** cut off, fly off, set off, set out; **4, 2** send up; **4, 3** chop off, lift off; **4, 3, 2** slip out of; **4, 4** take away; **5, 3** blast off, knock off, strip off UK; **5, 3, 6** leave the ground; **6, 3** strike out. See also **take away**

taker 4 user, wolf; **5** buyer, crook, leech, shark; **6** cadger, captor, client, locust, looter, mugger, patron, player, punter UK, raider, rapist, robber, sacker, seizer; **7** grabber, remover, spoiler, usurper, vampire, vulture; **8** abductor, customer, hijacker, marauder, parasite, pillager, predator, receiver, snatcher; **9** despoiler, embezzler, infringer, kidnapper, purchaser, racketeer, ransacker, skyjacker; **10** bootlegger, plagiarist; **11** blackmailer, confiscator, extortioner, participant; **12** appropriator, expropriator, extortionist, sequestrator; PHRASES: **3-8** bag-snatcher UK; **5-8** asset-stripper.

taking 4 coup, cute, rape; **5** greed, raped; **6** annexd, greedy, indent, merged, merger; **7** avarice, bumming, cadging, capture, getting, seizure, taxable, winning; **8** charming, grabbing UK, grasping, mooching, pleasing, rapacity, subduing, takeover, thieving, touching; **9** acquiring, assaulted, clutching, deceptive, deductive, indention, obtaining, plundered, predatory, rapacious, snatching, violation; **10** annexation, arrogation, assumption, attractive, avaricious, compelling, conquering, delightful, employment, enchanting, engagement, inheriting, intriguing, plagiarism, plundering, possession, possessive, ravishment, scrounging, subjection, usurpation; **11** acquisition, acquisitive, captivating, consumption, fascinating, inheritance, requisition, retrievable, subjugation; **12** appropriated, colonization, confiscation, confiscatory, deflowerment, extortionate, manipulative; **13** acquisitional, appropriation, commandeering, expropriatory; **14** requisitionary; **15** nationalization; PHRASES: **3-3** buy-out, rip-off; **3-7** tax-raising; **4, 5** coup d'état.

takings 3 tax; **4** haul, levy, plum, swag, take; **5** booty, catch, gross, prize, yield; **6** boodle, income, spoils; **7** capture, plunder, profits, returns, revenue, savings; **8** earnings, pickings, proceeds, receipts, turnover, winnings; **9** gleanings; PHRASES: **3-6, 5** ill-gotten gains; **4, 8** rich pickings; **6, 2, 3** spoils of war.

tale 3 lie; **5** rumor; **6** legend; **7** account, fiction, romance, untruth; **8** anecdote; **9** falsehood.

talent See **aptitude**

talisman 3 obi; **4** ankh, bell, book, juju, mojo, tiki; **5** amber, charm, jewel, relic, stone, totem; **6** amulet, emblem, fetish, fylfot, garlic, mascot, object, scarab, symbol; **7** mandala, periapt, trinket; **8** antidote, crucifix, familiar, shamrock, swastika, wishbone; **9** gammadion, horseshoe, lodestone, medallion; **10** bloodstone, phylactery; PHRASES: **2, 11** St Christopher; **4-4, 5** good-luck charm; **4-4, 6** four-leaf clover; **5, 3** black cat; **5, 4** fairy ring, lucky bean, magic belt, magic ring; **5, 5** lucky charm, magic sword; **5, 6** magic carpet, magic circle.

talk 3 gab, gas, jaw, rap, rat, yak; **4** blab, blah, chat, guff, sing, tell; **5** break, crack, rumor, slang, speak, utter, words; **6** babble, betray, confer, debate, double, gabble, gossip, inform, jabber, jargon, natter, parley, patter, reason, sermon, speech, squeal, waffle, witter UK; **7** address, blabber, chatter, chinwag, confess, consult, dialect, discuss, express, lecture, oration, palaver, prating, prattle; **8** chitchat, converse, dialogue, exchange, language, whispers; **9** discourse, jabbering, negotiate; **10** chattering, deliberate, discussion, vocabulary; **11** communicate, speculation; **12** conversation; PHRASES: **3, 3** hot air; **3-3** jaw-jaw *UK*; **4, 1, 4** have a word *UK*; **4-1-4** tête-à-tête; **4, 1, 10** have a discussion; **4, 2** give up; **4, 3, 3** chew the fat; **4, 4** baby ~, ~ show; **4-4** blah-blah; **4, 6** idle gossip; **5-2-5** heart-to-heart; **5, 4** empty ~, sales ~, small ~; **6, 4** pillow ~; **6-6** tittle-tattle; **7-3** yakkety-yak; **7, 5** compare notes.

talkative 4 glib; **5** gabby, gassy, windy, wordy; **6** chatty, fluent, prolix; **7** gossipy, verbose, voluble; **8** babbling, eloquent, gabbling; **9** garrulous, jabbering, jibbering; **10** articulate, chattering, loquacious; **12** multiloquent; **13** communicative; PHRASES: **4-6** long-winded; **7, 2** running on.

talkative (be talkative) 3 gab, gas, jaw; **4** blab, blah, chat, talk; **5** prate; **6** babble, gabble, gibber, jabber, natter, waffle, witter *UK*; **7** blabber, chatter; PHRASES: **2, 2, 3, 2** go on and on; **4, 2, 6** talk at length; **6, 2** rabbit on, ramble on, rattle on; **7, 2** prattle on.

talkativeness 4 blah; **5** spiel; **7** blarney, fluency; **8** bigmouth, verbiage; **9** eloquence, garrulity, logomania, logorrhea, loquacity, prolixity, verbosity; **10** multiloquy, volubility; **13** multiloquence; PHRASES: **4, 2, 3, 3** gift of the gab; **4, 2, 5** flow of words; **6, 6** fluent tongue; **6, 8** verbal diarrhea; **7, 6** runaway tongue. *See also* **talkative**

talker 3 jay; **6** gabber, gasbag, gasser, gossip, magpie, orator, ranter; **7** babbler *UK*, blabber, quacker, speaker, tattler, waffler, windbag; **8** bigmouth, driveler, informer, jabberer; **9** chatterer, raconteur, schmoozer; **10** chatterbox; **11** stoolpigeon; **12** blabbermouth, communicator; PHRASES: **5-5** motormouth; **6, 7** public speaker; **6-7** tittle-tattler.

talk nonsense 3 gag, pun; **4** blah, joke, quip, rant, rave; **6** gabble, garble; **7** blarney, romance; **10** rhapsodize; PHRASES: **4, 2, 5** play on words; **5, 5** crack jokes.

talks 5 panel; **6** parley, summit; **8** dialogue; **10** bargaining, conference, discussion; **11** discussions; **12** negotiations; PHRASES: **4-5, 5** high-level ~; **6, 5** summit ~; **6-6** treaty-making; **6, 7** summit meeting.

talk too much 4 bore, gush; **5** spout; **9** expatiate; **10** buttonhole; PHRASES: **3, 4, 6** oil one's tongue; **4, 3** spin out; **4, 4, 4, 3** talk one's head off; **4, 5** hold forth; **5, 2** drone on.

tall 3 big; **4** hard, high; **5** giant, lanky, large, leggy, lofty, rangy; **6** gangly, trying, untrue; **7** soaring; **8** colossal, elevated, gangling, gigantic, Olympian, towering, unlikely; **9** Amazonian, demanding, difficult; **10** incredible, monumental, statuesque; **11** complicated, exaggerated, substantial; **12** unbelievable; PHRASES: **3-7** far-fetched; **4-4** knee-high; **4-6** long-legged *UK*, long-limbed, long-necked; **5-4** chest-high, thigh-high, waist-high; **8-4** shoulder-high.

tall person 5 giant; **6** Amazon; **7** Goliath; **8** beanpole, colossus, longlegs; **11** highpockets; PHRASES: **3-6** six-footer; **5-6** seven-footer.

tall tale 4 yarn; **10** teratology; PHRASES: **4, 5** fish story; **6, 2, 5** flight of fancy; **6-3, 5** shaggy-dog story; **9, 4** traveler's tale; **10, 4** fisherman's tale.

tall thing 4 mast, pile, pole, post; **5** crane, pylon, shaft, spire, tower; **6** belfry, column, flèche, pagoda, pillar, turret; **7** chimney, derrick, giraffe, maypole, minaret, obelisk, redwood, sequoia, steeple; **8** barbican *UK*, elephant, lamppost, monument, pilaster, windmill, ziggurat; **9** campanile, flagstaff; **10** lighthouse, skyscraper, smokestack, watchtower; **11** streetlight; PHRASES: **4, 5** bell tower; **5, 4** radio mast; **5, 5** tower block *UK*, water tower; **6, 5** Eiffel Tower, office block; **6, 8** office building; **8, 5** Martello tower; **9, 4** telegraph pole, telephone pole.

tally 5 agree, check, count, match, score, total; **6** equate, reckon; **7** compute; **10** correspond; **11** calculation.

talon *See* **claw**

talus 9 anklebone.

tamarillo 4, 6 tree tomato.

tambourine 7 timbrel.

tame 4 dull, meek; **5** bland, train; **6** boring, broken, docile, pacify, subdue; **7** insipid, repress, subdued, trained; **8** overcome, suppress; **9** compliant, subjugate; **10** discipline; **11** disciplined, domesticate; **12** domesticated; PHRASES: **5, 2** break in.

Tamil Nadu 6 Madras.

tamp 4 cram, fill, pack; **5** stuff; **8** compress.

tamper 3 rig; 6 meddle; 7 corrupt; 9 influence, interfere; 10 manipulate; PHRASES: 4, 4 fool with; 6, 4 monkey with.

tan 3 dye; 4 burn, wash; 5 brown, color, toast, treat; 6 bronze, suntan; 7 process, sunburn; 8 preserve.

tangent 4 line; 5 angle, curve; 9 curvature; 10 refraction.

tangible 4 real; 5 handy, solid; 6 tender; 7 sensory, tactile, tactual; 8 concrete, gettable, material, palpable, sensuous; 9 reachable, touchable; 10 attainable; 11 perceptible, substantial; PHRASES: 3-2-4 get-at-able.

tangle 3 jam, mat, web; 4 face, hook, knot, mass, maze, mesh, mess, snag, trap, wind; 5 catch, ravel, snare, snarl, twist; 6 enmesh, jumble, jungle, oppose, tousle, welter; 7 confuse, ensnare, entwine; 8 confront, disorder, entangle; 9 labyrinth; 10 difficulty, intertwine, interweave; 12 complication; PHRASES: 3, 2 mix up; 3-2 mix-up; 4, 2, 7 come up against; 4, 4 mess with; 6, 2 square up.

tank 3 vat; 5 wagon; 6 boiler, engine; 7 cesspit, chamber, cistern, farming; 9 container, reservoir; PHRASES: 4, 3 ~ top; 4, 4 ~ trap.

tantrum See **outburst**

tap 3 bug, dab, hit, hot, pat, rap, tip, use; 4 bang, beat, blow, bung, cork, drum, flip, milk, mine, peck, pick; 5 brush, chuck, flick, knock, touch, whisk; 6 faucet, record, strike; 7 collect, exploit, extract, monitor, release, stopper, utilize; 8 overhear; 9 intercept; PHRASES: 4, 2 draw on; 4, 3 draw off, draw out; 4, 9, 2 take advantage of; 5, 3 screw ~; 6, 2, 2 listen in on; 9, 2 eavesdrop on.

tape 3 fix, tie; 4 band, bind, copy, grip, save; 5 stick, strip, video; 6 attach, fasten, record, ribbon, secure, string, ticker; 8 cassette, friction, magnetic, tapeline; 9 audiotape, cartridge, recording, videotape; 13 audiocassette; PHRASES: 3, 4 red ~; 4-6 tape-record; 4, 7 ~ measure; 4, 9 ~ recording; 5, 8 video cassette UK; 6, 4 gaffer ~, parcel ~ UK, Scotch ~, sticky ~; 7, 4 binding ~, masking ~, packing ~, punched ~ UK; 8, 4 adhesive ~, cassette ~, friction ~, magnetic ~; 9, 4 measuring ~; 10, 4 insulating ~ UK Can, perforated ~.

taper 5 light, point, torch; 6 candle, nar-

row, reduce; 7 dwindle; 8 diminish, elongate; 10 elongation, flashlight; PHRASES: 4, 2, 1, 5 come to a point; 4, 3 tail off; 4, 4 thin down; 5, 3 phase out.

tapered 4 thin; 6 peaked, shaped; 7 conical, pointed; 8 fusiform, lessened, tapering, thinning; 9 attenuate, decreased, dwindling, elongated, narrowing; 10 attenuated, convergent, diminished; PHRASES: 4-6 cone-shaped; 5-6 wedge-shaped; 6, 3 phased out, tailed off; 7, 3 petered out.

tar 2 AB UK; 4 salt, wood; 5 pitch; 6 sailor, Tarmac tm; 7 asphalt, bitumen, macadam, mineral; 8 creosote; PHRASES: 4, 3 coal ~, jack ~, pine ~, wood ~.

tardy See **late**

target 3 aim, end, pin, tee; 4 bull, butt, case, goal, mark, prey; 5 focus, inner, outer, prize; 6 object, quarry, trophy, vision, wreath; 9 objective; 11 destination; 13 disinterested; PHRASES: 3, 2, 4 end in view; 4, 5 Holy Grail; 5-3 bull's-eye; 6, 4 ~ area; 7, 4 winning post UK; 8, 4 Promised Land; 9, 4 finishing line, finishing tape.

tariff 3 due, tax; 4 cost, duty, levy, rate; 5 price; 6 charge, excise, PHRASES: 5, 4 price list.

tarnish 4 blot, dull, harm, mark, ruin, rust; 5 dirty, muddy, smear, spoil, stain, sully, taint; 6 damage, deaden, smudge; 7 blacken, blemish, corrode, destroy, oxidize; 8 discolor; PHRASES: 4, 4 tone down; 4, 5 lose shine.

tarragon 8 estragon.

tarry 3 lag; 4 stay, wait; 5 abide, dally, delay, pause, stall; 6 linger, sticky.

tart 3 pie; 4 acid, flan, sour; 5 sharp; 6 acidic, biting, bitter, pastry, quiche; 7 acerbic, tartlet. See also **loose woman**

tartan 5 check, inlay, pinto, plaid; 6 checkr, mosaic; 7 checked, patched, pattern, piebald; 8 fasciate, skewbald; 9 checkered, damascene, harlequin, marquetry, parquetry, patchwork; 12 tessellation.

task 3 job; 4 bout, deed, duty, feat, work; 5 brief, chore, place, shift, stint, trick, watch; 6 charge, errand, office, period; 7 calling, fatigue, mission, project, service, station, stretch; 8 business, exercise, function, overtime; 9 operation; 10 assignment, commission, engagement, profession; 11 undertaking; 14 responsibility; PHRASES: 3, 2, 4 job of work; 4, 2, 4 line of duty; 5, 4 hand's turn.

taste 3 bit, eat, get, sip, try; **4** bite, diet, feel, hint, lick, tang, test; **5** class, drink, enjoy, savor, smack, style; **6** degust, liking, nibble, notice, palate, reduce, relish, sample, taster; **7** discern, leaning, preview; **8** fondness, judgment, penchant, sapidity; **9** recognize, tastiness; **10** aftertaste, appreciate, experience, perception, preference, refinement; **11** discernment, estheticism, sensitivity; **12** palatability, predilection, tastefulness; **13** deliciousness; **14** discrimination, sophistication, unpalatability; PHRASES: **2, 7, 2** be exposed to; **3, 1, 4, 2** get a hint of; **3, 4, 4, 4** toy with one's food; **4, 2** peck at, pick at; **4, 5** acid ~, good ~, sour ~, tart ~; **5, 4** ~ buds; **5, 5** salty ~, sharp ~, spicy ~, sweet ~; **6, 5** bitter ~; **7, 5** pungent ~.

tasteful 4 chic; **6** classy; **7** elegant, refined, stylish; **8** artistic, charming, esthetic; **9** beautiful; **10** attractive, cultivated, discerning; **13** sophisticated; **14** discriminating.

tasteless 3 dry; **4** arid, dull, flat, loud, mild, tame, thin, weak; **5** banal, bland, cheap, crude, flash UK, gross, plain, rapid, stale, tacky, trite, vapid; **6** boring, cheesy, coarse, dilute, feeble, flashy, garish, jejune, tawdry, vulgar; **7** boorish, diluted, humdrum, insipid, obscene, watered; **8** lifeless, tactless, unsalted, unsavory; **9** offensive, sickening; **10** flavorless, indelicate, monotonous, unexciting, unflavored, uninspired, uninviting, unpleasant, unseasoned; **11** adulterated, distasteful, indifferent, nondescript; **12** unappetizing, unsatisfying; **13** characterless; PHRASES: **2, 3, 5** in bad taste; **2, 4, 5** in poor taste; **3, 2, 4** dry as dust; **4-3-5** milk-and-water; **4-7** foul-mouthed; **5-5** wishy-washy; **7-4** watered-down.

tasteless items 3 pap; **4** mash, pulp, slop; **5** gruel; **6** skilly UK; **9** dishwater; PHRASES: **4, 6** weak coffee; **5, 3, 4** bread and milk; **5, 3, 5** bread and water.

taster 5 buyer, diner, eater; **6** foodie; **7** analyst, blender, drinker, epicure, gourmet, nibbler; **8** gourmand; **9** appetizer; **10** specialist; **11** connoisseur; PHRASES: **3, 6** bon vivant; **4, 6** wine ~.

tasty 5 candy, juicy, salty, sapid, sharp, spicy, sweet, yummy; **6** dainty, edible, savory; **7** moreish UK, potable, pungent; **8** esculent, inviting, luscious, savorous, tastable, tasteful, tempting; **9** ambrosial, delicious, drinkable, epicurean, flavorful, palatable, succulent, toothsome; **10** appetizing, comestible, delectable, flavorsome, relishable; **11** scrumptious; **13** mouthwatering; PHRASES: **4, 2, 1, 4** done to a turn.

tattle See **gossip**

tattoo 4 show; **6** design, parade, signal; **7** display, pageant, pattern, summons; **10** tournament.

taunt 3 boo, dig, guy; **4** barb, gibe, goad, hiss, hoot, jeer, jibe, mock, twit; **5** chaff, scoff, sneer, sniff, snort, tease; **6** banter, deride, heckle, insult; **7** affront, barrack, catcall, provoke, teasing; **8** brickbat, derision, ridicule; **9** criticism, criticize, raspberry; **10** barracking; PHRASES: **3, 2** dig at; **3, 4** the bird; **4, 1, 9** blow a raspberry; **4, 2** jibe at, rail at; **4, 5** call names; **5, 2** laugh at; **5, 5** Bronx cheer.

taut 5 rigid, stiff, tense, tight; **7** anxious, nervous, worried; **8** stressed; **9** stretched.

tavern 3 bar, inn, pub UK; **5** local UK; **6** bodega, boozer; **8** alehouse, hostelry; PHRASES: **6, 5** public house.

tawdry 4 loud; **5** brash, cheap, crude, flash UK, gaudy, showy, tacky, tatty; **6** flashy, garish, kitsch, shoddy; **8** gimcrack; **9** cheapjack, tasteless; **10** flamboyant; **12** meretricious.

tax 3 ACT UK, GST, hit, VAT UK; **4** cess UK, dues, duty, levy, PAYE UK, rate, test, toll; **5** blame, drain, rates, taxes, tithe; **6** accuse, burden, charge, deduct, excise, impost, octroi UK, rating, return, strain, surtax, tariff, tenths; **7** customs, evasion, exhaust, itemize, millage, overtax, paystub, present, shelter, stretch; **8** confront, estimate, nuisance, overload, ratables, reproach, supertax, taxation; **9** avoidance, challenge, criticize, deduction; **10** assessment; **11** overstretch; **12** appraisement, overwithhold, valorization; PHRASES: **1-1** W-2; **2, 4** T4 slip; **3, 2, 3** pay as you earn; **3, 3, 4, 2** ask too much of; **3-3-5** off-the-books; **3, 4** ~ disk, ~ form, ~ owed, ~ rate; **3, 5** ~ exile UK, ~ haven; **3, 6** ~ demand, ~ office, ~ refund, ~ return, ~ system; **4, 3** city ~, gift ~, poll ~; **4-5** pass-along; **5, 3** cream off, local ~, sales ~, state ~; **5-3-4** above-the-line; **5, 4** death duty UK; **6, 3** combat pay, direct ~, estate ~, income ~; **6, 4** estate duty UK; **6, 5** Peter's pence; **6, 6** fiscal policy; **6, 7** Inland Revenue; **7, 3** company ~, council ~ UK; **7, 4** capital levy; **7, 5, 3** capital gains ~; **7, 6** college credit, revenue system, taxable income; **7, 10** special assessment; **8, 3** indirect ~, property ~, punitive ~, purchase ~ *UK*; **8, 5** assessed value, rateable value; **9, 3** amusement ~, corporate ~, municipal ~; **9, 6** community charge *UK*; **10, 3** capitation ~, collective ~, regressive ~; **11, 3** inheritance ~, progressive ~, withholding ~.

tax (historical taxes) 7 gabelle, scutage; **8** Danegeld; PHRASES: **4, 3** salt tax; **4, 3, 3** scot and lot *UK*; **5, 3** stamp tax; **6, 3** feudal tax, window tax *UK*.

taxation *See* **tax**

taxing 5 tough; **6** tiring; **7** levying, wearing; **8** draining; **9** demanding, difficult, strenuous; **10** exhausting; **11** challenging.

taxonomy, taxonomic group 4 form, race; **5** clade, class, genus, order, taxon, tribe; **6** family, phylum, series; **7** catalog *UK*, cladism, kingdom, section, species, variety; **8** cultivar, division, grouping, subclass, suborder, subtribe; **9** catalogue *UK*, subfamily, subphylum; **10** cladistics, subkingdom, subspecies, superclass; **11** arrangement, subdivision, superfamily, systematics; **12** cytotaxonomy, nomenclature, organization; **14** biosystematics, categorization, classification; PHRASES: **8, 6** Linnaean system.

tea 3 cha, tay *UK*; **4** brew, char, mate, rose; **5** Assam, bohea, hyson, pekoe; **6** Keemun, oolong, tisane; **8** infusion, pouchong; **9** chamomile *UK*, decoction, dishtowel; **10** Darjeeling; PHRASES: **3, 4** ~ cozy, ~ gown, ~ leaf; **3, 5** ~ cloth *UK*, ~ party, ~ towel; **3, 6** ~ garden; **3, 7** ~ biscuit, ~ service, ~ trolley; **4, 3** bush ~, high ~ *UK*, iced ~, leaf ~; **4, 4** Earl Grey; **5, 3** black ~, China ~ *UK*, fruit ~, green ~, lemon ~; **5, 4** yerba mate; **6, 3** Ceylon ~, herbal ~, Indian ~; **6, 5** orange pekoe; **7, 3** jasmine ~, Russian ~ *UK*; **7, 8** Lapsang Souchong; **8, 3** camomile ~; **9, 3** afternoon ~, gunpowder ~; **10, 3** peppermint ~.

teach 4 show; **5** brief, coach, drill, guide, train, tutor; **6** ground, school; **7** educate, instill; **8** instruct; **9** brainwash, enlighten, inculcate; **10** discipline; **12** indoctrinate.

teacher 3 Bed, don *UK*, sir; **4** amma, beak, guru, head, miss; **5** coach, guide, mufti, rabbi, tutor, usher; **6** fellow, master, mentor, mullah, reader, supply; **7** chalkie, dominie, sophist, trainer; **8** academic, educator, lecturer, mistress *UK*; **9** counselor,

governess, maharishi, pedagogue, preceptor, professor, schoolman *UK*; **10** instructor; **13** assistantship, schoolteacher; PHRASES: **6, 9** career counselor; **8, 7** visiting ~; **10, 7** substitute ~.

teaching 5 class, dogma; **6** gospel, lesson; **8** didactic, doctrine, tutelage; **9** education.

team 2 XI; **4** band, camp, cast, club, crew, duet, gang, side, span, trio, unit; **5** colts, corps, force, group, nonet, octet, panel, party, squad, staff; **6** circle, eleven, league, lineup, outfit, septet, sextet, troika, troupe; **7** company, coterie, fellows, fifteen, players, quartet, quintet; **8** partners, sorority; **9** community, orchestra, possibles, probables; **10** associates, colleagues, complement, duumvirate, federation, fraternity, sisterhood; **11** brotherhood, triumvirate; **12** congregation; **13** collaborators, confederation, confraternity; PHRASES: **2-7** co-workers.

tear 3 fly, rip, run, zip; **4** bead, dash, drip, drop, gash, grab, hole, hurt, pelt, pull, rend, rent, rush, slit; **5** cleft, force, hurry, pluck, rheum, seize, sheet, shred, slash, speed, split; **6** charge, cleave, damage, injure, remove, snatch, sprain, streak, wrench; **7** destroy, droplet, scratch; **8** lacerate, teardrop; PHRASES: **4, 3** ~ gas; **4, 4** ~ duct; **9, 5** crocodile tears.

tearful 3 sad; **6** crying, tragic; **7** howling, sobbing, unhappy, weeping; **8** mournful; **9** emotional; **10** lachrymose, melancholy; PHRASES: **2, 5** in tears.

tease 3 kid, rag, rib; **4** bait, goad, joke, josh, mock, twit; **5** annoy, chaff, clown, joker, laugh, scoff, taunt; **6** arouse, badger, bother, excite, harass, mocker *UK*, pester, teaser; **7** provoke, torment; **8** irritate, ridicule; **9** encourage, tantalize, tormentor; **10** manipulate; PHRASES: **3-6** leg-puller *UK*; **4, 3, 2** make fun of; **4, 5** mess about *UK*; **4, 6** mess around; **4, 8, 2** lead somebody on; **5, 2** laugh at.

teasing 3 coy; **5** jokey; **6** banter; **7** joshing, mocking, playful, ribbing; **8** raillery, repartee, tempting; **9** enigmatic; **10** coquettish, suggestive; **11** flirtatious, mischievous, provocative, tantalizing; PHRASES: **3-7** leg-pulling *UK*; **6-2-5** tongue-in-cheek.

technical 6 narrow, strict; **7** literal, nominal, precise; **8** official; **9** practical; **10** industrial, mechanical, methodical, procedural, scientific, specialist; **11** specialized; **12** professional; **13** technological; **14** methodological.

technical error 3 bug; **5** hitch, virus; **6** glitch; **8** gremlins.

technician 6 expert; **8** engineer, mechanic, operator; **10** specialist.

technique 2 MO; **3** way; **4** line, mode, tack; **5** skill, style, touch, trick; **6** method, system, tactic; **7** process; **8** strategy; **9** expertise, procedure; **PHRASES: 5, 8** modus operandi.

tedious 3 dry; **4** arid, dull, flat, slow; **5** banal, heavy, plain, prosy, stale, trite; **6** boring, deadly, draggy, dreary, dreich *UK*, leaden, prolix, stodgy, stuffy, tiring; **7** cloying, humdrum, insipid, irksome, prosaic, unfunny, uniform, wearing; **8** dragging, overlong, repeated, tiresome, wearying; **9** humorless, ponderous, satiating, soporific, tasteless, unvarying, wearisome; **10** invariable, monotonous, pedestrian, repetitive, unreadable; **11** commonplace, repetitious; **13** uninteresting; **PHRASES: 3, 2, 4** dry as dust; **4-6** long-winded; **5, 3** drawn out; **5-8** sleep-inducing.

teem 4 pelt, pour, rain; **5** crowd, swarm; **6** abound, stream.

teeth *See* **tooth**

teetotal 3 dry; **5** sober; **9** abstinent; **10** abstemious; **11** nondrinking.

telegram *See* **wire**

telephone 4 bell *UK*, buzz, call, ring *UK*; **5** phone; **6** blower *UK*, mobile, tinkle *UK*; **7** handset, headset; **8** earpiece, intercom, payphone, receiver; **9** cardphone, directory, extension, phonecard; **10** headphones, microphone, mouthpiece, radiophone, videophone; **11** switchboard; **PHRASES: 3, 3, 4** dog and bone *UK*; **3, 4** hot line; **3, 7** pay station; **4, 1, 4** make a call; **4, 2** hang up; **4, 3** ring off; **4, 4** chat line; **4, 5** cell phone; **5, 5** phone booth; **6, 9** mobile ~, public ~; **8, 5** cellular phone; **9, 3** ~ box; **9, 4** ~ pole, ~ wire; **9, 5** ~ booth, ~ kiosk.

telephone call 4 bell *UK*, buzz, call, ring *UK*; **6** tinkle *UK*; **PHRASES: 4, 4** toll call; **5, 4** local call, phone call; **7, 4** collect call; **8, 4** Freefone™ call, nuisance call, overseas call, personal call; **10, 4** conference call.

telescope 5 array, crush; **7** antenna, shorten; **8** compress, receiver; **9** heliostat, reflector, refractor; **10** almucantar, collimator, concertina; **PHRASES: 1-3, 9** X-ray ~; **5, 4** radio dish; **5, 9** radio ~, solar ~.

television 2 TV; **3** box, set, VCR; **4** tube; **5** color, telly *UK*, video; **6** screen, sweeps, zapper; **8** contrast, receiver; **9** colorcast, kinescope; **10** brightness, monochrome, telecamera; **PHRASES: 3, 3** the box; **3, 5** pay cable; **3, 10** pay ~; **4, 4** boob tube; **4, 7** test pattern; **5, 3** idiot box; **5-3-5** black-and-white; **5, 4** happy talk; **5, 6** audio signal, small screen, video signal; **5, 10** cable ~, color ~; **6-3** goggle-box *UK*; **6, 4** rabbit ears; **6, 7** remote control; **6, 10** public ~; **7-3, 4** cathode-ray tube; **10, 4** ~ tube.

tell 3 say; **4** know; **5** order, state, voice; **6** advise, charge, direct, expose, inform, relate, reveal; **7** command, divulge, express, narrate, recount; **8** describe, disclose, identify, instruct; **9** recognize; **11** communicate, distinguish; **12** discriminate; **13** differentiate.

temerity *See* **nerve**

temper 3 pet; **4** bate, bile, ease, fury, huff, mood, rage, tone; **5** allay, blood, paddy; **6** anneal, leaven, season, soften, spleen; **7** assuage; **8** mitigate, moderate; **9** fireworks.

temperament 5 humor; **6** makeup, nature, spirit, temper; **7** outlook; **9** character; **PHRASES: 11** disposition, personality.

temperance *See* **self-restraint**

temperate 4 calm, fair, mild; **5** balmy, sober; **8** balanced, moderate, teetotal; **9** abstinent, continent; **10** abstemious, restrained; **13** dispassionate.

temperature 1 C, F, T; **5** joule, therm; **6** Kelvin, Regulo *UK*; **11** calorimeter, thermograph, thermometer; **12** liquefaction, vaporization; **PHRASES: 5, 6** phase change; **7, 5** boiling point, Celsius scale, melting point, Réaumur scale; **8, 5** freezing point; **9, 5** calorific value; **10, 5** centigrade scale, Fahrenheit scale.

tempest 4 gale, riot; **5** storm, swell; **6** squall, tumult, uproar, vortex; **7** cyclone, tornado; **8** blizzard, brouhaha, upheaval; **9** commotion, hurricane, rainstorm, snowstorm, whirlwind; **11** disturbance; **12** atmospherics, thunderstorm; **PHRASES: 4, 5** high winds; **5, 3** heavy sea; **6, 5** ground swell; **8, 5** magnetic storm.

tempo 4 beat, pace, time; **5** meter, pulse, speed; **6** adagio, rhythm, timing, upbeat; **7** andante, measure, prosody; **8** downbeat; **9**

metronome; **10** polyrhythm, suspension; **11** rallentando, syncopation; **12** counterpoint; PHRASES: **4, 4** back beat, long note; **5, 4** short note; **5, 6** ~ rubato.

temporal 3 lay; **6** mortal; **7** earthly, mundane, profane, secular, worldly; **9** temporary; **10** historical, sequential; **11** progressive, terrestrial; **13** chronological; PHRASES: **4-5** time-based; **4-7** time-related.

temporary 4 temp; **5** brief, locum, short; **6** acting; **7** interim, stopgap; **9** ephemeral, makeshift, transient; **10** transitory; **11** provisional; PHRASES: **5-4** short-term.

tempt 4 coax, draw, lure, move; **5** tease; **6** allure, appeal, arouse, entice, excite, invite, seduce; **7** attract, ensnare, wheedle; **8** inveigle, motivate; **9** stimulate, tantalize, titillate; **10** facilitate; PHRASES: **4, 2** turn on; **4, 3, 4** gild the pill; **5, 3, 4** sugar the pill; **6, 2** pander to; **7, 3, 3** sweeten the pot; **7, 3, 4** sweeten the pill.

tempter, temptress 3 Eve; **4** rake, vamp; **5** Circe, Romeo, Satan, siren; **7** Lorelei, seducer; **8** Casanova; **9** temptress; **10** seductress, tantalizer; PHRASES: **4, 4** Mata Hari; **5, 6** femme fatale *Fr.*

tempting 9 seductive; **10** attractive, persuasive; **12** irresistible; **13** mouthwatering. *See also* **tempt**

ten 1 X; **2** IO; **5** tithe; **6** decade, tenner; **7** decagon, decapod; **8** decagram; **9** Decalogue, decathlon, decennium; **10** decahedron; PHRASES: **3, 12** T~ Commandments; **4, 3, 3** cock and hen; **7, 6** Downing Street.

tenacious 4 firm; **5** loyal; **6** clingy, dogged, urgent; **7** devoted, driving, earnest, serious, zealous; **8** attached, enduring, faithful, forceful, pressing, resolute, stubborn, thorough, tireless, vigorous; **9** committed, dedicated, dependent, desperate, energetic, insistent, obstinate, parasitic, steadfast; **10** determined, headstrong, inflexible, persistent, supportive; **11** persevering, sycophantic; **12** pertinacious, wholehearted; **13** indefatigable; PHRASES: **3-9** all-consuming; **4-6** bull-headed; **5-2-5** stick-to-itive; **5, 3** whole hog.

tenacious person 5 trier; **6** stayer; **9** workhorse; **10** workaholic; PHRASES: **3-4** die-hard; **3, 5** old guard; **5, 9** loyal supporter; **7, 6** willing worker.

tenacity 7 loyalty, resolve; **8** fidelity, firmness, hardness, pressure; **9** adherence, endurance, obstinacy, sternness; **10** attachment, compulsion, insistence, steeliness; **11** persistence; **12** perseverance, pertinacious, pitilessness, ruthlessness; **13** determination, implacability, inexorability, inflexibility, tenaciousness; **14** relentlessness; PHRASES: **7, 2** holding on. *See also* **tenacious**

tenant 6 lessee, lodger, renter; **8** occupier; **10** inhabitant; **11** leaseholder.

Ten Commandments 9 Decalogue.

tend 4 bend, lean, like, mind, veer; **5** nurse, verge, watch; **6** affect, manage, toward; **7** incline, prepare, redound; **8** approach, minister; **9** cultivate, influence, supervise; **10** contribute; PHRASES: **2, 2, 6, 2** be in charge of; **2, 3, 2** be apt to; **2, 4, 2** be wont to; **2, 6, 2** be likely to; **2, 8** be disposed; **3, 4** bid fair; **4, 1, 5, 2** have a habit of; **4, 1, 8, 2** have a tendency to; **4, 2** lead to, turn to; **4, 2, 3, 2** keep an eye on; **4, 3** care for; **4, 4, 2** take care of; **4, 5** look after; **4, 7** lean towards *UK*; **5, 2** point to; **5, 4** watch over; **6, 2** attend to; **7, 7** incline towards; **8, 2** minister to.

tendency 4 bent, bias, cast, tone, turn; **5** drift, knack, shift, swing, taste, tenor, trait, trend, trick; **6** course, stream; **7** bearing, climate, current, fashion, leaning, tending; **8** affinity, habitude, instinct, movement, penchant; **9** influence, mannerism, Zeitgeist; **10** partiality, proclivity, propensity; **11** disposition, inclination; **12** contribution, idiosyncrasy; **14** predisposition; PHRASES: **4, 2, 3, 5** sign of the times; **6, 2, 3, 3** spirit of the age.

tender 3 bid, put, red; **4** fond, give, kind, soft, sore, warm; **5** dough, money, offer, ready; **6** caring, gentle, kindly, loving, submit; **7** advance, present, proffer, propose; **8** delicate, estimate, inflamed, romantic; **9** emotional, quotation, sensitive; **11** sentimental, sympathetic; **12** affectionate; PHRASES: **3, 7** put forward; **4-7** soft-hearted.

tenderfoot *See* **novice**

tenderness 4 ache, love; **6** caring, warmth; **8** bruising, sympathy; **9** affection; **10** compassion; **11** sensitivity; **12** inflammation. *See also* **tender**

tending to 5 ready; **6** biased, likely, toward; **7** leading, leaning, partial; **8** prepared, probable, trending; **9** inclining, intending; **10** calculated, prejudiced; **11** prejudicial, tendentious; PHRASES: **3, 2** apt to; **5, 2** about to, prone to, ready to; **6, 2** aiming at, liable to; **7, 2** leading to; **7, 7** working towards; **8, 2** pointing to; **8, 7** inclined towards; **9, 2** conducive to.

tendril 4 coil, curl, lock, stem, vine, wisp; **5** frond, shoot, twist.

Tennessee 2 TN; **4** iris (flower); **9** Nashville (capital); **11** mockingbird (bird); **PHRASES: 3, 4, 5, 6, 2, 12, 9** Big Bend State, Mother of Southwestern Statesmen (nickname); **5, 6** tulip poplar (tree); **9, 5** Volunteer State (nickname); **11, 3, 8** Agriculture and Commerce (motto).

tennis 2 in; **3** ace, let, lob, LTA *UK*, net, out, set, van; **4** game, love, pair, seed; **5** deuce, drive, fault, match, rally, serve, smash, swing; **6** volley; **7** doubles, service, singles; **8** backhand, baseline, delivery, forehand; **9** advantage, frontenis, tramlines, Wimbledon; **PHRASES: 2, 4** US Open; **3, 2, 5** jeu de paume; **4, 3, 3, 5** game set and match; **4, 4** ping pong; **4, 5** foot fault; **4, 6** deck ~, lawn ~, real ~; **5, 3** Davis Cup; **5, 5** break point, match point; **5, 6** court ~, royal ~, table ~; **5, 7** slice service; **6, 4** French Open, ~ ball; **6, 5** ~ court; **6, 6** ground stroke, ~ racket; **6-7** follow-through; **7, 4** service line; **8, 3** Wightman Cup; **8, 5** overhead smash; **8, 6** platform ~.

tennis player 5 Budge (Don), Wills (Helen Newington); **6** Edberg (Stefan), Gibson (Althea), server, umpire; **8** Gonzales (Pancho), linesman, receiver, Rusedski (Greg), volleyer; **PHRASES: 3, 5** Rod Laver; **3, 6** net player, Tim Henman; **4, 3** ball boy; **4, 5** Fred Perry, Ivan Lendl; **4, 6** Bill Tilden; **4, 7** John McEnroe, Pete Sampras; **4, 8** John Newcombe; **5, 4** Björn Borg; **5, 5** Chris Evert; **5, 6** Andre Agassi, Boris Becker; **5, 7** Jimmy Connors; **5, 8** Venus Williams; **6, 4** Arthur Ashe, Steffi Graf; **6, 4, 4** Billie Jean King; **6, 5** Monica Seles; **6, 6** Leyton Hewitt; **6, 8** Serena Williams; **7, 6** Martina Hingis; **7, 8** Maureen Connolly; **8, 4** Virginia Wade; **8, 5** Margaret Smith.

tenor 4 gist, mood, tone; **5** drift; **7** meaning.

tense 4 edgy, taut; **5** brace, drawn, jumpy, rigid, stiff, tight; **6** aorist, future, tensed; **7** anxious, jittery, nervous, perfect, present, twitchy, uptight, worried; **8** strained, stressed; **9** imperfect; **10** pluperfect; **11** conditional, overwrought; **12** apprehensive; **PHRASES: 2, 4** on edge; **4, 8** past historic; **6, 7** future perfect; **8, 7** historic present.

tension 5 worry; **6** strain, stress; **7** anxiety; **8** conflict, friction, mistrust; **9** hostility; **PHRASES: 3, 7** ill feeling. *See also* **tense**

tent *See* **shelter**

tentative 3 shy; **5** pilot, rough, timid, trial; **6** unsure; **7** testing; **8** cautious, hesitant; **9** faltering, inquiring, searching, uncertain, unsettled; **10** indefinite; **11** exploratory, provisional, speculative, unconfirmed; **12** experimental, probationary; **PHRASES: 2, 5** on appro; **2, 8** on approval; **3, 5** not final.

tentative offer 6 chance, feeler, motion; **7** advance, opening; **8** overture; **10** submission, suggestion; **11** opportunity; **12** presentation; **PHRASES: 3, 2, 3, 5** toe in the water.

tenth 3 ten; **6** denary; **7** decimal, decuple, tenfold; **9** decagonal, decennial; **10** decahedral.

tenuous *See* **weak**

tenure 4 term; **5** lease; **7** tenancy; **8** freehold; **9** occupancy, trimester; **10** occupation.

tepid 4 warm; **8** lukewarm; **9** apathetic; **11** indifferent; **14** unenthusiastic; **PHRASES: 4-7** half-hearted.

tergiversate 6 recant, repent, resign; **7** forsake, reverse; **8** withdraw; **10** equivocate; **PHRASES: 4-5** back-pedal.

tergiversator 7 traitor; **8** apostate, deserter, recusant, renegade; **9** hypocrite; **11** equivocator; **12** tergiversant.

term 3 day, dub, eon, era, tag; **4** call, half, hour, Lent, name, span, time, week, word, year; **5** cycle, epoch, idiom, label, month, spell, stint; **6** decade, Hilary, minute, period, phrase, season, second, tenure; **7** century, inkhorn, quarter, stretch, Trinity; **8** duration, olympiad, semester, terminal, terminus; **9** designate, fortnight; **10** expression, Michaelmas, millennium, nanosecond; **11** microsecond, millisecond; **12** characterize; **PHRASES: 3, 4** law ~; **4, 4** half ~; **5, 5** lunar month; **8, 5** calendar month.

terminal 3 VDU *UK*; **4** load; **5** depot, fatal, noise; **6** deadly, lethal, mortal, signal; **7** airport, monitor, station; **8** computer, terminus, waveform; **9** incurable; **10** distortion; **11** workstation; **PHRASES: 4, 8** rail ~; **4-11** life-threatening.

terminate 2 ax; **3** end; **4** bump, fire, oust, sack, stop; **5** bench, cease, eject, lapse; **6** demote, depose, divest, expire, finish, remove, resign; **7** cashier, dismiss, suspend, unfrock; **8** conclude, dethrone; **9** discharge; **11** discontinue; PHRASES: 3, 3 lay off; 4, 2, 2, 3 come to an end; 4, 3 kiss off.

termination 3 end; **5** close; **6** expiry, finish, firing, recall; **7** closure, removal; **8** ejection, furlough, stoppage; **9** cessation, discharge, dismissal, expulsion, severance; **10** conclusion, expiration *UK*, redundancy *UK Can*, suspension; **11** dissolution, resignation; **14** discontinuance; PHRASES: 3, 2 the ax; 3-3 lay-off; 3, 3, 1 the big E; 3, 3, 5-2 the old heave-ho; 3, 4 the chop, the push, the sack; 3, 4, 3 the kiss off; 3, 5 the elbow *UK*, the shove; 3, 6 the bounce, the bullet; 4, 5 one's cards; 5, 8 nolle prosequi; 6, 9 golden handshake; 7, 6 walking papers; 8, 6 marching orders.

terminus 5 depot; **6** garage; **7** station; **8** terminal; **11** destination; PHRASES: 3, 2, 3, 4 end of the line; 4, 4 last stop; 8, 3 journey's end.

terms 5 lexis, offer; **6** clause, jargon; **7** article, footing, proviso, rapport, strings; **8** contract, language, position, provisos, standing; **9** provision, relations; **10** concession, conditions, provisions, requisites, vocabulary; **11** expressions, requirement, reservation, stipulation, terminology; **12** nomenclature, relationship, stipulations; **13** qualification; PHRASES: 3-3, 6 let-out clause; 4, 3, 3 sine qua non; 5, 5 small print; 6, 6 escape clause; 7, 5 written ~; 9, 6 essential clause.

terrace 3 row; **4** tier; **7** balcony, veranda.

terraced house 3, 5 row house.

terrain 4 land; **6** ground; **9** landscape, territory; **10** topography.

terrapin 8 tortoise.

terrestrial 4 land; **6** global; **7** earthly, worldly; **8** grounded, telluric; **9** surficial; **10** earthbound, geospheric, subsurface; **11** atmospheric, continental, underground; **12** hydrospheric, subterranean; **13** topographical; PHRASES: 4-8 land-dwelling; 7-8 surface-dwelling.

terrible 4 dire, grim; **5** awful, scary; **6** spooky; **7** awesome, fearful, ghastly, hideous, scaring; **8** alarming, daunting, dreadful, fearsome, horrible, horrific, menacing, shocking; **9** appalling, dismaying, frightful, startling, unnerving; **10** calamitous, enervating, formidable, horrendous, horrifying, petrifying, terrifying; **12** intimidating; PHRASES: 4-7 hair-raising.

terrific 2 A1; **3** ace, fab; **4** best, cool, huge; **5** awful, brill, dandy, grand, great, magic, swell; **6** classy, cosmic, exotic, groovy, superb, wizard; **7** amazing, awesome, corking *UK*, fearful, magical, topping, unusual; **8** dramatic, enormous, fabulous, gorgeous, shocking, smashing *UK*, spiffing *UK*, striking, stunning; **9** admirable, enigmatic, excellent, exquisite, fantastic, marvelous, monstrous; **10** astounding, impressive, incredible, miraculous, mysterious, phenomenal, prodigious, remarkable, shattering, stupendous, surprizing; **11** exceptional, frightening, scrumptious, sensational, unutterable; **12** breathtaking, overwhelming, unbelievable; **13** extraordinary; PHRASES: 3-5 top-notch; 3-9 awe-inspiring; 4-2 bang-on; 4-7 mind-blowing; 4-8 mind-boggling; 6, 8 record breaking.

terrified *See* **frightened**

terrify *See* **scare**

territory 4 area, beat, home, land, zone; **5** arena, field, patch, pitch, place, power, range, realm, space, state; **6** colony, domain, empire, ground, nation, region, sphere; **7** compass, country, kingdom, mandate, subject, terrain; **8** district, dominion, property, province, republic; **9** bailiwick, specialty, sultanate; **10** dependency, possession, speciality *UK*, superpower; **12** commonwealth, principality, protectorate.

terror 3 awe; **4** fear, funk; **5** dread, panic; **6** horror, phobia; **7** bugaboo, bugbear; **13** horrification; PHRASES: 3, 7 icy fingers; 4, 4 blue funk; 4, 5 cold sweat; 5, 5 blind panic; 8, 5 knocking knees; 10, 5 chattering teeth.

terrorism 6 terror; **7** bombing, sniping; **8** sabotage; **10** kidnapping, resistance; **12** intimidation; **13** assassination; PHRASES: 3, 7 car bombing; 6, 7 letter bombing, terror tactics; 7, 6 hostage taking; 9, 6 guerrilla attack.

terrorist 8 partisan, saboteur; **9** guerrilla; **12** bioterrorist; **14** cyberterrorist; PHRASES: 7, 7 freedom fighter; 8, 5 nonstate actor.

terse 4 curt; **5** brief, pithy, short; **6** abrupt; **7** brusque, clipped, concise; **8** succinct; PHRASES: 5, 3, 5 short and sweet.

test 3 MOT *UK*, try, vet; **4** exam, oral, quiz, scan; **5** assay, check, pilot, probe, proof, taste, trial; **6** assess, ordeal, review, sample, tryout; **7** analyze, examine, torment; **8** analysis, evidence, hardship, practice; **9** criterion, marketing, yardstick; **10** assessment, difficulty, experiment; **11** examination, investigate, tribulation; **13** investigation; PHRASES: **3, 1, 4** fly a kite; **3, 2, 3, 4** put to the ~; **3, 3** try out; **3-7** runthrough; **4, 3** T~ Act *UK*, ~ ban; **4, 4** acid ~, ~ case, ~ tube; **4, 5** ~ drive, ~ match *UK*, ~ paper; **5, 3** trial run; **6, 4** litmus ~; **10, 4** experiment with.

testament 5 proof; **7** witness; **8** evidence; **9** testimony; **13** demonstration.

tested 5 tried; **6** risked; **7** chanced, checked, essayed; **8** seasoned, ventured, verified; **9** confirmed, estimated; **10** determined, researched; **11** established, experienced.

testicles 4 nuts; **5** balls, pills, rocks; **7** cojones, goolies; **8** knackers.

testify 3 dob *UK*, lag, rat; **4** aver, avow, show, sing; **5** prove, state, swear; **6** affirm, allege, appear, assert, attest, inform, squeal; **7** confirm, declare, witness; **8** indicate; **11** demonstrate, stoolpigeon; PHRASES: **4, 3** bear out; **4, 7** bear witness; **4, 8** give evidence.

testimonial 5 honor; **6** reward; **7** tribute; **9** reference, statement; **11** celebration, endorsement; **12** confirmation; **14** acknowledgment, recommendation.

testimony 7 witness; **8** evidence; **9** affidavit, statement, testament; **10** deposition, indication; **11** declaration; **13** demonstration.

testing 4 hard; **5** tough; **6** taxing, trying; **9** difficult; **11** challenging.

testudo 8 tortoise.

testy *See* **irritable**

tether 4 lead, rein, rope; **5** chain, hitch; **6** fasten, secure; PHRASES: **3, 2** tie up.

Texas 2 TX; **5** pecan (tree); **6** Austin (capital); **10** bluebonnet (flower), Friendship (motto); **11** mockingbird (bird); PHRASES: **4, 4, 5** Lone Star State (nickname).

text 2 MS; **4** copy; **5** prose, topic, words; **6** record, script, thesis; **7** passage; **10** transcript; PHRASES: **4, 4** body ~; **4, 7** ~ message.

textbook 4 text; **5** model, prime; **6** manual, primer, reader; **7** classic, typical; **10** definitive, schoolbook.

textile 4 jute, knit, lace, silk, wool; **5** cloth, denim, drill, linen, satin, stuff, tweed, twill, voile, weave; **6** alpaca, angora, chintz, cotton, fabric, madras, merino, mohair, muslin, poplin, staple, tissue, velvet, vicuna; **7** chiffon, flannel, khaddar, sacking, suiting, taffeta, tussore; **8** cashmere, chenille, corduroy, homespun, material, moleskin, shantung, toweling; **9** sackcloth, velveteen; **10** broadcloth, seersucker; **11** cheesecloth, flannelette; PHRASES: **4, 5** yard goods; **5, 5** piece goods, woven cloth; **6, 6** cotton jersey.

texture 4 feel; **5** grain, touch; **6** finish; **7** quality, surface; **8** fineness; **9** roughness, sensation, structure; **10** coarseness, contexture, smoothness; **11** consistency; **12** constitution, intertexture; PHRASES: **7, 7** surface ~.

thank 3 tip; **6** praise, reward; **7** applaud; **9** attribute, recognize; **10** appreciate; **11** acknowledge; PHRASES: **2, 8** be grateful; **3, 7** pay tribute; **4, 6** give credit; **4, 9** show gratitude; **7, 6** express thanks.

thankful *See* **grateful**

thankless 6 trying; **7** useless; **9** difficult, fruitless; **11** unrewarding; **12** unprofitable, unrecognized; **13** unappreciated; **14** unacknowledged; PHRASES: **5, 3, 7** taken for granted; **7, 6** without credit, without thanks.

thank you! 2 ta!; **6** cheers!, thanks!; **8** gramercy!; PHRASES: **4, 6** many thanks!; **4, 7** much obliged!; **5, 2, 7** Allah be praised!; **5, 3** bless you!, thank God!; **5, 6** thank heaven!; **5, 8** thank goodness!; **6, 1, 3** thanks a lot!; **6, 2, 7** heaven be praised!.

thatch 3 mop; **4** hair, roof; **5** reeds, shock, straw; **6** rushes; **7** roofing, tresses.

thaw *See* **melt**

the (the French) 2 la, le; **3** les.

the (the German) 3 das, der, die.

the (the Italian) 2 il, la.

the (the northern) 1 T.

the (the old) 2 ye.

the (the Spanish) 2 el; **3** las, los.

theater 3 noh; **4** area, hall, site; **5** Abbey, arena, boîte, booth, drama, field, focus, Globe, house, odeon, odeum, opera, place, plays, realm, scene, venue; **6** acting, cinema, circus, kabuki, Lyceum, sphere; **7** cabaret, fleapit *UK*, stadium; **8** Broadway, pavilion, showboat, Windmill; **9** Criterion, dramatics, Haymarket, nightclub, nightspot, Palladium, playhouse; **10** auditorium, hippodrome, Hippodrome, Sheldonian, vaudeville; **11** Shaftesbury; **12** amphitheater, ediophusikon; PHRASES: **3, 3** big top, Old Vic; **3, 5** the stage; **4-3, 7** open-air ~; **4-7** role-playing; **4, 8** show business; **5, 2, 6** place of action; **5, 4** music hall; **5, 5** opera house; **5, 7** movie ~; **7, 4** concert hall; **7, 5** picture house *UK*; **7, 7** lecture ~, outdoor ~, variety ~.

theatergoer 3 fan, pit; **4** buff; **5** boxes, house, plant; **6** circle, claque, critic, stalls; **7** balcony, gallery, pittite, standee; **8** audience, claqueur, deadhead, filmgoer, literati, playgoer, reviewer, thespian; **9** operagoer, spectator; **10** balletgoer, enthusiast, groundling, promenader; **11** balletomane; PHRASES: **4, 5** full house, thin house; **4, 6** pass holder; **5, 4** opera buff; **5-4, 6** stage-door Johnny; **5-5** drama-lover; **5-7** first-nighter; **6, 5** packed house; **6, 7** talent spotter; **7, 7** culture vulture.

theatrical 4 camp; **5** hammy, showy, stage, stagy; **8** affected, dramatic, thespian; **10** histrionic; **12** melodramatic.

theatrical performance 3 hit; **4** bill, bomb, flop, show; **5** debut; **6** turkey; **7** benefit, failure, matinée, preview, success; **8** premiere; **10** exhibition, production; **11** presentment; PHRASES: **3-6, 3** box-office hit; **4, 3** long run; **4-3** sell-out; **4, 5** full house, gala night; **5, 3** short run, smash hit; **5, 5** first house, first night; **6, 5** second house; **7, 4** charity gala; **8, 7** critical success.

theft 3 job; **4** grab, lift; **5** caper, heist, pinch, steal; **6** holdup, piracy, snatch, taking; **7** hotting *UK*, larceny, lifting, mugging, nabbing, nicking *UK*, robbery, swiping; **8** boosting, burglary, fiddling, filching, hustling, pinching *UK*, poaching, rustling, stealing, thievery; **9** autotheft, hijacking, joyriding, pilferage, pilfering, pocketing, scrumping, snatching, snitching; **10** carjacking, purloining, skyjacking; **11** kleptomania, shoplifting; **12** embezzlement; **13** appropriation, housebreaking, pickpocketing; PHRASES: **3, 3** bag job; **3-4** ram-raid *UK*; **3, 5** car ~; **3-6** hot-wiring; **3-9** bag-snatching; **4, 7** bank robbery; **4-7** safe-blowing; **4-8** safe-breaking, safe-cracking; **5-2** break-in, stick-up; **5, 5** grand ~, petty ~; **5, 7** armed robbery, grand larceny, light fingers, petit larceny, train robbery; **5, 8** stock rustling; **5-9** purse-snatching; **6, 7** cattle raiding, sticky fingers; **6, 8** cattle rustling; **7,** **3, 4** robbing the till; **7, 7** highway robbery; **8, 5** unlawful entry; **8, 7** daylight robbery.

theme 4 idea, tune; **5** motif, topic, topos; **7** refrain, subject; **9** leitmotiv.

then 2 so; **3** and, too; **4** also, next; **5** later; **7** besides; **9** afterward, therefore; **11** nonetheless; **12** subsequently; PHRASES: **2, 4, 4** at that time, in that case; **2, 4, 5** at that point; **2, 4, 6** at that moment; **2, 8** in addition; **3, 4, 5** but ~ again; **4, 3, 5** ~ and there; **4, 5** ~ again.

theologian 2 DD; **6** divine; **8** canonist; **9** theologer, theologue; **10** scholastic, theologist; **11** hagiologist, hierologist, theologizer; **12** theologician; **13** eschatologist; **14** ecclesiologist.

theological 6 divine; **8** dogmatic, mystical; **9** canonical, doctrinal, patristic, religious, spiritual; **10** scriptural; **12** hagiological, hierological, metaphysical; **14** Christological, eschatological, hagiographical, hierographical, soteriological.

theology 2 RE *UK*, RI *UK*, RS; **8** divinity, doctrine, religion; **9** dogmatics, hagiology, hierology, Mariology, mysticism, scripture; **10** angelology, Buddhology, doctrinism, patristics, secularism; **11** apologetics, Christology, eschatology, hagiography, hierography, metaphysics, rationalism, soteriology; **12** doctrinalism, ecclesiology, ontotheology, spirituality; **15** physicotheology; PHRASES: **6, 8** crisis ~; **7, 8** natural ~.

theoretical 4 pure; **5** ideal; **6** formal; **7** applied, assumed; **8** abstract, academic, analytic(al), fanciful, mythical, notional, presumed, putative; **9** axiomatic, empirical, estimated, fictional, heuristic, imaginary, suspected, theoremic, theoretic; **10** conceptual, fictitious, indicative, perceptual, suggestive; **11** conjectural, speculative, theorematic; **12** experiential, experimental, guesstimated, hypothetical, mathematical; **13** observational, philosophical, propositional, suppositional; PHRASES: **4-2** made-up; **4-7** make-believe, self-evident.

theorist 6 boffin, critic; **7** gambler, guesser, planner, thinker; **8** academic, supposer, surmiser; **9** scientist, theorizer; **10** researcher, speculator; **11** doctrinaire, hypothesist, philosopher; **12** doctrinarian, experimenter, theoretician; PHRASES: **5, 7** model builder; **6, 7** theory builder; **8, 6** armchair critic, research worker.

theorize 5 guess, infer, opine, posit,

prove; **6** assume, deduce, derive, reason, reckon; **7** analyze, believe, imagine, presume, satisfy, suggest, suppose, suspect; **8** conceive, conclude, disprove, estimate, validate; **9** postulate, speculate; **10** conjecture, generalize, invalidate, presuppose; **11** demonstrate, guesstimate, hypothesize; **13** conceptualize; PHRASES: **3, 7** put forward.

theory 3 ism, law; **4** clue, hint, idea, rule; **5** axiom, fancy, guess, hunch, lemma, model; **6** belief, notion, scheme, system; **7** concept, feeling, formula, premise, program, theorem; **8** equation; **9** corollary, criterion, intuition, postulate, principle, suspicion, technique; **10** assumption, conjecture, hypothesis, indication, philosophy, simulation, suggestion; **11** abstraction, presumption, proposition, speculation, supposition; **12** idealization; **14** generalization, presupposition; PHRASES: **5, 10** first principles.

therapeutic 5 tonic; **7** calming, healing, helpful, nursing, tending; **8** curative, relaxing, remedial, salutary; **9** medicinal; **10** beneficial, corrective, preventive, satisfying; **11** restorative; **12** prophylactic.

therapy 3 ECT, HRT; **4** cure, diet, drip, help; **6** course, remedy; **7** dietary, healing, massage, nursing, regimen; **8** dialysis, medicine; **9** aftercare, allopathy, herbalism, orthotics, treatment; **10** homeopathy, medication, osteopathy, poulticing, psychiatry, psychology, rebirthing; **11** acupressure, acupuncture, fomentation, naturopathy, orthopedics; **12** chemotherapy, chiropractic, hydrotherapy, hypnotherapy, manipulation, osteotherapy, phototherapy, radiotherapy, therapeutics; **13** immunotherapy, physiotherapy *UK Can*, psychotherapy; **14** electrotherapy, psychoanalysis, rehabilitation; **15** catheterization, thalassotherapy; PHRASES: **4-4** drip-feed; **4-5, 4** cold-water cure; **4, 7** gene ~; **4-7** bone-setting; **4, 9** heat treatment; **5, 3** first aid; **5, 4** faith cure; **5, 7** group ~, shock ~; **5, 9** shock treatment; **5, 10** child psychology; **6, 4** nature cure; **6, 7** primal ~, speech ~; **7, 4** medical care; **7, 6** bedside manner; **7, 7** Gestalt ~, hormone ~; **8, 7** aversion ~, physical ~.

therefore 2 so; **4** ergo, thus; **5** argal, hence.

thereupon 8 directly; **11** accordingly, immediately; **12** consequently, subsequently.

thermometer 9 pyrometer; **10** thermopile; **11** calorimeter; **12** thermocouple; PHRASES: **3, 11** gas ~.

thesaurus *See* **dictionary**

thesis 4 case, idea, view; **5** claim, essay, issue, paper, point, topic; **6** notion, stance, theory; **7** grounds, opinion, premise, pretext; **8** argument, evidence, position, proposal, treatise; **9** assertion, monograph, postulate, statement, testimony; **10** hypothesis; **11** affirmation, attestation, composition, proposition; **12** dissertation.

thespian 5 actor, stagy; **6** player; **7** actress, artiste; **8** dramatic; **10** histrionic, theatrical; **11** personality; **12** melodramatic.

thick 3 dim, fat; **4** deep, dull, dumb, full, wide; **5** ample, broad, bulky, bushy, buxom, dense, gooey, gruff, heavy, lumpy, obese, plump, podgy *UK*, pudgy, round, solid, stiff, stout, tubby; **6** chubby, chunky, filled, flabby, hoarse, marked, obtuse, packed, padded, portly, rotund, stocky, stodgy, stupid, sturdy, syrupy; **7** clotted, copious, covered, crowded, curdled, densely, extreme, idiotic, massive, muffled, profuse, slurred, swelled, swollen, teeming, thickly, throaty, viscous; **8** abundant, bursting, coarsely, distinct, generous, thickset; **9** clabbered, corpulent, glutinous, thickened; **10** boneheaded, coagulated, gelatinous, incrassate, indistinct, overweight, potbellied, pronounced; **11** endomorphic, overflowing, substantial, thickheaded; **12** concentrated, impenetrable; **14** pachydermatous.

thicken 3 gel, set; **4** cake, clot, jell; **5** churn, crowd, crust, jelly, swarm; **6** cement, cohere, curdle, harden, lopper, reduce; **7** clabber, congeal, jellify, stiffen; **8** compress, condense, emulsify, solidify; **9** coagulate, intensify; **10** constipate, gelatinize, incrassate, inspissate; **11** consolidate; **12** conglomerate; PHRASES: **4, 2** firm up; **4, 4** boil down.

thickness 3 fat; **4** body, bulk, mass, slab; **5** depth, width; **7** blubber, breadth, density, obesity, padding, texture; **8** doorstep, potbelly, solidity; **9** rotundity, viscosity; **10** corpulence, upholstery; PHRASES: **5, 5** thick slice. *See also* **thick**

thickset *See* **stocky**

thick-skinned 4 hard; **6** coarse; **7** callous; **11** insensitive.

thief 3 dip; **4** yegg; **5** crimp, crook, taker; **6**

bandit, lifter, mugger, robber; **7** booster, burglar, filcher, poacher, prowler, rustler, stealer; **8** abductor, cutpurse, hijacker, intruder, peterman *UK*, picklock, pilferer; **9** cracksman *UK*, dognapper, kidnapper, larcenist, purloiner, scrounger, skyjacker, terrorist; **10** bushranger, highwayman, pickpocket, shanghaier, shoplifter; **12** housebreaker, kleptomaniac; PHRASES: **3, 7** cat burglar; **3-8** bag-snatcher *UK*; **4, 6** bank robber, Dick Turpin; **4-6** safe-blower; **4-7** safe-breaker, safe-cracker; **5, 4** Robin Hood *UK*; **5, 5** Jesse James, petty ~, sneak ~; **5, 6** train robber; **6, 5** cattle ~; **6, 6** Artful Dodger; **6, 7** cattle rustler; **7, 6** highway robber.

thighbone 5 femur.

thin 3 cut; **4** bony, fine, high, lamé, lean, puny, rare, slim, weak, wiry; **5** gauzy, gawky, lanky, light, rangy, reedy, runny, sheer, spare, tinny, weedy; **6** boyish, dilute, gasify, narrow, rarefy, scarce, shrill, skinny, slight, svelte, thinly, twiggy, watery, weaken; **7** cracked, diluted, exhaust, girlish, gracile, insipid, scraggy, scrawny, shallow, slender, squeaky, sylphic, tenuous, willowy; **8** delicate, disperse, gangling, meagrely, rawboned, scantily, skeletal, sparsely, vaporize; **9** attenuate, emaciated, scattered, sylphlike; **10** adulterate, diaphanous, leptosomic, threadlike; **11** ectomorphic, etherealize, lightweight, transparent, underweight; **14** undernourished; PHRASES: **4-6** lean-limbed, thin-legged; **4-7** flat-chested, wasp-waisted; **5, 4** water down; **5-4** wafer-thin; **5-6** small-framed; **6-7** narrow-waisted; **7-5** hatchet-faced, lantern-jawed; **7-6** spindle-legged *UK*; **8, 5** slightly built.

thin (become thin) 4 diet, slim; **6** reduce; **10** slenderize; PHRASES: **4, 4** slim down; **4, 6** lose weight; **5, 4, 6** watch one's weight.

thing 2 it; **3** fad; **4** body, idea, item; **5** being, craze, event, issue, mania, monad, point; **6** affair, detail, device, entity, factor, gadget, matter, object; **7** article, feature, machine; **8** business, fixation, incident; **9** happening, mechanism, obsession, something, substance; **10** occurrence, phenomenon; **11** contraption, fascination, thingamajig; **13** preoccupation.

think 4 deem, feel; **5** agree, judge, sense; **6** assume, deduce, ideate, induce, intuit, ponder, reason; **7** believe, cognize, imagine, reflect, suppose; **8** cogitate, consider, meditate, perceive, ruminate; **9** cerebrate, speculate; **10** apperceive, deliberate; **11** contemplate, ratiocinate, rationalize; **13** conceptualize; PHRASES: **3, 4, 4** use one's head; **3, 4, 5** use one's brain; **4, 4** mull over; **4, 4, 6** rack one's brains; **5, 2** weigh up *UK*.

thinker 4 sage; **6** genius; **7** dreamer, egghead, scholar, student; **8** academic, brainbox *UK*, highbrow, theorist; **9** professor; **10** ideologist; **11** philosopher; **12** intellectual; PHRASES: **4, 3** wise man; **7, 7** logical ~; **8, 6** rational person.

thinking 4 idea, view; **6** belief, theory; **7** opinion; **8** rational, thoughts; **10** assessment, discerning, philosophy, thoughtful; **11** intelligent; PHRASES: **8, 6** accepted wisdom.

thinking (ways of thinking) 5 logic; **6** acumen; **7** insight; **8** instinct; **9** deduction, induction, intuition, rationale, reasoning; **11** inspiration; **13** ratiocination; PHRASES: **5, 5** sixth sense; **6, 9** formal reasoning; **7, 4** quantum leap.

thinner 7 cleaner, diluent, diluter, solvent; **8** stripper; **10** turpentine.

thin person 4 runt, slip; **5** sylph; **6** dieter, shadow, wraith; **7** slimmer; **8** anorexic, beanpole, skeleton, weakling; **9** ectomorph, leptosome, scarecrow; **10** broomstick; **11** spindlelegs; PHRASES: **3, 2, 5** bag of bones; **6, 7** weight watcher; **7, 8** walking skeleton.

thin-skinned *See* **sensitive**

third 6 tierce; PHRASES: **5, 3** ~ age, ~ eye, ~ man *UK*; **5, 4** ~ part; **5, 5** major ~, minor ~, ~ class, ~ party, ~ power, T~ Reich, T~ World; **5, 6** ~ degree, ~ estate, ~ person; **7, 4** tertium quid.

third-rate 1 C.

thirst 4 ache, pine, want; **5** crave, parch; **6** desire, hunger; **7** craving, drought, dryness, longing; **8** appetite, yearning; **9** eagerness, thirsting; **10** xerostomia; **11** dehydration, thirstiness.

thirsty 3 dry; **4** avid, keen; **5** eager; **6** hungry; **7** athirst, craving, drouthy, gasping *UK*, longing, parched; **8** desiring, desirous, yearning; **9** thirsting, voracious; **10** dehydrated; PHRASES: **3, 2, 1, 4** dry as a bone.

thorn 3 awn; **4** barb, burr; **5** brier, point, spike, spine; **7** bristle, prickle, thistle.

thorough 4 full; **5** total, utter; **7** careful; **8** absolute, complete, detailed; **10** exhaustive, methodical, meticulous, systematic; **11** painstaking; PHRASES: **2-5** in-depth; **3-3-3** out-and-out.

thoroughbred 4 goer, pure; **5** pacer, punch, racer; **6** classy, fencer, hunter, jumper, stayer; **7** courser, hackney, hurdler, refined, speeder, stepper, trotter; **8** pedigree, purebred, sprinter; **9** carthorse *UK*, drayhorse, racehorse; **10** bloodstock, cultivated; **12** aristocratic; **13** steeplechaser; PHRASES: **3-6** fox-hunter; **4-4** well-bred; **4, 5** post horse *UK*; **4-7** blue-blooded, high-stepper; **5-5** blood-horse.

thoroughfare *See* **road, street**

thou 1 M; **3** mil.

though 3 yet; **5** while; **7** however; **8** although; **11** nonetheless; **12** nevertheless; PHRASES: **3, 3** and yet; **4, 2** even if; **4, 6** even ~.

thought 4 care, idea, plan; **5** ideas; **6** belief, design, notion, reason, theory; **7** concept, concern, notions, opinion; **8** planning, thinking; **9** attention, cognition, deduction, reasoning; **10** brainstorm, cogitation, conception, meditation, philosophy, reflection, rumination, suggestion; **11** cerebration, inspiration; **12** deliberation; **13** consideration, contemplation, ratiocination; PHRASES: **5, 4** brain wave *UK*; **6, 7** mental process; **6, 8** mental activity.

thoughtful 4 deep, kind; **5** sound; **6** caring, mental, musing; **7** careful, helpful, pensive, precise, sapient, wistful; **8** absorbed, accurate, brooding *UK*, cerebral, dreaming, profound, ruminant, selfless, sensible, studious, studying, thinking, thorough; **9** attentive, cognitive, judicious, reasoning, unselfish; **10** cogitative, meditative, meticulous, reasonable, reflective, ruminative, solicitous; **11** circumspect, considerate, painstaking, preoccupied, speculative, sympathetic; **12** concentrated, deliberative, intellectual; **13** concentrating, contemplative, introspective, philosophical; PHRASES: **2, 1, 5, 5** in a brown study; **4, 2, 7** deep in thought, lost in thought; **4-7** kind-hearted *UK*.

thoughtfulness 4 care; **7** thought; **8** accuracy, sympathy; **9** attention, precision; **10** meditation, reflection, solicitude; **13** consideration, contemplation, introspection. *See also* **thoughtful**

thoughtless 4 rude; **5** blank, inane; **6** stupid, unkind, vacant; **7** fatuous, foolish, selfish, vacuous; **8** carefree, careless, heedless, ignorant, impolite, mindless, reckless, tactless, uncaring; **9** easygoing, negligent, oblivious; **10** unthinking; **11** inattentive, insensitive; **12** unreflective; **13** inconsiderate; PHRASES: **5-2-5** happy-go-lucky; **5-3-4** devil-may-care; **5-6** empty-headed; **6-6** absent-minded.

thousand 1 G, K, M; **4** kilo, lakh, yard; **5** grand; **6** archer, myriad; **7** chiliad; **8** gigabyte, kilobyte, kilogram; **9** kilometer, millenary, millenial, milligram, millipede; **10** millennium, milliliter, millimeter, thousandth; **11** millenarian.

thousandth 9 millenary; **10** millennial; **11** millenarian; **12** thousandfold; PHRASES: **3-6** six-figure; **4-6** five-figure, four-figure.

thrash 3 lam; **4** beat, cane, flog, lash, lick, mash, whip; **5** baste, crush, flail, kevel, knead, pound, spank; **6** batter, defeat, hammer, kibble, pummel, squash, wallop; **7** leather, trounce; **8** lambaste; **9** pulverize; PHRASES: **4, 5, 4, 2** rain blows down on.

thread 4 clew, clue, cord, file, lace, link, tram, warp, weft, wire, woof, yarn; **5** fiber, floss, theme, thrum, twine; **6** cotton, strand, string, suture, tassel; **8** filament.

threadbare 4 thin; **5** banal, trite; **6** ragged, shabby; **7** clichéd, raggedy; **9** hackneyed; PHRASES: **4-3** worn-out; **4-4** well-worn.

threat 4 omen, risk; **5** fatwa, peril; **6** danger, hazard, menace; **7** portent, warning; **8** jeopardy; **9** ultimatum.

threaten 3 cow; **4** loom; **5** alarm, augur, bully, scare; **6** impend, menace; **7** imperil, portend, presage; **8** browbeat, endanger, frighten; **9** terrorize; **10** jeopardize, pressurize.

threatened *See* **endangered**

threatening 4 dark; **5** nasty; **7** hostile, ominous; **8** bullying, menacing, sinister; **10** aggressive, foreboding, portentous; **11** frightening; **12** inauspicious, intimidating.

three 4 cube, trey, trio; **5** cubed, third, triad, trine; **6** treble, trinal, triple, triune; **7** ternary, triadic, trifold, triform, trinary, trinity, triplex; **8** tertiary, triality; **9** threefold, threesome; **10** Musketeers, trebleness, trimorphic, tripleness, triplicate, triplicity; PHRASES: **11** trimorphism.

three-part (thing) 6 tripod, trivet, troika; **7** deltoid, trefoil, tricorn, trident, trilogy, triplet; **8** shamrock, triangle, tricycle, trigonal, trimaran, trimeter, tripedal, tripodic, triptych, tristich; **9** triennial, triennium, trihedral, trimester, trimetric, trinomial; **10** triangular, tridentate, trifoliate, trilateral, trilingual, trithedron; **11** trimestrial, triumvirate; **14** tridimensional, trihebdomadary; **5-6** three-decker, three-hander; **5-7** three-wheeler.

threshold **4** dawn, door, edge; **5** brink, entry, level, limit, verge; **7** ceiling, doorway, maximum, outside; **8** doorstep, entrance; PHRASES: **8, 5** starting point.

thrice **6** trebly, triply; **7** trinely; **9** threefold; PHRASES: **2, 10** in triplicate; **5, 5** three times.

thrift **7** caution, economy; **8** prudence; **9** austerity, frugality, parsimony; **11** carefulness, thriftiness; **12** cheeseparing; PHRASES: **4, 9** good husbandry; **4, 10** good management.

thrifty **5** canny; **6** frugal, meager, saving; **7** austere, careful, prudent, scrimpy, sparing, spartan, Spartan; **8** cautious, unlavish; **10** conserving, economical, unwasteful; **11** economizing; **12** cheeseparing, parsimonious; PHRASES: **4, 4, 5** good with money; **4-6** time-saving; **5-4** penny-wise; **5-6** labor-saving, money-saving.

thrifty (be thrifty) **6** budget; **7** husband; **8** conserve; PHRASES: **4, 2** make do; **4, 2, 1, 6** live on a budget.

thrill **3** joy; **6** excite, quiver; **7** delight, inspire; **8** pleasure; **9** adventure, electrify; **10** exhilarate.

thrive **4** boom; **5** bloom; **7** blossom, burgeon, improve, prosper, succeed; **8** flourish, increase; PHRASES: **2, 10** be successful; **4, 4** grow well.

throat **3** maw; **4** craw, crop; **5** gorge; **6** dewlap, gullet; **7** swallow, weasand, whistle; **8** thrapple UK, thropple, throttle, windpipe.

throb **4** thud; **5** pound, pulse, thump; **6** rhythm; **7** pulsate; **8** pounding; **9** pulsation.

throne **4** rule, seat; **5** chair, power; **7** command; **8** cathedra; **9** authority; **11** sovereignty.

throng **3** jam, mob, sea; **4** army, bevy, cram, fill, gang, hail, hive, host, mass, nest, pack, rout, ruck; **5** array, brood, bunch, cloud, covey, crowd, crush, drove, fleet, flock, flood, horde, press, shoal, swamp, swarm, troop; **6** colony, flight, gaggle, galaxy, legion; **7** clutter; **8** inundate; **9** multitude; **12** congregation.

throttle **3** gag; **5** check, choke; **6** adjust, muzzle, stifle, subdue; **7** control, correct, garrote, silence; **8** garrotte UK, regulate, strangle; **9** suffocate; **11** strangulate.

through **2** by, in; **3** per, via; **4** amid, over, past; **5** among, round; **6** across, amidst, around, beyond, during, within; **7** amongst; **10** throughout; PHRASES: **2, 1, 6, 2** as a result of; **2, 3, 2** by way of; **2, 5, 2** by means of; **3, 2** due to, out of; **5, 2** owing to; **7, 2** because of.

throw **3** lob, put, rug, shy; **4** bowl, bung UK, cast, dart, drop, emit, fire, flip, give, have, hold, host, hurl, jerk, kick, move, pass, pelt, pull, punt, snap, tilt, toss; **5** chuck, curve, flick, fling, heave, lance, pitch, serve, shawl, shine, sling; **6** baffle, direct, hurtle, launch, propel, puzzle; **7** arrange, blanket, cockshy UK, confuse, flummox, nonplus, perplex, project; **8** bewilder, catapult, coverlet, lapidate, organize, snowball, spitball, surprise; **9** bamboozle, slipcover; **10** disconcert, disconnect; PHRASES: **3, 3** let fly; **4, 3** send out; **4-3** shot-put.

throw away **3** bin UK; **4** blow, dump, junk, ruin; **5** chuck, ditch, scrap, spoil, waste; **6** reject; **7** discard; **8** jettison, squander; **11** precipitate; **12** defenestrate; PHRASES: **3, 3, 2** get rid of; **3, 4, 2** get shot of UK; **3, 7, 2** rid oneself of; **5, 3** throw out; **5, 9** throw overboard; **7, 2** dispose of; **7, 4** fritter away.

throwback **5** relic; **9** reversion; **10** regression; **11** resemblance.

throw down **3** sow; **4** drop, dust, pour, shed, slop, void; **5** fling, pitch, spill; **6** decant, shower; **7** moisten, scatter; **8** disperse, sprinkle; **9** broadcast; PHRASES: **3, 2** let go; **3, 4** let drop, let fall, let slip.

thrower **6** bowler, curler, heaver, hurler, server, tosser UK; **7** chucker, flinger, pitcher, slinger, striker; **10** discobolus, snowballer; PHRASES: **4-6** shot-putter; **5-7** knife-thrower, stone-slinger; **6, 7** discus ~; **7, 7** javelin ~.

thrush **5** mavis. *See also* **songbird**

thrust **4** gist, prod, push; **5** drive, focus, force, lunge, point, power, reach, shove; **6** attack, extend, propel; **7** assault, impetus, meaning, stretch; **8** momentum; **9** direction, offensive; **10** propulsion.

thud 4 bump, plop; **5** clunk, plonk, plump, plunk, thump; **7** tempest; **9** rainstorm.

thug 4 goon; **5** heavy, rough, tough; **6** mugger; **7** gorilla, hoodlum, ruffian; **8** hooligan.

thulium 2 TM.

thump *See* **punch**

thunder 3 din; **4** boom, clap, roar, yell; **5** shout; **6** bellow, rumble; **7** resound.

thunderstorm 5 storm, track; **6** deluge; **7** tempest, thunder; **8** downpour; **9** lightning, rainstorm; **10** cloudburst; **11** thunderbolt, thunderclap; PHRASES: **4, 2, 7** clap of thunder; **4, 2, 9** bolt of lightning; **4, 9** ball lightning, fork lightning; **5, 9** sheet lightning; **6, 9** summer lightning; **9, 3** lightning rod; **9, 5** lightning flash; **9, 6** lightning strike; **10, 5** electrical storm.

thus 2 so; **9** therefore; **11** accordingly; **12** consequently; PHRASES: **2, 1, 6** as a result; **2, 4, 3** in this way; **2, 4, 6** in this manner; **2, 7** as follows; **4, 2** like so.

thwart 4 balk *UK*, bilk, deny, foil, jilt, ruin, sour, stop; **5** spoil; **6** baffle, befool, hamper, hinder, humble, impede, refuse, reject; **7** prevent; **8** confound, obstruct; **9** frustrate, humiliate, stonewall; **10** disconcert, discontent; PHRASES: **3, 1, 4, 2** put a stop to; **3, 4, 2** put paid to *UK*; **4, 4** turn away; **5, 2** stand up.

thylacine 4 wolf; PHRASES: **9, 4** Tasmanian wolf.

Tibet 7 Sitsang.

tibia 8 shinbone.

tick 5 flash, jiffy, pulse, swing, throb, trice; **6** minute, moment, second; **7** instant; **8** undulate; **9** oscillate.

ticket 3 tab, tag; **5** label; **6** coupon, docket, marker, permit, return, season, single; **7** receipt, sticker, voucher; **9** roundtrip; PHRASES: **3-3, 6** one-way ~; **4, 6** meal ~, pawn ~; **5-4, 6** round-trip ~; **6, 8** travel document; **7, 6** parking ~; **8, 6** platform ~ *UK*.

tickle 4 itch; **5** amuse; **6** please; **7** delight, prickle, scratch; **8** irritate; **9** entertain.

ticklish 6 thorny, tricky; **7** awkward; **8** delicate; **11** problematic.

tide 3 ebb; **4** flow, flux, wave; **5** drift, flood, surge; **6** reflux, stream; **7** current, riptide, tideway; **8** tideland; **9** refluence, tidewater; **13** thalassometer; PHRASES: **3, 3, 4** ebb and flow; **3, 4** ebb ~, low ~, red ~; **3, 5** low water; **4, 3, 6** flux and reflux; **4, 4** full ~, high ~, neap ~, ~ gate, ~ race; **4, 5** high water, ~ chart, ~ gauge; **5, 4** flood ~, lunar ~, solar ~, tidal flow; **5, 5** tidal flood, tidal power, tidal range, tidal table; **5, 6** tidal stream; **5, 7** tidal current; **6, 4** direct ~, rising ~, spring ~; **8, 4** opposite ~; **10, 4** intertidal zone; **11, 4** equinoctial ~.

tidings *See* **news**

tidy 4 fair, neat, trim; **5** ample, clean, debug, groom, large, smart; **6** dapper, neaten, smooth, spruce; **7** arrange, correct, ordered, orderly, sizable, unravel, unsnarl; **8** organize, untangle; **9** organized, rearrange, shipshape; **10** immaculate, reasonable, straighten, worthwhile; **11** disentangle, substantial, uncluttered; **12** considerable; PHRASES: **2, 5** in order; **3, 2, 6** put to rights; **4, 3** iron out; **4, 4, 5** lick into shape; **4-6-3** well-turned-out *UK*; **4-7** well-groomed; **5, 2** clean up, clear up; **5, 3, 4** spick and span; **6, 2** spruce up; **7, 2** smarten up; **10, 2** straighten up.

tie 2 ha; **3** fix, ter; **4** band, bind, bond, draw, join, knot, lash, link, moor; **5** deuce, strap, truss, unite; **6** attach, cravat, fasten, secure, splice, string, tether; **7** windsor; **8** handicap, relation, restrain; **9** stalemate; **10** connection; PHRASES: **2, 4, 3, 4** be neck and neck; **2, 5** be equal; **3, 3** bow ~; **3, 6, 3** old school ~; **4, 4** dead heat; **4-6** even-steven; **5, 3** black ~, white ~; **8, 3** bootlace ~.

tied 5 bound, fixed, glued, yoked; **6** jammed, lashed, secure, wedged; **7** hitched, knotted, plaited, secured, spliced; **8** attached, fastened, stitched; **9** immovable; **10** interwoven.

tier *See* **level**

tiff *See* **quarrel**

tight 4 high, mean *UK*, snug, taut; **5** boozy, cheap, close, drunk, oiled, tense, tipsy, woozy; **6** loaded, stingy, strict; **7** pickled, squiffy *UK*; **9** niggardly, plastered; **11** constricted; **12** constricting.

tightness 7 tension; **8** rigidity. *See also* **tight**

tights *See* **legwear**

till 3 ATM, box, dig, hoe; **4** plow *UK*, rake, tray; **5** until; **6** drawer, plough *UK*; **7** prepare; **8** checkout; **9** cultivate; **12** Eulenspiegel; PHRASES: **4, 3** cash box; **4, 4** cash desk *UK*, turn over; **4, 7** slot machine; **4, 8** cash register; **4, 9** cash dispenser *UK*.

tillage **5** tilth; **6** sowing; **7** culture, dunging, hedging, plowing, weeding; **8** ethering, fruition, planting, plashing, silaging; **9** flowering, harrowing, pleaching, ploughing *UK*; **10** harvesting, heathering, irrigation; **11** cultivation, fertilizing; PHRASES: **3-6** hay-making; **4-8** crop-spraying; **4-9** muck-spreading; **5-6** hedge-laying.

tilt *See* **slope**

timber **4** bark, cord, cork, pole, wood; **6** flitch, lignin, lumber; **7** cordage, duramen *UK*, phellem, wetwood; **8** alburnum; PHRASES: **4, 4** late wood, tree ring; **4-4, 6** tree-ring dating; **5, 4** early wood; **6, 4** annual ring, growth ring. *See also* **tress and shrubs**

timber wolf **4** lobo; PHRASES: **4, 4** gray wolf.

timbre *See* **sound**

timbrel **10** tambourine.

time **1** T; **2** AM, mo *UK*, PM; **3** age, day, eon, era, min *UK*, sec; **4** beat, bird, date, hour, idle, pace, plan, week, year; **5** count, epoch, month, phase, point, speed, spell, stage, stint, tempo, trial, while; **6** decade, minute, moment, period, record, rhythm, season, second; **7** century, chiliad, chronon, instant, measure, midweek, monitor, program, quarter, stretch, tachyon, weekend; **8** duration, instance, interval, lifetime, occasion, organize, schedule, semester, timeslip, velocity; **9** calculate, decennium, fortnight *UK*, frequency, millenium, timetable *UK*, trimester; **10** generation, nanosecond; **11** microsecond, millisecond, synchronize; **12** acceleration, intermission, quinquennium; PHRASES: **3, 4** big ~; **3-4** two-four; **3-5** six-eight; **4, 4** beat ~, core ~, down ~, full ~, high ~, keep ~, leap year, mark ~, mean ~, slow ~ *UK*, ~ bomb, ~ warp, ~ zone; **4-4** four-four; **4, 5** ~ flies, ~ sheet; **4, 6** ~ travel, **4, 7** ~ capsule, ~ machine; **4, 9** ~ signature; **4, 10** ~ immemorial; **5, 2, 4** arrow of ~, march of ~, point in ~, river of ~; **5, 4** clock ~, extra ~, local ~, prime ~, quick ~, short ~ *UK*; **5-4** space-time, three-four; **5, 5** lunar month; **6, 2, 4** moment in ~; **6, 4** common ~, double ~, father ~, injury ~, summer ~ *UK*, triple ~; **6, 5** tempus fugit; **7, 2, 4** passage of ~; **7, 4** closing ~, opening ~ *UK*; **8-2, 4** drinking-up ~ *UK*, lighting-up ~ *UK*; **8, 4** borrowed ~, compound ~, question ~, response ~, standard ~; **8, 5** calendar month; **8-6** daylight-saving; **9, 4** quadruple ~, universal ~.

time (for the time being) **8** meantime; **9** meanwhile; PHRASES: **2, 3, 8** in the meantime; **3, 3, 5** for the nonce; **7, 6** between whiles.

time (keep time) **4** time; **5** clock, slate; **7** monitor; **8** schedule; **9** timetable; PHRASES: **3, 1, 4, 3** set a date for; **3, 3, 3** fix the day; **3, 3, 4** fix the date, fix the time.

time (little time) **1** T; **2** mo *UK*; **3** sec; **4** tick; **5** jiffy.

timekeeper **3** ref; **5** clock, watch; **6** ticker; **7** diarist, referee, sundial; **8** annalist, horologe; **9** conductor, hourglass, timepiece; **10** bandleader, chronicler, clockmaker, horologist, watchmaker; **11** calendarist, chronologer, chronometer; **12** chronologist; **13** chronographer; PHRASES: **4, 6** time beater; **5, 7** clock watcher; **8-5** calendar-maker.

timeless **2** nd; **7** abiding, ageless, endless, eternal, lasting, undying; **8** dateless, enduring, immortal, unending; **9** immutable, perpetual, unceasing; **10** changeless, continuous, unchanging; **11** everlasting, sempiternal.

timely **3** apt, fit; **5** happy, lucky; **6** suited; **7** apropos, fitting, welcome; **8** sensible, suitable; **9** befitting, favorable, fortunate, judicious, opportune; **10** auspicious, convenient, felicitous, propitious, seasonable; **11** appropriate; **12** providential; PHRASES: **3, 3, 8** for the occasion; **4-5** well-timed; **6-4** heaven-sent.

time off **5** break, leave, peace, quiet; **6** recess, relief; **7** holiday *UK*, leisure, respite; **8** breather, furlough, vacation; **10** recreation, sabbatical; PHRASES: **3, 3** day off; **3, 4** off duty; **4, 3** half day; **4-3** time-out; **4, 4** free time; **5, 4** spare time.

time period **3** age, day, eon, era; **4** hour, week, year; **5** epoch, month; **6** decade, minute, moment, second; **7** century, chiliad, instant, quarter, weekday; **9** decennium, fortnight; **10** generation, millennium, nanosecond; **11** microsecond, millisecond; **12** quinquennium.

timer **5** clock, diary, watch; **7** counter, daybook; **8** calendar, horologe; **9** timepiece; **10** chronogram; **11** chronograph, chronometer; PHRASES: **4, 5** time clock; **6, 6** timing device; **6, 8** Julian calendar.

timetable **8** schedule.

timid **3** coy, shy, wet; **4** weak; **5** jumpy,

nervy; **6** shaken; **7** bashful, fearful, insipid, jittery, nervous, panicky, rattled, wimpish; **8** cowardly, hesitant, reticent, retiring, timorous, unheroic; **9** diffident, nerveless, spineless, squeamish, tentative, tremulous; **10** frightened; **11** ineffectual; **12** apprehensive; **13** pusillanimous; PHRASES: **4-5** weak-kneed; **4-6** weak-minded, weak-willed; **5-5** wishy-washy; **5-7** faint-hearted.

timorous See **nervous**

tin 2 SN; **3** box, can; PHRASES: **3, 3** ~ can, ~ god, ~ hat; **3, 5** ~ plate; **3, 6** ~ lizzie; **3, 7** ~ soldier, ~ whistle; **4, 3** cake ~ *UK*; **7, 3** biscuit ~ *UK*.

tincal 5 borax.

tincture 4 hint, tint, tone; **5** tinge; **6** nuance; **7** essence, extract; **8** solution; **11** distilllate; **13** distilllation.

tinge 3 mix; **4** dash, drop, hint, tint; **5** color, shade, stain, touch, trace.

tingle 4 itch; **5** prick, sting; **6** tickle; **7** prickle.

tinker 3 fix, toy; **4** mend, play; **6** fiddle, repair, tamper; **9** interfere; PHRASES: **3, 5** put right; **4, 6** fool around, mess around *UK*; **6, 6** monkey around.

tinkle 4 ding; **5** chink, clink; **6** jingle.

tinny 4 high, poor, thin; **5** cheap; **6** shoddy, shrill; **7** ringing; **8** inferior, metallic; **9** worthless.

tinsel 5 glitz; **7** glitter, spangle; **8** streamer; **9** showiness; **10** decoration, flashiness; **15** pretentiousness.

tint 3 dye, hue; **5** color, rinse, shade, touch, trace; **6** streak; **8** colorant; **9** highlight.

tiny See **minute**

tip 3 cue, end, nib, nod, pay; **4** bend, clue, gift, give, hint, hole, idea, lean, list, pour, roll, slip, tilt; **5** angle, bonus, bribe, empty, extra, grade, imply, knock, point, slant, slope, spike, spill, spire, upend, upset; **6** advise, prompt, reward, signal, teeter, upturn; **7** breathe, capsize, garbage, incline, pointer, suggest, warning, whisper; **8** gradient, gratuity, indicate, intimate, overturn; **9** insinuate; **10** backhander *UK*, suggestion; **11** forewarning; PHRASES: **4, 6** turn turtle; **5, 4** knock over.

tipster 7 adviser, analyst; **8** informer; **9** informant; **10** consultant.

tipsy See **drunk**

tirade See **diatribe**

tire 3 sap, tax; **4** bush, flag, poop; **5** drain, weary, whack; **7** exhaust, fatigue, frazzle, knacker *UK*, shatter; **8** enervate; **9** prostrate; **10** debilitate. See also **attire**

tired 4 beat, dopy, dozy, weak; **5** bored, drawn, jaded, stale, weary, woozy; **6** bleary, bushed, drowsy, groggy, sleepy, zonked; **7** whacked *UK Can*; **8** flagging, footsore, listless; **9** lethargic; PHRASES: **6, 3** fagged out. See also **tire**

tiredness 7 fatigue, languor; **8** lethargy; **10** enervation, exhaustion. See also **tired**

tiring 7 tedious, wearing; **8** annoying; **9** demanding, laborious, wearisome; **10** monotonous. See also **tire**

tissue 3 net, web; **4** mass; **5** flesh; **6** matter, series; **7** network.

titan 5 giant; **6** genius; **8** superman; **10** superwoman.

titlark 5 pipit.

title 2 Mr; **3** cup, dub, sir; **4** call, deed, earl, lady, lord, name, page, role, term; **5** award, claim, count, deeds, label, right, style; **6** mister, rights, trophy; **7** entitle, heading; **8** identify; **9** designate, ownership; **11** designation, entitlement; **12** championship; PHRASES: **4, 3** call sir; **5, 2** refer to. See also **noble**

titleholder 4 lady, lord; **5** guest, owner; **6** holder, knight, vendor, winner; **7** honored; **8** champion, landlord; **9** cupholder, landowner, possessor; **10** proprietor.

to 4 shut, till; **6** closed, toward; **7** towards *UK*.

to (to the French) 1 a; **2** au; **3** aux; PHRASES: **1, 2** a la.

toast 4 burn, cook, heat, warm; **5** broil, brown, color, crisp, grill, skoal; **6** cheers, health, pledge, prosit, salute; **7** darling, delight, slainte, tribute; **8** favorite; **10** Gesundheit, sweetheart; PHRASES: **4-4** chin-chin *UK*; **5, 2** drink to; **5, 5** loyal ~, Melba ~.

tobacco 3 box, cig, fag *UK*, tar; **4** butt, chaw, plug, quid, shag, stem, stub; **5** baccy *UK*, cigar, flake, snuff; **6** ambeer, carton, ciggie, corona, Havana, hookah, packet; **7** ashtray, calumet, cheroot, humidor, menthol, smoking; **8** narghile, nicotine, snuffbox; **9** cigarette, cigarillo, panatella; **10** meerschaum; **12** churchwarden; PHRASES: **3, 3** dog end, fag end; **3-3** low-tar; **3, 4** the weed; **4, 2, 5** pipe of peace *UK*; **4-3** cork-tip, high-tar; **4, 4** clay pipe; **4-4** king-size; **4-4-3** roll-your-own; **5, 4** water pipe; **5-4** smoke-free; **6-3** filter-tip; **6, 4** coffin nail; **6, 5** cancer stick; **6-6** hubble-bubble; **7, 7** chewing ~, rolling ~, Turkish ~; **7-7** smoking-related; **8, 7** Virginia ~; **9, 3** cigarette end; **9, 4** cigarette case; **9, 5** cigarette paper.

toboggan 4 luge, sled, slip; **5** slide; **6** hurtle, sledge *UK*, sleigh, tumble; PHRASES: **7** bobsled.

tocsin *See* **alarm**

toddle *See* **walk**

to-do *See* **fuss**

toe 3 tae, tip; **5** digit, piggy; **6** pointe, tootsy; **6, 3** hammer ~.

together 4 calm, cool; **8** composed, mutually, unitedly; **9** collected, organized, unruffled; **11** inseparably; **12** collectively, concurrently; **14** simultaneously; PHRASES: **2, 1, 4** in a body, in a mass; **2, 1, 9** in a crocodile; **2, 3** as one, in tow; **2, 3, 4, 4** at the same time; **2, 4** at once, in sync; **2, 5** en masse; **2, 6** in convoy, in unison; **2, 7** in concert; **2, 8, 4** in someone's wake; **3, 8** all ~; **4-2** with-it; **4-4** laid-back; **4-9** self-possessed.

toggle 3 key, peg; **4** move; **5** clasp, lever; **6** buckle, button, change, switch; **7** command; **8** fastener, transfer.

togs *See* **clothes**

toil *See* **labor**

toilet 2 po *UK*, WC *UK*; **3** bog *UK*, can, loo *UK*, Men, pan, set; **4** head, john, soap; **5** heads, jakes, jerry, khazi *UK*, paper, potty, privy, stool, water, Women; **6** bedpan, lounge, throne, urinal; **7** bathing, chamber, commode, latrine, washing; **8** bathroom, dressing, gazunder *UK*, grooming, lavatory, outhouse, restroom, toilette, training; **9** ablutions; **10** closestool, thunderbox *UK*; **11** convenience, thunderbowl; PHRASES: **4, 4** Men's Room, rest room *UK*; **5, 6** earth closet *UK*, water closet; **6, 4** ~ bowl, Women's Room; **7, 3** chamber pot; **7, 5** getting ready; **7, 7** comfort station, getting dressed; **8, 4** lavatory bowl; **8, 6** chemical ~, portable ~.

toiletries 5 scent; **7** perfume; **8** smellies *UK*; PHRASES: **3, 2, 7** eau de cologne; **3, 2, 8** eau de toilette; **6, 5** toilet water; **7, 3** perfume oil; **9, 3** essential oil.

token 4 coin, mark, sign, slip; **5** empty; **6** coupon, symbol; **7** memento, nominal, voucher; **8** keepsake, reminder, souvenir,

symbolic; **10** indication; **11** perfunctory, remembrance; **13** demonstration.

tolerable 2 OK; **4** fair, okay; **5** fresh, sound; **7** average; **8** adequate, bearable, mediocre, middling, ordinary, passable, standard; **9** endurable; **10** acceptable, reasonable, sufficient; **11** indifferent, respectable, supportable; **12** satisfactory; **15** unexceptionable; PHRASES: **2-2** so-so; **3, 3** not bad; **3, 5** all right; **4-4** okey-doke; **5-5** fifty-fifty; **6, 4** pretty good.

tolerate 4 bear; **5** abide, allow, stand; **6** accept, endure; **7** forbear, stomach; PHRASES: **3, 2, 4** put up with; **4, 4** bear with; **5, 3** stand for.

toll 3 fee, tax; **4** call, ding, duty, levy, peal, ring; **5** clang; **7** payment; PHRASES: **4-4** ding-dong.

Tom 3 cat; **4** puss, Thos; **5** moggy; PHRASES: **3, 5** T~ Thumb; **3, 7** T~ Tiddler; **4, 3** long T~; **7, 3** peeping T~.

tomato 4, 5 love apple.

tome 4 book, work; **6** digest, volume.

tomfoolery 4 jape; **5** farce, prank, trick; **6** antics, banter, capers, joking, pranks, scrape, vagary; **8** clowning, drollery, mischief; **9** burlesque, horseplay, silliness; **10** buffoonery, skylarking; **11** shenanigans; **12** whimsicality; PHRASES: **4, 5** high jinks; **5, 6** silly season; **6, 8** monkey business; **7, 5** mucking about; **7, 6** fooling around, larking around *UK*, mucking around, playing around; **9, 4** practical joke.

ton 1 C, T; **3** lot; **4** chic, heap, mass; **5** ocean, stack; **8** mountain.

tonality *See* **sound**

tone 3 hue; **4** feel, tint; **5** color, drone, pitch, shade, sound, tinge; **6** manner, nature, timbre; **7** stridor; **8** ambiance, attitude, harmonic, language, monotone, overtone, register, tendency, tonality; **9** character, resonance, undertone; **10** atmosphere.

tongue 4 talk; **5** argot, idiom, slang; **6** glossa, jargon, lingua, patois, speech; **7** dialect, vulgate; **8** language, parlance, vocalism.

tonic 4 iron; **5** boost; **6** bracer, fillip, tisane; **7** alcohol, cordial, ginseng, livener, reviver, vitamin; **8** caffeine, infusion, nicotine, roborant; **9** energizer, hartshorn, refresher, stimulant; **10** Benzedrine *tm*; **11** amphetamine, restorative; PHRASES: **3, 4** pep pill; **3, 8** sal volatile; **4-2-2** pick-me-up; **4, 2,**

3, 3 shot in the arm; **4, 3** herb tea; **5, 5** royal jelly, ~ water; **8, 5** smelling salts.

too 4 also; 6 overly; 7 besides; 8 moreover; 9 extremely; 11 exceedingly, excessively; PHRASES: **2, 4** as well; **2, 8** in addition.

tool 2 ax; 3 adz, arm, awl, bit, jig, lug, nut, peg, ram, saw; 4 arms, bolt, clip, comb, file, fork, grip, haft, helm, hook, jack, nail, pole, prop, pump, rasp, rope, tack, vise; 5 cable, clamp, clasp, drill, gizmo, helve, jimmy, knife, lathe, lever, means, pedal, pivot, plane, poker, probe, punch, razor, screw, shaft, spade, tongs, wedge, wheel; 6 chisel, device, doodad, gadget, hammer, handle, hanger, jigsaw, lancet, mallet, pliers, pulley, rudder, sander, sheave, switch, tiller, trowel, weapon, wrench; 7 bellows, bradawl, crowbar, forceps, fretsaw, grapnel, hatchet, machine, nippers, nutpick, pincers, plunger, scalpel, spanner *UK*, stapler, support, syringe, trigger, utensil, whatnot, whatsit; 8 leverage, speculum, stopcock, tweezers; 9 apparatus, appliance, blowtorch, doohickey, fastening, hairbrush, handspike, implement, nailbrush, paperclip, thingummy; 10 instrument, perforator; 11 contraption, contrivance, screwdriver, stethoscope, thingumabob; PHRASES: **4, 3, 5** nuts and bolts; **4, 4** hand ~, nail file; **4, 5** fire tongs, hair dryer; **4, 6** pipe wrench; **4, 8** nail clippers, nail scissors; **5, 3** chain saw; **5, 4** edged ~, plumb line; **5, 5** craft knife, emery board; **5, 6** Allen wrench; **6, 3** church key, grease gun; **6, 6** monkey wrench, socket wrench, torque wrench; **6, 9** tongue depressor; **7, 4** curling iron, machine ~; **7, 5** shaving brush, Stanley knife *tm*; **8, 5** electric drill; **9, 4** precision ~, soldering iron; **10, 6** adjustable wrench.

tool (use tools) 3 hoe, mow, ram, saw; 4 chop, hook, nail, rake, tack; 5 drill, lever, punch, screw; 6 chisel, hammer, riddle, shovel, wrench; 7 crowbar; 9 mechanize.

tooth 3 cog; 4 fang, tine, tusk; 5 prong; 7 chopper; 10 projection; 11 indentation.

toothless 7 edental, useless; 8 biteless, edentate, impotent; 9 incapable, powerless, teethless; 10 edentulous; 11 ineffective, ineffectual.

tooth, teeth 3 cog; 4 fang, tine, tusk; 5 crown, fangs, molar, prong; 6 canine, cuspid, cutter, pearls, wisdom; 7 chopper, denture, grinder, incisor, ivories; 8 bicuspid, denticle, eyetooth, premolar; 9 bucktooth;

10 carnassial, projection; 11 indentation; 12 snaggletooth; PHRASES: **3, 5** egg tooth; **4, 5** baby tooth, gold tooth, milk tooth; **5, 5** false tooth, first tooth, sweet tooth; **6, 5** wisdom tooth; **9, 5** deciduous tooth *UK*, permanent tooth.

top 3 cap, end, lid; 4 acme, apex, arch, beat, best, boot, cork, head, kill, lead, peak, roof, slay; 5 chief, cover, crest, crown, excel, first, frost, gilet *UK*, icing, outdo; 6 apical, better, climax, double, drawer, exceed, murder, summit, tiptop, upmost, upside, zenith; 7 capital, eminent, execute, highest, hilltop, leading, maximal, maximum, overtop, stopper, supreme, surface, surpass, topmost, topping, topside, topsoil; 8 crowning, frosting, meridian, overarch, pinnacle, spinning, summital, surmount, surplice, ultimate, vertical, zenithal; 9 climactic, culminate, important, paramount, principal, slaughter, uppermost; 10 consummate, management, meridional; 11 culminating; 12 superstratum; PHRASES: **3, 3** big ~, ~ dog, ~ off, ~ out; **3, 5** ~ brass; **4, 3** hard ~, soft ~; **5, 3** screw ~ *UK*; **7, 2** improve on; **7, 3** humming ~ *UK*. *See also* **clothes**

topaz 7 citrine.

topee 4, 6 pith helmet.

top hat 6 topper; PHRASES: **4, 3** high hat.

topi 4, 6 pith helmet.

topic 4 gist, idea, meat, pith, plot, text; 5 angle, basis, drift, focus, issue, motif, point, theme, tract; 6 course, matter, rubric, thesis; 7 concern, essence, keynote, message, program, project, subject, theorem; 8 argument, contents, interest, treatise; 9 leitmotiv, statement; 10 foundation; 11 proposition, supposition; PHRASES: **4, 5** main point; **7, 6** subject matter.

topical 6 timely; 7 current, present; 8 relevant; 9 happening, immediate; 10 newsworthy; 11 interesting; 12 contemporary; PHRASES: **2-2-3-6** up-to-the-minute; **2-2-4** up-to-date; **2, 3, 4** in the news; **3, 3, 3, 5** hot off the press.

topmost *See* **top**

topping 5 icing; 6 upside; 7 surface, topside, topsoil; 8 frosting, meringue, piecrust; 12 superstratum; PHRASES: **3, 7** top surface; **3, 8** top dressing; **5, 4** upper side; **5, 7** upper surface.

topple 4 fall, oust; 6 depose, remove, tumble; 8 collapse; 9 overthrow; PHRASES: **3, 4**

tip over; **4, 4** fall over; **5, 4** bring down.

torch 4 lamp; **5** light; PHRASES: **3, 2, 4** set on fire; **3, 5, 2** set light to *UK*; **4, 4** burn down.

torment 3 nag, vex; **4** bane, bash, beat, harm, hell, hurt, pain, pest, rack; **5** abuse, agony, annoy, bully, harry, hound, scare, spite, taunt, tease; **6** attack, bother, demand, harass, injure, menace, molest, pester, plague, stress, thwart; **7** anguish, oppress, torture, trouble; **8** bullyrag, distress, frighten, maltreat, nuisance, threaten; **9** annoyance, blackmail, persecute, suffering, terrorize, tyrannize, victimize; **10** intimidate, irritation; PHRASES: **2, 4** do over; **3-5** ill-treat; **4, 2** bash up *UK*, beat up; **4, 2, 2, 3** have it in for; **4, 2, 3, 4** pain in the neck.

tormentor *See* **torturer**

tornado *See* **hurricane**

torpedo 4 ruin; **5** spoil, wreck; **6** thwart; **7** destroy.

torpid *See* **lazy**

torrent 4 flow, gush, rush, tide; **5** flood; **6** deluge, stream; **8** outburst.

torrid *See* **steamy**

tortoise 7 testudo; **8** terrapin.

tortuous 3 sly; **6** artful, crafty; **7** complex, devious, winding; **8** indirect, involved, twisting; **9** deceitful, difficult, intricate; **10** circuitous, convoluted; **11** complicated.

torture 4 pain, rack; **5** agony, press, wheel; **6** martyr, punish; **7** afflict, anguish, cruelty, kneecap, torment; **8** distress, mistreat, mutilate, triangle; **9** brutalize, martyrize, persecute, suffering, treadmill; **10** pilliwinks *UK*, thumbscrew; PHRASES: **3, 4, 7** the Star Chamber; **3, 11** the Inquisition; **4, 4** iron boot, work over; **4, 6** Iron Maiden; **7, 4** inflict pain; **7, 7** ~ chamber.

torturer 5 bully; **6** teaser; **8** harasser, pesterer; **9** oppressor, tormentor; **10** persecutor; **11** intimidator.

toss 3 lob, mix; **4** stir; **5** blend, fling, heave, pitch, throw.

total 3 add, all, lot, net, sum; **4** bill, full, make, nett; **5** count, equal, gross, score, tally, utter, whole; **6** entire, factor, number, result; **7** compute, product; **8** absolute, complete, entirety, quantity, totality, totalize; **9** aggregate, calculate, reckoning, summation; **10** unreserved; **11** unmitigated; PHRASES: **3, 2** add up, tot up; **3-3-3** out-and-

out; **3, 5, 5** the whole thing; **4, 2** come to; **4-5** full-blown; **4, 6** full amount; **5, 2** count up; **6, 2** amount to.

tote 3 lug; **4** bear, cart, haul, hold; **5** carry, heave, wield; **8** brandish.

totem 4 icon; **5** charm, image; **6** emblem, symbol; **14** representation.

touch 3 bit, dab, hit, jab, nip, pat, paw, pet, rub, tad, tap; **4** abut, dash, drop, feel, grab, grip, hint, hold, join, kick, kiss, link, maul, meet, move, poke, prod, pull, skim, slap, stir; **5** brush, catch, elbow, equal, flair, flick, goose, grasp, graze, grope, judge, knack, knead, knock, match, nudge, pinch, pluck, press, punch, rival, seize, shave, smash, stick, style, trace, tweak, upset; **6** adjoin, affect, border, caress, clutch, collar, fiddle, finger, fondle, fumble, handle, little, nuzzle, snatch, strike, stroke, talent, tickle, tinker, twitch; **7** ability, connect, contact, feeling, impress, massage, overlap, palpate, reality, soupçon, tactile, texture; **8** converge, esthesia, facility, football, maneuver, pressure, solidity; **9** aesthesis, intersect, sensation, tactility, vibration; **10** buttonhole, impression, manipulate; **11** consistency, palpability, sensitivity, tangibility; **12** concreteness; PHRASES: **3, 4** toy with; **3, 5** rub noses; **3, 5, 2** lay hands on; **4, 2** feel up, hold on, pick up; **4, 4** play with; **4, 4, 7** come into contact; **4, 5, 2** come close to; **6, 4** fiddle with, tamper with, tinker with; **7, 4** compete with.

touching 3 sad; **6** tender; **7** emotive, pitiful; **8** adjacent, glancing, poignant; **9** colliding, emotional; **10** contiguous, osteopathy; **11** interfacing; **12** chiropractic, heartrending; **13** heartbreaking; PHRASES: **4-2-4** hand-in-hand; **4-2-5** hand-in-glove; **6, 2, 2, 5** laying on of hands; **8, 7** physical contact. *See also* **touch**

touchy 3 raw; **4** sore; **5** cross, huffy, moody, sulky, testy; **6** grumpy, tetchy; **8** petulant; **9** impatient, irascible, irritable, sensitive; **12** cantankerous; PHRASES: **3-8** bad-tempered.

tough 4 firm, hard, hood, taut; **5** boned, chewy, hardy, harsh, rigid, rough, solid, stark, stern, stiff, tense, tight; **6** robust, rugged, severe, strict, strong, sturdy, taxing, tricky; **7** adamant, arduous, durable, fibrous, gristly, lasting, rubbery, starchy, stringy, testing; **8** daunting, exacting, gangster, leathery, muscular, starched, unsprung; **9** bombproof, dangerous, demanding, difficult, fireproof, inelastic, pokerlike, resilient, resistant, resisting, strenuous, stringent, unbending, unrelaxed; **10** hardheaded, inflexible, shockproof, untearable, whaleboned; **11** bulletproof, challenging, independent, infrangible, threatening, unbreakable; **12** indigestible, nonbreakable, shatterproof; **13** fractureproof, unshatterable; **14** indestructible, uncompromising; PHRASES: **4-5** chip-proof, rock-solid; **4-7** hard-hitting, hard-wearing, long-lasting; **5, 2, 1, 5** stiff as a board, stiff as a poker; **5, 2, 1, 6** stiff as a ramrod; **5, 2, 7** stiff as buckram; **6-5** muscle-bound.

toughen 3 tan; **6** anneal, harden, temper; **9** bombproof, fireproof, mercerize, ruggedize, vulcanize; **10** strengthen; **11** bulletproof; **12** shatterproof; PHRASES: **4-6** caseharden.

tough thing 3 nut; **7** coconut, gristle, leather; **9** cartilage; PHRASES: **3-4, 7** air-raid shelter; **11, 4** bulletproof vest.

toupee *See* **wig**

tour 4 trip; **6** outing, safari; **7** circuit; **9** excursion; PHRASES: **5, 4** grand ~; **7, 4** mystery ~ *UK*; **7-4, 4** whistle-stop ~.

tourist *See* **traveler**

tournament *See* **contest**

tourniquet 4 band; **5** strap; **7** bandage.

tousle 6 ruffle, rumple, tangle; **8** dishevel, disorder.

tout 4 hype, push; **6** flaunt, hawker, seller, vendor; **7** peddler; **9** advertise.

tow 3 lug, tug; **4** drag, draw, haul, pull.

towel 3 dab, dry; **4** wipe; **5** cloth; PHRASES: **3, 4** rub down; **4, 5** bath ~, hand ~.

tower 3 top, tug; **4** keep, loom, peel, rise, silo, soar; **5** broch *UK*, excel, outdo, spire; **6** belfry, donjon, exceed, nuragh, pagoda, turret; **7** bastion, command, minaret, mirador, overtop, surpass, tractor, tugboat; **8** barbican *UK*, Bastille, dominate, outclass, outstrip, overlook, surmount, ziggurat; **9** belvedere, campanile, transcend; **10** lighthouse, overshadow, skyscraper; PHRASES: **4, 5** rise above, shot ~; **5, 2, 5** ~ of Babel; **5, 5** clock ~, ivory ~, watch ~, water ~; **6, 5** Bloody T~, Eiffel T~; **7, 5** control ~, cooling ~; **8, 5** Martello ~, Victoria T~; **9, 5** Blackpool T~.

town 4 burg, city; **5** burgh; **7** borough; **9** community, townhouse; **10** metropolis, settlement; **11** megalopolis; **12** municipality; PHRASES: **3, 4** cow ~, new ~; **4, 4** boom ~, Cape T~, city hall, post ~, ~ hall, twin ~ *UK*; **4, 5** ~ clerk, ~ crier; **4, 7** ~ meeting; **5-2, 4** built-up area; **5, 4** ghost ~, urban area; **6, 4** county seat, county ~, garden city *UK*, market ~; **7, 4** country ~. *See also* **city**

townsperson 3 cit; **6** townee *UK*; **7** burgess, burgher, citizen, oppidan, slicker; **8** commuter, urbanite; **9** townsfolk; **10** townswoman; **11** suburbanite, townspeople; **12** metropolitan; PHRASES: **4, 7** city dweller, city slicker, town dweller.

toxic 6 deadly, lethal, septic; **7** noxious; **8** mephitic, poisoned, polluted, venomous; **9** pestilent, poisonous; **12** contaminated; PHRASES: **4-5** germ-laden.

toxin *See* **poison**

toxophilite 4 Eros; **6** archer.

toy 3 top; **4** doll, gonk, play, yoyo; **5** dally, dolly, golly, teddy; **6** bauble, dandle, gewgaw, rattle, trifle; **9** bagatelle, plaything, whirligig; **10** knickknack.

trace 3 bit, tug; **4** atom, copy, dash, draw, drop, find, hint, mark, sign; **5** tinge, touch, track, trail; **6** follow, leader, locate, sketch; **7** outline, remnant, residue, smidgen, vestige; **8** discover, evidence; **10** indication, smattering, suggestion; PHRASES: **3, 3** map out; **3, 4** pin down; **4, 3** mark out; **4, 4** hunt down; **5, 4** track down.

track 3 dog, row, rut, way; **4** hunt, lane, line, path, rail, road, song, spur; **5** chase, marks, orbit, print, route, scent, spoor, stalk, trace, trail; **6** course, follow, groove, pursue, siding, signal; **7** pathway, roadway; **8** footpath; **9** footsteps, sidetrack; **10** footprints, trajectory; PHRASES: **3, 5** paw marks; **4, 4** down line, hunt down, main line; **4, 5** hoof marks; **6, 4** branch line.

track events 3 leg, run; **4** heat, lane, race, walk; **5** baton, final, start; **6** hurdle, racing *UK*, sprint; **7** barrier, hurdles, running, walking; **8** obstacle; **9** finishing, sprinting; **10** changeover; **11** racewalking; **12** acceleration, steeplechase; PHRASES: **2-4, 4** 50-yard dash; **5, 4** relay race, water jump; **5, 5** false start; **5, 8** baton changing; **6, 4** sprint race; **6, 5, 4** medley relay race.

trackman 7 lineman; **10** platelayer *UK*.

tract 4 area, zone; **7** article, leaflet; **8** pamphlet, treatise; **9** territory.

trade 3 job; 4 deal, push, sell, swap; 5 craft, fence, float, skill, truck; 6 barter, dicker, export, handle, import, market, métier, peddle; 7 bargain, dealing, jobbing *UK*, operate, patrons, promote, smuggle, trading, traffic; 8 agiotage, business, carriage, commerce, dealings, exchange, industry, transact, vocation; 9 arbitrage, brokerage, brokering, clientele, customers, factorage, intervene, negotiate, patronage, profiteer, racketeer, smuggling; 10 acceptance, employment, factorship, occupation, profession; 11 incorporate, merchandise, trafficking, transaction; 12 profiteering, profitmaking, prostitution, racketeering, transactions; 13 commercialize, merchandising; PHRASES: 2, 8 do business; 3, 3, 4 buy and sell; 3, 5 rag ~; 4, 2 deal in, sell to; 4, 2, 4 line of work; 4, 4 deal with, turn over; 4, 5 free ~; 4, 8 fair exchange; 5, 4 ~ name, ~ wind; 5, 5 slave ~, ~ cycle, ~ union *UK*; 5, 6 black market, ~ secret; 5, 7 black economy; 5-7 share-pushing, stock-jobbing; 5, 8 ~ discount; 7, 2, 4 payment in kind; 8, 2, 5 exchange of goods; 8, 4 business deal.

trademark 4 logo; 5 brand, facet, trait; 6 emblem, symbol; 7 feature; 9 attribute; 14 characteristic.

trader 5 agent, buyer, fence; 6 broker, dealer, jobber, seller, vendor; 7 haggler; 8 barterer, exporter, importer, marketer, merchant, retailer *UK*; 9 profiteer, purchaser, racketeer; 10 negotiator, speculator, wholesaler; 11 businessman, distributor, stockbroker; 12 merchandiser; 13 businesswoman; PHRASES: 5, 6 white knight; 5-6 horse-trader, stock-jobber; 6, 5 market maker.

tradition 3 law; 4 form, lore, myth, rite; 5 habit, rules, Sunna, taboo; 6 belief, custom, legend, praxis, ritual, symbol, Talmud; 7 conduct, manners, Mishnah; 8 behavior, folklore, folksong, practice, protocol; 9 archetype, etiquette, formality, mythology, precedent; 10 consuetude, convention; 11 institution; 12 prescription; PHRASES: 3, 4, 5 the done thing; 9, 3 unwritten law.

traditional 3 old; 4 trad *UK*; 5 fixed, usual; 6 square; 8 accepted, cautious, habitual, moderate; 9 customary; 11 established; 12 conservative, conventional, heterosexual; PHRASES: 3-9 old-fashioned; 4-7 time-honored; 4-11 long-established; 8-4 buttoned-down.

traduce *See* **criticize**

traffic 3 run; 5 trade, truck; 6 handle, market, travel; 7 operate, smuggle; 8 business, commerce, dealings, movement, transfer; 9 transport; 11 circulation; 12 negotiations, transactions; 14 transportation; PHRASES: 2, 8 do business; 3, 3, 4 buy and sell; 4, 2 deal in; 4-4, 7 rush-hour ~; 4, 7 road ~; 5, 2 trade in; 5, 3, 6 toing and froing; 6, 2, 7 stream of ~; 7, 3 ~ cop, ~ jam; 7, 4 ~ flow; 7, 5 ~ light; 7, 6 ~ island, ~ warden; 8, 7 commuter ~.

traffic circle 8 junction; 10 crossroads; 12 intersection; PHRASES: 7, 6 traffic island; 7, 8 traffic junction.

traffic controller 9 metermaid; PHRASES: 4, 6 road patrol; 7, 3 traffic cop; 7, 6 traffic police, traffic warden; 7, 8 traffic engineer.

tragedy 6 buskin, hubris; 8 calamity, disaster, hamartia *Gk*; 9 catharsis, cothurnus, melodrama, Melpomene; 10 heartbreak, misfortune; 11 catastrophe, tragicomedy; PHRASES: 4, 7 high ~; 5, 7 Greek ~; 6, 4 tragic flaw, tragic muse; 7, 7 revenge ~, Senecan ~; 8, 7 domestic ~, Jacobean ~, romantic ~.

tragic 3 sad; 5 awful, comic, hammy; 7 miscast; 8 buskined, dreadful, farcical, romantic, terrible, typecast, wretched; 9 appalling, burlesque, cathartic, slapstick; 10 disastrous, knockabout, tragicomic; 11 sensational, unfortunate; 12 catastrophic, heartrending, vaudevillian; 13 heartbreaking, stereotypical; PHRASES: 6, 2 hammed up.

trail 5 Bruce, Cohos; 7 Buckeye, Freedom, Seaways; 8 Iditarod; 9 trailside, Tuscarora; 10 Wonderland; 11 Appalachian; 13 Susquehannock; PHRASES: 1, 3, 1, 5 C and O Canal; 3, 3 Ice Age; 4, 5, 8 East Coast Greenway; 4, 6 Long Island; 4, 8, 2, 4 Juan Bautista de Anza; 5, 3, 5 Lewis and Clark; 5, 3, 9 Civil War Discovery; 5-6 Trans-Canada; 5, 7 Great Western, North Country; 5, 9 Ozark Highlands; 6, 8 Unicoi Turnpike; 7, 5 Pacific Crest; 8-5 Hatfield-McCoy; 8, 5-2-5 Michigan Shore-to-Shore; 8, 6 Cascadia Marine, Superior Hiking; 8, 9 American Discovery; 9, 5 Sheltowee Trace; 10, 8 Undergound Railroad; 11, 5 Mississippi River; 11, 6 Continental Divide; 13, 7 International Express. *See* **track**

trailer 9 campervan; PHRASES: 6, 4 mobile home.

train 2 RY; 3 aim, dog; 4 file, line, tail; 5 bogie, chain, coach, focus, guide, point, teach, tutor, wagon; 6 convoy, direct, school, series, string; 7 drawbar, educate, express, freight, prepare; 8 coupling, exercise, instruct, practice, sequence; 10 procession, succession; 11 progression; PHRASES: 4, 2, 5 keep in shape; 4, 3 keep fit *UK*, work out; 4, 5 boat ~, gear ~, mail ~, milk ~, slow ~; 5, 4 night mail; 5, 5 goods ~, gravy ~; 6, 6 double header; 7, 5 freight ~; 8, 5 stopping ~; 9, 5 passenger ~.

training 5 drill; 7 tuition; 8 exercise, guidance, teaching; 9 education, schooling; 11 instruction, preparation; PHRASES: 4, 3 keep fit *UK*.

traitor 3 rat, spy; 5 Judas, snake; 6 Brutus; 7 serpent, trimmer; 8 betrayer, defector, deserter, informer, quisling, turncoat; 10 timeserver, treasonist; 11 archtraitor, conspirator; 12 collaborator; PHRASES: 5, 2, 3, 5 snake in the grass; 5, 8 Judas Iscariot; 6, 5 double agent; 6-6 double-dealer; 6-7 double-crosser; 8, 6 Benedict Arnold.

trajectory *See* **route**

tram 9 streetcar.

tramp 4 hike, hobo, trek; 5 march, tromp; 6 beggar, trudge; 7 traipse, vagrant; 8 vagabond; PHRASES: 8, 6 homeless person.

trample *See* **crush**

trance 4 daze; 5 dream, fugue, sleep, spell; 6 stupor; 7 amnesia, aphasia, aphonia, reverie; 8 daydream; 9 catalepsy, cataplexy; 10 meditation; 11 abstraction, daydreaming; 12 sleepwalking, somnambulism; PHRASES: 5, 5 dream state, fugue state.

tranquil *See* **calm**

transaction 4 deal; 6 matter; 8 business, contract; 9 operation.

transcendent 5 great; 6 divine, moving; 7 blessed, perfect, sublime, supreme; 8 heavenly, mystical, superior; 9 excellent, inspiring, unequaled, unlimited, unmatched, uplifting; 10 unconfined; 11 enlightened; 12 otherworldly, supernatural; 13 inspirational; 14 transcendental; PHRASES: 3-9 awe-inspiring.

transcendental 6 divine; 7 perfect; 8 heavenly, mystical; 9 uplifting; 12 otherworldly, supernatural; 13 inspirational; PHRASES: 3-9 awe-inspiring.

transcript *See* **text**

transfer 4 gift, move, pass, sale, swap; 5 decal, shift, trade; 6 assign, barter, castle, convey, decant, funnel, infect, moving, remove, siphon, spread, strain, switch; 7 channel, conduct, consign, convect, devolve, diffuse, perfuse, radiate, removal, shuffle; 8 delivery, disperse, exchange, handover, movement, reassign, relocate, shifting, transmit; 9 expulsion, reversion, transfuse, transpire, transport, transpose; 10 allocation, assignment, bequeathal, changeover, conversion, metathesis, relegation, relocation, removement, transition, transplant, transposal; 11 contaminate, deportation, disseminate, extradition, interchange, metastasize, metathesize, transferral *UK*, translocate, transmittal; 12 displacement, resettlement, substitution, transference, transmission; 13 translocation, transmittance, transposition; 14 delocalization, metempsychosis, transmigration, transplacement; 15 transplantation; PHRASES: 4, 2 hand on, pass on; 4, 4 hand over, make over, sign over, turn over.

transfiguration *See* **transformation**

transfigure *See* **transform**

transfix 4 gore, stab; 5 spike; 7 engross; 9 fascinate, hypnotize, mesmerize, spellbind.

transform 4 mold; 5 adapt, alter, morph, shape, twist; 6 change, deform, leaven, modify, mutate, reduce, reform, render, switch; 7 convert, distort, ferment, pervert, process, remodel, reshape; 8 decorate, renovate; 9 alchemize, interpret, translate, transmute; 10 metabolize, redecorate, reorganize; 11 rationalize, reinterpret, restructure, transfigure; 12 metamorphose, misinterpret, rehabilitate, transmogrify; PHRASES: 2-7 re-educate *UK*; 4, 4 make over, turn into; 4, 4, 5 lick into shape; 5, 4 paint over, paper over; 5, 4, 5 knock into shape.

transformation 6 change; 8 dilation, makeover, mutation, rotation; 9 homothety; 10 alteration, congruence, conversion, dilatation, metabolism, projection, reflection, renovation, revolution, similitude; 11 translation; 13 metamorphosis, transmutation; 14 metempsychosis; 15 transfiguration; PHRASES: 6, 5 mirror image.

transgress 3 err, sin; 4 fall; 5 lapse, poach, squat, usurp; 6 breach, impair, infest, invade; 7 deviate, disobey, impinge, intrude, overrun, violate; 8 encroach, entrench, infringe, trespass; **9** misbehave; **10** contravene; PHRASES: **2, 5** do wrong; **2, 6** go astray; **4, 7** make inroads; **5, 2** barge in; **5, 3, 5** break the rules; **5, 6** break bounds; **7, 3, 3** violate the law.

transgression 3 sin; **5** crime, lapse; **6** breach, plague; **7** offense; **8** invasion, trespass; **9** incursion, intrusion, violation; **10** infraction, usurpation, wrongdoing; **11** infestation, misbehavior, misdemeanor; **12** disobedience, encroachment, indiscretion, infringement; **13** contravention; PHRASES: **6, 9** taking liberties.

transient 5 brief, quick, short; **6** fading, flying, sudden; **7** passing; **8** decaying, fleeting, fugitive, meteoric, unstable, volatile; **9** ephemeral, fugacious, momentary, temporary; **10** evanescent, perishable, transitory; **12** disappearing; PHRASES: **5-4** short-term; **5-5** short-lived.

transient (be transient) 3 fly, rot; **4** fade, flit, melt, pass; **5** decay; **6** vanish; **7** shatter; **8** evanesce; **9** disappear, evaporate; PHRASES: **3, 4** fly away; **4, 2, 4** come to dust; **4, 2, 5** turn to ashes; **4, 2, 6** fall to pieces; **4, 4** melt away, pass away; **4, 5** fall apart; **7, 4** crumble away.

transit *See* **transport**

transitory *See* **fleeting**

translate 4 copy, edit, move, read, sign, turn; **5** adapt, gloss, shift; **6** change, cipher, decode, encode, redact, rehash, render, reword; **7** abridge, amplify, convert, explain, restate; **8** decipher, relocate, rephrase, simplify, transfer; **9** interpret, photocopy, transform, transmute; **10** paraphrase, plagiarize, transcribe; **13** transliterate; PHRASES: **3, 1, 4** use a crib, use a pony, use a trot; **3-4** lip-read; **3, 4, 4** put into code; **3, 4, 8** use sign language.

translated 4 free; **5** loose; **6** edited, verbal; **7** decoded, literal; **8** abridged, ciphered, decoding, faithful, redacted, restated, reworded; **9** rendering, restating, rewording; **10** deciphered, exegetical; **11** hermeneutic, paraphrased; **12** epigraphical, paraphrasing; **14** transliterated; PHRASES: **4-3-4** word-for-word.

translation 3 key; **4** crib, pony, trot; **7** copying, edition, epitome, version; **8** decoding, exegesis; **9** epigraphy, exegetics, redaction, rendering, rendition, rewording; **10** abridgment, adaptation, conversion, paraphrase, plagiarism; **11** paleography, re-

statement; **12** decipherment, hermeneutics, photocopying, transumption, unscrambling; **13** amplification, transcription; **14** interpretation, simplification; **15** transliteration; PHRASES: **3-7** lip-reading; **4, 11** free ~; **9, 4** bilingual text.

translator 7 decoder; **9** converter; **10** decipherer; **11** interpreter.

translucent 4 fine, thin; **5** clear, filmy, gauzy, lucid, sheer; **6** flimsy, lucent; **7** glowing, radiant, shining; **8** gleaming, luminous, lustrous, vaporous; **9** revealing; **10** diaphanous; **11** transparent; **13** insubstantial; **15** semitransparent; PHRASES: **3-7** see-through; **4-8** open-textured.

transmission 4 show; **6** spread; **7** contact, osmosis, program; **9** broadcast, contagion, diffusion, dispersal, infection, perfusion, spreading; **10** conduction, convection, diapedesis, dispersion, metastasis, throughput; **11** decantation, transfusion; **12** transduction; **13** communication, contamination, dissemination, transpiration.

transmit 3 air; **4** pipe, send; **5** relay; **6** convey, impart, spread; **7** consign, forward, gearbox, radiate; **8** dispatch, telecast, televize, transfer; **9** broadcast, circulate, propagate; **11** communicate, disseminate.

transparency 4 shot; **5** photo, slide; **6** purity; **7** clarity; **8** lucidity, openness; **9** cleanness, clearness, filminess, limpidity, plainness, sheerness; **10** candidness, directness, glassiness, limpidness, photograph, simplicity, vitreosity, wateriness; **11** obviousness, pellucidity; **12** pellucidness, translucence, vitreousness; **13** cloudlessness, colorlessness, crystallinity; **15** intelligibility, unambiguousness, unmistakability.

transparent 4 pure; **5** clear, plain; **6** glassy, limpid, liquid, patent, watery; **7** blatant, crystal, evident, hyaline, obvious, visible; **8** apparent, dioptric, pellucid, vitreous; **9** clarified, cloudless, colorless, unclouded; **10** diaphanous, refractive; **11** crystalline, translucent; **12** transpicuous, unobstructed; **13** nonreflective; **14** understandable; PHRASES: **3-7** see-through; **7, 5** crystal clear.

transparent thing 3 air, ice, net; **4** film, haze, lace, lens, mist; **5** gauze, glass, scrim, slide, smoke, vapor, voile, water; **6** hyalin, muslin, window; **7** chiffon, glasses, hyalite, organdy, organza, Perspex™, tiffany; **8** eyeglass, gossamer, negative, organdie, showcase; **9** clingfilm *UK*; **10** Cellophane™, glasshouse *UK*, greenhouse, Plexiglass™, spectacles; **12** conservatory, transparency; PHRASES: **5, 4** glass case *UK*; **5, 5** watch glass; **5, 6** sheer fabric, store window; **5, 7** clear varnish; **6, 4** bubble pack; **6, 8** window envelope; **7, 4** blister pack, crystal ball, display case, plastic wrap; **8, 4** goldfish bowl.

transpire *See* **happen**

transplant **4** move; **5** shift; **6** remove; **8** relocate, transfer.

transport **3** fit, fly, joy, lug; **4** bear, haul, hump, lift, load, move, pack, push, rail, ride, road, send, ship, sled, take, tote, waft, wing; **5** bring, carry, ferry, heave, remit, spasm, whisk; **6** convey, export, import, propel, remove, reship, schlep, unload; **7** airlift, commute, consign, delight, deliver, ecstasy, forward; **8** dispatch, expedite, transfer, transmit; **9** enrapture, manhandle, transship; **10** distribute; **14** transportation.

transport (by animal) **4** dray; **5** horse; **6** riding; **8** carriage; **9** carthorse *UK*, packhorse; PHRASES: **4, 5** mule train; **4, 6** pack animal; **4, 7** pony express; **5, 5** draft horse, wagon train; **5, 6** draft animal; **8, 5** dispatch rider *UK*.

transport (means of transport) **8** elevator, sidewalk; **9** escalator; **10** travolator *UK*; **12** rollerblades; PHRASES: **5, 6** cargo vessel; **5, 7** tramp steamer; **6, 6** roller skates; **6, 8** moving pavement; **7, 5** freight train; **8, 4** conveyor belt. *See also* **vehicle**

transportation **3** air, bus, car; **4** boat, cart, raft, rail, ship, sled, waft; **5** barge, carry, ferry, truck, water; **6** bridge, export, import, sledge *UK*; **7** airlift, cartage, carting, drayage, freight, haulage, hauling, humping, loading, mailing, passage, portage, posting, sending, transit, vection, vecture, vehicle, waftage; **8** carriage, delivery, dispatch, ferriage, handover, shipment, shipping, truckage; **9** commuting, porterage, transport *UK*, unloading, waggonage; **10** conveyance, expressage, forwarding, freightage, lighterage, telpherage, transition; **11** asportation, exportation, importation, vectitation; **12** distribution, transference; **13** palletization, transshipment; **16** containerization; PHRASES: **3, 7** air express, air freight; **7, 7** railway express.

transported thing **4** load, mail; **5** cargo, goods; **6** pallet; **7** baggage, freight, luggage, payload; **8** contents, shipment; **9** container; **11** consignment.

transporter *See* **carrier**

transpose **4** move; **5** alter; **6** invert, switch; **7** reorder; **8** transfer; **9** rearrange.

transposition **6** switch; **8** exchange, reversal; **9** inversion, recasting; **10** relocation, reordering; **12** substitution; **13** rearrangement.

transubstantiation *See* **conversion**

trap **3** con, gig, gin, gob *UK*, net, pit, web; **4** dupe, mine, ploy, reef, rock, ruse, sand, snag; **5** abyss, block, catch, chasm, decoy, mouth, setup, shoal, snare, trick; **6** ambush, bunker, corner, danger, entrap, hazard, kisser; **7** confine, deceive, dogcart, ensnare, pitfall, springe; **8** artifice, cakehole *UK*, carriage, deadfall, firetrap, flypaper, inveigle, obstacle, quagmire, surprise; **9** deathtrap, deception, minefield, quicksand, stratagem; **10** subterfuge; PHRASES: **3, 2** set up; **3, 2, 4** lie in wait; **3, 4** fly ~; **4, 2** lock in, shut in, take in; **4, 2, 8** take by surprise; **4, 3** sand bar, thin ice; **4, 4** tank ~, time bomb, ~ door; **4, 8** make mischief, pons asinorum; **5, 2** fence in; **5-2** catch-22; **5, 3** catch out; **5, 4** booby ~; **5, 8** catch unawares; **6, 3** powder keg; **7, 4** poverty ~ *UK*; **7, 5** dragon's teeth.

trappings **4** trap; **6** frills; **7** housing, symbols; **9** trimmings; **11** accessories; **13** accouterments, paraphernalia.

trash **3** pan; **4** ruin; **5** smash, wreck; **6** damage, drivel; **7** destroy, garbage, rubbish *UK*; **8** nonsense; **9** gibberish; PHRASES: **6, 4** double talk.

travel **2** go; **3** fly, ply; **4** hike, move, roam, rove, sail, tour, trek, wend; **5** drift, drive, motor, range, tramp; **6** cruise, voyage, wander; **7** commute, journey, migrate, proceed; **8** backpack, progress; **9** bushwhack, globetrot.

traveler **3** rep; **4** fare, hobo; **5** gipsy, gypsy, nomad, tramp; **7** migrant, pilgrim, tourist, tripper, tsigane, vagrant, voyager; **8** explorer, gadabout, motorist, wanderer, wayfarer; **9** itinerant, jetsetter, passenger; **10** backpacker; **12** excursionist, globetrotter; PHRASES: **6, 8** fellow ~.

traveling **6** mobile, moving; **7** migrant, nomadic, vagrant; **8** drifting, portable; **9** itinerant, migratory, wandering; **11** peripatetic.

traverse *See* **cross**

trawl **4** fish, hunt, scan, sift; **6** search; **7**

rummage; **13** investigation; PHRASES: **2, 7** go fishing; **5, 4** catch fish; **7, 6** rummage around.

tray 5 plate; **6** salver; **7** platter; **9** container; **10** receptacle; PHRASES: **2-4** in-tray; **3-4** out-tray *UK*; **7, 4** serving dish.

treacherous 5 dodgy *UK*, false, risky; **6** shifty, unsafe; **7** unsound; **8** disloyal, perilous, unstable; **9** betraying, dangerous, deceitful, faithless, hazardous, underhand; **10** inconstant, perfidious, precarious, traitorous, treasonous, unfaithful; **11** duplicitous; **13** untrustworthy; PHRASES: **3-5** two-faced; **5-7** false-hearted; **6-7** double-dealing; **6-8** double-crossing.

treachery 6 deceit; **7** treason; **8** sedition; **13** deceitfulness.

tread 4 pace, step, walk; **5** crush, stamp, stomp, tramp; **6** squash, stride; **7** flatten, trample; **8** footfall, footstep.

treason 8 betrayal, sedition; **9** treachery; **10** disloyalty, subversion.

treasure 3 gem; **4** star; **5** adore, money, pearl, prize, value; **6** riches, wealth; **7** cherish, paragon; **9** valuables.

treasurer 2 TR; **5** payer; **6** banker, bursar, minter, purser, teller; **7** almoner, cashier, steward, trustee; **8** quaestor; **9** consignee, financier, paymaster; **10** accountant, bookkeeper, controller, depositary; **11** stakeholder; PHRASES: **4, 6** mint master.

treasury 3 tag; **4** bank, bill, fund, safe; **5** store; **6** coffer; **7** almonry, bursary; **8** reserves; **9** exchequer, strongbox; **10** depository, strongroom; **13** countinghouse; PHRASES: **4, 2, 7** Bank of England; **4, 3** cash box; **5, 4** piggy bank; **6, 5** custom house, public money, public purse; **7, 4** savings bank; **8, 3** ~ tag *UK*; **8, 4** clearing bank, merchant bank, ~ bill, ~ bond, ~ note; **8, 5** treasure house.

treat 3 dye, set; **4** bind, cure, dope, dose, draw, drug, fill, gift, give, good, heal, pull, stop, tend, wash; **5** bleed, bonus, crown, dress, goody, nurse, purge, spoil; **6** advise, attend, bleach, doctor, drench, foment, handle, inject, luxury, pamper, pander, parley, physic, purify, regard, remedy, revive, toward, trepan; **7** bandage, control, curette, delight, discuss, extract, gratify, indulge, massage, operate, perfuse, plaster, process, staunch; **8** amputate, consider, delicacy, immunize, medicate, minister, pleasure,

poultice, sanitate, splendid, trephine; **9** cauterize, disinfect, entertain, inoculate, negotiate, prescribe, preshrink, rubberize, Sanforize™, sterilize, transfuse, vaccinate, vulcanize; **10** flameproof, indulgence, manipulate, pasteurize, waterproof; **11** hospitalize, showerproof *UK*; **12** anaesthetize, extravagance, phlebotomize; **13** antisepticize; PHRASES: **2, 9, 4** be concerned with; **3, 3** pay for; **3-3** tie-dye; **3, 3, 4** pay the bill; **4, 1, 4, 2** make a fuss of; **4, 2** take up, talk of; **4, 2, 3, 3** pick up the tab; **4, 2, 3, 5** pick up the check; **4, 3** care for; **4-3** Band-Aid; **4, 4** deal with, talk over; **4, 4, 2** take care of; **4, 5** talk about; **5, 2** think of, touch on; **6, 7** behave towards *UK*; **8, 2** minister to.

treatise *See* **dissertation**

treatment 4 boot, care, cure; **5** usage; **6** remedy; **7** conduct, control, dealing, healing, nursing, surgery, therapy; **8** analysis, behavior, guidance, handling, leniency, severity; **9** diplomacy, direction, operation, technique; **10** counseling, discipline, leadership, management, regulation; **11** arrangement, composition, supervision; **12** manipulation, organization, prescription, transactions; **13** draftsmanship, masterminding, orchestration; **14** administration, rehabilitation; PHRASES: **3, 6** kid gloves; **4, 2, 3, 3** kick in the ass; **4, 2, 3, 5** kick in the pants; **4, 4** iron hand; **5, 8** rough handling; **6, 5** velvet glove. *See also* **therapy**

treaty *See* **agreement**

treble 4 high; **6** piping, shrill; PHRASES: **4-7** high-pitched. *See also* **triple**

tree 4 bush, palm; **5** shrub, stool; **6** bonsai, maiden; **7** conifer, coppice, diagram, fruiter, graphic, pollard, pyramid, sapling; **8** hardwood, softwood, standard; **9** broadleaf, deciduous, evergreen, hierarchy; **10** ornamental; PHRASES: **3, 4** fan palm; **4, 4** ~ fern; **4, 6** ~ mallow; **4, 7** ~ diagram; **5, 4** dwarf ~, fruit ~, shade ~; **6, 4** bonsai ~, family ~, timber ~; **7, 4** amenity ~, feather palm; **8, 4** specimen ~; **9, 4** Christmas ~, deciduous ~; **10, 4** coniferous ~; **11, 4** broadleaved ~. *See also* **trees and shrubs**

tree disease 4 rust, wilt; **6** blight, canker, mildew, mosaic, mottle; **7** dieback; **11** defoliation; PHRASES: **3, 4** oak gall; **3, 5** oak apple; **4, 3** butt rot, soft rot; **4, 4** leaf cast, leaf curl, ring spot; **5, 3** heart rot; **5, 3, 7** Dutch elm disease; **5, 4** crown gall; **6, 3** pocket rot; **6, 4** needle cast; **7, 5** witches' broom.

tree-of-heaven 9 ailanthus.

tree part 4 bole, burl, burr, cone, fork, knot, leaf, limb, snag, spur, twig; **5** bough, crown, gnarl, stump, trunk; **6** branch, collar, crutch, leader, needle; PHRASES: 3, 4 fir cone; **4, 4** palm leaf, pine cone; **4, 5** palm frond, tree stump; **4, 6** pine needle.

tree product 3 gum, oil, wax; **4** nuts; **5** fruit, resin; **6** rubber; PHRASES: 3, 10 gum turpentine *UK*; **4, 3** palm oil, pine tar, wood tar; **4, 4** wood coal; **4, 5** wood pitch, wood sugar; **4, 6** wood spirit; **4, 7** wood alcohol, wood vinegar; **8, 3** pinewood oil.

trees and shrubs 3 ash, box, elm, fig, fir, may, oak, tea, yew; **4** acer, anil, coca, date, kava, kola, nipa, palm, pine, sloe, teak; **5** alder, aspen, balsa, beech, birch, broom, cacao, caper, cedar, ebony, elder, erica, furze, gorse, hazel, heath, holly, karri *UK*, larch, lilac, maple, orach, osier, papaw, pecan, rowan, salal, savin, wahoo, yucca; **6** acacia, azalea, bamboo, banyan, baobab, bonsai, cassia, daphne, datura, deodar, derris, durian, ginkgo, gomuti, jarrah, jinbul, jojoba, jujube, kalmia, laurel, locust, mimosa, moolar, myrtle, nutmeg, orache, poplar, privet, protea, redbud, sallow, salvia, sappan, spirea, spruce, tupelo, willow; **7** amboyna, arbutus, bebeeru, buckeye, catalpa, cypress, dogwood, durmast, fuchsia, heather, hemlock, hickory, jasmine, juniper, madroña, mugwort, palmyra, redwood, rhodora, rosebay, sequoia, soursop, syringa; **8** barberry, basswood, bayberry, berberis, bergamot, blackbox, calabash, camellia, chestnut, cinchona, coolabar, corkwood, euonymus, gardenia, guaiacum, hardhack, hawthorn, hornbeam, inkberry, ironwood, japonica, laburnum, lavender, magnolia, ninebark, oleander, quandong, rambutan, rosewood, saltbush, shagbark, sweetsop, sycamore, tamarack, tamarisk, viburnum, wisteria, woodbine, wormwood; **9** araucaria, bearberry, bitternut, blueberry, buckthorn, ceanothus, euphorbia, firethorn, forsythia, hackberry, jacaranda, kalanchoe, leadplant, mangroves, manzanita, mistletoe, mockernut, persimmon, poinciana, sagebrush, saskatoon, sassafras, satinwood, snowberry, spicebush, stinkwood, sweetwood, whitebeam *UK*; **10** arborvitae, brazilwood, buttonbush, chinquapin, chokeberry, coralberry, cottonwood, eucalyptus, frangipani,

greasewood, greenheart, hobblebush, mangosteen, poinsettia, pyracantha, sheepberry, yellowwood; **11** bitterbrush, bottlebrush, brittlebush, chaulmoogra, chokecherry, cotoneaster, leatherwood, liquidambar, phyllanthus, shittimwood, silverberry, stephanotis, winterberry; **12** checkerberry, serviceberry; **13** bougainvillea; PHRASES: 2, 4 bo tree; 2, 5, 5 St John's bread; **3, 3** red gum, red oak; **3, 4** gum tree, oil palm, red pine; **3, 5** box elder, red cedar, red maple, red osier; **3, 6** red spruce, wax myrtle; **4, 2, 6** rose of Sharon; **4-2-6** tree-of-heaven; **4, 3** blue gum, cork oak, holm oak, rock elm; **4, 4** jack pine, sago palm, tolu tree; **4, 6** bird cherry, blue spruce, mock orange; **4, 7** bald cypress, dawn redwood; **4, 11** bush honeysuckle; **5, 3** dwarf box, scrub oak, silky oak, sweet gum, white ash, white oak, withe rod; **5, 4** beach plum, carob tree, coral tree, flame tree, judas tree, kauri pine, pitch pine, plane tree, screw pine, stone pine, sugar pine, sweet fern, sweet gale, tulip tree, white pine; **5, 5** marsh elder, paper birch, sugar maple, white cedar, witch hazel; **5, 5, 6** Black Hills spruce; **5, 6** black cherry, black locust, black spruce, black walnut, honey locust, pussy willow, sitka spruce, white spruce; **5, 7** swamp cypress; **5, 8** horse chestnut, paper mulberry; **6, 3** balsam fir, poison ivy, willow oak; **6, 4** coffee tree, devil's club, dragon tree, golden rain, Joshua tree, pagoda tree *UK*, raffia palm, rubber tree; **6, 5** golden chain *UK*, pencil cedar, silver maple, yellow birch; **6, 6** balsam poplar, cherry laurel, temple flower; **6-6** monkey-puzzle; **6, 7** ground hemlock; **7, 3** douglas fir, Douglas fir, prickly ash; **7, 3, 5** western red cedar; **7, 4** cabbage palm, camphor tree, cypress pine *UK*, guelder rose, jumping bean, service tree, spindle tree, talipot palm; **7, 5** custard apple, incense cedar; **7, 6** peacock flower; **7, 7** western hemlock; **8, 3** American elm, chestnut oak, Labrador tea, mountain ash, slippery elm, stinking ash; **8, 4** creosote bush, cucumber tree, snowball tree, umbrella tree; **8, 5** butcher's broom, Japanese cedar, Japanese maple; **8, 6** mountain laurel; **8, 6, 4** Kentucky coffee tree; **8, 7** virginia creeper; **8, 9** highbush blueberry; **9, 4** butterfly bush, cranberry bush, lodgepole pine, ponderosa pine, toothache tree, traveler's tree, wayfaring tree; **9, 6** Jerusalem cherry; **10, 4** maidenhair tree, strawberry bush, strawberry tree, turpentine tree.

tree tomato 9 tamarillo.

trek 4 hike, walk; 5 climb, march, tramp; 6 ramble; 7 journey.

tremble 4 rock, sway; 5 quail, quake, shake, shock, waver; 6 dither, dodder, judder, quaver, quiver, shiver, tremor, twitch, wobble; 9 palpitate.

trembling 3 shy; 5 rocky, shaky, timid; 6 wobbly; 7 fearful, nervous; 8 timorous, unsteady; 9 confident, quavering, quivering, terrified, tremulous; 12 apprehensive.

tremendous *See* **great**

tremor *See* **quake**

tremulous *See* **trembling**

trench 3 sap; 5 ditch, drain; 6 dugout, furrow, gutter, trough; 7 channel; 10 trenchcoat; PHRASES: 6, 4 ~ foot; 6, 5 ~ fever, ~ knife; 6, 6 ~ mortar; 6, 7 ~ warfare.

trenchant *See* **incisive**

trend 3 fad, run; 4 mode, tend, tide; 5 craze, drift, mania, style, swing, thing, vogue; 6 course; 7 current, fashion; 8 futurism, tendency; 9 gravitate, modernism; 13 postmodernism; PHRASES: 3, 2, 5 the in thing; 3, 3 New Age; 3, 4 New Look, New Wave, the rage; 3, 4, 4 the last word; 3, 6, 5 the latest craze; 4, 7 high fashion; 8, 5 Nouvelle Vague.

trendy 2 in; 3 hip, mod; 4 chic, cool; 5 funky, natty, sharp; 6 groovy, modish, snazzy; 7 current; 8 swinging; 11 fashionable; 12 contemporary; PHRASES: 2, 7 in fashion; 4, 2 with it.

tress 4 curl, lock, tuft, wisp; 6 strand.

trestle *See* **support**

trial 4 pain, test; 5 pilot, worry; 6 appeal, assize, burden, misery, ordeal, sample, tryout *UK*; 7 anxiety, hearing, inquest, inquiry, retrial, sitting, torment, trouble, verdict; 8 audition, distress, hardship, judgment, sentence, sessions; 9 pleadings, probation, suffering; 10 assessment, difficulty, experiment; 11 examination, inquisition, prosecution, provisional, tribulation; 12 experimental, probationary; PHRASES: 5, 4 court case; 5, 6 legal action; 5-7 court-martial.

triangle 4 base, trio; 5 triad; 6 median, trigon; 7 trinity, triplet; 8 adjacent, altitude, centroid, circular, opposite; 9 spherical, threesome; 10 hypotenuse; 11 orthocenter; PHRASES: 5, 8 right ~; 6, 8 median ~; 7, 8 Bermuda ~, eternal ~, scalene ~.

triangular 7 deltoid; 10 trilateral; PHRASES: 5-5 three-sided; 5-6 wedge-shaped; 5-8 three-cornered.

tribe 4 clan; 6 family, people; 7 society; 9 community; 10 population; PHRASES: 6, 5 ethnic group.

tribunal 3 bar; 4 body; 5 bench, board, court, forum, panel; 6 throne; 7 council; 8 ecclesia, wardmote *UK*, woolsack; 9 Areopagus, committee; 10 electorate, judicatory; 12 confessional; PHRASES: 3, 2, 7 bar of justice; 3, 5 law court; 3, 6 vox populi; 5, 2, 3 court of law; 5, 2, 6 panel of judges; 5, 3, 4 judge and jury; 6, 7 public opinion; 8, 3 Judgment Day; 8, 4 judgment seat.

tributary 3 arm; 5 river; 6 branch, stream; 8 offshoot.

tribute 3 fee, tax; 4 duty, levy, toll; 5 award, honor, toast; 6 esteem, eulogy, excise, health, homage, praise, reward; 7 acclaim, payment; 8 accolade; 10 compliment; 11 acclamation, testimonial; 14 acknowledgment, congratulation; PHRASES: 4, 2, 7 mark of respect.

trice *See* **instant**

trick 3 con, kid, way; 4 dupe, fake, fool, hoax, joke, mock, pass, plan, ploy, ruse, scam, sham, snow, trap, wile; 5 blind, bluff, bogus, bunco, caper, catch, cheat, dodge, false, feint, fetch, fudge, habit, joker, knack, prank, quirk, shift, skill, spoof, sting *UK*, stunt, trait; 6 befool, betray, delude, design, device, devise, diddle, divert, enmesh, entrap, gambit, outwit, scheme, secret, wheeze; 7 chicane, collude, connive, deceive, defraud, ensnare, ficelle, gimmick, mislead, pretend, sleight, swindle, wrinkle; 8 artifice, conspire, contrive, entangle, flimflam, hoodwink, maneuver, outsmart, ridicule, strategy; 9 bamboozle, deception, diversion, machinate, mannerism, stratagem, technique, victimize, whitewash; 10 artificial, circumvent, confidence, manipulate; 11 contrivance, hornswoggle, outmaneuver; 14 characteristic; PHRASES: 3-2 put-on; 3-3 rip-off; 3, 5 hat ~; 4, 1, 4, 2 make a fool of; 4, 3, 1, 4 take for a ride; 4, 3, 2 make fun of; 4, 5 gold brick; 4, 9, 2 take advantage of; 5, 3, 4 wheel and deal; 5-4, 5 three-card ~ *UK*; 5, 5 dirty ~; 6, 5 artful dodge; 6-5 double-cross; 9, 4 practical joke; 10, 5 confidence ~ *UK*.

trickery *See* **deception**

trickle *See* **drip**

trickster *See* **cheat**

tricky 3 sly; **4** wily; **5** risky; **6** artful, crafty, fiddly *UK*, thorny; **7** awkward, complex, cunning, devious; **8** delicate, scheming, slippery; **9** deceitful, difficult; **11** complicated, problematic.

trifle 3 bit, dab, jot, pin, tad, tat *UK*, toy; **4** cake, cent, damn, dime, doit, drop, dust, gaud, iota, jest, joke, junk, rush, whit; **5** chaff, curio, farce, straw, tithe, touch; **6** bauble, bawbee *UK*, button, cobweb, detail, gewgaw, jumble, little, tittle, trivia; **7** details, feather, nothing, novelty, peanuts, pudding *UK*, scratch, smidgen, trickle, trinket; **8** fleabite, fraction, frippery, gimcrack, gossamer, kickshaw, minutiae, pinprick, sideshow, twopence; **9** accessory, amusement, bagatelle, brummagem, diversion, plaything; **10** knickknack, peccadillo, triviality; **11** chickenfeed, inessential; **12** nonessential, technicality; PHRASES: **2, 5, 6** no great shakes; **2, 6** no matter; **3, 7** red herring; **4-1-4** bric-a-brac; **4, 2, 3, 5** drop in the ocean; **5, 2, 1, 6** storm in a teacup; **5, 4** small beer; **5, 6** small change; **5, 8** brass farthing, small potatoes, white elephant; **6, 3** little bit, venial sin; **6, 4** child's play; **7, 6** plugged nickel; **9, 4** practical joke.

trifling *See* **trivial**

trigger *See* **activate**

trill 5 tweet; **6** chorus, quaver, shrill, warble; **7** tremolo, vibrate, vibrato; PHRASES: **4, 2, 1, 5** sing in a round.

trim 3 cut, lop; **4** clip, file, gimp, neat, pare, peel, slim, tidy; **5** braid, dinky, dress, prune, ruche, shave; **6** dapper, fettle, spruce, svelte; **7** garnish; **8** ornament; **9** shipshape.

trimming 4 edge; **5** braid, extra, frill, ruche; **6** fringe, luxury, ribbon, ruffle; **7** flounce, gaudery; **8** feathers, frippery, furbelow, spangles; **9** adornment, garniture, sparklers; **10** decoration; **11** knickknacks; **13** accompaniment; PHRASES: **3-2** add-on; **3-4** gew-gaws.

trinket *See* **bauble**

trip 3 hop; **4** fall, skip, slip, tour; **5** caper, crash, dance, jaunt, lurch, pitch, round, spree, visit; **6** career, falter, outing, prance, sprawl, topple, totter, tumble, voyage; **7** capsize, journey, stagger, stumble; **8** overturn; **9** excursion; **10** expedition; **11** hallucinate, overbalance; PHRASES: **2, 3, 1, 6** go for a burton; **3, 4** day ~, ego ~; **4, 1, 4** take a fall; **4, 1, 6** take a tumble; **4, 2** slip up; **4, 3, 4** bite the dust; **4, 4** fall down, fall over; **4, 4, 7** lose one's footing, miss one's footing; **4, 8** fall headlong; **4, 9** fall prostrate; **5, 4** field ~; **6, 4** topple over; **6-5** spread-eagle.

tripe *See* **rubbish**

triple 4 cube; **5** boost; **6** thrice, treble; **7** augment, trifold, triplex; **8** increase, multiple; **9** threefold; **10** tripartite, triplicate; PHRASES: **5-3** three-way; **5-7** three-layered; **6, 4** ~ bond, ~ jump, ~ time; **6-6** triple-decker; **6, 7** ~ entente; **6, 8** ~ alliance.

trite 5 banal, corny, hoary, stale, tired, vapid; **7** clichéd; **8** everyday, ordinary; **9** hackneyed; **11** commonplace, predictable; **12** conventional; PHRASES: **3, 3** old hat; **3, 8** old chestnut; **4-4** time-worn.

trite saying *See* **truism**

triumph 3 joy, win; **4** coup, crow, feat, glee; **5** boast, exult, gloat, glory; **7** delight, elation, prevail, rejoice, succeed, swagger, victory; **8** conquest; **9** celebrate; **10** exultation, jubilation; **11** achievement, masterpiece; **12** masterstroke; PHRASES: **4, 2, 5** tour de force.

triumph (expression of triumph) 2 ha; **3** aha, olé; **6** hooray, hurrah; **9** cowabunga.

trivet *See* **stand**

trivial 3 bad, toy; **4** airy, blah, poor, pulp, tiny; **5** cheap, dinky, minor, petty, small, teeny, token, usual, windy; **6** flimsy, frothy, grotty, paltry, shoddy, slight, tawdry, trashy; **7** foolish, limited, minimal, nominal, puerile, shallow, useless; **8** childish, fiddling, footling, gimcrack, inferior, marginal, mediocre, niggling, nugatory, ordinary, peddling, piddling, piffling, rubbishy, smallest, symbolic, trifling, trumpery, twopenny; **9** frivolous, jerkwater, parochial, pinchbeck, technical, valueless, worthless; **10** catchpenny, diminished, immaterial, irrelevant, negligible, potboiling, uneventful; **11** commonplace, lightweight, superficial, unimportant; **12** pettifogging; **13** featherheaded, insignificant, insubstantial; **14** featherbrained, inconsiderable; **15** inconsequential; PHRASES: **2, 5, 6** no great shakes; **3-3** two-bit; **3-5** one-horse; **3-7** nit-picking; **4-3-4** five-and-dime; **4-7** poor-quality; **5-4** ricky-tick, rinky-dink, small-time, small-town, third-rate; **5-5** jerry-built, teeny-weeny; **5, 6** chump change;

6-4 parish-pump, second-rate; **6, 5** Mickey Mouse; **6-6** teensy-weensy.

trivial error 4 slip; **5** lapse; **6** miscue; **8** omission; **9** oversight; PHRASES: **4-2** slip-up; **4, 2, 3, 3** slip of the pen; **4, 2, 3, 6** slip of the tongue; **6, 6** lapsus calami; **6, 7** lapsus linguae; **8, 4** Freudian slip.

triviality 6 trifle; **7** nothing; **8** frippery; **9** flippancy, frivolity, inutility; **10** mediocrity; **11** inferiority; **12** unimportance; **13** immateriality, inconsequence; **14** insignificance, superficiality. *See also* **trivial**

Trojan 5 Paris, Priam; **6** Dardan, Hector; **8** Teucrian *UK*; PHRASES: **6, 5** T~ horse.

troll 4 fish, lure, spin, walk; **5** amble, angle, drift, trail; **6** wander; **7** saunter. *See also* **mythical or imaginary being**

troop 4 army, band, herd, move, unit; **5** crowd, guard, horde, march, rally, squad; **6** detail, gather, guards, parade, patrol, stream, throng, trudge; **7** brigade, company, militia, traipse; **9** multitude; **10** detachment.

trophy 3 cup, pot; **4** gong *UK*, palm; **5** award, crown, honor, medal, plate, prize, scalp, spurs, title; **6** garter, plaque, reward, ribbon, shield, wreath; **7** chaplet, garland, laurels; **8** citation, figurine; **9** medallion, statuette; **10** decoration; PHRASES: **3, 5** war medal; **4, 3** gold cup; **4, 5** gold medal; **4, 6** blue ribbon; **5, 2, 5** order of merit; **5, 2, 6** Croix de Guerre; **5, 2, 8** order of chivalry; **5, 5** first prize; **6, 3** loving cup, silver cup; **6, 4** cordon bleu, honors list; **6, 5** bronze medal, George Cross *UK*, silver medal; **6, 6** laurel wreath; **6, 7** victor ludorum; **6, 8** Légion d'Honneur; **8, 5** Victoria Cross.

tropical disease 4 ague, yaws; **5** fever; **6** dengue; **7** cholera, leprosy, malaria; **8** beriberi, glaucoma, trachoma; **9** frambesia; **10** ascariasis; **11** kwashiorkor; **12** bilharziasis; **14** onchocerciasis; **15** ancylostomiasis, schistosomiasis, trypanosomiasis; PHRASES: **4-4** kala-azar; **5, 4** dhobi itch; **5, 5** ebola virus, Lassa fever; **5, 9** river blindness; **6, 5** yellow fever; **6, 7** Chagas' disease; **6, 8** sleepy sickness *UK*; **7, 5** miliary fever *UK*; **7, 7** Asiatic cholera, Hansen's disease; **8, 5** malarial fever; **8, 7** hookworm disease; **9, 5** breakbone fever; **10, 5** blackwater fever.

trot 3 jog, run; **4** pace; **5** hurry; **6** scurry; **7** dogtrot, scamper; PHRASES: **6, 4** rising ~, turkey ~; **7, 4** sitting ~.

trouble 3 ado, ail, bug, ill, irk, jam, vex, woe; **4** ache, bane, care, coil, fuss, mess, pain, pest, snag, stir, work; **5** aggro *UK*, alarm, annoy, fault, hitch, hydra, stink, trial, upset, worry; **6** bother, burden, danger, effort, harass, hassle, hinder, malady, molest, pester, scrape, strife, unrest; **7** agitate, ailment, anxiety, concern, dilemma, discord, disease, disrupt, disturb, illness, perturb, problem, thought, turmoil; **8** conflict, disorder, disquiet, distress, fighting, handicap, howdyedo, irritate, nuisance, obstruct, penalize; **9** attention, complaint, condition, embarrass, interrupt, suffering; **10** contention, difficulty, discommode, discontent, disruption, misfortune; **11** disturbance, tribulation; **12** disadvantage; **13** inconvenience; PHRASES: **3, 3** put out; **4, 2, 6** make an effort; **4, 5** take pains; **5, 4** weigh down; **5, 8** exert yourself. *See also* **disease, illness**

trouble (be in trouble) 3 die; **4** fail, lose, sink, slip; **6** grieve, regret, sorrow, suffer; **7** decline, founder; **8** miscarry; **10** degenerate; **11** deteriorate; PHRASES: **2, 2, 3** go to pot; **2, 2, 3, 4** go to the dogs; **2, 2, 4, 3, 4** go to rack and ruin; **2, 3** be ill; **2, 7** be unlucky; **2, 8** go downhill; **3, 1, 3, 5** hit a bad patch; **3, 2** cop it; **3, 3, 2** run out of luck; **3, 4, 6** hit (rock) bottom; **3, 7** run aground; **4, 2, 1, 3, 3** come to a bad end; **4, 2, 4, 5** fall on hard times; **4, 2, 5** come to grief; **4, 3, 5** bear the brunt; **4, 4, 2** fall foul of; **4, 4, 5** fall from grace; **4, 4, 7** burn one's fingers; **5, 2** catch it.

troubled 5 beset, stuck, upset, vexed; **6** tricky, uneasy; **7** annoyed, anxious, awkward, baffled, plagued, puzzled, stumped, violent, worried; **8** bothered, confused, harassed *UK*; **9** concerned, difficult, disturbed, mystified, perplexed, perturbed, snookered, turbulent, unsettled; **10** bewildered, deadlocked, distressed, nonplussed; **11** embarrassed, problematic; **14** inconvenienced; PHRASES: **2, 1, 3** in a fix, in a jam; **2, 1, 4** at a loss, in a mess, up a tree; **2, 1, 5, 4** in a tight spot; **2, 1, 7** in a dilemma; **2, 1, 8** in a quandary; **2, 1, 11** in a predicament; **2, 3, 4** in the soup, on the spot; **2, 3, 5** in hot water; **2, 4, 5** in deep water; **2, 12** in difficulties; **3, 3** put out.

trouble-free *See* **easy**

troublemaker 3 imp; **4** pest; **5** scamp; **6** menace, rascal, rioter, vandal; **7** handful, hellion, stirrer *UK*; **8** agitator, hooligan, irritant, nihilist, nuisance, scalawag *UK*; **9** amorality, anarchist, firebrand, miscreant, scallywag; **PHRASES: 4, 2, 3, 3** pain in the ass; **4, 2, 3, 4** pain in the neck; **4, 2, 7** lord of misrule; **6, 6** little monkey; **6-6** rabble-rouser; **7, 5** naughty child; **8-5** mischief-maker.

troublesome 4 hard; **5** fussy, moody, rowdy; **6** taxing, trying, unruly; **7** finicky, naughty, stroppy *UK*, wayward; **8** contrary, critical, grudging, niggling, obdurate, pedantic, perverse, stubborn, worrying; **9** demanding, difficult, obstinate, upsetting, wearisome; **10** bothersome, censorious, disorderly, disruptive, fastidious, headstrong, particular, pernickety *UK*, refractory; **11** disobedient, intractable, persnickety, problematic; **12** disapproving, discontented, obstreperous, overcritical, unmanageable; **13** hypercritical, uncooperative, undisciplined; **PHRASES: 3, 2, 4** out of hand; **3-7** ill-behaved, nit-picking; **4, 2, 6** hard to please; **4, 2, 7** hard to satisfy; **5, 7** badly behaved; **5-7** fault-finding; **6-6** bloody-minded *UK*; **6, 7** beyond control.

trough 3 low; **4** crib, rack; **5** ditch; **6** furrow, gutter, holder, manger, trench; **7** channel; **10** depression.

trounce *See* **beat**

trousers 7 pistols; **8** striders; **9** buckskins, coveralls; **PHRASES: 3, 5** gym pants; **3-7** hip-huggers; **4, 5** long pants; **5, 5** short pants; **6, 5** riding pants.

Troy 5 Ilion, Ilium.

truant 3 cut; **4** AWOL, dust, flit, scat; **5** mitch *UK*, scram, shirk, skive *UK*; **6** skiver *UK*; **7** shirker; **8** absentee, defected, deserted, malinger; **9** skedaddle; **10** malingerer; **PHRASES: 2, 1, 4** do a bunk *UK*; **2, 4** go AWOL; **3, 3** bug off; **3, 3, 3** cut and run; **4, 2** beat it *UK*; **4, 3** bunk off *UK*; **4, 3, 5** quit the scene; **4, 4** jump ship, turn tail; **4, 5** play hooky; **5, 3** slope off *UK*; **6, 2, 3, 2** bottle up and go.

truck 3 HGV *UK*, van; **4** cart, semi; **5** artic, lorry *UK*, trade, wagon; **6** tipper *UK*; **7** flatbed; **7** tractor, trailer; **8** dealings; **10** connection, juggernaut *UK*; **11** transporter; **12** pantechnicon; **13** communication; **PHRASES: 3, 6** van pickup; **3-6** low-loader *UK*; **7-7** tractor-trailer.

trudge 4 haul, hike, plod, slog, trek; **5** march, tramp; **7** traipse.

true 4 firm, real, sure; **5** exact, loyal, right, total, utter, valid; **6** actual, direct, gospel, proper; **7** certain, correct, devoted, dutiful, factual, genuine, sincere, staunch; **8** accurate, Biblical, constant, faithful, official, positive, reliable, revealed, rightful, straight; **9** authentic, confirmed, dedicated, veracious, veritable; **10** conclusive, legitimate, unmistaken; **12** unfictitious; **13** authenticated; **PHRASES: 4-2** spot-on *UK*; **4, 4** bona fide; **6-2-3** honest-to-God; **7, 4** holding good, holding ~; **7, 5** holding water; **8, 2** standing up; **8, 3, 4** standing the test.

truism 3 saw; **5** adage, axiom, maxim; **6** cliché, dictum, saying; **7** bromide, precept, proverb; **8** aphorism; **9** platitude, principle; **11** commonplace; **PHRASES: 3, 8** old chestnut; **5, 6** stock phrase.

truly 4 very; **6** indeed, really, verily; **7** greatly; **8** actually, forsooth, honestly; **9** extremely, factually, genuinely, sincerely, veritably; **10** enormously, faithfully *UK*; **13** exceptionally; **PHRASES: 2, 1, 6, 2, 4** as a matter of fact; **2, 3, 7** in all honesty; **2, 4** in fact, no buts; **2, 4, 3, 5** to tell the truth; **2, 5** in truth; **2, 5, 2, 4** in point of fact; **2, 7** in reality; **4, 5** with truth; **6, 5** beyond doubt; **6-5** really-truly.

truly (yours truly) 1 I; **2** me.

trump 4 beat, ruff; **5** outdo; **7** outplay, triumph; **9** undermine; **11** outmaneuver; **PHRASES: 2, 3, 6** go one better.

truncate *See* **shorten**

trundle 4 roll; **5** labor, trail, wheel; **6** lumber, rattle; **7** saunter, traipse.

trunk 3 box, STD; **4** body, bole, bulk, case, nose, road; **5** chest, crate, snout, stock, torso; **6** coffer, valise; **9** proboscis; **11** portmanteau.

truss 3 tie; **4** bind, prop; **5** brace, joist, sheaf, strut; **6** fetter, secure, tether; **7** support; **8** buttress.

trust 5 faith; **6** belief; **7** entrust; **8** reliance; **9** assurance, certainty, certitude; **10** confidence, conviction; **PHRASES: 4, 2** bank on, rely on; **5, 2** count on; **6, 2** depend on.

trustee 5 agent; **6** deputy; **8** director, executor; **14** representative.

trusting person 6 sucker; **7** ingenue; **8** innocent.

truth 4 fact; **5** facts, sooth; **6** gospel, verity; **7** honesty, reality; **8** fidelity, trueness, veracity; **9** actuality, certainty, integrity, rightness, sincerity; **10** revelation; **11** historicity, unfalseness; **12** authenticity; **14** unmistakenness, unspeciousness, unspuriousness, verisimilitude; **15** unerroneousness; PHRASES: **3, 2, 2** how it is; **3, 3-4** the low-down; **3, 4** the case; **3, 5** the facts; **4, 4** Holy Writ; **4, 5** God's ~; **4, 6** home truths; **5, 2, 4** facts of life; **6, 3** dinkum oil *Aus and NZ.*

truthful 4 bald, open, true; **5** blunt, exact, frank, naive, plain, right; **6** candid, direct, honest, proper, simple; **7** artless, correct, factual, literal, sincere; **8** accurate, faithful, reliable, straight, unbiased; **9** downright, guileless, ingenuous, objective, outspoken, realistic, veracious, veridical; **10** forthright, unaffected, unassuming; **11** openhearted, undisguised; **12** unflattering, unpretending; **13** unexaggerated, unpretentious; **15** straightforward; PHRASES: **5, 3, 3** warts and all; **5, 5** above board.

truthfulness 5 truth; **6** candor; **7** honesty, naiveté, naivety *UK*, probity; **8** accuracy, veracity; **9** sincerity; **10** exactitude; **11** objectivity, reliability; PHRASES: **4, 2, 4** lack of bias; **4, 2, 8** lack of disguise, lack of flattery, lack of pretense. *See also* **truthful**

try 2 do, go; **3** aim, tax, vex; **4** bash *UK*, hear, seek, shot, slog, stab, test, toil, work; **5** annoy, crack, judge, labor, score, slave, sweat, taste; **6** effort, sample, strain, strive, tackle; **7** attempt, examine, persist; **8** appraise, dispatch, endeavor, evaluate, irritate, overwork, struggle; **9** frustrate, persevere, undertake; **10** exasperate, experiment; **11** concentrate; PHRASES: **2, 3, 5, 3** go the whole hog; **2, 4, 9** do one's damnedest; **3, 2, 5** put on trial; **4, 1, 2** have a go; **4, 1, 5, 2** take a crack at; **4, 2, 1, 2** give it a go *UK*; **4, 2, 5** take to court; **4, 2, 6** make an effort; **4, 4** plug away; **4, 5** take pains; **4, 8** pass judgment; **5, 3** check out; **6, 4** buckle down; **6, 7** strain oneself; **10, 4** experiment with.

TT 4 race; **8** teetotal; **9** abstainer, Rechabite *UK*; PHRASES: **7, 6** Tourist Trophy.

tub 3 pot; **4** bath, drum; **6** barrel, carton; **9** container; PHRASES: **3, 3** hot ~; **6, 4** plunge bath *UK*.

tube 3 vas; **4** duct, hose, pipe, vein; **5** metro, sieve, spout, trunk; **6** artery, subway, tunnel, ureter; **7** conduit, grommet, picture; **8** bronchus, catheter, cylinder, electron, geissler, macaroni, speaking; **9** capillary, schnorkel; **10** television; PHRASES: **4, 4** test ~; **5, 4** drift ~, inner ~, Nixie ~, Pitot ~, shock ~; **6, 4** pollen ~, static ~, vacuum ~; **7-3, 4** cathode-ray ~; **9, 4** Fallopian ~; **10, 4** Eustachian ~.

tuck 3 put; **4** dart, fold, push, slip; **5** place, pleat; **6** gather, insert, pucker.

tug 3 jig, lug, tow; **4** boat, drag, draw, flip, hale, haul, jerk, jolt, pull, warp, yank, yerk; **5** heave, hitch, kedge, pluck, tweak; **6** handle, joggle, snatch, strain, twitch, wrench.

tulip tree 9 canoewood; PHRASES: **6, 6** yellow poplar.

tumble 6, 4 ~ weed; **6, 5** ~ dryer. *See also* **trip**

tumbledown 4 worn; **5** dingy, kaput, leaky, shaky, tatty, wonky *UK*; **6** broken, rotten, ruined, slummy; **7** cracked, decayed, rickety, ruinous, tottery; **8** decrepit, derelict, unsteady, weakened; **9** condemned; **10** ramshackle; **11** dilapidated; PHRASES: **2, 3, 4, 4** on its last legs; **2, 5** in ruins; **2, 9** in disrepair; **3-4** run-down; **3, 5, 3, 4** the worse for wear; **3-8** rat-infested; **4, 3** worn out; **6, 4** broken down; **7, 2, 6** falling to pieces; **7, 5** falling apart; **7-6** weather-beaten.

tumbler 5 glass; **6** beaker, goblet; **7** acrobat; **9** voltigeur.

tummy *See* **stomach**

tumour *See* **growth**

tumult 3 din; **4** moil, rout, rush, stir; **5** chaos, fever, furor *UK*, whirl; **6** bustle, clamor, flurry, frenzy, furore *UK*, hubbub, mayhem, racket, uproar; **7** bobbery, turmoil; **8** brouhaha, disorder; **9** commotion, confusion, maelstrom; **10** excitement, hullabaloo, turbulence; **11** disturbance, tumultation; PHRASES: **5-5** hurly-burly.

tune 3 air, lay; **4** aria, song, tone; **5** adapt, motif, theme, tweak; **6** adjust, melody, number, strain; **8** moderate, regulate. *See also* **song**

tungsten 1 W.

tunic 5 gippo *UK*, kurta; **6** caftan *UK*, jerkin, kaftan *UK*, tabard; **7** shalwar, tunicle; **8** chasuble, djellaba; **10** sticharion; **11** houppelande; PHRASES: **4-6** cote-hardie; **5, 5** apron ~. *See also* **clothes**

tunnel 3 den, dig, sap; **4** bore, hole, lair, mine, sett, tube; **5** drain, earth, métro, sewer, shaft; **6** burrow, cloaca, subway *UK*, warren; **7** channel, Chunnel, culvert; **8** excavate, railroad; **9** undermine, underpass; **10** passageway; **11** underground; PHRASES: **3, 4** dig down; **3, 5** way under; **4, 6** road ~; **5, 6** bored ~; **7, 6** Channel T~, railway ~.

turban 7 puggree *UK*.

turbid 5 dirty, muddy, murky; 6 cloudy, opaque; 7 chaotic, muddled; 8 confused; 9 scrambled; 12 disorganized.

turbulence 4 boil, fume, roil, stir; 5 chaos, churn, furor *UK*, havoc, swell, swirl; 6 furore *UK*, mayhem, seethe, squall, tumult, unrest, uproar; 7 boiling, ferment, rolling, turmoil; 8 disorder, pitching, seething, violence; 9 commotion, confusion, turbidity; 10 ebullition; 11 embroilment, instability; 12 fermentation; 13 effervescence; PHRASES: 5-5 hurly-burly. *See also* **turbulent**

turbulent 4 wild; 5 bumpy, rough, rowdy, windy; 6 bouncy, choppy, fuming, raging, stormy, unruly; 7 boiling, chaotic, riotous, rolling, violent; 8 blustery, confused, pitching, restless, seething, unstable; 9 unsettled; 10 changeable, disorderly, tumultuous; 11 quarrelsome, tempestuous; 12 effervescent; PHRASES: 2, 7 in turmoil.

turf 4 beat, lawn; 5 field, grass, orbit, patch; 6 meadow; 7 pasture, verdure; 9 territory; 12 neighborhood.

Turk 3 aga, bey; 4 agha, Omar; 5 Osman, Selim; 6 bashaw; 7 effendi, Ottoman; 8 Mameluke.

turkey 4 flop; 7 gobbler.

Turkey 2 TR.

Turkish 7 Ottoman; 9 Anatolian; PHRASES: 7, 4 T~ bath; 7, 7 T~ delight, T~ tobacco.

turmoil *See* **tumult, turbulence**

turn 1 U; 2 go; 3 act, aim, fit, PTO, rev, set, try; 4 bank, bend, bout, flip, fork, jink, jolt, kick, luff, ride, roll, shot, skit, sour, spin, stem, trip, veer, wind; 5 alter, churn, crack, crank, curve, drive, favor, focus, hinge, jaunt, pivot, point, round, scare, screw, shock, spasm, spoil, start, twirl, twist, wheel; 6 become, careen, chance, change, circle, corner, curdle, detour, direct, divert, errand, fright, gyrate, invert, number, outing, rotate, zigzag; 7 Christy, convert, crankle, deflect, deviate, innings, meander, revolve, roulade, seizure, service; 8 Christie, junction, rotation, surprise, telemark; 9 cartwheel, excursion, transform; 10 recitation, revolution; 11 concentrate, opportunity, performance; 12 metamorphose; PHRASES: 2, 3 go bad, go off *UK*; 2, 4 go sour; 2, 6 go around; 4, 4 good deed, good ~; 5, 4 funny ~; 5, 5 party piece *UK*; 5-5, 4 three-point ~ *UK*; 6, 9 change direction; 7, 4 Buggins ~, quarter ~; 9, 4 Immelmann ~.

turn around 4 veer; 5 boost, pivot, wheel; 6 double, finish, return, revert, swivel; 7 improve, process, reverse; 8 complete, increase; 9 roundtrip; 10 accomplish; PHRASES: 2, 4 go back; 4, 2 bump up; 4, 2, 1, 4 turn on a dime; 4, 2, 4, 4 turn on one's heel; 4, 3, 5, 3 face the other way; 4, 4 turn back, turn tail; 4, 4, 4 turn one's back; 4, 5 come about, face about *UK*; 5-4 about-face *UK*, about-turn, volte-face; 5, 4, 4 crane one's neck; 5, 5 swing round *UK*; 5-5-4 right-about-face.

turn back 4 turn; 6 double, return; 9 remigrate; PHRASES: 2, 4 go back; 3, 4 put back; 4, 4 fold back, fold down, fold over, turn down, turn over; 6, 4 double back.

turning 4 bend, exit, ramp, turn, whir *UK*; 6 corner, spiral, swivel, torque; 7 bowling, carving, joinery, reeling, rolling, souring, torsion; 8 junction, pivoting, spinning, swirling, trolling, twirling, twisting, wheeling, whirling, whirring; 9 carpentry, spiraling, trundling; 10 volutation; 11 pirouetting, woodworking; 13 cabinetmaking; 14 centrifugation; PHRASES: 3-4 off-ramp; 5, 4 minor road.

turning point 6 crisis, divide; 9 milestone, watershed; 10 crossroads; PHRASES: 4, 2, 3, 4 turn of the tide; 6, 5 crisis point; 7, 5 crucial point, pivotal point; 7, 6 crucial moment; 8, 6 decisive moment, defining moment.

turnip 4 neep *UK*; 5 navew.

turnover, turn over 2 TO; 3 p.t.o.; 4 flip, gain, till; 5 sales, trade, upend; 6 careen, income, profit, return; 7 capsize, revenue, takings; 8 business; 9 incomings; 10 somersault, throughput; PHRASES: 6, 4 bottom line; 6, 6 profit margin.

turnstile 4 gate; 7 barrier; 8 entrance, gatepost, turnpike; PHRASES: 4, 8 park entrance; 7, 4 kissing gate *UK*.

turn up 2 PU; 4 cock, come, show; 5 occur, raise; 6 appear, arrive, happen; 7 amplify, uncover, unearth; 8 discover, increase; PHRASES: 4, 2 crop up; 4, 2, 5 come to light; 5, 2, 5 bring to light.

tussle *See* **fight**

tutelary 7 keeping; 8 guardian, guarding, hygienic, vigilant, watchful; 9 custodial, surrogate; 10 antiseptic, preserving, protecting, protective; **12** disinfectant, prophylactic, shepherdlike.

tutor *See* **teach, teacher**

twaddle *See* **nonsense**

twang 4 ping; **5** drawl, plunk; **6** accent; **7** vibrate; **10** inflection, intonation; **11** reverberate.

tweak 3 nip; **4** jerk; **5** pinch, twist; **6** adjust, modify; **7** correct; **8** regulate; PHRASES: **4-4** fine-tune.

twelfth 9 duodenary; **10** duodecimal; PHRASES: **7, 3** T~ Day, ~ man *UK*; **7, 5** T~ Night; **8, 7** Glorious T~ *UK*.

twelve 4 noon; **5** dozen; **8** midnight; **9** dodecagon, duodecimo; **10** duodecimal; **11** twelvemonth; **12** dodecahedron; PHRASES: **6, 8** ~ apostles.

twenty 4 pony; **5** score; **8** vicenary; **9** vicennial, vigesimal.

twice 3 bis; **5** again; **6** double, doubly, dually, encore; **7** twofold; PHRASES: **2, 4, 5** as much again; **3, 5** two times, yet again; **4, 4** once more; **4, 5** over again; **5, 2, 4** ~ as much; **5, 4** ~ over.

twig 4 stem; **5** shoot, stick; **6** branch.

twin(s) 4 copy, dual, join, like, link, pair; **5** alike, clone, match; **6** double, Gemini, paired, relate, ringer; **7** connect, twofold; **8** Dioscuri, matching; **9** associate, duplicate, identical, photocopy; **11** counterpart; **12** doppelgänger; PHRASES: **4, 3** twin bed; **4, 4** dead spit *UK*, twin town *UK*; **4, 5** Twin Stars; **4-5** look-alike; **4, 6** dead ringer; **6, 3, 6** Castor and Pollux; **6, 4** carbon copy; **6, 5** mirror image; **7, 3, 5** Romulus and Remus; **7, 4** Siamese twin; **7, 5** Siamese twins; **8, 5** spitting image; **9, 4** identical twin; **9, 5** fraternal twins, identical twins.

twine 4 coil, cord, loop, wind, yarn; **5** snake, twist; **6** string, thread.

twinkle *See* **gleam**

twinkling 5 flash; **6** moment, second; **7** instant; PHRASES: **5, 6** split second.

twirl 4 bend, coil, curl, loop, spin, turn, wind; **5** twist, whirl; **6** rotate, spiral; **8** rotation; **10** revolution.

twist 4 bend, coil, curl, hurt, kink, loop, pull, rick *UK*, spin, turn, warp, wind; **5** alter, crook, curve, event, screw, snake, twine, twirl, weave, whirl, wring; **6** buckle, change, damage, deform, dogleg, injure, rotate, spiral, sprain, wrench, writhe, zig-

zag; **7** contort, crumple, distort, entwine, grimace, hairpin, meander, pervert, unscrew; **8** incident, rotation, surprise; **9** deviation, variation; **10** alteration, interweave, manipulate; **11** development; **12** misrepresent; PHRASES: **5, 3, 4** ~ and turn.

twisty 5 bendy *UK*; **7** snaking, winding; **8** tortuous, twisting; **10** meandering.

twit *See* **fool**

twitch 3 bob, jig, jog, tic; **4** flip, jerk, jolt, yerk; **5** flick, flirt, hitch, shake, spasm, tweak; **6** jiggle, joggle, snatch.

twitchy *See* **nervous**

two 2 II; **3** duo, twa; **4** both, dual, duet, dyad, pair, span, team, yoke; **5** brace, deuce, duple, mated, twain, yoked; **6** bifold, binary, couple, double, duplex, dyadic, paired, second, square; **7** coupled, doubled, matched, squared, twinned, twofold, twosome; **9** bracketed, dualistic, secondary; PHRASES: **1, 4** à deux; **2, 3, 3** me and you; **2, 4** in twos; **2, 5** in pairs; **3, 2, 3** ~ by ~; **5, 3, 4** Darby and Joan.

two-part 4 AC/DC; **5** biped; **6** biform; **7** bifocal, bipedal; **8** biannual, biennial, bisexual; **9** bicameral, bifurcate, bilateral, bilingual, binocular, bipartite; **12** ambidextrous; PHRASES: **3-3** two-ply, two-way; **3-5** two-level, two-story; **3-6** two-stroke; **3-11** two-dimensional; **4-7** dual-purpose; **6-5** double-sided.

tycoon *See* **magnate**

type 3 cap, hue, ilk, key; **4** bold, cast, face, font, form, kind, line, make, mark, mode, mold, sort; **5** brand, class, color, enter, fount, frame, genre, genus, grain, input, label, print, realm, Roman, shape, stamp, style; **6** domain, italic, kidney, league, manner, marque, nature, person, sphere, strain, stripe, uncial; **7** capital, cursive, feather, species, variety, version; **8** category, keyboard, printing, typeface; **9** character, lettering, majuscule, minuscule; **10** complexion, individual, persuasion, typography; PHRASES: **3, 2** key in; **4, 4** bold ~; **5-4, 6** lower-case letter, upper-case letter; **7, 6** capital letter. *See also* **typeface**

typefaces 3 dow; **4** bell, gill, zapf; **5** aster, bembo, block, doric, erbar, folio, goudy, ionic, kabel, lotus, mitra, sabon, times; **6** aachen, adroit, auriga, becket, bodoni, bulmer, caslon, cochin, cooper, corona, fenice, futura, glypha, gothic, horley, italia, janson, lucian, melior, modern, oliver, ondine, optima, romana; **7** antique, basilia, bauhaus, bernard, bookman, bramley, candida, century, coronet, cushing, electra, floreal, imprint, iridium, korinna, lubalin, madison, memphis, neuzeit, plantin, raleigh, spartan, stempel, tiffany, univers, wexford, windsor; **8** atheneum, benguiat, berkeley, breughel, cloister, concorde, egyptian, ehrhardt, fournier, franklin, frutiger, galliard, garamond, kennerly, novarese, olympian, palatino, perpetua, rockwell, souvenir; **9** americana, barcelona, britannic, caledonia, clarendon, clearface, criterion, dominante, eurostile, excelsior, fairfield, grotesque, helvetica, worcester; **10** cheltenham, churchward, devanagari, egyptienne, leamington; **11** baskerville, copperplate; PHRASES: **3, 7** old english; **4, 5** sans serif; **5, 5** avant garde; **5, 9** trump mediaeval.

typhoon *See* **storm**

typical 5 usual; **6** normal; **7** average, classic, generic, regular, special; **8** defining, expected, ordinary, peculiar, specific, standard; **10** archetypal, definitive, emblematic, mainstream, particular; **11** distinctive, predictable; **12** conventional; **13** stereotypical; **14** characteristic, representative.

typing error 4 typo; **7** erratum, literal; **8** misprint; **11** corrigendum; PHRASES: **8, 5** clerical error, printing error.

tyrant 4 czar, Nero, tsar; **5** Herod; **6** despot; **8** autocrat, dictator; **9** oppressor; **13** authoritarian; PHRASES: **3, 2, 9** man on horseback; **7, 8** tinhorn dictator.

tyro *See* **novice**

U

U **3** you; **5** uncle, upper; **9** universal.

ugly **4** drab, dull, foul, gory, loud, sour; **5** dingy, dowdy, gaudy, gross, mousy, nasty, plain, rough, seedy, tacky; **6** coarse, common, dreary, garish, grisly, grotty, homely, horrid, shabby, tawdry, vulgar; **7** awkward, defaced, hideous, hostile, squalid, uncouth, violent; **8** deformed, dreadful, gruesome, horrible, menacing, ungainly, unlovely, unseemly; **9** contorted, dangerous, graceless, inelegant, misshapen, monstrous, mutilated, obnoxious, repulsive, revolting, tasteless, unshapely, unsightly; **10** aggressive, disfigured, indelicate, unbecoming, unesthetic, unpleasant; **11** distasteful, distressing, misbegotten, overdressed, threatening; **12** disagreeable, intimidating, meretricious, unattractive; **13** unfashionable; **15** unprepossessing; PHRASES: **2, 3, 5** in bad taste; **3, 3, 2, 2, 4** not fit to be seen; **3-7** ill-favored; **3-8** bad-tempered; **4, 4** plug ~; **5, 7** badly dressed; **6, 2, 4** common as muck.

ugly (make ugly) **4** mask, scar; **5** spoil; **6** deface, deform, impair; **7** blemish, distort; **8** misshape, mutilate; **9** disfigure.

ugly person **3** dog; **6** fright, horror, howler; **7** monster; **8** gargoyle; **9** scarecrow; PHRASES: **3, 5** old witch; **4, 9** dog's breakfast; **5, 4** pizza face.

ugly place **4** slum; **7** blemish, eyesore; **9** carbuncle.

Ulan Bator **4** Urga; **5** Kulun.

ulcer **3** pus, rot; **4** boil, corn, cyst, kibe, sore, wolf; **5** blain, decay; **6** canker, matter; **7** abscess, fistula, pustule; **8** gangrene, swelling; **9** carbuncle, chilblain, discharge, festering, gathering, purulence; **10** ulceration; **12** inflammation; PHRASES: **4, 4** soft corn.

ULT **8** ultimate; PHRASES: **2, 3, 4, 5** in the last month (Latin: ultimo).

ulterior **6** hidden, secret; **7** unknown; **9** concealed, underhand.

ultimate **3** end, key; **4** best, last; **5** basic, final, ideal; **7** maximum, primary, supreme; **8** absolute, eventual, furthest, greatest; **10** concluding, conclusive; **11** fundamental.

ultra **7** extreme, radical; **9** excessive, extremist; **13** revolutionary.

Uluru **5, 4** Ayers Rock.

Ulysses **8** Odysseus.

umbrage *See* **offense**

umbrella **4** gamp *UK*; **5** aegis, cover; **6** brolly *UK*, canopy; **7** backing, parasol, support; **8** auspices, sunshade; **9** authority, patronage; **10** protection; **11** sponsorship, supervision; PHRASES: **8, 4** ~ bird, ~ pine, ~ tree; **8, 5** ~ plant, ~ stand.

umpire **3** ref, ump; **5** judge; **7** arbiter, decider, referee; **8** linesman, overseer.

unacceptable **3** bad, off, out; **4** poor; **11** intolerable; PHRASES: **3, 2** not on *UK*. *See also* **unsatisfactory**

unaccompanied **4** Lone, solo; **5** alone, solus; **6** single; **8** solitary; PHRASES: **2, 4, 3** on one's own, on one's tod; **2, 7** by oneself.

unaccustomed **3** new, raw; **4** wild; **5** alien, fresh, green, naive, rusty; **6** callow, unripe, unused; **7** strange, untamed, untried, unusual; **8** immature, innocent, unbroken, uncommon, untaught, unwonted; **9** different, untrained; **10** uneducated, unfamiliar, unseasoned, unskillful; **12** nonobservant, unacquainted, unhabituated, uninstructed; **13** disaccustomed, inexperienced; **14** undomesticated; PHRASES: **3, 2** new to; **3, 2, 3, 5** out of the habit; **3, 2, 3, 5, 2** not in the habit of; **3, 4** not used; **3, 4, 2** not used to.

unadorned 4 bald, bare; 5 plain; 6 purist, simple; 7 ascetic, austere, prudish, spartan; 9 uncolored, unpainted, untrimmed; 10 restrained; 11 puritanical, undecorated, ungarnished, unvarnished; 12 unornamented; 13 unembellished.

unadulterated *See* **pure**

unaffected 6 modest, simple; 7 artless, genuine, natural, sincere; 9 guileless, ingenuous; 10 unassuming, unofficial; 13 unconstrained, unpretentious.

unapproachable 4 cold; 5 aloof, erect, stiff; 6 remote, touchy; 7 distant, prickly, starchy; 8 hardened; 9 obstinate, unbending, withdrawn; 10 disdainful, unfriendly, unsociable; 11 independent, standoffish; PHRASES: 4-10 self-sufficient; 5-6 stiff-necked.

unattached 4 free; 6 single; 9 separated, unmarried; 11 uncommitted.

unauthorized 7 illegal, illicit; 8 informal, unlawful; 9 irregular; 10 injudicial, unlicensed, unofficial; 11 unchartered, unstatutory, unwarranted; 12 unlegislated, unsanctioned; 13 extrajudicial.

unavoidable 7 obvious; 8 manifest; 10 inevitable, obligatory; 11 inescapable.

unaware 8 ignorant.

unbalanced 6 biased, uneven, unfair; 7 crooked, unequal; 8 deranged, lopsided, unhinged, unstable; 9 disturbed; 10 prejudiced; 11 inequitable; PHRASES: 3-5 one-sided, top-heavy.

unbecoming *See* **improper**

unbelief 6 heresy; 7 atheism; 8 paganism; 9 misbelief, nonbelief; 10 heathenism, infidelity, irreligion, skepticism; 11 agnosticism, incredulity; PHRASES: 4, 2, 5 loss of faith.

unbelievable 4 tall; 5 great, weird; 6 superb, unreal; 7 amazing, bizarre, dubious; 8 doubtful, enormous, fabulous, fanciful, mystical, unlikely; 9 excellent, fantastic, ineffable, wonderful; 10 improbable, incredible, miraculous, mysterious, prodigious, staggering, suspicious, tremendous; 11 astonishing, implausible; 12 preposterous, questionable; 13 extraordinary; PHRASES: 3-7 far-fetched; 4-8 mind-boggling; 6, 6 beyond belief.

unbeliever 7 atheist, doubter, skeptic; 8 agnostic; 11 freethinker, nonbeliever.

unbiased *See* **impartial**

unbowed 5 proud; 6 raised, reared; 7 defiant, raising, rampant, rearing; 8 fearless, resolved, stubborn, unafraid, unbeaten, upraised, upreared; 9 undaunted; 10 determined, relentless, undefeated, unyielding; PHRASES: 6, 2 cocked up; 7, 2 pricked up.

unbridled *See* **unrestrained**

uncanny *See* **weird**

uncertain 4 iffy, moot; 5 vague; 6 unsure; 7 dubious, inexact, unclear, unknown; 8 agnostic, doubtful, hesitant; 9 ambiguous, skeptical, tentative, undecided, undefined; 10 changeable, disputable, indecisive, indefinite, suspicious, unreliable; 11 conjectural, contestable, distrustful, mistrustful, provisional, speculative, unbelieving; 12 hypothetical, questionable; 13 controversial, indeterminate; 14 controvertible; PHRASES: 2, 5 in doubt; 4-6 open-minded.

uncertain person 7 doubter, erratic, skeptic, worrier; 8 agnostic; 9 worrywart; 10 fussbudget, questioner; PHRASES: 8, 6 doubting Thomas.

uncertainty 2 if; 5 doubt, guess; 6 enigma; 8 distrust, mistrust, wavering; 9 ambiguity, guesswork, misgiving; 10 conjecture, hesitation, indecision, insecurity, Pyrrhonism, skepticism; 11 agnosticism, incertitude, questioning; 13 disputability, uncertainness; 14 contestability; PHRASES: 4, 4 open mind; 4, 5 wild guess; 4, 7 open verdict *UK*; 7, 5 anyone's guess; 8, 4 question mark; 8, 5 anybody's guess. *See also* **uncertain**

uncertified 7 untried; 8 unproved, unsigned, untested; 9 unchecked; 10 apocryphal, unofficial, unratified, unverified; 11 speculative; 12 experimental, undocumented; 13 unascertained; 14 uncorroborated; 15 unauthenticated.

unchangeable *See* **fixed**

unchanging 4 firm; 5 loyal, solid, total; 6 direct, stable; 7 eternal, undying; 8 absolute, constant, enduring, straight; 10 unshakable, unswerving; 11 unequivocal.

unchaste 4 fast; 5 frail, light, loose; 6 amoral, brazen, fallen, impure, wanton; 7 naughty, scarlet, seduced; 8 immodest; 9 flaunting, shameless; 10 unblushing, unvirtuous, womanizing; 11 promiscuous, prostituted; 12 meretricious, philandering; PHRASES: 2, 3, 4 on the game; 2, 4, 6 of easy virtue; **3-3** man-mad, sex-mad; **3-5** man-crazy.

uncivil *See* **rude**

uncle 3 Bob, oom *UK*; **10** pawnbroker; PHRASES: **3-4** pop-shop; **5, 3** U~ Sam; **5, 5** Dutch ~, U~ Remus, U~ Vanya.

unclean 4 foul, yuck; **5** dirty, dungy, fecal, fetid, grimy, lousy, mangy, manky, mucky, nasty, pongy *UK*, toxic, yucky; **6** coarse, filthy, grotty *UK*, grubby, impure, rotted, scabby, scurfy, septic, shabby, sinful, soiled, sordid, stinky *UK*, unholy; **7** beastly, carious, carrion, corrupt, hoggish, immoral, leprous, maggoty, noisome, ponging, profane, rotting, scruffy, squalid, stained, tainted; **8** crawling, flyblown, infected, nauseous, polluted, stinking, unchaste, unwashed, unworthy; **9** festering, offensive, poisonous, repulsive, uncleanly, unhealthy, unrefined; **10** abominable, disgusting, infectious, insanitary, malodorous, nauseating, nonsterile, pediculous, unhallowed, unhygienic, unpurified, unsanitary; **11** excremental; **12** contaminated, insalubrious, unfastidious, unsterilized; **13** stercoraceous; **15** excrementitious; PHRASES: **4-6** flea-bitten.

uncleanness 3 rot; **5** fetor, stink, taint; **6** sepsis, stench; **7** squalor; **8** impurity; **9** excretion, infection, profanity, wallowing; **10** corruption, immorality; **11** abomination, pediculosis, phthiriasis, putrescence; **12** putrefaction; **13** contamination, decomposition; PHRASES: **5, 6** dirty habits. *See also* **unclean**

unclear 4 hazy; **5** foggy, misty, vague; **6** arcane, fogged, unsure; **8** abstruse, nebulous, puzzling; **9** ambiguous, enigmatic, imprecise, uncertain; **10** perplexing *UK*.

unclothed *See* **bare, naked**

uncommon 3 few, odd; **4** rare; **6** scarce, superb; **7** curious, notable, unusual; **8** precious, singular, superior; **9** scattered; **10** infrequent, occasional; **11** exceptional, outstanding; PHRASES: **3-3** one-off; **4, 2, 3, 6** thin on the ground.

uncommunicative 5 cagey, close, vague; **6** silent; **7** evasive; **8** clamlike, discreet, reserved, reticent, taciturn; **9** secretive, withdrawn; **13** unforthcoming, uninformative; PHRASES: **5-5** poker-faced; **5-6** tight-lipped; **8-2** buttoned-up *UK*.

uncomplicated *See* **simple**

uncomplimentary *See* **disparaging**

uncompromising *See* **inflexible**

unconcealed *See* **open**

unconcerned 4 cold, cool, deaf; **5** aloof, bland, bored; **6** casual, remote; **8** detached, heedless, lukewarm; **9** apathetic; **10** insouciant; **11** indifferent; **12** uninterested.

unconditional *See* **unqualified**

unconnected *See* **separate**

unconscious 2 id; **3** ego, out; **4** mind, self; **6** asleep, psyche, reflex; **7** stunned, unaware; **8** comatose, ignorant, lifeless, superego; **9** automatic, catatonic, concussed, intuitive, oblivious, unwitting; **10** cataleptic, insensible, insentient, mechanical, subliminal, uninformed; **11** instinctive, involuntary; **12** subconscious; **13** unintentional; PHRASES: **2, 1, 4** in a coma; **3, 3, 3, 5** out for the count *UK*; **3, 4** out cold; **4, 2, 3, 5** dead to the world; **6, 3** wigged out, zonked out; **7, 3** knocked out.

unconsciousness 3 nap; **4** coma, doze; **5** faint, sleep, swoon; **6** catnap, snooze, stupor, torpor, trance; **8** blackout, daydream, etherism, numbness, oblivion; **9** catalepsy; **10** sleepiness, somnolence; **11** insentience, nothingness.

unconsidered *See* **hasty**

uncontrolled *See* **unrestrained**

unconventional 3 odd, off; **4** beat; **6** freaky, fringe, hippie, quirky; **7** nomadic, strange, unusual; **8** Bohemian, maverick, original, uncommon; **9** eccentric, irregular, traveling, wandering; **11** alternative, exceptional, independent, progressive; **12** experimental, freethinking; **13** nonconformist, unprecedented, untraditional; **15** individualistic; PHRASES: **3-1** non-U *UK*; **3, 3, 4** off the wall; **5-5** avant-garde.

unconvincing 4 lame, poor, thin; **6** forced; **8** fanciful, unlikely; **10** improbable; **11** implausible, transparent; PHRASES: **3-7** far-fetched.

uncooked 3 raw, red; **4** cold, pink, rare; **5** fresh; **6** bloody; **9** underdone; **10** unprepared; PHRASES: **4-5** half-baked; **4-6** half-cooked.

uncooperative 7 awkward *UK*; **8** contrary, negative, perverse, stubborn; **9** difficult, fractious, hindering, obstinate, oppugnant, resistant, truculent, unhelpful, unwilling; **10** refractory; **11** disobedient, disobliging, obstructive, reactionary, reactionist; **12** conservative, recalcitrant; **14** noncooperative; PHRASES: **6-6** bloody-minded *UK*.

uncoordinated *See* **clumsy**

uncouth 4 rude; **5** bawdy, brash, crude, rough; **6** cheeky, coarse, simple, vulgar; **7** boorish; **8** impolite, indecent, insolent; **9** offensive, primitive; **12** discourteous; **13** disrespectful; PHRASES: **3-8** bad-mannered, ill-mannered.

uncover 4 bare, find, open, undo; **5** strip; **6** divest, expose, reveal; **7** disrobe, exhibit, undress, unearth; **8** disclose, discover; PHRASES: **4, 3** find out, peel off, tear off; **4, 6** come across.

unction 3 oil; **4** balm, zeal; **5** salve; **6** fervor, lotion; **7** passion; **8** ointment; **10** enthusiasm; **11** earnestness.

unctuous 4 oily, smug; **5** fatty, phony *UK*, slimy; **6** creepy, greasy, phoney, smarmy; **8** slippery; **9** groveling; **10** obsequious; **11** sycophantic; **12** ingratiating; PHRASES: **4-6** well-coated.

uncultivated 6 coarse, fallow; **8** unfarmed, untilled; **9** unplanted, unrefined; **10** uncultured, unpolished; **15** unsophisticated.

uncut 4 pure; **6** entire, intact, unhurt, virgin; **7** perfect; **8** complete, flawless, unbroken, unedited, unharmed; **9** faultless, inviolate, undamaged, undivided, uninjured, unscathed, unspoiled, untouched; **10** unabridged, uncensored, unimpaired; **12** undiminished, unexpurgated; **13** unadulterated; **14** uncontaminated; PHRASES: **4-6** full-length.

undaunted 4 bold, game; **5** brave; **6** heroic; **7** armored, steeled; **8** carefree, fearless, unafraid, unbeaten, unshaken; **9** steadfast, unfearing, unworried; **10** impervious, undeterred, unhesitant, unshakable, unwavering; **11** indomitable, unconcerned, unconquered, undisturbed, unflinching, unshrinking; PHRASES: **7, 7** nothing daunted.

undecided 4 open; **5** vague; **7** anytime, unclear; **9** dithering, uncertain; **10** ambivalent, unresolved; **11** vacillating; PHRASES: **2, 3, 5** in two minds *UK*; **2, 5** in doubt.

undeniably 8 patently; **11** irrefutably; **13** incontestably.

under 3 sub; **4** down, sunk; **5** below, neath; **6** buried, subway; **7** bathyal, beneath, benthal, benthic, subaqua; **8** hypogeal, hypogene, immersed, undersea; **9** benthonic, hypogeous, submarine, submerged; **10** subaquatic, subaqueous, suboceanic, underneath, underwater; **11** underground; **12** bathypelagic, subterranean; **13** subterraneous; **14** subterrestrial; PHRASES: **4, 4** less than.

undercover 6 covert, hidden, secret; **9** disguised.

undercurrent 4 hint, pull, tide; **7** current, feeling; **8** undertow; **10** suggestion; **11** connotation.

underdog 5 loser; PHRASES: **5, 3** small fry; **6, 2** runner up; **6, 3** little guy; **6, 4** second best.

underestimate 5 scorn; **8** belittle, discount, minimize, misjudge, misprise; **9** disparage, patronize, underrate; **10** underprice, understate, undervalue; **11** underpraise; **12** miscalculate; PHRASES: **3, 2, 7, 2** not do justice to; **4, 4** mark down, play down; **4-4** pooh-pooh; **4, 5** hold cheap; **4-5** soft-pedal; **4, 5, 2** make light of; **4, 6, 2** make little of; **5, 3** shrug off.

underfed 4 lean, thin, weak; **5** frail, spare, unfed; **6** hungry, scurvy, skinny; **7** fasting, scraggy, starved, stunted, wasting; **8** anorexic, famished, ravening, ravenous, starving; **9** emaciated, macerated, voracious; **10** starveling; **12** malnourished; **14** undernourished; PHRASES: **2, 5, 7** on short commons; **4, 2, 1, 4** thin as a rail; **4-3** half-fed; **4-3-4** skin-and-bone; **4-7** half-starved; **6, 2, 1, 4** hungry as a bear; **6-8** famine-stricken.

underground 4 deep, tube *UK*; **5** metro; **6** arcane, buried, covert, hidden, secret, subway, tunnel; **7** covered; **8** basement, hypogeal, samizdat; **9** concealed, dissident, secretive, underpass; **10** resistance, subversive, undercover, underworld; **11** alternative, clandestine; **12** subterranean; PHRASES: **5, 6** below ground.

underground place 4 hell; **6** cellar, subway, tunnel; **7** pothole; **8** basement; **9** catacombs, underpass; **10** underworld; PHRASES: **6, 7** secret passage.

underhand 3 sly; **4** mean; **5** slyly; **6** sneaky; **8** sneakily; **9** deceitful, dishonest; **11** deceitfully, dishonestly.

undermine *See* **weaken**

undershirt 6 skivvy; **7** singlet; **9** undervest.

underside 4 base; 6 bottom; 8 basement; 10 foundation, underneath.

understand 3 dig, get, ken, see; 4 have, hold, know, read, twig *UK*; 5 colly, grasp, learn, savvy, seize; 6 absorb, fathom, follow, master, retain, rumble *UK*; 7 realize; 8 identify, remember; 9 apprehend, empathize, penetrate, recognize; 10 appreciate, comprehend, sympathize; PHRASES: 2, 2, 4, 4 be au fait with; 2, 4, 2 be with it; 2, 5, 2 be aware of; 2, 8, 4 be familiar with; 3, 2 get it; 3, 2, 3 see it all; 3, 2, 4 get to know; 3, 3, 4 get the idea; 3, 3, 4, 2 get the hang of; 3, 3, 5 see the light; 3, 3, 7 get the picture; 3, 5, 2 get ahold of; 3, 7 see through; 4, 2 take in; 4, 3 work out; 5, 2 catch on; 5, 2, 2 latch on to; 5, 3, 5, 2 catch the drift of; 5, 3, 7 grasp the meaning; 6, 2 cotton on, tumble to; 6, 3 figure out.

understanding 3 wit; 4 bond, deal, kind, mind, pact; 5 aware, grasp, sense; 6 accord, belief; 7 ability, empathy, harmony, insight, mastery, opinion, support; 8 contract, kindness, learning, sympathy, tolerant; 9 accepting, agreement, awareness, indulgent, intellect, knowledge, tolerance; 10 cleverness, compassion, conception, empathetic, estimation, indulgence, perception, settlement, supportive, thoughtful; 11 arrangement, considerate, discernment, realization, recognition, sympathetic; 12 appreciation, appreciative, apprehension, construction, intelligence; 13 comprehension, consideration; 14 identification, interpretation; PHRASES: 8, 7 personal feeling.

understate 7 devalue; 8 belittle, minimize; 9 underplay, underrate; 10 undervalue; 11 underreckon; 13 underestimate; 14 underemphasize; PHRASES: 4, 4 play down; 4, 5 sell short; 4, 6, 2 make little of.

understated 6 modest, simple; 7 unfussy; 8 discreet; 9 minimized; 10 minimalist, restrained, unassuming, underrated; 11 undervalued, unobtrusive; 12 conservative; 13 inconspicuous, underreckoned, unpretentious, unsubstantial; 14 underestimated; 15 underemphasized; PHRASES: 3-3 low-key.

understatement 5 irony; 7 dryness, litotes, meiosis, sarcasm; 9 euphemism; 12 minimization; 13 underemphasis; 14 underreckoning, undervaluation; 15 underestimation, unobtrusiveness.

understudy *See* **substitute**

undertake 2 do; 3 try, vow; 4 dare; 5 agree, begin, start; 6 accept, assume, commit, direct, engage, launch, manage, pledge, pursue, tackle; 7 attempt, execute, pioneer, promise, venture; 8 commence, confront, contract, endeavor, initiate, shoulder; 9 adventure, challenge, volunteer; PHRASES: 2, 2, 3 go in for; 2, 5 go about, go after; 3, 2 set to; 3, 4 get down; 3, 4, 2 get down to; 3, 4, 4, 4 get one's head down; 3, 5 get going; 3, 7 get weaving; 3, 8 get involved; 4, 1, 4, 2 take a shot at; 4, 1, 5, 2 take a crack at; 4, 2 fall to, sign up, take on, take up; 4, 2, 4 take in hand; 4, 2, 5, 4 come to grips with; 4, 3, 6 stir the possum; 4, 6, 2 take charge of; 5, 2 agree to; 5, 3 carry out; 5, 3, 6 grasp the nettle; 6, 2 buckle to *UK*, embark on, engage in; 6, 4 launch into, plunge into; 7, 2 venture on; 7, 4 grapple with.

undertaker 4 mute; 6 keener, sexton, weeper; 7 elegist, mourner; 8 embalmer, eulogist; 9 mortician; 10 epitaphist, pallbearer; 11 gravedigger, necrologist; PHRASES: 7, 8 funeral director; 8, 5 monument mason; 8, 6 obituary writer.

undertaking 3 job, try; 4 case, deal, deed, duty, feat, mise, pact, plan, seal, task, work; 5 cause, ideal, quest, topic; 6 accord, action, affair, assent, design, effort, matter, pledge, search; 7 attempt, compact, emprize, inquiry, mission, program, project, promise, purpose, subject, venture; 8 activity, alliance, business, campaign, contract, covenant, endeavor, exercise, security, struggle; 9 adventure, agreement, bartering, operation, principle, signature; 10 assignment, bargaining, commission, commitment, engagement, enterprise, obligation, occupation, pilgrimage, settlement; 11 arrangement, cooperation, negotiation, partnership, speculation; 12 ratification; 13 understanding; 14 responsibility; PHRASES: 1, 3, 2, 3 a lot to ask; 3, 11 big ~; 4, 4 hard task; 4, 5 tall order; 5, 2, 4 labor of love; 6, 2, 4 matter in hand.

undertone 4 hint; 5 tinge, trace; 10 suggestion; 12 undercurrent.

undervalue *See* **underestimate**

underwater 4 sunk; 6 marine, sunken; 7 benthic, flooded, subaqua; 8 immersed, undersea; 9 inundated, submarine, submerged; 10 subaquatic, subsurface; 12 bathypelagic; PHRASES: 3-7 sub-oceanic; 4-3 deep-sea; 4-4 Aqua-Lung™; 4-5 deep-water.

underwear 3 bra; **4** body *UK*, busk, BVD's, hoop, slip, vest *UK*; **5** jupon, lungi, pants *UK*, shift, smock, stays, teddy, thong; **6** basque, boxers, briefs, bustle, corset, garter, girdle, gusset, semmit, shorts, skivvy, smalls *UK*, trunks, undies; **7** caleçon, chemise, drawers, falsies, pannier, panties, singlet, smicket; **8** bloomers, bodysuit *UK*, camisole, corselet, knickers *UK*, lingerie, scanties, skivvies; **9** afterwelt, brassiere, crinoline, jockstrap, loincloth, pantalets, petticoat, supporter, undergown, undervest; **10** underdress, underlinen, underpants, undershirt, underskirt, waistcloth; **11** breechcloth, farthingale, undergirdle, undershorts, underthings; **12** camiknickers *UK*, combinations, underclothes, undergarment; **13** underclothing, undergarments; **14** unmentionables; PHRASES: **1-6** G-string, Y-fronts *UK*; **3, 4** fig leaf; **4-2** roll-on; **4-2, 6** roll-on girdle; **4, 3** crop top; **4-3** step-ins; **4-4** half-slip; **4, 5** long johns; **4, 8** body stocking; **4, 9** long ~; **5, 4** union suit; **5, 5** corps piqué; **5, 6** boxer shorts, panty girdle; **6, 4** garter belt, string vest *UK*; **6, 5** corset cover, skivvy shirt; **6, 6** corset bodice, jockey shorts; **6, 8** French knickers *UK*; **7, 1, 2, 5** chemise à la reine; **8, 7** envelope chemise; **9, 4** suspender belt.

underworld 7 illegal, illicit; **8** criminal, gangland, unlawful; PHRASES: **6, 5** nether world *UK*. See also **hell**

underwrite 4 back, fund; **7** endorse; **9** guarantee; **11** countersign.

undesirable 8 unwanted; **9** uninvited, unwelcome; **12** disagreeable; **13** objectionable.

undeveloped See **immature**

undiluted See **straight**

undirected 6 random; **7** aimless; **8** unguided, untaught; **9** pointless, unfocused, wandering; **10** unschooled; **11** purposeless; **13** directionless.

undisclosed See **secret**

undistinguished See **ordinary**

undivided See **complete**

undo 4 ruin; **5** annul, loose, untie; **6** defeat, repeal, revoke, unhook, unlock; **7** destroy, release, rescind, reverse, subvert, unravel; **8** overturn, unbutton, unfasten; **9** undermine.

undress 4 bare, doff, drop, moon, undo; **5** flash, strip, untie, unzip; **6** baring, change,

divest, expose, nudism, remove, reveal, streak, unhook, unlace, unrobe, unveil; **7** disrobe, mooning, uncloak, uncover, undrape; **8** bareness, denuding, disclose, exposing, exposure, flashing, naturism, unbutton, unclothe; **9** disrobing, revealing, streaking, stripping; **10** denudation, divestment, gymnosophy, striptease, unclothing, uncovering, undressing; **11** disrobement, toplessness; **13** exhibitionism; PHRASES: **3, 3** put off; **3, 4** lay bare, lay open; **4, 1, 5** wear a smile; **4, 3** peel off, slip off, take off; **4, 3, 2** slip out of; **5, 3** strip off *UK*; **5, 4** strip bare; **5, 5** strip poker; **5-6** strip-search; **6-3** skinny-dip; **6-7** skinny-dipping.

undressed 3 raw; **4** bare, nude; **5** bared, naked, nuddy *UK*; **6** nudist, unclad; **7** unrobed; **8** disrobed, starkers *UK*, stripped, undraped, ungarbed; **9** unattired, unclothed, uncovered; **10** naturistic; **11** clotheless; **13** gymnosophical; PHRASES: **2, 3, 3** in the raw; **2, 3, 4** in the buff, in the nude; **2, 3, 10** in the altogether; **2, 7** au naturel; **2, 7, 4** in nature's garb; **4-3** bare-ass; **4, 5** buck naked; **4-7** bare-bollock; **4, 7, 2** with nothing on; **5, 2, 1, 7** naked as a jaybird; **5-5** stark-naked; **5-8** strip-searched; **8, 5** stripped naked.

undue 8 unearned; **9** excessive, unmerited; **10** gratuitous, immoderate, undeserved, unexpected; **11** unjustified, unnecessary, unwarranted; **13** unjustifiable; PHRASES: **8-3** uncalled-for, unlooked-for.

undulate 4 roll; **5** heave, swell; **6** ripple; PHRASES: **4, 3, 4** rise and fall.

unearth 4 mine; **5** drill; **6** exhume, expose, quarry, reveal; **7** extract, uncover; **8** disclose, discover, disinter, excavate; **9** disentomb, publicize; PHRASES: **3, 2** dig up; **4, 6** come across; **5, 2, 5** bring to light; **6, 4** happen upon.

unemployed 4 free, idle; **6** fallow, unused; **7** jobless, resting, unwaged *UK*; **9** available, redundant *UK*, unengaged; **10** disengaged, unoccupied; PHRASES: **2, 3, 4** on the dole *UK*; **3, 2, 1, 3** out of a job; **3, 2, 4** out of work; **3, 7** not working; **4, 3** laid off; **4, 9** made redundant *UK*; **7, 2** signing on; **7, 4** between jobs.

unemployment 4 dole; **5** slump; **8** idleness, shutdown; **9** discharge, dismissal, recession, severance; **10** depression, redundancy *UK Can*, retirement; **11** joblessness, resignation, termination; PHRASES: **2, 4, 4** no more work; **3-3** lay-off; **3, 4** job loss, the sack.

unending *See* **endless**

unenlightened 7 unaware; 8 ignorant; 9 oblivious; 10 prejudiced, uninformed; 12 unacquainted; PHRASES: 6-6 closed-minded, narrow-minded.

unenthusiastic 4 cold, cool; 7 subdued; 8 lukewarm; 9 apathetic, unexcited, unhelpful; 11 indifferent, unimpressed; 12 uninterested, unresponsive; 13 uncooperative; PHRASES: 4-7 half-hearted.

unequal 5 unfit; 6 unable, uneven, unfair; 8 lopsided; 9 incapable; 10 asymmetric, inadequate, mismatched, unbalanced; 11 inequitable; 14 unsatisfactory; PHRASES: 3-5 one-sided.

unerring 4 sure; 7 certain; 8 absolute, definite, positive.

uneven 3 odd; 5 bitty *UK*, bumpy, jerky, jolty, rough; 6 choppy, dotted, jagged, patchy, rutted, spotty, unfair; 7 scrappy, snatchy, unequal; 8 lopsided, potholed; 9 irregular; 10 asymmetric, mismatched, unbalanced; 13 unsymmetrical; PHRASES: 3-5 one-sided, top-heavy.

unexceptional 4 fair; 6 boring; 7 trivial; 8 middling, passable; 9 tolerable; 10 irrelevant; 11 unimportant; PHRASES: 2-2 so-so.

unexpected 4 rare; 5 fluky; 6 chance, sudden; 8 freakish; 9 startling, unguessed; 10 accidental, fortuitous, miraculous, surprizing, unforeseen; 11 astonishing, unpredicted; 13 unanticipated, unforeseeable, unpredictable; PHRASES: 3, 2, 3, 4 out of the blue.

unexpectedly 2, 8 by accident; 7, 7 without warning. *See also* **unexpected**

unexpectedness 5 fluke; 6 chance, oddity, rarity, wonder; 7 miracle, prodigy; 8 surprise; PHRASES: 3, 10 the unforeseen; 5, 4 lucky shot; 5, 8 freak accident. *See also* **unexpected**

unexplained 6 arcane, secret; 8 baffling, unsolved; 9 enigmatic, insoluble, uncertain; 10 mysterious, unresolved, unsolvable; 12 impenetrable, inexplicable; PHRASES: 5, 6 never solved; 7, 1, 4 without a clue.

unfailing *See* **reliable**

unfair 4 mean; 5 dirty, false, wrong; 6 biased, uneven, unjust; 7 bigoted, crooked, partial, unequal; 8 partisan; 9 deceitful, dishonest, excessive; 10 exorbitant, fraudu-

lent, iniquitous, prejudiced; 11 inequitable, underhanded; 12 dishonorable, extortionate, unreasonable; 14 discriminating; PHRASES: 3-5 one-sided.

unfaithful 5 false; 6 fickle, untrue; 8 cheating, disloyal; 9 deceitful, faithless; 10 adulterous, traitorous; 11 treacherous; PHRASES: 3-6 two-timing; 6-8 double-crossing.

unfamiliar 3 new; 5 alien, novel; 6 exotic, unused; 7 foreign, strange, unaware, unknown, untried, unusual; 8 ignorant, unbeaten, untested, unversed; 9 different, unskilled, untrodden; 10 newfangled, unexplored; 12 unaccustomed, unacquainted; 13 inexperienced, unprecedented; 14 nontraditional; PHRASES: 3, 4, 6 not seen before; 4-8 mold-breaking; 7, 2 unheard of.

unfashionable 3 out; 5 dowdy, passé; 6 démodé; PHRASES: 3, 2, 3, 3 out of the ark.

unfavorable 3 bad; 7 adverse, harmful, hostile, opposed; 8 negative; 11 detrimental; 12 disapproving; 15 uncomplimentary.

unfeeling 4 cold, deaf, numb; 5 blind, cruel; 6 clumsy, stolid, unwary; 7 callous, inhuman, unaware; 8 blockish, hardened, heedless, pitiless, uncaring; 9 apathetic, forgetful, heartless, impassive, nerveless, oblivious, senseless, unmindful; 10 impervious, insentient; 11 hardhearted, indifferent, insensitive, unemotional; 12 unresponsive; 13 anaesthetized, unsympathetic; PHRASES: 4-7 cold-blooded; 5-6 heavy-handed.

unfeeling person 5 robot; 6 hearty, zombie; 7 android; 9 pachyderm; 11 sleepwalker; 12 somnambulist; PHRASES: 8, 6 Sleeping Beauty.

unfinished 3 raw; 5 crude, vague; 7 cursory, ongoing, partial, sketchy; 9 shapeless, unrefined; 10 incomplete, unpolished; 11 approximate, fragmentary, preliminary, rudimentary, uncompleted; PHRASES: 2, 8 in progress; 5-3-5 rough-and-ready.

unfit 2 US; 3 ill; 4 puny, weak; 5 frail, inapt, inept, wrong; 6 ailing, flabby; 7 useless; 8 hopeless, inexpert, unseemly, unsuited, untimely; 9 incapable, unhealthy, untrained; 10 inadequate, inapposite, ineligible, malapropos, unbecoming, unsuitable; 11 incompetent, inexpedient, unqualified; 12 inadmissible, inapplicable, incompatible, infelicitous, unacceptable; 13 inappropriate; PHRASES: 3, 2, 5 out of shape; 3, 2, 9 out of condition; **3-7** ill-adapted.

unfold 4 grow; **6** evolve, reveal, unfurl; **7** advance, clarify, develop, display, explain; **8** disclose, progress; PHRASES: **4, 2** open up; **4, 3** open out; **4, 5** make known; **6, 3** spread out.

unforced 7 natural; **9** unwitting, voluntary; **10** unprompted; **11** spontaneous.

unforeseen *See* **unexpected**

unfortunate 5 loser; **6** doomed, wretch; **7** fateful, unhappy, unlucky; **8** hopeless, luckless, underdog, untimely; **10** calamitous, disastrous; **11** inopportune; **12** unsuccessful; **13** inappropriate; PHRASES: **3-5** ill-fated, ill-timed; **4, 4** lame duck.

unfriendly *See* **hostile**

unfruitful *See* **infertile**

ungainly 5 heavy; **6** clumsy; **7** awkward; **8** unwieldy; **9** graceless, inelegant; **10** cumbersome, ungraceful; **12** inconvenient.

ungodly 4 late; **6** sinful, wicked; **7** corrupt, immoral, impious, profane; **8** depraved, unsocial; **9** unearthly; **10** irreverent, ridiculous; **11** blasphemous, irreligious; **12** unreasonable.

ungrateful 4 rude; **7** ingrate, selfish; **8** churlish, heedless; **9** forgetful, thankless, unmindful; **10** ungracious, unpleasant, unthankful; **11** thoughtless, unrewarding; **12** discourteous, unsatisfying; **13** inconsiderate; **14** unappreciative; PHRASES: **3-8** bad-mannered, ill-mannered.

unguent 3 oil; **4** balm; **5** cream, salve; **6** lotion; **8** chrismal, liniment, ointment; **10** unguentary, unguentous; **11** chrismatory.

unhappy 3 low, sad; **4** blue, down; **6** gloomy, moving, pining, somber, woeful; **7** doleful, forlorn, tearful, ululant; **8** dejected, desolate, dolorous, funereal, mournful, mourning, poignant, saddened, wretched; **9** cheerless, depressed, miserable, sorrowful, tormented, woebegone; **10** depressing, despondent, distressed, melancholy, sadhearted; **11** crestfallen, distressing, downhearted, heartbroken, languishing; **12** disconsolate, disheartened, heavyhearted, inconsolable; **13** heartbreaking; PHRASES: **3, 2** cut up; **5-8** grief-stricken; **6-7** broken-hearted.

unhealthy 3 ill, wan; **4** pale, sick, weak; **5** dirty, frail, green, mangy, peaky *UK Can*, tired, toxic, unfit, white; **6** anemic, infirm, morbid, pallid, peaked, sallow, sickly, un-

well, weakly, yellow; **7** bilious, corrupt, debased, harmful, invalid, noxious, unsound; **8** anorexic, damaging, decrepit, delicate, fatigued, ghoulish, polluted, underfed; **9** colorless, emaciated, exhausted, injurious, jaundiced, unnatural; **10** insanitary, unhygienic, unsanitary; **11** detrimental, unwholesome; **12** carcinogenic, insalubrious, malnourished; **13** hypochondriac; **14** undernourished, valetudinarian; PHRASES: **3, 2, 5** out of shape; **3, 2, 9** out of condition; **3, 4** run down; **4, 2, 1, 5** pale as a ghost; **5, 2, 1, 5** white as a sheet.

unhealthy (be unhealthy) 3 ail; **4** drop, fail, flag, peak, pine, sink; **5** catch, droop, faint, vomit; **6** sicken, suffer, weaken; **8** collapse, languish; **11** deteriorate; PHRASES: **2, 3** be ill; **2, 4, 4** go down with; **3, 5** get worse; **4, 3** fall ill, feel ill; **4, 4** fade away, fall sick, feel sick, grow weak; **4, 6** feel rotten; **5, 4** waste away.

unholy 7 immoral, profane, secular, ungodly; **8** shocking; **9** unblessed; **10** outrageous, scandalous, unhallowed; **11** blasphemous, disgraceful; **13** unconsecrated.

unhurried 4 calm, easy, idle, lazy, slow; **5** inert, slack; **6** Fabian, gentle; **7** gradual, languid, patient, precise, relaxed; **8** dawdling, indolent, listless, measured, moderate, slothful, sluggish, stealthy, thorough; **9** apathetic, easygoing, leisurely, lethargic; **10** deliberate, languorous, methodical, meticulous, phlegmatic, restrained, sluggardly; **11** circumspect, painstaking; **13** imperceptible; PHRASES: **6, 4, 4** taking one's time.

unhygienic 4 foul; **5** dirty, fuggy, fusty, humid, moldy, muggy, musty; **6** filthy, rotten, sordid, stuffy; **7** airless, baneful, harmful, miasmal, noxious, squalid, unclean; **8** flyblown, inedible, polluted; **9** injurious, poisonous, unhealthy; **10** insanitary, unsanitary; **11** undrinkable, unwholesome; **12** indigestible, insalubrious, unventilated; PHRASES: **3-8** rat-infested; **4-6** flea-bitten; **5-6** smoke-filled.

unidentified *See* **nameless**

uniform 3 tie; **4** even, flat, garb, kilt, like, same; **5** alike, dress, equal, level, plane; **6** attire, curved, ironed, jersey, livery, outfit, rolled, smooth, stable, steady, tartan; **7** costume, regalia, regular, rounded, routine, similar; **8** constant, edgeless, facemask, harrowed, straight, unbroken, unerring; **9** flattened, identical, immutable, permanent, steadfast, symmetric, unruffled, unvarying, waterworn; **10** consistent, continuing, continuous, equivalent, harmonious, harmonized, horizontal, inevitable, monotonous, persistent, unchanging, unwrinkled; **11** homogeneous, regimentals, steamrolled, undeviating; **12** bachelorette, sphragistics, standardized; PHRASES: **3, 3, 4** cap and gown; **3, 6, 3** old school tie; **4, 3** club tie; **4, 6** flak jacket; **5, 5** black dress; **5, 7** black armband; **6, 6** stable colors; **6, 7** school ~; **7, 6** jockey's colors; **8, 5** national dress, shoulder board.

uniform (make uniform) **5** align, level, liken, order; **8** equalize; **9** habituate, normalize; **10** assimilate, homogenize, regularize, stereotype; **11** standardize, systematize; **15** conventionalize; PHRASES: **4, 3** even out.

uniformity **5** habit; **7** harmony, routine; **8** equality, symmetry; **9** constancy, stability; **10** permanence, regularity, repetition, similarity; **11** consistency, equivalence, homogeneity, persistence; **13** inevitability; **15** standardization; PHRASES: **4, 2, 9** lack of deviation. *See also* **uniform**

unify *See* **unite**

unimaginative *See* **dull**

unimportant **5** light, minor, petty, small; **6** little, slight, venial; **7** trivial; **8** trifling; **10** expendable, forgivable, immaterial, irrelevant, negligible; **11** dispensable, forgettable, ineffectual, inessential, nondescript, superficial, unnecessary; **12** nonessential; **13** inappreciable, insignificant, insubstantial, uninfluential; **14** circumstantial, inconsiderable; **15** inconsequential; PHRASES: **2, 2, 11** of no consequence; **2, 5, 6** no great shakes; **5, 5** small stuff.

unimportant (be unimportant) **3, 2, 3** cut no ice; **4, 6** mean little; **5, 2, 6** carry no weight; **5, 3, 7** count for nothing.

uninformed **7** unaware; **8** ignorant; **10** uneducated; **12** unacquainted.

uninhibited **6** candid, wanton; **8** immodest, outgoing; **9** abandoned, dissolute; **10** licentious; **12** unrestrained; **13** unconstrained.

uninspired **3** dry, wan; **4** dull, flat, lame, limp, tame, thin, weak; **5** inane, loose, prosy, stale, vapid, wersh *UK*; **6** boring,

feeble, meager, smooth; **7** flaccid, insipid, languid, prosaic; **9** amorphous, colorless, pointless, schmaltzy, shapeless; **10** monotonous, undramatic, unexciting, unspirited; **11** commonplace, ineffective; **12** unconvincing; **13** unimpassioned; PHRASES: **5-5** wishy-washy.

unintelligence **5** folly; **7** fatuity, inanity; **8** hebetude; **9** ignorance, imitation, puerility, stolidity, stupidity; **10** immaturity; **12** illogicality; **13** unoriginality; **15** incomprehension; PHRASES: **4, 2, 3** lack of wit; **4, 2, 6** lack of wisdom; **4, 2, 9** lack of knowledge. *See also* **unintelligent**

unintelligent **3** dim; **4** daft, dull, dumb, soft; **5** dense, dopey, inane, nutty, silly, thick; **6** klutzy, oafish, obtuse, stolid, stupid, unwise; **7** boorish, doltish, fatuous, foolish, puerile, witless; **8** childish, ignorant, immature; **9** childlike, illogical, imitative, infantile; **10** unoriginal, unthinking; **11** blockheaded, thickheaded, thoughtless, uninventive; **12** unperceptive; **13** unimaginative; PHRASES: **3, 2, 5** out to lunch; **3, 3, 5** not all there; **3-6** dim-witted; **4, 2, 3, 4** soft in the head; **4-6** dull-witted; **5, 2, 1, 5** thick as a plank; **5-6** empty-headed.

unintelligent person **3** oaf; **4** boor, clod, ditz, dolt, dope, fool, prat, twit; **5** dumbo, dummy, dunce, idiot, klutz, ninny, wally; **6** cretin, dimwit, doofus, nitwit; **7** bumpkin, dullard, halfwit, pinhead, plonker *UK*, thickie *UK*; **8** dumbbell, dummkopf, imbecile, numskull *UK*, peabrain; **9** birdbrain, blockhead, ignoramus, lamebrain, numbskull, simpleton; **10** dunderhead, nincompoop; **12** scatterbrain; PHRASES: **5, 5** silly idiot; **6, 5** Simple Simon; **8, 5** complete idiot.

unintelligible **4** deep; **5** blank, muted; **6** arcane, hidden, mystic, occult, unseen; **7** crabbed, cramped, cryptic, deadpan, encoded, garbled, gnostic, jumbled, obscure, private, scrawly, unclear, unknown; **8** esoteric, mystical, oracular, profound, rambling; **9** enigmatic, gibbering, illegible, impassive, inaudible, ineffable, invisible, scrambled, scribbled; **10** incoherent, indistinct, mysterious, sphinxlike, unknowable, unreadable; **11** indefinable, inscrutable, meaningless, unspeakable, unutterable; **12** impenetrable, inarticulate, inexplicable, unbridgeable, unfathomable, unsearchable; **13** inconceivable, inexpressible, unaccountable, undiscernible, unexplainable; **14**

expressionless, incommunicable, indecipherable, transcendental, undecipherable, undiscoverable, untranslatable; **15** inapprehensible, unpronounceable; PHRASES: **2, 4, 8** so much nonsense; **3, 5** all Greek; **4, 6, 5** like double Dutch; **5-5** poker-faced; **6, 4, 5** beyond one's reach; **6, 5** double Dutch.

unintelligible (be unintelligible) 5 stump; **6** babble, baffle, doodle, gibber, puzzle, ramble, scrawl; **7** bedevil, confuse, flummox, mystify, perplex; **8** bewilder, confound, entangle, scribble; PHRASES: **4, 2, 7** talk in riddles; **4, 5** look blank; **4, 6, 5** talk double Dutch; **4, 8** talk nonsense; **5, 2, 7** speak in tongues.

unintelligible thing 4 code; **6** cipher, enigma, puzzle, riddle, scrawl, secret; **7** mystery, paradox, problem, puzzler; **8** idiolect, scribble; **9** conundrum, gibberish; PHRASES: **4, 3, 2, 5** hard nut to crack; **6, 4** secret book; **6, 5** double Dutch; **6, 7** knotty problem; **6, 8** secret language; **7, 5** obscure point.

unintentional *See* **accidental**

uninterested 4 cool; **5** aloof, blasé, bored; **6** casual, remote; **7** distant, unmoved; **8** detached, heedless, inactive, unbiased; **9** apathetic, impassive, objective; **10** complacent, disengaged, insensible, insouciant, nonchalant, phlegmatic, uninvolved, unthinking; **11** indifferent, unconcerned; **12** unresponsive; **13** dispassionate; **14** unenthusiastic; PHRASES: **3-8** non-partisan.

uninteresting *See* **boring**

uninterrupted *See* **continuous**

union 1 U; **3** tie; **4** bond, club, link; **5** crowd, guild, unity; **6** accord, coitus, fusion, league, merger, unison; **7** concord, harmony, joining, liaison, meeting, network, society, wedding, wedlock; **8** alliance, assembly, blending, cohesion, commerce, congress, exchange, junction, marriage, Teamster; **9** agreement, coalition, concourse, gathering, matrimony, synthesis; **10** collection, commonweal, concretion, confluence, connection, federation, rendezvous; **11** association, coagulation, coalescence, combination, concurrence, confederacy, convergence, intercourse, involvement, unification; **12** amalgamation, commonwealth; **13** agglutination, communication, concatenation, confederation, consolidation; **14** solidification; PHRASES: **5, 4** ~ card, ~ jack; **5, 5** labor ~, trade ~; **6, 4**

agency shop; **7, 8** walking delegate; **9, 5** Teamsters U~.

unique 3 one; **4** lone, only, rare, sole; **6** single; **8** nonesuch, peerless, singular; **9** matchless, nonpareil, unequaled; **10** individual, inimitable; **11** distinctive; **12** incomparable; PHRASES: **3-3** one-off *UK*.

unison *See* **agreement**

unit 1 I, K, L; **2** LB, OZ, ST; **3** amp, bel, bit, erg, kit, mil, ohm, one, set; **4** atom, baud, cell, deck, gram, gray, item, Lego™, pack, part, volt, watt; **5** brick, cadre, corps, farad, group, henry, joule, lumen, piece, squad, therm, thing, troop; **6** ampere, cohort, entity, factor, family, kelvin, legion, module, newton, outfit; **7** calorie, candela, company, coulomb, element, gestalt, integer, measure, Meccano™, poundal, section, voltage, wattage; **8** amperage, division, ensemble, entirety, kilowatt, megawatt, molecule, particle, regiment, totality; **9** component, inventory; **10** detachment; **11** constituent, singularity; **12** organization; PHRASES: **4-5** foot-pound; **8, 5** building block, building brick. *See also* **weights and measures**

unite 3 mix, tie, wed; **4** bond, fuse, grip, join, link, mass, meet, pack, pair, yoke; **5** blend, hitch, marry, match, merge, truss, unify; **6** adhere, clinch, cohere, couple, engage, gather, liaise, narrow, tauten; **7** bracket, collect, combine, compact, connect, embrace, grapple, include; **8** assemble, coalesce, compress, comprise, condense, converge, mobilize; **9** associate, constrict, hyphenate, integrate, interlock; **10** amalgamate; **11** concentrate, consolidate, incorporate; PHRASES: **4, 2, 7** join in wedlock; **4, 2, 9** join in matrimony; **4, 8** come together; **5, 8** bring together.

united 1 U; **3** one, UTD, wed; **5** joint; **7** unified; **8** cohesive, combined; **9** aggregate; **10** integrated; **11** amalgamated; PHRASES: **6, 7** U~ Kingdom, U~ Nations; **6, 9** U~ Provinces.

United States 4 Yank; **6** Yankee *Doodle*; **7** America; **8** Columbia; **9** Americana, Stateside; **11** Americanism; **15** Americanization; PHRASES: **2, 2, 1** US of A; **3, 6** the States; **3, 7, 3** the Melting Pot; **3, 9** the Americans; **4, 2, 7** Land of Liberty; **5, 3** Uncle Sam; **5, 3, 7** Stars and Stripes; **5, 5** Uncle Sugar; **8, 5** American eagle. *See also* **US**

unity *See* **agreement**

universal 1 U; 5 basic, total; 6 common, cosmic, entire, global, normal, simple, unique; 7 general, uniform; 8 complete, discrete, distinct, galactic, national, standard; 9 canonical, planetary, unanimous, unlimited, worldwide; 10 collective, continuous, nationwide, widespread; 11 countrywide, fundamental; 12 cosmopolitan; 13 comprehensive, international.

universe 3 all, sky; 4 life; 5 earth, ether, space, world; 6 cosmos, welkin; 7 heavens; 8 creation, empyrean, totality; 9 firmament, macrocosm; PHRASES: 4, 5 deep space; 5, 2, 6 vault of heaven; 5, 5 outer space.

university 1 U; 2 OU UK; 3 LSE UK, MIT, uni UK; 4 Yale; 6 campus, Oxford; 7 academe, academy, college, Harvard; 8 academia, Oxbridge, redbrick; 9 Cambridge; 11 polytechnic; PHRASES: 3, 6 Ivy League; 4, 5 alma mater.

unjust 5 fixed, undue, wrong; 6 ageist, biased, narrow, racist, sexist, unfair, warped; 7 bigoted, insular, partial, triable, twisted; 8 partisan, pedantic, snobbish, tortious, wrongful; 9 accusable, fanatical, hidebound, jaundiced, parochial, prejudged, sectarian, unmerited; 10 actionable, cognizable, homophobic, intolerant, prejudiced, provincial, punishable, subjective, undeserved, xenophobic; 11 inequitable, justiciable, predisposed, prejudicial, unwarranted; 12 chauvinistic, preconceived, preferential, undemocratic, unreasonable; 13 unimaginative, unwarrantable; 14 discriminatory; PHRASES: 3-5 one-sided; 4-7 anti-Semitic; 5-10 class-prejudiced, color-prejudiced; 6-6 narrow-minded.

unknown 1 n, x, y, z; 3 new; 4 anon; 5 alien, blank; 6 secret, unseen, untold, virgin; 7 foreign, mystery, obscure, strange, unnamed; 8 nameless, unspoken; 9 anonymous, ineffable, unbeknown, uncharted; 10 indefinite, mysterious, unexplored, unfamiliar, unknowable, unrealized; 11 unexplained, unperceived, unspecified; 12 undetermined, undiscovered, unidentified, unrecognized; PHRASES: 7, 2 unheard of.

unknown person 4 anon; 8 stranger; PHRASES: 1, 1, 5 A. N. Other; 2, 1 Mr X; 2, 6 Mr Nobody; 4, 3 John Doe; 4, 5 dark horse; 5, 4 blind date; 7, 7 person(s) unknown.

unknown thing 3 UFO; 6 enigma, secret; 7 mystery; 9 anonymity, guesswork, nonentity; PHRASES: 3, 2, 1, 4 pig in a poke;

3, 5 all Greek; 3, 7 the unknown; 5, 9 terra incognita; 6, 4 closed book; 7, 4 mystery tour UK; 7, 8 unknown quantity; 8, 5 anybody's guess, complete blank.

unlawful 6 banned; 7 illegal, illicit; 8 abnormal, criminal, improper, nonlegal, sadistic, wrongful; 9 dishonest, perverted; 10 incestuous, prohibited; 11 animalistic; 12 illegitimate, unauthorized; PHRASES: 4-11 sado-masochistic; 7, 3, 3 against the law.

unlike See **different**

unload 4 drop, dump; 5 empty; 6 unlade, unpack, unship; 7 deliver; 8 unburden; 9 disburden, discharge; PHRASES: 3-4 offload; 4, 3 drop off; 4, 4 take down.

unlock 4 open, undo; 5 solve; 6 answer, expose, reveal, unbolt; 7 release, unchain.

unlucky 6 doomed, tragic; 7 baleful, fateful, hapless, ominous; 8 accursed, luckless, wretched; 9 unblessed; 11 unfortunate; 12 inauspicious, unsuccessful; PHRASES: 3, 2, 4 out of luck; 3, 5 not lucky; 3-5 ill-fated; 3-6 ill-omened; 3-7 ill-starred; 4, 2, 4, 4 down on one's luck; 4-7 star-crossed; 5, 1, 5 under a cloud; 6-2 washed-up; 8-5 accident-prone.

unmannerly See **rude**

unmarried 4 free, solo; 5 widow; 6 chaste, single; 7 widowed, widower; 8 bachelor, celibate, divorced, divorcee UK, solitary, spinster, unwedded; 9 separated; 10 unattached.

unmatched See **supreme**

unmentionable See **taboo**

unmistakable 6 unique; 7 obvious; 8 definite; 11 distinctive, unambiguous.

unmitigated See **sheer**

unmoved 4 calm, cold, cool, dull, firm; 5 blank, blasé, still; 6 serene; 7 adamant; 8 composed, sanguine, tranquil; 9 apathetic, collected, impassive, oblivious, steadfast, unaroused, unexcited, unfeeling; 10 insouciant, nonchalant, phlegmatic, spiritless, unadmiring, unaffected, uninspired, unwavering, unyielding, wonderless; 11 indifferent, insensitive, unconcerned, unimpressed, unsurprised; 12 unresponsive; 13 disinterested, unimaginative; 14 unenthusiastic; PHRASES: 4-7 cold-blooded, cold-hearted.

unnatural 4 fake, mock, sham; 5 false, phony UK, quasi; 6 forced, phoney, pseudo; 7 pretend, virtual; 8 abnormal, affected, specious, spurious; **9** contrived, imitation, pretended, simulated, synthetic; **10** artificial; PHRASES: **2-6** so-called; **3-2** put-on; **3-4** man-made.

unnerve 5 alarm, scare, upset; **7** nonplus; **8** frighten.

unnerving 9 upsetting; **10** unsettling; **11** frightening; **12** demoralizing, intimidating.

unoccupied 4 free, idle; **5** empty; **6** unused, vacant; **7** disused; **8** deserted, forsaken, inactive, unfilled, unmanned; **9** abandoned, available, unpeopled, unsettled, unstaffed; **10** unemployed, untenanted; **11** depopulated, godforsaken, uninhabited, unpopulated; PHRASES: **2, 5, 4** at loose ends; **3, 2, 4** out of work; **7-2** unlived-in.

unorthodox *See* **unconventional**

unpaid 3 due; **4** free, owed; **5** owing; **7** amateur, overdue; **8** honorary; **9** unpayable, unsettled, voluntary; **10** unrewarded; **11** outstanding; **12** irredeemable; **13** uncompensated, unrecompensed, unremunerated; PHRASES: **2, 7** in arrears.

unpalatable 3 bad, off; **4** acid, dank, high, sour; **5** acrid, harsh, moldy, nasty, rough, stale, toxic; **6** bitter, corked, rancid, rotten, turned; **7** curdled, painful; **8** brackish, inedible, overripe, unsavory; **9** fermented, poisonous, revolting, uneatable; **10** disgusting, nauseating, uninviting, unpleasant; **11** distasteful, unappealing, undrinkable, unwholesome; **12** contaminated, disagreeable, indigestible, unacceptable, unappetizing, unattractive; PHRASES: **2, 3, 4** on the turn; **3-7** off-putting; **4-7** foul-tasting.

unperturbed *See* **calm**

unplanned 4 rash; **5** hasty; **6** rushed; **8** reckless; **9** impromptu, impulsive, makeshift, temporary; **10** accidental, unexpected, unforeseen, unintended, unprepared; **11** inadvertent, spontaneous, unscheduled; **12** coincidental; **13** unintentional; **14** unpremeditated; PHRASES: **2, 3** ad hoc; **3, 2, 3, 4** out of the blue; **4-2-3-6** spur-of-the-moment; **5-5** jerry-built.

unpleasant 3 bad; **4** base, cold, foul; **5** lowly, nasty, petty, small; **6** horrid, odious, shabby, sordid, trying, unkind; **7** beastly, hateful, hostile, hurtful, irksome, painful, squalid; **8** annoying, disliked, horrible, spiteful, unsavory; **9** invidious, loathsome, obnoxious, offensive, repulsive, revolting,

sickening, unlikable, unwelcome; **10** despicable, discordant, disgusting, nauseating, unfriendly, uninviting, unpleasing; **11** displeasing, distasteful, rebarbative, unpalatable; **12** disagreeable, discomfiting, unacceptable, unharmonious; **13** objectionable, uncomfortable; **14** discriminatory; PHRASES: **5-6** small-minded.

unpleasantness 4 fuss, pain; **5** spite, upset; **6** bother; **7** affront, dispute, offense, quarrel, scandal, squalor, trouble, umbrage; **8** argument, conflict; **9** hostility; **10** discomfort; **12** disagreement, discomfiture; **14** unpalatability; PHRASES: **3, 7** ill feeling. *See also* **unpleasant**

unpleasant person 3 cad, oaf; **4** boor, lout, pain, pest; **5** beast; **7** fighter; **8** hooligan, nuisance, wrangler; **9** aggressor, quarreler; **12** troublemaker; PHRASES: **4, 2, 3, 3** pain in the ass; **4, 2, 3, 4** pain in the neck; **8-5** mischief-maker.

unpredictable 5 dicey; **6** fickle, quirky, random; **7** erratic; **8** unstable, volatile; **9** illogical, impulsive, irregular, uncertain; **10** capricious, changeable, irrational; **12** inconsistent, inexplicable; **13** unaccountable.

unprepared 4 cold, late, slow; **6** behind, unwary; **7** exposed, unready; **8** backward; **9** impromptu, impulsive, surprised, unguarded, unplanned, untrained; **10** improvised, unarranged, vulnerable; **11** inexpectant, spontaneous, unqualified, unrehearsed; **12** disorganized, unsuspecting; PHRASES: **2, 3** ad hoc, ad lib; **2, 7** ad libitum; **3-3-4** off-the-cuff; **3-8** ill-equipped; **4-2-3-6** spur-of-the-moment; **6, 7** caught napping.

unpretentious 6 modest; **7** natural; **10** unaffected, unassuming; PHRASES: **2-6** aw-shucks; **4-8** self-effacing.

unprincipled *See* **dishonest**

unproductive 4 idle, lazy, slow; **6** barren; **7** blocked, sterile; **8** wasteful; **9** fruitless, infertile; **11** inefficient.

unprofitable 3 out; **4** bust, lean, poor, vain; **5** broke; **6** futile, ruined; **7** ruinous, useless; **8** bankrupt, prodigal, wasteful; **9** deficient, fruitless, insolvent, nonpaying, overdrawn, overspent, pointless, unhelpful; **10** charitable, lossmaking, profitless, uneconomic; **11** squandering; **12** impoverished, insufficient, overextended, unsuccessful; **14** unremunerative; **15** nonprofitmaking *UK*; PHRASES: **2, 3, 3** in the red; **3, 2, 6** out of pocket; **3-4** cut-rate; **3-5**

cut-price *UK*; **4-4** cash-poor; **4-7** loss-leading; **5, 2** belly up; **5-4** break-even; **7, 2, 1, 4** running at a loss.

unprotected 4 meek, nude; **7** exposed, subject, unarmed; **8** disarmed, harmless, innocent, insecure, isolated, orphaned; **9** dependent, pregnable, unguarded, untenable; **10** friendless, undefended, unshielded, vulnerable, weaponless; **11** defenseless, unfortified; **12** indefensible; PHRASES: **2, 4** at risk; **3-8** ill-equipped; **4, 2, 6** open to attack; **7, 8** without resource.

unprovided 4 bare, poor; **5** empty; **6** absent, greedy, vacant; **7** lacking, needing, skimped, stinted, unsated; **8** hindered, rationed, unfilled; **9** underpaid, unstocked; **10** insatiable, unsupplied; **11** underfunded, undermanned, unfulfilled, unfurnished, unsatisfied; **12** discontented, understaffed, unsuccessful; **13** underfinanced, unreplenished; **14** unaccommodated; PHRASES: **3-8** ill-equipped, ill-supplied; **3-9** ill-furnished; **4, 2** hard up; **5-6** empty-handed, short-handed; **5, 8** under strength; **7, 2** starved of; **8, 2** scraping by; **10, 3** ~ for.

unqualified 3 lay; **5** quack, sheer, total, utter; **8** absolute, outright, thorough; **11** categorical; **12** unrestricted; **13** unconditional.

unquestioning 8 absolute, obedient; **9** automatic; **10** unthinking; **12** wholehearted.

unravel 4 fail, undo; **5** solve, untie; **6** loosen, unknot; **7** crumble, resolve; **8** collapse; **11** disentangle; PHRASES: **4, 3** sort out; **4, 5** fall apart.

unreal 3 odd; **4** airy, fake, faux, hazy, mock, sham; **5** bogus, false, phony *UK*, vague, weird; **6** flimsy, forged, hollow, phoney; **7** blurred, elusive, ghostly, obscure, pretend, replica, shadowy, strange, tenuous; **8** ethereal, fanciful, fleeting, fugitive, illusory, invented, mythical, nebulous, spectral, spurious; **9** dreamlike, fantastic, imaginary, imitation, undefined, unnatural; **10** artificial, impalpable, incredible, indefinite, intangible, phantasmal; **11** counterfeit, fantastical, inauthentic, incorporeal, nonexistent; **12** reproduction; **13** indeterminate, insubstantial, unsubstantial; PHRASES: **3, 2, 4, 5** out of this world; **4-7** make-believe.

unrealistic 5 naive; **7** surreal, utopian; **8** abstract, romantic, unlikely; **9** fantastic, visionary; **10** idealistic, improbable, unworkable; **11** impractical; **13** impracticable.

unrealistic person 7 dreamer; **8** idealist, romantic; **9** theorizer, visionary; **10** speculator.

unreality 5 fancy; **7** fantasy, fiction; **8** delusion, illusion; **11** abnormality, ethereality, imagination, incongruity, unactuality; **12** nonexistence, subjectivity; **13** immaterialism, immateriality, impalpability, intangibility; **14** incorporeality; PHRASES: **4-7** make-believe; **4-8** self-delusion. *See also* **unreal**

unreasonable 3 OTT *UK*; **5** rabid, wrong; **6** biased, unfair, unjust; **7** bigoted, extreme, willful; **8** contrary, perverse; **9** excessive, illogical, misguided, obstinate; **10** exorbitant, immoderate, irrational, prejudiced; **11** extravagant, troublesome; **12** extortionate, unacceptable; **13** uncooperative.

unrecognizable 6 hidden; **7** altered, changed; **9** disguised, distorted, incognito, undefined; **10** indefinite, indistinct, unknowable; **12** incognizable; **14** unidentifiable; PHRASES: **6, 7** poorly defined; **6, 8** easily mistaken.

unrefined *See* **crude**

unrehearsed *See* **unprepared**

unrelated 4 free; **5** alien, apart, inapt, other; **6** exotic; **7** foreign, removed, strange; **8** carefree, detached, discrete, disjunct, distinct, divorced, floating, homeless, isolated, rootless, separate, singular, unallied; **9** disparate, reclusive, separated; **10** difference, disrelated, dissimilar, extraneous, inapposite, individual, irrelevant, segregated, unilateral, uninvolved; **11** impertinent, independent, unconnected; **12** disconnected, heterogenous, inapplicable, unaffiliated; **13** disassociated, inappropriate; PHRASES: **3, 7** red herring; **3, 8** non sequitur; **4, 3, 2, 5** fish out of water; **5-4** fancy-free; **5, 7, 2** owing nothing to; **6, 2, 3, 4** cuckoo in the nest; **6, 3, 5** beside the point.

unrelated (be unrelated) 5 labor; **6** ramble, strain, wander; **7** digress; PHRASES: **3, 6, 2** not relate to; **3, 7** not involve; **4, 3, 2** miss the point; **4, 3, 6** lose the thread.

unrelenting *See* **unyielding**

unreliable 4 iffy; **5** dodgy *UK*, gammy *UK*, risky, shaky; **6** fickle, flimsy, infirm, shifty, untrue; **7** erratic, unsound; **8** doubtful, fallible, insecure, perilous, slippery, unstable, unsteady, variable; **9** anecdotal, dangerous, dishonest, eccentric, erroneous, falsified, hazardous, irregular, transient; **10**

capricious, changeable, fallacious, inaccurate, perfidious, precarious, threadbare; **11** treacherous; **12** inconsistent, undependable; **13** insubstantial, unpredictable, untrustworthy; PHRASES: **3-2-5** fly-by-night.

unremitting *See* constant

unresponsive *See* unfeeling

unrestrained 3 lax; **4** free, wild; **5** showy; **6** wanton; **7** extreme, profuse, rampant; **8** perilous; **9** abandoned, excessive, hazardous, magnified, unbridled, unchecked; **10** hyperbolic, hysterical, immoderate, inordinate, outrageous, unreserved; **11** exaggerated, fantastical, uninhibited, unrepressed; **12** ostentatious, preposterous, uncontrolled, unrestricted.

unruffled *See* calm

unruly 5 rowdy; **7** chaotic, lawless, wayward; **8** anarchic, mutinous; **10** disorderly, disruptive, rebellious; **11** disobedient; **12** recalcitrant; **14** uncontrollable.

unsafe 4 weak; **5** crazy, dicey, dicky, frail, leaky, risky, shaky; **6** shoddy; **7** rickety, unsound; **8** critical, delicate, doubtful, gimcrack, insecure, slippery, ticklish, unsecure, unstable, unsteady; **9** condemned, crumbling, dangerous, tottering; **10** precarious, ramshackle, tumbledown, unbalanced, unreliable; **11** dilapidated, treacherous, waterlogged; **13** untrustworthy; PHRASES: **2, 3, 4** on the edge; **2, 3, 5** on the brink, on the verge; **3, 4** not safe; **3-5** top-heavy; **4-6** last-minute, last-second; **5, 3, 2** touch and go; **5-5** jerry-built; **5-7** nerve-racking; **5-8** heart-stopping; **7, 2, 6** falling to pieces.

unsaid 5 meant, tacit; **6** hinted, silent, unsung, untold; **7** implied; **8** implicit, inferred, unspoken, unstated, unvoiced; **9** indicated, intimated, suggested, unuttered, unwritten; **10** insinuated, undeclared, understood, undivulged, unpromoted; **11** unexpressed, unmentioned, unprofessed, unpublished; **12** unproclaimed, unpronounced; **13** unarticulated; PHRASES: **4-6** half-spoken.

unsatisfactory 3 bad; **4** lame, poor, weak; **5** lousy; **6** faulty, meager; **7** lacking; **8** inferior, mediocre, rejected; **9** defective, deficient, imperfect, unpopular; **10** inadequate, unapproved; **11** substandard; **12** insufficient, unacceptable; **13** disappointing, uncommendable; **15** dissatisfactory; PHRASES: **3, 2, 2, 7** not up to scratch; **3, 4, 6** not good enough; **5, 7** found wanting.

unsavory 5 shady; **7** immoral; **9** repellent, revolting; **10** disgusting, unpleasant, villainous; **12** disagreeable.

unscrupulous *See* dishonest

unseasonable 3 odd; **7** strange, unusual; **8** abnormal, untimely; **9** unwelcome; **10** unexpected; **11** inopportune; **12** inconvenient; PHRASES: **3-5** ill-timed.

unselfish 4 kind; **5** lofty, noble; **6** honest, humane, humble, modest; **7** liberal, sublime; **8** generous, martyred, selfless; **9** honorable; **10** altruistic, benevolent, charitable, idealistic, munificent, thoughtful; **11** considerate, magnanimous, sympathetic; **13** compassionate, philanthropic; PHRASES: **3-7** big-hearted; **4-6** high-minded, open-handed; **4-7** self-denying; **4-8** self-effacing; **4-10** self-abnegating; **4-11** self-sacrificing; **5, 2, 3, 3** ready to die for.

unsettled 5 upset; **7** anxious, worried; **8** variable; **9** disturbed, uncertain, undecided; **10** changeable, unresolved; **12** disconcerted, undetermined; **13** unpredictable; PHRASES: **4-5** open-ended.

unsexed 1 N; **6** barren, effete, gelded, spayed; **7** sexless, sterile; **8** neutered, unmanned; **9** caponized, castrated, infertile; **10** sterilized; **11** emasculated; **12** vasectomized.

unskilled 3 ham, lay, raw; **5** green, quack, young; **6** callow, pickup, unripe; **7** amateur, scratch, unsound; **8** affected, ignorant, immature, inexpert, quackish, specious, untaught, unversed; **9** charlatan, untrained, untutored; **10** amateurish, uneducable, uneducated, unfinished, unprepared, unseasoned, unskillful; **11** apprenticed, pretentious, semiskilled, undeveloped, uninitiated, unqualified, unteachable; **12** autodidactic, unconversant, uninstructed, unscientific; **13** inexperienced, nonspecialist; **15** nonprofessional; PHRASES: **2, 8** in training; **4-4** self-made; **4-6** self-taught; **4-7** half-skilled.

unskilled person 3 ass, ham, nit, oaf; **4** boob, bozo, butt, clod, colt, dolt, dude, fool, hack, hick, hulk, jerk, joke, lout, lump, muff, nerd, slob, swab; **5** booby, clown, looby *UK*, loser, quack, stick, wally; **6** cowboy, dauber, duffer, galoot, lubber, muffer, nitwit, novice, rookie, stooge, tinker; **7** amateur, botcher, buffoon, bumbler, bumpkin, bungler, dabbler, failure, fumbler, learner, marplot, student, trainee;

8 beginner, dipstick, imposter; **9** blunderer, charlatan, greenhorn, scribbler; **10** apprentice, landlubber, mismanager, mountebank; **11** blunderbuss, incompetent, probationer; **13** butterfingers; PHRASES: **3, 4** bad hand, bad shot; **3, 7** bad learner, raw recruit; **4, 4** poor hand, poor shot; **5, 6** horse marine; **6, 3** clumsy oaf; **7, 7** country bumpkin.

unskillful 4 dumb, wild; **5** gawky, giddy, inept, silly, unapt, unfit; **6** clumsy, failed, futile, stupid, unable, unwise; **7** awkward, foolish; **8** carefree, feckless, impotent, ungifted; **9** impolitic, impulsive, incapable, unadapted, unendowed, unskilled, untrained; **10** amateurish, inadequate, talentless, unequipped, uninformed, untalented; **11** inattentive, incompetent, ineffectual, inefficient, thoughtless, unpractical, unpromising; **12** disqualified, insufficient, undependable, undiplomatic, undiscerning, unimpressive, uninstructed, unremarkable, unsuccessful; **14** scatterbrained, unaccomplished, unbusinesslike, unprofessional; **15** unstatesmanlike; PHRASES: **3, 2, 2, 7** not up to scratch; **3-6** dim-witted, ham-fisted, ham-handed; **3-10** ill-considered; **4-5** easygoing; **5-2-5** happy-go-lucky; **5-6** lightminded.

unsociable 3 icy, shy; **4** cold, cool, mopy, rude; **5** aloof, apart, close; **6** chilly, frigid, frosty, morose, remote, silent, sullen; **7** distant, haughty, hostile, private, removed, uncivil; **8** autistic, detached, domestic, impolite, Olympian, reticent, retiring; **9** dissocial, exclusive, reclusive, seclusive, withdrawn; **10** antisocial, forbidding, unfriendly, ungracious, unmannerly; **11** dissociable, indifferent, standoffish, uncongenial, unwelcoming; **12** discourteous, inaccessible, ungregarious, unneighborly; **13** disrespectful, unforthcoming; **14** unapproachable; **15** uncommunicative, uncompanionable; PHRASES: **2, 4, 5** in one's shell; **4-9** self-contained; **4-10** self-sufficient.

unsocial person 4 monk; **5** loner; **6** hermit, misfit, oddity, santon; **7** ascetic, eremite, iceberg, recluse; **8** castaway, cenobite *UK*, homebody, marabout, outsider, sannyasi; **9** anchorite, coenobite, eccentric, guellemin; **10** troglodyte; **11** Hieronymite; PHRASES: **3, 3, 3** odd man out; **4-2-4** stay-at-home; **4, 3, 2, 5** fish out of water; **4, 4** lone wolf; **4, 7** cave dweller; **6, 3** square peg; **7, 3, 5** persona non grata; **8, 6** Robinson Crusoe.

unsolved 7 unknown; **8** baffling, untraced; **9** unguessed; **10** mysterious, undivulged, unresolved, unrevealed; **11** unexplained, unsuspected; **12** undiscovered.

unsophisticated 5 crude, naive; **6** simple; **8** homespun; **9** unrefined, unworldly; PHRASES: **4-3** corn-fed.

unsound 3 ill; **4** sick; **5** frail; **6** flawed, unsafe, unwell; **7** rickety; **8** specious, unstable; **9** illogical, unhealthy; **10** fallacious, ramshackle.

unsparing 5 cruel, harsh; **6** severe; **7** liberal; **8** generous; **9** merciless; **10** charitable, munificent, openhanded; **11** unforgiving.

unspeakable 4 foul; **5** awful; **9** appalling, revolting; **10** disgusting; **11** undefinable, unutterable; **12** overwhelming; **13** indescribable, inexpressible.

unspecified 3 few; **4** many; **5** vague; **7** several, unnamed; **10** indefinite; **11** unmentioned; **12** undetermined, unstipulated; **13** indeterminate.

unspoiled 4 pure; **7** natural, perfect; **8** innocent, pristine, unharmed; **9** untouched, wholesome; **11** uncorrupted.

unstable 5 dicky, shaky; **6** casual, groggy, infirm, labile, pliant, shifty, tickle, uneven, wobbly; **7** erratic, rickety, tottery; **8** doubtful, flexible, variable, volatile, wavering; **9** apathetic, irregular, teetering, tottering, trembling, tremulous, unstaunch; **10** changeable, inconstant, precarious, unbalanced, unreliable; **11** featureless, indifferent, suggestible, treacherous, unsteadfast, unsupported, vacillating; **12** questionable; **13** characterless, unpredictable; **14** impressionable.

unsteady See **unstable**

unstick 4 free, undo; **5** loose, prize, unpin; **6** detach, unglue, unseat; **7** release; **8** separate, unfasten; PHRASES: **4, 3** take off; **4, 4** take down; **4, 5** take apart; **5, 3** knock off, shake off.

unstressed See **relaxed**

unsuccessful 4 vain; **6** addled, failed, futile, manqué, wasted; **7** useless; **8** abortive; **9** fruitless; **10** disastrous; **11** ineffective; **12** unproductive.

unsuccessful thing 3 dud; **4** bomb, boob, flop; **5** lemon; **6** turkey; **7** washout, wipeout; **10** bankruptcy, nonstarter; **11** miscarriage; PHRASES: **3-3** boo-boo; **3, 4** bad idea; **3, 4, 3** bad hair day; **4-2** slip-up; **4, 3** faux pas; **4, 5** damp squib *UK*; **4-5, 5** wild-goose chase; **4, 7** crop failure; **4, 8** lost election; **6, 3** wasted day; **6, 7** engine failure; **10, 5** electrical fault.

unsymmetrical *See* **asymmetric**

unthinking 5 blunt; **7** selfish; **8** careless, heedless, tactless; **9** automatic, impulsive, intuitive, negligent, unmindful; **10** indiscreet, mechanical, neglectful, ungrateful; **11** inattentive, indifferent, instinctive, thoughtless; **12** disregarding, undiplomatic; **13** inconsiderate, unquestioning.

untidiness 4 mess; **5** chaos; **6** jumble, muddle; **7** clutter, neglect; **8** disarray, disorder; **10** negligence; **12** dishevelment. *See also* **untidy**

untidy 5 dirty, messy, slack; **6** filthy, grubby, ragged, shabby, shoddy, sloppy, sordid; **7** chaotic, jumbled, muddled, raggedy, ruffled, rumpled, scruffy, squalid, tousled, unclean, unkempt; **8** careless, crumpled, frumpish, slipshod, slobbish, slovenly, sluttish, uncombed; **9** cluttered, negligent, shambolic *UK*, unsightly, windblown; **10** bedraggled, disheveled, disorderly, neglectful, slatternly; PHRASES: **2, 1, 4** in a mess *UK*; **2, 1, 5** in a state *UK*; **2, 4** in rags; **5-5** topsy-turvy.

untie 4 free, undo; **6** loosen, unknot; **7** release, unleash, unravel; **8** unfasten; PHRASES: **3, 4** set free; **3, 5** let loose.

untimely 4 late; **5** early, inapt; **6** unripe; **7** advance, awkward, ominous; **8** immature, mistimed, unsuited; **9** intrusive, premature; **10** disrupting, disturbing, malapropos, precocious, unpunctual, unsuitable; **11** inexpedient, inopportune, unbefitting, unfavorable, unfortunate; **12** inauspicious, inconvenient, interrupting, unpropitious, unseasonable; **13** inappropriate; PHRASES: **3, 2, 4** not in time, out of sync, out of turn; **3, 2, 5** out of order; **3-5** ill-timed; **3-6** ill-omened; **3-7** ill-starred.

untold 6 myriad; **9** countless, ineffable; **10** numberless; **11** indefinable, innumerable, uncountable; **13** indescribable, inexpressible.

untouched 6 intact, unhurt; **7** unmoved; **8** unharmed; **9** undamaged; **10** unaffected; **11** indifferent, unconcerned, unimpressed; PHRASES: **4, 3, 5** safe and sound.

untrained 6 simple; **7** amateur, artless, natural; **8** ignorant, inexpert, untaught, unworked; **9** undrilled, unrefined, unskilled, untutored; **10** apprentice; **11** unexercised, unpracticed, unprocessed, unqualified; **12** uncultivated, uninstructed; **13** inexperienced; **15** unsophisticated.

untrue 5 false, wrong; **8** cheating, disloyal, imagined, libelous; **9** concocted, deceitful, distorted, erroneous, faithless, fictional, imaginary, incorrect, perverted; **10** fabricated, fallacious, fictitious, inaccurate, perjurious, slanderous, unfaithful, untruthful; **11** exaggerated, nonsensical, treacherous, understated; **13** fictionalized, untrustworthy; **14** misrepresented; PHRASES: **3-5** two-faced; **4-2** made-up; **7-2** dreamed-up.

untrustworthy *See* **unreliable**

untruth *See* **lie**

unusable 2 US; **6** broken; **7** useless; **10** unworkable; **11** impractical, ineffectual, inoperative; **12** unemployable; PHRASES: **3, 2, 10** out of commission.

unused 3 new; **4** idle; **5** extra, fresh, kaput, saved, spare; **6** absent, fallow, stored, vacant, wasted; **7** unspent, untried, useless; **8** deferred, pristine, reserved, unusable; **9** preserved, suspended, unapplied, unessayed; **10** unconsumed, unemployed, unfamiliar; **11** impractical, pigeonholed, unconverted, unexercised, unexploited; **12** unaccustomed, unacquainted, unemployable; **13** inexperienced, inoperational, nonreturnable *UK*; **14** nonconvertible; PHRASES: **2, 3, 5** on the blink, on the fritz; **2, 4** in hand; **2, 7** in reserve; **2, 8** in abeyance; **3, 5** out of order; **3, 2, 7** out of service; **4, 2, 3** left to rot; **5-3** brand-new. *See also* **unaccustomed**

unused thing 5 extra, spare, store; **6** reject; **7** discard, remains, savings; **8** castoffs; **9** remainder, stockpile.

unusual 3 odd, rum *UK*; **4** rare; **5** funny, kooky, moody, queer, weird; **6** exotic, freaky, scarce, unique; **7** bizarre, curious, erratic, oddball, strange; **8** aberrant, abnormal, atypical, freakish, original, peculiar, singular, uncommon, unwonted; **9** anomalous, eccentric, grotesque, monstrous, whimsical; **10** incoherent, individual, infrequent, outlandish, remarkable, unfamiliar, unorthodox; **11** exceptional, incongruous; **13** extraordinary, idiosyncratic, nonconforming; **14** unconventional; PHRASES: **3-3** far-out, way-out.

unveil *See* **reveal**

unwanted 4 free, idle; **5** fired; **6** otiose, sacked, unsold, vacant, waived; **7** jobless, resting, retired, shunned, surplus, useless; **8** annoying, inactive, leftover, unbought, unneeded; **9** discarded, dismissed, redundant, remaining, underused, uninvited, unwelcome; **10** discharged, unemployed, unrequired; **11** remaindered, superfluous, undesirable, unnecessary, unsolicited; **13** superannuated; PHRASES: **3, 2, 4** out of work; **3, 8** not required; **4, 3** laid off; **9, 4** dispensed with.

unwarranted 5 undue; **7** surplus; **8** needless; **9** excessive; **10** exorbitant, gratuitous, undeserved, unprovoked; **11** superfluous, unjustified, unnecessary; **12** overreaching; PHRASES: **8-3** uncalled-for.

unwelcome *See* **unwanted**

unwelcoming 7 hostile; **10** unfriendly; **11** standoffish, unreceptive.

unwell *See* **ill**

unwilling 4 loth, wary; **5** leery, loath; **6** averse; **8** grudging, hesitant; **9** demurring, reluctant; **10** indisposed; **11** disinclined; **14** unenthusiastic; PHRASES: **3, 2, 3, 4** not in the mood; **3, 2, 6** not so minded; **3, 5** not ready; **3, 7, 4** not feeling like; **3, 8** not prepared.

unwind 4 undo; **5** relax; **6** loosen; **7** unravel, untwist; **11** disentangle; PHRASES: **4, 4** slow down, wind down.

unwise *See* **foolish**

unwitting 7 unaware; **8** ignorant, innocent; **10** accidental; **11** involuntary, unconscious; **12** coincidental, unsuspecting; **13** unintentional.

unwonted *See* **unusual**

unworried *See* **calm**

unworthy 8 shameful; **9** degrading, worthless; **11** disgraceful, undeserving; **12** contemptible, dishonorable, disreputable.

unwritten 4 oral; **5** known, tacit, vocal; **6** spoken; **8** accepted; **9** unprinted; **10** understood, unrecorded; **11** traditional.

unyielding 4 dour, firm, grim; **5** rigid, solid, stiff, tough; **6** dogged, wooden; **7** adamant, chronic, durable, staunch, unmoved; **8** hardcore, hardened, obdurate, pitiless, resolute, stubborn; **9** immovable, incurable, inelastic, merciless, obstinate,

steadfast, tenacious, unbending; **10** determined, implacable, inexorable, inflexible, persistent; **11** irremovable, persevering, unrelenting; **12** intransigent, irreversible, unappeasable, uninfluenced; **14** uncompromising; PHRASES: **4, 2, 5** hard as nails; **4-5** hard-nosed; **4-6** hard-boiled, hardheaded; **4-8** case-hardened.

up 5 ahead, awake, happy; **6** active, cheery, higher, upbeat, uphill, uplong, uptown, upwith; **7** hopeful, leading, skyward, upalong, upwards, winning; **8** cheerful, positive, upstairs, upstream; **9** excelsior; **10** heavenward, optimistic, uphillward; PHRASES: **2, 3, 4** in the lead; **2, 3, 5** ~ and doing; **2, 3, 6** ~ and around; **2, 5** ~ north; **3, 2, 3** out of bed; **4, 4, 4** hand over fist; **4, 6** ever higher; **6, 3, 6** onward and upward.

upbeat *See* **optimistic**

upbraid *See* **scold**

update 5 renew; **6** inform, revise; **8** renovate; **9** modernize; PHRASES: **4, 2** fill in.

upheaval 7 turmoil; **8** disorder; **9** cataclysm, confusion; **11** disturbance.

uphill 4 hard; **5** tough; **6** rising; **7** arduous; **8** climbing, mounting; **9** ascending, demanding, difficult.

uphold *See* **support**

upholstery 6 covers, fabric; **8** material; **9** furniture; **11** furnishings.

upkeep 4 keep; **7** repairs; **11** maintenance; **12** conservation, preservation; PHRASES: **5, 7** child support.

upland 4 mesa, wold; **5** downs; **7** heights, plateau; **8** downland, highland, moorland; **9** tableland; PHRASES: **4, 6** high ground; **4, 7** high country; **10, 4** undulating land.

uplift 4 lift, move; **5** hoist, raise; **6** enrich; **7** elevate, hearten, improve, inspire.

Upper Volta 7-4 Burkina-Faso.

upright 5 moral; **6** decent, honest; **8** standing, straight, vertical; **9** honorable, righteous.

uprightness *See* **righteousness**

uprising 6 mutiny, revolt; **8** intifada; **9** overthrow, rebellion, secession; **10** insurgency, revolution; **12** insurrection.

uproar 5 chaos, noise; **8** upheaval; **11** disturbance, pandemonium.

uproot 8 displace, evacuate, relocate; **10** deracinate; PHRASES: **3, 2** dig up; **4, 2** move on, pull up.

upset 3 sad; 4 heel, hurt, lean, lilt, list, miss, rile, rock, skew, sway, tilt, vary; **5** shock, spill, spoil, swing, upend, wound; **6** change, defeat, dismay, grieve, offend, sadden; **7** affront, capsize, disrupt, disturb, letdown, reorder, reverse, setback, trouble, turmoil, unhappy, wounded; **8** disarray, dismayed, distress, offended, overturn, saddened, surprise, troubled; **9** commotion, confusion, displease, disturbed, fluctuate, unbalance; **10** disappoint, disconcert, disruption, distraught, distressed, traumatize; **11** destabilize, disorganize, disturbance; **12** disappointed; **14** disappointment, overcompensate; PHRASES: **3, 2** mix up; **3, 4** tip over; **4, 2** mess up; **4-2** turn-up *UK*; **5-2** shake-up; **5, 4** knock over.

upshot *See* **result**

upstart 6 nobody; 7 parvenu, unknown; 9 arriviste.

upsurge *See* **increase**

uptake 8 approval, interest; 9 agreement; **10** acceptance, commitment, perception; **12** appreciation, apprehension; PHRASES: **13** comprehension, understanding.

up-to-date 6 modern, trendy; 7 current, topical.

upturn 4 hill, ramp, rise; 5 grade, slope, spurt, surge, upend, upset; **6** growth, spiral, uplift, uprush; **7** capsize, improve, incline, revival, steepen, upcurve, updraft, upgrade, upsurge, upsweep, upswing, uptrend; **8** gradient, increase, overturn, recovery, upgrowth; **9** elevation, expansion; **10** upsurgence; **11** improvement; PHRASES: **3, 4** tip over; **3, 6** get better; **4, 2** turn up; **4, 6** turn turtle.

upwards *See* **up**

uranium 1 U.

urban 4 city, town; 5 civic, civil, local; **6** uptown; **7** borough, exurban, midtown, oppidan; **8** blighted, business, citified, communal, downtown, suburban; **9** municipal; **10** gentrified; **11** residential; **12** metropolitan, suburbanized; PHRASES: **5-2** built-up; **5-4** inner-city.

urban area 4 burg, city; 5 slums; 6 ghetto, Gotham, London, uptown; **8** downtown, precinct; **10** metropolis; **11** megalopolis; PHRASES: **2-2, 4** no-go area; **3, 4** new city, New York; **3, 5** Big Apple, big smoke, the Smoke; **4, 3** skid row; **4, 6** city center; **5-2, 4**

built-up area; **5, 4** inner city; **5, 6** urban sprawl; **6, 4** garden city *UK*; **7, 4** capital city, nowhere city; **9, 4** cathedral city.

urbanite 5 local; 6 townee *UK*, townie; **7** burgess, burgher, citizen, freeman, oppidan; **8** commuter, resident, townsman, uptowner, villager; **10** downtowner; **11** parishioner, suburbanite; **12** cosmopolitan, metropolitan; PHRASES: **4, 6** city father; **4, 7** city dweller, city manager, city slicker; **4-7** slum-dweller; **5, 7** urban dweller; **8, 7** suburban dweller.

urchin 3 imp, kid; 4 brat, tyke; 6 rascal; **8** hedgehog, hooligan, tearaway *UK*; **10** ragamuffin.

urge 3 egg, yen; 4 back, goad, itch, need, push, spur, whip, wish; **5** drive, force, impel, press; **6** advise, chivvy, compel, desire, exhort, incite, insist, pester; **7** commend, counsel, craving, impulse, longing, promote, support; **8** advocate, stampede, yearning; **9** encourage, impulsion, recommend; **10** compulsion; **11** inclination; PHRASES: **3, 2** egg on; **7, 2** prevail on.

urgent 5 vital; 7 burning, crucial, earnest, exigent, serious; **8** critical, pleading, pressing; **9** demanding, important, insistent; **10** beseeching, imperative, persuasive; **11** importunate.

urinary 8 diuretic, enuretic; 9 continent, urinative; **11** incontinent; PHRASES: **5-7** house-trained, potty-trained; **6-7** toilet-trained.

urinate 3 pee, wee, wet; 4 leak, make; 5 stale; **6** piddle, widdle *UK*; **9** micturate; PHRASES: **3-3** pee-pee, wee-wee; **4, 5** pass water, pump bilge; **5, 1, 5** spend a penny; **6, 3, 6** siphon the python.

urine 3 pee, wee; 4 urea; 5 water; 6 piddle, widdle *UK*; PHRASES: **3-3** pee-pee, wee-wee; **4, 4** uric acid; **6, 4** little jobs, number ones.

US 7 useless; PHRASES: **5, 3** Uncle Sam; **6, 6** United States.

usable 3 fit; 4 good; 5 valid; 6 useful; 7 current, working; **8** reusable, takeaway, workable; **9** available, operating, practical, throwaway; **10** applicable, consumable, disposable, employable, functional, profitable, recyclable, utilisable; **11** convertible, exploitable, functioning, operational, serviceable; **12** advantageous; PHRASES: **2, 4, 7** at one's service; **2, 7, 5** in working order; **2, 9** in operation; **3, 3, 3** fit for use; **8, 3, 3** approved for use.

usage 3 use; 4 norm; 5 habit, usury; 6 custom, usance; 7 control, running; 8 handling, practice; 9 procedure, tradition, treatment; 10 management; 12 manipulation.

use 3 aid, ply, tap, tax, try; 4 beat, form, good, help, mold, need, role, task, wear, wont, work; 5 abuse, adopt, allot, apply, avail, drive, enjoy, habit, point, power, reuse, spend, touch, tread, treat, usage, value, waste, wield, worth; 6 absorb, custom, demand, employ, expend, finger, follow, handle, manage, misuse, profit, resort, source; 7 benefit, consume, control, deplete, exhaust, exploit, fatigue, operate, purpose, routine, service, towards, utility, utilize, wastage; 8 brandish, disposal, exercise, function, handling, maneuver, mistreat, overwork, practice, recourse, squander, usufruct; 9 advantage, appliance, depletion, enjoyment, luxuriate, operation, procedure, recycling, treatment; 10 administer, assistance, conversion, deployment, employment, exhaustion, management, manipulate, possession, usefulness; 11 application, carefulness, consumption, expenditure, functioning, reclamation, utilization; 12 depreciation, dilapidation, exploitation, manipulation, practicality; 13 applicability; 14 convertibility, serviceability; PHRASES: 2, 7 go through; 3, 7 get through; 4, 2 draw on, take up; 4, 3 wear out; 4, 3, 4 wear and tear; 4, 9, 2 take advantage of; 5, 2, 4 bring to bear; 5, 4, 4 bring into play; 5, 8, 2 avail yourself of; 6, 6 behave toward; 7, 4 benefit from; 8, 2 dedicate to; 10, 2 consecrate to.

used 3 old; 4 worn; 5 known, spent, stale; 6 reused, shabby; 7 drained, misused; 8 consumed, depleted, employed, everyday, expended, finished, occupied, ordinary, recycled, shopworn, utilized; 9 exercised, exhausted, exploited, hackneyed, makeshift, practical, pragmatic, reclaimed; 10 convenient, secondhand, shopsoiled, threadbare; 11 dilapidated, manipulated, provisional, subservient, utilitarian; 12 instrumental; PHRASES: 2, 3 in use; 2, 7 in service; 2, 8 in practice; 3, 4 run down; 3-5 dog-eared, pre-owned; 4, 2 ~ up; 4-2-4 down-at-heel, hand-me-down; 4, 3 worn out; 4-3 cast-off; 4-4 well-used, well-worn; 4-5 well-known; 4-7 well-thumbed, well-trodden; 10, 5 previously owned.

useful 5 handy, nifty, ready; 7 applied, helpful; 8 positive, sensible, suitable, valuable; 9 adaptable, advisable, available, effective, expedient, operative, practical, pragmatic, throwaway, versatile; 10 applicable, beneficial, commodious, convenient, disposable, functional, worthwhile; 11 informative, practicable, serviceable, utilitarian; 12 advantageous, constructive, multipurpose; PHRASES: 2, 3 of use, on tap; 2, 4 at hand, of help, on call; 2-4 on-line; 2-6 on-stream; 2, 7 of service; 3-7 all-purpose; 3, 8, 3 for everyday use; 5, 3, 3 ready for use; 5, 3, 5 rough and ready.

useful (be useful) 3 aid; 4 help, work; 5 avail, serve; 6 answer; 7 advance, augment, operate, promote, suffice; 8 function, subserve; 10 supplement; PHRASES: 4, 2, 5 come in handy; 4, 2, 6 come in useful; 4, 3, 4 fill the bill; 4, 4, 7 suit one's purpose; 5, 4, 4 serve one's turn; 5, 7 prove helpful; 7, 7 produce results.

usefulness 3 aid, use; 4 good, help; 5 avail, point, usage, worth; 7 purpose, service, utility; 8 efficacy; 9 commodity; 10 employment, expediency; 11 application, convenience, suitability, utilization, versatility; 12 adaptability, availability, practicality; 13 applicability, functionalism; 14 utilitarianism; PHRASES: 4, 5 good stead. *See also* **useful**

useless 2 US; 3 dud, off; 4 down, duff *UK*, naff, null, void; 5 extra, inapt, inept, kaput, spent, unapt, unfit; 6 effete, feeble, futile, trashy, unable; 7 inutile, invalid; 8 bootless, feckless, hopeless, impotent, obsolete, outmoded, pathetic, rubbishy, unneeded, unusable, unwanted; 9 abrogated, excessive, pointless, powerless, redundant, throwaway, unhelpful, unskilled, valueless, worthless; 10 antiquated, disposable, expendable, inadequate, inoperable, ornamental, unavailing, unsaleable, unskillful, unsuitable, unworkable; 11 dispensable, impractical, incompetent, ineffective, ineffectual, inefficient, inexpedient, inoperative, superfluous, unnecessary, unpractical, unqualified; 12 functionless, inapplicable, inconvenient, unemployable, unsuccessful; 13 impracticable, nonfunctional, unserviceable; 14 nonfunctioning; PHRASES: 2-2 no-go; 2, 2, 3 of no use; 2, 4 no good; 2, 6, 4 no bloody good; 3, 2, 5 out of order; 3, 2, 6 out of action; 3, 3, 7 fit for nothing; 3, 7 not working; 3-9 old-fashioned; 4, 2 past it; 4, 2, 6 hors de combat; 4, 3 worn out; 4, 3, 4 null and void, over the hill; **4-3-7** good-for-nothing; **6, 4** broken down; **6, 5** Mickey Mouse; **7-2** screwed-up.

useless (make useless) 4 lame, undo; **5** unarm, unfit, unman, unrig; **6** deface, disarm, impair; **7** cheapen, destroy, devalue, disable, dismast, exhaust, pollute, unmount; **8** abrogate, castrate, obstruct, overfish, overwork, sabotage; **9** dismantle, sterilize; **10** deactivate, disqualify, emasculate, obliterate; **11** contaminate, disassemble; **12** decommission; PHRASES: **3, 2** lay up, use up; **3, 5** lay waste; **4, 2, 6** take to pieces; **4, 4, 5** clip one's wings; **5, 2** break up; **5, 4** break down; **5, 4, 5** cramp one's style; **6, 5** render unfit; **6, 8** render harmless.

user 5 owner; **6** abuser, client, driver, worker; **7** handler, manager, shopper; **8** consumer, customer, employer, operator; **9** exploiter; **11** manipulator.

usher 4 help, lead; **5** guide, pilot, steer; **6** escort, helper, leader; **7** conduct, doorman, marshal; **8** shepherd; **9** accompany, attendant, conductor; PHRASES: **5, 3** Black Rod.

usual 3 par; **6** common, normal; **7** general, regular, routine, typical; **8** frequent, habitual, ordinary, standard; **9** customary; **10** invariable.

usurp 4 grab, take; **5** seize, squat, steal; **6** assume, invade; **7** violate; **8** arrogate, encroach, infringe, trespass; **10** commandeer; **11** appropriate; PHRASES: **4, 4** take over.

Utah 2 UT; **8** Industry (motto); PHRASES: **4, 4** sego lily (flower); **4, 4, 4** Salt Lake City (capital); **4, 6** blue spruce (tree); **7, 5** Beehive State (nickname); **10, 4** California gull (bird).

utensil *See* **eating (eating utensils and dishes), tool**

utilitarian *See* **practical**

utility 5 worth; **7** benefit, service; **9** advantage, handiness; **10** efficiency, usefulness; **11** convenience; **12** practicality.

utmost 5 chief; **7** extreme, highest, supreme; **8** farthest, greatest, remotest; **11** farthermost; PHRASES: **4, 7** most distant.

utopia 5 ideal; **6** heaven; **8** paradise; PHRASES: **7-2** Shangri-la.

utter 3 cry, say; **4** aver, tell, view; **5** mouth, opine, reply, sheer, speak, state, total, voice; **6** convey, impart, reveal; **7** declare, exclaim, express; **8** absolute, disclose, indicate, outright, thorough; **9** pronounce, verbalize; **10** articulate; **11** unqualified.

utterance 4 gasp, note, word; **5** aside, crack, noise, sound, vowel; **6** answer, dictum, murmur, mutter, phrase, remark, speech, thesis; **7** address, comment, opinion, phoneme, thought, whisper; **8** averment, greeting, locution, question, response, sentence, syllable; **9** assertion, diphthong, statement; **10** allegation, expression, reflection; **11** affirmation, declaration, ejaculation, exclamation, observation; **12** announcement, contribution, interjection, vocalization; **13** communication, pronouncement; PHRASES: **4, 2, 5** word of mouth; **4, 3** one's bit; **4, 5** one's piece.

UV 11 ultraviolet.

V

V 3 via; **4** five, vein, verb; **5** verse; **6** versus, violin; **7** victory; **8** velocity.

vacancy *See* **job**

vacant 4 bare, free, open, void; 5 blank, clean, clear, empty, inane; 6 absent, barren, devoid, hollow, unused; 7 untaken, vacuous; 8 unfilled; 9 available; 10 unoccupied; 11 daydreaming, featureless, indifferent; 13 characterless; 14 expressionless; 15 uncomprehending; PHRASES: 3, 2, 3 not in use; 7, 7 without content.

vacation 4 rest, stay, trip; 5 break, leave, peace, quiet, relax; 6 recess, relief; 7 respite, retreat, sojourn; 8 breather, furlough; 10 familymoon, recreation, sabbatical; PHRASES: 3, 3 day off; 4, 3 time off; 4-3 timeout; 5, 2, 7 leave of absence; 9, 8 volunteer ~. *See* **holiday**

vacillate 4 dart, flit, sway, vary; 5 drift, flirt, float, hover, shift, stall, swing, tease, waver; 6 boggle, change, coquet, dither, fidget, palter, seesaw, teeter, wobble; 7 quibble, shuffle; 8 hesitate; 9 fluctuate, oscillate; 10 equivocate; 12 tergiversate; PHRASES: 2, 4, 3, 5 go back and forth; 3, 2, 3, 5 sit on the fence; 4, 3, 6 chop and change *UK*; 5, 5 think twice; 6, 4 trifle with; 6-6 shilly-shally, teeter-totter.

vacillating 6 fickle, shifty, unsure, wobbly; 7 evasive; 8 hesitant; 9 equivocal, uncertain, undecided; 10 ambivalent, indecisive, irresolute, unresolved; 11 uncommitted, vacillatory; 12 noncommittal, undetermined; PHRASES: 2, 3, 5 in two minds *UK*, of two minds. *See also* **vacillate**

vacillation 4 whim; 5 doubt; 7 caprice, dubiety; 8 wavering; 9 deviation, hesitancy; 10 hesitation, indecision; 11 ambivalence, uncertainty, versatility; 12 equivocation, irresolution; 13 inconsistency; 14 tergiversa-

tion; **15** nonperseverance. *See also* **vacillating**

vacuous *See* **stupid**

vacuum 4 void; 5 space; 7 vacuity; 9 blankness, emptiness; 11 nothingness; PHRASES: 6, 5 ~ flask; 6, 7 ~ cleaner.

vagrant 4 hobo; 5 tramp; 6 beggar, roving; 7 drifter, nomadic, roaming; 8 vagabond; 9 itinerant, wandering.

vague 4 hazy; 5 fuzzy; 6 dreamy; 7 blurred, distant, elusive, inexact, pensive, unclear; 8 formless, nebulous; 9 ambiguous, desultory, equivocal, imprecise, undefined; 10 abstracted, distracted, indefinite, indistinct, inexplicit; 11 indefinable; 14 scatterbrained; 15 interchangeable *UK*, undistinguished; PHRASES: 6-6 absent-minded.

vain 4 idle; 5 empty, proud; 6 futile, hollow, otiose, snooty, swanky; 7 useless; 8 abortive, arrogant, hopeless, immodest; 9 bigheaded, conceited, overproud, pointless, strutting, worthless; 10 swaggering; 11 ineffective; 12 megalomaniac, narcissistic, unproductive, unsuccessful, vainglorious; 13 insubstantial; PHRASES: 4, 2, 7 full of oneself; 4-9 self-important; 5-2 stuck-up; 7-6 swollen-headed *UK*.

vain (be vain) 4 brag; 5 boast, swank, swell; 7 swagger; PHRASES: 4, 3 talk big; 5, 3, 2, 2 think one is it; 7, 7 flatter oneself.

vain person 3 fop; 5 swank; 7 bighead, egotist, peacock; 8 braggart, smartass, wiseacre; 9 Narcissus; 10 toffeenose; 13 exhibitionist; PHRASES: 2, 6 Mr Clever; 4-2-3 know-it-all; 4, 3 wise guy; 4-3 know-all *UK*, show-off; 4, 4, 2, 5 God's gift to women; 4, 6 Miss Clever; 4-7 self-admirer; 5, 4 empty head; 5, 5 drama queen *UK*, smart aleck; 6, 4 clever dick, turkey cock; 6, 5 clever clogs *UK*, smarty pants; 7, 4 pompous twit, swelled head; **7, 5** stuffed shirt.

vale *See* **valley**

valediction 5 adieu; **7** goodbye, sendoff; **8** farewell; PHRASES: **4, 8** fond farewell; **5-6** leave-taking.

valedictory 4 last; **5** final; **7** goodbye, parting; **8** farewell.

valet 4 tidy; **5** clean; **6** batman, Jeeves, polish, vacuum; **7** dresser.

valetudinarian 5 frail; **6** feeble, sickly; **7** invalid, patient; **8** neurotic; **9** unhealthy; **12** convalescent, valetudinary; **13** hypochondriac.

valiant 5 brave, noble; **6** heroic; **8** fearless; **10** courageous.

valid 5 legal, sound; **6** cogent, lawful, usable; **7** binding; **8** endorsed, official, rational; **9** effective; **10** acceptable, authorized, compelling, convincing, legitimate, persuasive, reasonable; **11** justifiable; PHRASES: **2, 5** in force.

validate 4 sign; **5** check, prove; **6** assure, attest, clinch, ensure, ratify, record, second, uphold, verify; **7** certify, collate, confirm, endorse, justify, support, sustain, warrant; **8** document, legalize; **9** ascertain, authorize, establish, guarantee, reinforce, vindicate; **11** corroborate, demonstrate; **12** authenticate, substantiate; PHRASES: **4, 3** bear out.

valley 3 cwm *UK*, dip; **4** dale, dell, dene *UK*, glen, rift, vale; **5** basin, chine *UK*, coomb, ditch, fjord, gorge, gully; **6** canyon, cirque, clough, corrie *UK*, dingle, ravine; **7** chimney, couloir; **8** crevasse; **10** depression; PHRASES: **5, 6** Grand Canyon.

valour *See* **courage**

valuable 4 dear, rare, rich; **5** loved, solid, sound; **6** costly, golden, prized, scarce, unique, useful, valued; **7** helpful; **8** esteemed, precious, sterling; **9** cherished, effective, exclusive, expensive, important, priceless, respected, treasured; **10** beneficial, infrequent, invaluable, meaningful, worthwhile; **11** appreciated, inestimable, significant; **12** advantageous, constructive; **13** indispensable, irreplaceable; PHRASES: **2, 1, 7** at a premium; **4-4** blue-chip; **4, 4, 4** like gold dust; **4-5** gilt-edged, high-value; **5, 1, 4** worth a mint; **5, 1, 7** worth a fortune, worth a million; **5, 5** above price; **6, 5** beyond price.

valuation 5 prize; **6** bounty, reward, survey; **7** premium; **8** estimate, judgment; **9** appraisal; **10** assessment, estimation, evaluation.

value 3 use; **4** cost, rate; **5** merit, price, prize, worth; **6** assess, bounty, charge, esteem, profit, rarity, revere, reward, survey; **7** benefit, cherish, premium, respect; **8** appraise, estimate, evaluate, judgment, rareness, scarcity, treasure; **9** principle, valuation; **10** appreciate, assessment, importance, usefulness; **11** consequence; **12** preciousness, significance, valuableness; **13** pricelessness; **14** invaluableness; PHRASES: **3, 5** par ~; **3, 5, 2** set store by; **4, 5** face ~, fair ~, high ~; **5, 5** great worth, ~ added; **6, 5** money's worth; **6, 6** regard highly; **8, 5** exchange ~, monetary ~, scarcity ~.

values 6 ethics, ideals, morals, tenets; **7** beliefs; **9** standards; **10** principles.

valve 3 tap; **4** tube; **6** faucet, spigot; **8** stopcock; **9** regulator; **10** controller; PHRASES: **5, 5** radio ~; **6, 4** vacuum tube.

VAN 9 advantage.

vandal 4 thug; **8** criminal, hooligan; **10** delinquent, trespasser.

vanish 2 go; **3** die, end; **4** fade; **6** expire; **8** dissolve; **9** disappear, evaporate; PHRASES: **2, 5, 3** be wiped out; **2, 7** go missing; **2, 12** be exterminated; **3, 3** die out; **4, 4** fade away; **5, 2, 5** cease to exist; **5, 3** peter out; **6, 7** become extinct.

vanity 4 airs; **5** pride; **6** egoism; **7** conceit, egotism; **8** futility, vainness; **9** arrogance, emptiness, immodesty, pomposity, unreality; **10** hollowness, narcissism; **11** megalomania, uselessness; **13** bigheadedness, conceitedness, overproudness, pointlessness, worthlessness; **14** grandiloquence, ineffectuality, insignificance; **15** ineffectiveness; PHRASES: **4-10** self-importance.

vanquish 4 rout; **5** crush; **6** defeat, master, subdue; **7** capture, conquer, control, oppress, repress; **8** dominate, overcome, restrain, suppress; **9** constrain, overpower, subjugate, tyrannize; **10** annihilate, discipline, intimidate; PHRASES: **7, 4** triumph over.

vantage point 5 angle; **6** bridge; **7** cockpit, lookout; **8** position; **9** belvedere, viewpoint; **10** standpoint, watchtower; **11** perspective; PHRASES: **5, 2, 4** point of view; **5, 4** crow's nest; **7, 8** viewing platform; **11, 4** observation post.

vapor 3 air, fog, gas; 4 haze, mist; 5 cloud, ether, fumes, smoke, spray, steam; 6 clouds, miasma; 7 aerosol; PHRASES: 5, 5 water ~.

vaporize 4 boil, burn, heat; 6 dispel, vanish; 7 destroy, scatter; 8 decimate, disperse; 9 disappear, disembody, dissipate, evaporate, liquidate; 10 annihilate, incinerate, obliterate; PHRASES: 2, 4 go away; 4, 2, 5 turn to vapor; 4, 4 boil away, burn away, fade away; 5, 4 drive away.

vaporizer 3 CFC; 5 Freon™, spray, still; 6 retort; 7 aerosol, inhaler, steamer; 8 atomizer; 9 condenser, nebulizer; 10 propellant; PHRASES: 5, 3 spray can.

vapour trail 8 contrail.

variable 6 patchy, uneven; 7 erratic, mutable, varying; 8 changing, flexible; 9 irregular; 10 adjustable, capricious, changeable, inconstant; 11 fluctuating; 12 inconsistent; PHRASES: 2-3-4 up-and-down.

variance 5 clash; 6 change; 7 dispute, dissent; 8 conflict; 9 disparity; 10 adjustment, alteration, difference, divergence; 11 discrepancy; 12 modification; 13 inconsistency.

variant 8 abnormal, modified, optional; 9 departure, deviation, different, irregular; 11 alternative; 12 modification.

variation 9 departure, disparity, reworking; 10 adaptation, difference; 11 discrepancy, distinction; 13 dissimilarity.

varicella 10 chickenpox.

varied 6 florid, patchy; 7 diverse; 8 fasciate, nacreous; 10 iridescent, ornamental, reticulate; 13 heterogeneous, kaleidoscopic, polychromatic. *See also* **various**

variegate 3 bar, dot, fox; 4 band, blot, dust, spot, stud, vein; 5 check, cloud, crack, craze, inlay, patch, stain; 6 checkr, dapple, enamel, marble, mottle, pepper, powder, streak, stripe; 7 brindle, freckle, grizzle, pattern, spangle, speckle, stipple, striate; 8 discolor, maculate, sprinkle; 9 damascene, diversify; 10 tessellate.

variegated thing 4 opal; 5 agate, moiré, nacre, prism, tiger, zebra; 6 jaguar, jasper, motley, sequin, tartan; 7 collage, leopard, peacock, rainbow, spangle; 8 confetti, spectrum, tricolor; 9 chameleon, cymophane, Dalmatian, dragonfly, Harlequin; 10 chessboard, enamelwork, serpentine; 12 checkerboard, kaleidoscope;

13 tortoiseshell; PHRASES: 4, 4 shot silk; 5, 3 tabby cat; 5, 6 crazy paving *UK*; 6-2-5 mother-of-pearl; 6, 3 calico cat; 6-3 tiger's-eye; 7, 4 Joseph's coat, watered silk; 7, 5 cracked glass, dancing light, marbled paper, parquet floor, stained glass; 8, 3 mackerel sky; 8, 4 peacock's tail; 9, 5 patchwork quilt; 10, 3 buttermilk sky.

variety 4 form, kind, sort, type; 6 change; 8 category; 9 diversity, selection, variation; 10 assortment, collection; 11 variability; 12 multiplicity.

variola 8 smallpox.

various 4 many, some; 5 mixed; 6 divers, sundry, varied; 7 certain, diverse, several; 8 assorted, manifold, multiple, numerous, polyglot; 9 composite, countless, different, multiform, multirole, polygonal, versatile; 11 innumerable, multiracial; 12 multifaceted, multifarious, multilateral, multilingual, multipurpose, polymorphous; 13 miscellaneous, multinational; PHRASES: 1, 5, 2 a range of; 1, 6, 2 a choice of, a number of; 1, 7, 2 a mixture of, a variety of; 2, 10, 2 an assortment of; 4-5 many-sided.

varnish *See* **coat, coating**

vary 5 adapt, alter, waver; 6 adjust, change, differ, modify; 7 convert, deviate, distort, diverge; 8 contrast, disagree; 9 diversify, fluctuate; PHRASES: 2, 9 be different; 3, 3, 4 ebb and flow; 4, 3, 4 rise and fall.

vast 3 big, sea; 4 epic, huge; 5 great, large; 6 cosmic, mighty; 7 endless, immense, massive; 8 enormous, infinite; 9 limitless; 10 prodigious; 12 incalculable.

vat *See* **container**

vault 4 arch, dome, jump, leap, safe, tomb; 5 bound, crypt, grave; 6 cellar, cupola, hurdle, spring; 7 ossuary; 8 catacomb, treasury, vaulting, voussoir; 9 mausoleum, sepulcher; 10 strongroom, undercroft; PHRASES: 3, 5 fan ~, rib ~; 3, 8 fan vaulting; 5, 5 groin ~ *UK*; 6, 5 barrel ~, lierne ~; 6, 7 burial chamber; 7, 5 domical ~; 8, 5 treasure house.

vaulted 5 bowed; 6 curved, fanned, ribbed. *See also* **vault**

vector 4 path; 5 route; 6 course; 7 carrier; 9 direction; 10 trajectory; PHRASES: 6, 4 flight path.

vegetable 3 cep, pea, yam; 4 bean, beet, corn, eddo, herb, kale, leek, okra, root, taro; 5 chard, cress, enoki, gumbo, laver, morel, olive, onion, plant, pulse, swede *UK*, tuber; **6** blewit, carrot, celery, daikon, endive, fennel, garlic, greens, herbal, legume, manioc, potato, radish, sorrel, squash, tomato, turnip; **7** avocado, boletus, cabbage, cassava, chicory, collard, dasheen, gherkin, lettuce, parsnip, potherb, pumpkin, salsify, seaweed, shallot, spinach, truffle, vegetal; **8** brassica, broccoli, capsicum, celeriac, cucumber, earthnut, eggplant, escarole, kohlrabi, mushroom, rutabaga, samphire, scallion, zucchini; **9** artichoke, asparagus, aubergine *UK*, calabrese, courgette *UK*, radicchio, sweetcorn *UK*; **10** champignon; **11** cauliflower, chanterelle, horseradish; PHRASES: **3, 4** bok choy, pak choi *UK*; **3, 6** new potato; **3, 7** red cabbage; **4, 2, 3, 3** corn on the cob; **4, 5** home fries; **4, 6** bean sprout; **4, 9** root ~; **5, 4** sugar beet, sweet herb; **5, 5** green onion, laver bread *UK*, salad onion, snake gourd, Swiss chard; **5, 6** sweet potato; **5, 7** lady's fingers, savoy cabbage; **5, 8** field mushroom, horse mushroom *UK*; **5, 9** dried ~, green ~, salad ~; **6, 6** marrow squash, spring greens; **6-6** mangel-wurzel; **6, 8** button mushroom; **7, 5** Bermuda onion, cabbage salad; **7, 8** Chinese mushroom; **8, 3** Atlantic yam; **8, 6** Brussels sprout; **9, 3** elephant's ear; **9, 6** dandelion greens. *See also* **fruit, pulse**

vegetarian **5** vegan; **6** veggie; **10** fruitarian; **11** frugivorous, herbivorous; **13** graminivorous; **15** lactovegetarian.

vegetarian dish **6** fondue, hummus, omelet *UK*; **8** omelette; **9** chilladas; PHRASES: **3, 5** nut roast *UK*; **3, 6** nut cutlet *UK*; **5, 7** pease pudding *UK*; **7, 6** stuffed marrow; **8, 4** eggplant roll; **8, 6** macaroni cheese *UK*; **9, 4** vegetable flan; **9, 5** vegetable chili, vegetable curry.

vegetate **3** bud, veg; **4** grow, leaf, loaf, root; **5** shoot; **6** flower, sprout, unfold; **7** burgeon, dehisce, gemmate, overrun; **8** flourish, overgrow, stagnate; **9** germinate; **15** photosynthesize; PHRASES: **3, 2, 4** run to seed; **3, 3** veg out; **3, 6** sit around; **3, 7** lie dormant; **4, 4** kill time, take root; **4, 5** shed seeds; **5, 2** shoot up; **6, 2** sprout up.

vegetating **5** inert; **6** torpid; **7** dormant; **8** comatose, indolent, slothful, stagnant; **10** stagnating.

vehemence **3** vim; **4** fire; **5** ardor, gusto, vigor; **6** fervor; **7** feeling, passion; **8** strength, violence; **9** intensity; **10** enthusiasm; **11** inspiration; **12** forcefulness.

vehement **6** heated; **7** fervent, intense, violent; **8** vigorous; **10** passionate.

vehicle **3** BMX, bus, cab, fly, gig, van; **4** auto, axle, bike, cart, drag, dray, hack, hood, horn, hull, jeep, limo, luge, mini, pipa, shay, sled, tank, taxi, tire, tool, tram, trap, tube, wain, wing *UK*; **5** agent, araba, brake, buggy, choke, clash, coach, coupe, crane, crate, cycle, dandy, dooly, float, lorry *UK*, means, metro, moped, motor, palki, pedal, plate, Rolls, sedan, sulky, tonga, train, trike, truck, trunk, wagon, wheel; **6** amtrac, berlin, bumper, camper, chaise, clutch, diesel, digger, fender, fiacre, grille, hansom, hearse, hotrod, hubcap, hurdle, jalopy, jitney, junker, landau, limber, litter, maglev, medium, pickup, rocket, saloon, sledge *UK*, sleigh, snocat, subway, surrey, tandem, tanker, tourer, tricar, weasel; **7** airfoil, autobus, autocar, backhoe, bicycle, bobsled, britzka, browser, calèche, caravan *UK*, caroche, channel, chariot, chassis, coaster, combine, conduit, dogsled, droshky, flivver, freight, growler, hackery, machine, minibus, minicab *UK*, muffler, omnibus, phaeton, postbus, pullman, scooter, shunter, shuttle, spoiler, sunroof, tallyho, tilbury, tractor, trailer, trolley, tumbril, unicorn, whiskey *UK*, wrecker; **8** barouche, bodywork, brancard, brougham, carriage, carriole, clarence, curricle, dormeuse, headrest, kibitzka, microbus, monorail, mudguard, quadriga, railroad, rickshaw, roadster, runabout, silencer *UK*, snowplow, sociable, tailgate, toboggan, tricycle, unicycle, victoria; **9** ambulance, amphibian, bubblecar, buckboard, bulldozer, cabriolet, charabanc *UK*, coachwork, dashboard, diligence, freighter, funicular, headlight, indicator *UK*, limousine, milkfloat, monocycle, palankeen, palanquin, sidelight *UK*, streetcar, stretcher, taillight, tarantass, transport, wagonette; **10** automobile, beachwagon, bookmobile, conveyance, earthmover, instrument, jinricksha, juggernaut *UK*, locomotive, motorcycle, mouthpiece, paddywagon, rattletrap, roadroller, shandrydan, skateboard, snowmobile, velocipede, windshield; **11** convertible, jinrickshaw, landaulette, quadricycle, semitrailer, speedometer, steamroller, transporter, whitechapel; **12** désobligeant, intermediary, pantechnicon; **13** pennyfarthing; **14** transportation; PHRAS-

ES: 2-4 go-cart; 3-1-3 vis-à-vis; 3-2-3-3 sit-up-and-beg; 3, 3 air bag; 3, 4 mud flap; 3-4 bob-sled, dog-cart, two-door; 3, 5 fog light, gas gauge, gas pedal, old crock, sun visor; 3-5 ice-yacht; 3, 6 cup holder, tin lizzie; 3-6 two-seater; 3, 7 rev counter *UK*; 3-7 gas-guzzler, two-wheeler; 3-8 gun-carriage; 4-2-4 four-in-hand; 4, 3 race car; 4-3 hard-top, open-car, side-car, taxi-cab; 4, 4 back seat, golf cart, high beam, roof rack *UK Can*, seat belt; 4-4 cape-cart, dead-cart, four-door, pony-cart, push-bike *UK*; 4, 5 dump truck, dune buggy, fire truck, land yacht, milk train; 4-5 boat-train, kick-start, mail-coach; 4, 6 bail gharry, fire engine, side mirror, turn signal, wing mirror *UK*; 4-6 pony-engine, post-chaise; 4-7 bone-breaker, four-wheeler; 5-1 model-t; 5, 3 black cab *UK*, cable car, gypsy cab, panda car *UK*, squad car, staff car; 5-3 horse-bus, horse-cab, horse-van, motor-car, motor-van, steam-car; 5, 3, 4 coach and four; 5-3-4 horse-and-cart; 5, 4 chair lift, child seat, motor home; 5-4 horse-cart, motor-bike; 5, 5 black maria, brake light, goods train, local train, night train, panel truck, state coach, stick shift; 5-5 motor-coach, pedal-cycle, sedan-chair, stage-coach, stage-wagon; 5, 6 sound system; 5-6 steam-engine, thika-gharry; 5-7 steam-omnibus; 5-8 cycle-rickshaw, horse-carriage; 6, 3 camper van *UK*, moving van, police car, sports car; 6-3 estate-car, street-car; 6, 4 mobile home; 6, 5 diesel train, hazard light; 6-6 double-decker, single-decker *UK*; 6, 7 racing chariot; 6-8 riding-carriage; 7, 3 armored car, hackney cab *UK*, outside car; 7-3 trolley-bus, trolley-car; 7, 4 booster seat, driver's seat, exhaust pipe, luggage rack; 7-4 bullock-cart; 7, 5 covered wagon, express train, freight train, garbage truck, license plate, parking light, puffing billy, railway train, through train; 7-5 station-wagon; 7, 8 hackney carriage *UK*; 7-8 prairie-schooner; 8, 3 delivery van; 8-3 jaunting-car; 8, 5 steering wheel; 8-5 shooting-brake; 8, 6 rearview mirror, traction engine *UK*; 9, 4 passenger seat; 9-4 governess-cart; 9, 5 Conestoga wagon, passenger train; 10, 5 windscreen wiper *UK*.

veil 4 hide, mask, pall, vail; 5 burqa *UK*, cloak, cover, front, velum; 6 chador, domino, purdah, shroud; 7 blanket, conceal, curtain, envelop, obscure, yashmak; 8 covering, disguise; 10 camouflage.

vein 4 lode, mood; 5 iliac, renal; 6 tibial; 7 basilic, femoral, hepatic, jugular; 8 brachial, cephalic; 9 pulmonary, saphenous; 10 subclavian, suprarenal.

velocity *See* **speed**

venal 4 bent; 6 amoral; 7 corrupt, lawless; 8 bribable, decadent; 9 mercenary; 10 degenerate; 11 corruptible.

vend *See* **sell**

vendetta 3 war; 4 feud; 6 battle, grudge; 7 crusade, dispute, quarrel; 8 campaign; PHRASES: 4, 8 hate campaign.

veneer 5 cover, guise, layer, plate; 6 facing, finish; 7 conceal, surface; 8 covering, pretense; 9 semblance; 10 appearance.

venerable 3 old; 4 aged, Bede, gray, ripe, sage; 5 hoary, musty, stale; 6 mature, mellow, senile; 8 decrepit; 11 patriarchal.

venerate *See* **worship**

veneration *See* **worship**

Venetian 4 doge; 5 Gobbo; 7 Antonio, Shylock; PHRASES: 5, 4 Marco Polo; 8, 3 venetian red; 8, 5 V~ blind, V~ glass.

vengeance *See* **revenge**

vengeful *See* **vindictive**

venial 3 lax; 4 mild, weak; 5 frail, human, minor; 6 feeble, infirm, slight; 7 failing; 8 flagrant, trifling, unseemly; 9 allowable, defective, deficient, excusable, imperfect; 10 forgivable, indecorous, indiscreet, pardonable, scandalous, vulnerable; 12 scandalizing; 14 understandable; PHRASES: 3, 5 too human; 3, 7 not perfect; 4, 5 only human; 6, 7 easily tempted; 7, 4 morally weak.

venial sin 4 flaw; 5 fault; 6 defect, foible, laxity; 7 demerit, failing, frailty; 8 weakness; 9 indecorum, infirmity; 10 deficiency, limitation, peccadillo; 11 impropriety, shortcoming; 12 imperfection, indiscretion, unseemliness; PHRASES: 3, 5 bad taste; 4, 2, 9 lack of principle; 4, 5 weak point; 5, 4 fatal flaw; 5, 7 human frailty, minor offense; 5, 8 human weakness, moral weakness.

venom 4 bane; 5 spite, toxin; 6 malice, poison, rancor, spleen; 8 acrimony.

vent 5 voice; 6 escape, outlet; 7 exhaust, express, opening, release; 8 aperture, tailpipe.

ventilate 3 air; 6 aerate; 7 discuss, examine, express, freshen; 9 publicize; PHRASES: 3, 3 air out; 4, 5 make known; 4, 6 make public.

ventilated 4 airy; 5 aired, fresh; 6 cooled, fanned; PHRASES: 3-6 air-cooled; 3-11 air-conditioned.

ventilation 6 aerage, airing; 7 fanning; 8 aeration; 10 fumigation, perflation; 11 oxygenation, refreshment; 13 deodorization, oxygenization, refrigeration; PHRASES: 3, 7 air cooling; 3, 11 air circulation; 3, 12 air conditioning.

ventilator 2 AC; 3 fan; 4 duct, flue, vent; 5 shaft; 6 blower *UK*, louver, louvre; 7 aerator, opening; 8 aperture; 10 respirator; PHRASES: 3, 4 air duct; 3, 6 air cooler, air filter; 3, 7 air passage; 3, 11 air conditioner; 4, 4 iron lung.

venture 2 go; 3 aim, bid, say, try; 4 dare, goal, risk, shot, spec, stab; 5 brave, crack, fling, offer, quest, scout, trial, whack; 6 aiming, course, effort, gambit, gamble, hazard, scheme, submit; 7 capital, express, mission, presume, program, project, propose, seeking, suggest; 8 business, endeavor, exercise; 9 adventure, intention, objective, operation, undertake, volunteer; 10 enterprise, experiment; 11 speculation, undertaking; 13 perfectionism; PHRASES: 2, 2, 4 be so bold; 3, 7 put forward; 4, 2 take on; 4, 3, 5 have the cheek *UK*, have the nerve; 4, 3, 7 take the liberty; 4, 3, 8 have the audacity; 4, 8 high endeavor; 6, 2 embark on; 6, 3 worthy aim.

veracity *See* **truth, truthfulness**

veranda 5 porch; 6 loggia; 7 balcony, gallery, terrace.

verbal 4 oral; 5 vocal; 6 spoken, stated, voiced; 7 lingual, uttered; 8 speaking; 9 unwritten, vocalized; 10 enunciated, linguistic, pronounced.

verbiage 3 gas, jaw; 4 blah, guff, junk, line, wind; 5 drool, hooey, prate, spiel; 6 babble, bunkum, drivel, gabble, humbug, jabber, patter, waffle, yammer; 7 baloney, blarney, blather, eyewash, flannel, prattle; 8 claptrap, flimflam, flummery, malarkey, trumpery, vaporing; 9 moonshine, poppycock; 10 flapdoodle, galimatias; 12 gobbledygook, psychobabble; PHRASES: 5, 5 empty words; 7-3 yackety-yak.

verbose *See* **wordy**

verbosity *See* **long-windedness**

verdant 4 lush; 5 fresh, green, leafy, rural; 6 grassy; 7 fertile; 9 luxuriant.

verdict 3 act, law; 5 award, canon, edict, order; 6 decree, result, ruling; 7 finding, outcome; 8 decision, judgment, sentence; 9 acquittal, judgement; 10 conclusion; 11 legislation; 12 adjudication, condemnation; 13 pronouncement; 14 recapitulation; PHRASES: 6, 4 decree nisi; 6, 8 decree absolute *UK*; 7, 2 summing up.

verge 3 end, hem, lip, nib, rim, tip; 4 brim, edge, side, tend; 6 border, margin; 9 crossover.

verifiable 6 proved; 8 provable, recorded, seconded, showable; 9 authentic, witnessed; 10 documented; 11 certifiable, confirmable, supportable; 12 demonstrable.

verification 5 check, proof; 6 avowal, surety; 8 averment; 9 assurance, collation; 10 avouchment, crosscheck, validation; 11 affirmation, attestation; 12 confirmation, ratification; 13 ascertainment, certification, corroboration, determination, documentation; 14 authentication, substantiation; PHRASES: 6, 5 double check.

verify 4 sign; 5 check, prove; 6 assure, attest, ensure, ratify, record, second; 7 certify, collate, confirm, endorse, recheck, support, warrant; 8 document, validate; 9 ascertain, determine, guarantee, vindicate; 10 crosscheck; 11 corroborate, countersign; 12 authenticate, substantiate; PHRASES: 4, 3 bear out; 4, 4 make good, make sure; 4, 7 make certain; 6, 5 remove doubt; 6-5 double-check.

verisimilitude 5 truth; 11 credibility, reliability; 12 authenticity, plausibility.

verity *See* **truth**

vermin 4 lice, mice, rats, scum; 7 rodents.

verminous 5 alive, buggy, lousy, mothy; 6 grubby; 7 maggoty; 8 crawling, flyblown, infested, weevilly; PHRASES: 3-8 rat-infested; 4-5 moth-eaten; 4-6 flea-bitten, pest-ridden; 5-6 louse-ridden.

Vermont 2 VT; 10 Montpelier (capital); PHRASES: 3, 6 red clover (flower); 5, 5 sugar maple (tree); 5, 8, 5 Green Mountain State (nickname); 6, 6 hermit thrush (bird); 7, 3, 5 Freedom and Unity (motto).

vermouth 2 IT.

vernacular *See* **dialect**

versatile 7 Protean; 8 flexible; 9 adaptable; 11 resourceful; PHRASES: 3-6 all-around.

verse 1 e, V; 3 ode; 4 epic, poem; 5 canto, ditty, epode, haiku, lines, lyric, stave, tanka; 6 ballad, monody, sonnet, stanza; 7 Alcaics, ballade, couplet, epigram, iambics, rondeau, roundel, sestina, triolet, triplet, virelay; 8 Clerihew, doggerel, Leonines, limerick, madrigal, Sapphics; 9 dactylics, Pindarics, trochaics, vilanelle; 10 macaronics; 11 alexandrine, fourteeners; 12 Anacreontics; PHRASES: 4, 5 free ~; 5, 4 fixed form, terza rima; 5, 5 blank ~, chant royal, rhyme royal; 5, 6 Burns stanza; 6, 4 ottava rima.

versed in *See* **experienced**

version 4 form, kind, side, sort, type; 6 report; 7 account, edition, variety; 9 rendering; 10 adaptation; 11 description, translation.

vertebrate *See* **animal**

vertical 5 erect, plumb, sheer; 7 upended, upright; 8 plunging, standing, straight; 10 upstanding; 11 precipitous; 13 perpendicular; PHRASES: 2-3-4 up-and-down; 4, 5 very steep; 4, 7 bolt upright; 8, 2 standing up, straight up; 8, 4 straight down.

vertical (be vertical) 4 rear, rise; 5 arise, stand; 6 uprear, uprise; PHRASES: 2, 10 be upstanding; 3, 2 get up, sit up; 4, 2 rear up, rise up; 4, 2, 4, 4 rise to one's feet; 5, 2 stand up; 5, 2, 8 stand up straight; 5, 5 stand erect; 5, 7 stand upright; 10, 2 straighten up.

vertical (make vertical) 5 build, erect, pitch, plumb, raise, upend; 6 square; 7 bristle, elevate, upraise; 10 straighten; PHRASES: 3, 2 set up; 4, 2 cock up; 5, 2 prick up, raise up, stick up; 5, 2, 3 stand on end.

vertically 2 up; 7 endways, endwise, upright; 8 straight; PHRASES: 2, 3 on end; 2, 3, 8 on its hindlegs; 2, 4, 4 on one's feet; 4, 7 bolt upright. *See also* **vertical**

vertical thing 4 crag, face, pole, post, scar, wall; 5 bluff, cliff, newel, plumb, pylon, scarp, stack, stake; 6 column, normal, pillar; 7 upright; 8 palisade, vertical; 9 precipice; 10 escarpment, lighthouse, skyscraper, stalactite, stalagmite; 13 perpendicular; PHRASES: 5, 4 newel post; 5, 5 right angle; 8, 4 vertical axis, vertical line.

Verulamium 5, 6 Saint Albans.

verve *See* **vitality**

very 1 V.

very big 2 OS. *See also* **large**

very French 4 tres.

very good 2 A1, OK, pi, so, VG; 3 ace; 4 star; 5 boffo, right; 9 excellent, wonderful.

vespers 8 evensong.

vessel 2 SS; 3 bin, jar, jug, keg, pot, tun, urn, vat; 4 boat, bowl, cask, drum, ewer, pail, pipe, ship, silo, tank, vase; 5 barge, basin, caddy, craft, ferry, liner, skull, yacht; 6 barrel, bottle, bucket, firkin, hopper, tanker, whaler; 7 amphora, cistern, drifter, dustbin *UK*, garbage, pitcher, rowboat, scuttle, trawler, warship; 8 hogshead, puncheon, sailboat, trashcan; 9 container, freighter, steamboat, steamship; 10 receptacle; 11 merchantman; PHRASES: 3, 5 tea caddy; 4, 4 wine cask; 4, 6 beer barrel; 4, 7 coal scuttle; 5, 3 trash can; 5, 4 canal boat; 6, 3 kilner jar; 6, 4 narrow boat *UK*, rowing boat *UK*; 7, 3 garbage can, rubbish bin *UK*, wheelie bin *UK*; 7, 4 fishing boat, sailing boat *UK*; 8, 3 watering can; 8, 4 merchant ship, pleasure boat; 9, 4 passenger ship. *See also* **ship**

vest 5 lodge; 6 assign, bestow, confer, weskit; 7 consign, devolve, entrust.

vestige 4 hint, mark, sign; 5 piste, print, relic, scent, spoor, stain, trace, track, trail; 7 remains, remnant; 8 evidence, footstep, tidemark, tyremark; 9 footprint; 10 fingermark, indication, suggestion.

vestment 5 amice, crook, ephod, fanon, frock, habit, miter, robes, staff, stole, tiara; 6 mantle, tippet, turban, wimple; 7 apparel, biretta, calotte, capuche, cassock, crosier, garment, maniple, orphrey, pallium, regalia, soutane, tallith, tunicle, uniform, vesture; 8 chasuble, cingulum, scapular, skullcap, surplice, yarmulke; 9 clericals *UK*, headdress, zucchetto; 10 canonicals; 11 pontificals; 12 pontificalia; PHRASES: 3, 6 dog collar; 6, 3 prayer cap; 6, 5 triple crown; 7, 3 priest's cap; 8, 6 clerical collar; 9, 3 cardinal's hat; 9, 4 episcopal ring.

vet 5 check; 6 screen; 7 examine, farrier, inspect, monitor, veteran; 10 horseleech, veterinary, zootherapy; PHRASES: 5, 6 horse doctor; 6, 6 animal doctor.

veterinary disease 3 BSE; 5 bloat, farcy, mange, worms; 6 rabies, spavin, sweeny, thrust; 7 anthrax, megrims, murrain, scrapie; 8 blackleg, glanders, sheeprot, staggers, swinepox; 9 distemper, strangles; 10 rinderpest; 11 myxomatosis, psittacosis; PHRASES: 3-3, 7 mad-cow disease; 4, 3 hard pad; 5, 5 liver fluke, swine fever; 6, 5 parrot fever; 6, 9 canine distemper, equine distemper; **7, 7** variola porcina.

veto 2 no; **3** ban, bar; **4** deny; **5** annul, black, check, debar, order, taboo; **6** cancel, curfew, denial, forbid, impede, notice, outlaw, rebuff, refuse, reject, repeal, revoke; **7** abolish, censure, dissent, embargo, exclude, inhibit, prevent, refusal, suspend; **8** abrogate, disallow, obstacle, obstruct, prohibit, quashing, restrict, sanction, turndown; **9** abolition, annulment, blackball, crackdown, debarment, exclusion, interdict, interfere, ostracism, ostracize, proscribe, rejection, repealing, restraint; **10** abrogation, disapprove, forbidding, illegality, impediment, injunction, prevention, repression, suspension, temperance; **11** countermand, criminalize, illicitness, obstruction, prohibition, restriction, suppression; **12** cancellation, circumscribe, counterorder, disallowance, illegitimacy, interdiction, interference, proscription; **13** excommunicate; **15** circumscription, excommunication; PHRASES: **3, 2, 2** say no to; **3, 5** red light; **4, 2, 8** send to Coventry; **4, 3, 4, 2** shut the door on; **4, 3-6** make off-limits; **4, 4** turn down; **4, 7** make illegal; **5, 4, 2** crack down on; **6, 1, 3** impose a ban; **6, 3** zoning law; **6, 4** pocket ~, thumbs down; **6, 7** decide against; **8, 3** Volstead Act.

vetoed 5 taboo; **7** illegal, illicit, refused; **8** rejected, unlawful, verboten; **9** exclusive; **10** contraband, inhibiting, injunctive, preventive, repressive; **11** obstructive, prohibiting, prohibitive, prohibitory, restrictive, suppressive; **12** illegitimate, interdictive, preventative, unauthorized; **13** impermissible; **15** circumscriptive; PHRASES: **3-2-6** out-of-bounds; **3-6** off-limits; **3, 7** not allowed; **4, 3, 4** null and void. *See also* **veto**

vex 3 irk; **5** annoy, tease; **6** bother, puzzle; **7** agitate, confuse, perplex, torment, trouble; **8** confound, distress, irritate; **9** displease.

VF 4, 4 very fair; **5, 9** video frequency.

VG 4, 4 very good.

via 2 by; **3** per; **4** over; **6** toward; **7** through, towards; PHRASES: **2, 3, 2** by way of; **2, 3, 3, 2** on the way to; **2, 3, 4** on the road; **2, 5, 2** en route to, on route to; **2, 7, 2** in passage to, in transit to.

vibrant 5 alive, vivid; **6** bright; **8** dazzling; **9** brilliant, energetic, pulsating, vibrating; **10** flamboyant; **12** effervescent.

vibrate 4 beat, drum, pant, tick; **5** heave,

pulse, shake, throb; **6** judder, quiver, rattle, shiver; **7** agitate, flicker, flutter, pulsate, shudder, tremble; **8** resonate, ticktock; **9** oscillate, palpitate.

vibration 4 beat; **5** pulse, tempo, throb, trill; **6** rhythm, tremor; **7** beating, flutter, pitapat, shaking; **8** drumming, rataplan, staccato, vibrancy; **9** agitation, heartbeat, juddering *UK*, pulsation, quivering, resonance, shivering, throbbing, trembling; **10** arrhythmia, flickering, shuddering; **11** palpitation, vibratility; PHRASES: **3-1-3** rat-a-tat; **5-5** heart-throb; **6-6** pitter-patter.

vicar 3 rev; **6** curate, rector; **9** incumbent; PHRASES: **5, 6** ~ forane; **5, 7** ~ general.

vice 3 sin; **4** evil, flaw, lust, porn; **5** cramp, fault; **6** defect, foible; **7** admiral, badness, failing, gripper; **8** impurity, iniquity, weakness; **9** amoralism, amorality, carnality, depravity, indecency, president, turpitude, vulgarity; **10** chancellor, corruption, debauchery, degeneracy, immorality, perversion, profligacy, wickedness; **11** degradation, shortcoming; **12** degeneration, imperfection; **14** unvirtuousness; PHRASES: **2, 6** no morals; **4, 5** ~ squad, ~ versa; **5, 6** loose morals; **5, 9** moral turpitude.

vicepresident 4 Burr (Aaron), Bush (George), Ford (Gerald R.), Gore (Al); **5** Adams (John), Agnew (Spiro T.), Gerry (Elbridge), Nixon (Richard), Tyler (John); **6** Cheney (Dick), Colfax (Schuyler), Dallas (George), Garner (John N.), Hamlin (Hannibal), Quayle (Dan), Truman (Harry); **7** Barkley (Alben W.), Calhoun (John Caldwell), Johnson (Andrew), Johnson (Lyndon B.), Mondale (Walter), Wallace (Henry A.); **8** Coolidge (Calvin), Fillmore (Millard), Humphrey (Hubert H.); **9** Roosevelt (Theodore); **11** Rockefeller (Nelson A.); **12** Breckinridge (John C.).

vicinity *See* **neighborhood**

vicious 4 mean, wild; **6** fierce, savage; **7** brutish; **8** spiteful; **9** ferocious, malicious, rancorous; **10** backbiting.

victim 4 Abel, butt, dupe, prey; **5** patsy, slave; **6** martyr, quarry; **8** sufferer, underdog; **9** sacrifice, scapegoat; **11** unfortunate.

victor 5 champ, first; **6** winner; **7** subduer; **8** champion, defeater, medalist; **9** conqueror; **10** subjugator, vanquisher; **11** prizewinner, titleholder; PHRASES: **4-2** shoo-in; **4, 6** sure winner; **5-6** world-beater; **5, 8** world champion; **7, 8** Olympic champion.

Victoria 1 V; 2 VR; 3 VIR (Latin: V~ Imperatrix Regina); 7 station.

victorious 7 unbowed, winning; 8 champion, crushing, quelling, unbeaten; 9 triumphal; 10 conquering, invincible, successful, triumphant, unbeatable, undefeated; 12 prizewinning, unvanquished; 13 unconquerable; PHRASES: 2, 3 on top; 2, 3, 2, 3, 4 on top of the heap; 3, 2, 3, 6 top of the league; 3, 4 the best; 4-7 game-winning; 4-10 ever-victorious; 5-7 match-winning, world-beating.

victorious (be victorious) 3 win; 4 beat, take; 5 carry, check, crush, quell, storm; 6 defeat, subdue; 7 capture, conquer, prevail, subject, triumph; 8 suppress, vanquish; 9 checkmate, subjugate; PHRASES: 3, 1, 5 win a point; 3, 1, 7 win a victory; 3, 2, 1, 7 win by a whisker; 3, 2, 3, 4 pip at the post; 3, 3, 4 win the race; 3, 3, 5 win the match; 4, 2, 5 take by storm; 4, 3, 5 wear the crown; 4, 3, 7 wear the laurels; 5, 3, 3 carry the day; 5, 3, 6 sweep the boards; 6, 7 scrape through.

victory 1 V; 2 KO, VE; 3 set, win; 4 game, rout; 5 skunk; 6 hiding; 7 beating, licking, success, triumph; 8 conquest, knockout, pushover, walkaway, walkover, whipping; 9 thrashing, trouncing; 11 overrunning; PHRASES: 3, 5 and match; 4-2 walk-in; 4, 4 love game UK; 5, 2, 4 piece of cake; 6, 7 narrow ~; 7, 2, 1, 4 winning by a mile; 7, 7 Pyrrhic ~, runaway ~; 8, 7 crushing ~, military ~, overtime ~.

view 3 eye, see; 4 deem, gaze, peek, peer; 5 angle, facet, scene, sight, vista, watch; 6 aspect, assess, behold, eyeful, fright, notice, regard, survey, vision; 7 display, examine, eyesore, inspect, observe, opinion, outlook, pageant, picture, scenery, showing, tableau; 8 analysis, attitude, consider, overview, painting, panorama, peepshow, perceive, prospect, scrutiny, seascape; 9 cityscape, landscape, spectacle, townscape; 10 assessment, exhibition, inspection, photograph, scrutinize; 11 examination, observation, performance; 13 understanding; 14 interpretation; PHRASES: 3-6 eye-opener; 4, 2 look at, look on; 4, 4 look over; 5, 2 think of; 5-3, 4 bird's-eye ~, worm's-eye ~; 5, 4 check over; 9, 5 spectator sport.

viewpoint 4 bias, gods, view; 5 angle, slant, stand; 6 aspect, circle, gazebo, squint, stalls, stance, theory, window; 7 eyeshot, gallery, lookout, mirador, opinion, premise, spyhole UK, stadium, terrace, theater; 8 peephole, position; 9 belvedere, bleachers; 10 grandstand, impression, standpoint, watchtower, windshield; 11 observatory, perspective, planetarium; 12 amphitheater; PHRASES: 5, 2, 4 point of view; 5, 2, 6 field of vision; 5, 4 crow's nest, sight hole; 5, 6 dress circle, store window; 5-6 judas-window; 7, 5 conning tower, vantage point; 7, 6 picture window; 7, 8 viewing platform; 8, 4 ringside seat; 11, 3 observation car.

vigilant 4 wary; 5 alert, aware; 7 careful, heedful; 8 cautious, watchful; 9 attentive, observant; 10 prognostic; 12 apprehensive; PHRASES: 2, 3, 5 on the alert; 2, 4, 5 on your guard.

vignette 4 clip; 5 essay, piece, print, scene; 6 design; 7 article, drawing, extract, picture, snippet; 8 fragment, painting; 9 monograph; 10 decoration, photograph; 12 frontispiece, illustration.

vigor 2 go; 3 pep, vim, zip; 4 brio, dash, élan, guts UK, kick, life, snap, zest; 5 balls, drive, éclat, force, gusto, oomph, pluck, power, punch, spunk, verve, welly UK; 6 effort, energy, health, mettle, pepper, spirit, wallop; 7 impetus, pizzazz, potency, sparkle, stamina; 8 activity, dynamism, exertion, ferocity, keenness, strength, vitality; 9 animation, freshness, intensity, lustiness; 10 enthusiasm, excitement, exuberance, heartiness, liveliness, robustness; 11 inspiration, refreshment, stimulation; 12 exhilaration, forcefulness, invigoration; 14 revitalization; PHRASES: 3-2-3-2 get-up-and-go; 4, 3, 7 piss and vinegar; 7, 5 staying power; 8, 6 physical energy.

vigorous 4 hale, keen, spry; 5 brisk, hardy, lusty, nippy UK, peppy, pushy, vital, zippy; 6 active, feisty, hearty, lively, punchy, robust, snappy, spunky, strong, virile; 7 dynamic, growing, healthy, intense, vibrant, zestful; 8 animated, forceful, forcible, outgoing, powerful, spirited, vehement; 9 effective, efficient, energetic, extrovert, exuberant, strapping, strenuous, thrusting UK; 10 aggressive, mettlesome; 11 extroverted, flourishing; 12 enterprising, enthusiastic; PHRASES: 2-5 go-ahead; 2-7 go-getting; 3-7 red-blooded; 4, 2, 3 full of pep; 4, 2, 5 full of beans; 4, 3, 6 hale and hearty.

vigorous (be vigorous) 4 push; 5 drive; 6 thrive; 7 enthuse; PHRASES: 2, 2, 3, 5 be up and doing; **3, 4** hit hard; **4, 6** rush around; **5, 4** enjoy life, steam away; **5, 4, 6** burst with health; **6, 4** strike hard.

vigorously 4 hard; PHRASES: **2, 4, 4** at full tilt; **3, 3** all out; **3, 4** con brio; **4, 1, 4** with a will; **4, 1, 9** with a vengeance; **4, 3** flat out, like mad; **4, 4** full pelt, like hell; **4, 5** like crazy; **4, 5, 5** full steam ahead; **4, 11** like gangbusters; **6, 3, 5** hammer and tongs. *See also* **vigorous**

Viking 8 Norseman, Northman.

vile 3 bad; **4** base, evil, foul, grim; **5** awful, black, gross, nasty; **6** horrid, wicked; **7** beastly, crooked, ghastly, heinous, immoral, noisome, noxious; **8** accursed, criminal, depraved, dreadful, horrible, terrible; **9** execrable, obnoxious; **10** abominable, unpleasant, villainous; **11** unendurable, unspeakable; **12** disagreeable; **13** objectionable.

vilification 5 abuse, libel; **6** attack, threat; **7** calumny, obloquy, slander; **8** reproach; **9** abasement, criticism, onslaught; **10** backbiting, defamation, execration, opprobrium, revilement, scurrility, thundering; **11** denigration, fulmination; **12** denunciation, vituperation; **13** disparagement, maliciousness; PHRASES: **6, 2, 5** volley of abuse; **6, 5** verbal abuse; **8, 5** slanging match *UK*.

vilify 4 rail, slur; **5** abuse, blast, chide, libel, scold, slang; **6** accuse, attack, debase, defame, defile, gossip, malign, rebuke, revile; **7** asperse, condemn, degrade, inveigh, pillory, slander, thunder, whisper; **8** belittle, disgrace, execrate, reproach, threaten; **9** criticize, denigrate, disparage, fulminate, insinuate; **10** blackguard, denunciate, vituperate; PHRASES: **3, 4** run down; **4, 3, 5** damn and blast; **4, 5** call names, talk about; **4, 5, 4** heap abuse upon; **4, 7** rail against; **4, 7, 4** pour vitriol upon; **5, 3, 2** speak ill of; **5, 4** round upon; **6-4** tongue-lash; **7, 7** inveigh against.

village 4 dorp *SA*, wick; **5** thorp; **6** Auburn, hamlet, pueblo; **7** clachan *UK*; **8** tanktown; **9** community, homestead; **10** crossroads, settlement; PHRASES: **3-5, 4** one-horse town; **4, 4** hick town, rube town; **7, 4** whistle stop; **7, 5** ~ green; **9, 4** jerkwater town.

villain 3 cad, dog, rat; **4** Iago, ogre; **5** baddy, brute, cheat, crook, fiend, heavy, rogue; **7** dastard, traitor; **9** miscreant, scoundrel.

vim *See* **vitality**

vindicate 4 free; **5** claim, clear, prove, purge, remit; **6** acquit, assert, defend, excuse, pardon, uphold; **7** absolve, dismiss, justify, release, restore, support; **8** liberate, maintain; **9** discharge, exculpate, exonerate, reinstate; **12** rehabilitate; PHRASES: **3, 4** set free; **3, 5** set right; **4, 4** make good; **4, 4, 5** free from blame; **5, 3** allow for; **5, 4, 4** clear one's name; **6, 3, 5** assert the truth.

vindication 5 proof; **6** pardon; **7** purging, release; **8** evidence, remittal; **9** acquittal, assertion, clearance, discharge, dismissal, purgation, remission; **10** absolution; **11** exculpation, exoneration, restitution, restoration; **12** compurgation *UK*; **13** justification, reinstatement; **14** rehabilitation; PHRASES: **3, 2** the OK; **3, 5, 5** the green light.

vindicator 7 excuser, pleader; **8** advocate, champion, defender; **9** apologist, justifier, palliator, proponent; **11** whitewasher.

vindicatory 8 excusing, refuting; **9** defending, defensive, rebutting, rejoining, remissive, retorting; **10** apologetic, excusatory, justifying, mitigating, mitigative, palliative, qualifying, supportive; **11** exculpating, exculpatory, exonerating, exonerative, explanatory, extenuating, extenuatory, vindicating; **13** argumentative, corroborative.

vindictive 4 mean; **5** cruel, nasty; **6** bitter, unkind; **7** hurtful; **8** avenging, pitiless, punitive, spiteful, vengeful, venomous; **9** malicious, merciless, punishing, rancorous, requiting, resentful; **10** implacable, malevolent, revengeful; **11** retributive, unforgiving.

vinegar 6 acetum.

vingt-et-un 7 pontoon; **9** blackjack.

vintage 3 age, era, old; **4** time; **5** dated, epoch, prime; **6** period; **7** antique, classic, typical; **8** outmoded; **9** essential; **11** traditional; PHRASES: **3-2-4** out-of-date.

viola da gamba 4, 4 bass viol.

violate 4 defy, harm, ruin; **5** abuse, break, flout, spoil; **6** breach, damage, defile; **7** despoil, destroy, disobey, disrupt, disturb; **8** infringe; **9** desecrate, disregard, interrupt; **10** contravene; PHRASES: **5, 2** break up; **7, 4** intrude upon; **8, 4** encroach upon.

violation 4 rape, riot; **5** crime; **6** felony, murder, tumult; **7** rioting, robbery, turmoil; **8** disorder, homicide, regicide, trespass; **9**

extortion, sacrilege, vandalism; **10** infraction; **11** criminality, lawbreaking, lawlessness, tyrannicide; **12** infringement; **13** transgression; PHRASES: **4, 7** gang warfare; **6, 4** street riot; **6, 5** street fight.

violence **4** fury, rape; **5** force, might, power, vigor; **6** energy, excess, frenzy, murder, sadism; **7** bluster, carnage, cruelty, ferment, passion, torture; **8** ferocity, fighting, homicide, savagery, severity, strength, thuggery, wildness; **9** agitation, barbarity, bloodlust, bloodshed, brutality, harshness, intensity, pugnacity, roughness, slaughter, terrorism, vandalism, vehemence, violation, virulence; **10** aggression, bestiality, fierceness, storminess, turbulence; **11** hooliganism, impetuosity, viciousness; **12** forcefulness; **13** effervescence, murderousness; **14** boisterousness, pugnaciousness; **15** destructiveness; PHRASES: **5, 5** brute force; **5, 8** rough handling; **8, 5** physical force.

violence (instance of violence) **3** fit, row; **4** riot, rush; **5** blast, burst, clash, crash, flood, quake, shock, spasm, throe, twist; **6** attack, charge, fracas, murder, onrush, ruckus, rumpus, sortie, sprain, tremor, tumult, uproar, wrench; **7** assault, killing, outrage; **8** atrocity, brouhaha, eruption, fracture, massacre, outbreak, outburst, paroxysm; **9** bloodbath, cataclysm, commotion, explosion; **10** convulsion, detonation, earthquake, fisticuffs, roughhouse; **11** dislocation, dissilience, disturbance; PHRASES: **4-2** blow-up; **5-2** flare-up, punch-up; **5, 4** tidal wave.

violence (use violence) **3** hit, mug; **4** pull, rape; **5** abuse, break, force, shake, shock, smash, twist; **6** ravish, sprain, strain, strike, wrench; **7** assault, clobber, destroy, torture, violate; **8** fracture; **9** dislocate; PHRASES: **3, 5** use force; **3-5** ill-treat; **4, 2** beat up; **5, 2** break in; **5, 4** break open, force open.

violent **3** hot, mad; **4** rude, wild; **5** acute, angry, bluff, brisk, cruel, fiery, harsh, rabid, rough, sharp; **6** abrupt, ardent, bloody, brutal, crazed, fierce, fuming, heated, insane, mighty, raging, savage, severe, stormy, strong, unruly; **7** berserk, bestial, boiling, brusque, enraged, extreme, fervent, flaming, frantic, furious, howling, intense, kicking, rampant, riotous, roaring, ruinous, seismic, untamed, vicious, warlike, waspish; **8** agitated, blustery, bursting,

charging, eruptive, forceful, forcible, frenetic, frenzied, gnashing, inflamed, maddened, powerful, ravening, sadistic, tigerish, vehement, vigorous, virulent, volcanic; **9** barbarous, bellicose, desperate, disturbed, ebullient, energetic, excessive, explosive, ferocious, hotheaded, impetuous, murderous, scorching, spasmodic, thrashing, turbulent, unbridled; **10** aggressive, blustering, boisterous, convulsive, headstrong, hysterical, immoderate, infuriated, outrageous, passionate, pugnacious, struggling, tumultuous, tyrannical, uproarious; **11** cataclysmic, destructive, devastating, impassioned, intemperate, tempestuous, threatening, unmitigated; **12** bloodthirsty, catastrophic, effervescent, overwhelming, ungovernable, unrestrained; **13** irrepressible; **14** uncontrollable; PHRASES: **2, 3, 7** on the rampage, on the warpath; **2, 9** in hysterics; **3, 2, 7** out of control; **3-3** red-hot; **3-7** hot-blooded; **4, 1, 3, 3** like a mad dog; **4, 1, 3, 4** like a mad bull; **4, 1, 6, 4** like a raging bull; **4-4** slam-bang; **5-6** heavy-handed.

violent (be violent) **4** dash, rage, riot, roar; **5** rebel, storm; **6** charge, hurtle; **7** bluster, rampage; **8** stampede; **10** roughhouse; PHRASES: **2, 2, 3, 7** go on the rampage; **2, 7** go berserk; **3, 3** see red; **3, 4** run amok, run riot, run wild; **4, 2, 1, 3** kick up a row; **4, 2, 1, 7** kick up a shindig; **4, 2, 4** take up arms; **4, 7** lose control; **4, 8** rush headlong; **5, 2** crash in; **5, 3** break out, burst out; **5, 3, 5** break the peace.

violent creature or person **4** fury, hulk, thug, wolf; **5** beast, bravo, brute, bully, demon, devil, Herod, rough, tiger, tough; **6** Amazon, dragon, madcap, madman, mugger, rapist, savage, terror, vandal; **7** butcher, caveman, hangman, hellcat, hotspur, monster, ruffian, tigress; **8** agitator, arsonist, assassin, Boadicea, bullyboy, hooligan, militant, murderer, spitfire; **9** anarchist, barbarian, desperado, firebrand, hellhound, termagant, terrorist, thunderer; **10** psychopath, pyromaniac; **11** executioner, Neanderthal, slaughterer; **13** revolutionary; PHRASES: **3, 2, 5** man of blood; **3, 3** mad dog; **3-4** she-wolf; **4, 5** wild beast; **4-5** fireeater; **4, 6** fire raiser *UK*, holy terror *UK*; **4-6** hell-raiser; **4, 8** mass murderer; **5, 2, 4** hound of Hell; **5, 3** tough guy; **6, 3** bovver boy; **6, 5** savage beast; **6, 6** serial killer; **9, 6** homicidal maniac.

violently 6 bodily; **8** headlong; **11** tyrannously; **13** precipitately; PHRASES: **2, 3, 4, 5** at one fell swoop; **2, 5** by force, by storm; **2, 8** at gunpoint; **2, 10** at knifepoint; **4, 1, 9** with a vengeance; **4, 3** like mad; **4, 3, 4** neck and crop; **4, 5** head first; **4-8** high-handedly; **5, 3, 4** tooth and nail; **6, 3, 5** hammer and tongs; **6, 3, 6** beyond all reason. *See also* **violent**

violent weather 4 gale; **5** flood, storm; **6** squall; **7** cyclone, sirocco, tempest, thunder, tornado, typhoon, weather; **8** blizzard, downpour; **9** hailstorm, hurricane, rainstorm, sandstorm, snowstorm; **10** cloudburst; **11** fulguration; PHRASES: **3, 7** bad weather; **4, 5** dust storm; **4, 7** foul weather; **5, 5** flash flood; **5, 6** gully washer; **5, 7** dirty weather, rough weather; **6, 4** strong wind; **8, 5** magnetic storm.

VIP 3 nib, nob *UK*; **4** name, star, tuft; **5** nabob, swell; **6** bigwig, tycoon; **7** magnate, mugwump, someone; **8** luminary; **9** celebrity, dignitary, personage; PHRASES: **3, 4** big shot; **3, 6** big cheese; **6, 6** public figure; **8, 7** visiting fireman.

virgin 3 new; **4** maid; **6** chaste, maiden, vestal; **7** pucelle; PHRASES: **6, 4** V~ Mary, ~ wool; **6, 5** ~ birth; **6, 7** V~ Islands.

virginal 3 new; **4** pure; **6** chaste, intact, virgin; **8** innocent, maidenly; **9** abstinent, continent.

Virginia 2 VA; **7** dogwood (flower), dogwood (tree); **8** cardinal (bird), Richmond (capital); PHRASES: **3, 8, 5** Old Dominion State (nickname); **4, 6, 2, 7** Thus always to tyrants (motto).

Virginia creeper 8 woodbine; PHRASES: **6, 3** Boston ivy; **8, 3** Japanese ivy.

virginity 6 purity; **8** chastity; **9** freshness; **10** abstinence, continence, maidenhead, maidenhood.

virtual 4 near; **5** quasi; **6** almost; **8** implicit; **9** effective, essential, imaginary, practical, simulated; **10** artificial, cybernetic; **11** fundamental.

virtual reality 2 VR; **10** cyberspace, simulation.

virtue 3 pro; **4** duty, hope, love, plus; **5** asset, faith, grace, honor, skill; **6** purity; **7** benefit, charity, decency, feature, honesty, justice, probity, quality; **8** altruism, chastity, chivalry, idealism, morality, prudence, sanctity; **9** advantage, character, fortitude, innocence, integrity, obedience, rectitude,

virginity; **10** generosity, perfection, temperance; **11** benevolence, magnanimity; **12** philanthropy, spirituality, virtuousness; PHRASES: **4, 5** good point, plus point *UK*; **4-7** self-control; **4, 8** good behavior; **4, 10** good conscience; **5, 4** moral tone; **5, 8** moral strength; **5, 9** moral rectitude; **8, 5** personal honor. *See also* **virtuous**

virtuosity *See* **skill**

virtuoso 6 artist, genius; **7** maestro, prodigy; **8** musician; **10** wunderkind; PHRASES: **7, 6** bravura player.

virtuous 2 pi; **3** coy; **4** good, holy, prim; **5** godly, moral, noble, sober; **6** chaste, decent, honest, modest, proper, worthy; **7** angelic, perfect, saintly, sinless, upright; **8** generous, innocent, seraphic, spotless, unerring; **9** blameless, Christian, guiltless, honorable, righteous, saintlike, spiritual, stainless, uncorrupt, unselfish; **10** altruistic, benevolent, chivalrous, idealistic, immaculate, impeccable, sanctified; **11** magnanimous, uncorrupted; **13** disinterested, philanthropic; **14** irreproachable; PHRASES: **4, 2, 4** good as gold; **5, 8** above reproach; **5, 10** above temptation; **7, 7** without blemish.

virtuous (be virtuous) 6 behave; PHRASES: **2, 4** be good; **2, 8** go straight; **3, 2, 4** see no evil; **4, 2, 4** hear no evil; **5, 2, 4** speak no evil; **5, 3, 5** shame the devil; **8, 6** practice virtue.

virtuous person 6 martyr, priest; **8** altruist; PHRASES: **4, 6** good person; **4, 7** good example; **4, 9** Good Samaritan; **5-5** goodygoody; **5, 6** white knight; **6, 6** honest person; **7, 2, 6** paragon of virtue; **7, 5** shining light; **8, 5** straight arrow. *See also* **pure person**

virulent 6 bitter, fierce, lethal, strong; **8** venomous; **9** malicious, poisonous; **10** contagious, infectious; **12** vituperative.

virus 4 worm; **7** disease, illness; **8** sickness; **9** infection; PHRASES: **6, 5** Trojan horse; **8, 5** computer ~.

visceral 3 gut; **5** gutsy, renal, vital; **6** animal, bodily, rectal; **7** cardiac, colonic, enteric, gastric, jejunal, uterine; **8** duodenal, internal, primeval; **9** abdominal, glandular, heartfelt, intuitive, primitive, pulmonary; **10** intestinal, splanchnic; **11** instinctive, instinctual; **12** intrauterine; **14** cardiovascular.

viscosity 6 lentor; **8** gluiness, ropiness, tenacity; **9** gummosity, loppering, viscidity; **10** clabbering, gelatinity, spissitude, thickening; **11** glutinosity, viscousness; **12** colloidality, gluelikeness, incrassation, inspissation; **13** jellification. *See also* **viscous**

viscous 4 oily, ropy, waxy; **5** gaumy, gluey, gooey, gumbo, gummy, heavy, pasty, tacky, thick, tough; **6** clammy, doughy, slabby, sticky, stodgy, syrupy, viscid; **7** gumlike, gummous, stringy, treacly *UK*, viscose; **8** adhesive, emulsive, gluelike; **9** colloidal, glutenous, glutinose, glutinous, gumbolike, tenacious; **10** gelatinous, incrassate, inspissate; **12** mucilaginous; PHRASES: **5-4** jelly-like.

visibility 3 har; **5** image, range; **7** eyeshot, horizon, profile, skyline; **8** evidence, eyesight, haziness, presence; **9** fogginess, mistiness, overtness, sightline; **10** luminosity, prominence, revelation; **11** familiarity, tangibility, visibleness; **12** availability, distinctness; **13** detectability, observability; **14** discernibility, perceivability, perceptibility; **15** conspicuousness, identifiability, recognisability; PHRASES: **4, 2, 5** line of sight; **4, 7** high profile; **4, 10** good ~, poor ~; **5, 3** naked eye; **7, 7** visible horizon.

visible 3 out; **4** open; **5** clear, overt, plain; **6** patent, public; **7** evident, exposed, obvious, outward, present, seeable, showing, surface; **8** apparent, concrete, distinct, external, familiar, manifest, material, palpable, tangible, unhidden, viewable; **9** available, prominent, watchable; **10** detectable, noticeable, observable, ubiquitous; **11** conspicuous, discernible, perceivable, perceptible, spectacular, superficial, unconcealed, undisguised; **12** discoverable, identifiable, recognizable, unmistakable; **13** unmistakeable; **15** distinguishable; PHRASES: **2, 4** in view; **2, 4, 4** in full view; **2, 5** in focus, in sight; **2, 8** in evidence; **3-7** eye-opening; **3-8** eye-catching; **4, 2, 3, 3** easy on the eye; **4-7** high-profile; **5-3** clear-cut; **5, 3, 7** above the horizon; **5, 8** worth watching; **6, 4, 4** before one's eyes.

visible (become visible) 3 wax; **4** come, dawn, loom, peep, rise, show; **5** arise, begin, enter, issue; **6** appear, arrive, emerge; **7** surface; **11** materialize; PHRASES: **3, 2** pop up; **3, 3, 5** see the light; **4, 2** come up, crop up, fade in, show up, turn up; **4, 2, 3, 5** come on the scene; **4, 2, 5** come to light; **4, 3** come out, peep out; **4, 3, 4** rear its head; **4, 4, 5** come into sight; **4, 5** come forth; **4, 7** come forward; **5, 2, 5** heave in sight; **6, 6** reveal itself; **7, 6** present itself.

visible (be visible) 4 show; **6** appear, emerge; **7** emanate; **9** transpire; PHRASES: **2, 4** be seen; **2, 7** be obvious; **4, 2** loom up, show up; **4, 2, 5** come to light; **4, 4, 4** come into view; **4, 5** loom large; **5, 2, 6** stand to reason; **5, 3** stand out, stick out; **5, 3, 1, 4** stand out a mile; **5, 3, 3** catch the eye; **7, 6** attract notice.

visible (make visible) 4 open, show, sign; **5** focus, light; **6** expose, mirror, reveal, signal, unmask, unwrap; **7** clarify, display, exhibit, reflect, uncover; **8** disclose, indicate, manifest, signpost; **9** elucidate, highlight, spotlight, underline; **10** illuminate, illustrate; **11** demonstrate; PHRASES: **3, 2, 4** put on view; **3, 4** lay bare; **4, 2, 4** keep in view; **4, 2, 5** keep in sight; **4, 5, 2** keep sight of; **5, 2** focus on; **5, 2, 5** bring to light; **5, 3** point out.

visible thing 4 mark, sign, skin, wake; **5** badge, light, print, sight, trace; **6** façade, legacy, signal; **7** effects, exhibit, feature, impress, imprint, outcrop, outside, surface; **8** backwash, cynosure, exterior, insignia, landmark, property, signpost; **9** footprint, handiwork, packaging *UK*, signboard; **10** attraction, belongings; **11** fingerprint, inheritance; **12** hereditament, illustration; PHRASES: **4, 6** bold relief, high relief, side effect; **5, 2, 4** field of view; **5, 2, 6** field of vision; **8, 7** personal effects.

vision 4 idea, plan; **5** dream, ideal, image, sight; **6** mirage, seeing; **7** concept, fantasy; **8** eyesight, illusion, phantasm, prophecy, scotopia; **9** foresight; **10** apparition, perception, prescience, revelation; **11** forethought, imagination; **13** hallucination, manifestation, visualization; **14** farsightedness; PHRASES: **3, 5** far sight; **4, 5** long sight, near sight; **5, 5** short sight; **5, 6** night ~; **6, 5** visual sense; **6, 6** visual acuity; **6, 7** mental picture; **7, 2, 3** ability to see; **7, 6** perfect ~.

visionary 4 poet, seer; **5** crank; **6** artist; **7** avoider, diviner, dreamer, fantast, ostrich, prophet, thinker, Utopian; **8** creative, escapist, fanciful, idealist, original, quixotic, romancer, romantic; **9** eccentric, fantasist, farseeing, inventive, prescient, prophetic; **10** daydreamer *UK*, enthusiast, farsighted, idealistic, rhapsodist, unworkable; **11** imaginative, romanticist, unrealistic; **12** somnambulist, unrealizable; **13** impracticable; **14** philanthropist; PHRASES: **3, 7** Don

Quixote; **4-5** myth-maker; **5-5** lotus-eater; **6, 6** knight errant; **7, 7** wishful thinker; **8, 6** creative worker.

visit 3 see; **4** call, stay, trip; **5** break, haunt, relax; **6** outing, summer, unbend, winter; **7** holiday *UK*, layover, sojourn, weekend; **8** frequent, stopover, vacation; PHRASES: **2, 2** go to; **2, 2, 3** go to see; **3, 2** pop in; **4, 2** call on, drop by, look up, stay at, stay in, stop at; **4, 2, 2** call in on *UK*, drop in on; **4, 2, 4** keep up with; **4, 3** stop off; **4, 4** duty call, stop over, stop with; **5, 4** house call; **6, 4** social call; **7, 2** holiday at *UK*; **8, 5** official ~.

visor 3 cap. *See* **screen**

vista *See* **view**

Vistula 5 Wisla; **8** Weichsel; PHRASES: **7, 5** Wislany Zalew; **8, 4** Frisches Haff; **9, 5** Vislinsky Zaliv.

visual 5 chart, graph, optic; **6** filmic, ocular, scenic; **7** evident, eyelike, graphic, optical, picture, visible; **8** concrete, illusory, visional; **9** binocular, chromatic, graphical, imaginary, painterly, panoramic, pictorial; **10** observable, ophthalmic, photograph, reflecting, telescopic; **11** discernible, illusionary, microscopic; **12** illustration, photographic, stereoscopic; PHRASES: **3-11** two-dimensional; **6, 3** ~ aid; **6-4** mirror-like.

visual aid 3 VCR; **4** film; **5** chart, image, loupe, model, movie, specs, video; **6** frames, lenses, optics, shades, visual; **7** diagram, glasses, goggles, monocle; **8** bifocals, contacts, eyeglass, eyeshade, gunsight, spyglass; **9** backsight, foresight, lorgnette, magnifier, telescope, telescopy; **10** binoculars, microscope, microscopy, spectacles, sunglasses; **11** microreader, stereoscopy; **12** illustration, spectroscopy; **13** magnification; PHRASES: **4-4, 7** half-moon glasses; **4, 5** peep sight; **4, 6** hard lenses; **4, 7** dark glasses; **5-3** pince-nez; **5, 5** cross hairs; **5, 6** sight screen; **5, 7** field glasses, night glasses, opera glasses; **6, 7** granny glasses; **7, 6** contact lenses; **7, 7** reading glasses; **8, 7** polaroid glasses; **9, 6** microfilm reader; **10, 5** magnifying glass, telescopic sight.

visualization 5 image; **6** vision; **7** insight, picture, therapy; **8** planning; **9** awareness, foresight, imagining, picturing, prevision; **10** conception, meditation, perception; **11** discernment, imagination, perspicuity; **12** anticipation, perspicacity; **13** consideration, contemplation, hallucination, understanding; PHRASES: **3-11** far-

sightedness; **5, 3** mind's eye; **5, 8** image creation; **6, 5** mental image; **6, 7** mental picture; **9, 2** conjuring up.

visualize 4 plan; **7** discern, foresee, imagine, picture; **8** consider, envisage, envision, perceive; **10** anticipate, understand; **11** contemplate; PHRASES: **2, 5, 2** be aware of; **4, 5, 2** take stock of; **5, 2** dream of; **5, 5** think about.

vital 3 key; **4** live, real; **6** biotic, lively, viable; **7** crucial; **8** animated, critical; **9** essential, momentous, vivacious; **10** biological; **11** fundamental; **13** indispensable; PHRASES: **5, 5** ~ organ.

vitality 3 pep, vim, zip; **4** dash, life, zest; **5** drive, spunk, verve, vigor; **6** energy, spirit; **7** panache; **8** boldness, buoyancy, dynamism, raciness, strength, vivacity; **9** animation, vividness; **10** exuberance, liveliness; PHRASES: **3-2-3-2** get-up-and-go; **4, 2, 5** joie de vivre.

vitamin 1 A, B, C, D, E, K; **6** biotin; **7** choline; PHRASES: **5, 4** folic acid; **6, 4** lipoic acid; **9, 4** nicotinic acid; **11, 4** pantothenic acid.

vitamin deficiency disease 6 scurvy; **7** rickets; **8** beriberi; **12** osteomalacia; **13** xerophthalmia; PHRASES: **5, 9** night blindness.

vituperate 5 curse; **6** defame, revile, vilify; **7** blacken; **8** execrate; PHRASES: **4, 7** pour vitriol.

vituperative 7 abusive; **8** blasting, critical, libelous, reviling, scathing; **9** attacking, insulting, malicious, offensive, vilifying, vitriolic; **10** calumnious, censorious, defamatory, denouncing, slanderous; **11** ignominious, opprobrious, reproachful, threatening; **12** denunciatory.

vivid 4 rich; **5** clear, fresh, gaudy, lucid, plain; **6** active, bright, lively, strong; **7** glowing, graphic, intense, vibrant; **8** colorful, creative, distinct, original, poignant, powerful, striking; **9** brilliant, ingenious, inventive, realistic; **10** flamboyant; PHRASES: **4-4** life-like; **7, 5** crystal clear.

vixen 4 fury; **5** bitch, siren, witch; **7** hellcat, tigress, wildcat; PHRASES: **3-5** she-devil; **4-3** hell-hag.

VO 4, 3 very old; **9, 5** Victorian Order.

vocabulary 5 terms, words; **7** lexicon; **8** glossary, language; **10** dictionary; **11** expressions, terminology; PHRASES: **4, 4** word list.

vocal 5 frank; **6** spoken, verbal, voiced; **7** uttered, voluble; **9** insistent, outspoken, unwritten; **10** vociferous.

vocation 3 job; **4** bent, work; **6** career, talent; **8** aptitude; **10** occupation, profession; **11** inclination.

vociferous 4 loud; **5** noisy, vocal; **7** booming, raucous, roaring, voluble, yelling; **8** shouting, strident; **9** bellowing, clamorous, deafening, screaming, talkative; **10** stentorian, thundering, thunderous, uproarious; **11** loudmouthed; **12** enthusiastic, obstreperous; PHRASES: **4-8** full-throated.

vogue *See* **fashion**

voice 3 say; **4** alto, bass, vote; **5** opine, speak, tenor, utter; **6** active, assert, intone, larynx, middle, speech, treble; **7** declare, express, opinion, passive, soprano; **8** proclaim; **9** contralto, pronounce, utterance; **10** articulate, expression; **11** declaration; PHRASES: **5, 2, 6** power of speech, right of speech; **5, 3** ~ box; **5, 5** vocal sound; **5, 6** vocal chords; **7, 5** singing ~.

voice box 6 larynx.

voiceless 4 dumb, mute, surd; **6** infant, silent; **7** aphonic, ignored; **8** taciturn, unvoiced, wordless; **9** abandoned, dysphonic, forgotten, invisible; **10** overlooked, unspeaking; **13** disadvantaged, unrepresented; **15** disenfranchised, uncommunicative.

void 3 gut; **4** blow, bone, draw, hole, vent; **5** abyss, annul, drain, empty, purge, space; **6** cancel, cavity, fillet, reject, remove, unclog, unfoul, vacant, vacate, vacuum; **7** curette, deplete, exhaust, invalid, negated; **8** annulled, canceled, evacuate, infinity, obsolete, occupied; **9** eliminate, emptiness; **10** disembowel, eviscerate, hollowness, unoccupied; **11** nothingness; PHRASES: **3, 2, 3** not in use; **4, 3** blow out, pump out; **4, 3, 4** null and ~; **5, 2** drink up; **5, 2, 3, 5** drain to the dregs; **5, 3** clean out, clear off *UK*, clear out, empty out, sweep out, throw out; **5, 3, 5** clear the decks; **5, 4** clear away; **5, 5** empty space; **6, 3** siphon off.

volatile 6 fickle; **8** unstable; **9** dangerous, excitable, explosive, hazardous, impulsive, mercurial, vaporable, vaporific; **10** capricious, changeable, evaporable, precarious; **11** evaporative, vaporescent, vaporisable; **13** unpredictable, volatilisable; PHRASES: **3-7** hot-blooded; **3-8** hot-tempered.

volatility 11 instability, variability; **12** excitability, irascibility, vaporability; **13** changeability, evaporability; **14** vaporisability. *See also* **volatile**

volcanic 5 laval; **6** molten; **7** seismic; **8** eruptive; **9** explosive; **11** pyroclastic.

volcano 2 aa; **3** ash; **4** cone, Etna, Etna (Mount), Fuji (Mount), lava, melt, vent; **5** Hekla, Kenya (Mount), magma, Misti; **6** crater, ejecta, Erebus (Mount), geyser, Katmai (Mount), pumice, Shasta (Mount), tephra; **7** caldera, fissure, Kilauea, Rainier (Mount); **8** Cameroon, Cotopaxi, eruption, fumarole, Krakatau, Krakatoa, pahoehoe, Pinatubo (Mount), Vesuvius (Mount); **9** Stromboli, volcanism; **12** Popocatépetl; PHRASES: **2, 6** St. Helens (Mount); **3, 4** gas vent; **5, 3** Mauna Kea, Mauna Loa; **6, 7** active ~, shield ~; **8, 7** inactive ~; **9, 5, 7** Soufriere Hills V~.

vole 5, 5 field mouse; **6, 5** meadow mouse.

Volgograd 9 Tsaritsyn; **10** Stalingrad.

volition 4 will, wish; **6** choice, desire; **8** decision.

volley 3 hit, lob; **4** kick; **6** shower, stream, strike; **7** barrage, cascade, torrent.

voluble *See* **talkative**

volume 1 V; **2** CC, CL; **3** GAL, VOL; **4** book, bulk, mass, size, tome; **5** folio, quart, space; **6** quarto; **8** loudness.

voluntarily 6 freely, gladly; **7** happily; **9** willingly; PHRASES: **2, 4, 3, 6** of one's own accord; **3, 4, 3, 3** off one's own bat.

voluntary 6 chosen, unpaid; **7** charity, offered; **8** intended, offering, unbidden, unforced; **9** volunteer; **10** altruistic, charitable, controlled, deliberate, unprompted; **11** intentional, spontaneous; **12** humanitarian, volunteering; **13** philanthropic; PHRASES: **2, 4, 3, 6** on one's own accord; **3, 4, 3, 3** off one's own bat; **4, 6** with intent; **4-9** self-appointed.

volunteer 3 VSO (Voluntary Service Overseas); **4** give, lend, loan, tell; **5** offer; **6** advise, helper, inform, notify; **7** furnish, pioneer, present, provide; **8** acquaint, altruist; **9** candidate, innovator, undertake; **10** adventurer, benefactor, missionary, speculator, workaholic; **11** contributor *UK*; **12** entrepreneur, humanitarian; **14** philanthropist; PHRASES: **2-6** do-gooder, go-getter; **3, 7** put forward; **4, 2** step up, take on; **4, 6** hard worker; **4, 7** come forward; **4, 7, 3** work without pay; **4, 9** Good Samaritan; **5, 4** offer help; **5, 5** Peace Corps; **5, 7** candy striper; **5, 10** offer assistance; **6, 6** social worker, unpaid worker; **6, 7** public servant; **7, 6** charity worker; **9, 6** voluntary worker.

vomit 3 cat, gag; **4** barf, bile, emit, honk, hurl, puke, sick *UK*, spew, spit; **5** eject, expel, heave, retch; **7** chunder *UK*, upchuck, vomitus; **9** ejaculate; **11** regurgitate; PHRASES: **2, 4** be sick; **2, 8** be nauseous; **2, 9** be nauseated; **3, 6** cry Hughie; **4, 2** sick up *UK*; **4, 3** send out, spew out, spit out; **4, 5** send forth, spew forth; **5, 1, 3** shoot a cat; **5, 2** bring up, chuck up *UK*, throw up; **5, 3** throw out.

vortex 4 eddy; **5** flood, gurge, storm, surge, swirl, whirl; **6** morass; **7** cyclone, tornado, twister; **8** blizzard, quagmire; **9** charybdis, maelstrom, whirlpool, whirlwind; **10** turbulence, waterspout, whirlblast; PHRASES: **5, 4** tidal wave.

vote 2 no; **3** aye, nay, run, yea; **4** back, poll; **5** cross, elect, stand, voice; **6** ballot, choose, divide, reject, return; **7** canvass, support; **8** deselect, division *UK*, election; **10** plebiscite, referendum; **11** electioneer; **12** blackballing; PHRASES: **2, 2, 3, 7** go to the country; **3, 3** opt for; **3, 6** vox populi; **4, 1, 3** have a say; **4-2, 4** mail-in ~; **4, 2, 5** show of hands; **4, 4** card ~, cast ~, jury poll, open ~; **4, 4, 4** cast your ~; **5, 4** straw poll, voice ~; **5, 7** count ballots; **7, 4** opinion poll; **8, 4** absentee ~, deciding ~, majority ~; **8, 6** absentee ballot; **9, 4** blackball ~; **10, 4** cumulative ~.

vouchsafe 4 give; **5** agree, allow, grant, offer; **6** permit; **7** consent, promise.

vow 4 oath, test, word; **5** swear; **6** adjure, assert, assure, charge, commit, pledge; **7** declare, promise, testify; **8** charging; **9** affidavit, assurance, guarantee, statement, undertake; **10** adjuration, commitment, deposition; **11** declaration, undertaking; PHRASES: **4, 2, 5** word of honor; **4, 2, 6** oath of office; **4, 3, 4** kiss the book; **5, 4, 5** cross one's heart; **5, 9** sworn statement, sworn testimony.

voyage 2 go; **3** ply, run; **4** sail, trip; **6** cruise; **7** journey, odyssey, passage, proceed; **8** crossing.

voyeur 3 spy; **6** viewer; **7** watcher; **8** busybody, observer, onlooker; **10** rubberneck; PHRASES: **4, 6** nosy parker *UK*; **7, 3** Peeping Tom.

voyeurism 8 nosiness; **9** prurience; **12** ghoulishness; **13** lecherousness, rubbernecking, sexploitation.

vulcanite 7 ebonite.

vulgar 3 bad; **4** blue, loud, racy, rude, wild; **5** brash, cheap, crass, crude, gandy, gross, latin, rough, showy, tacky; **6** coarse, common, earthy, garish, gauche, glitzy, kitsch, plebby, savage, tawdry; **7** boorish, loutish, naughty, parvenu, uncouth; **8** barbaric, fraction, improper, plebeian; **9** inelegant, offensive, primitive, tasteless, unrefined; **10** outlandish, uncultured, unfeminine, unladylike; **12** discourteous, meretricious, ostentatious; **13** ungentlemanly; PHRASES: **3-1** non-U *UK*; **3-3** Day-Glo™; **3-4** ill-bred; **3-8** bad-mannered, ill-mannered; **5, 3** infra dig; **5, 10** infra dignitatem.

vulgar herd 4 scum; **6** rabble; PHRASES: **3, 4, 3, 5** Tom Dick and Harry; **3, 6** hoi polloi, the people, the proles; **4, 3, 4** rank and file; **4-4** riff-raff.

vulgarity 4 oath; **5** curse; **6** kitsch; **7** crudity; **9** expletive, indecency, obscenity, swearword, vulgarism; **13** insensitivity; PHRASES: **3, 5** bad taste; **3, 7** bad manners; **3, 8** bad language; **4, 4** rude word; **4-6, 4** four-letter word. *See also* **vulgar**

vulgarize 5 lower; **7** cheapen, coarsen; **10** popularize; **13** commercialize; PHRASES: **5, 3, 4** lower the tone.

vulgar person 3 cad, yob *UK*; **4** boor, lout, pleb, slob; **5** prole, yokel; **6** savage; **7** bounder, parvenu; **9** barbarian, vulgarian; **10** Philistine; PHRASES: **4-3** show-off; **7, 5** nouveau riche.

vulnerability 4 flaw; **6** defect; **7** failing, naiveté, naivety *UK*; **8** exposure; **9** innocence, liability; **10** insecurity; **11** instability, nonimmunity; **12** imperfection, pregnability; **14** susceptibility; PHRASES: **4, 2, 4** feet of clay; **4, 4** soft spot; **4, 6** easy target; **4, 10** soft underbelly; **5, 2, 3, 5** chink in the armor; **5, 4** fatal flaw; **6, 4** tender spot, tragic flaw; **7, 4** sitting duck; **7, 5** exposed flank; **7, 6** sitting target *UK*; **8, 4** Achilles' heel. *See also* **vulnerable**

vulnerable 4 bare, open, weak; **5** naive, naked; **6** liable; **7** exposed, unarmed, unaware, unready, unsound; **8** deserted, helpless, isolated, stranded, unwarned; **9** abandoned, guideless, pregnable, unarmored, uncovered, unflanked, unguarded; **10** expugnable, unattended, undefended, unescorted, unprepared, unshielded; **11** defenseless, shelterless, susceptible, unfortified, unprotected, unsupported; **12** unshepherded; PHRASES: **2, 3, 5, 2** at the mercy of; **2, 4** at risk; **2, 6** in danger; **3, 2, 1, 4** out on a limb; **3, 4, 5** off one's guard; **4-4** wide-open; **4, 4, 3, 3** left high and dry; **4, 6** clay pigeon.

W

W 4 watt, week, west, wife; **5** width; **6** wicket.

wad 3 gob, lag, pad; **4** chew, fill, lump, mass, pile, plug, roll; **5** clump, screw, sheaf, stack, stuff, twist; **6** bundle; **7** compact, cushion, portion, scrunch, squeeze; **8** compress.

waffle 6 babble, drivel, ramble; **7** blabber, rubbish; **8** nonsense; **10** balderdash; **12** gobbledygook. *See also* **cake**

waft 3 fan; **4** gust, puff, sail; **5** draft, drift, float, glide; **6** breath, breeze.

wag 3 wit; **4** flap, wave; **5** comic, joker, shake; **6** twitch, waggle, wiggle; **8** comedian, humorist.

wage 3 pay; **5** fight; **6** income, pursue, salary; **7** conduct; **8** earnings; PHRASES: **6, 2** engage in.

wager 3 bet; **4** ante, risk; **5** stake; **6** gamble; **7** venture.

wail 3 bay, cry; **4** fuss, howl, keen, moan, weep, yowl; **5** whine; **6** scream, shriek; **7** protest; **8** complain; **9** complaint; PHRASES: **4, 2, 1, 4** kick up a fuss.

waistcoat 4 vest.

wait 3 gap; **4** line, stay, stop; **5** await, dally, delay, pause, queue, tarry; **6** dawdle, expect, linger, loiter; **8** interval; **10** anticipate; **12** intermission, postponement; PHRASES: **4, 2** hang on, ~ up; **4-2** hold-up; **4, 3** time lag; **4, 3, 3** look out for; **4, 3, 4** pass the time; **4, 4** hang back, hang fire, kill time; **4, 4, 5** cool one's time, hold one's fire; **4, 4, 5** cool one's heels, kick one's heels; **4, 4, 6** hold one's horses; **4, 6** hang around; **5, 2** stand by.

waka 5 canoe.

wake 4 stir; **5** rouse; **6** arouse, awaken, kindle, rewake; **7** rewaken; PHRASES: **4, 2** come to, ~ up; **4, 6** come around.

Wales 5 Cymru; **7** Cambria; **8** Welshman; **9** Welshness; **10** Welshwoman; PHRASES: **3, 5** the Welsh; **3, 12** the Principality; **5, 5** North W~, South W~; **5, 6** North Walian, South Walian.

walk 3 jog, run; **4** chug, dart, dash, gait, hare, hike, lane, lope, pace, path, roam, roll, tour, trip; **5** amble, coast, dodge, drift, march, mince, shift, stray, strut, tramp, tread, weave; **6** cruise, motion, patter, potter *UK*, putter, stride, stroll, toddle, travel, waddle, wander; **7** saunter, shuffle, stagger, trundle, walkway; **9** promenade; **10** occupation; **11** perambulate.

walking 6 hiking, living; **7** outdoor; **8** rambling; PHRASES: **2, 3, 4** on the hoof; **2, 4** on foot; **4-7** hard-wearing; **5-4** heavy-duty; **5-7** cross-country; **7, 4** shanks's pony *UK*.

wall 3 sea; **4** cell, fire, mold; **5** fence, panel, party; **6** bricks, cavity, facing, mortar, parget, screen, stucco; **7** barrier, bulwark, chinese, curtain, divider, drapery, hanging, plaster, plywood, wailing, western; **8** abutment, antonine, boarding, bulkhead, buttress, cladding, hadrian's, paneling; **9** clapboard, partition, retaining, revetment, wallboard, wallpaper; **10** embankment; **12** weatherboard; PHRASES: **4, 5** ~ tiles; **5, 4** brick ~, stone ~; **6, 5** picket fence; **6, 8** flying buttress.

wallop 3 hit; **4** bash, beat, blow, buzz, fizz, whip; **5** clout, punch, smack, thump; **6** defeat, pizazz, strike, thwack; **7** destroy, trounce.

wallow *See* **flounder**

walrus 3, 3 sea cow; **3, 5** sea horse.

waltz 4 romp, sail, swan, walk; **5** cinch, steam, whizz; **6** breeze, stroll; **7** saunter; **8** pushover; PHRASES: **5, 2, 4** piece of cake. *See* *also* **dance**

wan 4 ashy, down, weak; 5 ashen, drawn; 6 feeble, pallid; 8 listless; 9 depressed.

wander 4 roam, walk; 5 amble, drift, mooch, mosey, stray; 6 ramble, stroll; 7 deviate, digress, meander; PHRASES: 4, 3, 5 lose the point; 4, 3, 6 lose the thread.

wandering 5 error, loose; 6 errant, roving; 7 devious, erratic, migrant, nomadic, vagrant; 8 errantry, excursus, homeless, rootless, vagrancy; 9 footloose, itinerant, stateless; 10 circuitous, digression, digressive, discursion, discursive, divagatory; 11 inattentive, pererration, peripatetic; 14 circuitousness, circumbendibus, circumlocution, discursiveness; PHRASES: 3, 3, 5 off the point; 3, 3, 7 off the subject. *See also* **wander**

wangle 3 fix, get; 6 obtain; 8 contrive, engineer.

want 4 lack, need, wish; 5 covet, crave, yearn; 6 dearth, desire; PHRASES: 4, 3 long for; 6, 5 hanker after.

wanton 5 cruel, nasty; 7 immoral, vicious; 8 heedless, immodest, needless, reckless; 9 abandoned, excessive, malicious; 10 gratuitous, licentious, malevolent, motiveless; 11 extravagant, meaningless; 12 unreasonable, unrestrained.

wapiti 3 elk.

war 3 cry, Tyr; 4 Ares, arms, baby, Eris, game, Mars, Odin; 5 bride, chest, civil, class, crime, dance, draft, Indra, jihad, paint, rally, whoop, Wotan; 6 action, Athena, bonnet; 7 Bellona, crusade, polemic, rivalry, warpath; 8 blackout, memorial; 9 enlisting, rationing; 10 Armageddon, blitzkrieg, Karttikeya, propaganda, revolution; 12 conscription, intervention, intimidation, mobilization; 13 correspondent; PHRASES: 2, 5, 6 no holds barred; 3, 2, 3, 3 ~ to the end; 3, 2, 3, 5 ~ to the knife; 3, 2, 3, 6 ~ on all fronts; 3, 2, 4 ~ on want; 3, 2, 5 ~ of words; 3, 2, 6 ~ of nerves; 3, 2, 9 ~ of attrition, ~ of expansion; 3, 2, 10 ~ of liberation; 3, 3 Cod ~, hot ~; 3-3, 3 all-out ~; 3, 4 ~ work; 3, 5 the draft, the sword; 3, 5, 3 The Great W~; 3, 6 ~ effort, ~ policy; 3, 7 ~ footing; 4-2 call-up; 4, 2, 4 call to arms; 4, 3 cold ~, holy ~, real ~; 4-3 half-war; 4-4, 3 high-tech ~; 4-7, 3 grim-visaged ~; 5, 3 trade ~, world ~; 5, 5 fiery cross; 5, 5, 3 First World W~; 5, 8 armed conflict; 5-8 saber-rattling; 5, 10 armed neutrality; 6, 2, 4 appeal to arms; 6, 3 atomic ~,

desert ~, global ~, phoney ~ *UK*; 6, 5 uneasy peace; 6, 5, 3 Second World W~; 7, 3 brother ~, general ~, limited ~; 7, 4 clarion call; 7, 5 horrida bella; 7, 7 victory gardens; 8, 3 computer ~, doubtful ~, economic ~; 8, 3, 2, 12 American W~ of Independence; 8, 4 military duty; 8, 7 Fortress America, national service; 8, 10 American Revolution; 9, 3 localized ~, religious ~, truceless ~; 10, 3 undeclared ~; 11, 3 ideological ~, imperialist ~, internecine ~, triphibious ~.

war (be at war) 4 kill, nuke, raid, rape, slay; 5 march; 6 ambush, attack, bloody, defend, invade, ravage, scorch; 7 besiege, counter, destroy, soldier; 8 blockade, campaign, demolish, maneuver; 9 beleaguer, slaughter; 12 countermarch; 13 counterattack; PHRASES: 3, 3 cut off; 3, 4 cut down, mow down, war upon; 3, 5 lay waste; 4, 3 ship out, wage war; 4, 3, 4 drop the bomb; 5, 2, 3 march to war; 5, 3, 6 press the button; 5, 4 stand firm; 5, 4, 5 flesh one's sword; 5, 6 smell powder, taste battle; 6, 3 starve out; 8, 1, 6 shoulder a musket.

war (go to war) 3 arm; 4 rise; 5 draft, fight, rally; 6 enlist, enroll, revolt; 7 recruit; 8 mobilize; 9 conscript; 10 commission, militarize; PHRASES: 3, 2, 4 fly to arms; 3, 4, 4 fly one's flag; 4, 2 call up, join up; 4, 2, 3, 6 call to the colors; 4, 2, 4 call to arms; 4, 3, 5 whet the sword; 4, 4, 6 show one's colors; 4, 11 open hostilities; 5, 4, 4 serve one's king; 5, 4, 6 raise one's banner; 6, 2, 4 appeal to arms; 6, 3, 4 answer the call; 7, 3 declare war; 7, 3, 4 display the flag.

war (to war) 10 militantly, militarily; 13 belligerently; PHRASES: 2, 4 at arms; 2, 6, 5 at sword's point.

warble *See* **sing**

warder *See* **prison officer**

wardrobe *See* **clothes**

warfare 4 raid; 5 blitz, order; 6 action, attack, combat, revolt, sieges; 7 battles, bombing, command, contest, defense, mission, rivalry, sniping, warring; 8 blockade, campaign, conflict, fighting, invasion, password, struggle, violence; 9 attrition, besieging, bloodshed, enclosure, incursion, operation, sanctions, watchword; 10 blockading, expedition, investment, operations, skirmishes, soldiering; 11 bombardment, campaigning, competition, hostilities; PHRASES: 3, 5, 7 air force service; 3, 7 gas ~, sea battles, sea raiding; 3, 10 air operations, sea operations; **3, 11** sea bombardment; **4, 2, 7** word of command; **4, 4** Star Wars; **4, 7** germ ~; **4-8** bush-fighting; **4, 9** arms sanctions; **4, 10** land operations; **5, 2, 5** deeds of blood; **5, 7** naval service, naval ~; **5, 8** fleet blockade; **5, 9** joint operation; **5, 10** naval operations; **6, 7** active service, aerial ~, atomic ~, carpet bombing, desert ~, jungle ~, mobile ~, static ~, trench ~; **6, 9** allied operation, ethnic cleansing; **7, 7** nuclear ~; **8, 7** chemical ~, infantry service, military service, mountain ~, tactical bombing, undersea ~.

warhorse **5** steed; **6** master; **7** charger, courser, Marengo, remount, veteran, warrior; **8** destrier, stalwart; **10** Bucephalus, campaigner, Copenhagen; PHRASES: **3, 4** old hand; **7, 5** cavalry horse.

wariness **4** care; **7** caution; **9** suspicion; **14** circumspection. *See also* **wary**

warlike **5** cruel; **6** fierce; **7** hawkish, hostile, martial, warring; **8** militant, military; **9** bellicose, combative, unpacific; **10** aggressive, pugilistic, pugnacious, Ramboesque; **11** belligerent; **12** bloodthirsty, militaristic, warmongering; PHRASES: **3-6** war-loving; **3-7** war-fevered; **4-2** gung-ho; **6-6** battle-hungry.

warlord *See* **military leader**

warm **3** hot; **4** cozy, fair, heat, kind, melt, mild, snug, thaw; **5** balmy, close, eager, fiery, humid, muggy, sunny, tepid; **6** cheery, genial, kindly, loving, reheat, steamy, sticky, sultry, tender, warmth; **7** amiable, clement, cordial, restful, summery; **8** cheerful, friendly, inviting, lukewarm, moderate, pleasant, sizzling, stifling, sunbaked, tropical; **9** congenial, convivial, heartfelt, temperate, welcoming; **10** equatorial, springlike, sweltering; **11** subtropical; **12** affectionate, enthusiastic, wholehearted; PHRASES: **3, 2, 3** hit it off; **3, 2, 4** get on with; **3, 7** get excited; **3, 7, 2** get stirred up; **4, 1, 5, 2** take a fancy to, take a shine to; **4, 1, 6, 2** take a liking to; **4, 2** heat up, take to; **4-7** kind-hearted *UK*.

warm-blooded *See* **passionate**

warmly **9** sincerely; **12** passionately; PHRASES: **4, 6** with fervor; **4, 10** with enthusiasm. *See also* **warm**

warmonger **4** hawk; **5** jingo; **8** crusader, jingoist; **9** aggressor, demagogue; **11** belligerent; PHRASES: **5-7** sabre-rattler *UK*; **6-6** rabble-rouser.

warmth **4** heat; **5** ardor; **6** fervor; **7** hotness; **10** cordiality, enthusiasm. *See also* **warm**

warn **4** hint, lour, wink; **5** alert, augur, lower, nudge, prime; **6** inform, menace; **7** caution, counsel, forearm, predict, reprove; **8** admonish, dissuade, forewarn, threaten; **11** remonstrate; PHRASES: **3, 3** tip off; **4, 6** give notice; **5, 1, 6** issue a caveat; **5, 6** spell danger; **5, 8** spell disaster; **6, 7** advise against.

warn (be warned) **6** beware; PHRASES: **4, 4** take heed; **5, 4, 4** watch one's step; **5, 4, 6** learn one's lesson; **6, 2, 7** profit by example.

warner **3** rat, spy; **4** mole; **5** guard, scout, watch; **6** sentry; **7** adviser, diviner, Ezekiel, lookout, prophet; **8** alarmist, caveator, sentinel, squealer, vanguard, watchdog; **9** Cassandra, cautioner, counselor, informant, rearguard, signaller; **10** admonisher; **11** Nostradamus, scaremonger.

warning **3** tip; **4** hint, omen, wink, word; **5** alarm, knell, nudge, siren; **6** advice, augury, caveat, danger, menace, signal, threat; **7** caution, counsel, ominous, portent, symptom; **8** menacing, minatory, monition, monitory; **9** deterrent, exemplary, indicator *UK*, reprimand, ultimatum; **10** admonition, admonitory, cautionary, dissuasive, foreboding, predicting, prediction, presageful, prognostic, protesting; **11** forewarning, premonition, premonitory, symptomatic, threatening; **12** admonishment, announcement, counsellable, intelligence, notification; **13** expostulation; PHRASES: **3-3** tip-off; **3, 4** bad omen; **3, 5** war cloud; **3-6** ill-omened; **4, 2, 3, 3** word in the ear; **4, 2, 3, 4** bird of ill omen, word to the wise; **4-2** wake-up call; **4, 2, 7** word of ~; **4, 4** evil omen; **5, 5** death knell; **5, 6** final demand, final notice; **6, 5** rising river; **6, 6** storm(y) petrel; **7, 6** advance notice; **9, 5** gathering storm; **9, 6** gathering clouds.

warp *See* **twist**

warrant **5** merit; **6** assure, demand, expect, insure, permit; **7** certify, deserve, justify, license; **9** authorize, guarantee; **11** certificate, necessitate; **13** authorization, certification; PHRASES: **4, 3** call for.

warren **4** hole, lair, maze; **5** earth *UK*; **6** burrow; **7** habitat; **8** catacomb; **9** labyrinth.

warring **5** armed; **7** arrayed, drafted, engaged, opposed; **8** battling, fighting, militant, opposing, sparring; **9** bellicose, combatant, defending, embattled, mobilized; **10** aggressive; **11** belligerent, campaigning, conscripted; PHRASES: **2, 2, 4** up in arms; **2, 3** at war; **2, 3, 5** at the front; **2, 3, 7** on the warpath; **2, 3, 9** on the defensive, on the offensive; **2, 5** at grips; **2, 6** in battle; **2, 6, 4** on active duty; **2, 11** at loggerheads; **5, 2, 4** sword in hand; **6-2** called-up; **6, 3** waging war.

warrior *See* **soldier**

warship 4 duck; **7** cruiser, flattop, frigate, gunboat; **8** corvette, flagship; **9** amphibian, blockship, destroyer, minelayer, storeship, submarine, troopship; **10** battleship, icebreaker; **11** dreadnought, minesweeper; PHRASES: **1-4** E-boat, Q-ship, U-boat; **2, 4** PT boat; **3-2-3** man-of-war; **3, 6** oil tanker, war vessel; **4, 4** fire ship, fuel ship; **5, 4** depot ship, guard ship; **5, 7** light cruiser; **6, 4** patrol boat, repair ship, supply ship; **6-6** hunter-killer; **6, 7** battle cruiser; **7, 4** capital ship, command ship, torpedo boat; **7, 5** landing craft; **7, 7** armored cruiser; **8, 4** hospital ship; **8, 6** flotilla leader; **8, 7** aircraft carrier; **9, 4** transport ship; **9, 6** destroyer escort, submarine chaser, submarine tender; **10, 4** ammunition ship, amphibious ship. *See also* **ship**

warship (historical naval ships) 6 bireme, raider; **7** galleon, Monitor, trireme, Victory, Warrior; **8** galleass, ironclad; **9** Merrimack, privateer; **11** Devastation, Dreadnought, quinquereme *UK*; PHRASES: **3, 6** war galley; **5-6** three-decker; **6, 4** pirate ship, turret ship.

wart 4 lump; **6** growth; **7** verruca.

wary 4 cagy, ware, waur *UK*; **5** chary; **7** careful, guarded; **8** cautious, watchful; **10** suspicious; **11** circumspect, mistrustful.

wash 3 dip; **4** bath, film, lave *UK*, swab, tint; **5** bathe, bidet, clean, enema, layer, rinse, stain, swish; **6** douche, shower, sluice, splash, sponge; **7** bathing, cleanse, clyster, coating, Jacuzzi™, launder, overlay, shampoo; **8** ablution, coloring; **9** suffusion; **10** balneation; PHRASES: **4, 3, 5** soap and water; **4, 4** bear away; **5, 2** clean up; **5, 4** carry away, sweep away; **6, 4** needle bath, shower bath, sponge down.

washer 4 ring, seal; **5** liner; **6** boiler, copper, gasket; **7** washtub; **9** washboard; **10** dishwasher, laundromat; PHRASES: **3, 4** car wash; **4-3** twin-tub *UK*; **6-5** washer-drier; **7, 7** washing machine.

washing 4 coat, film, soda; **5** layer; **7** coating, laundry, machine, overlay; PHRASES: **5, 5** dirty linen.

Washington 2 WA; **7** Olympia (capital); PHRASES: **3, 3, 3** Bye and bye (motto); **5, 12** coast rhododendron (flower); **6, 4, 5** willow gold finch (bird); **7, 7** western hemlock (tree); **9, 5** Evergreen State (nickname).

wastage *See* **waste**

waste 3 eat, ebb; **4** bare, blow, fade, gnaw, kill, leak, loss, melt, ruin, slag, slop, wane, wear, wilt; **5** abuse, decay, drain, dregs, erode, spare, spend, spill, spoil, spree, trash; **6** barren, devour, excess, expend, fallow, lavish, litter, misuse, murder, outlay, ravage, refuse, scraps, unused, weaken, wither; **7** atrophy, consume, decline, deplete, despoil, destroy, erosion, exhaust, expense, fritter, garbage, leakage, liquefy, outflow, rubbish *UK*, shrivel, spilled, splurge, surplus, useless, wastage; **8** decrease, deforest, desolate, diminish, disperse, drainage, emaciate, leftover, misspend, overcrop, overfish, overwork, remnants, spending, spillage, squander, unwanted, vaporize; **9** depletion, devastate, discarded, dissipate, evaporate, leftovers, overgraze, overspend, throwaway, worthless; **10** dispersion, emaciation, impoverish, lavishness; **11** consumption, deteriorate, dissipation, expenditure, prodigality, superfluity, superfluous; **12** extravagance, obsolescence, overspending, uncultivated; **13** deterioration, fruitlessness; **14** misapplication, overproduction, thriftlessness; PHRASES: **3, 2** dry up, use up; **3, 3** run low; **3, 4** ebb away; **3, 5** lay ~; **4, 3** burn out, milk dry, suck dry; **4, 4** burn down; **4, 5** gray water, vain labor; **5, 2, 4** labor in vain, ~ of time; **5, 2, 6** ~ of breath; **5, 2, 8** labor of Sisyphus; **5, 4** spilt milk, throw away, ~ away; **5, 6** fool's errand; **6, 2** gobble up; **6, 6** losing battle; **7, 4** fritter away.

waste (go to waste) 9 dissipate; PHRASES: **2, 2, 2, 5** go up in smoke; **2, 2, 3** go to pot; **2, 2, 3, 4** go to the dogs; **2, 2, 4** go to seed; **2, 4, 3, 5** go down the drain; **4, 2, 6** come to naught; **4, 2, 7** come to nothing.

wastebin 3 bin; **4** skip; **5** drain, sewer; **7** dredger, dustbin *UK*, garbage; **8** Dumpster, trashcan; **11** incinerator, wastebasket; PHRASES: **5, 8** waste disposer; **7, 3** garbage can, rubbish bin *UK*; **7, 4** rubbish scow; **7, 5** garbage truck, rubbish truck.

wasteful 6 lavish; **8** careless, prodigal, reckless; **10** profligate, thriftless, uneconomic; **11** extravagant, improvident, inefficient, spendthrift; **12** uneconomical.

wasteful (be wasteful) 8 squander; **9** dissipate; PHRASES: **4, 1, 5** draw a blank; **5, 2, 4** labor in vain; **5, 4** throw away, waste time; **5, 6** waste breath; **7, 4** fritter away.

waster 7 wastrel; **8** prodigal; **10** squanderer; **11** spendthrift; PHRASES: **3, 7** big spender.

watch 4 duty, fire, mind, view; **5** black, guard, night, shift, stalk, vigil; **6** beware, sentry, survey, turnip; **7** examine, inspect, lookout, monitor, observe, oversee, proctor; **8** consider, sentinel; **9** committee, supervise; **10** invigilate, scrutinize, wristwatch; **12** surveillance; PHRASES: **3, 2** spy on; **4, 2** gaze at, look at; **4, 2, 3, 2** keep an eye on; **4-3** bird-dog; **4, 5** clip ~, look after; **4-6** half-hunter; **5, 2** stare at; **6, 2** attend to; **6, 5** analog ~, pocket ~, quartz ~; **7, 5** digital ~.

watchful 4 wary; **5** alert; **7** careful, curious, guarded, heedful; **8** vigilant; **9** attentive, observant; **11** circumspect; PHRASES: **2, 3, 5** on the alert; **2, 3, 7** on the lookout; **2, 5** on guard; **5-4** sharp-eyed.

watchfully 8 sidelong, sideways; **10** glancingly. *See also* **watchful**

watchfulness 7 caution; **9** attention, vigilance; **10** observance; **11** finickiness; PHRASES: **4-7** baby-minding, baby-sitting; **5-3** stake-out; **5-4** guard-duty. *See also* **watchful**

water 3 eau, H20, ice, wet; **4** aqua, dunk, hose, pila, rain, soak, well; **5** brine, douse, drouk, drown, flood, fluid, souse, spray, swamp; **6** dampen, deluge, drench, hydrol, imbrue, liquid, sluice, spring, stream; **7** hydrate, immerse, moisten; **8** affusion, fountain, inundate, irrigate, moisture, permeate, saturate, sparging, sprinkle, submerge, submerse, swashing, waterlog; **9** aspersion, limewater, meltwater, percolate, rainwater; **10** irrigation; **11** aspergation; **13** spargefaction; PHRASES: **3, 5** ice ~, sea ~, tap ~, the briny; **4, 4** club soda; **4, 4, 5** fill with tears; **4, 5** bath ~, hard ~, rose ~, salt ~, soda ~, soft ~, well ~; **5, 3** Adam's ale; **5, 5** Adam's wine; **5, 5** fresh ~, heavy ~ (D2O); **6, 5** spring ~; **7, 5** mineral ~, quinine ~, running ~; **8, 5** standing ~.

water (on the water) 9 naturally; **10** underwater; **12** artificially; **13** competitively, piscatorially; PHRASES: **2, 3, 7** on the surface; **2, 8** by trolling.

water bird 3 auk, pen; **4** coot, duck, gull, ibis, loon, rail, ruff, shag, skua, smew, swan, teal, tern; **5** booby, crake, crane, diver, drake, egret, eider, goose, grebe, heron, scaup, snipe, stilt, stork, wader; **6** avocet, curlew, darter, dipper, dunlin, fulmar, gannet, godwit, jabiru, jacana, petrel, plover, puffin, scoter, wigeon; **7** bittern, finfoot, gadwall, lapwing, mallard, marabou, moorhen, pelican, penguin, pintail, pochard, seabird, seagull, skimmer, wrybill; **8** dabchick, dotterel, flamingo, redshank, shelduck, shoebill; **9** albatross, cormorant, corncrake, gallinule, goldeneye, guillemot, kittiwake, merganser, phalarope, razorbill, sandpiper, snakebird, spoonbill, waterfowl; **10** demoiselle, greenshank, hammerhead, kingfisher, muttonbird, sanderling, shearwater, sheathbill; **13** oystercatcher; PHRASES: **3, 3** mud hen; **3, 4** sea duck; **3, 5** sea eagle; **4, 4** mute swan; **5, 4** black swan, marsh bird, shore bird; **5, 5** brent goose; **5, 6** stone curlew, storm petrel; **6, 4** arctic tern, diving bird, diving duck, sacred ibis, wading bird; **6, 5** Canada goose; **7, 4** fishing bird, frigate bird, herring gull, muscovy duck, oceanic bird; **7, 5** graylag goose; **7, 7** emperor penguin; **8, 4** dabbling duck, perching duck; **8, 5** adjutant stork, barnacle goose, Hawaiian goose, whooping crane; **9, 4** harlequin duck, whistling duck; **10, 4** freshwater bird.

water buffalo 7 carabao; PHRASES: **5, 2** water ox.

water chestnut 7 caltrop.

water cycle 6 runoff; **11** evaporation, hydrometeor, hydrosphere, percolation; **13** precipitation, transpiration; PHRASES: **10, 5** hydrologic cycle.

waterfall 4 linn *UK*, weir; **5** chute, falls, nappe, sault, shoot; **6** rapids; **7** cascade, torrent; **8** cataract.

wateriness 3 fog, wet; **4** damp, haze, mist; **5** cloud, steam, vapor; **8** dampness, dewiness, rainfall; **9** raininess; **10** sloppiness; **12** condensation. *See also* **watery**

waterproof 4 seal; **5** caulk; **9** dampproof, leakproof, rainproof; **10** stormproof, watertight; **11** impermeable, showerproof *UK*; **13** moistureproof; PHRASES: **3-4** dry-shod; **5, 5**

flood proof; **5-9** water-resistant.

watershed *See* **turning point**

water system 4 dock, lock, mole, pier, port, quay; **5** canal, groin, jetty, wharf; **6** harbor; **7** barrage; **9** floodgate; **10** breakwater, sluicegate; PHRASES: **3, 4** sea wall; **6, 6** sewage system; **8, 6** drainage system.

waterway 5 canal, river; **6** seaway, stream; **7** channel; **8** aqueduct; **11** watercourse; PHRASES: **3, 4** sea lane; **5, 5** ocean track; **7, 5** steamer route; **8, 5** shipping canal; **9, 5** navigable water.

watery 3 dim, wan, wet; **4** hazy, pale, thin, weak; **5** bland, boggy, faint, fluid, moist, runny, soggy; **6** feeble, liquid; **7** aquatic, aqueous, diluted, hydrous, insipid; **8** hydrated, squelchy; **9** hydraulic, tasteless; **11** hydrometric, hydrostatic, waterlogged; **12** hydrodynamic; PHRASES: **7-4** watered-down.

wave 3 ray, wag; **4** beat, bore, curl, flap, foam, heat, kink, long, node, perm, rise, roll, sign, surf, sway; **5** brain, crest, crimp, eagre, flail, flood, froth, heave, light, radio, shake, shock, short, sound, spate, spume, surge, swell, tidal, trend, wield; **6** beckon, billow, comber, dumper, finger, medium, period, riffle, ripple, roller, seiche, series, signal, tremor, trough; **7** breaker, current, flutter, gesture, seismic, tsunami, upsurge, wavelet; **8** antinode, brandish, flounder, outbreak, overfall, undertow, undulate, waviness, whitecap; **9** oscillate, radiation, resonance, vibration, whitecaps; **10** choppiness, earthquake, seismicity, undulation; **11** diffraction, gesticulate, groundswell, oscillation; **12** longitudinal, undercurrent; **15** electromagnetic; PHRASES: **2, 5** in phase; **3, 2, 5** out of phase; **3, 6** air pocket; **5, 3** angry sea, heavy sea, rough sea; **5, 4** ocean ~, rogue ~, storm ~, white foam; **5, 5** heavy swell; **6, 3** choppy sea; **6, 4** guided ~; **6, 5** broken water; **7, 4** surface ~; **8, 4** acoustic ~, sawtooth ~, standing ~; **9, 3** turbulent sea; **9, 4** torsional ~, traveling ~; **10, 4** diffracted ~, mechanical ~, transverse ~.

waveform 5 hertz, pulse; **9** amplitude, frequency, waveshape; **10** wavelength; PHRASES: **4, 4** sine wave; **4, 5** wave crest, wave speed; **4, 6** wave number, wave trough; **5, 2, 5** speed of light, speed of sound; **5, 5** pulse train; **6, 4** square wave; **10, 4** sinusoidal wave.

waver 5 shake; **6** dither; **7** flicker, flutter,

shudder, tremble; **8** hesitate; **9** vacillate.

waving 7 seismic, sinuous; **8** undulant; **9** tremulous; **10** sinusoidal, successive, undulatory; **12** seismometric, succussatory, sussultatory; **13** seismographic, seismological. *See also* **wave**

wax 4 buff, grow, turn; **5** japan, shine, swell; **6** candle, expand, montan, polish, tallow; **7** cerumen, chinese, enlarge, sealing; **8** carnauba, cobbler's, increase, kerosene, paraffin; **9** vegetable; PHRASES: **3, 1, 5, 2** put a shine on.

wax myrtle 11 candleberry; PHRASES: **6-4** candle-tree.

way 3 rut; **4** form, lane, line, mode, path, road, tack, tone, wise; **5** alley, fosse, guise, means, milky, order, round, route, style, track; **6** Appian, avenue, custom, groove, manner, method, street, system, tactic; **7** conduct, fashion, passage, pathway, Pennine, process; **8** approach, behavior, progress; **9** algorithm, direction, Flaminian, operation, procedure, technique, tradition, tramlines; **10** proceeding; **11** methodology, progression; **14** constitutional; PHRASES: **3, 2, 4** ~ of life; **3, 3** the how; **3, 5** the drill; **4, 2, 6** line of action, line of attack; **4, 2, 9** mode of operation (MO); **4-3** know-how; **4, 3, 5** ways and means; **5, 5** daily grind; **5, 7** modus vivendi; **5, 8** modus operandi; **6, 5** beaten track.

way (by the way) 3 via; **6** across; **7** through; **12** incidentally; **14** transitionally; PHRASES: **2, 3, 2** by way of; **2, 5** en route; **2, 7** en passant, in transit.

way (make one's way) 5 climb; **6** toward; PHRASES: **4, 7** inch forward; **5, 4, 3** weave one's way; **5, 7** reach towards; **6, 7** muddle through.

wayfarer *See* **traveler**

Wayland 6 Völund; **7** Wieland.

way of life 5 ethos, mores; **6** habits, ideals, morals, praxis; **7** customs, manners; **9** lifestyle; **10** principles, traditions; **11** conventions; PHRASES: **5, 7** modus vivendi.

way out 4 door, exit, gate, path, port; **5** weird; **6** egress; **7** bizarre, outgate; **8** freakish, loophole; PHRASES: **4, 4** back door; **4, 6** fire escape; **6, 5** escape hatch, escape route.

way-out 3 odd; **5** great, weird; **7** strange, unusual; **8** peculiar, terrific; **9** excellent, fantastic, wonderful.

wayward 6 errant, unruly; **7** naughty,

willful.

WC **5, 6** water closet; **6, 8** London district; **7, 6** without change.

weak **3** dim, low; **4** limp, puny, thin; **5** bland, frail, seedy, shaky, slack, tired, wispy; **6** anemic, creaky, dilute, feeble, flimsy, floppy, infirm, shoddy, unsafe, watery, wobbly; **7** brittle, diluted, dithery, drained, exposed, flaccid, fragile, insipid, rickety, sagging, scrawny, tenuous, tottery; **8** cowardly, decrepit, delicate, gimcrack, helpless, impotent, unstrung; **9** breakable, enervated, enfeebled, exhausted, powerless, tasteless, teetering, tottering, unguarded, untenable; **10** flavorless, inadequate, indecisive, unhardened, untempered, vulnerable; **11** corruptible, debilitated, defenseless, ineffective, ineffectual, lightweight, unfortified, unprotected; **12** questionable, unconvincing; **13** imperceptible, insubstantial; PHRASES: **3, 4** run down; **4-6** weak-willed; **5-5** jerry-built; **5-7** faint-hearted; **6, 3** easily led; **7-4** watered-down.

weaken **3** mar, sag, sap; **4** dent, drop, fade, fail, fall, flag, flop, halt, harm, hurt, lame, maim, thin, tire, wane, wear, wilt; **5** abate, alarm, break, drain, droop, faint, shake, split, spoil, waver, wound, yield; **6** damage, denude, dilute, disarm, dodder, expose, falter, impair, injure, lessen, loosen, muffle, reduce, sicken, soften, sprain, starve, strain, teeter, totter; **7** consume, crumble, decline, deflate, deplete, deprive, disable, dwindle, exhaust, fatigue, slacken, stagger, subside, tremble, unnerve; **8** decimate, diminish, emaciate, enervate, enfeeble, hesitate, languish; **9** challenge, extenuate, undermine, vacillate; **10** debilitate, emasculate, impoverish, invalidate, neutralize; **11** destabilize, deteriorate; **12** incapacitate; PHRASES: **4, 2** cave in, give in; **4, 3** fall off, give way, thin out, wear off; **5, 4** strip bare, water down; **7, 4** detract from.

weakened **5** weary; **7** wearied; PHRASES: **2, 3, 4** on the wane; **4, 3** laid low, worn out; **5, 3** burnt out. *See also* **weaken**

weakling **3** wet; **4** baby, drip, nerd, weed, wimp; **5** pansy, patsy, softy; **6** coward, infant, kitten, victim; **7** chicken, doormat, milksop; **8** pushover; **9** jellyfish; **11** lightweight, milquetoast; **13** hypochondriac; PHRASES: **3-4** cry-baby; **4, 2, 4** babe in arms; **4, 3** lame dog, poor dab; **4, 4** easy mark,

easy meat *UK*, lame duck; **5, 3** small fry, straw man; **5-5** namby-pamby; **6, 3** mummy's boy; **6, 4** broken reed.

weakly **6** feebly, softly; **7** faintly, lightly, quietly, timidly; **8** slightly *UK*; **9** inaudibly, languidly, nervously; **10** sheepishly, unsteadily; **12** irresolutely, pathetically; **14** insufficiently; PHRASES: **4-9** half-heartedly; **7, 6** without effect. *See also* **weak**

weakness **4** flaw, rust; **5** decay, fault; **6** damage, defect, foible, liking; **7** failing, frailty; **8** appetite, debility, delicacy, dilution, drawback, fondness, paleness, penchant, puniness; **9** cowardice, faintness, fragility, impotence, infirmity, slackness; **10** difficulty, feebleness, flaccidity, flimsiness, impairment, incapacity, indecision, limitation, partiality, wateriness; **11** insipidness, instability, shortcoming; **12** dilapidation, disadvantage, enfeeblement, harmlessness, predilection; **13** powerlessness, vulnerability; PHRASES: **4, 2, 4** feet of clay; **4, 4** soft spot, weak spot; **8, 4** Achilles' heel. *See also* **weak**

weak thing **4** reed; **5** china, glass, paper, water; **6** cobweb, thread; **8** eggshell, gossamer; **9** dishwater; PHRASES: **4, 3, 5** milk and water; **4, 5** thin gruel; **4, 6** sand castle; **5, 2, 5** house of cards; **6, 2, 3, 3** castle in the air; **6, 2, 5** castle in Spain; **6, 5** tissue paper.

weak-willed **5** timid; **6** effete, scared, yellow; **7** chicken, gutless, nervous; **8** cowardly, hesitant, sheepish, timorous, unnerved, wavering; **9** nerveless, spineless; **10** indecisive; **13** pusillanimous; PHRASES: **4-5** weak-kneed; **4-7** half-hearted, lily-livered, limp-wristed; **5-5** namby-pamby; **5-7** mealy-mouthed.

wealth **4** gain; **5** array, funds, gains, means, money; **6** assets, choice, income, mammon, riches; **7** bonanza, capital, fortune, profits, savings, variety; **8** Golconda, plethora, richness, treasure; **9** abundance, affluence, multitude, profusion, resources; **10** cornucopia, prosperity; **11** investments; **12** multiplicity; PHRASES: **2, 6** El Dorado; **3, 2, 3, 7** end of the rainbow; **3, 2, 4** pot of gold *UK*; **4, 3** cash cow, nest egg; **4, 4** gold mine; **4-5, 5** well-lined purse; **4, 6** high income; **5, 5** Midas touch; **6, 5** golden goose, golden touch; **7, 5** worldly goods; **8, 5** material goods; **10, 5** bottomless purse.

wealthily **4** well; **6** richly; **8** lavishly; **9** opulently; **10** affluently; **11** comfortably, luxuriously; **12** prosperously; PHRASES: **2, 3, 5, 5** on the gravy train; **4, 2, 3, 3** high on the hog.

wealthy 4 rich; **5** flush; **6** loaded; **7** money-eyed, rolling; **8** affluent, dripping; **10** propertied, prosperous; **11** comfortable; PHRASES: **2, 3, 5** in the chips, in the dough, in the gravy, in the money; **2, 4, 6** in high cotton, on Easy Street; **2, 6** in clover; **4-2-2** well-to-do; **4, 2, 5** made of money; **4-3** well-off; **4-6** well-heeled; **5, 1, 4** worth a mint; **5, 1, 6** worth a bundle, worth a packet; **5, 2** quids in; **5, 8** worth millions; **6, 4** filthy rich; **7, 2, 2** rolling in it; **8, 4** stinking rich; **11, 3** comfortably off.

wealthy people 4 heir; **5** baron, Dives, Midas, nabob; **6** Plutus, tycoon, yuppie; **7** Croesus, heiress, magnate, parvenu, Sloanes, Solomon; **9** moneybags, plutocrat; **10** capitalist, glitterati, moneymaker; **11** beneficiary, billionaire, millionaire, Rockefeller; **13** millionairess; PHRASES: **3, 2, 5** man of means; **3, 2, 9** man of substance; **3, 3** fat cat; **3, 3, 3** the jet set; **3, 4-2-2** the well-to-do; **3, 4-6** the well-heeled; **3, 5** the haves; **3, 6** big earner; **3, 6, 3** the county set; **4, 3, 6** rich and famous; **4, 5** beau monde; **5, 2, 7** cream of society; **5, 5** upper class, upper crust; **5-7** money-spinner *UK*; **6, 6** Sloane Ranger *UK*; **8, 5** jeunesse dorée *Fr*, leisured class; **8, 6** nouveaux riches; **9, 6** beautiful people.

weapon 3 arm; **4** MOAB; **7** firearm; **8** armament, ordnance, weaponry; **9** artillery, bioweapon, deterrent; PHRASES: **6, 6** deadly ~, secret ~; **7, 6** natural ~, nuclear ~; **9, 6** defensive ~, offensive ~.

weapons 2 ax, v1, v2; **3** adz, bow, gun, gyn, tnt; **4** ball, barb, bill, bola, bolo, bolt, bomb, club, cosh *UK*, dart, dirk, fang, foil, kora *UK*, kris, mace, mine, pike, shot, tank, tuck, whip; **5** ancus, ankus *UK*, anlas, arrow, aswar, baton, bidag, bilbo, boson, brand, brick, estoc, flail, fusee, gupti, keris, khora, kilig, kilij, knife, kukri, kylie *UK*, lance, lasso, latch, pilum, prodd, saber, shaft, shell, sling, spear, stake, stave, stone, sword, tachi, waddy; **6** amukta, armlet, barkal, barong, baston, bodkin, bullet, cannon, carcas, cudgel, dagger, daisho, dragon, dusack, exocet, katana, kerrie, khanda, kikuki, kodogu, massue, mazule, mortar, napalm, parang, petard, qillij, quiver, ramrod, rapier, rocket, scythe, semtex, sumpit, talwar; **7** assegai, balasan, bayonet, belfrey,

biliong, bombard, bourdon, caliver, caltrap, caraben, carreau, chakram, chalcos, chopper, currier, cutlass, dudgeon, dussack, fauchon, grenade, halbart, halberd, harpoon, javelin, kastane, kindjal, longbow, missile, poniard, quarrel, shashqa, shinken, torpedo, trident, woomera *Aus*; **8** amusette, arbalest, arbalete, ballista, baselard, basilard, blowpipe, brickbat, calthorp, canister, carabine, catapult, chacheka, cladibas, claymore, crossbow, deringer, destrier, falchion, fauchard, hassegai, mangonel, ordnance, poignard, querquer, scimitar, shamshir, shrapnel, spontoon, sumpitan, tomahawk, weaponry; **9** arrowhead, badelaire, bandeleer, bandolier, bannerole, boomerang, cartouche, cartridge, detonator, falcastra, flagellum, flamberge, fléchette, gelignite, grapeshot, gunpowder, knobstick, mazzuelle, musketoon, slingshot, trebuchet, truncheon; **10** artillator, banderolle, brandestoc, broadsword, knobkerrie, powderhorn, sidewinder, throwstick; **11** misericorde, switchblade; **12** flamethrower; PHRASES: **1-4** a-bomb, h-bomb; **2-5** ax-knife; **3-3** dum-dum; **3-4** awl-pike; **3-6, 5** two-handed sword; **3-7** peashooter; **4-3** fire-pot; **4, 4** atom bomb, hail shot; **4-6** fire-sticks; **4, 7** hand grenade; **4, 8** fire carriage; **5, 4** chain shot, mills bomb, slung shot; **5, 5** broad arrow, small sword, sword stick; **5, 8** brass knuckles; **6-2** battle-ax; **6-3** doodle-bug; **6, 4** cannon ball, letter bomb, limpet mine; **6, 5** barbed arrow, boxing glove, khyber knife; **6, 6** breech loader, bridle cutter; **6, 7** guided missile; **6, 8** rocket launcher; **7, 4** neutron bomb; **7, 5** dueling sword; **7-6** knuckle-duster; **8, 4** hydrogen bomb; **8, 5** poisoned arrow, throwing knife; **9, 3** battering ram; **10, 4** incendiary bomb. *See also* **firearm**

wear 3 don, rub, tie; **4** bear, fray, garb; **5** carry, dress, erode, grind, scuff, sport; **7** costume, display, erasure, erosion, uniform; **8** abrasion, friction, garments; **9** attrition, corrosion, detrition; **12** obliteration, sandblasting; **13** deterioration; PHRASES: **3, 2** put on; **4, 2** have on, pull on, slip on; **4, 3** show off, ~ out; **4, 3, 4** ~ and tear; **4, 4** away, ~ down; **4, 7** ~ through.

weariness 6 apathy; **7** fatigue, inertia; **8** lethargy; **9** jadedness, tiredness; **10** exhaustion; **14** disenchantment; **15** disillusionment.

weary 3 sap; **4** tire; **5** drain, jaded, tired; **7**

exhaust; **8** fatigued; **9** exhausted; **12** disenchanted; **13** disillusioned; PHRASES: **3, 2** all in, fed up; **4, 3** worn out; **4, 4** worn down; **4, 8** lose patience; **5, 3** tired out.

weather 3 low, map; **4** damp, thaw, vane; **5** erode, front, spell; **6** endure, harden, mature, trough; **7** blister, climate, coarsen, corrode, crumble, sizzler, station, survive, thermal, toughen; **8** dampness, elements, humidity, interval, moisture, scorcher, sunshine, udometer *UK*, windsock; **9** anemogram, barograph, barometer, midsummer, nippiness, occlusion, withstand; **10** anemograph, anemometer, conditions, depression, hygrograph, hygrometer, inclemency, sultriness, summertime, wintriness; **11** anticyclone, pluviometer, temperature, thermograph, thermometer, weathercock; **12** psychrometer, weatherglass; PHRASES: **2, 4** El Niño; **2, 5, 6** St Luke's summer *UK*; **2, 7, 6** St Martin's summer *UK*; **2, 8, 3** St Swithin's day; **3, 3** dry air, ice age; **3, 4** air flow, air mass, dog days; **3, 5** dew point, hot spell; **3, 6** air stream; **3, 7** air density, get through; **3, 8** air pressure; **4, 3** last out, ride out, warm air; **4, 4** cold snap, heat haze, heat wave, wear away, wear down, wind cone, wind rose; **4, 5** cold front, cold spell, rain gauge, warm front, warm spell, wind gauge; **4-5, 6** wind-chill factor; **4, 6** high summer, warm sector, wind sleeve; **4, 7** come through, live through; **4, 9** cold occlusion, warm occlusion; **5, 3** moist air, polar air, stick out; **5, 5** polar front, storm glass; **5, 6** chill factor; **6, 2, 6** depths of winter; **6, 3** midday sun; **6, 4** Azores high; **6, 6** Indian summer; **6, 7** global warming, summer drought; **7, 4** flaming June, halcyon days; ~ lore; **7, 5** ~ radar; **7, 6** frontal system; **8, 3** tropical air; **8, 4** blocking high, tropical heat; **8, 5** occluded front; **8, 6** pressure system; **9, 3** Groundhog Day, Icelandic low; **9, 6** Stevenson screen; **10, 4** stationary high; **10, 5** greenhouse gases.

weathered 4 worn; **6** eroded; **7** abraded, scoured; **8** battered, striated; **9** windswept; PHRASES: **7-6** weather-beaten.

weather forecast 6 isobar, report; **7** outlook; **8** bulletin, forecast, isotherm; PHRASES: **2, 7, 6** US Weather Bureau; **4, 6** road report; **6, 6** travel report; **7, 3** weather map; **7, 5** tornado watch; **7, 6** weather bureau; **7, 7** general outlook, weather symbols; **7, 8** general synopsis; **8, 3** synoptic map.

weathering 7 erosion; **8** abrasion, chem-

ical; **9** striation; **10** denudation, mechanical; **13** sedimentation; PHRASES: **4, 7** rain erosion, wave erosion, wind erosion; **5, 7** river erosion; **7, 7** glacial erosion.

weather station 10 radiosonde; PHRASES: **4, 7** land station; **5, 7** field station; **6, 7** ground station; **7, 4** weather ship; **7, 7** coastal station, weather balloon; **9, 4** automatic buoy.

weave 3 mat, nap, web; **4** felt, knit, lace, pile, spin, tell, wind; **5** braid, merge, plait, snake, twist; **6** careen, create, invent, zigzag; **7** compose, concoct, entwine, meander, texture, weftage; **8** contrive; **9** construct, fabricate; **10** crisscross, intertwine, interweave; PHRASES: **3, 8** put together; **4, 2** make up; **5, 5** plain ~, twill ~.

weaving 3 nap, web; **4** lace, loom, warp, weft, woof; **6** bobbin, lacing, spider; **7** distaff, knitter, selvage, shuttle, spinner, texture, twining, webbing; **8** knitting, knotting *UK*; **10** weaverbird; **12** interweaving; PHRASES: **7, 5** ~ frame; **8, 4** Jacquard loom; **8, 5** spinning wheel.

web *See* **network**

wed *See* **marry**

wedding 4 cake, ring, vows; **6** golden, silver; **7** diamond, joining, linking, spousal, uniting; **8** espousal, hymeneal, marriage, nuptials; **9** betrothal, elopement, honeymoon; **10** invitation; **12** epithalamium, prothalamium; PHRASES: **3, 5, 7** Las Vegas ~; **5, 3, 4** tying the knot; **5, 7** quiet ~, white ~; **5, 8** civil ceremony; **6, 5** bridal suite, Gretna Green; **6, 7** bridal bouquet, bridal chamber, church ~; **7, 3** nuptial ode, ~ day; **7, 4** nuptial Mass, nuptial vows, saffron robe, saffron veil, ~ veil; **7, 5** ~ banns, ~ bells, ~ dress, ~ march, ~ music; **7, 6** ~ canopy, ~ shower *US and Aus*; **7, 7** shotgun ~, ~ present; **7, 8** ~ ceremony; **8, 4** marriage vows; **8, 5** hymeneal rites, marriage toast; **8, 6** registry office *UK*; **8, 7** forcible wedlock; **9, 5** honeymoon suite.

wedge 3 fix, jam, ram; **4** cram, hold, hunk, pack; **5** block, chock, lodge, stuff; **6** sliver; **7** segment.

wee *See* **small**

weedkiller 5 spray; **6** derris; **9** fungicide, herbicide, pesticide, pyrethrum; **10** dimethoate; **11** insecticide; PHRASES: **4, 6** moss killer, slug pellet; **8, 7** Bordeaux mixture.

week 8 hebdomad, sennight.

weep 3 cry, sob; 4 bawl, blub *UK*, leak, ooze, seep, wail; 5 exude; 6 boohoo, snivel; 7 blubber, ululate; 9 discharge, suppurate; PHRASES: 4, 5 shed tears.

weepy 3 sad; 5 mushy; 6 slushy, syrupy; 7 tearful; 9 emotional, miserable; 13 overemotional; 15 oversentimental.

weigh 4 heft; 6 assess, ponder; 7 measure; 8 consider, evaluate; 10 deliberate; 11 contemplate; PHRASES: 3, 2, 3, 5 lay on the scale; 4, 4 chew over, mull over; 5, 4 think over; 6, 1, 7 strike a balance; 7, 2 reflect on; 8, 2 meditate on.

weighing down 4 drag; 5 stone; 6 taxing; 7 incubus; 8 handicap, pressure, saddling; 9 burdening, cumbrance, millstone; 10 oppression; 11 encumbrance, onerousness, overbalance; 12 unwieldiness; 13 overburdening, ponderousness; 14 cumbersomeness, oppressiveness.

weigh on 5 crush; 7 oppress; 9 suffocate; PHRASES: 5, 4 press upon.

weight 4 bulk, lead, load, mass; 5 clout, plumb, power; 6 burden, import; 9 authority, heaviness, influence; 10 importance; 11 consequence, encumbrance; 12 significance; PHRASES: 3, 2, 6 ton of bricks; 4, 7 lead balloon.

weightless 4 airy; 5 light; 8 ethereal, feathery; 13 insubstantial.

weights and measures 2 cm, dr, ft, gr, hl, in, kg, km, lb, mg, ml, mm, oz, yd; 3 amp, are, bar, bel, bit, cwt, dwt, ell, erg, lux, mho, mil, mim *UK*, nit, ohm, rad, rem, rod, ton, tun; 4 acre, bale, barn, bolt, byte, cask, cord, cran, dram, dyne, foot, gill, gram, hand, hide, hour, inch, kilo, knot, line, link, mile, mole, nail, pace, peck, phon, phot, pica, pint, pipe, pole, pood, ream, rood, slug, span, torr, troy, volt, watt, yard; 5 cable, carat, chain, crith, cubit, curie, cusec, cycle, debye, farad, fermi, gauge, gauss, grain, henry, hertz, joule, liter, lumen, meter, minim, neper, ounce, perch, point, poise, pound, quart, quire, stade, stere, stilb, stoke, stone, tesla, therm, toise, tonne, verst, weber; 6 ampere, barrel, bushel, candle, cental, degree, denier, drachm, fathom, firkin, gallon, gramme *UK*, kelvin, league, megohm, micron, minute, newton, parsec, pascal, radian, réamur, second, stokes; 7 calorie, candela, centner, coulomb, decibel, diopter, faraday, furlong, gilbert, hectare, kilobar, kiloton, lambert, maxwell, megaton, oersted, poundal, quarter, quintal, röntgen, scruple, siemens; 8 ångstrom, chaldron, hogshead, kilogram, kilowatt, megawatt, microohm, quadrant; 9 centigram, decaliter, decameter, deciliter, decimeter, hectogram, kilocycle, kilohertz, kilolitre, kilometer, megacycle, megafarad, megahertz, microgram, microwatt, milligram, nanometer, scantling, steradian; 10 barleycorn *UK*, centiliter, centimeter, decagramme, decigramme, hectoliter, horsepower, kilogramme, microfarad, milliliter, millimeter, nanosecond, rutherford; 11 millisecond, millisteres, pennyweight; 13 hundredweight; PHRASES: 4-4 watt-hour; 4-5 foot-pound; 5, 4 cubic foot, cubic inch, cubic yard; 5-4 board-foot, light-year; 5, 5 cubic meter, fluid ounce; 6, 3 metric ton; 6, 4 square inch, square mile, square yard; 6, 9 square kilometer; 8, 4 nautical mile.

weir *See* **dam**

weird *See* **odd**

weird *See* **strange**

weka 7 woodhen; PHRASES: 5, 3 Maori hen *UK*.

welcome 3 hug; 4 hail, kiss; 5 cheer, comfy, greet; 6 accept, invite, salute, timely, warmth; 7 embrace, receive, relaxed, shelter; 8 friendly, greeting, inviting, pleasant; 9 convivial, handclasp, handshake, opportune, reception; 10 acceptable, appreciate, delightful, hospitable, salutation; 11 comfortable, hospitality, openhearted, pleasurable; 12 friendliness; PHRASES: 2, 4 at ease, at home; 3, 6 red carpet; 4, 2 jump at; 4-7 long-awaited; 4-8 backslapping; 6-3 longed-for; 6-4 heaven-sent.

weld 4 bond, fuse, join, seal, wold; 5 joint, woald; 6 solder.

welfare 4 alms, good; 6 health, safety; 9 interests, socialism, welfarism; 10 prosperity; PHRASES: 4-5 well-being; 6, 7 public ~, social ~.

welfare state 7 benefit; 10 assistance; PHRASES: 3, 4 the dole; 4, 6 food stamps, poor relief; 5, 5 nanny state *UK*; 5, 7 child support, child welfare; 6, 7 income support *UK*; 6, 8 social security, social services.

well 2 OK, so; 3 pit; 4 ably, bore, fine, grow, gush, okay, rise, very; 5 flood, fount, fully, sound, surge, swell; **6** anyhow, anyway, deeply, fairly, highly, source, spring; **7** capably, clearly, closely, glowing, healthy, totally, utterly; **8** borehole, expertly, fountain, genially, properly, suitably, superbly, thriving; **9** admirably, carefully, correctly, ethically, extremely, favorably, fittingly, fortunate, perfectly, precisely; **10** acceptably, completely, familiarly, graciously, intimately, peerlessly, personally, pleasantly, positively, skillfully, splendidly, thoroughly, virtuously, wellspring; **11** competently, courteously, effectively, efficiently, excellently, exquisitely; **12** benevolently, fountainhead, meticulously, satisfactory; **13** appropriately, magnificently; **14** satisfactorily; PHRASES: **2, 3, 4** in any case; **2, 4** on form *UK*; **2, 4, 6** in good health; **2, 6** in detail; **3, 4** now then; **3, 5** all right; **5, 6** water supply; **6, 2** spring up; **8, 3** fighting fit; **8, 4** artesian ~.

well (do well) 6 thrive; **7** prosper, succeed; **8** flourish; PHRASES: **3, 6** get better.

well-behaved 4 good; **5** suave; **6** docile, formal, polite, urbane; **7** dutiful, ethical, genteel, refined, willing; **8** cultured, gracious, ladylike, mannerly, obedient, polished, virtuous; **9** compliant, courteous, dignified; **10** cultivated, diplomatic, flattering, respectful; **11** gentlemanly; PHRASES: **2, 4, 8** on best behavior; **2, 7** de rigueur; **3-7** law-abiding; **4-4** well-bred; **4-8** well-mannered; **5-7** sweet-talking.

well-known 5 famed; **6** famous; **7** blatant, glaring, popular; **8** infamous, manifest, renowned; **9** notorious; **10** celebrated; **11** sensational; PHRASES: **2, 3, 9** in the headlines; **2, 9, 4** on everyone's lips.

well-made 7 cunning, elegant, stylish; **8** artistic, finished; **9** Daedalian; **12** professional; PHRASES: **4-4** deep-laid *UK*; **4-7** well-crafted.

well-off *See* **wealthy**

well-ordered 7 regular, uniform; **8** coherent; **10** methodical, meticulous, scientific, systematic; **11** punctilious; **12** businesslike; PHRASES: **4-9** well-organized.

well-rounded 3 fat; **5** curvy, plump, podgy, stout, tubby; **6** chubby, portly; **7** paunchy, shapely, sinuous; **9** corpulent; **10** curvaceous, potbellied, undulatory; PHRASES: **4-6** pear-shaped.

well-wisher *See* **supporter**

Welsh 4 harp; **5** corgi, poppy; **6** rabbit; **7** dresser, terrier; **8** mountain.

wend *See* **proceed**

West Indian dish 5 stoba; **6** asapao, féroce; **7** calalou, macadam; **8** pasteles, piononos; **12** chiquetaille.

West Virginia 2 WV; PHRASES: **0, 5, 5** sugar maple (tree); **8** cardinal (bird); **10** Charleston (capital); **8, 5** Mountain State (nickname); **12, 3, 6, 4** Mountaineers are always free (motto); **12, 7** rhododendron maximum (flower).

wet 4 damp, dank, fish, look, rain, soak, suit; **5** awash, douse, dream, humid, misty, moist, nurse, rainy, soggy, soppy, spray, steam, water; **6** bathed, dampen, dipped, drench, ducked, dunked, effete, feeble, liquid, soaked, sodden, soused, splash, watery; **7** blanket, drizzle, flooded, moisten, showery, soaking, sopping, steeped, swamped, wetness; **8** dampness, drenched, dripping, moisture, saturate, sprinkle, wringing; **9** saturated, streaming, submerged; **11** waterlogged, watersoaked; PHRASES: **3, 7** ~ through; **6, 2, 3, 4** soaked to the skin; **7, 3** drowned rat.

whack 3 hit; **4** blow, slap; **5** clout, thump; **6** strike, thwack.

whale 6 blower; **7** narwhal; PHRASES: **4, 5** blue ~, gray ~; **5, 5** minke ~, pilot ~, right ~, sperm ~, white ~; **6, 5** killer ~; **8, 5** humpback ~.

whatever 4 what; **5** which; **8** anything; **10** everything, whatsoever; PHRASES: **2, 3** at all; **2, 3, 4** of any kind; **2, 6, 4** no matter what; **4, 3, 4** what you will; **4, 4, 3** what have you.

wheal 4 mark, welt; **5** wound; **8** swelling; **9** contusion.

wheedle 4 coax; **5** charm; **6** cajole, obtain; **8** inveigle, persuade; PHRASES: **4, 3** coax out, draw out; **6, 3** winkle out *UK*.

wheel 3 big; **4** mill, roll, spur, turn; **5** crown, drive, idler, wagon, water; **6** escape, ferris, Ixion's, paddle, prayer, rotate; **7** balance, buffing, charkha, fortune, potter's, ratchet, trundle; **8** flywheel, pinwheel, roulette, spinning, sprocket, steering; **9** cartwheel, catherine, gearwheel.

wheel clamp 6, 4 Denver boot.

wheeze 4 gasp, hiss, joke, pant, ploy, rasp, ruse; **5** trick; **6** rattle; **7** whisper, whistle.

whelp 3 pup; PHRASES: 4, 5 bear young, give birth. *See also* **young animal**

when 3 now; 4 then; 5 today; 7 someday, tonight; 8 sometime, tomorrow; 9 whereupon, yesterday; PHRASES: 2, 3, 4 at the time; 2, 4, 6 at this moment; 3, 4 any time.

whenever 4 when; 7 whene'er; 10 whensoever; PHRASES: 4, 4 each time; 5, 4 every time.

where 4 here; 5 there; 6 hereat, passim; 7 thereat, thither, whither; 9 hereabout; 10 hereabouts; 11 thereabouts, whereabouts; PHRASES: 2, 3, 4 on the spot; 2, 3, 8 in the vicinity; 2, 4 in loco, in situ, on site; 2, 4, 5 at this point, in that place; 2, 6 in places; 2, 8 on location; 4, 3, 5 here and there; 4, 4 just here.

wherever 7 where'er; 11 wheresoever.

wherewithal *See* **means**

whet 4 file, hone; 5 grind, rouse; 6 arouse, kindle; 7 augment, sharpen; 9 stimulate.

whey 5 serum; 6 plasma.

whiff 3 hum *UK*; 4 hint, sign; 5 trace; 7 vestige.

while 2 as; 3 but; 4 time; 6 little, period, though; 7 however, whereas; 8 although, interval; 12 intermission; PHRASES: 2, 8 in contrast; 4, 2 even as; 4, 6 even though.

whim 3 fad; 4 idea, mood, urge; 5 craze, fancy, humor, quirk; 6 maggot, megrim, notion, vagary, whimsy; 7 boutade, caprice, impulse; 8 crotchet; 10 brainstorm; 11 peculiarity, temperament; 12 idiosyncrasy; PHRASES: 3, 2, 3, 6 bee in the bonnet; 3, 4-5 the whim-whams; 4-4 flip-flop; 4-5, 5 wild-goose chase; 6, 2, 4 change of mind; 7, 5 passing fancy.

whimper *See* **cry**

whimsical 3 fey; 5 witty; 6 fickle, quaint, quirky, random; 7 erratic, flighty, playful, wayward; 8 fanciful; 9 impulsive; 10 capricious; 11 imaginative; 13 temperamental, unpredictable; PHRASES: 3-3-4 off-the-wall; 3-9 old-fashioned.

whimsy 4 whim; 5 fancy; 6 oddity; 7 oddness; 10 quaintness, quirkiness; 12 eccentricity; PHRASES: 6, 2, 5 flight of fancy.

whine 3 cry, hum; 4 howl, moan, wail; 5 bleat, drone, gripe; 7 grumble, whimper; 8 complain; 9 complaint.

whinny *See* **neigh**

whip 3 rob; 4 beat, belt, flog, lash; 5 slash; 6 thrash; 7 scourge; 10 flagellate.

whirl 4 spin, turn; 5 twirl; 6 flurry, gyrate, vortex.

whirlwind 5 brief, rapid, swift; 7 cyclone, tornado; 9 hurricane; 10 tumultuous, waterspout; PHRASES: 5-5 short-lived.

whisk 4 beat, stir, whip; 6 aerate, bustle, hustle.

whiskey 4 corn, malt; 5 irish; 10 usquebaugh.

whisper 4 hint, hiss, purr, tale, word; 5 croon, mouth, rumor, utter; 6 gossip, murmur, mutter, rustle; 7 breathe, crackle; 9 susurrate.

whistle 3 tin; 4 hoot, toot, wolf; 5 penny, steam; 6 shriek.

white 3 icy, lie, out, tie, wan; 4 area, bear, ecru, fish, flag, gold, heat, lady, lead, meat, pale; 5 ashen, beige, birch, cream, drawn, horse, house, ivory, light, milky, paper, pasty, pearl, slave, snowy, stick, waxen, whale; 6 anemic, argent, chalky, creamy, ensign, frosty, frozen, greige, knight, marble, oyster, pallid, pearly, pepper, silver, spirit, undyed; 7 admiral, feather, graying, silvery, whitish; 8 argental, bleached, eggshell, elephant, freezing, magnolia, mushroom, platinum, silvered; 9 alabaster, albescent, albinotic, argentine, Caucasian; 10 albinistic, lactescent, unbleached; PHRASES: 3-5 off-white; 4-5 half-white, lily-white, milk-white, pure-white, snow-white; 4-7 fair-skinned *UK*; 5, 2, 1, 4 ~ as a lily; 5, 2, 4 ~ as milk; 5, 2, 6 ~ as marble; 6-3 washed-out.

white-eye 6 waxeye; PHRASES: 6-3 silvereye.

white-haired 4 fair, gray; 5 blond(e), hoary; 6 Nordic; 8 grizzled; 9 canescent; PHRASES: 3-5 ash-blond(e); 3-6 tow-headed; 4-3-6 salt-and-pepper; 6-6 flaxen-haired, golden-haired; 8-5 platinum-blond(e).

whitely 10 luminously; 14 achromatically. *See also* **white**

whiten 4 fade, pale; 5 clean, frost, white; 6 blanch, blanco, bleach, blench, silver; 7 grizzle; 8 etiolate; 9 calcimine, whitewash; 10 decolorize; PHRASES: 4, 4 pipe clay.

whitened 5 faded, hoary, soapy, spumy; 6 frosty; 7 foaming, frosted, lathery; 8 blanched, bleached; 11 decolorized, whitewashed; **PHRASES: 3-7** ice-covered; **4-6** snow-capped; **4-7** foam-flecked; **5-3** white-hot.

whitener 6 blanco; 7 whiting; 9 calcimine, whitewash; **PHRASES: 4, 4** pipe clay; **4, 5** Luma white, zinc white; **5, 4** white lead; **5, 5** flake white, Paris white, white paint; **5, 6** white alkali; **5, 7** white arsenic; **7, 5** Chinese white; **8, 5** titanium white.

whiteness 6 anemia, pallor; 8 albinism; 9 albinoism, hoariness; 10 albescence, canescence, etiolation, leucoderma, leukoderma, sallowness; 11 achromatism, lactescence; 13 colorlessness. *See also* **white**

white poplar 5 abele.

white thing 4 hoar, lily, milk, snow, swan; 5 chalk, flour, frost, ivory, paper, pearl, teeth; 6 marble, pewter, silver, whites; 8 platinum, whitecap, whitefly; 9 alabaster, whitebait, whitefish, whitetail; 10 whitethorn *UK*; 11 whitethroat; **PHRASES: 5, 3** white ant, white oak, white tie; **5, 4** white flag, white gold, white heat, white meat, white rose, white sale, white wall, white wine; **5, 5** white bread, white dwarf, White Friar, white goods, white horse *UK*, White House, white light, white metal, white paper, white sauce, white shark, white whale; **5, 5, 4** white blood cell; **5, 6** white clover, white coffee, white pepper, white poplar, white spruce; **5-6, 4** white-tailed deer; **5, 7** white admiral; **6, 2, 5** Cliffs of Dover; **6, 4** driven snow.

white walnut 9 butternut.

whitewash 4 beat, lime, plot, rout; 5 cover, paint, smear; 6 defeat; 7 conceal, trounce; 8 decorate; 9 deception, distemper, whitening; 10 conspiracy; 11 concealment; 12 misrepresent; **PHRASES: 3-5, 4** one-horse race; **5, 2** cover up; **5, 4** gloss over; **7, 4** explain away.

white whale 6 beluga.

whodunit *See* **mystery**

whoever 5 whoso; 8 whomever; 9 whosoever; 10 whomsoever; **PHRASES: 2, 6, 3** no matter who.

whole 3 all, one; 4 full, unit, well; 5 cured, gross, solid, sound, total, uncut, unity; 6 entire, global, healed, holism, intact, mended, single, united; 7 healthy, oneness, unified; 8 complete, ensemble, entirety, integral, totality, unbroken; 9 aggregate, integrity, undivided, universal; 10 integrated, unabridged, unimpaired; 11 indivisible, inseparable, integration; 12 completeness, indissoluble, universality; 13 comprehensive, inclusiveness, international; 14 indivisibility; **PHRASES: 2, 3, 5** in one piece; **3, 5** sum total; **3-9** all-embracing, all-inclusive; **6-3-5** across-the-board; **6, 4, 3** rolled into one.

whole (be whole) 5 total, unify, unite; 9 integrate; **PHRASES: 3, 2** sum up; **4, 2** come to; **6, 2** amount to.

whole (on the whole) 5 quite; 6 almost, mainly, mostly; 7 largely; 9 generally, virtually; 10 altogether; 11 effectively, essentially, practically; 13 predominantly; **PHRASES: 2, 1, 4** as a rule; **2, 3, 4** in the main; **2, 3, 5** by and large; **2, 4, 2** as good as; **2, 6** in effect; **2, 7** in essence, in general; **2, 9** in substance; **3, 2, 3** all in all; **3, 3, 4, 4** for the most part.

wholesale 4 bulk; 5 broad; 6 carpet, global; 7 broadly, general; 8 catholic; 9 generally, universal; 10 widespread; 13 comprehensive; 14 indiscriminate; **PHRASES: 3, 2, 4** all at once; **4-7** wide-ranging; **6-3-5** across-the-board.

wholesaler 5 agent; 6 banker, broker, dealer, trader, vendor; 7 cambist; 8 exporter, importer, marketer, merchant, operator, procurer, retailer *UK*, supplier; 9 financier, middleman, roundsman *UK*; 10 monopolist, speculator, trafficker; 11 oligopolist, stockbroker; 12 entrepreneur, merchandiser, moneychanger; **PHRASES: 6, 5** market maker.

wholesome 3 fit; 4 good, open; 5 clean, moral, ruddy; 6 decent, honest; 7 healthy; 8 sensible; 9 practical; 10 nourishing, nutritious; 14 commonsensical; **PHRASES: 5-3** clean-cut; **5-5** fresh-faced; **5-6** clean-living.

whole thing 3 sum; 4 unit; 5 globe, total, world; 6 corpus, cosmos; 7 gestalt, integer; 8 ensemble, entirety, totality, universe; 9 macrocosm, microcosm, summation; 10 Lebensraum; **PHRASES: 3, 5** sum total; **5, 6** whole number; **8, 5** complete works.

wholly 5 fully; 6 solely; 7 totally, utterly; 8 entirely; 10 absolutely, altogether, completely; 11 exclusively, unanimously, universally; **PHRASES: 2, 3** as one; **2, 4** in toto; **2, 5, 7** in every respect; **4, 3, 4** body and soul; **4, 3, 6** root and branch; **5, 3** every bit; **5, 3, 4** heart and soul; **5, 3, 5** pound for pound; **5, 4** every inch.

whoop *See* **shout**

whooping cough 9 pertussis.

whoosh 4 dash, hiss, roar, rush, whiz, zoom; 5 burst, spurt, surge, swish; 7 rushing, whistle.

whopper 3 lie; 4 tale; 5 giant; 7 monster, untruth; 8 elephant; 9 falsehood; 11 fabrication.

whopping 3 big; 4 huge; 6 defeat; 7 licking, pasting; 8 drubbing, enormous, gigantic; 9 monstrous, thrashing.

whortleberry 4 hurt; 8 fraughan; 9 blaeberry; 11 huckleberry.

WI 4, 6 West Indies.

wicked 3 bad; 4 base, cool, evil, mean, vile; 5 awful, cruel, great, wrong; 6 brutal, rotten, severe, sinful; 7 acerbic, beastly, callous, corrupt, cutting, heinous, hellish, immoral, impious, inhuman, knavish, naughty, roguish, teasing, vicious; 8 criminal, depraved, fiendish, improper, infamous, rascally, terrible, terrific; 9 appalling, atrocious, dishonest, evildoing, malicious, miscreant, nefarious, sarcastic, shameless; 10 abominable, delinquent, despicable, flagitious, impressive, inexpiable, iniquitous, maleficent, malevolent, misbehaved, outrageous, villainous, wrongdoing; 11 disgraceful, distressing, hardhearted, misbehaving, mischievous, unrighteous; 12 disreputable, incorrigible, irredeemable, irremissible, unforgivable, unpardonable, unprincipled, unscrupulous; 13 irreclaimable, reprehensible, transgressing; PHRASES: 6, 2, 3, 4 rotten to the core.

wicked (be wicked) 3 err, sin; 4 fall; 5 lapse, shock; 6 offend; 9 backslide, misbehave; 10 transgress; PHRASES: 2, 2, 3, 3 go to the bad; 2, 2, 3, 4 go to the dogs; 3, 4, 4 sow one's oats; 4, 1, 7 make a mistake; 4, 4, 4 ruin one's name; 4, 4, 5 fall from grace; 5, 2, 6 scoff at virtue; 8, 7 disgrace oneself.

wicked (make wicked) 5 tempt; 6 seduce; 7 corrupt, mislead, pervert; 9 brutalize, diabolize; 10 dehumanize; PHRASES: 4, 6 lead astray.

wickedness 3 sin; 4 evil, vice; 5 wrong; 6 infamy, malice; 7 cruelty, impiety, knavery, outrage, roguery; 8 atrocity, enormity, iniquity, trespass, villainy; 9 brutality, evildoing, flagrancy, improbity, obscenity, vitiation; 10 corruption, dishonesty, immorality, inhumanity, recidivism, wrongdoing; 11 abomination, criminality, delinquency, malevolence, misbehavior, peccability; 13 transgression; PHRASES: 3, 4 bad ways; 3, 7 bad conduct; 3, 8 bad behavior; 3, 9 bad character; 4, 2, 9 loss of innocence; 6, 4 wicked ways; 6, 6 fallen nature; 8, 2, 5 hardness of heart. *See also* **wicked**

wicked place 4 hell; 5 Hades; 7 brothel; 8 cathouse; PHRASES: 3, 2, 4 den of vice; 3, 2, 8 den of iniquity; 4, 2, 4 road to hell; 5, 3 opium den; 7, 4 robbers' lair; 8, 3 gambling den *UK*.

wicket 4 door, exit, gate; 5 stump; 7 opening; 8 aperture, entrance.

wide 5 ample, baggy, broad, large, loose, roomy, thick; 6 varied; 8 eclectic, spacious; 9 capacious, extensive, inclusive; 10 widespread; PHRASES: 3, 3, 4 off the mark; 3, 6 off course, off target.

wide-eyed 4 agog, dumb; 5 agape; 7 popeyed; 10 dumbstruck, speechless, transfixed; 11 dumbfounded; PHRASES: 3, 4 all agog; 4-7 open-mouthed; 5-4 round-eyed; 6, 2, 3, 4 rooted to the spot; 6, 4 struck dumb.

widen *See* **broaden**

widespread 4 rife; 6 common; 7 endemic, rampant; 8 epidemic, pandemic; 9 extensive, pervasive, prevalent; 10 ubiquitous; 11 omnipresent.

widow 6 relict; 7 bereave.

widowed 8 bereaved, widowish, wifeless; 9 widowered, widowlike; 11 husbandless.

widowhood 5 weeds; 11 widowerhood; PHRASES: 5, 9 grass ~; 6, 5 widow's weeds.

width *See* **breadth**

wield 3 ply, use; 4 have, hold, wave; 5 apply, carry, exert, sport; 6 employ, handle; 8 brandish, flourish; 10 manipulate.

wieldy 5 handy; 6 pliant; 7 ductile, pliable; 8 flexible, yielding; 9 adaptable, malleable, practical; 10 convenient, manageable; 12 maneuverable; 13 untroublesome; PHRASES: 4-5 well-oiled; 6-7 smooth-running.

wife 4 lady, mate; 5 bride, goody; 6 matron, missis, spouse; 7 consort, partner; 8 goodwife *UK*, newlywed; 9 concubine, homemaker, housewife; PHRASES: 4, 8 old lady; 3, 5 old dutch; 4-2-2 wife-to-be; 4, 4 good lady; 6-3, 4 common-law ~; 6, 4 better half; 6, 5 little woman *UK*.

wig 3 rug; 5 toupé; 6 toupee; 7 periwig; 8 lambaste; 9 hairpiece; PHRASES: 4, 9 hair extension; **5, 4** false hair.

wiggle 5 shake, twist; **6** jiggle, squirm, waggle; **7** wriggle.

wild 3 mad; **5** crazy, eager, feral, messy, rough, rowdy; **6** barren, madcap, remote, savage, stormy, unruly, untidy; **7** excited, natural, riotous, scruffy, squally, tousled, unkempt, untamed; **8** blustery, desolate, reckless; **9** turbulent, windswept; **10** disheveled, disorderly, irrational, outrageous; **11** tempestuous, uninhabited; **12** enthusiastic, uncultivated, unmanageable; **13** undisciplined; **14** uncontrollable, unconventional, undomesticated; PHRASES: **3-4** hog-wild.

wilderness 5 waste, wilds; **6** desert, sticks; **7** outback; **9** backwater, backwoods, wasteland; PHRASES: **5, 7** rough country.

wild pansy 10 heartsease; PHRASES: **4-2-8** love-in-idleness.

will 4 guts *UK*, mind, want, wish; **5** drive, fancy; **6** choice, desire, estate, intent, legacy, spirit; **7** bequest, bidding, codicil, command, longing, purpose, resolve; **8** ambition, backbone, conation, firmness, volition; **9** constancy, intention, stability, testament, willpower; **10** motivation, preference, steadiness; **11** disposition, inclination, inheritance, staunchness; **13** determination, steadfastness; PHRASES: **4, 4** iron ~.

will (at will) 2, 3 ad lib; **2, 3, 6, 3** as one thinks fit; **2, 3, 7** as one pleases; **2, 4, 8** at one's pleasure; **2, 7** ad libitum.

willed 7 willing; **8** conative, intended, volitive; **10** bequeathed, deliberate, volitional; **11** intentional.

willful 6 dogged, mulish, unruly; **7** wayward; **8** obdurate, perverse, stubborn; **9** conscious, difficult, malicious, obstinate, pigheaded; **10** bullheaded, deliberate, determined, headstrong, malevolent; **11** intentional; **12** intransigent, obstreperous; PHRASES: **4-6** self-willed; **6-6** bloody-minded *UK*.

willfulness 8 obduracy; **9** obstinacy; **10** perversity; **13** intransigence, premeditation; PHRASES: **4-4** self-will. *See also* **willful**

willing 4 game, keen; **5** eager, happy, prone, ready; **7** content, helpful; **8** disposed, prepared; **9** agreeable, assenting, receptive; **10** alacritous, consenting; **11** bequeathing, cooperative; **12** enthusiastic; PHRASES: **2, 5** in favor.

willing (be willing) 5 agree; **6** assent, comply; **7** consent; **9** acquiesce; PHRASES: **2, 3, 2, 4, 3** go out of one's way; **2, 5, 4** go along with; **4, 2** jump at, leap at.

willingly 6 freely, gladly; **10** cheerfully; **11** voluntarily; PHRASES: **2, 4, 3, 6** of one's own accord; **4, 4, 4** with open arms; **4, 4, 5** with good grace; **4, 5** with gusto; **7, 5** without demur. *See also* **willing**

willingness 7 consent; **8** alacrity; **10** enthusiasm; PHRASES: **11** disposition, inclination. *See also* **willing**

will-o'-the-wisp 8 wildfire; **5, 6** ignis fatuus; **6, 7** friar's lantern.

willowy 4 slim; **6** lissom *UK*, supple, svelte; **7** elegant, lissome, springy; **8** bendable, flexible, graceful; **9** malleable.

willpower 7 resolve; **8** tenacity; **10** resolution; **12** resoluteness; **13** determination, steadfastness; PHRASES: **4, 4** iron will; **4, 4, 6** mind over matter; **4-7** self-control; **4-10** self-discipline; **8, 2, 4** strength of mind, strength of will.

willy-nilly 6 anyway, random; **9** arbitrary, haphazard; **10** regardless; **11** unselective; **12** unsystematic; **15** unceremoniously; PHRASES: **2, 3, 4** in any case; **4, 2, 2, 3** like it or not.

wilt 4 fade, wane; **5** droop; **6** wither; **7** shrivel.

wily *See* **crafty**

win 6 attain; **7** prevail, succeed, triumph; **8** conquest.

wince 4 gasp, jump; **5** scowl, start; **6** cringe, flinch, recoil, shrink; **7** grimace, shudder.

winch 4 lift, pull; **5** crane, erect, heave, hoist, raise; **6** pulley; **7** capstan; **8** windlass; PHRASES: **4, 2** lift up.

wind 3 gas; **4** bend, berg, bise, bora, calm, coil, curl, eddy, föhn, gale, gust, head, hint, reel, roll, scud, tail; **5** blast, buran, curve, Eurus, foehn, gibli, snake, spool, storm, twine, twist, zonda; **6** Auster, austru, baguio *Philippines*, Boreas, breath, breeze, ghibli, haboob, saniel, simoom, solano, squall, Zephyr, zigzag; **7** baloney, chinook, cyclone (Indian Ocean), etesian, gregale, khamsin, meander, meltemi, mistral, monsoon, norther, pampero, sirocco, tornado, twister, typhoon (N Pacific), updraft; **8** easterly, encircle, headwind, levanter, libeccio, papagayo, tailwind, westerly, williwaw; **9** airstream, antitrade, crosswind, downdraft, harmattan, hurricane (US and West Indies), jetstream, libecchio, nor'easter, northerly, nor'wester, sandstorm, southerly, whirlwind; **10** euroclydon, flatulence, prevailing, tramontana, tramontane, waterspout; **11** information, northeaster, northwester, southeaster, southwester, tehuantepec; **12** brickfielder, crosscurrent; **13** northeasterly, northwesterly, southeasterly, southwesterly; PHRASES: 3, 2, 3, 5 eye of the storm; 3, 6 sea breeze; 3, 7 air current, wet chinook; 4, 4 full gale, near gale; 4, 5 dust devil, dust storm, snow eater, ~ force, ~ speed; 4-5 wind-chill; 4, 6 cape doctor, land breeze, sand column, wrap around; 5, 3 light air, Santa Ana; 5, 3, 4 twist and turn; 5, 4 brisk ~, fresh ~, stiff ~, trade ~, upper ~; 5-5 willy-willy UK; 5, 5, 3 storm force ten; 5, 6 fresh breeze, light breeze; 6, 2, 4 breath of ~; 6, 4 strong gale, valley ~; 6, 6 gentle breeze, strong breeze; 7, 2, 3 current of air; 7, 4 howling gale, onshore ~, surface ~; 8, 4 anabatic ~, mountain ~, offshore ~, variable ~; 8, 5 Beaufort scale, tropical storm; 8, 6 moderate breeze; 9, 4 favorable ~, following ~, katabatic ~; 9, 6 southerly buster UK; 10, 4 prevailing ~; 11, 4 geostrophic ~.

windmill 9 gustiness, propeller, whirligig; **10** helicopter.

window 3 bay, bow, box, gap, tax; 4 hole, pane, sash, seat, sill, slot; 5 gable, jesse, ledge, space; 6 chance, dormer, French, lancet, period; 7 display, graphic, opening, picture, transom; 8 envelope, fanlight, porthole, skylight; 9 interface; 11 opportunity; PHRASES: 5, 5 north light; 6, 3 dialog box; 7, 5 frosted glass, stained glass; 8, 3 dialogue box.

windsock 4 sock; 6 drogue; PHRASES: 4, 4 wind cone.

windsurfing terms 3 fin, gun, RAF; 4 boom, clew, ding, hull, pump, rail, sail, skeg, wing; 5 board, cleat, plane; 6 bumper, rocker, sinker, tandem, tridem; 7 bowline, customs, drysuit, fathead, floater, harness; 8 cavatate, downhaul, funboard, marginal, wishbone; 9 boardsail, boardsurf, flatboard, footstrap, freestyle, powerhead, sailboard, universal; 10 rotational, roundboard; 11 daggerboard, wavesailing; PHRASES: 1-5, 4 V-shape hull; 2, 4, 5 Le Mans start; 3-3 pop-out; 3-3-3 off-the-lip; 3, 4, 4 ins and outs; 3, 3, 5 tip the board; 3, 4 ice surf; 3, 5 GRP board; 3-5 sub-plane; 4, 2 hook in; 4, 3 spin

out, wipe out; 4, 4 free sail, wave jump, wave ride; 4, 5 foot steer; 5, 5 water start; 6, 2, 6 center of effort (CE); 6, 5 custom board; 6, 6 slalom course; 6, 7 camber inducer; 7, 4 harness line; 8, 4 downhaul line, wishbone boom; 9, 5 universal joint.

windup 4 joke; 5 prank, trick; 6 manual; 9 clockwork; 10 mechanical; PHRASES: 6-8 spring-operated.

windy 3 icy, raw; 4 cold; 5 blowy, brisk, fresh, gusty, wordy; 6 biting, bitter, boreal, breezy, eolian, stormy; 7 bracing, pompous, squally, verbose, voluble; 8 blustery, boastful, favonian, freezing, piercing; 9 bombastic, turbulent; 10 loquacious; 12 anemological; 13 insubstantial; PHRASES: 4-6 long-winded.

wine 3 bar, box; 4 hock, port, rosé, sack, vino; 5 plonk, rioja, Tokay; 6 bubbly, cellar, claret, cooler, sherry; 7 chablis, chianti, madeira, marsala, Martini™ UK, Moselle, retsina, semidry, tasting; 8 Bordeaux, burgundy, champers UK, frascati, Muscadet, riesling, spumante, vermouth; 9 champagne, Sauternes; 10 beaujolais, chardonnay; PHRASES: 3, 2, 4 vin du pays; 3, 2, 5 vin de table; 3, 4 dry ~, red ~, vin rosé; 3, 5 the grape; 3, 6 dry sherry; 3, 9 vin ordinaire; 4, 4 ruby port; 4-6, 4 full-bodied ~; 5, 2, 3, 5 blood of the grape, juice of the grape; 5, 4 Rhine ~, still ~, table ~, tawny port, white port, white ~; 5, 5 Bulls Blood, vinho verde UK; 5, 6 cream sherry; 5, 8 white Bordeaux; 7, 4 dessert ~, vintage port, vintage ~; 9, 4 fortified ~, sparkling ~.

wines 4 Fino, Hock, Port, rosé, sekt; 5 Byrrh, Crépy, Fitou, Médoc, Mosel, Rioja, Tavel, Tokay; 6 Alsace, Bandol, Barolo, Barsac, Beaune, Cahors, Cassis, Chinon, Claret, Frangy, Graves, Málaga, Saumur, Sherry, Volnay; 7 Aligoté, Campari, Chablis, Chianti, Crémant, Falerno, Gaillac, Madeira, Margaux, Marsala, Martini, Moselle, Orvieto, Pommard, Retsina, Vouvray; 8 Bordeaux, Brouilly, Dubonnet, Gigondas, Mercurey, Montagny, Montilla, Muscadet, Pauillac, Riesling, Sancerre, Santenay, Valençay, Vermouth; 9 Bourgueil, Champagne, Hermitage, Lambrusco, Meursault, Montlouis, Sauternes; 10 Barbaresco, Beaujolais, Manzanilla, Montrachet, Richebourg, Rivesaltes; 11 Amontillado, Monbazillac; 12 Valpolicella; 14 Gewürztraminer; PHRASES: 3, 2, 6 Vin de Paille; 3, 5 Vin Jaune; 4-5 Côte-Rôtie; 5-2-5

Côtes-du-Rhône; **5, 2, 7** Côtes du Ventoux; **5-4-4** Entre-Deux-Mers; **5, 5** Vinho Verde; **5, 6** Saint Julien; **5-6** Aloxe-Corton; **5, 7** Saint Estephe; **5-7** Saint-Emilion, Vosne-Romanée; **7-4** Pouilly-Fumé; **7-5** Romanée-Conti; **7, 6** Château d'Yquem, Château Lafite, Château Latour; **7-6** Pouilly-Fuissé; **7, 7** Château Margaux, Lacrima Christi.

wing 3 arm, nut, tip; **4** dash, hurt, part, whiz; **5** annex, hurry, shoot, speed, wound; **6** branch, collar, damage, fender, injure, pennon; **7** section; **8** division; **9** commander, extension; **10** department; **11** subdivision.

wink *See* **flash**

winning 4 best; **8** champion, charming; **9** endearing; **10** persuasive, successful, triumphant, victorious; **11** captivating.

winnings 3 cut; **4** draw, loot; **5** prize; **7** jackpot, takings; PHRASES: **4-3** rake-off.

winnow 7 examine, inspect; PHRASES: **2, 7** go through; **4, 4** pick over; **4, 7** sort through.

winter 4 yule; **5** close; **6** brumal, hiemal, wintry; **7** closing, wintery; **8** hibernal, twilight, yuletide; **9** Christmas, midwinter; **10** conclusion, winterlike, wintertide *UK*, wintertime; **11** hibernation; PHRASES: **3, 6** the Season; **6, 8** ~ solstice.

wintergreen 8 shinleaf, teaberry; **14** partridgeberry.

WIP 4, 2, 8 work in progress.

wipe 3 dab, mop; **4** dust, swab; **5** clean, erase, smear; **6** polish, tissue; **7** destroy.

wire 4 cord, flex *UK*, high, lead, line, live; **5** cable, equip, telex; **6** barbed; **7** chicken, connect, fencing, install, message; **8** filament, telegram; PHRASES: **4, 2** hook up.

wiry 4 lean, slim, thin; **5** rough, stiff; **6** coarse, sinewy; **7** bristly; **8** muscular, scratchy.

Wisconsin 2 WI; **5** robin (bird); **7** Forward (motto), Madison (capital); PHRASES: **4, 6** wood violet (flower); **5, 5** sugar maple (tree); **6, 5** Badger State (nickname).

wisdom 4 lore, tact; **5** sense; **6** acumen, reason; **7** insight; **8** learning, prudence, sagacity, sapience; **9** erudition, foresight, intuition, knowledge; **10** profundity; **11** discernment; **12** intelligence, perspicacity; **13** comprehension, understanding; **14** discrimination; PHRASES: **7, 2, 6** breadth of vision; **9, 2, 4** soundness of mind. *See also* **wise**

wise 3 owl; **4** just, sage, wily; **5** aware; **6** astute, crafty, shrewd; **7** erudite, knowing, learned, prudent, sapient, tactful; **8** discreet, educated, highbrow, informed, oracular, profound, rational, sensible; **9** judicious, objective, sagacious; **10** discerning, farsighted, perceptive, reflecting, thoughtful; **11** intelligent; **13** knowledgeable, perspicacious, statesmanlike; PHRASES: **2, 3, 4** in the know; **2, 4** au fait; **4-7** well-advised; **5-2** clued-in; **5-6** level-headed.

wise (be wise) 5 grasp, judge; **6** fathom, intuit; **7** discern; **10** understand; **11** distinguish; PHRASES: **3, 4, 4** use one's head; **4, 3, 5** know the score; **4, 5, 4** know what's what.

wisecrack *See* **joke**

wise person 4 guru, sage, seer; **5** sibyl, witch; **6** Athena, oracle, shaman; **7** prophet, Solomon, thinker; **11** philosopher.

wish 3 ask, bid; **4** hope, want, will; **5** covet, crave, fancy *UK*; **6** desire; **7** command, longing, request; **8** volition, yearning; **10** aspiration; **11** inclination.

wishbone 12 merrythought.

wishy-washy 4 weak; **5** bland; **6** feeble, watery; **7** insipid; **9** tasteless; **10** indecisive, irresolute.

wit 3 fun, wag; **5** clown, comic, humor, irony, joker; **6** banter, brains; **7** jesting, joshing, kidding, sarcasm; **8** badinage, clowning, comedian, humorist, quipping, repartee, satirist, wordplay; **9** intellect, sharpness, smartness; **10** cleverness, jocularity; **11** waggishness *UK*; **12** incisiveness, intelligence; **13** facetiousness; PHRASES: **3, 3** dry ~; **4, 5** blue humor; **5, 3** ready ~; **5, 5** black humor; **7, 5** gallows humor.

witchcraft 3 obi; **5** coven, magic, wanga, Wicca; **6** hoodoo, magism, obiism, voodoo; **7** alchemy, gramyre, jujuism, sorcery, theurgy; **8** totemism, witchery, wizardry; **9** diablerie, Hallowe'en, magianism, shamanism, sortilege, vampirism, voodooism, witchwork; **10** bewitchery, necromancy, spellcraft; **11** bedevilment, enchantment, thaumaturgy; **12** spellbinding, spellcasting, thaumaturgia; **13** thaumaturgics; PHRASES: **5, 3** black art; **5, 5** black magic, chaos magic, white magic; **7, 7** witches' Sabbath; **8, 4** witching hour; **9, 5** Walpurgis Night.

witch, wizard 4 mage *UK*; **5** Circe, hazel, lamia, magus, Medea, siren; **6** doctor,

Hecate, Medusa, Merlin, shaman, Stheno, wizard; **7** charmer, Euryale, lorelei, mermaid, warlock; **8** isangoma, magician, sorcerer, witchman; **9** bewitcher, enchanter, mundunugu, occultist, shamaness, shamanist, sorceress, theurgist, voodooist, wangateur; **10** witchwoman; **11** enchantress, necromancer, spellbinder, thaumaturge; **13** thaumaturgist; PHRASES: **5, 2, 5** Witch of Endor; **5, 5** water witch, white witch; **5, 6** obeah doctor, weird sister, witch doctor; **8, 3** medicine man.

with **3** and; **4** plus; **5** close; **6** beside; **9** alongside, including; PHRASES: **2, 4, 2** as well as; **2, 6, 4** in tandem ~; **2, 7, 4** in company ~, in concert ~; **2, 8, 2** in addition to; **4, 2** next to; **5, 4** along ~; **6, 4** paired ~; **7, 4** coupled ~, jointly ~; **8, 4** together ~.

withdraw **2** go; **3** die; **4** exit, jilt, quit, stop, void; **5** annul, cease, chuck, ditch, leave, unsay; **6** cancel, depart, desert, repeal, resign, retire, revoke, secede, shelve, strike, vacate; **7** abandon, abolish, decline, disavow, extract, forsake, rescind, retreat, scratch; **8** abdicate, abrogate, evacuate, renounce; **10** apostasize, invalidate, relinquish; **11** schismatize; **12** disaffiliate; PHRASES: **2, 4** go AWOL; **3, 3** bow out, cop out, cut out; **4, 1, 7** beat a retreat; **4, 2** jack in; **4, 3** drop out, move out, pull out, sell out, sign off, sign out, step out, take out, walk out; **4, 4** take back; **4, 4, 4** quit one's post; **4, 5** down tools, play hooky; **4, 6** play truant; **5, 2, 4, 4** throw in one's hand; **5, 3** check out, punch out; **5, 3, 5** leave the stage; **5, 4** stand down; **6, 5** change sides.

withdraw (a statement) **6** recant; **7** retract; **9** backtrack; PHRASES: **2, 1, 1-4** do a U-turn; **3, 4, 5** eat one's words; **3, 6, 3** eat humble pie.

withdrawal **7** leaving, removal, retreat; **8** symptoms; **9** departure, disavowal, secession; **10** abjuration, detachment, disclaimer, extraction, retirement, retraction, revocation, separation; **11** abandonment; **12** renunciation; PHRASES: **4, 6** cold turkey.

withdrawn **8** reserved, solitary; **9** inhibited; **11** introverted.

wither **4** fade, wane, wilt; **5** droop; **7** decline, shrivel; **8** languish.

withering *See* **contemptuous**

withhold **4** deny; **6** refuse; **8** suppress; PHRASES: **4, 4** hold back, keep back.

within *See* **inside**

withstand **4** bear, defy; **5** check; **6** endure, hinder, resist; **7** survive, weather; **8** tolerate; PHRASES: **3, 4, 5, 2** dig one's heels in; **4, 3** hold out; **4, 3, 4** stem the tide; **5, 4** stand firm; **5, 4, 6** stand one's ground; **6, 2, 5** refuse to budge; **6, 3, 5** breast the storm.

witness **3** see; **6** behold, expert; **7** endorse, observe, testify; **8** evidence, Jehovah's, onlooker; **9** bystander, spectator; **11** corroborate, countersign.

wizard *See* **witch, wizard**

WO **8** walkover; PHRASES: **3, 6** War Office; **7, 3** written off; **7, 7** welfare officer.

wobble **3** bob; **4** wave; **5** shake, waver; **6** dither, quaver, quiver; **7** tremble, vibrate; **8** hesitate; **9** vacillate; PHRASES: **6-6** shilly-shally.

woe **5** grief; **7** anguish, sadness, trouble; **8** calamity, disaster, distress; **10** affliction, misfortune.

wolf **3** cub; **4** bolt; **5** gorge, Romeo, scoff; **6** devour, gobble, guzzle, spider; **7** whistle; **8** Casanova, Lothario; **9** womanizer; **11** philanderer; PHRASES: **3, 4** Don Juan, put away; **4, 4** gulp down.

wolffish **7** catfish.

wolverine **7** glutton; **8** carcajou.

woman **4** aunt, babe, baby, bird, dame, doll, girl, lady, wife; **5** chick, fancy, mater, mommy, mummy, niece, widow, women; **6** auntie, female, granny, matron, mother, sister; **7** crumpet, madrina, painted, scarlet; **8** daughter; **9** godmother, homemaker, housewife, maternity, matriarch; **10** motherhood; **11** goddaughter, grandmother; **13** granddaughter, materfamilias; PHRASES: **2-4** ex-wife; **3, 3** old bag, old bat, old gal; **3, 4** old lady; **3, 5** old witch, old ~; **3, 8** old spinster; **4, 3, 5** ball and chain; **5, 2, 3, 5** ~ of the world; **7, 5** married ~.

woman soldier **4** WRAC *UK*, WRAF *UK*, Wren; **6** Amazon, Athena; **7** heroine; **8** Boadicea, Valkyrie; **10** battlemaid; **12** servicewoman; PHRASES: **4, 2, 3** Joan of Arc; **6, 7** female warrior.

womenfolk **5** harem; **6** purdah, zenana; **8** seraglio; **9** matronage; PHRASES: **3, 5** hen party *UK*, the girls; **3, 6, 3** the second sex *Offensive*; **3, 10** the sisterhood; **7, 4** distaff side.

wonder **3** awe; **4** fear, gape, gawk, gawp;

5 shock, sight, stare; **6** admire, marvel, stupor, vision; **7** fantasy, miracle, portent; **8** raptness, surprise; **9** amazement, curiosity, sensation, spectacle, speculate; **10** admiration, bafflement, conjecture, deliberate, phenomenon, puzzlement, wonderland, wonderment; **11** fascination, incredulity, masterpiece, uncertainty; **12** astonishment, bewilderment, masterstroke, stupefaction; **13** consternation, dumbfoundment; PHRASES: **3, 4, 4** rub one's eyes; **3-6** eye-opener; **4, 6** look aghast; **4-6** best-seller; **4, 7** hero worship; **4-7** chef-d'oeuvre; **5, 7** cause célèbre, seven wonders; **5, 9** annus mirabilis, quite something; **6, 2** goggle at.

wonderful 3 ace, fab; **4** best, rare; **5** brill, great, ideal, magic, outré, swell, weird; **6** cosmic, groovy, wizard; **7** amazing, awesome, bizarre, corking UK, perfect, strange, topping; **8** fabulous, peculiar, smashing UK, spiffing UK, splendid, striking, stunning, terrific, wondrous; **9** beguiling, brilliant, enigmatic, excellent, exquisite, fantastic, ineffable, marvelous; **10** astounding, delightful, impressive, improbable, incredible, miraculous, mysterious, noteworthy, outlandish, phenomenal, prodigious, remarkable, stupendous, surprizing; **11** astonishing, bewildering, exceptional, magnificent, scrumptious, sensational, unutterable; **12** breathtaking, overwhelming, thaumaturgic, unbelievable, unimaginable; **13** extraordinary, inconceivable, indescribable; PHRASES: **3-9** awe-inspiring; **4-2** bang-on; **4-7** mind-blowing; **4-8** mind-boggling; **5-4** hunky-dory.

wonderful (be wonderful) 3 awe; **4** daze, faze, stun; **5** amaze; **6** baffle, boggle, dazzle; **7** astound, bewitch, impress, stagger, startle, stupefy; **8** astonish, bewilder, confound; **9** dumbfound, electrify, spellbind; **11** flabbergast; PHRASES: **4, 4** bowl over; **4, 4, 4** blow one's mind, turn one's head; **6, 4** strike dumb.

wonderfully 2, 4, 8 to one's surprise; **4, 6, 5** with gaping mouth; **7, 2, 3** strange to say; **8, 5** mirabile dictu. See also **wonderful**

wondering 4 awed, rapt; **5** dazed, fazed; **6** aghast, amazed; **7** blinded, dazzled, puzzled, shocked; **8** admiring; **9** astounded, awestruck, impressed, marveling, stupefied, surprised; **10** astonished, bewildered, fascinated, gobsmacked, spellbound; **11** dumbfounded; **13** flabbergasted, thunderstruck; PHRASES: **6, 4** bowled over.

wonderment (sign of wonderment) 7 silence, whistle; **11** exclamation; PHRASES: **3, 2, 6** cry of wonder; **4, 2, 6** eyes on stalks; **4, 5** open mouth; **7, 4** popping eyes; **7, 7** shocked silence.

wont 4 used; **5** habit; **6** custom; **8** inclined, practice, tendency; **10** accustomed, preference.

woo See **court**

wood 3 log; **4** beam, pole, post, slat; **5** board, joist, plank, shook, stave, stick; **6** lumber, rafter, siding, timber; **7** baywood, lathing, plywood, sapwood; **8** boarding, cordwood, firewood, hardwood, kindling, lathwork, lighterd, mesquite, paneling, pulpwood, puncheon, softwood; **9** chipboard, clapboard, hardboard, heartwood, panelwork, primavera, trunkwood, woodgrain; **10** blockboard UK, branchwood, bulletwood, fiddlewood, panelboard, timberwork; **12** weatherboard; PHRASES: **3-2-4** two-by-four; **4, 7** ~ texture; **6, 4** Scotch pine; **7, 8** African mahogany. See also **woodland, timber**

wood alcohol 8 methanol.

woodbine 11 honeysuckle; PHRASES: **8, 7** Virginia creeper.

woodchuck 9 groundhog.

wooded 5 bosky, braky, copsy, shady, woody; **6** shaded, sylvan, woodsy; **8** arboreal, forestal, forested, sylvatic, timbered; **9** arboreous; **10** afforested, sylvestral; **12** reafforested; PHRASES: **4-7** tree-covered.

wooden 4 dull, flat; **5** stiff; **7** deadpan, paneled, stilted; **8** ligneous, straight, toneless; **9** impassive, lacquered; **11** emotionless, marquetried, parquetried; **12** inexpressive.

woodgrouse 12 capercaillie.

wood ibis 6 jabiru.

woodland 4 holt UK, wood; **5** arbor, bower, brake, brush, copse, hurst UK, stand, woods; **6** bocage, bosket, covert, forest; **7** coppice, spinney, thicket; **9** chaparral; **10** plantation, timberland.

wood pigeon 6 cushat UK; **8** ringdove.

wood spirit 8 methanol.

woodwork 3 bar, cut; **5** treen; **7** carving, joinery, woodcut; **8** crossbar, fittings UK, paneling, skirting, wainscot; **9** carpentry, engraving, marquetry, whittling, woodcraft, woodprint, xylograph; **10** pyrography, timberwork, woodenware, xylography; **11** lignography, pyrogravure, woodburning, woodcarving, woodworking; **13** cabinetmaking; **14** xylopyrography; PHRASES: **4, 5** wood block; **4, 7** wood turning; **4, 9** wood sculpture.

woodworking tool 3 adz, saw; **4** velo; **5** borer, burin, drill, lathe, plane; **6** chisel, graver, jigsaw, lamina, planer, router, sander, shaper; **7** jointer, tenoner; **8** mortiser; **9** drawknife, sandpaper; **10** spokeshave *UK*; PHRASES: **3, 3** rip saw; **4, 3** band saw; **4, 4** tint tool; **4, 5** jack plane; **4, 6** belt sander, disk sander; **5, 3** panel saw, tenon saw; **7, 6** spindle sander; **8, 3** circular saw, crosscut saw; **9, 5** smoothing plane.

woody 5 ashen, oaken, treen; **6** sylvan; **7** beechen, stilted; **8** arboreal, forested, hardwood, ligneous, softwood, timbered, woodland; **9** ligniform; PHRASES: **4-7** hardgrained, soft-grained.

woody nightshade 11 bittersweet.

wooly 4 hazy; **5** vague, woven; **6** woolen *UK*; **7** knitted, woollen; **8** confused; **9** crocheted.

word 3 cry; **4** buzz, chat, hail, name, news, oath, okay, sign, talk, term; **5** logos, rumor, shout, spell, story, write; **6** calque, define, etymon, gossip, hybrid, letter, Mayday, phrase, pledge, reword, slogan, verbum; **7** antonym, cognate, coinage, command, express, hearsay, homonym, meaning, metonym, paronym, promise, rewrite, synonym, tidings; **8** glosseme, morpheme, password, rephrase, syllable, tautonym; **9** assurance, catchword, formulate, guarantee, homograph, homophone, neologism, processor, statement, verbalize, watchword; **10** articulate, expression, invitation, jawbreaker, palindrome, pejorative, processing, shibboleth; **11** declaration, information; **12** announcement, conversation, monosyllable, polysyllable, proclamation; **13** authorization, communication; **14** sesquipedalian; PHRASES: **2-5** go-ahead; **3-2** say-so; **3, 3** war cry; **3, 3, 3** hue and cry; **3, 3, 4** cry for help; **3, 4, 5** put into words; **4, 4** code ~, loan ~, ~ form; **4, 9** back formation; **4, 11** loan translation; **5, 4** false root, ghost ~, magic ~, nonce ~; **6, 3** battle cry; **6, 4** spoken unit; **6-6** tittle-tattle; **7, 4** cognate ~, written unit.

worded 5 named, vogue, wordy; **6** coined, echoic, verbal; **7** archaic, argotic,

canting *UK*, clichéd, clipped, cognate, lexical, phrased, rhyming, verbose; **8** enclitic, obsolete; **9** corrupted, equivocal, hackneyed, homonymic, paronymic, redundant, synonymic(al), vocabular; **10** antonymous, glossarial, homophonic, loquacious, meaningful, newfangled, pejorative, pleonastic, proverbial, tautonymic; **11** cacographic(al), commonplace, homographic, palindromic, portmanteau, pretentious; **12** inflectional, onomatopoeic; **13** morphological, neologistical; **14** sesquipedalian; PHRASES: **4-4** well-worn; **4-6** back-formed.

wordy 6 prolix; **7** diffuse, verbose; **8** rambling, waffling; **10** loquacious; PHRASES: **4-6** long-winded.

work 2 op; **3** dig, erg, fag *UK*, job, run, tug; **4** camp, duty, haul, hump, lift, load, moil, opus, plod, pull, push, slog, toil; **5** drive, ethic, graft *UK*, grind, heave, knead, labor, shift, shove, slave, sweat, swink; **6** career, chores, corvee, drudge, effect, effort, oeuvre, strain; **7** control, legwork, operate, outwork, produce, product, succeed, travail; **8** creation, drudgery, exertion, farmwork, function, homework, industry, overwork, taskwork, vocation; **9** fieldwork, freelance, handiwork, housework, moonlight, persevere, piecework, spadework; **10** assignment, employment, grindstone, manipulate, occupation; **11** composition, journeywork, masterpiece, performance; PHRASES: **3, 2** set to; **3, 3, 3** ply the oar; **3, 4** peg away *UK*; **4, 2, 1, 5** ~ up a sweat; **4-2-4** nine-to-five; **4, 2, 4, 5** spit on one's palms; **4, 3** ~ out; **4, 3, 5** ~ all hours; **4, 4** hard ~, make ~; **4, 4, 1, 5** ~ like a horse; **4, 4, 1, 6** ~ like a Trojan; **4, 5** hard labor; **4, 5, 4, 2** make short ~ of; **4, 8** ~ overtime; **5, 2** clock in, punch in; **5, 2, 4, 4** labor of love, spell of duty; **5, 3** clock out, punch out; **5, 4** penal ~, slave away; **5, 5** bring about, daily grind, sweat blood; **6, 2** overdo it; **6, 4** beaver away, double time, manual ~, school ~, uphill ~; **6-4** donkey-work; **6, 5** forced labor, manual labor; **9, 4** thankless task.

workable 6 doable, viable; **8** feasible, operable, possible; **9** practical; **10** achievable, manageable; **11** practicable; **12** maneuverable.

worker 3 ant, bee, fag *UK*; **4** cook, hack, hand, help, maid; **5** actor, gofer, navvy *UK*, slave; **6** beaver, butler, docker, drudge, earner, farmer, flunky, ganger *UK*, menial, moiler, packer, porter, seller, toiler, wallah; **7** artisan, cleaner, laborer, newsman, roadman, sandhog, servant, teacher, workman; **8** dogsbody, domestic, employee, factotum, gardener, handyman, hausfrau; **9** anchorman, announcer, charwoman, chauffeur, excavator, executant, executive, homemaker, housewife, operative, performer, presenter *UK*, scientist, secretary, stevedore, volunteer; **10** freelancer, journalist, meatpacker, newscaster, salesclerk, workingman; **11** anchorwoman, breadwinner, businessman, pieceworker; **12** anchorperson, longshoreman, participator, Stakhanovite; **13** businesswoman; **14** philanthropist; PHRASES: **4, 2, 3, 6** jack of all trades; **4, 3** busy bee; **4, 4** farm hand, home help *UK*; **4, 5** wage slave; **4, 6** desk ~, farm ~, girl Friday, road ~; **4-6** blue-collar; **5, 2, 6** beast of burden; **5-4, 6** black-coat ~; **5-5** plate-layer; **5-6** white-collar; **5, 8** trade unionist; **6, 5** galley slave; **6, 6** manual ~, office ~, social ~; **6, 7** casual laborer; **7, 4** factory hand; **7, 6** charity ~, factory ~; **9, 6** voluntary ~.

work force 4 crew; **5** staff; **7** workers; **8** manpower; **9** personnel; PHRASES: **4, 5** shop floor; **5, 5** labor force; **7, 5** factory floor.

working 4 busy, week; **5** class, party, waged; **6** active; **7** running; **8** diligent, drudging, employed, grinding, laboring, operable, plodding, salaried, slogging, sweating, tireless; **9** assiduous, attentive, effective; **10** exercising, practicing; **11** functioning, industrious, operational, painstaking, persevering; PHRASES: **2, 3, 2** on the go; **2, 4** in work *UK*; **4, 2, 2** hard at it; **4-7** hard-working; **5-6** horny-handed.

working (not working) 3 off, out; PHRASES: **2, 1, 10** at a standstill; **2, 5, 4** at loose ends; **2, 6** on strike; **3, 2, 6** out of action; **3, 2, 10** out of commission; **3, 4** off duty, off work; **4, 2** laid up; **6, 4** broken down. *See also* **unemployed**

work of art 4 book, film, opus, play, poem; **5** movie, novel, opera, story; **6** ballet, oeuvre, sketch, sonata; **7** article, artwork, novella, picture; **8** concerto, creation, painting, symphony; **9** sculpture; **10** masterwork, production, travelogue; **11** composition, masterpiece, performance; PHRASES: **3, 6** old master; **4, 2, 5** tour de force; **4, 2, 6** work of genius; **4, 2, 7** work of fiction; **4-7** chef-d'oeuvre; **5, 2, 7** piece of writing; **5, 4** objet d'art; **6, 2, 5** object of virtu; **6, 4** magnum opus; **6, 5** museum piece; **7, 2, 5** article of virtu; **8, 4** literary work.

works 5 plant; **7** factory; **9** machinery, mechanism; **10** everything; **12** installation; PHRASES: **3, 3** the lot; **6, 5** moving parts; **10, 4** industrial unit.

workshop 3 den, lab, pit; **4** barn, dock, farm, firm, mill, mine, mint, shop, yard; **5** dairy, forge, plant, store, study, wharf, works; **6** armory, bureau, office, quarry, smithy, stable, stithy, studio; **7** arsenal, atelier, brewery, company, factory, foundry, furnace, kitchen, laundry, library, malting, nursery, offices, sawmill, smelter; **8** coalface, coalmine, colliery, creamery, dockyard, gasworks, refinery, shipyard, stannary *UK*, workroom; **9** steelyard, sweatshop, workplace; **10** brickworks, laboratory, metalworks, powerhouse, steelworks, waterworks; **11** distilllery, secretariat; PHRASES: **3, 4** tin mine; **4, 2, 8** hive of industry; **4, 4** Rust Belt, tree farm; **4, 5** malt house, shop floor; **4, 6** head office, main office; **5, 2, 4** place of work; **5, 4** paper mill, stock farm; **5, 5** power plant; **5, 7** blast furnace, power station *UK*; **6, 4** cotton mill, sewing room; **6, 6** branch office; **7, 4** laundry room, science park; **8, 4** assembly line, building site; **9, 6** executive office; **10, 4** brownfield site *UK*, excavation site, production line.

workshy *See* **lazy**

work wood 5 carve, inlay, paint; **6** veneer; **7** lacquer, whittle; **8** laminate; **9** upholster; PHRASES: **4, 4** turn wood.

world 5 earth, Earth, globe, realm; **6** circle, cosmos, domain, planet, sphere; **8** creation, humanity, universe; **9** biosphere, ecosphere, macrocosm, microcosm; PHRASES: **3, 5, 4** the human race; **5, 3, 5** flora and fauna; **7, 5** natural ~.

world music 3 jit, rai *UK*, ska, son; **4** soca, zouk; **5** benga, kwela *UK*, ragga, salsa; **6** marabi, reggae, zydeco; **7** bhangra, calypso, macumba, qawwali; **8** mariachi, mbaqanga, merengue; **9** marabenta.

worm 5 fluke, fluky, leech; **7** annelid, Cestoda, cestode, cestoid, rotifer; **8** Annelida, bookworm, flatworm, glowworm, helminth, mealworm, Nematoda, nematode, Nemertea, phoronid, Rotifera, silkworm, tapeworm, wireworm, woodworm; **9** annelidan, bloodworm, earthworm, Hirudinea, leechlike, nemertean, peripatus, Phoronida, planarian, roundworm, screwworm, segmented, Trematoda, trematode, vermiform; **10** helminthic, hirudinean, kinorhynch, lumbricoid, Polychaeta, polychaete, ribbonworm, sipunculid, vermicular; **11** aschelminth, caterpillar, chaetognath, gastrotrich, helminthoid, Kinorhyncha, nematomorph, Oligochaeta, oligochaete, Onychophora, Pogonophora, Sipunculida, Turbellaria; **12** Chaetognatha, Gastrotricha, hemichordate, Nematomorpha, onychophoran, pogonophoran, polychaetous, turbellarian; **13** oligochaetous, platyhelminth; **14** Acanthocephala; **15** acanthocephalan, Platyhelminthes, platyhelminthic; PHRASES: **4, 4** army ~; **5, 4** acorn ~, arrow ~, beard ~; **5, 5** blood fluke, liver fluke; **5-6, 4** spiny-headed ~; **5, 9** wheel animacule; **6, 4** peanut ~; **6, 5** insect larva; **7, 4** annelid ~, bristle ~ *UK*; **9, 4** horsehair ~, parasitic ~, segmented ~; **9, 5** medicinal leech.

worried 7 anxious, nervous; **8** fretting; **10** solicitous; **12** apprehensive. *See also* **worry**

worrier 6 fidget; **7** fusspot *UK*; **8** neurotic; **9** pessimist, worryguts *UK*, worrywart; **10** fussbudget.

worry 3 bug, irk, vex; **4** fret, fuss, stew; **5** angst, haunt, upset; **6** bother, harass, obsess, pester, plague, stress, unease; **7** agitate, agonize, anxiety, bugbear, concern, disturb, trouble; **8** disquiet; **9** preoccupy; **10** discomfort, solicitude, uneasiness; **12** apprehension; **13** preoccupation; PHRASES: **4, 2** claw at, tear at; **4, 4, 5** bite one's nails; **4, 5** lose sleep; **5, 5** sweat blood.

worry beads 8 kumbaloi.

worse 4 waur *UK*; **6** poorer; **8** downhill, inferior, shoddier; PHRASES: **3, 3, 5** for the ~.

worsen 4 sink; **6** impair, plunge; **7** decline, degrade, descend, inflame; **8** diminish; **9** aggravate; **10** degenerate, exacerbate; **11** deteriorate; PHRASES: **2, 8** go downhill; **3, 3, 5** hit the skids; **5, 3, 6** plumb the depths; **5, 4, 5** reach one's nadir; **5, 4, 6** touch rock bottom.

worship 3 awe, bow; **4** duty, hajj, laud, love, muda, obey, pray, puja; **5** adore, deify, exalt, extol, honor, kneel, piety; **6** bhakti, esteem, hallow, homage, praise, revere; **7** adulate, applaud, dignify, glorify, magnify, praying, respect; **8** devotion, humility, minister, oblation, offering, petition, venerate; **9** adoration, adulation, atonement, celebrate, extolment, genuflect, laudation,

penitence, reverence; **10** asceticism, dedication, exaltation, meditation, pilgrimage, veneration; **11** celebration, devotedness, prostration; **12** genuflection, propitiation, supplication, thanksgiving; **13** contemplation, dignification, glorification, magnification; PHRASES: **3, 6, 2** pay homage to; **3, 7** say prayers; **4, 2** pray to; **4, 3** fear God; **4, 5** sing hymns; **4, 7** sing praises; **5, 7** cross oneself; **7, 4, 3** commune with God.

worship (place of worship) 3 wat; **4** cell, fane, kirk, shul; **5** abbey, duomo; **6** chapel, church, masjid, mosque, pagoda, shrine, temple; **7** chantry, minster, mission, oratory; **8** basilica, pantheon, teocalli, ziggurat; **9** cathedral, oratorium, synagogue; **10** tabernacle; **11** conventicle; **12** meetinghouse; PHRASES: **4, 6** Lady chapel, side chapel; **5, 2, 3** house of God; **5, 2, 6** house of prayer; **6, 2, 4** chapel of rest *UK*.

worship (public worship) 4 azan, sext; **5** lauds, nones, prime, terce; **6** abodah, maarib, matins, musaph; **7** liturgy, minchah, prayers, vespers; **8** compline, evensong, yahrzeit; PHRASES: **4, 2, 6** call to prayer; **5, 2, 7** order of service; **6, 6** divine office; **6, 7** church service, divine service, prayer meeting; **7, 7** evening prayers, evening service, morning prayers, morning service; **8, 3** muezzin's cry; **8, 7** memorial service; **9, 4** canonical hour.

worshipful 6 humble, lordly; **7** adoring, ascetic, devoted, dutiful, honored, humbled; **8** majestic, princely, reverent; **9** prostrate; **10** devotional, meditative, respectful, supplicant; **11** deferential, reverential; **12** meditational, supplicating, supplicatory, venerational; **15** anthropolatrous; PHRASES: **4, 2, 7** full of praises; **4-11** hero-worshipping; **5, 9** right honorable.

worshipped 6 adored; **7** admired, blessed, honored, praised, revered; **8** esteemed, extolled, idolized, lionized; **9** glorified, venerated.

worshipper 3 fan; **4** fold; **5** flock, hajji, minyn, sheep; **6** adorer, sangha, votary; **7** admirer *UK*, devotee, groupie, pilgrim; **8** adherent, believer, congress, follower, idolizer, lionizer, penitent; **9** celebrant, venerator; **10** aficionado, chapelgoer, churchgoer, congregant, petitioner, suppliant; **11** communicant, parishioner, participant; **12** congregation; PHRASES: **4-9** hero-worshiper.

worth 4 cost, rate; 5 means, merit, price, skill, value; 6 appeal, assets, desert, virtue, wealth; 7 meaning, quality, respect, vintage; 8 eminence, nobility; 9 greatness, soundness; 10 admiration, attraction, costliness, excellence, importance, worthiness; 11 beneficence, preeminence, superiority; 12 flawlessness, magnificence, quintessence, significance; 13 pricelessness, supereminence; PHRASES: 4, 4 best foot, best side; 5, 2, 4 claim to fame; 6, 5 strong point; 7, 7 classic quality.

worthily 4 well; 5 nobly; 7 greatly, notably; 8 laudably; 9 admirably; 10 gloriously, profitably; 11 brilliantly, commendably, excellently; 13 meritoriously.

worthless 5 empty; 6 futile, hollow, paltry; 7 garbage, rubbish UK, trivial, useless; 9 pointless, valueless; 11 meaningless, unimportant; 13 insignificant; PHRASES: 2, 2, 5 of no value; 2, 3 no use; 2, 6, 5 of little value, of little worth; 3, 5, 1, 4 not worth a bean; 3, 5, 1, 5 not worth a light; 7, 5 without value.

worthlessness 8 futility; 10 triviality; 11 irrelevance; 12 unimportance; 14 insignificance. See also **worthless**

worthwhile 4 good, kind; 6 useful; 7 helpful; 8 edifying, harmless, salutary, valuable; 9 advisable, favorable, wholesome; 10 beneficial, meaningful, profitable, propitious, refreshing, salubrious; 12 advantageous.

worthy 3 ace, fab; 4 braw, fine, good, pure, rare; 5 grand, great, noble, prime, super; 6 choice, chosen, classy, famous, lovely, picked, select, superb, tested, valued; 7 admired, classic, corking UK, earnest, eminent, notable, perfect, quality, vintage; 8 approved, dazzling, esteemed, fabulous, flawless, glorious, laudable, selected, stunning, superior, topnotch, valuable, virtuous; 9 admirable, brilliant, deserving, estimable, excellent, exclusive, exemplary, exquisite, justified, marvelous, recherché, respected, superfine, topflight; 10 creditable, noteworthy; preferable, prodigious, worthwhile; 11 commendable, meritorious, outstanding, sensational, superlative; 12 praiseworthy; 13 distinguished; PHRASES: 1-2 A-OK; 3, 2, 5 out of sight; 3, 3 way out; 3-4 all-star; 4, 2, 4 good as gold; 4, 2, 4, 4 good as one's word; 4, 3 God's own UK; 4-6 hand-picked; 4, 7 good quality; 4-7 well-meaning; 5, 3 above par; 5, 4 alpha plus; 5-4

first-rate, hunky-dory; 5-5 first-class, super-duper; 7, 2, 4 couleur de rose.

worthy (be worthy) 3 vie; 4 pass; 5 equal, excel, merit, rival; 7 contend, deserve, qualify, suffice, surpass; 9 transcend; PHRASES: 4, 6 pass muster; 4, 10 bear comparison; 5, 3, 4 equal the best, stand the test; 5, 3, 5 sweep the board.

wound 3 cut; 4 gash, harm, hurt, sore; 5 upset; 6 damage, injure, injury, lesion, offend; 8 distress, mutilate.

woven 4 fine; 5 cloth, sheer, twill; 6 coarse, fabric, felted, looped, meshed, napped, netted; 7 brushed, knitted, tangled; 11 intertwined; PHRASES: 4, 5 ikat weave; 4-5 fine-weave, open-weave.

WP 4, 10 word processing.

WR 4, 7 King William (Latin: Willelmus Rex).

wraith See **ghost**

wrangle See **quarrel**

wrap 3 box, net; 4 bind, case, pack; 5 cloak, cover, drape, dress, scarf, shawl, stole; 6 encase, enfold, enwrap, rebozo, shroud, swathe; 7 bandage, enclose, envelop, package, sheathe, swaddle; 8 enshroud, giftwrap, pashmina, surround; 9 encompass; PHRASES: 4, 5 ~ round.

wrapper 4 cape, foil; 5 cover, shawl, stole; 6 binder, casing, folder, jacket, sheath, shroud; 7 binding, package; 8 covering, envelope, pashmina; 9 clingfilm UK, packaging UK, polythene UK, sheathing; 10 bubblewrap, Cellophane™; 12 giftwrapping UK, polyethylene; PHRASES: 3, 5 wax paper; 4, 5 book cover, dust cover; 4, 6 dust jacket; 6, 5 tissue paper; 7, 4 plastic wrap; 8, 4 aluminum foil; 8, 5 wrapping paper; 9, 5 wrapround skirt.

wrath See **anger**

wreak 2 do; 5 cause; 6 create; 7 inflict; PHRASES: 5, 5 bring about.

wreath 6 laurel; 7 circlet, garland; 9 headdress.

wreathe 4 coil, wind; 5 adorn, cover, twist; 6 swathe, writhe; 7 festoon, garland.

wreck See **ruin**

wrench 3 tug; 4 haul, hurt, jerk, pull; 5 crick, heave; 6 injure, injury, sprain, strain; PHRASES: 3, 6 box ~.

wrestle 5 brawl, fight; 6 tussle; 7 grapple;

8 struggle; PHRASES: **3, 7** pin someone; **4, 1, 5** last a round; **6, 1, 4** secure a fall.

wrestler **4** NCAA (National Collegiate Athletic Association); **8** grappler; PHRASES: **5-3-7** grunt-and-groaner; **6-5** Graeco-Roman; **7, 8** amateur ~, Olympic ~.

wrestling **3** pin; **4** fall, hold, judo, kick, ring, rope; **5** block, choke, gouge, match, punch, round; **6** corner; **7** amateur, armlock, grapple, Olympic, wrestle; **8** crescent, headlock; **9** freestyle; **10** strangling; **11** competitive, immobilized; **12** professional, recreational, stranglehold; PHRASES: **2-5-6** no-holds-barred; **3-2** all-in; **3-3** all-red; **3-3-5** red-and-white; **3-4** tag-team; **4, 4** body slam; **4, 6** full nelson, half nelson; **4-7** hair-pulling; **5-2-5-3** catch-as-catch-can; **5-3-5** grunt-and-groan; **6, 4** flying mare; **6-5** Graeco-Roman; **7, 4** illegal hold.

wretch **3** imp; **5** rogue; **6** horror *UK*, rascal, victim; **7** villain; **8** scalawag *UK*, sufferer; **9** scallywag, scoundrel; **10** blackguard, languisher; **11** unfortunate; PHRASES: **4, 5** poor thing.

wrinkle **3** rut; **4** bend, fold, furl, knit, line, plow *UK*, roll, ruck, seam, slit, slot; **5** canal, chink, crimp, ditch, flute, plica, score, track; **6** crease, furrow, gather, groove, gutter, plough *UK*, pucker, rumple, trough; **7** channel, crinkle, crumple, fissure, flexure, overlap, scrunch; **8** buckling *UK*, flection, scrumple, syncline; **9** anticline, corrugate, plication, plicature; PHRASES: **3-3** dog-ear; **5, 4** crow's foot; **8, 4** laughter line *UK*.

wrinkly **5** rough, rutty; **6** chinky, etched, rimose, rugged, rugose; **7** crinkly *UK*, crumply, wizened; **9** scratched; PHRASES: **5-7** wheel-tracked; **7-2** screwed-up. *See also* **wrinkle**

writ **7** summons; **10** injunction; PHRASES: **5, 5** court order.

write **3** pen; **5** carve, enter, prose, rhyme; **6** author, create, devise, inform, pencil, poetry, record, report, script; **7** compose, elegize, engrave, express, poetize, portray, prosify, versify; **8** describe, document, inscribe; **9** delineate, dramatize, represent; **10** correspond, transcribe; PHRASES: **3, 2, 5, 4** get in touch with; **3, 2, 7** put in writing; **3, 3, 2, 5** put pen to paper; **3, 4** jot down; **4, 4** note down; **5, 4** ~ down.

writer **2** Oz (Amos); **3** Ade (George), Day (Clarence), Lee (Harper), Nin (Anaïs), Paz (Octavio), Poe (Edgar Allan), Roy (Arundhati), Tan (Amy); **4** Agee (James), Amis (Sir Kingsley), Baum (L. Frank), Behn (Aphra), Buck (Pearl S.), Carr (Emily), Cobb (Irvin Shrewsbury), Dahl (Roald), Gide (André), Grey (Zane), Inge (William), King (Stephen), Luce (Clare Boothe), Mann (Heinrich), Mann (Thomas), Rand (Ayn), Rhys (Jean), Rice (Anne), Roth (Philip), Sand (George), Snow (C. P.), West (Dame Rebecca), West (Nathanael); **5** Agnon (Shmuel Yosef), Aiken (Conrad), Alger (Horatio), Barth (John), Bates (H. E.), Behan (Brendan), Benét (Stephen Vincent), Blume (Judy), Broun (Heywood), Čapek (Karel), Carey (Peter Philip), Crane (Stephen), Desai (Anita), Donne (John), Doyle (Roddy), Doyle (Sir Arthur Conan), Dumas (Alexandre), Eliot (George), Frank (Anne), Genet (Jean), Gogol (Nikolay Vasilyevich), Grass (Günter), Haley (Alex), Hardy (Thomas), Harte (Bret), Hearn (Lafcadio), Hecht (Ben), Henry (O.), Hesse (Hermann), James (Henry), James (P. D.), Joyce (James), Kumin (Maxine), Lewis (Sinclair), Lowry (Malcolm), Lurie (Alison), Marsh (Dame Ngaio), McKay (Claude), Milne (A. A.), Munro (Alice), Musil (Robert), Oates (Joyce Carol), Paton (Alan), Pound (Ezra), Scott (Sir Walter), Seuss (Dr.), Spark (Dame Muriel), Stein (Gertrude), Stowe (Harriet Beecher), Swift (Jonathan), Twain (Mark), Tyler (Anne), Verne (Jules), Vidal (Gore), Waugh (Evelyn), Wells (H. G.), Welty (Eudora), White (E. B.), Wilde (Oscar), Wolfe (Thomas), Wolfe (Tom), Woolf (Virginia); **6** Alcott (Louisa May), Algren (Nelson), Asimov (Isaac), Atwood (Margaret), Austen (Jane), author, Balzac (Honoré de), Barrie (Sir J. M.), Bellow (Saul), Bierce (Ambrose), Blixen (Karen), Borges (Jorge Luis), Bowles (Paul), Brontë (Ann), Brontë (Charlotte), Brontë (Emily), Brooks (Van Wyck), Capote (Truman), Carter (Angela), Cather (Willa), Chopin (Kate), Cicero (Marcus Tullius), Clancy (Tom), Conrad (Joseph), Cooper (James Fenimore), Coward (Sir Noel), Daudet (Alphonse), Dickey (James), Didion (Joan), Ferber (Edna), France (Anatole), Fuller (Margaret), Gaddis (William), Gilman (Charlotte Perkins), Goethe (Johann Wolfgang von), Greene (Graham), Harris (Joel Chandler), Heller (Joseph), Hughes (Langston), Irving (John), Irving (Washington), Jewett (Sarah

Orne), Kramer (Larry), Krutch (Joseph Wood), L'Engle (Madeleine), London (Jack), Mailer (Norman), Miller (Henry), Milosz (Czeslaw), Norton (Charles Eliot), Orwell (George), Parker (Dorothy), Porter (Katherine Anne), Potter (Beatrix), Proulx (E. Annie), Proust (Marcel), Runyon (Damon), Sayers (Dorothy L.), Schurz (Carl), Sendak (Maurice), Sewell (Anna), Singer (Isaac Bashevis), Smiley (Jane), Sontag (Susan), Sterne (Laurence), Stoker (Bram), Styron (William), Susann (Jacqueline), Tagore (Rabindranath), Updike (John), Walker (Alice), Warren (Robert Penn), Wiesel (Elie), Wilder (Laura Ingalls), Wilder (Thornton), Wilson (August), Wright (Richard); **7** Allende (Isabel), Angelou (Maya), Babbitt (Irving), Baldwin (James), Beckett (Samuel), Buckley (William F., Jr.), Burgess (Anthony), Burnett (Frances Hodgson), Canetti (Elias), Carroll (Lewis), Cheever (John), Chekhov (Anton Pavlovich), DeLillo (Don), Dickens (Charles), Dinesen (Isak), Drabble (Margaret), Dreiser (Theodore), Durrell (Lawrence), Ellison (Ralph), Farrell (James T.), Fleming (Ian), Forster (E. M.), Friedan (Betty), Fuentes (Carlos), Gallant (Mavis), Gardner (Erle Stanley), Grisham (John), Hammett (Dashiell), Howells (William Dean), Hurston (Zora Neale), Johnson (James Weldon), Kennedy (William), Kerouac (Jack), Kipling (Rudyard), Kundera (Milan), Lardner (Ring), Mahfouz (Naguib), Malamud (Bernard), Maugham (W. Somerset), Mitford (Jessica), Mitford (Nancy), Nabokov (Vladimir), Naipaul (V. S.), Narayan (R. K.), O'Connor (Flannery), Perkins (Maxwell), Pushkin (Aleksandr), Pynchon (Thomas), Richler (Mordecai), Rowling (J. K.), Saroyan (William), Shelley (Mary), Simenon (Georges), Soyinka (Wole), Stegner (Wallace), Theroux (Paul), Thoreau (Henry David), Thurber (James), Tolkien (J. R. R.), Tolstoy (Leo), Walcott (Derek), Walpole (Horace), Wharton (Edith); **8** Andersen (Hans Christian), Anderson (Sherwood), Asturias (Miguel Ángel), Beauvoir (Simone de), Beerbohm (Sir Max), Benchley (Robert), Bradbury (Ray), Brittain (Vera), Brookner (Anita), Caldwell (Erskine), Chandler (Raymond), Cortázar (Julio), Crichton (Michael), Deighton (Len), Doctorow (E. L.), Donleavy (J. P.), Faulkner (William), Fielding (Henry), Flaubert (Gustave), Gellhorn

(Martha), Heinlein (Robert), Koestler (Arthur), Lawrence (D. H.), Lawrence (T. E.), McCarthy (Mary), Melville (Herman), Meredith (George), Michener (James Albert), Mitchell (Margaret), Morrison (Toni), Murasaki (Shikibu), Ondaatje (Michael), Perrault (Charles), Rabelais (François), Rawlings (Marjorie Kinnan), Remarque (Erich Maria), Rousseau (Jean Jacques), Salinger (J. D.), Sillitoe (Alan), Sinclair (Upton), Spillane (Mickey), Stendhal, Strachey (Lytton), Trollope (Anthony), Turgenev (Ivan), Voltaire, Vonnegut (Kurt), Williams (William Carlos); **9** Blackmore (R. D.), Boccaccio (Giovanni), Burroughs (Edgar Rice), Burroughs (William S.), Cervantes (Miguel de), Charteris (Leslie), Chayefsky (Paddy), Goldsmith (Oliver), Hawthorne (Nathaniel), Hemingway (Ernest), Highsmith (Patricia), Isherwood (Christopher), Lampedusa (Giuseppe Tomasi di), Lindbergh (Anne), Linklater (Eric), Lovecraft (H. P.), Mansfield (Katherine), McCullers (Carson), Pasternak (Boris), Priestley (J. B.), Pritchett (Sir V. S.), Steinbeck (John), Stevenson (Robert Louis), Wodehouse (P. G.); **10** Carpentier (Alejo), Chesterton (G. K.), Fitzgerald (F. Scott), Galsworthy (John), Maupassant (Guy de), Montgomery (L. M.), Richardson (John), Tarkington (Booth); **11** Dostoyevsky (Fyodor), Kazantzakis (Nikos); **12** Solzhenitsyn (Aleksandr); **13** Chateaubriand (François Auguste René, Vicomte de); PHRASES: **2, 3** de Man (Paul); **2, 4** Le Guin (Ursula); **2, 7** Du Maurier; **2, 9** Ōe Kenzaburō; **3, 6** Dos Passos (John); **5-7** Robbe-Grillet (Alain), Saint-Exupéry (Antoine); **6, 6** Bulwer Lytton (Edward); **6, 7** García Márquez (Gabriel); **7-7** Brillat-Savarin (Anthelme); **9-4** Sackville-West (Vita). *See also* **poet**

writing **4** copy, text; **5** marks, prose; **6** script; **7** symbols; **10** characters, journalism, literature; **11** inscription.

wrong **3** sin; **4** evil, harm, hurt, vice; **5** abuse, amiss, crime, error, false, wound; **6** biased, damage, defame, felony, injure, injury, insult, malign, offend, uneven, unfair, unjust, untrue; **7** falsely, immoral, misdeed, offense, oppress; **8** improper, maltreat, mistaken, wrongful; **9** dishonest, erroneous, incorrect, unethical; **10** immorality, inaccurate, infraction, iniquitous, prejudiced, unbalanced, unsuitable, wickedness;

11 abomination, inequitable, misdemeanor; 12 infringement; 13 inappropriate, transgression; 14 discriminatory; 15 unsportsmanlike; PHRASES: 3, 2, 4 out of line; 3, 4 off beam; 3-5 ill-treat; 3, 7 not cricket; 4, 2, 3, 4 wide of the mark; 5, 3, 4 below the belt.

wrong (be wrong) 7 blunder; PHRASES: 4, 1, 7 make a mistake; 4, 2 slip up.

wrong (do wrong) 3 err, sin; 4 fall; 5 cheat, lapse, stray; 6 offend; 7 violate; 8 infringe, trespass; 10 degenerate, transgress; PHRASES: 2, 2, 3 go to pot; 2, 2, 3, 3 go to the bad; 2, 2, 3, 4 go to the dogs; 2, 2, 4, 3, 4 go to rack and ruin; 2, 6 go astray; 5, 3, 3 break the law; 5, 3, 5 break the rules; 6, 1, 5 commit a crime; 6, 2, 7 commit an offense.

wrong (go wrong) 4 fail; 11 malfunction; PHRASES: 2, 2, 3, 5 go on the blink; 2, 4 go phut; 2, 5 go kaput; 4, 3 conk out; 5, 4 break down.

wrong (in the wrong) 6 guilty, sinful, wicked; 7 abusive, crooked, harmful, hurtful, illegal, illicit, lawless, vicious; 8 criminal, culpable, unlawful; 9 felonious, injurious, offensive, violative; 10 abominable, delinquent, infringing; 11 blameworthy, unrighteous; 13 transgressive; PHRASES: 2, 5 at fault.

wrong (sense of wrong) 4 foul, tort; 5 gripe; 6 grouse, injury; 9 complaint, grievance, injustice; PHRASES: 3, 4 raw deal; 4, 4 foul play.

wrongdoer 4 crim *UK*; 5 crook, felon; 6 outlaw, sinner; 7 culprit, villain; 8 criminal, evildoer, offender; 9 infractor, miscreant, reprobate; 10 delinquent, lawbreaker, malefactor, trespasser; 12 transgressor.

wrongdoing 3 sin; 4 harm, vice; 5 abuse, crime, error; 6 felony, injury; 7 misdeed, offense; 8 trespass; 10 infraction, misconduct; 11 abomination, misdemeanor; 12 infringement; 13 transgression.

wrongly 4 awry; 5 amiss, badly; 7 loosely; 9 inexactly; 11 imperfectly, imprecisely; 12 accidentally; 13 approximately; PHRASES: 2, 7 by mistake; 3, 2, 4 out of true; 7, 8 without thinking. *See also* **wrong, wrong (in the wrong)**

wry 3 dry; 5 droll; 6 ironic; 7 cynical; 8 sardonic.

Wyoming 2 WY; 8 Cheyenne (capital); 10 cottonwood (tree), meadowlark (bird); PHRASES: 5, 6 Equal rights (motto); 6, 10 indian paintbrush (flower); 8, 3, 6, 5 Equality and Cowboy State (nickname).

XYZ

X 3 chi, ten; **4** kiss; **5** cross, error; **6** Christ; **8** multiply, treasure.

xenophobic 6 racist; **7** insular; **9** parochial; **10** intolerant, jingoistic, prejudiced; **13** nationalistic.

xerox™ 4 copy; PHRASES: **9** duplicate, photocopy, photostat™.

x-ray 8 Roentgen; **9** radiogram, screening.

Y 4 yard, year.

yak *See* **chat**

yank *See* **tug**

yap 3 bay, yak; **4** bark, chat, talk, woof, yelp; **6** baying, gossip, yammer; **7** chatter.

yard 4 area, lawn, plot; **5** court, patio, stick; **6** garden *UK*, ramada, stride; **7** terrace; **8** farmyard, Scotland; **9** courtyard, enclosure, flowerbed; **10** quadrangle; PHRASES: **4, 4** back ~, navy ~; **5, 7** water feature; **6, 3** raised bed.

yardstick *See* **benchmark**

yarn 4 tale, wool; **5** fiber, story; **6** thread; PHRASES: **4, 4** tall tale.

yawn 3 gap; **4** bore, gape, sigh; **5** crack, split; **7** stretch; **8** nonevent; PHRASES: **5, 2, 4** waste of time.

year 4 leap; **5** lunar, solar; **6** fiscal; **8** calendar; **9** financial; **10** sabbatical; **11** twelvemonth.

yearn for *See* **desire**

yell *See* **shout**

yellow 4 buff, gild, gilt, gold, sand, weld; **5** amber, beige, fever, honey, lemon, pages, straw, tawny; **6** canary, citron, creamy, fallow, flaxen, gilded, golden; **7** aureate, chamois, citrine, gamboge, luteous, mustard, saffron; **8** luteolin, massicot, orpiment, primrose, sunshine, xanthene, xanthous; **9** champagne, sulfurous; **10** chartreuse, flavescent; **11** xanthophyll; PHRASES: **6, 5** ~ ocher; **6, 6** Indian ~, Naples ~; **7, 6** Windsor ~.

yellow-haired 5 blond; PHRASES: **3-5** ash-blond; **3-6** tow-haired *UK*; **4-6** fair-haired; **5-5** honey-blond; **6-6** flaxen-haired, golden-haired; **8-5** platinum-blond; **10-5** strawberry-blond.

yellow thing 4 gold; **5** amber, honey, lemon, topaz; **6** banana, butter, citron, crocus, sulfur; **7** cowslip, mustard, sulphur *UK*; **8** daffodil, primrose; **9** brimstone, buttercup, dandelion; PHRASES: **6, 7** winter jasmine *UK*.

yelp 3 cry, sob, yap; **4** bark, crow, howl, wail; **5** growl, snarl, whine; **6** squeak, squeal.

yen *See* **urge**

yes 2 OK; **3** aye, nod, yah *UK*, yea, yup; **4** amen, okay, sure, yeah; **5** right; **6** indeed, surely; **9** certainly, naturally; **10** absolutely; **11** affirmative, endorsement; **12** ratification; PHRASES: **2, 6** of course; **6, 2** thumbs up.

yet 5 still; **7** however; **8** hitherto; **11** nonetheless; **12** nevertheless; PHRASES: **2, 3** so far; **2, 4, 3** up till now *UK*; **4, 3** thus far; **5, 3** until now.

yiddish 3 lox, -nik; **4** futz, gelt, nosh, putz, schm-, shul, tush; **5** bagel, dreck, golem, klutz, knish, kugel, latke, matzo, nudge, rebbe, shiva, yenta; **6** blintz, dybbuk, glitch, kibitz, kishke, kvetch, mazuma, mensch, mikvah, nudnik, pareve, schlep, schlub, shiksa, shtetl, shtick, zaftig; **7** chachka, dreidel, haimish, klezmer, meshuga, milchig, nebbish, schlock, schmeer, schmuck, shegetz, sheitel, tummler, tzimmes, Y~; **8** chutzpah, fleishig, kreplach, pastrami, schmaltz, schmooze, shammash, shidduch, shpilkes, Yahrzeit, yarmulke,

Yinglish; **9** rebbetzin, schlemiel, schnorrer, schnozzle, shemozzle, shmegegge, tchotchke; **10** hamantasch, schlimazel; **3, 3** yom tov; **3-3** hoo-hah; **7, 4** gefilte fish.

yield 4 bear, bend, cede, crop, give, obey; **5** adapt, agree, defer, fruit, grant; **6** comply, income, output, profit, relent, return, submit; **7** concede, consent, harvest, produce, product, revenue, succumb, vintage; **8** generate, proceeds; **9** acquiesce, surrender; **10** capitulate, production, relinquish; PHRASES: **3, 2** bow to, let go; **4, 2** give in, give up; **4, 3** give way; **4, 4** lose face; **5, 2** bring in; **5, 5** bring forth; **6, 4** second crop; **7, 4** vintage crop, vintage wine.

yielding 4 soft; **6** docile; **7** elastic, fertile, springy, squashy; **8** fruitful, prolific; **9** compliant, malleable; **10** productive; **13** accommodating. *See also* **yield**

yoke 4 bind, hook, join, link, loop; **5** lasso, leash, noose, reins, unite; **6** collar, halter, lariat, tether; **7** bondage, coupler, drawbar, harness; **8** coupling; **10** oppression, repression; **11** encumbrance.

Yom Kippur 3, 2, 9 Day of Atonement.

York 8 Eboracum.

Yorkshire 5 dales; **7** pudding *UK*, terrier.

you 2 tu, ye; **3** thy; **4** thee, thou; **5** thine.

young 3 new; **4** baby, kids, sons; **5** brood, early, fresh, hatch, issue, naive, spawn, youth; **6** babies, boyish, clutch, infant, junior, litter, little; **7** babyish, girlish, progeny; **8** childish, children, immature, innocent, juvenile, maidenly, underage, virginal, youthful; **9** beardless, childlike, daughters, embryonic, infantile, offspring, preschool, pubescent, underaged, unfledged; **10** adolescent; **11** juvenescent, undeveloped; PHRASES: **2, 3, 6** in the cradle; **2, 4, 7** in one's infancy; **3-7** new-fledged; **4-4** knee-high; **5, 3, 6** sweet and twenty; **5, 5** ~ blood; **5, 7** sweet sixteen.

young (have young) 3 cub, lay, pup; **4** drop, foal, lamb; **5** calve, hatch, spawn, whelp; **6** farrow, kitten, litter, sprout; **8** fructify; **9** germinate.

young (make young) 7 youthen; **10** rejuvenate; **12** reinvigorate.

young animal 3 cub, fry, kid, pup; **4** calf, colt, fawn, foal, grub, joey, lamb, pupa; **5** brood, chick, filly, larva, nymph, puppy, spawn, whelp, young; **6** clutch, cocoon, cygnet, farrow, heifer, kitten, litter, piglet;

7 bullock, lambkin, leveret, tadpole; **8** duckling, nestling, polliwog, yearling; **9** chrysalis, fledgling; **11** caterpillar.

young bird 4 eyas; **5** brood, chick, hatch, owlet, poult, squab; **6** clutch, cygnet, eaglet, pullet; **7** gosling; **8** duckling, nestling; **9** fledgling.

young fish 3 fry; **4** parr; **5** elver, smolt; **6** alevin, grilse; **10** fingerling.

young man 3 boy, cub, lad, pup; **5** youth; **6** laddie; **9** schoolboy, stripling.

young person 3 kid; **4** teen; **5** child, minor, youth; **6** junior; **7** groupie, young'un; **8** juvenile, teenager; **9** youngling, youngster; **10** adolescent; **11** teenybopper, weenybopper.

young plant 3 set; **5** scion, shoot, sprig; **6** sprout, sucker; **7** sapling; **8** offshoot, seedling.

young woman 4 baby, girl, lass, maid, miss; **5** chick, missy; **6** lassie, maiden, virgin; **10** schoolgirl; **12** mademoiselle; PHRASES: **4, 2, 1, 4** slip of a girl.

youth 3 kid; **5** child, minor, teens; **6** nonage; **7** boyhood, infancy, puberty; **8** babyhood, girlhood, minority, preteens, teenager, wardship; **9** childhood, puerility, pupillage, youngster; **10** immaturity, maidenhood, pubescence, schooldays; **11** adolescence; **14** apprenticeship; PHRASES: **3, 5, 2, 4** the prime of life; **5, 4** salad days; **6, 3** school age, tender age; **7, 3** awkward age; **9, 5** formative years.

youthful 5 fresh, young; **6** active, boyish, lively; **7** girlish; **8** childish, immature, maidenly, vigorous; **9** childlike, energetic, sprightly; **12** enthusiastic; PHRASES: **5, 2, 5** young at heart.

youthfulness 5 bloom, vigor; **6** energy; **7** newness; **8** radiance, vivacity; **10** enthusiasm, immaturity, juvenility; **12** juvenescence; PHRASES: **5, 5** young blood; **6, 5** boyish charm. *See also* **youthful**

yucky *See* **nasty**

Z 4 zero, zone.

zany 3 mad; **4** wild; **5** comic, crazy, silly, wacky; **6** madcap; **7** idiotic.

Zarathustra 9 Zoroaster.

zeal 4 fire, love, zest; **5** ardor, gusto, verve, vigor; **6** fervor, relish; **7** bigotry, passion; **8** devotion; **9** eagerness; **10** enthusiasm.

zealot 3 fan, nut; **5** bigot, ultra; **6** votary; **7**

devotee, diehard, fanatic; **8** activist, militant; **9** dogmatist, extremist, sectarian; **10** enthusiast.

zealous 4 avid, keen; **5** eager, fiery; **6** ardent, devout; **7** devoted, fervent; **8** vigorous; **9** committed, dedicated; **10** passionate; **12** enthusiastic.

zebra 6 quagga; **9** crosswalk; PHRASES: **5, 5** ~ finch, ~ plant.

zenith *See* **peak**

zeppelin *See* **airship**

zero 1 O; **2** no; **3** nil; **4** blob, duck, love, none; **5** squat, zilch; **6** cipher, cypher, naught; **7** nothing; PHRASES: **2, 5** no score; **3, 3** not any, not one; **3, 4** all gone; **5, 3** goose egg.

zero level 5 nadir; PHRASES: **4, 4** zero hour; **4, 6** last moment, rock bottom; **6, 5** crisis point, lowest point.

zest 4 peel, rind, skin, tang; **5** spice; **6** flavor; **8** piquancy; **9** sharpness. *See also* **zip**

zigzag 3 yaw; **4** tack, wavy, wind; **5** snake, twist, weave; **6** slalom, twisty, wander, wiggle; **7** chicane, crooked, meander, sinuous, stagger, winding; **8** tortuous; **10** meandering, serpentine; PHRASES: **3-3** ric-rac; **7-7** crinkle-crankle.

zinc 2 ZN.

zing *See* **zip**

zip 3 pep, vim; **4** brio, dash, fire, love, zeal, zing; **5** ardor, gusto, oomph, verve, vigor; **6** bounce, fervor, relish, spirit, zipper; **7** passion, pizzazz; **8** dynamism, vitality; **9** animation, eagerness; **10** enthusiasm, excitement, exuberance; PHRASES: **3-2-3-2**

get-up-and-go. *See also* **rush**

zodiac 3 Leo; **5** Aries, Libra, Virgo; **6** Cancer, Gemini, Pisces, Taurus; **7** Scorpio; **8** Aquarius; **9** Capricorn; **11** Sagittarius.

zone 4 area, belt; **6** region, sector; **7** equator, section, tropics; **9** territory; **10** subtropics; PHRASES: **4, 4** free ~, skip ~ *UK*, time ~; **5, 9** horse latitudes; **6, 4** frigid ~, torrid ~; **7-4, 4** nuclear-free ~; **7, 7** roaring forties; **8, 4** twilight ~; **9, 4** smokeless ~ *UK*, temperate ~; **10, 4** enterprise ~.

zoo 6 aviary; **7** reserve; **8** aquarium; **9** menagerie; **11** reservation; PHRASES: **6, 4** safari park.

zoological group 5 class, genus, order; **6** branch, family, gender, phylum; **7** species, variety; **8** subclass, subgenus, suborder; **9** subbranch, subfamily, subphylum; **10** subkingdom, subspecies, subvariety.

zoologist 9 zoonomist, zootomist; **10** ethologist, zoochemist, zoographer, zoometrist; **11** mammologist; **12** embryologist, entomologist, malacologist; **13** herpetologist, ichthyologist, ornithologist; **14** paleozoologist, parasitologist, protozoologist, zoopathologist; **15** helminthologist; PHRASES: **6, 9** animal ecologist, marine biologist.

zoom 4 rush, soar; **5** hurry, speed, whizz; PHRASES: **5-2** close-up.

Zoroaster 11 Zarathustra.

Zoroastrianism 8 Mazdaism.

zygomatic bone 5 jugal, malar.

zymurgy 7 brewing; **12** fermentation.